P9-DHA-384

ROGET'S II

The New Thesaurus

THIRD EDITION

ROGET'S II

The New Thesaurus

THIRD EDITION

By the Editors of
The American Heritage® Dictionaries

HOUGHTON MIFFLIN COMPANY
BOSTON NEW YORK

Library of Congress Cataloging-in-Publication Data
Roget's II : the new thesaurus. — 3rd ed.
p. cm.
Includes index.
ISBN 0-395-68722-5
1. English language — Synonyms and antonyms.
I. Houghton Mifflin Company. II. Title : Roget's 2.
III. Title : Roget's Two.
PE1591.R715 1995
423'.1 — dc20 94-42879
CIP

Deluxe Edition ISBN 0-395-73679-X

For information about this and other Houghton Mifflin trade and reference books and multimedia products, visit The Bookstore at Houghton Mifflin on the World Wide Web at http://www.hmco.com/trade/.

Manufactured in the United States of America

CONTENTS

EDITORIAL AND PRODUCTION STAFF

EDITORIAL STAFF

Vice President, Director of Lexical Publishing, Production, and Manufacturing Services
Margery S. Berube

Senior Lexicographer
David A. Jost
(Project Director)

Senior Coordinating Editor
Kaethe Ellis

Managing Editor
Marion Severynse

Senior Editor
Joseph P. Pickett

Editor
Martha F. Phelps

Associate Editors
James J. Boyle
Ann-Marie Imbornoni

Assistant Editors
Beth Gately Rowen
Susan E. Schwartz
So-Chung Shinn

Proofreading
Kathryn Blatt

Administrative Assistance
Lauren B. Hunnewell
Alisa Stepanian

Contributing Editor, Category Index
Patrick S. Diehl, Ph.D

PRODUCTION STAFF

Production and Manufacturing Manager
Christopher Leonesio

Production Supervisor
Patricia McTiernan

Senior Art and Production Coordinator
Margaret Anne Miles

Database Production Supervisor
Michael Rosenstein

Database Keyboarding
Miriam E. Palmerola (Supervisor)
Jane Ellin
Lori Galvin
Susan F. Harkins

Manufacturing Supervisor
Greg Mroczek

Production Coordinator
Nancy Priest

Senior Production Assistant
Christina Granados

Book Design
Melodie Wertelet

Administrative Assistance
Gladymir Veillard

PREFACE

Roget's II: The New Thesaurus, Third Edition, represents a significant improvement in thesaurus making. The lexicographic staff of Houghton Mifflin Company, publishers of *The American Heritage Dictionary of the English Language, Third Edition*, has designed *Roget's II* to provide rapid access to synonyms, facilitating the choice of appropriate words to express thoughts.

All entries are arranged in alphabetical order and are identified by part of speech. A definition precedes each list of synonyms, and each list is complete in itself. Synonyms with special applications are listed at the end of each synonym list and are labeled to provide usage guidance.

Roget's II is a source of appropriate words to express thoughts or ideas, guiding the user away from the common pitfall of selecting an unsuitable word. At times, however, one does not want only a synonym, and to provide the user with related words and words of opposite meaning to choose from, *Roget's II* contains a Category Index. Each synonym group closes with one or more cross-references to this Index. The Index then refers the user to related synonym groups, thus increasing one's choice of words substantially.

This thesaurus represents yet another major departure from traditional preparation of thesauruses. Every synonym and definition has been compared with the corresponding entry in *The American Heritage Dictionary of the English Language, Third Edition*, ensuring that the information in the Thesaurus is accurate and up to date.

An abiding objective of our reference publishing is to provide authoritative information about our language and guidance in its effective use. We believe *Roget's II: The New Thesaurus, Third Edition,* will serve the user well in selecting the right words to express thoughts precisely and add colorful variety to expression.

INTRODUCTION

Roget's II: The New Thesaurus, Third Edition, is a book devoted entirely to meaning. In contrast to the old-fashioned thesaurus, which groups undifferentiated words together with an entry word with no definition, this book provides an analysis — a definition — of the meaning or meanings of each entry word in the book. Synonyms are grouped according to meaning. What, then, *is* meaning?

MEANING

The meaning of even a single word is rather more complex than one might imagine. The most obvious aspect of meaning is *denotation*, that is, the thing meant, the concept or object referred to. The denotation of the word *chair*, for example, is that it is a piece of furniture, that it has a seat, legs, a back, and often arms, and that one person can sit on it. So long as it has these features, a chair can be identified as a chair irrespective of the fact that it may be big or small, made of chrome or wood, upholstered or caned — in short, no matter what other features it may have. Furthermore, a chair is distinct from all other pieces of furniture upon which one can sit. It is different from a stool because a stool is backless and armless. It is different from a couch, on which one or more may recline, and different from a chaise longue, which has a seat long enough to support the outstretched legs of the sitter. Thus the denotation of a word includes those features that are criterial and so serve to define and distinguish.

In addition to its denotation, a word may have a *connotation*, that is, the suggestive or associative implications of an expression beyond its literal sense. Differences, as of style or expressiveness, that cause a given term to convey a denotation more — or less — formally, colorfully, humorously, or the like, constitute the connotations of the word. For example, both *mouth* and *trap* denote the opening in the body through which food is ingested. *Mouth*, however, is what might be called a neutral term; it conveys information but has no connotations. *Trap*, on the other hand, is a slang word and is often considered to be somewhat vulgar.

Words expressive of emotion frequently have connotations, but many words that are not emotive also have them. Many sets of words of identical denotation can be arranged in a spectrum of greater to lesser formality. For example, of the synonym group *transpire*, *happen*, *occur*, *befall*, *betide*, and *hap*, all meaning "to take place, come to pass," *transpire* is the most formal; *happen* and *occur* are neutral — nonconnotative; and *befall, betide,* and *hap* have a somewhat archaic flavor. All of these facts beyond the bare denotation of the terms constitute the connotations of these words. In *Roget's II* labels such as *Informal*, *Regional*, and *Slang* identify restrictions with respect to level or style of usage.

Two or more words may have the same denotation and connotation and yet differ in their *range of applicability*; that is, they cannot be used interchangeably in the same context. *Cancel* and *vacate*, both having the same denotation ("to annul or invalidate") and both being nonconnotative, can nevertheless not be used interchangeably, because *vacate* is a legal term. One might *cancel* a magazine subscription, but one would hardly *vacate* it. *Slowly* and *adagio* have the same denotation, but *adagio* is a technical term in music. Terms of restricted range of applicability are identified in *Roget's II* by such labels as *Architecture*, *Music*, and *Psychiatry*.

SYNONYMY AND SYNONYMS

Given the complexity of meaning, a person searching for an alternative word must be sure that the synonym chosen is accurate and precise. Because of its emphasis on the meaning or meanings of a word *Roget's II* is specifically designed to offer the user a choice of synonyms that lie within the denotative range of the word or sense of the word with which they correspond.

In its strict sense, a *synonym* is a word with a meaning identical or very similar to that of another word. It is often said that in fact there is no such thing as an absolute synonym for any word, that is, a form that is identical in every aspect of meaning so that the two can be applied interchangeably. According to this extreme view the only true synonyms are terms having precisely the same denotation, connotation, and range of applicability. As it turns out, these so-called true synonyms are frequently technical terms and almost always concrete words coming from linguistically disparate sources. Good examples of such pairs are *celiac* (from Greek) and *abdominal* (from Latin); and *car* (from Latin) and *automobile* (from French). These meet the criteria for true synonymy: they have precisely the same denotations, connotations, and range of applicability, and they are used in identical contexts.

This view of synonomy is far too restrictive, however. In *Roget's II* synonymous terms are those having nearly identical denotations. English is rich in such words. Speakers very often have a choice from among a set of words of differing origin but the same denotation. A man may be *bearded* (from Old English), *barbate* (from Latin), *bewhiskered* (from Scandinavian), or *whiskered* (from Scandinavian). One may go to the *shore* (from Old English), the *coast* (from Latin), or the *littoral* (from Latin). One can refer to the sense of *hearing* (from Old English) or to the *acoustic* (from Greek), *auditory* (from Latin), *aural* (from Latin), or *auricular* (from Latin) sense. One can make clothing from *cloth* (from Old English), *fabric* (from Latin), *material* (from Latin), or *textiles* (from Latin). The reason for choosing one of these words over another is frequently stylistic: one may prefer a simpler or a more complex word; one may prefer a more formal or a less formal term. But the fact that these words share a denotation makes them synonymous and available as substitutes for words one has in mind so that one can be more precise, express oneself more colorfully, or avoid repetition. All of the terms included in the synonymies in *Roget's II* share the same denotation.

HOW TO USE THIS BOOK

THE ENTRIES

Roget's II: The New Thesaurus, Third Edition, contains three kinds of entries introduced by boldface headwords: main entries having synonym lists; indented subentries that consist either of a word spelled the same as the headword but with a different part of speech, or of a two-word verb derived from a single-word verb; and cross-reference entries from variant spellings to main entries:

fall *verb*
1. To move downward in response to gravity : descend, drop. *See* RISE.
fall down *verb Informal.* To be unsuccessful : choke, fail, fall through.
fall down *verb* See **fall.**

ENTRY ORDER

Main entries and cross-references are listed alphabetically. For instance, the first entry in this book is **A-1**. It is followed in turn by the separate entries **aback, abandon, abandoned, abandonment, abase,** and **abasement**.

Subentry order is as follows: two-word verbs derived from single-word verb headwords usually appear in alphabetical order as indented subentries directly under the base verbs. All verb entries precede the next part of speech, in the following example, the noun **fall**:

fall *verb*
fall back *verb*
fall down *verb*
fall off *verb*
fall on (or **upon**) *verb*
fall through *verb*
fall *noun*

Each of the two-word verb subentries shown above is also entered as a cross-reference at its own alphabetical place elsewhere in the book (see "**Cross-References**").

COMPONENTS OF MAIN ENTRIES

These are the components of a typical main entry:

> **destroy** *verb*
> **1.** To cause the complete ruin or wreckage of **:** bankrupt, break down, cross up, demolish, finish, ruin, shatter, sink, smash, spoil, torpedo, undo, wrack[2], wreck. *Slang:* total. ***Idiom:*** put the kibosh on. *See* HELP.

In the above example, the entry word **destroy** is followed by the italic part-of-speech label *verb*. A boldface sense number, in this case **1.**, appears in all multisense entries, followed by a definition of the meaning shared by the entry word and its synonyms. In this example the definition of **destroy** and its synonyms is "to cause the complete ruin or wreckage of." The synonyms are all substitutable for **destroy**.

A boldface colon introduces the list of words synonymous with **destroy**: *bankrupt, break down, cross up, demolish, finish, ruin, shatter, sink, smash, spoil, torpedo, undo, wrack*[2], and *wreck*. Labeled synonyms, in this case, *total* with its label *Slang*, appear after the main list of synonyms.

When appropriate, idioms equivalent to the synonyms are shown at the end of a synonym list. These idioms are phrases with the same meaning as the basic meaning shared by all the synonyms. In the entry shown here, *put the kibosh on* is an idiom that is equivalent to **destroy** and its synonyms. Idioms are not listed as main entries.

Each synonym list concludes with a Category reference, such as *See* HELP in the entry **destroy** shown above. For an explanation of this see "**Introduction to the Category Index**" on p. 1153.

SUBENTRIES

Words spelled the same as the entry words but with a different part of speech and also two-word verbs are indented subentries. For instance, the noun **abandon** is a subentry of the verb **abandon**, but **abandonment** is a separate entry. Two-word verbs derived from single-word verbs are shown as subentries of the single-word verbs, as in the case of **call down** at **call**.

CROSS-REFERENCES

Cross-references lead to subentries of main entries and variant spellings that differ markedly from the spellings of main entries. For example, **call down**, as already noted, is a subentry at **call**; hence **call down** is also entered at its own alphabetical place:

call down *verb* See **call.**

The variant spelling **aeon** is shown at its own alphabetical place:

aeon *noun* See **eon.**

VARIANTS

Equal and unequal variants are given following the main entry word. An equal variant is a spelling of a word that is just as acceptable as the entry word spelling. Equal variants are signaled by use of the connective *or*:

down-at-heel or **down-at-the-heel**

An unequal variant is a spelling that is less common than the entry word spelling but is nevertheless acceptable. Unequal variants are signaled by the connective *also*:

lese majesty also **lèse majesté**

When a single idiom can be worded in a variety of ways, the variant wordings are given parenthetically, as at **fall** *verb*:

Idioms: take a fall (*or* header *or* plunge *or* spill *or* tumble).

When variation exists between a verb and a two-word verb, the variation is shown parenthetically. For example, *run (around)* means that one can use either *run* or *run around* to mean "to be with as a companion."

HOMOGRAPHS

A homograph is a word that is spelled the same as another word but that differs in meaning and origin. Homographs are signaled by superscript numerals following the words to which they refer. Homograph numbers are used in main entries, synonym lists, and cross-references:

fell^{1} *verb*
1. To bring down, as with a saw or ax.
fell^{2} *adjective*
Showing or suggesting a disposition to be violently destructive without scruple or restraint.
fell^{3} *noun*
The skin of an animal : fur, hide^{2}.

In the synonym lists at **cut, fierce,** and **hide**^{2} the synonyms are styled as *fell*^{1}, *fell*^{2}, and *fell*[3], respectively. Notice also that *hide*[2] in the synonym list contains the proper homograph number for that main entry.

LABELS

All words requiring labels have been clearly tagged in synonym lists and in main and subentries. The kinds of labels used in this book are temporal labels (*Archiac, Obsolete*), usage labels (*Informal* and *Slang*), dialect labels (such as *Regional* and *Chiefly Regional*), and field labels (such as *Law*).

The label *Archaic* is used with words that were once common but are now rare. For example, *fright*, meaning "to fill with fear," is an archaic synonym of *frighten* and is labeled as such. *Obsolete* indicates that a term is no longer in active use, except, for example, in literary quotation. *Roget's II* contains very few archaic and obsolete terms.

Usage labels such as *Informal* and *Slang* indicate various levels of usage and styles of expression that may or may not be appropriate in all contexts or situations. *Informal* generally applies to those words that are commonly used in the spoken language and in ordinary writing but that might not be considered appropriate in very formal or official contexts or circumstances. The word *thick*, for example, carries an *Informal* label in the synonym list at **friendly**. *Slang*, on the other hand, is a style of language characteristic of very casual speech. Slang comprises words and special senses of words denoting things in an exceptionally vivid, humorous, irreverent, or sarcastic manner. For example, in the synonym list at **friendly** the word *tight* is labeled *Slang*.

Dialect labels such as *Regional* and *Chiefly Regional* indicate that a term is indigenous to a particular geographic area. For example, the word *afeard*, a synonym of *afraid*, is used by speakers only in a limited part of the United States. Hence it carries the label *Regional*. The word *mighty*, meaning "very," is labeled *Chiefly Regional* because it is used chiefly but not exclusively in the southern part of this country.

Language labels such as *British* distinguish between British English and American English. Examples of words that carry British labels include: *bobby* (*British*), a synonym at **policeman**; and *bonny* (*Scots*), a synonym at **beautiful**.

Some synonyms are labeled according to the fields of knowledge with which they are primarily associated. An example is the sense of **competence** meaning "conferred power" — a sense carrying the label *Law*.

Part-of-speech labels appear in italics at all boldface entries and subentries.

CATEGORY INDEX

The Category Index beginning on page 1155 is designed to provide the maximum number of word choices for the user. Each synonym group ends with one or more cross-references of the type *See* HAPPY. The word in small capital letters is a main entry in the Category Index. At the main entry word in the Index — in this instance *happy* — there appears a list of Thesaurus entries that are related to the synonym group with the cross-reference HAPPY.

HAPPY
unhappy

happy
noun
delight
elation
exultation
fulfillment
happiness
heaven
. . . .

unhappy
noun
complaint
disappointment
distress
gloom
grief
grouch
misery
mutter

This list contains words having related meanings or words of opposite meaning. Looking these words up in the Thesaurus proper offers the user many more word choices. This Index is especially helpful when the word sought for is only vaguely known. For a fuller explanation of the Category Index, see pp. 1153–1154.

A-1 *adjective* See **A-one.**

aback *adverb*

Without adequate preparation : short, unawarely, unawares. ***Idiom:*** by surprise. *See* PREPARED.

abandon *verb*

1. To give up or leave without intending to return or claim again : desert[3], forsake, leave[1], quit, throw over. ***Idioms:*** run out on, walk out on. *See* KEEP. **2.** To give up a possession, claim, or right : abdicate, cede, demit, forswear, hand over, quitclaim, relinquish, render, renounce, resign, surrender, waive, yield. *See* KEEP. **3.** To let (something) go : cede, forgo, lay down, relinquish, surrender, yield. *See* KEEP. **4.** To cease trying to accomplish or continue : break off, desist, discontinue, give up, leave off, quit, relinquish, remit, stop. *Informal:* swear off. *Slang:* lay off. ***Idioms:*** call it a day, call it quits, hang up one's fiddle, have done with, throw in the towel. *See* CONTINUE. **5.** To yield (oneself) unrestrainedly, as to a particular impulse : give over, give up, surrender. *See* RESIST.

abandon *noun* **1.** A complete surrender of inhibitions : abandonment, incontinence, unrestraint, wantonness, wildness. *See* RESTRAINT. **2.** A careless, often reckless disregard for consequences : carelessness, heedlessness, thoughtlessness. *See* CAREFUL.

abandoned *adjective*

1. Having been given up and left alone : bereft, derelict, deserted, desolate, forlorn, forsaken, lorn. *See* KEEP. **2.** Lacking in moral restraint : dissipated, dissolute, fast, gay, incontinent, licentious, profligate, rakish, unbridled, unconstrained, uncontrolled, ungoverned, uninhibited, unrestrained, wanton, wild. *See* RESTRAINT.

abandonment *noun*

1. The act of forsaking : desertion. *See* KEEP. **2.** A giving up of a possession, claim, or right : abdication, demission, quitclaim, relinquishment, renunciation, resignation, surrender, waiver. *See* KEEP. **3.** A complete surrender of inhibitions : abandon, incontinence, unrestraint, wantonness, wildness. *See* RESTRAINT.

abase *verb*

To deprive of esteem, self-worth, or effectiveness : degrade, demean[2], humble, humiliate, mortify. ***Idioms:*** bring low, take down a peg. *See* RESPECT, WIN.

abasement *noun*

A lowering in or deprivation of character or self-esteem : debasement, degradation, humiliation, mortification. *See* RESPECT, WIN.

abash *verb*

To cause (a person) to be self-consciously distressed : chagrin, confound, confuse, discomfit, discomfort, disconcert, discountenance, embarrass, faze, mortify. ***Idioms:*** put on the spot, throw for a loop. *See* PAIN.

abashment *noun*

Self-conscious distress : chagrin, confusion, discomfiture, discomposure, embarrassment. *See* PAIN.

abate *verb*

1. To grow or cause to grow gradually less : decrease, diminish, drain, dwindle, ebb, lessen, let up, peter (out), rebate, reduce, tail away (*or* off), taper (off). *See* INCREASE. **2.** To become or cause to become less active or intense : bate, die (away, down, off, *or* out), ease (off *or* up), ebb, fall, fall off, lapse, let up, moderate, remit, slacken, slack off, subside, wane. *See* INCREASE. **3.** To take away (a quantity) from another quantity : deduct, discount, rebate, subtract, take (off). *Informal:* knock off. *See* INCREASE.

abatement *noun*

1. The act or process of decreasing : curtailment, cut, cutback, decrease, decrement, diminishment, diminution, drain, reduction, slash, slowdown, taper. *See* INCREASE. **2.** The act or process of becoming less active or intense : ebb, letup, remission, slackening, subsidence, wane. *See* INCREASE. **3.** An amount deducted : deduction, discount, rebate, reduction. *See* INCREASE.

abbreviate *verb*
To make short or shorter the duration or extent of : abridge, condense, curtail, reduce, shorten. *See* INCREASE, LONG.

abdicate *verb*
To give up a possession, claim, or right : abandon, cede, demit, forswear, hand over, quitclaim, relinquish, render, renounce, resign, surrender, waive, yield. *See* KEEP.

abdication *noun*
A giving up of a possession, claim, or right : abandonment, demission, quitclaim, relinquishment, renunciation, resignation, surrender, waiver. *See* KEEP.

abduct *verb*
To seize and detain (a person) unlawfully : kidnap, snatch, spirit away. *See* CRIMES, FREE.

abecedarian *noun*
One who is just starting to learn or do something : beginner, fledgling, freshman, greenhorn, initiate, neophyte, novice, novitiate, tenderfoot, tyro. *Slang:* rookie. *See* START.

aberrance *noun*
The condition of being abnormal : aberrancy, aberration, abnormality, anomaly, deviance, deviancy, deviation, irregularity, preternaturalness, unnaturalness. *See* GOOD, USUAL.

aberrancy *noun*
The condition of being abnormal : aberrance, aberration, abnormality, anomaly, deviance, deviancy, deviation, irregularity, preternaturalness, unnaturalness. *See* GOOD, USUAL.

aberrant *adjective*
1. Straying from a proper course or standard : errant. *See* CORRECT. **2.** Departing from the normal : abnormal, anomalistic, anomalous, atypic, atypical, deviant, divergent, irregular, preternatural, unnatural. *See* GOOD, USUAL.

aberration *noun*
1. A departing from what is prescribed : departure, deviation, divergence, divergency, diversion. *See* APPROACH, CORRECT. **2.** The condition of being abnormal : aberrance, aberrancy, abnormality, anomaly, deviance, deviancy, deviation, irregularity, preternaturalness, unnaturalness. *See* GOOD, USUAL. **3.** *Psychology.* Serious mental illness or disorder impairing a person's capacity to function normally and safely : brainsickness, craziness, dementia, derangement, disturbance, insaneness, insanity, lunacy, madness, mental illness, psychopathy, unbalance. *Psychiatry:* mania. *Psychology:* alienation. *See* SANE.

abet *verb*
To give support or assistance : aid, assist, boost, help (out), relieve, succor. ***Idioms:*** give (*or* lend) a hand, give a leg up. *See* HELP.

abetment *noun*
The act or an instance of helping : aid, assist, assistance, hand, help, relief, succor, support. *See* HELP.

abetter *noun* See **abettor.**

abettor or **abetter** *noun*
A person who helps : aid, attendant, help, helper, reliever, succorer. *See* HELP.

abeyance *noun*
The condition of being temporarily inactive : abeyancy, dormancy, intermission, latency, quiescence, suspension. *See* ACTION.

abeyancy *noun*
The condition of being temporarily inactive : abeyance, dormancy, intermission, latency, quiescence, suspension. *See* ACTION.

abeyant *adjective*
Existing in a temporarily inactive form or state : dormant, inactive, latent, quiescent, sleeping. *See* ACTION, SHOW.

abhor *verb*
To regard with extreme dislike and hostility : abominate, despise, detest, execrate, hate, loathe. *See* LOVE.

abhorrence *noun*
1. An object of extreme dislike : abomination, anathema, aversion, bête noire, bugbear, detestation, execration, hate. *Informal:* horror. *See* LOVE. **2.** Extreme hostility and dislike : abomination, antipathy, aversion, detestation, hate, hatred, horror, loathing, repellence, repellency, repugnance, repugnancy, repulsion, revulsion. *See* LOVE.

abhorrent *adjective*
So objectionable as to elicit despisal or deserve condemnation : abominable, antipathetic, contemptible, despicable, despisable, detestable, disgusting, filthy, foul, infamous, loathsome, lousy, low, mean[2], nasty, nefarious, obnoxious, odious, repugnant, rotten, shabby, vile, wretched. *See* GOOD.

abide *verb*
1. To put up with : accept, bear, brook[2], endure, go, stand (for), stomach, suffer, support, sustain, swallow, take, tolerate, withstand. *Informal:* lump[2]. ***Idioms:*** take it, take it lying down. *See* ACCEPT. **2.** To continue to be in a place : bide, linger, remain, stay[1], tarry, wait. *Informal:* stick around. ***Idiom:*** stay put. *See* CONTINUE. **3.** To stop temporarily and remain, as if reluctant to leave : bide, linger, pause, stay[1], tarry, wait. *See* CONTINUE. **4.** To be in

existence or in a certain state for an indefinitely long time : continue, endure, go on, hold out, last[2], persist, remain, stay[1]. *See* CONTINUE.
5. To have as one's domicile, usually for an extended period : domicile, dwell, house, live[1], reside. *See* PLACE.
abide by *verb* To act in conformity with : adhere, carry out, comply, conform, follow, keep, mind, obey, observe. ***Idiom:*** toe the line (*or* mark). *See* ACCEPT, SAME.

abide by *verb* See **abide.**

abiding *adjective*
Existing or remaining in the same state for an indefinitely long time : continuing, durable, enduring, lasting, long-lasting, long-lived, longstanding, old, perdurable, perennial, permanent, persistent. *See* CONTINUE.

ability *noun*
1. Physical, mental, financial, or legal power to perform : capability, capacity, competence, competency, faculty, might. *See* ABILITY.
2. Natural or acquired facility in a specific activity : adeptness, art, command, craft, expertise, expertness, knack, mastery, proficiency, skill, technique. *Informal:* know-how. *See* ABILITY, KNOWLEDGE.

abjuration *noun*
A formal statement of disavowal : palinode, recantation, retractation, retraction, withdrawal. *See* ACCEPT.

abjure *verb*
To disavow (something previously written or said) irrevocably and usually formally : recall, recant, retract, take back, withdraw. *See* ACCEPT.

ablaze *adjective*
On fire : afire, aflame, alight[2], burning, conflagrant, fiery, flaming. ***Idioms:*** in a blaze, in flames. *See* HOT.

able *adjective*
Having the ability to perform well : capable, competent, good, skilled, skillful. *See* ABILITY.

able-bodied *adjective*
Full of vigor : iron, lusty, red-blooded, robust, strapping, sturdy, vigorous, vital. *See* STRONG.

abnormal *adjective*
Departing from the normal : aberrant, anomalistic, anomalous, atypic, atypical, deviant, divergent, irregular, preternatural, unnatural. *See* GOOD, USUAL.

abnormality *noun*
The condition of being abnormal : aberrance, aberrancy, aberration, anomaly, deviance, deviancy, deviation, irregularity, preternaturalness, unnaturalness. *See* GOOD, USUAL.

abode *noun*
A building or shelter where one lives : domicile, dwelling, habitation, home, house, lodging (often used in plural), place, residence. *Chiefly British:* dig (used in plural). *See* PROTECTION.

abolish *verb*
1. To put an end to, especially formally and with authority : abrogate, annihilate, annul, cancel, invalidate, negate, nullify, set aside, vitiate, void. *Law:* extinguish. *See* CONTINUE.
2. To destroy all traces of : annihilate, blot out, clear, eradicate, erase, exterminate, extinguish, extirpate, kill[1], liquidate, obliterate, remove, root[1] (out *or* up), rub out, snuff out, stamp out, uproot, wipe out. ***Idioms:*** do away with, make an end of, put an end to. *See* HELP, MAKE.

abolishment *noun*
An often formal act of putting an end to : abolition, abrogation, annihilation, annulment, cancellation, defeasance, invalidation, negation, nullification, voidance. *Law:* avoidance, extinguishment. *See* CONTINUE.

abolition *noun*
An often formal act of putting an end to : abolishment, abrogation, annihilation, annulment, cancellation, defeasance, invalidation, negation, nullification, voidance. *Law:* avoidance, extinguishment. *See* CONTINUE.

abominable *adjective*
So objectionable as to elicit despisal or deserve condemnation : abhorrent, antipathetic, contemptible, despicable, despisable, detestable, disgusting, filthy, foul, infamous, loathsome, lousy, low, mean[2], nasty, nefarious, obnoxious, odious, repugnant, rotten, shabby, vile, wretched. *See* GOOD.

abominate *verb*
To regard with extreme dislike and hostility : abhor, despise, detest, execrate, hate, loathe. *See* LOVE.

abomination *noun*
1. Extreme hostility and dislike : abhorrence, antipathy, aversion, detestation, hate, hatred, horror, loathing, repellence, repellency, repugnance, repugnancy, repulsion, revulsion. *See* LOVE. **2.** An object of extreme dislike : abhorrence, anathema, aversion, bête noire, bugbear, detestation, execration, hate. *Informal:* horror. *See* LOVE.

aboriginal *adjective*
Existing, born, or produced in a land or region : autochthonal, autochthonic, autochtho-

nous, endemic, indigenous, native. *See* NATIVE.

abort *verb*
To bring forth a nonviable fetus prematurely : miscarry, slip. *See* REPRODUCTION.

abound *verb*
To be abundantly filled or richly supplied : bristle, crawl, flow, overflow, pullulate, swarm, teem. *See* BIG, RICH.

about *adverb*
1. Near to in quantity or amount : almost, approximately, nearly, roughly. ***Idiom:*** on the order of. *See* NEAR. **2.** In or toward a former location or condition : around, back, backward, backwards, rearward, round. *See* APPROACH. **3.** Toward the back : around, back, backward, backwards, rearward. *See* PRECEDE.

about-face *verb*
To turn sharply around : double (back), reverse. *See* APPROACH.

abracadabra *noun*
1. Unintelligible or nonsensical talk or language : double talk, gibberish, gobbledygook, jabberwocky, mumbo jumbo. *See* CLEAR, WORDS. **2.** Esoteric, formulaic, and often incomprehensible speech relating to the occult : gibberish, hocus-pocus, mumbo jumbo. *See* CLEAR, SUPERNATURAL, WORDS.

abrade *verb*
To make (the skin) raw by or as if by friction : chafe, excoriate, fret, gall[2], irritate. *See* HELP.

abridge *verb*
To make short or shorter the duration or extent of : abbreviate, condense, curtail, reduce, shorten. *See* INCREASE, LONG.

abridgment *noun*
A short summary or version prepared by cutting down a larger work : abstract, brief, condensation, epitome, synopsis. *See* WORDS.

abrogate *verb*
To put an end to, especially formally and with authority : abolish, annihilate, annul, cancel, invalidate, negate, nullify, set aside, vitiate, void. *Law:* extinguish. *See* CONTINUE.

abrogation *noun*
An often formal act of putting an end to : abolishment, abolition, annihilation, annulment, cancellation, defeasance, invalidation, negation, nullification, voidance. *Law:* avoidance, extinguishment. *See* CONTINUE.

abrupt *adjective*
1. Happening quickly and without warning : hurried, precipitant, precipitate, sudden. *See* FAST, SURPRISE. **2.** Rudely unceremonious : blunt, brief, brusque, crusty, curt, gruff, short, short-spoken. *See* ATTITUDE. **3.** So sharply inclined as to be almost perpendicular : bold, precipitous, sheer[2], steep[1]. *See* HORIZONTAL.

abruptly *adverb*
Without any warning : short, suddenly. ***Idiom:*** all of a sudden. *See* FAST.

abscond *verb*
To break loose and leave suddenly, as from confinement or from a difficult or threatening situation : break out, decamp, escape, flee, fly, get away, run away. *Informal:* skip (out). *Slang:* lam. *Regional:* absquatulate. ***Idioms:*** cut and run, blow (*or* fly) the coop, give someone the slip, make a getaway, take flight, take it on the lam. *See* FREE.

absence *noun*
1. Failure to be present : nonattendance. *Law:* nonappearance. *See* ABSENCE. **2.** The condition of lacking a needed or usual amount : dearth, lack, want. *See* EXCESS.

absent *adjective*
1. Not present : away, gone, missing, wanting. *See* ABSENCE. **2.** Deficient in a usual or needed amount : lacking, wanting. *See* EXCESS. **3.** So lost in thought as to be unaware of one's surroundings : absent-minded, abstracted, bemused, distrait, faraway, inattentive, preoccupied. ***Idiom:*** a million miles away. *See* ABILITY, AWARENESS.

absent-minded *adjective*
So lost in thought as to be unaware of one's surroundings : absent, abstracted, bemused, distrait, faraway, inattentive, preoccupied. ***Idiom:*** a million miles away. *See* ABILITY, AWARENESS.

absent-mindedness *noun*
The condition of being so lost in solitary thought as to be unaware of one's surroundings : abstraction, bemusement, brown study, daydreaming, muse[2], reverie, study, trance. *See* AWARENESS.

absolute *adjective*
1. Supremely excellent in quality or nature : consummate, faultless, flawless, impeccable, indefectible, perfect, unflawed. *See* GOOD. **2.** Free from extraneous elements : perfect, plain, pure, sheer[2], simple, unadulterated, undiluted, unmixed. *See* CLEAN. **3.** Without limitations or mitigating conditions : unconditional, unconditioned, unqualified, unreserved. *See* LIMITED. **4.** Having no reservations : implicit, unconditional, undoubting, unfaltering, unhesitating, unquestioning, unreserved, wholehearted. *See* BIG, LIMITED. **5.** Completely such, without qualification or exception : all-out, arrant, complete, consummate, crashing,

damned, dead, downright, flat, out-and-out, outright, perfect, plain, pure, sheer², thorough, thoroughgoing, total, unbounded, unequivocal, unlimited, unmitigated, unqualified, unrelieved, unreserved, utter². *Informal:* flat-out, positive. *Chiefly British:* blooming. *See* BIG, LIMITED. **6.** Having and exercising complete political power and control : absolutistic, arbitrary, autarchic, autarchical, autocratic, autocratical, despotic, dictatorial, monocratic, totalitarian, tyrannic, tyrannical, tyrannous. *See* OVER, POLITICS.

absolutely *adverb*
1. Without question : certainly, doubtless, doubtlessly, positively, undoubtedly. *See* CERTAIN, LIMITED. **2.** To the fullest extent : all, altogether, completely, dead, entirely, flat, fully, just, perfectly, quite, thoroughly, totally, utterly, well², wholly. *Informal:* clean, clear. ***Idioms:*** in toto, through and through. *See* BIG, LIMITED. **3.** It is so; as you say or ask : agreed, all right, assuredly, aye, gladly, indubitably, roger, undoubtedly, unquestionably, willingly, yea, yes. *Informal:* OK, uh-huh, yeah, yep. *Slang:* right on. *See* AFFIRM.

absolution *noun*
The act or an instance of forgiving : amnesty, condonation, excuse, forgiveness, pardon, remission. *See* FORGIVENESS.

absolutism *noun*
1. A political doctrine advocating the principle of absolute rule : authoritarianism, autocracy, despotism, dictatorship, totalitarianism. *See* OVER, POLITICS. **2.** A government in which a single leader or party exercises absolute control over all citizens and every aspect of their lives : autarchy, autocracy, despotism, dictatorship, monocracy, tyranny. *See* OVER, POLITICS.

absolutistic *adjective*
Having and exercising complete political power and control : absolute, arbitrary, autarchic, autarchical, autocratic, autocratical, despotic, dictatorial, monocratic, totalitarian, tyrannic, tyrannical, tyrannous. *See* OVER, POLITICS.

absolve *verb*
1. To free from a charge or imputation of guilt : clear, exculpate, exonerate, vindicate. *Law:* acquit, purge. *See* LAW. **2.** To free from an obligation or duty : discharge, dispense, excuse, exempt, let off, relieve, spare. *See* FREE.

absorb *verb*
1. To take in (moisture or liquid) : drink, imbibe, soak (up), sop up, take up. *See* GIVE. **2.** To occupy the full attention of : consume, engross, immerse, monopolize, preoccupy. *See* AWARENESS, EXCITE. **3.** To take in and incorporate, especially mentally : assimilate, digest, imbibe, take up. *Informal:* soak (up). *See* ACCEPT.

absorbed *adjective*
Having one's thoughts fully occupied : deep, intent, preoccupied, rapt. ***Idiom:*** wrapped up in. *See* AWARENESS, EXCITE.

absorbent *adjective*
Having a capacity or tendency to absorb or soak up : absorptive, assimilative, bibulous. *See* DRY.

absorption *noun*
1. The process of absorbing and incorporating, especially mentally : assimilation, digestion. *See* ACCEPT. **2.** Total occupation of the attention or of the mind : engrossment, enthrallment, immersion, preoccupation, prepossession. *See* EXCITE.

absorptive *adjective*
Having a capacity or tendency to absorb or soak up : absorbent, assimilative, bibulous. *See* DRY.

absquatulate *verb*
Regional. To break loose and leave suddenly, as from confinement or from a difficult or threatening situation : abscond, break out, decamp, escape, flee, fly, get away, run away. *Informal:* skip (out). *Slang:* lam. ***Idioms:*** cut and run, blow (*or* fly) the coop, give someone the slip, make a getaway, take flight, take it on the lam. *See* FREE.

abstain *verb*
To hold oneself back : forbear, hold off, keep, refrain, withhold. *See* RESTRAINT.

abstemious *adjective*
Exercising moderation and self-restraint in appetites and behavior : continent, sober, temperate. *See* RESTRAINT.

abstinence *noun*
The practice of refraining from use of alcoholic liquors : dryness, soberness, sobriety, teetotalism, temperance. *See* DRUGS, RESTRAINT, USED.

abstract *adjective*
1. Existing only in concept and not in reality : hypothetic, hypothetical, ideal, theoretical, transcendent, transcendental. *See* REAL. **2.** Concerned primarily with theories rather than practical matters : academic, speculative, theoretical. *See* THOUGHTS.
abstract *noun* A short summary or version prepared by cutting down a larger work : abridgment, brief, condensation, epitome, synopsis. *See* WORDS.

abstract *verb* **1.** To remove from association with : detach, disassociate, disengage, dissociate, withdraw. *See* ASSEMBLE. **2.** To give a recapitulation of the salient facts of : epitomize, go over, recapitulate, review, run down, run through, summarize, sum up, synopsize, wrap up. *Informal:* recap. *See* THOUGHTS.

abstracted *adjective*
So lost in thought as to be unaware of one's surroundings : absent, absent-minded, bemused, distrait, faraway, inattentive, preoccupied. ***Idiom:*** a million miles away. *See* ABILITY, AWARENESS.

abstraction *noun*
The condition of being so lost in solitary thought as to be unaware of one's surroundings : absent-mindedness, bemusement, brown study, daydreaming, muse[2], reverie, study, trance. *See* AWARENESS.

abstruse *adjective*
Beyond the understanding of an average mind : deep, esoteric, profound, recondite. *Slang:* heavy. *See* EASY, SURFACE.

absurd *adjective*
So senseless as to be laughable : foolish, harebrained, idiotic, imbecilic, insane, lunatic, mad, moronic, nonsensical, preposterous, silly, soft-headed, tomfool, unearthly, zany. *Informal:* cockeyed, crazy, loony, loopy. *Slang:* balmy[2], dippy, dopey, jerky, sappy, wacky. *See* ABILITY, KNOWLEDGE.

absurdity *noun*
1. Something or someone uproariously funny or absurd : *Informal:* hoot, joke, laugh, scream. *Slang:* gas, howl, panic, riot. ***Idiom:*** a laugh a minute. *See* LAUGHTER. **2.** Foolish behavior : folly, foolery, foolishness, idiocy, imbecility, insanity, lunacy, madness, nonsense, preposterousness, senselessness, silliness, tomfoolery, zaniness. *Informal:* craziness. *See* ABILITY.

abundance *noun*
1. A great deal : mass, mountain, much, plenty, profusion, wealth, world. *Informal:* barrel, heap, lot, pack, peck[2], pile. *Regional:* power, sight. *See* BIG. **2.** Prosperity and a sufficiency of life's necessities : bounteousness, bountifulness, plenitude, plenteousness, plenty. *See* RICH.

abundant *adjective*
Characterized by abundance : ample, bounteous, bountiful, copious, generous, heavy, plenitudinous, plenteous, plentiful, substantial, voluminous. *See* BIG, GIVE, RICH.

abuse *verb*
1. To use wrongly and improperly : misapply, misappropriate, mishandle, misuse, pervert. *See* TREAT WELL. **2.** To take advantage of unfairly : exploit, impose, presume, use. *See* TREAT WELL. **3.** To hurt or injure by maltreatment : ill-treat, ill-use, maltreat, mishandle, mistreat, misuse. *See* HELP. **4.** To attack with harsh, often insulting language : assail, rail against (*or* at), revile, vituperate. *See* PRAISE.

abuse *noun* **1.** Wrong, often corrupt use : misapplication, misappropriation, mishandling, misuse, perversion. *See* TREAT WELL. **2.** Physically harmful treatment : ill-treatment, maltreatment, mishandling, mistreatment, misusage. *See* HELP. **3.** Harsh, often insulting language : billingsgate, contumely, invective, obloquy, railing, revilement, reviling, scurrility, scurrilousness, vituperation. *See* PRAISE.

abusive *adjective*
Of, relating to, or characterized by verbal abuse : contumelious, invective, opprobrious, scurrilous, vituperative. *See* ATTACK, ATTITUDE.

abut *verb*
To be contiguous or next to : adjoin, border, bound[2], butt[2], join, meet[1], neighbor, touch, verge. *See* NEAR.

abysm *noun*
Something of immeasurable and vast extent : abyss, chasm, deep, depth (often used in plural), gulf. *See* HIGH.

abysmal *adjective*
1. Extending far downward or inward from a surface : deep, profound. *See* SURFACE.
2. Open wide : abyssal, cavernous, gaping, yawning. *See* WIDE.

abyss *noun*
Something of immeasurable and vast extent : abysm, chasm, deep, depth (often used in plural), gulf. *See* HIGH.

abyssal *adjective*
Open wide : abysmal, cavernous, gaping, yawning. *See* WIDE.

academic *adjective*
1. Characterized by a narrow concern for book learning and formal rules, without knowledge or experience of practical matters : bookish, donnish, formalistic, inkhorn, literary, pedantic, pedantical, scholastic. *See* ATTITUDE, FLEXIBLE, TEACH. **2.** Concerned primarily with theories rather than practical matters : abstract, speculative, theoretical. *See* THOUGHTS.

accede *verb*
To respond affirmatively; receive with agreement or compliance : accept, acquiesce, agree,

assent, consent, nod, subscribe, yes. *See* AGREE.

accelerate *verb*
To increase the speed of : expedite, hasten, hurry, hustle, quicken, speed (up), step up. *See* FAST.

accent *noun*
1. A particular vocal quality that indicates some emotion or feeling : inflection, intonation, tone. ***Idiom:*** tone of voice. *See* SOUNDS. **2.** Special weight placed upon something considered important : accentuation, emphasis, stress. *See* IMPORTANT.
accent *verb* To accord emphasis to : accentuate, emphasize, feature, highlight, italicize, play up, point up, stress, underline, underscore. *See* IMPORTANT.

accentuate *verb*
To accord emphasis to : accent, emphasize, feature, highlight, italicize, play up, point up, stress, underline, underscore. *See* IMPORTANT.

accentuation *noun*
Special weight placed upon something considered important : accent, emphasis, stress. *See* IMPORTANT.

accept *verb*
1. To receive (something given or offered) willingly and gladly : embrace, take (up), welcome. *See* ACCEPT. **2.** To admit to one's possession, presence, or awareness : have, receive, take. *See* ACCEPT. **3.** To allow admittance, as to a group : admit, receive, take in. *See* ACCEPT. **4.** To regard (something) as true or real : believe. *Slang:* buy, swallow. *See* OPINION. **5.** To perceive and recognize the meaning of : apprehend, catch (on), compass, comprehend, conceive, fathom, follow, get, grasp, make out, read, see, sense, take, take in, understand. *Informal:* savvy. *Slang:* dig. *Chiefly British:* twig. *Scots:* ken. ***Idioms:*** get (*or* have) a handle on, get the picture. *See* UNDERSTAND. **6.** To put up with : abide, bear, brook[2], endure, go, stand (for), stomach, suffer, support, sustain, swallow, take, tolerate, withstand. *Informal:* lump[2]. ***Idioms:*** take it, take it lying down. *See* ACCEPT. **7.** To respond affirmatively; receive with agreement or compliance : accede, acquiesce, agree, assent, consent, nod, subscribe, yes. *See* AGREE.

acceptable *adjective*
1. Capable of being accepted : admissible, unobjectionable. *See* ACCEPT. **2.** Of moderately good quality but less than excellent : adequate, all right, average, common, decent, fair, fairish, goodish, moderate, passable, respectable, satisfactory, sufficient, tolerable. *Informal:* OK, tidy. *See* GOOD.

acceptance *noun*
1. The act or process of accepting : acquiescence, agreement, assent, consent, nod, yes. *Informal:* OK. *See* ACCEPT. **2.** Favorable regard : approbation, approval, favor. *See* ACCEPT, PRAISE.

acceptant *adjective*
Ready and willing to receive favorably, as new ideas : amenable, open, open-minded, receptive, responsive. *See* ACCEPT.

acceptation *noun*
That which is signified by a word or expression : connotation, denotation, import, intent, meaning, message, purport, sense, significance, significancy, signification, value. *See* MEANING.

accepted *adjective*
Generally approved or agreed upon : conventional, orthodox, received, recognized, sanctioned. *See* ACCEPT, AGREE, STRAIGHT, USUAL.

access *noun*
1. The right to enter or make use of : admission, admittance, entrance[1], entrée, entry, ingress. *See* ENTER. **2.** A sudden violent expression, as of emotion : blowup, burst, eruption, explosion, fit[2], flare-up, gust, outbreak, outburst. *See* EXPLOSION. **3.** A sudden and often acute manifestation of a disease : attack, fit[2], seizure. *Informal:* spell[3]. *See* HEALTH.

accessible *adjective*
1. Being within easy reach : convenient, handy, nearby. ***Idioms:*** close (*or* near) at hand, close by. *See* NEAR. **2.** Available for use : employable, open, operable, operative, practicable, usable, utilizable. *See* POSSIBLE. **3.** Easily approached : approachable, responsive, welcoming. *See* APPROACH, ATTITUDE.

accession *noun*
Something tending to augment something else : addition, acquisition, augmentation. *See* INCREASE.

accessory *noun*
1. A subordinate element added to another entity : adjunct, appendage, appurtenance, attachment, supplement. *See* INCREASE. **2.** One who assists a lawbreaker in a wrongful or criminal act : accomplice, confederate, conspirator. *See* CRIMES, HELP.
accessory *adjective* Giving or able to give help or support : ancillary, assistant, auxiliary, collateral, contributory, subsidiary, supportive. *See* HELP.

accident *noun*
1. An unexpected and usually undesirable event : casualty, contretemps, misadventure, mischance, misfortune, mishap. *See* HELP, SURPRISE. **2.** An unexpected random event : chance, fluke, fortuity, hap, happenchance, happenstance, hazard. *See* CERTAIN, SURPRISE.

accidental *adjective*
Occurring unexpectedly : casual, chance, contingent, fluky, fortuitous, inadvertent, odd. *See* SURPRISE.

acclaim *verb*
1. To express warm approval of : applaud, commend, compliment, laud, praise. *See* PRAISE. **2.** To pay tribute or homage to : celebrate, eulogize, exalt, extol, glorify, hail[2], honor, laud, magnify, panegyrize, praise. ***Idiom:*** sing someone's praises. *See* PRAISE.
acclaim *noun* An expression of warm approval : acclamation, applause, celebration, commendation, compliment, encomium, eulogy, kudos, laudation, panegyric, plaudit, praise. *See* PRAISE.

acclamation *noun*
An expression of warm approval : acclaim, applause, celebration, commendation, compliment, encomium, eulogy, kudos, laudation, panegyric, plaudit, praise. *See* PRAISE.

acclamatory *adjective*
Serving to compliment : approbatory, commendatory, complimentary, congratulatory, laudatory. *See* PRAISE.

acclimate *verb*
1. To make or become suitable to a particular situation or use : acclimatize, accommodate, adapt, adjust, conform, fashion, fit[1], reconcile, square, suit, tailor. *See* CHANGE. **2.** To make resistant to hardship, especially through continued exposure : acclimatize, caseharden, harden, indurate, season, toughen. *See* CONTINUE, RESIST.

acclimation *noun*
Adjustment to a changing environment : acclimatization. *Biology:* adaptation. *See* CHANGE.

acclimatization *noun*
Adjustment to a changing environment : acclimation. *Biology:* adaptation. *See* CHANGE.

acclimatize *verb*
1. To make or become suitable to a particular situation or use : acclimate, accommodate, adapt, adjust, conform, fashion, fit[1], reconcile, square, suit, tailor. *See* CHANGE. **2.** To make resistant to hardship, especially through continued exposure : acclimate, caseharden, harden, indurate, season, toughen. *See* CONTINUE, RESIST.

acclivity *noun*
An upward slope : ascent, rise. *See* RISE.

accolade *noun*
1. Recognition of achievement or superiority or a sign of this : distinction, honor, kudos, laurel (often used in plural). *See* RESPECT. **2.** Something given in return for a service or accomplishment : award, guerdon, honorarium, plum, premium, prize[1], reward. ***Idiom:*** token of appreciation (*or* esteem). *See* REWARD. **3.** A memento received as a symbol of excellence or victory : award, prize[1], trophy. *See* RESPECT.

accommodate *verb*
1. To perform a service or a courteous act for : favor, oblige. *See* HELP. **2.** To provide with often temporary lodging : bed (down), berth, bestow, billet, board, bunk[1], domicile, harbor, house, lodge, put up, quarter, room. *See* PROTECTION. **3.** To have the room or capacity for : contain, hold. *See* FULL. **4.** To make or become suitable to a particular situation or use : acclimate, acclimatize, adapt, adjust, conform, fashion, fit[1], reconcile, square, suit, tailor. *See* CHANGE. **5.** To bring into accord : attune, conform, coordinate, harmonize, integrate, proportion, reconcile, tune. *See* AGREE.

accommodating *adjective*
Ready to do favors for another : agreeable, complaisant, indulgent, obliging. *See* HELP, WILLING.

accommodation *noun*
1. The act of making suitable to an end or the condition of being made suitable to an end : adaptation, adaption, adjustment, conformation. *See* CHANGE. **2.** A settlement of differences through mutual concession : arrangement, compromise, give-and-take, medium, settlement. *Law:* composition. *See* AGREE.

accompaniment *noun*
1. One that accompanies another : associate, attendant, companion, concomitant. *See* ACCOMPANIED. **2.** Something added to another for embellishment or completion : complement, enhancement, enrichment. *See* ACCOMPANIED.

accompany *verb*
To be with or go with (another) : attend, companion, company, escort. *Obsolete:* consort. ***Idiom:*** go hand in hand with. *See* ACCOMPANIED.

accompanying *adjective*
Occurring or existing with : attendant, attend-

ing, coincident, concomitant, concurrent. *See* ACCOMPANIED.

accomplice *noun*
One who assists a lawbreaker in a wrongful or criminal act : accessory, confederate, conspirator. *See* CRIMES, HELP.

accomplish *verb*
To succeed in doing : achieve, attain, gain, reach, realize. *Slang:* score. *See* DO.

accomplished *adjective*
Proficient as a result of practice and study : finished, practiced. *See* ABILITY.

accomplishment *noun*
Something completed or attained successfully : achievement, acquirement, acquisition, attainment, effort, feat. *See* DO.

accord *verb*
1. To come to an understanding or to terms : agree, coincide, concur, get together, harmonize. *See* AGREE. **2.** To be compatible or in correspondence : agree, check, chime, comport with, conform, consist, correspond, fit[1], harmonize, match, square, tally. *Informal:* jibe[1]. *Archaic:* quadrate. *See* AGREE. **3.** To let have as a favor, prerogative, or privilege : award, concede, give, grant, vouchsafe. *See* GIVE. **4.** To give formally or officially : award, bestow, confer, grant, present[2]. *See* GIVE.

accord *noun* **1.** Harmonious mutual understanding : agreement, concord, concordance, concurrence, consonance, harmony, rapport, tune, unity. *Idiom:* meeting of the minds. *See* AGREE. **2.** Pleasing agreement, as of musical sounds : concert, concord, harmony, symphony, tune. *Music:* consonance. *See* BEAUTIFUL. **3.** An act or state of agreeing between parties regarding a course of action : agreement, arrangement, bargain, compact[2], deal, pact, understanding. *See* AGREE. **4.** A formal, usually written settlement between nations : agreement, concord, convention, pact, treaty. *See* AGREE, POLITICS.

accordance *noun*
1. The act or state of agreeing or conforming : agreement, chime, conformance, conformation, conformity, congruence, congruity, correspondence, harmonization, harmony, keeping. *See* AGREE. **2.** The act of conferring, as of an honor : bestowal, bestowment, conference, conferment, conferral, grant, presentation. *See* GIVE.

accordant *adjective*
In keeping with one's needs or expectations : agreeable, compatible, conformable, congenial, congruous, consistent, consonant, correspondent, corresponding, harmonious. *See* AGREE.

accost *verb*
1. To approach for the purpose of speech : greet, hail[2], salute. *See* APPROACH, GREETING, SEEK. **2.** To meet face-to-face, especially defiantly : confront, encounter, face, front. *See* MEET.

accouchement *noun*
The act or process of bringing forth young : birth, birthing, childbearing, childbirth, delivery, labor, lying-in, parturition, travail. *See* START.

account *noun*
1. A recounting of past events : chronicle, description, history, narration, narrative, report, statement, story, version. *See* WORDS. **2.** A statement of causes or motives : explanation, justification, rationale, rationalization, reason. *See* EXPLAIN. **3.** A precise list of fees or charges : bill[1], check, invoice, reckoning, statement. *Informal:* tab. *See* PAY. **4.** A feeling of deference, approval, and liking : admiration, appreciation, consideration, esteem, estimation, favor, honor, regard, respect. *See* RESPECT. **5.** A measure of those qualities that determine merit, desirability, usefulness, or importance : valuation, value, worth. *See* VALUE. **6.** The quality of being suitable or adaptable to an end : advantage, avail, benefit, profit, use, usefulness, utility. *See* USED.

account *verb* To look upon in a particular way : consider, deem, esteem, reckon, regard, see, view. *See* PERSPECTIVE.

account for *verb* To offer reasons for or a cause of : explain, justify, rationalize. *See* EXPLAIN.

accountable *adjective*
1. Legally obligated : amenable, answerable, liable, responsible. *See* LAW. **2.** Capable of being explained or accounted for : decipherable, explainable, explicable, illustratable, interpretable. *See* EXPLAIN.

account for *verb* See **account.**

accouter or **accoutre** *verb*
To supply what is needed for some activity or purpose : appoint, equip, fit[1], fit out (*or* up), furnish, gear, outfit, rig, turn out. *See* GIVE.

accouterment or **accoutrement** *noun*
Things needed for a task, journey, or other purpose. Often used in plural : apparatus, equipment, gear, material (used in plural), materiel, outfit, paraphernalia, rig, tackle, thing (used in plural), turnout. *See* MEANS.

accoutre *verb* See **accouter.**

accoutrement *noun* See **accouterment.**

accredit *verb*
1. To regard as belonging to or resulting from another : ascribe, assign, attribute, charge, credit, impute, lay[1], refer. *See* GIVE. **2.** To give authority to : authorize, commission, empower, enable, entitle, license, qualify. *See* ALLOW.

accretion *noun*
The result or product of building up : buildup, development, enlargement, multiplication, proliferation. *See* INCREASE.

accrue *verb*
To bring together so as to increase in mass or number : accumulate, agglomerate, aggregate, amass, collect[1], cumulate, garner, gather, hive, pile up, roll up. *See* COLLECT.

acculturate *verb*
To fit for companionship with others, especially in attitude or manners : civilize, humanize, socialize. *See* TEACH.

accumulate *verb*
To bring together so as to increase in mass or number : accrue, agglomerate, aggregate, amass, collect[1], cumulate, garner, gather, hive, pile up, roll up. *See* COLLECT.

accumulation *noun*
A quantity accumulated : aggregation, amassment, assemblage, collection, congeries, cumulation, gathering, mass. *See* COLLECT.

accumulative *adjective*
Increasing, as in force, by successive additions : additive, cumulative. *See* INCREASE.

accuracy *noun*
1. Correspondence with fact or truth : correctness, exactitude, exactness, fidelity, truth, veraciousness, veracity, veridicality, verity. *See* TRUE. **2.** Freedom from error : accurateness, correctness, exactitude, exactness, preciseness, precision, rightness. *See* CORRECT.

accurate *adjective*
1. Conforming to fact : correct, exact, faithful, precise, right, rigorous, true, veracious, veridical. *See* CORRECT, HONEST, REAL, TRUE.
2. Having no errors : correct, errorless, exact, precise, right, rigorous. *See* CORRECT, TRUE.

accurateness *noun*
Freedom from error : accuracy, correctness, exactitude, exactness, preciseness, precision, rightness. *See* CORRECT.

accursed *adjective*
So annoying or detestable as to deserve condemnation : blasted, blessed, bloody, confounded, cursed, damn, darn, execrable, infernal. *Informal:* blamed, damned. *Chiefly British:* blooming, ruddy. *See* LIKE.

accusation *noun*
A charging of someone with a misdeed : charge, denouncement, denunciation, imputation, incrimination. *Law:* indictment. *See* ATTACK, LAW, PRAISE.

accusatorial *adjective*
Containing, relating to, or involving an accusation : accusatory, denunciative, denunciatory. *See* ATTACK, ATTITUDE, PRAISE.

accusatory *adjective*
Containing, relating to, or involving an accusation : accusatorial, denunciative, denunciatory. *See* ATTACK, ATTITUDE, PRAISE.

accuse *verb*
To make an accusation against : arraign, charge, denounce, incriminate, indict, tax. *See* ATTACK, LAW, PRAISE.

accused *noun*
Law. A person against whom an action is brought : *Law:* defendant, respondent. *See* LAW.

accuser *noun*
1. One that accuses : denouncer, indicter. *See* ATTACK, LAW, PRAISE. **2.** One that makes a formal complaint, especially in court : claimant, complainant, plaintiff. *See* LAW.

accustom *verb*
To make familiar through constant practice or use : condition, habituate, inure, wont. *See* USUAL.

accustomed *adjective*
1. Commonly practiced or used : customary, habitual, regular, usual, wonted. *See* USUAL.
2. Familiar through repetition : chronic, habitual, routine. *See* USUAL. **3.** In the habit : habituated, used, wont. *See* USUAL.

ace *noun*
A person with a high degree of knowledge or skill in a particular field : adept, authority, dab hand, expert, master, past master, professional, proficient, wizard. *Informal:* whiz. *Slang:* crackerjack. *Chiefly British:* dab[2]. *See* ABILITY.

ace *adjective* Exceptionally good of its kind : banner, blue-ribbon, brag, capital, champion, excellent, fine[1], first-class, first-rate, prime, quality, splendid, superb, superior, terrific, tiptop, top. *Informal:* A-one, bully, dandy, great, swell, topflight, topnotch. *Slang:* boss. *Chiefly British:* tophole. *See* GOOD.

ace *verb Slang.* To win a victory over, as in battle or a competition : beat, best, conquer, defeat, master, overcome, prevail against (*or* over), rout, subdue, subjugate, surmount, triumph over, vanquish, worst. *Informal:* trim, whip. *Slang:* lick. ***Idioms:*** carry (*or* win) the day, get (*or* have) the best of, get (*or* have) the better of, go someone one better. *See* WIN.

acerb *adjective*
Having a taste characteristic of that produced by acids : acerbic, acetous, acid, acidulous, dry, sour, tangy, tart[1]. *See* TASTE.

acerbic *adjective*
1. Having a noticeably sharp pungent taste or smell : acrid, bitter, harsh, sour. *See* TASTE. **2.** Having a taste characteristic of that produced by acids : acerb, acetous, acid, acidulous, dry, sour, tangy, tart[1]. *See* TASTE. **3.** So sharp as to cause mental pain : acid, acidic, acrid, astringent, biting, caustic, corrosive, cutting, mordacious, mordant, pungent, scathing, sharp, slashing, stinging, trenchant, truculent, vitriolic. *See* ATTACK, RESPECT.

acerbity *noun*
Irony or bitterness, as of tone : acidity, acridity, causticity, corrosiveness, mordacity, mordancy, sarcasm, trenchancy. *See* LAUGHTER, RESPECT.

acetous *adjective*
Having a taste characteristic of that produced by acids : acerb, acerbic, acid, acidulous, dry, sour, tangy, tart[1]. *See* TASTE.

ache *verb*
1. To have or cause a feeling of physical pain or discomfort : hurt, pain, pang, twinge. *See* PAIN. **2.** To experience or express compassion : commiserate, compassionate, feel, pity, sympathize, yearn. ***Idioms:*** be sorry, have (*or* take) pity. *See* PITY. **3.** To have a strong longing for : covet, desire, hanker, long[2], pant, pine, want, wish, yearn. *Informal:* hone[2]. *See* DESIRE.

ache *noun* A sensation of physical discomfort occurring as the result of disease or injury : pain, pang, prick, prickle, smart, soreness, stab, sting, stitch, throe, twinge. *Informal:* misery. *See* PAIN.

achieve *verb*
To succeed in doing : accomplish, attain, gain, reach, realize. *Slang:* score. *See* DO.

achievement *noun*
1. Something completed or attained successfully : accomplishment, acquirement, acquisition, attainment, effort, feat. *See* DO. **2.** A great or heroic deed : exploit, feat, gest, masterstroke, stunt, tour de force. *See* ACTION.

aching *adjective*
Marked by, causing, or experiencing physical pain : achy, afflictive, hurtful, nagging, painful, smarting, sore. *See* PAIN.

acicula *noun*
A sharp or tapered end : acumination, apex, cusp, mucro, mucronation, point, tip[1]. *See* SHARP.

achy *adjective*
Marked by, causing, or experiencing physical pain : aching, afflictive, hurtful, nagging, painful, smarting, sore. *See* PAIN.

acicular *adjective*
Having an end that tapers to a point : aciculate, aciculated, acuminate, acute, cuspate, cuspated, cuspidate, cuspidated, mucronate, pointed, pointy, sharp. *See* SHARP.

aciculate *adjective*
Having an end that tapers to a point : acicular, aciculated, acuminate, acute, cuspate, cuspated, cuspidate, cuspidated, mucronate, pointed, pointy, sharp. *See* SHARP.

aciculated *adjective*
Having an end that tapers to a point : acicular, aciculate, acuminate, acute, cuspate, cuspated, cuspidate, cuspidated, mucronate, pointed, pointy, sharp. *See* SHARP.

acid *adjective*
1. Having a taste characteristic of that produced by acids : acerb, acerbic, acetous, acidulous, dry, sour, tangy, tart[1]. *See* TASTE. **2.** So sharp as to cause mental pain : acerbic, acidic, acrid, astringent, biting, caustic, corrosive, cutting, mordacious, mordant, pungent, scathing, sharp, slashing, stinging, trenchant, truculent, vitriolic. *See* ATTACK, RESPECT.

acidic *adjective*
So sharp as to cause mental pain : acerbic, acid, acrid, astringent, biting, caustic, corrosive, cutting, mordacious, mordant, pungent, scathing, sharp, slashing, stinging, trenchant, truculent, vitriolic. *See* ATTACK, RESPECT.

acidity *noun*
Irony or bitterness, as of tone : acerbity, acridity, causticity, corrosiveness, mordacity, mordancy, sarcasm, trenchancy. *See* LAUGHTER, RESPECT.

acidulous *adjective*
Having a taste characteristic of that produced by acids : acerb, acerbic, acetous, acid, dry, sour, tangy, tart[1]. *See* TASTE.

acknowledge *verb*
1. To recognize, often reluctantly, the reality or truth of : admit, avow, concede, confess, grant, own (up). *Slang:* fess up. *Chiefly Regional:* allow. *See* AFFIRM, KNOWLEDGE. **2.** To express

recognition of : admit, recognize. *See* AFFIRM, KNOWLEDGE.

acknowledgement *noun* See **acknowledgment.**

acknowledgment or **acknowledgement** *noun*
1. The act of admitting to something : admission, avowal, confession. *See* AFFIRM, KNOWLEDGE, SHOW. **2.** Favorable notice, as of an achievement : credit, recognition. *See* KNOWLEDGE.

acme *noun*
The highest point or state : apex, apogee, climax, crest, crown, culmination, height, meridian, peak, pinnacle, summit, top, zenith. *Informal:* payoff. *Medicine:* fastigium. *See* HIGH.

acquaint *verb*
1. To make known socially : introduce, present[2]. *See* KNOWLEDGE. **2.** To impart information to : advise, apprise, educate, enlighten, inform, notify, tell. *See* KNOWLEDGE, TEACH.

acquaintance *noun*
1. A person whom one knows casually : friend. *See* KNOWLEDGE. **2.** Personal knowledge derived from participation or observation : experience, familiarity. *See* KNOWLEDGE.

acquainted *adjective*
1. Having good knowledge of : conversant, familiar, versant, versed. ***Idiom:*** up on. *See* KNOWLEDGE. **2.** Provided with information; made aware : advised, educated, enlightened, informed, instructed, knowledgeable. *See* KNOWLEDGE.

acquiesce *verb*
To respond affirmatively; receive with agreement or compliance : accede, accept, agree, assent, consent, nod, subscribe, yes. *See* AGREE.

acquiescence *noun*
1. The act or process of accepting : acceptance, agreement, assent, consent, nod, yes. *Informal:* OK. *See* ACCEPT. **2.** The quality or state of willingly carrying out the wishes of others : amenability, amenableness, compliance, compliancy, deference, obedience, submission, submissiveness, tractability, tractableness. *See* RESIST.

acquiescent *adjective*
1. Submitting without objection or resistance : nonresistant, passive, resigned, submissive. *See* RESIST. **2.** Disposed to accept or agree : agreeable, game, minded, ready, willing. *Archaic:* fain. *See* WILLING.

acquirable *adjective*
Capable of being obtained or used : attainable, available, gettable, obtainable, procurable. *Idioms:* on hand, to be had. *See* GET.

acquire *verb*
1. To come into possession of : come by, gain, get, obtain, procure, secure, win. *Informal:* land, pick up. *See* GET. **2.** To come gradually to have : develop, form. *See* GET.

acquirement *noun*
Something completed or attained successfully : accomplishment, achievement, acquisition, attainment, effort, feat. *See* DO.

acquisition *noun*
1. Something completed or attained successfully : accomplishment, achievement, acquirement, attainment, effort, feat. *See* DO. **2.** Something tending to augment something else : accession, addition, augmentation. *See* INCREASE.

acquisitive *adjective*
Having a strong urge to obtain or possess something, especially material wealth, in quantity : avaricious, avid, covetous, grasping, greedy, hungry. *Informal:* grabby. *See* DESIRE, GIVE.

acquisitiveness *noun*
Excessive desire for more than one needs or deserves : avarice, avariciousness, avidity, covetousness, cupidity, graspingness, greed. *Informal:* grabbiness. *See* DESIRE, GIVE.

acquit *verb*
1. *Law.* To free from a charge or imputation of guilt : absolve, clear, exculpate, exonerate, vindicate. *Law:* purge. *See* LAW. **2.** To conduct oneself in a specified way : act, bear, behave, carry, comport, demean[1], deport, do, quit. *See* BE.

acquittal *noun*
Law. A freeing or clearing from accusation or guilt : exculpation, exoneration, vindication. *See* LAW.

acre *noun*
Usually extensive real estate. Often used in plural : estate, land, property. *See* OWNED.

acrid *adjective*
1. Having a noticeably sharp pungent taste or smell : acerbic, bitter, harsh, sour. *See* TASTE. **2.** So sharp as to cause mental pain : acerbic, acid, acidic, astringent, biting, caustic, corrosive, cutting, mordacious, mordant, pungent, scathing, sharp, slashing, stinging, trenchant, truculent, vitriolic. *See* ATTACK, RESPECT.

acridity *noun*
Irony or bitterness, as of tone : acerbity, acidity, causticity, corrosiveness, mordacity, mordancy, sarcasm, trenchancy. *See* LAUGHTER, RESPECT.

acrimonious *adjective*
Bitingly hostile : bitter, embittered, hard, rancorous, resentful, virulent. *See* ATTITUDE, LOVE.

acrimony *noun*
The quality or state of feeling bitter : bitterness, embitterment, gall[1], rancor, rancorousness, resentfulness, resentment, virulence, virulency. *See* FEELINGS.

act *noun*
1. The process of doing : action. *See* ACTION. **2.** Something done : action, deed, doing, thing, work. *See* DO. **3.** The formal product of a legislative or judicial body : assize, bill[1], enactment, law, legislation, lex, measure, statute. *See* LAW. **4.** A short theatrical piece within a larger production : sketch, skit. *See* PERFORMING ARTS. **5.** A display of insincere behavior : acting, disguise, dissemblance, masquerade, pretense, sham, show, simulation. *See* HONEST, TRUE.

act *verb* **1.** To conduct oneself in a specified way : acquit, bear, behave, carry, comport, demean[1], deport, do, quit. *See* BE. **2.** To behave affectedly or insincerely or take on a false or misleading appearance of : counterfeit, dissemble, fake, feign, play-act, pose, pretend, put on, sham, simulate. *See* HONEST, TRUE. **3.** To react in a specified way : behave, function, operate, perform, work. *See* ACTION. **4.** To perform the duties of another : function, officiate, serve. *See* DO, SUBSTITUTE. **5.** To play the part of : do, enact, impersonate, perform, play, play-act, portray, represent. *See* ACTION, PERFORMING ARTS, SUBSTITUTE. **6.** To produce on the stage. Also used with *out* : do, dramatize, enact, give, perform, present[2], put on, stage. *See* PERFORMING ARTS.

act up *verb* **1.** To behave in a rowdy, improper, or unruly fashion : carry on, misbehave. *Informal:* cut up, horse around. *See* GOOD. **2.** To work improperly due to mechanical difficulties : malfunction, misbehave. *See* THRIVE.

acting *adjective*
1. Temporarily assuming the duties of another : ad interim, interim, pro tem, provisional, temporary. *See* CONTINUE, SUBSTITUTE.

acting *noun* **1.** The art and occupation of an actor : dramatics, stage. *See* ACTION, PERFORMING ARTS, SUBSTITUTE. **2.** A display of insincere behavior : act, disguise, dissemblance, masquerade, pretense, sham, show, simulation. *See* HONEST, TRUE.

action *noun*
1. The process of doing : act. *See* ACTION. **2.** Something done : act, deed, doing, thing, work. *See* DO. **3.** The manner in which one behaves. Often used in plural : behavior, comportment, conduct, deportment, way. *See* BE. **4.** A legal proceeding to demand justice or enforce a right : case, cause, instance, lawsuit, suit. *See* LAW. **5.** A hostile encounter between opposing military forces : battle, combat, engagement. *See* CONFLICT.

actionable *adjective*
Subject to legal proceedings : *Law:* litigable, prosecutable, triable. *See* LAW.

activate *verb*
To arouse to action or put in motion : actuate, animate. *See* ACTION.

active *adjective*
1. In action or full operation : alive, functioning, going, operating, operative, running, working. *See* ACTION, AWARENESS. **2.** Disposed to action : brisk, driving, dynamic, dynamical, energetic, enterprising, lively, sprightly, spry, vigorous, zippy. *Informal:* peppy, snappy. *See* ACTION. **3.** Possessing, exerting, or displaying energy : brisk, dynamic, dynamical, energetic, forceful, kinetic, lively, sprightly, strenuous, vigorous. *Informal:* peppy. *See* ACTION.

activity *noun*
Energetic physical action : exercise, exertion. *See* ACTION.

actor *noun*
1. A theatrical performer : actress, player, thespian. *See* ACTION, PERFORMING ARTS, SUBSTITUTE. **2.** One who participates : participant, party, player. *See* PARTICIPATE.

actress *noun*
A theatrical performer : actor, player, thespian. *See* ACTION, PERFORMING ARTS, SUBSTITUTE.

actual *adjective*
1. Occurring or existing in act or fact : existent, extant. *See* BE, REAL. **2.** Not counterfeit or copied : authentic, bona fide, genuine, good, indubitable, original, real, true, undoubted, unquestionable. *See* TRUE. **3.** In agreement or correspondence with fact : real, true. *See* REAL.

actuality *noun*
1. The fact or state of existing or of being actual : being, entity, existence, reality. *See* BE, REAL. **2.** Something having real, demonstrable existence : event, fact, phenomenon, reality. *See* REAL. **3.** The quality of being actual or

factual : fact, factuality, factualness, reality, truth. *See* REAL.

actualization *noun*
The condition of being in full force or operation : being, effect, materialization, realization. *See* BE.

actualize *verb*
To make real or actual : materialize, realize. ***Idioms:*** bring to pass, carry into effect. *See* DO.

actually *adverb*
1. In truth : fairly, genuinely, indeed, positively, really, truly, truthfully, verily. ***Idiom:*** for fair. *See* REAL, TRUE. **2.** In point of fact : indeed, really. *See* REAL, TRUE. **3.** At this moment : currently, now. ***Idiom:*** even (*or* just *or* right) now. *See* TIME.

actuate *verb*
1. To arouse to action or put in motion : activate, animate. *See* ACTION. **2.** To set or keep going : drive, impel, mobilize, move, propel, run. *See* MOVE. **3.** To put into action or use : apply, employ, exercise, exploit, implement, practice, use, utilize. ***Idioms:*** avail oneself of, bring into play, bring to bear, make use of, put into practice, put to use. *See* USED.

act up *verb* See **act.**

acumen *noun*
Skill in perceiving, discriminating, or judging : astuteness, clear-sightedness, discernment, discrimination, eye, keenness, nose, penetration, perceptiveness, percipience, percipiency, perspicacity, sagacity, sageness, shrewdness, wit. *See* ABILITY, CAREFUL.

acuminate *adjective*
Having an end that tapers to a point : acicular, aciculate, aciculated, acute, cuspate, cuspated, cuspidate, cuspidated, mucronate, pointed, pointy, sharp. *See* SHARP.

acuminate *verb* To give a sharp edge to : edge, hone[1], sharpen, whet. *See* SHARP.

acumination *noun*
A sharp or tapered end : acicula, apex, cusp, mucro, mucronation, point, tip[1]. *See* SHARP.

acute *adjective*
1. Having an end that tapers to a point : acicular, aciculate, aciculated, acuminate, cuspate, cuspated, cuspidate, cuspidated, mucronate, pointed, pointy, sharp. *See* SHARP. **2.** Possessing or displaying perceptions of great accuracy and sensitivity : incisive, keen[1], penetrating, perceptive, probing, sensitive, sharp, trenchant. *See* CAREFUL, SHARP. **3.** So serious as to be at the point of crisis or necessary to resolve a crisis : climacteric, critical, crucial, desperate, dire. *See* SAFETY. **4.** Marked by severity or intensity : gnawing, knifelike, lancinating, piercing, sharp, shooting, stabbing. *See* BIG. **5.** *Music.* Elevated in pitch : high, high-pitched, piercing, piping, shrieky, shrill, shrilly, treble. *See* HIGH, SOUNDS.

adage *noun*
A usually pithy and familiar statement expressing an observation or principle generally accepted as wise or true : aphorism, byword, maxim, motto, proverb, saw, saying. *See* WORDS.

adamant *adjective*
Firmly, often unreasonably immovable in purpose or will : adamantine, brassbound, diehard, grim, implacable, incompliant, inexorable, inflexible, intransigent, iron, obdurate, relentless, remorseless, rigid, stubborn, unbendable, unbending, uncompliant, uncompromising, unrelenting, unyielding. ***Idiom:*** stubborn as a mule (*or* ox). *See* RESIST.

adamantine *adjective*
Firmly, often unreasonably immovable in purpose or will : adamant, brassbound, die-hard, grim, implacable, incompliant, inexorable, inflexible, intransigent, iron, obdurate, relentless, remorseless, rigid, stubborn, unbendable, unbending, uncompliant, uncompromising, unrelenting, unyielding. ***Idiom:*** stubborn as a mule (*or* ox). *See* RESIST.

adapt *verb*
To make or become suitable to a particular situation or use : acclimate, acclimatize, accommodate, adjust, conform, fashion, fit[1], reconcile, square, suit, tailor. *See* CHANGE.

adaptable *adjective*
Capable of adapting or being adapted : adaptive, adjustable, elastic, flexible, malleable, pliable, pliant, supple. *See* CHANGE.

adaptation *noun*
1. The act of making suitable to an end or the condition of being made suitable to an end : accommodation, adaption, adjustment, conformation. *See* CHANGE. **2.** *Biology.* Adjustment to a changing environment : acclimation, acclimatization. *See* CHANGE.

adaption *noun*
The act of making suitable to an end or the condition of being made suitable to an end : accommodation, adaptation, adjustment, conformation. *See* CHANGE.

adaptive *adjective*
Capable of adapting or being adapted : adaptable, adjustable, elastic, flexible, malleable, pliable, pliant, supple. *See* CHANGE.

add *verb*
To combine (figures) to form a sum. Also used with *up* : cast, foot (up), sum (up), tot[2] (up), total, totalize. *See* INCREASE.
added *adjective*
Being an addition : additional, extra, fresh, further, more, new, other. *See* INCREASE.
addition *noun*
1. The act or process of adding : summation, totalization. *See* INCREASE. **2.** Something tending to augment something else : accession, acquisition, augmentation. *See* INCREASE.
additional *adjective*
Being an addition : added, extra, fresh, further, more, new, other. *See* INCREASE.
additionally *adverb*
In addition : also, besides, further, furthermore, item, likewise, more, moreover, still, too, yet. ***Idioms:*** as well, to boot. *See* INCREASE.
additive *adjective*
Increasing, as in force, by successive additions : accumulative, cumulative. *See* INCREASE.
addle *verb*
To cause to be unclear in mind or intent : befuddle, bewilder, confound, confuse, discombobulate, dizzy, fuddle, jumble, mix up, muddle, mystify, perplex, puzzle. *Informal:* throw. ***Idiom:*** make one's head reel (*or* swim *or* whirl). *See* CLEAR, FEELINGS.
addled *adjective*
Mentally uncertain : addlepated, confounded, confused, confusional, muddle-headed, perplexed, turbid. *Informal:* mixed-up. *See* CLEAR.
addlepated *adjective*
Mentally uncertain : addled, confounded, confused, confusional, muddle-headed, perplexed, turbid. *Informal:* mixed-up. *See* CLEAR.
address *verb*
1. To direct speech to : speak, talk. *See* WORDS. **2.** To talk to an audience formally : lecture, prelect, speak. *Archaic:* bespeak. *See* WORDS. **3.** To bring an appeal or request, for example, to the attention of : appeal, apply, approach, petition. *Obsolete:* sue. *See* REQUEST. **4.** To mark (a written communication) with its destination : direct, superscribe. *See* START. **5.** To devote (oneself or one's efforts) : apply, bend, buckle down, concentrate, dedicate, devote, direct, focus, give, turn. *See* COLLECT, WORK. **6.** To cause (something) to be conveyed to a destination : consign, dispatch, forward, route, send, ship, transmit. *See* MOVE.
address *noun* **1.** A usually formal oral communication to an audience : allocution, declamation, lecture, oration, prelection, speech, talk. *See* WORDS. **2.** Romantic attentions. Often used in plural : courtship, suit. *See* SEEK, SEX. **3.** Behavior through which one reveals one's personality : air, bearing, demeanor, manner, mien, presence, style. *Archaic:* port. *See* BE, STYLE. **4.** The ability to say and do the right thing at the right time : diplomacy, savoir-faire, tact, tactfulness. *See* ABILITY, COURTESY.
adduce *verb*
To bring forward for formal consideration : cite, lay[1], present[2]. *Archaic:* allege. *See* LAW, WORDS.
adept *adjective*
Having or demonstrating a high degree of knowledge or skill : crack, expert, master, masterful, masterly, professional, proficient, skilled, skillful. *Slang:* crackerjack. *See* ABILITY.
adept *noun* A person with a high degree of knowledge or skill in a particular field : ace, authority, dab hand, expert, master, past master, professional, proficient, wizard. *Informal:* whiz. *Slang:* crackerjack. *Chiefly British:* dab[2]. *See* ABILITY.
adeptness *noun*
Natural or acquired facility in a specific activity : ability, art, command, craft, expertise, expertness, knack, mastery, proficiency, skill, technique. *Informal:* know-how. *See* ABILITY, KNOWLEDGE.
adequacy *noun*
An adequate quantity : enough, sufficiency. *See* EXCESS.
adequate *adjective*
1. Being what is needed without being in excess : comfortable, competent, decent, enough, satisfactory, sufficient. *See* EXCESS. **2.** Of moderately good quality but less than excellent : acceptable, all right, average, common, decent, fair, fairish, goodish, moderate, passable, respectable, satisfactory, sufficient, tolerable. *Informal:* OK, tidy. *See* GOOD.
adhere *verb*
1. To hold fast : bond, cleave[2], cling, cohere, stick. *See* CONNECT. **2.** To act in conformity with : abide by, carry out, comply, conform, follow, keep, mind, obey, observe. ***Idiom:*** toe the line (*or* mark). *See* ACCEPT, SAME.
adherence *noun*
The close physical union of two objects : adhesion, bond, cohesion. *See* CONNECT.
adherent *noun*
One who supports and adheres to another : co-

hort, disciple, follower, henchman, minion, partisan, satellite, supporter. *See* OVER, PRECEDE.

adhesion *noun*
The close physical union of two objects : adherence, bond, cohesion. *See* CONNECT.

adhesive *adjective*
Having the property of adhering : gluey, gooey, gummy, sticky, tacky[1]. *See* CLEAN, KEEP.

adieu *noun*
A separation of two or more people : farewell, good-bye, leave-taking, parting, valediction. *See* APPROACH.

ad interim *adjective*
Temporarily assuming the duties of another : acting, interim, pro tem, provisional, temporary. *See* CONTINUE, SUBSTITUTE.

adipose *adjective*
Having the qualities of fat : fat, fatty, greasy, oily, oleaginous, unctuous. *See* FAT.

adjacent *adjective*
1. Not far from another in space, time, or relation : close, contiguous, immediate, near, nearby, nigh, proximate. ***Idioms:*** at hand, under one's nose, within a stone's throw, within hailing distance. *See* NEAR. **2.** Sharing a common boundary : adjoining, conterminous, contiguous, next. *See* NEAR.

adjoin *verb*
To be contiguous or next to : abut, border, bound[2], butt[2], join, meet[1], neighbor, touch, verge. *See* NEAR.

adjoining *adjective*
Sharing a common boundary : adjacent, conterminous, contiguous, next. *See* NEAR.

adjourn *verb*
To put off until a later time : defer[1], delay, hold off, hold up, postpone, remit, shelve, stay[1], suspend, table, waive. *Informal:* wait. ***Idiom:*** put on ice. *See* DO.

adjournment *noun*
The act of putting off or the condition of being put off : deferment, deferral, delay, postponement, stay[1], suspension, waiver. *See* TIME.

adjudge *verb*
To make a decision about (a controversy or dispute, for example) after deliberation, as in a court of law : adjudicate, arbitrate, decide, decree, determine, judge, referee, rule, umpire. *See* DECIDE, LAW.

adjudicate *verb*
To make a decision about (a controversy or dispute, for example) after deliberation, as in a court of law : adjudge, arbitrate, decide, decree, determine, judge, referee, rule, umpire. *See* DECIDE, LAW.

adjunct *noun*
A subordinate element added to another entity : accessory, appendage, appurtenance, attachment, supplement. *See* INCREASE.

adjust *verb*
1. To make or become suitable to a particular situation or use : acclimate, acclimatize, accommodate, adapt, conform, fashion, fit[1], reconcile, square, suit, tailor. *See* CHANGE. **2.** To alter for proper functioning : fix, regulate, set[1], tune (up). *Music:* attune. *See* CHANGE, HELP.

adjustable *adjective*
Capable of adapting or being adapted : adaptable, adaptive, elastic, flexible, malleable, pliable, pliant, supple. *See* CHANGE.

adjustment *noun*
The act of making suitable to an end or the condition of being made suitable to an end : accommodation, adaptation, adaption, conformation. *See* CHANGE.

adjutant *noun*
A person who holds a position auxiliary to another and assumes some of the superior's responsibilities : aide, assistant, auxiliary, coadjutant, coadjutor, deputy, helper, lieutenant, second[2]. *See* HELP.

ad-lib *verb*
To compose or recite without preparation : extemporize, fake, improvise, make up. ***Idiom:*** wing it. *See* PLANNED, PREPARED.

ad-lib *noun* Something improvised : extemporization, impromptu, improvisation. *See* PLANNED, PREPARED.

ad-lib *adjective* Spoken, performed, or composed with little or no preparation or forethought : extemporaneous, extemporary, extempore, impromptu, improvised, offhand, snap, spur-of-the-moment, unrehearsed. *Informal:* off-the-cuff. *See* PREPARED.

admeasure *verb*
To set aside or distribute as a share : allocate, allot, allow, apportion, assign, give, lot, measure out, mete (out). *See* COLLECT.

admeasurement *noun*
The act of distributing or the condition of being distributed : allocation, assignment, apportionment, dispensation, distribution, division. *See* COLLECT.

administer *verb*
1. To have charge of (the affairs of others) : administrate, direct, govern, head, manage, run, superintend, supervise. *See* OVER. **2.** To oversee

the provision or execution of : administrate, carry out, dispense, execute. *See* OVER. **3.** To provide as a remedy : apply, dispense, give. *See* GIVE. **4.** To mete out by means of some action : deal, deliver, give. *See* GIVE.

administrable *adjective*

Capable of being governed : controllable, governable, manageable, rulable. *See* CONTROL.

administrant *noun*

A person having administrative or managerial authority in an organization : administrator, director, executive, manager, officer, official. *Informal:* exec. *See* OVER.

administrate *verb*

1. To have charge of (the affairs of others) : administer, direct, govern, head, manage, run, superintend, supervise. *See* OVER. **2.** To oversee the provision or execution of : administer, carry out, dispense, execute. *See* OVER.

administration *noun*

1. Authoritative control over the affairs of others : direction, government, management, superintendence, supervision. *See* OVER. **2.** The continuous exercise of authority over a political unit : control, direction, governance, government, rule. *See* CONTROL, POLITICS. **3.** The giving of a medication, especially by prescribed dosage : application, dispensation. *See* GIVE.

administrative *adjective*

Of, for, or relating to administration or administrators : directorial, executive, managerial, ministerial, supervisory. *See* OVER.

administrator *noun*

A person having administrative or managerial authority in an organization : administrant, director, executive, manager, officer, official. *Informal:* exec. *See* OVER.

admirable *adjective*

Deserving honor, respect, or admiration : commendable, creditable, deserving, estimable, exemplary, honorable, laudable, meritorious, praiseworthy, reputable, respectable, worthy. *See* GOOD, PRAISE, RESPECT, VALUE.

admiration *noun*

1. A feeling of deference, approval, and liking : account, appreciation, consideration, esteem, estimation, favor, honor, regard, respect. *See* RESPECT. **2.** *Archaic.* The emotion aroused by something awe-inspiring or astounding : amaze, amazement, astonishment, awe, marvel, wonder, wonderment. *Archaic:* dread. *See* EXCITE, FEELINGS.

admire *verb*

1. To regard with great pleasure or approval : appreciate. *See* LIKE, PRAISE. **2.** To have a high opinion of : consider, esteem, honor, regard, respect, value. ***Idioms:*** look up to, think highly (*or* much *or* well) of. *See* PRAISE.

admirer *noun*

1. One who ardently admires : devotee, enthusiast, fancier, lover. *Informal:* fan[2]. *See* LIKE, LOVE, PRAISE. **2.** A man who courts a woman : beau, courter, suitor, swain, wooer. *See* SEX.

admissible *adjective*

1. Capable of being accepted : acceptable, unobjectionable. *See* ACCEPT. **2.** Capable of being allowed : allowable, permissible. *Slang:* kosher. *See* ALLOW.

admission *noun*

1. The state of being allowed entry : admittance, entrance[1], ingress, ingression, introduction, intromission. *See* ACCEPT. **2.** The right to enter or make use of : access, admittance, entrance[1], entrée, entry, ingress. *See* ENTER. **3.** The act of admitting to something : acknowledgment, avowal, confession. *See* AFFIRM, KNOWLEDGE, SHOW.

admit *verb*

1. To allow admittance, as to a group : accept, receive, take in. *See* ACCEPT. **2.** To serve as a means of entrance for : intromit, let in. *See* ENTER. **3.** To afford an opportunity for : allow, let, permit. *See* ALLOW. **4.** To express recognition of : acknowledge, recognize. *See* AFFIRM, KNOWLEDGE. **5.** To recognize, often reluctantly, the reality or truth of : acknowledge, avow, concede, confess, grant, own (up). *Slang:* fess up. *Chiefly Regional:* allow. *See* AFFIRM, KNOWLEDGE.

admittance *noun*

1. The state of being allowed entry : admission, entrance[1], ingress, ingression, introduction, intromission. *See* ACCEPT. **2.** The right to enter or make use of : access, admission, entrance[1], entrée, entry, ingress. *See* ENTER.

admix *verb*

To put together into one mass so that the constituent parts are more or less homogeneous : amalgamate, blend, commingle, commix, fuse, intermingle, intermix, merge, mingle, mix, stir[1]. *See* ASSEMBLE.

admixture *noun*

Something produced by mixing : amalgam, amalgamation, blend, commixture, fusion, merger, mix, mixture. *See* ASSEMBLE.

admonish *verb*

1. To criticize for a fault or an offense : call down, castigate, chastise, chide, dress down, rap[1], rebuke, reprimand, reproach, reprove, scold, tax, upbraid. *Informal:* bawl out, lambaste. *Slang:* chew out. ***Idioms:*** call on the carpet, let someone have it, haul (*or* rake) over the coals, bring (*or* call *or* take) to task. *See* ATTACK, PRAISE. **2.** To notify (someone) of imminent danger or risk : alarm, alert, caution, forewarn, warn. *See* WARN.

admonishing *adjective*
Giving warning : admonitory, cautionary, monitory, warning. *See* WARN.

admonishment *noun*
1. Words expressive of strong disapproval : admonition, rebuke, reprimand, reproach, reproof, scolding. *Slang:* rap[1]. *See* PRAISE.
2. Advice to beware, as of a person or thing : admonition, caution, caveat, monition, warning. *See* WARN.

admonition *noun*
1. Words expressive of strong disapproval : admonishment, rebuke, reprimand, reproach, reproof, scolding. *Slang:* rap[1]. *See* PRAISE.
2. Advice to beware, as of a person or thing : admonishment, caution, caveat, monition, warning. *See* WARN.

admonitory *adjective*
Giving warning : admonishing, cautionary, monitory, warning. *See* WARN.

ado *noun*
Busy and useless activity : fuss. *Informal:* to-do. *See* ACTION, CALM.

adolescence *noun*
The time of life between childhood and maturity : greenness, juvenescence, juvenility, puberty, salad days, spring, youth, youthfulness. *See* YOUTH.

adolescent *noun*
A young person, usually between the ages of 13 and 19 : teen, teenager, youth. *Informal:* teener. *See* YOUTH.

adopt *verb*
1. To take, as another's idea, and make one's own : embrace, espouse, take on, take up. *See* ACCEPT, GIVE. **2.** To accept officially : affirm, approve, confirm, pass, ratify, sanction. *See* ACCEPT, LAW.

adoption *noun*
A ready taking up of something : embracement, espousal. *See* ACCEPT, GIVE.

adorable *adjective*
Easy to love : lovable, sweet. *See* GOOD, LIKE, LOVE.

adoration *noun*
1. The act of adoring, especially reverently : idolization, reverence, veneration, worship. *See* LIKE, LOVE, SACRED. **2.** Deep and ardent affection : devotion, love, worship. *See* LIKE, LOVE.

adore *verb*
1. To regard with great awe and devotion : idolize, revere, reverence, venerate, worship. *See* SACRED. **2.** To feel deep devoted love for : love, worship. *See* LOVE. **3.** To like or enjoy enthusiastically, often excessively : delight (in), dote on (*or* upon), love. *Slang:* eat up, groove on. *See* LIKE, LOVE.

adorn *verb*
1. To furnish with decorations : bedeck, deck[2] (out), decorate, dress (up), embellish, garnish, ornament, trim. *See* BEAUTIFUL. **2.** To endow with beauty and elegance by way of a notable addition : beautify, embellish, enhance, grace, set off. *See* BEAUTIFUL.

adornment *noun*
Something that adorns : decoration, embellishment, garnishment, garniture, ornament, ornamentation, trim, trimming. *See* BEAUTIFUL.

adroit *adjective*
1. Well done or executed : clean, deft, neat, skillful. *See* ABILITY, GOOD. **2.** Showing art or skill in performing or doing : artful, deft, dexterous, skillful. *See* ABILITY, KNOWLEDGE.
3. Exhibiting or possessing skill and ease in performance : clever, deft, dexterous, facile, handy, nimble, slick. *See* ABILITY.

adroitness *noun*
Skillfulness in the use of the hands or body : deftness, dexterity, dexterousness, prowess, skill, sleight. *See* ABILITY.

adscititious *adjective*
Not part of the real or essential nature of a thing : adventitious, incidental, supervenient. *See* SURFACE.

adulate *verb*
To compliment excessively and ingratiatingly : blandish, butter up, flatter, honey, slaver. *Informal:* soft-soap, sweet-talk. *See* PRAISE.

adulation *noun*
Excessive, ingratiating praise : blandishment, blarney, flattery, incense[2], oil, slaver. *Informal:* soft soap. ***Idiom:*** honeyed words. *See* PRAISE.

adulator *noun*
One who flatters another excessively : courtier, flatterer, sycophant, toady. *Informal:* apple-polisher. *See* OVER, PRAISE.

adult *adjective*
Having reached full growth and development : big, developed, full-blown, full-fledged, full-grown, grown, grown-up, mature, ripe. ***Idiom:*** of age. *See* YOUTH.

adulterant *noun*
One that contaminates : adulterator, contaminant, contamination, contaminator, impurity, poison, pollutant. *See* CLEAN.

adulterate *verb*
To make impure or inferior by deceptively adding foreign substances : debase, doctor, load, sophisticate. *See* CLEAN.

adulterated *adjective*
Mixed with other substances : alloyed, doctored, impure, loaded, sophisticated. *See* CLEAN.

adulteration *noun*
The state of being contaminated : contamination, pollution, sophistication. *See* CLEAN.

adulterator *noun*
One that contaminates : adulterant, contaminant, contamination, contaminator, impurity, poison, pollutant. *See* CLEAN.

adumbrate *verb*
1. To give an indication of something in advance : augur, bode, forecast, forerun, foreshadow, foretell, foretoken, portend, prefigure, presage, prognosticate. *See* FORESIGHT, SHOW. **2.** To draw up a preliminary plan or version of : block in (*or* out), draft, outline, rough in (*or* out), sketch. *See* PLANNED. **3.** To make dark or darker : darken, shade, shadow. *See* LIGHT.

advance *verb*
1. To go forward, especially toward a conclusion : come (along), get along, march[1], move, proceed, progress. *See* APPROACH. **2.** To state, as an idea, for consideration : offer, pose, propose, propound, put forward, set forth, submit, suggest. *See* OFFER. **3.** To cause to move forward or upward, as toward a goal : forward, further, promote. *See* FORWARD, HELP. **4.** To raise in rank : elevate, jump, promote, raise, upgrade. *See* RISE. **5.** To attain a higher status, rank, or condition : ascend, climb, mount, rise. ***Idiom:*** go up the ladder. *See* INCREASE, RISE. **6.** To supply (money), especially on credit : lend, loan. *See* GIVE.

advance *noun* **1.** Forward movement : advancement, furtherance, headway, march[1], progress, progression. *See* BETTER, FORWARD. **2.** The amount by which something is increased : boost, hike, increase, increment, jump, raise, rise. *See* INCREASE. **3.** A preliminary action intended to elicit a favorable response. Used in plural : approach, overture. *See* APPROACH.

advance *adjective* Going before : antecedent, anterior, earlier, precedent, preceding, previous, prior. *See* PRECEDE.

advanced *adjective*
1. Ahead of current trends or customs : forward, precocious, progressive. *See* PRECEDE. **2.** Far along in life or time : aged, elderly, old, senior. ***Idiom:*** getting along (*or* on) in years. *See* NEW.

advancement *noun*
1. A progression upward in rank : elevation, jump, promotion, rise, upgrade. *See* RISE. **2.** Forward movement : advance, furtherance, headway, march[1], progress, progression. *See* BETTER, FORWARD.

advantage *noun*
1. A factor conducive to superiority and success : handicap, head start, odds, start, vantage. *See* HELP. **2.** Something beneficial : avail, benefit, blessing, boon[1], favor, gain, profit. *See* HELP. **3.** Something that contributes to or increases one's well-being : benefit, good, interest (often used in plural), profit. *See* HELP. **4.** The quality of being suitable or adaptable to an end : account, avail, benefit, profit, use, usefulness, utility. *See* USED. **5.** A dominating position, as in a conflict : better[1], bulge, draw, drop, edge, superiority, upper hand, vantage. *Informal:* inside track, jump. *See* OVER.

advantage *verb* To be an advantage to : avail, benefit, profit, serve. *Archaic:* boot[2]. ***Idiom:*** stand someone in good stead. *See* HELP.

advantageous *adjective*
1. Affording benefit : benefic, beneficent, beneficial, benignant, favorable, good, helpful, profitable, propitious, salutary, toward, useful. *See* HELP. **2.** Affording profit : fat, lucrative, moneymaking, profitable, remunerative, rewarding. *See* GET.

advent *noun*
The act of arriving : appearance, arrival, coming. *See* START.

adventitious *adjective*
Not part of the real or essential nature of a thing : adscititious, incidental, supervenient. *See* SURFACE.

adventure *noun*
An exciting, often hazardous undertaking : emprise, enterprise, venture. *See* SAFETY.

adventure *verb* **1.** To run the risk of : chance, hazard, risk, venture. *See* SAFETY. **2.** To expose to possible loss or damage : compromise, hazard, risk, venture. *See* SAFETY.

adventurer *noun*
1. One who engages in exciting, risky pursuits :

daredevil, venturer. *See* SAFETY. **2.** A freelance fighter : Hessian, mercenary, soldier of fortune. *See* GET. **3.** One who speculates for quick profits : gambler, operator, speculator. *See* GAMBLING, MONEY.

adventuresome *adjective*
Taking or willing to take risks : adventurous, audacious, bold, daredevil, daring, enterprising, venturesome, venturous. *See* SAFETY.

adventuresomeness *noun*
Willingness to take risks : adventurousness, audaciousness, audacity, boldness, daredevilry, daredeviltry, daring, daringness, venturesomeness, venturousness. *See* SAFETY.

adventurous *adjective*
1. Taking or willing to take risks : adventuresome, audacious, bold, daredevil, daring, enterprising, venturesome, venturous. *See* SAFETY. **2.** Involving possible risk, loss, or injury : chancy, dangerous, hazardous, jeopardous, parlous, perilous, risky, treacherous, unsafe, venturesome, venturous. *Slang:* hairy. *See* SAFETY.

adventurousness *noun*
Willingness to take risks : adventuresomeness, audaciousness, audacity, boldness, daredevilry, daredeviltry, daring, daringness, venturesomeness, venturousness. *See* SAFETY.

adversarial *adjective*
Acting against or in opposition : adverse, antagonistic, antipathetic, opposed, opposing, oppositional. *See* SUPPORT.

adversary *noun*
One that opposes another in a battle, contest, controversy, or debate : antagonist, opponent, opposer, opposition, oppositionist, resister. *See* RESIST, SUPPORT.

adverse *adjective*
1. Acting against or in opposition : adversarial, antagonistic, antipathetic, opposed, opposing, oppositional. *See* SUPPORT. **2.** Tending to discourage, retard, or make more difficult : disadvantageous, negative, unadvantageous, unfavorable, unsatisfactory, untoward. *See* HELP.

adversity *noun*
Bad fortune : haplessness, misfortune, unfortunateness, unluckiness, untowardness. *See* LUCK.

advert *verb*
To call or direct attention to something : bring up, mention, point, point out, refer, touch (on *or* upon). *See* WORDS.

advertise *verb*
1. To make (information) generally known : blaze[2], blazon, broadcast, bruit, circulate, disseminate, noise, promulgate, propagate, spread. *Idioms:* spread far and wide, spread the word. *See* KNOWLEDGE. **2.** To make known vigorously the positive features of (a product) : ballyhoo, build up, cry (up), popularize, promote, publicize, talk up. *Informal:* pitch, plug. *Slang:* push. *See* KNOWLEDGE. **3.** To bring to public notice or make known publicly : announce, annunciate, broadcast, declare, proclaim, promulgate, publish. *See* KNOWLEDGE, WORDS.

advertisement *noun*
A systematic effort or part of this effort to increase the importance or reputation of by favorable publicity : ballyhoo, buildup, promotion, publicity, puffery. *Informal:* pitch, plug. *Slang:* hype. *See* KNOWLEDGE.

advertising *noun*
The act or profession of promoting something, as a product : promotion, publicity. *See* KNOWLEDGE.

advice *noun*
1. An opinion as to a decision or course of action : counsel, recommendation. *See* OPINION. **2.** New information, especially about recent events and happenings. Often used in plural : intelligence, news, tiding (often used in plural), word. *Informal:* scoop. *See* KNOWLEDGE, WORDS.

advisable *adjective*
Worth doing, especially for practical reasons : expedient, recommendable, well[2]. *See* WISE.

advise *verb*
1. To give recommendations to (someone) about a decision or course of action : counsel, recommend. *Informal:* mentor. *See* OPINION. **2.** To meet and exchange views to reach a decision : confer, consult, deliberate, parley, talk. *Informal:* powwow. *See* COLLECT, MEET, WORDS. **3.** To impart information to : acquaint, apprise, educate, enlighten, inform, notify, tell. *See* KNOWLEDGE, TEACH.

advised *adjective*
1. Resulting from deliberation and careful thought : calculated, considered, studied, studious. *See* WISE. **2.** Provided with information; made aware : acquainted, educated, enlightened, informed, instructed, knowledgeable. *See* KNOWLEDGE.

advisement *noun*
A careful considering of a matter : calculation, consideration, deliberation, lucubration, study. *See* THOUGHTS.

adviser or **advisor** *noun*
One who advises another, especially officially

or professionally : consultant, counselor, mentor. *Law:* counsel. *See* OPINION.

advisor *noun* See **adviser.**

advisory *adjective*
Giving advice : consultative, consultatory, consulting, consultive. *See* OPINION.

advocate *verb*
To aid the cause of by approving or favoring : back, champion, endorse, get behind, plump for, recommend, side with, stand behind, stand by, support, uphold. ***Idioms:*** align oneself with, go to bat for, take the part of. *See* SUPPORT.

aegis *noun*
Aid or support given by a patron : auspice (often used in plural), backing, patronage, patronization, sponsorship. *See* HELP.

aeon *noun* See **eon.**

aerate *verb*
To expose to circulating air : air, ventilate, wind[1]. *See* BREATH, OPEN.

aerial *adjective*
1. Of or relating to air : airy, atmospheric, pneumatic. *See* BREATH, HIGH. **2.** Imposingly high : airy, lofty, sky-high, soaring, towering. *See* HIGH. **3.** So light and insubstantial as to resemble air or a thin film : aery, airy, diaphanous, ethereal, filmy, gauzy, gossamer, gossamery, sheer[2], transparent, vaporous, vapory. *See* THICK.

aery *adjective*
So light and insubstantial as to resemble air or a thin film : aerial, airy, diaphanous, ethereal, filmy, gauzy, gossamer, gossamery, sheer[2], transparent, vaporous, vapory. *See* THICK.

aesthetic or **esthetic** *adjective*
Informal. Showing good taste : artistic, tasteful, tasty. *See* STYLE.

afeard also **afeared** *adjective*
Regional. Filled with fear or terror : afraid, aghast, apprehensive, fearful, fearsome, funky, panicky. *Regional:* ascared. *See* FEAR.

afeared *adjective* See **afeard.**

affability *noun*
The quality of being pleasant and friendly : agreeability, agreeableness, amenity, amiability, amiableness, congeniality, congenialness, cordiality, cordialness, friendliness, geniality, genialness, pleasantness, sociability, sociableness, warmth. *See* ATTITUDE, GOOD.

affable *adjective*
1. Pleasant and friendly in disposition : agreeable, amiable, congenial, cordial, genial, good-natured, good-tempered, pleasant, sociable, warm. *See* ATTITUDE, GOOD. **2.** Characterized by kindness and warm, unaffected courtesy : gracious, hospitable. *See* KIND.

affair *noun*
1. Something to be done, considered, or dealt with : business, matter, thing. *See* THING. **2.** A large or important social gathering : celebration, festivity, fete, function, gala, occasion, party, soiree. *Informal:* do. *Slang:* bash. *See* GROUP, WORK. **3.** Something that concerns or involves one personally : business, concern, lookout. *See* RELEVANT. **4.** An intimate sexual relationship between two people : amour, love, love affair, romance. *See* LOVE, SEX.

affect[1] *verb*
To evoke a usually strong mental or emotional response from : get (to), impress, move, strike, touch. *See* TOUCH.

affect[2] *verb*
To take on or give a false appearance of : assume, counterfeit, fake, feign, pretend, put on, sham, simulate. ***Idiom:*** make believe. *See* TRUE.

affectation *noun*
Artificial behavior adopted to impress others : affectedness, air (used in plural), mannerism, pose, pretense. *See* HONEST, TRUE.

affected *adjective*
1. Not genuine or sincere : artificial, feigned, insincere, phony, pretended. *See* TRUE. **2.** Artificially genteel : artificial, mannered, precious. *Informal:* la-di-da. *See* GOOD, HONEST, PLAIN, TRUE. **3.** Having concern : concerned, interested, involved. *See* CONCERN.

affectedness *noun*
Artificial behavior adopted to impress others : affectation, air (used in plural), mannerism, pose, pretense. *See* HONEST, TRUE.

affecting *adjective*
Exciting a deep, usually somber response : impressive, moving, poignant, stirring, touching. *See* TOUCH.

affection *noun*
1. The condition of being closely tied to another by affection or faith : attachment, devotion, fondness, liking, love, loyalty (used in plural). *See* CONNECT. **2.** A complex and usually strong subjective response, such as love or hate : affectivity, emotion, feeling, sentiment. *See* FEELINGS.

affectionate *adjective*
Feeling and expressing affection : devoted, doting, fond, loving. *See* ATTITUDE, LOVE.

affective *adjective*
Relating to, arising from, or appealing to the emotions : emotional, emotive. *See* FEELINGS.

affectivity *noun*
A complex and usually strong subjective response, such as love or hate : affection, emotion, feeling, sentiment. *See* FEELINGS.

afferent *adjective*
Transmitting impulses from sense organs to nerve centers : sensory. *See* BODY.

affianced *adjective*
Pledged to marry : betrothed, engaged, intended, plighted. *See* MARRIAGE.

affiliate *verb*
To unite or be united in a relationship : ally, associate, bind, combine, conjoin, connect, join, link, relate. *See* CONNECT.
affiliate *noun* **1.** One who is united in a relationship with another : ally, associate, cohort, colleague, confederate, copartner, fellow, partner. *See* CONNECT. **2.** A local unit of a business or an auxiliary controlled by such a business : branch, division, subsidiary. *See* PART.

affiliation *noun*
The state of being associated : alliance, association, combination, conjunction, connection, cooperation, partnership. *See* NEAR.

affinity *noun*
The quality or state of being alike : alikeness, analogy, comparison, correspondence, likeness, parallelism, resemblance, similarity, similitude, uniformity, uniformness. *See* SAME.

affirm *verb*
1. To put into words positively and with conviction : allege, argue, assert, asseverate, aver, avouch, avow, claim, contend, declare, hold, maintain, say, state. ***Idiom:*** have it. *See* AFFIRM. **2.** To accept officially : adopt, approve, confirm, pass, ratify, sanction. *See* ACCEPT, LAW.

affirmation *noun*
1. The act of asserting positively : allegation, assertion, asseveration, averment, claim, declaration, statement. *See* AFFIRM. **2.** An act of confirming officially : approval, confirmation, ratification, sanction. *See* LAW.

affirmative *adjective*
1. Giving assent : favorable, positive. *See* AFFIRM. **2.** Of a constructive nature : positive. *Informal:* upbeat. *See* HELP.

affix *verb*
1. To join one thing to another : attach, clip[2], connect, couple, fasten, fix, moor, secure. *See* ASSEMBLE. **2.** To ascribe (a misdeed or an error, for example) to : assign, blame, fasten, fix, impute, pin on, place. *See* GIVE. **3.** To add as a supplement or an appendix : annex, append, attach, subjoin. *See* INCREASE.

afflatus *noun*
Divine guidance and motivation imparted directly : inspiration. *See* RELIGION.

afflict *verb*
To bring great harm or suffering to : agonize, anguish, curse, excruciate, plague, rack, scourge, smite, strike, torment, torture. *See* ATTACK, HELP.

afflicted *adjective*
Having a painful ailment : miserable, suffering, wretched. *See* HAPPY.

affliction *noun*
1. A state of physical or mental suffering : agony, anguish, distress, hurt, misery, pain, torment, torture, woe, wound, wretchedness. *See* HAPPY. **2.** The condition of being sick : disorder, illness, indisposition, infirmity, sickness. *See* HEALTH. **3.** Something hard to bear physically or emotionally : burden[1], cross, trial, tribulation. *See* HEAVY, OVER. **4.** A cause of suffering or harm : bane, curse, evil, ill, plague, scourge, woe. *See* HELP.

afflictive *adjective*
Marked by, causing, or experiencing physical pain : aching, achy, hurtful, nagging, painful, smarting, sore. *See* PAIN.

affluence *noun*
A great amount of accumulated money and precious possessions : fortune, pelf, riches, treasure, wealth. *See* OWNED, RICH.

affluent *adjective*
Possessing a large amount of money, land, or other material possessions : flush, moneyed, rich, wealthy. *Slang:* loaded. ***Idioms:*** having money to burn, in the money, made of money, rolling in money. *See* RICH.

afford *verb*
To make (something) readily available : extend, offer, provide. ***Idiom:*** place (*or* put) at one's disposal. *See* OFFER.

affray *noun*
A quarrel, fight, or disturbance marked by very noisy, disorderly, and often violent behavior : brawl, broil[2], donnybrook, fray, free-for-all, melee, riot, row[2], ruction, tumult. *Informal:* fracas. *Slang:* rumble. *See* ATTACK.

affright *verb*
To fill with fear : alarm, frighten, panic, scare, scarify[2], startle, terrify, terrorize. *Archaic:* fright. ***Idioms:*** make one's blood run cold, make one's hair stand on end, scare silly (*or* stiff), scare the daylights out of. *See* FEAR.
affright *noun* Great agitation and anxiety caused by the expectation or the realization of danger : alarm, apprehension, dread, fear,

fearfulness, fright, funk, horror, panic, terror, trepidation. *Slang:* cold feet. ***Idiom:*** fear and trembling. *See* FEAR.

affront *verb*
To cause resentment or hurt by callous, rude behavior : huff, insult, miff, offend, outrage, pique. ***Idioms:*** add insult to injury, give offense to. *See* ATTACK, PAIN.
affront *noun* An act that offends a person's sense of pride or dignity : contumely, despite, indignity, insult, offense, outrage, slight. ***Idiom:*** slap in the face. *See* ATTACK.

afield *adverb*
Not in the right way or on the proper course : amiss, astray, awry, wrong. *See* THRIVE.

afire *adjective*
On fire : ablaze, aflame, alight[2], burning, conflagrant, fiery, flaming. ***Idioms:*** in a blaze, in flames. *See* HOT.

aflame *adjective*
On fire : ablaze, afire, alight[2], burning, conflagrant, fiery, flaming. ***Idioms:*** in a blaze, in flames. *See* HOT.

aforetime *adverb*
Archaic. At a time in the past : already, before, earlier, erstwhile, formerly, once, previously. *Archaic:* beforetime. *See* PRECEDE.

afraid *adjective*
Filled with fear or terror : aghast, apprehensive, fearful, fearsome, funky, panicky. *Regional:* afeard, ascared. *See* FEAR.

afresh *adverb*
Once more : again, anew. *See* REPETITION.

after *adverb*
At a subsequent time : afterward, afterwards, later, latterly, next, subsequently, ulteriorly. ***Idioms:*** after a while, by and by, later on. *See* PRECEDE.
after *adjective* **1.** Following something else in time : later, posterior, subsequent, ulterior. *See* PRECEDE. **2.** *Nautical.* Located in the rear : back, hind, hindmost, posterior, postern, rear[1]. *See* PRECEDE.

afterlife *noun*
Endless life after death : deathlessness, eternity, everlasting life, everlastingness, immortality. *See* CONTINUE, LIVE.

aftermath *noun*
Something brought about by a cause : consequence, corollary, effect, end product, event, fruit, harvest, issue, outcome, precipitate, ramification, result, resultant, sequel, sequence, sequent, upshot. *See* CAUSE.

afterward *adverb*
At a subsequent time : after, afterwards, later, latterly, next, subsequently, ulteriorly. ***Idioms:*** after a while, by and by, later on. *See* PRECEDE.

afterwards *adverb*
At a subsequent time : after, afterward, later, latterly, next, subsequently, ulteriorly. ***Idioms:*** after a while, by and by, later on. *See* PRECEDE.

again *adverb*
Once more : afresh, anew. *See* REPETITION.

age *noun*
1. Old age : agedness, elderliness, senectitude, senescence, year (used in plural). *See* YOUTH. **2.** A particular time notable for its distinctive characteristics : day, epoch, era, period, time (often used in plural). *See* TIME. **3.** *Informal.* A long time. Used in plural : eon, eternity, long[1], year (used in plural). *Informal:* blue moon. ***Idioms:*** forever and a day, forever and ever, month of Sundays. *See* TIME.
age *verb* **1.** To grow old : get along, get on. *See* YOUTH. **2.** To bring or come to full development : develop, grow, maturate, mature, mellow, ripen. *See* YOUTH.

aged *adjective*
1. Far along in life or time : advanced, elderly, old, senior. ***Idiom:*** getting along (*or* on) in years. *See* NEW. **2.** Brought to full flavor and richness by aging : mellow, ripe. *See* YOUTH.

agedness *noun*
Old age : age, elderliness, senectitude, senescence, year (used in plural). *See* YOUTH.

ageless *adjective*
Existing unchanged forever : dateless, eternal, timeless. *Archaic:* eterne. *See* CHANGE.

agency *noun*
1. That by which something is accomplished or some end achieved : agent, instrument, instrumentality, instrumentation, intermediary, mean[3] (used in plural), mechanism, medium, organ. *See* MEANS. **2.** A component of government that performs a given function : arm, branch, department, division, organ, wing. *See* PART.

agenda *noun*
An organized list, as of procedures, activities, or events : calendar, docket, lineup, order of the day (often used in plural), program, schedule, timetable. *See* PLANNED.

agent *noun*
1. That by which something is accomplished or some end achieved : agency, instrument, instrumentality, instrumentation, intermediary, mean[3] (used in plural), mechanism, medium, organ. *See* MEANS. **2.** A person who secretly

observes others to obtain information : operative, spy. *Informal:* spook. ***Idiom:*** secret (*or* undercover) agent. *See* INVESTIGATE.

age-old *adjective*
Belonging to, existing, or occurring in times long past : ancient, antediluvian, antiquated, antique, archaic, hoary, old, olden, old-time, timeworn, venerable. ***Idioms:*** old as Methuselah, old as the hills. *See* NEW.

agglomerate *verb*
To bring together so as to increase in mass or number : accrue, accumulate, aggregate, amass, collect[1], cumulate, garner, gather, hive, pile up, roll up. *See* COLLECT.

agglomeration *noun*
A group of things gathered haphazardly : bank[1], cumulus, drift, heap, hill, mass, mess, mound, mountain, pile, shock[2], stack, tumble. *See* ORDER.

aggrandize *verb*
1. To make or become greater or larger : amplify, augment, boost, build, build up, burgeon, enlarge, escalate, expand, extend, grow, increase, magnify, mount, multiply, proliferate, rise, run up, snowball, soar, swell, upsurge, wax. *Informal:* beef up. *See* INCREASE. **2.** To raise to a high position or status : apotheosize, dignify, elevate, ennoble, exalt, glorify, magnify, uplift. ***Idiom:*** put on a pedestal. *See* RISE.

aggrandizement *noun*
1. The act of increasing or rising : amplification, augment, augmentation, boost, buildup, enlargement, escalation, growth, hike, increase, jump, multiplication, proliferation, raise, rise, swell, upsurge, upswing, upturn. *See* INCREASE. **2.** The act of raising to a high position or status or the condition of being so raised : apotheosis, elevation, ennoblement, exaltation, glorification. *See* RISE.

aggravate *verb*
1. To make greater in intensity or severity : deepen, enhance, heighten, intensify, redouble. *See* INCREASE. **2.** To trouble the nerves or peace of mind of, especially by repeated vexations : annoy, bother, bug, chafe, disturb, exasperate, fret, gall[2], get, irk, irritate, nettle, peeve, provoke, put out, rile, ruffle, vex. ***Idioms:*** get in one's hair, get on one's nerves, get under one's skin. *See* FEELINGS, PAIN.

aggravation *noun*
1. Something that annoys : annoyance, besetment, bother, irritant, irritation, nuisance, peeve, plague, torment, vexation. *See* FEELINGS, PAIN. **2.** The feeling of being annoyed : annoyance, bother, botheration, exasperation, irritation, vexation. *See* FEELINGS, PAIN.

aggregate *noun*
1. A number or quantity obtained as a result of addition : amount, sum, summation, sum total, total, totality. *Archaic:* tale. *See* COUNT. **2.** An amount or quantity from which nothing is left out or held back : all, entirety, everything, gross, sum, total, totality, whole. *Informal:* work (used in plural). ***Idioms:*** everything but (*or* except) the kitchen sink; lock, stock, and barrel; the whole ball of wax (*or* kit and caboodle *or* megillah *or* nine yards *or* shebang). *See* PART.

aggregate *verb* **1.** To bring together so as to increase in mass or number : accrue, accumulate, agglomerate, amass, collect[1], cumulate, garner, gather, hive, pile up, roll up. *See* COLLECT. **2.** To come to in number or quantity : amount, number, reach, run into, total. ***Idiom:*** add up to. *See* INCREASE.

aggregation *noun*
A quantity accumulated : accumulation, amassment, assemblage, collection, congeries, cumulation, gathering, mass. *See* COLLECT.

aggress *verb*
To set upon with violent force : assail, assault, attack, beset, fall on (*or* upon), go at, have at, sail into, storm, strike. *Informal:* light into, pitch into. *See* ATTACK.

aggression *noun*
1. The act of attacking : assailment, assault, attack, attempt, offense, offensive, onrush, onset, onslaught, strike. *See* ATTACK. **2.** Hostile behavior : aggressiveness, belligerence, belligerency, combativeness, contentiousness, hostility, militance, militancy. *See* ATTACK.

aggressive *adjective*
1. Inclined to act in a hostile way : belligerent, combative, contentious, hostile, militant. *See* ATTACK, ATTITUDE. **2.** Marked by boldness and assertiveness : assertive. *See* ATTITUDE, TRY.

aggressiveness *noun*
Hostile behavior : aggression, belligerence, belligerency, combativeness, contentiousness, hostility, militance, militancy. *See* ATTACK.

aggressor *noun*
One who starts a hostile action : assailant, assailer, assaulter, attacker. *See* ATTACK.

aggrieve *verb*
1. To cause suffering or painful sorrow to : distress, grieve, hurt, injure, pain, wound. *See* HAPPY. **2.** To do a wrong to; treat unjustly : oppress, outrage, persecute, wrong. *See* RIGHT.

aghast *adjective*
Filled with fear or terror : afraid, apprehensive, fearful, fearsome, funky, panicky. *Regional:* afeard, ascared. *See* FEAR.

agile *adjective*
Moving or performing quickly, lightly, and easily : brisk, facile, nimble, quick, spry. *See* ABILITY.

agileness *noun*
The quality or state of being mentally agile : agility, dexterity, dexterousness, nimbleness, quickness. *See* ABILITY.

agility *noun*
The quality or state of being mentally agile : agileness, dexterity, dexterousness, nimbleness, quickness. *See* ABILITY.

agitate *verb*
1. To cause to move to and fro violently : churn, convulse, rock, shake. *See* CALM, REPETITION. **2.** To impair or destroy the composure of : bother, discompose, disquiet, distract, disturb, flurry, fluster, perturb, rock, ruffle, shake (up), toss, unsettle, upset. *Informal:* rattle. *See* CALM.

agitated *adjective*
In a state of anxiety or uneasiness : anxious, concerned, distressed, nervous, solicitous, uneasy, unsettled. *See* FEELINGS.

agitation *noun*
1. The condition of being physically agitated : commotion, convulsion, turbulence. *See* CALM. **2.** A state of discomposure : dither, fluster, flutter, perturbation, tumult, turmoil, upset. *Informal:* lather, stew. *See* CALM. **3.** An interruption of regular procedure or of public peace : commotion, disorder, disturbance, helter-skelter, stir[1], tumult, turbulence, turmoil, uproar. *Informal:* flap, to-do. *See* CALM, ORDER.

agitator *noun*
One who agitates, especially politically : fomenter, inciter, instigator. *See* CALM, CHANGE, POLITICS.

agnate *adjective*
Connected by or as if by kinship or common origin : akin, allied, cognate, connate, connatural, consanguine, consanguineous, kindred, related. *See* KIN.

agog *adjective*
Intensely desirous or interested : ardent, athirst, avid, bursting, eager, impatient, keen[1], solicitous, thirsting, thirsty. *Informal:* raring. ***Idioms:*** champing at the bit, ready and willing. *See* CONCERN.

agonize *verb*
1. To twist and turn, as in pain, struggle, or embarrassment : squirm, toss, turn, writhe. *See* REPETITION. **2.** To bring great harm or suffering to : afflict, anguish, curse, excruciate, plague, rack, scourge, smite, strike, torment, torture. *See* ATTACK, HELP.

agonizing *adjective*
Extraordinarily painful or distressing : anguishing, excruciating, harrowing, tormenting, torturous. *See* PAIN.

agony *noun*
A state of physical or mental suffering : affliction, anguish, distress, hurt, misery, pain, torment, torture, woe, wound, wretchedness. *See* HAPPY.

agree *verb*
1. To respond affirmatively; receive with agreement or compliance : accede, accept, acquiesce, assent, consent, nod, subscribe, yes. *See* AGREE. **2.** To come to an understanding or to terms : accord, coincide, concur, get together, harmonize. *See* AGREE. **3.** To be compatible or in correspondence : accord, check, chime, comport with, conform, consist, correspond, fit[1], harmonize, match, square, tally. *Informal:* jibe[1]. *Archaic:* quadrate. *See* AGREE.

agreeability *noun*
The quality of being pleasant and friendly : affability, agreeableness, amenity, amiability, amiableness, congeniality, congenialness, cordiality, cordialness, friendliness, geniality, genialness, pleasantness, sociability, sociableness, warmth. *See* ATTITUDE, GOOD.

agreeable *adjective*
1. To one's liking : congenial, favorable, good, grateful, gratifying, nice, pleasant, pleasing, pleasurable, satisfying, welcome. *See* LIKE. **2.** Pleasant and friendly in disposition : affable, amiable, congenial, cordial, genial, good-natured, good-tempered, pleasant, sociable, warm. *See* ATTITUDE, GOOD. **3.** In keeping with one's needs or expectations : accordant, compatible, conformable, congenial, congruous, consistent, consonant, correspondent, corresponding, harmonious. *See* AGREE. **4.** Disposed to accept or agree : acquiescent, game, minded, ready, willing. *Archaic:* fain. *See* WILLING. **5.** Ready to do favors for another : accommodating, complaisant, indulgent, obliging. *See* HELP, WILLING.

agreeableness *noun*
The quality of being pleasant and friendly : affability, agreeability, amenity, amiability, amiableness, congeniality, congenialness, cordiality,

cordialness, friendliness, geniality, genialness, pleasantness, sociability, sociableness, warmth. *See* ATTITUDE, GOOD.

agreed *adverb*
It is so; as you say or ask : absolutely, all right, assuredly, aye, gladly, indubitably, roger, undoubtedly, unquestionably, willingly, yea, yes. *Informal:* OK, uh-huh, yeah, yep. *Slang:* right on. *See* AFFIRM.

agreement *noun*
1. The act or process of accepting : acceptance, acquiescence, assent, consent, nod, yes. *Informal:* OK. *See* ACCEPT. **2.** The act or state of agreeing or conforming : accordance, chime, conformance, conformation, conformity, congruence, congruity, correspondence, harmonization, harmony, keeping. *See* AGREE. **3.** Harmonious mutual understanding : accord, concord, concordance, concurrence, consonance, harmony, rapport, tune, unity. ***Idiom:*** meeting of the minds. *See* AGREE. **4.** An act or state of agreeing between parties regarding a course of action : accord, arrangement, bargain, compact[2], deal, pact, understanding. *See* AGREE. **5.** A legally binding arrangement between parties : bond, compact[2], contract, convention, covenant, pact. *See* AGREE. **6.** A formal, usually written settlement between nations : accord, concord, convention, pact, treaty. *See* AGREE, POLITICS.

ahead *adverb*
Before the expected time : beforehand, betimes, early. ***Idioms:*** ahead of time, in advance, with time to spare. *See* TIME.

aid *verb*
To give support or assistance : abet, assist, boost, help (out), relieve, succor. ***Idioms:*** give (*or* lend) a hand, give a leg up. *See* HELP.
aid *noun* **1.** The act or an instance of helping : abetment, assist, assistance, hand, help, relief, succor, support. *See* HELP. **2.** Assistance, especially money, food, and other necessities, given to the needy or dispossessed : dole, handout, public assistance, relief, welfare. *See* HELP. **3.** A person who helps : abettor, attendant, help, helper, reliever, succorer. *See* HELP.

aide *noun*
A person who holds a position auxiliary to another and assumes some of the superior's responsibilities : adjutant, assistant, auxiliary, coadjutant, coadjutor, deputy, helper, lieutenant, second[2]. *See* HELP.

ail *verb*
To cause anxious uneasiness in : cark, concern, distress, trouble, worry. *See* CONCERN.

ailing *adjective*
Affected or tending to be affected with minor health problems : indisposed, low, mean[2], off-color, rocky, sickly. ***Idiom:*** under the weather. *See* HEALTH.

ailment *noun*
1. A pathological condition of mind or body : complaint, disease, disorder, ill, illness, infirmity, malady, sickness. *See* HEALTH. **2.** A minor illness, especially one of a temporary nature : bug, complaint, indisposition, malady. *See* HEALTH.

aim *verb*
1. To move (a weapon or blow, for example) in the direction of someone or something : cast, direct, head, level, point, set[1], train, turn, zero in. *Military:* lay[1]. *See* SEEK. **2.** To strive toward a goal : aspire, seek. ***Idiom:*** set one's sights on. *See* SEEK, START. **3.** To have in mind as a goal or purpose : contemplate, design, intend, mean[1], plan, project, propose, purpose, target. *Regional:* mind. *See* PLANNED, PURPOSE.
aim *noun* **1.** What one intends to do or achieve : ambition, design, end, goal, intent, intention, mark, meaning, object, objective, point, purpose, target, view, why. ***Idioms:*** end in view, why and wherefore. *See* PLANNED, PURPOSE. **2.** The thread or current of thought uniting or occurring in all the elements of a text or discourse : burden[2], drift, intent, meaning, purport, substance, tendency, tenor, thrust. *See* MEANING.

aimless *adjective*
Without aim, purpose, or intent : desultory, pointless, purposeless. *See* PURPOSE.

air *noun*
1. The gaseous mixture enveloping the earth : atmosphere. *See* HIGH, PLACE. **2.** The celestial regions as seen from the earth : firmament, heaven (often used in plural), sky. *Archaic:* welkin. *See* HIGH. **3.** A natural movement or current of air : blast, blow[1], breeze, gust, wind[1], zephyr. *Archaic:* gale. *See* BREATH. **4.** A general impression produced by a predominant quality or characteristic : ambiance, atmosphere, aura, feel, feeling, mood, smell, tone. *See* BE. **5.** Behavior through which one reveals one's personality : address, bearing, demeanor, manner, mien, presence, style. *Archaic:* port. *See* BE, STYLE. **6.** Artificial behavior adopted to impress others. Used in plural : affectation, affectedness, mannerism, pose, pretense. *See* HONEST, TRUE. **7.** A pleasing succession of musical tones forming a usually brief aesthetic

unit : aria, melody, strain[2], tune. *Obsolete:* note. *See* SOUNDS.

air *verb* **1.** To expose to circulating air : aerate, ventilate, wind[1]. *See* BREATH, OPEN. **2.** To utter publicly : express, put, state, vent, ventilate. ***Idiom:*** come out with. *See* SHOW, WORDS.

airless *adjective*
1. Oppressive due to a lack of fresh air : close, stifling, stuffy. *See* BREATH, OPEN. **2.** Marked by an absence of circulating air : breathless, breezeless, still, windless. *See* BREATH.

airy *adjective*
1. Of or relating to air : aerial, atmospheric, pneumatic. *See* BREATH, HIGH. **2.** Imposingly high : aerial, lofty, sky-high, soaring, towering. *See* HIGH. **3.** Exposed to or characterized by the presence of freely circulating air or wind : blowy, breezy, gusty, windy. *See* BREATH. **4.** So light and insubstantial as to resemble air or a thin film : aerial, aery, diaphanous, ethereal, filmy, gauzy, gossamer, gossamery, sheer[2], transparent, vaporous, vapory. *See* THICK. **5.** Displaying light-hearted nonchalance : breezy, buoyant, debonair, jaunty. *Informal:* corky. ***Idiom:*** free and easy. *See* ATTITUDE, CAREFUL, GOOD.

akin *adjective*
Connected by or as if by kinship or common origin : agnate, allied, cognate, connate, connatural, consanguine, consanguineous, kindred, related. *See* KIN.

alabaster *adjective*
Of a light color or complexion : fair, ivory, light[1], pale. *See* COLORS.

à la mode *adjective*
Being or in accordance with the current fashion : chic, dashing, fashionable, mod, modish, posh, smart, stylish, swank, swanky, trig. *Informal:* classy, in, sharp, snappy, swish, tony, trendy. *Slang:* with-it. ***Idioms:*** all the rage, up to the minute. *See* STYLE, USUAL.

alarm *noun*
1. Great agitation and anxiety caused by the expectation or the realization of danger : affright, apprehension, dread, fear, fearfulness, fright, funk, horror, panic, terror, trepidation. *Slang:* cold feet. ***Idiom:*** fear and trembling. *See* FEAR. **2.** A signal that warns of imminent danger : alarum, alert, tocsin, warning. *See* WARN.

alarm *verb* **1.** To fill with fear : affright, frighten, panic, scare, scarify[2], startle, terrify, terrorize. *Archaic:* fright. ***Idioms:*** make one's blood run cold, make one's hair stand on end, scare silly (*or* stiff), scare the daylights out of. *See* FEAR. **2.** To notify (someone) of imminent danger or risk : admonish, alert, caution, forewarn, warn. *See* WARN.

alarmist *noun*
One who needlessly alarms others : scaremonger. *See* POLITICS, WARN.

alarum *noun*
A signal that warns of imminent danger : alarm, alert, tocsin, warning. *See* WARN.

alcoholic *adjective*
Containing alcohol : hard, intoxicative, spirituous, strong. *See* INGESTION.

alert *adjective*
1. Vigilantly attentive : observant, open-eyed, vigilant, wakeful, wary, watchful, wide-awake. ***Idiom:*** on the ball. *See* AWARENESS. **2.** Mentally quick and original : bright, clever, intelligent, keen[1], quick, quick-witted, sharp, sharp-witted, smart. ***Idiom:*** smart as a whip. *See* ABILITY.

alert *noun* A signal that warns of imminent danger : alarm, alarum, tocsin, warning. *See* WARN.

alert *verb* To notify (someone) of imminent danger or risk : admonish, alarm, caution, forewarn, warn. *See* WARN.

alertness *noun*
The condition of being alert : vigilance, wakefulness, wariness, watchfulness. *See* AWARENESS.

alien *adjective*
1. Of, from, or characteristic of another place or part of the world : exotic, foreign, strange. *Archaic:* outlandish. *See* NATIVE. **2.** Not part of the essential nature of a thing : extraneous, extrinsic, foreign. *See* NATIVE.

alien *noun* A person coming from another country or into a new community : émigré, foreigner, newcomer, outlander, outsider, stranger. *See* NATIVE.

alien *verb* *Law.* To change the ownership of (property) by means of a legal document : cede, deed, grant, make over, sign over. *Law:* alienate, assign, convey, transfer. *See* GIVE, LAW.

alienate *verb*
1. To make distant, hostile, or unsympathetic : disaffect, disunite, estrange. ***Idiom:*** set at odds. *See* LOVE. **2.** *Law.* To change the ownership of (property) by means of a legal document : cede, deed, grant, make over, sign over. *Law:* alien, assign, convey, transfer. *See* GIVE, LAW.

alienation *noun*
1. The act of estranging or the condition of being estranged : disaffection, estrangement. *See*

LOVE. **2.** An interruption in friendly relations : breach, break, disaffection, estrangement, fissure, rent[2], rift, rupture, schism, split. *See* ASSEMBLE, HELP. **3.** *Psychology.* Serious mental illness or disorder impairing a person's capacity to function normally and safely : brainsickness, craziness, dementia, derangement, disturbance, insaneness, insanity, lunacy, madness, mental illness, psychopathy, unbalance. *Psychiatry:* mania. *Psychology:* aberration. *See* SANE. **4.** A making over of legal ownership or title : *Law:* assignment, conveyance, grant, transfer, transferal. *See* LAW.

alight[1] *verb*
To come to rest on the ground : land, light[2], set down, settle, touch down. *See* MOVE.
alight on (or upon) *verb Archaic.* To find or meet by chance : bump into, chance on (*or* upon), come across, come on (*or* upon), find, happen on (*or* upon), light on (*or* upon), run across, run into, stumble on (*or* upon), tumble on. ***Idiom:*** meet up with. *See* MEET.

alight[2] *adjective*
On fire : ablaze, afire, aflame, burning, conflagrant, fiery, flaming. ***Idioms:*** in a blaze, in flames. *See* HOT.

alight on or **upon** *verb* See **alight.**

align[1] also **aline** *verb*
1. To place in or form a line or lines : line (up), range. *See* ORDER. **2.** To be formally associated, as by treaty : ally, confederate, federate, league. *See* CONNECT, POLITICS.

alike *adjective*
Possessing the same or almost the same characteristics : analogous, comparable, corresponding, equivalent, like[2], parallel, similar, uniform. *See* SAME.

alikeness *noun*
The quality or state of being alike : affinity, analogy, comparison, correspondence, likeness, parallelism, resemblance, similarity, similitude, uniformity, uniformness. *See* SAME.

aliment *noun*
1. Something fit to be eaten : bread, comestible, diet, edible, esculent, fare, food, foodstuff, meat, nourishment, nurture, nutriment, nutrition, pabulum, pap, provender, provision (used in plural), sustenance, victual. *Slang:* chow, eats, grub. *See* INGESTION. **2.** That which sustains the mind or spirit : bread, food, nourishment, nutriment, pabulum, pap, sustenance. *See* CARE FOR, INGESTION.

alimentary *adjective*
1. Of or relating to food or nutrition : nutritional, nutritive. *See* INGESTION. **2.** Providing nourishment : nourishing, nutrient, nutritious, nutritive. *See* INGESTION.

alimentation *noun*
The means needed to support life : alimony, bread, bread and butter, keep, livelihood, living, maintenance, subsistence, support, sustenance, upkeep. *See* MONEY.

alimony *noun*
The means needed to support life : alimentation, bread, bread and butter, keep, livelihood, living, maintenance, subsistence, support, sustenance, upkeep. *See* MONEY.

aline *verb* See **align[1].**

alive *adjective*
1. Having existence or life : around, existent, existing, extant, living. *See* LIVE. **2.** Marked by or exhibiting life : animate, animated, live[2], living, vital. *See* LIVE. **3.** In action or full operation : active, functioning, going, operating, operative, running, working. *See* ACTION, AWARENESS. **4.** Full of animation and activity : replete, rife. *See* BIG, RICH. **5.** Marked by comprehension, cognizance, and perception : awake, aware, cognizant, sensible, sentient, wise[1]. *Slang:* hip. ***Idiom:*** on to. *See* KNOWLEDGE.

all *adjective*
Including every constituent or individual : complete, entire, gross, total, whole. *See* PART.
all *noun* An amount or quantity from which nothing is left out or held back : aggregate, entirety, everything, gross, sum, total, totality, whole. *Informal:* work (used in plural). ***Idioms:*** everything but (*or* except) the kitchen sink; lock, stock, and barrel; the whole ball of wax (*or* kit and caboodle *or* megillah *or* nine yards *or* shebang). *See* PART.
all *adverb* To the fullest extent : absolutely, altogether, completely, dead, entirely, flat, fully, just, perfectly, quite, thoroughly, totally, utterly, well[2], wholly. *Informal:* clean, clear. ***Idioms:*** in toto, through and through. *See* BIG, LIMITED.

all-around *adjective*
1. Covering a wide scope : all-inclusive, all-round, broad, broad-spectrum, comprehensive, expansive, extended, extensive, far-ranging, far-reaching, general, global, inclusive, large, overall, sweeping, wide-ranging, wide-reaching, widespread. *See* SPECIFIC. **2.** Having many aspects, uses, or abilities : all-round, many-sided, multifaceted, protean, various, versatile. *See* ABILITY, SAME.

allay *verb*
1. To make less severe or more bearable : alle-

viate, assuage, comfort, ease, lessen, lighten[2], mitigate, palliate, relieve. *See* INCREASE. **2.** To make or become calm : balm, becalm, calm (down), lull, quiet, settle, still, tranquilize. *See* CALM.

allegation *noun*
The act of asserting positively : affirmation, assertion, asseveration, averment, claim, declaration, statement. *See* AFFIRM.

allege *verb*
1. To put into words positively and with conviction : affirm, argue, assert, asseverate, aver, avouch, avow, claim, contend, declare, hold, maintain, say, state. ***Idiom:*** have it. *See* AFFIRM. **2.** *Archaic.* To bring forward for formal consideration : adduce, cite, lay[1], present[2]. *See* LAW, WORDS.

allegiance *noun*
Faithfulness or devotion to a person, a cause, obligations, or duties : constancy, faithfulness, fealty, fidelity, loyalty, steadfastness. *See* CONTINUE, OBLIGATION.

allegiant *adjective*
Adhering firmly and devotedly, as to a person, a cause, or a duty : constant, faithful, fast, firm[1], liege, loyal, staunch, steadfast, true. *See* CONTINUE, TRUST.

alleviate *verb*
To make less severe or more bearable : allay, assuage, comfort, ease, lessen, lighten[2], mitigate, palliate, relieve. *See* INCREASE.

alleviation *noun*
Freedom, especially from pain : assuagement, ease, mitigation, palliation, relief. *See* INCREASE.

alliance *noun*
1. An association, especially of nations for a common cause : Anschluss, bloc, cartel, coalition, confederacy, confederation, federation, league, organization, union. *See* CONNECT, GROUP, POLITICS. **2.** The state of being associated : affiliation, association, combination, conjunction, connection, cooperation, partnership. *See* NEAR.

allied *adjective*
1. Closely connected by or as if by a treaty : aligned, confederated, federated, unified. *See* CONNECT, POLITICS. **2.** Connected by or as if by kinship or common origin : agnate, akin, cognate, connate, connatural, consanguine, consanguineous, kindred, related. *See* KIN.

all-inclusive *adjective*
Covering a wide scope : all-around, all-round, broad, broad-spectrum, comprehensive, expansive, extended, extensive, far-ranging, far-reaching, general, global, inclusive, large, overall, sweeping, wide-ranging, wide-reaching, widespread. *See* SPECIFIC.

allocate *verb*
1. To set aside or apart for a specified purpose : appropriate, assign, designate, earmark. *See* COLLECT, MONEY. **2.** To set aside or distribute as a share : admeasure, allot, allow, apportion, assign, give, lot, measure out, mete (out). *See* COLLECT.

allocation *noun*
1. The act of distributing or the condition of being distributed : admeasurement, assignment, apportionment, dispensation, distribution, division. *See* COLLECT. **2.** That which is allotted : allotment, allowance, dole, lot, measure, part, portion, quantum, quota, ration, share, split. *Informal:* cut. *Slang:* divvy. *See* COLLECT.

allocution *noun*
A usually formal oral communication to an audience : address, declamation, lecture, oration, prelection, speech, talk. *See* WORDS.

allot *verb*
To set aside or distribute as a share : admeasure, allocate, allow, apportion, assign, give, lot, measure out, mete (out). *See* COLLECT.

allotment *noun*
That which is allotted : allocation, allowance, dole, lot, measure, part, portion, quantum, quota, ration, share, split. *Informal:* cut. *Slang:* divvy. *See* COLLECT.

all-out *adjective*
1. Covering all aspects with painstaking accuracy : complete, exhaustive, full-dress, intensive, thorough, thoroughgoing, thoroughpaced. *See* BIG, CAREFUL. **2.** Completely such, without qualification or exception : absolute, arrant, complete, consummate, crashing, damned, dead, downright, flat, out-and-out, outright, perfect, plain, pure, sheer[2], thorough, thoroughgoing, total, unbounded, unequivocal, unlimited, unmitigated, unqualified, unrelieved, unreserved, utter[2]. *Informal:* flat-out, positive. *Chiefly British:* blooming. *See* BIG, LIMITED.

all-overs *noun*
Informal. A state of nervous restlessness or agitation : fidget (often used in plural), jitter (used in plural), jump (used in plural), shiver[1] (used in plural), tremble (often used in plural). *Informal:* shake (used in plural). *Slang:* heebie-jeebies, jim-jams, willies. *See* CALM, FEAR.

allow *verb*
1. To neither forbid nor prevent : have, let, permit, suffer, tolerate. *See* ALLOW. **2.** To give one's consent to : approbate, approve, author-

ize, consent, endorse, let, permit, sanction. *Informal:* OK. *See* ALLOW. **3.** To afford an opportunity for : admit, let, permit. *See* ALLOW. **4.** To set aside or distribute as a share : admeasure, allocate, allot, apportion, assign, give, lot, measure out, mete (out). *See* COLLECT. **5.** *Chiefly Regional.* To recognize, often reluctantly, the reality or truth of : acknowledge, admit, avow, concede, confess, grant, own (up). *Slang:* fess up. *See* AFFIRM, KNOWLEDGE.

allowable *adjective*
Capable of being allowed : admissible, permissible. *Slang:* kosher. *See* ALLOW.

allowance *noun*
1. The approving of an action, especially when done by one in authority : approbation, approval, authorization, consent, endorsement, leave[2], license, permission, permit, sanction. *Informal:* OK. *See* ALLOW. **2.** That which is allotted : allocation, allotment, dole, lot, measure, part, portion, quantum, quota, ration, share, split. *Informal:* cut. *Slang:* divvy. *See* COLLECT. **3.** An accommodation made in the light of special or extenuating circumstances : concession. *See* AGREE.

alloyed *adjective*
Mixed with other substances : adulterated, doctored, impure, loaded, sophisticated. *See* CLEAN.

all right *adjective*
Of moderately good quality but less than excellent : acceptable, adequate, average, common, decent, fair, fairish, goodish, moderate, passable, respectable, satisfactory, sufficient, tolerable. *Informal:* OK, tidy. *See* GOOD.
all right *adverb* It is so; as you say or ask : absolutely, agreed, assuredly, aye, gladly, indubitably, roger, undoubtedly, unquestionably, willingly, yea, yes. *Informal:* OK, uh-huh, yeah, yep. *Slang:* right on. *See* AFFIRM.

all-round *adjective*
1. Covering a wide scope : all-around, all-inclusive, broad, broad-spectrum, comprehensive, expansive, extended, extensive, far-ranging, far-reaching, general, global, inclusive, large, overall, sweeping, wide-ranging, wide-reaching, widespread. *See* SPECIFIC. **2.** Having many aspects, uses, or abilities : all-around, many-sided, multifaceted, protean, various, versatile. *See* ABILITY, SAME.

all the same *adverb*
In spite of a preceding event or consideration : however, nevertheless, nonetheless, still, yet. *Informal:* still and all. ***Idiom:*** be that as it may. *See* AFFIRM.

allure *verb*
1. To direct or impel to oneself by some quality or action : appeal, attract, draw, entice, lure, magnetize, take. *Informal:* pull. *See* LIKE. **2.** To beguile or draw into a wrong or foolish course of action : entice, inveigle, lure, seduce, tempt. ***Idiom:*** lead astray. *See* PERSUASION.
allure *noun* The power or quality of attracting : allurement, appeal, attraction, attractiveness, call, charisma, charm, draw, enchantment, enticement, fascination, glamour, lure, magnetism, witchery. *Informal:* pull. *See* LIKE.

allurement *noun*
1. The power or quality of attracting : allure, appeal, attraction, attractiveness, call, charisma, charm, draw, enchantment, enticement, fascination, glamour, lure, magnetism, witchery. *Informal:* pull. *See* LIKE. **2.** Something that attracts, especially with the promise of pleasure or reward : bait, come-on, enticement, inducement, inveiglement, invitation, lure, seduction, temptation. *See* LIKE.

allurer *noun*
One that seduces : charmer, enticer, inveigler, lurer, seducer, tempter. *See* PERSUASION.

alluring *adjective*
Tending to seduce : bewitching, come-hither, enticing, inveigling, inviting, luring, seductive, siren, tempting, witching. *See* LIKE, PERSUASION, SEX.

allusive *adjective*
Tending to bring a memory, mood, or image, for example, subtly or indirectly to mind : connotative, evocative, impressionistic, reminiscent, suggestive. *See* SUGGEST.

alluvion *noun*
An abundant, usually overwhelming flow or fall, as of a river or rain : cataclysm, cataract, deluge, downpour, flood, freshet, inundation, Niagara, overflow, torrent. *Chiefly British:* spate. *See* BIG.

ally *verb*
1. To be formally associated, as by treaty : align, confederate, federate, league. *See* CONNECT, POLITICS. **2.** To unite or be united in a relationship : affiliate, associate, bind, combine, conjoin, connect, join, link, relate. *See* CONNECT.
ally *noun* **1.** One nation associated with another in a common cause : coalitionist, confederate, leaguer. *See* CONNECT, POLITICS. **2.** One who is united in a relationship with another : affiliate, associate, cohort, colleague, confederate, copartner, fellow, partner. *See* CONNECT.

almost *adverb*
Near to in quantity or amount : about, approximately, nearly, roughly. ***Idiom:*** on the order of. *See* NEAR.

alms *noun*
Something given to a charity or cause : benefaction, beneficence, charity, contribution, donation, gift, handout, offering, subscription. *See* GIVE.

almsman *noun*
One who begs habitually or for a living : almswoman, beggar, cadger, mendicant. *Informal:* panhandler. *Slang:* bummer, moocher. *See* REQUEST.

almswoman *noun*
One who begs habitually or for a living : almsman, beggar, cadger, mendicant. *Informal:* panhandler. *Slang:* bummer, moocher. *See* REQUEST.

alone *adjective*
1. Lacking the company of others : companionless, lone, lonely, lonesome, single, solitary, unaccompanied. *See* INCLUDE. **2.** Set away from all others : apart, detached, isolate, isolated, lone, removed, solitary. *See* INCLUDE. **3.** Without equal or rival : incomparable, matchless, nonpareil, only, peerless, singular, unequaled, unexampled, unique, unmatched, unparalleled, unrivaled. *See* SAME.
alone *adverb* **1.** Without the presence or aid of another : single-handedly, singly, solely, solitarily, solo. ***Idioms:*** all by one's lonesome, by oneself. *See* INCLUDE. **2.** To the exclusion of anyone or anything else : but, entirely, exclusively, only, solely. *See* INCLUDE.

aloneness *noun*
The quality or state of being alone : isolation, loneliness, singleness, solitariness, solitude. *See* INCLUDE.

aloof *adjective*
1. Not friendly, sociable, or warm in manner : chill, chilly, cool, distant, offish, remote, reserved, reticent, solitary, standoffish, unapproachable, uncommunicative, undemonstrative, withdrawn. *See* ATTITUDE, HOT. **2.** Lacking interest in one's surroundings or worldly affairs : detached, disinterested, incurious, indifferent, unconcerned, uninterested, uninvolved. *See* ATTITUDE, CONCERN.

aloofness *noun*
Dissociation from one's surroundings or worldly affairs : detachment, distance, remoteness. *See* ATTITUDE, CONCERN, INCLUDE, NEAR.

already *adverb*
At a time in the past : before, earlier, erstwhile, formerly, once, previously. *Archaic:* aforetime, beforetime. *See* PRECEDE.

also *adverb*
In addition : additionally, besides, further, furthermore, item, likewise, more, moreover, still, too, yet. ***Idioms:*** as well, to boot. *See* INCREASE.

alter *verb*
1. To make or become different : change, modify, mutate, turn, vary. *See* CHANGE. **2.** To render incapable of reproducing sexually : castrate, fix, geld, neuter, spay, sterilize, unsex. *See* REPRODUCTION, RICH.

alterable *adjective*
Capable of or liable to change : changeable, fluid, inconstant, mutable, uncertain, unsettled, unstable, unsteady, variable, variant. *Archaic:* various. *See* CHANGE.

alteration *noun*
The process or result of making or becoming different : change, modification, mutation, permutation, variation. *See* CHANGE.

altercation *noun*
A discussion, often heated, in which a difference of opinion is expressed : argument, bicker, clash, contention, controversy, debate, difficulty, disagreement, dispute, fight, hassle, polemic, quarrel, run-in, spat, squabble, tiff, word (used in plural), wrangle. *Informal:* rhubarb, tangle. *See* CONFLICT.

alternate *verb*
To do, use, or occur in successive turns : interchange, rotate. *See* CHANGE.
alternate *noun* One that takes the place of another : replacement, stand-in, substitute, surrogate. *Informal:* fill-in, pinch hitter, sub. *See* SUBSTITUTE.

alternation *noun*
Occurrence in successive turns : interchange, rotation. *See* CHANGE.

alternative *noun*
The power or right of choosing : choice, option. *See* CHOICE.

altitude *noun*
The distance of something from a given level : elevation, height. *See* HIGH.

alto *adjective*
Being a sound produced by a relatively small frequency of vibrations : bass, contralto, deep, low, low-pitched. *See* SOUNDS.

altogether *adverb*
To the fullest extent : absolutely, all, completely, dead, entirely, flat, fully, just, perfectly,

quite, thoroughly, totally, utterly, well[2], wholly. *Informal:* clean, clear. ***Idioms:*** in toto, through and through. *See* BIG, LIMITED.

altruism *noun*
Kindly, charitable interest in others : beneficence, benevolence, benignancy, benignity, charitableness, charity, goodwill, grace, kindheartedness, kindliness, kindness, philanthropy. *See* ATTITUDE, KIND.

altruistic *adjective*
1. Characterized by kindness and concern for others : beneficent, benevolent, benign, benignant, good, goodhearted, kind[1], kindhearted, kindly. *See* ATTITUDE, KIND. **2.** Of or concerned with charity : benevolent, charitable, eleemosynary, philanthropic, philanthropical. *See* GIVE, KIND.

amalgam *noun*
Something produced by mixing : admixture, amalgamation, blend, commixture, fusion, merger, mix, mixture. *See* ASSEMBLE.

amalgamate *verb*
To put together into one mass so that the constituent parts are more or less homogeneous : admix, blend, commingle, commix, fuse, intermingle, intermix, merge, mingle, mix, stir[1]. *See* ASSEMBLE.

amalgamation *noun*
Something produced by mixing : admixture, amalgam, blend, commixture, fusion, merger, mix, mixture. *See* ASSEMBLE.

amaranthine *adjective*
Enduring for all time : ceaseless, endless, eternal, everlasting, immortal, never-ending, perpetual, unending, world without end. *Archaic:* eterne. *See* CONTINUE.

amass *verb*
To bring together so as to increase in mass or number : accrue, accumulate, agglomerate, aggregate, collect[1], cumulate, garner, gather, hive, pile up, roll up. *See* COLLECT.

amassment *noun*
A quantity accumulated : accumulation, aggregation, assemblage, collection, congeries, cumulation, gathering, mass. *See* COLLECT.

amateur *noun*
One lacking professional skill and ease in a particular pursuit : dabbler, dilettante, nonprofessional, smatterer, uninitiate. *See* ABILITY.

amateurish *adjective*
Lacking the required professional skill : dilettante, dilettantish, nonprofessional, unprofessional, unskilled, unskillful. *See* ABILITY.

amative *adjective*
Feeling or devoted to sexual love or desire : amorous, concupiscent, erotic, lascivious, lecherous, lewd, libidinous, lustful, lusty, passionate, prurient, sexy. *See* SEX.

amativeness *noun*
Sexual hunger : concupiscence, desire, eroticism, erotism, itch, libidinousness, lust, lustfulness, passion, prurience, pruriency. *See* DESIRE, SEX.

amatory *adjective*
Of, concerning, or promoting sexual love or desire : amorous, aphrodisiac, erotic, lascivious, salacious, sexual, sexy. *See* SEX.

amaze *verb*
To impress strongly by what is unexpected or unusual : astonish, astound, awe, startle, surprise. ***Idioms:*** catch (*or* take) unawares, take aback. *See* SURPRISE.

amaze *noun* The emotion aroused by something awe-inspiring or astounding : amazement, astonishment, awe, marvel, wonder, wonderment. *Archaic:* admiration, dread. *See* EXCITE, FEELINGS.

amazement *noun*
The emotion aroused by something awe-inspiring or astounding : amaze, astonishment, awe, marvel, wonder, wonderment. *Archaic:* admiration, dread. *See* EXCITE, FEELINGS.

amazing *adjective*
So remarkable as to elicit disbelief : astonishing, astounding, fabulous, fantastic, fantastical, incredible, marvelous, miraculous, phenomenal, prodigious, stupendous, unbelievable, wonderful, wondrous. *See* GOOD.

ambiance also **ambience** *noun*
1. A general impression produced by a predominant quality or characteristic : air, atmosphere, aura, feel, feeling, mood, smell, tone. *See* BE. **2.** The totality of surrounding conditions and circumstances affecting growth or development : atmosphere, climate, environment, medium, milieu, mise en scène, surroundings, world. *See* BE, LIMITED, PLACE.

ambidexterity *noun*
Lack of sincerity : artificiality, disingenuousness, insincerity, phoniness. *See* HONEST.

ambidextrous *adjective*
Not being what one purports to be : disingenuous, insincere, left-handed, mala fide. *See* HONEST.

ambience *noun* See **ambiance.**

ambiguity *noun*
1. The quality or state of being ambiguous : ambiguousness, cloudiness, equivocalness, indefiniteness, nebulousness, obscureness, obscurity, uncertainty, unclearness, vagueness. *See*

CLEAR. **2.** An expression or term liable to more than one interpretation : double-entendre, equivocality, equivocation, equivoque, tergiversation. *See* CLEAR. **3.** The use or an instance of equivocal language : equivocation, equivoque, euphemism, hedge, prevarication, shuffle, tergiversation, weasel word. *Informal:* waffle. *See* CLEAR.

ambiguous *adjective*
1. Liable to more than one interpretation : cloudy, equivocal, inexplicit, nebulous, obscure, uncertain, unclear, vague. *See* CERTAIN, CLEAR. **2.** Not affording certainty : borderline, chancy, clouded, doubtful, dubious, dubitable, equivocal, inconclusive, indecisive, indeterminate, problematic, problematical, questionable, uncertain, unclear, unsure. *Informal:* iffy. ***Idioms:*** at issue, in doubt, in question. *See* CERTAIN, CLEAR.

ambiguousness *noun*
The quality or state of being ambiguous : ambiguity, cloudiness, equivocalness, indefiniteness, nebulousness, obscureness, obscurity, uncertainty, unclearness, vagueness. *See* CLEAR.

ambit *noun*
1. A line around a closed figure or area : circuit, circumference, compass, perimeter, periphery. *See* EDGE. **2.** An area within which something or someone exists, acts, or has influence or power : compass, extension, extent, orbit, purview, range, reach, realm, scope, sphere, sweep, swing. *See* TERRITORY.

ambition *noun*
1. A strong desire to achieve something : ambitiousness, aspiration, emulation. *See* DESIRE. **2.** What one intends to do or achieve : aim, design, end, goal, intent, intention, mark, meaning, object, objective, point, purpose, target, view, why. ***Idioms:*** end in view, why and wherefore. *See* PLANNED, PURPOSE.

ambitious *adjective*
Full of ambition : aspiring, emulous. *See* DESIRE.

ambitiousness *noun*
A strong desire to achieve something : ambition, aspiration, emulation. *See* DESIRE.

amble *verb*
To walk at a leisurely pace : meander, perambulate, promenade, ramble, saunter, stroll, wander. *Informal:* mosey. *See* MOVE.
amble *noun* An act of walking, especially for pleasure : meander (often used in plural), perambulation, promenade, ramble, saunter, stroll, walk, wander. *See* MOVE.

ambrosial *adjective*
Highly pleasing, especially to the sense of taste : appetizing, delectable, delicious, heavenly, luscious, savory, scrumptious, tasteful, tasty, toothsome. *Slang:* yummy. *See* GOOD, INGESTION.

ambulance chaser *noun*
Slang. A person who practices law : attorney, counsel, counselor, lawyer. *Chiefly British:* barrister. *See* LAW.

ambulate *verb*
To go on foot : foot, pace, step, tread, walk. *Slang:* hoof. ***Idiom:*** foot it. *See* MOVE.

ambuscade *noun*
An attack or stratagem for capturing or tricking an unsuspecting person : ambush, trap. *See* ATTACK.
ambuscade *verb* To attack suddenly and without warning : ambush, bushwhack, surprise, waylay. *See* ATTACK.

ambush *noun*
An attack or stratagem for capturing or tricking an unsuspecting person : ambuscade, trap. *See* ATTACK.
ambush *verb* To attack suddenly and without warning : ambuscade, bushwhack, surprise, waylay. *See* ATTACK.

ameliorate *verb*
To advance to a more desirable state : amend, better[1], help, improve, meliorate, upgrade. *See* HELP.

amelioration *noun*
1. The act of making better or the condition of being made better : amendment, betterment, improvement, melioration, upgrade. *See* BETTER. **2.** Steady improvement, as of an individual or a society : betterment, development, improvement, melioration, progress. *See* BETTER.

amenable *adjective*
1. Willing to carry out the wishes of others : biddable, compliant, conformable, docile, obedient, submissive, supple, tractable. *See* RESIST. **2.** Legally obligated : accountable, answerable, liable, responsible. *See* LAW. **3.** Ready and willing to receive favorably, as new ideas : acceptant, open, open-minded, receptive, responsive. *See* ACCEPT.

amenability *noun*
The quality or state of willingly carrying out the wishes of others : acquiescence, amenableness, compliance, compliancy, deference, obedience, submission, submissiveness, tractability, tractableness. *See* RESIST.

amenableness *noun*
The quality or state of willingly carrying out the

wishes of others : acquiescence, amenability, compliance, compliancy, deference, obedience, submission, submissiveness, tractability, tractableness. *See* RESIST.

amend *verb*

1. To advance to a more desirable state : ameliorate, better[1], help, improve, meliorate, upgrade. *See* HELP. **2.** To make right what is wrong : correct, emend, mend, rectify, redress, reform, remedy, right. *See* CORRECT. **3.** To prepare a new version of : emend, emendate, revamp, revise, rework, rewrite. *See* CHANGE.

amendatory *adjective*

Tending to correct : corrective, emendatory, reformative, reformatory, remedial. *See* CORRECT.

amendment *noun*

1. The act of making better or the condition of being made better : amelioration, betterment, improvement, melioration, upgrade. *See* BETTER. **2.** The act or process of revising : emendation, revision, rewrite. *See* CHANGE.

amends *noun*

Something to make up for loss or damage : compensation, indemnification, indemnity, offset, quittance, recompense, redress, reimbursement, remuneration, reparation, repayment, requital, restitution, satisfaction, setoff. *See* SUBSTITUTE.

amenity *noun*

1. The quality of being pleasant and friendly : affability, agreeability, agreeableness, amiability, amiableness, congeniality, congenialness, cordiality, cordialness, friendliness, geniality, genialness, pleasantness, sociability, sociableness, warmth. *See* ATTITUDE, GOOD. **2.** Anything that increases physical comfort : comfort, convenience, facility (often used in plural). *See* COMFORT. **3.** A courteous act or courteous acts that contribute to smoothness and ease in dealings and social relationships. Used in plural : civility, courtesy, pleasantry, politeness, propriety (used in plural). *See* COURTESY.

amerce *verb*

To impose a fine on : fine[2], mulct, penalize. *See* REWARD.

amercement *noun*

A sum of money levied as punishment for an offense : fine[2], mulct, penalty. *See* REWARD.

amiability *noun*

The quality of being pleasant and friendly : affability, agreeability, agreeableness, amenity, amiableness, congeniality, congenialness, cordiality, cordialness, friendliness, geniality, genialness, pleasantness, sociability, sociableness, warmth. *See* ATTITUDE, GOOD.

amiable *adjective*

Pleasant and friendly in disposition : affable, agreeable, congenial, cordial, genial, good-natured, good-tempered, pleasant, sociable, warm. *See* ATTITUDE, GOOD.

amiableness *noun*

The quality of being pleasant and friendly : affability, agreeability, agreeableness, amenity, amiability, congeniality, congenialness, cordiality, cordialness, friendliness, geniality, genialness, pleasantness, sociability, sociableness, warmth. *See* ATTITUDE, GOOD.

amicable *adjective*

Of or befitting a friend or friends : friendly, neighborly, warmhearted. *See* ATTITUDE, LOVE.

amigo *noun*

A person whom one knows well, likes, and trusts : brother, chum, confidant, confidante, familiar, friend, intimate[1], mate. *Informal:* bud[2], buddy, pal. *Slang:* sidekick. *See* LOVE.

amiss *adjective*

Not in accordance with what is usual or expected : astray, awry, sour, wrong. *See* SURPRISE, THRIVE.

amiss *adverb* Not in the right way or on the proper course : afield, astray, awry, wrong. *See* THRIVE.

amnesiac *adjective*

Unable to remember : amnesic, forgetful, oblivious. *See* REMEMBER.

amnesic *adjective*

Unable to remember : amnesiac, forgetful, oblivious. *See* REMEMBER.

amnesty *noun*

The act or an instance of forgiving : absolution, condonation, excuse, forgiveness, pardon, remission. *See* FORGIVENESS.

amok *adjective* See **amuck.**

amorist *noun*

A man amorously attentive to women : Casanova, Don Juan, gallant, lady's man, Lothario, Romeo. *See* SEX.

amorous *adjective*

1. Feeling or devoted to sexual love or desire : amative, concupiscent, erotic, lascivious, lecherous, lewd, libidinous, lustful, lusty, passionate, prurient, sexy. *See* SEX. **2.** Of, concerning, or promoting sexual love or desire : amatory, aphrodisiac, erotic, lascivious, salacious, sexual, sexy. *See* SEX.

amorousness *noun*

The passionate affection and desire felt by lovers for each other : fancy, love, passion, romance. *See* LOVE, SEX.

amorphous *adjective*
Having no distinct shape : formless, inchoate, shapeless, unformed, unshaped. *See* ORDER.

amount *noun*
1. A number or quantity obtained as a result of addition : aggregate, sum, summation, sum total, total, totality. *Archaic:* tale. *See* COUNT. **2.** The general sense or significance, as of an action or statement : burden[2], drift, import, purport, substance, tenor. ***Idioms:*** sum and substance, sum total. *See* MEANING. **3.** A measurable whole : body, budget, bulk, corpus, quantity, quantum. *See* BIG.
amount *verb* **1.** To come to in number or quantity : aggregate, number, reach, run into, total. ***Idiom:*** add up to. *See* INCREASE. **2.** To be equivalent or tantamount : constitute, correspond, equal. ***Idiom:*** have all the earmarks. *See* BE.

amour *noun*
An intimate sexual relationship between two people : affair, love, love affair, romance. *See* LOVE, SEX.

amour-propre *noun*
1. A sense of one's own dignity or worth : ego, pride, self-esteem, self-regard, self-respect. *See* RESPECT. **2.** A regarding of oneself with undue favor : conceit, ego, egoism, egotism, narcissism, pride, vainglory, vainness, vanity. *Slang:* ego trip. *See* SELF-LOVE.

ample *adjective*
1. Large in expanse : broad, expansive, extensive, spacious. *See* WIDE. **2.** Having plenty of room : capacious, commodious, roomy, spacious. *See* BIG. **3.** Of full measure; not narrow or restricted : capacious, full, voluminous, wide. *See* TIGHTEN. **4.** Characterized by abundance : abundant, bounteous, bountiful, copious, generous, heavy, plenitudinous, plenteous, plentiful, substantial, voluminous. *See* BIG, GIVE, RICH.

amplification *noun*
The act of increasing or rising : aggrandizement, augment, augmentation, boost, buildup, enlargement, escalation, growth, hike, increase, jump, multiplication, proliferation, raise, rise, swell, upsurge, upswing, upturn. *See* INCREASE.

amplify *verb*
1. To make or become greater or larger : aggrandize, augment, boost, build, build up, burgeon, enlarge, escalate, expand, extend, grow, increase, magnify, mount, multiply, proliferate, rise, run up, snowball, soar, swell, upsurge, wax. *Informal:* beef up. *See* INCREASE. **2.** To express at greater length or in greater detail : develop, dilate, elaborate, enlarge, expand, expatiate, labor. *See* EXPLAIN. **3.** To increase markedly in level or intensity, especially of sound : elevate, heighten, raise. *See* INCREASE.

amplitude *noun*
1. Great extent, amount, or dimension : bulk, magnitude, mass, size, volume (often used in plural). *See* BIG. **2.** The quality or state of being large in amount, extent, or importance : bigness, greatness, largeness, magnitude, sizableness, size. *See* BIG.

amuck also **amok** *adjective*
Out of control : runaway, uncontrolled. ***Idioms:*** out of hand, running wild. *See* CONTROL.

amulet *noun*
A small object worn or kept for its supposed magical power : charm, fetish, juju, periapt, phylactery, talisman. *See* SUPERNATURAL.

amuse *verb*
To occupy in an agreeable or pleasing way : divert, entertain, recreate, regale. *See* EXCITE.

amusement *noun*
1. The condition of being amused : entertainment, recreation. *See* EXCITE. **2.** Something, especially a performance or show, designed to entertain : distraction, diversion, entertainment, recreation. *See* EXCITE.

amusing *adjective*
1. Providing pleasure or entertainment : diverting, entertaining. *See* EXCITE. **2.** Arousing laughter : comic, comical, droll, funny, humorous, laughable, risible, zany. *See* LAUGHTER.

anaesthetic *adjective* See **anesthetic.**

analogize *verb*
To represent as similar : assimilate, compare, equate, identify, liken, match, parallel. *See* SAME.

analogous *adjective*
Possessing the same or almost the same characteristics : alike, comparable, corresponding, equivalent, like[2], parallel, similar, uniform. *See* SAME.

analogue *noun*
Something closely resembling or analogous to something else : congener, correlate, correlative, correspondent, counterpart, match, parallel. *See* SAME.

analogy *noun*
The quality or state of being alike : affinity, alikeness, comparison, correspondence, like-

ness, parallelism, resemblance, similarity, similitude, uniformity, uniformness. *See* SAME.

analysis *noun*
1. The separation of a whole into its parts for study : anatomy, breakdown, dissection. *See* ASSEMBLE, INVESTIGATE. 2. A close or systematic study : examination, inspection, investigation, review, survey. *See* INVESTIGATE.

analytic *adjective*
Able to reason validly : analytical, logical, ratiocinative, rational. *See* REASON.

analytical *adjective*
Able to reason validly : analytic, logical, ratiocinative, rational. *See* REASON.

analyze *verb*
1. To separate into parts for study : anatomize, break down, dissect, resolve. *See* ASSEMBLE, INVESTIGATE. 2. To study closely or systematically : examine, inspect, investigate. *See* INVESTIGATE.

anarchy *noun*
A lack of civil order or peace : disorder, lawlessness, misrule. *See* ORDER, PEACE.

anathema *noun*
1. A denunciation invoking a wish or threat of evil or injury : curse, damnation, execration, imprecation, malediction. *Archaic:* malison. *See* WORDS. 2. An object of extreme dislike : abhorrence, abomination, aversion, bête noire, bugbear, detestation, execration, hate. *Informal:* horror. *See* LOVE.

anathematize *verb*
To invoke evil or injury upon : curse, damn, imprecate. *Informal:* cuss. *Archaic:* execrate, maledict. *See* WORDS.

anatomize *verb*
To separate into parts for study : analyze, break down, dissect, resolve. *See* ASSEMBLE, INVESTIGATE.

anatomy *noun*
The separation of a whole into its parts for study : analysis, breakdown, dissection. *See* ASSEMBLE, INVESTIGATE.

ancestor *noun*
1. A person from whom one is descended : antecedent, ascendant, father, forebear, forefather, foremother, mother, parent, progenitor. *Archaic:* predecessor. *See* KIN, PRECEDE.
2. One that precedes, as in time : antecedent, forerunner, precursor, predecessor, progenitor. *See* PRECEDE.

ancestral *adjective*
Of or from one's ancestors : hereditary, inherited, patrimonial. *See* KIN, PRECEDE.

ancestry *noun*
One's ancestors or their character or one's ancestral derivation : birth, blood, bloodline, descent, extraction, family, genealogy, line, lineage, origin, parentage, pedigree, seed, stock. *See* KIN, PRECEDE.

anchor *verb*
To make secure : catch, fasten, fix, moor, secure. ***Idiom:*** make fast. *See* MOVE.

ancient *adjective*
1. Belonging to, existing, or occurring in times long past : age-old, antediluvian, antiquated, antique, archaic, hoary, old, olden, old-time, timeworn, venerable. ***Idioms:*** old as Methuselah, old as the hills. *See* NEW. 2. Of, existing, or occurring in a distant period : antediluvian, early, primitive. *See* START. 3. Long past : high, immemorial. *See* NEW.
ancient *noun* An elderly person : elder, golden ager, senior, senior citizen. *Informal:* oldster, old-timer. *See* YOUTH.

ancillary *adjective*
Giving or able to give help or support : accessory, assistant, auxiliary, collateral, contributory, subsidiary, supportive. *See* HELP.

anecdote *noun*
An entertaining and often oral account of a real or fictitious occurrence : fable, story, tale. *Informal:* tall tale, yarn. *See* WORDS.

anemic *adjective*
1. Of or associated with sickness : peaked, sick, sickly. *See* HEALTH. 2. Being weak in quality or substance : bloodless, pale, pallid, waterish, watery. *See* STRONG.

anesthetic also **anaesthetic** *adjective*
Lacking passion and emotion : bloodless, dull, insensate, insensible, insensitive. *See* ATTITUDE, FEELINGS.

anew *adverb*
Once more : afresh, again. *See* REPETITION.

anfractuous *adjective*
1. Repeatedly curving in alternate directions : flexuous, meandrous, serpentine, sinuous, snaky, tortuous, winding. *See* REPETITION, STRAIGHT. 2. Not taking a direct or straight line or course : circuitous, circular, devious, indirect, oblique, roundabout, tortuous. *See* STRAIGHT.

angel *noun*
1. A pure, uncorrupted person : innocent, lamb, virgin. *See* CLEAN, RIGHT. 2. *Informal.* One who assumes financial responsibility for another : backer, guarantor, guaranty, sponsor, surety, underwriter. *See* LAW, SUPPORT.
3. *Informal.* A person who supports or champi-

ons an activity, cause, or institution, for example : backer, benefactor, contributor, friend, patron, sponsor, supporter. *See* HELP.

angelic *adjective*
Free from evil and corruption : angelical, clean, innocent, lily-white, pure, sinless, unblemished, uncorrupted, undefiled, unstained, unsullied, untainted, virginal. ***Idiom:*** pure as the driven snow. *See* CLEAN, RIGHT, SEX.

angelical *adjective*
Free from evil and corruption : angelic, clean, innocent, lily-white, pure, sinless, unblemished, uncorrupted, undefiled, unstained, unsullied, untainted, virginal. ***Idiom:*** pure as the driven snow. *See* CLEAN, RIGHT, SEX.

anger *noun*
A strong feeling of displeasure or hostility : choler, indignation, irateness, ire. *See* FEELINGS.

anger *verb* **1.** To cause to feel or show anger : burn (up), enrage, incense[1], infuriate, madden, provoke. ***Idioms:*** make one hot under the collar, make one's blood boil, put one's back up. *See* FEELINGS. **2.** To be or become angry : blow up, boil over, bristle, burn, explode, flare up, foam, fume, rage, seethe. *Informal:* steam. ***Idioms:*** blow a fuse, blow a gasket, blow one's stack (*or* top), breathe fire, fly off the handle, get hot under the collar, hit the ceiling (*or* roof), lose one's temper, see red. *See* FEELINGS.

angle[1] *verb*
To try to obtain something, usually by subtleness and cunning : fish, hint. *See* ASK.

angle[2] *noun*
1. The particular angle from which something is considered : aspect, facet, frame of reference, hand, light[1], phase, regard, respect, side. *See* PERSPECTIVE. **2.** The position from which something is observed or considered : eye, outlook, point of view, slant, standpoint, vantage, viewpoint. *See* PERSPECTIVE. **3.** *Slang.* A clever, unexpected new trick or method : gimmick, twist. *Informal:* kicker, wrinkle. *Slang:* kick. *See* ABILITY, EXCITE, GOOD.

angle *verb* **1.** To swerve from a straight line : arc, arch, bend, bow[2], crook, curve, round, turn. *See* STRAIGHT. **2.** To cause to move, especially at an angle : bend, deflect, refract, turn. *See* STRAIGHT. **3.** *Informal.* To direct (material) to the interests of a particular group : bias, skew, slant. *See* STRAIGHT.

angry *adjective*
Feeling or showing anger : choleric, indignant, mad. *Informal:* sore. ***Idiom:*** hot under the collar. *See* FEELINGS.

angst *noun*
A troubled or anxious state of mind : anxiety, anxiousness, care, concern, disquiet, disquietude, distress, nervousness, solicitude, unease, uneasiness, worry. *See* FEELINGS.

anguish *noun*
A state of physical or mental suffering : affliction, agony, distress, hurt, misery, pain, torment, torture, woe, wound, wretchedness. *See* HAPPY.

anguish *verb* To bring great harm or suffering to : afflict, agonize, curse, excruciate, plague, rack, scourge, smite, strike, torment, torture. *See* ATTACK, HELP.

anguishing *adjective*
Extraordinarily painful or distressing : agonizing, excruciating, harrowing, tormenting, torturous. *See* PAIN.

angular *adjective*
Having little flesh or fat on the body : bony, fleshless, gaunt, lank, lanky, lean[2], meager, rawboned, scrawny, skinny, slender, slim, spare, thin, twiggy, weedy. ***Idioms:*** all skin and bones, thin as a rail. *See* FAT.

anhydrous *adjective*
Having little or no liquid or moisture : arid, bone-dry, dry, moistureless, sere, waterless. *See* DRY.

animal *adjective*
Relating to the desires and appetites of the body : carnal, fleshly, physical, sensual. *See* BODY.

animalism *noun*
A preoccupation with the body and satisfaction of its desires : animality, carnality, fleshliness, physicality, sensuality. *See* BODY.

animality *noun*
A preoccupation with the body and satisfaction of its desires : animalism, carnality, fleshliness, physicality, sensuality. *See* BODY.

animalize *verb*
To ruin utterly in character or quality : bastardize, bestialize, brutalize, canker, corrupt, debase, debauch, demoralize, deprave, pervert, stain, vitiate, warp. *See* CLEAN, HELP.

animate *verb*
1. To make alive : quicken, vitalize, vivify. *See* LIVE. **2.** To make lively or animated : brighten, enliven, light[1]. *See* HAPPY. **3.** To raise the spirits of : buoy (up), elate, elevate, exhilarate, flush, inspire, inspirit, lift, uplift. *Obsolete:* exalt. *See* HAPPY. **4.** To impart courage, inspiration, and resolution to : cheer (on), embolden, encourage, inspire, inspirit, motivate. *See*

HELP. **5.** To arouse the emotions of; make ardent : enkindle, fire, impassion, inspire, kindle, stir[1]. *See* EXCITE. **6.** To arouse to action or put in motion : activate, actuate. *See* ACTION.
animate *adjective* Marked by or exhibiting life : alive, animated, live[2], living, vital. *See* LIVE.

animated *adjective*
1. Marked by or exhibiting life : alive, animate, live[2], living, vital. *See* LIVE. **2.** Very brisk, alert, and full of high spirits : bouncy, chipper, dashing, high-spirited, lively, pert, spirited, vivacious. *Informal:* peppy. *Idioms:* bright-eyed and bushy-tailed, full of life. *See* ACTION.

animating *adjective*
Serving to enliven : enlivening, quickening, rousing, stimulating, vitalizing, vivifying. *See* EXCITE.

animation *noun*
1. A lively, emphatic, eager quality or manner : bounce, brio, dash, élan, esprit, life, liveliness, pertness, sparkle, spirit, verve, vigor, vim, vivaciousness, vivacity, zip. *Informal:* ginger, pep, peppiness. *Slang:* oomph. *See* ACTION. **2.** High spirits : elatedness, elation, euphoria, exaltation, exhilaration, inspiration, lift, uplift. *See* HAPPY. **3.** Capacity or power for work or vigorous activity : energy, force, might, potency, power, puissance, sprightliness, steam, strength. *Informal:* get-up-and-go, go, pep, peppiness, zip. *See* ACTION.

animosity *noun*
Deep-seated hatred, as between longtime opponents or rivals : animus, antagonism, antipathy, enmity, hostility, ill will. *See* LOVE.

animus *noun*
Deep-seated hatred, as between longtime opponents or rivals : animosity, antagonism, antipathy, enmity, hostility, ill will. *See* LOVE.

annals *noun*
A chronological record of past events : chronicle, history. *See* HAPPEN, WORDS.

annex *verb*
To add as a supplement or an appendix : affix, append, attach, subjoin. *See* INCREASE.
annex *noun* A part added to a main structure : arm, extension, wing. *See* PART.

annihilate *verb*
1. To destroy all traces of : abolish, blot out, clear, eradicate, erase, exterminate, extinguish, extirpate, kill[1], liquidate, obliterate, remove, root[1] (out *or* up), rub out, snuff out, stamp out, uproot, wipe out. *Idioms:* do away with, make an end of, put an end to. *See* HELP, MAKE. **2.** To kill savagely and indiscriminately : butcher, decimate, massacre, slaughter. *See* CRIMES, HELP, MAKE. **3.** To render totally ineffective by decisive defeat : crush, drub, overpower, overwhelm, smash, steamroller, thrash, trounce, vanquish. *Informal:* massacre, wallop. *Slang:* clobber, cream, shellac, smear. *See* WIN. **4.** To put an end to, especially formally and with authority : abolish, abrogate, annul, cancel, invalidate, negate, nullify, set aside, vitiate, void. *Law:* extinguish. *See* CONTINUE.

annihilation *noun*
1. Utter destruction : eradication, extermination, extinction, extinguishment, extirpation, liquidation, obliteration. *See* CRIMES, HELP, MAKE. **2.** An often formal act of putting an end to : abolishment, abolition, abrogation, annulment, cancellation, defeasance, invalidation, negation, nullification, voidance. *Law:* avoidance, extinguishment. *See* CONTINUE.

annotation *noun*
Critical explanation or analysis : comment, commentary, exegesis, interpretation, note. *See* WORDS.

announce *verb*
1. To bring to public notice or make known publicly : advertise, annunciate, broadcast, declare, proclaim, promulgate, publish. *See* KNOWLEDGE, WORDS. **2.** To make known the presence or arrival of : herald, introduce, proclaim, usher in. *See* KNOWLEDGE, START.

announcement *noun*
1. The act of announcing : annunciation, declaration, proclamation, promulgation, publication. *See* KNOWLEDGE. **2.** A public statement : annunciation, declaration, edict, manifesto, notice, proclamation, pronouncement. *See* KNOWLEDGE.

annoy *verb*
1. To trouble the nerves or peace of mind of, especially by repeated vexations : aggravate, bother, bug, chafe, disturb, exasperate, fret, gall[2], get, irk, irritate, nettle, peeve, provoke, put out, rile, ruffle, vex. *Idioms:* get in one's hair, get on one's nerves, get under one's skin. *See* FEELINGS, PAIN. **2.** To disturb by repeated attacks : bait, bedevil, beleaguer, beset, harass, harry, pester, plague, tease, torment, worry. *See* FEELINGS, PAIN.

annoyance *noun*
1. The act of annoying : botheration, bothering, exasperation, harassment, irritation, pestering, provocation, vexation. *See* FEELINGS, PAIN. **2.** The feeling of being annoyed : aggravation, bother, botheration, exasperation,

irritation, vexation. *See* FEELINGS, PAIN.
3. Something that annoys : aggravation, besetment, bother, irritant, irritation, nuisance, peeve, plague, torment, vexation. *See* FEELINGS, PAIN.

annoying *adjective*
Troubling the nerves or peace of mind, as by repeated vexations : bothersome, galling, irksome, irritating, nettlesome, plaguy, provoking, troublesome, vexatious. *See* PAIN.

annul *verb*
1. To put an end to, especially formally and with authority : abolish, abrogate, annihilate, cancel, invalidate, negate, nullify, set aside, vitiate, void. *Law:* extinguish. *See* CONTINUE.
2. To remove or invalidate by or as if by running a line through or wiping clean : blot (out), cancel, cross (off *or* out), delete, efface, erase, expunge, obliterate, rub (out), scratch (out), strike (out), undo, wipe (out), x (out). *Law:* vacate. *See* CONTINUE.

annular *adjective*
Having the shape of a curve everywhere equidistant from a fixed point : circular, globoid, globular, round, spheric, spherical. *See* GEOMETRY.

annulment *noun*
An often formal act of putting an end to : abolishment, abolition, abrogation, annihilation, cancellation, defeasance, invalidation, negation, nullification, voidance. *Law:* avoidance, extinguishment. *See* CONTINUE.

annunciate *verb*
To bring to public notice or make known publicly : advertise, announce, broadcast, declare, proclaim, promulgate, publish. *See* KNOWLEDGE, WORDS.

annunciation *noun*
1. The act of announcing : announcement, declaration, proclamation, promulgation, publication. *See* KNOWLEDGE. **2.** A public statement : announcement, declaration, edict, manifesto, notice, proclamation, pronouncement. *See* KNOWLEDGE.

anomalistic *adjective*
Departing from the normal : aberrant, abnormal, anomalous, atypic, atypical, deviant, divergent, irregular, preternatural, unnatural. *See* GOOD, USUAL.

anomalous *adjective*
Departing from the normal : aberrant, abnormal, anomalistic, atypic, atypical, deviant, divergent, irregular, preternatural, unnatural. *See* GOOD, USUAL.

anomaly *noun*
The condition of being abnormal : aberrance, aberrancy, aberration, abnormality, deviance, deviancy, deviation, irregularity, preternaturalness, unnaturalness. *See* GOOD, USUAL.

anonymity *noun*
The quality or state of being obscure : namelessness, obscurity. *See* KNOWLEDGE.

anonymous *adjective*
Having an unknown name or author : nameless, unnamed, unsigned. *See* KNOWLEDGE.

Anschluss *noun*
An association, especially of nations for a common cause : alliance, bloc, cartel, coalition, confederacy, confederation, federation, league, organization, union. *See* CONNECT, GROUP, POLITICS.

answer *noun*
1. Something spoken or written in return, as to a question or demand : rejoinder, reply, response. *See* ASK. **2.** Something worked out to explain, resolve, or provide a method for dealing with and settling a problem : determination, solution. *Mathematics:* result. *See* ASK.
answer *verb* **1.** To speak or act in response, as to a question : rejoin, reply, respond, retort, return, riposte. *See* ASK. **2.** To meet a need or requirement : do, serve, suffice, suit. *See* EXCESS, HELP. **3.** To supply fully or completely : fill, fulfill, meet[1], satisfy. *See* DO.

answerable *adjective*
Legally obligated : accountable, amenable, liable, responsible. *See* LAW.

antagonism *noun*
1. Deep-seated hatred, as between longtime opponents or rivals : animosity, animus, antipathy, enmity, hostility, ill will. *See* LOVE. **2.** The condition of being in conflict : antithesis, contradiction, contradistinction, contraposition, contrariety, contrariness, opposition, polarity. *See* SUPPORT.

antagonist *noun*
One that opposes another in a battle, contest, controversy, or debate : adversary, opponent, opposer, opposition, oppositionist, resister. *See* RESIST, SUPPORT.

antagonistic *adjective*
Acting against or in opposition : adversarial, adverse, antipathetic, opposed, opposing, oppositional. *See* SUPPORT.

ante *noun*
Something risked on an uncertain outcome : bet, pot, stake (often used in plural), wager. *See* GAMBLING.

antecede *verb*
To come, exist, or occur before in time : antedate, precede, predate. *See* PRECEDE.

antecedence *noun*
The act, condition, or right of preceding : precedence, precedency, priority, right of way. *See* PRECEDE.

antecedent *adjective*
1. Going before : advance, anterior, earlier, precedent, preceding, previous, prior. *See* PRECEDE. **2.** Just gone by or elapsed : anterior, earlier, foregoing, former, past, precedent, preceding, previous, prior. *See* TIME.

antecedent *noun* **1.** One that precedes, as in time : ancestor, forerunner, precursor, predecessor, progenitor. *See* PRECEDE. **2.** That which produces an effect : cause, occasion. *See* START. **3.** A person from whom one is descended : ancestor, ascendant, father, forebear, forefather, foremother, mother, parent, progenitor. *Archaic:* predecessor. *See* KIN, PRECEDE.

antedate *verb*
To come, exist, or occur before in time : antecede, precede, predate. *See* PRECEDE.

antediluvian *adjective*
1. Belonging to, existing, or occurring in times long past : age-old, ancient, antiquated, antique, archaic, hoary, old, olden, old-time, timeworn, venerable. ***Idioms:*** old as Methuselah, old as the hills. *See* NEW. **2.** Of, existing, or occurring in a distant period : ancient, early, primitive. *See* START.

anterior *adjective*
1. Going before : advance, antecedent, earlier, precedent, preceding, previous, prior. *See* PRECEDE. **2.** Just gone by or elapsed : antecedent, earlier, foregoing, former, past, precedent, preceding, previous, prior. *See* TIME.

anthropoid *adjective*
Resembling a human being : anthropomorphic, anthropomorphous, hominoid, humanoid, manlike. *See* CULTURE.

anthropomorphic *adjective*
Resembling a human being : anthropoid, anthropomorphous, hominoid, humanoid, manlike. *See* CULTURE.

anthropomorphous *adjective*
Resembling a human being : anthropoid, anthropomorphic, hominoid, humanoid, manlike. *See* CULTURE.

antic *noun*
A mischievous act : caper, frolic, joke, lark, prank[1], trick. *Informal:* shenanigan. *Slang:* monkeyshine (often used in plural). *See* GOOD, WORK.

antic *adjective* Conceived or done with no reference to reality or common sense : bizarre, fantastic, fantastical, far-fetched, grotesque. *See* TRUE, USUAL.

anticipant *adjective*
Having or marked by expectation : anticipative, anticipatory, expectant. *See* SURPRISE.

anticipate *verb*
1. To know in advance : divine, envision, foreknow, foresee, see. *See* FORESIGHT, SEE. **2.** To look forward to confidently : await, bargain for (*or* on), count on, depend on (*or* upon), expect, look for, wait (for). *Informal:* figure on. *See* SURPRISE.

anticipated *adjective*
Known to be about to arrive : due, expected, scheduled. *See* SURPRISE.

anticipation *noun*
1. The condition of looking forward to something, especially with eagerness : expectance, expectancy, expectation. *See* SURPRISE.
2. Something expected : expectancy, expectation, prospect. *See* SURPRISE.

anticipative *adjective*
Having or marked by expectation : anticipant, anticipatory, expectant. *See* SURPRISE.

anticipatory *adjective*
Having or marked by expectation : anticipant, anticipative, expectant. *See* SURPRISE.

antidote *noun*
Something that corrects or counteracts : corrective, countermeasure, curative, cure, remedy. *See* BETTER.

antipathetic *adjective*
1. Acting against or in opposition : adversarial, adverse, antagonistic, opposed, opposing, oppositional. *See* SUPPORT. **2.** So objectionable as to elicit despisal or deserve condemnation : abhorrent, abominable, contemptible, despicable, despisable, detestable, disgusting, filthy, foul, infamous, loathsome, lousy, low, mean[2], nasty, nefarious, obnoxious, odious, repugnant, rotten, shabby, vile, wretched. *See* GOOD.

antipathy *noun*
1. Deep-seated hatred, as between longtime opponents or rivals : animosity, animus, antagonism, enmity, hostility, ill will. *See* LOVE.
2. Extreme hostility and dislike : abhorrence, abomination, aversion, detestation, hate, hatred, horror, loathing, repellence, repellency, repugnance, repugnancy, repulsion, revulsion. *See* LOVE.

antipodal *adjective*
Diametrically opposed : antipodean, antithetical, antonymic, antonymous, contradictory,

contrary, converse[2], counter, diametric, diametrical, opposing, opposite, polar, reverse. *See* SUPPORT.

antipode *noun*
That which is diametrically opposed to another : antipodes, antithesis, antonym, contrary, converse[2], counter, opposite, reverse. *Logic:* contradictory, contrapositive. *See* SUPPORT.

antipodean *adjective*
Diametrically opposed : antipodal, antithetical, antonymic, antonymous, contradictory, contrary, converse[2], counter, diametric, diametrical, opposing, opposite, polar, reverse. *See* SUPPORT.

antipodes *noun*
That which is diametrically opposed to another : antipode, antithesis, antonym, contrary, converse[2], counter, opposite, reverse. *Logic:* contradictory, contrapositive. *See* SUPPORT.

antiquated *adjective*
1. Of a style or method formerly in vogue : antique, archaic, bygone, dated, dowdy, fusty, old, old-fashioned, old-time, outdated, outmoded, out-of-date, passé, vintage. *See* NEW.
2. Belonging to, existing, or occurring in times long past : age-old, ancient, antediluvian, antique, archaic, hoary, old, olden, old-time, timeworn, venerable. ***Idioms:*** old as Methuselah, old as the hills. *See* NEW.

antique *adjective*
1. Of a style or method formerly in vogue : antiquated, archaic, bygone, dated, dowdy, fusty, old, old-fashioned, old-time, outdated, outmoded, out-of-date, passé, vintage. *See* NEW.
2. Belonging to, existing, or occurring in times long past : age-old, ancient, antediluvian, antiquated, archaic, hoary, old, olden, old-time, timeworn, venerable. ***Idioms:*** old as Methuselah, old as the hills. *See* NEW.

antiseptic *adjective*
Free from dirt, stain, or impurities : clean, cleanly, immaculate, spotless, stainless, unsoiled, unsullied. *See* CLEAN.

antithesis *noun*
1. The condition of being in conflict : antagonism, contradiction, contradistinction, contraposition, contrariety, contrariness, opposition, polarity. *See* SUPPORT. **2.** That which is diametrically opposed to another : antipode, antipodes, antonym, contrary, converse[2], counter, opposite, reverse. *Logic:* contradictory, contrapositive. *See* SUPPORT.

antithetical *adjective*
Diametrically opposed : antipodal, antipodean, antonymic, antonymous, contradictory, contrary, converse[2], counter, diametric, diametrical, opposing, opposite, polar, reverse. *See* SUPPORT.

antonym *noun*
That which is diametrically opposed to another : antipode, antipodes, antithesis, contrary, converse[2], counter, opposite, reverse. *Logic:* contradictory, contrapositive. *See* SUPPORT.

antonymic *adjective*
Diametrically opposed : antipodal, antipodean, antithetical, antonymous, contradictory, contrary, converse[2], counter, diametric, diametrical, opposing, opposite, polar, reverse. *See* SUPPORT.

antonymous *adjective*
Diametrically opposed : antipodal, antipodean, antithetical, antonymic, contradictory, contrary, converse[2], counter, diametric, diametrical, opposing, opposite, polar, reverse. *See* SUPPORT.

anxiety *noun*
A troubled or anxious state of mind : angst, anxiousness, care, concern, disquiet, disquietude, distress, nervousness, solicitude, unease, uneasiness, worry. *See* FEELINGS.

anxious *adjective*
In a state of anxiety or uneasiness : agitated, concerned, distressed, nervous, solicitous, uneasy, unsettled. *See* FEELINGS.

anxiousness *noun*
A troubled or anxious state of mind : angst, anxiety, care, concern, disquiet, disquietude, distress, nervousness, solicitude, unease, uneasiness, worry. *See* FEELINGS.

A-one also **A-1** *adjective*
Informal. Exceptionally good of its kind : ace, banner, blue-ribbon, brag, capital, champion, excellent, fine[1], first-class, first-rate, prime, quality, splendid, superb, superior, terrific, tiptop, top. *Informal:* bully, dandy, great, swell, topflight, topnotch. *Slang:* boss. *Chiefly British:* tophole. *See* GOOD.

apace *adverb*
In a rapid way : fast, posthaste, quick, quickly. *Informal:* flat out, hell-for-leather, lickety-split, pronto. ***Idioms:*** full tilt, in a flash, in nothing flat, like a bat out of hell, like a blue streak, like a flash, like a house on fire, like a shot, like a streak, like greased lightning, like the wind, like wildfire. *See* FAST.

apanage *noun* See **appanage.**

apart *adverb*
As a separate unit : discretely, independently, individually, separately, singly. ***Idioms:*** one at a time, one by one. *See* INCLUDE.
apart *adjective* Set away from all others : alone, detached, isolate, isolated, lone, removed, solitary. *See* INCLUDE.

apartheid *noun*
The policy or practice of political, legal, economic, or social discrimination, as against the members of a minority group : segregation, separatism. *See* INCLUDE.

apathetic *adjective*
Without emotion or interest : detached, impassive, incurious, indifferent, insensible, lethargic, listless, phlegmatic, stolid, unconcerned, uninterested, unresponsive. *See* FEELINGS.

apathy *noun*
Lack of emotion or interest : disinterest, impassivity, incuriosity, incuriousness, indifference, insensibility, insensibleness, lassitude, lethargy, listlessness, phlegm, stolidity, stolidness, unconcern, uninterest, unresponsiveness. *See* FEELINGS.

ape *verb*
To copy (the manner or expression of another), especially in an exaggerated or mocking way : burlesque, caricature, imitate, mimic, mock, parody, travesty. ***Idiom:*** do a takeoff on. *See* SAME.

aperture *noun*
An open space allowing passage : hole, mouth, opening, orifice, outlet, vent. *See* OPEN.

apex *noun*
1. The highest point : cap, crest, crown, height, peak, roof, summit, top, vertex. *See* HIGH.
2. The highest point or state : acme, apogee, climax, crest, crown, culmination, height, meridian, peak, pinnacle, summit, top, zenith. *Informal:* payoff. *Medicine:* fastigium. *See* HIGH. **3.** A sharp or tapered end : acicula, acumination, cusp, mucro, mucronation, point, tip[1]. *See* SHARP.

aphonic *adjective*
Lacking the power or faculty of speech : dumb, inarticulate, mute, speechless, voiceless. *See* WORDS.

aphorism *noun*
A usually pithy and familiar statement expressing an observation or principle generally accepted as wise or true : adage, byword, maxim, motto, proverb, saw, saying. *See* WORDS.

aphoristic *adjective*
Precisely meaningful and tersely cogent : compact[1], epigrammatic, epigrammatical, marrowy, pithy. *Informal:* brass-tacks. ***Idioms:*** down to brass tacks, to the point. *See* MEANING, STYLE.

aphrodisiac *adjective*
Of, concerning, or promoting sexual love or desire : amatory, amorous, erotic, lascivious, salacious, sexual, sexy. *See* SEX.

aping *noun*
The act, practice, or art of copying the manner or expression of another : imitation, mimicry. *See* SAME.

apish *adjective*
Copying another in an inferior or obsequious way : emulative, imitative, slavish. *See* SAME.

aplomb *noun*
1. A firm belief in one's own powers : assurance, confidence, self-assurance, self-confidence, self-possession. *See* ATTITUDE, BELIEF. **2.** A stable, calm state of the emotions : balance, collectedness, composure, coolness, equanimity, imperturbability, imperturbableness, nonchalance, poise, sang-froid, self-possession, unflappability. *Slang:* cool. *See* CALM, FEELINGS.

apocalypse *noun*
Something disclosed, especially something not previously known or realized : disclosure, exposé, exposure, revelation. *Informal:* eye opener. *See* SHOW.

apocalyptic *adjective*
Portending future disaster : apocalyptical, baneful, dire, direful, fateful, fire-and-brimstone, grave[2], hellfire, ominous, portentous, unlucky. *See* LUCK, WARN.

apocalyptical *adjective*
Portending future disaster : apocalyptic, baneful, dire, direful, fateful, fire-and-brimstone, grave[2], hellfire, ominous, portentous, unlucky. *See* LUCK, WARN.

apogee *noun*
The highest point or state : acme, apex, climax, crest, crown, culmination, height, meridian, peak, pinnacle, summit, top, zenith. *Informal:* payoff. *Medicine:* fastigium. *See* HIGH.

apologetic *adjective*
Expressing or inclined to express an apology : contrite, penitent, regretful, repentant, sorry. *See* REGRET.
apologetic *noun* A statement that justifies or defends something, such as a past action or policy : apologia, apology, defense, justification, vindication. *See* ATTACK.

apologia *noun*
A statement that justifies or defends something,

such as a past action or policy : apologetic, apology, defense, justification, vindication. *See* ATTACK.

apologize *verb*
To support against arguments, attack, or criticism : defend, justify, maintain, vindicate. ***Idioms:*** speak up for, stand up for, stick up for. *See* SUPPORT.

apology *noun*
1. A statement of acknowledgment expressing regret or asking pardon : excuse, mea culpa, regret (used in plural). *See* REGRET. **2.** A statement that justifies or defends something, such as a past action or policy : apologetic, apologia, defense, justification, vindication. *See* ATTACK.

apostasy *noun*
An instance of defecting from or abandoning a cause : defection, recreance, recreancy, tergiversation. *See* APPROACH, TRUST.

apostate *noun*
A person who has defected : defector, deserter, recreant, renegade, runagate, tergiversator, turncoat. *Informal:* rat. *See* APPROACH.

apostatize *verb*
To abandon one's cause or party usually to join another : defect, desert[3], renegade, tergiversate, turn. *Slang:* rat. ***Idioms:*** change sides, turn one's coat. *See* APPROACH, TRUST.

apostle *noun*
A person doing religious or charitable work in a foreign country : evangelist, missionary, missioner. *See* RELIGION.

apostolic *adjective*
Of missionaries or their work : missionary. *See* RELIGION.

apotheosis *noun*
The act of raising to a high position or status or the condition of being so raised : aggrandizement, elevation, ennoblement, exaltation, glorification. *See* RISE.

apotheosize *verb*
To raise to a high position or status : aggrandize, dignify, elevate, ennoble, exalt, glorify, magnify, uplift. ***Idiom:*** put on a pedestal. *See* RISE.

appall *verb*
To deprive of courage or the power to act as a result of fear, anxiety, or disgust : consternate, daunt, dismay, horrify, shake, shock[1]. *See* FEAR.

appalling *adjective*
1. Very bad : awful, dreadful, fearful, frightful, ghastly, horrendous, horrible, shocking, terrible. *See* GOOD. **2.** Causing or able to cause fear : dire, direful, dreadful, fearful, fearsome, formidable, frightful, ghastly, redoubtable, scary, terrible, tremendous. *See* FEAR.

appanage also **apanage** *noun*
A privilege granted a person, as by virtue of birth : birthright, perquisite, prerogative, right. *Law:* droit. *See* OWNED.

apparatus *noun*
1. Something, as a machine, devised for a particular function : appliance, contraption, contrivance, device. *See* MACHINE. **2.** Things needed for a task, journey, or other purpose : accouterment (often used in plural), equipment, gear, material (used in plural), materiel, outfit, paraphernalia, rig, tackle, thing (used in plural), turnout. *See* MEANS.

apparel *noun*
Articles worn to cover the body : attire, clothes, clothing, dress, garment (used in plural), habiliment (often used in plural), raiment. *Informal:* dud (used in plural), tog (used in plural). *Slang:* thread (used in plural). *See* PUT ON.

apparel *verb* To put clothes on : attire, clothe, dress, garb, garment, invest. *Informal:* tog. *See* PUT ON.

apparent *adjective*
1. Readily seen, perceived, or understood : clear, clear-cut, crystal clear, distinct, evident, manifest, noticeable, observable, obvious, patent, plain, pronounced, visible. *See* SEE. **2.** Appearing as such but not necessarily so : external, ostensible, ostensive, outward, seeming, superficial. *See* SURFACE.

apparently *adverb*
On the surface : evidently, externally, ostensibly, ostensively, outwardly, seemingly, superficially. ***Idioms:*** on the face of it, to all appearances. *See* SURFACE.

apparition *noun*
A supernatural being, such as a ghost : bogey, bogeyman, bogle, eidolon, ghost, phantasm, phantasma, phantom, revenant, shade, shadow, specter, spirit, visitant, wraith. *Informal:* spook. *Regional:* haunt. *See* BEINGS, SUPERNATURAL.

appeal *noun*
1. An earnest or urgent request : entreaty, imploration, plea, prayer[1], supplication. *See* ASK. **2.** An application to a higher authority, as for sanction or a decision : petition. *Law:* prayer[1]. *See* ASK, LAW. **3.** The power or quality of attracting : allure, allurement, attraction, attractiveness, call, charisma, charm, draw, enchantment, enticement, fascination, glamour, lure, magnetism, witchery. *Informal:* pull. *See* LIKE.

appeal *verb* **1.** To make an earnest or urgent request : beg, beseech, crave, entreat, implore, plead, pray, sue, supplicate. *Archaic:* conjure. *See* ASK. **2.** To bring an appeal or request, for example, to the attention of : address, apply, approach, petition. *Obsolete:* sue. *See* REQUEST. **3.** *Law.* To make application to a higher authority, as to a court of law : petition. *Law:* sue. *See* LAW. **4.** To direct or impel to oneself by some quality or action : allure, attract, draw, entice, lure, magnetize, take. *Informal:* pull. *See* LIKE.

appealer *noun*
One that asks a higher authority for something, as a favor or redress : appellant, petitioner, suitor. *See* ASK, LAW.

appear *verb*
1. To come into view : emerge, issue, loom, materialize, show. ***Idioms:*** make (*or* put in) an appearance, meet the eye. *See* SEE. **2.** To begin to appear or develop : arise, commence, dawn, emerge, originate. *See* START. **3.** To have the appearance of : look, seem, sound[1]. ***Idiom:*** strike one as (being). *See* SURFACE.

appearance *noun*
1. The act of coming into view : emergence. *See* SEE. **2.** The act of arriving : advent, arrival, coming. *See* START. **3.** The way something or someone looks : aspect, look, mien. *See* SURFACE. **4.** The character projected or given by someone to the public : image, impression. *See* SURFACE.

appease *verb*
1. To ease the anger or agitation of : assuage, calm (down), conciliate, dulcify, gentle, mollify, pacify, placate, propitiate, soften, soothe, sweeten. ***Idiom:*** pour oil on troubled water. *See* CALM. **2.** To grant or have what is demanded by (a need or desire) : content, fulfill, gratify, indulge, satisfy. *See* GIVE.

appellant *noun*
One that asks a higher authority for something, as a favor or redress : appealer, petitioner, suitor. *See* ASK, LAW.

appellation *noun*
The word or words by which one is called and identified : appellative, cognomen, denomination, designation, epithet, name, nickname, style, tag, title. *Slang:* handle, moniker. *See* SPECIFIC, WORDS.

appellative *noun*
The word or words by which one is called and identified : appellation, cognomen, denomination, designation, epithet, name, nickname, style, tag, title. *Slang:* handle, moniker. *See* SPECIFIC, WORDS.

append *verb*
To add as a supplement or an appendix : affix, annex, attach, subjoin. *See* INCREASE.

appendage *noun*
A subordinate element added to another entity : accessory, adjunct, appurtenance, attachment, supplement. *See* INCREASE.

appertain *verb*
To be pertinent : apply, bear on (*or* upon), concern, pertain, refer, relate. ***Idioms:*** have a bearing on, have to do with. *See* RELEVANT.

appetence *noun*
A strong wanting of what promises enjoyment or pleasure : appetency, appetite, craving, desire, hunger, itch, longing, lust, thirst, wish, yearning, yen. *See* DESIRE.

appetency *noun*
A strong wanting of what promises enjoyment or pleasure : appetence, appetite, craving, desire, hunger, itch, longing, lust, thirst, wish, yearning, yen. *See* DESIRE.

appetite *noun*
1. A desire for food or drink : hunger, stomach, taste, thirst. *See* DESIRE. **2.** A strong wanting of what promises enjoyment or pleasure : appetence, appetency, craving, desire, hunger, itch, longing, lust, thirst, wish, yearning, yen. *See* DESIRE. **3.** A liking for something : fondness, partiality, preference, relish, taste, weakness. *See* LIKE.

appetizing *adjective*
Highly pleasing, especially to the sense of taste : ambrosial, delectable, delicious, heavenly, luscious, savory, scrumptious, tasteful, tasty, toothsome. *Slang:* yummy. *See* GOOD, INGESTION.

applaud *verb*
1. To express approval, especially by clapping : cheer, clap, root[2]. ***Idiom:*** give someone a hand. *See* PRAISE. **2.** To express warm approval of : acclaim, commend, compliment, laud, praise. *See* PRAISE.

applause *noun*
1. Approval expressed by clapping : hand, ovation, plaudit. *See* PRAISE. **2.** An expression of warm approval : acclaim, acclamation, celebration, commendation, compliment, encomium, eulogy, kudos, laudation, panegyric, plaudit, praise. *See* PRAISE.

apple-polish *verb*
Informal. To support slavishly every opinion or suggestion of a superior : bootlick, cringe, fawn, grovel, kowtow, slaver, toady, truckle.

Informal: brownnose, cotton. *Slang:* suck up. ***Idioms:*** curry favor, dance attendance, kiss someone's feet, lick someone's boots. *See* OVER.

apple-polisher *noun*
Informal. One who flatters another excessively : adulator, courtier, flatterer, sycophant, toady. *See* OVER, PRAISE.

applesauce *noun*
Slang. Something that does not have or make sense : balderdash, blather, bunkum, claptrap, drivel, garbage, idiocy, nonsense, piffle, poppycock, rigmarole, rubbish, tomfoolery, trash, twaddle. *Informal:* tommyrot. *Slang:* baloney, bilge, bull[1], bunk[2], crap, hooey, malarkey. *See* KNOWLEDGE.

appliance *noun*
Something, as a machine, devised for a particular function : apparatus, contraption, contrivance, device. *See* MACHINE.

applicability *noun*
The fact of being related to the matter at hand : application, appositeness, bearing, concernment, germaneness, materiality, pertinence, pertinency, relevance, relevancy. *See* RELEVANT.

applicable *adjective*
Related to the matter at hand : apposite, apropos, germane, material, pertinent, relevant. ***Idiom:*** to the point. *See* RELEVANT.

applicant *noun*
A person who applies for or seeks something, such as a job or position : aspirant, candidate, hopeful, petitioner, seeker. *See* SEEK.

application *noun*
1. The act of putting into play : employment, exercise, exertion, implementation, operation, play, usage, use, utilization. *See* USED. **2.** The condition of being put to use : duty, employment, service, use, utilization. *See* USED. **3.** The giving of a medication, especially by prescribed dosage : administration, dispensation. *See* GIVE. **4.** The fact of being related to the matter at hand : applicability, appositeness, bearing, concernment, germaneness, materiality, pertinence, pertinency, relevance, relevancy. *See* RELEVANT. **5.** Steady attention and effort, as to one's occupation : assiduity, assiduousness, diligence, industriousness, industry, sedulousness. *See* INDUSTRIOUS. **6.** A document used in applying, as for a job : form. *See* SEEK, WORDS.

apply *verb*
1. To provide as a remedy : administer, dispense, give. *See* GIVE. **2.** To put into action or use : actuate, employ, exercise, exploit, implement, practice, use, utilize. ***Idioms:*** avail oneself of, bring into play, bring to bear, make use of, put into practice, put to use. *See* USED. **3.** To devote (oneself or one's efforts) : address, bend, buckle down, concentrate, dedicate, devote, direct, focus, give, turn. *See* COLLECT, WORK. **4.** To be pertinent : appertain, bear on (*or* upon), concern, pertain, refer, relate. ***Idioms:*** have a bearing on, have to do with. *See* RELEVANT. **5.** To bring an appeal or request, for example, to the attention of : address, appeal, approach, petition. *Obsolete:* sue. *See* REQUEST. **6.** To look to when in need : go, refer, repair[2], resort, run, turn. ***Idioms:*** fall back on (*or* upon), have recourse to. *See* USED. **7.** To ask for employment, acceptance, or admission : petition, put in. *See* SEEK.

appoint *verb*
1. To select for an office or position : designate, make, name, nominate, tap[1]. *See* CHOICE. **2.** To supply what is needed for some activity or purpose : accouter, equip, fit[1], fit out (*or* up), furnish, gear, outfit, rig, turn out. *See* GIVE.

appointee *noun*
A person who is appointed to an office or position : designee, nominee. *See* CHOICE.

appointment *noun*
1. The act of appointing to an office or position : designation, nomination. *See* CHOICE. **2.** A post of employment : berth, billet, job, office, place, position, situation, slot, spot. *Slang:* gig. *See* PLACE. **3.** A commitment to appear at a certain time and place : assignation, date, engagement, rendezvous, tryst. *See* AGREE. **4.** A piece of equipment for comfort or convenience. Used in plural : furnishing, movable. *Chiefly British:* fitting (used in plural). *See* MACHINE.

apportion *verb*
To set aside or distribute as a share : admeasure, allocate, allot, allow, assign, give, lot, measure out, mete (out). *See* COLLECT.

apportionment *noun*
The act of distributing or the condition of being distributed : admeasurement, allocation, assignment, dispensation, distribution, division. *See* COLLECT.

apposite *adjective*
Related to the matter at hand : applicable, apropos, germane, material, pertinent, relevant. ***Idiom:*** to the point. *See* RELEVANT.

appositeness *noun*
The fact of being related to the matter at hand : applicability, application, bearing, concernment, germaneness, materiality, pertinence, per-

tinency, relevance, relevancy. *See* RELEVANT.

appraisal *noun*
The act or result of judging the worth or value of something or someone : appraisement, assessment, estimate, estimation, evaluation, judgment, valuation. *See* VALUE.

appraise *verb*
To make a judgment as to the worth or value of : assay, assess, calculate, estimate, evaluate, gauge, judge, rate[1], size up, valuate, value. ***Idiom:*** take the measure of. *See* VALUE.

appraisement *noun*
The act or result of judging the worth or value of something or someone : appraisal, assessment, estimate, estimation, evaluation, judgment, valuation. *See* VALUE.

appreciable *adjective*
Capable of being noticed or apprehended mentally : detectable, discernible, distinguishable, noticeable, observable, palpable, perceivable, perceptible, ponderable, sensible. *See* KNOWLEDGE.

appreciate *verb*
1. To recognize the worth, quality, importance, or magnitude of : cherish, esteem, prize[1], respect, treasure, value. ***Idiom:*** set store by. *See* PRAISE. **2.** To regard with great pleasure or approval : admire. *See* LIKE, PRAISE.

appreciation *noun*
1. A feeling of deference, approval, and liking : account, admiration, consideration, esteem, estimation, favor, honor, regard, respect. *See* RESPECT. **2.** A being grateful : gratefulness, gratitude, thankfulness, thanks. *See* GRATEFUL.

appreciative *adjective*
Showing or feeling gratitude : grateful, thankful. *See* GRATEFUL.

apprehend *verb*
1. To take into custody as a prisoner : arrest, seize. *Informal:* nab, pick up. *Slang:* bust, collar, pinch, run in. *See* LAW. **2.** To perceive directly with the intellect : compass, comprehend, fathom, grasp, know, understand. *Scots:* ken. *See* KNOWLEDGE. **3.** To perceive and recognize the meaning of : accept, catch (on), compass, comprehend, conceive, fathom, follow, get, grasp, make out, read, see, sense, take, take in, understand. *Informal:* savvy. *Slang:* dig. *Chiefly British:* twig. *Scots:* ken. ***Idioms:*** get (*or* have) a handle on, get the picture. *See* UNDERSTAND. **4.** To be intuitively aware of : feel, intuit, perceive, sense. ***Idioms:*** feel in one's bones, get vibrations. *See* KNOWLEDGE.

apprehension *noun*
1. Great agitation and anxiety caused by the expectation or the realization of danger : affright, alarm, dread, fear, fearfulness, fright, funk, horror, panic, terror, trepidation. *Slang:* cold feet. ***Idiom:*** fear and trembling. *See* FEAR. **2.** A seizing and holding by law : arrest, seizure. *Slang:* bust, collar, pickup, pinch. *See* LAW. **3.** Intellectual hold : comprehension, grasp, grip, hold, understanding. *Informal:* savvy. *See* KNOWLEDGE.

apprehensive *adjective*
Filled with fear or terror : afraid, aghast, fearful, fearsome, funky, panicky. *Regional:* afeard, ascared. *See* FEAR.

apprise *verb*
To impart information to : acquaint, advise, educate, enlighten, inform, notify, tell. *See* KNOWLEDGE, TEACH.

approach *verb*
1. To come near in space or time : near. ***Idioms:*** come close to, draw near to. *See* APPROACH. **2.** To come near, as in quality or amount : approximate, border on (*or* upon), challenge, rival, verge on. *See* SAME. **3.** To bring an appeal or request, for example, to the attention of : address, appeal, apply, petition. *Obsolete:* sue. *See* REQUEST. **4.** To go about the initial step in doing (something) : begin, commence, embark, enter, get off, inaugurate, initiate, institute, launch, lead off, open, set about, set out, set to, start, take on, take up, undertake. *Informal:* kick off. ***Idioms:*** get cracking, get going, get the show on the road. *See* START.

approach *noun* **1.** The act or fact of coming near : coming, convergence, imminence, nearness. *See* APPROACH. **2.** A method used in dealing with something : attack, course, line, modus operandi, plan, procedure, tack, technique. *See* MEANS. **3.** A preliminary action intended to elicit a favorable response : advance (used in plural), overture. *See* APPROACH.

approachable *adjective*
Easily approached : accessible, responsive, welcoming. *See* APPROACH, ATTITUDE.

approaching *adjective*
In the relatively near future : coming, forthcoming, upcoming. *See* NEAR.

approbate *verb*
To give one's consent to : allow, approve, authorize, consent, endorse, let, permit, sanction. *Informal:* OK. *See* ALLOW.

approbation *noun*
1. Favorable regard : acceptance, approval, favor. *See* ACCEPT, PRAISE. **2.** The approving of an action, especially when done by one in au-

thority : allowance, approval, authorization, consent, endorsement, leave[2], license, permission, permit, sanction. *Informal:* OK. *See* ALLOW.

approbatory *adjective*
Serving to compliment : acclamatory, commendatory, complimentary, congratulatory, laudatory. *See* PRAISE.

appropriate *adjective*
1. Suitable for a particular person, condition, occasion, or place : apt, becoming, befitting, correct, felicitous, fit[1], fitting, happy, meet[2], proper, right, tailor-made. *See* RIGHT. **2.** Suited to one's end or purpose : befitting, convenient, expedient, fit[1], good, meet[2], proper, suitable, tailor-made, useful. *See* AGREE, GOOD.
3. Consistent with prevailing or accepted standards or circumstances : deserved, due, fit[1], fitting, just, merited, proper, right, rightful, suitable. *See* RIGHT.
appropriate *verb* **1.** To set aside or apart for a specified purpose : allocate, assign, designate, earmark. *See* COLLECT, MONEY. **2.** To lay claim to for oneself or as one's right : arrogate, assume, commandeer, preempt, seize, take, usurp. *See* GIVE.

appropriation *noun*
1. Something, as a gift, granted for a definite purpose : grant, subsidy, subvention. *See* GIVE. **2.** The act of taking something for oneself : arrogation, assumption, preemption, seizure, usurpation. *See* GIVE.

approval *noun*
1. The approving of an action, especially when done by one in authority : allowance, approbation, authorization, consent, endorsement, leave[2], license, permission, permit, sanction. *Informal:* OK. *See* ALLOW. **2.** An act of confirming officially : affirmation, confirmation, ratification, sanction. *See* LAW. **3.** Favorable regard : acceptance, approbation, favor. *See* ACCEPT, PRAISE.

approve *verb*
1. To be favorably disposed toward : countenance, favor, hold with. *Informal:* go for. *Idiom:* take kindly to. *See* PRAISE. **2.** To give one's consent to : allow, approbate, authorize, consent, endorse, let, permit, sanction. *Informal:* OK. *See* ALLOW. **3.** To accept officially : adopt, affirm, confirm, pass, ratify, sanction. *See* ACCEPT, LAW.

approximate *verb*
1. To come near, as in quality or amount : approach, border on (*or* upon), challenge, rival, verge on. *See* SAME. **2.** To calculate approximately : estimate, place, put, reckon, set[1]. *See* PRECISE.

approximately *adverb*
Near to in quantity or amount : about, almost, nearly, roughly. *Idiom:* on the order of. *See* NEAR.

approximation *noun*
A rough or tentative calculation : estimate, estimation. *See* PRECISE.

appurtenance *noun*
A subordinate element added to another entity : accessory, adjunct, appendage, attachment, supplement. *See* INCREASE.

apropos *adjective*
Related to the matter at hand : applicable, apposite, germane, material, pertinent, relevant. *Idiom:* to the point. *See* RELEVANT.

apt *adjective*
1. Suitable for a particular person, condition, occasion, or place : appropriate, becoming, befitting, correct, felicitous, fit[1], fitting, happy, meet[2], proper, right, tailor-made. *See* RIGHT.
2. Having or showing a tendency or likelihood : disposed, given, inclined, liable, likely, prone. *See* LIKELY.

aptitude *noun*
An innate capability : aptness, bent, faculty, flair, genius, gift, head, instinct, knack, talent, turn. *See* ABILITY, APPROACH.

aptness *noun*
An innate capability : aptitude, bent, faculty, flair, genius, gift, head, instinct, knack, talent, turn. *See* ABILITY, APPROACH.

aquiver *adjective*
Marked by or affected with tremors : quaky, quivery, shaky, shivery, tremulant, tremulous, twittery. *See* REPETITION.

arbiter *noun*
A person, usually appointed, who decides the issues or results, or supervises the conduct, of a competition or conflict : arbitrator, judge, referee, umpire. *Sports:* ref, ump. *See* DECIDE.

arbitrary *adjective*
1. Determined or marked by whim or caprice rather than reason : capricious, whimsical. *See* SURPRISE. **2.** Based on individual judgment or discretion : discretionary, judgmental, personal, subjective. *See* OPINION, SURPRISE.
3. Having and exercising complete political power and control : absolute, absolutistic, autarchic, autarchical, autocratic, autocratical, despotic, dictatorial, monocratic, totalitarian, tyrannic, tyrannical, tyrannous. *See* OVER, POLITICS.

arbitrate *verb*
To make a decision about (a controversy or dispute, for example) after deliberation, as in a court of law : adjudge, adjudicate, decide, decree, determine, judge, referee, rule, umpire. *See* DECIDE, LAW.

arbitrator *noun*
A person, usually appointed, who decides the issues or results, or supervises the conduct, of a competition or conflict : arbiter, judge, referee, umpire. *Sports:* ref, ump. *See* DECIDE.

arc *verb*
To swerve from a straight line : angle[2], arch, bend, bow[2], crook, curve, round, turn. *See* STRAIGHT.

arcadian also **Arcadian** *adjective*
Of or relating to the countryside : bucolic, campestral, country, pastoral, provincial, rural, rustic. *Informal:* hick. *See* URBAN.

arcane *adjective*
Difficult to explain or understand : cabalistic, cryptic, enigmatic, mysterious, mystic, mystical, mystifying, occult, puzzling. *See* EXPLAIN, KNOWLEDGE.

arced *adjective*
Deviating from a straight line : arched, arciform, bent, bowed, curved, curvilinear, rounded. *See* STRAIGHT.

arch *verb*
1. To swerve from a straight line : angle[2], arc, bend, bow[2], crook, curve, round, turn. *See* STRAIGHT. **2.** To incline the body : bend, bow[1], hump, hunch, scrunch, stoop. *See* POSTURE.

archaic *adjective*
1. Belonging to, existing, or occurring in times long past : age-old, ancient, antediluvian, antiquated, antique, hoary, old, olden, old-time, timeworn, venerable. ***Idioms:*** old as Methuselah, old as the hills. *See* NEW. **2.** Of a style or method formerly in vogue : antiquated, antique, bygone, dated, dowdy, fusty, old, old-fashioned, old-time, outdated, outmoded, out-of-date, passé, vintage. *See* NEW.

arched *adjective*
Deviating from a straight line : arced, arciform, bent, bowed, curved, curvilinear, rounded. *See* STRAIGHT.

archenemy *noun*
One who is hostile to or opposes the purposes or interests of another : enemy, foe, nemesis. *See* LOVE.

archetypal *adjective*
Having the nature of, constituting, or serving as a type : archetypic, archetypical, classic, classical, model, paradigmatic, prototypal, prototypic, prototypical, quintessential, representative, typic, typical. *See* SAME, USUAL.

archetype *noun*
A first form from which varieties arise or imitations are made : father, master, original, protoplast, prototype. *See* START.

archetypic *adjective*
Having the nature of, constituting, or serving as a type : archetypal, archetypical, classic, classical, model, paradigmatic, prototypal, prototypic, prototypical, quintessential, representative, typic, typical. *See* SAME, USUAL.

archetypical *adjective*
Having the nature of, constituting, or serving as a type : archetypal, archetypic, classic, classical, model, paradigmatic, prototypal, prototypic, prototypical, quintessential, representative, typic, typical. *See* SAME, USUAL.

archfiend *noun*
A perversely bad, cruel, or wicked person : beast, devil, fiend, ghoul, monster, ogre, tiger, vampire. *See* KIND.

architect *noun*
One that creates, founds, or originates : author, creator, entrepreneur, father, founder[2], inventor, maker, originator, parent, patriarch. *See* START.

archive *noun*
A place where something is deposited for safekeeping : depository, magazine, repository, store, storehouse, warehouse. *See* KEEP.

arciform *adjective*
Deviating from a straight line : arced, arched, bent, bowed, curved, curvilinear, rounded. *See* STRAIGHT.

arctic *adjective*
Very cold : boreal, freezing, frigid, frosty, gelid, glacial, icy, polar, wintry. *Archaic:* frore. ***Idiom:*** bitter (*or* bitterly) cold. *See* HOT.

ardent *adjective*
1. Fired with intense feeling : blazing, burning, dithyrambic, fervent, fervid, fiery, flaming, glowing, heated, hot-blooded, impassioned, passionate, perfervid, red-hot, scorching, torrid. *See* FEELINGS. **2.** Showing or having enthusiasm : enthusiastic, fervent, keen[1], mad, rabid, warm, zealous. *Informal:* crazy. *Slang:* gung ho, nuts. *See* CONCERN. **3.** Intensely desirous or interested : agog, athirst, avid, bursting, eager, impatient, keen[1], solicitous, thirsting, thirsty. *Informal:* raring. ***Idioms:*** champing at the bit, ready and willing. *See* CONCERN. **4.** Marked by much heat : baking, blistering, boiling, broiling, burning, fiery, heated, hot, red-hot, roast-

ing, scalding, scorching, searing, sizzling, sultry, sweltering, torrid. *See* HOT.

ardor *noun*

1. Powerful, intense emotion : fervency, fervor, fire, passion. *See* FEELINGS. **2.** Passionate devotion to or interest in a cause or subject, for example : enthusiasm, fervor, fire, passion, zeal, zealousness. *See* CONCERN, FEELINGS.

ardorless *adjective*

Deficient in or lacking sexual desire : cold, frigid, inhibited, passionless, unresponsive. *See* SEX.

arduous *adjective*

1. Not easy to do, achieve, or master : difficult, hard, laborious, serious, tall, tough, uphill. *See* EASY. **2.** Requiring great or extreme bodily, mental, or spiritual strength : backbreaking, burdensome, demanding, difficult, effortful, exacting, exigent, formidable, hard, heavy, laborious, onerous, oppressive, rigorous, rough, severe, taxing, tough, trying, weighty. *See* HEAVY.

arduously *adverb*

With effort : difficultly, hard, heavily, laboriously. *See* EASY.

area *noun*

1. A part of the earth's surface : belt, district, locality, neighborhood, quarter, region, tract, zone. *Informal:* neck of the woods. *See* TERRITORY. **2.** A surrounding site : locality, neighborhood, vicinity. *See* NEAR, PLACE. **3.** A rather small part of a geographic unit considered in regard to its inhabitants or distinctive characteristics : district, neighborhood, quarter (often uppercase). *See* TERRITORY. **4.** A sphere of activity, experience, study, or interest : arena, bailiwick, circle, department, domain, field, orbit, province, realm, scene, subject, terrain, territory, world. *Slang:* bag. *See* TERRITORY.

arena *noun*

A sphere of activity, experience, study, or interest : area, bailiwick, circle, department, domain, field, orbit, province, realm, scene, subject, terrain, territory, world. *Slang:* bag. *See* TERRITORY.

argot *noun*

1. A variety of a language that differs from the standard form : cant[2], dialect, jargon, lingo, patois, vernacular. *See* WORDS. **2.** Specialized expressions indigenous to a particular field, subject, trade, or subculture : cant[2], dialect, idiom, jargon, language, lexicon, lingo, patois, terminology, vernacular, vocabulary. *See* WORDS.

arguable *adjective*

In doubt or dispute : contested, debatable, disputable, doubtful, exceptionable, moot, mootable, problematic, problematical, questionable, uncertain. *See* CERTAIN.

argue *verb*

1. To put forth reasons for or against something, often excitedly : contend, debate, dispute, moot. *See* AFFIRM, WORDS. **2.** To engage in a quarrel : bicker, contend, dispute, fight, quarrel, quibble, spat, squabble, tiff, wrangle. *Informal:* hassle, tangle. ***Idioms:*** cross swords, have it out, have words, lock horns. *See* CONFLICT. **3.** To put into words positively and with conviction : affirm, allege, assert, asseverate, aver, avouch, avow, claim, contend, declare, hold, maintain, say, state. ***Idiom:*** have it. *See* AFFIRM. **4.** To give grounds for believing in the existence or presence of : attest, bespeak, betoken, indicate, mark, point to, testify, witness. *See* SHOW.

argue into *verb* To succeed in causing (a person) to act in a certain way : bring, bring around (*or* round), convince, get, induce, persuade, prevail on (*or* upon), sell (on), talk into. *See* PERSUASION.

argue into *verb* See **argue.**

argument *noun*

1. A discussion, often heated, in which a difference of opinion is expressed : altercation, bicker, clash, contention, controversy, debate, difficulty, disagreement, dispute, fight, polemic, quarrel, run-in, spat, squabble, tiff, word (used in plural), wrangle. *Informal:* hassle, rhubarb, tangle. *See* CONFLICT. **2.** A course of reasoning : case, point. *See* REASON. **3.** A fact or circumstance that gives logical support to an assertion, claim, or proposal : ground (often used in plural), proof, reason, wherefore, why. ***Idiom:*** why and wherefore. *See* REASON.
4. What a speech, piece of writing, or artistic work is about : matter, point, subject, subject matter, text, theme, topic. *See* MEANING.

argumentation *noun*

The presentation of an argument or arguments : debate, disputation, forensics. *See* AFFIRM, WORDS.

argumentative *adjective*

Given to arguing : combative, contentious, disputatious, eristic, litigious, polemic, polemical, quarrelsome, scrappy. *See* CONFLICT.

argumentativeness *noun*

The quality or state of being argumentative : combativeness, contentiousness, disputatiousness, litigiousness, scrappiness. *See* CONFLICT.

aria *noun*
A pleasing succession of musical tones forming a usually brief aesthetic unit : air, melody, strain[2], tune. *Obsolete:* note. *See* SOUNDS.

arid *adjective*
1. Having little or no liquid or moisture : anhydrous, bone-dry, dry, moistureless, sere, waterless. *See* DRY. **2.** Having little or no precipitation : droughty, dry, rainless, thirsty. *See* DRY. **3.** Lacking liveliness, charm, or surprise : aseptic, colorless, drab, dry, dull, earthbound, flat, flavorless, lackluster, lifeless, lusterless, matter-of-fact, pedestrian, prosaic, spiritless, sterile, stodgy, unimaginative, uninspired. *See* EXCITE.

arise *verb*
1. To adopt a standing posture : get up, rise, stand (up), uprise, upspring. ***Idiom:*** get to one's feet. *See* RISE. **2.** To leave one's bed : get up, pile, rise, roll out. *Informal:* turn out. ***Idiom:*** rise and shine. *See* RISE. **3.** To move from a lower to a higher position : ascend, climb, lift, mount, rise, soar. *See* RISE. **4.** To begin to appear or develop : appear, commence, dawn, emerge, originate. *See* START. **5.** To come into being : begin, commence, originate, start. *See* START. **6.** To have as a source : come, derive, emanate, flow, issue, originate, proceed, rise, spring, stem, upspring. *See* START.

aristocracy *noun*
People of the highest social level : blue blood, crème de la crème, elite, flower, gentility, gentry, nobility, patriciate, quality, society, upper class, who's who. *Informal:* upper crust. *See* OVER.

aristocratic *adjective*
Of high birth or social position : blue-blooded, elite, highborn, highbred, noble, patrician, thoroughbred, upper-class, wellborn. *Informal:* upper-crust. *See* OVER.

arithmetic *noun*
Arithmetic calculations : computation, figure (used in plural), number (used in plural). *See* COUNT.

arm *noun*
1. Something resembling or structurally analogous to a tree branch : branch, fork, offshoot. *See* PART. **2.** A part added to a main structure : annex, extension, wing. *See* PART. **3.** A component of government that performs a given function : agency, branch, department, division, organ, wing. *See* PART.

armistice *noun*
A temporary cessation of hostilities by mutual consent of the contending parties : cease-fire, truce. *See* CONTINUE.

armpit *noun*
Slang. A place known for its great filth or corruption : cesspit, cesspool, pit[1], sink. *See* CLEAN, RIGHT.

army *noun*
A very large number of things grouped together : cloud, crowd, drove, flock, horde, host, legion, mass, mob, multitude, ruck[1], score (used in plural), swarm, throng. *See* BIG, GROUP.

aroma *noun*
1. A distinctive yet intangible quality deemed typical of a given thing : atmosphere, flavor, savor, smack[2]. *See* TASTE. **2.** A sweet or pleasant odor : bouquet, fragrance, perfume, redolence, scent. *See* SMELLS. **3.** The quality of something that may be perceived by the olfactory sense : odor, scent, smell. *See* SMELLS.

aromatic *adjective*
Having a pleasant odor : fragrant, redolent. *See* SMELLS.

aromatize *verb*
To fill with a pleasant odor : perfume, scent. *See* SMELLS.

around *adverb*
1. In or toward a former location or condition : about, back, backward, backwards, rearward, round. *See* APPROACH. **2.** Toward the back : about, back, backward, backwards, rearward. *See* PRECEDE. **3.** From one end to the other : over, round, through, throughout. *See* PART.
around *adjective* Having existence or life : alive, existent, existing, extant, living. *See* LIVE.

around-the-clock *adjective*
Existing or occurring without interruption or end : ceaseless, constant, continual, continuous, endless, eternal, everlasting, incessant, interminable, nonstop, ongoing, perpetual, persistent, relentless, round-the-clock, timeless, unceasing, unending, unfailing, uninterrupted, unremitting. *See* CONTINUE.

arouse *verb*
1. To cease sleeping : awake, awaken, rouse, stir[1], wake[1], waken. *See* AWARENESS. **2.** To induce or elicit (a reaction or emotion) : awake, awaken, kindle, raise, rouse, stir[1] (up), waken. *See* EXCITE.

arraign *verb*
To make an accusation against : accuse, charge, denounce, incriminate, indict, tax. *See* ATTACK, LAW, PRAISE.

arrange *verb*
1. To put into a deliberate order : array, deploy, dispose, marshal, order, organize, range, sort, systematize. *See* ORDER. **2.** To combine

and adapt in order to attain a particular effect : blend, coordinate, harmonize, integrate, orchestrate, synthesize, unify. *See* BEAUTIFUL. **3.** To plan the details or arrangements of : lay out, prepare, schedule, work out. *See* PLANNED. **4.** To bring about or come to an agreement concerning : conclude, fix, negotiate, set[1], settle. *See* AGREE. **5.** To put into correct or conclusive form : conclude, dispose of, fix, settle. *See* DO.

arrangement *noun*

1. A way or condition of being arranged : categorization, classification, deployment, disposal, disposition, distribution, formation, grouping, layout, lineup, order, organization, placement, sequence. *See* ORDER. **2.** A plan made in preparation for an undertaking. Often used in plural : preparation (often used in plural), provision (often used in plural). *See* PLANNED. **3.** An act or state of agreeing between parties regarding a course of action : accord, agreement, bargain, compact[2], deal, pact, understanding. *See* AGREE. **4.** A settlement of differences through mutual concession : accommodation, compromise, give-and-take, medium, settlement. *Law:* composition. *See* AGREE.

arrant *adjective*

1. Completely such, without qualification or exception : absolute, all-out, complete, consummate, crashing, damned, dead, downright, flat, out-and-out, outright, perfect, plain, pure, sheer[2], thorough, thoroughgoing, total, unbounded, unequivocal, unlimited, unmitigated, unqualified, unrelieved, unreserved, utter[2]. *Informal:* flat-out, positive. *Chiefly British:* blooming. *See* BIG, LIMITED. **2.** Conspicuously bad or offensive : capital, egregious, flagrant, glaring, gross, rank[2]. *See* GOOD.

array *verb*

1. To put into a deliberate order : arrange, deploy, dispose, marshal, order, organize, range, sort, systematize. *See* ORDER. **2.** To dress in formal or special clothing : attire, deck[2] (out), dress up, prank[2]. *Informal:* trick out (*or* up). *Slang:* doll up. *See* ORDER, PLAIN, PUT ON.

array *noun* **1.** An impressive or ostentatious exhibition : display, panoply, parade, pomp, show, spectacle. *See* SHOW. **2.** A number of individuals making up or considered a unit : band[2], batch, bevy, body, bunch, bundle, clump, cluster, clutch[2], collection, group, knot, lot, party, set[2]. *See* GROUP. **3.** Showy and elaborate clothing or apparel : attire, finery, frippery, regalia. *See* PUT ON.

arrearage *noun*

1. A condition of owing something to another : arrears, indebtedness, debt, liability, obligation. *See* PAY. **2.** Something, such as money, owed by one person to another : arrears, debt, due, indebtedness, liability, obligation. *See* OBLIGATION, PAY.

arrears *noun*

1. Something, such as money, owed by one person to another : arrearage, debt, due, indebtedness, liability, obligation. *See* OBLIGATION, PAY. **2.** A condition of owing something to another : arrearage, indebtedness, debt, liability, obligation. *See* PAY.

arrest *verb*

1. To prevent the occurrence or continuation of a movement, action, or operation : belay, cease, check, discontinue, halt[1], stall[1], stay[1], stop, surcease. ***Idioms:*** bring to a standstill, call a halt to, put a stop to. *See* CONTINUE. **2.** To come to a cessation : belay, cease, check, discontinue, halt[1], leave off, quit, stall[1], stop, surcease. ***Idiom:*** come to a halt (*or* standstill *or* stop). *See* CONTINUE. **3.** To take into custody as a prisoner : apprehend, seize. *Informal:* nab, pick up. *Slang:* bust, collar, pinch, run in. *See* LAW. **4.** To compel, as the attention, interest, or imagination, of : catch up, enthrall, fascinate, grip, hold, mesmerize, rivet, spellbind, transfix. *Slang:* grab. *See* EXCITE.

arrest *noun* A seizing and holding by law : apprehension, seizure. *Slang:* bust, collar, pickup, pinch. *See* LAW.

arresting *adjective*

Readily attracting notice : bold, conspicuous, eye-catching, marked, noticeable, observable, outstanding, pointed, prominent, pronounced, remarkable, salient, signal, striking. ***Idiom:*** sticking out like a sore thumb. *See* SEE.

arrival *noun*

1. The act of arriving : advent, appearance, coming. *See* START. **2.** One that arrives : comer, visitor. *See* ENTER. **3.** The achievement of something desired, planned, or attempted : success, successfulness. *See* THRIVE.

arrive *verb*

1. To come to a particular place : check in, get in, pull in, reach, show up, turn up. *Slang:* blow in. ***Idiom:*** make (*or* put in) an appearance. *See* START. **2.** To gain success : get ahead, get on, go far, rise, succeed. ***Idioms:*** go places, make good, make it. *See* THRIVE.

arrive at *verb* To reach (a goal or objective) : attain, come to, gain, get to. *Informal:* hit on (*or* upon). *See* START.

arrive at *verb* See **arrive.**

arrogance *noun*
The quality of being arrogant : haughtiness, hauteur, insolence, loftiness, lordliness, overbearingness, presumption, pride, pridefulness, proudness, superciliousness, superiority. *See* ATTITUDE.

arrogant *adjective*
Overly convinced of one's own superiority and importance : haughty, high-and-mighty, insolent, lofty, lordly, overbearing, overweening, prideful, proud, supercilious, superior. ***Idiom:*** on one's high horse. *See* ATTITUDE.

arrogate *verb*
To lay claim to for oneself or as one's right : appropriate, assume, commandeer, preempt, seize, take, usurp. *See* GIVE.

arrogation *noun*
The act of taking something for oneself : appropriation, assumption, preemption, seizure, usurpation. *See* GIVE.

art *noun*
1. Activity pursued as a livelihood : business, calling, career, craft, employment, job, line, métier, occupation, profession, pursuit, trade, vocation, work. *Slang:* racket. *Archaic:* employ. *See* ACTION. **2.** Natural or acquired facility in a specific activity : ability, adeptness, command, craft, expertise, expertness, knack, mastery, proficiency, skill, technique. *Informal:* know-how. *See* ABILITY, KNOWLEDGE. **3.** Deceitful cleverness : artfulness, artifice, craft, craftiness, cunning, foxiness, guile, slyness, wiliness. *See* HONEST, MEANS.

artful *adjective*
1. Showing art or skill in performing or doing : adroit, deft, dexterous, skillful. *See* ABILITY, KNOWLEDGE. **2.** Deceitfully clever : crafty, cunning, foxy, guileful, scheming, sharp, sly, tricky, wily. *See* ABILITY, HONEST, MEANS.

artfulness *noun*
Deceitful cleverness : art, artifice, craft, craftiness, cunning, foxiness, guile, slyness, wiliness. *See* HONEST, MEANS.

article *noun*
1. An individually considered portion of a whole : detail, element, item, particular, point. *See* PART. **2.** Something having material existence : item, object, thing. *See* THING.

articulacy *noun*
Vivid, effective, or persuasive communication in speech or artistic performance : articulateness, eloquence, eloquentness, expression, expressiveness, expressivity, facundity. *See* WORDS.

articulate *adjective*
1. Produced by the voice : oral, sonant, spoken, uttered, vocal, voiced. *See* SOUNDS.
2. Fluently persuasive and forceful : eloquent, facund, silver-tongued, smooth-spoken. *See* WORDS.

articulate *verb* **1.** To produce or make (speech sounds) : enunciate, pronounce, say, utter[1], vocalize. *See* WORDS. **2.** To put into words : communicate, convey, declare, express, say, state, talk, tell, utter[1], vent, verbalize, vocalize, voice. ***Idiom:*** give tongue (*or* vent *or* voice) to. *See* WORDS. **3.** To make into a whole by joining a system of parts : concatenate, integrate. *See* INCLUDE, PART.

articulateness *noun*
Vivid, effective, or persuasive communication in speech or artistic performance : articulacy, eloquence, eloquentness, expression, expressiveness, expressivity, facundity. *See* WORDS.

articulation *noun*
1. The act or an instance of expressing in words : expression, statement, utterance, verbalization, vocalization, voice. *See* WORDS.
2. The use of the speech organs to produce sounds : enunciation, utterance, vocalism, vocalization, voicing. *See* SOUNDS, WORDS.

artifice *noun*
1. An indirect, usually cunning means of gaining an end : deception, device, dodge, feint, gimmick, imposture, jig, maneuver, ploy, ruse, sleight, stratagem, subterfuge, trick, wile. *Informal:* shenanigan, take-in. *See* HONEST, MEANS. **2.** Deceitful cleverness : art, artfulness, craft, craftiness, cunning, foxiness, guile, slyness, wiliness. *See* HONEST, MEANS.

artificial *adjective*
1. Made by human beings instead of nature : manmade, manufactured, synthetic. *See* CULTURE. **2.** Made to imitate something else : imitation, manmade, mock, simulated, synthetic. *Informal:* pretend. *See* REAL. **3.** Not genuine or sincere : affected, feigned, insincere, phony, pretended. *See* TRUE. **4.** Artificially genteel : affected, mannered, precious. *Informal:* la-di-da. *See* GOOD, HONEST, PLAIN, TRUE.
5. Marked by unnaturalness, pretension, and often a slavish love of fads : factitious, plastic, synthetic, unnatural. *See* HONEST.

artificiality *noun*
Lack of sincerity : ambidexterity, disingenuousness, insincerity, phoniness. *See* HONEST.

artistic *adjective*
Showing good taste : tasteful, tasty. *Informal:* aesthetic. *See* STYLE.

artless *adjective*
1. Free from guile, cunning, or deceit : guileless, ingenuous, innocent, naive, natural, simple, unaffected, unsophisticated, unstudied, unworldly. *See* HONEST. **2.** Of a plain and unsophisticated nature : homely, homespun, natural, rustic, unadorned, unpolished. *See* PLAIN.

artsy-craftsy *adjective*
Informal. Pretentiously artistic : *Informal:* arty. *See* PLAIN.

arty *adjective*
Informal. Pretentiously artistic : *Informal:* artsy-craftsy. *See* PLAIN.

aruspex *noun* See **haruspex.**

ascared *adjective*
Regional. Filled with fear or terror : afraid, aghast, apprehensive, fearful, fearsome, funky, panicky. *Regional:* afeard. *See* FEAR.

ascend *verb*
1. To move from a lower to a higher position : arise, climb, lift, mount, rise, soar. *See* RISE. **2.** To move upward on or along : climb, go up, mount, scale[2]. *See* RISE. **3.** To attain a higher status, rank, or condition : advance, climb, mount, rise. ***Idiom:*** go up the ladder. *See* INCREASE, RISE.

ascendance *noun*
The condition or fact of being dominant : ascendancy, dominance, domination, paramountcy, predominance, preeminence, preponderance, preponderancy, prepotency, supremacy. *See* OVER.

ascendancy *noun*
The condition or fact of being dominant : ascendance, dominance, domination, paramountcy, predominance, preeminence, preponderance, preponderancy, prepotency, supremacy. *See* OVER.

ascendant *adjective*
Having preeminent significance : dominant, predominant, prepotent, prevailing, regnant, ruling, supreme. *See* IMPORTANT.
ascendant *noun* A person from whom one is descended : ancestor, antecedent, father, forebear, forefather, foremother, mother, parent, progenitor. *Archaic:* predecessor. *See* KIN, PRECEDE.

ascension *noun*
1. The act of rising or moving upward : ascent, rise, rising. *See* RISE. **2.** The act of moving upward on or along : ascent, climb. *See* RISE.

ascent *noun*
1. The act of rising or moving upward : ascension, rise, rising. *See* RISE. **2.** The act of moving upward on or along : ascension, climb. *See* RISE. **3.** An upward slope : acclivity, rise. *See* RISE.

ascertain *verb*
To obtain knowledge or awareness of something not known before, as through observation or study : determine, discover, find (out), hear, learn. *See* TEACH.

ascertainment *noun*
Something that has been discovered : discovery, find, finding, strike. *See* TEACH.

ascribe *verb*
To regard as belonging to or resulting from another : accredit, assign, attribute, charge, credit, impute, lay[1], refer. *See* GIVE.

ascription *noun*
The act of attributing : assignment, attribution, credit, imputation. *See* GIVE.

aseptic *adjective*
Lacking liveliness, charm, or surprise : arid, colorless, drab, dry, dull, earthbound, flat, flavorless, lackluster, lifeless, lusterless, matter-of-fact, pedestrian, prosaic, spiritless, sterile, stodgy, unimaginative, uninspired. *See* EXCITE.

asepticism *noun*
A lack of excitement, liveliness, or interest : blandness, colorlessness, drabness, dreariness, dryness, dullness, flatness, flavorlessness, insipidity, insipidness, jejuneness, lifelessness, sterileness, sterility, stodginess, vapidity, vapidness, weariness. *See* EXCITE.

ashen *adjective*
Lacking color : ashy, bloodless, cadaverous, colorless, livid, lurid, pale, pallid, pasty, sallow, wan, waxen. *See* COLORS.

ashy *adjective*
Lacking color : ashen, bloodless, cadaverous, colorless, livid, lurid, pale, pallid, pasty, sallow, wan, waxen. *See* COLORS.

aside *noun*
An instance of digressing : deviation, digression, divagation, divergence, divergency, excursion, excursus, irrelevancy, parenthesis, tangent. *See* APPROACH.

ask *verb*
1. To put a question to (someone) : examine, inquire, query, question, quiz. *See* ASK. **2.** To seek an answer to (a question) : pose, put, raise. *See* ASK. **3.** To endeavor to obtain (something) by expressing one's needs or desires. Also used with request, seek, solicit. *See* REQUEST. **4.** To have as a need or prerequisite : call for, demand, entail, involve, necessitate, require, take. *See* NECESSARY, OVER. **5.** To request

that someone take part in or be present at a particular occasion : bid, invite. *See* WARN.

askance *adverb*
With skepticism : doubtfully, dubiously, questioningly, skeptically. ***Idiom:*** with a grain of salt. *See* BELIEF.

asleep *adjective*
1. In a state of sleep : sleeping, unawake. ***Idioms:*** dead to the world, fast (*or* sound) asleep, in a sound (*or* wakeless) sleep, out like a light. *See* AWARENESS. **2.** Lacking physical feeling or sensitivity : dead, insensible, insensitive, numb, unfeeling. *See* AWARENESS. **3.** No longer alive : dead, deceased, defunct, departed, extinct, gone, late, lifeless. ***Idioms:*** at rest, pushing up daisies. *See* LIVE.

aspect *noun*
1. A disposition of the facial features that conveys meaning, feeling, or mood : cast, countenance, expression, face, look, visage. *See* EXPRESS. **2.** The way something or someone looks : appearance, look, mien. *See* SURFACE. **3.** An outward appearance : countenance, face, look, physiognomy, surface, visage. *See* SURFACE. **4.** The particular angle from which something is considered : angle[2], facet, frame of reference, hand, light[1], phase, regard, respect, side. *See* PERSPECTIVE.

asperity *noun*
Something that obstructs progress and requires great effort to overcome : difficulty, hardship, rigor, vicissitude (often used in plural). ***Idioms:*** a hard (*or* tough) nut to crack, a hard (*or* tough) row to hoe, heavy sledding. *See* EASY.

asperse *verb*
To make defamatory statements about : backbite, calumniate, defame, malign, slander, slur, tear down, traduce, vilify. *Law:* libel. ***Idiom:*** cast aspersions on. *See* ATTACK, CRIMES, LAW.

aspersion *noun*
The expression of injurious, malicious statements about someone : calumniation, calumny, character assassination, defamation, denigration, detraction, scandal, slander, traducement, vilification. *Law:* libel. *See* ATTACK, CRIMES, LAW.

asphyxiate *verb*
To stop the breathing of : choke, smother, stifle, suffocate. *See* BREATH.

aspirant *noun*
1. One who aspires : aspirer, hopeful. *See* SEEK. **2.** A person who applies for or seeks something, such as a job or position : applicant, candidate, hopeful, petitioner, seeker. *See* SEEK.

aspiration *noun*
1. A strong desire to achieve something : ambition, ambitiousness, emulation. *See* DESIRE. **2.** A fervent hope, wish, or goal : dream, ideal. *See* HOPE.

aspire *verb*
1. To have a fervent hope or aspiration : dream. ***Idioms:*** reach for the stars, set one's heart on. *See* SEEK. **2.** To strive toward a goal : aim, seek. ***Idiom:*** set one's sights on. *See* SEEK, START.

aspirer *noun*
One who aspires : aspirant, hopeful. *See* SEEK.

aspiring *adjective*
Full of ambition : ambitious, emulous. *See* DESIRE.

ass *noun*
One deficient in judgment and good sense : fool, idiot, imbecile, jackass, mooncalf, moron, nincompoop, ninny, nitwit, simple, simpleton, softhead, tomfool. *Informal:* dope, gander, goose. *Slang:* cretin, ding-dong, dip, goof, jerk, nerd, schmo, schmuck, turkey. *See* ABILITY.

assail *verb*
1. To hit heavily and repeatedly with violent blows : assault, baste, batter, beat, belabor, buffet, drub, hammer, pound, pummel, smash, thrash, thresh. *Informal:* lambaste. *Slang:* clobber. ***Idiom:*** rain blows on. *See* ATTACK, STRIKE. **2.** To attack with harsh, often insulting language : abuse, rail against (*or* at), revile, vituperate. *See* PRAISE. **3.** To set upon with violent force : aggress, assault, attack, beset, fall on (*or* upon), go at, have at, sail into, storm, strike. *Informal:* light into, pitch into. *See* ATTACK.

assailable *adjective*
Open to attack and capture because of a lack of protection : attackable, pregnable, vincible, vulnerable. *See* STRONG.

assailant *noun*
One who starts a hostile action : aggressor, assailer, assaulter, attacker. *See* ATTACK.

assailer *noun*
One who starts a hostile action : aggressor, assailant, assaulter, attacker. *See* ATTACK.

assailment *noun*
The act of attacking : aggression, assault, attack, attempt, offense, offensive, onrush, onset, onslaught, strike. *See* ATTACK.

assault *noun*
The act of attacking : aggression, assailment, attack, attempt, offense, offensive, on-

rush, onset, onslaught, strike. *See* ATTACK.
assault *verb* **1.** To set upon with violent force : aggress, assail, attack, beset, fall on (*or* upon), go at, have at, sail into, storm, strike. *Informal:* light into, pitch into. *See* ATTACK. **2.** To hit heavily and repeatedly with violent blows : assail, baste, batter, beat, belabor, buffet, drub, hammer, pound, pummel, smash, thrash, thresh. *Informal:* lambaste. *Slang:* clobber. ***Idiom:*** rain blows on. *See* ATTACK, STRIKE. **3.** To compel (another) to participate in or submit to a sexual act : force, rape, ravish, violate. *See* SEX.

assaulter *noun*
One who starts a hostile action : aggressor, assailant, assailer, attacker. *See* ATTACK.

assay *noun*
1. A procedure that ascertains effectiveness, value, proper function, or other quality : essay, proof, test, trial, tryout. *See* INVESTIGATE. **2.** *Archaic.* A trying to do or make something : attempt, crack, effort, endeavor, essay, go, offer, stab, trial, try. *Informal:* shot. *Slang:* take. *See* TRY.

assay *verb* **1.** To subject to a procedure that ascertains effectiveness, value, proper function, or other quality : check, essay, examine, prove, test, try, try out. ***Idioms:*** bring to the test, make trial of, put to the proof (*or* test). *See* INVESTIGATE. **2.** To make a judgment as to the worth or value of : appraise, assess, calculate, estimate, evaluate, gauge, judge, rate[1], size up, valuate, value. ***Idiom:*** take the measure of. *See* VALUE. **3.** To make an attempt to do or make : attempt, endeavor, essay, seek, strive, try. ***Idioms:*** have a go at, have (*or* make *or* take) a shot at, have (*or* take) a whack at, make a stab at, take a crack at. *See* TRY.

assemblage *noun*
1. A quantity accumulated : accumulation, aggregation, amassment, collection, congeries, cumulation, gathering, mass. *See* COLLECT. **2.** A number of persons who have come or been gathered together : assembly, body, company, conclave, conference, congregation, congress, convention, convocation, crowd, gathering, group, meeting, muster, troop. *Informal:* get-together. *See* COLLECT.

assemble *verb*
1. To bring together : call, cluster, collect[1], congregate, convene, convoke, gather, get together, group, muster, round up, summon. *See* COLLECT. **2.** To come together : cluster, collect[1], congregate, convene, forgather, gather, get together, group, muster. *See* COLLECT. **3.** To create by forming, combining, or altering materials : build, construct, fabricate, fashion, forge[1], frame, make, manufacture, mold, produce, put together, shape. *See* MAKE.

assembler *noun*
A person or business that makes or builds something : builder, constructor, erector, maker, manufacturer, producer. *See* MAKE.

assembly *noun*
1. A number of persons who have come or been gathered together : assemblage, body, company, conclave, conference, congregation, congress, convention, convocation, crowd, gathering, group, meeting, muster, troop. *Informal:* get-together. *See* COLLECT. **2.** A formal assemblage of the members of a group : conference, congress, convention, convocation, meeting. *See* ASSEMBLE.

assent *verb*
To respond affirmatively; receive with agreement or compliance : accede, accept, acquiesce, agree, consent, nod, subscribe, yes. *See* AGREE.

assent *noun* The act or process of accepting : acceptance, acquiescence, agreement, consent, nod, yes. *Informal:* OK. *See* ACCEPT.

assert *verb*
1. To put into words positively and with conviction : affirm, allege, argue, asseverate, aver, avouch, avow, claim, contend, declare, hold, maintain, say, state. ***Idiom:*** have it. *See* AFFIRM. **2.** To defend, maintain, or insist on the recognition of (one's rights, for example) : claim, vindicate. *See* ATTACK.

assertion *noun*
The act of asserting positively : affirmation, allegation, asseveration, averment, claim, declaration, statement. *See* AFFIRM.

assertive *adjective*
1. Marked by boldness and assertiveness : aggressive. *See* ATTITUDE, TRY. **2.** Bold and definite in character : emphatic, forceful, insistent. *See* STRONG.

assess *verb*
1. To establish and apply as compulsory : exact, impose, levy, put. *See* OBLIGATION, OVER, WILLING. **2.** To make a judgment as to the worth or value of : appraise, assay, calculate, estimate, evaluate, gauge, judge, rate[1], size up, valuate, value. ***Idiom:*** take the measure of. *See* VALUE.

assessment *noun*
1. The act or result of judging the worth or value of something or someone : appraisal, appraisement, estimate, estimation, evaluation,

judgment, valuation. *See* VALUE. **2.** A compulsory contribution, usually of money, that is required for the support of a government : duty, impost, levy, tariff, tax. *See* MONEY, PAY, POLITICS.

asset *noun*
All things, such as money, property, or goods, having economic value. Used in plural : capital, fortune, mean[3] (used in plural), resource (used in plural), wealth, wherewithal. *See* OWNED.

asseverate *verb*
To put into words positively and with conviction : affirm, allege, argue, assert, aver, avouch, avow, claim, contend, declare, hold, maintain, say, state. ***Idiom:*** have it. *See* AFFIRM.

asseveration *noun*
The act of asserting positively : affirmation, allegation, assertion, averment, claim, declaration, statement. *See* AFFIRM.

assiduity *noun*
Steady attention and effort, as to one's occupation : application, assiduousness, diligence, industriousness, industry, sedulousness. *See* INDUSTRIOUS.

assiduous *adjective*
Characterized by steady attention and effort : diligent, industrious, sedulous, studious. *See* INDUSTRIOUS.

assiduousness *noun*
Steady attention and effort, as to one's occupation : application, assiduity, diligence, industriousness, industry, sedulousness. *See* INDUSTRIOUS.

assign *verb*
1. To set aside or apart for a specified purpose : allocate, appropriate, designate, earmark. *See* COLLECT, MONEY. **2.** To set aside or distribute as a share : admeasure, allocate, allot, allow, apportion, give, lot, measure out, mete (out). *See* COLLECT. **3.** To regard as belonging to or resulting from another : accredit, ascribe, attribute, charge, credit, impute, lay[1], refer. *See* GIVE. **4.** To ascribe (a misdeed or an error, for example) to : affix, blame, fasten, fix, impute, pin on, place. *See* GIVE. **5.** *Law.* To change the ownership of (property) by means of a legal document : cede, deed, grant, make over, sign over. *Law:* alien, alienate, convey, transfer. *See* GIVE, LAW. **6.** To appoint and send to a particular place : post[2], set[1], station. *See* PLACE.

assignation *noun*
A commitment to appear at a certain time and place : appointment, date, engagement, rendezvous, tryst. *See* AGREE.

assignment *noun*
1. The act of distributing or the condition of being distributed : admeasurement, allocation, apportionment, dispensation, distribution, division. *See* COLLECT. **2.** The act of attributing : ascription, attribution, credit, imputation. *See* GIVE. **3.** A piece of work that has been assigned : chore, duty, job, office, stint, task. *See* WORK. **4.** A making over of legal ownership or title : *Law:* alienation, conveyance, grant, transfer, transferal. *See* LAW.

assimilate *verb*
1. To take in and incorporate, especially mentally : absorb, digest, imbibe, take up. *Informal:* soak (up). *See* ACCEPT. **2.** To represent as similar : analogize, compare, equate, identify, liken, match, parallel. *See* SAME.

assimilation *noun*
The process of absorbing and incorporating, especially mentally : absorption, digestion. *See* ACCEPT.

assimilative *adjective*
Having a capacity or tendency to absorb or soak up : absorbent, absorptive, bibulous. *See* DRY.

assist *verb*
To give support or assistance : abet, aid, boost, help (out), relieve, succor. ***Idioms:*** give (*or* lend) a hand, give a leg up. *See* HELP.
assist *noun* The act or an instance of helping : abetment, aid, assistance, hand, help, relief, succor, support. *See* HELP.

assistance *noun*
The act or an instance of helping : abetment, aid, assist, hand, help, relief, succor, support. *See* HELP.

assistant *noun*
A person who holds a position auxiliary to another and assumes some of the superior's responsibilities : adjutant, aide, auxiliary, coadjutant, coadjutor, deputy, helper, lieutenant, second[2]. *See* HELP.
assistant *adjective* Giving or able to give help or support : accessory, ancillary, auxiliary, collateral, contributory, subsidiary, supportive. *See* HELP.

assize *noun*
The formal product of a legislative or judicial body : act, bill[1], enactment, law, legislation, lex, measure, statute. *See* LAW.

associate *verb*
1. To unite or be united in a relationship : affiliate, ally, bind, combine, conjoin, connect, join,

link, relate. *See* CONNECT. **2.** To be with as a companion : consort, fraternize, hang around, hobnob, run (around), troop. *Slang:* hang out. ***Idiom:*** rub elbows (*or* shoulders) . *See* NEAR. **3.** To come or bring together in one's mind or imagination : bracket, connect, correlate, couple, identify, link. *See* SAME.

associate *noun* **1.** One who is united in a relationship with another : affiliate, ally, cohort, colleague, confederate, copartner, fellow, partner. *See* CONNECT. **2.** One who shares interests or activities with another : chum, companion, comrade, crony, fellow, mate. *Informal:* buddy, pal. *See* NEAR. **3.** One that accompanies another : accompaniment, attendant, companion, concomitant. *See* ACCOMPANIED.

association *noun*
1. The state of being associated : affiliation, alliance, combination, conjunction, connection, cooperation, partnership. *See* NEAR. **2.** A group of people united in a relationship and having some interest, activity, or purpose in common : club, confederation, congress, federation, fellowship, fraternity, guild, league, order, organization, society, sorority, union. *See* GROUP. **3.** A group of athletic teams that play each other : circuit, conference, league, loop. *See* GROUP. **4.** Something, such as a feeling, thought, or idea, associated in one's mind or imagination with a specific person or thing : connection, connotation, suggestion. *See* SUGGEST.

assort *verb*
To distribute into groups according to kinds : categorize, class, classify, group, pigeonhole, separate, sort (out). *See* COLLECT.

assorted *adjective*
Consisting of a number of different kinds : divers, diverse, diversified, heterogeneous, miscellaneous, mixed, motley, multifarious, multiform, sundry, varied, variegated, various. *Biology:* polymorphic, polymorphous. *See* SAME.

assortment *noun*
A collection of various things : conglomeration, gallimaufry, hodgepodge, jumble, medley, mélange, miscellany, mishmash, mixed bag, mixture, olio, patchwork, potpourri, salmagundi, variety. *Slang:* grab bag. *See* COLLECT.

assuage *verb*
1. To make less severe or more bearable : allay, alleviate, comfort, ease, lessen, lighten[2], mitigate, palliate, relieve. *See* INCREASE. **2.** To ease the anger or agitation of : appease, calm (down), conciliate, dulcify, gentle, mollify, pacify, placate, propitiate, soften, soothe, sweeten. ***Idiom:*** pour oil on troubled water. *See* CALM.

assuagement *noun*
Freedom, especially from pain : alleviation, ease, mitigation, palliation, relief. *See* INCREASE.

assume *verb*
1. To take upon oneself : incur, shoulder, tackle, take on, take over, undertake. *See* ACCEPT. **2.** To put (an article of clothing) on one's person : don, get on, pull on, put on, slip into, slip on. *See* PUT ON. **3.** To take on or give a false appearance of : affect[2], counterfeit, fake, feign, pretend, put on, sham, simulate. ***Idiom:*** make believe. *See* TRUE. **4.** To take for granted without proof : posit, postulate, premise, presume, presuppose, suppose. *Informal:* reckon. *See* BELIEF. **5.** To lay claim to for oneself or as one's right : appropriate, arrogate, commandeer, preempt, seize, take, usurp. *See* GIVE.

assumed *adjective*
Being fictitious and not real, as a name : made-up, pseudonymous. *See* TRUE.

assuming *adjective*
Rude and disrespectful : assumptive, audacious, bold, boldfaced, brash, brazen, cheeky, contumelious, familiar, forward, impertinent, impudent, insolent, malapert, nervy, overconfident, pert, presuming, presumptuous, pushy, sassy, saucy, smart. *Informal:* brassy, flip, fresh, smart-alecky, snippety, snippy, uppish, uppity. *Slang:* wise[1]. *See* ATTITUDE, COURTESY.

assumption *noun*
1. The act of taking something for oneself : appropriation, arrogation, preemption, seizure, usurpation. *See* GIVE. **2.** Something taken to be true without proof : postulate, postulation, premise, presupposition, supposition, theory, thesis. *See* REASON. **3.** The state or quality of being impudent or arrogantly self-confident : audaciousness, audacity, boldness, brashness, brazenness, cheek, cheekiness, chutzpah, discourtesy, disrespect, effrontery, face, familiarity, forwardness, gall[1], impertinence, impudence, impudency, incivility, insolence, nerve, nerviness, overconfidence, pertness, presumptuousness, pushiness, rudeness, sassiness, sauciness. *Informal:* brass, crust, sauce, uppishness, uppityness. *See* ATTITUDE, COURTESY.

assumptive *adjective*
1. Based on probability or presumption : likely, presumable, presumptive, probable, prospective. ***Idiom:*** taken for granted. *See* BELIEF, LIKELY. **2.** Rude and disrespectful : assuming, audacious, bold, boldfaced, brash, brazen,

cheeky, contumelious, familiar, forward, impertinent, impudent, insolent, malapert, nervy, overconfident, pert, presuming, presumptuous, pushy, sassy, saucy, smart. *Informal:* brassy, flip, fresh, smart-alecky, snippety, snippy, uppish, uppity. *Slang:* wise[1]. *See* ATTITUDE, COURTESY.

assurance *noun*
1. A declaration that one will or will not do a certain thing : covenant, engagement, guarantee, guaranty, pledge, plight[2], promise, solemn word, vow, warrant, word, word of honor. *See* OBLIGATION. **2.** The fact or condition of being without doubt : assuredness, certainty, certitude, confidence, conviction, positiveness, sureness, surety. *See* CERTAIN. **3.** The quality or state of being safe : safeness, safety, security. *See* SAFETY. **4.** A firm belief in one's own powers : aplomb, confidence, self-assurance, self-confidence, self-possession. *See* ATTITUDE, BELIEF.

assure *verb*
1. To cause (another) to believe or feel sure about something : convince, persuade, satisfy, win over. *See* PERSUASION. **2.** To render certain : ensure, guarantee, insure, secure, warrant. *Informal:* cinch. *See* CERTAIN.

assured *adjective*
1. Having no doubt : certain, confident, positive, sure, undoubting. *See* CERTAIN. **2.** Having a firm belief in one's own powers : confident, secure, self-assured, self-confident, self-possessed. *See* ATTITUDE, BELIEF.

assuredly *adverb*
It is so; as you say or ask : absolutely, agreed, all right, aye, gladly, indubitably, roger, undoubtedly, unquestionably, willingly, yea, yes. *Informal:* OK, uh-huh, yeah, yep. *Slang:* right on. *See* AFFIRM.

assuredness *noun*
The fact or condition of being without doubt : assurance, certainty, certitude, confidence, conviction, positiveness, sureness, surety. *See* CERTAIN.

astonish *verb*
To impress strongly by what is unexpected or unusual : amaze, astound, awe, startle, surprise. ***Idioms:*** catch (*or* take) unawares, take aback. *See* SURPRISE.

astonishing *adjective*
So remarkable as to elicit disbelief : amazing, astounding, fabulous, fantastic, fantastical, incredible, marvelous, miraculous, phenomenal, prodigious, stupendous, unbelievable, wonderful, wondrous. *See* GOOD.

astonishment *noun*
1. The emotion aroused by something awe-inspiring or astounding : amaze, amazement, awe, marvel, wonder, wonderment. *Archaic:* admiration, dread. *See* EXCITE, FEELINGS. **2.** One that evokes great surprise and admiration : marvel, miracle, phenomenon, prodigy, sensation, stunner, wonder, wonderment. ***Idioms:*** one for the books, the eighth wonder of the world. *See* GOOD.

astound *verb*
To impress strongly by what is unexpected or unusual : amaze, astonish, awe, startle, surprise. ***Idioms:*** catch (*or* take) unawares, take aback. *See* SURPRISE.

astounding *adjective*
So remarkable as to elicit disbelief : amazing, astonishing, fabulous, fantastic, fantastical, incredible, marvelous, miraculous, phenomenal, prodigious, stupendous, unbelievable, wonderful, wondrous. *See* GOOD.

astray *adverb*
Not in the right way or on the proper course : afield, amiss, awry, wrong. *See* THRIVE.
astray *adjective* **1.** Unable to find the correct way or place to go : disoriented, lost, stray. *See* SEEK. **2.** Not in accordance with what is usual or expected : amiss, awry, sour, wrong. *See* SURPRISE, THRIVE.

astringent *adjective*
So sharp as to cause mental pain : acerbic, acid, acidic, acrid, biting, caustic, corrosive, cutting, mordacious, mordant, pungent, scathing, sharp, slashing, stinging, trenchant, truculent, vitriolic. *See* ATTACK, RESPECT.

astute *adjective*
Having or showing a clever awareness and resourcefulness in practical matters : cagey, canny, knowing, perspicacious, shrewd, slick, smart, wise[1]. *Informal:* savvy. *See* ABILITY, CAREFUL.

astuteness *noun*
Skill in perceiving, discriminating, or judging : acumen, clear-sightedness, discernment, discrimination, eye, keenness, nose, penetration, perceptiveness, percipience, percipiency, perspicacity, sagacity, sageness, shrewdness, wit. *See* ABILITY, CAREFUL.

asylum *noun*
1. An institution that provides care and shelter : home, hospice, hospital, shelter. *See* PROTECTION. **2.** Something that physically protects, especially from danger : cover, covert, harbor, haven, protection, refuge, retreat, sanctuary,

shelter. *See* ATTACK, SAFETY. **3.** The state of being protected or safeguarded, as from danger or hardship : harborage, refuge, sanctuary, shelter. *See* SAFETY.

asymmetric *adjective*
Not straight, uniform, or symmetrical : asymmetrical, irregular. *See* SMOOTH, STRAIGHT.

asymmetrical *adjective*
Not straight, uniform, or symmetrical : asymmetric, irregular. *See* SMOOTH, STRAIGHT.

asymmetry *noun*
Lack of smoothness or regularity : crookedness, inequality, irregularity, jaggedness, roughness, unevenness. *See* SMOOTH, STRAIGHT.

athirst *adjective*
1. Intensely desirous or interested : agog, ardent, avid, bursting, eager, impatient, keen[1], solicitous, thirsting, thirsty. *Informal:* raring. *Idioms:* champing at the bit, ready and willing. *See* CONCERN. **2.** *Archaic.* Needing or desiring drink : dry, parched, thirsty. *See* DRY.

athletic *adjective*
Characterized by marked muscular development; powerfully built : brawny, burly, husky[2], muscular, robust, sinewy, sturdy. *See* STRONG.

atingle *adjective*
Feeling a very strong emotion : excited, fired up, thrilled, worked up. *Informal:* psyched. *Slang:* stoked, turned-on. *See* EXCITE.

atmosphere *noun*
1. The gaseous mixture enveloping the earth : air. *See* HIGH, PLACE. **2.** A general impression produced by a predominant quality or characteristic : air, ambiance, aura, feel, feeling, mood, smell, tone. *See* BE. **3.** The totality of surrounding conditions and circumstances affecting growth or development : ambiance, climate, environment, medium, milieu, mise en scène, surroundings, world. *See* BE, LIMITED, PLACE. **4.** A distinctive yet intangible quality deemed typical of a given thing : aroma, flavor, savor, smack[2]. *See* TASTE.

atmospheric *adjective*
Of or relating to air : aerial, airy, pneumatic. *See* BREATH, HIGH.

atrium *noun*
An area partially or entirely enclosed by walls or buildings : close, court, courtyard, enclosure, quad, quadrangle, yard. *See* PLACE.

atrocious *adjective*
1. Disgracefully and grossly offensive : heinous, monstrous, outrageous, scandalous, shocking. *Archaic:* enormous. *See* RIGHT. **2.** Extremely unpleasant to the senses or feelings : disgusting, foul, horrid, nasty, nauseating, offensive, repellent, repulsive, revolting, sickening, ugly, unwholesome, vile. *See* LIKE, PAIN.

atrociousness *noun*
1. The quality of passing all moral bounds : atrocity, enormity, heinousness, monstrousness. *See* GOOD. **2.** The quality or state of being flagrant : atrocity, egregiousness, enormity, flagrance, flagrancy, flagrantness, glaringness, grossness, outrageousness, rankness. *See* GOOD.

atrocity *noun*
1. The quality of passing all moral bounds : atrociousness, enormity, heinousness, monstrousness. *See* GOOD. **2.** The quality or state of being flagrant : atrociousness, egregiousness, enormity, flagrance, flagrancy, flagrantness, glaringness, grossness, outrageousness, rankness. *See* GOOD. **3.** A monstrous offense or evil : enormity, monstrosity, outrage. *See* RIGHT.

atrophy *noun*
Descent to a lower level or condition : decadence, declension, declination, decline, degeneracy, degeneration, deterioration. *See* BETTER.
atrophy *verb* To become lower in quality, character, or condition : decline, degenerate, descend, deteriorate, retrograde, sink, worsen. *Idioms:* go bad, go to pot, go to seed, go to the dogs. *See* BETTER.

attach *verb*
1. To join one thing to another : affix, clip[2], connect, couple, fasten, fix, moor, secure. *See* ASSEMBLE. **2.** To add as a supplement or an appendix : affix, annex, append, subjoin. *See* INCREASE.

attachment *noun*
1. The condition of being closely tied to another by affection or faith : affection, devotion, fondness, liking, love, loyalty (used in plural). *See* CONNECT. **2.** A subordinate element added to another entity : accessory, adjunct, appendage, appurtenance, supplement. *See* INCREASE.

attack *verb*
1. To set upon with violent force : aggress, assail, assault, beset, fall on (*or* upon), go at, have at, sail into, storm, strike. *Informal:* light into, pitch into. *See* ATTACK. **2.** To start work on vigorously : go at, sail in, tackle, wade in (*or* into). *Idiom:* hop to it. *See* WORK.
attack *noun* **1.** The act of attacking : aggression, assailment, assault, attempt, offense, offensive, onrush, onset, onslaught, strike. *See*

ATTACK. **2.** A method used in dealing with something : approach, course, line, modus operandi, plan, procedure, tack, technique. *See* MEANS. **3.** A sudden and often acute manifestation of a disease : access, fit[2], seizure. *Informal:* spell[3]. *See* HEALTH.

attackable *adjective*
Open to attack and capture because of a lack of protection : assailable, pregnable, vincible, vulnerable. *See* STRONG.

attacker *noun*
One who starts a hostile action : aggressor, assailant, assailer, assaulter. *See* ATTACK.

attain *verb*
1. To succeed in doing : accomplish, achieve, gain, reach, realize. *Slang:* score. *See* DO. **2.** To reach (a goal or objective) : arrive at, come to, gain, get to. *Informal:* hit on (*or* upon). *See* START.

attainable *adjective*
Capable of being obtained or used : acquirable, available, gettable, obtainable, procurable. ***Idioms:*** on hand, to be had. *See* GET.

attainment *noun*
Something completed or attained successfully : accomplishment, achievement, acquirement, acquisition, effort, feat. *See* DO.

attaint *noun*
Archaic. A mark of discredit or disgrace : black eye, blemish, blot, onus, spot, stain, stigma, taint, tarnish. ***Idiom:*** a blot on one's escutcheon. *See* MARKS, RESPECT.

attempt *verb*
To make an attempt to do or make : assay, endeavor, essay, seek, strive, try. ***Idioms:*** have a go at, have (*or* make *or* take) a shot at, have (*or* take) a whack at, make a stab at, take a crack at. *See* TRY.

attempt *noun* **1.** A trying to do or make something : crack, effort, endeavor, essay, go, offer, stab, trial, try. *Informal:* shot. *Slang:* take. *Archaic:* assay. *See* TRY. **2.** The act of attacking : aggression, assailment, assault, attack, offense, offensive, onrush, onset, onslaught, strike. *See* ATTACK.

attend *verb*
1. To occur as a consequence : ensue, follow, result. *See* CAUSE, PRECEDE. **2.** To be with or go with (another) : accompany, companion, company, escort. *Obsolete:* consort. ***Idiom:*** go hand in hand with. *See* ACCOMPANIED. **3.** To work and care for : do for, minister to, serve, wait on (*or* upon). *See* CARE FOR. **4.** To have the care and supervision of : care for, look after, mind, minister to, see to, tend[2], watch. ***Idioms:*** keep an eye on, look out for, take care (*or* charge) of, take under one's wing. *See* CARE FOR. **5.** To perceive by ear, usually attentively : hark, hear, heed, listen. *Archaic:* hearken. ***Idiom:*** give (*or* lend) one's ear. *See* SOUNDS.

attendant *noun*
A person who helps : abettor, aid, help, helper, reliever, succorer. *See* HELP. **2.** One that accompanies another : accompaniment, associate, companion, concomitant. *See* ACCOMPANIED.

attendant *adjective* Occurring or existing with : accompanying, attending, coincident, concomitant, concurrent. *See* ACCOMPANIED.

attending *adjective*
Occurring or existing with : accompanying, attendant, coincident, concomitant, concurrent. *See* ACCOMPANIED.

attention *noun*
1. Concentration of the mental powers on something : attentiveness, concentration, consideration, heedfulness, regardfulness. *See* EXCITE. **2.** The act of noting, observing, or taking into account : cognizance, espial, heed, mark, note, notice, observance, observation, regard, remark. *See* KNOWLEDGE, SEE.

attentive *adjective*
1. Concentrating the mental powers on something : heedful, intent, regardful. ***Idiom:*** all ears (*or* eyes). *See* EXCITE. **2.** Full of polite concern for the well-being of others : considerate, courteous, gallant, polite, solicitous, thoughtful. *See* CAREFUL, TREAT WELL.

attentiveness *noun*
1. Concentration of the mental powers on something : attention, concentration, consideration, heedfulness, regardfulness. *See* EXCITE. **2.** Thoughtful attention : concern, consideration, regard, solicitude, thoughtfulness. *See* ATTITUDE, CONCERN, KIND, TREAT WELL.

attenuate *verb*
1. To lessen or deplete the nerve, energy, or strength of : debilitate, devitalize, enervate, enfeeble, sap[2], undermine, undo, unnerve, weaken. *See* STRONG. **2.** To lessen the strength of by or as if by admixture : cut, dilute, thin, water (down), weaken. *See* STRONG. **3.** To become diffuse : rarefy, thin. *See* TIGHTEN.

attenuation *noun*
The depletion or sapping of strength or energy : debilitation, depletion, devitalization, enervation, enfeeblement, impoverishment. *See* STRONG.

attest *verb*
1. To assure the certainty or validity of : authenticate, back (up), bear out, confirm, corroborate, evidence, justify, substantiate, testify (to), validate, verify, warrant. *See* SUPPORT, TRUE. **2.** To confirm formally as true, accurate, or genuine : certify, testify, vouch (for), witness. ***Idiom:*** bear witness to. *See* AFFIRM. **3.** To give grounds for believing in the existence or presence of : argue, bespeak, betoken, indicate, mark, point to, testify, witness. *See* SHOW. **4.** To give evidence or testimony under oath : swear, testify, witness. *Law:* depone, depose. ***Idioms:*** bear witness, take the stand. *See* LAW.

attestant *noun*
One who testifies, especially in court : attester, testifier, witness. *Law:* deponent. *See* LAW.

attestation *noun*
That which confirms : authentication, confirmation, corroboration, demonstration, evidence, proof, substantiation, testament, testimonial, testimony, validation, verification, warrant. *See* TRUE.

attester or **attestor** *noun*
One who testifies, especially in court : attestant, testifier, witness. *Law:* deponent. *See* LAW.

attestor *noun* See **attester.**

attire *verb*
1. To put clothes on : apparel, clothe, dress, garb, garment, invest. *Informal:* tog. *See* PUT ON. **2.** To dress in formal or special clothing : array, deck² (out), dress up, prank². *Informal:* trick out (*or* up). *Slang:* doll up. *See* ORDER, PLAIN, PUT ON.

attire *noun* **1.** Articles worn to cover the body : apparel, clothes, clothing, dress, garment (used in plural), habiliment (often used in plural), raiment. *Informal:* dud (used in plural), tog (used in plural). *Slang:* thread (used in plural). *See* PUT ON. **2.** Showy and elaborate clothing or apparel : array, finery, frippery, regalia. *See* PUT ON.

attitude *noun*
1. The way in which one is placed or arranged : pose, position, posture. *See* POSTURE. **2.** The way in which a person holds or carries his or her body : carriage, pose, posture, stance. *See* POSTURE. **3.** A frame of mind affecting one's thoughts or behavior : outlook, position, posture, stance. *See* ATTITUDE. **4.** A general cast of mind with regard to something : feeling, sentiment. *See* ATTITUDE.

attitudinize *verb*
1. To assume an exaggerated or unnatural attitude or pose : pose, posture. ***Idiom:*** strike an attitude. *See* POSTURE. **2.** To represent oneself in a given character or as other than what one is : impersonate, masquerade, pass, pose, posture. ***Idiom:*** pass oneself off as. *See* HONEST.

attorney *noun*
A person who practices law : counsel, counselor, lawyer. *Slang:* ambulance chaser. *Chiefly British:* barrister. *See* LAW.

attract *verb*
1. To direct or impel to oneself by some quality or action : allure, appeal, draw, entice, lure, magnetize, take. *Informal:* pull. *See* LIKE. **2.** To arouse the interest and attention of : interest, intrigue. *Slang:* turn on. *See* EXCITE.

attraction *noun*
The power or quality of attracting : allure, allurement, appeal, attractiveness, call, charisma, charm, draw, enchantment, enticement, fascination, glamour, lure, magnetism, witchery. *Informal:* pull. *See* LIKE.

attractive *adjective*
1. Pleasing to the eye or mind : bewitching, enchanting, engaging, enticing, fascinating, fetching, glamorous, lovely, prepossessing, pretty, sweet, taking, tempting, winning, winsome. *See* LIKE. **2.** Having qualities that delight the eye : beauteous, beautiful, comely, fair, good-looking, gorgeous, handsome, lovely, pretty, pulchritudinous, ravishing, sightly, stunning. *Scots:* bonny. ***Idiom:*** easy on the eyes. *See* BEAUTIFUL. **3.** Pleasingly suited to the wearer : becoming, flattering. *See* BEAUTIFUL.

attractiveness *noun*
The power or quality of attracting : allure, allurement, appeal, attraction, call, charisma, charm, draw, enchantment, enticement, fascination, glamour, lure, magnetism, witchery. *Informal:* pull. *See* LIKE.

attribute *verb*
To regard as belonging to or resulting from another : accredit, ascribe, assign, charge, credit, impute, lay¹, refer. *See* GIVE.

attribute *noun* **1.** A distinctive element : character, characteristic, feature, mark, peculiarity, property, quality, savor, trait. *See* BE. **2.** An object associated with and serving to identify something else : emblem, symbol. *See* SUBSTITUTE.

attribution *noun*
The act of attributing : ascription, assignment, credit, imputation. *See* GIVE.

attrition *noun*
Theology. A feeling of regret for one's sins or misdeeds : compunction, contriteness,

contrition, penitence, penitency, remorse, remorsefulness, repentance, rue. *See* REGRET.

attune *verb*

1. To bring into accord : accommodate, conform, coordinate, harmonize, integrate, proportion, reconcile, tune. *See* AGREE. **2.** *Music.* To alter for proper functioning : adjust, fix, regulate, set[1], tune (up). *See* CHANGE, HELP.

atypic *adjective*

1. Departing from the normal : aberrant, abnormal, anomalistic, anomalous, atypical, deviant, divergent, irregular, preternatural, unnatural. *See* GOOD, USUAL. **2.** Not usual or ordinary : atypical, novel, unconventional, unordinary, unusual, unwonted. *Slang:* offbeat. *See* USUAL.

atypical *adjective*

1. Departing from the normal : aberrant, abnormal, anomalistic, anomalous, atypic, deviant, divergent, irregular, preternatural, unnatural. *See* GOOD, USUAL. **2.** Not usual or ordinary : atypic, novel, unconventional, unordinary, unusual, unwonted. *Slang:* offbeat. *See* USUAL.

au courant *adjective*

Characteristic of recent times or informed of what is current : contemporary, current, mod, modern, up-to-date, up-to-the-minute. *See* KNOWLEDGE, NEW.

audacious *adjective*

1. Having or showing courage : bold, brave, courageous, dauntless, doughty, fearless, fortitudinous, gallant, game, hardy, heroic, intrepid, mettlesome, plucky, stout, stouthearted, unafraid, undaunted, valiant, valorous. *Informal:* spunky. *Slang:* gutsy, gutty. *See* FEAR. **2.** Taking or willing to take risks : adventuresome, adventurous, bold, daredevil, daring, enterprising, venturesome, venturous. *See* SAFETY.
3. Rude and disrespectful : assuming, assumptive, bold, boldfaced, brash, brazen, cheeky, contumelious, familiar, forward, impertinent, impudent, insolent, malapert, nervy, overconfident, pert, presuming, presumptuous, pushy, sassy, saucy, smart. *Informal:* brassy, flip, fresh, smart-alecky, snippety, snippy, uppish, uppity. *Slang:* wise[1]. *See* ATTITUDE, COURTESY.

audaciousness *noun*

1. Willingness to take risks : adventuresomeness, adventurousness, audacity, boldness, daredevilry, daredeviltry, daring, daringness, venturesomeness, venturousness. *See* SAFETY.
2. The state or quality of being impudent or arrogantly self-confident : assumption, audacity, boldness, brashness, brazenness, cheek, cheekiness, chutzpah, discourtesy, disrespect, effrontery, face, familiarity, forwardness, gall[1], impertinence, impudence, impudency, incivility, insolence, nerve, nerviness, overconfidence, pertness, presumptuousness, pushiness, rudeness, sassiness, sauciness. *Informal:* brass, crust, sauce, uppishness, uppityness. *See* ATTITUDE, COURTESY.

audacity *noun*

1. Willingness to take risks : adventuresomeness, adventurousness, audaciousness, boldness, daredevilry, daredeviltry, daring, daringness, venturesomeness, venturousness. *See* SAFETY.
2. The state or quality of being impudent or arrogantly self-confident : assumption, audaciousness, boldness, brashness, brazenness, cheek, cheekiness, chutzpah, discourtesy, disrespect, effrontery, face, familiarity, forwardness, gall[1], impertinence, impudence, impudency, incivility, insolence, nerve, nerviness, overconfidence, pertness, presumptuousness, pushiness, rudeness, sassiness, sauciness. *Informal:* brass, crust, sauce, uppishness, uppityness. *See* ATTITUDE, COURTESY.

audience *noun*

1. The body of persons who admire a public personality, especially an entertainer : following, public. *See* LIKE. **2.** A chance to be heard : audition, hearing. *See* SOUNDS.

audition *noun*

1. The sense by which sound is perceived : ear, hearing. *See* SOUNDS. **2.** A chance to be heard : audience, hearing. *See* SOUNDS.

aught *noun*

Archaic. No thing; not anything : nil, nothing, null. *Informal:* zero. *Slang:* nix, zilch. *See* ABSENCE.

augment *verb*

To make or become greater or larger : aggrandize, amplify, boost, build, build up, burgeon, enlarge, escalate, expand, extend, grow, increase, magnify, mount, multiply, proliferate, rise, run up, snowball, soar, swell, upsurge, wax. *Informal:* beef up. *See* INCREASE.
augment *noun* The act of increasing or rising : aggrandizement, amplification, augmentation, boost, buildup, enlargement, escalation, growth, hike, increase, jump, multiplication, proliferation, raise, rise, swell, upsurge, upswing, upturn. *See* INCREASE.

augmentation *noun*

1. The act of increasing or rising : aggrandizement, amplification, augment, boost, buildup, enlargement, escalation, growth, hike, increase, jump, multiplication, proliferation, raise, rise, swell, upsurge, upswing, upturn. *See* INCREASE. **2.** Something tending to augment something else : accession, addition, acquisition. *See* INCREASE.

augur *noun*
A person who foretells future events by or as if by supernatural means : auspex, diviner, foreteller, haruspex, prophesier, prophet, prophetess, seer, sibyl, soothsayer, vaticinator. *See* FORESIGHT.

augur *verb* **1.** To tell about or make known (future events) by or as if by supernatural means : divine, foretell, prophesy, soothsay, vaticinate. *See* FORESIGHT. **2.** To give an indication of something in advance : adumbrate, bode, forecast, forerun, foreshadow, foretell, foretoken, portend, prefigure, presage, prognosticate. *See* FORESIGHT, SHOW.

augural *adjective*
Of or relating to the foretelling of events by or as if by supernatural means : divinitory, fatidic, fatidical, mantic, oracular, prophetic, sibylline, vatic, vatical, vaticinal, visionary. *See* FORESIGHT.

augury *noun*
A phenomenon that serves as a sign or warning of some future good or evil : forerunner, foretoken, omen, portent, prefigurement, presage, prognostic, prognostication, sign. ***Idiom:*** writing (*or* handwriting) on the wall. *See* FORESIGHT, WARN.

august *adjective*
1. Large and impressive in size, scope, or extent : baronial, grand, grandiose, imposing, lordly, magnific, magnificent, majestic, noble, princely, regal, royal, splendid, stately, sublime, superb. *See* BIG, GOOD. **2.** Raised to or occupying a high position or rank : elevated, exalted, grand, high-ranking, lofty. *See* RISE.

au naturel *adjective*
Not wearing any clothes : bare, naked, nude, unclad. *Chiefly British:* starkers. ***Idioms:*** in one's birthday suit, in the altogether (*or* buff *or* raw), naked as a jaybird, stark naked, without a stitch. *See* PUT ON, SHOW.

aura *noun*
A general impression produced by a predominant quality or characteristic : air, ambiance, atmosphere, feel, feeling, mood, smell, tone. *See* BE.

aureate *adjective*
Characterized by language that is elevated and sometimes pompous in style : bombastic, declamatory, flowery, fustian, grandiloquent, high-flown, high-sounding, magniloquent, orotund, overblown, rhetorical, sonorous, swollen. *See* PLAIN, STYLE, WORDS.

auricular *adjective*
Known about by very few : confidential, inside, private, secret. *Informal:* hush-hush. *See* SHOW.

aurora *noun*
The first appearance of daylight in the morning : cockcrow, dawn, dawning, daybreak, morn, morning, sunrise, sunup. *See* START.

auspex *noun*
A person who foretells future events by or as if by supernatural means : augur, diviner, foreteller, haruspex, prophesier, prophet, prophetess, seer, sibyl, soothsayer, vaticinator. *See* FORESIGHT.

auspice *noun*
Aid or support given by a patron. Often used in plural : aegis, backing, patronage, patronization, sponsorship. *See* HELP.

auspicious *adjective*
1. Occurring at a fitting or advantageous time : favorable, opportune, propitious, prosperous, seasonable, timely, well-timed. *See* LUCK. **2.** Indicative of future success or full of promise : benign, bright, brilliant, fair, favorable, fortunate, good, propitious. *See* LUCK.

austere *adjective*
Cold and forbidding : bleak, dour, grim, hard, harsh, severe, stark. *See* ATTITUDE, HOT.

austerity *noun*
The fact or condition of being rigorous and unsparing : hardness, harshness, rigidity, rigor, rigorousness, severity, sternness, strictness, stringency, toughness. *See* EASY.

autarchic *adjective*
Having and exercising complete political power and control : absolute, absolutistic, arbitrary, autarchical, autocratic, autocratical, despotic, dictatorial, monocratic, totalitarian, tyrannic, tyrannical, tyrannous. *See* OVER, POLITICS.

autarchical *adjective*
Having and exercising complete political power and control : absolute, absolutistic, arbitrary, autarchic, autocratic, autocratical, despotic, dictatorial, monocratic, totalitarian, tyrannic, tyrannical, tyrannous. *See* OVER, POLITICS.

autarchy *noun*
A government in which a single leader or party exercises absolute control over all citizens and every aspect of their lives : absolutism, autocracy, despotism, dictatorship, monocracy, tyranny. *See* OVER, POLITICS.

authentic *adjective*
1. Worthy of belief, as because of precision or

faithfulness to an original : authoritative, convincing, credible, faithful, true, trustworthy, valid. *See* TRUE. **2.** Not counterfeit or copied : actual, bona fide, genuine, good, indubitable, original, real, true, undoubted, unquestionable. *See* TRUE.

authenticate *verb*
1. To assure the certainty or validity of : attest, back (up), bear out, confirm, corroborate, evidence, justify, substantiate, testify (to), validate, verify, warrant. *See* SUPPORT, TRUE. **2.** To establish as true or genuine : bear out, confirm, corroborate, demonstrate, endorse, establish, evidence, prove, show, substantiate, validate, verify. *See* SHOW, SUPPORT.

authentication *noun*
That which confirms : attestation, confirmation, corroboration, demonstration, evidence, proof, substantiation, testament, testimonial, testimony, validation, verification, warrant. *See* TRUE.

authenticity *noun*
The quality of being authentic : genuineness, realness, truthfulness, validity. *See* TRUE.

author *noun*
One that creates, founds, or originates : architect, creator, entrepreneur, father, founder[2], inventor, maker, originator, parent, patriarch. *See* START.

authoritarian *adjective*
1. Characterized by or favoring absolute obedience to authority : autocratic, despotic, dictatorial, totalitarian, tyrannic, tyrannical. *See* OVER. **2.** Tending to dictate : bossy, dictatorial, dogmatic, domineering, imperious, magisterial, masterful, overbearing, peremptory. *See* OVER.

authoritarian *noun* One who imposes or favors absolute obedience to authority : autocrat, despot, dictator, martinet, totalitarian, tyrant. *See* OVER.

authoritarianism *noun*
A political doctrine advocating the principle of absolute rule : absolutism, autocracy, despotism, dictatorship, totalitarianism. *See* OVER, POLITICS.

authoritative *adjective*
1. Having or arising from authority : conclusive, official, sanctioned, standard. *See* TRUE. **2.** Worthy of belief, as because of precision or faithfulness to an original : authentic, convincing, credible, faithful, true, trustworthy, valid. *See* TRUE. **3.** Serving the function of deciding or settling with finality : conclusive, decisive, definitive, determinative, final. *See* DECIDE. **4.** Exercising authority : commanding, dominant, lordly, masterful. *See* OVER, STRONG.

authority *noun*
1. The right and power to command, decide, rule, or judge : command, control, domination, dominion, jurisdiction, mastery, might, power, prerogative, sovereignty, sway. *Informal:* say-so. *See* OVER. **2.** A person or group having the right and power to command, decide, rule, or judge : official. ***Idioms:*** powers that be, the Man. *See* OVER. **3.** Conferred power : faculty, mandate, right. *Law:* competence, competency. *See* ABILITY. **4.** A person with a high degree of knowledge or skill in a particular field : ace, adept, dab hand, expert, master, past master, professional, proficient, wizard. *Informal:* whiz. *Slang:* crackerjack. *Chiefly British:* dab[2]. *See* ABILITY.

authorization *noun*
The approving of an action, especially when done by one in authority : allowance, approbation, approval, consent, endorsement, leave[2], license, permission, permit, sanction. *Informal:* OK. *See* ALLOW.

authorize *verb*
1. To give authority to : accredit, commission, empower, enable, entitle, license, qualify. *See* ALLOW. **2.** To give one's consent to : allow, approbate, approve, consent, endorse, let, permit, sanction. *Informal:* OK. *See* ALLOW.

autochthonal *adjective*
Existing, born, or produced in a land or region : aboriginal, autochthonic, autochthonous, endemic, indigenous, native. *See* NATIVE.

autochthonic *adjective*
Existing, born, or produced in a land or region : aboriginal, autochthonal, autochthonous, endemic, indigenous, native. *See* NATIVE.

autochthonous *adjective*
Existing, born, or produced in a land or region : aboriginal, autochthonal, autochthonic, endemic, indigenous, native. *See* NATIVE.

autocracy *noun*
1. A government in which a single leader or party exercises absolute control over all citizens and every aspect of their lives : absolutism, autarchy, despotism, dictatorship, monocracy, tyranny. *See* OVER, POLITICS. **2.** A political doctrine advocating the principle of absolute rule : absolutism, authoritarianism, despotism, dictatorship, totalitarianism. *See* OVER, POLITICS. **3.** Absolute power, especially when exercised unjustly or cruelly : despotism, dictatorship, totalitarianism, tyranny. *See* OVER, POLITICS.

autocrat *noun*
One who imposes or favors absolute obedience to authority : authoritarian, despot, dictator, martinet, totalitarian, tyrant. *See* OVER.

autocratic *adjective*
1. Having and exercising complete political power and control : absolute, absolutistic, arbitrary, autarchic, autarchical, autocratical, despotic, dictatorial, monocratic, totalitarian, tyrannic, tyrannical, tyrannous. *See* OVER, POLITICS. **2.** Characterized by or favoring absolute obedience to authority : authoritarian, despotic, dictatorial, totalitarian, tyrannic, tyrannical. *See* OVER.

autocratical *adjective*
Having and exercising complete political power and control : absolute, absolutistic, arbitrary, autarchic, autarchical, autocratic, despotic, dictatorial, monocratic, totalitarian, tyrannic, tyrannical, tyrannous. *See* OVER, POLITICS.

autograph *verb*
To affix one's signature to : endorse, inscribe, sign, subscribe, undersign. ***Idioms:*** put one's John Hancock on, set one's hand to. *See* LAW.

automatic *adjective*
1. Acting or happening without apparent forethought, prompting, or planning : impulsive, instinctive, involuntary, reflex, spontaneous, unpremeditated. *See* PLANNED. **2.** Performed or performing automatically and impersonally : mechanical, perfunctory. *See* CONCERN.

autonomous *adjective*
Having political independence : free, independent, self-governing, sovereign. *See* DEPENDENCE, FREE.

autonomy *noun*
The condition of being politically free : freedom, independence, independency, liberty, self-government, sovereignty. *See* DEPENDENCE, FREE.

auxiliary *adjective*
1. Giving or able to give help or support : accessory, ancillary, assistant, collateral, contributory, subsidiary, supportive. *See* HELP.
2. Used or held in reserve : backup, emergency, reserve, secondary, standby, supplemental, supplementary. *See* INCREASE.
auxiliary *noun* A person who holds a position auxiliary to another and assumes some of the superior's responsibilities : adjutant, aide, assistant, coadjutant, coadjutor, deputy, helper, lieutenant, second[2]. *See* HELP.

avail *verb*
To be an advantage to : advantage, benefit, profit, serve. *Archaic:* boot[2]. ***Idiom:*** stand someone in good stead. *See* HELP.
avail *noun* **1.** The quality of being suitable or adaptable to an end : account, advantage, benefit, profit, use, usefulness, utility. *See* USED.
2. Something beneficial : advantage, benefit, blessing, boon[1], favor, gain, profit. *See* HELP.

available *adjective*
Capable of being obtained or used : acquirable, attainable, gettable, obtainable, procurable. ***Idioms:*** on hand, to be had. *See* GET.

avarice *noun*
Excessive desire for more than one needs or deserves : acquisitiveness, avariciousness, avidity, covetousness, cupidity, graspingness, greed. *Informal:* grabbiness. *See* DESIRE, GIVE.

avaricious *adjective*
Having a strong urge to obtain or possess something, especially material wealth, in quantity : acquisitive, avid, covetous, grasping, greedy, hungry. *Informal:* grabby. *See* DESIRE, GIVE.

avariciousness *noun*
Excessive desire for more than one needs or deserves : acquisitiveness, avarice, avidity, covetousness, cupidity, graspingness, greed. *Informal:* grabbiness. *See* DESIRE, GIVE.

avenge *verb*
To exact revenge for or from : pay back, pay off, redress, repay, requite, vindicate. *Informal:* fix. *Archaic:* wreak. ***Idioms:*** even the score, get back at, get even with, pay back in kind (*or* in one's own coin), settle (*or* square) accounts, take an eye for an eye. *See* FORGIVENESS.

avenue *noun*
A course affording passage from one place to another : boulevard, drive, expressway, freeway, highway, path, road, roadway, route, street, superhighway, thoroughfare, thruway, turnpike, way. *See* MOVE, OPEN.

aver *verb*
To put into words positively and with conviction : affirm, allege, argue, assert, asseverate, avouch, avow, claim, contend, declare, hold, maintain, say, state. ***Idiom:*** have it. *See* AFFIRM.

average *noun*
Something, as a type, number, quantity, or degree, that represents a midpoint between extremes on a scale of valuation : mean[3], median, medium, norm, par. *See* USUAL.
average *adjective* **1.** Of moderately good quality but less than excellent : acceptable, adequate, all right, common, decent, fair, fairish, goodish, moderate, passable, respectable, satisfactory, sufficient, tolerable. *Informal:* OK,

tidy. *See* GOOD. **2.** Commonly encountered : common, commonplace, general, normal, ordinary, typical, usual. *See* SURPRISE. **3.** Being of no special quality or type : common, commonplace, cut-and-dried, formulaic, garden, garden-variety, indifferent, mediocre, ordinary, plain, routine, run-of-the-mill, standard, stock, undistinguished, unexceptional, unremarkable. *See* GOOD, USUAL.

averment *noun*
The act of asserting positively : affirmation, allegation, assertion, asseveration, claim, declaration, statement. *See* AFFIRM.

averse *adjective*
Not inclined or willing to do or undertake : disinclined, indisposed, loath, reluctant, unwilling. *See* WILLING.

averseness *noun*
The state of not being disposed or inclined : disinclination, indisposition, reluctance, unwillingness. *See* WILLING.

aversion *noun*
1. Extreme hostility and dislike : abhorrence, abomination, antipathy, detestation, hate, hatred, horror, loathing, repellence, repellency, repugnance, repugnancy, repulsion, revulsion. *See* LOVE. **2.** An object of extreme dislike : abhorrence, abomination, anathema, bête noire, bugbear, detestation, execration, hate. *Informal:* horror. *See* LOVE.

avert *verb*
1. To change the direction or course of : deflect, deviate, divert, pivot, shift, swing, turn, veer. *See* CHANGE. **2.** To prohibit from occurring by advance planning or action : forestall, forfend, obviate, preclude, prevent, rule out, stave off, ward (off). ***Idiom:*** nip in the bud. *See* ALLOW.

avid *adjective*
1. Having an insatiable appetite for an activity or pursuit : edacious, gluttonous, greedy, omnivorous, rapacious, ravenous, unappeasable, voracious. *See* DESIRE. **2.** Having a strong urge to obtain or possess something, especially material wealth, in quantity : acquisitive, avaricious, covetous, grasping, greedy, hungry. *Informal:* grabby. *See* DESIRE, GIVE. **3.** Intensely desirous or interested : agog, ardent, athirst, bursting, eager, impatient, keen[1], solicitous, thirsting, thirsty. *Informal:* raring. ***Idioms:*** champing at the bit, ready and willing. *See* CONCERN.

avidity *noun*
1. The quality or condition of being voracious : edacity, omnivorousness, rapaciousness, rapacity, ravenousness, voracity. *See* DESIRE. **2.** Excessive desire for more than one needs or deserves : acquisitiveness, avarice, avariciousness, covetousness, cupidity, graspingness, greed. *Informal:* grabbiness. *See* DESIRE, GIVE.

avoid *verb*
To keep away from : burke, bypass, circumvent, dodge, duck, elude, escape, eschew, evade, get around, shun. ***Idioms:*** fight shy of, give a wide berth to, have no truck with, keep (*or* stay *or* steer) clear of. *See* SEEK.

avoidance *noun*
1. The act, an instance, or a means of avoiding : bypass, circumvention, escape, evasion. *See* SEEK. **2.** *Law.* An often formal act of putting an end to : abolishment, abolition, abrogation, annihilation, annulment, cancellation, defeasance, invalidation, negation, nullification, voidance. *Law:* extinguishment. *See* CONTINUE.

avoirdupois *noun*
Informal. The state or quality of being physically heavy : heaviness, heftiness, massiveness, ponderosity, ponderousness, weight, weightiness. *See* HEAVY.

avouch *verb*
To put into words positively and with conviction : affirm, allege, argue, assert, asseverate, aver, avow, claim, contend, declare, hold, maintain, say, state. ***Idiom:*** have it. *See* AFFIRM.

avow *verb*
1. To recognize, often reluctantly, the reality or truth of : acknowledge, admit, concede, confess, grant, own (up). *Slang:* fess up. *Chiefly Regional:* allow. *See* AFFIRM, KNOWLEDGE. **2.** To put into words positively and with conviction : affirm, allege, argue, assert, asseverate, aver, avouch, claim, contend, declare, hold, maintain, say, state. ***Idiom:*** have it. *See* AFFIRM.

avowal *noun*
The act of admitting to something : acknowledgment, admission, confession. *See* AFFIRM, KNOWLEDGE, SHOW.

await *verb*
To look forward to confidently : anticipate, bargain for (*or* on), count on, depend on (*or* upon), expect, look for, wait (for). *Informal:* figure on. *See* SURPRISE.

awake *verb*
1. To cease sleeping : arouse, awaken, rouse, stir[1], wake[1], waken. *See* AWARENESS. **2.** To

induce or elicit (a reaction or emotion) : arouse, awaken, kindle, raise, rouse, stir[1] (up), waken. *See* EXCITE.

awake *adjective* **1.** Not in a state of sleep : unsleeping, wakeful, wide-awake. *See* AWARENESS. **2.** Marked by comprehension, cognizance, and perception : alive, aware, cognizant, sensible, sentient, wise[1]. *Slang:* hip. ***Idiom:*** on to. *See* KNOWLEDGE.

awaken *verb*
1. To cease sleeping : arouse, awake, rouse, stir[1], wake[1], waken. *See* AWARENESS. **2.** To induce or elicit (a reaction or emotion) : arouse, awake, kindle, raise, rouse, stir[1] (up), waken. *See* EXCITE.

award *verb*
1. To give formally or officially : accord, bestow, confer, grant, present[2]. *See* GIVE. **2.** To let have as a favor, prerogative, or privilege : accord, concede, give, grant, vouchsafe. *See* GIVE.

award *noun* **1.** Something given in return for a service or accomplishment : accolade, guerdon, honorarium, plum, premium, prize[1], reward. ***Idiom:*** token of appreciation (*or* esteem). *See* REWARD. **2.** A memento received as a symbol of excellence or victory : accolade, prize[1], trophy. *See* RESPECT.

aware *adjective*
Marked by comprehension, cognizance, and perception : alive, awake, cognizant, sensible, sentient, wise[1]. *Slang:* hip. ***Idiom:*** on to. *See* KNOWLEDGE.

awareness *noun*
The condition of being aware : cognizance, consciousness, perception, sense. *See* KNOWLEDGE.

awash *adjective*
Full to the point of flowing over : big, brimful, brimming, overflowing. *See* BIG, RICH.

away *adjective*
Not present : absent, gone, missing, wanting. *See* ABSENCE.

awe *noun*
The emotion aroused by something awe-inspiring or astounding : amaze, amazement, astonishment, marvel, wonder, wonderment. *Archaic:* admiration, dread. *See* EXCITE, FEELINGS.

awe *verb* To impress strongly by what is unexpected or unusual : amaze, astonish, astound, startle, surprise. ***Idioms:*** catch (*or* take) unawares, take aback. *See* SURPRISE.

awesome *adjective*
Slang. Far beyond what is usual, normal, or customary : exceptional, extraordinary, magnificent, outstanding, preeminent, rare, remarkable, singular, towering, uncommon, unusual. *Informal:* standout. *Slang:* out of sight. *See* BETTER, USUAL.

awful *adjective*
Very bad : appalling, dreadful, fearful, frightful, ghastly, horrendous, horrible, shocking, terrible. *See* GOOD.

awful *adverb Informal.* To a high degree : awfully, dreadfully, eminently, exceedingly, exceptionally, extra, extremely, greatly, highly, most, notably, very. *Chiefly Regional:* mighty. *See* BIG.

awfully *adverb*
To a high degree : dreadfully, eminently, exceedingly, exceptionally, extra, extremely, greatly, highly, most, notably, very. *Informal:* awful. *Chiefly Regional:* mighty. *See* BIG.

awkward *adjective*
1. Lacking dexterity and grace in physical movement : clumsy, gawky, graceless, inept, lumpish, maladroit, ungainly, ungraceful. *Slang:* klutzy. ***Idiom:*** all thumbs. *See* ABILITY. **2.** Clumsily lacking in the ability to do or perform : bumbling, clumsy, gauche, heavy-handed, inept, maladroit, unskillful. *See* ABILITY. **3.** Characterized by inappropriateness and gracelessness, especially in expression : ill-chosen, inappropriate, inept, infelicitous, unfortunate, unhappy. *See* ABILITY, GOOD. **4.** Difficult to handle or manage : bulky, clumsy, ungainly, unhandy, unmanageable, unwieldy. *See* EASY. **5.** Characterized by embarrassment and discomfort : constrained, uncomfortable, uneasy. *See* FEELINGS.

awry *adverb*
Not in the right way or on the proper course : afield, amiss, astray, wrong. *See* THRIVE.

awry *adjective* Not in accordance with what is usual or expected : amiss, astray, sour, wrong. *See* SURPRISE, THRIVE.

ax *noun*
Informal. The act of dismissing or the condition of being dismissed from employment : discharge, dismissal, termination. *Slang:* boot[1], bounce, sack[1]. *See* KEEP.

ax *verb Informal.* To end the employment or service of : cashier, discharge, dismiss, drop, release, terminate. *Informal:* fire, pink-slip. *Slang:* boot[1], bounce, can, sack[1]. ***Idioms:*** give someone his or her walking papers, give someone the ax, give someone the gate, give someone the pink slip, let go, show someone the door. *See* KEEP.

axiom *noun*
A broad and basic rule or truth : fundamental, law, principle, theorem, universal. *See* ORDER.

ay *noun & adverb* See **aye.**

aye also **ay** *noun*
An affirmative vote or voter : yea, yes. *See* AFFIRM.
aye also **ay** *adverb* It is so; as you say or ask : absolutely, agreed, all right, assuredly, gladly, indubitably, roger, undoubtedly, unquestionably, willingly, yea, yes. *Informal:* OK, uh-huh, yeah, yep. *Slang:* right on. *See* AFFIRM.

·B·

babble *verb*
1. To talk rapidly, incoherently, or indistinctly : blather, chatter, gabble, gibber, jabber, prate, prattle. *See* WORDS. **2.** To talk volubly, persistently, and usually inconsequentially : blabber, chatter, chitchat, clack, jabber, palaver, prate, prattle, rattle (on), run on. *Informal:* go on, spiel. *Slang:* gab, gas, jaw, yak. ***Idioms:*** run off at the mouth, shoot the breeze (*or* bull). *See* WORDS.
babble *noun* **1.** Unintelligible or foolish talk : blather, blatherskite, double talk, gabble, gibberish, jabber, jabberwocky, jargon, nonsense, prate, prattle, twaddle. *See* WORDS. **2.** Incessant and usually inconsequential talk : blab, blabber, chat, chatter, chitchat, jabber, palaver, prate, prattle, small talk. *Slang:* gab, gas, yak. *See* WORDS.

babbling *adjective*
Emitting a murmuring sound felt to resemble a laugh : bubbling, burbling, gurgling, laughing, rippling. *See* LAUGHTER, SOUNDS.

babe *noun*
1. A very young child : baby, bambino, infant, neonate, newborn, nursling. ***Idiom:*** bundle of joy. *See* KIN, YOUTH. **2.** A guileless, unsophisticated person : child, ingénue, innocent, naive. ***Idiom:*** babe in the woods. *See* KNOWLEDGE. **3.** *Slang.* A person regarded as physically attractive : beauty, belle (used of a woman), lovely, stunner. *Slang:* doll, hunk (used of a man), knockout, looker, stud (used of a man). *See* BEAUTIFUL.

babel *noun*
Sounds or a sound, especially when loud, confused, or disagreeable : clamor, din, hubbub, hullabaloo, noise, pandemonium, racket, rumpus, tumult, uproar. *See* SOUNDS.

baby *noun*
1. A very young child : babe, bambino, infant, neonate, newborn, nursling. ***Idiom:*** bundle of joy. *See* KIN, YOUTH. **2.** A person who behaves in a childish, weak, or spoiled way : milksop, milquetoast, mollycoddle, weakling. ***Idiom:*** mama's boy (*or* girl). *See* YOUTH.
baby *verb* To treat with indulgence and often overtender care : cater, coddle, cosset, indulge, mollycoddle, overindulge, pamper, spoil. *See* TREAT WELL.

babyish *adjective*
1. Of or like a baby : cherubic, childlike, infantile, infantine. *See* YOUTH. **2.** Of or characteristic of a child, especially in immaturity : childish, immature, infantile, juvenile, puerile. *See* YOUTH.

back *noun*
The part or area farthest from the front : rear[1], rearward. *See* PRECEDE.
back *verb* **1.** To move in a reverse direction : backpedal, backtrack, fall back, retreat, retrocede, retrograde, retrogress. ***Idiom:*** retrace one's steps. *See* FORWARD. **2.** To supply capital to or for : capitalize, finance, fund, grubstake, stake, subsidize. *Informal:* bankroll. ***Idiom:*** put up money for. *See* HELP, MONEY. **3.** To aid the cause of by approving or favoring : advocate, champion, endorse, get behind, plump for, recommend, side with, stand behind, stand by, support, uphold. ***Idioms:*** align oneself with, go to bat for, take the part of. *See* SUPPORT. **4.** To present evidence in support of. Also used with *up* : buttress, corroborate, substantiate. *See* SUPPORT. **5.** To assure the certainty or validity of. Also used with *up* : attest, authenticate, bear out, confirm, corroborate, evidence, jus-

tify, substantiate, testify (to), validate, verify, warrant. *See* SUPPORT, TRUE.

back down (or **out**) *verb* To abandon a former position or commitment : renege, retreat. *Slang:* cop out, fink out. *See* RESIST.

back *adjective* **1.** Located in the rear : hind, hindmost, posterior, postern, rear[1]. *Nautical:* after. *See* PRECEDE. **2.** Far from centers of human population : insular, isolated, lonely, lonesome, obscure, outlying, out-of-the-way, remote, removed, secluded, solitary. ***Idiom:*** off the beaten path (*or* track). *See* NEAR.

back *adverb* **1.** Toward the back : about, around, backward, backwards, rearward. *See* PRECEDE. **2.** In or toward a former location or condition : about, around, backward, backwards, rearward, round. *See* APPROACH.

backbite *verb*
To make defamatory statements about : asperse, calumniate, defame, malign, slander, slur, tear down, traduce, vilify. *Law:* libel. ***Idiom:*** cast aspersions on. *See* ATTACK, CRIMES, LAW.

backbreaking *adjective*
Requiring great or extreme bodily, mental, or spiritual strength : arduous, burdensome, demanding, difficult, effortful, exacting, exigent, formidable, hard, heavy, laborious, onerous, oppressive, rigorous, rough, severe, taxing, tough, trying, weighty. *See* HEAVY.

back down or **out** *verb* See **back.**

backer *noun*
1. A person who supports or champions an activity, cause, or institution, for example : benefactor, contributor, friend, patron, sponsor, supporter. *Informal:* angel. *See* HELP. **2.** One who assumes financial responsibility for another : guarantor, guaranty, sponsor, surety, underwriter. *Informal:* angel. *See* LAW, SUPPORT.

backfire *verb*
To produce an unexpected and undesired result : boomerang. *See* SURPRISE.

background *noun*
Past events surrounding a person or thing : history, past. *See* HAPPEN.

backing *noun*
1. Aid or support given by a patron : aegis, auspice (often used in plural), patronage, patronization, sponsorship. *See* HELP. **2.** Money or property used to produce more wealth : capital, capitalization, financing, funding, grubstake, stake, subsidization. *See* HELP, MONEY. **3.** An indication of commendation or approval : endorsement, recommendation, support. *See* SUPPORT.

backlog *noun*
A supply stored or hidden for future use : cache, hoard, inventory, nest egg, reserve, reservoir, stock, stockpile, store, treasure. *Slang:* stash. *See* COLLECT.

backpack *verb*
To travel about or journey on foot : hike, march[1], peregrinate, traipse, tramp, trek. *See* MOVE.

backpedal *verb*
To move in a reverse direction : back, backtrack, fall back, retreat, retrocede, retrograde, retrogress. ***Idiom:*** retrace one's steps. *See* FORWARD.

backset *noun*
A change from better to worse : reversal, reverse, setback. *See* BETTER.

backside *noun*
Informal. The part of one's back on which one rests in sitting : buttock (used in plural), derrière, posterior, rump, seat. *Informal:* behind, bottom, rear[1]. *Slang:* bun (used in plural), fanny, tush. *Chiefly British:* bum[2]. *See* OVER.

backslide *verb*
To slip from a higher or better condition to a former, usually lower or poorer one : lapse, regress, relapse, retrogress, revert. *See* BETTER, REPETITION.

backslide *noun* A slipping from a higher or better condition to a lower or poorer one : backsliding, lapse, recidivation, recidivism, relapse. *See* BETTER, REPETITION.

backsliding *noun*
A slipping from a higher or better condition to a lower or poorer one : backslide, lapse, recidivation, recidivism, relapse. *See* BETTER, REPETITION.

backtrack *verb*
To move in a reverse direction : back, backpedal, fall back, retreat, retrocede, retrograde, retrogress. ***Idiom:*** retrace one's steps. *See* FORWARD.

backup *adjective*
Used or held in reserve : auxiliary, emergency, reserve, secondary, standby, supplemental, supplementary. *See* INCREASE.

backward *adjective*
1. Directed or facing toward the back or rear : retrograde, retrogressive. *See* PRECEDE. **2.** Not forward but reticent or reserved in manner : bashful, coy, demure, diffident, modest, retiring, self-effacing, shy[1], timid. *See* RESTRAINT. **3.** Exhibiting lack of education or knowledge :

benighted, ignorant, primitive, unenlightened. *See* KNOWLEDGE. **4.** Having only a limited ability to learn and understand : dull, simple, simple-minded, slow, slow-witted. *Informal:* soft. *Offensive:* feeble-minded, half-witted, retarded, weak-minded. *See* ABILITY. **5.** Not progressing and developing as fast as others, as in economic and social aspects : lagging, underdeveloped, undeveloped. *See* PRECEDE. **6.** Economically and socially below standard : depressed, deprived, disadvantaged, impoverished, underprivileged. *See* RICH. **7.** Clinging to obsolete ideas : conservative, reactionary, unprogressive. *See* POLITICS.

backward *adverb* **1.** Toward the back : about, around, back, backwards, rearward. *See* PRECEDE. **2.** In or toward a former location or condition : about, around, back, backwards, rearward, round. *See* APPROACH.

backwardness *noun*
An awkwardness or lack of self-confidence in the presence of others : bashfulness, coyness, retiringness, shyness, timidity, timidness. *See* RESTRAINT.

backwards *adverb*
1. Toward the back : about, around, back, backward, rearward. *See* PRECEDE. **2.** In or toward a former location or condition : about, around, back, backward, rearward, round. *See* APPROACH.

bad *adjective*
1. Below a standard of quality : bum[1], poor, unsatisfactory. ***Idioms:*** below par, not up to scratch (*or* snuff). *See* GOOD. **2.** Morally objectionable : black, evil, immoral, iniquitous, peccant, reprobate, sinful, vicious, wicked, wrong. *See* RIGHT. **3.** Misbehaving, often in a troublesome way : ill-behaved, naughty. *See* CONTROL, GOOD. **4.** Not pleasant or agreeable : disagreeable, displeasing, offensive, uncongenial, unpleasant, unsympathetic. *Informal:* icky. *Slang:* yucky. *See* GOOD, PAIN. **5.** Bringing, predicting, or characterized by misfortune : evil, ill, inauspicious, unfavorable, unpropitious. *See* LUCK. **6.** Impaired because of decay : putrid, rotten. *See* BETTER, TASTE, THRIVE. **7.** Causing harm or injury : deleterious, detrimental, evil, harmful, hurtful, ill, injurious, mischievous. *See* HELP.

bad *noun* Whatever is destructive or harmful : badness, evil, ill. *See* HELP.

badge *noun*
1. An emblem of honor worn on one's clothing : decoration, medal. *See* REWARD. **2.** Something visible or evident that gives grounds for believing in the existence or presence of something else : evidence, index, indication, indicator, manifestation, mark, note, sign, signification, stamp, symptom, token, witness. *See* SHOW.

badger *verb*
1. To trouble persistently from or as if from all sides : bedevil, beleaguer, beset, besiege, harass, harry, hound, importune, pester, plague, solicit. *See* ATTACK. **2.** To torment with persistent insult or ridicule : bait, bullyrag, heckle, hector, hound, taunt. *Informal:* needle, ride. ***Idiom:*** wave the red flag in front of the bull. *See* TREAT WELL.

badinage *noun*
Good-natured teasing : banter, chaff, raillery, taunt. *Informal:* ribbing. *See* LAUGHTER.

badlands *noun*
A tract of unproductive land : barren (often used in plural), desert[1], waste, wasteland, wilderness. *See* RICH.

bad name *noun*
Loss of or damage to one's reputation : bad odor, discredit, disgrace, dishonor, disrepute, humiliation, ignominy, ill repute, obloquy, odium, opprobrium, shame. *See* RESPECT.

badness *noun*
Whatever is destructive or harmful : bad, evil, ill. *See* HELP.

bad odor *noun*
Loss of or damage to one's reputation : bad name, discredit, disgrace, dishonor, disrepute, humiliation, ignominy, ill repute, obloquy, odium, opprobrium, shame. *See* RESPECT.

bad-tempered *adjective*
Having or showing a bad temper : cantankerous, crabbed, cranky, cross, disagreeable, fretful, grouchy, grumpy, ill-tempered, irascible, irritable, nasty, peevish, petulant, querulous, snappish, snappy, surly, testy, ugly, waspish. *Informal:* crabby, mean[2]. ***Idiom:*** out of sorts. *See* ATTITUDE.

baffle *verb*
To prevent from accomplishing a purpose : balk, check, checkmate, defeat, foil, frustrate, stymie, thwart. *Informal:* cross, stump. ***Idiom:*** cut the ground from under. *See* ALLOW.

bag *noun*
1. *Slang.* A sphere of activity, experience, study, or interest : area, arena, bailiwick, circle, department, domain, field, orbit, province, realm, scene, subject, terrain, territory, world. *See* TERRITORY. **2.** *Slang.* Something at which a person excels : forte, long suit, métier, spe-

cialty, strong point, strong suit. *Slang:* thing. *See* ABILITY.

bag *verb* **1.** To curve outward past the normal or usual limit : balloon, beetle, belly, bulge, jut, overhang, pouch, project, protrude, protuberate, stand out, stick out. *See* CONVEX. **2.** *Informal.* To gain possession of, especially after a struggle or chase : capture, catch, get, net[1], secure, take. *Slang:* nail. *See* GET.

baggage *noun*
A vulgar promiscuous woman who flouts propriety : hussy, jade, slattern, slut, tart[2], tramp, wanton, wench, whore. *Slang:* floozy. *See* SEX.

bail[1] *noun*
1. Money supplied for the temporary release of an arrested person that guarantees appearance of that person for trial : bond. *See* LAW. **2.** One who posts bond : bailsman, bondsman. *See* LAW.

bail[2] *verb*
To take a substance, as liquid, from a container by plunging the hand or a utensil into it : dip, lade, ladle, scoop (up). *See* GIVE.
bail out *verb* To catapult oneself from a disabled aircraft : eject, jump. *See* APPROACH.

bailiwick *noun*
A sphere of activity, experience, study, or interest : area, arena, circle, department, domain, field, orbit, province, realm, scene, subject, terrain, territory, world. *Slang:* bag. *See* TERRITORY.

bail out *verb* See **bail.**

bailsman[2] *noun*
One who posts bond : bail[1], bondsman. *See* LAW.

bairn *noun*
Scots. A young person between birth and puberty : bud[1], child, innocent, juvenile, moppet, tot[1], youngster. *Informal:* kid. *See* KIN, YOUTH.

bait *noun*
1. Something that attracts, especially with the promise of pleasure or reward : allurement, come-on, enticement, inducement, inveiglement, invitation, lure, seduction, temptation. *See* LIKE. **2.** Something that leads one into a place or situation from which escape is difficult : lure, snare, trap. *See* LIKE, SAFETY.
bait *verb* **1.** To torment with persistent insult or ridicule : badger, bullyrag, heckle, hector, hound, taunt. *Informal:* needle, ride. ***Idiom:*** wave the red flag in front of the bull. *See* TREAT WELL. **2.** To disturb by repeated attacks : annoy, bedevil, beleaguer, beset, harass, harry, pester, plague, tease, torment, worry. *See* FEELINGS, PAIN. **3.** To excite (another) by exposing something desirable while keeping it out of reach : tantalize, tease. *See* EXCITE.

bake *verb*
To feel or look hot : broil[1], burn, roast, swelter. *See* HOT.

baking *adjective*
Marked by much heat : ardent, blistering, boiling, broiling, burning, fiery, heated, hot, red-hot, roasting, scalding, scorching, searing, sizzling, sultry, sweltering, torrid. *See* HOT.

balance *noun*
1. A stable state characterized by the cancellation of all forces by equal opposing forces : counterpoise, equilibrium, equipoise, stasis. *See* ORDER. **2.** A stable, calm state of the emotions : aplomb, collectedness, composure, coolness, equanimity, imperturbability, imperturbableness, nonchalance, poise, sang-froid, self-possession, unflappability. *Slang:* cool. *See* CALM, FEELINGS. **3.** Satisfying arrangement marked by even distribution of elements, as in a design : harmony, proportion, symmetry. *See* BEAUTIFUL. **4.** What remains after a part has been used or subtracted : leavings, leftover, remainder, remains, remnant, residue, rest[2]. *See* LEFTOVER.
balance *verb* **1.** To examine in order to note the similarities and differences of : collate, compare. *See* SAME. **2.** To put in balance : counterbalance, equalize, stabilize, steady. *See* ORDER. **3.** To act as an equalizing weight or force to : compensate, counteract, counterbalance, counterpoise, countervail, make up, offset, set off. *See* ORDER. **4.** To make up for : compensate, counterbalance, counterpoise, countervail, neutralize, offset, outweigh, redeem, set off. *See* SUBSTITUTE. **5.** To place or be placed on a narrow or insecure surface : perch, poise. *See* POSTURE.

balanced *adjective*
1. Neither favorable or unfavorable : even[1], fifty-fifty. *See* FAIR. **2.** Possessing, proceeding from, or exhibiting good judgment and prudence : commonsensible, commonsensical, judicious, levelheaded, prudent, rational, reasonable, sagacious, sage, sane, sapient, sensible, sound[2], well-founded, well-grounded, wise[1]. *See* REASON, SANE. **3.** Characterized by or displaying symmetry, especially correspondence in scale or measure : proportional, proportionate, regular, symmetric, symmetrical. *See* SAME. **4.** Having components pleasingly combined : congruous, harmonious, symmetrical. *See* BEAUTIFUL.

bald *adjective*
1. Without the usual covering : bare, naked, nude. *See* PUT ON. 2. Without addition, decoration, or qualification : bare, dry, plain, simple, unadorned, unvarnished. *See* PLAIN.

balderdash *noun*
Something that does not have or make sense : blather, bunkum, claptrap, drivel, garbage, idiocy, nonsense, piffle, poppycock, rigmarole, rubbish, tomfoolery, trash, twaddle. *Informal:* tommyrot. *Slang:* applesauce, baloney, bilge, bull[1], bunk[2], crap, hooey, malarkey. *See* KNOWLEDGE.

bald-faced *adjective*
Characterized by or done without shame : barefaced, blatant, brazen, brazenfaced, shameless, unabashed, unblushing. *Informal:* brassy. *See* COURTESY, RESPECT, RIGHT.

baleful *adjective*
Strongly suggestive of great harm, menace, or evil : malign, sinister. *See* WARN.

balk *verb*
To prevent from accomplishing a purpose : baffle, check, checkmate, defeat, foil, frustrate, stymie, thwart. *Informal:* cross, stump. ***Idiom:*** cut the ground from under. *See* ALLOW.
balk *noun* A large, oblong piece of wood or other material, used especially for construction : beam, rafter, timber. *See* MATTER.

balky *adjective*
Given to acting in opposition to others : contrarious, contrary, difficult, froward, impossible, ornery, perverse, wayward. *See* ATTITUDE, SUPPORT.

ball *noun*
A party or gathering for dancing : dance. *Informal:* hop. *See* WORK.

balloon *verb*
To curve outward past the normal or usual limit : bag, beetle, belly, bulge, jut, overhang, pouch, project, protrude, protuberate, stand out, stick out. *See* CONVEX.

ballot *verb*
To select by vote for an office : elect, vote (in). *See* CHOICE, POLITICS.

balloter *noun*
One who votes : elector, voter. *See* CHOICE, POLITICS.

ball up *verb*
1. To harm irreparably through inept handling; make a mess : blunder, boggle, botch, bungle, foul up, fumble, gum up, mess up, mishandle, mismanage, muddle, muff, spoil. *Informal:* bollix up, muck up. *Slang:* blow[1], goof up, louse up, screw up, snafu. ***Idiom:*** make a muck of. *See* CORRECT, HELP. 2. To put into total disorder : confuse, disorder, jumble, mess up, muddle, scramble, snarl[2]. *Slang:* snafu. ***Idiom:*** play havoc with. *See* ORDER.

ballyhoo *noun*
A systematic effort or part of this effort to increase the importance or reputation of by favorable publicity : advertisement, buildup, promotion, publicity, puffery. *Informal:* pitch, plug. *Slang:* hype. *See* KNOWLEDGE.
ballyhoo *verb* 1. To make known vigorously the positive features of (a product) : advertise, build up, cry (up), popularize, promote, publicize, talk up. *Informal:* pitch, plug. *Slang:* push. *See* KNOWLEDGE. 2. To increase or seek to increase the importance or reputation of by favorable publicity : boost, build up, enhance, promote, publicize, puff, talk up, tout. *Informal:* plug. *Slang:* hype. *See* KNOWLEDGE.

balm *verb*
To make or become calm : allay, becalm, calm (down), lull, quiet, settle, still, tranquilize. *See* CALM.

balmy[1] *adjective*
Free from severity or violence, as in movement : delicate, faint, gentle, mild, smooth, soft. *See* CALM, STRONG.

balmy[2] *adjective*
Slang. So senseless as to be laughable : absurd, foolish, harebrained, idiotic, imbecilic, insane, lunatic, mad, moronic, nonsensical, preposterous, silly, softheaded, tomfool, unearthly, zany. *Informal:* cockeyed, crazy, loony, loopy. *Slang:* dippy, dopey, jerky, sappy, wacky. *See* ABILITY, KNOWLEDGE.

baloney *noun*
Slang. Something that does not have or make sense : balderdash, blather, bunkum, claptrap, drivel, garbage, idiocy, nonsense, piffle, poppycock, rigmarole, rubbish, tomfoolery, trash, twaddle. *Informal:* tommyrot. *Slang:* applesauce, bilge, bull[1], bunk[2], crap, hooey, malarkey. *See* KNOWLEDGE.

bambino *noun*
A very young child : babe, baby, infant, neonate, newborn, nursling. ***Idiom:*** bundle of joy. *See* KIN, YOUTH.

bamboozle *verb*
Informal. To cause to accept what is false, especially by trickery or misrepresentation : beguile, betray, bluff, cozen, deceive, delude, double-cross, dupe, fool, hoodwink, humbug, mislead, take in, trick. *Informal:* have. *Slang:* four-flush. ***Idioms:*** lead astray, play false, pull

the wool over someone's eyes, put something over on, take for a ride. *See* HONEST.

ban *verb*
1. To refuse to allow : debar, disallow, enjoin, forbid, inhibit, interdict, outlaw, prohibit, proscribe, taboo. *See* ALLOW. **2.** To keep from being published or transmitted : black out, censor, hush (up), stifle, suppress. ***Idiom:*** keep (*or* put) a lid on. *See* SHOW.
ban *noun* A refusal to allow : disallowance, forbiddance, inhibition, interdiction, prohibition, proscription, taboo. *See* ALLOW.

banal *adjective*
Without freshness or appeal because of overuse : bromidic, clichéd, commonplace, corny, hackneyed, musty, overused, overworked, platitudinal, platitudinous, shopworn, stale, stereotyped, stereotypic, stereotypical, threadbare, timeworn, tired, trite, warmed-over, well-worn, worn-out. *See* EXCITE, USUAL.

banality *noun*
A trite expression or idea : bromide, cliché, commonplace, platitude, stereotype, truism. *See* SURPRISE.

bananas *adjective*
Slang. Afflicted with or exhibiting irrationality and mental unsoundness : brainsick, crazy, daft, demented, disordered, distraught, dotty, insane, lunatic, mad, maniac, maniacal, mentally ill, moonstruck, off, touched, unbalanced, unsound, wrong. *Informal:* bonkers, cracked, daffy, gaga, loony. *Slang:* batty, buggy, cuckoo, fruity, loco, nuts, nutty, screwy, wacky. *Chiefly British:* crackers. *Law:* non compos mentis. ***Idioms:*** around the bend, crazy as a loon, mad as a hatter, not all there, nutty as a fruitcake, off (*or* out of) one's head, off one's rocker, of unsound mind, out of one's mind, sick in the head, stark raving mad. *See* SANE.

band[1] *noun*
1. A long narrow piece, as of material : bandeau, fillet, strip[2], stripe. *See* MATTER. **2.** A closed plane curve everywhere equidistant from a fixed point or something shaped like this : circle, circuit, disk, gyre, ring[1], wheel. *Archaic:* orb. *See* GEOMETRY.
band *verb* To encircle with or as if with a band : begird, belt, cincture, compass, encompass, engirdle, gird, girdle, girt, ring[1]. *Archaic:* engird. *See* EDGE.

band[2] *noun*
1. A number of individuals making up or considered a unit : array, batch, bevy, body, bunch, bundle, clump, cluster, clutch[2], collection, group, knot, lot, party, set[2]. *See* GROUP. **2.** A group of people acting together in a shared activity : company, corps, party, troop, troupe. *See* PERFORMING ARTS. **3.** An organized group of criminals, hoodlums, or wrongdoers : gang, pack, ring[1]. *Informal:* mob. *See* GROUP.
band *verb* To assemble or join in a group : combine, gang up, league, unite. *See* COLLECT.

bandage *verb*
To apply therapeutic materials to (a wound) : bind, dress. *See* CARE FOR.

bandeau *noun*
A long narrow piece, as of material : band[1], fillet, strip[2], stripe. *See* MATTER.

banderol *noun* See **banderole.**

banderole or **banderol** also **bannerol** *noun*
Fabric used especially as a symbol : banner, banneret, color (used in plural), ensign, flag[1], jack, oriflamme, pennant, pennon, standard, streamer. *See* SUBSTITUTE.

bandit *noun*
A person who steals : burglar, highwayman, housebreaker, larcener, larcenist, pilferer, purloiner, robber, stealer, thief. *See* CRIMES.

bandy *verb*
1. To give and receive : exchange, interchange. *See* GIVE. **2.** To speak together and exchange ideas and opinions about. Used with *about* : discuss, moot, talk over, thrash out (*or* over), thresh out (*or* over), toss around. *Informal:* hash (over), kick around, knock about (*or* around). *Slang:* rap[3]. ***Idiom:*** go into a huddle. *See* WORDS.

bane *noun*
1. The act of destroying or state of being destroyed : destruction, devastation, havoc, ruin, ruination, undoing, wrack[1], wreck, wreckage. *See* HELP, LEFTOVER. **2.** Anything that is injurious, destructive, or fatal : canker, contagion, poison, toxin, venom, virus. *See* HELP. **3.** Something that causes total loss or severe impairment, as of one's health, fortune, honor, or hopes : destroyer, destruction, downfall, ruin, ruination, undoing, wrecker. *See* HELP. **4.** A cause of suffering or harm : affliction, curse, evil, ill, plague, scourge, woe. *See* HELP.

baneful *adjective*
1. Extremely destructive or harmful : deadly, malignant, noxious, pernicious, pestilent, pestilential, virulent. *See* HELP. **2.** Portending future disaster : apocalyptic, apocalyptical, dire, direful, fateful, fire-and-brimstone, grave[2], hellfire, ominous, portentous, unlucky. *See* LUCK, WARN.

bang *noun*
1. An earsplitting, explosive noise : blast,

boom, roar, thunder. *See* SOUNDS. **2.** A sudden sharp, explosive noise : bark, clap, crack, explosion, pop[1], rat-a-tat-tat, report, snap. *See* SOUNDS. **3.** A forceful movement causing a loud noise : crash, slam, smash, wham. *See* STRIKE. **4.** A sudden sharp, powerful stroke : blow[2], clout, crack, hit, lick, pound, slug[3], sock, swat, thwack, welt, whack, wham, whop. *Informal:* bash, biff, bop, clip[1], wallop. *Slang:* belt, conk, paste. *See* ATTACK, STRIKE. **5.** *Slang.* A strong, pleasant feeling of excitement or stimulation : lift, thrill. *Informal:* wallop. *Slang:* boot[1], high, kick. *See* EXCITE.

bang *verb* **1.** To strike, set down, or close in such a way as to make a loud noise : clap, crash, slam, whack. *See* SOUNDS. **2.** To make an earsplitting explosive noise : blast, boom, roar, thunder. *See* SOUNDS.

bang *adverb* With precision or absolute conformity : dead, direct, directly, exactly, fair, flush, just, precisely, right, smack[1], square, squarely, straight. *Slang:* smack-dab. *See* PRECISE.

banish *verb*
1. To force to leave a country or place by official decree : deport, exile, expatriate, expel, ostracize, transport. *See* ACCEPT. **2.** To rid one's mind of : cast out, dismiss, dispel, shut out. *See* KEEP.

banishment *noun*
Enforced removal from one's native country by official decree : deportation, exile, expatriation, extradition, ostracism, transportation. *See* ACCEPT, REWARD.

bank[1] *noun*
A group of things gathered haphazardly : agglomeration, cumulus, drift, heap, hill, mass, mess, mound, mountain, pile, shock[2], stack, tumble. *See* ORDER.

bank *verb* To put into a disordered pile : drift, heap, hill, lump[1], mound, pile (up), stack. *See* ORDER.

bank[2] *verb*
To place (money) in a bank : deposit, lay away, salt away. *Informal:* sock away. *See* KEEP, MONEY.

bank on (or **upon)** *verb* To place trust or confidence in : believe in, count on (*or* upon), depend on (*or* upon), reckon on (*or* upon), rely on (*or* upon), trust (in). *See* TRUST.

bank on or **upon** *verb* See **bank.**

bankroll *verb*
Informal. To supply capital to or for : back, capitalize, finance, fund, grubstake, stake, subsidize. *Idiom:* put up money for. *See* HELP, MONEY.

bankrupt *verb*
1. To reduce to financial insolvency : break, bust, impoverish, pauperize, ruin. *Slang:* clean out. *See* MONEY. **2.** To cause the complete ruin or wreckage of : break down, cross up, demolish, destroy, finish, ruin, shatter, sink, smash, spoil, torpedo, undo, wash up, wrack[2], wreck. *Slang:* total. *Idiom:* put the kibosh on. *See* HELP.

bankruptcy *noun*
The condition of being financially insolvent : bust, failure, insolvency. *See* MONEY.

banner *noun*
Fabric used especially as a symbol : banderole, banneret, color (used in plural), ensign, flag[1], jack, oriflamme, pennant, pennon, standard, streamer. *See* SUBSTITUTE.

banner *adjective* Exceptionally good of its kind : ace, blue-ribbon, brag, capital, champion, excellent, fine[1], first-class, first-rate, prime, quality, splendid, superb, superior, terrific, tiptop, top. *Informal:* A-one, bully, dandy, great, swell, topflight, topnotch. *Slang:* boss. *Chiefly British:* tophole. *See* GOOD.

banneret *noun*
Fabric used especially as a symbol : banderole, banner, color (used in plural), ensign, flag[1], jack, oriflamme, pennant, pennon, standard, streamer. *See* SUBSTITUTE.

bannerol *noun* See **banderole.**

banquet *noun*
A large meal elaborately prepared or served : feast, junket. *Informal:* feed, spread. *See* INGESTION.

bantam *adjective*
Notably below average in amount, size, or scope : little, petite, small, smallish. *See* BIG.

banter *noun*
Good-natured teasing : badinage, chaff, raillery, taunt. *Informal:* ribbing. *See* LAUGHTER.

banter *verb* To tease : chaff, joke, josh. *Informal:* kid, rib, ride. *Slang:* jive, rag[2], razz. *See* LAUGHTER.

baptize *verb*
To give a name or title to : call, christen, denominate, designate, dub, entitle, name, style, term, title. *See* SPECIFIC, WORDS.

bar *noun*
1. A relatively long, straight, rigid piece of metal or other solid material : bloom[2], rod, shaft, slab, stick. *See* THING. **2.** Something that impedes or prevents entry or passage : barricade, barrier, block, blockage, clog, hamper, hin-

drance, hurdle, impediment, obstacle, obstruction, snag, stop, traverse, wall. *See* HELP, OPEN. **3.** A judicial assembly : court, tribunal. *See* LAW.

bar *verb* **1.** To shut in with or as if with bars : confine, lock, wall. *See* FREE. **2.** To stop or prevent passage of : block, dam, impede, obstruct. *Idiom:* be (*or* stand) in the way of. *See* OPEN. **3.** To keep from being admitted, included, or considered : count out, debar, eliminate, except, exclude, keep out, rule out, shut out. *See* INCLUDE.

barbarian *noun*
An unrefined, rude person : boor, chuff, churl, Philistine, vulgarian, yahoo. *See* GOOD.

barbarian *adjective* **1.** Not civilized : barbaric, barbarous, primitive, rude, savage, uncivilized, uncultivated, uncultured, wild. *Archaic:* uncivil. *See* CULTURE, WILD. **2.** Lacking in delicacy or refinement : barbaric, boorish, churlish, coarse, crass, crude, gross, ill-bred, indelicate, philistine, rough, rude, tasteless, uncivilized, uncouth, uncultivated, uncultured, unpolished, unrefined, vulgar. *See* COURTESY, SMOOTH.

barbaric *adjective*
1. Not civilized : barbarian, barbarous, primitive, rude, savage, uncivilized, uncultivated, uncultured, wild. *Archaic:* uncivil. *See* CULTURE, WILD. **2.** Lacking in delicacy or refinement : barbarian, boorish, churlish, coarse, crass, crude, gross, ill-bred, indelicate, philistine, rough, rude, tasteless, uncivilized, uncouth, uncultivated, uncultured, unpolished, unrefined, vulgar. *See* COURTESY, SMOOTH.

barbarism *noun*
A term that offends against established usage standards : corruption, solecism, vulgarism. *See* STYLE.

barbarity *noun*
A cruel act or an instance of cruel behavior : bestiality, brutality, cruelty, inhumanity, savagery, truculence, truculency. *See* ATTITUDE, KIND.

barbarous *adjective*
1. Not civilized : barbarian, barbaric, primitive, rude, savage, uncivilized, uncultivated, uncultured, wild. *Archaic:* uncivil. *See* CULTURE, WILD. **2.** Showing or suggesting a disposition to be violently destructive without scruple or restraint : bestial, cruel, fell[2], feral, ferocious, fierce, inhuman, savage, truculent, vicious, wolfish. *See* KIND.

bard *noun*
One who writes poetry : muse[2], poet, poetaster, poetess, rhymer, rhymester, versifier. *See* WORDS.

bare *adjective*
1. Without the usual covering : bald, naked, nude. *See* PUT ON. **2.** Not wearing any clothes : au naturel, naked, nude, unclad. *Chiefly British:* starkers. *Idioms:* in one's birthday suit, in the altogether (*or* buff *or* raw), naked as a jaybird, stark naked, without a stitch. *See* PUT ON, SHOW. **3.** Containing nothing : blank, clear, empty, vacant, vacuous, void. *See* FULL. **4.** Without addition, decoration, or qualification : bald, dry, plain, simple, unadorned, unvarnished. *See* PLAIN. **5.** Just sufficient : scant. *See* EXCESS.

bare *verb* **1.** To make bare : denude, disrobe, divest, expose, strip[1], uncover. *See* PUT ON. **2.** To make visible; bring to view : disclose, display, expose, reveal, show, unclothe, uncover, unmask, unveil. *Archaic:* discover. *Idioms:* bring to light, lay open, make plain. *See* SHOW.

barefaced *adjective*
Characterized by or done without shame : bald-faced, blatant, brazen, brazenfaced, shameless, unabashed, unblushing. *Informal:* brassy. *See* COURTESY, RESPECT, RIGHT.

barely *adverb*
By a very little; almost not : hardly, just, scarce, scarcely. *See* NEAR.

bareness *noun*
The state of being without clothes : nakedness, nudeness, nudity, undress. *See* PUT ON, SHOW.

bargain *noun*
1. An act or state of agreeing between parties regarding a course of action : accord, agreement, arrangement, compact[2], deal, pact, understanding. *See* AGREE. **2.** An agreement, especially one involving a sale or exchange : compact[2], contract, covenant, deal, transaction. *See* AGREE. **3.** Something offered or bought at a low price : *Informal:* buy, deal. *Slang:* steal. *See* MONEY, TRANSACTIONS.

bargain *verb* **1.** To argue about the terms, as of a sale : dicker, haggle, higgle, huckster, negotiate, palter. *See* AGREE. **2.** To enter into a formal agreement : contract, covenant. *See* AGREE.

bargain for or **on** *verb* To look forward to confidently : anticipate, await, count on, depend on (*or* upon), expect, look for, wait (for). *Informal:* figure on. *See* SURPRISE.

bargain for or **on** *verb* See **bargain.**

bark *noun*
A sudden sharp, explosive noise : bang, clap,

crack, explosion, pop[1], rat-a-tat-tat, report, snap. *See* SOUNDS.

bark *verb* **1.** To make a sudden sharp, explosive noise : bang, clap, crack, pop[1], snap. *See* SOUNDS. **2.** To speak abruptly and sharply : snap, snarl[1]. ***Idioms:*** bite someone's head off, snap someone's head (*or* nose) off. *See* WORDS.

barnyard *adjective*
Offensive to accepted standards of decency : bawdy, broad, coarse, dirty, Fescennine, filthy, foul, gross, lewd, nasty, obscene, profane, ribald, scatologic, scatological, scurrilous, smutty, vulgar. *Slang:* raunchy. *See* DECENT.

baronial *adjective*
Large and impressive in size, scope, or extent : august, grand, grandiose, imposing, lordly, magnific, magnificent, majestic, noble, princely, regal, royal, splendid, stately, sublime, superb. *See* BIG, GOOD.

baroque *adjective*
Elaborately and heavily ornamented : flamboyant, florid, ornate, rococo. *See* PLAIN.

barrage *noun*
A concentrated outpouring, as of missiles, words, or blows : bombardment, burst, cannonade, fusillade, hail[1], salvo, shower, storm, volley. *See* ATTACK.

barrage *verb* To direct a barrage at : bombard, cannonade, fusillade, pepper, shower. *See* ATTACK.

barrel *noun*
Informal. A great deal : abundance, mass, mountain, much, plenty, profusion, wealth, world. *Informal:* heap, lot, pack, peck[2], pile. *Regional:* power, sight. *See* BIG.

barrel *verb* *Slang.* To move swiftly : bolt, bucket, bustle, dart, dash, festinate, flash, fleet, flit, fly, haste, hasten, hurry, hustle, pelt[2], race, rocket, run, rush, sail, scoot, scour[2], shoot, speed, sprint, tear[1], trot, whirl, whisk, whiz, wing, zip, zoom. *Informal:* hotfoot, rip. *Slang:* highball. *Chiefly British:* nip[1]. ***Idioms:*** get a move on, get cracking, go like lightning, go like the wind, hotfoot it, make haste, make time, make tracks, run like the wind, shake a leg, step (*or* jump) on it. *See* MOVE.

barren *adjective*
1. Unable to produce offspring : childless, impotent, infertile, sterile, unfruitful. *See* RICH. **2.** Lacking or unable to produce growing plants or crops : infertile, sterile, unfruitful, unproductive. *See* RICH. **3.** Having no useful result : bootless, fruitless, futile, unavailing, unprofitable, unsuccessful, useless, vain. ***Idiom:*** in vain. *See* THRIVE, USED. **4.** Not having a desirable element : destitute, devoid, empty, innocent, lacking, void, wanting. ***Idiom:*** in want of. *See* FULL.

barren *noun* A tract of unproductive land. Often used in plural : badlands, desert[1], waste, wasteland, wilderness. *See* RICH.

barrenness *noun*
1. The state or condition of being unable to reproduce sexually : infertility, sterility, sterilization. *See* REPRODUCTION, RICH. **2.** Empty, unfilled space : emptiness, nothingness, vacancy, vacuity, vacuum, void. *See* FULL. **3.** Total lack of ideas, meaning, or substance : blankness, emptiness, hollowness, inanity, vacancy, vacuity, vacuousness. *See* FULL.

barricade *noun*
Something that impedes or prevents entry or passage : bar, barrier, block, blockage, clog, hamper, hindrance, hurdle, impediment, obstacle, obstruction, snag, stop, traverse, wall. *See* HELP, OPEN.

barrier *noun*
1. A solid structure that encloses an area or separates one area from another : partition, wall. *See* INCLUDE, THING. **2.** Something that impedes or prevents entry or passage : bar, barricade, block, blockage, clog, hamper, hindrance, hurdle, impediment, obstacle, obstruction, snag, stop, traverse, wall. *See* HELP, OPEN.

barrister *noun*
Chiefly British. A person who practices law : attorney, counsel, counselor, lawyer. *Slang:* ambulance chaser. *See* LAW.

basal *adjective*
1. Of or treating the most basic aspects : basic, beginning, elementary, rudimental, rudimentary. *See* SIMPLE, START. **2.** Arising from or going to the root or source : basic, foundational, fundamental, original, primary, radical, underlying. *See* SURFACE.

base[1] *noun*
1. The lowest or supporting part or structure : basis, bed, bottom, foot, footing, foundation, fundament, ground, groundwork, seat, substratum, underpinning (often used in plural). *See* OVER. **2.** That on which something immaterial, such as an argument or a charge, rests : basis, footing, foundation, fundament, ground (often used in plural), groundwork, underpinning (often used in plural). *See* OVER. **3.** A fundamental principle or underlying concept : basis, cornerstone, foundation, fundament, fundamental, root[1], rudiment (often used in plural). *See* OVER. **4.** A center of organization, supply, or activity : complex, headquarters, station.

Military: installation. *See* PLACE. **5.** The main part of a word to which affixes are attached : root[1], stem, theme. *See* WORDS.

base *verb* To provide a basis for : build, establish, found, ground, predicate, rest[1], root[1], underpin. *See* OVER.

base² *adjective*

1. Having or proceeding from low moral standards : ignoble, low, low-down, mean[2], sordid, squalid, vile. *See* RIGHT. **2.** Of decidedly inferior quality : cheap, lousy, miserable, paltry, poor, rotten, shoddy, sleazy, trashy. *Informal:* cheesy. *Slang:* crummy, schlocky. *See* GOOD. **3.** *Archaic.* Lacking high station or birth : baseborn, common, déclassé, declassed, humble, ignoble, lowly, mean[2], plebeian, unwashed, vulgar. *See* OVER.

baseborn *adjective*

1. Born to parents who are not married to each other : bastard, illegitimate, misbegotten, natural, spurious, unlawful. *See* KIN, LAW. **2.** Lacking high station or birth : common, déclassé, declassed, humble, ignoble, lowly, mean[2], plebeian, unwashed, vulgar. *Archaic:* base[2]. *See* OVER.

baseless *adjective*

Having no basis or foundation in fact : bottomless, groundless, idle, unfounded, unwarranted. *See* TRUE.

bash *verb*

To deliver a powerful blow to suddenly and sharply : catch, clout, hit, knock, pop[1], slam, slog, slug[3], smash, smite, sock, strike, swat, thwack, whack, wham, whop. *Informal:* biff, bop, clip[1], wallop. *Slang:* belt, conk, paste. ***Idioms:*** let someone have it, sock it to someone. *See* ATTACK, STRIKE.

bash *noun* **1.** *Informal.* A sudden sharp, powerful stroke : bang, blow[2], clout, crack, hit, lick, pound, slug[3], sock, swat, thwack, welt, whack, wham, whop. *Informal:* biff, bop, clip[1], wallop. *Slang:* belt, conk, paste. *See* ATTACK, STRIKE. **2.** *Slang.* A big, exuberant party : celebration, shindig, shindy. *Slang:* blast, blowout. *See* GROUP, RESTRAINT, WORK. **3.** *Slang.* A large or important social gathering : affair, celebration, festivity, fete, function, gala, occasion, party, soiree. *Informal:* do. *See* GROUP, WORK.

bashful *adjective*

Not forward but reticent or reserved in manner : backward, coy, demure, diffident, modest, retiring, self-effacing, shy[1], timid. *See* RESTRAINT.

bashfulness *noun*

An awkwardness or lack of self-confidence in the presence of others : backwardness, coyness, retiringness, shyness, timidity, timidness. *See* RESTRAINT.

basic *adjective*

1. Of or being an irreducible element : elemental, elementary, essential, fundamental, primitive, ultimate, underlying. *See* SURFACE. **2.** Constituting or forming part of the essence of something : constitutional, constitutive, essential, fundamental, integral, vital. *See* BE, SURFACE. **3.** Of or treating the most basic aspects : basal, beginning, elementary, rudimental, rudimentary. *See* SIMPLE, START. **4.** Arising from or going to the root or source : basal, foundational, fundamental, original, primary, radical, underlying. *See* SURFACE.

basic *noun* A fundamental irreducible constituent of a whole : element, essential, fundamental, rudiment (often used in plural). ***Idiom:*** part and parcel. *See* PART.

basically *adverb*

In regard to the essence of a matter : essentially, fundamentally. ***Idioms:*** at bottom, at heart, in essence. *See* SURFACE.

basin *noun*

1. The region drained by a river system : watershed. *See* TERRITORY. **2.** An area sunk below its surroundings : concavity, depression, dip, hollow, pit[1], sag, sink, sinkhole. *See* CONVEX.

basis *noun*

1. The lowest or supporting part or structure : base[1], bed, bottom, foot, footing, foundation, fundament, ground, groundwork, seat, substratum, underpinning (often used in plural). *See* OVER. **2.** That on which something immaterial, such as an argument or a charge, rests : base[1], footing, foundation, fundament, ground (often used in plural), groundwork, underpinning (often used in plural). *See* OVER. **3.** A justifying fact or consideration : foundation, justification, reason, warrant. *See* TRUE. **4.** An established position from which to operate or deal with others : footing, status, term (often used in plural). *See* CONNECT. **5.** A fundamental principle or underlying concept : base[1], cornerstone, foundation, fundament, fundamental, root[1], rudiment (often used in plural). *See* OVER.

bask *verb*

To take extravagant pleasure : indulge, luxuriate, revel, roll, rollick, wallow. *See* LIKE.

bass *adjective*

Being a sound produced by a relatively small

frequency of vibrations : alto, contralto, deep, low, low-pitched. *See* SOUNDS.

bastard *adjective*
Born to parents who are not married to each other : baseborn, illegitimate, misbegotten, natural, spurious, unlawful. *See* KIN, LAW.

bastardize *verb*
To ruin utterly in character or quality : animalize, bestialize, brutalize, canker, corrupt, debase, debauch, demoralize, deprave, pervert, stain, vitiate, warp. *See* CLEAN, HELP.

bastardy *noun*
The condition of being of illegitimate birth : illegitimacy. *See* KIN, LAW.

baste *verb*
To hit heavily and repeatedly with violent blows : assail, assault, batter, beat, belabor, buffet, drub, hammer, pound, pummel, smash, thrash, thresh. *Informal:* lambaste. *Slang:* clobber. ***Idiom:*** rain blows on. *See* ATTACK, STRIKE.

bat[1] *verb*
To open and close the eyes rapidly : blink, nictate, nictitate, twinkle, wink. *See* REPETITION, SEE.

bat[2] *noun*
Slang. A drinking bout : binge, brannigan, carousal, carouse, drunk, spree. *Slang:* bender, booze, jag, tear[1]. *See* DRUGS, RESTRAINT.

batch *noun*
A number of individuals making up or considered a unit : array, band[2], bevy, body, bunch, bundle, clump, cluster, clutch[2], collection, group, knot, lot, party, set[2]. *See* GROUP.

bate *verb*
To become or cause to become less active or intense : abate, die (away, down, off, *or* out), ease (off *or* up), ebb, fall, fall off, lapse, let up, moderate, remit, slacken, slack off, subside, wane. *See* INCREASE.

bathe *verb*
1. To make moist : dampen, moisten, wash, wet. *See* DRY. **2.** To flow against or along : lap, lave, lip, wash. *See* DRY.

bathetic *adjective*
Affectedly or extravagantly emotional : gushy, maudlin, mawkish, romantic, sentimental, slushy, sobby, soft, soppy. *Informal:* gooey, mushy, schmaltzy, sloppy, soupy. *Slang:* drippy, sappy, tear-jerking. *See* FEELINGS.

bathos *noun*
The quality or condition of being affectedly or overly emotional : maudlinism, mawkishness, sentimentalism, sentimentality. *Informal:* mush, mushiness, schmaltz, schmaltziness, sloppiness. *Slang:* sappiness. *See* FEELINGS.

batten *verb*
To make a large profit : profit. *Slang:* clean up. ***Idiom:*** make a killing. *See* MONEY.

batter *verb*
1. To hit heavily and repeatedly with violent blows : assail, assault, baste, beat, belabor, buffet, drub, hammer, pound, pummel, smash, thrash, thresh. *Informal:* lambaste. *Slang:* clobber. ***Idiom:*** rain blows on. *See* ATTACK, STRIKE. **2.** To injure or damage, as by abuse or heavy wear : knock about (*or* around), mangle[1], maul, rough up. *See* ATTACK, HELP, STRIKE.

battle *noun*
1. A hostile encounter between opposing military forces : action, combat, engagement. *See* CONFLICT. **2.** A vying with others for victory or supremacy : competition, contest, corrivalry, race, rivalry, strife, striving, struggle, tug of war, war, warfare. *See* CONFLICT.
battle *verb* To strive in opposition : combat, contend, duel, fight, struggle, tilt, war, wrestle. *See* CONFLICT.

battle-ax or **battle-axe** *noun*
Informal. A person, traditionally a woman, who persistently nags or criticizes : fishwife, fury, harpy, scold, shrew, termagant, virago, vixen. *See* PRAISE.

battle-axe *noun* See **battle-ax.**

battle cry *noun*
A rallying term used by proponents of a cause : call to arms, call to battle, cry, motto, rallying cry, war cry. *See* WORDS.

batty *adjective*
Slang. Afflicted with or exhibiting irrationality and mental unsoundness : brainsick, crazy, daft, demented, disordered, distraught, dotty, insane, lunatic, mad, maniac, maniacal, mentally ill, moonstruck, off, touched, unbalanced, unsound, wrong. *Informal:* bonkers, cracked, daffy, gaga, loony. *Slang:* bananas, buggy, cuckoo, fruity, loco, nuts, nutty, screwy, wacky. *Chiefly British:* crackers. *Law:* non compos mentis. ***Idioms:*** around the bend, crazy as a loon, mad as a hatter, not all there, nutty as a fruitcake, off (*or* out of) one's head, off one's rocker, of unsound mind, out of one's mind, sick in the head, stark raving mad. *See* SANE.

bauble *noun*
A small showy article : bibelot, gewgaw, gimcrack, knickknack, novelty, toy, trifle, trinket, whatnot. *See* THING.

bawd *noun*
A woman who engages in sexual intercourse for payment : call girl, camp follower, courtesan, harlot, prostitute, scarlet woman, streetwalker, strumpet, tart[2], whore. *Slang:* hooker, moll. ***Idioms:*** lady of easy virtue, lady of pleasure, lady of the night. *See* SEX.

bawdiness *noun*
The quality or state of being obscene : coarseness, dirtiness, filthiness, foulness, grossness, lewdness, obscenity, profaneness, profanity, scurrility, scurrilousness, smuttiness, vulgarity, vulgarness. *Slang:* raunch, raunchiness. *See* DECENT.

bawdry *noun*
Something that is offensive to accepted standards of decency : dirt, filth, obscenity, profanity, ribaldry, scatology, smut, vulgarity. *Slang:* raunch. *See* DECENT.

bawdy *adjective*
Offensive to accepted standards of decency : barnyard, broad, coarse, dirty, Fescennine, filthy, foul, gross, lewd, nasty, obscene, profane, ribald, scatologic, scatological, scurrilous, smutty, vulgar. *Slang:* raunchy. *See* DECENT.

bawl *verb*
1. To cry loudly, as a healthy child does from pain or distress : howl, wail, yowl. *See* SOUNDS. **2.** To make inarticulate sounds of grief or pain, usually accompanied by tears : blubber, cry, howl, keen[2], sob, wail, weep, yowl. *See* HAPPY, SOUNDS. **3.** To speak or say very loudly or with a shout : bellow, bluster, call, clamor, cry, halloo, holler, roar, shout, vociferate, whoop, yawp, yell. *See* SOUNDS.
bawl out *verb* **1.** *Informal.* To reprimand loudly or harshly : berate, rate[2]. *Informal:* tell off. ***Idioms:*** give hell to, give it to. *See* ATTACK. **2.** *Informal.* To criticize for a fault or an offense : admonish, call down, castigate, chastise, chide, dress down, rap[1], rebuke, reprimand, reproach, reprove, scold, tax, upbraid. *Informal:* lambaste. *Slang:* chew out. ***Idioms:*** call on the carpet, let someone have it, haul (*or* rake) over the coals, bring (*or* call *or* take) to task. *See* ATTACK, PRAISE.
bawl *noun* A loud, deep, prolonged sound : bellow, clamor, roar. *See* SOUNDS.

bawling *noun*
A fit of crying : blubbering, cry, sobbing, tear[2] (used in plural), wailing, weeping. *See* SOUNDS.

bawl out *verb* See **bawl.**

bay[1] *noun*
A body of water partly enclosed by land but having a wide outlet to the sea : bight, cove, inlet. *See* TERRITORY.

bay[2] *noun*
A long, mournful cry : howl, moan, ululation, wail, yowl. *See* SOUNDS.
bay *verb* To utter or emit a long, mournful, plaintive sound : howl, moan, ululate, wail, yowl. *See* SOUNDS.

be *verb*
1. To have reality or life : breathe, exist, live[1], subsist. *See* BE. **2.** To have being or actuality : exist, subsist. *See* BE.

beak *noun*
1. The horny projection forming a bird's jaws : bill[2]. *See* MOUTH. **2.** *Informal.* The structure on the human face that contains the nostrils and organs of smell and forms the beginning of the respiratory tract : nose, proboscis. *Informal:* snoot. *Slang:* nozzle, schnoz, schnozzle, snout. *See* BODY, CONVEX.

beam *noun*
1. A large, oblong piece of wood or other material, used especially for construction : balk, rafter, timber. *See* MATTER. **2.** A series of particles or waves traveling close together in parallel paths : ray, shaft. *See* LIGHT.
beam *verb* **1.** To emit a bright light : blaze[1], burn, gleam, glow, incandesce, radiate, shine. *See* LIGHT. **2.** To curve the lips upward in expressing amusement, pleasure, or happiness : grin, smile. ***Idioms:*** break into a smile, crack a smile. *See* EXPRESS.

beamy *adjective*
Giving off or reflecting light readily or in large amounts : bright, brilliant, effulgent, incandescent, irradiant, lambent, lucent, luminous, lustrous, radiant, refulgent, shiny. *See* LIGHT.

bean *noun*
Slang. The uppermost part of the body : head, noddle, pate, poll. *Slang:* block, conk, dome, noggin, noodle, nut. *See* BODY.

bear *verb*
1. To hold up : carry, support, sustain. *See* OVER. **2.** To sustain the weight of : carry, hold, support, uphold. *See* SUPPORT. **3.** To hold on one's person : carry, have, possess. *Informal:* pack. *See* OWNED. **4.** To move while supporting : carry, convey, lug[2], transport. *Informal:* tote. *Slang:* schlep. *See* OVER. **5.** To cause to come along with oneself : bring, carry, convey, fetch, take, transport. *See* ACCOMPANIED. **6.** To hold and turn over in the mind :

harbor, nourish, nurse. *See* THOUGHTS. **7.** To be endowed with as a visible characteristic or form : carry, display, exhibit, have, possess. *See* SHOW. **8.** To conduct oneself in a specified way : acquit, act, behave, carry, comport, demean[1], deport, do, quit. *See* BE. **9.** To put up with : abide, accept, brook[2], endure, go, stand (for), stomach, suffer, support, sustain, swallow, take, tolerate, withstand. *Informal:* lump[2]. ***Idioms:*** take it, take it lying down. *See* ACCEPT. **10.** To give birth to : bring forth, deliver, have. *Chiefly Regional:* birth. ***Idiom:*** be brought abed (*or* to bed) of. *See* RICH. **11.** To bring forth (a product) : give, produce, yield. *See* RICH. **12.** To exert pressure : press, push. *See* OVER. **13.** To proceed in a specified direction : go, head, make, set out, strike out. *See* APPROACH.

bear on (or **upon)** *verb* To be pertinent : appertain, apply, concern, pertain, refer, relate. ***Idioms:*** have a bearing on, have to do with. *See* RELEVANT.

bear out *verb* **1.** To assure the certainty or validity of : attest, authenticate, back (up), confirm, corroborate, evidence, justify, substantiate, testify (to), validate, verify, warrant. *See* SUPPORT, TRUE. **2.** To establish as true or genuine : authenticate, confirm, corroborate, demonstrate, endorse, establish, evidence, prove, show, substantiate, validate, verify. *See* SHOW, SUPPORT.

bear up *verb* To withstand stress or difficulty : endure, hold up, stand up. *See* CONTINUE.

bearable *adjective*
Capable of being tolerated : endurable, sufferable, tolerable. *See* CONTINUE.

beard *verb*
To confront boldly and courageously : brave, challenge, dare, defy, face, front. ***Idioms:*** fly in the face of, snap one's fingers at, stand up to, thumb one's nose at. *See* RESIST.

bearer *noun*
A person who carries messages or is sent on errands : carrier, conveyer, courier, envoy, messenger, runner, transporter. *See* OVER.

bearing *noun*
1. Behavior through which one reveals one's personality : address, air, demeanor, manner, mien, presence, style. *Archaic:* port. *See* BE, STYLE. **2.** The compass direction in which a ship or an aircraft moves : course, heading, vector. *See* APPROACH. **3.** One's place and direction relative to one's surroundings. Often used in plural : location, orientation, position, situation. *See* PLACE. **4.** The fact of being related to the matter at hand : applicability, application, appositeness, concernment, germaneness, materiality, pertinence, pertinency, relevance, relevancy. *See* RELEVANT.

bear on or **upon** *verb* See **bear.**

bear out *verb* See **bear.**

bear up *verb* See **bear.**

beast *noun*
A perversely bad, cruel, or wicked person : archfiend, devil, fiend, ghoul, monster, ogre, tiger, vampire. *See* KIND.

beat *verb*
1. To hit heavily and repeatedly with violent blows : assail, assault, baste, batter, belabor, buffet, drub, hammer, pound, pummel, smash, thrash, thresh. *Informal:* lambaste. *Slang:* clobber. ***Idiom:*** rain blows on. *See* ATTACK, STRIKE. **2.** To punish with blows or lashes : flog, hide[2], lash, thrash, whip. *Informal:* trim. *Slang:* lay into, lick. *See* ATTACK, REWARD. **3.** To move (one's arms or wings, for example) up and down : flap, flitter, flop, flutter, waggle, wave. *See* REPETITION. **4.** To indicate (time or rhythm), as with repeated gestures or sounds : count. ***Idioms:*** keep time, mark time. *See* REPETITION. **5.** To make rhythmic contractions, sounds, or movements : palpitate, pound, pulsate, pulse, throb. *See* REPETITION, SOUNDS. **6.** To shape, break, or flatten with repeated blows : forge[1], hammer, pound. *See* REPETITION, STRIKE. **7.** To mix rapidly to a frothy consistency : whip, whisk. *See* ASSEMBLE, REPETITION. **8.** To win a victory over, as in battle or a competition : best, conquer, defeat, master, overcome, prevail against (*or* over), rout, subdue, subjugate, surmount, triumph over, vanquish, worst. *Informal:* trim, whip. *Slang:* ace, lick. ***Idioms:*** carry (*or* win) the day, get (*or* have) the best of, get (*or* have) the better of, go someone one better. *See* WIN. **9.** *Informal.* To be greater or better than : best, better[1], exceed, excel, outdo, outmatch, outrun, outshine, outstrip, pass, surpass, top, transcend. ***Idioms:*** go beyond, go one better. *See* BIG. **10.** *Slang.* To make incapable of finding something to think, do, or say : confound, nonplus. *Informal:* flummox, stick, stump, throw. ***Idiom:*** put someone at a loss. *See* AFFECT, KNOWLEDGE.

beat down *verb* To be projected with blinding intensity : blaze[1], glare. *See* LIGHT.

beat off *verb* To turn or drive away : fend (off), keep off, parry, repel, repulse, ward off. *See* ALLOW, STRIKE.

beat *noun* **1.** A stroke or blow, especially one that produces a sound : clunk, pound, thud, thump. *See* ATTACK, SOUNDS, STRIKE. **2.** A periodic contraction or sound of something coursing : palpitation, pulsation, pulse, throb. *See* REPETITION, SOUNDS. **3.** The patterned, recurring alternation of contrasting elements, such as stressed and unstressed notes in music : cadence, cadency, measure, meter, rhythm, swing. *See* REPETITION. **4.** An area regularly covered, as by a policeman or reporter : circuit, round, route. *See* TERRITORY.

beat *adjective Informal.* Extremely tired : bleary, dead, drained, exhausted, fatigued, run-down, spent, tired out, wearied, weariful, weary, worn-down, worn-out. *Informal:* bushed, tuckered (out). *Slang:* done in, fagged (out), pooped (out). ***Idioms:*** all in, ready to drop. *See* HEALTH, TIRED.

beat down *verb* See **beat.**

beating *noun*
1. A punishment dealt with blows or lashes : flogging, hiding, lashing, thrashing, whipping. *Informal:* trimming. *Slang:* licking. *See* ATTACK, REWARD. **2.** The act of defeating or the condition of being defeated : defeat, drubbing, overthrow, rout, thrashing, vanquishment. *Informal:* massacre, trimming, whipping. *Slang:* dusting, licking. *See* WIN.

beatitude *noun*
A condition of good spirits : blessedness, bliss, cheer, cheerfulness, felicity, gladness, happiness, joy, joyfulness. *See* HAPPY.

beat off *verb* See **beat.**

beau *noun*
1. A man who is the favored companion of a woman : boyfriend. *Informal:* fellow. *See* CONNECT, SEX. **2.** A man who courts a woman : admirer, courter, suitor, swain, wooer. *See* SEX.

beau geste *noun*
An act requiring special generosity : compliment, courtesy, favor. *See* GIVE.

beau ideal *noun*
One that is worthy of imitation or duplication : example, exemplar, ideal, mirror, model, paradigm, pattern, standard. *See* GOOD.

beauteous *adjective*
Having qualities that delight the eye : attractive, beautiful, comely, fair, good-looking, gorgeous, handsome, lovely, pretty, pulchritudinous, ravishing, sightly, stunning. *Scots:* bonny. ***Idiom:*** easy on the eyes. *See* BEAUTIFUL.

beautiful *adjective*
Having qualities that delight the eye : attractive, beauteous, comely, fair, good-looking, gorgeous, handsome, lovely, pretty, pulchritudinous, ravishing, sightly, stunning. *Scots:* bonny. ***Idiom:*** easy on the eyes. *See* BEAUTIFUL.

beautify *verb*
To endow with beauty and elegance by way of a notable addition : adorn, embellish, enhance, grace, set off. *See* BEAUTIFUL.

beauty *noun*
1. A person regarded as physically attractive : belle (used of a woman), lovely, stunner. *Slang:* babe, doll, hunk (used of a man), knockout, looker, stud (used of a man). *See* BEAUTIFUL. **2.** A special feature or quality that confers superiority : distinction, excellence, merit, perfection, virtue. *See* GOOD.

becalm *verb*
To make or become calm : allay, balm, calm (down), lull, quiet, settle, still, tranquilize. *See* CALM.

becloud *verb*
To make dim or indistinct : bedim, befog, blear, blur, cloud, dim, dull, eclipse, fog, gloom, mist, obfuscate, obscure, overcast, overshadow, shadow. *See* CLEAR.

become *verb*
1. To come to be : come, get, grow, turn (out), wax. *See* CHANGE. **2.** To be appropriate or suitable to : befit, behoove, suit. *Archaic:* beseem. *See* AGREE. **3.** To be in keeping with : befit, conform, correspond, fit[1], go with, match, suit. *See* AGREE. **4.** To look good on or with : enhance, flatter, suit. ***Idiom:*** put in the best light. *See* AGREE, BEAUTIFUL.

becoming *adjective*
1. Suitable for a particular person, condition, occasion, or place : appropriate, apt, befitting, correct, felicitous, fit[1], fitting, happy, meet[2], proper, right, tailor-made. *See* RIGHT. **2.** Conforming to accepted standards : befitting, comely, comme il faut, correct, decent, decorous, de rigueur, nice, proper, respectable, right, seemly. *See* COURTESY. **3.** Pleasingly suited to the wearer : attractive, flattering. *See* BEAUTIFUL.

bed *noun*
The lowest or supporting part or structure : base[1], basis, bottom, foot, footing, foundation, fundament, ground, groundwork, seat, substratum, underpinning (often used in plural). *See* OVER.

bed *verb* **1.** To go to bed. Also used with *down* : retire. *Informal:* turn in. *Slang:* crash, flop. ***Idioms:*** call it a night, hit the hay (*or* sack). *See* AWARENESS. **2.** To provide with often temporary lodging. Also used with *down* : accommodate, berth, bestow, billet, board, bunk[1], domicile, harbor, house, lodge, put up, quarter, room. *See* PROTECTION. **3.** To engage in sexual relations with : copulate, couple, have, mate, sleep with, take. ***Idioms:*** go to bed with, make love, make whoopee, roll in the hay. *See* SEX.

bedaub *verb*
To spread with a greasy, sticky, or dirty substance : besmear, dab[1], daub, plaster, smear, smirch, smudge. *See* PUT ON.

bedaze *verb*
To dull the senses, as with a heavy blow, a shock, or fatigue : bemuse, benumb, daze, stun, stupefy. *Chiefly Regional:* maze. *See* AWARENESS.

bedazzle *verb*
To confuse with bright light : blind, daze, dazzle. *See* SEE.

bedeck *verb*
To furnish with decorations : adorn, deck[2] (out), decorate, dress (up), embellish, garnish, ornament, trim. *See* BEAUTIFUL.

bedevil *verb*
1. To trouble persistently from or as if from all sides : badger, beleaguer, beset, besiege, harass, harry, hound, importune, pester, plague, solicit. *See* ATTACK. **2.** To disturb by repeated attacks : annoy, bait, beleaguer, beset, harass, harry, pester, plague, tease, torment, worry. *See* FEELINGS, PAIN.

bedim *verb*
To make dim or indistinct : becloud, befog, blear, blur, cloud, dim, dull, eclipse, fog, gloom, mist, obfuscate, obscure, overcast, overshadow, shadow. *See* CLEAR.

bedraggled *adjective*
Showing signs of wear and tear or neglect : broken-down, decaying, decrepit, dilapidated, dingy, down-at-heel, faded, mangy, rundown, scrubby, scruffy, seedy, shabby, shoddy, sleazy, tattered, tatty, threadbare. *Informal:* tacky[2]. *Slang:* ratty. ***Idioms:*** all the worse for wear, gone to pot (*or* seed), past cure (*or* hope). *See* BETTER.

bee *noun*
An impulsive, often illogical turn of mind : boutade, caprice, conceit, fancy, freak, humor, impulse, megrim, notion, vagary, whim, whimsy. ***Idiom:*** bee in one's bonnet. *See* THOUGHTS.

beef *noun*
1. *Informal.* Solid and well-developed muscles : brawn, bulk, muscularity. *See* BODY. **2.** *Slang.* An expression of dissatisfaction or a circumstance regarded as a cause for such expression : complaint, grievance. *Informal:* gripe, grouse. *Slang:* kick. ***Idiom:*** bone to pick. *See* HAPPY.

beef *verb* *Slang.* To express negative feelings, especially of dissatisfaction or resentment : complain, grouch, grump, whine. *Informal:* crab, gripe, grouse, kick. *Slang:* bellyache, bitch. *See* FEELINGS, HAPPY.

beef up *verb* *Informal.* To make or become greater or larger : aggrandize, amplify, augment, boost, build, build up, burgeon, enlarge, escalate, expand, extend, grow, increase, magnify, mount, multiply, proliferate, rise, run up, snowball, soar, swell, upsurge, wax. *See* INCREASE.

beef up *verb* See **beef.**

beetle *verb*
To curve outward past the normal or usual limit : bag, balloon, belly, bulge, jut, overhang, pouch, project, protrude, protuberate, stand out, stick out. *See* CONVEX.

befall *verb*
1. To take place : betide, come, come about, come off, develop, hap, happen, occur, pass, transpire. ***Idiom:*** come to pass. *See* HAPPEN. **2.** To happen to one : betide, come. *See* HAPPEN. **3.** To take place by chance : chance, hap, happen. *See* HAPPEN.

befit *verb*
1. To be appropriate or suitable to : become, behoove, suit. *Archaic:* beseem. *See* AGREE. **2.** To be in keeping with : become, conform, correspond, fit[1], go with, match, suit. *See* AGREE.

befitting *adjective*
1. Suitable for a particular person, condition, occasion, or place : appropriate, apt, becoming, correct, felicitous, fit[1], fitting, happy, meet[2], proper, right, tailor-made. *See* RIGHT. **2.** Suited to one's end or purpose : appropriate, convenient, expedient, fit[1], good, meet[2], proper, suitable, tailor-made, useful. *See* AGREE, GOOD. **3.** Conforming to accepted standards : becoming, comely, comme il faut, correct, decent, decorous, de rigueur, nice, proper, respectable, right, seemly. *See* COURTESY.

befog *verb*
To make dim or indistinct : becloud, bedim, blear, blur, cloud, dim, dull, eclipse, fog, gloom, mist, obfuscate, obscure, overcast, overshadow, shadow. *See* CLEAR.

before *adverb*
1. At a time in the past : already, earlier, erstwhile, formerly, once, previously. *Archaic:* aforetime, beforetime. *See* PRECEDE. **2.** Up to this time : earlier, heretofore, previously, yet. *See* PRECEDE. **3.** Until then : beforehand, earlier. *See* PRECEDE.

beforehand *adverb*
1. Before the expected time : ahead, betimes, early. ***Idioms:*** ahead of time, in advance, with time to spare. *See* TIME. **2.** Until then : before, earlier. *See* PRECEDE.

beforetime *adverb*
Archaic. At a time in the past : already, before, earlier, erstwhile, formerly, once, previously. *Archaic:* aforetime. *See* PRECEDE.

befoul *verb*
1. To make dirty : begrime, besmirch, besoil, black, blacken, defile, dirty, smudge, smutch, soil, sully. *See* CLEAN. **2.** To contaminate the reputation of : besmear, besmirch, bespatter, blacken, cloud, denigrate, dirty, smear, smudge, smut, soil, spatter, stain, sully, taint, tarnish. ***Idioms:*** give a black eye to, sling (*or* throw) mud on. *See* ATTACK, CLEAN.

befuddle *verb*
1. To cause to be unclear in mind or intent : addle, bewilder, confound, confuse, discombobulate, dizzy, fuddle, jumble, mix up, muddle, mystify, perplex, puzzle. *Informal:* throw. ***Idiom:*** make one's head reel (*or* swim *or* whirl). *See* CLEAR, FEELINGS. **2.** To muddle or stupefy with or as if with alcoholic drink : besot, fuddle. *See* DRUGS.

befuddlement *noun*
A stunned or bewildered condition : bewilderedness, bewilderment, daze, discombobulation, fog, muddle, mystification, perplexity, puzzlement, stupefaction, stupor, trance. *See* AWARENESS.

beg *verb*
1. To ask or ask for as charity : bum[1], cadge. *Informal:* panhandle. *Slang:* mooch. *See* REQUEST. **2.** To make an earnest or urgent request : appeal, beseech, crave, entreat, implore, plead, pray, sue, supplicate. *Archaic:* conjure. *See* ASK.

beget *verb*
1. To be the biological father of : breed, father, get, procreate, sire. *See* KIN. **2.** To cause to come into existence : breed, create, engender, father, hatch, make, originate, parent, procreate, produce, sire, spawn. ***Idiom:*** give birth (*or* rise) to. *See* MAKE.

beggar *noun*
1. One who begs habitually or for a living : almsman, almswoman, cadger, mendicant. *Informal:* panhandler. *Slang:* bummer, moocher. *See* REQUEST. **2.** An impoverished person : down-and-out, down-and-outer, have-not, indigent, pauper. *See* RICH. **3.** One who humbly entreats : prayer[2], suitor, suppliant, supplicant. *See* REQUEST.

beggarly *adjective*
Having little or no money or wealth : destitute, down-and-out, impecunious, impoverished, indigent, necessitous, needy, penniless, penurious, poor, poverty-stricken. *Informal:* broke, strapped. ***Idioms:*** hard up, on one's uppers. *See* RICH.

beggary *noun*
1. The condition of being extremely poor : destitution, impecuniosity, impecuniousness, impoverishment, indigence, need, neediness, pennilessness, penuriousness, penury, poverty, privation, want. *See* RICH. **2.** The condition of being a beggar : mendicancy, mendicity. *See* RICH.

begin *verb*
1. To go about the initial step in doing (something) : approach, commence, embark, enter, get off, inaugurate, initiate, institute, launch, lead off, open, set about, set out, set to, start, take on, take up, undertake. *Informal:* kick off. ***Idioms:*** get cracking, get going, get the show on the road. *See* START. **2.** To come into being : arise, commence, originate, start. *See* START.

beginner *noun*
One who is just starting to learn or do something : abecedarian, fledgling, freshman, greenhorn, initiate, neophyte, novice, novitiate, tenderfoot, tyro. *Slang:* rookie. *See* START.

beginning *noun*
1. The act or process of bringing or being brought into existence : commencement, inauguration, inception, incipience, incipiency, initiation, launch, leadoff, opening, origination, start. *Informal:* kickoff. *See* START. **2.** The initial stage of a developmental process : birth, commencement, dawn, genesis, inception, nascence, nascency, onset, opening, origin, outset, spring, start. *See* START. **3.** A point of origination : derivation, fount, fountain, fountainhead, mother, origin, parent, provenance, provenience, root[1], rootstock, source, spring, well[1]. *See* START.

beginning *adjective* **1.** Of, relating to, or occurring at the start of something : inceptive, incipient, initial, initiatory, introductory, leadoff.

See START. **2.** At or near the start of a period, development, or series : early, first, initial. *See* START. **3.** Of or treating the most basic aspects : basal, basic, elementary, rudimental, rudimentary. *See* SIMPLE, START.

begird *verb*
1. To encircle with or as if with a band : band[1], belt, cincture, compass, encompass, engirdle, gird, girdle, girt, ring[1]. *Archaic:* engird. *See* EDGE. **2.** To shut in on all sides : beset, circle, compass, encircle, encompass, environ, gird, girdle, hedge, hem, ring[1], surround. *See* OPEN.

begrime *verb*
To make dirty : befoul, besmirch, besoil, black, blacken, defile, dirty, smudge, smutch, soil, sully. *See* CLEAN.

begrudge *verb*
To feel envy towards or for : covet, envy, grudge. *See* DESIRE.

beguile *verb*
1. To cause to accept what is false, especially by trickery or misrepresentation : betray, bluff, cozen, deceive, delude, double-cross, dupe, fool, hoodwink, humbug, mislead, take in, trick. *Informal:* bamboozle, have. *Slang:* four-flush. ***Idioms:*** lead astray, play false, pull the wool over someone's eyes, put something over on, take for a ride. *See* HONEST. **2.** To please greatly or irresistibly : bewitch, captivate, charm, enchant, entrance[2], fascinate. *See* LIKE.

behave *verb*
1. To conduct oneself in a specified way : acquit, act, bear, carry, comport, demean[1], deport, do, quit. *See* BE. **2.** To react in a specified way : act, function, operate, perform, work. *See* ACTION.

behavior *noun*
1. The manner in which one behaves : action (often used in plural), comportment, conduct, deportment, way. *See* BE. **2.** The way in which a machine or other thing performs or functions : functioning, operation, performance, reaction, working (often used in plural). *See* ACTION, MACHINE.

behemoth *noun*
One that is very large and powerful : giant, Goliath, jumbo, leviathan, mammoth, monster, titan. *Slang:* whopper. *See* BEINGS, BIG.
behemoth *adjective* Of extraordinary size and power : Brobdingnagian, Bunyanesque, colossal, cyclopean, elephantine, enormous, gargantuan, giant, gigantesque, gigantic, herculean, heroic, huge, immense, jumbo, mammoth, massive, massy, mastodonic, mighty, monster, monstrous, monumental, mountainous, prodigious, pythonic, stupendous, titanic, tremendous, vast. *Informal:* walloping. *Slang:* whopping. *See* BIG.

behest *noun*
An authoritative indication to be obeyed : bidding, charge, command, commandment, dictate, direction, directive, injunction, instruction (often used in plural), mandate, order, word. *See* OVER, WORDS.

behind *adverb*
1. Not on time : behindhand, belatedly, late, tardily. *See* TIME. **2.** So as to fall behind schedule : behindhand, late, slow. ***Idiom:*** behind time. *See* TIME.
behind *noun Informal.* The part of one's back on which one rests in sitting : buttock (used in plural), derrière, posterior, rump, seat. *Informal:* backside, bottom, rear[1]. *Slang:* bun (used in plural), fanny, tush. *Chiefly British:* bum[2]. *See* OVER.

behindhand *adjective*
Not being on time : belated, late, overdue, tardy. *See* TIME.
behindhand *adverb* **1.** Not on time : behind, belatedly, late, tardily. *See* TIME. **2.** So as to fall behind schedule : behind, late, slow. ***Idiom:*** behind time. *See* TIME.

behold *verb*
To apprehend (images) by use of the eyes : perceive, see. *Scots:* ken. *See* SEE.

beholden *adjective*
Owing something, such as gratitude or appreciation, to another : bound[3], indebted, obligated, obliged. *Archaic:* bounden. ***Idiom:*** under obligation. *See* OBLIGATION.

beholder *noun*
Someone who observes : bystander, looker-on, observer, onlooker, spectator, watcher. *See* AWARENESS, SEE.

behoove *verb*
To be appropriate or suitable to : become, befit, suit. *Archaic:* beseem. *See* AGREE.

being *noun*
1. The fact or state of existing or of being actual : actuality, entity, existence, reality. *See* BE, REAL. **2.** The condition of being in full force or operation : actualization, effect, materialization, realization. *See* BE. **3.** One that exists independently : entity, existence, existent, individual, object, something, thing. *See* BE, THING. **4.** A member of the human race : body, creature, homo, human, human being, individual, life, man, mortal, party, person, personage, soul. *See* BEINGS. **5.** A basic trait or set

of traits that define and establish the character of something : essence, essentiality, nature, quintessence, substance, texture. *See* SURFACE.

belabor *verb*
To hit heavily and repeatedly with violent blows : assail, assault, baste, batter, beat, buffet, drub, hammer, pound, pummel, smash, thrash, thresh. *Informal:* lambaste. *Slang:* clobber. ***Idiom:*** rain blows on. *See* ATTACK, STRIKE.

belated *adjective*
Not being on time : behindhand, late, overdue, tardy. *See* TIME.

belatedly *adverb*
Not on time : behind, behindhand, late, tardily. *See* TIME.

belatedness *noun*
The quality or condition of not being on time : lateness, tardiness. *See* TIME.

belay *verb*
1. To prevent the occurrence or continuation of a movement, action, or operation : arrest, cease, check, discontinue, halt[1], stall[1], stay[1], stop, surcease. ***Idioms:*** bring to a standstill, call a halt to, put a stop to. *See* CONTINUE. **2.** To come to a cessation : arrest, cease, check, discontinue, halt[1], leave off, quit, stall[1], stop, surcease. ***Idiom:*** come to a halt (*or* standstill *or* stop). *See* CONTINUE.

belch *verb*
To send forth (confined matter) violently : disgorge, eject, eruct, erupt, expel, spew. *Geology:* extravasate. *See* EXPLOSION.

beldam or **beldame** *noun*
An ugly, frightening old woman : crone, hag, witch. *Slang:* biddy. *Archaic:* trot. *See* BEAUTIFUL.

beldame *noun* See **beldam.**

beleaguer *verb*
1. To trouble persistently from or as if from all sides : badger, bedevil, beset, besiege, harass, harry, hound, importune, pester, plague, solicit. *See* ATTACK. **2.** To disturb by repeated attacks : annoy, bait, bedevil, beset, harass, harry, pester, plague, tease, torment, worry. *See* FEELINGS, PAIN. **3.** To surround with hostile troops : beset, besiege, blockade, invest, siege. ***Idiom:*** lay siege to. *See* ATTACK.

beleaguerment *noun*
A prolonged surrounding of an objective by hostile troops : besiegement, blockade, investment, siege. *See* ATTACK.

belie *verb*
1. To give an inaccurate view of by representing falsely or misleadingly : color, distort, falsify, load, misrepresent, misstate, pervert, twist, warp, wrench, wrest. ***Idiom:*** give a false coloring to. *See* TRUE. **2.** To prove or show to be false : confute, discredit, disprove, rebut, refute. *See* AFFIRM.

belief *noun*
1. Absolute certainty in the trustworthiness of another : confidence, dependence, faith, reliance, trust. *See* BELIEF. **2.** Mental acceptance of the truth or actuality of something : credence, credit, faith. *See* OPINION. **3.** Something accepted as true : conviction, feeling, idea, mind, notion, opinion, persuasion, position, sentiment, view. *See* OPINION.

believability *noun*
Appearance of truth or authenticity : color, credibility, credibleness, creditability, creditableness, plausibility, plausibleness, verisimilitude. *See* LIKELY.

believable *adjective*
Worthy of being believed : colorable, credible, creditable, plausible. *See* TRUE.

believe *verb*
1. To regard (something) as true or real : accept. *Slang:* buy, swallow. *See* OPINION. **2.** To have confidence in the truthfulness of : credit, trust. ***Idiom:*** take at one's word. *See* OPINION. **3.** To have an opinion : consider, deem, hold, opine, think. *Informal:* figure, judge. ***Idiom:*** be of the opinion. *See* OPINION. **4.** To view in a certain way : feel, hold, sense, think. *See* OPINION. **5.** To regard in an appraising way : repute, suppose, think. *See* BELIEF.
believe in *verb* To place trust or confidence in : bank on (*or* upon), count on (*or* upon), depend on (*or* upon), reckon on (*or* upon), rely on (*or* upon), trust (in). *See* TRUST.

believe in *verb* See **believe.**

belittle *verb*
To think, represent, or speak of as small or unimportant : decry, denigrate, deprecate, depreciate, derogate, detract, discount, disparage, downgrade, minimize, run down, slight, talk down. ***Idiom:*** make light (*or* little) of. *See* ATTACK, SHOW.

belittlement *noun*
The act or an instance of belittling : denigration, deprecation, depreciation, derogation, detraction, disparagement, minimization. *See* ATTACK, SHOW.

belle *noun*
A person regarded as physically attractive. Used of a woman : beauty, lovely, stunner. *Slang:* babe, doll, hunk (used of a man), knockout, looker, stud (used of a man). *See* BEAUTIFUL.

bellicose *adjective*
1. Having or showing an eagerness to fight : belligerent, combative, contentious, hostile, militant, pugnacious, quarrelsome, scrappy, truculent, warlike. *See* ATTACK. **2.** Of, relating to, or inclined toward war : martial, militaristic, military, warlike. *See* PEACE.

bellicoseness *noun*
1. Warlike or hostile attitude or nature : bellicosity, belligerence, belligerency, combativeness, contentiousness, hostility, militance, militancy, pugnaciousness, pugnacity, truculence, truculency. *See* ATTACK. **2.** The power or will to fight : bellicosity, belligerence, belligerency, combativeness, contentiousness, fight, pugnaciousness, pugnacity, truculence, truculency. *See* CONFLICT.

bellicosity *noun*
1. Warlike or hostile attitude or nature : bellicoseness, belligerence, belligerency, combativeness, contentiousness, hostility, militance, militancy, pugnaciousness, pugnacity, truculence, truculency. *See* ATTACK. **2.** The power or will to fight : bellicoseness, belligerence, belligerency, combativeness, contentiousness, fight, pugnaciousness, pugnacity, truculence, truculency. *See* CONFLICT.

belligerence *noun*
1. Warlike or hostile attitude or nature : bellicoseness, bellicosity, belligerency, combativeness, contentiousness, hostility, militance, militancy, pugnaciousness, pugnacity, truculence, truculency. *See* ATTACK. **2.** Hostile behavior : aggression, aggressiveness, belligerency, combativeness, contentiousness, hostility, militance, militancy. *See* ATTACK. **3.** The power or will to fight : bellicoseness, bellicosity, belligerency, combativeness, contentiousness, fight, pugnaciousness, pugnacity, truculence, truculency. *See* CONFLICT.

belligerency *noun*
1. A state of open, prolonged fighting : conflict, confrontation, hostility (used in plural), strife, struggle, war, warfare. *See* CONFLICT. **2.** Warlike or hostile attitude or nature : bellicoseness, bellicosity, belligerence, combativeness, contentiousness, hostility, militance, militancy, pugnaciousness, pugnacity, truculence, truculency. *See* ATTACK. **3.** Hostile behavior : aggression, aggressiveness, belligerence, combativeness, contentiousness, hostility, militance, militancy. *See* ATTACK. **4.** The power or will to fight : bellicoseness, bellicosity, belligerence, combativeness, contentiousness, fight, pugnaciousness, pugnacity, truculence, truculency. *See* CONFLICT.

belligerent *adjective*
1. Having or showing an eagerness to fight : bellicose, combative, contentious, hostile, militant, pugnacious, quarrelsome, scrappy, truculent, warlike. *See* ATTACK. **2.** Inclined to act in a hostile way : aggressive, combative, contentious, hostile, militant. *See* ATTACK, ATTITUDE. **3.** Of or engaged in warfare : combatant, hostile, militant. ***Idiom:*** at war. *See* ATTACK.

belligerent *noun* One who engages in a combat or struggle : combatant, fighter, soldier, warrior. *See* CONFLICT.

bellow *verb*
To speak or say very loudly or with a shout : bawl, bluster, call, clamor, cry, halloo, holler, roar, shout, vociferate, whoop, yawp, yell. *See* SOUNDS.

bellow *noun* A loud, deep, prolonged sound : bawl, clamor, roar. *See* SOUNDS.

belly *verb*
To curve outward past the normal or usual limit : bag, balloon, beetle, bulge, jut, overhang, pouch, project, protrude, protuberate, stand out, stick out. *See* CONVEX.

bellyache *verb*
Slang. To express negative feelings, especially of dissatisfaction or resentment : complain, grouch, grump, whine. *Informal:* crab, gripe, grouse, kick. *Slang:* beef, bitch. *See* FEELINGS, HAPPY.

bellyacher *noun*
Slang. A person who habitually complains or grumbles : complainer, crab, faultfinder, grouch, growler, grumbler, grump, murmurer, mutterer, whiner. *Informal:* crank, griper, grouser. *Slang:* sorehead, sourpuss. *See* HAPPY.

belong *verb*
To have a proper or suitable place : fit[1], go. *See* ORDER.

belonging *noun*
One's portable property. Often used in plural : effect (used in plural), good (used in plural), lares and penates, personal effects, personal property, possession (used in plural), property, thing (often used in plural). *Informal:* stuff. *Law:* chattel, movable (often used in plural). *See* OWNED.

beloved *adjective*
Regarded with much love and tenderness : darling, dear, loved, precious. *See* LOVE.

beloved *noun* A person who is much loved : darling, dear, honey, love, minion, precious, sweet, sweetheart, truelove. *Informal:* sweetie. ***Idiom:*** light of one's life. *See* LOVE.

belt *noun*

1. A part of the earth's surface : area, district, locality, neighborhood, quarter, region, tract, zone. *Informal:* neck of the woods. *See* TERRITORY. **2.** *Slang.* A sudden sharp, powerful stroke : bang, blow[2], clout, crack, hit, lick, pound, slug[3], sock, swat, thwack, welt, whack, wham, whop. *Informal:* bash, biff, bop, clip[1], wallop. *Slang:* conk, paste. *See* ATTACK, STRIKE. **3.** *Slang.* An act of drinking or the amount swallowed : draft, drink, potation, pull, quaff, sip, sup, swill. *Informal:* swig. *See* MOUTH.

belt *verb* **1.** To encircle with or as if with a band : band[1], begird, cincture, compass, encompass, engirdle, gird, girdle, girt, ring[1]. *Archaic:* engird. *See* EDGE. **2.** *Slang.* To deliver a powerful blow to suddenly and sharply : bash, catch, clout, hit, knock, pop[1], slam, slog, slug[3], smash, smite, sock, strike, swat, thwack, whack, wham, whop. *Informal:* biff, bop, clip[1], wallop. *Slang:* conk, paste. ***Idioms:*** let someone have it, sock it to someone. *See* ATTACK, STRIKE. **3.** *Slang.* To take into the mouth and swallow (a liquid) : drink, imbibe, pull on, quaff, sip, sup. *Informal:* swig, toss down (*or* off). ***Idiom:*** wet one's whistle. *See* MOUTH.

bemire *verb*

To soil with mud : mire, muck (up), mud, muddy, slush. *See* CLEAN.

bemuse *verb*

To dull the senses, as with a heavy blow, a shock, or fatigue : bedaze, benumb, daze, stun, stupefy. *Chiefly Regional:* maze. *See* AWARENESS.

bemused *adjective*

So lost in thought as to be unaware of one's surroundings : absent, absent-minded, abstracted, distrait, faraway, inattentive, preoccupied. ***Idiom:*** a million miles away. *See* ABILITY, AWARENESS.

bemusement *noun*

The condition of being so lost in solitary thought as to be unaware of one's surroundings : absent-mindedness, abstraction, brown study, daydreaming, muse[2], reverie, study, trance. *See* AWARENESS.

benchmark *noun*

A means by which individuals are compared and judged : criterion, gauge, mark, measure, standard, test, touchstone, yardstick. *See* USUAL.

bend *verb*

1. To swerve from a straight line : angle[2], arc, arch, bow[2], crook, curve, round, turn. *See* STRAIGHT. **2.** To cause to move, especially at an angle : angle[2], deflect, refract, turn. *See* STRAIGHT. **3.** To incline the body : arch, bow[1], hump, hunch, scrunch, stoop. *See* POSTURE. **4.** To be unable to hold up : give. *See* HELP. **5.** To devote (oneself or one's efforts) : address, apply, buckle down, concentrate, dedicate, devote, direct, focus, give, turn. *See* COLLECT, WORK.

bend *noun* Something bent : bow[2], crook, curvature, curve, round, turn. *See* STRAIGHT.

bender *noun*

Slang. A drinking bout : binge, brannigan, carousal, carouse, drunk, spree. *Slang:* bat[2], booze, jag, tear[1]. *See* DRUGS, RESTRAINT.

bending *adjective*

Having bends, curves, or angles : crooked, curved, curving. *See* STRAIGHT.

benediction *noun*

A short prayer said at meals : blessing, grace, thanks, thanksgiving. *See* GRATEFUL, RELIGION.

benefaction *noun*

1. Something given to a charity or cause : alms, beneficence, charity, contribution, donation, gift, handout, offering, subscription. *See* GIVE. **2.** A charitable deed : beneficence, benevolence, benignity, favor, kindliness, kindness, oblation, office (often used in plural), philanthropy. *See* GIVE, KIND.

benefactor *noun*

1. A person who supports or champions an activity, cause, or institution, for example : backer, contributor, friend, patron, sponsor, supporter. *Informal:* angel. *See* HELP. **2.** A person who gives to a charity or cause : benefactress, contributor, donator, donor, giver. *See* GIVE.

benefactress *noun*

A person who gives to a charity or cause : benefactor, contributor, donator, donor, giver. *See* GIVE.

benefic *adjective*

Affording benefit : advantageous, beneficent, beneficial, benignant, favorable, good, helpful, profitable, propitious, salutary, toward, useful. *See* HELP.

beneficence *noun*

1. Kindly, charitable interest in others : altruism, benevolence, benignancy, benignity, charitableness, charity, goodwill, grace, kindheartedness, kindliness, kindness, philanthropy. *See*

ATTITUDE, KIND. **2.** Something given to a charity or cause : alms, benefaction, charity, contribution, donation, gift, handout, offering, subscription. *See* GIVE. **3.** A charitable deed : benefaction, benevolence, benignity, favor, kindliness, kindness, oblation, office (often used in plural), philanthropy. *See* GIVE, KIND.

beneficent *adjective*
1. Characterized by kindness and concern for others : altruistic, benevolent, benign, benignant, good, goodhearted, kind[1], kindhearted, kindly. *See* ATTITUDE, KIND. **2.** Affording benefit : advantageous, benefic, beneficial, benignant, favorable, good, helpful, profitable, propitious, salutary, toward, useful. *See* HELP.

beneficial *adjective*
Affording benefit : advantageous, benefic, beneficent, benignant, favorable, good, helpful, profitable, propitious, salutary, toward, useful. *See* HELP.

benefit *noun*
1. Something beneficial : advantage, avail, blessing, boon[1], favor, gain, profit. *See* HELP. **2.** Something that contributes to or increases one's well-being : advantage, good, interest (often used in plural), profit. *See* HELP. **3.** The quality of being suitable or adaptable to an end : account, advantage, avail, profit, use, usefulness, utility. *See* USED. **4.** *Archaic.* A kindly act : favor, good turn, grace, indulgence, kindness, service. *See* HELP.
benefit *verb* **1.** To be an advantage to : advantage, avail, profit, serve. *Archaic:* boot[2]. ***Idiom:*** stand someone in good stead. *See* HELP. **2.** To derive advantage : capitalize, gain, profit. *See* HELP.

benevolence *noun*
1. Kindly, charitable interest in others : altruism, beneficence, benignancy, benignity, charitableness, charity, goodwill, grace, kindheartedness, kindliness, kindness, philanthropy. *See* ATTITUDE, KIND. **2.** A charitable deed : benefaction, beneficence, benignity, favor, kindliness, kindness, oblation, office (often used in plural), philanthropy. *See* GIVE, KIND.

benevolent *adjective*
1. Characterized by kindness and concern for others : altruistic, beneficent, benign, benignant, good, goodhearted, kind[1], kindhearted, kindly. *See* ATTITUDE, KIND. **2.** Of or concerned with charity : altruistic, charitable, eleemosynary, philanthropic, philanthropical. *See* GIVE, KIND.

benighted *adjective*
Exhibiting lack of education or knowledge : backward, ignorant, primitive, unenlightened. *See* KNOWLEDGE.

benightedness *noun*
The condition of being ignorant; lack of knowledge or learning : ignorance, illiteracy, illiterateness, nescience. *See* KNOWLEDGE.

benign *adjective*
1. Characterized by kindness and concern for others : altruistic, beneficent, benevolent, benignant, good, goodhearted, kind[1], kindhearted, kindly. *See* ATTITUDE, KIND. **2.** Indicative of future success or full of promise : auspicious, bright, brilliant, fair, favorable, fortunate, good, propitious. *See* LUCK.

benignancy *noun*
Kindly, charitable interest in others : altruism, beneficence, benevolence, benignity, charitableness, charity, goodwill, grace, kindheartedness, kindliness, kindness, philanthropy. *See* ATTITUDE, KIND.

benignant *adjective*
1. Affording benefit : advantageous, benefic, beneficent, beneficial, favorable, good, helpful, profitable, propitious, salutary, toward, useful. *See* HELP. **2.** Characterized by kindness and concern for others : altruistic, beneficent, benevolent, benign, good, goodhearted, kind[1], kindhearted, kindly. *See* ATTITUDE, KIND.

benignity *noun*
1. Kindly, charitable interest in others : altruism, beneficence, benevolence, benignancy, charitableness, charity, goodwill, grace, kindheartedness, kindliness, kindness, philanthropy. *See* ATTITUDE, KIND. **2.** A charitable deed : benefaction, beneficence, benevolence, favor, kindliness, kindness, oblation, office (often used in plural), philanthropy. *See* GIVE, KIND.

bent *adjective*
1. Deviating from a straight line : arced, arched, arciform, bowed, curved, curvilinear, rounded. *See* STRAIGHT. **2.** On an unwavering course of action : decided, determined, fixed, intent, resolute, set[1]. *See* DECIDE.
bent *noun* **1.** An inclination to something : bias, cast, disposition, leaning, partiality, penchant, predilection, predisposition, proclivity, proneness, propensity, squint, tendency, trend, turn. *See* APPROACH, LIKE. **2.** An innate capability : aptitude, aptness, faculty, flair, genius, gift, head, instinct, knack, talent, turn. *See* ABILITY, APPROACH.

benumb *verb*
1. To render less sensitive : blunt, deaden, desensitize, dull, numb. ***Idiom:*** take the edge off. *See* AWARENESS. **2.** To dull the senses, as with

a heavy blow, a shock, or fatigue : bedaze, bemuse, daze, stun, stupefy. *Chiefly Regional:* maze. *See* AWARENESS. **3.** To render helpless, as by emotion : numb, paralyze, petrify, stun, stupefy, wither. *See* AFFECT.

benumbed *adjective*
Lacking responsiveness or alertness : dull, insensible, insensitive, numb, stuporous, torpid, unresponsive, wooden. *See* AWARENESS.

bequeath *verb*
1. *Law.* To give (property) to another person after one's death : leave[1], will. *Law:* devise. *See* GIVE, LAW. **2.** To convey (something) from one generation to the next : hand down, hand on, pass (along *or* on), transmit. *See* GIVE.

berate *verb*
To reprimand loudly or harshly : bawl out, rate[2]. *Informal:* tell off. ***Idioms:*** give hell to, give it to. *See* ATTACK.

bereft *adjective*
Having been given up and left alone : abandoned, derelict, deserted, desolate, forlorn, forsaken, lorn. *See* KEEP.

berth *noun*
A post of employment : appointment, billet, job, office, place, position, situation, slot, spot. *Slang:* gig. *See* PLACE.
berth *verb* To provide with often temporary lodging : accommodate, bed (down), bestow, billet, board, bunk[1], domicile, harbor, house, lodge, put up, quarter, room. *See* PROTECTION.

beseech *verb*
To make an earnest or urgent request : appeal, beg, crave, entreat, implore, plead, pray, sue, supplicate. *Archaic:* conjure. *See* ASK.

beseem *verb*
Archaic. To be appropriate or suitable to : become, befit, behoove, suit. *See* AGREE.

beset *verb*
1. To set upon with violent force : aggress, assail, assault, attack, fall on (*or* upon), go at, have at, sail into, storm, strike. *Informal:* light into, pitch into. *See* ATTACK. **2.** To surround with hostile troops : beleaguer, besiege, blockade, invest, siege. ***Idiom:*** lay siege to. *See* ATTACK. **3.** To trouble persistently from or as if from all sides : badger, bedevil, beleaguer, besiege, harass, harry, hound, importune, pester, plague, solicit. *See* ATTACK. **4.** To disturb by repeated attacks : annoy, bait, bedevil, beleaguer, harass, harry, pester, plague, tease, torment, worry. *See* FEELINGS, PAIN. **5.** To shut in on all sides : begird, circle, compass, encircle, encompass, environ, gird, girdle, hedge, hem, ring[1], surround. *See* OPEN.

besetment *noun*
Something that annoys : aggravation, annoyance, bother, irritant, irritation, nuisance, peeve, plague, torment, vexation. *See* FEELINGS, PAIN.

besides *adverb*
In addition : additionally, also, further, furthermore, item, likewise, more, moreover, still, too, yet. ***Idioms:*** as well, to boot. *See* INCREASE.

besiege *verb*
1. To surround with hostile troops : beleaguer, beset, blockade, invest, siege. ***Idiom:*** lay siege to. *See* ATTACK. **2.** To surround and advance upon : close in, enclose, envelop, hedge, hem. *See* OPEN. **3.** To trouble persistently from or as if from all sides : badger, bedevil, beleaguer, beset, harass, harry, hound, importune, pester, plague, solicit. *See* ATTACK.

besiegement *noun*
A prolonged surrounding of an objective by hostile troops : beleaguerment, blockade, investment, siege. *See* ATTACK.

besmear *verb*
1. To spread with a greasy, sticky, or dirty substance : bedaub, dab[1], daub, plaster, smear, smirch, smudge. *See* PUT ON. **2.** To contaminate the reputation of : befoul, besmirch, bespatter, blacken, cloud, denigrate, dirty, smear, smudge, smut, soil, spatter, stain, sully, taint, tarnish. ***Idioms:*** give a black eye to, sling (*or* throw) mud on. *See* ATTACK, CLEAN.

besmirch *verb*
1. To contaminate the reputation of : befoul, besmear, bespatter, blacken, cloud, denigrate, dirty, smear, smudge, smut, soil, spatter, stain, sully, taint, tarnish. ***Idioms:*** give a black eye to, sling (*or* throw) mud on. *See* ATTACK, CLEAN. **2.** To make dirty : befoul, begrime, besoil, black, blacken, defile, dirty, smudge, smutch, soil, sully. *See* CLEAN.

besoil *verb*
To make dirty : befoul, begrime, besmirch, black, blacken, defile, dirty, smudge, smutch, soil, sully. *See* CLEAN.

besot *verb*
To muddle or stupefy with or as if with alcoholic drink : befuddle, fuddle. *See* DRUGS.

besotted *adjective*
Stupefied, excited, or muddled with alcoholic liquor : crapulent, crapulous, drunk, drunken, inebriate, inebriated, intoxicated, sodden, tipsy. *Informal:* cock-eyed, stewed. *Slang:* blind,

bombed, boozed, boozy, crocked, high, lit (up), loaded, looped, pickled, pixilated, plastered, potted, sloshed, smashed, soused, stinking, stinko, stoned, tight, zonked. ***Idioms:*** drunk as a skunk, half-seas over, high as a kite, in one's cups, three sheets in (*or* to) the wind. *See* DRUGS.

bespatter *verb*
1. To mark or soil with spots : blotch, spatter, splatter, splotch, spot. *See* MARKS. **2.** To hurl or scatter liquid upon : dash, slop, slosh, spatter, splash, splatter, spray, swash. *See* STRIKE. **3.** To contaminate the reputation of : befoul, besmear, besmirch, blacken, cloud, denigrate, dirty, smear, smudge, smut, soil, spatter, stain, sully, taint, tarnish. ***Idioms:*** give a black eye to, sling (*or* throw) mud on. *See* ATTACK, CLEAN.

bespeak *verb*
1. To give grounds for believing in the existence or presence of : argue, attest, betoken, indicate, mark, point to, testify, witness. *See* SHOW. **2.** To cause to be set aside, as for one's use, in advance : book, engage, reserve. *See* GET. **3.** *Archaic.* To talk to an audience formally : address, lecture, prelect, speak. *See* WORDS.

bespeckle *verb*
To mark with many small spots : besprinkle, dapple, dot, fleck, freckle, mottle, pepper, speck, speckle, sprinkle, stipple. *See* MARKS.

besprinkle *verb*
1. To scatter or release in drops or small particles : dust, powder, sprinkle. *See* STRIKE. **2.** To mark with many small spots : bespeckle, dapple, dot, fleck, freckle, mottle, pepper, speck, speckle, sprinkle, stipple. *See* MARKS.

best *adjective*
1. Surpassing all others in quality : optimal, optimum, superlative, unsurpassed. *See* BETTER. **2.** Much more than half : better[1], greater, larger, largest, most. *See* BETTER, BIG.

best *noun* **1.** The superlative or most preferable part of something : choice, cream, crème de la crème, elite, flower, pick, prize[1], top. ***Idioms:*** cream of the crop, flower of the flock, pick of the bunch (*or* crop) . *See* BETTER. **2.** Friendly greetings : regard (used in plural), respect (used in plural). *See* GREETING.

best *verb* **1.** To be greater or better than : better[1], exceed, excel, outdo, outmatch, outrun, outshine, outstrip, pass, surpass, top, transcend. *Informal:* beat. ***Idioms:*** go beyond, go one better. *See* BIG. **2.** To win a victory over, as in battle or a competition : beat, conquer, defeat, master, overcome, prevail against (*or* over), rout, subdue, subjugate, surmount, triumph over, vanquish, worst. *Informal:* trim, whip. *Slang:* ace, lick. ***Idioms:*** carry (*or* win) the day, get (*or* have) the best of, get (*or* have) the better of, go someone one better. *See* WIN.

bestain *verb*
To soil with foreign matter : discolor, smut, stain. *See* CLEAN, MARKS.

bestial *adjective*
Showing or suggesting a disposition to be violently destructive without scruple or restraint : barbarous, cruel, fell[2], feral, ferocious, fierce, inhuman, savage, truculent, vicious, wolfish. *See* KIND.

bestiality *noun*
1. Degrading, immoral acts or habits : corruption, depravity, flagitiousness, immorality, perversion, turpitude, vice, villainousness, villainy, wickedness. *See* CLEAN. **2.** A cruel act or an instance of cruel behavior : barbarity, brutality, cruelty, inhumanity, savagery, truculence, truculency. *See* ATTITUDE, KIND.

bestialize *verb*
To ruin utterly in character or quality : animalize, bastardize, brutalize, canker, corrupt, debase, debauch, demoralize, deprave, pervert, stain, vitiate, warp. *See* CLEAN, HELP.

bestow *verb*
1. To make a gift of : give (away), hand out, present[2]. *See* GIVE. **2.** To present as a gift to a charity or cause : contribute, donate, give, hand out. *See* GIVE. **3.** To give formally or officially : accord, award, confer, grant, present[2]. *See* GIVE. **4.** To provide with often temporary lodging : accommodate, bed (down), berth, billet, board, bunk[1], domicile, harbor, house, lodge, put up, quarter, room. *See* PROTECTION.

bestowal *noun*
The act of conferring, as of an honor : accordance, bestowment, conference, conferment, conferral, grant, presentation. *See* GIVE.

bestowment *noun*
The act of conferring, as of an honor : accordance, bestowal, conference, conferment, conferral, grant, presentation. *See* GIVE.

bestride *verb*
To sit or stand with a leg on each side of : straddle, stride. *See* POSTURE.

bet *noun*
1. Something risked on an uncertain outcome : ante, pot, stake (often used in plural), wager. *See* GAMBLING. **2.** A venture depending on chance : gamble, risk, speculation, wager. *See* GAMBLING.

bet *verb* **1.** To put up as a stake in a game or speculation : gamble, lay[1] (down), post[2], put, risk, stake, venture, wager. *Informal:* go. *See* GAMBLING. **2.** To make a bet : gamble, game, lay[1], play, wager. ***Idiom:*** put one's money on something. *See* GAMBLING.

bête noire *noun*
An object of extreme dislike : abhorrence, abomination, anathema, aversion, bugbear, detestation, execration, hate. *Informal:* horror. *See* LOVE.

bethink *verb*
To renew an image or thought in the mind : mind, recall, recollect, remember, reminisce, retain, revive, think. ***Idiom:*** bring to mind. *See* REMEMBER.

betide *verb*
1. To happen to one : befall, come. *See* HAPPEN. **2.** To take place : befall, come, come about, come off, develop, hap, happen, occur, pass, transpire. ***Idiom:*** come to pass. *See* HAPPEN.

betimes *adverb*
1. Before the expected time : ahead, beforehand, early. ***Idioms:*** ahead of time, in advance, with time to spare. *See* TIME. **2.** Once in a while; at times : intermittently, occasionally, periodically, sometimes, sporadically. ***Idioms:*** ever and again (*or* anon), now and again (*or* then). *See* CONTINUE.

betoken *verb*
To give grounds for believing in the existence or presence of : argue, attest, bespeak, indicate, mark, point to, testify, witness. *See* SHOW.

betray *verb*
1. To be treacherous to : double-cross. *Slang:* rat (on), sell out. ***Idiom:*** sell down the river. *See* TRUST. **2.** To disclose in a breach of confidence : blab, divulge, expose, give away, let out, reveal, tell, uncover, unveil. *Informal:* spill. *Archaic:* discover. ***Idioms:*** let slip, let the cat out of the bag, spill the beans, tell all. *See* SHOW. **3.** To cause to accept what is false, especially by trickery or misrepresentation : beguile, bluff, cozen, deceive, delude, double-cross, dupe, fool, hoodwink, humbug, mislead, take in, trick. *Informal:* bamboozle, have. *Slang:* four-flush. ***Idioms:*** lead astray, play false, pull the wool over someone's eyes, put something over on, take for a ride. *See* HONEST.

betrayal *noun*
An act of betraying : double cross, treachery. *Slang:* sellout. *See* TRUST.

betrayer *noun*
One who betrays : double-crosser, Judas, traitor. *Informal:* rat. *See* TRUST.

betrothal *noun*
The act or condition of being pledged to marry : engagement, espousal, troth. *See* MARRIAGE.

betrothed *adjective*
Pledged to marry : affianced, engaged, intended, plighted. *See* MARRIAGE.

betrothed *noun* A person to whom one is engaged to be married : fiancé, fiancée. *Informal:* intended. *See* MARRIAGE.

better[1] *adjective*
1. Of greater excellence than another : preferable, superior. *See* BETTER. **2.** Much more than half : best, greater, larger, largest, most. *See* BETTER, BIG.

better *adverb* To a greater extent : more. *See* BIG.

better *noun* **1.** One who stands above another in rank : elder, senior, superior. *Informal:* higher-up. *See* OVER. **2.** A dominating position, as in a conflict : advantage, bulge, draw, drop, edge, superiority, upper hand, vantage. *Informal:* inside track, jump. *See* OVER.

better *verb* **1.** To advance to a more desirable state : ameliorate, amend, help, improve, meliorate, upgrade. *See* HELP. **2.** To be greater or better than : best, exceed, excel, outdo, outmatch, outrun, outshine, outstrip, pass, surpass, top, transcend. *Informal:* beat. ***Idioms:*** go beyond, go one better. *See* BIG.

better[2] *noun* See **bettor.**

better half *noun*
Informal. A husband or wife : consort, mate, partner, spouse. *See* MARRIAGE.

betterment *noun*
1. The act of making better or the condition of being made better : amelioration, amendment, improvement, melioration, upgrade. *See* BETTER. **2.** Steady improvement, as of an individual or a society : amelioration, development, improvement, melioration, progress. *See* BETTER.

bettor also **better** *noun*
One who bets : gambler, gamester, player. *See* GAMBLING.

beveled *adjective*
Angled at a slant : bias, biased, diagonal, oblique, slanted, slanting. *See* STRAIGHT.

beverage *noun*
Any liquid that is fit for drinking : drink, drinkable, liquor, potable. *See* DRY.

bevy *noun*
A number of individuals making up or considered a unit : array, band², batch, body, bunch, bundle, clump, cluster, clutch², collection, group, knot, lot, party, set². *See* GROUP.

beware *verb*
To be careful : look out, mind, watch out. ***Idioms:*** be on guard, be on the lookout, keep an eye peeled, take care (*or* heed). *See* AWARENESS, CAREFUL.

bewilder *verb*
To cause to be unclear in mind or intent : addle, befuddle, confound, confuse, discombobulate, dizzy, fuddle, jumble, mix up, muddle, mystify, perplex, puzzle. *Informal:* throw. ***Idiom:*** make one's head reel (*or* swim *or* whirl). *See* CLEAR, FEELINGS.

bewilderedness *noun*
A stunned or bewildered condition : befuddlement, bewilderment, daze, discombobulation, fog, muddle, mystification, perplexity, puzzlement, stupefaction, stupor, trance. *See* AWARENESS.

bewilderment *noun*
A stunned or bewildered condition : befuddlement, bewilderedness, daze, discombobulation, fog, muddle, mystification, perplexity, puzzlement, stupefaction, stupor, trance. *See* AWARENESS.

bewitch *verb*
1. To act upon with or as if with magic : charm, enchant, enthrall, entrance², spell², spellbind, voodoo, witch. *See* PERSUASION.
2. To please greatly or irresistibly : beguile, captivate, charm, enchant, entrance², fascinate. *See* LIKE.

bewitching *adjective*
1. Pleasing to the eye or mind : attractive, enchanting, engaging, enticing, fascinating, fetching, glamorous, lovely, prepossessing, pretty, sweet, taking, tempting, winning, winsome. *See* LIKE. **2.** Tending to seduce : alluring, come-hither, enticing, inveigling, inviting, luring, seductive, siren, tempting, witching. *See* LIKE, PERSUASION, SEX.

bias *noun*
1. An inclination for or against that inhibits impartial judgment : one-sidedness, partiality, partisanship, prejudice, prepossession, tendentiousness. *See* AFFECT, LIKE, STRAIGHT.
2. An inclination to something : bent, cast, disposition, leaning, partiality, penchant, predilection, predisposition, proclivity, proneness, propensity, squint, tendency, trend, turn. *See* APPROACH, LIKE.

bias *adjective* Angled at a slant : beveled, biased, diagonal, oblique, slanted, slanting. *See* STRAIGHT.

bias *verb* **1.** To cause to have a prejudiced view : jaundice, prejudice, prepossess, warp. *See* AFFECT, STRAIGHT. **2.** To direct (material) to the interests of a particular group : skew, slant. *Informal:* angle². *See* STRAIGHT.

biased also **biassed** *adjective*
1. Exhibiting bias : one-sided, partial, partisan, prejudiced, prejudicial, prepossessed, tendentious. *See* LIKE, STRAIGHT. **2.** Angled at a slant : beveled, bias, diagonal, oblique, slanted, slanting. *See* STRAIGHT.

biassed *adjective* See **biased.**

bibelot *noun*
A small showy article : bauble, gewgaw, gimcrack, knickknack, novelty, toy, trifle, trinket, whatnot. *See* THING.

bibulous *adjective*
Having a capacity to soak up : absorbent, absorptive, assimilative. *See* DRY.

bicker *verb*
To engage in a quarrel : argue, contend, dispute, fight, quarrel, quibble, spat, squabble, tiff, wrangle. *Informal:* hassle, tangle. ***Idioms:*** cross swords, have it out, have words, lock horns. *See* CONFLICT.

bicker *noun* A discussion, often heated, in which a difference of opinion is expressed : altercation, argument, clash, contention, controversy, debate, difficulty, disagreement, dispute, fight, polemic, quarrel, run-in, spat, squabble, tiff, word (used in plural), wrangle. *Informal:* hassle, rhubarb, tangle. *See* CONFLICT.

bid *verb*
1. To give orders to : charge, command, direct, enjoin, instruct, order, tell. *See* OVER, WORDS.
2. To request that someone take part in or be present at a particular occasion : ask, invite. *See* WARN. **3.** To make an offer of : offer. *Informal:* go. *See* OFFER.

bid *noun* **1.** Something offered : offer, proffer, proposal, tender². *See* OFFER. **2.** A spoken or written request for someone to take part or be present : invitation. *Informal:* invite. *See* WARN.

biddable *adjective*
Willing to carry out the wishes of others : amenable, compliant, conformable, docile, obedient, submissive, supple, tractable. *See* RESIST.

biddie *noun* See **biddy.**

bidding *noun*
An authoritative indication to be obeyed : behest, charge, command, commandment, dictate,

direction, directive, injunction, instruction (often used in plural), mandate, order, word. *See* OVER, WORDS.

biddy also **biddie** *noun*
Slang. An ugly, frightening old woman : beldam, crone, hag, witch. *Archaic:* trot. *See* BEAUTIFUL.

bide *verb*
1. To continue to be in a place : abide, linger, remain, stay[1], tarry, wait. *Informal:* stick around. ***Idiom:*** stay put. *See* CONTINUE. **2.** To stop temporarily and remain, as if reluctant to leave : abide, linger, pause, stay[1], tarry, wait. *See* CONTINUE.

biff *verb*
Informal. To deliver a powerful blow to suddenly and sharply : bash, catch, clout, hit, knock, pop[1], slam, slog, slug[3], smash, smite, sock, strike, swat, thwack, whack, wham, whop. *Informal:* bop, clip[1], wallop. *Slang:* belt, conk, paste. ***Idioms:*** let someone have it, sock it to someone. *See* ATTACK, STRIKE.
biff *noun Informal.* A sudden sharp, powerful stroke : bang, blow[2], clout, crack, hit, lick, pound, slug[3], sock, swat, thwack, welt, whack, wham, whop. *Informal:* bash, bop, clip[1], wallop. *Slang:* belt, conk, paste. *See* ATTACK, STRIKE.

biform *adjective*
Composed of two parts or things : binary, double, dual, duple, duplex, duplicate, geminate, twofold. *See* PART.

bifurcate *verb*
To separate into branches or branchlike parts : branch (out), diverge, divide, fork, ramify, subdivide. *See* PART.

big *adjective*
1. Notably above average in amount, size, or scope : considerable, extensive, good, great, healthy, large, large-scale, sizable. *Informal:* tidy. *See* BIG. **2.** Having reached full growth and development : adult, developed, full-blown, full-fledged, full-grown, grown, grown-up, mature, ripe. ***Idiom:*** of age. *See* YOUTH. **3.** Carrying a developing fetus within the uterus : enceinte, expectant, expecting, gravid, parturient, pregnant. *Slang:* gone. *Archaic:* great. ***Idioms:*** in a family way, with child. *See* REPRODUCTION. **4.** Full to the point of flowing over : awash, brimful, brimming, overflowing. *See* BIG, RICH. **5.** Having great significance : consequential, considerable, historic, important, large, material, meaningful, monumental, significant, substantial. *See* IMPORTANT. **6.** Willing to give of oneself and one's possessions : big-hearted, generous, great-hearted, large-hearted, magnanimous, unselfish. *See* GIVE.

Big Brother *noun*
An absolute ruler, especially one who is harsh and oppressive : despot, dictator, führer, man on horseback, oppressor, strongman, totalitarian, tyrant. *See* OVER.

biggish *adjective*
Somewhat big : goodly, largish, respectable, sizable. *See* BIG.

bighead *noun*
Informal. An exaggerated belief in one's own importance : egoism, egotism, self-importance. *Informal:* bigheadedness, swelled head. *See* SELF-LOVE.

bigheaded *adjective*
Informal. Thinking too highly of oneself : conceited, egoistic, egoistical, egotistic, egotistical, narcissistic, vain, vainglorious. *Informal:* stuck-up, swellheaded. *See* SELF-LOVE.

bigheadedness *noun*
Informal. An exaggerated belief in one's own importance : egoism, egotism, self-importance. *Informal:* bighead, swelled head. *See* SELF-LOVE.

big-hearted *adjective*
Willing to give of oneself and one's possessions : big, generous, great-hearted, large-hearted, magnanimous, unselfish. *See* GIVE.

big-heartedness *noun*
The quality or state of being generous : bounteousness, bountifulness, freehandedness, generosity, generousness, great-heartedness, large-heartedness, lavishness, liberality, magnanimity, magnanimousness, munificence, openhandedness, unselfishness, unsparingness. *See* GIVE.

big house *noun*
Slang. A place for the confinement of persons in lawful detention : brig, house of correction, jail, keep, penitentiary, prison. *Informal:* lockup, pen[3]. *Slang:* can, clink, cooler, coop, hoosegow, joint, jug, pokey[1], slammer, stir[2]. *Chiefly Regional:* calaboose. *See* FREE.

bight *noun*
A body of water partly enclosed by land but having a wide outlet to the sea : bay[1], cove, inlet. *See* TERRITORY.

big-league *adjective*
Informal. Being among the leaders in one's field : blue-chip, major, major-league. *Informal:* bigtime, heavyweight. *See* IMPORTANT.

big name *noun*
Informal. A famous person : celebrity, hero, lion, luminary, name, notable, personage, personality. *See* KNOWLEDGE.

bigness *noun*
The quality or state of being large in amount, extent, or importance : amplitude, greatness, largeness, magnitude, sizableness, size. *See* BIG.

bigoted *adjective*
Not tolerant of the beliefs or opinions of others, for example : close-minded, hidebound, illiberal, intolerant, narrow-minded. *See* ACCEPT.

bigotry *noun*
Irrational suspicion or hatred of a particular group, race, or religion : intolerance, prejudice. *See* LIKE.

big shot *noun*
Slang. An important, influential person : character, dignitary, eminence, leader, lion, nabob, notability, notable, personage. *Informal:* big-timer, heavyweight, somebody, someone, VIP. *Slang:* big wheel, bigwig, muckamuck. *See* IMPORTANT.

bigtime or **big-time** *adjective*
Informal. Being among the leaders in one's field : blue-chip, major, major-league. *Informal:* big-league, heavyweight. *See* IMPORTANT.

big-timer *noun*
Informal. An important, influential person : character, dignitary, eminence, leader, lion, nabob, notability, notable, personage. *Informal:* heavyweight, somebody, someone, VIP. *Slang:* big shot, big wheel, bigwig, muckamuck. *See* IMPORTANT.

big wheel *noun*
Slang. An important, influential person : character, dignitary, eminence, leader, lion, nabob, notability, notable, personage. *Informal:* big-timer, heavyweight, somebody, someone, VIP. *Slang:* big shot, bigwig, muckamuck. *See* IMPORTANT.

bigwig *noun*
Slang. An important, influential person : character, dignitary, eminence, leader, lion, nabob, notability, notable, personage. *Informal:* big-timer, heavyweight, somebody, someone, VIP. *Slang:* big shot, big wheel, muckamuck. *See* IMPORTANT.

bilge *noun*
Slang. Something that does not have or make sense : balderdash, blather, bunkum, claptrap, drivel, garbage, idiocy, nonsense, piffle, poppycock, rigmarole, rubbish, tomfoolery, trash, twaddle. *Informal:* tommyrot. *Slang:* applesauce, baloney, bull[1], bunk[2], crap, hooey, malarkey. *See* KNOWLEDGE.

bilk *verb*
To get money or something else from by deceitful trickery : cheat, cozen, defraud, gull, mulct, rook, swindle, victimize. *Informal:* chisel, flimflam, take, trim. *Slang:* diddle[1], do, gyp, stick, sting. *See* HONEST.

bilk *noun* A person who cheats : cheat, cheater, cozener, defrauder, rook, sharper, swindler, trickster, victimizer. *Informal:* chiseler, crook, flimflammer. *Slang:* diddler, gyp, gypper. *See* HONEST.

bill[1] *noun*
1. A precise list of fees or charges : account, check, invoice, reckoning, statement. *Informal:* tab. *See* PAY. **2.** A document, such as a list or an outline, that gives, for example, the order of events in a public performance or the chief features of a stock offering : program, prospectus, syllabus. *See* PLANNED, WORDS. **3.** A usually public posting that conveys a message : billboard, notice, placard, poster, sign. *See* SHOW. **4.** The formal product of a legislative or judicial body : act, assize, enactment, law, legislation, lex, measure, statute. *See* LAW.

bill *verb* To present a statement of fees or charges to : invoice. *See* MONEY, REQUEST.

bill[2] *noun*
1. The horny projection forming a bird's jaws : beak. *See* MOUTH. **2.** The projecting rim on the front of a cap : brim, peak, visor. *See* CONVEX, PROTECTION.

billboard *noun*
A usually public posting that conveys a message : bill[1], notice, placard, poster, sign. *See* SHOW.

billet *noun*
A post of employment : appointment, berth, job, office, place, position, situation, slot, spot. *Slang:* gig. *See* PLACE.

billet *verb* To provide with often temporary lodging : accommodate, bed (down), berth, bestow, board, bunk[1], domicile, harbor, house, lodge, put up, quarter, room. *See* PROTECTION.

billingsgate *noun*
Harsh, often insulting language : abuse, contumely, invective, obloquy, railing, revilement, reviling, scurrility, scurrilousness, vituperation. *See* PRAISE.

binary *adjective*
Composed of two parts or things : biform, double, dual, duple, duplex, duplicate, geminate, twofold. *See* PART.

bind *verb*
1. To make fast or firmly fixed, as by means of a cord or rope : fasten, knot, secure, tie, tie up. *See* KEEP, TIGHTEN. **2.** To apply therapeutic materials to (a wound) : bandage, dress. *See* CARE FOR. **3.** To be morally bound to do : charge, commit, obligate, pledge. *See* OBLIGATION. **4.** To unite or be united in a relationship : affiliate, ally, associate, combine, conjoin, connect, join, link, relate. *See* CONNECT.
bind *noun Informal.* A difficult, often embarrassing situation or condition : box[1], corner, deep water, difficulty, dilemma, Dutch, fix, hole, hot spot, hot water, jam, plight[1], predicament, quagmire, scrape, soup, trouble. *Informal:* pickle, spot. *See* EASY.

bine *noun*
A young stemlike growth arising from a plant : offshoot, runner, shoot, sprig, sprout, tendril. *See* KIN.

binge *noun*
1. A drinking bout : brannigan, carousal, carouse, drunk, spree. *Slang:* bat[2], bender, booze, jag, tear[1]. *See* DRUGS, RESTRAINT. **2.** A period of uncontrolled self-indulgence : fling, orgy, rampage, spree. *Slang:* jag. *See* RESTRAINT.

bird *noun*
Slang. Any of various derisive sounds of disapproval : boo, catcall, hiss, hoot. *Slang:* Bronx cheer, raspberry, razz. *See* SOUNDS.

birdbrained *adjective*
Slang. Given to lighthearted silliness : emptyheaded, featherbrained, flighty, frivolous, frothy, giddy, harebrained, lighthearted, scatterbrained, silly. *Informal:* gaga. *Slang:* dizzy. *See* ABILITY.

bird-dog also **birddog** *verb*
Informal. To keep (another) under surveillance by moving along behind : dog, follow, shadow, track, trail. *Informal:* tail. *See* PRECEDE.

birth *noun*
1. The act or process of bringing forth young : accouchement, birthing, childbearing, childbirth, delivery, labor, lying-in, parturition, travail. *See* START. **2.** One's ancestors or their character or one's ancestral derivation : ancestry, blood, bloodline, descent, extraction, family, genealogy, line, lineage, origin, parentage, pedigree, seed, stock. *See* KIN, PRECEDE.
3. Noble rank or status by birth : blood, blue blood, nobility, noblesse. *See* KIN, OVER.
4. The initial stage of a developmental process : beginning, commencement, dawn, genesis, inception, nascence, nascency, onset, opening, origin, outset, spring, start. *See* START.
birth *verb Chiefly Regional.* To give birth to : bear, bring forth, deliver, have. ***Idiom:*** be brought abed (*or* to bed) of. *See* RICH.

birthing *noun*
The act or process of bringing forth young : accouchement, birth, childbearing, childbirth, delivery, labor, lying-in, parturition, travail. *See* START.

birthright *noun*
1. A privilege granted a person, as by virtue of birth : appanage, perquisite, prerogative, right. *Law:* droit. *See* OWNED. **2.** Any special privilege accorded a firstborn : heritage, inheritance, legacy, patrimony. *See* OWNED.

bistered *adjective*
Of a complexion tending toward brown or black : black-a-vised, brunet, dark, dusky, swarthy. *See* COLORS.

bit[1] *noun*
1. A tiny amount : crumb, dab[1], dash, dot, dram, drop, fragment, grain, iota, jot, minim, mite, modicum, molecule, ort, ounce, particle, scrap[1], scruple, shred, smidgen, speck, tittle, trifle, whit. *Chiefly British:* spot. *See* BIG. **2.** A small portion of food : crumb, morsel, mouthful, piece. *Informal:* bite. *See* BIG. **3.** A usually brief detail of news or information : item, paragraph, piece, squib, story. *See* WORDS. **4.** A rather short period : space, spell[3], time, while. *See* BIG. **5.** *Informal.* A particular kind of activity : *Slang:* routine. *See* ACTION.

bit[2] *noun*
An instrument or means of restraining : brake, bridle, leash, restraint, snaffle. *See* RESTRAINT.
bit *verb* To control, restrict, or arrest : brake, bridle, check, constrain, curb, hold, hold back, hold down, hold in, inhibit, keep, keep back, pull in, rein (back, in, *or* up), restrain. *See* RESTRAINT.

bitch *verb*
Slang. To express negative feelings, especially of dissatisfaction or resentment : complain, grouch, grump, whine. *Informal:* crab, gripe, grouse, kick. *Slang:* beef, bellyache. *See* FEELINGS, HAPPY.

bitchy *adjective*
Slang. Characterized by intense ill will or spite : black, despiteful, evil, hateful, malevolent, malicious, malign, malignant, mean[2], nasty, poisonous, spiteful, venomous, vicious, wicked. *See* ATTITUDE.

bite *verb*
1. To seize, as food, with the teeth : champ,

chomp, gnash, gnaw. *See* ATTACK, INGESTION. **2.** To consume gradually, as by chemical reaction or friction : corrode, eat, erode, gnaw, wear, wear away. *See* ATTACK. **3.** To feel or cause to feel a sensation of heat or discomfort : burn, smart, sting. *See* PAIN.

bite *noun* **1.** A cutting quality : edge, incisiveness, keenness, sharpness, sting. *See* SHARP. **2.** *Informal.* A small portion of food : bit[1], crumb, morsel, mouthful, piece. *See* BIG. **3.** A light meal : morsel, snack. *See* INGESTION.

biting *adjective*
So sharp as to cause mental pain : acerbic, acid, acidic, acrid, astringent, caustic, corrosive, cutting, mordacious, mordant, pungent, scathing, sharp, slashing, stinging, trenchant, truculent, vitriolic. *See* ATTACK, RESPECT.

bitter *adjective*
1. Having a noticeably sharp pungent taste or smell : acerbic, acrid, harsh, sour. *See* TASTE. **2.** Causing sharp, often prolonged discomfort : brutal, hard, harsh, rough, severe. *See* COMFORT. **3.** Difficult to accept : distasteful, indigestible, painful, unpalatable. *See* LIKE. **4.** Bitingly hostile : acrimonious, embittered, hard, rancorous, resentful, virulent. *See* ATTITUDE, LOVE.

bitterness *noun*
The quality or state of feeling bitter : acrimony, embitterment, gall[1], rancor, rancorousness, resentfulness, resentment, virulence, virulency. *See* FEELINGS.

bizarre *adjective*
1. Deviating from the customary : cranky, curious, eccentric, erratic, freakish, idiosyncratic, odd, outlandish, peculiar, quaint, queer, quirky, singular, strange, unnatural, unusual, weird. *Slang:* kooky, screwball. *British Slang:* rum, rummy[2]. *See* USUAL. **2.** Conceived or done with no reference to reality or common sense : antic, fantastic, fantastical, far-fetched, grotesque. *See* TRUE, USUAL.

blab *verb*
1. To disclose in a breach of confidence : betray, divulge, expose, give away, let out, reveal, tell, uncover, unveil. *Informal:* spill. *Archaic:* discover. ***Idioms:*** let slip, let the cat out of the bag, spill the beans, tell all. *See* SHOW. **2.** To engage in or spread gossip : gossip, noise, rumor, talk, tattle, tittle-tattle, whisper. ***Idioms:*** tell tales, tell tales out of school. *See* WORDS.

blab *noun* **1.** A person habitually engaged in idle talk about others : gossip, gossiper, gossipmonger, newsmonger, rumormonger, scandalmonger, tabby, talebearer, taleteller, tattle, tattler, tattletale, telltale, whisperer. *Slang:* yenta. *See* WORDS. **2.** Incessant and usually inconsequential talk : babble, blabber, chat, chatter, chitchat, jabber, palaver, prate, prattle, small talk. *Slang:* gab, gas, yak. *See* WORDS.

blabber *verb*
To talk volubly, persistently, and usually inconsequentially : babble, chatter, chitchat, clack, jabber, palaver, prate, prattle, rattle (on), run on. *Informal:* go on, spiel. *Slang:* gab, gas, jaw, yak. ***Idioms:*** run off at the mouth, shoot the breeze (*or* bull). *See* WORDS.

blabber *noun* Incessant and usually inconsequential talk : babble, blab, chat, chatter, chitchat, jabber, palaver, prate, prattle, small talk. *Slang:* gab, gas, yak. *See* WORDS.

blabby *adjective*
Inclined to gossip : gossipy, talebearing, taletelling. *See* WORDS.

black *adjective*
1. Of the darkest achromatic visual value : ebon, ebony, inky, jet[1], jetty, onyx, pitch-black, pitchy, sable, sooty. *See* COLORS. **2.** Having little or no light : dark, pitch-dark. *See* LIGHT. **3.** Covered or stained with or as if with dirt or other impurities : dirty, filthy, grimy, grubby, smutty, soiled, unclean, uncleanly. *See* CLEAN. **4.** Morally objectionable : bad, evil, immoral, iniquitous, peccant, reprobate, sinful, vicious, wicked, wrong. *See* RIGHT. **5.** Dark and depressing : bleak, blue, cheerless, dark, desolate, dismal, dreary, gloomy, glum, joyless, somber, tenebrific. *See* HAPPY, LIGHT. **6.** Characterized by intense ill will or spite : despiteful, evil, hateful, malevolent, malicious, malign, malignant, mean[2], nasty, poisonous, spiteful, venomous, vicious, wicked. *Slang:* bitchy. *See* ATTITUDE.

black *verb* To make dirty : befoul, begrime, besmirch, besoil, blacken, defile, dirty, smudge, smutch, soil, sully. *See* CLEAN.

black out *verb* **1.** To suffer temporary lack of consciousness : faint, keel over, pass out, swoon. *See* AWARENESS. **2.** To keep from being published or transmitted : ban, censor, hush (up), stifle, suppress. ***Idiom:*** keep (*or* put) a lid on. *See* SHOW.

black-a-vised *adjective*
Of a complexion tending toward brown or black : bistered, brunet, dark, dusky, swarthy. *See* COLORS.

blackball *verb*
1. To prevent or forbid authoritatively : negative, turn down, veto. *Slang:* nix. ***Idiom:*** turn thumbs down on. *See* ACCEPT. **2.** To exclude

from normal social or professional activities : blacklist, boycott, ostracize, shut out. *See* ACCEPT.

blacken *verb*
1. To make dirty : befoul, begrime, besmirch, besoil, black, defile, dirty, smudge, smutch, soil, sully. *See* CLEAN. **2.** To contaminate the reputation of : befoul, besmear, besmirch, bespatter, cloud, denigrate, dirty, smear, smudge, smut, soil, spatter, stain, sully, taint, tarnish. ***Idioms:*** give a black eye to, sling (*or* throw) mud on. *See* ATTACK, CLEAN.

black eye *noun*
1. A bruise surrounding the eye : *Informal:* mouse. *Slang:* shiner. *See* HEALTH, HELP. **2.** A mark of discredit or disgrace : blemish, blot, onus, spot, stain, stigma, taint, tarnish. *Archaic:* attaint. ***Idiom:*** a blot on one's escutcheon. *See* MARKS, RESPECT.

blackish *adjective*
Somewhat black : dark, dusky. *See* COLORS.

blackjack *verb*
To compel by pressure or threats : coerce, dragoon, force. *Informal:* hijack, strong-arm. *See* PERSUASION.

blacklist *verb*
To exclude from normal social or professional activities : blackball, boycott, ostracize, shut out. *See* ACCEPT.

black look *noun*
The act of wrinkling the brow, as in thought, puzzlement, or displeasure : frown, glower, lower[1], scowl. *See* EXPRESS.

blackout *noun*
A temporary loss of consciousness : faint, swoon. *Pathology:* syncope. *See* AWARENESS.

black out *verb* See **black.**

blade *noun*
The cutting part of a sharp instrument : edge. *See* SHARP.

blamable also **blameable** *adjective*
Deserving blame : blameful, blameworthy, censurable, culpable, guilty, reprehensible. ***Idiom:*** at fault. *See* PRAISE.

blame *verb*
1. To find fault with : censure, criticize, fault, rap[1]. *Informal:* cut up, pan. *Slang:* knock. *See* PRAISE. **2.** To ascribe (a misdeed or an error, for example) to : affix, assign, fasten, fix, impute, pin on, place. *See* GIVE.
blame *noun* **1.** Responsibility for an error or crime : culpability, fault, guilt, onus. *See* START. **2.** A comment expressing fault : censure, condemnation, criticism, denunciation, reprehension, reprobation. *Informal:* pan. *Slang:* knock. *See* PRAISE.

blameable *adjective* See **blamable.**

blamed *adjective*
Informal. So annoying or detestable as to deserve condemnation : accursed, blasted, blessed, bloody, confounded, cursed, damn, darn, execrable, infernal. *Informal:* damned. *Chiefly British:* blooming, ruddy. *See* LIKE.

blameful *adjective*
Deserving blame : blamable, blameworthy, censurable, culpable, guilty, reprehensible. ***Idiom:*** at fault. *See* PRAISE.

blameless *adjective*
1. Free from guilt or blame : faultless, guiltless, harmless, innocent, irreproachable, lily-white, unblamable. *Slang:* clean. ***Idiom:*** in the clear. *See* RIGHT. **2.** Beyond reproach : exemplary, good, irreprehensible, irreproachable, lily-white, unblamable. *See* RIGHT.

blameworthy *adjective*
Deserving blame : blamable, blameful, censurable, culpable, guilty, reprehensible. ***Idiom:*** at fault. *See* PRAISE.

blanch also **blench** *verb*
To lose normal coloration; turn pale : bleach, etiolate, pale, wan. *See* COLORS.

bland *adjective*
1. Effortlessly gracious and tactful in social manner : smooth, suave, urbane. *See* STYLE.
2. Lacking an appetizing flavor : flat, flavorless, insipid, tasteless, unsavory. *See* TASTE.
3. Lacking the qualities requisite for spiritedness and originality : innocuous, insipid, jejune, namby-pamby, vapid, washy, waterish, watery. *Informal:* wishy-washy. *See* EXCITE, GOOD.
4. Without definite or distinctive characteristics : colorless, indistinctive, neutral. *See* STRONG.

blandish *verb*
1. To persuade or try to persuade by gentle persistent urging or flattery : cajole, coax, honey, wheedle. *Informal:* soft-soap, sweet-talk. *See* PERSUASION. **2.** To compliment excessively and ingratiatingly : adulate, butter up, flatter, honey, slaver. *Informal:* soft-soap, sweet-talk. *See* PRAISE.

blandishment *noun*
Excessive, ingratiating praise : adulation, blarney, flattery, incense[2], oil, slaver. *Informal:* soft soap. ***Idiom:*** honeyed words. *See* PRAISE.

blandness *noun*
1. A lack of excitement, liveliness, or interest : asepticism, colorlessness, drabness, dreariness, dryness, dullness, flatness, flavorlessness, insi-

pidity, insipidness, jejuneness, lifelessness, sterileness, sterility, stodginess, vapidity, vapidness, weariness. *See* EXCITE. **2.** The state or quality of being insipid : innocuousness, insipidity, insipidness, jejuneness, vapidity, vapidness, washiness, wateriness. *Informal:* wishy-washiness. *See* EXCITE, TASTE.

blank *adjective*
1. Containing nothing : bare, clear, empty, vacant, vacuous, void. *See* FULL. **2.** Lacking expression : deadpan, expressionless, inexpressive, pokerfaced. *See* SHOW. **3.** Lacking intelligent thought or content : empty, empty-headed, inane, vacant, vacuous. *See* FULL.

blanket *verb*
To extend over the surface of : cap, cover, overlay, spread. *See* PUT ON.

blankness *noun*
1. Total lack of ideas, meaning, or substance : barrenness, emptiness, hollowness, inanity, vacancy, vacuity, vacuousness. *See* FULL. **2.** A desolate sense of loss : desolation, emptiness, hollowness, vacuum, void. *See* FULL.

blare *verb*
To proclaim in a blatantly startling way : scream, shout, shriek. *See* SHOW.

blaring *adjective*
Marked by extremely high volume and intensity of sound : deafening, earsplitting, loud, roaring, stentorian. *See* SOUNDS.

blarney *noun*
Excessive, ingratiating praise : adulation, blandishment, flattery, incense[2], oil, slaver. *Informal:* soft soap. ***Idiom:*** honeyed words. *See* PRAISE.

blaspheme *verb*
To use profane or obscene language : curse, damn, swear. *Informal:* cuss. *See* DECENT, SACRED, WORDS.

blasphemous *adjective*
Showing irreverence and contempt for something sacred : profane, sacrilegious. *See* SACRED.

blasphemy *noun*
1. An act of disrespect or impiety toward something regarded as sacred : desecration, profanation, sacrilege, violation. *See* SACRED. **2.** A profane or obscene term : curse, epithet, expletive, oath, swearword. *Informal:* cuss. *See* DECENT, SACRED, WORDS.

blast *noun*
1. A natural movement or current of air : air, blow[1], breeze, gust, wind[1], zephyr. *Archaic:* gale. *See* BREATH. **2.** An earsplitting, explosive noise : bang, boom, roar, thunder. *See* SOUNDS. **3.** A violent release of confined energy, usually accompanied by a loud sound and shock waves : blowout, blowup, burst, detonation, explosion, fulmination. *See* EXPLOSION. **4.** *Slang.* A big, exuberant party : celebration, shindig, shindy. *Slang:* bash, blowout. *See* GROUP, RESTRAINT, WORK.
blast *verb* **1.** To release or cause to release energy suddenly and violently, especially with a loud noise : blow[1] (up), burst, detonate, explode, fire, fulminate, go off, touch off. *See* EXPLOSION. **2.** To make an earsplitting explosive noise : bang, boom, roar, thunder. *See* SOUNDS. **3.** To spoil or destroy : blight, dash, nip[1]. *See* HELP.

blasted *adjective*
So annoying or detestable as to deserve condemnation : accursed, blessed, bloody, confounded, cursed, damn, darn, execrable, infernal. *Informal:* blamed, damned. *Chiefly British:* blooming, ruddy. *See* LIKE.

blatant *adjective*
1. Offensively loud and insistent : boisterous, clamorous, obstreperous, strident, vociferous. *Informal:* loudmouthed. *See* SOUNDS.
2. Characterized by or done without shame : bald-faced, barefaced, brazen, brazenfaced, shameless, unabashed, unblushing. *Informal:* brassy. *See* COURTESY, RESPECT, RIGHT.

blather *verb*
To talk rapidly, incoherently, or indistinctly : babble, chatter, gabble, gibber, jabber, prate, prattle. *See* WORDS.
blather *noun* **1.** Unintelligible or foolish talk : babble, blatherskite, double talk, gabble, gibberish, jabber, jabberwocky, jargon, nonsense, prate, prattle, twaddle. *See* WORDS. **2.** Something that does not have or make sense : balderdash, bunkum, claptrap, drivel, garbage, idiocy, nonsense, piffle, poppycock, rigmarole, rubbish, tomfoolery, trash, twaddle. *Informal:* tommyrot. *Slang:* applesauce, baloney, bilge, bull[1], bunk[2], crap, hooey, malarkey. *See* KNOWLEDGE.

blatherskite *noun*
Unintelligible or foolish talk : babble, blather, double talk, gabble, gibberish, jabber, jabberwocky, jargon, nonsense, prate, prattle, twaddle. *See* WORDS.

blaze[1] *noun*
1. The visible signs of combustion : conflagration, fire, flame, flare-up. *See* HOT. **2.** An intense blinding light : dazzle, glare. *See* LIGHT.
blaze *verb* **1.** To undergo combustion : burn, combust, flame, flare. *See* HOT. **2.** To emit a

bright light : beam, burn, gleam, glow, incandesce, radiate, shine. *See* LIGHT. **3.** To be projected with blinding intensity : beat down, glare. *See* LIGHT.

blaze² *verb*
To make (information) generally known : advertise, blazon, broadcast, bruit, circulate, disseminate, noise, promulgate, propagate, spread. ***Idioms:*** spread far and wide, spread the word. *See* KNOWLEDGE.

blazing *adjective*
Fired with intense feeling : ardent, burning, dithyrambic, fervent, fervid, fiery, flaming, glowing, heated, hot-blooded, impassioned, passionate, perfervid, red-hot, scorching, torrid. *See* FEELINGS.

blazon *verb*
To make (information) generally known : advertise, blaze², broadcast, bruit, circulate, disseminate, noise, promulgate, propagate, spread. ***Idioms:*** spread far and wide, spread the word. *See* KNOWLEDGE.

bleach *verb*
To lose normal coloration; turn pale : blanch, etiolate, pale, wan. *See* COLORS.

bleak *adjective*
1. Dark and depressing : black, blue, cheerless, dark, desolate, dismal, dreary, gloomy, glum, joyless, somber, tenebrific. *See* HAPPY, LIGHT. **2.** Cold and forbidding : austere, dour, grim, hard, harsh, severe, stark. *See* ATTITUDE, HOT.

blear *verb*
To make dim or indistinct : becloud, bedim, befog, blur, cloud, dim, dull, eclipse, fog, gloom, mist, obfuscate, obscure, overcast, overshadow, shadow. *See* CLEAR.
blear *adjective* Not clearly perceived or perceptible : bleary, cloudy, dim, faint, foggy, fuzzy, hazy, indefinite, indistinct, misty, obscure, shadowy, unclear, undistinct, vague. *See* CLEAR.

bleary *adjective*
1. Not clearly perceived or perceptible : blear, cloudy, dim, faint, foggy, fuzzy, hazy, indefinite, indistinct, misty, obscure, shadowy, unclear, undistinct, vague. *See* CLEAR. **2.** Extremely tired : dead, drained, exhausted, fatigued, rundown, spent, tired out, wearied, weariful, weary, worn-down, worn-out. *Informal:* beat, bushed, tuckered (out). *Slang:* done in, fagged (out), pooped (out). ***Idioms:*** all in, ready to drop. *See* HEALTH, TIRED.

bleed *verb*
To flow or leak out or emit something slowly : exude, leach, ooze, percolate, seep, transpire, transude, weep. *See* MOVE, SOLID.

blemish *verb*
To spoil the soundness or perfection of : damage, detract from, disserve, flaw, harm, hurt, impair, injure, mar, prejudice, tarnish, vitiate. *See* BETTER, HELP.
blemish *noun* **1.** Something that mars the appearance or causes inadequacy or failure : bug, defect, fault, flaw, imperfection, shortcoming. *See* BEAUTIFUL, BETTER, HELP. **2.** A mark of discredit or disgrace : black eye, blot, onus, spot, stain, stigma, taint, tarnish. *Archaic:* attaint. ***Idiom:*** a blot on (one's) escutcheon. *See* MARKS, RESPECT.

blench¹ *verb*
To draw away involuntarily, usually out of fear or disgust : cringe, flinch, quail, recoil, shrink, shy¹, start, wince. *See* APPROACH, SEEK.

blench² *verb* See **blanch.**

blend *verb*
1. To put together into one mass so that the constituent parts are more or less homogeneous : admix, amalgamate, commingle, commix, fuse, intermingle, intermix, merge, mingle, mix, stir¹. *See* ASSEMBLE. **2.** To combine and adapt in order to attain a particular effect : arrange, coordinate, harmonize, integrate, orchestrate, synthesize, unify. *See* BEAUTIFUL.
blend *noun* Something produced by mixing : admixture, amalgam, amalgamation, commixture, fusion, merger, mix, mixture. *See* ASSEMBLE.

bless *verb*
To make sacred by a religious rite : consecrate, hallow, sanctify. *See* RELIGION.

blessed *adjective*
1. Regarded with particular reverence or respect : hallowed, holy, sacred, sacrosanct. *See* RELIGION, RESPECT. **2.** So annoying or detestable as to deserve condemnation : accursed, blasted, bloody, confounded, cursed, damn, darn, execrable, infernal. *Informal:* blamed, damned. *Chiefly British:* blooming, ruddy. *See* LIKE.

blessedness *noun*
1. The quality of being holy or sacred : holiness, sacredness, sacrosanctity, sanctity. *See* RELIGION. **2.** A condition of supreme well-being and good spirits : beatitude, bliss, cheer, cheerfulness, felicity, gladness, happiness, joy, joyfulness. *See* HAPPY.

blessing *noun*
1. A short prayer said at meals : benediction, grace, thanks, thanksgiving. *See* GRATEFUL,

RELIGION. **2.** Something beneficial : advantage, avail, benefit, boon[1], favor, gain, profit. *See* HELP.

blight *verb*
To spoil or destroy : blast, dash, nip[1]. *See* HELP.

blind *adjective*
1. Without the sense of sight : eyeless, sightless, unseeing. *See* SEE. **2.** Unwilling or unable to perceive : dull, purblind, uncomprehending, unperceptive. *See* SEE. **3.** *Slang.* Stupefied, excited, or muddled with alcoholic liquor : besotted, crapulent, crapulous, drunk, drunken, inebriate, inebriated, intoxicated, sodden, tipsy. *Informal:* cock-eyed, stewed. *Slang:* bombed, boozed, boozy, crocked, high, lit (up), loaded, looped, pickled, pixilated, plastered, potted, sloshed, smashed, soused, stinking, stinko, stoned, tight, zonked. ***Idioms:*** drunk as a skunk, half-seas over, high as a kite, in one's cups, three sheets in (*or* to) the wind. *See* DRUGS. **4.** Screened from the view of oncoming drivers : concealed, hidden. *See* SHOW.
blind *verb* To confuse with bright light : bedazzle, daze, dazzle. *See* SEE.

blind alley *noun*
A course leading nowhere : cul-de-sac, dead end. *See* OPEN.

blindness *noun*
The condition of not being able to see : sightlessness. *See* SEE.

blink *verb*
1. To open and close the eyes rapidly : bat[1], nictate, nictitate, twinkle, wink. *See* REPETITION, SEE. **2.** To shine with intermittent gleams : flash, flicker, glimmer, twinkle, wink. *See* CONTINUE, LIGHT. **3.** To pretend not to see. Also used with *at* : connive at, disregard, ignore, pass over, wink at. ***Idioms:*** be blind to, close (*or* shut) one's eyes to, look the other way, turn a blind eye to. *See* SEE.
blink *noun* **1.** A brief closing of the eyes : nictation, nictitation, wink. *See* SEE. **2.** A sudden quick light : coruscation, flash, flicker, glance, gleam, glimmer, glint, spark[1], twinkle, wink. *See* LIGHT.

bliss *noun*
A condition of supreme well-being and good spirits : beatitude, blessedness, cheer, cheerfulness, felicity, gladness, happiness, joy, joyfulness. *See* HAPPY.

blister *verb*
To criticize harshly and devastatingly : drub, excoriate, flay, lash, rip into, scarify[1], scathe, scorch, score, scourge, slap, slash. *Informal:* roast. *Slang:* slam. ***Idioms:*** burn someone's ears, crawl all over, pin someone's ears back, put someone on the griddle, put someone on the hot seat, rake over the coals, read the riot act to. *See* PRAISE.

blistering *adjective*
Marked by much heat : ardent, baking, boiling, broiling, burning, fiery, heated, hot, red-hot, roasting, scalding, scorching, searing, sizzling, sultry, sweltering, torrid. *See* HOT.

blithe *adjective*
1. Free from care or worry : carefree, debonair, light[2], lighthearted. *See* CAREFUL, HAPPY. **2.** Characterized by joyful exuberance : blithesome, boon[2], convivial, gay, gleeful, jocund, jolly, jovial, merry, mirthful. *See* HAPPY.

blitheness *noun*
A state of joyful exuberance : blithesomeness, gaiety, glee, gleefulness, hilarity, jocoseness, jocosity, jocularity, jocundity, jolliness, jollity, joviality, lightheartedness, merriment, merriness, mirth, mirthfulness. *See* LAUGHTER.

blithesome *adjective*
Characterized by joyful exuberance : blithe, boon[2], convivial, gay, gleeful, jocund, jolly, jovial, merry, mirthful. *See* HAPPY.

blithesomeness *noun*
A state of joyful exuberance : blitheness, gaiety, glee, gleefulness, hilarity, jocoseness, jocosity, jocularity, jocundity, jolliness, jollity, joviality, lightheartedness, merriment, merriness, mirth, mirthfulness. *See* LAUGHTER.

blitzkrieg *noun*
A swift advance or attack : charge, rush. *See* APPROACH.

bloc *noun*
1. An association, especially of nations for a common cause : alliance, Anschluss, cartel, coalition, confederacy, confederation, federation, league, organization, union. *See* CONNECT, GROUP, POLITICS. **2.** A group of individuals united in a common cause : cartel, coalition, combination, combine, faction, party, ring[1]. *See* GROUP.

block *noun*
1. Something that impedes or prevents entry or passage : bar, barricade, barrier, blockage, clog, hamper, hindrance, hurdle, impediment, obstacle, obstruction, snag, stop, traverse, wall. *See* HELP, OPEN. **2.** *Slang.* The uppermost part of the body : head, noddle, pate, poll. *Slang:* bean, conk, dome, noggin, noodle, nut. *See* BODY.
block *verb* **1.** To stop or prevent passage of : bar, dam, impede, obstruct. ***Idiom:*** be (*or*

stand) in the way of. *See* OPEN. **2.** To plug up something, as a hole, space, or container : choke, clog, close, congest, cork, fill, plug, stop. *See* FULL. **3.** To cut off from sight. Also used with *out* : conceal, hide[1], obscure, obstruct, screen, shroud, shut off (*or* out). *See* SHOW.

block in (or **out)** *verb* To draw up a preliminary plan or version of : adumbrate, draft, outline, rough in (*or* out), sketch. *See* PLANNED.

blockade *noun*
A prolonged surrounding of an objective by hostile troops : beleaguerment, besiegement, investment, siege. *See* ATTACK.

blockade *verb* To surround with hostile troops : beleaguer, beset, besiege, invest, siege. *Idiom:* lay siege to. *See* ATTACK.

blockage *noun*
Something that impedes or prevents entry or passage : bar, barricade, barrier, block, clog, hamper, hindrance, hurdle, impediment, obstacle, obstruction, snag, stop, traverse, wall. *See* HELP, OPEN.

blockhead *noun*
A mentally dull person : chump[1], clod, dolt, dullard, dummkopf, dummy, dunce, numskull, thickhead. *Slang:* dimwit, dumbbell, dumbo. *See* ABILITY.

blockheaded *adjective*
Lacking in intelligence : dense, doltish, dumb, hebetudinous, obtuse, stupid, thickheaded, thick-witted. *Informal:* thick. *Slang:* dimwitted, dopey. *See* ABILITY.

block in or **out** *verb* See **block.**

blocky *adjective*
Short, heavy, and solidly built : chunky, compact[1], dumpy, heavyset, squat, stocky, stodgy, stubby, stumpy, thick, thickset. *See* FAT.

blond also **blonde** *adjective*
Having light hair : fair, fair-haired, towheaded. *See* COLORS.

blonde *adjective* See **blond.**

blood *noun*
1. The fluid circulated by the heart through the vascular system : gore. *See* BLOOD. **2.** The crime of murdering someone : homicide, killing, murder. *Slang:* hit. *See* HELP. **3.** One's ancestors or their character or one's ancestral derivation : ancestry, birth, bloodline, descent, extraction, family, genealogy, line, lineage, origin, parentage, pedigree, seed, stock. *See* KIN, PRECEDE. **4.** Noble rank or status by birth : birth, blue blood, nobility, noblesse. *See* KIN, OVER.

bloodbath also **blood bath** *noun*
The savage killing of many victims : bloodletting, bloodshed, butchery, carnage, massacre, pogrom, slaughter. *See* HELP.

bloodcurdling *adjective*
Causing great horror : hair-raising, horrible, horrid, horrific, terrific. *See* FEAR.

bloodless *adjective*
1. Lacking color : ashen, ashy, cadaverous, colorless, livid, lurid, pale, pallid, pasty, sallow, wan, waxen. *See* COLORS. **2.** Being weak in quality or substance : anemic, pale, pallid, waterish, watery. *See* STRONG. **3.** Lacking passion and emotion : anesthetic, dull, insensate, insensible, insensitive. *See* ATTITUDE, FEELINGS.

bloodletting *noun*
The savage killing of many victims : bloodbath, bloodshed, butchery, carnage, massacre, pogrom, slaughter. *See* HELP.

bloodline *noun*
One's ancestors or their character or one's ancestral derivation : ancestry, birth, blood, descent, extraction, family, genealogy, line, lineage, origin, parentage, pedigree, seed, stock. *See* KIN, PRECEDE.

bloodshed *noun*
The savage killing of many victims : bloodbath, bloodletting, butchery, carnage, massacre, pogrom, slaughter. *See* HELP.

bloodstain *verb*
To cover with blood : bloody, ensanguine, imbrue. *See* BLOOD.

bloodsucker *noun*
One who depends on another for support without reciprocating : hanger-on, leech, parasite, sponge. *Slang:* freeloader. *See* DEPENDENCE.

bloodsucking *adjective*
Of or characteristic of a parasite : parasitic, parasitical. *Slang:* freeloading. *See* DEPENDENCE.

bloodthirsty *adjective*
Eager for bloodshed : bloody, bloody-minded, cutthroat, homicidal, murderous, sanguinary, sanguineous, slaughterous. *See* HELP.

bloody *adjective*
1. Of or covered with blood : gory. *See* BLOOD. **2.** Attended by or causing bloodshed : gory, sanguinary, sanguineous. *See* BLOOD. **3.** Eager for bloodshed : bloodthirsty, bloody-minded, cutthroat, homicidal, murderous, sanguinary, sanguineous, slaughterous. *See* HELP. **4.** So annoying or detestable as to deserve condemnation : accursed, blasted, blessed, confounded, cursed, damn, darn, execrable, infernal. *Informal:* blamed, damned. *Chiefly British:* blooming, ruddy. *See* LIKE.

bloody *verb* To cover with blood : bloodstain, ensanguine, imbrue. *See* BLOOD.

bloody-minded *adjective*
Eager for bloodshed : bloodthirsty, bloody, cutthroat, homicidal, murderous, sanguinary, sanguineous, slaughterous. *See* HELP.

bloom¹ *noun*
1. The showy reproductive structure of a plant : blossom, floret, flower. *See* BETTER. **2.** A condition or time of vigor and freshness : blossom, efflorescence, florescence, flower, flush, prime. *See* BETTER. **3.** A fresh rosy complexion : blush, color, flush, glow. *See* BETTER.

bloom *verb* **1.** To bear flowers : blossom, blow³, burgeon, effloresce, flower. *See* BETTER, RICH. **2.** To grow rapidly and luxuriantly : blossom, flourish, thrive. *See* THRIVE.

bloom² *noun*
A relatively long, straight, rigid piece of metal or other solid material : bar, rod, shaft, slab, stick. *See* THING.

bloomer *noun*
Slang. A stupid, clumsy mistake : blunder, bull², bungle, foozle, fumble, muff, stumble. *Informal:* blooper, boner. *Slang:* goof. *See* CORRECT.

blooming *adjective*
1. Bright and clear in complexion; not dull or faded : creamy, fresh, glowing, peaches-and-cream. *See* BEAUTIFUL. **2.** Of a healthy reddish color : florid, flush, flushed, full-blooded, glowing, rosy, rubicund, ruddy, sanguine. *See* COLORS. **3.** *Chiefly British.* Completely such : absolute, all-out, arrant, complete, consummate, crashing, damned, dead, downright, flat, out-and-out, outright, perfect, plain, pure, sheer², thorough, thoroughgoing, total, unbounded, unequivocal, unlimited, unmitigated, unqualified, unrelieved, unreserved, utter². *Informal:* flat-out, positive. *See* BIG, LIMITED. **4.** *Chiefly British.* So annoying or detestable as to deserve condemnation : accursed, blasted, blessed, bloody, confounded, cursed, damn, darn, execrable, infernal. *Informal:* blamed, damned. *Chiefly British:* ruddy. *See* LIKE.

blooper *noun*
Informal. A stupid, clumsy mistake : blunder, bull², bungle, foozle, fumble, muff, stumble. *Informal:* boner. *Slang:* bloomer, goof. *See* CORRECT.

blossom *noun*
1. The showy reproductive structure of a plant : bloom¹, floret, flower. *See* BETTER. **2.** A condition or time of vigor and freshness : bloom¹, efflorescence, florescence, flower, flush, prime. *See* BETTER.

blossom *verb* **1.** To bear flowers : bloom¹, blow³, burgeon, effloresce, flower. *See* BETTER, RICH. **2.** To grow rapidly and luxuriantly : bloom¹, flourish, thrive. *See* THRIVE.

blot *noun*
1. A discolored mark made by smearing : blotch, daub, smear, smirch, smudge, smutch, splotch, stain. *See* MARKS. **2.** A mark of discredit or disgrace : black eye, blemish, onus, spot, stain, stigma, taint, tarnish. *Archaic:* attaint. ***Idiom:*** a blot on (one's) escutcheon. *See* MARKS, RESPECT.

blot *verb* To remove or invalidate by or as if by running a line through or wiping clean. Also used with *out* : annul, cancel, cross (off *or* out), delete, efface, erase, expunge, obliterate, rub (out), scratch (out), strike (out), undo, wipe (out), x (out). *Law:* vacate. *See* CONTINUE.

blot out *verb* To destroy all traces of : abolish, annihilate, clear, eradicate, erase, exterminate, extinguish, extirpate, kill¹, liquidate, obliterate, remove, root¹ (out *or* up), rub out, snuff out, stamp out, uproot, wipe out. ***Idioms:*** do away with, make an end of, put an end to. *See* HELP, MAKE.

blotch *noun*
A discolored mark made by smearing : blot, daub, smear, smirch, smudge, smutch, splotch, stain. *See* MARKS.

blotch *verb* To mark or soil with spots : bespatter, spatter, splatter, splotch, spot. *See* MARKS.

blot out *verb* See **blot.**

blow¹ *verb*
1. To be in a state of motion, as air : puff, winnow. *See* BREATH. **2.** To breathe hard : gasp, huff, pant, puff. *See* BREATH. **3.** To come open or fly apart suddenly and violently, as from internal pressure. Also used with *out* : burst, explode, pop¹. *Slang:* bust. *See* EXPLOSION. **4.** To release or cause to release energy suddenly and violently, especially with a loud noise. Also used with *up* : blast, burst, detonate, explode, fire, fulminate, go off, touch off. *See* EXPLOSION. **5.** *Informal.* To talk with excessive pride : boast, brag, crow, gasconade, rodomontade, vaunt. *See* PRAISE. **6.** *Slang.* To move or proceed away from a place : depart, exit, get away, get off, go, go away, leave¹, pull out, quit, retire, run (along), withdraw. *Informal:* cut out, push off, shove off. *Slang:* split, take off. ***Idioms:*** hit the road, take leave. *See* APPROACH. **7.** *Slang.* To spend (money)

excessively and usually foolishly : consume, dissipate, fool away, fritter away, riot away, squander, throw away, trifle away, waste. *See* SAVE. **8.** *Slang.* To pay for the food, drink, or entertainment of (another) : treat. *Informal:* set up, stand. ***Idiom:*** stand treat. *See* PAY. **9.** *Slang.* To harm irreparably through inept handling; make a mess : ball up, blunder, boggle, botch, bungle, foul up, fumble, gum up, mess up, mishandle, mismanage, muddle, muff, spoil. *Informal:* bollix up, muck up. *Slang:* goof up, louse up, screw up, snafu. ***Idiom:*** make a muck of. *See* CORRECT, HELP.

blow in *verb Slang.* To come to a particular place : arrive, check in, get in, pull in, reach, show up, turn up. ***Idiom:*** make (*or* put in) an appearance. *See* START.

blow up *verb* To be or become angry : anger, boil over, bristle, burn, explode, flare up, foam, fume, rage, seethe. *Informal:* steam. ***Idioms:*** blow a fuse, blow a gasket, blow one's stack (*or* top), breathe fire, fly off the handle, get hot under the collar, hit the ceiling (*or* roof), lose one's temper, see red. *See* FEELINGS.

blow *noun* **1.** A natural movement or current of air : air, blast, breeze, gust, wind¹, zephyr. *Archaic:* gale. *See* BREATH. **2.** *Informal.* An act of boasting : boast, brag, braggadocio, fanfaronade, gasconade, rodomontade, vaunt. *See* PRAISE.

blow² *noun*

1. A sudden sharp, powerful stroke : bang, clout, crack, hit, lick, pound, slug³, sock, swat, thwack, welt, whack, wham, whop. *Informal:* bash, biff, bop, clip¹, wallop. *Slang:* belt, conk, paste. *See* ATTACK, STRIKE. **2.** Something that jars the mind or emotions : jolt, shock¹. *Psychiatry:* trauma. *See* STRIKE.

blow³ *verb*

To bear flowers : bloom¹, blossom, burgeon, effloresce, flower. *See* BETTER, RICH.

blow-by-blow *adjective*

Characterized by attention to detail : circumstantial, detailed, full, minute², particular, thorough. *See* SPECIFIC.

blower *noun*

Slang. One given to boasting : boaster, brag, braggadocio, braggart, bragger, vaunter. *Informal:* blowhard. *See* PRAISE.

blowhard *noun*

Informal. One given to boasting : boaster, brag, braggadocio, braggart, bragger, vaunter. *Slang:* blower. *See* PRAISE.

blow in *verb* See **blow.**

blowout¹ *noun*

1. A violent release of confined energy, usually accompanied by a loud sound and shock waves : blast, blowup, burst, detonation, explosion, fulmination. *See* EXPLOSION. **2.** *Slang.* A big, exuberant party : celebration, shindig, shindy. *Slang:* bash, blast. *See* GROUP, RESTRAINT, WORK.

blowup *noun*

1. A violent release of confined energy, usually accompanied by a loud sound and shock waves : blast, blowout, burst, detonation, explosion, fulmination. *See* EXPLOSION. **2.** A sudden violent expression, as of emotion : accession, burst, eruption, explosion, fit², flare-up, gust, outbreak, outburst. *See* EXPLOSION.

blow up *verb* See **blow.**

blowy¹ *adjective*

Exposed to or characterized by the presence of freely circulating air or wind : airy, breezy, gusty, windy. *See* BREATH.

blubber *verb*

To make inarticulate sounds of grief or pain, usually accompanied by tears : bawl, cry, howl, keen², sob, wail, weep, yowl. *See* HAPPY, SOUNDS.

blubbering *noun*

A fit of crying : bawling, cry, sobbing, tear² (used in plural), wailing, weeping. *See* SOUNDS.

bludgeon *verb*

To domineer or drive into compliance by the use of as threats or force, for example : browbeat, bulldoze, bully, bullyrag, cow, hector, intimidate, menace, threaten. *Informal:* strong-arm. *See* OVER.

blue *adjective*

1. In low spirits : dejected, depressed, desolate, dispirited, down, downcast, downhearted, dull, dysphoric, gloomy, heavy-hearted, low, melancholic, melancholy, sad, spiritless, tristful, unhappy, wistful. ***Idiom:*** down at (*or* in) the mouth. *See* HAPPY. **2.** Dark and depressing : black, bleak, cheerless, dark, desolate, dismal, dreary, gloomy, glum, joyless, somber, tenebrific. *See* HAPPY, LIGHT. **3.** Tending to cause sadness or low spirits : cheerless, depressing, dismal, dispiriting, gloomy, joyless, melancholy, sad. *See* HAPPY. **4.** Bordering on indelicacy or impropriety : earthy, off-color, provocative, racy, risqué, salty, scabrous, spicy, suggestive. *See* DECENT.

blue blood *noun*

1. Noble rank or status by birth : birth, blood, nobility, noblesse. *See* KIN, OVER. **2.** People of the highest social level : aristocracy, crème de la crème, elite, flower, gentility, gentry, nobility, patriciate, quality, society, upper class, who's who. *Informal:* upper crust. *See* OVER.

blue-blooded *adjective*
Of high birth or social position : aristocratic, elite, highborn, highbred, noble, patrician, thoroughbred, upper-class, wellborn. *Informal:* upper-crust. *See* OVER.

blue-chip *adjective*
Being among the leaders in one's field : major, major-league. *Informal:* big-league, bigtime, heavyweight. *See* IMPORTANT.

bluecoat *noun*
A member of a law-enforcement agency : finest, officer, patrolman, patrolwoman, peace officer, police, policeman, police officer, policewoman. *Informal:* cop, law. *Slang:* bull[1], copper, flatfoot, fuzz, gendarme, heat, man (often uppercase). *Chiefly British:* bobby, constable, peeler. *See* LAW.

blue moon *noun*
Informal. A long time : eon, eternity, long[1], year (used in plural). *Informal:* age (used in plural). ***Idioms:*** forever and a day, forever and ever, month of Sundays. *See* TIME.

bluenose *noun*
A person who is too much concerned with being proper, modest, or righteous : Mrs. Grundy, prude, puritan, Victorian. *Informal:* old maid. *See* SEX.

bluenosed *adjective*
Marked by excessive concern for propriety and good form : genteel, old-maidish, precise, priggish, prim, prissy, proper, prudish, puritanical, strait-laced, stuffy, Victorian. ***Idiom:*** prim and proper. *See* PLAIN.

blueprint *noun*
A method for making, doing, or accomplishing something : design, game plan, idea, layout, plan, project, schema, scheme, strategy. *See* PLANNED.

blueprint *verb* **1.** To work out and arrange the parts or details of : design, lay out, map (out), plan, set out. *See* PLANNED. **2.** To form a strategy for : cast, chart, conceive, contrive, design, devise, formulate, frame, lay[1], plan, project, scheme, strategize, work out. *Informal:* dope out. ***Idiom:*** lay plans. *See* PLANNED.

blue-ribbon *adjective*
Exceptionally good of its kind : ace, banner, brag, capital, champion, excellent, fine[1], first-class, first-rate, prime, quality, splendid, superb, superior, terrific, tiptop, top. *Informal:* A-one, bully, dandy, great, swell, topflight, topnotch. *Slang:* boss. *Chiefly British:* tophole. *See* GOOD.

blues *noun*
A feeling or spell of dismally low spirits : dejection, depression, despondence, despondency, doldrums, dolefulness, downheartedness, dumps, dysphoria, funk, gloom, glumness, heavy-heartedness, melancholy, mope (used in plural), mournfulness, sadness, unhappiness. *See* FEELINGS, HAPPY.

bluff *verb*
To cause to accept what is false, especially by trickery or misrepresentation : beguile, betray, cozen, deceive, delude, double-cross, dupe, fool, hoodwink, humbug, mislead, take in, trick. *Informal:* bamboozle, have. *Slang:* four-flush. ***Idioms:*** lead astray, play false, pull the wool over someone's eyes, put something over on, take for a ride. *See* HONEST.

blunder *noun*
A stupid, clumsy mistake : bull[2], bungle, foozle, fumble, muff, stumble. *Informal:* blooper, boner. *Slang:* bloomer, goof. *See* CORRECT.

blunder *verb* **1.** To move awkwardly or clumsily : bumble[1], stumble. *See* ABILITY, MOVE. **2.** To proceed or perform in an unsteady, faltering manner : bumble[1], bungle, flounder, fudge, fumble, limp, muddle, shuffle, stagger, stumble. *See* THRIVE. **3.** To harm irreparably through inept handling; make a mess : ball up, boggle, botch, bungle, foul up, fumble, gum up, mess up, mishandle, mismanage, muddle, muff, spoil. *Informal:* bollix up, muck up. *Slang:* blow[1], goof up, louse up, screw up, snafu. ***Idiom:*** make a muck of. *See* CORRECT, HELP.

blunderer *noun*
A clumsy person : botcher, bungler, dub, foozler. *Slang:* screwup. ***Idiom:*** bull in a china shop. *See* ABILITY.

blunt *adjective*
1. Not physically sharp or keen : dull. *See* SHARP. **2.** Rudely unceremonious : abrupt, brief, brusque, crusty, curt, gruff, short, short-spoken. *See* ATTITUDE.

blunt *verb* **1.** To make or become less sharp-edged : dull, turn. ***Idiom:*** take the edge off. *See* SHARP. **2.** To render less sensitive : benumb, deaden, desensitize, dull, numb. ***Idiom:*** take the edge off. *See* AWARENESS.

blur *verb*
To make dim or indistinct : becloud, bedim, befog, blear, cloud, dim, dull, eclipse, fog, gloom, mist, obfuscate, obscure, overcast, overshadow, shadow. *See* CLEAR.

blurry *adjective*
Covered by or as if by a thin coating or film : cloudy, dim, filmy, hazy, misty. *See* CLEAR.

blurt *verb*
To speak suddenly or sharply, as from surprise or emotion. Also used with *out* : burst out, cry (out), ejaculate, exclaim, rap out. *See* WORDS.

blush *verb*
To become red in the face : color, crimson, flush, glow, mantle, redden. *See* EXPRESS.
blush *noun* **1.** A fresh rosy complexion : bloom[1], color, flush, glow. *See* BETTER. **2.** A quick look : glance, glimpse, peek, peep. *Informal:* gander. *See* SEE.

bluster *verb*
To speak or say very loudly or with a shout : bawl, bellow, call, clamor, cry, halloo, holler, roar, shout, vociferate, whoop, yawp, yell. *See* SOUNDS.

board *noun*
A raised platform on which theatrical performances are given. Used in plural : proscenium, stage. *See* PERFORMING ARTS.
board *verb* **1.** To provide with often temporary lodging : accommodate, bed (down), berth, bestow, billet, bunk[1], domicile, harbor, house, lodge, put up, quarter, room. *See* PROTECTION. **2.** To go aboard (a means of transport) : catch, take. *See* USED.

boast *verb*
1. To talk with excessive pride : brag, crow, gasconade, rodomontade, vaunt. *Informal:* blow[1]. *See* PRAISE. **2.** To have at one's disposal : command, enjoy, have, hold, possess. *See* OWNED.
boast *noun* An act of boasting : brag, braggadocio, fanfaronade, gasconade, rodomontade, vaunt. *Informal:* blow[1]. *See* PRAISE.

boaster *noun*
One given to boasting : brag, braggadocio, braggart, bragger, vaunter. *Informal:* blowhard. *Slang:* blower. *See* PRAISE.

boastful *adjective*
Characterized by or given to boasting : braggart, rodomontade. *See* ATTITUDE, PRAISE.

bobby *noun*
Chiefly British. A member of a law-enforcement agency : bluecoat, finest, officer, patrolman, patrolwoman, peace officer, police, policeman, police officer, policewoman. *Informal:* cop, law. *Slang:* bull[1], copper, flatfoot, fuzz, gendarme, heat, man (often uppercase). *Chiefly British:* constable, peeler. *See* LAW.

bode *verb*
To give an indication of something in advance : adumbrate, augur, forecast, forerun, foreshadow, foretell, foretoken, portend, prefigure, presage, prognosticate. *See* FORESIGHT, SHOW.

bodiless *adjective*
Having no body, form, or substance : discarnate, disembodied, immaterial, incorporeal, insubstantial, metaphysical, nonphysical, spiritual, unbodied, uncorporal, unsubstantial. *See* BODY.

bodily *adjective*
Of or relating to the human body : corporal, corporeal, fleshly, personal, physical, somatic. *See* BODY.

body *noun*
1. The physical frame of a dead person or animal : cadaver, carcass, corpse, remains. *Slang:* stiff. *See* BODY. **2.** A member of the human race : creature, homo, human, human being, individual, life, man, mortal, party, person, personage, soul. *See* BEINGS. **3.** A number of individuals making up or considered a unit : array, band[2], batch, bevy, bunch, bundle, clump, cluster, clutch[2], collection, group, knot, lot, party, set[2]. *See* GROUP. **4.** A group of people organized for a particular purpose : corps, crew, detachment, force, gang, team, unit. *See* GROUP. **5.** A number of persons who have come or been gathered together : assemblage, assembly, company, conclave, conference, congregation, congress, convention, convocation, crowd, gathering, group, meeting, muster, troop. *Informal:* get-together. *See* COLLECT. **6.** The main part : bulk. *Anatomy:* corpus. *See* BIG. **7.** A separate and distinct portion of matter : bulk, mass, object. *See* MATTER. **8.** A measurable whole : amount, budget, bulk, corpus, quantity, quantum. *See* BIG.
body forth *verb* To represent (an abstraction, for example) in or as if in bodily form : embody, exteriorize, externalize, incarnate, manifest, materialize, objectify, personalize, personify, substantiate. *See* SUBSTITUTE.

body politic *noun*
An organized geopolitical unit : country, land, nation, polity, state. *See* POLITICS, TERRITORY.

boff *noun*
Slang. A dazzling, often sudden instance of success : hit, sleeper. *Informal:* smash, smash hit, ten-strike, wow. *Slang:* boffo, boffola. *See* THRIVE.

boffo *noun*
Slang. A dazzling, often sudden instance of success : hit, sleeper. *Informal:* smash, smash hit,

ten-strike, wow. *Slang:* boff, boffola. *See* THRIVE.

boffola *noun*
Slang. A dazzling, often sudden instance of success : hit, sleeper. *Informal:* smash, smash hit, ten-strike, wow. *Slang:* boff, boffo. *See* THRIVE.

bog *noun*
A usually low-lying area of soft waterlogged ground and standing water : fen, marsh, marshland, mire, morass, muskeg, quag, quagmire, slough[1], swamp, swampland, wetland. *See* DRY.

bog *verb* To interfere with the progress of. Also used with *down* : encumber, hinder, hold back, impede, obstruct. ***Idiom:*** get in the way of. *See* HELP, OPEN.

bogey also **bogie** also **bogy** *noun*
A supernatural being, such as a ghost : apparition, bogeyman, bogle, eidolon, ghost, phantasm, phantasma, phantom, revenant, shade, shadow, specter, spirit, visitant, wraith. *Informal:* spook. *Regional:* haunt. *See* BEINGS, SUPERNATURAL.

bogeyman *noun*
A supernatural being, such as a ghost : apparition, bogey, bogle, eidolon, ghost, phantasm, phantasma, phantom, revenant, shade, shadow, specter, spirit, visitant, wraith. *Informal:* spook. *Regional:* haunt. *See* BEINGS, SUPERNATURAL.

boggle *verb*
1. To overwhelm with surprise, wonder, or bewilderment : bowl over, dumbfound, flabbergast, floor, stagger. *See* EXCITE, SURPRISE. **2.** To harm irreparably through inept handling; make a mess : ball up, blunder, botch, bungle, foul up, fumble, gum up, mess up, mishandle, mismanage, muddle, muff, spoil. *Informal:* bollix up, muck up. *Slang:* blow[1], goof up, louse up, screw up, snafu. ***Idiom:*** make a muck of. *See* CORRECT, HELP.

bogie *noun* See **bogey.**

bogle *noun*
A supernatural being, such as a ghost : apparition, bogey, bogeyman, eidolon, ghost, phantasm, phantasma, phantom, revenant, shade, shadow, specter, spirit, visitant, wraith. *Informal:* spook. *Regional:* haunt. *See* BEINGS, SUPERNATURAL.

bogus *adjective*
Fraudulently or deceptively imitative : counterfeit, fake, false, fraudulent, phony, sham, spurious, suppositious, supposititious. *See* TRUE.

bogy *noun* See **bogey.**

boil *verb*
1. To cook (food) in liquid heated to the point of steaming : parboil, simmer, stew. *See* INGESTION. **2.** To be in a state of emotional or mental turmoil : bubble, burn, churn, ferment, seethe, simmer, smolder. *See* CALM.

boil away *verb* To pass off as vapor, especially when heated : evaporate, vaporize, volatilize. *See* SOLID.

boil down *verb* To reduce in complexity or scope : simplify. *See* INCREASE, SIMPLE.

boil over *verb* To be or become angry : anger, blow up, bristle, burn, explode, flare up, foam, fume, rage, seethe. *Informal:* steam. ***Idioms:*** blow a fuse, blow a gasket, blow one's stack (*or* top), breathe fire, fly off the handle, get hot under the collar, hit the ceiling (*or* roof), lose one's temper, see red. *See* FEELINGS.

boil away *verb* See **boil.**

boil down *verb* See **boil.**

boiling *adjective*
Marked by much heat : ardent, baking, blistering, broiling, burning, fiery, heated, hot, red-hot, roasting, scalding, scorching, searing, sizzling, sultry, sweltering, torrid. *See* HOT.

boil over *verb* See **boil.**

boisterous *adjective*
Offensively loud and insistent : blatant, clamorous, obstreperous, strident, vociferous. *Informal:* loudmouthed. *See* SOUNDS.

bold *adjective*
1. Taking or willing to take risks : adventuresome, adventurous, audacious, daredevil, daring, enterprising, venturesome, venturous. *See* SAFETY. **2.** Having or showing courage : audacious, brave, courageous, dauntless, doughty, fearless, fortitudinous, gallant, game, hardy, heroic, intrepid, mettlesome, plucky, stout, stouthearted, unafraid, undaunted, valiant, valorous. *Informal:* spunky. *Slang:* gutsy, gutty. *See* FEAR. **3.** Rude and disrespectful : assuming, assumptive, audacious, boldfaced, brash, brazen, cheeky, contumelious, familiar, forward, impertinent, impudent, insolent, malapert, nervy, overconfident, pert, presuming, presumptuous, pushy, sassy, saucy, smart. *Informal:* brassy, flip, fresh, smart-alecky, snippety, snippy, uppish, uppity. *Slang:* wise[1]. *See* ATTITUDE, COURTESY. **4.** Readily attracting notice : arresting, conspicuous, eye-catching, marked, noticeable, observable, outstanding, pointed, prominent, pronounced, remarkable, salient, signal, striking. ***Idiom:*** sticking out like a sore thumb. *See* SEE. **5.** So sharply inclined as

to be almost perpendicular : abrupt, precipitous, sheer[2], steep[1]. *See* HORIZONTAL.

boldfaced *adjective*
Rude and disrespectful : assuming, assumptive, audacious, bold, brash, brazen, cheeky, contumelious, familiar, forward, impertinent, impudent, insolent, malapert, nervy, overconfident, pert, presuming, presumptuous, pushy, sassy, saucy, smart. *Informal:* brassy, flip, fresh, smart-alecky, snippety, snippy, uppish, uppity. *Slang:* wise[1]. *See* ATTITUDE, COURTESY.

boldness *noun*
1. Willingness to take risks : adventuresomeness, adventurousness, audaciousness, audacity, daredevilry, daredeviltry, daring, daringness, venturesomeness, venturousness. *See* SAFETY. **2.** The state or quality of being impudent or arrogantly self-confident : assumption, audaciousness, audacity, brashness, brazenness, cheek, cheekiness, chutzpah, discourtesy, disrespect, effrontery, face, familiarity, forwardness, gall[1], impertinence, impudence, impudency, incivility, insolence, nerve, nerviness, overconfidence, pertness, presumptuousness, pushiness, rudeness, sassiness, sauciness. *Informal:* brass, crust, sauce, uppishness, uppityness. *See* ATTITUDE, COURTESY.

bollix up *verb*
Informal. To harm irreparably through inept handling; make a mess : ball up, blunder, boggle, botch, bungle, foul up, fumble, gum up, mess up, mishandle, mismanage, muddle, muff, spoil. *Informal:* muck up. *Slang:* blow[1], goof up, louse up, screw up, snafu. ***Idiom:*** make a muck of. *See* CORRECT, HELP.

bolster *verb*
To keep from yielding or failing during stress or difficulty : buoy (up), prop, support, sustain, uphold. *See* HELP.

bolt *noun*
A sudden and involuntary movement : jump, start, startle. *See* MOVE.

bolt *verb* **1.** To move suddenly and involuntarily : jump, start. *See* MOVE. **2.** To leave hastily : get out, run. *Informal:* clear out, get, hotfoot, skedaddle. *Slang:* hightail, scram, vamoose. ***Idioms:*** beat it, hightail it, hotfoot it, make tracks. *See* APPROACH. **3.** To move swiftly : bucket, bustle, dart, dash, festinate, flash, fleet, flit, fly, haste, hasten, hurry, hustle, pelt[2], race, rocket, run, rush, sail, scoot, scour[2], shoot, speed, sprint, tear[1], trot, whirl, whisk, whiz, wing, zip, zoom. *Informal:* hotfoot, rip. *Slang:* barrel, highball. *Chiefly British:* nip[1]. ***Idioms:*** get a move on, get cracking, go like lightning, go like the wind, hotfoot it, make haste, make time, make tracks, run like the wind, shake a leg, step (*or* jump) on it. *See* MOVE. **4.** To swallow (food or drink) greedily or rapidly in large amounts : down, englut, engorge, gobble, gulp, guzzle, ingurgitate, swill, wolf. *See* INGESTION.

bomb *noun*
Slang. One that fails completely : bust, failure, fiasco, loser, washout. *Informal:* dud, flop, lemon. *See* THRIVE.

bomb *verb* *Slang.* To be unsuccessful : choke, fail, fall through. *Informal:* fall down, flop. ***Idioms:*** fail of success, fall short. *See* THRIVE.

bombard *verb*
To direct a barrage at : barrage, cannonade, fusillade, pepper, shower. *See* ATTACK.

bombardment *noun*
A concentrated outpouring, as of missiles, words, or blows : barrage, burst, cannonade, fusillade, hail[1], salvo, shower, storm, volley. *See* ATTACK.

bombast *noun*
Pretentious, pompous speech or writing : claptrap, fustian, grandiloquence, magniloquence, orotundity, rant, turgidity. *See* PLAIN, STYLE, WORDS.

bombastic *adjective*
Characterized by language that is elevated and sometimes pompous in style : aureate, declamatory, flowery, fustian, grandiloquent, high-flown, high-sounding, magniloquent, orotund, overblown, rhetorical, sonorous, swollen. *See* PLAIN, STYLE, WORDS.

bombed *adjective*
Slang. Stupefied, excited, or muddled with alcoholic liquor : besotted, crapulent, crapulous, drunk, drunken, inebriate, inebriated, intoxicated, sodden, tipsy. *Informal:* cock-eyed, stewed. *Slang:* blind, boozed, boozy, crocked, high, lit (up), loaded, looped, pickled, pixilated, plastered, potted, sloshed, smashed, soused, stinking, stinko, stoned, tight, zonked. ***Idioms:*** drunk as a skunk, half-seas over, high as a kite, in one's cups, three sheets in (*or* to) the wind. *See* DRUGS.

bona fide *adjective*
Not counterfeit or copied : actual, authentic, genuine, good, indubitable, original, real, true, undoubted, unquestionable. *See* TRUE.

bond *noun*
1. Something that physically confines the legs or arms : chain (used in plural), fetter, handcuff (often used in plural), hobble, iron (used in plural), manacle, restraint, shackle. *Archaic:* gyve.

See FREE. **2.** That which unites or binds : knot, ligament, ligature, link, nexus, tie, vinculum, yoke. *See* CONNECT. **3.** A legally binding arrangement between parties : agreement, compact[2], contract, convention, covenant, pact. *See* AGREE. **4.** The close physical union of two objects : adherence, adhesion, cohesion. *See* CONNECT. **5.** Money supplied for the temporary release of an arrested person that guarantees appearance of that person for trial : bail[1]. *See* LAW.

bond *verb* To hold fast : adhere, cleave[2], cling, cohere, stick. *See* CONNECT.

bondage *noun*
A state of subjugation to an owner or master : enslavement, helotry, serfdom, servileness, servility, servitude, slavery, thrall, thralldom, villeinage, yoke. *See* OVER.

bondsman *noun*
One who posts bond : bail[1], bailsman. *See* LAW.

bone *verb*
Informal. To study or work hard, especially when pressed for time. Also used with *up* : *Informal:* cram, grind. ***Idiom:*** burn the midnight oil. *See* WORK.

bone-dry *adjective*
Having little or no liquid or moisture : anhydrous, arid, dry, moistureless, sere, waterless. *See* DRY.

boner *noun*
Informal. A stupid, clumsy mistake : blunder, bull[2], bungle, foozle, fumble, muff, stumble. *Informal:* blooper. *Slang:* bloomer, goof. *See* CORRECT.

bong *verb*
To give forth or cause to give forth a clear, resonant sound : chime, knell, peal, ring[2], strike, toll[2]. *See* SOUNDS.

bonkers *adjective*
Informal. Afflicted with or exhibiting irrationality and mental unsoundness : brainsick, crazy, daft, demented, disordered, distraught, dotty, insane, lunatic, mad, maniac, maniacal, mentally ill, moonstruck, off, touched, unbalanced, unsound, wrong. *Informal:* cracked, daffy, gaga, loony. *Slang:* bananas, batty, buggy, cuckoo, fruity, loco, nuts, nutty, screwy, wacky. *Chiefly British:* crackers. *Law:* non compos mentis. ***Idioms:*** around the bend, crazy as a loon, mad as a hatter, not all there, nutty as a fruitcake, off (*or* out of) one's head, off one's rocker, of unsound mind, out of one's mind, sick in the head, stark raving mad. *See* SANE.

bonny *adjective*
1. *Scots.* Having qualities that delight the eye : attractive, beauteous, beautiful, comely, fair, good-looking, gorgeous, handsome, lovely, pretty, pulchritudinous, ravishing, sightly, stunning. ***Idiom:*** easy on the eyes. *See* BEAUTIFUL. **2.** *Scots.* Having pleasant desirable qualities : good, nice. *Scots:* braw. *See* GOOD.

bonus *noun*
A sum of money offered for a special service, such as the apprehension of a criminal : bounty, reward. *See* LAW, REWARD.

bony *adjective*
Having little flesh or fat on the body : angular, fleshless, gaunt, lank, lanky, lean[2], meager, rawboned, scrawny, skinny, slender, slim, spare, thin, twiggy, weedy. ***Idioms:*** all skin and bones, thin as a rail. *See* FAT.

boo *noun*
Any of various derisive sounds of disapproval : catcall, hiss, hoot. *Slang:* bird, Bronx cheer, raspberry, razz. *See* SOUNDS.

booby trap *noun*
A source of danger or difficulty not easily foreseen and avoided : pitfall, trap. *See* SAFETY.

boodle *noun*
1. *Slang.* Money, property, or a favor given, offered, or promised to a person or accepted by a person in a position of trust as an inducement to dishonest behavior : bribe, fix, graft, payola. *Informal:* payoff. *See* CRIMES, MONEY, PERSUASION. **2.** *Slang.* Goods or property seized unlawfully, especially by a victor in wartime : booty, loot, pillage, plunder, spoil (used in plural). *Nautical:* prize[2]. *See* CRIMES, GIVE.

book *noun*
A printed and bound work : tome, volume. *See* WORDS.

book *verb* **1.** To register in or as if in a book : catalog, enroll, inscribe, list[1], set down, write down. *See* REMEMBER. **2.** To cause to be set aside, as for one's use, in advance : bespeak, engage, reserve. *See* GET.

booking *noun*
A commitment, as for a performance by an entertainer : engagement. *Slang:* gig. *See* PERFORMING ARTS.

bookish *adjective*
1. Devoted to study or reading : scholarly, studious. *See* TEACH. **2.** Characterized by a narrow concern for book learning and formal rules, without knowledge or experience of practical matters : academic, donnish, formalistic, inkhorn, literary, pedantic, pedantical, scholastic. *See* ATTITUDE, FLEXIBLE, TEACH.

boom *verb*
1. To make a continuous deep reverberating sound : growl, grumble, roll, rumble. *See* SOUNDS. **2.** To make an earsplitting explosive noise : bang, blast, roar, thunder. *See* SOUNDS. **3.** To do or fare well : flourish, go, prosper, thrive. *Slang:* score. ***Idioms:*** get (*or* go) somewhere, go great guns, go strong. *See* THRIVE.
boom *noun* An earsplitting, explosive noise : bang, blast, roar, thunder. *See* SOUNDS.

boomerang *verb*
To produce an unexpected and undesired result : backfire. *See* SURPRISE.

booming *adjective*
Improving, growing, or succeeding steadily : boomy, flourishing, prospering, prosperous, roaring, thrifty, thriving. *See* THRIVE.

boomy *adjective*
Improving, growing, or succeeding steadily : booming, flourishing, prospering, prosperous, roaring, thrifty, thriving. *See* THRIVE.

boon[1] *noun*
Something beneficial : advantage, avail, benefit, blessing, favor, gain, profit. *See* HELP.

boon[2] *adjective*
Characterized by joyful exuberance : blithe, blithesome, convivial, gay, gleeful, jocund, jolly, jovial, merry, mirthful. *See* HAPPY.

boor *noun*
An unrefined, rude person : barbarian, chuff, churl, Philistine, vulgarian, yahoo. *See* GOOD.

boorish *adjective*
Lacking in delicacy or refinement : barbarian, barbaric, churlish, coarse, crass, crude, gross, ill-bred, indelicate, philistine, rough, rude, tasteless, uncivilized, uncouth, uncultivated, uncultured, unpolished, unrefined, vulgar. *See* COURTESY, SMOOTH.

boost *verb*
1. To move (something) to a higher position : elevate, heave, hoist, lift, pick up, raise, rear[2], take up, uphold, uplift, upraise, uprear. *See* RISE. **2.** To make or become greater or larger : aggrandize, amplify, augment, build, build up, burgeon, enlarge, escalate, expand, extend, grow, increase, magnify, mount, multiply, proliferate, rise, run up, snowball, soar, swell, upsurge, wax. *Informal:* beef up. *See* INCREASE. **3.** To increase in amount : hike, jack (up), jump, raise, up. *See* INCREASE. **4.** To give support or assistance : abet, aid, assist, help (out), relieve, succor. ***Idioms:*** give (*or* lend) a hand, give a leg up. *See* HELP. **5.** To increase or seek to increase the importance or reputation of by favorable publicity : ballyhoo, build up, enhance, promote, publicize, puff, talk up, tout. *Informal:* plug. *Slang:* hype. *See* KNOWLEDGE.
boost *noun* **1.** An instance of lifting or being lifted : heave, hoist, lift. *See* RISE. **2.** The act of increasing or rising : aggrandizement, amplification, augment, augmentation, buildup, enlargement, escalation, growth, hike, increase, jump, multiplication, proliferation, raise, rise, swell, upsurge, upswing, upturn. *See* INCREASE. **3.** The amount by which something is increased : advance, hike, increase, increment, jump, raise, rise. *See* INCREASE.

boot[1] *noun*
1. *Slang.* The act of dismissing or the condition of being dismissed from employment : discharge, dismissal, termination. *Informal:* ax. *Slang:* bounce, sack[1]. *See* KEEP. **2.** *Slang.* The act of ejecting or the state of being ejected : dismissal, ejection, ejectment, eviction, expulsion, ouster. *Slang:* bounce. *See* KEEP. **3.** *Slang.* A strong, pleasant feeling of excitement or stimulation : lift, thrill. *Informal:* wallop. *Slang:* bang, high, kick. *See* EXCITE.
boot *verb* **1.** *Slang.* To end the employment or service of : cashier, discharge, dismiss, drop, release, terminate. *Informal:* ax, fire, pink-slip. *Slang:* bounce, can, sack[1]. ***Idioms:*** give someone his or her walking papers, give someone the ax, give someone the gate, give someone the pink slip, let go, show someone the door. *See* KEEP. **2.** *Slang.* To put out by force. Also used with *out* : bump, dismiss, eject, evict, expel, oust, throw out. *Informal:* chuck. *Slang:* bounce, kick out. ***Idioms:*** give someone the boot, give someone the heave-ho (*or* old heave-ho), send packing, show someone the door, throw out on one's ear. *See* KEEP.

boot[2] *verb*
Archaic. To be an advantage to : advantage, avail, benefit, profit, serve. ***Idiom:*** stand someone in good stead. *See* HELP.

bootleg *verb*
To import or export secretly and illegally : run, smuggle. ***Idiom:*** run contraband. *See* CRIMES, MOVE.

bootlegger *noun*
A person who engages in smuggling : contrabandist, runner, smuggler. *See* CRIMES, MOVE.

bootless *adjective*
Having no useful result : barren, fruitless, futile, unavailing, unprofitable, unsuccessful, useless, vain. ***Idiom:*** in vain. *See* THRIVE, USED.

bootlessness *noun*
The condition or quality of being useless or

ineffective : fruitlessness, futility, unavailingness, unprofitableness, uselessness, vainness, vanity. *See* THRIVE, USED.

bootlick *verb*
To support slavishly every opinion or suggestion of a superior : cringe, fawn, grovel, kowtow, slaver, toady, truckle. *Informal:* apple-polish, brownnose, cotton. *Slang:* suck up. ***Idioms:*** curry favor, dance attendance, kiss someone's feet, lick someone's boots. *See* OVER.

booty *noun*
Goods or property seized unlawfully, especially by a victor in wartime : loot, pillage, plunder, spoil (used in plural). *Slang:* boodle. *Nautical:* prize[2]. *See* CRIMES, GIVE.

booze *noun*
Slang. A drinking bout : binge, brannigan, carousal, carouse, drunk, spree. *Slang:* bat[2], bender, jag, tear[1]. *See* DRUGS, RESTRAINT.
booze *verb Slang.* To take alcoholic liquor, especially excessively or habitually : drink, guzzle, imbibe, tipple. *Informal:* nip[2]. *Slang:* lush[2], soak, tank up. ***Idioms:*** bend the elbow, hit the bottle. *See* DRUGS.

boozed *adjective*
Slang. Stupefied, excited, or muddled with alcoholic liquor : besotted, crapulent, crapulous, drunk, drunken, inebriate, inebriated, intoxicated, sodden, tipsy. *Informal:* cock-eyed, stewed. *Slang:* blind, bombed, boozy, crocked, high, lit (up), loaded, looped, pickled, pixilated, plastered, potted, sloshed, smashed, soused, stinking, stinko, stoned, tight, zonked. ***Idioms:*** drunk as a skunk, half-seas over, high as a kite, in one's cups, three sheets in (*or* to) the wind. *See* DRUGS.

boozehound *noun*
Slang. A person who is habitually drunk : drunk, drunkard, inebriate, sot, tippler. *Slang:* boozer, lush[2], rummy[1], soak, souse, sponge, stiff. *See* DRUGS.

boozer *noun*
Slang. A person who is habitually drunk : drunk, drunkard, inebriate, sot, tippler. *Slang:* boozehound, lush[2], rummy[1], soak, souse, sponge, stiff. *See* DRUGS.

boozy *adjective*
Slang. Stupefied, excited, or muddled with alcoholic liquor : besotted, crapulent, crapulous, drunk, drunken, inebriate, inebriated, intoxicated, sodden, tipsy. *Informal:* cock-eyed, stewed. *Slang:* blind, bombed, boozed, crocked, high, lit (up), loaded, looped, pickled, pixilated, plastered, potted, sloshed, smashed, soused, stinking, stinko, stoned, tight, zonked. ***Idioms:*** drunk as a skunk, half-seas over, high as a kite, in one's cups, three sheets in (*or* to) the wind. *See* DRUGS.

bop *verb*
Informal. To deliver a powerful blow to suddenly and sharply : bash, catch, clout, hit, knock, pop[1], slam, slog, slug[3], smash, smite, sock, strike, swat, thwack, whack, wham, whop. *Informal:* biff, clip[1], wallop. *Slang:* belt, conk, paste. ***Idioms:*** let someone have it, sock it to someone. *See* ATTACK, STRIKE.
bop *noun Informal.* A sudden sharp, powerful stroke : bang, blow[2], clout, crack, hit, lick, pound, slug[3], sock, swat, thwack, welt, whack, wham, whop. *Informal:* bash, biff, clip[1], wallop. *Slang:* belt, conk, paste. *See* ATTACK, STRIKE.

border *noun*
1. A fairly narrow line or space forming a boundary : borderline, brim, brink, edge, edging, fringe, margin, periphery, rim, verge. *Chiefly Military:* perimeter. *See* EDGE. **2.** The line or area separating geopolitical units : borderland, boundary, frontier, march[2], marchland. *See* EDGE, TERRITORY.
border *verb* **1.** To put or form a border on : bound[2], edge, fringe, margin, rim, skirt, verge. *See* EDGE. **2.** To be contiguous or next to : abut, adjoin, bound[2], butt[2], join, meet[1], neighbor, touch, verge. *See* NEAR.
border on (or **upon)** *verb* To come near, as in quality or amount : approach, approximate, challenge, rival, verge on. *See* SAME.

borderland *noun*
The line or area separating geopolitical units : border, boundary, frontier, march[2], marchland. *See* EDGE, TERRITORY.

borderline *noun*
1. A fairly narrow line or space forming a boundary : border, brim, brink, edge, edging, fringe, margin, periphery, rim, verge. *Chiefly Military:* perimeter. *See* EDGE. **2.** A transitional interval beyond which some new action or different state of affairs is likely to begin or occur : brink, edge, point, threshold, verge. *See* EDGE.
borderline *adjective* Not affording certainty : ambiguous, chancy, clouded, doubtful, dubious, dubitable, equivocal, inconclusive, indecisive, indeterminate, problematic, problematical, questionable, uncertain, unclear, unsure. *Informal:* iffy. ***Idioms:*** at issue, in doubt, in question. *See* CERTAIN, CLEAR.

border on or **upon** *verb* See **border.**

bore *verb*
To fatigue with dullness or tedium : tire, weary. *See* EXCITE.
bore *noun* An unpleasant, tiresome person : *Slang:* drip, dweeb, jerk, nerd, pill, poop[2]. *See* LIKE.

boreal *adjective*
Very cold : arctic, freezing, frigid, frosty, gelid, glacial, icy, polar, wintry. *Archaic:* frore. ***Idiom:*** bitter (*or* bitterly) cold. *See* HOT.

boredom *noun*
The condition of being bored : ennui. *See* EXCITE.

boring *adjective*
Arousing no interest or curiosity : drear, dreary, dry, dull, humdrum, irksome, monotonous, stuffy, tedious, tiresome, uninteresting, weariful, wearisome, weary. *See* EXCITE.

bosom *noun*
The seat of a person's innermost emotions and feelings : breast, heart, soul. ***Idioms:*** bottom of one's heart, cockles of one's heart, one's heart of hearts. *See* FEELINGS.
bosom *verb Archaic.* To put one's arms around affectionately : clasp, embrace, enfold, hold, hug, press, squeeze. *Slang:* clinch. *Archaic:* clip[2], embosom. *See* TOUCH.

boss *noun*
1. Someone who directs and supervises workers : director, foreman, foreperson, forewoman, head, manager, overseer, superintendent, supervisor, taskmaster, taskmistress. *Informal:* straw boss. *Slang:* chief. *See* OVER. **2.** One who is highest in rank or authority : chief, chieftain, director, head, headman, hierarch, leader, master. *Slang:* honcho. ***Idiom:*** cock of the walk. *See* OVER. **3.** A professional politician who controls a party or political machine : chief, leader. *See* OVER.
boss *verb* **1.** To direct and watch over the work and performance of others : overlook, oversee, superintend, supervise, watch over. *See* OVER. **2.** To command or issue commands in an arrogant manner : dictate, dominate, domineer, order, rule, tyrannize. *See* OVER.
boss *adjective Slang.* Exceptionally good of its kind : ace, banner, blue-ribbon, brag, capital, champion, excellent, fine[1], first-class, first-rate, prime, quality, splendid, superb, superior, terrific, tiptop, top. *Informal:* A-one, bully, dandy, great, swell, topflight, topnotch. *Chiefly British:* tophole. *See* GOOD.

bossy *adjective*
Tending to dictate : authoritarian, dictatorial, dogmatic, domineering, imperious, magisterial, masterful, overbearing, peremptory. *See* OVER.

botch *verb*
To harm irreparably through inept handling; make a mess : ball up, blunder, boggle, bungle, foul up, fumble, gum up, mess up, mishandle, mismanage, muddle, muff, spoil. *Informal:* bollix up, muck up. *Slang:* blow[1], goof up, louse up, screw up, snafu. ***Idiom:*** make a muck of. *See* CORRECT, HELP.
botch *noun* A ruinous state of disorder : foul-up, mess, muddle, shambles. *Informal:* hash. *Slang:* screwup, snafu. *See* CORRECT, ORDER.

botcher *noun*
A clumsy person : blunderer, bungler, dub, foozler. *Slang:* screwup. ***Idiom:*** bull in a china shop. *See* ABILITY.

bother *verb*
1. To trouble the nerves or peace of mind of, especially by repeated vexations : aggravate, annoy, bug, chafe, disturb, exasperate, fret, gall[2], get, irk, irritate, nettle, peeve, provoke, put out, rile, ruffle, vex. ***Idioms:*** get in one's hair, get on one's nerves, get under one's skin. *See* FEELINGS, PAIN. **2.** To impair or destroy the composure of : agitate, discompose, disquiet, distract, disturb, flurry, fluster, perturb, rock, ruffle, shake (up), toss, unsettle, upset. *Informal:* rattle. *See* CALM.
bother *noun* **1.** Something that annoys : aggravation, annoyance, besetment, irritant, irritation, nuisance, peeve, plague, torment, vexation. *See* FEELINGS, PAIN. **2.** The feeling of being annoyed : aggravation, annoyance, botheration, exasperation, irritation, vexation. *See* FEELINGS, PAIN. **3.** Needless trouble : botheration, fuss, pother. *See* EASY.

botheration *noun*
1. The act of annoying : annoyance, bothering, exasperation, harassment, irritation, pestering, provocation, vexation. *See* FEELINGS, PAIN. **2.** The feeling of being annoyed : aggravation, annoyance, bother, exasperation, irritation, vexation. *See* FEELINGS, PAIN. **3.** Needless trouble : bother, fuss, pother. *See* EASY.

bothering *noun*
The act of annoying : annoyance, botheration, exasperation, harassment, irritation, pestering, provocation, vexation. *See* FEELINGS, PAIN.

bothersome *adjective*
Troubling the nerves or peace of mind, as by repeated vexations : annoying, galling, irksome, irritating, nettlesome, plaguy, provoking, troublesome, vexatious. *See* PAIN.

bottom *noun*
1. A side or surface that is below or under : un-

derneath, underside, undersurface. *See* OVER. **2.** The lowest or supporting part or structure : base[1], basis, bed, foot, footing, foundation, fundament, ground, groundwork, seat, substratum, underpinning (often used in plural). *See* OVER. **3.** A very low level, position, or degree : low, rock bottom. *See* HIGH. **4.** A point of origin from which ideas or influences, for example, originate : center, core, focus, heart, hub, quick, root[1]. *See* START. **5.** *Informal.* The part of one's back on which one rests in sitting : buttock (used in plural), derrière, posterior, rump, seat. *Informal:* backside, behind, rear[1]. *Slang:* bun (used in plural), fanny, tush. *Chiefly British:* bum[2]. *See* OVER.

bottom *adjective* Opposite to or farthest from the top : lowermost, lowest, nethermost, undermost. *See* OVER.

bottomless *adjective*
Having no basis or foundation in fact : baseless, groundless, idle, unfounded, unwarranted. *See* TRUE.

boulevard *noun*
A course affording passage from one place to another : avenue, drive, expressway, freeway, highway, path, road, roadway, route, street, superhighway, thoroughfare, thruway, turnpike, way. *See* MOVE, OPEN.

bounce *verb*
1. To spring back after colliding with something : rebound. *See* APPROACH, MOVE. **2.** To move in a lively way : bound[1], jump, leap, spring. *See* MOVE. **3.** *Slang.* To put out by force : bump, dismiss, eject, evict, expel, oust, throw out. *Informal:* chuck. *Slang:* boot[1] (out), kick out. ***Idioms:*** give someone the boot, give someone the heave-ho (*or* old heave-ho), send packing, show someone the door, throw out on one's ear. *See* KEEP. **4.** *Slang.* To end the employment or service of : cashier, discharge, dismiss, drop, release, terminate. *Informal:* ax, fire, pink-slip. *Slang:* boot[1], can, sack[1]. ***Idioms:*** give someone his or her walking papers, give someone the ax, give someone the gate, give someone the pink slip, let go, show someone the door. *See* KEEP.

bounce *noun* **1.** A lively, emphatic, eager quality or manner : animation, brio, dash, élan, esprit, life, liveliness, pertness, sparkle, spirit, verve, vigor, vim, vivaciousness, vivacity, zip. *Informal:* ginger, pep, peppiness. *Slang:* oomph. *See* ACTION. **2.** An act of bouncing or a bouncing movement : bound[1], rebound. *See* APPROACH, MOVE. **3.** A sudden lively movement : bound[1], jump, leap, spring. *See* MOVE. **4.** The quality or state of being flexible : ductility, elasticity, flexibility, flexibleness, give, malleability, malleableness, plasticity, pliability, pliableness, pliancy, pliantness, resilience, resiliency, spring, springiness, suppleness. *Obsolete:* flexure. *See* FLEXIBLE. **5.** The ability to recover quickly from depression or discouragement : buoyancy, elasticity, resilience, resiliency. *See* ABILITY. **6.** *Slang.* The act of ejecting or the state of being ejected : dismissal, ejection, ejectment, eviction, expulsion, ouster. *Slang:* boot[1]. *See* KEEP. **7.** *Slang.* The act of dismissing or the condition of being dismissed from employment : discharge, dismissal, termination. *Informal:* ax. *Slang:* boot[1], sack[1]. *See* KEEP.

bouncy *adjective*
Very brisk, alert, and full of high spirits : animated, chipper, dashing, high-spirited, lively, pert, spirited, vivacious. *Informal:* peppy. ***Idioms:*** bright-eyed and bushy-tailed, full of life. *See* ACTION.

bound[1] *verb*
To move in a lively way : bounce, jump, leap, spring. *See* MOVE.

bound *noun* **1.** A sudden lively movement : bounce, jump, leap, spring. *See* MOVE. **2.** An act of bouncing or a bouncing movement : bounce, rebound. *See* APPROACH, MOVE.

bound[2] *verb*
1. To put or form a border on : border, edge, fringe, margin, rim, skirt, verge. *See* EDGE. **2.** To be contiguous or next to : abut, adjoin, border, butt[2], join, meet[1], neighbor, touch, verge. *See* NEAR. **3.** To fix the limits of : delimit, delimitate, demarcate, determine, limit, mark (out *or* off), measure. *See* LIMITED.

bound *noun* **1.** A demarcation point or boundary beyond which something does not extend or occur. Often used in plural : confine (used in plural), end, limit. *See* EDGE. **2.** The boundary surrounding a certain area. Used in plural : confine (used in plural), limit (used in plural), precinct (often used in plural). *See* LIMITED.

bound[3] *adjective*
Owing something, such as gratitude or appreciation, to another : beholden, indebted, obligated, obliged. *Archaic:* bounden. ***Idiom:*** under obligation. *See* OBLIGATION.

boundary *noun*
The line or area separating geopolitical units : border, borderland, frontier, march[2], marchland. *See* EDGE, TERRITORY.

bounden *adjective*
Archaic. Owing something, such as gratitude or appreciation, to another : beholden, bound[3], indebted, obligated, obliged. ***Idiom:*** under obligation. *See* OBLIGATION.

boundless *adjective*
Having no ends or limits : endless, illimitable, immeasurable, infinite, limitless, measureless, unbounded, unlimited. *See* LIMITED.

boundlessness *noun*
The state or quality of being infinite : immeasurability, immeasurableness, inexhaustibility, inexhaustibleness, infiniteness, infinity, limitlessness, measurelessness, unboundedness, unlimitedness. *See* LIMITED.

bounteous *adjective*
Characterized by abundance : abundant, ample, bountiful, copious, generous, heavy, plenitudinous, plenteous, plentiful, substantial, voluminous. *See* BIG, GIVE, RICH.

bounteousness *noun*
1. The quality or state of being generous : big-heartedness, bountifulness, freehandedness, generosity, generousness, great-heartedness, large-heartedness, lavishness, liberality, magnanimity, magnanimousness, munificence, openhandedness, unselfishness, unsparingness. *See* GIVE. **2.** Prosperity and a sufficiency of life's necessities : abundance, bountifulness, plenitude, plenteousness, plenty. *See* RICH.

bountiful *adjective*
Characterized by abundance : abundant, ample, bounteous, copious, generous, heavy, plenitudinous, plenteous, plentiful, substantial, voluminous. *See* BIG, GIVE, RICH.

bountifulness *noun*
1. The quality or state of being generous : big-heartedness, bounteousness, freehandedness, generosity, generousness, great-heartedness, large-heartedness, lavishness, liberality, magnanimity, magnanimousness, munificence, openhandedness, unselfishness, unsparingness. *See* GIVE. **2.** Prosperity and a sufficiency of life's necessities : abundance, bounteousness, plenitude, plenteousness, plenty. *See* RICH.

bounty *noun*
A sum of money offered for a special service, such as the apprehension of a criminal : bonus, reward. *See* LAW, REWARD.

bouquet *noun*
1. Cut flowers that have been arranged in a usually small bunch : nosegay, posy. *See* THING.
2. A sweet or pleasant odor : aroma, fragrance, perfume, redolence, scent. *See* SMELLS.

bout *noun*
1. A limited, often assigned period of activity, duty, or opportunity : go, hitch, inning (often used in plural), shift, spell[3], stint, stretch, time, tour, trick, turn, watch. *See* TIME. **2.** An often prolonged period, as of illness : siege. *See* TIME.

boutade *noun*
An impulsive, often illogical turn of mind : bee, caprice, conceit, fancy, freak, humor, impulse, megrim, notion, vagary, whim, whimsy. ***Idiom:*** bee in one's bonnet. *See* THOUGHTS.

boutique *noun*
A retail establishment where merchandise is sold : emporium, outlet, shop, store. *See* TRANSACTIONS.

bow[1] *verb*
1. To incline the body : arch, bend, hump, hunch, scrunch, stoop. *See* POSTURE. **2.** To give in from or as if from a gradual loss of strength : buckle, capitulate, submit, succumb, surrender, yield. *Informal:* fold. *See* RESIST.
3. To conform to the will or judgment of another, especially out of respect or courtesy : defer[2], submit, yield. ***Idioms:*** give ground, give way. *See* PRECEDE, RESIST.
bow *noun* An inclination of the head or body, as in greeting, consent, courtesy, submission, or worship : curtsy, genuflection, kowtow, nod, obeisance. *See* COURTESY.

bow[2] *noun*
Something bent : bend, crook, curvature, curve, round, turn. *See* STRAIGHT.
bow *verb* To swerve from a straight line : angle, arc, arch, bend, crook, curve, round, turn. *See* STRAIGHT.

bowdlerize *verb*
To examine (material) and remove parts considered harmful or improper for publication or transmission : censor, expurgate, screen. *See* INCLUDE, SHOW.

bowed *adjective*
Deviating from a straight line : arced, arched, arciform, bent, curved, curvilinear, rounded. *See* STRAIGHT.

bowl over *verb*
To overwhelm with surprise, wonder, or bewilderment : boggle, dumbfound, flabbergast, floor, stagger. *See* EXCITE, SURPRISE.

box[1] *noun*
A difficult, often embarrassing situation or condition : corner, deep water, difficulty, dilemma, Dutch, fix, hole, hot spot, hot water, jam, plight[1], predicament, quagmire, scrape,

soup, trouble. *Informal:* bind, pickle, spot. *See* EASY.

box[2] *noun*
A quick, sharp blow, especially with the hand : buffet, bust, chop[1], cuff, punch, slap, smack[1], smacker, spank, swat, whack. *Informal:* clip[1], spat. *See* ATTACK, STRIKE.
box *verb* To hit with a quick, sharp blow of the hand : buffet, bust, cuff, punch, slap, smack[1], spank, swat, whack. *Informal:* clip[1], spat. *See* ATTACK, STRIKE.

box office *noun*
The amount of money collected as admission, especially to a sporting event : gate, take. *See* MONEY.

boy *noun*
Informal. A grown man referred to familiarly, jokingly, or as a member of one's set or group : fellow. *Informal:* chap. *See* BEINGS, CONNECT.

boycott *verb*
To exclude from normal social or professional activities : blackball, blacklist, ostracize, shut out. *See* ACCEPT.

boyfriend also **boy friend** *noun*
A man who is the favored companion of a woman : beau. *Informal:* fellow. *See* CONNECT, SEX.

brace *verb*
To prepare (oneself) for action : forearm, fortify, gird, ready, steel, strengthen. ***Idiom:*** gird (*or* gird up) one's loins. *See* PREPARED.
brace *noun* **1.** A means or device that keeps something erect, stable, or secure : buttress, crutch, prop, shore, stay[2], support, underpinning. *See* SUPPORT. **2.** Two items of the same kind together : couple, couplet, doublet, duet, duo, match, pair, two, twosome, yoke. *See* GROUP, SAME.

bracer *noun*
Informal. A medicine that restores or increases vigor : restorative, roborant, tonic. *Informal:* pick-me-up. *See* HELP.

bracing *adjective*
Producing or stimulating physical, mental, or emotional vigor : energizing, exhilarant, exhilarating, innerving, intoxicating, invigorating, refreshing, reinvigorating, renewing, restorative, roborant, stimulating, tonic. *See* HELP.

bracket *noun*
A division of persons or things by quality, rank, or grade : class, grade, league, order, rank[1], tier. *See* GROUP, VALUE.
bracket *verb* To come or bring together in one's mind or imagination : associate, connect, correlate, couple, identify, link. *See* SAME.

brag *verb*
To talk with excessive pride : boast, crow, gasconade, rodomontade, vaunt. *Informal:* blow[1]. *See* PRAISE.
brag *noun* **1.** An act of boasting : boast, braggadocio, fanfaronade, gasconade, rodomontade, vaunt. *Informal:* blow[1]. *See* PRAISE. **2.** One given to boasting : boaster, braggadocio, braggart, bragger, vaunter. *Informal:* blowhard. *Slang:* blower. *See* PRAISE.
brag *adjective* Exceptionally good of its kind : ace, banner, blue-ribbon, capital, champion, excellent, fine[1], first-class, first-rate, prime, quality, splendid, superb, superior, terrific, tiptop, top. *Informal:* A-one, bully, dandy, great, swell, topflight, topnotch. *Slang:* boss. *Chiefly British:* tophole. *See* GOOD.

braggadocio *noun*
1. One given to boasting : boaster, brag, braggart, bragger, vaunter. *Informal:* blowhard. *Slang:* blower. *See* PRAISE. **2.** An act of boasting : boast, brag, fanfaronade, gasconade, rodomontade, vaunt. *Informal:* blow[1]. *See* PRAISE.

braggart *noun*
One given to boasting : boaster, brag, braggadocio, bragger, vaunter. *Informal:* blowhard. *Slang:* blower. *See* PRAISE.
braggart *adjective* Characterized by or given to boasting : boastful, rodomontade. *See* ATTITUDE, PRAISE.

bragger *noun*
One given to boasting : boaster, brag, braggadocio, braggart, vaunter. *Informal:* blowhard. *Slang:* blower. *See* PRAISE.

brain *noun*
1. The seat of the faculty of intelligence and reason : head, mind. *Informal:* gray matter. *See* THOUGHTS. **2.** The faculty of thinking, reasoning, and acquiring and applying knowledge. Often used in plural : brainpower, intellect, intelligence, mentality, mind, sense, understanding, wit. *Slang:* smart (used in plural). *See* ABILITY, THOUGHTS. **3.** A person of great mental ability : intellect, intellectual, mind, thinker. *See* ABILITY.

brainchild *noun*
Something invented : contrivance, device, invention. *See* MACHINE, MAKE.

brainless *adjective*
Displaying a complete lack of forethought and good sense : fatuous, foolish, insensate, mindless, senseless, silly, unintelligent, weak-minded, witless. *See* ABILITY, PLANNED.

brainpower *noun*
The faculty of thinking, reasoning, and acquiring and applying knowledge : brain (often used in plural), intellect, intelligence, mentality, mind, sense, understanding, wit. *Slang:* smart (used in plural). *See* ABILITY, THOUGHTS.

brainsick *adjective*
Afflicted with or exhibiting irrationality and mental unsoundness : crazy, daft, demented, disordered, distraught, dotty, insane, lunatic, mad, maniac, maniacal, mentally ill, moonstruck, off, touched, unbalanced, unsound, wrong. *Informal:* bonkers, cracked, daffy, gaga, loony. *Slang:* bananas, batty, buggy, cuckoo, fruity, loco, nuts, nutty, screwy, wacky. *Chiefly British:* crackers. *Law:* non compos mentis. ***Idioms:*** around the bend, crazy as a loon, mad as a hatter, not all there, nutty as a fruitcake, off (*or* out of) one's head, off one's rocker, of unsound mind, out of one's mind, sick in the head, stark raving mad. *See* SANE.

brainsickness *noun*
Serious mental illness or disorder impairing a person's capacity to function normally and safely : craziness, dementia, derangement, disturbance, insaneness, insanity, lunacy, madness, mental illness, psychopathy, unbalance. *Psychiatry:* mania. *Psychology:* aberration, alienation. *See* SANE.

brainstorm *noun*
A sudden exciting thought : inspiration. *Informal:* brain wave. *See* THOUGHTS.

brainwash *verb*
To teach to accept a system of thought uncritically : indoctrinate, propagandize. *See* TEACH.

brain wave *noun*
Informal. A sudden exciting thought : brainstorm, inspiration. *See* THOUGHTS.

brainwork *noun*
The act or process of thinking : cerebration, cogitation, contemplation, deliberation, excogitation, meditation, reflection, rumination, speculation, thought. *See* THOUGHTS.

brainy *adjective*
Informal. Having or showing intelligence, often of a high order : brilliant, intellectual, intelligent, knowing, knowledgeable. *See* ABILITY.

brake *noun*
An instrument or means of restraining : bit[2], bridle, leash, restraint, snaffle. *See* RESTRAINT.
brake *verb* To control, restrict, or arrest : bit[2], bridle, check, constrain, curb, hold, hold back, hold down, hold in, inhibit, keep, keep back, pull in, rein (back, in, *or* up), restrain. *See* RESTRAINT.

branch *noun*
1. Something resembling or structurally analogous to a tree branch : arm, fork, offshoot. *See* PART. **2.** An area of academic study that is part of a larger body of learning : discipline, specialty. *See* PART. **3.** A local unit of a business or an auxiliary controlled by such a business : affiliate, division, subsidiary. *See* PART. **4.** A component of government that performs a given function : agency, arm, department, division, organ, wing. *See* PART. **5.** A part of a family, tribe, or other group, or of such a group's language, that is believed to stem from a common ancestor : division, offshoot, subdivision. *See* PART. **6.** *Chiefly Regional.* A small stream : brook[1], creek. *Chiefly Regional:* kill[2], run. *See* DRY.
branch *verb* To separate into branches or branchlike parts. Also used with *out* : bifurcate, diverge, divide, fork, ramify, subdivide. *See* PART.

brand *noun*
A name or other device placed on merchandise to signify its ownership or manufacture : colophon, label, mark, trademark. *See* MARKS.
brand *verb* **1.** To set off by or as if by a mark indicating ownership or manufacture : identify, label, mark, tag, trademark. *See* MARKS. **2.** To mark with disgrace or infamy : stigmatize. ***Idiom:*** give someone a bad name. *See* MARKS, RESPECT.

brandish *verb*
1. To wield boldly and dramatically : flourish, sweep, wave. *See* EXPRESS. **2.** To make a public and usually ostentatious show of : display, disport, exhibit, expose, flash, flaunt, parade, show (off), sport. *See* SHOW.

brand-new *adjective*
Not previously used : fresh, new. *See* NEW.

brannigan *noun*
A drinking bout : binge, carousal, carouse, drunk, spree. *Slang:* bat[2], bender, booze, jag, tear[1]. *See* DRUGS, RESTRAINT.

brash *adjective*
1. Characterized by unthinking boldness and haste : foolhardy, harum-scarum, hasty, headlong, hotheaded, ill-considered, impetuous, improvident, impulsive, incautious, madcap, precipitant, precipitate, rash[1], reckless, slapdash, temerarious, unconsidered. *See* CAREFUL. **2.** Lacking sensitivity and skill in dealing with others : clumsy, gauche, impolitic, indelicate, maladroit, tactless, undiplomatic, unpolitic, untactful. *See* ABILITY, COURTESY. **3.** Rude and disrespectful : assuming, assumptive, auda-

cious, bold, boldfaced, brazen, cheeky, contumelious, familiar, forward, impertinent, impudent, insolent, malapert, nervy, overconfident, pert, presuming, presumptuous, pushy, sassy, saucy, smart. *Informal:* brassy, flip, fresh, smart-alecky, snippety, snippy, uppish, uppity. *Slang:* wise[1]. *See* ATTITUDE, COURTESY.

brashness *noun*
1. Foolhardy boldness or disregard of danger : foolhardiness, incautiousness, rashness, recklessness, temerariousness, temerity. *See* CAREFUL. **2.** The state or quality of being impudent or arrogantly self-confident : assumption, audaciousness, audacity, boldness, brazenness, cheek, cheekiness, chutzpah, discourtesy, disrespect, effrontery, face, familiarity, forwardness, gall[1], impertinence, impudence, impudency, incivility, insolence, nerve, nerviness, overconfidence, pertness, presumptuousness, pushiness, rudeness, sassiness, sauciness. *Informal:* brass, crust, sauce, uppishness, uppityness. *See* ATTITUDE, COURTESY.

brass *noun*
1. *Informal.* The state or quality of being impudent or arrogantly self-confident : assumption, audaciousness, audacity, boldness, brashness, brazenness, cheek, cheekiness, chutzpah, discourtesy, disrespect, effrontery, face, familiarity, forwardness, gall[1], impertinence, impudence, impudency, incivility, insolence, nerve, nerviness, overconfidence, pertness, presumptuousness, pushiness, rudeness, sassiness, sauciness. *Informal:* crust, sauce, uppishness, uppityness. *See* ATTITUDE, COURTESY. **2.** *Chiefly British.* Something, such as coins or printed bills, used as a medium of exchange : cash, currency, lucre, money. *Informal:* wampum. *Slang:* bread, cabbage, dough, gelt, green, jack, lettuce, long green, mazuma, moola, scratch. *See* MONEY.

brassbound *adjective*
Firmly, often unreasonably immovable in purpose or will : adamant, adamantine, die-hard, grim, implacable, incompliant, inexorable, inflexible, intransigent, iron, obdurate, relentless, remorseless, rigid, stubborn, unbendable, unbending, uncompliant, uncompromising, unrelenting, unyielding. ***Idiom:*** stubborn as a mule (*or* ox). *See* RESIST.

brass ring *noun*
Slang. A person or thing worth catching : plum, prize[1]. *Informal:* catch. *See* DESIRE.

brass-tacks *adjective*
Informal. Precisely meaningful and tersely cogent : aphoristic, compact[1], epigrammatic, epigrammatical, marrowy, pithy. ***Idioms:*** down to brass tacks, to the point. *See* MEANING, STYLE.

brassy *adjective*
1. *Informal.* Rude and disrespectful : assuming, assumptive, audacious, bold, boldfaced, brash, brazen, cheeky, contumelious, familiar, forward, impertinent, impudent, insolent, malapert, nervy, overconfident, pert, presuming, presumptuous, pushy, sassy, saucy, smart. *Informal:* flip, fresh, smart-alecky, snippety, snippy, uppish, uppity. *Slang:* wise[1]. *See* ATTITUDE, COURTESY. **2.** *Informal.* Characterized by or done without shame : bald-faced, barefaced, blatant, brazen, brazenfaced, shameless, unabashed, unblushing. *See* COURTESY, RESPECT, RIGHT.

brattle *verb*
To make or cause to make a succession of short, sharp sounds : chatter, clack, clatter, rattle. *See* SOUNDS.

brave *adjective*
Having or showing courage : audacious, bold, courageous, dauntless, doughty, fearless, fortitudinous, gallant, game, hardy, heroic, intrepid, mettlesome, plucky, stout, stouthearted, unafraid, undaunted, valiant, valorous. *Informal:* spunky. *Slang:* gutsy, gutty. *See* FEAR.

brave *noun Archaic.* One who is habitually cruel to smaller or weaker people : browbeater, bulldozer, bully, hector, intimidator. *See* OVER.

brave *verb* To confront boldly and courageously : beard, challenge, dare, defy, face, front. ***Idioms:*** fly in the face of, snap one's fingers at, stand up to, thumb one's nose at. *See* RESIST.

braveness *noun*
The quality of mind enabling one to face danger or hardship resolutely : bravery, courage, courageousness, dauntlessness, doughtiness, fearlessness, fortitude, gallantry, gameness, heart, intrepidity, intrepidness, mettle, nerve, pluck, pluckiness, spirit, stoutheartedness, undauntedness, valiance, valiancy, valiantness, valor. *Informal:* spunk, spunkiness. *Slang:* gut (used in plural), gutsiness, moxie. *See* FEAR.

bravery *noun*
The quality of mind enabling one to face danger or hardship resolutely : braveness, courage, courageousness, dauntlessness, doughtiness, fearlessness, fortitude, gallantry, gameness, heart, intrepidity, intrepidness, mettle, nerve, pluck, pluckiness, spirit, stoutheartedness, undauntedness, valiance, valiancy, valiantness,

valor. *Informal:* spunk, spunkiness. *Slang:* gut (used in plural), gutsiness, moxie. *See* FEAR.

braw *adjective*
Scots. Having pleasant desirable qualities : good, nice. *Scots:* bonny. *See* GOOD.

brawl *noun*
A quarrel, fight, or disturbance marked by very noisy, disorderly, and often violent behavior : affray, broil[2], donnybrook, fray, free-for-all, melee, riot, row[2], ruction, tumult. *Informal:* fracas. *Slang:* rumble. *See* ATTACK.
brawl *verb* To quarrel noisily : broil[2], caterwaul, row[2], wrangle. *See* ATTACK.

brawn *noun*
1. Solid and well-developed muscles : bulk, muscularity. *Informal:* beef. *See* BODY. **2.** The state or quality of being physically strong : might, muscle, potence, potency, power, powerfulness, puissance, sinew, strength, thew (often used in plural). *See* STRONG.

brawny *adjective*
Characterized by marked muscular development; powerfully built : athletic, burly, husky[2], muscular, robust, sinewy, sturdy. *See* STRONG.

bray *verb*
To break up into tiny particles : crush, granulate, grind, mill, powder, pulverize, triturate. *See* HELP.

brazen *adjective*
1. Rude and disrespectful : assuming, assumptive, audacious, bold, boldfaced, brash, cheeky, contumelious, familiar, forward, impertinent, impudent, insolent, malapert, nervy, overconfident, pert, presuming, presumptuous, pushy, sassy, saucy, smart. *Informal:* brassy, flip, fresh, smart-alecky, snippety, snippy, uppish, uppity. *Slang:* wise[1]. *See* ATTITUDE, COURTESY. **2.** Characterized by or done without shame : bald-faced, barefaced, blatant, brazenfaced, shameless, unabashed, unblushing. *Informal:* brassy. *See* COURTESY, RESPECT, RIGHT.

brazenfaced *adjective*
Characterized by or done without shame : bald-faced, barefaced, blatant, brazen, shameless, unabashed, unblushing. *Informal:* brassy. *See* COURTESY, RESPECT, RIGHT.

brazenness *noun*
The state or quality of being impudent or arrogantly self-confident : assumption, audaciousness, audacity, boldness, brashness, cheek, cheekiness, chutzpah, discourtesy, disrespect, effrontery, face, familiarity, forwardness, gall[1], impertinence, impudence, impudency, incivility, insolence, nerve, nerviness, overconfidence, pertness, presumptuousness, pushiness, rudeness, sassiness, sauciness. *Informal:* brass, crust, sauce, uppishness, uppityness. *See* ATTITUDE, COURTESY.

breach *noun*
1. An opening, especially in a solid structure : break, gap, hole, perforation, rupture. *See* OPEN. **2.** An act or instance of breaking a law or regulation or of nonfulfillment of an obligation or promise, for example : contravention, infraction, infringement, transgression, trespass, violation. *See* RIGHT. **3.** An interruption in friendly relations : alienation, break, disaffection, estrangement, fissure, rent[2], rift, rupture, schism, split. *See* ASSEMBLE, HELP.
breach *verb* **1.** To make a hole or other opening in : break (through), gap, hole, perforate, pierce, puncture. *See* OPEN. **2.** To fail to fulfill (a promise) or conform to (a regulation) : break, contravene, infringe, transgress, violate. *See* DO.

bread *noun*
1. Something fit to be eaten : aliment, comestible, diet, edible, esculent, fare, food, foodstuff, meat, nourishment, nurture, nutriment, nutrition, pabulum, pap, provender, provision (used in plural), sustenance, victual. *Slang:* chow, eats, grub. *See* INGESTION. **2.** That which sustains the mind or spirit : aliment, food, nourishment, nutriment, pabulum, pap, sustenance. *See* CARE FOR, INGESTION. **3.** The means needed to support life : alimentation, alimony, bread and butter, keep, livelihood, living, maintenance, subsistence, support, sustenance, upkeep. *See* MONEY. **4.** *Slang.* Something, such as coins or printed bills, used as a medium of exchange : cash, currency, lucre, money. *Informal:* wampum. *Slang:* cabbage, dough, gelt, green, jack, lettuce, long green, mazuma, moola, scratch. *Chiefly British:* brass. *See* MONEY.

bread and butter *noun*
The means needed to support life : alimentation, alimony, bread, keep, livelihood, living, maintenance, subsistence, support, sustenance, upkeep. *See* MONEY.

breadth *noun*
The extent of something from side to side : broadness, wideness, width. *See* WIDE.

break *verb*
1. To crack or split into two or more fragments by means of or as a result of force, a blow, or strain : fracture, rift, rive, shatter, shiver[2], smash, splinter, sunder. *See* HELP. **2.** To become or cause to become apart one from an-

other : detach, disjoin, disjoint, disunite, divide, divorce, part, separate, split (up). ***Idioms:*** part company, set at odds. *See* ASSEMBLE. **3.** To make a hole or other opening in. Also used with *through* : breach, gap, hole, perforate, pierce, puncture. *See* OPEN. **4.** To pass into or through by overcoming resistance. Also used with *through* : enter, penetrate, perforate, pierce, puncture. *See* ENTER. **5.** To find the key to (a code, for example) : crack, decipher, decrypt, puzzle out. *See* KNOWLEDGE. **6.** To make known : carry, communicate, convey, disclose, get across, impart, pass, report, tell, transmit. *See* KNOWLEDGE. **7.** To be made public : come out, get out, out, transpire. *Informal:* leak (out). ***Idiom:*** come to light. *See* KNOWLEDGE, SHOW. **8.** To make or become unusable or inoperative : fail, ruin. *Slang:* bust. *See* HELP. **9.** To impair severely something such as the spirit, health, or effectiveness of : crush, destroy, overwhelm, ruin. *See* HELP. **10.** To give way mentally and emotionally. Also used with *down* : collapse, crack, snap. *Informal:* crack up, fold. *See* EXPLOSION. **11.** To suddenly lose all health or strength. Also used with *down* : cave in, collapse, crack, drop, give out, succumb. *Informal:* crack up. *Slang:* conk out. ***Idiom:*** give way. *See* HEALTH. **12.** To reduce to financial insolvency : bankrupt, bust, impoverish, pauperize, ruin. *Slang:* clean out. *See* MONEY. **13.** To undergo sudden financial failure : bust, collapse, crash, fail, go under. *Informal:* fold. ***Idioms:*** go belly up, go bust, go on the rocks, go to the wall. *See* MONEY. **14.** To lower in rank or grade : bump, degrade, demote, downgrade, reduce. *Slang:* bust. *See* RISE. **15.** To fail to fulfill (a promise) or conform to (a regulation) : breach, contravene, infringe, transgress, violate. *See* DO. **16.** To refuse or fail to obey : defy, disobey, flout, transgress, violate. ***Idiom:*** pay no attention to. *See* RESIST. **17.** To desist from, cease, or discontinue (a habit, for example) : cut out, give up, leave off, stop. *Slang:* kick. *See* CONTINUE. **18.** To interrupt regular activity for a short period : recess. ***Idioms:*** take a break, take a breather, take five (*or* ten). *See* CONTINUE. **19.** To make (an animal) docile : bust, gentle, master, tame. *See* WILD.

break down *verb* **1.** To cause the complete ruin or wreckage of : bankrupt, cross up, demolish, destroy, finish, ruin, shatter, sink, smash, spoil, torpedo, undo, wash up, wrack[2], wreck. *Slang:* total. ***Idiom:*** put the kibosh on. *See* HELP. **2.** To cease functioning properly : fail, give out. *Slang:* conk out. *See* THRIVE. **3.** To separate into parts for study : analyze, anatomize, dissect, resolve. *See* ASSEMBLE, INVESTIGATE. **4.** To take (something) apart : disassemble, dismantle, dismount, take down. *See* ASSEMBLE. **5.** To reduce or become reduced to pieces or components : break up, crumble, decompose, disintegrate, dissolve, fragment, fragmentize. *See* CONTINUE, HELP. **6.** To become or cause to become rotten or unsound : decay, decompose, deteriorate, disintegrate, molder, putrefy, rot, spoil, taint, turn. ***Idioms:*** go bad, go to pot, go to seed. *See* BETTER, THRIVE.

break in *verb* **1.** To enter forcibly or illegally : burglarize. *Law:* trespass. *See* CRIMES, ENTER. **2.** To interject remarks or questions into another's discourse : chime in, chip in, cut in, interrupt. *See* CONTINUE.

break off *verb* **1.** To stop suddenly, as a conversation, activity, or relationship : cease, discontinue, interrupt, suspend, terminate. *See* CONTINUE. **2.** To cease trying to accomplish or continue : abandon, desist, discontinue, give up, leave off, quit, relinquish, remit, stop. *Informal:* swear off. *Slang:* lay off. ***Idioms:*** call it a day, call it quits, hang up one's fiddle, have done with, throw in the towel. *See* CONTINUE. **3.** To terminate a relationship or an association by or as if by leaving one another : break up, part, separate. *Informal:* split (up). ***Idioms:*** call it quits, come to a parting of the ways, part company. *See* ASSEMBLE, CONTINUE.

break out *verb* **1.** To become manifest suddenly and in full force : burst (forth *or* out), erupt, explode, flare (up). *See* EXPLOSION, START. **2.** To break loose and leave suddenly, as from confinement or from a difficult or threatening situation : abscond, decamp, escape, flee, fly, get away, run away. *Informal:* skip (out). *Slang:* lam. *Regional:* absquatulate. ***Idioms:*** blow (*or* fly) the coop, cut and run, give someone the slip, make a getaway, take flight, take it on the lam. *See* FREE.

break up *verb* **1.** To make a division into parts, sections, or branches : dissever, divide, part, partition, section, segment, separate. *See* ASSEMBLE, PART. **2.** To reduce or become reduced to pieces or components : break down, crumble, decompose, disintegrate, dissolve, fragment, fragmentize. *See* CONTINUE, HELP. **3.** To terminate a relationship or an association by or as if by leaving one another : break off, part, separate. *Informal:* split (up). ***Idioms:*** call it quits, come to a parting of the ways, part company. *See* ASSEMBLE, CONTINUE. **4.** *Informal.* To express great amusement or mirth : guffaw, roar. *Slang:* howl. *See* LAUGHTER.

break *noun* **1.** An opening, especially in a solid structure : breach, gap, hole, perforation, rupture. *See* OPEN. **2.** A usually narrow partial opening caused by splitting and rupture : chink, cleavage, cleft, crack, crevice, fissure, rift, split. *See* OPEN. **3.** The act or an instance of escaping, as from confinement or difficulty : breakout, decampment, escape, escapement, flight, getaway. *Slang:* lam. *See* FREE. **4.** A cessation of continuity or regularity : discontinuance, discontinuation, discontinuity, disruption, interruption, pause, suspension. *See* CONTINUE. **5.** An interval during which continuity is suspended : gap, hiatus, interim, lacuna, void. *See* CONTINUE. **6.** A pause or interval, as from work or duty : intermission, recess, respite, rest[1], time-out. *Informal:* breather. *See* CONTINUE. **7.** A favorable or advantageous combination of circumstances : chance, occasion, opening, opportunity. *Informal:* shot. *See* LUCK. **8.** An interruption in friendly relations : alienation, breach, disaffection, estrangement, fissure, rent[2], rift, rupture, schism, split. *See* ASSEMBLE, HELP.

breakable *adjective*
Easily broken or damaged : brittle, delicate, fragile, frangible. *See* STRONG.

breakage *noun*
An act, instance, or consequence of breaking : damage, destruction, impairment, wreckage. *See* HELP.

breakdown *noun*
1. A cessation of proper mechanical functions : failure, outage. *See* THRIVE. **2.** An abrupt disastrous failure : collapse, crash, debacle, smash, smashup, wreck. *See* MONEY. **3.** A sudden sharp decline in mental, emotional, or physical health : collapse. *Informal:* crackup. *See* EXPLOSION. **4.** The separation of a whole into its parts for study : analysis, anatomy, dissection. *See* ASSEMBLE, INVESTIGATE. **5.** The condition of being decayed : decay, decomposition, deterioration, disintegration, putrefaction, putrescence, putridness, rot, rottenness, spoilage. *See* BETTER, THRIVE.

break down *verb* See **break.**

break in *verb* See **break.**

break-in *noun*
The act of entering a building or room with the intent to commit theft : burglary, trespass. *See* CRIMES.

breakneck *adjective*
Characterized by great celerity : expeditious, fast, fleet, quick, rapid, speedy, swift. *Informal:* hell-for-leather. ***Idiom:*** quick as a bunny (*or* wink). *See* FAST.

break off *verb* See **break.**

breakout *noun*
The act or an instance of escaping, as from confinement or difficulty : break, decampment, escape, escapement, flight, getaway. *Slang:* lam. *See* FREE.

break out *verb* See **break.**

break up *verb* See **break.**

breast *noun*
The seat of a person's innermost emotions and feelings : bosom, heart, soul. ***Idioms:*** bottom of one's heart, cockles of one's heart, one's heart of hearts. *See* FEELINGS.

breath *noun*
1. The vital principle or animating force within living beings : divine spark, élan vital, life force, psyche, soul, spirit, vital force, vitality. *See* BODY. **2.** The act or process of breathing : respiration. *See* BREATH. **3.** Air breathed out, evidenced by vapor, odor, or heat : exhalation. *See* BREATH. **4.** A slight amount or indication : dash, ghost, hair, hint, intimation, semblance, shade, shadow, soupçon, streak, suggestion, suspicion, taste, tinge, touch, trace, whiff, whisper. *Informal:* whisker. *See* BIG, SHOW.

breathe *verb*
1. To breathe in and out : respire. *See* BREATH. **2.** To draw air into the lungs in the process of respiration. Also used with *in* : inhale, inspire. *See* BREATH. **3.** To expel air in the process of respiration. Also used with *out* : exhale, expire. *See* BREATH. **4.** To have reality or life : be, exist, live[1], subsist. *See* BE. **5.** To tell in confidence : confide, whisper. *See* SHOW, WORDS.

breather *noun*
Informal. A pause or interval, as from work or duty : break, intermission, recess, respite, rest[1], time-out. *See* CONTINUE.

breathless *adjective*
Marked by an absence of circulating air : airless, breezeless, still, windless. *See* BREATH.

breed *verb*
1. To produce sexually or asexually others of one's kind : increase, multiply, procreate, proliferate, propagate, reproduce, spawn. *See* REPRODUCTION. **2.** To be the biological father of : beget, father, get, procreate, sire. *See* KIN.

3. To cause to come into existence : beget, create, engender, father, hatch, make, originate, parent, procreate, produce, sire, spawn. ***Idiom:*** give birth (*or* rise) to. *See* MAKE. **4.** To bring into existence and foster the development of : cultivate, grow, propagate, raise. *See* CARE FOR, REPRODUCTION.

breed *noun* A class that is defined by the common attribute or attributes possessed by all its members : cast, description, feather, ilk, kind², lot, manner, mold, nature, order, sort, species, stamp, stripe, type, variety. *Informal:* persuasion. *See* GROUP.

breeding *noun*
The process by which an organism produces others of its kind : multiplication, procreation, proliferation, propagation, reproduction, spawning. *Obsolete:* increase. *See* REPRODUCTION.

breeze *noun*
1. A gentle wind : zephyr. *See* BREATH. **2.** A natural movement or current of air : air, blast, blow¹, gust, wind¹, zephyr. *Archaic:* gale. *See* BREATH. **3.** *Informal.* An easily accomplished task : child's play, cinch, pushover, snap, walkaway, walkover. *Slang:* duck soup. *See* EASY.

breeze *verb Informal.* To move swiftly and effortlessly : zip. *Slang:* waltz. *See* EASY.

breezeless *adjective*
Marked by an absence of circulating air : airless, breathless, still, windless. *See* BREATH.

breezy *adjective*
1. Exposed to or characterized by the presence of freely circulating air or wind : airy, blowy, gusty, windy. *See* BREATH. **2.** Displaying lighthearted nonchalance : airy, buoyant, debonair, jaunty. *Informal:* corky. ***Idiom:*** free and easy. *See* ATTITUDE, CAREFUL, GOOD.

brew *verb*
To be imminent : hang over, impend, loom, lower¹, menace, overhang, threaten. *See* NEAR.

briary *adjective* See **briery.**

bribe *noun*
Money, property, or a favor given, offered, or promised to a person or accepted by a person in a position of trust as an inducement to dishonest behavior : fix, graft, payola. *Informal:* payoff. *Slang:* boodle. *See* CRIMES, MONEY, PERSUASION.

bribe *verb* To give, offer, or promise a bribe to : buy (off). *Informal:* pay off. ***Idiom:*** grease someone's palm (*or* hand). *See* CRIMES, MONEY, PERSUASION.

bridal *noun*
The act or ceremony by which two people become husband and wife : espousal, marriage, nuptial (often used in plural), spousal (often used in plural), wedding. *See* MARRIAGE.

bridle *noun*
An instrument or means of restraining : bit², brake, leash, restraint, snaffle. *See* RESTRAINT.

bridle *verb* To control, restrict, or arrest : bit², brake, check, constrain, curb, hold, hold back, hold down, hold in, inhibit, keep, keep back, pull in, rein (back, in, *or* up), restrain. *See* RESTRAINT.

brief *adjective*
1. Not long in time or duration : short. *See* BIG, FAST. **2.** Accomplished in very little time : expeditious, fast, flying, hasty, hurried, quick, rapid, short, speedy, swift. *See* FAST. **3.** Marked by or consisting of few words that are carefully chosen : compendious, concise, laconic, lean², short, succinct, summary, terse. *See* BIG, STYLE, WORDS. **4.** Rudely unceremonious : abrupt, blunt, brusque, crusty, curt, gruff, short, short-spoken. *See* ATTITUDE.

brief *noun* A short summary or version prepared by cutting down a larger work : abridgment, abstract, condensation, epitome, synopsis. *See* WORDS.

briery also **briary** *adjective*
Full of sharp needlelike protuberances : echinate, prickly, pricky, spiny, thistly, thorny. *See* SHARP.

brig *noun*
A place for the confinement of persons in lawful detention : house of correction, jail, keep, penitentiary, prison. *Informal:* lockup, pen³. *Slang:* big house, can, clink, cooler, coop, hoosegow, joint, jug, pokey¹, slammer, stir². *Chiefly Regional:* calaboose. *See* FREE.

bright *adjective*
1. Giving off or reflecting light readily or in large amounts : beamy, brilliant, effulgent, incandescent, irradiant, lambent, lucent, luminous, lustrous, radiant, refulgent, shiny. *See* LIGHT. **2.** Full of color : colorful, gay, rich, vivid. *See* COLORS. **3.** Indicative of future success or full of promise : auspicious, benign, brilliant, fair, favorable, fortunate, good, propitious. *See* LUCK. **4.** Being in or showing good spirits : cheerful, cheery, chipper, happy, lighthearted, sunny. *See* HAPPY. **5.** Mentally quick and original : alert, clever, intelligent, keen¹, quick, quick-witted, sharp, sharp-witted, smart. ***Idiom:*** smart as a whip. *See* ABILITY.

brighten *verb*
1. To become brighter or fairer : clear (up), lighten[1]. *See* CLEAR. **2.** To make lively or animated : animate, enliven, light[1]. *See* HAPPY.

brilliance *noun*
1. Exceptional brightness and clarity, as of a cut and polished stone : brilliancy, fire, luminosity, radiance. *See* LIGHT. **2.** Liveliness and vivacity of imagination : brilliancy, fire, genius, inspiration. *See* GOOD. **3.** Brilliant, showy splendor : brilliancy, glitter, glory, gorgeousness, magnificence, resplendence, resplendency, sparkle, sumptuousness. *Informal:* glitz. *See* BEAUTIFUL.

brilliancy *noun*
1. Exceptional brightness and clarity, as of a cut and polished stone : brilliance, fire, luminosity, radiance. *See* LIGHT. **2.** Liveliness and vivacity of imagination : brilliance, fire, genius, inspiration. *See* GOOD. **3.** Brilliant, showy splendor : brilliance, glitter, glory, gorgeousness, magnificence, resplendence, resplendency, sparkle, sumptuousness. *Informal:* glitz. *See* BEAUTIFUL.

brilliant *adjective*
1. Giving off or reflecting light readily or in large amounts : beamy, bright, effulgent, incandescent, irradiant, lambent, lucent, luminous, lustrous, radiant, refulgent, shiny. *See* LIGHT. **2.** Extemely bright : glaring, glary. *See* LIGHT. **3.** Marked by extraordinary elegance, beauty, and splendor : glorious, gorgeous, magnificent, proud, resplendent, splendid, splendorous. *See* BEAUTIFUL. **4.** Indicative of future success or full of promise : auspicious, benign, bright, fair, favorable, fortunate, good, propitious. *See* LUCK. **5.** Having or showing intelligence, often of a high order : intellectual, intelligent, knowing, knowledgeable. *Informal:* brainy. *See* ABILITY.

brim *noun*
1. The projecting rim on the front of a cap : bill[2], peak, visor. *See* CONVEX, PROTECTION. **2.** A fairly narrow line or space forming a boundary : border, borderline, brink, edge, edging, fringe, margin, periphery, rim, verge. *Chiefly Military:* perimeter. *See* EDGE.

brimful *adjective*
1. Full to the point of flowing over : awash, big, brimming, overflowing. *See* BIG, RICH. **2.** Completely filled : brimming, bursting, chockablock, full, packed, replete. *See* FULL.

brimming *adjective*
1. Full to the point of flowing over : awash, big, brimful, overflowing. *See* BIG, RICH. **2.** Completely filled : brimful, bursting, chockablock, full, packed, replete. *See* FULL.

bring *verb*
1. To cause to come along with oneself : bear, carry, convey, fetch, take, transport. *See* ACCOMPANIED. **2.** To succeed in causing (a person) to act in a certain way : argue into, bring around (*or* round), convince, get, induce, persuade, prevail on (*or* upon), sell (on), talk into. *See* PERSUASION. **3.** To be the cause of : bring about, bring on, cause, effect, effectuate, generate, induce, ingenerate, lead to, make, occasion, result in, secure, set off, stir[1] (up), touch off, trigger. ***Idioms:*** bring to pass (*or* effect), give rise to. *See* START. **4.** To achieve (a certain price). Also used with *in* : fetch, realize, sell for. *See* GET.

bring about *verb* To be the cause of : bring, bring on, cause, effect, effectuate, generate, induce, ingenerate, lead to, make, occasion, result in, secure, set off, stir[1] (up), touch off, trigger. *Idioms:* bring to pass (*or* effect), give rise to. *See* START.

bring around (or **round**) *verb* **1.** To succeed in causing (a person) to act in a certain way : argue into, bring, convince, get, induce, persuade, prevail on (*or* upon), sell (on), talk into. *See* PERSUASION. **2.** To cause to come back to life or consciousness : restore, resuscitate, revive, revivify. *See* LIVE.

bring down *verb* **1.** To cause to fall, as from a shot or blow : cut down, down, drop, fell[1], flatten, floor, ground, knock down, level, prostrate, strike down, throw. *Slang:* deck[1]. ***Idiom:*** lay low. *See* RISE. **2.** To bring about the downfall of : overthrow, overturn, subvert, topple, tumble, unhorse. *See* HELP.

bring forth *verb* To give birth to : bear, deliver, have. *Chiefly Regional:* birth. ***Idiom:*** be brought abed (*or* to bed) of. *See* RICH.

bring in *verb* To make as income or profit : clear, draw, earn, gain, gross, net[2], pay, produce, realize, repay, return, yield. *See* MONEY.

bring off *verb* To bring about and carry to a successful conclusion : carry out, carry through, effect, effectuate, execute, put through. *Informal:* swing. *See* DO.

bring on *verb* To be the cause of : bring, bring about, cause, effect, effectuate, generate, induce, ingenerate, lead to, make, occasion, result in, secure, set off, stir[1] (up), touch off, trigger. *Idioms:* bring to pass (*or* effect), give rise to. *See* START.

Informal: apple-polish, cotton. *Slang:* suck up. ***Idioms:*** curry favor, dance attendance, kiss someone's feet, lick someone's boots. *See* OVER.

brown study *noun*
The condition of being so lost in solitary thought as to be unaware of one's surroundings : absent-mindedness, abstraction, bemusement, daydreaming, muse[2], reverie, study, trance. *See* AWARENESS.

browse *verb*
To look through reading matter casually : dip into, flip through, glance at (*or* over *or* through), leaf (through), riffle (through), run through, scan, skim, thumb (through). *See* INVESTIGATE, WORDS.

bruise *verb*
To make a bruise or bruises on : contuse. *See* HELP.

bruit *verb*
To make (information) generally known : advertise, blaze[2], blazon, broadcast, circulate, disseminate, noise, promulgate, propagate, spread. ***Idioms:*** spread far and wide, spread the word. *See* KNOWLEDGE.

brume *noun*
A thick, heavy atmospheric condition offering reduced visibility because of the presence of suspended particles : fog, haze, mist, murk, smaze. *See* CLEAR.

brummagem *adjective*
Tastelessly showy : chintzy, flashy, garish, gaudy, glaring, loud, meretricious, tawdry, tinsel. *Informal:* tacky[2]. *See* STYLE.

brunet *adjective*
Of a complexion tending toward brown or black : bistered, black-a-vised, dark, dusky, swarthy. *See* COLORS.

brush[1] *noun*
Light and momentary contact with another person or thing : flick, graze, skim. *See* TOUCH.
brush *verb* To make light and momentary contact with, as in passing : flick, graze, kiss, shave, skim. *See* TOUCH.

brush[2] *noun*
A brief, hostile exposure to or contact with something such as danger or opposition : clash, encounter, run-in, skirmish. *See* TOUCH.

brusk *adjective* See **brusque.**

brusque also **brusk** *adjective*
Rudely unceremonious : abrupt, blunt, brief, crusty, curt, gruff, short, short-spoken. *See* ATTITUDE.

brutal *adjective*
Causing sharp, often prolonged discomfort : bitter, hard, harsh, rough, severe. *See* COMFORT.

brutality *noun*
A cruel act or an instance of cruel behavior : barbarity, bestiality, cruelty, inhumanity, savagery, truculence, truculency. *See* ATTITUDE, KIND.

brutalize *verb*
To ruin utterly in character or quality : animalize, bastardize, bestialize, canker, corrupt, debase, debauch, demoralize, deprave, pervert, stain, vitiate, warp. *See* CLEAN, HELP.

bubble *noun*
A fantastic, impracticable plan or desire : castle in the air, chimera, dream, fantasy, illusion, pipe dream, rainbow. *See* REAL.
bubble *verb* **1.** To form or cause to form foam : cream, effervesce, fizz, foam, froth, lather, spume, suds, yeast. *See* SOLID. **2.** To flow or move with a low slapping sound : burble, gurgle, lap, splash, swash, wash. *See* MOVE, SOUNDS. **3.** To be in a state of emotional or mental turmoil : boil, burn, churn, ferment, seethe, simmer, smolder. *See* CALM.

bubbling *adjective*
Emitting a murmuring sound felt to resemble a laugh : babbling, burbling, gurgling, laughing, rippling. *See* LAUGHTER, SOUNDS.

buck *verb*
To take a stand against : challenge, contest, dispute, oppose, resist, traverse. *See* SUPPORT.
buck up *verb* To impart strength and confidence to : cheer (up), encourage, hearten, nerve, perk up. *See* HELP.

bucket *verb*
To move swiftly : bolt, bustle, dart, dash, festinate, flash, fleet, flit, fly, haste, hasten, hurry, hustle, pelt[2], race, rocket, run, rush, sail, scoot, scour[2], shoot, speed, sprint, tear[1], trot, whirl, whisk, whiz, wing, zip, zoom. *Informal:* hotfoot, rip. *Slang:* barrel, highball. *Chiefly British:* nip[1]. ***Idioms:*** get a move on, get cracking, go like lightning, go like the wind, hotfoot it, make haste, make time, make tracks, run like the wind, shake a leg, step (*or* jump) on it. *See* MOVE.

buckle *verb*
1. To fall in : cave in, collapse, crumple, give, go. ***Idiom:*** give way. *See* EXPLOSION. **2.** To give in from or as if from a gradual loss of strength : bow[1], capitulate, submit, succumb, surrender, yield. *Informal:* fold. *See* RESIST.
buckle down *verb* To devote (oneself or one's efforts) : address, apply, bend, concentrate,

dedicate, devote, direct, focus, give, turn. *See* COLLECT, WORK.

buckle down *verb* See **buckle.**

buckram *adjective*
So rigidly constrained, formal, or awkward as to lack all grace and spontaneity : starchy, stiff, stilted, wooden. *See* FLEXIBLE.

buck up *verb* See **buck.**

bucolic *adjective*
Of or relating to the countryside : arcadian, campestral, country, pastoral, provincial, rural, rustic. *Informal:* hick. *See* URBAN.

bud[1] *noun*
1. A source of further growth and development : embryo, germ, kernel, nucleus, seed, spark[1]. *See* START. **2.** A young person between birth and puberty : child, innocent, juvenile, moppet, tot[1], youngster. *Informal:* kid. *Scots:* bairn. *See* KIN, YOUTH.

bud[2] *noun*
Informal. A person whom one knows well, likes, and trusts : amigo, brother, chum, confidant, confidante, familiar, friend, intimate[1], mate. *Informal:* buddy, pal. *Slang:* sidekick. *See* LOVE.

buddy *noun*
1. *Informal.* A person whom one knows well, likes, and trusts : amigo, brother, chum, confidant, confidante, familiar, friend, intimate[1], mate. *Informal:* bud[2], pal. *Slang:* sidekick. *See* LOVE. **2.** *Informal.* One who shares interests or activities with another : associate, chum, companion, comrade, crony, fellow, mate. *Informal:* pal. *See* NEAR.

budge *verb*
1. To make a slight movement : move, stir[1]. *See* MOVE. **2.** To impart slight movement to : move, stir[1]. *See* MOVE.

budget *noun*
A measurable whole : amount, body, bulk, corpus, quantity, quantum. *See* BIG.

buff[1] *verb*
To give a gleaming luster to, usually through friction : burnish, furbish, glaze, gloss, polish, shine, sleek. *See* LIGHT.

buff[2] *noun*
Informal. A person who is ardently devoted to a particular subject or activity : bug, devotee, enthusiast, fanatic, maniac, zealot. *Informal:* fan[2], fiend. *Slang:* freak, nut. *See* CONCERN.

buffet *noun*
A quick, sharp blow, especially with the hand : box[2], bust, chop[1], cuff, punch, slap, smack[1], smacker, spank, swat, whack. *Informal:* clip[1], spat. *See* ATTACK, STRIKE.

buffet *verb* **1.** To hit heavily and repeatedly with violent blows : assail, assault, baste, batter, beat, belabor, drub, hammer, pound, pummel, smash, thrash, thresh. *Informal:* lambaste. *Slang:* clobber. ***Idiom:*** rain blows on. *See* ATTACK, STRIKE. **2.** To hit with a quick, sharp blow of the hand : box[2], bust, cuff, punch, slap, smack[1], spank, swat, whack. *Informal:* clip[1], spat. *See* ATTACK, STRIKE.

bug *noun*
1. A minute organism usually producing disease : germ, microbe, microorganism. *See* BEINGS. **2.** A minor illness, especially one of a temporary nature : ailment, complaint, indisposition, malady. *See* HEALTH. **3.** Something that mars the appearance or causes inadequacy or failure : blemish, defect, fault, flaw, imperfection, shortcoming. *See* BEAUTIFUL, BETTER, HELP. **4.** A person who is ardently devoted to a particular subject or activity : devotee, enthusiast, fanatic, maniac, zealot. *Informal:* buff[2], fan[2], fiend. *Slang:* freak, nut. *See* CONCERN.

bug *verb* **1.** To trouble the nerves or peace of mind of, especially by repeated vexations : aggravate, annoy, bother, chafe, disturb, exasperate, fret, gall[2], get, irk, irritate, nettle, peeve, provoke, put out, rile, ruffle, vex. ***Idioms:*** get in one's hair, get on one's nerves, get under one's skin. *See* FEELINGS, PAIN. **2.** To monitor (telephone calls) with a concealed listening device connected to the circuit : tap[2], wiretap. *See* INVESTIGATE.

bugbear *noun*
An object of extreme dislike : abhorrence, abomination, anathema, aversion, bête noire, detestation, execration, hate. *Informal:* horror. *See* LOVE.

buggy *adjective*
Slang. Afflicted with or exhibiting irrationality and mental unsoundness : brainsick, crazy, daft, demented, disordered, distraught, dotty, insane, lunatic, mad, maniac, maniacal, mentally ill, moonstruck, off, touched, unbalanced, unsound, wrong. *Informal:* bonkers, cracked, daffy, gaga, loony. *Slang:* bananas, batty, cuckoo, fruity, loco, nuts, nutty, screwy, wacky. *Chiefly British:* crackers. *Law:* non compos mentis. ***Idioms:*** around the bend, crazy as a loon, mad as a hatter, not all there, nutty as a fruitcake, off (*or* out of) one's head, off one's rocker, of unsound mind, out of one's mind, sick in the head, stark raving mad. *See* SANE.

build *verb*
1. To make or form (a structure) : construct,

erect, put up, raise, rear[2]. *See* MAKE. **2.** To create by forming, combining, or altering materials : assemble, construct, fabricate, fashion, forge[1], frame, make, manufacture, mold, produce, put together, shape. *See* MAKE. **3.** To create by combining parts or elements : compose, configure, form, pattern, shape, structure. *See* MAKE. **4.** To make or become greater or larger : aggrandize, amplify, augment, boost, build up, burgeon, enlarge, escalate, expand, extend, grow, increase, magnify, mount, multiply, proliferate, rise, run up, snowball, soar, swell, upsurge, wax. *Informal:* beef up. *See* INCREASE. **5.** To provide a basis for : base[1], establish, found, ground, predicate, rest[1], root[1], underpin. *See* OVER.

build in *verb* To construct or include as an integral or permanent part : incorporate, integrate. *See* INCLUDE.

build up *verb* **1.** To achieve an increase of gradually : develop, gain. *See* INCREASE. **2.** To make or become greater or larger : aggrandize, amplify, augment, boost, build, burgeon, enlarge, escalate, expand, extend, grow, increase, magnify, mount, multiply, proliferate, rise, run up, snowball, soar, swell, upsurge, wax. *Informal:* beef up. *See* INCREASE. **3.** To make known vigorously the positive features of (a product) : advertise, ballyhoo, cry (up), popularize, promote, publicize, talk up. *Informal:* pitch, plug. *Slang:* push. *See* KNOWLEDGE. **4.** To increase or seek to increase the importance or reputation of by favorable publicity : ballyhoo, boost, enhance, promote, publicize, puff, talk up, tout. *Informal:* plug. *Slang:* hype. *See* KNOWLEDGE.

build *noun* The physical or constitutional characteristics of a person : constitution, habit, habitus, physique. *See* BODY.

builder *noun*
1. A person or business that makes or builds something : assembler, constructor, erector, maker, manufacturer, producer. *See* MAKE. **2.** A person instrumental in the growth of something, especially in its early stages : contributor, creator, developer, pioneer. *See* MAKE.

build in *verb* See **build.**

building *noun*
A usually permanent construction, such as a house or store : edifice, pile, structure. *See* MAKE.

building block *noun*
One of the individual entities contributing to a whole : component, constituent, element, factor, ingredient, integrant, part. *See* PART.

buildup also **build-up** *noun*
1. The act of increasing or rising : aggrandizement, amplification, augment, augmentation, boost, enlargement, escalation, growth, hike, increase, jump, multiplication, proliferation, raise, rise, swell, upsurge, upswing, upturn. *See* INCREASE. **2.** The result or product of building up : accretion, development, enlargement, multiplication, proliferation. *See* INCREASE. **3.** A systematic effort or part of this effort to increase the importance or reputation of by favorable publicity : advertisement, ballyhoo, promotion, publicity, puffery. *Informal:* pitch, plug. *Slang:* hype. *See* KNOWLEDGE.

build up *verb* See **build.**

built *adjective*
Informal. Having a full, voluptuous figure : buxom, curvaceous, curvy, shapely, well-developed. *Slang:* stacked. *See* BEAUTIFUL.

built-in *adjective*
1. Serving as part of a whole, as a nondetachable part of a larger unit : component, constituent, incorporated. *See* INCLUDE. **2.** Forming an essential element, as arising from the basic structure of an individual : congenital, connatural, constitutional, elemental, inborn, inbred, indigenous, indwelling, ingrained, inherent, innate, intrinsic, native, natural. *See* BE, NATIVE, START.

bulge *noun*
1. A part that protrudes or extends outward : jut, knob, knot, overhang, projection, protrusion, protuberance. *See* CONVEX. **2.** A dominating position, as in a conflict : advantage, better[1], draw, drop, edge, superiority, upper hand, vantage. *Informal:* inside track, jump. *See* OVER.

bulge *verb* To curve outward past the normal or usual limit : bag, balloon, beetle, belly, jut, overhang, pouch, project, protrude, protuberate, stand out, stick out. *See* CONVEX.

bulk *noun*
1. Great extent, amount, or dimension : amplitude, magnitude, mass, size, volume (often used in plural). *See* BIG. **2.** A measurable whole : amount, body, budget, corpus, quantity, quantum. *See* BIG. **3.** A separate and distinct portion of matter : body, mass, object. *See* MATTER. **4.** Solid and well-developed muscles : brawn, muscularity. *Informal:* beef. *See* BODY. **5.** The main part : body. *Anatomy:* corpus. *See* BIG. **6.** The greatest part or portion : mass, preponderance, preponderancy, weight. *See* BIG.

bulky *adjective*
1. Extremely large; having great mass : mas-

sive, oversize, oversized. *See* BIG. **2.** Having a large body, especially in girth : heavy, hefty, hulking, hulky, husky[2], stout. *See* BIG. **3.** Difficult to handle or manage : awkward, clumsy, ungainly, unhandy, unmanageable, unwieldy. *See* EASY.

bull[1] *noun*

1. *Slang.* A member of a law-enforcement agency : bluecoat, finest, officer, patrolman, patrolwoman, peace officer, police, policeman, police officer, policewoman. *Informal:* cop, law. *Slang:* copper, flatfoot, fuzz, gendarme, heat, man (often uppercase). *Chiefly British:* bobby, constable, peeler. *See* LAW. **2.** *Slang.* Something that does not have or make sense : balderdash, blather, bunkum, claptrap, drivel, garbage, idiocy, nonsense, piffle, poppycock, rigmarole, rubbish, tomfoolery, trash, twaddle. *Informal:* tommyrot. *Slang:* applesauce, baloney, bilge, bunk[2], crap, hooey, malarkey. *See* KNOWLEDGE.

bull[2] *noun*

A stupid, clumsy mistake : blunder, bungle, foozle, fumble, muff, stumble. *Informal:* blooper, boner. *Slang:* bloomer, goof. *See* CORRECT.

bulldoze *verb*

To domineer or drive into compliance by the use of as threats or force, for example : bludgeon, browbeat, bully, bullyrag, cow, hector, intimidate, menace, threaten. *Informal:* strong-arm. *See* OVER.

bulldozer *noun*

One who is habitually cruel to smaller or weaker people : browbeater, bully, hector, intimidator. *Archaic:* brave. *See* OVER.

bullheaded *adjective*

Tenaciously unwilling to yield : dogged, hardheaded, headstrong, mulish, obstinate, pertinacious, perverse, pigheaded, stiff-necked, tenacious, willful. *See* RESIST.

bullheadedness *noun*

The quality or state of being stubbornly unyielding : doggedness, hardheadedness, mulishness, obstinacy, obstinateness, pertinaciousness, pertinacity, perverseness, perversity, pigheadedness, tenaciousness, tenacity, willfulness. *See* RESIST.

bully *noun*

One who is habitually cruel to smaller or weaker people : browbeater, bulldozer, hector, intimidator. *Archaic:* brave. *See* OVER.

bully *verb* To domineer or drive into compliance by the use of as threats or force, for example : bludgeon, browbeat, bulldoze, bullyrag, cow, hector, intimidate, menace, threaten. *Informal:* strong-arm. *See* OVER.

bully *adjective Informal.* Exceptionally good of its kind : ace, banner, blue-ribbon, brag, capital, champion, excellent, fine[1], first-class, first-rate, prime, quality, splendid, superb, superior, terrific, tiptop, top. *Informal:* A-one, dandy, great, swell, topflight, topnotch. *Slang:* boss. *Chiefly British:* tophole. *See* GOOD.

bullyrag *verb*

1. To torment with persistent insult or ridicule : badger, bait, heckle, hector, hound, taunt. *Informal:* needle, ride. ***Idiom:*** wave the red flag in front of the bull. *See* TREAT WELL. **2.** To domineer or drive into compliance by the use of as threats or force, for example : bludgeon, browbeat, bulldoze, bully, cow, hector, intimidate, menace, threaten. *Informal:* strong-arm. *See* OVER.

bum[1] *noun*

A self-indulgent person who spends time avoiding work or other useful activity : drone[1], fainéant, good-for-nothing, idler, layabout, loafer, ne'er-do-well, no-good, slugabed, sluggard, wastrel. *Informal:* do-little, do-nothing, lazybones, slug[2]. *Slang:* slouch. *See* INDUSTRIOUS.

bum *verb* **1.** To ask or ask for as charity : beg, cadge. *Informal:* panhandle. *Slang:* mooch. *See* REQUEST. **2.** To pass time without working or in avoiding work. Also used with *around* : idle, laze, loaf, loiter, lounge, shirk. *Slang:* diddle[2], goldbrick, goof (off). *See* INDUSTRIOUS.

bum *adjective* Below a standard of quality : bad, poor, unsatisfactory. ***Idioms:*** below par, not up to scratch (*or* snuff). *See* GOOD.

bum[2] *noun*

Chiefly British. The part of one's back on which one rests in sitting : buttock (used in plural), derrière, posterior, rump, seat. *Informal:* backside, behind, bottom, rear[1]. *Slang:* bun (used in plural), fanny, tush. *See* OVER.

bumble[1] *verb*

1. To move awkwardly or clumsily : blunder[1], stumble. *See* ABILITY, MOVE. **2.** To proceed or perform in an unsteady, faltering manner : blunder, bungle, flounder, fudge, fumble, limp, muddle, shuffle, stagger, stumble. *See* THRIVE.

bumble[2] *verb*

To make a continuous low-pitched droning sound : burr, buzz, drone[2], hum, whir, whiz. *See* SOUNDS.

bumble *noun* A continuous low-pitched droning sound : burr, buzz, drone[2], hum, whir, whiz. *See* SOUNDS.

bumbling *adjective*
Clumsily lacking in the ability to do or perform : awkward, clumsy, gauche, heavy-handed, inept, maladroit, unskillful. *See* ABILITY.

bummer *noun*
1. *Slang.* A great disappointment or regrettable fact : crime, pity, shame. ***Idiom:*** a crying shame. *See* GOOD. **2.** *Slang.* One who begs habitually or for a living : almsman, almswoman, beggar, cadger, mendicant. *Informal:* panhandler. *Slang:* moocher. *See* REQUEST.

bump *verb*
1. To come together or come up against with force : collide, crash. *See* CONFLICT. **2.** To proceed with sudden, abrupt movements : jerk, jolt. *See* REPETITION. **3.** To put out by force : dismiss, eject, evict, expel, oust, throw out. *Informal:* chuck. *Slang:* boot¹ (out), bounce, kick out. ***Idioms:*** give someone the boot, give someone the heave-ho (*or* old heave-ho), send packing, show someone the door, throw out on one's ear. *See* KEEP. **4.** To lower in rank or grade : break, degrade, demote, downgrade, reduce. *Slang:* bust. *See* RISE.

bump into *verb* To find or meet by chance : chance on (*or* upon), come across, come on (*or* upon), find, happen on (*or* upon), light on (*or* upon), run across, run into, stumble on (*or* upon), tumble on. *Archaic:* alight on (*or* upon). ***Idiom:*** meet up with. *See* MEET.

bump off *verb Slang.* To take the life of (a person or persons) unlawfully : destroy, finish (off), kill¹, liquidate, murder, slay. *Informal:* put away. *Slang:* do in, knock off, off, rub out, waste, wipe out, zap. *See* HELP.

bump *noun* **1.** Violent forcible contact between two or more things : collision, concussion, crash, impact, jar, jolt, percussion, shock¹, smash. *See* CONFLICT. **2.** An unevenness or elevation on a surface : hump, knob, knot, lump¹, nub, protuberance. *See* CONVEX. **3.** A small raised area of skin resulting from a light blow or an insect sting, for example : bunch, knot, lump¹, swelling. *See* CONVEX.

bump into *verb* See **bump.**

bumpkin *noun*
A clumsy, unsophisticated person : clodhopper, rustic, yokel. *See* ABILITY.

bump off *verb* See **bump.**

bun *noun*
Slang. The part of one's back on which one rests in sitting. Used in plural : buttock (used in plural), derrière, posterior, rump, seat. *Informal:* backside, behind, bottom, rear¹. *Slang:* fanny, tush. *Chiefly British:* bum². *See* OVER.

bunch *noun*
1. A number of individuals making up or considered a unit : array, band², batch, bevy, body, bundle, clump, cluster, clutch², collection, group, knot, lot, party, set². *See* GROUP. **2.** *Informal.* A particular social group : circle, clique, coterie, crowd, set². *Informal:* gang. *See* GROUP. **3.** A small raised area of skin resulting from a light blow or an insect sting, for example : bump, knot, lump¹, swelling. *See* CONVEX.

buncombe *noun* See **bunkum.**

bundle *noun*
1. A number of individuals making up or considered a unit : array, band², batch, bevy, body, bunch, clump, cluster, clutch², collection, group, knot, lot, party, set². *See* GROUP. **2.** *Informal.* A large sum of money : fortune, mint. *Informal:* pretty penny, tidy sum, wad. *Slang:* pile. *See* RICH.

bundle up *verb* To put on warm clothes : wrap, wrap up. *See* PUT ON.

bundle up *verb* See **bundle.**

bungle *verb*
1. To proceed or perform in an unsteady, faltering manner : blunder, bumble¹, flounder, fudge, fumble, limp, muddle, shuffle, stagger, stumble. *See* THRIVE. **2.** To harm irreparably through inept handling; make a mess : ball up, blunder, boggle, botch, foul up, fumble, gum up, mess up, mishandle, mismanage, muddle, muff, spoil. *Informal:* bollix up, muck up. *Slang:* blow¹, goof up, louse up, screw up, snafu. ***Idiom:*** make a muck of. *See* CORRECT, HELP.

bungle *noun* A stupid, clumsy mistake : blunder, bull², foozle, fumble, muff, stumble. *Informal:* blooper, boner. *Slang:* bloomer, goof. *See* CORRECT.

bungler *noun*
A clumsy person : blunderer, botcher, dub, foozler. *Slang:* screwup. ***Idiom:*** bull in a china shop. *See* ABILITY.

bunk¹ *verb*
To provide with often temporary lodging : accommodate, bed (down), berth, bestow, billet, board, domicile, harbor, house, lodge, put up, quarter, room. *See* PROTECTION.

bunk² *noun*
Slang. Something that does not have or make sense : balderdash, blather, bunkum, claptrap,

drivel, garbage, idiocy, nonsense, piffle, poppycock, rigmarole, rubbish, tomfoolery, trash, twaddle. *Informal:* tommyrot. *Slang:* applesauce, baloney, bilge, bull[1], crap, hooey, malarkey. *See* KNOWLEDGE.

bunkum also **buncombe** *noun*
Something that does not have or make sense : balderdash, blather, claptrap, drivel, garbage, idiocy, nonsense, piffle, poppycock, rigmarole, rubbish, tomfoolery, trash, twaddle. *Informal:* tommyrot. *Slang:* applesauce, baloney, bilge, bull[1], bunk[2], crap, hooey, malarkey. *See* KNOWLEDGE.

Bunyanesque *adjective*
Of extraordinary size and power : behemoth, Brobdingnagian, colossal, cyclopean, elephantine, enormous, gargantuan, giant, gigantesque, gigantic, herculean, heroic, huge, immense, jumbo, mammoth, massive, massy, mastodonic, mighty, monster, monstrous, monumental, mountainous, prodigious, pythonic, stupendous, titanic, tremendous, vast. *Informal:* walloping. *Slang:* whopping. *See* BIG.

buoy *verb*
1. To keep from yielding or failing during stress or difficulty. Also used with *up* : bolster, prop, support, sustain, uphold. *See* HELP. **2.** To raise the spirits of. Also used with *up* : animate, elate, elevate, exhilarate, flush, inspire, inspirit, lift, uplift. *Obsolete:* exalt. *See* HAPPY.

buoyancy *noun*
The ability to recover quickly from depression or discouragement : bounce, elasticity, resilience, resiliency. *See* ABILITY.

buoyant *adjective*
Displaying light-hearted nonchalance : airy, breezy, debonair, jaunty. *Informal:* corky. ***Idiom:*** free and easy. *See* ATTITUDE, CAREFUL, GOOD.

bur *noun & verb* See **burr.**

burble *verb*
To flow or move with a low slapping sound : bubble, gurgle, lap, splash, swash, wash. *See* MOVE, SOUNDS.

burbling *adjective*
Emitting a murmuring sound felt to resemble a laugh : babbling, bubbling, gurgling, laughing, rippling. *See* LAUGHTER, SOUNDS.

burden[1] *noun*
1. Something carried physically : cargo, freight, haul, load. *Sports:* impost. *See* HEAVY, OVER. **2.** Something hard to bear physically or emotionally : affliction, cross, trial, tribulation. *See* HEAVY, OVER. **3.** A duty or responsibility that is a source of anxiety, worry, or hardship : millstone, onus, tax, weight. *Informal:* headache. *See* HEAVY, OVER. **4.** An act or course of action that is demanded of one, as by position, custom, law, or religion : charge, commitment, duty, imperative, must, need, obligation, responsibility. *See* OBLIGATION.

burden *verb* To place a burden or heavy load on : charge, cumber, encumber, freight, lade, load, saddle, tax, weight. *See* OVER.

burden[2] *noun*
1. The thread or current of thought uniting or occurring in all the elements of a text or discourse : aim, drift, intent, meaning, purport, substance, tendency, tenor, thrust. *See* MEANING. **2.** The general sense or significance, as of an action or statement : amount, drift, import, purport, substance, tenor. ***Idioms:*** sum and substance, sum total. *See* MEANING.

burdensome *adjective*
Requiring great or extreme bodily, mental, or spiritual strength : arduous, backbreaking, demanding, difficult, effortful, exacting, exigent, formidable, hard, heavy, laborious, onerous, oppressive, rigorous, rough, severe, taxing, tough, trying, weighty. *See* HEAVY.

burg *noun*
Informal. A large and important town : city, metropolis, municipality. *Informal:* town. *See* URBAN.

burgeon *verb*
1. To bear flowers : bloom[1], blossom, blow[3], effloresce, flower. *See* BETTER, RICH. **2.** To make or become greater or larger : aggrandize, amplify, augment, boost, build, build up, enlarge, escalate, expand, extend, grow, increase, magnify, mount, multiply, proliferate, rise, run up, snowball, soar, swell, upsurge, wax. *Informal:* beef up. *See* INCREASE.

burglar *noun*
A person who steals : bandit, highwayman, housebreaker, larcener, larcenist, pilferer, purloiner, robber, stealer, thief. *See* CRIMES.

burglarize *verb*
To enter forcibly or illegally : break in. *Law:* trespass. *See* CRIMES, ENTER.

burglary *noun*
The act of entering a building or room with the intent to commit theft : break-in, trespass. *See* CRIMES.

burial *noun*
An act of placing a body in a grave or tomb : entombment, inhumation, interment. *See* SHOW.

buried *adjective*
Lying beyond what is obvious or avowed : concealed, covert, hidden, obscured, ulterior. *Idiom:* under cover (*or* wraps). *See* SHOW.

burke *verb*
1. To hold (something requiring an outlet) in check : choke (back), gag, hold back, hold down, hush (up), muffle, quench, repress, smother, squelch, stifle, strangle, suppress, throttle. *Informal:* sit on (*or* upon). *See* RESTRAINT. **2.** To keep away from : avoid, bypass, circumvent, dodge, duck, elude, escape, eschew, evade, get around, shun. *Idioms:* fight shy of, give a wide berth to, have no truck with, keep (*or* stay *or* steer) clear of. *See* SEEK.

burlesque *noun*
A false, derisive, or impudent imitation of something : caricature, farce, mock, mockery, parody, sham, travesty. *See* RESPECT, SAME.
burlesque *verb* To copy (the manner or expression of another), especially in an exaggerated or mocking way : ape, caricature, imitate, mimic, mock, parody, travesty. *Idiom:* do a takeoff on. *See* SAME.

burly *adjective*
Characterized by marked muscular development; powerfully built : athletic, brawny, husky[2], muscular, robust, sinewy, sturdy. *See* STRONG.

burn *verb*
1. To undergo combustion : blaze[1], combust, flame, flare. *See* HOT. **2.** To undergo or cause to undergo damage by or as if by fire : char, scorch, sear, singe. *See* HOT. **3.** To emit a bright light : beam, blaze[1], gleam, glow, incandesce, radiate, shine. *See* LIGHT. **4.** To feel or look hot : bake, broil[1], roast, swelter. *See* HOT. **5.** To feel or cause to feel a sensation of heat or discomfort : bite, smart, sting. *See* PAIN. **6.** To cause to become sore or inflamed : inflame, irritate, sting. *See* HELP. **7.** To cause to feel or show anger. Also used with *up* : anger, enrage, incense[1], infuriate, madden, provoke. *Idioms:* make one hot under the collar, make one's blood boil, put one's back up. *See* FEELINGS. **8.** To be or become angry : anger, blow up, boil over, bristle, explode, flare up, foam, fume, rage, seethe. *Informal:* steam. *Idioms:* blow a fuse, blow a gasket, blow one's stack (*or* top), breathe fire, fly off the handle, get hot under the collar, hit the ceiling (*or* roof), lose one's temper, see red. *See* FEELINGS. **9.** To be in a state of emotional or mental turmoil : boil, bubble, churn, ferment, seethe, simmer, smolder. *See* CALM.
burn out *verb* To lose so much strength and power as to become ineffective or motionless : give out, run down. *Slang:* poop out[1]. *See* TIRED.
burn *noun* Damage or a damaged substance that results from burning : char, scorch, sear, singe. *See* HOT.

burning *adjective*
1. On fire : ablaze, afire, aflame, alight[2], conflagrant, fiery, flaming. *Idioms:* in a blaze, in flames. *See* HOT. **2.** Marked by much heat : ardent, baking, blistering, boiling, broiling, fiery, heated, hot, red-hot, roasting, scalding, scorching, searing, sizzling, sultry, sweltering, torrid. *See* HOT. **3.** Characterized by intense emotion and activity : fervid, fevered, feverish, heated, hectic. *See* EXCITE, FEELINGS, HOT. **4.** Fired with intense feeling : ardent, blazing, dithyrambic, fervent, fervid, fiery, flaming, glowing, heated, hot-blooded, impassioned, passionate, perfervid, red-hot, scorching, torrid. *See* FEELINGS. **5.** Compelling immediate attention : crying, dire, emergent, exigent, imperative, instant, pressing, urgent. *See* BIG.

burnish *verb*
To give a gleaming luster to, usually through friction : buff[1], furbish, glaze, gloss, polish, shine, sleek. *See* LIGHT.
burnish *noun* A radiant brightness or glow, usually due to light reflected from a smooth surface : glaze, gloss, luster, polish, sheen, shine, sleekness. *See* LIGHT.

burn out *verb* See **burn.**

burr also **bur** *noun*
A continuous low-pitched droning sound : bumble[2], buzz, drone[2], hum, whir, whiz. *See* SOUNDS.
burr also **bur** *verb* To make a continuous low-pitched droning sound : bumble[2], buzz, drone[2], hum, whir, whiz. *See* SOUNDS.

burrow *noun*
A place used as an animal's dwelling : den, hole, lair. *See* PROTECTION.

burst *verb*
1. To come open or fly apart suddenly and violently, as from internal pressure : blow[1] (out), explode, pop[1]. *Slang:* bust. *See* EXPLOSION. **2.** To release or cause to release energy suddenly and violently, especially with a loud noise : blast, blow[1] (up), detonate, explode, fire, fulminate, go off, touch off. *See* EXPLOSION. **3.** To become manifest suddenly and in full force. Also used with *forth* or *out* : break out, erupt, explode, flare (up). *See* EXPLOSION, START.

burst out *verb* To speak suddenly or sharply, as from surprise or emotion : blurt (out), cry (out), ejaculate, exclaim, rap out. *See* WORDS.

burst *noun* **1.** A violent release of confined energy, usually accompanied by a loud sound and shock waves : blast, blowout, blowup, detonation, explosion, fulmination. *See* EXPLOSION. **2.** A sudden violent expression, as of emotion : access, blowup, eruption, explosion, fit[1], flare-up, gust, outbreak, outburst. *See* EXPLOSION. **3.** A concentrated outpouring, as of missiles, words, or blows : barrage, bombardment, cannonade, fusillade, hail[1], salvo, shower, storm, volley. *See* ATTACK.

bursting *adjective*
1. Completely filled : brimful, brimming, chockablock, full, packed, replete. *See* FULL. **2.** Intensely desirous or interested : agog, ardent, athirst, avid, eager, impatient, keen[1], solicitous, thirsting, thirsty. *Informal:* raring. ***Idioms:*** champing at the bit, ready and willing. *See* CONCERN.

burst out *verb* See **burst.**

bury *verb*
1. To place (a corpse) in or as if in a grave : entomb, inhume, inter, lay[1]. ***Idiom:*** lay (*or* put) to rest. *See* SHOW. **2.** To put or keep out of sight : cache, conceal, ensconce, hide[1], occult, secrete. *Slang:* plant, stash. *See* SHOW.

bush *noun*
An uninhabited region left in its natural state : wild, wilderness, wildness. *See* WILD.

bushed *adjective*
Informal. Extremely tired : bleary, dead, drained, exhausted, fatigued, rundown, spent, tired out, wearied, weariful, weary, worn-down, worn-out. *Informal:* beat, tuckered (out). *Slang:* done in, fagged (out), pooped (out). ***Idioms:*** all in, ready to drop. *See* HEALTH, TIRED.

bushel *noun*
Informal. An indeterminately great amount or number : jillion, million (often used in plural), multiplicity, ream, trillion. *Informal:* gob[1] (often used in plural), heap (often used in plural), load (often used in plural), lot, oodles, passel, peck[2], scad (often used in plural), slew, wad, zillion. *See* BIG.

bushwhack *verb*
To attack suddenly and without warning : ambuscade, ambush, surprise, waylay. *See* ATTACK.

business *noun*
1. Activity pursued as a livelihood : art, calling, career, craft, employment, job, line, métier, occupation, profession, pursuit, trade, vocation, work. *Slang:* racket. *Archaic:* employ. *See* ACTION. **2.** Commercial, industrial, or professional activity in general : commerce, industry, trade, trading, traffic. *See* ACTION. **3.** A commercial organization : company, concern, corporation, enterprise, establishment, firm[2], house. *Informal:* outfit. *See* GROUP. **4.** The commercial transactions of customers with a supplier : custom, patronage, trade, traffic. *See* TRANSACTIONS. **5.** Something that concerns or involves one personally : affair, concern, lookout. *See* RELEVANT. **6.** Something to be done, considered, or dealt with : affair, matter, thing. *See* THING.

businesslike *adjective*
Marked by sober sincerity : earnest[1], no-nonsense, serious, sobersided. ***Idiom:*** in earnest. *See* HEAVY, WORK.

businessperson *noun*
A person engaged in buying and selling : dealer, merchandiser, merchant, speculator, trader, tradesman, trafficker. *See* TRANSACTIONS.

buss *verb*
To touch or caress with the lips, especially as a sign of passion or affection : kiss, osculate, smack[1]. *Informal:* peck[1]. *Slang:* smooch. *See* TOUCH.

buss *noun* The act or an instance of kissing : kiss, osculation, smack[1], smacker. *Informal:* peck[1]. *Slang:* smooch. *See* TOUCH.

bust *verb*
1. *Slang.* To make or become unusable or inoperative : break, fail, ruin. *See* HELP. **2.** *Slang.* To come open or fly apart suddenly and violently, as from internal pressure : blow[1] (out), burst, explode, pop[1]. *See* EXPLOSION. **3.** To make (an animal) docile : break, gentle, master, tame. *See* WILD. **4.** To reduce to financial insolvency : bankrupt, break, impoverish, pauperize, ruin. *Slang:* clean out. *See* MONEY. **5.** To undergo sudden financial failure : break, collapse, crash, fail, go under. *Informal:* fold. ***Idioms:*** go belly up, go bust, go on the rocks, go to the wall. *See* MONEY. **6.** *Slang.* To lower in rank or grade : break, bump, degrade, demote, downgrade, reduce. *See* RISE. **7.** To hit with a quick, sharp blow of the hand : box[2], buffet, cuff, punch, slap, smack[1], spank, swat, whack. *Informal:* clip[1], spat. *See* ATTACK, STRIKE. **8.** *Slang.* To take into custody as a prisoner : apprehend, arrest, seize. *Informal:* nab, pick up. *Slang:* collar, pinch, run in. *See* LAW.

bust *noun* 1. One that fails completely : failure, fiasco, loser, washout. *Informal:* dud, flop, lemon. *Slang:* bomb. *See* THRIVE. 2. The condition of being financially insolvent : bankruptcy, failure, insolvency. *See* MONEY. 3. A quick, sharp blow, especially with the hand : box[2], buffet, chop[1], cuff, punch, slap, smack[1], smacker, spank, swat, whack. *Informal:* clip[1], spat. *See* ATTACK, STRIKE. 4. *Slang.* A seizing and holding by law : apprehension, arrest, seizure. *Slang:* collar, pickup, pinch. *See* LAW.

bustle *verb*
1. To move swiftly : bolt, bucket, dart, dash, festinate, flash, fleet, flit, fly, haste, hasten, hurry, hustle, pelt[2], race, rocket, run, rush, sail, scoot, scour[2], shoot, speed, sprint, tear[1], trot, whirl, whisk, whiz, wing, zip, zoom. *Informal:* hotfoot, rip. *Slang:* barrel, highball. *Chiefly British:* nip[1]. ***Idioms:*** get a move on, get cracking, go like lightning, go like the wind, hotfoot it, make haste, make time, make tracks, run like the wind, shake a leg, step (*or* jump) on it. *See* MOVE. 2. To be nervously or uselessly active : fuss, putter. *Informal:* mess around. *See* ACTION, CALM.

bustle *noun* Agitated, excited movement and activity : flurry, stir[1], whirl, whirlpool. *See* CALM.

busy *adjective*
1. Involved in activity or work : employed, engaged, occupied. *See* ACTION. 2. Excessively filled with detail : cluttered, crowded, fussy. *See* SIMPLE.

busy *verb* To make busy : employ, engage, occupy. *See* ACTION.

busybody *noun*
A person given to intruding in other people's affairs : interloper, meddler, quidnunc. *Informal:* kibitzer. *Slang:* buttinsky. *Archaic:* pragmatic. *See* PARTICIPATE.

but *adverb*
To the exclusion of anyone or anything else : alone, entirely, exclusively, only, solely. *See* INCLUDE.

butcher *noun*
One who murders another : cutthroat, homicide, killer, manslayer, massacrer, murderer, murderess, slaughterer, slayer, triggerman. *See* HELP.

butcher *verb* To kill savagely and indiscriminately : annihilate, decimate, massacre, slaughter. *See* CRIMES, HELP, MAKE.

butchery *noun*
The savage killing of many victims : bloodbath, bloodletting, bloodshed, carnage, massacre, pogrom, slaughter. *See* HELP.

butt[1] *noun*
An act or instance of using force so as to propel ahead : push, shove, thrust. *See* PUSH.

butt[2] *verb*
To be contiguous or next to : abut, adjoin, border, bound[2], join, meet[1], neighbor, touch, verge. *See* NEAR.

butt[3] *noun*
1. One that is fired at, attacked, or abused : mark, target. *See* SEEK. 2. An object of amusement or laughter : jest, joke, laughingstock, mockery. *See* RESPECT. 3. A person who is easily deceived or victimized : dupe, fool, gull, lamb, pushover, victim. *Informal:* sucker. *Slang:* fall guy, gudgeon, mark, monkey, patsy, pigeon, sap[1]. *Chiefly British:* mug. *See* WISE.

butt[4] *noun*
Residual matter : end, fragment, ort (often used in plural), scrap[1], shard, stub. *See* LEFTOVER.

butter up *verb*
To compliment excessively and ingratiatingly : adulate, blandish, flatter, honey, slaver. *Informal:* soft-soap, sweet-talk. *See* PRAISE.

butt in *verb*
To intervene officiously or indiscreetly in the affairs of others : horn in, interfere, interlope, meddle. *See* PARTICIPATE.

buttinsky *noun*
Slang. A person given to intruding in other people's affairs : busybody, interloper, meddler, quidnunc. *Informal:* kibitzer. *Archaic:* pragmatic. *See* PARTICIPATE.

buttock *noun*
The part of one's back on which one rests in sitting. Used in plural : derrière, posterior, rump, seat. *Informal:* backside, behind, bottom, rear[1]. *Slang:* bun (used in plural), fanny, tush. *Chiefly British:* bum[2]. *See* OVER.

button-down also **buttoned-down** *adjective*
Conforming to established practice or standards : conformist, conventional, establishmentarian, orthodox, straight, traditional. *Slang:* square. *See* USUAL.

buttoned-down *adjective* See **button-down.**

buttress *noun*
A means or device that keeps something erect, stable, or secure : brace, crutch, prop, shore, stay[2], support, underpinning. *See* SUPPORT.

buttress *verb* To present evidence in support of : back (up), corroborate, substantiate. *See* SUPPORT.

buxom *adjective*
Having a full, voluptuous figure : curvaceous, curvy, shapely, well-developed. *Informal:* built. *Slang:* stacked. *See* BEAUTIFUL.

buy *verb*
1. To acquire in exchange for money or something of equal value : purchase. *See* GET, MONEY. **2.** To give, offer, or promise a bribe to. Also used with *off* : bribe. *Informal:* pay off. ***Idiom:*** grease someone's palm (*or* hand). *See* CRIMES, MONEY, PERSUASION. **3.** *Slang.* To regard (something) as true or real : accept, believe. *Slang:* swallow. *See* OPINION.

buy *noun* **1.** Something bought or capable of being bought : purchase. *See* GET, MONEY. **2.** *Informal.* Something offered or bought at a low price : bargain. *Informal:* deal. *Slang:* steal. *See* MONEY, TRANSACTIONS.

buyable *adjective*
Capable of being bribed : corruptible, purchasable, venal. *See* CRIMES, PERSUASION.

buyer *noun*
One who buys goods or services : client, customer, patron, purchaser. *See* TRANSACTIONS.

buzz *verb*
1. To make a continuous low-pitched droning sound : bumble[2], burr, drone[2], hum, whir, whiz. *See* SOUNDS. **2.** To communicate with (someone) by telephone : call, ring[2], telephone. *Informal:* dial, phone. ***Idioms:*** get someone on the horn, give someone a buzz (*or* call *or* ring). *See* WORDS.

buzz *noun* **1.** A continuous low-pitched droning sound : bumble[2], burr, drone[2], hum, whir, whiz. *See* SOUNDS. **2.** A telephone communication : call, ring[2]. *See* WORDS.

by-and-by *noun*
Time that is yet to be : future, hereafter. *Idiom:* time to come. *See* PRECEDE, TIME.

bygone *adjective*
Of a style or method formerly in vogue : antiquated, antique, archaic, dated, dowdy, fusty, old, old-fashioned, old-time, outdated, outmoded, out-of-date, passé, vintage. *See* NEW.

bypass *noun*
The act, an instance, or a means of avoiding : avoidance, circumvention, escape, evasion. *See* SEEK.

bypass *verb* **1.** To pass around but not through : circumnavigate, circumvent, detour, go around, skirt. *See* SEEK. **2.** To keep away from : avoid, burke, circumvent, dodge, duck, elude, escape, eschew, evade, get around, shun. ***Idioms:*** fight shy of, give a wide berth to, have no truck with, keep (*or* stay *or* steer) clear of. *See* SEEK.

byproduct or **by-product** *noun*
Something derived from another : derivation, derivative, descendant, offshoot, outgrowth, spinoff. *See* KIN.

bystander *noun*
Someone who observes : beholder, looker-on, observer, onlooker, spectator, watcher. *See* AWARENESS, SEE.

byword *noun*
A usually pithy and familiar statement expressing an observation or principle generally accepted as wise or true : adage, aphorism, maxim, motto, proverb, saw, saying. *See* WORDS.

byzantine also **Byzantine** *adjective*
Difficult to understand because of intricacy : complex, complicated, convoluted, daedal, Daedalian, elaborate, intricate, involute, involved, knotty, labyrinthine, tangled. *See* SIMPLE.

•C•

cabal *noun*
A secret plan to achieve an evil or illegal end : collusion, connivance, conspiracy, intrigue, machination, plot, scheme. *See* CRIMES, PLANNED.

cabalistic *adjective*
Difficult to explain or understand : arcane, cryptic, enigmatic, mysterious, mystic, mystical, mystifying, occult, puzzling. *See* EXPLAIN, KNOWLEDGE.

cabbage *noun*
Slang. Something, such as coins or printed bills, used as a medium of exchange : cash, currency, lucre, money. *Informal:* wampum. *Slang:* bread, dough, gelt, green, jack, lettuce, long green, mazuma, moola, scratch. *Chiefly British:* brass. *See* MONEY.

cache *noun*
A supply stored or hidden for future use : backlog, hoard, inventory, nest egg, reserve, reservoir, stock, stockpile, store, treasure. *Slang:* stash. *See* COLLECT.

cache *verb* To put or keep out of sight : bury, conceal, ensconce, hide[1], occult, secrete. *Slang:* plant, stash. *See* SHOW.

cachinnate *verb*
To express amusement, mirth, or scorn by smiling and emitting loud, inarticulate sounds : cackle, guffaw, laugh. *Informal:* heehaw. ***Idioms:*** die laughing, laugh one's head off, roll in the aisles, split one's sides. *See* LAUGHTER, SOUNDS.

cachinnation *noun*
An act of laughing : cackle, guffaw, laugh, laughter. *Informal:* heehaw. *See* LAUGHTER, SOUNDS.

cackle *verb*
To express amusement, mirth, or scorn by smiling and emitting loud, inarticulate sounds : cachinnate, guffaw, laugh. *Informal:* heehaw. ***Idioms:*** die laughing, laugh one's head off, roll in the aisles, split one's sides. *See* LAUGHTER, SOUNDS.

cackle *noun* An act of laughing : cachinnation, guffaw, laugh, laughter. *Informal:* heehaw. *See* LAUGHTER, SOUNDS.

cacophonous or **cacophonic** or **cacophonical** *adjective*
Characterized by unpleasant discordance of sound : discordant, disharmonious, dissonant, inharmonic, inharmonious, rude, unharmonious, unmusical. *See* AGREE, SOUNDS.

cadaver *noun*
The physical frame of a dead person or animal : body, carcass, corpse, remains. *Slang:* stiff. *See* BODY.

cadaverous *adjective*
1. Gruesomely suggestive of ghosts or death : deadly, deathlike, deathly, ghastly, ghostlike, ghostly, spectral. *See* LIVE. **2.** Lacking color : ashen, ashy, bloodless, colorless, livid, lurid, pale, pallid, pasty, sallow, wan, waxen. *See* COLORS. **3.** Physically haggard : drawn, emaciated, gaunt, shrunken, skeletal, wasted. ***Idiom:*** skin and bones. *See* BETTER, TIRED.

cadence *noun*
The patterned, recurring alternation of contrasting elements, such as stressed and unstressed notes in music : beat, cadency, measure, meter, rhythm, swing. *See* REPETITION.

cadenced *adjective*
Marked by a regular rhythm : measured, metrical, rhythmic, rhythmical. *See* REPETITION.

cadency *noun*
The patterned, recurring alternation of contrasting elements, such as stressed and unstressed notes in music : beat, cadence, measure, meter, rhythm, swing. *See* REPETITION.

cadge *verb*
To ask or ask for as charity : beg, bum[1]. *Informal:* panhandle. *Slang:* mooch. *See* REQUEST.

cadger *noun*
One who begs habitually or for a living : almsman, almswoman, beggar, mendicant. *Informal:* panhandler. *Slang:* bummer, moocher. *See* REQUEST.

caducity *noun*
The condition of being senile : dotage, senility. *See* YOUTH.

cage *verb*
To confine within a limited area : coop (in *or* up), enclose, fence (in), immure, mew (up), pen[2], shut in, shut up, wall (in *or* up). *See* FREE.

cagey also **cagy** *adjective*
Having or showing a clever awareness and resourcefulness in practical matters : astute,

canny, knowing, perspicacious, shrewd, slick, smart, wise[1]. *Informal:* savvy. *See* ABILITY, CAREFUL.

cagy *adjective* See **cagey.**

cajole *verb*
To persuade or try to persuade by gentle persistent urging or flattery : blandish, coax, honey, wheedle. *Informal:* soft-soap, sweet-talk. *See* PERSUASION.

cake *verb*
To make or become physically hard : concrete, congeal, dry, harden, indurate, petrify, set[1], solidify. *See* SOLID.

calaboose *noun*
Chiefly Regional. A place for the confinement of persons in lawful detention : brig, house of correction, jail, keep, penitentiary, prison. *Informal:* lockup, pen[3]. *Slang:* big house, can, clink, cooler, coop, hoosegow, joint, jug, pokey[1], slammer, stir[2]. *See* FREE.

calamitous *adjective*
Causing ruin or destruction : cataclysmal, cataclysmic, catastrophic, destructive, disastrous, fatal, fateful, ruinous. *See* HELP.

calamity *noun*
An occurrence inflicting widespread destruction and distress : cataclysm, catastrophe, disaster, tragedy. *See* HELP.

calculate *verb*
1. To ascertain by mathematics : cast, cipher, compute, figure, reckon. *See* REASON. **2.** To make a judgment as to the worth or value of : appraise, assay, assess, estimate, evaluate, gauge, judge, rate[1], size up, valuate, value. ***Idiom:*** take the measure of. *See* VALUE.

calculated *adjective*
1. Resulting from deliberation and careful thought : advised, considered, studied, studious. *See* WISE. **2.** Planned, weighed, or estimated in advance : considered, deliberate, intentional, premeditated. *See* PURPOSE.

calculating *adjective*
Coldly planning to achieve selfish aims : designing, scheming. *See* ATTITUDE.

calculation *noun*
1. The act, process, or result of calculating : computation, figuring, reckoning. *See* REASON. **2.** A careful considering of a matter : advisement, consideration, deliberation, lucubration, study. *See* THOUGHTS. **3.** Careful forethought to avoid harm or risk : care, carefulness, caution, chariness, gingerliness, precaution, wariness. *See* FEAR.

calendar *noun*
An organized list, as of procedures, activities, or events : agenda, docket, lineup, order of the day (often used in plural), program, schedule, timetable. *See* PLANNED.

caliber *noun*
1. A level of superiority that is usually high : merit, quality, stature, value, virtue, worth. *See* GOOD, VALUE. **2.** Degree of excellence : class, grade, quality. *See* BE, VALUE.

caliginous *adjective*
Deficient in brightness : dark, dim, dusky, murky, obscure. *See* LIGHT.

call *verb*
1. To speak or say very loudly or with a shout : bawl, bellow, bluster, clamor, cry, halloo, holler, roar, shout, vociferate, whoop, yawp, yell. *See* SOUNDS. **2.** To demand to appear, come, or assemble : convene, convoke, muster, send for, summon. *See* REQUEST. **3.** To bring together : assemble, cluster, collect[1], congregate, convene, convoke, gather, get together, group, muster, round up, summon. *See* COLLECT. **4.** To give a name or title to : baptize, christen, denominate, designate, dub, entitle, name, style, term, title. *See* SPECIFIC, WORDS. **5.** To describe with a word or term : characterize, designate, label, name, style, tag, term. *See* SPECIFIC, WORDS. **6.** To communicate with (someone) by telephone : buzz, ring[2], telephone. *Informal:* dial, phone. ***Idioms:*** get someone on the horn, give someone a buzz (*or* call *or* ring). *See* WORDS. **7.** To go to or seek out the company of in order to socialize : come by, come over, drop by, drop in, look in, look up, pop in, run in, see, stop (by *or* in), visit. ***Idiom:*** pay a visit. *See* SEEK. **8.** To tell about or make known (future events) in advance, especially by means of special knowledge or inference : forecast, foretell, predict, prognosticate, project. *See* FORESIGHT.

call down *verb* To criticize for a fault or an offense : admonish, castigate, chastise, chide, dress down, rap[1], rebuke, reprimand, reproach, reprove, scold, tax, upbraid. *Informal:* bawl out, lambaste. *Slang:* chew out. ***Idioms:*** bring (*or* call *or* take) to task, call on the carpet, haul (*or* rake) over the coals, let someone have it. *See* ATTACK, PRAISE.

call for *verb* **1.** To be a proper or sufficient occasion for : justify, occasion, warrant. *See* RIGHT. **2.** To have as a need or prerequisite : ask, demand, entail, involve, necessitate, require, take. *See* NECESSARY, OVER. **3.** To ask for urgently or insistently : claim, demand, exact, insist on (*or* upon), require, requisition. ***Idiom:*** cry out for. *See* REQUEST.

call off *verb* To decide not to go ahead with (something previously arranged) : cancel. *Slang:* scratch, scrub. *See* CONTINUE.

call *noun* **1.** A loud cry : halloo, holler, shout, yell. *See* SOUNDS. **2.** A telephone communication : buzz, ring[2]. *See* WORDS. **3.** That which provides a reason or justification : cause, ground (often used in plural), justification, necessity, occasion, reason, wherefore, why. ***Idiom:*** why and wherefore. *See* START. **4.** The act of demanding : claim, cry, demand, exaction, requisition. *See* REQUEST. **5.** An act or an instance of going or coming to see another : look-in, visit, visitation. *See* SEEK. **6.** The power or quality of attracting : allure, allurement, appeal, attraction, attractiveness, charisma, charm, draw, enchantment, enticement, fascination, glamour, lure, magnetism, witchery. *Informal:* pull. *See* LIKE.

call down *verb* See **call.**

call for *verb* See **call.**

call girl *noun*
A woman who engages in sexual intercourse for payment : bawd, camp follower, courtesan, harlot, prostitute, scarlet woman, streetwalker, strumpet, tart[2], whore. *Slang:* hooker, moll. ***Idioms:*** lady of easy virtue, lady of pleasure, lady of the night. *See* SEX.

calligraphic *adjective*
Of or relating to representation by means of writing : graphic, scriptural, written. *See* WORDS.

calling *noun*
1. An inner urge to pursue an activity or perform a service : mission, vocation. *See* DESIRE. **2.** Activity pursued as a livelihood : art, business, career, craft, employment, job, line, métier, occupation, profession, pursuit, trade, vocation, work. *Slang:* racket. *Archaic:* employ. *See* ACTION.

call off *verb* See **call.**

callous *adjective*
Completely lacking in compassion : cold-blooded, cold-hearted, compassionless, hard, hard-boiled, hardened, hardhearted, heartless, obdurate, stonyhearted, unfeeling. *See* ATTITUDE.

call to arms *noun*
A rallying term used by proponents of a cause : battle cry, call to battle, cry, motto, rallying cry, war cry. *See* WORDS.

call to battle *noun*
A rallying term used by proponents of a cause : battle cry, call to arms, cry, motto, rallying cry, war cry. *See* WORDS.

calm *adjective*
1. Motionless and undisturbed : halcyon, peaceful, placid, quiet, serene, still, stilly, tranquil, untroubled. *See* CALM. **2.** Not excited or emotionally agitated : peaceful, placid, serene, tranquil. *See* CALM. **3.** Not easily excited, even under pressure : collected, composed, cool, cool-headed, detached, even[1], even-tempered, imperturbable, nonchalant, possessed, unflappable, unruffled. *See* CALM.

calm *noun* **1.** An absence of motion or disturbance : calmness, hush, lull, peace, peacefulness, placidity, placidness, quiet, quietness, serenity, stillness, tranquillity, untroubledness. *See* CALM. **2.** Lack of emotional agitation : calmness, peace, peacefulness, placidity, placidness, quietude, serenity, tranquillity. *See* CALM.

calm *verb* **1.** To make or become calm. Also used with *down* : allay, balm, becalm, lull, quiet, settle, still, tranquilize. *See* CALM. **2.** To ease the anger or agitation of. Also used with *down* : appease, assuage, conciliate, dulcify, gentle, mollify, pacify, placate, propitiate, soften, soothe, sweeten. ***Idiom:*** pour oil on troubled water. *See* CALM.

calmness *noun*
1. An absence of motion or disturbance : calm, hush, lull, peace, peacefulness, placidity, placidness, quiet, quietness, serenity, stillness, tranquillity, untroubledness. *See* CALM. **2.** Lack of emotional agitation : calm, peace, peacefulness, placidity, placidness, quietude, serenity, tranquillity. *See* CALM.

calumniation *noun*
The expression of injurious, malicious statements about someone : aspersion, calumny, character assassination, defamation, denigration, detraction, scandal, slander, traducement, vilification. *Law:* libel. *See* ATTACK, CRIMES, LAW.

calumniate *verb*
To make defamatory statements about : asperse, backbite, defame, malign, slander, slur, tear down, traduce, vilify. *Law:* libel. ***Idiom:*** cast aspersions on. *See* ATTACK, CRIMES, LAW.

calumnious *adjective*
Damaging to the reputation : defamatory, detractive, injurious, invidious, scandalous, slanderous. *Law:* libelous. *See* ATTACK, CRIMES, LAW.

calumny *noun*
The expression of injurious, malicious statements about someone : aspersion, calumniation, character assassination, defamation, deni-

gration, detraction, scandal, slander, traducement, vilification. *Law:* libel. *See* ATTACK, CRIMES, LAW.

camouflage *verb*
To change or modify so as to prevent recognition of the true identity or character of : disguise, dissemble, dissimulate, mask, masquerade. *See* SHOW.

campaign *noun*
An organized effort to accomplish a purpose : crusade, drive, movement, push. *See* ACTION, SEEK.

campestral *adjective*
Of or relating to the countryside : arcadian, bucolic, country, pastoral, provincial, rural, rustic. *Informal:* hick. *See* URBAN.

camp follower *noun*
A woman who engages in sexual intercourse for payment : bawd, call girl, courtesan, harlot, prostitute, scarlet woman, streetwalker, strumpet, tart[2], whore. *Slang:* hooker, moll. ***Idioms:*** lady of easy virtue, lady of pleasure, lady of the night. *See* SEX.

can *noun*
Slang. A place for the confinement of persons in lawful detention : brig, house of correction, jail, keep, penitentiary, prison. *Informal:* lockup, pen[3]. *Slang:* big house, clink, cooler, coop, hoosegow, joint, jug, pokey[1], slammer, stir[2]. *Chiefly Regional:* calaboose. *See* FREE.

can *verb* **1.** To prepare (food) for storage and future use : conserve, preserve, put up. *See* KEEP. **2.** *Slang.* To end the employment or service of : cashier, discharge, dismiss, drop, release, terminate. *Informal:* ax, fire, pink-slip. *Slang:* boot[1], bounce, sack[1]. ***Idioms:*** give someone his or her walking papers, give someone the ax, give someone the gate, give someone the pink slip, let go, show someone the door. *See* KEEP.

canard *noun*
An untrue declaration : cock-and-bull story, falsehood, falsity, fib, fiction, inveracity, lie[2], misrepresentation, misstatement, prevarication, story, tale, untruth. *Informal:* fish story, tall tale. *Slang:* whopper. *See* TRUE.

cancel *verb*
1. To remove or invalidate by or as if by running a line through or wiping clean : annul, blot (out), cross (off *or* out), delete, efface, erase, expunge, obliterate, rub (out), scratch (out), strike (out), undo, wipe (out), x (out). *Law:* vacate. *See* CONTINUE. **2.** To put an end to, especially formally and with authority : abolish, abrogate, annihilate, annul, invalidate, negate, nullify, set aside, vitiate, void. *Law:* extinguish. *See* CONTINUE. **3.** To decide not to go ahead with (something previously arranged) : call off. *Slang:* scratch, scrub. *See* CONTINUE. **4.** To make ineffective by applying an opposite force or amount : counteract, negate, neutralize, nullify. *See* ACTION.

cancelation *noun* See **cancellation.**

cancellation also **cancelation** *noun*
1. The act of erasing or the condition of being erased : deletion, erasure, expunction, obliteration. *See* INCLUDE. **2.** An often formal act of ending : abolishment, abolition, abrogation, annihilation, annulment, defeasance, invalidation, negation, nullification, voidance. *Law:* avoidance, extinguishment. *See* CONTINUE.

candid *adjective*
Manifesting honesty and directness : direct, downright, forthright, frank, honest, ingenuous, man-to-man, open, plainspoken, straight, straightforward, straight-out, unreserved. *Informal:* straight-from-the-shoulder, straight-shooting. *See* CLEAR, SHOW.

candidate *noun*
A person who applies for or seeks something, such as a job or position : applicant, aspirant, hopeful, petitioner, seeker. *See* SEEK.

candy *verb*
To make superficially more acceptable or appealing : gild, honey, sugar, sugarcoat, sweeten. *See* LIKE.

cane *noun*
A fairly long straight piece of solid material used especially as a support in walking : staff, stave, stick, walking stick. *See* MACHINE.

canker *noun*
Anything that is injurious, destructive, or fatal : bane, contagion, poison, toxin, venom, virus. *See* HELP.

canker *verb* **1.** To have a destructive effect on : envenom, infect, poison. *Archaic:* empoison. *See* HELP. **2.** To ruin utterly in character or quality : animalize, bastardize, bestialize, brutalize, corrupt, debase, debauch, demoralize, deprave, pervert, stain, vitiate, warp. *See* CLEAN, HELP.

cannonade *verb*
To direct a barrage at : barrage, bombard, fusillade, pepper, shower. *See* ATTACK.

cannonade *noun* A concentrated outpouring, as of missiles, words, or blows : barrage, bombardment, burst, fusillade, hail[1], salvo, shower, storm, volley. *See* ATTACK.

canny *adjective*
1. Having or showing a clever awareness and

resourcefulness in practical matters : astute, cagey, knowing, perspicacious, shrewd, slick, smart, wise[1]. *Informal:* savvy. *See* ABILITY, CAREFUL. **2.** Careful in the use of material resources : chary, economical, frugal, provident, prudent, saving, Scotch, sparing, thrifty. *See* CAREFUL, SAVE.

can of worms *noun*
Informal. A situation that presents difficulty, uncertainty, or perplexity : hornets' nest, issue, problem, question. *See* EASY.

canon *noun*
A principle governing affairs within or among political units : decree, edict, institute, law, ordinance, precept, prescription, regulation, rule. *See* LAW.

canonical *adjective*
Adhering to beliefs or practices approved by authority or tradition : orthodox, received, sanctioned, time-honored. *See* USUAL.

cant[1] *noun*
Deviation from a particular direction : grade, gradient, heel[2], inclination, incline, lean[1], list[2], rake[2], slant, slope, tilt, tip[2]. *See* RISE, STRAIGHT.
cant *verb* To depart or cause to depart from true vertical or horizontal : heel[2], incline, lean[1], list[2], rake[2], slant, slope, tilt, tip[2]. *See* STRAIGHT.

cant[2] *noun*
1. A variety of a language that differs from the standard form : argot, dialect, jargon, lingo, patois, vernacular. *See* WORDS. **2.** Specialized expressions indigenous to a particular field, subject, trade, or subculture : argot, dialect, idiom, jargon, language, lexicon, lingo, patois, terminology, vernacular, vocabulary. *See* WORDS.

cantankerous *adjective*
Having or showing a bad temper : bad-tempered, crabbed, cranky, cross, disagreeable, fretful, grouchy, grumpy, ill-tempered, irascible, irritable, nasty, peevish, petulant, querulous, snappish, snappy, surly, testy, ugly, waspish. *Informal:* crabby, mean[2]. *Idiom:* out of sorts. *See* ATTITUDE.

cap *noun*
The highest point : apex, crest, crown, height, peak, roof, summit, top, vertex. *See* HIGH.
cap *verb* **1.** To put a topping on : crown, top, top off. *See* OVER, PUT ON. **2.** To extend over the surface of : blanket, cover, overlay, spread. *See* PUT ON. **3.** To reach or bring to a climax : climax, crest, crown, culminate, peak, top (off *or* out). *See* EXCITE.

capability *noun*
Physical, mental, financial, or legal power to perform : ability, capacity, competence, competency, faculty, might. *See* ABILITY.

capable *adjective*
Having the ability to perform well : able, competent, good, skilled, skillful. *See* ABILITY.

capacious *adjective*
1. Having plenty of room : ample, commodious, roomy, spacious. *See* BIG. **2.** Of full measure; not narrow or restricted : ample, full, voluminous, wide. *See* TIGHTEN.

capacity *noun*
1. Physical, mental, financial, or legal power to perform : ability, capability, competence, competency, faculty, might. *See* ABILITY. **2.** The ability or power to seize or attain : compass, grasp, range, reach, scope. *See* ABILITY.

caper *noun*
A mischievous act : antic, frolic, joke, lark, prank[1], trick. *Informal:* shenanigan. *Slang:* monkeyshine (often used in plural). *See* GOOD, WORK.
caper *verb* To leap and skip about playfully : cavort, dance, frisk, frolic, gambol, rollick, romp. *See* WORK.

capital *noun*
1. The monetary resources of a government, organization, or individual : finance (used in plural), fund (used in plural), money (often used in plural). *See* MONEY. **2.** Money or property used to produce more wealth : backing, capitalization, financing, funding, grubstake, stake, subsidization. *See* HELP, MONEY. **3.** All things, such as money, property, or goods, having economic value : asset (used in plural), fortune, mean[3] (used in plural), resource (used in plural), wealth, wherewithal. *See* OWNED.
capital *adjective* **1.** Most important, influential, or significant : cardinal, chief, first, foremost, key, leading, main, major, number one, paramount, premier, primary, prime, principal, top. *See* IMPORTANT. **2.** Exceptionally good of its kind : ace, banner, blue-ribbon, brag, champion, excellent, fine[1], first-class, first-rate, prime, quality, splendid, superb, superior, terrific, tiptop, top. *Informal:* A-one, bully, dandy, great, swell, topflight, topnotch. *Slang:* boss. *Chiefly British:* tophole. *See* GOOD. **3.** Conspicuously bad or offensive : arrrant, egregious, flagrant, glaring, gross, rank[2]. *See* GOOD.

capitalist *noun*
One who is occupied with or expert in large-

scale financial affairs : financier. *Informal:* moneyman. *See* MONEY.

capitalization *noun*
Money or property used to produce more wealth : backing, capital, financing, funding, grubstake, stake, subsidization. *See* HELP, MONEY.

capitalize *verb*
1. To supply capital to or for : back, finance, fund, grubstake, stake, subsidize. *Informal:* bankroll. ***Idiom:*** put up money for. *See* HELP, MONEY. **2.** To derive advantage : benefit, gain, profit. *See* HELP.

capitulate *verb*
To give in from or as if from a gradual loss of strength : bow[1], buckle, submit, succumb, surrender, yield. *Informal:* fold. *See* RESIST.

capitulation *noun*
The act of submitting or surrendering to the power of another : submission, surrender. *See* RESIST, WIN.

caprice *noun*
An impulsive, often illogical turn of mind : bee, boutade, conceit, fancy, freak, humor, impulse, megrim, notion, vagary, whim, whimsy. ***Idiom:*** bee in one's bonnet. *See* THOUGHTS.

capricious *adjective*
1. Determined or marked by whim or caprice rather than reason : arbitrary, whimsical. *See* SURPRISE. **2.** Following no predictable pattern : changeable, erratic, fantastic, fantastical, fickle, freakish, inconsistent, inconstant, mercurial, temperamental, ticklish, uncertain, unpredictable, unstable, unsteady, variable, volatile, whimsical. *See* CHANGE, CONTINUE.

capsize *verb*
To turn or cause to turn from a vertical or horizontal position : knock over, overthrow, overturn, topple, turn over, upset. *See* CHANGE, HORIZONTAL, MOVE.

capsized *adjective*
Turned over completely : inverted, overturned, upset, upside-down, upturned. *See* HORIZONTAL.

captain *verb*
To have authoritative charge of : command, lead. *See* PRECEDE.

captious *adjective*
Inclined to judge too severely : carping, censorious, critical, faultfinding, hypercritical, overcritical. *See* PRAISE.

captivate *verb*
To please greatly or irresistibly : beguile, bewitch, charm, enchant, entrance[2], fascinate. *See* LIKE.

capture *verb*
1. To gain possession of, especially after a struggle or chase : catch, get, net[1], secure, take. *Informal:* bag. *Slang:* nail. *See* GET. **2.** To obtain possession or control of : gain, get, take, win. *Slang:* cop. *See* GET.

carbon copy *noun*
Something closely resembling another : copy, duplicate, facsimile, image, likeness, reduplication, replica, replication, reproduction, simulacrum. *Archaic:* simulacre. *Law:* counterpart. *See* SAME.

carcass *noun*
The physical frame of a dead person or animal : body, cadaver, corpse, remains. *Slang:* stiff. *See* BODY.

card *noun*
1. *Informal.* A person who is appealingly odd or curious : character, oddity, original. *Informal:* oddball. *See* USUAL. **2.** *Informal.* A person whose words or actions provoke or are intended to provoke amusement or laughter : clown, comedian, comic, farceur, funnyman, humorist, jester, joker, jokester, quipster, wag[2], wit, zany. *See* LAUGHTER.

cardinal *adjective*
Most important, influential, or significant : capital, chief, first, foremost, key, leading, main, major, number one, paramount, premier, primary, prime, principal, top. *See* IMPORTANT.

care *noun*
1. A troubled or anxious state of mind : angst, anxiety, anxiousness, concern, disquiet, disquietude, distress, nervousness, solicitude, unease, uneasiness, worry. *See* FEELINGS. **2.** A cause of distress or anxiety : concern, trouble, worry. *See* CONCERN. **3.** Careful forethought to avoid harm or risk : calculation, carefulness, caution, chariness, gingerliness, precaution, wariness. *See* FEAR. **4.** Attentiveness to detail : carefulness, fastidiousness, meticulousness, pain (used in plural), painstaking, punctiliousness, scrupulousness, thoroughness. *See* CAREFUL. **5.** Cautious attentiveness : carefulness, caution, gingerliness, heed, heedfulness, mindfulness, regard. *See* CAREFUL. **6.** The function of watching, guarding, or overseeing : charge, custody, guardianship, keeping, superintendence, supervision, trust. *See* CARE FOR. **7.** The systematic application of remedies to effect a cure : regimen, rehabilitation, therapy, treatment. *Informal:* rehab. *See* HEALTH, HELP.

care *verb* To have an objection : mind, object. *See* CONCERN.

care for *verb* To have the care and supervision of : attend, look after, mind, minister to, see to, tend[2], watch. ***Idioms:*** keep an eye on, look out for, take care (*or* charge) of, take under one's wing. *See* CARE FOR.

career *noun*
Activity pursued as a livelihood : art, business, calling, craft, employment, job, line, métier, occupation, profession, pursuit, trade, vocation, work. *Slang:* racket. *Archaic:* employ. *See* ACTION.

care for *verb* See **care.**

carefree *adjective*
Free from care or worry : blithe, debonair, light[2], lighthearted. *See* CAREFUL, HAPPY.

careful *adjective*
1. Cautiously attentive : heedful, mindful, observant, watchful. *See* CAREFUL. **2.** Trying attentively to avoid danger, risk, or error : cautious, chary, circumspect, forehanded, gingerly, prudent, wary. *See* CAREFUL. **3.** Showing or marked by attentiveness to all aspects or details : fastidious, meticulous, painstaking, punctilious, scrupulous. *See* CAREFUL.

carefulness *noun*
1. Careful forethought to avoid harm or risk : calculation, care, caution, chariness, gingerliness, precaution, wariness. *See* FEAR. **2.** Attentiveness to detail : care, fastidiousness, meticulousness, pain (used in plural), painstaking, punctiliousness, scrupulousness, thoroughness. *See* CAREFUL. **3.** Cautious attentiveness : care, caution, gingerliness, heed, heedfulness, mindfulness, regard. *See* CAREFUL.

careless *adjective*
1. Lacking or marked by a lack of care : feckless, heedless, inattentive, irresponsible, reckless, thoughtless, unconcerned, unmindful, unthinking. *See* CAREFUL. **2.** Indifferent to correctness, accuracy, or neatness : messy, slapdash, slipshod, sloppy, slovenly, untidy. *See* CAREFUL. **3.** Showing no concern, attention, or regard : forgetful, heedless, mindless, unconcerned, unheeding, unmindful, unobservant, unthinking. *See* CAREFUL.

carelessness *noun*
A careless, often reckless disregard for consequences : abandon, heedlessness, thoughtlessness. *See* CAREFUL.

caress *verb*
To touch or stroke affectionately : cuddle, fondle, pat, pet[1]. *See* TOUCH.

caretaker *noun*
A person who is legally responsible for the person or property of another considered by law to be incompetent to manage his or her affairs : custodian, guardian, keeper. *Law:* conservator. *See* LAW.

careworn *adjective*
Pale and exhausted, as because of worry or sleeplessness : drawn, gaunt, haggard, hollow-eyed, wan, worn. *See* TIRED.

cargo *noun*
Something carried physically : burden[1], freight, haul, load. *Sports:* impost. *See* HEAVY, OVER.

caricature *noun*
A false, derisive, or impudent imitation of something : burlesque, farce, mock, mockery, parody, sham, travesty. *See* RESPECT, SAME.

caricature *verb* To copy (the manner or expression of another), especially in an exaggerated or mocking way : ape, burlesque, imitate, mimic, mock, parody, travesty. ***Idiom:*** do a takeoff on. *See* SAME.

cark *verb*
1. To cause anxious uneasiness in : ail, concern, distress, trouble, worry. *See* CONCERN. **2.** To focus the attention on something moodily and at length : brood, dwell, fret, mope, worry. *Informal:* stew. *See* CONCERN, THOUGHTS.

carnage *noun*
The savage killing of many victims : bloodbath, bloodletting, bloodshed, butchery, massacre, pogrom, slaughter. *See* HELP.

carnal *adjective*
Relating to the desires and appetites of the body : animal, fleshly, physical, sensual. *See* BODY.

carnality *noun*
A preoccupation with the body and satisfaction of its desires : animalism, animality, fleshliness, physicality, sensuality. *See* BODY.

carol *verb*
To utter words or sounds in musical tones : chant, sing, vocalize. *Archaic:* tune. *See* SOUNDS.

carom *verb*
To strike a surface at such an angle as to be deflected : dap, glance, graze, ricochet, skim, skip. *See* STRIKE.

carousal *noun*
A drinking bout : binge, brannigan, carouse, drunk, spree. *Slang:* bat[2], bender, booze, jag, tear[1]. *See* DRUGS, RESTRAINT.

carouse *noun*
A drinking bout : binge, brannigan, carousal, drunk, spree. *Slang:* bat[2], bender, booze, jag, tear[1]. *See* DRUGS, RESTRAINT.

carouse *verb* To behave riotously : frolic, revel, riot, roister. *Informal:* hell (around). *Idioms:* blow off steam, cut loose, kick over the traces, kick up one's heels, let go, let loose, make merry, make whoopee, paint the town red, raise Cain (*or* the devil *or* hell), whoop it up. *See* RESTRAINT.

carp *verb*
To raise unnecessary or trivial objections : cavil, niggle, nitpick, pettifog, quibble. *Idiom:* pick to pieces. *See* SUPPORT.
carp at *verb* To scold or find fault with constantly : fuss at, nag, peck at[1], pick on. *Informal:* henpeck. *See* PRAISE.

carp at *verb* See **carp.**

carper *noun*
A person who finds fault, often severely and willfully : caviler, critic, criticizer, faultfinder, hypercritic, niggler, nitpicker, quibbler. *See* PRAISE.

carping *adjective*
Inclined to judge too severely : captious, censorious, critical, faultfinding, hypercritical, overcritical. *See* PRAISE.

carriage *noun*
1. The moving of persons or goods from one place to another : conveyance, transit, transport, transportation. *See* MOVE. **2.** The way in which a person holds or carries his or her body : attitude, pose, posture, stance. *See* POSTURE.

carrier *noun*
A person who carries messages or is sent on errands : bearer, conveyer, courier, envoy, messenger, runner, transporter. *See* OVER.

carry *verb*
1. To move while supporting : bear, convey, lug[2], transport. *Informal:* tote. *Slang:* schlep. *See* OVER. **2.** To cause to come along with oneself : bear, bring, convey, fetch, take, transport. *See* ACCOMPANIED. **3.** To serve as a conduit : channel, conduct, convey, transmit. *See* ALLOW. **4.** To make known : break, communicate, convey, disclose, get across, impart, pass, report, tell, transmit. *See* KNOWLEDGE. **5.** To cause (a disease) to pass to another or others : communicate, convey, give, pass, spread, transmit. *See* MOVE. **6.** To hold up : bear, support, sustain. *See* OVER. **7.** To sustain the weight of : bear, hold, support, uphold. *See* SUPPORT. **8.** To hold on one's person : bear, have, possess. *Informal:* pack. *See* OWNED. **9.** To conduct oneself in a specified way : acquit, act, bear, behave, comport, demean[1], deport, do, quit. *See* BE. **10.** To proceed on a certain course or for a certain distance : extend, go, lead, reach, run, stretch. *See* REACH. **11.** To be accepted or approved : clear, pass. *See* ACCEPT. **12.** To be endowed with as a visible characteristic or form : bear, display, exhibit, have, possess. *See* SHOW. **13.** To have as an accompaniment, a condition, or a consequence : entail, involve. *See* START. **14.** To have for sale : keep, stock. *See* KEEP.
carry away *verb* To move or excite greatly : electrify, enrapture, thrill, transport. *Slang:* send. *See* EXCITE.
carry off *verb* To cause the death of : cut down, cut off, destroy, dispatch, finish (off), kill[1], slay. *Slang:* waste, zap. *Idioms:* put an end to, put to sleep. *See* HELP.
carry on *verb* **1.** To control the course of (an activity) : conduct, direct, manage, operate, run, steer. *See* OVER. **2.** To involve oneself in (an activity) : engage, have, indulge, partake, participate. *Idiom:* take part. *See* PARTICIPATE. **3.** To engage in (a war or campaign, for example) : carry out, conduct, wage. *See* DO. **4.** To continue without halting despite difficulties or setbacks : go on, hang on, keep on, persevere, persist. *Idioms:* hang in there, keep going, keep it up. *See* CONTINUE. **5.** To show enthusism : rave, rhapsodize. *See* FEELINGS. **6.** To behave in a rowdy, improper, or unruly fashion : act up, misbehave. *Informal:* cut up, horse around. *See* GOOD.
carry out *verb* **1.** To oversee the provision or execution of : administer, administrate, dispense, execute. *See* OVER. **2.** To engage in (a war or campaign, for example) : carry on, conduct, wage. *See* DO. **3.** To compel observance of : effect, enforce, execute, implement, invoke. *Idioms:* put in force, put into action. *See* OBLIGATION, OVER. **4.** To act in conformity with : abide by, adhere, comply, conform, follow, keep, mind, obey, observe. *Idiom:* toe the line (*or* mark). *See* ACCEPT, SAME. **5.** To bring about and carry to a successful conclusion : bring off, carry through, effect, effectuate, execute, put through. *Informal:* swing. *See* DO.
carry through *verb* To bring about and carry to a successful conclusion : bring off, carry out, effect, effectuate, execute, put through. *Informal:* swing. *See* DO.

carry away *verb* See **carry.**

carry off *verb* See **carry.**

carry on *verb* See **carry.**

carry out *verb* See **carry.**

carry through *verb* See **carry.**

cartel *noun*
1. A combination of businesses closely interconnected for common profit : combine, pool, syndicate, trust. *See* GROUP, MONEY. **2.** A group of individuals united in a common cause : bloc, coalition, combination, combine, faction, party, ring[1]. *See* GROUP. **3.** An association, especially of nations for a common cause : alliance, Anschluss, bloc, coalition, confederacy, confederation, federation, league, organization, union. *See* CONNECT, GROUP, POLITICS.

carve *verb*
1. To separate into parts with or as if with a sharp-edged instrument : cleave[1], cut, dissever, sever, slice, slit, split. *See* ASSEMBLE. **2.** To cut (a design or inscription) into a hard surface, especially for printing : engrave, etch, grave[3], incise. *See* MARKS.

Casanova *noun*
1. A man amorously attentive to women : amorist, Don Juan, gallant, lady's man, Lothario, Romeo. *See* SEX. **2.** A man who philanders : Don Juan, lady's man, philanderer, womanizer. *Slang:* lady-killer, wolf. ***Idioms:*** man on the make, skirt chaser. *See* SEX.

case *noun*
1. One that is representative of a group or class : example, illustration, instance, representative, sample, specimen. *See* SUBSTITUTE. **2.** A legal proceeding to demand justice or enforce a right : action, cause, instance, lawsuit, suit. *See* LAW. **3.** A course of reasoning : argument, point. *See* REASON.
case *verb Informal.* To look at carefully or critically : check (out), con, examine, go over, inspect, peruse, scrutinize, study, survey, traverse, view. ***Idiom:*** give a going-over. *See* INVESTIGATE.

caseharden *verb*
To make resistant to hardship, especially through continued exposure : acclimate, acclimatize, harden, indurate, season, toughen. *See* CONTINUE, RESIST.

cash *noun*
Something, such as coins or printed bills, used as a medium of exchange : currency, lucre, money. *Informal:* wampum. *Slang:* bread, cabbage, dough, gelt, green, jack, lettuce, long green, mazuma, moola, scratch. *Chiefly British:* brass. *See* MONEY.

cashier *verb*
To end the employment or service of : discharge, dismiss, drop, release, terminate. *Informal:* ax, fire, pink-slip. *Slang:* boot[1], bounce, can, sack[1]. ***Idioms:*** give someone his or her walking papers, give someone the ax, give someone the gate, give someone the pink slip, let go, show someone the door. *See* KEEP.

Cassandra *noun*
A prophet of misfortune or disaster : doomsayer, pessimist, worrywart. *See* HOPE.

cast *verb*
1. To send through the air with a motion of the hand or arm : dart, dash, fling, heave, hurl, hurtle, launch, pitch, shoot, shy[2], sling, throw, toss. *Informal:* fire. *See* MOVE. **2.** To move (a weapon or blow, for example) in the direction of someone or something : aim, direct, head, level, point, set[1], train, turn, zero in. *Military:* lay[1]. *See* SEEK. **3.** To send out heat, light, or energy : emit, irradiate, project, radiate, shed, throw. *See* MOVE. **4.** To form a strategy for : blueprint, chart, conceive, contrive, design, devise, formulate, frame, lay[1], plan, project, scheme, strategize, work out. *Informal:* dope out. ***Idiom:*** lay plans. *See* PLANNED. **5.** To ascertain by mathematics : calculate, cipher, compute, figure, reckon. *See* REASON. **6.** To combine (figures) to form a sum : add (up), foot (up), sum (up), tot[2] (up), total, totalize. *See* INCREASE.
cast about *verb* To try to find something : hunt, look, quest, search, seek. *See* SEEK.
cast out *verb* To rid one's mind of : banish, dismiss, dispel, shut out. *See* KEEP.
cast *noun* **1.** An act of throwing : fling, heave, hurl, launch, pitch, shy[2], sling, throw, toss. *See* MOVE. **2.** A disposition of the facial features that conveys meaning, feeling, or mood : aspect, countenance, expression, face, look, visage. *See* EXPRESS. **3.** A hollow device for shaping a fluid or plastic substance : form, matrix, mold. *See* SURFACE. **4.** The external outline of a thing : configuration, figure, form, pattern, shape. *See* SURFACE. **5.** A class that is defined by the common attribute or attributes possessed by all its members : breed, description, feather, ilk, kind[2], lot, manner, mold, nature, order, sort, species, stamp, stripe, type, variety. *Informal:* persuasion. *See* GROUP. **6.** An inclination to something : bent, bias, disposition, leaning, partiality, penchant, predilection, predisposition, proclivity, proneness, propensity, squint, tendency, trend, turn. *See* APPROACH, LIKE. **7.** A shade of a color, especially a pale or delicate variation : hue, tinge, tint, tone. *See* COLORS.

cast about *verb* See **cast**.

castigate *verb*
1. To subject (one) to a penalty for a wrong : chastise, correct, discipline, penalize, punish. *See* REWARD. **2.** To criticize for a fault or an offense : admonish, call down, chastise, chide, dress down, rap[1], rebuke, reprimand, reproach, reprove, scold, tax, upbraid. *Informal:* bawl out, lambaste. *Slang:* chew out. ***Idioms:*** bring (*or* call *or* take) to task, call on the carpet, haul (*or* rake) over the coals, let someone have it. *See* ATTACK, PRAISE.

castigation *noun*
Something, such as loss, pain, or confinement, imposed for wrongdoing : chastisement, correction, discipline, penalty, punishment. *See* REWARD.

castle in the air *noun*
A fantastic, impracticable plan or desire : bubble, chimera, dream, fantasy, illusion, pipe dream, rainbow. *See* REAL.

cast out *verb* See **cast.**

castrate *verb*
To render incapable of reproducing sexually : alter, fix, geld, neuter, spay, sterilize, unsex. *See* REPRODUCTION, RICH.

castration *noun*
The act or an instance of making one incapable of reproducing sexually : sterilization. *See* REPRODUCTION, RICH.

casual *adjective*
1. Occurring unexpectedly : accidental, chance, contingent, fluky, fortuitous, inadvertent, odd. *See* SURPRISE. **2.** Unconstrained by rigid standards or ceremony : easy, easygoing, informal, natural, relaxed, spontaneous, unceremonious, unrestrained. *Informal:* laid-back. *See* PLAIN, TIGHTEN.

casualness *noun*
Freedom from constraint, formality, embarrassment, or awkwardness : ease, easiness, informality, naturalness, poise, spontaneity, unceremoniousness, unrestraint. *See* RESTRAINT, TIGHTEN.

casualty *noun*
1. An unexpected and usually undesirable event : accident, contretemps, misadventure, mischance, misfortune, mishap. *See* HELP, SURPRISE. **2.** One that is made to suffer injury, loss, or death : prey, victim. *See* HELP. **3.** A termination of life, usually as the result of an accident or a disaster : death, fatality. *See* LIVE.

casuistry *noun*
Plausible but invalid reasoning : fallacy, sophism, sophistry, speciousness, spuriousness. *See* CORRECT, TRUE.

cataclysm *noun*
1. An occurrence inflicting widespread destruction and distress : calamity, catastrophe, disaster, tragedy. *See* HELP. **2.** A momentous or sweeping change : convulsion, revolution, upheaval. *See* CHANGE. **3.** An abundant, usually overwhelming flow or fall, as of a river or rain : alluvion, cataract, deluge, downpour, flood, freshet, inundation, Niagara, overflow, torrent. *Chiefly British:* spate. *See* BIG.

cataclysmal *adjective*
Causing ruin or destruction : calamitous, cataclysmic, catastrophic, destructive, disastrous, fatal, fateful, ruinous. *See* HELP.

cataclysmic *adjective*
Causing ruin or destruction : calamitous, cataclysmal, catastrophic, destructive, disastrous, fatal, fateful, ruinous. *See* HELP.

catacomb *noun*
A burial place or receptacle for human remains : cinerarium, crypt, grave[1], mausoleum, ossuary, sepulcher, sepulture, tomb, vault[1]. *See* KEEP, PLACE.

catalog or **catalogue** *noun*
A series, as of names or words, printed or written down : list[1], register, roll, roster, schedule. *See* REMEMBER.

catalog or **catalogue** *verb* To register in or as if in a book : book, enroll, inscribe, list[1], set down, write down. *See* REMEMBER.

catalogue *noun & verb* See **catalog.**

catalyst *noun*
An agent that stimulates or precipitates a reaction, development, or change : ferment, leaven, leavening, yeast. *See* CHANGE.

cataract *noun*
An abundant, usually overwhelming flow or fall, as of a river or rain : alluvion, cataclysm, deluge, downpour, flood, freshet, inundation, Niagara, overflow, torrent. *Chiefly British:* spate. *See* BIG.

catastrophe *noun*
An occurrence inflicting widespread destruction and distress : calamity, cataclysm, disaster, tragedy. *See* HELP.

catastrophic *adjective*
Causing ruin or destruction : calamitous, cataclysmal, cataclysmic, destructive, disastrous, fatal, fateful, ruinous. *See* HELP.

catcall *noun*
Any of various derisive sounds of disapproval : boo, hiss, hoot. *Slang:* bird, Bronx cheer, raspberry, razz. *See* SOUNDS.

catch *verb*
1. To gain possession of, especially after a struggle or chase : capture, get, net[1], secure, take. *Informal:* bag. *Slang:* nail. *See* GET. **2.** To come upon, especially suddenly or unexpectedly : hit on (*or* upon), surprise, take. *Informal:* hit. *See* SURPRISE. **3.** To perceive, especially barely or fleetingly : descry, detect, discern, espy, glimpse, spot, spy. *See* SEE. **4.** To get hold of (something moving) : clutch[1], grab, seize, snatch. *Informal:* nab. ***Idiom:*** lay hands on. *See* GET. **5.** To grasp at (something) eagerly, forcibly, and abruptly with the jaws : nip[1], snap, snatch, strike. *See* REACH. **6.** To have a sudden overwhelming effect on : seize, strike, take. *See* ATTACK, OVER. **7.** To go aboard (a means of transport) : board, take. *See* USED. **8.** To make secure : anchor, fasten, fix, moor, secure. ***Idiom:*** make fast. *See* MOVE. **9.** To become or cause to become stuck or lodged : fix, lodge, stick. *See* MOVE. **10.** To gain control of or an advantage over by or as if by trapping : enmesh, ensnare, ensnarl, entrap, snare, tangle, trammel, trap, web. *See* FREE. **11.** To deliver a powerful blow to suddenly and sharply : bash, clout, hit, knock, pop[1], slam, slog, slug[3], smash, smite, sock, strike, swat, thwack, whack, wham, whop. *Informal:* biff, bop, clip[1], wallop. *Slang:* belt, conk, paste. ***Idioms:*** let someone have it, sock it to someone. *See* ATTACK, STRIKE. **12.** To become affected with a disease : contract, develop, get, sicken, take. ***Idiom:*** come down with. *See* GET. **13.** To perceive and recognize the meaning of. Also used with *on* : accept, apprehend, compass, comprehend, conceive, fathom, follow, get, grasp, make out, read, see, sense, take, take in, understand. *Informal:* savvy. *Slang:* dig. *Chiefly British:* twig. *Scots:* ken. ***Idioms:*** get (*or* have) a handle on, get the picture. *See* UNDERSTAND.
catch up *verb* **1.** To come up even with another : overtake. *See* SEEK, WIN. **2.** To draw in so that extrication is difficult : embrangle, embroil, implicate, involve, mix up, suck. *See* FREE, PARTICIPATE. **3.** To compel, as the attention, interest, or imagination, of : arrest, enthrall, fascinate, grip, hold, mesmerize, rivet, spellbind, transfix. *Slang:* grab. *See* EXCITE.
catch *noun* **1.** The act of catching, especially a sudden taking and holding : clutch[1], grab, seizure, snatch. *See* GET. **2.** A device for fastening or for checking motion : clasp, fastener, hook. *See* MOVE. **3.** *Informal.* A person or thing worth catching : plum, prize[1]. *Slang:* brass ring. *See* DESIRE. **4.** *Informal.* A tricky or unsuspected condition : rub, snag. *See* LIMITED.

catching *adjective*
Capable of transmission by infection : communicable, contagious, infectious, taking. *See* MOVE.

catch up *verb* See **catch.**

catechism *noun*
A set of questions or exercises designed to determine knowledge or skill : catechization, exam, examination, quiz, test. *See* INVESTIGATE.

catechization *noun*
A set of questions or exercises designed to determine knowledge or skill : catechism, exam, examination, quiz, test. *See* INVESTIGATE.

categorical *adjective*
Clearly, fully, and sometimes emphatically expressed : clear, clear-cut, decided, definite, explicit, express, positive, precise, specific, unambiguous, unequivocal. *See* CLEAR.

categorization *noun*
A way or condition of being arranged : arrangement, classification, deployment, disposal, disposition, distribution, formation, grouping, layout, lineup, order, organization, placement, sequence. *See* ORDER.

categorize *verb*
1. To distribute into groups according to kinds : assort, class, classify, group, pigeonhole, separate, sort (out). *See* COLLECT. **2.** To assign to a class or classes : class, classify, distribute, grade, group, pigeonhole, place, range, rank[1], rate[1]. *See* GROUP, VALUE.

category *noun*
A subdivision of a larger group : class, classification, order, set[2]. *See* GROUP.

cater *verb*
1. To treat with indulgence and often overtender care : baby, coddle, cosset, indulge, mollycoddle, overindulge, pamper, spoil. *See* TREAT WELL. **2.** To comply with the wishes or ideas of (another) : gratify, humor, indulge. *See* RESIST.

caterwaul *verb*
To quarrel noisily : brawl, broil[2], row[2], wrangle. *See* ATTACK.

catharsis *noun*
Medicine. The act or process of discharging bodily wastes or foreign substances : elimination, evacuation, excretion, purgation. *See* KEEP.

cathartic *adjective*
Of, relating to, or tending to eliminate : elimi-

native, eliminatory, evacuant, evacuative, excretory, purgative. *See* KEEP.

catholic *adjective*

So pervasive and all-inclusive as to exist in or affect the whole world : cosmic, cosmopolitan, ecumenical, global, pandemic, planetary, universal, worldwide. *See* LIMITED, SPECIFIC.

catholicon *noun*

Something believed to cure all human disorders : cure-all, panacea. *See* HELP.

catlike *adjective*

So slow, deliberate, and secret as to escape observation : feline, furtive, slinky, sneaking, sneaky, stealthy. *See* MOVE.

catnap *noun*

A brief sleep : doze, nap, siesta, snooze. *See* AWARENESS.

catnap *verb* To sleep for a brief period : doze (off), nap, nod (off), siesta, snooze. ***Idiom:*** catch (*or* grab *or* take) forty winks. *See* AWARENESS.

cat's-paw also **cats-paw** *noun*

A person used or controlled by others : dupe, instrument, pawn[2], puppet, stooge, tool. *See* OVER.

cat's cradle *noun*

Something that is intricately and often bewilderingly complex : entanglement, jungle, knot, labyrinth, maze, mesh (often used in plural), morass, skein, snarl[2], tangle, web. *See* SIMPLE.

cause *noun*

1. That which produces an effect : antecedent, occasion. *See* START. **2.** A basis for an action or a decision : ground (often used in plural), motivation, motive, reason, spring. *See* START. **3.** That which provides a reason or justification : call, ground (often used in plural), justification, necessity, occasion, reason, wherefore, why. ***Idiom:*** why and wherefore. *See* START. **4.** A goal or set of interests served with dedication : crusade. *See* START. **5.** A legal proceeding to demand justice or enforce a right : action, case, instance, lawsuit, suit. *See* LAW.

cause *verb* To be the cause of : bring, bring about, bring on, effect, effectuate, generate, induce, ingenerate, lead to, make, occasion, result in, secure, set off, stir[1] (up), touch off, trigger. ***Idioms:*** bring to pass (*or* effect), give rise to. *See* START.

caustic *adjective*

So sharp as to cause mental pain : acerbic, acid, acidic, acrid, astringent, biting, corrosive, cutting, mordacious, mordant, pungent, scathing, sharp, slashing, stinging, trenchant, truculent, vitriolic. *See* ATTACK, RESPECT.

causticity *noun*

Irony or bitterness, as of tone : acerbity, acidity, acridity, corrosiveness, mordacity, mordancy, sarcasm, trenchancy. *See* LAUGHTER, RESPECT.

caution *noun*

1. Careful forethought to avoid harm or risk : calculation, care, carefulness, chariness, gingerliness, precaution, wariness. *See* FEAR. **2.** Cautious attentiveness : care, carefulness, gingerliness, heed, heedfulness, mindfulness, regard. *See* CAREFUL. **3.** The exercise of good judgment or common sense in practical matters : circumspection, discretion, forehandedness, foresight, foresightedness, forethought, forethoughtfulness, precaution, prudence. *See* CAREFUL. **4.** Advice to beware, as of a person or thing : admonishment, admonition, caveat, monition, warning. *See* WARN.

caution *verb* To notify (someone) of imminent danger or risk : admonish, alarm, alert, forewarn, warn. *See* WARN.

cautionary *adjective*

Giving warning : admonishing, admonitory, monitory, warning. *See* WARN.

cautious *adjective*

Trying attentively to avoid danger, risk, or error : careful, chary, circumspect, forehanded, gingerly, prudent, wary. *See* CAREFUL.

cave *noun*

A hollow beneath the earth's surface : cavern, grotto. *See* CONVEX.

cave in *verb* **1.** To fall in : buckle, collapse, crumple, give, go. ***Idiom:*** give way. *See* EXPLOSION. **2.** To suddenly lose all health or strength : break (down), collapse, crack, drop, give out, succumb. *Informal:* crack up. *Slang:* conk out. ***Idiom:*** give way. *See* HEALTH.

caveat *noun*

Advice to beware, as of a person or thing : admonishment, admonition, caution, monition, warning. *See* WARN.

cave in *verb* See **cave.**

cavern *noun*

A hollow beneath the earth's surface : cave, grotto. *See* CONVEX.

cavernous *adjective*

1. Curving inward : concave, hollow, indented, sunken. *See* CONVEX. **2.** Open wide : abysmal, abyssal, gaping, yawning. *See* WIDE.

cavil *verb*

To raise unnecessary or trivial objections : carp, niggle, nitpick, pettifog, quibble. ***Idiom:*** pick to pieces. *See* SUPPORT.

caviler *noun*
A person who finds fault, often severely and willfully : carper, critic, criticizer, faultfinder, hypercritic, niggler, nitpicker, quibbler. *See* PRAISE.

cavity *noun*
A space in an otherwise solid mass : hole, hollow, pocket, vacuity, void. *See* CONVEX.

cavort *verb*
To leap and skip about playfully : caper, dance, frisk, frolic, gambol, rollick, romp. *See* WORK.

cease *verb*
1. To prevent the occurrence or continuation of a movement, action, or operation : arrest, belay, check, discontinue, halt[1], stall[1], stay[1], stop, surcease. ***Idioms:*** bring to a standstill, call a halt to, put a stop to. *See* CONTINUE. **2.** To come to a cessation : arrest, belay, check, discontinue, halt[1], leave off, quit, stall[1], stop, surcease. ***Idiom:*** come to a halt (*or* standstill *or* stop). *See* CONTINUE. **3.** To stop suddenly, as a conversation, activity, or relationship : break off, discontinue, interrupt, suspend, terminate. *See* CONTINUE.
cease *noun* A concluding or terminating : cessation, close, closing, closure, completion, conclusion, consummation, end, ending, end of the line, finish, period, stop, stopping point, termination, terminus, wind-up, wrap-up. *See* CONTINUE.

cease-fire or **ceasefire** *noun*
A temporary cessation of hostilities by mutual consent of the contending parties : armistice, truce. *See* CONTINUE.

ceaseless *adjective*
1. Existing or occurring without interruption or end : around-the-clock, constant, continual, continuous, endless, eternal, everlasting, incessant, interminable, nonstop, ongoing, perpetual, persistent, relentless, round-the-clock, timeless, unceasing, unending, unfailing, uninterrupted, unremitting. *See* CONTINUE. **2.** Enduring for all time : amaranthine, endless, eternal, everlasting, immortal, never-ending, perpetual, unending, world without end. *Archaic:* eterne. *See* CONTINUE.

ceaselessness *noun*
The quality or state of having no end : endlessness, eternality, eternalness, eternity, everlastingness, perpetuity, world without end. *See* CONTINUE.

cede *verb*
1. To give up a possession, claim, or right : abandon, abdicate, demit, forswear, hand over, quitclaim, relinquish, render, renounce, resign, surrender, waive, yield. *See* KEEP. **2.** To let (something) go : abandon, forgo, lay down, relinquish, surrender, yield. *See* KEEP. **3.** To change the ownership of (property) by means of a legal document : deed, grant, make over, sign over. *Law:* alien, alienate, assign, convey, transfer. *See* GIVE, LAW.

ceiling *noun*
The greatest amount or number allowed : limit, limitation, maximum. *See* LIMITED.

celebrate *verb*
1. To mark (a day or an event) with ceremonies of respect, festivity, or rejoicing : commemorate, keep, observe, solemnize. *See* REMEMBER. **2.** To show joyful satisfaction in an event, especially by merrymaking : rejoice, revel. ***Idioms:*** kill the fatted calf, make merry. *See* LAUGHTER. **3.** To pay tribute or homage to : acclaim, eulogize, exalt, extol, glorify, hail[2], honor, laud, magnify, panegyrize, praise. ***Idiom:*** sing someone's praises. *See* PRAISE.

celebrated *adjective*
Widely known and esteemed : distinguished, eminent, famed, famous, great, illustrious, notable, noted, preeminent, prestigious, prominent, redoubtable, renowned. *See* KNOWLEDGE, RESPECT.

celebration *noun*
1. The act of observing a day or an event with ceremonies : commemoration, observance. *See* REMEMBER. **2.** The act of showing joyful satisfaction in an event : festivity, merrymaking, rejoicing, revel (often used in plural), revelry. *See* LAUGHTER. **3.** A big, exuberant party : shindig, shindy. *Slang:* bash, blast, blowout. *See* GROUP, RESTRAINT, WORK. **4.** A large or important social gathering : affair, festivity, fete, function, gala, occasion, party, soiree. *Informal:* do. *Slang:* bash. *See* GROUP, WORK. **5.** An expression of warm approval : acclaim, acclamation, applause, commendation, compliment, encomium, eulogy, kudos, laudation, panegyric, plaudit, praise. *See* PRAISE.

celebrity *noun*
1. A famous person : hero, lion, luminary, name, notable, personage, personality. *Informal:* big name. *See* KNOWLEDGE. **2.** Wide recognition for one's deeds : fame, famousness, notoriety, popularity, renown, reputation, repute. *See* KNOWLEDGE.

celerity *noun*
Rapidness of movement or activity : dispatch, expedition, expeditiousness, fleetness, haste,

hurry, hustle, quickness, rapidity, rapidness, speed, speediness, swiftness. *See* FAST.

celestial *adjective*
1. Of or relating to the heavens : empyreal, heavenly. *See* PLACE. **2.** Of or relating to heaven : divine, heavenly, paradisaic, paradisaical, paradisal, paradisiac, paradisiacal. *See* RELIGION.

censor *verb*
1. To examine (material) and remove parts considered harmful or improper for publication or transmission : bowdlerize, expurgate, screen. *See* INCLUDE, SHOW. **2.** To keep from being published or transmitted : ban, black out, hush (up), stifle, suppress. ***Idiom:*** keep (*or* put) a lid on. *See* SHOW.

censorious *adjective*
Inclined to judge too severely : captious, carping, critical, faultfinding, hypercritical, overcritical. *See* PRAISE.

censurable *adjective*
Deserving blame : blamable, blameful, blameworthy, culpable, guilty, reprehensible. ***Idiom:*** at fault. *See* PRAISE.

censure *noun*
A comment expressing fault : blame, condemnation, criticism, denunciation, reprehension, reprobation. *Informal:* pan. *Slang:* knock. *See* PRAISE.

censure *verb* **1.** To find fault with : blame, criticize, fault, rap[1]. *Informal:* cut up, pan. *Slang:* knock. *See* PRAISE. **2.** To feel or express strong disapproval of : condemn, denounce, deplore, reprehend, reprobate. *See* PRAISE.

center *noun*
1. A point or an area equidistant from all sides of something : median, middle, midpoint, midst. *See* EDGE. **2.** A place of concentrated activity, influence, or importance : focus, headquarters, heart, hub, seat. *See* EDGE. **3.** A point of origin from which ideas or influences, for example, originate : bottom, core, focus, heart, hub, quick, root[1]. *See* START.

center *verb* To direct toward a common center : channel, concentrate, converge, focalize, focus. *See* EDGE.

center *adjective* At, in, near, or being the center : central, medial, median, mid, middle. *See* EDGE.

central *adjective*
1. At, in, near, or being the center : center, medial, median, mid, middle. *See* EDGE. **2.** Not extreme : intermediate, mean[3], medial, median, mid, middle, middle-of-the-road, midway. *See* EDGE. **3.** Dominant in importance or influence : key, pivotal. *See* IMPORTANT.

cerebral *adjective*
1. Relating to or performed by the mind : intellective, intellectual, mental, psychic, psychical, psychological. *See* THOUGHTS. **2.** Appealing to or engaging the intellect : intellectual, sophisticated, thoughtful. *Informal:* highbrow. *See* THOUGHTS.

cerebrate *verb*
To use the powers of the mind, as in conceiving ideas, drawing inferences, and making judgments : cogitate, deliberate, ratiocinate, reflect, speculate, think. ***Idioms:*** put on one's thinking cap, use one's head. *See* THOUGHTS.

cerebration *noun*
The act or process of thinking : brainwork, cogitation, contemplation, deliberation, excogitation, meditation, reflection, rumination, speculation, thought. *See* THOUGHTS.

ceremonial *adjective*
Of or characterized by ceremony : ceremonious, formal, liturgical, ritual, ritualistic. *See* RITUAL.

ceremonial *noun* A formal act or set of acts prescribed by ritual : ceremony, liturgy, observance, office, rite, ritual, service. *See* RITUAL.

ceremonious *adjective*
1. Fond of or given to ceremony : conventional, courtly, formal, punctilious. *See* COURTESY. **2.** Of or characterized by ceremony : ceremonial, formal, liturgical, ritual, ritualistic. *See* RITUAL.

ceremoniousness *noun*
Strict observance of social conventions : ceremony, formality, protocol, punctiliousness. *See* COURTESY.

ceremony *noun*
1. A formal act or set of acts prescribed by ritual : ceremonial, liturgy, observance, office, rite, ritual, service. *See* RITUAL. **2.** A conventional social gesture or act without intrinsic purpose : form, formality, ritual. *See* RITUAL, USUAL. **3.** Strict observance of social conventions : ceremoniousness, formality, protocol, punctiliousness. *See* COURTESY.

certain *adjective*
1. In a definite and final form; not likely to change : firm[1], fixed, flat, set[1]. *See* CHANGE. **2.** Bound to happen : inescapable, inevitable, sure, unavoidable. *See* CERTAIN. **3.** Established beyond a doubt : hard, inarguable, incontestable, incontrovertible, indisputable, indubitable, irrefutable, positive, sure, unassailable, undeniable, undisputable, unquestionable. *See* CER-

TAIN, TRUE. **4.** Known positively : definite, positive, sure. *Idiom:* for certain. *See* CERTAIN. **5.** Such as could not possibly fail or disappoint : infallible, secure, sure, unerring, unfailing. *Informal:* sure-fire. *See* CERTAIN. **6.** Having no doubt : assured, confident, positive, sure, undoubting. *See* CERTAIN.

certainly *adverb*
Without question : absolutely, doubtless, doubtlessly, positively, undoubtedly. *See* CERTAIN, LIMITED.

certainty *noun*
1. The fact or condition of being without doubt : assurance, assuredness, certitude, confidence, conviction, positiveness, sureness, surety. *See* CERTAIN. **2.** A clearly established fact : cinch, sure thing. *See* CERTAIN, TRUE.

certify *verb*
1. To confirm formally as true, accurate, or genuine : attest, testify, vouch (for), witness. *Idiom:* bear witness to. *See* AFFIRM. **2.** To assume responsibility for the quality, worth, or durability of : guarantee, guaranty, warrant. *See* OBLIGATION.

certitude *noun*
The fact or condition of being without doubt : assurance, assuredness, certainty, confidence, conviction, positiveness, sureness, surety. *See* CERTAIN.

cessation *noun*
1. A concluding or terminating : cease, close, closing, closure, completion, conclusion, consummation, end, ending, end of the line, finish, period, stop, stopping point, termination, terminus, wind-up, wrap-up. *See* CONTINUE. **2.** The act of stopping : check, cut-off, discontinuance, discontinuation, halt[1], stay[1], stop, stoppage, surcease. *See* CONTINUE. **3.** The condition of being stopped : discontinuance, discontinuation, halt[1], standstill, stop, stoppage, surcease. *See* CONTINUE.

cesspit *noun*
A place known for its great filth or corruption : cesspool, pit[1], sink. *Slang:* armpit. *See* CLEAN, RIGHT.

cesspool *noun*
A place known for its great filth or corruption : cesspit, pit[1], sink. *Slang:* armpit. *See* CLEAN, RIGHT.

chafe *verb*
1. To make (the skin) raw by or as if by friction : abrade, excoriate, fret, gall[2], irritate. *See* HELP. **2.** To trouble the nerves or peace of mind of, especially by repeated vexations : aggravate, annoy, bother, bug, disturb, exasperate, fret, gall[2], get, irk, irritate, nettle, peeve, provoke, put out, rile, ruffle, vex. *Idioms:* get in one's hair, get on one's nerves, get under one's skin. *See* FEELINGS, PAIN. **3.** To worry over trifles : fuss, pother. *Informal:* take on. *See* CALM.

chaff *verb*
To tease or mock good-humoredly : banter, joke, josh. *Informal:* kid, rib, ride. *Slang:* jive, rag[2], razz. *See* LAUGHTER.
chaff *noun* Good-natured teasing : badinage, banter, raillery, taunt. *Informal:* ribbing. *See* LAUGHTER.

chagrin *noun*
Self-conscious distress : abashment, confusion, discomfiture, discomposure, embarrassment. *See* PAIN.
chagrin *verb* To cause (a person) to be self-consciously distressed : abash, confound, confuse, discomfit, discomfort, disconcert, discountenance, embarrass, faze, mortify. *Idioms:* put on the spot, throw for a loop. *See* PAIN.

chain *noun*
1. Something that physically confines the legs or arms. Used in plural : bond, fetter, handcuff (often used in plural), hobble, iron (used in plural), manacle, restraint, shackle. *Archaic:* gyve. *See* FREE. **2.** A number of things placed or occurring one after the other : consecution, course, order, procession, progression, round, run, sequence, series, string, succession, suite, train. *Informal:* streak. *See* ORDER.
chain *verb* To restrict the activity or free movement of : fetter, hamper, hamstring, handcuff, hobble, leash, manacle, shackle, tie, trammel. *Informal:* hog-tie. *See* FREE, HELP.

challenge *noun*
1. An act of taunting another to do something bold or rash : dare. *See* REQUEST. **2.** Behavior or an act that is intentionally provocative : defiance, provocation. *See* ATTACK. **3.** The act of expressing strong or reasoned opposition : demur, exception, expostulation, objection, protest, protestation, remonstrance, remonstration, squawk. *Slang:* kick. *See* SUPPORT.
challenge *verb* **1.** To call on another to do something requiring boldness : dare, defy. *Idiom:* throw down the gauntlet. *See* REQUEST. **2.** To confront boldly and courageously : beard, brave, dare, defy, face, front. *Idioms:* fly in the face of, snap one's fingers at, stand up to, thumb one's nose at. *See* RESIST. **3.** To come near, as in quality or amount : approach, approximate, border on (*or* upon), rival, verge on. *See* SAME. **4.** To express opposition, often by

argument : demur, except, expostulate, inveigh, object, protest, remonstrate. *Informal:* kick, squawk. ***Idioms:*** set up a squawk, take exception. *See* SUPPORT. **5.** To take a stand against : buck, contest, dispute, oppose, resist, traverse. *See* SUPPORT.

champ *verb*
1. To seize, as food, with the teeth : bite, chomp, gnash, gnaw. *See* ATTACK, INGESTION. **2.** To bite and grind with the teeth : chew, chomp, chump[2], crump, crunch, masticate, munch. *Regional:* chaw. *See* MOUTH.

champion *adjective*
Exceptionally good of its kind : ace, banner, blue-ribbon, brag, capital, excellent, fine[1], first-class, first-rate, prime, quality, splendid, superb, superior, terrific, tiptop, top. *Informal:* A-one, bully, dandy, great, swell, topflight, topnotch. *Slang:* boss. *Chiefly British:* tophole. *See* GOOD.

champion *verb* To aid the cause of by approving or favoring : advocate, back, endorse, get behind, plump for, recommend, side with, stand behind, stand by, support, uphold. ***Idioms:*** align oneself with, go to bat for, take the part of. *See* SUPPORT.

chance *noun*
1. The quality shared by random, unintended, or unpredictable events or this quality regarded as the cause of such events : fortuitousness, fortuity, fortune, hap, hazard, luck. *See* CERTAIN. **2.** The likeliness of a given event occurring : likelihood, odds, possibility, probability, prospect (used in plural). *See* LIKELY. **3.** An unexpected random event : accident, fluke, fortuity, hap, happenchance, happenstance, hazard. *See* CERTAIN, SURPRISE. **4.** A favorable or advantageous combination of circumstances : break, occasion, opening, opportunity. *Informal:* shot. *See* LUCK. **5.** A possibility of danger or harm : gamble, hazard, risk. *See* SAFETY.

chance *verb* **1.** To take place by chance : befall, hap, happen. *See* HAPPEN. **2.** To run the risk of : adventure, hazard, risk, venture. *See* SAFETY.

chance on (or **upon**) *verb* To find or meet by chance : bump into, come across, come on (*or* upon), find, happen on (*or* upon), light on (*or* upon), run across, run into, stumble on (*or* upon), tumble on. *Archaic:* alight on (*or* upon). ***Idiom:*** meet up with. *See* MEET.

chance *adjective* **1.** Occurring unexpectedly : accidental, casual, contingent, fluky, fortuitous, inadvertent, odd. *See* SURPRISE. **2.** Having no particular pattern, purpose, organization, or structure : desultory, haphazard, hit-or-miss, indiscriminate, random, spot, unplanned. *See* PLANNED.

chance on or **upon** *verb* See **chance.**

chancy *adjective*
1. Not affording certainty : ambiguous, borderline, clouded, doubtful, dubious, dubitable, equivocal, inconclusive, indecisive, indeterminate, problematic, problematical, questionable, uncertain, unclear, unsure. *Informal:* iffy. ***Idioms:*** at issue, in doubt, in question. *See* CERTAIN, CLEAR. **2.** Involving possible risk, loss, or injury : adventurous, dangerous, hazardous, jeopardous, parlous, perilous, risky, treacherous, unsafe, venturesome, venturous. *Slang:* hairy. *See* SAFETY.

change *verb*
1. To make or become different : alter, modify, mutate, turn, vary. *See* CHANGE. **2.** To give up in return for something else : commute, exchange, interchange, shift, substitute, switch, trade. *Informal:* swap. *See* CHANGE, SUBSTITUTE. **3.** To leave or discard for another : shift, switch. *See* CHANGE, SUBSTITUTE.

change *noun* **1.** The process or result of making or becoming different : alteration, modification, mutation, permutation, variation. *See* CHANGE. **2.** The act of exchanging or substituting : commutation, exchange, interchange, shift, substitution, switch, trade, transposition. *Informal:* swap. *See* CHANGE, SUBSTITUTE. **3.** The process or result of changing from one appearance, state, or phase to another : changeover, conversion, metamorphosis, mutation, shift, transfiguration, transformation, translation, transmogrification, transmutation, transubstantiation. *See* CHANGE. **4.** The process or an instance of passing from one form, state, or stage to another : passage, shift, transit, transition. *See* CHANGE.

changeable *adjective*
1. Capable of or liable to change : alterable, fluid, inconstant, mutable, uncertain, unsettled, unstable, unsteady, variable, variant. *Archaic:* various. *See* CHANGE. **2.** Following no predictable pattern : capricious, erratic, fantastic, fantastical, fickle, freakish, inconsistent, inconstant, mercurial, temperamental, ticklish, uncertain, unpredictable, unstable, unsteady, variable, volatile, whimsical. *See* CHANGE, CONTINUE. **3.** Changing easily, as in expression : fluid, mobile, plastic. *See* CHANGE.

changeless *adjective*
1. Remaining continually unchanged : consis-

tent, constant, invariable, same, unchanging, unfailing. *See* CHANGE. **2.** Having no change or variation : constant, equable, even[1], invariable, invariant, regular, same, steady, unchanging, uniform, unvarying. *See* SAME.

changeover *noun*
The process or result of changing from one appearance, state, or phase to another : change, conversion, metamorphosis, mutation, shift, transfiguration, transformation, translation, transmogrification, transmutation, transubstantiation. *See* CHANGE.

channel *verb*
1. To direct toward a common center : center, concentrate, converge, focalize, focus. *See* EDGE. **2.** To serve as a conduit : carry, conduct, convey, transmit. *See* ALLOW.

chant *verb*
To utter words or sounds in musical tones : carol, sing, vocalize. *Archaic:* tune. *See* SOUNDS.

chaos *noun*
A lack of order or regular arrangement : clutter, confusedness, confusion, derangement, disarrangement, disarray, disorder, disorderedness, disorderliness, disorganization, jumble, mess, mix-up, muddle, muss, scramble, topsy-turviness, tumble. *Slang:* snafu. *See* ORDER.

chaotic *adjective*
Characterized by physical confusion : confused, disordered, helter-skelter, higgledy-piggledy, topsy-turvy, upside-down. *Informal:* mixed-up. *See* ORDER.

chap *noun*
Informal. A grown man referred to familiarly, jokingly, or as a member of one's set or group : fellow. *Informal:* boy. *See* BEINGS, CONNECT.

char *verb*
To undergo or cause to undergo damage by or as if by fire : burn, scorch, sear, singe. *See* HOT.

char *noun* Damage or a damaged substance that results from burning : burn, scorch, sear, singe. *See* HOT.

character *noun*
1. The combination of emotional, intellectual, and moral qualities that distinguishes an individual : complexion, disposition, makeup, nature, personality. *See* BE. **2.** Moral or ethical strength : fiber, honesty, integrity, principle. *See* STRONG. **3.** A distinctive element : attribute, characteristic, feature, mark, peculiarity, property, quality, savor, trait. *See* BE. **4.** A statement attesting to personal qualifications, character, and dependability : recommendation, reference, testimonial. *See* SUPPORT. **5.** Public estimation of someone : name, report, reputation, repute. *Informal:* rep. *See* RESPECT. **6.** An important, influential person : dignitary, eminence, leader, lion, nabob, notability, notable, personage. *Informal:* big-timer, heavyweight, somebody, someone, VIP. *Slang:* big shot, big wheel, bigwig, muckamuck. *See* IMPORTANT. **7.** A person who is appealingly odd or curious : oddity, original. *Informal:* card, oddball. *See* USUAL. **8.** A person portrayed in fiction or drama : persona, personage. *See* REAL. **9.** A conventional mark used in a writing system : sign, symbol. *See* MARKS.

character assassination *noun*
The expression of injurious, malicious statements about someone : aspersion, calumniation, calumny, defamation, denigration, detraction, scandal, slander, traducement, vilification. *Law:* libel. *See* ATTACK, CRIMES, LAW.

characteristic *adjective*
Serving to identify or set apart an individual or group : distinctive, individual, peculiar, typical, vintage. *See* SAME.

characteristic *noun* A distinctive element : attribute, character, feature, mark, peculiarity, property, quality, savor, trait. *See* BE.

characterize *verb*
1. To describe with a word or term : call, designate, label, name, style, tag, term. *See* SPECIFIC, WORDS. **2.** To make noticeable or different : differentiate, discriminate, distinguish, individualize, mark, set apart, signalize, singularize. *See* SAME.

charade *noun*
The presentation of something false as true : make-believe, pretense. *See* HONEST, TRUE.

charge *verb*
1. To be morally bound to do : bind, commit, obligate, pledge. *See* OBLIGATION. **2.** To place a trust upon : entrust, trust. *See* TRUST. **3.** To make or become full; put as much into as can be held : fill, freight, heap, load, pack, pile. *See* FULL. **4.** To place a burden or heavy load on : burden[1], cumber, encumber, freight, lade, load, saddle, tax, weight. *See* OVER. **5.** To cause to be filled, as with a particular mood or tone : freight, imbue, impregnate, permeate, pervade, saturate, suffuse, transfuse. *See* FULL. **6.** To put (explosive material) into a weapon : load. *See* PUT IN. **7.** To give orders to : bid, command, direct, enjoin, instruct, order, tell. *See* OVER, WORDS. **8.** To make an accusation against : accuse, arraign, denounce, incriminate, indict, tax. *See* ATTACK, LAW, PRAISE. **9.** To regard as belonging to or resulting from another : ac-

credit, ascribe, assign, attribute, credit, impute, lay[1], refer. *See* GIVE.

charge *noun* **1.** An amount paid or to be paid for a purchase : cost, price. *Informal:* tab. *See* TRANSACTIONS. **2.** A fixed amount of money charged for a privilege or service : exaction, fee, toll[1]. *See* MONEY, PAY, TRANSACTIONS. **3.** A quantity of explosive put into a weapon : load. *See* EXPLOSION. **4.** An act or course of action that is demanded of one, as by position, custom, law, or religion : burden[1], commitment, duty, imperative, must, need, obligation, responsibility. *See* OBLIGATION. **5.** A person who relies on another for support : dependent, ward. *See* GIVE. **6.** The function of watching, guarding, or overseeing : care, custody, guardianship, keeping, superintendence, supervision, trust. *See* CARE FOR. **7.** The state of being detained by legal authority : confinement, custody, detention, ward. *See* FREE. **8.** An authoritative indication to be obeyed : behest, bidding, command, commandment, dictate, direction, directive, injunction, instruction (often used in plural), mandate, order, word. *See* OVER, WORDS. **9.** A charging of someone with a misdeed : accusation, denouncement, denunciation, imputation, incrimination. *Law:* indictment. *See* ATTACK, LAW, PRAISE. **10.** A swift advance or attack : blitzkrieg, rush. *See* APPROACH.

chariness *noun*
Careful forethought to avoid harm or risk : calculation, care, carefulness, caution, gingerliness, precaution, wariness. *See* FEAR.

charisma *noun*
The power or quality of attracting : allure, allurement, appeal, attraction, attractiveness, call, charm, draw, enchantment, enticement, fascination, glamour, lure, magnetism, witchery. *Informal:* pull. *See* LIKE.

charitable *adjective*
1. Of or concerned with charity : altruistic, benevolent, eleemosynary, philanthropic, philanthropical. *See* GIVE, KIND. **2.** Not strict or severe : clement, easy, forbearing, indulgent, lax, lenient, merciful, soft, tolerant. *See* ACCEPT. **3.** Concerned with human welfare and the alleviation of suffering : compassionate, human, humane, humanitarian, merciful. *See* ATTITUDE, KIND.

charitableness *noun*
1. Kindly, charitable interest in others : altruism, beneficence, benevolence, benignancy, benignity, charity, goodwill, grace, kindheartedness, kindliness, kindness, philanthropy. *See* ATTITUDE, KIND. **2.** Forbearing or lenient treatment : charity, forbearance, indulgence, lenience, leniency, lenity, tolerance, toleration. *See* ACCEPT.

charity *noun*
1. Something given to a charity or cause : alms, benefaction, beneficence, contribution, donation, gift, handout, offering, subscription. *See* GIVE. **2.** Kindly, charitable interest in others : altruism, beneficence, benevolence, benignancy, benignity, charitableness, goodwill, grace, kindheartedness, kindliness, kindness, philanthropy. *See* ATTITUDE, KIND. **3.** Kind, forgiving, or compassionate treatment of or disposition toward others : clemency, grace, lenience, leniency, lenity, mercifulness, mercy. *See* FORGIVENESS. **4.** Forbearing or lenient treatment : charitableness, forbearance, indulgence, lenience, leniency, lenity, tolerance, toleration. *See* ACCEPT.

charlatan *noun*
One who fakes : fake, faker, fraud, humbug, impostor, mountebank, phony, pretender, quack. *See* TRUE.

charm *noun*
1. The power or quality of attracting : allure, allurement, appeal, attraction, attractiveness, call, charisma, draw, enchantment, enticement, fascination, glamour, lure, magnetism, witchery. *Informal:* pull. *See* LIKE. **2.** A small object worn or kept for its supposed magical power : amulet, fetish, juju, periapt, phylactery, talisman. *See* SUPERNATURAL. **3.** An object or power that one uses to cause often evil events : evil eye, magic, spell[2]. *Slang:* whammy. *See* SUPERNATURAL.

charm *verb* **1.** To please greatly or irresistibly : beguile, bewitch, captivate, enchant, entrance[2], fascinate. *See* LIKE. **2.** To act upon with or as if with magic : bewitch, enchant, enthrall, entrance[2], spell[2], spellbind, voodoo, witch. *See* PERSUASION.

charmer *noun*
One that seduces : allurer, enticer, inveigler, lurer, seducer, tempter. *See* PERSUASION.

charming *adjective*
Giving great pleasure or delight : delectable, delicious, delightful, enchanting, heavenly, luscious. *Informal:* darling. *See* GOOD, HAPPY, LIKE.

chart *noun*
An orderly columnar display of data : table, tabulation. *See* KNOWLEDGE.

chart *verb* **1.** To show graphically the direction or location of, as by using coordinates : lay out, map (out), plot. *See* SHOW. **2.** To form a strategy for : blueprint, cast, conceive, contrive, design, devise, formulate, frame, lay[1], plan, project, scheme, strategize, work out. *Informal:* dope out. ***Idiom:*** lay plans. *See* PLANNED.

charter *verb*
To engage the temporary use of (something) for a fee : hire, lease, rent[1]. *See* GET, TRANSACTIONS.

chary *adjective*
1. Trying attentively to avoid danger, risk, or error : careful, cautious, circumspect, forehanded, gingerly, prudent, wary. *See* CAREFUL. **2.** Careful in the use of material resources : canny, economical, frugal, provident, prudent, saving, Scotch, sparing, thrifty. *See* CAREFUL, SAVE.

chase *verb*
1. To follow (another) with the intent of overtaking and capturing : pursue, run after. ***Idioms:*** be (*or* go) in pursuit, give chase. *See* SEEK. **2.** To look for and pursue (game) in order to capture or kill it : drive, hunt, run, stalk. *See* SEEK.

chase *noun* The following of another in an attempt to overtake and capture : hot pursuit, pursuit. *See* SEEK.

chasm *noun*
Something of immeasurable and vast extent : abysm, abyss, deep, depth (often used in plural), gulf. *See* HIGH.

chaste *adjective*
Morally beyond reproach, especially in sexual conduct : decent, modest, nice, pure, virgin, virginal, virtuous. *See* GOOD, RESTRAINT, SEX.

chasten *verb*
To castigate for the purpose of improving : correct. *See* PRAISE.

chastise *verb*
1. To subject (one) to a penalty for a wrong : castigate, correct, discipline, penalize, punish. *See* REWARD. **2.** To criticize for a fault or an offense : admonish, call down, castigate, chide, dress down, rap[1], rebuke, reprimand, reproach, reprove, scold, tax, upbraid. *Informal:* bawl out, lambaste. *Slang:* chew out. ***Idioms:*** bring (*or* call *or* take) to task, call on the carpet, haul (*or* rake) over the coals, let someone have it. *See* ATTACK, PRAISE.

chastisement *noun*
Something, such as loss, pain, or confinement, imposed for wrongdoing : castigation, correction, discipline, penalty, punishment. *See* REWARD.

chastity *noun*
The condition of being chaste : decency, innocence, modesty, purity, virginity, virtue, virtuousness. *See* GOOD, RESTRAINT, SEX.

chat *verb*
To engage in spoken exchange : confabulate, converse[1], discourse, speak, talk. *Informal:* confab, visit. *See* WORDS.

chat *noun* **1.** Spoken exchange : colloquy, confabulation, conversation, converse[1], dialogue, discourse, speech, talk. *Informal:* confab. *Slang:* jaw. *See* WORDS. **2.** Incessant and usually inconsequential talk : babble, blab, blabber, chatter, chitchat, jabber, palaver, prate, prattle, small talk. *Slang:* gab, gas, yak. *See* WORDS.

chattel *noun*
Law. One's portable property : belonging (often used in plural), effect (used in plural), good (used in plural), lares and penates, personal effects, personal property, possession (used in plural), property, thing (often used in plural). *Informal:* stuff. *Law:* movable (often used in plural). *See* OWNED.

chatter *verb*
1. To talk volubly, persistently, and usually inconsequentially : babble, blabber, chitchat, clack, jabber, palaver, prate, prattle, rattle (on), run on. *Informal:* go on, spiel. *Slang:* gab, gas, jaw, yak. ***Idioms:*** run off at the mouth, shoot the breeze (*or* bull). *See* WORDS. **2.** To talk rapidly, incoherently, or indistinctly : babble, blather, gabble, gibber, jabber, prate, prattle. *See* WORDS. **3.** To make or cause to make a succession of short, sharp sounds : brattle, clack, clatter, rattle. *See* SOUNDS.

chatter *noun* Incessant and usually inconsequential talk : babble, blab, blabber, chat, chitchat, jabber, palaver, prate, prattle, small talk. *Slang:* gab, gas, yak. *See* WORDS.

chatty *adjective*
1. Given to conversation : conversational, garrulous, loquacious, talkative, talky, voluble. *Slang:* gabby. *See* WORDS. **2.** In the style of conversation : colloquial, confabulatory, conversational, informal. *See* WORDS.

chaw *verb*
Regional. To bite and grind with the teeth : champ, chew, chomp, chump[2], crump, crunch, masticate, munch. *See* MOUTH.

cheap *adjective*
1. Low in price : inexpensive, low, low-cost, low-priced. *See* MONEY, VALUE. **2.** Of decid-

edly inferior quality : base[2], lousy, miserable, paltry, poor, rotten, shoddy, sleazy, trashy. *Informal:* cheesy. *Slang:* crummy, schlocky. *See* GOOD. **3.** Ungenerously or pettily reluctant to spend money : close, close-fisted, costive, hard-fisted, mean[2], miserly, niggard, niggardly, parsimonious, penny-pinching, penurious, petty, pinching, stingy, tight, tightfisted. *See* GIVE.

cheapen *verb*
1. To become or make less in price or value : depreciate, depress, devaluate, devalue, downgrade, lower[2], mark down, reduce, write down. *See* INCREASE, MONEY. **2.** To lower in character or quality : debase, degrade, demean[2], downgrade. *See* BETTER.

cheapskate *noun*
Slang. A stingy person : miser, niggard, Scrooge, skinflint. *Informal:* penny pincher. *Slang:* stiff, tightwad. *See* GIVE.

cheat *verb*
1. To get money or something else from by deceitful trickery : bilk, cozen, defraud, gull, mulct, rook, swindle, victimize. *Informal:* chisel, flimflam, take, trim. *Slang:* diddle[1], do, gyp, stick, sting. *See* HONEST. **2.** *Informal.* To be sexually unfaithful to another : philander, womanize. *Informal:* fool around, mess around, play around. *See* SEX.

cheat *noun* **1.** An act of cheating : fraud, swindle, victimization. *Informal:* flimflam. *Slang:* gyp. *See* HONEST. **2.** A person who cheats : bilk, cheater, cozener, defrauder, rook, sharper, swindler, trickster, victimizer. *Informal:* chiseler, crook, flimflammer. *Slang:* diddler, gyp, gypper. *See* HONEST.

cheater *noun*
A person who cheats : bilk, cheat, cozener, defrauder, rook, sharper, swindler, trickster, victimizer. *Informal:* chiseler, crook, flimflammer. *Slang:* diddler, gyp, gypper. *See* HONEST.

check *noun*
1. Something that limits or restricts : circumscription, constraint, cramp[2], curb, inhibition, limit, limitation, restraint, restriction, stricture, trammel. *See* LIMITED. **2.** The act of stopping : cessation, cut-off, discontinuance, discontinuation, halt[1], stay[1], stop, stoppage, surcease. *See* CONTINUE. **3.** The act of examining carefully : checkup, examination, inspection, perusal, scrutiny, study, view. *Informal:* going-over. *See* INVESTIGATE. **4.** A precise list of fees or charges : account, bill[1], invoice, reckoning, statement. *Informal:* tab. *See* PAY.

check *verb* **1.** To prevent the occurrence or continuation of a movement, action, or operation : arrest, belay, cease, discontinue, halt[1], stall[1], stay[1], stop, surcease. ***Idioms:*** bring to a standstill, call a halt to, put a stop to. *See* CONTINUE. **2.** To come to a cessation : arrest, belay, cease, discontinue, halt[1], leave off, quit, stall[1], stop, surcease. ***Idiom:*** come to a halt (*or* standstill *or* stop). *See* CONTINUE. **3.** To control, restrict, or arrest : bit[2], brake, bridle, constrain, curb, hold, hold back, hold down, hold in, inhibit, keep, keep back, pull in, rein (back, in, *or* up), restrain. *See* RESTRAINT. **4.** To prevent from accomplishing a purpose : baffle, balk, checkmate, defeat, foil, frustrate, stymie, thwart. *Informal:* cross, stump. ***Idiom:*** cut the ground from under. *See* ALLOW. **5.** To subject to a procedure that ascertains effectiveness, value, proper function, or other quality : assay, essay, examine, prove, test, try, try out. ***Idioms:*** bring to the test, make trial of, put to the proof (*or* test). *See* INVESTIGATE. **6.** To subject to a test of knowledge or skill : examine, quiz, test. *See* INVESTIGATE. **7.** To look at carefully or critically. Also used with *out* : con, examine, go over, inspect, peruse, scrutinize, study, survey, traverse, view. *Informal:* case. ***Idiom:*** give a going-over. *See* INVESTIGATE. **8.** To be compatible or in correspondence : accord, agree, chime, comport with, conform, consist, correspond, fit[1], harmonize, match, square, tally. *Informal:* jibe[1]. *Archaic:* quadrate. *See* AGREE.

check in *verb* To come to a particular place : arrive, get in, pull in, reach, show up, turn up. *Slang:* blow in. ***Idiom:*** make (*or* put in) an appearance. *See* START.

check out *verb* *Slang.* To cease living : decease, demise, depart, die, drop, expire, go, pass away, pass (on), perish, succumb. *Informal:* pop off. *Slang:* croak, kick in, kick off. ***Idioms:*** bite the dust, breathe one's last, cash in, give up the ghost, go to one's grave, kick the bucket, meet one's end (*or* Maker), pass on to the Great Beyond, turn up one's toes. *See* LIVE.

check in *verb* See **check.**

checkmate *verb*
To prevent from accomplishing a purpose : baffle, balk, check, defeat, foil, frustrate, stymie, thwart. *Informal:* cross, stump. ***Idiom:*** cut the ground from under. *See* ALLOW.

check out *verb* See **check.**

checkup *noun*
1. The act of examining carefully : check, examination, inspection, perusal, scrutiny, study, view. *Informal:* going-over. *See* INVESTIGATE.

2. A medical inquiry into a patient's state of health : exam, examination. *See* INVESTIGATE.

cheek *noun*
The state or quality of being impudent or arrogantly self-confident : assumption, audaciousness, audacity, boldness, brashness, brazenness, cheekiness, chutzpah, discourtesy, disrespect, effrontery, face, familiarity, forwardness, gall[1], impertinence, impudence, impudency, incivility, insolence, nerve, nerviness, overconfidence, pertness, presumptuousness, pushiness, rudeness, sassiness, sauciness. *Informal:* brass, crust, sauce, uppishness, uppityness. *See* ATTITUDE, COURTESY.

cheekiness *noun*
The state or quality of being impudent or arrogantly self-confident : assumption, audaciousness, audacity, boldness, brashness, brazenness, cheek, chutzpah, discourtesy, disrespect, effrontery, face, familiarity, forwardness, gall[1], impertinence, impudence, impudency, incivility, insolence, nerve, nerviness, overconfidence, pertness, presumptuousness, pushiness, rudeness, sassiness, sauciness. *Informal:* brass, crust, sauce, uppishness, uppityness. *See* ATTITUDE, COURTESY.

cheeky *adjective*
Rude and disrespectful : assuming, assumptive, audacious, bold, boldfaced, brash, brazen, contumelious, familiar, forward, impertinent, impudent, insolent, malapert, nervy, overconfident, pert, presuming, presumptuous, pushy, sassy, saucy, smart. *Informal:* brassy, flip, fresh, smart-alecky, snippety, snippy, uppish, uppity. *Slang:* wise[1]. *See* ATTITUDE, COURTESY.

cheer *noun*
A condition of supreme well-being and good spirits : beatitude, blessedness, bliss, cheerfulness, felicity, gladness, happiness, joy, joyfulness. *See* HAPPY.

cheer *verb* **1.** To give great or keen pleasure to : delight, enchant, gladden, gratify, overjoy, please, pleasure, tickle. *Archaic:* joy. *See* HAPPY, LIKE. **2.** To impart strength and confidence to. Also used with *up* : buck up, encourage, hearten, nerve, perk up. *See* HELP. **3.** To impart courage, inspiration, and resolution to. Also used with *on* : animate, embolden, encourage, inspire, inspirit, motivate. *See* HELP. **4.** To express approval, especially by clapping : applaud, clap, root[2]. ***Idiom:*** give someone a hand. *See* PRAISE.

cheerful *adjective*
1. Being in or showing good spirits : bright, cheery, chipper, happy, lighthearted, sunny. *See* HAPPY. **2.** Providing joy and pleasure : cheery, festive, glad, happy, joyful, joyous, pleasing. *See* HAPPY.

cheerfulness *noun*
A condition of supreme well-being and good spirits : beatitude, blessedness, bliss, cheer, felicity, gladness, happiness, joy, joyfulness. *See* HAPPY.

cheering *adjective*
Inspiring confidence or hope : encouraging, heartening, hopeful, likely, promising. *See* HELP.

cheerless *adjective*
1. Tending to cause sadness or low spirits : blue, depressing, dismal, dispiriting, gloomy, joyless, melancholy, sad. *See* HAPPY. **2.** Dark and depressing : black, bleak, blue, dark, desolate, dismal, dreary, gloomy, glum, joyless, somber, tenebrific. *See* HAPPY, LIGHT.

cheery *adjective*
1. Being in or showing good spirits : bright, cheerful, chipper, happy, lighthearted, sunny. *See* HAPPY. **2.** Providing joy and pleasure : cheerful, festive, glad, happy, joyful, joyous, pleasing. *See* HAPPY.

cheesy *adjective*
Informal. Of decidedly inferior quality : base[2], cheap, lousy, miserable, paltry, poor, rotten, shoddy, sleazy, trashy. *Slang:* crummy, schlocky. *See* GOOD.

chef *noun*
A person who prepares food for eating : cook. *See* INGESTION.

chef-d'oeuvre *noun*
An outstanding and ingenious work : magnum opus, masterpiece, masterwork. *See* GOOD.

cherish *verb*
1. To have the highest regard for : prize[1], treasure. ***Idiom:*** hold dear. *See* VALUE. **2.** To recognize the worth, quality, importance, or magnitude of : appreciate, esteem, prize[1], respect, treasure, value. ***Idiom:*** set store by. *See* PRAISE.

cherubic *adjective*
Of or like a baby : babyish, childlike, infantile, infantine. *See* YOUTH.

chew *verb*
To bite and grind with the teeth : champ, chomp, chump[2], crump, crunch, masticate, munch. *Regional:* chaw. *See* MOUTH.

chew on (or **over**) *verb* To think or think about carefully and at length : cogitate, consider, contemplate, deliberate, entertain, excogitate, meditate, mull, muse[1], ponder, reflect, revolve, ruminate, study, think, think out, think over, think through, turn over, weigh. ***Idioms:*** cudgel one's brains, put on one's thinking cap, rack one's brain. *See* THOUGHTS.

chew out *verb Slang.* To criticize for a fault or an offense : admonish, call down, castigate, chastise, chide, dress down, rap[1], rebuke, reprimand, reproach, reprove, scold, tax, upbraid. *Informal:* bawl out, lambaste. ***Idioms:*** bring (*or* call *or* take) to task, call on the carpet, haul (*or* rake) over the coals, let someone have it. *See* ATTACK, PRAISE.

chew on or **over** *verb* See **chew.**

chew out *verb* See **chew.**

chic *adjective*

Being or in accordance with the current fashion : à la mode, dashing, fashionable, mod, modish, posh, smart, stylish, swank, swanky, trig. *Informal:* classy, in, sharp, snappy, swish, tony, trendy. *Slang:* with-it. ***Idioms:*** all the rage, up to the minute. *See* STYLE, USUAL.

chicanery *noun*

Lack of straightforwardness and honesty in action : craft, craftiness, deviousness, dishonesty, indirection, shadiness, shiftiness, slyness, sneakiness, trickery, trickiness, underhandedness. *See* HONEST.

chicken *noun*

Slang. An ignoble, uncourageous person : coward, craven, dastard, funk, poltroon. *Slang:* yellow-belly. *See* FEAR.

chicken *adjective Slang.* Ignobly lacking in courage : chickenhearted, cowardly, craven, dastardly, faint-hearted, lily-livered, pusillanimous, unmanly. *Slang:* gutless, yellow, yellow-bellied. *See* FEAR.

chicken feed *noun*

Slang. A small or trifling amount of money : small change. *Informal:* peanut (used in plural). *Slang:* two bits. *See* BIG, MONEY.

chickenhearted *adjective*

Ignobly lacking in courage : cowardly, craven, dastardly, faint-hearted, lily-livered, pusillanimous, unmanly. *Slang:* chicken, gutless, yellow, yellow-bellied. *See* FEAR.

chickenheartedness *noun*

Ignoble lack of courage : cowardice, cowardliness, cravenness, dastardliness, faint-heartedness, funk, pusillanimity, unmanliness. *Slang:* gutlessness, yellowness, yellow streak. *See* FEAR.

chide *verb*

To criticize for a fault or an offense : admonish, call down, castigate, chastise, dress down, rap[1], rebuke, reprimand, reproach, reprove, scold, tax, upbraid. *Informal:* bawl out, lambaste. *Slang:* chew out. ***Idioms:*** bring (*or* call *or* take) to task, call on the carpet, haul (*or* rake) over the coals, let someone have it. *See* ATTACK, PRAISE.

chief *noun*

1. One who is highest in rank or authority : boss, chieftain, director, head, headman, hierarch, leader, master. *Slang:* honcho. ***Idiom:*** cock of the walk. *See* OVER. **2.** A professional politician who controls a party or political machine : boss, leader. *See* OVER. **3.** *Slang.* Someone who directs and supervises workers : boss, director, foreman, foreperson, forewoman, head, manager, overseer, superintendent, supervisor, taskmaster, taskmistress. *Informal:* straw boss. *See* OVER.

chief *adjective* **1.** Having or exercising authority : head, principal. *See* OVER. **2.** Most important, influential, or significant : capital, cardinal, first, foremost, key, leading, main, major, number one, paramount, premier, primary, prime, principal, top. *See* IMPORTANT.

chieftain *noun*

One who is highest in rank or authority : boss, chief, director, head, headman, hierarch, leader, master. *Slang:* honcho. ***Idiom:*** cock of the walk. *See* OVER.

child *noun*

1. A young person between birth and puberty : bud[1], innocent, juvenile, moppet, tot[1], youngster. *Informal:* kid. *Scots:* bairn. *See* KIN, YOUTH. **2.** One who is not yet legally of age : juvenile. *Law:* infant, minor. *See* LAW, YOUTH. **3.** A guileless, unsophisticated person : babe, ingénue, innocent, naive. ***Idiom:*** babe in the woods. *See* KNOWLEDGE. **4.** One descended directly from the same parents or ancestors : descendant, offspring, progeny, scion. *See* KIN.

childbearing *noun*

The act or process of bringing forth young : accouchement, birth, birthing, childbirth, delivery, labor, lying-in, parturition, travail. *See* START.

childbirth *noun*

The act or process of bringing forth young : accouchement, birth, birthing, childbearing, delivery, labor, lying-in, parturition, travail. *See* START.

childish *adjective*

Of or characteristic of a child, especially in immaturity : babyish, immature, infantile, juvenile, puerile. *See* YOUTH.

childless *adjective*
Unable to produce offspring : barren, impotent, infertile, sterile, unfruitful. *See* RICH.

childlike *adjective*
Of or like a baby : babyish, cherubic, infantile, infantine. *See* YOUTH.

child's play *noun*
An easily accomplished task : cinch, pushover, snap, walkaway, walkover. *Informal:* breeze. *Slang:* duck soup. *See* EASY.

chill *noun*
Relative lack of physical warmth : chilliness, cold, coldness, coolness. *See* HOT.

chill *adjective* **1.** Marked by a low temperature : chilly, cold, cool, nippy, shivery. *See* HOT. **2.** Not friendly, sociable, or warm in manner : aloof, chilly, cool, distant, offish, remote, reserved, reticent, solitary, standoffish, unapproachable, uncommunicative, undemonstrative, withdrawn. *See* ATTITUDE, HOT.

chilliness *noun*
Relative lack of physical warmth : chill, cold, coldness, coolness. *See* HOT.

chilly *adjective*
1. Marked by a low temperature : chill, cold, cool, nippy, shivery. *See* HOT. **2.** Not friendly, sociable, or warm in manner : aloof, chill, cool, distant, offish, remote, reserved, reticent, solitary, standoffish, unapproachable, uncommunicative, undemonstrative, withdrawn. *See* ATTITUDE, HOT.

chime *noun*
The act or state of agreeing or conforming : accordance, agreement, conformance, conformation, conformity, congruence, congruity, correspondence, harmonization, harmony, keeping. *See* AGREE.

chime *verb* **1.** To give forth or cause to give forth a clear, resonant sound : bong, knell, peal, ring[2], strike, toll[2]. *See* SOUNDS. **2.** To be compatible or in correspondence : accord, agree, check, comport with, conform, consist, correspond, fit[1], harmonize, match, square, tally. *Informal:* jibe[1]. *Archaic:* quadrate. *See* AGREE.

chime in *verb* To interject remarks or questions into another's discourse : break in, chip in, cut in, interrupt. *See* CONTINUE.

chime in *verb* See **chime.**

chimeric *adjective*
1. Of, relating to, or in the nature of an illusion; lacking reality : chimerical, delusive, delusory, dreamlike, hallucinatory, illusive, illusory, phantasmagoric, phantasmal, phantasmic, visionary. *See* REAL. **2.** Existing only in the imagination : chimerical, conceptual, fanciful, fantastic, fantastical, imaginary, notional, unreal, visionary. *See* REAL.

chimerical *adjective*
1. Of, relating to, or in the nature of an illusion; lacking reality : chimeric, delusive, delusory, dreamlike, hallucinatory, illusive, illusory, phantasmagoric, phantasmal, phantasmic, visionary. *See* REAL. **2.** Existing only in the imagination : chimeric, conceptual, fanciful, fantastic, fantastical, imaginary, notional, unreal, visionary. *See* REAL.

chink *noun*
A usually narrow partial opening caused by splitting and rupture : break, cleavage, cleft, crack, crevice, fissure, rift, split. *See* OPEN.

chintzy *adjective*
Tastelessly showy : brummagem, flashy, garish, gaudy, glaring, loud, meretricious, tawdry, tinsel. *Informal:* tacky[2]. *See* STYLE.

chip in *verb*
1. To give in common with others : contribute, donate, subscribe. *Informal:* kick in. *Slang:* come across. *See* GIVE. **2.** To interject remarks or questions into another's discourse : break in, chime in, cut in, interrupt. *See* CONTINUE.

chipper *adjective*
1. Very brisk, alert, and full of high spirits : animated, bouncy, dashing, high-spirited, lively, pert, spirited, vivacious. *Informal:* peppy. *Idioms:* bright-eyed and bushy-tailed, full of life. *See* ACTION. **2.** Being in or showing good spirits : bright, cheerful, cheery, happy, lighthearted, sunny. *See* HAPPY.

chisel *verb*
Informal. To get money or something else from by deceitful trickery : bilk, cheat, cozen, defraud, gull, mulct, rook, swindle, victimize. *Informal:* flimflam, take, trim. *Slang:* diddle[1], do, gyp, stick, sting. *See* HONEST.

chiseler *noun*
Informal. A person who cheats : bilk, cheat, cheater, cozener, defrauder, rook, sharper, swindler, trickster, victimizer. *Informal:* crook, flimflammer. *Slang:* diddler, gyp, gypper. *See* HONEST.

chitchat *noun*
Incessant and usually inconsequential talk : babble, blab, blabber, chat, chatter, jabber, palaver, prate, prattle, small talk. *Slang:* gab, gas, yak. *See* WORDS.

chitchat *verb* To talk volubly, persistently, and usually inconsequentially : babble, blabber, chatter, clack, jabber, palaver, prate, prattle,

rattle (on), run on. *Informal:* go on, spiel. *Slang:* gab, gas, jaw, yak. ***Idioms:*** run off at the mouth, shoot the breeze (*or* bull). *See* WORDS.

chivalric *adjective*
Respectfully attentive, especially to women : chivalrous, gallant. *See* ATTITUDE, COURTESY.

chivalrous *adjective*
1. Characterized by elaborate but usually formal courtesy : courtly, gallant, gracious, knightly, stately. *See* ATTITUDE, COURTESY. **2.** Respectfully attentive, especially to women : chivalric, gallant. *See* ATTITUDE, COURTESY.

chivalrousness *noun*
Respectful attention, especially toward women : chivalry, gallantry. *See* ATTITUDE, COURTESY.

chivalry *noun*
Respectful attention, especially toward women : chivalrousness, gallantry. *See* ATTITUDE, COURTESY.

chockablock *adjective*
Completely filled : brimful, brimming, bursting, full, packed, replete. *See* FULL.

choice *noun*
1. The act of choosing : election, option, preference, selection. *See* CHOICE. **2.** The power or right of choosing : alternative, option. *See* CHOICE. **3.** One that is selected : chosen, elect, pick, select. *See* CHOICE. **4.** The superlative or most preferable part of something : best, cream, crème de la crème, elite, flower, pick, prize[1], top. ***Idioms:*** cream of the crop, flower of the flock, pick of the bunch (*or* crop) . *See* BETTER.

choice *adjective* **1.** Of fine quality : fine[1], first-class, prime, select, superior. *See* BETTER. **2.** Appealing to refined taste : dainty, delicate, elegant, exquisite, fine[1]. *See* GOOD, INGESTION. **3.** Singled out in preference : chosen, elect, exclusive, select. *See* CHOICE, INCLUDE.

choke *verb*
1. To interfere with or stop the normal breathing of, especially by constricting the windpipe : strangle, throttle. *See* BREATH. **2.** To stop the breathing of : asphyxiate, smother, stifle, suffocate. *See* BREATH. **3.** To hold (something requiring an outlet) in check. Also used with *back* : burke, gag, hold back, hold down, hush (up), muffle, quench, repress, smother, squelch, stifle, strangle, suppress, throttle. *Informal:* sit on (*or* upon). *See* RESTRAINT. **4.** To plug up something, as a hole, space, or container : block, clog, close, congest, cork, fill, plug, stop. *See* FULL. **5.** To be unsuccessful : fail, fall through. *Informal:* fall down, flop. *Slang:* bomb. ***Idioms:*** fail of success, fall short. *See* THRIVE.

choke off *verb* To bring to an end forcibly as if by imposing a heavy weight : crush, extinguish, put down, quash, quell, quench, squash, squelch, suppress. ***Idiom:*** put the lid on. *See* CONTINUE, WIN.

choke *noun* Something used to fill a hole, space, or container : cork, fill, plug, stop, stopper. *See* FULL.

choke off *verb* See **choke.**

choler *noun*
A strong feeling of displeasure or hostility : anger, indignation, irateness, ire. *See* FEELINGS.

choleric *adjective*
1. Easily annoyed : irascible, peppery, quick-tempered, testy, tetchy, touchy. *See* FEELINGS. **2.** Feeling or showing anger : angry, indignant, mad. *Informal:* sore. ***Idiom:*** hot under the collar. *See* FEELINGS.

chomp *verb*
1. To bite and grind with the teeth : champ, chew, chump[2], crump, crunch, masticate, munch. *Regional:* chaw. *See* MOUTH. **2.** To seize, as food, with the teeth : bite, champ, gnash, gnaw. *See* ATTACK, INGESTION.

choose *verb*
1. To make a choice from a number of alternatives : cull, elect, opt (for), pick (out), select, single (out). *See* CHOICE. **2.** To have the desire or inclination to : desire, like[1], please, want, will, wish. ***Idioms:*** have a mind, see fit. *See* DESIRE.

choosy *adjective*
Very difficult to please : dainty, exacting, fastidious, finical, finicky, fussy, meticulous, nice, particular, persnickety, squeamish. *Informal:* picky. *See* ACCEPT.

chop[1] *verb*
To decrease, as in length or amount, by or as if by severing or excising : clip[1], crop, cut, cut back, cut down, lop[1], lower[2], pare, prune, shear, slash, trim, truncate. *See* INCREASE.

chop down *verb* To bring down, as with a saw or ax : cut (down), fell[1], hew. *See* RISE.

chop *noun* A quick, sharp blow, especially with the hand : box[2], buffet, bust, cuff, punch, slap, smack[1], smacker, spank, swat, whack. *Informal:* clip[1], spat. *See* ATTACK, STRIKE.

chop[2] *verb*
To turn aside sharply from a straight course : cut, sheer[1], skew, slue[1], swerve, veer. *Nautical:* yaw. *See* CHANGE.

chop down *verb* See **chop.**

chore *noun*
1. A piece of work that has been assigned : assignment, duty, job, office, stint, task. *See* WORK. **2.** A difficult or tedious undertaking : effort, task. *Informal:* job. *See* HEAVY, WORK.

chortle *verb*
To laugh quietly : chuckle. *See* LAUGHTER, SOUNDS.

chosen *adjective*
Singled out in preference : choice, elect, exclusive, select. *See* CHOICE, INCLUDE.
chosen *noun* One that is selected : choice, elect, pick, select. *See* CHOICE.

chow *noun*
Slang. Something fit to be eaten : aliment, bread, comestible, diet, edible, esculent, fare, food, foodstuff, meat, nourishment, nurture, nutriment, nutrition, pabulum, pap, provender, provision (used in plural), sustenance, victual. *Slang:* eats, grub. *See* INGESTION.
chow *verb Slang.* To take (food) into the body as nourishment : consume, devour, eat, fare, ingest, partake. ***Idioms:*** break bread, have (*or* take) a bite. *See* INGESTION.

christen *verb*
To give a name or title to : baptize, call, denominate, designate, dub, entitle, name, style, term, title. *See* SPECIFIC, WORDS.

chronic *adjective*
1. Of long duration : continuing, lingering, persistent, prolonged, protracted. *See* CONTINUE. **2.** Familiar through repetition : accustomed, habitual, routine. *See* USUAL. **3.** Subject to a disease or habit for a long time : confirmed, habitual, habituated, inveterate. *See* CONTINUE.

chronicle *noun*
1. A chronological record of past events : annals, history. *See* HAPPEN, WORDS. **2.** A recounting of past events : account, description, history, narration, narrative, report, statement, story, version. *See* WORDS.

chubby *adjective*
Well-rounded and full in form : plump[1], plumpish, pudgy, roly-poly, rotund, round, tubby, zaftig. *See* FAT.

chuck *verb*
1. *Informal.* To let go or get rid of as being useless or defective, for example : discard, dispose of, dump, junk, scrap[1], throw away, throw out. *Informal:* jettison, shuck (off). *Slang:* ditch. *See* KEEP. **2.** *Informal.* To put out by force : bump, dismiss, eject, evict, expel, oust, throw out. *Slang:* boot[1] (out), bounce, kick out. ***Idioms:*** give someone the boot, give someone the heave-ho (*or* old heave-ho), send packing, show someone the door, throw out on one's ear. *See* KEEP.

chuckle *verb*
To laugh quietly : chortle. *See* LAUGHTER, SOUNDS.

chuff *noun*
An unrefined, rude person : barbarian, boor, churl, Philistine, vulgarian, yahoo. *See* GOOD.

chum *noun*
1. A person whom one knows well, likes, and trusts : amigo, brother, confidant, confidante, familiar, friend, intimate[1], mate. *Informal:* bud[2], buddy, pal. *Slang:* sidekick. *See* LOVE. **2.** One who shares interests or activities with another : associate, companion, comrade, crony, fellow, mate. *Informal:* buddy, pal. *See* NEAR.

chumminess *noun*
The condition of being friends : closeness, companionship, comradeship, familiarity, fellowship, friendship, intimacy. *See* LOVE.

chummy *adjective*
Very closely associated : close, familiar, friendly, intimate[1]. *Informal:* thick. *Slang:* tight. ***Idiom:*** hand in glove with. *See* LOVE.

chump[1] *noun*
A mentally dull person : blockhead, clod, dolt, dullard, dummkopf, dummy, dunce, numskull, thickhead. *Slang:* dimwit, dumbbell, dumbo. *See* ABILITY.

chump[2] *verb*
To bite and grind with the teeth : champ, chew, chomp, crump, crunch, masticate, munch. *Regional:* chaw. *See* MOUTH.

chunk *noun*
An irregularly shaped mass of indefinite size : clod, clump, gob[1], hunch, lump[1], nugget, wad. *Informal:* hunk. *See* PART.

chunky *adjective*
Short, heavy, and solidly built : blocky, compact[1], dumpy, heavyset, squat, stocky, stodgy, stubby, stumpy, thick, thickset. *See* FAT.

church *noun*
Those who accept and practice a particular religious belief : communion, denomination, faith, persuasion, sect. *See* RELIGION.
church *adjective* Of or relating to a church or to an established religion : churchly, ecclesiastical, religious, spiritual. *See* RELIGION.

churchly *adjective*
Of or relating to a church or to an established religion : church, ecclesiastical, religious, spiritual. *See* RELIGION.

churchman *noun*
A person ordained for service in a Christian church : churchwoman, clergyman, clergywoman, cleric, clerical, clerk, divine, ecclesiastic, minister, parson, preacher. *Informal:* reverend. *See* RELIGION.

churchwoman *noun*
A person ordained for service in a Christian church : churchman, clergyman, clergywoman, cleric, clerical, clerk, divine, ecclesiastic, minister, parson, preacher. *Informal:* reverend. *See* RELIGION.

churl *noun*
An unrefined, rude person : barbarian, boor, chuff, Philistine, vulgarian, yahoo. *See* GOOD.

churlish *adjective*
Lacking in delicacy or refinement : barbarian, barbaric, boorish, coarse, crass, crude, gross, ill-bred, indelicate, philistine, rough, rude, tasteless, uncivilized, uncouth, uncultivated, uncultured, unpolished, unrefined, vulgar. *See* COURTESY, SMOOTH.

churn *verb*
1. To cause to move to and fro violently : agitate, convulse, rock, shake. *See* CALM, REPETITION. **2.** To be in a state of emotional or mental turmoil : boil, bubble, burn, ferment, seethe, simmer, smolder. *See* CALM.

chutzpah also **hutzpah** *noun*
Impudence; arrogant self-confidence : assumption, audaciousness, audacity, boldness, brashness, brazenness, cheek, cheekiness, discourtesy, disrespect, effrontery, face, familiarity, forwardness, gall[1], impertinence, impudence, impudency, incivility, insolence, nerve, nerviness, overconfidence, pertness, presumptuousness, pushiness, rudeness, sassiness, sauciness. *Informal:* brass, crust, sauce, uppishness, uppityness. *See* ATTITUDE, COURTESY.

cinch *noun*
1. An easily accomplished task : child's play, pushover, snap, walkaway, walkover. *Informal:* breeze. *Slang:* duck soup. *See* EASY. **2.** A clearly established fact : certainty, sure thing. *See* CERTAIN, TRUE.

cinch *verb Informal.* To render certain : assure, ensure, guarantee, insure, secure, warrant. *See* CERTAIN.

cincture *verb*
To encircle with or as if with a band : band[1], begird, belt, compass, encompass, engirdle, gird, girdle, girt, ring[1]. *Archaic:* engird. *See* EDGE.

cinerarium *noun*
A burial place or receptacle for human remains : catacomb, crypt, grave[1], mausoleum, ossuary, sepulcher, sepulture, tomb, vault[1]. *See* KEEP, PLACE.

cipher *noun*
A totally insignificant person : nebbish, nobody, nonentity, nothing. *Informal:* pipsqueak, zero. *Slang:* shrimp, zilch. *See* IMPORTANT.

cipher *verb* To ascertain by mathematics : calculate, cast, compute, figure, reckon. *See* REASON.

circle *noun*
1. A closed plane curve everywhere equidistant from a fixed point or something shaped like this : band[1], circuit, disk, gyre, ring[1], wheel. *Archaic:* orb. *See* GEOMETRY. **2.** A course, process, or journey that ends where it began or repeats itself : circuit, cycle, orbit, round, tour, turn. *See* REPETITION. **3.** A group of people sharing an interest, activity, or achievement : crowd, group, set[2]. *See* GROUP. **4.** A particular social group : clique, coterie, crowd, set[2]. *Informal:* bunch, gang. *See* GROUP. **5.** A sphere of activity, experience, study, or interest : area, arena, bailiwick, department, domain, field, orbit, province, realm, scene, subject, terrain, territory, world. *Slang:* bag. *See* TERRITORY.

circle *verb* **1.** To shut in on all sides : begird, beset, compass, encircle, encompass, environ, gird, girdle, hedge, hem, ring[1], surround. *See* OPEN. **2.** To move or cause to move in circles or around an axis : circumvolve, gyrate, orbit, revolve, rotate, turn, wheel. *See* MOVE, REPETITION.

circuit *noun*
1. A line around a closed figure or area : ambit, circumference, compass, perimeter, periphery. *See* EDGE. **2.** A closed plane curve everywhere equidistant from a fixed point or something shaped like this : band[1], circle, disk, gyre, ring[1], wheel. *Archaic:* orb. *See* GEOMETRY. **3.** A course, process, or journey that ends where it began or repeats itself : circle, cycle, orbit, round, tour, turn. *See* REPETITION. **4.** Circular movement around a point or about an axis : circulation, circumvolution, gyration, revolution, rotation, turn, wheel, whirl. *See* GEOMETRY, REPETITION. **5.** An area regularly covered, as by a policeman or reporter : beat, round, route. *See* TERRITORY. **6.** A group of athletic teams that play each other : association, conference, league, loop. *See* GROUP.

circuitous *adjective*
Not taking a direct or straight line or course :

anfractuous, circular, devious, indirect, oblique, roundabout, tortuous. *See* STRAIGHT.

circular *adjective*

1. Having the shape of a curve everywhere equidistant from a fixed point : annular, globoid, globular, round, spheric, spherical. *See* GEOMETRY. **2.** Not taking a direct or straight line or course : anfractuous, circuitous, devious, indirect, oblique, roundabout, tortuous. *See* STRAIGHT.

circulate *verb*

1. To move freely as a liquid : course, flow, run, stream. *See* MOVE. **2.** To extend over a wide area : diffuse, disperse, disseminate, distribute, radiate, scatter, spread, strew. *See* MOVE, WIDE. **3.** To become known far and wide : get around, go around, spread, travel. ***Idiom:*** go (*or* make) the rounds. *See* KNOWLEDGE. **4.** To make (information) generally known : advertise, blaze[2], blazon, broadcast, bruit, disseminate, noise, promulgate, propagate, spread. ***Idioms:*** spread far and wide, spread the word. *See* KNOWLEDGE. **5.** To pass (something) out : disperse, disseminate, distribute, hand out. *See* COLLECT.

circulation *noun*

1. Circular movement around a point or about an axis : circuit, circumvolution, gyration, revolution, rotation, turn, wheel, whirl. *See* GEOMETRY, REPETITION. **2.** The passing out or spreading about of something : dispersal, dispersion, dissemination, distribution. *See* COLLECT.

circumference *noun*

A line around a closed figure or area : ambit, circuit, compass, perimeter, periphery. *See* EDGE.

circumlocutionary *adjective*

Characterized by repetition and excessive wordiness : roundabout, tautological. *See* REPETITION, WORDS.

circumnavigate *verb*

To pass around but not through : bypass, circumvent, detour, go around, skirt. *See* SEEK.

circumscribe *verb*

To place a limit on : confine, limit, restrict. *See* LIMITED.

circumscription *noun*

1. The act of limiting or condition of being limited : confinement, constraint, limitation, restraint, restriction. *See* LIMITED. **2.** Something that limits or restricts : check, constraint, cramp[2], curb, inhibition, limit, limitation, restraint, restriction, stricture, trammel. *See* LIMITED.

circumspect *adjective*

Trying attentively to avoid danger, risk, or error : careful, cautious, chary, forehanded, gingerly, prudent, wary. *See* CAREFUL.

circumspection *noun*

The exercise of good judgment or common sense in practical matters : caution, discretion, forehandedness, foresight, foresightedness, forethought, forethoughtfulness, precaution, prudence. *See* CAREFUL.

circumstance *noun*

1. Existing surroundings that affect an activity. Often used in plural : condition (used in plural), environment. *Slang:* scene. *See* BE. **2.** One of the conditions or facts attending an event and having some bearing on it : detail, fact, factor, particular. *See* REAL. **3.** Something that happens : event, happening, incident, occasion, occurrence, thing. *See* HAPPEN. **4.** Something significant that happens : development, episode, event, happening, incident, news, occasion, occurrence, thing. *See* HAPPEN.

circumstantial *adjective*

Characterized by attention to detail : blow-by-blow, detailed, full, minute[2], particular, thorough. *See* SPECIFIC.

circumvent *verb*

1. To pass around but not through : bypass, circumnavigate, detour, go around, skirt. *See* SEEK. **2.** To keep away from : avoid, burke, bypass, dodge, duck, elude, escape, eschew, evade, get around, shun. ***Idioms:*** fight shy of, give a wide berth to, have no truck with, keep (*or* stay *or* steer) clear of. *See* SEEK.

circumvention *noun*

The act, an instance, or a means of avoiding : avoidance, bypass, escape, evasion. *See* SEEK.

circumvolution *noun*

Circular movement around a point or about an axis : circuit, circulation, gyration, revolution, rotation, turn, wheel, whirl. *See* GEOMETRY, REPETITION.

circumvolve *verb*

To move or cause to move in circles or around an axis : circle, gyrate, orbit, revolve, rotate, turn, wheel. *See* MOVE, REPETITION.

cite *verb*

1. To refer to by name : instance, mention, name, specify. *See* SPECIFIC. **2.** To bring forward for formal consideration : adduce, lay[1], present[2]. *Archaic:* allege. *See* LAW, WORDS.

citify *verb*

To imbue with city ways, manners, and customs : metropolitanize, urbanize. *See* URBAN.

citizen *noun*
A person owing loyalty to and entitled to the protection of a given state : national, subject. *See* GROUP, POLITICS.
city *noun*
A large and important town : metropolis, municipality. *Informal:* burg, town. *See* URBAN.
city *adjective* Of, in, or belonging to a city : metropolitan, municipal, urban. *See* URBAN.
civic *adjective*
Of, concerning, or affecting the community or the people : civil, national, public. *See* SPECIFIC.
civil *adjective*
1. Of, concerning, or affecting the community or the people : civic, national, public. *See* SPECIFIC. **2.** Characterized by good manners : courteous, genteel, mannerly, polite, well-bred, well-mannered. *See* COURTESY.
civility *noun*
1. Well-mannered behavior toward others : courteousness, courtesy, genteelness, gentility, mannerliness, politeness, politesse. *See* COURTESY. **2.** A courteous act or courteous acts that contribute to smoothness and ease in dealings and social relationships : amenity (used in plural), courtesy, pleasantry, politeness, propriety (used in plural). *See* COURTESY.
civilization *noun*
1. The total product of human creativity and intellect : culture, Kultur. *See* CULTURE. **2.** Enlightenment and excellent taste resulting from intellectual development : cultivation, culture, refinement. *See* CULTURE.
civilize *verb*
To fit for companionship with others, especially in attitude or manners : acculturate, humanize, socialize. *See* TEACH.
civilized *adjective*
Characterized by discriminating taste and broad knowledge as a result of development or education : cultivated, cultured, educated, polished, refined, urbane, well-bred. *See* CULTURE.
civilizing *adjective*
Promoting culture : cultural, edifying, enlightening, humanizing, refining. *See* CULTURE.
clack *verb*
1. To make a light, sharp noise : click, snap. *See* SOUNDS. **2.** To make or cause to make a succession of short, sharp sounds : brattle, chatter, clatter, rattle. *See* SOUNDS. **3.** To talk volubly, persistently, and usually inconsequentially : babble, blabber, chatter, chitchat, jabber, palaver, prate, prattle, rattle (on), run on. *Informal:* go on, spiel. *Slang:* gab, gas, jaw, yak. ***Idioms:*** run off at the mouth, shoot the breeze (*or* bull). *See* WORDS.
clack *noun* A light, sharp noise : click, snap. *See* SOUNDS.
clad *verb*
To furnish with a covering of a different material : cover, face, sheathe, side, skin. *See* SURFACE.
claim *verb*
1. To assert one's right to : demand. ***Idiom:*** lay claim to. *See* GIVE, OWNED, REQUEST. **2.** To defend, maintain, or insist on the recognition of (one's rights, for example) : assert, vindicate. *See* ATTACK. **3.** To put into words positively and with conviction : affirm, allege, argue, assert, asseverate, aver, avouch, avow, contend, declare, hold, maintain, say, state. ***Idiom:*** have it. *See* AFFIRM. **4.** To ask for urgently or insistently : call for, demand, exact, insist on (*or* upon), require, requisition. ***Idiom:*** cry out for. *See* REQUEST.
claim *noun* **1.** The act of demanding : call, cry, demand, exaction, requisition. *See* REQUEST. **2.** A legitimate or supposed right to demand something as one's rightful due : pretense, pretension, title. *Slang:* dibs. *See* OWNED, REQUEST. **3.** A right or legal share in something : interest, portion, stake, title. *See* PART. **4.** The act of asserting positively : affirmation, allegation, assertion, asseveration, averment, declaration, statement. *See* AFFIRM.
claimant *noun*
1. One who sets forth a claim to a royal title : claimer, pretender. *See* OWNED. **2.** One that makes a formal complaint, especially in court : accuser, complainant, plaintiff. *See* LAW.
claimer *noun*
One who sets forth a claim to a royal title : claimant, pretender. *See* OWNED.
clamber *verb*
To move or climb hurriedly, especially on all fours : scramble. *See* MOVE.
clamor *noun*
1. Sounds or a sound, especially when loud, confused, or disagreeable : babel, din, hubbub, hullabaloo, noise, pandemonium, racket, rumpus, tumult, uproar. *See* SOUNDS. **2.** Offensively loud and insistent utterances, especially of disapproval : hullabaloo, outcry, rumpus, uproar, vociferation. ***Idiom:*** hue and cry. *See* LIKE, SOUNDS. **3.** A loud, deep, prolonged sound : bawl, bellow, roar. *See* SOUNDS
clamor *verb* To speak or say very lou[illegible] with a shout : bawl, bellow, bluste[illegible]

halloo, holler, roar, shout, vociferate, whoop, yawp, yell. *See* SOUNDS.

clamorous *adjective*
Offensively loud and insistent : blatant, boisterous, obstreperous, strident, vociferous. *Informal:* loudmouthed. *See* SOUNDS.

clampdown *noun*
Sudden punitive action : crackdown, repression, suppression. *See* CONTINUE, WIN.

clan *noun*
A group of people sharing common ancestry : family, house, kindred, lineage, stock, tribe. ***Idioms:*** flesh and blood, kith and kin. *See* KIN.

clandestine *adjective*
Existing or operating in a way so as to ensure complete concealment and confidentiality : cloak-and-dagger, covert, huggermugger, secret, sub-rosa, undercover. *Informal:* hush-hush. ***Idiom:*** under wraps. *See* SHOW.

clandestinely *adverb*
In a secret way : covertly, huggermugger, secretly, sub rosa. ***Idioms:*** by stealth, on the sly, under cover. *See* SHOW.

clandestineness *noun*
The habit, practice, or policy of keeping secrets : clandestinity, concealment, covertness, huggermugger, huggermuggery, secrecy, secretiveness, secretness. *See* SHOW.

clandestinity *noun*
The habit, practice, or policy of keeping secrets : clandestineness, concealment, covertness, huggermugger, huggermuggery, secrecy, secretiveness, secretness. *See* SHOW.

clap *verb*
1. To express approval, especially by clapping : applaud, cheer, root[2]. ***Idiom:*** give someone a hand. *See* PRAISE. **2.** To make a sudden sharp, explosive noise : bang, bark, crack, pop[1], snap. *See* SOUNDS. **3.** To strike, set down, or close in such a way as to make a loud noise : bang[1], crash, slam, whack. *See* SOUNDS.
clap *noun* A sudden sharp, explosive noise : bang, bark, crack, explosion, pop[1], rat-a-tat-tat, report, snap. *See* SOUNDS.

claptrap *noun*
1. Pretentious, pompous speech or writing : bombast, fustian, grandiloquence, magniloquence, orotundity, rant, turgidity. *See* PLAIN, STYLE, WORDS. **2.** Something that does not ...e or make sense : balderdash, blather, bun... ...rivel, garbage, idiocy, nonsense, piffle, ho... rigmarole, rubbish, tomfoolery, ... *Informal:* tommyrot. *Slang:* ap... ...bilge, bull[1], bunk[2], crap, ...NOWLEDGE.

clarification *noun*
1. Something that serves to explain or clarify : construction, decipherment, elucidation, exegesis, explanation, explication, exposition, illumination, illustration, interpretation. *Archaic:* enucleation. *See* EXPLAIN. **2.** The act or process of removing physical impurities : purification, refinement. *See* CLEAN.

clarifier *noun*
Something that purifies or cleans : cleaner, cleanser, purifier, refiner, refinery. *See* CLEAN.

clarify *verb*
1. To make clear or clearer : clear (up), elucidate, illuminate, illustrate. ***Idiom:*** shed (*or* throw) light on (*or* upon). *See* CLEAR. **2.** To make or become clear by the removal of impurities : clean, cleanse, purify, refine. *See* CLEAN.

clarity *noun*
1. The condition of being clean and free of contaminants : cleanliness, cleanness, pureness, purity, taintlessness. *See* CLEAN. **2.** The quality of being clear and easy to perceive or understand : clearness, distinctness, limpidity, limpidness, lucidity, lucidness, pellucidity, pellucidness, perspicuity, perspicuousness, plainness. *See* CLEAR.

clash *verb*
1. To strike together with a loud, harsh noise : crash, smash. *See* SOUNDS. **2.** To fail to be in accord : conflict, contradict, disaccord, discord, jar. ***Idiom:*** go (*or* run) counter to. *See* AGREE.
clash *noun* **1.** A loud striking together : crash, smash. *See* SOUNDS. **2.** A state of disagreement and disharmony : conflict, confrontation, contention, difference, difficulty, disaccord, discord, discordance, dissension, dissent, dissentience, dissidence, dissonance, faction, friction, inharmony, schism, strife, variance, war, warfare. *See* CONFLICT. **3.** A discussion, often heated, in which a difference of opinion is expressed : altercation, argument, bicker, contention, controversy, debate, difficulty, disagreement, dispute, fight, polemic, quarrel, run-in, spat, squabble, tiff, word (used in plural), wrangle. *Informal:* hassle, rhubarb, tangle. *See* CONFLICT. **4.** A brief, hostile exposure to or contact with something such as danger or opposition : brush[2], encounter, run-in, skirmish. *See* TOUCH.

clasp *noun*
1. A device for fastening or for checking motion : catch, fastener, hook. *See* MOVE. **2.** The act of embracing : embrace, hug, squeeze. *Slang:* clinch. *See* TOUCH. **3.** An act or means

of holding something : clench, clutch[1], grasp, grip, hold. *Sports:* grapple. *See* KEEP.

clasp *verb* **1.** To put one's arms around affectionately : embrace, enfold, hold, hug, press, squeeze. *Slang:* clinch. *Archaic:* bosom, clip[2], embosom. *See* TOUCH. **2.** To take firmly with the hand and maintain a hold on : clench, clutch[1], grab, grapple, grasp, grip, seize. *See* KEEP.

class *noun*
1. A subdivision of a larger group : category, classification, order, set[2]. *See* GROUP. **2.** A division of persons or things by quality, rank, or grade : bracket, grade, league, order, rank[1], tier. *See* GROUP, VALUE. **3.** Degree of excellence : caliber, grade, quality. *See* BE, VALUE. **4.** *Informal.* High style in quality, manner, or dress : quality, refinement. *See* STYLE.

class *verb* **1.** To distribute into groups according to kinds : assort, categorize, classify, group, pigeonhole, separate, sort (out). *See* COLLECT. **2.** To assign to a class or classes : categorize, classify, distribute, grade, group, pigeonhole, place, range, rank[1], rate[1]. *See* GROUP, VALUE.

classic *adjective*
1. Having the nature of, constituting, or serving as a type : archetypal, archetypic, archetypical, classical, model, paradigmatic, prototypal, prototypic, prototypical, quintessential, representative, typic, typical. *See* SAME, USUAL.
2. Characterized by enduring excellence, appeal, and importance : classical, vintage. *See* GOOD.

classical *adjective*
1. Having the nature of, constituting, or serving as a type : archetypal, archetypic, archetypical, classic, model, paradigmatic, prototypal, prototypic, prototypical, quintessential, representative, typic, typical. *See* SAME, USUAL.
2. Characterized by enduring excellence, appeal, and importance : classic, vintage. *See* GOOD.

classification *noun*
1. A way or condition of being arranged : arrangement, categorization, deployment, disposal, disposition, distribution, formation, grouping, layout, lineup, order, organization, placement, sequence. *See* ORDER. **2.** A subdivision of a larger group : category, class, order, set[2]. *See* GROUP.

classified *adjective*
Of or being information available only to authorized persons : confidential, privileged, restricted. *See* SHOW.

classify *verb*
1. To distribute into groups according to kinds : assort, categorize, class, group, pigeonhole, separate, sort (out). *See* COLLECT. **2.** To assign to a class or classes : categorize, class, distribute, grade, group, pigeonhole, place, range, rank[1], rate[1]. *See* GROUP, VALUE.

classy *adjective*
Informal. Being or in accordance with the current fashion : à la mode, chic, dashing, fashionable, mod, modish, posh, smart, stylish, swank, swanky, trig. *Informal:* in, sharp, snappy, swish, tony, trendy. *Slang:* with-it. ***Idioms:*** all the rage, up to the minute. *See* STYLE, USUAL.

clatter *verb*
To make or cause to make a succession of short, sharp sounds : brattle, chatter, clack, rattle. *See* SOUNDS.

clean *adjective*
1. Free from dirt, stain, or impurities : antiseptic, cleanly, immaculate, spotless, stainless, unsoiled, unsullied. *See* CLEAN. **2.** Without imperfections or blemishes, as a line or contour : perfect, regular. *See* BEAUTIFUL. **3.** Well done or executed : adroit, deft, neat, skillful. *See* ABILITY, GOOD. **4.** Free from evil and corruption : angelic, angelical, innocent, lily-white, pure, sinless, unblemished, uncorrupted, undefiled, unstained, unsullied, untainted, virginal. ***Idiom:*** pure as the driven snow. *See* CLEAN, RIGHT, SEX. **5.** Not lewd or obscene : decent, modest, wholesome. *See* DECENT.
6. According to the rules : fair, sporting, sportsmanlike, sportsmanly. *See* FAIR. **7.** *Slang.* Free from guilt or blame : blameless, faultless, guiltless, harmless, innocent, irreproachable, lily-white, unblamable. ***Idiom:*** in the clear. *See* RIGHT.

clean *adverb* *Informal.* To the fullest extent : absolutely, all, altogether, completely, dead, entirely, flat, fully, just, perfectly, quite, thoroughly, totally, utterly, well[2], wholly.
Informal: clear. ***Idioms:*** in toto, through and through. *See* BIG, LIMITED.

clean *verb* **1.** To make or keep (an area) clean and orderly. Also used with *up* : clear (up), neaten (up), police, spruce (up), straighten (up), tidy (up). *See* ORDER. **2.** To make neat and trim; make presentable. Also used with *up* : freshen (up), groom, neaten (up), slick up, spruce (up), tidy (up), trig (out), trim. *See* O DER. **3.** To make or become clear by the moval of impurities : clarify, cleanse refine. *See* CLEAN.

clean out *verb* **1.** To remove the contents of : clear, empty (out), evacuate, vacate, void. *See* FULL. **2.** *Slang.* To reduce to financial insolvency : bankrupt, break, bust, impoverish, pauperize, ruin. *See* MONEY.

clean up *verb Slang.* To make a large profit : batten, profit. ***Idiom:*** make a killing. *See* MONEY.

cleaner *noun*
Something that purifies or cleans : clarifier, cleanser, purifier, refiner, refinery. *See* CLEAN.

cleanliness *noun*
The condition of being clean and free of contaminants : clarity, cleanness, pureness, purity, taintlessness. *See* CLEAN.

cleanly *adjective*
Free from dirt, stain, or impurities : antiseptic, clean, immaculate, spotless, stainless, unsoiled, unsullied. *See* CLEAN.

cleanly *adverb* In a fair, sporting manner : correctly, fair, fairly, properly. *See* FAIR.

cleanness *noun*
The condition of being clean and free of contaminants : clarity, cleanliness, pureness, purity, taintlessness. *See* CLEAN.

clean out *verb* See **clean.**

cleanse *verb*
1. To make or become clear by the removal of impurities : clarify, clean, purify, refine. *See* CLEAN. **2.** To free from sin, guilt, or defilement : lustrate, purge, purify. *See* CLEAN, RELIGION.

cleanser *noun*
Something that purifies or cleans : clarifier, cleaner, purifier, refiner, refinery. *See* CLEAN.

clean up *verb* See **clean.**

clear *adjective*
1. Free from clouds or mist, for example : cloudless, fair, fine[1], sunny, unclouded. *See* CLEAR. **2.** Free from what obscures or dims : crystal clear, crystalline, limpid, lucid, pellucid, see-through, transparent. *See* CLEAR. **3.** Admitting light so that objects beyond can be seen : crystal clear, crystalline, limpid, lucid, pellucid, see-through, translucent, transparent. *See* CLEAR. **4.** Free from flaws or blemishes : flawless, unblemished, unmarked. *See* BEAUTIFUL. **5.** Free from obstructions : free, open, unblocked, unimpeded, unobstructed. *See* OPEN. [illegible]eadily seen, perceived, or understood : ap- [illegible]clear-cut, crystal clear, distinct, evident, **7.** sharp [illegible]ticeable, observable, obvious, pat- [illegible]ounced, visible. *See* SEE. [illegible]ot ambiguous : distinct, [illegible]nequivocal, unmistakable. *See* CLEAR. **8.** Easily seen through due to a lack of subtlety : broad, obvious, patent, plain, unmistakable, unsubtle. *See* CLEAR, SEE. **9.** Without any doubt : clear-cut, decided, definite, distinct, pronounced, unquestionable. *See* CERTAIN. **10.** Clearly, fully, and sometimes emphatically expressed : categorical, clear-cut, decided, definite, explicit, express, positive, precise, specific, unambiguous, unequivocal. *See* CLEAR. **11.** Freed from contact or connection : free. *See* FREE, STRIKE. **12.** Containing nothing : bare, blank, empty, vacant, vacuous, void. *See* FULL.

clear *verb* **1.** To become brighter or fairer. Also used with *up* : brighten, lighten[1]. *See* CLEAR. **2.** To make clear or clearer. Also used with *up* : clarify, elucidate, illuminate, illustrate. ***Idiom:*** shed (*or* throw) light on (*or* upon). *See* CLEAR. **3.** To rid of obstructions : free, open, unblock. *See* OPEN. **4.** To make or keep (an area) clean and orderly. Also used with *up* : clean (up), neaten (up), police, spruce (up), straighten (up), tidy (up). *See* ORDER. **5.** To free from an entanglement : disengage, disentangle, disinvolve, extricate, untangle. *See* FREE. **6.** To remove the contents of : clean out, empty (out), evacuate, vacate, void. *See* FULL. **7.** To free from or cast out something objectionable or undesirable : disburden, disembarrass, disencumber, release, relieve, rid, shake off, throw off, unburden. *Slang:* shake. *See* KEEP. **8.** To destroy all traces of : abolish, annihilate, blot out, eradicate, erase, exterminate, extinguish, extirpate, kill[1], liquidate, obliterate, remove, root[1] (out *or* up), rub out, snuff out, stamp out, uproot, wipe out. ***Idioms:*** do away with, make an end of, put an end to. *See* HELP, MAKE. **9.** To free from a charge or imputation of guilt : absolve, exculpate, exonerate, vindicate. *Law:* acquit, purge. *See* LAW. **10.** To pass by or over safely or successfully : hurdle, negotiate, surmount. *See* THRIVE. **11.** To set right by giving what is due : discharge, liquidate, pay (off *or* up), satisfy, settle, square. *See* PAY. **12.** To make as income or profit : bring in, draw, earn, gain, gross, net[2], pay, produce, realize, repay, return, yield. *See* MONEY. **13.** To be accepted or approved : carry, pass. *See* ACCEPT.

clear out *verb Informal.* To leave hastily : bolt, get out, run. *Informal:* get, hotfoot, skedaddle. *Slang:* hightail, scram, vamoose. ***Idioms:*** beat it, hightail it, hotfoot it, make tracks. *See* APPROACH.

clear up *verb* To find a solution for : decipher, explain, resolve, solve, unravel. *Informal:* dope out, figure out. ***Idiom:*** get to the bottom of. *See* ASK, REASON.

clear *adverb Informal.* To the fullest extent : absolutely, all, altogether, completely, dead, entirely, flat, fully, just, perfectly, quite, thoroughly, totally, utterly, well[2], wholly. *Informal:* clean. ***Idioms:*** in toto, through and through. *See* BIG, LIMITED.

clearance *noun*
The act or process of eliminating : elimination, eradication, liquidation, purge, removal, riddance. *See* KEEP.

clear-cut *adjective*
1. Readily seen, perceived, or understood : apparent, clear, crystal clear, distinct, evident, manifest, noticeable, observable, obvious, patent, plain, pronounced, visible. *See* SEE. **2.** Without any doubt : clear, decided, definite, distinct, pronounced, unquestionable. *See* CERTAIN. **3.** Clearly, fully, and sometimes emphatically expressed : categorical, clear, decided, definite, explicit, express, positive, precise, specific, unambiguous, unequivocal. *See* CLEAR.

clearness *noun*
The quality of being clear and easy to perceive or understand : clarity, distinctness, limpidity, limpidness, lucidity, lucidness, pellucidity, pellucidness, perspicuity, perspicuousness, plainness. *See* CLEAR.

clear out *verb* See **clear.**

clear-sightedness *noun*
Skill in perceiving, discriminating, or judging : acumen, astuteness, discernment, discrimination, eye, keenness, nose, penetration, perceptiveness, percipience, percipiency, perspicacity, sagacity, sageness, shrewdness, wit. *See* ABILITY, CAREFUL.

clear up *verb* See **clear.**

cleavage *noun*
A usually narrow partial opening caused by splitting and rupture : break, chink, cleft, crack, crevice, fissure, rift, split. *See* OPEN.

cleave[1] *verb*
To separate into parts with or as if with a sharp-edged instrument : carve, cut, dissever, sever, slice, slit, split. *See* ASSEMBLE.

cleave[2] *verb*
To hold fast : adhere, bond, cling, cohere, stick. *See* CONNECT.

cleft *noun*
A usually narrow partial opening caused by splitting and rupture : break, chink, cleavage, crack, crevice, fissure, rift, split. *See* OPEN.

clemency *noun*
Kind, forgiving, or compassionate treatment of or disposition toward others : charity, grace, lenience, leniency, lenity, mercifulness, mercy. *See* FORGIVENESS.

clement *adjective*
Not strict or severe : charitable, easy, forbearing, indulgent, lax, lenient, merciful, soft, tolerant. *See* ACCEPT.

clench *verb*
To take firmly with the hand and maintain a hold on : clasp, clutch[1], grab, grapple, grasp, grip, seize. *See* KEEP.

clench *noun* An act or means of holding something : clasp, clutch[1], grasp, grip, hold. *Sports:* grapple. *See* KEEP.

clergyman *noun*
A person ordained for service in a Christian church : churchman, churchwoman, clergywoman, cleric, clerical, clerk, divine, ecclesiastic, minister, parson, preacher. *Informal:* reverend. *See* RELIGION.

clergywoman *noun*
A person ordained for service in a Christian church : churchman, churchwoman, clergyman, cleric, clerical, clerk, divine, ecclesiastic, minister, parson, preacher. *Informal:* reverend. *See* RELIGION.

cleric *noun*
A person ordained for service in a Christian church : churchman, churchwoman, clergyman, clergywoman, clerical, clerk, divine, ecclesiastic, minister, parson, preacher. *Informal:* reverend. *See* RELIGION.

clerical *noun*
A person ordained for service in a Christian church : churchman, churchwoman, clergyman, clergywoman, cleric, clerk, divine, ecclesiastic, minister, parson, preacher. *Informal:* reverend. *See* RELIGION.

clerk *noun*
1. One who sells : salesclerk, salesgirl, salesman, salesperson, saleswoman, seller, vender. *See* TRANSACTIONS. **2.** A person ordained for service in a Christian church : churchman, churchwoman, clergyman, clergywoman, cleric, clerical, divine, ecclesiastic, minister, parson, preacher. *Informal:* reverend. *See* RELIGION.

clever *adjective*
1. Mentally quick and original : alert, bright, intelligent, keen[1], quick, quick-witted, sharr sharp-witted, smart. ***Idiom:*** smart as a w *See* ABILITY. **2.** Exhibiting or possessi and ease in performance : adroit, d ous, facile, handy, nimble, slick.

3. Amusing or pleasing because of wit or originality : scintillating, smart, sparkling, witty. *See* LAUGHTER.

cliché *noun*
A trite expression or idea : banality, bromide, commonplace, platitude, stereotype, truism. *See* SURPRISE.

clichéd *adjective*
Without freshness or appeal because of overuse : banal, bromidic, commonplace, corny, hackneyed, musty, overused, overworked, platitudinal, platitudinous, shopworn, stale, stereotyped, stereotypic, stereotypical, threadbare, timeworn, tired, trite, warmed-over, well-worn, worn-out. *See* EXCITE, USUAL.

click *noun*
A light, sharp noise : clack, snap. *See* SOUNDS.
click *verb* **1.** To make a light, sharp noise : clack, snap. *See* SOUNDS. **2.** *Slang.* To turn out well : come off, go, go over, pan out, succeed, work, work out. *See* THRIVE. **3.** *Slang.* To interact with another or others in a meaningful fashion : communicate, connect, relate. ***Idioms:*** be on the same wavelength, hit it off. *See* CONNECT.

client *noun*
One who buys goods or services : buyer, customer, patron, purchaser. *See* TRANSACTIONS.

clientele *noun*
Customers or patrons collectively : patronage. *See* TRANSACTIONS.

climacteric *noun*
A decisive point : crisis, crossroad (used in plural), exigence, exigency, head, juncture, pass, turning point, zero hour. *See* DECIDE.
climacteric *adjective* So serious as to be at the point of crisis or necessary to resolve a crisis : acute, critical, crucial, desperate, dire. *See* SAFETY.

climactic *adjective*
Of or constituting a climax : crowning, culminating, peak. *See* HIGH, OVER.

climate *noun*
1. The totality of surrounding conditions and circumstances affecting growth or development : ambiance, atmosphere, environment, medium, milieu, mise en scène, surroundings, [illegible]orld. *See* BE, LIMITED, PLACE. **2.** A prevail[illegible] [illegible]uality, as of thought, behavior, or atti[illegible] [illegible]ood, spirit, temper, tone. *See* [illegible]

clima[illegible]
The hi[illegible] [illegible] state : acme, apex, apogee, cres[illegible] [illegible]nation, height, meridian, peak, pinnacle, summit, top, zenith. *Informal:* payoff. *Medicine:* fastigium. *See* HIGH.
climax *verb* To reach or bring to a climax : cap, crest, crown, culminate, peak, top (off *or* out). *See* EXCITE.

climb *verb*
1. To move upward on or along : ascend, go up, mount, scale². *See* RISE. **2.** To move from a lower to a higher position : arise, ascend, lift, mount, rise, soar. *See* RISE. **3.** To attain a higher status, rank, or condition : advance, ascend, mount, rise. ***Idiom:*** go up the ladder. *See* INCREASE, RISE.
climb *noun* The act of moving upward on or along : ascension, ascent. *See* RISE.

clinch *verb*
Slang. To put one's arms around affectionately : clasp, embrace, enfold, hold, hug, press, squeeze. *Archaic:* bosom, clip², embosom. *See* TOUCH.
clinch *noun* *Slang.* The act of embracing : clasp, embrace, hug, squeeze. *See* TOUCH.

clincher *noun*
Informal. Something, especially something held in reserve, that gives one a decisive advantage : trump, trump card. ***Idiom:*** ace in the hole. *See* HELP, WIN.

cling *verb*
To hold fast : adhere, bond, cleave², cohere, stick. *See* CONNECT.

clinging *adjective*
Persistently holding to something : fast, firm¹, secure, tenacious, tight. *See* FREE, TIGHTEN.

clink *noun*
Slang. A place for the confinement of persons in lawful detention : brig, house of correction, jail, keep, penitentiary, prison. *Informal:* lockup, pen³. *Slang:* big house, can, cooler, coop, hoosegow, joint, jug, pokey¹, slammer, stir². *Chiefly Regional:* calaboose. *See* FREE.

clip¹ *verb*
1. To decrease, as in length or amount, by or as if by severing or excising : chop¹, crop, cut, cut back, cut down, lop¹, lower², pare, prune, shear, slash, trim, truncate. *See* INCREASE.
2. *Informal.* To deliver a powerful blow to (someone) suddenly and sharply : bash, catch, clout, hit, knock, pop¹, slam, slog, slug³, smash, smite, sock, strike, swat, thwack, whack, wham, whop. *Informal:* biff, bop, wallop. *Slang:* belt, conk, paste. ***Idioms:*** let someone have it, sock it to someone. *See* ATTACK, STRIKE.
3. *Informal.* To hit with a quick, sharp blow of the hand : box², buffet, bust, cuff, punch, slap,

smack[1], spank, swat, whack. *Informal:* spat. *See* ATTACK, STRIKE. **4.** *Slang.* To exploit (another) by charging too much for something : fleece, overcharge. *Slang:* gouge, nick, rip off, scalp, skin, soak. ***Idioms:*** make someone pay through the nose, take someone for a ride, take someone to the cleaners. *See* HONEST.

clip *noun* **1.** *Informal.* A sudden sharp, powerful stroke : bang, blow[2], clout, crack, hit, lick, pound, slug[3], sock, swat, thwack, welt, whack, wham, whop. *Informal:* bash, biff, bop, wallop. *Slang:* belt, conk, paste. *See* ATTACK, STRIKE. **2.** *Informal.* A quick, sharp blow, especially with the hand : box[2], buffet, bust, chop[1], cuff, punch, slap, smack[1], smacker, spank, swat, whack. *Informal:* spat. *See* ATTACK, STRIKE. **3.** *Informal.* Rate of motion or performance : pace, speed, tempo, velocity. *See* FAST.

clip[2] *verb*
1. To join one thing to another : affix, attach, connect, couple, fasten, fix, moor, secure. *See* ASSEMBLE. **2.** *Archaic.* To put one's arms around affectionately : clasp, embrace, enfold, hold, hug, press, squeeze. *Slang:* clinch. *Archaic:* bosom, embosom. *See* TOUCH.

clique *noun*
A particular social group : circle, coterie, crowd, set[2]. *Informal:* bunch, gang. *See* GROUP.

cloak *noun*
1. A garment wrapped about a person : shawl, stole, wrap. *See* PUT ON. **2.** A deceptive outward appearance : color, coloring, cover, disguise, disguisement, façade, face, false colors, front, gloss, guise, mask, masquerade, pretense, pretext, semblance, show, veil, veneer, window-dressing. *Slang:* put-on. *See* SHOW.

cloak *verb* **1.** To cover as if with clothes : clothe, drape, mantle, robe. *See* PUT ON. **2.** To surround and cover completely so as to obscure : clothe, enfold, enshroud, envelop, enwrap, infold, invest, shroud, veil, wrap. *See* SHOW. **3.** To prevent (something) from being known : conceal, cover (up), enshroud, hide[1], hush (up), mask, shroud, veil. ***Idioms:*** keep under cover, keep under wraps. *See* SHOW.

cloak-and-dagger *adjective*
Existing or operating in a way so as to ensure complete concealment and confidentiality : clandestine, covert, huggermugger, secret, subrosa, undercover. *Informal:* hush-hush. ***Idiom:*** under wraps. *See* SHOW.

clobber *verb*
1. *Slang.* To hit heavily and repeatedly with violent blows : assail, assault, baste, batter, beat, belabor, buffet, drub, hammer, pound, pummel, smash, thrash, thresh. *Informal:* lambaste. ***Idiom:*** rain blows on. *See* ATTACK, STRIKE. **2.** *Slang.* To render totally ineffective by decisive defeat : annihilate, crush, drub, overpower, overwhelm, smash, steamroller, thrash, trounce, vanquish. *Informal:* massacre, wallop. *Slang:* cream, shellac, smear. *See* WIN.

clock *verb*
To record the speed or duration of : time. *See* REMEMBER, TIME.

clod *noun*
1. An irregularly shaped mass of indefinite size : chunk, clump, gob[1], hunch, lump[1], nugget, wad. *Informal:* hunk. *See* PART. **2.** A mentally dull person : blockhead, chump[1], dolt, dullard, dummkopf, dummy, dunce, numskull, thickhead. *Slang:* dimwit, dumbbell, dumbo. *See* ABILITY.

clodhopper *noun*
A clumsy, unsophisticated person : bumpkin, rustic, yokel. *See* ABILITY.

clog *noun*
Something that impedes or prevents entry or passage : bar, barricade, barrier, block, blockage, hamper, hindrance, hurdle, impediment, obstacle, obstruction, snag, stop, traverse, wall. *See* HELP, OPEN.

clog *verb* To plug up something, as a hole, space, or container : block, choke, close, congest, cork, fill, plug, stop. *See* FULL.

cloister *verb*
To put into solitude : seclude, sequester, sequestrate. *See* INCLUDE.

clomp *verb*
To make a dull sound by or as if by striking a surface with a heavy object : clump, clunk, thud. *See* SOUNDS.

close *adjective*
1. Not far from another in space, time, or relation : adjacent, contiguous, immediate, near, nearby, nigh, proximate. ***Idioms:*** at hand, under one's nose, within a stone's throw, within hailing distance. *See* NEAR. **2.** Very closely associated : chummy, familiar, friendly, intimate[1]. *Informal:* thick. *Slang:* tight. ***Idiom:*** hand in glove with. *See* LOVE. **3.** Having all parts near to each other : compact[1], crowded, dense, packed, thick, tight. *See* TIGHTEN. **4.** Nearly equivalent or even : neck and neck, nip [illegible] tuck, tight. *See* NEAR. **5.** Not deviatin[illegible] correctness, accuracy, or completen[illegible] faithful, full, rigorous, strict. *See* [illegible]

6. Affording little room for movement : confining, cramped, crowded, narrow, snug, tight. *See* TIGHTEN. **7.** Oppressive due to a lack of fresh air : airless, stifling, stuffy. *See* BREATH, OPEN. **8.** Not speaking freely or openly : close-mouthed, incommunicable, incommunicative, reserved, reticent, silent, taciturn, tightlipped, uncommunicable, uncommunicative. *See* RESTRAINT, SOUNDS. **9.** Ungenerously or pettily reluctant to spend money : cheap, close-fisted, costive, hard-fisted, mean[2], miserly, niggard, niggardly, parsimonious, penny-pinching, penurious, petty, pinching, stingy, tight, tightfisted. *See* GIVE.

close *verb* **1.** To move (a door, for example) in order to cover an opening : shut. *See* OPEN. **2.** To plug up something, as a hole, space, or container : block, choke, clog, congest, cork, fill, plug, stop. *See* FULL. **3.** To bring or come to a natural or proper end : complete, conclude, consummate, end, finish, terminate, wind up, wrap up. *See* START. **4.** To come together : converge, meet[1]. *See* OPEN.

close in *verb* To surround and advance upon : besiege, enclose, envelop, hedge, hem. *See* OPEN.

close off *verb* To set apart from a group : cut off, insulate, isolate, seclude, segregate, separate, sequester. *See* INCLUDE.

close out *verb* To get rid of completely by selling, especially in quantity or at a discount : dump, sell off, sell out, unload. *See* TRANSACTIONS.

close *noun* **1.** A concluding or terminating : cease, cessation, closing, closure, completion, conclusion, consummation, end, ending, end of the line, finish, period, stop, stopping point, termination, terminus, wind-up, wrap-up. *See* CONTINUE. **2.** The last part : conclusion, end, ending, finale, finish, last[1], termination, wind-up, wrap-up. *See* START. **3.** An area partially or entirely enclosed by walls or buildings : atrium, court, courtyard, enclosure, quad, quadrangle, yard. *See* PLACE.

close *adverb* To a point near in time, space, or relation : closely, hard, near, nearby, nigh. *See* NEAR.

'ose-fisted *adjective*
-enerously or pettily reluctant to spend
n. ous, cheap, close, costive, hard-fisted,
ing, st-rly, niggard, niggardly, parsimoni-
close in v-hing, penurious, petty, pinch-
-ghtfisted. *See* GIVE.

closely *adverb*
To a point near in time, space, or relation : close, hard, near, nearby, nigh. *See* NEAR.

close-minded *adjective*
Not tolerant of the beliefs or opinions of others, for example : bigoted, hidebound, illiberal, intolerant, narrow-minded. *See* ACCEPT.

close-mouthed *adjective*
Not speaking freely or openly : close, incommunicable, incommunicative, reserved, reticent, silent, taciturn, tightlipped, uncommunicable, uncommunicative. *See* RESTRAINT, SOUNDS.

closeness *noun*
The condition of being friends : chumminess, companionship, comradeship, familiarity, fellowship, friendship, intimacy. *See* LOVE.

close off *verb* See **close.**

close out *verb* See **close.**

closet *verb*
To enclose so as to hinder or prohibit escape : confine, imprison, shut up. *See* FREE.

closing *adjective*
Coming after all others : concluding, final, last[1], terminal. *See* START.

closing *noun* A concluding or terminating : cease, cessation, close, closure, completion, conclusion, consummation, end, ending, end of the line, finish, period, stop, stopping point, termination, terminus, wind-up, wrap-up. *See* CONTINUE.

closure *noun*
A concluding or terminating : cease, cessation, close, closing, completion, conclusion, consummation, end, ending, end of the line, finish, period, stop, stopping point, termination, terminus, wind-up, wrap-up. *See* CONTINUE.

clot *verb*
To change or be changed from a liquid into a soft, semisolid, or solid mass : coagulate, congeal, curdle, gelatinize, jell, jelly, set[1]. *See* SOLID.

clothe *verb*
1. To put clothes on : apparel, attire, dress, garb, garment, invest. *Informal:* tog. *See* PUT ON. **2.** To cover as if with clothes : cloak, drape, mantle, robe. *See* PUT ON. **3.** To surround and cover completely so as to obscure : cloak, enfold, enshroud, envelop, enwrap, infold, invest, shroud, veil, wrap. *See* SHOW.

clothes *noun*
Articles worn to cover the body : apparel, attire, clothing, dress, garment (used in plural), habiliment (often used in plural), raiment. *Informal:* dud (used in plural), tog (used in plural). *Slang:* thread (used in plural). *See* PUT ON.

clothing *noun*
Articles worn to cover the body : apparel, attire, clothes, dress, garment (used in plural), habiliment (often used in plural), raiment. *Informal:* dud (used in plural), tog (used in plural). *Slang:* thread (used in plural). *See* PUT ON.

cloud *noun*
A very large number of things grouped together : army, crowd, drove, flock, horde, host, legion, mass, mob, multitude, ruck[1], score (used in plural), swarm, throng. *See* BIG, GROUP.

cloud *verb* **1.** To make dim or indistinct : becloud, bedim, befog, blear, blur, dim, dull, eclipse, fog, gloom, mist, obfuscate, obscure, overcast, overshadow, shadow. *See* CLEAR. **2.** To contaminate the reputation of : befoul, besmear, besmirch, bespatter, blacken, denigrate, dirty, smear, smudge, smut, soil, spatter, stain, sully, taint, tarnish. ***Idioms:*** give a black eye to, sling (*or* throw) mud on. *See* ATTACK, CLEAN.

clouded *adjective*
Not affording certainty : ambiguous, borderline, chancy, doubtful, dubious, dubitable, equivocal, inconclusive, indecisive, indeterminate, problematic, problematical, questionable, uncertain, unclear, unsure. *Informal:* iffy. ***Idioms:*** at issue, in doubt, in question. *See* CERTAIN, CLEAR.

cloudiness *noun*
The quality or state of being ambiguous : ambiguity, ambiguousness, equivocalness, indefiniteness, nebulousness, obscureness, obscurity, uncertainty, unclearness, vagueness. *See* CLEAR.

cloudless *adjective*
Free from clouds or mist, for example : clear, fair, fine[1], sunny, unclouded. *See* CLEAR.

cloud nine *noun*
Informal. A state of elated bliss : ecstasy, heaven, paradise, rapture, seventh heaven, transport. *See* HAPPY.

cloudy *adjective*
1. Covered by or as if by a thin coating or film : blurry, dim, filmy, hazy, misty. *See* CLEAR. **2.** Having sediment or foreign particles stirred up or suspended : muddy, murky, roiled, roily, turbid. *See* CLEAR. **3.** Liable to more than one interpretation : ambiguous, equivocal, inexplicit, nebulous, obscure, uncertain, unclear, vague. *See* CERTAIN, CLEAR. **4.** Not clearly perceived or perceptible : blear, bleary, dim, faint, foggy, fuzzy, hazy, indefinite, indistinct, misty, obscure, shadowy, unclear, undistinct, vague. *See* CLEAR.

clout *noun*
1. A sudden sharp, powerful stroke : bang, blow[2], crack, hit, lick, pound, slug[3], sock, swat, thwack, welt, whack, wham, whop. *Informal:* bash, biff, bop, clip[1], wallop. *Slang:* belt, conk, paste. *See* ATTACK, STRIKE. **2.** *Informal.* The power to produce an effect by indirect means : influence, leverage, sway, weight. *Slang:* pull. *See* AFFECT. **3.** *Informal.* Effective means of influencing, compelling, or punishing : force, power, weight. *Informal:* muscle. *See* OVER, STRONG.

clout *verb* To deliver a powerful blow to suddenly and sharply : bash, catch, hit, knock, pop[1], slam, slog, slug[3], smash, smite, sock, strike, swat, thwack, whack, wham, whop. *Informal:* biff, bop, clip[1], wallop. *Slang:* belt, conk, paste. ***Idioms:*** let someone have it, sock it to someone. *See* ATTACK, STRIKE.

clown *noun*
A person whose words or actions provoke or are intended to provoke amusement or laughter : comedian, comic, farceur, funnyman, humorist, jester, joker, jokester, quipster, wag[2], wit, zany. *Informal:* card. *See* LAUGHTER.

clown *verb* *Informal.* To make jokes; behave playfully. Also used with *around* : jest, joke. *Informal:* fool around, fun. *See* LAUGHTER.

cloy *verb*
To satisfy to the full or to excess : engorge, glut, gorge, pall, sate, satiate, surfeit. *See* EXCESS, FULL.

club *noun*
A group of people united in a relationship and having some interest, activity, or purpose in common : association, confederation, congress, federation, fellowship, fraternity, guild, league, order, organization, society, sorority, union. *See* GROUP.

clue also **clew** *noun*
1. A piece of information useful in a search : lead, scent. *See* SHOW. **2.** A subtle pointing out : cue, hint, intimation, suggestion. *See* KNOWLEDGE, SUGGEST.

clump *noun*
1. An irregularly shaped mass of indefinite size : chunk, clod, gob[1], hunch, lump[1], nugget, wad. *Informal:* hunk. *See* PART. **2.** A number of individuals making up or considered a unit : array, band[2], batch, bevy, body, bunch, bundle, cluster, clutch[2], collection, group, knot, lot, party, set[2]. *See* GROUP.

clump *verb* **1.** To move heavily : galumph, hulk, lumber, lump[1], stump. *See* MOVE. **2.** To make a dull sound by or as if by striking a surface with a heavy object : clomp, clunk, thud. *See* SOUNDS.

clumsy *adjective*
1. Lacking dexterity and grace in physical movement : awkward, gawky, graceless, inept, lumpish, maladroit, ungainly, ungraceful. *Slang:* klutzy. ***Idiom:*** all thumbs. *See* ABILITY. **2.** Difficult to handle or manage : awkward, bulky, ungainly, unhandy, unmanageable, unwieldy. *See* EASY. **3.** Clumsily lacking in the ability to do or perform : awkward, bumbling, gauche, heavy-handed, inept, maladroit, unskillful. *See* ABILITY. **4.** Lacking sensitivity and skill in dealing with others : brash, gauche, impolitic, indelicate, maladroit, tactless, undiplomatic, unpolitic, untactful. *See* ABILITY, COURTESY.

clunk *noun*
A stroke or blow, especially one that produces a sound : beat, pound, thud, thump. *See* ATTACK, SOUNDS, STRIKE.
clunk *verb* To make a dull sound by or as if by striking a surface with a heavy object : clomp, clump, thud. *See* SOUNDS.

cluster *noun*
A number of individuals making up or considered a unit : array, band[2], batch, bevy, body, bunch, bundle, clump, clutch[2], collection, group, knot, lot, party, set[2]. *See* GROUP.
cluster *verb* **1.** To come together : assemble, collect[1], congregate, convene, forgather, gather, get together, group, muster. *See* COLLECT. **2.** To bring together : assemble, call, collect[1], congregate, convene, convoke, gather, get together, group, muster, round up, summon. *See* COLLECT.

clutch[1] *verb*
1. To take firmly with the hand and maintain a hold on : clasp, clench, grab, grapple, grasp, grip, seize. *See* KEEP. **2.** To get hold of (something moving) : catch, grab, seize, snatch. *Informal:* nab. ***Idiom:*** lay hands on. *See* GET.
clutch *noun* **1.** The act of catching, especially a sudden taking and holding : catch, grab, seizure, snatch. *See* GET. **2.** An act or means of holding something : clasp, clench, grasp, grip, hold. *Sports:* grapple. *See* KEEP.

clutch[2] *noun*
A number of individuals making up or considered a unit : array, band[2], batch, bevy, body, bunch, bundle, clump, cluster, collection, group, knot, lot, party, set[2]. *See* GROUP.

clutching *adjective*
Fearful of the loss of position or affection : jealous, possessive. *See* OWNED.

clutter *noun*
A lack of order or regular arrangement : chaos, confusedness, confusion, derangement, disarrangement, disarray, disorder, disorderedness, disorderliness, disorganization, jumble, mess, mix-up, muddle, muss, scramble, topsy-turviness, tumble. *Slang:* snafu. *See* ORDER.

cluttered *adjective*
Excessively filled with detail : busy, crowded, fussy. *See* SIMPLE.

coach *verb*
To impart knowledge and skill to : discipline, educate, instruct, school, teach, train, tutor. *See* TEACH.

coaction *noun*
Joint work toward a common end : collaboration, cooperation, synergy, teamwork. *See* CONFLICT.

coadjutant *noun*
A person who holds a position auxiliary to another and assumes some of the superior's responsibilities : adjutant, aide, assistant, auxiliary, coadjutor, deputy, helper, lieutenant, second[2]. *See* HELP.

coadjutor *noun*
A person who holds a position auxiliary to another and assumes some of the superior's responsibilities : adjutant, aide, assistant, auxiliary, coadjutant, deputy, helper, lieutenant, second[2]. *See* HELP.

coagulate *verb*
To change or be changed from a liquid into a soft, semisolid, or solid mass : clot, congeal, curdle, gelatinize, jell, jelly, set[1]. *See* SOLID.

coalesce *verb*
To bring or come together into a united whole : combine, compound, concrete, conjoin, conjugate, connect, consolidate, couple, join, link, marry, meld, unify, unite, wed, yoke. *See* ASSEMBLE.

coalition *noun*
1. An association, especially of nations for a common cause : alliance, Anschluss, bloc, cartel, confederacy, confederation, federation, league, organization, union. *See* CONNECT, GROUP, POLITICS. **2.** A group of individuals united in a common cause : bloc, cartel, combination, combine, faction, party, ring[1]. *See* GROUP. **3.** A bringing together into a whole : consolidation, unification, union, unity. *See* PART.

coalitionist *noun*
One nation associated with another in a common cause : ally, confederate, leaguer. *See* CONNECT, POLITICS.

coarse *adjective*
1. Lacking in delicacy or refinement : barbarian, barbaric, boorish, churlish, crass, crude, gross, ill-bred, indelicate, philistine, rough, rude, tasteless, uncivilized, uncouth, uncultivated, uncultured, unpolished, unrefined, vulgar. *See* COURTESY, SMOOTH. **2.** Offensive to accepted standards of decency : barnyard, bawdy, broad, dirty, Fescennine, filthy, foul, gross, lewd, nasty, obscene, profane, ribald, scatologic, scatological, scurrilous, smutty, vulgar. *Slang:* raunchy. *See* DECENT. **3.** Consisting of or covered with large particles : grainy, granular, gritty, rough. *See* SMOOTH. **4.** Having a surface that is not smooth : cragged, craggy, harsh, ironbound, jagged, ragged, rough, rugged, scabrous, uneven. *See* SMOOTH.

coarseness *noun*
The quality or state of being obscene : bawdiness, dirtiness, filthiness, foulness, grossness, lewdness, obscenity, profaneness, profanity, scurrility, scurrilousness, smuttiness, vulgarity, vulgarness. *Slang:* raunch, raunchiness. *See* DECENT.

coast *verb*
To pass smoothly, quietly, and undisturbed on or as if on a slippery surface : drift, slide. *See* MOVE.

coax *verb*
To persuade or try to persuade by gentle persistent urging or flattery : blandish, cajole, honey, wheedle. *Informal:* soft-soap, sweet-talk. *See* PERSUASION.

cock-and-bull story *noun*
An untrue declaration : canard, falsehood, falsity, fib, fiction, inveracity, lie[2], misrepresentation, misstatement, prevarication, story, tale, untruth. *Informal:* fish story, tall tale. *Slang:* whopper. *See* TRUE.

cockcrow *noun*
The first appearance of daylight in the morning : aurora, dawn, dawning, daybreak, morn, morning, sunrise, sunup. *See* START.

cockeyed *adjective*
1. *Informal.* So senseless as to be laughable : absurd, foolish, harebrained, idiotic, imbecilic, insane, lunatic, mad, moronic, nonsensical, preposterous, silly, softheaded, tomfool, unearthly, zany. *Informal:* crazy, loony, loopy. *Slang:* balmy[2], dippy, dopey, jerky, sappy, wacky. *See* ABILITY, KNOWLEDGE. **2.** *Informal.* Stupefied, excited, or muddled with alcoholic liquor : besotted, crapulent, crapulous, drunk, drunken, inebriate, inebriated, intoxicated, sodden, tipsy. *Informal:* stewed. *Slang:* blind, bombed, boozed, boozy, crocked, high, lit (up), loaded, looped, pickled, pixilated, plastered, potted, sloshed, smashed, soused, stinking, stinko, stoned, tight, zonked. ***Idioms:*** drunk as a skunk, half-seas over, high as a kite, in one's cups, three sheets in (*or* to) the wind. *See* DRUGS.

coddle *verb*
To treat with indulgence and often overtender care : baby, cater, cosset, indulge, mollycoddle, overindulge, pamper, spoil. *See* TREAT WELL.

coequal *noun*
One that is very similar to another in rank or position : colleague, compeer, equal, equivalent, fellow, peer[2]. *See* SAME.

coerce *verb*
1. To compel by pressure or threats : blackjack, dragoon, force. *Informal:* hijack, strong-arm. *See* PERSUASION. **2.** To cause (a person or thing) to act or move in spite of resistance : compel, constrain, force, make, obligate, oblige, pressure. *See* ATTACK.

coercion *noun*
Power used to overcome resistance : compulsion, constraint, duress, force, pressure, strength, violence. *See* ATTACK.

coercive *adjective*
Accomplished by force : forcible, violent. *Informal:* strong-arm. *See* ATTACK.

coetaneous *adjective*
Belonging to the same period of time as another : coeval, coexistent, concurrent, contemporaneous, contemporary, synchronic, synchronous. *See* TIME.

coeval *adjective*
Belonging to the same period of time as another : coetaneous, coexistent, concurrent, contemporaneous, contemporary, synchronic, synchronous. *See* TIME.
coeval *noun* One of the same time or age as another : contemporary. *See* TIME.

coexistent *adjective*
Belonging to the same period of time as another : coetaneous, coeval, concurrent, contemporaneous, contemporary, synchronic, synchronous. *See* TIME.

cogent *adjective*
1. Serving to convince : convincing, persuasive, satisfactory, telling. *See* PERSUASION. **2.** Based

on good judgment, reasoning, or evidence : just, solid, sound[2], tight, valid, well-founded, well-grounded. *See* GOOD, REASON.

cogitate *verb*
1. To think or think about carefully and at length : chew on (*or* over), consider, contemplate, deliberate, entertain, excogitate, meditate, mull, muse[1], ponder, reflect, revolve, ruminate, study, think, think out, think over, think through, turn over, weigh. ***Idioms:*** cudgel one's brains, put on one's thinking cap, rack one's brain. *See* THOUGHTS. **2.** To use the powers of the mind, as in conceiving ideas, drawing inferences, and making judgments : cerebrate, deliberate, ratiocinate, reflect, speculate, think. ***Idioms:*** put on one's thinking cap, use one's head. *See* THOUGHTS.

cogitation *noun*
The act or process of thinking : brainwork, cerebration, contemplation, deliberation, excogitation, meditation, reflection, rumination, speculation, thought. *See* THOUGHTS.

cogitative *adjective*
Of, characterized by, or disposed to thought : contemplative, deliberative, excogitative, meditative, pensive, reflective, ruminative, speculative, thinking, thoughtful. ***Idiom:*** in a brown study. *See* THOUGHTS.

cognate *adjective*
Connected by or as if by kinship or common origin : agnate, akin, allied, connate, connatural, consanguine, consanguineous, kindred, related. *See* KIN.

cognizance *noun*
1. The condition of being aware : awareness, consciousness, perception, sense. *See* KNOWLEDGE. **2.** The act of noting, observing, or taking into account : attention, espial, heed, mark, note, notice, observance, observation, regard, remark. *See* KNOWLEDGE, SEE.

cognizant *adjective*
Marked by comprehension, cognizance, and perception : alive, awake, aware, sensible, sentient, wise[1]. *Slang:* hip. ***Idiom:*** on to. *See* KNOWLEDGE.

cognomen *noun*
The word or words by which one is called and identified : appellation, appellative, denomination, designation, epithet, name, nickname, style, tag, title. *Slang:* handle, moniker. *See* SPECIFIC, WORDS.

cohere *verb*
To hold fast : adhere, bond, cleave[2], cling, stick. *See* CONNECT.

coherence *noun*
Logical agreement among parts : congruity, consistence, consistency. *See* AGREE.

cohesion *noun*
The close physical union of two objects : adherence, adhesion, bond. *See* CONNECT.

cohort *noun*
1. One who is united in a relationship with another : affiliate, ally, associate, colleague, confederate, copartner, fellow, partner. *See* CONNECT. **2.** One who supports and adheres to another : adherent, disciple, follower, henchman, minion, partisan, satellite, supporter. *See* OVER, PRECEDE.

coil *verb*
To move or proceed on a repeatedly curving course : corkscrew, curl, entwine, meander, snake, spiral, twine, twist, weave, wind[2], wreathe. *See* REPETITION, STRAIGHT.

coincide *verb*
1. To occur at the same time : concur, synchronize. *See* NEAR. **2.** To come to an understanding or to terms : accord, agree, concur, get together, harmonize. *See* AGREE.

coincident *adjective*
1. Existing or occurring at the same moment : contemporary, simultaneous. *See* TIME. **2.** Occurring or existing with : accompanying, attendant, attending, concomitant, concurrent. *See* ACCOMPANIED.

cold *adjective*
1. Marked by a low temperature : chill, chilly, cool, nippy, shivery. *See* HOT. **2.** Not affected by or showing emotion : cold-blooded, emotionless, unaffected, unemotional, unmoved. *See* ATTITUDE, HOT. **3.** Lacking all friendliness and warmth : frigid, frosty, glacial, icy. *See* ATTITUDE, HOT. **4.** Deficient in or lacking sexual desire : ardorless, frigid, inhibited, passionless, unresponsive. *See* SEX. **5.** Lacking consciousness : insensible, senseless, unconscious. ***Idioms:*** out cold, out like a light. *See* AWARENESS.

cold *noun* Relative lack of physical warmth : chill, chilliness, coldness, coolness. *See* HOT.

cold-blooded *adjective*
1. Completely lacking in compassion : callous, cold-hearted, compassionless, hard, hard-boiled, hardened, hardhearted, heartless, obdurate, stonyhearted, unfeeling. *See* ATTITUDE. **2.** Not affected by or showing emotion : cold, emotionless, unaffected, unemotional, unmoved. *See* ATTITUDE, HOT.

cold feet *noun*
Slang. Great agitation and anxiety caused by

the expectation or the realization of danger : affright, alarm, apprehension, dread, fear, fearfulness, fright, funk, horror, panic, terror, trepidation. ***Idiom:*** fear and trembling. *See* FEAR.

cold-hearted *adjective*
Completely lacking in compassion : callous, cold-blooded, compassionless, hard, hard-boiled, hardened, hardhearted, heartless, obdurate, stonyhearted, unfeeling. *See* ATTITUDE.

coldness *noun*
Relative lack of physical warmth : chill, chilliness, cold, coolness. *See* HOT.

coldshoulder *verb*
Informal. To slight (someone) deliberately : cut, rebuff, shun, snub, spurn. ***Idioms:*** close (*or* shut) the door on, give someone the cold shoulder, give someone the go-by, turn one's back on. *See* ACCEPT.
cold shoulder *noun Informal.* A deliberate slight : cut, rebuff, snub, spurn. *Informal:* go-by. *See* ACCEPT.

collaborate *verb*
To work together toward a common end : cooperate. *See* CONFLICT.

collaboration *noun*
Joint work toward a common end : coaction, cooperation, synergy, teamwork. *See* CONFLICT.

collaborative *adjective*
Working together toward a common end : cooperative, synergetic, synergic, synergistic. *See* CONFLICT.

collapse *verb*
1. To fall in : buckle, cave in, crumple, give, go. ***Idiom:*** give way. *See* EXPLOSION. **2.** To suddenly lose all health or strength : break (down), cave in, crack, drop, give out, succumb. *Informal:* crack up. *Slang:* conk out. ***Idiom:*** give way. *See* HEALTH. **3.** To give way mentally and emotionally : break (down), crack, snap. *Informal:* crack up, fold. *See* EXPLOSION.
4. To undergo sudden financial failure : break, bust, crash, fail, go under. *Informal:* fold. ***Idioms:*** go belly up, go bust, go on the rocks, go to the wall. *See* MONEY. **5.** To undergo capture, defeat, or ruin : fall, go down, go under, surrender, topple. *See* RESIST, WIN.
collapse *noun* **1.** A sudden sharp decline in mental, emotional, or physical health : breakdown. *Informal:* crackup. *See* EXPLOSION.
2. An abrupt disastrous failure : breakdown, crash, debacle, smash, smashup, wreck. *See* MONEY. **3.** A disastrous overwhelming defeat or ruin : downfall, fall, waterloo. *See* THRIVE.

collar *noun*
Slang. A seizing and holding by law : apprehension, arrest, seizure. *Slang:* bust, pickup, pinch. *See* LAW.
collar *verb Slang.* To take into custody as a prisoner : apprehend, arrest, seize. *Informal:* nab, pick up. *Slang:* bust, pinch, run in. *See* LAW.

collate *verb*
To examine in order to note the similarities and differences of : balance, compare. *See* SAME.

collateral *adjective*
1. Lying in the same plane and not intersecting : parallel. ***Idiom:*** side by side. *See* GEOMETRY. **2.** Giving or able to give help or support : accessory, ancillary, assistant, auxiliary, contributory, subsidiary, supportive. *See* HELP.
3. In a position of subordination : dependent, subject, subordinate, subservient. *See* OVER, PART.

colleague *noun*
1. One that is very similar to another in rank or position : coequal, compeer, equal, equivalent, fellow, peer[2]. *See* SAME. **2.** One who is united in a relationship with another : affiliate, ally, associate, cohort, confederate, copartner, fellow, partner. *See* CONNECT.

collect[1] *verb*
1. To bring together : assemble, call, cluster, congregate, convene, convoke, gather, get together, group, muster, round up, summon. *See* COLLECT. **2.** To bring together so as to increase in mass or number : accrue, accumulate, agglomerate, aggregate, amass, cumulate, garner, gather, hive, pile up, roll up. *See* COLLECT.
3. To come together : assemble, cluster, congregate, convene, forgather, gather, get together, group, muster. *See* COLLECT. **4.** To bring one's emotions under control : compose, contain, control, cool, simmer down. ***Idiom:*** cool it. *See* RESTRAINT.

collect[2] *noun*
A formula of words used in praying : litany, orison, prayer[1], rogation (often used in plural). *See* RELIGION.

collected *adjective*
Not easily excited, even under pressure : calm, composed, cool, cool-headed, detached, even[1], even-tempered, imperturbable, nonchalant, possessed, unflappable, unruffled. *See* CALM.

collectedness *noun*
A stable, calm state of the emotions : aplomb, balance, composure, coolness, equanimity, imperturbability, imperturbableness, nonchalance,

poise, sang-froid, self-possession, unflappability. *Slang:* cool. *See* CALM, FEELINGS.

collection *noun*
1. A number of individuals making up or considered a unit : array, band[2], batch, bevy, body, bunch, bundle, clump, cluster, clutch[2], group, knot, lot, party, set[2]. *See* GROUP. **2.** A quantity accumulated : accumulation, aggregation, amassment, assemblage, congeries, cumulation, gathering, mass. *See* COLLECT.

collide *verb*
To come together or come up against with force : bump, crash. *See* CONFLICT.

collision *noun*
Violent forcible contact between two or more things : bump, concussion, crash, impact, jar, jolt, percussion, shock[1], smash. *See* CONFLICT.

colloquial *adjective*
In the style of conversation : chatty, confabulatory, conversational, informal. *See* WORDS.

colloquium *noun*
A meeting for the exchange of views : conference, discussion, parley, seminar. *Informal:* powwow. *Slang:* rap session. *See* MEET, WORDS.

colloquy *noun*
Spoken exchange : chat, confabulation, conversation, converse[1], dialogue, discourse, speech, talk. *Informal:* confab. *Slang:* jaw. *See* WORDS.

collude *verb*
To work out a secret plan to achieve an evil or illegal end : connive, conspire, intrigue, machinate, plot, scheme. *See* CRIMES, PLANNED.

collusion *noun*
A secret plan to achieve an evil or illegal end : cabal, connivance, conspiracy, intrigue, machination, plot, scheme. *See* CRIMES, PLANNED.

colony *noun*
An area subject to rule by an outside power : dependency, possession, province, territory. *See* POLITICS.

colophon *noun*
A name or other device placed on merchandise to signify its ownership or manufacture : brand, label, mark, trademark. *See* MARKS.

color *noun*
1. The property by which the sense of vision can distinguish between objects, as a red apple and a green apple, that are very similar or identical in form and size : hue, shade, tint, tone. *See* COLORS. **2.** Something that imparts color : colorant, coloring, dye, dyestuff, pigment, stain, tincture. *See* COLORS. **3.** Skin tone, especially of the face : coloring, complexion. *See* COLORS. **4.** A fresh rosy complexion : bloom[1], blush, flush, glow. *See* BETTER. **5.** Fabric used especially as a symbol. Used in plural : banderole, banner, banneret, ensign, flag[1], jack, oriflamme, pennant, pennon, standard, streamer. *See* SUBSTITUTE. **6.** A deceptive outward appearance : cloak, coloring, cover, disguise, disguisement, façade, face, false colors, front, gloss, guise, mask, masquerade, pretense, pretext, semblance, show, veil, veneer, window-dressing. *Slang:* put-on. *See* SHOW. **7.** Appearance of truth or authenticity : believability, credibility, credibleness, creditability, creditableness, plausibility, plausibleness, verisimilitude. *See* LIKELY.

color *verb* **1.** To impart color to : dye, stain, tincture, tint. *See* COLORS. **2.** To immerse in a coloring solution : dip, dye. *See* COLORS, ENTER. **3.** To become red in the face : blush, crimson, flush, glow, mantle, redden. *See* EXPRESS. **4.** To give an inaccurate view of by representing falsely or misleadingly : belie, distort, falsify, load, misrepresent, misstate, pervert, twist, warp, wrench, wrest. ***Idiom:*** give a false coloring to. *See* TRUE. **5.** To give a deceptively attractive appearance to : gild, gloss (over), gloze (over), sugarcoat, varnish, veneer, whitewash. ***Idioms:*** paper over, put a good face on. *See* TRUE.

colorable *adjective*
Worthy of being believed : believable, credible, creditable, plausible. *See* TRUE.

colorant *noun*
Something that imparts color : color, coloring, dye, dyestuff, pigment, stain, tincture. *See* COLORS.

colorfast *adjective*
Permanently resistive to fading : fast, indelible. *See* CONTINUE.

colorful *adjective*
1. Full of color : bright, gay, rich, vivid. *See* COLORS. **2.** Evoking strong mental images through distinctiveness : picturesque, vivid. *See* STRONG.

coloring *noun*
1. Something that imparts color : color, colorant, dye, dyestuff, pigment, stain, tincture. *See* COLORS. **2.** Skin tone, especially of the face : color, complexion. *See* COLORS. **3.** A deceptive outward appearance : cloak, color, cover, disguise, disguisement, façade, face, false colors, front, gloss, guise, mask, masquerade, pretense, pretext, semblance, show, veil, veneer, window-dressing. *Slang:* put-on. *See* SHOW.

colorless *adjective*
1. Lacking color : ashen, ashy, bloodless, cadaverous, livid, lurid, pale, pallid, pasty, sallow, wan, waxen. *See* COLORS. **2.** Lacking liveliness, charm, or surprise : arid, aseptic, drab, dry, dull, earthbound, flat, flavorless, lackluster, lifeless, lusterless, matter-of-fact, pedestrian, prosaic, spiritless, sterile, stodgy, unimaginative, uninspired. *See* EXCITE. **3.** Without definite or distinctive characteristics : bland, indistinctive, neutral. *See* STRONG.

colorlessness *noun*
A lack of excitement, liveliness, or interest : asepticism, blandness, drabness, dreariness, dryness, dullness, flatness, flavorlessness, insipidity, insipidness, jejuneness, lifelessness, sterileness, sterility, stodginess, vapidity, vapidness, weariness. *See* EXCITE.

colossal *adjective*
Of extraordinary size and power : behemoth, Brobdingnagian, Bunyanesque, cyclopean, elephantine, enormous, gargantuan, giant, gigantesque, gigantic, herculean, heroic, huge, immense, jumbo, mammoth, massive, massy, mastodonic, mighty, monster, monstrous, monumental, mountainous, prodigious, pythonic, stupendous, titanic, tremendous, vast. *Informal:* walloping. *Slang:* whopping. *See* BIG.

column *noun*
A group of people or things arranged in a row : file, line, queue, rank[1], row[1], string, tier. *See* GROUP.

comb *verb*
To make a thorough search of : forage, ransack, rummage, scour[2]. *Slang:* shake down. ***Idioms:*** beat the bushes, leave no stone unturned, look (*or* search) high and low, look (*or* search) up and down, turn inside out, turn upside down. *See* INVESTIGATE.

combat *verb*
To strive in opposition : battle, contend, duel, fight, struggle, tilt, war, wrestle. *See* CONFLICT.

combat *noun* A hostile encounter between opposing military forces : action, battle, engagement. *See* CONFLICT.

combatant *noun*
One who engages in a combat or struggle : belligerent, fighter, soldier, warrior. *See* CONFLICT.

combatant *adjective* Of or engaged in warfare : belligerent, hostile, militant. ***Idiom:*** at war. *See* ATTACK.

combative *adjective*
1. Having or showing an eagerness to fight : bellicose, belligerent, contentious, hostile, militant, pugnacious, quarrelsome, scrappy, truculent, warlike. *See* ATTACK. **2.** Inclined to act in a hostile way : aggressive, belligerent, contentious, hostile, militant. *See* ATTACK, ATTITUDE. **3.** Given to arguing : argumentative, contentious, disputatious, eristic, litigious, polemic, polemical, quarrelsome, scrappy. *See* CONFLICT.

combativeness *noun*
1. Warlike or hostile attitude or nature : bellicoseness, bellicosity, belligerence, belligerency, contentiousness, hostility, militance, militancy, pugnaciousness, pugnacity, truculence, truculency. *See* ATTACK. **2.** Hostile behavior : aggression, aggressiveness, belligerence, belligerency, contentiousness, hostility, militance, militancy. *See* ATTACK. **3.** The power or will to fight : bellicoseness, bellicosity, belligerence, belligerency, contentiousness, fight, pugnaciousness, pugnacity, truculence, truculency. *See* CONFLICT. **4.** The quality or state of being argumentative : argumentativeness, contentiousness, disputatiousness, litigiousness, scrappiness. *See* CONFLICT.

combination *noun*
1. The state of being associated : affiliation, alliance, association, conjunction, connection, cooperation, partnership. *See* NEAR. **2.** The result of combining : composite, compound, conjugation, unification, union, unity. *See* ASSEMBLE. **3.** A group of individuals united in a common cause : bloc, cartel, coalition, combine, faction, party, ring[1]. *See* GROUP.

combinational *adjective*
Of, relating to, or tending to produce combination : combinative, combinatorial, conjugational, conjugative, conjunctional, connectional, connective. *See* ASSEMBLE.

combinative *adjective*
Of, relating to, or tending to produce combination : combinational, combinatorial, conjugational, conjugative, conjunctional, connectional, connective. *See* ASSEMBLE.

combinatorial *adjective*
Of, relating to, or tending to produce combination : combinational, combinative, conjugational, conjugative, conjunctional, connectional, connective. *See* ASSEMBLE.

combine *verb*
1. To bring or come together into a united whole : coalesce, compound, concrete, conjoin, conjugate, connect, consolidate, couple,

join, link, marry, meld, unify, unite, wed, yoke. *See* ASSEMBLE. **2.** To unite or be united in a relationship : affiliate, ally, associate, bind, conjoin, connect, join, link, relate. *See* CONNECT. **3.** To assemble or join in a group : band[2], gang up, league, unite. *See* COLLECT. **4.** To make a part of a united whole : embody, incorporate, integrate. *See* INCLUDE.

combine *noun* **1.** A group of individuals united in a common cause : bloc, cartel, coalition, combination, faction, party, ring[1]. *See* GROUP. **2.** A combination of businesses closely interconnected for common profit : cartel, pool, syndicate, trust. *See* GROUP, MONEY.

combust *verb*

To undergo combustion : blaze[1], burn, flame, flare. *See* HOT.

come *verb*

1. To go forward, especially toward a conclusion. Also used with *along* : advance, get along, march[1], move, proceed, progress. *See* APPROACH. **2.** To take place at a set time : fall, occur. *See* HAPPEN. **3.** To take place : befall, betide, come about, come off, develop, hap, happen, occur, pass, transpire. ***Idiom:*** come to pass. *See* HAPPEN. **4.** To happen to one : befall, betide. *See* HAPPEN. **5.** To have as a source : arise, derive, emanate, flow, issue, originate, proceed, rise, spring, stem, upspring. *See* START. **6.** To have as one's home or place of origin : hail[2], originate. *See* START. **7.** To come to be : become, get, grow, turn (out), wax. *See* CHANGE.

come about *verb* To take place : befall, betide, come, come off, develop, hap, happen, occur, pass, transpire. ***Idiom:*** come to pass. *See* HAPPEN.

come across *verb* **1.** To find or meet by chance : bump into, chance on (*or* upon), come on (*or* upon), find, happen on (*or* upon), light on (*or* upon), run across, run into, stumble on (*or* upon), tumble on. *Archaic:* alight on (*or* upon). ***Idiom:*** meet up with. *See* MEET. **2.** *Slang.* To give in common with others : chip in, contribute, donate, subscribe. *Informal:* kick in. *See* GIVE.

come around (or **round**) *verb* To regain one's health : convalesce, gain, improve, mend, perk up, rally, recover, recuperate. *See* HEALTH.

come back *verb* To go again to a former place : go back, return, revisit. *See* APPROACH.

come by *verb* **1.** To come into possession of : acquire, gain, get, obtain, procure, secure, win. *Informal:* land, pick up. *See* GET. **2.** To go to or seek out the company of in order to socialize : call, come over, drop by, drop in, look in, look up, pop in, run in, see, stop (by *or* in), visit. ***Idiom:*** pay a visit. *See* SEEK.

come in *verb* **1.** To come or go into (a place) : enter, go in, penetrate. *Nautical:* put in. ***Idioms:*** gain entrance (*or* entry), set foot in. *See* ENTER. **2.** To complete a race or competition in a specified position : finish, place, run. *See* BE.

come into *verb* To receive (property) from one who has died : inherit. *See* GET, LAW.

come off *verb* **1.** To take place : befall, betide, come, come about, develop, hap, happen, occur, pass, transpire. ***Idiom:*** come to pass. *See* HAPPEN. **2.** To turn out well : go, go over, pan out, succeed, work, work out. *Slang:* click. *See* THRIVE.

come on (or **upon**) *verb* To find or meet by chance : bump into, chance on (*or* upon), come across, find, happen on (*or* upon), light on (*or* upon), run across, run into, stumble on (*or* upon), tumble on. *Archaic:* alight on (*or* upon). ***Idiom:*** meet up with. *See* MEET.

come out *verb* **1.** To be made public : break, get out, out, transpire. *Informal:* leak (out). ***Idiom:*** come to light. *See* KNOWLEDGE, SHOW. **2.** To make one's formal entry, as into society : debut. ***Idiom:*** make one's bow. *See* KNOWLEDGE.

come over *verb* To go to or seek out the company of in order to socialize : call, come by, drop by, drop in, look in, look up, pop in, run in, see, stop (by *or* in), visit. ***Idiom:*** pay a visit. *See* SEEK.

come through *verb* To exist in spite of adversity : last[2], persist, pull through, ride out, survive, weather. *See* LIVE.

come to *verb* To reach (a goal or objective) : arrive at, attain, gain, get to. *Informal:* hit on (*or* upon). *See* START.

come about *verb* See **come.**

come across *verb* See **come.**

come around or **round** *verb* See **come.**

comeback *noun*

1. A return to former prosperity or status : recovery. *See* APPROACH, WIN. **2.** A spirited, incisive reply : repartee, retort, riposte. *See* ASK.

come back *verb* See **come.**

come by *verb* See **come.**

comedian *noun*

A person whose words or actions provoke or are intended to provoke amusement or laughter : clown, comic, farceur, funnyman, humorist, jester, joker, jokester, quipster, wag[2], wit, zany. *Informal:* card. *See* LAUGHTER.

comedic *adjective*
Intended to excite laughter or amusement : facetious, funny, humorous, jocose, jocular, witty. *See* LAUGHTER.

comedown *noun*
A sudden drop to a lower condition or status : descent, down, downfall, downgrade. *See* RISE.

comedy *noun*
The quality of being laughable or comical : comicality, comicalness, drollery, drollness, farcicality, funniness, humor, humorousness, jocoseness, jocosity, jocularity, ludicrousness, ridiculousness, wit, wittiness, zaniness. *See* LAUGHTER.

come-hither *adjective*
Tending to seduce : alluring, bewitching, enticing, inveigling, inviting, luring, seductive, siren, tempting, witching. *See* LIKE, PERSUASION, SEX.

come in *verb* See **come.**

come into *verb* See **come.**

comeliness *noun*
Conformity to recognized standards, as of conduct or appearance : correctness, decency, decentness, decorousness, decorum, properness, propriety, respectability, respectableness, seemliness. *See* USUAL.

comely *adjective*
1. Having qualities that delight the eye : attractive, beauteous, beautiful, fair, good-looking, gorgeous, handsome, lovely, pretty, pulchritudinous, ravishing, sightly, stunning. *Scots:* bonny. ***Idiom:*** easy on the eyes. *See* BEAUTIFUL. **2.** Conforming to accepted standards : becoming, befitting, comme il faut, correct, decent, decorous, de rigueur, nice, proper, respectable, right, seemly. *See* COURTESY.

come off *verb* See **come.**

come-on *noun*
Something that attracts, especially with the promise of pleasure or reward : allurement, bait, enticement, inducement, inveiglement, invitation, lure, seduction, temptation. *See* LIKE.

come on or **upon** *verb* See **come.**

come out *verb* See **come.**

come over *verb* See **come.**

comer *noun*
1. One that arrives : arrival, visitor. *See* ENTER. **2.** One showing much promise : rising star, up-and-comer. *See* ABILITY.

comestible *adjective*
Fit to be eaten : eatable, edible, esculent. *See* INGESTION.
comestible *noun* Something fit to be eaten : aliment, bread, diet, edible, esculent, fare, food, foodstuff, meat, nourishment, nurture, nutriment, nutrition, pabulum, pap, provender, provision (used in plural), sustenance, victual. *Slang:* chow, eats, grub. *See* INGESTION.

come through *verb* See **come.**

come to *verb* See **come.**

comeuppance *noun*
Something justly deserved : desert[2] (often used in plural), due, guerdon, recompense, reward, wage (often used in plural). *Informal:* lump[1] (used in plural). ***Idioms:*** what is coming to one, what one has coming. *See* REWARD.

comfort *verb*
1. To give hope to in time of grief or pain : console, solace, soothe. *See* HELP. **2.** To make less severe or more bearable : allay, alleviate, assuage, ease, lessen, lighten[2], mitigate, palliate, relieve. *See* INCREASE.
comfort *noun* **1.** Steady good fortune or financial security : ease, prosperity, prosperousness. *Informal:* easy street. ***Idioms:*** comfortable (*or* easy) circumstances, the good life. *See* RICH, THRIVE. **2.** A consoling in time of grief or pain : consolation, solace. *See* HELP. **3.** Anything that increases physical comfort : amenity, convenience, facility (often used in plural). *See* COMFORT.

comfortable *adjective*
1. Affording pleasurable ease : cozy, easeful, easy, snug. *Informal:* comfy, soft. *See* GOOD. **2.** Being what is needed without being in excess : adequate, competent, decent, enough, satisfactory, sufficient. *See* EXCESS. **3.** Enjoying steady good fortune or financial security : easy, prosperous, well-heeled, well-off, well-to-do. *Informal:* well-fixed. ***Idioms:*** comfortably off, in clover, on easy street. *See* RICH, THRIVE.

comfortless *adjective*
Causing discomfort : uncomfortable, uncomforting. *Informal:* uncomfy. *See* COMFORT.

comfy *adjective*
Informal. Affording pleasurable ease : comfortable, cozy, easeful, easy, snug. *Informal:* soft. *See* GOOD.

comic *adjective*
1. Arousing laughter : amusing, comical, droll, funny, humorous, laughable, risible, zany. *See* LAUGHTER. **2.** Deserving laughter : comical, farcical, funny, laughable, laughing, ludicrous, ridiculous, risible. *See* LAUGHTER.
comic *noun* A person whose words or actions provoke or are intended to provoke amusement or laughter : clown, comedian, farceur, funnyman, humorist, jester, joker, jokester, quipster,

wag[2], wit, zany. *Informal:* card. *See* LAUGHTER.

comical *adjective*

1. Arousing laughter : amusing, comic, droll, funny, humorous, laughable, risible, zany. *See* LAUGHTER. **2.** Deserving laughter : comic, farcical, funny, laughable, laughing, ludicrous, ridiculous, risible. *See* LAUGHTER.

comicality *noun*

The quality of being laughable or comical : comedy, comicalness, drollery, drollness, farcicality, funniness, humor, humorousness, jocoseness, jocosity, jocularity, ludicrousness, ridiculousness, wit, wittiness, zaniness. *See* LAUGHTER.

comicalness *noun*

The quality of being laughable or comical : comedy, comicality, drollery, drollness, farcicality, funniness, humor, humorousness, jocoseness, jocosity, jocularity, ludicrousness, ridiculousness, wit, wittiness, zaniness. *See* LAUGHTER.

coming *adjective*

1. In the relatively near future : approaching, forthcoming, upcoming. *See* NEAR. **2.** Being or occurring in the time ahead : future, later, subsequent. *See* PRECEDE, TIME. **3.** Occurring right after another : following, next. *See* PRECEDE, TIME. **4.** Showing great promise : promising, up-and-coming. ***Idiom:*** on the way up. *See* INCREASE.

coming *noun* **1.** The act of arriving : advent, appearance, arrival. *See* START. **2.** The act or fact of coming near : approach, convergence, imminence, nearness. *See* APPROACH.

coming-out *noun*

The instance or occasion of being presented for the first time to society : debut, presentation. *See* KNOWLEDGE.

command *verb*

1. To give orders to : bid, charge, direct, enjoin, instruct, order, tell. *See* OVER, WORDS. **2.** To have at one's disposal : boast, enjoy, have, hold, possess. *See* OWNED. **3.** To have authoritative charge of : captain, lead. *See* PRECEDE. **4.** To rise above, especially so as to afford a view of : dominate, overlook, tower above (*or* over). *See* OVER.

command *noun* **1.** An authoritative indication to be obeyed : behest, bidding, charge, commandment, dictate, direction, directive, injunction, instruction (often used in plural), mandate, order, word. *See* OVER, WORDS. **2.** The right and power to command, decide, rule, or judge : authority, control, domination, dominion, jurisdiction, mastery, might, power, prerogative, sovereignty, sway. *Informal:* say-so. *See* OVER. **3.** The act of exercising controlling power or the condition of being so controlled : control, dominance, domination, dominion, mastery, reign, rule, sway. *See* OVER. **4.** The capacity to lead others : lead, leadership. *See* PRECEDE. **5.** Natural or acquired facility in a specific activity : ability, adeptness, art, craft, expertise, expertness, knack, mastery, proficiency, skill, technique. *Informal:* know-how. *See* ABILITY, KNOWLEDGE.

commandeer *verb*

1. To take quick and forcible possession of : confiscate, expropriate, grab, seize, snatch. ***Idiom:*** help oneself to. *See* GIVE. **2.** To lay claim to for oneself or as one's right : appropriate, arrogate, assume, preempt, seize, take, usurp. *See* GIVE.

commanding *adjective*

1. Exercising authority : authoritative, dominant, lordly, masterful. *See* OVER, STRONG. **2.** Exercising controlling power or influence : controlling, dominant, dominating, dominative, governing, paramount, preponderant, regnant, reigning, ruling. *See* OVER.

commandment *noun*

An authoritative indication to be obeyed : behest, bidding, charge, command, dictate, direction, directive, injunction, instruction (often used in plural), mandate, order, word. *See* OVER, WORDS.

comme il faut *adjective*

Conforming to accepted standards : becoming, befitting, comely, correct, decent, decorous, de rigueur, nice, proper, respectable, right, seemly. *See* COURTESY.

commemorate *verb*

1. To honor or keep alive the memory of : memorialize. *See* REMEMBER. **2.** To mark (a day or an event) with ceremonies of respect, festivity, or rejoicing : celebrate, keep, observe, solemnize. *See* REMEMBER.

commemoration *noun*

1. The act of observing a day or an event with ceremonies : celebration, observance. *See* REMEMBER. **2.** Something, as a structure or custom, serving to honor or keep alive a memory : memorial, monument, remembrance. *See* REMEMBER.

commemorative *adjective*

Serving to honor or keep alive a memory : memorial. *See* REMEMBER.

commence *verb*

1. To go about the initial step in doing (something) : approach, begin, embark, enter, get off, inaugurate, initiate, institute, launch, lead off, open, set about, set out, set to, start, take on, take up, undertake. *Informal:* kick off. ***Idioms:*** get cracking, get going, get the show on the road. *See* START. **2.** To come into being : arise, begin, originate, start. *See* START. **3.** To begin to appear or develop : appear, arise, dawn, emerge, originate. *See* START.

commencement *noun*
1. The act or process of bringing or being brought into existence : beginning, inauguration, inception, incipience, incipiency, initiation, launch, leadoff, opening, origination, start. *Informal:* kickoff. *See* START. **2.** The initial stage of a developmental process : beginning, birth, dawn, genesis, inception, nascence, nascency, onset, opening, origin, outset, spring, start. *See* START.

commend *verb*
1. To express warm approval of : acclaim, applaud, compliment, laud, praise. *See* PRAISE. **2.** To pay a compliment to : compliment, congratulate, praise. ***Idiom:*** take off one's hat to. *See* PRAISE. **3.** To put in the charge of another for care, use, or performance : commit, confide, consign, entrust, give (over), hand over, relegate, trust, turn over. ***Idiom:*** give in trust (*or* charge). *See* GIVE.

commendable *adjective*
Deserving honor, respect, or admiration : admirable, creditable, deserving, estimable, exemplary, honorable, laudable, meritorious, praiseworthy, reputable, respectable, worthy. *See* GOOD, PRAISE, RESPECT, VALUE.

commendation *noun*
1. An expression of warm approval : acclaim, acclamation, applause, celebration, compliment, encomium, eulogy, kudos, laudation, panegyric, plaudit, praise. *See* PRAISE. **2.** An expression of admiration or congratulation : compliment, congratulation (often used in plural), praise, tribute. *See* PRAISE.

commendatory *adjective*
Serving to compliment : acclamatory, approbatory, complimentary, congratulatory, laudatory. *See* PRAISE.

commensurable *adjective*
Properly or correspondingly related in size, amount, or scale : commensurate, proportional, proportionate. ***Idiom:*** in proportion. *See* BIG.

commensurate *adjective*
Properly or correspondingly related in size, amount, or scale : commensurable, proportional, proportionate. ***Idiom:*** in proportion. *See* BIG.

comment *noun*
1. Critical explanation or analysis : annotation, commentary, exegesis, interpretation, note. *See* WORDS. **2.** An expression of fact or opinion : note, obiter dictum, observation, remark. *See* WORDS.
comment *verb* To state facts, opinions, or explanations : note, observe, remark. *See* WORDS.

commentary *noun*
1. Critical explanation or analysis : annotation, comment, exegesis, interpretation, note. *See* WORDS. **2.** A narrative of experiences undergone by the writer. Often used in plural : memoir, reminiscence (often used in plural). *See* WORDS.

commentator *noun*
A person who evaluates and reports on the worth of something : critic, judge, reviewer. *See* VALUE.

commerce *noun*
Commercial, industrial, or professional activity in general : business, industry, trade, trading, traffic. *See* ACTION.

commingle *verb*
To put together into one mass so that the constituent parts are more or less homogeneous : admix, amalgamate, blend, commix, fuse, intermingle, intermix, merge, mingle, mix, stir[1]. *See* ASSEMBLE.

commiserate *verb*
To experience or express compassion : ache, compassionate, feel, pity, sympathize, yearn. ***Idioms:*** be sorry, have (*or* take) pity. *See* PITY.

commiseration *noun*
Sympathetic, sad concern for someone in misfortune : compassion, condolence, empathy, pity, sympathy. *See* PITY.

commiserative *adjective*
Feeling or expressing pity : compassionate, condolatory, pitying, sympathetic. *Archaic:* piteous, pitiful. *See* FEELINGS, PITY.

commission *noun*
An assignment one is sent to carry out : errand, mission. *See* WORK.
commission *verb* To give authority to : accredit, authorize, empower, enable, entitle, license, qualify. *See* ALLOW.

commit *verb*
1. To be responsible for or guilty of (an error or crime) : perpetrate. *Informal:* pull off. *See* DO, LAW. **2.** To put in the charge of another for care, use, or performance : commend, confide,

consign, entrust, give (over), hand over, relegate, trust, turn over. ***Idiom:*** give in trust (*or* charge). *See* GIVE. **3.** To place officially in confinement : consign, institutionalize. *Informal:* send up. *See* FREE. **4.** To be morally bound to do : bind, charge, obligate, pledge. *See* OBLIGATION.

commitment *noun*
An act or course of action that is demanded of one, as by position, custom, law, or religion : burden[1], charge, duty, imperative, must, need, obligation, responsibility. *See* OBLIGATION.

commix *verb*
To put together into one mass so that the constituent parts are more or less homogeneous : admix, amalgamate, blend, commingle, fuse, intermingle, intermix, merge, mingle, mix, stir[1]. *See* ASSEMBLE.

commixture *noun*
Something produced by mixing : admixture, amalgam, amalgamation, blend, fusion, merger, mix, mixture. *See* ASSEMBLE.

commodious *adjective*
Having plenty of room : ample, capacious, roomy, spacious. *See* BIG.

commodity *noun*
A product or products bought and sold in commerce : good (used in plural), line, merchandise, ware. *See* MATTER, TRANSACTIONS.

common *adjective*
1. Belonging to, shared by, or applicable to all alike : communal, conjoint, general, joint, mutual, public. *See* GROUP. **2.** Belonging or relating to the whole : general, generic, universal. *See* SPECIFIC. **3.** Occurring quite often : everyday, familiar, frequent, regular, routine, widespread. *See* USUAL. **4.** Commonly encountered : average, commonplace, general, normal, ordinary, typical, usual. *See* SURPRISE. **5.** Lacking high station or birth : baseborn, déclassé, declassed, humble, ignoble, lowly, mean[2], plebeian, unwashed, vulgar. *Archaic:* base[2]. *See* OVER. **6.** Being of no special quality or type : average, commonplace, cut-and-dried, formulaic, garden, garden-variety, indifferent, mediocre, ordinary, plain, routine, run-of-the-mill, standard, stock, undistinguished, unexceptional, unremarkable. *See* GOOD, USUAL. **7.** Of moderately good quality but less than excellent : acceptable, adequate, all right, average, decent, fair, fairish, goodish, moderate, passable, respectable, satisfactory, sufficient, tolerable. *Informal:* OK, tidy. *See* GOOD. **8.** Of low or lower quality : inferior, low-grade, low-quality, mean[2], mediocre, second-class, second-rate, shabby, substandard. *See* BETTER. **9.** Known widely and unfavorably : infamous, notorious. *See* KNOWLEDGE.

common *noun* **1.** The common people. Used in plural : commonality, commonalty, commoner (used in plural), crowd, hoi polloi, mass (used in plural), mob, pleb (used in plural), plebeian (used in plural), populace, public, ruck[1], third estate. *See* OVER. **2.** A tract of cultivated land belonging to and used by a community : green. *See* GROUP.

commonality *noun*
The common people : common (used in plural), commonalty, commoner (used in plural), crowd, hoi polloi, mass (used in plural), mob, pleb (used in plural), plebeian (used in plural), populace, public, ruck[1], third estate. *See* OVER.

commonalty *noun*
The common people : common (used in plural), commonality, commoner (used in plural), crowd, hoi polloi, mass (used in plural), mob, pleb (used in plural), plebeian (used in plural), populace, public, ruck[1], third estate. *See* OVER.

commoner *noun*
The common people. Used in plural : common (used in plural), commonality, commonalty, crowd, hoi polloi, mass (used in plural), mob, pleb (used in plural), plebeian (used in plural), populace, public, ruck[1], third estate. *See* OVER.

commonly *adverb*
In an expected or customary manner; for the most part : consistently, customarily, frequently, generally, habitually, naturally, normally, often, regularly, routinely, typically, usually. ***Idioms:*** as usual, per usual. *See* BIG, USUAL.

commonplace *adjective*
1. Commonly encountered : average, common, general, normal, ordinary, typical, usual. *See* SURPRISE. **2.** Being of no special quality or type : average, common, cut-and-dried, formulaic, garden, garden-variety, indifferent, mediocre, ordinary, plain, routine, run-of-the-mill, standard, stock, undistinguished, unexceptional, unremarkable. *See* GOOD, USUAL. **3.** Without freshness or appeal because of overuse : banal, bromidic, clichéd, corny, hackneyed, musty, overused, overworked, platitudinal, platitudinous, shopworn, stale, stereotyped, stereotypic, stereotypical, threadbare, timeworn, tired, trite, warmed-over, well-worn, worn-out. *See* EXCITE, USUAL.

commonplace *noun* **1.** A trite expression or idea : banality, bromide, cliché, platitude, stereotype, truism. *See* SURPRISE. **2.** A regular or customary matter, condition, or course of events : norm, ordinary, rule, usual. *See* USUAL.

common sense *noun*
The ability to make sensible decisions : judgment, sense, wisdom. *Informal:* gumption, horse sense. *See* ABILITY.

commonsensible *adjective*
Possessing, proceeding from, or exhibiting good judgment and prudence : balanced, commonsensical, judicious, levelheaded, prudent, rational, reasonable, sagacious, sage, sane, sapient, sensible, sound[2], well-founded, well-grounded, wise[1]. *See* REASON, SANE.

commonsensical *adjective*
Possessing, proceeding from, or exhibiting good judgment and prudence : balanced, commonsensible, judicious, levelheaded, prudent, rational, reasonable, sagacious, sage, sane, sapient, sensible, sound[2], well-founded, well-grounded, wise[1]. *See* REASON, SANE.

commotion *noun*
1. The condition of being physically agitated : agitation, convulsion, turbulence. *See* CALM. **2.** An interruption of regular procedure or of public peace : agitation, disorder, disturbance, helter-skelter, stir[1], tumult, turbulence, turmoil, uproar. *Informal:* flap, to-do. *See* CALM, ORDER.

communal *adjective*
Belonging to, shared by, or applicable to all alike : common, conjoint, general, joint, mutual, public. *See* GROUP.

communalize *verb*
To place under government or group ownership or control : nationalize, socialize. *See* POLITICS, SPECIFIC.

communicable *adjective*
1. Capable of transmission by infection : catching, contagious, infectious, taking. *See* MOVE. **2.** Disposed to be open, sociable, and talkative : communicative, expansive, extraverted, extroverted, gregarious, outgoing, unreserved. *See* ATTITUDE.

communicate *verb*
1. To make known : break, carry, convey, disclose, get across, impart, pass, report, tell, transmit. *See* KNOWLEDGE. **2.** To give expression to, as by gestures, facial aspects, or bodily posture : convey, display, express, manifest. *See* SHOW. **3.** To put into words : articulate, convey, declare, express, say, state, talk, tell, utter[1], vent, verbalize, vocalize, voice. ***Idiom:*** give tongue (*or* vent *or* voice) to. *See* WORDS. **4.** To cause (a disease) to pass to another or others : carry, convey, give, pass, spread, transmit. *See* MOVE. **5.** To interact with another or others in a meaningful fashion : connect, relate. *Slang:* click. ***Idioms:*** be on the same wavelength, hit it off. *See* CONNECT.

communication *noun*
1. The exchange of ideas by writing, speech, or signals : communion, intercommunication, intercourse. *Obsolete:* converse[1]. *See* KNOWLEDGE. **2.** Something communicated, as information : message, word. *See* WORDS. **3.** A situation allowing exchange of ideas or messages : contact, intercommunication, touch. *See* CONNECT, TOUCH.

communicative *adjective*
Disposed to be open, sociable, and talkative : communicable, expansive, extraverted, extroverted, gregarious, outgoing, unreserved. *See* ATTITUDE.

communion *noun*
1. The exchange of ideas by writing, speech, or signals : communication, intercommunication, intercourse. *Obsolete:* converse[1]. *See* KNOWLEDGE. **2.** Those who accept and practice a particular religious belief : church, denomination, faith, persuasion, sect. *See* RELIGION.

community *noun*
Persons as an organized body : people, public, society. *See* SPECIFIC.

commutation *noun*
The act of exchanging or substituting : change, exchange, interchange, shift, substitution, switch, trade, transposition. *Informal:* swap. *See* CHANGE, SUBSTITUTE.

commute *verb*
To give up in return for something else : change, exchange, interchange, shift, substitute, switch, trade. *Informal:* swap. *See* CHANGE, SUBSTITUTE.

comp *noun*
Informal. A free ticket entitling one to transportation or admission : pass. *Slang:* freebie. *See* ENTER, TRANSACTIONS.

compact[1] *adjective*
1. Having all parts near to each other : close, crowded, dense, packed, thick, tight. *See* TIGHTEN. **2.** Precisely meaningful and tersely cogent : aphoristic, epigrammatic, epigrammatical, marrowy, pithy. *Informal:* brass-tacks. ***Idioms:*** down to brass tacks, to the point. *See* MEANING, STYLE. **3.** Short, heavy, and solidly built : blocky, chunky, dumpy, heavyset, squat, stocky, stodgy, stubby, stumpy, thick, thickset. *See* FAT.

compact *verb* **1.** To subject to compression : compress, constrict, constringe, squeeze. *See* TIGHTEN. **2.** To reduce in size, as by drawing together : compress, constrict, constringe, contract, shrink. *See* INCREASE.

compact² *noun*
1. An act or state of agreeing between parties regarding a course of action : accord, agreement, arrangement, bargain, deal, pact, understanding. *See* AGREE. **2.** A legally binding arrangement between parties : agreement, bond, contract, convention, covenant, pact. *See* AGREE. **3.** An agreement, especially one involving a sale or exchange : bargain, contract, covenant, deal, transaction. *See* AGREE.

compactness *noun*
The quality, condition, or degree of being thick : density, solidity, thickness. *See* THICK.

companion *noun*
1. One who shares interests or activities with another : associate, chum, comrade, crony, fellow, mate. *Informal:* buddy, pal. *See* NEAR. **2.** One that accompanies another : accompaniment, associate, attendant, concomitant. *See* ACCOMPANIED. **3.** One of a matched pair of things : counterpart, double, duplicate, fellow, match, mate, twin. *See* SAME.

companion *verb* To be with or go with (another) : accompany, attend, company, escort. *Obsolete:* consort. ***Idiom:*** go hand in hand with. *See* ACCOMPANIED.

companionable *adjective*
1. Liking company : convivial, sociable, social. *Chiefly British:* matey. *See* ATTITUDE. **2.** Spent, marked by, or enjoyed in the company of others : convivial, sociable, social. *See* ATTITUDE, PARTICIPATE.

companionless *adjective*
Lacking the company of others : alone, lone, lonely, lonesome, single, solitary, unaccompanied. *See* INCLUDE.

companionship *noun*
1. A pleasant association among people : company, fellowship, society. *See* CONNECT, GROUP. **2.** The condition of being friends : chumminess, closeness, comradeship, familiarity, fellowship, friendship, intimacy. *See* LOVE.

company *noun*
1. A number of persons who have come or been gathered together : assemblage, assembly, body, conclave, conference, congregation, congress, convention, convocation, crowd, gathering, group, meeting, muster, troop. *Informal:* get-together. *See* COLLECT. **2.** A person or persons visiting one : guest, visitant, visitor. *See* ACCOMPANIED. **3.** A pleasant association among people : companionship, fellowship, society. *See* CONNECT, GROUP. **4.** A commercial organization : business, concern, corporation, enterprise, establishment, firm², house. *Informal:* outfit. *See* GROUP. **5.** A group of people acting together in a shared activity : band², corps, party, troop, troupe. *See* PERFORMING ARTS.

company *verb* To be with or go with (another) : accompany, attend, companion, escort. *Obsolete:* consort. ***Idiom:*** go hand in hand with. *See* ACCOMPANIED.

comparable *adjective*
Possessing the same or almost the same characteristics : alike, analogous, corresponding, equivalent, like², parallel, similar, uniform. *See* SAME.

comparative *adjective*
Estimated by comparison : relative. *See* SAME.

compare *verb*
1. To represent as similar : analogize, assimilate, equate, identify, liken, match, parallel. *See* SAME. **2.** To examine in order to note the similarities and differences of : balance, collate. *See* SAME. **3.** To be equal or alike : correspond, equal, match, measure up, parallel, touch. *Informal:* stack up. *See* SAME.

comparison *noun*
The quality or state of being alike : affinity, alikeness, analogy, correspondence, likeness, parallelism, resemblance, similarity, similitude, uniformity, uniformness. *See* SAME.

compass *noun*
1. A line around a closed figure or area : ambit, circuit, circumference, perimeter, periphery. *See* EDGE. **2.** The ability or power to seize or attain : capacity, grasp, range, reach, scope. *See* ABILITY. **3.** An area within which something or someone exists, acts, or has influence or power : ambit, extension, extent, orbit, purview, range, reach, realm, scope, sphere, sweep, swing. *See* TERRITORY.

compass *verb* **1.** To encircle with or as if with a band : band¹, begird, belt, cincture, encompass, engirdle, gird, girdle, girt, ring¹. *Archaic:* engird. *See* EDGE. **2.** To shut in on all sides : begird, beset, circle, encircle, encompass, environ, gird, girdle, hedge, hem, ring¹, surround. *See* OPEN. **3.** To perceive and recognize the meaning of : accept, apprehend, catch (on), comprehend, conceive, fathom, follow, get, grasp, make out, read, see, sense, take, take in, understand. *Informal:* savvy. *Slang:* dig. *Chiefly British:* twig. *Scots:* ken. ***Idioms:*** get (*or* have) a handle on, get the picture. *See* UNDERSTAND. **4.** To perceive directly with the intellect : apprehend, comprehend, fathom, grasp, know, understand. *Scots:* ken. *See* KNOWLEDGE.

compassion *noun*
Sympathetic, sad concern for someone in misfortune : commiseration, condolence, empathy, pity, sympathy. *See* PITY.

compassionate *adjective*
1. Feeling or expressing pity : commiserative, condolatory, pitying, sympathetic. *Archaic:* piteous, pitiful. *See* FEELINGS, PITY. **2.** Concerned with human welfare and the alleviation of suffering : charitable, human, humane, humanitarian, merciful. *See* ATTITUDE, KIND.
compassionate *verb* To experience or express compassion : ache, commiserate, feel, pity, sympathize, yearn. ***Idioms:*** be sorry, have (*or* take) pity. *See* PITY.

compassionless *adjective*
Completely lacking in compassion : callous, cold-blooded, cold-hearted, hard, hard-boiled, hardened, hardhearted, heartless, obdurate, stonyhearted, unfeeling. *See* ATTITUDE.

compatible *adjective*
In keeping with one's needs or expectations : accordant, agreeable, conformable, congenial, congruous, consistent, consonant, correspondent, corresponding, harmonious. *See* AGREE.

compatriot *noun*
A person who is from one's own country : countryman, countrywoman, fellow citizen. *See* GROUP.

compeer *noun*
One that is very similar to another in rank or position : coequal, colleague, equal, equivalent, fellow, peer[2]. *See* SAME.

compel *verb*
To cause (a person or thing) to act or move in spite of resistance : coerce, constrain, force, make, obligate, oblige, pressure. *See* ATTACK.

compendious *adjective*
Marked by or consisting of few words that are carefully chosen : brief, concise, laconic, lean[2], short, succinct, summary, terse. *See* BIG, STYLE, WORDS.

compensate *verb*
1. To act as an equalizing weight or force to : balance, counteract, counterbalance, counterpoise, countervail, make up, offset, set off. *See* ORDER. **2.** To make up for : balance, counterbalance, counterpoise, countervail, neutralize, offset, outweigh, redeem, set off. *See* SUBSTITUTE. **3.** To give compensation to : indemnify, pay, recompense, redress, reimburse, remunerate, repay, requite. *See* PAY. **4.** To give payment to in return for goods or services rendered : pay, recompense, remunerate. *See* PAY. **5.** To give a satisfactory return to : indemnify, pay, recompense, remunerate, repay, requite, reward. *See* PAY.

compensation *noun*
1. Payment for work done : earnings, emolument, fee, hire, pay, remuneration, salary, stipend, wage. *See* PAY. **2.** Something given in exchange for goods or services rendered : consideration, payment, recompense, remuneration. *See* PAY. **3.** Something to make up for loss or damage : amends, indemnification, indemnity, offset, quittance, recompense, redress, reimbursement, remuneration, reparation, repayment, requital, restitution, satisfaction, setoff. *See* SUBSTITUTE.

compensative *adjective*
Affording compensation : compensatory, remunerative. *See* SUBSTITUTE.

compensatory *adjective*
Affording compensation : compensative, remunerative. *See* SUBSTITUTE.

compete *verb*
To strive against (others) for victory : contend, contest, emulate, rival, vie. *See* CONFLICT.

competence *noun*
1. Physical, mental, financial, or legal power to perform : ability, capability, capacity, competency, faculty, might. *See* ABILITY. **2.** *Law.* Conferred power : authority, faculty, mandate, right. *Law:* competency. *See* ABILITY.

competency *noun*
1. Physical, mental, financial, or legal power to perform : ability, capability, capacity, competence, faculty, might. *See* ABILITY. **2.** *Law.* Conferred power : authority, faculty, mandate, right. *Law:* competence. *See* ABILITY.

competent *adjective*
1. Having the ability to perform well : able, capable, good, skilled, skillful. *See* ABILITY.
2. Being what is needed without being in excess : adequate, comfortable, decent, enough, satisfactory, sufficient. *See* EXCESS.

competition *noun*
1. A vying with others for victory or supremacy : battle, contest, corrivalry, race, rivalry, strife, striving, struggle, tug of war, war, warfare. *See* CONFLICT. **2.** A trial of skill or ability : contest, meet[1]. *See* CONFLICT. **3.** One that competes : competitor, contender, contestant, corrival, opponent, rival. *See* CONFLICT.

competitive *adjective*
Given to competition : emulous. *See* CONFLICT.

competitor *noun*
One that competes : competition, contender, contestant, corrival, opponent, rival. *See* CONFLICT.

complain *verb*
To express negative feelings, especially of dissatisfaction or resentment : grouch, grump, whine. *Informal:* crab, gripe, grouse, kick. *Slang:* beef, bellyache, bitch. *See* FEELINGS, HAPPY.

complainant *noun*
One that makes a formal complaint, especially in court : accuser, claimant, plaintiff. *See* LAW.

complainer *noun*
A person who habitually complains or grumbles : crab, faultfinder, grouch, growler, grumbler, grump, murmurer, mutterer, whiner. *Informal:* crank, griper, grouser. *Slang:* bellyacher, sorehead, sourpuss. *See* HAPPY.

complaint *noun*
1. An expression of dissatisfaction or a circumstance regarded as a cause for such expression : grievance. *Informal:* gripe, grouse. *Slang:* beef, kick. ***Idiom:*** bone to pick. *See* HAPPY. **2.** A pathological condition of mind or body : ailment, disease, disorder, ill, illness, infirmity, malady, sickness. *See* HEALTH. **3.** A minor illness, especially one of a temporary nature : ailment, bug, indisposition, malady. *See* HEALTH.

complaisant *adjective*
Ready to do favors for another : accommodating, agreeable, indulgent, obliging. *See* HELP, WILLING.

complement *noun*
1. Something that completes another : supplement. *See* AGREE, PART. **2.** Something added to another for embellishment or completion : accompaniment, enhancement, enrichment. *See* ACCOMPANIED.
complement *verb* To supply what is lacking : complete, fill in (*or* out), round (off *or* out), supplement. *See* AGREE, PART.

complemental *adjective*
Forming or serving as a complement : complementary, supplemental. *See* AGREE, PART.

complementary *adjective*
Forming or serving as a complement : complemental, supplemental. *See* AGREE, PART.

complete *adjective*
1. Lacking nothing essential or normal : entire, full, intact, integral, perfect, whole. *See* PART. **2.** Including every constituent or individual : all, entire, gross, total, whole. *See* PART. **3.** Not shortened by omissions : unabbreviated, unabridged, uncensored, uncut, unexpurgated. *See* PART. **4.** Not more or less : entire, full, good, perfect, round, whole. *See* PART, PRECISE. **5.** Having reached completion : done, through. *See* PART. **6.** Covering all aspects with painstaking accuracy : all-out, exhaustive, full-dress, intensive, thorough, thoroughgoing, thoroughpaced. *See* BIG, CAREFUL. **7.** Completely such, without qualification or exception : absolute, all-out, arrant, consummate, crashing, damned, dead, downright, flat, out-and-out, outright, perfect, plain, pure, sheer[2], thorough, thoroughgoing, total, unbounded, unequivocal, unlimited, unmitigated, unqualified, unrelieved, unreserved, utter[2]. *Informal:* flat-out, positive. *Chiefly British:* blooming. *See* BIG, LIMITED.
complete *verb* **1.** To bring or come to a natural or proper end : close, conclude, consummate, end, finish, terminate, wind up, wrap up. *See* START. **2.** To supply what is lacking : complement, fill in (*or* out), round (off *or* out), supplement. *See* AGREE, PART.

completely *adverb*
1. To the fullest extent : absolutely, all, altogether, dead, entirely, flat, fully, just, perfectly, quite, thoroughly, totally, utterly, well[2], wholly. *Informal:* clean, clear. ***Idioms:*** in toto, through and through. *See* BIG, LIMITED. **2.** In a complete manner : exhaustively, intensively, thoroughly. ***Idioms:*** in and out, inside out, up and down. *See* PART, LIMITED.

completeness *noun*
The state of being entirely whole : entirety, integrity, oneness, totality, wholeness. *See* PART.

completion *noun*
A concluding or terminating : cease, cessation, close, closing, closure, conclusion, consummation, end, ending, end of the line, finish, period, stop, stopping point, termination, terminus, wind-up, wrap-up. *See* CONTINUE.

complex *adjective*
1. Consisting of two or more interconnected parts : composite, compound. *See* SIMPLE. **2.** Difficult to understand because of intricacy : byzantine, complicated, convoluted, daedal, Daedalian, elaborate, intricate, involute, involved, knotty, labyrinthine, tangled. *See* SIMPLE.
complex *noun* **1.** A usually large entity composed of interconnected parts : system. *See* PART. **2.** A center of organization, supply, or activity : base[1], headquarters, station.

Military: installation. *See* PLACE. **3.** An exaggerated concern : *Informal:* hang-up. *See* FEAR.

complexion *noun*

1. Skin tone, especially of the face : color, coloring. *See* COLORS. **2.** The combination of emotional, intellectual, and moral qualities that distinguishes an individual : character, disposition, makeup, nature, personality. *See* BE. **3.** A person's customary manner of emotional response : disposition, humor, nature, temper, temperament. *See* BE.

complexity *noun*

Something complex : complication, intricacy. *See* SIMPLE.

compliance *noun*

1. An act of willingly carrying out the wishes of others : obedience, observance. *See* RESIST. **2.** The quality or state of willingly carrying out the wishes of others : acquiescence, amenability, amenableness, compliancy, deference, obedience, submission, submissiveness, tractability, tractableness. *See* RESIST.

compliancy *noun*

The quality or state of willingly carrying out the wishes of others : acquiescence, amenability, amenableness, compliance, deference, obedience, submission, submissiveness, tractability, tractableness. *See* RESIST.

compliant *adjective*

Willing to carry out the wishes of others : amenable, biddable, conformable, docile, obedient, submissive, supple, tractable. *See* RESIST.

complicate *verb*

To make complex, intricate, or perplexing : embarrass, entangle, involve, perplex, ravel, snarl[2], tangle. *See* SIMPLE.

complicated *adjective*

1. Complexly detailed : elaborate, fancy, intricate. *See* PLAIN. **2.** Difficult to understand because of intricacy : byzantine, complex, convoluted, daedal, Daedalian, elaborate, intricate, involute, involved, knotty, labyrinthine, tangled. *See* SIMPLE.

complication *noun*

Something complex : complexity, intricacy. *See* SIMPLE.

compliment *noun*

1. An expression of admiration or congratulation : commendation, congratulation (often used in plural), praise, tribute. *See* PRAISE. **2.** An expression of warm approval : acclaim, acclamation, applause, celebration, commendation, encomium, eulogy, kudos, laudation, panegyric, plaudit, praise. *See* PRAISE. **3.** An act requiring special generosity : beau geste, courtesy, favor. *See* GIVE.

compliment *verb* **1.** To pay a compliment to : commend, congratulate, praise. ***Idiom:*** take off one's hat to. *See* PRAISE. **2.** To express warm approval of : acclaim, applaud, commend, laud, praise. *See* PRAISE.

complimentary *adjective*

1. Serving to compliment : acclamatory, approbatory, commendatory, congratulatory, laudatory. *See* PRAISE. **2.** Costing nothing : free, gratis, gratuitous. ***Idiom:*** on the house. *See* MONEY.

comply *verb*

To act in conformity with : abide by, adhere, carry out, conform, follow, keep, mind, obey, observe. ***Idiom:*** toe the line (*or* mark). *See* ACCEPT, SAME.

component *noun*

One of the individual entities contributing to a whole : building block, constituent, element, factor, ingredient, integrant, part. *See* PART.

component *adjective* Serving as part of a whole, as a nondetachable part of a larger unit : built-in, constituent, incorporated. *See* INCLUDE.

comport *verb*

To conduct oneself in a specified way : acquit, act, bear, behave, carry, demean[1], deport, do, quit. *See* BE.

comport with *verb* To be compatible or in correspondence : accord, agree, check, chime, conform, consist, correspond, fit[1], harmonize, match, square, tally. *Informal:* jibe[1]. *Archaic:* quadrate. *See* AGREE.

comportment *noun*

The manner in which one behaves : action (often used in plural), behavior, conduct, deportment, way. *See* BE.

comport with *verb* See **comport.**

compose *verb*

1. To be the constituent parts of : constitute, form, make (up). *See* BE. **2.** To create by combining parts or elements : build, configure, form, pattern, shape, structure. *See* MAKE. **3.** To form by artistic effort : create, indite, produce, write. *See* MAKE. **4.** To bring one's emotions under control : collect[1], contain, control, cool, simmer down. ***Idiom:*** cool it. *See* RESTRAINT.

composed *adjective*

Not easily excited, even under pressure : calm, collected, cool, cool-headed, detached, even[1], even-tempered, imperturbable, nonchalant, possessed, unflappable, unruffled. *See* CALM.

composite *adjective*
Consisting of two or more interconnected parts : complex, compound. *See* SIMPLE.
composite *noun* The result of combining : combination, compound, conjugation, unification, union, unity. *See* ASSEMBLE.

composition *noun*
1. Something that is the result of creative effort : opus, piece, production, work. *See* MAKE. **2.** A relatively brief discourse written especially as an exercise : essay, paper, theme. *See* WORDS. **3.** *Law.* A settlement of differences through mutual concession : accommodation, arrangement, compromise, give-and-take, medium, settlement. *See* AGREE.

compos mentis *adjective*
Mentally healthy : lucid, rational, sane. ***Idioms:*** all there, in one's right mind, of sound mind. *See* SANE.

composure *noun*
A stable, calm state of the emotions : aplomb, balance, collectedness, coolness, equanimity, imperturbability, imperturbableness, nonchalance, poise, sang-froid, self-possession, unflappability. *Slang:* cool. *See* CALM, FEELINGS.

compound *verb*
To bring or come together into a united whole : coalesce, combine, concrete, conjoin, conjugate, connect, consolidate, couple, join, link, marry, meld, unify, unite, wed, yoke. *See* ASSEMBLE.
compound *adjective* Consisting of two or more interconnected parts : complex, composite. *See* SIMPLE.
compound *noun* The result of combining : combination, composite, conjugation, unification, union, unity. *See* ASSEMBLE.

comprehend *verb*
1. To perceive and recognize the meaning of : accept, apprehend, catch (on), compass, conceive, fathom, follow, get, grasp, make out, read, see, sense, take, take in, understand. *Informal:* savvy. *Slang:* dig. *Chiefly British:* twig. *Scots:* ken. ***Idioms:*** get (*or* have) a handle on, get the picture. *See* UNDERSTAND. **2.** To perceive directly with the intellect : apprehend, compass, fathom, grasp, know, understand. *Scots:* ken. *See* KNOWLEDGE. **3.** To have as a part : comprise, contain, embody, embrace, encompass, have, include, involve, subsume, take in. *See* INCLUDE.

comprehensible *adjective*
Capable of being readily understood : fathomable, intelligible, knowable, understandable. *See* KNOWLEDGE.

comprehension *noun*
Intellectual hold : apprehension, grasp, grip, hold, understanding. *Informal:* savvy. *See* KNOWLEDGE.

comprehensive *adjective*
Covering a wide scope : all-around, all-inclusive, all-round, broad, broad-spectrum, expansive, extended, extensive, far-ranging, far-reaching, general, global, inclusive, large, overall, sweeping, wide-ranging, wide-reaching, widespread. *See* SPECIFIC.

compress *verb*
1. To subject to compression : compact[1], constrict, constringe, squeeze. *See* TIGHTEN. **2.** To reduce in size, as by drawing together : compact[1], constrict, constringe, contract, shrink. *See* INCREASE.

compression *noun*
A compressing of something : constriction, squeeze. *See* TIGHTEN.

comprise *verb*
To have as a part : comprehend, contain, embody, embrace, encompass, have, include, involve, subsume, take in. *See* INCLUDE.

compromise *noun*
A settlement of differences through mutual concession : accommodation, arrangement, give-and-take, medium, settlement. *Law:* composition. *See* AGREE.
compromise *verb* **1.** To make a concession : concede. ***Idioms:*** give and take, go fifty-fifty, meet someone halfway. *See* AGREE. **2.** To expose to possible loss or damage : adventure, hazard, risk, venture. *See* SAFETY.

compulsion *noun*
Power used to overcome resistance : coercion, constraint, duress, force, pressure, strength, violence. *See* ATTACK.

compulsory *adjective*
1. Imposed on one by authority, command, or convention : imperative, mandatory, necessary, obligatory, required, requisite. *See* OBLIGATION. **2.** Done under force : forced. *See* WILLING.

compunction *noun*
1. A feeling of regret for one's sins or misdeeds : contriteness, contrition, penitence, penitency, remorse, remorsefulness, repentance, rue. *Theology:* attrition. *See* REGRET. **2.** A feeling of uncertainty about the fitness or correctness of an action : misgiving, qualm, reservation, scruple. *See* CERTAIN.

compunctious *adjective*
Feeling or expressing regret for one's sins or misdeeds : contrite, penitent, penitential, re-

gretful, remorseful, repentant, sorry. *See* REGRET.

computation *noun*
1. The act, process, or result of calculating : calculation, figuring, reckoning. *See* REASON. **2.** Arithmetic calculations : arithmetic, figure (used in plural), number (used in plural). *See* COUNT.

compute *verb*
To ascertain by mathematics : calculate, cast, cipher, figure, reckon. *See* REASON.

comrade *noun*
One who shares interests or activities with another : associate, chum, companion, crony, fellow, mate. *Informal:* buddy, pal. *See* NEAR.

comradeship *noun*
The condition of being friends : chumminess, closeness, companionship, familiarity, fellowship, friendship, intimacy. *See* LOVE.

con *verb*
1. To apply one's mind to the acquisition or production of knowledge : lucubrate, study. *See* TEACH. **2.** To look at carefully or critically : check (out), examine, go over, inspect, peruse, scrutinize, study, survey, traverse, view. *Informal:* case. ***Idiom:*** give a going-over. *See* INVESTIGATE. **3.** To commit to memory : learn, memorize. *See* REMEMBER.

concatenate *verb*
To make into a whole by joining a system of parts : articulate, integrate. *See* INCLUDE, PART.

concave *adjective*
Curving inward : cavernous, hollow, indented, sunken. *See* CONVEX.

concavity *noun*
An area sunk below its surroundings : basin, depression, dip, hollow, pit[1], sag, sink, sinkhole. *See* CONVEX.

conceal *verb*
1. To cut off from sight : block (out), hide[1], obscure, obstruct, screen, shroud, shut off (*or* out). *See* SHOW. **2.** To prevent (something) from being known : cloak, cover (up), enshroud, hide[1], hush (up), mask, shroud, veil. ***Idioms:*** keep under cover, keep under wraps. *See* SHOW. **3.** To put or keep out of sight : bury, cache, ensconce, hide[1], occult, secrete. *Slang:* plant, stash. *See* SHOW.

concealed *adjective*
1. Screened from the view of oncoming drivers : blind, hidden. *See* SHOW. **2.** Lying beyond what is obvious or avowed : buried, covert, hidden, obscured, ulterior. ***Idiom:*** under cover (*or* wraps). *See* SHOW.

concealment *noun*
The habit, practice, or policy of keeping secrets : clandestineness, clandestinity, covertness, huggermugger, huggermuggery, secrecy, secretiveness, secretness. *See* SHOW.

concede *verb*
1. To recognize, often reluctantly, the reality or truth of : acknowledge, admit, avow, confess, grant, own (up). *Slang:* fess up. *Chiefly Regional:* allow. *See* AFFIRM, KNOWLEDGE. **2.** To let have as a favor, prerogative, or privilege : accord, award, give, grant, vouchsafe. *See* GIVE. **3.** To make a concession : compromise. ***Idioms:*** give and take, go fifty-fifty, meet someone halfway. *See* AGREE. **4.** To cease opposition : give in, yield. *See* WIN.

conceit *noun*
1. A regarding of oneself with undue favor : amour-propre, ego, egoism, egotism, narcissism, pride, vainglory, vainness, vanity. *Slang:* ego trip. *See* SELF-LOVE. **2.** An impulsive, often illogical turn of mind : bee, boutade, caprice, fancy, freak, humor, impulse, megrim, notion, vagary, whim, whimsy. ***Idiom:*** bee in one's bonnet. *See* THOUGHTS.

conceit *verb Chiefly British.* To find agreeable : fancy, like[1], take to. *See* LIKE.

conceited *adjective*
1. Thinking too highly of oneself : egoistic, egoistical, egotistic, egotistical, narcissistic, vain, vainglorious. *Informal:* bigheaded, stuck-up, swellheaded. *See* SELF-LOVE. **2.** Unduly preoccupied with one's own appearance : narcissistic, vain. *See* SELF-LOVE.

conceivable *adjective*
Capable of being anticipated, considered, or imagined : earthly, imaginable, likely, mortal, possible, thinkable. ***Idioms:*** humanly possible, within the bounds (*or* range *or* realm) of possibility. *See* POSSIBLE.

conceive *verb*
1. To form mental images of : envisage, envision, fancy, fantasize, image, imagine, picture, see, think, vision, visualize. *Informal:* feature. *See* THOUGHTS. **2.** To form a strategy for : blueprint, cast, chart, contrive, design, devise, formulate, frame, lay[1], plan, project, scheme, strategize, work out. *Informal:* dope out. ***Idiom:*** lay plans. *See* PLANNED. **3.** To perceive and recognize the meaning of : accept, apprehend, catch (on), compass, comprehend, fathom, follow, get, grasp, make out, read, see, sense, take, take in, understand. *Informal:* savvy. *Slang:* dig. *Chiefly British:* twig. *Scots:*

ken. ***Idioms:*** get (*or* have) a handle on, get the picture. *See* UNDERSTAND.

concentrate *verb*
1. To direct toward a common center : center, channel, converge, focalize, focus. *See* EDGE. **2.** To devote (oneself or one's efforts) : address, apply, bend, buckle down, dedicate, devote, direct, focus, give, turn. *See* COLLECT, WORK.

concentrated *adjective*
1. Not diffused or dispersed : exclusive, intensive, undivided, unswerving, whole. *See* EDGE, COLLECT, PART. **2.** Intensely sustained, especially in activity : fierce, heavy, heightened, intense, intensive. *See* STRONG. **3.** Having a high concentration of the distinguishing ingredient : potent, stiff, strong. *See* STRONG.

concentration *noun*
1. A converging at a common center : confluence, conflux, convergence. *See* EDGE. **2.** Concentration of the mental powers on something : attention, attentiveness, consideration, heedfulness, regardfulness. *See* EXCITE.

concept *noun*
That which exists in the mind as the product of careful mental activity : conception, idea, image, notion, perception, thought. *See* THOUGHTS.

conception *noun*
That which exists in the mind as the product of careful mental activity : concept, idea, image, notion, perception, thought. *See* THOUGHTS.

conceptual *adjective*
Existing only in the imagination : chimeric, chimerical, fanciful, fantastic, fantastical, imaginary, notional, unreal, visionary. *See* REAL.

concern *verb*
1. To be pertinent : appertain, apply, bear on (*or* upon), pertain, refer, relate. ***Idioms:*** have a bearing on, have to do with. *See* RELEVANT. **2.** To cause anxious uneasiness in : ail, cark, distress, trouble, worry. *See* CONCERN.

concern *noun* **1.** Something that concerns or involves one personally : affair, business, lookout. *See* RELEVANT. **2.** A cause of distress or anxiety : care, trouble, worry. *See* CONCERN. **3.** Thoughtful attention : attentiveness, consideration, regard, solicitude, thoughtfulness. *See* ATTITUDE, CONCERN, KIND, TREAT WELL. **4.** Curiosity about or attention to someone or something : concernment, interest, interestedness, regard. *See* CONCERN. **5.** The quality or state of being important : concernment, consequence, import, importance, moment, significance, significancy, weight, weightiness. *See* IMPORTANT. **6.** A troubled or anxious state of mind : angst, anxiety, anxiousness, care, disquiet, disquietude, distress, nervousness, solicitude, unease, uneasiness, worry. *See* FEELINGS. **7.** A commercial organization : business, company, corporation, enterprise, establishment, firm[2], house. *Informal:* outfit. *See* GROUP. **8.** A small specialized mechanical device : contraption, contrivance, gadget, gimmick, jigger, thing. *Informal:* doodad, doohickey, widget. *Slang:* gizmo. *See* MACHINE.

concerned *adjective*
1. Having concern : affected, interested, involved. *See* CONCERN. **2.** In a state of anxiety or uneasiness : agitated, anxious, distressed, nervous, solicitous, uneasy, unsettled. *See* FEELINGS.

concernment *noun*
1. The fact of being related to the matter at hand : applicability, application, appositeness, bearing, germaneness, materiality, pertinence, pertinency, relevance, relevancy. *See* RELEVANT. **2.** The quality or state of being important : concern, consequence, import, importance, moment, significance, significancy, weight, weightiness. *See* IMPORTANT. **3.** Curiosity about or attention to someone or something : concern, interest, interestedness, regard. *See* CONCERN.

concert *noun*
Pleasing agreement, as of musical sounds : accord, concord, harmony, symphony, tune. *Music:* consonance. *See* BEAUTIFUL.

concession *noun*
An accommodation made in the light of special or extenuating circumstances : allowance. *See* AGREE.

conciliate *verb*
1. To ease the anger or agitation of : appease, assuage, calm (down), dulcify, gentle, mollify, pacify, placate, propitiate, soften, soothe, sweeten. ***Idiom:*** pour oil on troubled water. *See* CALM. **2.** To reestablish friendship between : make up, reconcile, reunite. *See* LOVE.

conciliation *noun*
A reestablishment of friendship or harmony : rapprochement, reconcilement, reconciliation. *See* LOVE.

concise *adjective*
Marked by or consisting of few words that are carefully chosen : brief, compendious, laconic, lean[2], short, succinct, summary, terse. *See* BIG, STYLE, WORDS.

conclave *noun*
A number of persons who have come or been

gathered together : assemblage, assembly, body, company, conference, congregation, congress, convention, convocation, crowd, gathering, group, meeting, muster, troop. *Informal:* get-together. *See* COLLECT.

conclude *verb*
1. To bring or come to a natural or proper end : close, complete, consummate, end, finish, terminate, wind up, wrap up. *See* START. **2.** To bring about or come to an agreement concerning : arrange, fix, negotiate, set[1], settle. *See* AGREE. **3.** To put into correct or conclusive form : arrange, dispose of, fix, settle. *See* DO. **4.** To make up or cause to make up one's mind : decide, determine, resolve, settle. *See* DECIDE. **5.** To arrive at (a conclusion) from evidence or reasoning : deduce, deduct, draw, gather, infer, judge, understand. *See* REASON.

concluding *adjective*
Coming after all others : closing, final, last[1], terminal. *See* START.

conclusion *noun*
1. A concluding or terminating : cease, cessation, close, closing, closure, completion, consummation, end, ending, end of the line, finish, period, stop, stopping point, termination, terminus, wind-up, wrap-up. *See* CONTINUE. **2.** The last part : close, end, ending, finale, finish, last[1], termination, wind-up, wrap-up. *See* START. **3.** A position reached after consideration : decision, determination, resolution. *See* DECIDE. **4.** A position arrived at by reasoning from premises or general principles : deduction, illation, illative, inference, judgment. *See* REASON.

conclusive *adjective*
1. Determining or having the power to determine an outcome : crucial, deciding, decisive, determinative. *See* DECIDE, IMPORTANT. **2.** Serving the function of deciding or settling with finality : authoritative, decisive, definitive, determinative, final. *See* DECIDE. **3.** Having or arising from authority : authoritative, official, sanctioned, standard. *See* TRUE.

conclusively *adverb*
In conclusion : finally, last[1], lastly. *See* START.

concoct *verb*
To use ingenuity in making, developing, or achieving : contrive, devise, dream up, fabricate, formulate, hatch, invent, make up, think up. *Informal:* cook up. ***Idiom:*** come up with. *See* MAKE.

concomitant *adjective*
Occurring or existing with : accompanying, attendant, attending, coincident, concurrent. *See* ACCOMPANIED.

concomitant *noun* One that accompanies another : accompaniment, associate, attendant, companion. *See* ACCOMPANIED.

concord *noun*
1. Harmonious mutual understanding : accord, agreement, concordance, concurrence, consonance, harmony, rapport, tune, unity. ***Idiom:*** meeting of the minds. *See* AGREE. **2.** Pleasing agreement, as of musical sounds : accord, concert, harmony, symphony, tune. *Music:* consonance. *See* BEAUTIFUL. **3.** A formal, usually written settlement between nations : accord, agreement, convention, pact, treaty. *See* AGREE, POLITICS.

concordance *noun*
Harmonious mutual understanding : accord, agreement, concord, concurrence, consonance, harmony, rapport, tune, unity. ***Idiom:*** meeting of the minds. *See* AGREE.

concourse *noun*
The act or fact of coming together : confluence, convergence, gathering, junction, meeting. *See* CONNECT.

concrete *adjective*
1. Having verifiable existence : objective, real, substantial, substantive, tangible. *See* REAL. **2.** Composed of or relating to things that occupy space and can be perceived by the senses : corporeal, material, objective, phenomenal, physical, sensible, substantial, tangible. *See* BODY, MATTER.

concrete *verb* **1.** To bring or come together into a united whole : coalesce, combine, compound, conjoin, conjugate, connect, consolidate, couple, join, link, marry, meld, unify, unite, wed, yoke. *See* ASSEMBLE. **2.** To make or become physically hard : cake, congeal, dry, harden, indurate, petrify, set[1], solidify. *See* SOLID.

concupiscence *noun*
Sexual hunger : amativeness, desire, eroticism, erotism, itch, libidinousness, lust, lustfulness, passion, prurience, pruriency. *See* DESIRE, SEX.

concupiscent *adjective*
Feeling or devoted to sexual love or desire : amative, amorous, erotic, lascivious, lecherous, lewd, libidinous, lustful, lusty, passionate, prurient, sexy. *See* SEX.

concur *verb*
1. To come to an understanding or to terms : accord, agree, coincide, get together, harmo-

nize. *See* AGREE. **2.** To occur at the same time : coincide, synchronize. *See* NEAR.

concurrence *noun*
Harmonious mutual understanding : accord, agreement, concord, concordance, consonance, harmony, rapport, tune, unity. ***Idiom:*** meeting of the minds. *See* AGREE.

concurrent *adjective*
1. Belonging to the same period of time as another : coetaneous, coeval, coexistent, contemporaneous, contemporary, synchronic, synchronous. *See* TIME. **2.** Occurring or existing with : accompanying, attendant, attending, coincident, concomitant. *See* ACCOMPANIED.

concurrently *adverb*
At the same time : simultaneously, synchronously, together. ***Idioms:*** all at once, all together. *See* ACCOMPANIED, TIME.

concussion *noun*
Violent forcible contact between two or more things : bump, collision, crash, impact, jar, jolt, percussion, shock[1], smash. *See* CONFLICT.

condemn *verb*
1. To feel or express strong disapproval of : censure, denounce, deplore, reprehend, reprobate. *See* PRAISE. **2.** To pronounce judgment against : damn, doom, sentence. *See* LAW.

condemnable *adjective*
Worthy of severe disapproval : deplorable, disgraceful, shameful, unfortunate. *See* GOOD.

condemnation *noun*
A comment expressing fault : blame, censure, criticism, denunciation, reprehension, reprobation. *Informal:* pan. *Slang:* knock. *See* PRAISE.

condemned *adjective*
Sentenced to terrible, irrevocable punishment : doomed, fated, foredoomed, lost. *See* LAW, RELIGION.

condensation *noun*
A short summary or version prepared by cutting down a larger work : abridgment, abstract, brief, epitome, synopsis. *See* WORDS.

condense *verb*
1. To make short or shorter the duration or extent of : abbreviate, abridge, curtail, reduce, shorten. *See* INCREASE, LONG. **2.** To make thick or thicker, especially through evaporation or condensation : inspissate, thicken. *See* SOLID.

condescend *verb*
1. To descend to a level considered inappropriate to one's dignity : deign, stoop, vouchsafe. *See* OVER, RISE. **2.** To treat in a superciliously indulgent manner : patronize. *Informal:* high-hat. ***Idiom:*** speak (*or* talk) down to. *See* ATTITUDE, OVER, RESPECT, RISE.

condescendence *noun*
Superciliously indulgent treatment, especially of those considered inferior : condescension, patronization. *See* ATTITUDE, RESPECT, RISE.

condescension *noun*
Superciliously indulgent treatment, especially of those considered inferior : condescendence, patronization. *See* ATTITUDE, RESPECT, RISE.

condiment *noun*
A substance that imparts taste : flavor, flavoring, seasoner, seasoning, spice. *See* TASTE.

condition *noun*
1. Manner of being or form of existence : mode, situation, state, status. *See* BE. **2.** A state of sound readiness : fettle, fitness, form, kilter, order, shape, trim. *See* BETTER. **3.** Something indispensable : essential, must, necessity, need, precondition, prerequisite, requirement, requisite, sine qua non. *See* NECESSARY. **4.** A restricting or modifying element : provision, proviso, qualification, reservation, specification, stipulation, term (often used in plural). *Informal:* string (often used in plural). *See* LIMITED. **5.** Existing surroundings that affect an activity. Used in plural : circumstance (often used in plural), environment. *Slang:* scene. *See* BE.

condition *verb* To make familiar through constant practice or use : accustom, habituate, inure, wont. *See* USUAL.

conditional *adjective*
1. Depending on or containing a condition or conditions : provisional, provisory, tentative. *See* LIMITED. **2.** Determined or to be determined by someone or something else : conditioned, contingent, dependent, relative, reliant, subject. *See* START.

conditioned *adjective*
Determined or to be determined by someone or something else : conditional, contingent, dependent, relative, reliant, subject. *See* START.

condolatory *adjective*
Feeling or expressing pity : commiserative, compassionate, pitying, sympathetic. *Archaic:* piteous, pitiful. *See* FEELINGS, PITY.

condolence *noun*
Sympathetic, sad concern for someone in misfortune : commiseration, compassion, empathy, pity, sympathy. *See* PITY.

condonation *noun*
The act or an instance of forgiving : absolution, amnesty, excuse, forgiveness, pardon, remission. *See* FORGIVENESS.

condone *verb*
To grant forgiveness to or for : excuse, forgive, pardon, remit. ***Idiom:*** forgive and forget. *See* FORGIVENESS.

conduce *verb*
To have a share, as in an act or result; have a hand in : contribute, partake, participate, share. ***Idiom:*** take part. *See* PARTICIPATE, START.

conducive *adjective*
Tending to contribute to a result : contributive, contributory. *See* PARTICIPATE.

conduct *verb*
1. To control the course of (an activity) : carry on, direct, manage, operate, run, steer. *See* OVER. **2.** To engage in (a war or campaign, for example) : carry on, carry out, wage. *See* DO. **3.** To show the way to : direct, escort, guide, lead, pilot, route, shepherd, show, steer, usher. *See* SHOW. **4.** To serve as a conduit : carry, channel, convey, transmit. *See* ALLOW.
conduct *noun* The manner in which one behaves : action (often used in plural), behavior, comportment, deportment, way. *See* BE.

conductor *noun*
Something or someone that shows the way : director, escort, guide, lead, leader, pilot, shepherd, usher. *See* SHOW.

confab *noun*
Informal. Spoken exchange : chat, colloquy, confabulation, conversation, converse[1], dialogue, discourse, speech, talk. *Slang:* jaw. *See* WORDS.
confab *verb Informal.* To engage in spoken exchange : chat, confabulate, converse[1], discourse, speak, talk. *Informal:* visit. *See* WORDS.

confabulate *verb*
To engage in spoken exchange : chat, converse[1], discourse, speak, talk. *Informal:* confab, visit. *See* WORDS.

confabulation *noun*
Spoken exchange : chat, colloquy, conversation, converse[1], dialogue, discourse, speech, talk. *Informal:* confab. *Slang:* jaw. *See* WORDS.

confabulator *noun*
One given to conversation : conversationalist, conversationist, discourser, talker. *See* WORDS.

confabulatory *adjective*
In the style of conversation : chatty, colloquial, conversational, informal. *See* WORDS.

confederacy *noun*
An association, especially of nations for a common cause : alliance, Anschluss, bloc, cartel, coalition, confederation, federation, league, organization, union. *See* CONNECT, GROUP, POLITICS.

confederate *noun*
1. One nation associated with another in a common cause : ally, coalitionist, leaguer. *See* CONNECT, POLITICS. **2.** One who is united in a relationship with another : affiliate, ally, associate, cohort, colleague, copartner, fellow, partner. *See* CONNECT. **3.** One who assists a lawbreaker in a wrongful or criminal act : accessory, accomplice, conspirator. *See* CRIMES, HELP.
confederate *verb* To be formally associated, as by treaty : align, ally, federate, league. *See* CONNECT, POLITICS.

confederation *noun*
1. An association, especially of nations for a common cause : alliance, Anschluss, bloc, cartel, coalition, confederacy, federation, league, organization, union. *See* CONNECT, GROUP, POLITICS. **2.** A group of people united in a relationship and having some interest, activity, or purpose in common : association, club, congress, federation, fellowship, fraternity, guild, league, order, organization, society, sorority, union. *See* GROUP.

confer *verb*
1. To meet and exchange views to reach a decision : advise, consult, deliberate, parley, talk. *Informal:* powwow. *See* COLLECT, MEET, WORDS. **2.** To give formally or officially : accord, award, bestow, grant, present[2]. *See* GIVE.

conferee also **conferree** *noun*
One who participates in a conference : discussant, discusser. *See* MEET, WORDS.

conference *noun*
1. A meeting for the exchange of views : colloquium, discussion, parley, seminar. *Informal:* powwow. *Slang:* rap session. *See* MEET, WORDS. **2.** A number of persons who have come or been gathered together : assemblage, assembly, body, company, conclave, congregation, congress, convention, convocation, crowd, gathering, group, meeting, muster, troop. *Informal:* get-together. *See* COLLECT. **3.** A formal assemblage of the members of a group : assembly, congress, convention, convocation, meeting. *See* ASSEMBLE. **4.** An exchanging of views : discussion, ventilation. *Slang:* rap[3]. *See* WORDS. **5.** An exchange of views in an attempt to reach a decision : consultation, counsel, deliberation, parley. *See* WORDS. **6.** A group of athletic teams that play each other : association, circuit, league, loop. *See* GROUP. **7.** The act of conferring, as of an honor : accordance,

bestowal, bestowment, conferment, conferral, grant, presentation. *See* GIVE.

conferment *noun*
The act of conferring, as of an honor : accordance, bestowal, bestowment, conference, conferral, grant, presentation. *See* GIVE.

conferral *noun*
The act of conferring, as of an honor : accordance, bestowal, bestowment, conference, conferment, grant, presentation. *See* GIVE.

conferree *noun* See **conferee.**

confess *verb*
To recognize, often reluctantly, the reality or truth of : acknowledge, admit, avow, concede, grant, own (up). *Slang:* fess up. *Chiefly Regional:* allow. *See* AFFIRM, KNOWLEDGE.

confession *noun*
1. The act of admitting to something : acknowledgment, admission, avowal. *See* AFFIRM, KNOWLEDGE, SHOW. **2.** A system of religious belief : creed, denomination, faith, persuasion, religion, sect. *See* RELIGION.

confessor *noun*
One in whom secrets are confided : confidant, confidante, repository. *See* SHOW, WORDS.

confidant *noun*
1. One in whom secrets are confided : confessor, confidante, repository. *See* SHOW, WORDS. **2.** A person whom one knows well, likes, and trusts : amigo, brother, chum, confidante, familiar, friend, intimate[1], mate. *Informal:* bud[2], buddy, pal. *Slang:* sidekick. *See* LOVE.

confidante *noun*
1. One in whom secrets are confided : confessor, confidant, repository. *See* SHOW, WORDS. **2.** A person whom one knows well, likes, and trusts : amigo, brother, chum, confidant, familiar, friend, intimate[1], mate. *Informal:* bud[2], buddy, pal. *Slang:* sidekick. *See* LOVE.

confide *verb*
1. To tell in confidence : breathe, whisper. *See* SHOW, WORDS. **2.** To put in the charge of another for care, use, or performance : commend, commit, consign, entrust, give (over), hand over, relegate, trust, turn over. ***Idiom:*** give in trust (*or* charge). *See* GIVE.

confidence *noun*
1. Absolute certainty in the trustworthiness of another : belief, dependence, faith, reliance, trust. *See* BELIEF. **2.** A firm belief in one's own powers : aplomb, assurance, self-assurance, self-confidence, self-possession. *See* ATTITUDE, BELIEF. **3.** The fact or condition of being without doubt : assurance, assuredness, certainty, certitude, conviction, positiveness, sureness, surety. *See* CERTAIN.

confident *adjective*
1. Having no doubt : assured, certain, positive, sure, undoubting. *See* CERTAIN. **2.** Having a firm belief in one's own powers : assured, secure, self-assured, self-confident, self-possessed. *See* ATTITUDE, BELIEF.

confidential *adjective*
1. Known about by very few : auricular, inside, private, secret. *Informal:* hush-hush. *See* SHOW. **2.** Indicating intimacy and mutual trust : familiar, intimate[1]. *See* ATTITUDE, NEAR. **3.** Of or being information available only to authorized persons : classified, privileged, restricted. *See* SHOW.

configuration *noun*
The external outline of a thing : cast, figure, form, pattern, shape. *See* SURFACE.

configure *verb*
To create by combining parts : build, compose, form, pattern, shape, structure. *See* MAKE.

confine *verb*
1. To place a limit on : circumscribe, limit, restrict. *See* LIMITED. **2.** To shut in with or as if with bars : bar, lock, wall. *See* FREE. **3.** To enclose so as to hinder or prohibit escape : closet, imprison, shut up. *See* FREE. **4.** To put in jail : detain, immure, imprison, incarcerate, intern, jail, lock (up). *See* FREE.

confine *noun* **1.** A demarcation point or boundary beyond which something does not extend or occur. Used in plural : bound[2] (often used in plural), end, limit. *See* EDGE. **2.** The boundary surrounding a certain area. Used in plural : bound[2] (used in plural), limit (used in plural), precinct (often used in plural). *See* LIMITED.

confinement *noun*
1. The state of being detained by legal authority : charge, custody, detention, ward. *See* FREE. **2.** The act of limiting or condition of being limited : circumscription, constraint, limitation, restraint, restriction. *See* LIMITED.

confining *adjective*
Affording little room for movement : close, cramped, crowded, narrow, snug, tight. *See* TIGHTEN.

confirm *verb*
1. To assure the certainty or validity of : attest, authenticate, back (up), bear out, corroborate, evidence, justify, substantiate, testify (to), validate, verify, warrant. *See* SUPPORT, TRUE. **2.** To establish as true or genuine : authenti-

cate, bear out, corroborate, demonstrate, endorse, establish, evidence, prove, show, substantiate, validate, verify. *See* SHOW, SUPPORT. **3.** To make firmer in a particular conviction or habit : fortify, harden, strengthen. *See* STRONG. **4.** To accept officially : adopt, affirm, approve, pass, ratify, sanction. *See* ACCEPT, LAW.

confirmation *noun*
1. An act of confirming officially : affirmation, approval, ratification, sanction. *See* LAW. **2.** That which confirms : attestation, authentication, corroboration, demonstration, evidence, proof, substantiation, testament, testimonial, testimony, validation, verification, warrant. *See* TRUE.

confirmed *adjective*
1. Subject to a disease or habit for a long time : chronic, habitual, habituated, inveterate. *See* CONTINUE. **2.** Firmly established by long standing : deep-rooted, deep-seated, entrenched, hard-shell, ineradicable, ingrained, inveterate, irradicable, set[1], settled. *See* CONTINUE.

confiscate *verb*
To take quick and forcible possession of : commandeer, expropriate, grab, seize, snatch. *Idiom:* help oneself to. *See* GIVE.

confiscation *noun*
The act of taking quick and forcible possession of : expropriation, seizure. *See* GIVE.

conflagrant *adjective*
On fire : ablaze, afire, aflame, alight[2], burning, fiery, flaming. *Idioms:* in a blaze, in flames. *See* HOT.

conflagration *noun*
The visible signs of combustion : blaze[1], fire, flame, flare-up. *See* HOT.

conflict *noun*
1. A state of open, prolonged fighting : belligerency, confrontation, hostility (used in plural), strife, struggle, war, warfare. *See* CONFLICT. **2.** A state of disagreement and disharmony : clash, confrontation, contention, difference, difficulty, disaccord, discord, discordance, dissension, dissent, dissentience, dissidence, dissonance, faction, friction, inharmony, schism, strife, variance, war, warfare. *See* CONFLICT.
conflict *verb* To fail to be in accord : clash, contradict, disaccord, discord, jar. *Idiom:* go (*or* run) counter to. *See* AGREE.

confluence *noun*
1. A converging at a common center : concentration, conflux, convergence. *See* EDGE. **2.** The act or fact of coming together : concourse, convergence, gathering, junction, meeting. *See* CONNECT.

conflux *noun*
A converging at a common center : concentration, confluence, convergence. *See* EDGE.

conform *verb*
1. To be compatible or in correspondence : accord, agree, check, chime, comport with, consist, correspond, fit[1], harmonize, match, square, tally. *Informal:* jibe[1]. *Archaic:* quadrate. *See* AGREE. **2.** To be in keeping with : become, befit, correspond, fit[1], go with, match, suit. *See* AGREE. **3.** To make or become suitable to a particular situation or use : acclimate, acclimatize, accommodate, adapt, adjust, fashion, fit[1], reconcile, square, suit, tailor. *See* CHANGE. **4.** To bring into accord : accommodate, attune, coordinate, harmonize, integrate, proportion, reconcile, tune. *See* AGREE. **5.** To act in conformity with : abide by, adhere, carry out, comply, follow, keep, mind, obey, observe. *Idiom:* toe the line (*or* mark). *See* ACCEPT, SAME. **6.** To make conventional : conventionalize, stylize. *See* USUAL.

conformable *adjective*
1. In keeping with one's needs or expectations : accordant, agreeable, compatible, congenial, congruous, consistent, consonant, correspondent, corresponding, harmonious. *See* AGREE. **2.** Willing to carry out the wishes of others : amenable, biddable, compliant, docile, obedient, submissive, supple, tractable. *See* RESIST.

conformance *noun*
The act or state of agreeing or conforming : accordance, agreement, chime, conformation, conformity, congruence, congruity, correspondence, harmonization, harmony, keeping. *See* AGREE.

conformation *noun*
1. The act of making suitable to an end or the condition of being made suitable to an end : accommodation, adaptation, adaption, adjustment. *See* CHANGE. **2.** The act or state of agreeing or conforming : accordance, agreement, chime, conformance, conformity, congruence, congruity, correspondence, harmonization, harmony, keeping. *See* AGREE.

conformist *adjective*
Conforming to established practice or standards : button-down, conventional, establishmentarian, orthodox, straight, traditional. *Slang:* square. *See* USUAL.

conformity *noun*
The act or state of agreeing or conforming : accordance, agreement, chime, conformance,

conformation, congruence, congruity, correspondence, harmonization, harmony, keeping. *See* AGREE.

confound *verb*

1. To cause to be unclear in mind or intent : addle, befuddle, bewilder, confuse, discombobulate, dizzy, fuddle, jumble, mix up, muddle, mystify, perplex, puzzle. *Informal:* throw. ***Idiom:*** make one's head reel (*or* swim *or* whirl). *See* CLEAR, FEELINGS. **2.** To cause (a person) to be self-consciously distressed : abash, chagrin, confuse, discomfit, discomfort, disconcert, discountenance, embarrass, faze, mortify. ***Idioms:*** put on the spot, throw for a loop. *See* PAIN. **3.** To make incapable of finding something to think, do, or say : nonplus. *Informal:* flummox, stick, stump, throw. *Slang:* beat. ***Idiom:*** put someone at a loss. *See* AFFECT, KNOWLEDGE. **4.** To take (one thing) mistakenly for another : confuse, mistake, mix up. *See* CORRECT.

confounded *adjective*

1. Mentally uncertain : addled, addlepated, confused, confusional, muddle-headed, perplexed, turbid. *Informal:* mixed-up. *See* CLEAR. **2.** So annoying or detestable as to deserve condemnation : accursed, blasted, blessed, bloody, cursed, damn, darn, execrable, infernal. *Informal:* blamed, damned. *Chiefly British:* blooming, ruddy. *See* LIKE.

confront *verb*

1. To meet face-to-face, especially defiantly : accost, encounter, face, front. *See* MEET. **2.** To come up against : encounter, face, meet[1], run into. *See* MEET.

confrontation *noun*

1. A face-to-face, usually hostile meeting : encounter, face-off. *See* MEET. **2.** A state of open, prolonged fighting : belligerency, conflict, hostility (used in plural), strife, struggle, war, warfare. *See* CONFLICT. **3.** A state of disagreement and disharmony : clash, conflict, contention, difference, difficulty, disaccord, discord, discordance, dissension, dissent, dissentience, dissidence, dissonance, faction, friction, inharmony, schism, strife, variance, war, warfare. *See* CONFLICT.

confuse *verb*

1. To cause to be unclear in mind or intent : addle, befuddle, bewilder, confound, discombobulate, dizzy, fuddle, jumble, mix up, muddle, mystify, perplex, puzzle. *Informal:* throw. ***Idiom:*** make one's head reel (*or* swim *or* whirl). *See* CLEAR, FEELINGS. **2.** To cause (a person) to be self-consciously distressed : abash, chagrin, confound, discomfit, discomfort, disconcert, discountenance, embarrass, faze, mortify. ***Idioms:*** put on the spot, throw for a loop. *See* PAIN. **3.** To take (one thing) mistakenly for another : confound, mistake, mix up. *See* CORRECT. **4.** To put into total disorder : ball up, disorder, jumble, mess up, muddle, scramble, snarl[2]. *Slang:* snafu. ***Idiom:*** play havoc with. *See* ORDER.

confused *adjective*

1. Mentally uncertain : addled, addlepated, confounded, confusional, muddle-headed, perplexed, turbid. *Informal:* mixed-up. *See* CLEAR. **2.** Characterized by physical confusion : chaotic, disordered, helter-skelter, higgledy-piggledy, topsy-turvy, upside-down. *Informal:* mixed-up. *See* ORDER.

confusedness *noun*

A lack of order or regular arrangement : chaos, clutter, confusion, derangement, disarrangement, disarray, disorder, disorderedness, disorderliness, disorganization, jumble, mess, mix-up, muddle, muss, scramble, topsy-turviness, tumble. *Slang:* snafu. *See* ORDER.

confusion *noun*

1. Self-conscious distress : abashment, chagrin, discomfiture, discomposure, embarrassment. *See* PAIN. **2.** A lack of order or regular arrangement : chaos, clutter, confusedness, derangement, disarrangement, disarray, disorder, disorderedness, disorderliness, disorganization, jumble, mess, mix-up, muddle, muss, scramble, topsy-turviness, tumble. *Slang:* snafu. *See* ORDER.

confusional *adjective*

Mentally uncertain : addled, addlepated, confounded, confused, muddle-headed, perplexed, turbid. *Informal:* mixed-up. *See* CLEAR.

confute *verb*

To prove or show to be false : belie, discredit, disprove, rebut, refute. *See* AFFIRM.

congeal *verb*

1. To make or become physically hard : cake, concrete, dry, harden, indurate, petrify, set[1], solidify. *See* SOLID. **2.** To change or be changed from a liquid into a soft, semisolid, or solid mass : clot, coagulate, curdle, gelatinize, jell, jelly, set[1]. *See* SOLID.

congener *noun*

Something closely resembling or analogous to something else : analogue, correlate, correlative, correspondent, counterpart, match, parallel. *See* SAME.

congenial *adjective*

1. Pleasant and friendly in disposition : affable,

agreeable, amiable, cordial, genial, good-natured, good-tempered, pleasant, sociable, warm. *See* ATTITUDE, GOOD. **2.** To one's liking : agreeable, favorable, good, grateful, gratifying, nice, pleasant, pleasing, pleasurable, satisfying, welcome. *See* LIKE. **3.** In keeping with one's needs or expectations : accordant, agreeable, compatible, conformable, congruous, consistent, consonant, correspondent, corresponding, harmonious. *See* AGREE.

congeniality *noun*
The quality of being pleasant and friendly : affability, agreeability, agreeableness, amenity, amiability, amiableness, congenialness, cordiality, cordialness, friendliness, geniality, genialness, pleasantness, sociability, sociableness, warmth. *See* ATTITUDE, GOOD.

congenialness *noun*
The quality of being pleasant and friendly : affability, agreeability, agreeableness, amenity, amiability, amiableness, congeniality, cordiality, cordialness, friendliness, geniality, genialness, pleasantness, sociability, sociableness, warmth. *See* ATTITUDE, GOOD.

congenital *adjective*
1. Possessed at birth : hereditary, inborn, inherited, innate, native. *See* BE, NATIVE.
2. Forming an essential element, as arising from the basic structure of an individual : built-in, connatural, constitutional, elemental, inborn, inbred, indigenous, indwelling, ingrained, inherent, innate, intrinsic, native, natural. *See* BE, NATIVE, START.

congeries *noun*
A quantity accumulated : accumulation, aggregation, amassment, assemblage, collection, cumulation, gathering, mass. *See* COLLECT.

congest *verb*
To plug up something, as a hole, space, or container : block, choke, clog, close, cork, fill, plug, stop. *See* FULL.

conglomeration *noun*
A collection of various things : assortment, gallimaufry, hodgepodge, jumble, medley, mélange, miscellany, mishmash, mixed bag, mixture, olio, patchwork, potpourri, salmagundi, variety. *Slang:* grab bag. *See* COLLECT.

congratulate *verb*
1. To pay a compliment to : commend, compliment, praise. ***Idiom:*** take off one's hat to. *See* PRAISE. **2.** To be proud of (oneself), as for an accomplishment or achievement : plume, preen, pride. *See* RESPECT.

congratulation *noun*
An expression of admiration or congratulation. Often used in plural : commendation, compliment, praise, tribute. *See* PRAISE.

congratulatory *adjective*
Serving to compliment : acclamatory, approbatory, commendatory, complimentary, laudatory. *See* PRAISE.

congregate *verb*
1. To bring together : assemble, call, cluster, collect[1], convene, convoke, gather, get together, group, muster, round up, summon. *See* COLLECT. **2.** To come together : assemble, cluster, collect[1], convene, forgather, gather, get together, group, muster. *See* COLLECT.

congregation *noun*
A number of persons who have come or been gathered together : assemblage, assembly, body, company, conclave, conference, congress, convention, convocation, crowd, gathering, group, meeting, muster, troop. *Informal:* get-together. *See* COLLECT.

congress *noun*
1. A formal assemblage of the members of a group : assembly, conference, convention, convocation, meeting. *See* ASSEMBLE. **2.** A number of persons who have come or been gathered together : assemblage, body, company, conclave, conference, congregation, convention, convocation, crowd, gathering, group, meeting, muster, troop. *Informal:* get-together. *See* COLLECT.
3. A group of people united in a relationship and having some interest, activity, or purpose in common : association, club, confederation, federation, fellowship, fraternity, guild, league, order, organization, society, sorority, union. *See* GROUP.

congruence *noun*
The act or state of agreeing or conforming : accordance, agreement, chime, conformance, conformation, conformity, congruity, correspondence, harmonization, harmony, keeping. *See* AGREE.

congruity *noun*
1. The act or state of agreeing or conforming : accordance, agreement, chime, conformance, conformation, conformity, congruence, correspondence, harmonization, harmony, keeping. *See* AGREE. **2.** Logical agreement among parts : coherence, consistence, consistency. *See* AGREE.

congruous *adjective*
1. In keeping with one's needs or expectations : accordant, agreeable, compatible, conformable, congenial, consistent, consonant, correspondent, corresponding, harmonious. *See* AGREE.

2. Having components pleasingly combined : balanced, harmonious, symmetrical. *See* BEAUTIFUL.

conjectural *adjective*
Presumed to be true, real, or genuine, especially on inconclusive grounds : hypothetic, hypothetical, inferential, presumptive, supposed, suppositional, suppositious, supposititious, suppositive. *See* BELIEF.

conjecture *noun*
1. Abstract reasoning : speculation, theory. *See* BELIEF, THOUGHTS. 2. A judgment, estimate, or opinion arrived at by guessing : guess, guesswork, speculation, supposition, surmise. *See* OPINION.
conjecture *verb* To draw an inference on the basis of inconclusive evidence or insufficient information : guess, infer, speculate, suppose, surmise. *See* OPINION.

conjoin *verb*
1. To bring or come together into a united whole : coalesce, combine, compound, concrete, conjugate, connect, consolidate, couple, join, link, marry, meld, unify, unite, wed, yoke. *See* ASSEMBLE. 2. To unite or be united in a relationship : affiliate, ally, associate, bind, combine, connect, join, link, relate. *See* CONNECT.

conjoint *adjective*
Belonging to, shared by, or applicable to all alike : common, communal, general, joint, mutual, public. *See* GROUP.

conjugal *adjective*
Of, relating to, or typical of marriage : connubial, hymeneal, marital, married, matrimonial, nuptial, spousal, wedded. *See* MARRIAGE.

conjugality *noun*
The state of being united as husband and wife : connubiality, marriage, matrimony, wedlock. *See* MARRIAGE.

conjugate *verb*
To bring or come together into a united whole : coalesce, combine, compound, concrete, conjoin, connect, consolidate, couple, join, link, marry, meld, unify, unite, wed, yoke. *See* ASSEMBLE.

conjugation *noun*
The result of combining : combination, composite, compound, unification, union, unity. *See* ASSEMBLE.

conjugational *adjective*
Of, relating to, or tending to produce combination : combinational, combinative, combinatorial, conjugative, conjunctional, connectional, connective. *See* ASSEMBLE.

conjugative *adjective*
Of, relating to, or tending to produce combination : combinational, combinative, combinatorial, conjugational, conjunctional, connectional, connective. *See* ASSEMBLE.

conjunction *noun*
The state of being associated : affiliation, alliance, association, combination, connection, cooperation, partnership. *See* NEAR.

conjunctional *adjective*
Of, relating to, or tending to produce combination : combinational, combinative, combinatorial, conjugational, conjugative, connectional, connective. *See* ASSEMBLE.

conjuration *noun*
1. The use of skillful tricks and deceptions to produce entertainingly baffling effects : legerdemain, magic, prestidigitation, sleight of hand. *See* PERFORMING ARTS. 2. The use of supernatural powers to influence or predict events : magic, sorcery, sortilege, thaumaturgy, theurgy, witchcraft, witchery, witching, wizardry. *See* SUPERNATURAL.

conjure *verb*
Archaic. To make an earnest or urgent request : appeal, beg, beseech, crave, entreat, implore, plead, pray, sue, supplicate. *See* ASK.

conk *noun*
1. *Slang.* The uppermost part of the body : head, noddle, pate, poll. *Slang:* bean, block, dome, noggin, noodle, nut. *See* BODY.
2. *Slang.* A sudden sharp, powerful stroke : bang, blow[2], clout, crack, hit, lick, pound, slug[3], sock, swat, thwack, welt, whack, wham, whop. *Informal:* bash, biff, bop, clip[1], wallop. *Slang:* belt, paste. *See* ATTACK, STRIKE.
conk *verb* To deliver a powerful blow to suddenly and sharply : bash, catch, clout, hit, knock, pop[1], slam, slog, slug[3], smash, smite, sock, strike, swat, thwack, whack, wham, whop. *Informal:* biff, bop, clip[1], wallop. *Slang:* belt, paste. ***Idioms:*** let someone have it, sock it to someone. *See* ATTACK, STRIKE.
conk out *verb* 1. *Slang.* To cease functioning properly : break down, fail, give out. *See* THRIVE. 2. *Slang.* To suddenly lose all health or strength : break (down), cave in, collapse, crack, drop, give out, succumb. *Informal:* crack up. ***Idiom:*** give way. *See* HEALTH.

conk out *verb* See **conk.**

connate *adjective*
Connected by or as if by kinship or common origin : agnate, akin, allied, cognate, connatural, consanguine, consanguineous, kindred, related. *See* KIN.

connatural *adjective*
1. Forming an essential element, as arising from the basic structure of an individual : built-in, congenital, constitutional, elemental, inborn, inbred, indigenous, indwelling, ingrained, inherent, innate, intrinsic, native, natural. *See* BE, NATIVE, START. **2.** Connected by or as if by kinship or common origin : agnate, akin, allied, cognate, connate, consanguine, consanguineous, kindred, related. *See* KIN.

connect *verb*
1. To bring or come together into a united whole : coalesce, combine, compound, concrete, conjoin, conjugate, consolidate, couple, join, link, marry, meld, unify, unite, wed, yoke. *See* ASSEMBLE. **2.** To join one thing to another : affix, attach, clip², couple, fasten, fix, moor, secure. *See* ASSEMBLE. **3.** To come or bring together in one's mind or imagination : associate, bracket, correlate, couple, identify, link. *See* SAME. **4.** To unite or be united in a relationship : affiliate, ally, associate, bind, combine, conjoin, join, link, relate. *See* CONNECT. **5.** To interact with another or others in a meaningful fashion : communicate, relate. *Slang:* click. ***Idioms:*** be on the same wavelength, hit it off. *See* CONNECT.

connection *noun*
1. The state of being associated : affiliation, alliance, association, combination, conjunction, cooperation, partnership. *See* NEAR. **2.** A point or position at which two or more things are joined : coupling, joint, junction, juncture, seam, union. *See* CONNECT. **3.** A logical or natural association between two or more things : correlation, interconnection, interdependence, interrelationship, link, linkage, relation, relationship, tie-in. *Informal:* hookup. *See* CONNECT. **4.** Something, such as a feeling, thought, or idea, associated in one's mind or imagination with a specific person or thing : association, connotation, suggestion. *See* SUGGEST. **5.** An acquaintance who is in a position to help : contact, source. *See* CONNECT.

connectional *adjective*
Of, relating to, or tending to produce combination : combinational, combinative, combinatorial, conjugational, conjugative, conjunctional, connective. *See* ASSEMBLE.

connective *adjective*
Of, relating to, or tending to produce combination : combinational, combinative, combinatorial, conjugational, conjugative, conjunctional, connectional. *See* ASSEMBLE.

conniption *noun*
Informal. An angry outburst : fit², huff, passion, tantrum, temper. *Informal:* conniption fit. *See* FEELINGS.

conniption fit *noun*
Informal. An angry outburst : fit², huff, passion, tantrum, temper. *Informal:* conniption. *See* FEELINGS.

connivance also **connivence** *noun*
A secret plan to achieve an evil or illegal end : cabal, collusion, conspiracy, intrigue, machination, plot, scheme. *See* CRIMES, PLANNED.

connive *verb*
To work out a secret plan to achieve an evil or illegal end : collude, conspire, intrigue, machinate, plot, scheme. *See* CRIMES, PLANNED.
connive at *verb* To pretend not to see : blink (at), disregard, ignore, pass over, wink at. ***Idioms:*** be blind to, close (*or* shut) one's eyes to, look the other way, turn a blind eye to. *See* SEE.

connive at *verb* See **connive.**

connivence *noun* See **connivance.**

connotation *noun*
1. Something, such as a feeling, thought, or idea, associated in one's mind or imagination with a specific person or thing : association, connection, suggestion. *See* SUGGEST. **2.** That which is signified by a word or expression : acceptation, denotation, import, intent, meaning, message, purport, sense, significance, significancy, signification, value. *See* MEANING.

connotative *adjective*
Tending to bring a memory, mood, or image, for example, subtly or indirectly to mind : allusive, evocative, impressionistic, reminiscent, suggestive. *See* SUGGEST.

connote *verb*
To have or convey a particular idea : denote, import, intend, mean¹, signify, spell¹. ***Idiom:*** add up to. *See* MEANING.

connubial *adjective*
Of, relating to, or typical of marriage : conjugal, hymeneal, marital, married, matrimonial, nuptial, spousal, wedded. *See* MARRIAGE.

connubiality *noun*
The state of being united as husband and wife : conjugality, marriage, matrimony, wedlock. *See* MARRIAGE.

conquer *verb*
To win a victory over, as in battle or a competition : beat, best, defeat, master, overcome, prevail against (*or* over), rout, subdue, subjugate, surmount, triumph over, vanquish, worst. *Informal:* trim, whip. *Slang:* ace, lick. ***Idioms:***

carry (*or* win) the day, get (*or* have) the best of, get (*or* have) the better of, go someone one better. *See* WIN.

conquerer *noun* See **conqueror.**

conquering *adjective*
Relating to, having the nature of, or experiencing triumph : triumphal, triumphant, victorious, winning. *See* WIN.

conqueror also **conquerer** *noun*
One that conquers : conquistador, master, victor, winner. *See* WIN.

conquest *noun*
The act of conquering : triumph, victory, win. *See* WIN.

conquistador *noun*
One that conquers : conqueror, master, victor, winner. *See* WIN.

consanguine *adjective*
Connected by or as if by kinship or common origin : agnate, akin, allied, cognate, connate, connatural, consanguineous, kindred, related. *See* KIN.

consanguineous *adjective*
Connected by or as if by kinship or common origin : agnate, akin, allied, cognate, connate, connatural, consanguine, kindred, related. *See* KIN.

conscience *noun*
A sense of propriety or rightness : decency, grace. *See* RIGHT.

conscienceless *adjective*
Lacking scruples or principles : ruthless, unconscionable, unethical, unprincipled, unscrupulous. *See* HONEST.

conscious *adjective*
Tending toward awareness and appreciation : heedful, mindful, observant. *See* AWARENESS.

consciousness *noun*
The condition of being aware : awareness, cognizance, perception, sense. *See* KNOWLEDGE.

conscript *verb*
To enroll compulsorily in military service : draft, induct, levy. *See* GIVE.

conscription *noun*
Compulsory enrollment in military service : draft, induction, levy. *See* GIVE.

consecrate *verb*
1. To make sacred by a religious rite : bless, hallow, sanctify. *See* RELIGION. **2.** To give over by or as if by vow to a higher purpose : dedicate, devote, hallow. *See* GIVE.

consecrated *adjective*
Given over exclusively to a single use or purpose : dedicated, devoted, hallowed, sacred. *See* GIVE, INCLUDE.

consecution *noun*
1. A way in which things follow each other in space or time : order, procession, sequence, succession. *See* ORDER, PRECEDE. **2.** A number of things placed or occurring one after the other : chain, course, order, procession, progression, round, run, sequence, series, string, succession, suite, train. *Informal:* streak. *See* ORDER.

consecutive *adjective*
Following one after another in an orderly pattern : sequent, sequential, serial, subsequent, successional, successive. *See* PRECEDE, TIME.

consensus *noun*
The quality or condition of being in complete agreement or harmony : unanimity, unanimousness. *See* AGREE.

consent *verb*
1. To respond affirmatively; receive with agreement or compliance : accede, accept, acquiesce, agree, assent, nod, subscribe, yes. *See* AGREE. **2.** To give one's consent to : allow, approbate, approve, authorize, endorse, let, permit, sanction. *Informal:* OK. *See* ALLOW.

consent *noun* **1.** The act or process of accepting : acceptance, acquiescence, agreement, assent, nod, yes. *Informal:* OK. *See* ACCEPT.
2. The approving of an action, especially when done by one in authority : allowance, approbation, approval, authorization, endorsement, leave[2], license, permission, permit, sanction. *Informal:* OK. *See* ALLOW.

consequence *noun*
1. Something brought about by a cause : aftermath, corollary, effect, end product, event, fruit, harvest, issue, outcome, precipitate, ramification, result, resultant, sequel, sequence, sequent, upshot. *See* CAUSE. **2.** The quality or state of being important : concern, concernment, import, importance, moment, significance, significancy, weight, weightiness. *See* IMPORTANT.

consequent *adjective*
Consistent with reason and intellect : intelligent, logical, rational, reasonable. *See* REASON.

consequential *adjective*
1. Having great significance : big, considerable, historic, important, large, material, meaningful, monumental, significant, substantial. *See* IMPORTANT. **2.** Having or exercising influence : important, influential, powerful, weighty. *See* AFFECT, IMPORTANT, STRONG.

conservancy *noun*
The careful guarding of an asset : conserva-

tion, husbandry, management, preservation. *See* KEEP.

conservation *noun*
The careful guarding of an asset : conservancy, husbandry, management, preservation. *See* KEEP.

conservative *adjective*
1. Strongly favoring retention of the existing order : orthodox, right, rightist, right-wing, Tory, traditionalist, traditionalistic. *See* KEEP. **2.** Kept within sensible limits : discreet, moderate, reasonable, restrained, temperate. *See* PLAIN, RESTRAINT. **3.** Clinging to obsolete ideas : backward, reactionary, unprogressive. *See* POLITICS. **4.** Able to preserve : preservative, protective. *See* HELP.
conservative *noun* One who strongly favors retention of the existing order : orthodox, rightist, right-winger, Tory, traditionalist. *See* KEEP.

conservator *noun*
Law. A person who is legally responsible for the person or property of another considered by law to be incompetent to manage his or her affairs : caretaker, custodian, guardian, keeper. *See* LAW.

conserve *verb*
1. To protect (an asset) from loss or destruction : husband, preserve, save. *See* KEEP. **2.** To use without wasting : economize, save, spare. *See* SAVE. **3.** To prepare (food) for storage and future use : can, preserve, put up. *See* KEEP.

consider *verb*
1. To direct the eyes on an object : contemplate, eye, look, view. ***Idiom:*** clap (*or* lay *or* set) one's eyes on. *See* SEE. **2.** To think or think about carefully and at length : chew on (*or* over), cogitate, contemplate, deliberate, entertain, excogitate, meditate, mull, muse[1], ponder, reflect, revolve, ruminate, study, think, think out, think over, think through, turn over, weigh. ***Idioms:*** cudgel one's brains, put on one's thinking cap, rack one's brain. *See* THOUGHTS. **3.** To receive (an idea) and take it into consideration : entertain, hear of, think of. *See* THOUGHTS. **4.** To be occupied or concerned with : deal with, take up, treat. ***Idiom:*** have to do with. *See* RELEVANT. **5.** To look upon in a particular way : account, deem, esteem, reckon, regard, see, view. *See* PERSPECTIVE. **6.** To have an opinion : believe, deem, hold, opine, think. *Informal:* figure, judge. ***Idiom:*** be of the opinion. *See* OPINION. **7.** To have a high opinion of : admire, esteem, honor, regard, respect, value. ***Idioms:*** look up to, think highly (*or* much *or* well) of. *See* PRAISE.

considerable *adjective*
1. Notably above average in amount, size, or scope : big, extensive, good, great, healthy, large, large-scale, sizable. *Informal:* tidy. *See* BIG. **2.** Having great significance : big, consequential, historic, important, large, material, meaningful, monumental, significant, substantial. *See* IMPORTANT.

considerably *adverb*
To a considerable extent : far, much, quite, well[2]. ***Idioms:*** by a long shot (*or* way), by a wide margin, by far. *See* BIG.

considerate *adjective*
Full of polite concern for the well-being of others : attentive, courteous, gallant, polite, solicitous, thoughtful. *See* CAREFUL, TREAT WELL.

consideration *noun*
1. A careful considering of a matter : advisement, calculation, deliberation, lucubration, study. *See* THOUGHTS. **2.** Concentration of the mental powers on something : attention, attentiveness, concentration, heedfulness, regardfulness. *See* EXCITE. **3.** Thoughtful attention : attentiveness, concern, regard, solicitude, thoughtfulness. *See* ATTITUDE, CONCERN, KIND, TREAT WELL. **4.** A feeling of deference, approval, and liking : account, admiration, appreciation, esteem, estimation, favor, honor, regard, respect. *See* RESPECT. **5.** Something given in exchange for goods or services rendered : compensation, payment, recompense, remuneration. *See* PAY.

considered *adjective*
1. Resulting from deliberation and careful thought : advised, calculated, studied, studious. *See* WISE. **2.** Planned, weighed, or estimated in advance : calculated, deliberate, intentional, premeditated. *See* PURPOSE.

consign *verb*
1. To put in the charge of another for care, use, or performance : commend, commit, confide, entrust, give (over), hand over, relegate, trust, turn over. ***Idiom:*** give in trust (*or* charge). *See* GIVE. **2.** To place officially in confinement : commit, institutionalize. *Informal:* send up. *See* FREE. **3.** To cause (something) to be conveyed to a destination : address, dispatch, forward, route, send, ship, transmit. *See* MOVE.

consist *verb*
1. To have an inherent basis : dwell, exist, inhere, lie[1], repose, reside, rest[1]. *See* START. **2.** To be compatible or in correspondence : accord, agree, check, chime, comport with,

conform, correspond, fit[1], harmonize, match, square, tally. *Informal:* jibe[1]. *Archaic:* quadrate. *See* AGREE.

consistence *noun*
Logical agreement among parts : coherence, congruity, consistency. *See* AGREE.

consistency *noun*
Logical agreement among parts : coherence, congruity, consistence. *See* AGREE.

consistent *adjective*
1. In keeping with one's needs or expectations : accordant, agreeable, compatible, conformable, congenial, congruous, consonant, correspondent, corresponding, harmonious. *See* AGREE. **2.** Remaining continually unchanged : changeless, constant, invariable, same, unchanging, unfailing. *See* CHANGE.

consistently *adverb*
In an expected or customary manner; for the most part : commonly, customarily, frequently, generally, habitually, naturally, normally, often, regularly, routinely, typically, usually. ***Idioms:*** as usual, per usual. *See* BIG, USUAL.

consolation *noun*
A consoling in time of grief or pain : comfort, solace. *See* HELP.

console *verb*
To give hope to in time of grief or pain : comfort, solace, soothe. *See* HELP.

consolidate *verb*
To bring or come together into a united whole : coalesce, combine, compound, concrete, conjoin, conjugate, connect, couple, join, link, marry, meld, unify, unite, wed, yoke. *See* ASSEMBLE.

consolidation *noun*
A bringing together into a whole : coalition, unification, union, unity. *See* PART.

consonance *noun*
1. Harmonious mutual understanding : accord, agreement, concord, concordance, concurrence, harmony, rapport, tune, unity. ***Idiom:*** meeting of the minds. *See* AGREE. **2.** *Music.* Pleasing agreement, as of musical sounds : accord, concert, concord, harmony, symphony, tune. *See* BEAUTIFUL.

consonant *adjective*
1. In keeping with one's needs or expectations : accordant, agreeable, compatible, conformable, congenial, congruous, consistent, correspondent, corresponding, harmonious. *See* AGREE. **2.** Characterized by harmony of sound : harmonic, harmonious, musical, symphonic, symphonious. *See* BEAUTIFUL, SOUNDS.

consort *noun*
A husband or wife : mate, partner, spouse. *Informal:* better half. *See* MARRIAGE.

consort *verb* **1.** To be with as a companion : associate, fraternize, hang around, hobnob, run (around), troop. *Slang:* hang out. ***Idiom:*** rub elbows (*or* shoulders) . *See* NEAR. **2.** *Obsolete.* To be with or go with (another) : accompany, attend, companion, company, escort. ***Idiom:*** go hand in hand with. *See* ACCOMPANIED.

conspicuous *adjective*
Readily attracting notice : arresting, bold, eye-catching, marked, noticeable, observable, outstanding, pointed, prominent, pronounced, remarkable, salient, signal, striking. ***Idiom:*** sticking out like a sore thumb. *See* SEE.

conspiracy *noun*
A secret plan to achieve an evil or illegal end : cabal, collusion, connivance, intrigue, machination, plot, scheme. *See* CRIMES, PLANNED.

conspirator *noun*
One who assists a lawbreaker in a wrongful or criminal act : accessory, accomplice, confederate. *See* CRIMES, HELP.

conspire *verb*
To work out a secret plan to achieve an evil or illegal end : collude, connive, intrigue, machinate, plot, scheme. *See* CRIMES, PLANNED.

constable *noun*
Chiefly British. A member of a law-enforcement agency : bluecoat, finest, officer, patrolman, patrolwoman, peace officer, police, policeman, police officer, policewoman. *Informal:* cop, law. *Slang:* bull[1], copper, flatfoot, fuzz, gendarme, heat, man (often uppercase). *Chiefly British:* bobby, peeler. *See* LAW.

constancy *noun*
Faithfulness or devotion to a person, a cause, obligations, or duties : allegiance, faithfulness, fealty, fidelity, loyalty, steadfastness. *See* CONTINUE, OBLIGATION.

constant *adjective*
1. Existing or occurring without interruption or end : around-the-clock, ceaseless, continual, continuous, endless, eternal, everlasting, incessant, interminable, nonstop, ongoing, perpetual, persistent, relentless, round-the-clock, timeless, unceasing, unending, unfailing, uninterrupted, unremitting. *See* CONTINUE. **2.** Remaining continually unchanged : changeless, consistent, invariable, same, unchanging, unfailing. *See* CHANGE. **3.** Having no change or variation : changeless, equable, even[1], invariable, invariant, regular, same, steady, unchang-

ing, uniform, unvarying. *See* SAME. **4.** Indicating or possessing determination, resolution, or persistence : determined, firm[1], resolute, steadfast, steady, stiff, tough, unbending, uncompromising, unflinching, unwavering, unyielding. *See* PURPOSE. **5.** Adhering firmly and devotedly, as to a person, a cause, or a duty : allegiant, faithful, fast, firm[1], liege, loyal, staunch, steadfast, true. *See* CONTINUE, TRUST.

consternate *verb*
To deprive of courage or the power to act as a result of fear, anxiety, or disgust : appall, daunt, dismay, horrify, shake, shock[1]. *See* FEAR.

consternation *noun*
A sudden or complete loss of courage in the face of trouble or danger : dismay. *See* FEAR.

constituent *adjective*
Serving as part of a whole, as a nondetachable part of a larger unit : built-in, component, incorporated. *See* INCLUDE.
constituent *noun* One of the individual entities contributing to a whole : building block, component, element, factor, ingredient, integrant, part. *See* PART.

constitute *verb*
1. To be the constituent parts of : compose, form, make (up). *See* BE. **2.** To be equivalent or tantamount : amount, correspond, equal. ***Idiom:*** have all the earmarks. *See* BE. **3.** To put in force or cause to be by legal authority : enact, establish, legislate, make, promulgate. *See* ACTION, MAKE, POLITICS. **4.** To bring into existence formally : create, establish, found, institute, organize, originate, set up, start. *See* START.

constitution *noun*
1. The act of founding or establishing : creation, establishment, foundation, institution, organization, origination, start-up. *See* START. **2.** The physical or constitutional characteristics of a person : build, habit, habitus, physique. *See* BODY.

constitutional *adjective*
1. Forming an essential element, as arising from the basic structure of an individual : built-in, congenital, connatural, elemental, inborn, inbred, indigenous, indwelling, ingrained, inherent, innate, intrinsic, native, natural. *See* BE, NATIVE, START. **2.** Constituting or forming part of the essence of something : basic, constitutive, essential, fundamental, integral, vital. *See* BE, SURFACE.
constitutional *noun* A usually brief and regular journey on foot, especially for exercise : turn, walk. *See* MOVE.

constitutive *adjective*
Constituting or forming part of the essence of something : basic, constitutional, essential, fundamental, integral, vital. *See* BE, SURFACE.

constrain *verb*
1. To cause (a person or thing) to act or move in spite of resistance : coerce, compel, force, make, obligate, oblige, pressure. *See* ATTACK. **2.** To control, restrict, or arrest : bit[2], brake, bridle, check, curb, hold, hold back, hold down, hold in, inhibit, keep, keep back, pull in, rein (back, in, *or* up), restrain. *See* RESTRAINT. **3.** To check the freedom and spontaneity of : constrict, cramp[2], inhibit. *See* FREE, TIGHTEN.

constrained *adjective*
Characterized by embarrassment and discomfort : awkward, uncomfortable, uneasy. *See* FEELINGS.

constraint *noun*
1. Power used to overcome resistance : coercion, compulsion, duress, force, pressure, strength, violence. *See* ATTACK. **2.** The act of limiting or condition of being limited : circumscription, confinement, limitation, restraint, restriction. *See* LIMITED. **3.** Something that limits or restricts : check, circumscription, cramp[2], curb, inhibition, limit, limitation, restraint, restriction, stricture, trammel. *See* LIMITED.

constrict *verb*
1. To make smaller or narrower : constringe, narrow. *See* TIGHTEN, WIDE. **2.** To reduce in size, as by drawing together : compact[1], compress, constringe, contract, shrink. *See* INCREASE. **3.** To subject to compression : compact[1], compress, constringe, squeeze. *See* TIGHTEN. **4.** To check the freedom and spontaneity of : constrain, cramp[2], inhibit. *See* FREE, TIGHTEN.

constriction *noun*
1. A becoming narrow or narrower : *Pathology:* stricture. *See* WIDE. **2.** A compressing of something : compression, squeeze. *See* TIGHTEN.

constringe *verb*
1. To make smaller or narrower : constrict, narrow. *See* TIGHTEN, WIDE. **2.** To reduce in size, as by drawing together : compact[1], compress, constrict, contract, shrink. *See* INCREASE. **3.** To subject to compression : compact[1], compress, constrict, squeeze. *See* TIGHTEN.

construct *verb*
1. To create by forming, combining, or altering materials : assemble, build, fabricate, fashion, forge[1], frame, make, manufacture, mold, produce, put together, shape. *See* MAKE. **2.** To make or form (a structure) : build, erect, put up, raise, rear[2]. *See* MAKE.

constructer *noun* See **constructor.**

construction *noun*
Something that serves to explain or clarify : clarification, decipherment, elucidation, exegesis, explanation, explication, exposition, illumination, illustration, interpretation. *Archaic:* enucleation. *See* EXPLAIN.

constructor or **constructer** *noun*
A person or business that makes or builds something : assembler, builder, erector, maker, manufacturer, producer. *See* MAKE.

construe *verb*
1. To make understandable : decipher, explain, explicate, expound, interpret, spell out. *Archaic:* enucleate. ***Idiom:*** put into plain English. *See* EXPLAIN. **2.** To understand in a particular way : interpret, read, take. *See* UNDERSTAND. **3.** To express in another language, while systematically retaining the original sense : put, render, translate.
See WORDS.

consuetude *noun*
A habitual way of behaving : custom, habit, habitude, manner, practice, praxis, usage, usance, use, way, wont. *See* USUAL.

consult *verb*
To meet and exchange views to reach a decision : advise, confer, deliberate, parley, talk. *Informal:* powwow. *See* COLLECT, MEET, WORDS.

consultant *noun*
One who advises another, especially officially or professionally : adviser, counselor, mentor. *Law:* counsel. *See* OPINION.

consultation *noun*
An exchange of views in an attempt to reach a decision : conference, counsel, deliberation, parley. *See* WORDS.

consultative *adjective*
Giving advice : advisory, consultatory, consulting, consultive. *See* OPINION.

consultatory *adjective*
Giving advice : advisory, consultative, consulting, consultive. *See* OPINION.

consulting *adjective*
Giving advice : advisory, consultative, consultatory, consultive. *See* OPINION.

consultive *adjective*
Giving advice : advisory, consultative, consultatory, consulting. *See* OPINION.

consume *verb*
1. To take (food) into the body as nourishment : devour, eat, fare, ingest, partake. *Slang:* chow. ***Idioms:*** break bread, have (*or* take) a bite. *See* INGESTION. **2.** To eat completely or entirely : devour, dispatch, eat up. *Informal:* polish off, put away. *See* INGESTION. **3.** To use all of : drain, draw down, eat up, exhaust, expend, finish, play out, run through, spend, use up. *Informal:* polish off. *See* INCREASE. **4.** To be depleted : go, spend. ***Idiom:*** go down the drain. *See* INCREASE. **5.** To use up foolishly or needlessly : devour, dissipate, squander, waste. *See* SAVE. **6.** To spend (money) excessively and usually foolishly : dissipate, fool away, fritter away, riot away, squander, throw away, trifle away, waste. *Slang:* blow[1]. *See* SAVE. **7.** To do away with completely and destructively : devour, eat (up), swallow (up), waste. *See* HELP. **8.** To occupy the full attention of : absorb, engross, immerse, monopolize, preoccupy. *See* AWARENESS, EXCITE.

consumer *noun*
One who consumes goods and services : customer, user. *See* GIVE, USED.

consummate *verb*
To bring or come to a natural or proper end : close, complete, conclude, end, finish, terminate, wind up, wrap up. *See* START.
consummate *adjective* **1.** Supremely excellent in quality or nature : absolute, faultless, flawless, impeccable, indefectible, perfect, unflawed. *See* GOOD. **2.** Completely such, without qualification or exception : absolute, all-out, arrant, complete, crashing, damned, dead, downright, flat, out-and-out, outright, perfect, plain, pure, sheer[2], thorough, thoroughgoing, total, unbounded, unequivocal, unlimited, unmitigated, unqualified, unrelieved, unreserved, utter[2]. *Informal:* flat-out, positive. *Chiefly British:* blooming. *See* BIG, LIMITED.

consummation *noun*
1. A concluding or terminating : cease, cessation, close, closing, closure, completion, conclusion, end, ending, end of the line, finish, period, stop, stopping point, termination, terminus, wind-up, wrap-up. *See* CONTINUE. **2.** The condition of being fulfilled : culmination, fruition, fulfillment, materialization, realization. *See* DO, HAPPY.

consumption *noun*
1. A quantity consumed : usage, use. *See* GIVE,

USED. **2.** An infectious disease producing lesions especially of the lungs. No longer in scientific use : phthisic (no longer in scientific use), phthisis (no longer in scientific use), tuberculosis, white plague. *See* HEALTH.

consumptive *adjective*
Relating to or afflicted with tuberculosis. No longer in scientific use : phthisic (no longer in scientific use), phthisical (no longer in scientific use), tubercular, tuberculate, tuberculous. *See* HEALTH.

contact *noun*
1. A coming together so as to be touching : contingence, touch. *See* TOUCH. **2.** A situation allowing exchange of ideas or messages : communication, intercommunication, touch. *See* CONNECT, TOUCH. **3.** An acquaintance who is in a position to help : connection, source. *See* CONNECT.
contact *verb* **1.** To bring into or make contact with : touch. *See* TOUCH. **2.** To succeed in communicating with : get, reach. ***Idioms:*** catch up with, get hold of, get in touch with, get through to, get to. *See* REACH.

contagion *noun*
Anything that is injurious, destructive, or fatal : bane, canker, poison, toxin, venom, virus. *See* HELP.

contagious *adjective*
Capable of transmission by infection : catching, communicable, infectious, taking. *See* MOVE.

contain *verb*
1. To be filled by : have, hold. *See* INCLUDE. **2.** To have the room or capacity for : accommodate, hold. *See* FULL. **3.** To have as a part : comprehend, comprise, embody, embrace, encompass, have, include, involve, subsume, take in. *See* INCLUDE. **4.** To bring one's emotions under control : collect[1], compose, control, cool, simmer down. ***Idiom:*** cool it. *See* RESTRAINT.

contaminant *noun*
One that contaminates : adulterant, adulterator, contamination, contaminator, impurity, poison, pollutant. *See* CLEAN.

contaminate *verb* See **pollute, taint.**

contamination *noun*
1. The state of being contaminated : adulteration, pollution, sophistication. *See* CLEAN. **2.** One that contaminates : adulterant, adulterator, contaminant, contaminator, impurity, poison, pollutant. *See* CLEAN.

contaminative *adjective*
Morally detrimental : corruptive, demoralizing, unhealthy, unwholesome. *See* RIGHT.

contaminator *noun*
One that contaminates : adulterant, adulterator, contaminant, contamination, impurity, poison, pollutant. *See* CLEAN.

contemn *verb*
To regard with utter contempt and disdain : despise, disdain, scorn, scout[2]. ***Idioms:*** have no use for, look down on (*or* upon). *See* RESPECT.

contemplate *verb*
1. To direct the eyes on an object : consider, eye, look, view. ***Idiom:*** clap (*or* lay *or* set) one's eyes on. *See* SEE. **2.** To think or think about carefully and at length : chew on (*or* over), cogitate, consider, deliberate, entertain, excogitate, meditate, mull, muse[1], ponder, reflect, revolve, ruminate, study, think, think out, think over, think through, turn over, weigh. ***Idioms:*** cudgel one's brains, put on one's thinking cap, rack one's brain. *See* THOUGHTS. **3.** To have in mind as a goal or purpose : aim, design, intend, mean[1], plan, project, propose, purpose, target. *Regional:* mind. *See* PLANNED, PURPOSE.

contemplation *noun*
1. An act of directing the eyes on an object : look, regard, sight, view. *See* SEE. **2.** The act or process of thinking : brainwork, cerebration, cogitation, deliberation, excogitation, meditation, reflection, rumination, speculation, thought. *See* THOUGHTS.

contemplative *adjective*
Of, characterized by, or disposed to thought : cogitative, deliberative, excogitative, meditative, pensive, reflective, ruminative, speculative, thinking, thoughtful. ***Idiom:*** in a brown study. *See* THOUGHTS.

contemporaneous *adjective*
Belonging to the same period of time as another : coetaneous, coeval, coexistent, concurrent, contemporary, synchronic, synchronous. *See* TIME.

contemporary *adjective*
1. Belonging to the same period of time as another : coetaneous, coeval, coexistent, concurrent, contemporaneous, synchronic, synchronous. *See* TIME. **2.** Existing or occurring at the same moment : coincident, simultaneous. *See* TIME. **3.** In existence now : current, existent, existing, new, now, present[1], present-day. *See* TIME. **4.** Characteristic of recent times or informed of what is current : au courant, current, mod, modern, up-to-date, up-to-the-minute. *See* KNOWLEDGE, NEW.

contemporary *noun* **1.** One of the same time or age as another : coeval. *See* TIME. **2.** A person of the present age : modern. *See* NEW, TIME.

contempt *noun*
1. The feeling of despising : despisal, despite, disdain, scorn. *See* RESPECT. **2.** The disposition boldly to defy or resist authority or an opposing force : contumacy, defiance, despite, recalcitrance, recalcitrancy. *See* RESIST.

contemptible *adjective*
So objectionable as to elicit despisal or deserve condemnation : abhorrent, abominable, antipathetic, despicable, despisable, detestable, disgusting, filthy, foul, infamous, loathsome, lousy, low, mean[2], nasty, nefarious, obnoxious, odious, repugnant, rotten, shabby, vile, wretched. *See* GOOD.

contemptuous *adjective*
Showing scorn and disrespect toward (someone or something) : disdainful, scornful. ***Idiom:*** on one's high horse. *See* RESPECT.

contend *verb*
1. To strive in opposition : battle, combat, duel, fight, struggle, tilt, war, wrestle. *See* CONFLICT. **2.** *Informal.* To strive against (others) for victory : compete, contest, emulate, rival, vie. *See* CONFLICT. **3.** To put forth reasons for or against something, often excitedly : argue, debate, dispute, moot. *See* AFFIRM, WORDS. **4.** To engage in a quarrel : argue, bicker, dispute, fight, quarrel, quibble, spat, squabble, tiff, wrangle. *Informal:* hassle, tangle. ***Idioms:*** cross swords, have it out, have words, lock horns. *See* CONFLICT. **5.** To put into words positively and with conviction : affirm, allege, argue, assert, asseverate, aver, avouch, avow, claim, declare, hold, maintain, say, state. ***Idiom:*** have it. *See* AFFIRM.

contender *noun*
One that competes : competition, competitor, contestant, corrival, opponent, rival. *See* CONFLICT.

content *adjective*
Having achieved satisfaction, as of one's goal : fulfilled, gratified, happy, satisfied. *See* HAPPY.
content *verb* To grant or have what is demanded by (a need or desire) : appease, fulfill, gratify, indulge, satisfy. *See* GIVE.

contention *noun*
1. A discussion, often heated, in which a difference of opinion is expressed : altercation, argument, bicker, clash, controversy, debate, difficulty, disagreement, dispute, fight, polemic, quarrel, run-in, spat, squabble, tiff, word (used in plural), wrangle. *Informal:* hassle, rhubarb, tangle. *See* CONFLICT. **2.** A state of disagreement and disharmony : clash, conflict, confrontation, difference, difficulty, disaccord, discord, discordance, dissension, dissent, dissentience, dissidence, dissonance, faction, friction, inharmony, schism, strife, variance, war, warfare. *See* CONFLICT. **3.** A hypothetical controversial proposition : contestation, thesis. *See* OPINION.

contentious *adjective*
1. Given to arguing : argumentative, combative, disputatious, eristic, litigious, polemic, polemical, quarrelsome, scrappy. *See* CONFLICT. **2.** Having or showing an eagerness to fight : bellicose, belligerent, combative, hostile, militant, pugnacious, quarrelsome, scrappy, truculent, warlike. *See* ATTACK. **3.** Inclined to act in a hostile way : aggressive, belligerent, combative, hostile, militant. *See* ATTACK, ATTITUDE.

contentiousness *noun*
1. The quality or state of being argumentative : argumentativeness, combativeness, disputatiousness, litigiousness, scrappiness. *See* CONFLICT. **2.** Warlike or hostile attitude or nature : bellicoseness, bellicosity, belligerence, belligerency, combativeness, hostility, militance, militancy, pugnaciousness, pugnacity, truculence, truculency. *See* ATTACK. **3.** The power or will to fight : bellicoseness, bellicosity, belligerence, belligerency, combativeness, fight, pugnaciousness, pugnacity, truculence, truculency. *See* CONFLICT. **4.** Hostile behavior : aggression, aggressiveness, belligerence, belligerency, combativeness, hostility, militance, militancy. *See* ATTACK.

conterminous *adjective*
Sharing a common boundary : adjacent, adjoining, contiguous, next. *See* NEAR.

contest *noun*
1. A vying with others for victory or supremacy : battle, competition, corrivalry, race, rivalry, strife, striving, struggle, tug of war, war, warfare. *See* CONFLICT. **2.** A trial of skill or ability : competition, meet[1]. *See* CONFLICT.
contest *verb* **1.** To strive against (others) for victory : compete, contend, emulate, rival, vie. *See* CONFLICT. **2.** To take a stand against : buck, challenge, dispute, oppose, resist, traverse. *See* SUPPORT.

contestant *noun*
One that competes : competition, competitor, contender, corrival, opponent, rival. *See* CONFLICT.

contestation *noun*
A hypothetical controversial proposition : contention, thesis. *See* OPINION.

contested *adjective*
In doubt or dispute : arguable, debatable, disputable, doubtful, exceptionable, moot, mootable, problematic, problematical, questionable, uncertain. *See* CERTAIN.

contexture *noun*
A distinctive, complex underlying pattern or structure : fabric, fiber, texture, warp and woof, web. *See* BE.

contiguous *adjective*
1. Sharing a common boundary : adjacent, adjoining, conterminous, next. *See* NEAR. **2.** Not far from another in space, time, or relation : adjacent, close, immediate, near, nearby, nigh, proximate. ***Idioms:*** at hand, under one's nose, within a stone's throw, within hailing distance. *See* NEAR.

continent *adjective*
Exercising moderation and self-restraint in appetites and behavior : abstemious, sober, temperate. *See* RESTRAINT.

contingence *noun*
A coming together so as to be touching : contact, touch. *See* TOUCH.

contingency *noun*
Something that may occur or be done : eventuality, possibility. *See* POSSIBLE.

contingent *adjective*
1. Having a chance of happening or being true : likely, possible, probable. *See* LIKELY. **2.** Determined or to be determined by someone or something else : conditional, conditioned, dependent, relative, reliant, subject. *See* START. **3.** Occurring unexpectedly : accidental, casual, chance, fluky, fortuitous, inadvertent, odd. *See* SURPRISE.

continual *adjective*
Existing or occurring without interruption or end : around-the-clock, ceaseless, constant, continuous, endless, eternal, everlasting, incessant, interminable, nonstop, ongoing, perpetual, persistent, relentless, round-the-clock, timeless, unceasing, unending, unfailing, uninterrupted, unremitting. *See* CONTINUE.

continuance *noun*
Uninterrupted existence or succession : continuation, continuity, continuum, duration, endurance, persistence, persistency. *See* CONTINUE.

continuation *noun*
1. Uninterrupted existence or succession : continuance, continuity, continuum, duration, endurance, persistence, persistency. *See* CONTINUE. **2.** A continuing after interruption : renewal, resumption, resurgence, revival. *See* CONTINUE.

continue *verb*
1. To be in existence or in a certain state for an indefinitely long time : abide, endure, go on, hold out, last[2], persist, remain, stay[1]. *See* CONTINUE. **2.** To begin or go on after an interruption : pick up, renew, reopen, restart, resume, take up. *See* CONTINUE.

continuing *adjective*
1. Existing or remaining in the same state for an indefinitely long time : abiding, durable, enduring, lasting, long-lasting, long-lived, longstanding, old, perdurable, perennial, permanent, persistent. *See* CONTINUE. **2.** Of long duration : chronic, lingering, persistent, prolonged, protracted. *See* CONTINUE.

continuity *noun*
Uninterrupted existence or succession : continuance, continuation, continuum, duration, endurance, persistence, persistency. *See* CONTINUE.

continuous *adjective*
Existing or occurring without interruption or end : around-the-clock, ceaseless, constant, continual, endless, eternal, everlasting, incessant, interminable, nonstop, ongoing, perpetual, persistent, relentless, round-the-clock, timeless, unceasing, unending, unfailing, uninterrupted, unremitting. *See* CONTINUE.

continuum *noun*
Uninterrupted existence or succession : continuance, continuation, continuity, duration, endurance, persistence, persistency. *See* CONTINUE.

contort *verb*
To alter and spoil the natural form or appearance of : deform, disfigure, distort, misshape, twist. *See* BEAUTIFUL.

contour *noun*
A line marking and shaping the outer form of an object : delineation, outline, profile, silhouette. *See* EDGE, SURFACE.

contrabandist *noun*
A person who engages in smuggling : bootlegger, runner, smuggler. *See* CRIMES, MOVE.

contract *noun*
1. A legally binding arrangement between parties : agreement, bond, compact[2], convention, covenant, pact. *See* AGREE. **2.** An agreement, especially one involving a sale or exchange : bargain, compact[2], covenant, deal, transaction. *See* AGREE.

contract *verb* **1.** To enter into a formal agreement : bargain, covenant. *See* AGREE. **2.** To assume an obligation : engage, pledge, promise, undertake. *See* AGREE, OBLIGATION. **3.** To become affected with a disease : catch, develop, get, sicken, take. ***Idiom:*** come down with. *See* GET. **4.** To reduce in size, as by drawing together : compact[1], compress, constrict, constringe, shrink. *See* INCREASE.

contradict *verb*
1. To refuse to admit the truth, reality, value, or worth of : contravene, controvert, deny, disaffirm, gainsay, negate, negative, oppugn. *Law:* traverse. *See* AFFIRM. **2.** To fail to be in accord : clash, conflict, disaccord, discord, jar. ***Idiom:*** go (*or* run) counter to. *See* AGREE.

contradiction *noun*
1. The condition of being in conflict : antagonism, antithesis, contradistinction, contraposition, contrariety, contrariness, opposition, polarity. *See* SUPPORT. **2.** A refusal to grant the truth of a statement or charge : denial, disaffirmance, disaffirmation, disclaimer, negation, rejection. *Law:* traversal. *See* AFFIRM.

contradictory *adjective*
Diametrically opposed : antipodal, antipodean, antithetical, antonymic, antonymous, contrary, converse[2], counter, diametric, diametrical, opposing, opposite, polar, reverse. *See* SUPPORT.

contradictory *noun Logic.* That which is diametrically opposed to another : antipode, antipodes, antithesis, antonym, contrary, converse[2], counter, opposite, reverse. *Logic:* contrapositive. *See* SUPPORT.

contradistinction *noun*
The condition of being in conflict : antagonism, antithesis, contradiction, contraposition, contrariety, contrariness, opposition, polarity. *See* SUPPORT.

contralto *adjective*
Being a sound produced by a relatively small frequency of vibrations : alto, bass, deep, low, low-pitched. *See* SOUNDS.

contraposition *noun*
The condition of being in conflict : antagonism, antithesis, contradiction, contradistinction, contrariety, contrariness, opposition, polarity. *See* SUPPORT.

contrapositive *noun*
Logic. That which is diametrically opposed to another : antipode, antipodes, antithesis, antonym, contrary, converse[2], counter, opposite, reverse. *Logic:* contradictory. *See* SUPPORT.

contraption *noun*
1. Something, as a machine, devised for a particular function : apparatus, appliance, contrivance, device. *See* MACHINE. **2.** A small specialized mechanical device : concern, contrivance, gadget, gimmick, jigger, thing. *Informal:* doodad, doohickey, widget. *Slang:* gizmo. *See* MACHINE.

contrariety *noun*
The condition of being in conflict : antagonism, antithesis, contradiction, contradistinction, contraposition, contrariness, opposition, polarity. *See* SUPPORT.

contrariness *noun*
The condition of being in conflict : antagonism, antithesis, contradiction, contradistinction, contraposition, contrariety, opposition, polarity. *See* SUPPORT.

contrarious *adjective*
Given to acting in opposition to others : balky, contrary, difficult, froward, impossible, ornery, perverse, wayward. *See* ATTITUDE, SUPPORT.

contrary *adjective*
1. Diametrically opposed : antipodal, antipodean, antithetical, antonymic, antonymous, contradictory, converse[2], counter, diametric, diametrical, opposing, opposite, polar, reverse. *See* SUPPORT. **2.** Given to acting in opposition to others : balky, contrarious, difficult, froward, impossible, ornery, perverse, wayward. *See* ATTITUDE, SUPPORT.

contrary *noun* That which is diametrically opposed to another : antipode, antipodes, antithesis, antonym, converse[2], counter, opposite, reverse. *Logic:* contradictory, contrapositive. *See* SUPPORT.

contrast *noun*
Striking difference between compared individuals : counterpoint. *See* SAME.

contravene *verb*
1. To fail to fulfill (a promise) or conform to (a regulation) : breach, break, infringe, transgress, violate. *See* DO. **2.** To refuse to admit the truth, reality, value, or worth of : contradict, controvert, deny, disaffirm, gainsay, negate, negative, oppugn. *Law:* traverse. *See* AFFIRM.

contravention *noun*
An act or instance of breaking a law or regulation or of nonfulfillment of an obligation or promise, for example : breach, infraction, infringement, transgression, trespass, violation. *See* RIGHT.

contretemps *noun*
An unexpected and usually undesirable event :

accident, casualty, misadventure, mischance, misfortune, mishap. *See* HELP, SURPRISE.

contribute *verb*
1. To give in common with others : chip in, donate, subscribe. *Informal:* kick in. *Slang:* come across. *See* GIVE. **2.** To present as a gift to a charity or cause : bestow, donate, give, hand out. *See* GIVE. **3.** To have a share, as in an act or result; have a hand in : conduce, partake, participate, share. ***Idiom:*** take part. *See* PARTICIPATE, START.

contribution *noun*
Something given to a charity or cause : alms, benefaction, beneficence, charity, donation, gift, handout, offering, subscription. *See* GIVE.

contributive *adjective*
Tending to contribute to a result : conducive, contributory. *See* PARTICIPATE.

contributor *noun*
1. A person who gives to a charity or cause : benefactor, benefactress, donator, donor, giver. *See* GIVE. **2.** A person who supports or champions an activity, cause, or institution, for example : backer, benefactor, friend, patron, sponsor, supporter. *Informal:* angel. *See* HELP. **3.** A person instrumental in the growth of something, especially in its early stages : builder, creator, developer, pioneer. *See* MAKE.

contributory *adjective*
1. Giving or able to give help or support : accessory, ancillary, assistant, auxiliary, collateral, subsidiary, supportive. *See* HELP. **2.** Tending to contribute to a result : conducive, contributive. *See* PARTICIPATE.

contrite *adjective*
1. Feeling or expressing regret for one's sins or misdeeds : compunctious, penitent, penitential, regretful, remorseful, repentant, sorry. *See* REGRET. **2.** Expressing or inclined to express an apology : apologetic, penitent, regretful, repentant, sorry. *See* REGRET.

contriteness *noun*
A feeling of regret for one's sins or misdeeds : compunction, contrition, penitence, penitency, remorse, remorsefulness, repentance, rue. *Theology:* attrition. *See* REGRET.

contrition *noun*
A feeling of regret for one's sins or misdeeds : compunction, contriteness, penitence, penitency, remorse, remorsefulness, repentance, rue. *Theology:* attrition. *See* REGRET.

contrivance *noun*
1. Something, as a machine, devised for a particular function : apparatus, appliance, contraption, device. *See* MACHINE. **2.** A small specialized mechanical device : concern, contraption, gadget, gimmick, jigger, thing. *Informal:* doodad, doohickey, widget. *Slang:* gizmo. *See* MACHINE. **3.** Something invented : brainchild, device, invention. *See* MACHINE, MAKE.

contrive *verb*
1. To form a strategy for : blueprint, cast, chart, conceive, design, devise, formulate, frame, lay[1], plan, project, scheme, strategize, work out. *Informal:* dope out. ***Idiom:*** lay plans. *See* PLANNED. **2.** To use ingenuity in making, developing, or achieving : concoct, devise, dream up, fabricate, formulate, hatch, invent, make up, think up. *Informal:* cook up. ***Idiom:*** come up with. *See* MAKE.

contrived *adjective*
Not natural or spontaneous : effortful, forced, labored, strained. *See* TRUE.

control *verb*
1. To exercise authority or influence over : direct, dominate, govern, rule. ***Idioms:*** be at the helm, be in the driver's seat, hold sway over, hold the reins. *See* OVER. **2.** To bring one's emotions under control : collect[1], compose, contain, cool, simmer down. ***Idiom:*** cool it. *See* RESTRAINT. **3.** To keep the mechanical operation of (a device) within proper parameters : govern, regulate. *See* CONTROL, MACHINE.

control *noun* **1.** The right and power to command, decide, rule, or judge : authority, command, domination, dominion, jurisdiction, mastery, might, power, prerogative, sovereignty, sway. *Informal:* say-so. *See* OVER. **2.** The act of exercising controlling power or the condition of being so controlled : command, dominance, domination, dominion, mastery, reign, rule, sway. *See* OVER. **3.** The continuous exercise of authority over a political unit : administration, direction, governance, government, rule. *See* CONTROL, POLITICS. **4.** The keeping of one's thoughts and emotions to oneself : reserve, restraint, reticence, self-control, self-restraint, taciturnity, uncommunicativeness. *See* RESTRAINT.

controllable *adjective*
Capable of being governed : administrable, governable, manageable, rulable. *See* CONTROL.

controlled *adjective*
Tending to keep one's thoughts and emotions to oneself : inhibited, noncommittal, reserved, restrained, self-controlled, self-restrained. *See* RESTRAINT.

controlling *adjective*
Exercising controlling power or influence : commanding, dominant, dominating, dominative, governing, paramount, preponderant, regnant, reigning, ruling. *See* OVER.

controversy *noun*
A discussion, often heated, in which a difference of opinion is expressed : altercation, argument, bicker, clash, contention, debate, difficulty, disagreement, dispute, fight, polemic, quarrel, run-in, spat, squabble, tiff, word (used in plural), wrangle. *Informal:* hassle, rhubarb, tangle. *See* CONFLICT.

controvert *verb*
To refuse to admit the truth, reality, value, or worth of : contradict, contravene, deny, disaffirm, gainsay, negate, negative, oppugn. *Law:* traverse. *See* AFFIRM.

contumacious *adjective*
Marked by defiance : defiant, recalcitrant. *See* RESIST.

contumacy *noun*
The disposition boldly to defy or resist authority or an opposing force : contempt, defiance, despite, recalcitrance, recalcitrancy. *See* RESIST.

contumelious *adjective*
1. Rude and disrespectful : assuming, assumptive, audacious, bold, boldfaced, brash, brazen, cheeky, familiar, forward, impertinent, impudent, insolent, malapert, nervy, overconfident, pert, presuming, presumptuous, pushy, sassy, saucy, smart. *Informal:* brassy, flip, fresh, smart-alecky, snippety, snippy, uppish, uppity. *Slang:* wise[1]. *See* ATTITUDE, COURTESY. **2.** Of, relating to, or characterized by verbal abuse : abusive, invective, opprobrious, scurrilous, vituperative. *See* ATTACK, ATTITUDE.

contumely *noun*
1. An act that offends a person's sense of pride or dignity : affront, despite, indignity, insult, offense, outrage, slight. ***Idiom:*** slap in the face. *See* ATTACK. **2.** Harsh, often insulting language : abuse, billingsgate, invective, obloquy, railing, revilement, reviling, scurrility, scurrilousness, vituperation. *See* PRAISE.

contuse *verb*
To make a bruise or bruises on : bruise. *See* HELP.

conundrum *noun*
Anything that arouses curiosity or perplexes because it is unexplained, inexplicable, or secret : enigma, mystery, perplexity, puzzle, puzzler, riddle. *See* SHOW.

convalesce *verb*
To regain one's health : come around (*or* round), gain, improve, mend, perk up, rally, recover, recuperate. *See* HEALTH.

convene *verb*
1. To come together : assemble, cluster, collect[1], congregate, forgather, gather, get together, group, muster. *See* COLLECT. **2.** To bring together : assemble, call, cluster, collect[1], congregate, convoke, gather, get together, group, muster, round up, summon. *See* COLLECT. **3.** To demand to appear, come, or assemble : call, convoke, muster, send for, summon. *See* REQUEST.

convenience *noun*
Anything that increases physical comfort : amenity, comfort, facility (often used in plural). *See* COMFORT.

convenient *adjective*
1. Suited to one's end or purpose : appropriate, befitting, expedient, fit[1], good, meet[2], proper, suitable, tailor-made, useful. *See* AGREE, GOOD. **2.** Being within easy reach : accessible, handy, nearby. ***Idioms:*** close (*or* near) at hand, close by. *See* NEAR.

convention *noun*
1. A formal assemblage of the members of a group : assembly, conference, congress, convocation, meeting. *See* ASSEMBLE. **2.** A number of persons who have come or been gathered together : assemblage, assembly, body, company, conclave, conference, congregation, congress, convocation, crowd, gathering, group, meeting, muster, troop. *Informal:* get-together. *See* COLLECT. **3.** A legally binding arrangement between parties : agreement, bond, compact[2], contract, covenant, pact. *See* AGREE. **4.** A formal, usually written settlement between nations : accord, agreement, concord, pact, treaty. *See* AGREE, POLITICS. **5.** An accepted way of doing something : form. *See* USUAL.

conventional *adjective*
1. Generally approved or agreed upon : accepted, orthodox, received, recognized, sanctioned. *See* ACCEPT, AGREE, STRAIGHT, USUAL. **2.** Conforming to established practice or standards : button-down, conformist, establishmentarian, orthodox, straight, traditional. *Slang:* square. *See* USUAL. **3.** Fond of or given to ceremony : ceremonious, courtly, formal, punctilious. *See* COURTESY.

conventionalize *verb*
To make conventional : conform, stylize. *See* USUAL.

converge *verb*
1. To come together : close, meet[1]. *See* OPEN. **2.** To direct toward a common center : center, channel, concentrate, focalize, focus. *See* EDGE.

convergence *noun*
1. A converging at a common center : concentration, confluence, conflux. *See* EDGE. **2.** The act or fact of coming together : concourse, confluence, gathering, junction, meeting. *See* CONNECT. **3.** The act or fact of coming near : approach, coming, imminence, nearness. *See* APPROACH.

conversant *adjective*
Having good knowledge of : acquainted, familiar, versant, versed. ***Idiom:*** up on. *See* KNOWLEDGE.

conversation *noun*
Spoken exchange : chat, colloquy, confabulation, converse[1], dialogue, discourse, speech, talk. *Informal:* confab. *Slang:* jaw. *See* WORDS.

conversational *adjective*
1. In the style of conversation : chatty, colloquial, confabulatory, informal. *See* WORDS. **2.** Given to conversation : chatty, garrulous, loquacious, talkative, talky, voluble. *Slang:* gabby. *See* WORDS.

conversationalist *noun*
One given to conversation : confabulator, conversationist, discourser, talker. *See* WORDS.

conversationist *noun*
One given to conversation : confabulator, conversationalist, discourser, talker. *See* WORDS.

converse[1] *verb*
To engage in spoken exchange : chat, confabulate, discourse, speak, talk. *Informal:* confab, visit. *See* WORDS.

converse *noun* **1.** Spoken exchange : chat, colloquy, confabulation, conversation, dialogue, discourse, speech, talk. *Informal:* confab. *Slang:* jaw. *See* WORDS. **2.** *Obsolete.* The exchange of ideas by writing, speech, or signals : communication, communion, intercommunication, intercourse. *See* KNOWLEDGE.

converse[2] *adjective*
Diametrically opposed : antipodal, antipodean, antithetical, antonymic, antonymous, contradictory, contrary, counter, diametric, diametrical, opposing, opposite, polar, reverse. *See* SUPPORT.

converse *noun* That which is diametrically opposed to another : antipode, antipodes, antithesis, antonym, contrary, counter, opposite, reverse. *Logic:* contradictory, contrapositive. *See* SUPPORT.

conversion *noun*
1. The process or result of changing from one appearance, state, or phase to another : change, changeover, metamorphosis, mutation, shift, transfiguration, transformation, translation, transmogrification, transmutation, transubstantiation. *See* CHANGE. **2.** A fundamental change in one's beliefs : metanoia, rebirth, regeneration. *See* CHANGE.

convert *verb*
To change into a different form, substance, or state : metamorphose, mutate, transfigure, transform, translate, transmogrify, transmute, transpose, transubstantiate. *See* CHANGE.

convey *verb*
1. To cause to come along with oneself : bear, bring, carry, fetch, take, transport. *See* ACCOMPANIED. **2.** To move while supporting : bear, carry, lug[2], transport. *Informal:* tote. *Slang:* schlep. *See* OVER. **3.** To cause to be transferred from one to another : hand (over), pass, transmit. *See* GIVE. **4.** To serve as a conduit : carry, channel, conduct, transmit. *See* ALLOW. **5.** To cause (a disease) to pass to another or others : carry, communicate, give, pass, spread, transmit. *See* MOVE. **6.** To make known : break, carry, communicate, disclose, get across, impart, pass, report, tell, transmit. *See* KNOWLEDGE. **7.** To put into words : articulate, communicate, declare, express, say, state, talk, tell, utter[1], vent, verbalize, vocalize, voice. ***Idiom:*** give tongue (*or* vent *or* voice) to. *See* WORDS. **8.** To give expression to, as by gestures, facial aspects, or bodily posture : communicate, display, express, manifest. *See* SHOW. **9.** *Law.* To change the ownership of (property) by means of a legal document : cede, deed, grant, make over, sign over. *Law:* alien, alienate, assign, transfer. *See* GIVE, LAW.

conveyance *noun*
1. The moving of persons or goods from one place to another : carriage, transit, transport, transportation. *See* MOVE. **2.** A making over of legal ownership or title : *Law:* alienation, assignment, grant, transfer, transferal. *See* LAW.

conveyer *noun*
A person who carries messages or is sent on errands : bearer, carrier, courier, envoy, messenger, runner, transporter. *See* OVER.

conviction *noun*
1. The fact or condition of being without doubt : assurance, assuredness, certainty, certitude, confidence, positiveness, sureness, surety. *See* CERTAIN. **2.** Something believed or accepted as true by a person : belief, feeling, idea,

mind, notion, opinion, persuasion, position, sentiment, view. *See* OPINION.

convince *verb*
1. To cause (another) to believe or feel sure about something : assure, persuade, satisfy, win over. *See* PERSUASION. **2.** To succeed in causing (a person) to act in a certain way : argue into, bring, bring around (*or* round), get, induce, persuade, prevail on (*or* upon), sell (on), talk into. *See* PERSUASION.

convincing *adjective*
1. Serving to convince : cogent, persuasive, satisfactory, telling. *See* PERSUASION. **2.** Worthy of belief or trust, as because of precision or faithfulness to an original : authentic, authoritative, credible, faithful, true, trustworthy, valid. *See* TRUE.

convivial *adjective*
1. Liking company : companionable, sociable, social. *Chiefly British:* matey. *See* ATTITUDE. **2.** Characterized by joyful exuberance : blithe, blithesome, boon[2], gay, gleeful, jocund, jolly, jovial, merry, mirthful. *See* HAPPY. **3.** Spent, marked by, or enjoyed in the company of others : companionable, sociable, social. *See* ATTITUDE, PARTICIPATE.

conviviality *noun*
Joyful, exuberant activity : festival, festiveness, festivity, fun, gaiety, jollity, merriment, merrymaking, revel (often used in plural), revelry. *See* LAUGHTER.

convocation *noun*
1. A number of persons who have come or been gathered together : assemblage, assembly, body, company, conclave, conference, congregation, congress, convention, crowd, gathering, group, meeting, muster, troop. *Informal:* get-together. *See* COLLECT. **2.** A formal assemblage of the members of a group : assembly, conference, congress, convention, meeting. *See* ASSEMBLE.

convoke *verb*
1. To bring together : assemble, call, cluster, collect[1], congregate, convene, gather, get together, group, muster, round up, summon. *See* COLLECT. **2.** To demand to appear, come, or assemble : call, convene, muster, send for, summon. *See* REQUEST.

convoluted *adjective*
Difficult to understand because of intricacy : byzantine, complex, complicated, daedal, Daedalian, elaborate, intricate, involute, involved, knotty, labyrinthine, tangled. *See* SIMPLE.

convulse *verb*
To cause to move to and fro violently : agitate, churn, rock, shake. *See* CALM, REPETITION.

convulsion *noun*
1. The condition of being physically agitated : agitation, commotion, turbulence. *See* CALM. **2.** A momentous or sweeping change : cataclysm, revolution, upheaval. *See* CHANGE. **3.** A condition of anguished struggle and disorder : paroxysm, throe (used in plural). *See* CALM.

cook *verb*
To prepare (food) for eating by the use of heat : do. *See* INGESTION.
cook up *verb Informal.* To use ingenuity in making, developing, or achieving : concoct, contrive, devise, dream up, fabricate, formulate, hatch, invent, make up, think up. ***Idiom:*** come up with. *See* MAKE.
cook *noun* A person who prepares food for eating : chef. *See* INGESTION.

cook up *verb* See **cook.**

cool *adjective*
1. Marked by a low temperature : chill, chilly, cold, nippy, shivery. *See* HOT. **2.** Not easily excited, even under pressure : calm, collected, composed, cool-headed, detached, even[1], even-tempered, imperturbable, nonchalant, possessed, unflappable, unruffled. *See* CALM. **3.** Not friendly, sociable, or warm in manner : aloof, chill, chilly, distant, offish, remote, reserved, reticent, solitary, standoffish, unapproachable, uncommunicative, undemonstrative, withdrawn. *See* ATTITUDE, HOT. **4.** *Slang.* Particularly excellent : divine, fabulous, fantastic, fantastical, glorious, marvelous, sensational, splendid, superb, terrific, wonderful. *Informal:* dandy, dreamy, great, ripping, super, swell, tremendous. *Slang:* groovy, hot, keen[1], neat, nifty. ***Idiom:*** out of this world. *See* GOOD.
cool *verb* To bring one's emotions under control : collect[1], compose, contain, control, simmer down. ***Idiom:*** cool it. *See* RESTRAINT.
cool *noun Slang.* A stable, calm state of the emotions : aplomb, balance, collectedness, composure, coolness, equanimity, imperturbability, imperturbableness, nonchalance, poise, sang-froid, self-possession, unflappability. *See* CALM, FEELINGS.

cooler *noun*
Slang. A place for the confinement of persons in lawful detention : brig, house of correction, jail, keep, penitentiary, prison. *Informal:* lockup, pen[3]. *Slang:* big house, can, clink, coop, hoosegow, joint, jug, pokey[1], slammer, stir[2]. *Chiefly Regional:* calaboose. *See* FREE.

cool-headed *adjective*
Not easily excited, even under pressure : calm, collected, composed, cool, detached, even[1], even-tempered, imperturbable, nonchalant, possessed, unflappable, unruffled. *See* CALM.

coolness *noun*
1. Relative lack of physical warmth : chill, chilliness, cold, coldness. *See* HOT. **2.** A stable, calm state of the emotions : aplomb, balance, collectedness, composure, equanimity, imperturbability, imperturbableness, nonchalance, poise, sang-froid, self-possession, unflappability. *Slang:* cool. *See* CALM, FEELINGS.

coop *noun*
Slang. A place for the confinement of persons in lawful detention : brig, house of correction, jail, keep, penitentiary, prison. *Informal:* lockup, pen[3]. *Slang:* big house, can, clink, cooler, hoosegow, joint, jug, pokey[1], slammer, stir[2]. *Chiefly Regional:* calaboose. *See* FREE.
coop *verb* To confine within a limited area. Also used with *in* or *up* : cage, enclose, fence (in), immure, mew (up), pen[2], shut in, shut up, wall (in *or* up). *See* FREE.

cooperate *verb*
To work together toward a common end : collaborate. *See* CONFLICT.

cooperation *noun*
1. Joint work toward a common end : coaction, collaboration, synergy, teamwork. *See* CONFLICT. **2.** The state of being associated : affiliation, alliance, association, combination, conjunction, connection, partnership. *See* NEAR.

cooperative *adjective*
Working together toward a common end : collaborative, synergetic, synergic, synergistic. *See* CONFLICT.

coordinate *verb*
1. To bring into accord : accommodate, attune, conform, harmonize, integrate, proportion, reconcile, tune. *See* AGREE. **2.** To combine and adapt in order to attain a particular effect : arrange, blend, harmonize, integrate, orchestrate, synthesize, unify. *See* BEAUTIFUL.

cop *noun*
Informal. A member of a law-enforcement agency : bluecoat, finest, officer, patrolman, patrolwoman, peace officer, police, policeman, police officer, policewoman. *Informal:* law. *Slang:* bull[1], copper, flatfoot, fuzz, gendarme, heat, man (often uppercase). *Chiefly British:* bobby, constable, peeler. *See* LAW.
cop *verb* **1.** *Slang.* To take (another's property) without permission : filch, pilfer, purloin, snatch, steal, thieve. *Informal:* lift, swipe. *Slang:* heist, hook, nip[1], pinch, rip off, snitch. *Idiom:* make (*or* walk) off with. *See* CRIMES, GIVE. **2.** *Slang.* To obtain possession or control of : capture, gain, get, take, win. *See* GET.
cop out *verb* *Slang.* To abandon a former position or commitment : back down (*or* out), renege, retreat. *Slang:* fink out. *See* RESIST.

copartner *noun*
One who is united in a relationship with another : affiliate, ally, associate, cohort, colleague, confederate, fellow, partner. *See* CONNECT.

copious *adjective*
Characterized by abundance : abundant, ample, bounteous, bountiful, generous, heavy, plenitudinous, plenteous, plentiful, substantial, voluminous. *See* BIG, GIVE, RICH.

cop out *verb* See **cop.**

copper *noun*
Slang. A member of a law-enforcement agency : bluecoat, finest, officer, patrolman, patrolwoman, peace officer, police, policeman, police officer, policewoman. *Informal:* cop, law. *Slang:* bull[1], flatfoot, fuzz, gendarme, heat, man (often uppercase). *Chiefly British:* bobby, constable, peeler. *See* LAW.

copulate *verb*
To engage in sexual relations with : bed, couple, have, mate, sleep with, take. ***Idioms:*** go to bed with, make love, make whoopee, roll in the hay. *See* SEX.

copy *noun*
1. Something closely resembling another : carbon copy, duplicate, facsimile, image, likeness, reduplication, replica, replication, reproduction, simulacrum. *Archaic:* simulacre. *Law:* counterpart. *See* SAME. **2.** An inferior substitute imitating an original : ersatz, imitation, pinchbeck, simulation. *See* SUBSTITUTE.
copy *verb* **1.** To make a copy of : duplicate, imitate, replicate, reproduce, simulate. *See* SAME. **2.** To take as a model or make conform to a model : emulate, follow, imitate, model (on, upon, *or* after), pattern (on, upon, *or* after). ***Idioms:*** follow in the footsteps of, follow suit, follow the example of. *See* SAME.

coquet *verb*
To make amorous advances without serious intentions : dally, flirt, toy, trifle. *See* SEX.

coquetry *noun*
Flirting : dalliance, flirtation. *See* SEX.

coquette *noun*
A woman who is given to flirting : flirt. *Informal:* vamp. *See* SEX.

coquettish *adjective*
Given to flirting : coy, flirtatious, flirty. *See* SEX.

cordial *adjective*
Pleasant and friendly in disposition : affable, agreeable, amiable, congenial, genial, good-natured, good-tempered, pleasant, sociable, warm. *See* ATTITUDE, GOOD.

cordiality *noun*
The quality of being pleasant and friendly : affability, agreeability, agreeableness, amenity, amiability, amiableness, congeniality, congenialness, cordialness, friendliness, geniality, genialness, pleasantness, sociability, sociableness, warmth. *See* ATTITUDE, GOOD.

cordialness *noun*
The quality of being pleasant and friendly : affability, agreeability, agreeableness, amenity, amiability, amiableness, congeniality, congenialness, cordiality, friendliness, geniality, genialness, pleasantness, sociability, sociableness, warmth. *See* ATTITUDE, GOOD.

core *noun*
1. A point of origin from which ideas or influences, for example, originate : bottom, center, focus, heart, hub, quick, root[1]. *See* START.
2. The most central and material part : essence, gist, heart, kernel, marrow, meat, nub, pith, quintessence, root[1], soul, spirit, stuff, substance. *Law:* gravamen. *See* BE.

cork *noun*
Something used to fill a hole, space, or container : choke, fill, plug, stop, stopper. *See* FULL.
cork *verb* To plug up something, as a hole, space, or container : block, choke, clog, close, congest, fill, plug, stop. *See* FULL.

corkscrew *verb*
To move or proceed on a repeatedly curving course : coil, curl, entwine, meander, snake, spiral, twine, twist, weave, wind[2], wreathe. *See* REPETITION, STRAIGHT.

corky *adjective*
Informal. Displaying light-hearted nonchalance : airy, breezy, buoyant, debonair, jaunty. *Idiom:* free and easy. *See* ATTITUDE, CAREFUL, GOOD.

corner *noun*
1. A difficult, often embarrassing situation or condition : box[1], deep water, difficulty, dilemma, Dutch, fix, hole, hot spot, hot water, jam, plight[1], predicament, quagmire, scrape, soup, trouble. *Informal:* bind, pickle, spot. *See* EASY. **2.** Exclusive control or possession : monopoly. *See* CONTROL, OWNED.

cornerstone *noun*
A fundamental principle or underlying concept : base[1], basis, foundation, fundament, fundamental, root[1], rudiment (often used in plural). *See* OVER.

corny *adjective*
Without freshness or appeal because of overuse : banal, bromidic, clichéd, commonplace, hackneyed, musty, overused, overworked, platitudinal, platitudinous, shopworn, stale, stereotyped, stereotypic, stereotypical, threadbare, timeworn, tired, trite, warmed-over, well-worn, worn-out. *See* EXCITE, USUAL.

corollary *noun*
Something brought about by a cause : aftermath, consequence, effect, end product, event, fruit, harvest, issue, outcome, precipitate, ramification, result, resultant, sequel, sequence, sequent, upshot. *See* CAUSE.

corporal *adjective*
Of or relating to the human body : bodily, corporeal, fleshly, personal, physical, somatic. *See* BODY.

corporation *noun*
A commercial organization : business, company, concern, enterprise, establishment, firm[2], house. *Informal:* outfit. *See* GROUP.

corporeal *adjective*
1. Of or relating to the human body : bodily, corporal, fleshly, personal, physical, somatic. *See* BODY. **2.** Composed of or relating to things that occupy space and can be perceived by the senses : concrete, material, objective, phenomenal, physical, sensible, substantial, tangible. *See* BODY, MATTER.

corps *noun*
1. A group of people acting together in a shared activity : band[2], company, party, troop, troupe. *See* PERFORMING ARTS. **2.** A group of people organized for a particular purpose : body, crew, detachment, force, gang, team, unit. *See* GROUP.

corpse *noun*
The physical frame of a dead person or animal : body, cadaver, carcass, remains. *Slang:* stiff. *See* BODY.

corpulent *adjective*
Having too much flesh : fat, fatty, fleshy, gross, obese, overblown, overweight, porcine, portly, stout, weighty. *See* FAT.

corpus *noun*
1. A measurable whole : amount, body, budget, bulk, quantity, quantum. *See* BIG.
2. *Anatomy.* The main part : body, bulk. *See* BIG.

correct *verb*
1. To make right what is wrong : amend, emend, mend, rectify, redress, reform, remedy, right. *See* CORRECT. **2.** To subject (one) to a penalty for a wrong : castigate, chastise, discipline, penalize, punish. *See* REWARD. **3.** To castigate for the purpose of improving : chasten. *See* PRAISE.
correct *adjective* **1.** Having no errors : accurate, errorless, exact, precise, right, rigorous. *See* CORRECT, TRUE. **2.** Conforming to fact : accurate, exact, faithful, precise, right, rigorous, true, veracious, veridical. *See* CORRECT, HONEST, REAL, TRUE. **3.** Conforming to accepted standards : becoming, befitting, comely, comme il faut, decent, decorous, de rigueur, nice, proper, respectable, right, seemly. *See* COURTESY. **4.** Suitable for a particular person, condition, occasion, or place : appropriate, apt, becoming, befitting, felicitous, fit[1], fitting, happy, meet[2], proper, right, tailor-made. *See* RIGHT.

correction *noun*
Something, such as loss, pain, or confinement, imposed for wrongdoing : castigation, chastisement, discipline, penalty, punishment. *See* REWARD.

corrective *adjective*
Tending to correct : amendatory, emendatory, reformative, reformatory, remedial. *See* CORRECT.
corrective *noun* Something that corrects or counteracts : antidote, countermeasure, curative, cure, remedy. *See* BETTER.

correctly *adverb*
In a fair, sporting manner : cleanly, fair, fairly, properly. *See* FAIR.

correctness *noun*
1. Freedom from error : accuracy, accurateness, exactitude, exactness, preciseness, precision, rightness. *See* CORRECT. **2.** Correspondence with fact or truth : accuracy, exactitude, exactness, fidelity, truth, veraciousness, veracity, veridicality, verity. *See* TRUE. **3.** Conformity to recognized standards, as of conduct or appearance : comeliness, decency, decentness, decorousness, decorum, properness, propriety, respectability, respectableness, seemliness. *See* USUAL.

correlate *verb*
To come or bring together in one's mind or imagination : associate, bracket, connect, couple, identify, link. *See* SAME.
correlate *noun* Something closely resembling or analogous to something else : analogue, congener, correlative, correspondent, counterpart, match, parallel. *See* SAME.

correlation *noun*
A logical or natural association between two or more things : connection, interconnection, interdependence, interrelationship, link, linkage, relation, relationship, tie-in. *Informal:* hookup. *See* CONNECT.

correlative *noun*
Something closely resembling or analogous to something else : analogue, congener, correlate, correspondent, counterpart, match, parallel. *See* SAME.

correspond *verb*
1. To be compatible or in correspondence : accord, agree, check, chime, comport with, conform, consist, fit[1], harmonize, match, square, tally. *Informal:* jibe[1]. *Archaic:* quadrate. *See* AGREE. **2.** To be in keeping with : become, befit, conform, fit[1], go with, match, suit. *See* AGREE. **3.** To be equal or alike : compare, equal, match, measure up, parallel, touch. *Informal:* stack up. *See* SAME. **4.** To be equivalent or tantamount : amount, constitute, equal. ***Idiom:*** have all the earmarks. *See* BE.

correspondence *noun*
1. The act or state of agreeing or conforming : accordance, agreement, chime, conformance, conformation, conformity, congruence, congruity, harmonization, harmony, keeping. *See* AGREE. **2.** The quality or state of being alike : affinity, alikeness, analogy, comparison, likeness, parallelism, resemblance, similarity, similitude, uniformity, uniformness. *See* SAME.

correspondent *noun*
Something closely resembling or analogous to something else : analogue, congener, correlate, correlative, counterpart, match, parallel. *See* SAME.
correspondent *adjective* In keeping with one's needs or expectations : accordant, agreeable, compatible, conformable, congenial, congruous, consistent, consonant, corresponding, harmonious. *See* AGREE.

corresponding *adjective*
1. In keeping with one's needs or expectations : accordant, agreeable, compatible, conformable, congenial, congruous, consistent, consonant, correspondent, harmonious. *See* AGREE. **2.** Possessing the same or almost the same characteristics : alike, analogous, comparable, equivalent, like[2], parallel, similar, uniform. *See* SAME.

corrival *noun*
One that competes : competition, competitor,

contender, contestant, opponent, rival. *See* CONFLICT.

corrivalry *noun*
A vying with others for victory or supremacy : battle, competition, contest, race, rivalry, strife, striving, struggle, tug of war, war, warfare. *See* CONFLICT.

corroborate *verb*
1. To present evidence in support of : back (up), buttress, substantiate. *See* SUPPORT. **2.** To assure the certainty or validity of : attest, authenticate, back (up), bear out, confirm, evidence, justify, substantiate, testify (to), validate, verify, warrant. *See* SUPPORT, TRUE. **3.** To establish as true or genuine : authenticate, bear out, confirm, demonstrate, endorse, establish, evidence, prove, show, substantiate, validate, verify. *See* SHOW, SUPPORT.

corroboration *noun*
That which confirms : attestation, authentication, confirmation, demonstration, evidence, proof, substantiation, testament, testimonial, testimony, validation, verification, warrant. *See* TRUE.

corrode *verb*
To consume gradually, as by chemical reaction or friction : bite, eat, erode, gnaw, wear, wear away. *See* ATTACK.

corrosive *adjective*
So sharp as to cause mental pain : acerbic, acid, acidic, acrid, astringent, biting, caustic, cutting, mordacious, mordant, pungent, scathing, sharp, slashing, stinging, trenchant, truculent, vitriolic. *See* ATTACK, RESPECT.

corrosiveness *noun*
Irony or bitterness, as of tone : acerbity, acidity, acridity, causticity, mordacity, mordancy, sarcasm, trenchancy. *See* LAUGHTER, RESPECT.

corrupt *adjective*
1. Utterly reprehensible in nature or behavior : degenerate, depraved, flagitious, miscreant, perverse, rotten, unhealthy, villainous. *See* CLEAN, GOOD. **2.** Marked by dishonesty, especially in matters of public trust : dishonest, venal. *Informal:* crooked. *See* HONEST. **3.** Ruthlessly seeking personal advantage : mercenary, praetorian, venal. *Informal:* crooked. *See* SELF.

corrupt *verb* **1.** To ruin utterly in character or quality : animalize, bastardize, bestialize, brutalize, canker, debase, debauch, demoralize, deprave, pervert, stain, vitiate, warp. *See* CLEAN, HELP. **2.** To make morally impure : contaminate, defile, infect, pollute, soil, taint. *See* CLEAN.

corruptible *adjective*
Capable of being bribed : buyable, purchasable, venal. *See* CRIMES, PERSUASION.

corruption *noun*
1. Degrading, immoral acts or habits : bestiality, depravity, flagitiousness, immorality, perversion, turpitude, vice, villainousness, villainy, wickedness. *See* CLEAN. **2.** Departure from what is legally, ethically, and morally correct : corruptness, dishonesty, improbity. *Informal:* crookedness. *See* HONEST. **3.** A term that offends against established usage standards : barbarism, solecism, vulgarism. *See* STYLE.

corruptive *adjective*
Morally detrimental : contaminative, demoralizing, unhealthy, unwholesome. *See* RIGHT.

corruptness *noun*
Departure from what is legally, ethically, and morally correct : corruption, dishonesty, improbity. *Informal:* crookedness. *See* HONEST.

coruscate *verb*
To emit light suddenly in rays or sparks : flash, glance, gleam, glimmer, glint, glisten, glister, glitter, scintillate, shimmer, spangle, sparkle, twinkle, wink. *See* LIGHT.

coruscation *noun*
A sudden quick light : blink, flash, flicker, glance, gleam, glimmer, glint, spark[1], twinkle, wink. *See* LIGHT.

cosmic *adjective*
So pervasive and all-inclusive as to exist in or affect the whole world : catholic, cosmopolitan, ecumenical, global, pandemic, planetary, universal, worldwide. *See* LIMITED, SPECIFIC.

cosmopolitan *adjective*
1. So pervasive and all-inclusive as to exist in or affect the whole world : catholic, cosmic, ecumenical, global, pandemic, planetary, universal, worldwide. *See* LIMITED, SPECIFIC. **2.** Experienced in the ways of the world; lacking natural simplicity : sophisticated, worldly, worldly-wise. *See* KNOWLEDGE.

cosmos *noun*
The totality of all existing things : creation, macrocosm, nature, universe, world. *See* MATTER, PART.

cosset *verb*
To treat with indulgence and often overtender care : baby, cater, coddle, indulge, mollycoddle, overindulge, pamper, spoil. *See* TREAT WELL.

cost *noun*
1. An amount paid or to be paid for a purchase : charge, price. *Informal:* tab. *See* TRANSACTIONS. **2.** Something expended to obtain a

benefit or desired result : disbursement, expenditure, expense, outlay. *See* TRANSACTIONS. **3.** A loss sustained in the accomplishment of or as the result of something : expense, price, sacrifice, toll[1]. *See* TRANSACTIONS.

cost *verb* To require a specified price : go for, sell for. *See* TRANSACTIONS.

costive *adjective*
Ungenerously or pettily reluctant to spend money : cheap, close, close-fisted, hard-fisted, mean[2], miserly, niggard, niggardly, parsimonious, penny-pinching, penurious, petty, pinching, stingy, tight, tightfisted. *See* GIVE.

costly *adjective*
1. Bringing a high price : dear, expensive, high, high-priced. *See* TRANSACTIONS, VALUE.
2. Of great value : inestimable, invaluable, precious, priceless, valuable, worthy. ***Idioms:*** beyond price, of great price. *See* VALUE.

costume *noun*
1. A set or style of clothing : dress, garb, guise, habiliment (often used in plural), outfit, turnout. *Informal:* getup, rig. *See* PUT ON.
2. Clothes or other personal effects, such as makeup, worn to conceal one's identity : disguise. *See* SHOW.

cosy *adjective* See **cozy.**

coterie *noun*
A particular social group : circle, clique, crowd, set[2]. *Informal:* bunch, gang. *See* GROUP.

cotton *verb*
1. *Informal.* To live or act together in harmony : get along, get on, harmonize. ***Idiom:*** hit it off. *See* AGREE. **2.** *Informal.* To support slavishly every opinion or suggestion of a superior : bootlick, cringe, fawn, grovel, kowtow, slaver, toady, truckle. *Informal:* apple-polish, brownnose. *Slang:* suck up. ***Idioms:*** curry favor, dance attendance, kiss someone's feet, lick someone's boots. *See* OVER.

couch *verb*
To convey in language or words of a particular form : express, formulate, phrase, put, word. *See* WORDS.

counsel *noun*
1. An exchange of views in an attempt to reach a decision : conference, consultation, deliberation, parley. *See* WORDS. **2.** An opinion as to a decision or course of action : advice, recommendation. *See* OPINION. **3.** A person who practices law : attorney, counselor, lawyer. *Slang:* ambulance chaser. *Chiefly British:* barrister. *See* LAW. **4.** *Law.* One who advises another, especially officially or professionally : adviser, consultant, counselor, mentor. *See* OPINION.

counsel *verb* To give recommendations to (someone) about a decision or course of action : advise, recommend. *Informal:* mentor. *See* OPINION.

counsellor *noun* See **counselor.**

counselor also **counsellor** *noun*
1. One who advises another, especially officially or professionally : adviser, consultant, mentor. *Law:* counsel. *See* OPINION. **2.** A person who practices law : attorney, counsel, lawyer. *Slang:* ambulance chaser. *Chiefly British:* barrister. *See* LAW.

count *verb*
1. To note (items) one by one so as to get a total : enumerate, number, numerate, reckon, tally, tell. *See* COUNT. **2.** To be of significance or importance : import, matter, signify, weigh. *See* IMPORTANT. **3.** To indicate (time or rhythm), as with repeated gestures or sounds : beat. ***Idioms:*** keep time, mark time. *See* REPETITION.

count on *verb* **1.** To place trust or confidence in : bank on (*or* upon), believe in, depend on (*or* upon), reckon on (*or* upon), rely on (*or* upon), trust (in). *See* TRUST. **2.** To look forward to confidently : anticipate, await, bargain for (*or* on), depend on (*or* upon), expect, look for, wait (for). *Informal:* figure on. *See* SURPRISE.

count out *verb* To keep from being admitted, included, or considered : bar, debar, eliminate, except, exclude, keep out, rule out, shut out. *See* INCLUDE.

count *noun* A noting of items one by one : enumeration, numeration, reckoning, tally. *Archaic:* tale. *See* COUNT.

countenance *noun*
1. An outward appearance : aspect, face, look, physiognomy, surface, visage. *See* SURFACE. **2.** A disposition of the facial features that conveys meaning, feeling, or mood : aspect, cast, expression, face, look, visage. *See* EXPRESS.
3. The front surface of the head : face, feature (often used in plural), muzzle, visage. *Informal:* mug. *Slang:* kisser, map, pan, puss. *See* PRECEDE.

countenance *verb* **1.** To lend supportive approval to : encourage, favor, smile on (*or* upon). *See* SUPPORT. **2.** To be favorably disposed toward : approve, favor, hold with. *Informal:* go for. ***Idiom:*** take kindly to. *See* PRAISE.

counter *adjective*
Diametrically opposed : antipodal, antipodean, antithetical, antonymic, antonymous, contradictory, contrary, converse[2], diametric, diametrical, opposing, opposite, polar, reverse. *See* SUPPORT.
counter *noun* That which is diametrically opposed to another : antipode, antipodes, antithesis, antonym, contrary, converse[2], opposite, reverse. *Logic:* contradictory, contrapositive. *See* SUPPORT.
counter *verb* **1.** To return like for like : hit back, reciprocate, retaliate, retort, strike back. *See* ATTACK, FORGIVENESS. **2.** To place in opposition or be in opposition to : match, oppose, pit[1], play off. ***Idioms:*** bump heads with, meet head-on, set (*or* be) at odds, set (*or* be) at someone's throat, trade blows (*or* punches). *See* SUPPORT.

counteract *verb*
1. To act as an equalizing weight or force to : balance, compensate, counterbalance, counterpoise, countervail, make up, offset, set off. *See* ORDER. **2.** To make ineffective by applying an opposite force or amount : cancel, negate, neutralize, nullify. *See* ACTION.

counteraction *noun*
The act of retaliating : counterattack, counterblow, reciprocation, reprisal, requital, retaliation, retribution, revenge, tit for tat, vengeance. ***Idioms:*** an eye for an eye, a tooth for a tooth, like for like, measure for measure. *See* ATTACK, FORGIVENESS.

counterattack *noun*
The act of retaliating : counteraction, counterblow, reciprocation, reprisal, requital, retaliation, retribution, revenge, tit for tat, vengeance. ***Idioms:*** an eye for an eye, a tooth for a tooth, like for like, measure for measure. *See* ATTACK, FORGIVENESS.

counterbalance *verb*
1. To act as an equalizing weight or force to : balance, compensate, counteract, counterpoise, countervail, make up, offset, set off. *See* ORDER. **2.** To put in balance : balance, equalize, stabilize, steady. *See* ORDER. **3.** To make up for : balance, compensate, counterpoise, countervail, neutralize, offset, outweigh, redeem, set off. *See* SUBSTITUTE.

counterblow *noun*
The act of retaliating : counteraction, counterattack, reciprocation, reprisal, requital, retaliation, retribution, revenge, tit for tat, vengeance. ***Idioms:*** an eye for an eye, a tooth for a tooth, like for like, measure for measure. *See* ATTACK, FORGIVENESS.

counterfactual *adjective*
Devoid of truth : false, specious, spurious, truthless, untrue, untruthful, wrong. *See* TRUE.

counterfeit *verb*
1. To make a fraudulent copy of : fake, falsify, forge[1]. *See* TRUE. **2.** To take on or give a false appearance of : affect[2], assume, fake, feign, pretend, put on, sham, simulate. ***Idiom:*** make believe. *See* TRUE. **3.** To behave affectedly or insincerely or take on a false or misleading appearance of : act, dissemble, fake, feign, play-act, pose, pretend, put on, sham, simulate. *See* HONEST, TRUE. **4.** To contrive and present as genuine : fake, feign, pretend, simulate. ***Idioms:*** make believe, put on an act. *See* TRUE.
counterfeit *adjective* Fraudulently or deceptively imitative : bogus, fake, false, fraudulent, phony, sham, spurious, suppositious, supposititious. *See* TRUE.
counterfeit *noun* A fraudulent imitation : fake, forgery, phony, sham. *See* TRUE.

counterfeiter *noun*
One who makes a fraudulent copy of something : fabricator, faker, forger. *See* TRUE.

countermeasure *noun*
Something that corrects or counteracts : antidote, corrective, curative, cure, remedy. *See* BETTER.

counterpart *noun*
1. Something closely resembling or analogous to something else : analogue, congener, correlate, correlative, correspondent, match, parallel. *See* SAME. **2.** One that has the same functions and characteristics as another : opposite number, vis-à-vis. *See* SAME. **3.** *Law.* Something closely resembling another : carbon copy, copy, duplicate, facsimile, image, likeness, reduplication, replica, replication, reproduction, simulacrum. *Archaic:* simulacre. *See* SAME. **4.** One of a matched pair of things : companion, double, duplicate, fellow, match, mate, twin. *See* SAME.

counterpoint *noun*
Striking difference between compared individuals : contrast. *See* SAME.

counterpoise *noun*
A stable state characterized by the cancellation of all forces by equal opposing forces : balance, equilibrium, equipoise, stasis. *See* ORDER.
counterpoise *verb* **1.** To act as an equalizing weight or force to : balance, compensate, counteract, counterbalance, countervail, make up, offset, set off. *See* ORDER. **2.** To make up for : balance, compensate, counterbalance,

countervail, neutralize, offset, outweigh, redeem, set off. *See* SUBSTITUTE.

countervail *verb*

1. To act as an equalizing weight or force to : balance, compensate, counteract, counterbalance, counterpoise, make up, offset, set off. *See* ORDER. **2.** To make up for : balance, compensate, counterbalance, counterpoise, neutralize, offset, outweigh, redeem, set off. *See* SUBSTITUTE.

countless *adjective*

Too great to be calculated : immeasurable, incalculable, incomputable, inestimable, infinite, innumerable, measureless, uncountable. *See* BIG.

count on *verb* See **count.**

count out *verb* See **count.**

country *noun*

1. An organized geopolitical unit : body politic, land, nation, polity, state. *See* POLITICS, TERRITORY. **2.** A particular area used for or associated with a specific individual or activity : district, region, terrain, territory. *Slang:* turf. *See* TERRITORY. **3.** A rural area : countryside, God's country. *See* URBAN.

country *adjective* Of or relating to the countryside : arcadian, bucolic, campestral, pastoral, provincial, rural, rustic. *Informal:* hick. *See* URBAN.

countryman *noun*

A person who is from one's own country : compatriot, countrywoman, fellow citizen. *See* GROUP.

countryside *noun*

A rural area : country, God's country. *See* URBAN.

countrywoman *noun*

A person who is from one's own country : compatriot, countryman, fellow citizen. *See* GROUP.

couple *noun*

1. Two items of the same kind together : brace, couplet, doublet, duet, duo, match, pair, two, twosome, yoke. *See* GROUP, SAME. **2.** Two persons united, as by marriage : duo, pair, twosome. *See* GROUP.

couple *verb* **1.** To join one thing to another : affix, attach, clip[2], connect, fasten, fix, moor, secure. *See* ASSEMBLE. **2.** To bring or come together into a united whole : coalesce, combine, compound, concrete, conjoin, conjugate, connect, consolidate, join, link, marry, meld, unify, unite, wed, yoke. *See* ASSEMBLE. **3.** To come or bring together in one's mind or imagination : associate, bracket, connect, correlate, identify, link. *See* SAME. **4.** To engage in sexual relations with : bed, copulate, have, mate, sleep with, take. ***Idioms:*** go to bed with, make love, make whoopee, roll in the hay. *See* SEX.

couplet *noun*

Two items of the same kind together : brace, couple, doublet, duet, duo, match, pair, two, twosome, yoke. *See* GROUP, SAME.

coupling *noun*

A point or position at which two or more things are joined : connection, joint, junction, juncture, seam, union. *See* CONNECT.

courage *noun*

The quality of mind enabling one to face danger or hardship resolutely : braveness, bravery, courageousness, dauntlessness, doughtiness, fearlessness, fortitude, gallantry, gameness, heart, intrepidity, intrepidness, mettle, nerve, pluck, pluckiness, spirit, stoutheartedness, undauntedness, valiance, valiancy, valiantness, valor. *Informal:* spunk, spunkiness. *Slang:* gut (used in plural), gutsiness, moxie. *See* FEAR.

courageous *adjective*

Having or showing courage : audacious, bold, brave, dauntless, doughty, fearless, fortitudinous, gallant, game, hardy, heroic, intrepid, mettlesome, plucky, stout, stouthearted, unafraid, undaunted, valiant, valorous. *Informal:* spunky. *Slang:* gutsy, gutty. *See* FEAR.

courageousness *noun*

The quality of mind enabling one to face danger or hardship resolutely : braveness, bravery, courage, dauntlessness, doughtiness, fearlessness, fortitude, gallantry, gameness, heart, intrepidity, intrepidness, mettle, nerve, pluck, pluckiness, spirit, stoutheartedness, undauntedness, valiance, valiancy, valiantness, valor. *Informal:* spunk, spunkiness. *Slang:* gut (used in plural), gutsiness, moxie. *See* FEAR.

courier *noun*

A person who carries messages or is sent on errands : bearer, carrier, conveyer, envoy, messenger, runner, transporter. *See* OVER.

course *noun*

1. A method used in dealing with something : approach, attack, line, modus operandi, plan, procedure, tack, technique. *See* MEANS. **2.** A number of things placed or occurring one after the other : chain, consecution, order, procession, progression, round, run, sequence, series, string, succession, suite, train. *Informal:* streak. *See* ORDER. **3.** The compass direction in which a ship or an aircraft moves : bearing, heading, vector. *See* APPROACH.

course *verb* To move freely as a liquid : circulate, flow, run, stream. *See* MOVE.

court *noun*
1. An area partially or entirely enclosed by walls or buildings : atrium, close, courtyard, enclosure, quad, quadrangle, yard. *See* PLACE. **2.** A judicial assembly : bar, tribunal. *See* LAW.
court *verb* **1.** To behave so as to bring on (danger, for example) : invite, provoke, tempt. *See* SEEK. **2.** To attempt to gain the affection of : pursue, spark[2], woo. *Informal:* romance. *See* SEEK, SEX.

courteous *adjective*
1. Full of polite concern for the well-being of others : attentive, considerate, gallant, polite, solicitous, thoughtful. *See* CAREFUL, TREAT WELL. **2.** Characterized by good manners : civil, genteel, mannerly, polite, well-bred, well-mannered. *See* COURTESY.

courteousness *noun*
Well-mannered behavior toward others : civility, courtesy, genteelness, gentility, mannerliness, politeness, politesse. *See* COURTESY.

courter *noun*
A man who courts a woman : admirer, beau, suitor, swain, wooer. *See* SEX.

courtesan *noun*
A woman who engages in sexual intercourse for payment : bawd, call girl, camp follower, harlot, prostitute, scarlet woman, streetwalker, strumpet, tart[2], whore. *Slang:* hooker, moll. ***Idioms:*** lady of easy virtue, lady of pleasure, lady of the night. *See* SEX.

courtesy *noun*
1. Well-mannered behavior toward others : civility, courteousness, genteelness, gentility, mannerliness, politeness, politesse. *See* COURTESY. **2.** A courteous act or courteous acts that contribute to smoothness and ease in dealings and social relationships : amenity (used in plural), civility, pleasantry, politeness, propriety (used in plural). *See* COURTESY. **3.** An act requiring special generosity : beau geste, compliment, favor. *See* GIVE.

courtier *noun*
One who flatters another excessively : adulator, flatterer, sycophant, toady. *Informal:* apple-polisher. *See* OVER, PRAISE.

courtly *adjective*
1. Characterized by elaborate but usually formal courtesy : chivalrous, gallant, gracious, knightly, stately. *See* ATTITUDE, COURTESY.
2. Fond of or given to ceremony : ceremonious, conventional, formal, punctilious. *See* COURTESY.

courtship *noun*
Romantic attentions : address (often used in plural), suit. *See* SEEK, SEX.

courtyard *noun*
An area partially or entirely enclosed by walls or buildings : atrium, close, court, enclosure, quad, quadrangle, yard. *See* PLACE.

cove *noun*
A body of water partly enclosed by land but having a wide outlet to the sea : bay[1], bight, inlet. *See* TERRITORY.

covenant *noun*
1. A legally binding arrangement between parties : agreement, bond, compact[2], contract, convention, pact. *See* AGREE. **2.** An agreement, especially one involving a sale or exchange : bargain, compact[2], contract, deal, transaction. *See* AGREE. **3.** A declaration that one will or will not do a certain thing : assurance, engagement, guarantee, guaranty, pledge, plight[2], promise, solemn word, vow, warrant, word, word of honor. *See* OBLIGATION.
covenant *verb* **1.** To enter into a formal agreement : bargain, contract. *See* AGREE. **2.** To guarantee by a solemn promise : pledge, plight[2], promise, swear, vow. ***Idiom:*** give one's word of honor. *See* AGREE, OBLIGATION.

cover *verb*
1. To prevent (something) from being known. Also used with *up* : cloak, conceal, enshroud, hide[1], hush (up), mask, shroud, veil. ***Idioms:*** keep under cover, keep under wraps. *See* SHOW. **2.** To furnish with a covering of a different material : clad, face, sheathe, side, skin. *See* SURFACE. **3.** To extend over the surface of : blanket, cap, overlay, spread. *See* PUT ON. **4.** To journey over (a specified distance) : make. *Informal:* do. *See* MOVE. **5.** To observe, analyze, and relate the details of (an event) : report. *See* WORDS.
cover *noun* **1.** Something that physically protects, especially from danger : asylum, covert, harbor, haven, protection, refuge, retreat, sanctuary, shelter. *See* ATTACK, SAFETY. **2.** A deceptive outward appearance : cloak, color, coloring, disguise, disguisement, façade, face, false colors, front, gloss, guise, mask, masquerade, pretense, pretext, semblance, show, veil, veneer, window-dressing. *Slang:* put-on. *See* SHOW.

coverage *noun*
The reporting of news : reportage. *See* WORDS.

covert *adjective*
1. Existing or operating in a way so as to ensure complete concealment and confidentiality :

clandestine, cloak-and-dagger, huggermugger, secret, sub-rosa, undercover. *Informal:* hush-hush. ***Idiom:*** under wraps. *See* SHOW. **2.** Lying beyond what is obvious or avowed : buried, concealed, hidden, obscured, ulterior. ***Idiom:*** under cover (*or* wraps). *See* SHOW.
covert *noun* **1.** Something that physically protects, especially from danger : asylum, cover, harbor, haven, protection, refuge, retreat, sanctuary, shelter. *See* ATTACK, SAFETY. **2.** A hiding place : den, hideaway, hide-out, lair. *See* PLACE, SHOW.

covertly *adverb*
In a secret way : clandestinely, huggermugger, secretly, sub rosa. ***Idioms:*** by stealth, on the sly, under cover. *See* SHOW.

covertness *noun*
The habit, practice, or policy of keeping secrets : clandestineness, clandestinity, concealment, huggermugger, huggermuggery, secrecy, secretiveness, secretness. *See* SHOW.

covet *verb*
1. To feel envy towards or for : begrudge, envy, grudge. *See* DESIRE. **2.** To have a strong longing for : ache, desire, hanker, long[2], pant, pine, want, wish, yearn. *Informal:* hone[2]. *See* DESIRE.

covetous *adjective*
1. Resentfully or painfully desirous of another's advantages : envious, green-eyed, invidious, jealous. *See* DESIRE. **2.** Having a strong urge to obtain or possess something, especially material wealth, in quantity : acquisitive, avaricious, avid, grasping, greedy, hungry. *Informal:* grabby. *See* DESIRE, GIVE.

covetousness *noun*
1. Resentful or painful desire for another's advantages : enviousness, envy, jealousy. *See* DESIRE. **2.** Excessive desire for more than one needs or deserves : acquisitiveness, avarice, avariciousness, avidity, cupidity, graspingness, greed. *Informal:* grabbiness. *See* DESIRE, GIVE.

cow *verb*
To domineer or drive into compliance by the use of as threats or force, for example : bludgeon, browbeat, bulldoze, bully, bullyrag, hector, intimidate, menace, threaten. *Informal:* strong-arm. *See* OVER.

coward *noun*
An ignoble, uncourageous person : craven, dastard, funk, poltroon. *Slang:* chicken, yellow-belly. *See* FEAR.

cowardice *noun*
Ignoble lack of courage : chickenheartedness, cowardliness, cravenness, dastardliness, faint-heartedness, funk, pusillanimity, unmanliness. *Slang:* gutlessness, yellowness, yellow streak. *See* FEAR.

cowardliness *noun*
Ignoble lack of courage : chickenheartedness, cowardice, cravenness, dastardliness, faint-heartedness, funk, pusillanimity, unmanliness. *Slang:* gutlessness, yellowness, yellow streak. *See* FEAR.

cowardly *adjective*
Ignobly lacking in courage : chickenhearted, craven, dastardly, faint-hearted, lily-livered, pusillanimous, unmanly. *Slang:* chicken, gutless, yellow, yellow-bellied. *See* FEAR.

coy *adjective*
1. Not forward but reticent or reserved in manner : backward, bashful, demure, diffident, modest, retiring, self-effacing, shy[1], timid. *See* RESTRAINT. **2.** Given to flirting : coquettish, flirtatious, flirty. *See* SEX.

coyness *noun*
An awkwardness or lack of self-confidence in the presence of others : backwardness, bashfulness, retiringness, shyness, timidity, timidness. *See* RESTRAINT.

cozen *verb*
1. To cause to accept what is false, especially by trickery or misrepresentation : beguile, betray, bluff, deceive, delude, double-cross, dupe, fool, hoodwink, humbug, mislead, take in, trick. *Informal:* bamboozle, have. *Slang:* four-flush. ***Idioms:*** lead astray, play false, pull the wool over someone's eyes, put something over on, take for a ride. *See* HONEST. **2.** To get money or something else from by deceitful trickery : bilk, cheat, defraud, gull, mulct, rook, swindle, victimize. *Informal:* chisel, flimflam, take, trim. *Slang:* diddle[1], do, gyp, stick, sting. *See* HONEST.

cozener *noun*
A person who cheats : bilk, cheat, cheater, defrauder, rook, sharper, swindler, trickster, victimizer. *Informal:* chiseler, crook, flimflammer. *Slang:* diddler, gyp, gypper. *See* HONEST.

cozy also **cosy** *adjective*
Affording pleasurable ease : comfortable, easeful, easy, snug. *Informal:* comfy, soft. *See* GOOD.

crab *noun*
A person who habitually complains or grumbles : complainer, faultfinder, grouch, growler, grumbler, grump, murmurer, mutterer, whiner. *Informal:* crank, griper, grouser. *Slang:* bellyacher, sorehead, sourpuss. *See* HAPPY.

crab *verb Informal.* To express negative feelings, especially of dissatisfaction or resentment : complain, grouch, grump, whine. *Informal:* gripe, grouse, kick. *Slang:* beef, bellyache, bitch. *See* FEELINGS, HAPPY.

crabbed *adjective*
Having or showing a bad temper : bad-tempered, cantankerous, cranky, cross, disagreeable, fretful, grouchy, grumpy, ill-tempered, irascible, irritable, nasty, peevish, petulant, querulous, snappish, snappy, surly, testy, ugly, waspish. *Informal:* crabby, mean[2]. ***Idiom:*** out of sorts. *See* ATTITUDE.

crabby *adjective*
Informal. Having or showing a bad temper : bad-tempered, cantankerous, crabbed, cranky, cross, disagreeable, fretful, grouchy, grumpy, ill-tempered, irascible, irritable, nasty, peevish, petulant, querulous, snappish, snappy, surly, testy, ugly, waspish. *Informal:* mean[2]. ***Idiom:*** out of sorts. *See* ATTITUDE.

crack *verb*
1. To undergo partial breaking : fissure, fracture, rupture, split. *See* HELP. **2.** To make a sudden sharp, explosive noise : bang, bark, clap, pop[1], snap. *See* SOUNDS. **3.** To find the key to (a code, for example) : break, decipher, decrypt, puzzle out. *See* KNOWLEDGE. **4.** To give way mentally and emotionally : break (down), collapse, snap. *Informal:* crack up, fold. *See* EXPLOSION. **5.** To suddenly lose all health or strength : break (down), cave in, collapse, drop, give out, succumb. *Informal:* crack up. *Slang:* conk out. ***Idiom:*** give way. *See* HEALTH.

crack up *verb* **1.** *Informal.* To undergo wrecking : crash, smash. *Informal:* pile up. *See* HELP. **2.** *Informal.* To give way mentally and emotionally : break (down), collapse, crack, snap. *Informal:* fold. *See* EXPLOSION. **3.** *Informal.* To suddenly lose all health or strength : break (down), cave in, collapse, crack, drop, give out, succumb. *Slang:* conk out. ***Idiom:*** give way. *See* HEALTH.

crack *noun* **1.** A sudden sharp, explosive noise : bang, bark, clap, explosion, pop[1], rat-a-tat-tat, report, snap. *See* SOUNDS. **2.** A usually narrow partial opening caused by splitting and rupture : break, chink, cleavage, cleft, crevice, fissure, rift, split. *See* OPEN. **3.** A sudden sharp, powerful stroke : bang, blow[2], clout, hit, lick, pound, slug[3], sock, swat, thwack, welt, whack, wham, whop. *Informal:* bash, biff, bop, clip[1], wallop. *Slang:* belt, conk, paste. *See* ATTACK, STRIKE. **4.** A trying to do or make something : attempt, effort, endeavor, essay, go, offer, stab, trial, try. *Informal:* shot. *Slang:* take. *Archaic:* assay. *See* TRY. **5.** A brief trial : go, stab, try. *Informal:* fling, shot, whack, whirl. *See* TRY. **6.** A flippant or sarcastic remark : dig, quip. *Slang:* wisecrack. *See* RESPECT, WORDS. **7.** A very brief time : flash, instant, minute[1], moment, second[1], trice, twinkle, twinkling, wink. *Informal:* jiff, jiffy. *Chiefly British:* tick. *See* BIG, TIME.

crack *adjective* Having or demonstrating a high degree of knowledge or skill : adept, expert, master, masterful, masterly, professional, proficient, skilled, skillful. *Slang:* crackerjack. *See* ABILITY.

crackajack *adjective & noun* See **crackerjack.**

crackdown *noun*
Sudden punitive action : clampdown, repression, suppression. *See* CONTINUE, WIN.

cracked *adjective*
Informal. Afflicted with or exhibiting irrationality and mental unsoundness : brainsick, crazy, daft, demented, disordered, distraught, dotty, insane, lunatic, mad, maniac, maniacal, mentally ill, moonstruck, off, touched, unbalanced, unsound, wrong. *Informal:* bonkers, daffy, gaga, loony. *Slang:* bananas, batty, buggy, cuckoo, fruity, loco, nuts, nutty, screwy, wacky. *Chiefly British:* crackers. *Law:* non compos mentis. ***Idioms:*** around the bend, crazy as a loon, mad as a hatter, not all there, nutty as a fruitcake, off (*or* out of) one's head, off one's rocker, of unsound mind, out of one's mind, sick in the head, stark raving mad. *See* SANE.

crackerjack also **crackajack** *adjective*
Slang. Having or demonstrating a high degree of knowledge or skill : adept, crack, expert, master, masterful, masterly, professional, proficient, skilled, skillful. *See* ABILITY.

crackerjack also **crackajack** *noun Slang.* A person with a high degree of knowledge or skill in a particular field : ace, adept, authority, dab hand, expert, master, past master, professional, proficient, wizard. *Informal:* whiz. *Chiefly British:* dab[2]. *See* ABILITY.

crackers *adjective*
Chiefly British. Afflicted with or exhibiting irrationality and mental unsoundness : brainsick, crazy, daft, demented, disordered, distraught, dotty, insane, lunatic, mad, maniac, maniacal, mentally ill, moonstruck, off, touched, unbalanced, unsound, wrong. *Informal:* bonkers, cracked, daffy, gaga, loony. *Slang:* bananas, batty, buggy, cuckoo, fruity, loco, nuts, nutty,

screwy, wacky. *Law:* non compos mentis. ***Idioms:*** around the bend, crazy as a loon, mad as a hatter, not all there, nutty as a fruitcake, off (*or* out of) one's head, off one's rocker, of unsound mind, out of one's mind, sick in the head, stark raving mad. *See* SANE.

crackle *verb*
To make a series of short, sharp noises : crepitate, splutter, sputter. *See* SOUNDS.

crackpot *noun*
A person regarded as strange, eccentric, or crazy : crazy, eccentric, lunatic. *Informal:* crank, loon, loony. *Slang:* cuckoo, ding-a-ling, dingbat, kook, nut, screwball, weirdie, weirdo. *See* WISE.

crackup or **crack-up** *noun*
1. *Informal.* A wrecking of a vehicle : crash, smash, smashup, wreck. *Informal:* pileup. *See* HELP. **2.** *Informal.* A sudden sharp decline in mental, emotional, or physical health : breakdown, collapse. *See* EXPLOSION.

crack up *verb* See **crack.**

craft *noun*
1. Natural or acquired facility in a specific activity : ability, adeptness, art, command, expertise, expertness, knack, mastery, proficiency, skill, technique. *Informal:* know-how. *See* ABILITY, KNOWLEDGE. **2.** Deceitful cleverness : art, artfulness, artifice, craftiness, cunning, foxiness, guile, slyness, wiliness. *See* HONEST, MEANS. **3.** Lack of straightforwardness and honesty in action : chicanery, craftiness, deviousness, dishonesty, indirection, shadiness, shiftiness, slyness, sneakiness, trickery, trickiness, underhandedness. *See* HONEST. **4.** Activity pursued as a livelihood : art, business, calling, career, employment, job, line, métier, occupation, profession, pursuit, trade, vocation, work. *Slang:* racket. *Archaic:* employ. *See* ACTION.

craftiness *noun*
1. Deceitful cleverness : art, artfulness, artifice, craft, cunning, foxiness, guile, slyness, wiliness. *See* HONEST, MEANS. **2.** Lack of straightforwardness and honesty in action : chicanery, craft, deviousness, dishonesty, indirection, shadiness, shiftiness, slyness, sneakiness, trickery, trickiness, underhandedness. *See* HONEST.

craftsmanship *noun*
The technique, style, and quality of working : work, workmanship. *See* WORK.

crafty *adjective*
Deceitfully clever : artful, cunning, foxy, guileful, scheming, sharp, sly, tricky, wily. *See* ABILITY, HONEST, MEANS.

cragged *adjective*
Having a surface that is not smooth : coarse, craggy, harsh, ironbound, jagged, ragged, rough, rugged, scabrous, uneven. *See* SMOOTH.

craggy *adjective*
Having a surface that is not smooth : coarse, cragged, harsh, ironbound, jagged, ragged, rough, rugged, scabrous, uneven. *See* SMOOTH.

cram *verb*
1. To fill to excess by compressing or squeezing : crowd, jam, load, mob, pack, stuff. *Informal:* jam-pack. *See* FULL, TIGHTEN. **2.** *Informal.* To study or work hard, especially when pressed for time : *Informal:* bone (up), grind. ***Idiom:*** burn the midnight oil. *See* WORK.

cramp[1] *noun*
A violent, excruciating seizure of pain : paroxysm, shoot, spasm, throe. *See* PAIN.

cramp[2] *noun*
Something that limits or restricts : check, circumscription, constraint, curb, inhibition, limit, limitation, restraint, restriction, stricture, trammel. *See* LIMITED.
cramp *verb* To check the freedom and spontaneity of : constrain, constrict, inhibit. *See* FREE, TIGHTEN.

cramped *adjective*
Affording little room for movement : close, confining, crowded, narrow, snug, tight. *See* TIGHTEN.

crank *noun*
1. *Informal.* A person who habitually complains or grumbles : complainer, crab, faultfinder, grouch, growler, grumbler, grump, murmurer, mutterer, whiner. *Informal:* griper, grouser. *Slang:* bellyacher, sorehead, sourpuss. *See* HAPPY. **2.** *Informal.* A person regarded as strange, eccentric, or crazy : crackpot, crazy, eccentric, lunatic. *Informal:* loon, loony. *Slang:* cuckoo, ding-a-ling, dingbat, kook, nut, screwball, weirdie, weirdo. *See* WISE.

cranky *adjective*
1. Having or showing a bad temper : bad-tempered, cantankerous, crabbed, cross, disagreeable, fretful, grouchy, grumpy, ill-tempered, irascible, irritable, nasty, peevish, petulant, querulous, snappish, snappy, surly, testy, ugly, waspish. *Informal:* crabby, mean[2]. ***Idiom:*** out of sorts. *See* ATTITUDE. **2.** Deviating from the customary : bizarre, curious, eccentric, erratic, freakish, idiosyncratic, odd, outlandish, peculiar, quaint, queer, quirky, singular, strange, unnatural, unusual, weird. *Slang:* kooky, screwball. *British Slang:* rum, rummy[2]. *See* USUAL.

crap *noun*
Slang. Something that does not have or make sense : balderdash, blather, bunkum, claptrap, drivel, garbage, idiocy, nonsense, piffle, poppycock, rigmarole, rubbish, tomfoolery, trash, twaddle. *Informal:* tommyrot. *Slang:* applesauce, baloney, bilge, bull[1], bunk[2], hooey, malarkey. *See* KNOWLEDGE.

crapulence *noun*
The condition of being intoxicated with alcoholic liquor : drunkenness, inebriation, inebriety, insobriety, intoxication, tipsiness. *See* DRUGS.

crapulent *adjective*
Stupefied, excited, or muddled with alcoholic liquor : besotted, crapulous, drunk, drunken, inebriate, inebriated, intoxicated, sodden, tipsy. *Informal:* cock-eyed, stewed. *Slang:* blind, bombed, boozed, boozy, crocked, high, lit (up), loaded, looped, pickled, pixilated, plastered, potted, sloshed, smashed, soused, stinking, stinko, stoned, tight, zonked. ***Idioms:*** drunk as a skunk, half-seas over, high as a kite, in one's cups, three sheets in (*or* to) the wind. *See* DRUGS.

crapulous *adjective*
Stupefied, excited, or muddled with alcoholic liquor : besotted, crapulent, drunk, drunken, inebriate, inebriated, intoxicated, sodden, tipsy. *Informal:* cock-eyed, stewed. *Slang:* blind, bombed, boozed, boozy, crocked, high, lit (up), loaded, looped, pickled, pixilated, plastered, potted, sloshed, smashed, soused, stinking, stinko, stoned, tight, zonked. ***Idioms:*** drunk as a skunk, half-seas over, high as a kite, in one's cups, three sheets in (*or* to) the wind. *See* DRUGS.

crash *verb*
1. To undergo wrecking : smash. *Informal:* crack up, pile up. *See* HELP. **2.** To come together or come up against with force : bump, collide. *See* CONFLICT. **3.** To strike, set down, or close in such a way as to make a loud noise : bang[1], clap, slam, whack. *See* SOUNDS. **4.** To strike together with a loud, harsh noise : clash, smash. *See* SOUNDS. **5.** To undergo sudden financial failure : break, bust, collapse, fail, go under. *Informal:* fold. ***Idioms:*** go belly up, go bust, go on the rocks, go to the wall. *See* MONEY. **6.** *Slang.* To go to bed : bed (down), retire. *Informal:* turn in. *Slang:* flop. ***Idioms:*** call it a night, hit the hay (*or* sack). *See* AWARENESS.
crash *noun* **1.** A loud striking together : clash, smash. *See* SOUNDS. **2.** A forceful movement causing a loud noise : bang, slam, smash, wham. *See* STRIKE. **3.** A wrecking of a vehicle : smash, smashup, wreck. *Informal:* crack-up, pileup. *See* HELP. **4.** Violent forcible contact between two or more things : bump, collision, concussion, impact, jar, jolt, percussion, shock[1], smash. *See* CONFLICT. **5.** An abrupt disastrous failure : breakdown, collapse, debacle, smash, smashup, wreck. *See* MONEY.
crash *adjective Informal.* Designed to meet emergency needs as quickly as possible : *Informal:* hurry-up, rush. *See* FAST.

crashing *adjective*
Completely such, without qualification or exception : absolute, all-out, arrant, complete, consummate, damned, dead, downright, flat, out-and-out, outright, perfect, plain, pure, sheer[2], thorough, thoroughgoing, total, unbounded, unequivocal, unlimited, unmitigated, unqualified, unrelieved, unreserved, utter[2]. *Informal:* flat-out, positive. *Chiefly British:* blooming. *See* BIG, LIMITED.

crass *adjective*
Lacking in delicacy or refinement : barbarian, barbaric, boorish, churlish, coarse, crude, gross, ill-bred, indelicate, philistine, rough, rude, tasteless, uncivilized, uncouth, uncultivated, uncultured, unpolished, unrefined, vulgar. *See* COURTESY, SMOOTH.

crave *verb*
1. To have a greedy, obsessive desire : hunger, itch, lust, thirst. *See* DESIRE. **2.** To make an earnest or urgent request : appeal, beg, beseech, entreat, implore, plead, pray, sue, supplicate. *Archaic:* conjure. *See* ASK.

craven *adjective*
Ignobly lacking in courage : chickenhearted, cowardly, dastardly, faint-hearted, lily-livered, pusillanimous, unmanly. *Slang:* chicken, gutless, yellow, yellow-bellied. *See* FEAR.
craven *noun* An ignoble, uncourageous person : coward, dastard, funk, poltroon. *Slang:* chicken, yellow-belly. *See* FEAR.

cravenness *noun*
Ignoble lack of courage : chickenheartedness, cowardice, cowardliness, dastardliness, faint-heartedness, funk, pusillanimity, unmanliness. *Slang:* gutlessness, yellowness, yellow streak. *See* FEAR.

craving *noun*
A strong wanting of what promises enjoyment or pleasure : appetence, appetency, appetite, desire, hunger, itch, longing, lust, thirst, wish, yearning, yen. *See* DESIRE.

crawl *verb*
1. To move along in a crouching or prone position : creep, slide, snake, worm. *See* MOVE. **2.** To advance slowly : creep, drag, inch. *See* FAST. **3.** To be abundantly filled or richly supplied : abound, bristle, flow, overflow, pullulate, swarm, teem. *See* BIG, RICH. **4.** To experience a repugnant tingling sensation : creep. *See* FEAR, LIKE.
crawl *noun* A very slow rate of speed : creep, snail's pace. *See* FAST.

crawly *adjective*
Informal. Experiencing a repugnant tingling sensation : *Informal:* creepy. *See* FEAR, LIKE.

craze *verb*
To make insane : derange, madden, unbalance, unhinge. *See* SANE.
craze *noun* **1.** The current custom : fad, fashion, furor, mode, rage, style, trend, vogue. *Informal:* thing. ***Idioms:*** the in thing, the last word, the latest thing. *See* STYLE, USUAL. **2.** A subject or activity that inspires lively interest : enthusiasm, mania, passion, rage. *See* CONCERN.

craziness *noun*
1. Serious mental illness or disorder impairing a person's capacity to function normally and safely : brainsickness, dementia, derangement, disturbance, insaneness, insanity, lunacy, madness, mental illness, psychopathy, unbalance. *Psychiatry:* mania. *Psychology:* aberration, alienation. *See* SANE. **2.** *Informal.* Foolish behavior : absurdity, folly, foolery, foolishness, idiocy, imbecility, insanity, lunacy, madness, nonsense, preposterousness, senselessness, silliness, tomfoolery, zaniness. *See* ABILITY.

crazy *adjective*
1. Afflicted with or exhibiting irrationality and mental unsoundness : brainsick, daft, demented, disordered, distraught, dotty, insane, lunatic, mad, maniac, maniacal, mentally ill, moonstruck, off, touched, unbalanced, unsound, wrong. *Informal:* bonkers, cracked, daffy, gaga, loony. *Slang:* bananas, batty, buggy, cuckoo, fruity, loco, nuts, nutty, screwy, wacky. *Chiefly British:* crackers. *Law:* non compos mentis. ***Idioms:*** around the bend, crazy as a loon, mad as a hatter, not all there, nutty as a fruitcake, off (*or* out of) one's head, off one's rocker, of unsound mind, out of one's mind, sick in the head, stark raving mad. *See* SANE. **2.** *Informal.* Showing or having enthusiasm : ardent, enthusiastic, fervent, keen[1], mad, rabid, warm, zealous. *Slang:* gung ho, nuts. *See* CONCERN. **3.** *Informal.* So senseless as to be laughable : absurd, foolish, harebrained, idiotic, imbecilic, insane, lunatic, mad, moronic, nonsensical, preposterous, silly, softheaded, tomfool, unearthly, zany. *Informal:* cockeyed, loony, loopy. *Slang:* balmy[2], dippy, dopey, jerky, sappy, wacky. *See* ABILITY, KNOWLEDGE.
crazy *noun* A person regarded as strange, eccentric, or crazy : crackpot, eccentric, lunatic. *Informal:* crank, loon, loony. *Slang:* cuckoo, ding-a-ling, dingbat, kook, nut, screwball, weirdie, weirdo. *See* WISE.

cream *noun*
The superlative or most preferable part of something : best, choice, crème de la crème, elite, flower, pick, prize[1], top. ***Idioms:*** cream of the crop, flower of the flock, pick of the bunch (*or* crop) . *See* BETTER.
cream *verb* **1.** To form or cause to form foam : bubble, effervesce, fizz, foam, froth, lather, spume, suds, yeast. *See* SOLID. **2.** *Slang.* To render totally ineffective by decisive defeat : annihilate, crush, drub, overpower, overwhelm, smash, steamroller, thrash, trounce, vanquish. *Informal:* massacre, wallop. *Slang:* clobber, shellac, smear. *See* WIN.

creamy *adjective*
Bright and clear in complexion; not dull or faded : blooming, fresh, glowing, peaches-and-cream. *See* BEAUTIFUL.

crease *noun*
1. A line or an arrangement made by the doubling of one part over another : crimp, crinkle, crumple, fold, pleat, plica, plication, pucker, rimple, ruck[2], rumple, wrinkle. *See* SMOOTH. **2.** An indentation or seam on the skin, especially on the face : crinkle, furrow, line, wrinkle. *See* SMOOTH.
crease *verb* **1.** To bend together or make a crease in so that one part lies over another : double, fold, pleat, ply[1], ruck[2]. *See* ORDER, SMOOTH. **2.** To make irregular folds in, especially by pressing or twisting : crimp, crinkle, crumple, rimple, rumple, wrinkle. *See* SMOOTH.

create *verb*
1. To cause to come into existence : beget, breed, engender, father, hatch, make, originate, parent, procreate, produce, sire, spawn. ***Idiom:*** give birth (*or* rise) to. *See* MAKE. **2.** To bring into existence formally : constitute, establish, found, institute, organize, originate, set up, start. *See* START. **3.** To form by artistic effort : compose, indite, produce, write. *See* MAKE.

creation *noun*
1. The act of founding or establishing : constitution, establishment, foundation, institution, organization, origination, start-up. *See* START. 2. The totality of all existing things : cosmos, macrocosm, nature, universe, world. *See* MATTER, PART. 3. Any fictitious idea accepted as part of an ideology by an uncritical group; a received idea : fantasy, fiction, figment, invention, myth. *See* BELIEF, REAL.

creative *adjective*
Characterized by or productive of new things or new ideas : ingenious, innovative, innovatory, inventive, original. *See* ABILITY.

creativeness *noun*
The power or ability to invent : creativity, ingeniousness, ingenuity, invention, inventiveness, originality. *See* ABILITY, MAKE.

creativity *noun*
The power or ability to invent : creativeness, ingeniousness, ingenuity, invention, inventiveness, originality. *See* ABILITY, MAKE.

creator *noun*
1. One that creates, founds, or originates : architect, author, entrepreneur, father, founder[2], inventor, maker, originator, parent, patriarch. *See* START. 2. A person instrumental in the growth of something, especially in its early stages : builder, contributor, developer, pioneer. *See* MAKE.

creature *noun*
A member of the human race : being, body, homo, human, human being, individual, life, man, mortal, party, person, personage, soul. *See* BEINGS.

credence *noun*
Mental acceptance of the truth or actuality of something : belief, credit, faith. *See* OPINION.

credibility *noun*
Appearance of truth or authenticity : believability, color, credibleness, creditability, creditableness, plausibility, plausibleness, verisimilitude. *See* LIKELY.

credible *adjective*
1. Worthy of being believed : believable, colorable, creditable, plausible. *See* TRUE. 2. Worthy of belief, as because of precision or faithfulness to an original : authentic, authoritative, convincing, faithful, true, trustworthy, valid. *See* TRUE.

credibleness *noun*
Appearance of truth or authenticity : believability, color, credibility, creditability, creditableness, plausibility, plausibleness, verisimilitude. *See* LIKELY.

credit *noun*
1. Mental acceptance of the truth or actuality of something : belief, credence, faith. *See* OPINION. 2. Favorable notice, as of an achievement : acknowledgment, recognition. *See* KNOWLEDGE. 3. The act of attributing : ascription, assignment, attribution, imputation. *See* GIVE.

credit *verb* 1. To have confidence in the truthfulness of : believe, trust. ***Idiom:*** take at one's word. *See* OPINION. 2. To regard as belonging to or resulting from another : accredit, ascribe, assign, attribute, charge, impute, lay[1], refer. *See* GIVE.

creditability *noun*
Appearance of truth or authenticity : believability, color, credibility, credibleness, creditableness, plausibility, plausibleness, verisimilitude. *See* LIKELY.

creditable *adjective*
1. Deserving honor, respect, or admiration : admirable, commendable, deserving, estimable, exemplary, honorable, laudable, meritorious, praiseworthy, reputable, respectable, worthy. *See* GOOD, PRAISE, RESPECT, VALUE. 2. Worthy of being believed : believable, colorable, credible, plausible. *See* TRUE.

creditableness *noun*
Appearance of truth or authenticity : believability, color, credibility, credibleness, creditability, plausibility, plausibleness, verisimilitude. *See* LIKELY.

credulous *adjective*
Easily imposed on or tricked : dupable, easy, exploitable, gullible, naive, susceptible. *See* WISE.

creed *noun*
A system of religious belief : confession, denomination, faith, persuasion, religion, sect. *See* RELIGION.

creek *noun*
A small stream : brook[1]. *Chiefly Regional:* branch, kill[2], run. *See* DRY.

creep *verb*
1. To move along in a crouching or prone position : crawl, slide, snake, worm. *See* MOVE. 2. To move silently and furtively : glide, lurk, mouse, prowl, pussyfoot, skulk, slide, slink, slip, snake, sneak, steal. *Slang:* gumshoe. *See* MOVE. 3. To advance slowly : crawl, drag, inch. *See* FAST. 4. To experience a repugnant tingling sensation : crawl. *See* FEAR, LIKE.

creep *noun* A very slow rate of speed : crawl, snail's pace. *See* FAST.

creepy *adjective*
Informal. Experiencing a repugnant tingling sensation : *Informal:* crawly. *See* FEAR, LIKE.

crème de la crème *noun*
1. The superlative or most preferable part of something : best, choice, cream, elite, flower, pick, prize[1], top. ***Idioms:*** cream of the crop, flower of the flock, pick of the bunch (*or* crop) . *See* BETTER. **2.** People of the highest social level : aristocracy, blue blood, elite, flower, gentility, gentry, nobility, patriciate, quality, society, upper class, who's who. *Informal:* upper crust. *See* OVER.

crepitate *verb*
To make a series of short, sharp noises : crackle, splutter, sputter. *See* SOUNDS.

crest *noun*
1. The highest point : apex, cap, crown, height, peak, roof, summit, top, vertex. *See* HIGH. **2.** The highest point or state : acme, apex, apogee, climax, crown, culmination, height, meridian, peak, pinnacle, summit, top, zenith. *Informal:* payoff. *Medicine:* fastigium. *See* HIGH.
crest *verb* To reach or bring to a climax : cap, climax, crown, culminate, peak, top (off *or* out). *See* EXCITE.

cretin *noun*
Slang. One deficient in judgment and good sense : ass, fool, idiot, imbecile, jackass, mooncalf, moron, nincompoop, ninny, nitwit, simple, simpleton, softhead, tomfool. *Informal:* dope, gander, goose. *Slang:* ding-dong, dip, goof, jerk, nerd, schmo, schmuck, turkey. *See* ABILITY.

crevice *noun*
A usually narrow partial opening caused by splitting and rupture : break, chink, cleavage, cleft, crack, fissure, rift, split. *See* OPEN.

crew *noun*
A group of people organized for a particular purpose : body, corps, detachment, force, gang, team, unit. *See* GROUP.

crib *verb*
To reproduce (the artistic work of another, for example) illicitly : pirate, plagiarize. *See* GIVE, WORDS.

cribber *noun*
One who illicitly reproduces the artistic work, for example, of another : pirate, plagiarist, plagiarizer. *See* GIVE, WORDS.

crime *noun*
1. A serious breaking of the public law : illegality, misdeed, offense. *Law:* felony. *See* CRIMES. **2.** A wicked act or wicked behavior : deviltry, diablerie, evil, evildoing, immorality, iniquity, misdeed, offense, peccancy, sin, wickedness, wrong, wrongdoing. *See* RIGHT. **3.** Something that offends one's sense of propriety, fairness, or justice : offense, outrage, sin. *See* RIGHT. **4.** A great disappointment or regrettable fact : pity, shame. *Slang:* bummer. ***Idiom:*** a crying shame. *See* GOOD.

criminal *adjective*
Of, involving, or being a crime : illegal, illegitimate, illicit, lawless, unlawful, wrongful. *See* CRIMES.
criminal *noun* One who commits a crime : lawbreaker, malefactor, offender. *Law:* felon. *See* CRIMES.

criminate *verb*
To cause to appear involved in or guilty of a crime or fault : implicate, incriminate, inculpate. *See* ATTACK, CRIMES.

crimp *verb*
To make irregular folds in, especially by pressing or twisting : crease, crinkle, crumple, rimple, rumple, wrinkle. *See* SMOOTH.
crimp *noun* A line or an arrangement made by the doubling of one part over another : crease, crinkle, crumple, fold, pleat, plica, plication, pucker, rimple, ruck[2], rumple, wrinkle. *See* SMOOTH.

crimson *verb*
To become red in the face : blush, color, flush, glow, mantle, redden. *See* EXPRESS.

cringe *verb*
1. To draw away involuntarily, usually out of fear or disgust : blench[1], flinch, quail, recoil, shrink, shy[1], start, wince. *See* APPROACH, SEEK. **2.** To support slavishly every opinion or suggestion of a superior : bootlick, fawn, grovel, kowtow, slaver, toady, truckle. *Informal:* apple-polish, brownnose, cotton. *Slang:* suck up. ***Idioms:*** curry favor, dance attendance, kiss someone's feet, lick someone's boots. *See* OVER.
cringe *noun* An act of drawing back in an involuntary or instinctive fashion : flinch, recoil, shrink, wince. *See* APPROACH, SEEK.

crinkle *verb*
To make irregular folds in, especially by pressing or twisting : crease, crimp, crumple, rimple, rumple, wrinkle. *See* SMOOTH.
crinkle *noun* **1.** An indentation or seam on the skin, especially on the face : crease, furrow, line, wrinkle. *See* SMOOTH. **2.** A line or an arrangement made by the doubling of one part over another : crease, crimp, crumple, fold,

pleat, plica, plication, pucker, rimple, ruck[2], rumple, wrinkle. *See* SMOOTH.

cripple *verb*
1. To deprive of a limb or bodily member or its use : dismember, maim, mutilate. *See* HELP.
2. To render powerless or motionless, as by inflicting severe injury : disable, immobilize, incapacitate, knock out, paralyze. ***Idiom:*** put out of action (*or* commission). *See* HELP.

crisis *noun*
1. A decisive point : climacteric, crossroad (used in plural), exigence, exigency, head, juncture, pass, turning point, zero hour. *See* DECIDE. **2.** A highly volatile dangerous situation requiring immediate remedial action : emergency, extremity, flash point. *See* POLITICS, SAFETY.

crisscross *verb*
To pass through or over : cross, crosscut, cut across, decussate, intersect. *See* MEET.

criterion *noun*
A means by which individuals are compared and judged : benchmark, gauge, mark, measure, standard, test, touchstone, yardstick. *See* USUAL.

critic *noun*
1. A person who evaluates and reports on the worth of something : commentator, judge, reviewer. *See* VALUE. **2.** A person who finds fault, often severely and willfully : carper, caviler, criticizer, faultfinder, hypercritic, niggler, nitpicker, quibbler. *See* PRAISE.

critical *adjective*
1. Inclined to judge too severely : captious, carping, censorious, faultfinding, hypercritical, overcritical. *See* PRAISE. **2.** Characterized by careful and exact evaluation : discerning, discriminating. *See* CAREFUL, VALUE. **3.** So serious as to be at the point of crisis or necessary to resolve a crisis : acute, climacteric, crucial, desperate, dire. *See* SAFETY.

criticism *noun*
1. A comment expressing fault : blame, censure, condemnation, denunciation, reprehension, reprobation. *Informal:* pan. *Slang:* knock. *See* PRAISE. **2.** Evaluative and critical discourse : critique, notice, review. *See* OPINION, WORDS.

criticize *verb*
1. To find fault with : blame, censure, fault, rap[1]. *Informal:* cut up, pan. *Slang:* knock. *See* PRAISE. **2.** To write a critical report on : review. *See* OPINION, WORDS.

criticizer *noun*
A person who finds fault, often severely and willfully : carper, caviler, critic, faultfinder, hypercritic, niggler, nitpicker, quibbler. *See* PRAISE.

critique *noun*
Evaluative and critical discourse : criticism, notice, review. *See* OPINION, WORDS.

croak *verb*
Slang. To cease living : decease, demise, depart, die, drop, expire, go, pass away, pass (on), perish, succumb. *Informal:* pop off. *Slang:* check out, kick in, kick off. ***Idioms:*** bite the dust, breathe one's last, cash in, give up the ghost, go to one's grave, kick the bucket, meet one's end (*or* Maker), pass on to the Great Beyond, turn up one's toes. *See* LIVE.

croaking *adjective*
Low and grating in sound : croaky, gruff, hoarse, husky[1]. *See* SOUNDS.

croaky *adjective*
Low and grating in sound : croaking, gruff, hoarse, husky[1]. *See* SOUNDS.

crocked *adjective*
Slang. Stupefied, excited, or muddled with alcoholic liquor : besotted, crapulent, crapulous, drunk, drunken, inebriate, inebriated, intoxicated, sodden, tipsy. *Informal:* cock-eyed, stewed. *Slang:* blind, bombed, boozed, boozy, high, lit (up), loaded, looped, pickled, pixilated, plastered, potted, sloshed, smashed, soused, stinking, stinko, stoned, tight, zonked. ***Idioms:*** drunk as a skunk, half-seas over, high as a kite, in one's cups, three sheets in (*or* to) the wind. *See* DRUGS.

crone *noun*
An ugly, frightening old woman : beldam, hag, witch. *Slang:* biddy. *Archaic:* trot. *See* BEAUTIFUL.

crony *noun*
One who shares interests or activities with another : associate, chum, companion, comrade, fellow, mate. *Informal:* buddy, pal. *See* NEAR.

crook *noun*
1. Something bent : bend, bow[2], curvature, curve, round, turn. *See* STRAIGHT. **2.** *Informal.* A person who cheats : bilk, cheat, cheater, cozener, defrauder, rook, sharper, swindler, trickster, victimizer. *Informal:* chiseler, flimflammer. *Slang:* diddler, gyp, gypper. *See* HONEST.

crook *verb* To swerve from a straight line : angle[2], arc, arch, bend, bow[2], curve, round, turn. *See* STRAIGHT.

crooked *adjective*
1. Having bends, curves, or angles : bending, curved, curving. *See* STRAIGHT. **2.** *Informal.*

Marked by dishonesty, especially in matters of public trust : corrupt, dishonest, venal. *See* HONEST. **3.** *Informal.* Ruthlessly seeking personal advantage : corrupt, mercenary, praetorian, venal. *See* SELF.

crookedness *noun*
1. Lack of smoothness or regularity : asymmetry, inequality, irregularity, jaggedness, roughness, unevenness. *See* SMOOTH, STRAIGHT. **2.** *Informal.* Departure from what is legally, ethically, and morally correct : corruption, corruptness, dishonesty, improbity. *See* HONEST.

crop *noun*
The produce harvested from the land : fruit, fruitage, harvest, yield. *See* INGESTION.
crop *verb* **1.** To decrease, as in length or amount, by or as if by severing or excising : chop[1], clip[1], cut, cut back, cut down, lop[1], lower[2], pare, prune, shear, slash, trim, truncate. *See* INCREASE. **2.** To collect ripe crops : garner, gather, harvest, pick, reap. *See* COLLECT.

cross *noun*
Something hard to bear physically or emotionally : affliction, burden[1], trial, tribulation. *See* HEAVY, OVER.
cross *verb* **1.** To go across : pass, track, transit, traverse. *See* MOVE. **2.** To pass through or over : crisscross, crosscut, cut across, decussate, intersect. *See* MEET. **3.** To remove or invalidate by or as if by running a line through or wiping clean. Also used with *off* or *out* : annul, blot (out), cancel, delete, efface, erase, expunge, obliterate, rub (out), scratch (out), strike (out), undo, wipe (out), x (out). *Law:* vacate. *See* CONTINUE. **4.** *Informal.* To prevent from accomplishing a purpose : baffle, balk, check, checkmate, defeat, foil, frustrate, stymie, thwart. *Informal:* stump. ***Idiom:*** cut the ground from under. *See* ALLOW.
cross up *verb* To cause the complete ruin or wreckage of : bankrupt, break down, demolish, destroy, finish, ruin, shatter, sink, smash, spoil, torpedo, undo, wash up, wrack[2], wreck. *Slang:* total. ***Idiom:*** put the kibosh on. *See* HELP.
cross *adjective* Having or showing a bad temper : bad-tempered, cantankerous, crabbed, cranky, disagreeable, fretful, grouchy, grumpy, ill-tempered, irascible, irritable, nasty, peevish, petulant, querulous, snappish, snappy, surly, testy, ugly, waspish. *Informal:* crabby, mean[2]. ***Idiom:*** out of sorts. *See* ATTITUDE.

crosscut *verb*
To pass through or over : crisscross, cross, cut across, decussate, intersect. *See* MEET.

cross-examine *verb*
To question thoroughly and relentlessly to verify facts : interrogate. *Informal:* grill. ***Idiom:*** give someone the third degree. *See* INVESTIGATE.

cross-eye *noun*
The condition of not having the visual axes parallel : squint, strabismus. *See* SEE.

cross-eyed *adjective*
Marked by or affected with a squint : squint-eyed, squinty, strabismal, strabismic. *See* SEE.

crossing *adjective*
Situated or lying across : crosswise, thwart, transversal, transverse, traverse. *See* HORIZONTAL.

crossroad *noun*
A decisive point. Used in plural : climacteric, crisis, exigence, exigency, head, juncture, pass, turning point, zero hour. *See* DECIDE.

cross up *verb* See **cross.**

crosswise *adjective*
Situated or lying across : crossing, thwart, transversal, transverse, traverse. *See* HORIZONTAL.

crouch *verb*
To stoop low with the limbs pulled in close to the body : huddle, hunch, hunker (down), squat. *See* HIGH.

crow *verb*
1. To talk with excessive pride : boast, brag, gasconade, rodomontade, vaunt. *Informal:* blow[1]. *See* PRAISE. **2.** To feel or express an uplifting joy over a success or victory : exult, glory, jubilate, triumph. *See* HAPPY.

crowd *noun*
1. An enormous number of persons gathered together : crush, drove, flock, horde, mass, mob, multitude, press, ruck[1], swarm, throng. *See* BIG, GROUP. **2.** The common people : common (used in plural), commonality, commonalty, commoner (used in plural), hoi polloi, mass (used in plural), mob, pleb (used in plural), plebeian (used in plural), populace, public, ruck[1], third estate. *See* OVER. **3.** A group of people sharing an interest, activity, or achievement : circle, group, set[2]. *See* GROUP. **4.** A particular social group : circle, clique, coterie, set[2]. *Informal:* bunch, gang. *See* GROUP. **5.** A number of persons who have come or been gathered together : assemblage, assembly, body, company, conclave, conference, congregation, congress, convention, convocation, gathering, group, meeting, muster, troop. *Informal:* get-together. *See* COLLECT. **6.** A very large number of things grouped together :

army, cloud, drove, flock, horde, host, legion, mass, mob, multitude, ruck[1], score (used in plural), swarm, throng. *See* BIG, GROUP.

crowd *verb* **1.** To congregate, as around a person : flock, mob, press, throng. *See* COLLECT, TIGHTEN. **2.** To act on with a steady pushing force : crush, press. *See* PUSH. **3.** To fill to excess by compressing or squeezing tightly : cram, jam, load, mob, pack, stuff. *Informal:* jam-pack. *See* FULL, TIGHTEN.

crowded *adjective*

1. Affording little room for movement : close, confining, cramped, narrow, snug, tight. *See* TIGHTEN. **2.** Having all parts near to each other : close, compact[1], dense, packed, thick, tight. *See* TIGHTEN. **3.** Excessively filled with detail : busy, cluttered, fussy. *See* SIMPLE.

crown *noun*

1. The highest point : apex, cap, crest, height, peak, roof, summit, top, vertex. *See* HIGH.
2. The highest point or state : acme, apex, apogee, climax, crest, culmination, height, meridian, peak, pinnacle, summit, top, zenith. *Informal:* payoff. *Medicine:* fastigium. *See* HIGH.

crown *verb* **1.** To put a topping on : cap, top, top off. *See* OVER, PUT ON. **2.** To reach or bring to a climax : cap, climax, crest, culminate, peak, top (off *or* out). *See* EXCITE.

crowning *adjective*

Of or constituting a climax : climactic, culminating, peak. *See* HIGH, OVER.

crucial *adjective*

1. So serious as to be at the point of crisis or necessary to resolve a crisis : acute, climacteric, critical, desperate, dire. *See* SAFETY. **2.** Determining or having the power to determine an outcome : conclusive, deciding, decisive, determinative. *See* DECIDE, IMPORTANT.

crucible *noun*

A state of pain or anguish that tests a person : ordeal, trial, tribulation, visitation. *See* EASY.

crucify *verb*

To subject (another) to extreme physical cruelty, as in punishing : rack, torment, torture. *Idiom:* put on the rack (*or* wheel). *See* PAIN, REWARD.

crud *noun*

Slang. Foul or dirty matter : dirt, filth, grime, muck. *See* CLEAN.

crude *adjective*

1. In a natural state and still not prepared for use : native, raw, unprocessed, unrefined. *See* CLEAN. **2.** Lacking in delicacy or refinement : barbarian, barbaric, boorish, churlish, coarse, crass, gross, ill-bred, indelicate, philistine, rough, rude, tasteless, uncivilized, uncouth, uncultivated, uncultured, unpolished, unrefined, vulgar. *See* COURTESY, SMOOTH. **3.** Lacking expert, careful craftsmanship : primitive, raw, rough, rude, unpolished. *See* GOOD.

cruel *adjective*

1. Showing or suggesting a disposition to be violently destructive without scruple or restraint : barbarous, bestial, fell[2], feral, ferocious, fierce, inhuman, savage, truculent, vicious, wolfish. *See* KIND. **2.** So intense as to cause extreme suffering : ferocious, fierce, savage, vicious. *See* HELP, KIND.

cruelty *noun*

A cruel act or an instance of cruel behavior : barbarity, bestiality, brutality, inhumanity, savagery, truculence, truculency. *See* ATTITUDE, KIND.

crumb *noun*

1. A small portion of food : bit[1], morsel, mouthful, piece. *Informal:* bite. *See* BIG. **2.** A tiny amount : bit[1], dab[1], dash, dot, dram, drop, fragment, grain, iota, jot, minim, mite, modicum, molecule, ort, ounce, particle, scrap[1], scruple, shred, smidgen, speck, tittle, trifle, whit. *Chiefly British:* spot. *See* BIG.

crumble *verb*

To reduce or become reduced to pieces or components : break down, break up, decompose, disintegrate, dissolve, fragment, fragmentize. *See* CONTINUE, HELP.

crumby *adjective* See **crummy.**

crummy also **crumby** *adjective*

Slang. Of decidedly inferior quality : base[2], cheap, lousy, miserable, paltry, poor, rotten, shoddy, sleazy, trashy. *Informal:* cheesy. *Slang:* schlocky. *See* GOOD.

crump *verb*

To bite and grind with the teeth : champ, chew, chomp, chump[2], crunch, masticate, munch. *Regional:* chaw. *See* MOUTH.

crumple *verb*

1. To make irregular folds in, especially by pressing or twisting : crease, crimp, crinkle, rimple, rumple, wrinkle. *See* SMOOTH. **2.** To fall in : buckle, cave in, collapse, give, go. *Idiom:* give way. *See* EXPLOSION.

crumple *noun* A line or an arrangement made by the doubling of one part over another : crease, crimp, crinkle, fold, pleat, plica, plication, pucker, rimple, ruck[2], rumple, wrinkle. *See* SMOOTH.

crunch *verb*

1. To bite and grind with the teeth : champ,

chew, chomp, chump[2], crump, masticate, munch. *Regional:* chaw. *See* MOUTH. **2.** To rub together noisily : gnash, grind. *See* SOUNDS.

crusade *noun*

1. An organized effort to accomplish a purpose : campaign, drive, movement, push. *See* ACTION, SEEK. **2.** A goal or set of interests served with dedication : cause. *See* START.

crush *verb*

1. To press forcefully so as to break up into a pulpy mass : mash, mush, pulp, squash. *See* HELP. **2.** To break up into tiny particles : bray, granulate, grind, mill, powder, pulverize, triturate. *See* HELP. **3.** To bring to an end forcibly as if by imposing a heavy weight : choke off, extinguish, put down, quash, quell, quench, squash, squelch, suppress. ***Idiom:*** put the lid on. *See* CONTINUE, WIN. **4.** To render totally ineffective by decisive defeat : annihilate, drub, overpower, overwhelm, smash, steamroller, thrash, trounce, vanquish. *Informal:* massacre, wallop. *Slang:* clobber, cream, shellac, smear. *See* WIN. **5.** To impair severely something such as the spirit, health, or effectiveness of : break, destroy, overwhelm, ruin. *See* HELP. **6.** To affect deeply or completely, as with emotion : engulf, overcome, overpower, overwhelm, prostrate. *See* AFFECT. **7.** To act on with a steady pushing force : crowd, press. *See* PUSH. **8.** To extract from by applying pressure : express, press, squeeze. *See* TIGHTEN.

crush *noun* **1.** An enormous number of persons gathered together : crowd, drove, flock, horde, mass, mob, multitude, press, ruck[1], swarm, throng. *See* BIG, GROUP. **2.** *Informal.* An extravagant, short-lived romantic attachment : infatuation. *See* EXCITE, SEX.

crust *noun*

Informal. The state or quality of being impudent or arrogantly self-confident : assumption, audaciousness, audacity, boldness, brashness, brazenness, cheek, cheekiness, chutzpah, discourtesy, disrespect, effrontery, face, familiarity, forwardness, gall[1], impertinence, impudence, impudency, incivility, insolence, nerve, nerviness, overconfidence, pertness, presumptuousness, pushiness, rudeness, sassiness, sauciness. *Informal:* brass, sauce, uppishness, uppityness. *See* ATTITUDE, COURTESY.

crusty *adjective*

Rudely unceremonious : abrupt, blunt, brief, brusque, curt, gruff, short, short-spoken. *See* ATTITUDE.

crutch *noun*

A means or device that keeps something erect, stable, or secure : brace, buttress, prop, shore, stay[2], support, underpinning. *See* SUPPORT.

cry *verb*

1. To make inarticulate sounds of grief or pain, usually accompanied by tears : bawl, blubber, howl, keen[2], sob, wail, weep, yowl. *See* HAPPY, SOUNDS. **2.** To speak suddenly or sharply, as from surprise or emotion. Also used with *out* : blurt (out), burst out, ejaculate, exclaim, rap out. *See* WORDS. **3.** To speak or say very loudly or with a shout : bawl, bellow, bluster, call, clamor, halloo, holler, roar, shout, vociferate, whoop, yawp, yell. *See* SOUNDS. **4.** To make known vigorously the positive features of (a product). Also used with *up* : advertise, ballyhoo, build up, popularize, promote, publicize, talk up. *Informal:* pitch, plug. *Slang:* push. *See* KNOWLEDGE.

cry *noun* **1.** A sudden, sharp utterance : ejaculation, exclamation, outcry. *See* WORDS. **2.** A fit of crying : bawling, blubbering, sobbing, tear[2] (used in plural), wailing, weeping. *See* SOUNDS. **3.** The act of demanding : call, claim, demand, exaction, requisition. *See* REQUEST. **4.** A rallying term used by proponents of a cause : battle cry, call to arms, call to battle, motto, rallying cry, war cry. *See* WORDS.

crying *adjective*

Compelling immediate attention : burning, dire, emergent, exigent, imperative, instant, pressing, urgent. *See* BIG.

crypt *noun*

A burial place or receptacle for human remains : catacomb, cinerarium, grave[1], mausoleum, ossuary, sepulcher, sepulture, tomb, vault[1]. *See* KEEP, PLACE.

cryptic *adjective*

Difficult to explain or understand : arcane, cabalistic, enigmatic, mysterious, mystic, mystical, mystifying, occult, puzzling. *See* EXPLAIN, KNOWLEDGE.

crystal clear or **crystal-clear** *adjective*

1. Readily seen, perceived, or understood : apparent, clear, clear-cut, distinct, evident, manifest, noticeable, observable, obvious, patent, plain, pronounced, visible. *See* SEE. **2.** Free from what obscures or dims : clear, crystalline, limpid, lucid, pellucid, see-through, transparent. *See* CLEAR. **3.** Admitting light so that objects beyond can be seen : clear, crystalline, limpid, lucid, pellucid, see-through, translucent, transparent. *See* CLEAR.

crystalline *adjective*

1. Free from what obscures or dims : clear, crystal clear, limpid, lucid, pellucid, see-through, transparent. *See* CLEAR. **2.** Admitting light so that objects beyond can be seen : clear, crystal clear, limpid, lucid, pellucid, see-through, translucent, transparent. *See* CLEAR.

cuckoo *noun*
Slang. A person regarded as strange, eccentric, or crazy : crackpot, crazy, eccentric, lunatic. *Informal:* crank, loon, loony. *Slang:* ding-a-ling, dingbat, kook, nut, screwball, weirdie, weirdo. *See* WISE.
cuckoo *adjective Slang.* Afflicted with or exhibiting irrationality and mental unsoundness : brainsick, crazy, daft, demented, disordered, distraught, dotty, insane, lunatic, mad, maniac, maniacal, mentally ill, moonstruck, off, touched, unbalanced, unsound, wrong. *Informal:* bonkers, cracked, daffy, gaga, loony. *Slang:* bananas, batty, buggy, fruity, loco, nuts, nutty, screwy, wacky. *Chiefly British:* crackers. *Law:* non compos mentis. ***Idioms:*** around the bend, crazy as a loon, mad as a hatter, not all there, nutty as a fruitcake, off (*or* out of) one's head, off one's rocker, of unsound mind, out of one's mind, sick in the head, stark raving mad. *See* SANE.

cuddle *verb*
1. To touch or stroke affectionately : caress, fondle, pat, pet[1]. *See* TOUCH. **2.** To lie or press close together, usually with another person or thing : nestle, nuzzle, snug, snuggle. *See* NEAR.

cue *noun*
A subtle pointing out : clue, hint, intimation, suggestion. *See* KNOWLEDGE, SUGGEST.

cuff *verb*
To hit with a quick, sharp blow of the hand : box[2], buffet, bust, punch, slap, smack[1], spank, swat, whack. *Informal:* clip[1], spat. *See* ATTACK, STRIKE.
cuff *noun* A quick, sharp blow, especially with the hand : box[2], buffet, bust, chop[1], punch, slap, smack[1], smacker, spank, swat, whack. *Informal:* clip[1], spat. *See* ATTACK, STRIKE.

cul-de-sac *noun*
A course leading nowhere : blind alley, dead end. *See* OPEN.

cull *verb*
1. To make a choice from a number of alternatives : choose, elect, opt (for), pick (out), select, single (out). *See* CHOICE. **2.** To collect (something) bit by bit : extract, garner, gather, glean, pick up. *See* COLLECT.

culminate *verb*
To reach or bring to a climax : cap, climax, crest, crown, peak, top (off *or* out). *See* EXCITE.

culminating *adjective*
Of or constituting a climax : climactic, crowning, peak. *See* HIGH, OVER.

culmination *noun*
1. The highest point or state : acme, apex, apogee, climax, crest, crown, height, meridian, peak, pinnacle, summit, top, zenith. *Informal:* payoff. *Medicine:* fastigium. *See* HIGH. **2.** The condition of being fulfilled : consummation, fruition, fulfillment, materialization, realization. *See* DO, HAPPY.

culpability *noun*
Responsibility for an error or crime : blame, fault, guilt, onus. *See* START.

culpable *adjective*
Deserving blame : blamable, blameful, blameworthy, censurable, guilty, reprehensible. *Idiom:* at fault. *See* PRAISE.

cultivate *verb*
1. To prepare (soil) for the planting and raising of crops : culture, dress, tend[2], till, work. *See* PREPARED, TOUCH. **2.** To bring into existence and foster the development of : breed, grow, propagate, raise. *See* CARE FOR, REPRODUCTION. **3.** To promote and sustain the development of : foster, nourish, nurse, nurture. *See* CARE FOR.

cultivated *adjective*
Characterized by discriminating taste and broad knowledge as a result of development or education : civilized, cultured, educated, polished, refined, urbane, well-bred. *See* CULTURE.

cultivation *noun*
Enlightenment and excellent taste resulting from intellectual development : civilization, culture, refinement. *See* CULTURE.

cultural *adjective*
Promoting culture : civilizing, edifying, enlightening, humanizing, refining. *See* CULTURE.

culture *noun*
1. The total product of human creativity and intellect : civilization, Kultur. *See* CULTURE. **2.** Enlightenment and excellent taste resulting from intellectual development : civilization, cultivation, refinement. *See* CULTURE.
culture *verb* To prepare (soil) for the planting and raising of crops : cultivate, dress, tend[2], till, work. *See* PREPARED, TOUCH.

cultured *adjective*
Characterized by discriminating taste and broad knowledge as a result of development or education : civilized, cultivated, educated, polished, refined, urbane, well-bred. *See* CULTURE.

cumber *verb*
To place a burden or heavy load on : burden[1], charge, encumber, freight, lade, load, saddle, tax, weight. *See* OVER.

cumbersome *adjective*
Unwieldy or clumsy, especially due to excess weight : cumbrous, heavy, lumpish, lumpy, ponderous. *See* EASY, HEAVY.

cumbrous *adjective*
Unwieldy or clumsy, especially due to excess weight : cumbersome, heavy, lumpish, lumpy, ponderous. *See* EASY, HEAVY.

cumshaw *noun*
A material favor or gift, usually money, given in return for service : gratuity, largess, perquisite, tip[3]. *See* GIVE, TRANSACTIONS.

cumulate *verb*
To bring together so as to increase in mass or number : accrue, accumulate, agglomerate, aggregate, amass, collect[1], garner, gather, hive, pile up, roll up. *See* COLLECT.

cumulation *noun*
A quantity accumulated : accumulation, aggregation, amassment, assemblage, collection, congeries, gathering, mass. *See* COLLECT.

cumulative *adjective*
Increasing, as in force, by successive additions : accumulative, additive. *See* INCREASE.

cumulus *noun*
A group of things gathered haphazardly : agglomeration, bank[1], drift, heap, hill, mass, mess, mound, mountain, pile, shock[2], stack, tumble. *See* ORDER.

cunning *adjective*
Deceitfully clever : artful, crafty, foxy, guileful, scheming, sharp, sly, tricky, wily. *See* ABILITY, HONEST, MEANS.
cunning *noun* **1.** Deceitful cleverness : art, artfulness, artifice, craft, craftiness, foxiness, guile, slyness, wiliness. *See* HONEST, MEANS. **2.** The act or practice of deceiving : deceit, deceitfulness, deception, double-dealing, duplicity, guile, shiftiness. *See* HONEST.

cupidity *noun*
Excessive desire for more than one needs or deserves : acquisitiveness, avarice, avariciousness, avidity, covetousness, graspingness, greed. *Informal:* grabbiness. *See* DESIRE, GIVE.

curative *adjective*
Serving to cure : remedial, restorative, therapeutic. *See* HEALTH.
curative *noun* Something that corrects or counteracts : antidote, corrective, countermeasure, cure, remedy. *See* BETTER.

curb *noun*
Something that limits or restricts : check, circumscription, constraint, cramp[2], inhibition, limit, limitation, restraint, restriction, stricture, trammel. *See* LIMITED.
curb *verb* To control, restrict, or arrest : bit[2], brake, bridle, check, constrain, hold, hold back, hold down, hold in, inhibit, keep, keep back, pull in, rein (back, in, *or* up), restrain. *See* RESTRAINT.

curdle *verb*
To change or be changed from a liquid into a soft, semisolid, or solid mass : clot, coagulate, congeal, gelatinize, jell, jelly, set[1]. *See* SOLID.

cure *noun*
1. An agent used to restore health : elixir, medicament, medication, medicine, nostrum, physic, remedy. *See* HEALTH. **2.** Something that corrects or counteracts : antidote, corrective, countermeasure, curative, remedy. *See* BETTER.
cure *verb* To rectify (an undesirable or unhealthy condition) : heal, remedy. *See* HEALTH.

cure-all *noun*
Something believed to cure all human disorders : catholicon, panacea. *See* HELP.

cureless *adjective*
Offering no hope or expectation of improvement : hopeless, incurable, irremediable, irreparable. *See* HOPE.

curiosity *noun*
1. Mental acquisitiveness : curiousness, inquisitiveness, interest. ***Idiom:*** thirst for knowledge. *See* INVESTIGATE. **2.** Undue interest in the affairs of others : curiousness, inquisitiveness. *Informal:* nosiness, snoopiness. *See* INVESTIGATE.

curious *adjective*
1. Eager to acquire knowledge : inquiring, inquisitive, investigative, questioning. *See* INVESTIGATE. **2.** Unduly interested in the affairs of others : inquisitive, inquisitorial. *Informal:* nosy, snoopy. *See* INVESTIGATE. **3.** Causing puzzlement; perplexing : funny, odd, peculiar, queer, strange, weird. *See* USUAL. **4.** Deviating from the customary : bizarre, cranky, eccentric, erratic, freakish, idiosyncratic, odd, outlandish, peculiar, quaint, queer, quirky, singular, strange, unnatural, unusual, weird. *Slang:* kooky, screwball. *British Slang:* rum, rummy[2]. *See* USUAL.

curiousness *noun*
1. Mental acquisitiveness : curiosity, inquisitiveness, interest. ***Idiom:*** thirst for knowledge. *See* INVESTIGATE. **2.** Undue interest in the

affairs of others : curiosity, inquisitiveness. *Informal:* nosiness, snoopiness. *See* INVESTIGATE.

curl *verb*
1. To have or cause to have a curved or sinuous form or surface : curve, undulate, wave. *See* STRAIGHT. **2.** To move or proceed on a repeatedly curving course : coil, corkscrew, entwine, meander, snake, spiral, twine, twist, weave, wind[2], wreathe. *See* REPETITION, STRAIGHT.

currency *noun*
Something, such as coins or printed bills, used as a medium of exchange : cash, lucre, money. *Informal:* wampum. *Slang:* bread, cabbage, dough, gelt, green, jack, lettuce, long green, mazuma, moola, scratch. *Chiefly British:* brass. *See* MONEY.

current *adjective*
1. Characteristic of recent times or informed of what is current : au courant, contemporary, mod, modern, up-to-date, up-to-the-minute. *See* KNOWLEDGE, NEW. **2.** In existence now : contemporary, existent, existing, new, now, present[1], present-day. *See* TIME. **3.** Most generally existing or encountered at a given time : predominant, prevailing, prevalent, regnant, rife, widespread. *See* SPECIFIC.
current *noun* Something suggestive of running water : drift, flood, flow, flux, rush, spate, stream, surge, tide. *See* MOVE.

currently *adverb*
At this moment : actually, now. ***Idiom:*** even (*or* just *or* right) now. *See* TIME.

curse *noun*
1. A denunciation invoking a wish or threat of evil or injury : anathema, damnation, execration, imprecation, malediction. *Archaic:* malison. *See* WORDS. **2.** Something or someone believed to bring bad luck : hex, hoodoo. *Informal:* jinx. *See* LUCK. **3.** A cause of suffering or harm : affliction, bane, evil, ill, plague, scourge, woe. *See* HELP. **4.** A profane or obscene term : blasphemy, epithet, expletive, oath, swearword. *Informal:* cuss. *See* DECENT, SACRED, WORDS.
curse *verb* **1.** To invoke evil or injury upon : anathematize, damn, imprecate. *Informal:* cuss. *Archaic:* execrate, maledict. *See* WORDS. **2.** To bring bad luck or evil to : hex, hoodoo. *Informal:* jinx. *See* LUCK. **3.** To bring great harm or suffering to : afflict, agonize, anguish, excruciate, plague, rack, scourge, smite, strike, torment, torture. *See* ATTACK, HELP. **4.** To use profane or obscene language : blaspheme, damn, swear. *Informal:* cuss. *See* DECENT, SACRED, WORDS.

cursed also **curst** *adjective*
So annoying or detestable as to deserve condemnation : accursed, blasted, blessed, bloody, confounded, damn, darn, execrable, infernal. *Informal:* blamed, damned. *Chiefly British:* blooming, ruddy. *See* LIKE.

cursory *adjective*
Lacking in intellectual depth or thoroughness : one-dimensional, shallow, sketchy, skin-deep, superficial, uncritical. *See* SURFACE.

curst *adjective* See **cursed.**

curt *adjective*
Rudely unceremonious : abrupt, blunt, brief, brusque, crusty, gruff, short, short-spoken. *See* ATTITUDE.

curtail *verb*
To make short or shorter the duration or extent of : abbreviate, abridge, condense, reduce, shorten. *See* INCREASE, LONG.

curtailment *noun*
The act or process of decreasing : abatement, cut, cutback, decrease, decrement, diminishment, diminution, drain, reduction, slash, slowdown, taper. *See* INCREASE.

curtain *noun*
Slang. The act or fact of dying. Used in plural : death, decease, demise, dissolution, extinction, passing, quietus, rest[1]. *See* LIVE.

curtsy *noun*
An inclination of the head or body, as in greeting, consent, courtesy, submission, or worship : bow[1], genuflection, kowtow, nod, obeisance. *See* COURTESY.

curvaceous *adjective*
Having a full, voluptuous figure : buxom, curvy, shapely, well-developed. *Informal:* built. *Slang:* stacked. *See* BEAUTIFUL.

curvature *noun*
Something bent : bend, bow[2], crook, curve, round, turn. *See* STRAIGHT.

curve *noun*
Something bent : bend, bow[2], crook, curvature, round, turn. *See* STRAIGHT.
curve *verb* **1.** To swerve from a straight line : angle[2], arc, arch, bend, bow[2], crook, round, turn. *See* STRAIGHT. **2.** To have or cause to have a curved or sinuous form or surface : curl, undulate, wave. *See* STRAIGHT.

curved *adjective*
1. Deviating from a straight line : arced, arched, arciform, bent, bowed, curvilinear, rounded. *See* STRAIGHT. **2.** Having bends,

curves, or angles : bending, crooked, curving. *See* STRAIGHT.

curvilinear *adjective*
Deviating from a straight line : arced, arched, arciform, bent, bowed, curved, rounded. *See* STRAIGHT.

curving *adjective*
Having bends, curves, or angles : bending, crooked, curved. *See* STRAIGHT.

curvy *adjective*
Having a full, voluptuous figure : buxom, curvaceous, shapely, well-developed. *Informal:* built. *Slang:* stacked. *See* BEAUTIFUL.

cusp *noun*
A sharp or tapered end : acicula, acumination, apex, mucro, mucronation, point, tip[1]. *See* SHARP.

cuspate *adjective*
Having an end that tapers to a point : acicular, aciculate, aciculated, acuminate, acute, cuspated, cuspidate, cuspidated, mucronate, pointed, pointy, sharp. *See* SHARP.

cuspated *adjective*
Having an end that tapers to a point : acicular, aciculate, aciculated, acuminate, acute, cuspate, cuspidate, cuspidated, mucronate, pointed, pointy, sharp. *See* SHARP.

cuspidate *adjective*
Having an end that tapers to a point : acicular, aciculate, aciculated, acuminate, acute, cuspate, cuspated, cuspidated, mucronate, pointed, pointy, sharp. *See* SHARP.

cuspidated *adjective*
Having an end that tapers to a point : acicular, aciculate, aciculated, acuminate, acute, cuspate, cuspated, cuspidate, mucronate, pointed, pointy, sharp. *See* SHARP.

cuss *verb*
1. *Informal.* To invoke evil or injury upon : anathematize, curse, damn, imprecate. *Archaic:* execrate, maledict. *See* WORDS. **2.** *Informal.* To use profane or obscene language : blaspheme, curse, damn, swear. *See* DECENT, SACRED, WORDS.
cuss *noun Informal.* A profane or obscene term : blasphemy, curse, epithet, expletive, oath, swearword. *See* DECENT, SACRED, WORDS.

custodian *noun*
A person who is legally responsible for the person or property of another considered by law to be incompetent to manage his or her affairs : caretaker, guardian, keeper. *Law:* conservator. *See* LAW.

custody *noun*
1. The function of watching, guarding, or overseeing : care, charge, guardianship, keeping, superintendence, supervision, trust. *See* CARE FOR. **2.** The state of being detained by legal authority : charge, confinement, detention, ward. *See* FREE.

custom *noun*
1. A habitual way of behaving : consuetude, habit, habitude, manner, practice, praxis, usage, usance, use, way, wont. *See* USUAL. **2.** The commercial transactions of customers with a supplier : business, patronage, trade, traffic. *See* TRANSACTIONS.
custom *adjective* Made according to the specifications of the buyer : custom-built, customized, custom-made, made-to-order, tailor-made. *See* AGREE.

customarily *adverb*
In an expected or customary manner; for the most part : commonly, consistently, frequently, generally, habitually, naturally, normally, often, regularly, routinely, typically, usually. ***Idioms:*** as usual, per usual. *See* BIG, USUAL.

customariness *noun*
The quality or condition of being usual : habitualness, normalcy, normality, ordinariness, prevalence, regularity, routineness, usualness. *See* USUAL.

customary *adjective*
Commonly practiced or used : accustomed, habitual, regular, usual, wonted. *See* USUAL.

custom-built *adjective*
Made according to the specifications of the buyer : custom, customized, custom-made, made-to-order, tailor-made. *See* AGREE.

customer *noun*
1. One who buys goods or services : buyer, client, patron, purchaser. *See* TRANSACTIONS.
2. One who consumes goods and services : consumer, user. *See* GIVE, USED.

customized *adjective*
Made according to the specifications of the buyer : custom, custom-built, custom-made, made-to-order, tailor-made. *See* AGREE.

custom-made *adjective*
Made according to the specifications of the buyer : custom, custom-built, customized, made-to-order, tailor-made. *See* AGREE.

cut *verb*
1. To penetrate with a sharp edge : gash, incise, pierce, slash, slit. *See* ENTER, HELP. **2.** To separate into parts with or as if with a sharp-edged

instrument : carve, cleave[1], dissever, sever, slice, slit, split. *See* ASSEMBLE. **3.** To bring down, as with a saw or ax. Also used with *down* : chop down, fell[1], hew. *See* RISE. **4.** To turn aside sharply from a straight course : chop[2], sheer[1], skew, slue[1], swerve, veer. *Nautical:* yaw. *See* CHANGE. **5.** To decrease, as in length or amount, by or as if by severing or excising : chop[1], clip[1], crop, cut back, cut down, lop[1], lower[2], pare, prune, shear, slash, trim, truncate. *See* INCREASE. **6.** To lessen the strength of by or as if by admixture : attenuate, dilute, thin, water (down), weaken. *See* STRONG. **7.** To slight (someone) deliberately : rebuff, shun, snub, spurn. *Informal:* coldshoulder. ***Idioms:*** close (*or* shut) the door on, give someone the cold shoulder, give someone the go-by, turn one's back on. *See* ACCEPT. **8.** To fail to attend on purpose : truant. *Informal:* skip. ***Idioms:*** go AWOL, play hooky (*or* truant). *See* SEEK.

cut across *verb* To pass through or over : crisscross, cross, crosscut, decussate, intersect. *See* MEET.

cut back *verb* To decrease, as in length or amount, by or as if by severing or excising : chop[1], clip[1], crop, cut, cut down, lop[1], lower[2], pare, prune, shear, slash, trim, truncate. *See* INCREASE.

cut down *verb* **1.** To cause the death of : carry off, cut off, destroy, dispatch, finish (off), kill[1], slay. *Slang:* waste, zap. ***Idioms:*** put an end to, put to sleep. *See* HELP. **2.** To cause to fall, as from a shot or blow : bring down, down, drop, fell[1], flatten, floor, ground, knock down, level, prostrate, strike down, throw. *Slang:* deck[1]. ***Idiom:*** lay low. *See* RISE. **3.** To decrease, as in length or amount, by or as if by severing or excising : chop[1], clip[1], crop, cut, cut back, lop[1], lower[2], pare, prune, shear, slash, trim, truncate. *See* INCREASE.

cut in *verb* **1.** To force or come in as an improper or unwanted element : horn in, intrude, obtrude. *See* ENTER. **2.** To interject remarks or questions into another's discourse : break in, chime in, chip in, interrupt. *See* CONTINUE.

cut off *verb* **1.** To set apart from a group : close off, insulate, isolate, seclude, segregate, separate, sequester. *See* INCLUDE. **2.** To cause the death of : carry off, cut down, destroy, dispatch, finish (off), kill[1], slay. *Slang:* waste, zap. ***Idioms:*** put an end to, put to sleep. *See* HELP. **3.** To block the progress of and force to change direction : head off, intercept. *See* ALLOW.

cut out *verb* **1.** To take the place of (another) against the other's will : displace, supplant. *See* SUBSTITUTE. **2.** To desist from, cease, or discontinue (a habit, for example) : break, give up, leave off, stop. *Slang:* kick. *See* CONTINUE. **3.** *Informal.* To move or proceed away from a place : depart, exit, get away, get off, go, go away, leave[1], pull out, quit, retire, run (along), withdraw. *Informal:* push off, shove off. *Slang:* blow[1], split, take off. ***Idioms:*** hit the road, take leave. *See* APPROACH.

cut up *verb* **1.** *Informal.* To behave in a rowdy, improper, or unruly fashion : act up, carry on, misbehave. *Informal:* horse around. *See* GOOD. **2.** *Informal.* To find fault with : blame, censure, criticize, fault, rap[1]. *Informal:* pan. *Slang:* knock. *See* PRAISE.

cut *noun* **1.** The result of cutting : gash, incision, slash, slice, slit, split. *See* ENTER, HELP. **2.** A part severed from a whole : piece, portion, section, segment, slice. *See* PART. **3.** The act or process of decreasing : abatement, curtailment, cutback, decrease, decrement, diminishment, diminution, drain, reduction, slash, slowdown, taper. *See* INCREASE. **4.** *Informal.* That which is allotted : allocation, allotment, allowance, dole, lot, measure, part, portion, quantum, quota, ration, share, split. *Slang:* divvy. *See* COLLECT. **5.** A deliberate slight : rebuff, snub, spurn. *Informal:* cold shoulder, go-by. *See* ACCEPT. **6.** An unexcused absence : truancy, truantry. *Informal:* hooky. *See* SEEK.

cut across *verb* See **cut.**

cut-and-dried *adjective*
Being of no special quality or type : average, common, commonplace, formulaic, garden, garden-variety, indifferent, mediocre, ordinary, plain, routine, run-of-the-mill, standard, stock, undistinguished, unexceptional, unremarkable. *See* GOOD, USUAL.

cutback *noun*
The act or process of decreasing : abatement, curtailment, cut, decrease, decrement, diminishment, diminution, drain, reduction, slash, slowdown, taper. *See* INCREASE.

cut back *verb* See **cut.**

cut down *verb* See **cut.**

cut in *verb* See **cut.**

cut-off *noun*
The act of stopping : cessation, check, discontinuance, discontinuation, halt[1], stay[1], stop, stoppage, surcease. *See* CONTINUE.

cut off *verb* See **cut.**

cut out *verb* See **cut.**

cutthroat *noun*
One who murders another : butcher, homicide, killer, manslayer, massacrer, murderer, murderess, slaughterer, slayer, triggerman. *See* HELP.
cutthroat *adjective* Eager for bloodshed : bloodthirsty, bloody, bloody-minded, homicidal, murderous, sanguinary, sanguineous, slaughterous. *See* HELP.

cutting *adjective*
So sharp as to cause mental pain : acerbic, acid, acidic, acrid, astringent, biting, caustic, corrosive, mordacious, mordant, pungent, scathing, sharp, slashing, stinging, trenchant, truculent, vitriolic. *See* ATTACK, RESPECT.

cutup *noun*
Informal. One who causes minor trouble or damage : devil, imp, mischief, prankster, rascal, rogue, scamp. *See* GOOD.

cut up *verb* See **cut.**

cycle *noun*
A course, process, or journey that ends where it began or repeats itself : circle, circuit, orbit, round, tour, turn. *See* REPETITION.

cyclic *adjective*
Happening or appearing at regular intervals : cyclical, isochronal, isochronous, periodic, periodical, recurrent. ***Idiom:*** like clockwork. *See* REPETITION.

cyclical *adjective*
Happening or appearing at regular intervals : cyclic, isochronal, isochronous, periodic, periodical, recurrent. ***Idiom:*** like clockwork. *See* REPETITION.

cyclopean *adjective*
Of extraordinary size and power : behemoth, Brobdingnagian, Bunyanesque, colossal, elephantine, enormous, gargantuan, giant, gigantesque, gigantic, herculean, heroic, huge, immense, jumbo, mammoth, massive, massy, mastodonic, mighty, monster, monstrous, monumental, mountainous, prodigious, pythonic, stupendous, titanic, tremendous, vast. *Informal:* walloping. *Slang:* whopping. *See* BIG.

cynic *noun*
A person who expects only the worst from people : misanthrope, misanthropist. *See* ATTITUDE.
cynic *adjective* Marked by or displaying contemptuous mockery of the motives or virtues of others : cynical, ironic, ironical, sardonic, wry. *See* ATTITUDE, RESPECT.

cynical *adjective*
Marked by or displaying contemptuous mockery of the motives or virtues of others : cynic, ironic, ironical, sardonic, wry. *See* ATTITUDE, RESPECT.

·D·

dab¹ *verb*
To spread with a greasy, sticky, or dirty substance : bedaub, besmear, daub, plaster, smear, smirch, smudge. *See* PUT ON.
dab *noun* A tiny amount : bit¹, crumb, dash, dot, dram, drop, fragment, grain, iota, jot, minim, mite, modicum, molecule, ort, ounce, particle, scrap¹, scruple, shred, smidgen, speck, tittle, trifle, whit. *Chiefly British:* spot. *See* BIG.

dab² *noun*
Chiefly British. A person with a high degree of knowledge or skill in a particular field : ace, adept, authority, dab hand, expert, master, past master, professional, proficient, wizard. *Informal:* whiz. *Slang:* crackerjack. *See* ABILITY.

dabbler *noun*
One lacking professional skill and ease in a particular pursuit : amateur, dilettante, nonprofessional, smatterer, uninitiate. *See* ABILITY.

dab hand *noun*
A person with a high degree of knowledge or skill in a particular field : ace, adept, authority, expert, master, past master, professional, proficient, wizard. *Informal:* whiz. *Slang:* crackerjack. *Chiefly British:* dab². *See* ABILITY.

dad *noun*
Informal. A male parent : father, sire. *Informal:* daddy, pa, papa, pappy², pop². *Slang:* old man. *See* KIN.

daddy *noun*
Informal. A male parent : father, sire.

Informal: dad, pa, papa, pappy[2], pop[2]. *Slang:* old man. *See* KIN.

daedal *adjective*
Difficult to understand because of intricacy : byzantine, complex, complicated, convoluted, Daedalian, elaborate, intricate, involute, involved, knotty, labyrinthine, tangled. *See* SIMPLE.

Daedalian or **Daedalean** *adjective*
Difficult to understand because of intricacy : byzantine, complex, complicated, convoluted, daedal, elaborate, intricate, involute, involved, knotty, labyrinthine, tangled. *See* SIMPLE.

daffy *adjective*
Informal. Afflicted with or exhibiting irrationality and mental unsoundness : brainsick, crazy, daft, demented, disordered, distraught, dotty, insane, lunatic, mad, maniac, maniacal, mentally ill, moonstruck, off, touched, unbalanced, unsound, wrong. *Informal:* bonkers, cracked, gaga, loony. *Slang:* bananas, batty, buggy, cuckoo, fruity, loco, nuts, nutty, screwy, wacky. *Chiefly British:* crackers. *Law:* non compos mentis. ***Idioms:*** around the bend, crazy as a loon, mad as a hatter, not all there, nutty as a fruitcake, off (*or* out of) one's head, off one's rocker, of unsound mind, out of one's mind, sick in the head, stark raving mad. *See* SANE.

daft *adjective*
Afflicted with or exhibiting irrationality and mental unsoundness : brainsick, crazy, demented, disordered, distraught, dotty, insane, lunatic, mad, maniac, maniacal, mentally ill, moonstruck, off, touched, unbalanced, unsound, wrong. *Informal:* bonkers, cracked, daffy, gaga, loony. *Slang:* bananas, batty, buggy, cuckoo, fruity, loco, nuts, nutty, screwy, wacky. *Chiefly British:* crackers. *Law:* non compos mentis. ***Idioms:*** around the bend, crazy as a loon, mad as a hatter, not all there, nutty as a fruitcake, off (*or* out of) one's head, off one's rocker, of unsound mind, out of one's mind, sick in the head, stark raving mad. *See* SANE.

dainty *adjective*
1. Appealing to refined taste : choice, delicate, elegant, exquisite, fine[1]. *See* GOOD, INGESTION. **2.** Very difficult to please : choosy, exacting, fastidious, finical, finicky, fussy, meticulous, nice, particular, persnickety, squeamish. *Informal:* picky. *See* ACCEPT.

dainty *noun* Something fine and delicious, especially a food : delicacy, morsel, tidbit, treat. *Informal:* goody. *See* GOOD, INGESTION.

dalliance *noun*
1. The practice of flirting : coquetry, flirtation. *See* SEX. **2.** A usually brief romance entered into lightly or frivolously : flirtation. *See* SEX.

dally *verb*
1. To make amorous advances without serious intentions : coquet, flirt, toy, trifle. *See* SEX. **2.** To treat lightly or flippantly : flirt, play, toy, trifle. *See* WORK. **3.** To go or move slowly so that progress is hindered : dawdle, delay, dilly-dally, drag, lag, linger, loiter, poke, procrastinate, tarry, trail. ***Idioms:*** drag one's feet (*or* heels), mark time, take one's time. *See* FAST.

dam *verb*
To stop or prevent passage of : bar, block, impede, obstruct. ***Idiom:*** be (*or* stand) in the way of. *See* OPEN.

damage *noun*
1. An act, instance, or consequence of breaking : breakage, destruction, impairment, wreckage. *See* HELP. **2.** The action or result of inflicting loss or pain : detriment, harm, hurt, injury, mischief. *See* HELP.

damage *verb* To spoil the soundness or perfection of : blemish, detract from, disserve, flaw, harm, hurt, impair, injure, mar, prejudice, tarnish, vitiate. *See* BETTER, HELP.

damn *verb*
1. To pronounce judgment against : condemn, doom, sentence. *See* LAW. **2.** To invoke evil or injury upon : anathematize, curse, imprecate. *Informal:* cuss. *Archaic:* execrate, maledict. *See* WORDS. **3.** To use profane or obscene language : blaspheme, curse, swear. *Informal:* cuss. *See* DECENT, SACRED, WORDS.

damn *noun Informal.* The least bit : hoot, iota, jot, ounce, shred, whit. *Informal:* rap[2]. *Slang:* diddly. *See* BIG.

damn *adjective* So annoying or detestable as to deserve condemnation : accursed, blasted, blessed, bloody, confounded, cursed, darn, execrable, infernal. *Informal:* blamed, damned. *Chiefly British:* blooming, ruddy. *See* LIKE.

damnation *noun*
A denunciation invoking a wish or threat of evil or injury : anathema, curse, execration, imprecation, malediction. *Archaic:* malison. *See* WORDS.

damned *adjective*
1. Condemned, especially to hell : doomed, lost. ***Idiom:*** gone to blazes. *See* REWARD. **2.** *Informal.* So annoying or detestable as to deserve condemnation : accursed, blasted, blessed, bloody, confounded, cursed, damn, darn, execrable, infernal. *Informal:* blamed. *Chiefly British:* blooming, ruddy. *See* LIKE. **3.** Completely such, without qualification or ex-

ception : absolute, all-out, arrant, complete, consummate, crashing, dead, downright, flat, out-and-out, outright, perfect, plain, pure, sheer[2], thorough, thoroughgoing, total, unbounded, unequivocal, unlimited, unmitigated, unqualified, unrelieved, unreserved, utter[2]. *Informal:* flat-out, positive. *Chiefly British:* blooming. *See* BIG, LIMITED.

damp *adjective*
Slightly wet : dank, moist. *See* DRY.

dampen *verb*
1. To make moist : bathe, moisten, wash, wet. *See* DRY. **2.** To decrease or dull the sound of : deaden, muffle, mute, stifle. *See* INCREASE, SOUNDS.

dance *verb*
1. To move rhythmically to music, using patterns of steps or gestures : foot, step. *Slang:* hoof. ***Idioms:*** cut a rug, foot it, trip the light fantastic. *See* REPETITION, WORK. **2.** To leap and skip about playfully : caper, cavort, frisk, frolic, gambol, rollick, romp. *See* WORK.
dance *noun* A party or gathering for dancing : ball. *Informal:* hop. *See* WORK.

dancer *noun*
A person who dances, especially professionally : terpsichorean. *Slang:* hoofer. *See* REPETITION.

dander *noun*
Informal. A tendency to become angry or irritable : irascibility, irascibleness, spleen, temper, temperament, tetchiness. *Slang:* short fuse. ***Idiom:*** low boiling point. *See* FEELINGS.

dandy *adjective*
1. *Informal.* Exceptionally good of its kind : ace, banner, blue-ribbon, brag, capital, champion, excellent, fine[1], first-class, first-rate, prime, quality, splendid, superb, superior, terrific, tiptop, top. *Informal:* A-one, bully, great, swell, topflight, topnotch. *Slang:* boss. *Chiefly British:* tophole. *See* GOOD. **2.** *Informal.* Particularly excellent : divine, fabulous, fantastic, fantastical, glorious, marvelous, sensational, splendid, superb, terrific, wonderful. *Informal:* dreamy, great, ripping, super, swell, tremendous. *Slang:* cool, groovy, hot, keen[1], neat, nifty. ***Idiom:*** out of this world. *See* GOOD.

danger *noun*
Exposure to possible harm, loss, or injury : endangerment, hazard, imperilment, jeopardy, peril, risk. *See* SAFETY.

dangerous *adjective*
1. Involving possible risk, loss, or injury : adventurous, chancy, hazardous, jeopardous, parlous, perilous, risky, treacherous, unsafe, venturesome, venturous. *Slang:* hairy. *See* SAFETY. **2.** Causing or marked by danger or pain, for example : grave[2], grievous, serious, severe. *See* HELP.

dangle *verb*
To fasten or be fastened at one point with no support from below : depend, hang, sling, suspend, swing. *See* HANG.

dangly *adjective*
Hung or appearing to be hung from a support : hanging, pendulous, pensile. *See* HANG.

dank *adjective*
Slightly wet : damp, moist. *See* DRY.

dap *verb*
To strike a surface at such an angle as to be deflected : carom, glance, graze, ricochet, skim, skip. *See* STRIKE.

dapple *verb*
To mark with many small spots : bespeckle, besprinkle, dot, fleck, freckle, mottle, pepper, speck, speckle, sprinkle, stipple. *See* MARKS.

dare *verb*
1. To have the courage to put forward, as an idea, especially when rebuff or criticism is likely : hazard, presume, pretend, venture. *See* TRY. **2.** To call on another to do something requiring boldness : challenge, defy. ***Idiom:*** throw down the gauntlet. *See* REQUEST. **3.** To confront boldly and courageously : beard, brave, challenge, defy, face, front. ***Idioms:*** fly in the face of, snap one's fingers at, stand up to, thumb one's nose at. *See* RESIST.
dare *noun* An act of taunting another to do something bold or rash : challenge. *See* REQUEST.

daredevil *noun*
One who engages in exciting, risky pursuits : adventurer, venturer. *See* SAFETY.
daredevil *adjective* Taking or willing to take risks : adventuresome, adventurous, audacious, bold, daring, enterprising, venturesome, venturous. *See* SAFETY.

daredevilry *noun*
Willingness to take risks : adventuresomeness, adventurousness, audaciousness, audacity, boldness, daredeviltry, daring, daringness, venturesomeness, venturousness. *See* SAFETY.

daredeviltry *noun*
Willingness to take risks : adventuresomeness, adventurousness, audaciousness, audacity, boldness, daredevilry, daring, daringness, venturesomeness, venturousness. *See* SAFETY.

daring *adjective*
Taking or willing to take risks : adventuresome, adventurous, audacious, bold, daredevil,

enterprising, venturesome, venturous. *See* SAFETY.

daring *noun* Willingness to take risks : adventuresomeness, adventurousness, audaciousness, audacity, boldness, daredevilry, daredeviltry, daringness, venturesomeness, venturousness. *See* SAFETY.

daringness *noun*
Willingness to take risks : adventuresomeness, adventurousness, audaciousness, audacity, boldness, daredevilry, daredeviltry, daring, venturesomeness, venturousness. *See* SAFETY.

dark *adjective*
1. Having little or no light : black, pitch-dark. *See* LIGHT. **2.** Deficient in brightness : caliginous, dim, dusky, murky, obscure. *See* LIGHT. **3.** Somewhat black : blackish, dusky. *See* COLORS. **4.** Of a complexion tending toward brown or black : bistered, black-a-vised, brunet, dusky, swarthy. *See* COLORS. **5.** Dark and depressing : black, bleak, blue, cheerless, desolate, dismal, dreary, gloomy, glum, joyless, somber, tenebrific. *See* HAPPY, LIGHT. **6.** Characterized by or expressive of a foreboding somberness : lowery, sullen. *See* WARN. **7.** Marked by little hopefulness : dismal, gloomy, pessimistic. *See* HAPPY, HOPE.

dark *noun* Absence or deficiency of light : darkness, dimness, duskiness, murkiness, obscureness, obscurity. *See* LIGHT.

darken *verb*
To make dark or darker : adumbrate, shade, shadow. *See* LIGHT.

darkness *noun*
Absence or deficiency of light : dark, dimness, duskiness, murkiness, obscureness, obscurity. *See* LIGHT.

darling *noun*
1. A person who is much loved : beloved, dear, honey, love, minion, precious, sweet, sweetheart, truelove. *Informal:* sweetie. ***Idiom:*** light of one's life. *See* LOVE. **2.** One liked or preferred above all others : favorite, pet[1]. ***Idiom:*** apple of one's eye. *See* LIKE.

darling *adjective* **1.** Regarded with much love and tenderness : beloved, dear, loved, precious. *See* LOVE. **2.** Given special, usually doting treatment : fair-haired, favored, favorite, pet[1]. *See* TREAT WELL. **3.** *Informal.* Giving great pleasure or delight : charming, delectable, delicious, delightful, enchanting, heavenly, luscious. *See* GOOD, HAPPY, LIKE.

darn *adjective*
So annoying or detestable as to deserve condemnation : accursed, blasted, blessed, bloody, confounded, cursed, damn, execrable, infernal. *Informal:* blamed, damned. *Chiefly British:* blooming, ruddy. *See* LIKE.

dart *verb*
1. To move swiftly : bolt, bucket, bustle, dash, festinate, flash, fleet, flit, fly, haste, hasten, hurry, hustle, pelt[2], race, rocket, run, rush, sail, scoot, scour[2], shoot, speed, sprint, tear[1], trot, whirl, whisk, whiz, wing, zip, zoom. *Informal:* hotfoot, rip. *Slang:* barrel, highball. *Chiefly British:* nip[1]. ***Idioms:*** get a move on, get cracking, go like lightning, go like the wind, hotfoot it, make haste, make time, make tracks, run like the wind, shake a leg, step (*or* jump) on it. *See* MOVE. **2.** To pass quickly and lightly through the air : float, fly, sail, shoot, skim. *See* MOVE. **3.** To send through the air with a motion of the hand or arm : cast, dash, fling, heave, hurl, hurtle, launch, pitch, shoot, shy[2], sling, throw, toss. *Informal:* fire. *See* MOVE.

dash *verb*
1. To send through the air with a motion of the hand or arm : cast, dart, fling, heave, hurl, hurtle, launch, pitch, shoot, shy[2], sling, throw, toss. *Informal:* fire. *See* MOVE. **2.** To hurl or scatter liquid upon : bespatter, slop, slosh, spatter, splash, splatter, spray, swash. *See* STRIKE. **3.** To move swiftly : bolt, bucket, bustle, dart, festinate, flash, fleet, flit, fly, haste, hasten, hurry, hustle, pelt[2], race, rocket, run, rush, sail, scoot, scour[2], shoot, speed, sprint, tear[1], trot, whirl, whisk, whiz, wing, zip, zoom. *Informal:* hotfoot, rip. *Slang:* barrel, highball. *Chiefly British:* nip[1]. ***Idioms:*** get a move on, get cracking, go like lightning, go like the wind, hotfoot it, make haste, make time, make tracks, run like the wind, shake a leg, step (*or* jump) on it. *See* MOVE. **4.** To spoil or destroy : blast, blight, nip[1]. *See* HELP.

dash *noun* **1.** A lively, emphatic, eager quality or manner : animation, bounce, brio, élan, esprit, life, liveliness, pertness, sparkle, spirit, verve, vigor, vim, vivaciousness, vivacity, zip. *Informal:* ginger, pep, peppiness. *Slang:* oomph. *See* ACTION. **2.** A tiny amount : bit[1], crumb, dab[1], dot, dram, drop, fragment, grain, iota, jot, minim, mite, modicum, molecule, ort, ounce, particle, scrap[1], scruple, shred, smidgen, speck, tittle, trifle, whit. *Chiefly British:* spot. *See* BIG. **3.** A slight amount or indication : breath, ghost, hair, hint, intimation, semblance, shade, shadow, soupçon, streak, suggestion, suspicion, taste, tinge, touch, trace, whiff, whisper. *Informal:* whisker. *See* BIG, SHOW. **4.** A very small mark : dot, fleck, pinpoint, point, speck, spot. *See* MARKS. **5.** A quality of active mental and physical forcefulness : punch, starch, verve, vigor, vigorousness, vim, vitality. *Informal:* snap. ***Idiom:*** vim and vigor. *See* ACTION, TIRED.

dashing *adjective*
1. Very brisk, alert, and full of high spirits : animated, bouncy, chipper, high-spirited, lively, pert, spirited, vivacious. *Informal:* peppy. ***Idioms:*** bright-eyed and bushy-tailed, full of life. *See* ACTION. **2.** Being or in accordance with the current fashion : à la mode, chic, fashionable, mod, modish, posh, smart, stylish, swank, swanky, trig. *Informal:* classy, in, sharp, snappy, swish, tony, trendy. *Slang:* with-it. ***Idioms:*** all the rage, up to the minute. *See* STYLE, USUAL.

dastard *noun*
An ignoble, uncourageous person : coward, craven, funk, poltroon. *Slang:* chicken, yellowbelly. *See* FEAR.

dastardliness *noun*
Ignoble lack of courage : chickenheartedness, cowardice, cowardliness, cravenness, faintheartedness, funk, pusillanimity, unmanliness. *Slang:* gutlessness, yellowness, yellow streak. *See* FEAR.

dastardly *adjective*
Ignobly lacking in courage : chickenhearted, cowardly, craven, faint-hearted, lily-livered, pusillanimous, unmanly. *Slang:* chicken, gutless, yellow, yellow-bellied. *See* FEAR.

data *noun*
That which is known about a specific subject or situation : fact (used in plural), information, intelligence, knowledge, lore. *See* KNOWLEDGE.

date *noun*
A commitment to appear at a certain time and place : appointment, assignation, engagement, rendezvous, tryst. *See* AGREE.
date *verb* To be with another person socially on a regular basis : go out, see. *Informal:* take out. *See* CONNECT.

dated *adjective*
Of a style or method formerly in vogue : antiquated, antique, archaic, bygone, dowdy, fusty, old, old-fashioned, old-time, outdated, outmoded, out-of-date, passé, vintage. *See* NEW.

dateless *adjective*
Existing unchanged forever : ageless, eternal, timeless. *Archaic:* eterne. *See* CHANGE.

daub *verb*
To spread with a greasy, sticky, or dirty substance : bedaub, besmear, dab[1], plaster, smear, smirch, smudge. *See* PUT ON.
daub *noun* A discolored mark made by smearing : blot, blotch, smear, smirch, smudge, smutch, splotch, stain. *See* MARKS.

daunt *verb*
To deprive of courage or the power to act as a result of fear, anxiety, or disgust : appall, consternate, dismay, horrify, shake, shock[1]. *See* FEAR.

dauntless *adjective*
Having or showing courage : audacious, bold, brave, courageous, doughty, fearless, fortitudinous, gallant, game, hardy, heroic, intrepid, mettlesome, plucky, stout, stouthearted, unafraid, undaunted, valiant, valorous. *Informal:* spunky. *Slang:* gutsy, gutty. *See* FEAR.

dauntlessness *noun*
The quality of mind enabling one to face danger or hardship resolutely : braveness, bravery, courage, courageousness, doughtiness, fearlessness, fortitude, gallantry, gameness, heart, intrepidity, intrepidness, mettle, nerve, pluck, pluckiness, spirit, stoutheartedness, undauntedness, valiance, valiancy, valiantness, valor. *Informal:* spunk, spunkiness. *Slang:* gut (used in plural), gutsiness, moxie. *See* FEAR.

dawdle *verb*
1. To go or move slowly so that progress is hindered : dally, delay, dilly-dally, drag, lag, linger, loiter, poke, procrastinate, tarry, trail. ***Idioms:*** drag one's feet (*or* heels), mark time, take one's time. *See* FAST. **2.** To pass (time) without working or in avoiding work. Also used with *away* : fiddle away, idle (away), kill[1], trifle away, waste, while (away), wile (away). *See* INDUSTRIOUS.

dawdler *noun*
One that lags : dilly-dallier, lag, laggard, lagger, lingerer, loiterer, poke, procrastinator, straggler, tarrier. *Informal:* slowpoke. *See* FAST.

dawn *noun*
1. The first appearance of daylight in the morning : aurora, cockcrow, dawning, daybreak, morn, morning, sunrise, sunup. *See* START.
2. The initial stage of a developmental process : beginning, birth, commencement, genesis, inception, nascence, nascency, onset, opening, origin, outset, spring, start. *See* START.
dawn *verb* To begin to appear or develop : appear, arise, commence, emerge, originate. *See* START.

dawn on (or **upon**) *verb* To come as a realization : register, sink in, soak in. *See* KNOWLEDGE.

dawning *noun*
The first appearance of daylight in the morning : aurora, cockcrow, dawn, daybreak, morn, morning, sunrise, sunup. *See* START.

dawn on or **upon** *verb* See **dawn.**

day *noun*
1. The period during which someone or something exists. Often used in plural : duration, existence, life, lifetime, span, term. *See* LIVE, TIME. **2.** A particular time notable for its distinctive characteristics : age, epoch, era, period, time (often used in plural). *See* TIME.

daybreak *noun*
The first appearance of daylight in the morning : aurora, cockcrow, dawn, dawning, morn, morning, sunrise, sunup. *See* START.

daydream *noun*
An illusory mental image : dream, fancy, fantasy, fiction, figment, illusion, phantasm, phantasma, reverie, vision. *See* REAL.

daydream *verb* To experience dreams or daydreams : dream, fantasize, muse[1], woolgather. *See* REAL.

daydreaming *noun*
The condition of being so lost in solitary thought as to be unaware of one's surroundings : absent-mindedness, abstraction, bemusement, brown study, muse[2], reverie, study, trance. *See* AWARENESS.

daze *verb*
1. To dull the senses, as with a heavy blow, a shock, or fatigue : bedaze, bemuse, benumb, stun, stupefy. *Chiefly Regional:* maze. *See* AWARENESS. **2.** To confuse with bright light : bedazzle, blind, dazzle. *See* SEE.

daze *noun* A stunned or bewildered condition : befuddlement, bewilderedness, bewilderment, discombobulation, fog, muddle, mystification, perplexity, puzzlement, stupefaction, stupor, trance. *See* AWARENESS.

dazzle *verb*
To confuse with bright light : bedazzle, blind, daze. *See* SEE.

dazzle *noun* An intense blinding light : blaze[1], glare. *See* LIGHT.

dead *adjective*
1. No longer alive : asleep, deceased, defunct, departed, extinct, gone, late, lifeless. ***Idioms:*** at rest, pushing up daisies. *See* LIVE. **2.** Lacking physical feeling or sensitivity : asleep, insensible, insensitive, numb, unfeeling. *See* AWARENESS. **3.** Extremely tired : bleary, drained, exhausted, fatigued, rundown, spent, tired out, wearied, weariful, weary, worn-down, worn-out. *Informal:* beat, bushed, tuckered (out). *Slang:* done in, fagged (out), pooped (out). ***Idioms:*** all in, ready to drop. *See* HEALTH, TIRED. **4.** Completely lacking sensation or consciousness : inanimate, insensate, insentient. *See* LIVE. **5.** No longer in use, force, or operation : defunct, extinct, lost, vanished. *See* LIVE, NEW. **6.** Completely such, without qualification or exception : absolute, all-out, arrant, complete, consummate, crashing, damned, downright, flat, out-and-out, outright, perfect, plain, pure, sheer[2], thorough, thoroughgoing, total, unbounded, unequivocal, unlimited, unmitigated, unqualified, unrelieved, unreserved, utter[2]. *Informal:* flat-out, positive. *Chiefly British:* blooming. *See* BIG, LIMITED.

dead *adverb* **1.** To the fullest extent : absolutely, all, altogether, completely, entirely, flat, fully, just, perfectly, quite, thoroughly, totally, utterly, well[2], wholly. *Informal:* clean, clear. ***Idioms:*** in toto, through and through. *See* BIG, LIMITED. **2.** In a direct line : direct, directly, due, right, straight, straightaway. *See* STRAIGHT. **3.** With precision or absolute conformity : bang, direct, directly, exactly, fair, flush, just, precisely, right, smack[1], square, squarely, straight. *Slang:* smack-dab. *See* PRECISE.

deaden *verb*
1. To render less sensitive : benumb, blunt, desensitize, dull, numb. ***Idiom:*** take the edge off. *See* AWARENESS. **2.** To decrease or dull the sound of : dampen, muffle, mute, stifle. *See* INCREASE, SOUNDS.

dead end *noun*
A course leading nowhere : blind alley, cul-de-sac. *See* OPEN.

dead heat *noun*
An equality of scores, votes, or performances in a contest : deadlock, draw, stalemate, standoff, tie. *See* SAME.

deadliness *noun*
The quality or condition of causing death : fatality, lethality. *See* LIVE.

deadlock *noun*
An equality of scores, votes, or performances in a contest : dead heat, draw, stalemate, standoff, tie. *See* SAME.

deadly *adjective*
1. Causing or tending to cause death : deathly, fatal, lethal, mortal, vital. *See* LIVE. **2.** Gruesomely suggestive of ghosts or death : cadaverous, deathlike, deathly, ghastly, ghostlike,

ghostly, spectral. *See* LIVE. **3.** Extremely destructive or harmful : baneful, malignant, noxious, pernicious, pestilent, pestilential, virulent. *See* HELP.

deadpan *adjective*
Lacking expression : blank, expressionless, inexpressive, pokerfaced. *See* SHOW.

deafening *adjective*
Marked by extremely high volume and intensity of sound : blaring, earsplitting, loud, roaring, stentorian. *See* SOUNDS.

deal *verb*
1. To give out in portions or shares. Also used with *out* : dispense, distribute, divide, dole out, parcel out, portion (out), ration (out), share. *Slang:* divvy. *See* COLLECT. **2.** To offer for sale. Also used with *in* : handle, market, merchandise, merchant, peddle, retail, sell, trade (in), vend. *See* TRANSACTIONS. **3.** To engage in the illicit sale of (narcotics) : peddle. *Slang:* push. *See* TRANSACTIONS. **4.** To mete out by means of some action : administer, deliver, give. *See* GIVE.

deal with *verb* **1.** To be occupied or concerned with : consider, take up, treat. ***Idiom:*** have to do with. *See* RELEVANT. **2.** To behave in a specified way toward : handle, treat. *See* TREAT WELL.

deal *noun* **1.** An indefinite amount or extent : quantity. *Informal:* lot. *See* BIG. **2.** An act or state of agreeing between parties regarding a course of action : accord, agreement, arrangement, bargain, compact[2], pact, understanding. *See* AGREE. **3.** An agreement, especially one involving a sale or exchange : bargain, compact[2], contract, covenant, transaction. *See* AGREE. **4.** *Informal.* Something offered or bought at a low price : bargain. *Informal:* buy. *Slang:* steal. *See* MONEY, TRANSACTIONS.

dealer *noun*
1. A person engaged in buying and selling : businessperson, merchandiser, merchant, speculator, trader, tradesman, trafficker. *See* TRANSACTIONS. **2.** A person who sells narcotics illegally : peddler. *Slang:* pusher. *See* TRANSACTIONS.

deal with *verb* See **deal.**

dear *adjective*
1. Regarded with much love and tenderness : beloved, darling, loved, precious. *See* LOVE.
2. Bringing a high price : costly, expensive, high, high-priced. *See* TRANSACTIONS, VALUE.

dear *noun* A person who is much loved : beloved, darling, honey, love, minion, precious, sweet, sweetheart, truelove. *Informal:* sweetie. *Idiom:* light of one's life. *See* LOVE.

dearth *noun*
The condition of lacking a needed or usual amount : absence, lack, want. *See* EXCESS.

death *noun*
1. The act or fact of dying : decease, demise, dissolution, extinction, passing, quietus, rest[1]. *Slang:* curtain (used in plural). *See* LIVE. **2.** A termination of life, usually as the result of an accident or a disaster : casualty, fatality. *See* LIVE.

deathless *adjective*
Not being subject to death : immortal, undying. *See* CONTINUE, LIVE.

deathlessness *noun*
Endless life after death : afterlife, eternity, everlasting life, everlastingness, immortality. *See* CONTINUE, LIVE.

deathlike *adjective*
Gruesomely suggestive of ghosts or death : cadaverous, deadly, deathly, ghastly, ghostlike, ghostly, spectral. *See* LIVE.

deathly *adjective*
1. Gruesomely suggestive of ghosts or death : cadaverous, deadly, deathlike, ghastly, ghostlike, ghostly, spectral. *See* LIVE. **2.** Causing or tending to cause death : deadly, fatal, lethal, mortal, vital. *See* LIVE.

debacle *noun*
An abrupt disastrous failure : breakdown, collapse, crash, smash, smashup, wreck. *See* MONEY.

debar *verb*
1. To keep from being admitted, included, or considered : bar, count out, eliminate, except, exclude, keep out, rule out, shut out. *See* INCLUDE. **2.** To refuse to allow : ban, disallow, enjoin, forbid, inhibit, interdict, outlaw, prohibit, proscribe, taboo. *See* ALLOW.

debark *verb*
To come ashore from a seacraft : disembark, land. *See* MOVE.

debase *verb*
1. To lower in character or quality : cheapen, degrade, demean[2], downgrade. *See* BETTER.
2. To make impure or inferior by deceptively adding foreign substances : adulterate, doctor, load, sophisticate. *See* CLEAN. **3.** To ruin utterly in character or quality : animalize, bastardize, bestialize, brutalize, canker, corrupt, debauch, demoralize, deprave, pervert, stain, vitiate, warp. *See* CLEAN, HELP.

debasement *noun*
A lowering in or deprivation of character or

self-esteem : abasement, degradation, humiliation, mortification. *See* RESPECT, WIN.

debatable *adjective*
In doubt or dispute : arguable, contested, disputable, doubtful, exceptionable, moot, mootable, problematic, problematical, questionable, uncertain. *See* CERTAIN.

debate *verb*
To put forth reasons for or against something, often excitedly : argue, contend, dispute, moot. *See* AFFIRM, WORDS.
debate *noun* **1.** A discussion, often heated, in which a difference of opinion is expressed : altercation, argument, bicker, clash, contention, controversy, difficulty, disagreement, dispute, fight, polemic, quarrel, run-in, spat, squabble, tiff, word (used in plural), wrangle. *Informal:* hassle, rhubarb, tangle. *See* CONFLICT. **2.** The presentation of an argument or arguments : argumentation, disputation, forensics. *See* AFFIRM, WORDS.

debauch *verb*
1. To ruin utterly in character or quality : animalize, bastardize, bestialize, brutalize, canker, corrupt, debase, demoralize, deprave, pervert, stain, vitiate, warp. *See* CLEAN, HELP. **2.** To lure or persuade into a sexual relationship or a sexual act : seduce, undo. *See* SEX.

debaucher *noun*
A man who seduces women : Don Juan, Lothario, seducer. *See* SEX.

debilitate *verb*
To lessen or deplete the nerve, energy, or strength of : attenuate, devitalize, enervate, enfeeble, sap², undermine, undo, unnerve, weaken. *See* STRONG.

debilitation *noun*
The depletion or sapping of strength or energy : attenuation, depletion, devitalization, enervation, enfeeblement, impoverishment. *See* STRONG.

debility *noun*
The condition of being infirm or physically weak : decrepitude, delicacy, delicateness, feebleness, flimsiness, fragileness, fragility, frailness, frailty, infirmity, insubstantiality, puniness, unsoundness, unsubstantiality, weakliness, weakness. *See* STRONG.

debonair also **debonaire** *adjective*
1. Displaying light-hearted nonchalance : airy, breezy, buoyant, jaunty. *Informal:* corky. *Idiom:* free and easy. *See* ATTITUDE, CAREFUL, GOOD. **2.** Free from care or worry : blithe, carefree, light², lighthearted. *See* CAREFUL, HAPPY.

debonaire *adjective* See **debonair.**

debris *noun*
The remains of something destroyed, disintegrated, or decayed : rubble, ruin, wrack², wreck, wreckage. *See* LEFTOVER.

debt *noun*
1. Something, such as money, owed by one person to another : arrearage, arrears, due, indebtedness, liability, obligation. *See* OBLIGATION, PAY. **2.** A condition of owing something to another : arrearage, arrears, indebtedness, liability, obligation. *See* PAY.

debunk *verb*
To cause to be no longer believed or valued : deflate, discredit, explode, puncture. *Informal:* shoot down. *Idioms:* knock the bottom out of, shoot full of holes. *See* VALUE.

debut also **début** *noun*
The instance or occasion of being presented for the first time to society : coming-out, presentation. *See* KNOWLEDGE.
debut also **début** *verb* To make one's formal entry, as into society : come out. *Idiom:* make one's bow. *See* KNOWLEDGE.

decadence *noun*
Descent to a lower level or condition : atrophy, declension, declination, decline, degeneracy, degeneration, deterioration. *See* BETTER.

decamp *verb*
To break loose and leave suddenly, as from confinement or from a difficult or threatening situation : abscond, break out, escape, flee, fly, get away, run away. *Informal:* skip (out). *Slang:* lam. *Regional:* absquatulate. *Idioms:* blow (*or* fly) the coop, cut and run, give someone the slip, make a getaway, take flight, take it on the lam. *See* FREE.

decampment *noun*
The act or an instance of escaping, as from confinement or difficulty : break, breakout, escape, escapement, flight, getaway. *Slang:* lam. *See* FREE.

decant *verb*
To cause (a liquid) to flow in a steady stream : draw (off), effuse, pour. *See* MOVE.

decay *verb*
To become or cause to become rotten or unsound : break down, decompose, deteriorate, disintegrate, molder, putrefy, rot, spoil, taint, turn. *Idioms:* go bad, go to pot, go to seed. *See* BETTER, THRIVE.
decay *noun* The condition of being decayed : breakdown, decomposition, deterioration, disintegration, putrefaction, putrescence, putrid-

ness, rot, rottenness, spoilage. *See* BETTER, THRIVE.

decaying *adjective*
Showing signs of wear and tear or neglect : bedraggled, broken-down, decrepit, dilapidated, dingy, down-at-heel, faded, mangy, rundown, scrubby, scruffy, seedy, shabby, shoddy, sleazy, tattered, tatty, threadbare. *Informal:* tacky[2]. *Slang:* ratty. ***Idioms:*** all the worse for wear, gone to pot (*or* seed), past cure (*or* hope). *See* BETTER.

decease *verb*
To cease living : demise, depart, die, drop, expire, go, pass away, pass (on), perish, succumb. *Informal:* pop off. *Slang:* check out, croak, kick in, kick off. ***Idioms:*** bite the dust, breathe one's last, cash in, give up the ghost, go to one's grave, kick the bucket, meet one's end (*or* Maker), pass on to the Great Beyond, turn up one's toes. *See* LIVE.

decease *noun* The act or fact of dying : death, demise, dissolution, extinction, passing, quietus, rest[1]. *Slang:* curtain (used in plural). *See* LIVE.

deceased *adjective*
No longer alive : asleep, dead, defunct, departed, extinct, gone, late, lifeless. ***Idioms:*** at rest, pushing up daisies. *See* LIVE.

deceit *noun*
The act or practice of deceiving : cunning, deceitfulness, deception, double-dealing, duplicity, guile, shiftiness. *See* HONEST.

deceitful *adjective*
Given to or marked by deliberate concealment or misrepresentation of the truth : dishonest, lying, mendacious, untruthful. *See* HONEST.

deceitfulness *noun*
The act or practice of deceiving : cunning, deceit, deception, double-dealing, duplicity, guile, shiftiness. *See* HONEST.

deceive *verb*
To cause to accept what is false, especially by trickery or misrepresentation : beguile, betray, bluff, cozen, delude, double-cross, dupe, fool, hoodwink, humbug, mislead, take in, trick. *Informal:* bamboozle, have. *Slang:* four-flush. ***Idioms:*** lead astray, play false, pull the wool over someone's eyes, put something over on, take for a ride. *See* HONEST.

decency *noun*
1. A sense of propriety or rightness : conscience, grace. *See* RIGHT. **2.** Conformity to recognized standards, as of conduct or appearance : comeliness, correctness, decentness, decorousness, decorum, properness, propriety, respectability, respectableness, seemliness. *See* USUAL. **3.** The condition of being chaste : chastity, innocence, modesty, purity, virginity, virtue, virtuousness. *See* GOOD, RESTRAINT, SEX.

decent *adjective*
1. Conforming to accepted standards : becoming, befitting, comely, comme il faut, correct, decorous, de rigueur, nice, proper, respectable, right, seemly. *See* COURTESY. **2.** Not lewd or obscene : clean, modest, wholesome. *See* DECENT. **3.** Being what is needed without being in excess : adequate, comfortable, competent, enough, satisfactory, sufficient. *See* EXCESS. **4.** Of moderately good quality but less than excellent : acceptable, adequate, all right, average, common, fair, fairish, goodish, moderate, passable, respectable, satisfactory, sufficient, tolerable. *Informal:* OK, tidy. *See* GOOD. **5.** Morally beyond reproach, especially in sexual conduct : chaste, modest, nice, pure, virgin, virginal, virtuous. *See* GOOD, RESTRAINT, SEX. **6.** *Informal.* Proper in appearance : presentable, respectable. *See* GOOD, USUAL.

decentness *noun*
Conformity to recognized standards, as of conduct or appearance : comeliness, correctness, decency, decorousness, decorum, properness, propriety, respectability, respectableness, seemliness. *See* USUAL.

deception *noun*
1. The act or practice of deceiving : cunning, deceit, deceitfulness, double-dealing, duplicity, guile, shiftiness. *See* HONEST. **2.** An indirect, usually cunning means of gaining an end : artifice, device, dodge, feint, gimmick, imposture, jig, maneuver, ploy, ruse, sleight, stratagem, subterfuge, trick, wile. *Informal:* shenanigan, take-in. *See* HONEST, MEANS.

deceptive *adjective*
Tending to lead one into error : delusive, delusory, fallacious, illusive, illusory, misleading. *See* HONEST, REAL.

decide *verb*
1. To make a decision about (a controversy or dispute, for example) after deliberation, as in a court of law : adjudge, adjudicate, arbitrate, decree, determine, judge, referee, rule, umpire. *See* DECIDE, LAW. **2.** To make up or cause to make up one's mind : conclude, determine, resolve, settle. *See* DECIDE.

decided *adjective*
1. Without any doubt : clear, clear-cut, definite, distinct, pronounced, unquestionable. *See* CERTAIN. **2.** Clearly, fully, and sometimes em-

phatically expressed : categorical, clear, clear-cut, definite, explicit, express, positive, precise, specific, unambiguous, unequivocal. *See* CLEAR. **3.** Not hesitating or wavering : decisive, determined, firm[1], resolute. *See* DECIDE. **4.** On an unwavering course of action : bent, determined, fixed, intent, resolute, set[1]. *See* DECIDE.

decidedness *noun*
Unwavering firmness of character, action, or will : decision, decisiveness, determination, firmness, purpose, purposefulness, resoluteness, resolution, resolve, toughness, will, willpower. *See* CERTAIN, STRONG.

deciding *adjective*
Determining or having the power to determine an outcome : conclusive, crucial, decisive, determinative. *See* DECIDE, IMPORTANT.

decimate *verb*
To kill savagely and indiscriminately : annihilate, butcher, massacre, slaughter. *See* CRIMES, HELP, MAKE.

decipher *verb*
1. To make understandable : construe, explain, explicate, expound, interpret, spell out. *Archaic:* enucleate. ***Idiom:*** put into plain English. *See* EXPLAIN. **2.** To find a solution for : clear up, explain, resolve, solve, unravel. *Informal:* dope out, figure out. ***Idiom:*** get to the bottom of. *See* ASK, REASON. **3.** To find the key to (a code, for example) : break, crack, decrypt, puzzle out. *See* KNOWLEDGE.

decipherable *adjective*
Capable of being explained or accounted for : accountable, explainable, explicable, illustratable, interpretable. *See* EXPLAIN.

decipherment *noun*
Something that serves to explain or clarify : clarification, construction, elucidation, exegesis, explanation, explication, exposition, illumination, illustration, interpretation. *Archaic:* enucleation. *See* EXPLAIN.

decision *noun*
1. A position reached after consideration : conclusion, determination, resolution. *See* DECIDE. **2.** Unwavering firmness of character, action, or will : decidedness, decisiveness, determination, firmness, purpose, purposefulness, resoluteness, resolution, resolve, toughness, will, willpower. *See* CERTAIN, STRONG.

decisive *adjective*
1. Determining or having the power to determine an outcome : conclusive, crucial, deciding, determinative. *See* DECIDE, IMPORTANT. **2.** Serving the function of deciding or settling with finality : authoritative, conclusive, definitive, determinative, final. *See* DECIDE. **3.** Not hesitating or wavering : decided, determined, firm[1], resolute. *See* DECIDE.

decisiveness *noun*
Unwavering firmness of character, action, or will : decidedness, decision, determination, firmness, purpose, purposefulness, resoluteness, resolution, resolve, toughness, will, willpower. *See* CERTAIN, STRONG.

deck[1] *verb*
Slang. To cause to fall, as from a shot or blow : bring down, cut down, down, drop, fell[1], flatten, floor, ground, knock down, level, prostrate, strike down, throw. ***Idiom:*** lay low. *See* RISE.

deck[2] *verb*
1. To dress in formal or special clothing. Also used with *out* : array, attire, dress up, prank[2]. *Informal:* trick out (*or* up). *Slang:* doll up. *See* ORDER, PLAIN, PUT ON. **2.** To furnish with decorations. Also used with *out* : adorn, bedeck, decorate, dress (up), embellish, garnish, ornament, trim. *See* BEAUTIFUL.

declaim *verb*
To speak in a loud, pompous, or prolonged manner : harangue, mouth, perorate, rant, rave. *See* WORDS.

declaimer *noun*
One who delivers a public speech : lecturer, speaker, speechifier, speechmaker. *See* WORDS.

declamation *noun*
1. A usually formal oral communication to an audience : address, allocution, lecture, oration, prelection, speech, talk. *See* WORDS. **2.** The art of public speaking : elocution, oratory, rhetoric. *See* WORDS.

declamatory *adjective*
1. Of or relating to the art of public speaking : elocutionary, oratorical, rhetorical. *See* WORDS. **2.** Characterized by language that is elevated and sometimes pompous in style : aureate, bombastic, flowery, fustian, grandiloquent, high-flown, high-sounding, magniloquent, orotund, overblown, rhetorical, sonorous, swollen. *See* PLAIN, STYLE, WORDS.

declaration *noun*
1. The act of announcing : announcement, annunciation, proclamation, promulgation, publication. *See* KNOWLEDGE. **2.** A public statement : announcement, annunciation, edict, manifesto, notice, proclamation, pronouncement. *See* KNOWLEDGE. **3.** The act of asserting positively : affirmation, allegation, assertion,

asseveration, averment, claim, statement. *See* AFFIRM.

declare *verb*
1. To bring to public notice or make known publicly : advertise, announce, annunciate, broadcast, proclaim, promulgate, publish. *See* KNOWLEDGE, WORDS. 2. To put into words positively and with conviction : affirm, allege, argue, assert, asseverate, aver, avouch, avow, claim, contend, hold, maintain, say, state. ***Idiom:*** have it. *See* AFFIRM. 3. To put into words : articulate, communicate, convey, express, say, state, talk, tell, utter[1], vent, verbalize, vocalize, voice. ***Idiom:*** give tongue (*or* vent *or* voice) to. *See* WORDS.

déclassé *adjective*
Lacking high station or birth : baseborn, common, declassed, humble, ignoble, lowly, mean[2], plebeian, unwashed, vulgar. *Archaic:* base[2]. *See* OVER.

declassed *adjective*
Lacking high station or birth : baseborn, common, déclassé, humble, ignoble, lowly, mean[2], plebeian, unwashed, vulgar. *Archaic:* base[2]. *See* OVER.

declension *noun*
Descent to a lower level or condition : atrophy, decadence, declination, decline, degeneracy, degeneration, deterioration. *See* BETTER.

declination *noun*
1. Descent to a lower level or condition : atrophy, decadence, declension, decline, degeneracy, degeneration, deterioration. *See* BETTER. 2. A marked loss of strength or effectiveness : decline, deterioration, failure. *See* INCREASE.

decline *verb*
1. To be unwilling to accept, consider, or receive : dismiss, refuse, reject, spurn, turn down. *Slang:* nix. ***Idiom:*** turn thumbs down on. *See* ACCEPT. 2. To slope downward : descend, dip, drop, fall, pitch, sink. *See* RISE. 3. To become lower in quality, character, or condition : atrophy, degenerate, descend, deteriorate, retrograde, sink, worsen. ***Idioms:*** go bad, go to pot, go to seed, go to the dogs. *See* BETTER. 4. To lose strength or power : degenerate, deteriorate, fade, fail, flag[2], languish, sink, wane, waste (away), weaken. *Informal:* fizzle (out). ***Idioms:*** go downhill, hit the skids. *See* STRONG, INCREASE.

decline *noun* 1. Descent to a lower level or condition : atrophy, decadence, declension, declination, degeneracy, degeneration, deterioration. *See* BETTER. 2. A marked loss of strength or effectiveness : declination, deterioration, failure. *See* INCREASE. 3. A usually swift downward trend, as in prices : descent, dip, dive, downslide, downswing, downtrend, downturn, drop, drop-off, fall, nosedive, plunge, skid, slide, slump, tumble. *See* INCREASE. 4. A downward slope or distance : declivity, descent, drop, fall, pitch. *See* RISE.

declivity *noun*
A downward slope or distance : decline, descent, drop, fall, pitch. *See* RISE.

décolleté *adjective*
Cut to reveal the wearer's neck, chest, and back : low, low-cut, low-neck, low-necked, plunging. *See* HIGH.

decompose *verb*
1. To reduce or become reduced to pieces or components : break down, break up, crumble, disintegrate, dissolve, fragment, fragmentize. *See* CONTINUE, HELP. 2. To become or cause to become rotten or unsound : break down, decay, deteriorate, disintegrate, molder, putrefy, rot, spoil, taint, turn. ***Idioms:*** go bad, go to pot, go to seed. *See* BETTER, THRIVE.

decomposition *noun*
The condition of being decayed : breakdown, decay, deterioration, disintegration, putrefaction, putrescence, putridness, rot, rottenness, spoilage. *See* BETTER, THRIVE.

decontaminate *verb*
To render free of microorganisms : disinfect, sanitize, sterilize. *See* CLEAN.

decorate *verb*
To furnish with decorations : adorn, bedeck, deck[2] (out), dress (up), embellish, garnish, ornament, trim. *See* BEAUTIFUL.

decoration *noun*
1. Something that adorns : adornment, embellishment, garnishment, garniture, ornament, ornamentation, trim, trimming. *See* BEAUTIFUL. 2. An emblem of honor worn on one's clothing : badge, medal. *See* REWARD.

decorous *adjective*
Conforming to accepted standards : becoming, befitting, comely, comme il faut, correct, decent, de rigueur, nice, proper, respectable, right, seemly. *See* COURTESY.

decorousness *noun*
Conformity to recognized standards, as of conduct or appearance : comeliness, correctness, decency, decentness, decorum, properness, propriety, respectability, respectableness, seemliness. *See* USUAL.

decorticate *verb*
To remove the skin of : pare, peel, scale[1], skin, strip[1]. *See* PUT ON.

decorum *noun*
1. Conformity to recognized standards, as of conduct or appearance : comeliness, correctness, decency, decentness, decorousness, properness, propriety, respectability, respectableness, seemliness. *See* USUAL. **2.** Socially correct behavior : etiquette, good form, manner (used in plural), mores, propriety (also used in plural), p's and q's. *See* USUAL.

decrease *verb*
To grow or cause to grow gradually less : abate, diminish, drain, dwindle, ebb, lessen, let up, peter (out), rebate, reduce, tail away (*or* off), taper (off). *See* INCREASE.
decrease *noun* The act or process of decreasing : abatement, curtailment, cut, cutback, decrement, diminishment, diminution, drain, reduction, slash, slowdown, taper. *See* INCREASE.

decree *noun*
1. A principle governing affairs within or among political units : canon, edict, institute, law, ordinance, precept, prescription, regulation, rule. *See* LAW. **2.** An authoritative or official decision, especially one made by a court : determination, edict, judgment, pronouncement, ruling. *See* LAW.
decree *verb* **1.** To set forth expressly and authoritatively : dictate, fix, impose, lay down, ordain, prescribe. ***Idioms:*** call the shots (*or* tune), lay it on the line. *See* OVER. **2.** To make a decision about (a controversy or dispute, for example) after deliberation, as in a court of law : adjudge, adjudicate, arbitrate, decide, determine, judge, referee, rule, umpire. *See* DECIDE, LAW.

decrement *noun*
The act or process of decreasing : abatement, curtailment, cut, cutback, decrease, diminishment, diminution, drain, reduction, slash, slowdown, taper. *See* INCREASE.

decrepit *adjective*
1. Not physically strong : delicate, feeble, flimsy, fragile, frail, infirm, insubstantial, puny, unsound, unsubstantial, weak, weakly. *See* STRONG. **2.** Showing signs of wear and tear or neglect : bedraggled, broken-down, decaying, dilapidated, dingy, down-at-heel, faded, mangy, rundown, scrubby, scruffy, seedy, shabby, shoddy, sleazy, tattered, tatty, threadbare. *Informal:* tacky[2]. *Slang:* ratty. ***Idioms:*** all the worse for wear, gone to pot (*or* seed), past cure (*or* hope). *See* BETTER.

decrepitude *noun*
The condition of being infirm or physically weak : debility, delicacy, delicateness, feebleness, flimsiness, fragileness, fragility, frailness, frailty, infirmity, insubstantiality, puniness, unsoundness, unsubstantiality, weakliness, weakness. *See* STRONG.

decry *verb*
To think, represent, or speak of as small or unimportant : belittle, denigrate, deprecate, depreciate, derogate, detract, discount, disparage, downgrade, minimize, run down, slight, talk down. ***Idiom:*** make light (*or* little) of. *See* ATTACK, SHOW.

decrypt *verb*
To find the key to (a code, for example) : break, crack, decipher, puzzle out. *See* KNOWLEDGE.

decumbent *adjective*
Lying down : flat, horizontal, procumbent, prone, prostrate, recumbent. *See* HORIZONTAL.

decussate *verb*
To pass through or over : crisscross, cross, crosscut, cut across, intersect. *See* MEET.

dedicate *verb*
1. To give over by or as if by vow to a higher purpose : consecrate, devote, hallow. *See* GIVE. **2.** To devote (oneself or one's efforts) : address, apply, bend, buckle down, concentrate, devote, direct, focus, give, turn. *See* COLLECT, WORK.

dedicated *adjective*
Given over exclusively to a single use or purpose : consecrated, devoted, hallowed, sacred. *See* GIVE, INCLUDE.

deduce *verb*
To arrive at (a conclusion) from evidence or reasoning : conclude, deduct, draw, gather, infer, judge, understand. *See* REASON.

deduct *verb*
1. To take away (a quantity) from another quantity : abate, discount, rebate, subtract, take (off). *Informal:* knock off. *See* INCREASE. **2.** To arrive at (a conclusion) from evidence or reasoning : conclude, deduce, draw, gather, infer, judge, understand. *See* REASON.

deduction *noun*
1. An amount deducted : abatement, discount, rebate, reduction. *See* INCREASE. **2.** A position arrived at by reasoning from premises or general principles : conclusion, illation, illative, inference, judgment. *See* REASON.

deed *noun*
Something done : act, action, doing, thing, work. *See* DO.

deed *verb* To change the ownership of (property) by means of a legal document : cede, grant, make over, sign over. *Law:* alien, alienate, assign, convey, transfer. *See* GIVE, LAW.

deem *verb*
1. To have an opinion : believe, consider, hold, opine, think. *Informal:* figure, judge. ***Idiom:*** be of the opinion. *See* OPINION. **2.** To look upon in a particular way : account, consider, esteem, reckon, regard, see, view. *See* PERSPECTIVE.

de-emphasize *verb*
To make less emphatic or obvious : play down, tone down. *Informal:* soft-pedal. *See* SHOW.

deep *adjective*
1. Extending far downward or inward from a surface : abysmal, profound. *See* SURFACE. **2.** Beyond the understanding of an average mind : abstruse, esoteric, profound, recondite. *Slang:* heavy. *See* EASY, SURFACE. **3.** Having one's thoughts fully occupied : absorbed, intent, preoccupied, rapt. ***Idiom:*** wrapped up in. *See* AWARENESS, EXCITE. **4.** Resulting from or affecting one's innermost feelings : intense, profound, strong. *See* STRONG, SURFACE. **5.** Being a sound produced by a relatively small frequency of vibrations : alto, bass, contralto, low, low-pitched. *See* SOUNDS.
deep *noun* Something of immeasurable and vast extent : abysm, abyss, chasm, depth (often used in plural), gulf. *See* HIGH.

deepen *verb*
To make greater in intensity or severity : aggravate, enhance, heighten, intensify, redouble. *See* INCREASE.

deepness *noun*
1. The extent or measurement downward from a surface : depth, drop. *See* SURFACE. **2.** Intellectual penetration or range : depth, profoundness, profundity. *See* THOUGHTS.

deep-rooted *adjective*
Firmly established by long standing : confirmed, deep-seated, entrenched, hard-shell, ineradicable, ingrained, inveterate, irradicable, set[1], settled. *See* CONTINUE.

deep-seated *adjective*
Firmly established by long standing : confirmed, deep-rooted, entrenched, hard-shell, ineradicable, ingrained, inveterate, irradicable, set[1], settled. *See* CONTINUE.

deep water *noun*
A difficult, often embarrassing situation or condition : box[1], corner, difficulty, dilemma, Dutch, fix, hole, hot spot, hot water, jam, plight[1], predicament, quagmire, scrape, soup, trouble. *Informal:* bind, pickle, spot. *See* EASY.

defamation *noun*
The expression of injurious, malicious statements about someone : aspersion, calumniation, calumny, character assassination, denigration, detraction, scandal, slander, traducement, vilification. *Law:* libel. *See* ATTACK, CRIMES, LAW.

defamatory *adjective*
Damaging to the reputation : calumnious, detractive, injurious, invidious, scandalous, slanderous. *Law:* libelous. *See* ATTACK, CRIMES, LAW.

defame *verb*
To make defamatory statements about : asperse, backbite, calumniate, malign, slander, slur, tear down, traduce, vilify. *Law:* libel. ***Idiom:*** cast aspersions on. *See* ATTACK, CRIMES, LAW.

default *noun*
Nonperformance of what ought to be done : delinquency, dereliction, failure, neglect, omission. *Law:* nonfeasance. *See* DO.
default *verb* To not do (something necessary) : fail, neglect, omit. *See* DO.

defeasance *noun*
An often formal act of putting an end to : abolishment, abolition, abrogation, annihilation, annulment, cancellation, invalidation, negation, nullification, voidance. *Law:* avoidance, extinguishment. *See* CONTINUE.

defeat *verb*
1. To win a victory over, as in battle or a competition : beat, best, conquer, master, overcome, prevail against (*or* over), rout, subdue, subjugate, surmount, triumph over, vanquish, worst. *Informal:* trim, whip. *Slang:* ace, lick. ***Idioms:*** carry (*or* win) the day, get (*or* have) the best of, get (*or* have) the better of, go someone one better. *See* WIN. **2.** To prevent from accomplishing a purpose : baffle, balk, check, checkmate, foil, frustrate, stymie, thwart. *Informal:* cross, stump. ***Idiom:*** cut the ground from under. *See* ALLOW.
defeat *noun* The act of defeating or the condition of being defeated : beating, drubbing, overthrow, rout, thrashing, vanquishment. *Informal:* massacre, trimming, whipping. *Slang:* dusting, licking. *See* WIN.

defect *noun*
1. The condition or fact of being deficient : deficiency, deficit, inadequacy, insufficiency, lack, paucity, poverty, scantiness, scantness, scarceness, scarcity, shortage, shortcoming, shortfall, underage[1]. *See* EXCESS. **2.** Something that mars the appearance or causes inadequacy or fail-

ure : blemish, bug, fault, flaw, imperfection, shortcoming. *See* BEAUTIFUL, BETTER, HELP.

defect *verb* To abandon one's cause or party usually to join another : apostatize, desert[3], renegade, tergiversate, turn. *Slang:* rat. ***Idioms:*** change sides, turn one's coat. *See* APPROACH, TRUST.

defection *noun*
An instance of defecting from or abandoning a cause : apostasy, recreance, recreancy, tergiversation. *See* APPROACH, TRUST.

defective *adjective*
1. Having a defect or defects : faulty, imperfect. *See* BETTER. **2.** Lacking an essential element : deficient, incomplete, lacking, wanting. *See* BETTER, EXCESS.

defector *noun*
A person who has defected : apostate, deserter, recreant, renegade, runagate, tergiversator, turncoat. *Informal:* rat. *See* APPROACH.

defend *verb*
1. To keep safe from danger, attack, or harm : guard, preserve, protect, safeguard, secure, shield, ward. *Archaic:* fend. *See* ATTACK. **2.** To support against arguments, attack, or criticism : apologize, justify, maintain, vindicate. ***Idioms:*** speak up for, stand up for, stick up for. *See* SUPPORT.

defendable *adjective*
Capable of being defended against armed attack : defensible, tenable. *See* ATTACK.

defendant *noun*
A person against whom an action is brought : *Law:* accused, respondent. *See* LAW.

defense *noun*
1. The act or a means of defending : guard, preservation, protection, protector, safeguard, security, shield, ward. *See* ATTACK. **2.** A statement that justifies or defends something, such as a past action or policy : apologetic, apologia, apology, justification, vindication. *See* ATTACK.

defenseless *adjective*
Devoid of help or protection : helpless, unprotected. *See* SAFETY.

defensible *adjective*
1. Capable of being defended against armed attack : defendable, tenable. *See* ATTACK. **2.** Capable of being justified : excusable, justifiable, tenable. *See* FORGIVENESS, RIGHT.

defer[1] *verb*
To put off until a later time : adjourn, delay, hold off, hold up, postpone, remit, shelve, stay[1], suspend, table, waive. *Informal:* wait. ***Idiom:*** put on ice. *See* DO.

defer[2] *verb*
To conform to the will or judgment of another, especially out of respect or courtesy : bow[1], submit, yield. ***Idioms:*** give ground, give way. *See* PRECEDE, RESIST.

deference *noun*
1. The quality or state of willingly carrying out the wishes of others : acquiescence, amenability, amenableness, compliance, compliancy, obedience, submission, submissiveness, tractability, tractableness. *See* RESIST. **2.** Great respect or high public esteem accorded as a right or as due : homage, honor, obeisance. *See* RESPECT.

deferential *adjective*
Marked by courteous submission or respect : duteous, dutiful, obeisant, respectful. *See* RESIST.

deferment *noun*
The act of putting off or the condition of being put off : adjournment, deferral, delay, postponement, stay[1], suspension, waiver. *See* TIME.

deferral *noun*
The act of putting off or the condition of being put off : adjournment, deferment, delay, postponement, stay[1], suspension, waiver. *See* TIME.

defiance *noun*
1. Behavior or an act that is intentionally provocative : challenge, provocation. *See* ATTACK. **2.** The disposition boldly to defy or resist authority or an opposing force : contempt, contumacy, despite, recalcitrance, recalcitrancy. *See* RESIST.

defiant *adjective*
Marked by defiance : contumacious, recalcitrant. *See* RESIST.

deficiency *noun*
The condition or fact of being deficient : defect, deficit, inadequacy, insufficiency, lack, paucity, poverty, scantiness, scantness, scarceness, scarcity, shortage, shortcoming, shortfall, underage[1]. *See* EXCESS.

deficient *adjective*
1. Lacking an essential element : defective, incomplete, lacking, wanting. *See* BETTER, EXCESS. **2.** Not enough to meet a demand or requirement : inadequate, insufficient, scarce, short, shy[1], under, wanting. *See* BIG, EXCESS.

deficit *noun*
The condition or fact of being deficient : defect, deficiency, inadequacy, insufficiency, lack, paucity, poverty, scantiness, scantness,

scarceness, scarcity, shortage, shortcoming, shortfall, underage[1]. *See* EXCESS.

defile *verb*
1. To make dirty : befoul, begrime, besmirch, besoil, black, blacken, dirty, smudge, smutch, soil, sully. *See* CLEAN. **2.** To make physically impure : contaminate, foul, poison, pollute. *See* CLEAN. **3.** To make morally impure : contaminate, corrupt, infect, pollute, soil, taint. *See* CLEAN. **4.** To spoil or mar the sanctity of : desecrate, pollute, profane, violate. *See* CLEAN, RELIGION, SACRED. **5.** To deprive of virginity : deflower, violate. *See* SEX.

defilement *noun*
Impure condition : dirtiness, foulness, impurity, pollution, uncleanness, unwholesomeness. *See* CLEAN.

definite *adjective*
1. Having distinct limits : determinate, fixed, limited. *See* LIMITED. **2.** Without any doubt : clear, clear-cut, decided, distinct, pronounced, unquestionable. *See* CERTAIN. **3.** Known positively : certain, positive, sure. ***Idiom:*** for certain. *See* CERTAIN. **4.** Clearly, fully, and sometimes emphatically expressed : categorical, clear, clear-cut, decided, explicit, express, positive, precise, specific, unambiguous, unequivocal. *See* CLEAR.

definitive *adjective*
Serving the function of deciding or settling with finality : authoritative, conclusive, decisive, determinative, final. *See* DECIDE.

deflate *verb*
To cause to be no longer believed or valued : debunk, discredit, explode, puncture. *Informal:* shoot down. ***Idioms:*** knock the bottom out of, shoot full of holes. *See* VALUE.

deflect *verb*
1. To cause to move, especially at an angle : angle[2], bend, refract, turn. *See* STRAIGHT.
2. To change the direction or course of : avert, deviate, divert, pivot, shift, swing, turn, veer. *See* CHANGE.

deflower *verb*
To deprive of virginity : defile, violate. *See* SEX.

deform *verb*
To alter and spoil the natural form or appearance of : contort, disfigure, distort, misshape, twist. *See* BEAUTIFUL.

deformity *noun*
A disfiguring abnormality of shape or form : disfigurement, malformation. *See* BEAUTIFUL.

defraud *verb*
To get money or something else from by deceitful trickery : bilk, cheat, cozen, gull, mulct, rook, swindle, victimize. *Informal:* chisel, flimflam, take, trim. *Slang:* diddle[1], do, gyp, stick, sting. *See* HONEST.

defrauder *noun*
A person who cheats : bilk, cheat, cheater, cozener, rook, sharper, swindler, trickster, victimizer. *Informal:* chiseler, crook, flimflammer. *Slang:* diddler, gyp, gypper. *See* HONEST.

deft *adjective*
1. Showing art or skill in performing or doing : adroit, artful, dexterous, skillful. *See* ABILITY, KNOWLEDGE. **2.** Exhibiting or possessing skill and ease in performance : adroit, clever, dexterous, facile, handy, nimble, slick. *See* ABILITY. **3.** Well done or executed : adroit, clean, neat, skillful. *See* ABILITY, GOOD.

deftness *noun*
Skillfulness in the use of the hands or body : adroitness, dexterity, dexterousness, prowess, skill, sleight. *See* ABILITY.

defunct *adjective*
1. No longer alive : asleep, dead, deceased, departed, extinct, gone, late, lifeless. ***Idioms:*** at rest, pushing up daisies. *See* LIVE. **2.** No longer in use, force, or operation : dead, extinct, lost, vanished. *See* LIVE, NEW.

defy *verb*
1. To confront boldly and courageously : beard, brave, challenge, dare, face, front. ***Idioms:*** fly in the face of, snap one's fingers at, stand up to, thumb one's nose at. *See* RESIST.
2. To refuse or fail to obey : break, disobey, flout, transgress, violate. ***Idiom:*** pay no attention to. *See* RESIST. **3.** To call on another to do something requiring boldness : challenge, dare. ***Idiom:*** throw down the gauntlet. *See* REQUEST.

degeneracy *noun*
Descent to a lower level or condition : atrophy, decadence, declension, declination, decline, degeneration, deterioration. *See* BETTER.

degenerate *adjective*
Utterly reprehensible in nature or behavior : corrupt, depraved, flagitious, miscreant, perverse, rotten, unhealthy, villainous. *See* CLEAN, GOOD.

degenerate *verb* **1.** To become lower in quality, character, or condition : atrophy, decline, descend, deteriorate, retrograde, sink, worsen. ***Idioms:*** go bad, go to pot, go to seed, go to the dogs. *See* BETTER. **2.** To lose strength or power : decline, deteriorate, fade, fail, flag[2], languish, sink, wane, waste (away), weaken. *Informal:* fizzle (out). ***Idioms:*** go downhill, hit the skids. *See* STRONG, INCREASE.

degeneration *noun*
Descent to a lower level or condition : atrophy, decadence, declension, declination, decline, degeneracy, deterioration. *See* BETTER.

degradation *noun*
1. The act or an instance of demoting : demotion, reduction. *See* RISE. **2.** A lowering in or deprivation of character or self-esteem : abasement, debasement, humiliation, mortification. *See* RESPECT, WIN.

degrade *verb*
1. To lower in rank or grade : break, bump, demote, downgrade, reduce. *Slang:* bust. *See* RISE. **2.** To deprive of esteem, self-worth, or effectiveness : abase, demean², humble, humiliate, mortify. ***Idioms:*** bring low, take down a peg. *See* RESPECT, WIN. **3.** To lower in character or quality : cheapen, debase, demean², downgrade. *See* BETTER.

degree *noun*
1. One of the units in a course, as on an ascending or descending scale : grade, level, peg, point, rung, stage, step. *Informal:* notch. *See* BIG. **2.** Relative intensity or amount, as of a quality or attribute : extent, magnitude, measure, proportion. *See* BIG.

dehydrate *verb*
To make or become free of moisture : desiccate, dry (out), exsiccate, parch. *See* DRY.

deific *adjective*
Of, from, like, or being a god or God : divine, godlike, godly, heavenly, holy. *See* RELIGION.

deign *verb*
To descend to a level considered inappropriate to one's dignity : condescend, stoop, vouchsafe. *See* OVER, RISE.

deject *verb*
To make sad or gloomy : depress, dispirit, oppress, sadden, weigh down. *See* HAPPY.

dejected *adjective*
In low spirits : blue, depressed, desolate, dispirited, down, downcast, downhearted, dull, dysphoric, gloomy, heavy-hearted, low, melancholic, melancholy, sad, spiritless, tristful, unhappy, wistful. ***Idiom:*** down at (*or* in) the mouth. *See* HAPPY.

dejection *noun*
A feeling or spell of dismally low spirits : blues, depression, despondence, despondency, doldrums, dolefulness, downheartedness, dumps, dysphoria, funk, gloom, glumness, heavy-heartedness, melancholy, mope (used in plural), mournfulness, sadness, unhappiness. *See* FEELINGS, HAPPY.

delay *verb*
1. To put off until a later time : adjourn, defer¹, hold off, hold up, postpone, remit, shelve, stay¹, suspend, table, waive. *Informal:* wait. ***Idiom:*** put on ice. *See* DO. **2.** To cause to be later or slower than expected or desired : detain, hang up, hold up, lag, retard, set back, slow (down *or* up), stall². *See* HELP, TIME. **3.** To go or move slowly so that progress is hindered : dally, dawdle, dilly-dally, drag, lag, linger, loiter, poke, procrastinate, tarry, trail. ***Idioms:*** drag one's feet (*or* heels), mark time, take one's time. *See* FAST.

delay *noun* **1.** The act of putting off or the condition of being put off : adjournment, deferment, deferral, postponement, stay¹, suspension, waiver. *See* TIME. **2.** The condition or fact of being made late or slow : detainment, holdup, lag, retardation. *See* HELP, TIME.

delectable *adjective*
1. Giving great pleasure or delight : charming, delicious, delightful, enchanting, heavenly, luscious. *Informal:* darling. *See* GOOD, HAPPY, LIKE. **2.** Highly pleasing, especially to the sense of taste : ambrosial, appetizing, delicious, heavenly, luscious, savory, scrumptious, tasteful, tasty, toothsome. *Slang:* yummy. *See* GOOD, INGESTION.

delectation *noun*
1. A feeling of extreme gratification aroused by something good or desired : delight, enjoyment, joy, pleasure. *See* HAPPY, LIKE. **2.** The condition of responding pleasurably to something : enjoyment, pleasure. *See* PAIN.

delegate *noun*
One who stands for another : deputy, representative. *See* SUBSTITUTE.

delete *verb*
To remove or invalidate by or as if by running a line through or wiping clean : annul, blot (out), cancel, cross (off *or* out), efface, erase, expunge, obliterate, rub (out), scratch (out), strike (out), undo, wipe (out), x (out). *Law:* vacate. *See* CONTINUE.

deleterious *adjective*
Causing harm or injury : bad, detrimental, evil, harmful, hurtful, ill, injurious, mischievous. *See* HELP.

deletion *noun*
The act of erasing or the condition of being erased : cancellation, erasure, expunction, obliteration. *See* INCLUDE.

deliberate *adjective*
1. Done or said on purpose : intended, intentional, purposeful, voluntary, willful, witting.

See PURPOSE. **2.** Planned, weighed, or estimated in advance : calculated, considered, intentional, premeditated. *See* PURPOSE. **3.** Careful and slow in acting, moving, or deciding : leisurely, measured, unhurried. *See* FAST.

deliberate *verb* **1.** To think or think about carefully and at length : chew on (*or* over), cogitate, consider, contemplate, entertain, excogitate, meditate, mull, muse[1], ponder, reflect, revolve, ruminate, study, think, think out, think over, think through, turn over, weigh. ***Idioms:*** cudgel one's brains, put on one's thinking cap, rack one's brain. *See* THOUGHTS. **2.** To use the powers of the mind, as in conceiving ideas, drawing inferences, and making judgments : cerebrate, cogitate, ratiocinate, reflect, speculate, think. ***Idioms:*** put on one's thinking cap, use one's head. *See* THOUGHTS. **3.** To meet and exchange views to reach a decision : advise, confer, consult, parley, talk. *Informal:* powwow. *See* COLLECT, MEET, WORDS.

deliberation *noun*
1. A careful considering of a matter : advisement, calculation, consideration, lucubration, study. *See* THOUGHTS. **2.** The act or process of thinking : brainwork, cerebration, cogitation, contemplation, excogitation, meditation, reflection, rumination, speculation, thought. *See* THOUGHTS. **3.** An exchange of views in an attempt to reach a decision : conference, consultation, counsel, parley. *See* WORDS.

deliberative *adjective*
Of, characterized by, or disposed to thought : cogitative, contemplative, excogitative, meditative, pensive, reflective, ruminative, speculative, thinking, thoughtful. ***Idiom:*** in a brown study. *See* THOUGHTS.

delicacy *noun*
1. Something fine and delicious, especially a food : dainty, morsel, tidbit, treat. *Informal:* goody. *See* GOOD, INGESTION. **2.** The condition of being infirm or physically weak : debility, decrepitude, delicateness, feebleness, flimsiness, fragileness, fragility, frailness, frailty, infirmity, insubstantiality, puniness, unsoundness, unsubstantiality, weakliness, weakness. *See* STRONG.

delicate *adjective*
1. Appealing to refined taste : choice, dainty, elegant, exquisite, fine[1]. *See* GOOD, INGESTION. **2.** Not physically strong : decrepit, feeble, flimsy, fragile, frail, infirm, insubstantial, puny, unsound, unsubstantial, weak, weakly. *See* STRONG. **3.** Easily broken or damaged : breakable, brittle, fragile, frangible. *See* STRONG. **4.** Showing sensitivity and skill in dealing with others : diplomatic, discreet, politic, sensitive, tactful. *See* ABILITY. **5.** Requiring great tact or skill : sensitive, ticklish, touch-and-go, touchy, tricky. *See* EASY. **6.** Free from severity or violence, as in movement : balmy[1], faint, gentle, mild, smooth, soft. *See* CALM, STRONG. **7.** Able to make or detect effects of great subtlety or precision : fine[1], nice, subtle. *See* PRECISE. **8.** So slight as to be difficult to notice or appreciate : fine[1], finespun, nice, refined, subtle. *See* BIG.

delicateness *noun*
The condition of being infirm or physically weak : debility, decrepitude, delicacy, feebleness, flimsiness, fragileness, fragility, frailness, frailty, infirmity, insubstantiality, puniness, unsoundness, unsubstantiality, weakliness, weakness. *See* STRONG.

delicious *adjective*
1. Highly pleasing, especially to the sense of taste : ambrosial, appetizing, delectable, heavenly, luscious, savory, scrumptious, tasteful, tasty, toothsome. *Slang:* yummy. *See* GOOD, INGESTION. **2.** Giving great pleasure or delight : charming, delectable, delightful, enchanting, heavenly, luscious. *Informal:* darling. *See* GOOD, HAPPY, LIKE.

delight *noun*
A feeling of extreme gratification aroused by something good or desired : delectation, enjoyment, joy, pleasure. *See* HAPPY, LIKE.

delight *verb* **1.** To feel or take joy or pleasure : exult, joy, pleasure, rejoice. *See* HAPPY. **2.** To like or enjoy enthusiastically, often excessively. Also used with *in* : adore, dote on (*or* upon), love. *Slang:* eat up, groove on. *See* LIKE, LOVE. **3.** To give great or keen pleasure to : cheer, enchant, gladden, gratify, overjoy, please, pleasure, tickle. *Archaic:* joy. *See* HAPPY, LIKE.

delighted *adjective*
Eagerly compliant : glad, happy, pleased, tickled. *See* HAPPY.

delightful *adjective*
Giving great pleasure or delight : charming, delectable, delicious, enchanting, heavenly, luscious. *Informal:* darling. *See* GOOD, HAPPY, LIKE.

delimit *verb*
To fix the limits of : bound[2], delimitate, demarcate, determine, limit, mark (out *or* off), measure. *See* LIMITED.

delimitate *verb*
To fix the limits of : bound[2], delimit,

demarcate, determine, limit, mark (out *or* off), measure. *See* LIMITED.

delineate *verb*
To present a lifelike image of : depict, describe, express, image, limn, picture, portray, render, represent, show. *See* SHOW.

delineation *noun*
1. A line marking and shaping the outer form of an object : contour, outline, profile, silhouette. *See* EDGE, SURFACE. **2.** The act or process of describing in lifelike imagery : depiction, description, expression, portrayal, representation. *See* SHOW.

delineative *adjective*
Serving to describe : descriptive, graphic, representative. *See* WORDS.

delinquency *noun*
Nonperformance of what ought to be done : default, dereliction, failure, neglect, omission. *Law:* nonfeasance. *See* DO.

deliquesce *verb*
To change from a solid to a liquid : dissolve, flux, fuse, liquefy, melt, run, thaw. *See* SOLID.

delirious *adjective*
Marked by extreme excitement, confusion, or agitation : frantic, frenetic, frenzied, mad, wild. *Archaic:* madding. *See* CALM.

deliver *verb*
1. To relinquish to the possession or control of another : furnish, give, hand, hand over, provide, supply, transfer, turn over. *See* GIVE. **2.** To mete out by means of some action : administer, deal, give. *See* GIVE. **3.** To give birth to : bear, bring forth, have. *Chiefly Regional:* birth. ***Idiom:*** be brought abed (*or* to bed) of. *See* RICH. **4.** To extricate, as from danger or confinement : rescue, save. ***Idiom:*** come to the rescue of. *See* HELP.

deliverance *noun*
Extrication from danger or confinement : delivery, rescue, salvage, salvation. *See* HELP.

delivery *noun*
1. The act of delivering or the condition of being delivered : surrender, transfer. *See* GIVE. **2.** The act or process of bringing forth young : accouchement, birth, birthing, childbearing, childbirth, labor, lying-in, parturition, travail. *See* START. **3.** Extrication from danger or confinement : deliverance, rescue, salvage, salvation. *See* HELP.

delude *verb*
To cause to accept what is false, especially by trickery or misrepresentation : beguile, betray, bluff, cozen, deceive, double-cross, dupe, fool, hoodwink, humbug, mislead, take in, trick. *Informal:* bamboozle, have. *Slang:* four-flush. ***Idioms:*** lead astray, play false, pull the wool over someone's eyes, put something over on, take for a ride. *See* HONEST.

deluge *noun*
An abundant, usually overwhelming flow or fall, as of a river or rain : alluvion, cataclysm, cataract, downpour, flood, freshet, inundation, Niagara, overflow, torrent. *Chiefly British:* spate. *See* BIG.

deluge *verb* **1.** To flow over completely : drown, engulf, flood, flush, inundate, overflow, overwhelm, submerge, whelm. *See* FULL. **2.** To affect as if by an outpouring of water : flood, inundate, overwhelm, swamp, whelm. *See* FULL.

delusion *noun*
An erroneous perception of reality : hallucination, ignis fatuus, illusion, mirage, phantasm, phantasma, will-o'-the-wisp. *See* REAL.

delusive *adjective*
1. Tending to deceive; of the nature of an illusion : delusory, illusive, illusory. *See* REAL. **2.** Tending to lead one into error : deceptive, delusory, fallacious, illusive, illusory, misleading. *See* HONEST, REAL. **3.** Of, relating to, or in the nature of an illusion; lacking reality : chimeric, chimerical, delusory, dreamlike, hallucinatory, illusive, illusory, phantasmagoric, phantasmal, phantasmic, visionary. *See* REAL.

delusory *adjective*
1. Tending to deceive; of the nature of an illusion : delusive, illusive, illusory. *See* REAL. **2.** Tending to lead one into error : deceptive, delusive, fallacious, illusive, illusory, misleading. *See* HONEST, REAL. **3.** Of, relating to, or in the nature of an illusion; lacking reality : chimeric, chimerical, delusive, dreamlike, hallucina tory, illusive, illusory, phantasmagoric, phantasmal, phantasmic, visionary. *See* REAL.

delve *verb*
1. To go into or through for the purpose of making discoveries or acquiring information : dig, explore, inquire, investigate, look into, probe, reconnoiter, scout[1]. *See* INVESTIGATE. **2.** To break, turn over, or remove (earth or sand, for example) with or as if with a tool : dig, excavate, grub, scoop, shovel, spade. *See* ENTER.

demand *verb*
1. To ask for urgently or insistently : call for, claim, exact, insist on (*or* upon), require, requisition. ***Idiom:*** cry out for. *See* REQUEST. **2.** To assert one's right to : claim. ***Idiom:*** lay claim to. *See* GIVE, OWNED, REQUEST. **3.** To have

as a need or prerequisite : ask, call for, entail, involve, necessitate, require, take. *See* NECESSARY, OVER.
demand *noun* **1.** The act of demanding : call, claim, cry, exaction, requisition. *See* REQUEST. **2.** Something asked for or needed : exigence, exigency (often used in plural), need, want. *See* NECESSARY, OVER.

demanding *adjective*
1. Requiring great or extreme bodily, mental, or spiritual strength : arduous, backbreaking, burdensome, difficult, effortful, exacting, exigent, formidable, hard, heavy, laborious, onerous, oppressive, rigorous, rough, severe, taxing, tough, trying, weighty. *See* HEAVY. **2.** Rigorous and unsparing in treating others : exacting, hard, harsh, rigid, severe, stern, strict, tough, unyielding. *See* EASY.

demarcate *verb*
To fix the limits of : bound[2], delimit, delimitate, determine, limit, mark (out *or* off), measure. *See* LIMITED.

demean[1] *verb*
To conduct oneself in a specified way : acquit, act, bear, behave, carry, comport, deport, do, quit. *See* BE.

demean[2] *verb*
1. To deprive of esteem, self-worth, or effectiveness : abase, degrade, humble, humiliate, mortify. ***Idioms:*** bring low, take down a peg. *See* RESPECT, WIN. **2.** To lower in character or quality : cheapen, debase, degrade, downgrade. *See* BETTER.

demeanor *noun*
Behavior through which one reveals one's personality : address, air, bearing, manner, mien, presence, style. *Archaic:* port. *See* BE, STYLE.

demented *adjective*
Afflicted with or exhibiting irrationality and mental unsoundness : brainsick, crazy, daft, disordered, distraught, dotty, insane, lunatic, mad, maniac, maniacal, mentally ill, moonstruck, off, touched, unbalanced, unsound, wrong. *Informal:* bonkers, cracked, daffy, gaga, loony. *Slang:* bananas, batty, buggy, cuckoo, fruity, loco, nuts, nutty, screwy, wacky. *Chiefly British:* crackers. *Law:* non compos mentis. ***Idioms:*** around the bend, crazy as a loon, mad as a hatter, not all there, nutty as a fruitcake, off (*or* out of) one's head, off one's rocker, of unsound mind, out of one's mind, sick in the head, stark raving mad. *See* SANE.

dementia *noun*
Serious mental illness or disorder impairing a person's capacity to function normally and safely : brainsickness, craziness, derangement, disturbance, insaneness, insanity, lunacy, madness, mental illness, psychopathy, unbalance. *Psychiatry:* mania. *Psychology:* aberration, alienation. *See* SANE.

demise *noun*
The act or fact of dying : death, decease, dissolution, extinction, passing, quietus, rest[1]. *Slang:* curtain (used in plural). *See* LIVE.
demise *verb* To cease living : decease, depart, die, drop, expire, go, pass away, pass (on), perish, succumb. *Informal:* pop off. *Slang:* check out, croak, kick in, kick off. ***Idioms:*** bite the dust, breathe one's last, cash in, give up the ghost, go to one's grave, kick the bucket, meet one's end (*or* Maker), pass on to the Great Beyond, turn up one's toes. *See* LIVE.

demission *noun*
A giving up of a possession, claim, or right : abandonment, abdication, quitclaim, relinquishment, renunciation, resignation, surrender, waiver. *See* KEEP.

demit *verb*
1. To relinquish one's engagement in or occupation with : leave[1], quit, resign, terminate. *See* CONTINUE. **2.** To give up a possession, claim, or right : abandon, abdicate, cede, forswear, hand over, quitclaim, relinquish, render, renounce, resign, surrender, waive, yield. *See* KEEP.

demobilize *verb*
To release from military duty : discharge, muster out, separate. *See* FREE, KEEP.

democratic *adjective*
Of, representing, or carried on by people at large : general, popular, public. *See* POLITICS, SPECIFIC.

demolish *verb*
1. To pull down or break up so that reconstruction is impossible : destroy, dismantle, dynamite, knock down, level, pull down, pulverize, raze, tear down, wreck. *Aerospace:* destruct. *See* HELP. **2.** To cause the complete ruin or wreckage of : bankrupt, break down, cross up, destroy, finish, ruin, shatter, sink, smash, spoil, torpedo, undo, wash up, wrack[2], wreck. *Slang:* total. ***Idiom:*** put the kibosh on. *See* HELP.

demonstrate *verb*
1. To make manifest or apparent : display, evidence, evince, exhibit, manifest, proclaim, reveal, show. *See* SHOW. **2.** To establish as true or genuine : authenticate, bear out, confirm, corroborate, endorse, establish, evidence, prove, show, substantiate, validate, verify. *See* SHOW, SUPPORT.

demonstration *noun*
1. An act of showing or displaying : display, exhibit, exhibition, manifestation, show. *See* SHOW. 2. That which confirms : attestation, authentication, confirmation, corroboration, evidence, proof, substantiation, testament, testimonial, testimony, validation, verification, warrant. *See* TRUE.

demoralize *verb*
To ruin utterly in character or quality : animalize, bastardize, bestialize, brutalize, canker, corrupt, debase, debauch, deprave, pervert, stain, vitiate, warp. *See* CLEAN, HELP.

demoralizing *adjective*
Morally detrimental : contaminative, corruptive, unhealthy, unwholesome. *See* RIGHT.

demote *verb*
To lower in rank or grade : break, bump, degrade, downgrade, reduce. *Slang:* bust. *See* RISE.

demotion *noun*
The act or an instance of demoting : degradation, reduction. *See* RISE.

demur *verb*
To express opposition, often by argument : challenge, except, expostulate, inveigh, object, protest, remonstrate. *Informal:* kick, squawk. ***Idioms:*** set up a squawk, take exception. *See* SUPPORT.

demur *noun* The act of expressing strong or reasoned opposition : challenge, exception, expostulation, objection, protest, protestation, remonstrance, remonstration, squawk. *Slang:* kick. *See* SUPPORT.

demure *adjective*
Not forward but reticent or reserved in manner : backward, bashful, coy, diffident, modest, retiring, self-effacing, shy[1], timid. *See* RESTRAINT.

demureness *noun*
Reserve in speech, behavior, or dress : diffidence, modesty, reticence, self-effacement. *See* RESTRAINT.

den *noun*
1. A place used as an animal's dwelling : burrow, hole, lair. *See* PROTECTION. 2. A hiding place : covert, hideaway, hide-out, lair. *See* PLACE, SHOW.

denial *noun*
1. A turning down of a request : disallowance, refusal, rejection, turndown. *See* ACCEPT. 2. A refusal to grant the truth of a statement or charge : contradiction, disaffirmance, disaffirmation, disclaimer, negation, rejection. *Law:* traversal. *See* AFFIRM.

denigrate *verb*
1. To contaminate the reputation of : befoul, besmear, besmirch, bespatter, blacken, cloud, dirty, smear, smudge, smut, soil, spatter, stain, sully, taint, tarnish. ***Idioms:*** give a black eye to, sling (*or* throw) mud on. *See* ATTACK, CLEAN. 2. To think, represent, or speak of as small or unimportant : belittle, decry, deprecate, depreciate, derogate, detract, discount, disparage, downgrade, minimize, run down, slight, talk down. ***Idiom:*** make light (*or* little) of. *See* ATTACK, SHOW.

denigration *noun*
1. The expression of injurious, malicious statements about someone : aspersion, calumniation, calumny, character assassination, defamation, detraction, scandal, slander, traducement, vilification. *Law:* libel. *See* ATTACK, CRIMES, LAW. 2. The act or an instance of belittling : belittlement, deprecation, depreciation, derogation, detraction, disparagement, minimization. *See* ATTACK, SHOW.

denominate *verb*
To give a name or title to : baptize, call, christen, designate, dub, entitle, name, style, term, title. *See* SPECIFIC, WORDS.

denomination *noun*
1. Those who accept and practice a particular religious belief : church, communion, faith, persuasion, sect. *See* RELIGION. 2. A system of religious belief : confession, creed, faith, persuasion, religion, sect. *See* RELIGION. 3. The word or words by which one is called and identified : appellation, appellative, cognomen, designation, epithet, name, nickname, style, tag, title. *Slang:* handle, moniker. *See* SPECIFIC, WORDS.

denotation *noun*
That which is signified by a word or expression : acceptation, connotation, import, intent, meaning, message, purport, sense, significance, significancy, signification, value. *See* MEANING.

denotative *adjective*
Serving to designate or indicate : denotive, designative, designatory, exhibitive, exhibitory, indicative, indicatory. *See* SHOW.

denote *verb*
1. To make known or identify, as by signs : designate, indicate, mark, point out, show, specify. *See* SHOW. 2. To have or convey a particular idea : connote, import, intend, mean[1], signify, spell[1]. ***Idiom:*** add up to. *See* MEANING.

denotive *adjective*
Serving to designate or indicate : denotative, designative, designatory, exhibitive, exhibitory, indicative, indicatory. *See* SHOW.

denounce *verb*
1. To feel or express strong disapproval of : censure, condemn, deplore, reprehend, reprobate. *See* PRAISE. **2.** To make an accusation against : accuse, arraign, charge, incriminate, indict, tax. *See* ATTACK, LAW, PRAISE.

denouncement *noun*
A charging of someone with a misdeed : accusation, charge, denunciation, imputation, incrimination. *Law:* indictment. *See* ATTACK, LAW, PRAISE.

denouncer *noun*
One that accuses : accuser, indicter. *See* ATTACK, LAW, PRAISE.

dense *adjective*
1. Having all parts near to each other : close, compact[1], crowded, packed, thick, tight. *See* TIGHTEN. **2.** Growing profusely : heavy, lush[1], luxuriant, profuse, rank[2], thick. *See* BIG. **3.** Lacking in intelligence : blockheaded, doltish, dumb, hebetudinous, obtuse, stupid, thickheaded, thick-witted. *Informal:* thick. *Slang:* dimwitted, dopey. *See* ABILITY.

density *noun*
The quality, condition, or degree of being thick : compactness, solidity, thickness. *See* THICK.

denude *verb*
To make bare : bare, disrobe, divest, expose, strip[1], uncover. *See* PUT ON.

denunciation *noun*
1. A comment expressing fault : blame, censure, condemnation, criticism, reprehension, reprobation. *Informal:* pan. *Slang:* knock. *See* PRAISE. **2.** A charging of someone with a misdeed : accusation, charge, denouncement, imputation, incrimination. *Law:* indictment. *See* ATTACK, LAW, PRAISE.

denunciative *adjective*
Containing, relating to, or involving an accusation : accusatorial, accusatory, denunciatory. *See* ATTACK, ATTITUDE, PRAISE.

denunciatory *adjective*
Containing, relating to, or involving an accusation : accusatorial, accusatory, denunciative. *See* ATTACK, ATTITUDE, PRAISE.

deny *verb*
1. To refuse to admit the truth, reality, value, or worth of : contradict, contravene, controvert, disaffirm, gainsay, negate, negative, oppugn. *Law:* traverse. *See* AFFIRM. **2.** To be unwilling to grant : disallow, refuse, turn down, withhold. *See* ACCEPT. **3.** To refuse to recognize or acknowledge : disacknowledge, disavow, disclaim, disown, reject, renounce, repudiate. *Idiom:* turn one's back on. *See* ACCEPT.

depart *verb*
1. To move or proceed away from a place : exit, get away, get off, go, go away, leave[1], pull out, quit, retire, run (along), withdraw. *Informal:* cut out, push off, shove off. *Slang:* blow[1], split, take off. ***Idioms:*** hit the road, take leave. *See* APPROACH. **2.** To cease living : decease, demise, die, drop, expire, go, pass away, pass (on), perish, succumb. *Informal:* pop off. *Slang:* check out, croak, kick in, kick off. ***Idioms:*** bite the dust, breathe one's last, cash in, give up the ghost, go to one's grave, kick the bucket, meet one's end (*or* Maker), pass on to the Great Beyond, turn up one's toes. *See* LIVE. **3.** To turn away from a prescribed course of action or conduct : deviate, digress, diverge, stray, swerve, veer. *Archaic:* err. *See* APPROACH, CORRECT.

departed *adjective*
No longer alive : asleep, dead, deceased, defunct, extinct, gone, late, lifeless. ***Idioms:*** at rest, pushing up daisies. *See* LIVE.

departing *adjective*
Of, done, given, or said on departing : farewell, good-bye, parting, valedictory. *See* APPROACH.

department *noun*
1. A component of government that performs a given function : agency, arm, branch, division, organ, wing. *See* PART. **2.** A sphere of activity, experience, study, or interest : area, arena, bailiwick, circle, domain, field, orbit, province, realm, scene, subject, terrain, territory, world. *Slang:* bag. *See* TERRITORY.

departure *noun*
1. The act of leaving : egress, exit, exodus, going, withdrawal. *See* APPROACH. **2.** A departing from what is prescribed : aberration, deviation, divergence, divergency, diversion. *See* APPROACH, CORRECT.

depend *verb*
To fasten or be fastened at one point with no support from below : dangle, hang, sling, suspend, swing. *See* HANG.

depend on (or **upon**) *verb* **1.** To place trust or confidence in : bank on (*or* upon), believe in, count on (*or* upon), reckon on (*or* upon), rely on (*or* upon), trust (in). *See* TRUST. **2.** To look forward to confidently : anticipate, await, bargain for (*or* on), count on, expect, look for, wait (for). *Informal:* figure on. *See* SURPRISE. **3.** To be determined by or contingent on something unknown, uncertain, or changeable : hang on, hang upon, hinge on (*or* upon), rest on (*or* upon), turn on, turn upon. *See* START.

dependable *adjective*
Capable of being depended upon : reliable, responsible, solid, sound[2], trustworthy, trusty. *See* TRUST.

dependance *noun* See **dependence.**

dependant *noun* See **dependent.**

dependence also **dependance** *noun*
Absolute certainty in the trustworthiness of another : belief, confidence, faith, reliance, trust. *See* BELIEF.

dependency also **dependancy** *noun*
An area subject to rule by an outside power : colony, possession, province, territory. *See* POLITICS.

dependent *adjective*
1. Determined or to be determined by someone or something else : conditional, conditioned, contingent, relative, reliant, subject. *See* START. **2.** In a position of subordination : collateral, subject, subordinate, subservient. *See* OVER, PART.

dependent also **dependant** *noun* A person who relies on another for support : charge, ward. *See* GIVE.

depend on or **upon** *verb* See **depend.**

depict *verb*
To present a lifelike image of : delineate, describe, express, image, limn, picture, portray, render, represent, show. *See* SHOW.

depiction *noun*
The act or process of describing in lifelike imagery : delineation, description, expression, portrayal, representation. *See* SHOW.

deplete *verb*
1. To lessen or weaken severely, as by removing something essential : drain, exhaust, impoverish, sap[2], use up. *See* GIVE, INCREASE, RICH. **2.** To make or become no longer active or productive : desiccate, dry up, give out, play out, run out. *See* CONTINUE.

depletion *noun*
The depletion or sapping of strength or energy : attenuation, debilitation, devitalization, enervation, enfeeblement, impoverishment. *See* STRONG.

deplorable *adjective*
1. Worthy of severe disapproval : condemnable, disgraceful, shameful, unfortunate. *See* GOOD. **2.** Causing sorrow or regret : doleful, dolorous, grievous, lamentable, mournful, regrettable, rueful, sad, sorrowful, woeful. *See* HAPPY.

deplore *verb*
1. To feel or express strong disapproval of : censure, condemn, denounce, reprehend, reprobate. *See* PRAISE. **2.** To feel or express sorrow for : regret, repent, rue. *See* REGRET.

deploy *verb*
To put into a deliberate order : arrange, array, dispose, marshal, order, organize, range, sort, systematize. *See* ORDER.

deployment *noun*
A way or condition of being arranged : arrangement, categorization, classification, disposal, disposition, distribution, formation, grouping, layout, lineup, order, organization, placement, sequence. *See* ORDER.

depone *verb*
Law. To give evidence or testimony under oath : attest, swear, testify, witness. *Law:* depose. ***Idioms:*** bear witness, take the stand. *See* LAW.

deponent *noun*
Law. One who testifies, especially in court : attestant, attester, testifier, witness. *See* LAW.

deport *verb*
1. To force to leave a country or place by official decree : banish, exile, expatriate, expel, ostracize, transport. *See* ACCEPT. **2.** To conduct oneself in a specified way : acquit, act, bear, behave, carry, comport, demean[1], do, quit. *See* BE.

deportation *noun*
Enforced removal from one's native country by official decree : banishment, exile, expatriation, extradition, ostracism, transportation. *See* ACCEPT, REWARD.

deportee *noun*
One forced to emigrate, usually for political reasons : émigré, exile, expatriate, expellee. *See* APPROACH.

deportment *noun*
The manner in which one behaves : action (often used in plural), behavior, comportment, conduct, way. *See* BE.

depose *verb*
Law. To give evidence or testimony under oath : attest, swear, testify, witness. *Law:* depone. ***Idioms:*** bear witness, take the stand. *See* LAW.

deposit *verb*
1. To put down, especially in layers, by a natural process : precipitate. *See* INCREASE. **2.** To place (money) in a bank : bank[2], lay away, salt

away. *Informal:* sock away. *See* KEEP, MONEY.

deposit *noun* **1.** A partial or initial payment : down payment. *See* MONEY, PAY. **2.** Matter that settles on a bottom or collects on a surface by a natural process : dreg (often used in plural), lees, precipitate, precipitation, sediment. *See* LEFTOVER.

deposition *noun*
Law. A formal declaration of truth or fact given under oath : testimony, witness. *See* LAW.

depository *noun*
A place where something is deposited for safekeeping : archive, magazine, repository, store, storehouse, warehouse. *See* KEEP.

deprave *verb*
To ruin utterly in character or quality : animalize, bastardize, bestialize, brutalize, canker, corrupt, debase, debauch, demoralize, pervert, stain, vitiate, warp. *See* CLEAN, HELP.

depraved *adjective*
Utterly reprehensible in nature or behavior : corrupt, degenerate, flagitious, miscreant, perverse, rotten, unhealthy, villainous. *See* CLEAN, GOOD.

depravity *noun*
Degrading, immoral acts or habits : bestiality, corruption, flagitiousness, immorality, perversion, turpitude, vice, villainousness, villainy, wickedness. *See* CLEAN.

deprecate *verb*
1. To have or express an unfavorable opinion of : disapprove, discountenance, disesteem, disfavor, frown on (*or* upon), object. ***Idioms:*** hold no brief for, not go for, take a dim view of, take exception to. *See* LIKE. **2.** To think, represent, or speak of as small or unimportant : belittle, decry, denigrate, depreciate, derogate, detract, discount, disparage, downgrade, minimize, run down, slight, talk down. ***Idiom:*** make light (*or* little) of. *See* ATTACK, SHOW.

deprecation *noun*
The act or an instance of belittling : belittlement, denigration, depreciation, derogation, detraction, disparagement, minimization. *See* ATTACK, SHOW.

deprecative *adjective*
Tending or intending to belittle : deprecatory, depreciative, depreciatory, derogative, derogatory, detractive, disparaging, low, pejorative, slighting, uncomplimentary. *See* PRAISE.

deprecatory *adjective*
Tending or intending to belittle : deprecative, depreciative, depreciatory, derogative, derogatory, detractive, disparaging, low, pejorative, slighting, uncomplimentary. *See* PRAISE.

depreciate *verb*
1. To become or make less in price or value : cheapen, depress, devaluate, devalue, downgrade, lower[2], mark down, reduce, write down. *See* INCREASE, MONEY. **2.** To think, represent, or speak of as small or unimportant : belittle, decry, denigrate, deprecate, derogate, detract, discount, disparage, downgrade, minimize, run down, slight, talk down. ***Idiom:*** make light (*or* little) of. *See* ATTACK, SHOW.

depreciation *noun*
1. A lowering in price or value : devaluation, markdown, reduction, write-down. *See* INCREASE, MONEY. **2.** The act or an instance of belittling : belittlement, denigration, deprecation, derogation, detraction, disparagement, minimization. *See* ATTACK, SHOW.

depreciative *adjective*
Tending or intending to belittle : deprecative, deprecatory, depreciatory, derogative, derogatory, detractive, disparaging, low, pejorative, slighting, uncomplimentary. *See* PRAISE.

depreciatory *adjective*
Tending or intending to belittle : deprecative, deprecatory, depreciative, derogative, derogatory, detractive, disparaging, low, pejorative, slighting, uncomplimentary. *See* PRAISE.

depredate *verb*
To rob of goods by force, especially in time of war : despoil, havoc, loot, pillage, plunder, ransack, rape, ravage, sack[2], spoliate, strip[1]. *Archaic:* harrow, spoil. *See* CRIMES, GIVE.

depress *verb*
1. To make sad or gloomy : deject, dispirit, oppress, sadden, weigh down. *See* HAPPY. **2.** To cause to descend : drop, let down, lower[2], take down. *See* RISE. **3.** To become or make less in price or value : cheapen, depreciate, devaluate, devalue, downgrade, lower[2], mark down, reduce, write down. *See* INCREASE, MONEY.

depressed *adjective*
1. In low spirits : blue, dejected, desolate, dispirited, down, downcast, downhearted, dull, dysphoric, gloomy, heavy-hearted, low, melancholic, melancholy, sad, spiritless, tristful, unhappy, wistful. ***Idiom:*** down at (*or* in) the mouth. *See* HAPPY. **2.** Economically and socially below standard : backward, deprived, disadvantaged, impoverished, underprivileged. *See* RICH.

depressing *adjective*
Tending to cause sadness or low spirits : blue,

cheerless, dismal, dispiriting, gloomy, joyless, melancholy, sad. *See* HAPPY.

depression *noun*
1. An area sunk below its surroundings : basin, concavity, dip, hollow, pit[1], sag, sink, sinkhole. *See* CONVEX. 2. A feeling or spell of dismally low spirits : blues, dejection, despondence, despondency, doldrums, dolefulness, downheartedness, dumps, dysphoria, funk, gloom, glumness, heavy-heartedness, melancholy, mope (used in plural), mournfulness, sadness, unhappiness. *See* FEELINGS, HAPPY. 3. A period of decreased business activity and high unemployment : recession, slump. *See* RICH.

deprival *noun*
The condition of being deprived of what one once had or ought to have : deprivation, dispossession, divestiture, loss, privation. *See* GIVE, RICH.

deprivation *noun*
The condition of being deprived of what one once had or ought to have : deprival, dispossession, divestiture, loss, privation. *See* GIVE, RICH.

deprive *verb*
To take or keep something away from : dispossess, divest, rob, strip[1]. *See* GIVE.

deprived *adjective*
Economically and socially below standard : backward, depressed, disadvantaged, impoverished, underprivileged. *See* RICH.

depth *noun*
1. The extent or measurement downward from a surface : deepness, drop. *See* SURFACE. 2. Something of immeasurable and vast extent. Often used in plural : abysm, abyss, chasm, deep, gulf. *See* HIGH. 3. Exceptionally great concentration, power, or force, especially in activity. Often used in plural : ferociousness, ferocity, fierceness, fury, intensity, pitch, severity, vehemence, vehemency, violence. *See* BIG, STRONG. 4. Intellectual penetration or range : deepness, profoundness, profundity. *See* THOUGHTS.

deputy *noun*
1. One who stands for another : delegate, representative. *See* SUBSTITUTE. 2. A person who holds a position auxiliary to another and assumes some of the superior's responsibilities : adjutant, aide, assistant, auxiliary, coadjutant, coadjutor, helper, lieutenant, second[2]. *See* HELP.

derange *verb*
1. To put out of proper order : disarrange, disarray, disorder, disorganize, disrupt, disturb, jumble, mess up, mix up, muddle, tumble, unsettle, upset. *See* ORDER. 2. To disturb the health or physiological functioning of : disorder, turn, unsettle, upset. *See* HEALTH. 3. To make insane : craze, madden, unbalance, unhinge. *See* SANE.

derangement *noun*
1. A lack of order or regular arrangement : chaos, clutter, confusedness, confusion, disarrangement, disarray, disorder, disorderedness, disorderliness, disorganization, jumble, mess, mix-up, muddle, muss, scramble, topsy-turviness, tumble. *Slang:* snafu. *See* ORDER. 2. Serious mental illness or disorder impairing a person's capacity to function normally and safely : brainsickness, craziness, dementia, disturbance, insaneness, insanity, lunacy, madness, mental illness, psychopathy, unbalance. *Psychiatry:* mania. *Psychology:* aberration, alienation. *See* SANE.

derelict *adjective*
1. Having been given up and left alone : abandoned, bereft, deserted, desolate, forlorn, forsaken, lorn. *See* KEEP. 2. Guilty of neglect; lacking due care or concern : lax, neglectful, negligent, remiss, slack. *See* CAREFUL.

dereliction *noun*
Nonperformance of what ought to be done : default, delinquency, failure, neglect, omission. *Law:* nonfeasance. *See* DO.

deride *verb*
To make fun or make fun of : gibe, jeer, jest, laugh, mock, ridicule, scoff, scout[2], twit. *Chiefly British:* quiz. ***Idiom:*** poke fun at. *See* LAUGHTER, RESPECT.

de rigueur *adjective*
Conforming to accepted standards : becoming, befitting, comely, comme il faut, correct, decent, decorous, nice, proper, respectable, right, seemly. *See* COURTESY.

derision *noun*
Words or actions intended to evoke contemptuous laughter : mockery, ridicule. *See* LAUGHTER, RESPECT.

derisive *adjective*
Contemptuous or ironic in manner or wit : jeering, mocking, sarcastic, satiric, satirical, scoffing, sneering. *See* LAUGHTER, RESPECT.

derivation *noun*
1. Something derived from another : byproduct, derivative, descendant, offshoot, outgrowth, spinoff. *See* KIN. 2. A point of origination : beginning, fount, fountain, fountainhead, mother, origin, parent, prove-

nance, provenience, root[1], rootstock, source, spring, well[1]. *See* START.

derivational *adjective*
Stemming from an original source : derivative, derived, secondary. *See* KIN.

derivative *adjective*
Stemming from an original source : derivational, derived, secondary. *See* KIN.
derivative *noun* Something derived from another : byproduct, derivation, descendant, offshoot, outgrowth, spinoff. *See* KIN.

derive *verb*
1. To have as a source : arise, come, emanate, flow, issue, originate, proceed, rise, spring, stem, upspring. *See* START. **2.** To obtain from another source : draw, get, take. *See* KIN. **3.** To have hereditary derivation : descend, issue, spring. ***Idiom:*** trace one's descent. *See* KIN. **4.** To arrive at through reasoning : educe, evolve, excogitate. *See* REASON.

derived *adjective*
Stemming from an original source : derivational, derivative, secondary. *See* KIN.

derogate *verb*
To think, represent, or speak of as small or unimportant : belittle, decry, denigrate, deprecate, depreciate, detract, discount, disparage, downgrade, minimize, run down, slight, talk down. ***Idiom:*** make light (*or* little) of. *See* ATTACK, SHOW.

derogation *noun*
The act or an instance of belittling : belittlement, denigration, deprecation, depreciation, detraction, disparagement, minimization. *See* ATTACK, SHOW.

derogative *adjective*
Tending or intending to belittle : deprecative, deprecatory, depreciative, depreciatory, derogatory, detractive, disparaging, low, pejorative, slighting, uncomplimentary. *See* PRAISE.

derogatory *adjective*
Tending or intending to belittle : deprecative, deprecatory, depreciative, depreciatory, derogative, detractive, disparaging, low, pejorative, slighting, uncomplimentary. *See* PRAISE.

derrière *noun*
The part of one's back on which one rests in sitting : buttock (used in plural), posterior, rump, seat. *Informal:* backside, behind, bottom, rear[1]. *Slang:* bun (used in plural), fanny, tush. *Chiefly British:* bum[2]. *See* OVER.

descend *verb*
1. To move downward in response to gravity : drop, fall. *See* RISE. **2.** To slope downward : decline, dip, drop, fall, pitch, sink. *See* RISE. **3.** To have hereditary derivation : derive, issue, spring. ***Idiom:*** trace one's descent. *See* KIN. **4.** To bring oneself down to a lower level of behavior : lower[2], sink, stoop. *See* RISE. **5.** To become lower in quality, character, or condition : atrophy, decline, degenerate, deteriorate, retrograde, sink, worsen. ***Idioms:*** go bad, go to pot, go to seed, go to the dogs. *See* BETTER.

descendant *noun*
1. Something derived from another : byproduct, derivation, derivative, offshoot, outgrowth, spinoff. *See* KIN. **2.** One descended directly from the same parents or ancestors : child, offspring, progeny, scion. *See* KIN.
descendant *adjective* See **descendent.**

descendent also **descendant** *adjective*
Moving or sloping down : descending, downward. *See* RISE.

descending *adjective*
Moving or sloping down : descendent, downward. *See* RISE.

descent *noun*
1. The act of dropping from a height : drop, fall. *See* RISE. **2.** A downward slope or distance : decline, declivity, drop, fall, pitch. *See* RISE. **3.** One's ancestors or their character or one's ancestral derivation : ancestry, birth, blood, bloodline, extraction, family, genealogy, line, lineage, origin, parentage, pedigree, seed, stock. *See* KIN, PRECEDE. **4.** A sudden drop to a lower condition or status : comedown, down, downfall, downgrade. *See* RISE. **5.** A usually swift downward trend, as in prices : decline, dip, dive, downslide, downswing, downtrend, downturn, drop, drop-off, fall, nosedive, plunge, skid, slide, slump, tumble. *See* INCREASE.

describe *verb*
1. To give a verbal account of : narrate, recite, recount, rehearse, relate, report, tell. *See* WORDS. **2.** To present a lifelike image of : delineate, depict, express, image, limn, picture, portray, render, represent, show. *See* SHOW.

description *noun*
1. A recounting of past events : account, chronicle, history, narration, narrative, report, statement, story, version. *See* WORDS. **2.** The act or process of describing in lifelike imagery : delineation, depiction, expression, portrayal, representation. *See* SHOW. **3.** A class that is defined by the common attribute or attributes possessed by all its members : breed, cast, feather, ilk, kind[2], lot, manner, mold, nature, order, sort, species, stamp, stripe, type, variety. *Informal:* persuasion. *See* GROUP.

descriptive *adjective*
Serving to describe : delineative, graphic, representative. *See* WORDS.

descry *verb*
1. To perceive and fix the identity of, especially with difficulty : discern, distinguish, make out, pick out, spot. *See* SEE. **2.** To perceive, especially barely or fleetingly : catch, detect, discern, espy, glimpse, spot, spy. *See* SEE. **3.** To perceive with a special effort of the senses or the mind : detect, discern, distinguish, mark, mind, note, notice, observe, remark, see. *See* KNOWLEDGE, SEE.

desecrate *verb*
To spoil or mar the sanctity of : defile, pollute, profane, violate. *See* CLEAN, RELIGION, SACRED.

desecration *noun*
An act of disrespect or impiety toward something regarded as sacred : blasphemy, profanation, sacrilege, violation. *See* SACRED.

desegregate *verb*
To open to all people regardless of race : integrate. *See* INCLUDE, SAME.

desegregation *noun*
The act, process, or result of abolishing racial segregation : integration. *See* INCLUDE, SAME.

desensitize *verb*
To render less sensitive : benumb, blunt, deaden, dull, numb. ***Idiom:*** take the edge off. *See* AWARENESS.

desert[1] *noun*
A tract of unproductive land : badlands, barren (often used in plural), waste, wasteland, wilderness. *See* RICH.

desert[2] *noun*
Something justly deserved. Often used in plural : comeuppance, due, guerdon, recompense, reward, wage (often used in plural). *Informal:* lump[1] (used in plural). ***Idioms:*** what is coming to one, what one has coming. *See* REWARD.

desert[3] *verb*
1. To give up or leave without intending to return or claim again : abandon, forsake, leave[1], quit, throw over. ***Idioms:*** run out on, walk out on. *See* KEEP. **2.** To abandon one's cause or party usually to join another : apostatize, defect, renegade, tergiversate, turn. *Slang:* rat. ***Idioms:*** change sides, turn one's coat. *See* APPROACH, TRUST.

deserted *adjective*
1. Having been given up and left alone : abandoned, bereft, derelict, desolate, forlorn, forsaken, lorn. *See* KEEP. **2.** Empty of people : desolate, forlorn, godforsaken, lonely, lonesome, unfrequented. *See* FULL.

deserter *noun*
A person who has defected : apostate, defector, recreant, renegade, runagate, tergiversator, turncoat. *Informal:* rat. *See* APPROACH.

desertion *noun*
The act of forsaking : abandonment. *See* KEEP.

deserve *verb*
To acquire as a result of one's behavior or effort : earn, gain, get, merit, win. *Informal:* rate[1]. *See* GET.

deserved *adjective*
Consistent with prevailing or accepted standards or circumstances : appropriate, due, fit[1], fitting, just, merited, proper, right, rightful, suitable. *See* RIGHT.

deserving *adjective*
Deserving honor, respect, or admiration : admirable, commendable, creditable, estimable, exemplary, honorable, laudable, meritorious, praiseworthy, reputable, respectable, worthy. *See* GOOD, PRAISE, RESPECT, VALUE.

desiccate *verb*
1. To make or become free of moisture : dehydrate, dry (out), exsiccate, parch. *See* DRY.
2. To make or become no longer active or productive : deplete, dry up, give out, play out, run out. *See* CONTINUE.

design *verb*
1. To form a strategy for : blueprint, cast, chart, conceive, contrive, devise, formulate, frame, lay[1], plan, project, scheme, strategize, work out. *Informal:* dope out. ***Idiom:*** lay plans. *See* PLANNED. **2.** To work out and arrange the parts or details of : blueprint, lay out, map (out), plan, set out. *See* PLANNED. **3.** To have in mind as a goal or purpose : aim, contemplate, intend, mean[1], plan, project, propose, purpose, target. *Regional:* mind. *See* PLANNED, PURPOSE.

design *noun* **1.** An element or a component in a decorative composition : device, figure, motif, motive, pattern. *See* PART. **2.** A method for making, doing, or accomplishing something : blueprint, game plan, idea, layout, plan, project, schema, scheme, strategy. *See* PLANNED. **3.** What one intends to do or achieve : aim, ambition, end, goal, intent, intention, mark, meaning, object, objective, point, purpose, target, view, why. ***Idioms:*** end in view, why and wherefore. *See* PLANNED, PURPOSE.

designate *verb*
1. To make known or identify, as by signs : de-

note, indicate, mark, point out, show, specify. *See* SHOW. **2.** To set aside or apart for a specified purpose : allocate, appropriate, assign, earmark. *See* COLLECT, MONEY. **3.** To give a name or title to : baptize, call, christen, denominate, dub, entitle, name, style, term, title. *See* SPECIFIC, WORDS. **4.** To describe with a word or term : call, characterize, label, name, style, tag, term. *See* SPECIFIC, WORDS. **5.** To select for an office or position : appoint, make, name, nominate, tap[1]. *See* CHOICE.

designation *noun*
1. The act of appointing to an office or position : appointment, nomination. *See* CHOICE. **2.** The word or words by which one is called and identified : appellation, appellative, cognomen, denomination, epithet, name, nickname, style, tag, title. *Slang:* handle, moniker. *See* SPECIFIC, WORDS.

designative *adjective*
Serving to designate or indicate : denotative, denotive, designatory, exhibitive, exhibitory, indicative, indicatory. *See* SHOW.

designatory *adjective*
Serving to designate or indicate : denotative, denotive, designative, exhibitive, exhibitory, indicative, indicatory. *See* SHOW.

designee *noun*
A person who is appointed to an office or position : appointee, nominee. *See* CHOICE.

designing *adjective*
Coldly planning to achieve selfish aims : calculating, scheming. *See* ATTITUDE.

desirable *adjective*
Arousing erotic desire : sexy. *See* DESIRE, SEX.

desire *verb*
1. To have the desire or inclination to : choose, like[1], please, want, will, wish. ***Idioms:*** have a mind, see fit. *See* DESIRE. **2.** To have a strong longing for : ache, covet, hanker, long[2], pant, pine, want, wish, yearn. *Informal:* hone[2]. *See* DESIRE.
desire *noun* **1.** A strong wanting of what promises enjoyment or pleasure : appetence, appetency, appetite, craving, hunger, itch, longing, lust, thirst, wish, yearning, yen. *See* DESIRE. **2.** Sexual hunger : amativeness, concupiscence, eroticism, erotism, itch, libidinousness, lust, lustfulness, passion, prurience, pruriency. *See* DESIRE, SEX.

desist *verb*
To cease trying to accomplish or continue : abandon, break off, discontinue, give up, leave off, quit, relinquish, remit, stop. *Informal:* swear off. *Slang:* lay off. ***Idioms:*** call it a day, call it quits, hang up one's fiddle, have done with, throw in the towel. *See* CONTINUE.

desolate *adjective*
1. Empty of people : deserted, forlorn, godforsaken, lonely, lonesome, unfrequented. *See* FULL. **2.** Dark and depressing : black, bleak, blue, cheerless, dark, dismal, dreary, gloomy, glum, joyless, somber, tenebrific. *See* HAPPY, LIGHT. **3.** Having been given up and left alone : abandoned, bereft, derelict, deserted, forlorn, forsaken, lorn. *See* KEEP. **4.** Dejected due to the awareness of being alone : forlorn, lonely, lonesome, lorn. *See* HAPPY. **5.** In low spirits : blue, dejected, depressed, dispirited, down, downcast, downhearted, dull, dysphoric, gloomy, heavy-hearted, low, melancholic, melancholy, sad, spiritless, tristful, unhappy, wistful. ***Idiom:*** down at (*or* in) the mouth. *See* HAPPY.
desolate *verb* To destroy completely as or as if by conquering : devastate, ravage, waste. ***Idiom:*** lay waste. *See* HELP.

desolation *noun*
A desolate sense of loss : blankness, emptiness, hollowness, vacuum, void. *See* FULL.

despair *verb*
To lose all hope : despond, give up. *See* HOPE.
despair *noun* Utter lack of hope : desperateness, desperation, despond, despondence, despondency, hopelessness. *See* HOPE.

despairing *adjective*
Having lost all hope : desperate, despondent, forlorn, hopeless. *See* HOPE.

desperate *adjective*
1. Having lost all hope : despairing, despondent, forlorn, hopeless. *See* HOPE. **2.** So serious as to be at the point of crisis or necessary to resolve a crisis : acute, climacteric, critical, crucial, dire. *See* SAFETY. **3.** Extreme in degree, strength, or effect : fierce, furious, intense, terrible, vehement, violent. *See* BIG, STRONG.

desperateness *noun*
Utter lack of hope : despair, desperation, despond, despondence, despondency, hopelessness. *See* HOPE.

desperation *noun*
Utter lack of hope : despair, desperateness, despond, despondence, despondency, hopelessness. *See* HOPE.

despicable *adjective*
So objectionable as to elicit despisal or deserve condemnation : abhorrent, abominable, antipathetic, contemptible, despisable, detestable, disgusting, filthy, foul, infamous, loathsome,

lousy, low, mean[2], nasty, nefarious, obnoxious, odious, repugnant, rotten, shabby, vile, wretched. *See* GOOD.

despisable *adjective*
So objectionable as to elicit despisal or deserve condemnation : abhorrent, abominable, antipathetic, contemptible, despicable, detestable, disgusting, filthy, foul, infamous, loathsome, lousy, low, mean[2], nasty, nefarious, obnoxious, odious, repugnant, rotten, shabby, vile, wretched. *See* GOOD.

despisal *noun*
The feeling of despising : contempt, despite, disdain, scorn. *See* RESPECT.

despise *verb*
1. To regard with utter contempt and disdain : contemn, disdain, scorn, scout[2]. ***Idioms:*** have no use for, look down on (*or* upon). *See* RESPECT. **2.** To regard with extreme dislike and hostility : abhor, abominate, detest, execrate, hate, loathe. *See* LOVE.

despite *noun*
1. The disposition boldly to defy or resist authority or an opposing force : contempt, contumacy, defiance, recalcitrance, recalcitrancy. *See* RESIST. **2.** The feeling of despising : contempt, despisal, disdain, scorn. *See* RESPECT. **3.** An act that offends a person's sense of pride or dignity : affront, contumely, indignity, insult, offense, outrage, slight. ***Idiom:*** slap in the face. *See* ATTACK.

despiteful *adjective*
Characterized by intense ill will or spite : black, evil, hateful, malevolent, malicious, malign, malignant, mean[2], nasty, poisonous, spiteful, venomous, vicious, wicked. *Slang:* bitchy. *See* ATTITUDE.

despitefulness *noun*
A desire to harm others or to see others suffer : ill will, malevolence, malice, maliciousness, malignancy, malignity, meanness, nastiness, poisonousness, spite, spitefulness, venomousness, viciousness. *See* ATTITUDE.

despoil *verb*
To rob of goods by force, especially in time of war : depredate, havoc, loot, pillage, plunder, ransack, rape, ravage, sack[2], spoliate, strip[1]. *Archaic:* harrow, spoil. *See* CRIMES, GIVE.

despond *verb*
To lose all hope : despair, give up. *See* HOPE. **despond** *noun* Utter lack of hope : despair, desperateness, desperation, despondence, despondency, hopelessness. *See* HOPE.

despondence *noun*
1. Utter lack of hope : despair, desperateness, desperation, despond, despondency, hopelessness. *See* HOPE. **2.** A feeling or spell of dismally low spirits : blues, dejection, depression, despondency, doldrums, dolefulness, downheartedness, dumps, dysphoria, funk, gloom, glumness, heavy-heartedness, melancholy, mope (used in plural), mournfulness, sadness, unhappiness. *See* FEELINGS, HAPPY.

despondency *noun*
1. Utter lack of hope : despair, desperateness, desperation, despond, despondence, hopelessness. *See* HOPE. **2.** A feeling or spell of dismally low spirits : blues, dejection, depression, despondence, doldrums, dolefulness, downheartedness, dumps, dysphoria, funk, gloom, glumness, heavy-heartedness, melancholy, mope (used in plural), mournfulness, sadness, unhappiness. *See* FEELINGS, HAPPY.

despondent *adjective*
Having lost all hope : despairing, desperate, forlorn, hopeless. *See* HOPE.

despot *noun*
1. An absolute ruler, especially one who is harsh and oppressive : Big Brother, dictator, führer, man on horseback, oppressor, strongman, totalitarian, tyrant. *See* OVER. **2.** One who imposes or favors absolute obedience to authority : authoritarian, autocrat, dictator, martinet, totalitarian, tyrant. *See* OVER.

despotic *adjective*
1. Having and exercising complete political power and control : absolute, absolutistic, arbitrary, autarchic, autarchical, autocratic, autocratical, dictatorial, monocratic, totalitarian, tyrannic, tyrannical, tyrannous. *See* OVER, POLITICS. **2.** Characterized by or favoring absolute obedience to authority : authoritarian, autocratic, dictatorial, totalitarian, tyrannic, tyrannical. *See* OVER.

despotism *noun*
1. A government in which a single leader or party exercises absolute control over all citizens and every aspect of their lives : absolutism, autarchy, autocracy, dictatorship, monocracy, tyranny. *See* OVER, POLITICS. **2.** A political doctrine advocating the principle of absolute rule : absolutism, authoritarianism, autocracy, dictatorship, totalitarianism. *See* OVER, POLITICS. **3.** Absolute power, especially when exercised unjustly or cruelly : autocracy, dictatorship, totalitarianism, tyranny. *See* OVER, POLITICS.

destine *verb*
To determine the future of in advance : fate, foreordain, predestinate, predestine, predetermine, preordain. *See* CERTAIN.

destiny *noun*
That which is inevitably destined : fate, fortune, kismet, lot, portion, predestination. *See* CERTAIN.
destitute *adjective*
1. Not having a desirable element : barren, devoid, empty, innocent, lacking, void, wanting. *Idiom:* in want of. *See* FULL. **2.** Having little or no money or wealth : beggarly, down-and-out, impecunious, impoverished, indigent, necessitous, needy, penniless, penurious, poor, poverty-stricken. *Informal:* broke, strapped. *Idioms:* hard up, on one's uppers. *See* RICH.
destitution *noun*
The condition of being extremely poor : beggary, impecuniosity, impecuniousness, impoverishment, indigence, need, neediness, pennilessness, penuriousness, penury, poverty, privation, want. *See* RICH.
destroy *verb*
1. To cause the complete ruin or wreckage of : bankrupt, break down, cross up, demolish, finish, ruin, shatter, sink, smash, spoil, torpedo, undo, wash up, wrack[2], wreck. *Slang:* total. *Idiom:* put the kibosh on. *See* HELP. **2.** To pull down or break up so that reconstruction is impossible : demolish, dismantle, dynamite, knock down, level, pull down, pulverize, raze, tear down, wreck. *Aerospace:* destruct. *See* HELP. **3.** To cause the death of : carry off, cut down, cut off, dispatch, finish (off), kill[1], slay. *Slang:* waste, zap. *Idioms:* put an end to, put to sleep. *See* HELP. **4.** To take the life of (a person or persons) unlawfully : finish (off), kill[1], liquidate, murder, slay. *Informal:* put away. *Slang:* bump off, do in, knock off, off, rub out, waste, wipe out, zap. *See* HELP. **5.** To impair severely something such as the spirit, health, or effectiveness of : break, crush, overwhelm, ruin. *See* HELP.
destroyer *noun*
Something that causes total loss or severe impairment, as of one's health, fortune, honor, or hopes : bane, destruction, downfall, ruin, ruination, undoing, wrecker. *See* HELP.
destruct *verb*
Aerospace. To pull down or break up so that reconstruction is impossible : demolish, destroy, dismantle, dynamite, knock down, level, pull down, pulverize, raze, tear down, wreck. *See* HELP.
destruction *noun*
1. The act of destroying or state of being destroyed : bane, devastation, havoc, ruin, ruination, undoing, wrack[1], wreck, wreckage. *See* HELP, LEFTOVER. **2.** An act, instance, or consequence of breaking : breakage, damage, impairment, wreckage. *See* HELP. **3.** Something that causes total loss or severe impairment, as of one's health, fortune, honor, or hopes : bane, destroyer, downfall, ruin, ruination, undoing, wrecker. *See* HELP.
destructive *adjective*
1. Causing ruin or destruction : calamitous, cataclysmal, cataclysmic, catastrophic, disastrous, fatal, fateful, ruinous. *See* HELP. **2.** Having the capability or effect of damaging irreparably : pernicious, ruinous. *See* HELP.
desuetude *noun*
The quality or state of being obsolete : disuse, obsoleteness, obsoletism. *See* NEW, USED.
desultory *adjective*
1. Without aim, purpose, or intent : aimless, pointless, purposeless. *See* PURPOSE. **2.** Having no particular pattern, purpose, organization, or structure : chance, haphazard, hit-or-miss, indiscriminate, random, spot, unplanned. *See* PLANNED.
detach *verb*
1. To separate one thing from another thing : disconnect, disengage, uncouple. *See* ASSEMBLE. **2.** To become or cause to become apart one from another : break, disjoin, disjoint, disunite, divide, divorce, part, separate, split (up). *Idioms:* part company, set at odds. *See* ASSEMBLE. **3.** To remove from association with : abstract, disassociate, disengage, dissociate, withdraw. *See* ASSEMBLE.
detached *adjective*
1. Set away from all others : alone, apart, isolate, isolated, lone, removed, solitary. *See* INCLUDE. **2.** Lacking interest in one's surroundings or worldly affairs : aloof, disinterested, incurious, indifferent, unconcerned, uninterested, uninvolved. *See* ATTITUDE, CONCERN. **3.** Without emotion or interest : apathetic, impassive, incurious, indifferent, insensible, lethargic, listless, phlegmatic, stolid, unconcerned, uninterested, unresponsive. *See* FEELINGS. **4.** Not easily excited, even under pressure : calm, collected, composed, cool, cool-headed, even[1], even-tempered, imperturbable, nonchalant, possessed, unflappable, unruffled. *See* CALM. **5.** Feeling or showing no strong emotional involvement : disinterested, dispassionate, impersonal, indifferent, neutral. *See* FEELINGS.
detachment *noun*
1. The act or process of detaching : disconnection, disengagement, separation, uncoupling.

See ASSEMBLE. **2.** The act or an instance of separating one thing from another : disjunction, disjuncture, disseverance, disseverment, disunion, division, divorce, divorcement, parting, partition, separation, severance, split. *See* ASSEMBLE, PART. **3.** Dissociation from one's surroundings or worldly affairs : aloofness, distance, remoteness. *See* ATTITUDE, CONCERN, INCLUDE, NEAR. **4.** The quality or state of being just and unbiased : disinterest, disinterestedness, dispassion, dispassionateness, equitableness, fair-mindedness, fairness, impartiality, impartialness, justice, justness, nonpartisanship, objectiveness, objectivity. *See* FAIR. **5.** A group of people organized for a particular purpose : body, corps, crew, force, gang, team, unit. *See* GROUP. **6.** A unit of troops on special assignment : detail. *See* GROUP.

detail *noun*

1. An individually considered portion of a whole : article, element, item, particular, point. *See* PART. **2.** One of the conditions or facts attending an event and having some bearing on it : circumstance, fact, factor, particular. *See* REAL. **3.** A small, often specialized element of a whole : fine print, item, particular, technicality. *See* GROUP. **4.** A unit of troops on special assignment : detachment. *See* GROUP.

detail *verb* To make specific : particularize, specify, stipulate. *See* SPECIFIC.

detailed *adjective*

Characterized by attention to detail : blow-by-blow, circumstantial, full, minute[2], particular, thorough. *See* SPECIFIC.

detain *verb*

1. To cause to be later or slower than expected or desired : delay, hang up, hold up, lag, retard, set back, slow (down *or* up), stall[2]. *See* HELP, TIME. **2.** To keep in custody : hold. *See* FREE, LAW. **3.** To put in jail : confine, immure, imprison, incarcerate, intern, jail, lock (up). *See* FREE.

detainment *noun*

The condition or fact of being made late or slow : delay, holdup, lag, retardation. *See* HELP, TIME.

detect *verb*

1. To perceive, especially barely or fleetingly : catch, descry, discern, espy, glimpse, spot, spy. *See* SEE. **2.** To perceive with a special effort of the senses or the mind : descry, discern, distinguish, mark, mind, note, notice, observe, remark, see. *See* KNOWLEDGE, SEE.

detectable *adjective*

Capable of being noticed or apprehended mentally : appreciable, discernible, distinguishable, noticeable, observable, palpable, perceivable, perceptible, ponderable, sensible. *See* KNOWLEDGE.

detective *noun*

A person whose work is investigating crimes or obtaining hidden evidence or information : investigator, sleuth. *Informal:* eye. *Slang:* dick, gumshoe. *See* INVESTIGATE.

detention *noun*

The state of being detained by legal authority : charge, confinement, custody, ward. *See* FREE.

deter *verb*

To persuade (a person) not to do something : discourage, dissuade, divert. ***Idiom:*** talk out of. *See* PERSUASION.

deteriorate *verb*

1. To become lower in quality, character, or condition : atrophy, decline, degenerate, descend, retrograde, sink, worsen. ***Idioms:*** go bad, go to pot, go to seed, go to the dogs. *See* BETTER. **2.** To lose strength or power : decline, degenerate, fade, fail, flag[2], languish, sink, wane, waste (away), weaken. *Informal:* fizzle (out). ***Idioms:*** go downhill, hit the skids. *See* STRONG, INCREASE. **3.** To become or cause to become rotten or unsound : break down, decay, decompose, disintegrate, molder, putrefy, rot, spoil, taint, turn. ***Idioms:*** go bad, go to pot, go to seed. *See* BETTER, THRIVE.

deterioration *noun*

1. Descent to a lower level or condition : atrophy, decadence, declension, declination, decline, degeneracy, degeneration. *See* BETTER.
2. A marked loss of strength or effectiveness : declination, decline, failure. *See* INCREASE.
3. The condition of being decayed : breakdown, decay, decomposition, disintegration, putrefaction, putrescence, putridness, rot, rottenness, spoilage. *See* BETTER, THRIVE.

determent *noun*

The act of preventing : deterrence, forestallment, obviation, preclusion, prevention. *See* ALLOW.

determinate *adjective*

Having distinct limits : definite, fixed, limited. *See* LIMITED.

determination *noun*

1. A position reached after consideration : conclusion, decision, resolution. *See* DECIDE.
2. Unwavering firmness of character, action, or will : decidedness, decision, decisiveness, firmness, purpose, purposefulness, resoluteness, res-

olution, resolve, toughness, will, willpower. *See* CERTAIN, STRONG. **3.** An authoritative or official decision, especially one made by a court : decree, edict, judgment, pronouncement, ruling. *See* LAW. **4.** Something worked out to explain, resolve, or provide a method for dealing with and settling a problem : answer, solution. *Mathematics:* result. *See* ASK.

determinative *adjective*
1. Serving the function of deciding or settling with finality : authoritative, conclusive, decisive, definitive, final. *See* DECIDE. **2.** Determining or having the power to determine an outcome : conclusive, crucial, deciding, decisive. *See* DECIDE, IMPORTANT.

determine *verb*
1. To make a decision about (a controversy or dispute, for example) after deliberation, as in a court of law : adjudge, adjudicate, arbitrate, decide, decree, judge, referee, rule, umpire. *See* DECIDE, LAW. **2.** To obtain knowledge or awareness of something not known before, as through observation or study : ascertain, discover, find (out), hear, learn. *See* TEACH. **3.** To make up or cause to make up one's mind : conclude, decide, resolve, settle. *See* DECIDE. **4.** To fix the limits of : bound[2], delimit, delimitate, demarcate, limit, mark (out *or* off), measure. *See* LIMITED.

determined *adjective*
1. Indicating or possessing determination, resolution, or persistence : constant, firm[1], resolute, steadfast, steady, stiff, tough, unbending, uncompromising, unflinching, unwavering, unyielding. *See* PURPOSE. **2.** Not hesitating or wavering : decided, decisive, firm[1], resolute. *See* DECIDE. **3.** On an unwavering course of action : bent, decided, fixed, intent, resolute, set[1]. *See* DECIDE.

deterrence *noun*
The act of preventing : determent, forestallment, obviation, preclusion, prevention. *See* ALLOW.

deterrent *adjective*
Intended to prevent : preclusive, preventative, preventive. *See* ALLOW.

detest *verb*
To regard with extreme dislike and hostility : abhor, abominate, despise, execrate, hate, loathe. *See* LOVE.

detestable *adjective*
So objectionable as to elicit despisal or deserve condemnation : abhorrent, abominable, antipathetic, contemptible, despicable, despisable, disgusting, filthy, foul, infamous, loathsome, lousy, low, mean[2], nasty, nefarious, obnoxious, odious, repugnant, rotten, shabby, vile, wretched. *See* GOOD.

detestation *noun*
1. Extreme hostility and dislike : abhorrence, abomination, antipathy, aversion, hate, hatred, horror, loathing, repellence, repellency, repugnance, repugnancy, repulsion, revulsion. *See* LOVE. **2.** An object of extreme dislike : abhorrence, abomination, anathema, aversion, bête noire, bugbear, execration, hate. *Informal:* horror. *See* LOVE.

detonate *verb*
To release or cause to release energy suddenly and violently, especially with a loud noise : blast, blow[1] (up), burst, explode, fire, fulminate, go off, touch off. *See* EXPLOSION.

detonation *noun*
A violent release of confined energy, usually accompanied by a loud sound and shock waves : blast, blowout, blowup, burst, explosion, fulmination. *See* EXPLOSION.

detour *verb*
To pass around but not through : bypass, circumnavigate, circumvent, go around, skirt. *See* SEEK.

detract *verb*
To think, represent, or speak of as small or unimportant : belittle, decry, denigrate, deprecate, depreciate, derogate, discount, disparage, downgrade, minimize, run down, slight, talk down. *Idiom:* make light (*or* little) of. *See* ATTACK, SHOW.
detract from *verb* To spoil the soundness or perfection of : blemish, damage, disserve, flaw, harm, hurt, impair, injure, mar, prejudice, tarnish, vitiate. *See* BETTER, HELP.

detract from *verb* See **detract.**

detraction *noun*
1. The act or an instance of belittling : belittlement, denigration, deprecation, depreciation, derogation, disparagement, minimization. *See* ATTACK, SHOW. **2.** The expression of injurious, malicious statements about someone : aspersion, calumniation, calumny, character assassination, defamation, denigration, scandal, slander, traducement, vilification. *Law:* libel. *See* ATTACK, CRIMES, LAW.

detractive *adjective*
1. Tending or intending to belittle : deprecative, deprecatory, depreciative, depreciatory, derogative, derogatory, disparaging, low, pejorative, slighting, uncomplimentary. *See* PRAISE. **2.** Damaging to the reputation : calumnious, defamatory, injurious, invidious, scandalous,

slanderous. *Law:* libelous. *See* ATTACK, CRIMES, LAW.

detriment *noun*
1. The action or result of inflicting loss or pain : damage, harm, hurt, injury, mischief. *See* HELP. 2. An unfavorable condition, circumstance, or characteristic : disadvantage, drawback, handicap, minus. *See* HELP.

detrimental *adjective*
Causing harm or injury : bad, deleterious, evil, harmful, hurtful, ill, injurious, mischievous. *See* HELP.

de trop *adjective*
Being more than is needed, desired, or appropriate : excess, extra, spare, supererogatory, superfluous, supernumerary, surplus. *See* EXCESS.

devaluate *verb*
To become or make less in price or value : cheapen, depreciate, depress, devalue, downgrade, lower[2], mark down, reduce, write down. *See* INCREASE, MONEY.

devaluation *noun*
A lowering in price or value : depreciation, markdown, reduction, write-down. *See* INCREASE, MONEY.

devalue *verb*
To become or make less in price or value : cheapen, depreciate, depress, devaluate, downgrade, lower[2], mark down, reduce, write down. *See* INCREASE, MONEY.

devastate *verb*
To destroy completely as or as if by conquering : desolate, ravage, waste. *Idiom:* lay waste. *See* HELP.

devastation *noun*
The act of destroying or state of being destroyed : bane, destruction, havoc, ruin, ruination, undoing, wrack[1], wreck, wreckage. *See* HELP, LEFTOVER.

develop *verb*
1. To bring or come to full development : age, grow, maturate, mature, mellow, ripen. *See* YOUTH. 2. To bring (a product or idea, for example) into being : generate, produce. *See* KIN. 3. To take place : befall, betide, come, come about, come off, hap, happen, occur, pass, transpire. *Idiom:* come to pass. *See* HAPPEN. 4. To be disclosed gradually : evolve, unfold. *See* SHOW. 5. To express at greater length or in greater detail : amplify, dilate, elaborate, enlarge, expand, expatiate, labor. *See* EXPLAIN. 6. To disclose bit by bit : elaborate, evolve. *Idioms:* fill in the details, go into detail. *See* SHOW. 7. To come gradually to have : acquire, form. *See* GET. 8. To achieve an increase of gradually : build up, gain. *See* INCREASE. 9. To become affected with a disease : catch, contract, get, sicken, take. *Idiom:* come down with. *See* GET.

developed *adjective*
Having reached full growth and development : adult, big, full-blown, full-fledged, full-grown, grown, grown-up, mature, ripe. *Idiom:* of age. *See* YOUTH.

developer *noun*
A person instrumental in the growth of something, especially in its early stages : builder, contributor, creator, pioneer. *See* MAKE.

development *noun*
1. A progression from a simple form to a more complex one : evolution, evolvement, growth, progress, unfolding. *See* CHANGE. 2. The result or product of building up : accretion, buildup, enlargement, multiplication, proliferation. *See* INCREASE. 3. Steady improvement, as of an individual or a society : amelioration, betterment, improvement, melioration, progress. *See* BETTER. 4. Something significant that happens : circumstance, episode, event, happening, incident, news, occasion, occurrence, thing. *See* HAPPEN.

deviance *noun*
The condition of being abnormal : aberrance, aberrancy, aberration, abnormality, anomaly, deviancy, deviation, irregularity, preternaturalness, unnaturalness. *See* GOOD, USUAL.

deviancy *noun*
The condition of being abnormal : aberrance, aberrancy, aberration, abnormality, anomaly, deviance, deviation, irregularity, preternaturalness, unnaturalness. *See* GOOD, USUAL.

deviant *adjective*
Departing from the normal : aberrant, abnormal, anomalistic, anomalous, atypic, atypical, divergent, irregular, preternatural, unnatural. *See* GOOD, USUAL.

deviant *noun* One whose sexual behavior differs from the accepted norm : deviate, pervert. *See* SEX, USUAL.

deviate *verb*
1. To turn away from a prescribed course of action or conduct : depart, digress, diverge, stray, swerve, veer. *Archaic:* err. *See* APPROACH, CORRECT. 2. To turn aside, especially from the main subject in writing or speaking : digress, divagate, diverge, ramble, stray, wander. *Idiom:* go off at (*or* on) a tangent. *See* APPROACH. 3. To change the direction or

course of : avert, deflect, divert, pivot, shift, swing, turn, veer. *See* CHANGE.
deviate *noun* One whose sexual behavior differs from the accepted norm : deviant, pervert. *See* USUAL, SEX.
deviation *noun*
1. A departing from what is prescribed : aberration, departure, divergence, divergency, diversion. *See* APPROACH, CORRECT. **2.** An instance of digressing : aside, digression, divagation, divergence, divergency, excursion, excursus, irrelevancy, parenthesis, tangent. *See* APPROACH. **3.** The condition of being abnormal : aberrance, aberrancy, aberration, abnormality, anomaly, deviance, deviancy, irregularity, preternaturalness, unnaturalness. *See* GOOD, USUAL.
device *noun*
1. Something, as a machine, devised for a particular function : apparatus, appliance, contraption, contrivance. *See* MACHINE. **2.** Something invented : brainchild, contrivance, invention. *See* MACHINE, MAKE. **3.** An indirect, usually cunning means of gaining an end : artifice, deception, dodge, feint, gimmick, imposture, jig, maneuver, ploy, ruse, sleight, stratagem, subterfuge, trick, wile. *Informal:* shenanigan, take-in. *See* HONEST, MEANS. **4.** An element or a component in a decorative composition : design, figure, motif, motive, pattern. *See* PART.
devil *noun*
1. A perversely bad, cruel, or wicked person : archfiend, beast, fiend, ghoul, monster, ogre, tiger, vampire. *See* KIND. **2.** One who causes minor trouble or damage : imp, mischief, prankster, rascal, rogue, scamp. *Informal:* cutup. *See* GOOD.
devilish *adjective*
Perversely bad, cruel, or wicked : diabolic, diabolical, fiendish, ghoulish, hellish, infernal, ogreish, satanic, satanical. *See* KIND.
devilry *noun*
Annoying yet harmless, usually playful acts : deviltry, diablerie, high jinks, impishness, mischief, mischievousness, prankishness, rascality, roguery, roguishness, tomfoolery. *Informal:* shenanigan (often used in plural). *See* GOOD.
deviltry *noun*
1. Annoying yet harmless, usually playful acts : devilry, diablerie, high jinks, impishness, mischief, mischievousness, prankishness, rascality, roguery, roguishness, tomfoolery. *Informal:* shenanigan (often used in plural). *See* GOOD. **2.** A wicked act or wicked behavior : crime, diablerie, evil, evildoing, immorality, iniquity, misdeed, offense, peccancy, sin, wickedness, wrong, wrongdoing. *See* RIGHT.
devious *adjective*
1. Marked by treachery or deceit : disingenuous, duplicitous, guileful, indirect, lubricious, shifty, sneaky, underhand, underhanded. *See* HONEST. **2.** Not taking a direct or straight line or course : anfractuous, circuitous, circular, indirect, oblique, roundabout, tortuous. *See* STRAIGHT. **3.** Without a fixed or regular course : erratic, stray, wandering. *See* PURPOSE.
deviousness *noun*
Lack of straightforwardness and honesty in action : chicanery, craft, craftiness, dishonesty, indirection, shadiness, shiftiness, slyness, sneakiness, trickery, trickiness, underhandedness. *See* HONEST.
devise *verb*
1. To use ingenuity in making, developing, or achieving : concoct, contrive, dream up, fabricate, formulate, hatch, invent, make up, think up. *Informal:* cook up. ***Idiom:*** come up with. *See* MAKE. **2.** To form a strategy for : blueprint, cast, chart, conceive, contrive, design, formulate, frame, lay[1], plan, project, scheme, strategize, work out. *Informal:* dope out. ***Idiom:*** lay plans. *See* PLANNED. **3.** *Law.* To give (property) to another person after one's death : leave[1], will. *Law:* bequeath. *See* GIVE, LAW.
devitalization *noun*
The depletion or sapping of strength or energy : attenuation, debilitation, depletion, enervation, enfeeblement, impoverishment. *See* STRONG.
devitalize *verb*
To lessen or deplete the nerve, energy, or strength of : attenuate, debilitate, enervate, enfeeble, sap[2], undermine, undo, unnerve, weaken. *See* STRONG.
devoid *adjective*
Not having a desirable element : barren, destitute, empty, innocent, lacking, void, wanting. ***Idiom:*** in want of. *See* FULL.
devolve *verb*
To come as by lot or inheritance : fall, pass. *See* REACH.
devote *verb*
1. To devote (oneself or one's efforts) : address, apply, bend, buckle down, concentrate, dedicate, direct, focus, give, turn. *See* COLLECT, WORK. **2.** To give over by or as if by vow

to a higher purpose : consecrate, dedicate, hallow. *See* GIVE.

devoted *adjective*
1. Feeling and expressing affection : affectionate, doting, fond, loving. *See* ATTITUDE, LOVE. **2.** Given over exclusively to a single use or purpose : consecrated, dedicated, hallowed, sacred. *See* GIVE, INCLUDE.

devotee *noun*
1. A person who is ardently devoted to a particular subject or activity : bug, enthusiast, fanatic, maniac, zealot. *Informal:* buff[2], fan[2], fiend. *Slang:* freak, nut. *See* CONCERN. **2.** One who ardently admires : admirer, enthusiast, fancier, lover. *Informal:* fan[2]. *See* LIKE, LOVE, PRAISE. **3.** One zealously devoted to a religion : enthusiast, fanatic, sectary, votary, zealot. *See* BELIEF, LOVE, RELIGION.

devotion *noun*
1. Deep and ardent affection : adoration, love, worship. *See* LIKE, LOVE. **2.** The condition of being closely tied to another by affection or faith : affection, attachment, fondness, liking, love, loyalty (used in plural). *See* CONNECT. **3.** A state of often extreme religious ardour : devoutness, pietism, piety, piousness, religionism, religiosity, religiousness. *See* RELIGION.

devotional *adjective*
Deeply concerned with God and the beliefs and practice of religion : devout, godly, holy, pietistic, pietistical, pious, prayerful, religious, saintly. *See* RELIGION.

devour *verb*
1. To eat completely or entirely : consume, dispatch, eat up. *Informal:* polish off, put away. *See* INGESTION. **2.** To take (food) into the body as nourishment : consume, eat, fare, ingest, partake. *Slang:* chow. ***Idioms:*** break bread, have (*or* take) a bite. *See* INGESTION. **3.** To do away with completely and destructively : consume, eat (up), swallow (up), waste. *See* HELP. **4.** To use up foolishly or needlessly : consume, dissipate, squander, waste. *See* SAVE. **5.** To be avidly interested in : feast on, relish. *Slang:* eat up. *See* CONCERN.

devout *adjective*
Deeply concerned with God and the beliefs and practice of religion : devotional, godly, holy, pietistic, pietistical, pious, prayerful, religious, saintly. *See* RELIGION.

devoutness *noun*
A state of often extreme religious ardour : devotion, pietism, piety, piousness, religionism, religiosity, religiousness. *See* RELIGION.

dexterity *noun*
1. Skillfulness in the use of the hands or body : adroitness, deftness, dexterousness, prowess, skill, sleight. *See* ABILITY. **2.** The quality or state of being mentally agile : agileness, agility, dexterousness, nimbleness, quickness. *See* ABILITY.

dexterous *adjective*
1. Exhibiting or possessing skill and ease in performance : adroit, clever, deft, facile, handy, nimble, slick. *See* ABILITY. **2.** Showing art or skill in performing or doing : adroit, artful, deft, skillful. *See* ABILITY, KNOWLEDGE.

dexterousness *noun*
1. The quality or state of being mentally agile : agileness, agility, dexterity, nimbleness, quickness. *See* ABILITY. **2.** Skillfulness in the use of the hands or body : adroitness, deftness, dexterity, prowess, skill, sleight. *See* ABILITY.

diablerie *noun*
1. A wicked act or wicked behavior : crime, deviltry, evil, evildoing, immorality, iniquity, misdeed, offense, peccancy, sin, wickedness, wrong, wrongdoing. *See* RIGHT. **2.** *Informal.* Annoying yet harmless, usually playful acts : devilry, deviltry, high jinks, impishness, mischief, mischievousness, prankishness, rascality, roguery, roguishness, tomfoolery. *Informal:* shenanigan (often used in plural). *See* GOOD.

diabolic *adjective*
Perversely bad, cruel, or wicked : devilish, diabolical, fiendish, ghoulish, hellish, infernal, ogreish, satanic, satanical. *See* KIND.

diabolical *adjective*
Perversely bad, cruel, or wicked : devilish, diabolic, fiendish, ghoulish, hellish, infernal, ogreish, satanic, satanical. *See* KIND.

diagonal *adjective*
Angled at a slant : beveled, bias, biased, oblique, slanted, slanting. *See* STRAIGHT.

dial *noun*
The marked outer surface of an instrument : face. *See* PRECEDE.

dial *verb* *Informal.* To communicate with (someone) by telephone : buzz, call, ring[2], telephone. *Informal:* phone. ***Idioms:*** get someone on the horn, give someone a buzz (*or* call *or* ring). *See* WORDS.

dialect *noun*
1. A variety of a language that differs from the standard form : argot, cant[2], jargon, lingo, patois, vernacular. *See* WORDS. **2.** A system of terms used by a people sharing a history and culture : language, speech, tongue, vernacular.

Linguistics: langue. *See* WORDS. **3.** Specialized expressions indigenous to a particular field, subject, trade, or subculture : argot, cant[2], idiom, jargon, language, lexicon, lingo, patois, terminology, vernacular, vocabulary. *See* WORDS.

dialog *noun* See **dialogue.**

dialogue or **dialog** *noun*
Spoken exchange : chat, colloquy, confabulation, conversation, converse[1], discourse, speech, talk. *Informal:* confab. *Slang:* jaw. *See* WORDS.

diametric *adjective*
Diametrically opposed : antipodal, antipodean, antithetical, antonymic, antonymous, contradictory, contrary, converse[2], counter, diametrical, opposing, opposite, polar, reverse. *See* SUPPORT.

diametrical *adjective*
Diametrically opposed : antipodal, antipodean, antithetical, antonymic, antonymous, contradictory, contrary, converse[2], counter, diametric, opposing, opposite, polar, reverse. *See* SUPPORT.

diaphanous *adjective*
So light and insubstantial as to resemble air or a thin film : aërial, aery, airy, ethereal, filmy, gauzy, gossamer, gossamery, sheer[2], transparent, vaporous, vapory. *See* THICK.

diatribe *noun*
A long, violent, or blustering speech, usually of censure or denunciation : fulmination, harangue, jeremiad, philippic, tirade. *See* PRAISE.

dibs *noun*
Slang. A legitimate or supposed right to demand something as one's rightful due : claim, pretense, pretension, title. *See* OWNED, REQUEST.

dick *noun*
Slang. A person whose work is investigating crimes or obtaining hidden evidence or information : detective, investigator, sleuth. *Informal:* eye. *Slang:* gumshoe. *See* INVESTIGATE.

dicker *verb*
To argue about the terms, as of a sale : bargain, haggle, higgle, huckster, negotiate, palter. *See* AGREE.

dictate *verb*
1. To set forth expressly and authoritatively : decree, fix, impose, lay down, ordain, prescribe. *Idioms:* call the shots (*or* tune), lay it on the line. *See* OVER. **2.** To command or issue commands in an arrogant manner : boss, dominate, domineer, order, rule, tyrannize. *See* OVER.

dictate *noun* **1.** An authoritative indication to be obeyed : behest, bidding, charge, command, commandment, direction, directive, injunction, instruction (often used in plural), mandate, order, word. *See* OVER, WORDS. **2.** A code or set of codes governing action or procedure, for example : prescript, regulation, rubric, rule. *See* ORDER.

dictator *noun*
1. An absolute ruler, especially one who is harsh and oppressive : Big Brother, despot, führer, man on horseback, oppressor, strongman, totalitarian, tyrant. *See* OVER. **2.** One who imposes or favors absolute obedience to authority : authoritarian, autocrat, despot, martinet, totalitarian, tyrant. *See* OVER.

dictatorial *adjective*
1. Tending to dictate : authoritarian, bossy, dogmatic, domineering, imperious, magisterial, masterful, overbearing, peremptory. *See* OVER. **2.** Having and exercising complete political power and control : absolute, absolutistic, arbitrary, autarchic, autarchical, autocratic, autocratical, despotic, monocratic, totalitarian, tyrannic, tyrannical, tyrannous. *See* OVER, POLITICS. **3.** Characterized by or favoring absolute obedience to authority : authoritarian, autocratic, despotic, totalitarian, tyrannic, tyrannical. *See* OVER.

dictatorship *noun*
1. A government in which a single leader or party exercises absolute control over all citizens and every aspect of their lives : absolutism, autarchy, autocracy, despotism, monocracy, tyranny. *See* OVER, POLITICS. **2.** Absolute power, especially when exercised unjustly or cruelly : autocracy, despotism, totalitarianism, tyranny. *See* OVER, POLITICS. **3.** A political doctrine advocating the principle of absolute rule : absolutism, authoritarianism, autocracy, despotism, totalitarianism. *See* OVER, POLITICS.

diction *noun*
Choice of words and the way in which they are used : parlance, phrase, phraseology, phrasing, verbalism, wordage, wording. *See* WORDS.

dictionary *noun*
An alphabetical list of words often defined or translated : glossary, lexicon, vocabulary, wordbook. *See* WORDS.

didactic *adjective*
1. Teaching morality : didactical, moral, moralizing. *See* TEACH. **2.** Inclined to teach or

moralize excessively : didactical, preachy. *See* TEACH.

didactical *adjective*

1. Teaching morality : didactic, moral, moralizing. *See* TEACH. **2.** Inclined to teach or moralize excessively : didactic, preachy. *See* TEACH.

diddle[1] *verb*

Slang. To get money or something else from by deceitful trickery : bilk, cheat, cozen, defraud, gull, mulct, rook, swindle, victimize. *Informal:* chisel, flimflam, take, trim. *Slang:* do, gyp, stick, sting. *See* HONEST.

diddle[2] *verb*

Slang. To pass time without working or in avoiding work : bum[1] (around), idle, laze, loaf, loiter, lounge, shirk. *Slang:* goldbrick, goof (off). *See* INDUSTRIOUS.

diddler *noun*

Slang. A person who cheats : bilk, cheat, cheater, cozener, defrauder, rook, sharper, swindler, trickster, victimizer. *Informal:* chiseler, crook, flimflammer. *Slang:* gyp, gypper. *See* HONEST.

diddly *noun*

Slang. The least bit : hoot, iota, jot, ounce, shred, whit. *Informal:* damn, rap[2]. *See* BIG.

die *verb*

1. To cease living : decease, demise, depart, drop, expire, go, pass away, pass (on), perish, succumb. *Informal:* pop off. *Slang:* check out, croak, kick in, kick off. ***Idioms:*** bite the dust, breathe one's last, cash in, give up the ghost, go to one's grave, kick the bucket, meet one's end (*or* Maker), pass on to the Great Beyond, turn up one's toes. *See* LIVE. **2.** To cease to exist. Also used with *away* or *out* : disappear, expire. *See* LIVE. **3.** To become or cause to become less active or intense. Also used with *away, down, off,* or *out* : abate, bate, ease (off *or* up), ebb, fall, fall off, lapse, let up, moderate, remit, slacken, slack off, subside, wane. *See* INCREASE. **4.** To become inaudible. Also used with *away, out,* or *down* : fade, fade out. *See* INCREASE.

die-hard also **diehard** *adjective*

1. Firmly, often unreasonably immovable in purpose or will : adamant, adamantine, brassbound, grim, implacable, incompliant, inexorable, inflexible, intransigent, iron, obdurate, relentless, remorseless, rigid, stubborn, unbendable, unbending, uncompliant, uncompromising, unrelenting, unyielding. ***Idiom:*** stubborn as a mule (*or* ox). *See* RESIST. **2.** Vehemently, often fanatically opposing progress or reform : mossbacked, reactionary, ultraconservative. *See* POLITICS.

die-hard or **diehard** *noun* A person who vehemently, often fanatically opposes progress and favors return to a previous condition : mossback, reactionary, ultraconservative. *See* POLITICS.

die-hardism *noun*

The quality or state of being stubbornly inflexible : grimness, implacability, implacableness, incompliance, incompliancy, inexorability, inexorableness, inflexibility, inflexibleness, intransigence, intransigency, obduracy, obdurateness, relentlessness, remorselessness, rigidity, rigidness, stubbornness. *See* RESIST.

diet *noun*

Something fit to be eaten : aliment, bread, comestible, edible, esculent, fare, food, foodstuff, meat, nourishment, nurture, nutriment, nutrition, pabulum, pap, provender, provision (used in plural), sustenance, victual. *Slang:* chow, eats, grub. *See* INGESTION.

differ *verb*

1. To be unlike or dissimilar : disagree, diverge, vary. ***Idiom:*** be at variance. *See* SAME. **2.** To be of different opinion : disaccord, disagree, discord, dissent, vary. ***Idiom:*** join (*or* take) issue. *See* AGREE.

difference *noun*

1. The condition of being unlike or dissimilar : discrepance, discrepancy, disparity, dissimilarity, dissimilitude, distinction, divarication, divergence, divergency, unlikeness. *See* SAME. **2.** A marked lack of correspondence or agreement : disagreement, discrepance, discrepancy, disparity, gap, incompatibility, incongruity, inconsistency. *See* AGREE. **3.** The condition or fact of varying : variance, variation. *See* CHANGE, SAME. **4.** A state of disagreement and disharmony : clash, conflict, confrontation, contention, difficulty, disaccord, discord, discordance, dissension, dissent, dissentience, dissidence, dissonance, faction, friction, inharmony, schism, strife, variance, war, warfare. *See* CONFLICT.

different *adjective*

1. Not like another in nature, quality, amount, or form : disparate, dissimilar, divergent, diverse, unlike, variant, various. *See* SAME. **2.** Not the same as what was previously known or done : fresh, innovative, inventive, new, newfangled, novel, original, unfamiliar, unprecedented. *See* NEW.

differentiate *verb*

1. To recognize as being different : discern, discriminate, distinguish, know, separate, tell. *See* SAME. **2.** To make noticeable or different : characterize, discriminate, distinguish, individualize, mark, set apart, signalize, singularize. *See* SAME.

differentiation *noun*
The act or an instance of distinguishing : discrimination, distinction, separation. *See* SAME.

difficult *adjective*
1. Not easy to do, achieve, or master : arduous, hard, laborious, serious, tall, tough, uphill. *See* EASY. **2.** Requiring great or extreme bodily, mental, or spiritual strength : arduous, backbreaking, burdensome, demanding, effortful, exacting, exigent, formidable, hard, heavy, laborious, onerous, oppressive, rigorous, rough, severe, taxing, tough, trying, weighty. *See* HEAVY. **3.** Causing difficulty, trouble, or discomfort : incommodious, inconvenient, troublesome. *See* COMFORT. **4.** Given to acting in opposition to others : balky, contrarious, contrary, froward, impossible, ornery, perverse, wayward. *See* ATTITUDE, SUPPORT.

difficultly *adverb*
With effort : arduously, hard, heavily, laboriously. *See* EASY.

difficulty *noun*
1. Something that obstructs progress and requires great effort to overcome : asperity, hardship, rigor, vicissitude (often used in plural). ***Idioms:*** a hard (*or* tough) nut to crack, a hard (*or* tough) row to hoe, heavy sledding. *See* EASY. **2.** A difficult, often embarrassing situation or condition : box[1], corner, deep water, dilemma, Dutch, fix, hole, hot spot, hot water, jam, plight[1], predicament, quagmire, scrape, soup, trouble. *Informal:* bind, pickle, spot. *See* EASY. **3.** A state of disagreement and disharmony : clash, conflict, confrontation, contention, difference, disaccord, discord, discordance, dissension, dissent, dissentience, dissidence, dissonance, faction, friction, inharmony, schism, strife, variance, war, warfare. *See* CONFLICT. **4.** A discussion, often heated, in which a difference of opinion is expressed : altercation, argument, bicker, clash, contention, controversy, debate, disagreement, dispute, fight, polemic, quarrel, run-in, spat, squabble, tiff, word (used in plural), wrangle. *Informal:* hassle, rhubarb, tangle. *See* CONFLICT.

diffidence *noun*
Reserve in speech, behavior, or dress : demureness, modesty, reticence, self-effacement. *See* RESTRAINT.

diffident *adjective*
Not forward but reticent or reserved in manner : backward, bashful, coy, demure, modest, retiring, self-effacing, shy[1], timid. *See* RESTRAINT.

diffuse *verb*
To extend over a wide area : circulate, disperse, disseminate, distribute, radiate, scatter, spread, strew. *See* MOVE, WIDE.

diffuse *adjective* Using or containing an excessive number of words : long-winded, periphrastic, pleonastic, prolix, redundant, verbose, wordy. *See* EXCESS, STYLE, WORDS.

diffuseness *noun*
Words or the use of words in excess of those needed for clarity or precision : diffusion, long-windedness, pleonasm, prolixity, redundancy, verbiage, verboseness, verbosity, windiness, wordage, wordiness. *See* EXCESS, STYLE, WORDS.

diffusion *noun*
Words or the use of words in excess of those needed for clarity or precision : diffuseness, long-windedness, pleonasm, prolixity, redundancy, verbiage, verboseness, verbosity, windiness, wordage, wordiness. *See* EXCESS, STYLE, WORDS.

dig *verb*
1. To break, turn over, or remove (earth or sand, for example) with or as if with a tool : delve, excavate, grub, scoop, shovel, spade. *See* ENTER. **2.** To make by digging : excavate, scoop, shovel. *See* MAKE. **3.** To go into or through for the purpose of making discoveries or acquiring information : delve, explore, inquire, investigate, look into, probe, reconnoiter, scout[1]. *See* INVESTIGATE. **4.** To find by investigation. Also used with *out* or *up* : turn up, uncover, unearth. *See* SHOW. **5.** To cause to penetrate with force : drive, plunge, ram, run, sink, stab, stick, thrust. *See* PUT IN. **6.** To thrust against or into : jab, jog, nudge, poke, prod. *See* TOUCH. **7.** *Slang.* To perceive and recognize the meaning of : accept, apprehend, catch (on), compass, comprehend, conceive, fathom, follow, get, grasp, make out, read, see, sense, take, take in, understand. *Informal:* savvy. *Chiefly British:* twig. *Scots:* ken. ***Idioms:*** get (*or* have) a handle on, get the picture. *See* UNDERSTAND. **8.** *Slang.* To receive pleasure from : enjoy, like[1], relish, savor. *Informal:* go for. *See* LIKE.

dig *noun* **1.** An act of thrusting into or against, as to attract attention : jab, jog, nudge, poke.

See TOUCH. **2.** A flippant or sarcastic remark : crack, quip. *Slang:* wisecrack. *See* RESPECT, WORDS. **3.** *Chiefly British.* A building or shelter where one lives. Used in plural : abode, domicile, dwelling, habitation, home, house, lodging (often used in plural), place, residence. *See* PROTECTION.

digest *verb*
To take in and incorporate, especially mentally : absorb, assimilate, imbibe, take up. *Informal:* soak (up). *See* ACCEPT.

digestion *noun*
The process of absorbing and incorporating, especially mentally : absorption, assimilation. *See* ACCEPT.

dignify *verb*
1. To raise to a high position or status : aggrandize, apotheosize, elevate, ennoble, exalt, glorify, magnify, uplift. ***Idiom:*** put on a pedestal. *See* RISE. **2.** To lend dignity or honor to by an act or favor : grace, honor. *See* BEAUTIFUL.

dignitary *noun*
An important, influential person : character, eminence, leader, lion, nabob, notability, notable, personage. *Informal:* big-timer, heavyweight, somebody, someone, VIP. *Slang:* big shot, big wheel, bigwig, muckamuck. *See* IMPORTANT.

dignity *noun*
A person's high standing among others : good name, good report, honor, prestige, reputation, repute, respect, status. *See* RESPECT.

digress *verb*
1. To turn away from a prescribed course of action or conduct : depart, deviate, diverge, stray, swerve, veer. *Archaic:* err. *See* APPROACH, CORRECT. **2.** To turn aside, especially from the main subject in writing or speaking : deviate, divagate, diverge, ramble, stray, wander. ***Idiom:*** go off at (*or* on) a tangent. *See* APPROACH.

digression *noun*
An instance of digressing : aside, deviation, divagation, divergence, divergency, excursion, excursus, irrelevancy, parenthesis, tangent. *See* APPROACH.

digressive *adjective*
Marked by or given to digression : discursive, excursive, parenthetic, parenthetical, rambling, tangential. *See* APPROACH.

dilapidated *adjective*
1. Falling to ruin : ramshackle, ruinous, rundown, tumbledown. *See* BETTER. **2.** Showing signs of wear and tear or neglect : bedraggled, broken-down, decaying, decrepit, dingy, down-at-heel, faded, mangy, rundown, scrubby, scruffy, seedy, shabby, shoddy, sleazy, tattered, tatty, threadbare. *Informal:* tacky[2]. *Slang:* ratty. ***Idioms:*** all the worse for wear, gone to pot (*or* seed), past cure (*or* hope). *See* BETTER.

dilate *verb*
To express at greater length or in greater detail : amplify, develop, elaborate, enlarge, expand, expatiate, labor. *See* EXPLAIN.

dilatory *adjective*
Proceeding at a rate less than usual or desired : laggard, slow, slow-footed, slow-going, slow-paced, tardy. *Informal:* poky[1]. ***Idiom:*** slow as molasses in January. *See* FAST.

dilemma *noun*
A difficult, often embarrassing situation or condition : box[1], corner, deep water, difficulty, Dutch, fix, hole, hot spot, hot water, jam, plight[1], predicament, quagmire, scrape, soup, trouble. *Informal:* bind, pickle, spot. *See* EASY.

dilettante *noun*
One lacking professional skill and ease in a particular pursuit : amateur, dabbler, nonprofessional, smatterer, uninitiate. *See* ABILITY.
dilettante *adjective* Lacking the required professional skill : amateurish, dilettantish, nonprofessional, unprofessional, unskilled, unskillful. *See* ABILITY.

dilettantish *adjective*
Lacking the required professional skill : amateurish, dilettante, nonprofessional, unprofessional, unskilled, unskillful. *See* ABILITY.

diligence *noun*
Steady attention and effort, as to one's occupation : application, assiduity, assiduousness, industriousness, industry, sedulousness. *See* INDUSTRIOUS.

diligent *adjective*
Characterized by steady attention and effort : assiduous, industrious, sedulous, studious. *See* INDUSTRIOUS.

dilly-dallier *noun*
One that lags : dawdler, lag, laggard, lagger, lingerer, loiterer, poke, procrastinator, straggler, tarrier. *Informal:* slowpoke. *See* FAST.

dilly-dally *verb*
To go or move slowly so that progress is hindered : dally, dawdle, delay, drag, lag, linger, loiter, poke, procrastinate, tarry, trail. ***Idioms:*** drag one's feet (*or* heels), mark time, take one's time. *See* FAST.

dilute *verb*
To lessen the strength of by or as if by admix-

ture : attenuate, cut, thin, water (down), weaken. *See* STRONG.

dilute *adjective* Lower than normal in strength or concentration due to admixture : thin, washy, watered-down, waterish, watery, weak. *See* STRONG.

dim *adjective*
1. Deficient in brightness : caliginous, dark, dusky, murky, obscure. *See* LIGHT. **2.** Lacking vividness in color : drab, dull, flat, muddy, murky. *See* COLORS. **3.** Lacking gloss and luster : dull, flat, lackluster, lusterless, mat. *See* LIGHT. **4.** Covered by or as if by a thin coating or film : blurry, cloudy, filmy, hazy, misty. *See* CLEAR. **5.** Not clearly perceived or perceptible : blear, bleary, cloudy, faint, foggy, fuzzy, hazy, indefinite, indistinct, misty, obscure, shadowy, unclear, undistinct, vague. *See* CLEAR.

dim *verb* **1.** To make dim or indistinct : becloud, bedim, befog, blear, blur, cloud, dull, eclipse, fog, gloom, mist, obfuscate, obscure, overcast, overshadow, shadow. *See* CLEAR. **2.** To make or become less keen or responsive : dull, hebetate, stupefy. *See* AWARENESS.

dimension *noun*
The amount of space occupied by something : extent, magnitude, measure, proportion (often used in plural), size. *See* BIG.

diminish *verb*
To grow or cause to grow gradually less : abate, decrease, drain, dwindle, ebb, lessen, let up, peter (out), rebate, reduce, tail away (*or* off), taper (off). *See* INCREASE.

diminishment *noun*
The act or process of decreasing : abatement, curtailment, cut, cutback, decrease, decrement, diminution, drain, reduction, slash, slowdown, taper. *See* INCREASE.

diminution *noun*
The act or process of decreasing : abatement, curtailment, cut, cutback, decrease, decrement, diminishment, drain, reduction, slash, slowdown, taper. *See* INCREASE.

diminutive *adjective*
Extremely small : dwarf, Lilliputian, midget, miniature, minuscule, minute[2], pygmy, wee. *Informal:* peewee, pintsize, pintsized, teensy, teensy-weensy, teeny, teeny-weeny, tiny, weeny. *See* BIG.

dimness *noun*
Absence or deficiency of light : dark, darkness, duskiness, murkiness, obscureness, obscurity. *See* LIGHT.

dimwit *noun*
Slang. A mentally dull person : blockhead, chump[1], clod, dolt, dullard, dummkopf, dummy, dunce, numskull, thickhead. *Slang:* dumbbell, dumbo. *See* ABILITY.

dimwitted *adjective*
Slang. Lacking in intelligence : blockheaded, dense, doltish, dumb, hebetudinous, obtuse, stupid, thickheaded, thick-witted. *Informal:* thick. *Slang:* dopey. *See* ABILITY.

din *noun*
Sounds or a sound, especially when loud, confused, or disagreeable : babel, clamor, hubbub, hullabaloo, noise, pandemonium, racket, rumpus, tumult, uproar. *See* SOUNDS.

ding-a-ling *noun*
Slang. A person regarded as strange, eccentric, or crazy : crackpot, crazy, eccentric, lunatic. *Informal:* crank, loon, loony. *Slang:* cuckoo, dingbat, kook, nut, screwball, weirdie, weirdo. *See* WISE.

dingbat *noun*
Slang. A person regarded as strange, eccentric, or crazy : crackpot, crazy, eccentric, lunatic. *Informal:* crank, loon, loony. *Slang:* cuckoo, ding-a-ling, kook, nut, screwball, weirdie, weirdo. *See* WISE.

ding-dong *noun*
Slang. One deficient in judgment and good sense : ass, fool, idiot, imbecile, jackass, mooncalf, moron, nincompoop, ninny, nitwit, simple, simpleton, softhead, tomfool. *Informal:* dope, gander, goose. *Slang:* cretin, dip, goof, jerk, nerd, schmo, schmuck, turkey. *See* ABILITY.

dingy *adjective*
Showing signs of wear and tear or neglect : bedraggled, broken-down, decaying, decrepit, dilapidated, down-at-heel, faded, mangy, rundown, scrubby, scruffy, seedy, shabby, shoddy, sleazy, tattered, tatty, threadbare. *Informal:* tacky[2]. *Slang:* ratty. ***Idioms:*** all the worse for wear, gone to pot (*or* seed), past cure (*or* hope). *See* BETTER.

dip *verb*
1. To plunge briefly in or into a liquid : douse, duck, dunk, immerge, immerse, souse, submerge, submerse. *See* ENTER. **2.** To immerse in a coloring solution : color, dye. *See* COLORS, ENTER. **3.** To take a substance, as liquid, from a container by plunging the hand or a utensil into it : bail[2], lade, ladle, scoop (up). *See* GIVE. **4.** To slope downward : decline, descend, drop, fall, pitch, sink. *See* RISE.

dip into *verb* To look through reading matter casually : browse, flip through, glance at (*or* over *or* through), leaf (through), riffle (through), run through, scan, skim, thumb (through). *See* INVESTIGATE, WORDS.

dip *noun* **1.** The act of swimming : duck, dunk, plunge, swim. *See* WORK. **2.** A usually swift downward trend, as in prices : decline, descent, dive, downslide, downswing, downtrend, downturn, drop, drop-off, fall, nosedive, plunge, skid, slide, slump, tumble. *See* INCREASE. **3.** An area sunk below its surroundings : basin, concavity, depression, hollow, pit[1], sag, sink, sinkhole. *See* CONVEX. **4.** *Slang.* One deficient in judgment and good sense : ass, fool, idiot, imbecile, jackass, mooncalf, moron, nincompoop, ninny, nitwit, simple, simpleton, softhead, tomfool. *Informal:* dope, gander, goose. *Slang:* cretin, ding-dong, goof, jerk, nerd, schmo, schmuck, turkey. *See* ABILITY.

dip into *verb* See **dip.**

diplomacy *noun*
The ability to say and do the right thing at the right time : address, savoir-faire, tact, tactfulness. *See* ABILITY, COURTESY.

diplomatic *adjective*
Showing sensitivity and skill in dealing with others : delicate, discreet, politic, sensitive, tactful. *See* ABILITY.

dippy *adjective*
Slang. So senseless as to be laughable : absurd, foolish, harebrained, idiotic, imbecilic, insane, lunatic, mad, moronic, nonsensical, preposterous, silly, softheaded, tomfool, unearthly, zany. *Informal:* cockeyed, crazy, loony, loopy. *Slang:* balmy[2], dopey, jerky, sappy, wacky. *See* ABILITY, KNOWLEDGE.

dire *adjective*
1. Portending future disaster : apocalyptic, apocalyptical, baneful, direful, fateful, fire-and-brimstone, grave[2], hellfire, ominous, portentous, unlucky. *See* LUCK, WARN. **2.** Causing or able to cause fear : appalling, direful, dreadful, fearful, fearsome, formidable, frightful, ghastly, redoubtable, scary, terrible, tremendous. *See* FEAR. **3.** Compelling immediate attention : burning, crying, emergent, exigent, imperative, instant, pressing, urgent. *See* BIG. **4.** So serious as to be at the point of crisis or necessary to resolve a crisis : acute, climacteric, critical, crucial, desperate. *See* SAFETY.

direct *verb*
1. To have charge of (the affairs of others) : administer, administrate, govern, head, manage, run, superintend, supervise. *See* OVER. **2.** To control the course of (an activity) : carry on, conduct, manage, operate, run, steer. *See* OVER. **3.** To exercise authority or influence over : control, dominate, govern, rule. *Idioms:* be at the helm, be in the driver's seat, hold sway over, hold the reins. *See* OVER. **4.** To give orders to : bid, charge, command, enjoin, instruct, order, tell. *See* OVER, WORDS. **5.** To devote (oneself or one's efforts) : address, apply, bend, buckle down, concentrate, dedicate, devote, focus, give, turn. *See* COLLECT, WORK. **6.** To show the way to : conduct, escort, guide, lead, pilot, route, shepherd, show, steer, usher. *See* SHOW. **7.** To move (a weapon or blow, for example) in the direction of someone or something : aim, cast, head, level, point, set[1], train, turn, zero in. *Military:* lay[1]. *See* SEEK. **8.** To mark (a written communication) with its destination : address, superscribe. *See* START.

direct *adjective* **1.** Proceeding or lying in an uninterrupted line or course : straight, straightforward, through. *See* STRAIGHT. **2.** Manifesting honesty and directness, especially in speech : candid, downright, forthright, frank, honest, ingenuous, man-to-man, open, plainspoken, straight, straightforward, straight-out, unreserved. *Informal:* straight-from-the-shoulder, straight-shooting. *See* CLEAR, SHOW. **3.** Marked by the absence of any intervention : firsthand, immediate, primary. *See* CLEAR, NEAR. **4.** Of unbroken descent or lineage : lineal. *See* CONTINUE.

direct *adverb* **1.** In a direct line : dead, directly, due, right, straight, straightaway. *See* STRAIGHT. **2.** With precision or absolute conformity : bang, dead, directly, exactly, fair, flush, just, precisely, right, smack[1], square, squarely, straight. *Slang:* smack-dab. *See* PRECISE.

direction *noun*
1. Authoritative control over the affairs of others : administration, government, management, superintendence, supervision. *See* OVER. **2.** The continuous exercise of authority over a political unit : administration, control, governance, government, rule. *See* CONTROL, POLITICS. **3.** An act or instance of guiding : guidance, lead, leadership, management. *See* AFFECT. **4.** An authoritative indication to be obeyed : behest, bidding, charge, command, commandment, dictate, directive, injunction, instruction (often used in plural), mandate, order, word. *See* OVER, WORDS.

directive *noun*
An authoritative indication to be obeyed : behest, bidding, charge, command, commandment, dictate, direction, injunction, instruction

(often used in plural), mandate, order, word. *See* OVER, WORDS.

directly *adverb*

1. In a direct line : dead, direct, due, right, straight, straightaway. *See* STRAIGHT. **2.** Without intermediary : immediately. *See* CLEAR, NEAR. **3.** With precision or absolute conformity : bang, dead, direct, exactly, fair, flush, just, precisely, right, smack[1], square, squarely, straight. *Slang:* smack-dab. *See* PRECISE. **4.** Without delay : forthwith, immediately, instant, instantly, now, right away, right off, straightaway, straight off. ***Idioms:*** at once, first off. *See* TIME.

director *noun*

1. One who is highest in rank or authority : boss, chief, chieftain, head, headman, hierarch, leader, master. *Slang:* honcho. ***Idiom:*** cock of the walk. *See* OVER. **2.** Someone who directs and supervises workers : boss, foreman, foreperson, forewoman, head, manager, overseer, superintendent, supervisor, taskmaster, taskmistress. *Informal:* straw boss. *Slang:* chief. *See* OVER. **3.** A person having administrative or managerial authority in an organization : administrant, administrator, executive, manager, officer, official. *Informal:* exec. *See* OVER. **4.** Something or someone that shows the way : conductor, escort, guide, lead, leader, pilot, shepherd, usher. *See* SHOW.

directorial *adjective*

Of, for, or relating to administration or administrators : administrative, executive, managerial, ministerial, supervisory. *See* OVER.

direful *adjective*

1. Causing or able to cause fear : appalling, dire, dreadful, fearful, fearsome, formidable, frightful, ghastly, redoubtable, scary, terrible, tremendous. *See* FEAR. **2.** Portending future disaster : apocalyptic, apocalyptical, baneful, dire, fateful, fire-and-brimstone, grave[2], hellfire, ominous, portentous, unlucky. *See* LUCK, WARN.

dirt *noun*

1. Foul or dirty matter : filth, grime, muck. *Slang:* crud. *See* CLEAN. **2.** Something that is offensive to accepted standards of decency : bawdry, filth, obscenity, profanity, ribaldry, scatology, smut, vulgarity. *Slang:* raunch. *See* DECENT.

dirtiness *noun*

1. The condition or state of being dirty : filth, filthiness, foulness, griminess, grubbiness, smuttiness, squalor, uncleanliness, uncleanness. *See* CLEAN. **2.** Impure condition : defilement, foulness, impurity, pollution, uncleanness, unwholesomeness. *See* CLEAN. **3.** The quality or state of being obscene : bawdiness, coarseness, filthiness, foulness, grossness, lewdness, obscenity, profaneness, profanity, scurrility, scurrilousness, smuttiness, vulgarity, vulgarness. *Slang:* raunch, raunchiness. *See* DECENT.

dirty *adjective*

1. Covered or stained with or as if with dirt or other impurities : black, filthy, grimy, grubby, smutty, soiled, unclean, uncleanly. *See* CLEAN. **2.** Offensive to accepted standards of decency : barnyard, bawdy, broad, coarse, Fescennine, filthy, foul, gross, lewd, nasty, obscene, profane, ribald, scatologic, scatological, scurrilous, smutty, vulgar. *Slang:* raunchy. *See* DECENT. **3.** Violently disturbed or agitated, as by storms : heavy, raging, roiled, roily, rough, rugged, stormy, tempestuous, tumultuous, turbulent, ugly, violent, wild. *See* CALM.

dirty *verb* **1.** To make dirty : befoul, begrime, besmirch, besoil, black, blacken, defile, smudge, smutch, soil, sully. *See* CLEAN. **2.** To contaminate the reputation of : befoul, besmear, besmirch, bespatter, blacken, cloud, denigrate, smear, smudge, smut, soil, spatter, stain, sully, taint, tarnish. ***Idioms:*** give a black eye to, sling (*or* throw) mud on. *See* ATTACK, CLEAN.

dirty old man *noun*

Informal. An immoral or licentious man : lecher, roué, satyr. *Slang:* lech. *See* SEX.

disable *verb*

1. To render powerless or motionless, as by inflicting severe injury : cripple, immobilize, incapacitate, knock out, paralyze. ***Idiom:*** put out of action (*or* commission). *See* HELP. **2.** To make incapable, as of doing a job : disqualify, unfit. *See* ABILITY.

disaccord *noun*

A state of disagreement and disharmony : clash, conflict, confrontation, contention, difference, difficulty, discord, discordance, dissension, dissent, dissentience, dissidence, dissonance, faction, friction, inharmony, schism, strife, variance, war, warfare. *See* CONFLICT.

disaccord *verb* **1.** To fail to be in accord : clash, conflict, contradict, discord, jar. ***Idiom:*** go (*or* run) counter to. *See* AGREE. **2.** To be of different opinion : differ, disagree, discord, dissent, vary. ***Idiom:*** join (*or* take) issue. *See* AGREE.

disacknowledge *verb*

To refuse to recognize or acknowledge : deny, disavow, disclaim, disown, reject, renounce, repudiate. *Idiom:* turn one's back on. *See* ACCEPT.

disadvantage *noun*
An unfavorable condition, circumstance, or characteristic : detriment, drawback, handicap, minus. *See* HELP.

disadvantaged *adjective*
Economically and socially below standard : backward, depressed, deprived, impoverished, underprivileged. *See* RICH.

disadvantageous *adjective*
Tending to discourage, retard, or make more difficult : adverse, negative, unadvantageous, unfavorable, unsatisfactory, untoward. *See* HELP.

disaffect *verb*
To make distant, hostile, or unsympathetic : alienate, disunite, estrange. *Idiom:* set at odds. *See* LOVE.

disaffection *noun*
1. The act of estranging or the condition of being estranged : alienation, estrangement. *See* LOVE. **2.** An interruption in friendly relations : alienation, breach, break, estrangement, fissure, rent², rift, rupture, schism, split. *See* ASSEMBLE, HELP.

disaffirm *verb*
To refuse to admit the truth, reality, value, or worth of : contradict, contravene, controvert, deny, gainsay, negate, negative, oppugn. *Law:* traverse. *See* AFFIRM.

disaffirmance *noun*
A refusal to grant the truth of a statement or charge : contradiction, denial, disaffirmation, disclaimer, negation, rejection. *Law:* traversal. *See* AFFIRM.

disaffirmation *noun*
A refusal to grant the truth of a statement or charge : contradiction, denial, disaffirmance, disclaimer, negation, rejection. *Law:* traversal. *See* AFFIRM.

disagree *verb*
1. To be unlike or dissimilar : differ, diverge, vary. *Idiom:* be at variance. *See* SAME. **2.** To be of different opinion : differ, disaccord, discord, dissent, vary. *Idiom:* join (*or* take) issue. *See* AGREE.

disagreeable *adjective*
1. Not pleasant or agreeable : bad, displeasing, offensive, uncongenial, unpleasant, unsympathetic. *Informal:* icky. *Slang:* yucky. *See* GOOD, PAIN. **2.** Having or showing a bad temper : bad-tempered, cantankerous, crabbed, cranky, cross, fretful, grouchy, grumpy, ill-tempered, irascible, irritable, nasty, peevish, petulant, querulous, snappish, snappy, surly, testy, ugly, waspish. *Informal:* crabby, mean². *Idiom:* out of sorts. *See* ATTITUDE.

disagreement *noun*
1. A marked lack of correspondence or agreement : difference, discrepance, discrepancy, disparity, gap, incompatibility, incongruity, inconsistency. *See* AGREE. **2.** A discussion, often heated, in which a difference of opinion is expressed : altercation, argument, bicker, clash, contention, controversy, debate, difficulty, dispute, fight, polemic, quarrel, run-in, spat, squabble, tiff, word (used in plural), wrangle. *Informal:* hassle, rhubarb, tangle. *See* CONFLICT.

disallow *verb*
1. To refuse to allow : ban, debar, enjoin, forbid, inhibit, interdict, outlaw, prohibit, proscribe, taboo. *See* ALLOW. **2.** To be unwilling to grant : deny, refuse, turn down, withhold. *See* ACCEPT.

disallowance *noun*
1. A refusal to allow : ban, forbiddance, inhibition, interdiction, prohibition, proscription, taboo. *See* ALLOW. **2.** A turning down of a request : denial, refusal, rejection, turndown. *See* ACCEPT.

disappear *verb*
1. To pass out of sight either gradually or suddenly : evanesce, evaporate, fade, fade out, vanish. *See* SHOW. **2.** To cease to exist : die (away *or* out), expire. *See* LIVE.

disappearance *noun*
The act or an example of passing out of sight : evanescence, evaporation, fade-out, vanishment. *See* SHOW.

disappoint *verb*
To cause unhappiness by failing to satisfy the hopes, desires, or expectations of : discontent, disgruntle, dissatisfy, let down. *See* HAPPY.

disappointing *adjective*
Disturbing because of failure to measure up to a standard or produce the desired results : sorry, unlucky. *See* HAPPY.

disappointment *noun*
Unhappiness caused by the failure of one's hopes, desires, or expectations : discontent, discontentment, disgruntlement, dissatisfaction, letdown, regret. *See* HAPPY.

disapprobation *noun*
Unfavorable opinion or judgment : disapproval, disesteem, disfavor, displeasure. *See* LIKE.

disapproval *noun*
Unfavorable opinion or judgment : disappro-

bation, disesteem, disfavor, displeasure. *See* LIKE.

disapprove *verb*
To have or express an unfavorable opinion of : deprecate, discountenance, disesteem, disfavor, frown on (*or* upon), object. ***Idioms:*** hold no brief for, not go for, take a dim view of, take exception to. *See* LIKE.

disarrange *verb*
1. To put out of proper order : derange, disarray, disorder, disorganize, disrupt, disturb, jumble, mess up, mix up, muddle, tumble, unsettle, upset. *See* ORDER. **2.** To put (the hair or clothes) into a state of disarray : dishevel, disorder, mess (up), muss (up), rumple, tousle. *See* ORDER.

disarrangement *noun*
A lack of order or regular arrangement : chaos, clutter, confusedness, confusion, derangement, disarray, disorder, disorderedness, disorderliness, disorganization, jumble, mess, mix-up, muddle, muss, scramble, topsy-turviness, tumble. *Slang:* snafu. *See* ORDER.

disarray *noun*
A lack of order or regular arrangement : chaos, clutter, confusedness, confusion, derangement, disarrangement, disorder, disorderedness, disorderliness, disorganization, jumble, mess, mix-up, muddle, muss, scramble, topsy-turviness, tumble. *Slang:* snafu. *See* ORDER.

disarray *verb* To put out of proper order : derange, disarrange, disorder, disorganize, disrupt, disturb, jumble, mess up, mix up, muddle, tumble, unsettle, upset. *See* ORDER.

disassemble *verb*
To take (something) apart : break down, dismantle, dismount, take down. *See* ASSEMBLE.

disassociate *verb*
To remove from association with : abstract, detach, disengage, dissociate, withdraw. *See* ASSEMBLE.

disaster *noun*
An occurrence inflicting widespread destruction and distress : calamity, cataclysm, catastrophe, tragedy. *See* HELP.

disastrous *adjective*
Causing ruin or destruction : calamitous, cataclysmal, cataclysmic, catastrophic, destructive, fatal, fateful, ruinous. *See* HELP.

disavow *verb*
To refuse to recognize or acknowledge : deny, disacknowledge, disclaim, disown, reject, renounce, repudiate. ***Idiom:*** turn one's back on. *See* ACCEPT.

disbelief *noun*
The refusal or reluctance to believe : discredit, incredulity, incredulousness, unbelief. *See* BELIEF.

disbelieve *verb*
To give no credence to : discredit. ***Idiom:*** take no stock in. *See* BELIEF.

disbelieving *adjective*
Refusing or reluctant to believe : incredulous, questioning, skeptical, unbelieving. *See* BELIEF.

disburden *verb*
1. To free from or cast out something objectionable or undesirable : clear, disembarrass, disencumber, release, relieve, rid, shake off, throw off, unburden. *Slang:* shake. *See* KEEP. **2.** To remove the cargo or load from : discharge, dump, unlade, unload. *See* PUT IN.

disburse *verb*
To distribute (money) as payment : expend, give, lay out, outlay, pay (out), spend. *Informal:* fork out (*or* over *or* up), shell out. *See* SAVE.

disbursement *noun*
Something expended to obtain a benefit or desired result : cost, expenditure, expense, outlay. *See* TRANSACTIONS.

disc *noun* See **disk.**

discard *verb*
To let go or get rid of as being useless or defective, for example : dispose of, dump, junk, scrap[1], throw away, throw out. *Informal:* chuck, jettison, shuck (off). *Slang:* ditch. *See* KEEP.

discarnate *adjective*
Having no body, form, or substance : bodiless, disembodied, immaterial, incorporeal, insubstantial, metaphysical, nonphysical, spiritual, unbodied, uncorporal, unsubstantial. *See* BODY.

discern *verb*
1. To perceive and fix the identity of, especially with difficulty : descry, distinguish, make out, pick out, spot. *See* SEE. **2.** To perceive, especially barely or fleetingly : catch, descry, detect, espy, glimpse, spot, spy. *See* SEE. **3.** To perceive with a special effort of the senses or the mind : descry, detect, distinguish, mark, mind, note, notice, observe, remark, see. *See* KNOWLEDGE, SEE. **4.** To recognize as being different : differentiate, discriminate, distinguish, know, separate, tell. *See* SAME.

discernible *adjective*
1. Capable of being seen : perceivable, perceptible, seeable, viewable, visible, visual. *See* SEE.

2. Capable of being noticed or apprehended mentally : appreciable, detectable, distinguishable, noticeable, observable, palpable, perceivable, perceptible, ponderable, sensible. *See* KNOWLEDGE.

discerning *adjective*
Characterized by careful and exact evaluation : critical, discriminating. *See* CAREFUL, VALUE.

discernment *noun*
Skill in perceiving, discriminating, or judging : acumen, astuteness, clear-sightedness, discrimination, eye, keenness, nose, penetration, perceptiveness, percipience, percipiency, perspicacity, sagacity, sageness, shrewdness, wit. *See* ABILITY, CAREFUL.

discharge *verb*
1. To remove the cargo or load from : disburden, dump, unlade, unload. *See* PUT IN. **2.** To set at liberty : emancipate, free, liberate, loose, manumit, release. *Slang:* spring. ***Idiom:*** let loose. *See* FREE. **3.** To release from military duty : demobilize, muster out, separate. *See* FREE, KEEP. **4.** To free from an obligation or duty : absolve, dispense, excuse, exempt, let off, relieve, spare. *See* FREE. **5.** To pass or pour out : empty, flow, issue. *See* ENTER. **6.** To end the employment or service of : cashier, dismiss, drop, release, terminate. *Informal:* ax, fire, pink-slip. *Slang:* boot[1], bounce, can, sack[1]. ***Idioms:*** give someone his or her walking papers, give someone the ax, give someone the gate, give someone the pink slip, let go, show someone the door. *See* KEEP. **7.** To carry out the functions, requirements, or terms of : do, execute, exercise, fulfill, implement, keep, perform. ***Idiom:*** live up to. *See* DO. **8.** To set right by giving what is due : clear, liquidate, pay (off *or* up), satisfy, settle, square. *See* PAY.

discharge *noun* **1.** The act of beginning and carrying through to completion : effectuation, execution, performance, prosecution. *See* DO. **2.** The act of dismissing or the condition of being dismissed from employment : dismissal, termination. *Informal:* ax. *Slang:* boot[1], bounce, sack[1]. *See* KEEP.

disciple *noun*
One who supports and adheres to another : adherent, cohort, follower, henchman, minion, partisan, satellite, supporter. *See* OVER, PRECEDE.

disciplinary *adjective*
Inflicting or aiming to inflict punishment : punishing, punitive, punitory. *See* REWARD.

discipline *noun*
1. Something, such as loss, pain, or confinement, imposed for wrongdoing : castigation, chastisement, correction, penalty, punishment. *See* REWARD. **2.** An area of academic study that is part of a larger body of learning : branch, specialty. *See* PART.

discipline *verb* **1.** To impart knowledge and skill to : coach, educate, instruct, school, teach, train, tutor. *See* TEACH. **2.** To subject (one) to a penalty for a wrong : castigate, chastise, correct, penalize, punish. *See* REWARD.

disclaim *verb*
To refuse to recognize or acknowledge : deny, disacknowledge, disavow, disown, reject, renounce, repudiate. ***Idiom:*** turn one's back on. *See* ACCEPT.

disclaimer *noun*
A refusal to grant the truth of a statement or charge : contradiction, denial, disaffirmance, disaffirmation, negation, rejection. *Law:* traversal. *See* AFFIRM.

disclose *verb*
1. To make visible; bring to view : bare, display, expose, reveal, show, unclothe, uncover, unmask, unveil. *Archaic:* discover. ***Idioms:*** bring to light, lay open, make plain. *See* SHOW. **2.** To make known : break, carry, communicate, convey, get across, impart, pass, report, tell, transmit. *See* KNOWLEDGE.

disclosure *noun*
Something disclosed, especially something not previously known or realized : apocalypse, exposé, exposure, revelation. *Informal:* eye opener. *See* SHOW.

discolor *verb*
To soil with foreign matter : bestain, smut, stain. *See* CLEAN, MARKS.

discombobulate *verb*
To cause to be unclear in mind or intent : addle, befuddle, bewilder, confound, confuse, dizzy, fuddle, jumble, mix up, muddle, mystify, perplex, puzzle. *Informal:* throw. ***Idiom:*** make one's head reel (*or* swim *or* whirl). *See* CLEAR, FEELINGS.

discombobulation *noun*
A stunned or bewildered condition : befuddlement, bewilderedness, bewilderment, daze, fog, muddle, mystification, perplexity, puzzlement, stupefaction, stupor, trance. *See* AWARENESS.

discomfit *verb*
To cause (a person) to be self-consciously distressed : abash, chagrin, confound, confuse, discomfort, disconcert, discountenance, embarrass, faze, mortify. ***Idioms:*** put on the spot, throw for a loop. *See* PAIN.

discomfiture *noun*
Self-conscious distress : abashment, chagrin, confusion, discomposure, embarrassment. *See* PAIN.

discomfort *noun*
1. The state or quality of being inconvenient : incommodiousness, incommodity, inconvenience, trouble. *See* COMFORT. **2.** Something that causes difficulty, trouble, or lack of ease : incommodity, inconvenience. *See* COMFORT.
discomfort *verb* **1.** To cause inconvenience for : discommode, incommode, inconvenience, put out, trouble. *See* COMFORT. **2.** To cause (a person) to be self-consciously distressed : abash, chagrin, confound, confuse, discomfit, disconcert, discountenance, embarrass, faze, mortify. ***Idioms:*** put on the spot, throw for a loop. *See* PAIN.

discommode *verb*
To cause inconvenience for : discomfort, incommode, inconvenience, put out, trouble. *See* COMFORT.

discompose *verb*
To impair or destroy the composure of : agitate, bother, disquiet, distract, disturb, flurry, fluster, perturb, rock, ruffle, shake (up), toss, unsettle, upset. *Informal:* rattle. *See* CALM.

discomposure *noun*
Self-conscious distress : abashment, chagrin, confusion, discomfiture, embarrassment. *See* PAIN.

disconcert *verb*
To cause (a person) to be self-consciously distressed : abash, chagrin, confound, confuse, discomfit, discomfort, discountenance, embarrass, faze, mortify. ***Idioms:*** put on the spot, throw for a loop. *See* PAIN.

disconnect *verb*
To separate one thing from another thing : detach, disengage, uncouple. *See* ASSEMBLE.

disconnection *noun*
The act or process of detaching : detachment, disengagement, separation, uncoupling. *See* ASSEMBLE.

discontent *noun*
Unhappiness caused by the failure of one's hopes, desires, or expectations : disappointment, discontentment, disgruntlement, dissatisfaction, letdown, regret. *See* HAPPY.
discontent *verb* To cause unhappiness by failing to satisfy the hopes, desires, or expectations of : disappoint, disgruntle, dissatisfy, let down. *See* HAPPY.

discontentment *noun*
Unhappiness caused by the failure of one's hopes, desires, or expectations : disappointment, discontent, disgruntlement, dissatisfaction, letdown, regret. *See* HAPPY.

discontinuance *noun*
1. The act of stopping : cessation, check, cut-off, discontinuation, halt[1], stay[1], stop, stoppage, surcease. *See* CONTINUE. **2.** The condition of being stopped : cessation, discontinuation, halt[1], standstill, stop, stoppage, surcease. *See* CONTINUE. **3.** A cessation of continuity or regularity : break, discontinuation, discontinuity, disruption, interruption, pause, suspension. *See* CONTINUE.

discontinuation *noun*
1. The act of stopping : cessation, check, cut-off, discontinuance, halt[1], stay[1], stop, stoppage, surcease. *See* CONTINUE. **2.** The condition of being stopped : cessation, discontinuance, halt[1], standstill, stop, stoppage, surcease. *See* CONTINUE. **3.** A cessation of continuity or regularity : break, discontinuance, discontinuity, disruption, interruption, pause, suspension. *See* CONTINUE.

discontinue *verb*
1. To prevent the occurrence or continuation of a movement, action, or operation : arrest, belay, cease, check, halt[1], stall[1], stay[1], stop, surcease. ***Idioms:*** bring to a standstill, call a halt to, put a stop to. *See* CONTINUE. **2.** To stop suddenly, as a conversation, activity, or relationship : break off, cease, interrupt, suspend, terminate. *See* CONTINUE. **3.** To come to a cessation : arrest, belay, cease, check, halt[1], leave off, quit, stall[1], stop, surcease. ***Idiom:*** come to a halt (*or* standstill *or* stop). *See* CONTINUE.
4. To cease trying to accomplish or continue : abandon, break off, desist, give up, leave off, quit, relinquish, remit, stop. *Informal:* swear off. *Slang:* lay off. ***Idioms:*** call it a day, call it quits, hang up one's fiddle, have done with, throw in the towel. *See* CONTINUE.

discontinuity *noun*
A cessation of continuity or regularity : break, discontinuance, discontinuation, disruption, interruption, pause, suspension. *See* CONTINUE.

discord *noun*
A state of disagreement and disharmony : clash, conflict, confrontation, contention, difference, difficulty, disaccord, discordance, dissension, dissent, dissentience, dissidence, dissonance, faction, friction, inharmony, schism, strife, variance, war, warfare. *See* CONFLICT.
discord *verb* **1.** To fail to be in accord : clash, conflict, contradict, disaccord, jar. ***Idiom:*** go (*or* run) counter to. *See* AGREE. **2.** To be of

different opinion : differ, disaccord, disagree, dissent, vary. ***Idiom:*** join (*or* take) issue. *See* AGREE.

discordance *noun*
A state of disagreement and disharmony : clash, conflict, confrontation, contention, difference, difficulty, disaccord, discord, dissension, dissent, dissentience, dissidence, dissonance, faction, friction, inharmony, schism, strife, variance, war, warfare. *See* CONFLICT.

discordant *adjective*
1. Devoid of harmony and accord : inconsonant, inharmonious, uncongenial, unharmonious. *See* AGREE. **2.** Made up of parts or qualities that are disparate or otherwise markedly lacking in consistency : discrepant, dissonant, incompatible, incongruent, incongruous, inconsistent. *See* AGREE. **3.** Characterized by unpleasant discordance of sound : cacophonous, disharmonious, dissonant, inharmonic, inharmonious, rude, unharmonious, unmusical. *See* AGREE, SOUNDS.

discount *verb*
1. To take away (a quantity) from another quantity : abate, deduct, rebate, subtract, take (off). *Informal:* knock off. *See* INCREASE. **2.** To think, represent, or speak of as small or unimportant : belittle, decry, denigrate, deprecate, depreciate, derogate, detract, disparage, downgrade, minimize, run down, slight, talk down. ***Idiom:*** make light (*or* little) of. *See* ATTACK, SHOW.

discount *noun* An amount deducted : abatement, deduction, rebate, reduction. *See* INCREASE.

discountenance *verb*
1. To have or express an unfavorable opinion of : deprecate, disapprove, disesteem, disfavor, frown on (*or* upon), object. ***Idioms:*** hold no brief for, not go for, take a dim view of, take exception to. *See* LIKE. **2.** To cause (a person) to be self-consciously distressed : abash, chagrin, confound, confuse, discomfit, discomfort, disconcert, embarrass, faze, mortify. ***Idioms:*** put on the spot, throw for a loop. *See* PAIN.

discourage *verb*
1. To make less hopeful or enthusiastic : dishearten, dispirit. *See* HELP. **2.** To persuade (a person) not to do something : deter, dissuade, divert. ***Idiom:*** talk out of. *See* PERSUASION.

discourse *noun*
1. The faculty, act, or product of speaking : speech, talk, utterance, verbalization, vocalization. *See* WORDS. **2.** Spoken exchange : chat, colloquy, confabulation, conversation, converse[1], dialogue, speech, talk. *Informal:* confab. *Slang:* jaw. *See* WORDS. **3.** A formal, lengthy exposition of a topic : disquisition, dissertation, treatise. *See* WORDS.

discourse *verb* To engage in spoken exchange : chat, confabulate, converse[1], speak, talk. *Informal:* confab, visit. *See* WORDS.

discourser *noun*
One given to conversation : confabulator, conversationalist, conversationist, talker. *See* WORDS.

discourteous *adjective*
Lacking good manners : disrespectful, ill-bred, ill-mannered, impolite, rude, uncivil, ungracious, unmannerly, unpolished. *See* COURTESY.

discourtesy *noun*
The state or quality of being impudent or arrogantly self-confident : assumption, audaciousness, audacity, boldness, brashness, brazenness, cheek, cheekiness, chutzpah, disrespect, effrontery, face, familiarity, forwardness, gall[1], impertinence, impudence, impudency, incivility, insolence, nerve, nerviness, overconfidence, pertness, presumptuousness, pushiness, rudeness, sassiness, sauciness. *Informal:* brass, crust, sauce, uppishness, uppityness. *See* ATTITUDE, COURTESY.

discover *verb*
1. To obtain knowledge or awareness of something not known before, as through observation or study : ascertain, determine, find (out), hear, learn. *See* TEACH. **2.** *Archaic.* To make visible; bring to view : bare, disclose, display, expose, reveal, show, unclothe, uncover, unmask, unveil. ***Idioms:*** bring to light, lay open, make plain. *See* SHOW. **3.** *Archaic.* To disclose in a breach of confidence : betray, blab, divulge, expose, give away, let out, reveal, tell, uncover, unveil. *Informal:* spill. ***Idioms:*** let slip, let the cat out of the bag, spill the beans, tell all. *See* SHOW.

discovery *noun*
Something that has been discovered : ascertainment, find, finding, strike. *See* TEACH.

discredit *verb*
1. To damage in reputation : disgrace, dishonor, shame. ***Idiom:*** be a reproach to. *See* RESPECT. **2.** To cause to be no longer believed or valued : debunk, deflate, explode, puncture. *Informal:* shoot down. ***Idioms:*** knock the bottom out of, shoot full of holes. *See* VALUE. **3.** To prove or show to be false : belie, confute, disprove, rebut, refute. *See* AFFIRM. **4.** To give

no credence to : disbelieve. *Idiom:* take no stock in. *See* BELIEF.

discredit *noun* **1.** Loss of or damage to one's reputation : bad name, bad odor, disgrace, dishonor, disrepute, humiliation, ignominy, ill repute, obloquy, odium, opprobrium, shame. *See* RESPECT. **2.** The refusal or reluctance to believe : disbelief, incredulity, incredulousness, unbelief. *See* BELIEF.

discreditable *adjective*
Meriting or causing shame or dishonor : disgraceful, dishonorable, disreputable, ignominious, opprobrious, shameful. *See* RESPECT.

discreet *adjective*
1. Showing sensitivity and skill in dealing with others : delicate, diplomatic, politic, sensitive, tactful. *See* ABILITY. **2.** Kept within sensible limits : conservative, moderate, reasonable, restrained, temperate. *See* PLAIN, RESTRAINT.

discrepance *noun*
1. The condition of being unlike or dissimilar : difference, discrepancy, disparity, dissimilarity, dissimilitude, distinction, divarication, divergence, divergency, unlikeness. *See* SAME. **2.** A marked lack of correspondence or agreement : difference, disagreement, discrepancy, disparity, gap, incompatibility, incongruity, inconsistency. *See* AGREE.

discrepancy *noun*
1. The condition of being unlike or dissimilar : difference, discrepance, disparity, dissimilarity, dissimilitude, distinction, divarication, divergence, divergency, unlikeness. *See* SAME. **2.** A marked lack of correspondence or agreement : difference, disagreement, discrepance, disparity, gap, incompatibility, incongruity, inconsistency. *See* AGREE.

discrepant *adjective*
1. In sharp opposition : incompatible, incongruent, incongruous, inconsistent. *Logic:* repugnant. *See* AGREE. **2.** Made up of parts or qualities that are disparate or otherwise markedly lacking in consistency : discordant, dissonant, incompatible, incongruent, incongruous, inconsistent. *See* AGREE.

discrete *adjective*
1. Distinguished from others by nature or qualities : distinct, separate, several, various. *See* SAME. **2.** Being or related to a distinct entity : individual, particular, separate, single, singular. *See* INCLUDE.

discretely *adverb*
As a separate unit : apart, independently, individually, separately, singly. *Idioms:* one at a time, one by one. *See* INCLUDE.

discreteness *noun*
The quality of being individual : distinctiveness, individuality, particularity, separateness, singularity. *See* INCLUDE.

discretion *noun*
1. The exercise of good judgment or common sense in practical matters : caution, circumspection, forehandedness, foresight, foresightedness, forethought, forethoughtfulness, precaution, prudence. *See* CAREFUL.
2. Unrestricted freedom to choose : pleasure, will. *See* FREE.

discretionary *adjective*
1. Based on individual judgment or discretion : arbitrary, judgmental, personal, subjective. *See* OPINION, SURPRISE. **2.** Not compulsory or automatic : elective, facultative, optional. *See* CHOICE.

discriminate *verb*
1. To recognize as being different : differentiate, discern, distinguish, know, separate, tell. *See* SAME. **2.** To make noticeable or different : characterize, differentiate, distinguish, individualize, mark, set apart, signalize, singularize. *See* SAME.

discriminate *adjective* Able to recognize small differences or draw fine distinctions : discriminating, discriminative, discriminatory, select, selective. *See* PRECISE.

discriminating *adjective*
1. Able to recognize small differences or draw fine distinctions : discriminate, discriminative, discriminatory, select, selective. *See* PRECISE.
2. Characterized by careful and exact evaluation : critical, discerning. *See* CAREFUL, VALUE.

discrimination *noun*
1. The act or an instance of distinguishing : differentiation, distinction, separation. *See* SAME.
2. The ability to distinguish, especially to recognize small differences : refinement, selectiveness, selectivity. *See* PRECISE. **3.** Skill in perceiving, discriminating, or judging : acumen, astuteness, clear-sightedness, discernment, eye, keenness, nose, penetration, perceptiveness, percipience, percipiency, perspicacity, sagacity, sageness, shrewdness, wit. *See* ABILITY, CAREFUL.

discriminative *adjective*
Able to recognize small differences or draw fine distinctions : discriminate, discriminating, discriminatory, select, selective. *See* PRECISE.

discriminatory *adjective*
Able to recognize small differences or draw fine distinctions : discriminate, discriminating,

discriminative, select, selective. *See* PRECISE.

discursive *adjective*
Marked by or given to digression : digressive, excursive, parenthetic, parenthetical, rambling, tangential. *See* APPROACH.

discuss *verb*
To speak together and exchange ideas and opinions about : bandy (about), moot, talk over, thrash out (*or* over), thresh out (*or* over), toss around. *Informal:* hash (over), kick around, knock about (*or* around). *Slang:* rap³. *Idiom:* go into a huddle. *See* WORDS.

discussant *noun*
One who participates in a conference : conferee, discusser. *See* MEET, WORDS.

discusser *noun*
One who participates in a conference : conferee, discussant. *See* MEET, WORDS.

discussion *noun*
1. An exchanging of views : conference, ventilation. *Slang:* rap³. *See* WORDS. 2. A meeting for the exchange of views : colloquium, conference, parley, seminar. *Informal:* powwow. *Slang:* rap session. *See* MEET, WORDS.

disdain *verb*
To regard with utter contempt and disdain : contemn, despise, scorn, scout². *Idioms:* have no use for, look down on (*or* upon). *See* RESPECT.

disdain *noun* The feeling of despising : contempt, despisal, despite, scorn. *See* RESPECT.

disdainful *adjective*
Showing scorn and disrespect toward (someone or something) : contemptuous, scornful. *Idiom:* on one's high horse. *See* RESPECT.

disease *noun*
A pathological condition of mind or body : ailment, complaint, disorder, ill, illness, infirmity, malady, sickness. *See* HEALTH.

disembark *verb*
To come ashore from a seacraft : debark, land. *See* MOVE.

disembarrass *verb*
To free from or cast out something objectionable or undesirable : clear, disburden, disencumber, release, relieve, rid, shake off, throw off, unburden. *Slang:* shake. *See* KEEP.

disembodied *adjective*
Having no body, form, or substance : bodiless, discarnate, immaterial, incorporeal, insubstantial, metaphysical, nonphysical, spiritual, unbodied, uncorporal, unsubstantial. *See* BODY.

disencumber *verb*
To free from or cast out something objectionable or undesirable : clear, disburden, disembarrass, release, relieve, rid, shake off, throw off, unburden. *Slang:* shake. *See* KEEP.

disengage *verb*
1. To free from ties or fasteners : loose, loosen, slip, unbind, unclasp, undo, unfasten, unloose, unloosen, untie. *See* TIGHTEN. 2. To separate one thing from another thing : detach, disconnect, uncouple. *See* ASSEMBLE. 3. To remove from association with : abstract, detach, disassociate, dissociate, withdraw. *See* ASSEMBLE. 4. To free from an entanglement : clear, disentangle, disinvolve, extricate, untangle. *See* FREE.

disengagement *noun*
The act or process of detaching : detachment, disconnection, separation, uncoupling. *See* ASSEMBLE.

disentangle *verb*
To free from an entanglement : clear, disengage, disinvolve, extricate, untangle. *See* FREE.

disesteem *verb*
To have or express an unfavorable opinion of : deprecate, disapprove, discountenance, disfavor, frown on (*or* upon), object. *Idioms:* hold no brief for, not go for, take a dim view of, take exception to. *See* LIKE.

disesteem *noun* Unfavorable opinion or judgment : disapprobation, disapproval, disfavor, displeasure. *See* LIKE.

disfavor *noun*
Unfavorable opinion or judgment : disapprobation, disapproval, disesteem, displeasure. *See* LIKE.

disfavor *verb* To have or express an unfavorable opinion of : deprecate, disapprove, discountenance, disesteem, frown on (*or* upon), object. *Idioms:* hold no brief for, not go for, take a dim view of, take exception to. *See* LIKE.

disfigure *verb*
To alter and spoil the natural form or appearance of : contort, deform, distort, misshape, twist. *See* BEAUTIFUL.

disfigurement *noun*
A disfiguring abnormality of shape or form : deformity, malformation. *See* BEAUTIFUL.

disgorge *verb*
To send forth (confined matter) violently : belch, eject, eruct, erupt, expel, spew. *Geology:* extravasate. *See* EXPLOSION.

disgrace *noun*
Loss of or damage to one's reputation : bad name, bad odor, discredit, dishonor, disrepute, humiliation, ignominy, ill repute, obloquy,

odium, opprobrium, shame. *See* RESPECT.

disgrace *verb* To damage in reputation : discredit, dishonor, shame. ***Idiom:*** be a reproach to. *See* RESPECT.

disgraceful *adjective*
1. Meriting or causing shame or dishonor : discreditable, dishonorable, disreputable, ignominious, opprobrious, shameful. *See* RESPECT.
2. Worthy of severe disapproval : condemnable, deplorable, shameful, unfortunate. *See* GOOD.

disgracefulness *noun*
The condition of being infamous : dishonorableness, disreputability, disreputableness, ignominiousness, infamy, shamefulness. *See* GOOD, RESPECT, RIGHT.

disgruntle *verb*
To cause unhappiness by failing to satisfy the hopes, desires, or expectations of : disappoint, discontent, dissatisfy, let down. *See* HAPPY.

disgruntlement *noun*
Unhappiness caused by the failure of one's hopes, desires, or expectations : disappointment, discontent, discontentment, dissatisfaction, letdown, regret. *See* HAPPY.

disguise *verb*
To change or modify so as to prevent recognition of the true identity or character of : camouflage, dissemble, dissimulate, mask, masquerade. *See* SHOW.

disguise *noun* **1.** Clothes or other personal effects, such as makeup, worn to conceal one's identity : costume. *See* SHOW. **2.** A deceptive outward appearance : cloak, color, coloring, cover, disguisement, façade, face, false colors, front, gloss, guise, mask, masquerade, pretense, pretext, semblance, show, veil, veneer, window-dressing. *Slang:* put-on. *See* SHOW. **3.** A display of insincere behavior : act, acting, dissemblance, masquerade, pretense, sham, show, simulation. *See* HONEST, TRUE.

disguisement *noun*
A deceptive outward appearance : cloak, color, coloring, cover, disguise, façade, face, false colors, front, gloss, guise, mask, masquerade, pretense, pretext, semblance, show, veil, veneer, window-dressing. *Slang:* put-on. *See* SHOW.

disgust *verb*
To offend the senses or feelings of : nauseate, repel, revolt, sicken. ***Idiom:*** turn one's stomach. *See* LIKE.

disgust *noun* Extreme repugnance excited by something offensive : nausea. *See* LIKE.

disgusted *adjective*
Out of patience with : fed up, sick, tired, weary. ***Idiom:*** sick and tired.
See TIRED.

disgusting *adjective*
1. Extremely unpleasant to the senses or feelings : atrocious, foul, horrid, nasty, nauseating, offensive, repellent, repulsive, revolting, sickening, ugly, unwholesome, vile. *See* LIKE, PAIN. **2.** So objectionable as to elicit despisal or deserve condemnation : abhorrent, abominable, antipathetic, contemptible, despicable, despisable, detestable, filthy, foul, infamous, loathsome, lousy, low, mean[2], nasty, nefarious, obnoxious, odious, repugnant, rotten, shabby, vile, wretched. *See* GOOD.

disharmonious *adjective*
Characterized by unpleasant discordance of sound : cacophonous, discordant, dissonant, inharmonic, inharmonious, rude, unharmonious, unmusical. *See* AGREE, SOUNDS.

dishearten *verb*
To make less hopeful or enthusiastic : discourage, dispirit. *See* HELP.

dishevel *verb*
To put (the hair or clothes) into a state of disarray : disarrange, disorder, mess (up), muss (up), rumple, tousle. *See* ORDER.

disheveled *adjective*
Marked by an absence of cleanliness and order : messy, mussy, slipshod, sloppy, slovenly, unkempt, untidy. *See* ORDER.

dishonest *adjective*
1. Given to or marked by deliberate concealment or misrepresentation of the truth : deceitful, lying, mendacious, untruthful. *See* HONEST. **2.** Marked by dishonesty, especially in matters of public trust : corrupt, venal. *Informal:* crooked. *See* HONEST.

dishonesty *noun*
1. Lack of integrity : improbity. *See* HONEST.
2. Departure from what is legally, ethically, and morally correct : corruption, corruptness, improbity. *Informal:* crookedness. *See* HONEST.
3. Lack of straightforwardness and honesty in action : chicanery, craft, craftiness, deviousness, indirection, shadiness, shiftiness, slyness, sneakiness, trickery, trickiness, underhandedness. *See* HONEST.

dishonor *noun*
Loss of or damage to one's reputation : bad name, bad odor, discredit, disgrace, disrepute, humiliation, ignominy, ill repute, obloquy, odium, opprobrium, shame. *See* RESPECT.

dishonor *verb* To damage in reputation : discredit, disgrace, shame. ***Idiom:*** be a reproach to. *See* RESPECT.

dishonorable *adjective*
Meriting or causing shame or dishonor : discreditable, disgraceful, disreputable, ignominious, opprobrious, shameful. *See* RESPECT.

dishonorableness *noun*
The condition of being infamous : disgracefulness, disreputability, disreputableness, ignominiousness, infamy, shamefulness. *See* GOOD, RESPECT, RIGHT.

disinclination *noun*
1. An attitude or feeling of aversion : dislike, disrelish, distaste, mislike. *See* LIKE. **2.** The state of not being disposed or inclined : averseness, indisposition, reluctance, unwillingness. *See* WILLING.

disinclined *adjective*
Not inclined or willing to do or undertake : averse, indisposed, loath, reluctant, unwilling. *See* WILLING.

disinfect *verb*
To render free of microorganisms : decontaminate, sanitize, sterilize. *See* CLEAN.

disingenuous *adjective*
1. Not being what one purports to be : ambidextrous, insincere, left-handed, mala fide. *See* HONEST. **2.** Marked by treachery or deceit : devious, duplicitous, guileful, indirect, lubricious, shifty, sneaky, underhand, underhanded. *See* HONEST.

disingenuousness *noun*
Lack of sincerity : ambidexterity, artificiality, insincerity, phoniness. *See* HONEST.

disintegrate *verb*
1. To reduce or become reduced to pieces or components : break down, break up, crumble, decompose, dissolve, fragment, fragmentize. *See* CONTINUE, HELP. **2.** To become or cause to become rotten or unsound : break down, decay, decompose, deteriorate, molder, putrefy, rot, spoil, taint, turn. ***Idioms:*** go bad, go to pot, go to seed. *See* BETTER, THRIVE.

disintegration *noun*
The condition of being decayed : breakdown, decay, decomposition, deterioration, putrefaction, putrescence, putridness, rot, rottenness, spoilage. *See* BETTER, THRIVE.

disinterest *noun*
1. The quality or state of being just and unbiased : detachment, disinterestedness, dispassion, dispassionateness, equitableness, fair-mindedness, fairness, impartiality, impartialness, justice, justness, nonpartisanship, objectiveness, objectivity. *See* FAIR. **2.** Lack of emotion or interest : apathy, impassivity, incuriosity, incuriousness, indifference, insensibility, insensibleness, lassitude, lethargy, listlessness, phlegm, stolidity, stolidness, unconcern, uninterest, unresponsiveness. *See* FEELINGS.

disinterested *adjective*
1. Free from bias in judgment : dispassionate, equitable, fair, fair-minded, impartial, indifferent, just, nonpartisan, objective, square, unbiased, unprejudiced. ***Idiom:*** fair and square. *See* FAIR. **2.** Feeling or showing no strong emotional involvement : detached, dispassionate, impersonal, indifferent, neutral. *See* FEELINGS. **3.** Lacking interest in one's surroundings or worldly affairs : aloof, detached, incurious, indifferent, unconcerned, uninterested, uninvolved. *See* ATTITUDE, CONCERN.

disinterestedness *noun*
The quality or state of being just and unbiased : detachment, disinterest, dispassion, dispassionateness, equitableness, fair-mindedness, fairness, impartiality, impartialness, justice, justness, nonpartisanship, objectiveness, objectivity. *See* FAIR.

disinvolve *verb*
To free from an entanglement : clear, disengage, disentangle, extricate, untangle. *See* FREE.

disjoin *verb*
To become or cause to become apart one from another : break, detach, disjoint, disunite, divide, divorce, part, separate, split (up). ***Idioms:*** part company, set at odds. *See* ASSEMBLE.

disjoint *verb*
To become or cause to become apart one from another : break, detach, disjoin, disunite, divide, divorce, part, separate, split (up). ***Idioms:*** part company, set at odds. *See* ASSEMBLE.

disjunction *noun*
The act or an instance of separating one thing from another : detachment, disjuncture, disseverance, disseverment, disunion, division, divorce, divorcement, parting, partition, separation, severance, split. *See* ASSEMBLE, PART.

disjuncture *noun*
The act or an instance of separating one thing from another : detachment, disjunction, disseverance, disseverment, disunion, division, divorce, divorcement, parting, partition, separation, severance, split. *See* ASSEMBLE, PART.

disk also **disc** *noun*
A closed plane curve everywhere equidistant from a fixed point or something shaped like

this : band[1], circle, circuit, gyre, ring[1], wheel. *Archaic:* orb. *See* GEOMETRY.

dislike *verb*
To have a feeling of aversion for : disrelish, mislike. *Archaic:* distaste. ***Idiom:*** have no use for. *See* LIKE.

dislike *noun* An attitude or feeling of aversion : disinclination, disrelish, distaste, mislike. *See* LIKE.

dislocate *verb*
1. To alter the settled state or position of : displace, disturb, move, shake, shift. *See* MOVE. **2.** To displace (a bone) from a socket or joint : slip, throw out. ***Idiom:*** throw out of joint. *See* HELP.

dislocation *noun*
A change in normal place or position : displacement, disturbance, move, movement, rearrangement, shift. *See* MOVE.

disloyal *adjective*
Not true to duty or obligation : faithless, false, false-hearted, perfidious, recreant, traitorous, treacherous, unfaithful, untrue. *See* CONTINUE, TRUST.

disloyalty *noun*
Betrayal, especially of a moral obligation : faithlessness, false-heartedness, falseness, falsity, infidelity, perfidiousness, perfidy, traitorousness, treacherousness, treachery, unfaithfulness. *See* CONTINUE, TRUST.

dismal *adjective*
1. Tending to cause sadness or low spirits : blue, cheerless, depressing, dispiriting, gloomy, joyless, melancholy, sad. *See* HAPPY. **2.** Dark and depressing : black, bleak, blue, cheerless, dark, desolate, dreary, gloomy, glum, joyless, somber, tenebrific. *See* HAPPY, LIGHT. **3.** Marked by little hopefulness : dark, gloomy, pessimistic. *See* HAPPY, HOPE.

dismantle *verb*
1. To take (something) apart : break down, disassemble, dismount, take down. *See* ASSEMBLE. **2.** To pull down or break up so that reconstruction is impossible : demolish, destroy, dynamite, knock down, level, pull down, pulverize, raze, tear down, wreck. *Aerospace:* destruct. *See* HELP.

dismay *verb*
To deprive of courage or the power to act as a result of fear, anxiety, or disgust : appall, consternate, daunt, horrify, shake, shock[1]. *See* FEAR.

dismay *noun* A sudden or complete loss of courage in the face of trouble or danger : consternation. *See* FEAR.

dismember *verb*
To deprive of a limb or bodily member or its use : cripple, maim, mutilate. *See* HELP.

dismiss *verb*
1. To end the employment or service of : cashier, discharge, drop, release, terminate. *Informal:* ax, fire, pink-slip. *Slang:* boot[1], bounce, can, sack[1]. ***Idioms:*** give someone his or her walking papers, give someone the ax, give someone the gate, give someone the pink slip, let go, show someone the door. *See* KEEP. **2.** To direct or allow to leave : send (away). ***Idioms:*** send about one's business, send packing, show someone the door. *See* KEEP. **3.** To put out by force : bump, eject, evict, expel, oust, throw out. *Informal:* chuck. *Slang:* boot[1] (out), bounce, kick out. ***Idioms:*** give someone the boot, give someone the heave-ho (*or* old heave-ho), send packing, show someone the door, throw out on one's ear. *See* KEEP. **4.** To cease consideration or treatment of : drop, give over, give up, skip. ***Idioms:*** have done with, wash one's hands of. *See* KEEP. **5.** To rid one's mind of : banish, cast out, dispel, shut out. *See* KEEP. **6.** To be unwilling to accept, consider, or receive : decline, refuse, reject, spurn, turn down. *Slang:* nix. ***Idiom:*** turn thumbs down on. *See* ACCEPT.

dismissal *noun*
1. The act of dismissing or the condition of being dismissed from employment : discharge, termination. *Informal:* ax. *Slang:* boot[1], bounce, sack[1]. *See* KEEP. **2.** The act of ejecting or the state of being ejected : ejection, ejectment, eviction, expulsion, ouster. *Slang:* boot[1], bounce. *See* KEEP.

dismount *verb*
To take (something) apart : break down, disassemble, dismantle, take down. *See* ASSEMBLE.

disobedience *noun*
The condition or practice of not obeying : insubordination, noncompliance. *See* RESIST.

disobedient *adjective*
Refusing or failing to obey : insubordinate, noncompliant. *See* RESIST.

disobey *verb*
To refuse or fail to obey : break, defy, flout, transgress, violate. ***Idiom:*** pay no attention to. *See* RESIST.

disorder *noun*
1. A lack of order or regular arrangement : chaos, clutter, confusedness, confusion, derangement, disarrangement, disarray, disorderedness, disorderliness, disorganization, jumble, mess, mix-up, muddle, muss, scramble,

topsy-turviness, tumble. *Slang:* snafu. *See* ORDER. **2.** A lack of civil order or peace : anarchy, lawlessness, misrule. *See* ORDER, PEACE. **3.** An interruption of regular procedure or of public peace : agitation, commotion, disturbance, helter-skelter, stir[1], tumult, turbulence, turmoil, uproar. *Informal:* flap, to-do. *See* CALM, ORDER. **4.** A pathological condition of mind or body : ailment, complaint, disease, ill, illness, infirmity, malady, sickness. *See* HEALTH. **5.** The condition of being sick : affliction, illness, indisposition, infirmity, sickness. *See* HEALTH.

disorder *verb* **1.** To put out of proper order : derange, disarrange, disarray, disorganize, disrupt, disturb, jumble, mess up, mix up, muddle, tumble, unsettle, upset. *See* ORDER. **2.** To put into total disorder : ball up, confuse, jumble, mess up, muddle, scramble, snarl[2]. *Slang:* snafu. ***Idiom:*** play havoc with. *See* ORDER. **3.** To put (the hair or clothes) into a state of disarray : disarrange, dishevel, mess (up), muss (up), rumple, tousle. *See* ORDER. **4.** To disturb the health or physiological functioning of : derange, turn, unsettle, upset. *See* HEALTH.

disordered *adjective*
1. Characterized by physical confusion : chaotic, confused, helter-skelter, higgledy-piggledy, topsy-turvy, upside-down. *Informal:* mixed-up. *See* ORDER. **2.** Afflicted with or exhibiting irrationality and mental unsoundness : brainsick, crazy, daft, demented, distraught, dotty, insane, lunatic, mad, maniac, maniacal, mentally ill, moonstruck, off, touched, unbalanced, unsound, wrong. *Informal:* bonkers, cracked, daffy, gaga, loony. *Slang:* bananas, batty, buggy, cuckoo, fruity, loco, nuts, nutty, screwy, wacky. *Chiefly British:* crackers. *Law:* non compos mentis. ***Idioms:*** around the bend, crazy as a loon, mad as a hatter, not all there, nutty as a fruitcake, off (*or* out of) one's head, off one's rocker, of unsound mind, out of one's mind, sick in the head, stark raving mad. *See* SANE.

disorderedness *noun*
A lack of order or regular arrangement : chaos, clutter, confusedness, confusion, derangement, disarrangement, disarray, disorder, disorderliness, disorganization, jumble, mess, mix-up, muddle, muss, scramble, topsy-turviness, tumble. *Slang:* snafu. *See* ORDER.

disordering *noun*
The act or an example of upsetting : disorganization, disruption, upset. *See* ORDER.

disorderliness *noun*
1. A lack of order or regular arrangement : chaos, clutter, confusedness, confusion, derangement, disarrangement, disarray, disorder, disorderedness, disorganization, jumble, mess, mix-up, muddle, muss, scramble, topsy-turviness, tumble. *Slang:* snafu. *See* ORDER. **2.** The state of being messy or unkempt : messiness, sloppiness, slovenliness, untidiness. *See* ORDER. **3.** The quality or condition of being unruly : fractiousness, indocility, intractability, intractableness, obstinacy, obstinateness, obstreperousness, recalcitrance, recalcitrancy, refractoriness, uncontrollability, uncontrollableness, ungovernableness, unmanageability, unruliness, untowardness, wildness. *See* CONTROL, ORDER, PEACE, RESIST.

disorderly *adjective*
1. Lacking regular or logical order : messy, unsystematic. *See* ORDER. **2.** Not submitting to discipline or control : fractious, indocile, intractable, lawless, obstinate, obstreperous, recalcitrant, refractory, uncontrollable, undisciplined, ungovernable, unmanageable, unruly, untoward, wild. ***Idiom:*** out of line. *See* CONTROL, ORDER, PEACE, RESIST. **3.** *Law.* Upsetting civil order or peace : riotous, rowdy. *See* PEACE.

disorganization *noun*
1. A lack of order or regular arrangement : chaos, clutter, confusedness, confusion, derangement, disarrangement, disarray, disorder, disorderedness, disorderliness, jumble, mess, mix-up, muddle, muss, scramble, topsy-turviness, tumble. *Slang:* snafu. *See* ORDER. **2.** The act or an example of upsetting : disordering, disruption, upset. *See* ORDER.

disorganize *verb*
To put out of proper order : derange, disarrange, disarray, disorder, disrupt, disturb, jumble, mess up, mix up, muddle, tumble, unsettle, upset. *See* ORDER.

disoriented *adjective*
Unable to find the correct way or place to go : astray, lost, stray. *See* SEEK.

disown *verb*
To refuse to recognize or acknowledge : deny, disacknowledge, disavow, disclaim, reject, renounce, repudiate. ***Idiom:*** turn one's back on. *See* ACCEPT.

disparage *verb*
To think, represent, or speak of as small or unimportant : belittle, decry, denigrate, deprecate, depreciate, derogate, detract, discount, downgrade, minimize, run down, slight, talk down. ***Idiom:*** make light (*or* little) of. *See* ATTACK, SHOW.

disparagement *noun*
The act or an instance of belittling : belittlement, denigration, deprecation, depreciation, derogation, detraction, minimization. *See* ATTACK, SHOW.

disparaging *adjective*
Tending or intending to belittle : deprecative, deprecatory, depreciative, depreciatory, derogative, derogatory, detractive, low, pejorative, slighting, uncomplimentary. *See* PRAISE.

disparate *adjective*
Not like another in nature, quality, amount, or form : different, dissimilar, divergent, diverse, unlike, variant, various. *See* SAME.

disparity *noun*
1. The condition or fact of being unequal, as in age, rank, or degree : disproportion, disproportionateness, inequality. *See* SAME. **2.** The condition of being unlike or dissimilar : difference, discrepance, discrepancy, dissimilarity, dissimilitude, distinction, divarication, divergence, divergency, unlikeness. *See* SAME. **3.** A marked lack of correspondence or agreement : difference, disagreement, discrepance, discrepancy, gap, incompatibility, incongruity, inconsistency. *See* AGREE.

dispassion *noun*
The quality or state of being just and unbiased : detachment, disinterest, disinterestedness, dispassionateness, equitableness, fair-mindedness, fairness, impartiality, impartialness, justice, justness, nonpartisanship, objectiveness, objectivity. *See* FAIR.

dispassionate *adjective*
1. Feeling or showing no strong emotional involvement : detached, disinterested, impersonal, indifferent, neutral. *See* FEELINGS.
2. Free from bias in judgment : disinterested, equitable, fair, fair-minded, impartial, indifferent, just, nonpartisan, objective, square, unbiased, unprejudiced. ***Idiom:*** fair and square. *See* FAIR.

dispassionateness *noun*
The quality or state of being just and unbiased : detachment, disinterest, disinterestedness, dispassion, equitableness, fair-mindedness, fairness, impartiality, impartialness, justice, justness, nonpartisanship, objectiveness, objectivity. *See* FAIR.

dispatch *verb*
1. To cause (something) to be conveyed to a destination : address, consign, forward, route, send, ship, transmit. *See* MOVE. **2.** To eat completely or entirely : consume, devour, eat up. *Informal:* polish off, put away. *See* INGESTION. **3.** To cause the death of : carry off, cut down, cut off, destroy, finish (off), kill[1], slay. *Slang:* waste, zap. ***Idioms:*** put an end to, put to sleep. *See* HELP.

dispatch *noun* Rapidness of movement or activity : celerity, expedition, expeditiousness, fleetness, haste, hurry, hustle, quickness, rapidity, rapidness, speed, speediness, swiftness. *See* FAST.

dispel *verb*
1. To rid one's mind of : banish, cast out, dismiss, shut out. *See* KEEP. **2.** To cause to separate and go in various directions : disperse, dissipate, scatter. *See* COLLECT.

dispensable *adjective*
Not necessary : inessential, needless, nonessential, uncalled-for, unessential, unnecessary, unneeded, unrequired. *See* NECESSARY.

dispensation *noun*
1. The act of distributing or the condition of being distributed : admeasurement, allocation, assignment, apportionment, distribution, division. *See* COLLECT. **2.** The giving of a medication, especially by prescribed dosage : administration, application. *See* GIVE.

dispense *verb*
1. To give out in portions or shares : deal (out), distribute, divide, dole out, parcel out, portion (out), ration (out), share. *Slang:* divvy. *See* COLLECT. **2.** To provide as a remedy : administer, apply, give. *See* GIVE. **3.** To oversee the provision or execution of : administer, administrate, carry out, execute. *See* OVER. **4.** To free from an obligation or duty : absolve, discharge, excuse, exempt, let off, relieve, spare. *See* FREE.

dispersal *noun*
The passing out or spreading about of something : circulation, dispersion, dissemination, distribution. *See* COLLECT.

disperse *verb*
1. To cause to separate and go in various directions : dispel, dissipate, scatter. *See* COLLECT.
2. To pass (something) out : circulate, disseminate, distribute, hand out. *See* COLLECT. **3.** To extend over a wide area : circulate, diffuse, disseminate, distribute, radiate, scatter, spread, strew. *See* MOVE, WIDE. **4.** To disappear by or as if by rising : dissipate, lift, scatter. *See* COLLECT, RISE.

dispersion *noun*
The passing out or spreading about of something : circulation, dispersal, dissemination, distribution. *See* COLLECT.

dispirit *verb*
1. To make less hopeful or enthusiastic :

discourage, dishearten. *See* HELP. **2.** To make sad or gloomy : deject, depress, oppress, sadden, weigh down. *See* HAPPY.

dispirited *adjective*
In low spirits : blue, dejected, depressed, desolate, down, downcast, downhearted, dull, dysphoric, gloomy, heavy-hearted, low, melancholic, melancholy, sad, spiritless, tristful, unhappy, wistful. ***Idiom:*** down at (*or* in) the mouth. *See* HAPPY.

dispiriting *adjective*
Tending to cause sadness or low spirits : blue, cheerless, depressing, dismal, gloomy, joyless, melancholy, sad. *See* HAPPY.

displace *verb*
1. To alter the settled state or position of : dislocate, disturb, move, shake, shift. *See* MOVE. **2.** To take the place of (another) against the other's will : cut out, supplant. *See* SUBSTITUTE.

displacement *noun*
A change in normal place or position : dislocation, disturbance, move, movement, rearrangement, shift. *See* MOVE.

display *verb*
1. To make visible; bring to view : bare, disclose, expose, reveal, show, unclothe, uncover, unmask, unveil. *Archaic:* discover. ***Idioms:*** bring to light, lay open, make plain. *See* SHOW. **2.** To make manifest or apparent : demonstrate, evidence, evince, exhibit, manifest, proclaim, reveal, show. *See* SHOW. **3.** To make a public and usually ostentatious show of : brandish, disport, exhibit, expose, flash, flaunt, parade, show (off), sport. *See* SHOW. **4.** To be endowed with as a visible characteristic or form : bear, carry, exhibit, have, possess. *See* SHOW. **5.** To give expression to, as by gestures, facial aspects, or bodily posture : communicate, convey, express, manifest. *See* SHOW.
display *noun* **1.** An act of showing or displaying : demonstration, exhibit, exhibition, manifestation, show. *See* SHOW. **2.** An impressive or ostentatious exhibition : array, panoply, parade, pomp, show, spectacle. *See* SHOW.

displease *verb*
To be very disagreeable to : offend. *Slang:* turn off. ***Idioms:*** give offense to, not set right (*or* well) with. *See* LIKE, PAIN.

displeasing *adjective*
Not pleasant or agreeable : bad, disagreeable, offensive, uncongenial, unpleasant, unsympathetic. *Informal:* icky. *Slang:* yucky. *See* GOOD, PAIN.

displeasure *noun*
Unfavorable opinion or judgment : disapprobation, disapproval, disesteem, disfavor. *See* LIKE.

disport *verb*
1. To occupy oneself with amusement or diversion : play, recreate, sport. *See* WORK. **2.** To make a public and usually ostentatious show of : brandish, display, exhibit, expose, flash, flaunt, parade, show (off), sport. *See* SHOW.
disport *noun* Activity engaged in for relaxation and amusement : diversion, fun, play, recreation, sport. *See* WORK.

disposal *noun*
1. A way or condition of being arranged : arrangement, categorization, classification, deployment, disposition, distribution, formation, grouping, layout, lineup, order, organization, placement, sequence. *See* ORDER. **2.** The act of getting rid of something useless or used up : dumping, elimination, jettison, riddance. *See* KEEP.

dispose *verb*
1. To put into a deliberate order : arrange, array, deploy, marshal, order, organize, range, sort, systematize. *See* ORDER. **2.** To have an impact on in a certain way : incline, influence, predispose, sway. *See* AFFECT, LIKE.
dispose of *verb* **1.** To put into correct or conclusive form : arrange, conclude, fix, settle. *See* DO. **2.** To let go or get rid of as being useless or defective, for example : discard, dump, junk, scrap[1], throw away, throw out. *Informal:* chuck, jettison, shuck (off). *Slang:* ditch. *See* KEEP.

disposed *adjective*
Having or showing a tendency or likelihood : apt, given, inclined, liable, likely, prone. *See* LIKELY.

dispose of *verb* See **dispose.**

disposition *noun*
1. A person's customary manner of emotional response : complexion, humor, nature, temper, temperament. *See* BE. **2.** The combination of emotional, intellectual, and moral qualities that distinguishes an individual : character, complexion, makeup, nature, personality. *See* BE. **3.** An inclination to something : bent, bias, cast, leaning, partiality, penchant, predilection, predisposition, proclivity, proneness, propensity, squint, tendency, trend, turn. *See* APPROACH, LIKE. **4.** A way or condition of being arranged : arrangement, categorization, classification, deployment, disposal, distribution, formation, grouping, layout, lineup, order, or-

ganization, placement, sequence. *See* ORDER.

dispossess *verb*
To take or keep something away from : deprive, divest, rob, strip[1]. *See* GIVE.

dispossession *noun*
The condition of being deprived of what one once had or ought to have : deprival, deprivation, divestiture, loss, privation. *See* GIVE, RICH.

disproportion *noun*
The condition or fact of being unequal, as in age, rank, or degree : disparity, disproportionateness, inequality. *See* SAME.

disproportionateness *noun*
The condition or fact of being unequal, as in age, rank, or degree : disparity, disproportion, inequality. *See* SAME.

disprove *verb*
To prove or show to be false : belie, confute, discredit, rebut, refute. *See* AFFIRM.

disputable *adjective*
In doubt or dispute : arguable, contested, debatable, doubtful, exceptionable, moot, mootable, problematic, problematical, questionable, uncertain. *See* CERTAIN.

disputation *noun*
The presentation of an argument or arguments : argumentation, debate, forensics. *See* AFFIRM, WORDS.

disputatious *adjective*
Given to arguing : argumentative, combative, contentious, eristic, litigious, polemic, polemical, quarrelsome, scrappy. *See* CONFLICT.

disputatiousness *noun*
The quality or state of being argumentative : argumentativeness, combativeness, contentiousness, litigiousness, scrappiness. *See* CONFLICT.

dispute *verb*
1. To put forth reasons for or against something, often excitedly : argue, contend, debate, moot. *See* AFFIRM, WORDS. **2.** To engage in a quarrel : argue, bicker, contend, fight, quarrel, quibble, spat, squabble, tiff, wrangle. *Informal:* hassle, tangle. ***Idioms:*** cross swords, have it out, have words, lock horns. *See* CONFLICT. **3.** To take a stand against : buck, challenge, contest, oppose, resist, traverse. *See* SUPPORT.

dispute *noun* A discussion, often heated, in which a difference of opinion is expressed : altercation, argument, bicker, clash, contention, controversy, debate, difficulty, disagreement, fight, polemic, quarrel, run-in, spat, squabble, tiff, word (used in plural), wrangle. *Informal:* hassle, rhubarb, tangle. *See* CONFLICT.

disqualify *verb*
To make incapable, as of doing a job : disable, unfit. *See* ABILITY.

disquiet *verb*
To impair or destroy the composure of : agitate, bother, discompose, distract, disturb, flurry, fluster, perturb, rock, ruffle, shake (up), toss, unsettle, upset. *Informal:* rattle. *See* CALM.

disquiet *noun* **1.** A troubled or anxious state of mind : angst, anxiety, anxiousness, care, concern, disquietude, distress, nervousness, solicitude, unease, uneasiness, worry. *See* FEELINGS. **2.** An uneasy or nervous state : disquietude, inquietude, restiveness, restlessness, unease, uneasiness, unrest. *See* CALM.

disquieting *adjective*
Troubling to the mind or emotions : disruptive, distressful, distressing, disturbing, intrusive, perturbing, troublesome, troublous, unsettling, upsetting, worrisome. *See* HAPPY, PAIN.

disquietude *noun*
1. A troubled or anxious state of mind : angst, anxiety, anxiousness, care, concern, disquiet, distress, nervousness, solicitude, unease, uneasiness, worry. *See* FEELINGS. **2.** An uneasy or nervous state : disquiet, inquietude, restiveness, restlessness, unease, uneasiness, unrest. *See* CALM.

disquisition *noun*
A formal, lengthy exposition of a topic : discourse, dissertation, treatise. *See* WORDS.

disregard *verb*
1. To refuse to pay attention to (a person); treat with contempt : ignore, neglect, slight. *Regional:* igg. *See* CONCERN, THOUGHTS. **2.** To pretend not to see : blink (at), connive at, ignore, pass over, wink at. ***Idioms:*** be blind to, close (*or* shut) one's eyes to, look the other way, turn a blind eye to. *See* SEE. **3.** To fail to care for or give proper attention to : ignore, neglect, slight. *See* CARE FOR, CONCERN. **4.** To avoid the fulfillment of : neglect, shirk, slack. ***Idiom:*** let slide. *See* DO.

disregard *noun* **1.** An act or instance of neglecting : neglect, oversight, slight. *See* CARE FOR, CONCERN. **2.** A lack of consideration for others' feelings : inconsiderateness, inconsideration, thoughtlessness, unthoughtfulness. *See* COURTESY.

disregardful *adjective*
Devoid of consideration for others' feelings : inconsiderate, thoughtless, unthinking, unthoughtful. *See* CAREFUL, COURTESY.

disrelish *verb*
To have a feeling of aversion for : dislike, mislike. *Archaic:* distaste. ***Idiom:*** have no use for. *See* LIKE.
disrelish *noun* An attitude or feeling of aversion : disinclination, dislike, distaste, mislike. *See* LIKE.

disremember *verb*
Informal. To fail to remember : forget. ***Idiom:*** draw a blank. *See* REMEMBER.

disreputability *noun*
The condition of being infamous : disgracefulness, dishonorableness, disreputableness, ignominiousness, infamy, shamefulness. *See* GOOD, RESPECT, RIGHT.

disreputable *adjective*
Meriting or causing shame or dishonor : discreditable, disgraceful, dishonorable, ignominious, opprobrious, shameful. *See* RESPECT.

disreputableness *noun*
The condition of being infamous : disgracefulness, dishonorableness, disreputability, ignominiousness, infamy, shamefulness. *See* GOOD, RESPECT, RIGHT.

disrepute *noun*
Loss of or damage to one's reputation : bad name, bad odor, discredit, disgrace, dishonor, humiliation, ignominy, ill repute, obloquy, odium, opprobrium, shame. *See* RESPECT.

disrespect *noun*
1. Lack of proper respect : irreverence, lese majesty. *See* RESPECT. **2.** The state or quality of being impudent or arrogantly self-confident : assumption, audaciousness, audacity, boldness, brashness, brazenness, cheek, cheekiness, chutzpah, discourtesy, effrontery, face, familiarity, forwardness, gall[1], impertinence, impudence, impudency, incivility, insolence, nerve, nerviness, overconfidence, pertness, presumptuousness, pushiness, rudeness, sassiness, sauciness. *Informal:* brass, crust, sauce, uppishness, uppityness. *See* ATTITUDE, COURTESY.

disrespectful *adjective*
1. Having or showing a lack of respect : irreverent. *See* RESPECT. **2.** Lacking good manners : discourteous, ill-bred, ill-mannered, impolite, rude, uncivil, ungracious, unmannerly, unpolished. *See* COURTESY.

disrobe *verb*
1. To remove all the clothing from : strip[1], unclothe, undress. *See* PUT ON, SHOW. **2.** To make bare : bare, denude, divest, expose, strip[1], uncover. *See* PUT ON.

disrupt *verb*
1. To put out of proper order : derange, disarrange, disarray, disorder, disorganize, disturb, jumble, mess up, mix up, muddle, tumble, unsettle, upset. *See* ORDER. **2.** To break up the order or progress of : disturb, upset. *See* ORDER.

disruption *noun*
1. The act or an example of upsetting : disordering, disorganization, upset. *See* ORDER. **2.** A cessation of continuity or regularity : break, discontinuance, discontinuation, discontinuity, interruption, pause, suspension. *See* CONTINUE.

disruptive *adjective*
Troubling to the mind or emotions : disquieting, distressful, distressing, disturbing, intrusive, perturbing, troublesome, troublous, unsettling, upsetting, worrisome. *See* HAPPY, PAIN.

dissatisfaction *noun*
Unhappiness caused by the failure of one's hopes, desires, or expectations : disappointment, discontent, discontentment, disgruntlement, letdown, regret. *See* HAPPY.

dissatisfy *verb*
To cause unhappiness by failing to satisfy the hopes, desires, or expectations of : disappoint, discontent, disgruntle, let down. *See* HAPPY.

dissect *verb*
To separate into parts for study : analyze, anatomize, break down, resolve. *See* ASSEMBLE, INVESTIGATE.

dissection *noun*
The separation of a whole into its parts for study : analysis, anatomy, breakdown. *See* ASSEMBLE, INVESTIGATE.

dissemblance *noun*
A display of insincere behavior : act, acting, disguise, masquerade, pretense, sham, show, simulation. *See* HONEST, TRUE.

dissemble *verb*
1. To change or modify so as to prevent recognition of the true identity or character of : camouflage, disguise, dissimulate, mask, masquerade. *See* SHOW. **2.** To behave affectedly or insincerely or take on a false or misleading appearance of : act, counterfeit, fake, feign, playact, pose, pretend, put on, sham, simulate. *See* HONEST, TRUE.

disseminate *verb*
1. To extend over a wide area : circulate, diffuse, disperse, distribute, radiate, scatter, spread, strew. *See* MOVE, WIDE. **2.** To pass (something) out : circulate, disperse, distribute, hand out. *See* COLLECT. **3.** To make (information) generally known : advertise, blaze[2], blazon, broadcast, bruit, circulate, noise, promulgate, propagate, spread. ***Idioms:*** spread far and

wide, spread the word. *See* KNOWLEDGE.

dissemination *noun*
The passing out or spreading about of something : circulation, dispersal, dispersion, distribution. *See* COLLECT.

dissension *noun*
A state of disagreement and disharmony : clash, conflict, confrontation, contention, difference, difficulty, disaccord, discord, discordance, dissent, dissentience, dissidence, dissonance, faction, friction, inharmony, schism, strife, variance, war, warfare. *See* CONFLICT.

dissent *verb*
To be of different opinion : differ, disaccord, disagree, discord, vary. ***Idiom:*** join (*or* take) issue. *See* AGREE.
dissent *noun* A state of disagreement and disharmony : clash, conflict, confrontation, contention, difference, difficulty, disaccord, discord, discordance, dissension, dissentience, dissidence, dissonance, faction, friction, inharmony, schism, strife, variance, war, warfare. *See* CONFLICT.

dissenter *noun*
A person who dissents from the doctrine of an established church : dissident, heretic, nonconformist, schismatic, sectarian, sectary, separationist, separatist. *See* RELIGION.

dissentience *noun*
A state of disagreement and disharmony : clash, conflict, confrontation, contention, difference, difficulty, disaccord, discord, discordance, dissension, dissent, dissidence, dissonance, faction, friction, inharmony, schism, strife, variance, war, warfare. *See* CONFLICT.

dissertation *noun*
1. A formal, lengthy exposition of a topic : discourse, disquisition, treatise. *See* WORDS. **2.** A thorough, written presentation of an original point of view : thesis. *See* WORDS.

disserve *verb*
To spoil the soundness or perfection of : blemish, damage, detract from, flaw, harm, hurt, impair, injure, mar, prejudice, tarnish, vitiate. *See* BETTER, HELP.

disservice *noun*
An act that is not just : inequity, injustice, raw deal, wrong. *Law:* injury. *See* LAW, RIGHT.

dissever *verb*
1. To separate into parts with or as if with a sharp-edged instrument : carve, cleave[1], cut, sever, slice, slit, split. *See* ASSEMBLE. **2.** To make a division into parts, sections, or branches : break up, divide, part, partition, section, segment, separate. *See* ASSEMBLE, PART.

disseverance *noun*
The act or an instance of separating one thing from another : detachment, disjunction, disjuncture, disseverment, disunion, division, divorce, divorcement, parting, partition, separation, severance, split. *See* ASSEMBLE, PART.

disseverment *noun*
The act or an instance of separating one thing from another : detachment, disjunction, disjuncture, disseverance, disunion, division, divorce, divorcement, parting, partition, separation, severance, split. *See* ASSEMBLE, PART.

dissidence *noun*
A state of disagreement and disharmony : clash, conflict, confrontation, contention, difference, difficulty, disaccord, discord, discordance, dissension, dissent, dissentience, dissonance, faction, friction, inharmony, schism, strife, variance, war, warfare. *See* CONFLICT.

dissident *noun*
A person who dissents from the doctrine of an established church : dissenter, heretic, nonconformist, schismatic, sectarian, sectary, separationist, separatist. *See* RELIGION.

dissimilar *adjective*
Not like another in nature, quality, amount, or form : different, disparate, divergent, diverse, unlike, variant, various. *See* SAME.

dissimilarity *noun*
The condition of being unlike or dissimilar : difference, discrepance, discrepancy, disparity, dissimilitude, distinction, divarication, divergence, divergency, unlikeness. *See* SAME.

dissimilitude *noun*
The condition of being unlike or dissimilar : difference, discrepance, discrepancy, disparity, dissimilarity, distinction, divarication, divergence, divergency, unlikeness. *See* SAME.

dissimulate *verb*
To change or modify so as to prevent recognition of the true identity or character of : camouflage, disguise, dissemble, mask, masquerade. *See* SHOW.

dissipate *verb*
1. To cause to separate and go in various directions : dispel, disperse, scatter. *See* COLLECT. **2.** To disappear by or as if by rising : disperse, lift, scatter. *See* COLLECT, RISE. **3.** To spend (money) excessively and usually foolishly : consume, fool away, fritter away, riot away, squander, throw away, trifle away, waste. *Slang:* blow[1]. *See* SAVE. **4.** To use up foolishly

or needlessly : consume, devour, squander, waste. *See* SAVE.

dissipated *adjective*
Lacking in moral restraint : abandoned, dissolute, fast, gay, incontinent, licentious, profligate, rakish, unbridled, unconstrained, uncontrolled, ungoverned, uninhibited, unrestrained, wanton, wild. *See* RESTRAINT.

dissociate *verb*
To remove from association with : abstract, detach, disassociate, disengage, withdraw. *See* ASSEMBLE.

dissolute *adjective*
Lacking in moral restraint : abandoned, dissipated, fast, gay, incontinent, licentious, profligate, rakish, unbridled, unconstrained, uncontrolled, ungoverned, uninhibited, unrestrained, wanton, wild. *See* RESTRAINT.

dissoluteness *noun*
Excessive freedom; lack of restraint : dissolution, libertinism, license, licentiousness, profligacy. *See* RESTRAINT.

dissolution *noun*
1. Excessive freedom; lack of restraint : dissoluteness, libertinism, license, licentiousness, profligacy. *See* RESTRAINT. **2.** The act or fact of dying : death, decease, demise, extinction, passing, quietus, rest[1]. *Slang:* curtain (used in plural). *See* LIVE.

dissolve *verb*
1. To change from a solid to a liquid : deliquesce, flux, fuse, liquefy, melt, run, thaw. *See* SOLID. **2.** To reduce or become reduced to pieces or components : break down, break up, crumble, decompose, disintegrate, fragment, fragmentize. *See* CONTINUE, HELP. **3.** To disappear gradually by or as if by dispersal of particles : fade, melt (away). *See* INCREASE, SEE. **4.** To make (a film image) disappear gradually : fade out. *See* INCREASE, SEE.

dissolve *noun* A gradual disappearance, especially of a film image : fade, fadeaway, fadeout. *See* INCREASE, SEE.

dissonance *noun*
A state of disagreement and disharmony : clash, conflict, confrontation, contention, difference, difficulty, disaccord, discord, discordance, dissension, dissent, dissentience, dissidence, faction, friction, inharmony, schism, strife, variance, war, warfare. *See* CONFLICT.

dissonant *adjective*
1. Characterized by unpleasant discordance of sound : cacophonous, discordant, disharmonious, inharmonic, inharmonious, rude, unharmonious, unmusical. *See* AGREE, SOUNDS. **2.** Made up of parts or qualities that are disparate or otherwise markedly lacking in consistency : discordant, discrepant, incompatible, incongruent, incongruous, inconsistent. *See* AGREE.

dissuade *verb*
To persuade (a person) not to do something : deter, discourage, divert. ***Idiom:*** talk out of. *See* PERSUASION.

distaff *noun*
Women in general : femininity, muliebrity, womanhood, womankind, womenfolk. *See* GENDER.

distaff *adjective* Of, relating to, or characteristic of women : female, feminine, womanish, womanly. *See* GENDER.

distance *noun*
1. An extent, measured or unmeasured, of linear space : length, space, stretch. *Informal:* piece, way. *See* BIG. **2.** The fact or condition of being far removed or apart : farness, remoteness. *See* BIG, NEAR. **3.** A wide and open area, as of land, sky, or water : expanse, expansion, extent, reach, space, spread, stretch, sweep. *See* PLACE. **4.** Degree of separation, especially in time : remove. *See* NEAR. **5.** Dissociation from one's surroundings or worldly affairs : aloofness, detachment, remoteness. *See* ATTITUDE, CONCERN, INCLUDE, NEAR.

distant *adjective*
1. Far from others in space, time, or relationship : far, faraway, far-flung, far-off, remote, removed. ***Idiom:*** at a distance. *See* NEAR, TIME. **2.** Not friendly, sociable, or warm in manner : aloof, chill, chilly, cool, offish, remote, reserved, reticent, solitary, standoffish, unapproachable, uncommunicative, undemonstrative, withdrawn. *See* ATTITUDE, HOT.

distaste *noun*
An attitude or feeling of aversion : disinclination, dislike, disrelish, mislike. *See* LIKE.

distaste *verb Archaic.* To have a feeling of aversion for : dislike, disrelish, mislike. ***Idiom:*** have no use for. *See* LIKE.

distasteful *adjective*
1. Difficult to accept : bitter, indigestible, painful, unpalatable. *See* LIKE. **2.** So unpleasant in flavor as to be inedible : unappetizing, unpalatable, unsavory. *See* TASTE.

distill *verb*
To fall or let fall in drops of liquid : dribble, drip, drop, trickle, weep. *See* RISE.

distinct *adjective*
1. Distinguished from others by nature or qualities : discrete, separate, several, various. *See*

SAME. **2.** Readily seen, perceived, or understood : apparent, clear, clear-cut, crystal clear, evident, manifest, noticeable, observable, obvious, patent, plain, pronounced, visible. *See* SEE. **3.** Without any doubt : clear, clear-cut, decided, definite, pronounced, unquestionable. *See* CERTAIN. **4.** Clearly defined; not ambiguous : clear, sharp, unambiguous, unequivocal, unmistakable. *See* CLEAR.

distinction *noun*
1. The act or an instance of distinguishing : differentiation, discrimination, separation. *See* SAME. **2.** The condition of being unlike or dissimilar : difference, discrepance, discrepancy, disparity, dissimilarity, dissimilitude, divarication, divergence, divergency, unlikeness. *See* SAME. **3.** A position of exalted widely recognized importance : eminence, eminency, fame, glory, illustriousness, luster, mark, notability, note, preeminence, prestige, prominence, prominency, renown. *See* IMPORTANT, KNOWLEDGE, RESPECT. **4.** A special feature or quality that confers superiority : beauty, excellence, merit, perfection, virtue. *See* GOOD. **5.** Recognition of achievement or superiority or a sign of this : accolade, honor, kudos, laurel (often used in plural). *See* RESPECT.

distinctive *adjective*
Serving to identify or set apart an individual or group : characteristic, individual, peculiar, typical, vintage. *See* SAME.

distinctiveness *noun*
The quality of being individual : discreteness, individuality, particularity, separateness, singularity. *See* INCLUDE.

distinctness *noun*
The quality of being clear and easy to perceive or understand : clarity, clearness, limpidity, limpidness, lucidity, lucidness, pellucidity, pellucidness, perspicuity, perspicuousness, plainness. *See* CLEAR.

distinguish *verb*
1. To recognize as being different : differentiate, discern, discriminate, know, separate, tell. *See* SAME. **2.** To perceive and fix the identity of, especially with difficulty : descry, discern, make out, pick out, spot. *See* SEE. **3.** To perceive with a special effort of the senses or the mind : descry, detect, discern, mark, mind, note, notice, observe, remark, see. *See* KNOWLEDGE, SEE. **4.** To make noticeable or different : characterize, differentiate, discriminate, individualize, mark, set apart, signalize, singularize. *See* SAME. **5.** To cause to be eminent or recognized : elevate, ennoble, exalt, honor, signalize. *See* RESPECT.

distinguishable *adjective*
Capable of being noticed or apprehended mentally : appreciable, detectable, discernible, noticeable, observable, palpable, perceivable, perceptible, ponderable, sensible. *See* KNOWLEDGE.

distinguished *adjective*
Widely known and esteemed : celebrated, eminent, famed, famous, great, illustrious, notable, noted, preeminent, prestigious, prominent, redoubtable, renowned. *See* KNOWLEDGE, RESPECT.

distort *verb*
1. To alter and spoil the natural form or appearance of : contort, deform, disfigure, misshape, twist. *See* BEAUTIFUL. **2.** To give an inaccurate view of by representing falsely or misleadingly : belie, color, falsify, load, misrepresent, misstate, pervert, twist, warp, wrench, wrest. ***Idiom:*** give a false coloring to. *See* TRUE.

distract *verb*
To impair or destroy the composure of : agitate, bother, discompose, disquiet, disturb, flurry, fluster, perturb, rock, ruffle, shake (up), toss, unsettle, upset. *Informal:* rattle. *See* CALM.

distraction *noun*
Something, especially a performance or show, designed to entertain : amusement, diversion, entertainment, recreation. *See* EXCITE.

distrait *adjective*
So lost in thought as to be unaware of one's surroundings : absent, absent-minded, abstracted, bemused, faraway, inattentive, preoccupied. *Idiom:* a million miles away. *See* ABILITY, AWARENESS.

distraught *adjective*
Afflicted with or exhibiting irrationality and mental unsoundness : brainsick, crazy, daft, demented, disordered, dotty, insane, lunatic, mad, maniac, maniacal, mentally ill, moonstruck, off, touched, unbalanced, unsound, wrong. *Informal:* bonkers, cracked, daffy, gaga, loony. *Slang:* bananas, batty, buggy, cuckoo, fruity, loco, nuts, nutty, screwy, wacky. *Chiefly British:* crackers. *Law:* non compos mentis. *Idioms:* around the bend, crazy as a loon, mad as a hatter, not all there, nutty as a fruitcake, off (*or* out of) one's head, off one's rocker, of unsound mind, out of one's mind, sick in the head, stark raving mad. *See* SANE.

distress *verb*
1. To cause anxious uneasiness in : ail, cark,

concern, trouble, worry. *See* CONCERN. **2.** To cause suffering or painful sorrow to : aggrieve, grieve, hurt, injure, pain, wound. *See* HAPPY.

distress *noun* **1.** A troubled or anxious state of mind : angst, anxiety, anxiousness, care, concern, disquiet, disquietude, nervousness, solicitude, unease, uneasiness, worry. *See* FEELINGS. **2.** A state of physical or mental suffering : affliction, agony, anguish, hurt, misery, pain, torment, torture, woe, wound, wretchedness. *See* HAPPY. **3.** The condition of being in need of immediate assistance : exigence, exigency, hot water, trouble. *See* HELP.

distressed *adjective*
In a state of anxiety or uneasiness : agitated, anxious, concerned, nervous, solicitous, uneasy, unsettled. *See* FEELINGS.

distressful *adjective*
Troubling to the mind or emotions : disquieting, disruptive, distressing, disturbing, intrusive, perturbing, troublesome, troublous, unsettling, upsetting, worrisome. *See* HAPPY, PAIN.

distressing *adjective*
Troubling to the mind or emotions : disquieting, disruptive, distressful, disturbing, intrusive, perturbing, troublesome, troublous, unsettling, upsetting, worrisome. *See* HAPPY, PAIN.

distribute *verb*
1. To give out in portions or shares : deal (out), dispense, divide, dole out, parcel out, portion (out), ration (out), share. *Slang:* divvy. *See* COLLECT. **2.** To pass (something) out : circulate, disperse, disseminate, hand out. *See* COLLECT. **3.** To extend over a wide area : circulate, diffuse, disperse, disseminate, radiate, scatter, spread, strew. *See* MOVE, WIDE. **4.** To assign to a class or classes : categorize, class, classify, grade, group, pigeonhole, place, range, rank[1], rate[1]. *See* GROUP, VALUE.

distribution *noun*
1. The act of distributing or the condition of being distributed : admeasurement, allocation, assignment, apportionment, dispensation, division. *See* COLLECT. **2.** The passing out or spreading about of something : circulation, dispersal, dispersion, dissemination. *See* COLLECT. **3.** A way or condition of being arranged : arrangement, categorization, classification, deployment, disposal, disposition, formation, grouping, layout, lineup, order, organization, placement, sequence. *See* ORDER.

district *noun*
1. A part of the earth's surface : area, belt, locality, neighborhood, quarter, region, tract, zone. *Informal:* neck of the woods. *See* TERRITORY. **2.** A rather small part of a geographic unit considered in regard to its inhabitants or distinctive characteristics : area, neighborhood, quarter (often uppercase). *See* TERRITORY. **3.** A particular area used for or associated with a specific individual or activity : country, region, terrain, territory. *Slang:* turf. *See* TERRITORY.

distrust *noun*
Lack of trust : doubt, leeriness, mistrust, suspicion. *See* TRUST.

distrust *verb* **1.** To lack trust or confidence in : doubt, misdoubt, mistrust, suspect. *See* TRUST. **2.** To be uncertain, disbelieving, or skeptical about : doubt, misdoubt, mistrust, question, wonder. ***Idiom:*** have one's doubts. *See* CERTAIN.

distrustful *adjective*
Lacking trust or confidence : doubting, leery, mistrustful, suspicious, untrusting. *See* TRUST.

disturb *verb*
1. To alter the settled state or position of : dislocate, displace, move, shake, shift. *See* MOVE. **2.** To impair or destroy the composure of : agitate, bother, discompose, disquiet, distract, flurry, fluster, perturb, rock, ruffle, shake (up), toss, unsettle, upset. *Informal:* rattle. *See* CALM. **3.** To trouble the nerves or peace of mind of, especially by repeated vexations : aggravate, annoy, bother, bug, chafe, exasperate, fret, gall[2], get, irk, irritate, nettle, peeve, provoke, put out, rile, ruffle, vex. ***Idioms:*** get in one's hair, get on one's nerves, get under one's skin. *See* FEELINGS, PAIN. **4.** To break up the order or progress of : disrupt, upset. *See* ORDER. **5.** To put out of proper order : derange, disarrange, disarray, disorder, disorganize, disrupt, jumble, mess up, mix up, muddle, tumble, unsettle, upset. *See* ORDER.

disturbance *noun*
1. An interruption of regular procedure or of public peace : agitation, commotion, disorder, helter-skelter, stir[1], tumult, turbulence, turmoil, uproar. *Informal:* flap, to-do. *See* CALM, ORDER. **2.** A change in normal place or position : dislocation, displacement, move, movement, rearrangement, shift. *See* MOVE. **3.** Serious mental illness or disorder impairing a person's capacity to function normally and safely : brainsickness, craziness, dementia, derangement, insaneness, insanity, lunacy, madness, mental illness, psychopathy, unbalance. *Psychiatry:* mania. *Psychology:* aberration, alienation. *See* SANE.

disturbing *adjective*
Troubling to the mind or emotions : disquieting, disruptive, distressful, distressing, intrusive, perturbing, troublesome, troublous, unsettling, upsetting, worrisome. *See* HAPPY, PAIN.

disunion *noun*
1. The act or an instance of separating one thing from another : detachment, disjunction, disjuncture, disseverance, disseverment, division, divorce, divorcement, parting, partition, separation, severance, split. *See* ASSEMBLE, PART. **2.** The condition of being divided, as in opinion : disunity, divergence, divergency, division, schism. *See* ASSEMBLE.

disunite *verb*
1. To become or cause to become apart one from another : break, detach, disjoin, disjoint, divide, divorce, part, separate, split (up). ***Idioms:*** part company, set at odds. *See* ASSEMBLE. **2.** To make distant, hostile, or unsympathetic : alienate, disaffect, estrange. ***Idiom:*** set at odds. *See* LOVE.

disunity *noun*
The condition of being divided, as in opinion : disunion, divergence, divergency, division, schism. *See* ASSEMBLE.

disuse *noun*
The quality or state of being obsolete : desuetude, obsoleteness, obsoletism. *See* NEW, USED.

ditch *verb*
Slang. To let go or get rid of as being useless or defective, for example : discard, dispose of, dump, junk, scrap[1], throw away, throw out. *Informal:* chuck, jettison, shuck (off). *See* KEEP.

dither *noun*
A state of discomposure : agitation, fluster, flutter, perturbation, tumult, turmoil, upset. *Informal:* lather, stew. *See* CALM.
dither *verb* To be irresolute in acting or doing : falter, halt[2], hesitate, pause, shilly-shally, stagger, vacillate, waver, wobble. *See* DECIDE.

dithyrambic *adjective*
Fired with intense feeling : ardent, blazing, burning, fervent, fervid, fiery, flaming, glowing, heated, hot-blooded, impassioned, passionate, perfervid, red-hot, scorching, torrid. *See* FEELINGS.

divagate *verb*
To turn aside, especially from the main subject in writing or speaking : deviate, digress, diverge, ramble, stray, wander. ***Idiom:*** go off at (*or* on) a tangent. *See* APPROACH.

divagation *noun*
An instance of digressing : aside, deviation, digression, divergence, divergency, excursion, excursus, irrelevancy, parenthesis, tangent. *See* APPROACH.

divarication *noun*
The condition of being unlike or dissimilar : difference, discrepance, discrepancy, disparity, dissimilarity, dissimilitude, distinction, divergence, divergency, unlikeness. *See* SAME.

dive *verb*
1. To move or thrust at, under, or into the midst of with sudden force : lunge, plunge, wade in (*or* into). *See* ENTER. **2.** To undergo a sharp, rapid descent in value or price : drop, fall, nose-dive, plummet, plunge, sink, skid, slump, tumble. ***Idiom:*** take a sudden downtrend (*or* downturn). *See* INCREASE.
dive *noun* **1.** The act of plunging suddenly downward into or as if into water : nosedive, plunge, swoop. *Informal:* header. *See* ENTER. **2.** A sudden involuntary drop to the ground : fall, nosedive, pitch, plunge, spill, tumble. *Informal:* header. *See* RISE. **3.** A usually swift downward trend, as in prices : decline, descent, dip, downslide, downswing, downtrend, downturn, drop, drop-off, fall, nosedive, plunge, skid, slide, slump, tumble. *See* INCREASE. **4.** *Slang.* A disreputable or run-down bar or restaurant : *Slang:* honky-tonk, joint. *See* GOOD.

diverge *verb*
1. To separate into branches or branchlike parts : bifurcate, branch (out), divide, fork, ramify, subdivide. *See* PART. **2.** To be unlike or dissimilar : differ, disagree, vary. ***Idiom:*** be at variance. *See* SAME. **3.** To turn away from a prescribed course of action or conduct : depart, deviate, digress, stray, swerve, veer. *Archaic:* err. *See* APPROACH, CORRECT. **4.** To turn aside, especially from the main subject in writing or speaking : deviate, digress, divagate, ramble, stray, wander. ***Idiom:*** go off at (*or* on) a tangent. *See* APPROACH.

divergence *noun*
1. The condition of being unlike or dissimilar : difference, discrepance, discrepancy, disparity, dissimilarity, dissimilitude, distinction, divarication, divergency, unlikeness. *See* SAME. **2.** A departing from what is prescribed : aberration, departure, deviation, divergency, diversion. *See* APPROACH, CORRECT. **3.** An instance of digressing : aside, deviation, digression, divagation, divergency, excursion, excursus, irrelevancy, parenthesis, tangent. *See* APPROACH.

4. The condition of being divided, as in opinion : disunion, disunity, divergency, division, schism. *See* ASSEMBLE.

divergency *noun*

1. The condition of being unlike or dissimilar : difference, discrepance, discrepancy, disparity, dissimilarity, dissimilitude, distinction, divarication, divergence, unlikeness. *See* SAME. **2.** A departing from what is prescribed : aberration, departure, deviation, divergence, diversion. *See* APPROACH, CORRECT. **3.** An instance of digressing : aside, deviation, digression, divagation, divergence, excursion, excursus, irrelevancy, parenthesis, tangent. *See* APPROACH. **4.** The condition of being divided, as in opinion : disunion, disunity, divergence, division, schism. *See* ASSEMBLE.

divergent *adjective*

1. Departing from the normal : aberrant, abnormal, anomalistic, anomalous, atypic, atypical, deviant, irregular, preternatural, unnatural. *See* GOOD, USUAL. **2.** Not like another in nature, quality, amount, or form : different, disparate, dissimilar, diverse, unlike, variant, various. *See* SAME.

divers *adjective*

1. Consisting of a number more than two or three but less than many : several, some, sundry, various. *See* BIG. **2.** Consisting of a number of different kinds : assorted, diverse, diversified, heterogeneous, miscellaneous, mixed, motley, multifarious, multiform, sundry, varied, variegated, various. *Biology:* polymorphic, polymorphous. *See* SAME.

diverse *adjective*

1. Not like another in nature, quality, amount, or form : different, disparate, dissimilar, divergent, unlike, variant, various. *See* SAME. **2.** Consisting of a number of different kinds : assorted, divers, diversified, heterogeneous, miscellaneous, mixed, motley, multifarious, multiform, sundry, varied, variegated, various. *Biology:* polymorphic, polymorphous. *See* SAME.

diverseness *noun*

The quality of being made of many different elements, forms, kinds, or individuals : diversification, diversity, heterogeneity, heterogeneousness, miscellaneousness, multifariousness, multiformity, multiplicity, variegation, variety, variousness. *Biology:* polymorphism. *See* SAME.

diversification *noun*

The quality of being made of many different elements, forms, kinds, or individuals : diverseness, diversity, heterogeneity, heterogeneousness, miscellaneousness, multifariousness, multiformity, multiplicity, variegation, variety, variousness. *Biology:* polymorphism. *See* SAME.

diversified *adjective*

1. Consisting of a number of different kinds : assorted, divers, diverse, heterogeneous, miscellaneous, mixed, motley, multifarious, multiform, sundry, varied, variegated, various. *Biology:* polymorphic, polymorphous. *See* SAME. **2.** Not limited to a single class : general. *See* SPECIFIC.

diversion *noun*

1. A departing from what is prescribed : aberration, departure, deviation, divergence, divergency. *See* APPROACH, CORRECT. **2.** Activity engaged in for relaxation and amusement : disport, fun, play, recreation, sport. *See* WORK. **3.** Something, especially a performance or show, designed to entertain : amusement, distraction, entertainment, recreation. *See* EXCITE.

diversity *noun*

The quality of being made of many different elements, forms, kinds, or individuals : diverseness, diversification, heterogeneity, heterogeneousness, miscellaneousness, multifariousness, multiformity, multiplicity, variegation, variety, variousness. *Biology:* polymorphism. *See* SAME.

divert *verb*

1. To change the direction or course of : avert, deflect, deviate, pivot, shift, swing, turn, veer. *See* CHANGE. **2.** To persuade (a person) not to do something : deter, discourage, dissuade. ***Idiom:*** talk out of. *See* PERSUASION. **3.** To occupy in an agreeable or pleasing way : amuse, entertain, recreate, regale. *See* EXCITE.

diverting *adjective*

Providing pleasure or entertainment : amusing, entertaining. *See* EXCITE.

divest *verb*

1. To make bare : bare, denude, disrobe, expose, strip[1], uncover. *See* PUT ON. **2.** To take or keep something away from : deprive, dispossess, rob, strip[1]. *See* GIVE.

divestiture *noun*

The condition of being deprived of what one once had or ought to have : deprival, deprivation, dispossession, loss, privation. *See* GIVE, RICH.

divide *verb*

1. To make a division into parts, sections, or branches : break up, dissever, part, partition, section, segment, separate. *See* ASSEMBLE, PART. **2.** To separate into branches or branchlike parts : bifurcate, branch (out), diverge, fork, ramify, subdivide. *See* PART. **3.** To become or cause to become apart one from another : break, detach, disjoin, disjoint, disunite, divorce, part, separate, split (up). ***Idioms:*** part company, set at odds. *See* ASSEMBLE. **4.** To give out in portions or shares : deal (out), dispense, distribute, dole out, parcel out, portion (out), ration (out), share. *Slang:* divvy. *See* COLLECT.

divination *noun*
Something that is foretold by or as if by supernatural means : oracle, prophecy, soothsaying, vaticination, vision. *See* FORESIGHT.

divine *adjective*
1. Of, from, like, or being a god or God : deific, godlike, godly, heavenly, holy. *See* RELIGION. **2.** In the service or worship of God or a god : holy, religious, sacred. *See* RELIGION. **3.** Of or relating to heaven : celestial, heavenly, paradisaic, paradisaical, paradisal, paradisiac, paradisiacal. *See* RELIGION. **4.** Particularly excellent : fabulous, fantastic, fantastical, glorious, marvelous, sensational, splendid, superb, terrific, wonderful. *Informal:* dandy, dreamy, great, ripping, super, swell, tremendous. *Slang:* cool, groovy, hot, keen[1], neat, nifty. ***Idiom:*** out of this world. *See* GOOD.

divine *noun* A person ordained for service in a Christian church : churchman, churchwoman, clergyman, clergywoman, cleric, clerical, clerk, ecclesiastic, minister, parson, preacher. *Informal:* reverend. *See* RELIGION.

divine *verb* **1.** To tell about or make known (future events) by or as if by supernatural means : augur, foretell, prophesy, soothsay, vaticinate. *See* FORESIGHT. **2.** To know in advance : anticipate, envision, foreknow, foresee, see. *See* FORESIGHT, SEE.

diviner *noun*
A person who foretells future events by or as if by supernatural means : augur, auspex, foreteller, haruspex, prophesier, prophet, prophetess, seer, sibyl, soothsayer, vaticinator. *See* FORESIGHT.

divine spark *noun*
The vital principle or animating force that exists within living beings : breath, élan vital, life force, psyche, soul, spirit, vital force, vitality. *See* BODY.

divinitory *adjective*
Of or relating to the foretelling of events by or as if by supernatural means : augural, fatidic, fatidical, mantic, oracular, prophetic, sibylline, vatic, vatical, vaticinal, visionary. *See* FORESIGHT.

division *noun*
1. The act or an instance of separating one thing from another : detachment, disjunction, disjuncture, disseverance, disseverment, disunion, divorce, divorcement, parting, partition, separation, severance, split. *See* ASSEMBLE, PART. **2.** The act of distributing or the condition of being distributed : admeasurement, allocation, assignment, apportionment, dispensation, distribution. *See* COLLECT. **3.** One of the parts into which something is divided : member, part, piece, portion, section, segment, subdivision. *See* PART. **4.** A part of a family, tribe, or other group, or of such a group's language, that is believed to stem from a common ancestor : branch, offshoot, subdivision. *See* PART. **5.** A component of government that performs a given function : agency, arm, branch, department, organ, wing. *See* PART. **6.** A local unit of a business or an auxiliary controlled by such a business : affiliate, branch, subsidiary. *See* PART. **7.** The condition of being divided, as in opinion : disunion, disunity, divergence, divergency, schism. *See* ASSEMBLE.

divorce *noun*
The act or an instance of separating one thing from another : detachment, disjunction, disjuncture, disseverance, disseverment, disunion, division, divorcement, parting, partition, separation, severance, split. *See* ASSEMBLE, PART.

divorce *verb* To become or cause to become apart one from another : break, detach, disjoin, disjoint, disunite, divide, part, separate, split (up). ***Idioms:*** part company, set at odds. *See* ASSEMBLE.

divorcement *noun*
The act or an instance of separating one thing from another : detachment, disjunction, disjuncture, disseverance, disseverment, disunion, division, divorce, parting, partition, separation, severance, split. *See* ASSEMBLE, PART.

divulge *verb*
To disclose in a breach of confidence : betray, blab, expose, give away, let out, reveal, tell, uncover, unveil. *Informal:* spill. *Archaic:* discover. ***Idioms:*** let slip, let the cat out of the bag, spill the beans, tell all. *See* SHOW.

divvy *verb*
Slang. To give out in portions or shares : deal (out), dispense, distribute, divide, dole out,

parcel out, portion (out), ration (out), share. *See* COLLECT.

divvy *noun Slang.* That which is allotted : allocation, allotment, allowance, dole, lot, measure, part, portion, quantum, quota, ration, share, split. *Informal:* cut. *See* COLLECT.

dizziness *noun*
A sensation of whirling or falling : giddiness, lightheadedness, vertiginousness, vertigo, wooziness. *See* AWARENESS.

dizzy *adjective*
1. Having a sensation of whirling or falling : giddy, lightheaded, reeling, vertiginous, woozy. *See* AWARENESS. **2.** Producing dizziness or vertigo : dizzying, giddy, vertiginous. *See* AWARENESS. **3.** *Slang.* Given to lighthearted silliness : empty-headed, featherbrained, flighty, frivolous, frothy, giddy, harebrained, lighthearted, scatterbrained, silly. *Informal:* gaga. *Slang:* birdbrained. *See* ABILITY.

dizzy *verb* To cause to be unclear in mind or intent : addle, befuddle, bewilder, confound, confuse, discombobulate, fuddle, jumble, mix up, muddle, mystify, perplex, puzzle. *Informal:* throw. ***Idiom:*** make one's head reel (*or* swim *or* whirl). *See* CLEAR, FEELINGS.

dizzying *adjective*
Producing dizziness or vertigo : dizzy, giddy, vertiginous. *See* AWARENESS.

do *verb*
1. To begin and carry through to completion : execute, perform, prosecute. *Informal:* pull off. *See* DO. **2.** To carry out the functions, requirements, or terms of : discharge, execute, exercise, fulfill, implement, keep, perform. ***Idiom:*** live up to. *See* DO. **3.** To conduct oneself in a specified way : acquit, act, bear, behave, carry, comport, demean[1], deport, quit. *See* BE. **4.** To progress or perform adequately, especially in difficult circumstances : fare, fend, get along, get by, manage, muddle through, shift. *Informal:* make out. ***Idioms:*** make do, make shift. *See* THRIVE. **5.** To produce on the stage : act (out), dramatize, enact, give, perform, present[2], put on, stage. *See* PERFORMING ARTS. **6.** To play the part of : act, enact, impersonate, perform, play, play-act, portray, represent. *See* ACTION, PERFORMING ARTS, SUBSTITUTE. **7.** To prepare (food) for eating by the use of heat : cook. *See* INGESTION. **8.** *Informal.* To journey over (a specified distance) : cover, make. *See* MOVE. **9.** To meet a need or requirement : answer, serve, suffice, suit. *See* EXCESS, HELP. **10.** *Informal.* To spend or complete (time), as a prison term : put in, serve. *See* TIME. **11.** *Slang.* To get money or something else from by deceitful trickery : bilk, cheat, cozen, defraud, gull, mulct, rook, swindle, victimize. *Informal:* chisel, flimflam, take, trim. *Slang:* diddle[1], gyp, stick, sting. *See* HONEST.

do for *verb* To work and care for : attend, minister to, serve, wait on (*or* upon). *See* CARE FOR.

do in *verb* **1.** *Slang.* To make extremely tired : exhaust, fag (out), tire out, wear out. *Informal:* knock out, tucker (out). *Slang:* poop[1] (out). ***Idioms:*** run ragged, take it out of. *See* TIRED. **2.** *Slang.* To take the life of (a person or persons) unlawfully : destroy, finish (off), kill[1], liquidate, murder, slay. *Informal:* put away. *Slang:* bump off, knock off, off, rub out, waste, wipe out, zap. *See* HELP.

do up *verb* To cover and tie (something), as with paper and string : package, wrap. *See* PUT ON.

do *noun Informal.* A large or important social gathering : affair, celebration, festivity, fete, function, gala, occasion, party, soiree. *Slang:* bash. *See* GROUP, WORK.

docile *adjective*
1. Easily managed or handled : gentle, meek, mild, tame. *See* WILD. **2.** Willing to carry out the wishes of others : amenable, biddable, compliant, conformable, obedient, submissive, supple, tractable. *See* RESIST.

docket *noun*
An organized list, as of procedures, activities, or events : agenda, calendar, lineup, order of the day (often used in plural), program, schedule, timetable. *See* PLANNED.

doctor *verb*
1. *Informal.* To give medical aid to : treat. *See* HEALTH, HELP. **2.** To restore to proper condition or functioning : fix, fix up, mend, overhaul, patch, repair[1], revamp, right. ***Idiom:*** set right. *See* HELP. **3.** To impart a false character to (something) by alteration : fabricate, fake, falsify, fictionalize, fictionize. *See* TRUE. **4.** To make impure or inferior by deceptively adding foreign substances : adulterate, debase, load, sophisticate. *See* CLEAN.

doctored *adjective*
Mixed with other substances : adulterated, alloyed, impure, loaded, sophisticated. *See* CLEAN.

doctrinaire *adjective*
Devoted to certain doctrines without regard to practicability : dogmatic. *See* ABILITY.

doctrine *noun*
A principle taught or advanced for belief, as by

a religious or philosophical group : dogma, teaching, tenet. *See* BELIEF.

doddering *adjective*
Exhibiting the mental and physical deterioration often accompanying old age : doting, senile. *See* YOUTH.

dodge *verb*
1. To keep away from : avoid, burke, bypass, circumvent, duck, elude, escape, eschew, evade, get around, shun. ***Idioms:*** fight shy of, give a wide berth to, have no truck with, keep (*or* stay *or* steer) clear of. *See* SEEK. **2.** To avoid fulfilling or answering completely : duck, evade, hedge, sidestep, skirt. *See* SEEK.
dodge *noun* An indirect, usually cunning means of gaining an end : artifice, deception, device, feint, gimmick, imposture, jig, maneuver, ploy, ruse, sleight, stratagem, subterfuge, trick, wile. *Informal:* shenanigan, take-in. *See* HONEST, MEANS.

doff *verb*
To take from one's own person : remove, take off. *See* PUT ON.

do for *verb* See **do.**

dog *verb*
1. To keep (another) under surveillance by moving along behind : follow, shadow, track, trail. *Informal:* bird-dog, tail. *See* PRECEDE. **2.** To follow closely or persistently : heel[1], tag, trail. *See* PRECEDE.

dogged *adjective*
Tenaciously unwilling to yield : bullheaded, hardheaded, headstrong, mulish, obstinate, pertinacious, perverse, pigheaded, stiff-necked, tenacious, willful. *See* RESIST.

doggedness *noun*
The quality or state of being stubbornly unyielding : bullheadedness, hardheadedness, mulishness, obstinacy, obstinateness, pertinaciousness, pertinacity, perverseness, perversity, pigheadedness, tenaciousness, tenacity, willfulness. *See* RESIST.

dogma *noun*
A principle taught or advanced for belief, as by a religious or philosophical group : doctrine, teaching, tenet. *See* BELIEF.

dogmatic *adjective*
1. Devoted to certain doctrines without regard to practicability : doctrinaire. *See* ABILITY.
2. Tending to dictate : authoritarian, bossy, dictatorial, domineering, imperious, magisterial, masterful, overbearing, peremptory. *See* OVER.

do in *verb* See **do.**

doing *noun*
Something done : act, action, deed, thing, work. *See* DO.

doldrums *noun*
A feeling or spell of dismally low spirits : blues, dejection, depression, despondence, despondency, dolefulness, downheartedness, dumps, dysphoria, funk, gloom, glumness, heavy-heartedness, melancholy, mope (used in plural), mournfulness, sadness, unhappiness. *See* FEELINGS, HAPPY.

dole *noun*
1. Assistance, especially money, food, and other necessities, given to the needy or dispossessed : aid, handout, public assistance, relief, welfare. *See* HELP. **2.** That which is allotted : allocation, allotment, allowance, lot, measure, part, portion, quantum, quota, ration, share, split. *Informal:* cut. *Slang:* divvy. *See* COLLECT.
dole out *verb* To give out in portions or shares : deal (out), dispense, distribute, divide, parcel out, portion (out), ration (out), share. *Slang:* divvy. *See* COLLECT.

doleful *adjective*
1. Full of or expressive of sorrow : dolorous, lugubrious, mournful, plaintive, rueful, sad, sorrowful, woebegone, woeful. *See* HAPPY.
2. Causing sorrow or regret : deplorable, dolorous, grievous, lamentable, mournful, regrettable, rueful, sad, sorrowful, woeful. *See* HAPPY.

dolefulness *noun*
A feeling or spell of dismally low spirits : blues, dejection, depression, despondence, despondency, doldrums, downheartedness, dumps, dysphoria, funk, gloom, glumness, heavy-heartedness, melancholy, mope (used in plural), mournfulness, sadness, unhappiness. *See* FEELINGS, HAPPY.

dole out *verb* See **dole.**

do-little *noun*
Informal. A self-indulgent person who spends time avoiding work or other useful activity : bum[1], drone[1], fainéant, good-for-nothing, idler, layabout, loafer, ne'er-do-well, no-good, slugabed, sluggard, wastrel. *Informal:* do-nothing, lazybones, slug[2]. *Slang:* slouch. *See* INDUSTRIOUS.

doll *noun*
Slang. A person regarded as physically attractive : beauty, belle (used of a woman), lovely, stunner. *Slang:* babe, hunk (used of a man), knockout, looker, stud (used of a man). *See* BEAUTIFUL.

doll up *verb Slang.* To dress in formal or special clothing : array, attire, deck[2] (out), dress up, prank[2]. *Informal:* trick out (*or* up). *See* ORDER, PLAIN, PUT ON.

doll up *verb* See **doll.**

dolorous *adjective*
1. Full of or expressive of sorrow : doleful, lugubrious, mournful, plaintive, rueful, sad, sorrowful, woebegone, woeful. *See* HAPPY.
2. Causing sorrow or regret : deplorable, doleful, grievous, lamentable, mournful, regrettable, rueful, sad, sorrowful, woeful. *See* HAPPY.

dolt *noun*
A mentally dull person : blockhead, chump[1], clod, dullard, dummkopf, dummy, dunce, numskull, thickhead. *Slang:* dimwit, dumbbell, dumbo. *See* ABILITY.

doltish *adjective*
Lacking in intelligence : blockheaded, dense, dumb, hebetudinous, obtuse, stupid, thick-headed, thick-witted. *Informal:* thick. *Slang:* dimwitted, dopey. *See* ABILITY.

domain *noun*
A sphere of activity, experience, study, or interest : area, arena, bailiwick, circle, department, field, orbit, province, realm, scene, subject, terrain, territory, world. *Slang:* bag. *See* TERRITORY.

dome *noun*
Slang. The uppermost part of the body : head, noddle, pate, poll. *Slang:* bean, block, conk, noggin, noodle, nut. *See* BODY.

domestic *adjective*
1. Of or relating to the family or household : familial, family, home, homely, household. *See* GROUP, KIN. 2. Trained or bred to be of use to people : tame. *See* WILD. 3. Of, from, or within a country's own territory : home, internal, national, native. *See* NATIVE.

domesticate *verb*
To train to live with and be of use to man : domesticize, gentle, master, tame. *See* WILD.

domesticize *verb*
To train to live with and be of use to man : domesticate, gentle, master, tame. *See* WILD.

domicile *noun*
A building or shelter where one lives : abode, dwelling, habitation, home, house, lodging (often used in plural), place, residence. *Chiefly British:* dig (used in plural). *See* PROTECTION.

domicile *verb* 1. To provide with often temporary lodging : accommodate, bed (down), berth, bestow, billet, board, bunk[1], harbor, house, lodge, put up, quarter, room. *See* PROTECTION. 2. To have as one's domicile, usually for an extended period : abide, dwell, house, live[1], reside. *See* PLACE.

dominance *noun*
1. The condition or fact of being dominant : ascendance, ascendancy, domination, paramountcy, predominance, preeminence, preponderance, preponderancy, prepotency, supremacy. *See* OVER. 2. The act of exercising controlling power or the condition of being so controlled : command, control, domination, dominion, mastery, reign, rule, sway. *See* OVER.

dominant *adjective*
1. Exercising controlling power or influence : commanding, controlling, dominating, dominative, governing, paramount, preponderant, regnant, reigning, ruling. *See* OVER. 2. Exercising authority : authoritative, commanding, lordly, masterful. *See* OVER, STRONG. 3. Having preeminent significance : ascendant, predominant, prepotent, prevailing, regnant, ruling, supreme. *See* IMPORTANT.

dominate *verb*
1. To exercise authority or influence over : control, direct, govern, rule. ***Idioms:*** be at the helm, be in the driver's seat, hold sway over, hold the reins. *See* OVER. 2. To command or issue commands in an arrogant manner : boss, dictate, domineer, order, rule, tyrannize. *See* OVER. 3. To occupy the preeminent position in : predominate, preponderate, prevail, reign, rule. ***Idioms:*** have the ascendancy, reign supreme. *See* OVER. 4. To rise above, especially so as to afford a view of : command, overlook, tower above (*or* over). *See* OVER.

dominating *adjective*
Exercising controlling power or influence : commanding, controlling, dominant, dominative, governing, paramount, preponderant, regnant, reigning, ruling. *See* OVER.

domination *noun*
1. The condition or fact of being dominant : ascendance, ascendancy, dominance, paramountcy, predominance, preeminence, preponderance, preponderancy, prepotency, supremacy. *See* OVER. 2. The right and power to command, decide, rule, or judge : authority, command, control, dominion, jurisdiction, mastery, might, power, prerogative, sovereignty, sway. *Informal:* say-so. *See* OVER.
3. The act of exercising controlling power or the condition of being so controlled : command, control, dominance, dominion, mastery, reign, rule, sway. *See* OVER.

dominative *adjective*
Exercising controlling power or influence : commanding, controlling, dominant, dominating, governing, paramount, preponderant, regnant, reigning, ruling. *See* OVER.

domineer *verb*
To command arrogantly : boss, dictate, dominate, order, rule, tyrannize. *See* OVER.

domineering *adjective*
Tending to dictate : authoritarian, bossy, dictatorial, dogmatic, imperious, magisterial, masterful, overbearing, peremptory. *See* OVER.

dominion *noun*
1. The right and power to command, decide, rule, or judge : authority, command, control, domination, jurisdiction, mastery, might, power, prerogative, sovereignty, sway. *Informal:* say-so. *See* OVER. **2.** The fact of possessing or the legal right to possess something : ownership, possession, proprietorship, title. *See* OWNED. **3.** The act of exercising controlling power or the condition of being so controlled : command, control, dominance, domination, mastery, reign, rule, sway. *See* OVER.

don *verb*
To put (an article of clothing) on one's person : assume, get on, pull on, put on, slip into, slip on. *See* PUT ON.

donate *verb*
1. To present as a gift to a charity or cause : bestow, contribute, give, hand out. *See* GIVE. **2.** To give in common with others : chip in, contribute, subscribe. *Informal:* kick in. *Slang:* come across. *See* GIVE.

donation *noun*
Something given to a charity or cause : alms, benefaction, beneficence, charity, contribution, gift, handout, offering, subscription. *See* GIVE.

donator *noun*
A person who gives to a charity or cause : benefactor, benefactress, contributor, donor, giver. *See* GIVE.

done *adjective*
1. Having reached completion : complete, through. *See* PART. **2.** No longer effective, capable, or valuable : done for, finished, through, washed-up. *Informal:* kaput. ***Idioms:*** at the end of the line (*or* road), over the hill, past one's prime. *See* ABILITY, START. **3.** Having no further relationship : finished, through. *See* START.

done for *adjective*
No longer effective, capable, or valuable : done, finished, through, washed-up. *Informal:* kaput. ***Idioms:*** at the end of the line (*or* road), over the hill, past one's prime. *See* ABILITY, START.

done in *adjective*
Slang. Extremely tired : bleary, dead, drained, exhausted, fatigued, rundown, spent, tired out, wearied, wearyful, weary, worn-down, worn-out. *Informal:* beat, bushed, tuckered (out). *Slang:* fagged (out), pooped (out). ***Idioms:*** all in, ready to drop. *See* HEALTH, TIRED.

Don Juan *noun*
1. A man who seduces women : debaucher, Lothario, seducer. *See* SEX. **2.** A man amorously attentive to women : amorist, Casanova, gallant, lady's man, Lothario, Romeo. *See* SEX. **3.** A man who philanders : Casanova, lady's man, philanderer, womanizer. *Slang:* lady-killer, wolf. ***Idioms:*** man on the make, skirt chaser. *See* SEX.

donnish *adjective*
Characterized by a narrow concern for book learning and formal rules, without knowledge or experience of practical matters : academic, bookish, formalistic, inkhorn, literary, pedantic, pedantical, scholastic. *See* ATTITUDE, FLEXIBLE, TEACH.

donnybrook *noun*
A quarrel, fight, or disturbance marked by very noisy, disorderly, and often violent behavior : affray, brawl, broil[2], fray, free-for-all, melee, riot, row[2], ruction, tumult. *Informal:* fracas. *Slang:* rumble. *See* ATTACK.

donor *noun*
A person who gives to a charity or cause : benefactor, benefactress, contributor, donator, giver. *See* GIVE.

do-nothing *adjective*
Informal. Resistant to exertion and activity : fainéant, idle, indolent, lazy, shiftless, slothful, sluggard, sluggish. ***Idiom:*** bone lazy. *See* ACTION, INDUSTRIOUS.
do-nothing *noun Informal.* A self-indulgent person who spends time avoiding work or other useful activity : bum[1], drone[1], fainéant, good-for-nothing, idler, layabout, loafer, ne'er-do-well, no-good, slugabed, sluggard, wastrel. *Informal:* do-little, lazybones, slug[2]. *Slang:* slouch. *See* INDUSTRIOUS.

do-nothingism *noun*
Informal. The quality or state of being lazy : idleness, indolence, laziness, shiftlessness, sloth, slothfulness, sluggardness, sluggishness. *See* INDUSTRIOUS.

doodad *noun*
Informal. A small specialized mechanical device : concern, contraption, contrivance,

gadget, gimmick, jigger, thing. *Informal:* doohickey, widget. *Slang:* gizmo. *See* MACHINE.

doodle *verb*
To waste time by engaging in aimless activity : fool, putter. *Informal:* fool around, mess around. *See* THRIVE.

doohickey *noun*
Informal. A small specialized mechanical device : concern, contraption, contrivance, gadget, gimmick, jigger, thing. *Informal:* doodad, widget. *Slang:* gizmo. *See* MACHINE.

doom *noun*
A predestined tragic end : fate. *See* CERTAIN, LIVE, LUCK, START.
doom *verb* **1.** To pronounce judgment against : condemn, damn, sentence. *See* LAW. **2.** To predestine to a tragic end : fate, foredoom. *See* CERTAIN, LIVE, LUCK, START.

doomed *adjective*
1. Sentenced to terrible, irrevocable punishment : condemned, fated, foredoomed, lost. *See* LAW, RELIGION. **2.** Condemned, especially to hell : damned, lost. ***Idiom:*** gone to blazes. *See* REWARD.

doomsayer *noun*
A prophet of misfortune or disaster : Cassandra, pessimist, worrywart. *See* HOPE.

dope *noun*
1. *Informal.* A substance that affects the central nervous system and is often addictive : drug, hallucinogen, narcotic, opiate. *See* DRUGS. **2.** *Informal.* One deficient in judgment and good sense : ass, fool, idiot, imbecile, jackass, mooncalf, moron, nincompoop, ninny, nitwit, simple, simpleton, softhead, tomfool. *Informal:* gander, goose. *Slang:* cretin, ding-dong, dip, goof, jerk, nerd, schmo, schmuck, turkey. *See* ABILITY.
dope *verb Informal.* To administer or add a drug to. Also used with *up* : dose, drug, medicate, narcotize, opiate, physic. *See* DRUGS.
dope out *verb* **1.** *Informal.* To find a solution for : clear up, decipher, explain, resolve, solve, unravel. *Informal:* figure out. ***Idiom:*** get to the bottom of. *See* ASK, REASON. **2.** *Informal.* To form a strategy for : blueprint, cast, chart, conceive, contrive, design, devise, formulate, frame, lay[1], plan, project, scheme, strategize, work out. ***Idiom:*** lay plans. *See* PLANNED.

doped *adjective*
Informal. Stupefied, intoxicated, or otherwise influenced by the taking of drugs : drugged. *Slang:* high, hopped-up, lit (up), potted, spaced-out, stoned, turned-on, wiped-out, zonked. *See* DRUGS.

dope out *verb* See **dope.**

dopey also **dopy** *adjective*
1. *Slang.* Lacking mental and physical alertness and activity : hebetudinous, lethargic, sluggish, stupid, stuporous, torpid. *See* ACTION. **2.** *Slang.* Lacking in intelligence : blockheaded, dense, doltish, dumb, hebetudinous, obtuse, stupid, thickheaded, thick-witted. *Informal:* thick. *Slang:* dimwitted. *See* ABILITY. **3.** *Slang.* So senseless as to be laughable : absurd, foolish, harebrained, idiotic, imbecilic, insane, lunatic, mad, moronic, nonsensical, preposterous, silly, softheaded, tomfool, unearthly, zany. *Informal:* cockeyed, crazy, loony, loopy. *Slang:* balmy[2], dippy, jerky, sappy, wacky. *See* ABILITY, KNOWLEDGE.

dopy *adjective* See **dopey.**

dormancy *noun*
The condition of being temporarily inactive : abeyance, abeyancy, intermission, latency, quiescence, suspension. *See* ACTION.

dormant *adjective*
Existing in a temporarily inactive form or state : abeyant, inactive, latent, quiescent, sleeping. *See* ACTION, SHOW.

dose *verb*
To administer or add a drug to : drug, medicate, narcotize, opiate, physic. *Informal:* dope (up). *See* DRUGS.

dot *noun*
1. A very small mark : dash, fleck, pinpoint, point, speck, spot. *See* MARKS. **2.** A tiny amount : bit[1], crumb, dab[1], dash, dram, drop, fragment, grain, iota, jot, minim, mite, modicum, molecule, ort, ounce, particle, scrap[1], scruple, shred, smidgen, speck, tittle, trifle, whit. *Chiefly British:* spot. *See* BIG.
dot *verb* To mark with many small spots : bespeckle, besprinkle, dapple, fleck, freckle, mottle, pepper, speck, speckle, sprinkle, stipple. *See* MARKS.

dotage *noun*
The condition of being senile : caducity, senility. *See* YOUTH.

dote on *verb*
To like or enjoy enthusiastically, often excessively : adore, delight (in), love. *Slang:* eat up, groove on. *See* LIKE, LOVE.

doting *adjective*
1. Feeling and expressing affection : affectionate, devoted, fond, loving. *See* ATTITUDE, LOVE. **2.** Exhibiting the mental and physical deterioration often accompanying old age : doddering, senile. *See* YOUTH.

dotty *adjective*
Afflicted with or exhibiting irrationality and

mental unsoundness : brainsick, crazy, daft, demented, disordered, distraught, insane, lunatic, mad, maniac, maniacal, mentally ill, moonstruck, off, touched, unbalanced, unsound, wrong. *Informal:* bonkers, cracked, daffy, gaga, loony. *Slang:* bananas, batty, buggy, cuckoo, fruity, loco, nuts, nutty, screwy, wacky. *Chiefly British:* crackers. *Law:* non compos mentis. ***Idioms:*** around the bend, crazy as a loon, mad as a hatter, not all there, nutty as a fruitcake, off (*or* out of) one's head, off one's rocker, of unsound mind, out of one's mind, sick in the head, stark raving mad. *See* SANE.

double *adjective*
1. Twice as much or as large : twofold. *See* BIG. **2.** Consisting of two identical or similar related things, parts, or elements : dual, paired, twin. *See* SAME. **3.** Composed of two parts or things : biform, binary, dual, duple, duplex, duplicate, geminate, twofold. *See* PART. **4.** Being or acting so as to conceal one's real intentions : double-dealing, double-faced, two-faced. *See* HONEST.

double *noun* **1.** One exactly resembling another : duplicate, image, picture, portrait, spitting image. *Slang:* ringer. *See* SAME. **2.** One of a matched pair of things : companion, counterpart, duplicate, fellow, match, mate, twin. *See* SAME.

double *verb* **1.** To make or become twice as great : duplicate, geminate, redouble, twin. *See* BIG, INCREASE. **2.** To bend together or make a crease in so that one part lies over another : crease, fold, pleat, ply[1], ruck[2]. *See* ORDER, SMOOTH. **3.** To turn sharply around. Also used with *back* : about-face, reverse. *See* APPROACH.

double-cross *verb*
1. To be treacherous to : betray. *Slang:* rat (on), sell out. ***Idiom:*** sell down the river. *See* TRUST. **2.** To cause to accept what is false, especially by trickery or misrepresentation : beguile, betray, bluff, cozen, deceive, delude, dupe, fool, hoodwink, humbug, mislead, take in, trick. *Informal:* bamboozle, have. *Slang:* four-flush. ***Idioms:*** lead astray, play false, pull the wool over someone's eyes, put something over on, take for a ride. *See* HONEST.

double cross also **double-cross** *noun* An act of betraying : betrayal, treachery. *Slang:* sellout. *See* TRUST.

double-crosser *noun*
One who betrays : betrayer, Judas, traitor. *Informal:* rat. *See* TRUST.

double-dealing *adjective*
Being or acting so as to conceal one's real intentions : double, double-faced, two-faced. *See* HONEST.

double-dealing *noun* The act or practice of deceiving : cunning, deceit, deceitfulness, deception, duplicity, guile, shiftiness. *See* HONEST.

double-entendre *noun*
An expression or term liable to more than one interpretation : ambiguity, equivocality, equivocation, equivoque, tergiversation. *See* CLEAR.

double-faced *adjective*
Being or acting so as to conceal one's real intentions : double, double-dealing, two-faced. *See* HONEST.

doublet *noun*
Two items of the same kind together : brace, couple, couplet, duet, duo, match, pair, two, twosome, yoke. *See* GROUP, SAME.

double talk *noun*
1. Unintelligible or foolish talk : babble, blather, blatherskite, gabble, gibberish, jabber, jabberwocky, jargon, nonsense, prate, prattle, twaddle. *See* WORDS. **2.** Unintelligible or nonsensical talk or language : abracadabra, gibberish, gobbledygook, jabberwocky, mumbo jumbo. *See* CLEAR, WORDS.

doubt *verb*
1. To be uncertain, disbelieving, or skeptical about : distrust, misdoubt, mistrust, question, wonder. ***Idiom:*** have one's doubts. *See* CERTAIN. **2.** To lack trust or confidence in : distrust, misdoubt, mistrust, suspect. *See* TRUST.

doubt *noun* **1.** A lack of conviction or certainty : doubtfulness, dubiety, dubiousness, incertitude, mistrust, question, skepticism, suspicion, uncertainty, wonder. *See* CERTAIN. **2.** Lack of trust : distrust, leeriness, mistrust, suspicion. *See* TRUST.

doubter *noun*
One who habitually or instinctively doubts or questions : doubting Thomas, nonbeliever, skeptic, unbeliever. *See* BELIEF.

doubtful *adjective*
1. Not affording certainty : ambiguous, borderline, chancy, clouded, dubious, dubitable, equivocal, inconclusive, indecisive, indeterminate, problematic, problematical, questionable, uncertain, unclear, unsure. *Informal:* iffy. ***Idioms:*** at issue, in doubt, in question. *See* CERTAIN, CLEAR. **2.** Not likely : improbable, questionable, unapt, unlikely. *See* LIKELY. **3.** Experiencing doubt : dubious, skeptical, uncertain, undecided, unsure. ***Idiom:*** in doubt. *See*

CERTAIN. **4.** In doubt or dispute : arguable, contested, debatable, disputable, exceptionable, moot, mootable, problematic, problematical, questionable, uncertain. *See* CERTAIN. **5.** Of dubious character : equivocal, questionable, shady, suspect, suspicious, uncertain. *Informal:* fishy. *See* HONEST.

doubtfully *adverb*
With skepticism : askance, dubiously, questioningly, skeptically. *Idiom:* with a grain of salt. *See* BELIEF.

doubtfulness *noun*
A lack of conviction or certainty : doubt, dubiety, dubiousness, incertitude, mistrust, question, skepticism, suspicion, uncertainty, wonder. *See* CERTAIN.

doubting *adjective*
Lacking trust or confidence : distrustful, leery, mistrustful, suspicious, untrusting. *See* TRUST.

doubting Thomas *noun*
One who habitually or instinctively doubts or questions : doubter, nonbeliever, skeptic, unbeliever. *See* BELIEF.

doubtless *adverb*
Without question : absolutely, certainly, doubtlessly, positively, undoubtedly. *See* CERTAIN, LIMITED.

doubtlessly *adverb*
Without question : absolutely, certainly, doubtless, positively, undoubtedly. *See* CERTAIN, LIMITED.

dough *noun*
Slang. Something, such as coins or printed bills, used as a medium of exchange : cash, currency, lucre, money. *Informal:* wampum. *Slang:* bread, cabbage, gelt, green, jack, lettuce, long green, mazuma, moola, scratch. *Chiefly British:* brass. *See* MONEY.

doughtiness *noun*
The quality of mind enabling one to face danger or hardship resolutely : braveness, bravery, courage, courageousness, dauntlessness, fearlessness, fortitude, gallantry, gameness, heart, intrepidity, intrepidness, mettle, nerve, pluck, pluckiness, spirit, stoutheartedness, undauntedness, valiance, valiancy, valiantness, valor. *Informal:* spunk, spunkiness. *Slang:* gut (used in plural), gutsiness, moxie. *See* FEAR.

doughty *adjective*
Having or showing courage : audacious, bold, brave, courageous, dauntless, fearless, fortitudinous, gallant, game, hardy, heroic, intrepid, mettlesome, plucky, stout, stouthearted, unafraid, undaunted, valiant, valorous. *Informal:* spunky. *Slang:* gutsy, gutty. *See* FEAR.

do up *verb* See **do.**

dour *adjective*
1. Cold and forbidding : austere, bleak, grim, hard, harsh, severe, stark. *See* ATTITUDE, HOT. **2.** Broodingly and sullenly unhappy : gloomy, glum, moody, morose, saturnine, sour, sulky, sullen, surly. *See* HAPPY.

douse *verb*
1. To plunge briefly in or into a liquid : dip, duck, dunk, immerge, immerse, souse, submerge, submerse. *See* ENTER. **2.** To make thoroughly wet : drench, saturate, soak, sodden, sop, souse, wet. *See* DRY. **3.** To cause to stop burning or giving light : extinguish, put out, quench, snuff out. *See* CONTINUE.

dovetail *verb*
To conform to another, especially in size and shape : fit[1]. *See* AGREE.

dowdy *adjective*
1. Quite outmoded or unfashionable : frumpish. *Informal:* tacky[2]. *See* NEW. **2.** Of a style or method formerly in vogue : antiquated, antique, archaic, bygone, dated, fusty, old, old-fashioned, old-time, outdated, outmoded, out-of-date, passé, vintage. *See* NEW.

dower *verb*
To present with a quality, trait, or power : endow, endue, gift, gird, invest. *See* GIVE.

down *adjective*
1. Characterized by reduced economic activity : dull, off, slack, slow, sluggish, soft. *See* INCREASE. **2.** Suffering from or affected with an illness : ill, sick, unwell. *Informal:* laid up. *Chiefly Regional:* poorly. *See* HEALTH. **3.** In low spirits : blue, dejected, depressed, desolate, dispirited, downcast, downhearted, dull, dysphoric, gloomy, heavy-hearted, low, melancholic, melancholy, sad, spiritless, tristful, unhappy, wistful. *Idiom:* down at (*or* in) the mouth. *See* HAPPY.

down *noun* A sudden drop to a lower condition or status : comedown, descent, downfall, downgrade. *See* RISE.

down *verb* **1.** To cause to fall, as from a shot or blow : bring down, cut down, drop, fell[1], flatten, floor, ground, knock down, level, prostrate, strike down, throw. *Slang:* deck[1]. *Idiom:* lay low. *See* RISE. **2.** To swallow (food or drink) greedily or rapidly in large amounts : bolt, englut, engorge, gobble, gulp, guzzle, ingurgitate, swill, wolf. *See* INGESTION.

down-and-out or **down and out** *adjective*
Having little or no money or wealth : beggarly, destitute, impecunious, impoverished, indigent, necessitous, needy, penniless, penurious, poor,

poverty-stricken. *Informal:* broke, strapped. ***Idioms:*** hard up, on one's uppers. *See* RICH.

down-and-out or **down and out** *noun* An impoverished person : beggar, down-and-outer, have-not, indigent, pauper. *See* RICH.

down-and-outer *noun*
An impoverished person : beggar, down-and-out, have-not, indigent, pauper. *See* RICH.

down-at-heel or **down-at-the-heel** *adjective*
Showing signs of wear and tear or neglect : bedraggled, broken-down, decaying, decrepit, dilapidated, dingy, faded, mangy, rundown, scrubby, scruffy, seedy, shabby, shoddy, sleazy, tattered, tatty, threadbare. *Informal:* tacky[2]. *Slang:* ratty. ***Idioms:*** all the worse for wear, gone to pot (*or* seed), past cure (*or* hope). *See* BETTER.

down-at-the-heel *adjective* See **down-at-heel.**

downcast *adjective*
In low spirits : blue, dejected, depressed, desolate, dispirited, down, downhearted, dull, dysphoric, gloomy, heavy-hearted, low, melancholic, melancholy, sad, spiritless, tristful, unhappy, wistful. ***Idiom:*** down at (*or* in) the mouth. *See* HAPPY.

downfall *noun*
1. A sudden drop to a lower condition or status : comedown, descent, down, downgrade. *See* RISE. **2.** A disastrous overwhelming defeat or ruin : collapse, fall, waterloo. *See* THRIVE. **3.** Something that causes total loss or severe impairment, as of one's health, fortune, honor, or hopes : bane, destroyer, destruction, ruin, ruination, undoing, wrecker. *See* HELP.

downgrade *noun*
A sudden drop to a lower condition or status : comedown, descent, down, downfall. *See* RISE.

downgrade *verb* **1.** To lower in rank or grade : break, bump, degrade, demote, reduce. *Slang:* bust. *See* RISE. **2.** To lower in character or quality : cheapen, debase, degrade, demean[2]. *See* BETTER. **3.** To think, represent, or speak of as small or unimportant : belittle, decry, denigrate, deprecate, depreciate, derogate, detract, discount, disparage, minimize, run down, slight, talk down. ***Idiom:*** make light (*or* little) of. *See* ATTACK, SHOW. **4.** To become or make less in price or value : cheapen, depreciate, depress, devaluate, devalue, lower[2], mark down, reduce, write down. *See* INCREASE, MONEY.

downhearted *adjective*
In low spirits : blue, dejected, depressed, desolate, dispirited, down, downcast, dull, dysphoric, gloomy, heavy-hearted, low, melancholic, melancholy, sad, spiritless, tristful, unhappy, wistful. ***Idiom:*** down at (*or* in) the mouth. *See* HAPPY.

downheartedness *noun*
A feeling or spell of dismally low spirits : blues, dejection, depression, despondence, despondency, doldrums, dolefulness, dumps, dysphoria, funk, gloom, glumness, heavy-heartedness, melancholy, mope (used in plural), mournfulness, sadness, unhappiness. *See* FEELINGS, HAPPY.

down payment *noun*
A partial or initial payment : deposit. *See* MONEY, PAY.

downpour *noun*
An abundant, usually overwhelming flow or fall, as of a river or rain : alluvion, cataclysm, cataract, deluge, flood, freshet, inundation, Niagara, overflow, torrent. *Chiefly British:* spate. *See* BIG.

downright *adjective*
1. Completely such, without qualification or exception : absolute, all-out, arrant, complete, consummate, crashing, damned, dead, flat, out-and-out, outright, perfect, plain, pure, sheer[2], thorough, thoroughgoing, total, unbounded, unequivocal, unlimited, unmitigated, unqualified, unrelieved, unreserved, utter[2]. *Informal:* flat-out, positive. *Chiefly British:* blooming. *See* BIG, LIMITED. **2.** Manifesting honesty and directness, especially in speech : candid, direct, forthright, frank, honest, ingenuous, man-to-man, open, plainspoken, straight, straightforward, straight-out, unreserved. *Informal:* straight-from-the-shoulder, straight-shooting. *See* CLEAR, SHOW.

downslide *noun*
A usually swift downward trend, as in prices : decline, descent, dip, dive, downswing, downtrend, downturn, drop, drop-off, fall, nosedive, plunge, skid, slide, slump, tumble. *See* INCREASE.

downswing *noun*
A usually swift downward trend, as in prices : decline, descent, dip, dive, downslide, downtrend, downturn, drop, drop-off, fall, nosedive, plunge, skid, slide, slump, tumble. *See* INCREASE.

down-to-earth *adjective*
Having or indicating an awareness of things as they really are : hard, hardheaded, matter-of-fact, objective, practical, pragmatic, pragmatical, prosaic, realistic, sober, tough-minded, unromantic. *See* EXCITE, REAL.

downtrend *noun*
A usually swift downward trend, as in prices : decline, descent, dip, dive, downslide, downswing, downturn, drop, drop-off, fall, nosedive, plunge, skid, slide, slump, tumble. *See* INCREASE.

downturn *noun*
A usually swift downward trend, as in prices : decline, descent, dip, dive, downslide, downswing, downtrend, drop, drop-off, fall, nosedive, plunge, skid, slide, slump, tumble. *See* INCREASE.

downward *adjective*
Moving or sloping down : descendent, descending. *See* RISE.

doze *verb*
To sleep for a brief period. Also used with *off* : catnap, nap, nod (off), siesta, snooze. ***Idiom:*** catch (*or* grab *or* take) forty winks. *See* AWARENESS.
doze *noun* A brief sleep : catnap, nap, siesta, snooze. *See* AWARENESS.

dozy *adjective*
Ready for or needing sleep : drowsy, nodding, sleepy, slumberous, slumbery, somnolent, soporific. *See* AWARENESS.

drab *adjective*
1. Lacking vividness in color : dim, dull, flat, muddy, murky. *See* COLORS. **2.** Lacking liveliness, charm, or surprise : arid, aseptic, colorless, dry, dull, earthbound, flat, flavorless, lackluster, lifeless, lusterless, matter-of-fact, pedestrian, prosaic, spiritless, sterile, stodgy, unimaginative, uninspired. *See* EXCITE.

drabness *noun*
A lack of excitement, liveliness, or interest : asepticism, blandness, colorlessness, dreariness, dryness, dullness, flatness, flavorlessness, insipidity, insipidness, jejuneness, lifelessness, sterileness, sterility, stodginess, vapidity, vapidness, weariness. *See* EXCITE.

draft *noun*
1. The act of drawing or pulling a load : drag, draw, haul, pull, traction. *See* PUSH. **2.** An act of drinking or the amount swallowed : drink, potation, pull, quaff, sip, sup, swill. *Informal:* swig. *Slang:* belt. *See* MOUTH. **3.** Compulsory enrollment in military service : conscription, induction, levy. *See* GIVE. **4.** A preliminary plan or version, as of a written work : outline, rough, skeleton, sketch. *See* PLANNED, WORDS.
draft *verb* **1.** To enroll compulsorily in military service : conscript, induct, levy. *See* GIVE. **2.** To draw up a preliminary plan or version of : adumbrate, block in (*or* out), outline, rough in (*or* out), sketch. *See* PLANNED. **3.** To devise and set down : draw up, formulate, frame. *See* WORDS.

drag *verb*
1. To exert force so as to move (something) toward the source of the force : draw, haul, pull, tow, tug. *See* PUSH. **2.** To hang or cause to hang down and be pulled along behind : draggle, trail, train. *See* HANG. **3.** To advance slowly : crawl, creep, inch. *See* FAST. **4.** To go or move slowly so that progress is hindered : dally, dawdle, delay, dilly-dally, lag, linger, loiter, poke, procrastinate, tarry, trail. ***Idioms:*** drag one's feet (*or* heels), mark time, take one's time. *See* FAST.
drag *noun* **1.** The act of drawing or pulling a load : draft, draw, haul, pull, traction. *See* PUSH. **2.** An inhalation, as of a cigar, pipe, or cigarette : draw, puff, pull. *Slang:* hit. *See* BREATH.

dragging *adjective*
Extending tediously beyond a standard duration : drawn-out, lengthy, long[1], long-drawn-out, overlong, prolonged, protracted. *See* EXCITE, LONG.

draggle *verb*
To hang or cause to hang down and be pulled along behind : drag, trail, train. *See* HANG.

dragoon *verb*
To compel by pressure or threats : blackjack, coerce, force. *Informal:* hijack, strong-arm. *See* PERSUASION.

drain *verb*
1. To remove (a liquid) by a steady, gradual process : draw (off), let out, pump, tap[2]. *See* INCREASE. **2.** To grow or cause to grow gradually less : abate, decrease, diminish, dwindle, ebb, lessen, let up, peter (out), rebate, reduce, tail away (*or* off), taper (off). *See* INCREASE. **3.** To lessen or weaken severely, as by removing something essential : deplete, exhaust, impoverish, sap[2], use up. *See* GIVE, INCREASE, RICH. **4.** To use all of : consume, draw down, eat up, exhaust, expend, finish, play out, run through, spend, use up. *Informal:* polish off. *See* INCREASE. **5.** To diminish the strength and energy of : fatigue, jade, tire, wear, wear down, wear out, weary. *See* TIRED.
drain *noun* The act or process of decreasing : abatement, curtailment, cut, cutback, decrease, decrement, diminishment, diminution, reduction, slash, slowdown, taper. *See* INCREASE.

drained *adjective*
Extremely tired : bleary, dead, exhausted, fa-

tigued, rundown, spent, tired out, wearied, weariful, weary, worn-down, worn-out. *Informal:* beat, bushed, tuckered (out). *Slang:* done in, fagged (out), pooped (out). ***Idioms:*** all in, ready to drop. *See* HEALTH, TIRED.

draining *adjective*
Causing fatigue : exhausting, fatiguing, tiring, wearing, wearying. *See* TIRED.

dram *noun*
1. A small amount of liquor : drop, jigger, shot, sip, tot[1]. *Informal:* nip[2], slug[1]. *Slang:* snort. *See* BIG, INGESTION. **2.** A tiny amount : bit[1], crumb, dab[1], dash, dot, drop, fragment, grain, iota, jot, minim, mite, modicum, molecule, ort, ounce, particle, scrap[1], scruple, shred, smidgen, speck, tittle, trifle, whit. *Chiefly British:* spot. *See* BIG.

dramatic *adjective*
1. Of or relating to drama or the theater : dramaturgic, dramaturgical, histrionic, histrionical, theatric, theatrical, thespian. *See* PERFORMING ARTS. **2.** Suggesting drama or a stage performance, as in emotionality or suspense : histrionic, histrionical, melodramatic, sensational, spectacular, theatric, theatrical. *See* EXCITE, STYLE, SURPRISE.

dramatics *noun*
1. The art and occupation of an actor : acting, stage. *See* ACTION, PERFORMING ARTS, SUBSTITUTE. **2.** Overemotional exaggerated behavior calculated for effect : histrionics, melodramatics, theatrical (used in plural), theatrics. *See* FEELINGS, STYLE.

dramatize *verb*
To produce on the stage : act (out), do, enact, give, perform, present[2], put on, stage. *See* PERFORMING ARTS.

dramaturgic *adjective*
Of or relating to drama or the theater : dramatic, dramaturgical, histrionic, histrionical, theatric, theatrical, thespian. *See* PERFORMING ARTS.

dramaturgical *adjective*
Of or relating to drama or the theater : dramatic, dramaturgic, histrionic, histrionical, theatric, theatrical, thespian. *See* PERFORMING ARTS.

drape *verb*
1. To cover as if with clothes : cloak, clothe, mantle, robe. *See* PUT ON. **2.** To sit or lie with the limbs spread out awkwardly : loll, sprawl, spread-eagle, straddle. *See* POSTURE.

draw *verb*
1. To exert force so as to move (something) toward the source of the force : drag, haul, pull, tow, tug. *See* PUSH. **2.** To cause (a liquid) to flow in a steady stream. Also used with *off* : decant, effuse, pour. *See* MOVE. **3.** To remove (a liquid) by a steady, gradual process. Also used with *off* : drain, let out, pump, tap[2]. *See* INCREASE. **4.** To obtain from another source : derive, get, take. *See* KIN. **5.** To direct or impel to oneself by some quality or action : allure, appeal, attract, entice, lure, magnetize, take. *Informal:* pull. *See* LIKE. **6.** To call forth or bring out (something latent, hidden, or unexpressed). Also used with *out* : educe, elicit, evoke, summon. *See* SHOW. **7.** To make as income or profit : bring in, clear, earn, gain, gross, net[2], pay, produce, realize, repay, return, yield. *See* MONEY. **8.** To arrive at (a conclusion) from evidence or reasoning : conclude, deduce, deduct, gather, infer, judge, understand. *See* REASON.

draw back *verb* To move back in the face of enemy attack or after a defeat : fall back, pull back, pull out, retire, retreat, withdraw. ***Idioms:*** beat a retreat, give ground (*or* way). *See* FORWARD.

draw down *verb* To use all of : consume, drain, eat up, exhaust, expend, finish, play out, run through, spend, use up. *Informal:* polish off. *See* INCREASE.

draw in *verb* **1.** To pull back in : retract, withdraw. *See* SHOW. **2.** To involve (someone) in an activity : engage. *See* PARTICIPATE.

draw out *verb* To make or become longer : elongate, extend, lengthen, prolong, prolongate, protract, spin (out), stretch (out). *Mathematics:* produce. *See* INCREASE, LONG.

draw up *verb* To devise and set down : draft, formulate, frame. *See* WORDS.

draw *noun* **1.** The act of drawing or pulling a load : draft, drag, haul, pull, traction. *See* PUSH. **2.** An inhalation, as of a cigar, pipe, or cigarette : drag, puff, pull. *Slang:* hit. *See* BREATH. **3.** The power or quality of attracting : allure, allurement, appeal, attraction, attractiveness, call, charisma, charm, enchantment, enticement, fascination, glamour, lure, magnetism, witchery. *Informal:* pull. *See* LIKE. **4.** A dominating position, as in a conflict : advantage, better[1], bulge, drop, edge, superiority, upper hand, vantage. *Informal:* inside track, jump. *See* OVER. **5.** An equality of scores, votes, or performances in a contest : dead heat, deadlock, stalemate, standoff, tie. *See* SAME.

drawback *noun*
An unfavorable condition, circumstance, or

characteristic : detriment, disadvantage, handicap, minus. *See* HELP.

draw back *verb* See **draw.**

draw down *verb* See **draw.**

draw in *verb* See **draw.**

drawn *adjective*
1. Physically haggard : cadaverous, emaciated, gaunt, shrunken, skeletal, wasted. ***Idiom:*** skin and bones. *See* BETTER, TIRED. **2.** Pale and exhausted, as because of worry or sleeplessness : careworn, gaunt, haggard, hollow-eyed, wan, worn. *See* TIRED.

drawn-out *adjective*
Extending tediously beyond a standard duration : dragging, lengthy, long[1], long-drawn-out, overlong, prolonged, protracted. *See* EXCITE, LONG.

draw out *verb* See **draw.**

draw up *verb* See **draw.**

dread *verb*
To be afraid of : fear. ***Idiom:*** have one's heart in one's mouth. *See* FEAR.

dread *noun* **1.** Great agitation and anxiety caused by the expectation or the realization of danger : affright, alarm, apprehension, fear, fearfulness, fright, funk, horror, panic, terror, trepidation. *Slang:* cold feet. ***Idiom:*** fear and trembling. *See* FEAR. **2.** *Archaic.* The emotion aroused by something awe-inspiring or astounding : amaze, amazement, astonishment, awe, marvel, wonder, wonderment. *Archaic:* admiration. *See* EXCITE, FEELINGS.

dreadful *adjective*
1. Causing or able to cause fear : appalling, dire, direful, fearful, fearsome, formidable, frightful, ghastly, redoubtable, scary, terrible, tremendous. *See* FEAR. **2.** Very bad : appalling, awful, fearful, frightful, ghastly, horrendous, horrible, shocking, terrible. *See* GOOD.

dreadfully *adverb*
To a high degree : awfully, eminently, exceedingly, exceptionally, extra, extremely, greatly, highly, most, notably, very. *Informal:* awful. *Chiefly Regional:* mighty. *See* BIG.

dream *noun*
1. An illusory mental image : daydream, fancy, fantasy, fiction, figment, illusion, phantasm, phantasma, reverie, vision. *See* REAL. **2.** A fantastic, impracticable plan or desire : bubble, castle in the air, chimera, fantasy, illusion, pipe dream, rainbow. *See* REAL. **3.** A fervent hope, wish, or goal : aspiration, ideal. *See* HOPE.

dream *verb* **1.** To experience dreams or daydreams : daydream, fantasize, muse[1], woolgather. *See* REAL. **2.** To have a fervent hope or aspiration : aspire. ***Idioms:*** reach for the stars, set one's heart on. *See* SEEK.

dream up *verb* To use ingenuity in making, developing, or achieving : concoct, contrive, devise, fabricate, formulate, hatch, invent, make up, think up. *Informal:* cook up. ***Idiom:*** come up with. *See* MAKE.

dreamer *noun*
A person inclined to be imaginative or idealistic but impractical : idealist, utopian, visionary. *See* ABILITY, HOPE.

dreamlike *adjective*
Of, relating to, or in the nature of an illusion; lacking reality : chimeric, chimerical, delusive, delusory, hallucinatory, illusive, illusory, phantasmal, phantasmagoric, phantasmic, visionary. *See* REAL.

dream up *verb* See **dream.**

dreamy *adjective*
1. Given to daydreams or reverie : moony, visionary, woolgathering. *See* REAL. **2.** *Informal.* Particularly excellent : divine, fabulous, fantastic, fantastical, glorious, marvelous, sensational, splendid, superb, terrific, wonderful. *Informal:* dandy, great, ripping, super, swell, tremendous. *Slang:* cool, groovy, hot, keen[1], neat, nifty. ***Idiom:*** out of this world. *See* GOOD.

drear *adjective*
Arousing no interest or curiosity : boring, dreary, dry, dull, humdrum, irksome, monotonous, stuffy, tedious, tiresome, uninteresting, weariful, wearisome, weary. *See* EXCITE.

dreariness *noun*
A lack of excitement, liveliness, or interest : asepticism, blandness, colorlessness, drabness, dryness, dullness, flatness, flavorlessness, insipidity, insipidness, jejuneness, lifelessness, sterileness, sterility, stodginess, vapidity, vapidness, weariness. *See* EXCITE.

dreary *adjective*
1. Dark and depressing : black, bleak, blue, cheerless, dark, desolate, dismal, gloomy, glum, joyless, somber, tenebrific. *See* HAPPY, LIGHT. **2.** Arousing no interest or curiosity : boring, drear, dry, dull, humdrum, irksome, monotonous, stuffy, tedious, tiresome, uninteresting, weariful, wearisome, weary. *See* EXCITE.

dreg *noun*
1. Matter that settles on a bottom or collects on a surface by a natural process. Often used in plural : deposit, lees, precipitate, precipitation, sediment. *See* LEFTOVER. **2.** A group of persons regarded as the lowest class. Often used in plural : lumpenproletariat, rabble, ragtag and

bobtail, riffraff, trash. *Slang:* scum. ***Idioms:*** scum of the earth, tag and rag, the great unwashed. *See* OVER, RICH.

drench *verb*

To make thoroughly wet : douse, saturate, soak, sodden, sop, souse, wet. *See* DRY.

dress *verb*

1. To put clothes on : apparel, attire, clothe, garb, garment, invest. *Informal:* tog. *See* PUT ON. **2.** To furnish with decorations. Also used with *up* : adorn, bedeck, deck[2] (out), decorate, embellish, garnish, ornament, trim. *See* BEAUTIFUL. **3.** To apply therapeutic materials to (a wound) : bandage, bind. *See* CARE FOR. **4.** To prepare (soil) for the planting and raising of crops : cultivate, culture, tend[2], till, work. *See* PREPARED, TOUCH.

dress down *verb* To criticize for a fault or an offense : admonish, call down, castigate, chastise, chide, rap[1], rebuke, reprimand, reproach, reprove, scold, tax, upbraid. *Informal:* bawl out, lambaste. *Slang:* chew out. ***Idioms:*** call on the carpet, let someone have it, haul (*or* rake) over the coals, bring (*or* call *or* take) to task. *See* ATTACK, PRAISE.

dress up *verb* To dress in formal or special clothing : array, attire, deck[2] (out), prank[2]. *Informal:* trick out (*or* up). *Slang:* doll up. *See* ORDER, PLAIN, PUT ON.

dress *noun* **1.** Articles worn to cover the body : apparel, attire, clothes, clothing, garment (used in plural), habiliment (often used in plural), raiment. *Informal:* dud (used in plural), tog (used in plural). *Slang:* thread (used in plural). *See* PUT ON. **2.** A set or style of clothing : costume, garb, guise, habiliment (often used in plural), outfit, turnout. *Informal:* getup, rig. *See* PUT ON. **3.** A one-piece skirted outer garment for women and children : frock, gown. *See* PUT ON.

dress down *verb* See **dress.**

dress up *verb* See **dress.**

dressy *adjective*

Requiring elegant clothes and fine manners : formal, full-dress. *See* PLAIN.

dribble *verb*

1. To fall or let fall in drops of liquid : distill, drip, drop, trickle, weep. *See* RISE. **2.** To let saliva run from the mouth : drivel, drool, salivate, slaver, slobber. *See* DRY, MOUTH.

dribble *noun* The process or sound of dripping : drip, trickle. *See* RISE, SOUNDS.

driblet *noun*

A quantity of liquid falling or resting in a spherical mass : drop, droplet, globule. *See* DRY.

drift *verb*

1. To move along with or be carried away by the action of water : float, wash. *See* MOVE. **2.** To pass smoothly, quietly, and undisturbed on or as if on a slippery surface : coast, slide. *See* MOVE. **3.** To move about at random, especially over a wide area : gad, gallivant, meander, peregrinate, ramble, range, roam, rove, stray, traipse, wander. *See* MOVE. **4.** To put into a disordered pile : bank[1], heap, hill, lump[1], mound, pile (up), stack. *See* ORDER.

drift *noun* **1.** A group of things gathered haphazardly : agglomeration, bank[1], cumulus, heap, hill, mass, mess, mound, mountain, pile, shock[2], stack, tumble. *See* ORDER. **2.** Something suggestive of running water : current, flood, flow, flux, rush, spate, stream, surge, tide. *See* MOVE. **3.** The general sense or significance, as of an action or statement : amount, burden[2], import, purport, substance, tenor. ***Idioms:*** sum and substance, sum total. *See* MEANING. **4.** The thread or current of thought uniting or occurring in all the elements of a text or discourse : aim, burden[2], intent, meaning, purport, substance, tendency, tenor, thrust. *See* MEANING.

drill *noun*

Repetition of an action so as to develop or maintain one's skill : exercise, practice, rehearsal, study, training. *See* WORK.

drill *verb* **1.** To subject to or engage in forms of exertion in order to train, strengthen, or condition : exercise, practice, train, work out. *See* WORK. **2.** To instruct in a body of doctrine or belief : inculcate, indoctrinate. *See* TEACH. **3.** To fix (an idea, for example) in someone's mind by reemphasis and repetition : drive, implant, impress, inculcate, instill, pound. *See* TEACH.

drink *verb*

1. To take into the mouth and swallow (a liquid) : imbibe, pull on, quaff, sip, sup. *Informal:* swig, toss down (*or* off). *Slang:* belt. ***Idiom:*** wet one's whistle. *See* MOUTH. **2.** To take alcoholic liquor, especially excessively or habitually : guzzle, imbibe, tipple. *Informal:* nip[2]. *Slang:* booze, lush[2], soak, tank up. ***Idioms:*** bend the elbow, hit the bottle. *See* DRUGS. **3.** To take in (moisture or liquid) : absorb, imbibe, soak (up), sop up, take up. *See* GIVE. **4.** To salute by raising and drinking from a glass : pledge, toast. *See* DESIRE, REMEMBER.

drink *noun* **1.** Any liquid that is fit for drinking : beverage, drinkable, liquor, potable. *See*

DRY. **2.** An act of drinking or the amount swallowed : draft, potation, pull, quaff, sip, sup, swill. *Informal:* swig. *Slang:* belt. *See* MOUTH.

drinkable *noun*
Any liquid that is fit for drinking : beverage, drink, liquor, potable. *See* DRY.

drip *verb*
To fall or let fall in drops of liquid : distill, dribble, drop, trickle, weep. *See* RISE.
drip *noun* **1.** The process or sound of dripping : dribble, trickle. *See* RISE, SOUNDS. **2.** *Slang.* An unpleasant, tiresome person : bore. *Slang:* dweeb, jerk, nerd, pill, poop². *See* LIKE.

drippy *adjective*
Slang. Affectedly or extravagantly emotional : bathetic, gushy, maudlin, mawkish, romantic, sentimental, slushy, sobby, soft, soppy. *Informal:* gooey, mushy, schmaltzy, sloppy, soupy. *Slang:* sappy, tear-jerking. *See* FEELINGS.

drive *verb*
1. To force to move or advance with or as if with blows or pressure : propel, push, ram, shove, thrust. *See* MOVE. **2.** To urge to move along : herd, run. *See* MOVE. **3.** To move or advance against strong resistance : forge², lunge, plunge. *See* MOVE. **4.** To run and control (a motor vehicle) : motor, pilot, wheel. *Slang:* tool. *See* MOVE. **5.** To set or keep going : actuate, impel, mobilize, move, propel, run. *See* MOVE. **6.** To force to work : task, tax, work. ***Idiom:*** crack the whip. *See* WORK. **7.** To exert one's mental or physical powers, usually under difficulty and to the point of exhaustion : fag, labor, moil, strain¹, strive, sweat, toil, travail, tug, work. ***Idiom:*** break one's back (*or* neck). *See* WORK. **8.** To cause to penetrate with force : dig, plunge, ram, run, sink, stab, stick, thrust. *See* PUT IN. **9.** To fix (an idea, for example) in someone's mind by reemphasis and repetition : drill, implant, impress, inculcate, instill, pound. *See* TEACH. **10.** To look for and pursue (game) in order to capture or kill it : chase, hunt, run, stalk. *See* SEEK.
drive *noun* **1.** A trip in a motor vehicle : ride, run. *Informal:* spin, whirl. *See* MOVE. **2.** A course affording passage from one place to another : avenue, boulevard, expressway, freeway, highway, path, road, roadway, route, street, superhighway, thoroughfare, thruway, turnpike, way. *See* MOVE, OPEN. **3.** An organized effort to accomplish a purpose : campaign, crusade, movement, push. *See* ACTION, SEEK. **4.** An aggressive readiness along with energy to undertake taxing efforts : enterprise, hustle, initiative, punch. *Informal:* get-up-and-go, gumption, push. *See* ACTION, TIRED, TRY.

drivel *verb*
To let saliva run from the mouth : dribble, drool, salivate, slaver, slobber. *See* DRY, MOUTH.
drivel *noun* **1.** Saliva running from the mouth : drool, salivation, slaver, slobber. *See* DRY, MOUTH. **2.** Something that does not have or make sense : balderdash, blather, bunkum, claptrap, garbage, idiocy, nonsense, piffle, poppycock, rigmarole, rubbish, tomfoolery, trash, twaddle. *Informal:* tommyrot. *Slang:* applesauce, baloney, bilge, bull¹, bunk², crap, hooey, malarkey. *See* KNOWLEDGE.

driver *noun*
A person who operates a motor vehicle : motorist, operator. *See* MOVE.

driving *adjective*
Disposed to action : active, brisk, dynamic, dynamical, energetic, enterprising, lively, sprightly, spry, vigorous, zippy. *Informal:* peppy, snappy. *See* ACTION.

droit *noun*
Law. A privilege granted a person, as by virtue of birth : appanage, birthright, perquisite, prerogative, right. *See* OWNED.

droll *adjective*
Arousing laughter : amusing, comic, comical, funny, humorous, laughable, risible, zany. *See* LAUGHTER.

drollery *noun*
The quality of being laughable or comical : comedy, comicality, comicalness, drollness, farcicality, funniness, humor, humorousness, jocoseness, jocosity, jocularity, ludicrousness, ridiculousness, wit, wittiness, zaniness. *See* LAUGHTER.

drollness *noun*
The quality of being laughable or comical : comedy, comicality, comicalness, drollery, farcicality, funniness, humor, humorousness, jocoseness, jocosity, jocularity, ludicrousness, ridiculousness, wit, wittiness, zaniness. *See* LAUGHTER.

drone¹ *noun*
A self-indulgent person who spends time avoiding work or other useful activity : bum¹, fainéant, good-for-nothing, idler, layabout, loafer, ne'er-do-well, no-good, slugabed, sluggard, wastrel. *Informal:* do-little, do-nothing, lazybones, slug². *Slang:* slouch. *See* INDUSTRIOUS.

drone² *verb*
To make a continuous low-pitched droning

sound : bumble², burr, buzz, hum, whir, whiz. *See* SOUNDS.

drone *noun* A continuous low-pitched droning sound : bumble², burr, buzz, hum, whir, whiz. *See* SOUNDS.

drool *verb*

To let saliva run from the mouth : dribble, drivel, salivate, slaver, slobber. *See* DRY, MOUTH.

drool *noun* Saliva running from the mouth : drivel, salivation, slaver, slobber. *See* DRY, MOUTH.

droop *verb*

1. To hang limply, loosely, and carelessly : flop, loll, lop², sag, slouch, wilt. *See* HANG. **2.** To become limp, as from loss of freshness : flag², sag, wilt. *See* BETTER.

drop *noun*

1. A quantity of liquid falling or resting in a spherical mass : driblet, droplet, globule. *See* DRY. **2.** A small amount of liquor : dram, jigger, shot, sip, tot¹. *Informal:* nip², slug¹. *Slang:* snort. *See* BIG, INGESTION. **3.** A tiny amount : bit¹, crumb, dab¹, dash, dot, dram, fragment, grain, iota, jot, minim, mite, modicum, molecule, ort, ounce, particle, scrap¹, scruple, shred, smidgen, speck, tittle, trifle, whit. *Chiefly British:* spot. *See* BIG. **4.** The act of dropping from a height : descent, fall. *See* RISE. **5.** A usually swift downward trend, as in prices : decline, descent, dip, dive, downslide, downswing, downtrend, downturn, drop-off, fall, nosedive, plunge, skid, slide, slump, tumble. *See* INCREASE. **6.** The extent or measurement downward from a surface : deepness, depth. *See* SURFACE. **7.** A downward slope or distance : decline, declivity, descent, fall, pitch. *See* RISE. **8.** A dominating position, as in a conflict : advantage, better¹, bulge, draw, edge, superiority, upper hand, vantage. *Informal:* inside track, jump. *See* OVER.

drop *verb* **1.** To go from a more erect posture to a less erect posture : fall, sink, slump. *See* RISE. **2.** To undergo a sharp, rapid descent in value or price : dive, fall, nose-dive, plummet, plunge, sink, skid, slump, tumble. ***Idiom:*** take a sudden downtrend (*or* downturn). *See* INCREASE. **3.** To slope downward : decline, descend, dip, fall, pitch, sink. *See* RISE. **4.** To cause to fall, as from a shot or blow : bring down, cut down, down, fell¹, flatten, floor, ground, knock down, level, prostrate, strike down, throw. *Slang:* deck¹. ***Idiom:*** lay low. *See* RISE. **5.** To cease consideration or treatment of : dismiss, give over, give up, skip. ***Idioms:*** have done with, wash one's hands of. *See* KEEP. **6.** To take or leave out : eliminate, omit, remove. *See* INCLUDE. **7.** To suffer the loss of : forfeit, lose. ***Idiom:*** kiss good-by to. *See* GET. **8.** To suddenly lose all health or strength : break (down), cave in, collapse, crack, give out, succumb. *Informal:* crack up. *Slang:* conk out. ***Idiom:*** give way. *See* HEALTH. **9.** To cease living : decease, demise, depart, die, expire, go, pass away, pass (on), perish, succumb. *Informal:* pop off. *Slang:* check out, croak, kick in, kick off. ***Idioms:*** bite the dust, breathe one's last, cash in, give up the ghost, go to one's grave, kick the bucket, meet one's end (*or* Maker), pass on to the Great Beyond, turn up one's toes. *See* LIVE. **10.** To end the employment or service of : cashier, discharge, dismiss, release, terminate. *Informal:* ax, fire, pink-slip. *Slang:* boot¹, bounce, can, sack¹. ***Idioms:*** give someone his or her walking papers, give someone the ax, give someone the gate, give someone the pink slip, let go, show someone the door. *See* KEEP. **11.** To fall or let fall in drops of liquid : distill, dribble, drip, trickle, weep. *See* RISE. **12.** To move downward in response to gravity : descend, fall. *See* RISE. **13.** To come to the ground suddenly and involuntarily : fall, go down, nose-dive, pitch, plunge, spill, topple, tumble. ***Idiom:*** take a fall (*or* header *or* plunge *or* spill *or* tumble). *See* RISE. **14.** To cause to descend : depress, let down, lower², take down. *See* RISE.

drop by *verb* To go to or seek out the company of in order to socialize : call, come by, come over, drop in, look in, look up, pop in, run in, see, stop (by *or* in), visit. ***Idiom:*** pay a visit. *See* SEEK.

drop in *verb* To go to or seek out the company of in order to socialize : call, come by, come over, drop by, look in, look up, pop in, run in, see, stop (by *or* in), visit. ***Idiom:*** pay a visit. *See* SEEK.

drop off *verb* To decline, as in value or quantity, very gradually : fall off, sag, slip. *See* INCREASE.

drop by *verb* See **drop.**

drop in *verb* See **drop.**

droplet *noun*

A quantity of liquid falling or resting in a spherical mass : driblet, drop, globule. *See* DRY.

drop-off *noun*

A usually swift downward trend, as in prices : decline, descent, dip, dive, downslide, downswing, downtrend, downturn, drop, fall, nosedive, plunge, skid, slide, slump, tumble. *See* INCREASE.

drop off *verb* See **drop.**

drossy *adjective*
Lacking all worth and value : good-for-nothing, inutile, no-good, nothing, valueless, worthless. *Informal:* no-account. *See* VALUE.

droughty *adjective*
Having little or no precipitation : arid, dry, rainless, thirsty. *See* DRY.

drove *noun*
1. An enormous number of persons gathered together : crowd, crush, flock, horde, mass, mob, multitude, press, ruck[1], swarm, throng. *See* BIG, GROUP. **2.** A very large number of things grouped together : army, cloud, crowd, flock, horde, host, legion, mass, mob, multitude, ruck[1], score (used in plural), swarm, throng. *See* BIG, GROUP.

drown *verb*
To flow over completely : deluge, engulf, flood, flush, inundate, overflow, overwhelm, submerge, whelm. *See* FULL.

drowsy *adjective*
Ready for or needing sleep : dozy, nodding, sleepy, slumberous, slumbery, somnolent, soporific. *See* AWARENESS.

drub *verb*
1. To hit heavily and repeatedly with violent blows : assail, assault, baste, batter, beat, belabor, buffet, clobber, hammer, pound, pummel, smash, thrash, thresh. *Informal:* lambaste. *Slang:* clobber. ***Idiom:*** rain blows on. *See* ATTACK, STRIKE. **2.** To render totally ineffective by decisive defeat : annihilate, crush, overpower, overwhelm, smash, steamroller, thrash, trounce, vanquish. *Informal:* massacre, wallop. *Slang:* clobber, cream, shellac, smear. *See* WIN. **3.** To criticize harshly and devastatingly : blister, excoriate, flay, lash, rip into, scarify[1], scathe, scorch, score, scourge, slap, slash. *Informal:* roast. *Slang:* slam. ***Idioms:*** burn someone's ears, crawl all over, pin someone's ears back, put someone on the griddle, put someone on the hot seat, rake over the coals, read the riot act to. *See* PRAISE.

drubbing *noun*
The act of defeating or the condition of being defeated : beating, defeat, overthrow, rout, thrashing, vanquishment. *Informal:* massacre, trimming, whipping. *Slang:* dusting, licking. *See* WIN.

drudge *noun*
One who works or toils tirelessly : fag, grub, plodder, slave. *Informal:* grind, workhorse. *See* WORK.

drudge *verb* To do tedious, laborious, and sometimes menial work : grub, plod, slave, slog. *Informal:* grind. *See* WORK.

drudgery *noun*
Physical exertion that is usually difficult and exhausting : labor, moil, toil, travail, work. *Informal:* sweat. *Chiefly British:* fag. ***Idiom:*** sweat of one's brow. *See* WORK.

drug *noun*
1. A substance used in the treatment of disease : medicament, medication, medicine, pharmaceutical. *See* DRUGS. **2.** A substance that affects the central nervous system and is often addictive : hallucinogen, narcotic, opiate. *Informal:* dope. *See* DRUGS.

drug *verb* To administer or add a drug to : dose, medicate, narcotize, opiate, physic. *Informal:* dope (up). *See* DRUGS.

drugged *adjective*
Stupefied, intoxicated, or otherwise influenced by the taking of drugs : *Informal:* doped. *Slang:* high, hopped-up, lit (up), potted, spaced-out, stoned, turned-on, wiped-out, zonked. *See* DRUGS.

drunk *adjective*
Stupefied, excited, or muddled with alcoholic liquor : besotted, crapulent, crapulous, drunken, inebriate, inebriated, intoxicated, sodden, tipsy. *Informal:* cockeyed, stewed. *Slang:* blind, bombed, boozed, boozy, crocked, high, lit (up), loaded, looped, pickled, pixilated, plastered, potted, sloshed, smashed, soused, stinking, stinko, stoned, tight, zonked. ***Idioms:*** drunk as a skunk, half-seas over, high as a kite, in one's cups, three sheets in (*or* to) the wind. *See* DRUGS.

drunk *noun* **1.** A person who is habitually drunk : drunkard, inebriate, sot, tippler. *Slang:* boozehound, boozer, lush[2], rummy[1], soak, souse, sponge, stiff. *See* DRUGS. **2.** A drinking bout : binge, brannigan, carousal, carouse, spree. *Slang:* bat[2], bender, booze, jag, tear[1]. *See* DRUGS, RESTRAINT.

drunkard *noun*
A person who is habitually drunk : drunk, inebriate, sot, tippler. *Slang:* boozehound, boozer, lush[2], rummy[1], soak, souse, sponge, stiff. *See* DRUGS.

drunken *adjective*
Stupefied, excited, or muddled with alcoholic liquor : besotted, crapulent, crapulous, drunk, inebriate, inebriated, intoxicated, sodden, tipsy. *Informal:* cock-eyed, stewed. *Slang:* blind,

bombed, boozed, boozy, crocked, high, lit (up), loaded, looped, pickled, pixilated, plastered, potted, sloshed, smashed, soused, stinking, stinko, stoned, tight, zonked. ***Idioms:*** drunk as a skunk, half-seas over, high as a kite, in one's cups, three sheets in (*or* to) the wind. *See* DRUGS.

drunkenness *noun*
The condition of being intoxicated with alcoholic liquor : crapulence, inebriation, inebriety, insobriety, intoxication, tipsiness. *See* DRUGS.

dry *adjective*
1. Having little or no liquid or moisture : anhydrous, arid, bone-dry, moistureless, sere, waterless. *See* DRY. **2.** Having little or no precipitation : arid, droughty, rainless, thirsty. *See* DRY. **3.** Disagreeable to the sense of hearing : grating, harsh, hoarse, jarring, rasping, raspy, raucous, rough, scratchy, squawky, strident. *See* SOUNDS. **4.** Needing or desiring drink : parched, thirsty. *Archaic:* athirst. *See* DRY. **5.** Having a taste characteristic of that produced by acids : acerb, acerbic, acetous, acid, acidulous, sour, tangy, tart[1]. *See* TASTE. **6.** Without addition, decoration, or qualification : bald, bare, plain, simple, unadorned, unvarnished. *See* PLAIN. **7.** With little or no emotion or expression : impassive, matter-of-fact, unemotional. *See* ATTITUDE, EXCITE. **8.** Lacking liveliness, charm, or surprise : arid, aseptic, colorless, drab, dull, earthbound, flat, flavorless, lackluster, lifeless, lusterless, matter-of-fact, pedestrian, prosaic, spiritless, sterile, stodgy, unimaginative, uninspired. *See* EXCITE. **9.** Arousing no interest or curiosity : boring, drear, dreary, dull, humdrum, irksome, monotonous, stuffy, tedious, tiresome, uninteresting, weariful, wearisome, weary. *See* EXCITE.

dry *verb* **1.** To make or become free of moisture. Also used with *out* : dehydrate, desiccate, exsiccate, parch. *See* DRY. **2.** To make or become physically hard : cake, concrete, congeal, harden, indurate, petrify, set[1], solidify. *See* SOLID.

dry up *verb* **1.** To make or become no longer fresh or shapely because of loss of moisture : mummify, sear, shrivel, wither, wizen. *See* DRY. **2.** To make or become no longer active or productive : deplete, desiccate, give out, play out, run out. *See* CONTINUE.

dryness *noun*
1. A lack of excitement, liveliness, or interest : asepticism, blandness, colorlessness, drabness, dreariness, dullness, flatness, flavorlessness, insipidity, insipidness, jejuneness, lifelessness, sterileness, sterility, stodginess, vapidity, vapidness, weariness. *See* EXCITE. **2.** The practice of refraining from use of alcoholic liquors : abstinence, soberness, sobriety, teetotalism, temperance. *See* DRUGS, RESTRAINT, USED.

dry up *verb* See **dry.**

dual *adjective*
1. Composed of two parts or things : biform, binary, double, duple, duplex, duplicate, geminate, twofold. *See* PART. **2.** Consisting of two identical or similar related things, parts, or elements : double, paired, twin. *See* SAME.

dub *verb*
To give a name or title to : baptize, call, christen, denominate, designate, entitle, name, style, term, title. *See* SPECIFIC, WORDS.

dub *noun* A clumsy person : blunderer, botcher, bungler, foozler. *Slang:* screwup. *Idiom:* bull in a china shop. *See* ABILITY.

dubiety *noun*
A lack of conviction or certainty : doubt, doubtfulness, dubiousness, incertitude, mistrust, question, skepticism, suspicion, uncertainty, wonder. *See* CERTAIN.

dubious *adjective*
1. Experiencing doubt : doubtful, skeptical, uncertain, undecided, unsure. ***Idiom:*** in doubt. *See* CERTAIN. **2.** Not affording certainty : ambiguous, borderline, chancy, clouded, doubtful, dubitable, equivocal, inconclusive, indecisive, indeterminate, problematic, problematical, questionable, uncertain, unclear, unsure. *Informal:* iffy. ***Idioms:*** at issue, in doubt, in question. *See* CERTAIN, CLEAR.

dubiously *adverb*
With skepticism : askance, doubtfully, questioningly, skeptically. ***Idiom:*** with a grain of salt. *See* BELIEF.

dubiousness *noun*
A lack of conviction or certainty : doubt, doubtfulness, dubiety, incertitude, mistrust, question, skepticism, suspicion, uncertainty, wonder. *See* CERTAIN.

dubitable *adjective*
Not affording certainty : ambiguous, borderline, chancy, clouded, doubtful, dubious, equivocal, inconclusive, indecisive, indeterminate, problematic, problematical, questionable, uncertain, unclear, unsure. *Informal:* iffy. ***Idioms:*** at issue, in doubt, in question. *See* CERTAIN, CLEAR.

duck *verb*
1. To avoid fulfilling or answering completely : dodge, evade, hedge, sidestep, skirt. *See* SEEK.

2. To keep away from : avoid, burke, bypass, circumvent, dodge, elude, escape, eschew, evade, get around, shun. ***Idioms:*** fight shy of, give a wide berth to, have no truck with, keep (*or* stay *or* steer) clear of. *See* SEEK. **3.** To plunge briefly in or into a liquid : dip, douse, dunk, immerge, immerse, souse, submerge, submerse. *See* ENTER.

duck *noun* The act of swimming : dip, dunk, plunge, swim. *See* WORK.

duck soup *noun*
Slang. An easily accomplished task : child's play, cinch, pushover, snap, walkaway, walkover. *Informal:* breeze. *See* EASY.

ductile *adjective*
1. Capable of being shaped, bent, or drawn out, as by hammering or pressure : flexible, flexile, flexuous, malleable, moldable, plastic, pliable, pliant, supple, workable. *See* FLEXIBLE. **2.** Easily altered or influenced : elastic, flexible, flexile, impressionable, malleable, plastic, pliable, pliant, suggestible, supple. *See* FLEXIBLE.

ductility *noun*
The quality or state of being flexible : bounce, elasticity, flexibility, flexibleness, give, malleability, malleableness, plasticity, pliability, pliableness, pliancy, pliantness, resilience, resiliency, spring, springiness, suppleness. *Obsolete:* flexure. *See* FLEXIBLE.

dud *noun*
1. *Informal.* One that fails completely : bust, failure, fiasco, loser, washout. *Informal:* flop, lemon. *Slang:* bomb. *See* THRIVE. **2.** *Informal.* Articles worn to cover the body. Used in plural : apparel, attire, clothes, clothing, dress, garment (used in plural), habiliment (often used in plural), raiment. *Informal:* tog (used in plural). *Slang:* thread (used in plural). *See* PUT ON.

dudgeon *noun*
Extreme displeasure caused by an insult or slight : huff, miff, offense, pique, resentment, ruffled feathers, umbrage. *See* LIKE, PAIN.

due *adjective*
1. Owed as a debt : outstanding, owed, owing, payable, receivable, unpaid, unsettled. *See* PAY. **2.** Consistent with prevailing or accepted standards or circumstances : appropriate, deserved, fit[1], fitting, just, merited, proper, right, rightful, suitable. *See* RIGHT. **3.** Known to be about to arrive : anticipated, expected, scheduled. *See* SURPRISE.

due *noun* **1.** Something, such as money, owed by one person to another : arrearage, arrears, debt, indebtedness, liability, obligation. *See* OBLIGATION, PAY. **2.** Something justly deserved : comeuppance, desert[2] (often used in plural), guerdon, recompense, reward, wage (often used in plural). *Informal:* lump[1] (used in plural). ***Idioms:*** what is coming to one, what one has coming. *See* REWARD.

due *adverb* In a direct line : dead, direct, directly, right, straight, straightaway. *See* STRAIGHT.

duel *verb*
To strive in opposition : battle, combat, contend, fight, struggle, tilt, war, wrestle. *See* CONFLICT.

due process *noun*
The state, action, or principle of treating all persons equally in accordance with the law : equity, justice. *See* RIGHT.

duet *noun*
Two items of the same kind together : brace, couple, couplet, doublet, duo, match, pair, two, twosome, yoke. *See* GROUP, SAME.

dulcet *adjective*
Resembling or having the effect of music, especially pleasing music : euphonic, euphonious, melodic, melodious, musical, tuneful. *See* SOUNDS.

dulcify *verb*
To ease the anger or agitation of : appease, assuage, calm (down), conciliate, gentle, mollify, pacify, placate, propitiate, soften, soothe, sweeten. ***Idiom:*** pour oil on troubled water. *See* CALM.

dull *adjective*
1. Having only a limited ability to learn and understand : backward, simple, simple-minded, slow, slow-witted. *Informal:* soft. *Offensive:* feeble-minded, half-witted, retarded, weak-minded. *See* ABILITY. **2.** Lacking responsiveness or alertness : benumbed, insensible, insensitive, numb, stuporous, torpid, unresponsive, wooden. *See* AWARENESS. **3.** Unwilling or unable to perceive : blind, purblind, uncomprehending, unperceptive. *See* SEE. **4.** Lacking passion and emotion : anesthetic, bloodless, insensate, insensible, insensitive. *See* ATTITUDE, FEELINGS. **5.** In low spirits : blue, dejected, depressed, desolate, dispirited, down, downcast, downhearted, dysphoric, gloomy, heavy-hearted, low, melancholic, melancholy, sad, spiritless, tristful, unhappy, wistful. ***Idiom:*** down at (*or* in) the mouth. *See* HAPPY. **6.** Characterized by reduced economic activity : down, off, slack, slow, sluggish, soft. *See* INCREASE. **7.** Not physically sharp or keen : blunt. *See* SHARP. **8.** Arousing no interest or curiosity : boring, drear, dreary, dry, hum-

drum, irksome, monotonous, stuffy, tedious, tiresome, uninteresting, weariful, wearisome, weary. *See* EXCITE. **9.** Lacking liveliness, charm, or surprise : arid, aseptic, colorless, drab, dry, earthbound, flat, flavorless, lackluster, lifeless, lusterless, matter-of-fact, pedestrian, prosaic, spiritless, sterile, stodgy, unimaginative, uninspired. *See* EXCITE. **10.** Lacking vividness in color : dim, drab, flat, muddy, murky. *See* COLORS. **11.** Lacking gloss and luster : dim, flat, lackluster, lusterless, mat. *See* LIGHT.

dull *verb* **1.** To make or become less keen or responsive : dim, hebetate, stupefy. *See* AWARENESS. **2.** To render less sensitive : benumb, blunt, deaden, desensitize, numb. ***Idiom:*** take the edge off. *See* AWARENESS. **3.** To make or become less sharp-edged : blunt, turn. ***Idiom:*** take the edge off. *See* SHARP. **4.** To make dim or indistinct : becloud, bedim, befog, blear, blur, cloud, dim, eclipse, fog, gloom, mist, obfuscate, obscure, overcast, overshadow, shadow. *See* CLEAR.

dullard *noun*
A mentally dull person : blockhead, chump[1], clod, dolt, dummkopf, dummy, dunce, numskull, thickhead. *Slang:* dimwit, dumbbell, dumbo. *See* ABILITY.

dullness also **dulness** *noun*
1. A deficiency in mental and physical alertness and activity : hebetude, languidness, languor, lassitude, leadenness, lethargy, listlessness, sluggishness, stupor, torpidity, torpor. *See* ACTION. **2.** A lack of excitement, liveliness, or interest : asepticism, blandness, colorlessness, drabness, dreariness, dryness, flatness, flavorlessness, insipidity, insipidness, jejuneness, lifelessness, sterileness, sterility, stodginess, vapidity, vapidness, weariness. *See* EXCITE.

dulness *noun* See **dullness.**

dumb *adjective*
1. Lacking the power or faculty of speech : aphonic, inarticulate, mute, speechless, voiceless. *See* WORDS. **2.** Temporarily unable or unwilling to speak, as from shock or fear : inarticulate, mum, mute, silent, speechless, voiceless, wordless. *See* WORDS. **3.** Lacking in intelligence : blockheaded, dense, doltish, hebetudinous, obtuse, stupid, thickheaded, thick-witted. *Informal:* thick. *Slang:* dimwitted, dopey. *See* ABILITY.

dumbbell *noun*
Slang. A mentally dull person : blockhead, chump[1], clod, dolt, dullard, dummkopf, dummy, dunce, numskull, thickhead. *Slang:* dimwit, dumbo. *See* ABILITY.

dumbfound also **dumfound** *verb*
To overwhelm with surprise, wonder, or bewilderment : boggle, bowl over, flabbergast, floor, stagger. *See* EXCITE, SURPRISE.

dumbness *noun*
The avoidance of speech : muteness, silence, speechlessness, wordlessness. *See* WORDS.

dumbo *noun*
Slang. A mentally dull person : blockhead, chump[1], clod, dolt, dullard, dummkopf, dummy, dunce, numskull, thickhead. *Slang:* dimwit, dumbbell. *See* ABILITY.

dumfound *verb* See **dumbfound.**

dummkopf *noun*
A mentally dull person : blockhead, chump[1], clod, dolt, dullard, dummy, dunce, numskull, thickhead. *Slang:* dimwit, dumbbell, dumbo. *See* ABILITY.

dummy *noun*
A mentally dull person : blockhead, chump[1], clod, dolt, dullard, dummkopf, dunce, numskull, thickhead. *Slang:* dimwit, dumbbell, dumbo. *See* ABILITY.

dump *verb*
1. To remove the cargo or load from : disburden, discharge, unlade, unload. *See* PUT IN. **2.** To let go or get rid of as being useless or defective, for example : discard, dispose of, junk, scrap[1], throw away, throw out. *Informal:* chuck, jettison, shuck (off). *Slang:* ditch. *See* KEEP. **3.** To get rid of completely by selling, especially in quantity or at a discount : close out, sell off, sell out, unload. *See* TRANSACTIONS.

dumping *noun*
The act of getting rid of something useless or used up : disposal, elimination, jettison, riddance. *See* KEEP.

dumps *noun*
A feeling or spell of dismally low spirits : blues, dejection, depression, despondence, despondency, doldrums, dolefulness, downheartedness, dysphoria, funk, gloom, glumness, heavy-heartedness, melancholy, mope (used in plural), mournfulness, sadness, unhappiness. *See* FEELINGS, HAPPY.

dumpy *adjective*
Short, heavy, and solidly built : blocky, chunky, compact[1], heavyset, squat, stocky, stodgy, stubby, stumpy, thick, thickset. *See* FAT.

dunce *noun*
A mentally dull person : blockhead, chump[1], clod, dolt, dullard, dummkopf, dummy, num-

skull, thickhead. *Slang:* dimwit, dumbbell, dumbo. *See* ABILITY.

dunk *verb*
To plunge briefly in or into a liquid : dip, douse, duck, immerge, immerse, souse, submerge, submerse. *See* ENTER.
dunk *noun* The act of swimming : dip, duck, plunge, swim. *See* WORK.

duo *noun*
1. Two persons united, as by marriage : couple, pair, twosome. *See* GROUP. **2.** Two items of the same kind together : brace, couple, couplet, doublet, duet, match, pair, two, twosome, yoke. *See* GROUP, SAME.

dupable *adjective*
Easily imposed on or tricked : credulous, easy, exploitable, gullible, naive, susceptible. *See* WISE.

dupe *noun*
1. A person who is easily deceived or victimized : butt[3], fool, gull, lamb, pushover, victim. *Informal:* sucker. *Slang:* fall guy, gudgeon, mark, monkey, patsy, pigeon, sap[1]. *Chiefly British:* mug. *See* WISE. **2.** A person used or controlled by others : cat's-paw, instrument, pawn[2], puppet, stooge, tool. *See* OVER.
dupe *verb* To cause to accept what is false, especially by trickery or misrepresentation : beguile, betray, bluff, cozen, deceive, delude, double-cross, fool, hoodwink, humbug, mislead, take in, trick. *Informal:* bamboozle, have. *Slang:* four-flush. ***Idioms:*** lead astray, play false, pull the wool over someone's eyes, put something over on, take for a ride. *See* HONEST.

duple *adjective*
Composed of two parts or things : biform, binary, double, dual, duplex, duplicate, geminate, twofold. *See* PART.

duplex *adjective*
Composed of two parts or things : biform, binary, double, dual, duple, duplicate, geminate, twofold. *See* PART.

duplicate *adjective*
Composed of two parts or things : biform, binary, double, dual, duple, duplex, geminate, twofold. *See* PART.
duplicate *noun* **1.** Something closely resembling another : carbon copy, copy, facsimile, image, likeness, reduplication, plication, replica, replication, reproduction, simulacrum. *Archaic:* simulacre. *Law:* counterpart. *See* SAME. **2.** One exactly resembling another : double, image, picture, portrait, spitting image. *Slang:* ringer. *See* SAME. **3.** One of a matched pair of things : companion, counterpart, double, fellow, match, mate, twin. *See* SAME.
duplicate *verb* **1.** To make a copy of : copy, imitate, replicate, reproduce, simulate. *See* SAME. **2.** To make or become twice as great : double, geminate, redouble, twin. *See* BIG, INCREASE. **3.** To do or perform (an act) again : redo, repeat. *See* REPETITION.

duplicitous *adjective*
Marked by treachery or deceit : devious, disingenuous, guileful, indirect, lubricious, shifty, sneaky, underhand, underhanded. *See* HONEST.

duplicity *noun*
The act or practice of deceiving : cunning, deceit, deceitfulness, deception, double-dealing, guile, shiftiness. *See* HONEST.

durability *noun*
The condition of being free from defects or flaws : firmness, integrity, solidity, soundness, stability, strength, wholeness. *See* BETTER.

durable *adjective*
Existing or remaining in the same state for an indefinitely long time : abiding, continuing, enduring, lasting, long-lasting, long-lived, long-standing, old, perdurable, perennial, permanent, persistent. *See* CONTINUE.

duration *noun*
1. Uninterrupted existence or succession : continuance, continuation, continuity, continuum, endurance, persistence, persistency. *See* CONTINUE. **2.** A limited or specific period of time during which something happens, lasts, or extends : span, stretch, term, time. *See* TIME. **3.** The period during which someone or something exists : day (often used in plural), existence, life, lifetime, span, term. *See* LIVE, TIME.

duress *noun*
Power used to overcome resistance : coercion, compulsion, constraint, force, pressure, strength, violence. *See* ATTACK.

dusk *noun*
The period between afternoon and nighttime : eve, evening, eventide, gloaming, nightfall, twilight. *Archaic:* even[2], vesper. *See* START.

duskiness *noun*
Absence or deficiency of light : dark, darkness, dimness, murkiness, obscureness, obscurity. *See* LIGHT.

dusky *adjective*
1. Deficient in brightness : caliginous, dark, dim, murky, obscure. *See* LIGHT. **2.** Somewhat black : blackish, dark. *See* COLORS. **3.** Of a complexion tending toward brown or black :

bistered, black-a-vised, brunet, dark, swarthy. *See* COLORS.

dust *verb*
To scatter or release in drops or particles : besprinkle, powder, sprinkle. *See* STRIKE.

dusting *noun*
Slang. The act of defeating or the condition of being defeated : beating, defeat, drubbing, overthrow, rout, thrashing, vanquishment. *Informal:* massacre, trimming, whipping. *Slang:* licking. *See* WIN.

dusty *adjective*
Consisting of small particles : fine[1], powdery, pulverous, pulverulent. *See* BIG.

Dutch *noun*
A difficult, often embarrassing situation or condition : box[1], corner, deep water, difficulty, dilemma, fix, hole, hot spot, hot water, jam, plight[1], predicament, quagmire, scrape, soup, trouble. *Informal:* bind, pickle, spot. *See* EASY.

duteous *adjective*
Marked by courteous submission or respect : deferential, dutiful, obeisant, respectful. *See* RESIST.

dutiful *adjective*
Marked by courteous submission or respect : deferential, duteous, obeisant, respectful. *See* RESIST.

duty *noun*
1. An act or course of action that is demanded of one : burden[1], charge, commitment, imperative, must, need, obligation, responsibility. *See* OBLIGATION. **2.** A piece of work that has been assigned : assignment, chore, job, office, stint, task. *See* WORK. **3.** The condition of being put to use : application, employment, service, use, utilization. *See* USED. **4.** A compulsory contribution, usually of money, that is required for the support of a government : assessment, impost, levy, tariff, tax. *See* MONEY, PAY, POLITICS.

dwarf *adjective*
Extremely small : diminutive, Lilliputian, midget, miniature, minuscule, minute[2], pygmy, wee. *Informal:* peewee, pintsize, pintsized, teensy, teensy-weensy, teeny, teeny-weeny, tiny, weeny. *See* BIG.

dweeb *noun*
Slang. An unpleasant, tiresome person : bore. *Slang:* drip, jerk, nerd, pill, poop[2]. *See* LIKE.

dwell *verb*
1. To have as one's domicile, usually for an extended period : abide, domicile, house, live[1], reside. *See* PLACE. **2.** To have an inherent basis : consist, exist, inhere, lie[1], repose, reside, rest[1]. *See* START. **3.** To focus the attention on something moodily and at length : brood, cark, fret, mope, worry. *Informal:* stew. *See* CONCERN, THOUGHTS.

dwelling *noun*
A building or shelter where one lives : abode, domicile, habitation, home, house, lodging (often used in plural), place, residence. *Chiefly British:* dig (used in plural). *See* PROTECTION.

dwindle *verb*
To grow or cause to grow gradually less : abate, decrease, diminish, drain, ebb, lessen, let up, peter (out), rebate, reduce, tail away (*or* off), taper (off). *See* INCREASE.

dye *noun*
Something that imparts color : color, colorant, coloring, dyestuff, pigment, stain, tincture. *See* COLORS.

dye *verb* **1.** To impart color to : color, stain, tincture, tint. *See* COLORS. **2.** To immerse in a coloring solution : color, dip. *See* COLORS, ENTER.

dyestuff *noun*
Something that imparts color : color, colorant, coloring, dye, pigment, stain, tincture. *See* COLORS.

dynamic *adjective*
1. Possessing, exerting, or displaying energy : active, brisk, dynamical, energetic, forceful, kinetic, lively, sprightly, strenuous, vigorous. *Informal:* peppy. *See* ACTION. **2.** Full of or displaying force : dynamical, effective, forceful, forcible, hard-hitting, powerful, strong, vigorous. *See* STRONG. **3.** Disposed to action : active, brisk, driving, dynamical, energetic, enterprising, lively, sprightly, spry, vigorous, zippy. *Informal:* peppy, snappy. *See* ACTION.

dynamical *adjective*
1. Possessing, exerting, or displaying energy : active, brisk, dynamic, energetic, forceful, kinetic, lively, sprightly, strenuous, vigorous. *Informal:* peppy. *See* ACTION. **2.** Full of or displaying force : dynamic, effective, forceful, forcible, hard-hitting, powerful, strong, vigorous. *See* STRONG. **3.** Disposed to action : active, brisk, driving, dynamic, energetic, enterprising, lively, sprightly, spry, vigorous, zippy. *Informal:* peppy, snappy. *See* ACTION.

dynamite *verb*
To pull down or break up : demolish, destroy, dismantle, knock down, level, pull down, pulverize, raze, tear down, wreck. *Aerospace:* destruct. *See* HELP.

dynamo *noun*
An energetic person : hustler. *Informal:* eager beaver, go-getter, live wire. *See* CONCERN.

dysphoria *noun*
A feeling or spell of dismally low spirits : blues, dejection, depression, despondence, despondency, doldrums, dolefulness, downheartedness, dumps, funk, gloom, glumness, heavyheartedness, melancholy, mope (used in plural), mournfulness, sadness, unhappiness. *See* FEELINGS, HAPPY.

dysphoric *adjective*
In low spirits : blue, dejected, depressed, desolate, dispirited, down, downcast, downhearted, dull, gloomy, heavy-hearted, low, melancholic, melancholy, sad, spiritless, tristful, unhappy, wistful. ***Idiom:*** down at (*or* in) the mouth. *See* HAPPY.

• E •

eager *adjective*
Intensely desirous or interested : agog, ardent, athirst, avid, bursting, impatient, keen[1], solicitous, thirsting, thirsty. *Informal:* raring. ***Idioms:*** champing at the bit, ready and willing. *See* CONCERN.

eager beaver *noun*
Informal. An intensely energetic, enthusiastic person : dynamo, hustler. *Informal:* go-getter, live wire. *See* CONCERN.

ear *noun*
The sense by which sound is perceived : audition, hearing. *See* SOUNDS.

earlier *adjective*
1. Going before : advance, antecedent, anterior, precedent, preceding, previous, prior. *See* PRECEDE. **2.** Just gone by or elapsed : antecedent, anterior, foregoing, former, past, precedent, preceding, previous, prior. *See* TIME.
earlier *adverb* **1.** At a time in the past : already, before, erstwhile, formerly, once, previously. *Archaic:* aforetime, beforetime. *See* PRECEDE. **2.** Up to this time : before, heretofore, previously, yet. *See* PRECEDE. **3.** Until then : before, beforehand. *See* PRECEDE.

earliest *adjective*
Preceding all others in time : first, initial, maiden, original, pioneer, primary, prime, primordial. *See* START.

early *adjective*
1. At or near the start of a period, development, or series : beginning, first, initial. *See* START. **2.** Of, existing, or occurring in a distant period : ancient, antediluvian, primitive. *See* START. **3.** Developing, occurring, or appearing before the expected time : precocious, premature, untimely. *See* TIME.
early *adverb* Before the expected time : ahead, beforehand, betimes. ***Idioms:*** ahead of time, in advance, with time to spare. *See* TIME.

earmark *verb*
To set aside or apart for a specified purpose : allocate, appropriate, assign, designate. *See* COLLECT, MONEY.

earn *verb*
1. To receive, as wages, for one's labor : gain, get, make, win. *Informal:* pull down. ***Idioms:*** earn (*or* make) a living, earn one's keep. *See* GIVE, MONEY. **2.** To acquire as a result of one's behavior or effort : deserve, gain, get, merit, win. *Informal:* rate[1]. *See* GET. **3.** To make as income or profit : bring in, clear, draw, gain, gross, net[2], pay, produce, realize, repay, return, yield. *See* MONEY.

earnest[1] *adjective*
1. Marked by sober sincerity : businesslike, no-nonsense, serious, sobersided. ***Idiom:*** in earnest. *See* HEAVY, WORK. **2.** Full of or marked by dignity and seriousness : grave[2], sedate, serious, sober, solemn, somber, staid. *See* ATTITUDE, HEAVY. **3.** Having great consequence or weight : grave[2], heavy, momentous, serious, severe, weighty. *See* IMPORTANT.

earnest[2] *noun*
Something given to guarantee the repayment of a loan or the fulfillment of an obligation : guaranty, pawn[1], pledge, security, token, warrant. *See* TRANSACTIONS.

earnestness *noun*
Sober sincerity : seriousness, sobersidedness. *See* HEAVY, WORK.

earnings *noun*
1. Payment for work done : compensation, emolument, fee, hire, pay, remuneration, salary, stipend, wage. *See* PAY. **2.** Something earned,

won, or otherwise acquired : gain, profit, return. *See* GET, MONEY.

earshot *noun*
Range of audibility : hearing, sound[1]. *See* SOUNDS.

earsplitting *adjective*
Marked by extremely high volume and intensity of sound : blaring, deafening, loud, roaring, stentorian. *See* SOUNDS.

earth *noun*
1. The celestial body where humans live. Often uppercase : world. *See* PLACE. **2.** The human race : flesh, Homo sapiens, humanity, humankind, man, mankind, universe, world. *See* CULTURE.

earthbound also **earth-bound** *adjective*
1. Relating to or characteristic of the earth or of human life on earth : earthen, earthly, earthy, mundane, secular, tellurian, telluric, temporal, terrene, terrestrial, worldly. *See* BODY, CULTURE, PLACE. **2.** Lacking liveliness, charm, or surprise : arid, aseptic, colorless, drab, dry, dull, flat, flavorless, lackluster, lifeless, lusterless, matter-of-fact, pedestrian, prosaic, spiritless, sterile, stodgy, unimaginative, uninspired. *See* EXCITE.

earthen *adjective*
1. Consisting of or resembling soil : earthlike, earthy, terrestrial. *See* MATTER. **2.** Relating to or characteristic of the earth or of human life on earth : earthbound, earthly, earthy, mundane, secular, tellurian, telluric, temporal, terrene, terrestrial, worldly. *See* BODY, CULTURE, PLACE.

earthlike *adjective*
Consisting of or resembling soil : earthen, earthy, terrestrial. *See* MATTER.

earthly *adjective*
1. Relating to or characteristic of the earth or of human life on earth : earthbound, earthen, earthy, mundane, secular, tellurian, telluric, temporal, terrene, terrestrial, worldly. *See* BODY, CULTURE, PLACE. **2.** Capable of being anticipated, considered, or imagined : conceivable, imaginable, likely, mortal, possible, thinkable. ***Idioms:*** humanly possible, within the bounds (*or* range *or* realm) of possibility. *See* POSSIBLE.

earthquake *noun*
A shaking of the earth : quake, seism, temblor, tremblor, tremor. *Informal:* shake. *See* MOVE, REPETITION.

earthy *adjective*
1. Consisting of or resembling soil : earthen, earthlike, terrestrial. *See* MATTER. **2.** Relating to or characteristic of the earth or of human life on earth : earthbound, earthen, earthly, mundane, secular, tellurian, telluric, temporal, terrene, terrestrial, worldly. *See* BODY, CULTURE, PLACE. **3.** Bordering on indelicacy or impropriety : blue, off-color, provocative, racy, risqué, salty, scabrous, spicy, suggestive. *See* DECENT.

ease *noun*
1. Freedom, especially from pain : alleviation, assuagement, mitigation, palliation, relief. *See* INCREASE. **2.** Freedom from constraint, formality, embarrassment, or awkwardness : casualness, easiness, informality, naturalness, poise, spontaneity, unceremoniousness, unrestraint. *See* RESTRAINT, TIGHTEN. **3.** Freedom from labor, responsibility, or strain : leisure, relaxation, repose, rest[1]. *See* CONTINUE. **4.** The ability to perform without apparent effort : easiness, effortlessness, facileness, facility, readiness. *See* EASY. **5.** Steady good fortune or financial security : comfort, prosperity, prosperousness. *Informal:* easy street. ***Idioms:*** comfortable (*or* easy) circumstances, the good life. *See* RICH, THRIVE.

ease *verb* **1.** To make less severe or more bearable : allay, alleviate, assuage, comfort, lessen, lighten[2], mitigate, palliate, relieve. *See* INCREASE. **2.** To reduce in tension, pressure, or rigidity : let up, loose, loosen, relax, slack, slacken, untighten. *See* TIGHTEN. **3.** To become or cause to become less active or intense. Also used with *off* or *up* : abate, bate, die (away, down, off, *or* out), ebb, fall, fall off, lapse, let up, moderate, remit, slacken, slack off, subside, wane. *See* INCREASE. **4.** To make less difficult : expedite, facilitate. ***Idioms:*** clear (*or* prepare) the way for, grease the wheels, open the door for (*or* to). *See* EASY. **5.** To maneuver gently and slowly into place : glide, slide, slip. *See* CAREFUL, EASY. **6.** To advance carefully and gradually : edge, sidle. *See* CAREFUL, MOVE.

ease off *verb* To moderate or change a position or course of action as a result of pressure : relent, slacken, soften, weaken, yield. ***Idiom:*** give way (*or* ground). *See* STRONG.

easeful *adjective*
Affording pleasurable ease : comfortable, cozy, easy, snug. *Informal:* comfy, soft. *See* GOOD.

easiness *noun*
1. The ability to perform without apparent effort : ease, effortlessness, facileness, facility, readiness. *See* EASY. **2.** Freedom from constraint, formality, embarrassment, or

awkwardness : casualness, ease, informality, naturalness, poise, spontaneity, unceremoniousness, unrestraint. *See* RESTRAINT, TIGHTEN.

ease off *verb* See **ease.**

easy *adjective*

1. Posing no difficulty : effortless, facile, simple, smooth. *Informal:* snap. ***Idioms:*** easy as ABC, easy as falling off a log, easy as one-two-three, easy as pie, like taking candy from a baby, nothing to it. *See* EASY. **2.** Requiring little effort or exertion : light², moderate. *See* EASY. **3.** Marked by facility, especially of expression : effortless, flowing, fluent, fluid, graceful, smooth. *See* STYLE. **4.** Affording pleasurable ease : comfortable, cozy, easeful, snug. *Informal:* comfy, soft. *See* GOOD. **5.** Enjoying steady good fortune or financial security : comfortable, prosperous, well-heeled, well-off, well-to-do. *Informal:* well-fixed. ***Idioms:*** comfortably off, in clover, on easy street. *See* RICH, THRIVE. **6.** Unconstrained by rigid standards or ceremony : casual, easygoing, informal, natural, relaxed, spontaneous, unceremonious, unrestrained. *Informal:* laid-back. *See* PLAIN, TIGHTEN. **7.** Not strict or severe : charitable, clement, forbearing, indulgent, lax, lenient, merciful, soft, tolerant. *See* ACCEPT. **8.** Easily imposed on or tricked : credulous, dupable, exploitable, gullible, naive, susceptible. *See* WISE. **9.** Not steep or abrupt : gentle, gradual, moderate. *See* RISE. **10.** Marked by an absence of conventional restraint in sexual behavior; sexually unrestrained : fast, libertine, light², loose, wanton, whorish. *See* SEX.

easygoing also **easy-going** *adjective*

Unconstrained by rigid standards or ceremony : casual, easy, informal, natural, relaxed, spontaneous, unceremonious, unrestrained. *Informal:* laid-back. *See* PLAIN, TIGHTEN.

easy street *noun*

Informal. Steady good fortune or financial security : comfort, ease, prosperity, prosperousness. ***Idioms:*** comfortable (*or* easy) circumstances, the good life. *See* RICH, THRIVE.

eat *verb*

1. To take (food) into the body as nourishment : consume, devour, fare, ingest, partake. *Slang:* chow. ***Idioms:*** break bread, have (*or* take) a bite. *See* INGESTION. **2.** To do away with completely and destructively. Also used with *up* : consume, devour, swallow (up), waste. *See* HELP. **3.** To consume gradually, as by chemical reaction or friction : bite, corrode, erode, gnaw, wear, wear away. *See* ATTACK.

eat up *verb* **1.** To eat completely or entirely : consume, devour, dispatch. *Informal:* polish off, put away. *See* INGESTION. **2.** To use all of : consume, drain, draw down, exhaust, expend, finish, play out, run through, spend, use up. *Informal:* polish off. *See* INCREASE. **3.** *Slang.* To be avidly interested in : devour, feast on, relish. *See* CONCERN. **4.** *Slang.* To like or enjoy enthusiastically, often excessively : adore, delight (in), dote on (*or* upon), love. *Slang:* groove on. *See* LIKE, LOVE.

eatable *adjective*

Fit to be eaten : comestible, edible, esculent. *See* INGESTION.

eats *noun*

Slang. Something fit to be eaten : aliment, bread, comestible, diet, edible, esculent, fare, food, foodstuff, meat, nourishment, nurture, nutriment, nutrition, pabulum, pap, provender, provision (used in plural), sustenance, victual. *Slang:* chow, grub. *See* INGESTION.

eat up *verb* See **eat.**

eavesdrop *verb*

To observe or listen in secret to obtain information : spy. *See* INVESTIGATE.

ebb *noun*

The act or process of becoming less active or intense : abatement, letup, remission, slackening, subsidence, wane. *See* INCREASE.

ebb *verb* **1.** To grow or cause to grow gradually less : abate, decrease, diminish, drain, dwindle, lessen, let up, peter (out), rebate, reduce, tail away (*or* off), taper (off). *See* INCREASE. **2.** To move back or away from a point, limit, or mark : recede, retract, retreat, retrocede, retrograde, retrogress. *See* APPROACH. **3.** To become or cause to become less active or intense : abate, bate, die (away, down, off, *or* out), ease (off *or* up), fall, fall off, lapse, let up, moderate, remit, slacken, slack off, subside, wane. *See* INCREASE.

ebon *adjective*

Of the darkest achromatic visual value : black, ebony, inky, jet¹, jetty, onyx, pitch-black, pitchy, sable, sooty. *See* COLORS.

ebony *adjective*

Of the darkest achromatic visual value : black, ebon, inky, jet¹, jetty, onyx, pitch-black, pitchy, sable, sooty. *See* COLORS.

ebullient *adjective*

Full of joyful, unrestrained high spirits : effervescent, exuberant, sparkling. *See* HAPPY.

eccentric *adjective*

Deviating from the customary : bizarre, cranky, curious, erratic, freakish, idiosyncratic, odd, outlandish, peculiar, quaint, queer, quirky, singular, strange, unnatural, unusual, weird. *Slang:* kooky, screwball. *British Slang:* rum, rummy[2]. *See* USUAL.

eccentric *noun* A person regarded as strange, eccentric, or crazy : crackpot, crazy, lunatic. *Informal:* crank, loon, loony. *Slang:* cuckoo, ding-a-ling, dingbat, kook, nut, screwball, weirdie, weirdo. *See* WISE.

eccentricity *noun*
Peculiar behavior : idiosyncrasy, peculiarity, quirk, quirkiness, singularity. *See* USUAL.

ecclesiastic *noun*
A person ordained for service in a Christian church : churchman, churchwoman, clergyman, clergywoman, cleric, clerical, clerk, divine, minister, parson, preacher. *Informal:* reverend. *See* RELIGION.

ecclesiastical *adjective*
Of or relating to a church or to an established religion : church, churchly, religious, spiritual. *See* RELIGION.

echinate *adjective*
Full of sharp needlelike protuberances : briery, prickly, pricky, spiny, thistly, thorny. *See* SHARP.

echo *noun*
1. Repetition of sound via reflection from a surface : repercussion, reverberation. *See* SOUNDS. **2.** Imitative reproduction, as of the style of another : imitation, reflection, reflex, repetition. *See* SAME. **3.** One who mindlessly imitates another : imitator, mimic, parrot. *See* SAME.

echo *verb* **1.** To send back the sound of : rebound, reecho, reflect, repeat, resound, reverberate. *See* SOUNDS. **2.** To copy (another) slavishly : image, imitate, mimic, mirror, parrot, reflect, repeat. *See* SAME.

echoic *adjective*
Imitating sounds : imitative, onomatopoeic, onomatopoetic. *See* SAME, SOUNDS.

echoism *noun*
The formation of words in imitation of sounds : onomatopoeia. *See* SAME, SOUNDS.

eclipse *verb*
To make dim or indistinct : becloud, bedim, befog, blear, blur, cloud, dim, dull, fog, gloom, mist, obfuscate, obscure, overcast, overshadow, shadow. *See* CLEAR.

economical *adjective*
Careful in the use of material resources : canny, chary, frugal, provident, prudent, saving, Scotch, sparing, thrifty. *See* CAREFUL, SAVE.

economize *verb*
To use without wasting : conserve, save, spare. *See* SAVE.

economy *noun*
Careful use of material resources : frugality, providence, prudence, thrift, thriftiness. *See* SAVE.

ecstasy *noun*
A state of elated bliss : heaven, paradise, rapture, seventh heaven, transport. *Informal:* cloud nine. *See* HAPPY.

ecumenical *adjective*
So pervasive and all-inclusive as to exist in or affect the whole world : catholic, cosmic, cosmopolitan, global, pandemic, planetary, universal, worldwide. *See* LIMITED, SPECIFIC.

edacious *adjective*
1. Wanting to eat or drink more than one can reasonably consume : gluttonous, greedy, hoggish, piggish, ravenous, voracious. *See* DESIRE, INGESTION. **2.** Having an insatiable appetite for an activity or pursuit : avid, gluttonous, greedy, omnivorous, rapacious, ravenous, unappeasable, voracious. *See* DESIRE.

edacity *noun*
The quality or condition of being voracious : avidity, omnivorousness, rapaciousness, rapacity, ravenousness, voracity. *See* DESIRE.

eddy *verb*
To move or cause to move like a rapid rotary current of liquid : swirl, whirl. *See* MOVE, REPETITION.

edge *noun*
1. The cutting part of a sharp instrument : blade. *See* SHARP. **2.** A cutting quality : bite, incisiveness, keenness, sharpness, sting. *See* SHARP. **3.** A fairly narrow line or space forming a boundary : border, borderline, brim, brink, edging, fringe, margin, periphery, rim, verge. *Chiefly Military:* perimeter. *See* EDGE. **4.** The periphery of a city or town : environs, fringe, outskirt (often used in plural), skirt (used in plural), suburb (used in plural). *See* EDGE. **5.** A transitional interval beyond which some new action or different state of affairs is likely to begin or occur : borderline, brink, point, threshold, verge. *See* EDGE. **6.** A dominating position, as in a conflict : advantage, better[1], bulge, draw, drop, superiority, upper hand, vantage. *Informal:* inside track, jump. *See* OVER.

edge *verb* **1.** To give a sharp edge to : acuminate, hone[1], sharpen, whet. *See* SHARP. **2.** To put or form a border on : border, bound[2], fringe, margin, rim, skirt, verge. *See* EDGE. **3.** To advance carefully and gradually : ease, sidle. *See* CAREFUL, MOVE. **4.** To introduce gradually and slyly : foist, infiltrate, insinuate, wind[2], work, worm. *See* ENTER.

edging *noun*
A fairly narrow line or space forming a boundary : border, borderline, brim, brink, edge, fringe, margin, periphery, rim, verge. *Chiefly Military:* perimeter. *See* EDGE.

edgy *adjective*
Feeling or exhibiting nervous tension : fidgety, jittery, jumpy, nervous, restive, restless, skittish, tense, twitchy. *Slang:* uptight. ***Idioms:*** a bundle of nerves, all wound up, on edge. *See* TIGHTEN.

edible *adjective*
Fit to be eaten : comestible, eatable, esculent. *See* INGESTION.
edible *noun* Something fit to be eaten : aliment, bread, comestible, diet, esculent, fare, food, foodstuff, meat, nourishment, nurture, nutriment, nutrition, pabulum, pap, provender, provision (used in plural), sustenance, victual. *Slang:* chow, eats, grub. *See* INGESTION.

edict *noun*
1. A principle governing affairs within or among political units : canon, decree, institute, law, ordinance, precept, prescription, regulation, rule. *See* LAW. **2.** An authoritative or official decision, especially one made by a court : decree, determination, judgment, pronouncement, ruling. *See* LAW. **3.** A public statement : announcement, annunciation, declaration, manifesto, notice, proclamation, pronouncement. *See* KNOWLEDGE.

edification *noun*
The condition of being informed spiritually : enlightenment, illumination. *See* TEACH.

edifice *noun*
A usually permanent construction, such as a house or store : building, pile, structure. *See* MAKE.

edify *verb*
To enable (one) to understand, especially in a spiritual sense : enlighten, illume, illuminate, illumine. *See* TEACH.

edifying *adjective*
1. Promoting culture : civilizing, cultural, enlightening, humanizing, refining. *See* CULTURE. **2.** Serving to educate or inform : educational, educative, enlightening, illuminative, informative, instructional, instructive. *See* TEACH.

educable *adjective*
Capable of being educated : teachable, trainable. *See* TEACH.

educate *verb*
1. To impart knowledge and skill to : coach, discipline, instruct, school, teach, train, tutor. *See* TEACH. **2.** To impart information to : acquaint, advise, apprise, enlighten, inform, notify, tell. *See* KNOWLEDGE, TEACH.

educated *adjective*
1. Having an education : enlightened, informed, lettered, literate. *See* KNOWLEDGE. **2.** Characterized by discriminating taste and broad knowledge as a result of development or education : civilized, cultivated, cultured, polished, refined, urbane, well-bred. *See* CULTURE. **3.** Provided with information; made aware : acquainted, advised, enlightened, informed, instructed, knowledgeable. *See* KNOWLEDGE.

education *noun*
1. The act, process, or art of imparting knowledge and skill : instruction, pedagogics, pedagogy, schooling, teaching, training, tuition, tutelage, tutoring. *See* TEACH. **2.** Known facts, ideas, and skill that have been imparted : erudition, instruction, knowledge, learning, scholarship, science. *See* KNOWLEDGE.

educational *adjective*
Serving to educate or inform : edifying, educative, enlightening, illuminative, informative, instructional, instructive. *See* TEACH.

educative *adjective*
Serving to educate or inform : edifying, educational, enlightening, illuminative, informative, instructional, instructive. *See* TEACH.

educator *noun*
One who educates : instructor, pedagogue, teacher, trainer, tutor. *See* TEACH.

educe *verb*
1. To call forth or bring out (something latent, hidden, or unexpressed) : draw (out), elicit, evoke, summon. *See* SHOW. **2.** To arrive at through reasoning : derive, evolve, excogitate. *See* REASON.

eerie or **eery** *adjective*
Of a mysteriously strange and usually frightening nature : uncanny, unearthly, weird. *Informal:* spooky. *See* FEAR, USUAL.

eery *adjective* See **eerie.**

efface *verb*
To remove or invalidate by or as if by running a line through or wiping clean : annul, blot (out), cancel, cross (off *or* out), delete, erase, expunge, obliterate, rub (out), scratch (out),

strike (out), undo, wipe (out), x (out). *Law:* vacate. *See* CONTINUE.

effect *noun*

1. Something brought about by a cause : aftermath, consequence, corollary, end product, event, fruit, harvest, issue, outcome, precipitate, ramification, result, resultant, sequel, sequence, sequent, upshot. *See* CAUSE. **2.** The power or capacity to produce a desired result : effectiveness, effectuality, effectualness, efficaciousness, efficacy, efficiency, influence, potency. *See* AFFECT. **3.** The condition of being in full force or operation : actualization, being, materialization, realization. *See* BE. **4.** One's portable property. Used in plural : belonging (often used in plural), good (used in plural), lares and penates, personal effects, personal property, possession (used in plural), property, thing (often used in plural). *Informal:* stuff. *Law:* chattel, movable (often used in plural). *See* OWNED.

effect *verb* **1.** To be the cause of : bring, bring about, bring on, cause, effectuate, generate, induce, ingenerate, lead to, make, occasion, result in, secure, set off, stir[1] (up), touch off, trigger. ***Idioms:*** bring to pass (*or* effect), give rise to. *See* START. **2.** To bring about and carry to a successful conclusion : bring off, carry out, carry through, effectuate, execute, put through. *Informal:* swing. *See* DO. **3.** To compel observance of : carry out, enforce, execute, implement, invoke. ***Idioms:*** put in force, put into action. *See* OBLIGATION, OVER.

effective *adjective*

1. Producing or able to produce a desired effect : effectual, efficacious, efficient, productive. *See* THRIVE. **2.** Full of or displaying force : dynamic, dynamical, forceful, forcible, hard-hitting, powerful, strong, vigorous. *See* STRONG. **3.** In effect : operational, operative. *See* BE.

effectiveness *noun*

The power or capacity to produce a desired result : effect, effectuality, effectualness, efficaciousness, efficacy, efficiency, influence, potency. *See* AFFECT.

effectual *adjective*

Producing or able to produce a desired effect : effective, efficacious, efficient, productive. *See* THRIVE.

effectuality *noun*

The power or capacity to produce a desired result : effect, effectiveness, effectualness, efficaciousness, efficacy, efficiency, influence, potency. *See* AFFECT.

effectualness *noun*

The power or capacity to produce a desired result : effect, effectiveness, effectuality, efficaciousness, efficacy, efficiency, influence, potency. *See* AFFECT.

effectuate *verb*

1. To be the cause of : bring, bring about, bring on, cause, effect, generate, induce, ingenerate, lead to, make, occasion, result in, secure, set off, stir[1] (up), touch off, trigger. ***Idioms:*** bring to pass (*or* effect), give rise to. *See* START. **2.** To bring about and carry to a successful conclusion : bring off, carry out, carry through, effect, execute, put through. *Informal:* swing. *See* DO.

effectuation *noun*

The act of beginning and carrying through to completion : discharge, execution, performance, prosecution. *See* DO.

effeminacy *noun*

The quality of being effeminate : effeminateness, femininity, sissiness, unmanliness, womanishness. *See* GENDER.

effeminate *adjective*

Having qualities more appropriate to women than to men : epicene, feminine, sissified, sissyish, unmanly, womanish. *See* GENDER.

effeminateness *noun*

The quality of being effeminate : effeminacy, femininity, sissiness, unmanliness, womanishness. *See* GENDER.

effervesce *verb*

To form or cause to form foam : bubble, cream, fizz, foam, froth, lather, spume, suds, yeast. *See* SOLID.

effervescent *adjective*

Full of joyful, unrestrained high spirits : ebullient, exuberant, sparkling. *See* HAPPY.

efficacious *adjective*

Producing or able to produce a desired effect : effective, effectual, efficient, productive. *See* THRIVE.

efficaciousness *noun*

The power or capacity to produce a desired result : effect, effectiveness, effectuality, effectualness, efficacy, efficiency, influence, potency. *See* AFFECT.

efficacy *noun*

The power or capacity to produce a desired result : effect, effectiveness, effectuality, effectualness, efficaciousness, efficiency, influence, potency. *See* AFFECT.

efficiency *noun*

1. The quality of being efficient : productivity. *See* INDUSTRIOUS, THRIVE. **2.** The power or capacity to produce a desired result : effect, effectiveness, effectuality, effectualness, efficaciousness, efficacy, influence, potency. *See* AFFECT.

efficient *adjective*
1. Producing or able to produce a desired effect : effective, effectual, efficacious, productive. *See* THRIVE. **2.** Acting effectively with minimal waste : productive. *See* INDUSTRIOUS, THRIVE.

effloresce *verb*
To bear flowers : bloom[1], blossom, blow[3], burgeon, flower. *See* BETTER, RICH.

efflorescence *noun*
A condition or time of vigor and freshness : bloom[1], blossom, florescence, flower, flush, prime. *See* BETTER.

efflux *noun*
A sudden or rapid flowing outward : gush, outflow, outpour, outpouring, spate. *See* MOVE.

effort *noun*
1. The use of energy to do something : endeavor, exertion, pain (used in plural), strain[1], striving, struggle, trouble, while. *Informal:* elbow grease. *See* WORK. **2.** A difficult or tedious undertaking : chore, task. *Informal:* job. *See* HEAVY, WORK. **3.** A trying to do or make something : attempt, crack, endeavor, essay, go, offer, stab, trial, try. *Informal:* shot. *Slang:* take. *Archaic:* assay. *See* TRY. **4.** Something completed or attained successfully : accomplishment, achievement, acquirement, acquisition, attainment, feat. *See* DO.

effortful *adjective*
1. Requiring great or extreme bodily, mental, or spiritual strength : arduous, backbreaking, burdensome, demanding, difficult, exacting, exigent, formidable, hard, heavy, laborious, onerous, oppressive, rigorous, rough, severe, taxing, tough, trying, weighty. *See* HEAVY. **2.** Not natural or spontaneous : contrived, forced, labored, strained. *See* TRUE.

effortless *adjective*
1. Posing no difficulty : easy, facile, simple, smooth. *Informal:* snap. ***Idioms:*** easy as ABC, easy as falling off a log, easy as one-two-three, easy as pie, like taking candy from a baby, nothing to it. *See* EASY. **2.** Marked by facility, especially of expression : easy, flowing, fluent, fluid, graceful, smooth. *See* STYLE.

effortlessness *noun*
The ability to perform without apparent effort : ease, easiness, facileness, facility, readiness. *See* EASY.

effrontery *noun*
The state or quality of being impudent or arrogantly self-confident : assumption, audaciousness, audacity, boldness, brashness, brazenness, cheek, cheekiness, chutzpah, discourtesy, disrespect, face, familiarity, forwardness, gall[1], impertinence, impudence, impudency, incivility, insolence, nerve, nerviness, overconfidence, pertness, presumptuousness, pushiness, rudeness, sassiness, sauciness. *Informal:* brass, crust, sauce, uppishness, uppityness. *See* ATTITUDE, COURTESY.

effulgent *adjective*
Giving off or reflecting light readily or in large amounts : beamy, bright, brilliant, incandescent, irradiant, lambent, lucent, luminous, lustrous, radiant, refulgent, shiny. *See* LIGHT.

effuse *verb*
To cause (a liquid) to flow in a steady stream : decant, draw (off), pour. *See* MOVE.

egg on *verb*
To stir to action or feeling : excite, foment, galvanize, goad, impel, incite, inflame, inspire, instigate, motivate, move, pique, prick, prod, prompt, propel, provoke, set off, spur, stimulate, touch off, trigger, work up. *See* CAUSE, EXCITE.

ego *noun*
1. An individual's awareness of what constitutes his or her essential nature and distinguishes him or her from all others : self. *See* BE, SELF. **2.** A regarding of oneself with undue favor : amour-propre, conceit, egoism, egotism, narcissism, pride, vainglory, vainness, vanity. *Slang:* ego trip. *See* SELF-LOVE. **3.** A sense of one's own dignity or worth : amour-propre, pride, self-esteem, self-regard, self-respect. *See* RESPECT.

egocentric *adjective*
1. Concerned with the person rather than with society : egoistic, egoistical, individualistic. *See* SELF. **2.** Concerned only with oneself : egoistic, egoistical, egomaniacal, egotistic, egotistical, self-absorbed, self-centered, self-involved, selfish, self-seeking, self-serving. ***Idiom:*** wrapped up in oneself. *See* SELF.

egocentric *noun* A conceited, self-centered person : egoist, egomaniac, egotist, narcissist. *Informal:* swellhead. *See* SELF, SELF-LOVE.

egocentricity *noun*
Concern only for oneself : egocentrism, egoism, egomania, self-absorption, self-centeredness, self-involvement, selfishness. *See* SELF.

egocentrism *noun*
Concern only for oneself : egocentricity, egoism, egomania, self-absorption, self-centeredness, self-involvement, selfishness. *See* SELF.

egoism *noun*
1. Concern only for oneself : egocentricity, egocentrism, egomania, self-absorption, self-centeredness, self-involvement, selfishness. *See* SELF. **2.** An exaggerated belief in one's own importance : egotism, self-importance. *Informal:* bighead, bigheadedness, swelled head. *See* SELF-LOVE. **3.** A regarding of oneself with undue favor : amour-propre, conceit, ego, egotism, narcissism, pride, vainglory, vainness, vanity. *Slang:* ego trip. *See* SELF-LOVE.

egoist *noun*
A conceited, self-centered person : egocentric, egomaniac, egotist, narcissist. *Informal:* swellhead. *See* SELF, SELF-LOVE.

egoistic *adjective*
1. Concerned with the person rather than with society : egocentric, egoistical, individualistic. *See* SELF. **2.** Concerned only with oneself : egocentric, egoistical, egomaniacal, egotistic, egotistical, self-absorbed, self-centered, self-involved, selfish, self-seeking, self-serving. ***Idiom:*** wrapped up in oneself. *See* SELF. **3.** Thinking too highly of oneself : conceited, egoistical, egotistic, egotistical, narcissistic, vain, vainglorious. *Informal:* bigheaded, stuck-up, swellheaded. *See* SELF-LOVE.

egoistical *adjective*
1. Concerned with the person rather than with society : egocentric, egoistic, individualistic. *See* SELF. **2.** Concerned only with oneself : egocentric, egoistic, egomaniacal, egotistic, egotistical, self-absorbed, self-centered, self-involved, selfish, self-seeking, self-serving. ***Idiom:*** wrapped up in oneself. *See* SELF. **3.** Thinking too highly of oneself : conceited, egoistic, egotistic, egotistical, narcissistic, vain, vainglorious. *Informal:* bigheaded, stuck-up, swellheaded. *See* SELF-LOVE.

egomania *noun*
Concern only for oneself : egocentricity, egocentrism, egoism, self-absorption, self-centeredness, self-involvement, selfishness. *See* SELF.

egomaniac *noun*
A conceited, self-centered person : egocentric, egoist, egotist, narcissist. *Informal:* swellhead. *See* SELF, SELF-LOVE.

egomaniacal *adjective*
Concerned only with oneself : egocentric, egoistic, egoistical, egotistic, egotistical, self-absorbed, self-centered, self-involved, selfish, self-seeking, self-serving. ***Idiom:*** wrapped up in oneself. *See* SELF.

egotism *noun*
1. An exaggerated belief in one's own importance : egoism, self-importance. *Informal:* bighead, bigheadedness, swelled head. *See* SELF-LOVE. **2.** A regarding of oneself with undue favor : amour-propre, conceit, ego, egoism, narcissism, pride, vainglory, vainness, vanity. *Slang:* ego trip. *See* SELF-LOVE.

egotist *noun*
A conceited, self-centered person : egocentric, egoist, egomaniac, narcissist. *Informal:* swellhead. *See* SELF, SELF-LOVE.

egotistic *adjective*
1. Thinking too highly of oneself : conceited, egoistic, egoistical, egotistical, narcissistic, vain, vainglorious. *Informal:* bigheaded, stuck-up, swellheaded. *See* SELF-LOVE. **2.** Concerned only with oneself : egocentric, egoistic, egoistical, egomaniacal, egotistical, self-absorbed, self-centered, self-involved, selfish, self-seeking, self-serving. ***Idiom:*** wrapped up in oneself. *See* SELF.

egotistical *adjective*
1. Thinking too highly of oneself : conceited, egoistic, egoistical, egotistic, narcissistic, vain, vainglorious. *Informal:* bigheaded, stuck-up, swellheaded. *See* SELF-LOVE. **2.** Concerned only with oneself : egocentric, egoistic, egoistical, egomaniacal, egotistic, self-absorbed, self-centered, self-involved, selfish, self-seeking, self-serving. ***Idiom:*** wrapped up in oneself. *See* SELF.

ego trip *noun*
Slang. A regarding of oneself with undue favor : amour-propre, conceit, ego, egoism, egotism, narcissism, pride, vainglory, vainness, vanity. *See* SELF-LOVE.

egregious *adjective*
Conspicuously bad or offensive : arrant, capital, flagrant, glaring, gross, rank[2]. *See* GOOD.

egregiousness *noun*
The quality or state of being flagrant : atrociousness, atrocity, enormity, flagrance, flagrancy, flagrantness, glaringness, grossness, outrageousness, rankness. *See* GOOD.

egress *noun*
The act of leaving : departure, exit, exodus, going, withdrawal. *See* APPROACH.

eidolon *noun*
A supernatural being, such as a ghost : apparition, bogey, bogeyman, bogle, ghost, phantasm,

phantasma, phantom, revenant, shade, shadow, specter, spirit, visitant, wraith. *Informal:* spook. *Regional:* haunt. *See* BEINGS, SUPERNATURAL.

ejaculate *verb*
To speak suddenly or sharply, as from surprise or emotion : blurt (out), burst out, cry (out), exclaim, rap out. *See* WORDS.

ejaculation *noun*
A sudden, sharp utterance : cry, exclamation, outcry. *See* WORDS.

eject *verb*
1. To send forth (confined matter) violently : belch, disgorge, eruct, erupt, expel, spew. *Geology:* extravasate. *See* EXPLOSION. **2.** To put out by force : bump, dismiss, evict, expel, oust, throw out. *Informal:* chuck. *Slang:* boot[1] (out), bounce, kick out. ***Idioms:*** give someone the boot, give someone the heave-ho (*or* old heave-ho), send packing, show someone the door, throw out on one's ear. *See* KEEP. **3.** To catapult oneself from a disabled aircraft : bail out, jump. *See* APPROACH.

ejection *noun*
The act of ejecting or the state of being ejected : dismissal, ejectment, eviction, expulsion, ouster. *Slang:* boot[1], bounce. *See* KEEP.

ejectment *noun*
The act of ejecting or the state of being ejected : dismissal, ejection, eviction, expulsion, ouster. *Slang:* boot[1], bounce. *See* KEEP.

elaborate *adjective*
1. Complexly detailed : complicated, fancy, intricate. *See* PLAIN. **2.** Difficult to understand because of intricacy : byzantine, complex, complicated, convoluted, daedal, Daedalian, intricate, involute, involved, knotty, labyrinthine, tangled. *See* SIMPLE.
elaborate *verb* **1.** To express at greater length or in greater detail : amplify, develop, dilate, enlarge, expand, expatiate, labor. *See* EXPLAIN. **2.** To disclose bit by bit : develop, evolve. ***Idioms:*** fill in the details, go into detail. *See* SHOW.

élan *noun*
A lively, emphatic, eager quality or manner : animation, bounce, brio, dash, esprit, life, liveliness, pertness, sparkle, spirit, verve, vigor, vim, vivaciousness, vivacity, zip. *Informal:* ginger, pep, peppiness. *Slang:* oomph. *See* ACTION.

élan vital *noun*
The vital principle or animating force that is within living beings : breath, divine spark, life force, psyche, soul, spirit, vital force, vitality. *See* BODY.

elapse *verb*
To move past in time : go (by), lapse, pass. *See* TIME.

elastic *adjective*
1. Capable of withstanding stress without injury : flexible, flexile, resilient, springy, supple. *Physics:* plastic. *See* FLEXIBLE. **2.** Capable of adapting or being adapted : adaptable, adaptive, adjustable, flexible, malleable, pliable, pliant, supple. *See* CHANGE. **3.** Easily altered or influenced : ductile, flexible, flexile, impressionable, malleable, plastic, pliable, pliant, suggestible, supple. *See* FLEXIBLE.

elasticity *noun*
1. The quality or state of being flexible : bounce, ductility, flexibility, flexibleness, give, malleability, malleableness, plasticity, pliability, pliableness, pliancy, pliantness, resilience, resiliency, spring, springiness, suppleness. *Obsolete:* flexure. *See* FLEXIBLE. **2.** The ability to recover quickly from depression or discouragement : bounce, buoyancy, resilience, resiliency. *See* ABILITY.

elate *verb*
To raise the spirits of : animate, buoy (up), elevate, exhilarate, flush, inspire, inspirit, lift, uplift. *Obsolete:* exalt. *See* HAPPY.
elate *adjective* Feeling great delight and joy : elated, elevated, overjoyed. *Slang:* up. *See* HAPPY.

elated *adjective*
Feeling great delight and joy : elate, elevated, overjoyed. *Slang:* up. *See* HAPPY.

elatedness *noun*
High spirits : animation, elation, euphoria, exaltation, exhilaration, inspiration, lift, uplift. *See* HAPPY.

elation *noun*
High spirits : animation, elatedness, euphoria, exaltation, exhilaration, inspiration, lift, uplift. *See* HAPPY.

elbow grease *noun*
Informal. The use of energy to do something : effort, endeavor, exertion, pain (used in plural), strain[1], striving, struggle, trouble, while. *See* WORK.

elbowroom *noun*
1. Ease of or space for movement : freedom, play. *See* TIGHTEN. **2.** Suitable opportunity to accept or allow something : latitude, leeway, margin, play, room, scope. *See* PLACE, RESTRAINT.

elder *adjective*
Of greater age than another : older, senior. *See* YOUTH.

elder *noun* **1.** A person who is older than another : senior. *See* YOUTH. **2.** An elderly person : ancient, golden ager, senior, senior citizen. *Informal:* oldster, old-timer. *See* YOUTH. **3.** One who stands above another in rank : better[1], senior, superior. *Informal:* higher-up. *See* OVER.

elderliness *noun*
Old age : age, agedness, senectitude, senescence, year (used in plural). *See* YOUTH.

elderly *adjective*
Far along in life or time : advanced, aged, old, senior. ***Idiom:*** getting along (*or* on) in years. *See* NEW.

elect *verb*
1. To select by vote for an office : ballot, vote (in). *See* CHOICE, POLITICS. **2.** To make a choice from a number of alternatives : choose, cull, opt (for), pick (out), select, single (out). *See* CHOICE.

elect *adjective* Singled out in preference : choice, chosen, exclusive, select. *See* CHOICE, INCLUDE.

elect *noun* One that is selected : choice, chosen, pick, select. *See* CHOICE.

election *noun*
The act of choosing : choice, option, preference, selection. *See* CHOICE.

elective *adjective*
Not compulsory or automatic : discretionary, facultative, optional. *See* CHOICE.

elector *noun*
One who votes : balloter, voter. *See* CHOICE, POLITICS.

electrify *verb*
1. To cause to experience a sudden momentary shock : jolt, shock[1], startle. *See* EXCITE, SURPRISE. **2.** To move or excite greatly : carry away, enrapture, thrill, transport. *Slang:* send. *See* EXCITE.

eleemosynary *adjective*
Of or concerned with charity : altruistic, benevolent, charitable, philanthropic, philanthropical. *See* GIVE, KIND.

elegance *noun*
Refined, effortless beauty of manner, form, and style : elegancy, grace, polish, urbanity. *See* BEAUTIFUL, STYLE.

elegancy *noun*
Refined, effortless beauty of manner, form, and style : elegance, grace, polish, urbanity. *See* BEAUTIFUL, STYLE.

elegant *adjective*
1. Of such tasteful beauty as to elicit admiration : exquisite, graceful. *See* BEAUTIFUL, STYLE. **2.** Appealing to refined taste : choice, dainty, delicate, exquisite, fine[1]. *See* GOOD, INGESTION.

element *noun*
1. A fundamental irreducible constituent of a whole : basic, essential, fundamental, rudiment (often used in plural). ***Idiom:*** part and parcel. *See* PART. **2.** One of the individual entities contributing to a whole : building block, component, constituent, factor, ingredient, integrant, part. *See* PART. **3.** An individually considered portion of a whole : article, detail, item, particular, point. *See* PART.

elemental *adjective*
1. Of or being an irreducible element : basic, elementary, essential, fundamental, primitive, ultimate, underlying. *See* SURFACE. **2.** Forming an essential element, as arising from the basic structure of an individual : built-in, congenital, connatural, constitutional, inborn, inbred, indigenous, indwelling, ingrained, inherent, innate, intrinsic, native, natural. *See* BE, NATIVE, START.

elementary *adjective*
1. Of or being an irreducible element : basic, elemental, essential, fundamental, primitive, ultimate, underlying. *See* SURFACE. **2.** Of or treating the most basic aspects : basal, basic, beginning, rudimental, rudimentary. *See* SIMPLE, START.

elephantine *adjective*
1. Of extraordinary size and power : behemoth, Brobdingnagian, Bunyanesque, colossal, cyclopean, enormous, gargantuan, giant, gigantesque, gigantic, herculean, heroic, huge, immense, jumbo, mammoth, massive, massy, mastodonic, mighty, monster, monstrous, monumental, mountainous, prodigious, pythonic, stupendous, titanic, tremendous, vast. *Informal:* walloping. *Slang:* whopping. *See* BIG. **2.** Lacking fluency or gracefulness : heavy-handed, labored, ponderous. *See* GOOD.

elevate *verb*
1. To move (something) to a higher position : boost, heave, hoist, lift, pick up, raise, rear[2], take up, uphold, uplift, upraise, uprear. *See* RISE. **2.** To increase markedly in level or intensity, especially of sound : amplify, heighten, raise. *See* INCREASE. **3.** To raise in rank : advance, jump, promote, raise, upgrade. *See* RISE. **4.** To raise to a high position or status : aggrandize, apotheosize, dignify, ennoble, exalt, glorify, magnify, uplift. ***Idiom:*** put on a pedestal. *See* RISE. **5.** To cause to be eminent or recognized : distinguish, ennoble, exalt, honor,

signalize. *See* RESPECT. **6.** To raise the spirits of : animate, buoy (up), elate, exhilarate, flush, inspire, inspirit, lift, uplift. *Obsolete:* exalt. *See* HAPPY.

elevated *adjective*
1. Being positioned above a given level : raised. *See* RISE. **2.** Abnormally increased, especially in intensity : heightened, high, raised. *See* INCREASE. **3.** Raised to or occupying a high position or rank : august, exalted, grand, high-ranking, lofty. *See* RISE. **4.** Being on a high intellectual or moral level : high-minded, moral, noble. *See* HIGH. **5.** Exceedingly dignified in form, tone, or style : eloquent, exalted, grand, high, high-flown, lofty. *See* HIGH, STYLE. **6.** Feeling great delight and joy : elate, elated, overjoyed. *Slang:* up. *See* HAPPY.

elevation *noun*
1. The distance of something from a given level : altitude, height. *See* HIGH. **2.** The act of raising to a high position or status or the condition of being so raised : aggrandizement, apotheosis, ennoblement, exaltation, glorification. *See* RISE. **3.** A progression upward in rank : advancement, jump, promotion, rise, upgrade. *See* RISE.

elicit *verb*
To call forth or bring out (something latent, hidden, or unexpressed) : draw (out), educe, evoke, summon. *See* SHOW.

eligibility *noun*
The quality or state of being eligible : fitness, qualification, suitability, suitableness, worthiness. *See* ABILITY.

eligible *adjective*
1. Satisfying certain requirements, as for selection : fit[1], fitted, qualified, suitable, worthy. *See* ABILITY. **2.** Deemed suitable for marriage : marriageable. *Archaic:* marriable. *See* MARRIAGE.

eliminate *verb*
1. To get rid of, especially by banishment or execution : eradicate, liquidate, purge, remove, wipe out. ***Idioms:*** do away with, put an end to. *See* HELP, KEEP. **2.** To keep from being admitted, included, or considered : bar, count out, debar, except, exclude, keep out, rule out, shut out. *See* INCLUDE. **3.** To take or leave out : drop, omit, remove. *See* INCLUDE. **4.** To discharge (wastes or foreign substances) from the body : evacuate, excrete. *Medicine:* purge. *See* KEEP.

elimination *noun*
1. The act or process of eliminating : clearance, eradication, liquidation, purge, removal, riddance. *See* KEEP. **2.** The act of getting rid of something useless or used up : disposal, dumping, jettison, riddance. *See* KEEP. **3.** The act or process of discharging bodily wastes or foreign substances : evacuation, excretion, purgation. *Medicine:* catharsis. *See* KEEP.

eliminative *adjective*
Of, relating to, or tending to eliminate : cathartic, eliminatory, evacuant, evacuative, excretory, purgative. *See* KEEP.

eliminatory *adjective*
Of, relating to, or tending to eliminate : cathartic, eliminative, evacuant, evacuative, excretory, purgative. *See* KEEP.

elite or **élite** *noun*
1. People of the highest social level : aristocracy, blue blood, crème de la crème, flower, gentility, gentry, nobility, patriciate, quality, society, upper class, who's who. *Informal:* upper crust. *See* OVER. **2.** The superlative or most preferable part of something : best, choice, cream, crème de la crème, flower, pick, prize[1], top. ***Idioms:*** cream of the crop, flower of the flock, pick of the bunch (*or* crop) . *See* BETTER.

elite or **élite** *adjective* Of high birth or social position : aristocratic, blue-blooded, highborn, highbred, noble, patrician, thoroughbred, upper-class, wellborn. *Informal:* upper-crust. *See* OVER.

elitist or **élitist** *adjective*
Characteristic of or resembling a snob : snobbish, snobby. *Informal:* high-hat, snooty, stuck-up, uppish, uppity. *See* ATTITUDE, SELF-LOVE.

elitist or **élitist** *noun* One who despises people or things regarded as inferior, especially because of social or intellectual pretension : snob. *Informal:* snoot. *See* ATTITUDE, SELF-LOVE.

elixir *noun*
An agent used to restore health : cure, medicament, medication, medicine, nostrum, physic, remedy. *See* HEALTH.

elocution *noun*
The art of public speaking : declamation, oratory, rhetoric. *See* WORDS.

elocutionary *adjective*
Of or relating to the art of public speaking : declamatory, oratorical, rhetorical. *See* WORDS.

elongate *verb*
To make or become longer : draw out, extend, lengthen, prolong, prolongate, protract, spin

(out), stretch (out). *Mathematics:* produce. *See* INCREASE, LONG.

elongate *adjective* Having great physical length : elongated, extended, lengthy, long[1], prolonged. *See* LONG.

elongated *adjective*
Having great physical length : elongate, extended, lengthy, long[1], prolonged. *See* LONG.

elongation *noun*
The act of making something longer or the condition of being made longer : extension, prolongation, protraction. *See* LONG.

eloquence *noun*
Vivid, effective, or persuasive communication in speech or artistic performance : articulacy, articulateness, eloquentness, expression, expressiveness, expressivity, facundity. *See* WORDS.

eloquent *adjective*
1. Fluently persuasive and forceful : articulate, facund, silver-tongued, smooth-spoken. *See* WORDS. **2.** Exceedingly dignified in form, tone, or style : elevated, exalted, grand, high, high-flown, lofty. *See* HIGH, STYLE. **3.** Effectively conveying meaning, feeling, or mood : expressive, meaning, meaningful, significant. *See* EXPRESS, SHOW.

eloquentness *noun*
Vivid, effective, or persuasive communication in speech or artistic performance : articulacy, articulateness, eloquence, expression, expressiveness, expressivity, facundity. *See* WORDS.

elucidate *verb*
To make clear or clearer : clarify, clear (up), illuminate, illustrate. ***Idiom:*** shed (*or* throw) light on (*or* upon). *See* CLEAR.

elucidation *noun*
Something that serves to explain or clarify : clarification, construction, decipherment, exegesis, explanation, explication, exposition, illumination, illustration, interpretation. *Archaic:* enucleation. *See* EXPLAIN.

elucidative *adjective*
Serving to explain : exegetic, explanative, explanatory, explicative, expositive, expository, hermeneutic, hermeneutical, illustrative, interpretative, interpretive. *See* EXPLAIN.

elude *verb*
1. To keep away from : avoid, burke, bypass, circumvent, dodge, duck, escape, eschew, evade, get around, shun. ***Idioms:*** fight shy of, give a wide berth to, have no truck with, keep (*or* stay *or* steer) clear of. *See* SEEK. **2.** To get away from (a pursuer) : evade, lose, shake off, slip, throw off. *Slang:* shake. ***Idiom:*** give someone the shake (*or* slip). *See* SEEK. **3.** To fail to be fixed by the mind, memory, or senses of : escape. ***Idiom:*** slip away from. *See* OWNED.

elusive *adjective*
Characterized by or exhibiting evasion : evasive, slippery. *See* SEEK.

emaciated *adjective*
Physically haggard : cadaverous, drawn, gaunt, shrunken, skeletal, wasted. ***Idiom:*** skin and bones. *See* BETTER, TIRED.

emanate *verb*
To have as a source : arise, come, derive, flow, issue, originate, proceed, rise, spring, stem, upspring. *See* START.

emancipate *verb*
To set at liberty : discharge, free, liberate, loose, manumit, release. *Slang:* spring. ***Idiom:*** let loose. *See* FREE.

emancipation *noun*
The state of not being in confinement or servitude : freedom, liberation, liberty, manumission. *See* FREE.

embark *verb*
To go about the initial step in doing (something) : approach, begin, commence, enter, get off, inaugurate, initiate, institute, launch, lead off, open, set about, set out, set to, start, take on, take up, undertake. *Informal:* kick off. ***Idioms:*** get cracking, get going, get the show on the road. *See* START.

embarrass *verb*
1. To cause (a person) to be self-consciously distressed : abash, chagrin, confound, confuse, discomfit, discomfort, disconcert, discountenance, faze, mortify. ***Idioms:*** put on the spot, throw for a loop. *See* PAIN. **2.** To make complex, intricate, or perplexing : complicate, entangle, involve, perplex, ravel, snarl[2], tangle. *See* SIMPLE.

embarrassment *noun*
1. Self-conscious distress : abashment, chagrin, confusion, discomfiture, discomposure. *See* PAIN. **2.** A condition of going or being beyond what is needed, desired, or appropriate : excess, excessiveness, exorbitance, extravagance, extravagancy, extravagantness, overabundance, plethora, superabundance, superfluity, superfluousness, surfeit. *See* EXCESS.

embed also **imbed** *verb*
To implant so deeply as to make change nearly impossible : entrench, fasten, fix, infix, ingrain, lodge, root[1]. *See* MOVE.

embellish *verb*
1. To furnish with decorations : adorn, bedeck, deck[2] (out), decorate, dress (up), garnish,

ornament, trim. *See* BEAUTIFUL. **2.** To endow with beauty and elegance by way of a notable addition : adorn, beautify, enhance, grace, set off. *See* BEAUTIFUL.

embellishment *noun*
Something that adorns : adornment, decoration, garnishment, garniture, ornament, ornamentation, trim, trimming. *See* BEAUTIFUL.

embitter *verb*
To make or become bitter : sour. *See* HAPPY.

embittered *adjective*
Bitingly hostile : acrimonious, bitter, hard, rancorous, resentful, virulent. *See* ATTITUDE, LOVE.

embitterment *noun*
The quality or state of feeling bitter : acrimony, bitterness, gall[1], rancor, rancorousness, resentfulness, resentment, virulence, virulency. *See* FEELINGS.

emblem *noun*
An object associated with and serving to identify something else : attribute, symbol. *See* SUBSTITUTE.

emblematic *adjective*
Serving as a symbol : emblematical, representative, symbolic, symbolical. *See* SUBSTITUTE.

emblematical *adjective*
Serving as a symbol : emblematic, representative, symbolic, symbolical. *See* SUBSTITUTE.

embodiment *noun*
A physical entity typifying an abstraction : exteriorization, externalization, incarnation, manifestation, materialization, objectification, personalization, personification, substantiation, type. *Rhetoric:* prosopopeia. *See* SUBSTITUTE.

embody *verb*
1. To represent (an abstraction, for example) in or as if in bodily form : body forth, exteriorize, externalize, incarnate, manifest, materialize, objectify, personalize, personify, substantiate. *See* SUBSTITUTE. **2.** To make a part of a united whole : combine, incorporate, integrate. *See* INCLUDE. **3.** To have as a part : comprehend, comprise, contain, embrace, encompass, have, include, involve, subsume, take in. *See* INCLUDE.

embolden *verb*
To impart courage, inspiration, and resolution to : animate, cheer (on), encourage, inspire, inspirit, motivate. *See* HELP.

embosom *verb*
Archaic. To put one's arms around affectionately : clasp, embrace, enfold, hold, hug, press, squeeze. *Slang:* clinch. *Archaic:* bosom, clip[2]. *See* TOUCH.

embrace *verb*
1. To put one's arms around affectionately : clasp, enfold, hold, hug, press, squeeze. *Slang:* clinch. *Archaic:* bosom, clip[2], embosom. *See* TOUCH. **2.** To have as a part : comprehend, comprise, contain, embody, encompass, have, include, involve, subsume, take in. *See* INCLUDE. **3.** To receive (something given or offered) willingly and gladly : accept, take (up), welcome. *See* ACCEPT. **4.** To take, as another's idea, and make one's own : adopt, espouse, take on, take up. *See* ACCEPT, GIVE.
embrace *noun* The act of embracing : clasp, hug, squeeze. *Slang:* clinch. *See* TOUCH.

embracement *noun*
A ready taking up of something : adoption, espousal. *See* ACCEPT, GIVE.

embrangle *verb*
To draw in so that extrication is difficult : catch up, embroil, implicate, involve, mix up, suck. *See* FREE, PARTICIPATE.

embranglement *noun*
The condition of being entangled or implicated : embroilment, enmeshment, ensnarement, entanglement, involvement. *See* FREE, PARTICIPATE.

embroil *verb*
To draw in so that extrication is difficult : catch up, embrangle, implicate, involve, mix up, suck. *See* FREE, PARTICIPATE.

embroilment *noun*
The condition of being entangled or implicated : embranglement, enmeshment, ensnarement, entanglement, involvement. *See* FREE, PARTICIPATE.

embrue *verb* See **imbrue.**

embryo *noun*
A source of further growth and development : bud[1], germ, kernel, nucleus, seed, spark[1]. *See* START.

emend *verb*
1. To prepare a new version of : amend, emendate, revamp, revise, rework, rewrite. *See* CHANGE. **2.** To make right what is wrong : amend, correct, mend, rectify, redress, reform, remedy, right. *See* CORRECT.

emendate *verb*
To prepare a new version of : amend, emend, revamp, revise, rework, rewrite. *See* CHANGE.

emendation *noun*
The act or process of revising : amendment, revision, rewrite. *See* CHANGE.

emendatory *adjective*
Tending to correct : amendatory, corrective,

reformative, reformatory, remedial. *See* CORRECT.

emerge *verb*
1. To come into view : appear, issue, loom, materialize, show. ***Idioms:*** make (*or* put in) an appearance, meet the eye. *See* SEE. **2.** To begin to appear or develop : appear, arise, commence, dawn, originate. *See* START.

emergence *noun*
The act of coming into view : appearance. *See* SEE.

emergency *noun*
A highly volatile dangerous situation requiring immediate remedial action : crisis, extremity, flash point. *See* POLITICS, SAFETY.
emergency *adjective* Used or held in reserve : auxiliary, backup, reserve, secondary, standby, supplemental, supplementary. *See* INCREASE.

emergent *adjective*
Compelling immediate attention : burning, crying, dire, exigent, imperative, instant, pressing, urgent. *See* BIG.

emigrant *noun*
One who emigrates : immigrant, migrant, transmigrant. *See* APPROACH.

emigrate *verb*
To leave one's native land and settle in another : immigrate, migrate, transmigrate. *See* APPROACH.

emigration *noun*
Departure from one's native land to settle in another : exodus, immigration, migration, transmigration. *See* APPROACH.

émigré *noun*
1. One forced to emigrate, usually for political reasons : deportee, exile, expatriate, expellee. *See* APPROACH. **2.** A person coming from another country or into a new community : alien, foreigner, newcomer, outlander, outsider, stranger. *See* NATIVE.

eminence *noun*
1. A position of exalted widely recognized importance : distinction, eminency, fame, glory, illustriousness, luster, mark, notability, note, preeminence, prestige, prominence, prominency, renown. *See* IMPORTANT, KNOWLEDGE, RESPECT. **2.** A natural land elevation : hill, prominence, rise. *See* HIGH. **3.** An important, influential person : character, dignitary, leader, lion, nabob, notability, notable, personage. *Informal:* big-timer, heavyweight, somebody, someone, VIP. *Slang:* big shot, big wheel, bigwig, muckamuck. *See* IMPORTANT.

eminency *noun*
A position of exalted widely recognized importance : distinction, eminence, fame, glory, illustriousness, luster, mark, notability, note, preeminence, prestige, prominence, prominency, renown. *See* IMPORTANT, KNOWLEDGE, RESPECT.

eminent *adjective*
Widely known and esteemed : celebrated, distinguished, famed, famous, great, illustrious, notable, noted, preeminent, prestigious, prominent, redoubtable, renowned. *See* KNOWLEDGE, RESPECT.

eminently *adverb*
To a high degree : awfully, dreadfully, exceedingly, exceptionally, extra, extremely, greatly, highly, most, notably, very. *Informal:* awful. *Chiefly Regional:* mighty. *See* BIG.

emit *verb*
1. To discharge material, as vapor or fumes, usually suddenly and violently : give, give forth, give off, give out, issue, let off, let out, release, send forth, throw off, vent. *See* FREE, MOVE. **2.** To send out heat, light, or energy : cast, irradiate, project, radiate, shed, throw. *See* MOVE.

emolument *noun*
Payment for work done : compensation, earnings, fee, hire, pay, remuneration, salary, stipend, wage. *See* PAY.

emote *verb*
To make an emotional display : emotionalize, gush. *See* FEELINGS.

emotion *noun*
A complex and usually strong subjective response, such as love or hate : affection, affectivity, feeling, sentiment. *See* FEELINGS.

emotional *adjective*
1. Relating to, arising from, or appealing to the emotions : affective, emotive. *See* FEELINGS. **2.** Readily stirred by emotion : feeling, sensitive. *See* FEELINGS.

emotionalize *verb*
To make an emotional display : emote, gush. *See* FEELINGS.

emotionless *adjective*
Not affected by or showing emotion : cold, cold-blooded, unaffected, unemotional, unmoved. *See* ATTITUDE, HOT.

emotive *adjective*
Relating to, arising from, or appealing to the emotions : affective, emotional. *See* FEELINGS.

empathetic *adjective*
Cognizant of and comprehending the needs, feelings, problems, and views of others :

empathic, feeling, sympathetic, understanding. *See* UNDERSTAND.

empathic *adjective*
Cognizant of and comprehending the needs, feelings, problems, and views of others : empathetic, feeling, sympathetic, understanding. *See* UNDERSTAND.

empathize *verb*
1. To understand or be sensitive to another's feelings or ideas : sympathize. *See* UNDERSTAND. **2.** To associate or affiliate oneself closely with a person or group : identify, relate, sympathize. *See* SAME.

empathy *noun*
1. Sympathetic, sad concern for someone in misfortune : commiseration, compassion, condolence, pity, sympathy. *See* PITY. **2.** A very close understanding between persons : sympathy. *See* CONNECT, LOVE, UNDERSTAND.

emphasis *noun*
Special weight placed upon something considered important : accent, accentuation, stress. *See* IMPORTANT.

emphasize *verb*
To accord emphasis to : accent, accentuate, feature, highlight, italicize, play up, point up, stress, underline, underscore. *See* IMPORTANT.

emphatic *adjective*
1. Expressed or performed with emphasis : forceful, resounding. *See* STRONG. **2.** Bold and definite in character : assertive, forceful, insistent. *See* STRONG.

emphatically *adverb*
In a direct, positive manner : flat, flatly, positively. *Informal:* flat out. *See* STRONG.

emplace *verb*
To put in or assign to a certain position or location : install, locate, place, position, set[1], site, situate, spot. *See* PLACE.

emplacement *noun*
The place where a person or thing is located : location, locus, placement, position, site, situation. *See* PLACE.

employ *verb*
1. To obtain the use or services of : engage, hire, retain, take on. *Idiom:* put on the payroll. *See* GET, WORK. **2.** To make busy : busy, engage, occupy. *See* ACTION. **3.** To put into action or use : actuate, apply, exercise, exploit, implement, practice, use, utilize. *Idioms:* avail oneself of, bring into play, bring to bear, make use of, put into practice, put to use. *See* USED.
employ *noun* **1.** The state of being employed : employment, hire. *See* WORK. **2.** *Archaic.* Activity pursued as a livelihood : art, business, calling, career, craft, employment, job, line, métier, occupation, profession, pursuit, trade, vocation, work. *Slang:* racket. *See* ACTION.

employable *adjective*
1. Available for use : accessible, open, operable, operative, practicable, usable, utilizable. *See* POSSIBLE. **2.** In a condition to be used : serviceable, usable, utilizable. *See* USED.

employe *noun* See **employee.**

employed *adjective*
1. Having a job : hired, jobholding, retained, working. *See* WORK. **2.** Involved in activity or work : busy, engaged, occupied. *See* ACTION.

employee also **employe** *noun*
One who is employed by another : hireling, jobholder, worker. *Informal:* hire, hired hand. *See* OVER, WORK.

employer *noun*
One that employs persons for wages : hirer. *See* OVER, WORK.

employment *noun*
1. The act of employing for wages : engagement, hire. *See* GET, WORK. **2.** The state of being employed : employ, hire. *See* WORK. **3.** The act of putting into play : application, exercise, exertion, implementation, operation, play, usage, use, utilization. *See* USED. **4.** The condition of being put to use : application, duty, service, use, utilization. *See* USED. **5.** Activity pursued as a livelihood : art, business, calling, career, craft, job, line, métier, occupation, profession, pursuit, trade, vocation, work. *Slang:* racket. *Archaic:* employ. *See* ACTION.

empoison *verb*
Archaic. To have a destructive effect on : canker, envenom, infect, poison. *See* HELP.

emporium *noun*
A retail establishment where merchandise is sold : boutique, outlet, shop, store. *See* TRANSACTIONS.

empower *verb*
1. To give authority to : accredit, authorize, commission, enable, entitle, license, qualify. *See* ALLOW. **2.** To give the means, ability, or opportunity to do : enable, permit. *See* ALLOW.

emprise *noun*
An exciting, often hazardous undertaking : adventure, enterprise, venture. *See* SAFETY.

emptiness *noun*
1. Total absence of matter : vacancy, vacuity, vacuum, void. *See* FULL. **2.** Empty, unfilled space : barrenness, nothingness, vacancy, vacuity, vacuum, void. *See* FULL. **3.** Total lack

of ideas, meaning, or substance : barrenness, blankness, hollowness, inanity, vacancy, vacuity, vacuousness. *See* FULL. **4.** A desolate sense of loss : blankness, desolation, hollowness, vacuum, void. *See* FULL.

empty *adjective*
1. Containing nothing : bare, blank, clear, vacant, vacuous, void. *See* FULL. **2.** Lacking value, use, or substance : hollow, idle, otiose, vacant, vain. *See* FULL. **3.** Lacking intelligent thought or content : blank, empty-headed, inane, vacant, vacuous. *See* FULL. **4.** Not having a desirable element : barren, destitute, devoid, innocent, lacking, void, wanting. ***Idiom:*** in want of. *See* FULL.
empty *verb* **1.** To remove the contents of. Also used with *out* : clean out, clear, evacuate, vacate, void. *See* FULL. **2.** To pass or pour out : discharge, flow, issue. *See* ENTER.

empty-headed *adjective*
1. Lacking intelligent thought or content : blank, empty, inane, vacant, vacuous. *See* FULL. **2.** Given to lighthearted silliness : featherbrained, flighty, frivolous, frothy, giddy, harebrained, lighthearted, scatterbrained, silly. *Informal:* gaga. *Slang:* birdbrained, dizzy. *See* ABILITY.

empyreal *adjective*
Of or relating to the heavens : celestial, heavenly. *See* PLACE.

emulate *verb*
1. To take as a model or make conform to a model : copy, follow, imitate, model (on, upon, *or* after), pattern (on, upon, *or* after). ***Idioms:*** follow in the footsteps of, follow suit, follow the example of. *See* SAME. **2.** To strive against (others) for victory : compete, contend, contest, rival, vie. *See* CONFLICT.

emulation *noun*
A strong desire to achieve something : ambition, ambitiousness, aspiration. *See* DESIRE.

emulative *adjective*
Copying another in an inferior or obsequious way : apish, imitative, slavish. *See* SAME.

emulous *adjective*
1. Full of ambition : ambitious, aspiring. *See* DESIRE. **2.** Given to competition : competitive. *See* CONFLICT.

enable *verb*
1. To give the means, ability, or opportunity to do : empower, permit. *See* ALLOW. **2.** To give authority to : accredit, authorize, commission, empower, entitle, license, qualify. *See* ALLOW.

enact *verb*
1. To put in force or cause to be by legal authority : constitute, establish, legislate, make, promulgate. *See* ACTION, MAKE, POLITICS. **2.** To play the part of : act, do, impersonate, perform, play, play-act, portray, represent. *See* ACTION, PERFORMING ARTS, SUBSTITUTE. **3.** To produce on the stage : act (out), do, dramatize, give, perform, present[2], put on, stage. *See* PERFORMING ARTS.

enactment *noun*
The formal product of a legislative or judicial body : act, assize, bill[1], law, legislation, lex, measure, statute. *See* LAW.

enamored *adjective*
Affected with intense romantic attraction : infatuate, infatuated, smitten. *Slang:* gone. *See* EXCITE, SEX.

enceinte *adjective*
Carrying a developing fetus within the uterus : big, expectant, expecting, gravid, parturient, pregnant. *Slang:* gone. *Archaic:* great. ***Idioms:*** in a family way, with child. *See* REPRODUCTION.

enchant *verb*
1. To act upon with or as if with magic : bewitch, charm, enthrall, entrance[2], spell[2], spellbind, voodoo, witch. *See* PERSUASION. **2.** To please greatly or irresistibly : beguile, bewitch, captivate, charm, entrance[2], fascinate. *See* LIKE. **3.** To give great or keen pleasure to : cheer, delight, gladden, gratify, overjoy, please, pleasure, tickle. *Archaic:* joy. *See* HAPPY, LIKE.

enchanting *adjective*
1. Pleasing to the eye or mind : attractive, bewitching, engaging, enticing, fascinating, fetching, glamorous, lovely, prepossessing, pretty, sweet, taking, tempting, winning, winsome. *See* LIKE. **2.** Giving great pleasure or delight : charming, delectable, delicious, delightful, heavenly, luscious. *Informal:* darling. *See* GOOD, HAPPY, LIKE.

enchantment *noun*
The power or quality of attracting : allure, allurement, appeal, attraction, attractiveness, call, charisma, charm, draw, enticement, fascination, glamour, lure, magnetism, witchery. *Informal:* pull. *See* LIKE.

enchantress *noun*
1. A usually unscrupulous woman who seduces or exploits men : femme fatale, seductress, siren, temptress. *Informal:* vamp, witch. *See* SEX. **2.** A woman who practices magic : hag, lamia, sorceress, witch. *See* SUPERNATURAL.

encircle *verb*
To shut in on all sides : begird, beset, circle,

compass, encompass, environ, gird, girdle, hedge, hem, ring[1], surround. *See* OPEN.

enclose *verb*

1. To surround and advance upon : besiege, close in, envelop, hedge, hem. *See* OPEN. **2.** To confine within a limited area : cage, coop (in *or* up), fence (in), immure, mew (up), pen[2], shut in, shut up, wall (in *or* up). *See* FREE.

enclosure *noun*

An area partially or entirely enclosed by walls or buildings : atrium, close, court, courtyard, quad, quadrangle, yard. *See* PLACE.

encomium *noun*

An expression of warm approval : acclaim, acclamation, applause, celebration, commendation, compliment, eulogy, kudos, laudation, panegyric, plaudit, praise. *See* PRAISE.

encompass *verb*

1. To encircle with or as if with a band : band[1], begird, belt, cincture, compass, engirdle, gird, girdle, girt, ring[1]. *Archaic:* engird. *See* EDGE. **2.** To shut in on all sides : begird, beset, circle, compass, encircle, environ, gird, girdle, hedge, hem, ring[1], surround. *See* OPEN. **3.** To have as a part : comprehend, comprise, contain, embody, embrace, have, include, involve, subsume, take in. *See* INCLUDE.

encounter *verb*

1. To come up against : confront, face, meet[1], run into. *See* MEET. **2.** To meet face-to-face, especially defiantly : accost, confront, face, front. *See* MEET. **3.** To enter into conflict with : engage, meet[1], take on. ***Idiom:*** do (*or* join) battle with. *See* CONFLICT, MEET.

encounter *noun* **1.** A face-to-face, usually hostile meeting : confrontation, face-off. *See* MEET. **2.** A brief, hostile exposure to or contact with something such as danger or opposition : brush[2], clash, run-in, skirmish. *See* TOUCH.

encourage *verb*

1. To impart courage, inspiration, and resolution to : animate, cheer (on), embolden, inspire, inspirit, motivate. *See* HELP. **2.** To impart strength and confidence to : buck up, cheer (up), hearten, nerve, perk up. *See* HELP. **3.** To lend supportive approval to : countenance, favor, smile on (*or* upon). *See* SUPPORT. **4.** To help bring about : feed, foster, promote. *See* HELP.

encouragement *noun*

1. Something that encourages : inspiration, motivation, stimulation. *See* HELP. **2.** Something that causes and encourages a given response : fillip, impetus, impulse, incentive, inducement, motivation, prod, push, spur, stimulant, stimulation, stimulator, stimulus. *See* CAUSE.

encouraging *adjective*

Inspiring confidence or hope : cheering, heartening, hopeful, likely, promising. *See* HELP.

encroachment *noun*

An advance beyond proper or legal limits : entrenchment, impingement, infringement, intrusion, obtrusion, trespass. *See* ENTER.

encumber *verb*

1. To place a burden or heavy load on : burden[1], charge, cumber, freight, lade, load, saddle, tax, weight. *See* OVER. **2.** To interfere with the progress of : bog (down), hinder, hold back, impede, obstruct. ***Idiom:*** get in the way of. *See* HELP, OPEN.

end *noun*

1. The hindmost part of something : rear[1], tag end, tail, tail end. *See* PRECEDE. **2.** A demarcation point or boundary beyond which something does not extend or occur : bound[2] (often used in plural), confine (used in plural), limit. *See* EDGE. **3.** A concluding or terminating : cease, cessation, close, closing, closure, completion, conclusion, consummation, ending, end of the line, finish, period, stop, stopping point, termination, terminus, wind-up, wrap-up. *See* CONTINUE. **4.** The last part : close, conclusion, ending, finale, finish, last[1], termination, wind-up, wrap-up. *See* START. **5.** What one intends to do or achieve : aim, ambition, design, goal, intent, intention, mark, meaning, object, objective, point, purpose, target, view, why. ***Idioms:*** end in view, why and wherefore. *See* PLANNED, PURPOSE. **6.** The ultimate point to which an action, thought, discussion, or policy is carried : extreme, length, limit. *See* LIMITED. **7.** Residual matter : butt[4], fragment, ort (often used in plural), scrap[1], shard, stub. *See* LEFTOVER.

end *verb* To bring or come to a natural or proper end : close, complete, conclude, consummate, finish, terminate, wind up, wrap up. *See* START.

endanger *verb*

To subject to danger or destruction : imperil, jeopardize, menace, peril, risk, threaten. *See* SAFETY.

endangerment *noun*

Exposure to possible harm, loss, or injury : danger, hazard, imperilment, jeopardy, peril, risk. *See* SAFETY.

endeavor *noun*

1. A trying to do or make something : attempt, crack, effort, essay, go, offer, stab, trial, try.

Informal: shot. *Slang:* take. *Archaic:* assay. *See* TRY. **2.** The use of energy to do something : effort, exertion, pain (used in plural), strain[1], striving, struggle, trouble, while. *Informal:* elbow grease. *See* WORK.

endeavor *verb* To make an attempt to do or make : assay, attempt, essay, seek, strive, try. ***Idioms:*** have a go at, have (*or* make *or* take) a shot at, have (*or* take) a whack at, make a stab at, take a crack at. *See* TRY.

endemic *adjective*
Existing, born, or produced in a land or region : aboriginal, autochthonal, autochthonic, autochthonous, indigenous, native. *See* NATIVE.

ending *noun*
1. A concluding or terminating : cease, cessation, close, closing, closure, completion, conclusion, consummation, end, end of the line, finish, period, stop, stopping point, termination, terminus, wind-up, wrap-up. *See* CONTINUE.
2. The last part : close, conclusion, end, finale, finish, last[1], termination, wind-up, wrap-up. *See* START.

endless *adjective*
1. Having no ends or limits : boundless, illimitable, immeasurable, infinite, limitless, measureless, unbounded, unlimited. *See* LIMITED.
2. Enduring for all time : amaranthine, ceaseless, eternal, everlasting, immortal, never-ending, perpetual, unending, world without end. *Archaic:* eterne. *See* CONTINUE. **3.** Existing or occurring without interruption or end : around-the-clock, ceaseless, constant, continual, continuous, eternal, everlasting, incessant, interminable, nonstop, ongoing, perpetual, persistent, relentless, round-the-clock, timeless, unceasing, unending, unfailing, uninterrupted, unremitting. *See* CONTINUE.

endlessness *noun*
The quality or state of having no end : ceaselessness, eternality, eternalness, eternity, everlastingness, perpetuity, world without end. *See* CONTINUE.

endmost *adjective*
Bringing up the rear : hindermost, hindmost, last[1], lattermost, rearmost. *See* START.

end of the line *noun*
A concluding or terminating : cease, cessation, close, closing, closure, completion, conclusion, consummation, end, ending, finish, period, stop, stopping point, termination, terminus, wind-up, wrap-up. *See* CONTINUE.

endorse *verb*
1. To affix one's signature to : autograph, inscribe, sign, subscribe, undersign. ***Idioms:*** put one's John Hancock on, set one's hand to. *See* LAW. **2.** To give one's consent to : allow, approbate, approve, authorize, consent, let, permit, sanction. *Informal:* OK. *See* ALLOW.
3. To aid the cause of by approving or favoring : advocate, back, champion, get behind, plump for, recommend, side with, stand behind, stand by, support, uphold. ***Idioms:*** align oneself with, go to bat for, take the part of. *See* SUPPORT. **4.** To establish as true or genuine : authenticate, bear out, confirm, corroborate, demonstrate, establish, evidence, prove, show, substantiate, validate, verify. *See* SHOW, SUPPORT.

endorsement *noun*
1. The approving of an action, especially when done by one in authority : allowance, approbation, approval, authorization, consent, leave[2], license, permission, permit, sanction. *Informal:* OK. *See* ALLOW. **2.** An indication of commendation or approval : backing, recommendation, support. *See* SUPPORT.

endow *verb*
To present with a quality, trait, or power : dower, endue, gift, gird, invest. *See* GIVE.

endowed *adjective*
Having talent : gifted, talented. *See* ABILITY, GIVE.

end product *noun*
Something brought about by a cause : aftermath, consequence, corollary, effect, event, fruit, harvest, issue, outcome, precipitate, ramification, result, resultant, sequel, sequence, sequent, upshot. *See* CAUSE.

endue *verb*
To present with a quality, trait, or power : dower, endow, gift, gird, invest. *See* GIVE.

endurable *adjective*
Capable of being tolerated : bearable, sufferable, tolerable. *See* CONTINUE.

endurance *noun*
1. The quality or power of withstanding hardship or stress : stamina, staying power. *See* CONTINUE. **2.** Uninterrupted existence or succession : continuance, continuation, continuity, continuum, duration, persistence, persistency. *See* CONTINUE.

endure *verb*
1. To carry on through despite hardships : *Slang:* sweat out, tough out. *See* CONTINUE.
2. To put up with : abide, accept, bear, brook[2], go, stand (for), stomach, suffer, support, sustain, swallow, take, tolerate, withstand. *Informal:* lump[2]. ***Idioms:*** take it, take it

lying down. *See* ACCEPT. **3.** To be in existence or in a certain state for an indefinitely long time : abide, continue, go on, hold out, last[2], persist, remain, stay[1]. *See* CONTINUE. **4.** To withstand stress or difficulty : bear up, hold up, stand up. *See* CONTINUE.

enduring *adjective*
Existing or remaining in the same state for an indefinitely long time : abiding, continuing, durable, lasting, long-lasting, long-lived, long-standing, old, perdurable, perennial, permanent, persistent. *See* CONTINUE.

enemy *noun*
One who is hostile to or opposes the purposes or interests of another : archenemy, foe, nemesis. *See* LOVE.

energetic *adjective*
1. Possessing, exerting, or displaying energy : active, brisk, dynamic, dynamical, forceful, kinetic, lively, sprightly, strenuous, vigorous. *Informal:* peppy. *See* ACTION. **2.** Disposed to action : active, brisk, driving, dynamic, dynamical, enterprising, lively, sprightly, spry, vigorous, zippy. *Informal:* peppy, snappy. *See* ACTION.

energetically *adverb*
With intense energy and force : forcefully, forcibly, hard, powerfully, vigorously. ***Idioms:*** hammer and tongs, tooth and nail, with might and main. *See* STRONG.

energize *verb*
To give or impart vitality and energy to (someone or something) : exhilarate, invigorate, stimulate, vitalize. *See* HELP.

energizing *adjective*
Producing or stimulating physical, mental, or emotional vigor : bracing, exhilarant, exhilarating, innerving, intoxicating, invigorating, refreshing, reinvigorating, renewing, restorative, roborant, stimulating, tonic. *See* HELP.

energy *noun*
Capacity or power for work or vigorous activity : animation, force, might, potency, power, puissance, sprightliness, steam, strength. *Informal:* get-up-and-go, go, pep, peppiness, zip. *See* ACTION.

enervate *verb*
To lessen or deplete the nerve, energy, or strength of : attenuate, debilitate, devitalize, enfeeble, sap[2], undermine, undo, unnerve, weaken. *See* STRONG.

enervation *noun*
The depletion or sapping of strength or energy : attenuation, debilitation, depletion, devitalization, enfeeblement, impoverishment. *See* STRONG.

enfeeble *verb*
To lessen or deplete the nerve, energy, or strength of : attenuate, debilitate, devitalize, enervate, sap[2], undermine, undo, unnerve, weaken. *See* STRONG.

enfeeblement *noun*
The depletion or sapping of strength or energy : attenuation, debilitation, depletion, devitalization, enervation, impoverishment. *See* STRONG.

enfold *verb*
1. To cover completely and closely, as with clothing or bandages : envelop, enwrap, infold, invest, roll, swaddle, swathe, wrap, wrap up. *See* PUT ON. **2.** To surround and cover completely so as to obscure : cloak, clothe, enshroud, envelop, enwrap, infold, invest, shroud, veil, wrap. *See* SHOW. **3.** To put one's arms around affectionately : clasp, embrace, hold, hug, press, squeeze. *Slang:* clinch. *Archaic:* bosom, clip[2], embosom. *See* TOUCH.

enforce *verb*
To compel observance of : carry out, effect, execute, implement, invoke. ***Idioms:*** put in force, put into action. *See* OBLIGATION, OVER.

engage *verb*
1. To obtain the use or services of : employ, hire, retain, take on. ***Idiom:*** put on the payroll. *See* GET, WORK. **2.** To cause to be set aside, as for one's use, in advance : bespeak, book, reserve. *See* GET. **3.** To assume an obligation : contract, pledge, promise, undertake. *See* AGREE, OBLIGATION. **4.** To get and hold the attention of : involve, occupy. *See* EXCITE. **5.** To involve (someone) in an activity : draw in. *See* PARTICIPATE. **6.** To involve oneself in (an activity) : carry on, have, indulge, partake, participate. ***Idiom:*** take part. *See* PARTICIPATE. **7.** To make busy : busy, employ, occupy. *See* ACTION. **8.** To cause to be busy or in use : monopolize, occupy, preempt, tie up. *See* ACTION, USED. **9.** To enter into conflict with : encounter, meet[1], take on. ***Idiom:*** do (*or* join) battle with. *See* CONFLICT, MEET. **10.** To come or bring together and interlock : mesh. *See* CONNECT.

engaged *adjective*
1. Involved in activity or work : busy, employed, occupied. *See* ACTION. **2.** Pledged to marry : affianced, betrothed, intended, plighted. *See* MARRIAGE.

engagement *noun*
1. A commitment, as for a performance by an entertainer : booking. *Slang:* gig. *See* PERFORMING ARTS. **2.** The act or condition of being pledged to marry : betrothal, espousal, troth. *See* MARRIAGE. **3.** A declaration that one will or will not do a certain thing : assurance, covenant, guarantee, guaranty, pledge, plight[2], promise, solemn word, vow, warrant, word, word of honor. *See* OBLIGATION. **4.** A commitment to appear at a certain time and place : appointment, assignation, date, rendezvous, tryst. *See* AGREE. **5.** The act of employing for wages : employment, hire. *See* GET, WORK. **6.** A hostile encounter between opposing military forces : action, battle, combat. *See* CONFLICT.

engaging *adjective*
Pleasing to the eye or mind : attractive, bewitching, enchanting, enticing, fascinating, fetching, glamorous, lovely, prepossessing, pretty, sweet, taking, tempting, winning, winsome. *See* LIKE.

engender *verb*
To cause to come into existence : beget, breed, create, father, hatch, make, originate, parent, procreate, produce, sire, spawn. ***Idiom:*** give birth (*or* rise) to. *See* MAKE.

engineer *verb*
To make, achieve, or get through contrivance or guile : finesse, worm. *Informal:* finagle, wangle. *See* GET, MAKE.

engird *verb*
Archaic. To encircle with or as if with a band : band[1], begird, belt, cincture, compass, encompass, engirdle, gird, girdle, girt, ring.[1] *See* EDGE.

engirdle *verb*
To encircle with or as if with a band : band[1], begird, belt, cincture, compass, encompass, gird, girdle, girt, ring[1]. *Archaic:* engird. *See* EDGE.

englut *verb*
To swallow (food or drink) greedily or rapidly in large amounts : bolt, down, engorge, gobble, gulp, guzzle, ingurgitate, swill, wolf. *See* INGESTION.

engorge *verb*
1. To swallow (food or drink) greedily or rapidly in large amounts : bolt, down, englut, gobble, gulp, guzzle, ingurgitate, swill, wolf. *See* INGESTION. **2.** To satisfy to the full or to excess : cloy, glut, gorge, pall, sate, satiate, surfeit. *See* EXCESS, FULL.

engorgement *noun*
The condition of being full to or beyond satisfaction : repletion, satiation, satiety, surfeit. *See* EXCESS, FULL.

engrave *verb*
1. To cut (a design or inscription) into a hard surface, especially for printing : carve, etch, grave[3], incise. *See* MARKS. **2.** To produce a deep impression of : etch, fix, grave[3], impress, imprint, inscribe, stamp. *See* MARKS.

engross *verb*
1. To occupy the full attention of : absorb, consume, immerse, monopolize, preoccupy. *See* AWARENESS, EXCITE. **2.** To form letters, characters, or words on a surface with an instrument : indite, inscribe, scribe, write. *See* REMEMBER.

engrossment *noun*
Total occupation of the attention or of the mind : absorption, enthrallment, immersion, preoccupation, prepossession. *See* EXCITE.

engulf *verb*
1. To flow over completely : deluge, drown, flood, flush, inundate, overflow, overwhelm, submerge, whelm. *See* FULL. **2.** To affect deeply or completely, as with emotion : crush, overcome, overpower, overwhelm, prostrate. *See* AFFECT.

enhance *verb*
1. To endow with beauty and elegance by way of a notable addition : adorn, beautify, embellish, grace, set off. *See* BEAUTIFUL. **2.** To look good on or with : become, flatter, suit. ***Idiom:*** put in the best light. *See* AGREE, BEAUTIFUL. **3.** To make greater in intensity or severity : aggravate, deepen, heighten, intensify, redouble. *See* INCREASE. **4.** To increase or seek to increase the importance or reputation of by favorable publicity : ballyhoo, boost, build up, promote, publicize, puff, talk up, tout. *Informal:* plug. *Slang:* hype. *See* KNOWLEDGE.

enhancement *noun*
Something added to another for embellishment or completion : accompaniment, complement, enrichment. *See* ACCOMPANIED.

enigma *noun*
Anything that arouses curiosity or perplexes because it is unexplained, inexplicable, or secret : conundrum, mystery, perplexity, puzzle, puzzler, riddle. *See* SHOW.

enigmatic *adjective*
Difficult to explain or understand : arcane, cabalistic, cryptic, mysterious, mystic, mystical, mystifying, occult, puzzling. *See* EXPLAIN, KNOWLEDGE.

enjoin *verb*
1. To give orders to : bid, charge, command, direct, instruct, order, tell. *See* OVER, WORDS. **2.** To refuse to allow : ban, debar, disallow, forbid, inhibit, interdict, outlaw, prohibit, proscribe, taboo. *See* ALLOW.

enjoy *verb*
1. To receive pleasure from : like[1], relish, savor. *Informal:* go for. *Slang:* dig. *See* LIKE. **2.** To have the use or benefit of : have, hold, possess. *See* OWNED. **3.** To have at one's disposal : boast, command, have, hold, possess. *See* OWNED.

enjoyable *adjective*
Affording enjoyment : gratifying, pleasant, pleasing, pleasurable. *See* PAIN.

enjoyment *noun*
1. The condition of responding pleasurably to something : delectation, pleasure. *See* PAIN. **2.** A feeling of extreme gratification aroused by something good or desired : delectation, delight, joy, pleasure. *See* HAPPY, LIKE.

enkindle *verb*
1. To cause to burn or undergo combustion : fire, ignite, kindle, light[1]. *Slang:* torch. ***Idioms:*** set afire (*or* on fire), set fire to. *See* HOT, START. **2.** To arouse the emotions of; make ardent : animate, fire, impassion, inspire, kindle, stir[1]. *See* EXCITE.

enlarge *verb*
1. To make or become greater or larger : aggrandize, amplify, augment, boost, build, build up, burgeon, escalate, expand, extend, grow, increase, magnify, mount, multiply, proliferate, rise, run up, snowball, soar, swell, upsurge, wax. *Informal:* beef up. *See* INCREASE. **2.** To express at greater length or in greater detail : amplify, develop, dilate, elaborate, expand, expatiate, labor. *See* EXPLAIN.

enlargement *noun*
1. The act of increasing in dimensions, scope, or inclusiveness : expansion, extension, spread. *See* INCREASE. **2.** The act of increasing or rising : aggrandizement, amplification, augment, augmentation, boost, buildup, escalation, growth, hike, increase, jump, multiplication, proliferation, raise, rise, swell, upsurge, upswing, upturn. *See* INCREASE. **3.** The result or product of building up : accretion, buildup, development, multiplication, proliferation. *See* INCREASE.

enlighten *verb*
1. To enable (one) to understand, especially in a spiritual sense : edify, illume, illuminate, illumine. *See* TEACH. **2.** To impart information to : acquaint, advise, apprise, educate, inform, notify, tell. *See* KNOWLEDGE, TEACH.

enlightened *adjective*
1. Having an education : educated, informed, lettered, literate. *See* KNOWLEDGE. **2.** Provided with information; made aware : acquainted, advised, educated, informed, instructed, knowledgeable. *See* KNOWLEDGE.

enlightening *adjective*
1. Promoting culture : civilizing, cultural, edifying, humanizing, refining. *See* CULTURE. **2.** Serving to educate or inform : edifying, educational, educative, illuminative, informative, instructional, instructive. *See* TEACH.

enlightenment *noun*
The condition of being informed spiritually : edification, illumination. *See* TEACH.

enlist *verb*
To become a member of : enroll, enter, join, muster in, sign up. *Informal:* sign on. *See* PARTICIPATE.

enliven *verb*
To make lively or animated : animate, brighten, light[1]. *See* HAPPY.

enlivening *adjective*
Serving to enliven : animating, quickening, rousing, stimulating, vitalizing, vivifying. *See* EXCITE.

enmesh *verb*
To gain control of or an advantage over by or as if by trapping : catch, ensnare, ensnarl, entrap, snare, tangle, trammel, trap, web. *See* FREE.

enmeshment *noun*
The condition of being entangled or implicated : embranglement, embroilment, ensnarement, entanglement, involvement. *See* FREE, PARTICIPATE.

enmity *noun*
Deep-seated hatred, as between longtime opponents or rivals : animosity, animus, antagonism, antipathy, hostility, ill will. *See* LOVE.

ennoble *verb*
1. To cause to be eminent or recognized : distinguish, elevate, exalt, honor, signalize. *See* RESPECT. **2.** To raise to a high position or status : aggrandize, apotheosize, dignify, elevate, exalt, glorify, magnify, uplift. ***Idiom:*** put on a pedestal. *See* RISE.

ennoblement *noun*
The act of raising to a high position or status or the condition of being so raised : aggrandizement, apotheosis, elevation, exaltation, glorification. *See* RISE.

ennui *noun*
The condition of being bored : boredom. *See* EXCITE.

enormity *noun*
1. The quality of passing all moral bounds : atrociousness, atrocity, heinousness, monstrousness. *See* GOOD. **2.** The quality or state of being flagrant : atrociousness, atrocity, egregiousness, flagrance, flagrancy, flagrantness, glaringness, grossness, outrageousness, rankness. *See* GOOD. **3.** A monstrous offense or evil : atrocity, monstrosity, outrage. *See* RIGHT.

enormous *adjective*
1. Of extraordinary size and power : behemoth, Brobdingnagian, Bunyanesque, colossal, cyclopean, elephantine, gargantuan, giant, gigantesque, gigantic, herculean, heroic, huge, immense, jumbo, mammoth, massive, massy, mastodonic, mighty, monster, monstrous, monumental, mountainous, prodigious, pythonic, stupendous, titanic, tremendous, vast. *Informal:* walloping. *Slang:* whopping. *See* BIG. **2.** *Archaic.* Disgracefully and grossly offensive : atrocious, heinous, monstrous, outrageous, scandalous, shocking. *See* RIGHT.

enormousness *noun*
The quality of being enormous : hugeness, immenseness, immensity, prodigiousness, stupendousness, tremendousness, vastness. *See* BIG.

enough *adjective*
Being what is needed without being in excess : adequate, comfortable, competent, decent, satisfactory, sufficient. *See* EXCESS.
enough *noun* An adequate quantity : adequacy, sufficiency. *See* EXCESS.

enounce *verb*
To declare by way of a systematic statement : enunciate, state. *See* WORDS.

enquire *verb* See **inquire.**

enquirer *noun* See **inquirer.**

enquiring *adjective* See **inquiring.**

enquiry *noun* See **inquiry.**

enrage *verb*
To cause to feel or show anger : anger, burn (up), incense[1], infuriate, madden, provoke. ***Idioms:*** make one hot under the collar, make one's blood boil, put one's back up. *See* FEELINGS.

enrapture *verb*
To move or excite greatly : carry away, electrify, thrill, transport. *Slang:* send. *See* EXCITE.

enrich *verb*
To make fertile : fecundate, fertilize. *See* RICH.

enrichment *noun*
Something added to another for embellishment or completion : accompaniment, complement, enhancement. *See* ACCOMPANIED.

enroll *verb*
1. To register in or as if in a book : book, catalog, inscribe, list[1], set down, write down. *See* REMEMBER. **2.** To become a member of : enlist, enter, join, muster in, sign up. *Informal:* sign on. *See* PARTICIPATE.

ensanguine *verb*
To cover with blood : bloodstain, bloody, imbrue. *See* BLOOD.

ensconce *verb*
1. To place securely in a position or condition : establish, fix, install, seat, settle. *See* PUT IN.
2. To put or keep out of sight : bury, cache, conceal, hide[1], occult, secrete. *Slang:* plant, stash. *See* SHOW.

enshroud *verb*
1. To surround and cover completely so as to obscure : cloak, clothe, enfold, envelop, enwrap, infold, invest, shroud, veil, wrap. *See* SHOW. **2.** To prevent (something) from being known : cloak, conceal, cover (up), hide[1], hush (up), mask, shroud, veil. ***Idioms:*** keep under cover, keep under wraps. *See* SHOW.

ensign *noun*
Fabric used especially as a symbol : banderole, banner, banneret, color (used in plural), flag[1], jack, oriflamme, pennant, pennon, standard, streamer. *See* SUBSTITUTE.

enslave *verb*
To make subservient or subordinate : enthrall, subject, subjugate. *See* FREE.

enslavement *noun*
A state of subjugation to an owner or master : bondage, helotry, serfdom, servileness, servility, servitude, slavery, thrall, thralldom, villeinage, yoke. *See* OVER.

ensnare *verb*
To gain control of or an advantage over by or as if by trapping : catch, enmesh, ensnarl, entrap, snare, tangle, trammel, trap, web. *See* FREE.

ensnarement *noun*
The condition of being entangled or implicated : embranglement, embroilment, enmeshment, entanglement, involvement. *See* FREE, PARTICIPATE.

ensnarl *verb*
1. To twist together so that separation is

difficult : entangle, foul, snarl[2], tangle. *See* ORDER. **2.** To gain control of or an advantage over by or as if by trapping : catch, enmesh, ensnare, entrap, snare, tangle, trammel, trap, web. *See* FREE.

ensue *verb*
1. To occur as a consequence : attend, follow, result. *See* CAUSE, PRECEDE. **2.** To occur after in time : follow, succeed, supervene. ***Idiom:*** follow on (*or* upon) the heels of. *See* PRECEDE, TIME.

ensure *verb*
To render certain : assure, guarantee, insure, secure, warrant. *Informal:* cinch. *See* CERTAIN.

entail *verb*
1. To have as an accompaniment, a condition, or a consequence : carry, involve. *See* START. **2.** To have as a need or prerequisite : ask, call for, demand, involve, necessitate, require, take. *See* NECESSARY, OVER.

entangle *verb*
1. To twist together so that separation is difficult : ensnarl, foul, snarl[2], tangle. *See* ORDER. **2.** To make complex, intricate, or perplexing : complicate, embarrass, involve, perplex, ravel, snarl[2], tangle. *See* SIMPLE.

entanglement *noun*
1. The condition of being entangled or implicated : embranglement, embroilment, enmeshment, ensnarement, involvement. *See* FREE, PARTICIPATE. **2.** Something that is intricately and often bewilderingly complex : cat's cradle, jungle, knot, labyrinth, maze, mesh (often used in plural), morass, skein, snarl[2], tangle, web. *See* SIMPLE.

enter *verb*
1. To come or go into (a place) : come in, go in, penetrate. *Nautical:* put in. ***Idioms:*** gain entrance (*or* entry), set foot in. *See* ENTER. **2.** To pass into or through by overcoming resistance : break (through), penetrate, perforate, pierce, puncture. *See* ENTER. **3.** To become a member of : enlist, enroll, join, muster in, sign up. *Informal:* sign on. *See* PARTICIPATE. **4.** To go about the initial step in doing (something) : approach, begin, commence, embark, get off, inaugurate, initiate, institute, launch, lead off, open, set about, set out, set to, start, take on, take up, undertake. *Informal:* kick off. ***Idioms:*** get cracking, get going, get the show on the road. *See* START. **5.** To place on a list or in a record : insert, post[3], record, register. *See* REMEMBER.

enterprise *noun*
1. Something undertaken, especially something requiring extensive planning and work : project, undertaking, venture. *See* WORK. **2.** An exciting, often hazardous undertaking : adventure, emprise, venture. *See* SAFETY. **3.** A commercial organization : business, company, concern, corporation, establishment, firm[2], house. *Informal:* outfit. *See* GROUP. **4.** An aggressive readiness along with energy to undertake taxing efforts : drive, hustle, initiative, punch. *Informal:* get-up-and-go, gumption, push. *See* ACTION, TIRED, TRY.

enterprising *adjective*
1. Taking or willing to take risks : adventuresome, adventurous, audacious, bold, daredevil, daring, venturesome, venturous. *See* SAFETY. **2.** Disposed to action : active, brisk, driving, dynamic, dynamical, energetic, lively, sprightly, spry, vigorous, zippy. *Informal:* peppy, snappy. *See* ACTION.

entertain *verb*
1. To occupy in an agreeable or pleasing way : amuse, divert, recreate, regale. *See* EXCITE. **2.** To receive (an idea) and take it into consideration : consider, hear of, think of. *See* THOUGHTS. **3.** To think or think about carefully and at length : chew on (*or* over), cogitate, consider, contemplate, deliberate, excogitate, meditate, mull, muse[1], ponder, reflect, revolve, ruminate, study, think, think out, think over, think through, turn over, weigh. ***Idioms:*** cudgel one's brains, put on one's thinking cap, rack one's brain. *See* THOUGHTS.

entertaining *adjective*
Providing pleasure or entertainment : amusing, diverting. *See* EXCITE.

entertainment *noun*
1. Something, especially a performance or show, designed to entertain : amusement, distraction, diversion, recreation. *See* EXCITE. **2.** The condition of being amused : amusement, recreation. *See* EXCITE.

enthrall *verb*
1. To act upon with or as if with magic : bewitch, charm, enchant, entrance[2], spell[2], spellbind, voodoo, witch. *See* PERSUASION. **2.** To compel, as the attention, interest, or imagination, of : arrest, catch up, fascinate, grip, hold, mesmerize, rivet, spellbind, transfix. *Slang:* grab. *See* EXCITE. **3.** To make subservient or subordinate : enslave, subject, subjugate. *See* FREE.

enthrallment *noun*
Total occupation of the attention or of the mind : absorption, engrossment, immersion, preoccupation, prepossession. *See* EXCITE.

enthusiasm *noun*
1. Passionate devotion to or interest in a cause or subject, for example : ardor, fervor, fire, passion, zeal, zealousness. *See* CONCERN, FEELINGS. **2.** A subject or activity that inspires lively interest : craze, mania, passion, rage. *See* CONCERN.

enthusiast *noun*
1. One who ardently admires : admirer, devotee, fancier, lover. *Informal:* fan[2]. *See* LIKE, LOVE, PRAISE. **2.** A person who is ardently devoted to a particular subject or activity : bug, devotee, fanatic, maniac, zealot. *Informal:* buff[2], fan[2], fiend. *Slang:* freak, nut. *See* CONCERN. **3.** One zealously devoted to a religion : devotee, fanatic, sectary, votary, zealot. *See* BELIEF, LOVE, RELIGION.

enthusiastic *adjective*
Showing or having enthusiasm : ardent, fervent, keen[1], mad, rabid, warm, zealous. *Informal:* crazy. *Slang:* gung ho, nuts. *See* CONCERN.

entice *verb*
1. To direct or impel to oneself by some quality or action : allure, appeal, attract, draw, lure, magnetize, take. *Informal:* pull. *See* LIKE. **2.** To beguile or draw into a wrong or foolish course of action : allure, inveigle, lure, seduce, tempt. ***Idiom:*** lead astray. *See* PERSUASION.

enticement *noun*
1. The power or quality of attracting : allure, allurement, appeal, attraction, attractiveness, call, charisma, charm, draw, enchantment, fascination, glamour, lure, magnetism, witchery. *Informal:* pull. *See* LIKE. **2.** Something that attracts, especially with the promise of pleasure or reward : allurement, bait, come-on, inducement, inveiglement, invitation, lure, seduction, temptation. *See* LIKE.

enticer *noun*
One that seduces : allurer, charmer, inveigler, lurer, seducer, tempter. *See* PERSUASION.

enticing *adjective*
1. Pleasing to the eye or mind : attractive, bewitching, enchanting, engaging, fascinating, fetching, glamorous, lovely, prepossessing, pretty, sweet, taking, tempting, winning, winsome. *See* LIKE. **2.** Tending to seduce : alluring, bewitching, come-hither, inveigling, inviting, luring, seductive, siren, tempting, witching. *See* LIKE, PERSUASION, SEX.

entire *adjective*
1. Including every constituent or individual : all, complete, gross, total, whole. *See* PART. **2.** Lacking nothing essential or normal : complete, full, intact, integral, perfect, whole. *See* PART. **3.** Not more or less : complete, full, good, perfect, round, whole. *See* PART, PRECISE. **4.** In excellent condition : flawless, good, intact, perfect, sound[2], unblemished, unbroken, undamaged, unharmed, unhurt, unimpaired, uninjured, unmarred, whole. *See* THRIVE.

entirely *adverb*
1. To the fullest extent : absolutely, all, altogether, completely, dead, flat, fully, just, perfectly, quite, thoroughly, totally, utterly, well[2], wholly. *Informal:* clean, clear. ***Idioms:*** in toto, through and through. *See* BIG, LIMITED. **2.** To the exclusion of anyone or anything else : alone, but, exclusively, only, solely. *See* INCLUDE.

entirety *noun*
1. The state of being entirely whole : completeness, integrity, oneness, totality, wholeness. *See* PART. **2.** An amount or quantity from which nothing is left out or held back : aggregate, all, everything, gross, sum, total, totality, whole. *Informal:* work (used in plural). ***Idioms:*** everything but (*or* except) the kitchen sink; lock, stock, and barrel; the whole ball of wax (*or* kit and caboodle *or* megillah *or* nine yards *or* shebang). *See* PART.

entitle *verb*
1. To give a name or title to : baptize, call, christen, denominate, designate, dub, name, style, term, title. *See* SPECIFIC, WORDS. **2.** To give authority to : accredit, authorize, commission, empower, enable, license, qualify. *See* ALLOW.

entity *noun*
1. One that exists independently : being, existence, existent, individual, object, something, thing. *See* BE, THING. **2.** An organized array of individual elements and parts forming and working as a unit : integral, sum, system, totality, whole. *See* PART. **3.** The fact or state of existing or of being actual : actuality, being, existence, reality. *See* BE, REAL.

entomb *verb*
To place (a corpse) in or as if in a grave : bury, inhume, inter, lay[1]. ***Idiom:*** lay (*or* put) to rest. *See* SHOW.

entombment *noun*
An act of placing a body in a grave or tomb : burial, inhumation, interment. *See* SHOW.

entourage *noun*
A group of attendants or followers : following, retinue, suite, train. *See* OVER.

entrance¹ *noun*
1. The act of entering : entry, ingress. *See*

ENTER. **2.** The state of being allowed entry : admission, admittance, ingress, ingression, introduction, intromission. *See* ACCEPT. **3.** The right to enter or make use of : access, admission, admittance, entrée, entry, ingress. *See* ENTER.

entrance[2] *verb*
1. To act upon with or as if with magic : bewitch, charm, enchant, enthrall, spell[2], spellbind, voodoo, witch. *See* PERSUASION. **2.** To please greatly or irresistibly : beguile, bewitch, captivate, charm, enchant, fascinate. *See* LIKE.

entrap *verb*
To gain control of or an advantage over by or as if by trapping : catch, enmesh, ensnare, ensnarl, snare, tangle, trammel, trap, web. *See* FREE.

entreat *verb*
To make an earnest or urgent request : appeal, beg, beseech, crave, implore, plead, pray, sue, supplicate. *Archaic:* conjure. *See* ASK.

entreaty *noun*
An earnest or urgent request : appeal, imploration, plea, prayer[1], supplication. *See* ASK.

entrée *noun*
The right to enter or make use of : access, admission, admittance, entrance[1], entry, ingress. *See* ENTER.

entrench *verb*
To implant so deeply as to make change nearly impossible : embed, fasten, fix, infix, ingrain, lodge, root[1]. *See* MOVE.

entrenched *adjective*
Firmly established by long standing : confirmed, deep-rooted, deep-seated, hard-shell, ineradicable, ingrained, inveterate, irradicable, set[1], settled. *See* CONTINUE.

entrenchment *noun*
An advance beyond proper or legal limits : encroachment, impingement, infringement, intrusion, obtrusion, trespass. *See* ENTER.

entrepreneur *noun*
One that creates, founds, or originates : architect, author, creator, father, founder[2], inventor, maker, originator, parent, patriarch. *See* START.

entrust also **intrust** *verb*
1. To put in the charge of another for care, use, or performance : commend, commit, confide, consign, give (over), hand over, relegate, trust, turn over. ***Idiom:*** give in trust (*or* charge). *See* GIVE. **2.** To place a trust upon : charge, trust. *See* TRUST.

entry *noun*
1. The act of entering : entrance[1], ingress. *See* ENTER. **2.** The right to enter or make use of : access, admission, admittance, entrance[1], entrée, ingress. *See* ENTER. **3.** An item inserted, as in a diary, register, or reference book : insertion, posting. *See* WORDS.

entwine *verb*
To move or proceed on a repeatedly curving course : coil, corkscrew, curl, meander, snake, spiral, twine, twist, weave, wind[2], wreathe. *See* REPETITION, STRAIGHT.

enucleate *verb*
Archaic. To make understandable : construe, decipher, explain, explicate, expound, interpret, spell out. ***Idiom:*** put into plain English. *See* EXPLAIN.

enucleation *noun*
Archaic. Something that serves to explain or clarify : clarification, construction, decipherment, elucidation, exegesis, explanation, explication, exposition, illumination, illustration, interpretation. *See* EXPLAIN.

enumerate *verb*
1. To name or specify one by one : itemize, list[1], numerate, tick off. *See* COUNT, SPECIFIC. **2.** To note (items) one by one so as to get a total : count, number, numerate, reckon, tally, tell. *See* COUNT.

enumeration *noun*
A noting of items one by one : count, numeration, reckoning, tally. *Archaic:* tale. *See* COUNT.

enunciate *verb*
1. To produce or make (speech sounds) : articulate, pronounce, say, utter[1], vocalize. *See* WORDS. **2.** To declare by way of a systematic statement : enounce, state. *See* WORDS.

enunciation *noun*
The use of the speech organs to produce sounds : articulation, utterance, vocalism, vocalization, voicing. *See* SOUNDS, WORDS.

envelop *verb*
1. To cover completely and closely, as with clothing or bandages : enfold, enwrap, infold, invest, roll, swaddle, swathe, wrap, wrap up. *See* PUT ON. **2.** To surround and cover completely so as to obscure : cloak, clothe, enfold, enshroud, enwrap, infold, invest, shroud, veil, wrap. *See* SHOW. **3.** To surround and advance upon : besiege, close in, enclose, hedge, hem. *See* OPEN.

envenom *verb*
To have a destructive effect on : canker, infect, poison. *Archaic:* empoison. *See* HELP.

envious *adjective*
Resentfully or painfully desirous of another's

advantages : covetous, green-eyed, invidious, jealous. *See* DESIRE.

enviousness *noun*
Resentful or painful desire for another's advantages : covetousness, envy, jealousy. *See* DESIRE.

environ *verb*
To shut in on all sides : begird, beset, circle, compass, encircle, encompass, gird, girdle, hedge, hem, ring[1], surround. *See* OPEN.

environment *noun*
1. Existing surroundings that affect an activity : circumstance (often used in plural), condition (used in plural). *Slang:* scene. *See* BE. **2.** A surrounding area : environs, locale, locality, neighborhood, precinct (used in plural), surroundings, vicinity. *See* NEAR, PLACE. **3.** The totality of surrounding conditions and circumstances affecting growth or development : ambiance, atmosphere, climate, medium, milieu, mise en scène, surroundings, world. *See* BE, LIMITED, PLACE.

environs *noun*
1. A surrounding area : environment, locale, locality, neighborhood, precinct (used in plural), surroundings, vicinity. *See* NEAR, PLACE. **2.** The periphery of a city or town : edge, fringe, outskirt (often used in plural), skirt (used in plural), suburb (used in plural). *See* EDGE.

envisage *verb*
To form mental images of : conceive, envision, fancy, fantasize, image, imagine, picture, see, think, vision, visualize. *Informal:* feature. *See* THOUGHTS.

envision *verb*
1. To form mental images of : conceive, envisage, fancy, fantasize, image, imagine, picture, see, think, vision, visualize. *Informal:* feature. *See* THOUGHTS. **2.** To know in advance : anticipate, divine, foreknow, foresee, see. *See* FORESIGHT, SEE.

envoy *noun*
A person who carries messages or is sent on errands : bearer, carrier, conveyer, courier, messenger, runner, transporter. *See* OVER.

envy *noun*
Resentful or painful desire for another's advantages : covetousness, enviousness, jealousy. *See* DESIRE.
envy *verb* To feel envy towards or for : begrudge, covet, grudge. *See* DESIRE.

enwrap *verb*
1. To cover completely and closely, as with clothing or bandages : enfold, envelop, infold, invest, roll, swaddle, swathe, wrap, wrap up. *See* PUT ON. **2.** To surround and cover completely so as to obscure : cloak, clothe, enfold, enshroud, envelop, infold, invest, shroud, veil, wrap. *See* SHOW.

eon also **aeon** *noun*
A long time : eternity, long[1], year (used in plural). *Informal:* age (used in plural), blue moon. ***Idioms:*** forever and a day, forever and ever, month of Sundays. *See* TIME.

ephemeral *adjective*
Lasting or existing only for a short time : evanescent, fleet, fleeting, fugacious, fugitive, momentary, passing, short-lived, temporal, temporary, transient, transitory. *See* CONTINUE, TIME.

epicene *adjective*
Having qualities more appropriate to women than to men : effeminate, feminine, sissified, sissyish, unmanly, womanish. *See* GENDER.

epicure *noun*
A person devoted to pleasure and luxury : epicurean, hedonist, sensualist, sybarite, voluptuary. *See* PAIN.

epicurean *adjective*
1. Characterized by or devoted to pleasure and luxury as a lifestyle : hedonic, hedonistic, sybaritic, voluptuary, voluptuous. *See* PAIN. **2.** Relating to, suggestive of, or appealing to sense gratification : sensual, sensualistic, sensuous, voluptuous. *See* PAIN.
epicurean *noun* A person devoted to pleasure and luxury : epicure, hedonist, sensualist, sybarite, voluptuary. *See* PAIN.

epidemic *noun*
A sudden increase in something, as the occurrence of a disease : outbreak, plague, rash[2]. *See* INCREASE.

epidermis *noun*
The tissue forming the external covering of the body : integument, skin. *See* SURFACE.

epigrammatic *adjective*
Precisely meaningful and tersely cogent : aphoristic, compact[1], epigrammatical, marrowy, pithy. *Informal:* brass-tacks. ***Idioms:*** down to brass tacks, to the point. *See* MEANING, STYLE.

epigrammatical *adjective*
Precisely meaningful and tersely cogent : aphoristic, compact[1], epigrammatic, marrowy, pithy. *Informal:* brass-tacks. ***Idioms:*** down to brass tacks, to the point. *See* MEANING, STYLE.

episode *noun*
Something significant that happens :

circumstance, development, event, happening, incident, news, occasion, occurrence, thing. *See* HAPPEN.

epistle *noun*
A written communication directed to another : letter, missive, note. *See* WORDS.

epithet *noun*
1. The word or words by which one is called and identified : appellation, appellative, cognomen, denomination, designation, name, nickname, style, tag, title. *Slang:* handle, moniker. *See* SPECIFIC, WORDS. **2.** A profane or obscene term : blasphemy, curse, expletive, oath, swearword. *Informal:* cuss. *See* DECENT, SACRED, WORDS.

epitome *noun*
A short summary or version prepared by cutting down a larger work : abridgment, abstract, brief, condensation, synopsis. *See* WORDS.

epitomize *verb*
1. To give a recapitulation of the salient facts of : abstract, go over, recapitulate, review, run down, run through, summarize, sum up, synopsize, wrap up. *Informal:* recap. *See* THOUGHTS. **2.** To serve as an example, image, or symbol of : exemplify, illustrate, represent, stand for, symbol, symbolize, typify. *See* SUBSTITUTE.

epoch *noun*
A particular time notable for its distinctive characteristics : age, day, era, period, time (often used in plural). *See* TIME.

equable *adjective*
Having no change or variation : changeless, constant, even[1], invariable, invariant, regular, same, steady, unchanging, uniform, unvarying. *See* SAME.

equal *adjective*
1. Agreeing exactly in value, quantity, or effect : equivalent, even[1], identical, same, tantamount. ***Idioms:*** on a par, one and the same. *See* SAME. **2.** Having the necessary strength or ability : up to. *See* ABILITY. **3.** Just to all parties : equitable, even[1], evenhanded, fair. *See* SAME.

equal *noun* One that is very similar to another in rank or position : coequal, colleague, compeer, equivalent, fellow, peer[2]. *See* SAME.

equal *verb* **1.** To be equal or alike : compare, correspond, match, measure up, parallel, touch. *Informal:* stack up. *See* SAME. **2.** To be equivalent or tantamount : amount, constitute, correspond. ***Idiom:*** have all the earmarks. *See* BE. **3.** To do or make something equal to : match, meet[1], tie. *See* SAME.

equality *noun*
The state of being equivalent : equation, equivalence, equivalency, par, parity, sameness. *See* SAME.

equalize *verb*
1. To make equal : equate, even[1], level, square. *See* SAME. **2.** To put in balance : balance, counterbalance, stabilize, steady. *See* ORDER.

equanimity *noun*
A stable, calm state of the emotions : aplomb, balance, collectedness, composure, coolness, imperturbability, imperturbableness, nonchalance, poise, sang-froid, self-possession, unflappability. *Slang:* cool. *See* CALM, FEELINGS.

equate *verb*
1. To make equal : equalize, even[1], level, square. *See* SAME. **2.** To represent as similar : analogize, assimilate, compare, identify, liken, match, parallel. *See* SAME.

equation *noun*
The state of being equivalent : equality, equivalence, equivalency, par, parity, sameness. *See* SAME.

equilibrium *noun*
A stable state characterized by the cancellation of all forces by equal opposing forces : balance, counterpoise, equipoise, stasis. *See* ORDER.

equip *verb*
To supply what is needed for some activity or purpose : accouter, appoint, fit[1], fit out (*or* up), furnish, gear, outfit, rig, turn out. *See* GIVE.

equipment *noun*
Things needed for a task, journey, or other purpose : accouterment (often used in plural), apparatus, gear, material (used in plural), materiel, outfit, paraphernalia, rig, tackle, thing (used in plural), turnout. *See* MEANS.

equipoise *noun*
A stable state characterized by the cancellation of all forces by equal opposing forces : balance, counterpoise, equilibrium, stasis. *See* ORDER.

equitable *adjective*
1. Just to all parties : equal, even[1], evenhanded, fair. *See* SAME. **2.** Free from bias in judgment : disinterested, dispassionate, fair, fair-minded, impartial, indifferent, just, nonpartisan, objective, square, unbiased, unprejudiced. ***Idiom:*** fair and square. *See* FAIR.

equitableness *noun*
The quality or state of being just and unbiased :

detachment, disinterest, disinterestedness, dispassion, dispassionateness, fair-mindedness, fairness, impartiality, impartialness, justice, justness, nonpartisanship, objectiveness, objectivity. *See* FAIR.

equity *noun*
The state, action, or principle of treating all persons equally in accordance with the law : due process, justice. *See* RIGHT.

equivalence *noun*
The state of being equivalent : equality, equation, equivalency, par, parity, sameness. *See* SAME.

equivalency *noun*
The state of being equivalent : equality, equation, equivalence, par, parity, sameness. *See* SAME.

equivalent *adjective*
1. Agreeing exactly in value, quantity, or effect : equal, even[1], identical, same, tantamount. ***Idioms:*** on a par, one and the same. *See* SAME. **2.** Possessing the same or almost the same characteristics : alike, analogous, comparable, corresponding, like[2], parallel, similar, uniform. *See* SAME.
equivalent *noun* One that is very similar to another in rank or position : coequal, colleague, compeer, equal, fellow, peer[2]. *See* SAME.

equivocal *adjective*
1. Liable to more than one interpretation : ambiguous, cloudy, inexplicit, nebulous, obscure, uncertain, unclear, vague. *See* CERTAIN, CLEAR. **2.** Deliberately ambiguous or vague : evasive. *See* CLEAR. **3.** Not affording certainty : ambiguous, borderline, chancy, clouded, doubtful, dubious, dubitable, inconclusive, indecisive, indeterminate, problematic, problematical, questionable, uncertain, unclear, unsure. *Informal:* iffy. ***Idioms:*** at issue, in doubt, in question. *See* CERTAIN, CLEAR. **4.** Of dubious character : doubtful, questionable, shady, suspect, suspicious, uncertain. *Informal:* fishy. *See* HONEST.

equivocality *noun*
An expression or term liable to more than one interpretation : ambiguity, double-entendre, equivocation, equivoque, tergiversation. *See* CLEAR.

equivocalness *noun*
The quality or state of being ambiguous : ambiguity, ambiguousness, cloudiness, indefiniteness, nebulousness, obscureness, obscurity, uncertainty, unclearness, vagueness. *See* CLEAR.

equivocate *verb*
1. To use evasive or deliberately vague language : euphemize, hedge, shuffle, tergiversate, weasel. *Informal:* pussyfoot, waffle. ***Idioms:*** beat about (*or* around) the bush, mince words. *See* CLEAR. **2.** To stray from truthfulness or sincerity : palter, prevaricate, shuffle. *See* TRUE.

equivocation *noun*
1. The use or an instance of equivocal language : ambiguity, equivoque, euphemism, hedge, prevarication, shuffle, tergiversation, weasel word. *Informal:* waffle. *See* CLEAR.
2. An expression or term liable to more than one interpretation : ambiguity, double-entendre, equivocality, equivoque, tergiversation. *See* CLEAR.

equivoque also **equivoke** *noun*
1. An expression or term liable to more than one interpretation : ambiguity, double-entendre, equivocality, equivocation, tergiversation. *See* CLEAR. **2.** The use or an instance of equivocal language : ambiguity, equivocation, euphemism, hedge, prevarication, shuffle, tergiversation, weasel word. *Informal:* waffle. *See* CLEAR.

era *noun*
A particular time notable for its distinctive characteristics : age, day, epoch, period, time (often used in plural). *See* TIME.

eradicate *verb*
1. To destroy all traces of : abolish, annihilate, blot out, clear, erase, exterminate, extinguish, extirpate, kill[1], liquidate, obliterate, remove, root[1] (out *or* up), rub out, snuff out, stamp out, uproot, wipe out. ***Idioms:*** do away with, make an end of, put an end to. *See* HELP, MAKE.
2. To get rid of, especially by banishment or execution : eliminate, liquidate, purge, remove, wipe out. ***Idioms:*** do away with, put an end to. *See* HELP, KEEP.

eradication *noun*
1. The act or process of eliminating : clearance, elimination, liquidation, purge, removal, riddance. *See* KEEP. **2.** Utter destruction : annihilation, extermination, extinction, extinguishment, extirpation, liquidation, obliteration. *See* CRIMES, HELP, MAKE.

erase *verb*
1. To remove or invalidate by or as if by running a line through or wiping clean : annul, blot (out), cancel, cross (off *or* out), delete, efface, expunge, obliterate, rub (out), scratch (out), strike (out), undo, wipe (out), x (out). *Law:* vacate. *See* CONTINUE. **2.** To destroy all

traces of : abolish, annihilate, blot out, clear, eradicate, exterminate, extinguish, extirpate, kill[1], liquidate, obliterate, remove, root[1] (out *or* up), rub out, snuff out, stamp out, uproot, wipe out. ***Idioms:*** do away with, make an end of, put an end to. *See* HELP, MAKE.

erasure *noun*
The act of erasing or the condition of being erased : cancellation, deletion, expunction, obliteration. *See* INCLUDE.

erect *adjective*
Directed or pointed upward : raised, upright, upstanding. *See* HORIZONTAL.
erect *verb* **1.** To make or form (a structure) : build, construct, put up, raise, rear[2]. *See* MAKE. **2.** To raise upright : pitch, put up, raise, rear[2], set up, upraise, uprear. *See* HORIZONTAL, RISE.

erector *noun*
A person or business that makes or builds something : assembler, builder, constructor, maker, manufacturer, producer. *See* MAKE.

eristic *adjective*
Given to arguing : argumentative, combative, contentious, disputatious, litigious, polemic, polemical, quarrelsome, scrappy. *See* CONFLICT.

erode *verb*
To consume gradually, as by chemical reaction or friction : bite, corrode, eat, gnaw, wear, wear away. *See* ATTACK.

erotic *adjective*
1. Of, concerning, or promoting sexual love or desire : amatory, amorous, aphrodisiac, lascivious, salacious, sexual, sexy. *See* SEX. **2.** Feeling or devoted to sexual love or desire : amative, amorous, concupiscent, lascivious, lecherous, lewd, libidinous, lustful, lusty, passionate, prurient, sexy. *See* SEX.

eroticism *noun*
Sexual hunger : amativeness, concupiscence, desire, erotism, itch, libidinousness, lust, lustfulness, passion, prurience, pruriency. *See* DESIRE, SEX.

erotism *noun*
Sexual hunger : amativeness, concupiscence, desire, eroticism, itch, libidinousness, lust, lustfulness, passion, prurience, pruriency. *See* DESIRE, SEX.

err *verb*
1. To make an error or mistake : miscue, mistake, slip, slip up, stumble, trip up. *See* CORRECT. **2.** To violate a moral or divine law : offend, sin, transgress, trespass. *See* RIGHT. **3.** *Archaic.* To turn away from a prescribed course of action or conduct : depart, deviate, digress, diverge, stray, swerve, veer. *See* APPROACH, CORRECT.

errand *noun*
An assignment one is sent to carry out : commission, mission. *See* WORK.

errant *adjective*
1. Traveling about, especially in search of adventure : roaming, roving, wandering. *See* MOVE. **2.** Straying from a proper course or standard : aberrant. *See* CORRECT.

erratic *adjective*
1. Without a fixed or regular course : devious, stray, wandering. *See* PURPOSE. **2.** Lacking consistency or regularity in quality or performance : inconsistent, patchy, spotty, uneven, unsteady, variable. *See* CONTINUE, SAME. **3.** Following no predictable pattern : capricious, changeable, fantastic, fantastical, fickle, freakish, inconsistent, inconstant, mercurial, temperamental, ticklish, uncertain, unpredictable, unstable, unsteady, variable, volatile, whimsical. *See* CHANGE, CONTINUE. **4.** Deviating from the customary : bizarre, cranky, curious, eccentric, freakish, idiosyncratic, odd, outlandish, peculiar, quaint, queer, quirky, singular, strange, unnatural, unusual, weird. *Slang:* kooky, screwball. *British Slang:* rum, rummy[2]. *See* USUAL.

erratum *noun*
An act or thought that unintentionally deviates from what is correct, right, or true : error, inaccuracy, incorrectness, lapse, miscue, misstep, mistake, slip, slip-up, trip. *See* CORRECT.

erroneous *adjective*
Containing an error or errors : fallacious, false, inaccurate, incorrect, mistaken, off, unsound, untrue, wrong. ***Idioms:*** all wet, in error, off base, off (*or* wide of) the mark. *See* CORRECT.

erroneousness *noun*
An erroneous or false idea : error, fallacy, falsehood, falseness, falsity, untruth. *See* CORRECT, TRUE.

error *noun*
1. An act or thought that unintentionally deviates from what is correct, right, or true : erratum, inaccuracy, incorrectness, lapse, miscue, misstep, mistake, slip, slip-up, trip. *See* CORRECT. **2.** An erroneous or false idea : erroneousness, fallacy, falsehood, falseness, falsity, untruth. *See* CORRECT, TRUE.

errorless *adjective*
Having no errors : accurate, correct, exact, precise, right, rigorous. *See* CORRECT, TRUE.

ersatz *noun*
An inferior substitute imitating an original : copy, imitation, pinchbeck, simulation. *See* SUBSTITUTE.

erstwhile *adverb*
At a time in the past : already, before, earlier, formerly, once, previously. *Archaic:* aforetime, beforetime. *See* PRECEDE.
erstwhile *adjective* Having been such previously : former, late, old, once, onetime, past, previous, quondam, sometime, whilom. *See* PRECEDE.

eruct *verb*
To send forth (confined matter) violently : belch, disgorge, eject, erupt, expel, spew. *Geology:* extravasate. *See* EXPLOSION.

erudite *adjective*
Having or showing profound knowledge and scholarship : learned, lettered, scholarly, wise[1]. *See* KNOWLEDGE.

erudition *noun*
Known facts, ideas, and skill that have been imparted : education, instruction, knowledge, learning, scholarship, science. *See* KNOWLEDGE.

erupt *verb*
1. To become manifest suddenly and in full force : break out, burst (forth *or* out), explode, flare (up). *See* EXPLOSION, START. **2.** To send forth (confined matter) violently : belch, disgorge, eject, eruct, expel, spew. *Geology:* extravasate. *See* EXPLOSION.

eruption *noun*
1. The act of emerging violently from limits or restraints : explosion, outbreak, outburst. *See* EXPLOSION. **2.** A sudden violent expression, as of emotion : access, blowup, burst, explosion, fit[2], flare-up, gust, outbreak, outburst. *See* EXPLOSION.

escalate *verb*
To make or become greater or larger : aggrandize, amplify, augment, boost, build, build up, burgeon, enlarge, expand, extend, grow, increase, magnify, mount, multiply, proliferate, rise, run up, snowball, soar, swell, upsurge, wax. *Informal:* beef up. *See* INCREASE.

escalation *noun*
The act of increasing or rising : aggrandizement, amplification, augment, augmentation, boost, buildup, enlargement, growth, hike, increase, jump, multiplication, proliferation, raise, rise, swell, upsurge, upswing, upturn. *See* INCREASE.

escape *verb*
1. To break loose and leave suddenly, as from confinement or from a difficult or threatening situation : abscond, break out, decamp, flee, fly, get away, run away. *Informal:* skip (out). *Slang:* lam. *Regional:* absquatulate. ***Idioms:*** blow (*or* fly) the coop, cut and run, give someone the slip, make a getaway, take flight, take it on the lam. *See* FREE. **2.** To keep away from : avoid, burke, bypass, circumvent, dodge, duck, elude, eschew, evade, get around, shun. ***Idioms:*** fight shy of, give a wide berth to, have no truck with, keep (*or* stay *or* steer) clear of. *See* SEEK. **3.** To fail to be fixed by the mind, memory, or senses of : elude. ***Idiom:*** slip away from. *See* OWNED.
escape *noun* **1.** The act or an instance of escaping, as from confinement or difficulty : break, breakout, decampment, escapement, flight, getaway. *Slang:* lam. *See* FREE. **2.** The act, an instance, or a means of avoiding : avoidance, bypass, circumvention, evasion. *See* SEEK. **3.** Freedom from worry, care, or unpleasantness : forgetfulness, oblivion, obliviousness. *See* SEEK.

escaped *adjective*
Fleeing or having fled, as from home, confinement, captivity, or justice : fugitive, runaway. *See* SEEK.

escapee *noun*
One who flees, as from home, confinement, captivity, or justice : fugitive, refugee, runaway. *See* SEEK.

escapement *noun*
The act or an instance of escaping, as from confinement or difficulty : break, breakout, decampment, escape, flight, getaway. *Slang:* lam. *See* FREE.

eschew *verb*
To keep away from : avoid, burke, bypass, circumvent, dodge, duck, elude, escape, evade, get around, shun. ***Idioms:*** fight shy of, give a wide berth to, have no truck with, keep (*or* stay *or* steer) clear of. *See* SEEK.

escort *noun*
Something or someone that shows the way : conductor, director, guide, lead, leader, pilot, shepherd, usher. *See* SHOW.
escort *verb* **1.** To be with or go with (another) : accompany, attend, companion, company. *Obsolete:* consort. ***Idiom:*** go hand in hand with. *See* ACCOMPANIED. **2.** To show the way to : conduct, direct, guide, lead, pilot, route, shepherd, show, steer, usher. *See* SHOW.

esculent *adjective*
Fit to be eaten : comestible, eatable, edible. *See* INGESTION.

esculent *noun* Something fit to be eaten : aliment, bread, comestible, diet, edible, fare, food, foodstuff, meat, nourishment, nurture, nutriment, nutrition, pabulum, pap, provender, provision (used in plural), sustenance, victual. *Slang:* chow, eats, grub. *See* INGESTION.

esoteric *adjective*
Beyond the understanding of an average mind : abstruse, deep, profound, recondite. *Slang:* heavy. *See* EASY, SURFACE.

especial *adjective*
Of, relating to, or intended for a distinctive thing or group : individual, particular, special, specific. *See* SPECIFIC.

espial *noun*
The act of noting, observing, or taking into account : attention, cognizance, heed, mark, note, notice, observance, observation, regard, remark. *See* KNOWLEDGE, SEE.

espousal *noun*
1. The act or condition of being pledged to marry : betrothal, engagement, troth. *See* MARRIAGE. **2.** The act or ceremony by which two people become husband and wife : bridal, marriage, nuptial (often used in plural), spousal (often used in plural), wedding. *See* MARRIAGE. **3.** A ready taking up of something : adoption, embracement. *See* ACCEPT, GIVE.

espouse *verb*
1. To join or be joined in marriage : marry, mate, wed. *Slang:* hitch. ***Idiom:*** tie the knot. *See* MARRIAGE. **2.** To take, as another's idea, and make one's own : adopt, embrace, take on, take up. *See* ACCEPT, GIVE.

esprit *noun*
1. A lively, emphatic, eager quality or manner : animation, bounce, brio, dash, élan, life, liveliness, pertness, sparkle, spirit, verve, vigor, vim, vivaciousness, vivacity, zip. *Informal:* ginger, pep, peppiness. *Slang:* oomph. *See* ACTION. **2.** A strong sense of enthusiasm and dedication to a common goal that unites a group : esprit de corps, morale. *See* CONCERN, FEELINGS.

esprit de corps *noun*
A strong sense of enthusiasm and dedication to a common goal that unites a group : esprit, morale. *See* CONCERN, FEELINGS.

espy *verb*
To perceive, especially barely or fleetingly : catch, descry, detect, discern, glimpse, spot, spy. *See* SEE.

essay *noun*
1. A relatively brief discourse written especially as an exercise : composition, paper, theme. *See* WORDS. **2.** A procedure that ascertains effectiveness, value, proper function, or other quality : assay, proof, test, trial, tryout. *See* INVESTIGATE. **3.** A trying to do or make something : attempt, crack, effort, endeavor, go, offer, stab, trial, try. *Informal:* shot. *Slang:* take. *Archaic:* assay. *See* TRY.

essay *verb* **1.** To make an attempt to do or make : assay, attempt, endeavor, seek, strive, try. ***Idioms:*** have a go at, have (*or* make *or* take) a shot at, have (*or* take) a whack at, make a stab at, take a crack at. *See* TRY. **2.** To subject to a procedure that ascertains effectiveness, value, proper function, or other quality : assay, check, examine, prove, test, try, try out. ***Idioms:*** bring to the test, make trial of, put to the proof (*or* test). *See* INVESTIGATE.

essence *noun*
1. A basic trait or set of traits that define and establish the character of something : being, essentiality, nature, quintessence, substance, texture. *See* SURFACE. **2.** The most central and material part : core, gist, heart, kernel, marrow, meat, nub, pith, quintessence, root[1], soul, spirit, stuff, substance. *Law:* gravamen. *See* BE.

essential *adjective*
1. Constituting or forming part of the essence of something : basic, constitutional, constitutive, fundamental, integral, vital. *See* BE, SURFACE. **2.** Of or being an irreducible element : basic, elemental, elementary, fundamental, primitive, ultimate, underlying. *See* SURFACE. **3.** Incapable of being dispensed with : indispensable, necessary, needful, required, requisite. *See* IMPORTANT, NECESSARY.

essential *noun* **1.** A fundamental irreducible constituent of a whole : basic, element, fundamental, rudiment (often used in plural). ***Idiom:*** part and parcel. *See* PART. **2.** Something indispensable : condition, must, necessity, need, precondition, prerequisite, requirement, requisite, sine qua non. *See* NECESSARY.

essentiality *noun*
A basic trait or set of traits that define and establish the character of something : being, essence, nature, quintessence, substance, texture. *See* SURFACE.

essentially *adverb*
In regard to the essence of a matter : basically, fundamentally. ***Idioms:*** at bottom, at heart, in essence. *See* SURFACE.

establish *verb*
1. To bring into existence formally : constitute, create, found, institute, organize, originate, set up, start. *See* START. **2.** To place securely in a position or condition : ensconce, fix, install,

seat, settle. *See* PUT IN. **3.** To provide a basis for : base[1], build, found, ground, predicate, rest[1], root[1], underpin. *See* OVER. **4.** To put in force or cause to be by legal authority : constitute, enact, legislate, make, promulgate. *See* ACTION, MAKE, POLITICS. **5.** To establish as true or genuine : authenticate, bear out, confirm, corroborate, demonstrate, endorse, evidence, prove, show, substantiate, validate, verify. *See* SHOW, SUPPORT.

establishment *noun*
1. The act of founding or establishing : constitution, creation, foundation, institution, organization, origination, start-up. *See* START. **2.** A commercial organization : business, company, concern, corporation, enterprise, firm[2], house. *Informal:* outfit. *See* GROUP.

establishmentarian *adjective*
Conforming to established practice or standards : button-down, conformist, conventional, orthodox, straight, traditional. *Slang:* square. *See* USUAL.

estate *noun*
1. Usually extensive real estate : acre (often used in plural), land, property. *See* OWNED. **2.** Something, as land and assets, legally possessed : holding (often used in plural), possession (used in plural), property. *See* LAW, OWNED.

esteem *verb*
1. To have a high opinion of : admire, consider, honor, regard, respect, value. ***Idioms:*** look up to, think highly (*or* much *or* well) of. *See* PRAISE. **2.** To recognize the worth, quality, importance, or magnitude of : appreciate, cherish, prize[1], respect, treasure, value. ***Idiom:*** set store by. *See* PRAISE. **3.** To look upon in a particular way : account, consider, deem, reckon, regard, see, view. *See* PERSPECTIVE.
esteem *noun* A feeling of deference, approval, and liking : account, admiration, appreciation, consideration, estimation, favor, honor, regard, respect. *See* RESPECT.

esthetic *noun* See **aesthetic.**

estimable *adjective*
Deserving honor, respect, or admiration : admirable, commendable, creditable, deserving, exemplary, honorable, laudable, meritorious, praiseworthy, reputable, respectable, worthy. *See* GOOD, PRAISE, RESPECT, VALUE.

estimate *verb*
1. To calculate approximately : approximate, place, put, reckon, set[1]. *See* PRECISE. **2.** To make a judgment as to the worth or value of : appraise, assay, assess, calculate, evaluate, gauge, judge, rate[1], size up, valuate, value. ***Idiom:*** take the measure of. *See* VALUE.
estimate *noun* **1.** The act or result of judging the worth or value of something or someone : appraisal, appraisement, assessment, estimation, evaluation, judgment, valuation. *See* VALUE. **2.** A rough or tentative calculation : approximation, estimation. *See* PRECISE.

estimation *noun*
1. The act or result of judging the worth or value of something or someone : appraisal, appraisement, assessment, estimate, evaluation, judgment, valuation. *See* VALUE. **2.** A rough or tentative calculation : approximation, estimate. *See* PRECISE. **3.** A feeling of deference, approval, and liking : account, admiration, appreciation, consideration, esteem, favor, honor, regard, respect. *See* RESPECT.

estrange *verb*
To make distant, hostile, or unsympathetic : alienate, disaffect, disunite. ***Idiom:*** set at odds. *See* LOVE.

estrangement *noun*
1. The act of estranging or the condition of being estranged : alienation, disaffection. *See* LOVE. **2.** An interruption in friendly relations : alienation, breach, break, disaffection, fissure, rent[2], rift, rupture, schism, split. *See* ASSEMBLE, HELP.

estrus also **oestrus** *noun*
A regular period of sexual excitement in female mammals : heat, rut[2], season. *See* SEX.

etcetera *noun*
Articles too small or numerous to be specified. Used in plural : oddment (used in plural), odds and ends, sundries. *See* THING.

etch *verb*
1. To cut (a design or inscription) into a hard surface, especially for printing : carve, engrave, grave[3], incise. *See* MARKS. **2.** To produce a deep impression of : engrave, fix, grave[3], impress, imprint, inscribe, stamp. *See* MARKS.

eternal *adjective*
1. Without beginning or end : infinite, sempiternal. *See* LIMITED. **2.** Existing or occurring without interruption or end : around-the-clock, ceaseless, constant, continual, continuous, endless, everlasting, incessant, interminable, nonstop, ongoing, perpetual, persistent, relentless, round-the-clock, timeless, unceasing, unending, unfailing, uninterrupted, unremitting. *See* CONTINUE. **3.** Existing unchanged forever : ageless, dateless, timeless. *Archaic:* eterne. *See* CHANGE. **4.** Enduring for all time : amaranthine, ceaseless, endless, everlasting,

immortal, never-ending, perpetual, unending, world without end. *Archaic:* eterne. *See* CONTINUE.

eternality *noun*

1. The totality of time without beginning or end : eternalness, eternity, infinity, perpetuity, sempiternity. *See* LIMITED. **2.** The quality or state of having no end : ceaselessness, endlessness, eternalness, eternity, everlastingness, perpetuity, world without end. *See* CONTINUE.

eternalize *verb*

To cause to last endlessly : eternize, immortalize, perpetuate. *See* CONTINUE, REMEMBER.

eternalness *noun*

1. The totality of time without beginning or end : eternality, eternity, infinity, perpetuity, sempiternity. *See* LIMITED. **2.** The quality or state of having no end : ceaselessness, endlessness, eternality, eternity, everlastingness, perpetuity, world without end. *See* CONTINUE.

eterne *adjective*

1. *Archaic.* Existing unchanged forever : ageless, dateless, eternal, timeless. *See* CHANGE. **2.** *Archaic.* Enduring for all time : amaranthine, ceaseless, endless, eternal, everlasting, immortal, never-ending, perpetual, unending, world without end. *See* CONTINUE.

eternity *noun*

1. The totality of time without beginning or end : eternality, eternalness, infinity, perpetuity, sempiternity. *See* LIMITED. **2.** The quality or state of having no end : ceaselessness, endlessness, eternality, eternalness, everlastingness, perpetuity, world without end. *See* CONTINUE. **3.** Endless life after death : afterlife, deathlessness, everlasting life, everlastingness, immortality. *See* CONTINUE, LIVE. **4.** A long time : eon, long[1], year (used in plural). *Informal:* age (used in plural), blue moon. ***Idioms:*** forever and a day, forever and ever, month of Sundays. *See* TIME.

eternize *verb*

To cause to last endlessly : eternalize, immortalize, perpetuate. *See* CONTINUE, REMEMBER.

ethereal *adjective*

So light and insubstantial as to resemble air or a thin film : aerial, aery, airy, diaphanous, filmy, gauzy, gossamer, gossamery, sheer[2], transparent, vaporous, vapory. *See* THICK.

ethic *noun*

1. A rule or habit of conduct with regard to right and wrong or a body of such rules and habits : ethicality, moral (used in plural), morality. *See* RIGHT. **2.** The moral quality of a course of action. Used in plural : ethicality, ethicalness, morality, propriety, righteousness, rightfulness, rightness. *See* RIGHT.

ethical *adjective*

In accordance with principles of right or good conduct : moral, principled, proper, right, righteous, rightful, right-minded, virtuous. *See* RIGHT.

ethicality *noun*

1. A rule or habit of conduct with regard to right and wrong or a body of such rules and habits : ethic, moral (used in plural), morality. *See* RIGHT. **2.** The moral quality of a course of action : ethic (used in plural), ethicalness, morality, propriety, righteousness, rightfulness, rightness. *See* RIGHT.

ethicalness *noun*

The moral quality of a course of action : ethic (used in plural), ethicality, morality, propriety, righteousness, rightfulness, rightness. *See* RIGHT.

ethos *noun*

The thought processes characteristic of an individual or group : mentality, mind, mindset, psyche, psychology. ***Idiom:*** what makes someone tick. *See* THOUGHTS.

etiolate *verb*

To lose normal coloration; turn pale : blanch, bleach, pale, wan. *See* COLORS.

etiquette *noun*

Socially correct behavior : decorum, good form, manner (used in plural), mores, propriety (also used in plural), p's and q's. *See* USUAL.

eulogize *verb*

To pay tribute or homage to : acclaim, celebrate, exalt, extol, glorify, hail[2], honor, laud, magnify, panegyrize, praise. ***Idiom:*** sing someone's praises. *See* PRAISE.

euphemism *noun*

The use or an instance of equivocal language : ambiguity, equivocation, equivoque, hedge, prevarication, shuffle, tergiversation, weasel word. *Informal:* waffle. *See* CLEAR.

euphemize *verb*

To use evasive or deliberately vague language : equivocate, hedge, shuffle, tergiversate, weasel. *Informal:* pussyfoot, waffle. ***Idioms:*** beat about (*or* around) the bush, mince words. *See* CLEAR.

eulogy *noun*

An expression of warm approval : acclaim, acclamation, applause, celebration, commendation, compliment, encomium, kudos, laudation, panegyric, plaudit, praise. *See* PRAISE.

euphonic *adjective*

Resembling or having the effect of music, especially pleasing music : dulcet, euphonious, melodic, melodious, musical, tuneful. *See* SOUNDS.

euphonious *adjective*
Resembling or having the effect of music, especially pleasing music : dulcet, euphonic, melodic, melodious, musical, tuneful. *See* SOUNDS.

euphoria *noun*
High spirits : animation, elatedness, elation, exaltation, exhilaration, inspiration, lift, uplift. *See* HAPPY.

evacuant *adjective*
Of, relating to, or tending to eliminate : cathartic, eliminative, eliminatory, evacuative, excretory, purgative. *See* KEEP.

evacuate *verb*
1. To remove the contents of : clean out, clear, empty (out), vacate, void. *See* FULL. **2.** To discharge (wastes or foreign substances) from the body : eliminate, excrete. *Medicine:* purge. *See* KEEP.

evacuation *noun*
The act or process of discharging bodily wastes or foreign substances : elimination, excretion, purgation. *Medicine:* catharsis. *See* KEEP.

evacuative *adjective*
Of, relating to, or tending to eliminate : cathartic, eliminative, eliminatory, evacuant, excretory, purgative. *See* KEEP.

evade *verb*
1. To keep away from : avoid, burke, bypass, circumvent, dodge, duck, elude, escape, eschew, get around, shun. ***Idioms:*** fight shy of, give a wide berth to, have no truck with, keep (*or* stay *or* steer) clear of. *See* SEEK. **2.** To get away from (a pursuer) : elude, lose, shake off, slip, throw off. *Slang:* shake. ***Idiom:*** give someone the shake (*or* slip). *See* SEEK. **3.** To avoid fulfilling or answering completely : dodge, duck, hedge, sidestep, skirt. *See* SEEK.

evaluate *verb*
To make a judgment as to the worth or value of : appraise, assay, assess, calculate, estimate, gauge, judge, rate[1], size up, valuate, value. ***Idiom:*** take the measure of. *See* VALUE.

evaluation *noun*
The act or result of judging the worth or value of something or someone : appraisal, appraisement, assessment, estimate, estimation, judgment, valuation. *See* VALUE.

evanesce *verb*
To pass out of sight either gradually or suddenly : disappear, evaporate, fade, fade out, vanish. *See* SHOW.

evanescence *noun*
The act or an example of passing out of sight : disappearance, evaporation, fade-out, vanishment. *See* SHOW.

evanescent *adjective*
Lasting or existing only for a short time : ephemeral, fleet, fleeting, fugacious, fugitive, momentary, passing, short-lived, temporal, temporary, transient, transitory. *See* CONTINUE, TIME.

evangelist *noun*
A person doing religious or charitable work in a foreign country : apostle, missionary, missioner. *See* RELIGION.

evangelize *verb*
To deliver a sermon, especially as a vocation : preach, sermonize. *See* RELIGION.

evaporate *verb*
1. To pass off as vapor, especially when heated : boil away, vaporize, volatilize. *See* SOLID. **2.** To pass out of sight either gradually or suddenly : disappear, evanesce, fade, fade out, vanish. *See* SHOW.

evaporation *noun*
The act or an example of passing out of sight : disappearance, evanescence, fade-out, vanishment. *See* SHOW.

evasion *noun*
The act, an instance, or a means of avoiding : avoidance, bypass, circumvention, escape. *See* SEEK.

evasive *adjective*
1. Characterized by or exhibiting evasion : elusive, slippery. *See* SEEK. **2.** Deliberately ambiguous or vague : equivocal. *See* CLEAR.

eve *noun*
The period between afternoon and nighttime : dusk, evening, eventide, gloaming, nightfall, twilight. *Archaic:* even[2], vesper. *See* START.

even[1] *adjective*
1. Having no irregularities, roughness, or indentations : flat, flush, level, planar, plane[1], smooth, straight. *See* SMOOTH. **2.** On the same plane or line : flush, level. *See* SAME. **3.** Having no change or variation : changeless, constant, equable, invariable, invariant, regular, same, steady, unchanging, uniform, unvarying. *See* SAME. **4.** Not easily excited, even under pressure : calm, collected, composed, cool, cool-headed, detached, even-tempered, imperturbable, nonchalant, possessed, unflappable, unruffled. *See* CALM. **5.** Agreeing exactly in value, quantity, or effect : equal, equivalent, identical, same, tantamount. ***Idioms:*** on a par,

one and the same. *See* SAME. **6.** Just to all parties : equal, equitable, evenhanded, fair. *See* SAME. **7.** Owing or being owed nothing : quit, quits, square. *See* PAY. **8.** Neither favorable or unfavorable : balanced, fifty-fifty. *See* FAIR. **9.** Being an exact amount or number : exact. ***Idiom:*** on the nose. *See* PRECISE.

even *adverb* **1.** To a more extreme degree : still, yet. *See* BIG. **2.** Not just this but also : indeed. ***Idiom:*** not to mention. *See* TRUE. **3.** In an exact manner : exactly, just, precisely. *See* PRECISE, SAME.

even *verb* **1.** To make even, smooth, or level : flat, flatten, level, plane[2], smooth, straighten. *See* SMOOTH. **2.** To make equal : equalize, equate, level, square. *See* SAME.

even[2] *noun*
Archaic. The period between afternoon and nighttime : dusk, eve, evening, eventide, gloaming, nightfall, twilight. *Archaic:* vesper. *See* START.

evenhanded *adjective*
Just to all parties : equal, equitable, even[1], fair. *See* SAME.

evening *noun*
The period between afternoon and nighttime : dusk, eve, eventide, gloaming, nightfall, twilight. *Archaic:* even[2], vesper. *See* START.

event *noun*
1. Something that happens : circumstance, happening, incident, occasion, occurrence, thing. *See* HAPPEN. **2.** Something significant that happens : circumstance, development, episode, happening, incident, news, occasion, occurrence, thing. *See* HAPPEN. **3.** Something brought about by a cause : aftermath, consequence, corollary, effect, end product, fruit, harvest, issue, outcome, precipitate, ramification, result, resultant, sequel, sequence, sequent, upshot. *See* CAUSE. **4.** Something having real, demonstrable existence : actuality, fact, phenomenon, reality. *See* REAL.

even-tempered *adjective*
Not easily excited, even under pressure : calm, collected, composed, cool, cool-headed, detached, even[1], imperturbable, nonchalant, possessed, unflappable, unruffled. *See* CALM.

eventide *noun*
The period between afternoon and nighttime : dusk, eve, evening, gloaming, nightfall, twilight. *Archaic:* even[2], vesper. *See* START.

eventual *adjective*
Capable of being but not yet in existence : latent, possible, potential. *See* POSSIBLE.

eventuality *noun*
Something that may occur or be done : contingency, possibility. *See* POSSIBLE.

everlasting *adjective*
1. Enduring for all time : amaranthine, ceaseless, endless, eternal, immortal, never-ending, perpetual, unending, world without end. *Archaic:* eterne. *See* CONTINUE. **2.** Existing or occurring without interruption or end : around-the-clock, ceaseless, constant, continual, continuous, endless, eternal, incessant, interminable, nonstop, ongoing, perpetual, persistent, relentless, round-the-clock, timeless, unceasing, unending, unfailing, uninterrupted, unremitting. *See* CONTINUE.

everlasting life *noun*
Endless life after death : afterlife, deathlessness, eternity, everlastingness, immortality. *See* CONTINUE, LIVE.

everlastingness *noun*
1. The quality or state of having no end : ceaselessness, endlessness, eternality, eternalness, eternity, perpetuity, world without end. *See* CONTINUE. **2.** Endless life after death : afterlife, deathlessness, eternity, everlasting life, immortality. *See* CONTINUE, LIVE.

everyday *adjective*
1. Of or suitable for ordinary days or routine occasions : quotidian, workaday, workday. *See* GOOD, USUAL. **2.** Occurring quite often : common, familiar, frequent, regular, routine, widespread. *See* USUAL.

everything *noun*
An amount or quantity from which nothing is left out or held back : aggregate, all, entirety, gross, sum, total, totality, whole. *Informal:* work (used in plural). ***Idioms:*** everything but (*or* except) the kitchen sink; lock, stock, and barrel; the whole ball of wax (*or* kit and caboodle *or* megillah *or* nine yards *or* shebang). *See* PART.

evict *verb*
To put out by force : bump, dismiss, eject, expel, oust, throw out. *Informal:* chuck. *Slang:* boot[1] (out), bounce, kick out. ***Idioms:*** give someone the boot, give someone the heave-ho (*or* old heave-ho), send packing, show someone the door, throw out on one's ear. *See* KEEP.

eviction *noun*
The act of ejecting or the state of being ejected : dismissal, ejection, ejectment, expulsion, ouster. *Slang:* boot[1], bounce. *See* KEEP.

evidence *noun*
1. That which confirms : attestation, authentication, confirmation, corroboration, demon-

stration, proof, substantiation, testament, testimonial, testimony, validation, verification, warrant. *See* TRUE. **2.** Something visible or evident that gives grounds for believing in the existence or presence of something else : badge, index, indication, indicator, manifestation, mark, note, sign, signification, stamp, symptom, token, witness. *See* SHOW.

evidence *verb* **1.** To make manifest or apparent : demonstrate, display, evince, exhibit, manifest, proclaim, reveal, show. *See* SHOW. **2.** To establish as true or genuine : authenticate, bear out, confirm, corroborate, demonstrate, endorse, establish, prove, show, substantiate, validate, verify. *See* SHOW, SUPPORT. **3.** To assure the certainty or validity of : attest, authenticate, back (up), bear out, confirm, corroborate, justify, substantiate, testify (to), validate, verify, warrant. *See* SUPPORT, TRUE.

evident *adjective*
Readily seen, perceived, or understood : apparent, clear, clear-cut, crystal clear, distinct, manifest, noticeable, observable, obvious, patent, plain, pronounced, visible. *See* SEE.

evidently *adverb*
On the surface : apparently, externally, ostensibly, ostensively, outwardly, seemingly, superficially. ***Idioms:*** on the face of it, to all appearances. *See* SURFACE.

evil *adjective*
1. Morally objectionable : bad, black, immoral, iniquitous, peccant, reprobate, sinful, vicious, wicked, wrong. *See* RIGHT. **2.** Causing harm or injury : bad, deleterious, detrimental, harmful, hurtful, ill, injurious, mischievous. *See* HELP. **3.** Bringing, predicting, or characterized by misfortune : bad, ill, inauspicious, unfavorable, unpropitious. *See* LUCK. **4.** Characterized by intense ill will or spite : black, despiteful, hateful, malevolent, malicious, malign, malignant, mean[2], nasty, poisonous, spiteful, venomous, vicious, wicked. *Slang:* bitchy. *See* ATTITUDE.

evil *noun* **1.** That which is morally bad or objectionable : iniquity, peccancy, sin, wickedness, wrong. *See* RIGHT. **2.** A wicked act or wicked behavior : crime, deviltry, diablerie, evildoing, immorality, iniquity, misdeed, offense, peccancy, sin, wickedness, wrong, wrongdoing. *See* RIGHT. **3.** Whatever is destructive or harmful : bad, badness, ill. *See* HELP. **4.** A cause of suffering or harm : affliction, bane, curse, ill, plague, scourge, woe. *See* HELP.

evildoing *noun*
A wicked act or wicked behavior : crime, deviltry, diablerie, evil, immorality, iniquity, misdeed, offense, peccancy, sin, wickedness, wrong, wrongdoing. *See* RIGHT.

evil eye *noun*
An object or power that one uses to cause often evil events : charm, magic, spell[2]. *Slang:* whammy. *See* SUPERNATURAL.

evince *verb*
To make manifest or apparent : demonstrate, display, evidence, exhibit, manifest, proclaim, reveal, show. *See* SHOW.

evocative *adjective*
Tending to bring a memory, mood, or image, for example, subtly or indirectly to mind : allusive, connotative, impressionistic, reminiscent, suggestive. *See* SUGGEST.

evoke *verb*
To call forth or bring out (something latent, hidden, or unexpressed) : draw (out), educe, elicit, summon. *See* SHOW.

evolution *noun*
1. A progression from a simple form to a more complex one : development, evolvement, growth, progress, unfolding. *See* CHANGE. **2.** A calculated change in position : maneuver, move, movement, turn. *See* MOVE.

evolve *verb*
1. To be disclosed gradually : develop, unfold. *See* SHOW. **2.** To disclose bit by bit : develop, elaborate. ***Idioms:*** fill in the details, go into detail. *See* SHOW. **3.** To arrive at through reasoning : derive, educe, excogitate. *See* REASON.

evolvement *noun*
A progression from a simple form to a more complex one : development, evolution, growth, progress, unfolding. *See* CHANGE.

exact *adjective*
1. Conforming to fact : accurate, correct, faithful, precise, right, rigorous, true, veracious, veridical. *See* CORRECT, HONEST, REAL, TRUE. **2.** Strictly distinguished from others : precise, very. *See* PRECISE. **3.** Not deviating from correctness, accuracy, or completeness : close, faithful, full, rigorous, strict. *See* CAREFUL. **4.** Having no errors : accurate, correct, errorless, precise, right, rigorous. *See* CORRECT, TRUE. **5.** Being an exact amount or number : even[1]. ***Idiom:*** on the nose. *See* PRECISE. **6.** Conforming completely to established rule : rigorous, strict, uncompromising. *See* USUAL.

exact *verb* **1.** To obtain by coercion or intimidation : extort, squeeze, wrench, wrest, wring. *Slang:* shake down. *See* GET. **2.** To establish and apply as compulsory : assess, impose, levy, put. *See* OBLIGATION, OVER, WILLING. **3.** To ask for urgently or insistently : call for, claim, demand, insist on (*or* upon), require, requisition. ***Idiom:*** cry out for. *See* REQUEST.

exacting *adjective*
1. Rigorous and unsparing in treating others : demanding, hard, harsh, rigid, severe, stern, strict, tough, unyielding. *See* EASY. **2.** Very difficult to please : choosy, dainty, fastidious, finical, finicky, fussy, meticulous, nice, particular, persnickety, squeamish. *Informal:* picky. *See* ACCEPT. **3.** Requiring great or extreme bodily, mental, or spiritual strength : arduous, backbreaking, burdensome, demanding, difficult, effortful, exigent, formidable, hard, heavy, laborious, onerous, oppressive, rigorous, rough, severe, taxing, tough, trying, weighty. *See* HEAVY.

exaction *noun*
1. The act of demanding : call, claim, cry, demand, requisition. *See* REQUEST. **2.** A fixed amount of money charged for a privilege or service : charge, fee, toll[1]. *See* MONEY, PAY, TRANSACTIONS.

exactitude *noun*
1. Correspondence with fact or truth : accuracy, correctness, exactness, fidelity, truth, veraciousness, veracity, veridicality, verity. *See* TRUE. **2.** Freedom from error : accuracy, accurateness, correctness, exactness, preciseness, precision, rightness. *See* CORRECT.

exactly *adverb*
1. In an exact manner : even[1], just, precisely. *See* PRECISE, SAME. **2.** With precision or absolute conformity : bang, dead, direct, directly, fair, flush, just, precisely, right, smack[1], square, squarely, straight. *Slang:* smack-dab. *See* PRECISE.

exactness *noun*
1. Correspondence with fact or truth : accuracy, correctness, exactitude, fidelity, truth, veraciousness, veracity, veridicality, verity. *See* TRUE. **2.** Freedom from error : accuracy, accurateness, correctness, exactitude, preciseness, precision, rightness. *See* CORRECT.

exaggerate *verb*
To make (something) seem greater than is actually the case : hyperbolize, inflate, magnify, overcharge, overstate. ***Idioms:*** blow up out of proportion, lay it on thick, stretch the truth. *See* INCREASE.

exaggeration *noun*
The act or an instance of exaggerating : hyperbole, hyperbolism, overstatement, tall talk. *See* INCREASE.

exalt *verb*
1. To raise to a high position or status : aggrandize, apotheosize, dignify, elevate, ennoble, glorify, magnify, uplift. ***Idiom:*** put on a pedestal. *See* RISE. **2.** To cause to be eminent or recognized : distinguish, elevate, ennoble, honor, signalize. *See* RESPECT. **3.** To pay tribute or homage to : acclaim, celebrate, eulogize, extol, glorify, hail[2], honor, laud, magnify, panegyrize, praise. ***Idiom:*** sing someone's praises. *See* PRAISE. **4.** To honor (a deity) in religious worship : extol, glorify, laud, magnify, praise. *See* RELIGION. **5.** *Obsolete.* To raise the spirits of : animate, buoy (up), elate, elevate, exhilarate, flush, inspire, inspirit, lift, uplift. *See* HAPPY.

exaltation *noun*
1. The act of raising to a high position or status or the condition of being so raised : aggrandizement, apotheosis, elevation, ennoblement, glorification. *See* RISE. **2.** The honoring of a deity, as in worship : extolment, glorification, laudation, magnification, praise. *See* RELIGION. **3.** High spirits : animation, elatedness, elation, euphoria, exhilaration, inspiration, lift, uplift. *See* HAPPY.

exalted *adjective*
1. Raised to or occupying a high position or rank : august, elevated, grand, high-ranking, lofty. *See* RISE. **2.** Exceedingly dignified in form, tone, or style : elevated, eloquent, grand, high, high-flown, lofty. *See* HIGH, STYLE.

exam *noun*
1. A set of questions or exercises designed to determine knowledge or skill : catechism, catechization, examination, quiz, test. *See* INVESTIGATE. **2.** A medical inquiry into a patient's state of health : checkup, examination. *See* INVESTIGATE.

examination *noun*
1. The act of examining carefully : check, checkup, inspection, perusal, scrutiny, study, view. *Informal:* going-over. *See* INVESTIGATE. **2.** A close or systematic study : analysis, inspection, investigation, review, survey. *See* INVESTIGATE. **3.** A medical inquiry into a patient's state of health : checkup, exam. *See* INVESTIGATE. **4.** A set of questions or exercises designed to determine knowledge or skill :

catechism, catechization, exam, quiz, test. *See* INVESTIGATE.

examine *verb*

1. To look at carefully or critically : check (out), con, go over, inspect, peruse, scrutinize, study, survey, traverse, view. *Informal:* case. *Idiom:* give a going-over. *See* INVESTIGATE. **2.** To study closely or systematically : analyze, inspect, investigate. *See* INVESTIGATE. **3.** To subject to a procedure that ascertains effectiveness, value, proper function, or other quality : assay, check, essay, prove, test, try, try out. *Idioms:* bring to the test, make trial of, put to the proof (*or* test). *See* INVESTIGATE. **4.** To subject to a test of knowledge or skill : check, quiz, test. *See* INVESTIGATE. **5.** To put a question to (someone) : ask, inquire, query, question, quiz. *See* ASK.

example *noun*

1. One that is representative of a group or class : case, illustration, instance, representative, sample, specimen. *See* SUBSTITUTE. **2.** One that is worthy of imitation or duplication : beau ideal, exemplar, ideal, mirror, model, paradigm, pattern, standard. *See* GOOD. **3.** A closely similar case in existence or in the past : precedent. *See* SAME. **4.** An instance that warns or discourages prospective imitators : lesson, warning. *See* WARN.

exasperate *verb*

To trouble the nerves or peace of mind of, especially by repeated vexations : aggravate, annoy, bother, bug, chafe, disturb, fret, gall[2], get, irk, irritate, nettle, peeve, provoke, put out, rile, ruffle, vex. *Idioms:* get in one's hair, get on one's nerves, get under one's skin. *See* FEELINGS, PAIN.

exasperation *noun*

1. The act of annoying : annoyance, botheration, bothering, harassment, irritation, pestering, provocation, vexation. *See* FEELINGS, PAIN. **2.** The feeling of being annoyed : aggravation, annoyance, bother, botheration, irritation, vexation. *See* FEELINGS, PAIN.

excavate *verb*

1. To break, turn over, or remove (earth or sand, for example) with or as if with a tool : delve, dig, grub, scoop, shovel, spade. *See* ENTER. **2.** To make by digging : dig, scoop, shovel. *See* MAKE.

exceed *verb*

1. To be greater or better than : best, better[1], excel, outdo, outmatch, outrun, outshine, outstrip, pass, surpass, top, transcend. *Informal:* beat. *Idioms:* go beyond, go one better. *See* BIG. **2.** To go beyond the limits of : overreach, overrun, overstep, surpass, transcend. *See* EXCESS.

exceedingly *adverb*

To a high degree : awfully, dreadfully, eminently, exceptionally, extra, extremely, greatly, highly, most, notably, very. *Informal:* awful. *Chiefly Regional:* mighty. *See* BIG.

excel *verb*

To be greater or better than : best, better[1], exceed, outdo, outmatch, outrun, outshine, outstrip, pass, surpass, top, transcend. *Informal:* beat. *Idioms:* go beyond, go one better. *See* BIG.

excellence *noun*

1. The quality of being exceptionally good of its kind : fineness, superbness, superiority. *See* GOOD. **2.** A special feature or quality that confers superiority : beauty, distinction, merit, perfection, virtue. *See* GOOD.

excellent *adjective*

Exceptionally good of its kind : ace, banner, blue-ribbon, brag, capital, champion, fine[1], first-class, first-rate, prime, quality, splendid, superb, superior, terrific, tiptop, top. *Informal:* A-one, bully, dandy, great, swell, topflight, topnotch. *Slang:* boss. *Chiefly British:* tophole. *See* GOOD.

except *verb*

1. To keep from being admitted, included, or considered : bar, count out, debar, eliminate, exclude, keep out, rule out, shut out. *See* INCLUDE. **2.** To express opposition, often by argument : challenge, demur, expostulate, inveigh, object, protest, remonstrate. *Informal:* kick, squawk. *Idioms:* set up a squawk, take exception. *See* SUPPORT.

exception *noun*

The act of expressing strong or reasoned opposition : challenge, demur, expostulation, objection, protest, protestation, remonstrance, remonstration, squawk. *Slang:* kick. *See* SUPPORT.

exceptionable *adjective*

1. Arousing disapproval : ill-favored, inadmissible, objectionable, unacceptable, undesirable, unwanted, unwelcome. *See* LIKE. **2.** In doubt or dispute : arguable, contested, debatable, disputable, doubtful, moot, mootable, problematic, problematical, questionable, uncertain. *See* CERTAIN.

exceptional *adjective*

Far beyond what is usual, normal, or customary : extraordinary, magnificent, outstanding, preeminent, rare, remarkable, singular, towering, uncommon, unusual. *Informal:* standout. *Slang:* awesome, out of sight. *See* BETTER, USUAL.

exceptionally *adverb*
1. In a manner or to a degree that is unusual : extraordinarily, remarkably, singularly, uncommonly, unusually. *See* USUAL. **2.** To a high degree : awfully, dreadfully, eminently, exceedingly, extra, extremely, greatly, highly, most, notably, very. *Informal:* awful. *Chiefly Regional:* mighty. *See* BIG.

excess *noun*
1. A condition of going or being beyond what is needed, desired, or appropriate : embarrassment, excessiveness, exorbitance, extravagance, extravagancy, extravagantness, overabundance, plethora, superabundance, superfluity, superfluousness, surfeit. *See* EXCESS. **2.** An amount or quantity beyond what is needed, desired, or appropriate : fat, glut, overage, overflow, overmuch, overrun, overstock, oversupply, superfluity, surplus, surplusage. *See* EXCESS. **3.** Immoderate indulgence, as in food or drink : intemperance, overindulgence, surfeit. *See* EXCESS.
excess *adjective* Being more than is needed, desired, or appropriate : de trop, extra, spare, supererogatory, superfluous, supernumerary, surplus. *See* EXCESS.

excessive *adjective*
Exceeding a normal or reasonable limit : exorbitant, extravagant, extreme, immoderate, inordinate, overabundant, overmuch, undue. *See* EXCESS.

excessiveness *noun*
A condition of going or being beyond what is needed, desired, or appropriate : embarrassment, excess, exorbitance, extravagance, extravagancy, extravagantness, overabundance, plethora, superabundance, superfluity, superfluousness, surfeit. *See* EXCESS.

exchange *verb*
1. To give up in return for something else : change, commute, interchange, shift, substitute, switch, trade. *Informal:* swap. *See* CHANGE, SUBSTITUTE. **2.** To give and receive : bandy, interchange. *See* GIVE.
exchange *noun* The act of exchanging or substituting : change, commutation, interchange, shift, substitution, switch, trade, transposition. *Informal:* swap. *See* CHANGE, SUBSTITUTE.

excitation *noun*
Intensity of feeling or reaction : excitement, heat, warmth. *See* EXCITE, FEELINGS, HOT.

excite *verb*
To stir to action or feeling : egg on, foment, galvanize, goad, impel, incite, inflame, inspire, instigate, motivate, move, pique, prick, prod, prompt, propel, provoke, set off, spur, stimulate, touch off, trigger, work up. *See* CAUSE, EXCITE.

excited *adjective*
Feeling a very strong emotion : atingle, fired up, thrilled, worked up. *Informal:* psyched. *Slang:* stoked, turned-on. *See* EXCITE.

excitement *noun*
Intensity of feeling or reaction : excitation, heat, warmth. *See* EXCITE, FEELINGS, HOT.

exclaim *verb*
To speak suddenly or sharply, as from surprise or emotion : blurt (out), burst out, cry (out), ejaculate, rap out. *See* WORDS.

exclamation *noun*
A sudden, sharp utterance : cry, ejaculation, outcry. *See* WORDS.

exclude *verb*
To keep from being admitted, included, or considered : bar, count out, debar, eliminate, except, keep out, rule out, shut out. *See* INCLUDE.

exclusive *adjective*
1. Not divided among or shared with others : single, sole. *See* INCLUDE. **2.** Singled out in preference : choice, chosen, elect, select. *See* CHOICE, INCLUDE. **3.** Not diffused or dispersed : concentrated, intensive, undivided, unswerving, whole. *See* EDGE, COLLECT, PART. **4.** Catering to, used by, or admitting only the wealthy or socially superior : fancy, posh, swank, swanky. *Informal:* ritzy. *See* PLAIN.

exclusively *adverb*
To the exclusion of anyone or anything else : alone, but, entirely, only, solely. *See* INCLUDE.

excogitate *verb*
1. To think or think about carefully and at length : chew on (*or* over), cogitate, consider, contemplate, deliberate, entertain, meditate, mull, muse[1], ponder, reflect, revolve, ruminate, study, think, think out, think over, think through, turn over, weigh. ***Idioms:*** cudgel one's brains, put on one's thinking cap, rack one's brain. *See* THOUGHTS. **2.** To arrive at through reasoning : derive, educe, evolve. *See* REASON.

excogitation *noun*
The act or process of thinking : brainwork, cerebration, cogitation, contemplation, deliberation, meditation, reflection, rumination, speculation, thought. *See* THOUGHTS.

excogitative *adjective*
Of, characterized by, or disposed to thought : cogitative, contemplative, deliberative, meditative, pensive, reflective, ruminative, speculative, thinking, thoughtful. *Idiom:* in a brown study. *See* THOUGHTS.

excoriate *verb*
1. To make (the skin) raw by or as if by friction : abrade, chafe, fret, gall[2], irritate. *See* HELP. **2.** To criticize harshly and devastatingly : blister, drub, flay, lash, rip into, scarify[1], scathe, scorch, score, scourge, slap, slash. *Informal:* roast. *Slang:* slam. *Idioms:* burn someone's ears, crawl all over, pin someone's ears back, put someone on the griddle, put someone on the hot seat, rake over the coals, read the riot act to. *See* PRAISE.

excrete *verb*
To discharge (wastes or foreign substances) from the body : eliminate, evacuate. *Medicine:* purge. *See* KEEP.

excretion *noun*
The act or process of discharging bodily wastes or foreign substances : elimination, evacuation, purgation. *Medicine:* catharsis. *See* KEEP.

excretory *adjective*
Of, relating to, or tending to eliminate : cathartic, eliminative, eliminatory, evacuant, evacuative, purgative. *See* KEEP.

excruciate *verb*
To bring great harm or suffering to : afflict, agonize, anguish, curse, plague, rack, scourge, smite, strike, torment, torture. *See* ATTACK, HELP.

excruciating *adjective*
Extraordinarily painful or distressing : agonizing, anguishing, harrowing, tormenting, torturous. *See* PAIN.

exculpate *verb*
To free from a charge or imputation of guilt : absolve, clear, exonerate, vindicate. *Law:* acquit, purge. *See* LAW.

exculpation *noun*
A freeing or clearing from accusation or guilt : exoneration, vindication. *Law:* acquittal. *See* LAW.

excursion *noun*
1. A usually short journey taken for pleasure : jaunt, junket, outing, trip. *See* MOVE. **2.** An instance of digressing : aside, deviation, digression, divagation, divergence, divergency, excursus, irrelevancy, parenthesis, tangent. *See* APPROACH.

excursionist *noun*
One who travels for pleasure : sightseer, tourist. *Chiefly British:* tripper. *See* MOVE.

excursive *adjective*
Marked by or given to digression : digressive, discursive, parenthetic, parenthetical, rambling, tangential. *See* APPROACH.

excursus *noun*
An instance of digressing : aside, deviation, digression, divagation, divergence, divergency, excursion, irrelevancy, parenthesis, tangent. *See* APPROACH.

excusable *adjective*
1. Admitting of forgiveness or pardon : forgivable, pardonable, venial. *See* FORGIVENESS. **2.** Capable of being justified : defensible, justifiable, tenable. *See* FORGIVENESS, RIGHT.

excuse *verb*
1. To grant forgiveness to or for : condone, forgive, pardon, remit. *Idiom:* forgive and forget. *See* FORGIVENESS. **2.** To show to be just, right, or valid : justify, rationalize, vindicate. *Idiom:* make a case for. *See* RIGHT. **3.** To free from an obligation or duty : absolve, discharge, dispense, exempt, let off, relieve, spare. *See* FREE.

excuse *noun* **1.** An explanation offered to justify an action or make it better understood : plea, pretext. *See* EXPLAIN. **2.** A statement of acknowledgment expressing regret or asking pardon : apology, mea culpa, regret (used in plural). *See* REGRET. **3.** The act or an instance of forgiving : absolution, amnesty, condonation, forgiveness, pardon, remission. *See* FORGIVENESS.

exec *noun*
Informal. A person having administrative or managerial authority in an organization : administrant, administrator, director, executive, manager, officer, official. *See* OVER.

execrable *adjective*
So annoying or detestable as to deserve condemnation : accursed, blasted, blessed, bloody, confounded, cursed, damn, darn, infernal. *Informal:* blamed, damned. *Chiefly British:* blooming, ruddy. *See* LIKE.

execrate *verb*
1. To regard with extreme dislike and hostility : abhor, abominate, despise, detest, hate, loathe. *See* LOVE. **2.** *Archaic.* To invoke evil or injury upon : anathematize, curse, damn, imprecate. *Informal:* cuss. *Archaic:* maledict. *See* WORDS.

execration *noun*
1. A denunciation invoking a wish or threat of evil or injury : anathema, curse, damnation,

imprecation, malediction. *Archaic:* malison. *See* WORDS. **2.** An object of extreme dislike : abhorrence, abomination, anathema, aversion, bête noire, bugbear, detestation, hate. *Informal:* horror. *See* LOVE.

execute *verb*

1. To oversee the provision or execution of : administer, administrate, carry out, dispense. *See* OVER. **2.** To compel observance of : carry out, effect, enforce, implement, invoke. ***Idioms:*** put in force, put into action. *See* OBLIGATION, OVER. **3.** To begin and carry through to completion : do, perform, prosecute. *Informal:* pull off. *See* DO. **4.** To bring about and carry to a successful conclusion : bring off, carry out, carry through, effect, effectuate, put through. *Slang:* swing. *See* DO. **5.** To perform according to one's artistic conception : interpret, play, render. *See* PERFORMING ARTS. **6.** To carry out the functions, requirements, or terms of : discharge, do, exercise, fulfill, implement, keep, perform. ***Idiom:*** live up to. *See* DO.

execution *noun*

1. The act of beginning and carrying through to completion : discharge, effectuation, performance, prosecution. *See* DO. **2.** One's artistic conception as shown by the way in which something such as a dramatic role or musical composition is rendered : interpretation, performance, reading, realization, rendering, rendition. *See* PERFORMING ARTS.

executive *noun*

A person having administrative or managerial authority in an organization : administrant, administrator, director, manager, officer, official. *Informal:* exec. *See* OVER.

executive *adjective* Of, for, or relating to administration or administrators : administrative, directorial, managerial, ministerial, supervisory. *See* OVER.

exegesis *noun*

1. Critical explanation or analysis : annotation, comment, commentary, interpretation, note. *See* WORDS. **2.** Something that serves to explain or clarify : clarification, construction, decipherment, elucidation, explanation, explication, exposition, illumination, illustration, interpretation. *Archaic:* enucleation. *See* EXPLAIN.

exegetic *adjective*

Serving to explain : elucidative, explanative, explanatory, explicative, expositive, expository, hermeneutic, hermeneutical, illustrative, interpretative, interpretive. *See* EXPLAIN.

exemplar *noun*

One that is worthy of imitation or duplication : beau ideal, example, ideal, mirror, model, paradigm, pattern, standard. *See* GOOD.

exemplary *adjective*

1. Deserving honor, respect, or admiration : admirable, commendable, creditable, deserving, estimable, honorable, laudable, meritorious, praiseworthy, reputable, respectable, worthy. *See* GOOD, PRAISE, RESPECT, VALUE. **2.** Beyond reproach : blameless, good, irreprehensible, irreproachable, lily-white, unblamable. *See* RIGHT. **3.** Conforming to an ultimate form of perfection or excellence : ideal, model, perfect, supreme. *See* GOOD.

exemplify *verb*

1. To demonstrate and clarify with examples : illustrate, instance. *See* SHOW. **2.** To serve as an example, image, or symbol of : epitomize, illustrate, represent, stand for, symbol, symbolize, typify. *See* SUBSTITUTE.

exempt *verb*

To free from an obligation or duty : absolve, discharge, dispense, excuse, let off, relieve, spare. *See* FREE.

exercise *noun*

1. The act of putting into play : application, employment, exertion, implementation, operation, play, usage, use, utilization. *See* USED. **2.** Energetic physical action : activity, exertion. *See* ACTION. **3.** Repetition of an action so as to develop or maintain one's skill : drill, practice, rehearsal, study, training. *See* WORK.

exercise *verb* **1.** To put into action or use : actuate, apply, employ, exploit, implement, practice, use, utilize. ***Idioms:*** avail oneself of, bring into play, bring to bear, make use of, put into practice, put to use. *See* USED. **2.** To bring to bear steadily or forcefully : exert, ply^2, put out, throw, wield. *See* CAUSE. **3.** To subject to or engage in forms of exertion in order to train, strengthen, or condition : drill, practice, train, work out. *See* WORK. **4.** To carry out the functions, requirements, or terms of : discharge, do, execute, fulfill, implement, keep, perform. ***Idiom:*** live up to. *See* DO.

exert *verb*

To bring to bear steadily or forcefully : exercise, ply^2, put out, throw, wield. *See* CAUSE.

exertion *noun*

1. The act of putting into play : application, employment, exercise, implementation, operation, play, usage, use, utilization. *See* USED. **2.** The use of energy to do something : effort, endeavor, pain (used in plural), strain^1, striving, struggle, trouble, while. *Informal:* elbow grease. *See* WORK. **3.** Energetic physical action : activity, exercise. *See* ACTION.

exhalation *noun*
Air breathed out, evidenced by vapor, odor, or heat : breath. *See* BREATH.

exhale *verb*
To expel air in the process of respiration : breathe (out), expire. *See* BREATH.

exhaust *verb*
1. To make extremely tired : fag (out), tire out, wear out. *Informal:* knock out, tucker (out). *Slang:* do in, poop[1] (out). ***Idioms:*** run ragged, take it out of. *See* TIRED. **2.** To lessen or weaken severely, as by removing something essential : deplete, drain, impoverish, sap[2], use up. *See* GIVE, INCREASE, RICH. **3.** To use all of : consume, drain, draw down, eat up, expend, finish, play out, run through, spend, use up. *Informal:* polish off. *See* INCREASE.

exhausted *adjective*
Extremely tired : bleary, dead, drained, fatigued, rundown, spent, tired out, wearied, weariful, weary, worn-down, worn-out. *Informal:* beat, bushed, tuckered (out). *Slang:* done in, fagged (out), pooped (out). ***Idioms:*** all in, ready to drop. *See* HEALTH, TIRED.

exhausting *adjective*
Causing fatigue : draining, fatiguing, tiring, wearing, wearying. *See* TIRED.

exhaustion *noun*
The condition of being extremely tired : fatigue, tiredness, weariness. *See* TIRED.

exhaustive *adjective*
Covering all aspects with painstaking accuracy : all-out, complete, full-dress, intensive, thorough, thoroughgoing, thoroughpaced. *See* BIG, CAREFUL.

exhaustively *adverb*
In a complete manner : completely, intensively, thoroughly. ***Idioms:*** in and out, inside out, up and down. *See* LIMITED, PART.

exhibit *verb*
1. To make manifest or apparent : demonstrate, display, evidence, evince, manifest, proclaim, reveal, show. *See* SHOW. **2.** To make a public and usually ostentatious show of : brandish, display, disport, expose, flash, flaunt, parade, show (off), sport. *See* SHOW. **3.** To be endowed with as a visible characteristic or form : bear, carry, display, have, possess. *See* SHOW.

exhibit *noun* **1.** An act of showing or displaying : demonstration, display, exhibition, manifestation, show. *See* SHOW. **2.** A large public display, as of goods or works of art : exhibition, exposition, show. *See* SHOW.

exhibition *noun*
1. An act of showing or displaying : demonstration, display, exhibit, manifestation, show. *See* SHOW. **2.** A large public display, as of goods or works of art : exhibit, exposition, show. *See* SHOW.

exhibitionism *noun*
Showy mannerisms and behavior : staginess, theatricalism, theatricality, theatricalness. *See* PLAIN, STYLE.

exhibitive *adjective*
Serving to designate or indicate : denotative, denotive, designative, designatory, exhibitory, indicative, indicatory. *See* SHOW.

exhibitory *adjective*
Serving to designate or indicate : denotative, denotive, designative, designatory, exhibitive, indicative, indicatory. *See* SHOW.

exhilarant *adjective*
Producing or stimulating physical, mental, or emotional vigor : bracing, energizing, exhilarating, innerving, intoxicating, invigorating, refreshing, reinvigorating, renewing, restorative, roborant, stimulating, tonic. *See* HELP.

exhilarate *verb*
1. To raise the spirits of : animate, buoy (up), elate, elevate, flush, inspire, inspirit, lift, uplift. *Obsolete:* exalt. *See* HAPPY. **2.** To give or impart vitality and energy to (someone or something) : energize, invigorate, stimulate, vitalize. *See* HELP.

exhilarating *adjective*
Producing or stimulating physical, mental, or emotional vigor : bracing, energizing, exhilarant, innerving, intoxicating, invigorating, refreshing, reinvigorating, renewing, restorative, roborant, stimulating, tonic. *See* HELP.

exhilaration *noun*
High spirits : animation, elatedness, elation, euphoria, exaltation, inspiration, lift, uplift. *See* HAPPY.

exhort *verb*
To impel to action : press, urge. *See* CAUSE, PUSH.

exigence *noun*
1. The condition of being in need of immediate assistance : distress, exigency, hot water, trouble. *See* HELP. **2.** A condition in which something necessary or desirable is required or wanted : exigency, necessity, need. *See* NECESSARY. **3.** A decisive point : climacteric, crisis, crossroad (used in plural), exigency, head, juncture, pass, turning point, zero hour. *See*

DECIDE. **4.** Something asked for or needed : demand, exigency (often used in plural), need, want. *See* NECESSARY, OVER.

exigency *noun*

1. The condition of being in need of immediate assistance : distress, exigence, hot water, trouble. *See* HELP. **2.** A condition in which something necessary or desirable is required or wanted : exigence, necessity, need. *See* NECESSARY. **3.** A decisive point : climacteric, crisis, crossroad (used in plural), exigence, head, juncture, pass, turning point, zero hour. *See* DECIDE. **4.** Something asked for or needed. Often used in plural : demand, exigence, need, want. *See* NECESSARY, OVER.

exigent *adjective*

1. Compelling immediate attention : burning, crying, dire, emergent, imperative, instant, pressing, urgent. *See* BIG. **2.** Requiring great or extreme bodily, mental, or spiritual strength : arduous, backbreaking, burdensome, demanding, difficult, effortful, exacting, formidable, hard, heavy, laborious, onerous, oppressive, rigorous, rough, severe, taxing, tough, trying, weighty. *See* HEAVY.

exiguous *adjective*

Conspicuously deficient in quantity, fullness, or extent : meager, poor, puny, scant, scanty, skimpy, spare, sparse, stingy, thin. *Slang:* measly. *See* BIG, EXCESS.

exile *noun*

1. Enforced removal from one's native country by official decree : banishment, deportation, expatriation, extradition, ostracism, transportation. *See* ACCEPT, REWARD. **2.** One forced to emigrate, usually for political reasons : deportee, émigré, expatriate, expellee. *See* APPROACH.

exile *verb* To force to leave a country or place by official decree : banish, deport, expatriate, expel, ostracize, transport. *See* ACCEPT.

exist *verb*

1. To have being or actuality : be, subsist. *See* BE. **2.** To have an inherent basis : consist, dwell, inhere, lie[1], repose, reside, rest[1]. *See* START. **3.** To have reality or life : be, breathe, live[1], subsist. *See* BE.

existence *noun*

1. The fact or state of existing or of being actual : actuality, being, entity, reality. *See* BE, REAL. **2.** The period during which someone or something exists : day (often used in plural), duration, life, lifetime, span, term. *See* LIVE, TIME. **3.** One that exists independently : being, entity, existent, individual, object, something, thing. *See* BE, THING.

existent *adjective*

1. Occurring or existing in act or fact : actual, extant. *See* BE, REAL. **2.** Having existence or life : alive, around, existing, extant, living. *See* LIVE. **3.** In existence now : contemporary, current, existing, new, now, present[1], present-day. *See* TIME.

existent *noun* One that exists independently : being, entity, existence, individual, object, something, thing. *See* BE, THING.

existing *adjective*

1. Having existence or life : alive, around, existent, extant, living. *See* LIVE. **2.** In existence now : contemporary, current, existent, new, now, present[1], present-day. *See* TIME.

exit *noun*

The act of leaving : departure, egress, exodus, going, withdrawal. *See* APPROACH.

exit *verb* To move or proceed away from a place : depart, get away, get off, go, go away, leave[1], pull out, quit, retire, run (along), withdraw. *Informal:* cut out, push off, shove off. *Slang:* blow[1], split, take off. ***Idioms:*** hit the road, take leave. *See* APPROACH.

exodus *noun*

1. Departure from one's native land to settle in another : emigration, immigration, migration, transmigration. *See* APPROACH. **2.** The act of leaving : departure, egress, exit, going, withdrawal. *See* APPROACH.

exonerate *verb*

To free from a charge or imputation of guilt : absolve, clear, exculpate, vindicate. *Law:* acquit, purge. *See* LAW.

exoneration *noun*

A freeing or clearing from accusation or guilt : exculpation, vindication. *Law:* acquittal. *See* LAW.

exorbitance *noun*

A condition of going or being beyond what is needed, desired, or appropriate : embarrassment, excess, excessiveness, extravagance, extravagancy, extravagantness, overabundance, plethora, superabundance, superfluity, superfluousness, surfeit. *See* EXCESS.

exorbitant *adjective*

Exceeding a normal or reasonable limit : excessive, extravagant, extreme, immoderate, inordinate, overabundant, overmuch, undue. *See* EXCESS.

exotic *adjective*

Of, from, or characteristic of another place or

part of the world : alien, foreign, strange. *Archaic:* outlandish. *See* NATIVE.

expand *verb*

1. To make or become greater or larger : aggrandize, amplify, augment, boost, build, build up, burgeon, enlarge, escalate, extend, grow, increase, magnify, mount, multiply, proliferate, rise, run up, snowball, soar, swell, upsurge, wax. *Informal:* beef up. *See* INCREASE. **2.** To make or become more comprehensive or inclusive : broaden, extend, widen. *See* INCREASE. **3.** To express at greater length or in greater detail : amplify, develop, dilate, elaborate, enlarge, expatiate, labor. *See* EXPLAIN. **4.** To move or arrange so as to cover a larger area : extend, fan[1] (out), open (out *or* up), outstretch, spread, stretch, unfold, unroll. *See* MOVE.

expanse *noun*

A wide and open area, as of land, sky, or water : distance, expansion, extent, reach, space, spread, stretch, sweep. *See* PLACE.

expansible *adjective*

Capable of being extended or expanded : expansile, extendible, extensible, extensile, protractile, stretch, stretchable. *See* INCREASE.

expansile *adjective*

Capable of being extended or expanded : expansible, extendible, extensible, extensile, protractile, stretch, stretchable. *See* INCREASE.

expansion *noun*

1. The act of increasing in dimensions, scope, or inclusiveness : enlargement, extension, spread. *See* INCREASE. **2.** A wide and open area, as of land, sky, or water : distance, expanse, extent, reach, space, spread, stretch, sweep. *See* PLACE.

expansive *adjective*

1. Large in expanse : ample, broad, extensive, spacious. *See* WIDE. **2.** Covering a wide scope : all-around, all-inclusive, all-round, broad, broad-spectrum, comprehensive, extended, extensive, far-ranging, far-reaching, general, global, inclusive, large, overall, sweeping, wide-ranging, wide-reaching, widespread. *See* SPECIFIC. **3.** Disposed to be open, sociable, and talkative : communicable, communicative, extraverted, extroverted, gregarious, outgoing, unreserved. *See* ATTITUDE.

expatiate *verb*

To express at greater length or in greater detail : amplify, develop, dilate, elaborate, enlarge, expand, labor. *See* EXPLAIN.

expatriate *verb*

To force to leave a country or place by official decree : banish, deport, exile, expel, ostracize, transport. *See* ACCEPT.

expatriate *noun* One forced to emigrate, usually for political reasons : deportee, émigré, exile, expellee. *See* APPROACH.

expatriation *noun*

Enforced removal from one's native country by official decree : banishment, deportation, exile, extradition, ostracism, transportation. *See* ACCEPT, REWARD.

expect *verb*

1. To look forward to confidently : anticipate, await, bargain for (*or* on), count on, depend on (*or* upon), look for, wait (for). *Informal:* figure on. *See* SURPRISE. **2.** To oblige to do or not do by force of authority, propriety, or custom : require, suppose. *See* OBLIGATION.

expectance *noun*

The condition of looking forward to something, especially with eagerness : anticipation, expectancy, expectation. *See* SURPRISE.

expectancy *noun*

1. The condition of looking forward to something, especially with eagerness : anticipation, expectance, expectation. *See* SURPRISE.
2. Something expected : anticipation, expectation, prospect. *See* SURPRISE.

expectant *adjective*

1. Having or marked by expectation : anticipant, anticipative, anticipatory. *See* SURPRISE.
2. Carrying a developing fetus within the uterus : big, enceinte, expecting, gravid, parturient, pregnant. *Slang:* gone. *Archaic:* great. *Idioms:* in a family way, with child. *See* REPRODUCTION.

expectation *noun*

1. The condition of looking forward to something, especially with eagerness : anticipation, expectance, expectancy. *See* SURPRISE.
2. Something expected : anticipation, expectancy, prospect. *See* SURPRISE.

expected *adjective*

Known to be about to arrive : anticipated, due, scheduled. *See* SURPRISE.

expecting *adjective*

Carrying a developing fetus within the uterus : big, enceinte, expectant, gravid, parturient, pregnant. *Slang:* gone. *Archaic:* great. *Idioms:* in a family way, with child. *See* REPRODUCTION.

expediency *noun*

Something used temporarily or reluctantly when other means are not available :

expedient, makeshift, shift, stopgap. *See* HELP, SUBSTITUTE.

expedient *adjective*
1. Suited to one's end or purpose : appropriate, befitting, convenient, fit[1], good, meet[2], proper, suitable, tailor-made, useful. *See* AGREE, GOOD. **2.** Worth doing, especially for practical reasons : advisable, recommendable, well[2]. *See* WISE.

expedient *noun* Something used temporarily or reluctantly when other means are not available : expediency, makeshift, shift, stopgap. *See* HELP, SUBSTITUTE.

expedite *verb*
1. To make less difficult : ease, facilitate. ***Idioms:*** clear (*or* prepare) the way for, grease the wheels, open the door for (*or* to). *See* EASY. **2.** To increase the speed of : accelerate, hasten, hurry, hustle, quicken, speed (up), step up. *See* FAST.

expedition *noun*
1. A journey undertaken with a specific objective : pilgrimage, safari, tour, trek, voyage. *See* MOVE. **2.** Rapidness of movement or activity : celerity, dispatch, expeditiousness, fleetness, haste, hurry, hustle, quickness, rapidity, rapidness, speed, speediness, swiftness. *See* FAST.

expeditious *adjective*
1. Characterized by great celerity : breakneck, fast, fleet, quick, rapid, speedy, swift. *Informal:* hell-for-leather. ***Idiom:*** quick as a bunny (*or* wink). *See* FAST. **2.** Accomplished in very little time : brief, fast, flying, hasty, hurried, quick, rapid, short, speedy, swift. *See* FAST.

expeditiousness *noun*
Rapidness of movement or activity : celerity, dispatch, expedition, fleetness, haste, hurry, hustle, quickness, rapidity, rapidness, speed, speediness, swiftness. *See* FAST.

expel *verb*
1. To force to leave a country or place by official decree : banish, deport, exile, expatriate, ostracize, transport. *See* ACCEPT. **2.** To send forth (confined matter) violently : belch, disgorge, eject, eruct, erupt, spew. *Geology:* extravasate. *See* EXPLOSION. **3.** To put out by force : bump, dismiss, eject, evict, oust, throw out. *Informal:* chuck. *Slang:* boot[1] (out), bounce, kick out. ***Idioms:*** give someone the boot, give someone the heave-ho (*or* old heave-ho), send packing, show someone the door, throw out on one's ear. *See* KEEP.

expellee *noun*
One forced to emigrate, usually for political reasons : deportee, émigré, exile, expatriate. *See* APPROACH.

expend *verb*
1. To distribute (money) as payment : disburse, give, lay out, outlay, pay (out), spend. *Informal:* fork out (*or* over *or* up), shell out. *See* SAVE. **2.** To use all of : consume, drain, draw down, eat up, exhaust, finish, play out, run through, spend, use up. *Informal:* polish off. *See* INCREASE.

expenditure *noun*
Something expended to obtain a benefit or desired result : cost, disbursement, expense, outlay. *See* TRANSACTIONS.

expense *noun*
1. Something expended to obtain a benefit or desired result : cost, disbursement, expenditure, outlay. *See* TRANSACTIONS. **2.** A loss sustained in the accomplishment of or as the result of something : cost, price, sacrifice, toll[1]. *See* TRANSACTIONS.

expensive *adjective*
Bringing a high price : costly, dear, high, high-priced. *See* TRANSACTIONS, VALUE.

experience *noun*
Personal knowledge derived from participation or observation : acquaintance, familiarity. *See* KNOWLEDGE.

experience *verb* **1.** To participate in or partake of personally : feel, go through, have, know, meet[1] (with), see, suffer, taste (of), undergo. *Archaic:* prove. ***Idiom:*** run up against. *See* PARTICIPATE. **2.** To be physically aware of through the senses : feel, have. *See* KNOWLEDGE. **3.** To undergo an emotional reaction : feel, have, know, savor, taste. *See* FEELINGS.

experienced *adjective*
Skilled or knowledgeable through long practice : old, practiced, seasoned, versed, veteran. ***Idiom:*** knowing the ropes. *See* ABILITY.

experiment *noun*
An operation employed to resolve an uncertainty : experimentation, test, trial. *See* INVESTIGATE.

experiment *verb* To engage in experiments : test. *See* INVESTIGATE.

experimental *adjective*
Constituting a tentative model for future experiment or development : pilot, test, trial. *See* START.

experimentation *noun*
An operation employed to resolve an uncertainty : experiment, test, trial. *See* INVESTIGATE.

expert *noun*
A person with a high degree of knowledge or skill in a particular field : ace, adept, authority, dab hand, master, past master, professional, proficient, wizard. *Informal:* whiz. *Slang:* crackerjack. *Chiefly British:* dab[2]. *See* ABILITY.
expert *adjective* Having or demonstrating a high degree of knowledge or skill : adept, crack, master, masterful, masterly, professional, proficient, skilled, skillful. *Slang:* crackerjack. *See* ABILITY.

expertise *noun*
Natural or acquired facility in a specific activity : ability, adeptness, art, command, craft, expertness, knack, mastery, proficiency, skill, technique. *Informal:* know-how. *See* ABILITY, KNOWLEDGE.

expertness *noun*
Natural or acquired facility in a specific activity : ability, adeptness, art, command, craft, expertise, knack, mastery, proficiency, skill, technique. *Informal:* know-how. *See* ABILITY, KNOWLEDGE.

expiatory *adjective*
Serving to purify of sin : lustral, lustrative, purgative, purgatorial, purificatory. *See* CLEAN, RELIGION.

expire *verb*
1. To become void, especially through passage of time or an omission : lapse, run out. *See* CONTINUE, LAW. **2.** To cease to exist : die (away *or* out), disappear. *See* LIVE. **3.** To cease living : decease, demise, depart, die, drop, go, pass away, pass (on), perish, succumb. *Informal:* pop off. *Slang:* check out, croak, kick in, kick off. ***Idioms:*** bite the dust, breathe one's last, cash in, give up the ghost, go to one's grave, kick the bucket, meet one's end (*or* Maker), pass on to the Great Beyond, turn up one's toes. *See* LIVE. **4.** To expel air in the process of respiration : breathe (out), exhale. *See* BREATH.

explain *verb*
1. To make understandable : construe, decipher, explicate, expound, interpret, spell out. *Archaic:* enucleate. ***Idiom:*** put into plain English. *See* EXPLAIN. **2.** To find a solution for : clear up, decipher, resolve, solve, unravel. *Informal:* dope out, figure out. ***Idiom:*** get to the bottom of. *See* ASK, REASON. **3.** To offer reasons for or a cause of : account for, justify, rationalize. *See* EXPLAIN.
explain away *verb* To conceal or make light of a fault or offense : extenuate, gloss over, gloze (over), palliate, sleek over, whitewash. *See* SHOW.

explainable *adjective*
Capable of being explained or accounted for : accountable, decipherable, explicable, illustratable, interpretable. *See* EXPLAIN.

explain away *verb* See **explain.**

explanation *noun*
1. Something that serves to explain or clarify : clarification, construction, decipherment, elucidation, exegesis, explication, exposition, illumination, illustration, interpretation. *Archaic:* enucleation. *See* EXPLAIN. **2.** A statement of causes or motives : account, justification, rationale, rationalization, reason. *See* EXPLAIN.

explanative *adjective*
Serving to explain : elucidative, exegetic, explanatory, explicative, expositive, expository, hermeneutic, hermeneutical, illustrative, interpretative, interpretive. *See* EXPLAIN.

explanatory *adjective*
Serving to explain : elucidative, exegetic, explanative, explicative, expositive, expository, hermeneutic, hermeneutical, illustrative, interpretative, interpretive. *See* EXPLAIN.

expletive *noun*
A profane or obscene term : blasphemy, curse, epithet, oath, swearword. *Informal:* cuss. *See* DECENT, SACRED, WORDS.

explicable *adjective*
Capable of being explained or accounted for : accountable, decipherable, explainable, illustratable, interpretable. *See* EXPLAIN.

explicate *verb*
To make understandable : construe, decipher, explain, expound, interpret, spell out. *Archaic:* enucleate. ***Idiom:*** put into plain English. *See* EXPLAIN.

explication *noun*
Something that serves to explain or clarify : clarification, construction, decipherment, elucidation, exegesis, explanation, exposition, illumination, illustration, interpretation. *Archaic:* enucleation. *See* EXPLAIN.

explicative *adjective*
Serving to explain : elucidative, exegetic, explanative, explanatory, expositive, expository, hermeneutic, hermeneutical, illustrative, interpretative, interpretive. *See* EXPLAIN.

explicit *adjective*
Clearly, fully, and sometimes emphatically expressed : categorical, clear, clear-cut, decided, definite, express, positive, precise, specific, unambiguous, unequivocal. *See* CLEAR.

explode *verb*
1. To release or cause to release energy suddenly and violently, especially with a loud noise : blast, blow[1] (up), burst, detonate, fire, fulminate, go off, touch off. *See* EXPLOSION. **2.** To come open or fly apart suddenly and violently, as from internal pressure : blow[1] (out), burst, pop[1]. *Slang:* bust. *See* EXPLOSION. **3.** To become manifest suddenly and in full force : break out, burst (forth *or* out), erupt, flare (up). *See* EXPLOSION, START. **4.** To be or become angry : anger, blow up, boil over, bristle, burn, flare up, foam, fume, rage, seethe. *Informal:* steam. ***Idioms:*** blow a fuse, blow a gasket, blow one's stack (*or* top), breathe fire, fly off the handle, get hot under the collar, hit the ceiling (*or* roof), lose one's temper, see red. *See* FEELINGS. **5.** To increase or expand suddenly, rapidly, or without control : mushroom, snowball. *See* INCREASE. **6.** To cause to be no longer believed or valued : debunk, deflate, discredit, puncture. *Informal:* shoot down. ***Idioms:*** knock the bottom out of, shoot full of holes. *See* VALUE.

exploit *noun*
A great or heroic deed : achievement, feat, gest, masterstroke, stunt, tour de force. *See* ACTION.

exploit *verb* **1.** To put into action or use : actuate, apply, employ, exercise, implement, practice, use, utilize. ***Idioms:*** avail oneself of, bring into play, bring to bear, make use of, put into practice, put to use. *See* USED. **2.** To take advantage of unfairly : abuse, impose, presume, use. *See* TREAT WELL. **3.** To control to one's own advantage by artful or indirect means : maneuver, manipulate, play. *See* CONTROL, STRAIGHT.

exploitable *adjective*
Easily imposed on or tricked : credulous, dupable, easy, gullible, naive, susceptible. *See* WISE.

exploration *noun*
The act or an instance of exploring or investigating : investigation, probe, reconnaissance. *See* INVESTIGATE.

explore *verb*
To go into or through for the purpose of making discoveries or acquiring information : delve, dig, inquire, investigate, look into, probe, reconnoiter, scout[1]. *See* INVESTIGATE.

explosion *noun*
1. A violent release of confined energy, usually accompanied by a loud sound and shock waves : blast, blowout, blowup, burst, detonation, fulmination. *See* EXPLOSION. **2.** The act of emerging violently from limits or restraints : eruption, outbreak, outburst. *See* EXPLOSION. **3.** A sudden sharp, explosive noise : bang, bark, clap, crack, pop[1], rat-a-tat-tat, report, snap. *See* SOUNDS. **4.** A sudden violent expression, as of emotion : access, blowup, burst, eruption, fit[2], flare-up, gust, outbreak, outburst. *See* EXPLOSION.

expose *verb*
1. To lay open, as to something undesirable or injurious : subject. ***Idiom:*** open the door to. *See* PROTECTION. **2.** To make visible; bring to view : bare, disclose, display, reveal, show, unclothe, uncover, unmask, unveil. *Archaic:* discover. ***Idioms:*** bring to light, lay open, make plain. *See* SHOW. **3.** To make bare : bare, denude, disrobe, divest, strip[1], uncover. *See* PUT ON. **4.** To make a public and usually ostentatious show of : brandish, display, disport, exhibit, flash, flaunt, parade, show (off), sport. *See* SHOW. **5.** To disclose in a breach of confidence : betray, blab, divulge, give away, let out, reveal, tell, uncover, unveil. *Informal:* spill. *Archaic:* discover. ***Idioms:*** let slip, let the cat out of the bag, spill the beans, tell all. *See* SHOW.

exposé *noun*
Something disclosed, especially something not previously known or realized : apocalypse, disclosure, exposure, revelation. *Informal:* eye opener. *See* SHOW.

exposed *adjective*
Having no protecting or concealing cover : open, uncovered, unprotected. *See* PROTECTION.

exposition *noun*
1. Something that serves to explain or clarify : clarification, construction, decipherment, elucidation, exegesis, explanation, explication, illumination, illustration, interpretation. *Archaic:* enucleation. *See* EXPLAIN. **2.** A large public display, as of goods or works of art : exhibit, exhibition, show. *See* SHOW.

expositive *adjective*
Serving to explain : elucidative, exegetic, explanative, explanatory, explicative, expository, hermeneutic, hermeneutical, illustrative, interpretative, interpretive. *See* EXPLAIN.

expository *adjective*
Serving to explain : elucidative, exegetic, explanative, explanatory, explicative, expositive, hermeneutic, hermeneutical, illustrative, interpretative, interpretive. *See* EXPLAIN.

expostulate *verb*
To express opposition, often by argument : challenge, demur, except, inveigh, object, protest, remonstrate. *Informal:* kick, squawk. ***Idioms:*** set up a squawk, take exception. *See* SUPPORT.

expostulation *noun*
The act of expressing strong or reasoned opposition : challenge, demur, exception, objection, protest, protestation, remonstrance, remonstration, squawk. *Slang:* kick. *See* SUPPORT.

exposure *noun*
1. The condition of being laid open to something undesirable or injurious : liability, openness, susceptibility, susceptibleness, vulnerability, vulnerableness. *See* PROTECTION.
2. Something disclosed, especially something not previously known or realized : apocalypse, disclosure, exposé, revelation. *Informal:* eye opener. *See* SHOW.

expound *verb*
To make understandable : construe, decipher, explain, explicate, interpret, spell out. *Archaic:* enucleate. ***Idiom:*** put into plain English. *See* EXPLAIN.

express *verb*
1. To put into words : articulate, communicate, convey, declare, say, state, talk, tell, utter[1], vent, verbalize, vocalize, voice. ***Idiom:*** give tongue (*or* vent *or* voice) to. *See* WORDS.
2. To utter publicly : air, put, state, vent, ventilate. ***Idiom:*** come out with. *See* SHOW, WORDS. **3.** To give expression to, as by gestures, facial aspects, or bodily posture : communicate, convey, display, manifest. *See* SHOW. **4.** To present a lifelike image of : delineate, depict, describe, image, limn, picture, portray, render, represent, show. *See* SHOW. **5.** To convey in language or words of a particular form : couch, formulate, phrase, put, word. *See* WORDS. **6.** To extract from by applying pressure : crush, press, squeeze. *See* TIGHTEN.

express *adjective* **1.** Clearly, fully, and sometimes emphatically expressed : categorical, clear, clear-cut, decided, definite, explicit, positive, precise, specific, unambiguous, unequivocal. *See* CLEAR. **2.** Fixed and distinct from others : particular, set[1], special, specific. *See* SPECIFIC.

expression *noun*
1. The act or an instance of expressing in words : articulation, statement, utterance, verbalization, vocalization, voice. *See* WORDS.
2. Vivid, effective, or persuasive communication in speech or artistic performance : articulacy, articulateness, eloquence, eloquentness, expressiveness, expressivity, facundity. *See* WORDS.
3. The act or process of describing in lifelike imagery : delineation, depiction, description, portrayal, representation. *See* SHOW. **4.** Something that takes the place of words in communicating a thought or feeling : gesture, indication, sign, token. *See* SHOW. **5.** A sound or combination of sounds that symbolizes and communicates a meaning : locution, term, word. *See* WORDS. **6.** A word or group of words forming a unit and conveying meaning : locution, phrase. *See* WORDS. **7.** A disposition of the facial features that conveys meaning, feeling, or mood : aspect, cast, countenance, face, look, visage. *See* EXPRESS.

expressionless *adjective*
Lacking expression : blank, deadpan, inexpressive, pokerfaced. *See* SHOW.

expressive *adjective*
Effectively conveying meaning, feeling, or mood : eloquent, meaning, meaningful, significant. *See* EXPRESS, SHOW.

expressiveness *noun*
Vivid, effective, or persuasive communication in speech or artistic performance : articulacy, articulateness, eloquence, eloquentness, expression, expressivity, facundity. *See* WORDS.

expressivity *noun*
Vivid, effective, or persuasive communication in speech or artistic performance : articulacy, articulateness, eloquence, eloquentness, expression, expressiveness, facundity. *See* WORDS.

expressway *noun*
A course affording passage from one place to another : avenue, boulevard, drive, freeway, highway, path, road, roadway, route, street, superhighway, thoroughfare, thruway, turnpike, way. *See* MOVE, OPEN.

expropriate *verb*
To take quick and forcible possession of : commandeer, confiscate, grab, seize, snatch. ***Idiom:*** help oneself to. *See* GIVE.

expropriation *noun*
The act of taking quick and forcible possession of : confiscation, seizure. *See* GIVE.

expulsion *noun*
The act of ejecting or the state of being ejected : dismissal, ejection, ejectment, eviction, ouster. *Slang:* boot[1], bounce. *See* KEEP.

expunction *noun*
The act of erasing or the condition of being erased : cancellation, deletion, erasure, obliteration. *See* INCLUDE.

expunge *verb*
To remove or invalidate by or as if by running a line through or wiping clean : annul, blot (out), cancel, cross (off *or* out), delete, efface, erase, obliterate, rub (out), scratch (out), strike (out), undo, wipe (out), x (out). *Law:* vacate. *See* CONTINUE.

expurgate *verb*
To examine (material) and remove parts considered harmful or improper for publication or transmission : bowdlerize, censor, screen. *See* INCLUDE, SHOW.

exquisite *adjective*
1. Appealing to refined taste : choice, dainty, delicate, elegant, fine[1]. *See* GOOD, INGESTION. **2.** Of such tasteful beauty as to elicit admiration : elegant, graceful. *See* BEAUTIFUL, STYLE.

exsiccate *verb*
To make or become free of moisture : dehydrate, desiccate, dry (out), parch. *See* DRY.

extant *adjective*
1. Occurring or existing in act or fact : actual, existent. *See* BE, REAL. **2.** Having existence or life : alive, around, existent, existing, living. *See* LIVE.

extemporaneous *adjective*
Spoken, performed, or composed with little or no preparation or forethought : ad-lib, extemporary, extempore, impromptu, improvised, offhand, snap, spur-of-the-moment, unrehearsed. *Informal:* off-the-cuff. *See* PREPARED.

extemporary *adjective*
Spoken, performed, or composed with little or no preparation or forethought : ad-lib, extemporaneous, extempore, impromptu, improvised, offhand, snap, spur-of-the-moment, unrehearsed. *Informal:* off-the-cuff. *See* PREPARED.

extempore *adjective*
Spoken, performed, or composed with little or no preparation or forethought : ad-lib, extemporaneous, extemporary, impromptu, improvised, offhand, snap, spur-of-the-moment, unrehearsed. *Informal:* off-the-cuff. *See* PREPARED.

extemporization *noun*
Something improvised : ad-lib, impromptu, improvisation. *See* PLANNED, PREPARED.

extemporize *verb*
To compose or recite without preparation : ad-lib, fake, improvise, make up. ***Idiom:*** wing it. *See* PLANNED, PREPARED.

extend *verb*
1. To move or arrange so as to cover a larger area : expand, fan (out), open (out *or* up), outstretch, spread, stretch, unfold, unroll. *See* MOVE. **2.** To make or become longer : draw out, elongate, lengthen, prolong, prolongate, protract, spin (out), stretch (out). *Mathematics:* produce. *See* INCREASE, LONG. **3.** To make or become more comprehensive or inclusive : broaden, expand, widen. *See* INCREASE. **4.** To proceed on a certain course or for a certain distance : carry, go, lead, reach, run, stretch. *See* REACH. **5.** To change or fluctuate within limits : go, range, run, vary. *See* CHANGE. **6.** To make or become greater or larger : aggrandize, amplify, augment, boost, build, build up, burgeon, enlarge, escalate, expand, grow, increase, magnify, mount, multiply, proliferate, rise, run up, snowball, soar, swell, upsurge, wax. *Informal:* beef up. *See* INCREASE. **7.** To put before another for acceptance : offer, present[2], proffer, tender[2], volunteer. ***Idioms:*** come forward with, lay at someone's feet, lay before. *See* OFFER. **8.** To make (something) readily available : afford, offer, provide. ***Idiom:*** place (*or* put) at one's disposal. *See* OFFER. **9.** To arrange for the extension of : renew. *See* CONTINUE.

extended *adjective*
1. Having great physical length : elongate, elongated, lengthy, long[1], prolonged. *See* LONG. **2.** Covering a wide scope : all-around, all-inclusive, all-round, broad, broad-spectrum, comprehensive, expansive, extensive, far-ranging, far-reaching, general, global, inclusive, large, overall, sweeping, wide-ranging, wide-reaching, widespread. *See* SPECIFIC.

extendible *adjective*
Capable of being extended or expanded : expansible, expansile, extensible, extensile, protractile, stretch, stretchable. *See* INCREASE.

extensible *adjective*
Capable of being extended or expanded : expansible, expansile, extendible, extensile, protractile, stretch, stretchable. *See* INCREASE.

extensile *adjective*
Capable of being extended or expanded : expansible, expansile, extendible, extensible, protractile, stretch, stretchable. *See* INCREASE.

extension *noun*
1. The act of making something longer or the condition of being made longer : elongation, prolongation, protraction. *See* LONG. **2.** The act of increasing in dimensions, scope, or inclusiveness : enlargement, expansion, spread. *See* INCREASE. **3.** An area within which something or someone exists, acts, or has influence or power : ambit, compass, extent, orbit, pur-

view, range, reach, realm, scope, sphere, sweep, swing. *See* TERRITORY. **4.** A part added to a main structure : annex, arm, wing. *See* PART.

extensive *adjective*

1. Large in expanse : ample, broad, expansive, spacious. *See* WIDE. **2.** Notably above average in amount, size, or scope : big, considerable, good, great, healthy, large, large-scale, sizable. *Informal:* tidy. *See* BIG. **3.** Covering a wide scope : all-around, all-inclusive, all-round, broad, broad-spectrum, comprehensive, expansive, extended, far-ranging, far-reaching, general, global, inclusive, large, overall, sweeping, wide-ranging, wide-reaching, widespread. *See* SPECIFIC.

extent *noun*

1. The measure of how far or long something goes in space, time, or degree : length, reach, span, stretch. *See* BIG. **2.** An area within which something or someone exists, acts, or has influence or power : ambit, compass, extension, orbit, purview, range, reach, realm, scope, sphere, sweep, swing. *See* TERRITORY. **3.** The amount of space occupied by something : dimension, magnitude, measure, proportion (often used in plural), size. *See* BIG. **4.** Relative intensity or amount, as of a quality or attribute : degree, magnitude, measure, proportion. *See* BIG. **5.** A wide and open area, as of land, sky, or water : distance, expanse, expansion, reach, space, spread, stretch, sweep. *See* PLACE.

extenuate *verb*

1. To conceal or make light of a fault or offense : explain away, gloss over, gloze (over), palliate, sleek over, whitewash. *See* SHOW. **2.** *Archaic.* To make physically thin or thinner : slim, thin. *See* FAT, INCREASE.

exteriorization *noun*

A physical entity typifying an abstraction : embodiment, externalization, incarnation, manifestation, materialization, objectification, personalization, personification, substantiation, type. *Rhetoric:* prosopopeia. *See* SUBSTITUTE.

exteriorize *verb*

To represent (an abstraction, for example) in or as if in bodily form : body forth, embody, externalize, incarnate, manifest, materialize, objectify, personalize, personify, substantiate. *See* SUBSTITUTE.

exterminate *verb*

To destroy all traces of : abolish, annihilate, blot out, clear, eradicate, erase, extinguish, extirpate, kill[1], liquidate, obliterate, remove, root[1] (out *or* up), rub out, snuff out, stamp out, uproot, wipe out. *Idioms:* do away with, make an end of, put an end to. *See* HELP, MAKE.

extermination *noun*

Utter destruction : annihilation, eradication, extinction, extinguishment, extirpation, liquidation, obliteration. *See* CRIMES, HELP, MAKE.

external *adjective*

Appearing as such but not necessarily so : apparent, ostensible, ostensive, outward, seeming, superficial. *See* SURFACE.

externalization *noun*

A physical entity typifying an abstraction : embodiment, exteriorization, incarnation, manifestation, materialization, objectification, personalization, personification, substantiation, type. *Rhetoric:* prosopopeia. *See* SUBSTITUTE.

externally *adverb*

On the surface : apparently, evidently, ostensibly, ostensively, outwardly, seemingly, superficially. *Idioms:* on the face of it, to all appearances. *See* SURFACE.

externalize *verb*

To represent (an abstraction, for example) in or as if in bodily form : body forth, embody, exteriorize, incarnate, manifest, materialize, objectify, personalize, personify, substantiate. *See* SUBSTITUTE.

extinct *adjective*

1. No longer alive : asleep, dead, deceased, defunct, departed, gone, late, lifeless. *Idioms:* at rest, pushing up daisies. *See* LIVE. **2.** No longer in use, force, or operation : dead, defunct, lost, vanished. *See* LIVE, NEW.

extinction *noun*

1. Utter destruction : annihilation, eradication, extermination, extinguishment, extirpation, liquidation, obliteration. *See* CRIMES, HELP, MAKE. **2.** The act or fact of dying : death, decease, demise, dissolution, passing, quietus, rest[1]. *Slang:* curtain (used in plural). *See* LIVE.

extinguish *verb*

1. To cause to stop burning or giving light : douse, put out, quench, snuff out. *See* CONTINUE. **2.** To destroy all traces of : abolish, annihilate, blot out, clear, eradicate, erase, exterminate, extirpate, kill[1], liquidate, obliterate, remove, root[1] (out *or* up), rub out, snuff out, stamp out, uproot, wipe out. *Idioms:* do away with, make an end of, put an end to. *See* HELP, MAKE. **3.** To bring to an end forcibly as if by imposing a heavy weight : choke off, crush, put down, quash, quell, quench, squash, squelch, suppress. *Idiom:* put the lid on. *See* CONTINUE, WIN. **4.** *Law.* To put an end to, especially formally and with authority : abolish, abrogate, annihilate, annul, cancel, invalidate, negate, nullify, set aside, vitiate, void. *See* CONTINUE.

extinguishment *noun*
1. Utter destruction : annihilation, eradication, extermination, extinction, extirpation, liquidation, obliteration. *See* CRIMES, HELP, MAKE. **2.** *Law.* An often formal act of putting an end to : abolishment, abolition, abrogation, annihilation, annulment, cancellation, defeasance, invalidation, negation, nullification, voidance. *Law:* avoidance. *See* CONTINUE.

extirpate *verb*
To destroy all traces of : abolish, annihilate, blot out, clear, eradicate, erase, exterminate, extinguish, kill[1], liquidate, obliterate, remove, root (out *or* up), rub out, snuff out, stamp out, uproot, wipe out. ***Idioms:*** do away with, make an end of, put an end to. *See* HELP, MAKE.

extirpation *noun*
Utter destruction : annihilation, eradication, extermination, extinction, extinguishment, liquidation, obliteration. *See* CRIMES, HELP, MAKE.

extol *verb*
1. To pay tribute or homage to : acclaim, celebrate, eulogize, exalt, glorify, hail[2], honor, laud, magnify, panegyrize, praise. ***Idiom:*** sing someone's praises. *See* PRAISE. **2.** To honor (a deity) in religious worship : exalt, glorify, laud, magnify, praise. *See* RELIGION.

extolment *noun*
The honoring of a deity, as in worship : exaltation, glorification, laudation, magnification, praise. *See* RELIGION.

extort *verb*
To obtain by coercion or intimidation : exact, squeeze, wrench, wrest, wring. *Slang:* shake down. *See* GET.

extra *adjective*
1. Being more than is needed, desired, or appropriate : de trop, excess, spare, supererogatory, superfluous, supernumerary, surplus. *See* EXCESS. **2.** Being an addition : added, additional, fresh, further, more, new, other. *See* INCREASE.
extra *adverb* To a high degree : awfully, dreadfully, eminently, exceedingly, exceptionally, extremely, greatly, highly, most, notably, very. *Informal:* awful. *Chiefly Regional:* mighty. *See* BIG.

extract *verb*
1. To remove from a fixed position : pluck, pull, tear[1]. *See* PUT IN. **2.** To collect (something) bit by bit : cull, garner, gather, glean, pick up. *See* COLLECT.

extraction *noun*
One's ancestors or their character or one's ancestral derivation : ancestry, birth, blood, bloodline, descent, family, genealogy, line, lineage, origin, parentage, pedigree, seed, stock. *See* KIN, PRECEDE.

extradition *noun*
Enforced removal from one's native country by official decree : banishment, deportation, exile, expatriation, ostracism, transportation. *See* ACCEPT, REWARD.

extramundane *adjective*
Of, coming from, or relating to forces or beings that exist outside the natural world : extrasensory, metaphysical, miraculous, preternatural, superhuman, supernatural, superphysical, supersensible, transcendental, unearthly. *See* SUPERNATURAL.

extraneous *adjective*
1. Not part of the essential nature of a thing : alien, extrinsic, foreign. *See* NATIVE. **2.** Not relevant or pertinent to the subject; not applicable : immaterial, impertinent, inapplicable, irrelevant. ***Idioms:*** beside the point, neither here nor there. *See* RELEVANT.

extraordinarily *adverb*
In a manner or to a degree that is unusual : exceptionally, remarkably, singularly, uncommonly, unusually. *See* USUAL.

extraordinary *adjective*
Far beyond what is usual, normal, or customary : exceptional, magnificent, outstanding, preeminent, rare, remarkable, singular, towering, uncommon, unusual. *Informal:* standout. *Slang:* awesome, out of sight. *See* BETTER, USUAL.

extrasensory *adjective*
Of, coming from, or relating to forces or beings that exist outside the natural world : extramundane, metaphysical, miraculous, preternatural, superhuman, supernatural, superphysical, supersensible, transcendental, unearthly. *See* SUPERNATURAL.

extravagance *noun*
1. A condition of going or being beyond what is needed, desired, or appropriate : embarrassment, excess, excessiveness, exorbitance, extravagancy, extravagantness, overabundance, plethora, superabundance, superfluity, superfluousness, surfeit. *See* EXCESS. **2.** Excessive or imprudent expenditure : extravagancy, lavishness, prodigality, profligacy, profuseness, profusion, squander, waste, wastefulness. *See*

CAREFUL, SAVE. **3.** Something costly and unnecessary : extravagancy, frill, luxury. *See* SAVE.

extravagancy *noun*
1. A condition of going or being beyond what is needed, desired, or appropriate : embarrassment, excess, excessiveness, exorbitance, extravagance, extravagantness, overabundance, plethora, superabundance, superfluity, superfluousness, surfeit. *See* EXCESS. **2.** Excessive or imprudent expenditure : extravagance, lavishness, prodigality, profligacy, profuseness, profusion, squander, waste, wastefulness. *See* CAREFUL, SAVE. **3.** Something costly and unnecessary : extravagance, frill, luxury. *See* SAVE.

extravagant *adjective*
1. Characterized by excessive or imprudent spending : lavish, prodigal, profligate, profuse, spendthrift, wasteful. *See* CAREFUL, EXCESS, SAVE. **2.** Exceeding a normal or reasonable limit : excessive, exorbitant, extreme, immoderate, inordinate, overabundant, overmuch, undue. *See* EXCESS. **3.** Given to or marked by unrestrained abundance : exuberant, lavish, lush[1], luxuriant, opulent, prodigal, profuse, riotous, superabundant. *See* BIG, EXCESS.

extravagantness *noun*
A condition of going or being beyond what is needed, desired, or appropriate : embarrassment, excess, excessiveness, exorbitance, extravagance, extravagancy, overabundance, plethora, superabundance, superfluity, superfluousness, surfeit. *See* EXCESS.

extravasate *verb*
Geology. To send forth (confined matter) violently : belch, disgorge, eject, eruct, erupt, expel, spew. *See* EXPLOSION.

extraverted *adjective*
Disposed to be open, sociable, and talkative : communicable, communicative, expansive, extroverted, gregarious, outgoing, unreserved. *See* ATTITUDE.

extreme *adjective*
1. Most distant or remote, as from a center : farthermost, farthest, furthermost, furthest, outermost, outmost, ultimate, utmost, uttermost. *See* BIG, EDGE. **2.** Of the greatest possible degree, quality, or intensity : supreme, transcendent, ultimate, unsurpassable, utmost, uttermost. *See* BETTER, BIG. **3.** Exceeding a normal or reasonable limit : excessive, exorbitant, extravagant, immoderate, inordinate, overabundant, overmuch, undue. *See* EXCESS. **4.** Holding especially political views that deviate drastically and fundamentally from conventional or traditional beliefs : extremist, fanatic, fanatical, rabid, radical, revolutionary, ultra. *Slang:* far-out. *See* CONCERN, EDGE, POLITICS.

extreme *noun* **1.** The ultimate point to which an action, thought, discussion, or policy is carried : end, length, limit. *See* LIMITED. **2.** Either of the two points at the ends of a spectrum or range : limit. *See* EDGE.

extremely *adverb*
To a high degree : awfully, dreadfully, eminently, exceedingly, exceptionally, extra, greatly, highly, most, notably, very. *Informal:* awful. *Chiefly Regional:* mighty. *See* BIG.

extremist *noun*
One who holds extreme views or advocates extreme measures : fanatic, radical, revolutionary, revolutionist, ultra, zealot. *See* EDGE, CONCERN, POLITICS.

extremist *adjective* Holding especially political views that deviate drastically and fundamentally from conventional or traditional beliefs : extreme, fanatic, fanatical, rabid, radical, revolutionary, ultra. *Slang:* far-out. *See* CONCERN, EDGE, POLITICS.

extremity *noun*
A highly volatile dangerous situation requiring immediate remedial action : crisis, emergency, flash point. *See* POLITICS, SAFETY.

extricate *verb*
To free from an entanglement : clear, disengage, disentangle, disinvolve, untangle. *See* FREE.

extrinsic *adjective*
Not part of the essential nature of a thing : alien, extraneous, foreign. *See* NATIVE.

extroverted *adjective*
Disposed to be open, sociable, and talkative : communicable, communicative, expansive, extraverted, gregarious, outgoing, unreserved. *See* ATTITUDE.

exuberant *adjective*
1. Full of joyful, unrestrained high spirits : ebullient, effervescent, sparkling. *See* HAPPY. **2.** Given to or marked by unrestrained abundance : extravagant, lavish, lush[1], luxuriant, opulent, prodigal, profuse, riotous, superabundant. *See* BIG, EXCESS.

exude *verb*
To flow or leak out or emit something slowly : bleed, leach, ooze, percolate, seep, transpire, transude, weep. *See* MOVE, SOLID.

exult *verb*
1. To feel or express joy over a success or

victory : crow, glory, jubilate, triumph. *See* HAPPY. **2.** To feel or take joy or pleasure : delight, joy, pleasure, rejoice. *See* HAPPY.

exultance *noun*
The act or condition of feeling an uplifting joy over a success or victory : exultancy, exultation, jubilance, jubilation, triumph. *See* HAPPY.

exultancy *noun*
The act or condition of feeling an uplifting joy over a success or victory : exultance, exultation, jubilance, jubilation, triumph. *See* HAPPY.

exultant *adjective*
Feeling or expressing an uplifting joy over a success or victory : jubilant, triumphant. *See* HAPPY.

exultation *noun*
The act or condition of feeling an uplifting joy over a success or victory : exultance, exultancy, jubilance, jubilation, triumph. *See* HAPPY.

exuviate *verb*
To cast off by a natural process : molt, shed, slough[2], throw off. *See* PUT ON.

eye *noun*
1. An organ of vision : orb. *See* SEE. **2.** The faculty of seeing : eyesight, seeing, sight, vision. *Archaic:* light[1]. *See* SEE. **3.** Skill in perceiving, discriminating, or judging : acumen, astuteness, clear-sightedness, discernment, discrimination, keenness, nose, penetration, perceptiveness, percipience, percipiency, perspicacity, sagacity, sageness, shrewdness, wit. *See* ABILITY, CAREFUL. **4.** The position from which something is observed or considered : angle[2], outlook, point of view, slant, standpoint, vantage, viewpoint. *See* PERSPECTIVE. **5.** A length of line folded over and joined at the ends so as to form a curve or circle : loop, ring[1]. *See* STRAIGHT. **6.** The most intensely active central part : midst, thick. *See* EDGE. **7.** *Informal.* A person whose work is investigating crimes or obtaining hidden evidence or information : detective, investigator, sleuth. *Slang:* dick, gumshoe. *See* INVESTIGATE.

eye *verb* **1.** To direct the eyes on an object : consider, contemplate, look, view. ***Idiom:*** clap (*or* lay *or* set) one's eyes on. *See* SEE. **2.** To look intently and fixedly : gape, gawk, gaze, goggle, ogle, peer[1], stare. ***Idioms:*** gaze open-mouthed, rivet the eyes on. *See* SEE. **3.** To look at or on attentively or carefully : observe, regard, scrutinize, survey, watch. ***Idioms:*** have one's (*or* keep an) eye on, keep tabs on. *See* AWARENESS, SEE.

eye-catching *adjective*
Readily attracting notice : arresting, bold, conspicuous, marked, noticeable, observable, outstanding, pointed, prominent, pronounced, remarkable, salient, signal, striking. ***Idiom:*** sticking out like a sore thumb. *See* SEE.

eyeless *adjective*
Without the sense of sight : blind, sightless, unseeing. *See* SEE.

eye opener *noun*
Informal. Something disclosed, especially something not previously known or realized : apocalypse, disclosure, exposé, exposure, revelation. *See* SHOW.

eyesight *noun*
The faculty of seeing : eye, seeing, sight, vision. *Archaic:* light[1]. *See* SEE.

eyewitness *noun*
Someone who sees something occur : seer, viewer, witness. *See* SEE.

fable *noun*
1. A narrative not based on fact : fiction, story. *See* REAL. **2.** An entertaining and often oral account of a real or fictitious occurrence : anecdote, story, tale. *Informal:* tall tale, yarn. *See* WORDS. **3.** A traditional story or tale that has no proven factual basis : legend, myth. *See* BELIEF, REAL, RELIGION.

fabric *noun*
A distinctive, complex underlying pattern or structure : contexture, fiber, texture, warp and woof, web. *See* BE.

fabricate *verb*
1. To use ingenuity in making, developing, or achieving : concoct, contrive, devise, dream up, formulate, hatch, invent, make up, think

up. *Informal:* cook up. ***Idiom:*** come up with. *See* MAKE. **2.** To create by forming, combining, or altering materials : assemble, build, construct, fashion, forge[1], frame, make, manufacture, mold, produce, put together, shape. *See* MAKE. **3.** To impart a false character to (something) by alteration : doctor, fake, falsify, fictionalize, fictionize. *See* TRUE.

fabricator *noun*
1. One who makes a fraudulent copy of something : counterfeiter, faker, forger. *See* TRUE. **2.** One who tells lies : fabulist, falsifier, fibber, liar, prevaricator. *Informal:* storyteller. *Law:* perjurer. *See* TRUE.

fabulist *noun*
One who tells lies : fabricator, falsifier, fibber, liar, prevaricator. *Informal:* storyteller. *Law:* perjurer. *See* TRUE.

fabulous *adjective*
1. So remarkable as to elicit disbelief : amazing, astonishing, astounding, fantastic, fantastical, incredible, marvelous, miraculous, phenomenal, prodigious, stupendous, unbelievable, wonderful, wondrous. *See* GOOD. **2.** Particularly excellent : divine, fantastic, fantastical, glorious, marvelous, sensational, splendid, superb, terrific, wonderful. *Informal:* dandy, dreamy, great, ripping, super, swell, tremendous. *Slang:* cool, groovy, hot, keen[1], neat, nifty. ***Idiom:*** out of this world. *See* GOOD. **3.** Of or existing only in myths : legendary, mythic, mythical, mythologic, mythological. *See* REAL.

façade also **facade** *noun*
1. The forward outer surface of a building : face, front, frontage, frontal. *Architecture:* frontispiece. *See* PRECEDE. **2.** A deceptive outward appearance : cloak, color, coloring, cover, disguise, disguisement, face, false colors, front, gloss, guise, mask, masquerade, pretense, pretext, semblance, show, veil, veneer, window-dressing. *Slang:* put-on. *See* SHOW.

face *noun*
1. The front surface of the head : countenance, feature (often used in plural), muzzle, visage. *Informal:* mug. *Slang:* kisser, map, pan, puss. *See* PRECEDE. **2.** A disposition of the facial features that conveys meaning, feeling, or mood : aspect, cast, countenance, expression, look, visage. *See* EXPRESS. **3.** A facial contortion indicating displeasure, disgust, or pain : grimace, moue, mouth, pout. *Informal:* mug. *See* EXPRESS. **4.** An outward appearance : aspect, countenance, look, physiognomy, surface, visage. *See* SURFACE. **5.** The level of credit or respect at which one is regarded by others : prestige, standing, status. *See* RESPECT. **6.** The state or quality of being impudent or arrogantly self-confident : assumption, audaciousness, audacity, boldness, brashness, brazenness, cheek, cheekiness, chutzpah, discourtesy, disrespect, effrontery, familiarity, forwardness, gall[1], impertinence, impudence, impudency, incivility, insolence, nerve, nerviness, overconfidence, pertness, presumptuousness, pushiness, rudeness, sassiness, sauciness. *Informal:* brass, crust, sauce, uppishness, uppityness. *See* ATTITUDE, COURTESY. **7.** The forward outer surface of a building : façade, front, frontage, frontal. *Architecture:* frontispiece. *See* PRECEDE. **8.** A deceptive appearance : cloak, color, coloring, cover, disguise, disguisement, façade, false colors, front, gloss, guise, mask, masquerade, pretense, pretext, semblance, show, veil, veneer, window-dressing. *Slang:* put-on. *See* SHOW. **9.** The outer layer of an object : surface, top. *See* SURFACE. **10.** The marked outer surface of an instrument : dial. *See* PRECEDE.

face *verb* **1.** To have the face or front turned in a specific direction : front, look (on *or* upon). *See* PRECEDE. **2.** To confront boldly and courageously : beard, brave, challenge, dare, defy, front. ***Idioms:*** fly in the face of, snap one's fingers at, stand up to, thumb one's nose at. *See* RESIST. **3.** To meet face-to-face, especially defiantly : accost, confront, encounter, front. *See* MEET. **4.** To come up against : confront, encounter, meet[1], run into. *See* MEET. **5.** To furnish with a covering of a different material : clad, cover, sheathe, side, skin. *See* SURFACE.

face-lift *noun*
The act of making new or as if new again : facelifting, refurbishment, rejuvenation, renewal, renovation, restoration, revampment. *See* HELP, NEW.

facelifting *noun*
The act of making new or as if new again : face-lift, refurbishment, rejuvenation, renewal, renovation, restoration, revampment. *See* HELP, NEW.

face-off *noun*
A face-to-face, usually hostile meeting : confrontation, encounter. *See* MEET.

facet *noun*
The particular angle from which something is considered : angle[2], aspect, frame of reference, hand, light[1], phase, regard, respect, side. *See* PERSPECTIVE.

facetious *adjective*
Intended to excite laughter or amusement :

comedic, funny, humorous, jocose, jocular, witty. *See* LAUGHTER.

facile *adjective*

1. Posing no difficulty : easy, effortless, simple, smooth. *Informal:* snap. ***Idioms:*** easy as ABC, easy as falling off a log, easy as one-two-three, easy as pie, like taking candy from a baby, nothing to it. *See* EASY. **2.** Moving or performing quickly, lightly, and easily : agile, brisk, nimble, quick, spry. *See* ABILITY. **3.** Characterized by ready but often insincere or superficial discourse : glib, slick, smooth-tongued. *See* SURFACE, WORDS. **4.** Exhibiting or possessing skill and ease in performance : adroit, clever, deft, dexterous, handy, nimble, slick. *See* ABILITY.

facileness *noun*

The ability to perform without apparent effort : ease, easiness, effortlessness, facility, readiness. *See* EASY.

facilitate *verb*

To make less difficult : ease, expedite. ***Idioms:*** clear (*or* prepare) the way for, grease the wheels, open the door for (*or* to). *See* EASY.

facility *noun*

1. The ability to perform without apparent effort : ease, easiness, effortlessness, facileness, readiness. *See* EASY. **2.** Ready skill in expression : fluency, fluidity. *See* ABILITY. **3.** Anything that increases physical comfort. Often used in plural : amenity, comfort, convenience. *See* COMFORT.

facsimile *noun*

Something closely resembling another : carbon copy, copy, duplicate, image, likeness, reduplication, replica, replication, reproduction, simulacrum. *Archaic:* simulacre. *Law:* counterpart. *See* SAME.

fact *noun*

1. That which is known about a specific subject or situation. Used in plural : data, information, intelligence, knowledge, lore. *See* KNOWLEDGE. **2.** Something having real, demonstrable existence : actuality, event, phenomenon, reality. *See* REAL. **3.** One of the conditions or facts attending an event and having some bearing on it : circumstance, detail, factor, particular. *See* REAL. **4.** The quality of being actual or factual : actuality, factuality, factualness, reality, truth. *See* REAL.

faction *noun*

1. A group of individuals united in a common cause : bloc, cartel, coalition, combination, combine, party, ring[1]. *See* GROUP. **2.** A state of disagreement and disharmony : clash, conflict, confrontation, contention, difference, difficulty, disaccord, discord, discordance, dissension, dissent, dissentience, dissidence, dissonance, friction, inharmony, schism, strife, variance, war, warfare. *See* CONFLICT.

factitious *adjective*

Marked by unnaturalness, pretension, and often a slavish love of fads : artificial, plastic, synthetic, unnatural. *See* HONEST.

factor *noun*

1. One of the individual entities contributing to a whole : building block, component, constituent, element, ingredient, integrant, part. *See* PART. **2.** One of the conditions or facts attending an event and having some bearing on it : circumstance, detail, fact, particular. *See* REAL.

factory *noun*

A building or complex in which an industry is located : mill, plant, work (used in plural). *See* MAKE, PLACE.

factual *adjective*

Based on fact : hard. *See* REAL.

factuality *noun*

The quality of being actual or factual : actuality, fact, factualness, reality, truth. *See* REAL.

factualness *noun*

The quality of being actual or factual : actuality, fact, factuality, reality, truth. *See* REAL.

facultative *adjective*

Not compulsory or automatic : discretionary, elective, optional. *See* CHOICE.

faculty *noun*

1. An innate capability : aptitude, aptness, bent, flair, genius, gift, head, instinct, knack, talent, turn. *See* ABILITY, APPROACH. **2.** Physical, mental, financial, or legal power to perform : ability, capability, capacity, competence, competency, might. *See* ABILITY. **3.** Conferred power : authority, mandate, right. *Law:* competence, competency. *See* ABILITY.

facund *adjective*

Fluently persuasive and forceful : articulate, eloquent, silver-tongued, smooth-spoken. *See* WORDS.

facundity *noun*

Vivid, effective, or persuasive communication in speech or artistic performance : articulacy, articulateness, eloquence, eloquentness, expression, expressiveness, expressivity. *See* WORDS.

fad *noun*

The current custom : craze, fashion, furor, mode, rage, style, trend, vogue. *Informal:* thing. ***Idioms:*** the in thing, the last word, the latest thing. *See* STYLE, USUAL.

fade *verb*
1. To become inaudible : die (away, out, *or* down), fade out. *See* INCREASE. **2.** To lose strength or power : decline, degenerate, deteriorate, fail, flag[2], languish, sink, wane, waste (away), weaken. *Informal:* fizzle (out). ***Idioms:*** go downhill, hit the skids. *See* STRONG, INCREASE. **3.** To disappear gradually by or as if by dispersal of particles : dissolve, melt (away). *See* INCREASE, SEE. **4.** To pass out of sight either gradually or suddenly : disappear, evanesce, evaporate, fade out, vanish. *See* SHOW.
fade out *verb* **1.** To pass out of sight either gradually or suddenly : disappear, evanesce, evaporate, fade, vanish. *See* SHOW. **2.** To become inaudible : die (away, out, *or* down), fade. *See* INCREASE. **3.** To make (a film image) disappear gradually : dissolve. *See* INCREASE, SEE.
fade *noun* A gradual disappearance, especially of a film image : dissolve, fadeaway, fade-out. *See* INCREASE, SEE.

fadeaway *noun*
A gradual disappearance, especially of a film image : dissolve, fade, fade-out. *See* INCREASE, SEE.

faded *adjective*
Showing signs of wear and tear or neglect : bedraggled, broken-down, decaying, decrepit, dilapidated, dingy, down-at-heel, mangy, run-down, scrubby, scruffy, seedy, shabby, shoddy, sleazy, tattered, tatty, threadbare. *Informal:* tacky[2]. *Slang:* ratty. ***Idioms:*** all the worse for wear, gone to pot (*or* seed), past cure (*or* hope). *See* BETTER.

fade-out or **fadeout** *noun*
1. The act or an example of passing out of sight : disappearance, evanescence, evaporation, vanishment. *See* SHOW. **2.** A gradual disappearance, especially of a film image : dissolve, fade, fadeaway. *See* INCREASE, SEE.

fade out *verb* See **fade.**

fag *noun*
1. One who works or toils tirelessly : drudge, grub, plodder, slave. *Informal:* grind, workhorse. *See* WORK. **2.** *Chiefly British.* Physical exertion that is usually difficult and exhausting : drudgery, labor, moil, toil, travail, work. *Informal:* sweat. ***Idiom:*** sweat of one's brow. *See* WORK.
fag *verb* **1.** To exert one's mental or physical powers, usually under difficulty and to the point of exhaustion : drive, labor, moil, strain[1], strive, sweat, toil, travail, tug, work. ***Idiom:*** break one's back (*or* neck). *See* WORK. **2.** To make extremely tired. Also used with *out* : exhaust, tire out, wear out. *Informal:* knock out, tucker (out). *Slang:* do in, poop[1] (out). ***Idioms:*** run ragged, take it out of. *See* TIRED.

fagged *adjective*
Slang. Extremely tired. Used with *out* : bleary, dead, drained, exhausted, fatigued, rundown, spent, tired out, wearied, weariful, weary, worn-down, worn-out. *Informal:* beat, bushed, tuckered (out). *Slang:* done in, pooped (out). ***Idioms:*** all in, ready to drop. *See* HEALTH, TIRED.

fail *verb*
1. To prove deficient or insufficient : give out, run out. ***Idioms:*** fall short, run dry, run short. *See* EXCESS. **2.** To be unsuccessful : choke, fall through. *Informal:* fall down, flop. *Slang:* bomb. ***Idioms:*** fail of success, fall short. *See* THRIVE. **3.** To receive less than a passing grade : *Informal:* flunk. *See* THRIVE. **4.** To not do (something necessary) : default, neglect, omit. *See* DO. **5.** To lose strength or power : decline, degenerate, deteriorate, fade, flag[2], languish, sink, wane, waste (away), weaken. *Informal:* fizzle (out). ***Idioms:*** go downhill, hit the skids. *See* STRONG, INCREASE. **6.** To cease functioning properly : break down, give out. *Slang:* conk out. *See* THRIVE. **7.** To make or become unusable or inoperative : break, ruin. *Slang:* bust. *See* HELP. **8.** To undergo sudden financial failure : break, bust, collapse, crash, go under. *Informal:* fold. ***Idioms:*** go belly up, go bust, go on the rocks, go to the wall. *See* MONEY.

failing *noun*
An imperfection of character : fault, foible, frailty, infirmity, shortcoming, weakness, weak point. *See* BETTER, HELP.

fail-safe *adjective*
Designed so as to be impervious to human error or misuse : foolproof. *See* THRIVE.

failure *noun*
1. The condition of not achieving the desired end : unsuccess, unsuccessfulness. *See* THRIVE. **2.** One that fails completely : bust, fiasco, loser, washout. *Informal:* dud, flop, lemon. *Slang:* bomb. *See* THRIVE. **3.** A cessation of proper mechanical functions : breakdown, outage. *See* THRIVE. **4.** Nonperformance of what ought to be done : default, delinquency, dereliction, neglect, omission. *Law:* nonfeasance. *See* DO. **5.** A marked loss of strength or effectiveness : declination, decline,

deterioration. *See* INCREASE. **6.** The condition of being financially insolvent : bankruptcy, bust, insolvency. *See* MONEY.

fain *adjective*
Archaic. Disposed to accept or agree : acquiescent, agreeable, game, minded, ready, willing. *See* WILLING.

fainéant *adjective*
Resistant to exertion and activity : idle, indolent, lazy, shiftless, slothful, sluggard, sluggish. *Informal:* do-nothing. ***Idiom:*** bone lazy. *See* ACTION, INDUSTRIOUS.

fainéant *noun* A self-indulgent person who spends time avoiding work or other useful activity : bum[1], drone[1], good-for-nothing, idler, layabout, loafer, ne'er-do-well, no-good, slugabed, sluggard, wastrel. *Informal:* do-little, do-nothing, lazybones, slug[2]. *Slang:* slouch. *See* INDUSTRIOUS.

faint *adjective*
1. Free from severity or violence, as in movement : balmy[1], delicate, gentle, mild, smooth, soft. *See* CALM, STRONG. **2.** So lacking in strength as to be barely audible : feeble, weak. *See* STRONG. **3.** Small in degree, especially of probability : negligible, outside, remote, slender, slight, slim. *See* BIG. **4.** Not clearly perceived or perceptible : blear, bleary, cloudy, dim, foggy, fuzzy, hazy, indefinite, indistinct, misty, obscure, shadowy, unclear, undistinct, vague. *See* CLEAR.

faint *noun* A temporary loss of consciousness : blackout, swoon. *Pathology:* syncope. *See* AWARENESS.

faint *verb* To suffer temporary lack of consciousness : black out, keel over, pass out, swoon. *See* AWARENESS.

faint-hearted *adjective*
Ignobly lacking in courage : chickenhearted, cowardly, craven, dastardly, lily-livered, pusillanimous, unmanly. *Slang:* chicken, gutless, yellow, yellow-bellied. *See* FEAR.

faint-heartedness *noun*
Ignoble lack of courage : chickenheartedness, cowardice, cowardliness, cravenness, dastardliness, funk, pusillanimity, unmanliness. *Slang:* gutlessness, yellowness, yellow streak. *See* FEAR.

fair *adjective*
1. Having qualities that delight the eye : attractive, beauteous, beautiful, comely, good-looking, gorgeous, handsome, lovely, pretty, pulchritudinous, ravishing, sightly, stunning. *Scots:* bonny. ***Idiom:*** easy on the eyes. *See* BEAUTIFUL. **2.** Having light hair : blond, fair-haired, towheaded. *See* COLORS. **3.** Of a light color or complexion : alabaster, ivory, light[1], pale. *See* COLORS. **4.** Free from clouds or mist, for example : clear, cloudless, fine[1], sunny, unclouded. *See* CLEAR. **5.** Indicative of future success or full of promise : auspicious, benign, bright, brilliant, favorable, fortunate, good, propitious. *See* LUCK. **6.** Free from bias in judgment : disinterested, dispassionate, equitable, fair-minded, impartial, indifferent, just, nonpartisan, objective, square, unbiased, unprejudiced. ***Idiom:*** fair and square. *See* FAIR. **7.** Just to all parties : equal, equitable, even[1], evenhanded. *See* SAME. **8.** According to the rules : clean, sporting, sportsmanlike, sportsmanly. *See* FAIR. **9.** Of moderately good quality but less than excellent : acceptable, adequate, all right, average, common, decent, fairish, goodish, moderate, passable, respectable, satisfactory, sufficient, tolerable. *Informal:* OK, tidy. *See* GOOD.

fair *adverb* **1.** In a fair, sporting manner : cleanly, correctly, fairly, properly. *See* FAIR. **2.** With precision or absolute conformity : bang, dead, direct, directly, exactly, flush, just, precisely, right, smack[1], square, squarely, straight. *Slang:* smack-dab. *See* PRECISE.

fair-haired *adjective*
1. Having light hair : blond, fair, towheaded. *See* COLORS. **2.** Given special, usually doting treatment : darling, favored, favorite, pet[1]. *See* TREAT WELL.

fairish *adjective*
Of moderately good quality but less than excellent : acceptable, adequate, all right, average, common, decent, fair, goodish, moderate, passable, respectable, satisfactory, sufficient, tolerable. *Informal:* OK, tidy. *See* GOOD.

fairly *adverb*
1. In a fair, sporting manner : cleanly, correctly, fair, properly. *See* FAIR. **2.** In truth : actually, genuinely, indeed, positively, really, truly, truthfully, verily. ***Idiom:*** for fair. *See* REAL, TRUE. **3.** To some extent : pretty, rather. ***Idiom:*** more or less. *See* BIG.

fair-minded *adjective*
Free from bias in judgment : disinterested, dispassionate, equitable, fair, impartial, indifferent, just, nonpartisan, objective, square, unbiased, unprejudiced. ***Idiom:*** fair and square. *See* FAIR.

fair-mindedness *noun*
The quality or state of being just and unbiased : detachment, disinterest, disinterestedness, dispassion, dispassionateness, equitableness, fair-

ness, impartiality, impartialness, justice, justness, nonpartisanship, objectiveness, objectivity. *See* FAIR.

fairness *noun*
The quality or state of being just and unbiased : detachment, disinterest, disinterestedness, dispassion, dispassionateness, equitableness, fair-mindedness, impartiality, impartialness, justice, justness, nonpartisanship, objectiveness, objectivity. *See* FAIR.

faith *noun*
1. Absolute certainty in the trustworthiness of another : belief, confidence, dependence, reliance, trust. *See* BELIEF. **2.** Mental acceptance of the truth or actuality of something : belief, credence, credit. *See* OPINION. **3.** A system of religious belief : confession, creed, denomination, persuasion, religion, sect. *See* RELIGION. **4.** Those who accept and practice a particular religious belief : church, communion, denomination, persuasion, sect. *See* RELIGION.

faithful *adjective*
1. Adhering firmly and devotedly, as to a person, a cause, or a duty : allegiant, constant, fast, firm[1], liege, loyal, staunch, steadfast, true. *See* CONTINUE, TRUST. **2.** Worthy of belief, as because of precision or faithfulness to an original : authentic, authoritative, convincing, credible, true, trustworthy, valid. *See* TRUE. **3.** Not deviating from correctness, accuracy, or completeness : close, exact, full, rigorous, strict. *See* CAREFUL. **4.** Conforming to fact : accurate, correct, exact, precise, right, rigorous, true, veracious, veridical. *See* CORRECT, HONEST, REAL, TRUE.

faithfulness *noun*
Faithfulness or devotion to a person, a cause, obligations, or duties : allegiance, constancy, fealty, fidelity, loyalty, steadfastness. *See* CONTINUE, OBLIGATION.

faithless *adjective*
Not true to duty or obligation : disloyal, false, false-hearted, perfidious, recreant, traitorous, treacherous, unfaithful, untrue. *See* CONTINUE, TRUST.

faithlessness *noun*
Betrayal, especially of a moral obligation : disloyalty, false-heartedness, falseness, falsity, infidelity, perfidiousness, perfidy, traitorousness, treacherousness, treachery, unfaithfulness. *See* CONTINUE, TRUST.

fake *adjective*
Fraudulently or deceptively imitative : bogus, counterfeit, false, fraudulent, phony, sham, spurious, suppositious, supposititious. *See* TRUE.

fake *noun* **1.** One who fakes : charlatan, faker, fraud, humbug, impostor, mountebank, phony, pretender, quack. *See* TRUE. **2.** A fraudulent imitation : counterfeit, forgery, phony, sham. *See* TRUE.

fake *verb* **1.** To contrive and present as genuine : counterfeit, feign, pretend, simulate. ***Idioms:*** make believe, put on an act. *See* TRUE. **2.** To make a fraudulent copy of : counterfeit, falsify, forge[1]. *See* TRUE. **3.** To impart a false character to (something) by alteration : doctor, fabricate, falsify, fictionalize, fictionize. *See* TRUE. **4.** To take on or give a false appearance of : affect[2], assume, counterfeit, feign, pretend, put on, sham, simulate. ***Idiom:*** make believe. *See* TRUE. **5.** To behave affectedly or insincerely or take on a false or misleading appearance of : act, counterfeit, dissemble, feign, play-act, pose, pretend, put on, sham, simulate. *See* HONEST, TRUE. **6.** To compose or recite without preparation : ad-lib, extemporize, improvise, make up. ***Idiom:*** wing it. *See* PLANNED, PREPARED.

faker *noun*
1. One who fakes : charlatan, fake, fraud, humbug, impostor, mountebank, phony, pretender, quack. *See* TRUE. **2.** One who makes a fraudulent copy of something : counterfeiter, fabricator, forger. *See* TRUE.

fall *verb*
1. To move downward in response to gravity : descend, drop. *See* RISE. **2.** To go from a more erect posture to a less erect posture : drop, sink, slump. *See* RISE. **3.** To come to the ground suddenly and involuntarily : drop, go down, nose-dive, pitch, plunge, spill, topple, tumble. ***Idiom:*** take a fall (*or* header *or* plunge *or* spill *or* tumble). *See* RISE. **4.** To undergo capture, defeat, or ruin : collapse, go down, go under, surrender, topple. *See* RESIST, WIN. **5.** To slope downward : decline, descend, dip, drop, pitch, sink. *See* RISE. **6.** To become or cause to become less active or intense : abate, bate, die (away, down, off, *or* out), ease (off *or* up), ebb, fall off, lapse, let up, moderate, remit, slacken, slack off, subside, wane. *See* INCREASE. **7.** To undergo a sharp, rapid descent in value or price : dive, drop, nose-dive, plummet, plunge, sink, skid, slump, tumble. ***Idiom:*** take a sudden downtrend (*or* downturn). *See* INCREASE. **8.** To undergo moral deterioration : sink, slip. ***Idiom:*** go bad (*or* wrong). *See* RIGHT. **9.** To take place at a set time : come, occur. *See* HAPPEN. **10.** To come

as by lot or inheritance : devolve, pass. *See* REACH.

fall back *verb* **1.** To move back in the face of enemy attack or after a defeat : draw back, pull back, pull out, retire, retreat, withdraw. ***Idioms:*** beat a retreat, give ground (*or* way). *See* FORWARD. **2.** To move in a reverse direction : back, backpedal, backtrack, retreat, retrocede, retrograde, retrogress. ***Idiom:*** retrace one's steps. *See* FORWARD.

fall down *verb* *Informal.* To be unsuccessful : choke, fail, fall through. *Informal:* flop. *Slang:* bomb. ***Idioms:*** fail of success, fall short. *See* THRIVE.

fall off *verb* **1.** To decline, as in value or quantity, very gradually : drop off, sag, slip. *See* INCREASE. **2.** To become or cause to become less active or intense : abate, bate, die (away, down, off, *or* out), ease (off *or* up), ebb, fall, lapse, let up, moderate, remit, slacken, slack off, subside, wane. *See* INCREASE.

fall on (or **upon**) *verb* To set upon with violent force : aggress, assail, assault, attack, beset, go at, have at, sail into, storm, strike. *Informal:* light into, pitch into. *See* ATTACK.

fall through *verb* To be unsuccessful : choke, fail. *Informal:* fall down, flop. *Slang:* bomb. ***Idioms:*** fail of success, fall short. *See* THRIVE.

fall *noun* **1.** The act of dropping from a height : descent, drop. *See* RISE. **2.** A sudden involuntary drop to the ground : dive, nosedive, pitch, plunge, spill, tumble. *Informal:* header. *See* RISE. **3.** A downward slope or distance : decline, declivity, descent, drop, pitch. *See* RISE. **4.** A disastrous overwhelming defeat or ruin : collapse, downfall, waterloo. *See* THRIVE. **5.** A usually swift downward trend, as in prices : decline, descent, dip, dive, downslide, downswing, downtrend, downturn, drop, drop-off, nosedive, plunge, skid, slide, slump, tumble. *See* INCREASE.

fallacious *adjective*
1. Containing fundamental errors in reasoning : false, illogical, invalid, sophistic, specious, spurious, unsound. *See* CORRECT, TRUE. **2.** Containing an error or errors : erroneous, false, inaccurate, incorrect, mistaken, off, unsound, untrue, wrong. ***Idioms:*** all wet, in error, off base, off (*or* wide of) the mark. *See* CORRECT. **3.** Tending to lead one into error : deceptive, delusive, delusory, illusive, illusory, misleading. *See* HONEST, REAL.

fallacy *noun*
1. An erroneous or false idea : erroneousness, error, falsehood, falseness, falsity, untruth. *See* CORRECT, TRUE. **2.** Plausible but invalid reasoning : casuistry, sophism, sophistry, speciousness, spuriousness. *See* CORRECT, TRUE.

fallback *noun*
The moving back of a military force in the face of enemy attack or after a defeat : pullback, pullout, retirement, retreat, withdrawal. *See* FORWARD.

fall back *verb* See **fall.**

fall down *verb* See **fall.**

fall guy *noun*
1. *Slang.* One who is made an object of blame : goat, scapegoat, whipping boy. *Slang:* patsy. *See* PRAISE. **2.** *Slang.* A person who is easily deceived or victimized : butt[3], dupe, fool, gull, lamb, pushover, victim. *Informal:* sucker. *Slang:* gudgeon, mark, monkey, patsy, pigeon, sap[1]. *Chiefly British:* mug. *See* WISE.

fall off *verb* See **fall.**

fall on or **upon** *verb* See **fall.**

fall through *verb* See **fall.**

false *adjective*
1. Devoid of truth : counterfactual, specious, spurious, truthless, untrue, untruthful, wrong. *See* TRUE. **2.** Containing an error or errors : erroneous, fallacious, inaccurate, incorrect, mistaken, off, unsound, untrue, wrong. ***Idioms:*** all wet, in error, off base, off (*or* wide of) the mark. *See* CORRECT. **3.** Containing fundamental errors in reasoning : fallacious, illogical, invalid, sophistic, specious, spurious, unsound. *See* CORRECT, TRUE. **4.** Fraudulently or deceptively imitative : bogus, counterfeit, fake, fraudulent, phony, sham, spurious, suppositious, supposititious. *See* TRUE. **5.** Not true to duty or obligation : disloyal, faithless, false-hearted, perfidious, recreant, traitorous, treacherous, unfaithful, untrue. *See* CONTINUE, TRUST.

false colors *noun*
A deceptive outward appearance : cloak, color, coloring, cover, disguise, disguisement, façade, face, front, gloss, guise, mask, masquerade, pretense, pretext, semblance, show, veil, veneer, window-dressing. *Slang:* put-on. *See* SHOW.

false-hearted *adjective*
Not true to duty or obligation : disloyal, faithless, false, perfidious, recreant, traitorous, treacherous, unfaithful, untrue. *See* CONTINUE, TRUST.

false-heartedness *noun*
Betrayal, especially of a moral obligation : disloyalty, faithlessness, falseness, falsity, infidelity, perfidiousness, perfidy, traitorousness,

treacherousness, treachery, unfaithfulness. *See* CONTINUE, TRUST.

falsehood *noun*
1. An untrue declaration : canard, cock-and-bull story, falsity, fib, fiction, inveracity, lie[2], misrepresentation, misstatement, prevarication, story, tale, untruth. *Informal:* fish story, tall tale. *Slang:* whopper. *See* TRUE. **2.** An erroneous or false idea : erroneousness, error, fallacy, falseness, falsity, untruth. *See* CORRECT, TRUE. **3.** The practice of lying : inveracity, mendacity, perjury, truthlessness, untruthfulness. *See* TRUE.

false impression *noun*
A failure to understand correctly : misapprehension, misconception, misinterpretation, misunderstanding. *See* UNDERSTAND.

falseness *noun*
1. An erroneous or false idea : erroneousness, error, fallacy, falsehood, falsity, untruth. *See* CORRECT, TRUE. **2.** Betrayal, especially of a moral obligation : disloyalty, faithlessness, false-heartedness, falsity, infidelity, perfidiousness, perfidy, traitorousness, treacherousness, treachery, unfaithfulness. *See* CONTINUE, TRUST.

falsifier *noun*
One who tells lies : fabricator, fabulist, fibber, liar, prevaricator. *Informal:* storyteller. *Law:* perjurer. *See* TRUE.

falsify *verb*
1. To make untrue declarations : fib, forswear, lie[2], prevaricate. *Law:* perjure. *See* TRUE. **2.** To impart a false character to (something) by alteration : doctor, fabricate, fake, fictionalize, fictionize. *See* TRUE. **3.** To give an inaccurate view of by representing falsely or misleadingly : belie, color, distort, load, misrepresent, misstate, pervert, twist, warp, wrench, wrest. ***Idiom:*** give a false coloring to. *See* TRUE. **4.** To make a fraudulent copy of : counterfeit, fake, forge[1]. *See* TRUE.

falsity *noun*
1. Betrayal, especially of a moral obligation : disloyalty, faithlessness, false-heartedness, falseness, infidelity, perfidiousness, perfidy, traitorousness, treacherousness, treachery, unfaithfulness. *See* CONTINUE, TRUST. **2.** An erroneous or false idea : erroneousness, error, fallacy, falsehood, falseness, untruth. *See* CORRECT, TRUE. **3.** An untrue declaration : canard, cock-and-bull story, falsehood, fib, fiction, inveracity, lie[2], misrepresentation, misstatement, prevarication, story, tale, untruth. *Informal:* fish story, tall tale. *Slang:* whopper. *See* TRUE.

falter *verb*
1. To be irresolute in acting or doing : dither, halt[2], hesitate, pause, shilly-shally, stagger, vacillate, waver, wobble. *See* DECIDE. **2.** To walk unsteadily : lurch, reel, stagger, stumble, teeter, totter, weave, wobble. *See* MOVE.

fame *noun*
1. Wide recognition for one's deeds : celebrity, famousness, notoriety, popularity, renown, reputation, repute. *See* KNOWLEDGE. **2.** A position of exalted widely recognized importance : distinction, eminence, eminency, glory, illustriousness, luster, mark, notability, note, preeminence, prestige, prominence, prominency, renown. *See* IMPORTANT, KNOWLEDGE, RESPECT.

famed *adjective*
1. Widely known and esteemed : celebrated, distinguished, eminent, famous, great, illustrious, notable, noted, preeminent, prestigious, prominent, redoubtable, renowned. *See* KNOWLEDGE, RESPECT. **2.** Widely known and discussed : famous, leading, notorious, popular, well-known. *See* KNOWLEDGE.

familial *adjective*
Of or relating to the family or household : domestic, family, home, homely, household. *See* KIN, GROUP.

familiar *adjective*
1. Occurring quite often : common, everyday, frequent, regular, routine, widespread. *See* USUAL. **2.** Having good knowledge of : acquainted, conversant, versant, versed. ***Idiom:*** up on. *See* KNOWLEDGE. **3.** Very closely associated : chummy, close, friendly, intimate[1]. *Informal:* thick. *Slang:* tight. ***Idiom:*** hand in glove with. *See* LOVE. **4.** Indicating intimacy and mutual trust : confidential, intimate[1]. *See* ATTITUDE, NEAR. **5.** Rude and disrespectful : assuming, assumptive, audacious, bold, boldfaced, brash, brazen, cheeky, contumelious, forward, impertinent, impudent, insolent, malapert, nervy, overconfident, pert, presuming, presumptuous, pushy, sassy, saucy, smart. *Informal:* brassy, flip, fresh, smart-alecky, snippety, snippy, uppish, uppity. *Slang:* wise[1]. *See* ATTITUDE, COURTESY.
familiar *noun* A person whom one knows well, likes, and trusts : amigo, brother, chum, confidant, confidante, friend, intimate[1], mate. *Informal:* bud[2], buddy, pal. *Slang:* sidekick. *See* LOVE.

familiarity *noun*
1. Personal knowledge derived from participation or observation : acquaintance, experience.

See KNOWLEDGE. **2.** The condition of being friends : chumminess, closeness, companionship, comradeship, fellowship, friendship, intimacy. *See* LOVE. **3.** The state or quality of being impudent or arrogantly self-confident : assumption, audaciousness, audacity, boldness, brashness, brazenness, cheek, cheekiness, chutzpah, discourtesy, disrespect, effrontery, face, forwardness, gall[1], impertinence, impudence, impudency, incivility, insolence, nerve, nerviness, overconfidence, pertness, presumptuousness, pushiness, rudeness, sassiness, sauciness. *Informal:* brass, crust, sauce, uppishness, uppityness. *See* ATTITUDE, COURTESY.

family *noun*
1. A group of usually related people living together as a unit : house, household, ménage. *See* GROUP. **2.** A group of people sharing common ancestry : clan, house, kindred, lineage, stock, tribe. ***Idioms:*** flesh and blood, kith and kin. *See* KIN. **3.** One's relatives collectively : kin, kindred, kinfolk. *See* KIN. **4.** One's ancestors or their character or one's ancestral derivation : ancestry, birth, blood, bloodline, descent, extraction, genealogy, line, lineage, origin, parentage, pedigree, seed, stock. *See* KIN, PRECEDE.
family *adjective* Of or relating to the family or household : domestic, familial, home, homely, household. *See* KIN, GROUP.

family tree *noun*
A written record of ancestry : genealogy, pedigree. *See* KIN.

famished *adjective*
Desiring or craving food : hungry, ravenous, starving, voracious. *See* INGESTION.

famous *adjective*
1. Widely known and discussed : famed, leading, notorious, popular, well-known. *See* KNOWLEDGE. **2.** Widely known and esteemed : celebrated, distinguished, eminent, famed, great, illustrious, notable, noted, preeminent, prestigious, prominent, redoubtable, renowned. *See* KNOWLEDGE, RESPECT.

famousness *noun*
Wide recognition for one's deeds : celebrity, fame, notoriety, popularity, renown, reputation, repute. *See* KNOWLEDGE.

fan[1] *verb*
To move or arrange so as to cover a larger area. Also used with *out* : expand, extend, open (out *or* up), outstretch, spread, stretch, unfold, unroll. *See* MOVE.

fan[2] *noun*
1. *Informal.* One who ardently admires : admirer, devotee, enthusiast, fancier, lover. *See* LIKE, LOVE, PRAISE. **2.** *Informal.* A person who is ardently devoted to a particular subject or activity : bug, devotee, enthusiast, fanatic, maniac, zealot. *Informal:* buff[2], fiend. *Slang:* freak, nut. *See* CONCERN.

fanatic *noun*
1. One who holds extreme views or advocates extreme measures : extremist, radical, revolutionary, revolutionist, ultra, zealot. *See* EDGE, CONCERN, POLITICS. **2.** One zealously devoted to a religion : devotee, enthusiast, sectary, votary, zealot. *See* BELIEF, LOVE, RELIGION. **3.** A person who is ardently devoted to a particular subject or activity : bug, devotee, enthusiast, maniac, zealot. *Informal:* buff[2], fan[2], fiend. *Slang:* freak, nut. *See* CONCERN.
fanatic *adjective* Holding especially political views that deviate drastically and fundamentally from conventional or traditional beliefs : extreme, extremist, fanatical, rabid, radical, revolutionary, ultra. *Slang:* far-out. *See* CONCERN, EDGE, POLITICS.

fanatical *adjective*
Holding especially political views that deviate drastically and fundamentally from conventional or traditional beliefs : extreme, extremist, fanatic, rabid, radical, revolutionary, ultra. *Slang:* far-out. *See* CONCERN, EDGE, POLITICS.

fancier *noun*
One who ardently admires : admirer, devotee, enthusiast, lover. *Informal:* fan[2]. *See* LIKE, LOVE, PRAISE.

fanciful *adjective*
1. Existing only in the imagination : chimeric, chimerical, conceptual, fantastic, fantastical, imaginary, notional, unreal, visionary. *See* REAL. **2.** Consisting or suggestive of fiction : fantastic, fantastical, fictional, fictitious, fictive, invented, made-up. *See* REAL. **3.** Appealing to fancy : fancy, fantastic, fantastical, imaginative, whimsical. *See* PLAIN.

fancy *noun*
1. The power of the mind to form images : fantasy, imagination, imaginativeness. *See* REAL, THOUGHTS. **2.** An illusory mental image : daydream, dream, fantasy, fiction, figment, illusion, phantasm, phantasma, reverie, vision. *See* REAL. **3.** An impulsive, often illogical turn of mind : bee, boutade, caprice, conceit, freak, humor, impulse, megrim, notion, vagary, whim, whimsy. ***Idiom:*** bee in one's bonnet. *See* THOUGHTS. **4.** A desire for a particular thing or activity : liking, mind, pleasure, will. *See*

LIKE. **5.** The passionate affection and desire felt by lovers for each other : amorousness, love, passion, romance. *See* LOVE, SEX.

fancy *adjective* **1.** Appealing to fancy : fanciful, fantastic, fantastical, imaginative, whimsical. *See* PLAIN. **2.** Complexly detailed : complicated, elaborate, intricate. *See* PLAIN. **3.** Catering to, used by, or admitting only the wealthy or socially superior : exclusive, posh, swank, swanky. *Informal:* ritzy. *See* PLAIN.

fancy *verb* **1.** To form mental images of : conceive, envisage, envision, fantasize, image, imagine, picture, see, think, vision, visualize. *Informal:* feature. *See* THOUGHTS. **2.** To find agreeable : like[1], take to. *Chiefly British:* conceit. *See* LIKE.

fancy-free *adjective*
Without a spouse : footloose, lone, single, sole, spouseless, unattached, unmarried, unwed. ***Idiom:*** footloose and fancy-free. *See* MARRIAGE.

fanfaronade *noun*
An act of boasting : boast, brag, braggadocio, gasconade, rodomontade, vaunt. *Informal:* blow[1]. *See* PRAISE.

fanny *noun*
Slang. The part of one's back on which one rests in sitting : buttock (used in plural), derrière, posterior, rump, seat. *Informal:* backside, behind, bottom, rear[1]. *Slang:* bun (used in plural), tush. *Chiefly British:* bum[2]. *See* OVER.

fantasize[1] *verb*
1. To form mental images of : conceive, envisage, envision, fancy, image, imagine, picture, see, think, vision, visualize. *Informal:* feature. *See* THOUGHTS. **2.** To experience dreams or daydreams : daydream, dream, muse[1], woolgather. *See* REAL.

fantastic *adjective*
1. Appealing to fancy : fanciful, fancy, fantastical, imaginative, whimsical. *See* PLAIN. **2.** Existing only in the imagination : chimeric, chimerical, conceptual, fanciful, fantastical, imaginary, notional, unreal, visionary. *See* REAL. **3.** Following no predictable pattern : capricious, changeable, erratic, fantastical, fickle, freakish, inconsistent, inconstant, mercurial, temperamental, ticklish, uncertain, unpredictable, unstable, unsteady, variable, volatile, whimsical. *See* CHANGE, CONTINUE. **4.** So remarkable as to elicit disbelief : amazing, astonishing, astounding, fabulous, fantastical, incredible, marvelous, miraculous, phenomenal, prodigious, stupendous, unbelievable, wonderful, wondrous. *See* GOOD. **5.** Conceived or done with no reference to reality or common sense : antic, bizarre, fantastical, far-fetched, grotesque. *See* TRUE, USUAL. **6.** Consisting or suggestive of fiction : fanciful, fantastical, fictional, fictitious, fictive, invented, made-up. *See* REAL. **7.** Particularly excellent : divine, fabulous, fantastical, glorious, marvelous, sensational, splendid, superb, terrific, wonderful. *Informal:* dandy, dreamy, great, ripping, super, swell, tremendous. *Slang:* cool, groovy, hot, keen[1], neat, nifty. ***Idiom:*** out of this world. *See* GOOD.

fantastical *adjective*
1. Appealing to fancy : fanciful, fancy, fantastic, imaginative, whimsical. *See* PLAIN. **2.** Existing only in the imagination : chimeric, chimerical, conceptual, fanciful, fantastic, imaginary, notional, unreal, visionary. *See* REAL. **3.** Following no predictable pattern : capricious, changeable, erratic, fantastic, fickle, freakish, inconsistent, inconstant, mercurial, temperamental, ticklish, uncertain, unpredictable, unstable, unsteady, variable, volatile, whimsical. *See* CHANGE, CONTINUE. **4.** So remarkable as to elicit disbelief : amazing, astonishing, astounding, fabulous, fantastic, incredible, marvelous, miraculous, phenomenal, prodigious, stupendous, unbelievable, wonderful, wondrous. *See* GOOD. **5.** Conceived or done with no reference to reality or common sense : antic, bizarre, fantastic, far-fetched, grotesque. *See* TRUE, USUAL. **6.** Consisting or suggestive of fiction : fanciful, fantastic, fictional, fictitious, fictive, invented, made-up. *See* REAL. **7.** Particularly excellent : divine, fabulous, fantastic, glorious, marvelous, sensational, splendid, superb, terrific, wonderful. *Informal:* dandy, dreamy, great, ripping, super, swell, tremendous. *Slang:* cool, groovy, hot, keen[1], neat, nifty. ***Idiom:*** out of this world. *See* GOOD.

fantasy also **phantasy** *noun*
1. The power of the mind to form images : fancy, imagination, imaginativeness. *See* REAL, THOUGHTS. **2.** Any fictitious idea accepted as part of an ideology by an uncritical group; a received idea : creation, fiction, figment, invention, myth. *See* BELIEF, REAL. **3.** A fantastic, impracticable plan or desire : bubble, castle in the air, chimera, dream, illusion, pipe dream, rainbow. *See* REAL. **4.** An illusory mental image : daydream, dream, fancy, fiction, figment, illusion, phantasm, phantasma, reverie, vision. *See* REAL.

far *adverb*
To a considerable extent : considerably, much, quite, well[2]. ***Idioms:*** by a long shot (*or* way), by a wide margin, by far. *See* BIG.
far *adjective* Far from others in space, time, or relationship : distant, faraway, far-flung, far-off, remote, removed. ***Idiom:*** at a distance. *See* NEAR, TIME.

faraway *adjective*
1. Far from others in space, time, or relationship : distant, far, far-flung, far-off, remote, removed. ***Idiom:*** at a distance. *See* NEAR, TIME. **2.** So lost in thought as to be unaware of one's surroundings : absent, absent-minded, abstracted, bemused, distrait, inattentive, preoccupied. ***Idiom:*** a million miles away. *See* ABILITY, AWARENESS.

farce *noun*
A false, derisive, or impudent imitation of something : burlesque, caricature, mock, mockery, parody, sham, travesty. *See* RESPECT, SAME.

farceur *noun*
A person whose words or actions provoke or are intended to provoke amusement or laughter : clown, comedian, comic, funnyman, humorist, jester, joker, jokester, quipster, wag[2], wit, zany. *Informal:* card. *See* LAUGHTER.

farcical *adjective*
Deserving laughter : comic, comical, funny, laughable, laughing, ludicrous, ridiculous, risible. *See* LAUGHTER.

farcicality *noun*
The quality of being laughable or comical : comedy, comicality, comicalness, drollery, drollness, funniness, humor, humorousness, jocoseness, jocosity, jocularity, ludicrousness, ridiculousness, wit, wittiness, zaniness. *See* LAUGHTER.

fare *verb*
1. To progress or perform adequately, especially in difficult circumstances : do, fend, get along, get by, manage, muddle through, shift. *Informal:* make out. ***Idioms:*** make do, make shift. *See* THRIVE. **2.** To move along a particular course : go, journey, pass, proceed, push on, remove, travel, wend. ***Idiom:*** make one's way. *See* MOVE. **3.** To take (food) into the body as nourishment : consume, devour, eat, ingest, partake. *Slang:* chow. ***Idioms:*** break bread, have (*or* take) a bite. *See* INGESTION.
fare *noun* Something fit to be eaten : aliment, bread, comestible, diet, edible, esculent, food, foodstuff, meat, nourishment, nurture, nutriment, nutrition, pabulum, pap, provender, provision (used in plural), sustenance, victual. *Slang:* chow, eats, grub. *See* INGESTION.

farewell *noun*
A separation of two or more people : adieu, good-bye, leave-taking, parting, valediction. *See* APPROACH.
farewell *adjective* Of, done, given, or said on departing : departing, good-bye, parting, valedictory. *See* APPROACH.

far-fetched *adjective*
Conceived or done with no reference to reality or common sense : antic, bizarre, fantastic, fantastical, grotesque. *See* TRUE, USUAL.

far-flung *adjective*
1. Far from others in space, time, or relationship : distant, far, faraway, far-off, remote, removed. ***Idiom:*** at a distance. *See* NEAR, TIME. **2.** Spread out over a large area : widespread. *See* WIDE.

farness *noun*
The fact or condition of being far removed or apart : distance, remoteness. *See* BIG, NEAR.

far-off *adjective*
Far from others in space, time, or relationship : distant, far, faraway, far-flung, remote, removed. ***Idiom:*** at a distance. *See* NEAR, TIME.

far-out *adjective*
Slang. Holding especially political views that deviate drastically and fundamentally from conventional or traditional beliefs : extreme, extremist, fanatic, fanatical, rabid, radical, revolutionary, ultra. *See* CONCERN, EDGE, POLITICS.

far-ranging *adjective*
Covering a wide scope : all-around, all-inclusive, all-round, broad, broad-spectrum, comprehensive, expansive, extended, extensive, far-reaching, general, global, inclusive, large, overall, sweeping, wide-ranging, wide-reaching, widespread. *See* SPECIFIC.

far-reaching *adjective*
Covering a wide scope : all-around, all-inclusive, all-round, broad, broad-spectrum, comprehensive, expansive, extended, extensive, far-ranging, general, global, inclusive, large, overall, sweeping, wide-ranging, wide-reaching, widespread. *See* SPECIFIC.

farsighted or **far-sighted** *adjective*
Characterized by foresight : foresighted, prescient, visionary. *See* FORESIGHT.

farsightedness or **far-sightedness** *noun*
Unusual or creative discernment or perception : foresight, prescience, vision. *See* FORESIGHT.

farthermost *adjective*
Most distant or remote, as from a center : extreme, farthest, furthermost, furthest, outermost, outmost, ultimate, utmost, uttermost. *See* BIG, EDGE.

farthest *adjective*
Most distant or remote, as from a center : extreme, farthermost, furthermost, furthest, outermost, outmost, ultimate, utmost, uttermost. *See* BIG, EDGE.

fascinate *verb*
1. To please greatly or irresistibly : beguile, bewitch, captivate, charm, enchant, entrance[2]. *See* LIKE. **2.** To compel, as the attention, interest, or imagination, of : arrest, catch up, enthrall, grip, hold, mesmerize, rivet, spellbind, transfix. *Slang:* grab. *See* EXCITE.

fascinating *adjective*
Pleasing to the eye or mind : attractive, bewitching, enchanting, engaging, enticing, fetching, glamorous, lovely, prepossessing, pretty, sweet, taking, tempting, winning, winsome. *See* LIKE.

fascination *noun*
The power or quality of attracting : allure, allurement, appeal, attraction, attractiveness, call, charisma, charm, draw, enchantment, enticement, glamour, lure, magnetism, witchery. *Informal:* pull. *See* LIKE.

fashion *noun*
1. The current custom : craze, fad, furor, mode, rage, style, trend, vogue. *Informal:* thing. ***Idioms:*** the in thing, the last word, the latest thing. *See* STYLE, USUAL. **2.** The approach used to do something : manner, method, mode, modus operandi, style, system, way, wise[2]. *See* MEANS. **3.** A distinctive way of expressing oneself : manner, mode, style, tone, vein. *See* STYLE.

fashion *verb* **1.** To create by forming, combining, or altering materials : assemble, build, construct, fabricate, forge[1], frame, make, manufacture, mold, produce, put together, shape. *See* MAKE. **2.** To make or become suitable to a particular situation or use : acclimate, acclimatize, accommodate, adapt, adjust, conform, fit[1], reconcile, square, suit, tailor. *See* CHANGE.

fashionable *adjective*
Being or in accordance with the current fashion : à la mode, chic, dashing, mod, modish, posh, smart, stylish, swank, swanky, trig. *Informal:* classy, in, sharp, snappy, swish, tony, trendy. *Slang:* with-it. ***Idioms:*** all the rage, up to the minute. *See* STYLE, USUAL.

fast *adjective*
1. Characterized by great celerity : breakneck, expeditious, fleet, quick, rapid, speedy, swift. *Informal:* hell-for-leather. ***Idiom:*** quick as a bunny (*or* wink). *See* FAST. **2.** Accomplished in very little time : brief, expeditious, flying, hasty, hurried, quick, rapid, short, speedy, swift. *See* FAST. **3.** Lacking in moral restraint : abandoned, dissipated, dissolute, gay, incontinent, licentious, profligate, rakish, unbridled, unconstrained, uncontrolled, ungoverned, uninhibited, unrestrained, wanton, wild. *See* RESTRAINT. **4.** Marked by an absence of conventional restraint in sexual behavior; sexually unrestrained : easy, libertine, light[2], loose, wanton, whorish. *See* SEX. **5.** Permanently resistive to fading : colorfast, indelible. *See* CONTINUE. **6.** Persistently holding to something : clinging, firm[1], secure, tenacious, tight. *See* FREE, TIGHTEN. **7.** Firmly settled or positioned : firm[1], secure, stable, steady, strong, sure. *See* CONTINUE. **8.** Adhering firmly and devotedly, as to a person, a cause, or a duty : allegiant, constant, faithful, firm[1], liege, loyal, staunch, steadfast, true. *See* CONTINUE, TRUST.

fast *adverb* In a rapid way : apace, posthaste, quick, quickly. *Informal:* flat out, hell-for-leather, lickety-split, pronto. ***Idioms:*** full tilt, in a flash, in nothing flat, like a bat out of hell, like a blue streak, like a flash, like a house on fire, like a shot, like a streak, like greased lightning, like the wind, like wildfire. *See* FAST.

fasten *verb*
1. To join one thing to another : affix, attach, clip[2], connect, couple, fix, moor, secure. *See* ASSEMBLE. **2.** To make fast or firmly fixed, as by means of a cord or rope : bind, knot, secure, tie, tie up. *See* KEEP, TIGHTEN. **3.** To make secure : anchor, catch, fix, moor, secure. ***Idiom:*** make fast. *See* MOVE. **4.** To implant so deeply as to make change nearly impossible : embed, entrench, fix, infix, ingrain, lodge, root[1]. *See* MOVE. **5.** To ascribe (a misdeed or an error, for example) to : affix, assign, blame, fix, impute, pin on, place. *See* GIVE.

fastener *noun*
A device for fastening or for checking motion : catch, clasp, hook. *See* MOVE.

fastidious *adjective*
1. Showing or marked by attentiveness to all aspects or details : careful, meticulous, painstaking, punctilious, scrupulous. *See* CAREFUL. **2.** Very difficult to please : choosy, dainty, exacting, finical, finicky, fussy, meticulous,

nice, particular, persnickety, squeamish. *Informal:* picky. *See* ACCEPT.

fastidiousness *noun*
Attentiveness to detail : care, carefulness, meticulousness, pain (used in plural), painstaking, punctiliousness, scrupulousness, thoroughness. *See* CAREFUL.

fastigium *noun*
Medicine. The highest point or state : acme, apex, apogee, climax, crest, crown, culmination, height, meridian, peak, pinnacle, summit, top, zenith. *Informal:* payoff. *See* HIGH.

fastness *noun*
Reliability in withstanding pressure, force, or stress : firmness, hardness, security, soundness, stability, stableness, steadiness, strength, sturdiness, sureness. *See* BETTER, CHANGE, CONTINUE.

fat *noun*
1. Adipose tissue : suet. *See* FAT. **2.** An amount or quantity beyond what is needed, desired, or appropriate : excess, glut, overage, overflow, overmuch, overrun, overstock, oversupply, superfluity, surplus, surplusage. *See* EXCESS.
fat *adjective* **1.** Having too much flesh : corpulent, fatty, fleshy, gross, obese, overblown, overweight, porcine, portly, stout, weighty. *See* FAT. **2.** Having the qualities of fat : adipose, fatty, greasy, oily, oleaginous, unctuous. *See* FAT. **3.** Affording profit : advantageous, lucrative, moneymaking, profitable, remunerative, rewarding. *See* GET. **4.** Relatively great in extent from one surface to the opposite : thick. *See* THICK.

fatal *adjective*
1. So critically decisive as to affect the future : fateful, momentous. *See* DECIDE. **2.** Causing or tending to cause death : deadly, deathly, lethal, mortal, vital. *See* LIVE. **3.** Causing ruin or destruction : calamitous, cataclysmal, cataclysmic, catastrophic, destructive, disastrous, fateful, ruinous. *See* HELP.

fatality *noun*
1. A termination of life, usually as the result of an accident or a disaster : casualty, death. *See* LIVE. **2.** The quality or condition of causing death : deadliness, lethality. *See* LIVE.

fate *noun*
1. That which is inevitably destined : destiny, fortune, kismet, lot, portion, predestination. *See* CERTAIN. **2.** A predestined tragic end : doom. *See* CERTAIN, LIVE, LUCK, START.
fate *verb* **1.** To determine the future of in advance : destine, foreordain, predestinate, predestine, predetermine, preordain. *See* CERTAIN. **2.** To predestine to a tragic end : doom, foredoom. *See* CERTAIN, LIVE, LUCK, START.

fated *adjective*
1. Governed and decided by or as if by fate : fateful. *See* CERTAIN. **2.** Sentenced to terrible, irrevocable punishment : condemned, doomed, foredoomed, lost. *See* LAW, RELIGION.

fateful *adjective*
1. So critically decisive as to affect the future : fatal, momentous. *See* DECIDE. **2.** Governed and decided by or as if by fate : fated. *See* CERTAIN. **3.** Causing ruin or destruction : calamitous, cataclysmal, cataclysmic, catastrophic, destructive, disastrous, fatal, ruinous. *See* HELP. **4.** Portending future disaster : apocalyptic, apocalyptical, baneful, dire, direful, fire-and-brimstone, grave[2], hellfire, ominous, portentous, unlucky. *See* LUCK, WARN.

father *noun*
1. A male parent : sire. *Informal:* dad, daddy, pa, papa, pappy[2], pop[2]. *Slang:* old man. *See* KIN. **2.** A person from whom one is descended : ancestor, antecedent, ascendant, forebear, forefather, foremother, mother, parent, progenitor. *Archaic:* predecessor. *See* KIN, PRECEDE. **3.** One that creates, founds, or originates : architect, author, creator, entrepreneur, founder[2], inventor, maker, originator, parent, patriarch. *See* START. **4.** A first form from which varieties arise or imitations are made : archetype, master, original, protoplast, prototype. *See* START.
father *verb* **1.** To be the biological father of : beget, breed, get, procreate, sire. *See* KIN. **2.** To cause to come into existence : beget, breed, create, engender, hatch, make, originate, parent, procreate, produce, sire, spawn. ***Idiom:*** give birth (*or* rise) to. *See* MAKE.

fatherlike *adjective*
Like a father : fatherly, paternal. *See* KIN.

fatherly *adjective*
Like a father : fatherlike, paternal. *See* KIN.

fathom *verb*
1. To perceive and recognize the meaning of : accept, apprehend, catch (on), compass, comprehend, conceive, follow, get, grasp, make out, read, see, sense, take, take in, understand. *Informal:* savvy. *Slang:* dig. *Chiefly British:* twig. *Scots:* ken. ***Idioms:*** get (*or* have) a handle on, get the picture. *See* UNDERSTAND. **2.** To perceive directly with the intellect : apprehend, compass, comprehend, grasp, know, understand. *Scots:* ken. *See* KNOWLEDGE.

fathomable *adjective*
Capable of being readily understood : compre-

hensible, intelligible, knowable, understandable. *See* KNOWLEDGE.

fatidic *adjective*
Of or relating to the foretelling of events by or as if by supernatural means : augural, divinitory, fatidical, mantic, oracular, prophetic, sibylline, vatic, vatical, vaticinal, visionary. *See* FORESIGHT.

fatidical *adjective*
Of or relating to the foretelling of events by or as if by supernatural means : augural, divinitory, fatidic, mantic, oracular, prophetic, sibylline, vatic, vatical, vaticinal, visionary. *See* FORESIGHT.

fatigue *noun*
The condition of being extremely tired : exhaustion, tiredness, weariness. *See* TIRED.
fatigue *verb* To diminish the strength and energy of : drain, jade, tire, wear, wear down, wear out, weary. *See* TIRED.

fatigued *adjective*
Extremely tired : bleary, dead, drained, exhausted, rundown, spent, tired out, wearied, weariful, weary, worn-down, worn-out. *Informal:* beat, bushed, tuckered (out). *Slang:* done in, fagged (out), pooped (out). ***Idioms:*** all in, ready to drop. *See* HEALTH, TIRED.

fatiguing *adjective*
Causing fatigue : draining, exhausting, tiring, wearing, wearying. *See* TIRED.

fatty *adjective*
1. Having the qualities of fat : adipose, fat, greasy, oily, oleaginous, unctuous. *See* FAT. **2.** Having too much flesh : corpulent, fat, fleshy, gross, obese, overblown, overweight, porcine, portly, stout, weighty. *See* FAT.

fatuous *adjective*
Displaying a complete lack of forethought and good sense : brainless, foolish, insensate, mindless, senseless, silly, unintelligent, weak-minded, witless. *See* ABILITY, PLANNED.

fault *noun*
1. An imperfection of character : failing, foible, frailty, infirmity, shortcoming, weakness, weak point. *See* BETTER, HELP. **2.** Something that mars the appearance or causes inadequacy or failure : blemish, bug, defect, flaw, imperfection, shortcoming. *See* BEAUTIFUL, BETTER, HELP. **3.** Responsibility for an error or crime : blame, culpability, guilt, onus. *See* START.
fault *verb* To find fault with : blame, censure, criticize, rap[1]. *Informal:* cut up, pan. *Slang:* knock. *See* PRAISE.

faultfinder *noun*
1. A person who finds fault, often severely and willfully : carper, caviler, critic, criticizer, hypercritic, niggler, nitpicker, quibbler. *See* PRAISE. **2.** A person who habitually complains or grumbles : complainer, crab, grouch, growler, grumbler, grump, murmurer, mutterer, whiner. *Informal:* crank, griper, grouser. *Slang:* bellyacher, sorehead, sourpuss. *See* HAPPY.

faultfinding *adjective*
Inclined to judge too severely : captious, carping, censorious, critical, hypercritical, overcritical. *See* PRAISE.

faultless *adjective*
1. Free from guilt or blame : blameless, guiltless, harmless, innocent, irreproachable, lily-white, unblamable. *Slang:* clean. ***Idiom:*** in the clear. *See* RIGHT. **2.** Supremely excellent in quality or nature : absolute, consummate, flawless, impeccable, indefectible, perfect, unflawed. *See* GOOD.

faulty *adjective*
Having a defect or defects : defective, imperfect. *See* BETTER.

favor *noun*
1. A kindly act : good turn, grace, indulgence, kindness, service. *Archaic:* benefit. *See* HELP. **2.** A charitable deed : benefaction, beneficence, benevolence, benignity, kindliness, kindness, oblation, office (often used in plural), philanthropy. *See* GIVE, KIND. **3.** An act requiring special generosity : beau geste, compliment, courtesy. *See* GIVE. **4.** Favorable regard : acceptance, approbation, approval. *See* ACCEPT, PRAISE. **5.** A feeling of deference, approval, and liking : account, admiration, appreciation, consideration, esteem, estimation, honor, regard, respect. *See* RESPECT. **6.** Favorable or preferential bias : favoritism, partiality, partialness, preference. *See* FAIR. **7.** Something beneficial : advantage, avail, benefit, blessing, boon[1], gain, profit. *See* HELP.
favor *verb* **1.** To perform a service or a courteous act for : accommodate, oblige. *See* HELP. **2.** To be favorably disposed toward : approve, countenance, hold with. *Informal:* go for. ***Idiom:*** take kindly to. *See* PRAISE. **3.** To show partiality toward (someone) : prefer. ***Idiom:*** play favorites. *See* FAIR. **4.** To lend supportive approval to : countenance, encourage, smile on (*or* upon). *See* SUPPORT. **5.** To treat with inordinate gentleness and care : spare. ***Idiom:*** handle (*or* treat) with kid gloves. *See* TREAT WELL. **6.** *Chiefly Regional.* To be similar to, as in appearance : resemble, take after. *See* SAME.

favorable *adjective*
1. Affording benefit : advantageous, benefic, beneficent, beneficial, benignant, good, helpful, profitable, propitious, salutary, toward, useful. *See* HELP. **2.** Occurring at a fitting or advantageous time : auspicious, opportune, propitious, prosperous, seasonable, timely, well-timed. *See* LUCK. **3.** Indicative of future success or full of promise : auspicious, benign, bright, brilliant, fair, fortunate, good, propitious. *See* LUCK. **4.** To one's liking : agreeable, congenial, good, grateful, gratifying, nice, pleasant, pleasing, pleasurable, satisfying, welcome. *See* LIKE. **5.** Giving assent : affirmative, positive. *See* AFFIRM. **6.** Disposed to favor one over another : partial, preferential. *See* FAIR.

favored *adjective*
1. Given special, usually doting treatment : darling, fair-haired, favorite, pet[1]. *See* TREAT WELL. **2.** Being a favorite : favorite, popular, preferred, well-liked. *See* LIKE.

favorite *noun*
1. One liked or preferred above all others : darling, pet[1]. ***Idiom:*** apple of one's eye. *See* LIKE. **2.** A competitor regarded as the most likely winner : *Informal:* shoo-in. *See* WIN.

favorite *adjective* **1.** Being a favorite : favored, popular, preferred, well-liked. *See* LIKE. **2.** Given special, usually doting treatment : darling, fair-haired, favored, pet[1]. *See* TREAT WELL.

favoritism *noun*
Favorable or preferential bias : favor, partiality, partialness, preference. *See* FAIR.

fawn *verb*
To support slavishly every opinion or suggestion of a superior : bootlick, cringe, grovel, kowtow, slaver, toady, truckle. *Informal:* apple-polish, brownnose, cotton. *Slang:* suck up. ***Idioms:*** curry favor, dance attendance, kiss someone's feet, lick someone's boots. *See* OVER.

faze *verb*
To cause (a person) to be self-consciously distressed : abash, chagrin, confound, confuse, discomfit, discomfort, disconcert, discountenance, embarrass, mortify. ***Idioms:*** put on the spot, throw for a loop. *See* PAIN.

fealty *noun*
Faithfulness or devotion to a person, a cause, obligations, or duties : allegiance, constancy, faithfulness, fidelity, loyalty, steadfastness. *See* CONTINUE, OBLIGATION.

fear *noun*
Great agitation and anxiety caused by the expectation or the realization of danger : affright, alarm, apprehension, dread, fearfulness, fright, funk, horror, panic, terror, trepidation. *Slang:* cold feet. ***Idiom:*** fear and trembling. *See* FEAR.

fear *verb* To be afraid of : dread. ***Idiom:*** have one's heart in one's mouth. *See* FEAR.

fearful *adjective*
1. Causing or able to cause fear : appalling, dire, direful, dreadful, fearsome, formidable, frightful, ghastly, redoubtable, scary, terrible, tremendous. *See* FEAR. **2.** Filled with fear or terror : afraid, aghast, apprehensive, fearsome, funky, panicky. *Regional:* afeard, ascared. *See* FEAR. **3.** Very bad : appalling, awful, dreadful, frightful, ghastly, horrendous, horrible, shocking, terrible. *See* GOOD.

fearfulness *noun*
Great agitation and anxiety caused by the expectation or the realization of danger : affright, alarm, apprehension, dread, fear, fright, funk, horror, panic, terror, trepidation. *Slang:* cold feet. ***Idiom:*** fear and trembling. *See* FEAR.

fearless *adjective*
Having or showing courage : audacious, bold, brave, courageous, dauntless, doughty, fortitudinous, gallant, game, hardy, heroic, intrepid, mettlesome, plucky, stout, stouthearted, unafraid, undaunted, valiant, valorous. *Informal:* spunky. *Slang:* gutsy, gutty. *See* FEAR.

fearlessness *noun*
The quality of mind enabling one to face danger or hardship resolutely : braveness, bravery, courage, courageousness, dauntlessness, doughtiness, fortitude, gallantry, gameness, heart, intrepidity, intrepidness, mettle, nerve, pluck, pluckiness, spirit, stoutheartedness, undauntedness, valiance, valiancy, valiantness, valor. *Informal:* spunk, spunkiness. *Slang:* gut (used in plural), gutsiness, moxie. *See* FEAR.

fearsome *adjective*
1. Causing or able to cause fear : appalling, dire, direful, dreadful, fearful, formidable, frightful, ghastly, redoubtable, scary, terrible, tremendous. *See* FEAR. **2.** Filled with fear or terror : afraid, aghast, apprehensive, fearful, funky, panicky. *Regional:* afeard, ascared. *See* FEAR.

feasible *adjective*
Capable of occurring or being done : possible, practicable, viable, workable. ***Idiom:*** within reach. *See* POSSIBLE.

feast *noun*
A large meal elaborately prepared or served :

banquet, junket. *Informal:* feed, spread. *See* INGESTION.

feast on *verb* To be avidly interested in : devour, relish. *Slang:* eat up. *See* CONCERN.

feast on *verb* See **feast.**

feat *noun*
1. A great or heroic deed : achievement, exploit, gest, masterstroke, stunt, tour de force. *See* ACTION. **2.** Something completed or attained successfully : accomplishment, achievement, acquirement, acquisition, attainment, effort. *See* DO. **3.** A clever, dexterous act : stunt, trick. *See* ABILITY, EXCITE, GOOD.

feather *noun*
A class that is defined by the common attribute or attributes possessed by all its members : breed, cast, description, ilk, kind[2], lot, manner, mold, nature, order, sort, species, stamp, stripe, type, variety. *Informal:* persuasion. *See* GROUP.

featherbrained *adjective*
Given to lighthearted silliness : empty-headed, flighty, frivolous, frothy, giddy, harebrained, lighthearted, scatterbrained, silly. *Informal:* gaga. *Slang:* birdbrained, dizzy. *See* ABILITY.

feature *noun*
1. The front surface of the head. Often used in plural : countenance, face, muzzle, visage. *Informal:* mug. *Slang:* kisser, map, pan, puss. *See* PRECEDE. **2.** A distinctive element : attribute, character, characteristic, mark, peculiarity, property, quality, savor, trait. *See* BE. **3.** A prominent article in a periodical : lead. *Chiefly British:* leader. *See* WORDS.

feature *verb* **1.** To accord emphasis to : accent, accentuate, emphasize, highlight, italicize, play up, point up, stress, underline, underscore. *See* IMPORTANT. **2.** *Informal.* To form mental images of : conceive, envisage, envision, fancy, fantasize, image, imagine, picture, see, think, vision, visualize. *See* THOUGHTS.

febrific *adjective*
Being at a higher temperature than is normal or desirable : febrile, feverish, hectic, hot, pyretic. *See* HOT.

febrile *adjective*
Being at a higher temperature than is normal or desirable : febrific, feverish, hectic, hot, pyretic. *See* HOT.

feckless *adjective*
Lacking or marked by a lack of care : careless, heedless, inattentive, irresponsible, reckless, thoughtless, unconcerned, unmindful, unthinking. *See* CAREFUL.

fecund *adjective*
1. Capable of reproducing : fertile, fruitful, productive, prolific. *Biology:* proliferous. *See* RICH. **2.** Characterized by great productivity : fertile, fruitful, productive, prolific, rich. *See* RICH.

fecundate *verb*
To make fertile : enrich, fertilize. *See* RICH.

fecundity *noun*
The quality or state of being fertile : fertility, fruitfulness, productiveness, productivity, prolificacy, prolificness, richness. *See* RICH.

federate *verb*
To be formally associated, as by treaty : align, ally, confederate, league. *See* CONNECT, POLITICS.

federation *noun*
1. An association, especially of nations for a common cause : alliance, Anschluss, bloc, cartel, coalition, confederacy, confederation, league, organization, union. *See* CONNECT, GROUP, POLITICS. **2.** A group of people united in a relationship and having some interest, activity, or purpose in common : association, club, confederation, congress, fellowship, fraternity, guild, league, order, organization, society, sorority, union. *See* GROUP.

fed up *adjective*
Out of patience with : disgusted, sick, tired, weary. ***Idiom:*** sick and tired. *See* TIRED.

fee *noun*
1. A fixed amount of money charged for a privilege or service : charge, exaction, toll[1]. *See* MONEY, PAY, TRANSACTIONS. **2.** Payment for work done : compensation, earnings, emolument, hire, pay, remuneration, salary, stipend, wage. *See* PAY.

feeble *adjective*
1. Not physically strong : decrepit, delicate, flimsy, fragile, frail, infirm, insubstantial, puny, unsound, unsubstantial, weak, weakly. *See* STRONG. **2.** So lacking in strength as to be barely audible : faint, weak. *See* STRONG. **3.** Having little substance or significance; not solidly based : flimsy, insubstantial, tenuous, unsubstantial. *See* STRONG.

feeble-minded *adjective*
Offensive. Having only a limited ability to learn and understand : backward, dull, simple, simple-minded, slow, slow-witted. *Informal:* soft. *Offensive:* half-witted, retarded, weak-minded. *See* ABILITY.

feebleness *noun*
The condition of being infirm or physically weak : debility, decrepitude, delicacy,

delicateness, flimsiness, fragileness, fragility, frailness, frailty, infirmity, insubstantiality, puniness, unsoundness, unsubstantiality, weakliness, weakness. *See* STRONG.

feed *verb*
1. To sustain (a living organism) with food : nourish. *See* INGESTION. **2.** To maintain existence in a certain way : live[1], subsist. *See* INGESTION. **3.** To help bring about : encourage, foster, promote. *See* HELP.

feed *noun Informal.* A large meal elaborately prepared or served : banquet, feast, junket. *Informal:* spread. *See* INGESTION.

feel *verb*
1. To be physically aware of through the senses : experience, have. *See* KNOWLEDGE. **2.** To bring the hands or fingers, for example, into contact with so as to give or receive a physical sensation : finger, handle, palpate, touch. *See* TOUCH. **3.** To reach about or search blindly or uncertainly : fumble, grabble, grope, poke. *See* SEEK, TOUCH. **4.** To participate in or partake of personally : experience, go through, have, know, meet[1] (with), see, suffer, taste (of), undergo. *Archaic:* prove. ***Idiom:*** run up against. *See* PARTICIPATE. **5.** To be intuitively aware of : apprehend, intuit, perceive, sense. ***Idioms:*** feel in one's bones, get vibrations. *See* KNOWLEDGE. **6.** To undergo an emotional reaction : experience, have, know, savor, taste. *See* FEELINGS. **7.** To experience or express compassion : ache, commiserate, compassionate, pity, sympathize, yearn. ***Idioms:*** be sorry, have (*or* take) pity. *See* PITY. **8.** To view in a certain way : believe, hold, sense, think. *See* OPINION.

feel out *verb* To test the attitude of : probe, sound[3] (out). ***Idioms:*** put out feelers, send up a trial balloon. *See* INVESTIGATE.

feel *noun* **1.** A particular sensation conveyed by means of physical contact : feeling, touch. *See* TOUCH. **2.** The faculty or ability to perceive tactile stimulation : feeling, tactility, touch. *See* TOUCH. **3.** A general impression produced by a predominant quality or characteristic : air, ambiance, atmosphere, aura, feeling, mood, smell, tone. *See* BE. **4.** The proper method for doing, using, or handling something : knack, trick. *Informal:* hang. *See* ABILITY.

feeler *noun*
Something, as a remark, used to determine the attitude of another : probe. ***Idiom:*** trial balloon. *See* INVESTIGATE.

feeling *noun*
1. A particular sensation conveyed by means of physical contact : feel, touch. *See* TOUCH. **2.** The faculty or ability to perceive tactile stimulation : feel, tactility, touch. *See* TOUCH. **3.** An act of touching : palpation, touch. *See* TOUCH. **4.** The capacity for or an act of responding to a stimulus : sensation, sense, sensibility, sensitiveness, sensitivity, sentiment. *See* AWARENESS. **5.** A general cast of mind with regard to something : attitude, sentiment. *See* ATTITUDE. **6.** A complex and usually strong subjective response, such as love or hate : affection, affectivity, emotion, sentiment. *See* FEELINGS. **7.** The quality or condition of being emotionally and intuitively sensitive : sensibility, sensitiveness, sensitivity. *See* AWARENESS. **8.** Something believed or accepted as true by a person : belief, conviction, idea, mind, notion, opinion, persuasion, position, sentiment, view. *See* OPINION. **9.** A general impression produced by a predominant quality or characteristic : air, ambiance, atmosphere, aura, feel, mood, smell, tone. *See* BE. **10.** Intuitive cognition : hunch, idea, impression, intuition, suspicion. *See* THOUGHTS.

feeling *adjective* **1.** Cognizant of and comprehending the needs, feelings, problems, and views of others : empathetic, empathic, sympathetic, understanding. *See* UNDERSTAND. **2.** Readily stirred by emotion : emotional, sensitive. *See* FEELINGS.

feel out *verb* See **feel.**

feign *verb*
1. To take on or give a false appearance of : affect[2], assume, counterfeit, fake, pretend, put on, sham, simulate. ***Idiom:*** make believe. *See* TRUE. **2.** To behave affectedly or insincerely or take on a false or misleading appearance of : act, counterfeit, dissemble, fake, play-act, pose, pretend, put on, sham, simulate. *See* HONEST, TRUE. **3.** To contrive and present as genuine : counterfeit, fake, pretend, simulate. ***Idioms:*** make believe, put on an act. *See* TRUE. **4.** To claim or allege insincerely or falsely : pretend, profess. *See* TRUE.

feigned *adjective*
Not genuine or sincere : affected, artificial, insincere, phony, pretended. *See* TRUE.

feint *noun*
An indirect, usually cunning means of gaining an end : artifice, deception, device, dodge, gimmick, imposture, jig, maneuver, ploy, ruse, sleight, stratagem, subterfuge, trick, wile. *Informal:* shenanigan, take-in. *See* HONEST, MEANS.

felicitous *adjective*
Suitable for a particular person, condition, occasion, or place : appropriate, apt, becoming, befitting, correct, fit[1], fitting, happy, meet[2], proper, right, tailor-made. *See* RIGHT.

felicity *noun*
A condition of supreme well-being and good spirits : beatitude, blessedness, bliss, cheer, cheerfulness, gladness, happiness, joy, joyfulness. *See* HAPPY.

feline *adjective*
So slow, deliberate, and secret as to escape observation : catlike, furtive, slinky, sneaking, sneaky, stealthy. *See* MOVE.

fell[1] *verb*
1. To bring down, as with a saw or ax : chop down, cut (down), hew. *See* RISE. **2.** To cause to fall, as from a shot or blow : bring down, cut down, down, drop, flatten, floor, ground, knock down, level, prostrate, strike down, throw. *Slang:* deck[1]. ***Idiom:*** lay low. *See* RISE.

fell[2] *adjective*
Showing or suggesting a disposition to be violently destructive without scruple or restraint : barbarous, bestial, cruel, feral, ferocious, fierce, inhuman, savage, truculent, vicious, wolfish. *See* KIND.

fell[3] *noun*
The skin of an animal : fur, hide[2], jacket, pelt[1]. *See* SURFACE.

fellow *noun*
1. A grown man referred to familiarly, jokingly, or as a member of one's set or group : *Informal:* boy, chap. *See* BEINGS, CONNECT. **2.** *Informal.* A man who is the favored companion of a woman : beau, boyfriend. *See* CONNECT, SEX. **3.** One who is united in a relationship with another : affiliate, ally, associate, cohort, colleague, confederate, copartner, partner. *See* CONNECT. **4.** One who shares interests or activities with another : associate, chum, companion, comrade, crony, mate. *Informal:* buddy, pal. *See* NEAR. **5.** One that is very similar to another in rank or position : coequal, colleague, compeer, equal, equivalent, peer[2]. *See* SAME. **6.** One of a matched pair of things : companion, counterpart, double, duplicate, match, mate, twin. *See* SAME.

fellow citizen *noun*
A person who is from one's own country : compatriot, countryman, countrywoman. *See* GROUP.

fellowship *noun*
1. A pleasant association among people : companionship, company, society. *See* CONNECT, GROUP. **2.** A group of people united in a relationship and having some interest, activity, or purpose in common : association, club, confederation, congress, federation, fraternity, guild, league, order, organization, society, sorority, union. *See* GROUP. **3.** The condition of being friends : chumminess, closeness, companionship, comradeship, familiarity, friendship, intimacy. *See* LOVE.

felon *noun*
Law. One who commits a crime : criminal, lawbreaker, malefactor, offender. *See* CRIMES.

felony *noun*
Law. A serious breaking of the public law : crime, illegality, misdeed, offense. *See* CRIMES.

female *adjective*
Of, relating to, or characteristic of women : distaff, feminine, womanish, womanly. *See* GENDER.

femaleness *noun*
The quality or condition of being feminine : feminineness, femininity, womanliness. *See* GENDER.

feminine *adjective*
1. Of, relating to, or characteristic of women : distaff, female, womanish, womanly. *See* GENDER. **2.** Having qualities more appropriate to women than to men : effeminate, epicene, sissified, sissyish, unmanly, womanish. *See* GENDER.

feminineness *noun*
The quality or condition of being feminine : femaleness, femininity, womanliness. *See* GENDER.

femininity *noun*
1. The quality or condition of being feminine : femaleness, feminineness, womanliness. *See* GENDER. **2.** Women in general : distaff, muliebrity, womanhood, womankind, womenfolk. *See* GENDER. **3.** The quality of being effeminate : effeminacy, effeminateness, sissiness, unmanliness, womanishness. *See* GENDER.

femme fatale *noun*
A usually unscrupulous woman who seduces or exploits men : enchantress, seductress, siren, temptress. *Informal:* vamp, witch. *See* SEX.

fen *noun*
A usually low-lying area of soft waterlogged ground and standing water : bog, marsh, marshland, mire, morass, muskeg, quag, quagmire, slough[1], swamp, swampland, wetland. *See* DRY.

fence *verb*
1. To confine within a limited area. Also used

with *in* : cage, coop (in *or* up), enclose, immure, mew (up), pen[2], shut in, shut up, wall (in *or* up). *See* FREE. **2.** To separate with or as if with a wall : partition, wall. *See* INCLUDE.

fend *verb*
1. To turn or drive away. Also used with *off* : beat off, keep off, parry, repel, repulse, ward off. *See* ALLOW, STRIKE. **2.** *Archaic.* To keep safe from danger, attack, or harm : defend, guard, preserve, protect, safeguard, secure, shield, ward. *See* ATTACK. **3.** To progress or perform adequately, especially in difficult circumstances : do, fare, get along, get by, manage, muddle through, shift. *Informal:* make out. ***Idioms:*** make do, make shift. *See* THRIVE.

feral *adjective*
1. Of or relating to wild animals : savage, wild. *See* WILD. **2.** Showing or suggesting a disposition to be violently destructive without scruple or restraint : barbarous, bestial, cruel, fell[2], ferocious, fierce, inhuman, savage, truculent, vicious, wolfish. *See* KIND.

ferment *verb*
To be in a state of emotional or mental turmoil : boil, bubble, burn, churn, seethe, simmer, smolder. *See* CALM.
ferment *noun* **1.** An agent that stimulates or precipitates a reaction, development, or change : catalyst, leaven, leavening, yeast. *See* CHANGE. **2.** A state of uneasiness and usually resentment brewing to an eventual explosion : Sturm und Drang, turmoil, unrest. *See* CALM, PEACE.

ferocious *adjective*
1. Showing or suggesting a disposition to be violently destructive without scruple or restraint : barbarous, bestial, cruel, fell[2], feral, fierce, inhuman, savage, truculent, vicious, wolfish. *See* KIND. **2.** So intense as to cause extreme suffering : cruel, fierce, savage, vicious. *See* HELP, KIND.

ferociousness *noun*
Exceptionally great concentration, power, or force, especially in activity : depth (often used in plural), ferocity, fierceness, fury, intensity, pitch, severity, vehemence, vehemency, violence. *See* BIG, STRONG.

ferocity *noun*
Exceptionally great concentration, power, or force, especially in activity : depth (often used in plural), ferociousness, fierceness, fury, intensity, pitch, severity, vehemence, vehemency, violence. *See* BIG, STRONG.

fertile *adjective*
1. Capable of reproducing : fecund, fruitful, productive, prolific. *Biology:* proliferous. *See* RICH. **2.** Characterized by great productivity : fecund, fruitful, productive, prolific, rich. *See* RICH.

fertility *noun*
The quality or state of being fertile : fecundity, fruitfulness, productiveness, productivity, prolificacy, prolificness, richness. *See* RICH.

fertilize *verb*
To make fertile : enrich, fecundate. *See* RICH.

fervency *noun*
Powerful, intense emotion : ardor, fervor, fire, passion. *See* FEELINGS.

fervent *adjective*
1. Fired with intense feeling : ardent, blazing, burning, dithyrambic, fervid, fiery, flaming, glowing, heated, hot-blooded, impassioned, passionate, perfervid, red-hot, scorching, torrid. *See* FEELINGS. **2.** Showing or having enthusiasm : ardent, enthusiastic, keen[1], mad, rabid, warm, zealous. *Informal:* crazy. *Slang:* gung ho, nuts. *See* CONCERN.

fervid *adjective*
1. Fired with intense feeling : ardent, blazing, burning, dithyrambic, fervent, fiery, flaming, glowing, heated, hot-blooded, impassioned, passionate, perfervid, red-hot, scorching, torrid. *See* FEELINGS. **2.** Characterized by intense emotion and activity : burning, fevered, feverish, heated, hectic. *See* EXCITE, FEELINGS, HOT.

fervor *noun*
1. Powerful, intense emotion : ardor, fervency, fire, passion. *See* FEELINGS. **2.** Passionate devotion to or interest in a cause or subject, for example : ardor, enthusiasm, fire, passion, zeal, zealousness. *See* CONCERN, FEELINGS. **3.** Intense warmth : heat, hotness, torridity, torridness. *See* HOT.

Fescennine *adjective*
Offensive to accepted standards of decency : barnyard, bawdy, broad, coarse, dirty, filthy, foul, gross, lewd, nasty, obscene, profane, ribald, scatologic, scatological, scurrilous, smutty, vulgar. *Slang:* raunchy. *See* DECENT.

fess up *verb*
Slang. To recognize, often reluctantly, the reality or truth of : acknowledge, admit, avow, concede, confess, grant, own (up). *Chiefly Regional:* allow. *See* AFFIRM, KNOWLEDGE.

festinate *verb*
To move swiftly : bolt, bucket, bustle, dart, dash, flash, fleet, flit, fly, haste, hasten, hurry, hustle, pelt[2], race, rocket, run, rush, sail, scoot, scour[2], shoot, speed, sprint, tear[1], trot, whirl,

whisk, whiz, wing, zip, zoom. *Informal:* hotfoot, rip. *Slang:* barrel, highball. *Chiefly British:* nip[1]. ***Idioms:*** get a move on, get cracking, go like lightning, go like the wind, hotfoot it, make haste, make time, make tracks, run like the wind, shake a leg, step (*or* jump) on it. *See* MOVE.

festival *noun*
Joyful, exuberant activity : conviviality, festiveness, festivity, fun, gaiety, jollity, merriment, merrymaking, revel (often used in plural), revelry. *See* LAUGHTER.

festive *adjective*
1. Marked by festal celebration : gala, glad, gladsome, happy, joyful, joyous, merry. *See* HAPPY. **2.** Providing joy and pleasure : cheerful, cheery, glad, happy, joyful, joyous, pleasing. *See* HAPPY.

festiveness *noun*
Joyful, exuberant activity : conviviality, festival, festivity, fun, gaiety, jollity, merriment, merrymaking, revel (often used in plural), revelry. *See* LAUGHTER.

festivity *noun*
1. The act of showing joyful satisfaction in an event : celebration, merrymaking, rejoicing, revel (often used in plural), revelry. *See* LAUGHTER. **2.** A large or important social gathering : affair, celebration, fete, function, gala, occasion, party, soiree. *Informal:* do. *Slang:* bash. *See* GROUP, WORK. **3.** Joyful, exuberant activity : conviviality, festival, festiveness, fun, gaiety, jollity, merriment, merrymaking, revel (often used in plural), revelry. *See* LAUGHTER.

fetch *verb*
1. To cause to come along with oneself : bear, bring, carry, convey, take, transport. *See* ACCOMPANIED. **2.** To achieve (a certain price) : bring (in), realize, sell for. *See* GET.

fetching *adjective*
Pleasing to the eye or mind : attractive, bewitching, enchanting, engaging, enticing, fascinating, glamorous, lovely, prepossessing, pretty, sweet, taking, tempting, winning, winsome. *See* LIKE.

fete also **fête** *noun*
A large or important social gathering : affair, celebration, festivity, function, gala, occasion, party, soiree. *Informal:* do. *Slang:* bash. *See* GROUP, WORK.

fetid *adjective*
Having an unpleasant odor : foul, foul-smelling, malodorous, mephitic, noisome, reeky, stinking. *Informal:* smelly. *See* SMELLS.

fetish *noun*
1. A small object worn or kept for its supposed magical power : amulet, charm, juju, periapt, phylactery, talisman. *See* SUPERNATURAL.
2. An irrational preoccupation : fixation, mania, obsession. *Informal:* thing. *See* CONCERN.

fetter *noun*
Something that physically confines the legs or arms : bond, chain (used in plural), handcuff (often used in plural), hobble, iron (used in plural), manacle, restraint, shackle. *Archaic:* gyve. *See* FREE.

fetter *verb* To restrict the activity or free movement of : chain, hamper, hamstring, handcuff, hobble, leash, manacle, shackle, tie, trammel. *Informal:* hog-tie. *See* FREE, HELP.

fettle *noun*
A state of sound readiness : condition, fitness, form, kilter, order, shape, trim. *See* BETTER.

fevered *adjective*
Characterized by intense emotion and activity : burning, fervid, feverish, heated, hectic. *See* EXCITE, FEELINGS, HOT.

feverish *adjective*
1. Being at a higher temperature than is normal or desirable : febrific, febrile, hectic, hot, pyretic. *See* HOT. **2.** Characterized by intense emotion and activity : burning, fervid, fevered, heated, hectic. *See* EXCITE, FEELINGS, HOT.

fey *adjective*
Having, brought about by, or relating to supernatural powers or magic : magic, magical, talismanic, thaumaturgic, thaumaturgical, theurgic, theurgical, witching, wizardly. *See* SUPERNATURAL.

fiancé *noun*
A person to whom one is engaged to be married : betrothed, fiancée. *Informal:* intended. *See* MARRIAGE.

fiancée *noun*
A person to whom one is engaged to be married : betrothed, fiancé. *Informal:* intended. *See* MARRIAGE.

fiasco *noun*
One that fails completely : bust, failure, loser, washout. *Informal:* dud, flop, lemon. *Slang:* bomb. *See* THRIVE.

fib *noun*
An untrue declaration : canard, cock-and-bull story, falsehood, falsity, fiction, inveracity, lie[2], misrepresentation, misstatement, prevarication, story, tale, untruth. *Informal:* fish story, tall tale. *Slang:* whopper. *See* TRUE.

fib *verb* To make untrue declarations : falsify, forswear, lie[2], prevaricate. *Law:* perjure. *See* TRUE.

fibber *noun*
One who tells lies : fabricator, fabulist, falsifier, liar, prevaricator. *Informal:* storyteller. *Law:* perjurer. *See* TRUE.

fiber *noun*
1. A very fine continuous strand : fibril, filament, thread. *See* THING. **2.** A distinctive, complex underlying pattern or structure : contexture, fabric, texture, warp and woof, web. *See* BE. **3.** Moral or ethical strength : character, honesty, integrity, principle. *See* STRONG.

fibril *noun*
A very fine continuous strand : fiber, filament, thread. *See* THING.

fickle *adjective*
Following no predictable pattern : capricious, changeable, erratic, fantastic, fantastical, freakish, inconsistent, inconstant, mercurial, temperamental, ticklish, uncertain, unpredictable, unstable, unsteady, variable, volatile, whimsical. *See* CHANGE, CONTINUE.

fiction *noun*
1. An illusory mental image : daydream, dream, fancy, fantasy, figment, illusion, phantasm, phantasma, reverie, vision. *See* REAL.
2. Any fictitious idea accepted as part of an ideology by an uncritical group; a received idea : creation, fantasy, figment, invention, myth. *See* BELIEF, REAL. **3.** An untrue declaration : canard, cock-and-bull story, falsehood, falsity, fib, inveracity, lie[2], misrepresentation, misstatement, prevarication, story, tale, untruth. *Informal:* fish story, tall tale. *Slang:* whopper. *See* TRUE. **4.** A narrative not based on fact : fable, story. *See* REAL.

fictional *adjective*
Consisting or suggestive of fiction : fanciful, fantastic, fantastical, fictitious, fictive, invented, made-up. *See* REAL.

fictionalize *verb*
To impart a false character to (something) by alteration : doctor, fabricate, fake, falsify, fictionize. *See* TRUE.

fictionize *verb*
To impart a false character to (something) by alteration : doctor, fabricate, fake, falsify, fictionalize. *See* TRUE.

fictitious *adjective*
Consisting or suggestive of fiction : fanciful, fantastic, fantastical, fictional, fictive, invented, made-up. *See* REAL.

fictive *adjective*
Consisting or suggestive of fiction : fanciful, fantastic, fantastical, fictional, fictitious, invented, made-up. *See* REAL.

fiddle *verb*
1. To move one's fingers or hands in a nervous or aimless fashion : fidget, fool, monkey, play, putter, tinker, toy, trifle, twiddle. *See* TOUCH.
2. To handle something idly, ignorantly, or destructively : fool, meddle, mess, tamper, tinker. *Informal:* monkey. *See* HELP, TOUCH.
fiddle away *verb* To pass (time) without working or in avoiding work : dawdle (away), idle (away), kill[1], trifle away, waste, while (away), wile (away). *See* INDUSTRIOUS.

fiddle away *verb* See **fiddle.**

fiddle-faddle *noun*
Something or things that are unimportant : frippery, frivolity, froth, minutia, nonsense, small change, small potatoes, trifle, trivia, triviality. *See* IMPORTANT, SURFACE.

fidelity *noun*
1. Faithfulness or devotion to a person, a cause, obligations, or duties : allegiance, constancy, faithfulness, fealty, loyalty, steadfastness. *See* CONTINUE, OBLIGATION. **2.** Correspondence with fact or truth : accuracy, correctness, exactitude, exactness, truth, veraciousness, veracity, veridicality, verity. *See* TRUE.

fidget *verb*
To move one's fingers or hands in a nervous or aimless fashion : fiddle, fool, monkey, play, putter, tinker, toy, trifle, twiddle. *See* TOUCH.
fidget *noun* A state of nervous restlessness or agitation. Often used in plural : jitter (used in plural), jump (used in plural), shiver[1] (used in plural), tremble (often used in plural). *Informal:* all-overs, shake (used in plural). *Slang:* heebie-jeebies, jim-jams, willies. *See* CALM, FEAR.

fidgety *adjective*
Feeling or exhibiting nervous tension : edgy, jittery, jumpy, nervous, restive, restless, skittish, tense, twitchy. *Slang:* uptight. ***Idioms:*** a bundle of nerves, all wound up, on edge. *See* TIGHTEN.

field *noun*
A sphere of activity, experience, study, or interest : area, arena, bailiwick, circle, department, domain, orbit, province, realm, scene, subject, terrain, territory, world. *Slang:* bag. *See* TERRITORY.

fiend *noun*
1. A perversely bad, cruel, or wicked person : archfiend, beast, devil, ghoul, monster, ogre, tiger, vampire. *See* KIND. **2.** *Informal.* A per-

son who is ardently devoted to a particular subject or activity : bug, devotee, enthusiast, fanatic, maniac, zealot. *Informal:* buff[2], fan[2]. *Slang:* freak, nut. *See* CONCERN.

fiendish *adjective*
Perversely bad, cruel, or wicked : devilish, diabolic, diabolical, ghoulish, hellish, infernal, ogreish, satanic, satanical. *See* KIND.

fierce *adjective*
1. Showing or suggesting a disposition to be violently destructive without scruple or restraint : barbarous, bestial, cruel, fell[2], feral, ferocious, inhuman, savage, truculent, vicious, wolfish. *See* KIND. **2.** So intense as to cause extreme suffering : cruel, ferocious, savage, vicious. *See* HELP, KIND. **3.** Intensely violent in sustained velocity : furious, heavy, high, strong. *See* STRONG. **4.** Extreme in degree, strength, or effect : desperate, furious, intense, terrible, vehement, violent. *See* BIG, STRONG. **5.** Intensely sustained, especially in activity : concentrated, heavy, heightened, intense, intensive. *See* STRONG.

fiercely *adverb*
In a violent, strenuous way : frantically, frenziedly, furiously, hard, strenuously. *See* STRONG.

fierceness *noun*
Exceptionally great concentration, power, or force, especially in activity : depth (often used in plural), ferociousness, ferocity, fury, intensity, pitch, severity, vehemence, vehemency, violence. *See* BIG, STRONG.

fiery *adjective*
1. On fire : ablaze, afire, aflame, alight[2], burning, conflagrant, flaming. ***Idioms:*** in a blaze, in flames. *See* HOT. **2.** Marked by much heat : ardent, baking, blistering, boiling, broiling, burning, heated, hot, red-hot, roasting, scalding, scorching, searing, sizzling, sultry, sweltering, torrid. *See* HOT. **3.** Full of or characterized by a lively, emphatic, eager quality : high-spirited, mettlesome, peppery, spirited, vibrant. *Informal:* snappy. *See* ACTION, FEELINGS. **4.** Fired with intense feeling : ardent, blazing, burning, dithyrambic, fervent, fervid, flaming, glowing, heated, hot-blooded, impassioned, passionate, perfervid, red-hot, scorching, torrid. *See* FEELINGS.

fifty-fifty *adjective*
Neither favorable or unfavorable : balanced, even[1]. *See* FAIR.

fight *verb*
1. To engage in a quarrel : argue, bicker, contend, dispute, quarrel, quibble, spat, squabble, tiff, wrangle. *Informal:* hassle, tangle. ***Idioms:*** cross swords, have it out, have words, lock horns. *See* CONFLICT. **2.** To strive in opposition : battle, combat, contend, duel, struggle, tilt, war, wrestle. *See* CONFLICT.

fight *noun* **1.** A physical conflict involving two or more : fistfight, fisticuffs, scrap[2], scuffle, tussle. *Slang:* rumble. *See* CONFLICT. **2.** A discussion, often heated, in which a difference of opinion is expressed : altercation, argument, bicker, clash, contention, controversy, debate, difficulty, disagreement, dispute, polemic, quarrel, run-in, spat, squabble, tiff, word (used in plural), wrangle. *Informal:* hassle, rhubarb, tangle. *See* CONFLICT. **3.** The power or will to fight : bellicoseness, bellicosity, belligerence, belligerency, combativeness, contentiousness, pugnaciousness, pugnacity, truculence, truculency. *See* CONFLICT.

fighter *noun*
One who engages in a combat or struggle : belligerent, combatant, soldier, warrior. *See* CONFLICT.

figment *noun*
1. An illusory mental image : daydream, dream, fancy, fantasy, fiction, illusion, phantasm, phantasma, reverie, vision. *See* REAL. **2.** Any fictitious idea accepted as part of an ideology by an uncritical group; a received idea : creation, fantasy, fiction, invention, myth. *See* BELIEF, REAL.

figure *noun*
1. Arithmetic calculations. Used in plural : arithmetic, computation, number (used in plural). *See* COUNT. **2.** The external outline of a thing : cast, configuration, form, pattern, shape. *See* SURFACE. **3.** An element or a component in a decorative composition : design, device, motif, motive, pattern. *See* PART.

figure *verb* **1.** To ascertain by mathematics : calculate, cast, cipher, compute, reckon. *See* REASON. **2.** *Informal.* To have an opinion : believe, consider, deem, hold, opine, think. *Informal:* judge. ***Idiom:*** be of the opinion. *See* OPINION.

figure on *verb Informal.* To look forward to confidently : anticipate, await, bargain for (*or* on), count on, depend on (*or* upon), expect, look for, wait (for). *See* SURPRISE.

figure out *verb* **1.** *Informal.* To find a solution for : clear up, decipher, explain, resolve, solve, unravel. *Informal:* dope out. ***Idiom:*** get to the bottom of. *See* ASK, REASON. **2.** *Informal.* To arrive at an answer to (a mathematical problem) : solve, work, work out. *See* REASON.

figure on *verb* See **figure.**

figure out *verb* See **figure.**

figuring *noun*
The act, process, or result of calculating : calculation, computation, reckoning. *See* REASON.

filament *noun*
A very fine continuous strand : fiber, fibril, thread. *See* THING.

filch *verb*
To take (another's property) without permission : pilfer, purloin, snatch, steal, thieve. *Informal:* lift, swipe. *Slang:* cop, heist, hook, nip[1], pinch, rip off, snitch. ***Idiom:*** make (*or* walk) off with. *See* CRIMES, GIVE.

file *noun*
A group of people or things arranged in a row : column, line, queue, rank[1], row[1], string, tier. *See* GROUP.

fill *verb*
1. To make or become full; put as much into as can be held : charge, freight, heap, load, pack, pile. *See* FULL. **2.** To plug up something, as a hole, space, or container : block, choke, clog, close, congest, cork, plug, stop. *See* FULL. **3.** To supply fully or completely : answer, fulfill, meet[1], satisfy. *See* DO.
fill in (or **out**) *verb* **1.** To supply what is lacking : complement, complete, round (off *or* out), supplement. *See* AGREE, PART. **2.** To act as a substitute : stand in, substitute, supply. *Informal:* pinch-hit, sub. *See* SUBSTITUTE.
fill *noun* Something used to fill a hole, space, or container : choke, cork, plug, stop, stopper. *See* FULL.

fillet *noun*
A long narrow piece, as of material : band[1], bandeau, strip[2], stripe. *See* MATTER.

fill-in *noun*
Informal. One that takes the place of another : alternate, replacement, stand-in, substitute, surrogate. *Informal:* pinch hitter, sub. *See* SUBSTITUTE.

fill in or **out** *verb* See **fill.**

fillip *noun*
Something that causes and encourages a given response : encouragement, impetus, impulse, incentive, inducement, motivation, prod, push, spur, stimulant, stimulation, stimulator, stimulus. *See* CAUSE.

filmy *adjective*
1. So light and insubstantial as to resemble air or a thin film : aerial, aery, airy, diaphanous, ethereal, gauzy, gossamer, gossamery, sheer[2], transparent, vaporous, vapory. *See* THICK.
2. Covered by or as if by a thin coating or film : blurry, cloudy, dim, hazy, misty. *See* CLEAR.

filth *noun*
1. Foul or dirty matter : dirt, grime, muck. *Slang:* crud. *See* CLEAN. **2.** The condition or state of being dirty : dirtiness, filthiness, foulness, griminess, grubbiness, smuttiness, squalor, uncleanliness, uncleanness. *See* CLEAN.
3. Something that is offensive to accepted standards of decency : bawdry, dirt, obscenity, profanity, ribaldry, scatology, smut, vulgarity. *Slang:* raunch. *See* DECENT.

filthiness *noun*
1. The condition or state of being dirty : dirtiness, filth, foulness, griminess, grubbiness, smuttiness, squalor, uncleanliness, uncleanness. *See* CLEAN. **2.** The quality or state of being obscene : bawdiness, coarseness, dirtiness, foulness, grossness, lewdness, obscenity, profaneness, profanity, scurrility, scurrilousness, smuttiness, vulgarity, vulgarness. *Slang:* raunch, raunchiness. *See* DECENT.

filthy *adjective*
1. Covered or stained with or as if with dirt or other impurities : black, dirty, grimy, grubby, smutty, soiled, unclean, uncleanly. *See* CLEAN.
2. Heavily soiled; very dirty or unclean : foul, nasty, squalid, vile. *See* CLEAN. **3.** Offensive to accepted standards of decency : barnyard, bawdy, broad, coarse, dirty, Fescennine, foul, gross, lewd, nasty, obscene, profane, ribald, scatologic, scatological, scurrilous, smutty, vulgar. *Slang:* raunchy. *See* DECENT. **4.** So objectionable as to elicit despisal or deserve condemnation : abhorrent, abominable, antipathetic, contemptible, despicable, despisable, detestable, disgusting, foul, infamous, loathsome, lousy, low, mean[2], nasty, nefarious, obnoxious, odious, repugnant, rotten, shabby, vile, wretched. *See* GOOD.

finagle *verb*
1. *Informal.* To make, achieve, or get through contrivance or guile : engineer, finesse, worm. *Informal:* wangle. *See* GET, MAKE. **2.** *Informal.* To take clever or cunning steps to achieve one's goals : jockey, maneuver. ***Idiom:*** pull strings (*or* wires). *See* CONTROL, MEANS.

final *adjective*
1. Coming after all others : closing, concluding, last[1], terminal. *See* START. **2.** Of or relating to a terminative condition, stage, or point : last[1], latter, terminal, ultimate. *See* START.
3. Serving the function of deciding or settling

with finality : authoritative, conclusive, decisive, definitive, determinative. *See* DECIDE.

finale *noun*
The last part : close, conclusion, end, ending, finish, last[1], termination, wind-up, wrap-up. *See* START.

finally *adverb*
1. In conclusion : conclusively, last[1], lastly. *See* START. **2.** After a considerable length of time, usually after a delay : ultimately. ***Idioms:*** at last, at long last, in the end. *See* START, TIME.

finance *noun*
The monetary resources of a government, organization, or individual. Used in plural : capital, fund (used in plural), money (often used in plural). *See* MONEY.
finance *verb* To supply capital to or for : back, capitalize, fund, grubstake, stake, subsidize. *Informal:* bankroll. ***Idiom:*** put up money for. *See* HELP, MONEY.

financial *adjective*
Of or relating to finances or those who deal in finances : fiscal, monetary, pecuniary. *See* MONEY.

financier *noun*
One who is occupied with or expert in large-scale financial affairs : capitalist. *Informal:* moneyman. *See* MONEY.

financing *noun*
Money or property used to produce more wealth : backing, capital, capitalization, funding, grubstake, stake, subsidization. *See* HELP, MONEY.

find *verb*
1. To find or meet by chance : bump into, chance on (*or* upon), come across, come on (*or* upon), happen on (*or* upon), light on (*or* upon), run across, run into, stumble on (*or* upon), tumble on. *Archaic:* alight on (*or* upon). ***Idiom:*** meet up with. *See* MEET. **2.** To look for and discover : locate, pinpoint, spot. *See* GET. **3.** To obtain knowledge or awareness of something not known before, as through observation or study. Also used with *out* : ascertain, determine, discover, hear, learn. *See* TEACH.
find *noun* Something that has been discovered : ascertainment, discovery, finding, strike. *See* TEACH.

finding *noun*
Something that has been discovered : ascertainment, discovery, find, strike. *See* TEACH.

fine[1] *adjective*
1. Of fine quality : choice, first-class, prime, select, superior. *See* BETTER. **2.** Exceptionally good of its kind : ace, banner, blue-ribbon, brag, capital, champion, excellent, first-class, first-rate, prime, quality, splendid, superb, superior, terrific, tiptop, top. *Informal:* A-one, bully, dandy, great, swell, topflight, topnotch. *Slang:* boss. *Chiefly British:* tophole. *See* GOOD. **3.** Free from clouds or mist, for example : clear, cloudless, fair, sunny, unclouded. *See* CLEAR. **4.** Consisting of small particles : dusty, powdery, pulverous, pulverulent. *See* BIG. **5.** So slight as to be difficult to notice or appreciate : delicate, finespun, nice, refined, subtle. *See* BIG. **6.** Able to make or detect effects of great subtlety or precision : delicate, nice, subtle. *See* PRECISE. **7.** Appealing to refined taste : choice, dainty, delicate, elegant, exquisite. *See* GOOD, INGESTION.

fine[2] *noun*
A sum of money levied as punishment for an offense : amercement, mulct, penalty. *See* REWARD.
fine *verb* To impose a fine on : amerce, mulct, penalize. *See* REWARD.

fineness *noun*
The quality of being exceptionally good of its kind : excellence, superbness, superiority. *See* GOOD.

fine print *noun*
A small, often specialized element of a whole : detail, item, particular, technicality. *See* GROUP.

finery *noun*
Showy and elaborate clothing or apparel : array, attire, frippery, regalia. *See* PUT ON.

finespun *adjective*
So slight as to be difficult to notice or appreciate : delicate, fine[1], nice, refined, subtle. *See* BIG.

finesse *verb*
1. To make, achieve, or get through contrivance or guile : engineer, worm. *Informal:* finagle, wangle. *See* GET, MAKE. **2.** To outmaneuver (an opponent), especially with the aid of some extra resource : trump. *Informal:* one-up. *See* WIN.

finest *noun*
A member of a law-enforcement agency : bluecoat, officer, patrolman, patrolwoman, peace officer, police, policeman, police officer, policewoman. *Informal:* cop, law. *Slang:* bull[1], copper, flatfoot, fuzz, gendarme, heat, man (often uppercase). *Chiefly British:* bobby, constable, peeler. *See* LAW.

finger *verb*
1. To bring the hands or fingers, for example,

into contact with so as to give or receive a physical sensation : feel, handle, palpate, touch. *See* TOUCH. **2.** *Slang.* To establish the identification of : identify, pinpoint, place, recognize. ***Idiom:*** put one's finger on. *See* KNOWLEDGE.

finical *adjective*
Very difficult to please : choosy, dainty, exacting, fastidious, finicky, fussy, meticulous, nice, particular, persnickety, squeamish. *Informal:* picky. *See* ACCEPT.

finicky *adjective*
Very difficult to please : choosy, dainty, exacting, fastidious, finical, fussy, meticulous, nice, particular, persnickety, squeamish. *Informal:* picky. *See* ACCEPT.

finish *verb*
1. To complete a race or competition in a specified position : come in, place, run. *See* BE. **2.** To bring or come to a natural or proper end : close, complete, conclude, consummate, end, terminate, wind up, wrap up. *See* START. **3.** To use all of : consume, drain, draw down, eat up, exhaust, expend, play out, run through, spend, use up. *Informal:* polish off. *See* INCREASE. **4.** To cause the death of. Also used with *off* : carry off, cut down, cut off, destroy, dispatch, kill[1], slay. *Slang:* waste, zap. ***Idioms:*** put an end to, put to sleep. *See* HELP. **5.** To take the life of (a person or persons) unlawfully. Also used with *off* : destroy, kill[1], liquidate, murder, slay. *Informal:* put away. *Slang:* bump off, do in, knock off, off, rub out, waste, wipe out, zap. *See* HELP. **6.** To cause the complete ruin or wreckage of : bankrupt, break down, cross up, demolish, destroy, ruin, shatter, sink, smash, spoil, torpedo, undo, wash up, wrack[2], wreck. *Slang:* total. ***Idiom:*** put the kibosh on. *See* HELP.

finish *noun* **1.** A concluding or terminating : cease, cessation, close, closing, closure, completion, conclusion, consummation, end, ending, end of the line, period, stop, stopping point, termination, terminus, wind-up, wrap-up. *See* CONTINUE. **2.** The last part : close, conclusion, end, ending, finale, last[1], termination, wind-up, wrap-up. *See* START.

finished *adjective*
1. No longer effective, capable, or valuable : done, done for, through, washed-up. *Informal:* kaput. ***Idioms:*** at the end of the line (*or* road), over the hill, past one's prime. *See* ABILITY, START. **2.** Having no further relationship : done, through. *See* START. **3.** Proficient as a result of practice and study : accomplished, practiced. *See* ABILITY.

fink *noun*
Slang. One who gives incriminating information about others : informant, informer, tattler, tattletale. *Informal:* rat, tipster. *Slang:* snitch, snitcher, squealer, stoolie, stool pigeon. *See* KNOWLEDGE, LAW.

fink *verb Slang.* To give incriminating information about others, especially to the authorities : inform, talk, tattle, tip[3] (off). *Slang:* rat, sing, snitch, squeal, stool. ***Idiom:*** blow the whistle. *See* KNOWLEDGE, LAW.

fink out *verb Slang.* To abandon a former position or commitment : back down (*or* out), renege, retreat. *Slang:* cop out. *See* RESIST.

fink out *verb* See **fink.**

fire *noun*
1. The visible signs of combustion : blaze[1], conflagration, flame, flare-up. *See* HOT. **2.** Powerful, intense emotion : ardor, fervency, fervor, passion. *See* FEELINGS. **3.** Passionate devotion to or interest in a cause or subject, for example : ardor, enthusiasm, fervor, passion, zeal, zealousness. *See* CONCERN, FEELINGS. **4.** Exceptional brightness and clarity, as of a cut and polished stone : brilliance, brilliancy, luminosity, radiance. *See* LIGHT. **5.** Liveliness and vivacity of imagination : brilliance, brilliancy, genius, inspiration. *See* GOOD.

fire *verb* **1.** To cause to burn or undergo combustion : enkindle, ignite, kindle, light[1]. *Slang:* torch. ***Idioms:*** set afire (*or* on fire), set fire to. *See* HOT, START. **2.** To arouse the emotions of; make ardent : animate, enkindle, impassion, inspire, kindle, stir[1]. *See* EXCITE. **3.** To discharge a gun or firearm : shoot. ***Idiom:*** take a shot at. *See* ACTION. **4.** To release or cause to release energy suddenly and violently, especially with a loud noise : blast, blow[1] (up), burst, detonate, explode, fulminate, go off, touch off. *See* EXPLOSION. **5.** To launch with great force : hurtle, loose, project, propel, shoot. ***Idiom:*** let fly. *See* MOVE. **6.** *Informal.* To send through the air with a motion of the hand or arm : cast, dart, dash, fling, heave, hurl, hurtle, launch, pitch, shoot, shy[2], sling, throw, toss. *See* MOVE. **7.** *Informal.* To end the employment or service of : cashier, discharge, dismiss, drop, release, terminate. *Informal:* ax, pink-slip. *Slang:* boot[1], bounce, can, sack[1]. ***Idioms:*** give someone his or her walking papers, give someone the ax, give someone the gate, give someone the pink slip, let go, show someone the door. *See* KEEP.

fire-and-brimstone *adjective*
Portending future disaster : apocalyptic,

apocalyptical, baneful, dire, direful, fateful, grave[2], hellfire, ominous, portentous, unlucky. *See* LUCK, WARN.

fired up *adjective*
Feeling a very strong emotion : atingle, excited, thrilled, worked up. *Informal:* psyched. *Slang:* stoked, turned-on. *See* EXCITE.

firm[1] *adjective*
1. Unyielding to pressure or force : hard, incompressible, solid. *See* RESIST, STRONG. **2.** Firmly settled or positioned : fast, secure, stable, steady, strong, sure. *See* CONTINUE. **3.** Not easily moved or shaken : secure, solid, sound[2], stable, strong, sturdy, substantial, sure, unshakable. *See* CONTINUE, STRONG. **4.** Indicating or possessing determination, resolution, or persistence : constant, determined, resolute, steadfast, steady, stiff, tough, unbending, uncompromising, unflinching, unwavering, unyielding. *See* PURPOSE. **5.** Not hesitating or wavering : decided, decisive, determined, resolute. *See* DECIDE. **6.** Adhering firmly and devotedly, as to a person, a cause, or a duty : allegiant, constant, faithful, fast, liege, loyal, staunch, steadfast, true. *See* CONTINUE, TRUST. **7.** In a definite and final form; not likely to change : certain, fixed, flat, set[1]. *See* CHANGE. **8.** Persistently holding to something : clinging, fast, secure, tenacious, tight. *See* FREE, TIGHTEN.

firm[2] *noun*
A commercial organization : business, company, concern, corporation, enterprise, establishment, house. *Informal:* outfit. *See* GROUP.

firmament *noun*
The celestial regions as seen from the earth : air, heaven (often used in plural), sky. *Archaic:* welkin. *See* HIGH.

firmness *noun*
1. Reliability in withstanding pressure, force, or stress : fastness, hardness, security, soundness, stability, stableness, steadiness, strength, sturdiness, sureness. *See* BETTER, CHANGE, CONTINUE. **2.** Unwavering firmness of character, action, or will : decidedness, decision, decisiveness, determination, purpose, purposefulness, resoluteness, resolution, resolve, toughness, will, willpower. *See* CERTAIN, STRONG. **3.** The condition of being free from defects or flaws : durability, integrity, solidity, soundness, stability, strength, wholeness. *See* BETTER.

first *adjective*
1. Preceding all others in time : earliest, initial, maiden, original, pioneer, primary, prime, primordial. *See* START. **2.** At or near the start of a period, development, or series : beginning, early, initial. *See* START. **3.** Most important, influential, or significant : capital, cardinal, chief, foremost, key, leading, main, major, number one, paramount, premier, primary, prime, principal, top. *See* IMPORTANT.

first-class *adjective*
1. Exceptionally good of its kind : ace, banner, blue-ribbon, brag, capital, champion, excellent, fine[1], first-rate, prime, quality, splendid, superb, superior, terrific, tiptop, top. *Informal:* A-one, bully, dandy, great, swell, topflight, top-notch. *Slang:* boss. *Chiefly British:* tophole. *See* GOOD. **2.** Of fine quality : choice, fine[1], prime, select, superior. *See* BETTER.

firsthand *adjective*
Marked by the absence of any intervention : direct, immediate, primary. *See* CLEAR, NEAR.

first-rate *adjective*
Exceptionally good of its kind : ace, banner, blue-ribbon, brag, capital, champion, excellent, fine[1], first-class, prime, quality, splendid, superb, superior, terrific, tiptop, top. *Informal:* A-one, bully, dandy, great, swell, topflight, top-notch. *Slang:* boss. *Chiefly British:* tophole. *See* GOOD.

fiscal *adjective*
Of or relating to finances or those who deal in finances : financial, monetary, pecuniary. *See* MONEY.

fish *verb*
To try to obtain something, usually by subtleness and cunning : angle[1], hint. *See* ASK.

fish story *noun*
Informal. An untrue declaration : canard, cock-and-bull story, falsehood, falsity, fib, fiction, inveracity, lie[2], misrepresentation, misstatement, prevarication, story, tale, untruth. *Informal:* tall tale. *Slang:* whopper. *See* TRUE.

fishwife *noun*
A person, traditionally a woman, who persistently nags or criticizes : fury, harpy, scold, shrew, termagant, virago, vixen. *Informal:* battle-ax. *See* PRAISE.

fishy *adjective*
Informal. Of dubious character : doubtful, equivocal, questionable, shady, suspect, suspicious, uncertain. *See* HONEST.

fissure *noun*
1. A usually narrow partial opening caused by splitting and rupture : break, chink, cleavage, cleft, crack, crevice, rift, split. *See* OPEN. **2.** An interruption in friendly relations : alienation, breach, break, disaffection, estrangement,

rent[2], rift, rupture, schism, split. *See* ASSEMBLE, HELP.

fissure *verb* To undergo partial breaking : crack, fracture, rupture, split. *See* HELP.

fistfight *noun*
A physical conflict involving two or more : fight, fisticuffs, scrap[2], scuffle, tussle. *Slang:* rumble. *See* CONFLICT.

fisticuffs *noun*
A physical conflict involving two or more : fight, fistfight, scrap[2], scuffle, tussle. *Slang:* rumble. *See* CONFLICT.

fit[1] *verb*
1. To cause to be ready, as for use, consumption, or a special purpose : fix, make, prepare, prime, ready. *See* PREPARED. **2.** To supply what is needed for some activity or purpose : accouter, appoint, equip, fit out (*or* up), furnish, gear, outfit, rig, turn out. *See* GIVE. **3.** To have a proper or suitable place : belong, go. *See* ORDER. **4.** To be compatible or in correspondence : accord, agree, check, chime, comport with, conform, consist, correspond, harmonize, match, square, tally. *Informal:* jibe[1]. *Archaic:* quadrate. *See* AGREE. **5.** To make or become suitable to a particular situation or use : acclimate, acclimatize, accommodate, adapt, adjust, conform, fashion, reconcile, square, suit, tailor. *See* CHANGE. **6.** To conform to another, especially in size and shape : dovetail. *See* AGREE. **7.** To be in keeping with : become, befit, conform, correspond, go with, match, suit. *See* AGREE.

fit out (or **up**) *verb* To supply what is needed for some activity or purpose : accouter, appoint, equip, fit[1], furnish, gear, outfit, rig, turn out. *See* GIVE.

fit *adjective* **1.** Suitable for a particular person, condition, occasion, or place : appropriate, apt, becoming, befitting, correct, felicitous, fitting, happy, meet[2], proper, right, tailor-made. *See* RIGHT. **2.** Suited to one's end or purpose : appropriate, befitting, convenient, expedient, good, meet[2], proper, suitable, tailor-made, useful. *See* AGREE, GOOD. **3.** Satisfying certain requirements, as for selection : eligible, fitted, qualified, suitable, worthy. *See* ABILITY. **4.** Consistent with prevailing or accepted standards or circumstances : appropriate, deserved, due, fitting, just, merited, proper, right, rightful, suitable. *See* RIGHT. **5.** Having good health : hale, healthful, healthy, hearty, right, sound[2], well[2], whole, wholesome. ***Idioms:*** fit as a fiddle, hale and hearty, in fine fettle. *See* HEALTH.

fit[2] *noun*
1. A sudden and often acute manifestation of a disease : access, attack, seizure. *Informal:* spell[3]. *See* HEALTH. **2.** A sudden violent expression, as of emotion : access, blowup, burst, eruption, explosion, flare-up, gust, outbreak, outburst. *See* EXPLOSION. **3.** An angry outburst : huff, passion, tantrum, temper. *Informal:* conniption, conniption fit. *See* FEELINGS.

fitful *adjective*
Happening or appearing now and then : intermittent, occasional, periodic, periodical, sporadic. *Informal:* on-again, off-again. *See* CONTINUE.

fitness *noun*
1. The quality or state of being eligible : eligibility, qualification, suitability, suitableness, worthiness. *See* ABILITY. **2.** A state of sound readiness : condition, fettle, form, kilter, order, shape, trim. *See* BETTER.

fit out or **up** *verb* See **fit.**

fitted *adjective*
Satisfying certain requirements, as for selection : eligible, fit[1], qualified, suitable, worthy. *See* ABILITY.

fitting *adjective*
1. Suitable for a particular person, condition, occasion, or place : appropriate, apt, becoming, befitting, correct, felicitous, fit[1], happy, meet[2], proper, right, tailor-made. *See* RIGHT. **2.** Consistent with prevailing or accepted standards or circumstances : appropriate, deserved, due, fit[1], just, merited, proper, right, rightful, suitable. *See* RIGHT.

fitting *noun Chiefly British.* A piece of equipment for comfort or convenience. Used in plural : appointment (used in plural), furnishing, movable. *See* MACHINE.

fix *verb*
1. To place securely in a position or condition : ensconce, establish, install, seat, settle. *See* PUT IN. **2.** To make secure : anchor, catch, fasten, moor, secure. ***Idiom:*** make fast. *See* MOVE. **3.** To join one thing to another : affix, attach, clip[2], connect, couple, fasten, moor, secure. *See* ASSEMBLE. **4.** To become or cause to become stuck or lodged : catch, lodge, stick. *See* MOVE. **5.** To produce a deep impression of : engrave, etch, grave[3], impress, imprint, inscribe, stamp. *See* MARKS. **6.** To implant so deeply as to make change nearly impossible : embed, entrench, fasten, infix, ingrain, lodge, root[1]. *See* MOVE. **7.** To set forth expressly and authoritatively : decree, dictate, impose, lay

down, ordain, prescribe. ***Idioms:*** call the shots (*or* tune), lay it on the line. *See* OVER. **8.** To put into correct or conclusive form : arrange, conclude, dispose of, settle. *See* DO. **9.** To bring about or come to an agreement concerning : arrange, conclude, negotiate, set[1], settle. *See* AGREE. **10.** To ascribe (a misdeed or an error, for example) to : affix, assign, blame, fasten, impute, pin on, place. *See* GIVE. **11.** To restore to proper condition or functioning : doctor, fix up, mend, overhaul, patch, repair[1], revamp, right. ***Idiom:*** set right. *See* HELP. **12.** To alter for proper functioning : adjust, regulate, set[1], tune (up). *Music:* attune. *See* CHANGE, HELP. **13.** To cause to be ready, as for use, consumption, or a special purpose : fit[1], make, prepare, prime, ready. *See* PREPARED. **14.** To render incapable of reproducing sexually : alter, castrate, geld, neuter, spay, sterilize, unsex. *See* REPRODUCTION, RICH. **15.** *Informal.* To exact revenge for or from : avenge, pay back, pay off, redress, repay, requite, vindicate. *Archaic:* wreak. ***Idioms:*** even the score, get back at, get even with, pay back in kind (*or* in one's own coin), settle (*or* square) accounts, take an eye for an eye. *See* FORGIVENESS. **16.** To prearrange the outcome of (a contest) unlawfully : tamper. ***Idiom:*** stack the deck. *See* CRIMES.

fix up *verb* **1.** To improve in appearance, especially by refurbishing : smarten (up), spruce (up). *See* BETTER. **2.** To restore to proper condition or functioning : doctor, fix, mend, overhaul, patch, repair[1], revamp, right. ***Idiom:*** set right. *See* HELP.

fix *noun* **1.** Money, property, or a favor given, offered, or promised to a person or accepted by a person in a position of trust as an inducement to dishonest behavior : bribe, graft, payola. *Informal:* payoff. *Slang:* boodle. *See* CRIMES, MONEY, PERSUASION. **2.** A difficult, often embarrassing situation or condition : box[1], corner, deep water, difficulty, dilemma, Dutch, hole, hot spot, hot water, jam, plight[1], predicament, quagmire, scrape, soup, trouble. *Informal:* bind, pickle, spot. *See* EASY.

fixation *noun*
An irrational preoccupation : fetish, mania, obsession. *Informal:* thing. *See* CONCERN.

fixed *adjective*
1. Firmly in position : immobile, immovable, stationary, steadfast, steady, unmovable, unmoving. *See* MOVE. **2.** Having distinct limits : definite, determinate, limited. *See* LIMITED. **3.** In a definite and final form; not likely to change : certain, firm[1], flat, set[1]. *See* CHANGE. **4.** On an unwavering course of action : bent, decided, determined, intent, resolute, set[1]. *See* DECIDE.

fix up *verb* See **fix.**

fizz *verb*
1. To make a sharp sibilantsound : fizzle, hiss, sibilate, sizzle, swish, whiz, whoosh. *See* SOUNDS. **2.** To form or cause to form foam : bubble, cream, effervesce, foam, froth, lather, spume, suds, yeast. *See* SOLID.

fizzle *verb*
1. To make a sharp sibilant sound : fizz, hiss, sibilate, sizzle, swish, whiz, whoosh. *See* SOUNDS. **2.** *Informal.* To lose strength or power. Also used with *out* : decline, degenerate, deteriorate, fade, fail, flag[2], languish, sink, wane, waste (away), weaken. ***Idioms:*** go downhill, hit the skids. *See* STRONG, INCREASE.

flabbergast *verb*
To overwhelm with surprise, wonder, or bewilderment : boggle, bowl over, dumbfound, floor, stagger. *See* EXCITE, SURPRISE.

flabby *adjective*
Lacking in stiffness or firmness : flaccid, floppy, limp. *See* FLEXIBLE.

flaccid *adjective*
Lacking in stiffness or firmness : flabby, floppy, limp. *See* FLEXIBLE.

flag[1] *noun*
Fabric used especially as a symbol : banderole, banner, banneret, color (used in plural), ensign, jack, oriflamme, pennant, pennon, standard, streamer. *See* SUBSTITUTE.

flag *verb* To communicate by means of such devices as lights or signs : semaphore, signal. *See* EXPRESS, WORDS.

flag[2] *verb*
1. To become limp, as from loss of freshness : droop, sag, wilt. *See* BETTER. **2.** To lose strength or power : decline, degenerate, deteriorate, fade, fail, languish, sink, wane, waste (away), weaken. *Informal:* fizzle (out). ***Idioms:*** go downhill, hit the skids. *See* STRONG, INCREASE.

flagitious *adjective*
Utterly reprehensible in nature or behavior : corrupt, degenerate, depraved, miscreant, perverse, rotten, unhealthy, villainous. *See* CLEAN, GOOD.

flagitiousness *noun*
Degrading, immoral acts or habits : bestiality, corruption, depravity, immorality, perversion, turpitude, vice, villainousness, villainy, wickedness. *See* CLEAN.

flagrance *noun*
The quality or state of being flagrant : atrociousness, atrocity, egregiousness, enormity, flagrancy, flagrantness, glaringness, grossness, outrageousness, rankness. *See* GOOD.

flagrancy *noun*
The quality or state of being flagrant : atrociousness, atrocity, egregiousness, enormity, flagrance, flagrantness, glaringness, grossness, outrageousness, rankness. *See* GOOD.

flagrant *adjective*
Conspicuously bad or offensive : arrant, capital, egregious, glaring, gross, rank[2]. *See* GOOD.

flagrantness *noun*
The quality or state of being flagrant : atrociousness, atrocity, egregiousness, enormity, flagrance, flagrancy, glaringness, grossness, outrageousness, rankness. *See* GOOD.

flail *verb*
1. To swing about or strike at wildly : thrash, thresh, toss. ***Idiom:*** toss and turn. *See* ATTACK, MOVE, STRIKE. **2.** To beat (plants) with a machine or by hand to separate the grain from the straw : thrash, thresh. *See* ATTACK, STRIKE.

flair *noun*
An innate capability : aptitude, aptness, bent, faculty, genius, gift, head, instinct, knack, talent, turn. *See* ABILITY, APPROACH.

flamboyant *adjective*
1. Elaborately and heavily ornamented : baroque, florid, ornate, rococo. *See* PLAIN.
2. Marked by outward, often extravagant display : ostentatious, pretentious, showy, splashy, splurgy. *See* PLAIN.

flame *noun*
The visible signs of combustion : blaze[1], conflagration, fire, flare-up. *See* HOT.
flame *verb* To undergo combustion : blaze[1], burn, combust, flare. *See* HOT.

flaming *adjective*
1. On fire : ablaze, afire, aflame, alight[2], burning, conflagrant, fiery. ***Idioms:*** in a blaze, in flames. *See* HOT. **2.** Fired with intense feeling : ardent, blazing, burning, dithyrambic, fervent, fervid, fiery, glowing, heated, hot-blooded, impassioned, passionate, perfervid, red-hot, scorching, torrid. *See* FEELINGS.

flank *noun*
One of two or more contrasted parts or places identified by its location with respect to a center : hand, side. *See* PLACE.

flap *noun*
Informal. An interruption of regular procedure or of public peace : agitation, commotion, disorder, disturbance, helter-skelter, stir[1], tumult, turbulence, turmoil, uproar. *Informal:* to-do. *See* CALM, ORDER.
flap *verb* **1.** To move (one's arms or wings, for example) up and down : beat, flitter, flop, flutter, waggle, wave. *See* REPETITION. **2.** To move or cause to move about while being fixed at one edge : flutter, fly, wave. *See* REPETITION. **3.** To move through the air with or as if with wings : flit, flitter, flutter, fly, sail, wing. *See* MOVE.

flare *verb*
1. To undergo combustion : blaze[1], burn, combust, flame. *See* HOT. **2.** To become manifest suddenly and in full force. Also used with *up* : break out, burst (forth *or* out), erupt, explode. *See* EXPLOSION, START. **3.** To react explosively or suddenly. Also used with *up* : fly. *See* EXPLOSION.
flare up *verb* To be or become angry : anger, blow up, boil over, bristle, burn, explode, foam, fume, rage, seethe. *Informal:* steam. ***Idioms:*** blow a fuse, blow a gasket, blow one's stack (*or* top), breathe fire, fly off the handle, get hot under the collar, hit the ceiling (*or* roof), lose one's temper, see red. *See* FEELINGS.

flare-up *noun*
1. The visible signs of combustion : blaze[1], conflagration, fire, flame. *See* HOT. **2.** A sudden violent expression, as of emotion : access, blowup, burst, eruption, explosion, fit[2], gust, outbreak, outburst. *See* EXPLOSION.

flare up *verb* See **flare.**

flash *verb*
1. To emit light suddenly in rays or sparks : coruscate, glance, gleam, glimmer, glint, glisten, glister, glitter, scintillate, shimmer, spangle, sparkle, twinkle, wink. *See* LIGHT. **2.** To shine with intermittent gleams : blink, flicker, glimmer, twinkle, wink. *See* CONTINUE, LIGHT.
3. To move swiftly : bolt, bucket, bustle, dart, dash, festinate, fleet, flit, fly, haste, hasten, hurry, hustle, pelt[2], race, rocket, run, rush, sail, scoot, scour[2], shoot, speed, sprint, tear[1], trot, whirl, whisk, whiz, wing, zip, zoom. *Informal:* hotfoot, rip. *Slang:* barrel, highball. *Chiefly British:* nip[1]. ***Idioms:*** get a move on, get cracking, go like lightning, go like the wind, hotfoot it, make haste, make time, make tracks, run like the wind, shake a leg, step (*or* jump) on it. *See* MOVE. **4.** To make a public and usually ostentatious show of : brandish, display, disport, exhibit, expose, flaunt, parade, show (off), sport. *See* SHOW.

flash *noun* **1.** A sudden quick light : blink, coruscation, flicker, glance, gleam, glimmer, glint, spark[1], twinkle, wink. *See* LIGHT. **2.** Sparkling, brilliant light : glint, glisten, glister, glitter, scintillation, shimmer, sparkle. *See* BEAUTIFUL, LIGHT. **3.** A very brief time : crack, instant, minute[1], moment, second[1], trice, twinkle, twinkling, wink. *Informal:* jiff, jiffy. *Chiefly British:* tick. *See* BIG, TIME.

flash point also **flashpoint** *noun*
A highly volatile dangerous situation requiring immediate remedial action : crisis, emergency, extremity. *See* POLITICS, SAFETY.

flashy *adjective*
Tastelessly showy : brummagem, chintzy, garish, gaudy, glaring, loud, meretricious, tawdry, tinsel. *Informal:* tacky[2]. *See* STYLE.

flat *adjective*
1. Lying down : decumbent, horizontal, procumbent, prone, prostrate, recumbent. *See* HORIZONTAL. **2.** Lacking an appetizing flavor : bland, flavorless, insipid, tasteless, unsavory. *See* TASTE. **3.** Having lost tang or effervescence : stale. *See* SOLID, TASTE. **4.** Lacking liveliness, charm, or surprise : arid, aseptic, colorless, drab, dry, dull, earthbound, flavorless, lackluster, lifeless, lusterless, matter-of-fact, pedestrian, prosaic, spiritless, sterile, stodgy, unimaginative, uninspired. *See* EXCITE. **5.** Lacking gloss and luster : dim, dull, lackluster, lusterless, mat. *See* LIGHT. **6.** Lacking vividness in color : dim, drab, dull, muddy, murky. *See* COLOR. **7.** Having no irregularities, roughness, or indentations : even[1], flush, level, planar, plane[1], smooth, straight. *See* SMOOTH. **8.** In a definite and final form; not likely to change : certain, firm[1], fixed, set[1]. *See* CHANGE. **9.** Completely such, without qualification or exception : absolute, all-out, arrant, complete, consummate, crashing, damned, dead, downright, out-and-out, outright, perfect, plain, pure, sheer[2], thorough, thoroughgoing, total, unbounded, unequivocal, unlimited, unmitigated, unqualified, unrelieved, unreserved, utter[2]. *Informal:* flat-out, positive. *Chiefly British:* blooming. *See* BIG, LIMITED.

flat *adverb* **1.** To the fullest extent : absolutely, all, altogether, completely, dead, entirely, fully, just, perfectly, quite, thoroughly, totally, utterly, well[2], wholly. *Informal:* clean, clear. ***Idioms:*** in toto, through and through. *See* BIG, LIMITED. **2.** In a direct, positive manner : emphatically, flatly, positively. *Informal:* flat out. *See* STRONG.

flat *verb* To make even, smooth, or level : even[1], flatten, level, plane[2], smooth, straighten. *See* SMOOTH.

flatfoot *noun*
Slang. A member of a law-enforcement agency : bluecoat, finest, officer, patrolman, patrolwoman, peace officer, police, policeman, police officer, policewoman. *Informal:* cop, law. *Slang:* bull[1], copper, fuzz, gendarme, heat, man (often uppercase). *Chiefly British:* bobby, constable, peeler. *See* LAW.

flatly *adverb*
In a direct, positive manner : emphatically, flat, positively. *Informal:* flat out. *See* STRONG.

flatness *noun*
A lack of excitement, liveliness, or interest : asepticism, blandness, colorlessness, drabness, dreariness, dryness, dullness, flavorlessness, insipidity, insipidness, jejuneness, lifelessness, sterileness, sterility, stodginess, vapidity, vapidness, weariness. *See* EXCITE.

flat out *adverb*
1. *Informal.* In a direct, positive manner : emphatically, flat, flatly, positively. *See* STRONG. **2.** *Informal.* In a rapid way : apace, fast, posthaste, quick, quickly. *Informal:* hell-for-leather, lickety-split, pronto. ***Idioms:*** full tilt, in a flash, in nothing flat, like a bat out of hell, like a blue streak, like a flash, like a house on fire, like a shot, like a streak, like greased lightning, like the wind, like wildfire. *See* FAST.

flat-out *adjective Informal.* Completely such, without qualification or exception : absolute, all-out, arrant, complete, consummate, crashing, damned, dead, downright, flat, out-and-out, outright, perfect, plain, pure, sheer[2], thorough, thoroughgoing, total, unbounded, unequivocal, unlimited, unmitigated, unqualified, unrelieved, unreserved, utter[2]. *Informal:* positive. *Chiefly British:* blooming. *See* BIG, LIMITED.

flatten *verb*
1. To make even, smooth, or level : even[1], flat, level, plane[2], smooth, straighten. *See* SMOOTH. **2.** To cause to fall, as from a shot or blow : bring down, cut down, down, drop, fell[1], floor, ground, knock down, level, prostrate, strike down, throw. *Slang:* deck[1]. ***Idiom:*** lay low. *See* RISE.

flatter *verb*
1. To compliment excessively and ingratiatingly : adulate, blandish, butter up, honey, slaver. *Informal:* soft-soap, sweet-talk. *See* PRAISE. **2.** To look good on or with :

become, enhance, suit. ***Idiom:*** put in the best light. *See* AGREE, BEAUTIFUL.

flatterer *noun*
One who flatters another excessively : adulator, courtier, sycophant, toady. *Informal:* apple-polisher. *See* OVER, PRAISE.

flattering *adjective*
Pleasingly suited to the wearer : attractive, becoming. *See* BEAUTIFUL.

flattery *noun*
Excessive, ingratiating praise : adulation, blandishment, blarney, incense[2], oil, slaver. *Informal:* soft soap. ***Idiom:*** honeyed words. *See* PRAISE.

flatulent *adjective*
Filled up with or as if with something insubstantial : inflated, overblown, tumescent, tumid, turgid, windy. *See* INCREASE, PLAIN.

flaunt *verb*
To make a public and usually ostentatious show of : brandish, display, disport, exhibit, expose, flash, parade, show (off), sport. *See* SHOW.

flavor *noun*
1. A distinctive property of a substance affecting the gustatory sense : relish, sapor, savor, smack[2], tang, taste, zest. *See* TASTE. **2.** A distinctive yet intangible quality deemed typical of a given thing : aroma, atmosphere, savor, smack[2]. *See* TASTE. **3.** A substance that imparts taste : condiment, flavoring, seasoner, seasoning, spice. *See* TASTE.
flavor *verb* To impart flavor to : season. *See* TASTE.

flavoring *noun*
A substance that imparts taste : condiment, flavor, seasoner, seasoning, spice. *See* TASTE.

flavorless *adjective*
1. Lacking an appetizing flavor : bland, flat, insipid, tasteless, unsavory. *See* TASTE. **2.** Lacking liveliness, charm, or surprise : arid, aseptic, colorless, drab, dry, dull, earthbound, flat, lackluster, lifeless, lusterless, matter-of-fact, pedestrian, prosaic, spiritless, sterile, stodgy, unimaginative, uninspired. *See* EXCITE.

flavorlessness *noun*
A lack of excitement, liveliness, or interest : asepticism, blandness, colorlessness, drabness, dreariness, dryness, dullness, flatness, insipidity, insipidness, jejuneness, lifelessness, sterileness, sterility, stodginess, vapidity, vapidness, weariness. *See* EXCITE.

flaw *noun*
Something that mars the appearance or causes inadequacy or failure : blemish, bug, defect, fault, imperfection, shortcoming. *See* BEAUTIFUL, BETTER, HELP.
flaw *verb* To spoil the soundness or perfection of : blemish, damage, detract from, disserve, harm, hurt, impair, injure, mar, prejudice, tarnish, vitiate. *See* BETTER, HELP.

flawless *adjective*
1. Free from flaws or blemishes : clear, unblemished, unmarked. *See* BEAUTIFUL. **2.** In excellent condition : entire, good, intact, perfect, sound[2], unblemished, unbroken, undamaged, unharmed, unhurt, unimpaired, uninjured, unmarred, whole. *See* THRIVE.
3. Supremely excellent in quality or nature : absolute, consummate, faultless, impeccable, indefectible, perfect, unflawed. *See* GOOD.

flay *verb*
To criticize harshly and devastatingly : blister, drub, excoriate, lash, rip into, scarify[1], scathe, scorch, score, scourge, slap, slash. *Informal:* roast. *Slang:* slam. ***Idioms:*** burn someone's ears, crawl all over, pin someone's ears back, put someone on the griddle, put someone on the hot seat, rake over the coals, read the riot act to. *See* PRAISE.

fleck *noun*
A very small mark : dash, dot, pinpoint, point, speck, spot. *See* MARKS.
fleck *verb* To mark with many small spots : bespeckle, besprinkle, dapple, dot, freckle, mottle, pepper, speck, speckle, sprinkle, stipple. *See* MARKS.

fledgeling *noun* See **fledgling.**

fledgling also **fledgeling** *noun*
One who is just starting to learn or do something : abecedarian, beginner, freshman, greenhorn, initiate, neophyte, novice, novitiate, tenderfoot, tyro. *Slang:* rookie. *See* START.

flee *verb*
To break loose and leave suddenly, as from confinement or from a difficult or threatening situation : abscond, break out, decamp, escape, fly, get away, run away. *Informal:* skip (out). *Slang:* lam. *Regional:* absquatulate. ***Idioms:*** blow (*or* fly) the coop, cut and run, give someone the slip, make a getaway, take flight, take it on the lam. *See* FREE.

fleece *verb*
To exploit (another) by charging too much for something : overcharge. *Slang:* clip[1], gouge, nick, rip off, scalp, skin, soak. ***Idioms:*** make someone pay through the nose, take someone for a ride, take someone to the cleaners. *See* HONEST.

fleecy *adjective*
Covered with hair : furry, fuzzy, hairy, hirsute, pilose, woolly. *See* SMOOTH.

fleer *verb*
To smile or laugh scornfully or derisively : sneer, snicker, snigger. ***Idiom:*** curl one's lip. *See* EXPRESS, LAUGHTER, RESPECT.
fleer *noun* A facial expression or laugh conveying scorn or derision : sneer, snicker, snigger. *See* EXPRESS, LAUGHTER, RESPECT.

fleet *adjective*
1. Characterized by great celerity : breakneck, expeditious, fast, quick, rapid, speedy, swift. *Informal:* hell-for-leather. ***Idiom:*** quick as a bunny (*or* wink). *See* FAST. **2.** Lasting or existing only for a short time : ephemeral, evanescent, fleeting, fugacious, fugitive, momentary, passing, short-lived, temporal, temporary, transient, transitory. *See* CONTINUE, TIME.
fleet *verb* To move swiftly : bolt, bucket, bustle, dart, dash, festinate, flash, flit, fly, haste, hasten, hurry, hustle, pelt[2], race, rocket, run, rush, sail, scoot, scour[2], shoot, speed, sprint, tear[1], trot, whirl, whisk, whiz, wing, zip, zoom. *Informal:* hotfoot, rip. *Slang:* barrel, highball. *Chiefly British:* nip[1]. ***Idioms:*** get a move on, get cracking, go like lightning, go like the wind, hotfoot it, make haste, make time, make tracks, run like the wind, shake a leg, step (*or* jump) on it. *See* MOVE.

fleeting *adjective*
Lasting or existing only for a short time : ephemeral, evanescent, fleet, fugacious, fugitive, momentary, passing, short-lived, temporal, temporary, transient, transitory. *See* CONTINUE, TIME.

fleetness *noun*
Rapidness of movement or activity : celerity, dispatch, expedition, expeditiousness, haste, hurry, hustle, quickness, rapidity, rapidness, speed, speediness, swiftness. *See* FAST.

Fleet Street *noun*
British. Journalists and journalism in general : fourth estate, medium (used in plural **media**), press. *See* WORDS.

flesh *noun*
The human race : earth, Homo sapiens, humanity, humankind, man, mankind, universe, world. *See* CULTURE.

fleshless *adjective*
Having little flesh or fat on the body : angular, bony, gaunt, lank, lanky, lean[2], meager, rawboned, scrawny, skinny, slender, slim, spare, thin, twiggy, weedy. ***Idioms:*** all skin and bones, thin as a rail. *See* FAT.

fleshliness *noun*
A preoccupation with the body and satisfaction of its desires : animalism, animality, carnality, physicality, sensuality. *See* BODY.

fleshly *adjective*
1. Of or relating to the human body : bodily, corporal, corporeal, personal, physical, somatic. *See* BODY. **2.** Relating to the desires and appetites of the body : animal, carnal, physical, sensual. *See* BODY.

fleshy *adjective*
Having too much flesh : corpulent, fat, fatty, gross, obese, overblown, overweight, porcine, portly, stout, weighty. *See* FAT.

flexibility *noun*
The quality or state of being flexible : bounce, ductility, elasticity, flexibleness, give, malleability, malleableness, plasticity, pliability, pliableness, pliancy, pliantness, resilience, resiliency, spring, springiness, suppleness. *Obsolete:* flexure. *See* FLEXIBLE.

flexible *adjective*
1. Capable of being shaped, bent, or drawn out, as by hammering or pressure : ductile, flexile, flexuous, malleable, moldable, plastic, pliable, pliant, supple, workable. *See* FLEXIBLE.
2. Capable of withstanding stress without injury : elastic, flexile, resilient, springy, supple. *Physics:* plastic. *See* FLEXIBLE. **3.** Easily altered or influenced : ductile, elastic, flexile, impressionable, malleable, plastic, pliable, pliant, suggestible, supple. *See* FLEXIBLE.
4. Capable of adapting or being adapted : adaptable, adaptive, adjustable, elastic, malleable, pliable, pliant, supple. *See* CHANGE.

flexibleness *noun*
The quality or state of being flexible : bounce, ductility, elasticity, flexibility, give, malleability, malleableness, plasticity, pliability, pliableness, pliancy, pliantness, resilience, resiliency, spring, springiness, suppleness. *Obsolete:* flexure. *See* FLEXIBLE.

flexile *adjective*
1. Capable of being shaped, bent, or drawn out, as by hammering or pressure : ductile, flexible, flexuous, malleable, moldable, plastic, pliable, pliant, supple, workable. *See* FLEXIBLE.
2. Capable of withstanding stress without injury : elastic, flexible, resilient, springy, supple. *Physics:* plastic. *See* FLEXIBLE. **3.** Easily altered or influenced : ductile, elastic, flexible, impressionable, malleable, plastic, pliable, pliant, suggestible, supple. *See* FLEXIBLE.

flexuous *adjective*
1. Repeatedly curving in alternate directions :

anfractuous, meandrous, serpentine, sinuous, snaky, tortuous, winding. *See* REPETITION, STRAIGHT. **2.** Capable of being shaped, bent, or drawn out, as by hammering or pressure : ductile, flexible, flexile, malleable, moldable, plastic, pliable, pliant, supple, workable. *See* FLEXIBLE.

flexure *noun*
Obsolete. The quality or state of being flexible : bounce, ductility, elasticity, flexibility, flexibleness, give, malleability, malleableness, plasticity, pliability, pliableness, pliancy, pliantness, resilience, resiliency, spring, springiness, suppleness. *See* FLEXIBLE.

flick *noun*
Light and momentary contact with another person or thing : brush[1], graze, skim. *See* TOUCH.
flick *verb* To make light and momentary contact with, as in passing : brush[1], graze, kiss, shave, skim. *See* TOUCH.

flicker *verb*
1. To move quickly, lightly, and irregularly like a bird in flight : flit, flitter, flutter, hover. *See* REPETITION. **2.** To shine with intermittent gleams : blink, flash, glimmer, twinkle, wink. *See* CONTINUE, LIGHT.
flicker *noun* A sudden quick light : blink, coruscation, flash, glance, gleam, glimmer, glint, spark[1], twinkle, wink. *See* LIGHT.

flight *noun*
The act or an instance of escaping, as from confinement or difficulty : break, breakout, decampment, escape, escapement, getaway. *Slang:* lam. *See* FREE.

flighty *adjective*
Given to lighthearted silliness : empty-headed, featherbrained, frivolous, frothy, giddy, harebrained, lighthearted, scatterbrained, silly. *Informal:* gaga. *Slang:* birdbrained, dizzy. *See* ABILITY.

flimflam *noun*
Informal. An act of cheating : cheat, fraud, swindle, victimization. *Slang:* gyp. *See* HONEST.
flimflam *verb Informal.* To get money or something else from by deceitful trickery : bilk, cheat, cozen, defraud, gull, mulct, rook, swindle, victimize. *Informal:* chisel, take, trim. *Slang:* diddle[1], do, gyp, stick, sting. *See* HONEST.

flimflammer *noun*
Informal. A person who cheats : bilk, cheat, cheater, cozener, defrauder, rook, sharper, swindler, trickster, victimizer. *Informal:* chiseler, crook. *Slang:* diddler, gyp, gypper. *See* HONEST.

flimsiness *noun*
The condition of being infirm or physically weak : debility, decrepitude, delicacy, delicateness, feebleness, fragileness, fragility, frailness, frailty, infirmity, insubstantiality, puniness, unsoundness, unsubstantiality, weakliness, weakness. *See* STRONG.

flimsy *adjective*
1. Not physically strong : decrepit, delicate, feeble, fragile, frail, infirm, insubstantial, puny, unsound, unsubstantial, weak, weakly. *See* STRONG. **2.** Having little substance or significance; not solidly based : feeble, insubstantial, tenuous, unsubstantial. *See* STRONG. **3.** Not plausible or believable : implausible, improbable, inconceivable, incredible, shaky, thin, unbelievable, unconceivable, unconvincing, unsubstantial, weak. *See* LIKELY.

flinch *verb*
To draw away involuntarily, usually out of fear or disgust : blench[1], cringe, quail, recoil, shrink, shy[1], start, wince. *See* APPROACH, SEEK.
flinch *noun* An act of drawing back in an involuntary or instinctive fashion : cringe, recoil, shrink, wince. *See* APPROACH, SEEK.

fling *verb*
To send through the air with a motion of the hand or arm : cast, dart, dash, heave, hurl, hurtle, launch, pitch, shoot, shy[2], sling, throw, toss. *Informal:* fire. *See* MOVE.
fling *noun* **1.** An act of throwing : cast, heave, hurl, launch, pitch, shy[2], sling, throw, toss. *See* MOVE. **2.** A period of uncontrolled self-indulgence : binge, orgy, rampage, spree. *Slang:* jag. *See* RESTRAINT. **3.** *Informal.* A brief trial : crack, go, stab, try. *Informal:* shot, whack, whirl. *See* TRY.

flip *verb*
To throw (a coin) in order to decide something : toss. ***Idiom:*** call heads or tails. *See* LUCK, MOVE.
flip through *verb* To look through reading matter casually : browse, dip into, glance at (*or* over *or* through), leaf (through), riffle (through), run through, scan, skim, thumb (through). *See* INVESTIGATE, WORDS.
flip *adjective Informal.* Rude and disrespectful : assuming, assumptive, audacious, bold, boldfaced, brash, brazen, cheeky, contumelious, familiar, forward, impertinent, impudent, insolent, malapert, nervy, overconfident, pert, presuming, presumptuous, pushy,

sassy, saucy, smart. *Informal:* brassy, fresh, smart-alecky, snippety, snippy, uppish, uppity. *Slang:* wise[1]. *See* ATTITUDE, COURTESY.

flip through *verb* See **flip.**

flirt *verb*
1. To make amorous advances without serious intentions : coquet, dally, toy, trifle. *See* SEX.
2. To treat lightly or flippantly : dally, play, toy, trifle. *See* WORK.

flirt *noun* A woman who is given to flirting : coquette. *Informal:* vamp. *See* SEX.

flirtation *noun*
1. The practice of flirting : coquetry, dalliance. *See* SEX. **2.** A usually brief romance entered into lightly or frivolously : dalliance. *See* SEX.

flirtatious *adjective*
Given to flirting : coquettish, coy, flirty. *See* SEX.

flirty *adjective*
Given to flirting : coquettish, coy, flirtatious. *See* SEX.

flit *verb*
1. To move swiftly : bolt, bucket, bustle, dart, dash, festinate, flash, fleet, fly, haste, hasten, hurry, hustle, pelt[2], race, rocket, run, rush, sail, scoot, scour[2], shoot, speed, sprint, tear[1], trot, whirl, whisk, whiz, wing, zip, zoom. *Informal:* hotfoot, rip. *Slang:* barrel, highball. *Chiefly British:* nip[1]. ***Idioms:*** get a move on, get cracking, go like lightning, go like the wind, hotfoot it, make haste, make time, make tracks, run like the wind, shake a leg, step (*or* jump) on it. *See* MOVE. **2.** To move quickly, lightly, and irregularly like a bird in flight : flicker, flitter, flutter, hover. *See* REPETITION. **3.** To move through the air with or as if with wings : flap, flitter, flutter, fly, sail, wing. *See* MOVE.

flitter *verb*
1. To move (one's arms or wings, for example) up and down : beat, flap, flop, flutter, waggle, wave. *See* REPETITION. **2.** To move quickly, lightly, and irregularly like a bird in flight : flicker, flit, flutter, hover. *See* REPETITION.
3. To move through the air with or as if with wings : flap, flit, flutter, fly, sail, wing. *See* MOVE.

float *verb*
1. To move along with or be carried away by the action of water : drift, wash. *See* MOVE.
2. To pass quickly and lightly through the air : dart, fly, sail, shoot, skim. *See* MOVE.

flock *noun*
1. An enormous number of persons gathered together : crowd, crush, drove, horde, mass, mob, multitude, press, ruck[1], swarm, throng. *See* BIG, GROUP. **2.** A very large number of things grouped together : army, cloud, crowd, drove, horde, host, legion, mass, mob, multitude, ruck[1], score (used in plural), swarm, throng. *See* BIG, GROUP.

flock *verb* To congregate, as around a person : crowd, mob, press, throng. *See* COLLECT, TIGHTEN.

flog *verb*
To punish with blows or lashes : beat, hide[2], lash, thrash, whip. *Informal:* trim. *Slang:* lay into, lick. *See* ATTACK, REWARD.

flogging *noun*
A punishment dealt with blows or lashes : beating, hiding, lashing, thrashing, whipping. *Informal:* trimming. *Slang:* licking. *See* ATTACK, REWARD.

flood *noun*
1. An abundant, usually overwhelming flow or fall, as of a river or rain : alluvion, cataclysm, cataract, deluge, downpour, freshet, inundation, Niagara, overflow, torrent. *Chiefly British:* spate. *See* BIG. **2.** Something suggestive of running water : current, drift, flow, flux, rush, spate, stream, surge, tide. *See* MOVE.

flood *verb* **1.** To flow over completely : deluge, drown, engulf, flush, inundate, overflow, overwhelm, submerge, whelm. *See* FULL. **2.** To affect as if by an outpouring of water : deluge, inundate, overwhelm, swamp, whelm. *See* FULL. **3.** To come or go in large numbers : pour, swarm, throng, troop. *See* BIG, MOVE.

floor *verb*
1. To cause to fall, as from a shot or blow : bring down, cut down, down, drop, fell[1], flatten, ground, knock down, level, prostrate, strike down, throw. *Slang:* deck[1]. ***Idiom:*** lay low. *See* RISE. **2.** To overwhelm with surprise, wonder, or bewilderment : boggle, bowl over, dumbfound, flabbergast, stagger. *See* EXCITE, SURPRISE.

floozie *noun* See **floozy.**

floozy also **floozie** *noun*
Slang. A vulgar promiscuous woman who flouts propriety : baggage, hussy, jade, slattern, slut, tart[2], tramp, wanton, wench, whore. *See* SEX.

flop *verb*
1. To drop or sink heavily and noisily : plop, plump[2], plunk. *See* RISE. **2.** To hang limply, loosely, and carelessly : droop, loll, lop[2], sag, slouch, wilt. *See* HANG. **3.** To move (one's arms or wings, for example) up and down : beat, flap, flitter, flutter, waggle, wave. *See* REPETITION. **4.** *Informal.* To be unsuccessful : choke, fail, fall through. *Informal:* fall down.

Slang: bomb. ***Idioms:*** fail of success, fall short. *See* THRIVE. **5.** *Slang.* To go to bed : bed (down), retire. *Informal:* turn in. *Slang:* crash. ***Idioms:*** call it a night, hit the hay (*or* sack). *See* AWARENESS.

flop *noun Informal.* One that fails completely : bust, failure, fiasco, loser, washout. *Informal:* dud, lemon. *Slang:* bomb. *See* THRIVE.

floppy *adjective*
Lacking in stiffness or firmness : flabby, flaccid, limp. *See* FLEXIBLE.

florescence *noun*
A condition or time of vigor and freshness : bloom[1], blossom, efflorescence, flower, flush, prime. *See* BETTER.

floret *noun*
The showy reproductive structure of a plant : bloom[1], blossom, flower. *See* BETTER.

florid *adjective*
1. Of a healthy reddish color : blooming, flush, flushed, full-blooded, glowing, rosy, rubicund, ruddy, sanguine. *See* COLORS. **2.** Elaborately and heavily ornamented : baroque, flamboyant, ornate, rococo. *See* PLAIN.

flounce *verb*
To walk with exaggerated or unnatural motions expressive of self-importance or self-display : peacock, prance, strut, swagger, swank, swash. *Informal:* sashay. *See* MOVE, SELF-LOVE.

flounder *verb*
1. To proceed or perform in an unsteady, faltering manner : blunder, bumble[1], bungle, fudge, fumble, limp, muddle, shuffle, stagger, stumble. *See* THRIVE. **2.** To move about in an indolent or clumsy manner : wallow, welter. *See* MOVE.

flourish *verb*
1. To grow rapidly and luxuriantly : bloom[1], blossom, thrive. *See* THRIVE. **2.** To do or fare well : boom, go, prosper, thrive. *Slang:* score. ***Idioms:*** get (*or* go) somewhere, go great guns, go strong. *See* THRIVE. **3.** To be in one's prime : flower, shine. ***Idioms:*** cut a figure, make a splash. *See* THRIVE. **4.** To wield boldly and dramatically : brandish, sweep, wave. *See* EXPRESS.

flourishing *adjective*
Improving, growing, or succeeding steadily : booming, boomy, prospering, prosperous, roaring, thrifty, thriving. *See* THRIVE.

flout *verb*
To refuse or fail to obey : break, defy, disobey, transgress, violate. ***Idiom:*** pay no attention to. *See* RESIST.

flow *verb*
1. To move freely as a liquid : circulate, course, run, stream. *See* MOVE. **2.** To pass or pour out : discharge, empty, issue. *See* ENTER. **3.** To come forth or emit in abundance : gush, pour, run, rush, stream, surge, well[1]. *See* MOVE. **4.** To proceed with ease, especially of expression : glide, roll, sail. *See* MOVE. **5.** To have as a source : arise, come, derive, emanate, issue, originate, proceed, rise, spring, stem, upspring. *See* START. **6.** To be abundantly filled or richly supplied : abound, bristle, crawl, overflow, pullulate, swarm, teem. *See* BIG, RICH.

flow *noun* Something suggestive of running water : current, drift, flood, flux, rush, spate, stream, surge, tide. *See* MOVE.

flower *noun*
1. The showy reproductive structure of a plant : bloom[1], blossom, floret. *See* BETTER. **2.** A condition or time of vigor and freshness : bloom[1], blossom, efflorescence, florescence, flush, prime. *See* BETTER. **3.** The superlative or most preferable part of something : best, choice, cream, crème de la crème, elite, pick, prize[1], top. ***Idioms:*** cream of the crop, flower of the flock, pick of the bunch (*or* crop) . *See* BETTER. **4.** People of the highest social level : aristocracy, blue blood, crème de la crème, elite, gentility, gentry, nobility, patriciate, quality, society, upper class, who's who. *Informal:* upper crust. *See* OVER.

flower *verb* **1.** To bear flowers : bloom[1], blossom, blow[3], burgeon, effloresce. *See* BETTER, RICH. **2.** To be in one's prime : flourish, shine. ***Idioms:*** cut a figure, make a splash. *See* THRIVE.

flowery *adjective*
Characterized by language that is elevated and sometimes pompous in style : aureate, bombastic, declamatory, fustian, grandiloquent, high-flown, high-sounding, magniloquent, orotund, overblown, rhetorical, sonorous, swollen. *See* PLAIN, STYLE, WORDS.

flowing *adjective*
Marked by facility, especially of expression : easy, effortless, fluent, fluid, graceful, smooth. *See* STYLE.

fluency *noun*
Ready skill in expression : facility, fluidity. *See* ABILITY.

fluent *adjective*
Marked by facility, especially of expression : easy, effortless, flowing, fluid, graceful, smooth. *See* STYLE.

fluff *noun*
Informal. A minor mistake : lapse, slip, slip-up. *See* CORRECT.

fluid *adjective*
1. Changing easily, as in expression : changeable, mobile, plastic. *See* CHANGE. **2.** Marked by facility, especially of expression : easy, effortless, flowing, fluent, graceful, smooth. *See* STYLE. **3.** Capable of or liable to change : alterable, changeable, inconstant, mutable, uncertain, unsettled, unstable, unsteady, variable, variant. *Archaic:* various. *See* CHANGE.

fluidity *noun*
Ready skill in expression : facility, fluency. *See* ABILITY.

fluke *noun*
An unexpected random event : accident, chance, fortuity, hap, happenchance, happenstance, hazard. *See* CERTAIN, SURPRISE.

fluky *adjective*
Occurring unexpectedly : accidental, casual, chance, contingent, fortuitous, inadvertent, odd. *See* SURPRISE.

flummox *verb*
Informal. To make incapable of finding something to think, do, or say : confound, nonplus. *Informal:* stick, stump, throw. *Slang:* beat. ***Idiom:*** put someone at a loss. *See* AFFECT, KNOWLEDGE.

flunk *verb*
Informal. To receive less than a passing grade : fail. *See* THRIVE.

flurry *noun*
Agitated, excited movement and activity : bustle, stir[1], whirl, whirlpool. *See* CALM.

flurry *verb* To impair or destroy the composure of : agitate, bother, discompose, disquiet, distract, disturb, fluster, perturb, rock, ruffle, shake (up), toss, unsettle, upset. *Informal:* rattle. *See* CALM.

flush *verb*
1. To become red in the face : blush, color, crimson, glow, mantle, redden. *See* EXPRESS. **2.** To raise the spirits of : animate, buoy (up), elate, elevate, exhilarate, inspire, inspirit, lift, uplift. *Obsolete:* exalt. *See* HAPPY. **3.** To flow over completely : deluge, drown, engulf, flood, inundate, overflow, overwhelm, submerge, whelm. *See* FULL.

flush *noun* **1.** A fresh rosy complexion : bloom[1], blush, color, glow. *See* BETTER. **2.** A feeling of pervasive emotional warmth : glow. *See* FEELINGS. **3.** A condition or time of vigor and freshness : bloom[1], blossom, efflorescence, florescence, flower, prime. *See* BETTER.

flush *adjective* **1.** Of a healthy reddish color : blooming, florid, flushed, full-blooded, glowing, rosy, rubicund, ruddy, sanguine. *See* COLORS. **2.** Possessing a large amount of money, land, or other material possessions : affluent, moneyed, rich, wealthy. *Slang:* loaded. ***Idioms:*** having money to burn, in the money, made of money, rolling in money. *See* RICH. **3.** On the same plane or line : even[1], level. *See* SAME. **4.** Having no irregularities, roughness, or indentations : even[1], flat, level, planar, plane[1], smooth, straight. *See* SMOOTH.

flush *adverb* With precision or absolute conformity : bang, dead, direct, directly, exactly, fair, just, precisely, right, smack[1], square, squarely, straight. *Slang:* smack-dab. *See* PRECISE.

flushed *adjective*
Of a healthy reddish color : blooming, florid, flush, full-blooded, glowing, rosy, rubicund, ruddy, sanguine. *See* COLORS.

fluster *verb*
To impair or destroy the composure of : agitate, bother, discompose, disquiet, distract, disturb, flurry, perturb, rock, ruffle, shake (up), toss, unsettle, upset. *Informal:* rattle. *See* CALM.

fluster *noun* A state of discomposure : agitation, dither, flutter, perturbation, tumult, turmoil, upset. *Informal:* lather, stew. *See* CALM.

flutter *verb*
1. To move or cause to move about while being fixed at one edge : flap, fly, wave. *See* REPETITION. **2.** To move through the air with or as if with wings : flap, flit, flitter, fly, sail, wing. *See* MOVE. **3.** To move quickly, lightly, and irregularly like a bird in flight : flicker, flit, flitter, hover. *See* REPETITION. **4.** To move (one's arms or wings, for example) up and down : beat, flap, flitter, flop, waggle, wave. *See* REPETITION.

flutter *noun* A state of discomposure : agitation, dither, fluster, perturbation, tumult, turmoil, upset. *Informal:* lather, stew. *See* CALM.

flux *noun*
Something suggestive of running water : current, drift, flood, flow, rush, spate, stream, surge, tide. *See* MOVE.

flux *verb* To change from a solid to a liquid : deliquesce, dissolve, fuse, liquefy, melt, run, thaw. *See* SOLID.

fly *verb*
1. To move through the air with or as if with wings : flap, flit, flitter, flutter, sail, wing. *See* MOVE. **2.** To move or cause to move about

while being fixed at one edge : flap, flutter, wave. *See* REPETITION. **3.** To pass quickly and lightly through the air : dart, float, sail, shoot, skim. *See* MOVE. **4.** To move swiftly : bolt, bucket, bustle, dart, dash, festinate, flash, fleet, flit, haste, hasten, hurry, hustle, pelt[2], race, rocket, run, rush, sail, scoot, scour[2], shoot, speed, sprint, tear[1], trot, whirl, whisk, whiz, wing, zip, zoom. *Informal:* hotfoot, rip. *Slang:* barrel, highball. *Chiefly British:* nip[1]. ***Idioms:*** get a move on, get cracking, go like lightning, go like the wind, hotfoot it, make haste, make time, make tracks, run like the wind, shake a leg, step (*or* jump) on it. *See* MOVE. **5.** To break loose and leave suddenly, as from confinement or from a difficult or threatening situation : abscond, break out, decamp, escape, flee, get away, run away. *Informal:* skip (out). *Slang:* lam. *Regional:* absquatulate. ***Idioms:*** blow (*or* fly) the coop, cut and run, give someone the slip, make a getaway, take flight, take it on the lam. *See* FREE. **6.** To react explosively or suddenly : flare (up). *See* EXPLOSION.

flying *adjective*
Accomplished in very little time : brief, expeditious, fast, hasty, hurried, quick, rapid, short, speedy, swift. *See* FAST.

foam *noun*
A mass of bubbles in or on the surface of a liquid : froth, head, lather, spume, suds, yeast. *See* SOLID.

foam *verb* **1.** To form or cause to form foam : bubble, cream, effervesce, fizz, froth, lather, spume, suds, yeast. *See* SOLID. **2.** To be or become angry : anger, blow up, boil over, bristle, burn, explode, flare up, fume, rage, seethe. *Informal:* steam. ***Idioms:*** blow a fuse, blow a gasket, blow one's stack (*or* top), breathe fire, fly off the handle, get hot under the collar, hit the ceiling (*or* roof), lose one's temper, see red. *See* FEELINGS.

foamy *adjective*
Consisting of or resembling foam : frothy, lathery, spumous, spumy, sudsy, yeasty. *See* SOLID.

fob off *verb*
To offer or put into circulation (an inferior or spurious item) : foist, palm off, pass off, put off. *See* HONEST.

focalize *verb*
To direct toward a common center : center, channel, concentrate, converge, focus. *See* EDGE.

focus *noun*
1. A place of concentrated activity, influence, or importance : center, headquarters, heart, hub, seat. *See* EDGE. **2.** A point of origin from which ideas or influences, for example, originate : bottom, center, core, heart, hub, quick, root[1]. *See* START.

focus *verb* **1.** To direct toward a common center : center, channel, concentrate, converge, focalize. *See* EDGE. **2.** To devote (oneself or one's efforts) : address, apply, bend, buckle down, concentrate, dedicate, devote, direct, give, turn. *See* COLLECT, WORK.

foe *noun*
One who is hostile to or opposes the purposes or interests of another : archenemy, enemy, nemesis. *See* LOVE.

fog *noun*
1. A thick, heavy atmospheric condition offering reduced visibility because of the presence of suspended particles : brume, haze, mist, murk, smaze. *See* CLEAR. **2.** A stunned or bewildered condition : befuddlement, bewilderedness, bewilderment, daze, discombobulation, muddle, mystification, perplexity, puzzlement, stupefaction, stupor, trance. *See* AWARENESS.

fog *verb* To make dim or indistinct : becloud, bedim, befog, blear, blur, cloud, dim, dull, eclipse, gloom, mist, obfuscate, obscure, overcast, overshadow, shadow. *See* CLEAR.

foggy *adjective*
Not clearly perceived or perceptible : blear, bleary, cloudy, dim, faint, fuzzy, hazy, indefinite, indistinct, misty, obscure, shadowy, unclear, undistinct, vague. *See* CLEAR.

fogy *noun*
An old-fashioned person who is reluctant to change or innovate : fossil, fuddy-duddy, mossback. *Informal:* stick-in-the-mud. *Slang:* square. *See* NEW.

foible *noun*
An imperfection of character : failing, fault, frailty, infirmity, shortcoming, weakness, weak point. *See* BETTER, HELP.

foil *verb*
To prevent from accomplishing a purpose : baffle, balk, check, checkmate, defeat, frustrate, stymie, thwart. *Informal:* cross, stump. ***Idiom:*** cut the ground from under. *See* ALLOW.

foist *verb*
1. To offer or put into circulation (an inferior or spurious item) : fob off, palm off, pass off, put off. *See* HONEST. **2.** To force (another) to accept a burden : impose, inflict, saddle. *Informal:* stick. *See* GIVE, OVER, WILLING. **3.** To introduce gradually and slyly : edge,

infiltrate, insinuate, wind[2], work, worm. *See* ENTER.

fold *verb*
1. To bend together or make a crease in so that one part lies over another : crease, double, pleat, ply[1], ruck[2]. *See* ORDER, SMOOTH. **2.** *Informal.* To undergo sudden financial failure : break, bust, collapse, crash, fail, go under. ***Idioms:*** go belly up, go bust, go on the rocks, go to the wall. *See* MONEY. **3.** *Informal.* To give in from or as if from a gradual loss of strength : bow[1], buckle, capitulate, submit, succumb, surrender, yield. *See* RESIST. **4.** *Informal.* To give way mentally and emotionally : break (down), collapse, crack, snap. *Informal:* crack up. *See* EXPLOSION.
fold *noun* A line or an arrangement made by the doubling of one part over another : crease, crimp, crinkle, crumple, pleat, plica, plication, pucker, rimple, ruck[2], rumple, wrinkle. *See* SMOOTH.

folklore *noun*
A body of traditional beliefs and notions accumulated about a particular subject : legend, lore, myth, mythology, mythos, tradition. *See* KNOWLEDGE.

follow *verb*
1. To keep (another) under surveillance by moving along behind : dog, shadow, track, trail. *Informal:* bird-dog, tail. *See* PRECEDE. **2.** To act in conformity with : abide by, adhere, carry out, comply, conform, keep, mind, obey, observe. ***Idiom:*** toe the line (*or* mark). *See* ACCEPT, SAME. **3.** To take as a model or make conform to a model : copy, emulate, imitate, model (on, upon, *or* after), pattern (on, upon, *or* after). ***Idioms:*** follow in the footsteps of, follow suit, follow the example of. *See* SAME. **4.** To occur after in time : ensue, succeed, supervene. ***Idiom:*** follow on (*or* upon) the heels of. *See* PRECEDE, TIME. **5.** To occur as a consequence : attend, ensue, result. *See* CAUSE, PRECEDE. **6.** To perceive and recognize the meaning of : accept, apprehend, catch (on), compass, comprehend, conceive, fathom, get, grasp, make out, read, see, sense, take, take in, understand. *Informal:* savvy. *Slang:* dig. *Chiefly British:* twig. *Scots:* ken. ***Idioms:*** get (*or* have) a handle on, get the picture. *See* UNDERSTAND.
follow through *verb* To strengthen the effect of (an action) by further action : follow up, pursue. *See* CONTINUE.
follow up *verb* To strengthen the effect of (an action) by further action : follow through, pursue. *See* CONTINUE.

follower *noun*
One who supports and adheres to another : adherent, cohort, disciple, henchman, minion, partisan, satellite, supporter. *See* OVER, PRECEDE.

following *adjective*
Occurring right after another : coming, next. *See* PRECEDE, TIME.
following *noun* **1.** The body of persons who admire a public personality, especially an entertainer : audience, public. *See* LIKE. **2.** A group of attendants or followers : entourage, retinue, suite, train. *See* OVER.

follow through *verb* See **follow.**

follow up *verb* See **follow.**

folly *noun*
Foolish behavior : absurdity, foolery, foolishness, idiocy, imbecility, insanity, lunacy, madness, nonsense, preposterousness, senselessness, silliness, tomfoolery, zaniness. *Informal:* craziness. *See* ABILITY.

foment *verb*
To stir to action or feeling : egg on, excite, galvanize, goad, impel, incite, inflame, inspire, instigate, motivate, move, pique, prick, prod, prompt, propel, provoke, set off, spur, stimulate, touch off, trigger, work up. *See* CAUSE, EXCITE.

fomenter *noun*
One who agitates, especially politically : agitator, inciter, instigator. *See* CALM, CHANGE, POLITICS.

fond *adjective*
Feeling and expressing affection : affectionate, devoted, doting, loving. *See* ATTITUDE, LOVE.

fondle *verb*
To touch or stroke affectionately : caress, cuddle, pat, pet[1]. *See* TOUCH.

fondness *noun*
1. The condition of being closely tied to another by affection or faith : affection, attachment, devotion, liking, love, loyalty (used in plural). *See* CONNECT. **2.** A liking for something : appetite, partiality, preference, relish, taste, weakness. *See* LIKE.

food *noun*
1. Something fit to be eaten : aliment, bread, comestible, diet, edible, esculent, fare, foodstuff, meat, nourishment, nurture, nutriment, nutrition, pabulum, pap, provender, provision (used in plural), sustenance, victual. *Slang:* chow, eats, grub. *See* INGESTION. **2.** That

which sustains the mind or spirit : aliment, bread, nourishment, nutriment, pabulum, pap, sustenance. *See* CARE FOR, INGESTION.

foodstuff *noun*
Something fit to be eaten : aliment, bread, comestible, diet, edible, esculent, fare, food, meat, nourishment, nurture, nutriment, nutrition, pabulum, pap, provender, provision (used in plural), sustenance, victual. *Slang:* chow, eats, grub. *See* INGESTION.

fool *noun*
1. One deficient in judgment and good sense : ass, idiot, imbecile, jackass, mooncalf, moron, nincompoop, ninny, nitwit, simple, simpleton, softhead, tomfool. *Informal:* dope, gander, goose. *Slang:* cretin, ding-dong, dip, goof, jerk, nerd, schmo, schmuck, turkey. *See* ABILITY.
2. A person who is easily deceived or victimized : butt[3], dupe, gull, lamb, pushover, victim. *Informal:* sucker. *Slang:* fall guy, gudgeon, mark, monkey, patsy, pigeon, sap[1]. *Chiefly British:* mug. *See* WISE.

fool *verb* **1.** To cause to accept what is false, especially by trickery or misrepresentation : beguile, betray, bluff, cozen, deceive, delude, double-cross, dupe, hoodwink, humbug, mislead, take in, trick. *Informal:* bamboozle, have. *Slang:* four-flush. ***Idioms:*** lead astray, play false, pull the wool over someone's eyes, put something over on, take for a ride. *See* HONEST. **2.** To waste time by engaging in aimless activity : doodle, putter. *Informal:* fool around, mess around. *See* THRIVE. **3.** To handle something idly, ignorantly, or destructively : fiddle, meddle, mess, tamper, tinker. *Informal:* monkey. *See* HELP, TOUCH.
4. To move one's fingers or hands in a nervous or aimless fashion : fiddle, fidget, monkey, play, putter, tinker, toy, trifle, twiddle. *See* TOUCH.

fool around *verb* **1.** *Informal.* To waste time by engaging in aimless activity : doodle, fool, putter. *Informal:* mess around. *See* THRIVE. **2.** *Informal.* To make jokes; behave playfully : jest, joke. *Informal:* clown (around), fun. *See* LAUGHTER. **3.** *Informal.* To engage in kissing, caressing, and other amorous behavior : *Informal:* neck, pet[1], spoon. *Slang:* make out. *See* SEX. **4.** *Informal.* To be sexually unfaithful to another : philander, womanize. *Informal:* cheat, mess around, play around. *See* SEX.

fool away *verb* To spend (money) excessively and usually foolishly : consume, dissipate, fritter away, riot away, squander, throw away, trifle away, waste. *Slang:* blow[1]. *See* SAVE.

fool around *verb* See **fool.**

fool away *verb* See **fool.**

foolery *noun*
Foolish behavior : absurdity, folly, foolishness, idiocy, imbecility, insanity, lunacy, madness, nonsense, preposterousness, senselessness, silliness, tomfoolery, zaniness. *Informal:* craziness. *See* ABILITY.

foolhardiness *noun*
Foolhardy boldness or disregard of danger : brashness, incautiousness, rashness, recklessness, temerariousness, temerity. *See* CAREFUL.

foolhardy *adjective*
Characterized by unthinking boldness and haste : brash, harum-scarum, hasty, headlong, hotheaded, ill-considered, impetuous, improvident, impulsive, incautious, madcap, precipitant, precipitate, rash[1], reckless, slapdash, temerarious, unconsidered. *See* CAREFUL.

foolish *adjective*
1. Displaying a complete lack of forethought and good sense : brainless, fatuous, insensate, mindless, senseless, silly, unintelligent, weak-minded, witless. *See* ABILITY, PLANNED. **2.** So senseless as to be laughable : absurd, harebrained, idiotic, imbecilic, insane, lunatic, mad, moronic, nonsensical, preposterous, silly, softheaded, tomfool, unearthly, zany. *Informal:* cockeyed, crazy, loony, loopy. *Slang:* balmy[2], dippy, dopey, jerky, sappy, wacky. *See* ABILITY, KNOWLEDGE.

foolishness *noun*
Foolish behavior : absurdity, folly, foolery, idiocy, imbecility, insanity, lunacy, madness, nonsense, preposterousness, senselessness, silliness, tomfoolery, zaniness. *Informal:* craziness. *See* ABILITY.

foolproof *adjective*
Designed so as to be impervious to human error or misuse : fail-safe. *See* THRIVE.

foot *noun*
The lowest or supporting part or structure : base[1], basis, bed, bottom, footing, foundation, fundament, ground, groundwork, seat, substratum, underpinning (often used in plural). *See* OVER.

foot *verb* **1.** To go on foot : ambulate, pace, step, tread, walk. *Slang:* hoof. ***Idiom:*** foot it. *See* MOVE. **2.** To move rhythmically to music, using patterns of steps or gestures : dance, step. *Slang:* hoof. ***Idioms:*** cut a rug, foot it, trip the light fantastic. *See* REPETITION, WORK.
3. To combine (figures) to form a sum. Also used with *up* : add (up), cast, sum (up), tot[2] (up), total, totalize. *See* INCREASE.

footfall *noun*
The act or manner of going on foot : footstep, step, tread. *See* MOVE, SOUNDS.

footing *noun*
1. The lowest or supporting part or structure : base[1], basis, bed, bottom, foot, foundation, fundament, ground, groundwork, seat, substratum, underpinning (often used in plural). *See* OVER. **2.** That on which something immaterial, such as an argument or a charge, rests : base[1], basis, foundation, fundament, ground (often used in plural), groundwork, underpinning (often used in plural). *See* OVER. **3.** Positioning of one individual vis-à-vis others : place, position, rank[1], situation, standing, station, status. *See* PLACE. **4.** An established position from which to operate or deal with others : basis, status, term (often used in plural). *See* CONNECT.

footloose *adjective*
Without a spouse : fancy-free, lone, single, sole, spouseless, unattached, unmarried, unwed. ***Idiom:*** footloose and fancy-free. *See* MARRIAGE.

footstep *noun*
The act or manner of going on foot : footfall, step, tread. *See* MOVE, SOUNDS.

foozle *noun*
A stupid, clumsy mistake : blunder, bull[2], bungle, fumble, muff, stumble. *Informal:* blooper, boner. *Slang:* bloomer, goof. *See* CORRECT.

foozler *noun*
A clumsy person : blunderer, botcher, bungler, dub. *Slang:* screwup. ***Idiom:*** bull in a china shop. *See* ABILITY.

forage *verb*
To make a thorough search of : comb, ransack, rummage, scour[2]. *Slang:* shake down. ***Idioms:*** beat the bushes, leave no stone unturned, look (*or* search) high and low, look (*or* search) up and down, turn inside out, turn upside down. *See* INVESTIGATE.

foray *noun*
An act of invading, especially by military forces : incursion, inroad, invasion, raid. *See* ATTACK, ENTER.

foray *verb* To enter so as to attack, plunder, destroy, or conquer : invade, overrun, raid. *See* ATTACK, ENTER.

forbear *verb*
To hold oneself back : abstain, hold off, keep, refrain, withhold. *See* RESTRAINT.

forbearance *noun*
1. The capacity of enduring hardship or inconvenience without complaint : long-suffering, patience, resignation, tolerance. *See* ACCEPT. **2.** Forbearing or lenient treatment : charitableness, charity, indulgence, lenience, leniency, lenity, tolerance, toleration. *See* ACCEPT.

forbearing *adjective*
1. Enduring or capable of enduring hardship or inconvenience without complaint : long-suffering, patient, resigned. *See* ACCEPT. **2.** Not strict or severe : charitable, clement, easy, indulgent, lax, lenient, merciful, soft, tolerant. *See* ACCEPT.

forbid *verb*
To refuse to allow : ban, debar, disallow, enjoin, inhibit, interdict, outlaw, prohibit, proscribe, taboo. *See* ALLOW.

forbiddance *noun*
A refusal to allow : ban, disallowance, inhibition, interdiction, prohibition, proscription, taboo. *See* ALLOW.

forbidden *adjective*
Not allowed : impermissible, taboo, verboten. *See* ALLOW.

forbidding *adjective*
So disagreeable as to discourage approach : inhospitable, unhospitable, uninviting. *See* WARN.

force *noun*
1. Capacity or power for work or vigorous activity : animation, energy, might, potency, power, puissance, sprightliness, steam, strength. *Informal:* get-up-and-go, go, pep, peppiness, zip. *See* ACTION. **2.** Power used to overcome resistance : coercion, compulsion, constraint, duress, pressure, strength, violence. *See* ATTACK. **3.** Effective means of influencing, compelling, or punishing : power, weight. *Informal:* clout, muscle. *See* OVER, STRONG. **4.** The strong effect exerted by one person or thing on another : impact, impression, influence, repercussion. *See* AFFECT. **5.** The capacity to exert an influence : forcefulness, magnetism, power. *See* STRONG. **6.** A group of people organized for a particular purpose : body, corps, crew, detachment, gang, team, unit. *See* GROUP.

force *verb* **1.** To cause (a person or thing) to act or move in spite of resistance : coerce, compel, constrain, make, obligate, oblige, pressure. *See* ATTACK. **2.** To compel by pressure or threats : blackjack, coerce, dragoon. *Informal:* hijack, strong-arm. *See* PERSUASION. **3.** To compel (another) to participate in or submit to a sexual act : assault, rape, ravish, violate. *See* SEX.

forced *adjective*
1. Done under force : compulsory. *See* WILLING. **2.** Not natural or spontaneous : contrived, effortful, labored, strained. *See* TRUE.

forceful *adjective*
1. Full of or displaying force : dynamic, dynamical, effective, forcible, hard-hitting, powerful, strong, vigorous. *See* STRONG.
2. Possessing, exerting, or displaying energy : active, brisk, dynamic, dynamical, energetic, kinetic, lively, sprightly, strenuous, vigorous. *Informal:* peppy. *See* ACTION. **3.** Expressed or performed with emphasis : emphatic, resounding. *See* STRONG. **4.** Bold and definite in character : assertive, emphatic, insistent. *See* STRONG.

forcefully *adverb*
With intense energy and force : energetically, forcibly, hard, powerfully, vigorously. ***Idioms:*** hammer and tongs, tooth and nail, with might and main. *See* STRONG.

forcefulness *noun*
The capacity to exert an influence : force, magnetism, power. *See* STRONG.

forcible *adjective*
1. Accomplished by force : coercive, violent. *Informal:* strong-arm. *See* ATTACK. **2.** Full of or displaying force : dynamic, dynamical, effective, forceful, hard-hitting, powerful, strong, vigorous. *See* STRONG.

forcibly *adverb*
With intense energy and force : energetically, forcefully, hard, powerfully, vigorously. ***Idioms:*** hammer and tongs, tooth and nail, with might and main. *See* STRONG.

fore *noun*
The part of someone or something facing the viewer : forepart, front. *See* PRECEDE.

forearm *verb*
To prepare (oneself) for action : brace, fortify, gird, ready, steel, strengthen. ***Idiom:*** gird (*or* gird up) one's loins. *See* PREPARED.

forebear *noun*
A person from whom one is descended : ancestor, antecedent, ascendant, father, forefather, foremother, mother, parent, progenitor. *Archaic:* predecessor. *See* KIN, PRECEDE.

forebode *verb*
To give warning signs of (impending peril) : forewarn, threaten. *See* FORESIGHT.

foreboding *noun*
An indication of impending danger or harm : forewarning, threat, thundercloud. ***Idioms:*** gathering clouds, storm clouds. *See* FORESIGHT.

forecast *verb*
1. To tell about or make known (future events) in advance, especially by means of special knowledge or inference : call, foretell, predict, prognosticate, project. *See* FORESIGHT. **2.** To give an indication of something in advance : adumbrate, augur, bode, forerun, foreshadow, foretell, foretoken, portend, prefigure, presage, prognosticate. *See* FORESIGHT, SHOW.
forecast *noun* The act of predicting : outlook, prediction, prognosis, prognostication, projection. *See* FORESIGHT.

foredoom *verb*
To predestine to a tragic end : doom, fate. *See* CERTAIN, LIVE, LUCK, START.

foredoomed *adjective*
Sentenced to terrible, irrevocable punishment : condemned, doomed, fated, lost. *See* LAW, RELIGION.

forefather *noun*
A person from whom one is descended : ancestor, antecedent, ascendant, father, forebear, foremother, mother, parent, progenitor. *Archaic:* predecessor. *See* KIN, PRECEDE.

forefend *verb* See **forfend.**

foregather *verb* See **forgather.**

forego *verb* See **forgo.**

foregoing *adjective*
1. Next before the present one : last[1], latter, preceding, previous. *See* NEAR, PRECEDE.
2. Just gone by or elapsed : antecedent, anterior, earlier, former, past, precedent, preceding, previous, prior. *See* TIME.

forehanded *adjective*
Trying attentively to avoid danger, risk, or error : careful, cautious, chary, circumspect, gingerly, prudent, wary. *See* CAREFUL.

forehandedness *noun*
The exercise of good judgment or common sense in practical matters : caution, circumspection, discretion, foresight, foresightedness, forethought, forethoughtfulness, precaution, prudence. *See* CAREFUL.

foreign *adjective*
1. Of, from, or characteristic of another place or part of the world : alien, exotic, strange. *Archaic:* outlandish. *See* NATIVE. **2.** Not part of the essential nature of a thing : alien, extraneous, extrinsic. *See* NATIVE.

foreigner *noun*
A person coming from another country or into a new community : alien, émigré, newcomer, outlander, outsider, stranger. *See* NATIVE.

foreknow *verb*
To know in advance : anticipate, divine, envision, foresee, see. *See* FORESIGHT, SEE.

foreman *noun*
Someone who directs and supervises workers : boss, director, foreperson, forewoman, head, manager, overseer, superintendent, supervisor, taskmaster, taskmistress. *Informal:* straw boss. *Slang:* chief. *See* OVER.

foremost *adjective*
Most important, influential, or significant : capital, cardinal, chief, first, key, leading, main, major, number one, paramount, premier, primary, prime, principal, top. *See* IMPORTANT.

foremother *noun*
A person from whom one is descended : ancestor, antecedent, ascendant, father, forebear, forefather, mother, parent, progenitor. *Archaic:* predecessor. *See* KIN, PRECEDE.

forenoon *noun*
The time of day from sunrise to noon : morning. *See* TIME.

forensics *noun*
The presentation of an argument or arguments : argumentation, debate, disputation. *See* AFFIRM, WORDS.

foreordain *verb*
To determine the future of in advance : destine, fate, predestinate, predestine, predetermine, preordain. *See* CERTAIN.

forepart *noun*
The part of someone or something facing the viewer : fore, front. *See* PRECEDE.

foreperson *noun*
Someone who directs and supervises workers : boss, director, foreman, forewoman, head, manager, overseer, superintendent, supervisor, taskmaster, taskmistress. *Informal:* straw boss. *Slang:* chief. *See* OVER.

forerun *verb*
To give an indication of something in advance : adumbrate, augur, bode, forecast, foreshadow, foretell, foretoken, portend, prefigure, presage, prognosticate. *See* FORESIGHT, SHOW.

forerunner *noun*
1. One that precedes, as in time : ancestor, antecedent, precursor, predecessor, progenitor. *See* PRECEDE. **2.** A phenomenon that serves as a sign or warning of some future good or evil : augury, foretoken, omen, portent, prefigurement, presage, prognostic, prognostication, sign. ***Idiom:*** writing (*or* handwriting) on the wall. *See* FORESIGHT, WARN. **3.** One that indicates or announces someone or something to come : foreshadower, harbinger, herald, precursor, presager. *See* FORESIGHT, SHOW.

foresee *verb*
To know in advance : anticipate, divine, envision, foreknow, see. *See* FORESIGHT, SEE.

foreshadow *verb*
To give an indication of something in advance : adumbrate, augur, bode, forecast, forerun, foretell, foretoken, portend, prefigure, presage, prognosticate. *See* FORESIGHT, SHOW.

foreshadower *noun*
One that indicates or announces someone or something to come : forerunner, harbinger, herald, precursor, presager. *See* FORESIGHT, SHOW.

foresight *noun*
1. Unusual or creative discernment or perception : farsightedness, prescience, vision. *See* FORESIGHT. **2.** The exercise of good judgment or common sense in practical matters : caution, circumspection, discretion, forehandedness, foresightedness, forethought, forethoughtfulness, precaution, prudence. *See* CAREFUL.

foresighted *adjective*
Characterized by foresight : farsighted, prescient, visionary. *See* FORESIGHT.

foresightedness *noun*
The exercise of good judgment or common sense in practical matters : caution, circumspection, discretion, forehandedness, foresight, forethought, forethoughtfulness, precaution, prudence. *See* CAREFUL.

forestall *verb*
To prohibit from occurring by advance planning or action : avert, forfend, obviate, preclude, prevent, rule out, stave off, ward (off). *Idiom:* nip in the bud. *See* ALLOW.

forestallment *noun*
The act of preventing : determent, deterrence, obviation, preclusion, prevention. *See* ALLOW.

foreswear *verb* See **forswear.**

foresworn *adjective* See **forsworn.**

foretaste *noun*
A limited or anticipatory experience : sample, taste. *See* FORESIGHT.

foretell *verb*
1. To tell about or make known (future events) in advance, especially by means of special knowledge or inference : call, forecast, predict, prognosticate, project. *See* FORESIGHT. **2.** To tell about or make known (future events) by or as if by supernatural means : augur, divine, prophesy, soothsay, vaticinate. *See* FORESIGHT. **3.** To give an indication of something in

advance : adumbrate, augur, bode, forecast, forerun, foreshadow, foretoken, portend, prefigure, presage, prognosticate. *See* FORESIGHT, SHOW.

foreteller *noun*
A person who foretells future events by or as if by supernatural means : augur, auspex, diviner, haruspex, prophesier, prophet, prophetess, seer, sibyl, soothsayer, vaticinator. *See* FORESIGHT.

forethought *noun*
The exercise of good judgment or common sense in practical matters : caution, circumspection, discretion, forehandedness, foresight, foresightedness, forethoughtfulness, precaution, prudence. *See* CAREFUL.

forethoughtfulness *noun*
The exercise of good judgment or common sense in practical matters : caution, circumspection, discretion, forehandedness, foresight, foresightedness, forethought, precaution, prudence. *See* CAREFUL.

foretoken *verb*
To give an indication of something in advance : adumbrate, augur, bode, forecast, forerun, foreshadow, foretell, portend, prefigure, presage, prognosticate. *See* FORESIGHT, SHOW.
foretoken *noun* A phenomenon that serves as a sign or warning of some future good or evil : augury, forerunner, omen, portent, prefigurement, presage, prognostic, prognostication, sign. ***Idiom:*** writing (*or* handwriting) on the wall. *See* FORESIGHT, WARN.

forewarn *verb*
1. To notify (someone) of imminent danger or risk : admonish, alarm, alert, caution, warn. *See* WARN. **2.** To give warning signs of (impending peril) : forebode, threaten. *See* FORESIGHT.

forewarning *noun*
An indication of impending danger or harm : foreboding, threat, thundercloud. ***Idioms:*** gathering clouds, storm clouds. *See* FORESIGHT.

forewoman *noun*
Someone who directs and supervises workers : boss, director, foreman, foreperson, head, manager, overseer, superintendent, supervisor, taskmaster, taskmistress. *Informal:* straw boss. *Slang:* chief. *See* OVER.

foreword *noun*
A short section of preliminary remarks : induction, introduction, lead-in, overture, preamble, preface, prelude, prolegomenon, prologue. *See* START, WORDS.

forfeit *verb*
To suffer the loss of : drop, lose. ***Idiom:*** kiss good-by to. *See* GET.

forfend also **forefend** *verb*
To prohibit from occurring by advance planning or action : avert, forestall, obviate, preclude, prevent, rule out, stave off, ward (off). ***Idiom:*** nip in the bud. *See* ALLOW.

forgather also **foregather** *verb*
To come together : assemble, cluster, collect[1], congregate, convene, gather, get together, group, muster. *See* COLLECT.

forge[1] *verb*
1. To shape, break, or flatten with repeated blows : beat, hammer, pound. *See* REPETITION, STRIKE. **2.** To create by forming, combining, or altering materials : assemble, build, construct, fabricate, fashion, frame, make, manufacture, mold, produce, put together, shape. *See* MAKE. **3.** To make a fraudulent copy of : counterfeit, fake, falsify. *See* TRUE.

forge[2] *verb*
To move or advance against strong resistance : drive, lunge, plunge. *See* MOVE.

forger *noun*
One who makes a fraudulent copy of something : counterfeiter, fabricator, faker. *See* TRUE.

forgery *noun*
A fraudulent imitation : counterfeit, fake, phony, sham. *See* TRUE.

forget *verb*
To fail to remember : *Informal:* disremember. ***Idiom:*** draw a blank. *See* REMEMBER.

forgetful *adjective*
1. Unable to remember : amnesiac, amnesic, oblivious. *See* REMEMBER. **2.** Showing no concern, attention, or regard : careless, heedless, mindless, unconcerned, unheeding, unmindful, unobservant, unthinking. *See* CAREFUL.

forgetfulness *noun*
Freedom from worry, care, or unpleasantness : escape, oblivion, obliviousness. *See* SEEK.

forgivable *adjective*
Admitting of forgiveness or pardon : excusable, pardonable, venial. *See* FORGIVENESS.

forgive *verb*
To grant forgiveness to or for : condone, excuse, pardon, remit. ***Idiom:*** forgive and forget. *See* FORGIVENESS.

forgiveness *noun*
The act or an instance of forgiving : absolution, amnesty, condonation, excuse, pardon, remission. *See* FORGIVENESS.

forgo also **forego** *verb*
To let (something) go : abandon, cede, lay down, relinquish, surrender, yield. *See* KEEP.

fork *noun*
Something resembling or structurally analogous to a tree branch : arm, branch, offshoot. *See* PART.
fork *verb* To separate into branches or branch-like parts : bifurcate, branch (out), diverge, divide, ramify, subdivide. *See* PART.
fork out (or **over** or **up**) *verb Informal.* To distribute (money) as payment : disburse, expend, give, lay out, outlay, pay (out), spend. *Informal:* shell out. *See* SAVE.

fork out or **over** or **up** *verb* See **fork.**

forlorn *adjective*
1. Dejected due to the awareness of being alone : desolate, lonely, lonesome, lorn. *See* HAPPY. **2.** Having been given up and left alone : abandoned, bereft, derelict, deserted, desolate, forsaken, lorn. *See* KEEP. **3.** Empty of people : deserted, desolate, godforsaken, lonely, lonesome, unfrequented. *See* FULL. **4.** Having lost all hope : despairing, desperate, despondent, hopeless. *See* HOPE.

form *noun*
1. The external outline of a thing : cast, configuration, figure, pattern, shape. *See* SURFACE. **2.** A document used in applying, as for a job : application. *See* SEEK, WORDS. **3.** An accepted way of doing something : convention. *See* USUAL. **4.** A conventional social gesture or act without intrinsic purpose : ceremony, formality, ritual. *See* RITUAL, USUAL. **5.** A state of sound readiness : condition, fettle, fitness, kilter, order, shape, trim. *See* BETTER. **6.** A hollow device for shaping a fluid or plastic substance : cast, matrix, mold. *See* SURFACE.
form *verb* **1.** To give form to by or as if by pressing and kneading : model, mold, shape. *See* SURFACE. **2.** To create by combining parts or elements : build, compose, configure, pattern, shape, structure. *See* MAKE. **3.** To come gradually to have : acquire, develop. *See* GET. **4.** To be the constituent parts of : compose, constitute, make (up). *See* BE.

formal *adjective*
1. Fond of or given to ceremony : ceremonious, conventional, courtly, punctilious. *See* COURTESY. **2.** Of or characterized by ceremony : ceremonial, ceremonious, liturgical, ritual, ritualistic. *See* RITUAL. **3.** Requiring elegant clothes and fine manners : dressy, full-dress. *See* PLAIN.

formalistic *adjective*
Characterized by a narrow concern for book learning and formal rules, without knowledge or experience of practical matters : academic, bookish, donnish, inkhorn, literary, pedantic, pedantical, scholastic. *See* ATTITUDE, FLEXIBLE, TEACH.

formality *noun*
1. Strict observance of social conventions : ceremoniousness, ceremony, protocol, punctiliousness. *See* COURTESY. **2.** A conventional social gesture or act without intrinsic purpose : ceremony, form, ritual. *See* RITUAL, USUAL.

formation *noun*
A way or condition of being arranged : arrangement, categorization, classification, deployment, disposal, disposition, distribution, grouping, layout, lineup, order, organization, placement, sequence. *See* ORDER.

former *adjective*
1. Just gone by or elapsed : antecedent, anterior, earlier, foregoing, past, precedent, preceding, previous, prior. *See* TIME. **2.** Having been such previously : erstwhile, late, old, once, onetime, past, previous, quondam, sometime, whilom. *See* PRECEDE.

formerly *adverb*
At a time in the past : already, before, earlier, erstwhile, once, previously. *Archaic:* aforetime, beforetime. *See* PRECEDE.

formidable *adjective*
1. Causing or able to cause fear : appalling, dire, direful, dreadful, fearful, fearsome, frightful, ghastly, redoubtable, scary, terrible, tremendous. *See* FEAR. **2.** Requiring great or extreme bodily, mental, or spiritual strength : arduous, backbreaking, burdensome, demanding, difficult, effortful, exacting, exigent, hard, heavy, laborious, onerous, oppressive, rigorous, rough, severe, taxing, tough, trying, weighty. *See* HEAVY.

formless *adjective*
Having no distinct shape : amorphous, inchoate, shapeless, unformed, unshaped. *See* ORDER.

formula *noun*
A means or method of entering into or achieving something desirable : key, route, secret. *Informal:* ticket. *See* MEANS.

formulaic *adjective*
Being of no special quality or type : average, common, commonplace, cut-and-dried, garden, garden-variety, indifferent, mediocre, ordinary, plain, routine, run-of-the-mill, standard, stock,

undistinguished, unexceptional, unremarkable. *See* GOOD, USUAL.

formulate *verb*
1. To convey in language or words of a particular form : couch, express, phrase, put, word. *See* WORDS. **2.** To devise and set down : draft, draw up, frame. *See* WORDS. **3.** To form a strategy for : blueprint, cast, chart, conceive, contrive, design, devise, frame, lay[1], plan, project, scheme, strategize, work out. *Informal:* dope out. ***Idiom:*** lay plans. *See* PLANNED. **4.** To use ingenuity in making, developing, or achieving : concoct, contrive, devise, dream up, fabricate, hatch, invent, make up, think up. *Informal:* cook up. ***Idiom:*** come up with. *See* MAKE.

forsake *verb*
To give up or leave without intending to return or claim again : abandon, desert[3], leave[1], quit, throw over. ***Idioms:*** run out on, walk out on. *See* KEEP.

forsaken *adjective*
Having been given up and left alone : abandoned, bereft, derelict, deserted, desolate, forlorn, lorn. *See* KEEP.

forswear also **foreswear** *verb*
1. To give up a possession, claim, or right : abandon, abdicate, cede, demit, hand over, quitclaim, relinquish, render, renounce, resign, surrender, waive, yield. *See* KEEP. **2.** To make untrue declarations : falsify, fib, lie[2], prevaricate. *Law:* perjure. *See* TRUE.

forsworn or **foresworn** *adjective*
Marked by lying under oath : perjured, perjurious. *See* TRUE.

forte *noun*
Something at which a person excels : long suit, métier, specialty, strong point, strong suit. *Slang:* bag, thing. *See* ABILITY.

forthcoming *adjective*
In the relatively near future : approaching, coming, upcoming. *See* NEAR.

forthright *adjective*
Manifesting honesty and directness, especially in speech : candid, direct, downright, frank, honest, ingenuous, man-to-man, open, plainspoken, straight, straightforward, straight-out, unreserved. *Informal:* straight-from-the-shoulder, straight-shooting. *See* CLEAR, SHOW.

forthwith *adverb*
Without delay : directly, immediately, instant, instantly, now, right away, right off, straightaway, straight off. ***Idioms:*** at once, first off. *See* TIME.

fortify *verb*
1. To prepare (oneself) for action : brace, forearm, gird, ready, steel, strengthen. ***Idiom:*** gird (*or* gird up) one's loins. *See* PREPARED. **2.** To make firmer in a particular conviction or habit : confirm, harden, strengthen. *See* STRONG.

fortitude *noun*
The quality of mind enabling one to face danger or hardship resolutely : braveness, bravery, courage, courageousness, dauntlessness, doughtiness, fearlessness, gallantry, gameness, heart, intrepidity, intrepidness, mettle, nerve, pluck, pluckiness, spirit, stoutheartedness, undauntedness, valiance, valiancy, valiantness, valor. *Informal:* spunk, spunkiness. *Slang:* gut (used in plural), gutsiness, moxie. *See* FEAR.

fortitudinous *adjective*
Having or showing courage : audacious, bold, brave, courageous, dauntless, doughty, fearless, gallant, game, hardy, heroic, intrepid, mettlesome, plucky, stout, stouthearted, unafraid, undaunted, valiant, valorous. *Informal:* spunky. *Slang:* gutsy, gutty. *See* FEAR.

fortuitous *adjective*
Occurring unexpectedly : accidental, casual, chance, contingent, fluky, inadvertent, odd. *See* SURPRISE.

fortuitousness *noun*
The quality shared by random, unintended, or unpredictable events or this quality regarded as the cause of such events : chance, fortuity, fortune, hap, hazard, luck. *See* CERTAIN.

fortuity *noun*
1. An unexpected random event : accident, chance, fluke, hap, happenchance, happenstance, hazard. *See* CERTAIN, SURPRISE. **2.** The quality shared by random, unintended, or unpredictable events or this quality regarded as the cause of such events : chance, fortuitousness, fortune, hap, hazard, luck. *See* CERTAIN.

fortunate *adjective*
1. Indicative of future success or full of promise : auspicious, benign, bright, brilliant, fair, favorable, good, propitious. *See* LUCK. **2.** Characterized by luck or good fortune : happy, lucky, providential. *See* LUCK.

fortunateness *noun*
Success attained as a result of chance : fortune, luck, luckiness. ***Idiom:*** good fortune (*or* luck). *See* LUCK.

fortune *noun*
1. The quality shared by random, unintended, or unpredictable events or this quality regarded as the cause of such events : chance, fortuitous-

ness, fortuity, hap, hazard, luck. *See* CERTAIN. **2.** Success attained as a result of chance : fortunateness, luck, luckiness. ***Idiom:*** good fortune (*or* luck). *See* LUCK. **3.** All things, such as money, property, or goods, having economic value : asset (used in plural), capital, mean[3] (used in plural), resource (used in plural), wealth, wherewithal. *See* OWNED. **4.** A great amount of accumulated money and precious possessions : affluence, pelf, riches, treasure, wealth. *See* OWNED, RICH. **5.** A large sum of money : mint. *Informal:* bundle, pretty penny, tidy sum, wad. *Slang:* pile. *See* RICH. **6.** That which is inevitably destined : destiny, fate, kismet, lot, portion, predestination. *See* CERTAIN.

forward *adjective*
1. Rude and disrespectful : assuming, assumptive, audacious, bold, boldfaced, brash, brazen, cheeky, contumelious, familiar, impertinent, impudent, insolent, malapert, nervy, overconfident, pert, presuming, presumptuous, pushy, sassy, saucy, smart. *Informal:* brassy, flip, fresh, smart-alecky, snippety, snippy, uppish, uppity. *Slang:* wise[1]. *See* ATTITUDE, COURTESY. **2.** Ahead of current trends or customs : advanced, precocious, progressive. *See* PRECEDE.
forward *verb* **1.** To cause (something) to be conveyed to a destination : address, consign, dispatch, route, send, ship, transmit. *See* MOVE. **2.** To cause to move forward or upward, as toward a goal : advance, further, promote. *See* FORWARD, HELP.

forwardness *noun*
The state or quality of being impudent or arrogantly self-confident : assumption, audaciousness, audacity, boldness, brashness, brazenness, cheek, cheekiness, chutzpah, discourtesy, disrespect, effrontery, face, familiarity, gall[1], impertinence, impudence, impudency, incivility, insolence, nerve, nerviness, overconfidence, pertness, presumptuousness, pushiness, rudeness, sassiness, sauciness. *Informal:* brass, crust, sauce, uppishness, uppityness. *See* ATTITUDE, COURTESY.

fossil *noun*
An old-fashioned person who is reluctant to change or innovate : fogy, fuddy-duddy, mossback. *Informal:* stick-in-the-mud. *Slang:* square. *See* NEW.

foster *verb*
1. To promote and sustain the development of : cultivate, nourish, nurse, nurture. *See* CARE FOR. **2.** To help bring about : encourage, feed, promote. *See* HELP.

foul *adjective*
1. Extremely unpleasant to the senses or feelings : atrocious, disgusting, horrid, nasty, nauseating, offensive, repellent, repulsive, revolting, sickening, ugly, unwholesome, vile. *See* LIKE, PAIN. **2.** Having an unpleasant odor : fetid, foul-smelling, malodorous, mephitic, noisome, reeky, stinking. *Informal:* smelly. *See* SMELLS. **3.** Heavily soiled; very dirty or unclean : filthy, nasty, squalid, vile. *See* CLEAN. **4.** Offensive to accepted standards of decency : barnyard, bawdy, broad, coarse, dirty, Fescennine, filthy, gross, lewd, nasty, obscene, profane, ribald, scatologic, scatological, scurrilous, smutty, vulgar. *Slang:* raunchy. *See* DECENT. **5.** So objectionable as to elicit despisal or deserve condemnation : abhorrent, abominable, antipathetic, contemptible, despicable, despisable, detestable, disgusting, filthy, infamous, loathsome, lousy, low, mean[2], nasty, nefarious, obnoxious, odious, repugnant, rotten, shabby, vile, wretched. *See* GOOD.
foul *verb* **1.** To make physically impure : contaminate, defile, poison, pollute. *See* CLEAN. **2.** To twist together so that separation is difficult : ensnarl, entangle, snarl[2], tangle. *See* ORDER.
foul up *verb* To harm irreparably through inept handling; make a mess : ball up, blunder, boggle, botch, bungle, fumble, gum up, mess up, mishandle, mismanage, muddle, muff, spoil. *Informal:* bollix up, muck up. *Slang:* blow[1], goof up, louse up, screw up, snafu. ***Idiom:*** make a muck of. *See* CORRECT, HELP.

foulness *noun*
1. The condition or state of being dirty : dirtiness, filth, filthiness, griminess, grubbiness, smuttiness, squalor, uncleanliness, uncleanness. *See* CLEAN. **2.** Impure condition : defilement, dirtiness, impurity, pollution, uncleanness, unwholesomeness. *See* CLEAN. **3.** The quality or state of being obscene : bawdiness, coarseness, dirtiness, filthiness, grossness, lewdness, obscenity, profaneness, profanity, scurrility, scurrilousness, smuttiness, vulgarity, vulgarness. *Slang:* raunch, raunchiness. *See* DECENT.

foul-smelling *adjective*
Having an unpleasant odor : fetid, foul, malodorous, mephitic, noisome, reeky, stinking. *Informal:* smelly. *See* SMELLS.

foul-up *noun*
A ruinous state of disorder : botch, mess, muddle, shambles. *Informal:* hash. *Slang:* screwup, snafu. *See* CORRECT, ORDER.

foul up *verb* See **foul.**

found *verb*
1. To bring into existence formally : constitute, create, establish, institute, organize, originate, set up, start. *See* START. **2.** To provide a basis for : base[1], build, establish, ground, predicate, rest[1], root[1], underpin. *See* OVER.
foundation *noun*
1. The act of founding or establishing : constitution, creation, establishment, institution, organization, origination, start-up. *See* START. **2.** The lowest or supporting part or structure : base[1], basis, bed, bottom, foot, footing, fundament, ground, groundwork, seat, substratum, underpinning (often used in plural). *See* OVER. **3.** That on which something immaterial, such as an argument or a charge, rests : base[1], basis, footing, fundament, ground (often used in plural), groundwork, underpinning (often used in plural). *See* OVER. **4.** A fundamental principle or underlying concept : base[1], basis, cornerstone, fundament, fundamental, root[1], rudiment (often used in plural). *See* OVER. **5.** A justifying fact or consideration : basis, justification, reason, warrant. *See* TRUE.
foundational *adjective*
Arising from or going to the root or source : basal, basic, fundamental, original, primary, radical, underlying. *See* SURFACE.
founder[1] *verb*
To go beneath the surface or to the bottom of a liquid : sink, submerge, submerse. *See* RISE.
founder[2] *noun*
One that creates, founds, or originates : architect, author, creator, entrepreneur, father, inventor, maker, originator, parent, patriarch. *See* START.
fount *noun*
A point of origination : beginning, derivation, fountain, fountainhead, mother, origin, parent, provenance, provenience, root[1], rootstock, source, spring, well[1]. *See* START.
fountain *noun*
A point of origination : beginning, derivation, fount, fountainhead, mother, origin, parent, provenance, provenience, root[1], rootstock, source, spring, well[1]. *See* START.
fountainhead *noun*
A point of origination : beginning, derivation, fount, fountain, mother, origin, parent, provenance, provenience, root[1], rootstock, source, spring, well[1]. *See* START.
four-flush *verb*
Slang. To cause to accept what is false, especially by trickery or misrepresentation : beguile, betray, bluff, cozen, deceive, delude, double-cross, dupe, fool, hoodwink, humbug, mislead, take in, trick. *Informal:* bamboozle, have. ***Idioms:*** lead astray, play false, pull the wool over someone's eyes, put something over on, take for a ride. *See* HONEST.
fourth estate *noun*
Journalists and journalism in general : medium (used in plural **media**), press. *British:* Fleet Street. *See* WORDS.
foxiness *noun*
Deceitful cleverness : art, artfulness, artifice, craft, craftiness, cunning, guile, slyness, wiliness. *See* HONEST, MEANS.
foxy *adjective*
Deceitfully clever : artful, crafty, cunning, guileful, scheming, sharp, sly, tricky, wily. *See* ABILITY, HONEST, MEANS.
fracas *noun*
Informal. A quarrel, fight, or disturbance marked by very noisy, disorderly, and often violent behavior : affray, brawl, broil[2], donnybrook, fray, free-for-all, melee, riot, row[2], ruction, tumult. *Slang:* rumble. *See* ATTACK.
fractional *adjective*
Relating to or affecting only a part; not total : fragmentary, part, partial. *See* PART.
fractious *adjective*
Not submitting to discipline or control : disorderly, indocile, intractable, lawless, obstinate, obstreperous, recalcitrant, refractory, uncontrollable, undisciplined, ungovernable, unmanageable, unruly, untoward, wild. ***Idiom:*** out of line. *See* CONTROL, ORDER, PEACE, RESIST.
fractiousness *noun*
The quality or condition of being unruly : disorderliness, indocility, intractability, intractableness, obstinacy, obstinateness, obstreperousness, recalcitrance, recalcitrancy, refractoriness, uncontrollability, uncontrollableness, ungovernableness, unmanageability, unruliness, untowardness, wildness. *See* CONTROL, ORDER, PEACE, RESIST.
fracture *verb*
1. To crack or split into two or more fragments by means of or as a result of force, a blow, or strain : break, rift, rive, shatter, shiver[2], smash, splinter, sunder. *See* HELP. **2.** To undergo partial breaking : crack, fissure, rupture, split. *See* HELP.
fragile *adjective*
1. Easily broken or damaged : breakable, brittle, delicate, frangible. *See* STRONG. **2.** Not physically strong : decrepit, delicate, feeble, flimsy, frail, infirm, insubstantial, puny,

unsound, unsubstantial, weak, weakly. *See* STRONG.

fragileness *noun*
The condition of being infirm or physically weak : debility, decrepitude, delicacy, delicateness, feebleness, flimsiness, fragility, frailness, frailty, infirmity, insubstantiality, puniness, unsoundness, unsubstantiality, weakliness, weakness. *See* STRONG.

fragility *noun*
The condition of being infirm or physically weak : debility, decrepitude, delicacy, delicateness, feebleness, flimsiness, fragileness, frailness, frailty, infirmity, insubstantiality, puniness, unsoundness, unsubstantiality, weakliness, weakness. *See* STRONG.

fragment *noun*
1. Residual matter : butt[4], end, ort (often used in plural), scrap[1], shard, stub. *See* LEFTOVER. **2.** A tiny amount : bit[1], crumb, dab[1], dash, dot, dram, drop, grain, iota, jot, minim, mite, modicum, molecule, ort, ounce, particle, scrap[1], scruple, shred, smidgen, speck, tittle, trifle, whit. *Chiefly British:* spot. *See* BIG.
fragment *verb* To reduce or become reduced to pieces or components : break down, break up, crumble, decompose, disintegrate, dissolve, fragmentize. *See* CONTINUE, HELP.

fragmentary *adjective*
Relating to or affecting only a part; not total : fractional, part, partial. *See* PART.

fragmentize *verb*
To reduce or become reduced to pieces or components : break down, break up, crumble, decompose, disintegrate, dissolve, fragment. *See* CONTINUE, HELP.

fragrance *noun*
A sweet or pleasant odor : aroma, bouquet, perfume, redolence, scent. *See* SMELLS.

fragrant *adjective*
Having a pleasant odor : aromatic, redolent. *See* SMELLS.

frail *adjective*
Not physically strong : decrepit, delicate, feeble, flimsy, fragile, infirm, insubstantial, puny, unsound, unsubstantial, weak, weakly. *See* STRONG.

frailness *noun*
The condition of being infirm or physically weak : debility, decrepitude, delicacy, delicateness, feebleness, flimsiness, fragileness, fragility, frailty, infirmity, insubstantiality, puniness, unsoundness, unsubstantiality, weakliness, weakness. *See* STRONG.

frailty *noun*
1. The condition of being infirm or physically weak : debility, decrepitude, delicacy, delicateness, feebleness, flimsiness, fragileness, fragility, frailness, infirmity, insubstantiality, puniness, unsoundness, unsubstantiality, weakliness, weakness. *See* STRONG. **2.** An imperfection of character : failing, fault, foible, infirmity, shortcoming, weakness, weak point. *See* BETTER, HELP.

frame *verb*
1. To create by forming, combining, or altering materials : assemble, build, construct, fabricate, fashion, forge[1], make, manufacture, mold, produce, put together, shape. *See* MAKE. **2.** To form a strategy for : blueprint, cast, chart, conceive, contrive, design, devise, formulate, lay[1], plan, project, scheme, strategize, work out. *Informal:* dope out. ***Idiom:*** lay plans. *See* PLANNED. **3.** To devise and set down : draft, draw up, formulate. *See* WORDS.

frame of mind *noun*
A temporary state of mind or feeling : humor, mood, spirit (used in plural), temper, vein. *See* FEELINGS.

frame of reference *noun*
The particular angle from which something is considered : angle[2], aspect, facet, hand, light[1], phase, regard, respect, side. *See* PERSPECTIVE.

frangible *adjective*
Easily broken or damaged : breakable, brittle, delicate, fragile. *See* STRONG.

frank *adjective*
Manifesting honesty and directness, especially in speech : candid, direct, downright, forthright, honest, ingenuous, man-to-man, open, plainspoken, straight, straightforward, straight-out, unreserved. *Informal:* straight-from-the-shoulder, straight-shooting. *See* CLEAR, SHOW.

frantic *adjective*
Marked by extreme excitement, confusion, or agitation : delirious, frenetic, frenzied, mad, wild. *Archaic:* madding. *See* CALM.

frantically *adverb*
In a violent, strenuous way : fiercely, frenziedly, furiously, hard, strenuously. *See* STRONG.

fraternity *noun*
A group of people united in a relationship and having some interest, activity, or purpose in common : association, club, confederation, congress, federation, fellowship, guild, league, order, organization, society, sorority, union. *See* GROUP.

fraternize *verb*
To be with as a companion : associate, consort, hang around, hobnob, run (around), troop. *Slang:* hang out. ***Idiom:*** rub elbows (*or* shoulders) . *See* NEAR.

fraud *noun*
1. An act of cheating : cheat, swindle, victimization. *Informal:* flimflam. *Slang:* gyp. *See* HONEST. **2.** One who fakes : charlatan, fake, faker, humbug, impostor, mountebank, phony, pretender, quack. *See* TRUE.

fraudulent *adjective*
Fraudulently or deceptively imitative : bogus, counterfeit, fake, false, phony, sham, spurious, suppositious, supposititious. *See* TRUE.

fray *noun*
A quarrel, fight, or disturbance marked by very noisy, disorderly, and often violent behavior : affray, brawl, broil[2], donnybrook, free-for-all, melee, riot, row[2], ruction, tumult. *Informal:* fracas. *Slang:* rumble. *See* ATTACK.

freak *noun*
1. A person or animal that is abnormally formed : monster, monstrosity. *See* USUAL. **2.** An impulsive, often illogical turn of mind : bee, boutade, caprice, conceit, fancy, humor, impulse, megrim, notion, vagary, whim, whimsy. ***Idiom:*** bee in one's bonnet. *See* THOUGHTS. **3.** *Slang.* A person who is ardently devoted to a particular subject or activity : bug, devotee, enthusiast, fanatic, maniac, zealot. *Informal:* buff[2], fan[2], fiend. *Slang:* nut. *See* CONCERN.

freakish *adjective*
1. Deviating from the customary : bizarre, cranky, curious, eccentric, erratic, idiosyncratic, odd, outlandish, peculiar, quaint, queer, quirky, singular, strange, unnatural, unusual, weird. *Slang:* kooky, screwball. *British Slang:* rum, rummy[2]. *See* USUAL. **2.** Resembling a freak : freaky, grotesque, monstrous. *See* USUAL. **3.** Following no predictable pattern : capricious, changeable, erratic, fantastic, fantastical, fickle, inconsistent, inconstant, mercurial, temperamental, ticklish, uncertain, unpredictable, unstable, unsteady, variable, volatile, whimsical. *See* CHANGE, CONTINUE.

freaky *adjective*
Resembling a freak : freakish, grotesque, monstrous. *See* USUAL.

freckle *verb*
To mark with many small spots : bespeckle, besprinkle, dapple, dot, fleck, mottle, pepper, speck, speckle, sprinkle, stipple. *See* MARKS.

free *adjective*
1. Able to move about at will without bounds or restraint : loose, unconfined, unrestrained. ***Idioms:*** at large, at liberty, free as a bird, on the loose. *See* FREE. **2.** Having political independence : autonomous, independent, self-governing, sovereign. *See* DEPENDENCE, FREE. **3.** Lacking literal exactness : inexact, loose. *See* PRECISE. **4.** Costing nothing : complimentary, gratis, gratuitous. ***Idiom:*** on the house. *See* MONEY. **5.** Not spoken for or occupied : open, uninhabited, unoccupied, unreserved. *See* OWNED. **6.** Free from obstructions : clear, open, unblocked, unimpeded, unobstructed. *See* OPEN. **7.** Speaking or spoken without reserve : free-spoken, outspoken, vocal. *See* RESTRAINT. **8.** Characterized by bounteous giving : freehanded, generous, handsome, lavish, liberal, munificent, openhanded, unsparing, unstinting. *See* GIVE. **9.** Done by one's own choice : spontaneous, uncompelled, unforced, volitional, voluntary, willful. *See* WILLING. **10.** Freed from contact or connection : clear. *See* FREE, STRIKE.

free *verb* **1.** To set at liberty : discharge, emancipate, liberate, loose, manumit, release. *Slang:* spring. ***Idiom:*** let loose. *See* FREE. **2.** To rid of obstructions : clear, open, unblock. *See* OPEN.

freebee *noun* See **freebie.**

freebie also **freebee** *noun*
Slang. A free ticket entitling one to transportation or admission : pass. *Informal:* comp. *See* ENTER, TRANSACTIONS.

freedom *noun*
1. Departure from normal rules or procedures : liberty, license. *See* RESTRAINT. **2.** The state of not being in confinement or servitude : emancipation, liberation, liberty, manumission. *See* FREE. **3.** The condition of being politically free : autonomy, independence, independency, liberty, self-government, sovereignty. *See* DEPENDENCE, FREE. **4.** Ease of or space for movement : elbowroom, play. *See* TIGHTEN.

free-for-all *noun*
A quarrel, fight, or disturbance marked by very noisy, disorderly, and often violent behavior : affray, brawl, broil[2], donnybrook, fray, melee, riot, row[2], ruction, tumult. *Informal:* fracas. *Slang:* rumble. *See* ATTACK.

freehanded *adjective*
Characterized by bounteous giving : free, generous, handsome, lavish, liberal, munificent, openhanded, unsparing, unstinting. *See* GIVE.

freehandedness *noun*
The quality or state of being generous : bigheartedness, bounteousness, bountifulness, generosity, generousness, great-heartedness, large-heartedness, lavishness, liberality, magnanimity, magnanimousness, munificence, openhandedness, unselfishness, unsparingness. *See* GIVE.

freeload *verb*
Slang. To take advantage of the generosity of others : leech. *Informal:* sponge. *See* DEPENDENCE.

freeloader *noun*
Slang. One who depends on another for support without reciprocating : bloodsucker, hanger-on, leech, parasite, sponge. *See* DEPENDENCE.

freeloading *adjective*
Slang. Of or characteristic of a parasite : bloodsucking, parasitic, parasitical. *See* DEPENDENCE.

freely *adverb*
Of one's own free will : spontaneously, voluntarily, willfully, willingly. ***Idioms:*** of one's own accord, on one's own volition. *See* WILLING.

free-spoken *adjective*
Speaking or spoken without reserve : free, outspoken, vocal. *See* RESTRAINT.

freeway *noun*
A course affording passage from one place to another : avenue, boulevard, drive, expressway, highway, path, road, roadway, route, street, superhighway, thoroughfare, thruway, turnpike, way. *See* MOVE, OPEN.

freezing *adjective*
Very cold : arctic, boreal, frigid, frosty, gelid, glacial, icy, polar, wintry. *Archaic:* frore. ***Idiom:*** bitter (*or* bitterly) cold. *See* HOT.

freight *noun*
Something carried physically : burden[1], cargo, haul, load. *Sports:* impost. *See* HEAVY, OVER.
freight *verb* **1.** To place a burden or heavy load on : burden[1], charge, cumber, encumber, lade, load, saddle, tax, weight. *See* OVER. **2.** To make or become full; put as much into as can be held : charge, fill, heap, load, pack, pile. *See* FULL. **3.** To cause to be filled, as with a particular mood or tone : charge, imbue, impregnate, permeate, pervade, saturate, suffuse, transfuse. *See* FULL.

frenetic *adjective*
Marked by extreme excitement, confusion, or agitation : delirious, frantic, frenzied, mad, wild. *Archaic:* madding. *See* CALM.

frenzied *adjective*
Marked by extreme excitement, confusion, or agitation : delirious, frantic, frenetic, mad, wild. *Archaic:* madding. *See* CALM.

frenziedly *adverb*
In a violent, strenuous way : fiercely, frantically, furiously, hard, strenuously. *See* STRONG.

frequent *adjective*
Occurring quite often : common, everyday, familiar, regular, routine, widespread. *See* USUAL.
frequent *verb* To visit regularly : hang around, haunt, repair[2], resort. *Slang:* hang out. *See* PLACE.

frequently *adverb*
In an expected or customary manner; for the most part : commonly, consistently, customarily, generally, habitually, naturally, normally, often, regularly, routinely, typically, usually. ***Idioms:*** as usual, per usual. *See* BIG, USUAL.

fresh *adjective*
1. Not the same as what was previously known or done : different, innovative, inventive, new, newfangled, novel, original, unfamiliar, unprecedented. *See* NEW. **2.** Not previously used : brand-new, new. *See* NEW. **3.** Being an addition : added, additional, extra, further, more, new, other. *See* INCREASE. **4.** Bright and clear in complexion; not dull or faded : blooming, creamy, glowing, peaches-and-cream. *See* BEAUTIFUL. **5.** *Informal.* Rude and disrespectful : assuming, assumptive, audacious, bold, boldfaced, brash, brazen, cheeky, contumelious, familiar, forward, impertinent, impudent, insolent, malapert, nervy, overconfident, pert, presuming, presumptuous, pushy, sassy, saucy, smart. *Informal:* brassy, flip, smart-alecky, snippety, snippy, uppish, uppity. *Slang:* wise[1]. *See* ATTITUDE, COURTESY.

freshen *verb*
1. To make neat and trim; make presentable. Also used with *up* : clean (up), groom, neaten (up), slick up, spruce (up), tidy (up), trig (out), trim. *See* ORDER. **2.** To impart renewed energy and strength to (a person) : refresh, reinvigorate, rejuvenate, renew, restore, revitalize, revivify. *See* HELP, STRONG.

freshet *noun*
An abundant, usually overwhelming flow or fall, as of a river or rain : alluvion, cataclysm, cataract, deluge, downpour, flood, inundation, Niagara, overflow, torrent. *Chiefly British:* spate. *See* BIG.

freshman *noun*
One who is just starting to learn or do something : abecedarian, beginner, fledgling, greenhorn, initiate, neophyte, novice, novitiate, tenderfoot, tyro. *Slang:* rookie. *See* START.

freshness *noun*
The quality of being novel : innovativeness, newfangledness, newness, novelty, originality. *See* NEW.

fret *verb*
1. To trouble the nerves or peace of mind of, especially by repeated vexations : aggravate, annoy, bother, bug, chafe, disturb, exasperate, gall[2], get, irk, irritate, nettle, peeve, provoke, put out, rile, ruffle, vex. ***Idioms:*** get in one's hair, get on one's nerves, get under one's skin. *See* FEELINGS, PAIN. **2.** To focus the attention on something moodily and at length : brood, cark, dwell, mope, worry. *Informal:* stew. *See* CONCERN, THOUGHTS. **3.** To make (the skin) raw by or as if by friction : abrade, chafe, excoriate, gall[2], irritate. *See* HELP.

fretful *adjective*
1. Having or showing a bad temper : bad-tempered, cantankerous, crabbed, cranky, cross, disagreeable, grouchy, grumpy, ill-tempered, irascible, irritable, nasty, peevish, petulant, querulous, snappish, snappy, surly, testy, ugly, waspish. *Informal:* crabby, mean[2]. ***Idiom:*** out of sorts. *See* ATTITUDE. **2.** Being unable or unwilling to endure irritation or opposition, for example : impatient, intolerant, unforbearing. *See* ACCEPT, ATTITUDE, CALM.

friction *noun*
A state of disagreement and disharmony : clash, conflict, confrontation, contention, difference, difficulty, disaccord, discord, discordance, dissension, dissent, dissentience, dissidence, dissonance, faction, inharmony, schism, strife, variance, war, warfare. *See* CONFLICT.

friend *noun*
1. A person whom one knows well, likes, and trusts : amigo, brother, chum, confidant, confidante, familiar, intimate[1], mate. *Informal:* bud[2], buddy, pal. *Slang:* sidekick. *See* LOVE. **2.** A person whom one knows casually : acquaintance. *See* KNOWLEDGE. **3.** A person who supports or champions an activity, cause, or institution, for example : backer, benefactor, contributor, patron, sponsor, supporter. *Informal:* angel. *See* HELP.

friendliness *noun*
The quality of being pleasant and friendly : affability, agreeability, agreeableness, amenity, amiability, amiableness, congeniality, congenialness, cordiality, cordialness, geniality, genialness, pleasantness, sociability, sociableness, warmth. *See* ATTITUDE, GOOD.

friendly *adjective*
1. Of or befitting a friend or friends : amicable, neighborly, warmhearted. *See* ATTITUDE, LOVE. **2.** Very closely associated : chummy, close, familiar, intimate[1]. *Informal:* thick. *Slang:* tight. ***Idiom:*** hand in glove with. *See* LOVE.

friendship *noun*
The condition of being friends : chumminess, closeness, companionship, comradeship, familiarity, fellowship, intimacy. *See* LOVE.

fright *noun*
1. Great agitation and anxiety caused by the expectation or the realization of danger : affright, alarm, apprehension, dread, fear, fearfulness, funk, horror, panic, terror, trepidation. *Slang:* cold feet. ***Idiom:*** fear and trembling. *See* FEAR. **2.** *Informal.* An unsightly object : mess, monstrosity, ugliness. *Informal:* sight, ugly. *See* BEAUTIFUL.

fright *verb Archaic.* To fill with fear : affright, alarm, frighten, panic, scare, scarify[2], startle, terrify, terrorize. ***Idioms:*** make one's blood run cold, make one's hair stand on end, scare silly (*or* stiff), scare the daylights out of. *See* FEAR.

frighten *verb*
To fill with fear : affright, alarm, panic, scare, scarify[2], startle, terrify, terrorize. *Archaic:* fright. ***Idioms:*** make one's blood run cold, make one's hair stand on end, scare silly (*or* stiff), scare the daylights out of. *See* FEAR.

frightful *adjective*
1. Very bad : appalling, awful, dreadful, fearful, ghastly, horrendous, horrible, shocking, terrible. *See* GOOD. **2.** Causing or able to cause fear : appalling, dire, direful, dreadful, fearful, fearsome, formidable, ghastly, redoubtable, scary, terrible, tremendous. *See* FEAR.

frigid *adjective*
1. Very cold : arctic, boreal, freezing, frosty, gelid, glacial, icy, polar, wintry. *Archaic:* frore. ***Idiom:*** bitter (*or* bitterly) cold. *See* HOT. **2.** Lacking all friendliness and warmth : cold, frosty, glacial, icy. *See* ATTITUDE, HOT. **3.** Deficient in or lacking sexual desire : ardorless, cold, inhibited, passionless, unresponsive. *See* SEX.

frigidity *noun*
Extreme lack of warmth : frigidness, frosti-

ness, gelidity, gelidness, iciness, wintriness. *See* HOT.

frigidness *noun*
Extreme lack of warmth : frigidity, frostiness, gelidity, gelidness, iciness, wintriness. *See* HOT.

frill *noun*
Something costly and unnecessary : extravagance, extravagancy, luxury. *See* SAVE.

fringe *noun*
1. A fairly narrow line or space forming a boundary : border, borderline, brim, brink, edge, edging, margin, periphery, rim, verge. *Chiefly Military:* perimeter. *See* EDGE. **2.** The periphery of a city or town : edge, environs, outskirt (often used in plural), skirt (used in plural), suburb (used in plural). *See* EDGE.
fringe *verb* To put or form a border on : border, bound[2], edge, margin, rim, skirt, verge. *See* EDGE.

frippery *noun*
1. Showy and elaborate clothing or apparel : array, attire, finery, regalia. *See* PUT ON.
2. Something or things that are unimportant : fiddle-faddle, frivolity, froth, minutia, nonsense, small change, small potatoes, trifle, trivia, triviality. *See* IMPORTANT, SURFACE.

frisk *verb*
1. To leap and skip about playfully : caper, cavort, dance, frolic, gambol, rollick, romp. *See* WORK. **2.** To examine the person or personal effects of in order to find something lost or concealed : inspect, search. *Slang:* shake down. *See* INVESTIGATE.
frisk *noun* A thorough search of a place or persons : search. *Slang:* shakedown. *See* INVESTIGATE.

friskiness *noun*
The state of being full of high-spirited fun : frolicsomeness, playfulness, sportiveness, waggishness. *See* WORK.

frisky *adjective*
Full of high-spirited fun : frolicsome, impish, mischievous, playful, sportive, waggish. *See* WORK.

fritter away *verb*
To spend (money) excessively and usually foolishly : consume, dissipate, fool away, riot away, squander, throw away, trifle away, waste. *Slang:* blow[1]. *See* SAVE.

frivolity *noun*
Something or things that are unimportant : fiddle-faddle, frippery, froth, minutia, nonsense, small change, small potatoes, trifle, trivia, triviality. *See* IMPORTANT, SURFACE.

frivolous *adjective*
Given to lighthearted silliness : empty-headed, featherbrained, flighty, frothy, giddy, harebrained, lighthearted, scatterbrained, silly. *Informal:* gaga. *Slang:* birdbrained, dizzy. *See* ABILITY.

frock *noun*
A one-piece skirted outer garment for women and children : dress, gown. *See* PUT ON.

frolic *noun*
A mischievous act : antic, caper, joke, lark, prank[1], trick. *Informal:* shenanigan. *Slang:* monkeyshine (often used in plural). *See* GOOD, WORK.
frolic *verb* **1.** To leap and skip about playfully : caper, cavort, dance, frisk, gambol, rollick, romp. *See* WORK. **2.** To behave riotously : carouse, revel, riot, roister. *Informal:* hell (around). ***Idioms:*** blow off steam, cut loose, kick over the traces, kick up one's heels, let go, let loose, make merry, make whoopee, paint the town red, raise Cain (*or* the devil *or* hell), whoop it up. *See* RESTRAINT.

frolicsome *adjective*
Full of high-spirited fun : frisky, impish, mischievous, playful, sportive, waggish. *See* WORK.

frolicsomeness *noun*
The state of being full of high-spirited fun : friskiness, playfulness, sportiveness, waggishness. *See* WORK.

front *noun*
1. The part of someone or something facing the viewer : fore, forepart. *See* PRECEDE. **2.** The forward outer surface of a building : façade, face, frontage, frontal. *Architecture:* frontispiece. *See* PRECEDE. **3.** A deceptive outward appearance : cloak, color, coloring, cover, disguise, disguisement, façade, face, false colors, gloss, guise, mask, masquerade, pretense, pretext, semblance, show, veil, veneer, window-dressing. *Slang:* put-on. *See* SHOW.
front *verb* **1.** To have the face or front turned in a specific direction : face, look (on *or* upon). *See* PRECEDE. **2.** To meet face-to-face, especially defiantly : accost, confront, encounter, face. *See* MEET. **3.** To confront boldly and courageously : beard, brave, challenge, dare, defy, face. ***Idioms:*** fly in the face of, snap one's fingers at, stand up to, thumb one's nose at. *See* RESIST.

frontage *noun*
The forward outer surface of a building : façade, face, front, frontal. *Architecture:* frontispiece. *See* PRECEDE.

frontal *noun*
The forward outer surface of a building : façade, face, front, frontage. *Architecture:* frontispiece. *See* PRECEDE.

frontier *noun*
The line or area separating geopolitical units : border, borderland, boundary, march², marchland. *See* EDGE, TERRITORY.

frontispiece *noun*
Architecture. The forward outer surface of a building : façade, face, front, frontage, frontal. *See* PRECEDE.

front-runner also **frontrunner** *noun*
A leading contestant : leader, number one. *See* PRECEDE.

frore *adjective*
Archaic. Very cold : arctic, boreal, freezing, frigid, frosty, gelid, glacial, icy, polar, wintry. *Idiom:* bitter (*or* bitterly) cold. *See* HOT.

frostiness *noun*
Extreme lack of warmth : frigidity, frigidness, gelidity, gelidness, iciness, wintriness. *See* HOT.

frosty *adjective*
1. Very cold : arctic, boreal, freezing, frigid, gelid, glacial, icy, polar, wintry. *Archaic:* frore. *Idiom:* bitter (*or* bitterly) cold. *See* HOT.
2. Lacking all friendliness and warmth : cold, frigid, glacial, icy. *See* ATTITUDE, HOT.

froth *noun*
1. A mass of bubbles in or on the surface of a liquid : foam, head, lather, spume, suds, yeast. *See* SOLID. **2.** Something or things that are unimportant : fiddle-faddle, frippery, frivolity, minutia, nonsense, small change, small potatoes, trifle, trivia, triviality. *See* IMPORTANT, SURFACE.
froth *verb* To form or cause to form foam : bubble, cream, effervesce, fizz, foam, lather, spume, suds, yeast. *See* SOLID.

frothy *adjective*
1. Consisting of or resembling foam : foamy, lathery, spumous, spumy, sudsy, yeasty. *See* SOLID. **2.** Amusing but essentially empty and frivolous : light². *See* SURFACE. **3.** Given to lighthearted silliness : empty-headed, featherbrained, flighty, frivolous, giddy, harebrained, lighthearted, scatterbrained, silly. *Informal:* gaga. *Slang:* birdbrained, dizzy. *See* ABILITY.

froward *adjective*
Given to acting in opposition to others : balky, contrarious, contrary, difficult, impossible, ornery, perverse, wayward. *See* ATTITUDE, SUPPORT.

frown *verb*
To wrinkle one's brow, as in thought, puzzlement, or displeasure : glower, lower¹, scowl. *Idiom:* look black. *See* EXPRESS.
frown on (or **upon**) *verb* To have or express an unfavorable opinion of : deprecate, disapprove, discountenance, disesteem, disfavor, object. *Idioms:* hold no brief for, not go for, take a dim view of, take exception to. *See* LIKE.
frown *noun* The act of wrinkling the brow, as in thought, puzzlement, or displeasure : black look, glower, lower¹, scowl. *See* EXPRESS.

frown on or **upon** *verb* See **frown.**

frowsy *adjective* See **frowzy.**

frowzy also **frowsy** *adjective*
Smelling of mildew or decay : fusty, moldy, musty, putrid, rancid, rank², rotten. *See* SMELLS.

frugal *adjective*
Careful in the use of material resources : canny, chary, economical, provident, prudent, saving, Scotch, sparing, thrifty. *See* CAREFUL, SAVE.

frugality *noun*
Careful use of material resources : economy, providence, prudence, thrift, thriftiness. *See* SAVE.

fruit *noun*
1. The produce harvested from the land : crop, fruitage, harvest, yield. *See* INGESTION.
2. Something brought about by a cause : aftermath, consequence, corollary, effect, end product, event, harvest, issue, outcome, precipitate, ramification, result, resultant, sequel, sequence, sequent, upshot. *See* CAUSE.

fruitage *noun*
The produce harvested from the land : crop, fruit, harvest, yield. *See* INGESTION.

fruitful *adjective*
1. Capable of reproducing : fecund, fertile, productive, prolific. *Biology:* proliferous. *See* RICH. **2.** Characterized by great productivity : fecund, fertile, productive, prolific, rich. *See* RICH.

fruitfulness *noun*
The quality or state of being fertile : fecundity, fertility, productiveness, productivity, prolificacy, prolificness, richness. *See* RICH.

fruition *noun*
The condition of being fulfilled : consummation, culmination, fulfillment, materialization, realization. *See* DO, HAPPY.

fruitless *adjective*
Having no useful result : barren, bootless, futile, unavailing, unprofitable, unsuccessful, useless, vain. *Idiom:* in vain. *See* THRIVE, USED.

fruitlessness *noun*
The condition or quality of being useless or ineffective : bootlessness, futility, unavailingness, unprofitableness, uselessness, vainness, vanity. *See* THRIVE, USED.

fruity *adjective*
Slang. Afflicted with or exhibiting irrationality and mental unsoundness : brainsick, crazy, daft, demented, disordered, distraught, dotty, insane, lunatic, mad, maniac, maniacal, mentally ill, moonstruck, off, touched, unbalanced, unsound, wrong. *Informal:* bonkers, cracked, daffy, gaga, loony. *Slang:* bananas, batty, buggy, cuckoo, loco, nuts, nutty, screwy, wacky. *Chiefly British:* crackers. *Law:* non compos mentis. ***Idioms:*** around the bend, crazy as a loon, mad as a hatter, not all there, nutty as a fruitcake, off (*or* out of) one's head, off one's rocker, of unsound mind, out of one's mind, sick in the head, stark raving mad. *See* SANE.

frumpish *adjective*
Quite outmoded or unfashionable : dowdy. *Informal:* tacky[2]. *See* NEW.

frustrate *verb*
To prevent from accomplishing a purpose : baffle, balk, check, checkmate, defeat, foil, stymie, thwart. *Informal:* cross, stump. ***Idiom:*** cut the ground from under. *See* ALLOW.

fuddle *verb*
1. To cause to be unclear in mind or intent : addle, befuddle, bewilder, confound, confuse, discombobulate, dizzy, jumble, mix up, muddle, mystify, perplex, puzzle. *Informal:* throw. ***Idiom:*** make one's head reel (*or* swim *or* whirl). *See* CLEAR, FEELINGS. **2.** To muddle or stupefy with or as if with alcoholic drink : befuddle, besot. *See* DRUGS.

fuddy-duddy *noun*
An old-fashioned person who is reluctant to change or innovate : fogy, fossil, mossback. *Informal:* stick-in-the-mud. *Slang:* square. *See* NEW.

fudge *verb*
To proceed or perform in an unsteady, faltering manner : blunder, bumble[1], bungle, flounder, fumble, limp, muddle, shuffle, stagger, stumble. *See* THRIVE.

fuehrer *noun* See **führer.**

fugacious *adjective*
Lasting or existing only for a short time : ephemeral, evanescent, fleet, fleeting, fugitive, momentary, passing, short-lived, temporal, temporary, transient, transitory. *See* CONTINUE, TIME.

fugitive *adjective*
1. Fleeing or having fled, as from home, confinement, captivity, or justice : escaped, runaway. *See* SEEK. **2.** Lasting or existing only for a short time : ephemeral, evanescent, fleet, fleeting, fugacious, momentary, passing, short-lived, temporal, temporary, transient, transitory. *See* CONTINUE, TIME.
fugitive *noun* One who flees, as from home, confinement, captivity, or justice : escapee, refugee, runaway. *See* SEEK.

führer also **fuehrer** *noun*
An absolute ruler, especially one who is harsh and oppressive : Big Brother, despot, dictator, man on horseback, oppressor, strongman, totalitarian, tyrant. *See* OVER.

fulfil *verb* See **fulfill.**

fulfill also **fulfil** *verb*
1. To carry out the functions, requirements, or terms of : discharge, do, execute, exercise, implement, keep, perform. ***Idiom:*** live up to. *See* DO. **2.** To grant or have what is demanded by (a need or desire) : appease, content, gratify, indulge, satisfy. *See* GIVE. **3.** To supply fully or completely : answer, fill, meet[1], satisfy. *See* DO.

fulfilled *adjective*
Having achieved satisfaction, as of one's goal : content, gratified, happy, satisfied. *See* HAPPY.

fulfillment also **fulfilment** *noun*
The condition of being fulfilled : consummation, culmination, fruition, materialization, realization. *See* DO, HAPPY.

fulfilment *noun* See **fulfillment.**

full *adjective*
1. Completely filled : brimful, brimming, bursting, chockablock, packed, replete. *See* FULL. **2.** Lacking nothing essential or normal : complete, entire, intact, integral, perfect, whole. *See* PART. **3.** Not more or less : complete, entire, good, perfect, round, whole. *See* PART, PRECISE. **4.** Not deviating from correctness, accuracy, or completeness : close, exact, faithful, rigorous, strict. *See* CAREFUL. **5.** Characterized by attention to detail : blow-by-blow, circumstantial, detailed, minute[2], particular, thorough. *See* SPECIFIC. **6.** Of full measure; not narrow or restricted : ample, capacious, voluminous, wide. *See* TIGHTEN.

full-blooded *adjective*
1. Of pure breeding stock : highbred, pureblood, pureblooded, purebred, thoroughbred. *See* CLEAN. **2.** Of a healthy reddish color : blooming, florid, flush, flushed, glowing, rosy, rubicund, ruddy, sanguine. *See* COLORS.

full-blown *adjective*
Having reached full growth and development : adult, big, developed, full-fledged, full-grown, grown, grown-up, mature, ripe. *Idiom:* of age. *See* YOUTH.

full-dress *adjective*
1. Requiring elegant clothes and fine manners : dressy, formal. *See* PLAIN. 2. Covering all aspects with painstaking accuracy : all-out, complete, exhaustive, intensive, thorough, thoroughgoing, thoroughpaced. *See* BIG, CAREFUL.

full-fledged *adjective*
Having reached full growth and development : adult, big, developed, full-blown, full-grown, grown, grown-up, mature, ripe. *Idiom:* of age. *See* YOUTH.

full-grown *adjective*
Having reached full growth and development : adult, big, developed, full-blown, full-fledged, grown, grown-up, mature, ripe. *Idiom:* of age. *See* YOUTH.

full-strength *adjective*
Not diluted or mixed with other substances : neat, plain, pure, straight, unblended, undiluted, unmixed. *See* CLEAN, STRONG.

fully *adverb*
To the fullest extent : absolutely, all, altogether, completely, dead, entirely, flat, just, perfectly, quite, thoroughly, totally, utterly, well[2], wholly. *Informal:* clean, clear. *Idioms:* in toto, through and through. *See* BIG, LIMITED.

fulminate *verb*
To release or cause to release energy suddenly and violently, especially with a loud noise : blast, blow[1] (up), burst, detonate, explode, fire, go off, touch off. *See* EXPLOSION.

fulmination *noun*
1. A long, violent, or blustering speech, usually of censure or denunciation : diatribe, harangue, jeremiad, philippic, tirade. *See* PRAISE. 2. A violent release of confined energy, usually accompanied by a loud sound and shock waves : blast, blowout, blowup, burst, detonation, explosion. *See* EXPLOSION.

fulsome *adjective*
Affectedly and self-servingly earnest : oily, oleaginous, sleek, smarmy, unctuous. *See* ATTITUDE, HONEST.

fumble *verb*
1. To reach about or search blindly or uncertainly : feel, grabble, grope, poke. *See* SEEK, TOUCH. 2. To proceed or perform in an unsteady, faltering manner : blunder, bumble[1], bungle, flounder, fudge, limp, muddle, shuffle, stagger, stumble. *See* THRIVE. 3. To harm irreparably through inept handling; make a mess : ball up, blunder, boggle, botch, bungle, foul up, gum up, mess up, mishandle, mismanage, muddle, muff, spoil. *Informal:* bollix up, muck up. *Slang:* blow[1], goof up, louse up, screw up, snafu. *Idiom:* make a muck of. *See* CORRECT, HELP.

fumble *noun* A stupid, clumsy mistake : blunder, bull[2], bungle, foozle, muff, stumble. *Informal:* blooper, boner. *Slang:* bloomer, goof. *See* CORRECT.

fume *noun*
A condition of excited distress : *Informal:* snit, state, sweat, swivet. *Slang:* tizzy. *See* CALM.

fume *verb* To be or become angry : anger, blow up, boil over, bristle, burn, explode, flare up, foam, rage, seethe. *Informal:* steam. *Idioms:* blow a fuse, blow a gasket, blow one's stack (*or* top), breathe fire, fly off the handle, get hot under the collar, hit the ceiling (*or* roof), lose one's temper, see red. *See* FEELINGS.

fun *noun*
1. Joyful, exuberant activity : conviviality, festival, festiveness, festivity, gaiety, jollity, merriment, merrymaking, revel (often used in plural), revelry. *See* LAUGHTER. 2. Activity engaged in for relaxation and amusement : disport, diversion, play, recreation, sport. *See* WORK. 3. Actions taken as a joke : game, play, sport. *See* WORK.

fun *verb* *Informal.* To make jokes; behave playfully : jest, joke. *Informal:* clown (around), fool around. *See* LAUGHTER.

function *noun*
1. The proper activity of a person or thing : job, purpose, role, task. *See* DO. 2. A large or important social gathering : affair, celebration, festivity, fete, gala, occasion, party, soiree. *Informal:* do. *Slang:* bash. *See* GROUP, WORK.

function *verb* 1. To react in a specified way : act, behave, operate, perform, work. *See* ACTION. 2. To perform a function effectively : go, operate, run, take, work. *See* THRIVE. 3. To perform the duties of another : act, officiate, serve. *See* DO, SUBSTITUTE.

functional *adjective*
Serving or capable of serving a useful purpose : handy, practicable, practical, serviceable, useful, utilitarian. *See* USED.

functioning *noun*
The way in which a machine or other thing performs or functions : behavior, operation, per-

formance, reaction, working (often used in plural). *See* ACTION, MACHINE.

functioning *adjective* In action or full operation : active, alive, going, operating, operative, running, working. *See* ACTION, AWARENESS.

fund *noun*

The monetary resources of a government, organization, or individual. Used in plural : capital, finance (used in plural), money (often used in plural). *See* MONEY.

fund *verb* To supply capital to or for : back, capitalize, finance, grubstake, stake, subsidize. *Informal:* bankroll. ***Idiom:*** put up money for. *See* HELP, MONEY.

fundament *noun*

1. The lowest or supporting part or structure : base[1], basis, bed, bottom, foot, footing, foundation, ground, groundwork, seat, substratum, underpinning (often used in plural). *See* OVER. **2.** That on which something immaterial, such as an argument or a charge, rests : base[1], basis, footing, foundation, ground (often used in plural), groundwork, underpinning (often used in plural). *See* OVER. **3.** A fundamental principle or underlying concept : base[1], basis, cornerstone, foundation, fundamental, root[1], rudiment (often used in plural). *See* OVER.

fundamental *adjective*

1. Arising from or going to the root or source : basal, basic, foundational, original, primary, radical, underlying. *See* SURFACE. **2.** Of or being an irreducible element : basic, elemental, elementary, essential, primitive, ultimate, underlying. *See* SURFACE. **3.** Constituting or forming part of the essence of something : basic, constitutional, constitutive, essential, integral, vital. *See* BE, SURFACE.

fundamental *noun* **1.** A fundamental irreducible constituent of a whole : basic, element, essential, rudiment (often used in plural). ***Idiom:*** part and parcel. *See* PART. **2.** A fundamental principle or underlying concept : base[1], basis, cornerstone, foundation, fundament, root[1], rudiment (often used in plural). *See* OVER. **3.** A broad and basic rule or truth : axiom, law, principle, theorem, universal. *See* ORDER.

fundamentally *adverb*

In regard to the essence of a matter : basically, essentially. ***Idioms:*** at bottom, at heart, in essence. *See* SURFACE.

funding *noun*

Money or property used to produce more wealth : backing, capital, capitalization, financing, grubstake, stake, subsidization. *See* HELP, MONEY.

funk *noun*

1. Ignoble lack of courage : chickenheartedness, cowardice, cowardliness, cravenness, dastardliness, faint-heartedness, pusillanimity, unmanliness. *Slang:* gutlessness, yellowness, yellow streak. *See* FEAR. **2.** Great agitation and anxiety caused by the expectation or the realization of danger : affright, alarm, apprehension, dread, fear, fearfulness, fright, horror, panic, terror, trepidation. *Slang:* cold feet. ***Idiom:*** fear and trembling. *See* FEAR. **3.** A feeling or spell of dismally low spirits : blues, dejection, depression, despondence, despondency, doldrums, dolefulness, downheartedness, dumps, dysphoria, gloom, glumness, heavy-heartedness, melancholy, mope (used in plural), mournfulness, sadness, unhappiness. *See* FEELINGS, HAPPY. **4.** An ignoble, uncourageous person : coward, craven, dastard, poltroon. *Slang:* chicken, yellow-belly. *See* FEAR.

funky *adjective*

Filled with fear or terror : afraid, aghast, apprehensive, fearful, fearsome, panicky. *Regional:* afeard, ascared. *See* FEAR.

funniness *noun*

The quality of being laughable or comical : comedy, comicality, comicalness, drollery, drollness, farcicality, humor, humorousness, jocoseness, jocosity, jocularity, ludicrousness, ridiculousness, wit, wittiness, zaniness. *See* LAUGHTER.

funny *adjective*

1. Arousing laughter : amusing, comic, comical, droll, humorous, laughable, risible, zany. *See* LAUGHTER. **2.** Deserving laughter : comic, comical, farcical, laughable, laughing, ludicrous, ridiculous, risible. *See* LAUGHTER. **3.** Intended to excite laughter or amusement : comedic, facetious, humorous, jocose, jocular, witty. *See* LAUGHTER. **4.** Agreeably curious, especially in an old-fashioned or unusual way : odd, quaint. *See* USUAL. **5.** Causing puzzlement; perplexing : curious, odd, peculiar, queer, strange, weird. *See* USUAL.

funny *noun Informal.* Words or actions intended to excite laughter or amusement : gag, jape, jest, joke, quip, witticism. *Informal:* gag. *Slang:* ha-ha. *See* LAUGHTER.

funnyman *noun*

A person whose words or actions provoke or are intended to provoke amusement or laughter : clown, comedian, comic, farceur, humorist, jester, joker, jokester, quipster, wag[2], wit, zany. *Informal:* card. *See* LAUGHTER.

fur *noun*
The skin of an animal : fell[3], hide[2], jacket, pelt[1]. *See* SURFACE.

furbish *verb*
1. To give a gleaming luster to, usually through friction : buff[1], burnish, glaze, gloss, polish, shine, sleek. *See* LIGHT. **2.** To make new or as if new again : recondition, re-create, refresh, refurbish, rejuvenate, renew, renovate, restore, revamp. ***Idiom:*** give a new look to. *See* HELP, NEW.

furious *adjective*
1. Full of or marked by extreme anger : irate, ireful, rabid, wrathful. ***Idioms:*** fit to be tied, foaming at the mouth, in a rage (*or* temper), in a towering rage. *See* FEELINGS. **2.** Extreme in degree, strength, or effect : desperate, fierce, intense, terrible, vehement, violent. *See* BIG, STRONG. **3.** Intensely violent in sustained velocity : fierce, heavy, high, strong. *See* STRONG.

furiously *adverb*
In a violent, strenuous way : fiercely, frantically, frenziedly, hard, strenuously. *See* STRONG.

furlough *noun*
A regularly scheduled period spent away from work or duty, often in recreation : leave[2], vacation. *Chiefly British:* holiday. *See* WORK.

furnish *verb*
1. To supply what is needed for some activity or purpose : accouter, appoint, equip, fit[1], fit out (*or* up), gear, outfit, rig, turn out. *See* GIVE.
2. To relinquish to the possession or control of another : deliver, give, hand, hand over, provide, supply, transfer, turn over. *See* GIVE.

furnishing *noun*
A piece of equipment for comfort or convenience : appointment (used in plural), movable. *Chiefly British:* fitting (used in plural). *See* MACHINE.

furor *noun*
1. Violent or unrestrained anger : fury, irateness, ire, rage, wrath, wrathfulness. *See* FEELINGS. **2.** The current custom : craze, fad, fashion, mode, rage, style, trend, vogue. *Informal:* thing. ***Idioms:*** the in thing, the last word, the latest thing. *See* STYLE, USUAL.

furrow *noun*
An indentation or seam on the skin, especially on the face : crease, crinkle, line, wrinkle. *See* SMOOTH.

furry *adjective*
Covered with hair : fleecy, fuzzy, hairy, hirsute, pilose, woolly. *See* SMOOTH.

further *adjective*
Being an addition : added, additional, extra, fresh, more, new, other. *See* INCREASE.
further *adverb* In addition : additionally, also, besides, furthermore, item, likewise, more, moreover, still, too, yet. ***Idioms:*** as well, to boot. *See* INCREASE.
further *verb* To cause to move forward or upward, as toward a goal : advance, forward, promote. *See* FORWARD, HELP.

furtherance *noun*
Forward movement : advance, advancement, headway, march[1], progress, progression. *See* BETTER, FORWARD.

furthermore *adverb*
In addition : additionally, also, besides, further, item, likewise, more, moreover, still, too, yet. ***Idioms:*** as well, to boot. *See* INCREASE.

furthermost *adjective*
Most distant or remote, as from a center : extreme, farthermost, farthest, furthest, outermost, outmost, ultimate, utmost, uttermost. *See* BIG, EDGE.

furthest *adjective*
Most distant or remote, as from a center : extreme, farthermost, farthest, furthermost, outermost, outmost, ultimate, utmost, uttermost. *See* BIG, EDGE.

furtive *adjective*
1. So slow, deliberate, and secret as to escape observation : catlike, feline, slinky, sneaking, sneaky, stealthy. *See* MOVE. **2.** Trickily secret : secretive, sly, sneaking, sneaky, surreptitious. *See* HONEST.

furtiveness *noun*
The act of proceeding slowly, deliberately, and secretly to escape observation : slinkiness, sneakiness, stealth, stealthiness. *See* MOVE.

fury *noun*
1. Violent or unrestrained anger : furor, irateness, ire, rage, wrath, wrathfulness. *See* FEELINGS. **2.** Exceptionally great concentration, power, or force, especially in activity : depth (often used in plural), ferociousness, ferocity, fierceness, intensity, pitch, severity, vehemence, vehemency, violence. *See* BIG, STRONG. **3.** A person, traditionally a woman, who persistently nags or criticizes : fishwife, harpy, scold, shrew, termagant, virago, vixen. *Informal:* battle-ax. *See* PRAISE.

fuse *verb*
1. To change from a solid to a liquid : deli-

quesce, dissolve, flux, liquefy, melt, run, thaw. *See* SOLID. **2.** To put together into one mass so that the constituent parts are more or less homogeneous : admix, amalgamate, blend, commingle, commix, intermingle, intermix, merge, mingle, mix, stir[1]. *See* ASSEMBLE.

fusillade *noun*
A concentrated outpouring, as of missiles, words, or blows : barrage, bombardment, burst, cannonade, hail[1], salvo, shower, storm, volley. *See* ATTACK.
fusillade *verb* To direct a barrage at : barrage, bombard, cannonade, pepper, shower. *See* ATTACK.

fusion *noun*
Something produced by mixing : admixture, amalgam, amalgamation, blend, commixture, merger, mix, mixture. *See* ASSEMBLE.

fuss *noun*
1. Busy and useless activity : ado. *Informal:* to-do. *See* ACTION, CALM. **2.** Needless trouble : bother, botheration, pother. *See* EASY.
fuss *verb* **1.** To worry over trifles : chafe, pother. *Informal:* take on. *See* CALM. **2.** To be nervously or uselessly active : bustle, putter. *Informal:* mess around. *See* ACTION, CALM.
fuss at *verb* To scold or find fault with constantly : carp at, nag, peck at[1], pick on. *Informal:* henpeck. *See* PRAISE.

fuss at *verb* See **fuss.**

fussy *adjective*
1. Very difficult to please : choosy, dainty, exacting, fastidious, finical, finicky, meticulous, nice, particular, persnickety, squeamish. *Informal:* picky. *See* ACCEPT. **2.** Excessively filled with detail : busy, cluttered, crowded. *See* SIMPLE.

fustian *noun*
Pretentious, pompous speech or writing : bombast, claptrap, grandiloquence, magniloquence, orotundity, rant, turgidity. *See* PLAIN, STYLE, WORDS.
fustian *adjective* Characterized by language that is elevated and sometimes pompous in style : aureate, bombastic, declamatory, flowery, grandiloquent, high-flown, high-sounding, magniloquent, orotund, overblown, rhetorical, sonorous, swollen. *See* PLAIN, STYLE, WORDS.

fusty *adjective*
1. Smelling of mildew or decay : frowzy, moldy, musty, putrid, rancid, rank[2], rotten. *See* SMELLS. **2.** Of a style or method formerly in vogue : antiquated, antique, archaic, bygone, dated, dowdy, old, old-fashioned, old-time, outdated, outmoded, out-of-date, passé, vintage. *See* NEW.

futile *adjective*
Having no useful result : barren, bootless, fruitless, unavailing, unprofitable, unsuccessful, useless, vain. ***Idiom:*** in vain. *See* THRIVE, USED.

futility *noun*
The condition or quality of being useless or ineffective : bootlessness, fruitlessness, unavailingness, unprofitableness, uselessness, vainness, vanity. *See* USED, THRIVE.

future *noun*
1. Time that is yet to be : by-and-by, hereafter. ***Idiom:*** time to come. *See* PRECEDE, TIME. **2.** Chance of success or advancement : outlook, prospect (used in plural). *See* HOPE.
future *adjective* Being or occurring in the time ahead : coming, later, subsequent. *See* PRECEDE, TIME.

fuzz *noun*
Slang. A member of a law-enforcement agency : bluecoat, finest, officer, patrolman, patrolwoman, peace officer, police, policeman, police officer, policewoman. *Informal:* cop, law. *Slang:* bull[1], copper, flatfoot, gendarme, heat, man (often uppercase). *Chiefly British:* bobby, constable, peeler. *See* LAW.

fuzzy *adjective*
1. Covered with hair : fleecy, furry, hairy, hirsute, pilose, woolly. *See* SMOOTH. **2.** Not clearly perceived or perceptible : blear, bleary, cloudy, dim, faint, foggy, hazy, indefinite, indistinct, misty, obscure, shadowy, unclear, undistinct, vague. *See* CLEAR.

·G·

gab *verb*
Slang. To talk volubly, persistently, and usually inconsequentially : babble, blabber, chatter, chitchat, clack, jabber, palaver, prate, prattle, rattle (on), run on. *Informal:* go on, spiel. *Slang:* gas, jaw, yak. ***Idioms:*** run off at the mouth, shoot the breeze (*or* bull). *See* WORDS.
gab *noun Slang.* Incessant and usually inconsequential talk : babble, blab, blabber, chat, chatter, chitchat, jabber, palaver, prate, prattle, small talk. *Slang:* gas, yak. *See* WORDS.

gabble *verb*
To talk rapidly, incoherently, or indistinctly : babble, blather, chatter, gibber, jabber, prate, prattle. *See* WORDS.
gabble *noun* Unintelligible or foolish talk : babble, blather, blatherskite, double talk, gibberish, jabber, jabberwocky, jargon, nonsense, prate, prattle, twaddle. *See* WORDS.

gabby *adjective*
Slang. Given to conversation : chatty, conversational, garrulous, loquacious, talkative, talky, voluble. *See* WORDS.

gad *verb*
To move about at random, especially over a wide area : drift, gallivant, meander, peregrinate, ramble, range, roam, rove, stray, traipse, wander. *See* MOVE.

gadget *noun*
A small specialized mechanical device : concern, contraption, contrivance, gimmick, jigger, thing. *Informal:* doodad, doohickey, widget. *Slang:* gizmo. *See* MACHINE.

gag *noun*
Informal. Words or actions intended to excite laughter or amusement : jape, jest, joke, quip, witticism. *Informal:* funny. *Slang:* ha-ha. *See* LAUGHTER.
gag *verb* To hold (something requiring an outlet) in check : burke, choke (back), hold back, hold down, hush (up), muffle, quench, repress, smother, squelch, stifle, strangle, suppress, throttle. *Informal:* sit on (*or* upon). *See* RESTRAINT.

gaga *adjective*
1. *Informal.* Given to lighthearted silliness : empty-headed, featherbrained, flighty, frivolous, frothy, giddy, harebrained, lighthearted, scatterbrained, silly. *Slang:* birdbrained, dizzy. *See* ABILITY. **2.** *Informal.* Afflicted with or exhibiting irrationality and mental unsoundness : brainsick, crazy, daft, demented, disordered, distraught, dotty, insane, lunatic, mad, maniac, maniacal, mentally ill, moonstruck, off, touched, unbalanced, unsound, wrong. *Informal:* bonkers, cracked, daffy, loony. *Slang:* bananas, batty, buggy, cuckoo, fruity, loco, nuts, nutty, screwy, wacky. *Chiefly British:* crackers. *Law:* non compos mentis. ***Idioms:*** around the bend, crazy as a loon, mad as a hatter, not all there, nutty as a fruitcake, off (*or* out of) one's head, off one's rocker, of unsound mind, out of one's mind, sick in the head, stark raving mad. *See* SANE.

gage *noun & verb* See **gauge.**

gaiety *noun*
1. A state of joyful exuberance : blitheness, blithesomeness, glee, gleefulness, hilarity, jocoseness, jocosity, jocularity, jocundity, jolliness, jollity, joviality, lightheartedness, merriment, merriness, mirth, mirthfulness. *See* LAUGHTER. **2.** Joyful, exuberant activity : conviviality, festival, festiveness, festivity, fun, jollity, merriment, merrymaking, revel (often used in plural), revelry. *See* LAUGHTER.

gain *verb*
1. To come into possession of : acquire, come by, get, obtain, procure, secure, win. *Informal:* land, pick up. *See* GET. **2.** To obtain possession or control of : capture, get, take, win. *Slang:* cop. *See* GET. **3.** To acquire as a result of one's behavior or effort : deserve, earn, get, merit, win. *Informal:* rate[1]. *See* GET. **4.** To succeed in doing : accomplish, achieve, attain, reach, realize. *Slang:* score. *See* DO. **5.** To receive, as wages, for one's labor : earn, get, make, win. *Informal:* pull down. ***Idioms:*** earn (*or* make) a living, earn one's keep. *See* GIVE, MONEY. **6.** To make as income or profit : bring in, clear, draw, earn, gross, net[2], pay, produce, realize, repay, return, yield. *See* MONEY. **7.** To derive advantage : benefit, capitalize, profit. *See* HELP. **8.** To achieve an increase of gradually : build up, develop. *See* INCREASE. **9.** To reach (a goal or objective) : arrive at, attain, come to, get to. *Informal:* hit on (*or* upon). *See* START. **10.** To regain one's health : come around (*or* round), convalesce, improve,

mend, perk up, rally, recover, recuperate. *See* HEALTH.

gain *noun* **1.** Something earned, won, or otherwise acquired : earnings, profit, return. *See* GET, MONEY. **2.** Something beneficial : advantage, avail, benefit, blessing, boon[1], favor, profit. *See* HELP.

gainsay *verb*
To refuse to admit the truth, reality, value, or worth of : contradict, contravene, controvert, deny, disaffirm, negate, negative, oppugn. *Law:* traverse. *See* AFFIRM.

gala *noun*
A large or important social gathering : affair, celebration, festivity, fete, function, occasion, party, soiree. *Informal:* do. *Slang:* bash. *See* GROUP, WORK.

gala *adjective* Marked by festal celebration : festive, glad, gladsome, happy, joyful, joyous, merry. *See* HAPPY.

gale *noun*
Archaic. A natural movement or current of air : air, blast, blow[1], breeze, gust, wind[1], zephyr. *See* BREATH.

gall[1] *noun*
1. The quality or state of feeling bitter : acrimony, bitterness, embitterment, rancor, rancorousness, resentfulness, resentment, virulence, virulency. *See* FEELINGS. **2.** The state or quality of being impudent or arrogantly self-confident : assumption, audaciousness, audacity, boldness, brashness, brazenness, cheek, cheekiness, chutzpah, discourtesy, disrespect, effrontery, face, familiarity, forwardness, impertinence, impudence, impudency, incivility, insolence, nerve, nerviness, overconfidence, pertness, presumptuousness, pushiness, rudeness, sassiness, sauciness. *Informal:* brass, crust, sauce, uppishness, uppityness. *See* ATTITUDE, COURTESY.

gall[2] *verb*
1. To make (the skin) raw by or as if by friction : abrade, chafe, excoriate, fret, irritate. *See* HELP. **2.** To trouble the nerves or peace of mind of, especially by repeated vexations : aggravate, annoy, bother, bug, chafe, disturb, exasperate, fret, get, irk, irritate, nettle, peeve, provoke, put out, rile, ruffle, vex. ***Idioms:*** get in one's hair, get on one's nerves, get under one's skin. *See* FEELINGS, PAIN.

gallant *adjective*
1. Having or showing courage : audacious, bold, brave, courageous, dauntless, doughty, fearless, fortitudinous, game, hardy, heroic, intrepid, mettlesome, plucky, stout, stouthearted, unafraid, undaunted, valiant, valorous. *Informal:* spunky. *Slang:* gutsy, gutty. *See* FEAR. **2.** Respectfully attentive, especially to women : chivalric, chivalrous. *See* ATTITUDE, COURTESY. **3.** Characterized by elaborate but usually formal courtesy : chivalrous, courtly, gracious, knightly, stately. *See* ATTITUDE, COURTESY. **4.** Full of polite concern for the well-being of others : attentive, considerate, courteous, polite, solicitous, thoughtful. *See* CAREFUL, TREAT WELL.

gallant *noun* A man amorously attentive to women : amorist, Casanova, Don Juan, lady's man, Lothario, Romeo. *See* SEX.

gallantry *noun*
1. The quality of mind enabling one to face danger or hardship resolutely : braveness, bravery, courage, courageousness, dauntlessness, doughtiness, fearlessness, fortitude, gameness, heart, intrepidity, intrepidness, mettle, nerve, pluck, pluckiness, spirit, stoutheartedness, undauntedness, valiance, valiancy, valiantness, valor. *Informal:* spunk, spunkiness. *Slang:* gut (used in plural), gutsiness, moxie. *See* FEAR. **2.** The quality or state of being heroic : heroism, prowess, valiance, valiancy, valor. *See* FEAR. **3.** Respectful attention, especially toward women : chivalrousness, chivalry. *See* ATTITUDE, COURTESY.

gallimaufry *noun*
A collection of various things : assortment, conglomeration, hodgepodge, jumble, medley, mélange, miscellany, mishmash, mixed bag, mixture, olio, patchwork, potpourri, salmagundi, variety. *Slang:* grab bag. *See* COLLECT.

galling *adjective*
Troubling the nerves or peace of mind, as by repeated vexations : annoying, bothersome, irksome, irritating, nettlesome, plaguy, provoking, troublesome, vexatious. *See* PAIN.

gallivant *verb*
To move about at random, especially over a wide area : drift, gad, meander, peregrinate, ramble, range, roam, rove, stray, traipse, wander. *See* MOVE.

galumph *verb*
To move heavily : clump, hulk, lumber, lump[1], stump. *See* MOVE.

galvanize *verb*
To stir to action or feeling : egg on, excite, foment, goad, impel, incite, inflame, inspire, instigate, motivate, move, pique, prick, prod, prompt, propel, provoke, set off, spur, stimulate, touch off, trigger, work up. *See* CAUSE, EXCITE.

gamble *verb*
1. To make a bet : bet, game, lay[1], play, wager. ***Idiom:*** put one's money on something. *See* GAMBLING. **2.** To put up as a stake in a game or speculation : bet, lay[1] (down), post[2], put, risk, stake, venture, wager. *Informal:* go. *See* GAMBLING. **3.** To take a risk in the hope of gaining advantage : speculate, venture. ***Idiom:*** take a flyer. *See* GAMBLING.
gamble *noun* **1.** A venture depending on chance : bet, risk, speculation, wager. *See* GAMBLING. **2.** A possibility of danger or harm : chance, hazard, risk. *See* SAFETY.

gambler *noun*
1. One who bets : bettor, gamester, player. *See* GAMBLING. **2.** One who speculates for quick profits : adventurer, operator, speculator. *See* GAMBLING, MONEY.

gambol *verb*
To leap and skip about playfully : caper, cavort, dance, frisk, frolic, rollick, romp. *See* WORK.

game *noun*
Actions taken as a joke : fun, play, sport. *See* WORK.
game *verb* To make a bet : bet, gamble, lay[1], play, wager. ***Idiom:*** put one's money on something. *See* GAMBLING.
game *adjective* **1.** Having or showing courage : audacious, bold, brave, courageous, dauntless, doughty, fearless, fortitudinous, gallant, hardy, heroic, intrepid, mettlesome, plucky, stout, stouthearted, unafraid, undaunted, valiant, valorous. *Informal:* spunky. *Slang:* gutsy, gutty. *See* FEAR. **2.** Disposed to accept or agree : acquiescent, agreeable, minded, ready, willing. *Archaic:* fain. *See* WILLING.

gameness *noun*
The quality of mind enabling one to face danger or hardship resolutely : braveness, bravery, courage, courageousness, dauntlessness, doughtiness, fearlessness, fortitude, gallantry, heart, intrepidity, intrepidness, mettle, nerve, pluck, pluckiness, spirit, stoutheartedness, undauntedness, valiance, valiancy, valiantness, valor. *Informal:* spunk, spunkiness. *Slang:* gut (used in plural), gutsiness, moxie. *See* FEAR.

game plan *noun*
A method for making, doing, or accomplishing something : blueprint, design, idea, layout, plan, project, schema, scheme, strategy. *See* PLANNED.

gamester *noun*
One who bets : bettor, gambler, player. *See* GAMBLING.

gander *noun*
1. *Informal.* A quick look : blush, glance, glimpse, peek, peep. *See* SEE. **2.** *Informal.* One deficient in judgment and good sense : ass, fool, idiot, imbecile, jackass, mooncalf, moron, nincompoop, ninny, nitwit, simple, simpleton, softhead, tomfool. *Informal:* dope, goose. *Slang:* cretin, ding-dong, dip, goof, jerk, nerd, schmo, schmuck, turkey. *See* ABILITY.

gang *noun*
1. An organized group of criminals, hoodlums, or wrongdoers : band[2], pack, ring[1]. *Informal:* mob. *See* GROUP. **2.** *Informal.* A particular social group : circle, clique, coterie, crowd, set[2]. *Informal:* bunch. *See* GROUP. **3.** A group of people organized for a particular purpose : body, corps, crew, detachment, force, team, unit. *See* GROUP.
gang up *verb* To assemble or join in a group : band[2], combine, league, unite. *See* COLLECT.

gangling *adjective*
Tall, thin, and awkwardly built : gangly, lanky, rangy, spindling, spindly. *See* FAT.

gangly *adjective*
Tall, thin, and awkwardly built : gangling, lanky, rangy, spindling, spindly. *See* FAT.

gang up *verb* See **gang.**

gap *noun*
1. An opening, especially in a solid structure : breach, break, hole, perforation, rupture. *See* OPEN. **2.** A space or interval between objects or points : interspace, interstice, interval, separation. *See* OPEN. **3.** An interval during which continuity is suspended : break, hiatus, interim, lacuna, void. *See* CONTINUE. **4.** A marked lack of correspondence or agreement : difference, disagreement, discrepance, discrepancy, disparity, incompatibility, incongruity, inconsistency. *See* AGREE.
gap *verb* **1.** To make a hole or other opening in : breach, break (through), hole, perforate, pierce, puncture. *See* OPEN. **2.** To open wide : gape, yawn. *See* WIDE.

gape *verb*
1. To open the mouth wide with a deep inward breath, as when tired or bored : yawn. *See* MOUTH. **2.** To look intently and fixedly : eye, gawk, gaze, goggle, ogle, peer[1], stare. ***Idioms:*** gaze open-mouthed, rivet the eyes on. *See* SEE. **3.** To open wide : gap, yawn. *See* WIDE.
gape *noun* An intent fixed look : gaze, stare. *See* SEE.

gaping *adjective*
Open wide : abysmal, abyssal, cavernous, yawning. *See* WIDE.

garb *noun*
A set or style of clothing : costume, dress, guise, habiliment (often used in plural), outfit, turnout. *Informal:* getup, rig. *See* PUT ON.
garb *verb* To put clothes on : apparel, attire, clothe, dress, garment, invest. *Informal:* tog. *See* PUT ON.

garbage *noun*
Something that does not have or make sense : balderdash, blather, bunkum, claptrap, drivel, idiocy, nonsense, piffle, poppycock, rigmarole, rubbish, tomfoolery, trash, twaddle. *Informal:* tommyrot. *Slang:* applesauce, baloney, bilge, bull[1], bunk[2], crap, hooey, malarkey. *See* KNOWLEDGE.

garden *adjective*
Being of no special quality or type : average, common, commonplace, cut-and-dried, formulaic, garden-variety, indifferent, mediocre, ordinary, plain, routine, run-of-the-mill, standard, stock, undistinguished, unexceptional, unremarkable. *See* GOOD, USUAL.

garden-variety *adjective*
Being of no special quality or type : average, common, commonplace, cut-and-dried, formulaic, garden, indifferent, mediocre, ordinary, plain, routine, run-of-the-mill, standard, stock, undistinguished, unexceptional, unremarkable. *See* GOOD, USUAL.

gargantuan *adjective*
Of extraordinary size and power : behemoth, Brobdingnagian, Bunyanesque, colossal, cyclopean, elephantine, enormous, giant, gigantesque, gigantic, herculean, heroic, huge, immense, jumbo, mammoth, massive, massy, mastodonic, mighty, monster, monstrous, monumental, mountainous, prodigious, pythonic, stupendous, titanic, tremendous, vast. *Informal:* walloping. *Slang:* whopping. *See* BIG.

garish *adjective*
Tastelessly showy : brummagem, chintzy, flashy, gaudy, glaring, loud, meretricious, tawdry, tinsel. *Informal:* tacky[2]. *See* STYLE.

garment *noun*
Articles worn to cover the body. Used in plural : apparel, attire, clothes, clothing, dress, habiliment (often used in plural), raiment. *Informal:* dud (used in plural), tog (used in plural). *Slang:* thread (used in plural). *See* PUT ON.
garment *verb* To put clothes on : apparel, attire, clothe, dress, garb, invest. *Informal:* tog. *See* PUT ON.

garner *verb*
1. To collect ripe crops : crop, gather, harvest, pick, reap. *See* COLLECT. **2.** To collect (something) bit by bit : cull, extract, gather, glean, pick up. *See* COLLECT. **3.** To bring together so as to increase in mass or number : accrue, accumulate, agglomerate, aggregate, amass, collect[1], cumulate, gather, hive, pile up, roll up. *See* COLLECT.

garnish *verb*
To furnish with decorations : adorn, bedeck, deck[2] (out), decorate, dress (up), embellish, ornament, trim. *See* BEAUTIFUL.

garnishment *noun*
Something that adorns : adornment, decoration, embellishment, garniture, ornament, ornamentation, trim, trimming. *See* BEAUTIFUL.

garniture *noun*
Something that adorns : adornment, decoration, embellishment, garnishment, ornament, ornamentation, trim, trimming. *See* BEAUTIFUL.

garrulous *adjective*
Given to conversation : chatty, conversational, loquacious, talkative, talky, voluble. *Slang:* gabby. *See* WORDS.

gas *noun*
1. *Slang.* Incessant and usually inconsequential talk : babble, blab, blabber, chat, chatter, chitchat, jabber, palaver, prate, prattle, small talk. *Slang:* gab, yak. *See* WORDS. **2.** *Slang.* Something or someone uproariously funny or absurd : absurdity. *Informal:* hoot, joke, laugh, scream. *Slang:* howl, panic, riot. ***Idiom:*** a laugh a minute. *See* LAUGHTER.
gas *verb* *Slang.* To talk volubly, persistently, and usually inconsequentially : babble, blabber, chatter, chitchat, clack, jabber, palaver, prate, prattle, rattle (on), run on. *Informal:* go on, spiel. *Slang:* gab, jaw, yak. ***Idioms:*** run off at the mouth, shoot the breeze (*or* bull). *See* WORDS.

gasconade *noun*
An act of boasting : boast, brag, braggadocio, fanfaronade, rodomontade, vaunt. *Informal:* blow[1]. *See* PRAISE.
gasconade *verb* To talk with excessive pride : boast, brag, crow, rodomontade, vaunt. *Informal:* blow[1]. *See* PRAISE.

gash *verb*
To penetrate with a sharp edge : cut, incise, pierce, slash, slit. *See* ENTER, HELP.

gash *noun* The result of cutting : cut, incision, slash, slice, slit, split. *See* ENTER, HELP.

gasp *verb*
1. To breathe hard : blow[1], huff, pant, puff. *See* BREATH. **2.** To utter in a breathless manner : heave, pant. *See* BREATH, WORDS.

gate *noun*
The amount of money collected as admission, especially to a sporting event : box office, take. *See* MONEY.

gather *verb*
1. To collect (something) bit by bit : cull, extract, garner, glean, pick up. *See* COLLECT. **2.** To bring together so as to increase in mass or number : accrue, accumulate, agglomerate, aggregate, amass, collect[1], cumulate, garner, hive, pile up, roll up. *See* COLLECT. **3.** To collect ripe crops : crop, garner, harvest, pick, reap. *See* COLLECT. **4.** To bring together : assemble, call, cluster, collect[1], congregate, convene, convoke, get together, group, muster, round up, summon. *See* COLLECT. **5.** To come together : assemble, cluster, collect[1], congregate, convene, forgather, get together, group, muster. *See* COLLECT. **6.** To arrive at (a conclusion) from evidence or reasoning : conclude, deduce, deduct, draw, infer, judge, understand. *See* REASON.

gathering *noun*
1. A quantity accumulated : accumulation, aggregation, amassment, assemblage, collection, congeries, cumulation, mass. *See* COLLECT. **2.** A number of persons who have come or been gathered together : assemblage, assembly, body, company, conclave, conference, congregation, congress, convention, convocation, crowd, group, meeting, muster, troop. *Informal:* get-together. *See* COLLECT. **3.** The act or fact of coming together : concourse, confluence, convergence, junction, meeting. *See* CONNECT.

gauche *adjective*
1. Lacking sensitivity and skill in dealing with others : brash, clumsy, impolitic, indelicate, maladroit, tactless, undiplomatic, unpolitic, untactful. *See* ABILITY, COURTESY. **2.** Clumsily lacking in the ability to do or perform : awkward, bumbling, clumsy, heavy-handed, inept, maladroit, unskillful. *See* ABILITY.

gaudy *adjective*
Tastelessly showy : brummagem, chintzy, flashy, garish, glaring, loud, meretricious, tawdry, tinsel. *Informal:* tacky[2]. *See* STYLE.

gauge also **gage** *noun*
A means by which individuals are compared and judged : benchmark, criterion, mark, measure, standard, test, touchstone, yardstick. *See* USUAL.

gauge also **gage** *verb* **1.** To ascertain the dimensions, quantity, or capacity of : measure. *Archaic:* mete. ***Idiom:*** take the measure of. *See* BIG. **2.** To make a judgment as to the worth or value of : appraise, assay, assess, calculate, estimate, evaluate, judge, rate[1], size up, valuate, value. ***Idiom:*** take the measure of. *See* VALUE.

gaunt *adjective*
1. Having little flesh or fat on the body : angular, bony, fleshless, lank, lanky, lean[2], meager, rawboned, scrawny, skinny, slender, slim, spare, thin, twiggy, weedy. ***Idioms:*** all skin and bones, thin as a rail. *See* FAT. **2.** Pale and exhausted, as because of worry or sleeplessness : careworn, drawn, haggard, hollow-eyed, wan, worn. *See* TIRED. **3.** Physically haggard : cadaverous, drawn, emaciated, shrunken, skeletal, wasted. ***Idiom:*** skin and bones. *See* BETTER, TIRED.

gauzy *adjective*
So light and insubstantial as to resemble air or a thin film : aerial, aery, airy, diaphanous, ethereal, filmy, gossamer, gossamery, sheer[2], transparent, vaporous, vapory. *See* THICK.

gawk *noun*
A large, ungainly, and dull-witted person : hulk, lout, lump[1], oaf, ox. *Informal:* lummox. *Slang:* klutz, lug[1], meatball, meathead. *See* ABILITY.

gawk *verb* To look intently and fixedly : eye, gape, gaze, goggle, ogle, peer[1], stare. ***Idioms:*** gaze open-mouthed, rivet the eyes on. *See* SEE.

gawky *adjective*
Lacking dexterity and grace in physical movement : awkward, clumsy, graceless, inept, lumpish, maladroit, ungainly, ungraceful. *Slang:* klutzy. ***Idiom:*** all thumbs. *See* ABILITY.

gay *adjective*
1. Characterized by joyful exuberance : blithe, blithesome, boon[2], convivial, gleeful, jocund, jolly, jovial, merry, mirthful. *See* HAPPY. **2.** Full of color : bright, colorful, rich, vivid. *See* COLORS. **3.** Of, relating to, or having a sexual orientation to members of one's own sex : homophile, homosexual, lesbian. *See* SEX. **4.** Lacking in moral restraint : abandoned, dissipated, dissolute, fast, incontinent, licentious, profligate, rakish, unbridled, unconstrained, uncontrolled, ungoverned, uninhibited, unrestrained, wanton, wild. *See* RESTRAINT.

gaze *verb*
To look intently and fixedly : eye, gape, gawk,

goggle, ogle, peer[1], stare. ***Idioms:*** gaze open-mouthed, rivet the eyes on. *See* SEE.

gaze *noun* An intent fixed look : gape, stare. *See* SEE.

gear *noun*
Things needed for a task, journey, or other purpose : accouterment (often used in plural), apparatus, equipment, material (used in plural), materiel, outfit, paraphernalia, rig, tackle, thing (used in plural), turnout. *See* MEANS.

gear *verb* To supply what is needed for some activity or purpose : accouter, appoint, equip, fit[1], fit out (*or* up), furnish, outfit, rig, turn out. *See* GIVE.

gelatinize *verb*
To change or be changed from a liquid into a soft, semisolid, or solid mass : clot, coagulate, congeal, curdle, jell, jelly, set[1]. *See* SOLID.

gelatinous *adjective*
Having a dense or viscous consistency : heavy, stodgy, thick. *See* SOLID.

geld *verb*
To render incapable of reproducing sexually : alter, castrate, fix, neuter, spay, sterilize, unsex. *See* REPRODUCTION, RICH.

gelid *adjective*
Very cold : arctic, boreal, freezing, frigid, frosty, glacial, icy, polar, wintry. *Archaic:* frore. ***Idiom:*** bitter (*or* bitterly) cold. *See* HOT.

gelidity *noun*
Extreme lack of warmth : frigidity, frigidness, frostiness, gelidness, iciness, wintriness. *See* HOT.

gelt *noun*
Slang. Something, such as coins or printed bills, used as a medium of exchange : cash, currency, lucre, money. *Informal:* wampum. *Slang:* bread, cabbage, dough, green, jack, lettuce, long green, mazuma, moola, scratch. *Chiefly British:* brass. *See* MONEY.

gem *noun*
Someone or something considered exceptionally precious : pearl, prize[1], treasure. *See* VALUE.

geminate *verb*
To make or become twice as great : double, duplicate, redouble, twin. *See* BIG, INCREASE.

geminate *adjective* Composed of two parts or things : biform, binary, double, dual, duple, duplex, duplicate, twofold. *See* PART.

gendarme *noun*
Slang. A member of a law-enforcement agency : bluecoat, finest, officer, patrolman, patrolwoman, peace officer, police, policeman, police officer, policewoman. *Informal:* cop, law. *Slang:* bull[1], copper, flatfoot, fuzz, heat, man (often uppercase). *Chiefly British:* bobby, constable, peeler. *See* LAW.

genealogy *noun*
1. A written record of ancestry : family tree, pedigree. *See* KIN. **2.** One's ancestors or their character or one's ancestral derivation : ancestry, birth, blood, bloodline, descent, extraction, family, line, lineage, origin, parentage, pedigree, seed, stock. *See* KIN, PRECEDE.

general *adjective*
1. Belonging or relating to the whole : common, generic, universal. *See* SPECIFIC.
2. Belonging to, shared by, or applicable to all alike : common, communal, conjoint, joint, mutual, public. *See* GROUP. **3.** Of, representing, or carried on by people at large : democratic, popular, public. *See* POLITICS, SPECIFIC.
4. Commonly encountered : average, common, commonplace, normal, ordinary, typical, usual. *See* SURPRISE. **5.** Covering a wide scope : all-around, all-inclusive, all-round, broad, broad-spectrum, comprehensive, expansive, extended, extensive, far-ranging, far-reaching, global, inclusive, large, overall, sweeping, wide-ranging, wide-reaching, widespread. *See* SPECIFIC. **6.** Not limited to a single class : diversified. *See* SPECIFIC.

generalize *verb*
To make universal : universalize. *See* SPECIFIC.

generally *adverb*
In an expected or customary manner; for the most part : commonly, consistently, customarily, frequently, habitually, naturally, normally, often, regularly, routinely, typically, usually. ***Idioms:*** as usual, per usual. *See* BIG, USUAL.

generate *verb*
1. To bring (a product or idea, for example) into being : develop, produce. *See* KIN. **2.** To be the cause of : bring, bring about, bring on, cause, effect, effectuate, induce, ingenerate, lead to, make, occasion, result in, secure, set off, stir[1] (up), touch off, trigger. ***Idioms:*** bring to pass (*or* effect), give rise to. *See* START.

generic *adjective*
Belonging or relating to the whole : common, general, universal. *See* SPECIFIC.

generosity *noun*
The quality or state of being generous : big-heartedness, bounteousness, bountifulness, free-handedness, generousness, great-heartedness, large-heartedness, lavishness, liberality, magnanimity, magnanimousness, munificence,

openhandedness, unselfishness, unsparingness. *See* GIVE.

generous *adjective*

1. Characterized by bounteous giving : free, freehanded, handsome, lavish, liberal, munificent, openhanded, unsparing, unstinting. *See* GIVE. **2.** Willing to give of oneself and one's possessions : big, big-hearted, great-hearted, large-hearted, magnanimous, unselfish. *See* GIVE. **3.** Characterized by abundance : abundant, ample, bounteous, bountiful, copious, heavy, plenitudinous, plenteous, plentiful, substantial, voluminous. *See* BIG, GIVE, RICH.

generousness *noun*

The quality or state of being generous : big-heartedness, bounteousness, bountifulness, freehandedness, generosity, great-heartedness, large-heartedness, lavishness, liberality, magnanimity, magnanimousness, munificence, openhandedness, unselfishness, unsparingness. *See* GIVE.

genesis *noun*

The initial stage of a developmental process : beginning, birth, commencement, dawn, inception, nascence, nascency, onset, opening, origin, outset, spring, start. *See* START.

genial *adjective*

Pleasant and friendly in disposition : affable, agreeable, amiable, congenial, cordial, good-natured, good-tempered, pleasant, sociable, warm. *See* ATTITUDE, GOOD.

geniality *noun*

The quality of being pleasant and friendly : affability, agreeability, agreeableness, amenity, amiability, amiableness, congeniality, congenialness, cordiality, cordialness, friendliness, genialness, pleasantness, sociability, sociableness, warmth. *See* ATTITUDE, GOOD.

genialness *noun*

The quality of being pleasant and friendly : affability, agreeability, agreeableness, amenity, amiability, amiableness, congeniality, congenialness, cordiality, cordialness, friendliness, geniality, pleasantness, sociability, sociableness, warmth. *See* ATTITUDE, GOOD.

genius *noun*

1. Liveliness and vivacity of imagination : brilliance, brilliancy, fire, inspiration. *See* GOOD. **2.** An innate capability : aptitude, aptness, bent, faculty, flair, gift, head, instinct, knack, talent, turn. *See* ABILITY, APPROACH.

genteel *adjective*

1. Characterized by good manners : civil, courteous, mannerly, polite, well-bred, well-mannered. *See* COURTESY. **2.** Marked by excessive concern for propriety and good form : bluenosed, old-maidish, precise, priggish, prim, prissy, proper, prudish, puritanical, strait-laced, stuffy, Victorian. ***Idiom:*** prim and proper. *See* PLAIN.

genteelness *noun*

Well-mannered behavior toward others : civility, courteousness, courtesy, gentility, mannerliness, politeness, politesse. *See* COURTESY.

gentility *noun*

1. Well-mannered behavior toward others : civility, courteousness, courtesy, genteelness, mannerliness, politeness, politesse. *See* COURTESY. **2.** People of the highest social level : aristocracy, blue blood, crème de la crème, elite, flower, gentry, nobility, patriciate, quality, society, upper class, who's who. *Informal:* upper crust. *See* OVER.

gentle *adjective*

1. Of a kindly, considerate character : mild, soft, softhearted, tender[1], tenderhearted. *See* KIND. **2.** Free from severity or violence, as in movement : balmy[1], delicate, faint, mild, smooth, soft. *See* CALM, STRONG. **3.** Of small intensity : light[2], moderate, slight, soft. *See* STRONG. **4.** Easily managed or handled : docile, meek, mild, tame. *See* WILD. **5.** Not steep or abrupt : easy, gradual, moderate. *See* RISE.

gentle *verb* **1.** To ease the anger or agitation of : appease, assuage, calm (down), conciliate, dulcify, mollify, pacify, placate, propitiate, soften, soothe, sweeten. ***Idiom:*** pour oil on troubled water. *See* CALM. **2.** To train to live with and be of use to people : domesticate, domesticize, master, tame. *See* WILD. **3.** To make (an animal) docile : break, bust, master, tame. *See* WILD.

gentry *noun*

People of the highest social level : aristocracy, blue blood, crème de la crème, elite, flower, gentility, nobility, patriciate, quality, society, upper class, who's who. *Informal:* upper crust. *See* OVER.

genuflection *noun*

An inclination of the head or body, as in greeting, consent, courtesy, submission, or worship : bow[1], curtsy, kowtow, nod, obeisance. *See* COURTESY.

genuine *adjective*

1. Not counterfeit or copied : actual, authentic, bona fide, good, indubitable, original, real, true, undoubted, unquestionable. *See* TRUE. **2.** Devoid of any hypocrisy or pretense : heartfelt, hearty, honest, natural, real, sincere, true, unaffected, unfeigned, unmannered. *See* TRUE.

genuinely *adverb*
In truth : actually, fairly, indeed, positively, really, truly, truthfully, verily. ***Idiom:*** for fair. *See* REAL, TRUE.

genuineness *noun*
The quality of being authentic : authenticity, realness, truthfulness, validity. *See* TRUE.

germ *noun*
1. A minute organism usually producing disease : bug, microbe, microorganism. *See* BEINGS. **2.** A source of further growth and development : bud[1], embryo, kernel, nucleus, seed, spark[1]. *See* START.

germane *adjective*
Related to the matter at hand : applicable, apposite, apropos, material, pertinent, relevant. ***Idiom:*** to the point. *See* RELEVANT.

germaneness *noun*
The fact of being related to the matter at hand : applicability, application, appositeness, bearing, concernment, materiality, pertinence, pertinency, relevance, relevancy. *See* RELEVANT.

gest or **geste** *noun*
A great or heroic deed : achievement, exploit, feat, masterstroke, stunt, tour de force. *See* ACTION.

gestation *noun*
The condition of carrying a developing fetus within the uterus : gravidity, gravidness, parturiency, pregnancy. *See* REPRODUCTION.

geste *noun* See **gest.**

gesticulate *verb*
To make bodily motions so as to convey an idea or complement speech : gesture, motion, sign, signal, signalize. ***Idiom:*** give the high sign. *See* EXPRESS.

gesticulation *noun*
An expressive, meaningful bodily movement : gesture, indication, motion, sign, signal. *Informal:* high sign. *See* EXPRESS.

gesture *noun*
1. An expressive, meaningful bodily movement : gesticulation, indication, motion, sign, signal. *Informal:* high sign. *See* EXPRESS. **2.** Something that takes the place of words in communicating a thought or feeling : expression, indication, sign, token. *See* SHOW.
gesture *verb* To make bodily motions so as to convey an idea or complement speech : gesticulate, motion, sign, signal, signalize. ***Idiom:*** give the high sign. *See* EXPRESS.

get *verb*
1. To come into possession of : acquire, come by, gain, obtain, procure, secure, win. *Informal:* land, pick up. *See* GET. **2.** To obtain from another source : derive, draw, take. *See* KIN. **3.** To acquire as a result of one's behavior or effort : deserve, earn, gain, merit, win. *Informal:* rate[1]. *See* GET. **4.** To gain possession of, especially after a struggle or chase : capture, catch, net[1], secure, take. *Informal:* bag. *Slang:* nail. *See* GET. **5.** To receive, as wages, for one's labor : earn, gain, make, win. *Informal:* pull down. ***Idioms:*** earn (*or* make) a living, earn one's keep. *See* GIVE, MONEY. **6.** To succeed in communicating with : contact, reach. ***Idioms:*** catch up with, get hold of, get in touch with, get through to, get to. *See* REACH. **7.** To become affected with a disease : catch, contract, develop, sicken, take. ***Idiom:*** come down with. *See* GET. **8.** To perceive and recognize the meaning of : accept, apprehend, catch (on), compass, comprehend, conceive, fathom, follow, grasp, make out, read, see, sense, take, take in, understand. *Informal:* savvy. *Slang:* dig. *Chiefly British:* twig. *Scots:* ken. ***Idioms:*** get (*or* have) a handle on, get the picture. *See* UNDERSTAND. **9.** To gain knowledge or mastery of by study : learn, master. *Informal:* pick up. *See* TEACH. **10.** To be the biological father of : beget, breed, father, procreate, sire. *See* KIN. **11.** To cause to be in a certain state or to undergo a particular experience or action : have, make. *See* CAUSE. **12.** *Informal.* To leave hastily : bolt, get out, run. *Informal:* clear out, hotfoot, skedaddle. *Slang:* hightail, scram, vamoose. ***Idioms:*** beat it, hightail it, hotfoot it, make tracks. *See* APPROACH. **13.** To succeed in causing (a person) to act in a certain way : argue into, bring, bring around (*or* round), convince, induce, persuade, prevail on (*or* upon), sell (on), talk into. *See* PERSUASION. **14.** To obtain possession or control of : capture, gain, take, win. *Slang:* cop. *See* GET. **15.** To evoke a usually strong mental or emotional response from. Also used with *to* : affect[1], impress, move, strike, touch. *See* TOUCH. **16.** To trouble the nerves or peace of mind of, especially by repeated vexations : aggravate, annoy, bother, bug, chafe, disturb, exasperate, fret, gall[2], irk, irritate, nettle, peeve, provoke, put out, rile, ruffle, vex. ***Idioms:*** get in one's hair, get on one's nerves, get under one's skin. *See* FEELINGS, PAIN. **17.** To come to be : become, come, grow, turn (out), wax. *See* CHANGE.

get across *verb* To make known : break, carry, communicate, convey, disclose, impart, pass, report, tell, transmit. *See* KNOWLEDGE.

get ahead *verb* To gain success : arrive, get on, go far, rise, succeed. ***Idioms:*** go places, make good, make it. *See* THRIVE.
get along *verb* **1.** To live or act together in harmony : get on, harmonize. *Informal:* cotton. ***Idiom:*** hit it off. *See* AGREE. **2.** To go forward, especially toward a conclusion : advance, come (along), march[1], move, proceed, progress. *See* APPROACH. **3.** To progress or perform adequately, especially in difficult circumstances : do, fare, fend, get by, manage, muddle through, shift. *Informal:* make out. ***Idioms:*** make do, make shift. *See* THRIVE. **4.** To grow old : age, get on. *See* YOUTH.
get around *verb* **1.** To keep away from : avoid, burke, bypass, circumvent, dodge, duck, elude, escape, eschew, evade, shun. ***Idioms:*** fight shy of, give a wide berth to, have no truck with, keep (*or* stay *or* steer) clear of. *See* SEEK. **2.** To become known far and wide : circulate, go around, spread, travel. ***Idiom:*** go (*or* make) the rounds. *See* KNOWLEDGE.
get away *verb* **1.** To break loose and leave suddenly, as from confinement or from a difficult or threatening situation : abscond, break out, decamp, escape, flee, fly, run away. *Informal:* skip (out). *Slang:* lam. *Regional:* absquatulate. ***Idioms:*** blow (*or* fly) the coop, cut and run, give someone the slip, make a getaway, take flight, take it on the lam. *See* FREE. **2.** To move or proceed away from a place : depart, exit, get off, go, go away, leave[1], pull out, quit, retire, run (along), withdraw. *Informal:* cut out, push off, shove off. *Slang:* blow[1], split, take off. ***Idioms:*** hit the road, take leave. *See* APPROACH.
get behind *verb* To aid the cause of by approving or favoring : advocate, back, champion, endorse, plump for, recommend, side with, stand behind, stand by, support, uphold. ***Idioms:*** align oneself with, go to bat for, take the part of. *See* SUPPORT.
get by *verb* To progress or perform adequately, especially in difficult circumstances : do, fare, fend, get along, manage, muddle through, shift. *Informal:* make out. ***Idioms:*** make do, make shift. *See* THRIVE.
get in *verb* To come to a particular place : arrive, check in, pull in, reach, show up, turn up. *Slang:* blow in. ***Idiom:*** make (*or* put in) an appearance. *See* START.
get off *verb* **1.** To go about the initial step in doing (something) : approach, begin, commence, embark, enter, inaugurate, initiate, institute, launch, lead off, open, set about, set out, set to, start, take on, take up, undertake. *Informal:* kick off. ***Idioms:*** get cracking, get going, get the show on the road. *See* START. **2.** To move or proceed away from a place : depart, exit, get away, go, go away, leave[1], pull out, quit, retire, run (along), withdraw. *Informal:* cut out, push off, shove off. *Slang:* blow[1], split, take off. ***Idioms:*** hit the road, take leave. *See* APPROACH.
get on *verb* **1.** To put (an article of clothing) on one's person : assume, don, pull on, put on, slip into, slip on. *See* PUT ON. **2.** To live or act together in harmony : get along, harmonize. *Informal:* cotton. ***Idiom:*** hit it off. *See* AGREE. **3.** To gain success : arrive, get ahead, go far, rise, succeed. ***Idioms:*** go places, make good, make it. *See* THRIVE. **4.** To grow old : age, get along. *See* YOUTH.
get out *verb* **1.** To leave hastily : bolt, run. *Informal:* clear out, get, hotfoot, skedaddle. *Slang:* hightail, scram, vamoose. ***Idioms:*** beat it, hightail it, hotfoot it, make tracks. *See* APPROACH. **2.** To be made public : break, come out, out, transpire. *Informal:* leak (out). ***Idiom:*** come to light. *See* KNOWLEDGE, SHOW.
get to *verb* To reach (a goal or objective) : arrive at, attain, come to, gain. *Informal:* hit on (*or* upon). *See* START.
get together *verb* **1.** To bring together : assemble, call, cluster, collect[1], congregate, convene, convoke, gather, group, muster, round up, summon. *See* COLLECT. **2.** To come together : assemble, cluster, collect[1], congregate, convene, forgather, gather, group, muster. *See* COLLECT. **3.** To come together face-to-face by arrangement : meet[1], rendezvous. *See* MEET. **4.** To come to an understanding or to terms : accord, agree, coincide, concur, harmonize. *See* AGREE.
get up *verb* **1.** To leave one's bed : arise, pile, rise, roll out. *Informal:* turn out. ***Idiom:*** rise and shine. *See* RISE. **2.** To adopt a standing posture : arise, rise, stand (up), uprise, upspring. ***Idiom:*** get to one's feet. *See* RISE.
get *noun* A group consisting of those descended directly from the same parents or ancestors : brood, issue, offspring, posterity, progeny, seed. *See* KIN.
get across *verb* See **get.**
get ahead *verb* See **get.**
get along *verb* See **get.**
get around *verb* See **get.**
getaway *noun*
The act or an instance of escaping, as from con-

finement or difficulty : break, breakout, decampment, escape, escapement, flight. *Slang:* lam. *See* FREE.

get away *verb* See **get.**

get behind *verb* See **get.**

get by *verb* See **get.**

get in *verb* See **get.**

get off *verb* See **get.**

get on *verb* See **get.**

get out *verb* See **get.**

gettable *adjective*
Capable of being obtained or used : acquirable, attainable, available, obtainable, procurable. ***Idioms:*** on hand, to be had. *See* GET.

get to *verb* See **get.**

get-together *noun*
Informal. A number of persons who have come or been gathered together : assemblage, assembly, body, company, conclave, conference, congregation, congress, convention, convocation, crowd, gathering, group, meeting, muster, troop. *See* COLLECT.

get together *verb* See **get.**

getup *noun*
Informal. A set or style of clothing : costume, dress, garb, guise, habiliment (often used in plural), outfit, turnout. *Informal:* rig. *See* PUT ON.

get up *verb* See **get.**

get-up-and-go *noun*
1. *Informal.* An aggressive readiness along with energy to undertake taxing efforts : drive, enterprise, hustle, initiative, punch. *Informal:* gumption, push. *See* ACTION, TIRED, TRY. **2.** *Informal.* Capacity or power for work or vigorous activity : animation, energy, force, might, potency, power, puissance, sprightliness, steam, strength. *Informal:* go, pep, peppiness, zip. *See* ACTION.

gewgaw *noun*
A small showy article : bauble, bibelot, gimcrack, knickknack, novelty, toy, trifle, trinket, whatnot. *See* THING.

ghastly *adjective*
1. Shockingly repellent : grim, grisly, gruesome, hideous, horrible, horrid, lurid, macabre. *See* BEAUTIFUL. **2.** Causing or able to cause fear : appalling, dire, direful, dreadful, fearful, fearsome, formidable, frightful, redoubtable, scary, terrible, tremendous. *See* FEAR. **3.** Gruesomely suggestive of ghosts or death : cadaverous, deadly, deathlike, deathly, ghostlike, ghostly, spectral. *See* LIVE. **4.** Very bad : appalling, awful, dreadful, fearful, frightful, horrendous, horrible, shocking, terrible. *See* GOOD.

ghost *noun*
1. A supernatural being, such as a ghost : apparition, bogey, bogeyman, bogle, eidolon, phantasm, phantasma, phantom, revenant, shade, shadow, specter, spirit, visitant, wraith. *Informal:* spook. *Regional:* haunt. *See* BEINGS, SUPERNATURAL. **2.** A slight amount or indication : breath, dash, hair, hint, intimation, semblance, shade, shadow, soupçon, streak, suggestion, suspicion, taste, tinge, touch, trace, whiff, whisper. *Informal:* whisker. *See* BIG, SHOW.
ghost *verb* *Informal.* To write for and credit authorship to another : ghostwrite. *See* WORDS.

ghostlike *adjective*
Gruesomely suggestive of ghosts or death : cadaverous, deadly, deathlike, deathly, ghastly, ghostly, spectral. *See* LIVE.

ghostly *adjective*
Gruesomely suggestive of ghosts or death : cadaverous, deadly, deathlike, deathly, ghastly, ghostlike, spectral. *See* LIVE.

ghostwrite *verb*
To write for and credit authorship to another : *Informal:* ghost. *See* WORDS.

ghoul *noun*
A perversely bad, cruel, or wicked person : archfiend, beast, devil, fiend, monster, ogre, tiger, vampire. *See* KIND.

ghoulish *adjective*
Perversely bad, cruel, or wicked : devilish, diabolic, diabolical, fiendish, hellish, infernal, ogreish, satanic, satanical. *See* KIND.

giant *noun*
One that is extraordinarily large and powerful : behemoth, Goliath, jumbo, leviathan, mammoth, monster, titan. *Slang:* whopper. *See* BEINGS, BIG.
giant *adjective* Of extraordinary size and power : behemoth, Brobdingnagian, Bunyanesque, colossal, cyclopean, elephantine, enormous, gargantuan, gigantesque, gigantic, herculean, heroic, huge, immense, jumbo, mammoth, massive, massy, mastodonic, mighty, monster, monstrous, monumental, mountainous, prodigious, pythonic, stupendous, titanic, tremendous, vast. *Informal:* walloping. *Slang:* whopping. *See* BIG.

gibber *verb*
To talk rapidly, incoherently, or indistinctly : babble, blather, chatter, gabble, jabber, prate, prattle. *See* WORDS.

gibberish *noun*
1. Unintelligible or nonsensical talk or

language : abracadabra, double talk, gobbledygook, jabberwocky, mumbo jumbo. *See* CLEAR, WORDS. **2.** Unintelligible or foolish talk : babble, blather, blatherskite, double talk, gabble, jabber, jabberwocky, jargon, nonsense, prate, prattle, twaddle. *See* WORDS. **3.** Esoteric, formulaic, and often incomprehensible speech relating to the occult : abracadabra, hocus-pocus, mumbo jumbo. *See* CLEAR, SUPERNATURAL, WORDS.

gibbet *verb*
To execute by suspending by the neck : hang. *Informal:* string up. *Slang:* swing. *See* HELP.

gibe also **jibe** *verb*
To make fun or make fun of : deride, jeer, jest, laugh, mock, ridicule, scoff, scout[2], twit. *Chiefly British:* quiz. ***Idiom:*** poke fun at. *See* LAUGHTER, RESPECT.
gibe *noun* An instance of mockery or derision : insult, jeer, scoff, taunt, twit. *See* LAUGHTER, RESPECT.

giddiness *noun*
A sensation of whirling or falling : dizziness, lightheadedness, vertiginousness, vertigo, wooziness. *See* AWARENESS.

giddy *adjective*
1. Having a sensation of whirling or falling : dizzy, lightheaded, reeling, vertiginous, woozy. *See* AWARENESS. **2.** Producing dizziness or vertigo : dizzy, dizzying, vertiginous. *See* AWARENESS. **3.** Given to lighthearted silliness : empty-headed, featherbrained, flighty, frivolous, frothy, harebrained, lighthearted, scatterbrained, silly. *Informal:* gaga. *Slang:* birdbrained, dizzy. *See* ABILITY.

gift *noun*
1. Something bestowed freely : present[2], presentation. *Chiefly British:* handsel. *See* GIVE. **2.** Something given to a charity or cause : alms, benefaction, beneficence, charity, contribution, donation, handout, offering, subscription. *See* GIVE. **3.** An innate capability : aptitude, aptness, bent, faculty, flair, genius, head, instinct, knack, talent, turn. *See* ABILITY, APPROACH.
gift *verb* To present with a quality, trait, or power : dower, endow, endue, gird, invest. *See* GIVE.

gifted *adjective*
Having talent : endowed, talented. *See* ABILITY, GIVE.

gig *noun*
1. *Slang.* A post of employment : appointment, berth, billet, job, office, place, position, situation, slot, spot. *See* PLACE. **2.** *Slang.* A commitment, as for a performance by an entertainer : booking, engagement. *See* PERFORMING ARTS.

gigantesque *adjective*
Of extraordinary size and power : behemoth, Brobdingnagian, Bunyanesque, colossal, cyclopean, elephantine, enormous, gargantuan, giant, gigantic, herculean, heroic, huge, immense, jumbo, mammoth, massive, massy, mastodonic, mighty, monster, monstrous, monumental, mountainous, prodigious, pythonic, stupendous, titanic, tremendous, vast. *Informal:* walloping. *Slang:* whopping. *See* BIG.

gigantic *adjective*
Of extraordinary size and power : behemoth, Brobdingnagian, Bunyanesque, colossal, cyclopean, elephantine, enormous, gargantuan, giant, gigantesque, herculean, heroic, huge, immense, jumbo, mammoth, massive, massy, mastodonic, mighty, monster, monstrous, monumental, mountainous, prodigious, pythonic, stupendous, titanic, tremendous, vast. *Informal:* walloping. *Slang:* whopping. *See* BIG.

giggle *verb*
To laugh in a stifled way : snicker, snigger, titter. *See* LAUGHTER.
giggle *noun* A stifled laugh : snicker, snigger, titter. *See* LAUGHTER.

gild *verb*
1. To give a deceptively attractive appearance to : color, gloss (over), gloze (over), sugarcoat, varnish, veneer, whitewash. ***Idioms:*** paper over, put a good face on. *See* TRUE. **2.** To make superficially more acceptable or appealing : candy, honey, sugar, sugarcoat, sweeten. *See* LIKE.

gimcrack *noun*
A small showy article : bauble, bibelot, gewgaw, knickknack, novelty, toy, trifle, trinket, whatnot. *See* THING.

gimmick *noun*
1. An indirect, usually cunning means of gaining an end : artifice, deception, device, dodge, feint, imposture, jig, maneuver, ploy, ruse, sleight, stratagem, subterfuge, trick, wile. *Informal:* shenanigan, take-in. *See* HONEST, MEANS. **2.** A small specialized mechanical device : concern, contraption, contrivance, gadget, jigger, thing. *Informal:* doodad, doohickey, widget. *Slang:* gizmo. *See* MACHINE. **3.** A clever, unexpected new trick or method : twist. *Informal:* kicker, wrinkle. *Slang:* angle[2], kick. *See* ABILITY, EXCITE, GOOD.

ginger *noun*
Informal. A lively, emphatic, eager quality or

manner : animation, bounce, brio, dash, élan, esprit, life, liveliness, pertness, sparkle, spirit, verve, vigor, vim, vivaciousness, vivacity, zip. *Informal:* pep, peppiness. *Slang:* oomph. *See* ACTION.

gingerliness *noun*
1. Cautious attentiveness : care, carefulness, caution, heed, heedfulness, mindfulness, regard. *See* CAREFUL. **2.** Careful forethought to avoid risk : calculation, care, carefulness, caution, chariness, precaution, wariness. *See* FEAR.

gingerly *adjective*
Trying attentively to avoid danger, risk, or error : careful, cautious, chary, circumspect, forehanded, prudent, wary. *See* CAREFUL.

gip *verb* See **gyp.**

gird *verb*
1. To encircle with or as if with a band : band[1], begird, belt, cincture, compass, encompass, engirdle, girdle, girt, ring[1]. *Archaic:* engird. *See* EDGE. **2.** To shut in on all sides : begird, beset, circle, compass, encircle, encompass, environ, girdle, hedge, hem, ring[1], surround. *See* OPEN. **3.** To present with a quality, trait, or power : dower, endow, endue, gift, invest. *See* GIVE. **4.** To prepare (oneself) for action : brace, forearm, fortify, ready, steel, strengthen. ***Idiom:*** gird (*or* gird up) one's loins. *See* PREPARED.

girdle *verb*
1. To encircle with or as if with a band : band[1], begird, belt, cincture, compass, encompass, engirdle, gird, girt, ring[1]. *Archaic:* engird. *See* EDGE. **2.** To shut in on all sides : begird, beset, circle, compass, encircle, encompass, environ, gird, hedge, hem, ring[1], surround. *See* OPEN.

girt *verb*
To encircle with or as if with a band : band[1], begird, belt, cincture, compass, encompass, engirdle, gird, girdle, ring[1]. *Archaic:* engird. *See* EDGE.

gismo *noun* See **gizmo.**

gist *noun*
The most central and material part : core, essence, heart, kernel, marrow, meat, nub, pith, quintessence, root[1], soul, spirit, stuff, substance. *Law:* gravamen. *See* BE.

give *verb*
1. To make a gift of. Also used with *away* : bestow, hand out, present[2]. *See* GIVE. **2.** To present as a gift to a charity or cause : bestow, contribute, donate, hand out. *See* GIVE. **3.** To relinquish to the possession or control of another : deliver, furnish, hand, hand over, provide, supply, transfer, turn over. *See* GIVE. **4.** To distribute (money) as payment : disburse, expend, lay out, outlay, pay (out), spend. *Informal:* fork out (*or* over *or* up), shell out. *See* SAVE. **5.** To provide as a remedy : administer, apply, dispense. *See* GIVE. **6.** To mete out by means of some action : administer, deal, deliver. *See* GIVE. **7.** To let have as a favor, prerogative, or privilege : accord, award, concede, grant, vouchsafe. *See* GIVE. **8.** To put in the charge of another for care, use, or performance. Also used with *over* : commend, commit, confide, consign, entrust, hand over, relegate, trust, turn over. ***Idiom:*** give in trust (*or* charge). *See* GIVE. **9.** To devote (oneself or one's efforts) : address, apply, bend, buckle down, concentrate, dedicate, devote, direct, focus, turn. *See* COLLECT, WORK. **10.** To set aside or distribute as a share : admeasure, allocate, allot, allow, apportion, assign, lot, measure out, mete (out). *See* COLLECT. **11.** To produce on the stage : act (out), do, dramatize, enact, perform, present[2], put on, stage. *See* PERFORMING ARTS. **12.** To organize and carry out (an activity) : have, hold, stage. *See* CONTROL, PLANNED. **13.** To cause (a disease) to pass to another or others : carry, communicate, convey, pass, spread, transmit. *See* MOVE. **14.** To bring forth (a product) : bear, produce, yield. *See* RICH. **15.** To discharge material, as vapor or fumes, usually suddenly and violently : emit, give forth, give off, give out, issue, let off, let out, release, send forth, throw off, vent. *See* FREE, MOVE. **16.** To be unable to hold up : bend. *See* HELP. **17.** To fall in : buckle, cave in, collapse, crumple, go. ***Idiom:*** give way. *See* EXPLOSION.

give away *verb* To disclose in a breach of confidence : betray, blab, divulge, expose, let out, reveal, tell, uncover, unveil. *Informal:* spill. *Archaic:* discover. ***Idioms:*** let slip, let the cat out of the bag, spill the beans, tell all. *See* SHOW.

give back *verb* **1.** To put (someone) in the possession of a prior position or office : reinstate, replace, restore, return. *See* INCREASE, KEEP. **2.** To send, put, or carry back to a former location : restore, return, take back. *See* INCREASE, KEEP.

give forth *verb* To discharge material, as vapor or fumes, usually suddenly and violently : emit, give, give off, give out, issue, let off, let out, release, send forth, throw off, vent. *See* FREE, MOVE.

give in *verb* To cease opposition : concede, yield. *See* WIN.

give off *verb* To discharge material, as vapor or fumes, usually suddenly and violently : emit, give, give forth, give out, issue, let off, let out, release, send forth, throw off, vent. *See* FREE, MOVE.

give out *verb* **1.** To discharge material, as vapor or fumes, usually suddenly and violently : emit, give, give forth, give off, issue, let off, let out, release, send forth, throw off, vent. *See* FREE, MOVE. **2.** To cease functioning properly : break down, fail. *Slang:* conk out. *See* THRIVE. **3.** To suddenly lose all health or strength : break (down), cave in, collapse, crack, drop, succumb. *Informal:* crack up. *Slang:* conk out. ***Idiom:*** give way. *See* HEALTH. **4.** To lose so much strength and power as to become ineffective or motionless : burn out, run down. *Slang:* poop out[1]. *See* TIRED. **5.** To make or become no longer active or productive : deplete, desiccate, dry up, play out, run out. *See* CONTINUE. **6.** To prove deficient or insufficient : fail, run out. ***Idioms:*** fall short, run dry, run short. *See* EXCESS.

give over *verb* **1.** To yield (oneself) unrestrainedly, as to a particular impulse : abandon, give up, surrender. *See* RESIST. **2.** To cease consideration or treatment of : dismiss, drop, give up, skip. ***Idioms:*** have done with, wash one's hands of. *See* KEEP.

give up *verb* **1.** To yield (oneself) unrestrainedly, as to a particular impulse : abandon, give over, surrender. *See* RESIST. **2.** To cease trying to accomplish or continue : abandon, break off, desist, discontinue, leave off, quit, relinquish, remit, stop. *Informal:* swear off. *Slang:* lay off. ***Idioms:*** call it a day, call it quits, hang up one's fiddle, have done with, throw in the towel. *See* CONTINUE. **3.** To desist from, cease, or discontinue (a habit, for example) : break, cut out, leave off, stop. *Slang:* kick. *See* CONTINUE. **4.** To cease consideration or treatment of : dismiss, drop, give over, skip. ***Idioms:*** have done with, wash one's hands of. *See* KEEP. **5.** To lose all hope : despair, despond. *See* HOPE.

give *noun* The quality or state of being flexible : bounce, ductility, elasticity, flexibility, flexibleness, malleability, malleableness, plasticity, pliability, pliableness, pliancy, pliantness, resilience, resiliency, spring, springiness, suppleness. *Obsolete:* flexure. *See* FLEXIBLE.

give-and-take also **give and take** *noun*
A settlement of differences through mutual concession : accommodation, arrangement, compromise, medium, settlement. *Law:* composition. *See* AGREE.

give away *verb* See **give.**

give back *verb* See **give.**

give forth *verb* See **give.**

give in *verb* See **give.**

given *adjective*
Having or showing a tendency or likelihood : apt, disposed, inclined, liable, likely, prone. *See* LIKELY.

give off *verb* See **give.**

give out *verb* See **give.**

give over *verb* See **give.**

giver *noun*
A person who gives to a charity or cause : benefactor, benefactress, contributor, donator, donor. *See* GIVE.

give up *verb* See **give.**

gizmo also **gismo** *noun*
Slang. A small specialized mechanical device : concern, contraption, contrivance, gadget, gimmick, jigger, thing. *Informal:* doodad, doohickey, widget. *See* MACHINE.

glacial *adjective*
1. Very cold : arctic, boreal, freezing, frigid, frosty, gelid, icy, polar, wintry. *Archaic:* frore. ***Idiom:*** bitter (*or* bitterly) cold. *See* HOT.
2. Lacking all friendliness and warmth : cold, frigid, frosty, icy. *See* ATTITUDE, HOT.

glad *adjective*
1. Providing joy and pleasure : cheerful, cheery, festive, happy, joyful, joyous, pleasing. *See* HAPPY. **2.** Marked by festal celebration : festive, gala, gladsome, happy, joyful, joyous, merry. *See* HAPPY. **3.** Eagerly compliant : delighted, happy, pleased, tickled. *See* HAPPY.

gladden *verb*
To give great or keen pleasure to : cheer, delight, enchant, gratify, overjoy, please, pleasure, tickle. *Archaic:* joy. *See* HAPPY, LIKE.

gladly *adverb*
It is so; as you say or ask : absolutely, agreed, all right, assuredly, aye, indubitably, roger, undoubtedly, unquestionably, willingly, yea, yes. *Informal:* OK, uh-huh, yeah, yep. *Slang:* right on. *See* AFFIRM.

gladness *noun*
A condition of supreme well-being and good spirits : beatitude, blessedness, bliss, cheer, cheerfulness, felicity, happiness, joy, joyfulness. *See* HAPPY.

gladsome *adjective*
Marked by festal celebration : festive, gala, glad, happy, joyful, joyous, merry. *See* HAPPY.

glamor *noun* See **glamour.**

glamorous also **glamourous** *adjective*
Pleasing to the eye or mind : attractive, bewitching, enchanting, engaging, enticing, fascinating, fetching, lovely, prepossessing, pretty, sweet, taking, tempting, winning, winsome. *See* LIKE.

glamour also **glamor** *noun*
The power or quality of attracting : allure, allurement, appeal, attraction, attractiveness, call, charisma, charm, draw, enchantment, enticement, fascination, lure, magnetism, witchery. *Informal:* pull. *See* LIKE.

glamourous *adjective* See **glamorous.**

glance *verb*
1. To look briefly and quickly : glimpse, peek, peep. *See* SEE. **2.** To emit light suddenly in rays or sparks : coruscate, flash, gleam, glimmer, glint, glisten, glister, glitter, scintillate, shimmer, spangle, sparkle, twinkle, wink. *See* LIGHT. **3.** To strike a surface at such an angle as to be deflected : carom, dap, graze, ricochet, skim, skip. *See* STRIKE.

glance at (or **over** or **through**) *verb* To look through reading matter casually : browse, dip into, flip through, leaf (through), riffle (through), run through, scan, skim, thumb (through). *See* INVESTIGATE, WORDS.

glance *noun* **1.** A quick look : blush, glimpse, peek, peep. *Informal:* gander. *See* SEE. **2.** A sudden quick light : blink, coruscation, flash, flicker, gleam, glimmer, glint, spark[1], twinkle, wink. *See* LIGHT.

glance at or **over** or **through** *verb* See **glance.**

glare *verb*
1. To stare fixedly and angrily : glower, lower[1], scowl. ***Idiom:*** look daggers at. *See* EXPRESS, SEE. **2.** To be projected with blinding intensity : beat down, blaze[1]. *See* LIGHT. **3.** To be obtrusively conspicuous : stand out, stick out. ***Idioms:*** stare someone in the face, stick out like a sore thumb. *See* SEE.

glare *noun* **1.** A fixed angry stare : glower, lower, scowl. *See* EXPRESS, SEE. **2.** An intense blinding light : blaze[1], dazzle. *See* LIGHT.

glaring *adjective*
1. Extemely bright : brilliant, glary. *See* LIGHT. **2.** Tastelessly showy : brummagem, chintzy, flashy, garish, gaudy, loud, meretricious, tawdry, tinsel. *Informal:* tacky[2]. *See* STYLE. **3.** Conspicuously bad or offensive : arrant, capital, egregious, flagrant, gross, rank[2]. *See* GOOD.

glaringness *noun*
The quality or state of being flagrant : atrociousness, atrocity, egregiousness, enormity, flagrance, flagrancy, flagrantness, grossness, outrageousness, rankness. *See* GOOD.

glary *adjective*
Extemely bright : brilliant, glaring. *See* LIGHT.

glassy *adjective*
Having a high, radiant sheen : gleaming, glistening, glossy, lustrous, polished, shining, shiny. *See* LIGHT.

glaze *noun*
A radiant brightness or glow, usually due to light reflected from a smooth surface : burnish, gloss, luster, polish, sheen, shine, sleekness. *See* LIGHT.

glaze *verb* To give a gleaming luster to, usually through friction : buff[1], burnish, furbish, gloss, polish, shine, sleek. *See* LIGHT.

gleam *noun*
A sudden quick light : blink, coruscation, flash, flicker, glance, glimmer, glint, spark[1], twinkle, wink. *See* LIGHT.

gleam *verb* **1.** To emit a bright light : beam, blaze[1], burn, glow, incandesce, radiate, shine. *See* LIGHT. **2.** To emit light suddenly in rays or sparks : coruscate, flash, glance, glimmer, glint, glisten, glister, glitter, scintillate, shimmer, spangle, sparkle, twinkle, wink. *See* LIGHT. **3.** To shine brightly and steadily but without a flame : glow, incandesce, luminesce. *See* LIGHT.

gleaming *adjective*
Having a high, radiant sheen : glassy, glistening, glossy, lustrous, polished, shining, shiny. *See* LIGHT.

glean *verb*
To collect (something) bit by bit : cull, extract, garner, gather, pick up. *See* COLLECT.

glee *noun*
A state of joyful exuberance : blitheness, blithesomeness, gaiety, gleefulness, hilarity, jocoseness, jocosity, jocularity, jocundity, jolliness, jollity, joviality, lightheartedness, merriment, merriness, mirth, mirthfulness. *See* LAUGHTER.

gleeful *adjective*
Characterized by joyful exuberance : blithe, blithesome, boon[2], convivial, gay, jocund, jolly, jovial, merry, mirthful. *See* HAPPY.

gleefulness *noun*
A state of joyful exuberance : blitheness, blithesomeness, gaiety, glee, hilarity, jocoseness, jocosity, jocularity, jocundity, jolliness, jollity, joviality, lightheartedness, merriment, merriness, mirth, mirthfulness. *See* LAUGHTER.

glib *adjective*
Characterized by ready but often insincere or

superficial discourse : facile, slick, smooth-tongued. *See* SURFACE, WORDS.

glide *verb*

1. To move smoothly, continuously, and effortlessly : glissade, lapse, slide, slip, slither. *See* MOVE. **2.** To maneuver gently and slowly into place : ease, slide, slip. *See* CAREFUL, EASY. **3.** To proceed with ease, especially of expression : flow, roll, sail. *See* MOVE. **4.** To move silently and furtively : creep, lurk, mouse, prowl, pussyfoot, skulk, slide, slink, slip, snake, sneak, steal. *Slang:* gumshoe. *See* MOVE.

glimmer *noun*

A sudden quick light : blink, coruscation, flash, flicker, glance, gleam, glint, spark[1], twinkle, wink. *See* LIGHT.

glimmer *verb* **1.** To shine with intermittent gleams : blink, flash, flicker, twinkle, wink. *See* CONTINUE, LIGHT. **2.** To emit light suddenly in rays or sparks : coruscate, flash, glance, gleam, glint, glisten, glister, glitter, scintillate, shimmer, spangle, sparkle, twinkle, wink. *See* LIGHT.

glimpse *noun*

A quick look : blush, glance, peek, peep. *Informal:* gander. *See* SEE.

glimpse *verb* **1.** To perceive, especially barely or fleetingly : catch, descry, detect, discern, espy, spot, spy. *See* SEE. **2.** To look briefly and quickly : glance, peek, peep. *See* SEE.

glint *noun*

1. A sudden quick light : blink, coruscation, flash, flicker, glance, gleam, glimmer, spark[1], twinkle, wink. *See* LIGHT. **2.** Sparkling, brilliant light : flash, glisten, glister, glitter, scintillation, shimmer, sparkle. *See* BEAUTIFUL, LIGHT.

glint *verb* To emit light suddenly in rays or sparks : coruscate, flash, glance, gleam, glimmer, glisten, glister, glitter, scintillate, shimmer, spangle, sparkle, twinkle, wink. *See* LIGHT.

glissade *verb*

To move smoothly, continuously, and effortlessly : glide, lapse, slide, slip, slither. *See* MOVE.

glisten *verb*

To emit light suddenly in rays or sparks : coruscate, flash, glance, gleam, glimmer, glint, glister, glitter, scintillate, shimmer, spangle, sparkle, twinkle, wink. *See* LIGHT.

glisten *noun* Sparkling, brilliant light : flash, glint, glister, glitter, scintillation, shimmer, sparkle. *See* BEAUTIFUL, LIGHT.

glistening *adjective*

Having a high, radiant sheen : glassy, gleaming, glossy, lustrous, polished, shining, shiny. *See* LIGHT.

glister *verb*

To emit light suddenly in rays or sparks : coruscate, flash, glance, gleam, glimmer, glint, glisten, glitter, scintillate, shimmer, spangle, sparkle, twinkle, wink. *See* LIGHT.

glister *noun* Sparkling, brilliant light : flash, glint, glisten, glitter, scintillation, shimmer, sparkle. *See* BEAUTIFUL, LIGHT.

glitter *noun*

1. Sparkling, brilliant light : flash, glint, glisten, glister, scintillation, shimmer, sparkle. *See* BEAUTIFUL, LIGHT. **2.** Brilliant, showy splendor : brilliance, brilliancy, glory, gorgeousness, magnificence, resplendence, resplendency, sparkle, sumptuousness. *Informal:* glitz. *See* BEAUTIFUL. **3.** A small sparkling decoration : sequin, spangle. *See* BEAUTIFUL.

glitter *verb* To emit light suddenly in rays or sparks : coruscate, flash, glance, gleam, glimmer, glint, glisten, glister, scintillate, shimmer, spangle, sparkle, twinkle, wink. *See* LIGHT.

glitz *noun*

Informal. Brilliant, showy splendor : brilliance, brilliancy, glitter, glory, gorgeousness, magnificence, resplendence, resplendency, sparkle, sumptuousness. *See* BEAUTIFUL.

gloaming *noun*

The period between afternoon and nighttime : dusk, eve, evening, eventide, nightfall, twilight. *Archaic:* even[2], vesper. *See* START.

global *adjective*

1. So pervasive and all-inclusive as to exist in or affect the whole world : catholic, cosmic, cosmopolitan, ecumenical, pandemic, planetary, universal, worldwide. *See* LIMITED, SPECIFIC. **2.** Covering a wide scope : all-around, all-inclusive, all-round, broad, broad-spectrum, comprehensive, expansive, extended, extensive, far-ranging, far-reaching, general, inclusive, large, overall, sweeping, wide-ranging, wide-reaching, widespread. *See* SPECIFIC.

globoid *adjective*

Having the shape of a curve everywhere equidistant from a fixed point : annular, circular, globular, round, spheric, spherical. *See* GEOMETRY.

globular *adjective*

Having the shape of a curve everywhere equidistant from a fixed point : annular, circular, globoid, round, spheric, spherical. *See* GEOMETRY.

globule *noun*
A quantity of liquid falling or resting in a spherical mass : driblet, drop, droplet. *See* DRY.

gloom *noun*
A feeling or spell of dismally low spirits : blues, dejection, depression, despondence, despondency, doldrums, dolefulness, downheartedness, dumps, dysphoria, funk, glumness, heavy-heartedness, melancholy, mope (used in plural), mournfulness, sadness, unhappiness. *See* FEELINGS, HAPPY.
gloom *verb* To make dim or indistinct : becloud, bedim, befog, blear, blur, cloud, dim, dull, eclipse, fog, mist, obfuscate, obscure, overcast, overshadow, shadow. *See* CLEAR.

gloomy *adjective*
1. Dark and depressing : black, bleak, blue, cheerless, dark, desolate, dismal, dreary, glum, joyless, somber, tenebrific. *See* HAPPY, LIGHT. **2.** Broodingly and sullenly unhappy : dour, glum, moody, morose, saturnine, sour, sulky, sullen, surly. *See* HAPPY. **3.** In low spirits : blue, dejected, depressed, desolate, dispirited, down, downcast, downhearted, dull, dysphoric, heavy-hearted, low, melancholic, melancholy, sad, spiritless, tristful, unhappy, wistful. ***Idiom:*** down at (*or* in) the mouth. *See* HAPPY. **4.** Tending to cause sadness or low spirits : blue, cheerless, depressing, dismal, dispiriting, joyless, melancholy, sad. *See* HAPPY. **5.** Marked by little hopefulness : dark, dismal, pessimistic. *See* HAPPY, HOPE.

glorification *noun*
1. The act of raising to a high position or status or the condition of being so raised : aggrandizement, apotheosis, elevation, ennoblement, exaltation. *See* RISE. **2.** The honoring of a deity, as in worship : exaltation, extolment, laudation, magnification, praise. *See* RELIGION.

glorify *verb*
1. To raise to a high position or status : aggrandize, apotheosize, dignify, elevate, ennoble, exalt, magnify, uplift. ***Idiom:*** put on a pedestal. *See* RISE. **2.** To pay tribute or homage to : acclaim, celebrate, eulogize, exalt, extol, hail[2], honor, laud, magnify, panegyrize, praise. ***Idiom:*** sing someone's praises. *See* PRAISE. **3.** To honor (a deity) in religious worship : exalt, extol, laud, magnify, praise. *See* RELIGION.

glorious *adjective*
1. Marked by extraordinary elegance, beauty, and splendor : brilliant, gorgeous, magnificent, proud, resplendent, splendid, splendorous. *See* BEAUTIFUL. **2.** Particularly excellent : divine, fabulous, fantastic, fantastical, marvelous, sensational, splendid, superb, terrific, wonderful. *Informal:* dandy, dreamy, great, ripping, super, swell, tremendous. *Slang:* cool, groovy, hot, keen[1], neat, nifty. ***Idiom:*** out of this world. *See* GOOD.

glory *noun*
1. A position of exalted widely recognized importance : distinction, eminence, eminency, fame, illustriousness, luster, mark, notability, note, preeminence, prestige, prominence, prominency, renown. *See* IMPORTANT, KNOWLEDGE, RESPECT. **2.** Something meriting the highest praise or regard : grandeur, grandiosity, grandness, greatness, majesty, splendor. *See* PRAISE. **3.** Brilliant, showy splendor : brilliance, brilliancy, glitter, gorgeousness, magnificence, resplendence, resplendency, sparkle, sumptuousness. *Informal:* glitz. *See* BEAUTIFUL.
glory *verb* To feel or express an uplifting joy over a success or victory : crow, exult, jubilate, triumph. *See* HAPPY.

gloss *noun*
1. A radiant brightness or glow, usually due to light reflected from a smooth surface : burnish, glaze, luster, polish, sheen, shine, sleekness. *See* LIGHT. **2.** A deceptive outward appearance : cloak, color, coloring, cover, disguise, disguisement, façade, face, false colors, front, guise, mask, masquerade, pretense, pretext, semblance, show, veil, veneer, window-dressing. *Slang:* put-on. *See* SHOW.
gloss *verb* **1.** To give a gleaming luster to, usually through friction : buff[1], burnish, furbish, glaze, polish, shine, sleek. *See* LIGHT. **2.** To give a deceptively attractive appearance to. Also used with *over* : color, gild, gloze (over), sugarcoat, varnish, veneer, whitewash. ***Idioms:*** paper over, put a good face on. *See* TRUE.
gloss over *verb* To conceal or make light of a fault or offense : explain away, extenuate, gloze (over), palliate, sleek over, whitewash. *See* SHOW.

glossary *noun*
An alphabetical list of words often defined or translated : dictionary, lexicon, vocabulary, wordbook. *See* WORDS.

gloss over *verb* See **gloss.**

glossy *adjective*
Having a high, radiant sheen : glassy, gleam-

ing, glistening, lustrous, polished, shining, shiny. *See* LIGHT.

glow *verb*

1. To shine brightly and steadily but without a flame : gleam, incandesce, luminesce. *See* LIGHT. **2.** To emit a bright light : beam, blaze[1], burn, gleam, incandesce, radiate, shine. *See* LIGHT. **3.** To become red in the face : blush, color, crimson, flush, mantle, redden. *See* EXPRESS.

glow *noun* **1.** A fresh rosy complexion : bloom[1], blush, color, flush. *See* BETTER. **2.** A feeling of pervasive emotional warmth : flush. *See* FEELINGS.

glower *verb*

1. To stare fixedly and angrily : glare, lower[1], scowl. ***Idiom:*** look daggers at. *See* EXPRESS, SEE. **2.** To wrinkle one's brow, as in thought, puzzlement, or displeasure : frown, lower[1], scowl. ***Idiom:*** look black. *See* EXPRESS.

glower *noun* **1.** A fixed angry stare : glare, lower, scowl. *See* EXPRESS, SEE. **2.** The act of wrinkling the brow, as in thought, puzzlement, or displeasure : black look, frown, lower[1], scowl. *See* EXPRESS.

glowing *adjective*

1. Bright and clear in complexion; not dull or faded : blooming, creamy, fresh, peaches-and-cream. *See* BEAUTIFUL. **2.** Of a healthy reddish color : blooming, florid, flush, flushed, full-blooded, rosy, rubicund, ruddy, sanguine. *See* COLORS. **3.** Fired with intense feeling : ardent, blazing, burning, dithyrambic, fervent, fervid, fiery, flaming, heated, hot-blooded, impassioned, passionate, perfervid, red-hot, scorching, torrid. *See* FEELINGS.

gloze *verb*

1. To conceal or make light of a fault or offense. Also used with *over* : explain away, extenuate, gloss over, palliate, sleek over, whitewash. *See* SHOW. **2.** To give a deceptively attractive appearance to. Also used with *over* : color, gild, gloss (over), sugarcoat, varnish, veneer, whitewash. ***Idioms:*** paper over, put a good face on. *See* TRUE.

gluey *adjective*

Having the property of adhering : adhesive, gooey, gummy, sticky, tacky[1]. *See* CLEAN, KEEP.

glum *adjective*

1. Broodingly and sullenly unhappy : dour, gloomy, moody, morose, saturnine, sour, sulky, sullen, surly. *See* HAPPY. **2.** Dark and depressing : black, bleak, blue, cheerless, dark, desolate, dismal, dreary, gloomy, joyless, somber, tenebrific. *See* HAPPY, LIGHT.

glumness *noun*

A feeling or spell of dismally low spirits : blues, dejection, depression, despondence, despondency, doldrums, dolefulness, downheartedness, dumps, dysphoria, funk, gloom, heavy-heartedness, melancholy, mope (used in plural), mournfulness, sadness, unhappiness. *See* FEELINGS, HAPPY.

glut *verb*

To satisfy to the full or to excess : cloy, engorge, gorge, pall, sate, satiate, surfeit. *See* EXCESS, FULL.

glut *noun* An amount or quantity beyond what is needed, desired, or appropriate : excess, fat, overage, overflow, overmuch, overrun, overstock, oversupply, superfluity, surplus, surplusage. *See* EXCESS.

glutinous *adjective*

Having a heavy, gluey quality : mucilaginous, viscid, viscose, viscous. *See* SOLID.

glutinousness *noun*

The physical property of being viscous : viscidity, viscosity. *See* SOLID.

gluttonous *adjective*

1. Wanting to eat or drink more than one can reasonably consume : edacious, greedy, hoggish, piggish, ravenous, voracious. *See* DESIRE, INGESTION. **2.** Having an insatiable appetite for an activity or pursuit : avid, edacious, greedy, omnivorous, rapacious, ravenous, unappeasable, voracious. *See* DESIRE.

gnash *verb*

1. To rub together noisily : crunch, grind. *See* SOUNDS. **2.** To seize, as food, with the teeth : bite, champ, chomp, gnaw. *See* ATTACK, INGESTION.

gnaw *verb*

1. To seize, as food, with the teeth : bite, champ, chomp, gnash. *See* ATTACK, INGESTION. **2.** To consume gradually, as by chemical reaction or friction : bite, corrode, eat, erode, wear, wear away. *See* ATTACK.

gnawing *adjective*

Marked by severity or intensity : acute, knifelike, lancinating, piercing, sharp, shooting, stabbing. *See* BIG.

go *verb*

1. To move along a particular course : fare, journey, pass, proceed, push on, remove, travel, wend. ***Idiom:*** make one's way. *See* MOVE. **2.** To proceed in a specified direction : bear, head, make, set out, strike out. *See* APPROACH. **3.** To move or proceed away from a place :

depart, exit, get away, get off, go away, leave[1], pull out, quit, retire, run (along), withdraw. *Informal:* cut out, push off, shove off. *Slang:* blow[1], split, take off. ***Idioms:*** hit the road, take leave. *See* APPROACH. **4.** To look to when in need : apply, refer, repair[2], resort, run, turn. ***Idioms:*** fall back on (*or* upon), have recourse to. *See* USED. **5.** To proceed on a certain course or for a certain distance : carry, extend, lead, reach, run, stretch. *See* REACH. **6.** To change or fluctuate within limits : extend, range, run, vary. *See* CHANGE. **7.** To perform a function effectively : function, operate, run, take, work. *See* THRIVE. **8.** To move toward a termination : go away, pass, pass away. *See* APPROACH, INCREASE, TIME. **9.** To have a proper or suitable place : belong, fit[1]. *See* ORDER. **10.** To move past in time. Also used with *by* : elapse, lapse, pass. *See* TIME. **11.** To be depleted : consume, spend. ***Idiom:*** go down the drain. *See* INCREASE. **12.** To fall in : buckle, cave in, collapse, crumple, give. ***Idiom:*** give way. *See* EXPLOSION. **13.** To cease living : decease, demise, depart, die, drop, expire, pass away, pass (on), perish, succumb. *Informal:* pop off. *Slang:* check out, croak, kick in, kick off. ***Idioms:*** bite the dust, breathe one's last, cash in, give up the ghost, go to one's grave, kick the bucket, meet one's end (*or* Maker), pass on to the Great Beyond, turn up one's toes. *See* LIVE. **14.** To do or fare well : boom, flourish, prosper, thrive. *Slang:* score. ***Idioms:*** get (*or* go) somewhere, go great guns, go strong. *See* THRIVE. **15.** To turn out well : come off, go over, pan out, succeed, work, work out. *Slang:* click. *See* THRIVE. **16.** To put up with : abide, accept, bear, brook[2], endure, stand (for), stomach, suffer, support, sustain, swallow, take, tolerate, withstand. *Informal:* lump[2]. ***Idioms:*** take it, take it lying down. *See* ACCEPT. **17.** *Informal.* To put up as a stake in a game or speculation : bet, gamble, lay[1] (down), post[2], put, risk, stake, venture, wager. *See* GAMBLING. **18.** *Informal.* To make an offer of : bid, offer. *See* OFFER.

go along *verb* To agree to cooperate or participate : *Informal:* play along. *See* PARTICIPATE.

go around *verb* **1.** To pass around but not through : bypass, circumnavigate, circumvent, detour, skirt. *See* SEEK. **2.** To become known far and wide : circulate, get around, spread, travel. ***Idiom:*** go (*or* make) the rounds. *See* KNOWLEDGE.

go at *verb* **1.** To set upon with violent force : aggress, assail, assault, attack, beset, fall on (*or* upon), have at, sail into, storm, strike. *Informal:* light into, pitch into. *See* ATTACK. **2.** To start work on vigorously : attack, sail in, tackle, wade in (*or* into). ***Idiom:*** hop to it. *See* WORK.

go away *verb* **1.** To move or proceed away from a place : depart, exit, get away, get off, go, leave[1], pull out, quit, retire, run (along), withdraw. *Informal:* cut out, push off, shove off. *Slang:* blow[1], split, take off. ***Idioms:*** hit the road, take leave. *See* APPROACH. **2.** To move toward a termination : go, pass, pass away. *See* APPROACH, INCREASE, TIME.

go back *verb* To go again to a former place : come back, return, revisit. *See* APPROACH.

go down *verb* **1.** To come to the ground suddenly and involuntarily : drop, fall, nose-dive, pitch, plunge, spill, topple, tumble. ***Idiom:*** take a fall (*or* header *or* plunge *or* spill *or* tumble). *See* RISE. **2.** To undergo capture, defeat, or ruin : collapse, fall, go under, surrender, topple. *See* RESIST, WIN.

go far *verb* To gain success : arrive, get ahead, get on, rise, succeed. ***Idioms:*** go places, make good, make it. *See* THRIVE.

go for *verb* **1.** *Informal.* To be favorably disposed toward : approve, countenance, favor, hold with. ***Idiom:*** take kindly to. *See* PRAISE. **2.** *Informal.* To receive pleasure from : enjoy, like[1], relish, savor. *Slang:* dig. *See* LIKE. **3.** To require a specified price : cost, sell for. *See* TRANSACTIONS.

go in *verb* To come or go into (a place) : come in, enter, penetrate. *Nautical:* put in. ***Idioms:*** gain entrance (*or* entry), set foot in. *See* ENTER.

go off *verb* To release or cause to release energy suddenly and violently, especially with a loud noise : blast, blow[1] (up), burst, detonate, explode, fire, fulminate, touch off. *See* EXPLOSION.

go on *verb* **1.** To be in existence or in a certain state for an indefinitely long time : abide, continue, endure, hold out, last[2], persist, remain, stay[1]. *See* CONTINUE. **2.** To continue without halting despite difficulties or setbacks : carry on, hang on, keep on, persevere, persist. ***Idioms:*** hang in there, keep going, keep it up. *See* CONTINUE. **3.** *Informal.* To talk volubly, persistently, and usually inconsequentially : babble, blabber, chatter, chitchat, clack, jabber, palaver, prate, prattle, rattle (on), run on. *Informal:* spiel. *Slang:* gab, gas, jaw, yak.

Idioms: run off at the mouth, shoot the breeze (*or* bull). *See* WORDS.
go out *verb* To be with another person socially on a regular basis : date, see. *Informal:* take out. *See* CONNECT.
go over *verb* **1.** To turn out well : come off, go, pan out, succeed, work, work out. *Slang:* click. *See* THRIVE. **2.** To look at carefully or critically : check (out), con, examine, inspect, peruse, scrutinize, study, survey, traverse, view. *Informal:* case. *Idiom:* give a going-over. *See* INVESTIGATE. **3.** To give a recapitulation of the salient facts of : abstract, epitomize, recapitulate, review, run down, run through, summarize, sum up, synopsize, wrap up. *Informal:* recap. *See* THOUGHTS.
go through *verb* To participate in or partake of personally : experience, feel, have, know, meet (with), see, suffer, taste (of), undergo. *Archaic:* prove. *Idiom:* run up against. *See* PARTICIPATE.
go under *verb* **1.** To undergo capture, defeat, or ruin : collapse, fall, go down, surrender, topple. *See* RESIST, WIN. **2.** To undergo sudden financial failure : break, bust, collapse, crash, fail. *Informal:* fold. *Idioms:* go belly up, go bust, go on the rocks, go to the wall. *See* MONEY.
go up *verb* To move upward on or along : ascend, climb, mount, scale[2]. *See* RISE.
go with *verb* To be in keeping with : become, befit, conform, correspond, fit[1], match, suit. *See* AGREE.
go *noun* **1.** A trying to do or make something : attempt, crack, effort, endeavor, essay, offer, stab, trial, try. *Informal:* shot. *Slang:* take. *Archaic:* assay. *See* TRY. **2.** A brief trial : crack, stab, try. *Informal:* fling, shot, whack, whirl. *See* TRY. **3.** A limited, often assigned period of activity, duty, or opportunity : bout, hitch, inning (often used in plural), shift, spell[3], stint, stretch, time, tour, trick, turn, watch. *See* TIME. **4.** *Informal.* Capacity or power for work or vigorous activity : animation, energy, force, might, potency, power, puissance, sprightliness, steam, strength. *Informal:* get-up-and-go, pep, peppiness, zip. *See* ACTION.
go *adjective Informal.* In a state of preparedness : ready, set[1]. *Slang:* together. *Idioms:* all set, in working order. *See* PREPARED.
goad *noun*
Something that incites especially a violent response : incitation, incitement, instigation, provocation, stimulus, trigger. *See* CAUSE.
goad *verb* To stir to action or feeling : egg on, excite, foment, galvanize, impel, incite, inflame, inspire, instigate, motivate, move, pique, prick, prod, prompt, propel, provoke, set off, spur, stimulate, touch off, trigger, work up. *See* CAUSE, EXCITE.
goal *noun*
What one intends to do or achieve : aim, ambition, design, end, intent, intention, mark, meaning, object, objective, point, purpose, target, view, why. *Idioms:* end in view, why and wherefore. *See* PLANNED, PURPOSE.
go along *verb* See **go.**
go around *verb* See **go.**
goat *noun*
One who is made an object of blame : scapegoat, whipping boy. *Slang:* fall guy, patsy. *See* PRAISE.
go at *verb* See **go.**
go away *verb* See **go.**
gob[1] *noun*
1. An irregularly shaped mass of indefinite size : chunk, clod, clump, hunch, lump[1], nugget, wad. *Informal:* hunk. *See* PART.
2. *Informal.* An indeterminately great amount or number. Often used in plural : jillion, million (often used in plural), multiplicity, ream, trillion. *Informal:* bushel, heap (often used in plural), load (often used in plural), lot, oodles, passel, peck[2], scad (often used in plural), slew, wad, zillion. *See* BIG.
gob[2] *noun*
Slang. The opening in the body through which food is ingested : mouth. *Slang:* puss, trap. *See* MOUTH.
gob[3] *noun*
Slang. A person engaged in sailing or working on a ship : jack (uppercase), jack-tar, mariner, navigator, sailor, sea dog, seafarer, seaman. *Informal:* salt, tar. *See* SEA.
go back *verb* See **go.**
gobble *verb*
To swallow (food or drink) greedily or rapidly in large amounts : bolt, down, englut, engorge, gulp, guzzle, ingurgitate, swill, wolf. *See* INGESTION.
gobbledegook *noun* See **gobbledygook.**
gobbledygook also **gobbledegook** *noun*
Unintelligible or nonsensical talk or language : abracadabra, double talk, gibberish, jabberwocky, mumbo jumbo. *See* CLEAR, WORDS.
go-between *noun*
Someone who acts as an intermediate agent in a transaction or helps to resolve differences : broker, interceder, intercessor, intermediary,

intermediate, intermediator, mediator, middleman. *See* MEANS.

go-by *noun*
Informal. A deliberate slight : cut, rebuff, snub, spurn. *Informal:* cold shoulder. *See* ACCEPT.

godforsaken also **Godforsaken** *adjective*
Empty of people : deserted, desolate, forlorn, lonely, lonesome, unfrequented. *See* FULL.

godlike *adjective*
Of, from, like, or being a god or God : deific, divine, godly, heavenly, holy. *See* RELIGION.

godly *adjective*
1. Deeply concerned with God and the beliefs and practice of religion : devotional, devout, holy, pietistic, pietistical, pious, prayerful, religious, saintly. *See* RELIGION. **2.** Of, from, like, or being a god or God : deific, divine, godlike, heavenly, holy. *See* RELIGION.

go down *verb* See **go.**

God's country *noun*
A rural area : country, countryside. *See* URBAN.

go far *verb* See **go.**

go for *verb* See **go.**

go-getter *noun*
Informal. An intensely energetic, enthusiastic person : dynamo, hustler. *Informal:* eager beaver, live wire. *See* CONCERN.

goggle *verb*
To look intently and fixedly : eye, gape, gawk, gaze, ogle, peer[1], stare. ***Idioms:*** gaze openmouthed, rivet the eyes on. *See* SEE.

go in *verb* See **go.**

going *noun*
The act of leaving : departure, egress, exit, exodus, withdrawal. *See* APPROACH.
going *adjective* In action or full operation : active, alive, functioning, operating, operative, running, working. *See* ACTION, AWARENESS.

going-over *noun*
Informal. The act of examining carefully : check, checkup, examination, inspection, perusal, scrutiny, study, view. *See* INVESTIGATE.

goldbrick *verb*
Slang. To pass time without working or in avoiding work : bum[1] (around), idle, laze, loaf, loiter, lounge, shirk. *Slang:* diddle[2], goof (off). *See* INDUSTRIOUS.

golden ager *noun*
An elderly person : ancient, elder, senior, senior citizen. *Informal:* oldster, old-timer. *See* YOUTH.

Goliath *noun*
One that is extraordinarily large and powerful : behemoth, giant, jumbo, leviathan, mammoth, monster, titan. *Slang:* whopper. *See* BEINGS, BIG.

gone *adjective*
1. Not present : absent, away, missing, wanting. *See* ABSENCE. **2.** No longer in one's possession : lost, missing. *See* GET. **3.** No longer alive : asleep, dead, deceased, defunct, departed, extinct, late, lifeless. ***Idioms:*** at rest, pushing up daisies. *See* LIVE. **4.** *Slang.* Affected with intense romantic attraction : enamored, infatuate, infatuated, smitten. *See* EXCITE, SEX. **5.** *Slang.* Carrying a developing fetus within the uterus : big, enceinte, expectant, expecting, gravid, parturient, pregnant. *Archaic:* great. ***Idioms:*** in a family way, with child. *See* REPRODUCTION.

good *adjective*
1. Having pleasant desirable qualities : nice. *Scots:* bonny, braw. *See* GOOD. **2.** To one's liking : agreeable, congenial, favorable, grateful, gratifying, nice, pleasant, pleasing, pleasurable, satisfying, welcome. *See* LIKE. **3.** Suited to one's end or purpose : appropriate, befitting, convenient, expedient, fit[1], meet[2], proper, suitable, tailor-made, useful. *See* AGREE, GOOD. **4.** In excellent condition : entire, flawless, intact, perfect, sound[2], unblemished, unbroken, undamaged, unharmed, unhurt, unimpaired, uninjured, unmarred, whole. *See* THRIVE. **5.** Well above average : high-grade, nice. *See* GOOD, ABILITY. **6.** Affording benefit : advantageous, benefic, beneficent, beneficial, benignant, favorable, helpful, profitable, propitious, salutary, toward, useful. *See* HELP. **7.** Having the ability to perform well : able, capable, competent, skilled, skillful. *See* ABILITY. **8.** Not counterfeit or copied : actual, authentic, bona fide, genuine, indubitable, original, real, true, undoubted, unquestionable. *See* TRUE. **9.** Notably above average in amount, size, or scope : big, considerable, extensive, great, healthy, large, large-scale, sizable. *Informal:* tidy. *See* BIG. **10.** Not more or less : complete, entire, full, perfect, round, whole. *See* PART, PRECISE. **11.** Indicative of future success or full of promise : auspicious, benign, bright, brilliant, fair, favorable, fortunate, propitious. *See* LUCK. **12.** Beyond reproach : blameless, exemplary, irreprehensible, irreproachable, lilywhite, unblamable. *See* RIGHT. **13.** Having or marked by uprightness in principle and action : honest, honorable, incorruptible, righteous,

true, upright, upstanding. *Informal:* straight-shooting. ***Idiom:*** on the up-and-up (*or* up and up). *See* HONEST. **14.** Characterized by kindness and concern for others : altruistic, beneficent, benevolent, benign, benignant, goodhearted, kind[1], kindhearted, kindly. *See* ATTITUDE, KIND.

good *noun* **1.** Something that contributes to or increases one's well-being : advantage, benefit, interest (often used in plural), profit. *See* HELP. **2.** The quality or state of being morally sound : goodness, morality, probity, rectitude, righteousness, rightness, uprightness, virtue, virtuousness. *See* RIGHT. **3.** A product or products bought and sold in commerce. Used in plural : commodity, line, merchandise, ware. *See* MATTER, TRANSACTIONS. **4.** One's portable property. Used in plural : belonging (often used in plural), effect (used in plural), lares and penates, personal effects, personal property, possession (used in plural), property, thing (often used in plural). *Informal:* stuff. *Law:* chattel, movable (often used in plural). *See* OWNED.

good-by *noun & adjective* See **good-bye.**

good-bye or **goodbye** also **good-by** *noun*
A separation of two or more people : adieu, farewell, leave-taking, parting, valediction. *See* APPROACH.
good-bye or **goodbye** also **good-by** *adjective* Of, done, given, or said on departing : departing, farewell, parting, valedictory. *See* APPROACH.

good form *noun*
Socially correct behavior : decorum, etiquette, manner (used in plural), mores, propriety (also used in plural), p's and q's. *See* USUAL.

good-for-nothing *noun*
A self-indulgent person who spends time avoiding work or other useful activity : bum[1], drone[1], fainéant, idler, layabout, loafer, ne'er-do-well, no-good, slugabed, sluggard, wastrel. *Informal:* do-little, do-nothing, lazybones, slug[2]. *Slang:* slouch. *See* INDUSTRIOUS.
good-for-nothing *adjective* Lacking all worth and value : drossy, inutile, no-good, nothing, valueless, worthless. *Informal:* no-account. *See* VALUE.

goodhearted *adjective*
Characterized by kindness and concern for others : altruistic, beneficent, benevolent, benign, benignant, good, kind[1], kindhearted, kindly. *See* ATTITUDE, KIND.

goodish *adjective*
Of moderately good quality but less than excellent : acceptable, adequate, all right, average, common, decent, fair, fairish, moderate, passable, respectable, satisfactory, sufficient, tolerable. *Informal:* OK, tidy. *See* GOOD.

good-looking *adjective*
Having qualities that delight the eye : attractive, beauteous, beautiful, comely, fair, gorgeous, handsome, lovely, pretty, pulchritudinous, ravishing, sightly, stunning. *Scots:* bonny. *Idiom:* easy on the eyes. *See* BEAUTIFUL.

goodly *adjective*
Somewhat big : biggish, largish, respectable, sizable. *See* BIG.

good name *noun*
A person's high standing among others : dignity, good report, honor, prestige, reputation, repute, respect, status. *See* RESPECT.

good-natured *adjective*
Pleasant and friendly in disposition : affable, agreeable, amiable, congenial, cordial, genial, good-tempered, pleasant, sociable, warm. *See* ATTITUDE, GOOD.

goodness *noun*
The quality or state of being morally sound : good, morality, probity, rectitude, righteousness, rightness, uprightness, virtue, virtuousness. *See* RIGHT.

good report *noun*
A person's high standing among others : dignity, good name, honor, prestige, reputation, repute, respect, status. *See* RESPECT.

good-tempered *adjective*
Pleasant and friendly in disposition : affable, agreeable, amiable, congenial, cordial, genial, good-natured, pleasant, sociable, warm. *See* ATTITUDE, GOOD.

good turn *noun*
A kindly act : favor, grace, indulgence, kindness, service. *Archaic:* benefit. *See* HELP.

goodwill also **good will** *noun*
Kindly, charitable interest in others : altruism, beneficence, benevolence, benignancy, benignity, charitableness, charity, grace, kindheartedness, kindliness, kindness, philanthropy. *See* ATTITUDE, KIND.

goody *noun*
Informal. Something fine and delicious, especially a food : dainty, delicacy, morsel, tidbit, treat. *See* GOOD, INGESTION.

gooey *adjective*
1. Having the property of adhering : adhesive, gluey, gummy, sticky, tacky[1]. *See* CLEAN, KEEP. **2.** *Informal.* Affectedly or extravagantly emotional : bathetic, gushy, maudlin, mawkish, romantic, sentimental, slushy, sobby, soft, soppy. *Informal:* mushy, schmaltzy, sloppy,

soupy. *Slang:* drippy, sappy, tear-jerking. *See* FEELINGS.

goof *noun*
1. *Slang.* One deficient in judgment and good sense : ass, fool, idiot, imbecile, jackass, mooncalf, moron, nincompoop, ninny, nitwit, simple, simpleton, softhead, tomfool. *Informal:* dope, gander, goose. *Slang:* cretin, ding-dong, dip, jerk, nerd, schmo, schmuck, turkey. *See* ABILITY. **2.** *Slang.* A stupid, clumsy mistake : blunder, bull[2], bungle, foozle, fumble, muff, stumble. *Informal:* blooper, boner. *Slang:* bloomer. *See* CORRECT.
goof *verb* *Slang.* To pass time without working or in avoiding work. Also used with *off* : bum[1] (around), idle, laze, loaf, loiter, lounge, shirk. *Slang:* diddle[2], goldbrick. *See* INDUSTRIOUS.
goof up *verb* *Slang.* To harm irreparably through inept handling; make a mess : ball up, blunder, boggle, botch, bungle, foul up, fumble, gum up, mess up, mishandle, mismanage, muddle, muff, spoil. *Informal:* bollix up, muck up. *Slang:* blow[1], louse up, screw up, snafu. ***Idiom:*** make a muck of. *See* CORRECT, HELP.

go off *verb* See **go.**

goof up *verb* See **goof.**

goon *noun*
Slang. A person who treats others violently and roughly, especially for hire : hoodlum, ruffian, thug, tough. *Informal:* hooligan. *Slang:* gorilla, hood. *See* ATTACK, CRIMES.

go on *verb* See **go.**

goose *noun*
Informal. One deficient in judgment and good sense : ass, fool, idiot, imbecile, jackass, mooncalf, moron, nincompoop, ninny, nitwit, simple, simpleton, softhead, tomfool. *Informal:* dope, gander. *Slang:* cretin, ding-dong, dip, goof, jerk, nerd, schmo, schmuck, turkey. *See* ABILITY.

go out *verb* See **go.**

go over *verb* See **go.**

gore *noun*
The fluid circulated by the heart through the vascular system : blood. *See* BLOOD.

gorge *verb*
To satisfy to the full or to excess : cloy, engorge, glut, pall, sate, satiate, surfeit. *See* EXCESS, FULL.

gorgeous *adjective*
1. Having qualities that delight the eye : attractive, beauteous, beautiful, comely, fair, good-looking, handsome, lovely, pretty, pulchritudinous, ravishing, sightly, stunning. *Scots:* bonny. ***Idiom:*** easy on the eyes. *See* BEAUTIFUL. **2.** Marked by extraordinary elegance, beauty, and splendor : brilliant, glorious, magnificent, proud, resplendent, splendid, splendorous. *See* BEAUTIFUL.

gorgeousness *noun*
Brilliant, showy splendor : brilliance, brilliancy, glitter, glory, magnificence, resplendence, resplendency, sparkle, sumptuousness. *Informal:* glitz. *See* BEAUTIFUL.

gorilla *noun*
Slang. A person who treats others violently and roughly, especially for hire : hoodlum, ruffian, thug, tough. *Informal:* hooligan. *Slang:* goon, hood. *See* ATTACK, CRIMES.

gory *adjective*
1. Of or covered with blood : bloody. *See* BLOOD. **2.** Attended by or causing bloodshed : bloody, sanguinary, sanguineous. *See* BLOOD.

gossamer *adjective*
So light and insubstantial as to resemble air or a thin film : aerial, aery, airy, diaphanous, ethereal, filmy, gauzy, gossamery, sheer[2], transparent, vaporous, vapory. *See* THICK.

gossamery *adjective*
So light and insubstantial as to resemble air or a thin film : aerial, aery, airy, diaphanous, ethereal, filmy, gauzy, gossamer, sheer[2], transparent, vaporous, vapory. *See* THICK.

gossip *noun*
1. Idle, often sensational and groundless talk about others : gossipry, hearsay, report, rumor, talebearing, tattle, tittle-tattle, word. *Slang:* scuttlebutt. *See* WORDS. **2.** A person habitually engaged in idle talk about others : blab, gossiper, gossipmonger, newsmonger, rumormonger, scandalmonger, tabby, talebearer, taleteller, tattle, tattler, tattletale, telltale, whisperer. *Slang:* yenta. *See* WORDS.
gossip *verb* To engage in or spread gossip : blab, noise, rumor, talk, tattle, tittle-tattle, whisper. ***Idioms:*** tell tales, tell tales out of school. *See* WORDS.

gossiper *noun*
A person habitually engaged in idle talk about others : blab, gossip, gossipmonger, newsmonger, rumormonger, scandalmonger, tabby, talebearer, taleteller, tattle, tattler, tattletale, telltale, whisperer. *Slang:* yenta. *See* WORDS.

gossipmonger *noun*
A person habitually engaged in idle talk about others : blab, gossip, gossiper, newsmonger, rumormonger, scandalmonger, tabby, talebearer, taleteller, tattle, tattler, tattletale, telltale, whisperer. *Slang:* yenta. *See* WORDS.

gossipry *noun*
Idle, often sensational and groundless talk about others : gossip, hearsay, report, rumor, talebearing, tattle, tittle-tattle, word. *Slang:* scuttlebutt. *See* WORDS.

gossipy *adjective*
Inclined to gossip : blabby, talebearing, taletelling. *See* WORDS.

go through *verb* See **go.**

gouge *verb*
Slang. To exploit (another) by charging too much for something : fleece, overcharge. *Slang:* clip[1], nick, rip off, scalp, skin, soak. ***Idioms:*** make someone pay through the nose, take someone for a ride, take someone to the cleaners. *See* HONEST.

go under *verb* See **go.**

go up *verb* See **go.**

govern *verb*
1. To have charge of (the affairs of others) : administer, administrate, direct, head, manage, run, superintend, supervise. *See* OVER. **2.** To exercise the authority of a sovereign : reign, rule. *Archaic:* sway. ***Idiom:*** wear the crown (*or* purple). *See* OVER. **3.** To keep the mechanical operation of (a device) within proper parameters : control, regulate. *See* CONTROL, MACHINE. **4.** To exercise authority or influence over : control, direct, dominate, rule. ***Idioms:*** be at the helm, be in the driver's seat, hold sway over, hold the reins. *See* OVER.

governable *adjective*
Capable of being governed : administrable, controllable, manageable, rulable. *See* CONTROL.

governance *noun*
1. The continuous exercise of authority over a political unit : administration, control, direction, government, rule. *See* CONTROL, POLITICS. **2.** A system by which a political unit is controlled : government, regime, rule. *See* POLITICS.

governing *adjective*
Exercising controlling power or influence : commanding, controlling, dominant, dominating, dominative, paramount, preponderant, regnant, reigning, ruling. *See* OVER.

government *noun*
1. The continuous exercise of authority over a political unit : administration, control, direction, governance, rule. *See* CONTROL, POLITICS. **2.** A system by which a political unit is controlled : governance, regime, rule. *See* POLITICS. **3.** Authoritative control over the affairs of others : administration, direction, management, superintendence, supervision. *See* OVER.

governmental *adjective*
Of or relating to government : gubernatorial, regulatory. *See* POLITICS.

go with *verb* See **go.**

gown *noun*
A one-piece skirted outer garment for women and children : dress, frock. *See* PUT ON.

grab *verb*
1. To get hold of (something moving) : catch, clutch[1], seize, snatch. *Informal:* nab. ***Idiom:*** lay hands on. *See* GET. **2.** To take firmly with the hand and maintain a hold on : clasp, clench, clutch[1], grapple, grasp, grip, seize. *See* KEEP. **3.** To take quick and forcible possession of : commandeer, confiscate, expropriate, seize, snatch. ***Idiom:*** help oneself to. *See* GIVE. **4.** *Slang.* To compel, as the attention, interest, or imagination, of : arrest, catch up, enthrall, fascinate, grip, hold, mesmerize, rivet, spellbind, transfix. *See* EXCITE.

grab *noun* The act of catching, especially a sudden taking and holding : catch, clutch[1], seizure, snatch. *See* GET.

grab bag *noun*
Slang. A collection of various things : assortment, conglomeration, gallimaufry, hodgepodge, jumble, medley, mélange, miscellany, mishmash, mixed bag, mixture, olio, patchwork, potpourri, salmagundi, variety. *See* COLLECT.

grabbiness *noun*
Informal. Excessive desire for more than one needs or deserves : acquisitiveness, avarice, avariciousness, avidity, covetousness, cupidity, graspingness, greed. *See* DESIRE, GIVE.

grabble *verb*
To reach about or search blindly or uncertainly : feel, fumble, grope, poke. *See* SEEK, TOUCH.

grabby *adjective*
Informal. Having a strong urge to obtain or possess something, especially material wealth, in quantity : acquisitive, avaricious, avid, covetous, grasping, greedy, hungry. *See* DESIRE, GIVE.

grace *noun*
1. Refined, effortless beauty of manner, form, and style : elegance, elegancy, polish, urbanity. *See* BEAUTIFUL, STYLE. **2.** A sense of propriety or rightness : conscience, decency. *See* RIGHT. **3.** Kindly, charitable interest in others : altruism, beneficence, benevolence, benignancy, benignity, charitableness, charity, goodwill, kindheartedness, kindliness, kindness, philan-

thropy. *See* ATTITUDE, KIND. **4.** Kind, forgiving, or compassionate treatment of or disposition toward others : charity, clemency, lenience, leniency, lenity, mercifulness, mercy. *See* FORGIVENESS. **5.** A kindly act : favor, good turn, indulgence, kindness, service. *Archaic:* benefit. *See* HELP. **6.** Temporary immunity from penalties : reprieve, respite. *See* CONTINUE. **7.** A short prayer said at meals : benediction, blessing, thanks, thanksgiving. *See* GRATEFUL, RELIGION.

grace *verb* **1.** To lend dignity or honor to by an act or favor : dignify, honor. *See* BEAUTIFUL. **2.** To endow with beauty and elegance by way of a notable addition : adorn, beautify, embellish, enhance, set off. *See* BEAUTIFUL.

graceful *adjective*
1. Of such tasteful beauty as to elicit admiration : elegant, exquisite. *See* BEAUTIFUL, STYLE. **2.** Marked by facility, especially of expression : easy, effortless, flowing, fluent, fluid, smooth. *See* STYLE.

graceless *adjective*
Lacking dexterity and grace in physical movement : awkward, clumsy, gawky, inept, lumpish, maladroit, ungainly, ungraceful. *Slang:* klutzy. ***Idiom:*** all thumbs. *See* ABILITY.

gracious *adjective*
1. Characterized by kindness and warm, unaffected courtesy : affable, hospitable. *See* KIND. **2.** Characterized by elaborate but usually formal courtesy : chivalrous, courtly, gallant, knightly, stately. *See* ATTITUDE, COURTESY.

gradation *noun*
1. The degree of vividness of a color, as when modified by the addition of black or white pigment : hue, shade, tinge, tint. *See* COLORS. **2.** A slight variation between nearly identical entities : nuance, shade. *See* BIG.

gradational *adjective*
Proceeding very slowly by degrees : gradual, piecemeal, step-by-step. *See* FAST.

grade *noun*
1. One of the units in a course, as on an ascending or descending scale : degree, level, peg, point, rung, stage, step. *Informal:* notch. *See* BIG. **2.** Degree of excellence : caliber, class, quality. *See* BE, VALUE. **3.** A division of persons or things by quality, rank, or grade : bracket, class, league, order, rank[1], tier. *See* GROUP, VALUE. **4.** Deviation from a particular direction : cant[1], gradient, heel[2], inclination, incline, lean[1], list[2], rake[2], slant, slope, tilt, tip[2]. *See* RISE, STRAIGHT.

grade *verb* **1.** To assign to a class or classes : categorize, class, classify, distribute, group, pigeonhole, place, range, rank[1], rate[1]. *See* GROUP, VALUE. **2.** To evaluate and assign a grade to : mark, score. *See* VALUE.

gradient *noun*
Deviation from a particular direction : cant[1], grade, heel[2], inclination, incline, lean[1], list[2], rake[2], slant, slope, tilt, tip[2]. *See* RISE, STRAIGHT.

gradual *adjective*
1. Proceeding very slowly by degrees : gradational, piecemeal, step-by-step. *See* FAST. **2.** Not steep or abrupt : easy, gentle, moderate. *See* RISE.

graft *noun*
Money, property, or a favor given, offered, or promised to a person or accepted by a person in a position of trust as an inducement to dishonest behavior : bribe, fix, payola. *Informal:* payoff. *Slang:* boodle. *See* CRIMES, MONEY, PERSUASION.

grain *noun*
A tiny amount : bit[1], crumb, dab[1], dash, dot, dram, drop, fragment, iota, jot, minim, mite, modicum, molecule, ort, ounce, particle, scrap[1], scruple, shred, smidgen, speck, tittle, trifle, whit. *Chiefly British:* spot. *See* BIG.

grainy *adjective*
Consisting of or covered with large particles : coarse, granular, gritty, rough. *See* SMOOTH.

grand *adjective*
1. Large and impressive in size, scope, or extent : august, baronial, grandiose, imposing, lordly, magnific, magnificent, majestic, noble, princely, regal, royal, splendid, stately, sublime, superb. *See* BIG, GOOD. **2.** Exceedingly dignified in form, tone, or style : elevated, eloquent, exalted, high, high-flown, lofty. *See* HIGH, STYLE. **3.** Raised to or occupying a high position or rank : august, elevated, exalted, high-ranking, lofty. *See* RISE.

grandeur *noun*
Something meriting the highest praise or regard : glory, grandiosity, grandness, greatness, majesty, splendor. *See* PRAISE.

grandiloquence *noun*
Pretentious, pompous speech or writing : bombast, claptrap, fustian, magniloquence, orotundity, rant, turgidity. *See* PLAIN, STYLE, WORDS.

grandiloquent *adjective*
Characterized by language that is elevated and sometimes pompous in style : aureate, bombastic, declamatory, flowery, fustian,

high-flown, high-sounding, magniloquent, orotund, overblown, rhetorical, sonorous, swollen. *See* PLAIN, STYLE, WORDS.

grandiose *adjective*

1. Large and impressive in size, scope, or extent : august, baronial, grand, imposing, lordly, magnific, magnificent, majestic, noble, princely, regal, royal, splendid, stately, sublime, superb. *See* BIG, GOOD. **2.** Characterized by an exaggerated show of dignity or self-importance : hoity-toity, pompous, pretentious, puffed-up, puffy, self-important. *Informal:* highfalutin. *See* PLAIN.

grandioseness *noun*

Boastful self-importance or display : grandiosity, ostentation, pomposity, pompousness, pretension, pretentiousness. *See* PLAIN.

grandiosity *noun*

1. Something meriting the highest praise or regard : glory, grandeur, grandness, greatness, majesty, splendor. *See* PRAISE. **2.** Boastful self-importance or display : grandioseness, ostentation, pomposity, pompousness, pretension, pretentiousness. *See* PLAIN.

grandness *noun*

Something meriting the highest praise or regard : glory, grandeur, grandiosity, greatness, majesty, splendor. *See* PRAISE.

grant *verb*

1. To let have as a favor, prerogative, or privilege : accord, award, concede, give, vouchsafe. *See* GIVE. **2.** To give formally or officially : accord, award, bestow, confer, present[2]. *See* GIVE. **3.** To change the ownership of (property) by means of a legal document : cede, deed, make over, sign over. *Law:* alien, alienate, assign, convey, transfer. *See* GIVE, LAW. **4.** To recognize, often reluctantly, the reality or truth of : acknowledge, admit, avow, concede, confess, own (up). *Slang:* fess up. *Chiefly Regional:* allow. *See* AFFIRM, KNOWLEDGE.

grant *noun* **1.** The act of conferring, as of an honor : accordance, bestowal, bestowment, conference, conferment, conferral, presentation. *See* GIVE. **2.** Something, as a gift, granted for a definite purpose : appropriation, subsidy, subvention. *See* GIVE. **3.** *Law.* A making over of legal ownership or title : *Law:* alienation, assignment, conveyance, transfer, transferal. *See* LAW.

granular *adjective*

Consisting of or covered with large particles : coarse, grainy, gritty, rough. *See* SMOOTH.

granulate *verb*

To break up into tiny particles : bray, crush, grind, mill, powder, pulverize, triturate. *See* HELP.

graphic *adjective*

1. Of or relating to representation by means of writing : calligraphic, scriptural, written. *See* WORDS. **2.** Of or relating to representation by drawings or pictures : hieroglyphic, illustrative, photographic, pictographic, pictorial. *See* SEE. **3.** Described verbally in sharp and accurate detail : lifelike, photographic, pictorial, picturesque, realistic, vivid. *See* SPECIFIC, WORDS. **4.** Serving to describe : delineative, descriptive, representative. *See* WORDS.

grapple *noun*

Sports. An act or means of holding something : clasp, clench, clutch[1], grasp, grip, hold. *See* KEEP.

grapple *verb* **1.** To take firmly with the hand and maintain a hold on : clasp, clench, clutch[1], grab, grasp, grip, seize. *See* KEEP. **2.** To contend with an opponent at close quarters, as by attempting to throw him or her : scuffle, tussle, wrestle. ***Idiom:*** go to the mat with. *See* CONFLICT, TOUCH.

grasp *verb*

1. To take firmly with the hand and maintain a hold on : clasp, clench, clutch[1], grab, grapple, grip, seize. *See* KEEP. **2.** To perceive directly with the intellect : apprehend, compass, comprehend, fathom, know, understand. *Scots:* ken. *See* KNOWLEDGE. **3.** To perceive and recognize the meaning of : accept, apprehend, catch (on), compass, comprehend, conceive, fathom, follow, get, make out, read, see, sense, take, take in, understand. *Informal:* savvy. *Slang:* dig. *Chiefly British:* twig. *Scots:* ken. ***Idioms:*** get (*or* have) a handle on, get the picture. *See* UNDERSTAND.

grasp *noun* **1.** An act or means of holding something : clasp, clench, clutch[1], grip, hold. *Sports:* grapple. *See* KEEP. **2.** Firm control : grip, hold. *See* CONTROL. **3.** A strong or powerful influence : grip, hold. *See* AFFECT. **4.** The ability or power to seize or attain : capacity, compass, range, reach, scope. *See* ABILITY. **5.** Intellectual hold : apprehension, comprehension, grip, hold, understanding. *Informal:* savvy. *See* KNOWLEDGE.

grasping *adjective*

Having a strong urge to obtain or possess something, especially material wealth, in quantity : acquisitive, avaricious, avid, covetous, greedy, hungry. *Informal:* grabby. *See* DESIRE, GIVE.

graspingness *noun*
Excessive desire for more than one needs or deserves : acquisitiveness, avarice, avariciousness, avidity, covetousness, cupidity, greed. *Informal:* grabbiness. *See* DESIRE, GIVE.

grate *verb*
To bring or come into abrasive contact, often with a harsh grating sound : rasp, scrape, scratch. *See* SOUNDS.

grateful *adjective*
1. Showing or feeling gratitude : appreciative, thankful. *See* GRATEFUL. **2.** To one's liking : agreeable, congenial, favorable, good, gratifying, nice, pleasant, pleasing, pleasurable, satisfying, welcome. *See* LIKE.

gratefulness *noun*
A being grateful : appreciation, gratitude, thankfulness, thanks. *See* GRATEFUL.

gratified *adjective*
Having achieved satisfaction, as of one's goal : content, fulfilled, happy, satisfied. *See* HAPPY.

gratify *verb*
1. To give great or keen pleasure to : cheer, delight, enchant, gladden, overjoy, please, pleasure, tickle. *Archaic:* joy. *See* HAPPY, LIKE. **2.** To grant or have what is demanded by (a need or desire) : appease, content, fulfill, indulge, satisfy. *See* GIVE. **3.** To comply with the wishes or ideas of (another) : cater, humor, indulge. *See* RESIST.

gratifying *adjective*
1. To one's liking : agreeable, congenial, favorable, good, grateful, nice, pleasant, pleasing, pleasurable, satisfying, welcome. *See* LIKE. **2.** Affording enjoyment : enjoyable, pleasant, pleasing, pleasurable. *See* PAIN.

grating *adjective*
Disagreeable to the sense of hearing : dry, harsh, hoarse, jarring, rasping, raspy, raucous, rough, scratchy, squawky, strident. *See* SOUNDS.

gratis *adjective*
Costing nothing : complimentary, free, gratuitous. ***Idiom:*** on the house. *See* MONEY.

gratitude *noun*
A being grateful : appreciation, gratefulness, thankfulness, thanks. *See* GRATEFUL.

gratuitous *adjective*
1. Costing nothing : complimentary, free, gratis. ***Idiom:*** on the house. *See* MONEY. **2.** Not required, necessary, or warranted by the circumstances of the case : supererogative, supererogatory, uncalled-for, wanton. *See* NECESSARY.

gratuity *noun*
A material favor or gift, usually money, given in return for service : cumshaw, largess, perquisite, tip[3]. *See* GIVE, TRANSACTIONS.

gravamen *noun*
Law. The most central and material part : core, essence, gist, heart, kernel, marrow, meat, nub, pith, quintessence, root[1], soul, spirit, stuff, substance. *See* BE.

grave[1] *noun*
A burial place or receptacle for human remains : catacomb, cinerarium, crypt, mausoleum, ossuary, sepulcher, sepulture, tomb, vault[1]. *See* KEEP, PLACE.

grave[2] *adjective*
1. Having great consequence or weight : earnest[1], heavy, momentous, serious, severe, weighty. *See* IMPORTANT. **2.** Causing or marked by danger or pain, for example : dangerous, grievous, serious, severe. *See* HELP. **3.** Portending future disaster : apocalyptic, apocalyptical, baneful, dire, direful, fateful, fire-and-brimstone, hellfire, ominous, portentous, unlucky. *See* LUCK, WARN. **4.** Full of or marked by dignity and seriousness : earnest[1], sedate, serious, sober, solemn, somber, staid. *See* ATTITUDE, HEAVY.

grave[3] *verb*
1. To cut (a design or inscription) into a hard surface, especially for printing : carve, engrave, etch, incise. *See* MARKS. **2.** To produce a deep impression of : engrave, etch, fix, impress, imprint, inscribe, stamp. *See* MARKS.

graveness *noun*
1. The condition of being grave and of involving serious consequences : gravity, momentousness, seriousness, weightiness. *See* IMPORTANT. **2.** High seriousness of manner or bearing : gravity, sedateness, sobriety, solemnity, solemnness, staidness. *See* ATTITUDE, HEAVY, STYLE.

gravid *adjective*
Carrying a developing fetus within the uterus : big, enceinte, expectant, expecting, parturient, pregnant. *Slang:* gone. *Archaic:* great. ***Idioms:*** in a family way, with child. *See* REPRODUCTION.

gravidity *noun*
The condition of carrying a developing fetus within the uterus : gestation, gravidness, parturiency, pregnancy. *See* REPRODUCTION.

gravidness *noun*
The condition of carrying a developing fetus within the uterus : gestation, gravidity, parturiency, pregnancy. *See* REPRODUCTION.

gravitate *verb*
To fall or drift down to the bottom : settle, sink. *See* RISE.

gravity *noun*
1. The condition of being grave and of involving serious consequences : graveness, momentousness, seriousness, weightiness. *See* IMPORTANT. **2.** High seriousness of manner or bearing : graveness, sedateness, sobriety, solemnity, solemnness, staidness. *See* ATTITUDE, HEAVY, STYLE.

gray matter *noun*
Informal. The seat of the faculty of intelligence and reason : brain, head, mind. *See* THOUGHTS.

graze *verb*
1. To make light and momentary contact with, as in passing : brush[1], flick, kiss, shave, skim. *See* TOUCH. **2.** To strike a surface at such an angle as to be deflected : carom, dap, glance, ricochet, skim, skip.
See STRIKE.
graze *noun* Light and momentary contact with another person or thing : brush[1], flick, skim. *See* TOUCH.

greasy *adjective*
Having the qualities of fat : adipose, fat, fatty, oily, oleaginous, unctuous. *See* FAT.

great *adjective*
1. Notably above average in amount, size, or scope : big, considerable, extensive, good, healthy, large, large-scale, sizable. *Informal:* tidy. *See* BIG. **2.** Widely known and esteemed : celebrated, distinguished, eminent, famed, famous, illustrious, notable, noted, preeminent, prestigious, prominent, redoubtable, renowned. *See* KNOWLEDGE, RESPECT. **3.** *Informal.* Exceptionally good of its kind : ace, banner, blue-ribbon, brag, capital, champion, excellent, fine[1], first-class, first-rate, prime, quality, splendid, superb, superior, terrific, tiptop, top. *Informal:* A-one, bully, dandy, swell, topflight, topnotch. *Slang:* boss. *Chiefly British:* tophole. *See* GOOD. **4.** *Informal.* Particularly excellent : divine, fabulous, fantastic, fantastical, glorious, marvelous, sensational, splendid, superb, terrific, wonderful. *Informal:* dandy, dreamy, ripping, super, swell, tremendous. *Slang:* cool, groovy, hot, keen[1], neat, nifty. ***Idiom:*** out of this world. *See* GOOD. **5.** *Archaic.* Carrying a developing fetus within the uterus : big, enceinte, expectant, expecting, gravid, parturient, pregnant. *Slang:* gone. ***Idioms:*** in a family way, with child. *See* REPRODUCTION.

greater *adjective*
Much more than half : best, better[1], larger, largest, most. *See* BETTER, BIG.

great-hearted *adjective*
Willing to give of oneself and one's possessions : big, big-hearted, generous, large-hearted, magnanimous, unselfish. *See* GIVE.

great-heartedness *noun*
The quality or state of being generous : big-heartedness, bounteousness, bountifulness, free-handedness, generosity, generousness, large-heartedness, lavishness, liberality, magnanimity, magnanimousness, munificence, openhandedness, unselfishness, unsparingness. *See* GIVE.

greatly *adverb*
To a high degree : awfully, dreadfully, eminently, exceedingly, exceptionally, extra, extremely, highly, most, notably, very. *Informal:* awful. *Chiefly Regional:* mighty. *See* BIG.

greatness *noun*
1. The quality or state of being large in amount, extent, or importance : amplitude, bigness, largeness, magnitude, sizableness, size. *See* BIG. **2.** Something meriting the highest praise or regard : glory, grandeur, grandiosity, grandness, majesty, splendor. *See* PRAISE.

greed *noun*
Excessive desire for more than one needs or deserves : acquisitiveness, avarice, avariciousness, avidity, covetousness, cupidity, graspingness. *Informal:* grabbiness. *See* DESIRE, GIVE.

greedy *adjective*
1. Having a strong urge to obtain or possess something, especially material wealth, in quantity : acquisitive, avaricious, avid, covetous, grasping, hungry. *Informal:* grabby. *See* DESIRE, GIVE. **2.** Wanting to eat or drink more than one can reasonably consume : edacious, gluttonous, hoggish, piggish, ravenous, voracious. *See* DESIRE, INGESTION. **3.** Having an insatiable appetite for an activity or pursuit : avid, edacious, gluttonous, omnivorous, rapacious, ravenous, unappeasable, voracious. *See* DESIRE.

green *noun*
1. A tract of cultivated land belonging to and used by a community : common. *See* GROUP. **2.** *Slang.* Something, such as coins or printed bills, used as a medium of exchange : cash, currency, lucre, money. *Informal:* wampum. *Slang:* bread, cabbage, dough, gelt, jack, lettuce, long green, mazuma, moola, scratch. *Chiefly British:* brass. *See* MONEY.

green *adjective* **1.** Being in an early period of growth or development : immature, infant, juvenile, young, youthful. *See* YOUTH. **2.** Lacking experience and the knowledge gained from it : inexperienced, inexpert, raw, uninitiate, uninitiated, unpracticed, unseasoned, untried, unversed. *See* ABILITY.

green-eyed *adjective*
Resentfully or painfully desirous of another's advantages : covetous, envious, invidious, jealous. *See* DESIRE.

greenhorn *noun*
One who is just starting to learn or do something : abecedarian, beginner, fledgling, freshman, initiate, neophyte, novice, novitiate, tenderfoot, tyro. *Slang:* rookie. *See* START.

greenness *noun*
1. The time of life between childhood and maturity : adolescence, juvenescence, juvenility, puberty, salad days, spring, youth, youthfulness. *See* YOUTH. **2.** Lack of experience and the knowledge gained from it : inexperience, inexpertness, rawness. *See* ABILITY.

greet *verb*
1. To address in a friendly and respectful way : hail[2], salute, welcome. *See* GREETING. **2.** To approach for the purpose of speech : accost, hail[2], salute. *See* APPROACH, GREETING, SEEK. **3.** To present with a specified reaction : meet[1], react, respond. *See* FEELINGS, GREETING.

greeting *noun*
An expression, in words or gestures, marking a meeting of persons : hail[2], salutation, salute, welcome. *See* GREETING.

gregarious *adjective*
1. Disposed to be open, sociable, and talkative : communicable, communicative, expansive, extraverted, extroverted, outgoing, unreserved. *See* ATTITUDE. **2.** Of, characterized by, or inclined to living together in communities : social. *See* CONNECT, GROUP.

gridlock *noun*
A cessation of normal activity, caused by an accident or strike, for example : immobilization, jam, stoppage, tie-up. *See* CONTINUE.

grief *noun*
Mental anguish or pain caused by loss or despair : heartache, heartbreak, sorrow. *See* HAPPY.

grievance *noun*
An expression of dissatisfaction or a circumstance regarded as a cause for such expression : complaint. *Informal:* gripe, grouse. *Slang:* beef, kick. ***Idiom:*** bone to pick. *See* HAPPY.

grieve *verb*
1. To cause suffering or painful sorrow to : aggrieve, distress, hurt, injure, pain, wound. *See* HAPPY. **2.** To feel, show, or express grief : lament, mourn, sorrow, suffer. *See* HAPPY.

grievous *adjective*
1. Causing sorrow or regret : deplorable, doleful, dolorous, lamentable, mournful, regrettable, rueful, sad, sorrowful, woeful. *See* HAPPY. **2.** Causing or marked by danger or pain, for example : dangerous, grave[2], serious, severe. *See* HELP.

grill *verb*
Informal. To question thoroughly and relentlessly to verify facts : cross-examine, interrogate. ***Idiom:*** give someone the third degree. *See* INVESTIGATE.

grim *adjective*
1. Firmly, often unreasonably immovable in purpose or will : adamant, adamantine, brass-bound, die-hard, implacable, incompliant, inexorable, inflexible, intransigent, iron, obdurate, relentless, remorseless, rigid, stubborn, unbendable, unbending, uncompliant, uncompromising, unrelenting, unyielding. ***Idiom:*** stubborn as a mule (*or* ox). *See* RESIST. **2.** Cold and forbidding : austere, bleak, dour, hard, harsh, severe, stark. *See* ATTITUDE, HOT. **3.** Shockingly repellent : ghastly, grisly, gruesome, hideous, horrible, horrid, lurid, macabre. *See* BEAUTIFUL.

grimace *noun*
A facial contortion indicating displeasure, disgust, or pain : face, moue, mouth, pout. *Informal:* mug. *See* EXPRESS.
grimace *verb* To contort one's face to indicate displeasure, disgust, or pain, for example : mouth, mug. ***Idioms:*** make a face, make faces. *See* EXPRESS.

grime *noun*
Foul or dirty matter : dirt, filth, muck. *Slang:* crud. *See* CLEAN.

griminess *noun*
The condition or state of being dirty : dirtiness, filth, filthiness, foulness, grubbiness, smuttiness, squalor, uncleanliness, uncleanness. *See* CLEAN.

grimness *noun*
The quality or state of being stubbornly inflexible : die-hardism, implacability, implacableness, incompliance, incompliancy, inexorability, inexorableness, inflexibility, inflexibleness, intransigence, intransigency, obduracy, obdurateness, relentlessness, remorselessness, rigidity, rigidness, stubbornness. *See* RESIST.

grimy *adjective*
Covered or stained with or as if with dirt or other impurities : black, dirty, filthy, grubby, smutty, soiled, unclean, uncleanly. *See* CLEAN.

grin *verb*
To curve the lips upward in expressing amusement, pleasure, or happiness : beam, smile. ***Idioms:*** break into a smile, crack a smile. *See* EXPRESS.
grin *noun* A facial expression marked by an upward curving of the lips : smile. *See* EXPRESS.

grind *verb*
1. To break up into tiny particles : bray, crush, granulate, mill, powder, pulverize, triturate. *See* HELP. **2.** To rub together noisily : crunch, gnash. *See* SOUNDS. **3.** *Informal.* To do tedious, laborious, and sometimes menial work : drudge, grub, plod, slave, slog. *See* WORK. **4.** *Informal.* To study or work hard, especially when pressed for time : *Informal:* bone (up), cram. ***Idiom:*** burn the midnight oil. *See* WORK. **5.** To treat arbitrarily or cruelly : trample, tyrannize. *See* OVER.
grind *noun* **1.** *Informal.* A habitual, laborious, often tiresome course of action : routine, rut[1], treadmill. *Slang:* groove. *See* USUAL. **2.** *Informal.* One who works or toils tirelessly : drudge, fag, grub, plodder, slave. *Informal:* workhorse. *See* WORK.

grip *noun*
1. Firm control : grasp, hold. *See* CONTROL. **2.** An act or means of holding something : clasp, clench, clutch[1], grasp, hold. *Sports:* grapple. *See* KEEP. **3.** A strong or powerful influence : grasp, hold. *See* AFFECT. **4.** Intellectual hold : apprehension, comprehension, grasp, hold, understanding. *Informal:* savvy. *See* KNOWLEDGE.
grip *verb* **1.** To take firmly with the hand and maintain a hold on : clasp, clench, clutch[1], grab, grapple, grasp, seize. *See* KEEP. **2.** To compel, as the attention, interest, or imagination, of : arrest, catch up, enthrall, fascinate, hold, mesmerize, rivet, spellbind, transfix. *Slang:* grab. *See* EXCITE.

gripe *verb*
Informal. To express negative feelings, especially of dissatisfaction or resentment : complain, grouch, grump, whine. *Informal:* crab, grouse, kick. *Slang:* beef, bellyache, bitch. *See* FEELINGS, HAPPY.
gripe *noun Informal.* An expression of dissatisfaction or a circumstance regarded as a cause for such expression : complaint, grievance. *Informal:* grouse. *Slang:* beef, kick. ***Idiom:*** bone to pick. *See* HAPPY.

griper *noun*
Informal. A person who habitually complains or grumbles : complainer, crab, faultfinder, grouch, growler, grumbler, grump, murmurer, mutterer, whiner. *Informal:* crank, grouser. *Slang:* bellyacher, sorehead, sourpuss. *See* HAPPY.

grisly *adjective*
Shockingly repellent : ghastly, grim, gruesome, hideous, horrible, horrid, lurid, macabre. *See* BEAUTIFUL.

gritty *adjective*
Consisting of or covered with large particles : coarse, grainy, granular, rough. *See* SMOOTH.

groom *verb*
To make neat and trim; make presentable : clean (up), freshen (up), neaten (up), slick up, spruce (up), tidy (up), trig (out), trim. *See* ORDER.

groove *noun*
Slang. A habitual, laborious, often tiresome course of action : routine, rut[1], treadmill. *Informal:* grind. *See* USUAL.
groove on *verb Slang.* To like or enjoy enthusiastically, often excessively : adore, delight (in), dote on (*or* upon), love. *Slang:* eat up. *See* LIKE, LOVE.

groove on *verb* See **groove.**

groovy *adjective*
Slang. Particularly excellent : divine, fabulous, fantastic, fantastical, glorious, marvelous, sensational, splendid, superb, terrific, wonderful. *Informal:* dandy, dreamy, great, ripping, super, swell, tremendous. *Slang:* cool, hot, keen[1], neat, nifty. ***Idiom:*** out of this world. *See* GOOD.

grope *verb*
To reach about or search blindly or uncertainly : feel, fumble, grabble, poke. *See* SEEK, TOUCH.

gross *adjective*
1. Including every constituent or individual : all, complete, entire, total, whole. *See* PART. **2.** Conspicuously bad or offensive : arrant, capital, egregious, flagrant, glaring, rank[2]. *See* GOOD. **3.** Lacking in delicacy or refinement : barbarian, barbaric, boorish, churlish, coarse, crass, crude, ill-bred, indelicate, philistine, rough, rude, tasteless, uncivilized, uncouth, uncultivated, uncultured, unpolished, unrefined, vulgar. *See* COURTESY, SMOOTH. **4.** Offensive to accepted standards of decency : barnyard, bawdy, broad, coarse, dirty, Fescennine, filthy,

foul, lewd, nasty, obscene, profane, ribald, scatologic, scatological, scurrilous, smutty, vulgar. *Slang:* raunchy. *See* DECENT. **5.** Having too much flesh : corpulent, fat, fatty, fleshy, obese, overblown, overweight, porcine, portly, stout, weighty. *See* FAT.

gross *noun* An amount or quantity from which nothing is left out or held back : aggregate, all, entirety, everything, sum, total, totality, whole. *Informal:* work (used in plural). ***Idioms:*** everything but (*or* except) the kitchen sink; lock, stock, and barrel; the whole ball of wax (*or* kit and caboodle *or* megillah *or* nine yards *or* shebang). *See* PART.

gross *verb* To make as income or profit : bring in, clear, draw, earn, gain, net[2], pay, produce, realize, repay, return, yield. *See* MONEY.

grossness *noun*
1. The quality or state of being flagrant : atrociousness, atrocity, egregiousness, enormity, flagrance, flagrancy, flagrantness, glaringness, outrageousness, rankness. *See* GOOD. **2.** The quality or state of being obscene : bawdiness, coarseness, dirtiness, filthiness, foulness, lewdness, obscenity, profaneness, profanity, scurrility, scurrilousness, smuttiness, vulgarity, vulgarness. *Slang:* raunch, raunchiness. *See* DECENT.

grotesque *adjective*
1. Resembling a freak : freakish, freaky, monstrous. *See* USUAL. **2.** Conceived or done with no reference to reality or common sense : antic, bizarre, fantastic, fantastical, far-fetched. *See* TRUE, USUAL.

grotto *noun*
A hollow beneath the earth's surface : cave, cavern. *See* CONVEX.

grouch *noun*
A person who habitually complains or grumbles : complainer, crab, faultfinder, growler, grumbler, grump, murmurer, mutterer, whiner. *Informal:* crank, griper, grouser. *Slang:* bellyacher, sorehead, sourpuss. *See* HAPPY.

grouch *verb* To express negative feelings, especially of dissatisfaction or resentment : complain, grump, whine. *Informal:* crab, gripe, grouse, kick. *Slang:* beef, bellyache, bitch. *See* FEELINGS, HAPPY.

grouchy *adjective*
Having or showing a bad temper : bad-tempered, cantankerous, crabbed, cranky, cross, disagreeable, fretful, grumpy, ill-tempered, irascible, irritable, nasty, peevish, petulant, querulous, snappish, snappy, surly, testy, ugly, waspish. *Informal:* crabby, mean[2]. *Idiom:* out of sorts. *See* ATTITUDE.

ground *noun*
1. The lowest or supporting part or structure : base[1], basis, bed, bottom, foot, footing, foundation, fundament, groundwork, seat, substratum, underpinning (often used in plural). *See* OVER. **2.** That on which something immaterial, such as an argument or a charge, rests. Often used in plural : base[1], basis, footing, foundation, fundament, groundwork, underpinning (often used in plural). *See* OVER. **3.** A basis for an action or a decision. Often used in plural : cause, motivation, motive, reason, spring. *See* START. **4.** A fact or circumstance that gives logical support to an assertion, claim, or proposal. Often used in plural : argument, proof, reason, wherefore, why. ***Idiom:*** why and wherefore. *See* REASON. **5.** That which provides a reason or justification. Often used in plural : call, cause, justification, necessity, occasion, reason, wherefore, why. ***Idiom:*** why and wherefore. *See* START.

ground *verb* **1.** To cause to fall, as from a shot or blow : bring down, cut down, down, drop, fell[1], flatten, floor, knock down, level, prostrate, strike down, throw. *Slang:* deck[1]. ***Idiom:*** lay low. *See* RISE. **2.** To provide a basis for : base[1], build, establish, found, predicate, rest[1], root[1], underpin. *See* OVER.

groundless *adjective*
Having no basis or foundation in fact : baseless, bottomless, idle, unfounded, unwarranted. *See* TRUE.

groundlessly *adverb*
Without basis or foundation in fact : unfoundedly, unwarrantedly. *See* REASON.

groundwork *noun*
1. The lowest or supporting part or structure : base[1], basis, bed, bottom, foot, footing, foundation, fundament, ground, seat, substratum, underpinning (often used in plural). *See* OVER. **2.** That on which something immaterial, such as an argument or a charge, rests : base[1], basis, footing, foundation, fundament, ground (often used in plural), underpinning (often used in plural). *See* OVER.

group *noun*
1. A number of individuals making up or considered a unit : array, band[2], batch, bevy, body, bunch, bundle, clump, cluster, clutch[2], collection, knot, lot, party, set[2]. *See* GROUP. **2.** A number of persons who have come or been gathered together : assemblage, assembly, body, company, conclave, conference, congre-

gation, congress, convention, convocation, crowd, gathering, meeting, muster, troop. *Informal:* get-together. *See* COLLECT. **3.** A group of people sharing an interest, activity, or achievement : circle, crowd, set[2]. *See* GROUP.

group *verb* **1.** To bring together : assemble, call, cluster, collect[1], congregate, convene, convoke, gather, get together, muster, round up, summon. *See* COLLECT. **2.** To come together : assemble, cluster, collect[1], congregate, convene, forgather, gather, get together, muster. *See* COLLECT. **3.** To distribute into groups according to kinds : assort, categorize, class, classify, pigeonhole, separate, sort (out). *See* COLLECT. **4.** To assign to a class or classes : categorize, class, classify, distribute, grade, pigeonhole, place, range, rank[1], rate[1]. *See* GROUP, VALUE.

grouping *noun*
A way or condition of being arranged : arrangement, categorization, classification, deployment, disposal, disposition, distribution, formation, layout, lineup, order, organization, placement, sequence. *See* ORDER.

grouse *verb*
Informal. To express negative feelings, especially of dissatisfaction or resentment : complain, grouch, grump, whine. *Informal:* crab, gripe, kick. *Slang:* beef, bellyache, bitch. *See* FEELINGS, HAPPY.

grouse *noun* *Informal.* An expression of dissatisfaction or a circumstance regarded as a cause for such expression : complaint, grievance. *Informal:* gripe. *Slang:* beef, kick. ***Idiom:*** bone to pick. *See* HAPPY.

grouser *noun*
Informal. A person who habitually complains or grumbles : complainer, crab, faultfinder, grouch, growler, grumbler, grump, murmurer, mutterer, whiner. *Informal:* crank, griper. *Slang:* bellyacher, sorehead, sourpuss. *See* HAPPY.

grovel *verb*
To support slavishly every opinion or suggestion of a superior : bootlick, cringe, fawn, kowtow, slaver, toady, truckle. *Informal:* apple-polish, brownnose, cotton. *Slang:* suck up. ***Idioms:*** curry favor, dance attendance, kiss someone's feet, lick someone's boots. *See* OVER.

grow *verb*
1. To make or become greater or larger : aggrandize, amplify, augment, boost, build, build up, burgeon, enlarge, escalate, expand, extend, increase, magnify, mount, multiply, proliferate, rise, run up, snowball, soar, swell, upsurge, wax. *Informal:* beef up. *See* INCREASE. **2.** To bring into existence and foster the development of : breed, cultivate, propagate, raise. *See* CARE FOR, REPRODUCTION. **3.** To bring or come to full development : age, develop, maturate, mature, mellow, ripen. *See* YOUTH. **4.** To come to be : become, come, get, turn (out), wax. *See* CHANGE.

growl *verb*
To make a continuous deep reverberating sound : boom, grumble, roll, rumble. *See* SOUNDS.

growler *noun*
A person who habitually complains or grumbles : complainer, crab, faultfinder, grouch, grumbler, grump, murmurer, mutterer, whiner. *Informal:* crank, griper, grouser. *Slang:* bellyacher, sorehead, sourpuss. *See* HAPPY.

grown *adjective*
Having reached full growth and development : adult, big, developed, full-blown, full-fledged, full-grown, grown-up, mature, ripe. ***Idiom:*** of age. *See* YOUTH.

grown-up *adjective*
Having reached full growth and development : adult, big, developed, full-blown, full-fledged, full-grown, grown, mature, ripe. ***Idiom:*** of age. *See* YOUTH.

growth *noun*
1. A progression from a simple form to a more complex one : development, evolution, evolvement, progress, unfolding. *See* CHANGE. **2.** The act of increasing or rising : aggrandizement, amplification, augment, augmentation, boost, buildup, enlargement, escalation, hike, increase, jump, multiplication, proliferation, raise, rise, swell, upsurge, upswing, upturn. *See* INCREASE.

grub *verb*
1. To break, turn over, or remove (earth or sand, for example) with or as if with a tool : delve, dig, excavate, scoop, shovel, spade. *See* ENTER. **2.** To do tedious, laborious, and sometimes menial work : drudge, plod, slave, slog. *Informal:* grind. *See* WORK.

grub *noun* **1.** One who works or toils tirelessly : drudge, fag, plodder, slave. *Informal:* grind, workhorse. *See* WORK. **2.** *Slang.* Something fit to be eaten : aliment, bread, comestible, diet, edible, esculent, fare, food, foodstuff, meat, nourishment, nurture, nutriment, nutrition, pabulum, pap, provender, provision (used in plural), sustenance, victual. *Slang:* chow, eats. *See* INGESTION.

grubbiness *noun*
The condition or state of being dirty : dirtiness, filth, filthiness, foulness, griminess, smuttiness, squalor, uncleanliness, uncleanness. *See* CLEAN.

grubby *adjective*
Covered or stained with or as if with dirt or other impurities : black, dirty, filthy, grimy, smutty, soiled, unclean, uncleanly. *See* CLEAN.

grubstake *noun*
Money or property used to produce more wealth : backing, capital, capitalization, financing, funding, stake, subsidization. *See* HELP, MONEY.
grubstake *verb* To supply capital to or for : back, capitalize, finance, fund, stake, subsidize. *Informal:* bankroll. ***Idiom:*** put up money for. *See* HELP, MONEY.

grudge *verb*
To feel envy towards or for : begrudge, covet, envy. *See* DESIRE.

gruesome *adjective*
Shockingly repellent : ghastly, grim, grisly, hideous, horrible, horrid, lurid, macabre. *See* BEAUTIFUL.

gruff *adjective*
1. Rudely unceremonious : abrupt, blunt, brief, brusque, crusty, curt, short, short-spoken. *See* ATTITUDE. **2.** Low and grating in sound : croaking, croaky, hoarse, husky[1]. *See* SOUNDS.

grumble *verb*
1. To complain in low indistinct tones : grunt, murmur, mutter. *See* HAPPY, SOUNDS. **2.** To make a continuous deep reverberating sound : boom, growl, roll, rumble. *See* SOUNDS.
grumble *noun* A low indistinct utterance of complaint : grunt, murmur, mutter. *See* HAPPY, SOUNDS.

grumbler *noun*
A person who habitually complains or grumbles : complainer, crab, faultfinder, grouch, growler, grump, murmurer, mutterer, whiner. *Informal:* crank, griper, grouser. *Slang:* bellyacher, sorehead, sourpuss. *See* HAPPY.

grump *noun*
A person who habitually complains or grumbles : complainer, crab, faultfinder, grouch, growler, grumbler, murmurer, mutterer, whiner. *Informal:* crank, griper, grouser. *Slang:* bellyacher, sorehead, sourpuss. *See* HAPPY.
grump *noun Informal.* An expression of dissatisfaction or a circumstance regarded as a cause for such expression : complaint, grievance. *Informal:* gripe. *Slang:* beef, kick. ***Idiom:*** bone to pick. *See* HAPPY.

grumpy *adjective*
Having or showing a bad temper : bad-tempered, cantankerous, crabbed, cranky, cross, disagreeable, fretful, grouchy, ill-tempered, irascible, irritable, nasty, peevish, petulant, querulous, snappish, snappy, surly, testy, ugly, waspish. *Informal:* crabby, mean[2]. ***Idiom:*** out of sorts. *See* ATTITUDE.

grunt *verb*
To complain in low indistinct tones : grumble, murmur, mutter. *See* HAPPY, SOUNDS.
grunt *noun* A low indistinct utterance of complaint : grumble, murmur, mutter. *See* HAPPY, SOUNDS.

guarantee *noun*
1. An assumption of responsibility, as one given by a manufacturer, for the quality, worth, or durability of a product : guaranty, surety, warrant, warranty. *See* OBLIGATION. **2.** A declaration that one will or will not do a certain thing : assurance, covenant, engagement, guaranty, pledge, plight[2], promise, solemn word, vow, warrant, word, word of honor. *See* OBLIGATION.
guarantee *verb* **1.** To give a promise of payment of : secure. *See* MONEY, OBLIGATION. **2.** To assume responsibility for the quality, worth, or durability of : certify, guaranty, warrant. *See* OBLIGATION. **3.** To render certain : assure, ensure, insure, secure, warrant. *Informal:* cinch. *See* CERTAIN.

guarantor *noun*
One who assumes financial responsibility for another : backer, guaranty, sponsor, surety, underwriter. *Informal:* angel. *See* LAW, SUPPORT.

guaranty *noun*
1. Something given to guarantee the repayment of a loan or the fulfillment of an obligation : earnest[2], pawn[1], pledge, security, token, warrant. *See* TRANSACTIONS. **2.** An assumption of responsibility, as one given by a manufacturer, for the quality, worth, or durability of a product : guarantee, surety, warrant, warranty. *See* OBLIGATION. **3.** A declaration that one will or will not do a certain thing : assurance, covenant, engagement, guarantee, pledge, plight[2], promise, solemn word, vow, warrant, word, word of honor. *See* OBLIGATION. **4.** One who assumes financial responsibility for another : backer, guarantor, sponsor, surety, underwriter. *Informal:* angel. *See* LAW, SUPPORT.

guaranty *verb* To assume responsibility for the quality, worth, or durability of : certify, guarantee, warrant. *See* OBLIGATION.

guard *verb*
To keep safe from danger, attack, or harm : defend, preserve, protect, safeguard, secure, shield, ward. *Archaic:* fend. *See* ATTACK.

guard *noun* **1.** A person or special body of persons assigned to provide protection or keep watch over, for example : lookout, picket, protector, sentinel, sentry, ward, watch. *See* AWARENESS, SAFETY. **2.** The act or a means of defending : defense, preservation, protection, protector, safeguard, security, shield, ward. *See* ATTACK.

guardian *noun*
A person who is legally responsible for the person or property of another considered by law to be incompetent to manage his or her affairs : caretaker, custodian, keeper. *Law:* conservator. *See* LAW.

guardianship *noun*
The function of watching, guarding, or overseeing : care, charge, custody, keeping, superintendence, supervision, trust. *See* CARE FOR.

gubernatorial *adjective*
Of or relating to government : governmental, regulatory. *See* POLITICS.

gudgeon *noun*
Slang. A person who is easily deceived or victimized : butt[3], dupe, fool, gull, lamb, pushover, victim. *Informal:* sucker. *Slang:* fall guy, mark, monkey, patsy, pigeon, sap[1]. *Chiefly British:* mug. *See* WISE.

guerdon *noun*
1. Something given in return for a service or accomplishment : accolade, award, honorarium, plum, premium, prize[1], reward. ***Idiom:*** token of appreciation (*or* esteem). *See* REWARD. **2.** Something justly deserved : comeuppance, desert[2] (often used in plural), due, recompense, reward, wage (often used in plural). *Informal:* lump[1] (used in plural). ***Idioms:*** what is coming to one, what one has coming. *See* REWARD.

guerdon *verb* To bestow a reward on : reward. *See* REWARD.

guess *verb*
To draw an inference on the basis of inconclusive evidence or insufficient information : conjecture, infer, speculate, suppose, surmise. *See* OPINION.

guess *noun* A judgment, estimate, or opinion arrived at by guessing : conjecture, guesswork, speculation, supposition, surmise. *See* OPINION.

guesswork *noun*
A judgment, estimate, or opinion arrived at by guessing : conjecture, guess, speculation, supposition, surmise. *See* OPINION.

guest *noun*
A person or persons visiting one : company, visitant, visitor. *See* ACCOMPANIED.

guffaw *noun*
An act of laughing : cachinnation, cackle, laugh, laughter. *Informal:* heehaw. *See* LAUGHTER, SOUNDS.

guffaw *verb* **1.** To express great amusement or mirth : roar. *Informal:* break up. *Slang:* howl. *See* LAUGHTER. **2.** To express amusement, mirth, or scorn by smiling and emitting loud, inarticulate sounds : cachinnate, cackle, laugh. *Informal:* heehaw. ***Idioms:*** die laughing, laugh one's head off, roll in the aisles, split one's sides. *See* LAUGHTER, SOUNDS.

guidance *noun*
An act or instance of guiding : direction, lead, leadership, management. *See* AFFECT.

guide *noun*
Something or someone that shows the way : conductor, director, escort, lead, leader, pilot, shepherd, usher. *See* SHOW.

guide *verb* **1.** To show the way to : conduct, direct, escort, lead, pilot, route, shepherd, show, steer, usher. *See* SHOW. **2.** To direct the course of carefully : jockey, maneuver, navigate, pilot, steer. ***Idiom:*** back and fill. *See* CONTROL, MOVE.

guild *noun*
A group of people united in a relationship and having some interest, activity, or purpose in common : association, club, confederation, congress, federation, fellowship, fraternity, league, order, organization, society, sorority, union. *See* GROUP.

guile *noun*
1. Deceitful cleverness : art, artfulness, artifice, craft, craftiness, cunning, foxiness, slyness, wiliness. *See* HONEST, MEANS. **2.** The act or practice of deceiving : cunning, deceit, deceitfulness, deception, double-dealing, duplicity, shiftiness. *See* HONEST.

guileful *adjective*
1. Deceitfully clever : artful, crafty, cunning, foxy, scheming, sharp, sly, tricky, wily. *See* ABILITY, HONEST, MEANS. **2.** Marked by

treachery or deceit : devious, disingenuous, duplicitous, indirect, lubricious, shifty, sneaky, underhand, underhanded. *See* HONEST.

guileless *adjective*
Free from guile, cunning, or deceit : artless, ingenuous, innocent, naive, natural, simple, unaffected, unsophisticated, unstudied, unworldly. *See* HONEST.

guilt *noun*
Responsibility for an error or crime : blame, culpability, fault, onus. *See* START.

guiltless *adjective*
Free from guilt or blame : blameless, faultless, harmless, innocent, irreproachable, lily-white, unblamable. *Slang:* clean. ***Idiom:*** in the clear. *See* RIGHT.

guilty *adjective*
Deserving blame : blamable, blameful, blameworthy, censurable, culpable, reprehensible. ***Idiom:*** at fault. *See* PRAISE.

guise *noun*
1. A deceptive outward appearance : cloak, color, coloring, cover, disguise, disguisement, façade, face, false colors, front, gloss, mask, masquerade, pretense, pretext, semblance, show, veil, veneer, window-dressing. *Slang:* put-on. *See* SHOW. **2.** A set or style of clothing : costume, dress, garb, habiliment (often used in plural), outfit, turnout. *Informal:* getup, rig. *See* PUT ON.

gulf *noun*
Something of immeasurable and vast extent : abysm, abyss, chasm, deep, depth (often used in plural). *See* HIGH.

gull *noun*
A person who is easily deceived or victimized : butt[3], dupe, fool, lamb, pushover, victim. *Informal:* sucker. *Slang:* fall guy, gudgeon, mark, monkey, patsy, pigeon, sap[1]. *Chiefly British:* mug. *See* WISE.
gull *verb* To get money or something else from by deceitful trickery : bilk, cheat, cozen, defraud, mulct, rook, swindle, victimize. *Informal:* chisel, flimflam, take, trim. *Slang:* diddle[1], do, gyp, stick, sting. *See* HONEST.

gullible *adjective*
Easily imposed on or tricked : credulous, dupable, easy, exploitable, naive, susceptible. *See* WISE.

gulp *verb*
To swallow (food or drink) greedily or rapidly in large amounts : bolt, down, englut, engorge, gobble, guzzle, ingurgitate, swill, wolf. *See* INGESTION.
gulp *noun* An act of swallowing : ingestion, swallow. *See* MOUTH.

gummy *adjective*
Having the property of adhering : adhesive, gluey, gooey, sticky, tacky[1]. *See* CLEAN, KEEP.

gumption *noun*
1. *Informal.* An aggressive readiness along with energy to undertake taxing efforts : drive, enterprise, hustle, initiative, punch. *Informal:* get-up-and-go, push. *See* ACTION, TIRED, TRY. **2.** *Informal.* The ability to make sensible decisions : common sense, judgment, sense, wisdom. *Informal:* horse sense. *See* ABILITY.

gumshoe *noun*
Slang. A person whose work is investigating crimes or obtaining hidden evidence or information : detective, investigator, sleuth. *Informal:* eye. *Slang:* dick. *See* INVESTIGATE.
gumshoe *verb Slang.* To move silently and furtively : creep, glide, lurk, mouse, prowl, pussyfoot, skulk, slide, slink, slip, snake, sneak, steal. *See* MOVE.

gum up *verb*
To harm irreparably through inept handling; make a mess : ball up, blunder, boggle, botch, bungle, foul up, fumble, mess up, mishandle, mismanage, muddle, muff, spoil. *Informal:* bollix up, muck up. *Slang:* blow[1], goof up, louse up, screw up, snafu. ***Idiom:*** make a muck of. *See* CORRECT, HELP.

gun *verb*
To wound or kill with a firearm. Often used with *down* : pick off, shoot. *Slang:* plug. *See* HELP.

gung ho *adjective*
Slang. Showing or having enthusiasm : ardent, enthusiastic, fervent, keen[1], mad, rabid, warm, zealous. *Informal:* crazy. *Slang:* nuts. *See* CONCERN.

gurgle *verb*
To flow or move with a low slapping sound : bubble, burble, lap, splash, swash, wash. *See* MOVE, SOUNDS.

gurgling *adjective*
Emitting a murmuring sound felt to resemble a laugh : babbling, bubbling, burbling, laughing, rippling. *See* LAUGHTER, SOUNDS.

gush *verb*
1. To come forth or emit in abundance : flow, pour, run, rush, stream, surge, well[1]. *See* MOVE. **2.** To make an emotional display : emote, emotionalize. *See* FEELINGS.
gush *noun* A sudden or rapid flowing outward : efflux, outflow, outpour, outpouring, spate. *See* MOVE.

gushy *adjective*
Affectedly or extravagantly emotional : bathetic, maudlin, mawkish, romantic, sentimental, slushy, sobby, soft, soppy. *Informal:* gooey, mushy, schmaltzy, sloppy, soupy. *Slang:* drippy, sappy, tear-jerking. *See* FEELINGS.

gust *noun*
1. A natural movement or current of air : air, blast, blow[1], breeze, wind[1], zephyr. *Archaic:* gale. *See* BREATH. **2.** A sudden violent expression, as of emotion : access, blowup, burst, eruption, explosion, fit[2], flare-up, outbreak, outburst. *See* EXPLOSION.

gusto *noun*
Spirited enjoyment : relish, zest. *See* PAIN.

gusty *adjective*
Exposed to or characterized by the presence of freely circulating air or wind : airy, blowy, breezy, windy. *See* BREATH.

gut *noun*
Slang. The quality of mind enabling one to face danger or hardship resolutely. Used in plural : braveness, bravery, courage, courageousness, dauntlessness, doughtiness, fearlessness, fortitude, gallantry, gameness, heart, intrepidity, intrepidness, mettle, nerve, pluck, pluckiness, spirit, stoutheartedness, undauntedness, valiance, valiancy, valiantness, valor. *Informal:* spunk, spunkiness. *Slang:* gutsiness, moxie. *See* FEAR.

gut *adjective Slang.* Of, relating to, or arising from one's mental or spiritual being : inner, interior, internal, intimate[1], inward, visceral. *See* BODY.

gutless *adjective*
Slang. Ignobly lacking in courage : chicken-hearted, cowardly, craven, dastardly, faint-hearted, lily-livered, pusillanimous, unmanly. *Slang:* chicken, yellow, yellow-bellied. *See* FEAR.

gutlessness *noun*
Slang. Ignoble lack of courage : chickenheartedness, cowardice, cowardliness, cravenness, dastardliness, faint-heartedness, funk, pusillanimity, unmanliness. *Slang:* yellowness, yellow streak. *See* FEAR.

gutsiness *noun*
Slang. The quality of mind enabling one to face danger or hardship resolutely : braveness, bravery, courage, courageousness, dauntlessness, doughtiness, fearlessness, fortitude, gallantry, gameness, heart, intrepidity, intrepidness, mettle, nerve, pluck, pluckiness, spirit, stoutheartedness, undauntedness, valiance, valiancy, valiantness, valor. *Informal:* spunk, spunkiness. *Slang:* gut (used in plural), moxie. *See* FEAR.

gutsy *adjective*
Slang. Having or showing courage : audacious, bold, brave, courageous, dauntless, doughty, fearless, fortitudinous, gallant, game, gutty, hardy, heroic, intrepid, mettlesome, plucky, stout, stouthearted, unafraid, undaunted, valiant, valorous. *Informal:* spunky. *Slang:* gutty. *See* FEAR.

gutty *adjective*
Slang. Having or showing courage : audacious, bold, brave, courageous, dauntless, doughty, fearless, fortitudinous, gallant, game, hardy, heroic, intrepid, mettlesome, plucky, stout, stouthearted, unafraid, undaunted, valiant, valorous. *Informal:* spunky. *Slang:* gutsy. *See* FEAR.

guzzle *verb*
1. To swallow (food or drink) greedily or rapidly in large amounts : bolt, down, englut, engorge, gobble, gulp, ingurgitate, swill, wolf. *See* INGESTION. **2.** To take alcoholic liquor, especially excessively or habitually : drink, imbibe, tipple. *Informal:* nip[2]. *Slang:* booze, lush[2], soak, tank up. ***Idioms:*** bend the elbow, hit the bottle. *See* DRUGS.

gyp also **gip** *verb*
Slang. To get money or something else from by deceitful trickery : bilk, cheat, cozen, defraud, gull, mulct, rook, swindle, victimize. *Informal:* chisel, flimflam, take, trim. *Slang:* diddle[1], do, stick, sting. *See* HONEST.

gyp also **gip** *noun* **1.** *Slang.* An act of cheating : cheat, fraud, swindle, victimization. *Informal:* flimflam. *See* HONEST. **2.** *Slang.* A person who cheats : bilk, cheat, cheater, cozener, defrauder, rook, sharper, swindler, trickster, victimizer. *Informal:* chiseler, crook, flimflammer. *Slang:* diddler, gypper. *See* HONEST.

gypper *noun*
Slang. A person who cheats : bilk, cheat, cheater, cozener, defrauder, rook, sharper, swindler, trickster, victimizer. *Informal:* chiseler, crook, flimflammer. *Slang:* diddler, gyp. *See* HONEST.

gyrate *verb*
To move or cause to move in circles or around an axis : circle, circumvolve, orbit, revolve, rotate, turn, wheel. *See* MOVE, REPETITION.

gyration *noun*
Circular movement around a point or about an axis : circuit, circulation, circumvolution, revolution, rotation, turn, wheel, whirl. *See* GEOMETRY, REPETITION.

gyre *noun*
A closed plane curve that is everywhere equidistant from a fixed point or something that is shaped like such a closed plane curve : band[1], circle, circuit, disk, ring[1], wheel. *Archaic:* orb. *See* GEOMETRY.

gyve *noun*
Archaic. Something that physically confines the legs or arms : bond, chain (used in plural), fetter, handcuff (often used in plural), hobble, iron (used in plural), manacle, restraint, shackle. *See* FREE.

·H·

habiliment *noun*
1. A set or style of clothing. Often used in plural : costume, dress, garb, guise, outfit, turnout. *Informal:* getup, rig. *See* PUT ON. **2.** Articles worn to cover the body. Often used in plural : apparel, attire, clothes, clothing, dress, garment (used in plural), raiment. *Informal:* dud (used in plural), tog (used in plural). *Slang:* thread (used in plural). *See* PUT ON.

habit *noun*
1. A habitual way of behaving : consuetude, custom, habitude, manner, practice, praxis, usage, usance, use, way, wont. *See* USUAL. **2.** The physical or constitutional characteristics of a person : build, constitution, habitus, physique. *See* BODY. **3.** Clothing worn by members of a religious order : robe, vestment. *See* PUT ON.

habitable *adjective*
Fit to live in : inhabitable, livable. *See* COMFORT.

habitat *noun*
The natural environment of an animal or plant : haunt, home, stamping ground. *See* TERRITORY.

habitation *noun*
A building or shelter where one lives : abode, domicile, dwelling, home, house, lodging (often used in plural), place, residence. *Chiefly British:* dig (used in plural). *See* PROTECTION.

habitual *adjective*
1. Subject to a disease or habit for a long time : chronic, confirmed, habituated, inveterate. *See* CONTINUE. **2.** Familiar through repetition : accustomed, chronic, routine. *See* USUAL. **3.** Commonly practiced or used : accustomed, customary, regular, usual, wonted. *See* USUAL.

habitually *adverb*
In an expected or customary manner; for the most part : commonly, consistently, customarily, frequently, generally, naturally, normally, often, regularly, routinely, typically, usually. ***Idioms:*** as usual, per usual. *See* BIG, USUAL.

habitualness *noun*
The quality or condition of being usual : customariness, normalcy, normality, ordinariness, prevalence, regularity, routineness, usualness. *See* USUAL.

habituate *verb*
To make familiar through constant practice or use : accustom, condition, inure, wont. *See* USUAL.

habituated *adjective*
1. In the habit : accustomed, used, wont. *See* USUAL. **2.** Subject to a disease or habit for a long time : chronic, confirmed, habitual, inveterate. *See* CONTINUE.

habitude *noun*
A habitual way of behaving : consuetude, custom, habit, manner, practice, praxis, usage, usance, use, way, wont. *See* USUAL.

habitus *noun*
The physical or constitutional characteristics of a person : build, constitution, habit, physique. *See* BODY.

hackneyed *adjective*
Without freshness or appeal because of overuse : banal, bromidic, clichéd, commonplace, corny, musty, overused, overworked, platitudinal, platitudinous, shopworn, stale, stereotyped, stereotypic, stereotypical, threadbare, timeworn, tired, trite, warmed-over, well-worn, worn-out. *See* EXCITE, USUAL.

hag *noun*
1. An ugly, frightening old woman : beldam, crone, witch. *Slang:* biddy. *Archaic:* trot. *See* BEAUTIFUL. **2.** A woman who practices magic : enchantress, lamia, sorceress, witch. *See* SUPERNATURAL.

haggard *adjective*
Pale and exhausted, as because of worry or sleeplessness : careworn, drawn, gaunt, hollow-eyed, wan, worn. *See* TIRED.

he terms, as of a sale : bar-
le, huckster, negotiate, palter.

ctions intended to excite
amusement : gag, jape, jest, joke, quip, witticism. *Informal:* funny, gag. *See* LAUGHTER.

hail[1] *noun*
A concentrated outpouring, as of missiles, words, or blows : barrage, bombardment, burst, cannonade, fusillade, salvo, shower, storm, volley. *See* ATTACK.

hail[2] *verb*
1. To approach for the purpose of speech : accost, greet, salute. *See* APPROACH, GREETING, SEEK. **2.** To address in a friendly and respectful way : greet, salute, welcome. *See* GREETING. **3.** To pay tribute or homage to : acclaim, celebrate, eulogize, exalt, extol, glorify, honor, laud, magnify, panegyrize, praise. ***Idiom:*** sing someone's praises. *See* PRAISE. **4.** To have as one's home or place of origin : come, originate. *See* START.
hail *noun* An expression, in words or gestures, marking a meeting of persons : greeting, salutation, salute, welcome. *See* GREETING.

hair *noun*
A slight amount or indication : breath, dash, ghost, hint, intimation, semblance, shade, shadow, soupçon, streak, suggestion, suspicion, taste, tinge, touch, trace, whiff, whisper. *Informal:* whisker. *See* BIG, SHOW.

hair-raising *adjective*
Causing great horror : bloodcurdling, horrible, horrid, horrific, terrific. *See* FEAR.

hairy *adjective*
1. Covered with hair : fleecy, furry, fuzzy, hirsute, pilose, woolly. *See* SMOOTH. **2.** *Slang.* Involving possible risk, loss, or injury : adventurous, chancy, dangerous, hazardous, jeopardous, parlous, perilous, risky, treacherous, unsafe, venturesome, venturous. *See* SAFETY.

halcyon *adjective*
Motionless and undisturbed : calm, peaceful, placid, quiet, serene, still, stilly, tranquil, untroubled. *See* CALM.

hale *adjective*
Having good health : fit[1], healthful, healthy, hearty, right, sound[2], well[2], whole, wholesome. ***Idioms:*** fit as a fiddle, hale and hearty, in fine fettle. *See* HEALTH.

haleness *noun*
The condition of being physically and mentally sound : health, healthiness, heartiness, soundness, wholeness. *See* HEALTH.

halfhearted *adjective*
Lacking warmth, interest, enthusiasm, or involvement : lukewarm, tepid, unenthusiastic. *See* ATTITUDE, HOT.

half-witted *adjective*
Offensive. Having only a limited ability to learn and understand : backward, dull, simple, simple-minded, slow, slow-witted. *Informal:* soft. *Offensive:* feeble-minded, retarded, weak-minded. *See* ABILITY.

halloa *noun & verb* See **halloo.**

halloo also **halloa** *noun*
A loud cry : call, holler, shout, yell. *See* SOUNDS.
halloo also **halloa** *verb* To speak or say very loudly or with a shout : bawl, bellow, bluster, call, clamor, cry, holler, roar, shout, vociferate, whoop, yawp, yell. *See* SOUNDS.

hallow *verb*
1. To give over by or as if by vow to a higher purpose : consecrate, dedicate, devote. *See* GIVE. **2.** To make sacred by a religious rite : bless, consecrate, sanctify. *See* RELIGION.

hallowed *adjective*
1. Given over exclusively to a single use or purpose : consecrated, dedicated, devoted, sacred. *See* GIVE, INCLUDE. **2.** Regarded with particular reverence or respect : blessed, holy, sacred, sacrosanct. *See* RELIGION, RESPECT.

hallucination *noun*
1. An erroneous perception of reality : delusion, ignis fatuus, illusion, mirage, phantasm, phantasma, will-o'-the-wisp. *See* REAL. **2.** An illusion of perceiving something that does not really exist : phantasmagoria, phantasmagory. *Slang:* trip. *See* REAL.

hallucinatory *adjective*
Of, relating to, or in the nature of an illusion; lacking reality : chimeric, chimerical, delusive, delusory, dreamlike, illusive, illusory, phantasmagoric, phantasmal, phantasmic, visionary. *See* REAL.

hallucinogen *noun*
A substance that affects the central nervous system and is often addictive : drug, narcotic, opiate. *Informal:* dope. *See* DRUGS.

halt[1] *noun*
1. The act of stopping : cessation, check, cutoff, discontinuance, discontinuation, stay[1], stop, stoppage, surcease. *See* CONTINUE.
2. The condition of being stopped : cessation, discontinuance, discontinuation, standstill, stop, stoppage, surcease. *See* CONTINUE.

halt *verb* **1.** To prevent the occurrence or continuation of a movement, action, or operation : arrest, belay, cease, check, discontinue, stall[1], stay[1], stop, surcease. ***Idioms:*** bring to a standstill, call a halt to, put a stop to. *See* CONTINUE. **2.** To come to a cessation : arrest, belay, cease, check, discontinue, leave off, quit, stall[1], stop, surcease. ***Idiom:*** come to a halt (*or* standstill *or* stop). *See* CONTINUE.

halt[2] *verb*
1. To be irresolute in acting or doing : dither, falter, hesitate, pause, shilly-shally, stagger, vacillate, waver, wobble. *See* DECIDE. **2.** To walk in a lame way : hitch, hobble, limp. *See* MOVE.

halting *adjective*
Given to or exhibiting hesitation : hesitant, indecisive, irresolute, pendulous, shilly-shally, tentative, timid, vacillant, vacillatory. *See* DECIDE.

hammer *verb*
1. To hit heavily and repeatedly with violent blows : assail, assault, baste, batter, beat, belabor, buffet, drub, pound, pummel, smash, thrash, thresh. *Informal:* lambaste. *Slang:* clobber. ***Idiom:*** rain blows on. *See* ATTACK, STRIKE. **2.** To shape, break, or flatten with repeated blows : beat, forge[1], pound. *See* REPETITION, STRIKE.

hamper *verb*
To restrict the activity or free movement of : chain, fetter, hamstring, handcuff, hobble, leash, manacle, shackle, tie, trammel. *Informal:* hog-tie. *See* FREE, HELP.

hamper *noun* Something that impedes or prevents entry or passage : bar, barricade, barrier, block, blockage, clog, hindrance, hurdle, impediment, obstacle, obstruction, snag, stop, traverse, wall. *See* HELP, OPEN.

hamstring *verb*
To restrict the activity or free movement of : chain, fetter, hamper, handcuff, hobble, leash, manacle, shackle, tie, trammel. *Informal:* hog-tie. *See* FREE, HELP.

hand *noun*
1. Approval expressed by clapping : applause, ovation, plaudit. *See* PRAISE. **2.** The act or an instance of helping : abetment, aid, assist, assistance, help, relief, succor, support. *See* HELP. **3.** One who labors : laborer, operative, roustabout, worker, working girl, workingman, workingwoman, workman, workwoman. *See* WORK. **4.** The particular angle from which something is considered : angle[2], aspect, facet, frame of reference, light[1], phase, regard, respect, side. *See* PERSPECTIVE. **5.** One of two or more contrasted parts or places identified by its location with respect to a center : flank, side. *See* PLACE.

hand *verb* **1.** To relinquish to the possession or control of another : deliver, furnish, give, hand over, provide, supply, transfer, turn over. *See* GIVE. **2.** To cause to be transferred from one to another. Also used with *over* : convey, pass, transmit. *See* GIVE.

hand down *verb* **1.** To convey (something) from one generation to the next : bequeath, hand on, pass (along *or* on), transmit. *See* GIVE. **2.** To deliver (an indictment or verdict, for example) : render, return. *See* LAW.

hand on *verb* To convey (something) from one generation to the next : bequeath, hand down, pass (along *or* on), transmit. *See* GIVE.

hand out *verb* **1.** To pass (something) out : circulate, disperse, disseminate, distribute. *See* COLLECT. **2.** To make a gift of : bestow, give (away), present[2]. *See* GIVE. **3.** To present as a gift to a charity or cause : bestow, contribute, donate, give. *See* GIVE.

hand over *verb* **1.** To relinquish to the possession or control of another : deliver, furnish, give, hand, provide, supply, transfer, turn over. *See* GIVE. **2.** To put in the charge of another for care, use, or performance : commend, commit, confide, consign, entrust, give (over), relegate, trust, turn over. ***Idiom:*** give in trust (*or* charge). *See* GIVE. **3.** To give up a possession, claim, or right : abandon, abdicate, cede, demit, forswear, quitclaim, relinquish, render, renounce, resign, surrender, waive, yield. *See* KEEP.

handcuff *noun*
Something that physically confines the legs or arms. Often used in plural : bond, chain (used in plural), fetter, hobble, iron (used in plural), manacle, restraint, shackle. *Archaic:* gyve. *See* FREE.

handcuff *verb* To restrict the activity or free movement of : chain, fetter, hamper, hamstring, hobble, leash, manacle, shackle, tie, trammel. *Informal:* hog-tie. *See* FREE, HELP.

hand down *verb* See **hand.**

handicap *noun*
1. A factor conducive to superiority and success : advantage, head start, odds, start, vantage. *See* HELP. **2.** An unfavorable condition, circumstance, or characteristic : detriment, disadvantage, drawback, minus. *See* HELP.

handle *verb*
1. To bring the hands or fingers, for example, into contact with so as to give or receive a

physical sensation : feel, finger, palpate, touch. *See* TOUCH. **2.** To use with or as if with the hands : manipulate, ply², wield. *See* CONTROL, USED. **3.** To behave in a specified way toward : deal with, treat. *See* TREAT WELL. **4.** To offer for sale : deal (in), market, merchandise, merchant, peddle, retail, sell, trade (in), vend. *See* TRANSACTIONS.

handle *noun Slang.* The word or words by which one is called and identified : appellation, appellative, cognomen, denomination, designation, epithet, name, nickname, style, tag, title. *Slang:* moniker. *See* SPECIFIC, WORDS.

hand on *verb* See **hand.**

handout *noun*
1. Something given to a charity or cause : alms, benefaction, beneficence, charity, contribution, donation, gift, offering, subscription. *See* GIVE. **2.** Assistance, especially money, food, and other necessities, given to the needy : aid, dole, public assistance, relief, welfare. *See* HELP.

hand out *verb* See **hand.**

hand over *verb* See **hand.**

handsel also **hansel** *noun*
Chiefly British. Something bestowed freely : gift, present², presentation. *See* GIVE.

handsome *adjective*
1. Having qualities that delight the eye : attractive, beauteous, beautiful, comely, fair, good-looking, gorgeous, lovely, pretty, pulchritudinous, ravishing, sightly, stunning. *Scots:* bonny. ***Idiom:*** easy on the eyes. *See* BEAUTIFUL. **2.** Characterized by bounteous giving : free, freehanded, generous, lavish, liberal, munificent, openhanded, unsparing, unstinting. *See* GIVE.

handy *adjective*
1. Exhibiting or possessing skill and ease in performance : adroit, clever, deft, dexterous, facile, nimble, slick. *See* ABILITY. **2.** Being within easy reach : accessible, convenient, nearby. ***Idioms:*** close (*or* near) at hand, close by. *See* NEAR. **3.** Serving or capable of serving a useful purpose : functional, practicable, practical, serviceable, useful, utilitarian. *See* USED.

hang *verb*
1. To fasten or be fastened at one point with no support from below : dangle, depend, sling, suspend, swing. *See* HANG. **2.** To execute by suspending by the neck : gibbet. *Informal:* string up. *Slang:* swing. *See* HELP. **3.** To remain stationary over a place or object : hover, poise. *See* HANG.

hang around *verb* **1.** To visit regularly : frequent, haunt, repair², resort. *Slang:* hang out. *See* PLACE. **2.** To be with as a companion : associate, consort, fraternize, hobnob, run (around), troop. *Slang:* hang out. ***Idiom:*** rub elbows (*or* shoulders). *See* NEAR.

hang on *verb* **1.** To be determined by or contingent on something unknown, uncertain, or changeable : depend on (*or* upon), hang upon, hinge on (*or* upon), rest on (*or* upon), turn on, turn upon. *See* START. **2.** To continue without halting despite difficulties or setbacks : carry on, go on, keep on, persevere, persist. ***Idioms:*** hang in there, keep going, keep it up. *See* CONTINUE.

hang out *verb* **1.** *Slang.* To visit regularly : frequent, hang around, haunt, repair², resort. *See* PLACE. **2.** *Slang.* To be with as a companion : associate, consort, fraternize, hang around, hobnob, run (around), troop. ***Idiom:*** rub elbows (*or* shoulders). *See* NEAR.

hang over *verb* To be imminent : brew, impend, loom, lower¹, menace, overhang, threaten. *See* NEAR.

hang up *verb* To cause to be later or slower than expected or desired : delay, detain, hold up, lag, retard, set back, slow (down *or* up), stall². *See* HELP, TIME.

hang upon *verb* To be determined by or contingent on something unknown, uncertain, or changeable : depend on (*or* upon), hang on, hinge on (*or* upon), rest on (*or* upon), turn on, turn upon. *See* START.

hang *noun Informal.* The proper method for doing, using, or handling something : feel, knack, trick. *See* ABILITY.

hang around *verb* See **hang.**

hanger-on *noun*
One who depends on another for support without reciprocating : bloodsucker, leech, parasite, sponge. *Slang:* freeloader. *See* DEPENDENCE.

hanging *adjective*
Hung or appearing to be hung from a support : dangly, pendulous, pensile. *See* HANG.

hang on *verb* See **hang.**

hangout *noun*
Slang. A frequently visited place : haunt, rendezvous, resort, stamping ground. *See* PLACE, REPETITION.

hang out *verb* See **hang.**

hang over *verb* See **hang.**

hang-up *noun*
Informal. An exaggerated concern : complex. *See* FEAR.

hang up *verb* See **hang.**

hang upon *verb* See **hang.**

hanker *verb*
To have a strong longing for : ache, covet, desire, long[2], pant, pine, want, wish, yearn. *Informal:* hone[2]. *See* DESIRE.

hansel *noun* See **handsel.**

hap *noun*
1. The quality shared by random, unintended, or unpredictable events or this quality regarded as the cause of such events : chance, fortuitousness, fortuity, fortune, hazard, luck. *See* CERTAIN. **2.** An unexpected random event : accident, chance, fluke, fortuity, happenchance, happenstance, hazard. *See* CERTAIN, SURPRISE.
hap *verb* **1.** To take place : befall, betide, come, come about, come off, develop, happen, occur, pass, transpire. ***Idiom:*** come to pass. *See* HAPPEN. **2.** To take place by chance : befall, chance, happen. *See* HAPPEN.

haphazard *adjective*
Having no particular pattern, purpose, organization, or structure : chance, desultory, hit-or-miss, indiscriminate, random, spot, unplanned. *See* PLANNED.

hapless *adjective*
Involving or undergoing chance misfortune : ill-fated, ill-starred, luckless, star-crossed, unfortunate, unhappy, unlucky, untoward. *See* LUCK.

haplessness *noun*
Bad fortune : adversity, misfortune, unfortunateness, unluckiness, untowardness. *See* LUCK.

happen *verb*
1. To take place : befall, betide, come, come about, come off, develop, hap, occur, pass, transpire. ***Idiom:*** come to pass. *See* HAPPEN. **2.** To take place by chance : befall, chance, hap. *See* HAPPEN.
happen on (or **upon)** *verb* To find or meet by chance : bump into, chance on (*or* upon), come across, come on (*or* upon), find, light on (*or* upon), run across, run into, stumble on (*or* upon), tumble on. *Archaic:* alight on (*or* upon). ***Idiom:*** meet up with. *See* MEET.

happenchance *noun*
An unexpected random event : accident, chance, fluke, fortuity, hap, happenstance, hazard. *See* CERTAIN, SURPRISE.

happening *noun*
1. Something that happens : circumstance, event, incident, occasion, occurrence, thing. *See* HAPPEN. **2.** Something significant that happens : circumstance, development, episode, event, incident, news, occasion, occurrence, thing. *See* HAPPEN.

happen on or **upon** *verb* See **happen.**

happenstance *noun*
An unexpected random event : accident, chance, fluke, fortuity, hap, happenchance, hazard. *See* CERTAIN, SURPRISE.

happiness *noun*
A condition of supreme well-being and good spirits : beatitude, blessedness, bliss, cheer, cheerfulness, felicity, gladness, joy, joyfulness. *See* HAPPY.

happy *adjective*
1. Characterized by luck or good fortune : fortunate, lucky, providential. *See* LUCK. **2.** Being in or showing good spirits : bright, cheerful, cheery, chipper, lighthearted, sunny. *See* HAPPY. **3.** Having achieved satisfaction, as of one's goal : content, fulfilled, gratified, satisfied. *See* HAPPY. **4.** Providing joy and pleasure : cheerful, cheery, festive, glad, joyful, joyous, pleasing. *See* HAPPY. **5.** Marked by festal celebration : festive, gala, glad, gladsome, joyful, joyous, merry. *See* HAPPY. **6.** Suitable for a particular person, condition, occasion, or place : appropriate, apt, becoming, befitting, correct, felicitous, fit[1], fitting, meet[2], proper, right, tailor-made. *See* RIGHT. **7.** Eagerly compliant : delighted, glad, pleased, tickled. *See* HAPPY.

harangue *noun*
A long, violent, or blustering speech, usually of censure or denunciation : diatribe, fulmination, jeremiad, philippic, tirade. *See* PRAISE.
harangue *verb* To speak in a loud, pompous, or prolonged manner : declaim, mouth, perorate, rant, rave. *See* WORDS.

harass *verb*
1. To trouble persistently from or as if from all sides : badger, bedevil, beleaguer, beset, besiege, harry, hound, importune, pester, plague, solicit. *See* ATTACK. **2.** To disturb by repeated attacks : annoy, bait, bedevil, beleaguer, beset, harry, pester, plague, tease, torment, worry. *See* FEELINGS, PAIN.

harassment *noun*
The act of annoying : annoyance, botheration, bothering, exasperation, irritation, pestering, provocation, vexation. *See* FEELINGS, PAIN.

harbinger *noun*
One that indicates someone or something to come : forerunner, foreshadower, herald, precursor, presager. *See* FORESIGHT, SHOW.

harbor *noun*
Something that physically protects, especially

from danger : asylum, cover, covert, haven, protection, refuge, retreat, sanctuary, shelter. *See* ATTACK, SAFETY.

harbor *verb* **1.** To give refuge to : haven, house, shelter. *See* PROTECTION. **2.** To provide with often temporary lodging : accommodate, bed (down), berth, bestow, billet, board, bunk[1], domicile, house, lodge, put up, quarter, room. *See* PROTECTION. **3.** To hold and turn over in the mind : bear, nourish, nurse. *See* THOUGHTS.

harborage *noun*

The state of being protected or safeguarded, as from danger or hardship : asylum, refuge, sanctuary, shelter. *See* SAFETY.

hard *adjective*

1. Unyielding to pressure or force : firm[1], incompressible, solid. *See* RESIST, STRONG. **2.** Physically toughened so as to have great endurance : hard-bitten, hard-handed, hardy, rugged, tough. ***Idiom:*** hard as nails. *See* CONTINUE, STRONG. **3.** Not easy to do, achieve, or master : arduous, difficult, laborious, serious, tall, tough, uphill. *See* EASY. **4.** Requiring great or extreme bodily, mental, or spiritual strength : arduous, backbreaking, burdensome, demanding, difficult, effortful, exacting, exigent, formidable, heavy, laborious, onerous, oppressive, rigorous, rough, severe, taxing, tough, trying, weighty. *See* HEAVY. **5.** Conveying great physical force : heavy, hefty, powerful, severe. *See* BIG. **6.** Indulging in drink to an excessive degree : heavy. *Informal:* two-fisted. *See* EXCESS. **7.** Rigorous and unsparing in treating others : demanding, exacting, harsh, rigid, severe, stern, strict, tough, unyielding. *See* EASY. **8.** Cold and forbidding : austere, bleak, dour, grim, harsh, severe, stark. *See* ATTITUDE, HOT. **9.** Causing sharp, often prolonged discomfort : bitter, brutal, harsh, rough, severe. *See* COMFORT. **10.** Completely lacking in compassion : callous, cold-blooded, cold-hearted, compassionless, hard-boiled, hardened, hardhearted, heartless, obdurate, stonyhearted, unfeeling. *See* ATTITUDE. **11.** Bitingly hostile : acrimonious, bitter, embittered, rancorous, resentful, virulent. *See* ATTITUDE, LOVE. **12.** Established beyond a doubt : certain, inarguable, incontestable, incontrovertible, indisputable, indubitable, irrefutable, positive, sure, unassailable, undeniable, undisputable, unquestionable. *See* CERTAIN, TRUE. **13.** Based on fact : factual. *See* REAL. **14.** Having or indicating an awareness of things as they really are : down-to-earth, hardheaded, matter-of-fact, objective, practical, pragmatic, pragmatical, prosaic, realistic, sober, tough-minded, unromantic. *See* EXCITE, REAL. **15.** Containing alcohol : alcoholic, intoxicative, spirituous, strong. *See* INGESTION.

hard *adverb* **1.** In a violent, strenuous way : fiercely, frantically, frenziedly, furiously, strenuously. *See* STRONG. **2.** With effort : arduously, difficultly, heavily, laboriously. *See* EASY. **3.** With intense energy and force : energetically, forcefully, forcibly, powerfully, vigorously. ***Idioms:*** hammer and tongs, tooth and nail, with might and main. *See* STRONG. **4.** To a point near in time, space, or relation : close, closely, near, nearby, nigh. *See* NEAR.

hard-bitten *adjective*

Physically toughened so as to have great endurance : hard, hard-handed, hardy, rugged, tough. ***Idiom:*** hard as nails. *See* CONTINUE, STRONG.

hard-boiled *adjective*

Completely lacking in compassion : callous, cold-blooded, cold-hearted, compassionless, hard, hardened, hardhearted, heartless, obdurate, stonyhearted, unfeeling. *See* ATTITUDE.

harden *verb*

1. To make or become physically hard : cake, concrete, congeal, dry, indurate, petrify, set[1], solidify. *See* SOLID. **2.** To make firmer in a particular conviction or habit : confirm, fortify, strengthen. *See* STRONG. **3.** To make resistant to hardship, especially through continued exposure : acclimate, acclimatize, caseharden, indurate, season, toughen. *See* CONTINUE, RESIST.

hardened *adjective*

Completely lacking in compassion : callous, cold-blooded, cold-hearted, compassionless, hard, hard-boiled, hardhearted, heartless, obdurate, stonyhearted, unfeeling. *See* ATTITUDE.

hard-fisted *adjective*

Ungenerously or pettily reluctant to spend money : cheap, close, close-fisted, costive, mean[2], miserly, niggard, niggardly, parsimonious, penny-pinching, penurious, petty, pinching, stingy, tight, tightfisted. *See* GIVE.

hard-handed *adjective*

Physically toughened so as to have great endurance : hard, hard-bitten, hardy, rugged, tough. ***Idiom:*** hard as nails. *See* CONTINUE, STRONG.

hardheaded *adjective*

1. Tenaciously unwilling to yield : bullheaded, dogged, headstrong, mulish, obstinate, pertinacious, perverse, pigheaded, stiff-necked, tenacious, willful. *See* RESIST. **2.** Having or indicating an awareness of things as they really are : down-to-earth, hard, matter-of-fact, objective, practical, pragmatic, pragmatical, prosaic, realistic, sober, tough-minded, unromantic. *See* EXCITE, REAL.

hardheadedness *noun*
The quality or state of being stubbornly unyielding : bullheadedness, doggedness, mulishness, obstinacy, obstinateness, pertinaciousness, pertinacity, perverseness, perversity, pigheadedness, tenaciousness, tenacity, willfulness. *See* RESIST.

hardhearted *adjective*
Completely lacking in compassion : callous, cold-blooded, cold-hearted, compassionless, hard, hard-boiled, hardened, heartless, obdurate, stonyhearted, unfeeling. *See* ATTITUDE.

hard-hitting *adjective*
Full of or displaying force : dynamic, dynamical, effective, forceful, forcible, powerful, strong, vigorous. *See* STRONG.

hardly *adverb*
By a very little; almost not : barely, just, scarce, scarcely. *See* NEAR.

hardness *noun*
1. Reliability in withstanding pressure, force, or stress : fastness, firmness, security, soundness, stability, stableness, steadiness, strength, sturdiness, sureness. *See* BETTER, CHANGE, CONTINUE. **2.** The fact or condition of being rigorous and unsparing : austerity, harshness, rigidity, rigor, rigorousness, severity, sternness, strictness, stringency, toughness. *See* EASY.

hard-shell *adjective*
Firmly established by long standing : confirmed, deep-rooted, deep-seated, entrenched, ineradicable, ingrained, inveterate, irradicable, set[1], settled. *See* CONTINUE.

hardship *noun*
Something that obstructs progress and requires great effort to overcome : asperity, difficulty, rigor, vicissitude (often used in plural). ***Idioms:*** a hard (*or* tough) nut to crack, a hard (*or* tough) row to hoe, heavy sledding. *See* EASY.

hardy *adjective*
1. Physically toughened so as to have great endurance : hard, hard-bitten, hard-handed, rugged, tough. ***Idiom:*** hard as nails. *See* CONTINUE, STRONG. **2.** Capable of exerting considerable effort or of withstanding considerable stress or hardship : stalwart, stout, strong, sturdy, tough. *See* STRONG. **3.** Having or showing courage : audacious, bold, brave, courageous, dauntless, doughty, fearless, fortitudinous, gallant, game, heroic, intrepid, mettlesome, plucky, stout, stouthearted, unafraid, undaunted, valiant, valorous. *Informal:* spunky. *Slang:* gutsy, gutty. *See* FEAR.

harebrained *adjective*
1. So senseless as to be laughable : absurd, foolish, idiotic, imbecilic, insane, lunatic, mad, moronic, nonsensical, preposterous, silly, soft-headed, tomfool, unearthly, zany. *Informal:* cockeyed, crazy, loony, loopy. *Slang:* balmy[2], dippy, dopey, jerky, sappy, wacky. *See* ABILITY, KNOWLEDGE. **2.** Given to lighthearted silliness : empty-headed, featherbrained, flighty, frivolous, frothy, giddy, lighthearted, scatterbrained, silly. *Informal:* gaga. *Slang:* birdbrained, dizzy. *See* ABILITY.

hark *verb*
1. To perceive by ear, usually attentively : attend, hear, heed, listen. *Archaic:* hearken. ***Idiom:*** give (*or* lend) one's ear. *See* SOUNDS. **2.** To make an effort to hear something : hearken, listen. *Archaic:* list[3]. ***Idiom:*** give (*or* lend) an ear. *See* SOUNDS.

harken *verb* See **hearken.**

harlot *noun*
A woman who engages in sexual intercourse for payment : bawd, call girl, camp follower, courtesan, prostitute, scarlet woman, streetwalker, strumpet, tart[2], whore. *Slang:* hooker, moll. ***Idioms:*** lady of easy virtue, lady of pleasure, lady of the night. *See* SEX.

harm *noun*
The action or result of inflicting loss or pain : damage, detriment, hurt, injury, mischief. *See* HELP.

harm *verb* To spoil the soundness or perfection of : blemish, damage, detract from, disserve, flaw, hurt, impair, injure, mar, prejudice, tarnish, vitiate. *See* BETTER, HELP.

harmful *adjective*
Causing harm or injury : bad, deleterious, detrimental, evil, hurtful, ill, injurious, mischievous. *See* HELP.

harmless *adjective*
1. Devoid of hurtful qualities : hurtless, innocent, innocuous, inoffensive, unoffensive. *See* HELP. **2.** Free from guilt or blame : blameless, faultless, guiltless, innocent, irreproachable, lily-white, unblamable. *Slang:* clean. ***Idiom:*** in the clear. *See* RIGHT.

harmonic *adjective*
Characterized by harmony of sound : consonant, harmonious, musical, symphonic, symphonious. *See* BEAUTIFUL, SOUNDS.

harmonious *adjective*
1. In keeping with one's needs or expectations : accordant, agreeable, compatible, conformable, congenial, congruous, consistent, consonant, correspondent, corresponding. *See* AGREE. **2.** Having components pleasingly combined : balanced, congruous, symmetrical. *See* BEAUTIFUL. **3.** Characterized by harmony of sound : consonant, harmonic, musical, symphonic, symphonious. *See* BEAUTIFUL, SOUNDS.

harmonization *noun*
The act or state of agreeing or conforming : accordance, agreement, chime, conformance, conformation, conformity, congruence, congruity, correspondence, harmony, keeping. *See* AGREE.

harmonize *verb*
1. To bring into accord : accommodate, attune, conform, coordinate, integrate, proportion, reconcile, tune. *See* AGREE. **2.** To combine and adapt in order to attain a particular effect : arrange, blend, coordinate, integrate, orchestrate, synthesize, unify. *See* BEAUTIFUL. **3.** To come to an understanding or to terms : accord, agree, coincide, concur, get together. *See* AGREE. **4.** To be compatible or in correspondence : accord, agree, check, chime, comport with, conform, consist, correspond, fit[1], match, square, tally. *Informal:* jibe[1]. *Archaic:* quadrate. *See* AGREE. **5.** To live or act together in harmony : get along, get on. *Informal:* cotton. ***Idiom:*** hit it off. *See* AGREE.

harmony *noun*
1. The act or state of agreeing or conforming : accordance, agreement, chime, conformance, conformation, conformity, congruence, congruity, correspondence, harmonization, keeping. *See* AGREE. **2.** Harmonious mutual understanding : accord, agreement, concord, concordance, concurrence, consonance, rapport, tune, unity. ***Idiom:*** meeting of the minds. *See* AGREE. **3.** Satisfying arrangement marked by even distribution of elements, as in a design : balance, proportion, symmetry. *See* BEAUTIFUL. **4.** Pleasing agreement, as of musical sounds : accord, concert, concord, symphony, tune. *Music:* consonance. *See* BEAUTIFUL.

harpy *noun*
A person, traditionally a woman, who persistently nags or criticizes : fishwife, fury, scold, shrew, termagant, virago, vixen. *Informal:* battle-ax. *See* PRAISE.

harrow *verb*
Archaic. To rob of goods by force, especially in time of war : depredate, despoil, havoc, loot, pillage, plunder, ransack, rape, ravage, sack[2], spoliate, strip[1]. *Archaic:* spoil. *See* CRIMES, GIVE.

harrowing *adjective*
Extraordinarily painful or distressing : agonizing, anguishing, excruciating, tormenting, torturous. *See* PAIN.

harry *verb*
1. To disturb by repeated attacks : annoy, bait, bedevil, beleaguer, beset, harass, pester, plague, tease, torment, worry. *See* FEELINGS, PAIN. **2.** To trouble persistently from or as if from all sides : badger, bedevil, beleaguer, beset, besiege, harass, hound, importune, pester, plague, solicit. *See* ATTACK. **3.** To make a surprise attack on : maraud, raid. *See* ATTACK.

harsh *adjective*
1. Having a surface that is not smooth : coarse, cragged, craggy, ironbound, jagged, ragged, rough, rugged, scabrous, uneven. *See* SMOOTH. **2.** Disagreeable to the sense of hearing : dry, grating, hoarse, jarring, rasping, raspy, raucous, rough, scratchy, squawky, strident. *See* SOUNDS. **3.** Having a noticeably sharp pungent taste or smell : acerbic, acrid, bitter, sour. *See* TASTE. **4.** Rigorous and unsparing in treating others : demanding, exacting, hard, rigid, severe, stern, strict, tough, unyielding. *See* EASY. **5.** Cold and forbidding : austere, bleak, dour, grim, hard, severe, stark. *See* ATTITUDE, HOT. **6.** Causing sharp, often prolonged discomfort : bitter, brutal, hard, rough, severe. *See* COMFORT.

harshness *noun*
The fact or condition of being rigorous and unsparing : austerity, hardness, rigidity, rigor, rigorousness, severity, sternness, strictness, stringency, toughness. *See* EASY.

harum-scarum *adjective*
Characterized by unthinking boldness and haste : brash, foolhardy, hasty, headlong, hotheaded, ill-considered, impetuous, improvident, impulsive, incautious, madcap, precipitant, precipitate, rash[1], reckless, slapdash, temerarious, unconsidered. *See* CAREFUL.

haruspex also **aruspex** *noun*
A person who foretells future events by or as if by supernatural means : augur, auspex, diviner, foreteller, prophesier, prophet, prophetess, seer, sibyl, soothsayer, vaticinator. *See* FORESIGHT.

harvest *noun*
1. The produce harvested from the land : crop, fruit, fruitage, yield. *See* INGESTION. **2.** Some-

thing brought about by a cause : aftermath, consequence, corollary, effect, end product, event, fruit, issue, outcome, precipitate, ramification, result, resultant, sequel, sequence, sequent, upshot. *See* CAUSE.

harvest *verb* To collect ripe crops : crop, garner, gather, pick, reap. *See* COLLECT.

hash *noun*

Informal. A ruinous state of disorder : botch, foul-up, mess, muddle, shambles. *Slang:* screwup, snafu. *See* CORRECT, ORDER.

hash *verb Informal.* To speak together and exchange ideas and opinions about. Also used with *over* : bandy (about), discuss, moot, talk over, thrash out (*or* over), thresh out (*or* over), toss around. *Informal:* kick around, knock about (*or* around). *Slang:* rap[3]. ***Idiom:*** go into a huddle. *See* WORDS.

hassle *noun*

Informal. A discussion, often heated, in which a difference of opinion is expressed : altercation, argument, bicker, clash, contention, controversy, debate, difficulty, disagreement, dispute, fight, polemic, quarrel, run-in, spat, squabble, tiff, word (used in plural), wrangle. *Informal:* rhubarb, tangle. *See* CONFLICT.

hassle *verb Informal.* To engage in a quarrel : argue, bicker, contend, dispute, fight, quarrel, quibble, spat, squabble, tiff, wrangle. *Informal:* tangle. ***Idioms:*** cross swords, have it out, have words, lock horns. *See* CONFLICT.

haste *noun*

1. Rapidness of movement or activity : celerity, dispatch, expedition, expeditiousness, fleetness, hurry, hustle, quickness, rapidity, rapidness, speed, speediness, swiftness. *See* FAST. **2.** Careless headlong action : hastiness, hurriedness, precipitance, precipitancy, precipitateness, precipitation, rashness, rush. *See* CAREFUL.

haste *verb* To move swiftly : bolt, bucket, bustle, dart, dash, festinate, flash, fleet, flit, fly, hasten, hurry, hustle, pelt[2], race, rocket, run, rush, sail, scoot, scour[2], shoot, speed, sprint, tear[1], trot, whirl, whisk, whiz, wing, zip, zoom. *Informal:* hotfoot, rip. *Slang:* barrel, highball. *Chiefly British:* nip[1]. ***Idioms:*** get a move on, get cracking, go like lightning, go like the wind, hotfoot it, make haste, make time, make tracks, run like the wind, shake a leg, step (*or* jump) on it. *See* MOVE.

hasten *verb*

1. To move swiftly : bolt, bucket, bustle, dart, dash, festinate, flash, fleet, flit, fly, haste, hurry, hustle, pelt[2], race, rocket, run, rush, sail, scoot, scour[2], shoot, speed, sprint, tear[1], trot, whirl, whisk, whiz, wing, zip, zoom. *Informal:* hotfoot, rip. *Slang:* barrel, highball. *Chiefly British:* nip[1]. ***Idioms:*** get a move on, get cracking, go like lightning, go like the wind, hotfoot it, make haste, make time, make tracks, run like the wind, shake a leg, step (*or* jump) on it. *See* MOVE. **2.** To increase the speed of : accelerate, expedite, hurry, hustle, quicken, speed (up), step up. *See* FAST.

hastiness *noun*

Careless headlong action : haste, hurriedness, precipitance, precipitancy, precipitateness, precipitation, rashness, rush. *See* CAREFUL.

hasty *adjective*

1. Accomplished in very little time : brief, expeditious, fast, flying, hurried, quick, rapid, short, speedy, swift. *See* FAST. **2.** Characterized by unthinking boldness and haste : brash, foolhardy, harum-scarum, headlong, hotheaded, ill-considered, impetuous, improvident, impulsive, incautious, madcap, precipitant, precipitate, rash[1], reckless, slapdash, temerarious, unconsidered. *See* CAREFUL.

hatch *verb*

1. To cause to come into existence : beget, breed, create, engender, father, make, originate, parent, procreate, produce, sire, spawn. ***Idiom:*** give birth (*or* rise) to. *See* MAKE. **2.** To use ingenuity in making, developing, or achieving : concoct, contrive, devise, dream up, fabricate, formulate, invent, make up, think up. *Informal:* cook up. ***Idiom:*** come up with. *See* MAKE.

hate *verb*

To regard with extreme dislike and hostility : abhor, abominate, despise, detest, execrate, loathe. *See* LOVE.

hate *noun* **1.** Extreme hostility and dislike : abhorrence, abomination, antipathy, aversion, detestation, hatred, horror, loathing, repellence, repellency, repugnance, repugnancy, repulsion, revulsion. *See* LOVE. **2.** An object of extreme dislike : abhorrence, abomination, anathema, aversion, bête noire, bugbear, detestation, execration. *Informal:* horror. *See* LOVE.

hateable *adjective*

Eliciting or deserving hate : hateful. *See* LOVE.

hateful *adjective*

1. Eliciting or deserving hate : hateable. *See* LOVE. **2.** Characterized by intense ill will or spite : black, despiteful, evil, malevolent, malicious, malign, malignant, mean[2], nasty, poisonous, spiteful, venomous, vicious, wicked. *Slang:* bitchy. *See* ATTITUDE.

hatred *noun*

Extreme hostility and dislike : abhorrence,

abomination, antipathy, aversion, detestation, hate, horror, loathing, repellence, repellency, repugnance, repugnancy, repulsion, revulsion. *See* LOVE.

haughtiness *noun*
The quality of being arrogant : arrogance, hauteur, insolence, loftiness, lordliness, overbearingness, presumption, pride, pridefulness, proudness, superciliousness, superiority. *See* ATTITUDE.

haughty *adjective*
Overly convinced of one's own superiority and importance : arrogant, high-and-mighty, insolent, lofty, lordly, overbearing, overweening, prideful, proud, supercilious, superior. ***Idiom:*** on one's high horse. *See* ATTITUDE.

haul *verb*
To exert force so as to move (something) toward the source of the force : drag, draw, pull, tow, tug. *See* PUSH.
haul *noun* **1.** The act of drawing or pulling a load : draft, drag, draw, pull, traction. *See* PUSH. **2.** Something carried physically : burden[1], cargo, freight, load. *Sports:* impost. *See* HEAVY, OVER.

haunt *verb*
1. To visit regularly : frequent, hang around, repair[2], resort. *Slang:* hang out. *See* PLACE. **2.** To come to mind continually : obsess, torment, trouble, weigh on (*or* upon). *See* REPETITION.
haunt *noun* **1.** A frequently visited place : rendezvous, resort, stamping ground. *Slang:* hangout. *See* PLACE, REPETITION. **2.** The natural environment of an animal or plant : habitat, home, stamping ground. *See* TERRITORY. **3.** *Regional.* A supernatural being, such as a ghost : apparition, bogey, bogeyman, bogle, eidolon, ghost, phantasm, phantasma, phantom, revenant, shade, shadow, specter, spirit, visitant, wraith. *Informal:* spook. *See* BEINGS, SUPERNATURAL.

hauteur *noun*
The quality of being arrogant : arrogance, haughtiness, insolence, loftiness, lordliness, overbearingness, presumption, pride, pridefulness, proudness, superciliousness, superiority. *See* ATTITUDE.

have *verb*
1. To keep at one's disposal : hold, own, possess, retain. *See* KEEP. **2.** To hold on one's person : bear, carry, possess. *Informal:* pack. *See* OWNED. **3.** To have at one's disposal : boast, command, enjoy, hold, possess. *See* OWNED. **4.** To have the use or benefit of : enjoy, hold, possess. *See* OWNED. **5.** To be endowed with as a visible characteristic or form : bear, carry, display, exhibit, possess. *See* SHOW. **6.** To have as a part : comprehend, comprise, contain, embody, embrace, encompass, include, involve, subsume, take in. *See* INCLUDE. **7.** To be filled by : contain, hold. *See* INCLUDE. **8.** To admit to one's possession, presence, or awareness : accept, receive, take. *See* ACCEPT. **9.** To participate in or partake of personally : experience, feel, go through, know, meet[1] (with), see, suffer, taste (of), undergo. *Archaic:* prove. ***Idiom:*** run up against. *See* PARTICIPATE. **10.** To be physically aware of through the senses : experience, feel. *See* KNOWLEDGE. **11.** To undergo an emotional reaction : experience, feel, know, savor, taste. *See* FEELINGS. **12.** To cause to be in a certain state or to undergo a particular experience or action : get, make. *See* CAUSE. **13.** To neither forbid nor prevent : allow, let, permit, suffer, tolerate. *See* ALLOW. **14.** To organize and carry out (an activity) : give, hold, stage. *See* CONTROL, PLANNED. **15.** To involve oneself in (an activity) : carry on, engage, indulge, partake, participate. ***Idiom:*** take part. *See* PARTICIPATE. **16.** *Informal.* To cause to accept what is false, especially by trickery or misrepresentation : beguile, betray, bluff, cozen, deceive, delude, double-cross, dupe, fool, hoodwink, humbug, mislead, take in, trick. *Informal:* bamboozle. *Slang:* four-flush. ***Idioms:*** lead astray, play false, pull the wool over someone's eyes, put something over on, take for a ride. *See* HONEST. **17.** To give birth to : bear, bring forth, deliver. *Chiefly Regional:* birth. ***Idiom:*** be brought abed (*or* to bed) of. *See* RICH. **18.** To engage in sexual relations with : bed, copulate, couple, mate, sleep with, take. ***Idioms:*** go to bed with, make love, make whoopee, roll in the hay. *See* SEX.
have at *verb* To set upon with violent force : aggress, assail, assault, attack, beset, fall on (*or* upon), go at, sail into, storm, strike. *Informal:* light into, pitch into. *See* ATTACK.

have at *verb* See **have.**

haven *noun*
Something that physically protects, especially from danger : asylum, cover, covert, harbor, protection, refuge, retreat, sanctuary, shelter. *See* ATTACK, SAFETY.
haven *verb* To give refuge to : harbor, house, shelter. *See* PROTECTION.

have-not *noun*
An impoverished person : beggar, down-and-

out, down-and-outer, indigent, pauper. *See* RICH.

havoc *noun*
The act of destroying or state of being destroyed : bane, destruction, devastation, ruin, ruination, undoing, wrack[1], wreck, wreckage. *See* HELP, LEFTOVER.
havoc *verb* To rob of goods by force, especially in time of war : depredate, despoil, loot, pillage, plunder, ransack, rape, ravage, sack[2], spoliate, strip[1]. *Archaic:* harrow, spoil. *See* CRIMES, GIVE.

hawk *verb*
To travel about selling goods : huckster, peddle, vend. *See* TRANSACTIONS.

hazard *noun*
1. An unexpected random event : accident, chance, fluke, fortuity, hap, happenchance, happenstance. *See* CERTAIN, SURPRISE. **2.** The quality shared by random, unintended, or unpredictable events or this quality regarded as the cause of such events : chance, fortuitousness, fortuity, fortune, hap, luck. *See* CERTAIN. **3.** Exposure to possible harm, loss, or injury : danger, endangerment, imperilment, jeopardy, peril, risk. *See* SAFETY. **4.** A possibility of danger or harm : chance, gamble, risk. *See* SAFETY.
hazard *verb* **1.** To expose to possible loss or damage : adventure, compromise, risk, venture. *See* SAFETY. **2.** To run the risk of : adventure, chance, risk, venture. *See* SAFETY. **3.** To have the courage to put forward, as an idea, especially when rebuff or criticism is likely : dare, presume, pretend, venture. *See* TRY.

hazardous *adjective*
Involving possible risk, loss, or injury : adventurous, chancy, dangerous, jeopardous, parlous, perilous, risky, treacherous, unsafe, venturesome, venturous. *Slang:* hairy. *See* SAFETY.

haze *noun*
A thick, heavy atmospheric condition offering reduced visibility because of the presence of suspended particles : brume, fog, mist, murk, smaze. *See* CLEAR.

hazy *adjective*
1. Covered by or as if by a thin coating or film : blurry, cloudy, dim, filmy, misty. *See* CLEAR. **2.** Heavy, dark, or dense, especially with impurities : murky, smoggy, turbid. *See* CLEAR. **3.** Not clearly perceived or perceptible : blear, bleary, cloudy, dim, faint, foggy, fuzzy, indefinite, indistinct, misty, obscure, shadowy, unclear, undistinct, vague. *See* CLEAR.

head *noun*
1. The uppermost part of the body : noddle, pate, poll. *Slang:* bean, block, conk, dome, noggin, noodle, nut. *See* BODY. **2.** The seat of the faculty of intelligence and reason : brain, mind. *Informal:* gray matter. *See* THOUGHTS. **3.** An innate capability : aptitude, aptness, bent, faculty, flair, genius, gift, instinct, knack, talent, turn. *See* ABILITY, APPROACH. **4.** One who is highest in rank or authority : boss, chief, chieftain, director, headman, hierarch, leader, master. *Slang:* honcho. ***Idiom:*** cock of the walk. *See* OVER. **5.** Someone who directs and supervises workers : boss, director, foreman, foreperson, forewoman, manager, overseer, superintendent, supervisor, taskmaster, taskmistress. *Informal:* straw boss. *Slang:* chief. *See* OVER. **6.** A mass of bubbles in or on the surface of a liquid : foam, froth, lather, spume, suds, yeast. *See* SOLID. **7.** A decisive point : climacteric, crisis, crossroad (used in plural), exigence, exigency, juncture, pass, turning point, zero hour. *See* DECIDE. **8.** A term or terms in large type introducing a text : heading, headline. *See* WORDS.
head *adjective* Having or exercising authority : chief, principal. *See* OVER.
head *verb* **1.** To have charge of (the affairs of others) : administer, administrate, direct, govern, manage, run, superintend, supervise. *See* OVER. **2.** To move (a weapon or blow, for example) in the direction of someone or something : aim, cast, direct, level, point, set[1], train, turn, zero in. *Military:* lay[1]. *See* SEEK. **3.** To proceed in a specified direction : bear, go, make, set out, strike out. *See* APPROACH.
head off *verb* To block the progress of and force to change direction : cut off, intercept. *See* ALLOW.

headache *noun*
Informal. A duty or responsibility that is a source of anxiety, worry, or hardship : burden[1], millstone, onus, tax, weight. *See* HEAVY, OVER.

header *noun*
1. *Informal.* The act of plunging suddenly downward into or as if into water : dive, nosedive, plunge, swoop. *See* ENTER. **2.** *Informal.* A sudden involuntary drop to the ground : dive, fall, nosedive, pitch, plunge, spill, tumble. *See* RISE.

heading *noun*
1. A term or terms in large type introducing a

text : head, headline. *See* WORDS. **2.** The compass direction in which a ship or an aircraft moves : bearing, course, vector. *See* APPROACH.

headline *noun*
A term or terms in large type introducing a text : head, heading. *See* WORDS.

headlong *adjective*
Characterized by unthinking boldness and haste : brash, foolhardy, harum-scarum, hasty, hotheaded, ill-considered, impetuous, improvident, impulsive, incautious, madcap, precipitant, precipitate, rash[1], reckless, slapdash, temerarious, unconsidered. *See* CAREFUL.

headman *noun*
One who is highest in rank or authority : boss, chief, chieftain, director, head, hierarch, leader, master. *Slang:* honcho. ***Idiom:*** cock of the walk. *See* OVER.

head off *verb* See **head.**

headquarters *noun*
1. A center of organization, supply, or activity : base[1], complex, station. *Military:* installation. *See* PLACE. **2.** A place of concentrated activity, influence, or importance : center, focus, heart, hub, seat. *See* EDGE.

head start *noun*
A factor conducive to superiority and success : advantage, handicap, odds, start, vantage. *See* HELP.

headstrong *adjective*
Tenaciously unwilling to yield : bullheaded, dogged, hardheaded, mulish, obstinate, pertinacious, perverse, pigheaded, stiff-necked, tenacious, willful. *See* RESIST.

headway *noun*
Forward movement : advance, advancement, furtherance, march[1], progress, progression. *See* BETTER, FORWARD.

heal *verb*
To rectify (an undesirable or unhealthy condition) : cure, remedy. *See* HEALTH.

health *noun*
The condition of being physically and mentally sound : haleness, healthiness, heartiness, soundness, wholeness. *See* HEALTH.

healthful *adjective*
1. Promoting good health : healthsome, healthy, hygienic, salubrious, salutary, wholesome. *See* HEALTH. **2.** Having good health : fit[1], hale, healthy, hearty, right, sound[2], well[2], whole, wholesome. ***Idioms:*** fit as a fiddle, hale and hearty, in fine fettle. *See* HEALTH.

healthiness *noun*
The condition of being physically and mentally sound : haleness, health, heartiness, soundness, wholeness. *See* HEALTH.

healthsome *adjective*
Promoting good health : healthful, healthy, hygienic, salubrious, salutary, wholesome. *See* HEALTH.

healthy *adjective*
1. Having good health : fit[1], hale, healthful, hearty, right, sound[2], well[2], whole, wholesome. ***Idioms:*** fit as a fiddle, hale and hearty, in fine fettle. *See* HEALTH. **2.** Promoting good health : healthful, healthsome, hygienic, salubrious, salutary, wholesome. *See* HEALTH. **3.** Notably above average in amount, size, or scope : big, considerable, extensive, good, great, large, large-scale, sizable. *Informal:* tidy. *See* BIG.

heap *noun*
1. A group of things gathered haphazardly : agglomeration, bank[1], cumulus, drift, hill, mass, mess, mound, mountain, pile, shock[2], stack, tumble. *See* ORDER. **2.** *Informal.* A great deal : abundance, mass, mountain, much, plenty, profusion, wealth, world. *Informal:* barrel, lot, pack, peck[2], pile. *Regional:* power, sight. *See* BIG. **3.** *Informal.* An indeterminately great amount or number. Often used in plural : jillion, million (often used in plural), multiplicity, ream, trillion. *Informal:* bushel, gob[1] (often used in plural), load (often used in plural), lot, oodles, passel, peck[2], scad (often used in plural), slew, wad, zillion. *See* BIG.

heap *verb* **1.** To put into a disordered pile : bank[1], drift, hill, lump[1], mound, pile (up), stack. *See* ORDER. **2.** To make or become full; put as much into as can be held : charge, fill, freight, load, pack, pile. *See* FULL. **3.** To fill to overflowing : lade, load, pile. *See* FULL. **4.** To give in great abundance : lavish, rain, shower. *See* BIG, GIVE.

hear *verb*
1. To perceive by ear, usually attentively : attend, hark, heed, listen. *Archaic:* hearken. ***Idiom:*** give (*or* lend) one's ear. *See* SOUNDS. **2.** To obtain knowledge or awareness of something not known before, as through observation or study : ascertain, determine, discover, find (out), learn. *See* TEACH.

hear of *verb* To receive (an idea) and take it into consideration : consider, entertain, think of. *See* THOUGHTS.

hearing *noun*
1. The sense by which sound is perceived : audition, ear. *See* SOUNDS. **2.** Range of audibility : earshot, sound[1]. *See* SOUNDS. **3.** A

chance to be heard : audience, audition. *See* SOUNDS. **4.** The examination and deciding upon evidence, charges, and claims in court : trial. *See* LAW.

hearken also **harken** *verb*
1. To make an effort to hear something : hark, listen. *Archaic:* list[3]. ***Idiom:*** give (*or* lend) an ear. *See* SOUNDS. **2.** *Archaic.* To perceive by ear, usually attentively : attend, hark, hear, heed, listen. ***Idiom:*** give (*or* lend) one's ear. *See* SOUNDS.

hear of *verb* See **hear.**

hearsay *noun*
Idle, often sensational and groundless talk about others : gossip, gossipry, report, rumor, talebearing, tattle, tittle-tattle, word. *Slang:* scuttlebutt. *See* WORDS.

heart *noun*
1. The circulatory organ of the body : *Slang:* ticker. *See* BODY. **2.** The seat of a person's innermost emotions and feelings : bosom, breast, soul. ***Idioms:*** bottom of one's heart, cockles of one's heart, one's heart of hearts. *See* FEELINGS. **3.** The quality of mind enabling one to face danger or hardship resolutely : braveness, bravery, courage, courageousness, dauntlessness, doughtiness, fearlessness, fortitude, gallantry, gameness, intrepidity, intrepidness, mettle, nerve, pluck, pluckiness, spirit, stoutheartedness, undauntedness, valiance, valiancy, valiantness, valor. *Informal:* spunk, spunkiness. *Slang:* gut (used in plural), gutsiness, moxie. *See* FEAR. **4.** The most central and material part : core, essence, gist, kernel, marrow, meat, nub, pith, quintessence, root[1], soul, spirit, stuff, substance. *Law:* gravamen. *See* BE. **5.** A place of concentrated activity, influence, or importance : center, focus, headquarters, hub, seat. *See* EDGE. **6.** A point of origin from which ideas or influences, for example, originate : bottom, center, core, focus, hub, quick, root[1]. *See* START.

heartache *noun*
Mental anguish or pain caused by loss or despair : grief, heartbreak, sorrow. *See* HAPPY.

heartbreak *noun*
Mental anguish or pain caused by loss or despair : grief, heartache, sorrow. *See* HAPPY.

hearten *verb*
To impart strength and confidence to : buck up, cheer (up), encourage, nerve, perk up. *See* HELP.

heartening *adjective*
Inspiring confidence or hope : cheering, encouraging, hopeful, likely, promising. *See* HELP.

heartfelt *adjective*
Devoid of any hypocrisy or pretense : genuine, hearty, honest, natural, real, sincere, true, unaffected, unfeigned, unmannered. *See* TRUE.

heartiness *noun*
The condition of being physically and mentally sound : haleness, health, healthiness, soundness, wholeness. *See* HEALTH.

heartless *adjective*
Completely lacking in compassion : callous, cold-blooded, cold-hearted, compassionless, hard, hard-boiled, hardened, hardhearted, obdurate, stonyhearted, unfeeling. *See* ATTITUDE.

hearty *adjective*
1. Devoid of any hypocrisy or pretense : genuine, heartfelt, honest, natural, real, sincere, true, unaffected, unfeigned, unmannered. *See* TRUE. **2.** Having good health : fit[1], hale, healthful, healthy, right, sound[2], well[2], whole, wholesome. ***Idioms:*** fit as a fiddle, hale and hearty, in fine fettle. *See* HEALTH.

heat *noun*
1. Intense warmth : fervor, hotness, torridity, torridness. *See* HOT. **2.** Intensity of feeling or reaction : excitation, excitement, warmth. *See* EXCITE, FEELINGS, HOT. **3.** A regular period of sexual excitement in female mammals : estrus, rut[2], season. *See* SEX. **4.** *Slang.* A member of a law-enforcement agency : bluecoat, finest, officer, patrolman, patrolwoman, peace officer, police, policeman, police officer, policewoman. *Informal:* cop, law. *Slang:* bull[1], copper, flatfoot, fuzz, gendarme, man (often uppercase). *Chiefly British:* bobby, constable, peeler. *See* LAW.

heated *adjective*
1. Marked by much heat : ardent, baking, blistering, boiling, broiling, burning, fiery, hot, red-hot, roasting, scalding, scorching, searing, sizzling, sultry, sweltering, torrid. *See* HOT. **2.** Characterized by intense emotion and activity : burning, fervid, fevered, feverish, hectic. *See* EXCITE, FEELINGS, HOT. **3.** Fired with intense feeling : ardent, blazing, burning, dithyrambic, fervent, fervid, fiery, flaming, glowing, hot-blooded, impassioned, passionate, perfervid, red-hot, scorching, torrid. *See* FEELINGS.

heave *verb*
1. To move (something) to a higher position : boost, elevate, hoist, lift, pick up, raise, rear[2], take up, uphold, uplift, upraise, uprear. *See*

RISE. **2.** To move vigorously from side to side or up and down : pitch, rock, roll, toss. *See* REPETITION. **3.** To send through the air with a motion of the hand or arm : cast, dart, dash, fling, hurl, hurtle, launch, pitch, shoot, shy[2], sling, throw, toss. *Informal:* fire. *See* MOVE. **4.** To utter in a breathless manner : gasp, pant. *See* BREATH, WORDS. **5.** To eject the contents of the stomach through the mouth : throw up, vomit. *Slang:* puke. *See* MOUTH.

heave *noun* **1.** An instance of lifting or being lifted : boost, hoist, lift. *See* RISE. **2.** An act of throwing : cast, fling, hurl, launch, pitch, shy[2], sling, throw, toss. *See* MOVE.

heaven *noun*
1. The celestial regions as seen from the earth. Often used in plural : air, firmament, sky. *Archaic:* welkin. *See* HIGH. **2.** A state of elated bliss : ecstasy, paradise, rapture, seventh heaven, transport. *Informal:* cloud nine. *See* HAPPY.

heavenly *adjective*
1. Giving great pleasure or delight : charming, delectable, delicious, delightful, enchanting, luscious. *Informal:* darling. *See* GOOD, HAPPY, LIKE. **2.** Highly pleasing, especially to the sense of taste : ambrosial, appetizing, delectable, delicious, luscious, savory, scrumptious, tasteful, tasty, toothsome. *Slang:* yummy. *See* GOOD, INGESTION. **3.** Of or relating to the heavens : celestial, empyreal. *See* PLACE. **4.** Of or relating to heaven : celestial, divine, paradisaic, paradisaical, paradisal, paradisiac, paradisiacal. *See* RELIGION. **5.** Of, from, like, or being a god or God : deific, divine, godlike, godly, holy. *See* RELIGION.

heavily *adverb*
With effort : arduously, difficultly, hard, laboriously. *See* EASY.

heaviness *noun*
The state or quality of being physically heavy : heftiness, massiveness, ponderosity, ponderousness, weight, weightiness. *Informal:* avoirdupois. *See* HEAVY.

heavy *adjective*
1. Having a relatively great weight : heavyweight, hefty, massive, ponderous, weighty. *See* HEAVY. **2.** Unwieldy or clumsy, especially due to excess weight : cumbersome, cumbrous, lumpish, lumpy, ponderous. *See* EASY, HEAVY. **3.** Having a large body, especially in girth : bulky, hefty, hulking, hulky, husky[2], stout. *See* BIG. **4.** Characterized by abundance : abundant, ample, bounteous, bountiful, copious, generous, plenitudinous, plenteous, plentiful, substantial, voluminous. *See* BIG, GIVE, RICH. **5.** Intensely sustained, especially in activity : concentrated, fierce, heightened, intense, intensive. *See* STRONG. **6.** Conveying great physical force : hard, hefty, powerful, severe. *See* BIG. **7.** Intensely violent in sustained velocity : fierce, furious, high, strong. *See* STRONG. **8.** Violently disturbed or agitated, as by storms : dirty, raging, roiled, roily, rough, rugged, stormy, tempestuous, tumultuous, turbulent, ugly, violent, wild. *See* CALM. **9.** Indulging in drink to an excessive degree : hard. *Informal:* two-fisted. *See* EXCESS. **10.** Having great consequence or weight : earnest[1], grave[2], momentous, serious, severe, weighty. *See* IMPORTANT. **11.** Having a dense or viscous consistency : gelatinous, stodgy, thick. *See* SOLID. **12.** Not readily digested because of richness : rich. *See* INGESTION. **13.** Growing profusely : dense, lush[1], luxuriant, profuse, rank[2], thick. *See* BIG. **14.** Burdened by a weighty load : heavy-laden, laden, loaded. *See* FULL. **15.** Requiring great or extreme bodily, mental, or spiritual strength : arduous, backbreaking, burdensome, demanding, difficult, effortful, exacting, exigent, formidable, hard, laborious, onerous, oppressive, rigorous, rough, severe, taxing, tough, trying, weighty. *See* HEAVY. **16.** *Slang.* Beyond the understanding of an average mind : abstruse, deep, esoteric, profound, recondite. *See* EASY, SURFACE.

heavy *noun* *Slang.* A mean, worthless character in a story or play : villain. *See* RIGHT.

heavy-handed *adjective*
1. Clumsily lacking in the ability to do or perform : awkward, bumbling, clumsy, gauche, inept, maladroit, unskillful. *See* ABILITY. **2.** Lacking fluency or gracefulness : elephantine, labored, ponderous. *See* GOOD.

heavy-hearted *adjective*
In low spirits : blue, dejected, depressed, desolate, dispirited, down, downcast, downhearted, dull, dysphoric, gloomy, low, melancholic, melancholy, sad, spiritless, tristful, unhappy, wistful. ***Idiom:*** down at (*or* in) the mouth. *See* HAPPY.

heavy-heartedness *noun*
A feeling or spell of dismally low spirits : blues, dejection, depression, despondence, despondency, doldrums, dolefulness, downheartedness, dumps, dysphoria, funk, gloom, glumness, melancholy, mope (used in plural), mournfulness, sadness, unhappiness. *See* FEELINGS, HAPPY.

heavy-laden *adjective*
Burdened by a weighty load : heavy, laden, loaded. *See* FULL.

heavyset *adjective*
Short, heavy, and solidly built : blocky, chunky, compact[1], dumpy, squat, stocky, stodgy, stubby, stumpy, thick, thickset. *See* FAT.

heavyweight *noun*
Informal. An important, influential person : character, dignitary, eminence, leader, lion, nabob, notability, notable, personage. *Informal:* big-timer, somebody, someone, VIP. *Slang:* big shot, big wheel, bigwig, muckamuck. *See* IMPORTANT.

heavyweight *adjective*
1. Having a relatively great weight : heavy, hefty, massive, ponderous, weighty. *See* HEAVY. **2.** *Informal.* Being among the leaders in one's field : blue-chip, major, major-league. *Informal:* big-league, bigtime. *See* IMPORTANT.

hebetate *verb*
To make or become less keen or responsive : dim, dull, stupefy. *See* AWARENESS.

hebetude *noun*
A deficiency in mental and physical alertness and activity : dullness, languidness, languor, lassitude, leadenness, lethargy, listlessness, sluggishness, stupor, torpidity, torpor. *See* ACTION.

hebetudinous *adjective*
1. Lacking mental and physical alertness and activity : lethargic, sluggish, stupid, stuporous, torpid. *Slang:* dopey. *See* ACTION. **2.** Lacking in intelligence : blockheaded, dense, doltish, dumb, obtuse, stupid, thickheaded, thick-witted. *Informal:* thick. *Slang:* dimwitted, dopey. *See* ABILITY.

hecatomb *noun*
One or more living creatures slain and offered to a deity as part of a religious rite : immolation, offering, sacrifice, victim. *See* RELIGION.

heckle *verb*
To torment with persistent insult or ridicule : badger, bait, bullyrag, hector, hound, taunt. *Informal:* needle, ride. ***Idiom:*** wave the red flag in front of the bull. *See* TREAT WELL.

hectic *adjective*
1. Characterized by intense emotion and activity : burning, fervid, fevered, feverish, heated. *See* EXCITE, FEELINGS, HOT. **2.** Being at a higher temperature than is normal or desirable : febrific, febrile, feverish, hot, pyretic. *See* HOT.

hector *noun*
One who is habitually cruel to smaller or weaker people : browbeater, bulldozer, bully, intimidator. *Archaic:* brave. *See* OVER.
hector *verb* **1.** To domineer or drive into compliance by the use of as threats or force, for example : bludgeon, browbeat, bulldoze, bully, bullyrag, cow, intimidate, menace, threaten. *Informal:* strong-arm. *See* OVER. **2.** To torment with persistent insult or ridicule : badger, bait, bullyrag, heckle, hound, taunt. *Informal:* needle, ride. ***Idiom:*** wave the red flag in front of the bull. *See* TREAT WELL.

hedge *noun*
The use or an instance of equivocal language : ambiguity, equivocation, equivoque, euphemism, prevarication, shuffle, tergiversation, weasel word. *Informal:* waffle. *See* CLEAR.
hedge *verb* **1.** To shut in on all sides : begird, beset, circle, compass, encircle, encompass, environ, gird, girdle, hem, ring[1], surround. *See* OPEN. **2.** To surround and advance upon : besiege, close in, enclose, envelop, hem. *See* OPEN. **3.** To use evasive or deliberately vague language : equivocate, euphemize, shuffle, tergiversate, weasel. *Informal:* pussyfoot, waffle. ***Idioms:*** beat about (*or* around) the bush, mince words. *See* CLEAR. **4.** To avoid fulfilling or answering completely : dodge, duck, evade, sidestep, skirt. *See* SEEK.

hedonic *adjective*
Characterized by or devoted to pleasure and luxury as a lifestyle : epicurean, hedonistic, sybaritic, voluptuary, voluptuous. *See* PAIN.

hedonist *noun*
A person devoted to pleasure and luxury : epicure, epicurean, sensualist, sybarite, voluptuary. *See* PAIN.

hedonistic *adjective*
Characterized by or devoted to pleasure and luxury as a lifestyle : epicurean, hedonic, sybaritic, voluptuary, voluptuous. *See* PAIN.

heebie-jeebies *noun*
Slang. A state of nervous restlessness or agitation : fidget (often used in plural), jitter (used in plural), jump (used in plural), shiver[1] (used in plural), tremble (often used in plural). *Informal:* all-overs, shake (used in plural). *Slang:* jim-jams, willies. *See* CALM, FEAR.

heed *verb*
To perceive by ear, usually attentively : attend, hark, hear, listen. *Archaic:* hearken. ***Idiom:*** give (*or* lend) one's ear. *See* SOUNDS.
heed *noun* **1.** Cautious attentiveness : care, carefulness, caution, gingerliness, heedfulness, mindfulness, regard. *See* CAREFUL. **2.** The act of noting, observing, or taking into account :

attention, cognizance, espial, mark, note, notice, observance, observation, regard, remark. *See* KNOWLEDGE, SEE.

heedful *adjective*

1. Concentrating the mental powers on something : attentive, intent, regardful. ***Idiom:*** all ears (*or* eyes). *See* EXCITE. 2. Cautiously attentive : careful, mindful, observant, watchful. *See* CAREFUL. 3. Tending toward awareness and appreciation : conscious, mindful, observant. *See* AWARENESS.

heedfulness *noun*

1. Concentration of the mental powers on something : attention, attentiveness, concentration, consideration, regardfulness. *See* EXCITE. 2. Cautious attentiveness : care, carefulness, caution, gingerliness, heed, mindfulness, regard. *See* CAREFUL.

heedless *adjective*

1. Showing no concern, attention, or regard : careless, forgetful, mindless, unconcerned, unheeding, unmindful, unobservant, unthinking. *See* CAREFUL. 2. Lacking or marked by a lack of care : careless, feckless, inattentive, irresponsible, reckless, thoughtless, unconcerned, unmindful, unthinking. *See* CAREFUL.

heedlessness *noun*

A careless, often reckless disregard for consequences : abandon, carelessness, thoughtlessness. *See* CAREFUL.

heehaw *noun*

Informal. An act of laughing : cachinnation, cackle, guffaw, laugh, laughter. *See* LAUGHTER, SOUNDS.

heehaw *verb Informal.* To express amusement, mirth, or scorn by smiling and emitting loud, inarticulate sounds : cachinnate, cackle, guffaw, laugh. ***Idioms:*** die laughing, laugh one's head off, roll in the aisles, split one's sides. *See* LAUGHTER, SOUNDS.

heel¹ *verb*

To follow closely or persistently : dog, tag, trail. *See* PRECEDE.

heel² *verb*

To depart or cause to depart from true vertical or horizontal : cant¹, incline, lean¹, list², rake², slant, slope, tilt, tip². *See* STRAIGHT.

heel *noun* Deviation from a particular direction : cant¹, grade, gradient, inclination, incline, lean¹, list², rake², slant, slope, tilt, tip². *See* RISE, STRAIGHT.

heftiness *noun*

The state or quality of being physically heavy : heaviness, massiveness, ponderosity, ponderousness, weight, weightiness. *Informal:* avoirdupois. *See* HEAVY.

hefty *adjective*

1. Having a relatively great weight : heavy, heavyweight, massive, ponderous, weighty. *See* HEAVY. 2. Having a large body, especially in girth : bulky, heavy, hulking, hulky, husky², stout. *See* BIG. 3. Conveying great physical force : hard, heavy, powerful, severe. *See* BIG.

height *noun*

1. The distance of something from a given level : altitude, elevation. *See* HIGH. 2. The highest point : apex, cap, crest, crown, peak, roof, summit, top, vertex. *See* HIGH. 3. The highest point or state : acme, apex, apogee, climax, crest, crown, culmination, meridian, peak, pinnacle, summit, top, zenith. *Informal:* payoff. *Medicine:* fastigium. *See* HIGH.

heighten *verb*

1. To make greater in intensity or severity : aggravate, deepen, enhance, intensify, redouble. *See* INCREASE. 2. To increase markedly in level or intensity, especially of sound : amplify, elevate, raise. *See* INCREASE.

heightened *adjective*

1. Intensely sustained, especially in activity : concentrated, fierce, heavy, intense, intensive. *See* STRONG. 2. Abnormally increased, especially in intensity : elevated, high, raised. *See* INCREASE.

heinous *adjective*

Disgracefully and grossly offensive : atrocious, monstrous, outrageous, scandalous, shocking. *Archaic:* enormous. *See* RIGHT.

heinousness *noun*

The quality of passing all moral bounds : atrociousness, atrocity, enormity, monstrousness. *See* GOOD.

heist *verb*

1. *Slang.* To take (another's property) without permission : filch, pilfer, purloin, snatch, steal, thieve. *Informal:* lift, swipe. *Slang:* cop, hook, nip¹, pinch, rip off, snitch. ***Idiom:*** make (*or* walk) off with. *See* CRIMES, GIVE. 2. *Slang.* To take property or possessions from (a person or company, for example) unlawfully and usually forcibly : hold up, rob, stick up. *Slang:* knock off. *See* CRIMES, GIVE.

heist *noun Slang.* The act or crime of taking another's property unlawfully and by force : holdup, robbery. *Slang:* stickup. *See* CRIMES, GIVE.

hell *noun*

Excruciating punishment : living hell, persecution, torment, torture. ***Idiom:*** tortures of the damned. *See* REWARD.

hell *verb Informal.* To behave riotously. Used with *around* : carouse, frolic, revel, riot, roister. ***Idioms:*** blow off steam, cut loose, kick over the traces, kick up one's heels, let go, let loose, make merry, make whoopee, paint the town red, raise Cain (*or* the devil *or* hell), whoop it up. *See* RESTRAINT.

hellfire *adjective*
Portending future disaster : apocalyptic, apocalyptical, baneful, dire, direful, fateful, fire-and-brimstone, grave[2], ominous, portentous, unlucky. *See* LUCK, WARN.

hell-for-leather *adverb*
Informal. In a rapid way : apace, fast, posthaste, quick, quickly. *Informal:* flat out, lickety-split, pronto. ***Idioms:*** full tilt, in a flash, in nothing flat, like a bat out of hell, like a blue streak, like a flash, like a house on fire, like a shot, like a streak, like greased lightning, like the wind, like wildfire. *See* FAST.

hell-for-leather *adjective Informal.* Characterized by great celerity : breakneck, expeditious, fast, fleet, quick, rapid, speedy, swift. ***Idiom:*** quick as a bunny (*or* wink). *See* FAST.

hellish *adjective*
Perversely bad, cruel, or wicked : devilish, diabolic, diabolical, fiendish, ghoulish, infernal, ogreish, satanic, satanical. *See* KIND.

helotry *noun*
A state of subjugation to an owner or master : bondage, enslavement, serfdom, servileness, servility, servitude, slavery, thrall, thralldom, villeinage, yoke. *See* OVER.

help *verb*
1. To give support or assistance. Also used with *out* : abet, aid, assist, boost, relieve, succor. ***Idioms:*** give (*or* lend) a hand, give a leg up. *See* HELP. **2.** To advance to a more desirable state : ameliorate, amend, better[1], improve, meliorate, upgrade. *See* HELP.

help *noun* **1.** The act or an instance of helping : abetment, aid, assist, assistance, hand, relief, succor, support. *See* HELP. **2.** A person who helps : abettor, aid, attendant, helper, reliever, succorer. *See* HELP.

helper *noun*
1. A person who helps : abettor, aid, attendant, help, reliever, succorer. *See* HELP. **2.** A person who holds a position auxiliary to another and assumes some of the superior's responsibilities : adjutant, aide, assistant, auxiliary, coadjutant, coadjutor, deputy, lieutenant, second[2]. *See* HELP.

helpful *adjective*
Affording benefit : advantageous, benefic, beneficent, beneficial, benignant, favorable, good, profitable, propitious, salutary, toward, useful. *See* HELP.

helping *noun*
An individual quantity of food : mess, portion, serving. *See* INGESTION.

helpless *adjective*
1. Devoid of help or protection : defenseless, unprotected. *See* SAFETY. **2.** Lacking power or strength : impotent, powerless. *See* ABILITY, HELP. **3.** Not capable of accomplishing anything : impotent, inadequate, incapable, ineffectual, powerless, weak. *See* ABILITY, STRONG.

helplessly *adverb*
Without regard to desire or inclination : involuntarily, perforce, willy-nilly. *See* WILLING.

helplessness *noun*
The condition or state of being incapable of accomplishing or effecting anything : impotence, inadequacy, incapability, ineffectiveness, ineffectuality, ineffectualness, inefficacy, powerlessness, uselessness. *See* AFFECT, STRONG.

helter-skelter *adjective*
Characterized by physical confusion : chaotic, confused, disordered, higgledy-piggledy, topsy-turvy, upside-down. *Informal:* mixed-up. *See* ORDER.

helter-skelter *noun* An interruption of regular procedure or of public peace : agitation, commotion, disorder, disturbance, stir[1], tumult, turbulence, turmoil, uproar. *Informal:* flap, to-do. *See* CALM, ORDER.

hem *verb*
1. To shut in on all sides : begird, beset, circle, compass, encircle, encompass, environ, gird, girdle, hedge, ring[1], surround. *See* OPEN. **2.** To surround and advance upon : besiege, close in, enclose, envelop, hedge. *See* OPEN.

henchman *noun*
One who supports and adheres to another : adherent, cohort, disciple, follower, minion, partisan, satellite, supporter. *See* OVER, PRECEDE.

henpeck *verb*
Informal. To scold or find fault with constantly : carp at, fuss at, nag, peck at, pick on. *See* PRAISE.

herald *noun*
One that indicates or announces someone or

something to come : forerunner, foreshadower, harbinger, precursor, presager. *See* FORESIGHT, SHOW.
herald *verb* To make known the presence or arrival of : announce, introduce, proclaim, usher in. *See* KNOWLEDGE, START.

herculean *adjective*
Of extraordinary size and power : behemoth, Brobdingnagian, Bunyanesque, colossal, cyclopean, elephantine, enormous, gargantuan, giant, gigantesque, gigantic, heroic, huge, immense, jumbo, mammoth, massive, massy, mastodonic, mighty, monster, monstrous, monumental, mountainous, prodigious, pythonic, stupendous, titanic, tremendous, vast. *Informal:* walloping. *Slang:* whopping. *See* BIG.

herd *verb*
To urge to move along : drive, run. *See* MOVE.

hereafter *noun*
Time that is yet to be : by-and-by, future. *Idiom:* time to come. *See* PRECEDE, TIME.

hereditary *adjective*
1. Of or from one's ancestors : ancestral, inherited, patrimonial. *See* KIN, PRECEDE. **2.** Possessed at birth : congenital, inborn, inherited, innate, native. *See* BE, NATIVE.

heretic *noun*
A person who dissents from the doctrine of an established church : dissenter, dissident, nonconformist, schismatic, sectarian, sectary, separationist, separatist. *See* RELIGION.

heretofore *adverb*
Up to this time : before, earlier, previously, yet. *See* PRECEDE.

heritage *noun*
1. Something immaterial, as a style or philosophy, that is passed from one generation to another : inheritance, legacy, tradition. *See* AFFECT. **2.** Any special privilege accorded a firstborn : birthright, inheritance, legacy, patrimony. *See* OWNED.

hermeneutic *adjective*
Serving to explain : elucidative, exegetic, explanative, explanatory, explicative, expositive, expository, hermeneutical, illustrative, interpretative, interpretive. *See* EXPLAIN.

hero *noun*
1. A person revered especially for noble courage : paladin. *See* FEAR. **2.** A famous person : celebrity, lion, luminary, name, notable, personage, personality. *Informal:* big name. *See* KNOWLEDGE.

heroic *adjective*
1. Having or showing courage : audacious, bold, brave, courageous, dauntless, doughty, fearless, fortitudinous, gallant, game, hardy, intrepid, mettlesome, plucky, stout, stouthearted, unafraid, undaunted, valiant, valorous. *Informal:* spunky. *Slang:* gutsy, gutty. *See* FEAR. **2.** Of extraordinary size and power : behemoth, Brobdingnagian, Bunyanesque, colossal, cyclopean, elephantine, enormous, gargantuan, giant, gigantesque, gigantic, herculean, huge, immense, jumbo, mammoth, massive, massy, mastodonic, mighty, monster, monstrous, monumental, mountainous, prodigious, pythonic, stupendous, titanic, tremendous, vast. *Informal:* walloping. *Slang:* whopping. *See* BIG.

heroism *noun*
The quality or state of being heroic : gallantry, prowess, valiance, valiancy, valor. *See* FEAR.

hesitancy *noun*
The act of hesitating or state of being hesitant : hesitation, indecision, indecisiveness, irresoluteness, irresolution, pause, shilly-shally, tentativeness, timidity, timidness, to-and-fro, vacillation. *See* DECIDE.

hesitant *adjective*
Given to or exhibiting hesitation : halting, indecisive, irresolute, pendulous, shilly-shally, tentative, timid, vacillant, vacillatory. *See* DECIDE.

hesitate *verb*
To be irresolute in acting or doing : dither, falter, halt[2], pause, shilly-shally, stagger, vacillate, waver, wobble. *See* DECIDE.

hesitation *noun*
The act of hesitating or state of being hesitant : hesitancy, indecision, indecisiveness, irresoluteness, irresolution, pause, shilly-shally, tentativeness, timidity, timidness, to-and-fro, vacillation. *See* DECIDE.

Hessian *noun*
A freelance fighter : adventurer, mercenary, soldier of fortune. *See* GET.

heterogeneity *noun*
The quality of being made of many different elements, forms, kinds, or individuals : diverseness, diversification, diversity, heterogeneousness, miscellaneousness, multifariousness, multiformity, multiplicity, variegation, variety, variousness. *Biology:* polymorphism. *See* SAME.

heterogeneous *adjective*
Consisting of a number of different kinds : assorted, divers, diverse, diversified, miscellaneous, mixed, motley, multifarious, multiform,

sundry, varied, variegated, various. *Biology:* polymorphic, polymorphous. *See* SAME.

heterogeneousness *noun*
The quality of being made of many different elements, forms, kinds, or individuals : diverseness, diversification, diversity, heterogeneity, miscellaneousness, multifariousness, multiformity, multiplicity, variegation, variety, variousness. *Biology:* polymorphism. *See* SAME.

hew *verb*
To bring down, as with a saw or ax : chop down, cut (down), fell[1]. *See* RISE.

hex *noun*
Something or someone believed to bring bad luck : curse, hoodoo. *Informal:* jinx. *See* LUCK.
hex *verb* To bring bad luck or evil to : curse, hoodoo. *Informal:* jinx. *See* LUCK.

hiatus *noun*
An interval during which continuity is suspended : break, gap, interim, lacuna, void. *See* CONTINUE.

hick *adjective*
Informal. Of or relating to the countryside : arcadian, bucolic, campestral, country, pastoral, provincial, rural, rustic. *See* URBAN.

hidden *adjective*
1. Concealed from view : screened, secluded, secret. *See* SHOW. **2.** Screened from the view of oncoming drivers : blind, concealed. *See* SHOW. **3.** Lying beyond what is obvious or avowed : buried, concealed, covert, obscured, ulterior. ***Idiom:*** under cover (*or* wraps). *See* SHOW.

hide[1] *verb*
1. To put or keep out of sight : bury, cache, conceal, ensconce, occult, secrete. *Slang:* plant, stash. *See* SHOW. **2.** To prevent (something) from being known : cloak, conceal, cover (up), enshroud, hush (up), mask, shroud, veil. ***Idioms:*** keep under cover, keep under wraps. *See* SHOW. **3.** To conceal in obscurity : obscure, submerge. *See* SHOW. **4.** To cut off from sight : block (out), conceal, obscure, obstruct, screen, shroud, shut off (*or* out). *See* SHOW.
hide out *verb* To shut oneself up in secrecy : *Informal:* hole up. ***Idioms:*** go underground, lay (*or* lie) low. *See* SHOW.

hide[2] *noun*
The skin of an animal : fell[3], fur, jacket, pelt[1]. *See* SURFACE.
hide *verb* To punish with blows or lashes : beat, flog, lash, thrash, whip. *Informal:* trim. *Slang:* lay into, lick. *See* ATTACK, REWARD.

hideaway *noun*
A hiding place : covert, den, hide-out, lair. *See* PLACE, SHOW.

hidebound *adjective*
Not tolerant of the beliefs or opinions of others, for example : bigoted, close-minded, illiberal, intolerant, narrow-minded. *See* ACCEPT.

hideous *adjective*
1. Extremely displeasing to the eye : ill-favored, ugly, unsightly. ***Idiom:*** ugly as sin. *See* BEAUTIFUL. **2.** Shockingly repellent : ghastly, grim, grisly, gruesome, horrible, horrid, lurid, macabre. *See* BEAUTIFUL.

hideousness *noun*
The quality or condition of being ugly : ugliness, unsightliness. *See* BEAUTIFUL.

hide-out *noun*
A hiding place : covert, den, hideaway, lair. *See* PLACE, SHOW.

hide out *verb* See **hide.**

hiding *noun*
A punishment dealt with blows or lashes : beating, flogging, lashing, thrashing, whipping. *Informal:* trimming. *Slang:* licking. *See* ATTACK, REWARD.

hierarch *noun*
One who is highest in rank or authority : boss, chief, chieftain, director, head, headman, leader, master. *Slang:* honcho. ***Idiom:*** cock of the walk. *See* OVER.

hieroglyphic *adjective*
Of or relating to representation by drawings or pictures : graphic, illustrative, photographic, pictographic, pictorial. *See* SEE.

hifalutin *adjective* See **highfalutin.**

higgle *verb*
To argue about the terms, as of a sale : bargain, dicker, haggle, huckster, negotiate, palter. *See* AGREE.

higgledy-piggledy *adjective*
Characterized by physical confusion : chaotic, confused, disordered, helter-skelter, topsy-turvy, upside-down. *Informal:* mixed-up. *See* ORDER.

high *adjective*
1. Extending to a great height : tall. *See* HIGH. **2.** Having a rather great upward projection : long[1], tall. *See* HIGH. **3.** Long past : ancient, immemorial. *See* NEW. **4.** Elevated in pitch : high-pitched, piercing, piping, shrieky, shrill, shrilly, treble. *Music:* acute. *See* HIGH, SOUNDS. **5.** Exceedingly dignified in form, tone, or style : elevated, eloquent, exalted, grand, high-flown, lofty. *See* HIGH, STYLE. **6.** Abnormally increased, especially in intensity : elevated,

heightened, raised. *See* INCREASE. **7.** Bringing a high price : costly, dear, expensive, high-priced. *See* TRANSACTIONS, VALUE. **8.** Intensely violent in sustained velocity : fierce, furious, heavy, strong. *See* STRONG. **9.** *Slang.* Stupefied, excited, or muddled with alcoholic liquor : besotted, crapulent, crapulous, drunk, drunken, inebriate, inebriated, intoxicated, sodden, tipsy. *Informal:* cock-eyed, stewed. *Slang:* blind, bombed, boozed, boozy, crocked, lit (up), loaded, looped, pickled, pixilated, plastered, potted, sloshed, smashed, soused, stinking, stinko, stoned, tight, zonked. ***Idioms:*** drunk as a skunk, half-seas over, high as a kite, in one's cups, three sheets in (*or* to) the wind. *See* DRUGS. **10.** *Slang.* Stupefied, intoxicated, or otherwise influenced by the taking of drugs : drugged. *Informal:* doped. *Slang:* hopped-up, lit (up), potted, spaced-out, stoned, turned-on, wiped-out, zonked. *See* DRUGS.

high *noun Slang.* A strong, pleasant feeling of excitement or stimulation : lift, thrill. *Informal:* wallop. *Slang:* bang, boot[1], kick. *See* EXCITE.

high-and-mighty *adjective*
Overly convinced of one's own superiority and importance : arrogant, haughty, insolent, lofty, lordly, overbearing, overweening, prideful, proud, supercilious, superior. ***Idiom:*** on one's high horse. *See* ATTITUDE.

highball *verb*
Slang. To move swiftly : bolt, bucket, bustle, dart, dash, festinate, flash, fleet, flit, fly, haste, hasten, hurry, hustle, pelt[2], race, rocket, run, rush, sail, scoot, scour[2], shoot, speed, sprint, tear[1], trot, whirl, whisk, whiz, wing, zip, zoom. *Informal:* hotfoot, rip. *Slang:* barrel. *Chiefly British:* nip[1]. ***Idioms:*** get a move on, get cracking, go like lightning, go like the wind, hotfoot it, make haste, make time, make tracks, run like the wind, shake a leg, step (*or* jump) on it. *See* MOVE.

highborn *adjective*
Of high birth or social position : aristocratic, blue-blooded, elite, highbred, noble, patrician, thoroughbred, upper-class, wellborn. *Informal:* upper-crust. *See* OVER.

highbred *adjective*
1. Of pure breeding stock : full-blooded, pure-blood, pureblooded, purebred, thoroughbred. *See* CLEAN. **2.** Of high birth or social position : aristocratic, blue-blooded, elite, highborn, noble, patrician, thoroughbred, upper-class, wellborn. *Informal:* upper-crust. *See* OVER.

highbrow *adjective*
Informal. Appealing to or engaging the intellect : cerebral, intellectual, sophisticated, thoughtful. *See* THOUGHTS.

higher *adjective*
1. Being at a height or level above another : superior, upper. *See* HIGH. **2.** Being at a rank above another : senior, superior. *See* OVER.

higher-up *noun*
Informal. One who stands above another in rank : better[1], elder, senior, superior. *See* OVER.

highest *adjective*
1. Of, being, located at, or forming the top : loftiest, top, topmost, upmost, uppermost. *See* HIGH. **2.** Preeminent in rank or position : top, top-drawer. *See* OVER.

highfalutin or **hifalutin** also **highfaluting** *adjective*
Informal. Characterized by an exaggerated show of dignity or self-importance : grandiose, hoity-toity, pompous, pretentious, puffed-up, puffy, self-important. *See* PLAIN.

highfaluting *adjective* See **highfalutin.**

high-flown *adjective*
1. Exceedingly dignified in form, tone, or style : elevated, eloquent, exalted, grand, high, lofty. *See* HIGH, STYLE. **2.** Characterized by language that is elevated and sometimes pompous in style : aureate, bombastic, declamatory, flowery, fustian, grandiloquent, high-sounding, magniloquent, orotund, overblown, rhetorical, sonorous, swollen. *See* PLAIN, STYLE, WORDS.

high-grade *adjective*
Well above average : good, nice. *See* GOOD, ABILITY.

high-hat *verb*
Informal. To treat in a superciliously indulgent manner : condescend, patronize. ***Idiom:*** speak (*or* talk) down to. *See* ATTITUDE, OVER, RESPECT, RISE.

high-hat *adjective Informal.* Characteristic of or resembling a snob : elitist, snobbish, snobby. *Informal:* snooty, stuck-up, uppish, uppity. *See* ATTITUDE, SELF-LOVE.

highjack *verb* See **hijack.**

high jinks *noun*
Annoying yet harmless, usually playful acts : devilry, deviltry, diablerie, impishness, mischief, mischievousness, prankishness, rascality, roguery, roguishness, tomfoolery. *Informal:* shenanigan (often used in plural). *See* GOOD.

highlight *verb*
To accord emphasis to : accent, accentuate,

emphasize, feature, italicize, play up, point up, stress, underline, underscore. *See* IMPORTANT.

highly *adverb*
To a high degree : awfully, dreadfully, eminently, exceedingly, exceptionally, extra, extremely, greatly, most, notably, very. *Informal:* awful. *Chiefly Regional:* mighty. *See* BIG.

high-minded *adjective*
Being on a high intellectual or moral level : elevated, moral, noble. *See* HIGH.

high-pitched *adjective*
Elevated in pitch : high, piercing, piping, shrieky, shrill, shrilly, treble. *Music:* acute. *See* HIGH, SOUNDS.

high-priced *adjective*
Bringing a high price : costly, dear, expensive, high. *See* TRANSACTIONS, VALUE.

high-ranking *adjective*
Raised to or occupying a high position or rank : august, elevated, exalted, grand, lofty. *See* RISE.

high sign *noun*
Informal. An expressive, meaningful bodily movement : gesticulation, gesture, indication, motion, sign, signal. *See* EXPRESS.

high-sounding *adjective*
Characterized by language that is elevated and sometimes pompous in style : aureate, bombastic, declamatory, flowery, fustian, grandiloquent, high-flown, magniloquent, orotund, overblown, rhetorical, sonorous, swollen. *See* PLAIN, STYLE, WORDS.

high-spirited *adjective*
1. Very brisk, alert, and full of high spirits : animated, bouncy, chipper, dashing, lively, pert, spirited, vivacious. *Informal:* peppy. ***Idioms:*** bright-eyed and bushy-tailed, full of life. *See* ACTION. **2.** Full of or characterized by a lively, emphatic, eager quality : fiery, mettlesome, peppery, spirited, vibrant. *Informal:* snappy. *See* ACTION, FEELINGS.

hightail *verb*
Slang. To leave hastily : bolt, get out, run. *Informal:* clear out, get, hotfoot, skedaddle. *Slang:* scram, vamoose. ***Idioms:*** beat it, hightail it, hotfoot it, make tracks. *See* APPROACH.

highway *noun*
A course affording passage from one place to another : avenue, boulevard, drive, expressway, freeway, path, road, roadway, route, street, superhighway, thoroughfare, thruway, turnpike, way. *See* MOVE, OPEN.

highwayman *noun*
A person who steals : bandit, burglar, housebreaker, larcener, larcenist, pilferer, purloiner, robber, stealer, thief. *See* CRIMES.

hijack also **highjack** *verb*
Informal. To compel by pressure or threats : blackjack, coerce, dragoon, force. *Informal:* strong-arm. *See* PERSUASION.

hike *verb*
1. To travel about or journey on foot : backpack, march[1], peregrinate, traipse, tramp, trek. *See* MOVE. **2.** To increase in amount : boost, jack (up), jump, raise, up. *See* INCREASE.
hike *noun* **1.** The act of increasing or rising : aggrandizement, amplification, augment, augmentation, boost, buildup, enlargement, escalation, growth, increase, jump, multiplication, proliferation, raise, rise, swell, upsurge, upswing, upturn. *See* INCREASE. **2.** The amount by which something is increased : advance, boost, increase, increment, jump, raise, rise. *See* INCREASE.

hilarious *adjective*
Extremely funny : priceless, sidesplitting. *Informal:* killing, rich. *See* LAUGHTER.

hilarity *noun*
A state of joyful exuberance : blitheness, blithesomeness, gaiety, glee, gleefulness, jocoseness, jocosity, jocularity, jocundity, jolliness, jollity, joviality, lightheartedness, merriment, merriness, mirth, mirthfulness. *See* LAUGHTER.

hill *noun*
1. A natural land elevation : eminence, prominence, rise. *See* HIGH. **2.** A group of things gathered haphazardly : agglomeration, bank[1], cumulus, drift, heap, mass, mess, mound, mountain, pile, shock[2], stack, tumble. *See* ORDER.
hill *verb* To put into a disordered pile : bank[1], drift, heap, lump[1], mound, pile (up), stack. *See* ORDER.

hind *adjective*
Located in the rear : back, hindmost, posterior, postern, rear[1]. *Nautical:* after. *See* PRECEDE.

hinder *verb*
To interfere with the progress of : bog (down), encumber, hold back, impede, obstruct. ***Idiom:*** get in the way of. *See* HELP, OPEN.

hindermost *adjective*
Bringing up the rear : endmost, hindmost, last[1], lattermost, rearmost. *See* START.

hindmost *adjective*
1. Located in the rear : back, hind, posterior, postern, rear[1]. *Nautical:* after. *See* PRECEDE.
2. Bringing up the rear : endmost, hindermost, last[1], lattermost, rearmost. *See* START.

hindrance *noun*
Something that impedes or prevents entry or passage : bar, barricade, barrier, block, blockage, clog, hamper, hurdle, impediment, obstacle, obstruction, snag, stop, traverse, wall. *See* HELP, OPEN.

hinge on or **upon** *verb*
To be determined by or contingent on something unknown, uncertain, or changeable : depend on (*or* upon), hang on, hang upon, rest on (*or* upon), turn on, turn upon. *See* START.

hint *noun*
1. A subtle quality underlying or felt to underlie a situation, action, or person : implication, inkling, suspicion, undercurrent, undertone. *See* SHOW, SUGGEST. **2.** A subtle pointing out : clue, cue, intimation, suggestion. *See* KNOWLEDGE, SUGGEST. **3.** A slight amount or indication : breath, dash, ghost, hair, intimation, semblance, shade, shadow, soupçon, streak, suggestion, suspicion, taste, tinge, touch, trace, whiff, whisper. *Informal:* whisker. *See* BIG, SHOW.
hint *verb* **1.** To convey an idea by indirect, subtle means : imply, insinuate, intimate[2], suggest. ***Idiom:*** drop a hint. *See* SHOW, SUGGEST. **2.** To try to obtain something, usually by subtleness and cunning : angle[1], fish. *See* ASK.

hip *adjective*
Slang. Marked by comprehension, cognizance, and perception : alive, awake, aware, cognizant, sensible, sentient, wise[1]. ***Idiom:*** on to. *See* KNOWLEDGE.

hire *verb*
1. To obtain the use or services of : employ, engage, retain, take on. ***Idiom:*** put on the payroll. *See* GET, WORK. **2.** To engage the temporary use of (something) for a fee : charter, lease, rent[1]. *See* GET, TRANSACTIONS. **3.** To give temporary use of in return for payment. Also used with *out* : lease, let, rent[1]. *See* TRANSACTIONS.
hire *noun* **1.** The act of employing for wages : employment, engagement. *See* GET, WORK. **2.** The state of being employed : employ, employment. *See* WORK. **3.** Payment for work done : compensation, earnings, emolument, fee, pay, remuneration, salary, stipend, wage. *See* PAY. **4.** *Informal.* One who is employed by another : employee, hireling, jobholder, worker. *Informal:* hired hand. *See* OVER, WORK.

hired *adjective*
Having a job : employed, jobholding, retained, working. *See* WORK.

hired hand *noun*
Informal. One who is employed by another : employee, hireling, jobholder, worker. *Informal:* hire. *See* OVER, WORK.

hireling *noun*
One who is employed by another : employee, jobholder, worker. *Informal:* hire, hired hand. *See* OVER, WORK.

hirer *noun*
One that employs persons for wages : employer. *See* OVER, WORK.

hirsute *adjective*
Covered with hair : fleecy, furry, fuzzy, hairy, pilose, woolly. *See* SMOOTH.

hiss *noun*
Any of various derisive sounds of disapproval : boo, catcall, hoot. *Slang:* bird, Bronx cheer, raspberry, razz. *See* SOUNDS.
hiss *verb* To make a sharp sibilant sound : fizz, fizzle, sibilate, sizzle, swish, whiz, whoosh. *See* SOUNDS.

historic *adjective*
Having great significance : big, consequential, considerable, important, large, material, meaningful, monumental, significant, substantial. *See* IMPORTANT.

history *noun*
1. A recounting of past events : account, chronicle, description, narration, narrative, report, statement, story, version. *See* WORDS. **2.** A chronological record of past events : annals, chronicle. *See* HAPPEN, WORDS. **3.** Past events surrounding a person or thing : background, past. *See* HAPPEN.

histrionic *adjective*
1. Of or relating to drama or the theater : dramatic, dramaturgic, dramaturgical, histrionical, theatric, theatrical, thespian. *See* PERFORMING ARTS. **2.** Suggesting drama or a stage performance, as in emotionality or suspense : dramatic, histrionical, melodramatic, sensational, spectacular, theatric, theatrical. *See* EXCITE, STYLE, SURPRISE.

histrionical *adjective*
1. Of or relating to drama or the theater : dramatic, dramaturgic, dramaturgical, histrionic, theatric, theatrical, thespian. *See* PERFORMING ARTS. **2.** Suggesting drama or a stage performance, as in emotionality or suspense : dramatic, histrionic, melodramatic, sensational, spectacular, theatric, theatrical. *See* EXCITE, STYLE, SURPRISE.

histrionics *noun*
Overemotional exaggerated behavior calculated for effect : dramatics, melodramatics, theatri-

cal (used in plural), theatrics. *See* FEELINGS, STYLE.

hit *verb*
1. To deliver a powerful blow to suddenly and sharply : bash, catch, clout, knock, pop[1], slam, slog, slug[3], smash, smite, sock, strike, swat, thwack, whack, wham, whop. *Informal:* biff, bop, clip[1], wallop. *Slang:* belt, conk, paste. ***Idioms:*** let someone have it, sock it to someone. *See* ATTACK, STRIKE. **2.** To enter a person's mind : occur, strike. ***Idiom:*** cross one's mind. *See* HAPPEN. **3.** *Informal.* To come upon, especially suddenly or unexpectedly : catch, hit on (*or* upon), surprise, take. *See* SURPRISE.
hit back *verb* To return like for like, especially to return an unfriendly or hostile action with a similar one : counter, reciprocate, retaliate, retort, strike back. *See* ATTACK, FORGIVENESS.
hit on (or **upon**) *verb* **1.** To come upon, especially suddenly or unexpectedly : catch, surprise, take. *Informal:* hit. *See* SURPRISE. **2.** *Informal.* To reach (a goal or objective) : arrive at, attain, come to, gain, get to. *See* START.
hit *noun* **1.** A sudden sharp, powerful stroke : bang, blow[2], clout, crack, lick, pound, slug[3], sock, swat, thwack, welt, whack, wham, whop. *Informal:* bash, biff, bop, clip[1], wallop. *Slang:* belt, conk, paste. *See* ATTACK, STRIKE. **2.** A dazzling, often sudden instance of success : sleeper. *Informal:* smash, smash hit, ten-strike, wow. *Slang:* boff, boffo, boffola. *See* THRIVE. **3.** *Slang.* An inhalation, as of a cigar, pipe, or cigarette : drag, draw, puff, pull. *See* BREATH. **4.** *Slang.* The crime of murdering someone : blood, homicide, killing, murder. *See* HELP.

hit back *verb* See **hit.**

hitch *verb*
1. To walk in a lame way : halt[2], hobble, limp. *See* MOVE. **2.** *Slang.* To join or be joined in marriage : espouse, marry, mate, wed. ***Idiom:*** tie the knot. *See* MARRIAGE.
hitch *noun* **1.** A term of service, as in the military or in prison : stretch, time, tour. *See* TIME. **2.** A limited, often assigned period of activity, duty, or opportunity : bout, go, inning (often used in plural), shift, spell[3], stint, stretch, time, tour, trick, turn, watch. *See* TIME.

hit on or **upon** *verb* See **hit.**

hit-or-miss *adjective*
Having no particular pattern, purpose, organization, or structure : chance, desultory, haphazard, indiscriminate, random, spot, unplanned. *See* PLANNED.

hive *verb*
To bring together so as to increase in mass or number : accrue, accumulate, agglomerate, aggregate, amass, collect[1], cumulate, garner, gather, pile up, roll up. *See* COLLECT.

hoard *noun*
A supply stored or hidden for future use : backlog, cache, inventory, nest egg, reserve, reservoir, stock, stockpile, store, treasure. *Slang:* stash. *See* COLLECT.
hoard *verb* To store up (supplies or money), usually well beyond one's needs : squirrel (away), stockpile, treasure. *Slang:* stash. *See* COLLECT, GIVE.

hoarse *adjective*
1. Low and grating in sound : croaking, croaky, gruff, husky[1]. *See* SOUNDS. **2.** Disagreeable to the sense of hearing : dry, grating, harsh, jarring, rasping, raspy, raucous, rough, scratchy, squawky, strident. *See* SOUNDS.

hoary *adjective*
Belonging to, existing, or occurring in times long past : age-old, ancient, antediluvian, antiquated, antique, archaic, old, olden, old-time, timeworn, venerable. ***Idioms:*** old as Methuselah, old as the hills. *See* NEW.

hobble *verb*
1. To walk in a lame way : halt[2], hitch, limp. *See* MOVE. **2.** To restrict the activity or free movement of : chain, fetter, hamper, hamstring, handcuff, leash, manacle, shackle, tie, trammel. *Informal:* hog-tie. *See* FREE, HELP.
hobble *noun* Something that physically confines the legs or arms : bond, chain (used in plural), fetter, handcuff (often used in plural), iron (used in plural), manacle, restraint, shackle. *Archaic:* gyve. *See* FREE.

hobnob *verb*
To be with as a companion : associate, consort, fraternize, hang around, run (around), troop. *Slang:* hang out. ***Idiom:*** rub elbows (*or* shoulders) . *See* NEAR.

hock *verb*
Slang. To give or deposit as a pawn : hypothecate, mortgage, pawn[1], pledge. *See* TRANSACTIONS.

hocus-pocus *noun*
Esoteric, formulaic, and often incomprehensible speech relating to the occult : abracadabra, gibberish, mumbo jumbo. *See* CLEAR, SUPERNATURAL, WORDS.

hodgepodge *noun*
A collection of various things : assortment, conglomeration, gallimaufry, jumble, medley, mélange, miscellany, mishmash, mixed bag,

mixture, olio, patchwork, potpourri, salmagundi, variety. *Slang:* grab bag. *See* COLLECT.

hoggish *adjective*
Wanting to eat or drink more than one can reasonably consume : edacious, gluttonous, greedy, piggish, ravenous, voracious. *See* DESIRE, INGESTION.

hog-tie also **hogtie** *verb*
Informal. To restrict the activity or free movement of : chain, fetter, hamper, hamstring, handcuff, hobble, leash, manacle, shackle, tie, trammel. *See* FREE, HELP.

hoi polloi *noun*
The common people : common (used in plural), commonality, commonalty, commoner (used in plural), crowd, mass (used in plural), mob, pleb (used in plural), plebeian (used in plural), populace, public, ruck[1], third estate. *See* OVER.

hoist *verb*
To move (something) to a higher position : boost, elevate, heave, lift, pick up, raise, rear[2], take up, uphold, uplift, upraise, uprear. *See* RISE.
hoist *noun* An instance of lifting or being lifted : boost, heave, lift. *See* RISE.

hoity-toity *adjective*
Characterized by an exaggerated show of dignity or self-importance : grandiose, pompous, pretentious, puffed-up, puffy, self-important. *Informal:* highfalutin. *See* PLAIN.

hold *verb*
1. To put one's arms around affectionately : clasp, embrace, enfold, hug, press, squeeze. *Slang:* clinch. *Archaic:* bosom, clip[2], embosom. *See* TOUCH. **2.** To sustain the weight of : bear, carry, support, uphold. *See* SUPPORT. **3.** To keep in custody : detain. *See* FREE, LAW. **4.** To compel, as the attention, interest, or imagination, of : arrest, catch up, enthrall, fascinate, grip, mesmerize, rivet, spellbind, transfix. *Slang:* grab. *See* EXCITE. **5.** To be filled by : contain, have. *See* INCLUDE. **6.** To have the room or capacity for : accommodate, contain. *See* FULL. **7.** To have and maintain in one's possession : hold back, keep, keep back, reserve, retain, withhold. *See* KEEP. **8.** To have at one's disposal : boast, command, enjoy, have, possess. *See* OWNED. **9.** To have the use or benefit of : enjoy, have, possess. *See* OWNED. **10.** To control, restrict, or arrest : bit[2], brake, bridle, check, constrain, curb, hold back, hold down, hold in, inhibit, keep, keep back, pull in, rein (back, in, *or* up), restrain. *See* RESTRAINT. **11.** To keep at one's disposal : have, own, possess, retain. *See* KEEP. **12.** To have an opinion : believe, consider, deem, opine, think. *Informal:* figure, judge. ***Idiom:*** be of the opinion. *See* OPINION. **13.** To put into words positively and with conviction : affirm, allege, argue, assert, asseverate, aver, avouch, avow, claim, contend, declare, maintain, say, state. ***Idiom:*** have it. *See* AFFIRM. **14.** To view in a certain way : believe, feel, sense, think. *See* OPINION. **15.** To prove valid under scrutiny. Also used with *up* : prove out, stand up. *Informal:* wash. ***Idioms:*** hold water, pass muster, ring true. *See* TRUE. **16.** To organize and carry out (an activity) : give, have, stage. *See* CONTROL, PLANNED.

hold back *verb* **1.** To have and maintain in one's possession : hold, keep, keep back, reserve, retain, withhold. *See* KEEP. **2.** To interfere with the progress of : bog (down), encumber, hinder, impede, obstruct. ***Idiom:*** get in the way of. *See* HELP, OPEN. **3.** To hold (something requiring an outlet) in check : burke, choke (back), gag, hold down, hush (up), muffle, quench, repress, smother, squelch, stifle, strangle, suppress, throttle. *Informal:* sit on (*or* upon). *See* RESTRAINT. **4.** To control, restrict, or arrest : bit[2], brake, bridle, check, constrain, curb, hold, hold down, hold in, inhibit, keep, keep back, pull in, rein (back, in, *or* up), restrain. *See* RESTRAINT.

hold down *verb* **1.** To hold (something requiring an outlet) in check : burke, choke (back), gag, hold back, hush (up), muffle, quench, repress, smother, squelch, stifle, strangle, suppress, throttle. *Informal:* sit on (*or* upon). *See* RESTRAINT. **2.** To control, restrict, or arrest : bit[2], brake, bridle, check, constrain, curb, hold, hold back, hold in, inhibit, keep, keep back, pull in, rein (back, in, *or* up), restrain. *See* RESTRAINT.

hold in *verb* To control, restrict, or arrest : bit[2], brake, bridle, check, constrain, curb, hold, hold back, hold down, inhibit, keep, keep back, pull in, rein (back, in, *or* up), restrain. *See* RESTRAINT.

hold off *verb* **1.** To put off until a later time : adjourn, defer[1], delay, hold up, postpone, remit, shelve, stay[1], suspend, table, waive. *Informal:* wait. ***Idiom:*** put on ice. *See* DO. **2.** To hold oneself back : abstain, forbear, keep, refrain, withhold. *See* RESTRAINT.

hold out *verb* To be in existence or in a certain state for an indefinitely long time : abide, continue, endure, go on, last[2], persist, remain, stay[1]. *See* CONTINUE.

hold up *verb* **1.** To put off until a later time : adjourn, defer[1], delay, hold off, postpone, remit, shelve, stay[1], suspend, table, waive. *Informal:* wait. ***Idiom:*** put on ice. *See* DO. **2.** To cause to be later or slower than expected or desired : delay, detain, hang up, lag, retard, set back, slow (down *or* up), stall[2]. *See* HELP, TIME. **3.** To take property or possessions from (a person or company, for example) unlawfully and usually forcibly : rob, stick up. *Slang:* heist, knock off. *See* CRIMES, GIVE. **4.** To withstand stress or difficulty : bear up, endure, stand up. *See* CONTINUE.

hold with *verb* To be favorably disposed toward : approve, countenance, favor. *Informal:* go for. ***Idiom:*** take kindly to. *See* PRAISE.

hold *noun* **1.** An act or means of holding something : clasp, clench, clutch[1], grasp, grip. *Sports:* grapple. *See* KEEP. **2.** A strong or powerful influence : grasp, grip. *See* AFFECT. **3.** Firm control : grasp, grip. *See* CONTROL. **4.** Intellectual hold : apprehension, comprehension, grasp, grip, understanding. *Informal:* savvy. *See* KNOWLEDGE.

hold back *verb* See **hold.**

hold down *verb* See **hold.**

holder *noun*

A person who has legal title to property : master, owner, possessor, proprietor. *See* OWNED.

hold in *verb* See **hold.**

holding *noun*

Something, as land and assets, legally possessed. Used in plural : estate, possession (used in plural), property. *See* LAW, OWNED.

hold off *verb* See **hold.**

hold out *verb* See **hold.**

holdup *noun*

1. The condition or fact of being made late or slow : delay, detainment, lag, retardation. *See* HELP, TIME. **2.** The act or crime of taking another's property unlawfully and by force : robbery. *Slang:* heist, stickup. *See* CRIMES, GIVE.

hold up *verb* See **hold.**

hold with *verb* See **hold.**

hole *noun*

1. A space in an otherwise solid mass : cavity, hollow, pocket, vacuity, void. *See* CONVEX. **2.** An opening, especially in a solid structure : breach, break, gap, perforation, rupture. *See* OPEN. **3.** An open space allowing passage : aperture, mouth, opening, orifice, outlet, vent. *See* OPEN. **4.** A place used as an animal's dwelling : burrow, den, lair. *See* PROTECTION. **5.** An ugly, squalid dwelling : hovel, hut, shack, shanty. *See* GOOD, RICH. **6.** A difficult, often embarrassing situation or condition : box[1], corner, deep water, difficulty, dilemma, Dutch, fix, hot spot, hot water, jam, plight[1], predicament, quagmire, scrape, soup, trouble. *Informal:* bind, pickle, spot. *See* EASY.

hole *verb* To make a hole or other opening in : breach, break (through), gap, perforate, pierce, puncture. *See* OPEN.

hole up *verb* *Informal.* To shut oneself up in secrecy : hide out. ***Idioms:*** go underground, lay (*or* lie) low. *See* SHOW.

hole up *verb* See **hole.**

holiday *noun*

Chiefly British. A regularly scheduled period spent away from work or duty, often in recreation : furlough, leave[2], vacation. *See* WORK.

holiness *noun*

The quality of being holy or sacred : blessedness, sacredness, sacrosanctity, sanctity. *See* RELIGION.

holler *verb*

To speak or say very loudly or with a shout : bawl, bellow, bluster, call, clamor, cry, halloo, roar, shout, vociferate, whoop, yawp, yell. *See* SOUNDS.

holler *noun* A loud cry : call, halloo, shout, yell. *See* SOUNDS.

hollow *adjective*

1. Curving inward : cavernous, concave, indented, sunken. *See* CONVEX. **2.** Lacking value, use, or substance : empty, idle, otiose, vacant, vain. *See* FULL.

hollow *noun* **1.** A space in an otherwise solid mass : cavity, hole, pocket, vacuity, void. *See* CONVEX. **2.** An area sunk below its surroundings : basin, concavity, depression, dip, pit[1], sag, sink, sinkhole. *See* CONVEX.

hollow-eyed *adjective*

Pale and exhausted, as because of worry or sleeplessness : careworn, drawn, gaunt, haggard, wan, worn. *See* TIRED.

hollowness *noun*

1. Total lack of ideas, meaning, or substance : barrenness, blankness, emptiness, inanity, vacancy, vacuity, vacuousness. *See* FULL. **2.** A desolate sense of loss : blankness, desolation, emptiness, vacuum, void. *See* FULL.

holy *adjective*

1. Of, from, like, or being a god or God : deific, divine, godlike, godly, heavenly. *See* RELIGION. **2.** In the service or worship of God or a god : divine, religious, sacred. *See* RELIGION. **3.** Regarded with particular reverence or respect : blessed, hallowed, sacred, sacrosanct. *See* RELIGION, RESPECT. **4.** Deeply concerned with God and the beliefs and practice of religion : devotional, devout, godly, pietistic, pietistical, pious, prayerful, religious, saintly. *See* RELIGION.

homage *noun*
Great respect or high public esteem accorded as a right or as due : deference, honor, obeisance. *See* RESPECT.

home *noun*
1. A building or shelter where one lives : abode, domicile, dwelling, habitation, house, lodging (often used in plural), place, residence. *Chiefly British:* dig (used in plural). *See* PROTECTION. **2.** The natural environment of an animal or plant : habitat, haunt, stamping ground. *See* TERRITORY. **3.** An institution that provides care and shelter : asylum, hospice, hospital, shelter. *See* PROTECTION.
home *adjective* **1.** Of or relating to the family or household : domestic, familial, family, homely, household. *See* KIN, GROUP. **2.** Of, from, or within a country's own territory : domestic, internal, national, native. *See* NATIVE.

homely *adjective*
1. Not handsome or beautiful : plain, unattractive, uncomely, unlovely. ***Idioms:*** not much for looks, not much to look at, short on looks. *See* BEAUTIFUL. **2.** Of a plain and unsophisticated nature : artless, homespun, natural, rustic, unadorned, unpolished. *See* PLAIN. **3.** Of or relating to the family or household : domestic, familial, family, home, household. *See* KIN, GROUP.

homespun *adjective*
Of a plain and unsophisticated nature : artless, homely, natural, rustic, unadorned, unpolished. *See* PLAIN.

homicidal *adjective*
Eager for bloodshed : bloodthirsty, bloody, bloody-minded, cutthroat, murderous, sanguinary, sanguineous, slaughterous. *See* HELP.

homicide *noun*
1. The crime of murdering someone : blood, killing, murder. *Slang:* hit. *See* HELP. **2.** One who murders another : butcher, cutthroat, killer, manslayer, massacrer, murderer, murderess, slaughterer, slayer, triggerman. *See* HELP.

hominoid *adjective*
Resembling a human being : anthropoid, anthropomorphic, anthropomorphous, humanoid, manlike. *See* CULTURE.

homo *noun*
A member of the human race : being, body, creature, human, human being, individual, life, man, mortal, party, person, personage, soul. *See* BEINGS.

homophile *adjective*
Of, relating to, or having a sexual orientation to members of one's own sex : gay, homosexual, lesbian. *See* SEX.

Homo sapiens *noun*
The human race : earth, flesh, humanity, humankind, man, mankind, universe, world. *See* CULTURE.

homosexual *adjective*
Of, relating to, or having a sexual orientation to members of one's own sex : gay, homophile, lesbian. *See* SEX.

honcho *noun*
Slang. One who is highest in rank or authority : boss, chief, chieftain, director, head, headman, hierarch, leader, master. ***Idiom:*** cock of the walk. *See* OVER.

hone[1] *verb*
To give a sharp edge to : acuminate, edge, sharpen, whet. *See* SHARP.

hone[2] *verb*
Informal. To have a strong longing for : ache, covet, desire, hanker, long[2], pant, pine, want, wish, yearn. *See* DESIRE.

honest *adjective*
1. Having or marked by uprightness in principle and action : good, honorable, incorruptible, righteous, true, upright, upstanding. *Informal:* straight-shooting. ***Idiom:*** on the up-and-up (*or* up and up). *See* HONEST. **2.** Manifesting honesty and directness, especially in speech : candid, direct, downright, forthright, frank, ingenuous, man-to-man, open, plainspoken, straight, straightforward, straight-out, unreserved. *Informal:* straight-from-the-shoulder, straight-shooting. *See* CLEAR, SHOW. **3.** Devoid of any hypocrisy or pretense : genuine, heartfelt, hearty, natural, real, sincere, true, unaffected, unfeigned, unmannered. *See* TRUE.

honesty *noun*
1. The quality of being honest : honor, honorableness, incorruptibility, integrity, upstandingness. *See* HONEST. **2.** Moral or ethical strength : character, fiber, integrity, principle. *See* STRONG.

honey *noun*
A person who is much loved : beloved, darling, dear, love, minion, precious, sweet, sweetheart,

truelove. *Informal:* sweetie. *Idiom:* light of one's life. *See* LOVE.

honey *verb* **1.** To make superficially more acceptable or appealing : candy, gild, sugar, sugarcoat, sweeten. *See* LIKE. **2.** To compliment excessively and ingratiatingly : adulate, blandish, butter up, flatter, slaver. *Informal:* soft-soap, sweet-talk. *See* PRAISE. **3.** To persuade or try to persuade by gentle persistent urging or flattery : blandish, cajole, coax, wheedle. *Informal:* soft-soap, sweet-talk. *See* PERSUASION.

honky-tonk *noun*

Slang. A disreputable or run-down bar or restaurant : *Slang:* dive, joint. *See* GOOD.

honor *noun*

1. Great respect or high public esteem accorded as a right or as due : deference, homage, obeisance. *See* RESPECT. **2.** A feeling of deference, approval, and liking : account, admiration, appreciation, consideration, esteem, estimation, favor, regard, respect. *See* RESPECT. **3.** A person's high standing among others : dignity, good name, good report, prestige, reputation, repute, respect, status. *See* RESPECT. **4.** Recognition of achievement or superiority or a sign of this : accolade, distinction, kudos, laurel (often used in plural). *See* RESPECT. **5.** The quality of being honest : honesty, honorableness, incorruptibility, integrity, upstandingness. *See* HONEST.

honor *verb* **1.** To have a high opinion of : admire, consider, esteem, regard, respect, value. *Idioms:* look up to, think highly (*or* much *or* well) of. *See* PRAISE. **2.** To pay tribute or homage to : acclaim, celebrate, eulogize, exalt, extol, glorify, hail[2], laud, magnify, panegyrize, praise. *Idiom:* sing someone's praises. *See* PRAISE. **3.** To cause to be eminent or recognized : distinguish, elevate, ennoble, exalt, signalize. *See* RESPECT. **4.** To lend dignity or honor to by an act or favor : dignify, grace. *See* BEAUTIFUL.

honorable *adjective*

1. Deserving honor, respect, or admiration : admirable, commendable, creditable, deserving, estimable, exemplary, laudable, meritorious, praiseworthy, reputable, respectable, worthy. *See* GOOD, PRAISE, RESPECT, VALUE.
2. Having or marked by uprightness in principle and action : good, honest, incorruptible, righteous, true, upright, upstanding. *Informal:* straight-shooting. *Idiom:* on the up-and-up (*or* up and up). *See* HONEST.

honorableness *noun*

The quality of being honest : honesty, honor, incorruptibility, integrity, upstandingness. *See* HONEST.

honorarium *noun*

Something given in return for a service or accomplishment : accolade, award, guerdon, plum, premium, prize[1], reward. *Idiom:* token of appreciation (*or* esteem). *See* REWARD.

hood *noun*

1. *Slang.* A person who treats others violently and roughly, especially for hire : hoodlum, ruffian, thug, tough. *Informal:* hooligan. *Slang:* goon, gorilla. *See* ATTACK, CRIMES. **2.** *Slang.* A rough, violent person who engages in destructive actions : hoodlum, mug, roughneck, rowdy, ruffian, tough. *Informal:* toughie. *Slang:* punk. *See* ATTACK, CRIMES.

hoodlum *noun*

1. A person who treats others violently and roughly, especially for hire : ruffian, thug, tough. *Informal:* hooligan. *Slang:* goon, gorilla, hood. *See* ATTACK, CRIMES. **2.** A rough, violent person who engages in destructive actions : mug, roughneck, rowdy, ruffian, tough. *Informal:* toughie. *Slang:* hood, punk. *See* ATTACK, CRIMES.

hoodoo *noun*

Something or someone believed to bring bad luck : curse, hex. *Informal:* jinx. *See* LUCK.

hoodoo *verb* To bring bad luck or evil to : curse, hex. *Informal:* jinx. *See* LUCK.

hoodwink *verb*

To cause to accept what is false, especially by trickery or misrepresentation : beguile, betray, bluff, cozen, deceive, delude, double-cross, dupe, fool, humbug, mislead, take in, trick. *Informal:* bamboozle, have. *Slang:* four-flush. *Idioms:* lead astray, play false, pull the wool over someone's eyes, put something over on, take for a ride. *See* HONEST.

hooey *noun*

Slang. Something that does not have or make sense : balderdash, blather, bunkum, claptrap, drivel, garbage, idiocy, nonsense, piffle, poppycock, rigmarole, rubbish, tomfoolery, trash, twaddle. *Informal:* tommyrot. *Slang:* applesauce, baloney, bilge, bull[1], bunk[2], crap, malarkey. *See* KNOWLEDGE.

hoof *verb*

1. *Slang.* To move rhythmically to music, using patterns of steps or gestures : dance, foot, step. *Idioms:* cut a rug, foot it, trip the light fantastic. *See* REPETITION, WORK. **2.** *Slang.* To go on foot : ambulate, foot, pace, step, tread, walk. ***Idiom:*** foot it. *See* MOVE.

hoofer *noun*
Slang. A person who dances, especially professionally : dancer, terpsichorean. *See* REPETITION.

hoo-hah *noun*
Slang. A condition of intense public interest or excitement : brouhaha, sensation, stir[1], uproar. *Informal:* to-do. *See* EXCITE.

hook *noun*
A device for fastening or for checking motion : catch, clasp, fastener. *See* MOVE.
hook *verb Slang.* To take (another's property) without permission : filch, pilfer, purloin, snatch, steal, thieve. *Informal:* lift, swipe. *Slang:* cop, heist, nip[1], pinch, rip off, snitch. ***Idiom:*** make (*or* walk) off with. *See* CRIMES, GIVE.

hooker *noun*
Slang. A woman who engages in sexual intercourse for payment : bawd, call girl, camp follower, courtesan, harlot, prostitute, scarlet woman, streetwalker, strumpet, tart[2], whore. *Slang:* moll. ***Idioms:*** lady of easy virtue, lady of pleasure, lady of the night. *See* SEX.

hookup *noun*
Informal. A logical or natural association between two or more things : connection, correlation, interconnection, interdependence, interrelationship, link, linkage, relation, relationship, tie-in. *See* CONNECT.

hooky *noun*
Informal. An unexcused absence : cut, truancy, truantry. *See* SEEK.

hooligan *noun*
Informal. A person who treats others violently and roughly, especially for hire : hoodlum, ruffian, thug, tough. *Slang:* goon, gorilla, hood. *See* ATTACK, CRIMES.

hoosegow *noun*
Slang. A place for the confinement of persons in lawful detention : brig, house of correction, jail, keep, penitentiary, prison. *Informal:* lockup, pen[3]. *Slang:* big house, can, clink, cooler, coop, joint, jug, pokey[1], slammer, stir[2]. *Chiefly Regional:* calaboose. *See* FREE.

hoot *noun*
1. Any of various derisive sounds of disapproval : boo, catcall, hiss. *Slang:* bird, Bronx cheer, raspberry, razz. *See* SOUNDS. **2.** *Informal.* Something or someone uproariously funny or absurd : absurdity. *Informal:* joke, laugh, scream. *Slang:* gas, howl, panic, riot. ***Idiom:*** a laugh a minute. *See* LAUGHTER. **3.** The least bit : iota, jot, ounce, shred, whit. *Informal:* damn, rap[2]. *Slang:* diddly. *See* BIG.

hop *verb*
To bound lightly : skip, skitter, spring, trip. *See* MOVE.
hop *noun* **1.** A light bounding movement : skip, spring. *See* MOVE. **2.** *Informal.* A party or gathering for dancing : ball, dance. *See* WORK.

hopeful *adjective*
Inspiring confidence or hope : cheering, encouraging, heartening, likely, promising. *See* HELP.
hopeful *noun* **1.** One who aspires : aspirant, aspirer. *See* SEEK. **2.** A person who applies for or seeks something, such as a job or position : applicant, aspirant, candidate, petitioner, seeker. *See* SEEK.

hopeless *adjective*
1. Having lost all hope : despairing, desperate, despondent, forlorn. *See* HOPE. **2.** Offering no hope or expectation of improvement : cureless, incurable, irremediable, irreparable. *See* HOPE.

hopelessness *noun*
Utter lack of hope : despair, desperateness, desperation, despond, despondence, despondency. *See* HOPE.

hopped-up *adjective*
Slang. Stupefied, intoxicated, or otherwise influenced by the taking of drugs : drugged. *Informal:* doped. *Slang:* high, lit (up), potted, spaced-out, stoned, turned-on, wiped-out, zonked. *See* DRUGS.

horde *noun*
1. An enormous number of persons gathered together : crowd, crush, drove, flock, mass, mob, multitude, press, ruck[1], swarm, throng. *See* BIG, GROUP. **2.** A very large number of things grouped together : army, cloud, crowd, drove, flock, host, legion, mass, mob, multitude, ruck[1], score (used in plural), swarm, throng. *See* BIG, GROUP.

horizon *noun*
The extent of one's perception, understanding, knowledge, or vision : ken, purview, range, reach, scope. *See* ABILITY, KNOWLEDGE, SEE.

horizontal *adjective*
Lying down : decumbent, flat, procumbent, prone, prostrate, recumbent. *See* HORIZONTAL.

hornets' nest *noun*
A situation that presents difficulty, uncertainty, or perplexity : issue, problem, question. *Informal:* can of worms. *See* EASY.

horn in *verb*
1. To force or come in as an improper or

unwanted element : cut in, intrude, obtrude. *See* ENTER. **2.** To intervene officiously or indiscreetly in the affairs of others : butt in, interfere, interlope, meddle. *See* PARTICIPATE.

horrendous *adjective*
Very bad : appalling, awful, dreadful, fearful, frightful, ghastly, horrible, shocking, terrible. *See* GOOD.

horrible *adjective*
1. Causing great horror : bloodcurdling, hair-raising, horrid, horrific, terrific. *See* FEAR. **2.** Shockingly repellent : ghastly, grim, grisly, gruesome, hideous, horrid, lurid, macabre. *See* BEAUTIFUL. **3.** Very bad : appalling, awful, dreadful, fearful, frightful, ghastly, horrendous, shocking, terrible. *See* GOOD.

horrid *adjective*
1. Causing great horror : bloodcurdling, hair-raising, horrible, horrific, terrific. *See* FEAR. **2.** Extremely unpleasant to the senses or feelings : atrocious, disgusting, foul, nasty, nauseating, offensive, repellent, repulsive, revolting, sickening, ugly, unwholesome, vile. *See* LIKE, PAIN. **3.** Shockingly repellent : ghastly, grim, grisly, gruesome, hideous, horrible, lurid, macabre. *See* BEAUTIFUL.

horrific *adjective*
Causing great horror : bloodcurdling, hair-raising, horrible, horrid, terrific. *See* FEAR.

horrify *verb*
To deprive of courage or the power to act as a result of fear, anxiety, or disgust : appall, consternate, daunt, dismay, shake, shock[1]. *See* FEAR.

horror *noun*
1. Great agitation and anxiety caused by the expectation or the realization of danger : affright, alarm, apprehension, dread, fear, fearfulness, fright, funk, panic, terror, trepidation. *Slang:* cold feet. ***Idiom:*** fear and trembling. *See* FEAR. **2.** Extreme hostility and dislike : abhorrence, abomination, antipathy, aversion, detestation, hate, hatred, loathing, repellence, repellency, repugnance, repugnancy, repulsion, revulsion. *See* LOVE. **3.** *Informal.* An object of extreme dislike : abhorrence, abomination, anathema, aversion, bête noire, bugbear, detestation, execration, hate. *See* LOVE.

horse around *verb*
Informal. To behave in a rowdy, improper, or unruly fashion : act up, carry on, misbehave. *Informal:* cut up. *See* GOOD.

horseplay *noun*
Improper, often rude behavior : misbehavior, misconduct, misdoing, naughtiness, wrongdoing. *See* GOOD.

horse sense *noun*
Informal. The ability to make sensible decisions : common sense, judgment, sense, wisdom. *Informal:* gumption. *See* ABILITY.

hospice *noun*
An institution that provides care and shelter : asylum, home, hospital, shelter. *See* PROTECTION.

hospitable *adjective*
Characterized by kindness and warm, unaffected courtesy : affable, gracious. *See* KIND.

hospital *noun*
An institution that provides care and shelter : asylum, home, hospice, shelter. *See* PROTECTION.

host *noun*
A very large number of things grouped together : army, cloud, crowd, drove, flock, horde, legion, mass, mob, multitude, ruck[1], score (used in plural), swarm, throng. *See* BIG, GROUP.

hostile *adjective*
1. Of or engaged in warfare : belligerent, combatant, militant. ***Idiom:*** at war. *See* ATTACK. **2.** Having or showing an eagerness to fight : bellicose, belligerent, combative, contentious, militant, pugnacious, quarrelsome, scrappy, truculent, warlike. *See* ATTACK. **3.** Inclined to act in a hostile way : aggressive, belligerent, combative, contentious, militant. *See* ATTACK, ATTITUDE. **4.** Feeling or showing unfriendliness : inimical, unfriendly. *See* LOVE.

hostility *noun*
1. Warlike or hostile attitude or nature : bellicoseness, bellicosity, belligerence, belligerency, combativeness, contentiousness, militance, militancy, pugnaciousness, pugnacity, truculence, truculency. *See* ATTACK. **2.** Deep-seated hatred, as between longtime opponents or rivals : animosity, animus, antagonism, antipathy, enmity, ill will. *See* LOVE. **3.** Hostile behavior : aggression, aggressiveness, belligerence, belligerency, combativeness, contentiousness, militance, militancy. *See* ATTACK. **4.** A state of open, prolonged fighting. Used in plural : belligerency, conflict, confrontation, strife, struggle, war, warfare. *See* CONFLICT.

hot *adjective*
1. Marked by much heat : ardent, baking, blistering, boiling, broiling, burning, fiery, heated, red-hot, roasting, scalding, scorching, searing, sizzling, sultry, sweltering, torrid. *See* HOT.

2. Being at a higher temperature than is normal or desirable : febrific, febrile, feverish, hectic, pyretic. *See* HOT. **3.** *Informal.* Of great current interest : live[2], red-hot. *See* EXCITE. **4.** *Slang.* Particularly excellent : divine, fabulous, fantastic, fantastical, glorious, marvelous, sensational, splendid, superb, terrific, wonderful. *Informal:* dandy, dreamy, great, ripping, super, swell, tremendous. *Slang:* cool, groovy, keen[1], neat, nifty. ***Idiom:*** out of this world. *See* GOOD.

hot-blooded *adjective*
Fired with intense feeling : ardent, blazing, burning, dithyrambic, fervent, fervid, fiery, flaming, glowing, heated, impassioned, passionate, perfervid, red-hot, scorching, torrid. *See* FEELINGS.

hotfoot *verb*
1. *Informal.* To leave hastily : bolt, get out, run. *Informal:* clear out, get, skedaddle. *Slang:* hightail, scram, vamoose. ***Idioms:*** beat it, hightail it, hotfoot it, make tracks. *See* APPROACH. **2.** *Informal.* To move swiftly : bolt, bucket, bustle, dart, dash, festinate, flash, fleet, flit, fly, haste, hasten, hurry, hustle, pelt[2], race, rocket, run, rush, sail, scoot, scour[2], shoot, speed, sprint, tear[1], trot, whirl, whisk, whiz, wing, zip, zoom. *Informal:* rip. *Slang:* barrel, highball. *Chiefly British:* nip[1]. ***Idioms:*** get a move on, get cracking, go like lightning, go like the wind, hotfoot it, make haste, make time, make tracks, run like the wind, shake a leg, step (*or* jump) on it. *See* MOVE.

hotheaded *adjective*
Characterized by unthinking boldness and haste : brash, foolhardy, harum-scarum, hasty, headlong, ill-considered, impetuous, improvident, impulsive, incautious, madcap, precipitant, precipitate, rash[1], reckless, slapdash, temerarious, unconsidered. *See* CAREFUL.

hotness *noun*
Intense warmth : fervor, heat, torridity, torridness. *See* HOT.

hot pursuit *noun*
The following of another in an attempt to overtake and capture : chase, pursuit. *See* SEEK.

hot spot *noun*
A difficult, often embarrassing situation or condition : box[1], corner, deep water, difficulty, dilemma, Dutch, fix, hole, hot water, jam, plight[1], predicament, quagmire, scrape, soup, trouble. *Informal:* bind, pickle, spot. *See* EASY.

hot water *noun*
1. The condition of being in need of immediate assistance : distress, exigence, exigency, trouble. *See* HELP. **2.** A difficult, often embarrassing situation or condition : box[1], corner, deep water, difficulty, dilemma, Dutch, fix, hole, hot spot, jam, plight[1], predicament, quagmire, scrape, soup, trouble. *Informal:* bind, pickle, spot. *See* EASY.

hound *verb*
1. To trouble persistently from or as if from all sides : badger, bedevil, beleaguer, beset, besiege, harass, harry, importune, pester, plague, solicit. *See* ATTACK. **2.** To torment with persistent insult or ridicule : badger, bait, bullyrag, heckle, hector, taunt. *Informal:* needle, ride. ***Idiom:*** wave the red flag in front of the bull. *See* TREAT WELL.

house *noun*
1. A building or shelter where one lives : abode, domicile, dwelling, habitation, home, lodging (often used in plural), place, residence. *Chiefly British:* dig (used in plural). *See* PROTECTION. **2.** A group of usually related people living together as a unit : family, household, ménage. *See* GROUP. **3.** A commercial organization : business, company, concern, corporation, enterprise, establishment, firm[2]. *Informal:* outfit. *See* GROUP. **4.** A group of people sharing common ancestry : clan, family, kindred, lineage, stock, tribe. ***Idioms:*** flesh and blood, kith and kin. *See* KIN.

house *verb* **1.** To provide with often temporary lodging : accommodate, bed (down), berth, bestow, billet, board, bunk[1], domicile, harbor, lodge, put up, quarter, room. *See* PROTECTION. **2.** To have as one's domicile, usually for an extended period : abide, domicile, dwell, live[1], reside. *See* PLACE. **3.** To give refuge to : harbor, haven, shelter. *See* PROTECTION.

housebreaker *noun*
A person who steals : bandit, burglar, highwayman, larcener, larcenist, pilferer, purloiner, robber, stealer, thief. *See* CRIMES.

housecleaning *noun*
Informal. A thorough or drastic reorganization : overhaul, shakeup. *See* CHANGE.

household *noun*
A group of usually related people living together as a unit : family, house, ménage. *See* GROUP.

household *adjective* Of or relating to the family or household : domestic, familial, family, home, homely. *See* KIN, GROUP.

house of correction *noun*
A place for the confinement of persons in lawful detention : brig, jail, keep, penitentiary, prison. *Informal:* lockup, pen[3]. *Slang:* big house, can, clink, cooler, coop, hoosegow, joint, jug, pokey[1], slammer, stir[2]. *Chiefly Regional:* calaboose. *See* FREE.

housing *noun*
Dwellings in general : lodging, shelter. ***Idiom:*** a roof over one's head. *See* PROTECTION.

hovel *noun*
An ugly, squalid dwelling : hole, hut, shack, shanty. *See* GOOD, RICH.

hover *verb*
1. To remain stationary over a place or object : hang, poise. *See* HANG. **2.** To move quickly, lightly, and irregularly like a bird in flight : flicker, flit, flitter, flutter. *See* REPETITION.

however *adverb*
In spite of a preceding event or consideration : all the same, nevertheless, nonetheless, still, yet. *Informal:* still and all. ***Idiom:*** be that as it may. *See* AFFIRM.

howl *verb*
1. To utter or emit a long, mournful, plaintive sound : bay[2], moan, ululate, wail, yowl. *See* SOUNDS. **2.** To cry loudly, as a healthy child does from pain or distress : bawl, wail, yowl. *See* SOUNDS. **3.** To make inarticulate sounds of grief or pain, usually accompanied by tears : bawl, blubber, cry, keen[2], sob, wail, weep, yowl. *See* HAPPY, SOUNDS. **4.** *Slang.* To express great amusement or mirth : guffaw, roar. *Informal:* break up. *See* LAUGHTER.
howl *noun* **1.** A long, mournful cry : bay[2], moan, ululation, wail, yowl. *See* SOUNDS. **2.** *Slang.* Something or someone uproariously funny or absurd : absurdity. *Informal:* hoot, joke, laugh, scream. *Slang:* gas, panic, riot. ***Idiom:*** a laugh a minute. *See* LAUGHTER.

hub *noun*
1. A point of origin from which ideas or influences, for example, originate : bottom, center, core, focus, heart, quick, root[1]. *See* START. **2.** A place of concentrated activity, influence, or importance : center, focus, headquarters, heart, seat. *See* EDGE.

hubbub *noun*
Sounds or a sound, especially when loud, confused, or disagreeable : babel, clamor, din, hullabaloo, noise, pandemonium, racket, rumpus, tumult, uproar. *See* SOUNDS.

huckster *verb*
1. To travel about selling goods : hawk, peddle, vend. *See* TRANSACTIONS. **2.** To argue about the terms, as of a sale : bargain, dicker, haggle, higgle, negotiate, palter. *See* AGREE.

huddle *verb*
To stoop low with the limbs pulled in close to the body : crouch, hunch, hunker (down), squat. *See* HIGH.

hue *noun*
1. The property by which the sense of vision can distinguish between objects, as a red apple and a green apple, that are very similar or identical in form and size : color, shade, tint, tone. *See* COLORS. **2.** The degree of vividness of a color, as when modified by the addition of black or white pigment : gradation, shade, tinge, tint. *See* COLORS. **3.** A shade of a color, especially a pale or delicate variation : cast, tinge, tint, tone. *See* COLORS.

huff *noun*
1. An angry outburst : fit[2], passion, tantrum, temper. *Informal:* conniption, conniption fit. *See* FEELINGS. **2.** Extreme displeasure caused by an insult or slight : dudgeon, miff, offense, pique, resentment, ruffled feathers, umbrage. *See* LIKE, PAIN.
huff *verb* **1.** To breathe hard : blow[1], gasp, pant, puff. *See* BREATH. **2.** To cause resentment or hurt by callous, rude behavior : affront, insult, miff, offend, outrage, pique. ***Idioms:*** add insult to injury, give offense to. *See* ATTACK, PAIN.

hug *verb*
To put one's arms around affectionately : clasp, embrace, enfold, hold, press, squeeze. *Slang:* clinch. *Archaic:* bosom, clip[2], embosom. *See* TOUCH.
hug *noun* The act of embracing : clasp, embrace, squeeze. *Slang:* clinch. *See* TOUCH.

huge *adjective*
Of extraordinary size and power : behemoth, Brobdingnagian, Bunyanesque, colossal, cyclopean, elephantine, enormous, gargantuan, giant, gigantesque, gigantic, herculean, heroic, immense, jumbo, mammoth, massive, massy, mastodonic, mighty, monster, monstrous, monumental, mountainous, prodigious, pythonic, stupendous, titanic, tremendous, vast. *Informal:* walloping. *Slang:* whopping. *See* BIG.

hugeness *noun*
The quality of being enormous : enormousness, immenseness, immensity, prodigiousness, stupendousness, tremendousness, vastness. *See* BIG.

huggermugger or **hugger-mugger** *noun*
The habit, practice, or policy of keeping

secrets : clandestineness, clandestinity, concealment, covertness, huggermuggery, secrecy, secretiveness, secretness. *See* SHOW.

huggermugger or **hugger-mugger** *adjective* Existing or operating in a way so as to ensure complete concealment and confidentiality : clandestine, cloak-and-dagger, covert, secret, sub-rosa, undercover. *Informal:* hush-hush. *Idiom:* under wraps. *See* SHOW.

huggermugger or **hugger-mugger** *adverb* In a secret way : clandestinely, covertly, secretly, sub rosa. *Idioms:* by stealth, on the sly, under cover. *See* SHOW.

huggermuggery or **hugger-muggery** *noun*
The habit, practice, or policy of keeping secrets : clandestineness, clandestinity, concealment, covertness, huggermugger, secrecy, secretiveness, secretness. *See* SHOW.

hulk *noun*
A large, ungainly, and dull-witted person : gawk, lout, lump[1], oaf, ox. *Informal:* lummox. *Slang:* klutz, lug[1], meatball, meathead. *See* ABILITY.

hulk *verb* To move heavily : clump, galumph, lumber, lump[1], stump. *See* MOVE.

hulking *adjective*
Having a large body, especially in girth : bulky, heavy, hefty, hulky, husky[2], stout. *See* BIG.

hulky *adjective*
Having a large body, especially in girth : bulky, heavy, hefty, hulking, husky[2], stout. *See* BIG.

hullaballoo *noun* See **hullabaloo.**

hullabaloo also **hullaballoo** *noun*
1. Sounds or a sound, especially when loud, confused, or disagreeable : babel, clamor, din, hubbub, noise, pandemonium, racket, rumpus, tumult, uproar. *See* SOUNDS. **2.** Offensively loud and insistent utterances, especially of disapproval : clamor, outcry, rumpus, uproar, vociferation. *Idiom:* hue and cry. *See* LIKE, SOUNDS.

hum *verb*
To make a continuous low-pitched droning sound : bumble[2], burr, buzz, drone[2], whir, whiz. *See* SOUNDS.

hum *noun* A continuous low-pitched droning sound : bumble[2], burr, buzz, drone[2], whir, whiz. *See* SOUNDS.

human *adjective*
1. Of or characteristic of human beings or mankind : mortal. *See* BEINGS. **2.** Concerned with human welfare and the alleviation of suffering : charitable, compassionate, humane, humanitarian, merciful. *See* ATTITUDE, KIND.

human *noun* A member of the human race : being, body, creature, homo, human being, individual, life, man, mortal, party, person, personage, soul. *See* BEINGS.

human being *noun*
A member of the human race : being, body, creature, homo, human, individual, life, man, mortal, party, person, personage, soul. *See* BEINGS.

humane *adjective*
Concerned with human welfare and the alleviation of suffering : charitable, compassionate, human, humanitarian, merciful. *See* ATTITUDE, KIND.

humanitarian *adjective*
Concerned with human welfare and the alleviation of suffering : charitable, compassionate, human, humane, merciful. *See* ATTITUDE, KIND.

humanity *noun*
The human race : earth, flesh, Homo sapiens, humankind, man, mankind, universe, world. *See* CULTURE.

humanize *verb*
To fit for companionship with others, especially in attitude or manners : acculturate, civilize, socialize. *See* TEACH.

humanizing *adjective*
Promoting culture : civilizing, cultural, edifying, enlightening, refining. *See* CULTURE.

humankind *noun*
The human race : earth, flesh, Homo sapiens, humanity, man, mankind, universe, world. *See* CULTURE.

humanoid *adjective*
Resembling a human being : anthropoid, anthropomorphic, anthropomorphous, hominoid, manlike. *See* CULTURE.

humble *adjective*
1. Having or expressing feelings of humility : lowly, meek, modest. *See* ATTITUDE, BIG, SELF-LOVE. **2.** Lacking high station or birth : baseborn, common, déclassé, declassed, ignoble, lowly, mean[2], plebeian, unwashed, vulgar. *Archaic:* base[2]. *See* OVER. **3.** Of little distinction : lowly, mean[2], simple. *See* PLAIN.

humble *verb* To deprive of esteem, self-worth, or effectiveness : abase, degrade, demean[2], humiliate, mortify. *Idioms:* bring low, take down a peg. *See* RESPECT, WIN.

humbleness *noun*
Lack of vanity or self-importance : humility, lowliness, meekness, modesty. *See* ATTITUDE, BIG, SELF-LOVE.

humbug *noun*
One who fakes : charlatan, fake, faker, fraud, impostor, mountebank, phony, pretender, quack. *See* TRUE.
humbug *verb* To cause to accept what is false, especially by trickery or misrepresentation : beguile, betray, bluff, cozen, deceive, delude, double-cross, dupe, fool, hoodwink, mislead, take in, trick. *Informal:* bamboozle, have. *Slang:* four-flush. ***Idioms:*** lead astray, play false, pull the wool over someone's eyes, put something over on, take for a ride. *See* HONEST.

humdrum *adjective*
Arousing no interest or curiosity : boring, drear, dreary, dry, dull, irksome, monotonous, stuffy, tedious, tiresome, uninteresting, wearisome, wearisome, weary. *See* EXCITE.
humdrum *noun* A tiresome lack of variety : monotone, monotonousness, monotony, sameness. *See* CHANGE, EXCITE.

humid *adjective*
Damp and warm : muggy, soggy, sticky, sultry. *See* DRY, HOT.

humiliate *verb*
To deprive of esteem, self-worth, or effectiveness : abase, degrade, demean[2], humble, mortify. ***Idioms:*** bring low, take down a peg. *See* RESPECT, WIN.

humiliation *noun*
1. A lowering in or deprivation of character or self-esteem : abasement, debasement, degradation, mortification. *See* RESPECT, WIN. **2.** Loss of or damage to one's reputation : bad name, bad odor, discredit, disgrace, dishonor, disrepute, ignominy, ill repute, obloquy, odium, opprobrium, shame. *See* RESPECT.

humility *noun*
Lack of vanity or self-importance : humbleness, lowliness, meekness, modesty. *See* ATTITUDE, BIG, SELF-LOVE.

humor *noun*
1. The quality of being laughable or comical : comedy, comicality, comicalness, drollery, drollness, farcicality, funniness, humorousness, jocoseness, jocosity, jocularity, ludicrousness, ridiculousness, wit, wittiness, zaniness. *See* LAUGHTER. **2.** A person's customary manner of emotional response : complexion, disposition, nature, temper, temperament. *See* BE. **3.** A temporary state of mind or feeling : frame of mind, mood, spirit (used in plural), temper, vein. *See* FEELINGS. **4.** An impulsive, often illogical turn of mind : bee, boutade, caprice, conceit, fancy, freak, impulse, megrim, notion, vagary, whim, whimsy. ***Idiom:*** bee in one's bonnet. *See* THOUGHTS.
humor *verb* To comply with the wishes or ideas of (another) : cater, gratify, indulge. *See* RESIST.

humorist *noun*
A person whose words or actions provoke or are intended to provoke amusement or laughter : clown, comedian, comic, farceur, funnyman, jester, joker, jokester, quipster, wag[2], wit, zany. *Informal:* card. *See* LAUGHTER.

humorous *adjective*
1. Intended to excite laughter or amusement : comedic, facetious, funny, jocose, jocular, witty. *See* LAUGHTER. **2.** Arousing laughter : amusing, comic, comical, droll, funny, laughable, risible, zany. *See* LAUGHTER.

humorousness *noun*
The quality of being laughable or comical : comedy, comicality, comicalness, drollery, drollness, farcicality, funniness, humor, jocoseness, jocosity, jocularity, ludicrousness, ridiculousness, wit, wittiness, zaniness. *See* LAUGHTER.

hump *noun*
An unevenness or elevation on a surface : bump, knob, knot, lump[1], nub, protuberance. *See* CONVEX.
hump *verb* To incline the body : arch, bend, bow[1], hunch, scrunch, stoop. *See* POSTURE.

hunch *noun*
1. Intuitive cognition : feeling, idea, impression, intuition, suspicion. *See* THOUGHTS. **2.** An irregularly shaped mass of indefinite size : chunk, clod, clump, gob[1], lump[1], nugget, wad. *Informal:* hunk. *See* PART.
hunch *verb* **1.** To stoop low with the limbs pulled in close to the body : crouch, huddle, hunker (down), squat. *See* HIGH. **2.** To incline the body : arch, bend, bow[1], hump, scrunch, stoop. *See* POSTURE.

hunger *noun*
1. A desire for food or drink : appetite, stomach, taste, thirst. *See* DESIRE. **2.** A strong wanting of what promises enjoyment or pleasure : appetence, appetency, appetite, craving, desire, itch, longing, lust, thirst, wish, yearning, yen. *See* DESIRE.
hunger *verb* To have a greedy, obsessive desire : crave, itch, lust, thirst. *See* DESIRE.

hungry *adjective*
1. Desiring or craving food : famished, ravenous, starving, voracious. *See* INGESTION. **2.** Having a strong urge to obtain or possess

something, especially material wealth, in quantity : acquisitive, avaricious, avid, covetous, grasping, greedy. *Informal:* grabby. *See* DESIRE, GIVE.

hunk *noun*
1. *Informal.* An irregularly shaped mass of indefinite size : chunk, clod, clump, gob[1], hunch, lump[1], nugget, wad. *See* PART.
2. *Slang.* A person regarded as physically attractive. Used of a man : beauty, belle (used of a woman), lovely, stunner. *Slang:* babe, doll, knockout, looker, stud (used of a man). *See* BEAUTIFUL.

hunker *verb*
1. To stoop low with the limbs pulled in close to the body. Also used with *down* : crouch, huddle, hunch, squat. *See* HIGH. 2. To sit on one's heels. Also used with *down* : squat. *See* POSTURE.

hunt *verb*
1. To look for and pursue (game) in order to capture or kill it : chase, drive, run, stalk. *See* SEEK. 2. To try to find something : cast about, look, quest, search, seek. *See* SEEK.
hunt down *verb* To pursue and locate : nose out, run down, trace, track down. ***Idiom:*** run to earth (*or* ground). *See* GET.

hunt down *verb* See **hunt.**

hurdle *noun*
Something that impedes or prevents entry or passage : bar, barricade, barrier, block, blockage, clog, hamper, hindrance, impediment, obstacle, obstruction, snag, stop, traverse, wall. *See* HELP, OPEN.
hurdle *verb* 1. To pass by or over safely or successfully : clear, negotiate, surmount. *See* THRIVE. 2. To move off the ground by a muscular effort of the legs and feet : jump, leap, spring, vault[2]. *See* MOVE, RISE.

hurl *verb*
To send through the air with a motion of the hand or arm : cast, dart, dash, fling, heave, hurtle, launch, pitch, shoot, shy[2], sling, throw, toss. *Informal:* fire. *See* MOVE.
hurl *noun* An act of throwing : cast, fling, heave, launch, pitch, shy[2], sling, throw, toss. *See* MOVE.

hurried *adjective*
1. Happening quickly and without warning : abrupt, precipitant, precipitate, sudden. *See* FAST, SURPRISE. 2. Accomplished in very little time : brief, expeditious, fast, flying, hasty, quick, rapid, short, speedy, swift. *See* FAST.

hurriedness *noun*
Careless headlong action : haste, hastiness, precipitance, precipitancy, precipitateness, precipitation, rashness, rush. *See* CAREFUL.

hurry *verb*
1. To move swiftly : bolt, bucket, bustle, dart, dash, festinate, flash, fleet, flit, fly, haste, hasten, hustle, pelt[2], race, rocket, run, rush, sail, scoot, scour[2], shoot, speed, sprint, tear[1], trot, whirl, whisk, whiz, wing, zip, zoom. *Informal:* hotfoot, rip. *Slang:* barrel, highball. *Chiefly British:* nip[1]. ***Idioms:*** get a move on, get cracking, go like lightning, go like the wind, hotfoot it, make haste, make time, make tracks, run like the wind, shake a leg, step (*or* jump) on it. *See* MOVE. 2. To increase the speed of : accelerate, expedite, hasten, hustle, quicken, speed (up), step up. *See* FAST.
hurry *noun* Rapidness of movement or activity : celerity, dispatch, expedition, expeditiousness, fleetness, haste, hustle, quickness, rapidity, rapidness, speed, speediness, swiftness. *See* FAST.

hurry-up *adjective*
Designed to meet emergency needs as quickly as possible : *Informal:* crash, rush. *See* FAST.

hurt *verb*
1. To cause physical damage to : injure, wound. *See* HELP. 2. To have or cause a feeling of physical pain or discomfort : ache, pain, pang, twinge. *See* PAIN. 3. To cause suffering or painful sorrow to : aggrieve, distress, grieve, injure, pain, wound. *See* HAPPY. 4. To spoil the soundness or perfection of : blemish, damage, detract from, disserve, flaw, harm, impair, injure, mar, prejudice, tarnish, vitiate. *See* BETTER, HELP.
hurt *noun* 1. A state of physical or mental suffering : affliction, agony, anguish, distress, misery, pain, torment, torture, woe, wound, wretchedness. *See* HAPPY. 2. The action or result of inflicting loss or pain : damage, detriment, harm, injury, mischief. *See* HELP.

hurtful *adjective*
1. Marked by, causing, or experiencing physical pain : aching, achy, afflictive, nagging, painful, smarting, sore. *See* PAIN. 2. Causing harm or injury : bad, deleterious, detrimental, evil, harmful, ill, injurious, mischievous. *See* HELP.

hurtle *verb*
1. To send through the air with a motion of the hand or arm : cast, dart, dash, fling, heave, hurl, launch, pitch, shoot, shy[2], sling, throw, toss. *Informal:* fire. *See* MOVE. 2. To launch with great force : fire, loose, project, propel, shoot. ***Idiom:*** let fly. *See* MOVE.

hurtless *adjective*
Devoid of hurtful qualities : harmless, innocent, innocuous, inoffensive, unoffensive. *See* HELP.

husband *verb*
To protect (an asset) from loss or destruction : conserve, preserve, save. *See* KEEP.

husbandry *noun*
The careful guarding of an asset : conservancy, conservation, management, preservation. *See* KEEP.

hush *verb*
1. To cause to become silent : quiet, quieten, shush, shut up, silence, still. *See* SOUNDS. **2.** To hold (something requiring an outlet) in check. Also used with *up* : burke, choke (back), gag, hold back, hold down, muffle, quench, repress, smother, squelch, stifle, strangle, suppress, throttle. *Informal:* sit on (*or* upon). *See* RESTRAINT. **3.** To prevent (something) from being known. Also used with *up* : cloak, conceal, cover (up), enshroud, hide[1], mask, shroud, veil. ***Idioms:*** keep under cover, keep under wraps. *See* SHOW. **4.** To keep from being published or transmitted. Also used with *up* : ban, black out, censor, stifle, suppress. ***Idiom:*** keep (*or* put) a lid on. *See* SHOW.
hush *noun* **1.** The absence of sound or noise : noiselessness, quiet, quietness, silence, soundlessness, still, stillness. *See* SOUNDS. **2.** An absence of motion or disturbance : calm, calmness, lull, peace, peacefulness, placidity, placidness, quiet, quietness, serenity, stillness, tranquillity, untroubledness. *See* CALM.
hush *adjective Archaic.* Marked by, done with, or making no sound or noise : hushed, noiseless, quiet, silent, soundless, still, stilly. *See* SOUNDS.

hushed *adjective*
1. Marked by, done with, or making no sound or noise : noiseless, quiet, silent, soundless, still, stilly. *Archaic:* hush. *See* SOUNDS. **2.** Not irritating, strident, or loud : low, low-key, low-keyed, quiet, small, soft, subdued, whispery. *See* SOUNDS.

hush-hush *adjective*
1. *Informal.* Known about by very few : auricular, confidential, inside, private, secret. *See* SHOW. **2.** *Informal.* Existing or operating in a way so as to ensure complete concealment and confidentiality : clandestine, cloak-and-dagger, covert, huggermugger, secret, sub-rosa, undercover. ***Idiom:*** under wraps. *See* SHOW.

husky[1] *adjective*
Low and grating in sound : croaking, croaky, gruff, hoarse. *See* SOUNDS.

husky[2] *adjective*
1. Characterized by marked muscular development; powerfully built : athletic, brawny, burly, muscular, robust, sinewy, sturdy. *See* STRONG. **2.** Having a large body, especially in girth : bulky, heavy, hefty, hulking, hulky, stout. *See* BIG.

hussy *noun*
A vulgar promiscuous woman who flouts propriety : baggage, jade, slattern, slut, tart[2], tramp, wanton, wench, whore. *Slang:* floozy. *See* SEX.

hustle *verb*
1. To increase the speed of : accelerate, expedite, hasten, hurry, quicken, speed (up), step up. *See* FAST. **2.** To move swiftly : bolt, bucket, bustle, dart, dash, festinate, flash, fleet, flit, fly, haste, hasten, hurry, pelt[2], race, rocket, run, rush, sail, scoot, scour[2], shoot, speed, sprint, tear[1], trot, whirl, whisk, whiz, wing, zip, zoom. *Informal:* hotfoot, rip. *Slang:* barrel, highball. *Chiefly British:* nip[1]. ***Idioms:*** get a move on, get cracking, go like lightning, go like the wind, hotfoot it, make haste, make time, make tracks, run like the wind, shake a leg, step (*or* jump) on it. *See* MOVE.
hustle *noun* **1.** An aggressive readiness along with energy to undertake taxing efforts : drive, enterprise, initiative, punch. *Informal:* get-up-and-go, gumption, push. *See* ACTION, TIRED, TRY. **2.** Rapidness of movement or activity : celerity, dispatch, expedition, expeditiousness, fleetness, haste, hurry, quickness, rapidity, rapidness, speed, speediness, swiftness. *See* FAST.

hustler *noun*
An intensely energetic, enthusiastic person : dynamo. *Informal:* eager beaver, go-getter, live wire. *See* CONCERN.

hut *noun*
An ugly, squalid dwelling : hole, hovel, shack, shanty. *See* GOOD, RICH.

hutzpah *noun* See **chutzpah.**

hygienic *adjective*
Promoting good health : healthful, healthsome, healthy, salubrious, salutary, wholesome. *See* HEALTH.

hymeneal *adjective*
Of, relating to, or typical of marriage : conjugal, connubial, marital, married, matrimonial, nuptial, spousal, wedded. *See* MARRIAGE.

hype *noun*
Slang. A systematic effort or part of this effort to increase the importance or reputation of by favorable publicity : advertisement, ballyhoo, buildup, promotion, publicity, puffery. *Informal:* pitch, plug. *See* KNOWLEDGE.
hype *verb Slang.* To increase or seek to increase the importance or reputation of by favorable publicity : ballyhoo, boost, build up, enhance, promote, publicize, puff, talk up, tout. *Informal:* plug. *See* KNOWLEDGE.

hyperbole *noun*
The act or an instance of exaggerating : exaggeration, hyperbolism, overstatement, tall talk. *See* INCREASE.

hyperbolism *noun*
The act or an instance of exaggerating : exaggeration, hyperbole, overstatement, tall talk. *See* INCREASE.

hyperbolize *verb*
To make (something) seem greater than is actually the case : exaggerate, inflate, magnify, overcharge, overstate. ***Idioms:*** blow up out of proportion, lay it on thick, stretch the truth. *See* INCREASE.

hypercritic *noun*
A person who finds fault, often severely and willfully : carper, caviler, critic, criticizer, faultfinder, niggler, nitpicker, quibbler. *See* PRAISE.

hypercritical *adjective*
Inclined to judge too severely : captious, carping, censorious, critical, faultfinding, overcritical. *See* PRAISE.

hypnotic *adjective*
Inducing sleep or sedation : narcotic, opiate, sedative, sleepy, slumberous, somnifacient, somniferous, somnific, somnolent, soporific. *See* AWARENESS.
hypnotic *noun* Something that induces sleep or sedation : narcotic, opiate, sedative, somnifacient, soporific. *See* AWARENESS.

hypocrisy *noun*
A show or expression of feelings or beliefs one does not actually hold or possess : pharisaism, phoniness, sanctimoniousness, sanctimony, tartuffery, two-facedness. *See* HONEST.

hypocrite *noun*
A person who practices hypocrisy : pharisee, phony, tartuffe. *See* HONEST.

hypocritical *adjective*
Of or practicing hypocrisy : Pecksniffian, pharisaic, pharisaical, phony, sanctimonious, two-faced. *See* HONEST.

hypogeal *adjective*
Located or operating beneath the earth's surface : hypogean, hypogeous, subterranean, subterrestrial, underground. *See* SURFACE.

hypogean *adjective*
Located or operating beneath the earth's surface : hypogeal, hypogeous, subterranean, subterrestrial, underground. *See* SURFACE.

hypogeous *adjective*
Located or operating beneath the earth's surface : hypogeal, hypogean, subterranean, subterrestrial, underground. *See* SURFACE.

hypothecate *verb*
To give or deposit as a pawn : mortgage, pawn[1], pledge. *Slang:* hock. *See* TRANSACTIONS.

hypothesis *noun*
A belief used as the basis for action : theory. *See* BELIEF, THOUGHTS.

hypothesize *verb*
To formulate or assert as a tentative explanation : speculate, theorize. *See* BELIEF, THOUGHTS.

hypothetic *adjective*
1. Existing only in concept and not in reality : abstract, hypothetical, ideal, theoretical, transcendent, transcendental. *See* REAL. **2.** Presumed to be true, real, or genuine, especially on inconclusive grounds : conjectural, hypothetical, inferential, presumptive, supposed, suppositional, suppositious, supposititious, suppositive. *See* BELIEF.

hypothetical *adjective*
1. Existing only in concept and not in reality : abstract, hypothetic, ideal, theoretical, transcendent, transcendental. *See* REAL. **2.** Presumed to be true, real, or genuine, especially on inconclusive grounds : conjectural, hypothetic, inferential, presumptive, supposed, suppositional, suppositious, supposititious, suppositive. *See* BELIEF.

·I·

iciness *noun*
Extreme lack of warmth : frigidity, frigidness, frostiness, gelidity, gelidness, wintriness. *See* HOT.

icky *adjective*
Informal. Not pleasant or agreeable : bad, disagreeable, displeasing, offensive, uncongenial, unpleasant, unsympathetic. *Slang:* yucky. *See* GOOD, PAIN.

icy *adjective*
1. Very cold : arctic, boreal, freezing, frigid, frosty, gelid, glacial, polar, wintry. *Archaic:* frore. ***Idiom:*** bitter (*or* bitterly) cold. *See* HOT. **2.** Lacking all friendliness and warmth : cold, frigid, frosty, glacial. *See* ATTITUDE, HOT.

idea *noun*
1. That which exists in the mind as the product of careful mental activity : concept, conception, image, notion, perception, thought. *See* THOUGHTS. **2.** Something believed or accepted as true by a person : belief, conviction, feeling, mind, notion, opinion, persuasion, position, sentiment, view. *See* OPINION. **3.** Intuitive cognition : feeling, hunch, impression, intuition, suspicion. *See* THOUGHTS. **4.** A method for making, doing, or accomplishing something : blueprint, design, game plan, layout, plan, project, schema, scheme, strategy. *See* PLANNED. **5.** The gist of a specific action or situation : import, meaning, point, purport, significance, significancy. *See* MEANING.

ideal *noun*
1. One that is worthy of imitation or duplication : beau ideal, example, exemplar, mirror, model, paradigm, pattern, standard. *See* GOOD. **2.** A fervent hope, wish, or goal : aspiration, dream. *See* HOPE.

ideal *adjective* **1.** Conforming to an ultimate form of perfection or excellence : exemplary, model, perfect, supreme. *See* GOOD. **2.** Existing only in concept and not in reality : abstract, hypothetic, hypothetical, theoretical, transcendent, transcendental. *See* REAL.

idealist *noun*
A person inclined to be imaginative or idealistic but impractical : dreamer, utopian, visionary. *See* ABILITY, HOPE.

idealistic *adjective*
1. Showing a tendency to envision things in perfect but unrealistic form : utopian, visionary. *See* HOPE, REAL. **2.** Not compatible with reality : quixotic, romantic, starry-eyed, unrealistic, utopian, visionary. *See* HOPE, REAL.

identic *adjective*
Being one and not another or others; not different in nature or identity : identical, same, selfsame, very. *See* SAME.

identical *adjective*
1. Being one and not another or others; not different in nature or identity : identic, same, selfsame, very. *See* SAME. **2.** Agreeing exactly in value, quantity, or effect : equal, equivalent, even[1], same, tantamount. ***Idioms:*** on a par, one and the same. *See* SAME.

identicalness *noun*
The quality or condition of being exactly the same as something else : identity, oneness, sameness, selfsameness. *See* SAME.

identify *verb*
1. To set off by or as if by a mark indicating ownership or manufacture : brand, label, mark, tag, trademark. *See* MARKS. **2.** To establish the identification of : pinpoint, place, recognize. *Slang:* finger. ***Idiom:*** put one's finger on. *See* KNOWLEDGE. **3.** To represent as similar : analogize, assimilate, compare, equate, liken, match, parallel. *See* SAME. **4.** To come or bring together in one's mind or imagination : associate, bracket, connect, correlate, couple, link. *See* SAME. **5.** To associate or affiliate oneself closely with a person or group : empathize, relate, sympathize. *See* SAME.

identity *noun*
1. The set of behavioral or personal characteristics by which an individual is recognizable : individualism, individuality, selfhood. *See* BE. **2.** The quality or condition of being exactly the same as something else : identicalness, oneness, sameness, selfsameness. *See* SAME.

idiocy *noun*
1. Foolish behavior : absurdity, folly, foolery, foolishness, imbecility, insanity, lunacy, madness, nonsense, preposterousness, senselessness, silliness, tomfoolery, zaniness. *Informal:* craziness. *See* ABILITY. **2.** Something that does not have or make sense : balderdash, blather, bunkum, claptrap, drivel, garbage, nonsense, piffle,

poppycock, rigmarole, rubbish, tomfoolery, trash, twaddle. *Informal:* tommyrot. *Slang:* applesauce, baloney, bilge, bull[1], bunk[2], crap, hooey, malarkey. *See* KNOWLEDGE.

idiom *noun*
Specialized expressions indigenous to a particular field, subject, trade, or subculture : argot, cant[2], dialect, jargon, language, lexicon, lingo, patois, terminology, vernacular, vocabulary. *See* WORDS.

idiosyncrasy *noun*
Peculiar behavior : eccentricity, peculiarity, quirk, quirkiness, singularity. *See* USUAL.

idiosyncratic *adjective*
Deviating from the customary : bizarre, cranky, curious, eccentric, erratic, freakish, odd, outlandish, peculiar, quaint, queer, quirky, singular, strange, unnatural, unusual, weird. *Slang:* kooky, screwball. *British Slang:* rum, rummy[2]. *See* USUAL.

idiot *noun*
One deficient in judgment and good sense : ass, fool, imbecile, jackass, mooncalf, moron, nincompoop, ninny, nitwit, simple, simpleton, softhead, tomfool. *Informal:* dope, gander, goose. *Slang:* cretin, ding-dong, dip, goof, jerk, nerd, schmo, schmuck, turkey. *See* ABILITY.

idiotic *adjective*
So senseless as to be laughable : absurd, foolish, harebrained, imbecilic, insane, lunatic, mad, moronic, nonsensical, preposterous, silly, softheaded, tomfool, unearthly, zany. *Informal:* cockeyed, crazy, loony, loopy. *Slang:* balmy[2], dippy, dopey, jerky, sappy, wacky. *See* ABILITY, KNOWLEDGE.

idle *adjective*
1. Marked by a lack of action or activity : inactive, inert, inoperative. *See* ACTION. **2.** Resistant to exertion and activity : fainéant, indolent, lazy, shiftless, slothful, sluggard, sluggish. *Informal:* do-nothing. ***Idiom:*** bone lazy. *See* ACTION, INDUSTRIOUS. **3.** Not occupied or put to use : inactive, unemployed, unused, vacant. *See* USED. **4.** Lacking value, use, or substance : empty, hollow, otiose, vacant, vain. *See* FULL. **5.** Having no basis or foundation in fact : baseless, bottomless, groundless, unfounded, unwarranted. *See* TRUE.
idle *verb* **1.** To pass time without working or in avoiding work : bum[1] (around), laze, loaf, loiter, lounge, shirk. *Slang:* diddle[2], goldbrick, goof (off). *See* INDUSTRIOUS. **2.** To pass (time) without working or in avoiding work. Also used with *away* : dawdle (away), fiddle away, kill[1], trifle away, waste, while (away), wile (away). *See* INDUSTRIOUS. **3.** To cause to cease regular activity : immobilize, stop, tie up. ***Idiom:*** bring to a screeching halt. *See* CONTINUE.

idleness *noun*
1. A lack of action or activity : inaction, inactivity, inertness, inoperativeness, stagnation. *See* ACTION. **2.** The quality or state of being lazy : indolence, laziness, shiftlessness, sloth, slothfulness, sluggardness, sluggishness. *Informal:* do-nothingism. *See* INDUSTRIOUS.

idler *noun*
A self-indulgent person who spends time avoiding work or other useful activity : bum[1], drone[1], fainéant, good-for-nothing, layabout, loafer, ne'er-do-well, no-good, slugabed, sluggard, wastrel. *Informal:* do-little, do-nothing, lazybones, slug[2]. *Slang:* slouch. *See* INDUSTRIOUS.

idolization *noun*
The act of adoring, especially reverently : adoration, reverence, veneration, worship. *See* LIKE, LOVE, SACRED.

idolize *verb*
To regard with great awe and devotion : adore, revere, reverence, venerate, worship. *See* SACRED.

idyllic *adjective*
Charmingly simple and carefree : pastoral. *See* CALM, SIMPLE.

iffy *adjective*
Informal. Not affording certainty : ambiguous, borderline, chancy, clouded, doubtful, dubious, dubitable, equivocal, inconclusive, indecisive, indeterminate, problematic, problematical, questionable, uncertain, unclear, unsure. ***Idioms:*** at issue, in doubt, in question. *See* CERTAIN, CLEAR.

igg *verb*
Regional. To refuse to pay attention to (a person); treat with contempt : disregard, ignore, neglect, slight. *See* CONCERN, THOUGHTS.

ignis fatuus *noun*
An erroneous perception of reality : delusion, hallucination, illusion, mirage, phantasm, phantasma, will-o'-the-wisp. *See* REAL.

ignite *verb*
To cause to burn or undergo combustion : enkindle, fire, kindle, light[1]. *Slang:* torch. ***Idioms:*** set afire (*or* on fire), set fire to. *See* HOT, START.

ignoble *adjective*
1. Having or proceeding from low moral standards : base[2], low, low-down, mean[2], sordid, squalid, vile. *See* RIGHT. **2.** Lacking high

station or birth : baseborn, common, déclassé, declassed, humble, lowly, mean[2], plebeian, unwashed, vulgar. *Archaic:* base[2]. *See* OVER.

ignominious *adjective*
Meriting or causing shame or dishonor : discreditable, disgraceful, dishonorable, disreputable, opprobrious, shameful. *See* RESPECT.

ignominiousness *noun*
The condition of being infamous : disgracefulness, dishonorableness, disreputability, disreputableness, infamy, shamefulness. *See* GOOD, RESPECT, RIGHT.

ignominy *noun*
Loss of or damage to one's reputation : bad name, bad odor, discredit, disgrace, dishonor, disrepute, humiliation, ill repute, obloquy, odium, opprobrium, shame. *See* RESPECT.

ignorance *noun*
1. The condition of being ignorant; lack of knowledge or learning : benightedness, illiteracy, illiterateness, nescience. *See* KNOWLEDGE. **2.** The condition of being uninformed or unaware : innocence, nescience, obliviousness, unawareness, unconsciousness, unfamiliarity. *See* KNOWLEDGE.

ignorant *adjective*
1. Without education or knowledge : illiterate, nescient, uneducated, uninstructed, unlearned, unschooled, untaught. *See* KNOWLEDGE. **2.** Exhibiting lack of education or knowledge : backward, benighted, primitive, unenlightened. *See* KNOWLEDGE. **3.** Not aware or informed : innocent, oblivious, unacquainted, unaware, unconscious, unenlightened, unfamiliar, uninformed, unknowing, unwitting. ***Idiom:*** in the dark. *See* KNOWLEDGE.

ignore *verb*
1. To refuse to pay attention to (a person); treat with contempt : disregard, neglect, slight. *Regional:* igg. *See* CONCERN, THOUGHTS. **2.** To pretend not to see : blink (at), connive at, disregard, pass over, wink at. ***Idioms:*** be blind to, close (*or* shut) one's eyes to, look the other way, turn a blind eye to. *See* SEE. **3.** To fail to care for or give proper attention to : disregard, neglect, slight. *See* CARE FOR, CONCERN.

ilk *noun*
A class that is defined by the common attribute or attributes possessed by all its members : breed, cast, description, feather, kind[2], lot, manner, mold, nature, order, sort, species, stamp, stripe, type, variety. *Informal:* persuasion. *See* GROUP.

ill *adjective*
1. Suffering from or affected with an illness : down, sick, unwell. *Informal:* laid up. *Chiefly Regional:* poorly. *See* HEALTH. **2.** Causing harm or injury : bad, deleterious, detrimental, evil, harmful, hurtful, injurious, mischievous. *See* HELP. **3.** Bringing, predicting, or characterized by misfortune : bad, evil, inauspicious, unfavorable, unpropitious. *See* LUCK.

ill *noun* **1.** Whatever is destructive or harmful : bad, badness, evil. *See* HELP. **2.** A pathological condition of mind or body : ailment, complaint, disease, disorder, illness, infirmity, malady, sickness. *See* HEALTH. **3.** A cause of suffering or harm : affliction, bane, curse, evil, plague, scourge, woe. *See* HELP.

ill-advised *adjective*
Not wise : ill-considered, impolitic, imprudent, indiscreet, injudicious, unsound, unwise. *See* WISE.

illation *noun*
A position arrived at by reasoning from premises or general principles : conclusion, deduction, illative, inference, judgment. *See* REASON.

illative *noun*
A position arrived at by reasoning from premises or general principles : conclusion, deduction, illation, inference, judgment. *See* REASON.

ill-behaved *adjective*
Misbehaving, often in a troublesome way : bad, naughty. *See* CONTROL, GOOD.

ill-bred *adjective*
1. Lacking in delicacy or refinement : barbarian, barbaric, boorish, churlish, coarse, crass, crude, gross, indelicate, philistine, rough, rude, tasteless, uncivilized, uncouth, uncultivated, uncultured, unpolished, unrefined, vulgar. *See* COURTESY, SMOOTH. **2.** Lacking good manners : discourteous, disrespectful, ill-mannered, impolite, rude, uncivil, ungracious, unmannerly, unpolished. *See* COURTESY.

ill-chosen *adjective*
Characterized by inappropriateness and gracelessness, especially in expression : awkward, inappropriate, inept, infelicitous, unfortunate, unhappy. *See* ABILITY, GOOD.

ill-considered *adjective*
1. Characterized by unthinking boldness and haste : brash, foolhardy, harum-scarum, hasty, headlong, hotheaded, impetuous, improvident, impulsive, incautious, madcap, precipitant, precipitate, rash[1], reckless, slapdash, temerarious, unconsidered. *See* CAREFUL. **2.** Not wise : ill-advised, impolitic, imprudent, indiscreet, injudicious, unsound, unwise. *See* WISE.

illegal *adjective*
1. Prohibited by law : illegitimate, illicit, law-

less, outlawed, unlawful, wrongful. *See* CRIMES, LAW. **2.** Of, involving, or being a crime : criminal, illegitimate, illicit, lawless, unlawful, wrongful. *See* CRIMES.

illegality *noun*
1. The state or quality of being illegal : illegitimacy, illicitness, unlawfulness. *See* CRIMES, LAW. **2.** A serious breaking of the public law : crime, misdeed, offense. *Law:* felony. *See* CRIMES.

illegitimacy *noun*
1. The state or quality of being illegal : illegality, illicitness, unlawfulness. *See* CRIMES, LAW. **2.** The condition of being of illegitimate birth : bastardy. *See* KIN, LAW.

illegitimate *adjective*
1. Prohibited by law : illegal, illicit, lawless, outlawed, unlawful, wrongful. *See* CRIMES, LAW. **2.** Of, involving, or being a crime : criminal, illegal, illicit, lawless, unlawful, wrongful. *See* CRIMES. **3.** Born to parents who are not married to each other : baseborn, bastard, misbegotten, natural, spurious, unlawful. *See* KIN, LAW.

ill-fated *adjective*
Involving or undergoing chance misfortune : hapless, ill-starred, luckless, star-crossed, unfortunate, unhappy, unlucky, untoward. *See* LUCK.

ill-favored *adjective*
1. Extremely displeasing to the eye : hideous, ugly, unsightly. ***Idiom:*** ugly as sin. *See* BEAUTIFUL. **2.** Arousing disapproval : exceptionable, inadmissible, objectionable, unacceptable, undesirable, unwanted, unwelcome. *See* LIKE.

illiberal *adjective*
Not tolerant of the beliefs or opinions of others, for example : bigoted, close-minded, hidebound, intolerant, narrow-minded. *See* ACCEPT.

illicit *adjective*
1. Contrary to accepted, especially moral conventions : unlawful. *See* RIGHT. **2.** Prohibited by law : illegal, illegitimate, lawless, outlawed, unlawful, wrongful. *See* CRIMES, LAW. **3.** Of, involving, or being a crime : criminal, illegal, illegitimate, lawless, unlawful, wrongful. *See* CRIMES.

illicitness *noun*
The state or quality of being illegal : illegality, illegitimacy, unlawfulness. *See* CRIMES, LAW.

illimitable *adjective*
Having no ends or limits : boundless, endless, immeasurable, infinite, limitless, measureless, unbounded, unlimited. *See* LIMITED.

illiteracy *noun*
The condition of being ignorant; lack of knowledge or learning : benightedness, ignorance, illiterateness, nescience. *See* KNOWLEDGE.

illiterate *adjective*
Without education or knowledge : ignorant, nescient, uneducated, uninstructed, unlearned, unschooled, untaught. *See* KNOWLEDGE.

illiterateness *noun*
The condition of being ignorant; lack of knowledge or learning : benightedness, ignorance, illiteracy, nescience. *See* KNOWLEDGE.

ill-mannered *adjective*
Lacking good manners : discourteous, disrespectful, ill-bred, impolite, rude, uncivil, ungracious, unmannerly, unpolished. *See* COURTESY.

illness *noun*
1. The condition of being sick : affliction, disorder, indisposition, infirmity, sickness. *See* HEALTH. **2.** A pathological condition of mind or body : ailment, complaint, disease, disorder, ill, infirmity, malady, sickness. *See* HEALTH.

illogical *adjective*
1. Containing fundamental errors in reasoning : fallacious, false, invalid, sophistic, specious, spurious, unsound. *See* CORRECT, TRUE. **2.** Not governed by or predicated on reason : irrational, unreasonable, unreasoned. ***Idiom:*** out of bounds. *See* REASON.

illogicality *noun*
The absence of reason : illogicalness, irrationality, unreason, unreasonableness. *See* REASON.

illogicalness *noun*
The absence of reason : illogicality, irrationality, unreason, unreasonableness. *See* REASON.

ill repute *noun*
Loss of or damage to one's reputation : bad name, bad odor, discredit, disgrace, dishonor, disrepute, humiliation, ignominy, obloquy, odium, opprobrium, shame. *See* RESPECT.

ill-starred *adjective*
Involving or undergoing chance misfortune : hapless, ill-fated, luckless, star-crossed, unfortunate, unhappy, unlucky, untoward. *See* LUCK.

ill-suited *adjective*
Not suited to a given purpose : inappropriate, inapt, unfit, unsuitable, unsuited. *See* ABILITY.

ill-tempered *adjective*
Having or showing a bad temper : bad-tempered, cantankerous, crabbed, cranky, cross, disagreeable, fretful, grouchy, grumpy,

irascible, irritable, nasty, peevish, petulant, querulous, snappish, snappy, surly, testy, ugly, waspish. *Informal:* crabby, mean². ***Idiom:*** out of sorts. *See* ATTITUDE.

ill-timed *adjective*
Not occurring at a favorable time : inconvenient, inopportune, untimely. *See* TIME.

ill-treat *verb*
To hurt or injure by maltreatment : abuse, ill-use, maltreat, mishandle, mistreat, misuse. *See* HELP.

ill-treatment *noun*
Physically harmful treatment : abuse, maltreatment, mishandling, mistreatment, misusage. *See* HELP.

illume *verb*
1. To provide, cover, or fill with light : illuminate, illumine, light¹, lighten¹. *See* LIGHT.
2. To enable (one) to understand, especially in a spiritual sense : edify, enlighten, illuminate, illumine. *See* TEACH.

illuminate *verb*
1. To provide, cover, or fill with light : illume, illumine, light¹, lighten¹. *See* LIGHT. **2.** To make clear or clearer : clarify, clear (up), elucidate, illustrate. ***Idiom:*** shed (*or* throw) light on (*or* upon). *See* CLEAR. **3.** To enable (one) to understand, especially in a spiritual sense : edify, enlighten, illume, illumine. *See* TEACH.

illumination *noun*
1. The act of physically illuminating or the condition of being filled with light : light¹, lighting. *See* LIGHT. **2.** Electromagnetic radiation that makes vision possible : light¹. *See* LIGHT.
3. The condition of being informed spiritually : edification, enlightenment. *See* TEACH.
4. Something that serves to explain or clarify : clarification, construction, decipherment, elucidation, exegesis, explanation, explication, exposition, illustration, interpretation. *Archaic:* enucleation. *See* EXPLAIN.

illuminative *adjective*
Serving to educate or inform : edifying, educational, educative, enlightening, informative, instructional, instructive. *See* TEACH.

illumine *verb*
1. To provide, cover, or fill with light : illume, illuminate, light¹, lighten¹. *See* LIGHT. **2.** To enable (one) to understand, especially in a spiritual sense : edify, enlighten, illume, illuminate. *See* TEACH.

ill-use *verb*
To hurt or injure by maltreatment : abuse, ill-treat, maltreat, mishandle, mistreat, misuse. *See* HELP.

illusion *noun*
1. An erroneous perception of reality : delusion, hallucination, ignis fatuus, mirage, phantasm, phantasma, will-o'-the-wisp. *See* REAL.
2. An illusory mental image : daydream, dream, fancy, fantasy, fiction, figment, phantasm, phantasma, reverie, vision. *See* REAL.
3. A fantastic, impracticable plan or desire : bubble, castle in the air, chimera, dream, fantasy, pipe dream, rainbow. *See* REAL.

illusive *adjective*
1. Of, relating to, or in the nature of an illusion; lacking reality : chimeric, chimerical, delusive, delusory, dreamlike, hallucinatory, illusory, phantasmagoric, phantasmal, phantasmic, visionary. *See* REAL. **2.** Tending to lead one into error : deceptive, delusive, delusory, fallacious, illusory, misleading. *See* HONEST, REAL.
3. Tending to deceive; of the nature of an illusion : delusive, delusory, illusory. *See* REAL.

illusory *adjective*
1. Of, relating to, or in the nature of an illusion; lacking reality : chimeric, chimerical, delusive, delusory, dreamlike, hallucinatory, illusive, phantasmagoric, phantasmal, phantasmic, visionary. *See* REAL. **2.** Tending to lead one into error : deceptive, delusive, delusory, fallacious, illusive, misleading. *See* HONEST, REAL.
3. Tending to deceive; of the nature of an illusion : delusive, delusory, illusive. *See* REAL.

illustratable *adjective*
Capable of being explained or accounted for : accountable, decipherable, explainable, explicable, interpretable. *See* EXPLAIN.

illustrate *verb*
1. To demonstrate and clarify with examples : exemplify, instance. *See* SHOW. **2.** To serve as an example, image, or symbol of : epitomize, exemplify, represent, stand for, symbol, symbolize, typify. *See* SUBSTITUTE. **3.** To make clear or clearer : clarify, clear (up), elucidate, illuminate. ***Idiom:*** shed (*or* throw) light on (*or* upon). *See* CLEAR.

illustration *noun*
1. Something that serves to explain or clarify : clarification, construction, decipherment, elucidation, exegesis, explanation, explication, exposition, illumination, interpretation. *Archaic:* enucleation. *See* EXPLAIN. **2.** One that is representative of a group or class : case, example, instance, representative, sample, specimen. *See* SUBSTITUTE.

illustrative *adjective*
1. Serving to explain : elucidative, exegetic,

explanative, explanatory, explicative, expositive, expository, hermeneutic, hermeneutical, interpretative, interpretive. *See* EXPLAIN. **2.** Of or relating to representation by drawings or pictures : graphic, hieroglyphic, photographic, pictographic, pictorial. *See* SEE.

illustrious *adjective*
Widely known and esteemed : celebrated, distinguished, eminent, famed, famous, great, notable, noted, preeminent, prestigious, prominent, redoubtable, renowned. *See* KNOWLEDGE, RESPECT.

illustriousness *noun*
A position of exalted widely recognized importance : distinction, eminence, eminency, fame, glory, luster, mark, notability, note, preeminence, prestige, prominence, prominency, renown. *See* IMPORTANT, KNOWLEDGE, RESPECT.

ill will *noun*
1. Deep-seated hatred, as between longtime opponents or rivals : animosity, animus, antagonism, antipathy, enmity, hostility. *See* LOVE. **2.** A desire to harm others or to see others suffer : despitefulness, malevolence, malice, maliciousness, malignancy, malignity, meanness, nastiness, poisonousness, spite, spitefulness, venomousness, viciousness. *See* ATTITUDE.

image *noun*
1. Something that is reflected : reflection. *See* SHOW. **2.** Something closely resembling another : carbon copy, copy, duplicate, facsimile, likeness, reduplication, replica, replication, reproduction, simulacrum. *Archaic:* simulacre. *Law:* counterpart. *See* SAME. **3.** One exactly resembling another : double, duplicate, picture, portrait, spitting image. *Slang:* ringer. *See* SAME. **4.** The character projected or given by someone to the public : appearance, impression. *See* SURFACE. **5.** That which exists in the mind as the product of careful mental activity : concept, conception, idea, notion, perception, thought. *See* THOUGHTS.

image *verb* **1.** To present a lifelike image of : delineate, depict, describe, express, limn, picture, portray, render, represent, show. *See* SHOW. **2.** To copy (another) slavishly : echo, imitate, mimic, mirror, parrot, reflect, repeat. *See* SAME. **3.** To send back or form an image of : mirror, reflect. *See* SHOW. **4.** To form mental images of : conceive, envisage, envision, fancy, fantasize, imagine, picture, see, think, vision, visualize. *Informal:* feature. *See* THOUGHTS.

imaginable *adjective*
Capable of being anticipated, considered, or imagined : conceivable, earthly, likely, mortal, possible, thinkable. ***Idioms:*** humanly possible, within the bounds (*or* range *or* realm) of possibility. *See* POSSIBLE.

imaginary *adjective*
Existing only in the imagination : chimeric, chimerical, conceptual, fanciful, fantastic, fantastical, notional, unreal, visionary. *See* REAL.

imagination *noun*
The power of the mind to form images : fancy, fantasy, imaginativeness. *See* REAL, THOUGHTS.

imaginative *adjective*
Appealing to fancy : fanciful, fancy, fantastic, fantastical, whimsical. *See* PLAIN.

imaginativeness *noun*
The power of the mind to form images : fancy, fantasy, imagination. *See* REAL, THOUGHTS.

imagine *verb*
To form mental images of : conceive, envisage, envision, fancy, fantasize, image, picture, see, think, vision, visualize. *Informal:* feature. *See* THOUGHTS.

imbecile *noun*
One deficient in judgment and good sense : ass, fool, idiot, jackass, mooncalf, moron, nincompoop, ninny, nitwit, simple, simpleton, softhead, tomfool. *Informal:* dope, gander, goose. *Slang:* cretin, ding-dong, dip, goof, jerk, nerd, schmo, schmuck, turkey. *See* ABILITY.

imbecilic *adjective*
So senseless as to be laughable : absurd, foolish, harebrained, idiotic, insane, lunatic, mad, moronic, nonsensical, preposterous, silly, softheaded, tomfool, unearthly, zany. *Informal:* cockeyed, crazy, loony, loopy. *Slang:* balmy[2], dippy, dopey, jerky, sappy, wacky. *See* ABILITY, KNOWLEDGE.

imbecility *noun*
Foolish behavior : absurdity, folly, foolery, foolishness, idiocy, insanity, lunacy, madness, nonsense, preposterousness, senselessness, silliness, tomfoolery, zaniness. *Informal:* craziness. *See* ABILITY.

imbed *verb* See **embed.**

imbibe *verb*
1. To take into the mouth and swallow (a liquid) : drink, pull on, quaff, sip, sup. *Informal:* swig, toss down (*or* off). *Slang:* belt. ***Idiom:*** wet one's whistle. *See* MOUTH. **2.** To take alcoholic liquor, especially excessively or habitually : drink, guzzle, tipple. *Informal:* nip[2]. *Slang:* booze, lush[2], soak, tank up.

Idioms: bend the elbow, hit the bottle. *See* DRUGS. **3.** To take in (moisture or liquid) : absorb, drink, soak (up), sop up, take up. *See* GIVE. **4.** To take in and incorporate, especially mentally : absorb, assimilate, digest, take up. *Informal:* soak (up). *See* ACCEPT.

imbrue also **embrue** *verb*
To cover with blood : bloodstain, bloody, ensanguine. *See* BLOOD.

imbue *verb*
To cause to be filled, as with a particular mood or tone : charge, freight, impregnate, permeate, pervade, saturate, suffuse, transfuse. *See* FULL.

imitate *verb*
1. To take as a model or make conform to a model : copy, emulate, follow, model (on, upon, *or* after), pattern (on, upon, *or* after). *Idioms:* follow in the footsteps of, follow suit, follow the example of. *See* SAME. **2.** To copy (the manner or expression of another), especially in an exaggerated or mocking way : ape, burlesque, caricature, mimic, mock, parody, travesty. *Idiom:* do a takeoff on. *See* SAME. **3.** To copy (another) slavishly : echo, image, mimic, mirror, parrot, reflect, repeat. *See* SAME. **4.** To make a copy of : copy, duplicate, replicate, reproduce, simulate. *See* SAME.

imitation *noun*
1. The act, practice, or art of copying the manner or expression of another : aping, mimicry. *See* SAME. **2.** Imitative reproduction, as of the style of another : echo, reflection, reflex, repetition. *See* SAME. **3.** A usually amusing caricature of another : parody. *Informal:* takeoff. *See* LAUGHTER, RESPECT, SAME. **4.** An inferior substitute imitating an original : copy, ersatz, pinchbeck, simulation. *See* SUBSTITUTE.

imitation *adjective* Made to imitate something else : artificial, manmade, mock, simulated, synthetic. *Informal:* pretend. *See* REAL.

imitative *adjective*
1. Copying another in an inferior or obsequious way : apish, emulative, slavish. *See* SAME. **2.** Imitating sounds : echoic, onomatopoeic, onomatopoetic. *See* SAME, SOUNDS.

imitator *noun*
One who mindlessly imitates another : echo, mimic, parrot. *See* SAME.

immaculate *adjective*
Free from dirt, stain, or impurities : antiseptic, clean, cleanly, spotless, stainless, unsoiled, unsullied. *See* CLEAN.

immaterial *adjective*
1. Not relevant or pertinent to the subject; not applicable : extraneous, impertinent, inapplicable, irrelevant. *Idioms:* beside the point, neither here nor there. *See* RELEVANT. **2.** Having no body, form, or substance : bodiless, discarnate, disembodied, incorporeal, insubstantial, metaphysical, nonphysical, spiritual, unbodied, uncorporal, unsubstantial. *See* BODY.

immature *adjective*
1. Being in an early period of growth or development : green, infant, juvenile, young, youthful. *See* YOUTH. **2.** Of or characteristic of a child, especially in immaturity : babyish, childish, infantile, juvenile, puerile. *See* YOUTH.

immeasurability *noun*
The state or quality of being infinite : boundlessness, immeasurableness, inexhaustibility, inexhaustibleness, infiniteness, infinity, limitlessness, measurelessness, unboundedness, unlimitedness. *See* LIMITED.

immeasurable *adjective*
1. Too great to be calculated : countless, incalculable, incomputable, inestimable, infinite, innumerable, measureless, uncountable. *See* BIG. **2.** Having no ends or limits : boundless, endless, illimitable, infinite, limitless, measureless, unbounded, unlimited. *See* LIMITED.

immeasurableness *noun*
The state or quality of being infinite : boundlessness, immeasurability, inexhaustibility, inexhaustibleness, infiniteness, infinity, limitlessness, measurelessness, unboundedness, unlimitedness. *See* LIMITED.

immediate *adjective*
1. Occurring at once : instant, instantaneous. *See* TIME. **2.** Not far from another in space, time, or relation : adjacent, close, contiguous, near, nearby, nigh, proximate. *Idioms:* at hand, under one's nose, within a stone's throw, within hailing distance. *See* NEAR. **3.** Marked by the absence of any intervention : direct, firsthand, primary. *See* CLEAR, NEAR.

immediately *adverb*
1. Without delay : directly, forthwith, instant, instantly, now, right away, right off, straightaway, straight off. *Idioms:* at once, first off. *See* TIME. **2.** Without intermediary : directly. *See* CLEAR, NEAR.

immemorial *adjective*
Long past : ancient, high. *See* NEW.

immense *adjective*
Of extraordinary size and power : behemoth, Brobdingnagian, Bunyanesque, colossal, cyclo-

pean, elephantine, enormous, gargantuan, giant, gigantesque, gigantic, herculean, heroic, huge, jumbo, mammoth, massive, massy, mastodonic, mighty, monster, monstrous, monumental, mountainous, prodigious, pythonic, stupendous, titanic, tremendous, vast. *Informal:* walloping. *Slang:* whopping. *See* BIG.

immenseness *noun*
The quality of being enormous : enormousness, hugeness, immensity, prodigiousness, stupendousness, tremendousness, vastness. *See* BIG.

immensity *noun*
The quality of being enormous : enormousness, hugeness, immenseness, prodigiousness, stupendousness, tremendousness, vastness. *See* BIG.

immerge *verb*
To plunge briefly in or into a liquid : dip, douse, duck, dunk, immerse, souse, submerge, submerse. *See* ENTER.

immerse *verb*
1. To plunge briefly in or into a liquid : dip, douse, duck, dunk, immerge, souse, submerge, submerse. *See* ENTER. **2.** To occupy the full attention of : absorb, consume, engross, monopolize, preoccupy. *See* AWARENESS, EXCITE.

immersion *noun*
Total occupation of the attention or of the mind : absorption, engrossment, enthrallment, preoccupation, prepossession. *See* EXCITE.

immigrant *noun*
One who emigrates : emigrant, migrant, transmigrant. *See* APPROACH.

immigrate *verb*
To leave one's native land and settle in another : emigrate, migrate, transmigrate. *See* APPROACH.

immigration *noun*
Departure from one's native land to settle in another : emigration, exodus, migration, transmigration. *See* APPROACH.

imminence *noun*
The act or fact of coming near : approach, coming, convergence, nearness. *See* APPROACH.

imminent *adjective*
About to occur at any moment : impending, momentary, proximate. *See* NEAR.

immobile *adjective*
1. Firmly in position : fixed, immovable, stationary, steadfast, steady, unmovable, unmoving. *See* MOVE. **2.** Not moving : motionless, stationary, still, stock-still, unmoving. *See* MOVE.

immobilization *noun*
A cessation of normal activity, caused by an accident or strike, for example : gridlock, jam, stoppage, tie-up. *See* CONTINUE.

immobilize *verb*
1. To render powerless or motionless, as by inflicting severe injury : cripple, disable, incapacitate, knock out, paralyze. ***Idiom:*** put out of action (*or* commission). *See* HELP. **2.** To cause to cease regular activity : idle, stop, tie up. ***Idiom:*** bring to a screeching halt. *See* CONTINUE.

immoderate *adjective*
Exceeding a normal or reasonable limit : excessive, exorbitant, extravagant, extreme, inordinate, overabundant, overmuch, undue. *See* EXCESS.

immodest *adjective*
Not in keeping with conventional mores : improper, indecent, indecorous, indelicate, naughty, unbecoming, unbefitting, unseemly, untoward. ***Idiom:*** out of line. *See* USUAL.

immolate *verb*
To offer as a sacrifice : sacrifice, victimize. *See* GIVE, RELIGION.

immolation *noun*
One or more living creatures slain and offered to a deity as part of a religious rite : hecatomb, offering, sacrifice, victim. *See* RELIGION.

immoral *adjective*
1. Morally objectionable : bad, black, evil, iniquitous, peccant, reprobate, sinful, vicious, wicked, wrong. *See* RIGHT. **2.** Not chaste or moral : impure, unchaste, unclean, uncleanly. *See* GOOD, RESTRAINT, SEX.

immorality *noun*
1. A wicked act or wicked behavior : crime, deviltry, diablerie, evil, evildoing, iniquity, misdeed, offense, peccancy, sin, wickedness, wrong, wrongdoing. *See* RIGHT. **2.** Degrading, immoral acts or habits : bestiality, corruption, depravity, flagitiousness, perversion, turpitude, vice, villainousness, villainy, wickedness. *See* CLEAN.

immortal *adjective*
1. Not being subject to death : deathless, undying. *See* CONTINUE, LIVE. **2.** Enduring for all time : amaranthine, ceaseless, endless, eternal, everlasting, never-ending, perpetual, unending, world without end. *Archaic:* eterne. *See* CONTINUE.

immortality *noun*
Endless life after death : afterlife, deathless-

ness, eternity, everlasting life, everlastingness. *See* CONTINUE, LIVE.

immortalize *verb*
To cause to last endlessly : eternalize, eternize, perpetuate. *See* CONTINUE, REMEMBER.

immovable *adjective*
Firmly in position : fixed, immobile, stationary, steadfast, steady, unmovable, unmoving. *See* MOVE.

immune *adjective*
Having the capacity to withstand : impervious, insusceptible, proof, resistant, resistive, unsusceptible. *See* RESIST.

immunity *noun*
The capacity to withstand : imperviousness, insusceptibility, resistance, unsusceptibility. *See* RESIST.

immure *verb*
1. To confine within a limited area : cage, coop (in *or* up), enclose, fence (in), mew (up), pen[2], shut in, shut up, wall (in *or* up). *See* FREE. **2.** To put in jail : confine, detain, imprison, incarcerate, intern, jail, lock (up). *See* FREE.

immutable *adjective*
Incapable of changing or being modified : inalterable, inflexible, invariable, ironclad, rigid, unalterable, unchangeable. *See* FLEXIBLE.

imp *noun*
One who causes minor trouble or damage : devil, mischief, prankster, rascal, rogue, scamp. *Informal:* cutup. *See* GOOD.

impact *noun*
1. Violent forcible contact between two or more things : bump, collision, concussion, crash, jar, jolt, percussion, shock[1], smash. *See* CONFLICT. **2.** The strong effect exerted by one person or thing on another : force, impression, influence, repercussion. *See* AFFECT. **3.** The capacity to create a powerful effect : *Informal:* punch, wallop. *See* AFFECT.

impair *verb*
To spoil the soundness or perfection of : blemish, damage, detract from, disserve, flaw, harm, hurt, injure, mar, prejudice, tarnish, vitiate. *See* BETTER, HELP.

impairment *noun*
An act, instance, or consequence of breaking : breakage, damage, destruction, wreckage. *See* HELP.

impalpable *adjective*
Incapable of being apprehended by the mind or the senses : imperceptible, imponderable, inappreciable, indiscernible, indistinguishable, insensible, intangible, invisible, unnoticeable, unobservable. *See* KNOWLEDGE.

impart *verb*
To make known : break, carry, communicate, convey, disclose, get across, pass, report, tell, transmit. *See* KNOWLEDGE.

impartial *adjective*
1. Free from bias in judgment : disinterested, dispassionate, equitable, fair, fair-minded, indifferent, just, nonpartisan, objective, square, unbiased, unprejudiced. ***Idiom:*** fair and square. *See* FAIR. **2.** Not inclining toward or actively taking either side in a matter under dispute : neuter, neutral, nonaligned, nonpartisan, unbiased, uncommitted, uninvolved, unprejudiced. *Idiom:* on the fence. *See* FAIR.

impartiality *noun*
The quality or state of being just and unbiased : detachment, disinterest, disinterestedness, dispassion, dispassionateness, equitableness, fair-mindedness, fairness, impartialness, justice, justness, nonpartisanship, objectiveness, objectivity. *See* FAIR.

impartialness *noun*
The quality or state of being just and unbiased : detachment, disinterest, disinterestedness, dispassion, dispassionateness, equitableness, fair-mindedness, fairness, impartiality, justice, justness, nonpartisanship, objectiveness, objectivity. *See* FAIR.

impassable *adjective*
Incapable of being negotiated or overcome : insuperable, insurmountable. *See* DO.

impassible *adjective*
Not capable of being affected or impressed : impassive, insensitive, insusceptible, unimpressionable, unsusceptible. *See* AFFECT.

impassion *verb*
To arouse the emotions of; make ardent : animate, enkindle, fire, inspire, kindle, stir[1]. *See* EXCITE.

impassioned *adjective*
Fired with intense feeling : ardent, blazing, burning, dithyrambic, fervent, fervid, fiery, flaming, glowing, heated, hot-blooded, passionate, perfervid, red-hot, scorching, torrid. *See* FEELINGS.

impassive *adjective*
1. Without emotion or interest : apathetic, detached, incurious, indifferent, insensible, lethargic, listless, phlegmatic, stolid, unconcerned, uninterested, unresponsive. *See* FEELINGS. **2.** With little or no emotion or expression : dry, matter-of-fact, unemotional. *See* ATTITUDE, EXCITE. **3.** Not capable of being affected or impressed : impassible, insen-

sitive, insusceptible, unimpressionable, unsusceptible. *See* AFFECT.

impassivity *noun*
Lack of emotion or interest : apathy, disinterest, incuriosity, incuriousness, indifference, insensibility, insensibleness, lassitude, lethargy, listlessness, phlegm, stolidity, stolidness, unconcern, uninterest, unresponsiveness. *See* FEELINGS.

impatient *adjective*
1. Being unable or unwilling to endure irritation or opposition, for example : fretful, intolerant, unforbearing. *See* ACCEPT, ATTITUDE, CALM. **2.** Intensely desirous or interested : agog, ardent, athirst, avid, bursting, eager, keen[1], solicitous, thirsting, thirsty. *Informal:* raring. *Idioms:* champing at the bit, ready and willing. *See* CONCERN.

impeccable *adjective*
Supremely excellent in quality or nature : absolute, consummate, faultless, flawless, indefectible, perfect, unflawed. *See* GOOD.

impecuniosity *noun*
The condition of being extremely poor : beggary, destitution, impecuniousness, impoverishment, indigence, need, neediness, pennilessness, penuriousness, penury, poverty, privation, want. *See* RICH.

impecunious *adjective*
Having little or no money or wealth : beggarly, destitute, down-and-out, impoverished, indigent, necessitous, needy, penniless, penurious, poor, poverty-stricken. *Informal:* broke, strapped. *Idioms:* hard up, on one's uppers. *See* RICH.

impecuniousness *noun*
The condition of being extremely poor : beggary, destitution, impecuniosity, impoverishment, indigence, need, neediness, pennilessness, penuriousness, penury, poverty, privation, want. *See* RICH.

impede *verb*
1. To interfere with the progress of : bog (down), encumber, hinder, hold back, obstruct. *Idiom:* get in the way of. *See* HELP, OPEN. **2.** To stop or prevent passage of : bar, block, dam, obstruct. *Idiom:* be (*or* stand) in the way of. *See* OPEN.

impediment *noun*
Something that impedes or prevents entry or passage : bar, barricade, barrier, block, blockage, clog, hamper, hindrance, hurdle, obstacle, obstruction, snag, stop, traverse, wall. *See* HELP, OPEN.

impel *verb*
1. To stir to action or feeling : egg on, excite, foment, galvanize, goad, incite, inflame, inspire, instigate, motivate, move, pique, prick, prod, prompt, propel, provoke, set off, spur, stimulate, touch off, trigger, work up. *See* CAUSE, EXCITE. **2.** To set or keep going : actuate, drive, mobilize, move, propel, run. *See* MOVE.

impend *verb*
To be imminent : brew, hang over, loom, lower[1], menace, overhang, threaten. *See* NEAR.

impending *adjective*
About to occur at any moment : imminent, momentary, proximate. *See* NEAR.

impenetrable *adjective*
Incapable of being grasped by the intellect or understanding : incomprehensible, inscrutable, uncomprehensible, unfathomable, unintelligible. *See* KNOWLEDGE.

impenitent *adjective*
Devoid of remorse : remorseless, unrepentant. *See* REGRET.

imperative *adjective*
1. Compelling immediate attention : burning, crying, dire, emergent, exigent, instant, pressing, urgent. *See* BIG. **2.** Imposed on one by authority, command, or convention : compulsory, mandatory, necessary, obligatory, required, requisite. *See* OBLIGATION.
imperative *noun* An act or course of action that is demanded of one, as by position, custom, law, or religion : burden[1], charge, commitment, duty, must, need, obligation, responsibility. *See* OBLIGATION.

imperceptible *adjective*
1. Incapable of being apprehended by the mind or the senses : impalpable, imponderable, inappreciable, indiscernible, indistinguishable, insensible, intangible, invisible, unnoticeable, unobservable. *See* KNOWLEDGE. **2.** So minute as not to be discernible : infinitesimal, microscopic. *See* BIG.

imperfect *adjective*
Having a defect or defects : defective, faulty. *See* BETTER.

imperfection *noun*
Something that mars the appearance or causes inadequacy or failure : blemish, bug, defect, fault, flaw, shortcoming. *See* BEAUTIFUL, BETTER, HELP.

imperil *verb*
To subject to danger : endanger, jeopardize, menace, peril, risk, threaten. *See* SAFETY.

imperilment *noun*
Exposure to possible harm, loss, or injury :

danger, endangerment, hazard, jeopardy, peril, risk. *See* SAFETY.

imperious *adjective*
Tending to dictate : authoritarian, bossy, dictatorial, dogmatic, domineering, magisterial, masterful, overbearing, peremptory. *See* OVER.

impermanent *adjective*
Intended, used, or present for a limited time : interim, provisional, short-range, short-term, temporary. *See* CONTINUE.

impermissible *adjective*
Not allowed : forbidden, taboo, verboten. *See* ALLOW.

impersonal *adjective*
Feeling or showing no strong emotional involvement : detached, disinterested, dispassionate, indifferent, neutral. *See* FEELINGS.

impersonate *verb*
1. To represent oneself in a given character or as other than what one is : attitudinize, masquerade, pass, pose, posture. *Idiom:* pass oneself off as. *See* HONEST. **2.** To play the part of : act, do, enact, perform, play, play-act, portray, represent. *See* ACTION, PERFORMING ARTS, SUBSTITUTE.

impersonator *noun*
A performer skilled at copying the manner or expression of another : mime, mimic. *See* PERFORMING ARTS, SAME.

impertinence *noun*
The state or quality of being impudent or arrogantly self-confident : assumption, audaciousness, audacity, boldness, brashness, brazenness, cheek, cheekiness, chutzpah, discourtesy, disrespect, effrontery, face, familiarity, forwardness, gall[1], impudence, impudency, incivility, insolence, nerve, nerviness, overconfidence, pertness, presumptuousness, pushiness, rudeness, sassiness, sauciness. *Informal:* brass, crust, sauce, uppishness, uppityness. *See* ATTITUDE, COURTESY.

impertinent *adjective*
1. Rude and disrespectful : assuming, assumptive, audacious, bold, boldfaced, brash, brazen, cheeky, contumelious, familiar, forward, impudent, insolent, malapert, nervy, overconfident, pert, presuming, presumptuous, pushy, sassy, saucy, smart. *Informal:* brassy, flip, fresh, smart-alecky, snippety, snippy, uppish, uppity. *Slang:* wise[1]. *See* ATTITUDE, COURTESY.
2. Not relevant or pertinent to the subject; not applicable : extraneous, immaterial, inapplicable, irrelevant. *Idioms:* beside the point, neither here nor there. *See* RELEVANT.

imperturbability *noun*
A stable, calm state of the emotions : aplomb, balance, collectedness, composure, coolness, equanimity, imperturbableness, nonchalance, poise, sang-froid, self-possession, unflappability. *Slang:* cool. *See* CALM, FEELINGS.

imperturbable *adjective*
Not easily excited, even under pressure : calm, collected, composed, cool, cool-headed, detached, even[1], even-tempered, nonchalant, possessed, unflappable, unruffled. *See* CALM.

imperturbableness *noun*
A stable, calm state of the emotions : aplomb, balance, collectedness, composure, coolness, equanimity, imperturbability, nonchalance, poise, sang-froid, self-possession, unflappability. *Slang:* cool. *See* CALM, FEELINGS.

impervious *adjective*
Having the capacity to withstand : immune, insusceptible, proof, resistant, resistive, unsusceptible. *See* RESIST.

imperviousness *noun*
The capacity to withstand : immunity, insusceptibility, resistance, unsusceptibility. *See* RESIST.

impetuous *adjective*
Characterized by unthinking boldness and haste : brash, foolhardy, harum-scarum, hasty, headlong, hotheaded, ill-considered, improvident, impulsive, incautious, madcap, precipitant, precipitate, rash[1], reckless, slapdash, temerarious, unconsidered. *See* CAREFUL.

impetus *noun*
Something that causes and encourages a given response : encouragement, fillip, impulse, incentive, inducement, motivation, prod, push, spur, stimulant, stimulation, stimulator, stimulus. *See* CAUSE.

impingement *noun*
An advance beyond proper or legal limits : encroachment, entrenchment, infringement, intrusion, obtrusion, trespass. *See* ENTER.

impish *adjective*
Full of high-spirited fun : frisky, frolicsome, mischievous, playful, sportive, waggish. *See* WORK.

impishness *noun*
Annoying yet harmless, usually playful acts : devilry, deviltry, diablerie, high jinks, mischief, mischievousness, prankishness, rascality, roguery, roguishness, tomfoolery. *Informal:* shenanigan (often used in plural). *See* GOOD.

implacability *noun*
The quality or state of being stubbornly

inflexible : die-hardism, grimness, implacableness, incompliance, incompliancy, inexorability, inexorableness, inflexibility, inflexibleness, intransigence, intransigency, obduracy, obdurateness, relentlessness, remorselessness, rigidity, rigidness, stubbornness. *See* RESIST.

implacable *adjective*
Firmly, often unreasonably immovable in purpose or will : adamant, adamantine, brassbound, die-hard, grim, incompliant, inexorable, inflexible, intransigent, iron, obdurate, relentless, remorseless, rigid, stubborn, unbendable, unbending, uncompliant, uncompromising, unrelenting, unyielding. ***Idiom:*** stubborn as a mule (*or* ox). *See* RESIST.

implacableness *noun*
The quality or state of being stubbornly inflexible : die-hardism, grimness, implacability, incompliance, incompliancy, inexorability, inexorableness, inflexibility, inflexibleness, intransigence, intransigency, obduracy, obdurateness, relentlessness, remorselessness, rigidity, rigidness, stubbornness. *See* RESIST.

implant *verb*
To fix (an idea, for example) in someone's mind by reemphasis and repetition : drill, drive, impress, inculcate, instill, pound. *See* TEACH.

implausible *adjective*
Not plausible or believable : flimsy, improbable, inconceivable, incredible, shaky, thin, unbelievable, unconceivable, unconvincing, unsubstantial, weak. *See* LIKELY.

implement *noun*
A device used to do work or perform a task : instrument, tool, utensil. *See* MACHINE, MEANS.

implement *verb* **1.** To put into action or use : actuate, apply, employ, exercise, exploit, practice, use, utilize. ***Idioms:*** avail oneself of, bring into play, bring to bear, make use of, put into practice, put to use. *See* USED. **2.** To carry out the functions, requirements, or terms of : discharge, do, execute, exercise, fulfill, keep, perform. ***Idiom:*** live up to. *See* DO. **3.** To compel observance of : carry out, effect, enforce, execute, invoke. ***Idioms:*** put in force, put into action. *See* OBLIGATION, OVER.

implementation *noun*
The act of putting into play : application, employment, exercise, exertion, operation, play, usage, use, utilization. *See* USED.

implicate *verb*
1. To draw in so that extrication is difficult : catch up, embrangle, embroil, involve, mix up, suck. *See* FREE, PARTICIPATE. **2.** To cause to appear involved in or guilty of a crime or fault : criminate, incriminate, inculpate. *See* ATTACK, CRIMES.

implication *noun*
A subtle quality underlying or felt to underlie a situation, action, or person : hint, inkling, suspicion, undercurrent, undertone. *See* SHOW, SUGGEST.

implicit *adjective*
1. Conveyed indirectly without words or speech : implied, inferred, tacit, understood, unsaid, unspoken, unuttered, wordless. ***Idiom:*** taken for granted. *See* SHOW. **2.** Involved in the essential nature of something but not shown or developed : practical, virtual. *See* BE, SHOW. **3.** Having no reservations : absolute, unconditional, undoubting, unfaltering, unhesitating, unquestioning, unreserved, wholehearted. *See* BIG, LIMITED.

implied *adjective*
Conveyed indirectly without words or speech : implicit, inferred, tacit, understood, unsaid, unspoken, unuttered, wordless. ***Idiom:*** taken for granted. *See* SHOW.

imploration *noun*
An earnest or urgent request : appeal, entreaty, plea, prayer[1], supplication. *See* ASK.

implore *verb*
To make an earnest or urgent request : appeal, beg, beseech, crave, entreat, plead, pray, sue, supplicate. *Archaic:* conjure. *See* ASK.

imply *verb*
1. To lead to by logical inference : indicate, point to, suggest. *See* MEANING. **2.** To convey an idea by indirect, subtle means : hint, insinuate, intimate[2], suggest. ***Idiom:*** drop a hint. *See* SHOW, SUGGEST.

impolite *adjective*
Lacking good manners : discourteous, disrespectful, ill-bred, ill-mannered, rude, uncivil, ungracious, unmannerly, unpolished. *See* COURTESY.

impolitic *adjective*
1. Not wise : ill-advised, ill-considered, imprudent, indiscreet, injudicious, unsound, unwise. *See* WISE. **2.** Lacking sensitivity and skill in dealing with others : brash, clumsy, gauche, indelicate, maladroit, tactless, undiplomatic, unpolitic, untactful. *See* ABILITY, COURTESY.

imponderable *adjective*
Incapable of being apprehended by the mind or the senses : impalpable, imperceptible, inappreciable, indiscernible, indistinguishable, insensible, intangible, invisible, unnoticeable, unobservable. *See* KNOWLEDGE.

import *verb*
1. To have or convey a particular idea : connote, denote, intend, mean[1], signify, spell[1]. *Idiom:* add up to. *See* MEANING. **2.** To be of significance or importance : count, matter, signify, weigh. *See* IMPORTANT.
import *noun* **1.** That which is signified by a word or expression : acceptation, connotation, denotation, intent, meaning, message, purport, sense, significance, significancy, signification, value. *See* MEANING. **2.** The general sense or significance, as of an action or statement : amount, burden[2], drift, purport, substance, tenor. *Idioms:* sum and substance, sum total. *See* MEANING. **3.** The gist of a specific action or situation : idea, meaning, point, purport, significance, significancy. *See* MEANING. **4.** The quality or state of being important : concern, concernment, consequence, importance, moment, significance, significancy, weight, weightiness. *See* IMPORTANT.

importance *noun*
The quality or state of being important : concern, concernment, consequence, import, moment, significance, significancy, weight, weightiness. *See* IMPORTANT.

important *adjective*
1. Having great significance : big, consequential, considerable, historic, large, material, meaningful, monumental, significant, substantial. *See* IMPORTANT. **2.** Having or exercising influence : consequential, influential, powerful, weighty. *See* AFFECT, IMPORTANT, STRONG.

importunate *adjective*
Firm or obstinate, as in making a demand or maintaining a stand : importune, insistent, persistent, urgent. *See* CONTINUE.

importune *verb*
To trouble persistently from or as if from all sides : badger, bedevil, beleaguer, beset, besiege, harass, harry, hound, pester, plague, solicit. *See* ATTACK.
importune *adjective* Firm or obstinate, as in making a demand or maintaining a stand : importunate, insistent, persistent, urgent. *See* CONTINUE.

impose *verb*
1. To establish and apply as compulsory : assess, exact, levy, put. *See* OBLIGATION, OVER, WILLING. **2.** To set forth expressly and authoritatively : decree, dictate, fix, lay down, ordain, prescribe. *Idioms:* call the shots (*or* tune), lay it on the line. *See* OVER. **3.** To cause to undergo or bear (something unwelcome or damaging, for example) : inflict, play, visit, wreak. *See* GIVE, OVER, WILLING. **4.** To force (another) to accept a burden : foist, inflict, saddle. *Informal:* stick. *See* GIVE, OVER, WILLING. **5.** To take advantage of unfairly : abuse, exploit, presume, use. *See* TREAT WELL.

imposing *adjective*
Large and impressive in size, scope, or extent : august, baronial, grand, grandiose, lordly, magnific, magnificent, majestic, noble, princely, regal, royal, splendid, stately, sublime, superb. *See* BIG, GOOD.

imposition *noun*
An excessive, unwelcome burden : infliction, intrusion. *See* LIKE, WILLING.

impossible *adjective*
1. Not capable of happening or being done : impracticable, impractical, unattainable, unrealizable, unthinkable, unworkable. *Idiom:* out of the question. *See* POSSIBLE. **2.** So unpleasant or painful as not to be endured or tolerated : insufferable, insupportable, intolerable, unbearable, unendurable, unsufferable, unsupportable. *See* PAIN. **3.** Given to acting in opposition to others : balky, contrarious, contrary, difficult, froward, ornery, perverse, wayward. *See* ATTITUDE, SUPPORT.

impost *noun*
1. A compulsory contribution, usually of money, that is required for the support of a government : assessment, duty, levy, tariff, tax. *See* MONEY, PAY, POLITICS. **2.** *Sports.* Something carried physically : burden[1], cargo, freight, haul, load. *See* HEAVY, OVER.

impostor *noun*
One who fakes : charlatan, fake, faker, fraud, humbug, mountebank, phony, pretender, quack. *See* TRUE.

imposture *noun*
An indirect, usually cunning means of gaining an end : artifice, deception, device, dodge, feint, gimmick, jig, maneuver, ploy, ruse, sleight, stratagem, subterfuge, trick, wile. *Informal:* shenanigan, take-in. *See* HONEST, MEANS.

impotence *noun*
The condition or state of being incapable of accomplishing or effecting anything : helplessness, inadequacy, incapability, ineffectiveness, ineffectuality, ineffectualness, inefficacy, powerlessness, uselessness. *See* AFFECT, STRONG.

impotent *adjective*
1. Lacking power or strength : helpless, powerless. *See* ABILITY, HELP. **2.** Not capable of

accomplishing anything : helpless, inadequate, incapable, ineffectual, powerless, weak. *See* ABILITY, STRONG. **3.** Unable to produce offspring : barren, childless, infertile, sterile, unfruitful. *See* RICH.

impoverish *verb*
1. To reduce to financial insolvency : bankrupt, break, bust, pauperize, ruin. *Slang:* clean out. *See* MONEY. **2.** To lessen or weaken severely, as by removing something essential : deplete, drain, exhaust, sap^2, use up. *See* GIVE, INCREASE, RICH.

impoverished *adjective*
1. Having little or no money or wealth : beggarly, destitute, down-and-out, impecunious, indigent, necessitous, needy, penniless, penurious, poor, poverty-stricken. *Informal:* broke, strapped. ***Idioms:*** hard up, on one's uppers. *See* RICH. **2.** Economically and socially below standard : backward, depressed, deprived, disadvantaged, underprivileged. *See* RICH.

impoverishment *noun*
1. The condition of being extremely poor : beggary, destitution, impecuniosity, impecuniousness, indigence, need, neediness, pennilessness, penuriousness, penury, poverty, privation, want. *See* RICH. **2.** The depletion or sapping of strength or energy : attenuation, debilitation, depletion, devitalization, enervation, enfeeblement. *See* STRONG.

impracticable *adjective*
1. Not capable of happening or being done : impossible, impractical, unattainable, unrealizable, unthinkable, unworkable. ***Idiom:*** out of the question. *See* POSSIBLE. **2.** Incapable of being used or availed of to advantage : impractical, unnegotiable, unserviceable, unusable, unworkable, useless. *See* USED.

impractical *adjective*
1. Not capable of happening or being done : impossible, impracticable, unattainable, unrealizable, unthinkable, unworkable. ***Idiom:*** out of the question. *See* POSSIBLE. **2.** Incapable of dealing efficiently with practical matters : ivory-tower. *See* THRIVE. **3.** Incapable of being used or availed of to advantage : impracticable, unnegotiable, unserviceable, unusable, unworkable, useless. *See* USED.

imprecate *verb*
To invoke evil or injury upon : anathematize, curse, damn. *Informal:* cuss. *Archaic:* execrate, maledict. *See* WORDS.

imprecation *noun*
A denunciation invoking a wish or threat of evil or injury : anathema, curse, damnation, execration, malediction. *Archaic:* malison. *See* WORDS.

impregnable *adjective*
Incapable of being conquered, overrun, or subjugated : indomitable, invincible, unconquerable. *See* DO, WIN.

impregnate *verb*
To cause to be filled, as with a particular mood or tone : charge, freight, imbue, permeate, pervade, saturate, suffuse, transfuse. *See* FULL.

impress *verb*
1. To evoke a usually strong mental or emotional response from : affect^1, get (to), move, strike, touch. *See* TOUCH. **2.** To fix (an idea, for example) in someone's mind by reemphasis and repetition : drill, drive, implant, inculcate, instill, pound. *See* TEACH. **3.** To produce a deep impression of : engrave, etch, fix, grave^3, imprint, inscribe, stamp. *See* MARKS.
impress *noun* The visible effect made on a surface by pressure : impression, imprint, indent, indentation, mark, print, stamp. *See* MARKS.

impressible *adjective*
Able to receive and respond to external stimuli : impressionable, responsive, sensible, sensitive, sentient, susceptible, susceptive. *See* AWARENESS.

impression *noun*
1. The strong effect exerted by one person or thing on another : force, impact, influence, repercussion. *See* AFFECT. **2.** The character projected or given by someone to the public : appearance, image. *See* SURFACE. **3.** Intuitive cognition : feeling, hunch, idea, intuition, suspicion. *See* THOUGHTS. **4.** The visible effect made on a surface by pressure : impress, imprint, indent, indentation, mark, print, stamp. *See* MARKS. **5.** The entire number of copies of a publication printed from a single typesetting : printing. *See* WORDS.

impressionable *adjective*
1. Easily altered or influenced : ductile, elastic, flexible, flexile, malleable, plastic, pliable, pliant, suggestible, supple. *See* FLEXIBLE. **2.** Able to receive and respond to external stimuli : impressible, responsive, sensible, sensitive, sentient, susceptible, susceptive. *See* AWARENESS.

impressionistic *adjective*
Tending to bring a memory, mood, or image, for example, subtly or indirectly to mind : allusive, connotative, evocative, reminiscent, suggestive. *See* SUGGEST.

impressive *adjective*
Exciting a deep, usually somber response :

affecting, moving, poignant, stirring, touching. *See* TOUCH.

imprint *verb*
To produce a deep impression of : engrave, etch, fix, grave[3], impress, inscribe, stamp. *See* MARKS.
imprint *noun* The visible effect made on a surface by pressure : impress, impression, indent, indentation, mark, print, stamp. *See* MARKS.

imprison *verb*
1. To put in jail : confine, detain, immure, incarcerate, intern, jail, lock (up). *See* FREE.
2. To enclose so as to hinder or prohibit escape : closet, confine, shut up. *See* FREE.

improbable *adjective*
1. Not likely : doubtful, questionable, unapt, unlikely. *See* LIKELY. **2.** Not plausible or believable : flimsy, implausible, inconceivable, incredible, shaky, thin, unbelievable, unconceivable, unconvincing, unsubstantial, weak. *See* LIKELY.

improbity *noun*
1. Departure from what is legally, ethically, and morally correct : corruption, corruptness, dishonesty. *Informal:* crookedness. *See* HONEST.
2. Lack of integrity : dishonesty. *See* HONEST.

impromptu *adjective*
Spoken, performed, or composed with little or no preparation or forethought : ad-lib, extemporaneous, extemporary, extempore, improvised, offhand, snap, spur-of-the-moment, unrehearsed. *Informal:* off-the-cuff. *See* PREPARED.
impromptu *noun* Something improvised : ad-lib, extemporization, improvisation. *See* PLANNED, PREPARED.

improper *adjective*
1. Not suited to circumstances : inappropriate, inapt, incongruous, inept, malapropos, unapt, unbecoming, unbefitting, unfit, unseemly, unsuitable. ***Idiom:*** out of place. *See* AGREE, USUAL. **2.** Not in keeping with conventional mores : immodest, indecent, indecorous, indelicate, naughty, unbecoming, unbefitting, unseemly, untoward. ***Idiom:*** out of line. *See* USUAL.

improperness *noun*
The condition of being improper : impropriety, inappropriateness, unbecomingness, unfitness, unseemliness, unsuitability, unsuitableness. *See* AGREE, USUAL.

impropriety *noun*
1. The condition of being improper : improperness, inappropriateness, unbecomingness, unfitness, unseemliness, unsuitability, unsuitableness. *See* AGREE, USUAL. **2.** An improper act or statement : indecency, indecorum, indelicacy. *See* USUAL.

improve *verb*
1. To advance to a more desirable state : ameliorate, amend, better[1], help, meliorate, upgrade. *See* HELP. **2.** To regain one's health : come around (*or* round), convalesce, gain, mend, perk up, rally, recover, recuperate. *See* HEALTH.

improvement *noun*
1. The act of making better or the condition of being made better : amelioration, amendment, betterment, melioration, upgrade. *See* BETTER.
2. Steady improvement, as of an individual or a society : amelioration, betterment, development, melioration, progress. *See* BETTER.

improvident *adjective*
1. Reckless, especially in the use of material resources : thriftless, unthrifty. *See* CAREFUL.
2. Characterized by unthinking boldness and haste : brash, foolhardy, harum-scarum, hasty, headlong, hotheaded, ill-considered, impetuous, impulsive, incautious, madcap, precipitant, precipitate, rash[1], reckless, slapdash, temerarious, unconsidered. *See* CAREFUL.

improvisation *noun*
Something improvised : ad-lib, extemporization, impromptu. *See* PLANNED, PREPARED.

improvise *verb*
To compose or recite without preparation : ad-lib, extemporize, fake, make up. ***Idiom:*** wing it. *See* PLANNED, PREPARED.

improvised *adjective*
Spoken, performed, or composed with little or no preparation or forethought : ad-lib, extemporaneous, extemporary, extempore, impromptu, offhand, snap, spur-of-the-moment, unrehearsed. *Informal:* off-the-cuff. *See* PREPARED.

imprudent *adjective*
Not wise : ill-advised, ill-considered, impolitic, indiscreet, injudicious, unsound, unwise. *See* WISE.

impudence *noun*
The state or quality of being impudent or arrogantly self-confident : assumption, audaciousness, audacity, boldness, brashness, brazenness, cheek, cheekiness, chutzpah, discourtesy, disrespect, effrontery, face, familiarity, forwardness, gall[1], impertinence, impudency, incivility, insolence, nerve, nerviness, overconfidence, pertness, presumptuousness, pushiness, rudeness, sassiness, sauciness. *Informal:* brass, crust,

sauce, uppishness, uppityness. *See* ATTITUDE, COURTESY.

impudency *noun*
The state or quality of being impudent or arrogantly self-confident : assumption, audaciousness, audacity, boldness, brashness, brazenness, cheek, cheekiness, chutzpah, discourtesy, disrespect, effrontery, face, familiarity, forwardness, gall[1], impertinence, impudence, incivility, insolence, nerve, nerviness, overconfidence, pertness, presumptuousness, pushiness, rudeness, sassiness, sauciness. *Informal:* brass, crust, sauce, uppishness, uppityness. *See* ATTITUDE, COURTESY.

impudent *adjective*
Rude and disrespectful : assuming, assumptive, audacious, bold, boldfaced, brash, brazen, cheeky, contumelious, familiar, forward, impertinent, insolent, malapert, nervy, overconfident, pert, presuming, presumptuous, pushy, sassy, saucy, smart, snippety, snippy. *Informal:* brassy, flip, fresh, smart-alecky, uppish, uppity. *Slang:* wise[1]. *See* ATTITUDE, COURTESY.

impulse *noun*
1. Something that causes and encourages a given response : encouragement, fillip, impetus, incentive, inducement, motivation, prod, push, spur, stimulant, stimulation, stimulator, stimulus. *See* CAUSE. **2.** An impulsive, often illogical turn of mind : bee, boutade, caprice, conceit, fancy, freak, humor, megrim, notion, vagary, whim, whimsy. ***Idiom:*** bee in one's bonnet. *See* THOUGHTS.

impulsive *adjective*
1. Characterized by unthinking boldness and haste : brash, foolhardy, harum-scarum, hasty, headlong, hotheaded, ill-considered, impetuous, improvident, incautious, madcap, precipitant, precipitate, rash[1], reckless, slapdash, temerarious, unconsidered. *See* CAREFUL. **2.** Acting or happening without apparent forethought, prompting, or planning : automatic, instinctive, involuntary, reflex, spontaneous, unpremeditated. *See* PLANNED.

impure *adjective*
1. Ceremonially or religiously unfit : unclean. *See* CLEAN, RELIGION, SACRED. **2.** Not chaste or moral : immoral, unchaste, unclean, uncleanly. *See* GOOD, RESTRAINT, SEX. **3.** Mixed with other substances : adulterated, alloyed, doctored, loaded, sophisticated. *See* CLEAN.

impurity *noun*
1. Impure condition : defilement, dirtiness, foulness, pollution, uncleanness, unwholesomeness. *See* CLEAN. **2.** One that contaminates : adulterant, adulterator, contaminant, contamination, contaminator, poison, pollutant. *See* CLEAN.

imputation *noun*
1. A charging of someone with a misdeed : accusation, charge, denouncement, denunciation, incrimination. *Law:* indictment. *See* ATTACK, LAW, PRAISE. **2.** The act of attributing : ascription, assignment, attribution, credit. *See* GIVE.

impute *verb*
1. To ascribe (a misdeed or an error, for example) to : affix, assign, blame, fasten, fix, pin on, place. *See* GIVE. **2.** To regard as belonging to or resulting from another : accredit, ascribe, assign, attribute, charge, credit, lay[1], refer. *See* GIVE.

in *adjective*
Informal. Being or in accordance with the current fashion : à la mode, chic, dashing, fashionable, mod, modish, posh, smart, stylish, swank, swanky, trig. *Informal:* classy, sharp, snappy, swish, tony, trendy. *Slang:* with-it. ***Idioms:*** all the rage, up to the minute. *See* STYLE, USUAL.

inability *noun*
Lack of ability or capacity : incapability, incapacity, incompetence, incompetency, powerlessness. *See* ABILITY.

inaccessible *adjective*
1. Unable to be reached : inapproachable, unapproachable, unattainable, unavailable, unreachable. ***Idioms:*** beyond reach, out of the way. *See* REACH. **2.** Not accessible or handy : inconvenient. *See* REACH.

inaccuracy *noun*
An act or thought that unintentionally deviates from what is correct, right, or true : erratum, error, incorrectness, lapse, miscue, misstep, mistake, slip, slip-up, trip. *See* CORRECT.

inaccurate *adjective*
Containing an error or errors : erroneous, fallacious, false, incorrect, mistaken, off, unsound, untrue, wrong. ***Idioms:*** all wet, in error, off base, off (*or* wide of) the mark. *See* CORRECT.

inaction *noun*
A lack of action or activity : idleness, inactivity, inertness, inoperativeness, stagnation. *See* ACTION.

inactive *adjective*
1. Marked by a lack of action or activity : idle, inert, inoperative. *See* ACTION. **2.** Not occupied or put to use : idle, unemployed, unused, vacant. *See* USED. **3.** Existing in a temporarily

inactive form or state : abeyant, dormant, latent, quiescent, sleeping. *See* ACTION, SHOW.

inactivity *noun*
A lack of action or activity : idleness, inaction, inertness, inoperativeness, stagnation. *See* ACTION.

inadequacy *noun*
1. The condition or state of being incapable of accomplishing or effecting anything : helplessness, impotence, incapability, ineffectiveness, ineffectuality, ineffectualness, inefficacy, powerlessness, uselessness. *See* AFFECT, STRONG. **2.** The condition or fact of being deficient : defect, deficiency, deficit, insufficiency, lack, paucity, poverty, scantiness, scantness, scarceness, scarcity, shortage, shortcoming, shortfall, underage[1]. *See* EXCESS.

inadequate *adjective*
1. Not enough to meet a demand or requirement : deficient, insufficient, scarce, short, shy[1], under, wanting. *See* BIG, EXCESS. **2.** Lacking capability : incapable, incompetent, unequal, unfit, unqualified. *See* ABILITY, EXCESS. **3.** Not capable of accomplishing anything : helpless, impotent, incapable, ineffectual, powerless, weak. *See* ABILITY, STRONG.

inadmissible *adjective*
Arousing disapproval : exceptionable, ill-favored, objectionable, unacceptable, undesirable, unwanted, unwelcome. *See* LIKE.

inadvertent *adjective*
1. Not intended : undesigned, undevised, unintended, unintentional, unmeant, unplanned, unwitting. *See* PLANNED. **2.** Occurring unexpectedly : accidental, casual, chance, contingent, fluky, fortuitous, odd. *See* SURPRISE.

inalterable *adjective*
Incapable of changing or being modified : immutable, inflexible, invariable, ironclad, rigid, unalterable, unchangeable. *See* FLEXIBLE.

inane *adjective*
Lacking intelligent thought or content : blank, empty, empty-headed, vacant, vacuous. *See* FULL.

inanimate *adjective*
Completely lacking sensation or consciousness : dead, insensate, insentient. *See* LIVE.

inanity *noun*
Total lack of ideas, meaning, or substance : barrenness, blankness, emptiness, hollowness, vacancy, vacuity, vacuousness. *See* FULL.

inapplicable *adjective*
Not relevant or pertinent to the subject; not applicable : extraneous, immaterial, impertinent, irrelevant. ***Idioms:*** beside the point, neither here nor there. *See* RELEVANT.

inappreciable *adjective*
Incapable of being apprehended by the mind or the senses : impalpable, imperceptible, imponderable, indiscernible, indistinguishable, insensible, intangible, invisible, unnoticeable, unobservable. *See* KNOWLEDGE.

inapproachable *adjective*
Unable to be reached : inaccessible, unapproachable, unattainable, unavailable, unreachable. ***Idioms:*** beyond reach, out of the way. *See* REACH.

inappropriate *adjective*
1. Not suited to circumstances : improper, inapt, incongruous, inept, malapropos, unapt, unbecoming, unbefitting, unfit, unseemly, unsuitable. ***Idiom:*** out of place. *See* AGREE, USUAL. **2.** Not suited to a given purpose : ill-suited, inapt, unfit, unsuitable, unsuited. *See* ABILITY. **3.** Characterized by inappropriateness and gracelessness, especially in expression : awkward, ill-chosen, inept, infelicitous, unfortunate, unhappy. *See* ABILITY, GOOD.

inappropriateness *noun*
The condition of being improper : improperness, impropriety, unbecomingness, unfitness, unseemliness, unsuitability, unsuitableness. *See* AGREE, USUAL.

inapt *adjective*
1. Not suited to circumstances : improper, inappropriate, incongruous, inept, malapropos, unapt, unbecoming, unbefitting, unfit, unseemly, unsuitable. ***Idiom:*** out of place. *See* AGREE, USUAL. **2.** Not suited to a given purpose : ill-suited, inappropriate, unfit, unsuitable, unsuited. *See* ABILITY. **3.** Lacking the qualities, as efficiency or skill, required to produce desired results : incapable, incompetent, inefficient, inept, inexpert, unskilled, unskillful, unworkmanlike. *See* ABILITY.

inarguable *adjective*
Established beyond a doubt : certain, hard, incontestable, incontrovertible, indisputable, indubitable, irrefutable, positive, sure, unassailable, undeniable, undisputable, unquestionable. *See* CERTAIN, TRUE.

inarticulate *adjective*
1. Lacking the power or faculty of speech : aphonic, dumb, mute, speechless, voiceless. *See* WORDS. **2.** Temporarily unable or unwilling to speak, as from shock or fear : dumb, mum,

mute, silent, speechless, voiceless, wordless. *See* WORDS.

inattentive *adjective*
1. So lost in thought as to be unaware of one's surroundings : absent, absent-minded, abstracted, bemused, distrait, faraway, preoccupied. ***Idiom:*** a million miles away. *See* ABILITY, AWARENESS. 2. Lacking or marked by a lack of care : careless, feckless, heedless, irresponsible, reckless, thoughtless, unconcerned, unmindful, unthinking. *See* CAREFUL.

inaugural *noun*
The act or process of formally admitting a person to membership or office : inauguration, induction, initiation, installation, instatement, investiture. *See* ACCEPT.

inaugurate *verb*
1. To admit formally into membership or office, as with ritual : induct, initiate, install, instate, invest. *See* ACCEPT. 2. To go about the initial step in doing (something) : approach, begin, commence, embark, enter, get off, initiate, institute, launch, lead off, open, set about, set out, set to, start, take on, take up, undertake. *Informal:* kick off. ***Idioms:*** get cracking, get going, get the show on the road. *See* START.

inauguration *noun*
1. The act or process of formally admitting a person to membership or office : inaugural, induction, initiation, installation, instatement, investiture. *See* ACCEPT. 2. The act or process of bringing or being brought into existence : beginning, commencement, inception, incipience, incipiency, initiation, launch, leadoff, opening, origination, start. *Informal:* kickoff. *See* START.

inauspicious *adjective*
Bringing, predicting, or characterized by misfortune : bad, evil, ill, unfavorable, unpropitious. *See* LUCK.

inborn *adjective*
1. Possessed at birth : congenital, hereditary, inherited, innate, native. *See* BE, NATIVE.
2. Forming an essential element, as arising from the basic structure of an individual : built-in, congenital, connatural, constitutional, elemental, inbred, indigenous, indwelling, ingrained, inherent, innate, intrinsic, native, natural. *See* BE, NATIVE, START.

inbred *adjective*
Forming an essential element, as arising from the basic structure of an individual : built-in, congenital, connatural, constitutional, elemental, inborn, indigenous, indwelling, ingrained, inherent, innate, intrinsic, native, natural. *See* BE, NATIVE, START.

incalculable *adjective*
Too great to be calculated : countless, immeasurable, incomputable, inestimable, infinite, innumerable, measureless, uncountable. *See* BIG.

incandesce *verb*
1. To emit a bright light : beam, blaze[1], burn, gleam, glow, radiate, shine. *See* LIGHT. 2. To shine brightly and steadily but without a flame : gleam, glow, luminesce. *See* LIGHT.

incandescent *adjective*
Giving off or reflecting light readily or in large amounts : beamy, bright, brilliant, effulgent, irradiant, lambent, lucent, luminous, lustrous, radiant, refulgent, shiny. *See* LIGHT.

incapability *noun*
1. Lack of ability or capacity : inability, incapacity, incompetence, incompetency, powerlessness. *See* ABILITY. 2. The condition or state of being incapable of accomplishing or effecting anything : helplessness, impotence, inadequacy, ineffectiveness, ineffectuality, ineffectualness, inefficacy, powerlessness, uselessness. *See* AFFECT, STRONG.

incapable *adjective*
1. Lacking capability : inadequate, incompetent, unequal, unfit, unqualified. *See* ABILITY, EXCESS. 2. Lacking the qualities, as efficiency or skill, required to produce desired results : inapt, incompetent, inefficient, inept, inexpert, unskilled, unskillful, unworkmanlike. *See* ABILITY. 3. Not capable of accomplishing anything : helpless, impotent, inadequate, ineffectual, powerless, weak. *See* ABILITY, STRONG.

incapacitate *verb*
To render powerless or motionless, as by inflicting severe injury : cripple, disable, immobilize, knock out, paralyze. ***Idiom:*** put out of action (*or* commission). *See* HELP.

incapacity *noun*
Lack of ability or capacity : inability, incapability, incompetence, incompetency, powerlessness. *See* ABILITY.

incarcerate *verb*
To put in jail : confine, detain, immure, imprison, intern, jail, lock (up). *See* FREE.

incarnate *verb*
To represent (an abstraction, for example) in or as if in bodily form : body forth, embody, exteriorize, externalize, manifest, materialize, objectify, personalize, personify, substantiate. *See* SUBSTITUTE.

incarnation *noun*
A physical entity typifying an abstraction : embodiment, exteriorization, externalization, manifestation, materialization, objectification, personalization, personification, substantiation, type. *Rhetoric:* prosopopeia. *See* SUBSTITUTE.

incautious *adjective*
Characterized by unthinking boldness and haste : brash, foolhardy, harum-scarum, hasty, headlong, hotheaded, ill-considered, impetuous, improvident, impulsive, madcap, precipitant, precipitate, rash[1], reckless, slapdash, temerarious, unconsidered. *See* CAREFUL.

incautiousness *noun*
Foolhardy boldness or disregard of danger : brashness, foolhardiness, rashness, recklessness, temerariousness, temerity. *See* CAREFUL.

incense[1] *verb*
To cause to feel or show anger : anger, burn (up), enrage, infuriate, madden, provoke. ***Idioms:*** make one hot under the collar, make one's blood boil, put one's back up. *See* FEELINGS.

incense[2] *noun*
Excessive, ingratiating praise : adulation, blandishment, blarney, flattery, oil, slaver. *Informal:* soft soap. ***Idiom:*** honeyed words. *See* PRAISE.

incentive *noun*
Something that causes and encourages a given response : encouragement, fillip, impetus, impulse, inducement, motivation, prod, push, spur, stimulant, stimulation, stimulator, stimulus. *See* CAUSE.

inception *noun*
1. The act or process of bringing or being brought into existence : beginning, commencement, inauguration, incipience, incipiency, initiation, launch, leadoff, opening, origination, start. *Informal:* kickoff. *See* START. **2.** The initial stage of a developmental process : beginning, birth, commencement, dawn, genesis, nascence, nascency, onset, opening, origin, outset, spring, start. *See* START.

inceptive *adjective*
Of, relating to, or occurring at the start of something : beginning, incipient, initial, initiatory, introductory, leadoff. *See* START.

incertitude *noun*
A lack of conviction or certainty : doubt, doubtfulness, dubiety, dubiousness, mistrust, question, skepticism, suspicion, uncertainty, wonder. *See* CERTAIN.

incessant *adjective*
Existing or occurring without interruption or end : around-the-clock, ceaseless, constant, continual, continuous, endless, eternal, everlasting, interminable, nonstop, ongoing, perpetual, persistent, relentless, round-the-clock, timeless, unceasing, unending, unfailing, uninterrupted, unremitting. *See* CONTINUE.

inch *verb*
To advance slowly : crawl, creep, drag. *See* FAST.

inchoate *adjective*
Having no distinct shape : amorphous, formless, shapeless, unformed, unshaped. *See* ORDER.

incident *noun*
1. Something that happens : circumstance, event, happening, occasion, occurrence, thing. *See* HAPPEN. **2.** Something significant that happens : circumstance, development, episode, event, happening, news, occasion, occurrence, thing. *See* HAPPEN.

incidental *adjective*
Not part of the real or essential nature of a thing : adscititious, adventitious, supervenient. *See* SURFACE.

incipience *noun*
The act or process of bringing or being brought into existence : beginning, commencement, inauguration, inception, incipiency, initiation, launch, leadoff, opening, origination, start. *Informal:* kickoff. *See* START.

incipiency *noun*
The act or process of bringing or being brought into existence : beginning, commencement, inauguration, inception, incipience, initiation, launch, leadoff, opening, origination, start. *Informal:* kickoff. *See* START.

incipient *adjective*
Of, relating to, or occurring at the start of something : beginning, inceptive, initial, initiatory, introductory, leadoff. *See* START.

incise *verb*
1. To penetrate with a sharp edge : cut, gash, pierce, slash, slit. *See* ENTER, HELP. **2.** To cut (a design or inscription) into a hard surface, especially for printing : carve, engrave, etch, grave[3]. *See* MARKS.

incision *noun*
The result of cutting : cut, gash, slash, slice, slit, split. *See* ENTER, HELP.

incisive *adjective*
Possessing or displaying perceptions of great accuracy and sensitivity : acute, keen[1], penetrating, perceptive, probing, sensitive, sharp, trenchant. *See* CAREFUL, SHARP.

incisiveness *noun*
A cutting quality : bite, edge, keenness, sharpness, sting. *See* SHARP.

incitation *noun*
Something that incites especially a violent response : goad, incitement, instigation, provocation, stimulus, trigger. *See* CAUSE.

incite *verb*
To stir to action or feeling : egg on, excite, foment, galvanize, goad, impel, inflame, inspire, instigate, motivate, move, pique, prick, prod, prompt, propel, provoke, set off, spur, stimulate, touch off, trigger, work up. *See* CAUSE, EXCITE.

incitement *noun*
Something that incites especially a violent response : goad, incitation, instigation, provocation, stimulus, trigger. *See* CAUSE.

inciter *noun*
One who agitates, especially politically : agitator, fomenter, instigator. *See* CALM, CHANGE, POLITICS.

incivility *noun*
The state or quality of being impudent or arrogantly self-confident : assumption, audaciousness, audacity, boldness, brashness, brazenness, cheek, cheekiness, chutzpah, discourtesy, disrespect, effrontery, face, familiarity, forwardness, gall[1], impertinence, impudence, impudency, insolence, nerve, nerviness, overconfidence, pertness, presumptuousness, pushiness, rudeness, sassiness, sauciness. *Informal:* brass, crust, sauce, uppishness, uppityness. *See* ATTITUDE, COURTESY.

inclination *noun*
Deviation from a particular direction : cant[1], grade, gradient, heel[2], incline, lean[1], list[2], rake[2], slant, slope, tilt, tip[2]. *See* RISE, STRAIGHT.

incline *verb*
1. To depart or cause to depart from true vertical or horizontal : cant[1], heel[2], lean[1], list[2], rake[2], slant, slope, tilt, tip[2]. *See* STRAIGHT. **2.** To have a tendency or inclination : lean[1], slant, squint, tend[1], trend. *See* LIKELY. **3.** To have an impact on in a certain way : dispose, influence, predispose, sway. *See* AFFECT, LIKE.
incline *noun* Deviation from a particular direction : cant[1], grade, gradient, heel[2], inclination, lean[1], list[2], rake[2], slant, slope, tilt, tip[2]. *See* RISE, STRAIGHT.

inclined *adjective*
Having or showing a tendency or likelihood : apt, disposed, given, liable, likely, prone. *See* LIKELY.

include *verb*
To have as a part : comprehend, comprise, contain, embody, embrace, encompass, have, involve, subsume, take in. *See* INCLUDE.

inclusive *adjective*
Covering a wide scope : all-around, all-inclusive, all-round, broad, broad-spectrum, comprehensive, expansive, extended, extensive, far-ranging, far-reaching, general, global, large, overall, sweeping, wide-ranging, wide-reaching, widespread. *See* SPECIFIC.

incommode *verb*
To cause inconvenience for : discomfort, discommode, inconvenience, put out, trouble. *See* COMFORT.

incommodious *adjective*
Causing difficulty, trouble, or discomfort : difficult, inconvenient, troublesome. *See* COMFORT.

incommodiousness *noun*
The state or quality of being inconvenient : discomfort, incommodity, inconvenience, trouble. *See* COMFORT.

incommodity *noun*
1. The state or quality of being inconvenient : discomfort, incommodiousness, inconvenience, trouble. *See* COMFORT. **2.** Something that causes difficulty, trouble, or lack of ease : discomfort, inconvenience. *See* COMFORT.

incommunicable *adjective*
1. Not speaking freely or openly : close, close-mouthed, incommunicative, reserved, reticent, silent, taciturn, tightlipped, uncommunicable, uncommunicative. *See* RESTRAINT, SOUNDS. **2.** That cannot be described : indefinable, indescribable, ineffable, inexpressible, undescribable, unspeakable, unutterable. ***Idioms:*** beyond description (*or* words), defying description. *See* WORDS.

incommunicative *adjective*
Not speaking freely or openly : close, close-mouthed, incommunicable, reserved, reticent, silent, taciturn, tightlipped, uncommunicable, uncommunicative. *See* RESTRAINT, SOUNDS.

incomparable *adjective*
Without equal or rival : alone, matchless, nonpareil, only, peerless, singular, unequaled, unexampled, unique, unmatched, unparalleled, unrivaled. *See* SAME.

incompatibility *noun*
A marked lack of correspondence or agreement : difference, disagreement, discrepance, discrepancy, disparity, gap, incongruity, inconsistency. *See* AGREE.

incompatible *adjective*
1. Made up of parts or qualities that are disparate or otherwise markedly lacking in consistency : discordant, discrepant, dissonant, incongruent, incongruous, inconsistent. *See* AGREE. **2.** In sharp opposition : discrepant, incongruent, incongruous, inconsistent. *Logic:* repugnant. *See* AGREE.

incompetence *noun*
Lack of ability or capacity : inability, incapability, incapacity, incompetency, powerlessness. *See* ABILITY.

incompetency *noun*
Lack of ability or capacity : inability, incapability, incapacity, incompetence, powerlessness. *See* ABILITY.

incompetent *adjective*
1. Lacking capability : inadequate, incapable, unequal, unfit, unqualified. *See* ABILITY, EXCESS. **2.** Totally incapable of doing a job : unable, unfit, unqualified. *See* ABILITY. **3.** Lacking the qualities, as efficiency or skill, required to produce desired results : inapt, incapable, inefficient, inept, inexpert, unskilled, unskillful, unworkmanlike. *See* ABILITY.

incomplete *adjective*
Lacking an essential element : defective, deficient, lacking, wanting. *See* BETTER, EXCESS.

incompliance *noun*
The quality or state of being stubbornly inflexible : die-hardism, grimness, implacability, implacableness, incompliancy, inexorability, inexorableness, inflexibility, inflexibleness, intransigence, intransigency, obduracy, obdurateness, relentlessness, remorselessness, rigidity, rigidness, stubbornness. *See* RESIST.

incompliancy *noun*
The quality or state of being stubbornly inflexible : die-hardism, grimness, implacability, implacableness, incompliance, inexorability, inexorableness, inflexibility, inflexibleness, intransigence, intransigency, obduracy, obdurateness, relentlessness, remorselessness, rigidity, rigidness, stubbornness. *See* RESIST.

incompliant *adjective*
Firmly, often unreasonably immovable in purpose or will : adamant, adamantine, brassbound, die-hard, grim, implacable, inexorable, inflexible, intransigent, iron, obdurate, relentless, remorseless, rigid, stubborn, unbendable, unbending, uncompliant, uncompromising, unrelenting, unyielding. ***Idiom:*** stubborn as a mule (*or* ox). *See* RESIST.

incomprehensible *adjective*
Incapable of being grasped by the intellect or understanding : impenetrable, inscrutable, uncomprehensible, unfathomable, unintelligible. *See* KNOWLEDGE.

incompressible *adjective*
Unyielding to pressure or force : firm[1], hard, solid. *See* RESIST, STRONG.

incomputable *adjective*
Too great to be calculated : countless, immeasurable, incalculable, inestimable, infinite, innumerable, measureless, uncountable. *See* BIG.

inconceivable *adjective*
1. Not to be believed : incredible, unbelievable, unimaginable, unthinkable. ***Idioms:*** beyond belief, contrary to all reason. *See* BELIEF.
2. Not plausible or believable : flimsy, implausible, improbable, incredible, shaky, thin, unbelievable, unconceivable, unconvincing, unsubstantial, weak. *See* LIKELY.

inconclusive *adjective*
Not affording certainty : ambiguous, borderline, chancy, clouded, doubtful, dubious, dubitable, equivocal, indecisive, indeterminate, problematic, problematical, questionable, uncertain, unclear, unsure. *Informal:* iffy. ***Idioms:*** at issue, in doubt, in question. *See* CERTAIN, CLEAR.

incongruent *adjective*
1. Made up of parts or qualities that are disparate or otherwise markedly lacking in consistency : discordant, discrepant, dissonant, incompatible, incongruous, inconsistent. *See* AGREE. **2.** In sharp opposition : discrepant, incompatible, incongruous, inconsistent. *Logic:* repugnant. *See* AGREE.

incongruity *noun*
A marked lack of correspondence or agreement : difference, disagreement, discrepance, discrepancy, disparity, gap, incompatibility, inconsistency. *See* AGREE.

incongruous *adjective*
1. Made up of parts or qualities that are disparate or otherwise markedly lacking in consistency : discordant, discrepant, dissonant, incompatible, incongruent, inconsistent. *See* AGREE. **2.** In sharp opposition : discrepant, incompatible, incongruent, inconsistent. *Logic:* repugnant. *See* AGREE. **3.** Not suited to circumstances : improper, inappropriate, inapt, inept, malapropos, unapt, unbecoming, unbefitting, unfit, unseemly, unsuitable. ***Idiom:*** out of place. *See* AGREE, USUAL.

inconsequence *noun*
Lack of importance : inconsequentiality, inconsequentialness, indifference, insignifi-

cance, insignificancy, unimportance. *See* CONCERN.

inconsequent *adjective*
Not of great importance : inconsequential, insignificant, little, trivial, unimportant. *See* BIG.

inconsequential *adjective*
Not of great importance : inconsequent, insignificant, little, trivial, unimportant. *See* BIG.

inconsequentiality *noun*
Lack of importance : inconsequence, inconsequentialness, indifference, insignificance, insignificancy, unimportance. *See* CONCERN.

inconsequentialness *noun*
Lack of importance : inconsequence, inconsequentiality, indifference, insignificance, insignificancy, unimportance. *See* CONCERN.

inconsiderable *adjective*
Contemptibly unimportant : negligible, niggling, nugatory, paltry, petty, picayune, piddling, small, small-minded, trifling. *Slang:* measly. ***Idiom:*** of no account. *See* IMPORTANT.

inconsiderableness *noun*
Contemptible unimportance : negligibility, negligibleness, paltriness, pettiness, smallness, triviality, trivialness. *See* IMPORTANT.

inconsiderate *adjective*
Devoid of consideration for others' feelings : disregardful, thoughtless, unthinking, unthoughtful. *See* CAREFUL, COURTESY.

inconsiderateness *noun*
A lack of consideration for others' feelings : disregard, inconsideration, thoughtlessness, unthoughtfulness. *See* COURTESY.

inconsideration *noun*
A lack of consideration for others' feelings : disregard, inconsiderateness, thoughtlessness, unthoughtfulness. *See* COURTESY.

inconsistency *noun*
A marked lack of correspondence or agreement : difference, disagreement, discrepance, discrepancy, disparity, gap, incompatibility, incongruity. *See* AGREE.

inconsistent *adjective*
1. Lacking consistency or regularity in quality or performance : erratic, patchy, spotty, uneven, unsteady, variable. *See* CONTINUE, SAME. **2.** Following no predictable pattern : capricious, changeable, erratic, fantastic, fantastical, fickle, freakish, inconstant, mercurial, temperamental, ticklish, uncertain, unpredictable, unstable, unsteady, variable, volatile, whimsical. *See* CHANGE, CONTINUE. **3.** In sharp opposition : discrepant, incompatible, incongruent, incongruous. *Logic:* repugnant. *See* AGREE. **4.** Made up of parts or qualities that are disparate or otherwise markedly lacking in consistency : discordant, discrepant, dissonant, incompatible, incongruent, incongruous. *See* AGREE.

inconsonant *adjective*
Devoid of harmony and accord : discordant, inharmonious, uncongenial, unharmonious. *See* AGREE.

inconspicuous *adjective*
Not readily noticed or seen : obscure, unconspicuous, unnoticeable, unobtrusive. ***Idiom:*** having (*or* keeping) a low profile. *See* SEE.

inconstant *adjective*
1. Capable of or liable to change : alterable, changeable, fluid, mutable, uncertain, unsettled, unstable, unsteady, variable, variant. *Archaic:* various. *See* CHANGE. **2.** Following no predictable pattern : capricious, changeable, erratic, fantastic, fantastical, fickle, freakish, inconsistent, mercurial, temperamental, ticklish, uncertain, unpredictable, unstable, unsteady, variable, volatile, whimsical. *See* CHANGE, CONTINUE.

incontestable *adjective*
Established beyond a doubt : certain, hard, inarguable, incontrovertible, indisputable, indubitable, irrefutable, positive, sure, unassailable, undeniable, undisputable, unquestionable. *See* CERTAIN, TRUE.

incontinence *noun*
A complete surrender of inhibitions : abandon, abandonment, unrestraint, wantonness, wildness. *See* RESTRAINT.

incontinent *adjective*
Lacking in moral restraint : abandoned, dissipated, dissolute, fast, gay, licentious, profligate, rakish, unbridled, unconstrained, uncontrolled, ungoverned, uninhibited, unrestrained, wanton, wild. *See* RESTRAINT.

incontrovertible *adjective*
Established beyond a doubt : certain, hard, inarguable, incontestable, indisputable, indubitable, irrefutable, positive, sure, unassailable, undeniable, undisputable, unquestionable. *See* CERTAIN, TRUE.

inconvenience *noun*
1. The state or quality of being inconvenient : discomfort, incommodiousness, incommodity, trouble. *See* COMFORT. **2.** Something that causes difficulty, trouble, or lack of ease : discomfort, incommodity. *See* COMFORT.
inconvenience *verb* To cause inconvenience for : discomfort, discommode, incommode, put out, trouble. *See* COMFORT.

inconvenient *adjective*
1. Not accessible or handy : inaccessible. *See* REACH. 2. Causing difficulty, trouble, or discomfort : difficult, incommodious, troublesome. *See* COMFORT. 3. Not occurring at a favorable time : ill-timed, inopportune, untimely. *See* TIME.

incorporate *verb*
1. To construct or include as an integral or permanent part : build in, integrate. *See* INCLUDE. 2. To make a part of a united whole : combine, embody, integrate. *See* INCLUDE.

incorporated *adjective*
Serving as part of a whole, as a nondetachable part of a larger unit : built-in, component, constituent. *See* INCLUDE.

incorporeal *adjective*
Having no body, form, or substance : bodiless, discarnate, disembodied, immaterial, insubstantial, metaphysical, nonphysical, spiritual, unbodied, uncorporal, unsubstantial. *See* BODY.

incorrect *adjective*
Containing an error or errors : erroneous, fallacious, false, inaccurate, mistaken, off, unsound, untrue, wrong. ***Idioms:*** all wet, in error, off base, off (*or* wide of) the mark. *See* CORRECT.

incorrectness *noun*
An act or thought that unintentionally deviates from what is correct, right, or true : erratum, error, inaccuracy, lapse, miscue, misstep, mistake, slip, slip-up, trip. *See* CORRECT.

incorruptibility *noun*
The quality of being honest : honesty, honor, honorableness, integrity, upstandingness. *See* HONEST.

incorruptible *adjective*
Having or marked by uprightness in principle and action : good, honest, honorable, righteous, true, upright, upstanding. *Informal:* straight-shooting. ***Idiom:*** on the up-and-up (*or* up and up). *See* HONEST.

increase *verb*
1. To make or become greater or larger : aggrandize, amplify, augment, boost, build, build up, burgeon, enlarge, escalate, expand, extend, grow, magnify, mount, multiply, proliferate, rise, run up, snowball, soar, swell, upsurge, wax. *Informal:* beef up. *See* INCREASE. 2. To produce sexually or asexually others of one's kind : breed, multiply, procreate, proliferate, propagate, reproduce, spawn. *See* REPRODUCTION.

increase *noun* 1. The act of increasing or rising : aggrandizement, amplification, augment, augmentation, boost, buildup, enlargement, escalation, growth, hike, jump, multiplication, proliferation, raise, rise, swell, upsurge, upswing, upturn. *See* INCREASE. 2. The amount by which something is increased : advance, boost, hike, increment, jump, raise, rise. *See* INCREASE. 3. *Obsolete.* The process by which an organism produces others of its kind : breeding, multiplication, procreation, proliferation, propagation, reproduction, spawning. *See* REPRODUCTION.

incredible *adjective*
1. Not plausible or believable : flimsy, implausible, improbable, inconceivable, shaky, thin, unbelievable, unconceivable, unconvincing, unsubstantial, weak. *See* LIKELY. 2. Not to be believed : inconceivable, unbelievable, unimaginable, unthinkable. ***Idioms:*** beyond belief, contrary to all reason. *See* BELIEF. 3. So remarkable as to elicit disbelief : amazing, astonishing, astounding, fabulous, fantastic, fantastical, marvelous, miraculous, phenomenal, prodigious, stupendous, unbelievable, wonderful, wondrous. *See* GOOD.

incredulity *noun*
The refusal or reluctance to believe : disbelief, discredit, incredulousness, unbelief. *See* BELIEF.

incredulous *adjective*
Refusing or reluctant to believe : disbelieving, questioning, skeptical, unbelieving. *See* BELIEF.

incredulousness *noun*
The refusal or reluctance to believe : disbelief, discredit, incredulity, unbelief. *See* BELIEF.

increment *noun*
The amount by which something is increased : advance, boost, hike, increase, jump, raise, rise. *See* INCREASE.

incriminate *verb*
1. To make an accusation against : accuse, arraign, charge, denounce, indict, tax. *See* ATTACK, LAW, PRAISE. 2. To cause to appear involved in or guilty of a crime or fault : criminate, implicate, inculpate. *See* ATTACK, CRIMES.

incrimination *noun*
A charging of someone with a misdeed : accusation, charge, denouncement, denunciation, imputation. *Law:* indictment. *See* ATTACK, LAW, PRAISE.

inculcate *verb*
1. To fix (an idea, for example) in someone's

mind by reemphasis and repetition : drill, drive, implant, impress, instill, pound. *See* TEACH. **2.** To instruct in a body of doctrine or belief : drill, indoctrinate. *See* TEACH.

inculpate *verb*
To cause to appear involved in or guilty of a crime or fault : criminate, implicate, incriminate. *See* ATTACK, CRIMES.

incumbency *noun*
The holding of something, such as a position : occupancy, occupation, tenure. *See* PLACE.

incur *verb*
To take upon oneself : assume, shoulder, tackle, take on, take over, undertake. *See* ACCEPT.

incurable *adjective*
Offering no hope or expectation of improvement : cureless, hopeless, irremediable, irreparable. *See* HOPE.

incuriosity *noun*
Lack of emotion or interest : apathy, disinterest, impassivity, incuriousness, indifference, insensibility, insensibleness, lassitude, lethargy, listlessness, phlegm, stolidity, stolidness, unconcern, uninterest, unresponsiveness. *See* FEELINGS.

incurious *adjective*
1. Lacking interest in one's surroundings or worldly affairs : aloof, detached, disinterested, indifferent, unconcerned, uninterested, uninvolved. *See* ATTITUDE, CONCERN. **2.** Without emotion or interest : apathetic, detached, impassive, indifferent, insensible, lethargic, listless, phlegmatic, stolid, unconcerned, uninterested, unresponsive. *See* FEELINGS.

incuriousness *noun*
Lack of emotion or interest : apathy, disinterest, impassivity, incuriosity, indifference, insensibility, insensibleness, lassitude, lethargy, listlessness, phlegm, stolidity, stolidness, unconcern, uninterest, unresponsiveness. *See* FEELINGS.

incursion *noun*
An act of invading, especially by military forces : foray, inroad, invasion, raid. *See* ATTACK, ENTER.

indebted *adjective*
Owing something, such as gratitude or appreciation, to another : beholden, bound[3], obligated, obliged. *Archaic:* bounden. ***Idiom:*** under obligation. *See* OBLIGATION.

indebtedness *noun*
1. A condition of owing something to another : arrearage, arrears, debt, liability, obligation. *See* PAY. **2.** Something, such as money, owed by one person to another : arrearage, arrears, debt, due, liability, obligation. *See* OBLIGATION, PAY.

indecency *noun*
An improper act or statement : impropriety, indecorum, indelicacy. *See* USUAL.

indecent *adjective*
Not in keeping with conventional mores : immodest, improper, indecorous, indelicate, naughty, unbecoming, unbefitting, unseemly, untoward. ***Idiom:*** out of line. *See* USUAL.

indecision *noun*
The act of hesitating or state of being hesitant : hesitancy, hesitation, indecisiveness, irresoluteness, irresolution, pause, shilly-shally, tentativeness, timidity, timidness, to-and-fro, vacillation. *See* DECIDE.

indecisive *adjective*
1. Given to or exhibiting hesitation : halting, hesitant, irresolute, pendulous, shilly-shally, tentative, timid, vacillant, vacillatory. *See* DECIDE. **2.** Not affording certainty : ambiguous, borderline, chancy, clouded, doubtful, dubious, dubitable, equivocal, inconclusive, indeterminate, problematic, problematical, questionable, uncertain, unclear, unsure. *Informal:* iffy. ***Idioms:*** at issue, in doubt, in question. *See* CERTAIN, CLEAR.

indecisiveness *noun*
The act of hesitating or state of being hesitant : hesitancy, hesitation, indecision, irresoluteness, irresolution, pause, shilly-shally, tentativeness, timidity, timidness, to-and-fro, vacillation. *See* DECIDE.

indecorous *adjective*
Not in keeping with conventional mores : immodest, improper, indecent, indelicate, naughty, unbecoming, unbefitting, unseemly, untoward. ***Idiom:*** out of line. *See* USUAL.

indecorum *noun*
An improper act or statement : impropriety, indecency, indelicacy. *See* USUAL.

indeed *adverb*
1. In truth : actually, fairly, genuinely, positively, really, truly, truthfully, verily. ***Idiom:*** for fair. *See* REAL, TRUE. **2.** In point of fact : actually, really. *See* REAL, TRUE. **3.** Not just this but also : even[1]. ***Idiom:*** not to mention. *See* TRUE.

indefatigable *adjective*
Having or showing a capacity for protracted effort, regardless of difficulty or frustration : inexhaustible, tireless, unfailing, unflagging, untiring, unwearied, weariless. *See* CONTINUE, TIRED.

indefectible *adjective*
Supremely excellent in quality or nature : absolute, consummate, faultless, flawless, impeccable, perfect, unflawed. *See* GOOD.

indefensible *adjective*
Impossible to excuse, pardon, or justify : inexcusable, unforgivable, unjustifiable, unpardonable. *See* FORGIVENESS.

indefinable *adjective*
That cannot be described : incommunicable, indescribable, ineffable, inexpressible, undescribable, unspeakable, unutterable. ***Idioms:*** beyond description (*or* words), defying description. *See* WORDS.

indefinite *adjective*
1. Not clearly perceived or perceptible : blear, bleary, cloudy, dim, faint, foggy, fuzzy, hazy, indistinct, misty, obscure, shadowy, unclear, undistinct, vague. *See* CLEAR. **2.** Lacking precise limits : indeterminate, inexact, undetermined. *See* LIMITED. **3.** Marked by lack of firm decision or commitment; of questionable outcome : open, uncertain, undecided, undetermined, unresolved, unsettled, unsure, vague. ***Idiom:*** up in the air. *See* CERTAIN.

indefiniteness *noun*
The quality or state of being ambiguous : ambiguity, ambiguousness, cloudiness, equivocalness, nebulousness, obscureness, obscurity, uncertainty, unclearness, vagueness. *See* CLEAR.

indelible *adjective*
Permanently resistive to fading : colorfast, fast. *See* CONTINUE.

indelicacy *noun*
An improper act or statement : impropriety, indecency, indecorum. *See* USUAL.

indelicate *adjective*
1. Not in keeping with conventional mores : immodest, improper, indecent, indecorous, naughty, unbecoming, unbefitting, unseemly, untoward. ***Idiom:*** out of line. *See* USUAL. **2.** Lacking in delicacy or refinement : barbarian, barbaric, boorish, churlish, coarse, crass, crude, gross, ill-bred, philistine, rough, rude, tasteless, uncivilized, uncouth, uncultivated, uncultured, unpolished, unrefined, vulgar. *See* COURTESY, SMOOTH. **3.** Lacking sensitivity and skill in dealing with others : brash, clumsy, gauche, impolitic, maladroit, tactless, undiplomatic, unpolitic, untactful. *See* ABILITY, COURTESY.

indemnification *noun*
Something to make up for loss or damage : amends, compensation, indemnity, offset, quittance, recompense, redress, reimbursement, remuneration, reparation, repayment, requital, restitution, satisfaction, setoff. *See* SUBSTITUTE.

indemnify *verb*
1. To give compensation to : compensate, pay, recompense, redress, reimburse, remunerate, repay, requite. *See* PAY. **2.** To give a satisfactory return to : compensate, pay, recompense, remunerate, repay, requite, reward. *See* PAY.

indemnity *noun*
Something to make up for loss or damage : amends, compensation, indemnification, offset, quittance, recompense, redress, reimbursement, remuneration, reparation, repayment, requital, restitution, satisfaction, setoff. *See* SUBSTITUTE.

indent *noun*
The visible effect made on a surface by pressure : impress, impression, imprint, indentation, mark, print, stamp. *See* MARKS.

indentation *noun*
The visible effect made on a surface by pressure : impress, impression, imprint, indent, mark, print, stamp. *See* MARKS.

indented *adjective*
Curving inward : cavernous, concave, hollow, sunken. *See* CONVEX.

independence *noun*
1. The condition of being politically free : autonomy, freedom, independency, liberty, self-government, sovereignty. *See* DEPENDENCE, FREE. **2.** The capacity to manage one's own affairs, make one's own judgments, and provide for oneself : self-determination, self-reliance, self-sufficiency. *See* DEPENDENCE.

independency *noun*
The condition of being politically free : autonomy, freedom, independence, liberty, self-government, sovereignty. *See* DEPENDENCE, FREE.

independent *adjective*
1. Having political independence : autonomous, free, self-governing, sovereign. *See* DEPENDENCE, FREE. **2.** Free from the influence, guidance, or control of others : self-contained, self-reliant, self-sufficient. *See* DEPENDENCE. **3.** Able to support oneself financially : self-sufficient, self-supporting. *See* DEPENDENCE, MONEY.

independently *adverb*
As a separate unit : apart, discretely, individually, separately, singly. ***Idioms:*** one at a time, one by one. *See* INCLUDE.

indescribable *adjective*
That cannot be described : incommunicable, indefinable, ineffable, inexpressible, undescribable, unspeakable, unutterable. ***Idioms:*** beyond description (*or* words), defying description. *See* WORDS.

indeterminate *adjective*
1. Not affording certainty : ambiguous, borderline, chancy, clouded, doubtful, dubious, dubitable, equivocal, inconclusive, indecisive, problematic, problematical, questionable, uncertain, unclear, unsure. *Informal:* iffy. *Idioms:* at issue, in doubt, in question. *See* CERTAIN, CLEAR. **2.** Lacking precise limits : indefinite, inexact, undetermined. *See* LIMITED.

index *noun*
Something visible or evident that gives grounds for believing in the existence or presence of something else : badge, evidence, indication, indicator, manifestation, mark, note, sign, signification, stamp, symptom, token, witness. *See* SHOW.

indicate *verb*
1. To make known or identify, as by signs : denote, designate, mark, point out, show, specify. *See* SHOW. **2.** To give a precise indication of, as on a register or scale : mark, read, record, register, show. *See* SHOW. **3.** To give grounds for believing in the existence or presence of : argue, attest, bespeak, betoken, mark, point to, testify, witness. *See* SHOW. **4.** To lead to by logical inference : imply, point to, suggest. *See* MEANING.

indication *noun*
1. Something that takes the place of words in communicating a thought or feeling : expression, gesture, sign, token. *See* SHOW. **2.** An expressive, meaningful bodily movement : gesticulation, gesture, motion, sign, signal. *Informal:* high sign. *See* EXPRESS. **3.** Something visible or evident that gives grounds for believing in the existence or presence of something else : badge, evidence, index, indicator, manifestation, mark, note, sign, signification, stamp, symptom, token, witness. *See* SHOW.

indicative *adjective*
Serving to designate or indicate : denotative, denotive, designative, designatory, exhibitive, exhibitory, indicatory. *See* SHOW.

indicator *noun*
Something visible or evident that gives grounds for believing in the existence or presence of something else : badge, evidence, index, indication, manifestation, mark, note, sign, signification, stamp, symptom, token, witness. *See* SHOW.

indicatory *adjective*
Serving to designate or indicate : denotative, denotive, designative, designatory, exhibitive, exhibitory, indicative. *See* SHOW.

indict *verb*
To make an accusation against : accuse, arraign, charge, denounce, incriminate, tax. *See* ATTACK, LAW, PRAISE.

indicter or **indictor** *noun*
One that accuses : accuser, denouncer. *See* ATTACK, LAW, PRAISE.

indictment *noun*
Law. A charging of someone with a misdeed : accusation, charge, denouncement, denunciation, imputation, incrimination. *See* ATTACK, LAW, PRAISE.

indictor *noun* See **indicter.**

indifference *noun*
1. Lack of importance : inconsequence, inconsequentiality, inconsequentialness, insignificance, insignificancy, unimportance. *See* CONCERN. **2.** Lack of emotion or interest : apathy, disinterest, impassivity, incuriosity, incuriousness, insensibility, insensibleness, lassitude, lethargy, listlessness, phlegm, stolidity, stolidness, unconcern, uninterest, unresponsiveness. *See* FEELINGS.

indifferent *adjective*
1. Free from bias in judgment : disinterested, dispassionate, equitable, fair, fair-minded, impartial, just, nonpartisan, objective, square, unbiased, unprejudiced. ***Idiom:*** fair and square. *See* FAIR. **2.** Feeling or showing no strong emotional involvement : detached, disinterested, dispassionate, impersonal, neutral. *See* FEELINGS. **3.** Without emotion or interest : apathetic, detached, impassive, incurious, insensible, lethargic, listless, phlegmatic, stolid, unconcerned, uninterested, unresponsive. *See* FEELINGS. **4.** Lacking interest in one's surroundings or worldly affairs : aloof, detached, disinterested, incurious, unconcerned, uninterested, uninvolved. *See* ATTITUDE, CONCERN. **5.** Being of no special quality or type : average, common, commonplace, cut-and-dried, formulaic, garden, garden-variety, mediocre, ordinary, plain, routine, run-of-the-mill, standard, stock, undistinguished, unexceptional, unremarkable. *See* GOOD, USUAL.

indigence *noun*
The condition of being extremely poor : beggary, destitution, impecuniosity, impecuniousness, impoverishment, need, neediness, penni-

lessness, penuriousness, penury, poverty, privation, want. *See* RICH.

indigenous *adjective*
1. Existing, born, or produced in a land or region : aboriginal, autochthonal, autochthonic, autochthonous, endemic, native. *See* NATIVE. **2.** Forming an essential element, as arising from the basic structure of an individual : built-in, congenital, connatural, constitutional, elemental, inborn, inbred, indwelling, ingrained, inherent, innate, intrinsic, native, natural. *See* BE, NATIVE, START.

indigent *adjective*
Having little or no money or wealth : beggarly, destitute, down-and-out, impecunious, impoverished, necessitous, needy, penniless, penurious, poor, poverty-stricken. *Informal:* broke, strapped. ***Idioms:*** hard up, on one's uppers. *See* RICH.
indigent *noun* An impoverished person : beggar, down-and-out, down-and-outer, have-not, pauper. *See* RICH.

indigestible *adjective*
Difficult to accept : bitter, distasteful, painful, unpalatable. *See* LIKE.

indignant *adjective*
Feeling or showing anger : angry, choleric, mad. *Informal:* sore. ***Idiom:*** hot under the collar. *See* FEELINGS.

indignation *noun*
A strong feeling of displeasure or hostility : anger, choler, irateness, ire. *See* FEELINGS.

indignity *noun*
An act that offends a person's sense of pride or dignity : affront, contumely, despite, insult, offense, outrage, slight. ***Idiom:*** slap in the face. *See* ATTACK.

indirect *adjective*
1. Not taking a direct or straight line or course : anfractuous, circuitous, circular, devious, oblique, roundabout, tortuous. *See* STRAIGHT. **2.** Marked by treachery or deceit : devious, disingenuous, duplicitous, guileful, lubricious, shifty, sneaky, underhand, underhanded. *See* HONEST.

indirection *noun*
Lack of straightforwardness and honesty in action : chicanery, craft, craftiness, deviousness, dishonesty, shadiness, shiftiness, slyness, sneakiness, trickery, trickiness, underhandedness. *See* HONEST.

indiscernible *adjective*
Incapable of being apprehended by the mind or the senses : impalpable, imperceptible, imponderable, inappreciable, indistinguishable, insensible, intangible, invisible, unnoticeable, unobservable. *See* KNOWLEDGE.

indiscreet *adjective*
Not wise : ill-advised, ill-considered, impolitic, imprudent, injudicious, unsound, unwise. *See* WISE.

indiscriminate *adjective*
Having no particular pattern, purpose, organization, or structure : chance, desultory, haphazard, hit-or-miss, random, spot, unplanned. *See* PLANNED.

indispensable *adjective*
Incapable of being dispensed with : essential, necessary, needful, required, requisite. *See* IMPORTANT, NECESSARY.

indisposed *adjective*
1. Affected or tending to be affected with minor health problems : ailing, low, mean[2], off-color, rocky, sickly. ***Idiom:*** under the weather. *See* HEALTH. **2.** Not inclined or willing to do or undertake : averse, disinclined, loath, reluctant, unwilling. *See* WILLING.

indisposition *noun*
1. The state of not being disposed or inclined : averseness, disinclination, reluctance, unwillingness. *See* WILLING. **2.** A minor illness, especially one of a temporary nature : ailment, bug, complaint, malady. *See* HEALTH. **3.** The condition of being sick : affliction, disorder, illness, infirmity, sickness. *See* HEALTH.

indisputable *adjective*
Established beyond a doubt : certain, hard, inarguable, incontestable, incontrovertible, indubitable, irrefutable, positive, sure, unassailable, undeniable, undisputable, unquestionable. *See* CERTAIN, TRUE.

indistinct *adjective*
Not clearly perceived or perceptible : blear, bleary, cloudy, dim, faint, foggy, fuzzy, hazy, indefinite, misty, obscure, shadowy, unclear, undistinct, vague. *See* CLEAR.

indistinctive *adjective*
Without definite or distinctive characteristics : bland, colorless, neutral. *See* STRONG.

indistinguishable *adjective*
Incapable of being apprehended by the mind or the senses : impalpable, imperceptible, imponderable, inappreciable, indiscernible, insensible, intangible, invisible, unnoticeable, unobservable. *See* KNOWLEDGE.

indite *verb*
1. To form by artistic effort : compose, create, produce, write. *See* MAKE. **2.** To form letters, characters, or words on a surface with an

instrument : engross, inscribe, scribe, write. *See* REMEMBER.

individual *adjective*
1. Belonging to, relating to, or affecting a particular person : personal, private. *See* SPECIFIC. **2.** Being or related to a distinct entity : discrete, particular, separate, single, singular. *See* INCLUDE. **3.** Serving to identify or set apart an individual or group : characteristic, distinctive, peculiar, typical, vintage. *See* SAME. **4.** Of, relating to, or intended for a distinctive thing or group : especial, particular, special, specific. *See* SPECIFIC.
individual *noun* **1.** A member of the human race : being, body, creature, homo, human, human being, life, man, mortal, party, person, personage, soul. *See* BEINGS. **2.** One that exists independently : being, entity, existence, existent, object, something, thing. *See* BE, THING.

individualism *noun*
The set of behavioral or personal characteristics by which an individual is recognizable : identity, individuality, selfhood. *See* BE.

individualistic *adjective*
Concerned with the person rather than with society : egocentric, egoistic, egoistical. *See* SELF.

individuality *noun*
1. The set of behavioral or personal characteristics by which an individual is recognizable : identity, individualism, selfhood. *See* BE. **2.** The quality of being individual : discreteness, distinctiveness, particularity, separateness, singularity. *See* INCLUDE.

individualize *verb*
To make noticeable or different : characterize, differentiate, discriminate, distinguish, mark, set apart, signalize, singularize. *See* SAME.

individually *adverb*
As a separate unit : apart, discretely, independently, separately, singly. ***Idioms:*** one at a time, one by one. *See* INCLUDE.

indocile *adjective*
Not submitting to discipline or control : disorderly, fractious, intractable, lawless, obstinate, obstreperous, recalcitrant, refractory, uncontrollable, undisciplined, ungovernable, unmanageable, unruly, untoward, wild. ***Idiom:*** out of line. *See* CONTROL, ORDER, PEACE, RESIST.

indocility *noun*
The quality or condition of being unruly : disorderliness, fractiousness, intractability, intractableness, obstinacy, obstinateness, obstreperousness, recalcitrance, recalcitrancy, refractoriness, uncontrollability, uncontrollableness, ungovernableness, unmanageability, unruliness, untowardness, wildness. *See* CONTROL, ORDER, PEACE, RESIST.

indoctrinate *verb*
1. To instruct in a body of doctrine or belief : drill, inculcate. *See* TEACH. **2.** To teach to accept a system of thought uncritically : brainwash, propagandize. *See* TEACH.

indolence *noun*
The quality or state of being lazy : idleness, laziness, shiftlessness, sloth, slothfulness, sluggardness, sluggishness. *Informal:* do-nothingism. *See* INDUSTRIOUS.

indolent *adjective*
Resistant to exertion and activity : fainéant, idle, lazy, shiftless, slothful, sluggard, sluggish. *Informal:* do-nothing. ***Idiom:*** bone lazy. *See* ACTION, INDUSTRIOUS.

indomitable *adjective*
Incapable of being conquered, overrun, or subjugated : impregnable, invincible, unconquerable. *See* DO, WIN.

indubitable *adjective*
1. Established beyond a doubt : certain, hard, inarguable, incontestable, incontrovertible, indisputable, irrefutable, positive, sure, unassailable, undeniable, undisputable, unquestionable. *See* CERTAIN, TRUE. **2.** Not counterfeit or copied : actual, authentic, bona fide, genuine, good, original, real, true, undoubted, unquestionable. *See* TRUE.

indubitably *adverb*
It is so; as you say or ask : absolutely, agreed, all right, assuredly, aye, gladly, roger, undoubtedly, unquestionably, willingly, yea, yes. *Informal:* OK, uh-huh, yeah, yep. *Slang:* right on. *See* AFFIRM.

induce *verb*
1. To succeed in causing (a person) to act in a certain way : argue into, bring, bring around (*or* round), convince, get, persuade, prevail on (*or* upon), sell (on), talk into. *See* PERSUASION. **2.** To be the cause of : bring, bring about, bring on, cause, effect, effectuate, generate, ingenerate, lead to, make, occasion, result in, secure, set off, stir[1] (up), touch off, trigger. ***Idioms:*** bring to pass (*or* effect), give rise to. *See* START.

inducement *noun*
1. Something that causes and encourages a given response : encouragement, fillip, impetus, impulse, incentive, motivation, prod, push, spur, stimulant, stimulation, stimulator, stimulus. *See* CAUSE. **2.** Something that attracts,

especially with the promise of pleasure or reward : allurement, bait, come-on, enticement, inveiglement, invitation, lure, seduction, temptation. *See* LIKE.

induct *verb*
1. To admit formally into membership or office, as with ritual : inaugurate, initiate, install, instate, invest. *See* ACCEPT. **2.** To enroll compulsorily in military service : conscript, draft, levy. *See* GIVE.

induction *noun*
1. The act or process of formally admitting a person to membership or office : inaugural, inauguration, initiation, installation, instatement, investiture. *See* ACCEPT. **2.** Compulsory enrollment in military service : conscription, draft, levy. *See* GIVE. **3.** A short section of preliminary remarks : foreword, introduction, lead-in, overture, preamble, preface, prelude, prolegomenon, prologue. *See* START, WORDS.

inductive *adjective*
Before or in preparation for the main matter, action, or business : introductory, prefatory, preliminary, preparatory, prolegomenous. *See* START.

indulge *verb*
1. To comply with the wishes or ideas of (another) : cater, gratify, humor. *See* RESIST. **2.** To treat with indulgence and often overtender care : baby, cater, coddle, cosset, mollycoddle, overindulge, pamper, spoil. *See* TREAT WELL. **3.** To grant or have what is demanded by (a need or desire) : appease, content, fulfill, gratify, satisfy. *See* GIVE. **4.** To take extravagant pleasure : bask, luxuriate, revel, roll, rollick, wallow. *See* LIKE. **5.** To involve oneself in (an activity) : carry on, engage, have, partake, participate. ***Idiom:*** take part. *See* PARTICIPATE.

indulgence *noun*
1. A kindly act : favor, good turn, grace, kindness, service. *Archaic:* benefit. *See* HELP. **2.** Forbearing or lenient treatment : charitableness, charity, forbearance, lenience, leniency, lenity, tolerance, toleration. *See* ACCEPT.

indulgent *adjective*
1. Ready to do favors for another : accommodating, agreeable, complaisant, obliging. *See* HELP, WILLING. **2.** Not strict or severe : charitable, clement, easy, forbearing, lax, lenient, merciful, soft, tolerant. *See* ACCEPT.

indurate *verb*
1. To make or become physically hard : cake, concrete, congeal, dry, harden, petrify, set[1], solidify. *See* SOLID. **2.** To make resistant to hardship, especially through continued exposure : acclimate, acclimatize, caseharden, harden, season, toughen. *See* CONTINUE, RESIST.

industrious *adjective*
Characterized by steady attention and effort : assiduous, diligent, sedulous, studious. *See* INDUSTRIOUS.

industriousness *noun*
Steady attention and effort, as to one's occupation : application, assiduity, assiduousness, diligence, industry, sedulousness. *See* INDUSTRIOUS.

industry *noun*
1. Commercial, industrial, or professional activity in general : business, commerce, trade, trading, traffic. *See* ACTION. **2.** Steady attention and effort, as to one's occupation : application, assiduity, assiduousness, diligence, industriousness, sedulousness. *See* INDUSTRIOUS.

indwelling *adjective*
Forming an essential element, as arising from the basic structure of an individual : built-in, congenital, connatural, constitutional, elemental, inborn, inbred, indigenous, ingrained, inherent, innate, intrinsic, native, natural. *See* BE, NATIVE, START.

inebriate *adjective* Stupefied, excited, or muddled with alcoholic liquor : besotted, crapulent, crapulous, drunk, drunken, inebriated, intoxicated, sodden, tipsy. *Informal:* cock-eyed, stewed. *Slang:* blind, bombed, boozed, boozy, crocked, high, lit (up), loaded, looped, pickled, pixilated, plastered, potted, sloshed, smashed, soused, stinking, stinko, stoned, tight, zonked. ***Idioms:*** drunk as a skunk, half-seas over, high as a kite, in one's cups, three sheets in (*or* to) the wind. *See* DRUGS.

inebriate *noun* A person who is habitually drunk : drunk, drunkard, sot, tippler. *Slang:* boozehound, boozer, lush[2], rummy[1], soak, souse, sponge, stiff. *See* DRUGS.

inebriated *adjective*
Stupefied, excited, or muddled with alcoholic liquor : besotted, crapulent, crapulous, drunk, drunken, inebriate, intoxicated, sodden, tipsy. *Informal:* cock-eyed, stewed. *Slang:* blind, bombed, boozed, boozy, crocked, high, lit (up), loaded, looped, pickled, pixilated, plastered, potted, sloshed, smashed, soused, stinking, stinko, stoned, tight, zonked. ***Idioms:*** drunk as a skunk, half-seas over, high as a kite, in one's

cups, three sheets in (*or* to) the wind. *See* DRUGS.

inebriation *noun*
The condition of being intoxicated with alcoholic liquor : crapulence, drunkenness, inebriety, insobriety, intoxication, tipsiness. *See* DRUGS.

inebriety *noun*
The condition of being intoxicated with alcoholic liquor : crapulence, drunkenness, inebriation, insobriety, intoxication, tipsiness. *See* DRUGS.

ineffable *adjective*
That cannot be described : incommunicable, indefinable, indescribable, inexpressible, undescribable, unspeakable, unutterable. ***Idioms:*** beyond description (*or* words), defying description. *See* WORDS.

ineffective *adjective*
Not having the desired effect : ineffectual, inefficacious, inefficient, useless. *See* AFFECT.

ineffectiveness *noun*
The condition or state of being incapable of accomplishing or effecting anything : helplessness, impotence, inadequacy, incapability, ineffectuality, ineffectualness, inefficacy, powerlessness, uselessness. *See* AFFECT, STRONG.

ineffectual *adjective*
1. Not having the desired effect : ineffective, inefficacious, inefficient, useless. *See* AFFECT. **2.** Having no useful purpose : inutile, unusable, useless, worthless. *See* USED. **3.** Not capable of accomplishing anything : helpless, impotent, inadequate, incapable, powerless, weak. *See* ABILITY, STRONG.

ineffectuality *noun*
The condition or state of being incapable of accomplishing or effecting anything : helplessness, impotence, inadequacy, incapability, ineffectiveness, ineffectualness, inefficacy, powerlessness, uselessness. *See* AFFECT, STRONG.

ineffectualness *noun*
The condition or state of being incapable of accomplishing or effecting anything : helplessness, impotence, inadequacy, incapability, ineffectiveness, ineffectuality, inefficacy, powerlessness, uselessness. *See* AFFECT, STRONG.

inefficacious *adjective*
Not having the desired effect : ineffective, ineffectual, inefficient, useless. *See* AFFECT.

inefficacy *noun*
The condition or state of being incapable of accomplishing or effecting anything : helplessness, impotence, inadequacy, incapability, ineffectiveness, ineffectuality, ineffectualness, powerlessness, uselessness. *See* AFFECT, STRONG.

inefficient *adjective*
1. Lacking the qualities, as efficiency or skill, required to produce desired results : inapt, incapable, incompetent, inept, inexpert, unskilled, unskillful, unworkmanlike. *See* ABILITY. **2.** Not having the desired effect : ineffective, ineffectual, inefficacious, useless. *See* AFFECT.

inelastic *adjective*
Not changing shape or bending : inflexible, rigid, stiff, unbending, unyielding. *See* FLEXIBLE.

inelegant *adjective*
Lacking style and good taste : tasteless, unbecoming. *Informal:* tacky[2]. *See* STYLE.

inept *adjective*
1. Not suited to circumstances : improper, inappropriate, inapt, incongruous, malapropos, unapt, unbecoming, unbefitting, unfit, unseemly, unsuitable. ***Idiom:*** out of place. *See* AGREE, USUAL. **2.** Characterized by inappropriateness and gracelessness, especially in expression : awkward, ill-chosen, inappropriate, infelicitous, unfortunate, unhappy. *See* ABILITY, GOOD. **3.** Lacking the qualities, as efficiency or skill, required to produce desired results : inapt, incapable, incompetent, inefficient, inexpert, unskilled, unskillful, unworkmanlike. *See* ABILITY. **4.** Clumsily lacking in the ability to do or perform : awkward, bumbling, clumsy, gauche, heavy-handed, maladroit, unskillful. *See* ABILITY. **5.** Lacking dexterity and grace in physical movement : awkward, clumsy, gawky, graceless, lumpish, maladroit, ungainly, ungraceful. *Slang:* klutzy. ***Idiom:*** all thumbs. *See* ABILITY.

inequality *noun*
1. The condition or fact of being unequal, as in age, rank, or degree : disparity, disproportion, disproportionateness. *See* SAME. **2.** Lack of smoothness or regularity : asymmetry, crookedness, irregularity, jaggedness, roughness, unevenness. *See* SMOOTH, STRAIGHT.

inequitable *adjective*
Not fair, right, or just : unequal, unfair, unjust. *See* FAIR.

inequity *noun*
1. Lack of justice : iniquity, injustice, unfairness, unjustness, wrong. *See* LAW, RIGHT. **2.** An act that is not just : disservice, injustice, raw deal, wrong. *Law:* injury. *See* LAW, RIGHT.

ineradicable *adjective*
Firmly established by long standing : con-

firmed, deep-rooted, deep-seated, entrenched, hard-shell, ingrained, inveterate, irradicable, set[1], settled. *See* CONTINUE.

inert *adjective*
Marked by a lack of action or activity : idle, inactive, inoperative. *See* ACTION.

inertness *noun*
A lack of action or activity : idleness, inaction, inactivity, inoperativeness, stagnation. *See* ACTION.

inescapable *adjective*
Bound to happen : certain, inevitable, sure, unavoidable. *See* CERTAIN.

inessential *adjective*
Not necessary : dispensable, needless, nonessential, uncalled-for, unessential, unnecessary, unneeded, unrequired. *See* NECESSARY.

inestimable *adjective*
1. Too great to be calculated : countless, immeasurable, incalculable, incomputable, infinite, innumerable, measureless, uncountable. *See* BIG. **2.** Of great value : costly, invaluable, precious, priceless, valuable, worthy. ***Idioms:*** beyond price, of great price. *See* VALUE.

inevitable *adjective*
Bound to happen : certain, inescapable, sure, unavoidable. *See* CERTAIN.

inexact *adjective*
1. Lacking precise limits : indefinite, indeterminate, undetermined. *See* LIMITED. **2.** Lacking literal exactness : free, loose. *See* PRECISE.

inexcusable *adjective*
Impossible to excuse, pardon, or justify : indefensible, unforgivable, unjustifiable, unpardonable. *See* FORGIVENESS.

inexhaustibility *noun*
The state or quality of being infinite : boundlessness, immeasurability, immeasurableness, inexhaustibleness, infiniteness, infinity, limitlessness, measurelessness, unboundedness, unlimitedness. *See* LIMITED.

inexhaustible *adjective*
Having or showing a capacity for protracted effort, regardless of difficulty or frustration : indefatigable, tireless, unfailing, unflagging, untiring, unwearied, weariless. *See* CONTINUE, TIRED.

inexhaustibleness *noun*
The state or quality of being infinite : boundlessness, immeasurability, immeasurableness, inexhaustibility, infiniteness, infinity, limitlessness, measurelessness, unboundedness, unlimitedness. *See* LIMITED.

inexorability *noun*
The quality or state of being stubbornly inflexible : die-hardism, grimness, implacability, implacableness, incompliance, incompliancy, inexorableness, inflexibility, inflexibleness, intransigence, intransigency, obduracy, obdurateness, relentlessness, remorselessness, rigidity, rigidness, stubbornness. *See* RESIST.

inexorable *adjective*
Firmly, often unreasonably immovable in purpose or will : adamant, adamantine, brassbound, die-hard, grim, implacable, incompliant, inflexible, intransigent, iron, obdurate, relentless, remorseless, rigid, stubborn, unbendable, unbending, uncompliant, uncompromising, unrelenting, unyielding. ***Idiom:*** stubborn as a mule (*or* ox). *See* RESIST.

inexorableness *noun*
The quality or state of being stubbornly inflexible : die-hardism, grimness, implacability, implacableness, incompliance, incompliancy, inexorability, inflexibility, inflexibleness, intransigence, intransigency, obduracy, obdurateness, relentlessness, remorselessness, rigidity, rigidness, stubbornness. *See* RESIST.

inexpensive *adjective*
Low in price : cheap, low, low-cost, low-priced. *See* MONEY, VALUE.

inexperience *noun*
Lack of experience and the knowledge gained from it : greenness, inexpertness, rawness. *See* ABILITY.

inexperienced *adjective*
Lacking experience and the knowledge gained from it : green, inexpert, raw, uninitiate, uninitiated, unpracticed, unseasoned, untried, unversed. *See* ABILITY.

inexpert *adjective*
1. Lacking the qualities, as efficiency or skill, required to produce desired results : inapt, incapable, incompetent, inefficient, inept, unskilled, unskillful, unworkmanlike. *See* ABILITY. **2.** Lacking experience and the knowledge gained from it : green, inexperienced, raw, uninitiate, uninitiated, unpracticed, unseasoned, untried, unversed. *See* ABILITY.

inexpertness *noun*
Lack of experience and the knowledge gained from it : greenness, inexperience, rawness. *See* ABILITY.

inexplicable *adjective*
That cannot be explained : unaccountable, unexplainable. *See* EXPLAIN.

inexplicit *adjective*
Liable to more than one interpretation : ambiguous, cloudy, equivocal, nebulous,

obscure, uncertain, unclear, vague. *See* CERTAIN, CLEAR.

inexpressible *adjective*
That cannot be described : incommunicable, indefinable, indescribable, ineffable, undescribable, unspeakable, unutterable. ***Idioms:*** beyond description (*or* words), defying description. *See* WORDS.

inexpressive *adjective*
Lacking expression : blank, deadpan, expressionless, pokerfaced. *See* SHOW.

infallible *adjective*
Such as could not possibly fail or disappoint : certain, secure, sure, unerring, unfailing. *Informal:* sure-fire. *See* CERTAIN.

infamous *adjective*
1. Known widely and unfavorably : common, notorious. *See* KNOWLEDGE. **2.** So objectionable as to elicit despisal or deserve condemnation : abhorrent, abominable, antipathetic, contemptible, despicable, despisable, detestable, disgusting, filthy, foul, loathsome, lousy, low, mean[2], nasty, nefarious, obnoxious, odious, repugnant, rotten, shabby, vile, wretched. *See* GOOD.

infamousness *noun*
Unfavorable, usually unsavory renown : infamy, notoriety, notoriousness. *See* KNOWLEDGE.

infamy *noun*
1. Unfavorable, usually unsavory renown : infamousness, notoriety, notoriousness. *See* KNOWLEDGE. **2.** The condition of being infamous : disgracefulness, dishonorableness, disreputability, disreputableness, ignominiousness, shamefulness. *See* GOOD, RESPECT, RIGHT.

infancy *noun*
Law. The state or period of being under legal age : minority, nonage. *See* LAW, YOUTH.

infant *noun*
1. A very young child : babe, baby, bambino, neonate, newborn, nursling. ***Idiom:*** bundle of joy. *See* KIN, YOUTH. **2.** *Law.* One who is not yet legally of age : child, juvenile. *Law:* minor. *See* LAW, YOUTH.

infant *adjective* Being in an early period of growth or development : green, immature, juvenile, young, youthful. *See* YOUTH.

infantile *adjective*
1. Of or like a baby : babyish, cherubic, childlike, infantine. *See* YOUTH. **2.** Of or characteristic of a child, especially in immaturity : babyish, childish, immature, juvenile, puerile. *See* YOUTH.

infantine *adjective*
Of or like a baby : babyish, cherubic, childlike, infantile. *See* YOUTH.

infatuate *adjective*
Affected with intense romantic attraction : enamored, infatuated, smitten. *Slang:* gone. *See* EXCITE, SEX.

infatuated *adjective*
Affected with intense romantic attraction : enamored, infatuate, smitten. *Slang:* gone. *See* EXCITE, SEX.

infatuation *noun*
An extravagant, short-lived romantic attachment : *Informal:* crush. *See* EXCITE, SEX.

infect *verb*
1. To have a destructive effect on : canker, envenom, poison. *Archaic:* empoison. *See* HELP. **2.** To make morally impure : contaminate, corrupt, defile, pollute, soil, taint. *See* CLEAN.

infectious *adjective*
Capable of transmission by infection : catching, communicable, contagious, taking. *See* MOVE.

infelicitous *adjective*
Characterized by inappropriateness and gracelessness, especially in expression : awkward, ill-chosen, inappropriate, inept, unfortunate, unhappy. *See* ABILITY, GOOD.

infer *verb*
1. To arrive at (a conclusion) from evidence or reasoning : conclude, deduce, deduct, draw, gather, judge, understand. *See* REASON. **2.** To draw an inference on the basis of inconclusive evidence or insufficient information : conjecture, guess, speculate, suppose, surmise. *See* OPINION.

inference *noun*
A position arrived at by reasoning from premises or general principles : conclusion, deduction, illation, illative, judgment. *See* REASON.

inferential *adjective*
Presumed to be true, real, or genuine, especially on inconclusive grounds : conjectural, hypothetic, hypothetical, presumptive, supposed, suppositional, suppositious, supposititious, suppositive. *See* BELIEF.

inferior *adjective*
1. Below another in standing or importance : junior, lesser, low, lower[2], minor, minor-league, petty, secondary, small, subaltern, subordinate, under. *Informal:* smalltime. *See* OVER. **2.** Of low or lower quality : common,

low-grade, low-quality, mean[2], mediocre, second-class, second-rate, shabby, substandard. *See* BETTER.

inferior *noun* One belonging to a lower class or rank : junior, secondary, subaltern, subordinate, underling. *See* OVER.

infernal *adjective*

1. Perversely bad, cruel, or wicked : devilish, diabolic, diabolical, fiendish, ghoulish, hellish, ogreish, satanic, satanical. *See* KIND.

2. So annoying or detestable as to deserve condemnation : accursed, blasted, blessed, bloody, confounded, cursed, damn, darn, execrable. *Informal:* blamed, damned. *Chiefly British:* blooming, ruddy. *See* LIKE.

inferred *adjective*

Conveyed indirectly without words or speech : implicit, implied, tacit, understood, unsaid, unspoken, unuttered, wordless. *Idiom:* taken for granted. *See* SHOW.

infertile *adjective*

1. Lacking or unable to produce growing plants or crops : barren, sterile, unfruitful, unproductive. *See* RICH. **2.** Unable to produce offspring : barren, childless, impotent, sterile, unfruitful. *See* RICH.

infertility *noun*

The state or condition of being unable to reproduce sexually : barrenness, sterility, sterilization. *See* REPRODUCTION, RICH.

infidelity *noun*

Betrayal, especially of a moral obligation : disloyalty, faithlessness, false-heartedness, falseness, falsity, perfidiousness, perfidy, traitorousness, treacherousness, treachery, unfaithfulness. *See* CONTINUE, TRUST.

infiltrate *verb*

To introduce gradually and slyly : edge, foist, insinuate, wind[2], work, worm. *See* ENTER.

infinite *adjective*

1. Having no ends or limits : boundless, endless, illimitable, immeasurable, limitless, measureless, unbounded, unlimited. *See* LIMITED.

2. Without beginning or end : eternal, sempiternal. *See* LIMITED. **3.** Too great to be calculated : countless, immeasurable, incalculable, incomputable, inestimable, innumerable, measureless, uncountable. *See* BIG.

infiniteness *noun*

The state or quality of being infinite : boundlessness, immeasurability, immeasurableness, inexhaustibility, inexhaustibleness, infinity, limitlessness, measurelessness, unboundedness, unlimitedness. *See* LIMITED.

infinitesimal *adjective*

So minute as not to be discernible : imperceptible, microscopic. *See* BIG.

infinity *noun*

1. The state or quality of being infinite : boundlessness, immeasurability, immeasurableness, inexhaustibility, inexhaustibleness, infiniteness, limitlessness, measurelessness, unboundedness, unlimitedness. *See* LIMITED.

2. The totality of time without beginning or end : eternality, eternalness, eternity, perpetuity, sempiternity. *See* LIMITED.

infirm *adjective*

1. Not physically strong : decrepit, delicate, feeble, flimsy, fragile, frail, insubstantial, puny, unsound, unsubstantial, weak, weakly. *See* STRONG. **2.** Lacking stability : insecure, precarious, shaky, tottering, tottery, unstable, unsteady, unsure, weak, wobbly. *See* CHANGE, STRONG.

infirmity *noun*

1. A pathological condition of mind or body : ailment, complaint, disease, disorder, ill, illness, malady, sickness. *See* HEALTH. **2.** The condition of being infirm or physically weak : debility, decrepitude, delicacy, delicateness, feebleness, flimsiness, fragileness, fragility, frailness, frailty, insubstantiality, puniness, unsoundness, unsubstantiality, weakliness, weakness. *See* STRONG. **3.** The condition of being sick : affliction, disorder, illness, indisposition, sickness. *See* HEALTH. **4.** An imperfection of character : failing, fault, foible, frailty, shortcoming, weakness, weak point. *See* BETTER, HELP.

infix *verb*

To implant so deeply as to make change nearly impossible : embed, entrench, fasten, fix, ingrain, lodge, root[1]. *See* MOVE.

inflame *verb*

1. To stir to action or feeling : egg on, excite, foment, galvanize, goad, impel, incite, inspire, instigate, motivate, move, pique, prick, prod, prompt, propel, provoke, set off, spur, stimulate, touch off, trigger, work up. *See* CAUSE, EXCITE. **2.** To cause to become sore or inflamed : burn, irritate, sting. *See* HELP.

inflammation *noun*

An instance of being irritated, as in a part of the body : irritation, soreness. *See* HELP.

inflate *verb*

To make (something) seem greater than is actually the case : exaggerate, hyperbolize, magnify, overcharge, overstate. *Idioms:* blow up out of proportion, lay it on thick, stretch the truth. *See* INCREASE.

inflated *adjective*
Filled up with or as if with something insubstantial : flatulent, overblown, tumescent, tumid, turgid, windy. *See* INCREASE, PLAIN.

inflection *noun*
A particular vocal quality that indicates some emotion or feeling : accent, intonation, tone. *Idiom:* tone of voice. *See* SOUNDS.

inflexibility *noun*
The quality or state of being stubbornly inflexible : die-hardism, grimness, implacability, implacableness, incompliance, incompliancy, inexorability, inexorableness, inflexibleness, intransigence, intransigency, obduracy, obdurateness, relentlessness, remorselessness, rigidity, rigidness, stubbornness. *See* RESIST.

inflexible *adjective*
1. Not changing shape or bending : inelastic, rigid, stiff, unbending, unyielding. *See* FLEXIBLE. **2.** Incapable of changing or being modified : immutable, inalterable, invariable, ironclad, rigid, unalterable, unchangeable. *See* FLEXIBLE. **3.** Firmly, often unreasonably immovable in purpose or will : adamant, adamantine, brassbound, die-hard, grim, implacable, incompliant, inexorable, intransigent, iron, obdurate, relentless, remorseless, rigid, stubborn, unbendable, unbending, uncompliant, uncompromising, unrelenting, unyielding. *Idiom:* stubborn as a mule (*or* ox). *See* RESIST.

inflexibleness *noun*
The quality or state of being stubbornly inflexible : die-hardism, grimness, implacability, implacableness, incompliance, incompliancy, inexorability, inexorableness, inflexibility, intransigence, intransigency, obduracy, obdurateness, relentlessness, remorselessness, rigidity, rigidness, stubbornness. *See* RESIST.

inflict *verb*
1. To cause to undergo or bear (something unwelcome or damaging, for example) : impose, play, visit, wreak. *See* GIVE, OVER, WILLING. **2.** To force (another) to accept a burden : foist, impose, saddle. *Informal:* stick. *See* GIVE, OVER, WILLING.

infliction *noun*
An excessive, unwelcome burden : imposition, intrusion. *See* LIKE, WILLING.

influence *noun*
1. The power or capacity to produce a desired result : effect, effectiveness, effectuality, effectualness, efficaciousness, efficacy, efficiency, potency. *See* AFFECT. **2.** The power to produce an effect by indirect means : leverage, sway, weight. *Informal:* clout. *Slang:* pull. *See* AFFECT. **3.** The strong effect exerted by one person or thing on another : force, impact, impression, repercussion. *See* AFFECT.

influence *verb* To have an impact on in a certain way : dispose, incline, predispose, sway. *See* AFFECT, LIKE.

influential *adjective*
Having or exercising influence : consequential, important, powerful, weighty. *See* AFFECT, IMPORTANT, STRONG.

infold *verb*
1. To cover completely and closely, as with clothing or bandages : enfold, envelop, enwrap, invest, roll, swaddle, swathe, wrap, wrap up. *See* PUT ON. **2.** To surround and cover completely so as to obscure : cloak, clothe, enfold, enshroud, envelop, enwrap, invest, shroud, veil, wrap. *See* SHOW.

inform *verb*
1. To impart information to : acquaint, advise, apprise, educate, enlighten, notify, tell. *See* KNOWLEDGE, TEACH. **2.** To give incriminating information about others, especially to the authorities : talk, tattle, tip[3] (off). *Slang:* fink, rat, sing, snitch, squeal, stool. *Idiom:* blow the whistle. *See* KNOWLEDGE, LAW.

informal *adjective*
1. Unconstrained by rigid standards or ceremony : casual, easy, easygoing, natural, relaxed, spontaneous, unceremonious, unrestrained. *Informal:* laid-back. *See* PLAIN, TIGHTEN. **2.** In the style of conversation : chatty, colloquial, confabulatory, conversational. *See* WORDS.

informality *noun*
Freedom from constraint, formality, embarrassment, or awkwardness : casualness, ease, easiness, naturalness, poise, spontaneity, unceremoniousness, unrestraint. *See* RESTRAINT, TIGHTEN.

informant *noun*
One who gives incriminating information about others : informer, tattler, tattletale. *Informal:* rat, tipster. *Slang:* fink, snitch, snitcher, squealer, stoolie, stool pigeon. *See* KNOWLEDGE, LAW.

information *noun*
1. That which is known; the sum of what has been perceived, discovered, or inferred : knowledge, lore, wisdom. *See* KNOWLEDGE.

2. That which is known about a specific subject or situation : data, fact (used in plural), intelligence, knowledge, lore. *See* KNOWLEDGE.

informative *adjective*
Serving to educate or inform : edifying, educational, educative, enlightening, illuminative, instructional, instructive. *See* TEACH.

informed *adjective*
1. Provided with information; made aware : acquainted, advised, educated, enlightened, instructed, knowledgeable. *See* KNOWLEDGE. **2.** Having an education : educated, enlightened, lettered, literate. *See* KNOWLEDGE.

informer *noun*
One who gives incriminating information about others : informant, tattler, tattletale. *Informal:* rat, tipster. *Slang:* fink, snitch, snitcher, squealer, stoolie, stool pigeon. *See* KNOWLEDGE, LAW.

infraction *noun*
An act or instance of breaking a law or regulation or of nonfulfillment of an obligation or promise, for example : breach, contravention, infringement, transgression, trespass, violation. *See* RIGHT.

infrequent *adjective*
Rarely occurring or appearing : occasional, rare, scarce, sporadic, uncommon, unusual. ***Idiom:*** few and far between. *See* USUAL.

infrequently *adverb*
At rare intervals : little, occasionally, rarely, seldom, sporadically. ***Idioms:*** hardly (*or* scarcely) ever, once in a blue moon. *See* USUAL.

infringe *verb*
To fail to fulfill (a promise) or conform to (a regulation) : breach, break, contravene, transgress, violate. *See* DO.

infringement *noun*
1. An act or instance of breaking a law or regulation or of nonfulfillment of an obligation or promise, for example : breach, contravention, infraction, transgression, trespass, violation. *See* RIGHT. **2.** An advance beyond proper or legal limits : encroachment, entrenchment, impingement, intrusion, obtrusion, trespass. *See* ENTER.

infuriate *verb*
To cause to feel or show anger : anger, burn (up), enrage, incense[1], madden, provoke. ***Idioms:*** make one hot under the collar, make one's blood boil, put one's back up. *See* FEELINGS.

infuse *verb*
Chemistry. To saturate (something) with a liquid : soak, steep[2]. *See* DRY.

ingenerate *verb*
To be the cause of : bring, bring about, bring on, cause, effect, effectuate, generate, induce, lead to, make, occasion, result in, secure, set off, stir[1] (up), touch off, trigger. ***Idioms:*** bring to pass (*or* effect), give rise to. *See* START.

ingenious *adjective*
1. Characterized by or productive of new things or new ideas : creative, innovative, innovatory, inventive, original. *See* ABILITY. **2.** Able to use the means at one's disposal to meet situations effectively : inventive, resourceful. *See* ABILITY.

ingeniousness *noun*
The power or ability to invent : creativeness, creativity, ingenuity, invention, inventiveness, originality. *See* ABILITY, MAKE.

ingénue *noun*
A guileless, unsophisticated person : babe, child, innocent, naive. ***Idiom:*** babe in the woods. *See* KNOWLEDGE.

ingenuity *noun*
The power or ability to invent : creativeness, creativity, ingeniousness, invention, inventiveness, originality. *See* ABILITY, MAKE.

ingenuous *adjective*
1. Free from guile, cunning, or deceit : artless, guileless, innocent, naive, natural, simple, unaffected, unsophisticated, unstudied, unworldly. *See* HONEST. **2.** Manifesting honesty and directness, especially in speech : candid, direct, downright, forthright, frank, honest, man-to-man, open, plainspoken, straight, straightforward, straight-out, unreserved. *Informal:* straight-from-the-shoulder, straight-shooting. *See* CLEAR, SHOW.

ingest *verb*
1. To cause to pass from the mouth into the stomach : swallow, take. *See* MOUTH. **2.** To take (food) into the body as nourishment : consume, devour, eat, fare, partake. *Slang:* chow. ***Idioms:*** break bread, have (*or* take) a bite. *See* INGESTION.

ingestion *noun*
An act of swallowing : gulp, swallow. *See* MOUTH.

ingrain *verb*
To implant so deeply as to make change nearly impossible : embed, entrench, fasten, fix, infix, lodge, root[1]. *See* MOVE.

ingrained *adjective*
1. Firmly established by long standing : confirmed, deep-rooted, deep-seated, entrenched, hard-shell, ineradicable, inveterate, irradicable, set[1], settled. *See* CONTINUE. **2.** Forming an

essential element, as arising from the basic structure of an individual : built-in, congenital, connatural, constitutional, elemental, inborn, inbred, indigenous, indwelling, inherent, innate, intrinsic, native, natural. *See* BE, NATIVE, START.

ingratiating *adjective*
Purposefully contrived to gain favor : ingratiatory, insinuating, saccharine, sugary. *See* PAIN.

ingratiatory *adjective*
Purposefully contrived to gain favor : ingratiating, insinuating, saccharine, sugary. *See* PAIN.

ingredient *noun*
One of the individual entities contributing to a whole : building block, component, constituent, element, factor, integrant, part. *See* PART.

ingress *noun*
1. The act of entering : entrance[1], entry. *See* ENTER. **2.** The right to enter or make use of : access, admission, admittance, entrance[1], entrée, entry. *See* ENTER. **3.** The state of being allowed entry : admission, admittance, entrance[1], ingression, introduction, intromission. *See* ACCEPT.

ingression *noun*
The state of being allowed entry : admission, admittance, entrance[1], ingress, introduction, intromission. *See* ACCEPT.

ingurgitate *verb*
To swallow (food or drink) greedily or rapidly in large amounts : bolt, down, englut, engorge, gobble, gulp, guzzle, swill, wolf. *See* INGESTION.

inhabit *verb*
To live in (a place), as does a people : occupy, people, populate. *See* PLACE.

inhabitable *adjective*
Fit to live in : habitable, livable. *See* COMFORT.

inhalation *noun*
The act of breathing in : inspiration. *See* BREATH.

inhale *verb*
To draw air into the lungs in the process of respiration : breathe (in), inspire. *See* BREATH.

inharmonic *adjective*
Characterized by unpleasant discordance of sound : cacophonous, discordant, disharmonious, dissonant, inharmonious, rude, unharmonious, unmusical. *See* AGREE, SOUNDS.

inharmonious *adjective*
1. Devoid of harmony and accord : discordant, inconsonant, uncongenial, unharmonious. *See* AGREE. **2.** Characterized by unpleasant discordance of sound : cacophonous, discordant, disharmonious, dissonant, inharmonic, rude, unharmonious, unmusical. *See* AGREE, SOUNDS.

inharmony *noun*
A state of disagreement and disharmony : clash, conflict, confrontation, contention, difference, difficulty, disaccord, discord, discordance, dissension, dissent, dissentience, dissidence, dissonance, faction, friction, schism, strife, variance, war, warfare. *See* CONFLICT.

inhere *verb*
To have an inherent basis : consist, dwell, exist, lie[1], repose, reside, rest[1]. *See* START.

inherent *adjective*
Forming an essential element, as arising from the basic structure of an individual : built-in, congenital, connatural, constitutional, elemental, inborn, inbred, indigenous, indwelling, ingrained, innate, intrinsic, native, natural. *See* BE, NATIVE, START.

inherit *verb*
To receive (property) from one who has died : come into. *See* GET, LAW.

inheritance *noun*
1. Any special privilege accorded a firstborn : birthright, heritage, legacy, patrimony. *See* OWNED. **2.** Something immaterial, as a style or philosophy, that is passed from one generation to another : heritage, legacy, tradition. *See* AFFECT.

inherited *adjective*
1. Of or from one's ancestors : ancestral, hereditary, patrimonial. *See* KIN, PRECEDE.
2. Possessed at birth : congenital, hereditary, inborn, innate, native. *See* BE, NATIVE.

inhibit *verb*
1. To control, restrict, or arrest : bit[2], brake, bridle, check, constrain, curb, hold, hold back, hold down, hold in, keep, keep back, pull in, rein (back, in, *or* up), restrain. *See* RESTRAINT.
2. To check the freedom and spontaneity of : constrain, constrict, cramp[2]. *See* FREE, TIGHTEN. **3.** To refuse to allow : ban, debar, disallow, enjoin, forbid, interdict, outlaw, prohibit, proscribe, taboo. *See* ALLOW.

inhibited *adjective*
1. Tending to keep one's thoughts and emotions to oneself : controlled, noncommittal, reserved, restrained, self-controlled, self-restrained. *See* RESTRAINT. **2.** Deficient in or lacking sexual desire : ardorless, cold, frigid, passionless, unresponsive. *See* SEX.

inhibition *noun*
1. A refusal to allow : ban, disallowance, for-

biddance, interdiction, prohibition, proscription, taboo. *See* ALLOW. **2.** Something that limits or restricts : check, circumscription, constraint, cramp[2], curb, limit, limitation, restraint, restriction, stricture, trammel. *See* LIMITED.

inhospitable *adjective*
So disagreeable as to discourage approach : forbidding, unhospitable, uninviting. *See* WARN.

inhospitableness *noun*
Lack of cordiality and hospitableness : inhospitality, ungraciousness, unreceptiveness, unwelcome, unwelcomeness. *See* LIKE.

inhospitality *noun*
Lack of cordiality and hospitableness : inhospitableness, ungraciousness, unreceptiveness, unwelcome, unwelcomeness. *See* LIKE.

inhuman *adjective*
Showing or suggesting a disposition to be violently destructive without scruple or restraint : barbarous, bestial, cruel, fell[2], feral, ferocious, fierce, savage, truculent, vicious, wolfish. *See* KIND.

inhumanity *noun*
A cruel act or an instance of cruel behavior : barbarity, bestiality, brutality, cruelty, savagery, truculence, truculency. *See* ATTITUDE, KIND.

inhumation *noun*
An act of placing a body in a grave or tomb : burial, entombment, interment. *See* SHOW.

inhume *verb*
To place (a corpse) in or as if in a grave : bury, entomb, inter, lay[1]. ***Idiom:*** lay (*or* put) to rest. *See* SHOW.

inimical *adjective*
Feeling or showing unfriendliness : hostile, unfriendly. *See* LOVE.

iniquitous *adjective*
Morally objectionable : bad, black, evil, immoral, peccant, reprobate, sinful, vicious, wicked, wrong. *See* RIGHT.

iniquity *noun*
1. That which is morally bad or objectionable : evil, peccancy, sin, wickedness, wrong. *See* RIGHT. **2.** Lack of justice : inequity, injustice, unfairness, unjustness, wrong. *See* LAW, RIGHT. **3.** A wicked act or wicked behavior : crime, deviltry, diablerie, evil, evildoing, immorality, misdeed, offense, peccancy, sin, wickedness, wrong, wrongdoing. *See* RIGHT.

initial *adjective*
1. Of, relating to, or occurring at the start of something : beginning, inceptive, incipient, initiatory, introductory, leadoff. *See* START. **2.** At or near the start of a period, development, or series : beginning, early, first. *See* START. **3.** Preceding all others in time : earliest, first, maiden, original, pioneer, primary, prime, primordial. *See* START.

initiate *verb*
1. To go about the initial step in doing (something) : approach, begin, commence, embark, enter, get off, inaugurate, institute, launch, lead off, open, set about, set out, set to, start, take on, take up, undertake. *Informal:* kick off. ***Idioms:*** get cracking, get going, get the show on the road. *See* START. **2.** To admit formally into membership or office, as with ritual : inaugurate, induct, install, instate, invest. *See* ACCEPT.

initiate *noun* One who is just starting to learn or do something : abecedarian, beginner, fledgling, freshman, greenhorn, neophyte, novice, novitiate, tenderfoot, tyro. *Slang:* rookie. *See* START.

initiation *noun*
1. The act or process of bringing or being brought into existence : beginning, commencement, inauguration, inception, incipience, incipiency, launch, leadoff, opening, origination, start. *Informal:* kickoff. *See* START. **2.** The act or process of formally admitting a person to membership or office : inaugural, inauguration, induction, installation, instatement, investiture. *See* ACCEPT.

initiative *noun*
An aggressive readiness along with energy to undertake taxing efforts : drive, enterprise, hustle, punch. *Informal:* get-up-and-go, gumption, push. *See* ACTION, TIRED, TRY.

initiatory *adjective*
Of, relating to, or occurring at the start of something : beginning, inceptive, incipient, initial, introductory, leadoff. *See* START.

inject *verb*
To put or set into, between, or among another or other things : insert, interject, interlard, interpolate, interpose, introduce. *See* PUT IN.

injudicious *adjective*
Not wise : ill-advised, ill-considered, impolitic, imprudent, indiscreet, unsound, unwise. *See* WISE.

injunction *noun*
An authoritative indication to be obeyed : behest, bidding, charge, command, commandment, dictate, direction, directive, instruction (often used in plural), mandate, order, word. *See* OVER, WORDS.

injure *verb*
1. To cause physical damage to : hurt, wound. *See* HELP. **2.** To spoil the soundness or perfection of : blemish, damage, detract from, disserve, flaw, harm, hurt, impair, mar, prejudice, tarnish, vitiate. *See* BETTER, HELP. **3.** To cause suffering or painful sorrow to : aggrieve, distress, grieve, hurt, pain, wound. *See* HAPPY.

injurious *adjective*
1. Causing harm or injury : bad, deleterious, detrimental, evil, harmful, hurtful, ill, mischievous. *See* HELP. **2.** Damaging to the reputation : calumnious, defamatory, detractive, invidious, scandalous, slanderous. *Law:* libelous. *See* ATTACK, CRIMES, LAW.

injury *noun*
1. The action or result of inflicting loss or pain : damage, detriment, harm, hurt, mischief. *See* HELP. **2.** *Law.* An act that is not just : disservice, inequity, injustice, raw deal, wrong. *See* LAW, RIGHT.

injustice *noun*
1. Lack of justice : inequity, iniquity, unfairness, unjustness, wrong. *See* LAW, RIGHT.
2. An act that is not just : disservice, inequity, raw deal, wrong. *Law:* injury. *See* LAW, RIGHT.

inkhorn *adjective*
Characterized by a narrow concern for book learning and formal rules, without knowledge or experience of practical matters : academic, bookish, donnish, formalistic, literary, pedantic, pedantical, scholastic. *See* ATTITUDE, FLEXIBLE, TEACH.

inkling *noun*
A subtle quality underlying or felt to underlie a situation, action, or person : hint, implication, suspicion, undercurrent, undertone. *See* SHOW, SUGGEST.

inky *adjective*
Of the darkest achromatic visual value : black, ebon, ebony, jet[1], jetty, onyx, pitch-black, pitchy, sable, sooty. *See* COLORS.

inlet *noun*
A body of water partly enclosed by land but having a wide outlet to the sea : bay[1], bight, cove. *See* TERRITORY.

inlying *adjective*
Located inside or farther in : inner, inside, interior, internal. *See* EDGE.

innate *adjective*
1. Possessed at birth : congenital, hereditary, inborn, inherited, native. *See* BE, NATIVE.
2. Forming an essential element, as arising from the basic structure of an individual : built-in, congenital, connatural, constitutional, elemental, inborn, inbred, indigenous, indwelling, ingrained, inherent, intrinsic, native, natural. *See* BE, NATIVE, START.

inner *adjective*
1. Located inside or farther in : inlying, inside, interior, internal. *See* EDGE. **2.** Of, relating to, or arising from one's mental or spiritual being : interior, internal, intimate[1], inward, visceral. *Slang:* gut. *See* BODY. **3.** Being closer to a center of power and influence : inside. *See* EDGE, POLITICS.

innerving *adjective*
Producing or stimulating physical, mental, or emotional vigor : bracing, energizing, exhilarant, exhilarating, invigorating, intoxicating, refreshing, reinvigorating, renewing, restorative, roborant, stimulating, tonic. *See* HELP.

inning *noun*
A limited, often assigned period of activity, duty, or opportunity. Often used in plural : bout, go, hitch, shift, spell[3], stint, stretch, time, tour, trick, turn, watch. *See* TIME.

innocence *noun*
1. The condition of being chaste : chastity, decency, modesty, purity, virginity, virtue, virtuousness. *See* GOOD, RESTRAINT, SEX.
2. The condition of being uninformed or unaware : ignorance, nescience, obliviousness, unawareness, unconsciousness, unfamiliarity. *See* KNOWLEDGE.

innocent *adjective*
1. Free from evil and corruption : angelic, angelical, clean, lily-white, pure, sinless, unblemished, uncorrupted, undefiled, unstained, unsullied, untainted, virginal. ***Idiom:*** pure as the driven snow. *See* CLEAN, RIGHT, SEX. **2.** Free from guilt or blame : blameless, faultless, guiltless, harmless, irreproachable, lily-white, unblamable. *Slang:* clean. ***Idiom:*** in the clear. *See* RIGHT. **3.** Within, allowed by, or sanctioned by the law : lawful, legal, legitimate, licit. *Slang:* legit. *See* LAW. **4.** Devoid of hurtful qualities : harmless, hurtless, innocuous, inoffensive, unoffensive. *See* HELP. **5.** Free from guile, cunning, or deceit : artless, guileless, ingenuous, naive, natural, simple, unaffected, unsophisticated, unstudied, unworldly. *See* HONEST. **6.** Not aware or informed : ignorant, oblivious, unacquainted, unaware, unconscious, unenlightened, unfamiliar, uninformed, unknowing, unwitting. ***Idiom:*** in the dark. *See* KNOWLEDGE. **7.** Not having a desirable element : barren, destitute, devoid, empty,

lacking, void, wanting. *Idiom:* in want of. *See* FULL.

innocent *noun* **1.** A pure, uncorrupted person : angel, lamb, virgin. *See* CLEAN, RIGHT. **2.** A guileless, unsophisticated person : babe, child, ingénue, naive. *Idiom:* babe in the woods. *See* KNOWLEDGE. **3.** A young person between birth and puberty : bud[1], child, juvenile, moppet, tot[1], youngster. *Informal:* kid. *Scots:* bairn. *See* KIN, YOUTH.

innocuous *adjective*
1. Devoid of hurtful qualities : harmless, hurtless, innocent, inoffensive, unoffensive. *See* HELP. **2.** Lacking the qualities requisite for spiritedness and originality : bland, insipid, jejune, namby-pamby, vapid, washy, waterish, watery. *Informal:* wishy-washy. *See* EXCITE, GOOD.

innocuousness *noun*
The state or quality of being insipid : blandness, insipidity, insipidness, jejuneness, vapidity, vapidness, washiness, wateriness. *Informal:* wishy-washiness. *See* EXCITE, TASTE.

innovation *noun*
A new and unusual thing : novelty. *See* NEW.

innovative *adjective*
1. Characterized by or productive of new things or new ideas : creative, ingenious, innovatory, inventive, original. *See* ABILITY. **2.** Not the same as what was previously known or done : different, fresh, inventive, new, newfangled, novel, original, unfamiliar, unprecedented. *See* NEW.

innovativeness *noun*
The quality of being novel : freshness, newfangledness, newness, novelty, originality. *See* NEW.

innovatory *adjective*
Characterized by or productive of new things or new ideas : creative, ingenious, innovative, inventive, original. *See* ABILITY.

innuendo *noun*
An artful, indirect, often derogatory hint : insinuation. *See* SUGGEST.

innumerable *adjective*
Too great to be calculated : countless, immeasurable, incalculable, incomputable, inestimable, infinite, measureless, uncountable. *See* BIG.

inobtrusive *adjective*
Not showy or obtrusive : quiet, restrained, subdued, tasteful, unobtrusive. *See* PLAIN.

inoffensive *adjective*
Devoid of hurtful qualities : harmless, hurtless, innocent, innocuous, unoffensive. *See* HELP.

inoperative *adjective*
Marked by a lack of action or activity : idle, inactive, inert. *See* ACTION.

inoperativeness *noun*
A lack of action or activity : idleness, inaction, inactivity, inertness, stagnation. *See* ACTION.

inopportune *adjective*
Not occurring at a favorable time : ill-timed, inconvenient, untimely. *See* TIME.

inordinate *adjective*
Exceeding a normal or reasonable limit : excessive, exorbitant, extravagant, extreme, immoderate, overabundant, overmuch, undue. *See* EXCESS.

inquest *noun*
A seeking of knowledge, data, or the truth about something : inquiry, inquisition, investigation, probe, research. *See* INVESTIGATE.

inquietude *noun*
An uneasy or nervous state : disquiet, disquietude, restiveness, restlessness, unease, uneasiness, unrest. *See* CALM.

inquire also **enquire** *verb*
1. To put a question to (someone) : ask, examine, query, question, quiz. *See* ASK. **2.** To go into or through for the purpose of making discoveries or acquiring information : delve, dig, explore, investigate, look into, probe, reconnoiter, scout[1]. *See* INVESTIGATE.

inquirer also **enquirer** *noun*
One who inquires : inquisitor, investigator, prober, querier, quester, questioner, researcher. *See* ASK, INVESTIGATE.

inquiring also **enquiring** *adjective*
Eager to acquire knowledge : curious, inquisitive, investigative, questioning. *See* INVESTIGATE.

inquiry also **enquiry** *noun*
1. A request for data : interrogation, query, question. *Law:* interrogatory. *See* ASK, INVESTIGATE. **2.** A seeking of knowledge, data, or the truth about something : inquest, inquisition, investigation, probe, research. *See* INVESTIGATE.

inquisition *noun*
A seeking of knowledge, data, or the truth about something : inquest, inquiry, investigation, probe, research. *See* INVESTIGATE.

inquisitive *adjective*
1. Unduly interested in the affairs of others : curious, inquisitorial. *Informal:* nosy, snoopy. *See* INVESTIGATE. **2.** Eager to acquire knowledge : curious, inquiring, investigative, questioning. *See* INVESTIGATE.

inquisitiveness *noun*
1. Undue interest in the affairs of others : curiosity, curiousness. *Informal:* nosiness, snoopiness. *See* INVESTIGATE. **2.** Mental acquisitiveness : curiosity, curiousness, interest. ***Idiom:*** thirst for knowledge. *See* INVESTIGATE.

inquisitor *noun*
1. One who inquires : inquirer, investigator, prober, querier, quester, questioner, researcher. *See* ASK, INVESTIGATE. **2.** One who conducts an official inquiry, usually with no regard for human rights : interrogator, questioner. *See* ASK, INVESTIGATE.

inquisitorial *adjective*
Unduly interested in the affairs of others : curious, inquisitive. *Informal:* nosy, snoopy. *See* INVESTIGATE.

inroad *noun*
An act of invading, especially by military forces : foray, incursion, invasion, raid. *See* ATTACK, ENTER.

insalubrious *adjective*
Not sustaining or promoting health : unhealthy, unsalutary, unwholesome. *See* HEALTH.

insane *adjective*
1. Afflicted with or exhibiting irrationality and mental unsoundness : brainsick, crazy, daft, demented, disordered, distraught, dotty, lunatic, mad, maniac, maniacal, mentally ill, moonstruck, off, touched, unbalanced, unsound, wrong. *Informal:* bonkers, cracked, daffy, gaga, loony. *Slang:* bananas, batty, buggy, cuckoo, fruity, loco, nuts, nutty, screwy, wacky. *Chiefly British:* crackers. *Law:* non compos mentis. ***Idioms:*** around the bend, crazy as a loon, mad as a hatter, not all there, nutty as a fruitcake, off (*or* out of) one's head, off one's rocker, of unsound mind, out of one's mind, sick in the head, stark raving mad. *See* SANE. **2.** So senseless as to be laughable : absurd, foolish, harebrained, idiotic, imbecilic, lunatic, mad, moronic, nonsensical, preposterous, silly, softheaded, tomfool, unearthly, zany. *Informal:* cockeyed, crazy, loony, loopy. *Slang:* balmy[2], dippy, dopey, jerky, sappy, wacky. *See* ABILITY, KNOWLEDGE.

insaneness *noun*
Serious mental illness or disorder impairing a person's capacity to function normally and safely : brainsickness, craziness, dementia, derangement, disturbance, insanity, lunacy, madness, mental illness, psychopathy, unbalance. *Psychiatry:* mania. *Psychology:* aberration, alienation. *See* SANE.

insanity *noun*
1. Serious mental illness or disorder impairing a person's capacity to function normally and safely : brainsickness, craziness, dementia, derangement, disturbance, insaneness, lunacy, madness, mental illness, psychopathy, unbalance. *Psychiatry:* mania. *Psychology:* aberration, alienation. *See* SANE. **2.** Foolish behavior : absurdity, folly, foolery, foolishness, idiocy, imbecility, lunacy, madness, nonsense, preposterousness, senselessness, silliness, tomfoolery, zaniness. *Informal:* craziness. *See* ABILITY.

inscribe *verb*
1. To form letters, characters, or words on a surface with an instrument : engross, indite, scribe, write. *See* REMEMBER. **2.** To produce a deep impression of : engrave, etch, fix, grave[3], impress, imprint, stamp. *See* MARKS. **3.** To register in or as if in a book : book, catalog, enroll, list[1], set down, write down. *See* REMEMBER. **4.** To affix one's signature to : autograph, endorse, sign, subscribe, undersign. ***Idioms:*** put one's John Hancock on, set one's hand to. *See* LAW.

inscrutable *adjective*
Incapable of being grasped by the intellect or understanding : impenetrable, incomprehensible, uncomprehensible, unfathomable, unintelligible. *See* KNOWLEDGE.

insecure *adjective*
1. Inadequately protected : unguarded, unprotected, unsafe. *See* SAFETY. **2.** Lacking stability : infirm, precarious, shaky, tottering, tottery, unstable, unsteady, unsure, weak, wobbly. *See* CHANGE, STRONG.

insecureness *noun*
The quality or condition of being erratic and undependable : insecurity, instability, precariousness, shakiness, unstableness, unsteadiness, unsureness. *See* CHANGE, STRONG.

insecurity *noun*
The quality or condition of being erratic and undependable : insecureness, instability, precariousness, shakiness, unstableness, unsteadiness, unsureness. *See* CHANGE, STRONG.

insensate *adjective*
1. Completely lacking sensation or consciousness : dead, inanimate, insentient. *See* LIVE. **2.** Lacking passion and emotion : anesthetic, bloodless, dull, insensible, insensitive. *See* ATTITUDE, FEELINGS. **3.** Displaying a com-

plete lack of forethought and good sense : brainless, fatuous, foolish, mindless, senseless, silly, unintelligent, weak-minded, witless. *See* ABILITY, PLANNED.

insensibility *noun*
Lack of emotion or interest : apathy, disinterest, impassivity, incuriosity, incuriousness, indifference, insensibleness, lassitude, lethargy, listlessness, phlegm, stolidity, stolidness, unconcern, uninterest, unresponsiveness. *See* FEELINGS.

insensible *adjective*
1. Incapable of being apprehended by the mind or the senses : impalpable, imperceptible, imponderable, inappreciable, indiscernible, indistinguishable, intangible, invisible, unnoticeable, unobservable. *See* KNOWLEDGE. **2.** Lacking consciousness : cold, senseless, unconscious. ***Idioms:*** out cold, out like a light. *See* AWARENESS. **3.** Lacking physical feeling or sensitivity : asleep, dead, insensitive, numb, unfeeling. *See* AWARENESS. **4.** Lacking responsiveness or alertness : benumbed, dull, insensitive, numb, stuporous, torpid, unresponsive, wooden. *See* AWARENESS. **5.** Without emotion or interest : apathetic, detached, impassive, incurious, indifferent, lethargic, listless, phlegmatic, stolid, unconcerned, uninterested, unresponsive. *See* FEELINGS. **6.** Lacking passion and emotion : anesthetic, bloodless, dull, insensate, insensitive. *See* ATTITUDE, FEELINGS.

insensibleness *noun*
Lack of emotion or interest : apathy, disinterest, impassivity, incuriosity, incuriousness, indifference, insensibility, lassitude, lethargy, listlessness, phlegm, stolidity, stolidness, unconcern, uninterest, unresponsiveness. *See* FEELINGS.

insensitive *adjective*
1. Lacking physical feeling or sensitivity : asleep, dead, insensible, numb, unfeeling. *See* AWARENESS. **2.** Not capable of being affected or impressed : impassible, impassive, insusceptible, unimpressionable, unsusceptible. *See* AFFECT. **3.** Lacking passion and emotion : anesthetic, bloodless, dull, insensate, insensible. *See* ATTITUDE, FEELINGS. **4.** Lacking responsiveness or alertness : benumbed, dull, insensible, numb, stuporous, torpid, unresponsive, wooden. *See* AWARENESS.

insentient *adjective*
Completely lacking sensation or consciousness : dead, inanimate, insensate. *See* LIVE.

insert *verb*
1. To put or set into, between, or among another or other things : inject, interject, interlard, interpolate, interpose, introduce. *See* PUT IN. **2.** To place on a list or in a record : enter, post[3], record, register. *See* REMEMBER.

insertion *noun*
An item inserted, as in a diary, register, or reference book : entry, posting. *See* WORDS.

inside *adjective*
1. Located inside or farther in : inlying, inner, interior, internal. *See* EDGE. **2.** Known about by very few : auricular, confidential, private, secret. *Informal:* hush-hush. *See* SHOW. **3.** Being closer to a center of power and influence : inner. *See* EDGE, POLITICS. **4.** Characterized by a close and thorough acquaintance : intimate[1], personal. *See* NEAR.

inside track *noun*
Informal. A dominating position, as in a conflict : advantage, better[1], bulge, draw, drop, edge, superiority, upper hand, vantage. *Informal:* jump. *See* OVER.

insight *noun*
1. The power to discern the true nature of a person or situation : instinct, intuition, intuitiveness, penetration, sixth sense. *See* THOUGHTS. **2.** Deep, thorough, or mature understanding : profundity, sagaciousness, sagacity, sageness, sapience, wisdom. *See* WISE.

insignificance *noun*
Lack of importance : inconsequence, inconsequentiality, inconsequentialness, indifference, insignificancy, unimportance. *See* CONCERN.

insignificancy *noun*
Lack of importance : inconsequence, inconsequentiality, inconsequentialness, indifference, insignificance, unimportance. *See* CONCERN.

insignificant *adjective*
Not of great importance : inconsequent, inconsequential, little, trivial, unimportant. *See* BIG.

insincere *adjective*
1. Not genuine or sincere : affected, artificial, feigned, phony, pretended. *See* TRUE. **2.** Not being what one purports to be : ambidextrous, disingenuous, left-handed, mala fide. *See* HONEST.

insincerity *noun*
Lack of sincerity : ambidexterity, artificiality, disingenuousness, phoniness. *See* HONEST.

insinuate *verb*
1. To introduce gradually and slyly : edge, foist, infiltrate, wind[2], work, worm. *See* ENTER. **2.** To convey an idea by indirect, subtle

means : hint, imply, intimate[2], suggest. *Idiom:* drop a hint. *See* SHOW, SUGGEST.

insinuating *adjective*
1. Provoking a change of outlook and especially gradual doubt and suspicion : insinuative, insinuatory, suggestive. *See* SUGGEST. 2. Purposefully contrived to gain favor : ingratiating, ingratiatory, saccharine, sugary. *See* PAIN.

insinuation *noun*
An artful, indirect, often derogatory hint : innuendo. *See* SUGGEST.

insinuative *adjective*
Provoking a change of outlook and especially gradual doubt and suspicion : insinuating, insinuatory, suggestive. *See* SUGGEST.

insinuatory *adjective*
Provoking a change of outlook and especially gradual doubt and suspicion : insinuating, insinuative, suggestive. *See* SUGGEST.

insipid *adjective*
1. Lacking an appetizing flavor : bland, flat, flavorless, tasteless, unsavory. *See* TASTE.
2. Lacking the qualities requisite for spiritedness and originality : bland, innocuous, jejune, namby-pamby, vapid, washy, waterish, watery. *Informal:* wishy-washy. *See* EXCITE, GOOD.

insipidity *noun*
1. The state or quality of being insipid : blandness, innocuousness, insipidness, jejuneness, vapidity, vapidness, washiness, wateriness. *Informal:* wishy-washiness. *See* EXCITE, TASTE. 2. A lack of excitement, liveliness, or interest : asepticism, blandness, colorlessness, drabness, dreariness, dryness, dullness, flatness, flavorlessness, insipidness, jejuneness, lifelessness, sterileness, sterility, stodginess, vapidity, vapidness, weariness. *See* EXCITE.

insipidness *noun*
1. The state or quality of being insipid : blandness, innocuousness, insipidity, jejuneness, vapidity, vapidness, washiness, wateriness. *Informal:* wishy-washiness. *See* EXCITE, TASTE. 2. A lack of excitement, liveliness, or interest : asepticism, blandness, colorlessness, drabness, dreariness, dryness, dullness, flatness, flavorlessness, insipidity, jejuneness, lifelessness, sterileness, sterility, stodginess, vapidity, vapidness, weariness. *See* EXCITE.

insist *verb*
1. To take and maintain a stand obstinately : persevere, persist. *See* CONTINUE. 2. To solicit (something) insistently : press, urge. *See* CONTINUE, SEEK.
insist on (or **upon**) *verb* To ask for urgently or insistently : call for, claim, demand, exact, require, requisition. *Idiom:* cry out for. *See* REQUEST.

insistence *noun*
1. The state or quality of being insistent : insistency, perseverance, persistence, persistency. *See* CONTINUE. 2. Urgent solicitation : insistency, pressing. *Archaic:* instance. *See* CONTINUE, SEEK.

insistency *noun*
1. The state or quality of being insistent : insistence, perseverance, persistence, persistency. *See* CONTINUE. 2. Urgent solicitation : insistence, pressing. *Archaic:* instance. *See* CONTINUE, SEEK.

insistent *adjective*
1. Firm or obstinate, as in making a demand or maintaining a stand : importunate, importune, persistent, urgent. *See* CONTINUE. 2. Bold and definite in character : assertive, emphatic, forceful. *See* STRONG.

insist on or **upon** *verb* See **insist.**

insobriety *noun*
The condition of being intoxicated with alcoholic liquor : crapulence, drunkenness, inebriation, inebriety, intoxication, tipsiness. *See* DRUGS.

insolence *noun*
1. The quality of being arrogant : arrogance, haughtiness, hauteur, loftiness, lordliness, overbearingness, presumption, pride, pridefulness, proudness, superciliousness, superiority. *See* ATTITUDE. 2. The state or quality of being impudent or arrogantly self-confident : assumption, audaciousness, audacity, boldness, brashness, brazenness, cheek, cheekiness, chutzpah, discourtesy, disrespect, effrontery, face, familiarity, forwardness, gall[1], impertinence, impudence, impudency, incivility, nerve, nerviness, overconfidence, pertness, presumptuousness, pushiness, rudeness, sassiness, sauciness. *Informal:* brass, crust, sauce, uppishness, uppityness. *See* ATTITUDE, COURTESY.

insolent *adjective*
1. Overly convinced of one's own superiority and importance : arrogant, haughty, high-and-mighty, lofty, lordly, overbearing, overweening, prideful, proud, supercilious, superior. *Idiom:* on one's high horse. *See* ATTITUDE. 2. Rude and disrespectful : assuming, assumptive, audacious, bold, boldfaced, brash, brazen, cheeky, contumelious, familiar, forward, impertinent, impudent, malapert, nervy, overconfident, pert, presuming, presumptuous, pushy, sassy, saucy, smart. *Informal:* brassy, flip, fresh, smart-alecky, snippety, snippy, uppish, uppity.

Slang: wise[1]. *See* ATTITUDE, COURTESY.

insolvency *noun*

The condition of being financially insolvent : bankruptcy, bust, failure. *See* MONEY.

inspect *verb*

1. To study closely or systematically : analyze, examine, investigate. *See* INVESTIGATE. **2.** To look at carefully or critically : check (out), con, examine, go over, peruse, scrutinize, study, survey, traverse, view. *Informal:* case. *Idiom:* give a going-over. *See* INVESTIGATE. **3.** To examine the person or personal effects of in order to find something lost or concealed : frisk, search. *Slang:* shake down. *See* INVESTIGATE.

inspection *noun*

1. The act of examining carefully : check, checkup, examination, perusal, scrutiny, study, view. *Informal:* going-over. *See* INVESTIGATE. **2.** A close or systematic study : analysis, examination, investigation, review, survey. *See* INVESTIGATE.

inspiration *noun*

1. High spirits : animation, elatedness, elation, euphoria, exaltation, exhilaration, lift, uplift. *See* HAPPY. **2.** Liveliness and vivacity of imagination : brilliance, brilliancy, fire, genius. *See* GOOD. **3.** Something that encourages : encouragement, motivation, stimulation. *See* HELP. **4.** A sudden exciting thought : brainstorm. *Informal:* brain wave. *See* THOUGHTS. **5.** Divine guidance and motivation imparted directly : afflatus. *See* RELIGION. **6.** The act of breathing in : inhalation. *See* BREATH.

inspire *verb*

1. To arouse the emotions of; make ardent : animate, enkindle, fire, impassion, kindle, stir[1]. *See* EXCITE. **2.** To raise the spirits of : animate, buoy (up), elate, elevate, exhilarate, flush, inspirit, lift, uplift. *Obsolete:* exalt. *See* HAPPY. **3.** To impart courage, inspiration, and resolution to : animate, cheer (on), embolden, encourage, inspirit, motivate. *See* HELP. **4.** To stir to action or feeling : egg on, excite, foment, galvanize, goad, impel, incite, inflame, instigate, motivate, move, pique, prick, prod, prompt, propel, provoke, set off, spur, stimulate, touch off, trigger, work up. *See* CAUSE, EXCITE. **5.** To draw air into the lungs in the process of respiration : breathe (in), inhale. *See* BREATH.

inspirit *verb*

1. To impart courage, inspiration, and resolution to : animate, cheer (on), embolden, encourage, inspire, motivate. *See* HELP. **2.** To raise the spirits of : animate, buoy (up), elate, elevate, exhilarate, flush, inspire, lift, uplift. *Obsolete:* exalt. *See* HAPPY.

inspissate *verb*

To make thick or thicker, especially through evaporation or condensation : condense, thicken. *See* SOLID.

instability *noun*

1. The quality or condition of being physically unsteady : precariousness, ricketiness, shakiness, unstableness, unsteadiness, wobbliness. *See* FLEXIBLE. **2.** The quality or condition of being erratic and undependable : insecureness, insecurity, precariousness, shakiness, unstableness, unsteadiness, unsureness. *See* CHANGE, STRONG.

instal *verb* See **install.**

install also **instal** *verb*

1. To put in or assign to a certain position or location : emplace, locate, place, position, set[1], site, situate, spot. *See* PLACE. **2.** To admit formally into membership or office, as with ritual : inaugurate, induct, initiate, instate, invest. *See* ACCEPT. **3.** To place securely in a position or condition : ensconce, establish, fix, seat, settle. *See* PUT IN.

installation *noun*

1. The act or process of formally admitting a person to membership or office : inaugural, inauguration, induction, initiation, instatement, investiture. *See* ACCEPT. **2.** *Military.* A center of organization, supply, or activity : base[1], complex, headquarters, station. *See* PLACE.

instance *noun*

1. One that is representative of a group or class : case, example, illustration, representative, sample, specimen. *See* SUBSTITUTE. **2.** A legal proceeding to demand justice or enforce a right : action, case, cause, lawsuit, suit. *See* LAW. **3.** *Archaic.* Urgent solicitation : insistence, insistency, pressing. *See* CONTINUE, SEEK.

instance *verb* **1.** To refer to by name : cite, mention, name, specify. *See* SPECIFIC. **2.** To demonstrate and clarify with examples : exemplify, illustrate. *See* SHOW.

instant *noun*

1. A very brief time : crack, flash, minute[1], moment, second[1], trice, twinkle, twinkling, wink. *Informal:* jiff, jiffy. *Chiefly British:* tick. *See* BIG, TIME. **2.** A particular interval of time that is limited and often crucial : juncture, moment, point. *See* TIME.

instant *adjective* **1.** Occurring at once : immediate, instantaneous. *See* TIME. **2.** Compelling immediate attention : burning, crying, dire, emergent, exigent, imperative, pressing, urgent. *See* BIG.

instant *adverb* Without delay : directly, forthwith, immediately, instantly, now, right away, right off, straightaway, straight off. ***Idioms:*** at once, first off. *See* TIME.

instantaneous *adjective*
Occurring at once : immediate, instant. *See* TIME.

instantly *adverb*
Without delay : directly, forthwith, immediately, instant, now, right away, right off, straightaway, straight off. ***Idioms:*** at once, first off. *See* TIME.

instate *verb*
To admit formally into membership or office, as with ritual : inaugurate, induct, initiate, install, invest. *See* ACCEPT.

instatement *noun*
The act or process of formally admitting a person to membership or office : inaugural, inauguration, induction, initiation, installation, investiture. *See* ACCEPT.

instigate *verb*
To stir to action or feeling : egg on, excite, foment, galvanize, goad, impel, incite, inflame, inspire, motivate, move, pique, prick, prod, prompt, propel, provoke, set off, spur, stimulate, touch off, trigger, work up. *See* CAUSE, EXCITE.

instigation *noun*
Something that incites especially a violent response : goad, incitation, incitement, provocation, stimulus, trigger. *See* CAUSE.

instigator *noun*
One who agitates, especially politically : agitator, fomenter, inciter. *See* CALM, CHANGE, POLITICS.

instil *verb* See **instill.**

instill also **instil** *verb*
To fix (an idea, for example) in someone's mind by reemphasis and repetition : drill, drive, implant, impress, inculcate, pound. *See* TEACH.

instinct *noun*
1. An innate capability : aptitude, aptness, bent, faculty, flair, genius, gift, head, knack, talent, turn. *See* ABILITY, APPROACH. **2.** The power to discern the true nature of a person or situation : insight, intuition, intuitiveness, penetration, sixth sense. *See* THOUGHTS.

instinctive *adjective*
1. Derived from or prompted by a natural tendency or impulse : instinctual, intuitive, visceral. *See* THOUGHTS. **2.** Acting or happening without apparent forethought, prompting, or planning : automatic, impulsive, involuntary, reflex, spontaneous, unpremeditated. *See* PLANNED.

instinctual *adjective*
Derived from or prompted by a natural tendency or impulse : instinctive, intuitive, visceral. *See* THOUGHTS.

institute *verb*
1. To bring into existence formally : constitute, create, establish, found, organize, originate, set up, start. *See* START. **2.** To go about the initial step in doing (something) : approach, begin, commence, embark, enter, get off, inaugurate, initiate, launch, lead off, open, set about, set out, set to, start, take on, take up, undertake. *Informal:* kick off. ***Idioms:*** get cracking, get going, get the show on the road. *See* START.

institute *noun* A principle governing affairs within or among political units : canon, decree, edict, law, ordinance, precept, prescription, regulation, rule. *See* LAW.

institution *noun*
The act of founding or establishing : constitution, creation, establishment, foundation, organization, origination, start-up. *See* START.

institutionalize *verb*
To place officially in confinement : commit, consign. *Informal:* send up. *See* FREE.

instruct *verb*
1. To impart knowledge and skill to : coach, discipline, educate, school, teach, train, tutor. *See* TEACH. **2.** To give orders to : bid, charge, command, direct, enjoin, order, tell. *See* OVER, WORDS.

instructed *adjective*
Provided with information; made aware : acquainted, advised, educated, enlightened, informed, knowledgeable. *See* KNOWLEDGE.

instruction *noun*
1. The act, process, or art of imparting knowledge and skill : education, pedagogics, pedagogy, schooling, teaching, training, tuition, tutelage, tutoring. *See* TEACH. **2.** Known facts, ideas, and skill that have been imparted : education, erudition, knowledge, learning, scholarship, science. *See* KNOWLEDGE. **3.** An authoritative indication to be obeyed. Often used in plural : behest, bidding, charge, command, commandment, dictate, direction, directive, injunction, mandate, order, word. *See* OVER, WORDS.

instructional *adjective*
Serving to educate or inform : edifying, educational, educative, enlightening, illuminative, informative, instructive. *See* TEACH.

instructive *adjective*
Serving to educate or inform : edifying, educational, educative, enlightening, illuminative, informative, instructional. *See* TEACH.

instructor *noun*
One who educates : educator, pedagogue, teacher, trainer, tutor. *See* TEACH.

instrument *noun*
1. That by which something is accomplished or some end achieved : agency, agent, instrumentality, instrumentation, intermediary, mean[3] (used in plural), mechanism, medium, organ. *See* MEANS. **2.** A person used or controlled by others : cat's-paw, dupe, pawn[2], puppet, stooge, tool. *See* OVER. **3.** A device used to do work or perform a task : implement, tool, utensil. *See* MACHINE, MEANS.

instrumentality *noun*
That by which something is accomplished or some end achieved : agency, agent, instrument, instrumentation, intermediary, mean[3] (used in plural), mechanism, medium, organ. *See* MEANS.

instrumentation *noun*
That by which something is accomplished or some end achieved : agency, agent, instrument, instrumentality, intermediary, mean[3] (used in plural), mechanism, medium, organ. *See* MEANS.

insubordinate *adjective*
Refusing or failing to obey : disobedient, noncompliant. *See* RESIST.

insubordination *noun*
The condition or practice of not obeying : disobedience, noncompliance. *See* RESIST.

insubstantial *adjective*
1. Having no body, form, or substance : bodiless, discarnate, disembodied, immaterial, incorporeal, metaphysical, nonphysical, spiritual, unbodied, uncorporal, unsubstantial. *See* BODY. **2.** Having little substance or significance; not solidly based : feeble, flimsy, tenuous, unsubstantial. *See* STRONG. **3.** Not physically strong : decrepit, delicate, feeble, flimsy, fragile, frail, infirm, puny, unsound, unsubstantial, weak, weakly. *See* STRONG.

insubstantiality *noun*
The condition of being infirm or physically weak : debility, decrepitude, delicacy, delicateness, feebleness, flimsiness, fragileness, fragility, frailness, frailty, infirmity, puniness, unsoundness, unsubstantiality, weakliness, weakness. *See* STRONG.

insufferable *adjective*
So unpleasant or painful as not to be endured or tolerated : impossible, insupportable, intolerable, unbearable, unendurable, unsufferable, unsupportable. *See* PAIN.

insufficiency *noun*
The condition or fact of being deficient : defect, deficiency, deficit, inadequacy, lack, paucity, poverty, scantiness, scantness, scarceness, scarcity, shortage, shortcoming, shortfall, underage[1]. *See* EXCESS.

insufficient *adjective*
Not enough to meet a demand or requirement : deficient, inadequate, scarce, short, shy[1], under, wanting. *See* BIG, EXCESS.

insular *adjective*
1. Far from centers of human population : back, isolated, lonely, lonesome, obscure, outlying, out-of-the-way, remote, removed, secluded, solitary. *Idiom:* off the beaten path (*or* track). *See* NEAR. **2.** Having the restricted outlook often characteristic of geographic isolation : limited, local, narrow, narrow-minded, parochial, provincial, small-town. *See* LIMITED.

insulate *verb*
To set apart from a group : close off, cut off, isolate, seclude, segregate, separate, sequester. *See* INCLUDE.

insulation *noun*
The act or process of isolating : isolation, segregation, separation, sequestration. *See* INCLUDE.

insult *verb*
To cause resentment or hurt by callous, rude behavior : affront, huff, miff, offend, outrage, pique. *Idioms:* add insult to injury, give offense to. *See* ATTACK, PAIN.
insult *noun* **1.** An act that offends a person's sense of pride or dignity : affront, contumely, despite, indignity, offense, outrage, slight. *Idiom:* slap in the face. *See* ATTACK. **2.** An instance of mockery or derision : gibe, jeer, scoff, taunt, twit. *See* LAUGHTER, RESPECT.

insuperable *adjective*
Incapable of being negotiated or overcome : impassable, insurmountable. *See* DO.

insupportable *adjective*
So unpleasant or painful as not to be endured or tolerated : impossible, insufferable, intolerable, unbearable, unendurable, unsufferable, unsupportable. *See* PAIN.

insure *verb*
To render certain : assure, ensure, guarantee, secure, warrant. *Informal:* cinch. *See* CERTAIN.

insurgence *noun*
Organized opposition intended to change or overthrow existing authority : insurgency,

insurrection, mutiny, rebellion, revolt, revolution, sedition, uprising. *See* RESIST.

insurgency *noun*
Organized opposition intended to change or overthrow existing authority : insurgence, insurrection, mutiny, rebellion, revolt, revolution, sedition, uprising. *See* RESIST.

insurgent *adjective*
Participating in open revolt against a government or ruling authority : mutinous, rebellious, revolutionary. *See* RESIST.
insurgent *noun* A person who rebels : insurrectionary, insurrectionist, mutineer, rebel, revolutionary, revolutionist. *See* RESIST.

insurmountable *adjective*
Incapable of being negotiated or overcome : impassable, insuperable. *See* DO.

insurrection *noun*
Organized opposition intended to change or overthrow existing authority : insurgence, insurgency, mutiny, rebellion, revolt, revolution, sedition, uprising. *See* RESIST.

insurrectionary *noun*
A person who rebels : insurgent, insurrectionist, mutineer, rebel, revolutionary, revolutionist. *See* RESIST.

insurrectionist *noun*
A person who rebels : insurgent, insurrectionary, mutineer, rebel, revolutionary, revolutionist. *See* RESIST.

insusceptibility *noun*
The capacity to withstand : immunity, imperviousness, resistance, unsusceptibility. *See* RESIST.

insusceptible *adjective*
1. Not capable of being affected or impressed : impassible, impassive, insensitive, unimpressionable, unsusceptible. *See* AFFECT. **2.** Having the capacity to withstand : immune, impervious, proof, resistant, resistive, unsusceptible. *See* RESIST.

intact *adjective*
1. Lacking nothing essential or normal : complete, entire, full, integral, perfect, whole. *See* PART. **2.** In excellent condition : entire, flawless, good, perfect, sound[2], unblemished, unbroken, undamaged, unharmed, unhurt, unimpaired, uninjured, unmarred, whole. *See* THRIVE.

intangible *adjective*
Incapable of being apprehended by the mind or the senses : impalpable, imperceptible, imponderable, inappreciable, indiscernible, indistinguishable, insensible, invisible, unnoticeable, unobservable. *See* KNOWLEDGE.

integral *adjective*
1. Constituting or forming part of the essence of something : basic, constitutional, constitutive, essential, fundamental, vital. *See* BE, SURFACE. **2.** Lacking nothing essential or normal : complete, entire, full, intact, perfect, whole. *See* PART.
integral *noun* An organized array of individual elements and parts forming and working as a unit : entity, sum, system, totality, whole. *See* PART.

integrant *noun*
One of the individual entities contributing to a whole : building block, component, constituent, element, factor, ingredient, part. *See* PART.

integrate *verb*
1. To make into a whole by joining a system of parts : articulate, concatenate. *See* INCLUDE, PART. **2.** To combine and adapt in order to attain a particular effect : arrange, blend, coordinate, harmonize, orchestrate, synthesize, unify. *See* BEAUTIFUL. **3.** To bring into accord : accommodate, attune, conform, coordinate, harmonize, proportion, reconcile, tune. *See* AGREE. **4.** To construct or include as an integral or permanent part : build in, incorporate. *See* INCLUDE. **5.** To make a part of a united whole : combine, embody, incorporate. *See* INCLUDE. **6.** To open to all people regardless of race : desegregate. *See* INCLUDE, SAME.

integration *noun*
The act, process, or result of abolishing racial segregation : desegregation. *See* INCLUDE, SAME.

integrity *noun*
1. Moral or ethical strength : character, fiber, honesty, principle. *See* STRONG. **2.** The quality of being honest : honesty, honor, honorableness, incorruptibility, upstandingness. *See* HONEST. **3.** The condition of being free from defects or flaws : durability, firmness, solidity, soundness, stability, strength, wholeness. *See* BETTER. **4.** The state of being entirely whole : completeness, entirety, oneness, totality, wholeness. *See* PART.

integument *noun*
The tissue forming the external covering of the body : epidermis, skin. *See* SURFACE.

intellect *noun*
1. The faculty of thinking, reasoning, and acquiring and applying knowledge : brain (often used in plural), brainpower, intelligence, mentality, mind, sense, understanding, wit. *Slang:* smart (used in plural). *See* ABILITY,

THOUGHTS. **2.** A person of great mental ability : brain, intellectual, mind, thinker. *See* ABILITY.

intellective *adjective*
Relating to or performed by the mind : cerebral, intellectual, mental, psychic, psychical, psychological. *See* THOUGHTS.

intellectual *adjective*
1. Relating to or performed by the mind : cerebral, intellective, mental, psychic, psychical, psychological. *See* THOUGHTS. **2.** Appealing to or engaging the intellect : cerebral, sophisticated, thoughtful. *Informal:* highbrow. *See* THOUGHTS. **3.** Having or showing intelligence, often of a high order : brilliant, intelligent, knowing, knowledgeable. *Informal:* brainy. *See* ABILITY.
intellectual *noun* A person of great mental ability : brain, intellect, mind, thinker. *See* ABILITY.

intelligence *noun*
1. The faculty of thinking, reasoning, and acquiring and applying knowledge : brain (often used in plural), brainpower, intellect, mentality, mind, sense, understanding, wit. *Slang:* smart (used in plural). *See* ABILITY, THOUGHTS. **2.** That which is known about a specific subject or situation : data, fact (used in plural), information, knowledge, lore. *See* KNOWLEDGE. **3.** New information, especially about recent events and happenings : advice (often used in plural), news, tiding (often used in plural), word. *Informal:* scoop. *See* KNOWLEDGE, WORDS.

intelligent *adjective*
1. Having or showing intelligence, often of a high order : brilliant, intellectual, knowing, knowledgeable. *Informal:* brainy. *See* ABILITY. **2.** Mentally quick and original : alert, bright, clever, keen[1], quick, quick-witted, sharp, sharp-witted, smart. ***Idiom:*** smart as a whip. *See* ABILITY. **3.** Consistent with reason and intellect : consequent, logical, rational, reasonable. *See* REASON.

intelligible *adjective*
Capable of being readily understood : comprehensible, fathomable, knowable, understandable. *See* KNOWLEDGE.

intemperance *noun*
Immoderate indulgence, as in food or drink : excess, overindulgence, surfeit. *See* EXCESS.

intend *verb*
1. To have in mind as a goal or purpose : aim, contemplate, design, mean[1], plan, project, propose, purpose, target. *Regional:* mind. *See* PLANNED, PURPOSE. **2.** To have or convey a particular idea : connote, denote, import, mean[1], signify, spell[1]. ***Idiom:*** add up to. *See* MEANING.

intended *adjective*
1. Done or said on purpose : deliberate, intentional, purposeful, voluntary, willful, witting. *See* PURPOSE. **2.** Pledged to marry : affianced, betrothed, engaged, plighted. *See* MARRIAGE.
intended *noun Informal.* A person to whom one is engaged to be married : betrothed, fiancé, fiancée. *See* MARRIAGE.

intense *adjective*
1. Extreme in degree, strength, or effect : desperate, fierce, furious, terrible, vehement, violent. *See* BIG, STRONG. **2.** Intensely sustained, especially in activity : concentrated, fierce, heavy, heightened, intensive. *See* STRONG. **3.** Resulting from or affecting one's innermost feelings : deep, profound, strong. *See* STRONG, SURFACE.

intensify *verb*
To make greater in intensity or severity : aggravate, deepen, enhance, heighten, redouble. *See* INCREASE.

intensity *noun*
Exceptionally great concentration, power, or force, especially in activity : depth (often used in plural), ferociousness, ferocity, fierceness, fury, pitch, severity, vehemence, vehemency, violence. *See* BIG, STRONG.

intensive *adjective*
1. Intensely sustained, especially in activity : concentrated, fierce, heavy, heightened, intense. *See* STRONG. **2.** Covering all aspects with painstaking accuracy : all-out, complete, exhaustive, full-dress, thorough, thoroughgoing, thoroughpaced. *See* BIG, CAREFUL. **3.** Not diffused or dispersed : concentrated, exclusive, undivided, unswerving, whole. *See* COLLECT, EDGE, PART.

intensively *adverb*
In a complete manner : completely, exhaustively, thoroughly. ***Idioms:*** in and out, inside out, up and down. *See* LIMITED, PART.

intent *noun*
1. What one intends to do or achieve : aim, ambition, design, end, goal, intention, mark, meaning, object, objective, point, purpose, target, view, why. ***Idioms:*** end in view, why and wherefore. *See* PLANNED, PURPOSE. **2.** The thread or current of thought uniting or occurring in all the elements of a text or discourse : aim, burden[2], drift, meaning, purport, substance, tendency, tenor, thrust. *See*

MEANING. **3.** That which is signified by a word or expression : acceptation, connotation, denotation, import, meaning, message, purport, sense, significance, significancy, signification, value. *See* MEANING.

intent *adjective* **1.** Concentrating the mental powers on something : attentive, heedful, regardful. ***Idiom:*** all ears (*or* eyes). *See* EXCITE. **2.** Having one's thoughts fully occupied : absorbed, deep, preoccupied, rapt. ***Idiom:*** wrapped up in. *See* AWARENESS, EXCITE. **3.** On an unwavering course of action : bent, decided, determined, fixed, resolute, set[1]. *See* DECIDE.

intention *noun*
What one intends to do or achieve : aim, ambition, design, end, goal, intent, mark, meaning, object, objective, point, purpose, target, view, why. ***Idioms:*** end in view, why and wherefore. *See* PLANNED, PURPOSE.

intentional *adjective*
1. Done or said on purpose : deliberate, intended, purposeful, voluntary, willful, witting. *See* PURPOSE. **2.** Planned, weighed, or estimated in advance : calculated, considered, deliberate, premeditated. *See* PURPOSE.

inter *verb*
To place (a corpse) in or as if in a grave : bury, entomb, inhume, lay[1]. ***Idiom:*** lay (*or* put) to rest. *See* SHOW.

interceder *noun*
Someone who acts as an intermediate agent in a transaction or helps to resolve differences : broker, go-between, intercessor, intermediary, intermediate, intermediator, mediator, middleman. *See* MEANS.

intercept *verb*
To block the progress of and force to change direction : cut off, head off. *See* ALLOW.

intercessor *noun*
Someone who acts as an intermediate agent in a transaction or helps to resolve differences : broker, go-between, interceder, intermediary, intermediate, intermediator, mediator, middleman. *See* MEANS.

interchange *verb*
1. To give up in return for something else : change, commute, exchange, shift, substitute, switch, trade. *Informal:* swap. *See* CHANGE, SUBSTITUTE. **2.** To give and receive : bandy, exchange. *See* GIVE. **3.** To do, use, or occur in successive turns : alternate, rotate. *See* CHANGE.

interchange *noun* **1.** The act of exchanging or substituting : change, commutation, exchange, shift, substitution, switch, trade, transposition. *Informal:* swap. *See* CHANGE, SUBSTITUTE. **2.** Occurrence in successive turns : alternation, rotation. *See* CHANGE.

intercommunication *noun*
1. The exchange of ideas by writing, speech, or signals : communication, communion, intercourse. *Obsolete:* converse[1]. *See* KNOWLEDGE. **2.** A situation allowing exchange of ideas or messages : communication, contact, touch. *See* CONNECT, TOUCH.

interconnection *noun*
A logical or natural association between two or more things : connection, correlation, interdependence, interrelationship, link, linkage, relation, relationship, tie-in. *Informal:* hookup. *See* CONNECT.

intercourse *noun*
The exchange of ideas by writing, speech, or signals : communication, communion, intercommunication. *Obsolete:* converse[1]. *See* KNOWLEDGE.

interdependence *noun*
A logical or natural association between two or more things : connection, correlation, interconnection, interrelationship, link, linkage, relation, relationship, tie-in. *Informal:* hookup. *See* CONNECT.

interdict *verb*
To refuse to allow : ban, debar, disallow, enjoin, forbid, inhibit, outlaw, prohibit, proscribe, taboo. *See* ALLOW.

interdict *noun* A coercive measure intended to ensure compliance or conformity : interdiction, penalty, sanction. *See* REWARD.

interdiction *noun*
1. A refusal to allow : ban, disallowance, forbiddance, inhibition, prohibition, proscription, taboo. *See* ALLOW. **2.** A coercive measure intended to ensure compliance or conformity : interdict, penalty, sanction. *See* REWARD.

interest *noun*
1. Mental acquisitiveness : curiosity, curiousness, inquisitiveness. ***Idiom:*** thirst for knowledge. *See* INVESTIGATE. **2.** Curiosity about or attention to someone or something : concern, concernment, interestedness, regard. *See* CONCERN. **3.** Something that contributes to or increases one's well-being. Often used in plural : advantage, benefit, good, profit. *See* HELP. **4.** A right or legal share in something : claim, portion, stake, title. *See* PART.

interest *verb* To arouse the interest and attention of : attract, intrigue. *Slang:* turn on. *See* EXCITE.

interested *adjective*
Having concern : affected, concerned, involved. *See* CONCERN.

interestedness *noun*
Curiosity about or attention to someone or something : concern, concernment, interest, regard. *See* CONCERN.

interfere *verb*
To intervene officiously or indiscreetly in the affairs of others : butt in, horn in, interlope, meddle. *See* PARTICIPATE.

interference *noun*
The act or an instance of interfering or intruding : intervention, intrusion, meddling, obtrusion. *See* PARTICIPATE.

interfering *adjective*
Given to intruding in other people's affairs : intrusive, meddlesome, meddling, obtrusive, officious. *See* PARTICIPATE.

interim *noun*
An interval during which continuity is suspended : break, gap, hiatus, lacuna, void. *See* CONTINUE.

interim *adjective* **1.** Intended, used, or present for a limited time : impermanent, provisional, short-range, short-term, temporary. *See* CONTINUE. **2.** Temporarily assuming the duties of another : acting, ad interim, pro tem, provisional, temporary. *See* CONTINUE, SUBSTITUTE.

interior *adjective*
1. Located inside or farther in : inlying, inner, inside, internal. *See* EDGE. **2.** Of, relating to, or arising from one's mental or spiritual being : inner, internal, intimate[1], inward, visceral. *Slang:* gut. *See* BODY.

interject *verb*
To put or set into, between, or among another or other things : inject, insert, interlard, interpolate, interpose, introduce. *See* PUT IN.

interlard *verb*
To put or set into, between, or among another or other things : inject, insert, interject, interpolate, interpose, introduce. *See* PUT IN.

interlope *verb*
To intervene officiously or indiscreetly in the affairs of others : butt in, horn in, interfere, meddle. *See* PARTICIPATE.

interloper *noun*
A person given to intruding in other people's affairs : busybody, meddler, quidnunc. *Informal:* kibitzer. *Slang:* buttinsky. *Archaic:* pragmatic. *See* PARTICIPATE.

intermediary *noun*
1. Someone who acts as an intermediate agent in a transaction or helps to resolve differences : broker, go-between, interceder, intercessor, intermediate, intermediator, mediator, middleman. *See* MEANS. **2.** That by which something is accomplished or some end achieved : agency, agent, instrument, instrumentality, instrumentation, mean[3] (used in plural), mechanism, medium, organ. *See* MEANS.

intermediate *adjective*
Not extreme : central, mean[3], medial, median, mid, middle, middle-of-the-road, midway. *See* EDGE.

intermediate *noun* Someone who acts as an intermediate agent in a transaction or helps to resolve differences : broker, go-between, interceder, intercessor, intermediary, intermediator, mediator, middleman. *See* MEANS.

intermediator *noun*
Someone who acts as an intermediate agent in a transaction or helps to resolve differences : broker, go-between, interceder, intercessor, intermediary, intermediate, mediator, middleman. *See* MEANS.

interment *noun*
An act of placing a body in a grave or tomb : burial, entombment, inhumation. *See* SHOW.

interminable *adjective*
Existing or occurring without interruption or end : around-the-clock, ceaseless, constant, continual, continuous, endless, eternal, everlasting, incessant, nonstop, ongoing, perpetual, persistent, relentless, round-the-clock, timeless, unceasing, unending, unfailing, uninterrupted, unremitting. *See* CONTINUE.

intermingle *verb*
To put together into one mass so that the constituent parts are more or less homogeneous : admix, amalgamate, blend, commingle, commix, fuse, intermix, merge, mingle, mix, stir[1]. *See* ASSEMBLE.

intermission *noun*
1. The condition of being temporarily inactive : abeyance, abeyancy, dormancy, latency, quiescence, suspension. *See* ACTION. **2.** A pause or interval, as from work or duty : break, recess, respite, rest[1], time-out. *Informal:* breather. *See* CONTINUE.

intermittent *adjective*
Happening or appearing now and then : fitful, occasional, periodic, periodical, sporadic. *Informal:* on-again, off-again. *See* CONTINUE.

intermittently *adverb*
Once in a while; at times : betimes, occasionally, periodically, sometimes, sporadically.

Idioms: ever and again (*or* anon), now and again (*or* then). *See* CONTINUE.

intermix *verb*
To put together into one mass so that the constituent parts are more or less homogeneous : admix, amalgamate, blend, commingle, commix, fuse, intermingle, merge, mingle, mix, stir[1]. *See* ASSEMBLE.

intern *verb*
To put in jail : confine, detain, immure, imprison, incarcerate, jail, lock (up). *See* FREE.

internal *adjective*
1. Located inside or farther in : inlying, inner, inside, interior. *See* EDGE. **2.** Of, relating to, or arising from one's mental or spiritual being : inner, interior, intimate[1], inward, visceral. *Slang:* gut. *See* BODY. **3.** Of, from, or within a country's own territory : domestic, home, national, native. *See* NATIVE.

interpolate *verb*
To put or set into, between, or among another or other things : inject, insert, interject, interlard, interpose, introduce. *See* PUT IN.

interpose *verb*
To put or set into, between, or among another or other things : inject, insert, interject, interlard, interpolate, introduce. *See* PUT IN.

interpret *verb*
1. To make understandable : construe, decipher, explain, explicate, expound, spell out. *Archaic:* enucleate. *Idiom:* put into plain English. *See* EXPLAIN. **2.** To understand in a particular way : construe, read, take. *See* UNDERSTAND. **3.** To perform according to one's artistic conception : execute, play, render. *See* PERFORMING ARTS.

interpretable *adjective*
Capable of being explained or accounted for : accountable, decipherable, explainable, explicable, illustratable. *See* EXPLAIN.

interpretation *noun*
1. Something that serves to explain or clarify : clarification, construction, decipherment, elucidation, exegesis, explanation, explication, exposition, illumination, illustration. *Archaic:* enucleation. *See* EXPLAIN. **2.** Critical explanation or analysis : annotation, comment, commentary, exegesis, note. *See* WORDS. **3.** One's artistic conception as shown by the way in which something such as a dramatic role or musical composition is rendered : execution, performance, reading, realization, rendering, rendition. *See* PERFORMING ARTS.

interpretative *adjective*
Serving to explain : elucidative, exegetic, explanative, explanatory, explicative, expositive, expository, hermeneutic, hermeneutical, illustrative, interpretive. *See* EXPLAIN.

interpretive *adjective*
Serving to explain : elucidative, exegetic, explanative, explanatory, explicative, expositive, expository, hermeneutic, hermeneutical, illustrative, interpretative. *See* EXPLAIN.

interrelationship *noun*
A logical or natural association between two or more things : connection, correlation, interconnection, interdependence, link, linkage, relation, relationship, tie-in. *Informal:* hookup. *See* CONNECT.

interrogate *verb*
To question thoroughly and relentlessly to verify facts : cross-examine. *Informal:* grill. *Idiom:* give someone the third degree. *See* INVESTIGATE.

interrogation *noun*
A request for data : inquiry, query, question. *Law:* interrogatory. *See* ASK, INVESTIGATE.

interrogator *noun*
One who conducts an official inquiry, usually with no regard for human rights : inquisitor, questioner. *See* ASK, INVESTIGATE.

interrogatory *noun*
Law. A request for data : inquiry, interrogation, query, question. *See* ASK, INVESTIGATE.

interrupt *verb*
1. To stop suddenly, as a conversation, activity, or relationship : break off, cease, discontinue, suspend, terminate. *See* CONTINUE. **2.** To interject remarks or questions into another's discourse : break in, chime in, chip in, cut in. *See* CONTINUE.

interruption *noun*
A cessation of continuity or regularity : break, discontinuance, discontinuation, discontinuity, disruption, pause, suspension. *See* CONTINUE.

intersect *verb*
To pass through or over : crisscross, cross, crosscut, cut across, decussate. *See* MEET.

interspace *noun*
A space or interval between objects or points : gap, interstice, interval, separation. *See* OPEN.

interstice *noun*
A space or interval between objects or points : gap, interspace, interval, separation. *See* OPEN.

interval *noun*
A space or interval between objects or points : gap, interspace, interstice, separation. *See* OPEN.

intervention *noun*
The act or an instance of interfering or

intruding : interference, intrusion, meddling, obtrusion. *See* PARTICIPATE.

intimacy *noun*
The condition of being friends : chumminess, closeness, companionship, comradeship, familiarity, fellowship, friendship. *See* LOVE.

intimate[1] *adjective*
1. Very closely associated : chummy, close, familiar, friendly. *Informal:* thick. *Slang:* tight. *Idiom:* hand in glove with. *See* LOVE.
2. Characterized by a close and thorough acquaintance : inside, personal. *See* NEAR.
3. Of, relating to, or arising from one's mental or spiritual being : inner, interior, internal, inward, visceral. *Slang:* gut. *See* BODY. **4.** Indicating intimacy and mutual trust : confidential, familiar. *See* ATTITUDE, NEAR.
intimate *noun* A person whom one knows well, likes, and trusts : amigo, brother, chum, confidant, confidante, familiar, friend, mate. *Informal:* bud[2], buddy, pal. *Slang:* sidekick. *See* LOVE.

intimate[2] *verb*
To convey an idea by indirect, subtle means : hint, imply, insinuate, suggest. *Idiom:* drop a hint. *See* SHOW, SUGGEST.

intimation *noun*
1. A subtle pointing out : clue, cue, hint, suggestion. *See* KNOWLEDGE, SUGGEST. **2.** A slight amount or indication : breath, dash, ghost, hair, hint, semblance, shade, shadow, soupçon, streak, suggestion, suspicion, taste, tinge, touch, trace, whiff, whisper. *Informal:* whisker. *See* BIG, SHOW.

intimidate *verb*
To domineer or drive into compliance by the use of as threats or force, for example : bludgeon, browbeat, bulldoze, bully, bullyrag, cow, hector, menace, threaten. *Informal:* strong-arm. *See* OVER.

intimidation *noun*
An expression of the intent to hurt or punish another : menace, threat. *See* WARN.

intimidator *noun*
One who is habitually cruel to smaller or weaker people : browbeater, bulldozer, bully, hector. *Archaic:* brave. *See* OVER.

intolerable *adjective*
So unpleasant or painful as not to be endured or tolerated : impossible, insufferable, insupportable, unbearable, unendurable, unsufferable, unsupportable. *See* PAIN.

intolerance *noun*
Irrational suspicion or hatred of a particular group, race, or religion : bigotry, prejudice. *See* LIKE.

intolerant *adjective*
1. Not tolerant of the beliefs or opinions of others, for example : bigoted, close-minded, hidebound, illiberal, narrow-minded. *See* ACCEPT.
2. Being unable or unwilling to endure irritation or opposition, for example : fretful, impatient, unforbearing. *See* ACCEPT, ATTITUDE, CALM.

intonation *noun*
A particular vocal quality that indicates some emotion or feeling : accent, inflection, tone. *Idiom:* tone of voice. *See* SOUNDS.

intoxicated *adjective*
Stupefied, excited, or muddled with alcoholic liquor : besotted, crapulent, crapulous, drunk, drunken, inebriate, inebriated, sodden, tipsy. *Informal:* cock-eyed, stewed. *Slang:* blind, bombed, boozed, boozy, crocked, high, lit (up), loaded, looped, pickled, pixilated, plastered, potted, sloshed, smashed, soused, stinking, stinko, stoned, tight, zonked. *Idioms:* drunk as a skunk, half-seas over, high as a kite, in one's cups, three sheets in (*or* to) the wind. *See* DRUGS.

intoxicating *adjective*
Producing or stimulating physical, mental, or emotional vigor : bracing, energizing, exhilarant, exhilarating, innerving, invigorating, refreshing, reinvigorating, renewing, restorative, roborant, stimulating, tonic. *See* HELP.

intoxication *noun*
The condition of being intoxicated with alcoholic liquor : crapulence, drunkenness, inebriation, inebriety, insobriety, tipsiness. *See* DRUGS.

intoxicative *adjective*
Containing alcohol : alcoholic, hard, spirituous, strong. *See* INGESTION.

intractability *noun*
The quality or condition of being unruly : disorderliness, fractiousness, indocility, intractableness, obstinacy, obstinateness, obstreperousness, recalcitrance, recalcitrancy, refractoriness, uncontrollability, uncontrollableness, ungovernableness, unmanageability, unruliness, untowardness, wildness. *See* CONTROL, ORDER, PEACE, RESIST.

intractable *adjective*
Not submitting to discipline or control : disorderly, fractious, indocile, lawless, obstinate, obstreperous, recalcitrant, refractory, uncontrollable, undisciplined, ungovernable, unmanageable, unruly, untoward, wild. *Idiom:* out of line. *See* CONTROL, ORDER, PEACE, RESIST.

intractableness *noun*
The quality or condition of being unruly : disorderliness, fractiousness, indocility, intractability, obstinacy, obstinateness, obstreperousness, recalcitrance, recalcitrancy, refractoriness, uncontrollability, uncontrollableness, ungovernableness, unmanageability, unruliness, untowardness, wildness. *See* CONTROL, ORDER, PEACE, RESIST.

intransigence *noun*
The quality or state of being stubbornly inflexible : die-hardism, grimness, implacability, implacableness, incompliance, incompliancy, inexorability, inexorableness, inflexibility, inflexibleness, intransigency, obduracy, obdurateness, relentlessness, remorselessness, rigidity, rigidness, stubbornness. *See* RESIST.

intransigency *noun*
The quality or state of being stubbornly inflexible : die-hardism, grimness, implacability, implacableness, incompliance, incompliancy, inexorability, inexorableness, inflexibility, inflexibleness, intransigence, obduracy, obdurateness, relentlessness, remorselessness, rigidity, rigidness, stubbornness. *See* RESIST.

intransigent *adjective*
Firmly, often unreasonably immovable in purpose or will : adamant, adamantine, brassbound, die-hard, grim, implacable, incompliant, inexorable, inflexible, iron, obdurate, relentless, remorseless, rigid, stubborn, unbendable, unbending, uncompliant, uncompromising, unrelenting, unyielding. ***Idiom:*** stubborn as a mule (*or* ox). *See* RESIST.

intrepid *adjective*
Having or showing courage : audacious, bold, brave, courageous, dauntless, doughty, fearless, fortitudinous, gallant, game, gutty, hardy, heroic, mettlesome, plucky, stout, stouthearted, unafraid, undaunted, valiant, valorous. *Informal:* spunky. *Slang:* gutsy. *See* FEAR.

intrepidity *noun*
The quality of mind enabling one to face danger or hardship resolutely : braveness, bravery, courage, courageousness, dauntlessness, doughtiness, fearlessness, fortitude, gallantry, gameness, heart, intrepidness, mettle, nerve, pluck, pluckiness, spirit, stoutheartedness, undauntedness, valiance, valiancy, valiantness, valor. *Informal:* spunk, spunkiness. *Slang:* gut (used in plural), gutsiness, moxie. *See* FEAR.

intrepidness *noun*
The quality of mind enabling one to face danger or hardship resolutely : braveness, bravery, courage, courageousness, dauntlessness, doughtiness, fearlessness, fortitude, gallantry, gameness, heart, intrepidity, mettle, nerve, pluck, pluckiness, spirit, stoutheartedness, undauntedness, valiance, valiancy, valiantness, valor. *Informal:* spunk, spunkiness. *Slang:* gut (used in plural), gutsiness, moxie. *See* FEAR.

intricacy *noun*
Something complex : complexity, complication. *See* SIMPLE.

intricate *adjective*
1. Complexly detailed : complicated, elaborate, fancy. *See* PLAIN. **2.** Difficult to understand because of intricacy : byzantine, complex, complicated, convoluted, daedal, Daedalian, elaborate, involute, involved, knotty, labyrinthine, tangled. *See* SIMPLE.

intrigue *noun*
A secret plan to achieve an evil or illegal end : cabal, collusion, connivance, conspiracy, machination, plot, scheme. *See* CRIMES, PLANNED.
intrigue *verb* **1.** To work out a secret plan to achieve an evil or illegal end : collude, connive, conspire, machinate, plot, scheme. *See* CRIMES, PLANNED. **2.** To arouse the interest and attention of : attract, interest. *Slang:* turn on. *See* EXCITE.

intrinsic *adjective*
Forming an essential element, as arising from the basic structure of an individual : built-in, congenital, connatural, constitutional, elemental, inborn, inbred, indigenous, indwelling, ingrained, inherent, innate, native, natural. *See* BE, NATIVE, START.

introduce *verb*
1. To make known socially : acquaint, present[2]. *See* KNOWLEDGE. **2.** To make known the presence or arrival of : announce, herald, proclaim, usher in. *See* KNOWLEDGE, START. **3.** To put forward (a topic) for discussion : bring up, broach, moot, put forth, raise. *See* START. **4.** To bring into currency, use, fashion, or practice : launch, originate. *See* START. **5.** To put or set into, between, or among another or other things : inject, insert, interject, interlard, interpolate, interpose. *See* PUT IN. **6.** To begin (something) with preliminary or prefatory material : lead, precede, preface, usher in. *See* START, WORDS.

introduction *noun*
1. The state of being allowed entry : admission, admittance, entrance[1], ingress, ingression, intromission. *See* ACCEPT. **2.** A short section of preliminary remarks : foreword, induction, lead-in, overture, preamble, preface, prelude, prolegomenon, prologue. *See* START, WORDS.

introductory *adjective*
1. Of, relating to, or occurring at the start of something : beginning, inceptive, incipient, initial, initiatory, leadoff. *See* START. **2.** Before or in preparation for the main matter, action, or business : inductive, prefatory, preliminary, preparatory, prolegomenous. *See* START.
3. Serving to introduce a subject or person, for example : prefatory, preliminary, preparatory, prolegomenous. *See* START, WORDS.

intromission *noun*
The state of being allowed entry : admission, admittance, entrance[1], ingress, ingression, introduction. *See* ACCEPT.

intromit *verb*
To serve as a means of entrance for : admit, let in. *See* ENTER.

intrude *verb*
To force or come in as an improper or unwanted element : cut in, horn in, obtrude. *See* ENTER.

intrusion *noun*
1. The act or an instance of interfering or intruding : interference, intervention, meddling, obtrusion. *See* PARTICIPATE. **2.** An advance beyond proper or legal limits : encroachment, entrenchment, impingement, infringement, obtrusion, trespass. *See* ENTER.
3. An excessive, unwelcome burden : imposition, infliction. *See* LIKE, WILLING.

intrusive *adjective*
1. Troubling to the mind or emotions : disquieting, disruptive, distressful, distressing, disturbing, perturbing, troublesome, troublous, unsettling, upsetting, worrisome. *See* HAPPY, PAIN. **2.** Given to intruding in other people's affairs : interfering, meddlesome, meddling, obtrusive, officious. *See* PARTICIPATE.

intrust *verb* See **entrust.**

intuit *verb*
To be intuitively aware of : apprehend, feel, perceive, sense. ***Idioms:*** feel in one's bones, get vibrations. *See* KNOWLEDGE.

intuition *noun*
1. Intuitive cognition : feeling, hunch, idea, impression, suspicion. *See* THOUGHTS. **2.** The power to discern the true nature of a person or situation : insight, instinct, intuitiveness, penetration, sixth sense. *See* THOUGHTS.

intuitive *adjective*
Derived from or prompted by a natural tendency or impulse : instinctive, instinctual, visceral. *See* THOUGHTS.

intuitiveness *noun*
The power to discern the true nature of a person or situation : insight, instinct, intuition, penetration, sixth sense. *See* THOUGHTS.

inundate *verb*
1. To flow over completely : deluge, drown, engulf, flood, flush, overflow, overwhelm, submerge, whelm. *See* FULL. **2.** To affect as if by an outpouring of water : deluge, flood, overwhelm, swamp, whelm. *See* FULL.

inundation *noun*
An abundant, usually overwhelming flow or fall, as of a river or rain : alluvion, cataclysm, cataract, deluge, downpour, flood, freshet, Niagara, overflow, torrent. *Chiefly British:* spate. *See* BIG.

inure *verb*
To make familiar through constant practice or use : accustom, condition, habituate, wont. *See* USUAL.

inutile *adjective*
1. Having no useful purpose : ineffectual, unusable, useless, worthless. *See* USED.
2. Lacking all worth and value : drossy, good-for-nothing, no-good, nothing, valueless, worthless. *Informal:* no-account. *See* VALUE.

invade *verb*
To enter so as to attack, plunder, destroy, or conquer : foray, overrun, raid. *See* ATTACK, ENTER.

invalid *adjective*
Containing fundamental errors in reasoning : fallacious, false, illogical, sophistic, specious, spurious, unsound. *See* CORRECT, TRUE.

invalidate *verb*
To put an end to, especially formally and with authority : abolish, abrogate, annihilate, annul, cancel, negate, nullify, set aside, vitiate, void. *Law:* extinguish. *See* CONTINUE.

invalidation *noun*
An often formal act of putting an end to : abolishment, abolition, abrogation, annihilation, annulment, cancellation, defeasance, negation, nullification, voidance. *Law:* avoidance, extinguishment. *See* CONTINUE.

invaluable *adjective*
Of great value : costly, inestimable, precious, priceless, valuable, worthy. ***Idioms:*** beyond price, of great price. *See* VALUE.

invariable *adjective*
1. Having no change or variation : changeless, constant, equable, even[1], invariant, regular, same, steady, unchanging, uniform, unvarying. *See* SAME. **2.** Remaining continually unchanged : changeless, consistent, constant, same, unchanging, unfailing. *See* CHANGE.
3. Incapable of changing or being modified :

immutable, inalterable, inflexible, ironclad, rigid, unalterable, unchangeable. *See* FLEXIBLE.

invariant *adjective*
Having no change or variation : changeless, constant, equable, even[1], invariable, regular, same, steady, unchanging, uniform, unvarying. *See* SAME.

invasion *noun*
An act of invading, especially by military forces : foray, incursion, inroad, raid. *See* ATTACK, ENTER.

invective *noun*
Harsh, often insulting language : abuse, billingsgate, contumely, obloquy, railing, revilement, reviling, scurrility, scurrilousness, vituperation. *See* PRAISE.
invective *adjective* Of, relating to, or characterized by verbal abuse : abusive, contumelious, opprobrious, scurrilous, vituperative. *See* ATTACK, ATTITUDE.

inveigh *verb*
To express opposition, often by argument : challenge, demur, except, expostulate, object, protest, remonstrate. *Informal:* kick, squawk. ***Idioms:*** set up a squawk, take exception. *See* SUPPORT.

inveigle *verb*
To beguile or draw into a wrong or foolish course of action : allure, entice, lure, seduce, tempt. ***Idiom:*** lead astray. *See* PERSUASION.

inveiglement *noun*
Something that attracts, especially with the promise of pleasure or reward : allurement, bait, come-on, enticement, inducement, invitation, lure, seduction, temptation. *See* LIKE.

inveigler *noun*
One that seduces : allurer, charmer, enticer, lurer, seducer, tempter. *See* PERSUASION.

inveigling *adjective*
Tending to seduce : alluring, bewitching, come-hither, enticing, inviting, luring, seductive, siren, tempting, witching. *See* LIKE, PERSUASION, SEX.

invent *verb*
To use ingenuity in making, developing, or achieving : concoct, contrive, devise, dream up, fabricate, formulate, hatch, make up, think up. *Informal:* cook up. ***Idiom:*** come up with. *See* MAKE.

invented *adjective*
Consisting or suggestive of fiction : fanciful, fantastic, fantastical, fictional, fictitious, fictive, made-up. *See* REAL.

invention *noun*
1. The power or ability to invent : creativeness, creativity, ingeniousness, ingenuity, inventiveness, originality. *See* ABILITY, MAKE. **2.** Something invented : brainchild, contrivance, device. *See* MACHINE, MAKE. **3.** Any fictitious idea accepted as part of an ideology by an uncritical group; a received idea : creation, fantasy, fiction, figment, myth. *See* BELIEF, REAL.

inventive *adjective*
1. Characterized by or productive of new things or new ideas : creative, ingenious, innovative, innovatory, original. *See* ABILITY. **2.** Not the same as what was previously known or done : different, fresh, innovative, new, newfangled, novel, original, unfamiliar, unprecedented. *See* NEW. **3.** Able to use the means at one's disposal to meet situations effectively : ingenious, resourceful. *See* ABILITY.

inventiveness *noun*
The power or ability to invent : creativeness, creativity, ingeniousness, ingenuity, invention, originality. *See* ABILITY, MAKE.

inventor *noun*
One that creates, founds, or originates : architect, author, creator, entrepreneur, father, founder[2], maker, originator, parent, patriarch. *See* START.

inventory *noun*
A supply stored or hidden for future use : backlog, cache, hoard, nest egg, reserve, reservoir, stock, stockpile, store, treasure. *Slang:* stash. *See* COLLECT.

inveracity *noun*
1. The practice of lying : falsehood, mendacity, perjury, truthlessness, untruthfulness. *See* TRUE. **2.** An untrue declaration : canard, cock-and-bull story, falsehood, falsity, fib, fiction, lie[2], misrepresentation, misstatement, prevarication, story, tale, untruth. *Informal:* fish story, tall tale. *Slang:* whopper. *See* TRUE.

inversion *noun*
The act of changing or being changed from one position, direction, or course to the opposite : reversal, transposition, turnabout, turnaround. *See* CHANGE.

invert *verb*
To change to the opposite position, direction, or course : reverse, transpose, turn (about, around, over, *or* round). *See* CHANGE.

inverted *adjective*
Turned over completely : capsized, overturned, upset, upside-down, upturned. *See* HORIZONTAL.

invest *verb*
1. To admit formally into membership or office, as with ritual : inaugurate, induct, initiate, install, instate. *See* ACCEPT. **2.** To present with a quality, trait, or power : dower, endow, endue, gift, gird. *See* GIVE. **3.** To put clothes on : apparel, attire, clothe, dress, garb, garment. *Informal:* tog. *See* PUT ON. **4.** To cover completely and closely, as with clothing or bandages : enfold, envelop, enwrap, infold, roll, swaddle, swathe, wrap, wrap up. *See* PUT ON. **5.** To surround and cover completely so as to obscure : cloak, clothe, enfold, enshroud, envelop, enwrap, infold, shroud, veil, wrap. *See* SHOW. **6.** To surround with hostile troops : beleaguer, beset, besiege, blockade, siege. *Idiom:* lay siege to. *See* ATTACK.

investigate *verb*
1. To study closely or systematically : analyze, examine, inspect. *See* INVESTIGATE. **2.** To go into or through for the purpose of making discoveries or acquiring information : delve, dig, explore, inquire, look into, probe, reconnoiter, scout[1]. *See* INVESTIGATE.

investigation *noun*
1. The act or an instance of exploring or investigating : exploration, probe, reconnaissance. *See* INVESTIGATE. **2.** A seeking of knowledge, data, or the truth about something : inquest, inquiry, inquisition, probe, research. *See* INVESTIGATE. **3.** A close or systematic study : analysis, examination, inspection, review, survey. *See* INVESTIGATE.

investigative *adjective*
Eager to acquire knowledge : curious, inquiring, inquisitive, questioning. *See* INVESTIGATE.

investigator *noun*
1. One who inquires : inquirer, inquisitor, prober, querier, quester, questioner, researcher. *See* ASK, INVESTIGATE. **2.** A person whose work is investigating crimes or obtaining hidden evidence or information : detective, sleuth. *Informal:* eye. *Slang:* dick, gumshoe. *See* INVESTIGATE.

investiture *noun*
The act or process of formally admitting a person to membership or office : inaugural, inauguration, induction, initiation, installation, instatement. *See* ACCEPT.

investment *noun*
A prolonged surrounding of an objective by hostile troops : beleaguerment, besiegement, blockade, siege. *See* ATTACK.

inveterate *adjective*
1. Firmly established by long standing : confirmed, deep-rooted, deep-seated, entrenched, hard-shell, ineradicable, ingrained, irradicable, set[1], settled. *See* CONTINUE. **2.** Subject to a disease or habit for a long time : chronic, confirmed, habitual, habituated. *See* CONTINUE.

invidious *adjective*
1. Damaging to the reputation : calumnious, defamatory, detractive, injurious, scandalous, slanderous. *Law:* libelous. *See* ATTACK, CRIMES, LAW. **2.** Resentfully or painfully desirous of another's advantages : covetous, envious, green-eyed, jealous. *See* DESIRE.

invigorate *verb*
To give or impart vitality and energy to (someone or something) : energize, exhilarate, stimulate, vitalize. *See* HELP.

invigorating *adjective*
Producing or stimulating physical, mental, or emotional vigor : bracing, energizing, exhilarant, exhilarating, innerving, intoxicating, refreshing, reinvigorating, renewing, restorative, roborant, stimulating, tonic. *See* HELP.

invincible *adjective*
Incapable of being conquered, overrun, or subjugated : impregnable, indomitable, unconquerable. *See* DO, WIN.

inviolability *noun*
The quality or condition of being safe from assault, trespass, or violation : sacredness, sacrosanctity, sanctity. *See* SAFETY.

inviolable *adjective*
Protected from violation or abuse by custom, law, or feelings of reverence : sacred, sacrosanct. *See* SACRED.

invisible *adjective*
Incapable of being apprehended by the mind or the senses : impalpable, imperceptible, imponderable, inappreciable, indiscernible, indistinguishable, insensible, intangible, unnoticeable, unobservable. *See* KNOWLEDGE.

invitation *noun*
1. A spoken or written request for someone to take part or be present : bid. *Informal:* invite. *See* WARN. **2.** Something that attracts, especially with the promise of pleasure or reward : allurement, bait, come-on, enticement, inducement, inveiglement, lure, seduction, temptation. *See* LIKE.

invite *verb*
1. To request that someone take part in or be present at a particular occasion : ask, bid. *See* WARN. **2.** To behave so as to bring on (danger,

for example) : court, provoke, tempt. *See* SEEK.

invite *noun Informal.* A spoken or written request for someone to take part or be present : bid, invitation. *See* WARN.

inviting *adjective*
Tending to seduce : alluring, bewitching, come-hither, enticing, inveigling, luring, seductive, siren, tempting, witching. *See* LIKE, PERSUASION, SEX.

invocation *noun*
The act of praying : prayer[1], supplication. *See* RELIGION.

invoice *noun*
A precise list of fees or charges : account, bill[1], check, reckoning, statement. *Informal:* tab. *See* PAY.

invoice *verb* To present a statement of fees or charges to : bill[1]. *See* MONEY, REQUEST.

invoke *verb*
To compel observance of : carry out, effect, enforce, execute, implement. ***Idioms:*** put in force, put into action. *See* OBLIGATION, OVER.

involuntarily *adverb*
Without regard to desire or inclination : helplessly, perforce, willy-nilly. *See* WILLING.

involuntary *adjective*
Acting or happening without apparent forethought, prompting, or planning : automatic, impulsive, instinctive, reflex, spontaneous, unpremeditated. *See* PLANNED.

involute *adjective*
Difficult to understand because of intricacy : byzantine, complex, complicated, convoluted, daedal, Daedalian, elaborate, intricate, involved, knotty, labyrinthine, tangled. *See* SIMPLE.

involve *verb*
1. To have as a part : comprehend, comprise, contain, embody, embrace, encompass, have, include, subsume, take in. *See* INCLUDE. **2.** To have as an accompaniment, a condition, or a consequence : carry, entail. *See* START. **3.** To have as a need or prerequisite : ask, call for, demand, entail, necessitate, require, take. *See* NECESSARY, OVER. **4.** To draw in so that extrication is difficult : catch up, embrangle, embroil, implicate, mix up, suck. *See* FREE, PARTICIPATE. **5.** To get and hold the attention of : engage, occupy. *See* EXCITE. **6.** To make complex, intricate, or perplexing : complicate, embarrass, entangle, perplex, ravel, snarl[2], tangle. *See* SIMPLE.

involved *adjective*
1. Difficult to understand because of intricacy : byzantine, complex, complicated, convoluted, daedal, Daedalian, elaborate, intricate, involute, knotty, labyrinthine, tangled. *See* SIMPLE. **2.** Having concern : affected, concerned, interested. *See* CONCERN.

involvement *noun*
1. The act or fact of participating : participation, sharing. *See* PARTICIPATE. **2.** The condition of being entangled or implicated : embranglement, embroilment, enmeshment, ensnarement, entanglement. *See* FREE, PARTICIPATE.

inward *adjective*
Of, relating to, or arising from one's mental or spiritual being : inner, interior, internal, intimate[1], visceral. *Slang:* gut. *See* BODY.

iota *noun*
1. A tiny amount : bit[1], crumb, dab[1], dash, dot, dram, drop, fragment, grain, jot, minim, mite, modicum, molecule, ort, ounce, particle, scrap[1], scruple, shred, smidgen, speck, tittle, trifle, whit. *Chiefly British:* spot. *See* BIG. **2.** The least bit : hoot, jot, ounce, shred, whit. *Informal:* damn, rap[2]. *Slang:* diddly. *See* BIG.

irascibility *noun*
A tendency to become angry or irritable : irascibleness, spleen, temper, temperament, tetchiness. *Informal:* dander. *Slang:* short fuse. ***Idiom:*** low boiling point. *See* FEELINGS.

irascible *adjective*
1. Having or showing a bad temper : bad-tempered, cantankerous, crabbed, cranky, cross, disagreeable, fretful, grouchy, grumpy, ill-tempered, irritable, nasty, peevish, petulant, querulous, snappish, snappy, surly, testy, ugly, waspish. *Informal:* crabby, mean[2]. ***Idiom:*** out of sorts. *See* ATTITUDE. **2.** Easily annoyed : choleric, peppery, quick-tempered, testy, tetchy, touchy. *See* FEELINGS.

irascibleness *noun*
A tendency to become angry or irritable : irascibility, spleen, temper, temperament, tetchiness. *Informal:* dander. *Slang:* short fuse. ***Idiom:*** low boiling point. *See* FEELINGS.

irate *adjective*
Full of or marked by extreme anger : furious, ireful, rabid, wrathful. ***Idioms:*** fit to be tied, foaming at the mouth, in a rage (*or* temper), in a towering rage. *See* FEELINGS.

irateness *noun*
1. Violent or unrestrained anger : furor, fury, ire, rage, wrath, wrathfulness. *See* FEELINGS.

2. A strong feeling of displeasure or hostility : anger, choler, indignation, ire. *See* FEELINGS.

ire *noun*

1. Violent or unrestrained anger : furor, fury, irateness, rage, wrath, wrathfulness. *See* FEELINGS. 2. A strong feeling of displeasure or hostility : anger, choler, indignation, irateness. *See* FEELINGS.

ireful *adjective*

Full of or marked by extreme anger : furious, irate, rabid, wrathful. ***Idioms:*** fit to be tied, foaming at the mouth, in a rage (*or* temper), in a towering rage. *See* FEELINGS.

irenic *adjective*

Inclined or disposed to peace; not quarrelsome or unruly : pacific, pacifical, pacifist, pacifistic, peaceable, peaceful. *See* PEACE.

irk *verb*

To trouble the nerves or peace of mind of, especially by repeated vexations : aggravate, annoy, bother, bug, chafe, disturb, exasperate, fret, gall[2], get, irritate, nettle, peeve, provoke, put out, rile, ruffle, vex. ***Idioms:*** get in one's hair, get on one's nerves, get under one's skin. *See* FEELINGS, PAIN.

irksome *adjective*

1. Troubling the nerves or peace of mind, as by repeated vexations : annoying, bothersome, galling, irritating, nettlesome, plaguy, provoking, troublesome, vexatious. *See* PAIN.
2. Arousing no interest or curiosity : boring, drear, dreary, dry, dull, humdrum, monotonous, stuffy, tedious, tiresome, uninteresting, weariful, wearisome, weary. *See* EXCITE.

iron *noun*

Something that physically confines the legs or arms. Used in plural : bond, chain (used in plural), fetter, handcuff (often used in plural), hobble, manacle, restraint, shackle. *Archaic:* gyve. *See* FREE.

iron *adjective* 1. Full of vigor : able-bodied, lusty, red-blooded, robust, strapping, sturdy, vigorous, vital. *See* STRONG. 2. Firmly, often unreasonably immovable in purpose or will : adamant, adamantine, brassbound, die-hard, grim, implacable, incompliant, inexorable, inflexible, intransigent, obdurate, relentless, remorseless, rigid, stubborn, unbendable, unbending, uncompliant, uncompromising, unrelenting, unyielding. ***Idiom:*** stubborn as a mule (*or* ox). *See* RESIST.

iron *verb* To smooth by applying heat and pressure : mangle[2], press. *See* SMOOTH.

ironbound *adjective*

Having a surface that is not smooth : coarse, cragged, craggy, harsh, jagged, ragged, rough, rugged, scabrous, uneven. *See* SMOOTH.

ironclad *adjective*

Incapable of changing or being modified : immutable, inalterable, inflexible, invariable, rigid, unalterable, unchangeable. *See* FLEXIBLE.

ironic *adjective*

Marked by or displaying contemptuous mockery of others : cynic, cynical, ironical, sardonic, wry. *See* ATTITUDE, RESPECT.

ironical *adjective*

Marked by or displaying contemptuous mockery of others : cynic, cynical, ironic, sardonic, wry. *See* ATTITUDE, RESPECT.

irradiant *adjective*

Giving off or reflecting light readily or in large amounts : beamy, bright, brilliant, effulgent, incandescent, lambent, lucent, luminous, lustrous, radiant, refulgent, shiny. *See* LIGHT.

irradiate *verb*

To send out heat, light, or energy : cast, emit, project, radiate, shed, throw. *See* MOVE.

irradicable *adjective*

Firmly established by long standing : confirmed, deep-rooted, deep-seated, entrenched, hard-shell, ineradicable, ingrained, inveterate, set[1], settled. *See* CONTINUE.

irrational *adjective*

Not governed by or predicated on reason : illogical, unreasonable, unreasoned. ***Idiom:*** out of bounds. *See* REASON.

irrationality *noun*

The absence of reason : illogicality, illogicalness, unreason, unreasonableness. *See* REASON.

irrefutable *adjective*

Established beyond a doubt : certain, hard, inarguable, incontestable, incontrovertible, indisputable, indubitable, positive, sure, unassailable, undeniable, undisputable, unquestionable. *See* CERTAIN, TRUE.

irregular *adjective*

1. Not straight, uniform, or symmetrical : asymmetric, asymmetrical. *See* SMOOTH, STRAIGHT. 2. Departing from the normal : aberrant, abnormal, anomalistic, anomalous, atypic, atypical, deviant, divergent, preternatural, unnatural. *See* GOOD, USUAL.

irregularity *noun*

1. Lack of smoothness or regularity : asymmetry, crookedness, inequality, jaggedness, roughness, unevenness. *See* SMOOTH, STRAIGHT.
2. The condition of being abnormal : aberrance, aberrancy, aberration, abnormality,

anomaly, deviance, deviancy, deviation, preternaturalness, unnaturalness. *See* GOOD, USUAL.

irrelevancy *noun*
An instance of digressing : aside, deviation, digression, divagation, divergence, divergency, excursion, excursus, parenthesis, tangent. *See* APPROACH.

irrelevant *adjective*
Not relevant or pertinent to the subject; not applicable : extraneous, immaterial, impertinent, inapplicable. ***Idioms:*** beside the point, neither here nor there. *See* RELEVANT.

irremediable *adjective*
Offering no hope or expectation of improvement : cureless, hopeless, incurable, irreparable. *See* HOPE.

irreparable *adjective*
Offering no hope or expectation of improvement : cureless, hopeless, incurable, irremediable. *See* HOPE.

irreprehensible *adjective*
Beyond reproach : blameless, exemplary, good, irreproachable, lily-white, unblamable. *See* RIGHT.

irreproachable *adjective*
1. Beyond reproach : blameless, exemplary, good, irreprehensible, lily-white, unblamable. *See* RIGHT. **2.** Free from guilt or blame : blameless, faultless, guiltless, harmless, innocent, lily-white, unblamable. *Slang:* clean. ***Idiom:*** in the clear. *See* RIGHT.

irresolute *adjective*
Given to or exhibiting hesitation : halting, hesitant, indecisive, pendulous, shilly-shally, tentative, timid, vacillant, vacillatory. *See* DECIDE.

irresoluteness *noun*
The act of hesitating or state of being hesitant : hesitancy, hesitation, indecision, indecisiveness, irresolution, pause, shilly-shally, tentativeness, timidity, timidness, to-and-fro, vacillation. *See* DECIDE.

irresolution *noun*
The act of hesitating or state of being hesitant : hesitancy, hesitation, indecision, indecisiveness, irresoluteness, pause, shilly-shally, tentativeness, timidity, timidness, to-and-fro, vacillation. *See* DECIDE.

irresponsible *adjective*
Lacking or marked by a lack of care : careless, feckless, heedless, inattentive, reckless, thoughtless, unconcerned, unmindful, unthinking. *See* CAREFUL.

irreverence *noun*
Lack of proper respect : disrespect, lese majesty. *See* RESPECT.

irreverent *adjective*
Having or showing a lack of respect : disrespectful. *See* RESPECT.

irreversible *adjective*
That cannot be revoked or undone : irrevocable, unalterable. ***Idiom:*** beyond recall. *See* CHANGE.

irrevocable *adjective*
That cannot be revoked or undone : irreversible, unalterable. ***Idiom:*** beyond recall. *See* CHANGE.

irritable *adjective*
Having or showing a bad temper : bad-tempered, cantankerous, crabbed, cranky, cross, disagreeable, fretful, grouchy, grumpy, ill-tempered, irascible, nasty, peevish, petulant, querulous, snappish, snappy, surly, testy, ugly, waspish. *Informal:* crabby, mean². ***Idiom:*** out of sorts. *See* ATTITUDE.

irritant *noun*
Something that annoys : aggravation, annoyance, besetment, bother, irritation, nuisance, peeve, plague, torment, vexation. *See* FEELINGS, PAIN.

irritate *verb*
1. To trouble the nerves or peace of mind of, especially by repeated vexations : aggravate, annoy, bother, bug, chafe, disturb, exasperate, fret, gall², get, irk, nettle, peeve, provoke, put out, rile, ruffle, vex. ***Idioms:*** get in one's hair, get on one's nerves, get under one's skin. *See* FEELINGS, PAIN. **2.** To make (the skin) raw by or as if by friction : abrade, chafe, excoriate, fret, gall². *See* HELP. **3.** To cause to become sore or inflamed : burn, inflame, sting. *See* HELP.

irritating *adjective*
Troubling the nerves or peace of mind, as by repeated vexations : annoying, bothersome, galling, irksome, nettlesome, plaguy, provoking, troublesome, vexatious. *See* PAIN.

irritation *noun*
1. The act of annoying : annoyance, botheration, bothering, exasperation, harassment, pestering, provocation, vexation. *See* FEELINGS, PAIN. **2.** The feeling of being annoyed : aggravation, annoyance, bother, botheration, exasperation, vexation. *See* FEELINGS, PAIN. **3.** Something that annoys : aggravation, annoyance, besetment, bother, irritant, nuisance, peeve, plague, torment, vexation. *See*

FEELINGS, PAIN. **4.** An instance of being irritated, as in a part of the body : inflammation, soreness. *See* HELP.

isochronal *adjective*
Happening or appearing at regular intervals : cyclic, cyclical, isochronous, periodic, periodical, recurrent. ***Idiom:*** like clockwork. *See* REPETITION.

isochronous *adjective*
Happening or appearing at regular intervals : cyclic, cyclical, isochronal, periodic, periodical, recurrent. ***Idiom:*** like clockwork. *See* REPETITION.

isolate *verb*
To set apart from a group : close off, cut off, insulate, seclude, segregate, separate, sequester. *See* INCLUDE.
isolate *adjective* Set away from all others : alone, apart, detached, isolated, lone, removed, solitary. *See* INCLUDE.

isolated *adjective*
1. Set away from all others : alone, apart, detached, isolate, lone, removed, solitary. *See* INCLUDE. **2.** Far from centers of human population : back, insular, lonely, lonesome, obscure, outlying, out-of-the-way, remote, removed, secluded, solitary. ***Idiom:*** off the beaten path (*or* track). *See* NEAR.

isolation *noun*
1. The act or process of isolating : insulation, segregation, separation, sequestration. *See* INCLUDE. **2.** The quality or state of being alone : aloneness, loneliness, singleness, solitariness, solitude. *See* INCLUDE.

issue *noun*
1. The act or process of publishing printed matter : printing, publication, publishing. *See* WORDS. **2.** Something brought about by a cause : aftermath, consequence, corollary, effect, end product, event, fruit, harvest, outcome, precipitate, ramification, result, resultant, sequel, sequence, sequent, upshot. *See* CAUSE. **3.** A group consisting of those descended directly from the same parents or ancestors : brood, get, offspring, posterity, progeny, seed. *See* KIN. **4.** A situation that presents difficulty, uncertainty, or perplexity : hornets' nest, problem, question. *Informal:* can of worms. *See* EASY.
issue *verb* **1.** To pass or pour out : discharge, empty, flow. *See* ENTER. **2.** To discharge material, as vapor or fumes, usually suddenly and violently : emit, give, give forth, give off, give out, let off, let out, release, send forth, throw off, vent. *See* FREE, MOVE. **3.** To come into view : appear, emerge, loom, materialize, show. ***Idioms:*** make (*or* put in) an appearance, meet the eye. *See* SEE. **4.** To have hereditary derivation : derive, descend, spring. ***Idiom:*** trace one's descent. *See* KIN. **5.** To present for circulation, exhibit, or sale : bring out, publish, put out. *See* WORDS. **6.** To have as a source : arise, come, derive, emanate, flow, originate, proceed, rise, spring, stem, upspring. *See* START.

italicize *verb*
To accord emphasis to : accent, accentuate, emphasize, feature, highlight, play up, point up, stress, underline, underscore. *See* IMPORTANT.

itch *noun*
1. A strong wanting of what promises enjoyment or pleasure : appetence, appetency, appetite, craving, desire, hunger, longing, lust, thirst, wish, yearning, yen. *See* DESIRE. **2.** Sexual hunger : amativeness, concupiscence, desire, eroticism, erotism, libidinousness, lust, lustfulness, passion, prurience, pruriency. *See* DESIRE, SEX.
itch *verb* To have a greedy, obsessive desire : crave, hunger, lust, thirst. *See* DESIRE.

item *noun*
1. An individually considered portion of a whole : article, detail, element, particular, point. *See* PART. **2.** A small, often specialized element of a whole : detail, fine print, particular, technicality. *See* GROUP. **3.** Something having material existence : article, object, thing. *See* THING. **4.** A usually brief detail of news or information : bit[1], paragraph, piece, squib, story. *See* WORDS.
item *adverb* In addition : additionally, also, besides, further, furthermore, likewise, more, moreover, still, too, yet. ***Idioms:*** as well, to boot. *See* INCREASE.

itemize *verb*
To name or specify one by one : enumerate, list[1], numerate, tick off. *See* COUNT, SPECIFIC.

iterate *verb*
To state again : reiterate, repeat, restate. *See* REPETITION.

iteration *noun*
The act or process of repeating : reiteration, repetition, restatement. *See* REPETITION.

iterative *adjective*
Characterized by repetition : reiterative, repetitious, repetitive. *See* REPETITION.

itinerant *adjective*
1. Leading the life of a person without a fixed domicile; moving from place to place : nomadic, peripatetic, vagabond, vagrant. *See* MOVE. **2.** Moving from one area to another in search of work : migrant, migratory. *See* MOVE.

ivory *adjective*
Of a light color or complexion : alabaster, fair, light[1], pale. *See* COLORS.

ivory-tower *adjective*
Incapable of dealing efficiently with practical matters : impractical. *See* THRIVE.

• J •

jab *verb*
To thrust against or into : dig, jog, nudge, poke, prod. *See* TOUCH.
jab *noun* An act of thrusting into or against, as to attract attention : dig, jog, nudge, poke. *See* TOUCH.

jabber *verb*
1. To talk rapidly, incoherently, or indistinctly : babble, blather, chatter, gabble, gibber, prate, prattle. *See* WORDS. **2.** To talk volubly, persistently, and usually inconsequentially : babble, blabber, chatter, chitchat, clack, palaver, prate, prattle, rattle (on), run on. *Informal:* go on, spiel. *Slang:* gab, gas, jaw, yak. ***Idioms:*** run off at the mouth, shoot the breeze (*or* bull). *See* WORDS.
jabber *noun* **1.** Unintelligible or foolish talk : babble, blather, blatherskite, double talk, gabble, gibberish, jabberwocky, jargon, nonsense, prate, prattle, twaddle. *See* WORDS. **2.** Incessant and usually inconsequential talk : babble, blab, blabber, chat, chatter, chitchat, palaver, prate, prattle, small talk. *Slang:* gab, gas, yak. *See* WORDS.

jabberwocky *noun*
1. Unintelligible or nonsensical talk or language : abracadabra, double talk, gibberish, gobbledygook, mumbo jumbo. *See* CLEAR, WORDS. **2.** Unintelligible or foolish talk : babble, blather, blatherskite, double talk, gabble, gibberish, jabber, jargon, nonsense, prate, prattle, twaddle. *See* WORDS.

jack *noun*
1. A person engaged in sailing or working on a ship. Uppercase : jack-tar, mariner, navigator, sailor, sea dog, seafarer, seaman. *Informal:* salt, tar. *Slang:* gob[3]. *See* SEA. **2.** Fabric used especially as a symbol : banderole, banner, banneret, color (used in plural), ensign, flag[1], oriflamme, pennant, pennon, standard, streamer. *See* SUBSTITUTE. **3.** *Slang.* Something, such as coins or printed bills, used as a medium of exchange : cash, currency, lucre, money. *Informal:* wampum. *Slang:* bread, cabbage, dough, gelt, green, lettuce, long green, mazuma, moola, scratch. *Chiefly British:* brass. *See* MONEY.
jack *verb* To increase in amount. Also used with *up* : boost, hike, jump, raise, up. *See* INCREASE.

jackass *noun*
One deficient in judgment and good sense : ass, fool, idiot, imbecile, mooncalf, moron, nincompoop, ninny, nitwit, simple, simpleton, softhead, tomfool. *Informal:* dope, gander, goose. *Slang:* cretin, ding-dong, dip, goof, jerk, nerd, schmo, schmuck, turkey. *See* ABILITY.

jacket *noun*
The skin of an animal : fell[3], fur, hide[2], pelt[1]. *See* SURFACE.

jack-tar *noun*
A person engaged in sailing or working on a ship : jack (uppercase), mariner, navigator, sailor, sea dog, seafarer, seaman. *Informal:* salt, tar. *Slang:* gob[3]. *See* SEA.

jade *noun*
A vulgar promiscuous woman who flouts propriety : baggage, hussy, slattern, slut, tart[2], tramp, wanton, wench, whore. *Slang:* floozy. *See* SEX.
jade *verb* To diminish the strength and energy of : drain, fatigue, tire, wear, wear down, wear out, weary. *See* TIRED.

jag *noun*
1. *Slang.* A drinking bout : binge, brannigan, carousal, carouse, drunk, spree. *Slang:* bat[2], bender, booze, tear[1]. *See* DRUGS, RESTRAINT. **2.** *Slang.* A period of uncontrolled self-indulgence : binge, fling, orgy, rampage, spree. *See* RESTRAINT.

jagged *adjective*
Having a surface that is not smooth : coarse, cragged, craggy, harsh, ironbound, ragged, rough, rugged, scabrous, uneven. *See* SMOOTH.

jaggedness *noun*
Lack of smoothness or regularity : asymmetry, crookedness, inequality, irregularity, roughness, unevenness. *See* SMOOTH, STRAIGHT.

jail *noun*
A place for the confinement of persons in lawful detention : brig, house of correction, keep, penitentiary, prison. *Informal:* lockup, pen[3]. *Slang:* big house, can, clink, cooler, coop, hoosegow, joint, jug, pokey[1], slammer, stir[2]. *Chiefly Regional:* calaboose. *See* FREE.
jail *verb* To put in jail : confine, detain, immure, imprison, incarcerate, intern, lock (up). *See* FREE.

jailer also **jailor** *noun*
A guard or keeper of a prison : turnkey, warden. *British:* warder. *See* FREE.

jailor *noun* See **jailer.**

jam *verb*
To fill to excess by compressing or squeezing tightly : cram, crowd, load, mob, pack, stuff. *Informal:* jam-pack. *See* FULL, TIGHTEN.
jam *noun* **1.** A cessation of normal activity, caused by an accident or strike, for example : gridlock, immobilization, stoppage, tie-up. *See* CONTINUE. **2.** A difficult, often embarrassing situation or condition : box[1], corner, deep water, difficulty, dilemma, Dutch, fix, hole, hot spot, hot water, plight[1], predicament, quagmire, scrape, soup, trouble. *Informal:* bind, pickle, spot. *See* EASY.

jam-pack *verb*
Informal. To fill to excess by compressing or squeezing tightly : cram, crowd, jam, load, mob, pack, stuff. *See* FULL, TIGHTEN.

jape *noun*
Words or actions intended to excite laughter or amusement : gag, jest, joke, quip, witticism. *Informal:* funny, gag. *Slang:* ha-ha. *See* LAUGHTER.

jar *verb*
To fail to be in accord : clash, conflict, contradict, disaccord, discord. ***Idiom:*** go (*or* run) counter to. *See* AGREE.
jar *noun* Violent forcible contact between two or more things : bump, collision, concussion, crash, impact, jolt, percussion, shock[1], smash. *See* CONFLICT.

jargon *noun*
1. Unintelligible or foolish talk : babble, blather, blatherskite, double talk, gabble, gibberish, jabber, jabberwocky, nonsense, prate, prattle, twaddle. *See* WORDS. **2.** A variety of a language that differs from the standard form : argot, cant[2], dialect, lingo, patois, vernacular. *See* WORDS. **3.** Specialized expressions indigenous to a particular field, subject, trade, or subculture : argot, cant[2], dialect, idiom, language, lexicon, lingo, patois, terminology, vernacular, vocabulary. *See* WORDS.

jarring *adjective*
Disagreeable to the sense of hearing : dry, grating, harsh, hoarse, rasping, raspy, raucous, rough, scratchy, squawky, strident. *See* SOUNDS.

jaundice *verb*
To cause to have a prejudiced view : bias, prejudice, prepossess, warp. *See* AFFECT, STRAIGHT.

jaunt *noun*
A usually short journey taken for pleasure : excursion, junket, outing, trip. *See* MOVE.

jaunty *adjective*
Displaying light-hearted nonchalance : airy, breezy, buoyant, debonair. *Informal:* corky. ***Idiom:*** free and easy. *See* ATTITUDE, CAREFUL, GOOD.

jaw *verb*
Slang. To talk volubly, persistently, and usually inconsequentially : babble, blabber, chatter, chitchat, clack, jabber, palaver, prate, prattle, rattle (on), run on. *Informal:* go on, spiel. *Slang:* gab, gas, yak. ***Idioms:*** run off at the mouth, shoot the breeze (*or* bull). *See* WORDS.
jaw *noun Slang.* Spoken exchange : chat, colloquy, confabulation, conversation, converse[1], dialogue, discourse, speech, talk. *Informal:* confab. *See* WORDS.

jealous *adjective*
1. Fearful of the loss of position or affection : clutching, possessive. *See* OWNED. **2.** Resentfully or painfully desirous of another's advantages : covetous, envious, green-eyed, invidious. *See* DESIRE.

jealousy *noun*
Resentful or painful desire for another's advantages : covetousness, enviousness, envy. *See* DESIRE.

jeer *verb*
To make fun or make fun of : deride, gibe, jest, laugh, mock, ridicule, scoff, scout[2], twit. *Chiefly British:* quiz. ***Idiom:*** poke fun at. *See* LAUGHTER, RESPECT.
jeer *noun* An instance of mockery or derision : gibe, insult, scoff, taunt, twit. *See* LAUGHTER, RESPECT.

jeering *adjective*
Contemptuous or ironic in manner or wit : derisive, mocking, sarcastic, satiric, satirical, scoffing, sneering. *See* LAUGHTER, RESPECT.

jejune *adjective*
Lacking the qualities requisite for spiritedness and originality : bland, innocuous, insipid, namby-pamby, vapid, washy, waterish, watery. *Informal:* wishy-washy. *See* EXCITE, GOOD.

jejuneness *noun*
1. The state or quality of being insipid : blandness, dullness, innocuousness, insipidity, insipidness, vapidity, vapidness, washiness, wateriness. *Informal:* wishy-washiness. *See* EXCITE, TASTE. **2.** A lack of excitement, liveliness, or interest : asepticism, blandness, colorlessness, drabness, dreariness, dryness, flatness, flavorlessness, insipidity, insipidness, lifelessness, sterileness, sterility, stodginess, vapidity, vapidness, weariness. *See* EXCITE.

jell *verb*
To change or be changed from a liquid into a soft, semisolid, or solid mass : clot, coagulate, congeal, curdle, gelatinize, jelly, set[1]. *See* SOLID.

jelly *verb*
To change or be changed from a liquid into a soft, semisolid, or solid mass : clot, coagulate, congeal, curdle, gelatinize, jell, set[1]. *See* SOLID.

jeopardize *verb*
To subject to danger or destruction : endanger, imperil, menace, peril, risk, threaten. *See* SAFETY.

jeopardous *adjective*
Involving possible risk, loss, or injury : adventurous, chancy, dangerous, hazardous, parlous, perilous, risky, treacherous, unsafe, venturesome, venturous. *Slang:* hairy. *See* SAFETY.

jeopardy *noun*
Exposure to possible harm, loss, or injury : danger, endangerment, hazard, imperilment, peril, risk. *See* SAFETY.

jeremiad *noun*
A long, violent, or blustering speech, usually of censure or denunciation : diatribe, fulmination, harangue, philippic, tirade. *See* PRAISE.

jerk *verb*
1. To move or cause to move with a sudden abrupt motion : lurch, snap, twitch, wrench, yank. *See* MOVE, PUSH. **2.** To proceed with sudden, abrupt movements : bump, jolt. *See* REPETITION.

jerk *noun* **1.** A sudden motion, such as a pull : lurch, snap, tug, twitch, wrench, yank. *See* MOVE, PUSH. **2.** *Slang.* One deficient in judgment and good sense : ass, fool, idiot, imbecile, jackass, mooncalf, moron, nincompoop, ninny, nitwit, simple, simpleton, softhead, tomfool. *Informal:* dope, gander, goose. *Slang:* cretin, ding-dong, dip, goof, nerd, schmo, schmuck, turkey. *See* ABILITY. **3.** *Slang.* An unpleasant, tiresome person : bore. *Slang:* drip, dweeb, nerd, pill, poop[2]. *See* LIKE.

jerky *adjective*
Slang. So senseless as to be laughable : absurd, foolish, harebrained, idiotic, imbecilic, insane, lunatic, mad, moronic, nonsensical, preposterous, silly, softheaded, tomfool, unearthly, zany. *Informal:* cockeyed, crazy, loony, loopy. *Slang:* balmy[2], dippy, dopey, sappy, wacky. *See* ABILITY, KNOWLEDGE.

jest *noun*
1. An object of amusement or laughter : butt[3], joke, laughingstock, mockery. *See* RESPECT. **2.** Words or actions intended to excite laughter or amusement : gag, jape, joke, quip, witticism. *Informal:* funny, gag. *Slang:* ha-ha. *See* LAUGHTER.

jest *verb* **1.** To make jokes; behave playfully : joke. *Informal:* clown (around), fool around, fun. *See* LAUGHTER. **2.** To make fun or make fun of : deride, gibe, jeer, laugh, mock, ridicule, scoff, scout[2], twit. *Chiefly British:* quiz. *Idiom:* poke fun at. *See* LAUGHTER, RESPECT.

jester *noun*
A person whose words or actions provoke or are intended to provoke amusement or laughter : clown, comedian, comic, farceur, funnyman, humorist, joker, jokester, quipster, wag[2], wit, zany. *Informal:* card. *See* LAUGHTER.

jet[1] *adjective*
Of the darkest achromatic visual value : black, ebon, ebony, inky, jetty, onyx, pitch-black, pitchy, sable, sooty. *See* COLORS.

jet[2] *noun*
A sudden swift stream of ejected liquid : spout, spray, spurt, squirt. *See* MOVE.

jet *verb* To eject or be ejected in a sudden thin, swift stream : spout, spray, spurt, squirt. *See* MOVE.

jettison *verb*
Informal. To let go or get rid of as being useless or defective, for example : discard, dispose of, dump, junk, scrap[1], throw away, throw out. *Informal:* chuck, shuck (off). *Slang:* ditch. *See* KEEP.

jettison *noun* The act of getting rid of something useless or used up : disposal, dumping, elimination, riddance. *See* KEEP.

jetty *adjective*
Of the darkest achromatic visual value : black, ebon, ebony, inky, jet[1], onyx, pitch-black, pitchy, sable, sooty. *See* COLORS.

jibe[1] *verb*
Informal. To be compatible or in correspondence : accord, agree, check, chime, comport with, conform, consist, correspond, fit[1], harmonize, match, square, tally. *Archaic:* quadrate. *See* AGREE.

jibe[2] *verb* See **gibe.**

jiff *noun*
Informal. A very brief time : crack, flash, instant, minute[1], moment, second[1], trice, twinkle, twinkling, wink. *Informal:* jiffy. *Chiefly British:* tick. *See* BIG, TIME.

jiffy *noun*
Informal. A very brief time : crack, flash, instant, minute[1], moment, second[1], trice, twinkle, twinkling, wink. *Informal:* jiff. *Chiefly British:* tick. *See* BIG, TIME.

jig *noun*
An indirect, usually cunning means of gaining an end : artifice, deception, device, dodge, feint, gimmick, imposture, maneuver, ploy, ruse, sleight, stratagem, subterfuge, trick, wile. *Informal:* shenanigan, take-in. *See* HONEST, MEANS.

jigger *noun*
1. A small amount of liquor : dram, drop, shot, sip, tot[1]. *Informal:* nip[2], slug[1]. *Slang:* snort. *See* BIG, INGESTION. **2.** A small specialized mechanical device : concern, contraption, contrivance, gadget, gimmick, thing. *Informal:* doodad, doohickey, widget. *Slang:* gizmo. *See* MACHINE.

jiggle *verb*
To cause to move to and fro with short, jerky movements : joggle, shake. *See* REPETITION.

jillion *noun*
An indeterminately great amount or number : million (often used in plural), multiplicity, ream, trillion. *Informal:* bushel, gob[1] (often used in plural), heap (often used in plural), load (often used in plural), lot, oodles, passel, peck[2], scad (often used in plural), slew, wad, zillion. *See* BIG.

jim-jams *noun*
Slang. A state of nervous restlessness or agitation : fidget (often used in plural), jitter (used in plural), jump (used in plural), shiver[1] (used in plural), tremble (often used in plural). *Informal:* all-overs, shake (used in plural). *Slang:* heebie-jeebies, willies. *See* CALM, FEAR.

jinx *noun*
Informal. Something or someone believed to bring bad luck : curse, hex, hoodoo. *See* LUCK.

jinx *verb* *Informal.* To bring bad luck or evil to : curse, hex, hoodoo. *See* LUCK.

jitter *noun*
A state of nervous restlessness or agitation. Used in plural : fidget (often used in plural), jump (used in plural), shiver[1] (used in plural), tremble (often used in plural). *Informal:* all-overs, shake (used in plural). *Slang:* heebie-jeebies, jim-jams, willies. *See* CALM, FEAR.

jittery *adjective*
Feeling or exhibiting nervous tension : edgy, fidgety, jumpy, nervous, restive, restless, skittish, tense, twitchy. *Slang:* uptight. ***Idioms:*** a bundle of nerves, all wound up, on edge. *See* TIGHTEN.

jive *verb*
Slang. To tease or mock good-humoredly : banter, chaff, joke, josh. *Informal:* kid, rib, ride. *Slang:* rag[2], razz. *See* LAUGHTER.

job *noun*
1. Activity pursued as a livelihood : art, business, calling, career, craft, employment, line, métier, occupation, profession, pursuit, trade, vocation, work. *Slang:* racket. *Archaic:* employ. *See* ACTION. **2.** A post of employment : appointment, berth, billet, office, place, position, situation, slot, spot. *Slang:* gig. *See* PLACE. **3.** A piece of work that has been assigned : assignment, chore, duty, office, stint, task. *See* WORK. **4.** The proper activity of a person or thing : function, purpose, role, task. *See* DO. **5.** *Informal.* A difficult or tedious undertaking : chore, effort, task. *See* HEAVY, WORK.

jobholder *noun*
One who is employed by another : employee, hireling, worker. *Informal:* hire, hired hand. *See* OVER, WORK.

jobholding *adjective*
Having a job : employed, hired, retained, working. *See* WORK.

jobless *adjective*
Out of work : unemployed, workless. *See* WORK.

jockey *verb*
1. To direct the course of carefully : guide, maneuver, navigate, pilot, steer. ***Idiom:*** back and fill. *See* CONTROL, MOVE. **2.** To take clever or cunning steps to achieve one's goals : maneuver. *Informal:* finagle. ***Idiom:*** pull strings (*or* wires). *See* CONTROL, MEANS.

jocose *adjective*
Intended to excite laughter or amusement : comedic, facetious, funny, humorous, jocular, witty. *See* LAUGHTER.

jocoseness *noun*
1. A state of joyful exuberance : blitheness, blithesomeness, gaiety, glee, gleefulness, hilarity, jocosity, jocularity, jocundity, jolliness, jollity, joviality, lightheartedness, merriment, merriness, mirth, mirthfulness. *See* LAUGHTER.
2. The quality of being laughable or comical : comedy, comicality, comicalness, drollery, drollness, farcicality, funniness, humor, humorousness, jocosity, jocularity, ludicrousness, ridiculousness, wit, wittiness, zaniness. *See* LAUGHTER.

jocosity *noun*
1. A state of joyful exuberance : blitheness, blithesomeness, gaiety, glee, gleefulness, hilarity, jocoseness, jocularity, jocundity, jolliness, jollity, joviality, lightheartedness, merriment, merriness, mirth, mirthfulness. *See* LAUGHTER.
2. The quality of being laughable or comical : comedy, comicality, comicalness, drollery, drollness, farcicality, funniness, humor, humorousness, jocoseness, jocularity, ludicrousness, ridiculousness, wit, wittiness, zaniness. *See* LAUGHTER.

jocular *adjective*
Intended to excite laughter or amusement : comedic, facetious, funny, humorous, jocose, witty. *See* LAUGHTER.

jocularity *noun*
1. The quality of being laughable or comical : comedy, comicality, comicalness, drollery, drollness, farcicality, funniness, humor, humorousness, jocoseness, jocosity, ludicrousness, ridiculousness, wit, wittiness, zaniness. *See* LAUGHTER. **2.** A state of joyful exuberance : blitheness, blithesomeness, gaiety, glee, gleefulness, hilarity, jocoseness, jocosity, jocundity, jolliness, jollity, joviality, lightheartedness, merriment, merriness, mirth, mirthfulness. *See* LAUGHTER.

jocund *adjective*
Characterized by joyful exuberance : blithe, blithesome, boon[2], convivial, gay, gleeful, jolly, jovial, merry, mirthful. *See* HAPPY.

jocundity *noun*
A state of joyful exuberance : blitheness, blithesomeness, gaiety, glee, gleefulness, hilarity, jocoseness, jocosity, jocularity, jolliness, jollity, joviality, lightheartedness, merriment, merriness, mirth, mirthfulness. *See* LAUGHTER.

jog *verb*
1. To thrust against or into : dig, jab, nudge, poke, prod. *See* TOUCH. **2.** To move with a steady easy gait faster than a walk but slower than a run : lope, trot. *See* MOVE.
jog *noun* **1.** An act of thrusting into or against, as to attract attention : dig, jab, nudge, poke. *See* TOUCH. **2.** A person's steady easy gait that is faster than a walk but slower than a run : lope, trot. *See* MOVE.

joggle *verb*
To cause to move to and fro with short, jerky movements : jiggle, shake. *See* REPETITION.

join *verb*
1. To be contiguous or next to : abut, adjoin, border, bound[2], butt[2], meet[1], neighbor, touch, verge. *See* NEAR. **2.** To bring or come together into a united whole : coalesce, combine, compound, concrete, conjoin, conjugate, connect, consolidate, couple, link, marry, meld, unify, unite, wed, yoke. *See* ASSEMBLE. **3.** To unite or be united in a relationship : affiliate, ally, associate, bind, combine, conjoin, connect, link, relate. *See* CONNECT. **4.** To become a member of : enlist, enroll, enter, muster in, sign up. *Informal:* sign on. *See* PARTICIPATE.

joint *noun*
1. A point or position at which two or more things are joined : connection, coupling, junction, juncture, seam, union. *See* CONNECT.
2. *Slang.* A disreputable or run-down bar or restaurant : *Slang:* dive, honky-tonk. *See* GOOD. **3.** *Slang.* A place for the confinement of persons in lawful detention : brig, house of correction, jail, keep, penitentiary, prison. *Informal:* lockup, pen[3]. *Slang:* big house, can, clink, cooler, coop, hoosegow, jug, pokey[1], slammer, stir[2]. *Chiefly Regional:* calaboose. *See* FREE.
joint *adjective* Belonging to, shared by, or applicable to all alike : common, communal, conjoint, general, mutual, public. *See* GROUP.

jointly *adverb*
In, into, or as a single body : together. ***Idioms:*** as one, in one breath, in the same breath, in unison, with one accord, with one voice. *See* ACCOMPANIED.

joke *noun*
1. Words or actions intended to excite laughter or amusement : gag, jape, jest, quip, witticism. *Informal:* funny, gag. *Slang:* ha-ha. *See* LAUGHTER. **2.** A mischievous act : antic, caper, frolic, lark, prank[1], trick. *Informal:* shenanigan. *Slang:* monkeyshine (often used in plural). *See* GOOD, WORK. **3.** *Informal.* Something or

someone uproariously funny or absurd : absurdity. *Informal:* hoot, laugh, scream. *Slang:* gas, howl, panic, riot. ***Idiom:*** a laugh a minute. *See* LAUGHTER. **4.** An object of amusement or laughter : butt[3], jest, laughingstock, mockery. *See* RESPECT.

joke *verb* **1.** To make jokes; behave playfully : jest. *Informal:* clown (around), fool around, fun. *See* LAUGHTER. **2.** To tease or mock good-humoredly : banter, chaff, josh. *Informal:* kid, rib, ride. *Slang:* jive, rag[2], razz. *See* LAUGHTER.

joker *noun*
A person who provokes or intends to provoke amusement or laughter : clown, comedian, comic, farceur, funnyman, humorist, jester, jokester, quipster, wag[2], wit, zany. *Informal:* card. *See* LAUGHTER.

jokester *noun*
A person whose words or actions provoke or are intended to provoke amusement or laughter : clown, comedian, comic, farceur, funnyman, humorist, jester, joker, quipster, wag[2], wit, zany. *Informal:* card. *See* LAUGHTER.

jolliness *noun*
A state of joyful exuberance : blitheness, blithesomeness, gaiety, glee, gleefulness, hilarity, jocoseness, jocosity, jocularity, jocundity, jollity, joviality, lightheartedness, merriment, merriness, mirth, mirthfulness. *See* LAUGHTER.

jollity *noun*
1. A state of joyful exuberance : blitheness, blithesomeness, gaiety, glee, gleefulness, hilarity, jocoseness, jocosity, jocularity, jocundity, jolliness, joviality, lightheartedness, merriment, merriness, mirth, mirthfulness. *See* LAUGHTER. **2.** Joyful, exuberant activity : conviviality, festival, festiveness, festivity, fun, gaiety, merriment, merrymaking, revel (often used in plural), revelry. *See* LAUGHTER.

jolly *adjective*
Characterized by joyful exuberance : blithe, blithesome, boon[2], convivial, gay, gleeful, jocund, jovial, merry, mirthful. *See* HAPPY.

jolt *verb*
1. To cause to experience a sudden momentary shock : electrify, shock[1], startle. *See* EXCITE, SURPRISE. **2.** To proceed with sudden, abrupt movements : bump, jerk. *See* REPETITION.

jolt *noun* **1.** Violent forcible contact between two or more things : bump, collision, concussion, crash, impact, jar, percussion, shock[1], smash. *See* CONFLICT. **2.** Something that jars the mind or emotions : blow[2], shock[1]. *Psychiatry:* trauma. *See* STRIKE.

josh *verb*
To tease or mock good-humoredly : banter, chaff, joke. *Informal:* kid, rib, ride. *Slang:* jive, rag[2], razz. *See* LAUGHTER.

jot *noun*
1. A tiny amount : bit[1], crumb, dab[1], dash, dot, dram, drop, fragment, grain, iota, minim, mite, modicum, molecule, ort, ounce, particle, scrap[1], scruple, shred, smidgen, speck, tittle, trifle, whit. *Chiefly British:* spot. *See* BIG. **2.** The least bit : hoot, iota, ounce, shred, whit. *Informal:* damn, rap[2]. *Slang:* diddly. *See* BIG.

journey *verb*
1. To make or go on a journey : pass, peregrinate, travel, trek, trip. ***Idiom:*** hit the road. *See* MOVE. **2.** To move along a particular course : fare, go, pass, proceed, push on, remove, travel, wend. ***Idiom:*** make one's way. *See* MOVE.

joust *noun*
Any competition or test of opposing wills likened to the sport in which knights fought with lances : tilt, tournament, tourney. *See* CONFLICT.

jovial *adjective*
Characterized by joyful exuberance : blithe, blithesome, boon[2], convivial, gay, gleeful, jocund, jolly, merry, mirthful. *See* HAPPY.

joviality *noun*
A state of joyful exuberance : blitheness, blithesomeness, gaiety, glee, gleefulness, hilarity, jocoseness, jocosity, jocularity, jocundity, jolliness, jollity, lightheartedness, merriment, merriness, mirth, mirthfulness. *See* LAUGHTER.

joy *noun*
1. A feeling of extreme gratification aroused by something good or desired : delectation, delight, enjoyment, pleasure. *See* HAPPY, LIKE. **2.** A condition of supreme well-being and good spirits : beatitude, blessedness, bliss, cheer, cheerfulness, felicity, gladness, happiness, joyfulness. *See* HAPPY.

joy *verb* **1.** To feel or take joy or pleasure : delight, exult, pleasure, rejoice. *See* HAPPY. **2.** *Archaic.* To give great or keen pleasure to : cheer, delight, enchant, gladden, gratify, overjoy, please, pleasure, tickle. *See* HAPPY, LIKE.

joyful *adjective*
1. Providing joy and pleasure : cheerful, cheery, festive, glad, happy, joyous, pleasing. *See* HAPPY. **2.** Marked by festal celebration : festive, gala, glad, gladsome, happy, joyous, merry. *See* HAPPY.

joyfulness *noun*
A condition of supreme well-being and good spirits : beatitude, blessedness, bliss, cheer, cheerfulness, felicity, gladness, happiness, joy. *See* HAPPY.

joyless *adjective*
1. Tending to cause sadness or low spirits : blue, cheerless, depressing, dismal, dispiriting, gloomy, melancholy, sad. *See* HAPPY. **2.** Dark and depressing : black, bleak, blue, cheerless, dark, desolate, dismal, dreary, gloomy, glum, somber, tenebrific. *See* HAPPY, LIGHT.

joyous *adjective*
1. Providing joy and pleasure : cheerful, cheery, festive, glad, happy, joyful, pleasing. *See* HAPPY. **2.** Marked by festal celebration : festive, gala, glad, gladsome, happy, joyful, merry. *See* HAPPY.

jubilance *noun*
The act or condition of feeling an uplifting joy over a success or victory : exultance, exultancy, exultation, jubilation, triumph. *See* HAPPY.

jubilant *adjective*
Feeling or expressing an uplifting joy over a success or victory : exultant, triumphant. *See* HAPPY.

jubilate *verb*
To feel or express an uplifting joy over a success or victory : crow, exult, glory, triumph. *See* HAPPY.

jubilation *noun*
The act or condition of feeling an uplifting joy over a success or victory : exultance, exultancy, exultation, jubilance, triumph. *See* HAPPY.

Judas *noun*
One who betrays : betrayer, double-crosser, traitor. *Informal:* rat. *See* TRUST.

judge *verb*
1. To arrive at (a conclusion) from evidence or reasoning : conclude, deduce, deduct, draw, gather, infer, understand. *See* REASON. **2.** To make a judgment as to the worth or value of : appraise, assay, assess, calculate, estimate, evaluate, gauge, rate[1], size up, valuate, value. ***Idiom:*** take the measure of. *See* VALUE. **3.** To make a decision about (a controversy or dispute, for example) after deliberation, as in a court of law : adjudge, adjudicate, arbitrate, decide, decree, determine, referee, rule, umpire. *See* DECIDE, LAW. **4.** *Informal.* To have an opinion : believe, consider, deem, hold, opine, think. *Informal:* figure. ***Idiom:*** be of the opinion. *See* OPINION.

judge *noun* **1.** A person who evaluates and reports on the worth of something : commentator, critic, reviewer. *See* VALUE. **2.** A public official who decides cases brought before a court of law in order to administer justice : jurisprudent, jurist, justice, justice of the peace, magistrate. *See* DECIDE, LAW. **3.** A person, usually appointed, who decides the issues or results, or supervises the conduct, of a competition or conflict : arbiter, arbitrator, referee, umpire. *Sports:* ref, ump. *See* DECIDE.

judgement *noun* See **judgment.**

judgment also **judgement** *noun*
1. A position arrived at by reasoning from premises or general principles : conclusion, deduction, illation, illative, inference. *See* REASON. **2.** The ability to make sensible decisions : common sense, sense, wisdom. *Informal:* gumption, horse sense. *See* ABILITY. **3.** The act or result of judging the worth or value of something or someone : appraisal, appraisement, assessment, estimate, estimation, evaluation, valuation. *See* VALUE. **4.** An authoritative or official decision, especially one made by a court : decree, determination, edict, pronouncement, ruling. *See* LAW. **5.** A judicial decision, especially one setting the punishment to be inflicted on a convicted person : sentence. *Slang:* rap[1]. *See* LAW.

judgmental *adjective*
Based on individual judgment or discretion : arbitrary, discretionary, personal, subjective. *See* OPINION, SURPRISE.

judicious *adjective*
Possessing, proceeding from, or exhibiting good judgment and prudence : balanced, commonsensible, commonsensical, levelheaded, prudent, rational, reasonable, sagacious, sage, sane, sapient, sensible, sound[2], well-founded, well-grounded, wise[1]. *See* REASON, SANE.

jug *noun*
Slang. A place for the confinement of persons in lawful detention : brig, house of correction, jail, keep, penitentiary, prison. *Informal:* lockup, pen[3]. *Slang:* big house, can, clink, cooler, coop, hoosegow, joint, pokey[1], slammer, stir[2]. *Chiefly Regional:* calaboose. *See* FREE.

juju *noun*
A small object worn or kept for its supposed magical power : amulet, charm, fetish, periapt, phylactery, talisman. *See* SUPERNATURAL.

jumble *verb*
1. To put into total disorder : ball up, confuse, disorder, mess up, muddle, scramble, snarl[2].

Slang: snafu. ***Idiom:*** play havoc with. *See* ORDER. **2.** To put out of proper order : derange, disarrange, disarray, disorder, disorganize, disrupt, disturb, mess up, mix up, muddle, tumble, unsettle, upset. *See* ORDER. **3.** To mix together so as to change the order of arrangement : scramble, shuffle. *Games:* riffle. *See* CHANGE, ORDER. **4.** To cause to be unclear in mind or intent : addle, befuddle, bewilder, confound, confuse, discombobulate, dizzy, fuddle, mix up, muddle, mystify, perplex, puzzle. *Informal:* throw. ***Idiom:*** make one's head reel (*or* swim *or* whirl). *See* CLEAR, FEELINGS.

jumble *noun* **1.** A collection of various things : assortment, conglomeration, gallimaufry, hodgepodge, medley, mélange, miscellany, mishmash, mixed bag, mixture, olio, patchwork, potpourri, salmagundi, variety. *Slang:* grab bag. *See* COLLECT. **2.** A lack of order or regular arrangement : chaos, clutter, confusedness, confusion, derangement, disarrangement, disarray, disorder, disorderedness, disorderliness, disorganization, mess, mix-up, muddle, muss, scramble, topsy-turviness, tumble. *Slang:* snafu. *See* ORDER.

jumbo *noun*
One that is extraordinarily large and powerful : behemoth, giant, Goliath, leviathan, mammoth, monster, titan. *Slang:* whopper. *See* BEINGS, BIG.

jumbo *adjective* Of extraordinary size and power : behemoth, Brobdingnagian, Bunyanesque, colossal, cyclopean, elephantine, enormous, gargantuan, giant, gigantesque, gigantic, herculean, heroic, huge, immense, mammoth, massive, massy, mastodonic, mighty, monster, monstrous, monumental, mountainous, prodigious, pythonic, stupendous, titanic, tremendous, vast. *Informal:* walloping. *Slang:* whopping. *See* BIG.

jump *verb*
1. To move off the ground by a muscular effort of the legs and feet : hurdle, leap, spring, vault[2]. *See* MOVE, RISE. **2.** To move in a lively way : bounce, bound[1], leap, spring. *See* MOVE. **3.** To move suddenly and involuntarily : bolt, start. *See* MOVE. **4.** To catapult oneself from a disabled aircraft : bail out, eject. *See* APPROACH. **5.** To increase in amount : boost, hike, jack (up), raise, up. *See* INCREASE. **6.** To raise in rank : advance, elevate, promote, raise, upgrade. *See* RISE.

jump *noun* **1.** The act of jumping : leap, spring, vault[2]. *See* MOVE, RISE. **2.** A sudden lively movement : bounce, bound[1], leap, spring. *See* MOVE. **3.** A sudden and involuntary movement : bolt, start, startle. *See* MOVE. **4.** *Informal.* A dominating position, as in a conflict : advantage, better[1], bulge, draw, drop, edge, superiority, upper hand, vantage. *Informal:* inside track. *See* OVER. **5.** The act of increasing or rising : aggrandizement, amplification, augment, augmentation, boost, buildup, enlargement, escalation, growth, hike, increase, multiplication, proliferation, raise, rise, swell, upsurge, upswing, upturn. *See* INCREASE. **6.** The amount by which something is increased : advance, boost, hike, increase, increment, raise, rise. *See* INCREASE. **7.** A progression upward in rank : advancement, elevation, promotion, rise, upgrade. *See* RISE. **8.** A state of nervous restlessness or agitation. Used in plural : fidget (often used in plural), jitter (used in plural), shiver[1] (used in plural), tremble (often used in plural). *Informal:* all-overs, shake (used in plural). *Slang:* heebie-jeebies, jim-jams, willies. *See* CALM, FEAR.

jumpy *adjective*
Feeling or exhibiting nervous tension : edgy, fidgety, jittery, nervous, restive, restless, skittish, tense, twitchy. *Slang:* uptight. ***Idioms:*** a bundle of nerves, all wound up, on edge. *See* TIGHTEN.

junction *noun*
1. The act or fact of coming together : concourse, confluence, convergence, gathering, meeting. *See* CONNECT. **2.** A point or position at which two or more things are joined : connection, coupling, joint, juncture, seam, union. *See* CONNECT.

juncture *noun*
1. A point or position at which two or more things are joined : connection, coupling, joint, junction, seam, union. *See* CONNECT. **2.** A particular interval of time that is limited and often crucial : instant, moment, point. *See* TIME. **3.** A decisive point : climacteric, crisis, crossroad (used in plural), exigence, exigency, head, pass, turning point, zero hour. *See* DECIDE.

jungle *noun*
Something that is intricately and often bewilderingly complex : cat's cradle, entanglement, knot, labyrinth, maze, mesh (often used in plural), morass, skein, snarl[2], tangle, web. *See* SIMPLE.

junior *adjective*
Below another in standing or importance : inferior, lesser, low, lower[2], minor, minor-league, petty, secondary, small, subaltern,

subordinate, under. *Informal:* smalltime. *See* OVER.

junior *noun* One belonging to a lower class or rank : inferior, secondary, subaltern, subordinate, underling. *See* OVER.

junk *verb*
To let go or get rid of as being useless or defective, for example : discard, dispose of, dump, scrap[1], throw away, throw out. *Informal:* chuck, jettison, shuck (off). *Slang:* ditch. *See* KEEP.

junket *noun*
1. A large meal elaborately prepared or served : banquet, feast. *Informal:* feed, spread. *See* INGESTION. **2.** A usually short journey taken for pleasure : excursion, jaunt, outing, trip. *See* MOVE.

jurisdiction *noun*
The right and power to command, decide, rule, or judge : authority, command, control, domination, dominion, mastery, might, power, prerogative, sovereignty, sway. *Informal:* say-so. *See* OVER.

jurisprudent *noun*
A public official who decides cases brought before a court of law in order to administer justice : judge, jurist, justice, justice of the peace, magistrate. *See* DECIDE, LAW.

jurist *noun*
A public official who decides cases brought before a court of law in order to administer justice : judge, jurisprudent, justice, justice of the peace, magistrate. *See* DECIDE, LAW.

just *adjective*
1. Free from bias in judgment : disinterested, dispassionate, equitable, fair, fair-minded, impartial, indifferent, nonpartisan, objective, square, unbiased, unprejudiced. ***Idiom:*** fair and square. *See* FAIR. **2.** Consistent with prevailing or accepted standards or circumstances : appropriate, deserved, due, fit[1], fitting, merited, proper, right, rightful, suitable. *See* RIGHT. **3.** Based on good judgment, reasoning, or evidence : cogent, solid, sound[2], tight, valid, well-founded, well-grounded. *See* GOOD, REASON.

just *adverb* **1.** In an exact manner : even[1], exactly, precisely. *See* PRECISE, SAME. **2.** With precision or absolute conformity : bang, dead, direct, directly, exactly, fair, flush, precisely, right, smack[1], square, squarely, straight. *Slang:* smack-dab. *See* PRECISE. **3.** To the fullest extent : absolutely, all, altogether, completely, dead, entirely, flat, fully, perfectly, quite, thoroughly, totally, utterly, well[2], wholly. *Informal:* clean, clear. ***Idioms:*** in toto, through and through. *See* BIG, LIMITED. **4.** Only a moment ago : newly, recently. *See* TIME. **5.** By a very little; almost not : barely, hardly, scarce, scarcely. *See* NEAR. **6.** Nothing more than : merely, only. *See* INCLUDE, SPECIFIC.

justice *noun*
1. The quality or state of being just and unbiased : detachment, disinterest, disinterestedness, dispassion, dispassionateness, equitableness, fair-mindedness, fairness, impartiality, impartialness, justness, nonpartisanship, objectiveness, objectivity. *See* FAIR. **2.** The state, action, or principle of treating all persons equally in accordance with the law : due process, equity. *See* RIGHT. **3.** A public official who decides cases brought before a court of law in order to administer justice : judge, jurisprudent, jurist, justice of the peace, magistrate. *See* DECIDE, LAW.

justice of the peace *noun*
A public official who decides cases brought before a court of law in order to administer justice : judge, jurisprudent, jurist, justice, magistrate. *See* DECIDE, LAW.

justifiable *adjective*
Capable of being justified : defensible, excusable, tenable. *See* FORGIVENESS, RIGHT.

justification *noun*
1. A statement that justifies or defends something, such as a past action or policy : apologetic, apologia, apology, defense, vindication. *See* ATTACK. **2.** A statement of causes or motives : account, explanation, rationale, rationalization, reason. *See* EXPLAIN. **3.** A justifying fact or consideration : basis, foundation, reason, warrant. *See* TRUE. **4.** That which provides a reason or justification : call, cause, ground (often used in plural), necessity, occasion, reason, wherefore, why. ***Idiom:*** why and wherefore. *See* START.

justify *verb*
1. To show to be just, right, or valid : excuse, rationalize, vindicate. ***Idiom:*** make a case for. *See* RIGHT. **2.** To be a proper or sufficient occasion for : call for, occasion, warrant. *See* RIGHT. **3.** To assure the certainty or validity of : attest, authenticate, back (up), bear out, confirm, corroborate, evidence, substantiate, testify (to), validate, verify, warrant. *See* SUPPORT, TRUE. **4.** To support against arguments, attack, or criticism : apologize, defend, maintain, vindicate. ***Idioms:*** speak up for, stand up for, stick up for. *See* SUPPORT. **5.** To offer rea-

sons for or a cause of : account for, explain, rationalize. *See* EXPLAIN.

justness *noun*
The quality or state of being just and unbiased : detachment, disinterest, disinterestedness, dispassion, dispassionateness, equitableness, fair-mindedness, fairness, impartiality, impartialness, justice, nonpartisanship, objectiveness, objectivity. *See* FAIR.

jut *verb*
To curve outward past the normal or usual limit : bag, balloon, beetle, belly, bulge, overhang, pouch, project, protrude, protuberate, stand out, stick out. *See* CONVEX.
jut *noun* A part that protrudes or extends outward : bulge, knob, knot, overhang, projection, protrusion, protuberance. *See* CONVEX.

juvenescence *noun*
The time of life between childhood and maturity : adolescence, greenness, juvenility, puberty, salad days, spring, youth, youthfulness. *See* YOUTH.

juvenile *adjective*
1. Being in an early period of growth or development : green, immature, infant, young, youthful. *See* YOUTH. **2.** Of or characteristic of a child, especially in immaturity : babyish, childish, immature, infantile, puerile. *See* YOUTH.
juvenile *noun* **1.** A young person between birth and puberty : bud[1], child, innocent, moppet, tot[1], youngster. *Informal:* kid. *Scots:* bairn. *See* KIN, YOUTH. **2.** One who is not yet legally of age : child. *Law:* infant, minor. *See* LAW, YOUTH.

juvenility *noun*
The time of life between childhood and maturity : adolescence, greenness, juvenescence, puberty, salad days, spring, youth, youthfulness. *See* YOUTH.

•K•

kaput *adjective*
Informal. No longer effective, capable, or valuable : done, done for, finished, through, washed-up. ***Idioms:*** at the end of the line (*or* road), over the hill, past one's prime. *See* ABILITY, START.

keel over *verb*
To suffer temporary lack of consciousness : black out, faint, pass out, swoon. *See* AWARENESS.

keen[1] *adjective*
1. Having a fine edge, as for cutting : sharp. *See* SHARP. **2.** Mentally quick and original : alert, bright, clever, intelligent, quick, quick-witted, sharp, sharp-witted, smart. ***Idiom:*** smart as a whip. *See* ABILITY. **3.** Possessing or displaying perceptions of great accuracy and sensitivity : acute, incisive, penetrating, perceptive, probing, sensitive, sharp, trenchant. *See* CAREFUL, SHARP. **4.** Showing or having enthusiasm : ardent, enthusiastic, fervent, mad, rabid, warm, zealous. *Informal:* crazy. *Slang:* gung ho, nuts. *See* CONCERN.
5. Intensely desirous or interested : agog, ardent, athirst, avid, bursting, eager, impatient, solicitous, thirsting, thirsty. *Informal:* raring. *Idioms:* champing at the bit, ready and willing. *See* CONCERN. **6.** *Slang.* Particularly excellent : divine, fabulous, fantastic, fantastical, glorious, marvelous, sensational, splendid, superb, terrific, wonderful. *Informal:* dandy, dreamy, great, ripping, super, swell, tremendous. *Slang:* cool, groovy, hot, neat, nifty. *Idiom:* out of this world. *See* GOOD.

keen[2] *verb*
To make inarticulate sounds of grief or pain, usually accompanied by tears : bawl, blubber, cry, howl, sob, wail, weep, yowl. *See* HAPPY, SOUNDS.

keenness *noun*
1. A cutting quality : bite, edge, incisiveness, sharpness, sting. *See* SHARP. **2.** Skill in perceiving, discriminating, or judging : acumen, astuteness, clear-sightedness, discernment, discrimination, eye, nose, penetration, perceptiveness, percipience, percipiency, perspicacity, sagacity, sageness, shrewdness, wit. *See* ABILITY, CAREFUL.

keep *verb*
1. To have and maintain in one's possession : hold, hold back, keep back, reserve, retain, withhold. *See* KEEP. **2.** To have for sale : carry,

stock. *See* KEEP. **3.** To supply with the necessities of life : maintain, provide for, support. ***Idiom:*** take care of. *See* CARE FOR. **4.** To have or put in a customary place : store. *See* PLACE. **5.** To remain fresh and unspoiled : last[2]. *See* CHANGE. **6.** To persevere in some condition, action, or belief : maintain, retain, stay with. *See* CONTINUE. **7.** To control, restrict, or arrest : bit[2], brake, bridle, check, constrain, curb, hold, hold back, hold down, hold in, inhibit, keep back, pull in, rein (back, in, *or* up), restrain. *See* RESTRAINT. **8.** To hold oneself back : abstain, forbear, hold off, refrain, withhold. *See* RESTRAINT. **9.** To reserve for the future : lay aside, lay away, lay by, lay in, lay up, put by, salt away, save (up), set by. *See* KEEP, SAVE. **10.** To carry out the functions, requirements, or terms of : discharge, do, execute, exercise, fulfill, implement, perform. ***Idiom:*** live up to. *See* DO. **11.** To act in conformity with : abide by, adhere, carry out, comply, conform, follow, mind, obey, observe. ***Idiom:*** toe the line (*or* mark). *See* ACCEPT, SAME. **12.** To mark (a day or an event) with ceremonies of respect, festivity, or rejoicing : celebrate, commemorate, observe, solemnize. *See* REMEMBER.

keep back *verb* **1.** To have and maintain in one's possession : hold, hold back, keep, reserve, retain, withhold. *See* KEEP. **2.** To control, restrict, or arrest : bit[2], brake, bridle, check, constrain, curb, hold, hold back, hold down, hold in, inhibit, keep, pull in, rein (back, in, *or* up), restrain. *See* RESTRAINT.

keep off *verb* To turn or drive away : beat off, fend (off), parry, repel, repulse, ward off. *See* ALLOW, STRIKE.

keep on *verb* To continue without halting despite difficulties or setbacks : carry on, go on, hang on, persevere, persist. ***Idioms:*** hang in there, keep going, keep it up. *See* CONTINUE.

keep out *verb* To keep from being admitted, included, or considered : bar, count out, debar, eliminate, except, exclude, rule out, shut out. *See* INCLUDE.

keep up *verb* To keep in a condition of good repair, efficiency, or use : maintain, preserve, sustain. *See* KEEP.

keep *noun* **1.** The means needed to support life : alimentation, alimony, bread, bread and butter, livelihood, living, maintenance, subsistence, support, sustenance, upkeep. *See* MONEY. **2.** A place for the confinement of persons in lawful detention : brig, house of correction, jail, penitentiary, prison. *Informal:* lockup, pen[3]. *Slang:* big house, can, clink, cooler, coop, hoosegow, joint, jug, pokey[1], slammer, stir[2]. *Chiefly Regional:* calaboose. *See* FREE.

keep back *verb* See **keep.**

keeper *noun*
A person who is legally responsible for the person or property of another considered by law to be incompetent to manage his or her affairs : caretaker, custodian, guardian. *Law:* conservator. *See* LAW.

keeping *noun*
1. The function of watching, guarding, or overseeing : care, charge, custody, guardianship, superintendence, supervision, trust. *See* CARE FOR. **2.** The act or state of agreeing or conforming : accordance, agreement, chime, conformance, conformation, conformity, congruence, congruity, correspondence, harmonization, harmony. *See* AGREE.

keep off *verb* See **keep.**

keep on *verb* See **keep.**

keep out *verb* See **keep.**

keepsake *noun*
Something that causes one to remember : memento, remembrance, reminder, souvenir, token, trophy. *See* REMEMBER.

keep up *verb* See **keep.**

ken *noun*
The extent of one's perception, understanding, knowledge, or vision : horizon, purview, range, reach, scope. *See* ABILITY, KNOWLEDGE, SEE.

ken *verb* **1.** *Scots.* To perceive directly with the intellect : apprehend, compass, comprehend, fathom, grasp, know, understand. *See* KNOWLEDGE. **2.** *Scots.* To apprehend (images) by use of the eyes : behold, perceive, see. *See* SEE. **3.** *Scots.* To perceive and recognize the meaning of : accept, apprehend, catch (on), compass, comprehend, conceive, fathom, follow, get, grasp, make out, read, see, sense, take, take in, understand. *Informal:* savvy. *Slang:* dig. *Chiefly British:* twig. ***Idioms:*** get (*or* have) a handle on, get the picture. *See* UNDERSTAND.

kernel *noun*
1. A fertilized plant ovule capable of germinating : pip, pit[2], seed. *See* START. **2.** A source of further growth and development : bud[1], embryo, germ, nucleus, seed, spark[1]. *See* START. **3.** The most central and material part : core, essence, gist, heart, marrow, meat, nub, pith, quintessence, root[1], soul, spirit, stuff, substance. *Law:* gravamen. *See* BE.

key *noun*
A means or method of entering into or achieving something desirable : formula, route, secret. *Informal:* ticket. *See* MEANS.
key *adjective* **1.** Most important, influential, or significant : capital, cardinal, chief, first, foremost, leading, main, major, number one, paramount, premier, primary, prime, principal, top. *See* IMPORTANT. **2.** Dominant in importance or influence : central, pivotal. *See* IMPORTANT.

kibitzer *noun*
Informal. A person given to intruding in other people's affairs : busybody, interloper, meddler, quidnunc. *Slang:* buttinsky. *Archaic:* pragmatic. *See* PARTICIPATE.

kick *verb*
1. *Informal.* To express negative feelings, especially of dissatisfaction or resentment : complain, grouch, grump, whine. *Informal:* crab, gripe, grouse. *Slang:* beef, bellyache, bitch. *See* FEELINGS, HAPPY. **2.** *Informal.* To express opposition, often by argument : challenge, demur, except, expostulate, inveigh, object, protest, remonstrate. *Informal:* squawk. *Idioms:* set up a squawk, take exception. *See* SUPPORT. **3.** *Slang.* To desist from, cease, or discontinue (a habit, for example) : break, cut out, give up, leave off, stop. *See* CONTINUE.
kick around *verb Informal.* To speak together and exchange ideas and opinions about : bandy (about), discuss, moot, talk over, thrash out (*or* over), thresh out (*or* over), toss around. *Informal:* hash (over), knock about (*or* around). *Slang:* rap[3]. *Idiom:* go into a huddle. *See* WORDS.
kick in *verb* **1.** *Informal.* To give in common with others : chip in, contribute, donate, subscribe. *Slang:* come across. *See* GIVE. **2.** *Slang.* To cease living : decease, demise, depart, die, drop, expire, go, pass away, pass (on), perish, succumb. *Informal:* pop off. *Slang:* check out, croak, kick off. *Idioms:* bite the dust, breathe one's last, cash in, give up the ghost, go to one's grave, kick the bucket, meet one's end (*or* Maker), pass on to the Great Beyond, turn up one's toes. *See* LIVE.
kick off *verb* **1.** *Informal.* To go about the initial step in doing (something) : approach, begin, commence, embark, enter, get off, inaugurate, initiate, institute, launch, lead off, open, set about, set out, set to, start, take on, take up, undertake. *Idioms:* get cracking, get going, get the show on the road. *See* START. **2.** *Slang.* To cease living : decease, demise, depart, die, drop, expire, go, pass away, pass (on), perish, succumb. *Informal:* pop off. *Slang:* check out, croak, kick in. *Idioms:* bite the dust, breathe one's last, cash in, give up the ghost, go to one's grave, kick the bucket, meet one's end (*or* Maker), pass on to the Great Beyond, turn up one's toes. *See* LIVE.
kick out *verb Slang.* To put out by force : bump, dismiss, eject, evict, expel, oust, throw out. *Informal:* chuck. *Slang:* boot[1] (out), bounce. *Idioms:* give someone the boot, give someone the heave-ho (*or* old heave-ho), send packing, show someone the door, throw out on one's ear. *See* KEEP.
kick *noun* **1.** *Slang.* An expression of dissatisfaction or a circumstance regarded as a cause for such expression : complaint, grievance. *Informal:* gripe, grouse. *Slang:* beef. *Idiom:* bone to pick. *See* HAPPY. **2.** *Slang.* The act of expressing strong or reasoned opposition : challenge, demur, exception, expostulation, objection, protest, protestation, remonstrance, remonstration, squawk. *See* SUPPORT.
3. *Slang.* A stimulating or intoxicating effect : *Informal:* punch, sting, wallop. *See* DRUGS.
4. *Slang.* A strong, pleasant feeling of excitement or stimulation : lift, thrill. *Informal:* wallop. *Slang:* bang, boot[1], high. *See* EXCITE. **5.** *Slang.* A temporary concentration of interest : *Slang:* trip. *See* EXCITE. **6.** *Slang.* A clever, unexpected new trick or method : gimmick, twist. *Informal:* kicker, wrinkle. *Slang:* angle[2]. *See* ABILITY, EXCITE, GOOD.

kick around *verb* See **kick.**

kicker *noun*
Informal. A clever, unexpected new trick or method : gimmick, twist. *Informal:* wrinkle. *Slang:* angle[2], kick. *See* ABILITY, EXCITE, GOOD.

kick in *verb* See **kick.**

kickoff *noun*
Informal. The act or process of bringing or being brought into existence : beginning, commencement, inauguration, inception, incipience, incipiency, initiation, launch, leadoff, opening, origination, start. *See* START.

kick off *verb* See **kick.**

kick out *verb* See **kick.**

kid *noun*
Informal. A young person between birth and puberty : bud[1], child, innocent, juvenile, moppet, tot[1], youngster. *Scots:* bairn. *See* KIN, YOUTH.
kid *verb Informal.* To tease or mock good-humoredly : banter, chaff, joke, josh.

Informal: rib, ride. *Slang:* jive, rag², razz. *See* LAUGHTER.

kidnap *verb*
To seize and detain (a person) unlawfully : abduct, snatch, spirit away. *See* CRIMES, FREE.

kill¹ *verb*
1. To cause the death of : carry off, cut down, cut off, destroy, dispatch, finish (off), slay. *Slang:* waste, zap. ***Idioms:*** put an end to, put to sleep. *See* HELP. **2.** To take the life of (a person or persons) unlawfully : destroy, finish (off), liquidate, murder, slay. *Informal:* put away. *Slang:* bump off, do in, knock off, off, rub out, waste, wipe out, zap. *See* HELP. **3.** To destroy all traces of : abolish, annihilate, blot out, clear, eradicate, erase, exterminate, extinguish, extirpate, liquidate, obliterate, remove, root¹ (out *or* up), rub out, snuff out, stamp out, uproot, wipe out. ***Idioms:*** do away with, make an end of, put an end to. *See* HELP, MAKE. **4.** To pass (time) without working or in avoiding work : dawdle (away), fiddle away, idle (away), trifle away, waste, while (away), wile (away). *See* INDUSTRIOUS.

kill² *noun*
Chiefly Regional. A small stream : brook¹, creek. *Chiefly Regional:* branch, run. *See* DRY.

killer *noun*
One who murders another : butcher, cutthroat, homicide, manslayer, massacrer, murderer, murderess, slaughterer, slayer, triggerman. *See* HELP.

killing *noun*
The crime of murdering someone : blood, homicide, murder. *Slang:* hit. *See* HELP.
killing *adjective Informal.* Extremely funny : hilarious, priceless, sidesplitting. *Informal:* rich. *See* LAUGHTER.

kilter *noun*
A state of sound readiness : condition, fettle, fitness, form, order, shape, trim. *See* BETTER.

kin *noun*
1. One's relatives collectively : family, kindred, kinfolk. *See* KIN. **2.** A person connected to another person by blood or marriage : kinsman, kinswoman, relation, relative. *See* KIN.

kind¹ *adjective*
Characterized by kindness and concern for others : altruistic, beneficent, benevolent, benign, benignant, good, goodhearted, kindhearted, kindly. *See* ATTITUDE, KIND.

kind² *noun*
A class that is defined by the common attribute or attributes possessed by all its members : breed, cast, description, feather, ilk, lot, manner, mold, nature, order, sort, species, stamp, stripe, type, variety. *Informal:* persuasion. *See* GROUP.

kindhearted *adjective*
Characterized by kindness and concern for others : altruistic, beneficent, benevolent, benign, benignant, good, goodhearted, kind¹, kindly. *See* ATTITUDE, KIND.

kindheartedness *noun*
Kindly, charitable interest in others : altruism, beneficence, benevolence, benignancy, benignity, charitableness, charity, goodwill, grace, kindliness, kindness, philanthropy. *See* ATTITUDE, KIND.

kindle *verb*
1. To cause to burn or undergo combustion : enkindle, fire, ignite, light¹. *Slang:* torch. ***Idioms:*** set afire (*or* on fire), set fire to. *See* HOT, START. **2.** To arouse the emotions of; make ardent : animate, enkindle, fire, impassion, inspire, stir¹. *See* EXCITE. **3.** To induce or elicit (a reaction or emotion) : arouse, awake, awaken, raise, rouse, stir¹ (up), waken. *See* EXCITE.

kindliness *noun*
1. Kindly, charitable interest in others : altruism, beneficence, benevolence, benignancy, benignity, charitableness, charity, goodwill, grace, kindheartedness, kindness, philanthropy. *See* ATTITUDE, KIND. **2.** A charitable deed : benefaction, beneficence, benevolence, benignity, favor, kindness, oblation, office (often used in plural), philanthropy. *See* GIVE, KIND.

kindly *adjective*
Characterized by kindness and concern for others : altruistic, beneficent, benevolent, benign, benignant, good, goodhearted, kind¹, kindhearted. *See* ATTITUDE, KIND.

kindness *noun*
1. Kindly, charitable interest in others : altruism, beneficence, benevolence, benignancy, benignity, charitableness, charity, goodwill, grace, kindheartedness, kindliness, philanthropy. *See* ATTITUDE, KIND. **2.** A charitable deed : benefaction, beneficence, benevolence, benignity, favor, kindliness, oblation, office (often used in plural), philanthropy. *See* GIVE, KIND. **3.** A kindly act : favor, good turn, grace, indulgence, service. *Archaic:* benefit. *See* HELP.

kindred *noun*
1. A group of people sharing common ancestry : clan, family, house, lineage, stock,

tribe. *Idioms:* flesh and blood, kith and kin. *See* KIN. **2.** One's relatives collectively : family, kin, kinfolk. *See* KIN.

kindred *adjective* Connected by or as if by kinship or common origin : agnate, akin, allied, cognate, connate, connatural, consanguine, consanguineous, related. *See* KIN.

kinetic *adjective*
Possessing, exerting, or displaying energy : active, brisk, dynamic, dynamical, energetic, forceful, lively, sprightly, strenuous, vigorous. *Informal:* peppy. *See* ACTION.

kinfolk also **kinsfolk** or **kinfolks** *noun*
One's relatives collectively : family, kin, kindred. *See* KIN.

kinfolks *noun* See **kinfolk.**

kinsfolk *noun* See **kinfolk.**

kinsman *noun*
A person connected to another person by blood or marriage : kin, kinswoman, relation, relative. *See* KIN.

kinswoman *noun*
A person connected to another person by blood or marriage : kin, kinsman, relation, relative. *See* KIN.

kismet *noun*
That which is inevitably destined : destiny, fate, fortune, lot, portion, predestination. *See* CERTAIN.

kiss *verb*
1. To touch or caress with the lips, especially as a sign of passion or affection : buss, osculate, smack[1]. *Informal:* peck[1]. *Slang:* smooch. *See* TOUCH. **2.** To make light and momentary contact with, as in passing : brush[1], flick, graze, shave, skim. *See* TOUCH.

kiss *noun* The act or an instance of kissing : buss, osculation, smack[1], smacker. *Informal:* peck[1]. *Slang:* smooch. *See* TOUCH.

kisser *noun*
Slang. The front surface of the head : countenance, face, feature (often used in plural), muzzle, visage. *Informal:* mug. *Slang:* map, pan, puss. *See* PRECEDE.

klutz *noun*
Slang. A large, ungainly, and dull-witted person : gawk, hulk, lout, lump[1], oaf, ox. *Informal:* lummox. *Slang:* lug[1], meatball, meathead. *See* ABILITY.

klutzy *adjective*
Slang. Lacking dexterity and grace in physical movement : awkward, clumsy, gawky, graceless, inept, lumpish, maladroit, ungainly, ungraceful. *Idiom:* all thumbs. *See* ABILITY.

knack *noun*
1. The proper method for doing, using, or handling something : feel, trick. *Informal:* hang. *See* ABILITY. **2.** Natural or acquired facility in a specific activity : ability, adeptness, art, command, craft, expertise, expertness, mastery, proficiency, skill, technique. *Informal:* know-how. *See* ABILITY, KNOWLEDGE. **3.** An innate capability : aptitude, aptness, bent, faculty, flair, genius, gift, head, instinct, talent, turn. *See* ABILITY, APPROACH.

knead *verb*
To handle in a way so as to mix, form, and shape : manipulate, work. *See* TOUCH.

knell *verb*
To give forth or cause to give forth a clear, resonant sound : bong, chime, peal, ring[2], strike, toll[2]. *See* SOUNDS.

knickknack *noun*
A small showy article : bauble, bibelot, gewgaw, gimcrack, novelty, toy, trifle, trinket, whatnot. *See* THING.

knifelike *adjective*
Marked by severity or intensity : acute, gnawing, lancinating, piercing, sharp, shooting, stabbing. *See* BIG.

knightly *adjective*
Characterized by elaborate but usually formal courtesy : chivalrous, courtly, gallant, gracious, stately. *See* ATTITUDE, COURTESY.

knob *noun*
1. A part that protrudes or extends outward : bulge, jut, knot, overhang, projection, protrusion, protuberance. *See* CONVEX. **2.** An unevenness or elevation on a surface : bump, hump, knot, lump[1], nub, protuberance. *See* CONVEX.

knock *verb*
1. To deliver a powerful blow to suddenly and sharply : bash, catch, clout, hit, pop[1], slam, slog, slug[3], smash, smite, sock, strike, swat, thwack, whack, wham, whop. *Informal:* biff, bop, clip[1], wallop. *Slang:* belt, conk, paste. *Idioms:* let someone have it, sock it to someone. *See* ATTACK, STRIKE. **2.** To make a noise by striking : rap[1], tap[1]. *See* SOUNDS. **3.** *Slang.* To find fault with : blame, censure, criticize, fault, rap[1]. *Informal:* cut up, pan. *See* PRAISE.

knock about (or **around**) *verb* **1.** To be rough or brutal with : manhandle, rough (up), slap around. *Slang:* mess up. *See* ATTACK, STRIKE. **2.** To injure or damage, as by abuse or heavy wear : batter, mangle[1], maul, rough up. *See* ATTACK, HELP, STRIKE. **3.** *Informal.* To speak together and exchange ideas and opinions about : bandy (about), discuss, moot, talk over, thrash out (*or* over), thresh out (*or* over), toss around. *Informal:* hash (over), kick around. *Slang:* rap[3]. ***Idiom:*** go into a huddle. *See* WORDS.

knock down *verb* **1.** To cause to fall, as from a shot or blow : bring down, cut down, down, drop, fell[1], flatten, floor, ground, level, prostrate, strike down, throw. *Slang:* deck[1]. ***Idiom:*** lay low. *See* RISE. **2.** To pull down or break up so that reconstruction is impossible : demolish, destroy, dismantle, dynamite, level, pull down, pulverize, raze, tear down, wreck. *Aerospace:* destruct. *See* HELP.

knock off *verb* **1.** *Informal.* To take away (a quantity) from another quantity : abate, deduct, discount, rebate, subtract, take (off). *See* INCREASE. **2.** *Slang.* To take the life of (a person or persons) unlawfully : destroy, finish (off), kill[1], liquidate, murder, slay. *Informal:* put away. *Slang:* bump off, do in, off, rub out, waste, wipe out, zap. *See* HELP. **3.** *Slang.* To take property or possessions from (a person or company, for example) unlawfully and usually forcibly : hold up, rob, stick up. *Slang:* heist. *See* CRIMES, GIVE.

knock out *verb* **1.** To render powerless or motionless, as by inflicting severe injury : cripple, disable, immobilize, incapacitate, paralyze. ***Idiom:*** put out of action (*or* commission). *See* HELP. **2.** *Informal.* To make extremely tired : exhaust, fag (out), tire out, wear out. *Informal:* tucker (out). *Slang:* do in, poop[1] (out). ***Idioms:*** run ragged, take it out of. *See* TIRED.

knock over *verb* To turn or cause to turn from a vertical or horizontal position : capsize, overthrow, overturn, topple, turn over, upset. *See* CHANGE, HORIZONTAL, MOVE.

knock *noun* **1.** The sound made by a light blow : rap[1], tap[1]. *See* SOUNDS. **2.** *Slang.* A comment expressing fault : blame, censure, condemnation, criticism, denunciation, reprehension, reprobation. *Informal:* pan. *See* PRAISE.

knockabout *adjective*
Marked by vigorous physical exertion : rough, rough-and-tumble, rugged, strenuous, tough. *See* ACTION.

knock about or **around** *verb* See **knock.**

knock down *verb* See **knock.**

knock off *verb* See **knock.**

knockout *noun*
Slang. A person regarded as physically attractive : beauty, belle (used of a woman), lovely, stunner. *Slang:* babe, doll, hunk (used of a man), looker, stud (used of a man). *See* BEAUTIFUL.

knock out *verb* See **knock.**

knock over *verb* See **knock.**

knot *noun*
1. That which unites or binds : bond, ligament, ligature, link, nexus, tie, vinculum, yoke. *See* CONNECT. **2.** A number of individuals making up or considered a unit : array, band[2], batch, bevy, body, bunch, bundle, clump, cluster, clutch[2], collection, group, lot, party, set[2]. *See* GROUP. **3.** Something that is intricately and often bewilderingly complex : cat's cradle, entanglement, jungle, labyrinth, maze, mesh (often used in plural), morass, skein, snarl[2], tangle, web. *See* SIMPLE. **4.** A part that protrudes or extends outward : bulge, jut, knob, overhang, projection, protrusion, protuberance. *See* CONVEX. **5.** An unevenness or elevation on a surface : bump, hump, knob, lump[1], nub, protuberance. *See* CONVEX. **6.** A small raised area of skin resulting from a light blow or an insect sting, for example : bump, bunch, lump[1], swelling. *See* CONVEX.

knot *verb* To make fast or firmly fixed, as by means of a cord or rope : bind, fasten, secure, tie, tie up. *See* KEEP, TIGHTEN.

knotty *adjective*
Difficult to understand because of intricacy : byzantine, complex, complicated, convoluted, daedal, Daedalian, elaborate, intricate, involute, involved, labyrinthine, tangled. *See* SIMPLE.

know *verb*
1. To perceive directly with the intellect : apprehend, compass, comprehend, fathom, grasp, understand. *Scots:* ken. *See* KNOWLEDGE. **2.** To participate in or partake of personally : experience, feel, go through, have, meet[1] (with), see, suffer, taste (of), undergo. *Archaic:* prove. ***Idiom:*** run up against. *See* PARTICIPATE. **3.** To undergo an emotional reaction : experience, feel, have, savor, taste. *See* FEELINGS. **4.** To perceive to be identical with something held in the memory : recognize. *See* KNOWLEDGE, REMEMBER. **5.** To recognize as being different : differentiate, discern, discriminate, distinguish, separate, tell. *See* SAME.

knowable *adjective*
Capable of being readily understood : comprehensible, fathomable, intelligible, understandable. *See* KNOWLEDGE.

know-how *noun*
Informal. Natural or acquired facility in a spe-

cific activity : ability, adeptness, art, command, craft, expertise, expertness, knack, mastery, proficiency, skill, technique. *See* ABILITY, KNOWLEDGE.

knowing *adjective*

1. Having or showing intelligence, often of a high order : brilliant, intellectual, intelligent, knowledgeable. *Informal:* brainy. *See* ABILITY. **2.** Possessing or showing sound judgment and keen perception : sagacious, sage, sapient, wise[1]. *See* WISE. **3.** Having or showing a clever awareness and resourcefulness in practical matters : astute, cagey, canny, perspicacious, shrewd, slick, smart, wise[1]. *Informal:* savvy. *See* ABILITY, CAREFUL.

know-it-all *noun*

Informal. One who is obnoxiously self-assertive and arrogant : malapert, witling. *Informal:* saucebox, smart aleck, smarty, smarty-pants, wisenheimer. *Slang:* wiseacre, wisecracker, wise guy. *See* GOOD.

knowledge *noun*

1. That which is known; the sum of what has been perceived, discovered, or inferred : information, lore, wisdom. *See* KNOWLEDGE. **2.** Known facts, ideas, and skill that have been imparted : education, erudition, instruction, learning, scholarship, science. *See* KNOWLEDGE. **3.** That which is known about a specific subject or situation : data, fact (used in plural), information, intelligence, lore. *See* KNOWLEDGE.

knowledgeable *adjective*

1. Provided with information; made aware : acquainted, advised, educated, enlightened, informed, instructed. *See* KNOWLEDGE. **2.** Having or showing intelligence, often of a high order : brilliant, intellectual, intelligent, knowing. *Informal:* brainy. *See* ABILITY.

kook *noun*

Slang. A person regarded as strange, eccentric, or crazy : crackpot, crazy, eccentric, lunatic. *Informal:* crank, loon, loony. *Slang:* cuckoo, ding-a-ling, dingbat, nut, screwball, weirdie, weirdo. *See* WISE.

kooky *adjective*

Slang. Deviating from the customary : bizarre, cranky, curious, eccentric, erratic, freakish, idiosyncratic, odd, outlandish, peculiar, quaint, queer, quirky, singular, strange, unnatural, unusual, weird. *Slang:* screwball. *British Slang:* rum, rummy[2]. *See* USUAL.

kowtow *verb*

To support slavishly every opinion or suggestion of a superior : bootlick, cringe, fawn, grovel, slaver, toady, truckle. *Informal:* apple-polish, brownnose, cotton. *Slang:* suck up. *Idioms:* curry favor, dance attendance, kiss someone's feet, lick someone's boots. *See* OVER.

kowtow *noun* An inclination of the head or body, as in greeting, consent, courtesy, submission, or worship : bow[1], curtsy, genuflection, nod, obeisance. *See* COURTESY.

kosher *adjective*

Slang. Capable of being allowed : admissible, allowable, permissible. *See* ALLOW.

kudos *noun*

1. Recognition of achievement or superiority or a sign of this : accolade, distinction, honor, laurel (often used in plural). *See* RESPECT. **2.** An expression of warm approval : acclaim, acclamation, applause, celebration, commendation, compliment, encomium, eulogy, laudation, panegyric, plaudit, praise. *See* PRAISE.

Kultur *noun*

The total product of human creativity and intellect : civilization, culture. *See* CULTURE.

·L·

label *noun*
1. An identifying or descriptive slip : tag, ticket. *See* MARKS. 2. A name or other device placed on merchandise to signify its ownership or manufacture : brand, colophon, mark, trademark. *See* MARKS.
label *verb* 1. To attach a ticket to : mark, tag, ticket. *See* MARKS. 2. To set off by or as if by a mark indicating ownership or manufacture : brand, identify, mark, tag, trademark. *See* MARKS. 3. To describe with a word or term : call, characterize, designate, name, style, tag, term. *See* SPECIFIC, WORDS.

labor *noun*
1. Physical exertion that is usually difficult and exhausting : drudgery, moil, toil, travail, work. *Informal:* sweat. *Chiefly British:* fag. ***Idiom:*** sweat of one's brow. *See* WORK. 2. The act or process of bringing forth young : accouchement, birth, birthing, childbearing, childbirth, delivery, lying-in, parturition, travail. *See* START.
labor *verb* 1. To exert one's mental or physical powers, usually under difficulty and to the point of exhaustion : drive, fag, moil, strain[1], strive, sweat, toil, travail, tug, work. ***Idiom:*** break one's back (*or* neck). *See* WORK. 2. To express at greater length or in greater detail : amplify, develop, dilate, elaborate, enlarge, expand, expatiate. *See* EXPLAIN.

labored *adjective*
1. Not natural or spontaneous : contrived, effortful, forced, strained. *See* TRUE. 2. Lacking fluency or gracefulness : elephantine, heavy-handed, ponderous. *See* GOOD.

laborer *noun*
One who labors : hand, operative, roustabout, worker, working girl, workingman, workingwoman, workman, workwoman. *See* WORK.

laborious *adjective*
1. Requiring great or extreme bodily, mental, or spiritual strength : arduous, backbreaking, burdensome, demanding, difficult, effortful, exacting, exigent, formidable, hard, heavy, onerous, oppressive, rigorous, rough, severe, taxing, tough, trying, weighty. *See* HEAVY.
2. Not easy to do, achieve, or master : arduous, difficult, hard, serious, tall, tough, uphill. *See* EASY.

laboriously *adverb*
With effort : arduously, difficultly, hard, heavily. *See* EASY.

labyrinth *noun*
Something that is intricately and often bewilderingly complex : cat's cradle, entanglement, jungle, knot, maze, mesh (often used in plural), morass, skein, snarl[2], tangle, web. *See* SIMPLE.

labyrinthine *adjective*
Difficult to understand because of intricacy : byzantine, complex, complicated, convoluted, daedal, Daedalian, elaborate, intricate, involute, involved, knotty, tangled. *See* SIMPLE.

lachrymose *adjective*
Filled with or shedding tears : tearful, teary, weeping, weepy. ***Idiom:*** in tears. *See* HAPPY.

lack *noun*
1. The condition or fact of being deficient : defect, deficiency, deficit, inadequacy, insufficiency, paucity, poverty, scantiness, scantness, scarceness, scarcity, shortage, shortcoming, shortfall, underage[1]. *See* EXCESS. 2. The condition of lacking a needed or usual amount : absence, dearth, want. *See* EXCESS.
lack *verb* To be without what is needed, required, or essential : need, require, want. *See* OWNED.

lackadaisical *adjective*
Lacking energy and vitality or showing such a lack : flagging, languid, languorous, leaden, limp, listless, lymphatic, spiritless. *See* ACTION, TIRED.

lacking *adjective*
1. Lacking an essential element : defective, deficient, incomplete, wanting. *See* BETTER, EXCESS. 2. Deficient in a usual or needed amount : absent, wanting. *See* EXCESS. 3. Not having a desirable element : barren, destitute, devoid, empty, innocent, void, wanting. ***Idiom:*** in want of. *See* FULL.

lackluster *adjective*
1. Lacking gloss and luster : dim, dull, flat, lusterless, mat. *See* LIGHT. 2. Lacking liveliness, charm, or surprise : arid, aseptic, colorless, drab, dry, dull, earthbound, flat, flavorless, lifeless, lusterless, matter-of-fact, pedestrian, prosaic, spiritless, sterile, stodgy, unimaginative, uninspired. *See* EXCITE.

laconic *adjective*
Marked by or consisting of few words that are carefully chosen : brief, compendious, concise, lean[2], short, succinct, summary, terse. *See* BIG, STYLE, WORDS.

lacuna *noun*
An interval during which continuity is suspended : break, gap, hiatus, interim, void. *See* CONTINUE.

lade *verb*
1. To place a burden or heavy load on : burden[1], charge, cumber, encumber, freight, load, saddle, tax, weight. *See* OVER. **2.** To fill to overflowing : heap, load, pile. *See* FULL. **3.** To take a substance, as liquid, from a container by plunging the hand or a utensil into it : bail[2], dip, ladle, scoop (up). *See* GIVE.

la-de-da *adjective* See **la-di-da.**

laden *adjective*
Burdened by a weighty load : heavy, heavy-laden, loaded. *See* FULL.

la-di-da also **la-de-da** *adjective*
Informal. Artificially genteel : affected, artificial, mannered, precious. *See* GOOD, HONEST, PLAIN, TRUE.

ladies' man *noun* See **lady's man.**

ladle *verb*
To take a substance, as liquid, from a container by plunging the hand or a utensil into it : bail[2], dip, lade, scoop (up). *See* GIVE.

lady-killer *noun*
Slang. A man who philanders : Casanova, Don Juan, lady's man, philanderer, womanizer. *Slang:* wolf. ***Idioms:*** man on the make, skirt chaser. *See* SEX.

lady's man also **ladies' man** *noun*
1. A man amorously attentive to women : amorist, Casanova, Don Juan, gallant, Lothario, Romeo. *See* SEX. **2.** A man who philanders : Casanova, Don Juan, philanderer, womanizer. *Slang:* lady-killer, wolf. ***Idioms:*** man on the make, skirt chaser. *See* SEX.

lag *verb*
1. To go or move slowly so that progress is hindered : dally, dawdle, delay, dilly-dally, drag, linger, loiter, poke, procrastinate, tarry, trail. ***Idioms:*** drag one's feet (*or* heels), mark time, take one's time. *See* FAST. **2.** To cause to be later or slower than expected or desired : delay, detain, hang up, hold up, retard, set back, slow (down *or* up), stall[2]. *See* HELP, TIME.

lag *noun* **1.** The condition or fact of being made late or slow : delay, detainment, holdup, retardation. *See* HELP, TIME. **2.** One that lags : dawdler, dilly-dallier, laggard, lagger, lingerer, loiterer, poke, procrastinator, straggler, tarrier. *Informal:* slowpoke. *See* FAST.

laggard *noun*
One that lags : dawdler, dilly-dallier, lag, lagger, lingerer, loiterer, poke, procrastinator, straggler, tarrier. *Informal:* slowpoke. *See* FAST.

laggard *adjective* Proceeding at a rate less than usual or desired : dilatory, slow, slow-footed, slow-going, slow-paced, tardy. *Informal:* poky[1]. ***Idiom:*** slow as molasses in January. *See* FAST.

lagger *noun*
One that lags : dawdler, dilly-dallier, lag, laggard, lingerer, loiterer, poke, procrastinator, straggler, tarrier. *Informal:* slowpoke. *See* FAST.

lagging *adjective*
Not progressing and developing as fast as others, as in economic and social aspects : backward, underdeveloped, undeveloped. *See* PRECEDE.

laid-back *adjective*
Informal. Unconstrained by rigid standards or ceremony : casual, easy, easygoing, informal, natural, relaxed, spontaneous, unceremonious, unrestrained. *See* PLAIN, TIGHTEN.

laid up *adjective*
Informal. Suffering from or affected with an illness : down, ill, sick, unwell. *Chiefly Regional:* poorly. *See* HEALTH.

lair *noun*
1. A place used as an animal's dwelling : burrow, den, hole. *See* PROTECTION. **2.** A hiding place : covert, den, hideaway, hide-out. *See* PLACE, SHOW.

lam *verb*
Slang. To break loose and leave suddenly, as from confinement or from a difficult or threatening situation : abscond, break out, decamp, escape, flee, fly, get away, run away. *Informal:* skip (out). *Regional:* absquatulate. ***Idioms:*** blow (*or* fly) the coop, cut and run, give someone the slip, make a getaway, take flight, take it on the lam. *See* FREE.

lam *noun* *Slang.* The act or an instance of escaping, as from confinement or difficulty : break, breakout, decampment, escape, escapement, flight, getaway. *See* FREE.

lamb *noun*
1. A pure, uncorrupted person : angel, innocent, virgin. *See* CLEAN, RIGHT. **2.** A person who is easily deceived or victimized : butt[3], dupe, fool, gull, pushover, victim. *Informal:*

sucker. *Slang:* fall guy, gudgeon, mark, monkey, patsy, pigeon, sap[1]. *Chiefly British:* mug. *See* WISE.

lambaste *verb*

1. *Informal.* To hit heavily and repeatedly with violent blows : assail, assault, baste, batter, beat, belabor, buffet, drub, hammer, pound, pummel, smash, thrash, thresh. *Slang:* clobber. ***Idiom:*** rain blows on. *See* ATTACK, STRIKE. **2.** *Informal.* To criticize for a fault or an offense : admonish, call down, castigate, chastise, chide, dress down, rap[1], rebuke, reprimand, reproach, reprove, scold, tax, upbraid. *Informal:* bawl out. *Slang:* chew out. ***Idioms:*** bring (*or* call *or* take) to task, call on the carpet, haul (*or* rake) over the coals, let someone have it. *See* ATTACK, PRAISE.

lambent *adjective*

Giving off or reflecting light readily or in large amounts : beamy, bright, brilliant, effulgent, incandescent, irradiant, lucent, luminous, lustrous, radiant, refulgent, shiny. *See* LIGHT.

lament *verb*

To feel, show, or express grief : grieve, mourn, sorrow, suffer. *See* HAPPY.

lamentable *adjective*

Causing sorrow or regret : deplorable, doleful, dolorous, grievous, mournful, regrettable, rueful, sad, sorrowful, woeful. *See* HAPPY.

lamia *noun*

A woman who practices magic : enchantress, hag, sorceress, witch. *See* SUPERNATURAL.

lamina *noun*

A thin outer covering of an object : membrane, sheath, sheathing, skin. *See* SURFACE.

lampoon *noun*

A work, as a novel or play, that exposes folly by the use of humor or irony : lampoonery, satire. *See* LAUGHTER, RESPECT.

lampoonery *noun*

A work, as a novel or play, that exposes folly by the use of humor or irony : lampoon, satire. *See* LAUGHTER, RESPECT.

lancinating *adjective*

Marked by severity or intensity : acute, gnawing, knifelike, piercing, sharp, shooting, stabbing. *See* BIG.

land *noun*

1. An organized geopolitical unit : body politic, country, nation, polity, state. *See* POLITICS, TERRITORY. **2.** Usually extensive real estate : acre (often used in plural), estate, property. *See* OWNED.

land *verb* **1.** To come ashore from a seacraft : debark, disembark. *See* MOVE. **2.** To come to rest on the ground : alight[1], light[2], set down, settle, touch down. *See* MOVE. **3.** *Informal.* To come into possession of : acquire, come by, gain, get, obtain, pick up, procure, secure, win. *Informal:* pick up. *See* GET.

language *noun*

1. A system of terms used by a people sharing a history and culture : dialect, speech, tongue, vernacular. *Linguistics:* langue. *See* WORDS. **2.** Specialized expressions indigenous to a particular field, subject, trade, or subculture : argot, cant[2], dialect, idiom, jargon, lexicon, lingo, patois, terminology, vernacular, vocabulary. *See* WORDS.

langue *noun*

Linguistics. A system of terms used by a people sharing a history and culture : dialect, language, speech, tongue, vernacular. *See* WORDS.

languid *adjective*

Lacking energy and vitality or showing such a lack : flagging, lackadaisical, languorous, leaden, limp, listless, lymphatic, spiritless. *See* ACTION, TIRED.

languidness *noun*

A deficiency in mental and physical alertness and activity : dullness, hebetude, languor, lassitude, leadenness, lethargy, listlessness, sluggishness, stupor, torpidity, torpor. *See* ACTION.

languish *verb*

1. To lose strength or power : decline, degenerate, deteriorate, fade, fail, flag[2], sink, wane, waste (away), weaken. *Informal:* fizzle (out). ***Idioms:*** go downhill, hit the skids. *See* INCREASE, STRONG. **2.** To waste away from longing or grief : pine (away), wither. *See* HEALTH.

languor *noun*

A deficiency in mental and physical alertness and activity : dullness, hebetude, languidness, lassitude, leadenness, lethargy, listlessness, sluggishness, stupor, torpidity, torpor. *See* ACTION.

languorous *adjective*

Lacking energy and vitality or showing such a lack : flagging, lackadaisical, languid, leaden, limp, listless, lymphatic, spiritless. *See* ACTION, TIRED.

lank *adjective*

Having little flesh or fat on the body : angular, bony, fleshless, gaunt, lanky, lean[2], meager, rawboned, scrawny, skinny, slender, slim, spare, thin, twiggy, weedy. ***Idioms:*** all skin and bones, thin as a rail. *See* FAT.

lanky *adjective*

1. Tall, thin, and awkwardly built : gangling, gangly, rangy, spindling, spindly. *See* FAT.

2. Having little flesh or fat on the body : angular, bony, fleshless, gaunt, lank, lean[2], meager, rawboned, scrawny, skinny, slender, slim, spare, thin, twiggy, weedy. *Idioms:* all skin and bones, thin as a rail. *See* FAT.

lap *verb*
1. To flow against or along : bathe, lave, lip, wash. *See* DRY. **2.** To flow or move with a low slapping sound : bubble, burble, gurgle, splash, swash, wash. *See* MOVE, SOUNDS.

lapse *verb*
1. To slip from a higher or better condition to a former, usually lower or poorer one : backslide, regress, relapse, retrogress, revert. *See* BETTER, REPETITION. **2.** To become or cause to become less active or intense : abate, bate, die (away, down, off, *or* out), ease (off *or* up), ebb, fall, fall off, let up, moderate, remit, slacken, slack off, subside, wane. *See* INCREASE. **3.** To move smoothly, continuously, and effortlessly : glide, glissade, slide, slip, slither. *See* MOVE. **4.** To become void, especially through passage of time or an omission : expire, run out. *See* CONTINUE, LAW. **5.** To move past in time : elapse, go (by), pass. *See* TIME.

lapse *noun* **1.** A minor mistake : slip, slip-up. *Informal:* fluff. *See* CORRECT. **2.** An act or thought that unintentionally deviates from what is correct, right, or true : erratum, error, inaccuracy, incorrectness, miscue, misstep, mistake, slip, slip-up, trip. *See* CORRECT. **3.** A slipping from a higher or better condition to a lower or poorer one : backslide, backsliding, recidivation, recidivism, relapse. *See* BETTER, REPETITION.

larcener *noun*
A person who steals : bandit, burglar, highwayman, housebreaker, larcenist, pilferer, purloiner, robber, stealer, thief. *See* CRIMES.

larcenist *noun*
A person who steals : bandit, burglar, highwayman, housebreaker, larcener, pilferer, purloiner, robber, stealer, thief. *See* CRIMES.

larcenous *adjective*
Tending to larceny : thievish. *See* CRIMES.

larceny *noun*
The crime of taking someone else's property without consent : pilferage, steal, theft, thievery. *Slang:* rip-off. *See* CRIMES.

lares and penates *noun*
One's portable property : belonging (often used in plural), effect (used in plural), good (used in plural), personal effects, personal property, possession (used in plural), property, thing (often used in plural). *Informal:* stuff. *Law:* chattel, movable (often used in plural). *See* OWNED.

large *adjective*
1. Notably above average in amount, size, or scope : big, considerable, extensive, good, great, healthy, large-scale, sizable. *Informal:* tidy. *See* BIG. **2.** Covering a wide scope : all-around, all-inclusive, all-round, broad, broad-spectrum, comprehensive, expansive, extended, extensive, far-ranging, far-reaching, general, global, inclusive, overall, sweeping, wide-ranging, wide-reaching, widespread. *See* SPECIFIC. **3.** Having great significance : big, consequential, considerable, historic, important, material, meaningful, monumental, significant, substantial. *See* IMPORTANT.

large-hearted *adjective*
Willing to give of oneself and one's possessions : big, big-hearted, generous, great-hearted, magnanimous, unselfish. *See* GIVE.

large-heartedness *noun*
The quality or state of being generous : big-heartedness, bounteousness, bountifulness, free-handedness, generosity, generousness, great-heartedness, lavishness, liberality, magnanimity, magnanimousness, munificence, openhandedness, unselfishness, unsparingness. *See* GIVE.

largeness *noun*
The quality or state of being large in amount, extent, or importance : amplitude, bigness, greatness, magnitude, sizableness, size. *See* BIG.

larger *adjective*
Much more than half : best, better[1], greater, largest, most. *See* BETTER, BIG.

large-scale *adjective*
Notably above average in amount, size, or scope : big, considerable, extensive, good, great, healthy, large, sizable. *Informal:* tidy. *See* BIG.

largess also **largesse** *noun*
A material favor or gift, usually money, given in return for service : cumshaw, gratuity, perquisite, tip[3]. *See* GIVE, TRANSACTIONS.

largesse *noun* See **largess.**

largest *adjective*
Much more than half : best, better[1], greater, larger, most. *See* BETTER, BIG.

largish *adjective*
Somewhat big : biggish, goodly, respectable, sizable. *See* BIG.

lark *noun*
A mischievous act : antic, caper, frolic, joke, prank[1], trick. *Informal:* shenanigan. *Slang:*

monkeyshine (often used in plural). *See* GOOD, WORK.

lascivious *adjective*

1. Feeling or devoted to sexual love or desire : amative, amorous, concupiscent, erotic, lecherous, lewd, libidinous, lustful, lusty, passionate, prurient, sexy. *See* SEX. **2.** Of, concerning, or promoting sexual love or desire : amatory, amorous, aphrodisiac, erotic, salacious, sexual, sexy. *See* SEX.

lash *verb*

1. To punish with blows or lashes : beat, flog, hide[2], thrash, whip. *Informal:* trim. *Slang:* lay into, lick. *See* ATTACK, REWARD. **2.** To criticize harshly and devastatingly : blister, drub, excoriate, flay, rip into, scarify[1], scathe, scorch, score, scourge, slap, slash. *Informal:* roast. *Slang:* slam. ***Idioms:*** burn someone's ears, crawl all over, pin someone's ears back, put someone on the griddle, put someone on the hot seat, rake over the coals, read the riot act to. *See* PRAISE.

lashing *noun*

A punishment dealt with blows or lashes : beating, flogging, hiding, thrashing, whipping. *Informal:* trimming. *Slang:* licking. *See* ATTACK, REWARD.

lassitude *noun*

1. A deficiency in mental and physical alertness and activity : dullness, hebetude, languidness, languor, leadenness, lethargy, listlessness, sluggishness, stupor, torpidity, torpor. *See* ACTION. **2.** Lack of emotion or interest : apathy, disinterest, impassivity, incuriosity, incuriousness, indifference, insensibility, insensibleness, lethargy, listlessness, phlegm, stolidity, stolidness, unconcern, uninterest, unresponsiveness. *See* FEELINGS.

last[1] *adjective*

1. Coming after all others : closing, concluding, final, terminal. *See* START. **2.** Bringing up the rear : endmost, hindermost, hindmost, lattermost, rearmost. *See* START. **3.** Next before the present one : foregoing, latter, preceding, previous. *See* NEAR, PRECEDE. **4.** Of or relating to a terminative condition, stage, or point : final, latter, terminal, ultimate. *See* START.

last *adverb* In conclusion : conclusively, finally, lastly. *See* START.

last *noun* The last part : close, conclusion, end, ending, finale, finish, termination, wind-up, wrap-up. *See* START.

last[2] *verb*

1. To be in existence or in a certain state for an indefinitely long time : abide, continue, endure, go on, hold out, persist, remain, stay[1]. *See* CONTINUE. **2.** To exist in spite of adversity : come through, persist, pull through, ride out, survive, weather. *See* LIVE. **3.** To remain fresh and unspoiled : keep. *See* CHANGE.

lasting *adjective*

Existing or remaining in the same state for an indefinitely long time : abiding, continuing, durable, enduring, long-lasting, long-lived, long-standing, old, perdurable, perennial, permanent, persistent. *See* CONTINUE.

lastly *adverb*

In conclusion : conclusively, finally, last[1]. *See* START.

late *adjective*

1. Not being on time : behindhand, belated, overdue, tardy. *See* TIME. **2.** Having been such previously : erstwhile, former, old, once, onetime, past, previous, quondam, sometime, whilom. *See* PRECEDE. **3.** No longer alive : asleep, dead, deceased, defunct, departed, extinct, gone, lifeless. ***Idioms:*** at rest, pushing up daisies. *See* LIVE.

late *adverb* **1.** Not on time : behind, behindhand, belatedly, tardily. *See* TIME. **2.** So as to fall behind schedule : behind, behindhand, slow. ***Idiom:*** behind time. *See* TIME. **3.** Not long ago : lately, latterly, recently. ***Idiom:*** of late. *See* NEAR, PRECEDE, TIME.

lately *adverb*

Not long ago : late, latterly, recently. ***Idiom:*** of late. *See* NEAR, PRECEDE, TIME.

latency *noun*

The condition of being temporarily inactive : abeyance, abeyancy, dormancy, intermission, quiescence, suspension. *See* ACTION.

lateness *noun*

The quality or condition of not being on time : belatedness, tardiness. *See* TIME.

latent *adjective*

1. Capable of being but not yet in existence : eventual, possible, potential. *See* POSSIBLE. **2.** Existing in a temporarily inactive form or state : abeyant, dormant, inactive, quiescent, sleeping. *See* ACTION, SHOW.

later *adjective*

1. Following something else in time : after, posterior, subsequent, ulterior. *See* PRECEDE. **2.** Being or occurring in the time ahead : coming, future, subsequent. *See* PRECEDE, TIME.

later *adverb* At a subsequent time : after, afterward, afterwards, latterly, next, subsequently, ulteriorly. ***Idioms:*** after a while, by and by, later on. *See* PRECEDE.

lather *noun*
1. A mass of bubbles in or on the surface of a liquid : foam, froth, head, spume, suds, yeast. *See* SOLID. **2.** Moisture excreted through the pores of the skin : perspiration, sweat. *See* DRY. **3.** *Informal.* A state of discomposure : agitation, dither, fluster, flutter, perturbation, tumult, turmoil, upset. *Informal:* stew. *See* CALM.
lather *verb* **1.** To form or cause to form foam : bubble, cream, effervesce, fizz, foam, froth, spume, suds, yeast. *See* SOLID. **2.** To excrete moisture through the pores of the skin : perspire, sweat. *See* DRY.

lathery *adjective*
Consisting of or resembling foam : foamy, frothy, spumous, spumy, sudsy, yeasty. *See* SOLID.

latitude *noun*
Suitable opportunity to accept or allow something : elbowroom, leeway, margin, play, room, scope. *See* PLACE, RESTRAINT.

latter *adjective*
1. Of or relating to a terminative condition, stage, or point : final, last[1], terminal, ultimate. *See* START. **2.** Next before the present one : foregoing, last[1], preceding, previous. *See* NEAR, PRECEDE.

latter-day *adjective*
Of or relating to the present or times close to the present : modern, recent. *See* NEW, TIME.

latterly *adverb*
1. At a subsequent time : after, afterward, afterwards, later, next, subsequently, ulteriorly. ***Idioms:*** after a while, by and by, later on. *See* PRECEDE. **2.** Not long ago : late, lately, recently. ***Idiom:*** of late. *See* NEAR, PRECEDE, TIME.

lattermost *adjective*
Bringing up the rear : endmost, hindermost, hindmost, last[1], rearmost. *See* START.

laud *verb*
1. To pay tribute or homage to : acclaim, celebrate, eulogize, exalt, extol, glorify, hail[2], honor, magnify, panegyrize, praise. ***Idiom:*** sing someone's praises. *See* PRAISE. **2.** To express warm approval of : acclaim, applaud, commend, compliment, praise. *See* PRAISE. **3.** To honor (a deity) in religious worship : exalt, extol, glorify, magnify, praise. *See* RELIGION.

laudable *adjective*
Deserving honor, respect, or admiration : admirable, commendable, creditable, deserving, estimable, exemplary, honorable, meritorious, praiseworthy, reputable, respectable, worthy. *See* GOOD, PRAISE, RESPECT, VALUE.

laudation *noun*
1. An expression of warm approval : acclaim, acclamation, applause, celebration, commendation, compliment, encomium, eulogy, kudos, panegyric, plaudit, praise. *See* PRAISE. **2.** The honoring of a deity, as in worship : exaltation, extolment, glorification, magnification, praise. *See* RELIGION.

laudatory *adjective*
Serving to compliment : acclamatory, approbatory, commendatory, complimentary, congratulatory. *See* PRAISE.

laugh *verb*
1. To express amusement, mirth, or scorn by smiling and emitting loud, inarticulate sounds : cachinnate, cackle, guffaw. *Informal:* heehaw. ***Idioms:*** die laughing, laugh one's head off, roll in the aisles, split one's sides. *See* LAUGHTER, SOUNDS. **2.** To make fun or make fun of : deride, gibe, jeer, jest, mock, ridicule, scoff, scout[2], twit. *Chiefly British:* quiz. ***Idiom:*** poke fun at. *See* LAUGHTER, RESPECT.
laugh *noun* **1.** An act of laughing : cachinnation, cackle, guffaw, laughter. *Informal:* heehaw. *See* LAUGHTER, SOUNDS. **2.** *Informal.* Something or someone uproariously funny or absurd : absurdity. *Informal:* hoot, joke, scream. *Slang:* gas, howl, panic, riot. ***Idiom:*** a laugh a minute. *See* LAUGHTER.

laughable *adjective*
1. Arousing laughter : amusing, comic, comical, droll, funny, humorous, risible, zany. *See* LAUGHTER. **2.** Deserving laughter : comic, comical, farcical, funny, laughing, ludicrous, ridiculous, risible. *See* LAUGHTER.

laughing *adjective*
1. Deserving laughter : comic, comical, farcical, funny, laughable, ludicrous, ridiculous, risible. *See* LAUGHTER. **2.** Emitting a murmuring sound felt to resemble a laugh : babbling, bubbling, burbling, gurgling, rippling. *See* LAUGHTER, SOUNDS.

laughingstock *noun*
An object of amusement or laughter : butt[3], jest, joke, mockery. *See* RESPECT.

laughter *noun*
An act of laughing : cachinnation, cackle, guffaw, laugh. *Informal:* heehaw. *See* LAUGHTER, SOUNDS.

launch *verb*
1. To send through the air with a motion of the hand or arm : cast, dart, dash, fling, heave, hurl, hurtle, pitch, shoot, shy[2], sling, throw,

toss. *Informal:* fire. *See* MOVE. **2.** To go about the initial step in doing (something) : approach, begin, commence, embark, enter, get off, inaugurate, initiate, institute, lead off, open, set about, set out, set to, start, take on, take up, undertake. *Informal:* kick off. ***Idioms:*** get cracking, get going, get the show on the road. *See* START. **3.** To bring into currency, use, fashion, or practice : introduce, originate. *See* START.

launch *noun* **1.** An act of throwing : cast, fling, heave, hurl, pitch, shy[2], sling, throw, toss. *See* MOVE. **2.** The act or process of bringing or being brought into existence : beginning, commencement, inauguration, inception, incipience, incipiency, initiation, leadoff, opening, origination, start. *Informal:* kickoff. *See* START.

laurel *noun*
Recognition of achievement or superiority or a sign of this. Often used in plural : accolade, distinction, honor, kudos. *See* RESPECT.

lave *verb*
To flow against or along : bathe, lap, lip, wash. *See* DRY.

lavish *adjective*
1. Characterized by extravagant, ostentatious magnificence : lush[1], luxuriant, luxurious, opulent, palatial, plush, rich, sumptuous. *Informal:* plushy. *See* RICH. **2.** Characterized by excessive or imprudent spending : extravagant, prodigal, profligate, profuse, spendthrift, wasteful. *See* CAREFUL, EXCESS, SAVE. **3.** Given to or marked by unrestrained abundance : extravagant, exuberant, lush[1], luxuriant, opulent, prodigal, profuse, riotous, superabundant. *See* BIG, EXCESS. **4.** Characterized by bounteous giving : free, freehanded, generous, handsome, liberal, munificent, openhanded, unsparing, unstinting. *See* GIVE.

lavish *verb* To give in great abundance : heap, rain, shower. *See* BIG, GIVE.

lavishness *noun*
1. Excessive or imprudent expenditure : extravagance, extravagancy, prodigality, profligacy, profuseness, profusion, squander, waste, wastefulness. *See* CAREFUL, SAVE. **2.** The quality or state of being generous : big-heartedness, bounteousness, bountifulness, freehandedness, generosity, generousness, great-heartedness, large-heartedness, liberality, magnanimity, magnanimousness, munificence, openhandedness unselfishness, unsparingness. *See* GIVE.

law *noun*
1. A principle governing affairs within or among political units : canon, decree, edict, institute, ordinance, precept, prescription, regulation, rule. *See* LAW. **2.** The formal product of a legislative or judicial body : act, assize, bill[1], enactment, legislation, lex, measure, statute. *See* LAW. **3.** *Informal.* A member of a law-enforcement agency : bluecoat, finest, officer, patrolman, patrolwoman, peace officer, police, policeman, police officer, policewoman. *Informal:* cop. *Slang:* bull[1], copper, flatfoot, fuzz, gendarme, heat, man (often uppercase). *Chiefly British:* bobby, constable, peeler. *See* LAW. **4.** A broad and basic rule or truth : axiom, fundamental, principle, theorem, universal. *See* ORDER.

law *verb* To institute or subject to legal proceedings : litigate, prosecute, sue. ***Idiom:*** bring suit. *See* LAW.

lawbreaker *noun*
One who commits a crime : criminal, malefactor, offender. *Law:* felon. *See* CRIMES.

lawful *adjective*
Within, allowed by, or sanctioned by the law : innocent, legal, legitimate, licit. *Slang:* legit. *See* LAW.

lawfulness *noun*
The state or quality of being within the law : legality, legitimacy, legitimateness, licitness. *See* LAW.

lawless *adjective*
1. Prohibited by law : illegal, illegitimate, illicit, outlawed, unlawful, wrongful. *See* CRIMES, LAW. **2.** Of, involving, or being a crime : criminal, illegal, illegitimate, illicit, unlawful, wrongful. *See* CRIMES. **3.** Not submitting to discipline or control : disorderly, fractious, indocile, intractable, obstinate, obstreperous, recalcitrant, refractory, uncontrollable, undisciplined, ungovernable, unmanageable, unruly, untoward, wild. ***Idiom:*** out of line. *See* CONTROL, ORDER, PEACE, RESIST.

lawlessness *noun*
A lack of civil order or peace : anarchy, disorder, misrule. *See* ORDER, PEACE.

lawsuit *noun*
A legal proceeding to demand justice or enforce a right : action, case, cause, instance, suit. *See* LAW.

lawyer *noun*
A person who practices law : attorney, counsel, counselor. *Slang:* ambulance chaser. *Chiefly British:* barrister. *See* LAW.

lax *adjective*
1. Not strict or severe : charitable, clement, easy, forbearing, indulgent, lenient, merciful, soft, tolerant. *See* ACCEPT. **2.** Guilty of neglect;

lacking due care or concern : derelict, neglectful, negligent, remiss, slack. *See* CAREFUL. **3.** Not tautly bound, held, or fastened : loose, relaxed, slack. *See* TIGHTEN.

laxity *noun*
The state or quality of being negligent : laxness, negligence, remissness, slackness. *See* CAREFUL.

laxness *noun*
The state or quality of being negligent : laxity, negligence, remissness, slackness. *See* CAREFUL.

lay[1] *verb*
1. To place (a story, for example) in a designated setting : set[1]. *See* PLACE. **2.** To deposit in a specified place : place, put, set[1], stick. *See* PLACE, RISE. **3.** To place (a corpse) in or as if in a grave : bury, entomb, inhume, inter. ***Idiom:*** lay (*or* put) to rest. *See* SHOW. **4.** To regard as belonging to or resulting from another : accredit, ascribe, assign, attribute, charge, credit, impute, refer. *See* GIVE. **5.** To arrange tableware upon (a table) in preparation for a meal : set[1], spread. *See* ORDER. **6.** To form a strategy for : blueprint, cast, chart, conceive, contrive, design, devise, formulate, frame, plan, project, scheme, strategize, work out. *Informal:* dope out. ***Idiom:*** lay plans. *See* PLANNED. **7.** To bring forward for formal consideration : adduce, cite, present[2]. *Archaic:* allege. *See* LAW, WORDS. **8.** To put up as a stake in a game or speculation. Also used with *down* : bet, gamble, post[2], put, risk, stake, venture, wager. *Informal:* go. *See* GAMBLING. **9.** To make a bet : bet, gamble, game, play, wager. ***Idiom:*** put one's money on something. *See* GAMBLING. **10.** *Military.* To move (a weapon or blow, for example) in the direction of someone or something : aim, cast, direct, head, level, point, set[1], train, turn, zero in. *See* SEEK.

lay aside *verb* To reserve for the future : keep, lay away, lay by, lay in, lay up, put by, salt away, save (up), set by. *See* KEEP, SAVE.

lay away *verb* **1.** To reserve for the future : keep, lay aside, lay by, lay in, lay up, put by, salt away, save (up), set by. *See* KEEP, SAVE. **2.** To place (money) in a bank : bank[2], deposit, salt away. *Informal:* sock away. *See* KEEP, MONEY.

lay by *verb* To reserve for the future : keep, lay aside, lay away, lay in, lay up, put by, salt away, save (up), set by. *See* KEEP, SAVE.

lay down *verb* **1.** To let (something) go : abandon, cede, forgo, relinquish, surrender, yield. *See* KEEP. **2.** To set forth expressly and authoritatively : decree, dictate, fix, impose, ordain, prescribe. ***Idioms:*** call the shots (*or* tune), lay it on the line. *See* OVER.

lay for *verb Informal.* To wait concealed in order to attack (someone) : ***Idioms:*** lay wait for, lie in wait for. *See* ATTACK, SHOW.

lay in *verb* **1.** To reserve for the future : keep, lay aside, lay away, lay by, lay up, put by, salt away, save (up), set by. *See* KEEP, SAVE. **2.** To accumulate and set aside for future use : lay up, save (up), stockpile, store (up). *See* KEEP.

lay into *verb Slang.* To punish with blows or lashes : beat, flog, hide[2], lash, thrash, whip. *Informal:* trim. *Slang:* lick. *See* ATTACK, REWARD.

lay off *verb Slang.* To cease trying to accomplish or continue : abandon, break off, desist, discontinue, give up, leave off, quit, relinquish, remit, stop. *Informal:* swear off. ***Idioms:*** call it a day, call it quits, hang up one's fiddle, have done with, throw in the towel. *See* CONTINUE.

lay out *verb* **1.** To plan the details or arrangements of : arrange, prepare, schedule, work out. *See* PLANNED. **2.** To work out and arrange the parts or details of : blueprint, design, map (out), plan, set out. *See* PLANNED. **3.** To show graphically the direction or location of, as by using coordinates : chart, map (out), plot. *See* SHOW. **4.** To distribute (money) as payment : disburse, expend, give, outlay, pay (out), spend. *Informal:* fork out (*or* over *or* up), shell out. *See* SAVE.

lay up *verb* **1.** To reserve for the future : keep, lay aside, lay away, lay by, lay in, put by, salt away, save (up), set by. *See* KEEP, SAVE. **2.** To accumulate and set aside for future use : lay in, save (up), stockpile, store (up). *See* KEEP.

lay[2] *adjective*
Not religious in subject matter, form, or use : profane, secular, temporal, worldly. *See* SACRED.

layabout *noun*
A self-indulgent person who spends time avoiding work or other useful activity : bum[1], drone[1], fainéant, good-for-nothing, idler, loafer, ne'er-do-well, no-good, slugabed, sluggard, wastrel. *Informal:* do-little, do-nothing, lazybones, slug[2]. *Slang:* slouch. *See* INDUSTRIOUS.

lay aside *verb* See **lay[1]**.
lay away *verb* See **lay[1]**.
lay by *verb* See **lay[1]**.
lay down *verb* See **lay[1]**.
lay for *verb* See **lay[1]**.

lay in *verb* See **lay**[1].
lay into *verb* See **lay**[1].
lay off *verb* See **lay**[1].
layout *noun*
1. A method for making, doing, or accomplishing something : blueprint, design, game plan, idea, plan, project, schema, scheme, strategy. *See* PLANNED. **2.** A way or condition of being arranged : arrangement, categorization, classification, deployment, disposal, disposition, distribution, formation, grouping, lineup, order, organization, placement, sequence. *See* ORDER.
lay out *verb* See **lay**[1].
lay up *verb* See **lay**[1].
laze *verb*
To pass time without working or in avoiding work : bum[1] (around), idle, loaf, loiter, lounge, shirk. *Slang:* diddle[2], goldbrick, goof (off). *See* INDUSTRIOUS.
laziness *noun*
The quality or state of being lazy : idleness, indolence, shiftlessness, sloth, slothfulness, sluggardness, sluggishness. *Informal:* do-nothingism. *See* INDUSTRIOUS.
lazy *adjective*
Resistant to exertion and activity : fainéant, idle, indolent, shiftless, slothful, sluggard, sluggish. *Informal:* do-nothing. ***Idiom:*** bone lazy. *See* ACTION, INDUSTRIOUS.
lazybones *noun*
Informal. A self-indulgent person who spends time avoiding work or other useful activity : bum[1], drone[1], fainéant, good-for-nothing, idler, layabout, loafer, ne'er-do-well, no-good, slugabed, sluggard, wastrel. *Informal:* do-little, do-nothing, slug[2]. *Slang:* slouch. *See* INDUSTRIOUS.
leach *verb*
To flow or leak out or emit something slowly : bleed, exude, ooze, percolate, seep, transpire, transude, weep. *See* MOVE, SOLID.
lead *verb*
1. To show the way to : conduct, direct, escort, guide, pilot, route, shepherd, show, steer, usher. *See* SHOW. **2.** To proceed on a certain course or for a certain distance : carry, extend, go, reach, run, stretch. *See* REACH. **3.** To have authoritative charge of : captain, command. *See* PRECEDE. **4.** To go through (life) in a certain way : live[1], pass, pursue. *See* BE. **5.** To begin (something) with preliminary or prefatory material : introduce, precede, preface, usher in. *See* START, WORDS.
lead off *verb* To go about the initial step in doing (something) : approach, begin, commence, embark, enter, get off, inaugurate, initiate, institute, launch, open, set about, set out, set to, start, take on, take up, undertake. *Informal:* kick off. ***Idioms:*** get cracking, get going, get the show on the road. *See* START.
lead to *verb* To be the cause of : bring, bring about, bring on, cause, effect, effectuate, generate, induce, ingenerate, make, occasion, result in, secure, set off, stir[1] (up), touch off, trigger. ***Idioms:*** bring to pass (*or* effect), give rise to. *See* START.
lead *noun* **1.** Something or someone that shows the way : conductor, director, escort, guide, leader, pilot, shepherd, usher. *See* SHOW. **2.** A piece of information useful in a search : clue, scent. *See* SHOW. **3.** An act or instance of guiding : direction, guidance, leadership, management. *See* AFFECT. **4.** The capacity to lead others : command, leadership. *See* PRECEDE. **5.** The main performer in a theatrical production : principal, protagonist, star. *See* PERFORMING ARTS. **6.** A prominent article in a periodical : feature. *Chiefly British:* leader. *See* WORDS.
leaden *adjective*
Lacking energy and vitality or showing such a lack : flagging, lackadaisical, languid, languorous, limp, listless, lymphatic, spiritless. *See* ACTION, TIRED.
leadenness *noun*
A deficiency in mental and physical alertness and activity : dullness, hebetude, languidness, languor, lassitude, lethargy, listlessness, sluggishness, stupor, torpidity, torpor. *See* ACTION.
leader *noun*
1. Something or someone that shows the way : conductor, director, escort, guide, lead, pilot, shepherd, usher. *See* SHOW. **2.** A leading contestant : front-runner, number one. *See* PRECEDE. **3.** One who is highest in rank or authority : boss, chief, chieftain, director, head, headman, hierarch, master. *Slang:* honcho. ***Idiom:*** cock of the walk. *See* OVER. **4.** A professional politician who controls a party or political machine : boss, chief. *See* OVER. **5.** An important, influential person : character, dignitary, eminence, lion, nabob, notability, notable, personage. *Informal:* big-timer, heavyweight, somebody, someone, VIP. *Slang:* big shot, big wheel, bigwig, muckamuck. *See* IMPORTANT. **6.** *Chiefly British.* A prominent article in a periodical : feature, lead. *See* WORDS.
leadership *noun*
1. The capacity to lead others : command,

lead. *See* PRECEDE. **2.** An act or instance of guiding : direction, guidance, lead, management. *See* AFFECT.

lead-in *noun*
A short section of preliminary remarks : foreword, induction, introduction, overture, preamble, preface, prelude, prolegomenon, prologue. *See* START, WORDS.

leading *adjective*
1. Most important, influential, or significant : capital, cardinal, chief, first, foremost, key, main, major, number one, paramount, premier, primary, prime, principal, top. *See* IMPORTANT. **2.** Widely known and discussed : famed, famous, notorious, popular, well-known. *See* KNOWLEDGE.

leadoff *noun*
The act or process of bringing or being brought into existence : beginning, commencement, inauguration, inception, incipience, incipiency, initiation, launch, opening, origination, start. *Informal:* kickoff. *See* START.
leadoff *adjective* Of, relating to, or occurring at the start of something : beginning, inceptive, incipient, initial, initiatory, introductory. *See* START.

lead off *verb* See **lead.**

lead to *verb* See **lead.**

leaf *verb*
To look through reading matter casually. Also used with *through* : browse, dip into, flip through, glance at (*or* over *or* through), riffle (through), run through, scan, skim, thumb (through). *See* INVESTIGATE, WORDS.

league *noun*
1. An association, especially of nations for a common cause : alliance, Anschluss, bloc, cartel, coalition, confederacy, confederation, federation, organization, union. *See* CONNECT, GROUP, POLITICS. **2.** A group of people united in a relationship and having some interest, activity, or purpose in common : association, club, confederation, congress, federation, fellowship, fraternity, guild, order, organization, society, sorority, union. *See* GROUP. **3.** A group of athletic teams that play each other : association, circuit, conference, loop. *See* GROUP. **4.** A division of persons or things by quality, rank, or grade : bracket, class, grade, order, rank[1], tier. *See* GROUP, VALUE.
league *verb* **1.** To be formally associated, as by treaty : align, ally, confederate, federate. *See* CONNECT, POLITICS. **2.** To assemble or join in a group : band[2], combine, gang up, unite. *See* COLLECT.

leaguer *noun*
One nation associated with another in a common cause : ally, coalitionist, confederate. *See* CONNECT, POLITICS.

leak *verb*
Informal. To be made public. Also used with *out* : break, come out, get out, out, transpire. *Idiom:* come to light. *See* KNOWLEDGE, SHOW.

lean[1] *verb*
1. To depart or cause to depart from true vertical or horizontal : cant[1], heel[2], incline, list[2], rake[2], slant, slope, tilt, tip[2]. *See* STRAIGHT. **2.** To have a tendency or inclination : incline, slant, squint, tend[1], trend. *See* LIKELY.
lean *noun* Deviation from a particular direction : cant[1], grade, gradient, heel[2], inclination, incline, list[2], rake[2], slant, slope, tilt, tip[2]. *See* RISE, STRAIGHT.

lean[2] *adjective*
1. Having little flesh or fat on the body : angular, bony, fleshless, gaunt, lank, lanky, meager, rawboned, scrawny, skinny, slender, slim, spare, thin, twiggy, weedy. *Idioms:* all skin and bones, thin as a rail. *See* FAT. **2.** Marked by or consisting of few words that are carefully chosen : brief, compendious, concise, laconic, short, succinct, summary, terse. *See* BIG, STYLE, WORDS. **3.** Characterized by an economy of artistic expression : spare, tight. *See* STYLE.

leaning *noun*
An inclination to something : bent, bias, cast, disposition, partiality, penchant, predilection, predisposition, proclivity, proneness, propensity, squint, tendency, trend, turn. *See* APPROACH, LIKE.

leap *verb*
1. To move off the ground by a muscular effort of the legs and feet : hurdle, jump, spring, vault[2]. *See* MOVE, RISE. **2.** To move in a lively way : bounce, bound[1], jump, spring. *See* MOVE.
leap *noun* **1.** The act of jumping : jump, spring, vault[2]. *See* MOVE, RISE. **2.** A sudden lively movement : bounce, bound[1], jump, spring. *See* MOVE.

learn *verb*
1. To gain knowledge or mastery of by study : get, master. *Informal:* pick up. *See* TEACH. **2.** To commit to memory : con, memorize. *See* REMEMBER. **3.** To obtain knowledge or awareness of something not known before, as through observation or study : ascertain,

determine, discover, find (out), hear. *See* TEACH.

learned *adjective*
Having or showing profound knowledge and scholarship : erudite, lettered, scholarly, wise[1]. *See* KNOWLEDGE.

learner *noun*
One who is being educated : pupil, scholar, student. *See* TEACH.

learning *noun*
Known facts, ideas, and skill that have been imparted : education, erudition, instruction, knowledge, scholarship, science. *See* KNOWLEDGE.

lease *verb*
1. To give temporary use of in return for payment : hire (out), let, rent[1]. *See* TRANSACTIONS. **2.** To engage the temporary use of (something) for a fee : charter, hire, rent[1]. *See* GET, TRANSACTIONS.

leash *verb*
To restrict the activity or free movement of : chain, fetter, hamper, hamstring, handcuff, hobble, manacle, shackle, tie, trammel. *Informal:* hog-tie. *See* FREE, HELP.
leash *noun* An instrument or means of restraining : bit[2], brake, bridle, restraint, snaffle. *See* RESTRAINT.

leave[1] *verb*
1. To move or proceed away from a place : depart, exit, get away, get off, go, go away, pull out, quit, retire, run (along), withdraw. *Informal:* cut out, push off, shove off. *Slang:* blow[1], split, take off. ***Idioms:*** hit the road, take leave. *See* APPROACH. **2.** To give (property) to another person after one's death : will. *Law:* bequeath, devise. *See* GIVE, LAW. **3.** To give up or leave without intending to return or claim again : abandon, desert[3], forsake, quit, throw over. ***Idioms:*** run out on, walk out on. *See* KEEP. **4.** To relinquish one's engagement in or occupation with : demit, quit, resign, terminate. *See* CONTINUE.
leave off *verb* **1.** To come to a cessation : arrest, belay, cease, check, discontinue, halt[1], quit, stall[1], stop, surcease. ***Idiom:*** come to a halt (*or* standstill *or* stop). *See* CONTINUE. **2.** To cease trying to accomplish or continue : abandon, break off, desist, discontinue, give up, quit, relinquish, remit, stop. *Informal:* swear off. *Slang:* lay off. ***Idioms:*** call it a day, call it quits, hang up one's fiddle, have done with, throw in the towel. *See* CONTINUE. **3.** To desist from, cease, or discontinue (a habit, for example) : break, cut out, give up, stop. *Slang:* kick. *See* CONTINUE.

leave[2] *noun*
1. The approving of an action, especially when done by one in authority : allowance, approbation, approval, authorization, consent, endorsement, license, permission, permit, sanction. *Informal:* OK. *See* ALLOW. **2.** A regularly scheduled period spent away from work or duty, often in recreation : furlough, vacation. *Chiefly British:* holiday. *See* WORK.

leaven *noun*
An agent that stimulates or precipitates a reaction, development, or change : catalyst, ferment, leavening, yeast. *See* CHANGE.

leavening *noun*
An agent that stimulates or precipitates a reaction, development, or change : catalyst, ferment, leaven, yeast. *See* CHANGE.

leave off *verb* See **leave.**

leave-taking *noun*
A separation of two or more people : adieu, farewell, good-bye, parting, valediction. *See* APPROACH.

leavings *noun*
What remains after a part has been used or subtracted : balance, leftover, remainder, remains, remnant, residue, rest[2]. *See* LEFTOVER.

lech *noun*
Slang. An immoral or licentious man : lecher, roué, satyr. *Informal:* dirty old man. *See* SEX.

lecher *noun*
An immoral or licentious man : roué, satyr. *Informal:* dirty old man. *Slang:* lech. *See* SEX.

lecherous *adjective*
Feeling or devoted to sexual love or desire : amative, amorous, concupiscent, erotic, lascivious, lewd, libidinous, lustful, lusty, passionate, prurient, sexy. *See* SEX.

lecture *noun*
A usually formal oral communication to an audience : address, allocution, declamation, oration, prelection, speech, talk. *See* WORDS.
lecture *verb* To talk to an audience formally : address, prelect, speak. *Archaic:* bespeak. *See* WORDS.

lecturer *noun*
One who delivers a public speech : declaimer, speaker, speechifier, speechmaker. *See* WORDS.

leech *noun*
One who depends on another for support without reciprocating : bloodsucker, hanger-on, parasite, sponge. *Slang:* freeloader. *See* DEPENDENCE.

leech *verb* To take advantage of the generosity of others : *Informal:* sponge. *Slang:* freeload. *See* DEPENDENCE.

leeriness *noun*
Lack of trust : distrust, doubt, mistrust, suspicion. *See* TRUST.

leery *adjective*
Lacking trust or confidence : distrustful, doubting, mistrustful, suspicious, untrusting. *See* TRUST.

lees *noun*
Matter that settles on a bottom or collects on a surface by a natural process : deposit, dreg (often used in plural), precipitate, precipitation, sediment. *See* LEFTOVER.

leeway *noun*
Suitable opportunity to accept or allow something : elbowroom, latitude, margin, play, room, scope. *See* PLACE, RESTRAINT.

left-handed *adjective*
Not being what one purports to be : ambidextrous, disingenuous, insincere, mala fide. *See* HONEST.

leftover *adjective*
Being what remains, especially after a part has been removed : remaining. *See* LEFTOVER.
leftover *noun* What remains after a part has been used or subtracted : balance, leavings, remainder, remains, remnant, residue, rest[2]. *See* LEFTOVER.

legacy *noun*
1. Any special privilege accorded a firstborn : birthright, heritage, inheritance, patrimony. *See* OWNED. **2.** Something immaterial, as a style or philosophy, that is passed from one generation to another : heritage, inheritance, tradition. *See* AFFECT.

legal *adjective*
Within, allowed by, or sanctioned by the law : innocent, lawful, legitimate, licit. *Slang:* legit. *See* LAW.

legality *noun*
The state or quality of being within the law : lawfulness, legitimacy, legitimateness, licitness. *See* LAW.

legalize *verb*
To make lawful : legitimate, legitimatize, legitimize. *See* LAW.

legation *noun*
A diplomatic office or headquarters in a foreign country : mission. *See* POLITICS.

legend *noun*
1. A traditional story or tale that has no proven factual basis : fable, myth. *See* BELIEF, REAL, RELIGION. **2.** A body of traditional beliefs and notions accumulated about a particular subject : folklore, lore, myth, mythology, mythos, tradition. *See* KNOWLEDGE.

legendary *adjective*
Of or existing only in myths : fabulous, mythic, mythical, mythologic, mythological. *See* REAL.

legerdemain *noun*
The use of skillful tricks and deceptions to produce entertainingly baffling effects : conjuration, magic, prestidigitation, sleight of hand. *See* PERFORMING ARTS.

legion *noun*
A very large number of things grouped together : army, cloud, crowd, drove, flock, horde, host, mass, mob, multitude, ruck[1], score (used in plural), swarm, throng. *See* BIG, GROUP.
legion *adjective* Amounting to or consisting of a large, indefinite number : many, multitudinous, myriad, numerous. ***Idiom:*** quite a few. *See* BIG.

legislate *verb*
To put in force or cause to be by legal authority : constitute, enact, establish, make, promulgate. *See* ACTION, MAKE, POLITICS.

legislation *noun*
The formal product of a legislative or judicial body : act, assize, bill[1], enactment, law, lex, measure, statute. *See* LAW.

legit *adjective*
Slang. Within, allowed by, or sanctioned by the law : innocent, lawful, legal, legitimate, licit. *See* LAW.

legitimacy *noun*
The state or quality of being within the law : lawfulness, legality, legitimateness, licitness. *See* LAW.

legitimate *adjective*
1. Within, allowed by, or sanctioned by the law : innocent, lawful, legal, licit. *Slang:* legit. *See* LAW. **2.** Being so legitimately : rightful, true. *See* TRUE.
legitimate *verb* To make lawful : legalize, legitimatize, legitimize. *See* LAW.

legitimateness *noun*
The state or quality of being within the law : lawfulness, legality, legitimacy, licitness. *See* LAW.

legitimatize *verb*
To make lawful : legalize, legitimate, legitimize. *See* LAW.

legitimize *verb*
To make lawful : legalize, legitimate, legitimatize. *See* LAW.

leisure *noun*
Freedom from labor, responsibility, or strain : ease, relaxation, repose, rest[1]. *See* CONTINUE.
leisurely *adjective*
Careful and slow in acting, moving, or deciding : deliberate, measured, unhurried. *See* FAST.
lemon *noun*
Informal. One that fails completely : bust, failure, fiasco, loser, washout. *Informal:* dud, flop. *Slang:* bomb. *See* THRIVE.
lend *verb*
To supply (money), especially on credit : advance, loan. *See* GIVE.
length *noun*
1. The measure of how far or long something goes in space, time, or degree : extent, reach, span, stretch. *See* BIG. **2.** An extent, measured or unmeasured, of linear space : distance, space, stretch. *Informal:* piece, way. *See* BIG. **3.** The ultimate point to which an action, thought, discussion, or policy is carried : end, extreme, limit. *See* LIMITED.
lengthen *verb*
To make or become longer : draw out, elongate, extend, prolong, prolongate, protract, spin (out), stretch (out). *Mathematics:* produce. *See* INCREASE, LONG.
lengthy *adjective*
1. Having great physical length : elongate, elongated, extended, long[1], prolonged. *See* LONG. **2.** Extending tediously beyond a standard duration : dragging, drawn-out, long[1], long-drawn-out, overlong, prolonged, protracted. *See* EXCITE, LONG.
lenience *noun*
1. Kind, forgiving, or compassionate treatment of or disposition toward others : charity, clemency, grace, leniency, lenity, mercifulness, mercy. *See* FORGIVENESS. **2.** Forbearing or lenient treatment : charitableness, charity, forbearance, indulgence, leniency, lenity, tolerance, toleration. *See* ACCEPT.
leniency *noun*
1. Kind, forgiving, or compassionate treatment of or disposition toward others : charity, clemency, grace, lenience, lenity, mercifulness, mercy. *See* FORGIVENESS. **2.** Forbearing or lenient treatment : charitableness, charity, forbearance, indulgence, lenience, lenity, tolerance, toleration. *See* ACCEPT.
lenient *adjective*
Not strict or severe : charitable, clement, easy, forbearing, indulgent, lax, merciful, soft, tolerant. *See* ACCEPT.
lenity *noun*
1. Kind, forgiving, or compassionate treatment of or disposition toward others : charity, clemency, grace, lenience, leniency, mercifulness, mercy. *See* FORGIVENESS. **2.** Forbearing or lenient treatment : charitableness, charity, forbearance, indulgence, lenience, leniency, tolerance, toleration. *See* ACCEPT.
lesbian *adjective*
Of, relating to, or having a sexual orientation to members of one's own sex : gay, homophile, homosexual. *See* SEX.
lese majesty also **lèse majesté** *noun*
Lack of proper respect : disrespect, irreverence. *See* RESPECT.
lessen *verb*
1. To grow or cause to grow gradually less : abate, decrease, diminish, drain, dwindle, ebb, let up, peter (out), rebate, reduce, tail away (*or* off), taper (off). *See* INCREASE. **2.** To make less severe or more bearable : allay, alleviate, assuage, comfort, ease, lighten[2], mitigate, palliate, relieve. *See* INCREASE.
lesser *adjective*
Below another in standing or importance : inferior, junior, low, lower[2], minor, minor-league, petty, secondary, small, subaltern, subordinate, under. *Informal:* smalltime. *See* OVER.
lesson *noun*
1. The principle taught by a fable or parable, for example : moral. *See* MEANING. **2.** An instance that warns or discourages prospective imitators : example, warning. *See* WARN.
let *verb*
1. To give one's consent to : allow, approbate, approve, authorize, consent, endorse, permit, sanction. *Informal:* OK. *See* ALLOW. **2.** To afford an opportunity for : admit, allow, permit. *See* ALLOW. **3.** To neither forbid nor prevent : allow, have, permit, suffer, tolerate. *See* ALLOW. **4.** To give temporary use of in return for payment : hire (out), lease, rent[1]. *See* TRANSACTIONS.
let down *verb* **1.** To cause to descend : depress, drop, lower[2], take down. *See* RISE. **2.** To cause unhappiness by failing to satisfy the hopes, desires, or expectations of : disappoint, discontent, disgruntle, dissatisfy. *See* HAPPY.
let in *verb* To serve as a means of entrance for : admit, intromit. *See* ENTER.
let off *verb* **1.** To discharge material, as vapor or fumes, usually suddenly and violently : emit, give, give forth, give off, give out, issue, let out, release, send forth, throw off, vent. *See*

FREE, MOVE. **2.** To free from an obligation or duty : absolve, discharge, dispense, excuse, exempt, relieve, spare. *See* FREE.

let out *verb* **1.** To discharge material, as vapor or fumes, usually suddenly and violently : emit, give, give forth, give off, give out, issue, let off, release, send forth, throw off, vent. *See* FREE, MOVE. **2.** To remove (a liquid) by a steady, gradual process : drain, draw (off), pump, tap[2]. *See* INCREASE. **3.** To disclose in a breach of confidence : betray, blab, divulge, expose, give away, reveal, tell, uncover, unveil. *Informal:* spill. *Archaic:* discover. ***Idioms:*** let slip, let the cat out of the bag, spill the beans, tell all. *See* SHOW.

let up *verb* **1.** To grow or cause to grow gradually less : abate, decrease, diminish, drain, dwindle, ebb, lessen, peter (out), rebate, reduce, tail away (*or* off), taper (off). *See* INCREASE. **2.** To become or cause to become less active or intense : abate, bate, die (away, down, off, *or* out), ease (off *or* up), ebb, fall, fall off, lapse, moderate, remit, slacken, slack off, subside, wane. *See* INCREASE. **3.** To reduce in tension, pressure, or rigidity : ease, loose, loosen, relax, slack, slacken, untighten. *See* TIGHTEN.

letdown *noun*
Unhappiness caused by the failure of one's hopes, desires, or expectations : disappointment, discontent, discontentment, disgruntlement, dissatisfaction, regret. *See* HAPPY.

let down *verb* See **let.**

lethal *adjective*
Causing or tending to cause death : deadly, deathly, fatal, mortal, vital. *See* LIVE.

lethality *noun*
The quality or condition of causing death : deadliness, fatality. *See* LIVE.

lethargic *adjective*
1. Lacking mental and physical alertness and activity : hebetudinous, sluggish, stupid, stuporous, torpid. *Slang:* dopey. *See* ACTION. **2.** Without emotion or interest : apathetic, detached, impassive, incurious, indifferent, insensible, listless, phlegmatic, stolid, unconcerned, uninterested, unresponsive. *See* FEELINGS.

lethargy *noun*
1. A deficiency in mental and physical alertness and activity : dullness, hebetude, languidness, languor, lassitude, leadenness, listlessness, sluggishness, stupor, torpidity, torpor. *See* ACTION. **2.** Lack of emotion or interest : apathy, disinterest, impassivity, incuriosity, incuriousness, indifference, insensibility, insensibleness, lassitude, listlessness, phlegm, stolidity, stolidness, unconcern, uninterest, unresponsiveness. *See* FEELINGS.

let in *verb* See **let.**

let off *verb* See **let.**

let out *verb* See **let.**

letter *noun*
A written communication directed to another : epistle, missive, note. *See* WORDS.

lettered *adjective*
1. Having an education : educated, enlightened, informed, literate. *See* KNOWLEDGE. **2.** Having or showing profound knowledge and scholarship : erudite, learned, scholarly, wise[1]. *See* KNOWLEDGE.

lettuce *noun*
Slang. Something, such as coins or printed bills, used as a medium of exchange : cash, currency, lucre, money. *Informal:* wampum. *Slang:* bread, cabbage, dough, gelt, green, jack, long green, mazuma, moola, scratch. *Chiefly British:* brass. *See* MONEY.

letup *noun*
The act or process of becoming less active or intense : abatement, ebb, remission, slackening, subsidence, wane. *See* INCREASE.

let up *verb* See **let.**

level *noun*
One of the units in a course, as on an ascending or descending scale : degree, grade, peg, point, rung, stage, step. *Informal:* notch. *See* BIG.

level *adjective* **1.** Having no irregularities, roughness, or indentations : even[1], flat, flush, planar, plane[1], smooth, straight. *See* SMOOTH. **2.** On the same plane or line : even[1], flush. *See* SAME.

level *verb* **1.** To make even, smooth, or level : even[1], flat, flatten, plane[2], smooth, straighten. *See* SMOOTH. **2.** To pull down or break up so that reconstruction is impossible : demolish, destroy, dismantle, dynamite, knock down, pull down, pulverize, raze, tear down, wreck. *Aerospace:* destruct. *See* HELP. **3.** To cause to fall, as from a shot or blow : bring down, cut down, down, drop, fell[1], flatten, floor, ground, knock down, prostrate, strike down, throw. *Slang:* deck[1]. ***Idiom:*** lay low. *See* RISE. **4.** To make equal : equalize, equate, even[1], square. *See* SAME. **5.** To move (a weapon or blow, for example) in the direction of someone or something : aim, cast, direct, head, point, set[1], train, turn, zero in. *Military:* lay[1]. *See* SEEK.

levelheaded *adjective*
Possessing, proceeding from, or exhibiting good judgment : balanced, commonsensible,

commonsensical, judicious, prudent, rational, reasonable, sagacious, sage, sane, sapient, sensible, sound[2], well-founded, well-grounded, wise[1]. *See* REASON, SANE.

leverage *noun*
The power to produce an effect by indirect means : influence, sway, weight. *Informal:* clout. *Slang:* pull. *See* AFFECT.

leviathan *noun*
One that is extraordinarily large and powerful : behemoth, giant, Goliath, jumbo, mammoth, monster, titan. *Slang:* whopper. *See* BEINGS, BIG.

levy *verb*
1. To establish and apply as compulsory : assess, exact, impose, put. *See* OBLIGATION, OVER, WILLING. **2.** To enroll compulsorily in military service : conscript, draft, induct. *See* GIVE.

levy *noun* **1.** Compulsory enrollment in military service : conscription, draft, induction. *See* GIVE. **2.** A compulsory contribution, usually of money, that is required for the support of a government : assessment, duty, impost, tariff, tax. *See* MONEY, PAY, POLITICS.

lewd *adjective*
1. Feeling or devoted to sexual love or desire : amative, amorous, concupiscent, erotic, lascivious, lecherous, libidinous, lustful, lusty, passionate, prurient, sexy. *See* SEX. **2.** Offensive to accepted standards of decency : barnyard, bawdy, broad, coarse, dirty, Fescennine, filthy, foul, gross, nasty, obscene, profane, ribald, scatologic, scatological, scurrilous, smutty, vulgar. *Slang:* raunchy. *See* DECENT.

lewdness *noun*
The quality or state of being obscene : bawdiness, coarseness, dirtiness, filthiness, foulness, grossness, obscenity, profaneness, profanity, scurrility, scurrilousness, smuttiness, vulgarity, vulgarness. *Slang:* raunch, raunchiness. *See* DECENT.

lex *noun*
The formal product of a legislative or judicial body : act, assize, bill[1], enactment, law, legislation, measure, statute. *See* LAW.

lexicon *noun*
1. An alphabetical list of words often defined or translated : dictionary, glossary, vocabulary, wordbook. *See* WORDS. **2.** Specialized expressions indigenous to a particular field, subject, trade, or subculture : argot, cant[2], dialect, idiom, jargon, language, lingo, patois, terminology, vernacular, vocabulary. *See* WORDS. **3.** All the words of a language : vocabulary, word-hoard. *See* WORDS.

liability *noun*
1. A condition of owing something to another : arrearage, arrears, indebtedness, debt, obligation. *See* PAY. **2.** The condition of being laid open to something undesirable or injurious : exposure, openness, susceptibility, susceptibleness, vulnerability, vulnerableness. *See* PROTECTION. **3.** Something, such as money, owed by one person to another : arrearage, arrears, debt, due, indebtedness, obligation. *See* OBLIGATION, PAY.

liable *adjective*
1. Legally obligated : accountable, amenable, answerable, responsible. *See* LAW. **2.** Tending to incur : open, prone, subject, susceptible, susceptive, vulnerable. *See* LIKELY. **3.** Having or showing a tendency or likelihood : apt, disposed, given, inclined, likely, prone. *See* LIKELY.

liar *noun*
One who tells lies : fabricator, fabulist, falsifier, fibber, prevaricator. *Informal:* storyteller. *Law:* perjurer. *See* TRUE.

libel *noun*
Law. The expression of injurious, malicious statements about someone : aspersion, calumniation, calumny, character assassination, defamation, denigration, detraction, scandal, slander, traducement, vilification. *See* ATTACK, CRIMES, LAW.

libel *verb* *Law.* To make defamatory statements about : asperse, backbite, calumniate, defame, malign, slander, slur, tear down, traduce, vilify. ***Idiom:*** cast aspersions on. *See* ATTACK, CRIMES, LAW.

libelous *adjective*
Law. Damaging to the reputation : calumnious, defamatory, detractive, injurious, invidious, scandalous, slanderous. *See* ATTACK, CRIMES, LAW.

liberal *adjective*
1. Not narrow or conservative in thought, expression, or conduct : broad, broad-minded, open-minded, progressive, tolerant. *See* ATTITUDE, WIDE. **2.** Favoring civil liberties and social progress : liberalistic, progressive. *See* POLITICS. **3.** Characterized by bounteous giving : free, freehanded, generous, handsome, lavish, munificent, openhanded, unsparing, unstinting. *See* GIVE.

liberal *noun* A person with liberal political opinions : liberalist, progressive. *See* POLITICS.

liberalist *noun*
A person with liberal political opinions : liberal, progressive. *See* POLITICS.

liberalistic *adjective*
Favoring civil liberties and social progress : liberal, progressive. *See* POLITICS.

liberality *noun*
The quality or state of being generous : bigheartedness, bounteousness, bountifulness, freehandedness, generosity, generousness, greatheartedness, large-heartedness, lavishness, magnanimity, magnanimousness, munificence, openhandedness, unselfishness, unsparingness. *See* GIVE.

liberate *verb*
To set at liberty : discharge, emancipate, free, loose, manumit, release. *Slang:* spring. ***Idiom:*** let loose. *See* FREE.

liberation *noun*
The state of not being in confinement or servitude : emancipation, freedom, liberty, manumission. *See* FREE.

libertine *noun*
An immoral or licentious person : profligate, rake[1], wanton. *See* SEX.

libertine *adjective* Marked by an absence of conventional restraint in sexual behavior; sexually unrestrained : easy, fast, light[2], loose, wanton, whorish. *See* SEX.

libertinism *noun*
Excessive freedom; lack of restraint : dissoluteness, dissolution, license, licentiousness, profligacy. *See* RESTRAINT.

liberty *noun*
1. The state of not being in confinement or servitude : emancipation, freedom, liberation, manumission. *See* FREE. **2.** The condition of being politically free : autonomy, freedom, independence, independency, self-government, sovereignty. *See* DEPENDENCE, FREE.
3. Departure from normal rules or procedures : freedom, license. *See* RESTRAINT.

libidinous *adjective*
Feeling or devoted to sexual love or desire : amative, amorous, concupiscent, erotic, lascivious, lecherous, lewd, lustful, lusty, passionate, prurient, sexy. *See* SEX.

libidinousness *noun*
Sexual hunger : amativeness, concupiscence, desire, eroticism, erotism, itch, lust, lustfulness, passion, prurience, pruriency. *See* DESIRE, SEX.

license *noun*
1. The approving of an action, especially when done by one in authority : allowance, approbation, approval, authorization, consent, endorsement, leave[2], permission, permit, sanction. *Informal:* OK. *See* ALLOW. **2.** Proof of legal permission to do something : permit, warrant. ***Idiom:*** piece of paper. *See* ALLOW, LAW.
3. Departure from normal rules or procedures : freedom, liberty. *See* RESTRAINT. **4.** Excessive freedom; lack of restraint : dissoluteness, dissolution, libertinism, licentiousness, profligacy. *See* RESTRAINT.

license *verb* To give authority to : accredit, authorize, commission, empower, enable, entitle, qualify. *See* ALLOW.

licentious *adjective*
Lacking in moral restraint : abandoned, dissipated, dissolute, fast, gay, incontinent, profligate, rakish, unbridled, unconstrained, uncontrolled, ungoverned, uninhibited, unrestrained, wanton, wild. *See* RESTRAINT.

licentiousness *noun*
Excessive freedom; lack of restraint : dissoluteness, dissolution, libertinism, license, profligacy. *See* RESTRAINT.

licit *adjective*
Within, allowed by, or sanctioned by the law : innocent, lawful, legal, legitimate. *Slang:* legit. *See* LAW.

licitness *noun*
The state or quality of being within the law : lawfulness, legality, legitimacy, legitimateness. *See* LAW.

lick *verb*
1. *Slang.* To punish with blows or lashes : beat, flog, hide[2], lash, thrash, whip. *Informal:* trim. *Slang:* lay into. *See* ATTACK, REWARD.
2. *Slang.* To win a victory over, as in battle or a competition : beat, best, conquer, defeat, master, overcome, prevail against (*or* over), rout, subdue, subjugate, surmount, triumph over, vanquish, worst. *Informal:* trim, whip. *Slang:* ace. ***Idioms:*** carry (*or* win) the day, get (*or* have) the best of, get (*or* have) the better of, go someone one better. *See* WIN.

lick *noun* A sudden sharp, powerful stroke : bang, blow[2], clout, crack, hit, pound, slug[3], sock, swat, thwack, welt, whack, wham, whop. *Informal:* bash, biff, bop, clip[1], wallop. *Slang:* belt, conk, paste. *See* ATTACK, STRIKE.

lickety-split *adverb*
Informal. In a rapid way : apace, fast, posthaste, quick, quickly. *Informal:* flat out, hell-for-leather, pronto. ***Idioms:*** full tilt, in a flash, in nothing flat, like a bat out of hell, like a blue streak, like a flash, like a house on fire, like a

shot, like a streak, like greased lightning, like the wind, like wildfire. *See* FAST.

licking *noun*
1. *Slang.* A punishment dealt with blows or lashes : beating, flogging, hiding, lashing, thrashing, whipping. *Informal:* trimming. *See* ATTACK, REWARD. **2.** *Slang.* The act of defeating or the condition of being defeated : beating, defeat, drubbing, overthrow, rout, thrashing, vanquishment. *Informal:* massacre, trimming, whipping. *Slang:* dusting. *See* WIN.

lie[1] *verb*
1. To be or place oneself in a prostrate or recumbent position. Also used with *down* : recline, repose, stretch (out). *See* HORIZONTAL. **2.** To take repose, as by sleeping or lying quietly. Also used with *down* : recline, repose, rest[1], stretch (out). *See* CONTINUE. **3.** To have an inherent basis : consist, dwell, exist, inhere, repose, reside, rest[1]. *See* START.

lie[2] *noun*
An untrue declaration : canard, cock-and-bull story, falsehood, falsity, fib, fiction, inveracity, misrepresentation, misstatement, prevarication, story, tale, untruth. *Informal:* fish story, tall tale. *Slang:* whopper. *See* TRUE.
lie *verb* To make untrue declarations : falsify, fib, forswear, prevaricate. *Law:* perjure. *See* TRUE.

liege *adjective*
Adhering firmly and devotedly, as to a person, a cause, or a duty : allegiant, constant, faithful, fast, firm[1], loyal, staunch, steadfast, true. *See* CONTINUE, TRUST.

lieu *noun*
Archaic. The function or position customarily occupied by another : place, stead. *See* PLACE, SUBSTITUTE.

lieutenant *noun*
A person who holds a position auxiliary to another and assumes some of the superior's responsibilities : adjutant, aide, assistant, auxiliary, coadjutant, coadjutor, deputy, helper, second[2]. *See* HELP.

life *noun*
1. A lively, emphatic, eager quality or manner : animation, bounce, brio, dash, élan, esprit, liveliness, pertness, sparkle, spirit, verve, vigor, vim, vivaciousness, vivacity, zip. *Informal:* ginger, pep, peppiness. *Slang:* oomph. *See* ACTION. **2.** A member of the human race : being, body, creature, homo, human, human being, individual, man, mortal, party, person, personage, soul. *See* BEINGS. **3.** The period during which someone or something exists : day (often used in plural), duration, existence, lifetime, span, term. *See* LIVE, TIME.

life force *noun*
The vital principle or animating force within living beings : breath, divine spark, élan vital, psyche, soul, spirit, vital force, vitality. *See* BODY.

lifeless *adjective*
1. No longer alive : asleep, dead, deceased, defunct, departed, extinct, gone, late. ***Idioms:*** at rest, pushing up daisies. *See* LIVE. **2.** Lacking liveliness, charm, or surprise : arid, aseptic, colorless, drab, dry, dull, earthbound, flat, flavorless, lackluster, lusterless, matter-of-fact, pedestrian, prosaic, spiritless, sterile, stodgy, unimaginative, uninspired. *See* EXCITE.

lifelessness *noun*
A lack of excitement, liveliness, or interest : asepticism, blandness, colorlessness, drabness, dreariness, dryness, dullness, flatness, flavorlessness, insipidity, insipidness, jejuneness, sterileness, sterility, stodginess, vapidity, vapidness, weariness. *See* EXCITE.

lifelike *adjective*
1. Accurately representing what is depicted or described : natural, naturalistic, realistic, true, true-life, truthful. *See* REAL. **2.** Described verbally in sharp and accurate detail : graphic, photographic, pictorial, picturesque, realistic, vivid. *See* SPECIFIC, WORDS.

lifetime *noun*
The period during which someone or something exists : day (often used in plural), duration, existence, life, span, term. *See* LIVE, TIME.

lift *verb*
1. To move (something) to a higher position : boost, elevate, heave, hoist, pick up, raise, rear[2], take up, uphold, uplift, upraise, uprear. *See* RISE. **2.** To move from a lower to a higher position : arise, ascend, climb, mount, rise, soar. *See* RISE. **3.** To rise up in flight. Also used with *off* : take off. *See* RISE. **4.** To disappear by or as if by rising : disperse, dissipate, scatter. *See* COLLECT, RISE. **5.** To take back or remove : recall, repeal, rescind, reverse, revoke. *See* CONTINUE, LAW, MAKE. **6.** To raise the spirits of : animate, buoy (up), elate, elevate, exhilarate, flush, inspire, inspirit, uplift. *Obsolete:* exalt. *See* HAPPY. **7.** *Informal.* To take (another's property) without permission : filch, pilfer, purloin, snatch, steal, thieve. *Informal:* swipe. *Slang:* cop, heist, hook, nip[1], pinch, rip off, snitch. ***Idiom:*** make (*or* walk) off with. *See* CRIMES, GIVE.

lift *noun* **1.** An instance of lifting or being

lifted : boost, heave, hoist. *See* RISE. **2.** High spirits : animation, elatedness, elation, euphoria, exaltation, exhilaration, inspiration, uplift. *See* HAPPY. **3.** A strong, pleasant feeling of excitement or stimulation : thrill. *Informal:* wallop. *Slang:* bang, boot[1], high, kick. *See* EXCITE.

liftoff *noun*
The act of rising in flight : takeoff. *See* RISE.

ligament *noun*
That which unites or binds : bond, knot, ligature, link, nexus, tie, vinculum, yoke. *See* CONNECT.

ligature *noun*
That which unites or binds : bond, knot, ligament, link, nexus, tie, vinculum, yoke. *See* CONNECT.

light[1] *noun*
1. Electromagnetic radiation that makes vision possible : illumination. *See* LIGHT. **2.** The act of physically illuminating or the condition of being filled with light : illumination, lighting. *See* LIGHT. **3.** The particular angle from which something is considered : angle[2], aspect, facet, frame of reference, hand, phase, regard, respect, side. *See* PERSPECTIVE. **4.** *Archaic.* The faculty of seeing : eye, eyesight, seeing, sight, vision. *See* SEE.
light *verb* **1.** To cause to burn or undergo combustion : enkindle, fire, ignite, kindle. *Slang:* torch. ***Idioms:*** set afire (*or* on fire), set fire to. *See* HOT, START. **2.** To provide, cover, or fill with light : illume, illuminate, illumine, lighten[1]. *See* LIGHT. **3.** To make lively or animated : animate, brighten, enliven. *See* HAPPY.
light *adjective* Of a light color or complexion : alabaster, fair, ivory, pale. *See* COLOR.

light[2] *adjective*
1. Having little weight; not heavy : lightweight, weightless. ***Idiom:*** light as a feather. *See* HEAVY. **2.** Of small intensity : gentle, moderate, slight, soft. *See* STRONG. **3.** Requiring little effort or exertion : easy, moderate. *See* EASY. **4.** Amusing but essentially empty and frivolous : frothy. *See* SURFACE. **5.** Free from care or worry : blithe, carefree, debonair, lighthearted. *See* CAREFUL, HAPPY. **6.** Marked by an absence of conventional restraint in sexual behavior; sexually unrestrained : easy, fast, libertine, loose, wanton, whorish. *See* SEX.
light *verb* To come to rest on the ground : alight[1], land, set down, settle, touch down. *See* MOVE.
light into *verb* *Informal.* To set upon with violent force : aggress, assail, assault, attack, beset, fall on (*or* upon), go at, have at, sail into, storm, strike. *Informal:* pitch into. *See* ATTACK.
light on (or **upon**) *verb* To find or meet by chance : bump into, chance on (*or* upon), come across, come on (*or* upon), find, happen on (*or* upon), run across, run into, stumble on (*or* upon), tumble on. *Archaic:* alight on (*or* upon). *Idiom:* meet up with. *See* MEET.

lighten[1] *verb*
1. To provide, cover, or fill with light : illume, illuminate, illumine, light[1]. *See* LIGHT. **2.** To become brighter or fairer : brighten, clear (up). *See* CLEAR.

lighten[2] *verb*
To make less severe or more bearable : allay, alleviate, assuage, comfort, ease, lessen, mitigate, palliate, relieve. *See* INCREASE.

lightheaded *adjective*
Having a sensation of whirling or falling : dizzy, giddy, reeling, vertiginous, woozy. *See* AWARENESS.

lightheadedness *noun*
A sensation of whirling or falling : dizziness, giddiness, vertiginousness, vertigo, wooziness. *See* AWARENESS.

lighthearted *adjective*
1. Free from care or worry : blithe, carefree, debonair, light[2]. *See* CAREFUL, HAPPY. **2.** Being in or showing good spirits : bright, cheerful, cheery, chipper, happy, sunny. *See* HAPPY. **3.** Given to lighthearted silliness : empty-headed, featherbrained, flighty, frivolous, frothy, giddy, harebrained, scatterbrained, silly. *Informal:* gaga. *Slang:* birdbrained, dizzy. *See* ABILITY.

lightheartedness *noun*
A state of joyful exuberance : blitheness, blithesomeness, gaiety, glee, gleefulness, hilarity, jocoseness, jocosity, jocularity, jocundity, jolliness, jollity, joviality, merriment, merriness, mirth, mirthfulness. *See* LAUGHTER.

lighting *noun*
The act of physically illuminating or the condition of being filled with light : illumination, light[1]. *See* LIGHT.

light into *verb* See **light[2]**.

light on or **upon** *verb* See **light[2]**.

lightweight *adjective*
Having little weight; not heavy : light[2], weightless. ***Idiom:*** light as a feather. *See* HEAVY.

like[1] *verb*
1. To receive pleasure from : enjoy, relish,

savor. *Informal:* go for. *Slang:* dig. *See* LIKE. **2.** To find agreeable : fancy, take to. *Chiefly British:* conceit. *See* LIKE. **3.** To have the desire or inclination to : choose, desire, please, want, will, wish. ***Idioms:*** have a mind, see fit. *See* DESIRE.

like² *adjective*
Possessing the same or almost the same characteristics : alike, analogous, comparable, corresponding, equivalent, parallel, similar, uniform. *See* SAME.

likelihood *noun*
The likeliness of a given event occurring : chance, odds, possibility, probability, prospect (used in plural). *See* LIKELY.

likely *adjective*
1. Having a chance of happening or being true : contingent, possible, probable. *See* LIKELY. **2.** Based on probability or presumption : assumptive, presumable, presumptive, probable, prospective. ***Idiom:*** taken for granted. *See* BELIEF, LIKELY. **3.** Capable of being anticipated, considered, or imagined : conceivable, earthly, imaginable, mortal, possible, thinkable. ***Idioms:*** humanly possible, within the bounds (*or* range *or* realm) of possibility. *See* POSSIBLE. **4.** Inspiring confidence or hope : cheering, encouraging, heartening, hopeful, promising. *See* HELP. **5.** Having or showing a tendency or likelihood : apt, disposed, given, inclined, liable, prone. *See* LIKELY.

liken *verb*
To represent as similar : analogize, assimilate, compare, equate, identify, match, parallel. *See* SAME.

likeness *noun*
1. The quality or state of being alike : affinity, alikeness, analogy, comparison, correspondence, parallelism, resemblance, similarity, similitude, uniformity, uniformness. *See* SAME. **2.** Something closely resembling another : carbon copy, copy, duplicate, facsimile, image, reduplication, replica, replication, reproduction, simulacrum. *Archaic:* simulacre. *Law:* counterpart. *See* SAME.

likewise *adverb*
In addition : additionally, also, besides, further, furthermore, item, more, moreover, still, too, yet. ***Idioms:*** as well, to boot. *See* INCREASE.

liking *noun*
1. The condition of being closely tied to another by affection or faith : affection, attachment, devotion, fondness, love, loyalty (used in plural). *See* CONNECT. **2.** A desire for a particular thing or activity : fancy, mind, pleasure, will. *See* LIKE.

Lilliputian also **lilliputian** *adjective*
Extremely small : diminutive, dwarf, midget, miniature, minuscule, minute², pygmy, wee. *Informal:* peewee, pintsize, pintsized, teensy, teensy-weensy, teeny, teeny-weeny, weeny. *See* BIG.

lily-livered *adjective*
Ignobly lacking in courage : chickenhearted, cowardly, craven, dastardly, faint-hearted, pusillanimous, unmanly. *Slang:* chicken, gutless, yellow, yellow-bellied. *See* FEAR.

lily-white *adjective*
1. Beyond reproach : blameless, exemplary, good, irreprehensible, irreproachable, unblamable. *See* RIGHT. **2.** Free from evil and corruption : angelic, angelical, clean, innocent, pure, sinless, unblemished, uncorrupted, undefiled, unstained, unsullied, untainted, virginal. ***Idiom:*** pure as the driven snow. *See* CLEAN, RIGHT, SEX. **3.** Free from guilt or blame : blameless, faultless, guiltless, harmless, innocent, irreproachable, unblamable. *Slang:* clean. ***Idiom:*** in the clear. *See* RIGHT.

limit *noun*
1. A demarcation point or boundary beyond which something does not extend or occur : bound² (often used in plural), confine (used in plural), end. *See* EDGE. **2.** Either of the two points at the ends of a spectrum or range : extreme. *See* EDGE. **3.** The boundary surrounding a certain area. Used in plural : bound² (used in plural), confine (used in plural), precinct (often used in plural). *See* LIMITED. **4.** Something that limits or restricts : check, circumscription, constraint, cramp², curb, inhibition, limitation, restraint, restriction, stricture, trammel. *See* LIMITED. **5.** The greatest amount or number allowed : ceiling, limitation, maximum. *See* LIMITED. **6.** The ultimate point to which an action, thought, discussion, or policy is carried : end, extreme, length. *See* LIMITED.

limit *verb* **1.** To place a limit on : circumscribe, confine, restrict. *See* LIMITED. **2.** To fix the limits of : bound², delimit, delimitate, demarcate, determine, mark (out *or* off), measure. *See* LIMITED.

limitation *noun*
1. The act of limiting or condition of being limited : circumscription, confinement, constraint, restraint, restriction. *See* LIMITED. **2.** Something that limits or restricts : check, circumscription, constraint, cramp², curb, inhi-

bition, limit, restraint, restriction, stricture, trammel. *See* LIMITED. **3.** The greatest amount or number allowed : ceiling, limit, maximum. *See* LIMITED.

limited *adjective*
1. Kept within certain limits : restricted. *See* LIMITED. **2.** Having distinct limits : definite, determinate, fixed. *See* LIMITED. **3.** Not broad or elevated in scope or understanding : little, narrow, narrow-minded, petty, small, small-minded. *See* LIMITED, WIDE. **4.** Having the restricted outlook often characteristic of geographic isolation : insular, local, narrow, narrow-minded, parochial, provincial, small-town. *See* LIMITED. **5.** Not total, unlimited, or wholehearted : modified, qualified, reserved, restricted. *See* BIG, LIMITED.

limitless *adjective*
Having no ends or limits : boundless, endless, illimitable, immeasurable, infinite, measureless, unbounded, unlimited. *See* LIMITED.

limitlessness *noun*
The state or quality of being infinite : boundlessness, immeasurability, immeasurableness, inexhaustibility, inexhaustibleness, infiniteness, infinity, measurelessness, unboundedness, unlimitedness. *See* LIMITED.

limn *verb*
To present a lifelike image of : delineate, depict, describe, express, image, picture, portray, render, represent, show. *See* SHOW.

limp *verb*
1. To walk in a lame way : halt[2], hitch, hobble. *See* MOVE. **2.** To proceed or perform in an unsteady, faltering manner : blunder, bumble[1], bungle, flounder, fudge, fumble, muddle, shuffle, stagger, stumble. *See* THRIVE.

limp *adjective* **1.** Lacking in stiffness or firmness : flabby, flaccid, floppy. *See* FLEXIBLE. **2.** Lacking energy and vitality or showing such a lack : flagging, lackadaisical, languid, languorous, leaden, listless, lymphatic, spiritless. *See* ACTION, TIRED.

limpid *adjective*
1. Admitting light so that objects beyond can be seen : clear, crystal clear, crystalline, lucid, pellucid, see-through, translucent, transparent. *See* CLEAR. **2.** Free from what obscures or dims : clear, crystal clear, crystalline, lucid, pellucid, see-through, transparent. *See* CLEAR.

limpidity *noun*
The quality of being clear and easy to perceive or understand : clarity, clearness, distinctness, limpidness, lucidity, lucidness, pellucidity, pellucidness, perspicuity, perspicuousness, plainness. *See* CLEAR.

limpidness *noun*
The quality of being clear and easy to perceive or understand : clarity, clearness, distinctness, limpidity, lucidity, lucidness, pellucidity, pellucidness, perspicuity, perspicuousness, plainness. *See* CLEAR.

line *noun*
1. An indentation or seam on the skin, especially on the face : crease, crinkle, furrow, wrinkle. *See* SMOOTH. **2.** A method used in dealing with something : approach, attack, course, modus operandi, plan, procedure, tack, technique. *See* MEANS. **3.** An official or prescribed plan or course of action : policy, procedure, program. *See* PLANNED. **4.** Activity pursued as a livelihood : art, business, calling, career, craft, employment, job, métier, occupation, profession, pursuit, trade, vocation, work. *Slang:* racket. *Archaic:* employ. *See* ACTION. **5.** A product or products bought and sold in commerce : commodity, good (used in plural), merchandise, ware. *See* MATTER, TRANSACTIONS. **6.** A group of people or things arranged in a row : column, file, queue, rank[1], row[1], string, tier. *See* GROUP. **7.** One's ancestors or their character or one's ancestral derivation : ancestry, birth, blood, bloodline, descent, extraction, family, genealogy, lineage, origin, parentage, pedigree, seed, stock. *See* KIN, PRECEDE.

line *verb* To place in or form a line or lines. Also used with *up* : align, range. *See* ORDER.

lineage *noun*
1. One's ancestors or their character or one's ancestral derivation : ancestry, birth, blood, bloodline, descent, extraction, family, genealogy, line, origin, parentage, pedigree, seed, stock. *See* KIN, PRECEDE. **2.** A group of people sharing common ancestry : clan, family, house, kindred, stock, tribe. ***Idioms:*** flesh and blood, kith and kin. *See* KIN.

lineal *adjective*
Of unbroken descent or lineage : direct. *See* CONTINUE.

lineup also **line-up** *noun*
1. A way or condition of being arranged : arrangement, categorization, classification, deployment, disposal, disposition, distribution, formation, grouping, layout, order, organization, placement, sequence. *See* ORDER. **2.** An organized list, as of procedures, activities, or events : agenda, calendar, docket, order of the day (often used in plural), program, schedule,

timetable. *See* PLANNED. **3.** A list of candidates proposed or endorsed by a political party : slate, ticket. *See* POLITICS.

linger *verb*
1. To stop temporarily and remain, as if reluctant to leave : abide, bide, pause, stay[1], tarry, wait. *See* CONTINUE. **2.** To continue to be in a place : abide, bide, remain, stay[1], tarry, wait. *Informal:* stick around. ***Idiom:*** stay put. *See* CONTINUE. **3.** To go or move slowly so that progress is hindered : dally, dawdle, delay, dilly-dally, drag, lag, loiter, poke, procrastinate, tarry, trail. ***Idioms:*** drag one's feet (*or* heels), mark time, take one's time. *See* FAST.

lingerer *noun*
One that lags : dawdler, dilly-dallier, lag, laggard, lagger, loiterer, poke, procrastinator, straggler, tarrier. *Informal:* slowpoke. *See* FAST.

lingering *adjective*
Of long duration : chronic, continuing, persistent, prolonged, protracted. *See* CONTINUE.

lingo *noun*
1. A variety of a language that differs from the standard form : argot, cant[2], dialect, jargon, patois, vernacular. *See* WORDS. **2.** Specialized expressions indigenous to a particular field, subject, trade, or subculture : argot, cant[2], dialect, idiom, jargon, language, lexicon, patois, terminology, vernacular, vocabulary. *See* WORDS.

link *noun*
1. That which unites or binds : bond, knot, ligament, ligature, nexus, tie, vinculum, yoke. *See* CONNECT. **2.** A logical or natural association between two or more things : connection, correlation, interconnection, interdependence, interrelationship, linkage, relation, relationship, tie-in. *Informal:* hookup. *See* CONNECT.
link *verb* **1.** To unite or be united in a relationship : affiliate, ally, associate, bind, combine, conjoin, connect, join, relate. *See* CONNECT. **2.** To bring or come together into a united whole : coalesce, combine, compound, concrete, conjoin, conjugate, connect, consolidate, couple, join, marry, meld, unify, unite, wed, yoke. *See* ASSEMBLE. **3.** To come or bring together in one's mind or imagination : associate, bracket, connect, correlate, couple, identify. *See* SAME.

linkage *noun*
A logical or natural association between two or more things : connection, correlation, interconnection, interdependence, interrelationship, link, relation, relationship, tie-in. *Informal:* hookup. *See* CONNECT.

lion *noun*
1. A famous person : celebrity, hero, luminary, name, notable, personage, personality. *Informal:* big name. *See* KNOWLEDGE. **2.** An important, influential person : character, dignitary, eminence, leader, nabob, notability, notable, personage. *Informal:* big-timer, heavyweight, somebody, someone, VIP. *Slang:* big shot, big wheel, bigwig, muckamuck. *See* IMPORTANT.

lip *verb*
To flow against or along : bathe, lap, lave, wash. *See* DRY.

liquefy *verb*
To change from a solid to a liquid : deliquesce, dissolve, flux, fuse, melt, run, thaw. *See* SOLID.

liquidate *verb*
1. To set right by giving what is due : clear, discharge, pay (off *or* up), satisfy, settle, square. *See* PAY. **2.** To destroy all traces of : abolish, annihilate, blot out, clear, eradicate, erase, exterminate, extinguish, extirpate, kill[1], obliterate, remove, root[1] (out *or* up), rub out, snuff out, stamp out, uproot, wipe out. ***Idioms:*** do away with, make an end of, put an end to. *See* HELP, MAKE. **3.** To get rid of, especially by banishment or execution : eliminate, eradicate, purge, remove, wipe out. ***Idioms:*** do away with, put an end to. *See* HELP, KEEP. **4.** To take the life of (a person or persons) unlawfully : destroy, finish (off), kill[1], murder, slay. *Informal:* put away. *Slang:* bump off, do in, knock off, off, rub out, waste, wipe out, zap. *See* HELP.

liquidation *noun*
1. The act or process of eliminating : clearance, elimination, eradication, purge, removal, riddance. *See* KEEP. **2.** Utter destruction : annihilation, eradication, extermination, extinction, extinguishment, extirpation, obliteration. *See* CRIMES, HELP, MAKE.

liquor *noun*
Any liquid that is fit for drinking : beverage, drink, drinkable, potable. *See* DRY.

list[1] *noun*
A series, as of names or words, printed or written down : catalog, register, roll, roster, schedule. *See* REMEMBER.
list *verb* **1.** To name or specify one by one : enumerate, itemize, numerate, tick off. *See* COUNT, SPECIFIC. **2.** To register in or as if in a book : book, catalog, enroll, inscribe, set down, write down. *See* REMEMBER.

list² *noun*
Deviation from a particular direction : cant¹, grade, gradient, heel², inclination, incline, lean¹, rake², slant, slope, tilt, tip². *See* RISE, STRAIGHT.
list *verb* To depart or cause to depart from true vertical or horizontal : cant¹, heel², incline, lean¹, rake², slant, slope, tilt, tip². *See* STRAIGHT.

list³ *verb*
Archaic. To make an effort to hear something : hark, hearken, listen. ***Idiom:*** give (*or* lend) an ear. *See* SOUNDS.

listen *verb*
1. To make an effort to hear something : hark, hearken. *Archaic:* list³. ***Idiom:*** give (*or* lend) an ear. *See* SOUNDS. **2.** To perceive by ear, usually attentively : attend, hark, hear, heed. *Archaic:* hearken. ***Idiom:*** give (*or* lend) one's ear. *See* SOUNDS.

listless *adjective*
1. Lacking energy and vitality or showing such a lack : flagging, lackadaisical, languid, languorous, leaden, limp, lymphatic, spiritless. *See* ACTION, TIRED. **2.** Without emotion or interest : apathetic, detached, impassive, incurious, indifferent, insensible, lethargic, phlegmatic, stolid, unconcerned, uninterested, unresponsive. *See* FEELINGS.

listlessness *noun*
1. A deficiency in mental and physical alertness and activity : dullness, hebetude, languidness, languor, lassitude, leadenness, lethargy, sluggishness, stupor, torpidity, torpor. *See* ACTION. **2.** Lack of emotion or interest : apathy, disinterest, impassivity, incuriosity, incuriousness, indifference, insensibility, insensibleness, lassitude, lethargy, phlegm, stolidity, stolidness, unconcern, uninterest, unresponsiveness. *See* FEELINGS.

lit *adjective*
1. *Slang.* Stupefied, excited, or muddled with alcoholic liquor. Also used with *up* : besotted, crapulent, crapulous, drunk, drunken, inebriate, inebriated, intoxicated, sodden, tipsy. *Informal:* cock-eyed, stewed. *Slang:* blind, bombed, boozed, boozy, crocked, high, loaded, looped, pickled, pixilated, plastered, potted, sloshed, smashed, soused, stinking, stinko, stoned, tight, zonked. ***Idioms:*** drunk as a skunk, half-seas over, high as a kite, in one's cups, three sheets in (*or* to) the wind. *See* DRUGS. **2.** *Slang.* Stupefied, intoxicated, or otherwise influenced by the taking of drugs. Also used with *up* : drugged. *Informal:* doped. *Slang:* high, hopped-up, potted, spaced-out, stoned, turned-on, wiped-out, zonked. *See* DRUGS.

litany *noun*
A formula of words used in praying : collect², orison, prayer¹, rogation (often used in plural). *See* RELIGION.

literal *adjective*
Employing the very same words as another : verbal, verbatim, word-for-word. *See* SAME.

literary *adjective*
Characterized by a narrow concern for book learning and formal rules, without knowledge or experience of practical matters : academic, bookish, donnish, formalistic, inkhorn, pedantic, pedantical, scholastic. *See* ATTITUDE, FLEXIBLE, TEACH.

literate *adjective*
Having an education : educated, enlightened, informed, lettered. *See* KNOWLEDGE.

litigable *adjective*
Law. Subject to legal proceedings : *Law:* actionable, prosecutable, triable. *See* LAW.

litigate *verb*
To institute or subject to legal proceedings : law, prosecute, sue. ***Idiom:*** bring suit. *See* LAW.

litigious *adjective*
Given to arguing : argumentative, combative, contentious, disputatious, eristic, polemic, polemical, quarrelsome, scrappy. *See* CONFLICT.

litigiousness *noun*
The quality or state of being argumentative : argumentativeness, combativeness, contentiousness, disputatiousness, scrappiness. *See* CONFLICT.

litter *noun*
The offspring, as of an animal or a bird, for example, that are the result of one breeding season : brood, young. *See* KIN.

little *adjective*
1. Notably below average in amount, size, or scope : bantam, petite, small, smallish. *See* BIG. **2.** Not of great importance : inconsequent, inconsequential, insignificant, trivial, unimportant. *See* BIG. **3.** Not broad or elevated in scope or understanding : limited, narrow, narrow-minded, petty, small, small-minded. *See* LIMITED, WIDE. **4.** Not yet large in size because of incomplete growth : small. *See* YOUTH.
little *adverb* At rare intervals : infrequently, occasionally, rarely, seldom, sporadically. ***Idioms:*** hardly (*or* scarcely) ever, once in a blue moon. *See* USUAL.

littlest *adjective*
Comprising the least possible : minimal, minimum, smallest. *See* BIG.
liturgical *adjective*
Of or characterized by ceremony : ceremonial, ceremonious, formal, ritual, ritualistic. *See* RITUAL.
liturgy *noun*
A formal act or set of acts prescribed by ritual : ceremonial, ceremony, observance, office, rite, ritual, service. *See* RITUAL.
livable also **liveable** *adjective*
Fit to live in : habitable, inhabitable. *See* COMFORT.
live[1] *verb*
1. To have reality or life : be, breathe, exist, subsist. *See* BE. **2.** To have as one's domicile, usually for an extended period : abide, domicile, dwell, house, reside. *See* PLACE. **3.** To maintain existence in a certain way : feed, subsist. *See* INGESTION. **4.** To go through (life) in a certain way : lead, pass, pursue. *See* BE.
live[2] *adjective*
1. Marked by or exhibiting life : alive, animate, animated, living, vital. *See* LIVE. **2.** Of great current interest : red-hot. *Informal:* hot. *See* EXCITE.
liveable *adjective* See **livable.**
livelihood *noun*
The means needed to support life : alimentation, alimony, bread, bread and butter, keep, living, maintenance, subsistence, support, sustenance, upkeep. *See* MONEY.
liveliness *noun*
A lively, emphatic, eager quality or manner : animation, bounce, brio, dash, élan, esprit, life, pertness, sparkle, spirit, verve, vigor, vim, vivaciousness, vivacity, zip. *Informal:* ginger, pep, peppiness. *Slang:* oomph. *See* ACTION.
lively *adjective*
1. Possessing, exerting, or displaying energy : active, brisk, dynamic, dynamical, energetic, forceful, kinetic, sprightly, strenuous, vigorous. *Informal:* peppy. *See* ACTION. **2.** Very brisk, alert, and full of high spirits : animated, bouncy, chipper, dashing, high-spirited, pert, spirited, vivacious. *Informal:* peppy. ***Idioms:*** bright-eyed and bushy-tailed, full of life. *See* ACTION. **3.** Disposed to action : active, brisk, driving, dynamic, dynamical, energetic, enterprising, sprightly, spry, vigorous, zippy. *Informal:* peppy, snappy. *See* ACTION.
live wire *noun*
Informal. An intensely energetic, enthusiastic person : dynamo, hustler. *Informal:* eager beaver, go-getter. *See* CONCERN.
livid *adjective*
Lacking color : ashen, ashy, bloodless, cadaverous, colorless, lurid, pale, pallid, pasty, sallow, wan, waxen. *See* COLORS.
living *adjective*
1. Having existence or life : alive, around, existent, existing, extant. *See* LIVE. **2.** Marked by or exhibiting life : alive, animate, animated, live[2], vital. *See* LIVE.
living *noun* The means needed to support life : alimentation, alimony, bread, bread and butter, keep, livelihood, maintenance, subsistence, support, sustenance, upkeep. *See* MONEY.
living hell *noun*
Excruciating punishment : hell, persecution, torment, torture. ***Idiom:*** tortures of the damned. *See* REWARD.
load *noun*
1. Something carried physically : burden[1], cargo, freight, haul. *Sports:* impost. *See* HEAVY, OVER. **2.** A quantity of explosive put into a weapon : charge. *See* EXPLOSION. **3.** *Informal.* An indeterminately great amount or number. Often used in plural : jillion, million (often used in plural), multiplicity, ream, trillion. *Informal:* bushel, gob[1] (often used in plural), heap (often used in plural), lot, oodles, passel, peck[2], scad (often used in plural), slew, wad, zillion. *See* BIG.
load *verb* **1.** To place a burden or heavy load on : burden[1], charge, cumber, encumber, freight, lade, saddle, tax, weight. *See* OVER. **2.** To make or become full; put as much into as can be held : charge, fill, freight, heap, pack, pile. *See* FULL. **3.** To fill to overflowing : heap, lade, pile. *See* FULL. **4.** To fill to excess by compressing or squeezing tightly : cram, crowd, jam, mob, pack, stuff. *Informal:* jam-pack. *See* FULL, TIGHTEN. **5.** To put (explosive material) into a weapon : charge. *See* PUT IN. **6.** To give an inaccurate view of by representing falsely or misleadingly : belie, color, distort, falsify, misrepresent, misstate, pervert, twist, warp, wrench, wrest. ***Idiom:*** give a false coloring to. *See* TRUE. **7.** To make impure or inferior by deceptively adding foreign substances : adulterate, debase, doctor, sophisticate. *See* CLEAN.
loaded *adjective*
1. Burdened by a weighty load : heavy, heavy-laden, laden. *See* FULL. **2.** Mixed with other substances : adulterated, alloyed, doctored, impure, sophisticated. *See* CLEAN. **3.** *Slang.* Stupefied, excited, or muddled with alcoholic

liquor : besotted, crapulent, crapulous, drunk, drunken, inebriate, inebriated, intoxicated, sodden, tipsy. *Informal:* cock-eyed, stewed. *Slang:* blind, bombed, boozed, boozy, crocked, high, lit (up), looped, pickled, pixilated, plastered, potted, sloshed, smashed, soused, stinking, stinko, stoned, tight, zonked. ***Idioms:*** drunk as a skunk, half-seas over, high as a kite, in one's cups, three sheets in (*or* to) the wind. *See* DRUGS. **4.** *Slang.* Possessing a large amount of money, land, or other material possessions : affluent, flush, moneyed, rich, wealthy. ***Idioms:*** having money to burn, in the money, made of money, rolling in money. *See* RICH.

loaf *verb*
To pass time without working or in avoiding work : bum[1] (around), idle, laze, loiter, lounge, shirk. *Slang:* diddle[2], goldbrick, goof (off). *See* INDUSTRIOUS.

loafer *noun*
A self-indulgent person who spends time avoiding work or other useful activity : bum[1], drone[1], fainéant, good-for-nothing, idler, layabout, ne'er-do-well, no-good, slugabed, sluggard, wastrel. *Informal:* do-little, do-nothing, lazybones, slug[2]. *Slang:* slouch. *See* INDUSTRIOUS.

loan *verb*
To supply (money), especially on credit : advance, lend. *See* GIVE.

loath also **loth** *adjective*
Not inclined or willing to do or undertake : averse, disinclined, indisposed, reluctant, unwilling. *See* WILLING.

loathe *verb*
To regard with extreme dislike and hostility : abhor, abominate, despise, detest, execrate, hate. *See* LOVE.

loathing *noun*
Extreme hostility and dislike : abhorrence, abomination, antipathy, aversion, detestation, hate, hatred, horror, repellence, repellency, repugnance, repugnancy, repulsion, revulsion. *See* LOVE.

loathsome *adjective*
So objectionable as to elicit despisal or deserve condemnation : abhorrent, abominable, antipathetic, contemptible, despicable, despisable, detestable, disgusting, filthy, foul, infamous, lousy, low, mean[2], nasty, nefarious, obnoxious, odious, repugnant, rotten, shabby, vile, wretched. *See* GOOD.

local *adjective*
1. Confined to a particular location or site : localized. *See* LIMITED. **2.** Having the restricted outlook often characteristic of geographic isolation : insular, limited, narrow, narrow-minded, parochial, provincial, small-town. *See* LIMITED.

locale *noun*
1. A surrounding area : environment, environs, locality, neighborhood, precinct (used in plural), surroundings, vicinity. *See* NEAR, PLACE. **2.** A particular geographic area : locality, location, place. *See* PLACE. **3.** The place where an action or event occurs : scene, setting, site, stage. *See* PLACE.

locality *noun*
1. A particular geographic area : locale, location, place. *See* PLACE. **2.** A part of the earth's surface : area, belt, district, neighborhood, quarter, region, tract, zone. *Informal:* neck of the woods. *See* TERRITORY. **3.** A surrounding site : area, neighborhood, vicinity. *See* NEAR, PLACE. **4.** A surrounding area : environment, environs, locale, neighborhood, precinct (used in plural), surroundings, vicinity. *See* NEAR, PLACE.

localized *adjective*
Confined to a particular location or site : local. *See* LIMITED.

locate *verb*
1. To look for and discover : find, pinpoint, spot. *See* GET. **2.** To put in or assign to a certain position or location : emplace, install, place, position, set[1], site, situate, spot. *See* PLACE.

location *noun*
1. One's place and direction relative to one's surroundings : bearing (often used in plural), orientation, position, situation. *See* PLACE. **2.** A particular geographic area : locale, locality, place. *See* PLACE. **3.** The place where a person or thing is located : emplacement, locus, placement, position, site, situation. *See* PLACE. **4.** A particular portion of space chosen for something : locus, place, point, spot. *See* PLACE.

lock *verb*
1. To shut in with or as if with bars : bar, confine, wall. *See* FREE. **2.** To put in jail. Also used with *up* : confine, detain, immure, imprison, incarcerate, intern, jail. *See* FREE.

lockup *noun*
Informal. A place for the confinement of persons in lawful detention : brig, house of correction, jail, keep, penitentiary, prison. *Informal:* pen[3]. *Slang:* big house, can, clink, cooler, coop, hoosegow, joint, jug, pokey[1], slammer, stir[2]. *Chiefly Regional:* calaboose. *See* FREE.

loco *adjective*
Slang. Afflicted with or exhibiting irrationality and mental unsoundness : brainsick, crazy, daft, demented, disordered, distraught, dotty, insane, lunatic, mad, maniac, maniacal, mentally ill, moonstruck, off, touched, unbalanced, unsound, wrong. *Informal:* bonkers, cracked, daffy, gaga, loony. *Slang:* bananas, batty, buggy, cuckoo, fruity, nuts, nutty, screwy, wacky. *Chiefly British:* crackers. *Law:* non compos mentis. *Idioms:* around the bend, crazy as a loon, mad as a hatter, not all there, nutty as a fruitcake, off (*or* out of) one's head, off one's rocker, of unsound mind, out of one's mind, sick in the head, stark raving mad. *See* SANE.

locus *noun*
1. The place where a person or thing is located : emplacement, location, placement, position, site, situation. *See* PLACE. **2.** A particular portion of space chosen for something : location, place, point, spot. *See* PLACE.

locution *noun*
1. A sound or combination of sounds that symbolizes and communicates a meaning : expression, term, word. *See* WORDS. **2.** A word or group of words forming a unit and conveying meaning : expression, phrase. *See* WORDS.

lodge *verb*
1. To provide with often temporary lodging : accommodate, bed (down), berth, bestow, billet, board, bunk[1], domicile, harbor, house, put up, quarter, room. *See* PROTECTION. **2.** To remain as a guest or lodger : sojourn, stay[1], visit. *See* PLACE. **3.** To become or cause to become stuck or lodged : catch, fix, stick. *See* MOVE. **4.** To implant so deeply as to make change nearly impossible : embed, entrench, fasten, fix, infix, ingrain, root[1]. *See* MOVE.

lodging *noun*
1. Dwellings in general : housing, shelter. *Idiom:* a roof over one's head. *See* PROTECTION. **2.** A building or shelter where one lives. Often used in plural : abode, domicile, dwelling, habitation, home, house, place, residence. *Chiefly British:* dig (used in plural). *See* PROTECTION.

loftiest *adjective*
Of, being, located at, or forming the top : highest, top, topmost, upmost, uppermost. *See* HIGH.

loftiness *noun*
The quality of being arrogant : arrogance, haughtiness, hauteur, insolence, lordliness, overbearingness, presumption, pride, pridefulness, proudness, superciliousness, superiority. *See* ATTITUDE.

lofty *adjective*
1. Imposingly high : aerial, airy, sky-high, soaring, towering. *See* HIGH. **2.** Exceedingly dignified in form, tone, or style : elevated, eloquent, exalted, grand, high, high-flown. *See* HIGH, STYLE. **3.** Raised to or occupying a high position or rank : august, elevated, exalted, grand, high-ranking. *See* RISE. **4.** Overly convinced of one's own superiority and importance : arrogant, haughty, high-and-mighty, insolent, lordly, overbearing, overweening, prideful, proud, supercilious, superior. *Idiom:* on one's high horse. *See* ATTITUDE.

logic *noun*
1. Exact, valid, and rational reasoning : ratiocination, rationality, reason. *See* REASON.
2. What is sound or reasonable : rationale, rationality, rationalness, reason, sense. *Idiom:* rhyme or reason. *See* REASON.

logical *adjective*
1. Consistent with reason and intellect : consequent, intelligent, rational, reasonable. *See* REASON. **2.** Able to reason validly : analytic, analytical, ratiocinative, rational. *See* REASON.

loiter *verb*
1. To go or move slowly so that progress is hindered : dally, dawdle, delay, dilly-dally, drag, lag, linger, poke, procrastinate, tarry, trail. *Idioms:* drag one's feet (*or* heels), mark time, take one's time. *See* FAST. **2.** To pass time without working or in avoiding work : bum[1] (around), idle, laze, loaf, lounge, shirk. *Slang:* diddle[2], goldbrick, goof (off). *See* INDUSTRIOUS.

loiterer *noun*
One that lags : dawdler, dilly-dallier, lag, laggard, lagger, lingerer, poke, procrastinator, straggler, tarrier. *Informal:* slowpoke. *See* FAST.

loll *verb*
1. To take on or move with an awkward, slovenly posture : slouch, slump. *See* MOVE, POSTURE. **2.** To hang limply, loosely, and carelessly : droop, flop, lop[2], sag, slouch, wilt. *See* HANG. **3.** To sit or lie with the limbs spread out awkwardly : drape, sprawl, spread-eagle, straddle. *See* POSTURE.

lone *adjective*
1. Lacking the company of others : alone, companionless, lonely, lonesome, single, solitary, unaccompanied. *See* INCLUDE. **2.** Without a spouse : fancy-free, footloose, single, sole,

spouseless, unattached, unmarried, unwed. *Idiom:* footloose and fancy-free. *See* MARRIAGE. **3.** Alone in a given category : one, only, particular, separate, single, singular, sole, solitary, unique. ***Idioms:*** first and last, one and only. *See* INCLUDE. **4.** Set away from all others : alone, apart, detached, isolate, isolated, removed, solitary. *See* INCLUDE.

loneliness *noun*
The quality or state of being alone : aloneness, isolation, singleness, solitariness, solitude. *See* INCLUDE.

lonely *adjective*
1. Lacking the company of others : alone, companionless, lone, lonesome, single, solitary, unaccompanied. *See* INCLUDE. **2.** Empty of people : deserted, desolate, forlorn, godforsaken, lonesome, unfrequented. *See* FULL. **3.** Far from centers of human population : back, insular, isolated, lonesome, obscure, outlying, out-of-the-way, remote, removed, secluded, solitary. ***Idiom:*** off the beaten path (*or* track). *See* NEAR. **4.** Dejected due to the awareness of being alone : desolate, forlorn, lonesome, lorn. *See* HAPPY.

lonesome *adjective*
1. Dejected due to the awareness of being alone : desolate, forlorn, lonely, lorn. *See* HAPPY. **2.** Lacking the company of others : alone, companionless, lone, lonely, single, solitary, unaccompanied. *See* INCLUDE. **3.** Empty of people : deserted, desolate, forlorn, godforsaken, lonely, unfrequented. *See* FULL. **4.** Far from centers of human population : back, insular, isolated, lonely, obscure, outlying, out-of-the-way, remote, removed, secluded, solitary. ***Idiom:*** off the beaten path (*or* track). *See* NEAR.

long¹ *adjective*
1. Having great physical length : elongate, elongated, extended, lengthy, prolonged. *See* LONG. **2.** Having a rather great upward projection : high, tall. *See* HIGH. **3.** Having many syllables : polysyllabic, sesquipedal, sesquipedalian. *See* LONG. **4.** Extending tediously beyond a standard duration : dragging, drawn-out, lengthy, long-drawn-out, overlong, prolonged, protracted. *See* EXCITE, LONG.
long *noun* A long time : eon, eternity, year (used in plural). *Informal:* age (used in plural), blue moon. ***Idioms:*** forever and a day, forever and ever, month of Sundays. *See* TIME.

long² *verb*
To have a strong longing for : ache, covet, desire, hanker, pant, pine, want, wish, yearn. *Informal:* hone². *See* DESIRE.

long-drawn-out *adjective*
Extending tediously beyond a standard duration : dragging, drawn-out, lengthy, long¹, overlong, prolonged, protracted. *See* EXCITE, LONG.

long green *noun*
Slang. Something, such as coins or printed bills, used as a medium of exchange : cash, currency, lucre, money. *Informal:* wampum. *Slang:* bread, cabbage, dough, gelt, green, jack, lettuce, mazuma, moola, scratch. *Chiefly British:* brass. *See* MONEY.

longing *noun*
A strong wanting of what promises enjoyment or pleasure : appetence, appetency, appetite, craving, desire, hunger, itch, lust, thirst, wish, yearning, yen. *See* DESIRE.

long-lasting *adjective*
Existing or remaining in the same state for an indefinitely long time : abiding, continuing, durable, enduring, lasting, long-lived, long-standing, old, perdurable, perennial, permanent, persistent. *See* CONTINUE.

long-lived *adjective*
Existing or remaining in the same state for an indefinitely long time : abiding, continuing, durable, enduring, lasting, long-lasting, long-standing, old, perdurable, perennial, permanent, persistent. *See* CONTINUE.

long-standing *adjective*
Existing or remaining in the same state for an indefinitely long time : abiding, continuing, durable, enduring, lasting, long-lasting, long-lived, old, perdurable, perennial, permanent, persistent. *See* CONTINUE.

long-suffering *adjective*
Enduring or capable of enduring hardship or inconvenience without complaint : forbearing, patient, resigned. *See* ACCEPT.
long-suffering *noun* The capacity of enduring hardship or inconvenience without complaint : forbearance, patience, resignation, tolerance. *See* ACCEPT.

long suit *noun*
Something at which a person excels : forte, métier, specialty, strong point, strong suit. *Slang:* bag, thing. *See* ABILITY.

long-winded *adjective*
Using or containing an excessive number of words : diffuse, periphrastic, pleonastic, prolix, redundant, verbose, wordy. *See* EXCESS, STYLE, WORDS.

long-windedness *noun*
Words or the use of words in excess of those needed for clarity or precision : diffuseness, diffusion, pleonasm, prolixity, redundancy, verbiage, verboseness, verbosity, windiness, wordage, wordiness. *See* EXCESS, STYLE, WORDS.

look *verb*
1. To direct the eyes on an object : consider, contemplate, eye, view. ***Idiom:*** clap (*or* lay *or* set) one's eyes on. *See* SEE. **2.** To try to find something : cast about, hunt, quest, search, seek. *See* SEEK. **3.** To have the appearance of : appear, seem, sound[1]. ***Idiom:*** strike one as (being). *See* SURFACE.
look after *verb* To have the care and supervision of : attend, care for, mind, minister to, see to, tend[2], watch. ***Idioms:*** keep an eye on, look out for, take care (*or* charge) of, take under one's wing. *See* CARE FOR.
look for *verb* To look forward to confidently : anticipate, await, bargain for (*or* on), count on, depend on (*or* upon), expect, wait (for). *Informal:* figure on. *See* SURPRISE.
look in *verb* To go to or seek out the company of in order to socialize : call, come by, come over, drop by, drop in, look up, pop in, run in, see, stop (by *or* in), visit. ***Idiom:*** pay a visit. *See* SEEK.
look into *verb* To go into or through for the purpose of making discoveries or acquiring information : delve, dig, explore, inquire, investigate, probe, reconnoiter, scout[1]. *See* INVESTIGATE.
look on (or **upon)** *verb* To have the face or front turned in a specific direction : face, front. *See* PRECEDE.
look out *verb* To be careful : beware, mind, watch out. ***Idioms:*** be on guard, be on the lookout, keep an eye peeled, take care (*or* heed). *See* AWARENESS, CAREFUL.
look over *verb* To view broadly or from a height : overlook, scan, survey. *See* SEE.
look up *verb* To go to or seek out the company of in order to socialize : call, come by, come over, drop by, drop in, look in, pop in, run in, see, stop (by *or* in), visit. ***Idiom:*** pay a visit. *See* SEEK.
look *noun* **1.** An act of directing the eyes on an object : contemplation, regard, sight, view. *See* SEE. **2.** A disposition of the facial features that conveys meaning, feeling, or mood : aspect, cast, countenance, expression, face, visage. *See* EXPRESS. **3.** An outward appearance : aspect, countenance, face, physiognomy, surface, visage. *See* SURFACE. **4.** The way something or someone looks : appearance, aspect, mien. *See* SURFACE.

look after *verb* See **look.**

looker *noun*
Slang. A person regarded as physically attractive : beauty, belle (used of a woman), lovely, stunner. *Slang:* babe, doll, hunk (used of a man), knockout, stud (used of a man). *See* BEAUTIFUL.

looker-on *noun*
Someone who observes : beholder, bystander, observer, onlooker, spectator, watcher. *See* AWARENESS, SEE.

look for *verb* See **look.**

look-in *noun*
An act or an instance of going or coming to see another : call, visit, visitation. *See* SEEK.

look in *verb* See **look.**

look into *verb* See **look.**

look on or **upon** *verb* See **look.**

lookout *noun*
1. The act of carefully watching : surveillance, vigil, vigilance, watch. ***Idiom:*** watch and ward. *See* AWARENESS. **2.** A high structure or place commanding a wide view : observatory, outlook, overlook. *See* AWARENESS. **3.** A person or special body of persons assigned to provide protection or keep watch over, for example : guard, picket, protector, sentinel, sentry, ward, watch. *See* AWARENESS, SAFETY. **4.** That which is or can be seen : outlook, panorama, perspective, prospect, scene, sight, view, vista. *See* SEE. **5.** Something that concerns or involves one personally : affair, business, concern. *See* RELEVANT.

look out *verb* See **look.**

look over *verb* See **look.**

look up *verb* See **look.**

loom *verb*
1. To come into view : appear, emerge, issue, materialize, show. ***Idioms:*** make (*or* put in) an appearance, meet the eye. *See* SEE. **2.** To be imminent : brew, hang over, impend, lower[1], menace, overhang, threaten. *See* NEAR.

loon *noun*
Informal. A person regarded as strange, eccentric, or crazy : crackpot, crazy, eccentric, lunatic. *Informal:* crank, loony. *Slang:* cuckoo, ding-a-ling, dingbat, kook, nut, screwball, weirdie, weirdo. *See* WISE.

looney *adjective & noun* See **loony.**

loony or **looney** also **luny** *adjective*
1. *Informal.* So senseless as to be laughable : absurd, foolish, harebrained, idiotic, imbecilic, insane, lunatic, mad, moronic, nonsensical, pre-

posterous, silly, softheaded, tomfool, unearthly, zany. *Informal:* cockeyed, crazy, loopy. *Slang:* balmy², dippy, dopey, jerky, sappy, wacky. *See* ABILITY, KNOWLEDGE. **2.** *Informal.* Afflicted with or exhibiting irrationality and mental unsoundness : brainsick, crazy, daft, demented, disordered, distraught, dotty, insane, lunatic, mad, maniac, maniacal, mentally ill, moonstruck, off, touched, unbalanced, unsound, wrong. *Informal:* bonkers, cracked, daffy, gaga. *Slang:* bananas, batty, buggy, cuckoo, fruity, loco, nuts, nutty, screwy, wacky. *Chiefly British:* crackers. *Law:* non compos mentis. ***Idioms:*** around the bend, crazy as a loon, mad as a hatter, not all there, nutty as a fruitcake, off (*or* out of) one's head, off one's rocker, of unsound mind, out of one's mind, sick in the head, stark raving mad. *See* SANE.

loony or **looney** also **luny** *noun Informal.* A person regarded as strange, eccentric, or crazy : crackpot, crazy, eccentric, lunatic. *Informal:* crank, loon. *Slang:* cuckoo, ding-a-ling, dingbat, kook, nut, screwball, weirdie, weirdo. *See* WISE.

loop *noun*

1. A length of line folded over and joined at the ends so as to form a curve or circle : eye, ring¹. *See* STRAIGHT. **2.** A group of athletic teams that play each other : association, circuit, conference, league. *See* GROUP.

looped *adjective*

Slang. Stupefied, excited, or muddled with alcoholic liquor : besotted, crapulent, crapulous, drunk, drunken, inebriate, inebriated, intoxicated, sodden, tipsy. *Informal:* cock-eyed, stewed. *Slang:* blind, bombed, boozed, boozy, crocked, high, lit (up), loaded, pickled, pixilated, plastered, potted, sloshed, smashed, soused, stinking, stinko, stoned, tight, zonked. ***Idioms:*** drunk as a skunk, half-seas over, high as a kite, in one's cups, three sheets in (*or* to) the wind. *See* DRUGS.

loopy *adjective*

Informal. So senseless as to be laughable : absurd, foolish, harebrained, idiotic, imbecilic, insane, lunatic, mad, moronic, nonsensical, preposterous, silly, softheaded, tomfool, unearthly, zany. *Informal:* cockeyed, crazy, loony. *Slang:* balmy², dippy, dopey, jerky, sappy, wacky. *See* ABILITY, KNOWLEDGE.

loose *adjective*

1. Not tautly bound, held, or fastened : lax, relaxed, slack. *See* TIGHTEN. **2.** Able to move about at will without bounds or restraint : free, unconfined, unrestrained. ***Idioms:*** at large, at liberty, free as a bird, on the loose. *See* FREE. **3.** Marked by an absence of conventional restraint in sexual behavior; sexually unrestrained : easy, fast, libertine, light², wanton, whorish. *See* SEX. **4.** Lacking literal exactness : free, inexact. *See* PRECISE.

loose *verb* **1.** To set at liberty : discharge, emancipate, free, liberate, manumit, release. *Slang:* spring. ***Idiom:*** let loose. *See* FREE. **2.** To free from ties or fasteners : disengage, loosen, slip, unbind, unclasp, undo, unfasten, unloose, unloosen, untie. *See* TIGHTEN. **3.** To launch with great force : fire, hurtle, project, propel, shoot. ***Idiom:*** let fly. *See* MOVE. **4.** To reduce in tension, pressure, or rigidity : ease, let up, loosen, relax, slack, slacken, untighten. *See* TIGHTEN.

loosen *verb*

1. To free from ties or fasteners : disengage, loose, slip, unbind, unclasp, undo, unfasten, unloose, unloosen, untie. *See* TIGHTEN. **2.** To reduce in tension, pressure, or rigidity : ease, let up, loose, relax, slack, slacken, untighten. *See* TIGHTEN.

loot *noun*

Goods or property seized unlawfully, especially by a victor in wartime : booty, pillage, plunder, spoil (used in plural). *Slang:* boodle. *Nautical:* prize². *See* CRIMES, GIVE.

loot *verb* To rob of goods by force, especially in time of war : depredate, despoil, havoc, pillage, plunder, ransack, rape, ravage, sack², spoliate, strip¹. *Archaic:* harrow, spoil. *See* CRIMES, GIVE.

lop¹ *verb*

To decrease, as in length or amount, by or as if by severing or excising : chop¹, clip¹, crop, cut, cut back, cut down, lower², pare, prune, shear, slash, trim, truncate. *See* INCREASE.

lop² *verb*

To hang limply, loosely, and carelessly : droop, flop, loll, sag, slouch, wilt. *See* HANG.

lope *verb*

To move with a steady easy gait faster than a walk but slower than a run : jog, trot. *See* MOVE.

lope *noun* A person's steady easy gait that is faster than a walk but slower than a run : jog, trot. *See* MOVE.

loquacious *adjective*

Given to conversation : chatty, conversational, garrulous, talkative, talky, voluble. *Slang:* gabby. *See* WORDS.

lordliness *noun*

The quality of being arrogant : arrogance,

haughtiness, hauteur, insolence, loftiness, overbearingness, presumption, pride, pridefulness, proudness, superciliousness, superiority. *See* ATTITUDE.

lordly *adjective*

1. Exercising authority : authoritative, commanding, dominant, masterful. *See* OVER, STRONG. **2.** Large and impressive in size, scope, or extent : august, baronial, grand, grandiose, imposing, magnific, magnificent, majestic, noble, princely, regal, royal, splendid, stately, sublime, superb. *See* BIG, GOOD. **3.** Overly convinced of one's own superiority and importance : arrogant, haughty, high-and-mighty, insolent, lofty, overbearing, overweening, prideful, proud, supercilious, superior. ***Idiom:*** on one's high horse. *See* ATTITUDE.

lore *noun*

1. That which is known about a specific subject or situation : data, fact (used in plural), information, intelligence, knowledge. *See* KNOWLEDGE. **2.** A body of traditional beliefs and notions accumulated about a particular subject : folklore, legend, myth, mythology, mythos, tradition. *See* KNOWLEDGE. **3.** That which is known; the sum of what has been perceived, discovered, or inferred : information, knowledge, wisdom. *See* KNOWLEDGE.

lorn *adjective*

1. Having been given up and left alone : abandoned, bereft, derelict, deserted, desolate, forlorn, forsaken. *See* KEEP. **2.** Dejected due to the awareness of being alone : desolate, forlorn, lonely, lonesome. *See* HAPPY.

lose *verb*

1. To be unable to find : mislay, misplace. *See* GET. **2.** To suffer the loss of : drop, forfeit. ***Idiom:*** kiss good-by to. *See* GET. **3.** To fail to take advantage of : miss, waste. ***Idioms:*** let slip, let slip through one's fingers, lose out on. *See* USED. **4.** To get away from (a pursuer) : elude, evade, shake off, slip, throw off. *Slang:* shake. ***Idiom:*** give someone the shake (*or* slip). *See* SEEK.

loser *noun*

1. One that fails completely : bust, failure, fiasco, washout. *Informal:* dud, flop, lemon. *Slang:* bomb. *See* THRIVE. **2.** A person living under very unhappy circumstances : miserable, underdog, underprivileged, unfortunate, wretch. *See* RICH.

losing *noun*

The act or an instance of losing something : loss, misplacement. *See* GET.

loss *noun*

1. The act or an instance of losing something : losing, misplacement. *See* GET. **2.** The condition of being deprived of what one once had or ought to have : deprival, deprivation, dispossession, divestiture, privation. *See* GIVE, RICH.

lost *adjective*

1. Unable to find the correct way or place to go : astray, disoriented, stray. *See* SEEK. **2.** No longer in one's possession : gone, missing. *See* GET. **3.** No longer in use, force, or operation : dead, defunct, extinct, vanished. *See* LIVE, NEW. **4.** Sentenced to terrible, irrevocable punishment : condemned, doomed, fated, foredoomed. *See* LAW, RELIGION. **5.** Condemned, especially to hell : damned, doomed. ***Idiom:*** gone to blazes. *See* REWARD.

lot *noun*

1. That which is allotted : allocation, allotment, allowance, dole, measure, part, portion, quantum, quota, ration, share, split. *Informal:* cut. *Slang:* divvy. *See* COLLECT. **2.** That which is inevitably destined : destiny, fate, fortune, kismet, portion, predestination. *See* CERTAIN. **3.** A number of individuals making up or considered a unit : array, band[2], batch, bevy, body, bunch, bundle, clump, cluster, clutch[2], collection, group, knot, party, set[2]. *See* GROUP. **4.** A class that is defined by the common attribute or attributes possessed by all its members : breed, cast, description, feather, ilk, kind[2], manner, mold, nature, order, sort, species, stamp, stripe, type, variety. *Informal:* persuasion. *See* GROUP. **5.** *Informal.* A great deal : abundance, mass, mountain, much, plenty, profusion, wealth, world. *Informal:* barrel, heap, pack, peck[2], pile. *Regional:* power, sight. *See* BIG. **6.** *Informal.* An indeterminately great amount or number : jillion, million (often used in plural), multiplicity, ream, trillion. *Informal:* bushel, gob[1] (often used in plural), heap (often used in plural), load (often used in plural), oodles, passel, peck[2], scad (often used in plural), slew, wad, zillion. *See* BIG. **7.** *Informal.* An indefinite amount or extent : deal, quantity. *See* BIG. **8.** A piece of land : parcel, plot, tract. *See* TERRITORY.

lot *verb* To set aside or distribute as a share : admeasure, allocate, allot, allow, apportion, assign, give, measure out, mete (out). *See* COLLECT.

loth *adjective* See **loath.**

Lothario also **lothario** *noun*

1. A man amorously attentive to women :

amorist, Casanova, Don Juan, gallant, lady's man, Romeo. *See* SEX. **2.** A man who seduces women : debaucher, Don Juan, seducer. *See* SEX.

loud *adjective*

1. Marked by extremely high volume and intensity of sound : blaring, deafening, earsplitting, roaring, stentorian. *See* SOUNDS. **2.** Tastelessly showy : brummagem, chintzy, flashy, garish, gaudy, glaring, meretricious, tawdry, tinsel. *Informal:* tacky[2]. *See* STYLE.

loudmouthed *adjective*

Informal. Offensively loud and insistent : blatant, boisterous, clamorous, obstreperous, strident, vociferous. *See* SOUNDS.

lounge *verb*

To pass time without working or in avoiding work : bum[1] (around), idle, laze, loaf, loiter, shirk. *Slang:* diddle[2], goldbrick, goof (off). *See* INDUSTRIOUS.

lour *verb & noun* See **lower[1].**

loury *adjective* See **lowery.**

louse up *verb*

Slang. To harm irreparably through inept handling; make a mess : ball up, blunder, boggle, botch, bungle, foul up, fumble, gum up, mess up, mishandle, mismanage, muddle, muff, spoil. *Informal:* bollix up, muck up. *Slang:* blow[1], goof up, screw up, snafu. *Idiom:* make a muck of. *See* CORRECT, HELP.

lousy *adjective*

1. So objectionable as to elicit despisal or deserve condemnation : abhorrent, abominable, antipathetic, contemptible, despicable, despisable, detestable, disgusting, filthy, foul, infamous, loathsome, low, mean[2], nasty, nefarious, obnoxious, odious, repugnant, rotten, shabby, vile, wretched. *See* GOOD. **2.** Of decidedly inferior quality : base[2], cheap, miserable, paltry, poor, rotten, shoddy, sleazy, trashy. *Informal:* cheesy. *Slang:* crummy, schlocky. *See* GOOD.

lout *noun*

A large, ungainly, and dull-witted person : gawk, hulk, lump[1], oaf, ox. *Informal:* lummox. *Slang:* klutz, lug[1], meatball, meathead. *See* ABILITY.

lovable *adjective*

Easy to love : adorable, sweet. *See* GOOD, LIKE, LOVE.

love *noun*

1. Deep and ardent affection : adoration, devotion, worship. *See* LIKE, LOVE. **2.** The passionate affection and desire felt by lovers for each other : amorousness, fancy, passion, romance. *See* LOVE, SEX. **3.** An intimate sexual relationship between two people : affair, amour, love affair, romance. *See* LOVE, SEX. **4.** The condition of being closely tied to another by affection or faith : affection, attachment, devotion, fondness, liking, loyalty (used in plural). *See* CONNECT. **5.** A person who is much loved : beloved, darling, dear, honey, minion, precious, sweet, sweetheart, truelove. *Informal:* sweetie. *Idiom:* light of one's life. *See* LOVE. **6.** A strong, enthusiastic liking for something : love affair, passion, romance. *See* LOVE.

love *verb* To feel deep devoted love for : adore, worship. *See* LOVE.

love affair *noun*

1. An intimate sexual relationship between two people : affair, amour, love, romance. *See* LOVE, SEX. **2.** A strong, enthusiastic liking for something : love, passion, romance. *See* LOVE.

loved *adjective*

Regarded with much love and tenderness : beloved, darling, dear, precious. *See* LOVE.

lovely *adjective*

1. Pleasing to the eye or mind : attractive, bewitching, enchanting, engaging, enticing, fascinating, fetching, glamorous, prepossessing, pretty, sweet, taking, tempting, winning, winsome. *See* LIKE. **2.** Having qualities that delight the eye : attractive, beauteous, beautiful, comely, fair, good-looking, gorgeous, handsome, pretty, pulchritudinous, ravishing, sightly, stunning. *Scots:* bonny. *Idiom:* easy on the eyes. *See* BEAUTIFUL.

lovely *noun* A person regarded as physically attractive : beauty, belle (used of a woman), stunner. *Slang:* babe, doll, hunk (used of a man), knockout, looker, stud (used of a man). *See* BEAUTIFUL.

lover *noun*

1. A person's regular sexual partner : paramour. *See* SEX. **2.** One who ardently admires : admirer, devotee, enthusiast, fancier. *Informal:* fan[2]. *See* LIKE, LOVE, PRAISE.

loving *adjective*

Feeling and expressing affection : affectionate, devoted, doting, fond. *See* ATTITUDE, LOVE.

low *adjective*

1. Cut to reveal the wearer's neck, chest, and back : décolleté, low-cut, low-neck, low-necked, plunging. *See* HIGH. **2.** Below another in standing or importance : inferior, junior, lesser, lower[2], minor, minor-league, petty, secondary, small, subaltern, subordinate, under. *Informal:* smalltime. *See* OVER. **3.** So objectionable as to elicit despisal or deserve condemnation : abhorrent, abominable, antipathetic, contemptible, despicable, despisable, detestable, disgusting, filthy, foul, infamous, loathsome, lousy, mean², nasty, nefarious, obnoxious, odious, repugnant, rotten, shabby, vile, wretched. *See* GOOD. **4.** Having or proceeding from low moral standards : base², ignoble, low-down, mean², sordid, squalid, vile. *See* RIGHT. **5.** In low spirits : blue, dejected, depressed, desolate, dispirited, down, downcast, downhearted, dull, dysphoric, gloomy, heavy-hearted, melancholic, melancholy, sad, spiritless, tristful, unhappy, wistful. *Idiom:* down at (*or* in) the mouth. *See* HAPPY. **6.** Low in price : cheap, inexpensive, low-cost, low-priced. *See* MONEY, VALUE. **7.** Being a sound produced by a relatively small frequency of vibrations : alto, bass, contralto, deep, low-pitched. *See* SOUNDS. **8.** Not irritating, strident, or loud : hushed, low-key, low-keyed, quiet, small, soft, subdued, whispery. *See* SOUNDS. **9.** Tending or intending to belittle : deprecative, deprecatory, depreciative, depreciatory, derogative, derogatory, detractive, disparaging, pejorative, slighting, uncomplimentary. *See* PRAISE. **10.** Affected or tending to be affected with minor health problems : ailing, indisposed, mean², off-color, rocky, sickly. *Idiom:* under the weather. *See* HEALTH.

low *noun* A very low level, position, or degree : bottom, rock bottom. *See* HIGH.

low-cost *adjective*
Low in price : cheap, inexpensive, low, low-priced. *See* MONEY, VALUE.

low-cut *adjective*
Cut to reveal the wearer's neck, chest, and back : décolleté, low, low-neck, low-necked, plunging. *See* HIGH.

low-down *adjective*
Having or proceeding from low moral standards : base², ignoble, low, mean², sordid, squalid, vile. *See* RIGHT.

lower¹ also **lour** *verb*
1. To wrinkle one's brow, as in thought, puzzlement, or displeasure : frown, glower, scowl. *Idiom:* look black. *See* EXPRESS. **2.** To stare fixedly and angrily : glare, glower, scowl. *Idiom:* look daggers at. *See* EXPRESS, SEE. **3.** To be imminent : brew, hang over, impend, loom, menace, overhang, threaten. *See* NEAR.

lower also **lour** *noun* The act of wrinkling the brow, as in thought, puzzlement, or displeasure : black look, frown, glower, scowl. *See* EXPRESS.

lower² *adjective*
Below another in standing or importance : inferior, junior, lesser, low, minor, minor-league, petty, secondary, small, subaltern, subordinate, under. *Informal:* smalltime. *See* OVER.

lower *verb* **1.** To cause to descend : depress, drop, let down, take down. *See* RISE. **2.** To decrease, as in length or amount, by or as if by severing or excising : chop¹, clip¹, crop, cut, cut back, cut down, lop¹, pare, prune, shear, slash, trim, truncate. *See* INCREASE. **3.** To become or make less in price or value : cheapen, depreciate, depress, devaluate, devalue, downgrade, mark down, reduce, write down. *See* INCREASE, MONEY. **4.** To bring oneself down to a lower level of behavior : descend, sink, stoop. *See* RISE.

lowermost *adjective*
Opposite to or farthest from the top : bottom, lowest, nethermost, undermost. *See* OVER.

lowery also **loury** *adjective*
Characterized by or expressive of a foreboding somberness : dark, sullen. *See* WARN.

lowest *adjective*
Opposite to or farthest from the top : bottom, lowermost, nethermost, undermost. *See* OVER.

low-grade *adjective*
Of low or lower quality : common, inferior, low-quality, mean², mediocre, second-class, second-rate, shabby, substandard. *See* BETTER.

low-key *adjective*
Not irritating, strident, or loud : hushed, low, low-keyed, quiet, small, soft, subdued, whispery. *See* SOUNDS.

low-keyed *adjective*
Not irritating, strident, or loud : hushed, low, low-key, quiet, small, soft, subdued, whispery. *See* SOUNDS.

lowliness *noun*
Lack of vanity or self-importance : humbleness, humility, meekness, modesty. *See* ATTITUDE, BIG, SELF-LOVE.

lowly *adjective*
1. Lacking high station or birth : baseborn, common, déclassé, declassed, humble, ignoble, mean², plebeian, unwashed, vulgar. *Archaic:* base². *See* OVER. **2.** Of little distinction : humble, mean², simple. *See* PLAIN. **3.** Having or expressing feelings of humility : humble, meek, modest. *See* ATTITUDE, BIG, SELF-LOVE.

low-neck *adjective*
Cut to reveal the wearer's neck, chest, and back : décolleté, low, low-cut, low-necked, plunging. *See* HIGH.

low-necked *adjective*
Cut to reveal the wearer's neck, chest, and back : décolleté, low, low-cut, low-neck, plunging. *See* HIGH.

low-pitched *adjective*
Being a sound produced by a relatively small frequency of vibrations : alto, bass, contralto, deep, low. *See* SOUNDS.

low-priced *adjective*
Low in price : cheap, inexpensive, low, low-cost. *See* MONEY, VALUE.

low-quality *adjective*
Of low or lower quality : common, inferior, low-grade, mean[2], mediocre, second-class, second-rate, shabby, substandard. *See* BETTER.

loyal *adjective*
Adhering firmly and devotedly, as to a person, a cause, or a duty : allegiant, constant, faithful, fast, firm[1], liege, staunch, steadfast, true. *See* CONTINUE, TRUST.

loyalty *noun*
1. Faithfulness or devotion to a person, a cause, obligations, or duties : allegiance, constancy, faithfulness, fealty, fidelity, steadfastness. *See* CONTINUE, OBLIGATION. **2.** The condition of being closely tied to another by affection or faith. Used in plural : affection, attachment, devotion, fondness, liking, love. *See* CONNECT.

lubricious *adjective*
1. So smooth and glassy as to offer insecure hold or footing : slick, slippery, slithery. *Idiom:* slippery as an eel. *See* SMOOTH.
2. Marked by treachery or deceit : devious, disingenuous, duplicitous, guileful, indirect, shifty, sneaky, underhand, underhanded. *See* HONEST.

lucent *adjective*
Giving off or reflecting light readily or in large amounts : beamy, bright, brilliant, effulgent, incandescent, irradiant, lambent, luminous, lustrous, radiant, refulgent, shiny. *See* LIGHT.

lucid *adjective*
1. Mentally healthy : compos mentis, rational, sane. *Idioms:* all there, in one's right mind, of sound mind. *See* SANE. **2.** Admitting light so that objects beyond can be seen : clear, crystal clear, crystalline, limpid, pellucid, see-through, translucent, transparent. *See* CLEAR. **3.** Free from what obscures or dims : clear, crystal clear, crystalline, limpid, pellucid, see-through, transparent. *See* CLEAR.

lucidity *noun*
1. The quality of being clear and easy to perceive or understand : clarity, clearness, distinctness, limpidity, limpidness, lucidness, pellucidity, pellucidness, perspicuity, perspicuousness, plainness. *See* CLEAR. **2.** A healthy mental state : lucidness, mind, reason, saneness, sanity, sense (often used in plural), soundness, wit (used in plural). *Slang:* marble (used in plural). *See* SANE.

lucidness *noun*
1. The quality of being clear and easy to perceive or understand : clarity, clearness, distinctness, limpidity, limpidness, lucidity, pellucidity, pellucidness, perspicuity, perspicuousness, plainness. *See* CLEAR. **2.** A healthy mental state : lucidity, mind, reason, saneness, sanity, sense (often used in plural), soundness, wit (used in plural). *Slang:* marble (used in plural). *See* SANE.

luck *noun*
1. The quality shared by random, unintended, or unpredictable events or this quality regarded as the cause of such events : chance, fortuitousness, fortuity, fortune, hap, hazard. *See* CERTAIN. **2.** Success attained as a result of chance : fortunateness, fortune, luckiness. *Idiom:* good fortune (*or* luck). *See* LUCK.

luckiness *noun*
Success attained as a result of chance : fortunateness, fortune, luck. *Idiom:* good fortune (*or* luck). *See* LUCK.

luckless *adjective*
Involving or undergoing chance misfortune : hapless, ill-fated, ill-starred, star-crossed, unfortunate, unhappy, unlucky, untoward. *See* LUCK.

lucky *adjective*
Characterized by luck or good fortune : fortunate, happy, providential. *See* LUCK.

lucrative *adjective*
Affording profit : advantageous, fat, moneymaking, profitable, remunerative, rewarding. *See* GET.

lucre *noun*
Something, such as coins or printed bills, used as a medium of exchange : cash, currency, money. *Informal:* wampum. *Slang:* bread, cabbage, dough, gelt, green, jack, lettuce, long green, mazuma, moola, scratch. *Chiefly British:* brass. *See* MONEY.

lucubrate *verb*
To apply one's mind to the acquisition or production of knowledge : con, study. *See* TEACH.

lucubration *noun*
A careful considering of a matter : advisement, calculation, consideration, deliberation, study. *See* THOUGHTS.

ludicrous *adjective*
Deserving laughter : comic, comical, farcical, funny, laughable, laughing, ridiculous, risible. *See* LAUGHTER.

ludicrousness *noun*
The quality of being laughable or comical : comedy, comicality, comicalness, drollery, drollness, farcicality, funniness, humor, humorousness, jocoseness, jocosity, jocularity, ridiculousness, wit, wittiness, zaniness. *See* LAUGHTER.

lug[1] *noun*
Slang. A large, ungainly, and dull-witted person : gawk, hulk, lout, oaf, ox. *Informal:* lummox. *Slang:* klutz, meatball, meathead. *See* ABILITY.

lug[2] *verb*
To move while supporting : bear, carry, convey, transport. *Informal:* tote. *Slang:* schlep. *See* OVER.

lugubrious *adjective*
Full of or expressive of sorrow : doleful, dolorous, mournful, plaintive, rueful, sad, sorrowful, woebegone, woeful. *See* HAPPY.

lukewarm *adjective*
Lacking warmth, interest, enthusiasm, or involvement : halfhearted, tepid, unenthusiastic. *See* ATTITUDE, HOT.

lull *verb*
To make or become calm : allay, balm, becalm, calm (down), quiet, settle, still, tranquilize. *See* CALM.
lull *noun* An absence of motion or disturbance : calm, calmness, hush, peace, peacefulness, placidity, placidness, quiet, quietness, serenity, stillness, tranquillity, untroubledness. *See* CALM.

lumber *verb*
To move heavily : clump, galumph, hulk, lump[1], stump. *See* MOVE.

luminary *noun*
A famous person : celebrity, hero, lion, name, notable, personage, personality. *Informal:* big name. *See* KNOWLEDGE.

luminesce *verb*
To shine brightly and steadily but without a flame : gleam, glow, incandesce. *See* LIGHT.

luminosity *noun*
Exceptional brightness and clarity, as of a cut and polished stone : brilliance, brilliancy, fire, radiance. *See* LIGHT.

luminous *adjective*
Giving off or reflecting light readily or in large amounts : beamy, bright, brilliant, effulgent, incandescent, irradiant, lambent, lucent, lustrous, radiant, refulgent, shiny. *See* LIGHT.

lummox *noun*
Informal. A large, ungainly, and dull-witted person : gawk, hulk, lout, lump[1], oaf, ox. *Slang:* klutz, lug[1], meatball, meathead. *See* ABILITY.

lump[1] *noun*
1. An irregularly shaped mass of indefinite size : chunk, clod, clump, gob[1], hunch, nugget, wad. *Informal:* hunk. *See* PART. **2.** An unevenness or elevation on a surface : bump, hump, knob, knot, nub, protuberance. *See* CONVEX. **3.** A small raised area of skin resulting from a light blow or an insect sting, for example : bump, bunch, knot, swelling. *See* CONVEX. **4.** A large, ungainly, and dull-witted person : gawk, hulk, lout, oaf, ox. *Informal:* lummox. *Slang:* klutz, lug, meatball, meathead. *See* ABILITY. **5.** *Informal.* Something justly deserved. Used in plural : comeuppance, desert[2] (often used in plural), due, guerdon, recompense, reward, wage (often used in plural). ***Idioms:*** what is coming to one, what one has coming. *See* REWARD.
lump *verb* **1.** To put into a disordered pile : bank[1], drift, heap, hill, mound, pile (up), stack. *See* ORDER. **2.** To move heavily : clump, galumph, hulk, lumber, stump. *See* MOVE.

lump[2] *verb*
Informal. To put up with : abide, accept, bear, brook[2], endure, go, stand (for), stomach, suffer, support, sustain, swallow, take, tolerate, withstand. ***Idioms:*** take it, take it lying down. *See* ACCEPT.

lumpenproletariat *noun*
A group of persons regarded as the lowest class : dreg (often used in plural), rabble, ragtag and bobtail, riffraff, trash. *Slang:* scum. ***Idioms:*** scum of the earth, tag and rag, the great unwashed. *See* OVER, RICH.

lumpish *adjective*
1. Lacking dexterity and grace in physical movement : awkward, clumsy, gawky, graceless, inept, maladroit, ungainly, ungraceful. *Slang:* klutzy. ***Idiom:*** all thumbs. *See* ABILITY. **2.** Unwieldy or clumsy, especially due to excess weight : cumbersome, cumbrous, heavy, lumpy, ponderous. *See* EASY, HEAVY.

lumpy *adjective*
Unwieldy or clumsy, especially due to excess weight : cumbersome, cumbrous, heavy, lumpish, ponderous. *See* EASY, HEAVY.

lunacy *noun*
1. Serious mental illness or disorder impairing a person's capacity to function normally and

safely : brainsickness, craziness, dementia, derangement, disturbance, insaneness, insanity, madness, mental illness, psychopathy, unbalance. *Psychiatry:* mania. *Psychology:* aberration, alienation. *See* SANE. **2.** Foolish behavior : absurdity, folly, foolery, foolishness, idiocy, imbecility, insanity, madness, nonsense, preposterousness, senselessness, silliness, tomfoolery, zaniness. *Informal:* craziness. *See* ABILITY.

lunatic *adjective*
1. Afflicted with or exhibiting irrationality and mental unsoundness : brainsick, crazy, daft, demented, disordered, distraught, dotty, insane, mad, maniac, maniacal, mentally ill, moonstruck, off, touched, unbalanced, unsound, wrong. *Informal:* bonkers, cracked, daffy, gaga, loony. *Slang:* bananas, batty, buggy, cuckoo, fruity, loco, nuts, nutty, screwy, wacky. *Chiefly British:* crackers. *Law:* non compos mentis. *Idioms:* around the bend, crazy as a loon, mad as a hatter, not all there, nutty as a fruitcake, off (*or* out of) one's head, off one's rocker, of unsound mind, out of one's mind, sick in the head, stark raving mad. *See* SANE. **2.** So senseless as to be laughable : absurd, foolish, harebrained, idiotic, imbecilic, insane, mad, moronic, nonsensical, preposterous, silly, softheaded, tomfool, unearthly, zany. *Informal:* cockeyed, crazy, loony, loopy. *Slang:* balmy[2], dippy, dopey, jerky, sappy, wacky. *See* ABILITY, KNOWLEDGE.
lunatic *noun* A person regarded as strange, eccentric, or crazy : crackpot, crazy, eccentric. *Informal:* crank, loon, loony. *Slang:* cuckoo, ding-a-ling, dingbat, kook, nut, screwball, weirdie, weirdo. *See* WISE.

lunge *verb*
1. To move or thrust at, under, or into the midst of with sudden force : dive, plunge, wade in (*or* into). *See* ENTER. **2.** To move or advance against strong resistance : drive, forge[2], plunge. *See* MOVE.

luny *adjective & noun* See **loony.**

lurch *verb*
1. To walk unsteadily : falter, reel, stagger, stumble, teeter, totter, weave, wobble. *See* MOVE. **2.** To lean suddenly, unsteadily, and erratically from the vertical axis : pitch, roll, seesaw, yaw. *See* MOVE, STRAIGHT. **3.** To move or cause to move with a sudden abrupt motion : jerk, snap, twitch, wrench, yank. *See* MOVE, PUSH.
lurch *noun* A sudden motion, such as a pull : jerk, snap, tug, twitch, wrench, yank. *See* MOVE, PUSH.

lure *noun*
1. Something that attracts, especially with the promise of pleasure or reward : allurement, bait, come-on, enticement, inducement, inveiglement, invitation, seduction, temptation. *See* LIKE. **2.** Something that leads one into a place or situation from which escape is difficult : bait, snare, trap. *See* LIKE, SAFETY. **3.** The power or quality of attracting : allure, allurement, appeal, attraction, attractiveness, call, charisma, charm, draw, enchantment, enticement, fascination, glamour, magnetism, witchery. *Informal:* pull. *See* LIKE.
lure *verb* **1.** To beguile or draw into a wrong or foolish course of action : allure, entice, inveigle, seduce, tempt. *Idiom:* lead astray. *See* PERSUASION. **2.** To direct or impel to oneself by some quality or action : allure, appeal, attract, draw, entice, magnetize, take. *Informal:* pull. *See* LIKE.

lurer *noun*
One that seduces : allurer, charmer, enticer, inveigler, seducer, tempter. *See* PERSUASION.

lurid *adjective*
1. Shockingly repellent : ghastly, grim, grisly, gruesome, hideous, horrible, horrid, macabre. *See* BEAUTIFUL. **2.** Lacking color : ashen, ashy, bloodless, cadaverous, colorless, livid, pale, pallid, pasty, sallow, wan, waxen. *See* COLORS.

luring *adjective*
Tending to seduce : alluring, bewitching, come-hither, enticing, inveigling, inviting, seductive, siren, tempting, witching. *See* LIKE, PERSUASION, SEX.

lurk *verb*
To move silently and furtively : creep, glide, mouse, prowl, pussyfoot, skulk, slide, slink, slip, snake, sneak, steal. *Slang:* gumshoe. *See* MOVE.

luscious *adjective*
1. Highly pleasing, especially to the sense of taste : ambrosial, appetizing, delectable, delicious, heavenly, savory, scrumptious, tasteful, tasty, toothsome. *Slang:* yummy. *See* GOOD, INGESTION. **2.** Giving great pleasure or delight : charming, delectable, delicious, delightful, enchanting, heavenly. *Informal:* darling. *See* GOOD, HAPPY, LIKE.

lush[1] *noun*
1. Growing profusely : dense, heavy, luxuriant, profuse, rank[2], thick. *See* BIG. **2.** Marked by unrestrained abundance : extravagant,

exuberant, lavish, luxuriant, opulent, prodigal, profuse, riotous, superabundant. *See* BIG, EXCESS. **3.** Characterized by extravagant, ostentatious magnificence : lavish, luxuriant, luxurious, opulent, palatial, plush, rich, sumptuous. *Informal:* plushy. *See* RICH.

lush² *noun*
Slang. A person who is habitually drunk : drunk, drunkard, inebriate, sot, tippler. *Slang:* boozehound, boozer, rummy¹, soak, souse, sponge, stiff. *See* DRUGS.
lush *verb Slang.* To take alcoholic liquor, especially excessively or habitually : drink, guzzle, imbibe, tipple. *Informal:* nip². *Slang:* booze, soak, tank up. *Idioms:* bend the elbow, hit the bottle. *See* DRUGS.

lust *noun*
1. Sexual hunger : amativeness, concupiscence, desire, eroticism, erotism, itch, libidinousness, lustfulness, passion, prurience, pruriency. *See* DESIRE, SEX. **2.** A strong wanting of what promises enjoyment or pleasure : appetence, appetency, appetite, craving, desire, hunger, itch, longing, thirst, wish, yearning, yen. *See* DESIRE.
lust *verb* To have a greedy, obsessive desire : crave, hunger, itch, thirst. *See* DESIRE.

luster *noun*
1. A radiant brightness or glow, usually due to light reflected from a smooth surface : burnish, glaze, gloss, polish, sheen, shine, sleekness. *See* LIGHT. **2.** A position of exalted widely recognized importance : distinction, eminence, eminency, fame, glory, illustriousness, mark, notability, note, preeminence, prestige, prominence, prominency, renown. *See* IMPORTANT, KNOWLEDGE, RESPECT.

lusterless *adjective*
1. Lacking gloss and luster : dim, dull, flat, lackluster, mat. *See* LIGHT. **2.** Lacking liveliness, charm, or surprise : arid, aseptic, colorless, drab, dry, dull, earthbound, flat, flavorless, lackluster, lifeless, matter-of-fact, pedestrian, prosaic, spiritless, sterile, stodgy, unimaginative, uninspired. *See* EXCITE.

lustful *adjective*
Feeling or devoted to sexual love or desire : amative, amorous, concupiscent, erotic, lascivious, lecherous, lewd, libidinous, lusty, passionate, prurient, sexy. *See* SEX.

lustfulness *noun*
Sexual hunger : amativeness, concupiscence, desire, eroticism, erotism, itch, libidinousness, lust, passion, prurience, pruriency. *See* DESIRE, SEX.

lustral *adjective*
Serving to purify of sin : expiatory, lustrative, purgative, purgatorial, purificatory. *See* CLEAN, RELIGION.

lustrate *verb*
To free from sin, guilt, or defilement : cleanse, purge, purify. *See* CLEAN, RELIGION.

lustration *noun*
A freeing from sin, guilt, or defilement : purgation, purification. *See* CLEAN, RELIGION.

lustrative *adjective*
Serving to purify of sin : expiatory, lustral, purgative, purgatorial, purificatory. *See* CLEAN, RELIGION.

lustrous *adjective*
1. Having a high, radiant sheen : glassy, gleaming, glistening, glossy, polished, shining, shiny. *See* LIGHT. **2.** Giving off or reflecting light readily or in large amounts : beamy, bright, brilliant, effulgent, incandescent, irradiant, lambent, lucent, luminous, radiant, refulgent, shiny. *See* LIGHT.

lusty *adjective*
1. Full of vigor : able-bodied, iron, red-blooded, robust, strapping, sturdy, vigorous, vital. *See* STRONG. **2.** Feeling or devoted to sexual love or desire : amative, amorous, concupiscent, erotic, lascivious, lecherous, lewd, libidinous, lustful, passionate, prurient, sexy. *See* SEX.

luxuriant *adjective*
1. Growing profusely : dense, heavy, lush¹, profuse, rank², thick. *See* BIG. **2.** Given to or marked by unrestrained abundance : extravagant, exuberant, lavish, lush¹, opulent, prodigal, profuse, riotous, superabundant. *See* BIG, EXCESS. **3.** Characterized by extravagant, ostentatious magnificence : lavish, lush¹, luxurious, opulent, palatial, plush, rich, sumptuous. *Informal:* plushy. *See* RICH.

luxuriate *verb*
To take extravagant pleasure : bask, indulge, revel, roll, rollick, wallow. *See* LIKE.

luxurious *adjective*
Characterized by extravagant, ostentatious magnificence : lavish, lush¹, luxuriant, opulent, palatial, plush, rich, sumptuous. *Informal:* plushy. *See* RICH.

luxury *noun*
Something costly and unnecessary : extravagance, extravagancy, frill. *See* SAVE.

lying *adjective*
Given to or marked by deliberate concealment or misrepresentation of the truth : deceitful,

dishonest, mendacious, untruthful. *See* HONEST.

lying-in *noun*
The act or process of bringing forth young : accouchement, birth, birthing, childbearing, childbirth, delivery, labor, parturition, travail. *See* START.

lymphatic *adjective*
Lacking energy and vitality or showing such a lack : flagging, lackadaisical, languid, languorous, leaden, limp, listless, spiritless. *See* ACTION, TIRED.

lyric *adjective*
Of, relating to, or having the characteristics of poetry : poetic, poetical. *See* WORDS.

lyricism *noun*
Something likened to poetry, as in form or style : poem, poetry. *See* STYLE, WORDS.

·M·

macabre *adjective*
1. Susceptible to or marked by preoccupation with unwholesome matters : morbid, sick, unhealthy, unwholesome. *See* GOOD. **2.** Shockingly repellent : ghastly, grim, grisly, gruesome, hideous, horrible, horrid, lurid. *See* BEAUTIFUL.

machinate *verb*
To work out a secret plan to achieve an evil or illegal end : collude, connive, conspire, intrigue, plot, scheme. *See* CRIMES, PLANNED.

machination *noun*
A secret plan to achieve an evil or illegal end : cabal, collusion, connivance, conspiracy, intrigue, plot, scheme. *See* CRIMES, PLANNED.

macho *adjective*
Of, characteristic of, or befitting the male sex : male, manful, manlike, manly, mannish, masculine, virile. *See* GENDER.

macrocosm *noun*
The totality of all existing things : cosmos, creation, nature, universe, world. *See* MATTER, PART.

mad *adjective*
1. Feeling or showing anger : angry, choleric, indignant. *Informal:* sore. *Idiom:* hot under the collar. *See* FEELINGS. **2.** Afflicted with or exhibiting irrationality and mental unsoundness : brainsick, crazy, daft, demented, disordered, distraught, dotty, insane, lunatic, maniac, maniacal, mentally ill, moonstruck, off, touched, unbalanced, unsound, wrong. *Informal:* bonkers, cracked, daffy, gaga, loony. *Slang:* bananas, batty, buggy, cuckoo, fruity, loco, nuts, nutty, screwy, wacky. *Chiefly British:* crackers. *Law:* non compos mentis. *Idioms:* around the bend, crazy as a loon, mad as a hatter, not all there, nutty as a fruitcake, off (*or* out of) one's head, off one's rocker, of unsound mind, out of one's mind, sick in the head, stark raving mad. *See* SANE. **3.** So senseless as to be laughable : absurd, foolish, harebrained, idiotic, imbecilic, insane, lunatic, moronic, nonsensical, preposterous, silly, softheaded, tomfool, unearthly, zany. *Informal:* cockeyed, crazy, loony, loopy. *Slang:* balmy[2], dippy, dopey, jerky, sappy, wacky. *See* ABILITY, KNOWLEDGE. **4.** Showing or having enthusiasm : ardent, enthusiastic, fervent, keen[1], rabid, warm, zealous. *Informal:* crazy. *Slang:* gung ho, nuts. *See* CONCERN. **5.** Marked by extreme excitement, confusion, or agitation : delirious, frantic, frenetic, frenzied, wild. *Archaic:* madding. *See* CALM.

madcap *adjective*
Characterized by unthinking boldness and haste : brash, foolhardy, harum-scarum, hasty, headlong, hotheaded, ill-considered, impetuous, improvident, impulsive, incautious, precipitant, precipitate, rash[1], reckless, slapdash, temerarious, unconsidered. *See* CAREFUL.

madden *verb*
1. To cause to feel or show anger : anger, burn (up), enrage, incense[1], infuriate, provoke. *Idioms:* make one hot under the collar, make one's blood boil, put one's back up. *See* FEELINGS. **2.** To make insane : craze, derange, unbalance, unhinge. *See* SANE.

madding *adjective*
Archaic. Marked by extreme excitement, confusion, or agitation : delirious, frantic, frenetic, frenzied, mad, wild. *See* CALM.

made-to-order *adjective*
Made according to the specifications of the

buyer : custom, custom-built, customized, custom-made, tailor-made. *See* AGREE.

made-up *adjective*
1. Consisting or suggestive of fiction : fanciful, fantastic, fantastical, fictional, fictitious, fictive, invented. *See* REAL. **2.** Being fictitious and not real, as a name : assumed, pseudonymous. *See* TRUE.

madness *noun*
1. Serious mental illness or disorder impairing a person's capacity to function normally and safely : brainsickness, craziness, dementia, derangement, disturbance, insaneness, insanity, lunacy, mental illness, psychopathy, unbalance. *Psychiatry:* mania. *Psychology:* aberration, alienation. *See* SANE. **2.** Foolish behavior : absurdity, folly, foolery, foolishness, idiocy, imbecility, insanity, lunacy, nonsense, preposterousness, senselessness, silliness, tomfoolery, zaniness. *Informal:* craziness. *See* ABILITY.

magazine *noun*
A place where something is deposited for safekeeping : archive, depository, repository, store, storehouse, warehouse. *See* KEEP.

magic *noun*
1. The use of supernatural powers to influence or predict events : conjuration, sorcery, sortilege, thaumaturgy, theurgy, witchcraft, witchery, witching, wizardry. *See* SUPERNATURAL. **2.** An object or power that one uses to cause often evil events : charm, evil eye, spell[2]. *Slang:* whammy. *See* SUPERNATURAL. **3.** The use of skillful tricks and deceptions to produce entertainingly baffling effects : conjuration, legerdemain, prestidigitation, sleight of hand. *See* PERFORMING ARTS.
magic also **magical** *adjective* Having, brought about by, or relating to supernatural powers or magic : fey, magical, talismanic, thaumaturgic, thaumaturgical, theurgic, theurgical, witching, wizardly. *See* SUPERNATURAL.

magical *adjective*
Having, brought about by, or relating to supernatural powers or magic : fey, magic, talismanic, thaumaturgic, thaumaturgical, theurgic, theurgical, witching, wizardly. *See* SUPERNATURAL.

magisterial *adjective*
Tending to dictate : authoritarian, bossy, dictatorial, dogmatic, domineering, imperious, masterful, overbearing, peremptory. *See* OVER.

magistrate *noun*
A public official who decides cases brought before a court of law in order to administer justice : judge, jurisprudent, jurist, justice, justice of the peace. *See* DECIDE, LAW.

magnanimity *noun*
The quality or state of being generous : bigheartedness, bounteousness, bountifulness, freehandedness, generosity, generousness, greatheartedness, large-heartedness, lavishness, liberality, magnanimousness, munificence, openhandedness, unselfishness, unsparingness. *See* GIVE.

magnanimous *adjective*
Willing to give of oneself and one's possessions : big, big-hearted, generous, greathearted, large-hearted, unselfish. *See* GIVE.

magnanimousness *noun*
The quality or state of being generous : bigheartedness, bounteousness, bountifulness, freehandedness, generosity, generousness, greatheartedness, large-heartedness, lavishness, liberality, magnanimity, munificence, openhandedness, unselfishness, unsparingness. *See* GIVE.

magnetism *noun*
1. The power or quality of attracting : allure, allurement, appeal, attraction, attractiveness, call, charisma, charm, draw, enchantment, enticement, fascination, glamour, lure, witchery. *Informal:* pull. *See* LIKE. **2.** The capacity to exert an influence : force, forcefulness, power. *See* STRONG.

magnetize *verb*
To direct or impel to oneself by some quality or action : allure, appeal, attract, draw, entice, lure, take. *Informal:* pull. *See* LIKE.

magnific *adjective*
Large and impressive in size, scope, or extent : august, baronial, grand, grandiose, imposing, lordly, magnificent, majestic, noble, princely, regal, royal, splendid, stately, sublime, superb. *See* BIG, GOOD.

magnification *noun*
The honoring of a deity, as in worship : exaltation, extolment, glorification, laudation, praise. *See* RELIGION.

magnificence *noun*
Brilliant, showy splendor : brilliance, brilliancy, glitter, glory, gorgeousness, resplendence, resplendency, sparkle, sumptuousness. *Informal:* glitz. *See* BEAUTIFUL.

magnificent *adjective*
1. Marked by extraordinary elegance, beauty, and splendor : brilliant, glorious, gorgeous, proud, resplendent, splendid, splendorous. *See* BEAUTIFUL. **2.** Large and impressive in size, scope, or extent : august, baronial, grand,

grandiose, imposing, lordly, magnific, majestic, noble, princely, regal, royal, splendid, stately, sublime, superb. *See* BIG, GOOD. **3.** Far beyond what is usual, normal, or customary : exceptional, extraordinary, outstanding, preeminent, rare, remarkable, singular, towering, uncommon, unusual. *Informal:* standout. *Slang:* awesome, out of sight. *See* BETTER, USUAL.

magnify *verb*
1. To make or become greater or larger : aggrandize, amplify, augment, boost, build, build up, burgeon, enlarge, escalate, expand, extend, grow, increase, mount, multiply, proliferate, rise, run up, snowball, soar, swell, upsurge, wax. *Informal:* beef up. *See* INCREASE. **2.** To make (something) seem greater than is actually the case : exaggerate, hyperbolize, inflate, overcharge, overstate. ***Idioms:*** blow up out of proportion, lay it on thick, stretch the truth. *See* INCREASE. **3.** To pay tribute or homage to : acclaim, celebrate, eulogize, exalt, extol, glorify, hail[2], honor, laud, panegyrize, praise. ***Idiom:*** sing someone's praises. *See* PRAISE. **4.** To honor (a deity) in religious worship : exalt, extol, glorify, laud, praise. *See* RELIGION. **5.** To raise to a high position or status : aggrandize, apotheosize, dignify, elevate, ennoble, exalt, glorify, uplift. ***Idiom:*** put on a pedestal. *See* RISE.

magniloquent *adjective*
Characterized by language that is elevated and sometimes pompous in style : aureate, bombastic, declamatory, flowery, fustian, grandiloquent, high-flown, high-sounding, orotund, overblown, rhetorical, sonorous, swollen. *See* PLAIN, STYLE, WORDS.

magniloquence *noun*
Pretentious, pompous speech or writing : bombast, claptrap, fustian, grandiloquence, orotundity, rant, turgidity. *See* PLAIN, STYLE, WORDS.

magnitude *noun*
1. Great extent, amount, or dimension : amplitude, bulk, mass, size, volume (often used in plural). *See* BIG. **2.** The quality or state of being large in amount, extent, or importance : amplitude, bigness, greatness, largeness, sizableness, size. *See* BIG. **3.** Relative intensity or amount, as of a quality or attribute : degree, extent, measure, proportion. *See* BIG. **4.** The amount of space occupied by something : dimension, extent, measure, proportion (often used in plural), size. *See* BIG.

magnum opus *noun*
An outstanding and ingenious work : chef-d'oeuvre, masterpiece, masterwork. *See* GOOD.

maiden *adjective*
Preceding all others in time : earliest, first, initial, original, pioneer, primary, prime, primordial. *See* START.

maim *verb*
To deprive of a limb or bodily member or its use : cripple, dismember, mutilate. *See* HELP.

main *adjective*
Most important, influential, or significant : capital, cardinal, chief, first, foremost, key, leading, major, number one, paramount, premier, primary, prime, principal, top. *See* IMPORTANT.

maintain *verb*
1. To persevere in some condition, action, or belief : keep, retain, stay with. *See* CONTINUE. **2.** To keep in a condition of good repair, efficiency, or use : keep up, preserve, sustain. *See* KEEP. **3.** To supply with the necessities of life : keep, provide for, support. ***Idiom:*** take care of. *See* CARE FOR. **4.** To support against arguments, attack, or criticism : apologize, defend, justify, vindicate. ***Idioms:*** speak up for, stand up for, stick up for. *See* SUPPORT. **5.** To put into words positively and with conviction : affirm, allege, argue, assert, asseverate, aver, avouch, avow, claim, contend, declare, hold, say, state. ***Idiom:*** have it. *See* AFFIRM.

maintenance *noun*
The means needed to support life : alimentation, alimony, bread, bread and butter, keep, livelihood, living, subsistence, support, sustenance, upkeep. *See* MONEY.

majestic *adjective*
Large and impressive in size, scope, or extent : august, baronial, grand, grandiose, imposing, lordly, magnific, magnificent, noble, princely, regal, royal, splendid, stately, sublime, superb. *See* BIG, GOOD.

majesty *noun*
Something meriting the highest praise or regard : glory, grandeur, grandiosity, grandness, greatness, splendor. *See* PRAISE.

major *adjective*
1. Being among the leaders in one's field : blue-chip, major-league. *Informal:* big-league, big-time, heavyweight. *See* IMPORTANT. **2.** Most important, influential, or significant : capital, cardinal, chief, first, foremost, key, leading, main, number one, paramount, premier, primary, prime, principal, top. *See* IMPORTANT.

major-league *adjective*
Being among the leaders in one's field :

blue-chip, major. *Informal:* big-league, bigtime, heavyweight. *See* IMPORTANT.

make *verb*

1. To cause to come into existence : beget, breed, create, engender, father, hatch, originate, parent, procreate, produce, sire, spawn. ***Idiom:*** give birth (*or* rise) to. *See* MAKE. **2.** To be the cause of : bring, bring about, bring on, cause, effect, effectuate, generate, induce, ingenerate, lead to, occasion, result in, secure, set off, stir[1] (up), touch off, trigger. ***Idioms:*** bring to pass (*or* effect), give rise to. *See* START. **3.** To create by forming, combining, or altering materials : assemble, build, construct, fabricate, fashion, forge[1], frame, manufacture, mold, produce, put together, shape. *See* MAKE. **4.** To cause to be in a certain state or to undergo a particular experience or action : get, have. *See* CAUSE. **5.** To select for an office or position : appoint, designate, name, nominate, tap[1]. *See* CHOICE. **6.** To cause (a person or thing) to act or move in spite of resistance : coerce, compel, constrain, force, obligate, oblige, pressure. *See* ATTACK. **7.** To cause to be ready, as for use, consumption, or a special purpose : fit[1], fix, prepare, prime, ready. *See* PREPARED. **8.** To put in force or cause to be by legal authority : constitute, enact, establish, legislate, promulgate. *See* ACTION, MAKE, POLITICS. **9.** To journey over (a specified distance) : cover. *Informal:* do. *See* MOVE. **10.** To proceed in a specified direction : bear, go, head, set out, strike out. *See* APPROACH. **11.** To receive, as wages, for one's labor : earn, gain, get, win. *Informal:* pull down. ***Idioms:*** earn (*or* make) a living, earn one's keep. *See* GIVE, MONEY. **12.** To be the constituent parts of. Also used with *up* : compose, constitute, form. *See* BE.

make out *verb* **1.** To perceive and fix the identity of, especially with difficulty : descry, discern, distinguish, pick out, spot. *See* SEE. **2.** To perceive and recognize the meaning of : accept, apprehend, catch (on), compass, comprehend, conceive, fathom, follow, get, grasp, read, see, sense, take, take in, understand. *Informal:* savvy. *Slang:* dig. *Chiefly British:* twig. *Scots:* ken. ***Idioms:*** get (*or* have) a handle on, get the picture. *See* UNDERSTAND. **3.** *Informal.* To progress or perform adequately, especially in difficult circumstances : do, fare, fend, get along, get by, manage, muddle through, shift. ***Idioms:*** make do, make shift. *See* THRIVE. **4.** *Slang.* To engage in kissing, caressing, and other amorous behavior : *Informal:* fool around, neck, pet[1], spoon. *See* SEX.

make over *verb* To change the ownership of (property) by means of a legal document : cede, deed, grant, sign over. *Law:* alien, alienate, assign, convey, transfer. *See* GIVE, LAW.

make up *verb* **1.** To use ingenuity in making, developing, or achieving : concoct, contrive, devise, dream up, fabricate, formulate, hatch, invent, think up. *Informal:* cook up. ***Idiom:*** come up with. *See* MAKE. **2.** To compose or recite without preparation : ad-lib, extemporize, fake, improvise. ***Idiom:*** wing it. *See* PLANNED, PREPARED. **3.** To act as an equalizing weight or force to : balance, compensate, counteract, counterbalance, counterpoise, countervail, offset, set off. *See* ORDER. **4.** To reestablish friendship between : conciliate, reconcile, reunite. *See* LOVE.

make-believe *noun*

The presentation of something false as true : charade, pretense. *See* HONEST, TRUE.

make out *verb* See **make.**

make over *verb* See **make.**

maker *noun*

1. One that creates, founds, or originates : architect, author, creator, entrepreneur, father, founder[2], inventor, originator, parent, patriarch. *See* START. **2.** A person or business that makes or builds something : assembler, builder, constructor, erector, manufacturer, producer. *See* MAKE.

makeshift *noun*

Something used temporarily or reluctantly when other means are not available : expediency, expedient, shift, stopgap. *See* HELP, SUBSTITUTE.

makeup or **make-up** *noun*

The combination of emotional, intellectual, and moral qualities that distinguishes an individual : character, complexion, disposition, nature, personality. *See* BE.

make up *verb* See **make.**

maladroit *adjective*

1. Lacking dexterity and grace in physical movement : awkward, clumsy, gawky, graceless, inept, lumpish, ungainly, ungraceful. *Slang:* klutzy. ***Idiom:*** all thumbs. *See* ABILITY. **2.** Clumsily lacking in the ability to do or perform : awkward, bumbling, clumsy, gauche, heavy-handed, inept, unskillful. *See* ABILITY. **3.** Lacking sensitivity and skill in dealing with others : brash, clumsy, gauche, impolitic, indelicate, tactless, undiplomatic, unpolitic, untactful. *See* ABILITY, COURTESY.

malady *noun*

1. A pathological condition of mind or body :

ailment, complaint, disease, disorder, ill, illness, infirmity, sickness. *See* HEALTH. **2.** A minor illness, especially one of a temporary nature : ailment, bug, complaint, indisposition. *See* HEALTH.

mala fide *adjective*
Not being what one purports to be : ambidextrous, disingenuous, insincere, left-handed. *See* HONEST.

malapert *adjective*
Rude and disrespectful : assuming, assumptive, audacious, bold, boldfaced, brash, brazen, cheeky, contumelious, familiar, forward, impertinent, impudent, insolent, nervy, overconfident, pert, presuming, presumptuous, pushy, sassy, saucy, smart. *Informal:* brassy, flip, fresh, smart-alecky, snippety, snippy, uppish, uppity. *Slang:* wise[1]. *See* ATTITUDE, COURTESY.
malapert *noun* One who is obnoxiously self-assertive and arrogant : witling. *Informal:* know-it-all, saucebox, smart aleck, smarty, smarty-pants, wisenheimer. *Slang:* wiseacre, wisecracker, wise guy. *See* GOOD.

malapropos *adjective*
Not suited to circumstances : improper, inappropriate, inapt, incongruous, inept, unapt, unbecoming, unbefitting, unfit, unseemly, unsuitable. ***Idiom:*** out of place. *See* AGREE, USUAL.

malarkey also **malarky** *noun*
Slang. Something that does not have or make sense : balderdash, blather, bunkum, claptrap, drivel, garbage, idiocy, nonsense, piffle, poppycock, rigmarole, rubbish, tomfoolery, trash, twaddle. *Informal:* tommyrot. *Slang:* applesauce, baloney, bilge, bull[1], bunk[2], crap, hooey. *See* KNOWLEDGE.

malarky *noun* See **malarkey.**

male *adjective*
Of, characteristic of, or befitting the male sex : macho, manful, manlike, manly, mannish, masculine, virile. *See* GENDER.

maledict *verb*
Archaic. To invoke evil or injury upon : anathematize, curse, damn, imprecate. *Informal:* cuss. *Archaic:* execrate. *See* WORDS.

malediction *noun*
A denunciation invoking a wish or threat of evil or injury : anathema, curse, damnation, execration, imprecation. *Archaic:* malison. *See* WORDS.

malefactor *noun*
One who commits a crime : criminal, lawbreaker, offender. *Law:* felon. *See* CRIMES.

malevolence *noun*
A desire to harm others or to see others suffer : despitefulness, ill will, malice, maliciousness, malignancy, malignity, meanness, nastiness, poisonousness, spite, spitefulness, venomousness, viciousness. *See* ATTITUDE.

malevolent *adjective*
Characterized by intense ill will or spite : black, despiteful, evil, hateful, malicious, malign, malignant, mean[2], nasty, poisonous, spiteful, venomous, vicious, wicked. *Slang:* bitchy. *See* ATTITUDE.

malformation *noun*
A disfiguring abnormality of shape or form : deformity, disfigurement. *See* BEAUTIFUL.

malfunction *verb*
To work improperly due to mechanical difficulties : act up, misbehave. *See* THRIVE.

malice *noun*
A desire to harm others or to see others suffer : despitefulness, ill will, malevolence, maliciousness, malignancy, malignity, meanness, nastiness, poisonousness, spite, spitefulness, venomousness, viciousness. *See* ATTITUDE.

malicious *adjective*
Characterized by intense ill will or spite : black, despiteful, evil, hateful, malevolent, malign, malignant, mean[2], nasty, poisonous, spiteful, venomous, vicious, wicked. *Slang:* bitchy. *See* ATTITUDE.

maliciousness *noun*
A desire to harm others or to see others suffer : despitefulness, ill will, malevolence, malice, malignancy, malignity, meanness, nastiness, poisonousness, spite, spitefulness, venomousness, viciousness. *See* ATTITUDE.

malign *verb*
To make defamatory statements about : asperse, backbite, calumniate, defame, slander, slur, tear down, traduce, vilify. *Law:* libel. ***Idiom:*** cast aspersions on. *See* ATTACK, CRIMES, LAW.
malign *adjective* **1.** Strongly suggestive of great harm, menace, or evil : baleful, sinister. *See* WARN. **2.** Characterized by intense ill will or spite : black, despiteful, evil, hateful, malevolent, malicious, malignant, mean[2], nasty, poisonous, spiteful, venomous, vicious, wicked. *Slang:* bitchy. *See* ATTITUDE.

malignancy *noun*
A desire to harm others or to see others suffer : despitefulness, ill will, malevolence, malice, maliciousness, malignity, meanness, nastiness, poisonousness, spite, spitefulness, venomousness, viciousness. *See* ATTITUDE.

malignant *adjective*
1. Characterized by intense ill will or spite : black, despiteful, evil, hateful, malevolent, malicious, malign, mean², nasty, poisonous, spiteful, venomous, vicious, wicked. *Slang:* bitchy. *See* ATTITUDE. **2.** Extremely destructive or harmful : baneful, deadly, noxious, pernicious, pestilent, pestilential, virulent. *See* HELP.

malignity *noun*
A desire to harm others or to see others suffer : despitefulness, ill will, malevolence, malice, maliciousness, malignancy, meanness, nastiness, poisonousness, spite, spitefulness, venomousness, viciousness. *See* ATTITUDE.

malison *noun*
Archaic. A denunciation invoking a wish or threat of evil or injury : anathema, curse, damnation, execration, imprecation, malediction. *See* WORDS.

malleability *noun*
The quality or state of being flexible : bounce, ductility, elasticity, flexibility, flexibleness, give, malleableness, plasticity, pliability, pliableness, pliancy, pliantness, resilience, resiliency, spring, springiness, suppleness. *Obsolete:* flexure. *See* FLEXIBLE.

malleable *adjective*
1. Capable of being shaped, bent, or drawn out, as by hammering or pressure : ductile, flexible, flexile, flexuous, moldable, plastic, pliable, pliant, supple, workable. *See* FLEXIBLE. **2.** Easily altered or influenced : ductile, elastic, flexible, flexile, impressionable, plastic, pliable, pliant, suggestible, supple. *See* FLEXIBLE. **3.** Capable of adapting or being adapted : adaptable, adaptive, adjustable, elastic, flexible, pliable, pliant, supple. *See* CHANGE.

malleableness *noun*
The quality or state of being flexible : bounce, ductility, elasticity, flexibility, flexibleness, give, malleability, plasticity, pliability, pliableness, pliancy, pliantness, resilience, resiliency, spring, springiness, suppleness. *Obsolete:* flexure. *See* FLEXIBLE.

malodorous *adjective*
Having an unpleasant odor : fetid, foul, foul-smelling, mephitic, noisome, reeky, stinking. *Informal:* smelly. *See* SMELLS.

maltreat *verb*
To hurt or injure by maltreatment : abuse, ill-treat, ill-use, mishandle, mistreat, misuse. *See* HELP.

maltreatment *noun*
Physically harmful treatment : abuse, ill-treatment, mishandling, mistreatment, misusage. *See* HELP.

mammoth *noun*
One that is extraordinarily large and powerful : behemoth, giant, Goliath, jumbo, leviathan, monster, titan. *Slang:* whopper. *See* BEINGS, BIG.

mammoth *adjective* Of extraordinary size and power : behemoth, Brobdingnagian, Bunyanesque, colossal, cyclopean, elephantine, enormous, gargantuan, giant, gigantesque, gigantic, herculean, heroic, huge, immense, jumbo, massive, massy, mastodonic, mighty, monster, monstrous, monumental, mountainous, prodigious, pythonic, stupendous, titanic, tremendous, vast. *Informal:* walloping. *Slang:* whopping. *See* BIG.

man *noun*
1. A member of the human race : being, body, creature, homo, human, human being, individual, life, mortal, party, person, personage, soul. *See* BEINGS. **2.** The human race : earth, flesh, Homo sapiens, humanity, humankind, mankind, universe, world. *See* CULTURE. **3.** *Slang.* A member of a law-enforcement agency. Often uppercase : bluecoat, finest, officer, patrolman, patrolwoman, peace officer, police, policeman, police officer, policewoman. *Informal:* cop, law. *Slang:* bull¹, copper, flatfoot, fuzz, gendarme, heat. *Chiefly British:* bobby, constable, peeler. *See* LAW.

manacle *noun*
Something that physically confines the legs or arms : bond, chain (used in plural), fetter, handcuff (often used in plural), hobble, iron (used in plural), restraint, shackle. *Archaic:* gyve. *See* FREE.

manacle *verb* To restrict the activity or free movement of : chain, fetter, hamper, hamstring, handcuff, hobble, leash, shackle, tie, trammel. *Informal:* hog-tie. *See* FREE, HELP.

manage *verb*
1. To control or direct the functioning of : operate, run, use, work. *See* CONTROL. **2.** To control the course of (an activity) : carry on, conduct, direct, operate, run, steer. *See* OVER. **3.** To have charge of (the affairs of others) : administer, administrate, direct, govern, head, run, superintend, supervise. *See* OVER. **4.** To progress or perform adequately, especially in difficult circumstances : do, fare, fend, get along, get by, muddle through, shift. *Informal:* make out. *Idioms:* make do, make shift. *See* THRIVE.

manageable *adjective*
Capable of being governed : administrable, controllable, governable, rulable. *See* CONTROL.

management *noun*
1. Authoritative control over the affairs of others : administration, direction, government, superintendence, supervision. *See* OVER. **2.** The careful guarding of an asset : conservancy, conservation, husbandry, preservation. *See* KEEP. **3.** An act or instance of guiding : direction, guidance, lead, leadership. *See* AFFECT.

manager *noun*
1. A person having administrative or managerial authority in an organization : administrant, administrator, director, executive, officer, official. *Informal:* exec. *See* OVER. **2.** Someone who directs and supervises workers : boss, director, foreman, foreperson, forewoman, head, overseer, superintendent, supervisor, taskmaster, taskmistress. *Informal:* straw boss. *Slang:* chief. *See* OVER.

managerial *adjective*
Of, for, or relating to administration or administrators : administrative, directorial, executive, ministerial, supervisory. *See* OVER.

mandate *noun*
1. An authoritative indication to be obeyed : behest, bidding, charge, command, commandment, dictate, direction, directive, injunction, instruction (often used in plural), order, word. *See* OVER, WORDS. **2.** Conferred power : authority, faculty, right. *Law:* competence, competency. *See* ABILITY.

mandatory *adjective*
Imposed on one by authority, command, or convention : compulsory, imperative, necessary, obligatory, required, requisite. *See* OBLIGATION.

maneuver *noun*
1. A method of deploying troops and equipment in combat : stratagem, tactic. *See* MEANS. **2.** A calculated change in position : evolution, move, movement, turn. *See* MOVE. **3.** An action calculated to achieve an end : measure (often used in plural), move, procedure, step, tactic. *See* ACTION. **4.** An indirect, usually cunning means of gaining an end : artifice, deception, device, dodge, feint, gimmick, imposture, jig, ploy, ruse, sleight, stratagem, subterfuge, trick, wile. *Informal:* shenanigan, take-in. *See* HONEST, MEANS.

maneuver *verb* **1.** To go or cause to go from one place to another : move, remove, shift, transfer. *See* MOVE. **2.** To direct the course of carefully : guide, jockey, navigate, pilot, steer. ***Idiom:*** back and fill. *See* CONTROL, MOVE. **3.** To take clever or cunning steps to achieve one's goals : jockey. *Informal:* finagle. ***Idiom:*** pull strings (*or* wires). *See* CONTROL, MEANS. **4.** To control to one's own advantage by artful or indirect means : exploit, manipulate, play. *See* CONTROL, STRAIGHT.

manful *adjective*
Of, characteristic of, or befitting the male sex : macho, male, manlike, manly, mannish, masculine, virile. *See* GENDER.

mangle[1] *verb*
To injure or damage, as by abuse or heavy wear : batter, knock about (*or* around), maul, rough up. *See* ATTACK, HELP, STRIKE.

mangle[2] *verb*
To smooth by applying heat and pressure : iron, press. *See* SMOOTH.

mangy *adjective*
Showing signs of wear and tear or neglect : bedraggled, broken-down, decaying, decrepit, dilapidated, dingy, down-at-heel, faded, run-down, scrubby, scruffy, seedy, shabby, shoddy, sleazy, tattered, tatty, threadbare. *Informal:* tacky[2]. *Slang:* ratty. ***Idioms:*** all the worse for wear, gone to pot (*or* seed), past cure (*or* hope). *See* BETTER.

manhandle *verb*
To be rough or brutal with : knock about (*or* around), rough (up), slap around. *Slang:* mess up. *See* ATTACK, STRIKE.

mania *noun*
1. A subject or activity that inspires lively interest : craze, enthusiasm, passion, rage. *See* CONCERN. **2.** An irrational preoccupation : fetish, fixation, obsession. *Informal:* thing. *See* CONCERN. **3.** *Psychiatry.* Serious mental illness or disorder impairing a person's capacity to function normally and safely : brainsickness, craziness, dementia, derangement, disturbance, insaneness, insanity, lunacy, madness, mental illness, psychopathy, unbalance. *Psychology:* aberration, alienation. *See* SANE.

maniac *noun*
A person who is ardently devoted to a particular subject or activity : bug, devotee, enthusiast, fanatic, zealot. *Informal:* buff[2], fan[2], fiend. *Slang:* freak, nut. *See* CONCERN.

maniac *adjective* Afflicted with or exhibiting irrationality and mental unsoundness : brainsick, crazy, daft, demented, disordered, distraught, dotty, insane, lunatic, mad, maniacal, mentally ill, moonstruck, off, touched, unbalanced, unsound, wrong. *Informal:* bonkers, cracked, daffy, gaga, loony. *Slang:* bananas, batty, buggy, cuckoo, fruity, loco, nuts, nutty, screwy, wacky. *Chiefly British:* crackers. *Law:* non compos mentis. ***Idioms:*** around the bend, crazy as a loon, mad as a hatter, not all there, nutty as a fruitcake, off (*or* out of) one's head, off one's rocker, of unsound mind, out of one's mind, sick in the head, stark raving mad. *See* SANE.

maniacal *adjective*
Afflicted with or exhibiting irrationality and mental unsoundness : brainsick, crazy, daft, demented, disordered, distraught, dotty, insane, lunatic, mad, maniac, mentally ill, moonstruck, off, touched, unbalanced, unsound, wrong. *Informal:* bonkers, cracked, daffy, gaga, loony. *Slang:* bananas, batty, buggy, cuckoo, fruity, loco, nuts, nutty, screwy, wacky. *Chiefly British:* crackers. *Law:* non compos mentis. ***Idioms:*** around the bend, crazy as a loon, mad as a hatter, not all there, nutty as a fruitcake, off (*or* out of) one's head, off one's rocker, of unsound mind, out of one's mind, sick in the head, stark raving mad. *See* SANE.

manifest *adjective*
Readily seen, perceived, or understood : apparent, clear, clear-cut, crystal clear, distinct, evident, noticeable, observable, obvious, patent, plain, pronounced, visible. *See* SEE.
manifest *verb* **1.** To make manifest or apparent : demonstrate, display, evidence, evince, exhibit, proclaim, reveal, show. *See* SHOW. **2.** To give expression to, as by gestures, facial aspects, or bodily posture : communicate, convey, display, express. *See* SHOW. **3.** To represent (an abstraction, for example) in or as if in bodily form : body forth, embody, exteriorize, externalize, incarnate, materialize, objectify, personalize, personify, substantiate. *See* SUBSTITUTE.

manifestation *noun*
1. An act of showing or displaying : demonstration, display, exhibit, exhibition, show. *See* SHOW. **2.** Something visible or evident that gives grounds for believing in the existence or presence of something else : badge, evidence, index, indication, indicator, mark, note, sign, signification, stamp, symptom, token, witness. *See* SHOW. **3.** A physical entity typifying an abstraction : embodiment, exteriorization, externalization, incarnation, materialization, objectification, personalization, personification, substantiation, type. *Rhetoric:* prosopopeia. *See* SUBSTITUTE.

manifesto *noun*
A public statement : announcement, annunciation, declaration, edict, notice, proclamation, pronouncement. *See* KNOWLEDGE.

manipulate *verb*
1. To use with or as if with the hands : handle, ply[2], wield. *See* CONTROL, USED. **2.** To handle in a way so as to mix, form, and shape : knead, work. *See* TOUCH. **3.** To control to one's own advantage by artful or indirect means : exploit, maneuver, play. *See* CONTROL, STRAIGHT.

mankind *noun*
The human race : earth, flesh, Homo sapiens, humanity, humankind, man, universe, world. *See* CULTURE.

manlike *adjective*
1. Resembling a human being : anthropoid, anthropomorphic, anthropomorphous, hominoid, humanoid. *See* CULTURE. **2.** Of, characteristic of, or befitting the male sex : macho, male, manful, manly, mannish, masculine, virile. *See* GENDER.

manly *adjective*
Of, characteristic of, or befitting the male sex : macho, male, manful, manlike, mannish, masculine, virile. *See* GENDER.

manmade *adjective*
1. Made by human beings instead of nature : artificial, manufactured, synthetic. *See* CULTURE. **2.** Made to imitate something else : artificial, imitation, mock, simulated, synthetic. *Informal:* pretend. *See* REAL.

manner *noun*
1. The approach used to do something : fashion, method, mode, modus operandi, style, system, way, wise[2]. *See* MEANS. **2.** Behavior through which one reveals one's personality : address, air, bearing, demeanor, mien, presence, style. *Archaic:* port. *See* BE, STYLE. **3.** A habitual way of behaving : consuetude, custom, habit, habitude, practice, praxis, usage, usance, use, way, wont. *See* USUAL. **4.** Socially correct behavior. Used in plural : decorum, etiquette, good form, mores, propriety (also used in plural), p's and q's. *See* USUAL. **5.** A distinctive way of expressing oneself : fashion, mode, style, tone, vein. *See* STYLE. **6.** A class that is defined by the common attribute or attributes possessed by all its members : breed, cast, description, feather, ilk, kind[2], lot, mold, nature, order, sort, species, stamp, stripe, type, variety. *Informal:* persuasion. *See* GROUP.

mannered *adjective*
Artificially genteel : affected, artificial, pre-

cious. *Informal:* la-di-da. *See* GOOD, HONEST, PLAIN, TRUE.

mannerism *noun*
Artificial behavior adopted to impress others : affectation, affectedness, air (used in plural), pose, pretense. *See* HONEST, TRUE.

mannerliness *noun*
Well-mannered behavior toward others : civility, courteousness, courtesy, genteelness, gentility, politeness, politesse. *See* COURTESY.

mannerly *adjective*
Characterized by good manners : civil, courteous, genteel, polite, well-bred, well-mannered. *See* COURTESY.

mannish *adjective*
Of, characteristic of, or befitting the male sex : macho, male, manful, manlike, manly, masculine, virile. *See* GENDER.

man on horseback *noun*
An absolute ruler, especially one who is harsh and oppressive : Big Brother, despot, dictator, führer, oppressor, strongman, totalitarian, tyrant. *See* OVER.

manslayer *noun*
One who murders another : butcher, cutthroat, homicide, killer, massacrer, murderer, murderess, slaughterer, slayer, triggerman. *See* HELP.

mantic *adjective*
Of or relating to the foretelling of events by or as if by supernatural means : augural, divinitory, fatidic, fatidical, oracular, prophetic, sibylline, vatic, vatical, vaticinal, visionary. *See* FORESIGHT.

mantle *verb*
1. To cover as if with clothes : cloak, clothe, drape, robe. *See* PUT ON. **2.** To become red in the face : blush, color, crimson, flush, glow, redden. *See* EXPRESS.

man-to-man *adjective*
Manifesting honesty and directness, especially in speech : candid, direct, downright, forthright, frank, honest, ingenuous, open, plainspoken, straight, straightforward, straight-out, unreserved. *Informal:* straight-from-the-shoulder, straight-shooting. *See* CLEAR, SHOW.

manufacture *verb*
To create by forming, combining, or altering materials : assemble, build, construct, fabricate, fashion, forge¹, frame, make, mold, produce, put together, shape. *See* MAKE.

manufactured *adjective*
Made by human beings instead of nature : artificial, manmade, synthetic. *See* CULTURE.

manufacturer *noun*
A person or business that makes or builds something : assembler, builder, constructor, erector, maker, producer. *See* MAKE.

manumission *noun*
The state of not being in confinement or servitude : emancipation, freedom, liberation, liberty. *See* FREE.

manumit *verb*
To set at liberty : discharge, emancipate, free, liberate, loose, release. *Slang:* spring. ***Idiom:*** let loose. *See* FREE.

many *adjective*
Amounting to or consisting of a large, indefinite number : legion, multitudinous, myriad, numerous. ***Idiom:*** quite a few. *See* BIG.

many-sided *adjective*
Having many aspects, uses, or abilities : all-around, all-round, multifaceted, protean, various, versatile. *See* ABILITY, SAME.

map *noun*
Slang. The front surface of the head : countenance, face, feature (often used in plural), muzzle, visage. *Informal:* mug. *Slang:* kisser, pan, puss. *See* PRECEDE.

map *verb* **1.** To show graphically the direction or location of, as by using coordinates. Also used with *out* : chart, lay out, plot. *See* SHOW. **2.** To work out and arrange the parts or details of. Also used with *out* : blueprint, design, lay out, plan, set out. *See* PLANNED.

mar *verb*
To spoil the soundness or perfection of : blemish, damage, detract from, disserve, flaw, harm, hurt, impair, injure, prejudice, tarnish, vitiate. *See* BETTER, HELP.

maraud *verb*
To make a surprise attack on : harry, raid. *See* ATTACK.

marble *noun*
Slang. A healthy mental state. Used in plural : lucidity, lucidness, mind, reason, saneness, sanity, sense (often used in plural), soundness, wit (used in plural). *See* SANE.

march¹ *verb*
1. To walk with long steps, especially in a vigorous manner : stalk, stride. *See* MOVE. **2.** To travel about or journey on foot : backpack, hike, peregrinate, traipse, tramp, trek. *See* MOVE. **3.** To go forward, especially toward a conclusion : advance, come (along), get along, move, proceed, progress. *See* APPROACH.

march *noun* Forward movement : advance, advancement, furtherance, headway, progress, progression. *See* BETTER, FORWARD.

march² *noun*
The line or area separating geopolitical units : border, borderland, boundary, frontier, marchland. *See* EDGE, TERRITORY.

marchland *noun*
The line or area separating geopolitical units : border, borderland, boundary, frontier, march². *See* EDGE, TERRITORY.

margin *noun*
1. A fairly narrow line or space forming a boundary : border, borderline, brim, brink, edge, edging, fringe, periphery, rim, verge. *Chiefly Military:* perimeter. *See* EDGE. **2.** Suitable opportunity to accept or allow something : elbowroom, latitude, leeway, play, room, scope. *See* PLACE, RESTRAINT.
margin *verb* To put or form a border on : border, bound², edge, fringe, rim, skirt, verge. *See* EDGE.

marine *adjective*
1. Of or relating to the seas or oceans : maritime, oceanic, pelagic, thalassic. *See* SEA. **2.** Of or relating to sea navigation : maritime, nautical, navigational. *See* SEA.

mariner *noun*
A person engaged in sailing or working on a ship : jack (uppercase), jack-tar, navigator, sailor, sea dog, seafarer, seaman. *Informal:* salt, tar. *Slang:* gob³. *See* SEA.

marital *adjective*
Of, relating to, or typical of marriage : conjugal, connubial, hymeneal, married, matrimonial, nuptial, spousal, wedded. *See* MARRIAGE.

maritime *adjective*
1. Of or relating to the seas or oceans : marine, oceanic, pelagic, thalassic. *See* SEA. **2.** Of or relating to sea navigation : marine, nautical, navigational. *See* SEA.

mark *noun*
1. The visible effect made on a surface by pressure : impress, impression, imprint, indent, indentation, print, stamp. *See* MARKS. **2.** Something visible or evident that gives grounds for believing in the existence or presence of something else : badge, evidence, index, indication, indicator, manifestation, note, sign, signification, stamp, symptom, token, witness. *See* SHOW. **3.** A name or other device placed on merchandise to signify its ownership or manufacture : brand, colophon, label, trademark. *See* MARKS. **4.** A distinctive element : attribute, character, characteristic, feature, peculiarity, property, quality, savor, trait. *See* BE. **5.** A means by which individuals are compared and judged : benchmark, criterion, gauge, measure, standard, test, touchstone, yardstick. *See* USUAL. **6.** A position of exalted widely recognized importance : distinction, eminence, eminency, fame, glory, illustriousness, luster, notability, note, preeminence, prestige, prominence, prominency, renown. *See* IMPORTANT, KNOWLEDGE, RESPECT. **7.** The act of noting, observing, or taking into account : attention, cognizance, espial, heed, note, notice, observance, observation, regard, remark. *See* KNOWLEDGE, SEE. **8.** One that is fired at, attacked, or abused : butt³, target. *See* SEEK. **9.** What one intends to do or achieve : aim, ambition, design, end, goal, intent, intention, meaning, object, objective, point, purpose, target, view, why. ***Idioms:*** end in view, why and wherefore. *See* PLANNED, PURPOSE. **10.** *Slang.* A person who is easily deceived or victimized : butt³, dupe, fool, gull, lamb, pushover, victim. *Informal:* sucker. *Slang:* fall guy, gudgeon, monkey, patsy, pigeon, sap¹. *Chiefly British:* mug. *See* WISE.
mark *verb* **1.** To make known or identify, as by signs : denote, designate, indicate, point out, show, specify. *See* SHOW. **2.** To give a precise indication of, as on a register or scale : indicate, read, record, register, show. *See* SHOW. **3.** To make a target of : target. ***Idiom:*** draw (*or* get) a bead on. *See* SEEK. **4.** To give grounds for believing in the existence or presence of : argue, attest, bespeak, betoken, indicate, point to, testify, witness. *See* SHOW. **5.** To make noticeable or different : characterize, differentiate, discriminate, distinguish, individualize, set apart, signalize, singularize. *See* SAME. **6.** To fix the limits of. Also used with *off* or *out* : bound², delimit, delimitate, demarcate, determine, limit, measure. *See* LIMITED. **7.** To set off by or as if by a mark indicating ownership or manufacture : brand, identify, label, tag, trademark. *See* MARKS. **8.** To attach a ticket to : label, tag, ticket. *See* MARKS. **9.** To evaluate and assign a grade to : grade, score. *See* VALUE. **10.** To perceive with a special effort of the senses or the mind : descry, detect, discern, distinguish, mind, note, notice, observe, remark, see. *See* KNOWLEDGE, SEE.
mark down *verb* To become or make less in price or value : cheapen, depreciate, depress, devaluate, devalue, downgrade, lower², reduce, write down. *See* INCREASE, MONEY.

markdown *noun*
A lowering in price or value : depreciation, devaluation, reduction, write-down. *See* INCREASE, MONEY.

mark down *verb* See **mark.**

marked *adjective*
Readily attracting notice : arresting, bold, conspicuous, eye-catching, noticeable, observable, outstanding, pointed, prominent, pronounced, remarkable, salient, signal, striking. ***Idiom:*** sticking out like a sore thumb. *See* SEE.

market *verb*
To offer for sale : deal (in), handle, merchandise, merchant, peddle, retail, sell, trade (in), vend. *See* TRANSACTIONS.

marketability *noun*
Market appeal : marketableness, salability, salableness. *Slang:* sell. *See* DESIRE.

marketableness *noun*
Market appeal : marketability, salability, salableness. *Slang:* sell. *See* DESIRE.

marriable *adjective*
Archaic. Deemed suitable for marriage : eligible, marriageable. *See* MARRIAGE.

marriage *noun*
1. The state of being united as husband and wife : conjugality, connubiality, matrimony, wedlock. *See* MARRIAGE. **2.** The act or ceremony by which two people become husband and wife : bridal, espousal, nuptial (often used in plural), spousal (often used in plural), wedding. *See* MARRIAGE.

marriageable *adjective*
Deemed suitable for marriage : eligible. *Archaic:* marriable. *See* MARRIAGE.

married *adjective*
Of, relating to, or typical of marriage : conjugal, connubial, hymeneal, marital, matrimonial, nuptial, spousal, wedded. *See* MARRIAGE.

marrow *noun*
The most central and material part : core, essence, gist, heart, kernel, meat, nub, pith, quintessence, root[1], soul, spirit, stuff, substance. *Law:* gravamen. *See* BE.

marrowy *adjective*
Precisely meaningful and tersely cogent : aphoristic, compact[1], epigrammatic, epigrammatical, pithy. *Informal:* brass-tacks. ***Idioms:*** down to brass tacks, to the point. *See* MEANING, STYLE.

marry *verb*
1. To join or be joined in marriage : espouse, mate, wed. *Slang:* hitch. ***Idiom:*** tie the knot. *See* MARRIAGE. **2.** To bring or come together into a united whole : coalesce, combine, compound, concrete, conjoin, conjugate, connect, consolidate, couple, join, link, meld, unify, unite, wed, yoke. *See* ASSEMBLE.

marsh *noun*
A usually low-lying area of soft waterlogged ground and standing water : bog, fen, marshland, mire, morass, muskeg, quag, quagmire, slough[1], swamp, swampland, wetland. *See* DRY.

marshal *verb*
1. To assemble, prepare, or put into operation, as for war or a similar emergency : mobilize, muster, organize, rally. *See* MOVE. **2.** To put into a deliberate order : arrange, array, deploy, dispose, order, organize, range, sort, systematize. *See* ORDER.

marshland *noun*
A usually low-lying area of soft waterlogged ground and standing water : bog, fen, marsh, mire, morass, muskeg, quag, quagmire, slough[1], swamp, swampland, wetland. *See* DRY.

martial *adjective*
1. Of, relating to, or inclined toward war : bellicose, militaristic, military, warlike. *See* PEACE. **2.** Relating to, characteristic of, or performed by troops : military, soldierly. *See* PEACE.

martinet *noun*
One who imposes or favors absolute obedience to authority : authoritarian, autocrat, despot, dictator, totalitarian, tyrant. *See* OVER.

marvel *noun*
1. One that evokes great surprise and admiration : astonishment, miracle, phenomenon, prodigy, sensation, stunner, wonder, wonderment. ***Idioms:*** one for the books, the eighth wonder of the world. *See* GOOD. **2.** The emotion aroused by something awe-inspiring or astounding : amaze, amazement, astonishment, awe, wonder, wonderment. *Archaic:* admiration, dread. *See* EXCITE, FEELINGS.

marvel *verb* To have a feeling of great awe and rapt admiration : wonder. *See* EXCITE, FEELINGS.

marvellous *adjective* See **marvelous.**

marvelous also **marvellous** *adjective*
1. So remarkable as to elicit disbelief : amazing, astonishing, astounding, fabulous, fantastic, fantastical, incredible, miraculous, phenomenal, prodigious, stupendous, unbelievable, wonderful, wondrous. *See* GOOD. **2.** Particularly excellent : divine, fabulous, fantastic, fantastical, glorious, sensational, splendid, superb, terrific, wonderful. *Informal:* dandy, dreamy, great, ripping, super, swell, tremendous. *Slang:* cool, groovy, hot, keen[1], neat, nifty. ***Idiom:*** out of this world. *See* GOOD.

masculine *adjective*
Of, characteristic of, or befitting the male sex : macho, male, manful, manlike, manly, mannish, virile. *See* GENDER.

mash *verb*
To press forcefully so as to break up into a pulpy mass : crush, mush, pulp, squash. *See* HELP.

mask *noun*
A deceptive outward appearance : cloak, color, coloring, cover, disguise, disguisement, façade, face, false colors, front, gloss, guise, masquerade, pretense, pretext, semblance, show, veil, veneer, window-dressing. *Slang:* put-on. *See* SHOW.

mask *verb* **1.** To prevent (something) from being known : cloak, conceal, cover (up), enshroud, hide[1], hush (up), shroud, veil. *Idioms:* keep under cover, keep under wraps. *See* SHOW. **2.** To change or modify so as to prevent recognition of the true identity or character of : camouflage, disguise, dissemble, dissimulate, masquerade. *See* SHOW.

masquerade *noun*
1. A deceptive outward appearance : cloak, color, coloring, cover, disguise, disguisement, façade, face, false colors, front, gloss, guise, mask, pretense, pretext, semblance, show, veil, veneer, window-dressing. *Slang:* put-on. *See* SHOW. **2.** A display of insincere behavior : act, acting, disguise, dissemblance, pretense, sham, show, simulation. *See* HONEST, TRUE.

masquerade *verb* **1.** To change or modify so as to prevent recognition of the true identity or character of : camouflage, disguise, dissemble, dissimulate, mask. *See* SHOW. **2.** To represent oneself in a given character or as other than what one is : attitudinize, impersonate, pass, pose, posture. *Idiom:* pass oneself off as. *See* HONEST.

mass *noun*
1. A separate and distinct portion of matter : body, bulk, object. *See* MATTER. **2.** A quantity accumulated : accumulation, aggregation, amassment, assemblage, collection, congeries, cumulation, gathering. *See* COLLECT. **3.** A group of things gathered haphazardly : agglomeration, bank[1], cumulus, drift, heap, hill, mess, mound, mountain, pile, shock[2], stack, tumble. *See* ORDER. **4.** A great deal : abundance, mountain, much, plenty, profusion, wealth, world. *Informal:* barrel, heap, lot, pack, peck[2], pile. *Regional:* power, sight. *See* BIG. **5.** An enormous number of persons gathered together : crowd, crush, drove, flock, horde, mob, multitude, press, ruck[1], swarm, throng. *See* BIG, GROUP. **6.** A very large number of things grouped together : army, cloud, crowd, drove, flock, horde, host, legion, mob, multitude, ruck[1], score (used in plural), swarm, throng. *See* BIG, GROUP. **7.** The greatest part or portion : bulk, preponderance, preponderancy, weight. *See* BIG. **8.** Great extent, amount, or dimension : amplitude, bulk, magnitude, size, volume (often used in plural). *See* BIG. **9.** The common people. Used in plural : common (used in plural), commonality, commonalty, commoner (used in plural), crowd, hoi polloi, mob, pleb (used in plural), plebeian (used in plural), populace, public, ruck[1], third estate. *See* OVER.

massacre *noun*
1. The savage killing of many victims : bloodbath, bloodletting, bloodshed, butchery, carnage, pogrom, slaughter. *See* HELP. **2.** *Informal.* The act of defeating or the condition of being defeated : beating, defeat, drubbing, overthrow, rout, thrashing, vanquishment. *Informal:* trimming, whipping. *Slang:* dusting, licking. *See* WIN.

massacre *verb* **1.** To kill savagely and indiscriminately : annihilate, butcher, decimate, slaughter. *See* CRIMES, HELP, MAKE. **2.** *Informal.* To render totally ineffective by decisive defeat : annihilate, crush, drub, overpower, overwhelm, smash, steamroller, thrash, trounce, vanquish. *Informal:* wallop. *Slang:* clobber, cream, shellac, smear. *See* WIN.

massacrer *noun*
One who murders another : butcher, cutthroat, homicide, killer, manslayer, murderer, murderess, slaughterer, slayer, triggerman. *See* HELP.

massive *adjective*
1. Extremely large; having great mass : bulky, oversize, oversized. *See* BIG. **2.** Having a relatively great weight : heavy, heavyweight, hefty, ponderous, weighty. *See* HEAVY. **3.** Of extraordinary size and power : behemoth, Brobdingnagian, Bunyanesque, colossal, cyclopean, elephantine, enormous, gargantuan, giant, gigantesque, gigantic, herculean, heroic, huge, immense, jumbo, mammoth, massy, mastodonic, mighty, monster, monstrous, monumental, mountainous, prodigious, pythonic, stupendous, titanic, tremendous, vast. *Informal:* walloping. *Slang:* whopping. *See* BIG.

massiveness *noun*
The state or quality of being physically heavy : heaviness, heftiness, ponderosity, ponderous-

ness, weight, weightiness. *Informal:* avoirdupois. *See* HEAVY.

massy *adjective*
Of extraordinary size and power : behemoth, Brobdingnagian, Bunyanesque, colossal, cyclopean, elephantine, enormous, gargantuan, giant, gigantesque, gigantic, herculean, heroic, huge, immense, jumbo, mammoth, massive, mastodonic, mighty, monster, monstrous, monumental, mountainous, prodigious, pythonic, stupendous, titanic, tremendous, vast. *Informal:* walloping. *Slang:* whopping. *See* BIG.

master *noun*
1. One who is highest in rank or authority : boss, chief, chieftain, director, head, headman, hierarch, leader. *Slang:* honcho. ***Idiom:*** cock of the walk. *See* OVER. **2.** A person who has legal title to property : holder, owner, possessor, proprietor. *See* OWNED. **3.** One that conquers : conqueror, conquistador, victor, winner. *See* WIN. **4.** A person with a high degree of knowledge or skill in a particular field : ace, adept, authority, dab hand, expert, past master, professional, proficient, wizard. *Informal:* whiz. *Slang:* crackerjack. *Chiefly British:* dab[2]. *See* ABILITY. **5.** A first form from which varieties arise or imitations are made : archetype, father, original, protoplast, prototype. *See* START.

master *adjective* Having or demonstrating a high degree of knowledge or skill : adept, crack, expert, masterful, masterly, professional, proficient, skilled, skillful. *Slang:* crackerjack. *See* ABILITY.

master *verb* **1.** To gain knowledge or mastery of by study : get, learn. *Informal:* pick up. *See* TEACH. **2.** To win a victory over, as in battle or a competition : beat, best, conquer, defeat, overcome, prevail against (*or* over), rout, subdue, subjugate, surmount, triumph over, vanquish, worst. *Informal:* trim, whip. *Slang:* ace, lick. ***Idioms:*** carry (*or* win) the day, get (*or* have) the best of, get (*or* have) the better of, go someone one better. *See* WIN. **3.** To train to live with and be of use to people : domesticate, domesticize, gentle, tame. *See* WILD. **4.** To make (an animal) docile : break, bust, gentle, tame. *See* WILD.

masterful *adjective*
1. Tending to dictate : authoritarian, bossy, dictatorial, dogmatic, domineering, imperious, magisterial, overbearing, peremptory. *See* OVER. **2.** Exercising authority : authoritative, commanding, dominant, lordly. *See* OVER, STRONG. **3.** Having or demonstrating a high degree of knowledge or skill : adept, crack, expert, master, masterly, professional, proficient, skilled, skillful. *Slang:* crackerjack. *See* ABILITY.

masterly *adjective*
Having or demonstrating a high degree of knowledge or skill : adept, crack, expert, master, masterful, professional, proficient, skilled, skillful. *Slang:* crackerjack. *See* ABILITY.

masterpiece *noun*
An outstanding and ingenious work : chef-d'oeuvre, magnum opus, masterwork. *See* GOOD.

masterstroke *noun*
A great or heroic deed : achievement, exploit, feat, gest, stunt, tour de force. *See* ACTION.

masterwork *noun*
An outstanding and ingenious work : chef-d'oeuvre, magnum opus, masterpiece. *See* GOOD.

mastery *noun*
1. Natural or acquired facility in a specific activity : ability, adeptness, art, command, craft, expertise, expertness, knack, proficiency, skill, technique. *Informal:* know-how. *See* ABILITY, KNOWLEDGE. **2.** The right and power to command, decide, rule, or judge : authority, command, control, domination, dominion, jurisdiction, might, power, prerogative, sovereignty, sway. *Informal:* say-so. *See* OVER. **3.** The act of exercising controlling power or the condition of being so controlled : command, control, dominance, domination, dominion, reign, rule, sway. *See* OVER.

masticate *verb*
To bite and grind with the teeth : champ, chew, chomp, chump[2], crump, crunch, munch. *Regional:* chaw. *See* MOUTH.

mastodonic *adjective*
Of extraordinary size and power : behemoth, Brobdingnagian, Bunyanesque, colossal, cyclopean, elephantine, enormous, gargantuan, giant, gigantesque, gigantic, herculean, heroic, huge, immense, jumbo, mammoth, massive, massy, mighty, monster, monstrous, monumental, mountainous, prodigious, pythonic, stupendous, titanic, tremendous, vast. *Informal:* walloping. *Slang:* whopping. *See* BIG.

mat also **matte** *adjective*
Lacking gloss and luster : dim, dull, flat, lackluster, lusterless. *See* LIGHT.

match *noun*
1. One of a matched pair of things : companion, counterpart, double, duplicate, fellow,

mate, twin. *See* SAME. **2.** Something closely resembling or analogous to something else : analogue, congener, correlate, correlative, correspondent, counterpart, parallel. *See* SAME. **3.** Two items of the same kind together : brace, couple, couplet, doublet, duet, duo, pair, two, twosome, yoke. *See* GROUP, SAME.

match *verb* **1.** To be equal or alike : compare, correspond, equal, measure up, parallel, touch. *Informal:* stack up. *See* SAME. **2.** To be compatible or in correspondence : accord, agree, check, chime, comport with, conform, consist, correspond, fit[1], harmonize, square, tally. *Informal:* jibe[1]. *Archaic:* quadrate. *See* AGREE. **3.** To be in keeping with : become, befit, conform, correspond, fit[1], go with, suit. *See* AGREE. **4.** To place in opposition or be in opposition to : counter, oppose, pit[1], play off. ***Idioms:*** bump heads with, meet head-on, set (*or* be) at odds, set (*or* be) at someone's throat, trade blows (*or* punches). *See* SUPPORT. **5.** To do or make something equal to : equal, meet[1], tie. *See* SAME. **6.** To represent as similar : analogize, assimilate, compare, equate, identify, liken, parallel. *See* SAME.

matchless *adjective*

Without equal or rival : alone, incomparable, nonpareil, only, peerless, singular, unequaled, unexampled, unique, unmatched, unparalleled, unrivaled. *See* SAME.

mate *noun*

1. One of a matched pair of things : companion, counterpart, double, duplicate, fellow, match, twin. *See* SAME. **2.** A husband or wife : consort, partner, spouse. *Informal:* better half. *See* MARRIAGE. **3.** One who shares interests or activities with another : associate, chum, companion, comrade, crony, fellow. *Informal:* buddy, pal. *See* NEAR. **4.** A person whom one knows well, likes, and trusts : amigo, brother, chum, confidant, confidante, familiar, friend, intimate[1]. *Informal:* bud[2], buddy, pal. *Slang:* sidekick. *See* LOVE.

mate *verb* **1.** To join or be joined in marriage : espouse, marry, wed. *Slang:* hitch. ***Idiom:*** tie the knot. *See* MARRIAGE. **2.** To engage in sexual relations with : bed, copulate, couple, have, sleep with, take. ***Idioms:*** go to bed with, make love, make whoopee, roll in the hay. *See* SEX.

material *noun*

1. That from which things are or can be made : matter, stuff, substance. ***Idiom:*** grist for one's mill. *See* MATTER. **2.** Things needed for a task, journey, or other purpose. Used in plural : accouterment (often used in plural), apparatus, equipment, gear, materiel, outfit, paraphernalia, rig, tackle, thing (used in plural), turnout. *See* MEANS. **3.** The basic substance or essential elements of character that qualify a person for a specified role : stuff, timber. *See* BE.

material *adjective* **1.** Composed of or relating to things that occupy space and can be perceived by the senses : concrete, corporeal, objective, phenomenal, physical, sensible, substantial, tangible. *See* BODY, MATTER. **2.** Of or preoccupied with material rather than spiritual or intellectual things : materialistic, sensual. *See* BODY. **3.** Related to the matter at hand : applicable, apposite, apropos, germane, pertinent, relevant. ***Idiom:*** to the point. *See* RELEVANT. **4.** Having great significance : big, consequential, considerable, historic, important, large, meaningful, monumental, significant, substantial. *See* IMPORTANT.

materialistic *adjective*

Of or preoccupied with material rather than spiritual or intellectual things : material, sensual. *See* BODY.

materiality *noun*

1. The fact of being related to the matter at hand : applicability, application, appositeness, bearing, concernment, germaneness, pertinence, pertinency, relevance, relevancy. *See* RELEVANT. **2.** That which occupies space and can be perceived by the senses : matter, substance. *See* BODY.

materialization *noun*

1. The condition of being in full force or operation : actualization, being, effect, realization. *See* BE. **2.** The condition of being fulfilled : consummation, culmination, fruition, fulfillment, realization. *See* DO, HAPPY. **3.** A physical entity typifying an abstraction : embodiment, exteriorization, externalization, incarnation, manifestation, objectification, personalization, personification, substantiation, type. *Rhetoric:* prosopopeia. *See* SUBSTITUTE.

materialize *verb*

1. To make real or actual : actualize, realize. ***Idioms:*** bring to pass, carry into effect. *See* DO. **2.** To represent (an abstraction, for example) in or as if in bodily form : body forth, embody, exteriorize, externalize, incarnate, manifest, objectify, personalize, personify, substantiate. *See* SUBSTITUTE. **3.** To come into view : appear, emerge, issue, loom, show. ***Idioms:*** make (*or* put in) an appearance, meet the eye. *See* SEE.

materiel or **matériel** *noun*
Things needed for a task, journey, or other purpose : accouterment (often used in plural), apparatus, equipment, gear, material (used in plural), outfit, paraphernalia, rig, tackle, thing (used in plural), turnout. *See* MEANS.

matey *adjective*
Chiefly British. Liking company : companionable, convivial, sociable, social. *See* ATTITUDE.

matrimonial *adjective*
Of, relating to, or typical of marriage : conjugal, connubial, hymeneal, marital, married, nuptial, spousal, wedded. *See* MARRIAGE.

matrimony *noun*
The state of being united as husband and wife : conjugality, connubiality, marriage, wedlock. *See* MARRIAGE.

matrix *noun*
A hollow device for shaping a fluid or plastic substance : cast, form, mold. *See* SURFACE.

matte *adjective* See **mat.**

matter *noun*
1. That which occupies space and can be perceived by the senses : materiality, substance. *See* BODY. **2.** That from which things are or can be made : material, stuff, substance. ***Idiom:*** grist for one's mill. *See* MATTER. **3.** What a speech, piece of writing, or artistic work is about : argument, point, subject, subject matter, text, theme, topic. *See* MEANING. **4.** Something to be done, considered, or dealt with : affair, business, thing. *See* THING.

matter *verb* To be of significance or importance : count, import, signify, weigh. *See* IMPORTANT.

matter-of-fact *adjective*
1. Lacking liveliness, charm, or surprise : arid, aseptic, colorless, drab, dry, dull, earthbound, flat, flavorless, lackluster, lifeless, lusterless, pedestrian, prosaic, spiritless, sterile, stodgy, unimaginative, uninspired. *See* EXCITE. **2.** Having or indicating an awareness of things as they really are : down-to-earth, hard, hardheaded, objective, practical, pragmatic, pragmatical, prosaic, realistic, sober, tough-minded, unromantic. *See* EXCITE, REAL. **3.** With little or no emotion or expression : dry, impassive, unemotional. *See* ATTITUDE, EXCITE.

maturate *verb*
To bring or come to full development : age, develop, grow, mature, mellow, ripen. *See* YOUTH.

mature *adjective*
Having reached full growth and development : adult, big, developed, full-blown, full-fledged, full-grown, grown, grown-up, ripe. *Idiom:* of age. *See* YOUTH.

mature *verb* To bring or come to full development : age, develop, grow, maturate, mellow, ripen. *See* YOUTH.

maudlin *adjective*
Affectedly or extravagantly emotional : bathetic, gushy, mawkish, romantic, sentimental, slushy, sobby, soft, soppy. *Informal:* gooey, mushy, schmaltzy, sloppy, soupy. *Slang:* drippy, sappy, tear-jerking. *See* FEELINGS.

maudlinism *noun*
The quality or condition of being affectedly or overly emotional : bathos, mawkishness, sentimentalism, sentimentality. *Informal:* mush, mushiness, schmaltz, schmaltziness, sloppiness. *Slang:* sappiness. *See* FEELINGS.

maul *verb*
To injure or damage, as by abuse or heavy wear : batter, knock about (*or* around), mangle[1], rough up. *See* ATTACK, HELP, STRIKE.

mausoleum *noun*
A burial place or receptacle for human remains : catacomb, cinerarium, crypt, grave[1], ossuary, sepulcher, sepulture, tomb, vault[1]. *See* KEEP, PLACE.

mawkish *adjective*
Affectedly or extravagantly emotional : bathetic, gushy, maudlin, romantic, sentimental, slushy, sobby, soft, soppy. *Informal:* gooey, mushy, schmaltzy, sloppy, soupy. *Slang:* drippy, sappy, tear-jerking. *See* FEELINGS.

mawkishness *noun*
The quality or condition of being affectedly or overly emotional : bathos, maudlinism, sentimentalism, sentimentality. *Informal:* mush, mushiness, schmaltz, schmaltziness, sloppiness. *Slang:* sappiness. *See* FEELINGS.

maxim *noun*
A usually pithy and familiar statement expressing an observation or principle generally accepted as wise or true : adage, aphorism, byword, motto, proverb, saw, saying. *See* WORDS.

maximal *adjective*
Greatest in quantity or highest in degree that has been or can be attained : maximum, top, topmost, ultimate, utmost, uttermost. *See* HIGH, LIMITED.

maximum *noun*
1. The greatest quantity or highest degree attainable : outside, top, ultimate, utmost, uttermost. ***Idiom:*** ne plus ultra. *See* HIGH, LIMITED. **2.** The greatest amount or number

allowed : ceiling, limit, limitation. *See* LIMITED.

maximum *adjective* Greatest in quantity or highest in degree that has been or can be attained : maximal, top, topmost, ultimate, utmost, uttermost. *See* HIGH, LIMITED.

maybe *adverb*
Possibly but not certainly : mayhap, perchance, perhaps. *See* CERTAIN.

mayhap *adverb*
Possibly but not certainly : maybe, perchance, perhaps. *See* CERTAIN.

maze *noun*
Something that is intricately and often bewilderingly complex : cat's cradle, entanglement, jungle, knot, labyrinth, mesh (often used in plural), morass, skein, snarl[2], tangle, web. *See* SIMPLE.

maze *verb Chiefly Regional.* To dull the senses, as with a heavy blow, a shock, or fatigue : bedaze, bemuse, benumb, daze, stun, stupefy. *See* AWARENESS.

mazuma *noun*
Slang. Something, such as coins or printed bills, used as a medium of exchange : cash, currency, lucre, money. *Informal:* wampum. *Slang:* bread, cabbage, dough, gelt, green, jack, lettuce, long green, moola, scratch. *Chiefly British:* brass. *See* MONEY.

mea culpa *noun*
A statement of acknowledgment expressing regret or asking pardon : apology, excuse, regret (used in plural). *See* REGRET.

meager *adjective*
1. Conspicuously deficient in quantity, fullness, or extent : exiguous, poor, puny, scant, scanty, skimpy, spare, sparse, stingy, thin. *Slang:* measly. *See* BIG, EXCESS. **2.** Having little flesh or fat on the body : angular, bony, fleshless, gaunt, lank, lanky, lean[2], rawboned, scrawny, skinny, slender, slim, spare, thin, twiggy, weedy. ***Idioms:*** all skin and bones, thin as a rail. *See* FAT.

mean[1] *verb*
1. To have or convey a particular idea : connote, denote, import, intend, signify, spell[1]. *Idiom:* add up to. *See* MEANING. **2.** To have in mind as a goal or purpose : aim, contemplate, design, intend, plan, project, propose, purpose, target. *Regional:* mind. *See* PLANNED, PURPOSE.

mean[2] *adjective*
1. Characterized by intense ill will or spite : black, despiteful, evil, hateful, malevolent, malicious, malign, malignant, nasty, poisonous, spiteful, venomous, vicious, wicked. *Slang:* bitchy. *See* ATTITUDE. **2.** Having or proceeding from low moral standards : base[2], ignoble, low, low-down, sordid, squalid, vile. *See* RIGHT. **3.** Ungenerously or pettily reluctant to spend money : cheap, close, close-fisted, costive, hard-fisted, miserly, niggard, niggardly, parsimonious, penny-pinching, penurious, petty, pinching, stingy, tight, tightfisted. *See* GIVE. **4.** Of low or lower quality : common, inferior, low-grade, low-quality, mediocre, second-class, second-rate, shabby, substandard. *See* BETTER. **5.** Of little distinction : humble, lowly, simple. *See* PLAIN. **6.** Lacking high station or birth : baseborn, common, déclassé, declassed, humble, ignoble, lowly, plebeian, unwashed, vulgar. *Archaic:* base[2]. *See* OVER. **7.** Affected or tending to be affected with minor health problems : ailing, indisposed, low, off-color, rocky, sickly. ***Idiom:*** under the weather. *See* HEALTH. **8.** So objectionable as to elicit despisal or deserve condemnation : abhorrent, abominable, antipathetic, contemptible, despicable, despisable, detestable, disgusting, filthy, foul, infamous, loathsome, lousy, low, nasty, nefarious, obnoxious, odious, repugnant, rotten, shabby, vile, wretched. *See* GOOD. **9.** *Informal.* Having or showing a bad temper : bad-tempered, cantankerous, crabbed, cranky, cross, disagreeable, fretful, grouchy, grumpy, ill-tempered, irascible, irritable, nasty, peevish, petulant, querulous, snappish, snappy, surly, testy, ugly, waspish. *Informal:* crabby. ***Idiom:*** out of sorts. *See* ATTITUDE. **10.** *Slang.* Hard to treat, manage, or cope with : troublesome, wicked. *Informal:* pesky. *See* EASY.

mean[3] *noun*
1. Something, as a type, number, quantity, or degree, that represents a midpoint between extremes on a scale of valuation : average, median, medium, norm, par. *See* USUAL. **2.** That by which something is accomplished or some end achieved. Used in plural : agency, agent, instrument, instrumentality, instrumentation, intermediary, mechanism, medium, organ. *See* MEANS. **3.** All things, such as money, property, or goods, having economic value. Used in plural : asset (used in plural), capital, fortune, resource (used in plural), wealth, wherewithal. *See* OWNED.

mean *adjective* Not extreme : central, intermediate, medial, median, mid, middle, middle-of-the-road, midway. *See* EDGE.

meander *verb*
1. To move or proceed on a repeatedly curving

course : coil, corkscrew, curl, entwine, snake, spiral, twine, twist, weave, wind[2], wreathe. *See* REPETITION, STRAIGHT. **2.** To move about at random, especially over a wide area : drift, gad, gallivant, peregrinate, ramble, range, roam, rove, stray, traipse, wander. *See* MOVE. **3.** To walk at a leisurely pace : amble, perambulate, promenade, ramble, saunter, stroll, wander. *Informal:* mosey. *See* MOVE.

meander *noun* An act of walking, especially for pleasure. Often used in plural : amble, perambulation, promenade, ramble, saunter, stroll, walk, wander. *See* MOVE.

meandrous *adjective*

Repeatedly curving in alternate directions : anfractuous, flexuous, serpentine, sinuous, snaky, tortuous, winding. *See* REPETITION, STRAIGHT.

meaning *noun*

1. That which is signified by a word or expression : acceptation, connotation, denotation, import, intent, message, purport, sense, significance, significancy, signification, value. *See* MEANING. **2.** The thread or current of thought uniting or occurring in all the elements of a text or discourse : aim, burden[2], drift, intent, purport, substance, tendency, tenor, thrust. *See* MEANING. **3.** What one intends to do or achieve : aim, ambition, design, end, goal, intent, intention, mark, object, objective, point, purpose, target, view, why. ***Idioms:*** end in view, why and wherefore. *See* PLANNED, PURPOSE. **4.** The gist of a specific action or situation : idea, import, point, purport, significance, significancy. *See* MEANING.

meaning *adjective* Effectively conveying meaning, feeling, or mood : eloquent, expressive, meaningful, significant. *See* EXPRESS, SHOW.

meaningful *adjective*

1. Effectively conveying meaning, feeling, or mood : eloquent, expressive, meaning, significant. *See* EXPRESS, SHOW. **2.** Conveying hidden or unexpressed meaning : pregnant, significant, suggestive. *See* MEANING. **3.** Having great significance : big, consequential, considerable, historic, important, large, material, monumental, significant, substantial. *See* IMPORTANT.

meaningless *adjective*

Lacking rational direction or purpose : mindless, pointless, purposeless, senseless. ***Idiom:*** without rhyme or reason. *See* PURPOSE.

meanness *noun*

A desire to harm others or to see others suffer : despitefulness, ill will, malevolence, malice, maliciousness, malignancy, malignity, nastiness, poisonousness, spite, spitefulness, venomousness, viciousness. *See* ATTITUDE.

measly *adjective*

1. *Slang.* Conspicuously deficient in quantity, fullness, or extent : exiguous, meager, poor, puny, scant, scanty, skimpy, spare, sparse, stingy, thin. *See* BIG, EXCESS. **2.** *Slang.* Contemptibly unimportant : inconsiderable, negligible, niggling, nugatory, paltry, petty, picayune, piddling, small, small-minded, trifling. ***Idiom:*** of no account. *See* IMPORTANT.

measure *noun*

1. The amount of space occupied by something : dimension, extent, magnitude, proportion (often used in plural), size. *See* BIG. **2.** Relative intensity or amount, as of a quality or attribute : degree, extent, magnitude, proportion. *See* BIG. **3.** A means by which individuals are compared and judged : benchmark, criterion, gauge, mark, standard, test, touchstone, yardstick. *See* USUAL. **4.** The act or process of ascertaining dimensions, quantity, or capacity : measurement, mensuration, metrology. *See* BIG. **5.** That which is allotted : allocation, allotment, allowance, dole, lot, part, portion, quantum, quota, ration, share, split. *Informal:* cut. *Slang:* divvy. *See* COLLECT. **6.** Avoidance of extremes of opinion, feeling, or personal conduct : moderateness, moderation, temperance. *See* EDGE. **7.** An action calculated to achieve an end. Often used in plural : maneuver, move, procedure, step, tactic. *See* ACTION. **8.** The formal product of a legislative or judicial body : act, assize, bill[1], enactment, law, legislation, lex, statute. *See* LAW. **9.** The patterned, recurring alternation of contrasting elements, such as stressed and unstressed notes in music : beat, cadence, cadency, meter, rhythm, swing. *See* REPETITION.

measure *verb* **1.** To ascertain the dimensions, quantity, or capacity of : gauge. *Archaic:* mete. ***Idiom:*** take the measure of. *See* BIG. **2.** To fix the limits of : bound[2], delimit, delimitate, demarcate, determine, limit, mark (out *or* off). *See* LIMITED.

measure out *verb* To set aside or distribute as a share : admeasure, allocate, allot, allow, apportion, assign, give, lot, mete (out). *See* COLLECT.

measure up *verb* To be equal or alike : compare, correspond, equal, match, parallel, touch. *Informal:* stack up. *See* SAME.

measured *adjective*
1. Careful and slow in acting, moving, or deciding : deliberate, leisurely, unhurried. *See* FAST. **2.** Marked by a regular rhythm : cadenced, metrical, rhythmic, rhythmical. *See* REPETITION.

measureless *adjective*
1. Too great to be calculated : countless, immeasurable, incalculable, incomputable, inestimable, infinite, innumerable, uncountable. *See* BIG. **2.** Having no ends or limits : boundless, endless, illimitable, immeasurable, infinite, limitless, unbounded, unlimited. *See* LIMITED.

measurelessness *noun*
The state or quality of being infinite : boundlessness, immeasurability, immeasurableness, inexhaustibility, inexhaustibleness, infiniteness, infinity, limitlessness, unboundedness, unlimitedness. *See* LIMITED.

measurement *noun*
The act or process of ascertaining dimensions, quantity, or capacity : measure, mensuration, metrology. *See* BIG.

measure out *verb* See **measure.**

measure up *verb* See **measure.**

meat *noun*
1. Something fit to be eaten : aliment, bread, comestible, diet, edible, esculent, fare, food, foodstuff, nourishment, nurture, nutriment, nutrition, pabulum, pap, provender, provision (used in plural), sustenance, victual. *Slang:* chow, eats, grub. *See* INGESTION. **2.** The most central and material part : core, essence, gist, heart, kernel, marrow, nub, pith, quintessence, root[1], soul, spirit, stuff, substance. *Law:* gravamen. *See* BE.

meatball *noun*
Slang. A large, ungainly, and dull-witted person : gawk, hulk, lout, lump[1], oaf, ox. *Informal:* lummox. *Slang:* klutz, lug[1], meathead. *See* ABILITY.

meathead *noun*
Slang. A large, ungainly, and dull-witted person : gawk, hulk, lout, lump[1], oaf, ox. *Informal:* lummox. *Slang:* klutz, lug[1], meatball. *See* ABILITY.

mechanical *adjective*
Performed or performing automatically and impersonally : automatic, perfunctory. *See* CONCERN.

mechanism *noun*
That by which something is accomplished or some end achieved : agency, agent, instrument, instrumentality, instrumentation, intermediary, mean[3] (used in plural), medium, organ. *See* MEANS.

medal *noun*
An emblem of honor worn on one's clothing : badge, decoration. *See* REWARD.

meddle *verb*
1. To intervene officiously or indiscreetly in the affairs of others : butt in, horn in, interfere, interlope. *See* PARTICIPATE. **2.** To handle something idly, ignorantly, or destructively : fiddle, fool, mess, tamper, tinker. *Informal:* monkey. *See* HELP, TOUCH.

meddler *noun*
A person given to intruding in other people's affairs : busybody, interloper, quidnunc. *Informal:* kibitzer. *Slang:* buttinsky. *Archaic:* pragmatic. *See* PARTICIPATE.

meddlesome *adjective*
Given to intruding in other people's affairs : interfering, intrusive, meddling, obtrusive, officious. *See* PARTICIPATE.

meddling *noun*
The act or an instance of interfering or intruding : interference, intervention, intrusion, obtrusion. *See* PARTICIPATE.
meddling *adjective* Given to intruding in other people's affairs : interfering, intrusive, meddlesome, obtrusive, officious. *See* PARTICIPATE.

medial *adjective*
1. At, in, near, or being the center : center, central, median, mid, middle. *See* EDGE. **2.** Not extreme : central, intermediate, mean[3], median, mid, middle, middle-of-the-road, midway. *See* EDGE.

median *adjective*
1. At, in, near, or being the center : center, central, medial, mid, middle. *See* EDGE. **2.** Not extreme : central, intermediate, mean[3], medial, mid, middle, middle-of-the-road, midway. *See* EDGE.
median *noun* **1.** A point or an area equidistant from all sides of something : center, middle, midpoint, midst. *See* EDGE. **2.** Something, as a type, number, quantity, or degree, that represents a midpoint between extremes on a scale of valuation : average, mean[3], medium, norm, par. *See* USUAL.

mediator *noun*
Someone who acts as an intermediate agent in a transaction or helps to resolve differences : broker, go-between, interceder, intercessor, intermediary, intermediate, intermediator, middleman. *See* MEANS.

medicament *noun*
1. An agent used to restore health : cure, elixir,

medication, medicine, nostrum, physic, remedy. *See* HEALTH. **2.** A substance used in the treatment of disease : drug, medication, medicine, pharmaceutical. *See* DRUGS.

medicate *verb*
To administer or add a drug to : dose, drug, narcotize, opiate, physic. *Informal:* dope (up). *See* DRUGS.

medication *noun*
1. An agent used to restore health : cure, elixir, medicament, medicine, nostrum, physic, remedy. *See* HEALTH. **2.** A substance used in the treatment of disease : drug, medicament, medicine, pharmaceutical. *See* DRUGS.

medicine *noun*
1. An agent used to restore health : cure, elixir, medicament, medication, nostrum, physic, remedy. *See* HEALTH. **2.** A substance used in the treatment of disease : drug, medicament, medication, pharmaceutical. *See* DRUGS.

mediocre *adjective*
1. Being of no special quality or type : average, common, commonplace, cut-and-dried, formulaic, garden, garden-variety, indifferent, ordinary, plain, routine, run-of-the-mill, standard, stock, undistinguished, unexceptional, unremarkable. *See* GOOD, USUAL. **2.** Of low or lower quality : common, inferior, low-grade, low-quality, mean², second-class, second-rate, shabby, substandard. *See* BETTER.

meditate *verb*
To think or think about carefully and at length : chew on (*or* over), cogitate, consider, contemplate, deliberate, entertain, excogitate, mull, muse¹, ponder, reflect, revolve, ruminate, study, think, think out, think over, think through, turn over, weigh. ***Idioms:*** cudgel one's brains, put on one's thinking cap, rack one's brain. *See* THOUGHTS.

meditation *noun*
The act or process of thinking : brainwork, cerebration, cogitation, contemplation, deliberation, excogitation, reflection, rumination, speculation, thought. *See* THOUGHTS.

meditative *adjective*
Of, characterized by, or disposed to thought : cogitative, contemplative, deliberative, excogitative, pensive, reflective, ruminative, speculative, thinking, thoughtful. ***Idiom:*** in a brown study. *See* THOUGHTS.

medium *noun*
1. Something, as a type, number, quantity, or degree, that represents a midpoint between extremes on a scale of valuation : average, mean³, median, norm, par. *See* USUAL. **2.** A settlement of differences through mutual concession : accommodation, arrangement, compromise, give-and-take, settlement. *Law:* composition. *See* AGREE. **3.** That by which something is accomplished or some end achieved : agency, agent, instrument, instrumentality, instrumentation, intermediary, mean³ (used in plural), mechanism, organ. *See* MEANS. **4.** Journalists and journalism in general. Used in plural (**media**) : fourth estate, press. *British:* Fleet Street. *See* WORDS. **5.** The totality of surrounding conditions and circumstances affecting growth or development : ambiance, atmosphere, climate, environment, milieu, mise en scène, surroundings, world. *See* BE, LIMITED, PLACE.

medley *noun*
A collection of various things : assortment, conglomeration, gallimaufry, hodgepodge, jumble, mélange, miscellany, mishmash, mixed bag, mixture, olio, patchwork, potpourri, salmagundi, variety. *Slang:* grab bag. *See* COLLECT.

meek *adjective*
1. Having or expressing feelings of humility : humble, lowly, modest. *See* ATTITUDE, BIG, SELF-LOVE. **2.** Easily managed or handled : docile, gentle, mild, tame. *See* WILD.

meekness *noun*
Lack of vanity or self-importance : humbleness, humility, lowliness, modesty. *See* ATTITUDE, BIG, SELF-LOVE.

meet¹ *verb*
1. To come up against : confront, encounter, face, run into. *See* MEET. **2.** To come together face-to-face by arrangement : get together, rendezvous. *See* MEET. **3.** To be contiguous or next to : abut, adjoin, border, bound², butt², join, neighbor, touch, verge. *See* NEAR. **4.** To come together : close, converge. *See* OPEN. **5.** To participate in or partake of personally. Also used with *with* : experience, feel, go through, have, know, see, suffer, taste (of), undergo. *Archaic:* prove. ***Idiom:*** run up against. *See* PARTICIPATE. **6.** To enter into conflict with : encounter, engage, take on. ***Idiom:*** do (*or* join) battle with. *See* CONFLICT, MEET. **7.** To present with a specified reaction : greet, react, respond. *See* FEELINGS, GREETING. **8.** To do or make something equal to : equal, match, tie. *See* SAME. **9.** To supply fully or completely : answer, fill, fulfill, satisfy. *See* DO.

meet *noun* A trial of skill or ability : competition, contest. *See* CONFLICT.

meet² *adjective*
1. Suitable for a particular person, condition,

occasion, or place : appropriate, apt, becoming, befitting, correct, felicitous, fit[1], fitting, happy, proper, right, tailor-made. *See* RIGHT. **2.** Suited to one's end or purpose : appropriate, befitting, convenient, expedient, fit[1], good, proper, suitable, tailor-made, useful. *See* AGREE, GOOD.

meeting *noun*
1. The act or fact of coming together : concourse, confluence, convergence, gathering, junction. *See* CONNECT. **2.** A number of persons who have come or been gathered together : assemblage, assembly, body, company, conclave, conference, congregation, congress, convention, convocation, crowd, gathering, group, muster, troop. *Informal:* get-together. *See* COLLECT. **3.** A formal assemblage of the members of a group : assembly, conference, congress, convention, convocation. *See* ASSEMBLE.

megrim *noun*
An impulsive, often illogical turn of mind : bee, boutade, caprice, conceit, fancy, freak, humor, impulse, notion, vagary, whim, whimsy. ***Idiom:*** bee in one's bonnet. *See* THOUGHTS.

melancholic *adjective*
In low spirits : blue, dejected, depressed, desolate, dispirited, down, downcast, downhearted, dull, dysphoric, gloomy, heavy-hearted, low, melancholy, sad, spiritless, tristful, unhappy, wistful. ***Idiom:*** down at (*or* in) the mouth. *See* HAPPY.

melancholy *noun*
A feeling or spell of dismally low spirits : blues, dejection, depression, despondence, despondency, doldrums, dolefulness, downheartedness, dumps, dysphoria, funk, gloom, glumness, heavy-heartedness, mope (used in plural), mournfulness, sadness, unhappiness. *See* FEELINGS, HAPPY.
melancholy *adjective* **1.** In low spirits : blue, dejected, depressed, desolate, dispirited, down, downcast, downhearted, dull, dysphoric, gloomy, heavy-hearted, low, melancholic, sad, spiritless, tristful, unhappy, wistful. ***Idiom:*** down at (*or* in) the mouth. *See* HAPPY. **2.** Tending to cause sadness or low spirits : blue, cheerless, depressing, dismal, dispiriting, gloomy, joyless, sad. *See* HAPPY.

mélange also **melange** *noun*
A collection of various things : assortment, conglomeration, gallimaufry, hodgepodge, jumble, medley, miscellany, mishmash, mixed bag, mixture, olio, patchwork, potpourri, salmagundi, variety. *Slang:* grab bag. *See* COLLECT.

meld *verb*
To bring or come together into a united whole : coalesce, combine, compound, concrete, conjoin, conjugate, connect, consolidate, couple, join, link, marry, unify, unite, wed, yoke. *See* ASSEMBLE.

melee also **mêlée** *noun*
A quarrel, fight, or disturbance marked by very noisy, disorderly, and often violent behavior : affray, brawl, broil[2], donnybrook, fray, free-for-all, riot, row[2], ruction, tumult. *Informal:* fracas. *Slang:* rumble. *See* ATTACK.

meliorate *verb*
To advance to a more desirable state : ameliorate, amend, better[1], help, improve, upgrade. *See* HELP.

melioration *noun*
1. The act of making better or the condition of being made better : amelioration, amendment, betterment, improvement, upgrade. *See* BETTER. **2.** Steady improvement, as of an individual or a society : amelioration, betterment, development, improvement, progress. *See* BETTER.

mellow *adjective*
1. Brought to full flavor and richness by aging : aged, ripe. *See* YOUTH. **2.** Having or producing a full, deep, or rich sound : orotund, plangent, resonant, resounding, ringing, rotund, round, sonorous, vibrant. *See* SOUNDS.
mellow *verb* To bring or come to full development : age, develop, grow, maturate, mature, ripen. *See* YOUTH.

melodic *adjective*
1. Having or producing a pleasing melody : melodious, musical, tuneful. *See* SOUNDS. **2.** Resembling or having the effect of music, especially pleasing music : dulcet, euphonic, euphonious, melodious, musical, tuneful. *See* SOUNDS.

melodious *adjective*
1. Having or producing a pleasing melody : melodic, musical, tuneful. *See* SOUNDS. **2.** Resembling or having the effect of music, especially pleasing music : dulcet, euphonic, euphonious, melodic, musical, tuneful. *See* SOUNDS.

melodramatic *adjective*
Suggesting drama or a stage performance, as in emotionality or suspense : dramatic, histrionic, histrionical, sensational, spectacular, theatric, theatrical. *See* EXCITE, STYLE, SURPRISE.

melodramatics *noun*
Overemotional exaggerated behavior calculated

for effect : dramatics, histrionics, theatrical (used in plural), theatrics. *See* FEELINGS, STYLE.

melody *noun*

A pleasing succession of musical tones forming a usually brief aesthetic unit : air, aria, strain[2], tune. *Obsolete:* note. *See* SOUNDS.

melt *verb*

1. To change from a solid to a liquid : deliquesce, dissolve, flux, fuse, liquefy, run, thaw. *See* SOLID. **2.** To disappear gradually by or as if by dispersal of particles. Also used with *away* : dissolve, fade. *See* INCREASE, SEE.

member *noun*

One of the parts into which something is divided : division, part, piece, portion, section, segment, subdivision. *See* PART.

membrane *noun*

A thin outer covering of an object : lamina, sheath, sheathing, skin. *See* SURFACE.

memento *noun*

Something that causes one to remember : keepsake, remembrance, reminder, souvenir, token, trophy. *See* REMEMBER.

memo *noun*

Informal. A brief record written as an aid to the memory : memorandum, notation, note. *See* WORDS.

memoir *noun*

A narrative of experiences undergone by the writer : commentary (often used in plural), reminiscence (often used in plural). *See* WORDS.

memorandum *noun*

A brief record written as an aid to the memory : notation, note. *Informal:* memo. *See* WORDS.

memorial *noun*

Something, as a structure or custom, serving to honor or keep alive a memory : commemoration, monument, remembrance. *See* REMEMBER.

memorial *adjective* Serving to honor or keep alive a memory : commemorative. *See* REMEMBER.

memorialize *verb*

To honor or keep alive the memory of : commemorate. *See* REMEMBER.

memorize *verb*

To commit to memory : con, learn. *See* REMEMBER.

memory *noun*

1. The power of retaining and recalling past experience : recall, recollection, remembrance, reminiscence. *See* REMEMBER. **2.** An act or instance of remembering : recollection, remembrance, reminiscence. *See* REMEMBER.

menace *noun*

1. One regarded as an imminent danger : sword of Damocles, threat. ***Idiom:*** clear and present danger. *See* SAFETY. **2.** An expression of the intent to hurt or punish another : intimidation, threat. *See* WARN.

menace *verb* **1.** To domineer or drive into compliance by the use of as threats or force, for example : bludgeon, browbeat, bulldoze, bully, bullyrag, cow, hector, intimidate, threaten. *Informal:* strong-arm. *See* OVER. **2.** To subject to danger or destruction : endanger, imperil, jeopardize, peril, risk, threaten. *See* SAFETY. **3.** To be imminent : brew, hang over, impend, loom, lower[1], overhang, threaten. *See* NEAR.

ménage *noun*

A group of usually related people living together as a unit : family, house, household. *See* GROUP.

mend *verb*

1. To restore to proper condition or functioning : doctor, fix, fix up, overhaul, patch, repair[1], revamp, right. ***Idiom:*** set right. *See* HELP. **2.** To make right what is wrong : amend, correct, emend, rectify, redress, reform, remedy, right. *See* CORRECT. **3.** To regain one's health : come around (*or* round), convalesce, gain, improve, perk up, rally, recover, recuperate. *See* HEALTH.

mendacious *adjective*

Given to or marked by deliberate concealment or misrepresentation of the truth : deceitful, dishonest, lying, untruthful. *See* HONEST.

mendacity *noun*

The practice of lying : falsehood, inveracity, perjury, truthlessness, untruthfulness. *See* TRUE.

mendicancy *noun*

The condition of being a beggar : beggary, mendicity. *See* RICH.

mendicant *noun*

One who begs habitually or for a living : almsman, almswoman, beggar, cadger. *Informal:* panhandler. *Slang:* bummer, moocher. *See* REQUEST.

mendicity *noun*

The condition of being a beggar : beggary, mendicancy. *See* RICH.

menial *adjective*

Excessively eager to serve or obey : obsequious, servile, slavish, subservient. *See* OVER.

mensuration *noun*
The act or process of ascertaining dimensions, quantity, or capacity : measure, measurement, metrology. *See* BIG.

mental *adjective*
Relating to or performed by the mind : cerebral, intellective, intellectual, psychic, psychical, psychological. *See* THOUGHTS.

mental illness *noun*
Serious mental illness or disorder impairing a person's capacity to function normally and safely : brainsickness, craziness, dementia, derangement, disturbance, insaneness, insanity, lunacy, madness, psychopathy, unbalance. *Psychiatry:* mania. *Psychology:* aberration, alienation. *See* SANE.

mentality *noun*
1. The thought processes characteristic of an individual or group : ethos, mind, mindset, psyche, psychology. ***Idiom:*** what makes someone tick. *See* THOUGHTS. **2.** The faculty of thinking, reasoning, and acquiring and applying knowledge : brain (often used in plural), brainpower, intellect, intelligence, mind, sense, understanding, wit. *Slang:* smart (used in plural). *See* ABILITY, THOUGHTS.

mentally ill *adjective*
Afflicted with or exhibiting irrationality and mental unsoundness : brainsick, crazy, daft, demented, disordered, distraught, dotty, insane, lunatic, mad, maniac, maniacal, moonstruck, off, touched, unbalanced, unsound, wrong. *Informal:* bonkers, cracked, daffy, gaga, loony. *Slang:* bananas, batty, buggy, cuckoo, fruity, loco, nuts, nutty, screwy, wacky. *Chiefly British:* crackers. *Law:* non compos mentis. ***Idioms:*** around the bend, crazy as a loon, mad as a hatter, not all there, nutty as a fruitcake, off (*or* out of) one's head, off one's rocker, of unsound mind, out of one's mind, sick in the head, stark raving mad. *See* SANE.

mention *verb*
1. To call or direct attention to something : advert, bring up, point, point out, refer, touch (on *or* upon). *See* WORDS. **2.** To refer to by name : cite, instance, name, specify. *See* SPECIFIC.

mentor *noun*
One who advises another, especially officially or professionally : adviser, consultant, counselor. *Law:* counsel. *See* OPINION.
mentor *verb Informal.* To give recommendations to (someone) about a decision or course of action : advise, counsel, recommend. *See* OPINION.

mephitic *adjective*
1. Capable of injuring or killing by poison : mephitical, poison, poisonous, toxic, toxicant, venomous, virulent. *See* HELP. **2.** Having an unpleasant odor : fetid, foul, foul-smelling, malodorous, noisome, reeky, stinking. *Informal:* smelly. *See* SMELLS.

mephitical *adjective*
Capable of injuring or killing by poison : mephitic, poison, poisonous, toxic, toxicant, venomous, virulent. *See* HELP.

mercenary *adjective*
Ruthlessly seeking personal advantage : corrupt, praetorian, venal. *Informal:* crooked. *See* SELF.
mercenary *noun* A freelance fighter : adventurer, Hessian, soldier of fortune. *See* GET.

merchandise *noun*
A product or products bought and sold in commerce : commodity, good (used in plural), line, ware. *See* MATTER, TRANSACTIONS.
merchandise *verb* To offer for sale : deal (in), handle, market, merchant, peddle, retail, sell, trade (in), vend. *See* TRANSACTIONS.

merchandiser *noun*
A person engaged in buying and selling : businessperson, dealer, merchant, speculator, trader, tradesman, trafficker. *See* TRANSACTIONS.

merchant *noun*
A person engaged in buying and selling : businessperson, dealer, merchandiser, speculator, trader, tradesman, trafficker. *See* TRANSACTIONS.
merchant *verb* To offer for sale : deal (in), handle, market, merchandise, peddle, retail, sell, trade (in), vend. *See* TRANSACTIONS.

merciful *adjective*
1. Concerned with human welfare and the alleviation of suffering : charitable, compassionate, human, humane, humanitarian. *See* ATTITUDE, KIND. **2.** Not strict or severe : charitable, clement, easy, forbearing, indulgent, lax, lenient, soft, tolerant. *See* ACCEPT.

mercifulness *noun*
Kind, forgiving, or compassionate treatment of or disposition toward others : charity, clemency, grace, lenience, leniency, lenity, mercy. *See* FORGIVENESS.

merciless *adjective*
Having or showing no mercy : pitiless, remorseless, unmerciful. *See* KIND.

mercurial *adjective*
Following no predictable pattern : capricious, changeable, erratic, fantastic, fantastical, fickle,

freakish, inconsistent, inconstant, temperamental, ticklish, uncertain, unpredictable, unstable, unsteady, variable, volatile, whimsical. *See* CHANGE, CONTINUE.

mercy *noun*
Kind, forgiving, or compassionate treatment of or disposition toward others : charity, clemency, grace, lenience, leniency, lenity, mercifulness. *See* FORGIVENESS.

mere *adjective*
Considered apart from anything else : very. *See* INCLUDE, SPECIFIC.

merely *adverb*
Nothing more than : just, only. *See* INCLUDE, SPECIFIC.

meretricious *adjective*
Tastelessly showy : brummagem, chintzy, flashy, garish, gaudy, glaring, loud, tawdry, tinsel. *Informal:* tacky[2]. *See* STYLE.

merge *verb*
To put together into one mass so that the constituent parts are more or less homogeneous : admix, amalgamate, blend, commingle, commix, fuse, intermingle, intermix, mingle, mix, stir[1]. *See* ASSEMBLE.

merger *noun*
Something produced by mixing : admixture, amalgam, amalgamation, blend, commixture, fusion, mix, mixture. *See* ASSEMBLE.

meridian *noun*
The highest point or state : acme, apex, apogee, climax, crest, crown, culmination, height, peak, pinnacle, summit, top, zenith. *Informal:* payoff. *Medicine:* fastigium. *See* HIGH.

merit *noun*
1. A level of superiority that is usually high : caliber, quality, stature, value, virtue, worth. *See* GOOD, VALUE. **2.** A special feature or quality that confers superiority : beauty, distinction, excellence, perfection, virtue. *See* GOOD.
merit *verb* To acquire as a result of one's behavior or effort : deserve, earn, gain, get, win. *Informal:* rate[1]. *See* GET.

merited *adjective*
Consistent with prevailing or accepted standards or circumstances : appropriate, deserved, due, fit[1], fitting, just, proper, right, rightful, suitable. *See* RIGHT.

meritorious *adjective*
Deserving honor, respect, or admiration : admirable, commendable, creditable, deserving, estimable, exemplary, honorable, laudable, praiseworthy, reputable, respectable, worthy. *See* GOOD, PRAISE, RESPECT, VALUE.

merriment *noun*
1. A state of joyful exuberance : blitheness, blithesomeness, gaiety, glee, gleefulness, hilarity, jocoseness, jocosity, jocularity, jocundity, jolliness, jollity, joviality, lightheartedness, merriness, mirth, mirthfulness. *See* LAUGHTER.
2. Joyful, exuberant activity : conviviality, festival, festiveness, festivity, fun, gaiety, jollity, merrymaking, revel (often used in plural), revelry. *See* LAUGHTER.

merriness *noun*
A state of joyful exuberance : blitheness, blithesomeness, gaiety, glee, gleefulness, hilarity, jocoseness, jocosity, jocularity, jocundity, jolliness, jollity, joviality, lightheartedness, merriment, mirth, mirthfulness. *See* LAUGHTER.

merry *adjective*
1. Characterized by joyful exuberance : blithe, blithesome, boon[2], convivial, gay, gleeful, jocund, jolly, jovial, mirthful. *See* HAPPY.
2. Marked by festal celebration : festive, gala, glad, gladsome, happy, joyful, joyous. *See* HAPPY.

merrymaking *noun*
1. The act of showing joyful satisfaction in an event : celebration, festivity, rejoicing, revel (often used in plural), revelry. *See* LAUGHTER.
2. Joyful, exuberant activity : conviviality, festival, festiveness, festivity, fun, gaiety, jollity, merriment, revel (often used in plural), revelry. *See* LAUGHTER.

mesh *noun*
1. An open fabric woven of strands that are interlaced and knotted at usually regular intervals : net[1], netting, network, web. *See* THING. **2.** Something that is intricately and often bewilderingly complex. Often used in plural : cat's cradle, entanglement, jungle, knot, labyrinth, maze, morass, skein, snarl[2], tangle, web. *See* SIMPLE.
mesh *verb* To come or bring together and interlock : engage. *See* CONNECT.

mesmerize *verb*
To compel, as the attention, interest, or imagination, of : arrest, catch up, enthrall, fascinate, grip, hold, rivet, spellbind, transfix. *Slang:* grab. *See* EXCITE.

mess *noun*
1. A group of things gathered haphazardly : agglomeration, bank[1], cumulus, drift, heap, hill, mass, mound, mountain, pile, shock[2], stack, tumble. *See* ORDER. **2.** A lack of order or regular arrangement : chaos, clutter, confusedness, confusion, derangement, disarrangement, disarray, disorder, disorderedness,

disorderliness, disorganization, jumble, mix-up, muddle, muss, scramble, topsy-turviness, tumble. *Slang:* snafu. *See* ORDER. **3.** A ruinous state of disorder : botch, foul-up, muddle, shambles. *Informal:* hash. *Slang:* screwup, snafu. *See* CORRECT, ORDER. **4.** An unsightly object : monstrosity, ugliness. *Informal:* fright, sight, ugly. *See* BEAUTIFUL. **5.** An individual quantity of food : helping, portion, serving. *See* INGESTION.

mess *verb* **1.** To handle something idly, ignorantly, or destructively : fiddle, fool, meddle, tamper, tinker. *Informal:* monkey. *See* HELP, TOUCH. **2.** To put (the hair or clothes) into a state of disarray. Also used with *up* : disarrange, dishevel, disorder, muss (up), rumple, tousle. *See* ORDER.

mess around *verb* **1.** *Informal.* To waste time by engaging in aimless activity : doodle, fool, putter. *Informal:* fool around. *See* THRIVE. **2.** *Informal.* To be nervously or uselessly active : bustle, fuss, putter. *See* ACTION, CALM. **3.** *Informal.* To be sexually unfaithful to another : philander, womanize. *Informal:* cheat, fool around, play around. *See* SEX.

mess up *verb* **1.** To harm irreparably through inept handling; make a mess : ball up, blunder, boggle, botch, bungle, foul up, fumble, gum up, mishandle, mismanage, muddle, muff, spoil. *Informal:* bollix up, muck up. *Slang:* blow[1], goof up, louse up, screw up, snafu. ***Idiom:*** make a muck of. *See* CORRECT, HELP. **2.** To put into total disorder : ball up, confuse, disorder, jumble, muddle, scramble, snarl[2]. *Slang:* snafu. ***Idiom:*** play havoc with. *See* ORDER. **3.** To put out of proper order : derange, disarrange, disarray, disorder, disorganize, disrupt, disturb, jumble, mix up, muddle, tumble, unsettle, upset. *See* ORDER. **4.** *Slang.* To be rough or brutal with : knock about (*or* around), manhandle, rough (up), slap around. *See* ATTACK, STRIKE.

message *noun*

1. Something communicated, as information : communication, word. *See* WORDS. **2.** That which is signified by a word or expression : acceptation, connotation, denotation, import, intent, meaning, purport, sense, significance, significancy, signification, value. *See* MEANING.

mess around *verb* See **mess.**

messenger *noun*

A person who carries messages or is sent on errands : bearer, carrier, conveyer, courier, envoy, runner, transporter. *See* OVER.

messiness *noun*

The state of being messy or unkempt : disorderliness, sloppiness, slovenliness, untidiness. *See* ORDER.

mess up *verb* See **mess.**

messy *adjective*

1. Marked by an absence of cleanliness and order : disheveled, mussy, slipshod, sloppy, slovenly, unkempt, untidy. *See* ORDER. **2.** Indifferent to correctness, accuracy, or neatness : careless, slapdash, slipshod, sloppy, slovenly, untidy. *See* CAREFUL. **3.** Lacking regular or logical order : disorderly, unsystematic. *See* ORDER.

metamorphose *verb*

1. To change into a different form, substance, or state : convert, mutate, transfigure, transform, translate, transmogrify, transmute, transpose, transubstantiate. *See* CHANGE. **2.** To bring about a radical change in : revolutionize, transform. *See* CHANGE.

metamorphosis *noun*

The process or result of changing from one appearance, state, or phase to another : change, changeover, conversion, mutation, shift, transfiguration, transformation, translation, transmogrification, transmutation, transubstantiation. *See* CHANGE.

metanoia *noun*

A fundamental change in one's beliefs : conversion, rebirth, regeneration. *See* CHANGE.

metaphysical *adjective*

1. Having no body, form, or substance : bodiless, discarnate, disembodied, immaterial, incorporeal, insubstantial, nonphysical, spiritual, unbodied, uncorporal, unsubstantial. *See* BODY. **2.** Of, coming from, or relating to forces or beings that exist outside the natural world : extramundane, extrasensory, miraculous, preternatural, superhuman, supernatural, superphysical, supersensible, transcendental, unearthly. *See* SUPERNATURAL.

mete *verb*

1. To set aside or distribute as a share. Also used with *out* : admeasure, allocate, allot, allow, apportion, assign, give, lot, measure out. *See* COLLECT. **2.** *Archaic.* To ascertain the dimensions, quantity, or capacity of : gauge, measure. ***Idiom:*** take the measure of. *See* BIG.

meter *noun*

The patterned, recurring alternation of contrasting elements, such as stressed and unstressed notes in music : beat, cadence, cadency, measure, rhythm, swing. *See* REPETITION.

method *noun*
1. The approach used to do something : fashion, manner, mode, modus operandi, style, system, way, wise[2]. *See* MEANS. **2.** Systematic arrangement and design : order, orderliness, organization, pattern, plan, system, systematization, systemization. *See* ORDER.

methodic *adjective*
Arranged or proceeding in a set, systematized pattern : methodical, orderly, regular, systematic, systematical. *See* ABILITY, ORDER.

methodical *adjective*
Arranged or proceeding in a set, systematized pattern : methodic, orderly, regular, systematic, systematical. *See* ABILITY, ORDER.

methodize *verb*
To arrange in an orderly manner : order, organize, systematize, systemize. *See* ORDER.

meticulous *adjective*
1. Showing or marked by attentiveness to all aspects or details : careful, fastidious, painstaking, punctilious, scrupulous. *See* CAREFUL. **2.** Very difficult to please : choosy, dainty, exacting, fastidious, finical, finicky, fussy, nice, particular, persnickety, squeamish. *Informal:* picky. *See* ACCEPT.

meticulousness *noun*
Attentiveness to detail : care, carefulness, fastidiousness, pain (used in plural), painstaking, punctiliousness, scrupulousness, thoroughness. *See* CAREFUL.

métier *noun*
1. Activity pursued as a livelihood : art, business, calling, career, craft, employment, job, line, occupation, profession, pursuit, trade, vocation, work. *Slang:* racket. *Archaic:* employ. *See* ACTION. **2.** Something at which a person excels : forte, long suit, specialty, strong point, strong suit. *Slang:* bag, thing. *See* ABILITY.

metrical *adjective*
Marked by a regular rhythm : cadenced, measured, rhythmic, rhythmical. *See* REPETITION.

metrology *noun*
The act or process of ascertaining dimensions, quantity, or capacity : measure, measurement, mensuration. *See* BIG.

metropolis *noun*
A large and important town : city, municipality. *Informal:* burg, town. *See* URBAN.

metropolitan *adjective*
Of, in, or belonging to a city : city, municipal, urban. *See* URBAN.

metropolitanize *verb*
To imbue with city ways, manners, and customs : citify, urbanize. *See* URBAN.

mettle *noun*
The quality of mind enabling one to face danger or hardship resolutely : braveness, bravery, courage, courageousness, dauntlessness, doughtiness, fearlessness, fortitude, gallantry, gameness, heart, intrepidity, intrepidness, nerve, pluck, pluckiness, spirit, stoutheartedness, undauntedness, valiance, valiancy, valiantness, valor. *Informal:* spunk, spunkiness. *Slang:* gut (used in plural), gutsiness, moxie. *See* FEAR.

mettlesome *adjective*
1. Having or showing courage : audacious, bold, brave, courageous, dauntless, doughty, fearless, fortitudinous, gallant, game, hardy, heroic, intrepid, plucky, stout, stouthearted, unafraid, undaunted, valiant, valorous. *Informal:* spunky. *Slang:* gutsy, gutty. *See* FEAR. **2.** Full of or characterized by a lively, emphatic, eager quality : fiery, high-spirited, peppery, spirited, vibrant. *Informal:* snappy. *See* ACTION, FEELINGS.

mew *verb*
To confine within a limited area. Also used with *up* : cage, coop (in *or* up), enclose, fence (in), immure, pen[2], shut in, shut up, wall (in *or* up). *See* FREE.

microbe *noun*
A minute organism usually producing disease : bug, germ, microorganism. *See* BEINGS.

microorganism also **micro-organism** *noun*
A minute organism usually producing disease : bug, germ, microbe. *See* BEINGS.

microscopic *adjective*
So minute as not to be discernible : imperceptible, infinitesimal. *See* BIG.

mid *adjective*
1. At, in, near, or being the center : center, central, medial, median, middle. *See* EDGE. **2.** Not extreme : central, intermediate, mean[3], medial, median, middle, middle-of-the-road, midway. *See* EDGE.

middle *adjective*
1. At, in, near, or being the center : center, central, medial, median, mid. *See* EDGE. **2.** Not extreme : central, intermediate, mean[3], medial, median, mid, middle-of-the-road, midway. *See* EDGE.
middle *noun* A point or an area equidistant from all sides of something : center, median, midpoint, midst. *See* EDGE.

middleman *noun*
Someone who acts as an intermediate agent in a transaction or helps to resolve differences : broker, go-between, interceder, intercessor,

intermediary, intermediate, intermediator, mediator. *See* MEANS.

middle-of-the-road *adjective*
Not extreme : central, intermediate, mean[3], medial, median, mid, middle, midway. *See* EDGE.

midget *adjective*
Extremely small : diminutive, dwarf, Lilliputian, miniature, minuscule, minute[2], pygmy, tiny, wee. *Informal:* peewee, pintsize, pintsized, teensy, teensy-weensy, teeny, teeny-weeny, weeny. *See* BIG.

midpoint *noun*
A point or an area equidistant from all sides of something : center, median, middle, midst. *See* EDGE.

midst *noun*
1. A point or an area equidistant from all sides of something : center, median, middle, midpoint. *See* EDGE. **2.** The most intensely active central part : eye, thick. *See* EDGE.

midway *adjective*
Not extreme : central, intermediate, mean[3], medial, median, mid, middle, middle-of-the-road. *See* EDGE.

mien *noun*
1. Behavior through which one reveals one's personality : address, air, bearing, demeanor, manner, presence, style. *Archaic:* port. *See* BE, STYLE. **2.** The way something or someone looks : appearance, aspect, look. *See* SURFACE.

miff *noun*
Extreme displeasure caused by an insult or slight : dudgeon, huff, offense, pique, resentment, ruffled feathers, umbrage. *See* LIKE, PAIN.

miff *verb* To cause resentment or hurt by callous, rude behavior : affront, huff, insult, offend, outrage, pique. ***Idioms:*** add insult to injury, give offense to. *See* ATTACK, PAIN.

might *noun*
1. Physical, mental, financial, or legal power to perform : ability, capability, capacity, competence, competency, faculty. *See* ABILITY.
2. The right and power to command, decide, rule, or judge : authority, command, control, domination, dominion, jurisdiction, mastery, power, prerogative, sovereignty, sway. *Informal:* say-so. *See* OVER. **3.** The state or quality of being physically strong : brawn, muscle, potence, potency, power, powerfulness, puissance, sinew, strength, thew (often used in plural). *See* STRONG. **4.** Capacity or power for work or vigorous activity : animation, energy, force, potency, power, puissance, sprightliness, steam, strength. *Informal:* get-up-and-go, go, pep, peppiness, zip. *See* ACTION.

mighty *adjective*
1. Having or able to exert great power : potent, powerful, puissant. *See* STRONG. **2.** Having great physical strength : potent, powerful, puissant, strong. *See* STRONG. **3.** Of extraordinary size and power : behemoth, Brobdingnagian, Bunyanesque, colossal, cyclopean, elephantine, enormous, gargantuan, giant, gigantesque, gigantic, herculean, heroic, huge, immense, jumbo, mammoth, massive, massy, mastodonic, monster, monstrous, monumental, mountainous, prodigious, pythonic, stupendous, titanic, tremendous, vast. *Informal:* walloping. *Slang:* whopping. *See* BIG.

mighty *adverb Chiefly Regional.* To a high degree : awfully, dreadfully, eminently, exceedingly, exceptionally, extra, extremely, greatly, highly, most, notably, very. *Informal:* awful. *See* BIG.

migrant *noun*
One who emigrates : emigrant, immigrant, transmigrant. *See* APPROACH.

migrant *adjective* **1.** Moving from one habitat to another on a seasonal basis : migrational, migratory, transmigratory. *See* MOVE. **2.** Moving from one area to another in search of work : itinerant, migratory. *See* MOVE.

migrate *verb*
1. To leave one's native land and settle in another : emigrate, immigrate, transmigrate. *See* APPROACH. **2.** To change habitat seasonally : transmigrate. *See* MOVE.

migration *noun*
Departure from one's native land to settle in another : emigration, exodus, immigration, transmigration. *See* APPROACH.

migrational *adjective*
Moving from one habitat to another on a seasonal basis : migrant, migratory, transmigratory. *See* MOVE.

migratory *adjective*
1. Moving from one habitat to another on a seasonal basis : migrant, migrational, transmigratory. *See* MOVE. **2.** Moving from one area to another in search of work : itinerant, migrant. *See* MOVE.

mild *adjective*
1. Of a kindly, considerate character : gentle, soft, softhearted, tender[1], tenderhearted. *See* KIND. **2.** Easily managed or handled : docile, gentle, meek, tame. *See* WILD. **3.** Free from extremes in temperature : moderate, temper-

minimization *noun*
The act or an instance of belittling : belittlement, denigration, deprecation, depreciation, derogation, detraction, disparagement. *See* ATTACK, SHOW.

minimize *verb*
To think, represent, or speak of as small or unimportant : belittle, decry, denigrate, deprecate, depreciate, derogate, detract, discount, disparage, downgrade, run down, slight, talk down. ***Idiom:*** make light (*or* little) of. *See* ATTACK, SHOW.

minimum *adjective*
Comprising the least possible : littlest, minimal, smallest. *See* BIG.

minion *noun*
1. One who supports and adheres to another : adherent, cohort, disciple, follower, henchman, partisan, satellite, supporter. *See* OVER, PRECEDE. **2.** A person who is much loved : beloved, darling, dear, honey, love, precious, sweet, sweetheart, truelove. *Informal:* sweetie. ***Idiom:*** light of one's life. *See* LOVE.

miniscule *adjective* See **minuscule.**

minister *noun*
A person ordained for service in a Christian church : churchman, churchwoman, clergyman, clergywoman, cleric, clerical, clerk, divine, ecclesiastic, parson, preacher. *Informal:* reverend. *See* RELIGION.

minister to *verb* **1.** To have the care and supervision of : attend, care for, look after, mind, see to, tend[2], watch. ***Idioms:*** keep an eye on, look out for, take care (*or* charge) of, take under one's wing. *See* CARE FOR. **2.** To work and care for : attend, do for, serve, wait on (*or* upon). *See* CARE FOR.

ministerial *adjective*
Of, for, or relating to administration or administrators : administrative, directorial, executive, managerial, supervisory. *See* OVER.

minister to *verb* See **minister.**

minor *adjective*
1. Below another in standing or importance : inferior, junior, lesser, low, lower[2], minor-league, petty, secondary, small, subaltern, subordinate, under. *Informal:* smalltime. *See* OVER. **2.** *Law.* Not yet a legal adult : underage[2]. *See* LAW, YOUTH.

minor *noun Law.* One who is not yet legally of age : child, juvenile. *Law:* infant. *See* LAW, YOUTH.

minority *noun*
The state or period of being under legal age : nonage. *Law:* infancy. *See* LAW, YOUTH.

minor-league *adjective*
Below another in standing or importance : inferior, junior, lesser, low, lower[2], minor, petty, secondary, small, subaltern, subordinate, under. *Informal:* smalltime. *See* OVER.

mint *noun*
A large sum of money : fortune. *Informal:* bundle, pretty penny, tidy sum, wad. *Slang:* pile. *See* RICH.

minus *noun*
An unfavorable condition, circumstance, or characteristic : detriment, disadvantage, drawback, handicap. *See* HELP.

minuscule also **miniscule** *adjective*
Extremely small : diminutive, dwarf, Lilliputian, midget, miniature, minute[2], pygmy, tiny, wee. *Informal:* peewee, pintsize, pintsized, teensy, teensy-weensy, teeny, teeny-weeny, weeny. *See* BIG.

minute[1] *noun*
A very brief time : crack, flash, instant, moment, second[1], trice, twinkle, twinkling, wink. *Informal:* jiff, jiffy. *Chiefly British:* tick. *See* BIG, TIME.

minute[2] *adjective*
1. Extremely small : diminutive, dwarf, Lilliputian, midget, miniature, minuscule, pygmy, tiny, wee. *Informal:* peewee, pintsize, pintsized, teensy, teensy-weensy, teeny, teeny-weeny, weeny. *See* BIG. **2.** Characterized by attention to detail : blow-by-blow, circumstantial, detailed, full, particular, thorough. *See* SPECIFIC.

minutia *noun*
Something or things that are unimportant : fiddle-faddle, frippery, frivolity, froth, nonsense, small change, small potatoes, trifle, trivia, triviality. *See* IMPORTANT, SURFACE.

miracle *noun*
1. An event inexplicable by the laws of nature : wonder. *See* SUPERNATURAL. **2.** One that evokes great surprise and admiration : astonishment, marvel, phenomenon, prodigy, sensation, stunner, wonder, wonderment. ***Idioms:*** one for the books, the eighth wonder of the world. *See* GOOD.

miraculous *adjective*
1. Of, coming from, or relating to forces or beings that exist outside the natural world : extramundane, extrasensory, metaphysical, preternatural, superhuman, supernatural, superphysical, supersensible, transcendental, unearthly. *See* SUPERNATURAL. **2.** So remarkable as to elicit disbelief : amazing, astonishing, astounding, fabulous, fantastic, fantastical, incredible, marvelous, phenomenal, prodigious,

miscellaneous *adjective*
Consisting of a number of different kinds : assorted, divers, diverse, diversified, heterogeneous, mixed, motley, multifarious, multiform, sundry, varied, variegated, various. *Biology:* polymorphic, polymorphous. *See* SAME.

miscellaneousness *noun*
The quality of being made of many different elements, forms, kinds, or individuals : diverseness, diversification, diversity, heterogeneity, heterogeneousness, multifariousness, multiformity, multiplicity, variegation, variety, variousness. *Biology:* polymorphism. *See* SAME.

miscellany *noun*
A collection of various things : assortment, conglomeration, gallimaufry, hodgepodge, jumble, medley, mélange, mishmash, mixed bag, mixture, olio, patchwork, potpourri, salmagundi, variety. *Slang:* grab bag. *See* COLLECT.

mischance *noun*
An unexpected and usually undesirable event : accident, casualty, contretemps, misadventure, misfortune, mishap. *See* HELP, SURPRISE.

mischief *noun*
1. Annoying yet harmless, usually playful acts : devilry, deviltry, diablerie, high jinks, impishness, mischievousness, prankishness, rascality, roguery, roguishness, tomfoolery. *Informal:* shenanigan (often used in plural). *See* GOOD. **2.** One who causes minor trouble or damage : devil, imp, prankster, rascal, rogue, scamp. *Informal:* cutup. *See* GOOD. **3.** The action or result of inflicting loss or pain : damage, detriment, harm, hurt, injury. *See* HELP.

mischievous *adjective*
1. Causing harm or injury : bad, deleterious, detrimental, evil, harmful, hurtful, ill, injurious. *See* HELP. **2.** Full of high-spirited fun : frisky, frolicsome, impish, playful, sportive, waggish. *See* WORK.

mischievousness *noun*
Annoying yet harmless, usually playful acts : devilry, deviltry, diablerie, high jinks, impishness, mischief, prankishness, rascality, roguery, roguishness, tomfoolery. *Informal:* shenanigan (often used in plural). *See* GOOD.

misconceive *verb*
To understand incorrectly : misapprehend, misconstrue, misinterpret, misread, mistake, misunderstand. *See* UNDERSTAND.

misconception *noun*
A failure to understand correctly : false impression, misapprehension, misinterpretation, misunderstanding. *See* UNDERSTAND.

misconduct *noun*
Improper, often rude behavior : horseplay, misbehavior, misdoing, naughtiness, wrongdoing. *See* GOOD.

misconstrue *verb*
To understand incorrectly : misapprehend, misconceive, misinterpret, misread, mistake, misunderstand. *See* UNDERSTAND.

miscreant *adjective*
Utterly reprehensible in nature or behavior : corrupt, degenerate, depraved, flagitious, perverse, rotten, unhealthy, villainous. *See* CLEAN, GOOD.

miscue *noun*
An act or thought that unintentionally deviates from what is correct, right, or true : erratum, error, inaccuracy, incorrectness, lapse, misstep, mistake, slip, slip-up, trip. *See* CORRECT.
miscue *verb* To make an error or mistake : err, mistake, slip, slip up, stumble, trip up. *See* CORRECT.

misdeed *noun*
1. A wicked act or wicked behavior : crime, deviltry, diablerie, evil, evildoing, immorality, iniquity, offense, peccancy, sin, wickedness, wrong, wrongdoing. *See* RIGHT. **2.** A serious breaking of the public law : crime, illegality, offense. *Law:* felony. *See* CRIMES.

misdoing *noun*
Improper, often rude behavior : horseplay, misbehavior, misconduct, naughtiness, wrongdoing. *See* GOOD.

misdoubt *verb*
1. To be uncertain, disbelieving, or skeptical about : distrust, doubt, mistrust, question, wonder. ***Idiom:*** have one's doubts. *See* CERTAIN. **2.** To lack trust or confidence in : distrust, doubt, mistrust, suspect. *See* TRUST.

mise en scène *noun*
1. The properties, backdrops, and other objects arranged for a dramatic presentation : scene, scenery, set[2], setting. *See* PERFORMING ARTS. **2.** The totality of surrounding conditions and circumstances affecting growth or development : ambiance, atmosphere, climate, environment, medium, milieu, surroundings, world. *See* BE, LIMITED, PLACE.

miser *noun*
A stingy person : niggard, Scrooge, skinflint. *Informal:* penny pincher. *Slang:* cheapskate, stiff, tightwad. *See* GIVE.

miserable *adjective*
1. Suffering from usually prolonged anguish : woebegone, woeful, wretched. *See* HAPPY. **2.** Having a painful ailment : afflicted,

suffering, wretched. *See* HAPPY. **3.** Of decidedly inferior quality : base[2], cheap, lousy, paltry, poor, rotten, shoddy, sleazy, trashy. *Informal:* cheesy. *Slang:* crummy, schlocky. *See* GOOD.

miserable *noun* A person living under very unhappy circumstances : loser, underdog, underprivileged, unfortunate, wretch. *See* RICH.

miserly *adjective*
Ungenerously or pettily reluctant to spend money : cheap, close, close-fisted, costive, hard-fisted, mean[2], niggard, niggardly, parsimonious, penny-pinching, penurious, petty, pinching, stingy, tight, tightfisted. *See* GIVE.

misery *noun*
1. A state of prolonged anguish and privation : suffering, woe, wretchedness. *See* HAPPY. **2.** A state of physical or mental suffering : affliction, agony, anguish, distress, hurt, pain, torment, torture, woe, wound, wretchedness. *See* HAPPY. **3.** *Informal.* A sensation of physical discomfort occurring as the result of disease or injury : ache, pain, pang, prick, prickle, smart, soreness, stab, sting, stitch, throe, twinge. *See* PAIN.

misestimate *verb*
1. To calculate wrongly : miscalculate, misjudge, misreckon. *See* CORRECT. **2.** To make a mistake in judging : misjudge. *See* CORRECT.
misestimate *noun* A wrong calculation : miscalculation, misestimation, misjudgment, misreckoning. *See* CORRECT.

misestimation *noun*
A wrong calculation : miscalculation, misestimate, misjudgment, misreckoning. *See* CORRECT.

misfire *verb*
To go wrong, be unsuccessful, or fail to attain a goal : miscarry, miss. ***Idioms:*** fall short, miss fire, miss the mark. *See* THRIVE.

misfortune *noun*
1. Bad fortune : adversity, haplessness, unfortunateness, unluckiness, untowardness. *See* LUCK. **2.** An unexpected and usually undesirable event : accident, casualty, contretemps, misadventure, mischance, mishap. *See* HELP, SURPRISE.

misgiving *noun*
A feeling of uncertainty about the fitness or correctness of an action : compunction, qualm, reservation, scruple. *See* CERTAIN.

mishandle *verb*
1. To use wrongly and improperly : abuse, misapply, misappropriate, misuse, pervert. *See* TREAT WELL. **2.** To harm irreparably through inept handling; make a mess : ball up, blunder, boggle, botch, bungle, foul up, fumble, gum up, mess up, mismanage, muddle, muff, spoil. *Informal:* bollix up, muck up. *Slang:* blow[1], goof up, louse up, screw up, snafu. ***Idiom:*** make a muck of. *See* CORRECT, HELP. **3.** To hurt or injure by maltreatment : abuse, ill-treat, ill-use, maltreat, mistreat, misuse. *See* HELP.

mishandling *noun*
1. Physically harmful treatment : abuse, ill-treatment, maltreatment, mistreatment, misusage. *See* HELP. **2.** Wrong, often corrupt use : abuse, misapplication, misappropriation, misuse, perversion. *See* TREAT WELL.

mishap *noun*
An unexpected and usually undesirable event : accident, casualty, contretemps, misadventure, mischance, misfortune. *See* HELP, SURPRISE.

mishmash *noun*
A collection of various things : assortment, conglomeration, gallimaufry, hodgepodge, jumble, medley, mélange, miscellany, mixed bag, mixture, olio, patchwork, potpourri, salmagundi, variety. *Slang:* grab bag. *See* COLLECT.

misinterpret *verb*
To understand incorrectly : misapprehend, misconceive, misconstrue, misread, mistake, misunderstand. *See* UNDERSTAND.

misinterpretation *noun*
A failure to understand correctly : false impression, misapprehension, misconception, misunderstanding. *See* UNDERSTAND.

misjudge *verb*
1. To make a mistake in judging : misestimate. *See* CORRECT. **2.** To calculate wrongly : miscalculate, misestimate, misreckon. *See* CORRECT.

misjudgment *noun*
A wrong calculation : miscalculation, misestimate, misestimation, misreckoning. *See* CORRECT.

mislay *verb*
To be unable to find : lose, misplace. *See* GET.

mislead *verb*
To cause to accept what is false, especially by trickery or misrepresentation : beguile, betray, bluff, cozen, deceive, delude, double-cross, dupe, fool, hoodwink, humbug, take in, trick. *Informal:* bamboozle, have. *Slang:* four-flush. ***Idioms:*** lead astray, play false, pull the wool over someone's eyes, put something over on, take for a ride. *See* HONEST.

misleading *adjective*
Tending to lead one into error : deceptive,

delusive, delusory, fallacious, illusive, illusory. *See* HONEST, REAL.

mislike *verb*
To have a feeling of aversion for : dislike, disrelish. *Archaic:* distaste. ***Idiom:*** have no use for. *See* LIKE.

mislike *noun* An attitude or feeling of aversion : disinclination, dislike, disrelish, distaste. *See* LIKE.

mismanage *verb*
To harm irreparably through inept handling; make a mess : ball up, blunder, boggle, botch, bungle, foul up, fumble, gum up, mess up, mishandle, muddle, muff, spoil. *Informal:* bollix up, muck up. *Slang:* blow[1], goof up, louse up, screw up, snafu. ***Idiom:*** make a muck of. *See* CORRECT, HELP.

misplace *verb*
To be unable to find : lose, mislay. *See* GET.

misplacement *noun*
The act or an instance of losing something : losing, loss. *See* GET.

misread *verb*
To understand incorrectly : misapprehend, misconceive, misconstrue, misinterpret, mistake, misunderstand. *See* UNDERSTAND.

misreckon *verb*
To calculate wrongly : miscalculate, misestimate, misjudge. *See* CORRECT.

misreckoning *noun*
A wrong calculation : miscalculation, misestimate, misestimation, misjudgment. *See* CORRECT.

misrepresent *verb*
To give an inaccurate view of by representing falsely or misleadingly : belie, color, distort, falsify, load, misstate, pervert, twist, warp, wrench, wrest. ***Idiom:*** give a false coloring to. *See* TRUE.

misrepresentation *noun*
An untrue declaration : canard, cock-and-bull story, falsehood, falsity, fib, fiction, inveracity, lie[2], misstatement, prevarication, story, tale, untruth. *Informal:* fish story, tall tale. *Slang:* whopper. *See* TRUE.

misrule *noun*
A lack of civil order or peace : anarchy, disorder, lawlessness. *See* ORDER, PEACE.

miss *verb*
1. To go wrong, be unsuccessful, or fail to attain a goal : miscarry, misfire. ***Idioms:*** fall short, miss fire, miss the mark. *See* THRIVE. **2.** To fail to take advantage of : lose, waste. ***Idioms:*** let slip, let slip through one's fingers, lose out on. *See* USED.

misshape *verb*
To alter and spoil the natural form or appearance of : contort, deform, disfigure, distort, twist. *See* BEAUTIFUL.

missing *adjective*
1. Not present : absent, away, gone, wanting. *See* ABSENCE. **2.** No longer in one's possession : gone, lost. *See* GET.

mission *noun*
1. A diplomatic office or headquarters in a foreign country : legation. *See* POLITICS. **2.** An assignment one is sent to carry out : commission, errand. *See* WORK. **3.** An inner urge to pursue an activity or perform a service : calling, vocation. *See* DESIRE.

missionary *noun*
A person doing religious or charitable work in a foreign country : apostle, evangelist, missioner. *See* RELIGION.

missionary *adjective* Of missionaries or their work : apostolic. *See* RELIGION.

missioner *noun*
A person doing religious or charitable work in a foreign country : apostle, evangelist, missionary. *See* RELIGION.

missive *noun*
A written communication directed to another : epistle, letter, note. *See* WORDS.

misstate *verb*
To give an inaccurate view of by representing falsely or misleadingly : belie, color, distort, falsify, load, misrepresent, pervert, twist, warp, wrench, wrest. ***Idiom:*** give a false coloring to. *See* TRUE.

misstatement *noun*
An untrue declaration : canard, cock-and-bull story, falsehood, falsity, fib, fiction, inveracity, lie[2], misrepresentation, prevarication, story, tale, untruth. *Informal:* fish story, tall tale. *Slang:* whopper. *See* TRUE.

misstep *noun*
An act or thought that unintentionally deviates from what is correct, right, or true : erratum, error, inaccuracy, incorrectness, lapse, miscue, mistake, slip, slip-up, trip. *See* CORRECT.

mist *noun*
A thick, heavy atmospheric condition offering reduced visibility because of the presence of suspended particles : brume, fog, haze, murk, smaze. *See* CLEAR.

mist *verb* To make dim or indistinct : becloud, bedim, befog, blear, blur, cloud, dim, dull, eclipse, fog, gloom, obfuscate, obscure, overcast, overshadow, shadow. *See* CLEAR.

mistake *noun*
An act or thought that unintentionally deviates from what is correct, right, or true : erratum, error, inaccuracy, incorrectness, lapse, miscue, misstep, slip, slip-up, trip. *See* CORRECT.
mistake *verb* **1.** To make an error or mistake : err, miscue, slip, slip up, stumble, trip up. *See* CORRECT. **2.** To understand incorrectly : misapprehend, misconceive, misconstrue, misinterpret, misread, misunderstand. *See* UNDERSTAND. **3.** To take (one thing) mistakenly for another : confound, confuse, mix up. *See* CORRECT.

mistaken *adjective*
Containing an error or errors : erroneous, fallacious, false, inaccurate, incorrect, off, unsound, untrue, wrong. ***Idioms:*** all wet, in error, off base, off (*or* wide of) the mark. *See* CORRECT.

mistreat *verb*
To hurt or injure by maltreatment : abuse, ill-treat, ill-use, maltreat, mishandle, misuse. *See* HELP.

mistreatment *noun*
Physically harmful treatment : abuse, ill-treatment, maltreatment, mishandling, misusage. *See* HELP.

mistrust *noun*
1. Lack of trust : distrust, doubt, leeriness, suspicion. *See* TRUST. **2.** A lack of conviction or certainty : doubt, doubtfulness, dubiety, dubiousness, incertitude, question, skepticism, suspicion, uncertainty, wonder. *See* CERTAIN.
mistrust *verb* **1.** To lack trust or confidence in : distrust, doubt, misdoubt, suspect. *See* TRUST. **2.** To be uncertain, disbelieving, or skeptical about : distrust, doubt, misdoubt, question, wonder. ***Idiom:*** have one's doubts. *See* CERTAIN.

mistrustful *adjective*
Lacking trust or confidence : distrustful, doubting, leery, suspicious, untrusting. *See* TRUST.

misty *adjective*
1. Covered by or as if by a thin coating or film : blurry, cloudy, dim, filmy, hazy. *See* CLEAR. **2.** Not clearly perceived or perceptible : blear, bleary, cloudy, dim, faint, foggy, fuzzy, hazy, indefinite, indistinct, obscure, shadowy, unclear, undistinct, vague. *See* CLEAR.

misunderstand *verb*
To understand incorrectly : misapprehend, misconceive, misconstrue, misinterpret, misread, mistake. *See* UNDERSTAND.

misunderstanding *noun*
A failure to understand correctly : false impression, misapprehension, misconception, misinterpretation. *See* UNDERSTAND.

misusage *noun*
Physically harmful treatment : abuse, ill-treatment, maltreatment, mishandling, mistreatment. *See* HELP.

misuse *noun*
Wrong, often corrupt use : abuse, misapplication, misappropriation, mishandling, perversion. *See* TREAT WELL.
misuse *verb* **1.** To use wrongly and improperly : abuse, misapply, misappropriate, mishandle, pervert. *See* TREAT WELL. **2.** To hurt or injure by maltreatment : abuse, ill-treat, ill-use, maltreat, mishandle, mistreat. *See* HELP.

mite *noun*
A tiny amount : bit[1], crumb, dab[1], dash, dot, dram, drop, fragment, grain, iota, jot, minim, modicum, molecule, ort, ounce, particle, scrap[1], scruple, shred, smidgen, speck, tittle, trifle, whit. *Chiefly British:* spot. *See* BIG.

mitigate *verb*
To make less severe or more bearable : allay, alleviate, assuage, comfort, ease, lessen, lighten[2], palliate, relieve. *See* INCREASE.

mitigation *noun*
Freedom, especially from pain : alleviation, assuagement, ease, palliation, relief. *See* INCREASE.

mix *verb*
1. To put together into one mass so that the constituent parts are more or less homogeneous : admix, amalgamate, blend, commingle, commix, fuse, intermingle, intermix, merge, mingle, stir[1]. *See* ASSEMBLE. **2.** To take part in social activities : mingle, socialize. *See* GROUP.
mix up *verb* **1.** To cause to be unclear in mind or intent : addle, befuddle, bewilder, confound, confuse, discombobulate, dizzy, fuddle, jumble, muddle, mystify, perplex, puzzle. *Informal:* throw. ***Idiom:*** make one's head reel (*or* swim *or* whirl). *See* CLEAR, FEELINGS. **2.** To take (one thing) mistakenly for another : confound, confuse, mistake. *See* CORRECT. **3.** To put out of proper order : derange, disarrange, disarray, disorder, disorganize, disrupt, disturb, jumble, mess up, muddle, tumble, unsettle, upset. *See* ORDER. **4.** To draw in so that extrication is difficult : catch up, embrangle, embroil, implicate, involve, suck. *See* FREE, PARTICIPATE.

mix *noun* Something produced by mixing : admixture, amalgam, amalgamation, blend, commixture, fusion, merger, mixture. *See* ASSEMBLE.

mixed *adjective*
Consisting of a number of different kinds : assorted, divers, diverse, diversified, heterogeneous, miscellaneous, motley, multifarious, multiform, sundry, varied, variegated, various. *Biology:* polymorphic, polymorphous. *See* SAME.

mixed bag *noun*
A collection of various things : assortment, conglomeration, gallimaufry, hodgepodge, jumble, medley, mélange, miscellany, mishmash, mixture, olio, patchwork, potpourri, salmagundi, variety. *Slang:* grab bag. *See* COLLECT.

mixed-up *adjective*
1. *Informal.* Characterized by physical confusion : chaotic, confused, disordered, helter-skelter, higgledy-piggledy, topsy-turvy, upside-down. *See* ORDER. **2.** *Informal.* Mentally uncertain : addled, addlepated, confounded, confused, confusional, muddle-headed, perplexed, turbid. *See* CLEAR.

mixture *noun*
1. Something produced by mixing : admixture, amalgam, amalgamation, blend, commixture, fusion, merger, mix. *See* ASSEMBLE. **2.** A collection of various things : assortment, conglomeration, gallimaufry, hodgepodge, jumble, medley, mélange, miscellany, mishmash, mixed bag, olio, patchwork, potpourri, salmagundi, variety. *Slang:* grab bag. *See* COLLECT.

mix-up also **mixup** *noun*
A lack of order or regular arrangement : chaos, clutter, confusedness, confusion, derangement, disarrangement, disarray, disorder, disorderedness, disorderliness, disorganization, jumble, mess, muddle, muss, scramble, topsy-turviness, tumble. *Slang:* snafu. *See* ORDER.

mix up *verb* See **mix.**

moan *noun*
A long, mournful cry : bay[2], howl, ululation, wail, yowl. *See* SOUNDS.

moan *verb* To utter or emit a long, mournful, plaintive sound : bay[2], howl, ululate, wail, yowl. *See* SOUNDS.

mob *noun*
1. An enormous number of persons gathered together : crowd, crush, drove, flock, horde, mass, multitude, press, ruck[1], swarm, throng. *See* BIG, GROUP. **2.** The common people : common (used in plural), commonality, commonalty, commoner (used in plural), crowd, hoi polloi, mass (used in plural), pleb (used in plural), plebeian (used in plural), populace, public, ruck[1], third estate. *See* OVER. **3.** *Informal.* An organized group of criminals, hoodlums, or wrongdoers : band[2], gang, pack, ring[1]. *See* GROUP. **4.** A very large number of things grouped together : army, cloud, crowd, drove, flock, horde, host, legion, mass, multitude, ruck[1], score (used in plural), swarm, throng. *See* BIG, GROUP.

mob *verb* **1.** To congregate, as around a person : crowd, flock, press, throng. *See* COLLECT, TIGHTEN. **2.** To fill to excess by compressing or squeezing tightly : cram, crowd, jam, load, pack, stuff. *Informal:* jam-pack. *See* FULL, TIGHTEN.

mobile *adjective*
1. Capable of moving or being moved from place to place : movable, moving, transportable, traveling. *See* MOVE. **2.** Changing easily, as in expression : changeable, fluid, plastic. *See* CHANGE.

mobilize *verb*
1. To set or keep going : actuate, drive, impel, move, propel, run. *See* MOVE. **2.** To assemble, equip, and train for war : militarize. *See* PEACE. **3.** To assemble, prepare, or put into operation, as for war or a similar emergency : marshal, muster, organize, rally. *See* MOVE.

mock *verb*
1. To make fun or make fun of : deride, gibe, jeer, jest, laugh, ridicule, scoff, scout[2], twit. *Chiefly British:* quiz. ***Idiom:*** poke fun at. *See* LAUGHTER, RESPECT. **2.** To copy (the manner or expression of another), especially in an exaggerated or mocking way : ape, burlesque, caricature, imitate, mimic, parody, travesty. ***Idiom:*** do a takeoff on. *See* SAME.

mock *noun* A false, derisive, or impudent imitation of something : burlesque, caricature, farce, mockery, parody, sham, travesty. *See* RESPECT, SAME.

mock *adjective* Made to imitate something else : artificial, imitation, manmade, simulated, synthetic. *Informal:* pretend. *See* REAL.

mockery *noun*
1. Words or actions intended to evoke contemptuous laughter : derision, ridicule. *See* LAUGHTER, RESPECT. **2.** A false, derisive, or impudent imitation of something : burlesque, caricature, farce, mock, parody, sham, travesty. *See* RESPECT, SAME. **3.** An object of amusement or laughter : butt[3], jest, joke, laughingstock. *See* RESPECT.

mocking *adjective*
Contemptuous or ironic in manner or wit : derisive, jeering, sarcastic, satiric, satirical, scoffing, sneering. *See* LAUGHTER, RESPECT.

mod *adjective*
1. Being or in accordance with the current fashion : à la mode, chic, dashing, fashionable, modish, posh, smart, stylish, swank, swanky, trig. *Informal:* classy, in, sharp, snappy, swish, tony, trendy. *Slang:* with-it. ***Idioms:*** all the rage, up to the minute. *See* STYLE, USUAL.
2. Characteristic of recent times or informed of what is current : au courant, contemporary, current, modern, up-to-date, up-to-the-minute. *See* KNOWLEDGE, NEW.

mode *noun*
1. The approach used to do something : fashion, manner, method, modus operandi, style, system, way, wise[2]. *See* MEANS. **2.** A distinctive way of expressing oneself : fashion, manner, style, tone, vein. *See* STYLE. **3.** Manner of being or form of existence : condition, situation, state, status. *See* BE. **4.** The current custom : craze, fad, fashion, furor, rage, style, trend, vogue. *Informal:* thing. ***Idioms:*** the in thing, the last word, the latest thing. *See* STYLE, USUAL.

model *noun*
1. A small-scale representation of something : miniature. *See* SAME. **2.** One that is worthy of imitation or duplication : beau ideal, example, exemplar, ideal, mirror, paradigm, pattern, standard. *See* GOOD.
model *verb* **1.** To take as a model or make conform to a model. Also used with *on*, *upon*, or *after* : copy, emulate, follow, imitate, pattern (on, upon, *or* after). ***Idioms:*** follow in the footsteps of, follow suit, follow the example of. *See* SAME. **2.** To give form to by or as if by pressing and kneading : form, mold, shape. *See* SURFACE.
model *adjective* **1.** Having the nature of, constituting, or serving as a type : archetypal, archetypic, archetypical, classic, classical, paradigmatic, prototypal, prototypic, prototypical, quintessential, representative, typic, typical. *See* SAME, USUAL. **2.** Conforming to an ultimate form of perfection or excellence : exemplary, ideal, perfect, supreme. *See* GOOD.

moderate *adjective*
1. Not excessive or extreme in amount, degree, or force : modest, reasonable, temperate. *See* BIG, EDGE. **2.** Kept within sensible limits : conservative, discreet, reasonable, restrained, temperate. *See* PLAIN, RESTRAINT. **3.** Suited to or within the means of ordinary people : modest, popular, reasonable. *See* MONEY. **4.** Not steep or abrupt : easy, gentle, gradual. *See* RISE. **5.** Requiring little effort or exertion : easy, light[2]. *See* EASY. **6.** Free from extremes in temperature : mild, temperate. *See* EDGE. **7.** Of small intensity : gentle, light[2], slight, soft. *See* STRONG. **8.** Of moderately good quality but less than excellent : acceptable, adequate, all right, average, common, decent, fair, fairish, goodish, passable, respectable, satisfactory, sufficient, tolerable. *Informal:* OK, tidy. *See* GOOD.
moderate *verb* **1.** To make or become less severe or extreme : mute, qualify, soften, subdue, tame, temper, tone down. *See* INCREASE. **2.** To become or cause to become less active or intense : abate, bate, die (away, down, off, *or* out), ease (off *or* up), ebb, fall, fall off, lapse, let up, remit, slacken, slack off, subside, wane. *See* INCREASE.

moderateness *noun*
Avoidance of extremes of opinion, feeling, or personal conduct : measure, moderation, temperance. *See* EDGE.

moderation *noun*
Avoidance of extremes of opinion, feeling, or personal conduct : measure, moderateness, temperance. *See* EDGE.

modern *adjective*
1. Of or relating to the present or times close to the present : latter-day, recent. *See* NEW, TIME. **2.** Characteristic of recent times or informed of what is current : au courant, contemporary, current, mod, up-to-date, up-to-the-minute. *See* KNOWLEDGE, NEW.
modern *noun* A person of the present age : contemporary. *See* NEW, TIME.

modernize *verb*
To make modern in appearance or style : update. *See* NEW.

modest *adjective*
1. Having or expressing feelings of humility : humble, lowly, meek. *See* ATTITUDE, BIG, SELF-LOVE. **2.** Not forward but reticent or reserved in manner : backward, bashful, coy, demure, diffident, retiring, self-effacing, shy[1], timid. *See* RESTRAINT. **3.** Morally beyond reproach, especially in sexual conduct : chaste, decent, nice, pure, virgin, virginal, virtuous. *See* GOOD, RESTRAINT, SEX. **4.** Not lewd or obscene : clean, decent, wholesome. *See* DECENT. **5.** Not elaborate or showy, as in appearance or style : plain, simple, unassuming, unostentatious, unpretentious. *See* PLAIN. **6.** Not excessive or extreme in amount, degree,

or force : moderate, reasonable, temperate. *See* BIG, EDGE. **7.** Suited to or within the means of ordinary people : moderate, popular, reasonable. *See* MONEY.

modesty *noun*
1. Lack of vanity or self-importance : humbleness, humility, lowliness, meekness. *See* ATTITUDE, BIG, SELF-LOVE. **2.** Reserve in speech, behavior, or dress : demureness, diffidence, reticence, self-effacement. *See* RESTRAINT.
3. The condition of being chaste : chastity, decency, innocence, purity, virginity, virtue, virtuousness. *See* GOOD, RESTRAINT, SEX.
4. Lack of ostentation or pretension : plainness, simpleness, simplicity, unassumingness, unostentatiousness, unpretentiousness. *See* PLAIN.

modicum *noun*
A tiny amount : bit[1], crumb, dab[1], dash, dot, dram, drop, fragment, grain, iota, jot, minim, mite, molecule, ort, ounce, particle, scrap[1], scruple, shred, smidgen, speck, tittle, trifle, whit. *Chiefly British:* spot. *See* BIG.

modification *noun*
The process or result of making or becoming different : alteration, change, mutation, permutation, variation. *See* CHANGE.

modified *adjective*
Not total, unlimited, or wholehearted : limited, qualified, reserved, restricted. *See* BIG, LIMITED.

modify *verb*
To make or become different : alter, change, mutate, turn, vary. *See* CHANGE.

modish *adjective*
Being or in accordance with the current fashion : à la mode, chic, dashing, fashionable, mod, posh, smart, stylish, swank, swanky, trig. *Informal:* classy, in, sharp, snappy, swish, tony, trendy. *Slang:* with-it. ***Idioms:*** all the rage, up to the minute. *See* STYLE, USUAL.

modus operandi *noun*
1. A method used in dealing with something : approach, attack, course, line, plan, procedure, tack, technique. *See* MEANS. **2.** The approach used to do something : fashion, manner, method, mode, style, system, way, wise[2]. *See* MEANS.

moil *verb*
To exert one's mental or physical powers, usually under difficulty and to the point of exhaustion : drive, fag, labor, strain[1], strive, sweat, toil, travail, tug, work. ***Idiom:*** break one's back (*or* neck). *See* WORK.

moil *noun* Physical exertion that is usually difficult and exhausting : drudgery, labor, toil, travail, work. *Informal:* sweat. *Chiefly British:* fag. ***Idiom:*** sweat of one's brow. *See* WORK.

moist *adjective*
Slightly wet : damp, dank. *See* DRY.

moisten *verb*
To make moist : bathe, dampen, wash, wet. *See* DRY.

moistureless *adjective*
Having little or no liquid or moisture : anhydrous, arid, bone-dry, dry, sere, waterless. *See* DRY.

mold *noun*
1. A hollow device for shaping a fluid or plastic substance : cast, form, matrix. *See* SURFACE.
2. A class that is defined by the common attribute or attributes possessed by all its members : breed, cast, description, feather, ilk, kind[2], lot, manner, nature, order, sort, species, stamp, stripe, type, variety. *Informal:* persuasion. *See* GROUP.

mold *verb* **1.** To create by forming, combining, or altering materials : assemble, build, construct, fabricate, fashion, forge[1], frame, make, manufacture, produce, put together, shape. *See* MAKE. **2.** To give form to by or as if by pressing and kneading : form, model, shape. *See* SURFACE.

moldable *adjective*
Capable of being shaped, bent, or drawn out, as by hammering or pressure : ductile, flexible, flexile, flexuous, malleable, plastic, pliable, pliant, supple, workable. *See* FLEXIBLE.

molder *verb*
To become or cause to become rotten or unsound : break down, decay, decompose, deteriorate, disintegrate, putrefy, rot, spoil, taint, turn. ***Idioms:*** go bad, go to pot, go to seed. *See* BETTER, THRIVE.

moldy *adjective*
Smelling of mildew or decay : frowzy, fusty, musty, putrid, rancid, rank[2], rotten. *See* SMELLS.

molecule *noun*
A tiny amount : bit[1], crumb, dab[1], dash, dot, dram, drop, fragment, grain, iota, jot, minim, mite, modicum, ort, ounce, particle, scrap[1], scruple, shred, smidgen, speck, tittle, trifle, whit. *Chiefly British:* spot. *See* BIG.

moll *noun*
Slang. A woman who engages in sexual intercourse for payment : bawd, call girl, camp follower, courtesan, harlot, prostitute, scarlet woman, streetwalker, strumpet, tart[2], whore.

Slang: hooker. ***Idioms:*** lady of easy virtue, lady of pleasure, lady of the night. *See* SEX.

mollify *verb*
To ease the anger or agitation of : appease, assuage, calm (down), conciliate, dulcify, gentle, pacify, placate, propitiate, soften, soothe, sweeten. ***Idiom:*** pour oil on troubled water. *See* CALM.

mollycoddle *verb*
To treat with indulgence and often overtender care : baby, cater, coddle, cosset, indulge, overindulge, pamper, spoil. *See* TREAT WELL.
mollycoddle *noun* A person who behaves in a childish, weak, or spoiled way : baby, milksop, milquetoast, weakling. ***Idiom:*** mama's boy (*or* girl). *See* YOUTH.

molt *verb*
To cast off by a natural process : exuviate, shed, slough[2], throw off. *See* PUT ON.

moment *noun*
1. A very brief time : crack, flash, instant, minute[1], second[1], trice, twinkle, twinkling, wink. *Informal:* jiff, jiffy. *Chiefly British:* tick. *See* BIG, TIME. **2.** A particular interval of time that is limited and often crucial : instant, juncture, point. *See* TIME. **3.** The quality or state of being important : concern, concernment, consequence, import, importance, significance, significancy, weight, weightiness. *See* IMPORTANT.

momentary *adjective*
1. Lasting or existing only for a short time : ephemeral, evanescent, fleet, fleeting, fugacious, fugitive, passing, short-lived, temporal, temporary, transient, transitory. *See* CONTINUE, TIME. **2.** About to occur at any moment : imminent, impending, proximate. *See* NEAR.

momentous *adjective*
1. Having great consequence or weight : earnest[1], grave[2], heavy, serious, severe, weighty. *See* IMPORTANT. **2.** So critically decisive as to affect the future : fatal, fateful. *See* DECIDE.

momentousness *noun*
The condition of being grave and of involving serious consequences : graveness, gravity, seriousness, weightiness. *See* IMPORTANT.

monetary *adjective*
Of or relating to finances or those who deal in finances : financial, fiscal, pecuniary. *See* MONEY.

money *noun*
1. Something, such as coins or printed bills, used as a medium of exchange : cash, currency, lucre. *Informal:* wampum. *Slang:* bread, cabbage, dough, gelt, green, jack, lettuce, long green, mazuma, moola, scratch. *Chiefly British:* brass. *See* MONEY. **2.** The monetary resources of a government, organization, or individual. Often used in plural : capital, finance (used in plural), fund (used in plural). *See* MONEY.

moneyed *adjective*
Possessing a large amount of money, land, or other material possessions : affluent, flush, rich, wealthy. *Slang:* loaded. ***Idioms:*** having money to burn, in the money, made of money, rolling in money. *See* RICH.

moneymaking *adjective*
Affording profit : advantageous, fat, lucrative, profitable, remunerative, rewarding. *See* GET.

moneyman *noun*
Informal. One who is occupied with or expert in large-scale financial affairs : capitalist, financier. *See* MONEY.

monicker *noun* See **moniker.**

moniker or **monicker** *noun*
Slang. The word or words by which one is called and identified : appellation, appellative, cognomen, denomination, designation, epithet, name, nickname, style, tag, title. *Slang:* handle. *See* SPECIFIC, WORDS.

monition *noun*
Advice to beware, as of a person or thing : admonishment, admonition, caution, caveat, warning. *See* WARN.

monitory *adjective*
Giving warning : admonishing, admonitory, cautionary, warning. *See* WARN.

monkey *noun*
Slang. A person who is easily deceived or victimized : butt[3], dupe, fool, gull, lamb, pushover, victim. *Informal:* sucker. *Slang:* fall guy, gudgeon, mark, patsy, pigeon, sap[1]. *Chiefly British:* mug. *See* WISE.
monkey *verb* **1.** *Informal.* To handle something idly, ignorantly, or destructively : fiddle, fool, meddle, mess, tamper, tinker. *See* HELP, TOUCH. **2.** To move one's fingers or hands in a nervous or aimless fashion : fiddle, fidget, fool, play, putter, tinker, toy, trifle, twiddle. *See* TOUCH.

monkeyshine *noun*
Slang. A mischievous act. Often used in plural : antic, caper, frolic, joke, lark, prank[1], trick. *Informal:* shenanigan. *See* GOOD, WORK.

monocracy *noun*
A government in which a single leader or party exercises absolute control over all citizens and every aspect of their lives : absolutism, autarchy, autocracy, despotism, dictatorship, tyranny. *See* OVER, POLITICS.

monocratic *adjective*
Having and exercising complete political power and control : absolute, absolutistic, arbitrary, autarchic, autarchical, autocratic, autocratical, despotic, dictatorial, totalitarian, tyrannic, tyrannical, tyrannous. *See* OVER, POLITICS.

monopolize *verb*
1. To cause to be busy or in use : engage, occupy, preempt, tie up. *See* ACTION, USED. **2.** To occupy the full attention of : absorb, consume, engross, immerse, preoccupy. *See* AWARENESS, EXCITE.

monopoly *noun*
Exclusive control or possession : corner. *See* CONTROL, OWNED.

monotone *noun*
A tiresome lack of variety : humdrum, monotonousness, monotony, sameness. *See* CHANGE, EXCITE.

monotonous *adjective*
Arousing no interest or curiosity : boring, drear, dreary, dry, dull, humdrum, irksome, stuffy, tedious, tiresome, uninteresting, weariful, wearisome, weary. *See* EXCITE.

monotonousness *noun*
A tiresome lack of variety : humdrum, monotone, monotony, sameness. *See* CHANGE, EXCITE.

monotony *noun*
A tiresome lack of variety : humdrum, monotone, monotonousness, sameness. *See* CHANGE, EXCITE.

monster *noun*
1. A person or animal that is abnormally formed : freak, monstrosity. *See* USUAL. **2.** One that is extraordinarily large and powerful : behemoth, giant, Goliath, jumbo, leviathan, mammoth, titan. *Slang:* whopper. *See* BEINGS, BIG. **3.** A perversely bad, cruel, or wicked person : archfiend, beast, devil, fiend, ghoul, ogre, tiger, vampire. *See* KIND.

monster *adjective* Of extraordinary size and power : behemoth, Brobdingnagian, Bunyanesque, colossal, cyclopean, elephantine, enormous, gargantuan, giant, gigantesque, gigantic, herculean, heroic, huge, immense, jumbo, mammoth, massive, massy, mastodonic, mighty, monstrous, monumental, mountainous, prodigious, pythonic, stupendous, titanic, tremendous, vast. *Informal:* walloping. *Slang:* whopping. *See* BIG.

monstrosity *noun*
1. An unsightly object : mess, ugliness. *Informal:* fright, sight, ugly. *See* BEAUTIFUL. **2.** A monstrous offense or evil : atrocity, enormity, outrage. *See* RIGHT. **3.** A person or animal that is abnormally formed : freak, monster. *See* USUAL.

monstrous *adjective*
1. Disgracefully and grossly offensive : atrocious, heinous, outrageous, scandalous, shocking. *Archaic:* enormous. *See* RIGHT. **2.** Of extraordinary size and power : behemoth, Brobdingnagian, Bunyanesque, colossal, cyclopean, elephantine, enormous, gargantuan, giant, gigantesque, gigantic, herculean, heroic, huge, immense, jumbo, mammoth, massive, massy, mastodonic, mighty, monster, monumental, mountainous, prodigious, pythonic, stupendous, titanic, tremendous, vast. *Informal:* walloping. *Slang:* whopping. *See* BIG. **3.** Resembling a freak : freakish, freaky, grotesque. *See* USUAL.

monstrousness *noun*
The quality of passing all moral bounds : atrociousness, atrocity, enormity, heinousness. *See* GOOD.

monument *noun*
Something, as a structure or custom, serving to honor or keep alive a memory : commemoration, memorial, remembrance. *See* REMEMBER.

monumental *adjective*
1. Of extraordinary size and power : behemoth, Brobdingnagian, Bunyanesque, colossal, cyclopean, elephantine, enormous, gargantuan, giant, gigantesque, gigantic, herculean, heroic, huge, immense, jumbo, mammoth, massive, massy, mastodonic, mighty, monster, monstrous, mountainous, prodigious, pythonic, stupendous, titanic, tremendous, vast. *Informal:* walloping. *Slang:* whopping. *See* BIG. **2.** Having great significance : big, consequential, considerable, historic, important, large, material, meaningful, significant, substantial. *See* IMPORTANT.

mooch *verb*
Slang. To ask or ask for as charity : beg, bum[1], cadge. *Informal:* panhandle. *See* REQUEST.

moocher *noun*
Slang. One who begs habitually or for a living : almsman, almswoman, beggar, cadger, mendicant. *Informal:* panhandler. *Slang:* bummer. *See* REQUEST.

mood *noun*
1. A temporary state of mind or feeling : frame of mind, humor, spirit (used in plural), temper, vein. *See* FEELINGS. **2.** A general impression produced by a predominant quality or characteristic : air, ambiance, atmosphere, aura, feel, feeling, smell, tone. *See* BE. **3.** A

prevailing quality, as of thought, behavior, or attitude : climate, spirit, temper, tone. *See* ATTITUDE.

moody *adjective*
1. Given to changeable emotional states, especially of anger or gloom : temperamental. *See* FEELINGS. **2.** Broodingly and sullenly unhappy : dour, gloomy, glum, morose, saturnine, sour, sulky, sullen, surly. *See* HAPPY.

moola or **moolah** *noun*
Slang. Something, such as coins or printed bills, used as a medium of exchange : cash, currency, lucre, money. *Informal:* wampum. *Slang:* bread, cabbage, dough, gelt, green, jack, lettuce, long green, mazuma, scratch. *Chiefly British:* brass. *See* MONEY.

moolah *noun* See **moola.**

mooncalf *noun*
One deficient in judgment and good sense : ass, fool, idiot, imbecile, jackass, moron, nincompoop, ninny, nitwit, simple, simpleton, softhead, tomfool. *Informal:* dope, gander, goose. *Slang:* cretin, ding-dong, dip, goof, jerk, nerd, schmo, schmuck, turkey. *See* ABILITY.

moonstricken *adjective* See **moonstruck.**

moonstruck also **moonstricken** *adjective*
Afflicted with or exhibiting irrationality and mental unsoundness : brainsick, crazy, daft, demented, disordered, distraught, dotty, insane, lunatic, mad, maniac, maniacal, mentally ill, off, touched, unbalanced, unsound, wrong. *Informal:* bonkers, cracked, daffy, gaga, loony. *Slang:* bananas, batty, buggy, cuckoo, fruity, loco, nuts, nutty, screwy, wacky. *Chiefly British:* crackers. *Law:* non compos mentis. *Idioms:* around the bend, crazy as a loon, mad as a hatter, not all there, nutty as a fruitcake, off (*or* out of) one's head, off one's rocker, of unsound mind, out of one's mind, sick in the head, stark raving mad. *See* SANE.

moony *adjective*
Given to daydreams or reverie : dreamy, visionary, woolgathering. *See* REAL.

moor *verb*
1. To join one thing to another : affix, attach, clip[2], connect, couple, fasten, fix, secure. *See* ASSEMBLE. **2.** To make secure : anchor, catch, fasten, fix, secure. *Idiom:* make fast. *See* MOVE.

moot *verb*
1. To put forward (a topic) for discussion : bring up, broach, introduce, put forth, raise. *See* START. **2.** To speak together and exchange ideas and opinions about : bandy (about), discuss, talk over, thrash out (*or* over), thresh out (*or* over), toss around. *Informal:* hash (over), kick around, knock about (*or* around). *Slang:* rap[3]. *Idiom:* go into a huddle. *See* WORDS. **3.** To put forth reasons for or against something, often excitedly : argue, contend, debate, dispute. *See* AFFIRM, WORDS.

moot *adjective* In doubt or dispute : arguable, contested, debatable, disputable, doubtful, exceptionable, mootable, problematic, problematical, questionable, uncertain. *See* CERTAIN.

mootable *adjective*
In doubt or dispute : arguable, contested, debatable, disputable, doubtful, exceptionable, moot, problematic, problematical, questionable, uncertain. *See* CERTAIN.

mope *verb*
1. To focus the attention on something moodily and at length : brood, cark, dwell, fret, worry. *Informal:* stew. *See* CONCERN, THOUGHTS. **2.** To be sullenly aloof or withdrawn, as in silent resentment or protest : pet[2], pout, sulk. *See* HAPPY.

mope *noun* A feeling or spell of dismally low spirits. Used in plural : blues, dejection, depression, despondence, despondency, doldrums, dolefulness, downheartedness, dumps, dysphoria, funk, gloom, glumness, heavyheartedness, melancholy, mournfulness, sadness, unhappiness. *See* FEELINGS, HAPPY.

moppet *noun*
A young person between birth and puberty : bud[1], child, innocent, juvenile, tot[1], youngster. *Informal:* kid. *Scots:* bairn. *See* KIN, YOUTH.

moral *adjective*
1. Teaching morality : didactic, didactical, moralizing. *See* TEACH. **2.** In accordance with principles of right or good conduct : ethical, principled, proper, right, righteous, rightful, right-minded, virtuous. *See* RIGHT. **3.** Being on a high intellectual or moral level : elevated, high-minded, noble. *See* HIGH.

moral *noun* **1.** The principle taught by a fable or parable, for example : lesson. *See* MEANING. **2.** A rule or habit of conduct with regard to right and wrong or a body of such rules and habits. Used in plural : ethic, ethicality, morality. *See* RIGHT.

morale *noun*
A strong sense of enthusiasm and dedication to a common goal that unites a group : esprit, esprit de corps. *See* CONCERN, FEELINGS.

morality *noun*
1. The quality or state of being morally sound : good, goodness, probity, rectitude, righteousness, rightness, uprightness, virtue, virtuous-

ness. *See* RIGHT. **2.** The moral quality of a course of action : ethic (used in plural), ethicality, ethicalness, propriety, righteousness, rightfulness, rightness. *See* RIGHT. **3.** A rule or habit of conduct with regard to right and wrong or a body of such rules and habits : ethic, ethicality, moral (used in plural). *See* RIGHT.

moralize *verb*
To indulge in moral reflection, usually pompously : preach, sermonize. *See* TEACH.

moralizing *adjective*
Teaching morality : didactic, didactical, moral. *See* TEACH.

morass *noun*
1. A usually low-lying area of soft waterlogged ground and standing water : bog, fen, marsh, marshland, mire, muskeg, quag, quagmire, slough[1], swamp, swampland, wetland. *See* DRY. **2.** Something that is intricately and often bewilderingly complex : cat's cradle, entanglement, jungle, knot, labyrinth, maze, mesh (often used in plural), skein, snarl[2], tangle, web. *See* SIMPLE.

morbid *adjective*
Susceptible to or marked by preoccupation with unwholesome matters : macabre, sick, unhealthy, unwholesome. *See* GOOD.

mordacious *adjective*
So sharp as to cause mental pain : acerbic, acid, acidic, acrid, astringent, biting, caustic, corrosive, cutting, mordant, pungent, scathing, sharp, slashing, stinging, trenchant, truculent, vitriolic. *See* ATTACK, RESPECT.

mordacity *noun*
Irony or bitterness, as of tone : acerbity, acidity, acridity, causticity, corrosiveness, mordancy, sarcasm, trenchancy. *See* LAUGHTER, RESPECT.

mordancy *noun*
Irony or bitterness, as of tone : acerbity, acidity, acridity, causticity, corrosiveness, mordacity, sarcasm, trenchancy. *See* LAUGHTER, RESPECT.

mordant *adjective*
So sharp as to cause mental pain : acerbic, acid, acidic, acrid, astringent, biting, caustic, corrosive, cutting, mordacious, pungent, scathing, sharp, slashing, stinging, trenchant, truculent, vitriolic. *See* ATTACK, RESPECT.

more *adjective*
Being an addition : added, additional, extra, fresh, further, new, other. *See* INCREASE.
more *adverb* **1.** To a greater extent : better[1]. *See* BIG. **2.** In addition : additionally, also, besides, further, furthermore, item, likewise, moreover, still, too, yet. ***Idioms:*** as well, to boot. *See* INCREASE.

moreover *adverb*
In addition : additionally, also, besides, further, furthermore, item, likewise, more, still, too, yet. ***Idioms:*** as well, to boot. *See* INCREASE.

mores *noun*
Socially correct behavior : decorum, etiquette, good form, manner (used in plural), propriety (also used in plural), p's and q's. *See* USUAL.

morn *noun*
The first appearance of daylight in the morning : aurora, cockcrow, dawn, dawning, daybreak, morning, sunrise, sunup. *See* START.

morning *noun*
1. The time of day from sunrise to noon : forenoon. *See* TIME. **2.** The first appearance of daylight in the morning : aurora, cockcrow, dawn, dawning, daybreak, morn, sunrise, sunup. *See* START.

moron *noun*
One deficient in judgment and good sense : ass, fool, idiot, imbecile, jackass, mooncalf, nincompoop, ninny, nitwit, simple, simpleton, softhead, tomfool. *Informal:* dope, gander, goose. *Slang:* cretin, ding-dong, dip, goof, jerk, nerd, schmo, schmuck, turkey. *See* ABILITY.

moronic *adjective*
So senseless as to be laughable : absurd, foolish, harebrained, idiotic, imbecilic, insane, lunatic, mad, nonsensical, preposterous, silly, softheaded, tomfool, unearthly, zany. *Informal:* cockeyed, crazy, loony, loopy. *Slang:* balmy[2], dippy, dopey, jerky, sappy, wacky. *See* ABILITY, KNOWLEDGE.

morose *adjective*
Broodingly and sullenly unhappy : dour, gloomy, glum, moody, saturnine, sour, sulky, sullen, surly. *See* HAPPY.

morsel *noun*
1. A small portion of food : bit[1], crumb, mouthful, piece. *Informal:* bite. *See* BIG. **2.** A light meal : bite, snack. *See* INGESTION. **3.** Something fine and delicious, especially a food : dainty, delicacy, tidbit, treat. *Informal:* goody. *See* GOOD, INGESTION.

mortal *adjective*
1. Of or characteristic of human beings or mankind : human. *See* BEINGS. **2.** Causing or tending to cause death : deadly, deathly, fatal, lethal, vital. *See* LIVE. **3.** Capable of being anticipated, considered, or imagined : conceivable, earthly, imaginable, likely, possible, thinkable. ***Idioms:*** humanly possible, within the

bounds (*or* range *or* realm) of possibility. *See* POSSIBLE.

mortal *noun* A member of the human race : being, body, creature, homo, human, human being, individual, life, man, party, person, personage, soul. *See* BEINGS.

mortgage *verb*
To give or deposit as a pawn : hypothecate, pawn[1], pledge. *Slang:* hock. *See* TRANSACTIONS.

mortification *noun*
A lowering in or deprivation of character or self-esteem : abasement, debasement, degradation, humiliation. *See* RESPECT, WIN.

mortify *verb*
1. To deprive of esteem, self-worth, or effectiveness : abase, degrade, demean[2], humable, humiliate. ***Idioms:*** bring low, take down a peg. *See* RESPECT, WIN. **2.** To cause (a person) to be self-consciously distressed : abash, chagrin, confound, confuse, discomfit, discomfort, disconcert, discountenance, embarrass, faze. ***Idioms:*** put on the spot, throw for a loop. *See* PAIN.

mosey *verb*
Informal. To walk at a leisurely pace : amble, meander, perambulate, promenade, ramble, saunter, stroll, wander. *See* MOVE.

mossback *noun*
1. A person who vehemently, often fanatically opposes progress and favors return to a previous condition : die-hard, reactionary, ultraconservative. *See* POLITICS. **2.** An old-fashioned person who is reluctant to change or innovate : fogy, fossil, fuddy-duddy. *Informal:* stick-in-the-mud. *Slang:* square. *See* NEW.

mossbacked *adjective*
Vehemently, often fanatically opposing progress or reform : die-hard, reactionary, ultraconservative. *See* POLITICS.

most *adjective*
Much more than half : best, better[1], greater, larger, largest. *See* BETTER, BIG.

most *adverb* To a high degree : awfully, dreadfully, eminently, exceedingly, exceptionally, extra, extremely, greatly, highly, notably, very. *Informal:* awful. *Chiefly Regional:* mighty. *See* BIG.

mother *noun*
1. A person from whom one is descended : ancestor, antecedent, ascendant, father, forebear, forefather, foremother, parent, progenitor. *Archaic:* predecessor. *See* KIN, PRECEDE. **2.** A point of origination : beginning, derivation, fount, fountain, fountainhead, origin, parent, provenance, provenience, root[1], rootstock, source, spring, well[1]. *See* START.

motif *noun*
An element or a component in a decorative composition : design, device, figure, motive, pattern. *See* PART.

motion *noun*
1. The act or process of moving : move, movement, stir[1]. *See* MOVE. **2.** An expressive, meaningful bodily movement : gesticulation, gesture, indication, sign, signal. *Informal:* high sign. *See* EXPRESS.

motion *verb* To make bodily motions so as to convey an idea or complement speech : gesticulate, gesture, sign, signal, signalize. ***Idiom:*** give the high sign. *See* EXPRESS.

motionless *adjective*
Not moving : immobile, stationary, still, stockstill, unmoving. *See* MOVE.

motivate *verb*
1. To stir to action or feeling : egg on, excite, foment, galvanize, goad, impel, incite, inflame, inspire, instigate, move, pique, prick, prod, prompt, propel, provoke, set off, spur, stimulate, touch off, trigger, work up. *See* CAUSE, EXCITE. **2.** To impart courage, inspiration, and resolution to : animate, cheer (on), embolden, encourage, inspire, inspirit. *See* HELP.

motivation *noun*
1. Something that encourages : encouragement, inspiration, stimulation. *See* HELP. **2.** Something that causes and encourages a given response : encouragement, fillip, impetus, impulse, incentive, inducement, prod, push, spur, stimulant, stimulation, stimulator, stimulus. *See* CAUSE. **3.** A basis for an action or a decision : cause, ground (often used in plural), motive, reason, spring. *See* START.

motive *noun*
1. A basis for an action or a decision : cause, ground (often used in plural), motivation, reason, spring. *See* START. **2.** An element or a component in a decorative composition : design, device, figure, motif, pattern. *See* PART.

motley *adjective*
1. Consisting of a number of different kinds : assorted, divers, diverse, diversified, heterogeneous, miscellaneous, mixed, multifarious, multiform, sundry, varied, variegated, various. *Biology:* polymorphic, polymorphous. *See* SAME. **2.** Having many different colors : multicolor, multicolored, polychromatic, polychrome, polychromic, polychromous, varicolored, variegated, versicolor, versicolored. *See* COLORS.

motor *verb*
To run and control (a motor vehicle) : drive, pilot, wheel. *Slang:* tool. *See* MOVE.

motorist *noun*
A person who operates a motor vehicle : driver, operator. *See* MOVE.

mottle *verb*
To mark with many small spots : bespeckle, besprinkle, dapple, dot, fleck, freckle, pepper, speck, speckle, sprinkle, stipple. *See* MARKS.

motto *noun*
1. A usually pithy and familiar statement expressing an observation or principle generally accepted as wise or true : adage, aphorism, byword, maxim, proverb, saw, saying. *See* WORDS. **2.** A rallying term used by proponents of a cause : battle cry, call to arms, call to battle, cry, rallying cry, war cry. *See* WORDS.

moue *noun*
A facial contortion indicating displeasure, disgust, or pain : face, grimace, mouth, pout. *Informal:* mug. *See* EXPRESS.

mound *noun*
A group of things gathered haphazardly : agglomeration, bank[1], cumulus, drift, heap, hill, mass, mess, mountain, pile, shock[2], stack, tumble. *See* ORDER.

mound *verb* To put into a disordered pile : bank[1], drift, heap, hill, lump[1], pile (up), stack. *See* ORDER.

mount *verb*
1. To move upward on or along : ascend, climb, go up, scale[2]. *See* RISE. **2.** To move from a lower to a higher position : arise, ascend, climb, lift, rise, soar. *See* RISE. **3.** To make or become greater or larger : aggrandize, amplify, augment, boost, build, build up, burgeon, enlarge, escalate, expand, extend, grow, increase, magnify, multiply, proliferate, rise, run up, snowball, soar, swell, upsurge, wax. *Informal:* beef up. *See* INCREASE. **4.** To attain a higher status, rank, or condition : advance, ascend, climb, rise. ***Idiom:*** go up the ladder. *See* INCREASE, RISE.

mountain *noun*
1. A group of things gathered haphazardly : agglomeration, bank[1], cumulus, drift, heap, hill, mass, mess, mound, pile, shock[2], stack, tumble. *See* ORDER. **2.** A great deal : abundance, mass, much, plenty, profusion, wealth, world. *Informal:* barrel, heap, lot, pack, peck[2], pile. *Regional:* power, sight. *See* BIG.

mountainous *adjective*
Of extraordinary size and power : behemoth, Brobdingnagian, Bunyanesque, colossal, cyclopean, elephantine, enormous, gargantuan, giant, gigantesque, gigantic, herculean, heroic, huge, immense, jumbo, mammoth, massive, massy, mastodonic, mighty, monster, monstrous, monumental, prodigious, pythonic, stupendous, titanic, tremendous, vast. *Informal:* walloping. *Slang:* whopping. *See* BIG.

mountebank *noun*
One who fakes : charlatan, fake, faker, fraud, humbug, impostor, phony, pretender, quack. *See* TRUE.

mourn *verb*
To feel, show, or express grief : grieve, lament, sorrow, suffer. *See* HAPPY.

mournful *adjective*
1. Full of or expressive of sorrow : doleful, dolorous, lugubrious, plaintive, rueful, sad, sorrowful, woebegone, woeful. *See* HAPPY.
2. Causing sorrow or regret : deplorable, doleful, dolorous, grievous, lamentable, regrettable, rueful, sad, sorrowful, woeful. *See* HAPPY.

mournfulness *noun*
A feeling or spell of dismally low spirits : blues, dejection, depression, despondence, despondency, doldrums, dolefulness, downheartedness, dumps, dysphoria, funk, gloom, glumness, heavy-heartedness, melancholy, mope (used in plural), sadness, unhappiness. *See* FEELINGS, HAPPY.

mouse *noun*
Informal. A bruise surrounding the eye : black eye. *Slang:* shiner. *See* HEALTH, HELP.

mouse *verb* To move silently and furtively : creep, glide, lurk, prowl, pussyfoot, skulk, slide, slink, slip, snake, sneak, steal. *Slang:* gumshoe. *See* MOVE.

mouth *noun*
1. The opening in the body through which food is ingested : *Slang:* gob[2], puss, trap. *See* MOUTH. **2.** A facial contortion indicating displeasure, disgust, or pain : face, grimace, moue, pout. *Informal:* mug. *See* EXPRESS. **3.** A person who speaks on behalf of another or others : speaker, spokesman, spokesperson, spokeswoman. *Informal:* mouthpiece. *See* SUBSTITUTE. **4.** An open space allowing passage : aperture, hole, opening, orifice, outlet, vent. *See* OPEN.

mouth *verb* **1.** To speak in a loud, pompous, or prolonged manner : declaim, harangue, perorate, rant, rave. *See* WORDS. **2.** To contort one's face to indicate displeasure, disgust, or pain, for example : grimace, mug. ***Idioms:*** make a face, make faces. *See* EXPRESS.

mouthful *noun*
A small portion of food : bit[1], crumb, morsel, piece. *Informal:* bite. *See* BIG.

mouthpiece *noun*
Informal. A person who speaks on behalf of another or others : mouth, speaker, spokesman, spokesperson, spokeswoman. *See* SUBSTITUTE.

movable also **moveable** *adjective*
Capable of moving or being moved from place to place : mobile, moving, transportable, traveling. *See* MOVE.
movable also **moveable** *noun* **1.** A piece of equipment for comfort or convenience : appointment (used in plural), furnishing. *Chiefly British:* fitting (used in plural). *See* MACHINE. **2.** *Law.* One's portable property. Often used in plural : belonging (often used in plural), effect (used in plural), good (used in plural), lares and penates, personal effects, personal property, possession (used in plural), property, thing (often used in plural). *Informal:* stuff. *Law:* chattel. *See* OWNED.

move *verb*
1. To go or cause to go from one place to another : maneuver, remove, shift, transfer. *See* MOVE. **2.** To alter the settled state or position of : dislocate, displace, disturb, shake, shift. *See* MOVE. **3.** To go forward, especially toward a conclusion : advance, come (along), get along, march[1], proceed, progress. *See* APPROACH. **4.** To change one's residence or place of business, for example : relocate, remove, transfer. *See* MOVE. **5.** To make a slight movement : budge, stir[1]. *See* MOVE. **6.** To impart slight movement to : budge, stir[1]. *See* MOVE. **7.** To stir to action or feeling : egg on, excite, foment, galvanize, goad, impel, incite, inflame, inspire, instigate, motivate, pique, prick, prod, prompt, propel, provoke, set off, spur, stimulate, touch off, trigger, work up. *See* CAUSE, EXCITE. **8.** To set or keep going : actuate, drive, impel, mobilize, propel, run. *See* MOVE. **9.** To evoke a usually strong mental or emotional response from : affect[1], get (to), impress, strike, touch. *See* TOUCH.
move *noun* **1.** The act or process of moving : motion, movement, stir[1]. *See* MOVE. **2.** A change in normal place or position : dislocation, displacement, disturbance, movement, rearrangement, shift. *See* MOVE. **3.** The act or process of moving from one place to another : relocation, remotion, removal. *See* MOVE. **4.** A calculated change in position : evolution, maneuver, movement, turn. *See* MOVE. **5.** An action calculated to achieve an end : maneuver, measure (often used in plural), procedure, step, tactic. *See* ACTION.

moveable *adjective & noun* See **movable.**

movement *noun*
1. The act or process of moving : motion, move, stir[1]. *See* MOVE. **2.** A change in normal place or position : dislocation, displacement, disturbance, move, rearrangement, shift. *See* MOVE. **3.** A calculated change in position : evolution, maneuver, move, turn. *See* MOVE. **4.** An organized effort to accomplish a purpose : campaign, crusade, drive, push. *See* ACTION, SEEK.

moving *adjective*
1. Capable of moving or being moved from place to place : mobile, movable, transportable, traveling. *See* MOVE. **2.** Exciting a deep, usually somber response : affecting, impressive, poignant, stirring, touching. *See* TOUCH.

moxie *noun*
Slang. The quality of mind enabling one to face danger or hardship resolutely : braveness, bravery, courage, courageousness, dauntlessness, doughtiness, fearlessness, fortitude, gallantry, gameness, heart, intrepidity, intrepidness, mettle, nerve, pluck, pluckiness, spirit, stoutheartedness, undauntedness, valiance, valiancy, valiantness, valor. *Informal:* spunk, spunkiness. *Slang:* gut (used in plural), gutsiness. *See* FEAR.

Mrs. Grundy *noun*
A person who is too much concerned with being proper, modest, or righteous : bluenose, prude, puritan, Victorian. *Informal:* old maid. *See* SEX.

much *noun*
A great deal : abundance, mass, mountain, plenty, profusion, wealth, world. *Informal:* barrel, heap, lot, pack, peck[2], pile. *Regional:* power, sight. *See* BIG.
much *adverb* To a considerable extent : considerably, far, quite, well[2]. ***Idioms:*** by a long shot (*or* way), by a wide margin, by far. *See* BIG.

mucilaginous *adjective*
Having a heavy, gluey quality : glutinous, viscid, viscose, viscous. *See* SOLID.

muck *noun*
1. A viscous, usually offensively dirty substance : mire, ooze, slime, slop, sludge, slush. *See* CLEAN. **2.** Foul or dirty matter : dirt, filth, grime. *Slang:* crud. *See* CLEAN.

muck *verb* To soil with mud. Also used with *up* : bemire, mire, mud, muddy, slush. *See* CLEAN.

muck up *verb Informal.* To harm irreparably through inept handling; make a mess : ball up, blunder, boggle, botch, bungle, foul up, fumble, gum up, mess up, mishandle, mismanage, muddle, muff, spoil. *Informal:* bollix up. *Slang:* blow[1], goof up, louse up, screw up, snafu. *Idiom:* make a muck of. *See* CORRECT, HELP.

muckamuck *noun*
Slang. An important, influential person : character, dignitary, eminence, leader, lion, nabob, notability, notable, personage. *Informal:* bigtimer, heavyweight, somebody, someone, VIP. *Slang:* big shot, big wheel, bigwig. *See* IMPORTANT.

muck up *verb* See **muck.**

mucky *adjective*
Of, relating to, or covered with slime : miry, oozy, slimy, sludgy, slushy. *See* CLEAN.

mucro *noun*
A sharp or tapered end : acicula, acumination, apex, cusp, mucronation, point, tip[1]. *See* SHARP.

mucronate *adjective*
Having an end that tapers to a point : acicular, aciculate, aciculated, acuminate, acute, cuspate, cuspated, cuspidate, cuspidated, pointed, pointy, sharp. *See* SHARP.

mucronation *noun*
A sharp or tapered end : acicula, acumination, apex, cusp, mucro, point, tip[1]. *See* SHARP.

mud *verb*
To soil with mud : bemire, mire, muck (up), muddy, slush. *See* CLEAN.

muddle *verb*
1. To put out of proper order : derange, disarrange, disarray, disorder, disorganize, disrupt, disturb, jumble, mess up, mix up, tumble, unsettle, upset. *See* ORDER. **2.** To put into total disorder : ball up, confuse, disorder, jumble, mess up, scramble, snarl[2]. *Slang:* snafu. *Idiom:* play havoc with. *See* ORDER. **3.** To cause to be unclear in mind or intent : addle, befuddle, bewilder, confound, confuse, discombobulate, dizzy, fuddle, jumble, mix up, mystify, perplex, puzzle. *Informal:* throw. *Idiom:* make one's head reel (*or* swim *or* whirl). *See* CLEAR, FEELINGS. **4.** To harm irreparably through inept handling; make a mess : ball up, blunder, boggle, botch, bungle, foul up, fumble, gum up, mess up, mishandle, mismanage, muff, spoil. *Informal:* bollix up, muck up. *Slang:* blow[1], goof up, louse up, screw up, snafu. *Idiom:* make a muck of. *See* CORRECT, HELP. **5.** To proceed or perform in an unsteady, faltering manner : blunder, bumble[1], bungle, flounder, fudge, fumble, limp, shuffle, stagger, stumble. *See* THRIVE.

muddle through *verb* To progress or perform adequately, especially in difficult circumstances : do, fare, fend, get along, get by, manage, shift. *Informal:* make out. *Idioms:* make do, make shift. *See* THRIVE.

muddle *noun* **1.** A lack of order or regular arrangement : chaos, clutter, confusedness, confusion, derangement, disarrangement, disarray, disorder, disorderedness, disorderliness, disorganization, jumble, mess, mix-up, muss, scramble, topsy-turviness, tumble. *Slang:* snafu. *See* ORDER. **2.** A ruinous state of disorder : botch, foul-up, mess, shambles. *Informal:* hash. *Slang:* screwup, snafu. *See* CORRECT, ORDER. **3.** A stunned or bewildered condition : befuddlement, bewilderedness, bewilderment, daze, discombobulation, fog, mystification, perplexity, puzzlement, stupefaction, stupor, trance. *See* AWARENESS.

muddle-headed *adjective*
Mentally uncertain : addled, addlepated, confounded, confused, confusional, perplexed, turbid. *Informal:* mixed-up. *See* CLEAR.

muddle through *verb* See **muddle.**

muddy *adjective*
1. Covered or soiled with mud : miry. *See* CLEAN. **2.** Having sediment or foreign particles stirred up or suspended : cloudy, murky, roiled, roily, turbid. *See* CLEAR. **3.** Lacking vividness in color : dim, drab, dull, flat, murky. *See* COLORS.

muddy *verb* To soil with mud : bemire, mire, muck (up), mud, slush. *See* CLEAN.

mudslinging *noun*
An attempt to destroy someone's reputation : smear, smear campaign. *See* PRAISE.

muff *verb*
To harm irreparably through inept handling; make a mess : ball up, blunder, boggle, botch, bungle, foul up, fumble, gum up, mess up, mishandle, mismanage, muddle, spoil. *Informal:* bollix up, muck up. *Slang:* blow[1], goof up, louse up, screw up, snafu. *Idiom:* make a muck of. *See* CORRECT, HELP.

muff *noun* A stupid, clumsy mistake : blunder, bull[2], bungle, foozle, fumble, stumble. *Informal:* blooper, boner. *Slang:* bloomer, goof. *See* CORRECT.

muffle *verb*
1. To decrease or dull the sound of : dampen,

deaden, mute, stifle. *See* INCREASE, SOUNDS. **2.** To hold (something requiring an outlet) in check : burke, choke (back), gag, hold back, hold down, hush (up), quench, repress, smother, squelch, stifle, strangle, suppress, throttle. *Informal:* sit on (*or* upon). *See* RESTRAINT.

mug *noun*
1. *Informal.* The front surface of the head : countenance, face, feature (often used in plural), muzzle, visage. *Slang:* kisser, map, pan, puss. *See* PRECEDE. **2.** *Informal.* A facial contortion indicating displeasure, disgust, or pain : face, grimace, moue, mouth, pout. *See* EXPRESS. **3.** A rough, violent person who engages in destructive actions : hoodlum, roughneck, rowdy, ruffian, tough. *Informal:* toughie. *Slang:* hood, punk. *See* ATTACK, CRIMES. **4.** *Chiefly British.* A person who is easily deceived or victimized : butt[3], dupe, fool, gull, lamb, pushover, victim. *Informal:* sucker. *Slang:* fall guy, gudgeon, mark, monkey, patsy, pigeon, sap[1]. *See* WISE.
mug *verb* To contort one's face to indicate displeasure, disgust, or pain, for example : grimace, mouth. ***Idioms:*** make a face, make faces. *See* EXPRESS.

muggy *adjective*
Damp and warm : humid, soggy, sticky, sultry. *See* DRY, HOT.

mulct *noun*
A sum of money levied as punishment for an offense : amercement, fine[2], penalty. *See* REWARD.
mulct *verb* **1.** To impose a fine on : amerce, fine[2], penalize. *See* REWARD. **2.** To get money or something else from by deceitful trickery : bilk, cheat, cozen, defraud, gull, rook, swindle, victimize. *Informal:* chisel, flimflam, take, trim. *Slang:* diddle[1], do, gyp, stick, sting. *See* HONEST.

muliebrity *noun*
Women in general : distaff, femininity, womanhood, womankind, womenfolk. *See* GENDER.

mulish *adjective*
Tenaciously unwilling to yield : bullheaded, dogged, hardheaded, headstrong, obstinate, pertinacious, perverse, pigheaded, stiff-necked, tenacious, willful. *See* RESIST.

mulishness *noun*
The quality or state of being stubbornly unyielding : bullheadedness, doggedness, hardheadedness, obstinacy, obstinateness, pertinaciousness, pertinacity, perverseness, perversity, pigheadedness, tenaciousness, tenacity, willfulness. *See* RESIST.

mull *verb*
To think or think about carefully and at length : chew on (*or* over), cogitate, consider, contemplate, deliberate, entertain, excogitate, meditate, muse[1], ponder, reflect, revolve, ruminate, study, think, think out, think over, think through, turn over, weigh. ***Idioms:*** cudgel one's brains, put on one's thinking cap, rack one's brain. *See* THOUGHTS.

multicolor *adjective*
Having many different colors : motley, multicolored, polychromatic, polychrome, polychromic, polychromous, varicolored, variegated, versicolor, versicolored. *See* COLORS.

multicolored *adjective*
Having many different colors : motley, multicolor, polychromatic, polychrome, polychromic, polychromous, varicolored, variegated, versicolor, versicolored. *See* COLORS.

multifaceted *adjective*
Having many aspects, uses, or abilities : all-around, all-round, many-sided, protean, various, versatile. *See* ABILITY, SAME.

multifarious *adjective*
Consisting of a number of different kinds : assorted, divers, diverse, diversified, heterogeneous, miscellaneous, mixed, motley, multiform, sundry, varied, variegated, various. *Biology:* polymorphic, polymorphous. *See* SAME.

multifariousness *noun*
The quality of being made of many different elements, forms, kinds, or individuals : diverseness, diversification, diversity, heterogeneity, heterogeneousness, miscellaneousness, multiformity, multiplicity, variegation, variety, variousness. *Biology:* polymorphism. *See* SAME.

multiform *adjective*
Consisting of a number of different kinds : assorted, divers, diverse, diversified, heterogeneous, miscellaneous, mixed, motley, multifarious, sundry, varied, variegated, various. *Biology:* polymorphic, polymorphous. *See* SAME.

multiformity *noun*
The quality of being made of many different elements, forms, kinds, or individuals : diverseness, diversification, diversity, heterogeneity, heterogeneousness, miscellaneousness, multifariousness, multiplicity, variegation, variety, variousness. *Biology:* polymorphism. *See* SAME.

multiplication *noun*
1. The act of increasing or rising : aggrandizement, amplification, augment, augmentation, boost, buildup, enlargement, escalation, growth, hike, increase, jump, proliferation, raise, rise, swell, upsurge, upswing, upturn. *See* INCREASE. **2.** The result or product of building up : accretion, buildup, development, enlargement, proliferation. *See* INCREASE. **3.** The process by which an organism produces others of its kind : breeding, procreation, proliferation, propagation, reproduction, spawning. *Obsolete:* increase. *See* REPRODUCTION.

multiplicity *noun*
1. The quality of being made of many different elements, forms, kinds, or individuals : diverseness, diversification, diversity, heterogeneity, heterogeneousness, miscellaneousness, multifariousness, multiformity, variegation, variety, variousness. *Biology:* polymorphism. *See* SAME. **2.** An indeterminately great amount or number : jillion, million (often used in plural), ream, trillion. *Informal:* bushel, gob[1] (often used in plural), heap (often used in plural), load (often used in plural), lot, oodles, passel, peck[2], scad (often used in plural), slew, wad, zillion. *See* BIG.

multiply *verb*
1. To make or become greater or larger : aggrandize, amplify, augment, boost, build, build up, burgeon, enlarge, escalate, expand, extend, grow, increase, magnify, mount, proliferate, rise, run up, snowball, soar, swell, upsurge, wax. *Informal:* beef up. *See* INCREASE. **2.** To produce sexually or asexually others of one's kind : breed, increase, procreate, proliferate, propagate, reproduce, spawn. *See* REPRODUCTION.

multitude *noun*
1. An enormous number of persons gathered together : crowd, crush, drove, flock, horde, mass, mob, press, ruck[1], swarm, throng. *See* BIG, GROUP. **2.** A very large number of things grouped together : army, cloud, crowd, drove, flock, horde, host, legion, mass, mob, ruck[1], score (used in plural), swarm, throng. *See* BIG, GROUP.

multitudinous *adjective*
Amounting to or consisting of a large, indefinite number : legion, many, myriad, numerous. ***Idiom:*** quite a few. *See* BIG.

mum *adjective*
Temporarily unable or unwilling to speak, as from shock or fear : dumb, inarticulate, mute, silent, speechless, voiceless, wordless. *See* WORDS.

mumble *verb*
To speak or utter indistinctly, as by lowering the voice or partially closing the mouth : murmur, mutter, whisper. *See* SOUNDS.
mumble *noun* A low, indistinct, and often continuous sound : murmur, sigh, sough, susurration, susurrus, whisper. *See* SOUNDS.

mumbo jumbo *noun*
1. Unintelligible or nonsensical talk or language : abracadabra, double talk, gibberish, gobbledygook, jabberwocky. *See* CLEAR, WORDS. **2.** Esoteric, formulaic, and often incomprehensible speech relating to the occult : abracadabra, gibberish, hocus-pocus. *See* CLEAR, SUPERNATURAL, WORDS.

mummify *verb*
To make or become no longer fresh or shapely because of loss of moisture : dry up, sear, shrivel, wither, wizen. *See* DRY.

munch *verb*
To bite and grind with the teeth : champ, chew, chomp, chump[2], crump, crunch, masticate. *Regional:* chaw. *See* MOUTH.

mundane *adjective*
Relating to or characteristic of the earth or of human life on earth : earthbound, earthen, earthly, earthy, secular, tellurian, telluric, temporal, terrene, terrestrial, worldly. *See* BODY, CULTURE, PLACE.

municipal *adjective*
Of, in, or belonging to a city : city, metropolitan, urban. *See* URBAN.

municipality *noun*
A large and important town : city, metropolis. *Informal:* burg, town. *See* URBAN.

munificence *noun*
The quality or state of being generous : bigheartedness, bounteousness, bountifulness, freehandedness, generosity, generousness, great-heartedness, large-heartedness, lavishness, liberality, magnanimity, magnanimousness, openhandedness, unselfishness, unsparingness. *See* GIVE.

munificent *adjective*
Characterized by bounteous giving : free, freehanded, generous, handsome, lavish, liberal, openhanded, unsparing, unstinting. *See* GIVE.

murder *noun*
The crime of murdering someone : blood, homicide, killing. *Slang:* hit. *See* HELP.
murder *verb* To take the life of (a person or persons) unlawfully : destroy, finish (off), kill[1], liquidate, slay. *Informal:* put away. *Slang:*

bump off, do in, knock off, off, rub out, waste, wipe out, zap. *See* HELP.

murderer *noun*
One who murders another : butcher, cutthroat, homicide, killer, manslayer, massacrer, murderess, slaughterer, slayer, triggerman. *See* HELP.

murderess *noun*
One who murders another : butcher, cutthroat, homicide, killer, manslayer, massacrer, murderer, slaughterer, slayer, triggerman. *See* HELP.

murderous *adjective*
Eager for bloodshed : bloodthirsty, bloody, bloody-minded, cutthroat, homicidal, sanguinary, sanguineous, slaughterous. *See* HELP.

murk also **mirk** *noun*
A thick, heavy atmospheric condition offering reduced visibility because of the presence of suspended particles : brume, fog, haze, mist, smaze. *See* CLEAR.

murkiness *noun*
Absence or deficiency of light : dark, darkness, dimness, duskiness, obscureness, obscurity. *See* LIGHT.

murky also **mirky** *adjective*
1. Deficient in brightness : caliginous, dark, dim, dusky, obscure. *See* LIGHT. **2.** Lacking vividness in color : dim, drab, dull, flat, muddy. *See* COLORS. **3.** Heavy, dark, or dense, especially with impurities : hazy, smoggy, turbid. *See* CLEAR. **4.** Having sediment or foreign particles stirred up or suspended : cloudy, muddy, roiled, roily, turbid. *See* CLEAR.

murmur *noun*
1. A low, indistinct, and often continuous sound : mumble, sigh, sough, susurration, susurrus, whisper. *See* SOUNDS. **2.** A low indistinct utterance of complaint : grumble, grunt, mutter. *See* HAPPY, SOUNDS.
murmur *verb* **1.** To make a low, continuous, and indistinct sound : sigh, sough, whisper. *See* SOUNDS. **2.** To complain in low indistinct tones : grumble, grunt, mutter. *See* HAPPY, SOUNDS. **3.** To speak or utter indistinctly, as by lowering the voice or partially closing the mouth : mumble, mutter, whisper. *See* SOUNDS.

murmurer *noun*
A person who habitually complains or grumbles : complainer, crab, faultfinder, grouch, growler, grumbler, grump, mutterer, whiner. *Informal:* crank, griper, grouser. *Slang:* bellyacher, sorehead, sourpuss. *See* HAPPY.

muscle *noun*
1. The state or quality of being physically strong : brawn, might, potence, potency, power, powerfulness, puissance, sinew, strength, thew (often used in plural). *See* STRONG. **2.** *Informal.* Effective means of influencing, compelling, or punishing : force, power, weight. *Informal:* clout. *See* OVER, STRONG.
muscle *verb Informal.* To force one's way into a place or situation : push, shove. *See* ENTER, PUSH.

muscular *adjective*
Characterized by marked muscular development; powerfully built : athletic, brawny, burly, husky[2], robust, sinewy, sturdy. *See* STRONG.

muscularity *noun*
Solid and well-developed muscles : brawn, bulk. *Informal:* beef. *See* BODY.

muse[1] *verb*
1. To experience dreams or daydreams : daydream, dream, fantasize, woolgather. *See* REAL. **2.** To think or think about carefully and at length : chew on (*or* over), cogitate, consider, contemplate, deliberate, entertain, excogitate, meditate, mull, ponder, reflect, revolve, ruminate, study, think, think out, think over, think through, turn over, weigh. ***Idioms:*** cudgel one's brains, put on one's thinking cap, rack one's brain. *See* THOUGHTS.

muse[2] *noun*
1. One who writes poetry : bard, poet, poetaster, poetess, rhymer, rhymester, versifier. *See* WORDS. **2.** The condition of being so lost in solitary thought as to be unaware of one's surroundings : absent-mindedness, abstraction, bemusement, brown study, daydreaming, reverie, study, trance. *See* AWARENESS.

mush *noun*
Informal. The quality or condition of being affectedly or overly emotional : bathos, maudlinism, mawkishness, sentimentalism, sentimentality. *Informal:* mushiness, schmaltz, schmaltziness, sloppiness. *Slang:* sappiness. *See* FEELINGS.
mush *verb* To press forcefully so as to break up into a pulpy mass : crush, mash, pulp, squash. *See* HELP.

mushiness *noun*
Informal. The quality or condition of being affectedly or overly emotional : bathos, maudlinism, mawkishness, sentimentalism, sentimentality. *Informal:* mush, schmaltz, schmaltziness, sloppiness. *Slang:* sappiness. *See* FEELINGS.

mushroom *verb*
To increase or expand suddenly, rapidly, or without control : explode, snowball. *See* INCREASE.

mushy *adjective*
1. Yielding easily to pressure or weight; not firm : pappy[1], pulpous, pulpy, quaggy, soft, spongy, squashy, squishy, yielding. *See* RESIST. **2.** *Informal.* Affectedly or extravagantly emotional : bathetic, gushy, maudlin, mawkish, romantic, sentimental, slushy, sobby, soft, soppy. *Informal:* gooey, schmaltzy, sloppy, soupy. *Slang:* drippy, sappy, tear-jerking. *See* FEELINGS.

musical *adjective*
1. Characterized by harmony of sound : consonant, harmonic, harmonious, symphonic, symphonious. *See* BEAUTIFUL, SOUNDS. **2.** Having or producing a pleasing melody : melodic, melodious, tuneful. *See* SOUNDS. **3.** Resembling or having the effect of music, especially pleasing music : dulcet, euphonic, euphonious, melodic, melodious, tuneful. *See* SOUNDS.

musician *noun*
One who plays a musical instrument : performer, player. *See* PERFORMING ARTS.

muskeg *noun*
A usually low-lying area of soft waterlogged ground and standing water : bog, fen, marsh, marshland, mire, morass, quag, quagmire, slough[1], swamp, swampland, wetland. *See* DRY.

muss *verb*
To put (the hair or clothes) into a state of disarray. Also used with *up* : disarrange, dishevel, disorder, mess (up), rumple, tousle. *See* ORDER.

muss *noun* A lack of order or regular arrangement : chaos, clutter, confusedness, confusion, derangement, disarrangement, disarray, disorder, disorderedness, disorderliness, disorganization, jumble, mess, mix-up, muddle, scramble, topsy-turviness, tumble. *Slang:* snafu. *See* ORDER.

mussy *adjective*
Marked by an absence of cleanliness and order : disheveled, messy, slipshod, sloppy, slovenly, unkempt, untidy. *See* ORDER.

must *verb*
To be required or compelled to do : need. ***Idioms:*** have got to, have to, must needs. *See* NECESSARY.

must *noun* **1.** An act or course of action that is demanded of one, as by position, custom, law, or religion : burden[1], charge, commitment, duty, imperative, need, obligation, responsibility. *See* OBLIGATION. **2.** Something indispensable : condition, essential, necessity, need, precondition, prerequisite, requirement, requisite, sine qua non. *See* NECESSARY.

muster *verb*
1. To assemble, prepare, or put into operation, as for war or a similar emergency : marshal, mobilize, organize, rally. *See* MOVE. **2.** To bring together : assemble, call, cluster, collect[1], congregate, convene, convoke, gather, get together, group, round up, summon. *See* COLLECT. **3.** To demand to appear, come, or assemble : call, convene, convoke, send for, summon. *See* REQUEST. **4.** To come together : assemble, cluster, collect[1], congregate, convene, forgather, gather, get together, group. *See* COLLECT.

muster in *verb* To become a member of : enlist, enroll, enter, join, sign up. *Informal:* sign on. *See* PARTICIPATE.

muster out *verb* To release from military duty : demobilize, discharge, separate. *See* FREE, KEEP.

muster *noun* A number of persons who have come or been gathered together : assemblage, assembly, body, company, conclave, conference, congregation, congress, convention, convocation, crowd, gathering, group, meeting, troop. *Informal:* get-together. *See* COLLECT.

muster in *verb* See **muster.**

muster out *verb* See **muster.**

musty *adjective*
1. Smelling of mildew or decay : frowzy, fusty, moldy, putrid, rancid, rank[2], rotten. *See* SMELLS. **2.** Without freshness or appeal because of overuse : banal, bromidic, clichéd, commonplace, corny, hackneyed, overused, overworked, platitudinal, platitudinous, shopworn, stale, stereotyped, stereotypic, stereotypical, threadbare, timeworn, tired, trite, warmed-over, well-worn, worn-out. *See* EXCITE, USUAL.

mutable *adjective*
Capable of or liable to change : alterable, changeable, fluid, inconstant, uncertain, unsettled, unstable, unsteady, variable, variant. *Archaic:* various. *See* CHANGE.

mutate *verb*
1. To make or become different : alter, change, modify, turn, vary. *See* CHANGE. **2.** To change into a different form, substance, or state : convert, metamorphose, transfigure, transform, translate, transmogrify, transmute, transpose, transubstantiate. *See* CHANGE.

mutation *noun*
1. The process or result of making or becoming different : alteration, change, modification, permutation, variation. *See* CHANGE. **2.** The process or result of changing from one appearance, state, or phase to another : change, changeover, conversion, metamorphosis, shift, transfiguration, transformation, translation, transmogrification, transmutation, transubstantiation. *See* CHANGE.

mute *adjective*
1. Temporarily unable or unwilling to speak, as from shock or fear : dumb, inarticulate, mum, silent, speechless, voiceless, wordless. *See* WORDS. **2.** Lacking the power or faculty of speech : aphonic, dumb, inarticulate, speechless, voiceless. *See* WORDS.
mute *verb* **1.** To decrease or dull the sound of : dampen, deaden, muffle, stifle. *See* INCREASE, SOUNDS. **2.** To make or become less severe or extreme : moderate, qualify, soften, subdue, tame, temper, tone down. *See* INCREASE.

muteness *noun*
The avoidance of speech : dumbness, silence, speechlessness, wordlessness. *See* WORDS.

mutilate *verb*
To deprive of a limb or bodily member or its use : cripple, dismember, maim. *See* HELP.

mutineer *noun*
A person who rebels : insurgent, insurrectionary, insurrectionist, rebel, revolutionary, revolutionist. *See* RESIST.

mutinous *adjective*
Participating in open revolt against a government or ruling authority : insurgent, rebellious, revolutionary. *See* RESIST.

mutiny *noun*
Organized opposition intended to change or overthrow existing authority : insurgence, insurgency, insurrection, rebellion, revolt, revolution, sedition, uprising. *See* RESIST.
mutiny *verb* To refuse allegiance to and oppose by force a government or ruling authority : rebel, revolt, rise (up). *See* RESIST.

mutter *verb*
1. To speak or utter indistinctly, as by lowering the voice or partially closing the mouth : mumble, murmur, whisper. *See* SOUNDS. **2.** To complain in low indistinct tones : grumble, grunt, murmur. *See* HAPPY, SOUNDS.
mutter *noun* A low indistinct utterance of complaint : grumble, grunt, murmur. *See* HAPPY, SOUNDS.

mutterer *noun*
A person who habitually complains or grumbles : complainer, crab, faultfinder, grouch, growler, grumbler, grump, murmurer, whiner. *Informal:* crank, griper, grouser. *Slang:* bellyacher, sorehead, sourpuss. *See* HAPPY.

mutual *adjective*
1. Having the same relationship each to the other : reciprocal, reciprocative. *See* CONNECT. **2.** Belonging to, shared by, or applicable to all alike : common, communal, conjoint, general, joint, public. *See* GROUP.

muzzle *noun*
The front surface of the head : countenance, face, feature (often used in plural), visage. *Informal:* mug. *Slang:* kisser, map, pan, puss. *See* PRECEDE.

myriad *adjective*
Amounting to or consisting of a large, indefinite number : legion, many, multitudinous, numerous. *Idiom:* quite a few. *See* BIG.

mysterious *adjective*
Difficult to explain or understand : arcane, cabalistic, cryptic, enigmatic, mystic, mystical, mystifying, occult, puzzling. *See* EXPLAIN, KNOWLEDGE.

mystery *noun*
Anything that arouses curiosity or perplexes because it is unexplained, inexplicable, or secret : conundrum, enigma, perplexity, puzzle, puzzler, riddle. *See* SHOW.

mystic *adjective*
Difficult to explain or understand : arcane, cabalistic, cryptic, enigmatic, mysterious, mystical, mystifying, occult, puzzling. *See* EXPLAIN, KNOWLEDGE.

mystical *adjective*
Difficult to explain or understand : arcane, cabalistic, cryptic, enigmatic, mysterious, mystic, mystifying, occult, puzzling. *See* EXPLAIN, KNOWLEDGE.

mystification *noun*
A stunned or bewildered condition : befuddlement, bewilderedness, bewilderment, daze, discombobulation, fog, muddle, perplexity, puzzlement, stupefaction, stupor, trance. *See* AWARENESS.

mystify *verb*
To cause to be unclear in mind or intent : addle, befuddle, bewilder, confound, confuse, discombobulate, dizzy, fuddle, jumble, mix up, muddle, perplex, puzzle. *Informal:* throw. *Idiom:* make one's head reel (*or* swim *or* whirl). *See* CLEAR, FEELINGS.

mystifying *adjective*
Difficult to explain or understand : arcane, cabalistic, cryptic, enigmatic, mysterious, mystic, mystical, occult, puzzling. *See* EXPLAIN, KNOWLEDGE.

myth *noun*
1. A traditional story or tale that has no proven factual basis : fable, legend. *See* BELIEF, REAL, RELIGION. **2.** A body of traditional beliefs and notions that has accumulated about a particular subject : folklore, legend, lore, mythology, mythos, tradition. *See* KNOWLEDGE. **3.** Any idea of a fictitious nature that is accepted as part of an ideology by a group that is uncritical; a received idea : creation, fantasy, fiction, figment, invention. *See* BELIEF, REAL.

mythic *adjective*
Of or existing only in myths : fabulous, legendary, mythical, mythologic, mythological. *See* REAL.

mythical *adjective*
Of or existing only in myths : fabulous, legendary, mythic, mythologic, mythological. *See* REAL.

mythologic *adjective*
Of or existing only in myths : fabulous, legendary, mythic, mythical, mythological. *See* REAL.

mythological *adjective*
Of or existing only in myths : fabulous, legendary, mythic, mythical, mythologic. *See* REAL.

mythology *noun*
A body of traditional beliefs and notions accumulated about a particular subject : folklore, legend, lore, myth, mythos, tradition. *See* KNOWLEDGE.

mythos *noun*
A body of traditional beliefs and notions accumulated about a particular subject : folklore, legend, lore, myth, mythology, tradition. *See* KNOWLEDGE.

·N·

nab *verb*
1. *Informal.* To take into custody as a prisoner : apprehend, arrest, seize. *Informal:* pick up. *Slang:* bust, collar, pinch, run in. *See* LAW. **2.** *Informal.* To get hold of (something moving) : catch, clutch[1], grab, seize, snatch. ***Idiom:*** lay hands on. *See* GET.

nabob *noun*
An important, influential person : character, dignitary, eminence, leader, lion, notability, notable, personage. *Informal:* big-timer, heavyweight, somebody, someone, VIP. *Slang:* big shot, big wheel, bigwig, muckamuck. *See* IMPORTANT.

nag *verb*
To scold or find fault with constantly : carp at, fuss at, peck at[1], pick on. *Informal:* henpeck. *See* PRAISE.

nagging *adjective*
Marked by, causing, or experiencing physical pain : aching, achy, afflictive, hurtful, painful, smarting, sore. *See* PAIN.

naif or **naïf** *adjective & noun* See **naive.**

nail *verb*
Slang. To gain possession of, especially after a struggle or chase : capture, catch, get, net[1], secure, take. *Informal:* bag. *See* GET.

naive or **naïve** also **naif** or **naïf** *adjective*
1. Free from guile, cunning, or deceit : artless, guileless, ingenuous, innocent, natural, simple, unaffected, unsophisticated, unstudied, unworldly. *See* HONEST. **2.** Easily imposed on or tricked : credulous, dupable, easy, exploitable, gullible, susceptible. *See* WISE.
naive or **naïve** also **naif** or **naïf** *noun* A guileless, unsophisticated person : babe, child, ingénue, innocent. ***Idiom:*** babe in the woods. *See* KNOWLEDGE.

naked *adjective*
1. Not wearing any clothes : au naturel, bare, nude, unclad. *Chiefly British:* starkers. ***Idioms:*** in one's birthday suit, in the altogether (*or* buff *or* raw), naked as a jaybird, stark naked, without a stitch. *See* PUT ON, SHOW. **2.** Without the usual covering : bald, bare, nude. *See* PUT ON.

nakedness *noun*
The state of being without clothes : bareness, nudeness, nudity, undress. *See* PUT ON, SHOW.

namby-pamby *adjective*
Lacking the qualities requisite for spiritedness and originality : bland, innocuous, insipid, jejune, vapid, washy, waterish, watery. *Informal:* wishy-washy. *See* EXCITE, GOOD.

name *noun*
1. The word or words by which one is called and identified : appellation, appellative, cognomen, denomination, designation, epithet, nickname, style, tag, title. *Slang:* handle, moniker. *See* SPECIFIC, WORDS. **2.** Public estimation of someone : character, report, reputation, repute. *Informal:* rep. *See* RESPECT. **3.** A famous person : celebrity, hero, lion, luminary, notable, personage, personality. *Informal:* big name. *See* KNOWLEDGE.
name *verb* **1.** To give a name or title to : baptize, call, christen, denominate, designate, dub, entitle, style, term, title. *See* SPECIFIC, WORDS. **2.** To refer to by name : cite, instance, mention, specify. *See* SPECIFIC. **3.** To describe with a word or term : call, characterize, designate, label, style, tag, term. *See* SPECIFIC, WORDS. **4.** To select for an office or position : appoint, designate, make, nominate, tap[1]. *See* CHOICE.

nameless *adjective*
1. Not known or not widely known by name : obscure, unheard-of, unknown. *See* KNOWLEDGE. **2.** Having an unknown name or author : anonymous, unnamed, unsigned. *See* KNOWLEDGE.

namelessness *noun*
The quality or state of being obscure : anonymity, obscurity. *See* KNOWLEDGE.

namely *adverb*
That is to say : scilicet, specifically, videlicet. ***Idiom:*** to wit. *See* SPECIFIC.

nap *noun*
A brief sleep : catnap, doze, siesta, snooze. *See* AWARENESS.
nap *verb* To sleep for a brief period : catnap, doze (off), nod (off), siesta, snooze. ***Idiom:*** catch (*or* grab *or* take) forty winks. *See* AWARENESS.

narcism *noun* See **narcissism.**

narcissism also **narcism** *noun*
A regarding of oneself with undue favor : amour-propre, conceit, ego, egoism, egotism, pride, vainglory, vainness, vanity. *Slang:* ego trip. *See* SELF-LOVE.

narcissist *noun*
A conceited, self-centered person : egocentric, egoist, egomaniac, egotist. *Informal:* swellhead. *See* SELF, SELF-LOVE.

narcissistic *adjective*
1. Thinking too highly of oneself : conceited, egoistic, egoistical, egotistic, egotistical, vain, vainglorious. *Informal:* bigheaded, stuck-up, swellheaded. *See* SELF-LOVE. **2.** Unduly preoccupied with one's own appearance : conceited, vain. *See* SELF-LOVE.

narcotic *noun*
1. A substance that affects the central nervous system and is often addictive : drug, hallucinogen, opiate. *Informal:* dope. *See* DRUGS.
2. Something that induces sleep or sedation : hypnotic, opiate, sedative, somnifacient, soporific. *See* AWARENESS.
narcotic *adjective* Inducing sleep or sedation : hypnotic, opiate, sedative, sleepy, slumberous, somnifacient, somniferous, somnific, somnolent, soporific. *See* AWARENESS.

narcotize *verb*
To administer or add a drug to : dose, drug, medicate, opiate, physic. *Informal:* dope (up). *See* DRUGS.

narrate *verb*
To give a verbal account of : describe, recite, recount, rehearse, relate, report, tell. *See* WORDS.

narration *noun*
A recounting of past events : account, chronicle, description, history, narrative, report, statement, story, version. *See* WORDS.

narrative *noun*
A recounting of past events : account, chronicle, description, history, narration, report, statement, story, version. *See* WORDS.

narrow *adjective*
1. Affording little room for movement : close, confining, cramped, crowded, snug, tight. *See* TIGHTEN. **2.** Not broad or elevated in scope or understanding : limited, little, narrow-minded, petty, small, small-minded. *See* LIMITED, WIDE. **3.** Having the restricted outlook often characteristic of geographic isolation : insular, limited, local, narrow-minded, parochial, provincial, small-town. *See* LIMITED.
narrow *verb* To make smaller or narrower : constrict, constringe. *See* TIGHTEN, WIDE.

narrow-minded *adjective*
1. Not tolerant of the beliefs or opinions of others, for example : bigoted, close-minded, hidebound, illiberal, intolerant. *See* ACCEPT. **2.** Not broad or elevated in scope or understanding : limited, little, narrow, petty, small, small-minded. *See* LIMITED, WIDE. **3.** Having the restricted outlook often characteristic of geographic isolation : insular, limited, local, nar-

row, parochial, provincial, small-town. *See* LIMITED.

nascence *noun*
The initial stage of a developmental process : beginning, birth, commencement, dawn, genesis, inception, nascency, onset, opening, origin, outset, spring, start. *See* START.

nascency *noun*
The initial stage of a developmental process : beginning, birth, commencement, dawn, genesis, inception, nascence, onset, opening, origin, outset, spring, start. *See* START.

nastiness *noun*
A desire to harm others or to see others suffer : despitefulness, ill will, malevolence, malice, maliciousness, malignancy, malignity, meanness, poisonousness, spite, spitefulness, venomousness, viciousness. *See* ATTITUDE.

nasty *adjective*
1. Heavily soiled; very dirty or unclean : filthy, foul, squalid, vile. *See* CLEAN. **2.** Extremely unpleasant to the senses or feelings : atrocious, disgusting, foul, horrid, nauseating, offensive, repellent, repulsive, revolting, sickening, ugly, unwholesome, vile. *See* LIKE, PAIN. **3.** Offensive to accepted standards of decency : barnyard, bawdy, broad, coarse, dirty, Fescennine, filthy, foul, gross, lewd, obscene, profane, ribald, scatologic, scatological, scurrilous, smutty, vulgar. *Slang:* raunchy. *See* DECENT.
4. Characterized by intense ill will or spite : black, despiteful, evil, hateful, malevolent, malicious, malign, malignant, mean[2], poisonous, spiteful, venomous, vicious, wicked. *Slang:* bitchy. *See* ATTITUDE. **5.** Having or showing a bad temper : bad-tempered, cantankerous, crabbed, cranky, cross, disagreeable, fretful, grouchy, grumpy, ill-tempered, irascible, irritable, peevish, petulant, querulous, snappish, snappy, surly, testy, ugly, waspish. *Informal:* crabby, mean[2]. ***Idiom:*** out of sorts. *See* ATTITUDE. **6.** So objectionable as to elicit despisal or deserve condemnation : abhorrent, abominable, antipathetic, contemptible, despicable, despisable, detestable, disgusting, filthy, foul, infamous, loathsome, lousy, low, mean[2], nefarious, obnoxious, odious, repugnant, rotten, shabby, vile, wretched. *See* GOOD.

nation *noun*
An organized geopolitical unit : body politic, country, land, polity, state. *See* POLITICS, TERRITORY.

national *adjective*
1. Of, concerning, or affecting the community or the people : civic, civil, public. *See* SPECIFIC. **2.** Of, from, or within a country's own territory : domestic, home, internal, native. *See* NATIVE.

national *noun* A person owing loyalty to and entitled to the protection of a given state : citizen, subject. *See* GROUP, POLITICS.

nationalize *verb*
To place under government or group ownership or control : communalize, socialize. *See* POLITICS, SPECIFIC.

native *adjective*
1. Possessed at birth : congenital, hereditary, inborn, inherited, innate. *See* BE, NATIVE.
2. Forming an essential element, as arising from the basic structure of an individual : built-in, congenital, connatural, constitutional, elemental, inborn, inbred, indigenous, indwelling, ingrained, inherent, innate, intrinsic, natural. *See* BE, NATIVE, START. **3.** Of, from, or within a country's own territory : domestic, home, internal, national. *See* NATIVE. **4.** Existing, born, or produced in a land or region : aboriginal, autochthonal, autochthonic, autochthonous, endemic, indigenous. *See* NATIVE. **5.** In a primitive state; not domesticated or cultivated; produced by nature : natural, rough, uncultivated, undomesticated, untamed, wild. *See* WILD. **6.** In a natural state and still not prepared for use : crude, raw, unprocessed, unrefined. *See* CLEAN.

natural *adjective*
1. Produced by nature; not artificial or manmade : organic, unadulterated. ***Idiom:*** pure as the driven snow. *See* CULTURE. **2.** In a primitive state; not domesticated or cultivated; produced by nature : native, rough, uncultivated, undomesticated, untamed, wild. *See* WILD. **3.** Forming an essential element, as arising from the basic structure of an individual : built-in, congenital, connatural, constitutional, elemental, inborn, inbred, indigenous, indwelling, ingrained, inherent, innate, intrinsic, native. *See* BE, NATIVE, START. **4.** Devoid of any hypocrisy or pretense : genuine, heartfelt, hearty, honest, real, sincere, true, unaffected, unfeigned, unmannered. *See* TRUE. **5.** Free from guile, cunning, or deceit : artless, guileless, ingenuous, innocent, naive, simple, unaffected, unsophisticated, unstudied, unworldly. *See* HONEST. **6.** Unconstrained by rigid standards or ceremony : casual, easy, easygoing, informal, relaxed, spontaneous, unceremonious, unrestrained. *Informal:* laid-back. *See* PLAIN, TIGHTEN. **7.** Of a plain and unsophisticated nature : artless, homely, homespun, rustic,

unadorned, unpolished. *See* PLAIN. **8.** Accurately representing what is depicted or described : lifelike, naturalistic, realistic, true, true-life, truthful. *See* REAL. **9.** Born to parents who are not married to each other : baseborn, bastard, illegitimate, misbegotten, spurious, unlawful. *See* KIN, LAW.

naturalistic *adjective*
Accurately representing what is depicted or described : lifelike, natural, realistic, true, true-life, truthful. *See* REAL.

naturally *adverb*
In an expected or customary manner; for the most part : commonly, consistently, customarily, frequently, generally, habitually, normally, often, regularly, routinely, typically, usually. ***Idioms:*** as usual, per usual. *See* BIG, USUAL.

naturalness *noun*
Freedom from constraint, formality, embarrassment, or awkwardness : casualness, ease, easiness, informality, poise, spontaneity, unceremoniousness, unrestraint. *See* RESTRAINT, TIGHTEN.

nature *noun*
1. The totality of all existing things : cosmos, creation, macrocosm, universe, world. *See* MATTER, PART. **2.** A class that is defined by the common attribute or attributes possessed by all its members : breed, cast, description, feather, ilk, kind[2], lot, manner, mold, order, sort, species, stamp, stripe, type, variety. *Informal:* persuasion. *See* GROUP. **3.** The combination of emotional, intellectual, and moral qualities that distinguishes an individual : character, complexion, disposition, makeup, personality. *See* BE. **4.** A basic trait or set of traits that define and establish the character of something : being, essence, essentiality, quintessence, substance, texture. *See* SURFACE. **5.** A person's customary manner of emotional response : complexion, disposition, humor, temper, temperament. *See* BE.

naughtiness *noun*
Improper, often rude behavior : horseplay, misbehavior, misconduct, misdoing, wrongdoing. *See* GOOD.

naughty *adjective*
1. Misbehaving, often in a troublesome way : bad, ill-behaved. *See* CONTROL, GOOD. **2.** Not in keeping with conventional mores : immodest, improper, indecent, indecorous, indelicate, unbecoming, unbefitting, unseemly, untoward. ***Idiom:*** out of line. *See* USUAL.

nausea *noun*
Extreme repugnance excited by something offensive : disgust. *See* LIKE.

nauseate *verb*
To offend the senses or feelings of : disgust, repel, revolt, sicken. ***Idiom:*** turn one's stomach. *See* LIKE.

nauseating *adjective*
Extremely unpleasant to the senses or feelings : atrocious, disgusting, foul, horrid, nasty, offensive, repellent, repulsive, revolting, sickening, ugly, unwholesome, vile. *See* LIKE, PAIN.

nautical *adjective*
Of or relating to sea navigation : marine, maritime, navigational. *See* SEA.

navigable *adjective*
Capable of being passed, traversed, or crossed : negotiable, passable. *See* OPEN.

navigate *verb*
To direct the course of carefully : guide, jockey, maneuver, pilot, steer. ***Idiom:*** back and fill. *See* CONTROL, MOVE.

navigational *adjective*
Of or relating to sea navigation : marine, maritime, nautical. *See* SEA.

navigator *noun*
A person engaged in sailing or working on a ship : jack (uppercase), jack-tar, mariner, sailor, sea dog, seafarer, seaman. *Informal:* salt, tar. *Slang:* gob[3]. *See* SEA.

nay *adverb*
Not so : no. *Informal:* nope. *Slang:* nix. ***Idiom:*** nothing doing. *See* AFFIRM.

nay *noun* **1.** A negative response : no, refusal, rejection. *See* AFFIRM. **2.** A negative vote or voter : no. *See* AFFIRM.

near *adverb*
To a point near in time, space, or relation : close, closely, hard, nearby, nigh. *See* NEAR.

near *adjective* Not far from another in space, time, or relation : adjacent, close, contiguous, immediate, nearby, nigh, proximate. ***Idioms:*** at hand, under one's nose, within a stone's throw, within hailing distance. *See* NEAR.

near *verb* To come near in space or time : approach. ***Idioms:*** come close to, draw near to. *See* APPROACH.

nearby *adjective*
1. Not far from another in space, time, or relation : adjacent, close, contiguous, immediate, near, nigh, proximate. ***Idioms:*** at hand, under one's nose, within a stone's throw, within hailing distance. *See* NEAR. **2.** Being within easy reach : accessible, convenient, handy. ***Idioms:*** close (*or* near) at hand, close by. *See* NEAR.

nearby *adverb* To a point near in time, space, or relation : close, closely, hard, near, nigh. *See* NEAR.

nearly *adverb*
Near to in quantity or amount : about, almost, approximately, roughly. ***Idiom:*** on the order of. *See* NEAR.

nearness *noun*
The act or fact of coming near : approach, coming, convergence, imminence. *See* APPROACH.

neat *adjective*
1. In good order or clean condition : orderly, shipshape, snug, spick-and-span, spruce, taut, tidy, trig, trim, well-groomed. *Chiefly British:* tight. ***Idiom:*** neat as a pin. *See* CLEAN, ORDER. **2.** Well done or executed : adroit, clean, deft, skillful. *See* ABILITY, GOOD. **3.** Not diluted or mixed with other substances : full-strength, plain, pure, straight, unblended, undiluted, unmixed. *See* CLEAN, STRONG. **4.** *Slang.* Particularly excellent : divine, fabulous, fantastic, fantastical, glorious, marvelous, sensational, splendid, superb, terrific, wonderful. *Informal:* dandy, dreamy, great, ripping, super, swell, tremendous. *Slang:* cool, groovy, hot, keen[1], nifty. ***Idiom:*** out of this world. *See* GOOD.

neaten *verb*
1. To make or keep (an area) clean and orderly. Also used with *up* : clean (up), clear (up), police, spruce (up), straighten (up), tidy (up). *See* ORDER. **2.** To make neat and trim; make presentable. Also used with *up* : clean (up), freshen (up), groom, slick up, spruce (up), tidy (up), trig (out), trim. *See* ORDER.

nebbish *noun*
A totally insignificant person : cipher, nobody, nonentity, nothing. *Informal:* pip-squeak, zero. *Slang:* shrimp, zilch. *See* IMPORTANT.

nebulous *adjective*
Liable to more than one interpretation : ambiguous, cloudy, equivocal, inexplicit, obscure, uncertain, unclear, vague. *See* CERTAIN, CLEAR.

nebulousness *noun*
The quality or state of being ambiguous : ambiguity, ambiguousness, cloudiness, equivocalness, indefiniteness, obscureness, obscurity, uncertainty, unclearness, vagueness. *See* CLEAR.

necessary *adjective*
1. Incapable of being dispensed with : essential, indispensable, needful, required, requisite. *See* IMPORTANT, NECESSARY. **2.** Imposed on one by authority, command, or convention : compulsory, imperative, mandatory, obligatory, required, requisite. *See* OBLIGATION.

necessitate *verb*
To have as a need or prerequisite : ask, call for, demand, entail, involve, require, take. *See* NECESSARY, OVER.

necessitous *adjective*
Having little or no money or wealth : beggarly, destitute, down-and-out, impecunious, impoverished, indigent, needy, penniless, penurious, poor, poverty-stricken. *Informal:* broke, strapped. ***Idioms:*** hard up, on one's uppers. *See* RICH.

necessity *noun*
1. That which provides a reason or justification : call, cause, ground (often used in plural), justification, occasion, reason, wherefore, why. ***Idiom:*** why and wherefore. *See* START. **2.** Something indispensable : condition, essential, must, need, precondition, prerequisite, requirement, requisite, sine qua non. *See* NECESSARY. **3.** A condition in which something necessary or desirable is required or wanted : exigence, exigency, need. *See* NECESSARY.

neck *verb*
Informal. To engage in kissing, caressing, and other amorous behavior : *Informal:* fool around, pet[1], spoon. *Slang:* make out. *See* SEX.

neck and neck *adjective*
Nearly equivalent or even : close, nip and tuck, tight. *See* NEAR.

neck of the woods *noun*
Informal. A part of the earth's surface : area, belt, district, locality, neighborhood, quarter, region, tract, zone. *See* TERRITORY.

need *noun*
1. A condition in which something necessary or desirable is required or wanted : exigence, exigency, necessity. *See* NECESSARY. **2.** Something indispensable : condition, essential, must, necessity, precondition, prerequisite, requirement, requisite, sine qua non. *See* NECESSARY. **3.** Something asked for or needed : demand, exigence, exigency (often used in plural), want. *See* NECESSARY, OVER. **4.** An act or course of action that is demanded of one, as by position, custom, law, or religion : burden[1], charge, commitment, duty, imperative, must, obligation, responsibility. *See* OBLIGATION. **5.** The condition of being extremely poor : beggary, destitution, impecuniosity, impecuniousness, impoverishment, indigence, neediness, pennilessness, penuriousness, penury, poverty, privation, want. *See* RICH.

need *verb* **1.** To be required or compelled to do : must. ***Idioms:*** have got to, have to, must needs. *See* NECESSARY. **2.** To be without what is needed, required, or essential : lack, require, want. *See* OWNED.

needful *adjective*
Incapable of being dispensed with : essential, indispensable, necessary, required, requisite. *See* IMPORTANT, NECESSARY.

neediness *noun*
The condition of being extremely poor : beggary, destitution, impecuniosity, impecuniousness, impoverishment, indigence, need, pennilessness, penuriousness, penury, poverty, privation, want. *See* RICH.

needle *noun*
A sharp, pointed object : prick, prickle, spine, thorn. *See* SHARP.

needle *verb Informal.* To torment with persistent insult or ridicule : badger, bait, bullyrag, heckle, hector, hound, taunt. *Informal:* ride. ***Idiom:*** wave the red flag in front of the bull. *See* TREAT WELL.

needless *adjective*
Not necessary : dispensable, inessential, nonessential, uncalled-for, unessential, unnecessary, unneeded, unrequired. *See* NECESSARY.

needy *adjective*
Having little or no money or wealth : beggarly, destitute, down-and-out, impecunious, impoverished, indigent, necessitous, penniless, penurious, poor, poverty-stricken. *Informal:* broke, strapped. ***Idioms:*** hard up, on one's uppers. *See* RICH.

ne'er-do-well *noun*
A self-indulgent person who spends time avoiding work or other useful activity : bum[1], drone[1], fainéant, good-for-nothing, idler, layabout, loafer, no-good, slugabed, sluggard, wastrel. *Informal:* do-little, do-nothing, lazybones, slug[2]. *Slang:* slouch. *See* INDUSTRIOUS.

nefarious *adjective*
So objectionable as to elicit despisal or deserve condemnation : abhorrent, abominable, antipathetic, contemptible, despicable, despisable, detestable, disgusting, filthy, foul, infamous, loathsome, lousy, low, mean[2], nasty, obnoxious, odious, repugnant, rotten, shabby, vile, wretched. *See* GOOD.

negate *verb*
1. To make ineffective by applying an opposite force or amount : cancel, counteract, neutralize, nullify. *See* ACTION. **2.** To put an end to, especially formally and with authority : abolish, abrogate, annihilate, annul, cancel, invalidate, nullify, set aside, vitiate, void. *Law:* extinguish. *See* CONTINUE. **3.** To refuse to admit the truth, reality, value, or worth of : contradict, contravene, controvert, deny, disaffirm, gainsay, negative, oppugn. *Law:* traverse. *See* AFFIRM.

negation *noun*
1. An often formal act of putting an end to : abolishment, abolition, abrogation, annihilation, annulment, cancellation, defeasance, invalidation, nullification, voidance. *Law:* avoidance, extinguishment. *See* CONTINUE. **2.** A refusal to grant the truth of a statement or charge : contradiction, denial, disaffirmance, disaffirmation, disclaimer, rejection. *Law:* traversal. *See* AFFIRM.

negative *adjective*
Tending to discourage, retard, or make more difficult : adverse, disadvantageous, unadvantageous, unfavorable, unsatisfactory, untoward. *See* HELP.

negative *verb* **1.** To prevent or forbid authoritatively : blackball, turn down, veto. *Slang:* nix. ***Idiom:*** turn thumbs down on. *See* ACCEPT. **2.** To refuse to admit the truth, reality, value, or worth of : contradict, contravene, controvert, deny, disaffirm, gainsay, negate, oppugn. *Law:* traverse. *See* AFFIRM.

neglect *verb*
1. To refuse to pay attention to (a person); treat with contempt : disregard, ignore, slight. *Regional:* igg. *See* CONCERN, THOUGHTS. **2.** To fail to care for or give proper attention to : disregard, ignore, slight. *See* CARE FOR, CONCERN. **3.** To not do (something necessary) : default, fail, omit. *See* DO. **4.** To avoid the fulfillment of : disregard, shirk, slack. ***Idiom:*** let slide. *See* DO.

neglect *noun* **1.** An act or instance of neglecting : disregard, oversight, slight. *See* CARE FOR, CONCERN. **2.** Nonperformance of what ought to be done : default, delinquency, dereliction, failure, omission. *Law:* nonfeasance. *See* DO.

neglectful *adjective*
Guilty of neglect; lacking due care or concern : derelict, lax, negligent, remiss, slack. *See* CAREFUL.

negligence *noun*
The state or quality of being negligent : laxity, laxness, remissness, slackness. *See* CAREFUL.

negligent *adjective*
Guilty of neglect; lacking due care or concern : derelict, lax, neglectful, remiss, slack. *See* CAREFUL.

negligibility *noun*
Contemptible unimportance : inconsiderableness, negligibleness, paltriness, pettiness, smallness, triviality, trivialness. *See* IMPORTANT.

negligible *adjective*
1. Contemptibly unimportant : inconsiderable, niggling, nugatory, paltry, petty, picayune, piddling, small, small-minded, trifling. *Slang:* measly. ***Idiom:*** of no account. *See* IMPORTANT.
2. Small in degree, especially of probability : faint, outside, remote, slender, slight, slim. *See* BIG.

negligibleness *noun*
Contemptible unimportance : inconsiderableness, negligibility, paltriness, pettiness, smallness, triviality, trivialness. *See* IMPORTANT.

negotiable *adjective*
Capable of being passed, traversed, or crossed : navigable, passable. *See* OPEN.

negotiate *verb*
1. To argue about the terms, as of a sale : bargain, dicker, haggle, higgle, huckster, palter. *See* AGREE. **2.** To bring about or come to an agreement concerning : arrange, conclude, fix, set[1], settle. *See* AGREE. **3.** To pass by or over safely or successfully : clear, hurdle, surmount. *See* THRIVE.

negotiation *noun*
The act or process of dealing with another to reach an agreement : parley, talk (often used in plural). *See* WORDS.

neighbor *verb*
To be contiguous or next to : abut, adjoin, border, bound[2], butt[2], join, meet[1], touch, verge. *See* NEAR.

neighborhood *noun*
1. A rather small part of a geographic unit considered in regard to its inhabitants or distinctive characteristics : area, district, quarter (often uppercase). *See* TERRITORY. **2.** A part of the earth's surface : area, belt, district, locality, quarter, region, tract, zone. *Informal:* neck of the woods. *See* TERRITORY. **3.** A surrounding area : environment, environs, locale, locality, precinct (used in plural), surroundings, vicinity. *See* NEAR, PLACE. **4.** A surrounding site : area, locality, vicinity. *See* NEAR, PLACE.
5. *Informal.* Approximate size or amount : range, vicinity. *See* NEAR.

neighborly *adjective*
Of or befitting a friend or friends : amicable, friendly, warmhearted. *See* ATTITUDE, LOVE.

nemesis *noun*
One who is hostile to or opposes the purposes or interests of another : archenemy, enemy, foe. *See* LOVE.

neonate *noun*
A very young child : babe, baby, bambino, infant, newborn, nursling. ***Idiom:*** bundle of joy. *See* KIN, YOUTH.

neophyte *noun*
One who is just starting to learn or do something : abecedarian, beginner, fledgling, freshman, greenhorn, initiate, novice, novitiate, tenderfoot, tyro. *Slang:* rookie. *See* START.

nerd also **nurd** *noun*
1. *Slang.* One deficient in judgment and good sense : ass, fool, idiot, imbecile, jackass, mooncalf, moron, nincompoop, ninny, nitwit, simple, simpleton, softhead, tomfool. *Informal:* dope, gander, goose. *Slang:* cretin, ding-dong, dip, goof, jerk, schmo, schmuck, turkey. *See* ABILITY. **2.** *Slang.* An unpleasant, tiresome person : bore. *Slang:* drip, dweeb, jerk, pill, poop[2]. *See* LIKE.

nerve *noun*
1. The quality of mind enabling one to face danger or hardship resolutely : braveness, bravery, courage, courageousness, dauntlessness, doughtiness, fearlessness, fortitude, gallantry, gameness, heart, intrepidity, intrepidness, mettle, pluck, pluckiness, spirit, stoutheartedness, undauntedness, valiance, valiancy, valiantness, valor. *Informal:* spunk, spunkiness. *Slang:* gut (used in plural), gutsiness, moxie. *See* FEAR.
2. The state or quality of being impudent or arrogantly self-confident : assumption, audaciousness, audacity, boldness, brashness, brazenness, cheek, cheekiness, chutzpah, discourtesy, disrespect, effrontery, face, familiarity, forwardness, gall[1], impertinence, impudence, impudency, incivility, insolence, nerviness, overconfidence, pertness, presumptuousness, pushiness, rudeness, sassiness, sauciness. *Informal:* brass, crust, sauce, uppishness, uppityness. *See* ATTITUDE, COURTESY.
nerve *verb* To impart strength and confidence to : buck up, cheer (up), encourage, hearten, perk up. *See* HELP.

nerviness *noun*
The state or quality of being impudent or arrogantly self-confident : assumption, audaciousness, audacity, boldness, brashness, brazenness, cheek, cheekiness, chutzpah, discourtesy, disrespect, effrontery, face, familiarity, forwardness, gall[1], impertinence, impudence, impudency, incivility, insolence, nerve, overconfidence, pertness, presumptuousness, pushiness, rudeness, sassiness, sauciness. *Informal:* brass, crust,

sauce, uppishness, uppityness. *See* ATTITUDE, COURTESY.

nervous *adjective*
1. In a state of anxiety or uneasiness : agitated, anxious, concerned, distressed, solicitous, uneasy, unsettled. *See* FEELINGS. **2.** Feeling or exhibiting nervous tension : edgy, fidgety, jittery, jumpy, restive, restless, skittish, tense, twitchy. *Slang:* uptight. ***Idioms:*** a bundle of nerves, all wound up, on edge. *See* TIGHTEN.

nervousness *noun*
A troubled or anxious state of mind : angst, anxiety, anxiousness, care, concern, disquiet, disquietude, distress, solicitude, unease, uneasiness, worry. *See* FEELINGS.

nervy *adjective*
Rude and disrespectful : assuming, assumptive, audacious, bold, boldfaced, brash, brazen, cheeky, contumelious, familiar, forward, impertinent, impudent, insolent, malapert, overconfident, pert, presuming, presumptuous, pushy, sassy, saucy, smart. *Informal:* brassy, flip, fresh, smart-alecky, snippety, snippy, uppish, uppity. *Slang:* wise[1]. *See* ATTITUDE, COURTESY.

nescience *noun*
1. The condition of being ignorant; lack of knowledge or learning : benightedness, ignorance, illiteracy, illiterateness. *See* KNOWLEDGE. **2.** The condition of being uninformed or unaware : ignorance, innocence, obliviousness, unawareness, unconsciousness, unfamiliarity. *See* KNOWLEDGE.

nescient *adjective*
Without education or knowledge : ignorant, illiterate, uneducated, uninstructed, unlearned, unschooled, untaught. *See* KNOWLEDGE.

nest egg *noun*
A supply stored or hidden for future use : backlog, cache, hoard, inventory, reserve, reservoir, stock, stockpile, store, treasure. *Slang:* stash. *See* COLLECT.

nestle *verb*
To lie or press close together, usually with another person or thing : cuddle, nuzzle, snug, snuggle. *See* NEAR.

net[1] *noun*
An open fabric woven of strands that are interlaced and knotted at usually regular intervals : mesh, netting, network, web. *See* THING.
net *verb* To gain possession of, especially after a struggle or chase : capture, catch, get, secure, take. *Informal:* bag. *Slang:* nail. *See* GET.

net[2] *verb*
To make as income or profit : bring in, clear, draw, earn, gain, gross, pay, produce, realize, repay, return, yield. *See* MONEY.

nethermost *adjective*
Opposite to or farthest from the top : bottom, lowermost, lowest, undermost. *See* OVER.

netting *noun*
An open fabric woven of strands that are interlaced and knotted at usually regular intervals : mesh, net[1], network, web. *See* THING.

nettle *verb*
To trouble the nerves or peace of mind of, especially by repeated vexations : aggravate, annoy, bother, bug, chafe, disturb, exasperate, fret, gall[2], get, irk, irritate, peeve, provoke, put out, rile, ruffle, vex. ***Idioms:*** get in one's hair, get on one's nerves, get under one's skin. *See* FEELINGS, PAIN.

nettlesome *adjective*
1. Troubling the nerves or peace of mind, as by repeated vexations : annoying, bothersome, galling, irksome, irritating, plaguy, provoking, troublesome, vexatious. *See* PAIN. **2.** So replete with interlocking points and complications as to be painfully irritating : prickly, spiny, thorny. *See* EASY, PAIN.

network *noun*
1. An open fabric woven of strands that are interlaced and knotted at usually regular intervals : mesh, net[1], netting, web. *See* THING. **2.** An interwoven or interrelated number of things : tissue, web. *See* GROUP.

neuter *adjective*
Not inclining toward or actively taking either side in a matter under dispute : impartial, neutral, nonaligned, nonpartisan, unbiased, uncommitted, uninvolved, unprejudiced. ***Idiom:*** on the fence. *See* FAIR.
neuter *verb* To render incapable of reproducing sexually : alter, castrate, fix, geld, spay, sterilize, unsex. *See* REPRODUCTION, RICH.

neutral *adjective*
1. Not inclining toward or actively taking either side in a matter under dispute : impartial, neuter, nonaligned, nonpartisan, unbiased, uncommitted, uninvolved, unprejudiced. ***Idiom:*** on the fence. *See* FAIR. **2.** Feeling or showing no strong emotional involvement : detached, disinterested, dispassionate, impersonal, indifferent. *See* FEELINGS. **3.** Without definite or distinctive characteristics : bland, colorless, indistinctive. *See* STRONG.

neutralize *verb*
1. To make up for : balance, compensate, counterbalance, counterpoise, countervail, offset, outweigh, redeem, set off. *See* SUBSTI-

TUTE. **2.** To make ineffective by applying an opposite force or amount : cancel, counteract, negate, nullify. *See* ACTION.

never-ending *adjective*
Enduring for all time : amaranthine, ceaseless, endless, eternal, everlasting, immortal, perpetual, unending, world without end. *Archaic:* eterne. *See* CONTINUE.

nevertheless *adverb*
In spite of a preceding event or consideration : all the same, however, nonetheless, still, yet. *Informal:* still and all. ***Idiom:*** be that as it may. *See* AFFIRM.

new *adjective*
1. In existence now : contemporary, current, existent, existing, now, present[1], present-day. *See* TIME. **2.** Not previously used : brand-new, fresh. *See* NEW. **3.** Not the same as what was previously known or done : different, fresh, innovative, inventive, newfangled, novel, original, unfamiliar, unprecedented. *See* NEW.
4. Being an addition : added, additional, extra, fresh, further, more, other. *See* INCREASE.

newborn *noun*
A very young child : babe, baby, bambino, infant, neonate, nursling. ***Idiom:*** bundle of joy. *See* KIN, YOUTH.

newcomer *noun*
A person coming from another country or into a new community : alien, émigré, foreigner, outlander, outsider, stranger. *See* NATIVE.

newfangled *adjective*
Not the same as what was previously known or done : different, fresh, innovative, inventive, new, novel, original, unfamiliar, unprecedented. *See* NEW.

newfangledness *noun*
The quality of being novel : freshness, innovativeness, newness, novelty, originality. *See* NEW.

newly *adverb*
Only a moment ago : just, recently. *See* TIME.

newness *noun*
The quality of being novel : freshness, innovativeness, newfangledness, novelty, originality. *See* NEW.

news *noun*
1. New information, especially about recent events and happenings : advice (often used in plural), intelligence, tiding (often used in plural), word. *Informal:* scoop. *See* KNOWLEDGE, WORDS. **2.** Something significant that happens : circumstance, development, episode, event, happening, incident, occasion, occurrence, thing. *See* HAPPEN.

newsmonger *noun*
A person habitually engaged in idle talk about others : blab, gossip, gossiper, gossipmonger, rumormonger, scandalmonger, tabby, talebearer, taleteller, tattle, tattler, tattletale, telltale, whisperer. *Slang:* yenta. *See* WORDS.

next *adjective*
1. Sharing a common boundary : adjacent, adjoining, conterminous, contiguous. *See* NEAR. **2.** Occurring right after another : coming, following. *See* PRECEDE, TIME.
next *adverb* At a subsequent time : after, afterward, afterwards, later, latterly, subsequently, ulteriorly. ***Idioms:*** after a while, by and by, later on. *See* PRECEDE.

nexus *noun*
That which unites or binds : bond, knot, ligament, ligature, link, tie, vinculum, yoke. *See* CONNECT.

Niagara *noun*
An abundant, usually overwhelming flow or fall, as of a river or rain : alluvion, cataclysm, cataract, deluge, downpour, flood, freshet, inundation, overflow, torrent. *Chiefly British:* spate. *See* BIG.

nice *adjective*
1. To one's liking : agreeable, congenial, favorable, good, grateful, gratifying, pleasant, pleasing, pleasurable, satisfying, welcome. *See* LIKE.
2. Having pleasant desirable qualities : good. *Scots:* bonny, braw. *See* GOOD. **3.** Well above average : good, high-grade. *See* GOOD, ABILITY. **4.** Conforming to accepted standards : becoming, befitting, comely, comme il faut, correct, decent, decorous, de rigueur, proper, respectable, right, seemly. *See* COURTESY.
5. Morally beyond reproach, especially in sexual conduct : chaste, decent, modest, pure, virgin, virginal, virtuous. *See* GOOD, RESTRAINT, SEX. **6.** Very difficult to please : choosy, dainty, exacting, fastidious, finical, finicky, fussy, meticulous, particular, persnickety, squeamish. *Informal:* picky. *See* ACCEPT.
7. Able to make or detect effects of great subtlety or precision : delicate, fine[1], subtle. *See* PRECISE. **8.** So slight as to be difficult to notice or appreciate : delicate, fine[1], finespun, refined, subtle. *See* BIG.

niche *noun*
The proper or designated location : place. *See* PLACE.

nick *verb*
Slang. To exploit (another) by charging too much for something : fleece, overcharge. *Slang:* clip[1], gouge, rip off, scalp, skin, soak.

Idioms: make someone pay through the nose, take someone for a ride, take someone to the cleaners. *See* HONEST.

nickname *noun*
The word or words by which one is called and identified : appellation, appellative, cognomen, denomination, designation, epithet, name, style, tag, title. *Slang:* handle, moniker. *See* SPECIFIC, WORDS.

nictate *verb*
To open and close the eyes rapidly : bat[1], blink, nictitate, twinkle, wink. *See* REPETITION, SEE.

nictation *noun*
A brief closing of the eyes : blink, nictitation, wink. *See* SEE.

nictitate *verb*
To open and close the eyes rapidly : bat[1], blink, nictate, twinkle, wink. *See* REPETITION, SEE.

nictitation *noun*
A brief closing of the eyes : blink, nictation, wink. *See* SEE.

nifty *adjective*
Slang. Particularly excellent : divine, fabulous, fantastic, fantastical, glorious, marvelous, sensational, splendid, superb, terrific, wonderful. *Informal:* dandy, dreamy, great, ripping, super, swell, tremendous. *Slang:* cool, groovy, hot, keen[1], neat. *Idiom:* out of this world. *See* GOOD.

niggard *noun*
A stingy person : miser, Scrooge, skinflint. *Informal:* penny pincher. *Slang:* cheapskate, stiff, tightwad. *See* GIVE.

niggard *adjective* Ungenerously or pettily reluctant to spend money : cheap, close, close-fisted, costive, hard-fisted, mean[2], miserly, niggardly, parsimonious, penny-pinching, penurious, petty, pinching, stingy, tight, tightfisted. *See* GIVE.

niggardly *adjective*
Ungenerously or pettily reluctant to spend money : cheap, close, close-fisted, costive, hard-fisted, mean[2], miserly, niggard, parsimonious, penny-pinching, penurious, petty, pinching, stingy, tight, tightfisted. *See* GIVE.

niggle *verb*
To raise unnecessary or trivial objections : carp, cavil, nitpick, pettifog, quibble. *Idiom:* pick to pieces. *See* SUPPORT.

niggler *noun*
A person who finds fault, often severely and willfully : carper, caviler, critic, criticizer, faultfinder, hypercritic, nitpicker, quibbler. *See* PRAISE.

niggling *adjective*
Contemptibly unimportant : inconsiderable, negligible, nugatory, paltry, petty, picayune, piddling, small, small-minded, trifling. *Slang:* measly. *Idiom:* of no account. *See* IMPORTANT.

nigh *adverb*
To a point near in time, space, or relation : close, closely, hard, near, nearby. *See* NEAR.

nigh *adjective* Not far from another in space, time, or relation : adjacent, close, contiguous, immediate, near, nearby, proximate. *Idioms:* at hand, under one's nose, within a stone's throw, within hailing distance. *See* NEAR.

night *noun*
The period of time between sunset and sunrise : nighttime. *See* LIGHT.

night *adjective* Of or occurring during the night : nightly, nocturnal. *See* LIGHT.

nightfall *noun*
The period between afternoon and nighttime : dusk, eve, evening, eventide, gloaming, twilight. *Archaic:* even[2], vesper. *See* START.

nightly *adjective*
Of or occurring during the night : night, nocturnal. *See* LIGHT.

nighttime *noun*
The period of time between sunset and sunrise : night. *See* LIGHT.

nihility *noun*
The condition of not existing : nonexistence, nothing, nothingness. *See* ABSENCE.

nil *noun*
No thing; not anything : nothing, null. *Informal:* zero. *Slang:* nix, zilch. *Archaic:* aught. *See* ABSENCE.

nimble *adjective*
1. Moving or performing quickly, lightly, and easily : agile, brisk, facile, quick, spry. *See* ABILITY. **2.** Exhibiting or possessing skill and ease in performance : adroit, clever, deft, dexterous, facile, handy, slick. *See* ABILITY.

nimbleness *noun*
The quality or state of being mentally agile : agileness, agility, dexterity, dexterousness, quickness. *See* ABILITY.

nincompoop *noun*
One deficient in judgment and good sense : ass, fool, idiot, imbecile, jackass, mooncalf, moron, ninny, nitwit, simple, simpleton, softhead, tomfool. *Informal:* dope, gander, goose. *Slang:* cretin, ding-dong, dip, goof, jerk, nerd, schmo, schmuck, turkey. *See* ABILITY.

ninny *noun*
One deficient in judgment and good sense : ass, fool, idiot, imbecile, jackass, mooncalf, moron, nincompoop, nitwit, simple, simpleton, softhead, tomfool. *Informal:* dope, gander, goose. *Slang:* cretin, ding-dong, dip, goof, jerk, nerd, schmo, schmuck, turkey. *See* ABILITY.

nip[1] *verb*
1. To grasp at (something) eagerly, forcibly, and abruptly with the jaws : catch, snap, snatch, strike. *See* REACH. **2.** To spoil or destroy : blast, blight, dash. *See* HELP. **3.** *Slang.* To take (another's property) without permission : filch, pilfer, purloin, snatch, steal, thieve. *Informal:* lift, swipe. *Slang:* cop, heist, hook, pinch, rip off, snitch. ***Idiom:*** make (*or* walk) off with. *See* CRIMES, GIVE. **4.** *Chiefly British.* To move swiftly : bolt, bucket, bustle, dart, dash, festinate, flash, fleet, flit, fly, haste, hasten, hurry, hustle, pelt[2], race, rocket, run, rush, sail, scoot, scour[2], shoot, speed, sprint, tear[1], trot, whirl, whisk, whiz, wing, zip, zoom. *Informal:* hotfoot, rip. *Slang:* barrel, highball. ***Idioms:*** get a move on, get cracking, go like lightning, go like the wind, hotfoot it, make haste, make time, make tracks, run like the wind, shake a leg, step (*or* jump) on it. *See* MOVE.

nip[2] *noun*
Informal. A small amount of liquor : dram, drop, jigger, shot, sip, tot[1]. *Informal:* slug[1]. *Slang:* snort. *See* BIG, INGESTION.
nip *verb Informal.* To take alcoholic liquor, especially excessively or habitually : drink, guzzle, imbibe, tipple. *Slang:* booze, lush[2], soak, tank up. ***Idioms:*** bend the elbow, hit the bottle. *See* DRUGS.

nip and tuck *adjective*
Nearly equivalent or even : close, neck and neck, tight. *See* NEAR.

nippy *adjective*
Marked by a low temperature : chill, chilly, cold, cool, shivery. *See* HOT.

nitpick *verb*
To raise unnecessary or trivial objections : carp, cavil, niggle, pettifog, quibble. ***Idiom:*** pick to pieces. *See* SUPPORT.

nitpicker *noun*
A person who finds fault, often severely and willfully : carper, caviler, critic, criticizer, faultfinder, hypercritic, niggler, quibbler. *See* PRAISE.

nitwit *noun*
One deficient in judgment and good sense : ass, fool, idiot, imbecile, jackass, mooncalf, moron, nincompoop, ninny, simple, simpleton, softhead, tomfool. *Informal:* dope, gander, goose. *Slang:* cretin, ding-dong, dip, goof, jerk, nerd, schmo, schmuck, turkey. *See* ABILITY.

nix *noun*
Slang. No thing; not anything : nil, nothing, null. *Informal:* zero. *Slang:* zilch. *Archaic:* aught. *See* ABSENCE.
nix *adverb Slang.* Not so : nay, no. *Informal:* nope. ***Idiom:*** nothing doing. *See* AFFIRM.
nix *verb* **1.** *Slang.* To prevent or forbid authoritatively : blackball, negative, turn down, veto. ***Idiom:*** turn thumbs down on. *See* ACCEPT. **2.** *Slang.* To be unwilling to accept, consider, or receive : decline, dismiss, refuse, reject, spurn, turn down. ***Idiom:*** turn thumbs down on. *See* ACCEPT.

no *adverb*
Not so : nay. *Informal:* nope. *Slang:* nix. ***Idiom:*** nothing doing. *See* AFFIRM.
no *noun* **1.** A negative response : nay, refusal, rejection. *See* AFFIRM. **2.** A negative vote or voter : nay. *See* AFFIRM.

no-account *adjective*
Informal. Lacking all worth and value : drossy, good-for-nothing, inutile, no-good, nothing, valueless, worthless. *See* VALUE.

nobility *noun*
1. People of the highest social level : aristocracy, blue blood, crème de la crème, elite, flower, gentility, gentry, patriciate, quality, society, upper class, who's who. *Informal:* upper crust. *See* OVER. **2.** Noble rank or status by birth : birth, blood, blue blood, noblesse. *See* KIN, OVER.

noble *adjective*
1. Of high birth or social position : aristocratic, blue-blooded, elite, highborn, highbred, patrician, thoroughbred, upper-class, wellborn. *Informal:* upper-crust. *See* OVER. **2.** Being on a high intellectual or moral level : elevated, high-minded, moral. *See* HIGH. **3.** Large and impressive in size, scope, or extent : august, baronial, grand, grandiose, imposing, lordly, magnific, magnificent, majestic, princely, regal, royal, splendid, stately, sublime, superb. *See* BIG, GOOD.

noblesse *noun*
Noble rank or status by birth : birth, blood, blue blood, nobility. *See* KIN, OVER.

nobody *pronoun*
No person : none, no one. *See* ABSENCE.
nobody *noun* A totally insignificant person : cipher, nebbish, nonentity, nothing. *Informal:* pip-squeak, zero. *Slang:* shrimp, zilch. *See* IMPORTANT.

nocturnal *adjective*
Of or occurring during the night : night, nightly. *See* LIGHT.

nod *verb*
1. To respond affirmatively; receive with agreement or compliance : accede, accept, acquiesce, agree, assent, consent, subscribe, yes. *See* AGREE. **2.** To sleep for a brief period. Also used with *off* : catnap, doze (off), nap, siesta, snooze. ***Idiom:*** catch (*or* grab *or* take) forty winks. *See* AWARENESS.

nod *noun* **1.** An inclination of the head or body, as in greeting, consent, courtesy, submission, or worship : bow[1], curtsy, genuflection, kowtow, obeisance. *See* COURTESY. **2.** The act or process of accepting : acceptance, acquiescence, agreement, assent, consent, yes. *Informal:* OK. *See* ACCEPT.

nodding *adjective*
Ready for or needing sleep : dozy, drowsy, sleepy, slumberous, slumbery, somnolent, soporific. *See* AWARENESS.

noddle *noun*
The uppermost part of the body : head, pate, poll. *Slang:* bean, block, conk, dome, noggin, noodle, nut. *See* BODY.

noggin *noun*
Slang. The uppermost part of the body : head, noddle, pate, poll. *Slang:* bean, block, conk, dome, noodle, nut. *See* BODY.

no-good *adjective*
Lacking all worth and value : drossy, good-for-nothing, inutile, nothing, valueless, worthless. *Informal:* no-account. *See* VALUE.

no-good *noun* A self-indulgent person who spends time avoiding work or other useful activity : bum[1], drone[1], fainéant, good-for-nothing, idler, layabout, loafer, ne'er-do-well, slugabed, sluggard, wastrel. *Informal:* do-little, do-nothing, lazybones, slug[2]. *Slang:* slouch. *See* INDUSTRIOUS.

noise *noun*
1. Sounds or a sound, especially when loud, confused, or disagreeable : babel, clamor, din, hubbub, hullabaloo, pandemonium, racket, rumpus, tumult, uproar. *See* SOUNDS. **2.** The sensation caused by vibrating wave motion that is perceived by the organs of hearing : sonance, sound[1]. *See* SOUNDS.

noise *verb* **1.** To make (information) generally known : advertise, blaze[2], blazon, broadcast, bruit, circulate, disseminate, promulgate, propagate, spread. ***Idioms:*** spread far and wide, spread the word. *See* KNOWLEDGE. **2.** To engage in or spread gossip : blab, gossip, rumor, talk, tattle, tittle-tattle, whisper. ***Idioms:*** tell tales, tell tales out of school. *See* WORDS.

noiseless *adjective*
Marked by, done with, or making no sound or noise : hushed, quiet, silent, soundless, still, stilly. *Archaic:* hush. *See* SOUNDS.

noiselessness *noun*
The absence of sound or noise : hush, quiet, quietness, silence, soundlessness, still, stillness. *See* SOUNDS.

noisome *adjective*
Having an unpleasant odor : fetid, foul, foul-smelling, malodorous, mephitic, reeky, stinking. *Informal:* smelly. *See* SMELLS.

nomadic *adjective*
Leading the life of a person without a fixed domicile; moving from place to place : itinerant, peripatetic, vagabond, vagrant. *See* MOVE.

nominate *verb*
To select for an office or position : appoint, designate, make, name, tap[1]. *See* CHOICE.

nomination *noun*
The act of appointing to an office or position : appointment, designation. *See* CHOICE.

nominee *noun*
A person who is appointed to an office or position : appointee, designee. *See* CHOICE.

nonage *noun*
The state or period of being under legal age : minority. *Law:* infancy. *See* LAW, YOUTH.

nonaligned *adjective*
Not inclining toward or actively taking either side in a matter under dispute : impartial, neuter, neutral, nonpartisan, unbiased, uncommitted, uninvolved, unprejudiced. ***Idiom:*** on the fence. *See* FAIR.

nonappearance *noun*
Law. Failure to be present : absence, nonattendance. *See* ABSENCE.

nonattendance *noun*
Failure to be present : absence. *Law:* nonappearance. *See* ABSENCE.

nonbeliever *noun*
One who habitually or instinctively doubts or questions : doubter, doubting Thomas, skeptic, unbeliever. *See* BELIEF.

nonchalance *noun*
A stable, calm state of the emotions : aplomb, balance, collectedness, composure, coolness, equanimity, imperturbability, imperturbableness, poise, sang-froid, self-possession, unflappability. *Slang:* cool. *See* CALM, FEELINGS.

nonchalant *adjective*
Not easily excited, even under pressure : calm, collected, composed, cool, cool-headed,

detached, even[1], even-tempered, imperturbable, possessed, unflappable, unruffled. *See* CALM.

noncommittal *adjective*
Tending to keep one's thoughts and emotions to oneself : controlled, inhibited, reserved, restrained, self-controlled, self-restrained. *See* RESTRAINT.

noncompliance *noun*
The condition or practice of not obeying : disobedience, insubordination. *See* RESIST.

noncompliant *adjective*
Refusing or failing to obey : disobedient, insubordinate. *See* RESIST.

non compos mentis *adjective*
Law. Afflicted with or exhibiting irrationality and mental unsoundness : brainsick, crazy, daft, demented, disordered, distraught, dotty, insane, lunatic, mad, maniac, maniacal, mentally ill, moonstruck, off, touched, unbalanced, unsound, wrong. *Informal:* bonkers, cracked, daffy, gaga, loony. *Slang:* bananas, batty, buggy, cuckoo, fruity, loco, nuts, nutty, screwy, wacky. *Chiefly British:* crackers. ***Idioms:*** around the bend, crazy as a loon, mad as a hatter, not all there, nutty as a fruitcake, off (*or* out of) one's head, off one's rocker, of unsound mind, out of one's mind, sick in the head, stark raving mad. *See* SANE.

nonconformist *noun*
A person who dissents from the doctrine of an established church : dissenter, dissident, heretic, schismatic, sectarian, sectary, separationist, separatist. *See* RELIGION.

none *pronoun*
No person : nobody, no one. *See* ABSENCE.

nonentity *noun*
A totally insignificant person : cipher, nebbish, nobody, nothing. *Informal:* pip-squeak, zero. *Slang:* shrimp, zilch. *See* IMPORTANT.

nonessential *adjective*
Not necessary : dispensable, inessential, needless, uncalled-for, unessential, unnecessary, unneeded, unrequired. *See* NECESSARY.

nonesuch *noun*
A person or thing so excellent as to have no equal or match : nonpareil, paragon, phoenix. *See* GOOD.

nonetheless *adverb*
In spite of a preceding event or consideration : all the same, however, nevertheless, still, yet. *Informal:* still and all. ***Idiom:*** be that as it may. *See* AFFIRM.

nonexistence *noun*
The condition of not existing : nihility, nothing, nothingness. *See* ABSENCE.

nonfeasance *noun*
Law. Nonperformance of what ought to be done : default, delinquency, dereliction, failure, neglect, omission. *See* DO.

no-nonsense *adjective*
Marked by sober sincerity : businesslike, earnest[1], serious, sobersided. ***Idiom:*** in earnest. *See* HEAVY, WORK.

nonpareil *adjective*
Without equal or rival : alone, incomparable, matchless, only, peerless, singular, unequaled, unexampled, unique, unmatched, unparalleled, unrivaled. *See* SAME.

nonpareil *noun* A person or thing so excellent as to have no equal or match : nonesuch, paragon, phoenix. *See* GOOD.

nonpartisan *adjective*
1. Not inclining toward or actively taking either side in a matter under dispute : impartial, neuter, neutral, nonaligned, unbiased, uncommitted, uninvolved, unprejudiced. ***Idiom:*** on the fence. *See* FAIR. **2.** Free from bias in judgment : disinterested, dispassionate, equitable, fair, fair-minded, impartial, indifferent, just, objective, square, unbiased, unprejudiced. ***Idiom:*** fair and square. *See* FAIR.

nonpartisanship *noun*
The quality or state of being just and unbiased : detachment, disinterest, disinterestedness, dispassion, dispassionateness, equitableness, fair-mindedness, fairness, impartiality, impartialness, justice, justness, objectiveness, objectivity. *See* FAIR.

nonphysical *adjective*
Having no body, form, or substance : bodiless, discarnate, disembodied, immaterial, incorporeal, insubstantial, metaphysical, spiritual, unbodied, uncorporal, unsubstantial. *See* BODY.

nonplus *verb*
To make incapable of finding something to think, do, or say : confound. *Informal:* flummox, stick, stump, throw. *Slang:* beat. ***Idiom:*** put someone at a loss. *See* AFFECT, KNOWLEDGE.

nonprofessional *noun*
One lacking professional skill and ease in a particular pursuit : amateur, dabbler, dilettante, smatterer, uninitiate. *See* ABILITY.

nonprofessional *adjective* Lacking the required professional skill : amateurish, dilettante, dilettantish, unprofessional, unskilled, unskillful. *See* ABILITY.

nonresistant *adjective*
Submitting without objection or resistance :

acquiescent, passive, resigned, submissive. *See* RESIST.

nonsense *noun*
1. Unintelligible or foolish talk : babble, blather, blatherskite, double talk, gabble, gibberish, jabber, jabberwocky, jargon, prate, prattle, twaddle. *See* WORDS. **2.** Something that does not have or make sense : balderdash, blather, bunkum, claptrap, drivel, garbage, idiocy, piffle, poppycock, rigmarole, rubbish, tomfoolery, trash, twaddle. *Informal:* tommyrot. *Slang:* applesauce, baloney, bilge, bull[1], bunk[2], crap, hooey, malarkey. *See* KNOWLEDGE. **3.** Foolish behavior : absurdity, folly, foolery, foolishness, idiocy, imbecility, insanity, lunacy, madness, preposterousness, senselessness, silliness, tomfoolery, zaniness. *Informal:* craziness. *See* ABILITY. **4.** Something or things that are unimportant : fiddle-faddle, frippery, frivolity, froth, minutia, small change, small potatoes, trifle, trivia, triviality. *See* IMPORTANT, SURFACE.

nonsensical *adjective*
So senseless as to be laughable : absurd, foolish, harebrained, idiotic, imbecilic, insane, lunatic, mad, moronic, preposterous, silly, softheaded, tomfool, unearthly, zany. *Informal:* cockeyed, crazy, loony, loopy. *Slang:* balmy[2], dippy, dopey, jerky, sappy, wacky. *See* ABILITY, KNOWLEDGE.

nonstop *adjective*
Existing or occurring without interruption or end : around-the-clock, ceaseless, constant, continual, continuous, endless, eternal, everlasting, incessant, interminable, ongoing, perpetual, persistent, relentless, round-the-clock, timeless, unceasing, unending, unfailing, uninterrupted, unremitting. *See* CONTINUE.

noodle *noun*
Slang. The uppermost part of the body : head, noddle, pate, poll. *Slang:* bean, block, conk, dome, noggin, nut. *See* BODY.

no one *pronoun*
No person : nobody, none. *See* ABSENCE.

nope *adverb*
Informal. Not so : nay, no. *Slang:* nix. ***Idiom:*** nothing doing. *See* AFFIRM.

norm *noun*
1. A regular or customary matter, condition, or course of events : commonplace, ordinary, rule, usual. *See* USUAL. **2.** Something, as a type, number, quantity, or degree, that represents a midpoint between extremes on a scale of valuation : average, mean[3], median, medium, par. *See* USUAL.

normal *adjective*
Commonly encountered : average, common, commonplace, general, ordinary, typical, usual. *See* SURPRISE.

normalcy *noun*
The quality or condition of being usual : customariness, habitualness, normality, ordinariness, prevalence, regularity, routineness, usualness. *See* USUAL.

normality *noun*
The quality or condition of being usual : customariness, habitualness, normalcy, ordinariness, prevalence, regularity, routineness, usualness. *See* USUAL.

normally *adverb*
In an expected or customary manner; for the most part : commonly, consistently, customarily, frequently, generally, habitually, naturally, often, regularly, routinely, typically, usually. ***Idioms:*** as usual, per usual. *See* BIG, USUAL.

nose *noun*
1. The structure on the human face that contains the nostrils and organs of smell and forms the beginning of the respiratory tract : proboscis. *Informal:* beak, snoot. *Slang:* nozzle, schnoz, schnozzle, snout. *See* BODY, CONVEX. **2.** The sense by which odors are perceived : olfaction, scent, smell. *See* SMELLS. **3.** Skill in perceiving, discriminating, or judging : acumen, astuteness, clear-sightedness, discernment, discrimination, eye, keenness, penetration, perceptiveness, percipience, percipiency, perspicacity, sagacity, sageness, shrewdness, wit. *See* ABILITY, CAREFUL.

nose *verb* **1.** To perceive with the olfactory sense : scent, smell, sniff, snuff, whiff. ***Idiom:*** catch (*or* get) a whiff of. *See* SMELLS. **2.** *Informal.* To look into or inquire about curiously, inquisitively, or in a meddlesome fashion. Also used with *around* : poke, pry, snoop. ***Idiom:*** stick one's nose into. *See* INVESTIGATE, PARTICIPATE.

nose out *verb* To pursue and locate : hunt down, run down, trace, track down. ***Idiom:*** run to earth (*or* ground). *See* GET.

nosedive *noun*
1. A sudden involuntary drop to the ground : dive, fall, pitch, plunge, spill, tumble. *Informal:* header. *See* RISE. **2.** The act of plunging suddenly downward into or as if into water : dive, plunge, swoop. *Informal:* header. *See* ENTER. **3.** A usually swift downward trend, as in prices : decline, descent, dip, dive, downslide, downswing, downtrend, downturn, drop, drop-

off, fall, plunge, skid, slide, slump, tumble. *See* INCREASE.

nose-dive *verb* **1.** To come to the ground suddenly and involuntarily : drop, fall, go down, pitch, plunge, spill, topple, tumble. ***Idiom:*** take a fall (*or* header *or* plunge *or* spill *or* tumble). *See* RISE. **2.** To undergo a sharp, rapid descent in value or price : dive, drop, fall, plummet, plunge, sink, skid, slump, tumble. ***Idiom:*** take a sudden downtrend (*or* downturn). *See* INCREASE.

nosegay *noun*
Cut flowers that have been arranged in a usually small bunch : bouquet, posy. *See* THING.

nose out *verb* See **nose.**

nosey *adjective* See **nosy.**

nosiness *noun*
Informal. Undue interest in the affairs of others : curiosity, curiousness, inquisitiveness. *Informal:* snoopiness. *See* INVESTIGATE.

nostrum *noun*
An agent used to restore health : cure, elixir, medicament, medication, medicine, physic, remedy. *See* HEALTH.

nosy or **nosey** *adjective*
Informal. Unduly interested in the affairs of others : curious, inquisitive, inquisitorial. *Informal:* snoopy. *See* INVESTIGATE.

notability *noun*
1. A position of exalted widely recognized importance : distinction, eminence, eminency, fame, glory, illustriousness, luster, mark, note, preeminence, prestige, prominence, prominency, renown. *See* IMPORTANT, KNOWLEDGE, RESPECT. **2.** An important, influential person : character, dignitary, eminence, leader, lion, nabob, notable, personage. *Informal:* big-timer, heavyweight, somebody, someone, VIP. *Slang:* big shot, big wheel, bigwig, muckamuck. *See* IMPORTANT.

notable *adjective*
Widely known and esteemed : celebrated, distinguished, eminent, famed, famous, great, illustrious, noted, preeminent, prestigious, prominent, redoubtable, renowned. *See* KNOWLEDGE, RESPECT.

notable *noun* **1.** An important, influential person : character, dignitary, eminence, leader, lion, nabob, notability, personage. *Informal:* big-timer, heavyweight, somebody, someone, VIP. *Slang:* big shot, big wheel, bigwig, muckamuck. *See* IMPORTANT. **2.** A famous person : big name, celebrity, hero, lion, luminary, name, personage, personality. *See* KNOWLEDGE.

notably *adverb*
To a high degree : awfully, dreadfully, eminently, exceedingly, exceptionally, extra, extremely, greatly, highly, most, very. *Informal:* awful. *Chiefly Regional:* mighty. *See* BIG.

notation *noun*
A brief record written as an aid to the memory : memorandum, note. *Informal:* memo. *See* WORDS.

notch *noun*
Informal. One of the units in a course, as on an ascending or descending scale : degree, grade, level, peg, point, rung, stage, step. *See* BIG.

notch *verb* *Informal.* To gain (a point or points) in a game or contest : post[1], score, tally. *See* DO.

note *noun*
1. A brief record written as an aid to the memory : memorandum, notation. *Informal:* memo. *See* WORDS. **2.** A written communication directed to another : epistle, letter, missive. *See* WORDS. **3.** An expression of fact or opinion : comment, obiter dictum, observation, remark. *See* WORDS. **4.** Critical explanation or analysis : annotation, comment, commentary, exegesis, interpretation. *See* WORDS. **5.** Something visible or evident that gives grounds for believing in the existence or presence of something else : badge, evidence, index, indication, indicator, manifestation, mark, sign, signification, stamp, symptom, token, witness. *See* SHOW. **6.** A position of exalted widely recognized importance : distinction, eminence, eminency, fame, glory, illustriousness, luster, mark, notability, preeminence, prestige, prominence, prominency, renown. *See* IMPORTANT, KNOWLEDGE, RESPECT. **7.** The act of noting, observing, or taking into account : attention, cognizance, espial, heed, mark, notice, observance, observation, regard, remark. *See* KNOWLEDGE, SEE. **8.** *Obsolete.* A pleasing succession of musical tones forming a usually brief aesthetic unit : air, aria, melody, strain[2], tune. *See* SOUNDS.

note *verb* **1.** To perceive with a special effort of the senses or the mind : descry, detect, discern, distinguish, mark, mind, notice, observe, remark, see. *See* KNOWLEDGE, SEE. **2.** To state facts, opinions, or explanations : comment, observe, remark. *See* WORDS.

noted *adjective*
Widely known and esteemed : celebrated, distinguished, eminent, famed, famous, great, illustrious, notable, preeminent, prestigious,

prominent, redoubtable, renowned. *See* KNOWLEDGE, RESPECT.

nothing *noun*
1. No thing; not anything : nil, null. *Informal:* zero. *Slang:* nix, zilch. *Archaic:* aught. *See* ABSENCE. **2.** A totally insignificant person : cipher, nebbish, nobody, nonentity. *Informal:* pip-squeak, zero. *Slang:* shrimp, zilch. *See* IMPORTANT. **3.** The condition of not existing : nihility, nonexistence, nothingness. *See* ABSENCE.
nothing *adjective* Lacking all worth and value : drossy, good-for-nothing, inutile, no-good, valueless, worthless. *Informal:* no-account. *See* VALUE.

nothingness *noun*
1. The condition of not existing : nihility, nonexistence, nothing. *See* ABSENCE. **2.** Empty, unfilled space : barrenness, emptiness, vacancy, vacuity, vacuum, void. *See* FULL.

notice *noun*
1. The act of noting, observing, or taking into account : attention, cognizance, espial, heed, mark, note, observance, observation, regard, remark. *See* KNOWLEDGE, SEE. **2.** A usually public posting that conveys a message : bill[1], billboard, placard, poster, sign. *See* SHOW. **3.** A public statement : announcement, annunciation, declaration, edict, manifesto, proclamation, pronouncement. *See* KNOWLEDGE. **4.** Evaluative and critical discourse : criticism, critique, review. *See* OPINION, WORDS.
notice *verb* To perceive with a special effort of the senses or the mind : descry, detect, discern, distinguish, mark, mind, note, observe, remark, see. *See* KNOWLEDGE, SEE.

noticeable *adjective*
1. Readily seen, perceived, or understood : apparent, clear, clear-cut, crystal clear, distinct, evident, manifest, observable, obvious, patent, plain, pronounced, visible. *See* SEE. **2.** Capable of being noticed or apprehended mentally : appreciable, detectable, discernible, distinguishable, observable, palpable, perceivable, perceptible, ponderable, sensible. *See* KNOWLEDGE. **3.** Readily attracting notice : arresting, bold, conspicuous, eye-catching, marked, observable, outstanding, pointed, prominent, pronounced, remarkable, salient, signal, striking. ***Idiom:*** sticking out like a sore thumb. *See* SEE.

notify *verb*
To impart information to : acquaint, advise, apprise, educate, enlighten, inform, tell. *See* KNOWLEDGE, TEACH.

notion *noun*
1. Something believed or accepted as true by a person : belief, conviction, feeling, idea, mind, opinion, persuasion, position, sentiment, view. *See* OPINION. **2.** That which exists in the mind as the product of careful mental activity : concept, conception, idea, image, perception, thought. *See* THOUGHTS. **3.** An impulsive, often illogical turn of mind : bee, boutade, caprice, conceit, fancy, freak, humor, impulse, megrim, vagary, whim, whimsy. ***Idiom:*** bee in one's bonnet. *See* THOUGHTS.

notional *adjective*
Existing only in the imagination : chimeric, chimerical, conceptual, fanciful, fantastic, fantastical, imaginary, unreal, visionary. *See* REAL.

notoriety *noun*
1. Unfavorable, usually unsavory renown : infamousness, infamy, notoriousness. *See* KNOWLEDGE. **2.** Wide recognition for one's deeds : celebrity, fame, famousness, popularity, renown, reputation, repute. *See* KNOWLEDGE.

notorious *adjective*
1. Known widely and unfavorably : common, infamous. *See* KNOWLEDGE. **2.** Widely known and discussed : famed, famous, leading, popular, well-known. *See* KNOWLEDGE.

notoriousness *noun*
Unfavorable, usually unsavory renown : infamousness, infamy, notoriety. *See* KNOWLEDGE.

nourish *verb*
1. To sustain (a living organism) with food : feed. *See* INGESTION. **2.** To promote and sustain the development of : cultivate, foster, nurse, nurture. *See* CARE FOR. **3.** To hold and turn over in the mind : bear, harbor, nurse. *See* THOUGHTS.

nourishing *adjective*
Providing nourishment : alimentary, nutrient, nutritious, nutritive. *See* INGESTION.

nourishment *noun*
1. Something fit to be eaten : aliment, bread, comestible, diet, edible, esculent, fare, food, foodstuff, meat, nurture, nutriment, nutrition, pabulum, pap, provender, provision (used in plural), sustenance, victual. *Slang:* chow, eats, grub. *See* INGESTION. **2.** That which sustains the mind or spirit : aliment, bread, food, nutriment, pabulum, pap, sustenance. *See* CARE FOR, INGESTION.

novel *adjective*
1. Not the same as what was previously known

or done : different, fresh, innovative, inventive, new, newfangled, original, unfamiliar, unprecedented. *See* NEW. **2.** Not usual or ordinary : atypic, atypical, unconventional, unordinary, unusual, unwonted. *Slang:* offbeat. *See* USUAL.

novelty *noun*

1. The quality of being novel : freshness, innovativeness, newfangledness, newness, originality. *See* NEW. **2.** A new and unusual thing : innovation. *See* NEW. **3.** A small showy article : bauble, bibelot, gewgaw, gimcrack, knickknack, toy, trifle, trinket, whatnot. *See* THING.

novice *noun*

1. One who is just starting to learn or do something : abecedarian, beginner, fledgling, freshman, greenhorn, initiate, neophyte, novitiate, tenderfoot, tyro. *Slang:* rookie. *See* START. **2.** An entrant who has not yet taken the final vows of a religious order : novitiate. *See* RELIGION.

noviciate *noun* See **novitiate.**

novitiate also **noviciate** *noun*

1. An entrant who has not yet taken the final vows of a religious order : novice. *See* RELIGION. **2.** One who is just starting to learn or do something : abecedarian, beginner, fledgling, freshman, greenhorn, initiate, neophyte, novice, tenderfoot, tyro. *Slang:* rookie. *See* START.

now *adverb*

1. At this moment : actually, currently. ***Idiom:*** even (*or* just *or* right) now. *See* TIME. **2.** Without delay : directly, forthwith, immediately, instant, instantly, right away, right off, straightaway, straight off. ***Idioms:*** at once, first off. *See* TIME. **3.** At times : sometimes. *See* TIME. **4.** At the present; these days : nowadays, today. *See* TIME.

now *noun* The current time : nowadays, present[1], today. *See* TIME.

now *adjective* In existence now : contemporary, current, existent, existing, new, present[1], present-day. *See* TIME.

nowadays *adverb*

At the present; these days : now, today. *See* TIME.

nowadays *noun* The current time : now, present[1], today. *See* TIME.

noxious *adjective*

Extremely destructive or harmful : baneful, deadly, malignant, pernicious, pestilent, pestilential, virulent. *See* HELP.

nozzle *noun*

Slang. The structure on the human face that contains the nostrils and organs of smell and forms the beginning of the respiratory tract : nose, proboscis. *Informal:* beak, snoot. *Slang:* schnoz, schnozzle, snout. *See* BODY, CONVEX.

nuance *noun*

A slight variation between nearly identical entities : gradation, shade. *See* BIG.

nub *noun*

1. An unevenness or elevation on a surface : bump, hump, knob, knot, lump[1], protuberance. *See* CONVEX. **2.** The most central and material part : core, essence, gist, heart, kernel, marrow, meat, pith, quintessence, root[1], soul, spirit, stuff, substance. *Law:* gravamen. *See* BE.

nucleus *noun*

A source of further growth and development : bud[1], embryo, germ, kernel, seed, spark[1]. *See* START.

nude *adjective*

1. Not wearing any clothes : au naturel, bare, naked, unclad. *Chiefly British:* starkers. ***Idioms:*** in one's birthday suit, in the altogether (*or* buff *or* raw), naked as a jaybird, stark naked, without a stitch. *See* PUT ON, SHOW. **2.** Without the usual covering : bald, bare, naked. *See* PUT ON.

nudeness *noun*

The state of being without clothes : bareness, nakedness, nudity, undress. *See* PUT ON, SHOW.

nudge *verb*

To thrust against or into : dig, jab, jog, poke, prod. *See* TOUCH.

nudge *noun* An act of thrusting into or against, as to attract attention : dig, jab, jog, poke. *See* TOUCH.

nudity *noun*

The state of being without clothes : bareness, nakedness, nudeness, undress. *See* PUT ON, SHOW.

nugatory *adjective*

Contemptibly unimportant : inconsiderable, negligible, niggling, paltry, petty, picayune, piddling, small, small-minded, trifling. *Slang:* measly. ***Idiom:*** of no account. *See* IMPORTANT.

nugget *noun*

An irregularly shaped mass of indefinite size : chunk, clod, clump, gob[1], hunch, lump[1], wad. *Informal:* hunk. *See* PART.

nuisance *noun*

Something that annoys : aggravation, annoyance, besetment, bother, irritant, irritation, peeve, plague, torment, vexation. *See* FEELINGS, PAIN.

null *noun*

No thing; not anything : nil, nothing.

Informal: zero. *Slang:* nix, zilch. *Archaic:* aught. *See* ABSENCE.

nullification *noun*
An often formal act of putting an end to : abolishment, abolition, abrogation, annihilation, annulment, cancellation, defeasance, invalidation, negation, voidance. *Law:* avoidance, extinguishment. *See* CONTINUE.

nullify *verb*
1. To put an end to, especially formally and with authority : abolish, abrogate, annihilate, annul, cancel, invalidate, negate, set aside, vitiate, void. *Law:* extinguish. *See* CONTINUE.
2. To make ineffective by applying an opposite force or amount : cancel, counteract, negate, neutralize. *See* ACTION.

numb *adjective*
1. Lacking physical feeling or sensitivity : asleep, dead, insensible, insensitive, unfeeling. *See* AWARENESS. **2.** Lacking responsiveness or alertness : benumbed, dull, insensible, insensitive, stuporous, torpid, unresponsive, wooden. *See* AWARENESS.
numb *verb* **1.** To render less sensitive : benumb, blunt, deaden, desensitize, dull. ***Idiom:*** take the edge off. *See* AWARENESS. **2.** To render helpless, as by emotion : benumb, paralyze, petrify, stun, stupefy, wither. *See* AFFECT.

number *noun*
Arithmetic calculations. Used in plural : arithmetic, computation, figure (used in plural). *See* COUNT.
number *verb* **1.** To note (items) one by one so as to get a total : count, enumerate, numerate, reckon, tally, tell. *See* COUNT. **2.** To come to in number or quantity : aggregate, amount, reach, run into, total. ***Idiom:*** add up to. *See* INCREASE.

number one *noun*
A leading contestant : front-runner, leader. *See* PRECEDE.
number one *adjective* Most important, influential, or significant : capital, cardinal, chief, first, foremost, key, leading, main, major, paramount, premier, primary, prime, principal, top. *See* IMPORTANT.

numbskull *noun* See **numskull.**

numerate *verb*
1. To note (items) one by one so as to get a total : count, enumerate, number, reckon, tally, tell. *See* COUNT. **2.** To name or specify one by one : enumerate, itemize, list[1], tick off. *See* COUNT, SPECIFIC.

numeration *noun*
A noting of items one by one : count, enumeration, reckoning, tally. *Archaic:* tale. *See* COUNT.

numerous *adjective*
Amounting to or consisting of a large, indefinite number : legion, many, multitudinous, myriad. ***Idiom:*** quite a few. *See* BIG.

numinous *adjective*
Of or concerned with the spirit rather than the body or material things : otherworldly, spiritual, unworldly. *See* BODY.

numskull also **numbskull** *noun*
A mentally dull person : blockhead, chump[1], clod, dolt, dullard, dummkopf, dummy, dunce, thickhead. *Slang:* dimwit, dumbbell, dumbo. *See* ABILITY.

nuptial *adjective*
Of, relating to, or typical of marriage : conjugal, connubial, hymeneal, marital, married, matrimonial, spousal, wedded. *See* MARRIAGE.
nuptial *noun* The act or ceremony by which two people become husband and wife. Often used in plural : bridal, espousal, marriage, spousal (often used in plural), wedding. *See* MARRIAGE.

nurd *noun* See **nerd.**

nurse *verb*
1. To promote and sustain the development of : cultivate, foster, nourish, nurture. *See* CARE FOR. **2.** To hold and turn over in the mind : bear, harbor, nourish. *See* THOUGHTS.

nursling *noun*
A very young child : babe, baby, bambino, infant, neonate, newborn. ***Idiom:*** bundle of joy. *See* KIN, YOUTH.

nurture *noun*
Something fit to be eaten : aliment, bread, comestible, diet, edible, esculent, fare, food, foodstuff, meat, nourishment, nutriment, nutrition, pabulum, pap, provender, provision (used in plural), sustenance, victual. *Slang:* chow, eats, grub. *See* INGESTION.
nurture *verb* To promote and sustain the development of : cultivate, foster, nourish, nurse. *See* CARE FOR.

nut *noun*
1. *Slang.* A person regarded as strange, eccentric, or crazy : crackpot, crazy, eccentric, lunatic. *Informal:* crank, loon, loony. *Slang:* cuckoo, ding-a-ling, dingbat, kook, screwball, weirdie, weirdo. *See* WISE. **2.** *Slang.* A person who is ardently devoted to a particular subject or activity : bug, devotee, enthusiast, fanatic, maniac, zealot. *Informal:* buff[2], fan[2], fiend. *Slang:* freak. *See* CONCERN. **3.** *Slang.* The uppermost part of the body : head, noddle,

pate, poll. *Slang:* bean, block, conk, dome, noggin, noodle. *See* BODY.

nutrient *adjective*

Providing nourishment : alimentary, nourishing, nutritious, nutritive. *See* INGESTION.

nutriment *noun*

1. Something fit to be eaten : aliment, bread, comestible, diet, edible, esculent, fare, food, foodstuff, meat, nourishment, nurture, nutrition, pabulum, pap, provender, provision (used in plural), sustenance, victual. *Slang:* chow, eats, grub. *See* INGESTION. **2.** That which sustains the mind or spirit : aliment, bread, food, nourishment, pabulum, pap, sustenance. *See* CARE FOR, INGESTION.

nutrition *noun*

Something fit to be eaten : aliment, bread, comestible, diet, edible, esculent, fare, food, foodstuff, meat, nourishment, nurture, nutriment, pabulum, pap, provender, provision (used in plural), sustenance, victual. *Slang:* chow, eats, grub. *See* INGESTION.

nutritional *adjective*

Of or relating to food or nutrition : alimentary, nutritive. *See* INGESTION.

nutritious *adjective*

Providing nourishment : alimentary, nourishing, nutrient, nutritive. *See* INGESTION.

nutritive *adjective*

1. Providing nourishment : alimentary, nourishing, nutrient, nutritious. *See* INGESTION. **2.** Of or relating to food or nutrition : alimentary, nutritional. *See* INGESTION.

nuts *adjective*

1. *Slang.* Afflicted with or exhibiting irrationality and mental unsoundness : brainsick, crazy, daft, demented, disordered, distraught, dotty, insane, lunatic, mad, maniac, maniacal, mentally ill, moonstruck, off, touched, unbalanced, unsound, wrong. *Informal:* bonkers, cracked, daffy, gaga, loony. *Slang:* bananas, batty, buggy, cuckoo, fruity, loco, nutty, screwy, wacky. *Chiefly British:* crackers. *Law:* non compos mentis. ***Idioms:*** around the bend, crazy as a loon, mad as a hatter, not all there, nutty as a fruitcake, off (*or* out of) one's head, off one's rocker, of unsound mind, out of one's mind, sick in the head, stark raving mad. *See* SANE. **2.** *Slang.* Showing or having enthusiasm : ardent, enthusiastic, fervent, keen[1], mad, rabid, warm, zealous. *Informal:* crazy. *Slang:* gung ho. *See* CONCERN.

nutty *adjective*

Slang. Afflicted with or exhibiting irrationality and mental unsoundness : brainsick, crazy, daft, demented, disordered, distraught, dotty, insane, lunatic, mad, maniac, maniacal, mentally ill, moonstruck, off, touched, unbalanced, unsound, wrong. *Informal:* bonkers, cracked, daffy, gaga, loony. *Slang:* bananas, batty, buggy, cuckoo, fruity, loco, nuts, screwy, wacky. *Chiefly British:* crackers. *Law:* non compos mentis. ***Idioms:*** around the bend, crazy as a loon, mad as a hatter, not all there, nutty as a fruitcake, off (*or* out of) one's head, off one's rocker, of unsound mind, out of one's mind, sick in the head, stark raving mad. *See* SANE.

nuzzle *verb*

To lie or press close together, usually with another person or thing : cuddle, nestle, snug, snuggle. *See* NEAR.

oaf *noun*

A large, ungainly, and dull-witted person : gawk, hulk, lout, lump[1], ox. *Informal:* lummox. *Slang:* klutz, lug[1], meatball, meathead. *See* ABILITY.

oath *noun*

A profane or obscene term : blasphemy, curse, epithet, expletive, swearword. *Informal:* cuss. *See* DECENT, SACRED, WORDS.

obduracy *noun*

The quality or state of being stubbornly inflexible : die-hardism, grimness, implacability, implacableness, incompliance, incompliancy, inexorability, inexorableness, inflexibility, inflexibleness, intransigence, intransigency, obdurateness, relentlessness, remorselessness, rigidity, rigidness, stubbornness. *See* RESIST.

obdurate *adjective*

1. Completely lacking in compassion : callous,

cold-blooded, cold-hearted, compassionless, hard, hard-boiled, hardened, hardhearted, heartless, stonyhearted, unfeeling. *See* ATTITUDE. **2.** Firmly, often unreasonably immovable in purpose or will : adamant, adamantine, brassbound, die-hard, grim, implacable, incompliant, inexorable, inflexible, intransigent, iron, relentless, remorseless, rigid, stubborn, unbendable, unbending, uncompliant, uncompromising, unrelenting, unyielding. ***Idiom:*** stubborn as a mule (*or* ox). *See* RESIST.

obdurateness *noun*
The quality or state of being stubbornly inflexible : die-hardism, grimness, implacability, implacableness, incompliance, incompliancy, inexorability, inexorableness, inflexibility, inflexibleness, intransigence, intransigency, obduracy, relentlessness, remorselessness, rigidity, rigidness, stubbornness. *See* RESIST.

obedience *noun*
1. The quality or state of willingly carrying out the wishes of others : acquiescence, amenability, amenableness, compliance, compliancy, deference, submission, submissiveness, tractability, tractableness. *See* RESIST. **2.** An act of willingly carrying out the wishes of others : compliance, observance. *See* RESIST.

obedient *adjective*
Willing to carry out the wishes of others : amenable, biddable, compliant, conformable, docile, submissive, supple, tractable. *See* RESIST.

obeisance *noun*
1. An inclination of the head or body, as in greeting, consent, courtesy, submission, or worship : bow[1], curtsy, genuflection, kowtow, nod. *See* COURTESY. **2.** Great respect or high public esteem accorded as a right or as due : deference, homage, honor. *See* RESPECT.

obeisant *adjective*
Marked by courteous submission or respect : deferential, duteous, dutiful, respectful. *See* RESIST.

obese *adjective*
Having too much flesh : corpulent, fat, fatty, fleshy, gross, overblown, overweight, porcine, portly, stout, weighty. *See* FAT.

obey *verb*
To act in conformity with : abide by, adhere, carry out, comply, conform, follow, keep, mind, observe. ***Idiom:*** toe the line (*or* mark). *See* ACCEPT, SAME.

obfuscate *verb*
To make dim or indistinct : becloud, bedim, befog, blear, blur, cloud, dim, dull, eclipse, fog, gloom, mist, obscure, overcast, overshadow, shadow. *See* CLEAR.

obiter dictum *noun*
An expression of fact or opinion : comment, note, observation, remark. *See* WORDS.

object *noun*
1. Something having material existence : article, item, thing. *See* THING. **2.** One that exists independently : being, entity, existence, existent, individual, something, thing. *See* BE, THING. **3.** A separate and distinct portion of matter : body, bulk, mass. *See* MATTER. **4.** What one intends to do or achieve : aim, ambition, design, end, goal, intent, intention, mark, meaning, objective, point, purpose, target, view, why. ***Idioms:*** end in view, why and wherefore. *See* PLANNED, PURPOSE.

object *verb* **1.** To express opposition, often by argument : challenge, demur, except, expostulate, inveigh, protest, remonstrate. *Informal:* kick, squawk. ***Idioms:*** set up a squawk, take exception. *See* SUPPORT. **2.** To have an objection : care, mind. *See* CONCERN. **3.** To have or express an unfavorable opinion of : deprecate, disapprove, discountenance, disesteem, disfavor, frown on (*or* upon). ***Idioms:*** hold no brief for, not go for, take a dim view of, take exception to. *See* LIKE.

objectification *noun*
A physical entity typifying an abstraction : embodiment, exteriorization, externalization, incarnation, manifestation, materialization, personalization, personification, substantiation, type. *Rhetoric:* prosopopeia. *See* SUBSTITUTE.

objectify *verb*
To represent (an abstraction, for example) in or as if in bodily form : body forth, embody, exteriorize, externalize, incarnate, manifest, materialize, personalize, personify, substantiate. *See* SUBSTITUTE.

objection *noun*
The act of expressing strong or reasoned opposition : challenge, demur, exception, expostulation, protest, protestation, remonstrance, remonstration, squawk. *Slang:* kick. *See* SUPPORT.

objectionable *adjective*
Arousing disapproval : exceptionable, ill-favored, inadmissible, unacceptable, undesirable, unwanted, unwelcome. *See* LIKE.

objective *adjective*
1. Composed of or relating to things that occupy space and can be perceived by the senses : concrete, corporeal, material, phenomenal, physical, sensible, substantial, tangible.

See BODY, MATTER. **2.** Having verifiable existence : concrete, real, substantial, substantive, tangible. *See* REAL. **3.** Free from bias in judgment : disinterested, dispassionate, equitable, fair, fair-minded, impartial, indifferent, just, nonpartisan, square, unbiased, unprejudiced. ***Idiom:*** fair and square. *See* FAIR. **4.** Having or indicating an awareness of things as they really are : down-to-earth, hard, hardheaded, matter-of-fact, practical, pragmatic, pragmatical, prosaic, realistic, sober, tough-minded, unromantic. *See* EXCITE, REAL.

objective *noun* What one intends to do or achieve : aim, ambition, design, end, goal, intent, intention, mark, meaning, object, point, purpose, target, view, why. ***Idioms:*** end in view, why and wherefore. *See* PLANNED, PURPOSE.

objectiveness *noun*
The quality or state of being just and unbiased : detachment, disinterest, disinterestedness, dispassion, dispassionateness, equitableness, fair-mindedness, fairness, impartiality, impartialness, justice, justness, nonpartisanship, objectivity. *See* FAIR.

objectivity *noun*
The quality or state of being just and unbiased : detachment, disinterest, disinterestedness, dispassion, dispassionateness, equitableness, fair-mindedness, fairness, impartiality, impartialness, justice, justness, nonpartisanship, objectiveness. *See* FAIR.

oblation *noun*
1. A presentation made to a deity as an act of worship : offering. *See* OFFER, RELIGION.
2. A charitable deed : benefaction, beneficence, benevolence, benignity, favor, kindliness, kindness, office (often used in plural), philanthropy. *See* GIVE, KIND.

obligate *verb*
1. To be morally bound to do : bind, charge, commit, pledge. *See* OBLIGATION. **2.** To cause (a person or thing) to act or move in spite of resistance : coerce, compel, constrain, force, make, oblige, pressure. *See* ATTACK.

obligated *adjective*
Owing something, such as gratitude or appreciation, to another : beholden, bound[3], indebted, obliged. *Archaic:* bounden. ***Idiom:*** under obligation. *See* OBLIGATION.

obligation *noun*
1. An act or course of action that is demanded of one, as by position, custom, law, or religion : burden[1], charge, commitment, duty, imperative, must, need, responsibility. *See* OBLIGATION. **2.** Something, such as money, owed by one person to another : arrearage, arrears, debt, due, indebtedness, liability. *See* OBLIGATION, PAY. **3.** A condition of owing something to another : arrearage, arrears, indebtedness, debt, liability. *See* PAY.

obligatory *adjective*
Imposed on one by authority, command, or convention : compulsory, imperative, mandatory, necessary, required, requisite. *See* OBLIGATION.

oblige *verb*
1. To cause (a person or thing) to act or move in spite of resistance : coerce, compel, constrain, force, make, obligate, pressure. *See* ATTACK.
2. To perform a service or a courteous act for : accommodate, favor. *See* HELP.

obliged *adjective*
Owing something, such as gratitude or appreciation, to another : beholden, bound[3], indebted, obligated. *Archaic:* bounden. ***Idiom:*** under obligation. *See* OBLIGATION.

obliging *adjective*
Ready to do favors for another : accommodating, agreeable, complaisant, indulgent. *See* HELP, WILLING.

oblique *adjective*
1. Angled at a slant : beveled, bias, biased, diagonal, slanted, slanting. *See* STRAIGHT.
2. Not taking a direct or straight line or course : anfractuous, circuitous, circular, devious, indirect, roundabout, tortuous. *See* STRAIGHT.

obliterate *verb*
1. To destroy all traces of : abolish, annihilate, blot out, clear, eradicate, erase, exterminate, extinguish, extirpate, kill[1], liquidate, remove, root[1] (out *or* up), rub out, snuff out, stamp out, uproot, wipe out. ***Idioms:*** do away with, make an end of, put an end to. *See* HELP, MAKE.
2. To remove or invalidate by or as if by running a line through or wiping clean : annul, blot (out), cancel, cross (off *or* out), delete, efface, erase, expunge, rub (out), scratch (out), strike (out), undo, wipe (out), x (out). *Law:* vacate. *See* CONTINUE.

obliteration *noun*
1. Utter destruction : annihilation, eradication, extermination, extinction, extinguishment, extirpation, liquidation. *See* CRIMES, HELP, MAKE. **2.** The act of erasing or the condition of being erased : cancellation, deletion, erasure, expunction. *See* INCLUDE.

oblivion *noun*
Freedom from worry, care, or unpleasantness : escape, forgetfulness, obliviousness. *See* SEEK.

oblivious *adjective*
1. Unable to remember : amnesiac, amnesic, forgetful. *See* REMEMBER. **2.** Not aware or informed : ignorant, innocent, unacquainted, unaware, unconscious, unenlightened, unfamiliar, uninformed, unknowing, unwitting. ***Idiom:*** in the dark. *See* KNOWLEDGE.

obliviousness *noun*
1. The condition of being uninformed or unaware : ignorance, innocence, nescience, unawareness, unconsciousness, unfamiliarity. *See* KNOWLEDGE. **2.** Freedom from worry, care, or unpleasantness : escape, forgetfulness, oblivion. *See* SEEK.

obloquy *noun*
1. Harsh, often insulting language : abuse, billingsgate, contumely, invective, railing, revilement, reviling, scurrility, scurrilousness, vituperation. *See* PRAISE. **2.** Loss of or damage to one's reputation : bad name, bad odor, discredit, disgrace, dishonor, disrepute, humiliation, ignominy, ill repute, odium, opprobrium, shame. *See* RESPECT.

obnoxious *adjective*
So objectionable as to elicit despisal or deserve condemnation : abhorrent, abominable, antipathetic, contemptible, despicable, despisable, detestable, disgusting, filthy, foul, infamous, loathsome, lousy, low, mean[2], nasty, nefarious, odious, repugnant, rotten, shabby, vile, wretched. *See* GOOD.

obscene *adjective*
1. Offensive to accepted standards of decency : barnyard, bawdy, broad, coarse, dirty, Fescennine, filthy, foul, gross, lewd, nasty, profane, ribald, scatologic, scatological, scurrilous, smutty, vulgar. *Slang:* raunchy. *See* DECENT. **2.** Beyond all reason : outrageous, preposterous, ridiculous, shocking, unconscionable, unreasonable. ***Idioms:*** out of bounds, out of sight. *See* USUAL.

obscenity *noun*
1. The quality or state of being obscene : bawdiness, coarseness, dirtiness, filthiness, foulness, grossness, lewdness, profaneness, profanity, scurrility, scurrilousness, smuttiness, vulgarity, vulgarness. *Slang:* raunch, raunchiness. *See* DECENT. **2.** Something that is offensive to accepted standards of decency : bawdry, dirt, filth, profanity, ribaldry, scatology, smut, vulgarity. *Slang:* raunch. *See* DECENT.

obscure *adjective*
1. Deficient in brightness : caliginous, dark, dim, dusky, murky. *See* LIGHT. **2.** Not clearly perceived or perceptible : blear, bleary, cloudy, dim, faint, foggy, fuzzy, hazy, indefinite, indistinct, misty, shadowy, unclear, undistinct, vague. *See* CLEAR. **3.** Far from centers of human population : back, insular, isolated, lonely, lonesome, outlying, out-of-the-way, remote, removed, secluded, solitary. ***Idiom:*** off the beaten path (*or* track). *See* NEAR. **4.** Not readily noticed or seen : inconspicuous, unconspicuous, unnoticeable, unobtrusive. ***Idiom:*** having (*or* keeping) a low profile. *See* SEE. **5.** Not known or not widely known by name : nameless, unheard-of, unknown. *See* KNOWLEDGE. **6.** Liable to more than one interpretation : ambiguous, cloudy, equivocal, inexplicit, nebulous, uncertain, unclear, vague. *See* CERTAIN, CLEAR.

obscure *verb* **1.** To make dim or indistinct : becloud, bedim, befog, blear, blur, cloud, dim, dull, eclipse, fog, gloom, mist, obfuscate, overcast, overshadow, shadow. *See* CLEAR. **2.** To conceal in obscurity : hide[1], submerge. *See* SHOW. **3.** To cut off from sight : block (out), conceal, hide[1], obstruct, screen, shroud, shut off (*or* out). *See* SHOW.

obscured *adjective*
Lying beyond what is obvious or avowed : buried, concealed, covert, hidden, ulterior. ***Idiom:*** under cover (*or* wraps). *See* SHOW.

obscureness *noun*
1. Absence or deficiency of light : dark, darkness, dimness, duskiness, murkiness, obscurity. *See* LIGHT. **2.** The quality or state of being ambiguous : ambiguity, ambiguousness, cloudiness, equivocalness, indefiniteness, nebulousness, obscurity, uncertainty, unclearness, vagueness. *See* CLEAR.

obscurity *noun*
1. Absence or deficiency of light : dark, darkness, dimness, duskiness, murkiness, obscureness. *See* LIGHT. **2.** The quality or state of being obscure : anonymity, namelessness. *See* KNOWLEDGE. **3.** The quality or state of being ambiguous : ambiguity, ambiguousness, cloudiness, equivocalness, indefiniteness, nebulousness, obscureness, uncertainty, unclearness, vagueness. *See* CLEAR.

obsequious *adjective*
Excessively eager to serve or obey : menial, servile, slavish, subservient. *See* OVER.

observable *adjective*
1. Readily seen, perceived, or understood : apparent, clear, clear-cut, crystal clear, distinct, evident, manifest, noticeable, obvious, patent, plain, pronounced, visible. *See* SEE. **2.** Capable of being noticed or apprehended mentally :

appreciable, detectable, discernible, distinguishable, noticeable, palpable, perceivable, perceptible, ponderable, sensible. *See* KNOWLEDGE. **3.** Readily attracting notice : arresting, bold, conspicuous, eye-catching, marked, noticeable, outstanding, pointed, prominent, pronounced, remarkable, salient, signal, striking. ***Idiom:*** sticking out like a sore thumb. *See* SEE.

observance *noun*

1. An act of willingly carrying out the wishes of others : compliance, obedience. *See* RESIST. **2.** The act of observing a day or an event with ceremonies : celebration, commemoration. *See* REMEMBER. **3.** A formal act or set of acts prescribed by ritual : ceremonial, ceremony, liturgy, office, rite, ritual, service. *See* RITUAL. **4.** The act of noting, observing, or taking into account : attention, cognizance, espial, heed, mark, note, notice, observation, regard, remark. *See* KNOWLEDGE, SEE. **5.** The act of observing, often for an extended time : observation, scrutiny, watch. *See* AWARENESS, SEE.

observant *adjective*

1. Vigilantly attentive : alert, open-eyed, vigilant, wakeful, wary, watchful, wide-awake. ***Idiom:*** on the ball. *See* AWARENESS. **2.** Cautiously attentive : careful, heedful, mindful, watchful. *See* CAREFUL. **3.** Tending toward awareness and appreciation : conscious, heedful, mindful. *See* AWARENESS.

observation *noun*

1. The act of noting, observing, or taking into account : attention, cognizance, espial, heed, mark, note, notice, observance, regard, remark. *See* KNOWLEDGE, SEE. **2.** The act of observing, often for an extended time : observance, scrutiny, watch. *See* AWARENESS, SEE. **3.** An expression of fact or opinion : comment, note, obiter dictum, remark. *See* WORDS.

observatory *noun*

A high structure or place commanding a wide view : lookout, outlook, overlook. *See* AWARENESS.

observe *verb*

1. To perceive with a special effort of the senses or the mind : descry, detect, discern, distinguish, mark, mind, note, notice, remark, see. *See* KNOWLEDGE, SEE. **2.** To look at or on attentively or carefully : eye, regard, scrutinize, survey, watch. ***Idioms:*** have one's (*or* keep an) eye on, keep tabs on. *See* AWARENESS, SEE. **3.** To state facts, opinions, or explanations : comment, note, remark. *See* WORDS. **4.** To act in conformity with : abide by, adhere, carry out, comply, conform, follow, keep, mind, obey. ***Idiom:*** toe the line (*or* mark). *See* ACCEPT, SAME. **5.** To mark (a day or an event) with ceremonies of respect, festivity, or rejoicing : celebrate, commemorate, keep, solemnize. *See* REMEMBER.

observer *noun*

Someone who observes : beholder, bystander, looker-on, onlooker, spectator, watcher. *See* AWARENESS, SEE.

obsess *verb*

1. To dominate the mind or thoughts of : possess. *See* CONTROL. **2.** To come to mind continually : haunt, torment, trouble, weigh on (*or* upon). *See* REPETITION.

obsession *noun*

An irrational preoccupation : fetish, fixation, mania. *Informal:* thing. *See* CONCERN.

obsolesce *verb*

To make or become obsolete : obsolete, outdate, superannuate. *See* NEW, USED.

obsolete *adjective*

No longer in use : superseded. ***Idioms:*** in mothballs, on the shelf. *See* NEW, USED.

obsolete *verb* To make or become obsolete : obsolesce, outdate, superannuate. *See* NEW, USED.

obsolete *noun* Something that is obsolete : obsoletism. *See* NEW, USED.

obsoleteness *noun*

The quality or state of being obsolete : desuetude, disuse, obsoletism. *See* NEW, USED.

obsoletism *noun*

1. The quality or state of being obsolete : desuetude, disuse, obsoleteness. *See* NEW, USED. **2.** Something that is obsolete : obsolete. *See* NEW, USED.

obstacle *noun*

Something that impedes or prevents entry or passage : bar, barricade, barrier, block, blockage, clog, hamper, hindrance, hurdle, impediment, obstruction, snag, stop, traverse, wall. *See* HELP, OPEN.

obstinacy *noun*

1. The quality or state of being stubbornly unyielding : bullheadedness, doggedness, hardheadedness, mulishness, obstinateness, pertinaciousness, pertinacity, perverseness, perversity, pigheadedness, tenaciousness, tenacity, willfulness. *See* RESIST. **2.** The quality or condition of being unruly : disorderliness, fractiousness, indocility, intractability, intractableness, obstinateness, obstreperousness, recalcitrance, recalcitrancy, refractoriness, uncontrollability, uncontrollableness, ungovernableness, unmanageability, unruliness, untowardness, wildness. *See* CONTROL, ORDER, PEACE, RESIST.

obstinate *adjective*
1. Tenaciously unwilling to yield : bullheaded, dogged, hardheaded, headstrong, mulish, pertinacious, perverse, pigheaded, stiff-necked, tenacious, willful. *See* RESIST. **2.** Not submitting to discipline or control : disorderly, fractious, indocile, intractable, lawless, obstreperous, recalcitrant, refractory, uncontrollable, undisciplined, ungovernable, unmanageable, unruly, untoward, wild. ***Idiom:*** out of line. *See* CONTROL, ORDER, PEACE, RESIST. **3.** Difficult to alleviate or cure : persistent, pertinacious, stubborn. *See* CONTINUE.

obstinateness *noun*
1. The quality or state of being stubbornly unyielding : bullheadedness, doggedness, hardheadedness, mulishness, obstinacy, pertinaciousness, pertinacity, perverseness, perversity, pigheadedness, tenaciousness, tenacity, willfulness. *See* RESIST. **2.** The quality or condition of being unruly : disorderliness, fractiousness, indocility, intractability, intractableness, obstinacy, obstreperousness, recalcitrance, recalcitrancy, refractoriness, uncontrollability, uncontrollableness, ungovernableness, unmanageability, unruliness, untowardness, wildness. *See* CONTROL, ORDER, PEACE, RESIST.

obstreperous *adjective*
1. Not submitting to discipline or control : disorderly, fractious, indocile, intractable, lawless, obstinate, recalcitrant, refractory, uncontrollable, undisciplined, ungovernable, unmanageable, unruly, untoward, wild. ***Idiom:*** out of line. *See* CONTROL, ORDER, PEACE, RESIST. **2.** Offensively loud and insistent : blatant, boisterous, clamorous, strident, vociferous. *Informal:* loudmouthed. *See* SOUNDS.

obstreperousness *noun*
The quality or condition of being unruly : disorderliness, fractiousness, indocility, intractability, intractableness, obstinacy, obstinateness, recalcitrance, recalcitrancy, refractoriness, uncontrollability, uncontrollableness, ungovernableness, unmanageability, unruliness, untowardness, wildness. *See* CONTROL, ORDER, PEACE, RESIST.

obstruct *verb*
1. To interfere with the progress of : bog (down), encumber, hinder, hold back, impede. ***Idiom:*** get in the way of. *See* HELP, OPEN. **2.** To stop or prevent passage of : bar, block, dam, impede. ***Idiom:*** be (*or* stand) in the way of. *See* OPEN. **3.** To cut off from sight : block (out), conceal, hide[1], obscure, screen, shroud, shut off (*or* out). *See* SHOW.

obstruction *noun*
Something that impedes or prevents entry or passage : bar, barricade, barrier, block, blockage, clog, hamper, hindrance, hurdle, impediment, obstacle, snag, stop, traverse, wall. *See* HELP, OPEN.

obtain *verb*
To come into possession of : acquire, come by, gain, get, procure, secure, win. *Informal:* land, pick up. *See* GET.

obtainable *adjective*
Capable of being obtained or used : acquirable, attainable, available, gettable, procurable. ***Idioms:*** on hand, to be had. *See* GET.

obtrude *verb*
To force or come in as an improper or unwanted element : cut in, horn in, intrude. *See* ENTER.

obtrusion *noun*
1. The act or an instance of interfering or intruding : interference, intervention, intrusion, meddling. *See* PARTICIPATE. **2.** An advance beyond proper or legal limits : encroachment, entrenchment, impingement, infringement, intrusion, trespass. *See* ENTER.

obtrusive *adjective*
Given to intruding in other people's affairs : interfering, intrusive, meddlesome, meddling, officious. *See* PARTICIPATE.

obtuse *adjective*
Lacking in intelligence : blockheaded, dense, doltish, dumb, hebetudinous, stupid, thickheaded, thick-witted. *Informal:* thick. *Slang:* dimwitted, dopey. *See* ABILITY.

obviate *verb*
To prohibit from occurring by advance planning or action : avert, forestall, forfend, preclude, prevent, rule out, stave off, ward (off). ***Idiom:*** nip in the bud. *See* ALLOW.

obviation *noun*
The act of preventing : determent, deterrence, forestallment, preclusion, prevention. *See* ALLOW.

obvious *adjective*
1. Readily seen, perceived, or understood : apparent, clear, clear-cut, crystal clear, distinct, evident, manifest, noticeable, observable, patent, plain, pronounced, visible. *See* SEE. **2.** Easily seen through due to a lack of subtlety : broad, clear, patent, plain, unmistakable, unsubtle. *See* CLEAR, SEE.

occasion *noun*
1. Something that happens : circumstance, event, happening, incident, occurrence, thing. *See* HAPPEN. 2. The general point at which an event occurs : time. ***Idiom:*** point in time. *See* TIME. 3. Something significant that happens : circumstance, development, episode, event, happening, incident, news, occurrence, thing. *See* HAPPEN. 4. A favorable or advantageous combination of circumstances : break, chance, opening, opportunity. *Informal:* shot. *See* LUCK. 5. That which produces an effect : antecedent, cause. *See* START. 6. That which provides a reason or justification : call, cause, ground (often used in plural), justification, necessity, reason, wherefore, why. ***Idiom:*** why and wherefore. *See* START. 7. A large or important social gathering : affair, celebration, festivity, fete, function, gala, party, soiree. *Informal:* do. *Slang:* bash. *See* GROUP, WORK.
occasion *verb* 1. To be the cause of : bring, bring about, bring on, cause, effect, effectuate, generate, induce, ingenerate, lead to, make, result in, secure, set off, stir[1] (up), touch off, trigger. ***Idioms:*** bring to pass (*or* effect), give rise to. *See* START. 2. To be a proper or sufficient occasion for : call for, justify, warrant. *See* RIGHT.

occasional *adjective*
1. Happening or appearing now and then : fitful, intermittent, periodic, periodical, sporadic. *Informal:* on-again, off-again. *See* CONTINUE. 2. Rarely occurring or appearing : infrequent, rare, scarce, sporadic, uncommon, unusual. ***Idiom:*** few and far between. *See* USUAL.

occasionally *adverb*
1. Once in a while; at times : betimes, intermittently, periodically, sometimes, sporadically. ***Idioms:*** ever and again (*or* anon), now and again (*or* then). *See* CONTINUE. 2. At rare intervals : infrequently, little, rarely, seldom, sporadically. ***Idioms:*** hardly (*or* scarcely) ever, once in a blue moon. *See* USUAL.

occult *adjective*
Difficult to explain or understand : arcane, cabalistic, cryptic, enigmatic, mysterious, mystic, mystical, mystifying, puzzling. *See* EXPLAIN, KNOWLEDGE.
occult *verb* To put or keep out of sight : bury, cache, conceal, ensconce, hide[1], secrete. *Slang:* plant, stash. *See* SHOW.

occupancy *noun*
The holding of something, such as a position : incumbency, occupation, tenure. *See* PLACE.

occupation *noun*
1. Activity pursued as a livelihood : art, business, calling, career, craft, employment, job, line, métier, profession, pursuit, trade, vocation, work. *Slang:* racket. *Archaic:* employ. *See* ACTION. 2. The holding of something, such as a position : incumbency, occupancy, tenure. *See* PLACE.

occupied *adjective*
Involved in activity or work : busy, employed, engaged. *See* ACTION.

occupy *verb*
1. To live in (a place), as does a people : inhabit, people, populate. *See* PLACE. 2. To seize and move into by force : take over. *See* ATTACK. 3. To cause to be busy or in use : engage, monopolize, preempt, tie up. *See* ACTION, USED. 4. To make busy : busy, employ, engage. *See* ACTION. 5. To get and hold the attention of : engage, involve. *See* EXCITE.

occur *verb*
1. To take place : befall, betide, come, come about, come off, develop, hap, happen, pass, transpire. ***Idiom:*** come to pass. *See* HAPPEN. 2. To take place at a set time : come, fall. *See* HAPPEN. 3. To enter a person's mind : hit, strike. ***Idiom:*** cross one's mind. *See* HAPPEN.

occurrence *noun*
1. The condition or fact of being present : presence. *See* BE. 2. Something that happens : circumstance, event, happening, incident, occasion, thing. *See* HAPPEN. 3. Something significant that happens : circumstance, development, episode, event, happening, incident, news, occasion, thing. *See* HAPPEN.

oceanic *adjective*
Of or relating to the seas or oceans : marine, maritime, pelagic, thalassic. *See* SEA.

odd *adjective*
1. Deviating from the customary : bizarre, cranky, curious, eccentric, erratic, freakish, idiosyncratic, outlandish, peculiar, quaint, queer, quirky, singular, strange, unnatural, unusual, weird. *Slang:* kooky, screwball. *British Slang:* rum, rummy[2]. *See* USUAL. 2. Causing puzzlement; perplexing : curious, funny, peculiar, queer, strange, weird. *See* USUAL. 3. Agreeably curious, especially in an old-fashioned or unusual way : funny, quaint. *See* USUAL. 4. Occurring unexpectedly : accidental, casual, chance, contingent, fluky, fortuitous, inadvertent. *See* SURPRISE.

oddball *noun*
Informal. A person who is appealingly odd or

curious : character, oddity, original. *Informal:* card. *See* USUAL.

oddity *noun*
A person who is appealingly odd or curious : character, original. *Informal:* card, oddball. *See* USUAL.

oddment *noun*
Articles too small or numerous to be specified. Used in plural : etcetera (used in plural), odds and ends, sundries. *See* THING.

odds *noun*
1. A factor conducive to superiority and success : advantage, handicap, head start, start, vantage. *See* HELP. **2.** The likeliness of a given event occurring : chance, likelihood, possibility, probability, prospect (used in plural). *See* LIKELY.

odds and ends *noun*
Articles too small or numerous to be specified : etcetera (used in plural), oddment (used in plural), sundries. *See* THING.

odious *adjective*
So objectionable as to elicit despisal or deserve condemnation : abhorrent, abominable, antipathetic, contemptible, despicable, despisable, detestable, disgusting, filthy, foul, infamous, loathsome, lousy, low, mean², nasty, nefarious, obnoxious, repugnant, rotten, shabby, vile, wretched. *See* GOOD.

odium *noun*
Loss of or damage to one's reputation : bad name, bad odor, discredit, disgrace, dishonor, disrepute, humiliation, ignominy, ill repute, obloquy, opprobrium, shame. *See* RESPECT.

odor *noun*
The quality of something that may be perceived by the olfactory sense : aroma, scent, smell. *See* SMELLS.

oestrus *noun* See **estrus.**

off *adjective*
1. Characterized by reduced economic activity : down, dull, slack, slow, sluggish, soft. *See* INCREASE. **2.** Containing an error or errors : erroneous, fallacious, false, inaccurate, incorrect, mistaken, unsound, untrue, wrong. *Idioms:* all wet, in error, off base, off (*or* wide of) the mark. *See* CORRECT. **3.** Afflicted with or exhibiting irrationality and mental unsoundness : brainsick, crazy, daft, demented, disordered, distraught, dotty, insane, lunatic, mad, maniac, maniacal, mentally ill, moonstruck, touched, unbalanced, unsound, wrong. *Informal:* bonkers, cracked, daffy, gaga, loony. *Slang:* bananas, batty, buggy, cuckoo, fruity, loco, nuts, nutty, screwy, wacky. *Chiefly British:* crackers. *Law:* non compos mentis. *Idioms:* around the bend, crazy as a loon, mad as a hatter, not all there, nutty as a fruitcake, off (*or* out of) one's head, off one's rocker, of unsound mind, out of one's mind, sick in the head, stark raving mad. *See* SANE.

off *verb Slang.* To take the life of (a person or persons) unlawfully : destroy, finish (off), kill¹, liquidate, murder, slay. *Informal:* put away. *Slang:* bump off, do in, knock off, rub out, waste, wipe out, zap. *See* HELP.

offbeat *adjective*
Slang. Not usual or ordinary : atypic, atypical, novel, unconventional, unordinary, unusual, unwonted. *See* USUAL.

off-color *adjective*
1. Bordering on indelicacy or impropriety : blue, earthy, provocative, racy, risqué, salty, scabrous, spicy, suggestive. *See* DECENT. **2.** Affected or tending to be affected with minor health problems : ailing, indisposed, low, mean², rocky, sickly. *Idiom:* under the weather. *See* HEALTH.

offend *verb*
1. To cause resentment or hurt by callous, rude behavior : affront, huff, insult, miff, outrage, pique. *Idioms:* add insult to injury, give offense to. *See* ATTACK, PAIN. **2.** To be very disagreeable to : displease. *Slang:* turn off. *Idioms:* give offense to, not set right (*or* well) with. *See* LIKE, PAIN. **3.** To violate a moral or divine law : err, sin, transgress, trespass. *See* RIGHT.

offender *noun*
One who commits a crime : criminal, lawbreaker, malefactor. *Law:* felon. *See* CRIMES.

offense *noun*
1. An act that offends a person's sense of pride or dignity : affront, contumely, despite, indignity, insult, outrage, slight. *Idiom:* slap in the face. *See* ATTACK. **2.** Extreme displeasure caused by an insult or slight : dudgeon, huff, miff, pique, resentment, ruffled feathers, umbrage. *See* LIKE, PAIN. **3.** A wicked act or wicked behavior : crime, deviltry, diablerie, evil, evildoing, immorality, iniquity, misdeed, peccancy, sin, wickedness, wrong, wrongdoing. *See* RIGHT. **4.** Something that offends one's sense of propriety, fairness, or justice : crime, outrage, sin. *See* RIGHT. **5.** A serious breaking of the public law : crime, illegality, misdeed. *Law:* felony. *See* CRIMES. **6.** The act of attacking : aggression, assailment, assault, attack, attempt, offensive, onrush, onset, onslaught, strike. *See* ATTACK.

offensive *adjective*
1. Extremely unpleasant to the senses or feelings : atrocious, disgusting, foul, horrid, nasty, nauseating, repellent, repulsive, revolting, sickening, ugly, unwholesome, vile. *See* LIKE, PAIN. **2.** Not pleasant or agreeable : bad, disagreeable, displeasing, uncongenial, unpleasant, unsympathetic. *Informal:* icky. *Slang:* yucky. *See* GOOD, PAIN.
offensive *noun* The act of attacking : aggression, assailment, assault, attack, attempt, offense, onrush, onset, onslaught, strike. *See* ATTACK.

offer *verb*
1. To put before another for acceptance : extend, present[2], proffer, tender[2], volunteer. ***Idioms:*** come forward with, lay at someone's feet, lay before. *See* OFFER. **2.** To state, as an idea, for consideration : advance, pose, propose, propound, put forward, set forth, submit, suggest. *See* OFFER. **3.** To make (something) readily available : afford, extend, provide. ***Idiom:*** place (*or* put) at one's disposal. *See* OFFER. **4.** To make an offer of : bid. *Informal:* go. *See* OFFER.
offer *noun* **1.** Something offered : bid, proffer, proposal, tender[2]. *See* OFFER. **2.** A trying to do or make something : attempt, crack, effort, endeavor, essay, go, stab, trial, try. *Informal:* shot. *Slang:* take. *Archaic:* assay. *See* TRY.

offering *noun*
1. A presentation made to a deity as an act of worship : oblation. *See* OFFER, RELIGION. **2.** One or more living creatures slain and offered to a deity as part of a religious rite : hecatomb, immolation, sacrifice, victim. *See* RELIGION. **3.** Something given to a charity or cause : alms, benefaction, beneficence, charity, contribution, donation, gift, handout, subscription. *See* GIVE.

offhand *adjective*
Spoken, performed, or composed with little or no preparation or forethought : ad-lib, extemporaneous, extemporary, extempore, impromptu, improvised, snap, spur-of-the-moment, unrehearsed. *Informal:* off-the-cuff. *See* PREPARED.

office *noun*
1. A piece of work that has been assigned : assignment, chore, duty, job, stint, task. *See* WORK. **2.** A post of employment : appointment, berth, billet, job, place, position, situation, slot, spot. *Slang:* gig. *See* PLACE. **3.** A charitable deed. Often used in plural : benefaction, beneficence, benevolence, benignity, favor, kindliness, kindness, oblation, philanthropy. *See* GIVE, KIND. **4.** A formal act or set of acts prescribed by ritual : ceremonial, ceremony, liturgy, observance, rite, ritual, service. *See* RITUAL.

officer *noun*
1. A person having administrative or managerial authority in an organization : administrant, administrator, director, executive, manager, official. *Informal:* exec. *See* OVER. **2.** A member of a law-enforcement agency : bluecoat, finest, patrolman, patrolwoman, peace officer, police, policeman, police officer, policewoman. *Informal:* cop, law. *Slang:* bull[1], copper, flatfoot, fuzz, gendarme, heat, man (often uppercase). *Chiefly British:* bobby, constable, peeler. *See* LAW.

official *adjective*
Having or arising from authority : authoritative, conclusive, sanctioned, standard. *See* TRUE.
official *noun* **1.** A person or group having the right and power to command, decide, rule, or judge : authority. ***Idioms:*** powers that be, the Man. *See* OVER. **2.** A person having administrative or managerial authority in an organization : administrant, administrator, director, executive, manager, officer. *Informal:* exec. *See* OVER.

officiate *verb*
To perform the duties of another : act, function, serve. *See* DO, SUBSTITUTE.

officious *adjective*
Given to intruding in other people's affairs : interfering, intrusive, meddlesome, meddling, obtrusive. *See* PARTICIPATE.

offish *adjective*
Not friendly, sociable, or warm in manner : aloof, chill, chilly, cool, distant, remote, reserved, reticent, solitary, standoffish, unapproachable, uncommunicative, undemonstrative, withdrawn. *See* ATTITUDE, HOT.

offset *noun*
Something to make up for loss or damage : amends, compensation, indemnification, indemnity, quittance, recompense, redress, reimbursement, remuneration, reparation, repayment, requital, restitution, satisfaction, setoff. *See* SUBSTITUTE.
offset *verb* **1.** To act as an equalizing weight or force to : balance, compensate, counteract, counterbalance, counterpoise, countervail, make up, set off. *See* ORDER. **2.** To make up for : balance, compensate, counterbalance,

counterpoise, countervail, neutralize, outweigh, redeem, set off. *See* SUBSTITUTE.

offshoot *noun*

1. Something resembling or structurally analogous to a tree branch : arm, branch, fork. *See* PART. **2.** Something derived from another : byproduct, derivation, derivative, descendant, outgrowth, spinoff. *See* KIN. **3.** A part of a family, tribe, or other group, or of such a group's language, that is believed to stem from a common ancestor : branch, division, subdivision. *See* PART. **4.** A young stemlike growth arising from a plant : bine, runner, shoot, sprig, sprout, tendril. *See* KIN.

offspring *noun*

1. A group consisting of those descended directly from the same parents or ancestors : brood, get, issue, posterity, progeny, seed. *See* KIN. **2.** One descended directly from the same parents or ancestors : child, descendant, progeny, scion. *See* KIN.

off-the-cuff *adjective*

Informal. Spoken, performed, or composed with little or no preparation or forethought : ad-lib, extemporaneous, extemporary, extempore, impromptu, improvised, offhand, snap, spur-of-the-moment, unrehearsed. *See* PREPARED.

often *adverb*

In an expected or customary manner; for the most part : commonly, consistently, customarily, frequently, generally, habitually, naturally, normally, regularly, routinely, typically, usually. ***Idioms:*** as usual, per usual. *See* BIG, USUAL.

ogle *verb*

To look intently and fixedly : eye, gape, gawk, gaze, goggle, peer[1], stare. ***Idioms:*** gaze openmouthed, rivet the eyes on. *See* SEE.

ogre *noun*

A perversely bad, cruel, or wicked person : archfiend, beast, devil, fiend, ghoul, monster, tiger, vampire. *See* KIND.

ogreish *adjective*

Perversely bad, cruel, or wicked : devilish, diabolic, diabolical, fiendish, ghoulish, hellish, infernal, satanic, satanical. *See* KIND.

oil *noun*

Excessive, ingratiating praise : adulation, blandishment, blarney, flattery, incense[2], slaver. *Informal:* soft soap. ***Idiom:*** honeyed words. *See* PRAISE.

oily *adjective*

1. Having the qualities of fat : adipose, fat, fatty, greasy, oleaginous, unctuous. *See* FAT. **2.** Affectedly and self-servingly earnest : fulsome, oleaginous, sleek, smarmy, unctuous. *See* ATTITUDE, HONEST.

OK or **O.K.** or **okay** *noun*

1. *Informal.* The approving of an action, especially when done by one in authority : allowance, approbation, approval, authorization, consent, endorsement, leave[2], license, permission, permit, sanction. *See* ALLOW. **2.** *Informal.* The act or process of accepting : acceptance, acquiescence, agreement, assent, consent, nod, yes. *See* ACCEPT.

OK or **O.K.** or **okay** *verb Informal.* To give one's consent to : allow, approbate, approve, authorize, consent, endorse, let, permit, sanction. *See* ALLOW.

OK or **O.K.** or **okay** *adverb Informal.* It is so; as you say or ask : absolutely, agreed, all right, assuredly, aye, gladly, indubitably, roger, undoubtedly, unquestionably, willingly, yea, yes. *Informal:* uh-huh, yeah, yep. *Slang:* right on. *See* AFFIRM.

OK or **O.K.** or **okay** *adjective Informal.* Of moderately good quality but less than excellent : acceptable, adequate, all right, average, common, decent, fair, fairish, goodish, moderate, passable, respectable, satisfactory, sufficient, tolerable. *Informal:* tidy. *See* GOOD.

okay *noun & verb & adverb & adjective* See **OK.**

old *adjective*

1. Existing or remaining in the same state for an indefinitely long time : abiding, continuing, durable, enduring, lasting, long-lasting, long-lived, long-standing, perdurable, perennial, permanent, persistent. *See* CONTINUE. **2.** Far along in life or time : advanced, aged, elderly, senior. ***Idiom:*** getting along (*or* on) in years. *See* NEW. **3.** Belonging to, existing, or occurring in times long past : age-old, ancient, antediluvian, antiquated, antique, archaic, hoary, olden, old-time, timeworn, venerable. ***Idioms:*** old as Methuselah, old as the hills. *See* NEW. **4.** Having been such previously : erstwhile, former, late, once, onetime, past, previous, quondam, sometime, whilom. *See* PRECEDE. **5.** Of a style or method formerly in vogue : antiquated, antique, archaic, bygone, dated, dowdy, fusty, old-fashioned, old-time, outdated, outmoded, out-of-date, passé, vintage. *See* NEW. **6.** Skilled or knowledgeable through long practice : experienced, practiced, seasoned, versed, veteran. ***Idiom:*** knowing the ropes. *See* ABILITY.

olden *adjective*

Belonging to, existing, or occurring in times

long past : age-old, ancient, antediluvian, antiquated, antique, archaic, hoary, old, old-time, timeworn, venerable. ***Idioms:*** old as Methuselah, old as the hills. *See* NEW.

older *adjective*
Of greater age than another : elder, senior. *See* YOUTH.

old-fashioned *adjective*
Of a style or method formerly in vogue : antiquated, antique, archaic, bygone, dated, dowdy, fusty, old, old-time, outdated, outmoded, out-of-date, passé, vintage. *See* NEW.

old hand *noun*
One who has had long experience in a given activity or capacity : veteran. *Informal:* old-timer, vet. *See* ABILITY, KNOWLEDGE.

old maid *noun*
Informal. A person who is too much concerned with being proper, modest, or righteous : bluenose, Mrs. Grundy, prude, puritan, Victorian. *See* SEX.

old-maidish *adjective*
Marked by excessive concern for propriety and good form : bluenosed, genteel, precise, priggish, prim, prissy, proper, prudish, puritanical, strait-laced, stuffy, Victorian. ***Idiom:*** prim and proper. *See* PLAIN.

old man *noun*
Slang. A male parent : father, sire. *Informal:* dad, daddy, pa, papa, pappy², pop². *See* KIN.

oldster *noun*
Informal. An elderly person : ancient, elder, golden ager, senior, senior citizen. *Informal:* old-timer. *See* YOUTH.

old-time *adjective*
1. Belonging to, existing, or occurring in times long past : age-old, ancient, antediluvian, antiquated, antique, archaic, hoary, old, olden, timeworn, venerable. ***Idioms:*** old as Methuselah, old as the hills. *See* NEW. **2.** Of a style or method formerly in vogue : antiquated, antique, archaic, bygone, dated, dowdy, fusty, old, old-fashioned, outdated, outmoded, out-of-date, passé, vintage. *See* NEW.

old-timer *noun*
1. *Informal.* An elderly person : ancient, elder, golden ager, senior, senior citizen. *Informal:* oldster. *See* YOUTH. **2.** *Informal.* One who has had long experience in a given activity or capacity : old hand, veteran. *Informal:* vet. *See* ABILITY, KNOWLEDGE.

oleaginous *adjective*
1. Having the qualities of fat : adipose, fat, fatty, greasy, oily, unctuous. *See* FAT. **2.** Affectedly and self-servingly earnest : fulsome, oily, sleek, smarmy, unctuous. *See* ATTITUDE, HONEST.

olfaction *noun*
The sense by which odors are perceived : nose, scent, smell. *See* SMELLS.

olio *noun*
A collection of various things : assortment, conglomeration, gallimaufry, hodgepodge, jumble, medley, mélange, miscellany, mishmash, mixed bag, mixture, patchwork, potpourri, salmagundi, variety. *Slang:* grab bag. *See* COLLECT.

omen *noun*
A phenomenon that serves as a sign or warning of some future good or evil : augury, forerunner, foretoken, portent, prefigurement, presage, prognostic, prognostication, sign. ***Idiom:*** writing (*or* handwriting) on the wall. *See* FORESIGHT, WARN.

ominous *adjective*
Portending future disaster : apocalyptic, apocalyptical, baneful, dire, direful, fateful, fire-and-brimstone, grave², hellfire, portentous, unlucky. *See* LUCK, WARN.

omission *noun*
Nonperformance of what ought to be done : default, delinquency, dereliction, failure, neglect. *Law:* nonfeasance. *See* DO.

omit *verb*
1. To take or leave out : drop, eliminate, remove. *See* INCLUDE. **2.** To not do (something necessary) : default, fail, neglect. *See* DO.

omnipresent *adjective*
Ever present in all places : ubiquitous, universal. *See* LIMITED, SPECIFIC.

omnivorous *adjective*
Having an insatiable appetite for an activity or pursuit : avid, edacious, gluttonous, greedy, rapacious, ravenous, unappeasable, voracious. *See* DESIRE.

omnivorousness *noun*
The quality or condition of being voracious : avidity, edacity, rapaciousness, rapacity, ravenousness, voracity. *See* DESIRE.

on-again, off-again *adjective*
Informal. Happening or appearing now and then : fitful, intermittent, occasional, periodic, periodical, sporadic. *See* CONTINUE.

once *adverb*
At a time in the past : already, before, earlier, erstwhile, formerly, previously. *Archaic:* aforetime, beforetime. *See* PRECEDE.

once *adjective* Having been such previously : erstwhile, former, late, old, onetime, past, previous, quondam, sometime, whilom. *See* PRECEDE.

one *adjective*
Alone in a given category : lone, only, particular, separate, single, singular, sole, solitary, unique. ***Idioms:*** first and last, one and only. *See* INCLUDE.

one-dimensional *adjective*
Lacking in intellectual depth or thoroughness : cursory, shallow, sketchy, skin-deep, superficial, uncritical. *See* SURFACE.

oneness *noun*
1. The condition of being one : singleness, singularity, unity. *See* PART. **2.** The quality or condition of being unique : singleness, singularity, uniqueness. *See* SAME. **3.** The state of being entirely whole : completeness, entirety, integrity, totality, wholeness. *See* PART. **4.** The quality or condition of being exactly the same as something else : identicalness, identity, sameness, selfsameness. *See* SAME. **5.** An identity or coincidence of interests, purposes, or sympathies among the members of a group : solidarity, union, unity. *See* AGREE.

onerous *adjective*
Requiring great or extreme bodily, mental, or spiritual strength : arduous, backbreaking, burdensome, demanding, difficult, effortful, exacting, exigent, formidable, hard, heavy, laborious, oppressive, rigorous, rough, severe, taxing, tough, trying, weighty. *See* HEAVY.

one-sided *adjective*
Exhibiting bias : biased, partial, partisan, prejudiced, prejudicial, prepossessed, tendentious. *See* LIKE, STRAIGHT.

one-sidedness *noun*
An inclination for or against that inhibits impartial judgment : bias, partiality, partisanship, prejudice, prepossession, tendentiousness. *See* AFFECT, LIKE, STRAIGHT.

onetime *adjective*
Having been such previously : erstwhile, former, late, old, once, past, previous, quondam, sometime, whilom. *See* PRECEDE.

one-up *verb*
Informal. To outmaneuver (an opponent), especially with the aid of some extra resource : finesse, trump. *See* WIN.

ongoing *adjective*
Existing or occurring without interruption or end : around-the-clock, ceaseless, constant, continual, continuous, endless, eternal, everlasting, incessant, interminable, nonstop, perpetual, persistent, relentless, round-the-clock, timeless, unceasing, unending, unfailing, uninterrupted, unremitting. *See* CONTINUE.

onlooker *noun*
Someone who observes : beholder, bystander, looker-on, observer, spectator, watcher. *See* AWARENESS, SEE.

only *adjective*
1. Alone in a given category : lone, one, particular, separate, single, singular, sole, solitary, unique. ***Idioms:*** first and last, one and only. *See* INCLUDE. **2.** Without equal or rival : alone, incomparable, matchless, nonpareil, peerless, singular, unequaled, unexampled, unique, unmatched, unparalleled, unrivaled. *See* SAME.

only *adverb* **1.** To the exclusion of anyone or anything else : alone, but, entirely, exclusively, solely. *See* INCLUDE. **2.** Nothing more than : just, merely. *See* INCLUDE, SPECIFIC.

onomatopoeia *noun*
The formation of words in imitation of sounds : echoism. *See* SAME, SOUNDS.

onomatopoeic *adjective*
Imitating sounds : echoic, imitative, onomatopoetic. *See* SAME, SOUNDS.

onomatopoetic *adjective*
Imitating sounds : echoic, imitative, onomatopoeic. *See* SAME, SOUNDS.

onrush *noun*
The act of attacking : aggression, assailment, assault, attack, attempt, offense, offensive, onset, onslaught, strike. *See* ATTACK.

onset *noun*
1. The act of attacking : aggression, assailment, assault, attack, attempt, offense, offensive, onrush, onslaught, strike. *See* ATTACK.
2. The initial stage of a developmental process : beginning, birth, commencement, dawn, genesis, inception, nascence, nascency, opening, origin, outset, spring, start. *See* START.

onslaught *noun*
The act of attacking : aggression, assailment, assault, attack, attempt, offense, offensive, onrush, onset, strike. *See* ATTACK.

onus *noun*
1. A duty or responsibility that is a source of anxiety, worry, or hardship : burden[1], millstone, tax, weight. *Informal:* onus. *See* HEAVY, OVER. **2.** A mark of discredit or disgrace : black eye, blemish, blot, spot, stain, stigma, taint, tarnish. *Archaic:* attaint. ***Idiom:*** a blot on one's escutcheon. *See* MARKS, RESPECT.
3. Responsibility for an error or crime : blame, culpability, fault, guilt. *See* START.

onyx *adjective*
Of the darkest achromatic visual value : black,

ebon, ebony, inky, jet[1], jetty, pitch-black, pitchy, sable, sooty. *See* COLORS.

oodles *noun*
Informal. An indeterminately great amount or number : jillion, million (often used in plural), multiplicity, ream, trillion. *Informal:* bushel, gob[1] (often used in plural), heap (often used in plural), load (often used in plural), lot, passel, peck[2], scad (often used in plural), slew, wad, zillion. *See* BIG.

oomph *noun*
Slang. A lively, emphatic, eager quality or manner : animation, bounce, brio, dash, élan, esprit, life, liveliness, pertness, sparkle, spirit, verve, vigor, vim, vivaciousness, vivacity, zip. *Informal:* ginger, pep, peppiness. *See* ACTION.

ooze *verb*
To flow or leak out or emit something slowly : bleed, exude, leach, percolate, seep, transpire, transude, weep. *See* MOVE, SOLID.
ooze *noun* A viscous, usually offensively dirty substance : mire, muck, slime, slop, sludge, slush. *See* CLEAN.

oozy *adjective*
Of, relating to, or covered with slime : miry, mucky, slimy, sludgy, slushy. *See* CLEAN.

open *adjective*
1. Free from obstructions : clear, free, unblocked, unimpeded, unobstructed. *See* OPEN. **2.** Having no protecting or concealing cover : exposed, uncovered, unprotected. *See* PROTECTION. **3.** Not restricted or confined to few : open-door, public, unrestricted. *See* OPEN. **4.** Tending to incur : liable, prone, subject, susceptible, susceptive, vulnerable. *See* LIKELY. **5.** Ready and willing to receive favorably, as new ideas : acceptant, amenable, open-minded, receptive, responsive. *See* ACCEPT. **6.** Available for use : accessible, employable, operable, operative, practicable, usable, utilizable. *See* POSSIBLE. **7.** Not spoken for or occupied : free, uninhabited, unoccupied, unreserved. *See* OWNED. **8.** Marked by lack of firm decision or commitment; of questionable outcome : indefinite, uncertain, undecided, undetermined, unresolved, unsettled, unsure, vague. ***Idiom:*** up in the air. *See* CERTAIN. **9.** Manifesting honesty and directness, especially in speech : candid, direct, downright, forthright, frank, honest, ingenuous, man-to-man, plainspoken, straight, straightforward, straight-out, unreserved. *Informal:* straight-from-the-shoulder, straight-shooting. *See* CLEAR, SHOW.
open *verb* **1.** To become or cause to become open : unclose, undo. *See* OPEN. **2.** To rid of obstructions : clear, free, unblock. *See* OPEN. **3.** To move or arrange so as to cover a larger area. Also used with *out* or *up* : expand, extend, fan (out), outstretch, spread, stretch, unfold, unroll. *See* MOVE. **4.** To go about the initial step in doing (something) : approach, begin, commence, embark, enter, get off, inaugurate, initiate, institute, launch, lead off, set about, set out, set to, start, take on, take up, undertake. *Informal:* kick off. ***Idioms:*** get cracking, get going, get the show on the road. *See* START.

open-door *adjective*
Not restricted or confined to few : open, public, unrestricted. *See* OPEN.

open-eyed *adjective*
Vigilantly attentive : alert, observant, vigilant, wakeful, wary, watchful, wide-awake. ***Idiom:*** on the ball. *See* AWARENESS.

openhanded *adjective*
Characterized by bounteous giving : free, freehanded, generous, handsome, lavish, liberal, munificent, unsparing, unstinting. *See* GIVE.

openhandedness *noun*
The quality or state of being generous : bigheartedness, bounteousness, bountifulness, freehandedness, generosity, generousness, greatheartedness, large-heartedness, lavishness, liberality, magnanimity, magnanimousness, munificence, unselfishness, unsparingness. *See* GIVE.

opening *noun*
1. An open space allowing passage : aperture, hole, mouth, orifice, outlet, vent. *See* OPEN. **2.** The initial stage of a developmental process : beginning, birth, commencement, dawn, genesis, inception, nascence, nascency, onset, origin, outset, spring, start. *See* START. **3.** The act or process of bringing or being brought into existence : beginning, commencement, inauguration, inception, incipience, incipiency, initiation, launch, leadoff, origination, start. *Informal:* kickoff. *See* START. **4.** A favorable or advantageous combination of circumstances : break, chance, occasion, opportunity. *Informal:* shot. *See* LUCK.

open-minded *adjective*
1. Ready and willing to receive favorably, as new ideas : acceptant, amenable, open, receptive, responsive. *See* ACCEPT. **2.** Not narrow or conservative in thought, expression, or conduct : broad, broad-minded, liberal, progressive, tolerant. *See* ATTITUDE, WIDE.

open-mindedness *noun*
Ready acceptance of often new suggestions, ideas, influences, or opinions : openness, receptiveness, receptivity, responsiveness. *See* ACCEPT.

openness *noun*
1. The condition of being laid open to something undesirable or injurious : exposure, liability, susceptibility, susceptibleness, vulnerability, vulnerableness. *See* PROTECTION. **2.** Ready acceptance of often new suggestions, ideas, influences, or opinions : open-mindedness, receptiveness, receptivity, responsiveness. *See* ACCEPT.

operable *adjective*
Available for use : accessible, employable, open, operative, practicable, usable, utilizable. *See* POSSIBLE.

operate *verb*
1. To perform a function effectively : function, go, run, take, work. *See* THRIVE. **2.** To control or direct the functioning of : manage, run, use, work. *See* CONTROL. **3.** To control the course of (an activity) : carry on, conduct, direct, manage, run, steer. *See* OVER. **4.** To react in a specified way : act, behave, function, perform, work. *See* ACTION.

operating *adjective*
In action or full operation : active, alive, functioning, going, operative, running, working. *See* ACTION, AWARENESS.

operation *noun*
1. The way in which a machine or other thing performs or functions : behavior, functioning, performance, reaction, working (often used in plural). *See* ACTION, MACHINE. **2.** The act of putting into play : application, employment, exercise, exertion, implementation, play, usage, use, utilization. *See* USED.

operational *adjective*
In effect : effective, operative. *See* BE.

operative *adjective*
1. In effect : effective, operational. *See* BE. **2.** Available for use : accessible, employable, open, operable, practicable, usable, utilizable. *See* POSSIBLE. **3.** In action or full operation : active, alive, functioning, going, operating, running, working. *See* ACTION, AWARENESS.
operative *noun* **1.** One who labors : hand, laborer, roustabout, worker, working girl, workingman, workingwoman, workman, workwoman. *See* WORK. **2.** A person who secretly observes others to obtain information : agent, spy. *Informal:* spook. ***Idiom:*** secret (*or* undercover) agent. *See* INVESTIGATE.

operator *noun*
1. A person who operates a motor vehicle : driver, motorist. *See* MOVE. **2.** One who speculates for quick profits : adventurer, gambler, speculator. *See* GAMBLING, MONEY.

opiate *noun*
1. A substance that affects the central nervous system and is often addictive : drug, hallucinogen, narcotic. *Informal:* dope. *See* DRUGS. **2.** Something that induces sleep or sedation : hypnotic, narcotic, sedative, somnifacient, soporific. *See* AWARENESS.
opiate *adjective* Inducing sleep or sedation : hypnotic, narcotic, sedative, sleepy, slumberous, somnifacient, somniferous, somnific, somnolent, soporific. *See* AWARENESS.
opiate *verb* To administer or add a drug to : dose, drug, medicate, narcotize, physic. *Informal:* dope (up). *See* DRUGS.

opine *verb*
To have an opinion : believe, consider, deem, hold, think. *Informal:* figure, judge. ***Idiom:*** be of the opinion. *See* OPINION.

opinion *noun*
Something believed or accepted as true by a person : belief, conviction, feeling, idea, mind, notion, persuasion, position, sentiment, view. *See* OPINION.

opponent *noun*
1. One that opposes another in a battle, contest, controversy, or debate : adversary, antagonist, opposer, opposition, oppositionist, resister. *See* RESIST, SUPPORT. **2.** One that competes : competition, competitor, contender, contestant, corrival, rival. *See* CONFLICT.

opportune *adjective*
Occurring at a fitting or advantageous time : auspicious, favorable, propitious, prosperous, seasonable, timely, well-timed. *See* LUCK.

opportunity *noun*
A favorable or advantageous combination of circumstances : break, chance, occasion, opening. *Informal:* shot. *See* LUCK.

oppose *verb*
1. To place in opposition or be in opposition to : counter, match, pit[1], play off. ***Idioms:*** bump heads with, meet head-on, set (*or* be) at odds, set (*or* be) at someone's throat, trade blows (*or* punches). *See* SUPPORT. **2.** To take a stand against : buck, challenge, contest, dispute, resist, traverse. *See* SUPPORT.

opposed *adjective*
Acting against or in opposition : adversarial, adverse, antagonistic, antipathetic, opposing, oppositional. *See* SUPPORT.

opposer *noun*
One that opposes another in a battle, contest, controversy, or debate : adversary, antagonist, opponent, opposition, oppositionist, resister. *See* RESIST, SUPPORT.

opposing *adjective*
1. Acting against or in opposition : adversarial, adverse, antagonistic, antipathetic, opposed, oppositional. *See* SUPPORT. **2.** Diametrically opposed : antipodal, antipodean, antithetical, antonymic, antonymous, contradictory, contrary, converse², counter, diametric, diametrical, opposite, polar, reverse. *See* SUPPORT.

opposite *adjective*
Diametrically opposed : antipodal, antipodean, antithetical, antonymic, antonymous, contradictory, contrary, converse², counter, diametric, diametrical, opposing, polar, reverse. *See* SUPPORT.
opposite *noun* That which is diametrically opposed to another : antipode, antipodes, antithesis, antonym, contrary, converse², counter, reverse. *Logic:* contradictory, contrapositive. *See* SUPPORT.

opposite number *noun*
One that has the same functions and characteristics as another : counterpart, vis-à-vis. *See* SAME.

opposition *noun*
1. The act of resisting : renitence, renitency, resistance. *See* RESIST. **2.** The condition of being in conflict : antagonism, antithesis, contradiction, contradistinction, contraposition, contrariety, contrariness, polarity. *See* SUPPORT. **3.** One that opposes another in a battle, contest, controversy, or debate : adversary, antagonist, opponent, opposer, oppositionist, resister. *See* RESIST, SUPPORT.

oppositional *adjective*
Acting against or in opposition : adversarial, adverse, antagonistic, antipathetic, opposed, opposing. *See* SUPPORT.

oppositionist *noun*
One that opposes another in a battle, contest, controversy, or debate : adversary, antagonist, opponent, opposer, opposition, resister. *See* RESIST, SUPPORT.

oppress *verb*
1. To do a wrong to; treat unjustly : aggrieve, outrage, persecute, wrong. *See* RIGHT. **2.** To make sad or gloomy : deject, depress, dispirit, sadden, weigh down. *See* HAPPY.

oppressive *adjective*
Requiring great or extreme bodily, mental, or spiritual strength : arduous, backbreaking, burdensome, demanding, difficult, effortful, exacting, exigent, formidable, hard, heavy, laborious, onerous, rigorous, rough, severe, taxing, tough, trying, weighty. *See* HEAVY.

oppressor *noun*
An absolute ruler, especially one who is harsh and oppressive : Big Brother, despot, dictator, führer, man on horseback, strongman, totalitarian, tyrant. *See* OVER.

opprobrious *adjective*
1. Of, relating to, or characterized by verbal abuse : abusive, contumelious, invective, scurrilous, vituperative. *See* ATTACK, ATTITUDE. **2.** Meriting or causing shame or dishonor : discreditable, disgraceful, dishonorable, disreputable, ignominious, shameful. *See* RESPECT.

opprobrium *noun*
Loss of or damage to one's reputation : bad name, bad odor, discredit, disgrace, dishonor, disrepute, humiliation, ignominy, ill repute, obloquy, odium, shame. *See* RESPECT.

oppugn *verb*
To refuse to admit the truth, reality, value, or worth of : contradict, contravene, controvert, deny, disaffirm, gainsay, negate, negative. *Law:* traverse. *See* AFFIRM.

opt *verb*
To make a choice from a number of alternatives. Also used with *for* : choose, cull, elect, pick (out), select, single (out). *See* CHOICE.

optic *adjective*
Serving, resulting from, or relating to the sense of sight : optical, visual. *See* SEE.

optical *adjective*
Serving, resulting from, or relating to the sense of sight : optic, visual. *See* SEE.

optimal *adjective*
Surpassing all others in quality : best, optimum, superlative, unsurpassed. *See* BETTER.

optimism *noun*
A tendency to expect a favorable outcome or to dwell on hopeful aspects : sanguineness, sanguinity. *See* HOPE.

optimist *noun*
One who expects a favorable outcome or dwells on hopeful aspects : Pollyanna. *See* HOPE.

optimistic *adjective*
Expecting a favorable outcome or dwelling on hopeful aspects : Panglossian, roseate, rose-colored, rosy, sanguine. *Informal:* upbeat. *Idioms:* looking on the bright side, looking through rose-colored glasses. *See* HOPE.

optimum *adjective*
Surpassing all others in quality : best, optimal, superlative, unsurpassed. *See* BETTER.

option *noun*
1. The act of choosing : choice, election, preference, selection. *See* CHOICE. **2.** The power or right of choosing : alternative, choice. *See* CHOICE.

optional *adjective*
Not compulsory or automatic : discretionary, elective, facultative. *See* CHOICE.

opulent *adjective*
1. Characterized by extravagant, ostentatious magnificence : lavish, lush[1], luxuriant, luxurious, palatial, plush, rich, sumptuous. *Informal:* plushy. *See* RICH. **2.** Given to or marked by unrestrained abundance : extravagant, exuberant, lavish, lush[1], luxuriant, prodigal, profuse, riotous, superabundant. *See* BIG, EXCESS.

opus *noun*
1. Something that is the result of creative effort : composition, piece, production, work. *See* MAKE. **2.** An issue of printed material offered for sale or distribution : publication, title, volume, work. *See* WORDS.

oracle *noun*
Something that is foretold by or as if by supernatural means : divination, prophecy, soothsaying, vaticination, vision. *See* FORESIGHT.

oracular *adjective*
Of or relating to the foretelling of events by or as if by supernatural means : augural, divinitory, fatidic, fatidical, mantic, prophetic, sibylline, vatic, vatical, vaticinal, visionary. *See* FORESIGHT.

oral *adjective*
1. Produced by the voice : articulate, sonant, spoken, uttered, vocal, voiced. *See* SOUNDS.
2. Expressed or transmitted in speech : spoken, unwritten, verbal, word-of-mouth. *See* WORDS.

oration *noun*
A usually formal oral communication to an audience : address, allocution, declamation, lecture, prelection, speech, talk. *See* WORDS.

orator *noun*
A public speaker : rhetorician. *See* WORDS.

oratorical *adjective*
Of or relating to the art of public speaking : declamatory, elocutionary, rhetorical. *See* WORDS.

oratory *noun*
The art of public speaking : declamation, elocution, rhetoric. *See* WORDS.

orb *noun*
1. An organ of vision : eye. *See* SEE. **2.** *Archaic.* A closed plane curve everywhere equidistant from a fixed point or something shaped like this : band[1], circle, circuit, disk, gyre, ring[1], wheel. *See* GEOMETRY.

orbit *noun*
1. A course, process, or journey that ends where it began or repeats itself : circle, circuit, cycle, round, tour, turn. *See* REPETITION. **2.** A sphere of activity, experience, study, or interest : area, arena, bailiwick, circle, department, domain, field, province, realm, scene, subject, terrain, territory, world. *Slang:* bag. *See* TERRITORY.
3. An area within which something or someone exists, acts, or has influence or power : ambit, compass, extension, extent, purview, range, reach, realm, scope, sphere, sweep, swing. *See* TERRITORY.
orbit *verb* To move or cause to move in circles or around an axis : circle, circumvolve, gyrate, revolve, rotate, turn, wheel. *See* MOVE, REPETITION.

orchestrate *verb*
To combine and adapt in order to attain a particular effect : arrange, blend, coordinate, harmonize, integrate, synthesize, unify. *See* BEAUTIFUL.

ordain *verb*
To set forth expressly and authoritatively : decree, dictate, fix, impose, lay down, prescribe. ***Idioms:*** call the shots (*or* tune), lay it on the line. *See* OVER.

ordeal *noun*
A state of pain or anguish that tests one's resiliency and character : crucible, trial, tribulation, visitation. *See* EASY.

order *noun*
1. A way or condition of being arranged : arrangement, categorization, classification, deployment, disposal, disposition, distribution, formation, grouping, layout, lineup, organization, placement, sequence. *See* ORDER. **2.** Systematic arrangement and design : method, orderliness, organization, pattern, plan, system, systematization, systemization. *See* ORDER.
3. A state of sound readiness : condition, fettle, fitness, form, kilter, shape, trim. *See* BETTER.
4. A way in which things follow each other in space or time : consecution, procession, sequence, succession. *See* ORDER, PRECEDE.
5. A number of things placed or occurring one after the other : chain, consecution, course, procession, progression, round, run, sequence, series, string, succession, suite, train. *Informal:* streak. *See* ORDER. **6.** An authoritative indication to be obeyed : behest, bidding, charge, command, commandment, dictate, direction, directive, injunction, instruction (often used in

plural), mandate, word. *See* OVER, WORDS. **7.** A group of people united in a relationship and having some interest, activity, or purpose in common : association, club, confederation, congress, federation, fellowship, fraternity, guild, league, organization, society, sorority, union. *See* GROUP. **8.** A class that is defined by the common attribute or attributes possessed by all its members : breed, cast, description, feather, ilk, kind[2], lot, manner, mold, nature, sort, species, stamp, stripe, type, variety. *Informal:* persuasion. *See* GROUP. **9.** A division of persons or things by quality, rank, or grade : bracket, class, grade, league, rank[1], tier. *See* GROUP, VALUE. **10.** A subdivision of a larger group : category, class, classification, set[2]. *See* GROUP.

order *verb* **1.** To give orders to : bid, charge, command, direct, enjoin, instruct, tell. *See* OVER, WORDS. **2.** To command or issue commands in an arrogant manner : boss, dictate, dominate, domineer, rule, tyrannize. *See* OVER. **3.** To put into a deliberate order : arrange, array, deploy, dispose, marshal, organize, range, sort, systematize. *See* ORDER. **4.** To arrange in an orderly manner : methodize, organize, systematize, systemize. *See* ORDER.

orderliness *noun*
Systematic arrangement and design : method, order, organization, pattern, plan, system, systematization, systemization. *See* ORDER.

orderly *adjective*
1. In good order or clean condition : neat, shipshape, snug, spick-and-span, spruce, taut, tidy, trig, trim, well-groomed. *Chiefly British:* tight. ***Idiom:*** neat as a pin. *See* CLEAN, ORDER. **2.** Arranged or proceeding in a set, systematized pattern : methodic, methodical, regular, systematic, systematical. *See* ABILITY, ORDER.

order of the day *noun*
An organized list, as of procedures, activities, or events. Often used in plural : agenda, calendar, docket, lineup, program, schedule, timetable. *See* PLANNED.

ordinance *noun*
A principle governing affairs within or among political units : canon, decree, edict, institute, law, precept, prescription, regulation, rule. *See* LAW.

ordinariness *noun*
The quality or condition of being usual : customariness, habitualness, normalcy, normality, prevalence, regularity, routineness, usualness. *See* USUAL.

ordinary *adjective*
1. Commonly encountered : average, common, commonplace, general, normal, typical, usual. *See* SURPRISE. **2.** Being of no special quality or type : average, common, commonplace, cut-and-dried, formulaic, garden, garden-variety, indifferent, mediocre, plain, routine, run-of-the-mill, standard, stock, undistinguished, unexceptional, unremarkable. *See* GOOD, USUAL.

ordinary *noun* A regular or customary matter, condition, or course of events : commonplace, norm, rule, usual. *See* USUAL.

organ *noun*
1. A component of government that performs a given function : agency, arm, branch, department, division, wing. *See* PART. **2.** That by which something is accomplished or some end achieved : agency, agent, instrument, instrumentality, instrumentation, intermediary, mean[3] (used in plural), mechanism, medium. *See* MEANS.

organic *adjective*
Produced by nature; not artificial or manmade : natural, unadulterated. ***Idiom:*** pure as the driven snow. *See* CULTURE.

organization *noun*
1. The act of founding or establishing : constitution, creation, establishment, foundation, institution, origination, start-up. *See* START. **2.** A way or condition of being arranged : arrangement, categorization, classification, deployment, disposal, disposition, distribution, formation, grouping, layout, lineup, order, placement, sequence. *See* ORDER. **3.** Systematic arrangement and design : method, order, orderliness, pattern, plan, system, systematization, systemization. *See* ORDER. **4.** A group of people united in a relationship and having some interest, activity, or purpose in common : association, club, confederation, congress, federation, fellowship, fraternity, guild, league, order, society, sorority, union. *See* GROUP. **5.** An association, especially of nations for a common cause : alliance, Anschluss, bloc, cartel, coalition, confederacy, confederation, federation, league, union. *See* CONNECT, GROUP, POLITICS.

organize *verb*
1. To put into a deliberate order : arrange, array, deploy, dispose, marshal, order, range, sort, systematize. *See* ORDER. **2.** To arrange in an orderly manner : methodize, order, systematize, systemize. *See* ORDER. **3.** To assemble, prepare, or put into operation, as for war or a similar emergency : marshal, mobilize, muster,

rally. *See* MOVE. **4.** To bring into existence formally : constitute, create, establish, found, institute, originate, set up, start. *See* START.

orgy *noun*
A period of uncontrolled self-indulgence : binge, fling, rampage, spree. *Slang:* jag. *See* RESTRAINT.

orientation *noun*
One's place and direction relative to one's surroundings : bearing (often used in plural), location, position, situation. *See* PLACE.

orifice *noun*
An open space allowing passage : aperture, hole, mouth, opening, outlet, vent. *See* OPEN.

oriflamme *noun*
Fabric used especially as a symbol : banderole, banner, banneret, color (used in plural), ensign, flag[1], jack, pennant, pennon, standard, streamer. *See* SUBSTITUTE.

origin *noun*
1. A point of origination : beginning, derivation, fount, fountain, fountainhead, mother, parent, provenance, provenience, root[1], rootstock, source, spring, well[1]. *See* START. **2.** The initial stage of a developmental process : beginning, birth, commencement, dawn, genesis, inception, nascence, nascency, onset, opening, outset, spring, start. *See* START. **3.** One's ancestors or their character or one's ancestral derivation : ancestry, birth, blood, bloodline, descent, extraction, family, genealogy, line, lineage, parentage, pedigree, seed, stock. *See* KIN, PRECEDE.

original *adjective*
1. Preceding all others in time : earliest, first, initial, maiden, pioneer, primary, prime, primordial. *See* START. **2.** Arising from or going to the root or source : basal, basic, foundational, fundamental, primary, radical, underlying. *See* SURFACE. **3.** Not derived from something else : primary, prime, primitive. *See* START. **4.** Not counterfeit or copied : actual, authentic, bona fide, genuine, good, indubitable, real, true, undoubted, unquestionable. *See* TRUE. **5.** Not the same as what was previously known or done : different, fresh, innovative, inventive, new, newfangled, novel, unfamiliar, unprecedented. *See* NEW. **6.** Characterized by or productive of new things or new ideas : creative, ingenious, innovative, innovatory, inventive. *See* ABILITY.
original *noun* **1.** A first form from which varieties arise or imitations are made : archetype, father, master, protoplast, prototype. *See* START. **2.** A person who is appealingly odd or curious : character, oddity. *Informal:* card, oddball. *See* USUAL.

originality *noun*
1. The quality of being novel : freshness, innovativeness, newfangledness, newness, novelty. *See* NEW. **2.** The power or ability to invent : creativeness, creativity, ingeniousness, ingenuity, invention, inventiveness. *See* ABILITY, MAKE.

originate *verb*
1. To cause to come into existence : beget, breed, create, engender, father, hatch, make, parent, procreate, produce, sire, spawn. ***Idiom:*** give birth (*or* rise) to. *See* MAKE. **2.** To bring into existence formally : constitute, create, establish, found, institute, organize, set up, start. *See* START. **3.** To bring into currency, use, fashion, or practice : introduce, launch. *See* START. **4.** To come into being : arise, begin, commence, start. *See* START. **5.** To begin to appear or develop : appear, arise, commence, dawn, emerge. *See* START. **6.** To have as a source : arise, come, derive, emanate, flow, issue, proceed, rise, spring, stem, upspring. *See* START. **7.** To have as one's home or place of origin : come, hail[2]. *See* START.

origination *noun*
1. The act or process of bringing or being brought into existence : beginning, commencement, inauguration, inception, incipience, incipiency, initiation, launch, leadoff, opening, start. *Informal:* kickoff. *See* START. **2.** The act of founding or establishing : constitution, creation, establishment, foundation, institution, organization, start-up. *See* START.

originator *noun*
One that creates, founds, or originates : architect, author, creator, entrepreneur, father, founder[2], inventor, maker, parent, patriarch. *See* START.

orison *noun*
A formula of words used in praying : collect[2], litany, prayer[1], rogation (often used in plural). *See* RELIGION.

ornament *noun*
Something that adorns : adornment, decoration, embellishment, garnishment, garniture, ornamentation, trim, trimming. *See* BEAUTIFUL.
ornament *verb* To furnish with decorations : adorn, bedeck, deck[2] (out), decorate, dress (up), embellish, garnish, trim. *See* BEAUTIFUL.

ornamentation *noun*
Something that adorns : adornment, decoration, embellishment, garnishment, garniture,

ornament, trim, trimming. *See* BEAUTIFUL.

ornate *adjective*
Elaborately and heavily ornamented : baroque, flamboyant, florid, rococo. *See* PLAIN.

ornery *adjective*
Given to acting in opposition to others : balky, contrarious, contrary, difficult, froward, impossible, perverse, wayward. *See* ATTITUDE, SUPPORT.

orotund *adjective*
1. Characterized by language that is elevated and sometimes pompous in style : aureate, bombastic, declamatory, flowery, fustian, grandiloquent, high-flown, high-sounding, magniloquent, overblown, rhetorical, sonorous, swollen. *See* PLAIN, STYLE, WORDS. **2.** Having or producing a full, deep, or rich sound : mellow, plangent, resonant, resounding, ringing, rotund, round, sonorous, vibrant. *See* SOUNDS.

orotundity *noun*
Pretentious, pompous speech or writing : bombast, claptrap, fustian, grandiloquence, magniloquence, rant, turgidity. *See* PLAIN, STYLE, WORDS.

ort *noun*
1. Residual matter. Often used in plural : butt[4], end, fragment, scrap[1], shard, stub. *See* LEFTOVER. **2.** A tiny amount : bit[1], crumb, dab[1], dash, dot, dram, drop, fragment, grain, iota, jot, minim, mite, modicum, molecule, ounce, particle, scrap[1], scruple, shred, smidgen, speck, tittle, trifle, whit. *Chiefly British:* spot. *See* BIG.

orthodox *adjective*
1. Adhering to beliefs or practices approved by authority or tradition : canonical, received, sanctioned, time-honored. *See* USUAL. **2.** Conforming to established practice or standards : button-down, conformist, conventional, establishmentarian, straight, traditional. *Slang:* square. *See* USUAL. **3.** Generally approved or agreed upon : accepted, conventional, received, recognized, sanctioned. *See* ACCEPT, AGREE, STRAIGHT, USUAL. **4.** Strongly favoring retention of the existing order : conservative, right, rightist, right-wing, Tory, traditionalist, traditionalistic. *See* KEEP.

orthodox *noun* One who strongly favors retention of the existing order : conservative, rightist, right-winger, Tory, traditionalist. *See* KEEP.

oscillate *verb*
To move rhythmically back and forth suspended or as if suspended from above : sway, swing. *See* MOVE, REPETITION.

osculate *verb*
To touch or caress with the lips, especially as a sign of passion or affection : buss, kiss, smack[1]. *Informal:* peck[1]. *Slang:* smooch. *See* TOUCH.

osculation *noun*
The act or an instance of kissing : buss, kiss, smack[1], smacker. *Informal:* peck[1]. *Slang:* smooch. *See* TOUCH.

ossuary *noun*
A burial place or receptacle for human remains : catacomb, cinerarium, crypt, grave[1], mausoleum, sepulcher, sepulture, tomb, vault[1]. *See* KEEP, PLACE.

ostensible *adjective*
Appearing as such but not necessarily so : apparent, external, ostensive, outward, seeming, superficial. *See* SURFACE.

ostensibly *adverb*
On the surface : apparently, evidently, externally, ostensively, outwardly, seemingly, superficially. ***Idioms:*** on the face of it, to all appearances. *See* SURFACE.

ostensive *adjective*
Appearing as such but not necessarily so : apparent, external, ostensible, outward, seeming, superficial. *See* SURFACE.

ostensively *adverb*
On the surface : apparently, evidently, externally, ostensibly, outwardly, seemingly, superficially. ***Idioms:*** on the face of it, to all appearances. *See* SURFACE.

ostentation *noun*
Boastful self-importance or display : grandioseness, grandiosity, pomposity, pompousness, pretension, pretentiousness. *See* PLAIN.

ostentatious *adjective*
Marked by outward, often extravagant display : flamboyant, pretentious, showy, splashy, splurgy. *See* PLAIN.

ostracism *noun*
Enforced removal from one's native country by official decree : banishment, deportation, exile, expatriation, extradition, transportation. *See* ACCEPT, REWARD.

ostracize *verb*
1. To exclude from normal social or professional activities : blackball, blacklist, boycott, shut out. *See* ACCEPT. **2.** To force to leave a country or place by official decree : banish, deport, exile, expatriate, expel, transport. *See* ACCEPT.

other *adjective*
Being an addition : added, additional, extra, fresh, further, more, new. *See* INCREASE.

otherworldly *adjective*
Of or concerned with the spirit rather than the body or material things : numinous, spiritual, unworldly. *See* BODY.

otiose *adjective*
Lacking value, use, or substance : empty, hollow, idle, vacant, vain. *See* FULL.

ounce *noun*
1. A tiny amount : bit[1], crumb, dab[1], dash, dot, dram, drop, fragment, grain, iota, jot, minim, mite, modicum, molecule, ort, particle, scrap[1], scruple, shred, smidgen, speck, tittle, trifle, whit. *Chiefly British:* spot. *See* BIG.
2. The least bit : hoot, iota, jot, shred, whit. *Informal:* damn, rap[2]. *Slang:* diddly. *See* BIG.

oust *verb*
To put out by force : bump, dismiss, eject, evict, expel, throw out. *Informal:* chuck. *Slang:* boot[1] (out), bounce, kick out. ***Idioms:*** give someone the boot, give someone the heave-ho (*or* old heave-ho), send packing, show someone the door, throw out on one's ear. *See* KEEP.

ouster *noun*
The act of ejecting or the state of being ejected : dismissal, ejection, ejectment, eviction, expulsion. *Slang:* boot[1], bounce. *See* KEEP.

out *verb*
To be made public : break, come out, get out, transpire. *Informal:* leak (out). ***Idiom:*** come to light. *See* KNOWLEDGE, SHOW.

outage *noun*
A cessation of proper mechanical functions : breakdown, failure. *See* THRIVE.

out-and-out *adjective*
Completely such, without qualification or exception : absolute, all-out, arrant, complete, consummate, crashing, damned, dead, downright, flat, outright, perfect, plain, pure, sheer[2], thorough, thoroughgoing, total, unbounded, unequivocal, unlimited, unmitigated, unqualified, unrelieved, unreserved, utter[2]. *Informal:* flat-out, positive. *Chiefly British:* blooming. *See* BIG, LIMITED.

outbreak *noun*
1. A sudden increase in something, as the occurrence of a disease : epidemic, plague, rash[2]. *See* INCREASE. **2.** The act of emerging violently from limits or restraints : eruption, explosion, outburst. *See* EXPLOSION. **3.** A sudden violent expression, as of emotion : access, blowup, burst, eruption, explosion, fit[2], flare-up, gust, outburst. *See* EXPLOSION.

outburst *noun*
1. The act of emerging violently from limits or restraints : eruption, explosion, outbreak. *See* EXPLOSION. **2.** A sudden violent expression, as of emotion : access, blowup, burst, eruption, explosion, fit[2], flare-up, gust, outbreak. *See* EXPLOSION.

outcome *noun*
Something brought about by a cause : aftermath, consequence, corollary, effect, end product, event, fruit, harvest, issue, precipitate, ramification, result, resultant, sequel, sequence, sequent, upshot. *See* CAUSE.

outcry *noun*
1. A sudden, sharp utterance : cry, ejaculation, exclamation. *See* WORDS. **2.** Offensively loud and insistent utterances, especially of disapproval : clamor, hullabaloo, rumpus, uproar, vociferation. ***Idiom:*** hue and cry. *See* LIKE, SOUNDS.

outdate *verb*
To make or become obsolete : obsolesce, obsolete, superannuate. *See* NEW, USED.

outdated *adjective*
Of a style or method formerly in vogue : antiquated, antique, archaic, bygone, dated, dowdy, fusty, old, old-fashioned, old-time, outmoded, out-of-date, passé, vintage. *See* NEW.

outdo *verb*
To be greater or better than : best, better[1], exceed, excel, outmatch, outrun, outshine, outstrip, pass, surpass, top, transcend. *Informal:* beat. ***Idioms:*** go beyond, go one better. *See* BIG.

outermost *adjective*
Most distant or remote, as from a center : extreme, farthermost, farthest, furthermost, furthest, outmost, ultimate, utmost, uttermost. *See* BIG, EDGE.

outfit *noun*
1. Things needed for a task, journey, or other purpose : accouterment (often used in plural), apparatus, equipment, gear, material (used in plural), materiel, paraphernalia, rig, tackle, thing (used in plural), turnout. *See* MEANS. **2.** A set or style of clothing : costume, dress, garb, guise, habiliment (often used in plural), turnout. *Informal:* getup, rig. *See* PUT ON. **3.** *Informal.* A commercial organization : business, company, concern, corporation, enterprise, establishment, firm[2], house. *See* GROUP.
outfit *verb* To supply what is needed for some activity or purpose : accouter, appoint, equip, fit[1], fit out (*or* up), furnish, gear, rig, turn out. *See* GIVE.

outflow *noun*
A sudden or rapid flowing outward : efflux, gush, outpour, outpouring, spate. *See* MOVE.

outgoing *adjective*
Disposed to be open, sociable, and talkative : communicable, communicative, expansive, extraverted, extroverted, gregarious, unreserved. *See* ATTITUDE.

outgrowth *noun*
Something derived from another : byproduct, derivation, derivative, descendant, offshoot, spinoff. *See* KIN.

outing *noun*
A usually short journey taken for pleasure : excursion, jaunt, junket, trip. *See* MOVE.

outlander *noun*
A person coming from another country or into a new community : alien, émigré, foreigner, newcomer, outsider, stranger. *See* NATIVE.

outlandish *adjective*
1. Deviating from the customary : bizarre, cranky, curious, eccentric, erratic, freakish, idiosyncratic, odd, peculiar, quaint, queer, quirky, singular, strange, unnatural, unusual, weird. *Slang:* kooky, screwball. *British Slang:* rum, rummy[2]. *See* USUAL. **2.** *Archaic.* Of, from, or characteristic of another place or part of the world : alien, exotic, foreign, strange. *See* NATIVE.

outlast *verb*
To live, exist, or remain longer than : outlive, outwear, survive. *See* CONTINUE.

outlaw *verb*
To refuse to allow : ban, debar, disallow, enjoin, forbid, inhibit, interdict, prohibit, proscribe, taboo. *See* ALLOW.

outlawed *adjective*
Prohibited by law : illegal, illegitimate, illicit, lawless, unlawful, wrongful. *See* CRIMES, LAW.

outlay *noun*
Something expended to obtain a benefit or desired result : cost, disbursement, expenditure, expense. *See* TRANSACTIONS.
outlay *verb* To distribute (money) as payment : disburse, expend, give, lay out, pay (out), spend. *Informal:* fork out (*or* over *or* up), shell out. *See* SAVE.

outlet *noun*
1. An open space allowing passage : aperture, hole, mouth, opening, orifice, vent. *See* OPEN. **2.** A retail establishment where merchandise is sold : boutique, emporium, shop, store. *See* TRANSACTIONS.

outline *noun*
1. A line marking and shaping the outer form of an object : contour, delineation, profile, silhouette. *See* EDGE, SURFACE. **2.** A preliminary plan or version, as of a written work : draft, rough, skeleton, sketch. *See* PLANNED, WORDS.
outline *verb* To draw up a preliminary plan or version of : adumbrate, block in (*or* out), draft, rough in (*or* out), sketch. *See* PLANNED.

outlive *verb*
To live, exist, or remain longer than : outlast, outwear, survive. *See* CONTINUE.

outlook *noun*
1. The position from which something is observed or considered : angle[2], eye, point of view, slant, standpoint, vantage, viewpoint. *See* PERSPECTIVE. **2.** A frame of mind affecting one's thoughts or behavior : attitude, position, posture, stance. *See* ATTITUDE. **3.** Chance of success or advancement : future, prospect (used in plural). *See* HOPE. **4.** The act of predicting : forecast, prediction, prognosis, prognostication, projection. *See* FORESIGHT. **5.** A high structure or place commanding a wide view : lookout, observatory, overlook. *See* AWARENESS. **6.** That which is or can be seen : lookout, panorama, perspective, prospect, scene, sight, view, vista. *See* SEE.

outlying *adjective*
Far from centers of human population : back, insular, isolated, lonely, lonesome, obscure, out-of-the-way, remote, removed, secluded, solitary. ***Idiom:*** off the beaten path (*or* track). *See* NEAR.

outmaneuver *verb*
To get the better of by cleverness or cunning : outsmart, outthink, outwit, overreach. *See* WIN.

outmatch *verb*
To be greater or better than : best, better[1], exceed, excel, outdo, outrun, outshine, outstrip, pass, surpass, top, transcend. *Informal:* beat. ***Idioms:*** go beyond, go one better. *See* BIG.

outmoded *adjective*
Of a style or method formerly in vogue : antiquated, antique, archaic, bygone, dated, dowdy, fusty, old, old-fashioned, old-time, outdated, out-of-date, passé, vintage. *See* NEW.

outmost *adjective*
Most distant or remote, as from a center : extreme, farthermost, farthest, furthermost, furthest, outermost, ultimate, utmost, uttermost. *See* BIG, EDGE.

out-of-date *adjective*
Of a style or method formerly in vogue : antiquated, antique, archaic, bygone, dated, dowdy, fusty, old, old-fashioned, old-time, outdated, outmoded, passé, vintage. *See* NEW.

out of sight *adjective*
Slang. Far beyond what is usual, normal, or customary : exceptional, extraordinary, magnificent, outstanding, preeminent, rare, remarkable, singular, towering, uncommon, unusual. *Informal:* standout. *Slang:* awesome. *See* BETTER, USUAL.

out-of-the-way *adjective*
Far from centers of human population : back, insular, isolated, lonely, lonesome, obscure, outlying, remote, removed, secluded, solitary. ***Idiom:*** off the beaten path (*or* track). *See* NEAR.

outpour *noun*
A sudden or rapid flowing outward : efflux, gush, outflow, outpouring, spate. *See* MOVE.

outpouring *noun*
A sudden or rapid flowing outward : efflux, gush, outflow, outpour, spate. *See* MOVE.

output *noun*
The amount or quantity produced : production, yield. *See* BIG.

outrage *noun*
1. A monstrous offense or evil : atrocity, enormity, monstrosity. *See* RIGHT. **2.** Something that offends one's sense of propriety, fairness, or justice : crime, offense, sin. *See* RIGHT. **3.** An act that offends a person's sense of pride or dignity : affront, contumely, despite, indignity, insult, offense, slight. ***Idiom:*** slap in the face. *See* ATTACK.

outrage *verb* **1.** To cause resentment or hurt by callous, rude behavior : affront, huff, insult, miff, offend, pique. ***Idioms:*** add insult to injury, give offense to. *See* ATTACK, PAIN. **2.** To do a wrong to; treat unjustly : aggrieve, oppress, persecute, wrong. *See* RIGHT.

outrageous *adjective*
1. Disgracefully and grossly offensive : atrocious, heinous, monstrous, scandalous, shocking. *Archaic:* enormous. *See* RIGHT. **2.** Beyond all reason : obscene, preposterous, ridiculous, shocking, unconscionable, unreasonable. ***Idioms:*** out of bounds, out of sight. *See* USUAL.

outrageousness *noun*
The quality or state of being flagrant : atrociousness, atrocity, egregiousness, enormity, flagrance, flagrancy, flagrantness, glaringness, grossness, rankness. *See* GOOD.

outright *adjective*
Completely such, without qualification or exception : absolute, all-out, arrant, complete, consummate, crashing, damned, dead, downright, flat, out-and-out, perfect, plain, pure, sheer[2], thorough, thoroughgoing, total, unbounded, unequivocal, unlimited, unmitigated, unqualified, unrelieved, unreserved, utter[2]. *Informal:* flat-out, positive. *Chiefly British:* blooming. *See* BIG, LIMITED.

outrun *verb*
To be greater or better than : best, better[1], exceed, excel, outdo, outmatch, outshine, outstrip, pass, surpass, top, transcend. *Informal:* beat. ***Idioms:*** go beyond, go one better. *See* BIG.

outset *noun*
The initial stage of a developmental process : beginning, birth, commencement, dawn, genesis, inception, nascence, nascency, onset, opening, origin, spring, start. *See* START.

outshine *verb*
To be greater or better than : best, better[1], exceed, excel, outdo, outmatch, outrun, outstrip, pass, surpass, top, transcend. *Informal:* beat. ***Idioms:*** go beyond, go one better. *See* BIG.

outside *noun*
The greatest quantity or highest degree attainable : maximum, top, ultimate, utmost, uttermost. ***Idiom:*** ne plus ultra. *See* HIGH, LIMITED.

outside *adjective* Small in degree, especially of probability : faint, negligible, remote, slender, slight, slim. *See* BIG.

outsider *noun*
A person coming from another country or into a new community : alien, émigré, foreigner, newcomer, outlander, stranger. *See* NATIVE.

outskirt *noun*
The periphery of a city or town. Often used in plural : edge, environs, fringe, skirt (used in plural), suburb (used in plural). *See* EDGE.

outsmart *verb*
To get the better of by cleverness or cunning : outmaneuver, outthink, outwit, overreach. *See* WIN.

outspoken *adjective*
Speaking or spoken without reserve : free, free-spoken, vocal. *See* RESTRAINT.

outstanding *adjective*
1. Readily attracting notice : arresting, bold, conspicuous, eye-catching, marked, noticeable, observable, pointed, prominent, pronounced, remarkable, salient, signal, striking. ***Idiom:*** sticking out like a sore thumb. *See* SEE. **2.** Far beyond what is usual, normal, or customary : exceptional, extraordinary, magnificent, preeminent, rare, remarkable, singular, towering, uncommon, unusual. *Informal:* standout. *Slang:* awesome, out of sight. *See* BETTER, USUAL. **3.** Owed as a debt : due, owed, owing,

payable, receivable, unpaid, unsettled. *See* PAY.

outstretch *verb*
1. To extend, especially an appendage : reach, stretch (out). *See* REACH. **2.** To move or arrange so as to cover a larger area : expand, extend, fan (out), open (out *or* up), spread, stretch, unfold, unroll. *See* MOVE.

outstrip *verb*
To be greater or better than : best, better[1], exceed, excel, outdo, outmatch, outrun, outshine, pass, surpass, top, transcend. *Informal:* beat. ***Idioms:*** go beyond, go one better. *See* BIG.

outthink *verb*
To get the better of by cleverness or cunning : outmaneuver, outsmart, outwit, overreach. *See* WIN.

outward *adjective*
Appearing as such but not necessarily so : apparent, external, ostensible, ostensive, seeming, superficial. *See* SURFACE.

outwardly *adverb*
On the surface : apparently, evidently, externally, ostensibly, ostensively, seemingly, superficially. ***Idioms:*** on the face of it, to all appearances. *See* SURFACE.

outwear *verb*
To live, exist, or remain longer than : outlast, outlive, survive. *See* CONTINUE.

outweigh *verb*
To make up for : balance, compensate, counterbalance, counterpoise, countervail, neutralize, offset, redeem, set off. *See* SUBSTITUTE.

outwit *verb*
To get the better of by cleverness or cunning : outmaneuver, outsmart, outthink, overreach. *See* WIN.

oval *adjective*
Resembling an egg in shape : ovate, oviform, ovoid, ovoidal. *See* GEOMETRY.

ovate *adjective*
Resembling an egg in shape : oval, oviform, ovoid, ovoidal. *See* GEOMETRY.

ovation *noun*
Approval expressed by clapping : applause, hand, plaudit. *See* PRAISE.

over *adverb*
1. From one end to the other : around, round, through, throughout. *See* PART. **2.** To an end or conclusion : through. *See* START.

overabundance *noun*
A condition of going or being beyond what is needed, desired, or appropriate : embarrassment, excess, excessiveness, exorbitance, extravagance, extravagancy, extravagantness, plethora, superabundance, superfluity, superfluousness, surfeit. *See* EXCESS.

overabundant *adjective*
Exceeding a normal or reasonable limit : excessive, exorbitant, extravagant, extreme, immoderate, inordinate, overmuch, undue. *See* EXCESS.

overage *noun*
An amount or quantity beyond what is needed, desired, or appropriate : excess, fat, glut, overflow, overmuch, overrun, overstock, oversupply, superfluity, surplus, surplusage. *See* EXCESS.

overall *adjective*
Covering a wide scope : all-around, all-inclusive, all-round, broad, broad-spectrum, comprehensive, expansive, extended, extensive, far-ranging, far-reaching, general, global, inclusive, large, sweeping, wide-ranging, wide-reaching, widespread. *See* SPECIFIC.

overbearing *adjective*
1. Overly convinced of one's own superiority and importance : arrogant, haughty, high-and-mighty, insolent, lofty, lordly, overweening, prideful, proud, supercilious, superior. ***Idiom:*** on one's high horse. *See* ATTITUDE. **2.** Tending to dictate : authoritarian, bossy, dictatorial, dogmatic, domineering, imperious, magisterial, masterful, peremptory. *See* OVER.

overbearingness *noun*
The quality of being arrogant : arrogance, haughtiness, hauteur, insolence, loftiness, lordliness, presumption, pride, pridefulness, proudness, superciliousness, superiority. *See* ATTITUDE.

overblown *adjective*
1. Characterized by language that is elevated and sometimes pompous in style : aureate, bombastic, declamatory, flowery, fustian, grandiloquent, high-flown, high-sounding, magniloquent, orotund, rhetorical, sonorous, swollen. *See* PLAIN, STYLE, WORDS. **2.** Filled up with or as if with something insubstantial : flatulent, inflated, tumescent, tumid, turgid, windy. *See* INCREASE, PLAIN. **3.** Having too much flesh : corpulent, fat, fatty, fleshy, gross, obese, overweight, porcine, portly, stout, weighty. *See* FAT.

overcast *verb*
To make dim or indistinct : becloud, bedim, befog, blear, blur, cloud, dim, dull, eclipse, fog, gloom, mist, obfuscate, obscure, overshadow, shadow. *See* CLEAR.

overcharge *verb*
1. To exploit (another) by charging too much

for something : fleece. *Slang:* clip[1], gouge, nick, rip off, scalp, skin, soak. ***Idioms:*** make someone pay through the nose, take someone for a ride, take someone to the cleaners. *See* HONEST. **2.** To make (something) seem greater than is actually the case : exaggerate, hyperbolize, inflate, magnify, overstate. ***Idioms:*** blow up out of proportion, lay it on thick, stretch the truth. *See* INCREASE.

overcome *verb*
1. To win a victory over, as in battle or a competition : beat, best, conquer, defeat, master, prevail against (*or* over), rout, subdue, subjugate, surmount, triumph over, vanquish, worst. *Informal:* trim, whip. *Slang:* ace, lick. ***Idioms:*** carry (*or* win) the day, get (*or* have) the best of, get (*or* have) the better of, go someone one better. *See* WIN. **2.** To affect deeply or completely, as with emotion : crush, engulf, overpower, overwhelm, prostrate. *See* AFFECT.

overconfidence *noun*
Arrogant self-confidence; impudence : assumption, audaciousness, audacity, boldness, brashness, brazenness, cheek, cheekiness, chutzpah, discourtesy, disrespect, effrontery, face, familiarity, forwardness, gall[1], impertinence, impudence, impudency, incivility, insolence, nerve, nerviness, pertness, presumptuousness, pushiness, rudeness, sassiness, sauciness. *Informal:* brass, crust, sauce, uppishness, uppityness. *See* ATTITUDE, COURTESY.

overconfident *adjective*
Rude and disrespectful : assuming, assumptive, audacious, bold, boldfaced, brash, brazen, cheeky, contumelious, familiar, forward, impertinent, impudent, insolent, malapert, nervy, pert, presuming, presumptuous, pushy, sassy, saucy, smart. *Informal:* brassy, flip, fresh, smart-alecky, snippety, snippy, uppish, uppity. *Slang:* wise[1]. *See* ATTITUDE, COURTESY.

overcritical *adjective*
Inclined to judge too severely : captious, carping, censorious, critical, faultfinding, hypercritical. *See* PRAISE.

overdue *adjective*
Not being on time : behindhand, belated, late, tardy. *See* TIME.

overflow *verb*
1. To flow over completely : deluge, drown, engulf, flood, flush, inundate, overwhelm, submerge, whelm. *See* FULL. **2.** To be abundantly filled or richly supplied : abound, bristle, crawl, flow, pullulate, swarm, teem. *See* BIG, RICH.

overflow *noun* **1.** An abundant, usually overwhelming flow or fall, as of a river or rain : alluvion, cataclysm, cataract, deluge, downpour, flood, freshet, inundation, Niagara, torrent. *Chiefly British:* spate. *See* BIG. **2.** An amount or quantity beyond what is needed, desired, or appropriate : excess, fat, glut, overage, overmuch, overrun, overstock, oversupply, superfluity, surplus, surplusage. *See* EXCESS.

overflowing *adjective*
Full to the point of flowing over : awash, big, brimful, brimming. *See* BIG, RICH.

overhang *verb*
1. To curve outward past the normal or usual limit : bag, balloon, beetle, belly, bulge, jut, pouch, project, protrude, protuberate, stand out, stick out. *See* CONVEX. **2.** To be imminent : brew, hang over, impend, loom, lower[1], menace, threaten. *See* NEAR.

overhang *noun* A part that protrudes or extends outward : bulge, jut, knob, knot, projection, protrusion, protuberance. *See* CONVEX.

overhaul *verb*
1. To restore to proper condition or functioning : doctor, fix, fix up, mend, patch, repair[1], revamp, right. ***Idiom:*** set right. *See* HELP. **2.** To catch up with and move past : overtake, pass. *See* APPROACH.

overhaul *noun* A thorough or drastic reorganization : shakeup. *Informal:* housecleaning. *See* CHANGE.

overindulge *verb*
To treat with indulgence and often overtender care : baby, cater, coddle, cosset, indulge, mollycoddle, pamper, spoil. *See* TREAT WELL.

overindulgence *noun*
Immoderate indulgence, as in food or drink : excess, intemperance, surfeit. *See* EXCESS.

overjoy *verb*
To give great or keen pleasure to : cheer, delight, enchant, gladden, gratify, please, pleasure, tickle. *Archaic:* joy. *See* HAPPY, LIKE.

overjoyed *adjective*
Feeling great delight and joy : elate, elated, elevated. *Slang:* up. *See* HAPPY.

overlay *verb*
To extend over the surface of : blanket, cap, cover, spread. *See* PUT ON.

overlong *adjective*
Extending tediously beyond a standard duration : dragging, drawn-out, lengthy, long[1], long-drawn-out, prolonged, protracted. *See* EXCITE, LONG.

overlook *verb*
1. To view broadly or from a height : look

over, scan, survey. *See* SEE. **2.** To rise above, especially so as to afford a view of : command, dominate, tower above (*or* over). *See* OVER. **3.** To direct and watch over the work and performance of others : boss, oversee, superintend, supervise, watch over. *See* OVER.

overlook *noun* A high structure or place commanding a wide view : lookout, observatory, outlook. *See* AWARENESS.

overly *adverb*
Too much : overmuch, unduly. *Informal:* super. *See* EXCESS.

overmuch *adjective*
Exceeding a normal or reasonable limit : excessive, exorbitant, extravagant, extreme, immoderate, inordinate, overabundant, undue. *See* EXCESS.

overmuch *adverb* Too much : overly, unduly. *Informal:* super. *See* EXCESS.

overmuch *noun* An amount or quantity beyond what is needed, desired, or appropriate : excess, fat, glut, overage, overflow, overrun, overstock, oversupply, superfluity, surplus, surplusage. *See* EXCESS.

overpower *verb*
1. To render totally ineffective by decisive defeat : annihilate, crush, drub, overwhelm, smash, steamroller, thrash, trounce, vanquish. *Informal:* massacre, wallop. *Slang:* clobber, cream, shellac, smear. *See* WIN. **2.** To affect deeply or completely, as with emotion : crush, engulf, overcome, overwhelm, prostrate. *See* AFFECT.

overpowering *adjective*
Awesomely or forbiddingly intense : overwhelming, staggering, towering. *See* BIG.

overreach *verb*
1. To go beyond the limits of : exceed, overrun, overstep, surpass, transcend. *See* EXCESS. **2.** To get the better of by cleverness or cunning : outmaneuver, outsmart, outthink, outwit. *See* WIN.

overrun *verb*
1. To enter so as to attack, plunder, destroy, or conquer : foray, invade, raid. *See* ATTACK, ENTER. **2.** To go beyond the limits of : exceed, overreach, overstep, surpass, transcend. *See* EXCESS.

overrun *noun* An amount or quantity beyond what is needed, desired, or appropriate : excess, fat, glut, overage, overflow, overmuch, overstock, oversupply, superfluity, surplus, surplusage. *See* EXCESS.

oversee *verb*
To direct and watch over the work and performance of others : boss, overlook, superintend, supervise, watch over. *See* OVER.

overseer *noun*
Someone who directs and supervises workers : boss, director, foreman, foreperson, forewoman, head, manager, superintendent, supervisor, taskmaster, taskmistress. *Informal:* straw boss. *Slang:* chief. *See* OVER.

overshadow *verb*
To make dim or indistinct : becloud, bedim, befog, blear, blur, cloud, dim, dull, eclipse, fog, gloom, mist, obfuscate, obscure, overcast, shadow. *See* CLEAR.

oversight *noun*
An act or instance of neglecting : disregard, neglect, slight. *See* CARE FOR, CONCERN.

oversize *adjective*
Extremely large; having great mass : bulky, massive, oversized. *See* BIG.

oversized *adjective*
Extremely large; having great mass : bulky, massive, oversize. *See* BIG.

oversleep *verb*
To sleep longer than intended : sleep in. *See* AWARENESS.

overstate *verb*
To make (something) seem greater than is actually the case : exaggerate, hyperbolize, inflate, magnify, overcharge. ***Idioms:*** blow up out of proportion, lay it on thick, stretch the truth. *See* INCREASE.

overstatement *noun*
The act or an instance of exaggerating : exaggeration, hyperbole, hyperbolism, tall talk. *See* INCREASE.

overstep *verb*
To go beyond the limits of : exceed, overreach, overrun, surpass, transcend. *See* EXCESS.

overstock *noun*
An amount or quantity beyond what is needed, desired, or appropriate : excess, fat, glut, overage, overflow, overmuch, overrun, oversupply, superfluity, surplus, surplusage. *See* EXCESS.

oversupply *noun*
An amount or quantity beyond what is needed, desired, or appropriate : excess, fat, glut, overage, overflow, overmuch, overrun, overstock, superfluity, surplus, surplusage. *See* EXCESS.

overtake *verb*
1. To come up even with another : catch up. *See* SEEK, WIN. **2.** To catch up with and move past : overhaul, pass. *See* APPROACH.

overthrow *verb*
1. To turn or cause to turn from either a vertical or horizontal position : capsize, knock over,

overturn, topple, turn over, upset. *See* CHANGE, HORIZONTAL, MOVE. **2.** To bring about the downfall of : bring down, overturn, subvert, topple, tumble, unhorse. *See* HELP.

overthrow *noun* The act of defeating or the condition of being defeated : beating, defeat, drubbing, rout, thrashing, vanquishment. *Informal:* massacre, trimming, whipping. *Slang:* dusting, licking. *See* WIN.

overture *noun*
1. A short section of preliminary remarks : foreword, induction, introduction, lead-in, preamble, preface, prelude, prolegomenon, prologue. *See* START, WORDS. **2.** A preliminary action intended to elicit a favorable response : advance (used in plural), approach. *See* APPROACH.

overturn *verb*
1. To turn or cause to turn from a vertical or horizontal position : capsize, knock over, overthrow, topple, turn over, upset. *See* CHANGE, HORIZONTAL, MOVE. **2.** To bring about the downfall of : bring down, overthrow, subvert, topple, tumble, unhorse. *See* HELP.

overturned *adjective*
Turned over completely : capsized, inverted, upset, upside-down, upturned. *See* HORIZONTAL.

overused *adjective*
Without freshness or appeal because of overuse : banal, bromidic, clichéd, commonplace, corny, hackneyed, musty, overworked, platitudinal, platitudinous, shopworn, stale, stereotyped, stereotypic, stereotypical, threadbare, timeworn, tired, trite, warmed-over, well-worn, worn-out. *See* EXCITE, USUAL.

overview *noun*
A general or comprehensive view or treatment : survey. *See* THOUGHTS.

overweening *adjective*
Overly convinced of one's own superiority and importance : arrogant, haughty, high-and-mighty, insolent, lofty, lordly, overbearing, prideful, proud, supercilious, superior. ***Idiom:*** on one's high horse. *See* ATTITUDE.

overweight *adjective*
Having too much flesh : corpulent, fat, fatty, fleshy, gross, obese, overblown, porcine, portly, stout, weighty. *See* FAT.

overwhelm *verb*
1. To flow over completely : deluge, drown, engulf, flood, flush, inundate, overflow, submerge, whelm. *See* FULL. **2.** To render totally ineffective by decisive defeat : annihilate, crush, drub, overpower, smash, steamroller, thrash, trounce, vanquish. *Informal:* massacre, wallop. *Slang:* clobber, cream, shellac, smear. *See* WIN. **3.** To affect deeply or completely, as with emotion : crush, engulf, overcome, overpower, prostrate. *See* AFFECT. **4.** To impair severely something such as the spirit, health, or effectiveness of : break, crush, destroy, ruin. *See* HELP. **5.** To affect as if by an outpouring of water : deluge, flood, inundate, swamp, whelm. *See* FULL.

overwhelming *adjective*
Awesomely or forbiddingly intense : overpowering, staggering, towering. *See* BIG.

overworked *adjective*
Without freshness or appeal because of overuse : banal, bromidic, clichéd, commonplace, corny, hackneyed, musty, overused, platitudinal, platitudinous, shopworn, stale, stereotyped, stereotypic, stereotypical, threadbare, timeworn, tired, trite, warmed-over, well-worn, worn-out. *See* EXCITE, USUAL.

oviform *adjective*
Resembling an egg in shape : oval, ovate, ovoid, ovoidal. *See* GEOMETRY.

ovoid *adjective*
Resembling an egg in shape : oval, ovate, oviform, ovoidal. *See* GEOMETRY.

ovoidal *adjective*
Resembling an egg in shape : oval, ovate, oviform, ovoid. *See* GEOMETRY.

owed *adjective*
Owed as a debt : due, outstanding, owing, payable, receivable, unpaid, unsettled. *See* PAY.

owing *adjective*
Owed as a debt : due, outstanding, owed, payable, receivable, unpaid, unsettled. *See* PAY.

own *verb*
1. To keep at one's disposal : have, hold, possess, retain. *See* KEEP. **2.** To recognize, often reluctantly, the reality or truth of. Also used with *up* : acknowledge, admit, avow, concede, confess, grant. *Slang:* fess up. *Chiefly Regional:* allow. *See* AFFIRM, KNOWLEDGE.

owner *noun*
A person who has legal title to property : holder, master, possessor, proprietor. *See* OWNED.

ownership *noun*
The fact of possessing or the legal right to possess something : dominion, possession, proprietorship, title. *See* OWNED.

ox *noun*
A large, ungainly, and dull-witted person : gawk, hulk, lout, lump[1], oaf. *Informal:* lummox. *Slang:* klutz, lug[1], meatball, meathead. *See* ABILITY.

·P·

pa *noun*
Informal. A male parent : father, sire. *Informal:* dad, daddy, papa, pappy[2], pop[2]. *Slang:* old man. *See* KIN.

pabulum *noun*
1. Something fit to be eaten : aliment, bread, comestible, diet, edible, esculent, fare, food, foodstuff, meat, nourishment, nurture, nutriment, nutrition, pap, provender, provision (used in plural), sustenance, victual. *Slang:* chow, eats, grub. *See* INGESTION. **2.** That which sustains the mind or spirit : aliment, bread, food, nourishment, nutriment, pap, sustenance. *See* CARE FOR, INGESTION.

pace *noun*
Rate of motion or performance : speed, tempo, velocity. *Informal:* clip[1]. *See* FAST.
pace *verb* To go on foot : ambulate, foot, step, tread, walk. *Slang:* hoof. ***Idiom:*** foot it. *See* MOVE.

pacific *adjective*
Inclined or disposed to peace; not quarrelsome or unruly : irenic, pacifical, pacifist, pacifistic, peaceable, peaceful. *See* PEACE.

pacifical *adjective*
Inclined or disposed to peace; not quarrelsome or unruly : irenic, pacific, pacifist, pacifistic, peaceable, peaceful. *See* PEACE.

pacifist *adjective*
Inclined or disposed to peace; not quarrelsome or unruly : irenic, pacific, pacifical, pacifistic, peaceable, peaceful. *See* PEACE.

pacifistic *adjective*
Inclined or disposed to peace; not quarrelsome or unruly : irenic, pacific, pacifical, pacifist, peaceable, peaceful. *See* PEACE.

pacify *verb*
To ease the anger or agitation of : appease, assuage, calm (down), conciliate, dulcify, gentle, mollify, placate, propitiate, soften, soothe, sweeten. ***Idiom:*** pour oil on troubled water. *See* CALM.

pack *noun*
1. *Informal.* A great deal : abundance, mass, mountain, much, plenty, profusion, wealth, world. *Informal:* barrel, heap, lot, peck[2], pile. *Regional:* power, sight. *See* BIG. **2.** An organized group of criminals, hoodlums, or wrongdoers : band[2], gang, ring[1]. *Informal:* mob. *See* GROUP.
pack *verb* **1.** To make or become full; put as much into as can be held : charge, fill, freight, heap, load, pile. *See* FULL. **2.** To fill to excess by compressing or squeezing tightly : cram, crowd, jam, load, mob, stuff. *Informal:* jam-pack. *See* FULL, TIGHTEN. **3.** *Informal.* To hold on one's person : bear, carry, have, possess. *See* OWNED.

package *verb*
To cover and tie (something), as with paper and string : do up, wrap. *See* PUT ON.

packed *adjective*
1. Completely filled : brimful, brimming, bursting, chockablock, full, replete. *See* FULL. **2.** Having all parts near to each other : close, compact[1], crowded, dense, thick, tight. *See* TIGHTEN.

pact *noun*
1. An act or state of agreeing between parties regarding a course of action : accord, agreement, arrangement, bargain, compact[2], deal, understanding. *See* AGREE. **2.** A formal, usually written settlement between nations : accord, agreement, concord, convention, treaty. *See* AGREE, POLITICS. **3.** A legally binding arrangement between parties : agreement, bond, compact[2], contract, convention, covenant. *See* AGREE.

pain *noun*
1. A sensation of physical discomfort occurring as the result of disease or injury : ache, pang, prick, prickle, smart, soreness, stab, sting, stitch, throe, twinge. *Informal:* misery. *See* PAIN. **2.** A state of physical or mental suffering : affliction, agony, anguish, distress, hurt, misery, torment, torture, woe, wound, wretchedness. *See* HAPPY. **3.** Attentiveness to detail. Used in plural : care, carefulness, fastidiousness, meticulousness, painstaking, punctiliousness, scrupulousness, thoroughness. *See* CAREFUL. **4.** The use of energy to do something. Used in plural : effort, endeavor, exertion, strain[1], striving, struggle, trouble, while. *Informal:* elbow grease. *See* WORK. **5.** *Informal.* One that makes another totally miserable by causing sharp pain and irritation :

thorn, trial. *Idioms:* pain in the neck, thorn in the flesh (*or* side). *See* PAIN.

pain *verb* **1.** To cause suffering or painful sorrow to : aggrieve, distress, grieve, hurt, injure, wound. *See* HAPPY. **2.** To have or cause a feeling of physical pain or discomfort : ache, hurt, pang, twinge. *See* PAIN.

painful *adjective*
1. Marked by, causing, or experiencing physical pain : aching, achy, afflictive, hurtful, nagging, smarting, sore. *See* PAIN. **2.** Difficult to accept : bitter, distasteful, indigestible, unpalatable. *See* LIKE.

painstaking *adjective*
Showing or marked by attentiveness to all aspects or details : careful, fastidious, meticulous, punctilious, scrupulous. *See* CAREFUL.

painstaking *noun* Attentiveness to detail : care, carefulness, fastidiousness, meticulousness, pain (used in plural), punctiliousness, scrupulousness, thoroughness. *See* CAREFUL.

pair *noun*
1. Two items of the same kind together : brace, couple, couplet, doublet, duet, duo, match, two, twosome, yoke. *See* GROUP, SAME. **2.** Two persons united, as by marriage : couple, duo, twosome. *See* GROUP.

paired *adjective*
Consisting of two identical or similar related things, parts, or elements : double, dual, twin. *See* SAME.

pal *noun*
1. *Informal.* A person whom one knows well, likes, and trusts : amigo, brother, chum, confidant, confidante, familiar, friend, intimate[1], mate. *Informal:* bud[2], buddy. *Slang:* sidekick. *See* LOVE. **2.** *Informal.* One who shares interests or activities with another : associate, chum, companion, comrade, crony, fellow, mate. *Informal:* buddy. *See* NEAR.

paladin *noun*
A person revered especially for noble courage : hero. *See* FEAR.

palatial *adjective*
Characterized by extravagant, ostentatious magnificence : lavish, lush[1], luxuriant, luxurious, opulent, plush, rich, sumptuous. *Informal:* plushy. *See* RICH.

palaver *noun*
Incessant and usually inconsequential talk : babble, blab, blabber, chat, chatter, chitchat, jabber, prate, prattle, small talk. *Slang:* gab, gas, yak. *See* WORDS.

palaver *verb* To talk volubly, persistently, and usually inconsequentially : babble, blabber, chatter, chitchat, clack, jabber, prate, prattle, rattle (on), run on. *Informal:* go on, spiel. *Slang:* gab, gas, jaw, yak. *Idioms:* run off at the mouth, shoot the breeze (*or* bull). *See* WORDS.

pale *adjective*
1. Lacking color : ashen, ashy, bloodless, cadaverous, colorless, livid, lurid, pallid, pasty, sallow, wan, waxen. *See* COLORS. **2.** Of a light color or complexion : alabaster, fair, ivory, light[1]. *See* COLORS. **3.** Being weak in quality or substance : anemic, bloodless, pallid, waterish, watery. *See* STRONG.

pale *verb* To lose normal coloration; turn pale : blanch, bleach, etiolate, wan. *See* COLORS.

palinode *noun*
A formal statement of disavowal : abjuration, recantation, retractation, retraction, withdrawal. *See* ACCEPT.

pall *verb*
To satisfy to the full or to excess : cloy, engorge, glut, gorge, sate, satiate, surfeit. *See* EXCESS, FULL.

palliate *verb*
1. To conceal or make light of a fault or offense : explain away, extenuate, gloss over, gloze (over), sleek over, whitewash. *See* SHOW. **2.** To make less severe or more bearable : allay, alleviate, assuage, comfort, ease, lessen, lighten[2], mitigate, relieve. *See* INCREASE.

palliation *noun*
Freedom, especially from pain : alleviation, assuagement, ease, mitigation, relief. *See* INCREASE.

pallid *adjective*
1. Lacking color : ashen, ashy, bloodless, cadaverous, colorless, livid, lurid, pale, pasty, sallow, wan, waxen. *See* COLORS. **2.** Being weak in quality or substance : anemic, bloodless, pale, waterish, watery. *See* STRONG.

palm off *verb*
To offer or put into circulation (an inferior or spurious item) : fob off, foist, pass off, put off. *See* HONEST.

palpability *noun*
The quality or condition of being discernible by touch : tactility, tangibility, tangibleness, touchableness. *See* TOUCH.

palpable *adjective*
1. Discernible by touch : tactile, tangible, touchable. *See* TOUCH. **2.** Capable of being noticed or apprehended mentally : appreciable, detectable, discernible, distinguishable, noticeable, observable, perceivable, perceptible, ponderable, sensible. *See* KNOWLEDGE.

palpate *verb*
To bring the hands or fingers, for example, into contact with so as to give or receive a physical sensation : feel, finger, handle, touch. *See* TOUCH.

palpation *noun*
An act of touching : feeling, touch. *See* TOUCH.

palpitate *verb*
To make rhythmic contractions, sounds, or movements : beat, pound, pulsate, pulse, throb. *See* REPETITION, SOUNDS.

palpitation *noun*
A periodic contraction or sound of something coursing : beat, pulsation, pulse, throb. *See* REPETITION, SOUNDS.

palter *verb*
1. To stray from truthfulness or sincerity : equivocate, prevaricate, shuffle. *See* TRUE.
2. To argue about the terms, as of a sale : bargain, dicker, haggle, higgle, huckster, negotiate. *See* AGREE.

paltriness *noun*
Contemptible unimportance : inconsiderableness, negligibility, negligibleness, pettiness, smallness, triviality, trivialness. *See* IMPORTANT.

paltry *adjective*
1. Contemptibly unimportant : inconsiderable, negligible, niggling, nugatory, petty, picayune, piddling, small, small-minded, trifling. *Slang:* measly. ***Idiom:*** of no account. *See* IMPORTANT. **2.** Of decidedly inferior quality : base[2], cheap, lousy, miserable, poor, rotten, shoddy, sleazy, trashy. *Informal:* cheesy. *Slang:* crummy, schlocky. *See* GOOD.

pamper *verb*
To treat with indulgence and often overtender care : baby, cater, coddle, cosset, indulge, mollycoddle, overindulge, spoil. *See* TREAT WELL.

pan *noun*
1. *Slang.* The front surface of the head : countenance, face, feature (often used in plural), muzzle, visage. *Informal:* mug. *Slang:* kisser, map, puss. *See* PRECEDE. **2.** *Informal.* A comment expressing fault : blame, censure, condemnation, criticism, denunciation, reprehension, reprobation. *Slang:* knock. *See* PRAISE.
pan *verb Informal.* To find fault with : blame, censure, criticize, fault, rap[1]. *Informal:* cut up. *Slang:* knock. *See* PRAISE.
pan out *verb* To turn out well : come off, go, go over, succeed, work, work out. *Slang:* click. *See* THRIVE.

panacea *noun*
Something believed to cure all human disorders : catholicon, cure-all. *See* HELP.

pandemic *adjective*
So pervasive and all-inclusive as to exist in or affect the whole world : catholic, cosmic, cosmopolitan, ecumenical, global, planetary, universal, worldwide. *See* LIMITED, SPECIFIC.

pandemonium *noun*
Sounds or a sound, especially when loud, confused, or disagreeable : babel, clamor, din, hubbub, hullabaloo, noise, racket, rumpus, tumult, uproar. *See* SOUNDS.

panegyric *noun*
An expression of warm approval : acclaim, acclamation, applause, celebration, commendation, compliment, encomium, eulogy, kudos, laudation, plaudit, praise. *See* PRAISE.

panegyrize *verb*
To pay tribute or homage to : acclaim, celebrate, eulogize, exalt, extol, glorify, hail[2], honor, laud, magnify, praise. ***Idiom:*** sing someone's praises. *See* PRAISE.

pang *noun*
A sensation of physical discomfort occurring as the result of disease or injury : ache, pain, prick, prickle, smart, soreness, stab, sting, stitch, throe, twinge. *Informal:* misery. *See* PAIN.
pang *verb* To have or cause a feeling of physical pain or discomfort : ache, hurt, pain, twinge. *See* PAIN.

Panglossian *adjective*
Expecting a favorable outcome or dwelling on hopeful aspects : optimistic, roseate, rose-colored, rosy, sanguine. *Informal:* upbeat. ***Idioms:*** looking on the bright side, looking through rose-colored glasses. *See* HOPE.

panhandle *verb*
Informal. To ask or ask for as charity : beg, bum[1], cadge. *Slang:* mooch. *See* REQUEST.

panhandler *noun*
Informal. One who begs habitually or for a living : almsman, almswoman, beggar, cadger, mendicant. *Slang:* bummer, moocher. *See* REQUEST.

panic *noun*
1. Great agitation and anxiety caused by the expectation or the realization of danger : affright, alarm, apprehension, dread, fear, fearfulness, fright, funk, horror, terror, trepidation. *Slang:* cold feet. ***Idiom:*** fear and trembling. *See* FEAR. **2.** *Slang.* Something or someone uproariously funny or absurd : absurdity. *Informal:* hoot, joke, laugh, scream. *Slang:* gas, howl,

riot. *Idiom:* a laugh a minute. *See* LAUGHTER.

panic *verb* To fill with fear : affright, alarm, frighten, scare, scarify[2], startle, terrify, terrorize. *Archaic:* fright. *Idioms:* make one's blood run cold, make one's hair stand on end, scare silly (*or* stiff), scare the daylights out of. *See* FEAR.

panicky *adjective*
Filled with fear or terror : afraid, aghast, apprehensive, fearful, fearsome, funky. *Regional:* afeard, ascared. *See* FEAR.

panoply *noun*
An impressive or ostentatious exhibition : array, display, parade, pomp, show, spectacle. *See* SHOW.

panorama *noun*
That which is or can be seen : lookout, outlook, perspective, prospect, scene, sight, view, vista. *See* SEE.

pan out *verb* See **pan.**

pant *verb*
1. To breathe hard : blow[1], gasp, huff, puff. *See* BREATH. **2.** To utter in a breathless manner : gasp, heave. *See* BREATH, WORDS. **3.** To have a strong longing for : ache, covet, desire, hanker, long[2], pine, want, wish, yearn. *Informal:* hone[2]. *See* DESIRE.

pap *noun*
1. Something fit to be eaten : aliment, bread, comestible, diet, edible, esculent, fare, food, foodstuff, meat, nourishment, nurture, nutriment, nutrition, pabulum, provender, provision (used in plural), sustenance, victual. *Slang:* chow, eats, grub. *See* INGESTION. **2.** That which sustains the mind or spirit : aliment, bread, food, nourishment, nutriment, pabulum, sustenance. *See* CARE FOR, INGESTION.

papa *noun*
Informal. A male parent : father, sire. *Informal:* dad, daddy, pa, pappy[2], pop[2]. *Slang:* old man. *See* KIN.

paper *noun*
A relatively brief discourse written especially as an exercise : composition, essay, theme. *See* WORDS.

pappy[1] *adjective*
Yielding easily to pressure or weight; not firm : mushy, pulpous, pulpy, quaggy, soft, spongy, squashy, squishy, yielding. *See* RESIST.

pappy[2] *noun*
Informal. A male parent : father, sire. *Informal:* dad, daddy, pa, papa, pop[2]. *Slang:* old man. *See* KIN.

par *noun*
1. Something, as a type, number, quantity, or degree, that represents a midpoint between extremes on a scale of valuation : average, mean[3], median, medium, norm. *See* USUAL. **2.** The state of being equivalent : equality, equation, equivalence, equivalency, parity, sameness. *See* SAME.

parade *noun*
1. A formal military inspection : review. *See* INVESTIGATE. **2.** An impressive or ostentatious exhibition : array, display, panoply, pomp, show, spectacle. *See* SHOW.

parade *verb* To make a public and usually ostentatious show of : brandish, display, disport, exhibit, expose, flash, flaunt, show (off), sport. *See* SHOW.

paradigm *noun*
One that is worthy of imitation or duplication : beau ideal, example, exemplar, ideal, mirror, model, pattern, standard. *See* GOOD.

paradigmatic *adjective*
Having the nature of, constituting, or serving as a type : archetypal, archetypic, archetypical, classic, classical, model, prototypal, prototypic, prototypical, quintessential, representative, typic, typical. *See* SAME, USUAL.

paradisaic *adjective*
Of or relating to heaven : celestial, divine, heavenly, paradisaical, paradisal, paradisiac, paradisiacal. *See* RELIGION.

paradisaical *adjective*
Of or relating to heaven : celestial, divine, heavenly, paradisaic, paradisal, paradisiac, paradisiacal. *See* RELIGION.

paradisal *adjective*
Of or relating to heaven : celestial, divine, heavenly, paradisaic, paradisaical, paradisiac, paradisiacal. *See* RELIGION.

paradise *noun*
A state of elated bliss : ecstasy, heaven, rapture, seventh heaven, transport. *Informal:* cloud nine. *See* HAPPY.

paradisiac *adjective*
Of or relating to heaven : celestial, divine, heavenly, paradisaic, paradisaical, paradisal, paradisiacal. *See* RELIGION.

paradisiacal *adjective*
Of or relating to heaven : celestial, divine, heavenly, paradisaic, paradisaical, paradisal, paradisiac. *See* RELIGION.

paragon *noun*
A person or thing so excellent as to have no equal or match : nonesuch, nonpareil, phoenix. *See* GOOD.

paragraph *noun*
A usually brief detail of news or information :

bit[1], item, piece, squib, story. *See* WORDS.

parallel *adjective*
1. Lying in the same plane and not intersecting : collateral. ***Idiom:*** side by side. *See* GEOMETRY. **2.** Possessing the same or almost the same characteristics : alike, analogous, comparable, corresponding, equivalent, like[2], similar, uniform. *See* SAME.
parallel *noun* Something closely resembling or analogous to something else : analogue, congener, correlate, correlative, correspondent, counterpart, match. *See* SAME.
parallel *verb* **1.** To be equal or alike : compare, correspond, equal, match, measure up, touch. *Informal:* stack up. *See* SAME. **2.** To represent as similar : analogize, assimilate, compare, equate, identify, liken, match. *See* SAME.

parallelism *noun*
The quality or state of being alike : affinity, alikeness, analogy, comparison, correspondence, likeness, resemblance, similarity, similitude, uniformity, uniformness. *See* SAME.

paralyze *verb*
1. To render powerless or motionless, as by inflicting severe injury : cripple, disable, immobilize, incapacitate, knock out. ***Idiom:*** put out of action (*or* commission). *See* HELP. **2.** To render helpless, as by emotion : benumb, numb, petrify, stun, stupefy, wither. *See* AFFECT.

paramount *adjective*
1. Most important, influential, or significant : capital, cardinal, chief, first, foremost, key, leading, main, major, number one, premier, primary, prime, principal, top. *See* IMPORTANT. **2.** Exercising controlling power or influence : commanding, controlling, dominant, dominating, dominative, governing, preponderant, regnant, reigning, ruling. *See* OVER.

paramountcy *noun*
The condition or fact of being dominant : ascendance, ascendancy, dominance, domination, predominance, preeminence, preponderance, preponderancy, prepotency, supremacy. *See* OVER.

paramour *noun*
A person's regular sexual partner : lover. *See* SEX.

paraphernalia *noun*
Things needed for a task, journey, or other purpose : accouterment (often used in plural), apparatus, equipment, gear, material (used in plural), materiel, outfit, rig, tackle, thing (used in plural), turnout. *See* MEANS.

paraphrase *noun*
A restating of something in other, especially simpler, words : rendering, restatement, translation, version. *See* WORDS.
paraphrase *verb* To express the meaning of in other, especially simpler, words : render, rephrase, restate, reword, translate. *See* WORDS.

parasite *noun*
One who depends on another for support without reciprocating : bloodsucker, hanger-on, leech, sponge. *Slang:* freeloader. *See* DEPENDENCE.

parasitic *adjective*
Of or characteristic of a parasite : bloodsucking, parasitical. *Slang:* freeloading. *See* DEPENDENCE.

parasitical *adjective*
Of or characteristic of a parasite : bloodsucking, parasitic. *Slang:* freeloading. *See* DEPENDENCE.

parboil *verb*
To cook (food) in liquid heated to the point of steaming : boil, simmer, stew. *See* INGESTION.

parcel *noun*
A piece of land : lot, plot, tract. *See* TERRITORY.
parcel out *verb* To give out in portions or shares : deal (out), dispense, distribute, divide, dole out, portion (out), ration (out), share. *Slang:* divvy. *See* COLLECT.

parcel out *verb* See **parcel.**

parch *verb*
To make or become free of moisture : dehydrate, desiccate, dry (out), exsiccate. *See* DRY.

parched *adjective*
Needing or desiring drink : dry, thirsty. *Archaic:* athirst. *See* DRY.

pardon *verb*
To grant forgiveness to or for : condone, excuse, forgive, remit. ***Idiom:*** forgive and forget. *See* FORGIVENESS.
pardon *noun* The act or an instance of forgiving : absolution, amnesty, condonation, excuse, forgiveness, remission. *See* FORGIVENESS.

pardonable *adjective*
Admitting of forgiveness or pardon : excusable, forgivable, venial. *See* FORGIVENESS.

pare *verb*
1. To remove the skin of : decorticate, peel, scale[1], skin, strip[1]. *See* PUT ON. **2.** To decrease, as in length or amount, by or as if by severing or excising : chop[1], clip[1], crop, cut, cut back, cut down, lop[1], lower[2], prune, shear, slash, trim, truncate. *See* INCREASE.

parent *noun*
1. A person from whom one is descended : ancestor, antecedent, ascendant, father, forebear, forefather, foremother, mother, progenitor. *Archaic:* predecessor. *See* KIN, PRECEDE. **2.** One that creates, founds, or originates : architect, author, creator, entrepreneur, father, founder[2], inventor, maker, originator, patriarch. *See* START. **3.** A point of origination : beginning, derivation, fount, fountain, fountainhead, mother, origin, provenance, provenience, root[1], rootstock, source, spring, well[1]. *See* START.
parent *verb* To cause to come into existence : beget, breed, create, engender, father, hatch, make, originate, procreate, produce, sire, spawn. ***Idiom:*** give birth (*or* rise) to. *See* MAKE.

parentage *noun*
One's ancestors or their character or one's ancestral derivation : ancestry, birth, blood, bloodline, descent, extraction, family, genealogy, line, lineage, origin, pedigree, seed, stock. *See* KIN, PRECEDE.

parenthesis *noun*
An instance of digressing : aside, deviation, digression, divagation, divergence, divergency, excursion, excursus, irrelevancy, tangent. *See* APPROACH.

parenthetic *adjective*
Marked by or given to digression : digressive, discursive, excursive, parenthetical, rambling, tangential. *See* APPROACH.

parenthetical *adjective*
Marked by or given to digression : digressive, discursive, excursive, parenthetic, rambling, tangential. *See* APPROACH.

parity *noun*
The state of being equivalent : equality, equation, equivalence, equivalency, par, sameness. *See* SAME.

parlance *noun*
Choice of words and the way in which they are used : diction, phrase, phraseology, phrasing, verbalism, wordage, wording. *See* WORDS.

parley *noun*
1. The act or process of dealing with another to reach an agreement : negotiation, talk (often used in plural). *See* WORDS. **2.** An exchange of views in an attempt to reach a decision : conference, consultation, counsel, deliberation. *See* WORDS. **3.** A meeting for the exchange of views : colloquium, conference, discussion, seminar. *Informal:* powwow. *Slang:* rap session. *See* MEET, WORDS.
parley *verb* To meet and exchange views to reach a decision : advise, confer, consult, deliberate, talk. *Informal:* powwow. *See* COLLECT, MEET, WORDS.

parlous *adjective*
Involving possible risk, loss, or injury : adventurous, chancy, dangerous, hazardous, jeopardous, perilous, risky, treacherous, unsafe, venturesome, venturous. *Slang:* hairy. *See* SAFETY.

parochial *adjective*
Having the restricted outlook often characteristic of geographic isolation : insular, limited, local, narrow, narrow-minded, provincial, small-town. *See* LIMITED.

parody *noun*
1. A usually amusing caricature of another : imitation. *Informal:* takeoff. *See* LAUGHTER, RESPECT, SAME. **2.** A false, derisive, or impudent imitation of something : burlesque, caricature, farce, mock, mockery, sham, travesty. *See* RESPECT, SAME.
parody *verb* To copy (the manner or expression of another), especially in an exaggerated or mocking way : ape, burlesque, caricature, imitate, mimic, mock, travesty. ***Idiom:*** do a takeoff on. *See* SAME.

paroxysm *noun*
1. A condition of anguished struggle and disorder : convulsion, throe (used in plural). *See* CALM. **2.** A violent, excruciating seizure of pain : cramp[1], shoot, spasm, throe. *See* PAIN.

parrot *noun*
One who mindlessly imitates another : echo, imitator, mimic. *See* SAME.
parrot *verb* To copy (another) slavishly : echo, image, imitate, mimic, mirror, reflect, repeat. *See* SAME.

parry *verb*
To turn or drive away : beat off, fend (off), keep off, repel, repulse, ward off. *See* ALLOW, STRIKE.

parsimonious *adjective*
Ungenerously or pettily reluctant to spend money : cheap, close, close-fisted, costive, hard-fisted, mean[2], miserly, niggard, niggardly, penny-pinching, penurious, petty, pinching, stingy, tight, tightfisted. *See* GIVE.

parson *noun*
A person ordained for service in a Christian church : churchman, churchwoman, clergyman, clergywoman, cleric, clerical, clerk, divine, ecclesiastic, minister, preacher. *Informal:* reverend. *See* RELIGION.

part *noun*
1. One of the parts into which something is

divided : division, member, piece, portion, section, segment, subdivision. *See* PART. **2.** That which is allotted : allocation, allotment, allowance, dole, lot, measure, portion, quantum, quota, ration, share, split. *Informal:* cut. *Slang:* divvy. *See* COLLECT. **3.** One of the individual entities contributing to a whole : building block, component, constituent, element, factor, ingredient, integrant. *See* PART. **4.** A particular subdivision of a written work : passage, section, segment. *See* PART. **5.** One's proper or expected function in a common effort : piece, role, share. *See* DO, PARTICIPATE. **6.** One of two or more opposing opinions, actions, or attitudes, as in a disagreement : side. *See* PERSPECTIVE.

part *verb* **1.** To make a division into parts, sections, or branches : break up, dissever, divide, partition, section, segment, separate. *See* ASSEMBLE, PART. **2.** To become or cause to become apart one from another : break, detach, disjoin, disjoint, disunite, divide, divorce, separate, split (up). ***Idioms:*** part company, set at odds. *See* ASSEMBLE. **3.** To terminate a relationship or an association by or as if by leaving one another : break off, break up, separate. *Informal:* split (up). ***Idioms:*** call it quits, come to a parting of the ways, part company. *See* ASSEMBLE, CONTINUE.

part *adjective* Relating to or affecting only a part; not total : fractional, fragmentary, partial. *See* PART.

partake *verb*

1. To have a share, as in an act or result; have a hand in : conduce, contribute, participate, share. ***Idiom:*** take part. *See* PARTICIPATE, START. **2.** To involve oneself in (an activity) : carry on, engage, have, indulge, participate. ***Idiom:*** take part. *See* PARTICIPATE. **3.** To take (food) into the body as nourishment : consume, devour, eat, fare, ingest. *Slang:* chow. ***Idioms:*** break bread, have (*or* take) a bite. *See* INGESTION.

partial *adjective*

1. Relating to or affecting only a part; not total : fractional, fragmentary, part. *See* PART. **2.** Disposed to favor one over another : favorable, preferential. *See* FAIR. **3.** Exhibiting bias : biased, one-sided, partisan, prejudiced, prejudicial, prepossessed, tendentious. *See* LIKE, STRAIGHT.

partiality *noun*

1. Favorable or preferential bias : favor, favoritism, partialness, preference. *See* FAIR. **2.** An inclination for or against that inhibits impartial judgment : bias, one-sidedness, partisanship, prejudice, prepossession, tendentiousness. *See* AFFECT, LIKE, STRAIGHT. **3.** A liking for something : appetite, fondness, preference, relish, taste, weakness. *See* LIKE. **4.** An inclination to something : bent, bias, cast, disposition, leaning, penchant, predilection, predisposition, proclivity, proneness, propensity, squint, tendency, trend, turn. *See* APPROACH, LIKE.

partialness *noun*

Favorable or preferential bias : favor, favoritism, partiality, preference. *See* FAIR.

participant *noun*

One who participates : actor, party, player. *See* PARTICIPATE.

participate *verb*

1. To involve oneself in (an activity) : carry on, engage, have, indulge, partake. ***Idiom:*** take part. *See* PARTICIPATE. **2.** To have a share, as in an act or result; have a hand in : conduce, contribute, partake, share. ***Idiom:*** take part. *See* PARTICIPATE, START.

participation *noun*

The act or fact of participating : involvement, sharing. *See* PARTICIPATE.

particle *noun*

A tiny amount : bit[1], crumb, dab[1], dash, dot, dram, drop, fragment, grain, iota, jot, minim, mite, modicum, molecule, ort, ounce, scrap[1], scruple, shred, smidgen, speck, tittle, trifle, whit. *Chiefly British:* spot. *See* BIG.

particular *adjective*

1. Being or related to a distinct entity : discrete, individual, separate, single, singular. *See* INCLUDE. **2.** Of, relating to, or intended for a distinctive thing or group : especial, individual, special, specific. *See* SPECIFIC. **3.** Alone in a given category : lone, one, only, separate, single, singular, sole, solitary, unique. ***Idioms:*** first and last, one and only. *See* INCLUDE. **4.** Fixed and distinct from others : express, set[1], special, specific. *See* SPECIFIC. **5.** Characterized by attention to detail : blow-by-blow, circumstantial, detailed, full, minute[2], thorough. *See* SPECIFIC. **6.** Very difficult to please : choosy, dainty, exacting, fastidious, finical, finicky, fussy, meticulous, nice, persnickety, squeamish. *Informal:* picky. *See* ACCEPT.

particular *noun* **1.** An individually considered portion of a whole : article, detail, element, item, point. *See* PART. **2.** A small, often specialized element of a whole : detail, fine print, item, technicality. *See* GROUP. **3.** One of the conditions or facts attending an event and having some bearing on it : circumstance, detail, fact, factor. *See* REAL.

particularity *noun*
The quality of being individual : discreteness, distinctiveness, individuality, separateness, singularity. *See* INCLUDE.

particularize *verb*
To make specific : detail, specify, stipulate. *See* SPECIFIC.

parting *noun*
1. The act or an instance of separating one thing from another : detachment, disjunction, disjuncture, disseverance, disseverment, disunion, division, divorce, divorcement, partition, separation, severance, split. *See* ASSEMBLE, PART. **2.** A separation of two or more people : adieu, farewell, good-bye, leave-taking, valediction. *See* APPROACH.
parting *adjective* Of, done, given, or said on departing : departing, farewell, good-bye, valedictory. *See* APPROACH.

partisan *noun*
One who supports and adheres to another : adherent, cohort, disciple, follower, henchman, minion, satellite, supporter. *See* OVER, PRECEDE.
partisan *adjective* Exhibiting bias : biased, one-sided, partial, prejudiced, prejudicial, prepossessed, tendentious. *See* LIKE, STRAIGHT.

partisanship *noun*
An inclination for or against that inhibits impartial judgment : bias, one-sidedness, partiality, prejudice, prepossession, tendentiousness. *See* AFFECT, LIKE, STRAIGHT.

partition *noun*
1. The act or an instance of separating one thing from another : detachment, disjunction, disjuncture, disseverance, disseverment, disunion, division, divorce, divorcement, parting, separation, severance, split. *See* ASSEMBLE, PART. **2.** A solid structure that encloses an area or separates one area from another : barrier, wall. *See* INCLUDE, THING.
partition *verb* **1.** To make a division into parts, sections, or branches : break up, dissever, divide, part, section, segment, separate. *See* ASSEMBLE, PART. **2.** To separate with or as if with a wall : fence, wall. *See* INCLUDE.

partner *noun*
1. One who is united in a relationship with another : affiliate, ally, associate, cohort, colleague, confederate, copartner, fellow. *See* CONNECT. **2.** A husband or wife : consort, mate, spouse. *Informal:* better half. *See* MARRIAGE.

partnership *noun*
The state of being associated : affiliation, alliance, association, combination, conjunction, connection, cooperation. *See* NEAR.

parturiency *noun*
The condition of carrying a developing fetus within the uterus : gestation, gravidity, gravidness, pregnancy. *See* REPRODUCTION.

parturient *adjective*
Carrying a developing fetus within the uterus : big, enceinte, expectant, expecting, gravid, pregnant. *Slang:* gone. *Archaic:* great. ***Idioms:*** in a family way, with child. *See* REPRODUCTION.

parturition *noun*
The act or process of bringing forth young : accouchement, birth, birthing, childbearing, childbirth, delivery, labor, lying-in, travail. *See* START.

party *noun*
1. A large or important social gathering : affair, celebration, festivity, fete, function, gala, occasion, soiree. *Informal:* do. *Slang:* bash. *See* GROUP, WORK. **2.** A group of people acting together in a shared activity : band², company, corps, troop, troupe. *See* PERFORMING ARTS. **3.** A group of individuals united in a common cause : bloc, cartel, coalition, combination, combine, faction, ring¹. *See* GROUP. **4.** One who participates : actor, participant, player. *See* PARTICIPATE. **5.** A member of the human race : being, body, creature, homo, human, human being, individual, life, man, mortal, person, personage, soul. *See* BEINGS. **6.** A number of individuals making up or considered a unit : array, band², batch, bevy, body, bunch, bundle, clump, cluster, clutch², collection, group, knot, lot, set². *See* GROUP.

pass *verb*
1. To move along a particular course : fare, go, journey, proceed, push on, remove, travel, wend. ***Idiom:*** make one's way. *See* MOVE. **2.** To make or go on a journey : journey, peregrinate, travel, trek, trip. ***Idiom:*** hit the road. *See* MOVE. **3.** To catch up with and move past : overhaul, overtake. *See* APPROACH. **4.** To be greater or better than : best, better¹, exceed, excel, outdo, outmatch, outrun, outshine, outstrip, surpass, top, transcend. *Informal:* beat. ***Idioms:*** go beyond, go one better. *See* BIG. **5.** To go across : cross, track, transit, traverse. *See* MOVE. **6.** To move past in time : elapse, go (by), lapse. *See* TIME. **7.** To cause to be transferred from one to another : convey, hand (over), transmit. *See* GIVE. **8.** To make known :

break, carry, communicate, convey, disclose, get across, impart, report, tell, transmit. *See* KNOWLEDGE. **9.** To cause (a disease) to pass to another or others : carry, communicate, convey, give, spread, transmit. *See* MOVE. **10.** To come as by lot or inheritance : devolve, fall. *See* REACH. **11.** To convey (something) from one generation to the next. Also used with *along* or *on* : bequeath, hand down, hand on, transmit. *See* GIVE. **12.** To move toward a termination : go, go away, pass away. *See* APPROACH, INCREASE, TIME. **13.** To cease living. Also used with *on* : decease, demise, depart, die, drop, expire, go, pass away, perish, succumb. *Informal:* pop off. *Slang:* check out, croak, kick in, kick off. ***Idioms:*** bite the dust, breathe one's last, cash in, give up the ghost, go to one's grave, kick the bucket, meet one's end (*or* Maker), pass on to the Great Beyond, turn up one's toes. *See* LIVE. **14.** To take place : befall, betide, come, come about, come off, develop, hap, happen, occur, transpire. ***Idiom:*** come to pass. *See* HAPPEN. **15.** To use time in a particular way : put in, spend. *See* TIME. **16.** To go through (life) in a certain way : lead, live[1], pursue. *See* BE. **17.** To represent oneself in a given character or as other than what one is : attitudinize, impersonate, masquerade, pose, posture. ***Idiom:*** pass oneself off as. *See* HONEST. **18.** To be accepted or approved : carry, clear. *See* ACCEPT. **19.** To accept officially : adopt, affirm, approve, confirm, ratify, sanction. *See* ACCEPT, LAW.

pass away *verb* **1.** To move toward a termination : go, go away, pass. *See* APPROACH, INCREASE, TIME. **2.** To cease living : decease, demise, depart, die, drop, expire, go, pass (on), perish, succumb. *Informal:* pop off. *Slang:* check out, croak, kick in, kick off. ***Idioms:*** bite the dust, breathe one's last, cash in, give up the ghost, go to one's grave, kick the bucket, meet one's end (*or* Maker), pass on to the Great Beyond, turn up one's toes. *See* LIVE.

pass off *verb* To offer or put into circulation (an inferior or spurious item) : fob off, foist, palm off, put off. *See* HONEST.

pass out *verb* To suffer temporary lack of consciousness : black out, faint, keel over, swoon. *See* AWARENESS.

pass over *verb* To pretend not to see : blink (at), connive at, disregard, ignore, wink at. ***Idioms:*** be blind to, close (*or* shut) one's eyes to, look the other way, turn a blind eye to. *See* SEE.

pass *noun* **1.** A free ticket entitling one to transportation or admission : *Informal:* comp. *Slang:* freebie. *See* ENTER, TRANSACTIONS. **2.** A decisive point : climacteric, crisis, crossroad (used in plural), exigence, exigency, head, juncture, turning point, zero hour. *See* DECIDE.

passable *adjective*
1. Capable of being passed, traversed, or crossed : navigable, negotiable. *See* OPEN. **2.** Of moderately good quality but less than excellent : acceptable, adequate, all right, average, common, decent, fair, fairish, goodish, moderate, respectable, satisfactory, sufficient, tolerable. *Informal:* OK, tidy. *See* GOOD.

passage *noun*
1. The process or an instance of passing from one form, state, or stage to another : change, shift, transit, transition. *See* CHANGE. **2.** A particular subdivision of a written work : part, section, segment. *See* PART.

pass away *verb* See **pass.**

passé *adjective*
Of a style or method formerly in vogue : antiquated, antique, archaic, bygone, dated, dowdy, fusty, old, old-fashioned, old-time, outdated, outmoded, out-of-date, vintage. *See* NEW.

passel *noun*
Informal. An indeterminately great amount or number : jillion, million (often used in plural), multiplicity, ream, trillion. *Informal:* bushel, gob[1] (often used in plural), heap (often used in plural), load (often used in plural), lot, oodles, peck[2], scad (often used in plural), slew, wad, zillion. *See* BIG.

passing *adjective*
Lasting or existing only for a short time : ephemeral, evanescent, fleet, fleeting, fugacious, fugitive, momentary, short-lived, temporal, temporary, transient, transitory. *See* CONTINUE, TIME.

passing *noun* The act or fact of dying : death, decease, demise, dissolution, extinction, quietus, rest[1]. *Slang:* curtain (used in plural). *See* LIVE.

passion *noun*
1. Powerful, intense emotion : ardor, fervency, fervor, fire. *See* FEELINGS. **2.** The passionate affection and desire felt by lovers for each other : amorousness, fancy, love, romance. *See* LOVE, SEX. **3.** Sexual hunger : amativeness, concupiscence, desire, eroticism, erotism, itch, libidinousness, lust, lustfulness, prurience, pruriency. *See* DESIRE, SEX. **4.** A strong,

enthusiastic liking for something : love, love affair, romance. *See* LOVE. **5.** Passionate devotion to or interest in a cause or subject, for example : ardor, enthusiasm, fervor, fire, zeal, zealousness. *See* CONCERN, FEELINGS. **6.** A subject or activity that inspires lively interest : craze, enthusiasm, mania, rage. *See* CONCERN. **7.** An angry outburst : fit[2], huff, tantrum, temper. *Informal:* conniption, conniption fit. *See* FEELINGS.

passionate *adjective*
1. Feeling or devoted to sexual love or desire : amative, amorous, concupiscent, erotic, lascivious, lecherous, lewd, libidinous, lustful, lusty, prurient, sexy. *See* SEX. **2.** Fired with intense feeling : ardent, blazing, burning, dithyrambic, fervent, fervid, fiery, flaming, glowing, heated, hot-blooded, impassioned, perfervid, red-hot, scorching, torrid. *See* FEELINGS.

passionless *adjective*
Deficient in or lacking sexual desire : ardorless, cold, frigid, inhibited, unresponsive. *See* SEX.

passive *adjective*
Submitting without objection or resistance : acquiescent, nonresistant, resigned, submissive. *See* RESIST.

pass off *verb* See **pass.**
pass out *verb* See **pass.**
pass over *verb* See **pass.**

past *adjective*
1. Just gone by or elapsed : antecedent, anterior, earlier, foregoing, former, precedent, preceding, previous, prior. *See* TIME. **2.** Having been such previously : erstwhile, former, late, old, once, onetime, previous, quondam, sometime, whilom. *See* PRECEDE.
past *noun* **1.** Past events surrounding a person or thing : background, history. *See* HAPPEN. **2.** A former period of time or of one's life : yesterday, yesteryear, yore. ***Idioms:*** bygone days, days gone by, the good old days, the old days. *See* TIME.

past master *noun*
A person with a high degree of knowledge or skill in a particular field : ace, adept, authority, dab hand, expert, master, professional, proficient, wizard. *Informal:* whiz. *Slang:* crackerjack. *Chiefly British:* dab[2]. *See* ABILITY.

paste *verb*
Slang. To deliver a powerful blow to suddenly and sharply : bash, catch, clout, hit, knock, pop[1], slam, slog, slug[3], smash, smite, sock, strike, swat, thwack, whack, wham, whop. *Informal:* biff, bop, clip[1], wallop. *Slang:* belt, conk. *Idioms:* let someone have it, sock it to someone. *See* ATTACK, STRIKE.
paste *noun Slang.* A sudden sharp, powerful stroke : bang, blow[2], clout, crack, hit, lick, pound, slug[3], sock, swat, thwack, welt, whack, wham, whop. *Informal:* bash, biff, bop, clip[1], wallop. *Slang:* belt, conk. *See* ATTACK, STRIKE.

pastoral *adjective*
1. Of or relating to the countryside : arcadian, bucolic, campestral, country, provincial, rural, rustic. *Informal:* hick. *See* URBAN. **2.** Charmingly simple and carefree : idyllic. *See* CALM, SIMPLE.

pasty *adjective*
Lacking color : ashen, ashy, bloodless, cadaverous, colorless, livid, lurid, pale, pallid, sallow, wan, waxen. *See* COLORS.

pat *verb*
To touch or stroke affectionately : caress, cuddle, fondle, pet[1]. *See* TOUCH.

patch *verb*
To restore to proper condition or functioning : doctor, fix, fix up, mend, overhaul, repair[1], revamp, right. ***Idiom:*** set right. *See* HELP.

patchwork *noun*
A collection of various things : assortment, conglomeration, gallimaufry, hodgepodge, jumble, medley, mélange, miscellany, mishmash, mixed bag, mixture, olio, potpourri, salmagundi, variety. *Slang:* grab bag. *See* COLLECT.

patchy *adjective*
Lacking consistency or regularity in quality or performance : erratic, inconsistent, spotty, uneven, unsteady, variable. *See* CONTINUE, SAME.

pate *noun*
The uppermost part of the body : head, noddle, poll. *Slang:* bean, block, conk, dome, noggin, noodle, nut. *See* BODY.

patent *adjective*
1. Readily seen, perceived, or understood : apparent, clear, clear-cut, crystal clear, distinct, evident, manifest, noticeable, observable, obvious, plain, pronounced, visible. *See* SEE. **2.** Easily seen through due to a lack of subtlety : broad, clear, obvious, plain, unmistakable, unsubtle. *See* CLEAR, SEE.

paternal *adjective*
Like a father : fatherlike, fatherly. *See* KIN.

path *noun*
A course affording passage from one place to another : avenue, boulevard, drive, expressway, freeway, highway, road, roadway, route,

street, superhighway, thoroughfare, thruway, turnpike, way. *See* MOVE, OPEN.

pathetic *adjective*
Arousing or deserving pity : piteous, pitiable, pitiful, poor, rueful, ruthful. *See* PITY.

patience *noun*
The capacity of enduring hardship or inconvenience without complaint : forbearance, long-suffering, resignation, tolerance. *See* ACCEPT.

patient *adjective*
Enduring or capable of enduring hardship or inconvenience without complaint : forbearing, long-suffering, resigned. *See* ACCEPT.

patois *noun*
1. A variety of a language that differs from the standard form : argot, cant[2], dialect, jargon, lingo, vernacular. *See* WORDS. **2.** Specialized expressions indigenous to a particular field, subject, trade, or subculture : argot, cant[2], dialect, idiom, jargon, language, lexicon, lingo, terminology, vernacular, vocabulary. *See* WORDS.

patriarch *noun*
One that creates, founds, or originates : architect, author, creator, entrepreneur, father, founder[2], inventor, maker, originator, parent. *See* START.

patrician *adjective*
Of high birth or social position : aristocratic, blue-blooded, elite, highborn, highbred, noble, thoroughbred, upper-class, wellborn. *Informal:* upper-crust. *See* OVER.

patriciate *noun*
People of the highest social level : aristocracy, blue blood, crème de la crème, elite, flower, gentility, gentry, nobility, quality, society, upper class, who's who. *Informal:* upper crust. *See* OVER.

patrimonial *adjective*
Of or from one's ancestors : ancestral, hereditary, inherited. *See* KIN, PRECEDE.

patrimony *noun*
Any special privilege accorded a firstborn : birthright, heritage, inheritance, legacy. *See* OWNED.

patrol *verb*
To maintain or keep in order with or as if with police : police. *See* LAW.

patrolman *noun*
A member of a law-enforcement agency : bluecoat, finest, officer, patrolwoman, peace officer, police, policeman, police officer, policewoman. *Informal:* cop, law. *Slang:* bull[1], copper, flatfoot, fuzz, gendarme, heat, man (often uppercase). *Chiefly British:* bobby, constable, peeler. *See* LAW.

patrolwoman *noun*
A member of a law-enforcement agency : bluecoat, finest, officer, patrolman, peace officer, police, policeman, police officer, policewoman. *Informal:* cop, law. *Slang:* bull[1], copper, flatfoot, fuzz, gendarme, heat, man (often uppercase). *Chiefly British:* bobby, constable, peeler. *See* LAW.

patron *noun*
1. A person who supports or champions an activity, cause, or institution, for example : backer, benefactor, contributor, friend, sponsor, supporter. *Informal:* angel. *See* HELP.
2. One who buys goods or services : buyer, client, customer, purchaser. *See* TRANSACTIONS.

patronage *noun*
1. Aid or support given by a patron : aegis, auspice (often used in plural), backing, patronization, sponsorship. *See* HELP. **2.** The commercial transactions of customers with a supplier : business, custom, trade, traffic. *See* TRANSACTIONS. **3.** Customers or patrons collectively : clientele. *See* TRANSACTIONS. **4.** The political appointments or jobs that are at the disposal of those in power : spoil (used in plural). *Slang:* pork. *See* POLITICS.

patronization *noun*
1. Aid or support given by a patron : aegis, auspice (often used in plural), backing, patronage, sponsorship. *See* HELP. **2.** Superciliously indulgent treatment, especially of those considered inferior : condescendence, condescension. *See* ATTITUDE, RESPECT, RISE.

patronize *verb*
1. To act as a patron to : sponsor, support. *See* HELP. **2.** To treat in a superciliously indulgent manner : condescend. *Informal:* high-hat. ***Idiom:*** speak (*or* talk) down to. *See* ATTITUDE, OVER, RESPECT, RISE.

patsy *noun*
1. *Slang.* A person who is easily deceived or victimized : butt[3], dupe, fool, gull, lamb, pushover, victim. *Informal:* sucker. *Slang:* fall guy, gudgeon, mark, monkey, pigeon, sap[1]. *Chiefly British:* mug. *See* WISE. **2.** *Slang.* One who is made an object of blame : goat, scapegoat, whipping boy. *Slang:* fall guy. *See* PRAISE.

pattern *noun*
1. One that is worthy of imitation or duplication : beau ideal, example, exemplar, ideal, mirror, model, paradigm, standard. *See* GOOD.
2. The external outline of a thing : cast, configuration, figure, form, shape. *See* SURFACE.
3. An element or a component in a decorative composition : design, device, figure, motif,

motive. *See* PART. **4.** Systematic arrangement and design : method, order, orderliness, organization, plan, system, systematization, systemization. *See* ORDER.

pattern *verb* **1.** To take as a model or make conform to a model. Also used with *after, on,* or *upon* : copy, emulate, follow, imitate, model (on, upon, *or* after). ***Idioms:*** follow in the footsteps of, follow suit, follow the example of. *See* SAME. **2.** To create by combining parts or elements : build, compose, configure, form, shape, structure. *See* MAKE.

paucity *noun*

The condition or fact of being deficient : defect, deficiency, deficit, inadequacy, insufficiency, lack, poverty, scantiness, scantness, scarceness, scarcity, shortage, shortcoming, shortfall, underage[1]. *See* EXCESS.

pauper *noun*

An impoverished person : beggar, down-and-out, down-and-outer, have-not, indigent. *See* RICH.

pauperize *verb*

To reduce to financial insolvency : bankrupt, break, bust, impoverish, ruin. *Slang:* clean out. *See* MONEY.

pause *verb*

1. To stop temporarily and remain, as if reluctant to leave : abide, bide, linger, stay[1], tarry, wait. *See* CONTINUE. **2.** To be irresolute in acting or doing : dither, falter, halt[2], hesitate, shilly-shally, stagger, vacillate, waver, wobble. *See* DECIDE.

pause *noun* **1.** A cessation of continuity or regularity : break, discontinuance, discontinuation, discontinuity, disruption, interruption, suspension. *See* CONTINUE. **2.** The act of hesitating or state of being hesitant : hesitancy, hesitation, indecision, indecisiveness, irresoluteness, irresolution, shilly-shally, tentativeness, timidity, timidness, to-and-fro, vacillation. *See* DECIDE.

pawn[1] *noun*

Something given to guarantee the repayment of a loan or the fulfillment of an obligation : earnest[2], guaranty, pledge, security, token, warrant. *See* TRANSACTIONS.

pawn *verb* To give or deposit as a pawn : hypothecate, mortgage, pledge. *Slang:* hock. *See* TRANSACTIONS.

pawn[2] *noun*

A person used or controlled by others : cat's-paw, dupe, instrument, puppet, stooge, tool. *See* OVER.

pay *verb*

1. To give payment to in return for goods or services rendered : compensate, recompense, remunerate. *See* PAY. **2.** To give compensation to : compensate, indemnify, recompense, redress, reimburse, remunerate, repay, requite. *See* PAY. **3.** To distribute (money) as payment. Also used with *out* : disburse, expend, give, lay out, outlay, spend. *Informal:* fork out (*or* over *or* up), shell out. *See* SAVE. **4.** To set right by giving what is due. Also used with *off* or *up* : clear, discharge, liquidate, satisfy, settle, square. *See* PAY. **5.** To make as income or profit : bring in, clear, draw, earn, gain, gross, net[2], produce, realize, repay, return, yield. *See* MONEY. **6.** To give a satisfactory return to : compensate, indemnify, recompense, remunerate, repay, requite, reward. *See* PAY.

pay back *verb* To exact revenge for or from : avenge, pay off, redress, repay, requite, vindicate. *Informal:* fix. *Archaic:* wreak. ***Idioms:*** even the score, get back at, get even with, pay back in kind (*or* in one's own coin), settle (*or* square) accounts, take an eye for an eye. *See* FORGIVENESS.

pay off *verb* **1.** To exact revenge for or from : avenge, pay back, redress, repay, requite, vindicate. *Informal:* fix. *Archaic:* wreak. ***Idioms:*** even the score, get back at, get even with, pay back in kind (*or* in one's own coin), settle (*or* square) accounts, take an eye for an eye. *See* FORGIVENESS. **2.** *Informal.* To give, offer, or promise a bribe to : bribe, buy (off). ***Idiom:*** grease someone's palm (*or* hand). *See* CRIMES, MONEY, PERSUASION.

pay *noun* Payment for work done : compensation, earnings, emolument, fee, hire, remuneration, salary, stipend, wage. *See* PAY.

payable *adjective*

Owed as a debt : due, outstanding, owed, owing, receivable, unpaid, unsettled. *See* PAY.

pay back *verb* See **pay.**

payment *noun*

Something given in exchange for goods or services rendered : compensation, consideration, recompense, remuneration. *See* PAY.

payoff *noun*

1. *Informal.* The highest point or state : acme, apex, apogee, climax, crest, crown, culmination, height, meridian, peak, pinnacle, summit, top, zenith. *Medicine:* fastigium. *See* HIGH. **2.** *Informal.* Money, property, or a favor given, offered, or promised to a person or accepted by a person in a position of trust as an inducement to dishonest behavior : bribe, fix, graft, payola. *Slang:* boodle. *See* CRIMES, MONEY, PERSUASION.

pay off *verb* See **pay.**

payola *noun*
Money, property, or a favor given, offered, or promised to a person or accepted by a person in a position of trust as an inducement to dishonest behavior : bribe, fix, graft. *Informal:* payoff. *Slang:* boodle. *See* CRIMES, MONEY, PERSUASION.

peace *noun*
1. Lack of emotional agitation : calm, calmness, peacefulness, placidity, placidness, quietude, serenity, tranquillity. *See* CALM. **2.** An absence of motion or disturbance : calm, calmness, hush, lull, peacefulness, placidity, placidness, quiet, quietness, serenity, stillness, tranquillity, untroubledness. *See* CALM.

peaceable *adjective*
Inclined or disposed to peace; not quarrelsome or unruly : irenic, pacific, pacifical, pacifist, pacifistic, peaceful. *See* PEACE.

peaceful *adjective*
1. Not excited or emotionally agitated : calm, placid, serene, tranquil. *See* CALM. **2.** Motionless and undisturbed : calm, halcyon, placid, quiet, serene, still, stilly, tranquil, untroubled. *See* CALM. **3.** Inclined or disposed to peace; not quarrelsome or unruly : irenic, pacific, pacifical, pacifist, pacifistic, peaceable. *See* PEACE.

peacefulness *noun*
1. Lack of emotional agitation : calm, calmness, peace, placidity, placidness, quietude, serenity, tranquillity. *See* CALM. **2.** An absence of motion or disturbance : calm, calmness, hush, lull, peace, placidity, placidness, quiet, quietness, serenity, stillness, tranquillity, untroubledness. *See* CALM.

peace officer *noun*
A member of a law-enforcement agency : bluecoat, finest, officer, patrolman, patrolwoman, police, policeman, police officer, policewoman. *Informal:* cop, law. *Slang:* bull¹, copper, flatfoot, fuzz, gendarme, heat, man (often uppercase). *Chiefly British:* bobby, constable, peeler. *See* LAW.

peaches-and-cream *adjective*
Bright and clear in complexion; not dull or faded : blooming, creamy, fresh, glowing. *See* BEAUTIFUL.

peacock *verb*
To walk with exaggerated or unnatural motions expressive of self-importance or self-display : flounce, prance, strut, swagger, swank, swash. *Informal:* sashay. *See* MOVE, SELF-LOVE.

peak *noun*
1. The projecting rim on the front of a cap : bill², brim, visor. *See* CONVEX, PROTECTION. **2.** The highest point : apex, cap, crest, crown, height, roof, summit, top, vertex. *See* HIGH. **3.** The highest point or state : acme, apex, apogee, climax, crest, crown, culmination, height, meridian, pinnacle, summit, top, zenith. *Informal:* payoff. *Medicine:* fastigium. *See* HIGH.
peak *verb* To reach or bring to a climax : cap, climax, crest, crown, culminate, top (off *or* out). *See* EXCITE.
peak *adjective* Of or constituting a climax : climactic, crowning, culminating. *See* HIGH, OVER.

peaked *adjective*
Of or associated with sickness : anemic, sick, sickly. *See* HEALTH.

peal *verb*
To give forth or cause to give forth a clear, resonant sound : bong, chime, knell, ring², strike, toll². *See* SOUNDS.

peanut *noun*
Informal. A small or trifling amount of money. Used in plural : small change. *Slang:* chicken feed, two bits. *See* BIG, MONEY.

pearl *noun*
Someone or something considered exceptionally precious : gem, prize¹, treasure. *See* VALUE.

peccancy *noun*
1. A wicked act or wicked behavior : crime, deviltry, diablerie, evil, evildoing, immorality, iniquity, misdeed, offense, sin, wickedness, wrong, wrongdoing. *See* RIGHT. **2.** That which is morally bad or objectionable : evil, iniquity, sin, wickedness, wrong. *See* RIGHT.

peccant *adjective*
Morally objectionable : bad, black, evil, immoral, iniquitous, reprobate, sinful, vicious, wicked, wrong. *See* RIGHT.

peck¹ *verb*
Informal. To touch or caress with the lips, especially as a sign of passion or affection : buss, kiss, osculate, smack¹. *Slang:* smooch. *See* TOUCH.
peck at *verb* To scold or find fault with constantly : carp at, fuss at, nag, pick on. *Informal:* henpeck. *See* PRAISE.
peck *noun* *Informal.* The act or an instance of kissing : buss, kiss, osculation, smack¹, smacker. *Slang:* smooch. *See* TOUCH.

peck² *noun*
1. *Informal.* A great deal : abundance, mass,

mountain, much, plenty, profusion, wealth, world. *Informal:* barrel, heap, lot, pack, pile. *Regional:* power, sight. *See* BIG. **2.** *Informal.* An indeterminately great amount or number : jillion, million (often used in plural), multiplicity, ream, trillion. *Informal:* bushel, gob[1] (often used in plural), heap (often used in plural), load (often used in plural), lot, oodles, passel, scad (often used in plural), slew, wad, zillion. *See* BIG.

peck at *verb* See **peck[1]**.

Pecksniffian *adjective*
Of or practicing hypocrisy : hypocritical, pharisaic, pharisaical, phony, sanctimonious, two-faced. *See* HONEST.

peculiar *adjective*
1. Deviating from the customary : bizarre, cranky, curious, eccentric, erratic, freakish, idiosyncratic, odd, outlandish, quaint, queer, quirky, singular, strange, unnatural, unusual, weird. *Slang:* kooky, screwball. *British Slang:* rum, rummy[2]. *See* USUAL. **2.** Causing puzzlement; perplexing : curious, funny, odd, queer, strange, weird. *See* USUAL. **3.** Serving to identify or set apart an individual or group : characteristic, distinctive, individual, typical, vintage. *See* SAME.

peculiarity *noun*
1. A distinctive element : attribute, character, characteristic, feature, mark, property, quality, savor, trait. *See* BE. **2.** Peculiar behavior : eccentricity, idiosyncrasy, quirk, quirkiness, singularity. *See* USUAL.

pecuniary *adjective*
Of or relating to finances or those who deal in finances : financial, fiscal, monetary. *See* MONEY.

pedagogics *noun*
The act, process, or art of imparting knowledge and skill : education, instruction, pedagogy, schooling, teaching, training, tuition, tutelage, tutoring. *See* TEACH.

pedagogue *noun*
One who educates : educator, instructor, teacher, trainer, tutor. *See* TEACH.

pedagogy *noun*
The act, process, or art of imparting knowledge and skill : education, instruction, pedagogics, schooling, teaching, training, tuition, tutelage, tutoring. *See* TEACH.

pedantic *adjective*
Characterized by a narrow concern for book learning and formal rules, without knowledge or experience of practical matters : academic, bookish, donnish, formalistic, inkhorn, literary, pedantical, scholastic. *See* ATTITUDE, FLEXIBLE, TEACH.

pedantical *adjective*
Characterized by a narrow concern for book learning and formal rules, without knowledge or experience of practical matters : academic, bookish, donnish, formalistic, inkhorn, literary, pedantic, scholastic. *See* ATTITUDE, FLEXIBLE, TEACH.

peddle *verb*
1. To travel about selling goods : hawk, huckster, vend. *See* TRANSACTIONS. **2.** To offer for sale : deal (in), handle, market, merchandise, merchant, retail, sell, trade (in), vend. *See* TRANSACTIONS. **3.** To engage in the illicit sale of (narcotics) : deal. *Slang:* push. *See* TRANSACTIONS.

peddler *noun*
A person who sells narcotics illegally : dealer. *Slang:* pusher. *See* TRANSACTIONS.

pedestrian *adjective*
Lacking liveliness, charm, or surprise : arid, aseptic, colorless, drab, dry, dull, earthbound, flat, flavorless, lackluster, lifeless, lusterless, matter-of-fact, prosaic, spiritless, sterile, stodgy, unimaginative, uninspired. *See* EXCITE.

pedigree *noun*
1. One's ancestors or their character or one's ancestral derivation : ancestry, birth, blood, bloodline, descent, extraction, family, genealogy, line, lineage, origin, parentage, seed, stock. *See* KIN, PRECEDE. **2.** A written record of ancestry : family tree, genealogy. *See* KIN.

peek *verb*
To look briefly and quickly : glance, glimpse, peep. *See* SEE.
peek *noun* A quick look : blush, glance, glimpse, peep. *Informal:* gander. *See* SEE.

peel *noun*
The outer covering of a fruit : rind, skin. *See* SURFACE.
peel *verb* To remove the skin of : decorticate, pare, scale[1], skin, strip[1]. *See* PUT ON.

peeler *noun*
Chiefly British. A member of a law-enforcement agency : bluecoat, finest, officer, patrolman, patrolwoman, peace officer, police, policeman, police officer, policewoman. *Informal:* cop, law. *Slang:* bull[1], copper, flatfoot, fuzz, gendarme, heat, man (often uppercase). *Chiefly British:* bobby, constable. *See* LAW.

peep *verb*
To look briefly and quickly : glance, glimpse, peek. *See* SEE.

peep *noun* A quick look : blush, glance, glimpse, peek. *Informal:* gander. *See* SEE.

peer[1] *verb*
To look intently and fixedly : eye, gape, gawk, gaze, goggle, ogle, stare. ***Idioms:*** gaze open-mouthed, rivet the eyes on. *See* SEE.

peer[2] *noun*
One that is very similar to another in rank or position : coequal, colleague, compeer, equal, equivalent, fellow. *See* SAME.

peerless *adjective*
Without equal or rival : alone, incomparable, matchless, nonpareil, only, singular, unequaled, unexampled, unique, unmatched, unparalleled, unrivaled. *See* SAME.

peeve *verb*
To trouble the nerves or peace of mind of, especially by repeated vexations : aggravate, annoy, bother, bug, chafe, disturb, exasperate, fret, gall[2], get, irk, irritate, nettle, provoke, put out, rile, ruffle, vex. ***Idioms:*** get in one's hair, get on one's nerves, get under one's skin. *See* FEELINGS, PAIN.

peeve *noun* Something that annoys : aggravation, annoyance, besetment, bother, irritant, irritation, nuisance, plague, torment, vexation. *See* FEELINGS, PAIN.

peevish *adjective*
Having or showing a bad temper : bad-tempered, cantankerous, crabbed, cranky, cross, disagreeable, fretful, grouchy, grumpy, ill-tempered, irascible, irritable, nasty, petulant, querulous, snappish, snappy, surly, testy, ugly, waspish. *Informal:* crabby, mean[2]. ***Idiom:*** out of sorts. *See* ATTITUDE.

peewee *adjective*
Informal. Extremely small : diminutive, dwarf, Lilliputian, midget, miniature, minuscule, minute[2], pygmy, tiny, wee. *Informal:* pintsize, pintsized, teensy, teensy-weensy, teeny, teeny-weeny, weeny. *See* BIG.

peg *noun*
One of the units in a course, as on an ascending or descending scale : degree, grade, level, point, rung, stage, step. *Informal:* notch. *See* BIG.

pejorative *adjective*
Tending or intending to belittle : deprecative, deprecatory, depreciative, depreciatory, derogative, derogatory, detractive, disparaging, low, slighting, uncomplimentary. *See* PRAISE.

pelagic *adjective*
Of or relating to the seas or oceans : marine, maritime, oceanic, thalassic. *See* SEA.

pelf *noun*
A great amount of accumulated money and precious possessions : affluence, fortune, riches, treasure, wealth. *See* OWNED, RICH.

pellucid *adjective*
1. Admitting light so that objects beyond can be seen : clear, crystal clear, crystalline, limpid, lucid, see-through, translucent, transparent. *See* CLEAR. **2.** Free from what obscures or dims : clear, crystal clear, crystalline, limpid, lucid, see-through, transparent. *See* CLEAR.

pellucidity *noun*
The quality of being clear and easy to perceive or understand : clarity, clearness, distinctness, limpidity, limpidness, lucidity, lucidness, pellucidness, perspicuity, perspicuousness, plainness. *See* CLEAR.

pellucidness *noun*
The quality of being clear and easy to perceive or understand : clarity, clearness, distinctness, limpidity, limpidness, lucidity, lucidness, pellucidity, perspicuity, perspicuousness, plainness. *See* CLEAR.

pelt[1] *noun*
The skin of an animal : fell[3], fur, hide[2], jacket. *See* SURFACE.

pelt[2] *verb*
To move swiftly : bolt, bucket, bustle, dart, dash, festinate, flash, fleet, flit, fly, haste, hasten, hurry, hustle, race, rocket, run, rush, sail, scoot, scour[2], shoot, speed, sprint, tear[1], trot, whirl, whisk, whiz, wing, zip, zoom. *Informal:* hotfoot, rip. *Slang:* barrel, highball. *Chiefly British:* nip[1]. ***Idioms:*** get a move on, get cracking, go like lightning, go like the wind, hotfoot it, make haste, make time, make tracks, run like the wind, shake a leg, step (*or* jump) on it. *See* MOVE.

pen[1] *verb*
To be the author of (a published work or works) : publish, write. *See* WORDS.

pen[2] *verb*
To confine within a limited area : cage, coop (in *or* up), enclose, fence (in), immure, mew (up), shut in, shut up, wall (in *or* up). *See* FREE.

pen[3] *noun*
Informal. A place for the confinement of persons in lawful detention : brig, house of correction, jail, keep, penitentiary, prison. *Informal:* lockup. *Slang:* big house, can, clink, cooler, coop, hoosegow, joint, jug, pokey[1], slammer, stir[2]. *Chiefly Regional:* calaboose. *See* FREE.

penalize *verb*
1. To subject (one) to a penalty for a wrong : castigate, chastise, correct, discipline, punish.

See REWARD. **2.** To impose a fine on : amerce, fine[2], mulct. *See* REWARD.

penalty *noun*
1. Something, such as loss, pain, or confinement, imposed for wrongdoing : castigation, chastisement, correction, discipline, punishment. *See* REWARD. **2.** A sum of money levied as punishment for an offense : amercement, fine[2], mulct. *See* REWARD. **3.** A coercive measure intended to ensure compliance or conformity : interdict, interdiction, sanction. *See* REWARD.

penchant *noun*
An inclination to something : bent, bias, cast, disposition, leaning, partiality, predilection, predisposition, proclivity, proneness, propensity, squint, tendency, trend, turn. *See* APPROACH, LIKE.

pendulous *adjective*
1. Hung or appearing to be hung from a support : dangly, hanging, pensile. *See* HANG. **2.** Given to or exhibiting hesitation : halting, hesitant, indecisive, irresolute, shilly-shally, tentative, timid, vacillant, vacillatory. *See* DECIDE.

penetrate *verb*
1. To pass into or through by overcoming resistance : break (through), enter, perforate, pierce, puncture. *See* ENTER. **2.** To come or go into (a place) : come in, enter, go in. *Nautical:* put in. ***Idioms:*** gain entrance (*or* entry), set foot in. *See* ENTER.

penetrating *adjective*
Possessing or displaying perceptions of great accuracy and sensitivity : acute, incisive, keen[1], perceptive, probing, sensitive, sharp, trenchant. *See* CAREFUL, SHARP.

penetration *noun*
1. Skill in perceiving, discriminating, or judging : acumen, astuteness, clear-sightedness, discernment, discrimination, eye, keenness, nose, perceptiveness, percipience, percipiency, perspicacity, sagacity, sageness, shrewdness, wit. *See* ABILITY, CAREFUL. **2.** The power to discern the true nature of a person or situation : insight, instinct, intuition, intuitiveness, sixth sense. *See* THOUGHTS.

penitence *noun*
A feeling of regret for one's sins or misdeeds : compunction, contriteness, contrition, penitency, remorse, remorsefulness, repentance, rue. *Theology:* attrition. *See* REGRET.

penitency *noun*
A feeling of regret for one's sins or misdeeds : compunction, contriteness, contrition, penitence, remorse, remorsefulness, repentance, rue. *Theology:* attrition. *See* REGRET.

penitent *adjective*
1. Feeling or expressing regret for one's sins or misdeeds : compunctious, contrite, penitential, regretful, remorseful, repentant, sorry. *See* REGRET. **2.** Expressing or inclined to express an apology : apologetic, contrite, regretful, repentant, sorry. *See* REGRET.

penitential *adjective*
Feeling or expressing regret for one's sins or misdeeds : compunctious, contrite, penitent, regretful, remorseful, repentant, sorry. *See* REGRET.

penitentiary *noun*
A place for the confinement of persons in lawful detention : brig, house of correction, jail, keep, prison. *Informal:* lockup, pen[3]. *Slang:* big house, can, clink, cooler, coop, hoosegow, joint, jug, pokey[1], slammer, stir[2]. *Chiefly Regional:* calaboose. *See* FREE.

pennant *noun*
Fabric used especially as a symbol : banderole, banner, banneret, color (used in plural), ensign, flag[1], jack, oriflamme, pennon, standard, streamer. *See* SUBSTITUTE.

penniless *adjective*
Having little or no money or wealth : beggarly, destitute, down-and-out, impecunious, impoverished, indigent, necessitous, needy, penurious, poor, poverty-stricken. *Informal:* broke, strapped. ***Idioms:*** hard up, on one's uppers. *See* RICH.

pennilessness *noun*
The condition of being extremely poor : beggary, destitution, impecuniosity, impecuniousness, impoverishment, indigence, need, neediness, penuriousness, penury, poverty, privation, want. *See* RICH.

pennon *noun*
Fabric used especially as a symbol : banderole, banner, banneret, color (used in plural), ensign, flag[1], jack, oriflamme, pennant, standard, streamer. *See* SUBSTITUTE.

penny pincher *noun*
Informal. A stingy person : miser, niggard, Scrooge, skinflint. *Slang:* cheapskate, stiff, tightwad. *See* GIVE.

penny-pinching *adjective*
Ungenerously or pettily reluctant to spend money : cheap, close, close-fisted, costive, hard-fisted, mean[2], miserly, niggard, niggardly, parsimonious, penurious, petty, pinching, stingy, tight, tightfisted. *See* GIVE.

pensile *adjective*
Hung or appearing to be hung from a support : dangly, hanging, pendulous. *See* HANG.

pension *verb*
To remove from active service. Also used with *off* : retire, superannuate. ***Idiom:*** put out to pasture. *See* KEEP.

pensive *adjective*
Of, characterized by, or disposed to thought : cogitative, contemplative, deliberative, excogitative, meditative, reflective, ruminative, speculative, thinking, thoughtful. ***Idiom:*** in a brown study. *See* THOUGHTS.

penumbra *noun*
Comparative darkness that results from the blocking of light rays : shade, shadow, umbra, umbrage. *See* LIGHT.

penurious *adjective*
1. Ungenerously or pettily reluctant to spend money : cheap, close, close-fisted, costive, hard-fisted, mean[2], miserly, niggard, niggardly, parsimonious, penny-pinching, petty, pinching, stingy, tight, tightfisted. *See* GIVE. **2.** Having little or no money or wealth : beggarly, destitute, down-and-out, impecunious, impoverished, indigent, necessitous, needy, penniless, poor, poverty-stricken. *Informal:* broke, strapped. ***Idioms:*** hard up, on one's uppers. *See* RICH.

penuriousness *noun*
The condition of being extremely poor : beggary, destitution, impecuniosity, impecuniousness, impoverishment, indigence, need, neediness, pennilessness, penury, poverty, privation, want. *See* RICH.

penury *noun*
The condition of being extremely poor : beggary, destitution, impecuniosity, impecuniousness, impoverishment, indigence, need, neediness, pennilessness, penuriousness, poverty, privation, want. *See* RICH.

people *noun*
Persons as an organized body : community, public, society. *See* SPECIFIC.
people *verb* To live in (a place), as does a people : inhabit, occupy, populate. *See* PLACE.

pep *noun*
1. *Informal.* A lively, emphatic, eager quality or manner : animation, bounce, brio, dash, élan, esprit, life, liveliness, pertness, sparkle, spirit, verve, vigor, vim, vivaciousness, vivacity, zip. *Informal:* ginger, peppiness. *Slang:* oomph. *See* ACTION. **2.** *Informal.* Capacity or power for work or vigorous activity : animation, energy, force, might, potency, power, puissance, sprightliness, steam, strength. *Informal:* get-up-and-go, go, peppiness, zip. *See* ACTION.

pepper *verb*
1. To mark with many small spots : bespeckle, besprinkle, dapple, dot, fleck, freckle, mottle, speck, speckle, sprinkle, stipple. *See* MARKS.
2. To direct a barrage at : barrage, bombard, cannonade, fusillade, shower. *See* ATTACK.

peppery *adjective*
1. Easily annoyed : choleric, irascible, quick-tempered, testy, tetchy, touchy. *See* FEELINGS.
2. Full of or characterized by a lively, emphatic, eager quality : fiery, high-spirited, mettlesome, spirited, vibrant. *Informal:* snappy. *See* ACTION, FEELINGS.

peppiness *noun*
1. *Informal.* A lively, emphatic, eager quality or manner : animation, bounce, brio, dash, élan, esprit, life, liveliness, pertness, sparkle, spirit, verve, vigor, vim, vivaciousness, vivacity, zip. *Informal:* ginger, pep. *Slang:* oomph. *See* ACTION. **2.** *Informal.* Capacity or power for work or vigorous activity : animation, energy, force, might, potency, power, puissance, sprightliness, steam, strength. *Informal:* get-up-and-go, go, pep, zip. *See* ACTION.

peppy *adjective*
1. *Informal.* Possessing, exerting, or displaying energy : active, brisk, dynamic, dynamical, energetic, forceful, kinetic, lively, sprightly, strenuous, vigorous. *See* ACTION. **2.** *Informal.* Very brisk, alert, and full of high spirits : animated, bouncy, chipper, dashing, high-spirited, lively, pert, spirited, vivacious. ***Idioms:*** bright-eyed and bushy-tailed, full of life. *See* ACTION.
3. *Informal.* Disposed to action : active, brisk, driving, dynamic, dynamical, energetic, enterprising, lively, sprightly, spry, vigorous, zippy. *Informal:* snappy. *See* ACTION.

perambulate *verb*
To walk at a leisurely pace : amble, meander, promenade, ramble, saunter, stroll, wander. *Informal:* mosey. *See* MOVE.

perambulation *noun*
An act of walking, especially for pleasure : amble, meander (often used in plural), promenade, ramble, saunter, stroll, walk, wander. *See* MOVE.

perceivable *adjective*
1. Capable of being seen : discernible, perceptible, seeable, viewable, visible, visual. *See* SEE.
2. Capable of being noticed or apprehended mentally : appreciable, detectable, discernible, distinguishable, noticeable, observable,

palpable, perceptible, ponderable, sensible. *See* KNOWLEDGE.

perceive *verb*
1. To apprehend (images) by use of the eyes : behold, see. *Scots:* ken. *See* SEE. **2.** To be intuitively aware of : apprehend, feel, intuit, sense. ***Idioms:*** feel in one's bones, get vibrations. *See* KNOWLEDGE.

perceptibility *noun*
The quality, condition, or degree of being visible : visibility, visuality, visualness. *See* SEE.

perceptible *adjective*
1. Capable of being seen : discernible, perceivable, seeable, viewable, visible, visual. *See* SEE. **2.** Capable of being noticed or apprehended mentally : appreciable, detectable, discernible, distinguishable, noticeable, observable, palpable, perceivable, ponderable, sensible. *See* KNOWLEDGE.

perception *noun*
1. The condition of being aware : awareness, cognizance, consciousness, sense. *See* KNOWLEDGE. **2.** That which exists in the mind as the product of careful mental activity : concept, conception, idea, image, notion, thought. *See* THOUGHTS.

perceptive *adjective*
Possessing or displaying perceptions of great accuracy and sensitivity : acute, incisive, keen[1], penetrating, probing, sensitive, sharp, trenchant. *See* CAREFUL, SHARP.

perceptiveness *noun*
Skill in perceiving, discriminating, or judging : acumen, astuteness, clear-sightedness, discernment, discrimination, eye, keenness, nose, penetration, percipience, percipiency, perspicacity, sagacity, sageness, shrewdness, wit. *See* ABILITY, CAREFUL.

perch *verb*
To place or be placed on a narrow or insecure surface : balance, poise. *See* POSTURE.

perchance *adverb*
Possibly but not certainly : maybe, mayhap, perhaps. *See* CERTAIN.

percipience *noun*
Skill in perceiving, discriminating, or judging : acumen, astuteness, clear-sightedness, discernment, discrimination, eye, keenness, nose, penetration, perceptiveness, percipiency, perspicacity, sagacity, sageness, shrewdness, wit. *See* ABILITY, CAREFUL.

percipiency *noun*
Skill in perceiving, discriminating, or judging : acumen, astuteness, clear-sightedness, discernment, discrimination, eye, keenness, nose, penetration, perceptiveness, percipience, perspicacity, sagacity, sageness, shrewdness, wit. *See* ABILITY, CAREFUL.

percolate *verb*
To flow or leak out or emit something slowly : bleed, exude, leach, ooze, seep, transpire, transude, weep. *See* MOVE, SOLID.

percussion *noun*
Violent forcible contact between two or more things : bump, collision, concussion, crash, impact, jar, jolt, shock[1], smash. *See* CONFLICT.

perdurable *adjective*
Existing or remaining in the same state for an indefinitely long time : abiding, continuing, durable, enduring, lasting, long-lasting, long-lived, long-standing, old, perennial, permanent, persistent. *See* CONTINUE.

peregrinate *verb*
1. To make or go on a journey : journey, pass, travel, trek, trip. ***Idiom:*** hit the road. *See* MOVE. **2.** To travel about or journey on foot : backpack, hike, march[1], traipse, tramp, trek. *See* MOVE. **3.** To move about at random, especially over a wide area : drift, gad, gallivant, meander, ramble, range, roam, rove, stray, traipse, wander. *See* MOVE.

peremptory *adjective*
Tending to dictate : authoritarian, bossy, dictatorial, dogmatic, domineering, imperious, magisterial, masterful, overbearing. *See* OVER.

perennial *adjective*
Existing or remaining in the same state for an indefinitely long time : abiding, continuing, durable, enduring, lasting, long-lasting, long-lived, long-standing, old, perdurable, permanent, persistent. *See* CONTINUE.

perfect *adjective*
1. Lacking nothing essential or normal : complete, entire, full, intact, integral, whole. *See* PART. **2.** In excellent condition : entire, flawless, good, intact, sound[2], unblemished, unbroken, undamaged, unharmed, unhurt, unimpaired, uninjured, unmarred, whole. *See* THRIVE. **3.** Without imperfections or blemishes, as a line or contour : clean, regular. *See* BEAUTIFUL. **4.** Conforming to an ultimate form of perfection or excellence : exemplary, ideal, model, supreme. *See* GOOD. **5.** Not more or less : complete, entire, full, good, round, whole. *See* PART, PRECISE. **6.** Completely such, without qualification or exception : absolute, all-out, arrant, complete, consummate, crashing, damned, dead, downright, flat,

out-and-out, outright, plain, pure, sheer[2], thorough, thoroughgoing, total, unbounded, unequivocal, unlimited, unmitigated, unqualified, unrelieved, unreserved, utter[2]. *Informal:* flat-out, positive. *Chiefly British:* blooming. *See* BIG, LIMITED. **7.** Free from extraneous elements : absolute, plain, pure, sheer[2], simple, unadulterated, undiluted, unmixed. *See* CLEAN. **8.** Supremely excellent in quality or nature : absolute, consummate, faultless, flawless, impeccable, indefectible, unflawed. *See* GOOD.

perfect *verb* To bring to perfection or completion : polish, refine, smooth. ***Idiom:*** smooth off the rough edges. *See* BETTER.

perfection *noun*
A special feature or quality that confers superiority : beauty, distinction, excellence, merit, virtue. *See* GOOD.

perfectly *adverb*
To the fullest extent : absolutely, all, altogether, completely, dead, entirely, flat, fully, just, quite, thoroughly, totally, utterly, well[2], wholly. *Informal:* clean, clear. ***Idioms:*** in toto, through and through. *See* BIG, LIMITED.

perfervid *adjective*
Fired with intense feeling : ardent, blazing, burning, dithyrambic, fervent, fervid, fiery, flaming, glowing, heated, hot-blooded, impassioned, passionate, red-hot, scorching, torrid. *See* FEELINGS.

perfidious *adjective*
Not true to duty or obligation : disloyal, faithless, false, false-hearted, recreant, traitorous, treacherous, unfaithful, untrue. *See* CONTINUE, TRUST.

perfidiousness *noun*
Betrayal, especially of a moral obligation : disloyalty, faithlessness, false-heartedness, falseness, falsity, infidelity, perfidy, traitorousness, treacherousness, treachery, unfaithfulness. *See* CONTINUE, TRUST.

perfidy *noun*
1. Betrayal, especially of a moral obligation : disloyalty, faithlessness, false-heartedness, falseness, falsity, infidelity, perfidiousness, traitorousness, treacherousness, treachery, unfaithfulness. *See* CONTINUE, TRUST. **2.** Willful betrayal of fidelity, confidence, or trust : treacherousness, treachery, treason. *See* TRUST.

perforate *verb*
1. To make a hole or other opening in : breach, break (through), gap, hole, pierce, puncture. *See* OPEN. **2.** To pass into or through by overcoming resistance : break (through), enter, penetrate, pierce, puncture. *See* ENTER.

perforation *noun*
1. An opening, especially in a solid structure : breach, break, gap, hole, rupture. *See* OPEN. **2.** A small mark or hole made by a sharp, pointed object : prick, puncture, stab. *See* MARKS, OPEN.

perforce *adverb*
Without regard to desire or inclination : helplessly, involuntarily, willy-nilly. *See* WILLING.

perform *verb*
1. To begin and carry through to completion : do, execute, prosecute. *Informal:* pull off. *See* DO. **2.** To react in a specified way : act, behave, function, operate, work. *See* ACTION. **3.** To carry out the functions, requirements, or terms of : discharge, do, execute, exercise, fulfill, implement, keep. ***Idiom:*** live up to. *See* DO. **4.** To play the part of : act, do, enact, impersonate, play, play-act, portray, represent. *See* ACTION, PERFORMING ARTS, SUBSTITUTE. **5.** To produce on the stage : act (out), do, dramatize, enact, give, present[2], put on, stage. *See* PERFORMING ARTS. **6.** To make music : play. *See* PERFORMING ARTS.

performance *noun*
1. The act of beginning and carrying through to completion : discharge, effectuation, execution, prosecution. *See* DO. **2.** One's artistic conception, as of a dramatic role : execution, interpretation, reading, realization, rendering, rendition. *See* PERFORMING ARTS. **3.** The way in which a machine or other thing performs or functions : behavior, functioning, operation, reaction, working (often used in plural). *See* ACTION, MACHINE.

performer *noun*
One who plays a musical instrument : musician, player. *See* PERFORMING ARTS.

perfume *noun*
A sweet or pleasant odor : aroma, bouquet, fragrance, redolence, scent. *See* SMELLS.

perfume *verb* To fill with a pleasant odor : aromatize, scent. *See* SMELLS.

perfunctory *adjective*
Performed or performing automatically and impersonally : automatic, mechanical. *See* CONCERN.

perhaps *adverb*
Possibly but not certainly : maybe, mayhap, perchance. *See* CERTAIN.

periapt *noun*
A small object worn or kept for its supposed magical power : amulet, charm, fetish, juju, phylactery, talisman. *See* SUPERNATURAL.

peril *noun*
Exposure to possible harm, loss, or injury : danger, endangerment, hazard, imperilment, jeopardy, risk. *See* SAFETY.
peril *verb* To subject to danger or destruction : endanger, imperil, jeopardize, menace, risk, threaten. *See* SAFETY.

perilous *adjective*
Involving possible risk, loss, or injury : adventurous, chancy, dangerous, hazardous, jeopardous, parlous, risky, treacherous, unsafe, venturesome, venturous. *Slang:* hairy. *See* SAFETY.

perimeter *noun*
1. A line around a closed figure or area : ambit, circuit, circumference, compass, periphery. *See* EDGE. **2.** *Chiefly Military.* A fairly narrow line or space forming a boundary : border, borderline, brim, brink, edge, edging, fringe, margin, periphery, rim, verge. *See* EDGE.

period *noun*
1. A specific length of time characterized by the occurrence of certain conditions or events : season, span, stretch, term. *See* TIME. **2.** A particular time notable for its distinctive characteristics : age, day, epoch, era, time (often used in plural). *See* TIME. **3.** An interval regarded as a distinct evolutionary or developmental unit : phase, stage. *See* TIME. **4.** A span designated for a given activity : season, time. *See* TIME. **5.** A concluding or terminating : cease, cessation, close, closing, closure, completion, conclusion, consummation, end, ending, end of the line, finish, stop, stopping point, termination, terminus, wind-up, wrap-up. *See* CONTINUE.

periodic *adjective*
1. Happening or appearing at regular intervals : cyclic, cyclical, isochronal, isochronous, periodical, recurrent. ***Idiom:*** like clockwork. *See* REPETITION. **2.** Happening or appearing now and then : fitful, intermittent, occasional, periodical, sporadic. *Informal:* on-again, off-again. *See* CONTINUE.

periodical *adjective*
1. Happening or appearing at regular intervals : cyclic, cyclical, isochronal, isochronous, periodic, recurrent. ***Idiom:*** like clockwork. *See* REPETITION. **2.** Happening or appearing now and then : fitful, intermittent, occasional, periodic, sporadic. *Informal:* on-again, off-again. *See* CONTINUE.

periodically *adverb*
Once in a while; at times : betimes, intermittently, occasionally, sometimes, sporadically. ***Idioms:*** ever and again (*or* anon), now and again (*or* then). *See* CONTINUE.

peripatetic *adjective*
Leading the life of a person without a fixed domicile; moving from place to place : itinerant, nomadic, vagabond, vagrant. *See* MOVE.

periphery *noun*
1. A line around a closed figure or area : ambit, circuit, circumference, compass, perimeter. *See* EDGE. **2.** A fairly narrow line or space forming a boundary : border, borderline, brim, brink, edge, edging, fringe, margin, rim, verge. *Chiefly Military:* perimeter. *See* EDGE.

periphrastic *adjective*
Using or containing an excessive number of words : diffuse, long-winded, pleonastic, prolix, redundant, verbose, wordy. *See* EXCESS, STYLE, WORDS.

perish *verb*
To cease living : decease, demise, depart, die, drop, expire, go, pass away, pass (on), succumb. *Informal:* pop off. *Slang:* check out, croak, kick in, kick off. ***Idioms:*** bite the dust, breathe one's last, cash in, give up the ghost, go to one's grave, kick the bucket, meet one's end (*or* Maker), pass on to the Great Beyond, turn up one's toes. *See* LIVE.

perjure *verb*
Law. To make untrue declarations : falsify, fib, forswear, lie[2], prevaricate. *See* TRUE.

perjured *adjective*
Marked by lying under oath : forsworn, perjurious. *See* TRUE.

perjurer *noun*
Law. One who tells lies : fabricator, fabulist, falsifier, fibber, liar, prevaricator. *Informal:* storyteller. *See* TRUE.

perjurious *adjective*
Marked by lying under oath : forsworn, perjured. *See* TRUE.

perjury *noun*
The practice of lying : falsehood, inveracity, mendacity, truthlessness, untruthfulness. *See* TRUE.

perk up *verb*
1. To impart strength and confidence to : buck up, cheer (up), encourage, hearten, nerve. *See* HELP. **2.** To regain one's health : come around (*or* round), convalesce, gain, improve, mend, rally, recover, recuperate. *See* HEALTH.

permanent *adjective*
Existing or remaining in the same state for an indefinitely long time : abiding, continuing, durable, enduring, lasting, long-lasting, long-lived, long-standing, old, perdurable, perennial, persistent. *See* CONTINUE.

permeate *verb*
To cause to be filled, as with a particular mood or tone : charge, freight, imbue, impregnate, pervade, saturate, suffuse, transfuse. *See* FULL.

permissible *adjective*
Capable of being allowed : admissible, allowable. *Slang:* kosher. *See* ALLOW.

permission *noun*
The approving of an action, especially when done by one in authority : allowance, approbation, approval, authorization, consent, endorsement, leave[2], license, permit, sanction. *Informal:* OK. *See* ALLOW.

permit *verb*
1. To neither forbid nor prevent : allow, have, let, suffer, tolerate. *See* ALLOW. **2.** To give one's consent to : allow, approbate, approve, authorize, consent, endorse, let, sanction. *Informal:* OK. *See* ALLOW. **3.** To afford an opportunity for : admit, allow, let. *See* ALLOW. **4.** To give the means, ability, or opportunity to do : empower, enable. *See* ALLOW.

permit *noun* **1.** The approving of an action, especially when done by one in authority : allowance, approbation, approval, authorization, consent, endorsement, leave[2], license, permission, sanction. *Informal:* OK. *See* ALLOW. **2.** Proof of legal permission to do something : license, warrant. ***Idiom:*** piece of paper. *See* ALLOW, LAW.

permutation *noun*
The process or result of making or becoming different : alteration, change, modification, mutation, variation. *See* CHANGE.

pernicious *adjective*
1. Extremely destructive or harmful : baneful, deadly, malignant, noxious, pestilent, pestilential, virulent. *See* HELP. **2.** Having the capability or effect of damaging irreparably : destructive, ruinous. *See* HELP.

perorate *verb*
To speak in a loud, pompous, or prolonged manner : declaim, harangue, mouth, rant, rave. *See* WORDS.

perpendicular *adjective*
At right angles to the horizon or to level ground : plumb, upright, vertical. *See* HORIZONTAL.

perpetrate *verb*
To be responsible for or guilty of (an error or crime) : commit. *Informal:* pull off. *See* DO, LAW.

perpetual *adjective*
1. Enduring for all time : amaranthine, ceaseless, endless, eternal, everlasting, immortal, never-ending, unending, world without end. *Archaic:* eterne. *See* CONTINUE. **2.** Existing or occurring without interruption or end : around-the-clock, ceaseless, constant, continual, continuous, endless, eternal, everlasting, incessant, interminable, nonstop, ongoing, persistent, relentless, round-the-clock, timeless, unceasing, unending, unfailing, uninterrupted, unremitting. *See* CONTINUE.

perpetuate *verb*
To cause to last endlessly : eternalize, eternize, immortalize. *See* CONTINUE, REMEMBER.

perpetuity *noun*
1. The quality or state of having no end : ceaselessness, endlessness, eternality, eternalness, eternity, everlastingness, world without end. *See* CONTINUE. **2.** The totality of time without beginning or end : eternality, eternalness, eternity, infinity, sempiternity. *See* LIMITED.

perplex *verb*
1. To cause to be unclear in mind or intent : addle, befuddle, bewilder, confound, confuse, discombobulate, dizzy, fuddle, jumble, mix up, muddle, mystify, puzzle. *Informal:* throw. ***Idiom:*** make one's head reel (*or* swim *or* whirl). *See* CLEAR, FEELINGS. **2.** To make complex, intricate, or perplexing : complicate, embarrass, entangle, involve, ravel, snarl[2], tangle. *See* SIMPLE.

perplexed *adjective*
Mentally uncertain : addled, addlepated, confounded, confused, confusional, muddleheaded, turbid. *Informal:* mixed-up. *See* CLEAR.

perplexity *noun*
1. A stunned or bewildered condition : befuddlement, bewilderedness, bewilderment, daze, discombobulation, fog, muddle, mystification, puzzlement, stupefaction, stupor, trance. *See* AWARENESS. **2.** Anything that arouses curiosity or perplexes because it is unexplained, inexplicable, or secret : conundrum, enigma, mystery, puzzle, puzzler, riddle. *See* SHOW.

perquisite *noun*
1. A material favor or gift, usually money, given in return for service : cumshaw, gratuity, largess, tip[3]. *See* GIVE, TRANSACTIONS. **2.** A privilege granted a person, as by virtue of birth : appanage, birthright, prerogative, right. *Law:* droit. *See* OWNED.

persecute *verb*
To do a wrong to; treat unjustly : aggrieve, oppress, outrage, wrong. *See* RIGHT.

persecution *noun*
Excruciating punishment : hell, living hell, torment, torture. ***Idiom:*** tortures of the damned. *See* REWARD.

perseverance *noun*
The state or quality of being insistent : insistence, insistency, persistence, persistency. *See* CONTINUE.

persevere *verb*
1. To continue without halting despite difficulties or setbacks : carry on, go on, hang on, keep on, persist. ***Idioms:*** hang in there, keep going, keep it up. *See* CONTINUE. **2.** To take and maintain a stand obstinately : insist, persist. *See* CONTINUE.

persist *verb*
1. To take and maintain a stand obstinately : insist, persevere. *See* CONTINUE. **2.** To continue without halting despite difficulties or setbacks : carry on, go on, hang on, keep on, persevere. ***Idioms:*** hang in there, keep going, keep it up. *See* CONTINUE. **3.** To exist in spite of adversity : come through, last², pull through, ride out, survive, weather. *See* LIVE. **4.** To be in existence or in a certain state for an indefinitely long time : abide, continue, endure, go on, hold out, last², remain, stay¹. *See* CONTINUE.

persistence *noun*
1. The state or quality of being insistent : insistence, insistency, perseverance, persistency. *See* CONTINUE. **2.** Uninterrupted existence or succession : continuance, continuation, continuity, continuum, duration, endurance, persistency. *See* CONTINUE.

persistency *noun*
1. The state or quality of being insistent : insistence, insistency, perseverance, persistence. *See* CONTINUE. **2.** Uninterrupted existence or succession : continuance, continuation, continuity, continuum, duration, endurance, persistence. *See* CONTINUE.

persistent *adjective*
1. Firm or obstinate, as in making a demand or maintaining a stand : importunate, importune, insistent, urgent. *See* CONTINUE. **2.** Existing or occurring without interruption or end : around-the-clock, ceaseless, constant, continual, continuous, endless, eternal, everlasting, incessant, interminable, nonstop, ongoing, perpetual, relentless, round-the-clock, timeless, unceasing, unending, unfailing, uninterrupted, unremitting. *See* CONTINUE. **3.** Existing or remaining in the same state for an indefinitely long time : abiding, continuing, durable, enduring, lasting, long-lasting, long-lived, longstanding, old, perdurable, perennial, permanent. *See* CONTINUE. **4.** Of long duration : chronic, continuing, lingering, prolonged, protracted. *See* CONTINUE. **5.** Difficult to alleviate or cure : obstinate, pertinacious, stubborn. *See* CONTINUE.

persnickety *adjective*
Very difficult to please : choosy, dainty, exacting, fastidious, finical, finicky, fussy, meticulous, nice, particular, squeamish. *Informal:* picky. *See* ACCEPT.

person *noun*
A member of the human race : being, body, creature, homo, human, human being, individual, life, man, mortal, party, personage, soul. *See* BEINGS.

persona *noun*
A person portrayed in fiction or drama : character, personage. *See* REAL.

personage *noun*
1. A person portrayed in fiction or drama : character, persona. *See* REAL. **2.** A member of the human race : being, body, creature, homo, human, human being, individual, life, man, mortal, party, person, soul. *See* BEINGS. **3.** An important, influential person : character, dignitary, eminence, leader, lion, nabob, notability, notable. *Informal:* big-timer, heavyweight, somebody, someone, VIP. *Slang:* big shot, big wheel, bigwig, muckamuck. *See* IMPORTANT. **4.** A famous person : celebrity, hero, lion, luminary, name, notable, personality. *Informal:* big name. *See* KNOWLEDGE.

personal *adjective*
1. Belonging to, relating to, or affecting a particular person : individual, private. *See* SPECIFIC. **2.** Belonging or confined to a particular person or group as opposed to the public or the government : private, privy. *See* SPECIFIC. **3.** Based on individual judgment or discretion : arbitrary, discretionary, judgmental, subjective. *See* OPINION, SURPRISE. **4.** Characterized by a close and thorough acquaintance : inside, intimate¹. *See* NEAR. **5.** Of or relating to the human body : bodily, corporal, corporeal, fleshly, physical, somatic. *See* BODY.

personal effects *noun*
One's portable property : belonging (often used in plural), effect (used in plural), good (used in plural), lares and penates, personal property, possession (used in plural), property, thing (often used in plural). *Informal:* stuff. *Law:* chattel, movable (often used in plural). *See* OWNED.

personality *noun*
1. The combination of emotional, intellectual, and moral qualities that distinguishes an individual : character, complexion, disposition, makeup, nature. *See* BE. **2.** A famous person : celebrity, hero, lion, luminary, name, notable, personage. *Informal:* big name. *See* KNOWLEDGE.

personalization *noun*
A physical entity typifying an abstraction : embodiment, exteriorization, externalization, incarnation, manifestation, materialization, objectification, personification, substantiation, type. *Rhetoric:* prosopopeia. *See* SUBSTITUTE.

personalize *verb*
To represent (an abstraction, for example) in or as if in bodily form : body forth, embody, exteriorize, externalize, incarnate, manifest, materialize, objectify, personify, substantiate. *See* SUBSTITUTE.

personal property *noun*
One's portable property : belonging (often used in plural), effect (used in plural), good (used in plural), lares and penates, personal effects, possession (used in plural), property, thing (often used in plural). *Informal:* stuff. *Law:* chattel, movable (often used in plural). *See* OWNED.

personification *noun*
A physical entity typifying an abstraction : embodiment, exteriorization, externalization, incarnation, manifestation, materialization, objectification, personalization, substantiation, type. *Rhetoric:* prosopopeia. *See* SUBSTITUTE.

personify *verb*
To represent (an abstraction, for example) in or as if in bodily form : body forth, embody, exteriorize, externalize, incarnate, manifest, materialize, objectify, personalize, substantiate. *See* SUBSTITUTE.

perspective *noun*
That which is or can be seen : lookout, outlook, panorama, prospect, scene, sight, view, vista. *See* SEE.

perspicacious *adjective*
Having or showing a clever awareness and resourcefulness in practical matters : astute, cagey, canny, knowing, shrewd, slick, smart, wise[1]. *Informal:* savvy. *See* ABILITY, CAREFUL.

perspicacity *noun*
Skill in perceiving, discriminating, or judging : acumen, astuteness, clear-sightedness, discernment, discrimination, eye, keenness, nose, penetration, perceptiveness, percipience, percipiency, sagacity, sageness, shrewdness, wit. *See* ABILITY, CAREFUL.

perspicuity *noun*
The quality of being clear and easy to perceive or understand : clarity, clearness, distinctness, limpidity, limpidness, lucidity, lucidness, pellucidity, pellucidness, perspicuousness, plainness. *See* CLEAR.

perspicuousness *noun*
The quality of being clear and easy to perceive or understand : clarity, clearness, distinctness, limpidity, limpidness, lucidity, lucidness, pellucidity, pellucidness, perspicuity, plainness. *See* CLEAR.

perspiration *noun*
Moisture excreted through the pores of the skin : lather, sweat. *See* DRY.

perspire *verb*
To excrete moisture through the pores of the skin : lather, sweat. *See* DRY.

perspiring *adjective*
Producing or covered with sweat : sudoriferous, sweating, sweaty. *See* DRY.

persuade *verb*
1. To succeed in causing (a person) to act in a certain way : argue into, bring, bring around (*or* round), convince, get, induce, prevail on (*or* upon), sell (on), talk into. *See* PERSUASION. **2.** To cause (another) to believe or feel sure about something : assure, convince, satisfy, win over. *See* PERSUASION.

persuasion *noun*
1. Something believed or accepted as true by a person : belief, conviction, feeling, idea, mind, notion, opinion, position, sentiment, view. *See* OPINION. **2.** A system of religious belief : confession, creed, denomination, faith, religion, sect. *See* RELIGION. **3.** Those who accept and practice a particular religious belief : church, communion, denomination, faith, sect. *See* RELIGION. **4.** *Informal.* A class that is defined by the common attribute or attributes possessed by all its members : breed, cast, description, feather, ilk, kind[2], lot, manner, mold, nature, order, sort, species, stamp, stripe, type, variety. *See* GROUP.

persuasive *adjective*
Serving to convince : cogent, convincing, satisfactory, telling. *See* PERSUASION.

pert *adjective*
1. Very brisk, alert, and full of high spirits : animated, bouncy, chipper, dashing, high-spirited, lively, spirited, vivacious. *Informal:* peppy. ***Idioms:*** bright-eyed and bushy-tailed, full of life. *See* ACTION. **2.** Disrespectful and

rude : assuming, assumptive, audacious, bold, boldfaced, brash, brazen, cheeky, contumelious, familiar, forward, impertinent, impudent, insolent, malapert, nervy, overconfident, presuming, presumptuous, pushy, sassy, saucy, smart. *Informal:* brassy, flip, fresh, smart-alecky, snippety, snippy, uppish, uppity. *Slang:* wise[1]. *See* ATTITUDE, COURTESY.

pertain *verb*
To be pertinent : appertain, apply, bear on (*or* upon), concern, refer, relate. ***Idioms:*** have a bearing on, have to do with. *See* RELEVANT.

pertinacious *adjective*
1. Tenaciously unwilling to yield : bullheaded, dogged, hardheaded, headstrong, mulish, obstinate, perverse, pigheaded, stiff-necked, tenacious, willful. *See* RESIST. **2.** Difficult to alleviate or cure : obstinate, persistent, stubborn. *See* CONTINUE.

pertinaciousness *noun*
The quality or state of being stubbornly unyielding : bullheadedness, doggedness, hardheadedness, mulishness, obstinacy, obstinateness, pertinacity, perverseness, perversity, pigheadedness, tenaciousness, tenacity, willfulness. *See* RESIST.

pertinacity *noun*
The quality or state of being stubbornly unyielding : bullheadedness, doggedness, hardheadedness, mulishness, obstinacy, obstinateness, pertinaciousness, perverseness, perversity, pigheadedness, tenaciousness, tenacity, willfulness. *See* RESIST.

pertinence *noun*
The fact of being related to the matter at hand : applicability, application, appositeness, bearing, concernment, germaneness, materiality, pertinency, relevance, relevancy. *See* RELEVANT.

pertinency *noun*
The fact of being related to the matter at hand : applicability, application, appositeness, bearing, concernment, germaneness, materiality, pertinence, relevance, relevancy. *See* RELEVANT.

pertinent *adjective*
Related to the matter at hand : applicable, apposite, apropos, germane, material, relevant. ***Idiom:*** to the point. *See* RELEVANT.

pertness *noun*
1. A lively, emphatic, eager quality or manner : animation, bounce, brio, dash, élan, esprit, life, liveliness, sparkle, spirit, verve, vigor, vim, vivaciousness, vivacity, zip. *Informal:* ginger, pep, peppiness. *Slang:* oomph. *See* ACTION. **2.** The state or quality of being impudent or arrogantly self-confident : assumption, audaciousness, audacity, boldness, brashness, brazenness, cheek, cheekiness, chutzpah, discourtesy, disrespect, effrontery, face, familiarity, forwardness, gall[1], impertinence, impudence, impudency, incivility, insolence, nerve, nerviness, overconfidence, presumptuousness, pushiness, rudeness, sassiness, sauciness. *Informal:* brass, crust, sauce, uppishness, uppityness. *See* ATTITUDE, COURTESY.

perturb *verb*
To impair or destroy the composure of : agitate, bother, discompose, disquiet, distract, disturb, flurry, fluster, rock, ruffle, shake (up), toss, unsettle, upset. *Informal:* rattle. *See* CALM.

perturbation *noun*
A state of discomposure : agitation, dither, fluster, flutter, tumult, turmoil, upset. *Informal:* lather, stew. *See* CALM.

perturbing *adjective*
Troubling to the mind or emotions : disquieting, disruptive, distressful, distressing, disturbing, intrusive, troublesome, troublous, unsettling, upsetting, worrisome. *See* HAPPY, PAIN.

perusal *noun*
The act of examining carefully : check, checkup, examination, inspection, scrutiny, study, view. *Informal:* going-over. *See* INVESTIGATE.

peruse *verb*
To look at carefully or critically : check (out), con, examine, go over, inspect, scrutinize, study, survey, traverse, view. *Informal:* case. ***Idiom:*** give a going-over. *See* INVESTIGATE.

pervade *verb*
To cause to be filled, as with a particular mood or tone : charge, freight, imbue, impregnate, permeate, saturate, suffuse, transfuse. *See* FULL.

perverse *adjective*
1. Utterly reprehensible in nature or behavior : corrupt, degenerate, depraved, flagitious, miscreant, rotten, unhealthy, villainous. *See* CLEAN, GOOD. **2.** Tenaciously unwilling to yield : bullheaded, dogged, hardheaded, headstrong, mulish, obstinate, pertinacious, pigheaded, stiff-necked, tenacious, willful. *See* RESIST. **3.** Given to acting in opposition to others : balky, contrarious, contrary, difficult, froward, impossible, ornery, wayward. *See* ATTITUDE, SUPPORT.

perverseness *noun*
The quality or state of being stubbornly

unyielding : bullheadedness, doggedness, hardheadedness, mulishness, obstinacy, obstinateness, pertinaciousness, pertinacity, perversity, pigheadedness, tenaciousness, tenacity, willfulness. *See* RESIST.

perversion *noun*
1. Wrong, often corrupt use : abuse, misapplication, misappropriation, mishandling, misuse. *See* TREAT WELL. **2.** Degrading, immoral acts or habits : bestiality, corruption, depravity, flagitiousness, immorality, turpitude, vice, villainousness, villainy, wickedness. *See* CLEAN.

perversity *noun*
The quality or state of being stubbornly unyielding : bullheadedness, doggedness, hardheadedness, mulishness, obstinacy, obstinateness, pertinaciousness, pertinacity, perverseness, pigheadedness, tenaciousness, tenacity, willfulness. *See* RESIST.

pervert *verb*
1. To ruin utterly in character or quality : animalize, bastardize, bestialize, brutalize, canker, corrupt, debase, debauch, demoralize, deprave, stain, vitiate, warp. *See* CLEAN, HELP. **2.** To use wrongly and improperly : abuse, misapply, misappropriate, mishandle, misuse. *See* TREAT WELL. **3.** To give an inaccurate view of by representing falsely or misleadingly : belie, color, distort, falsify, load, misrepresent, misstate, twist, warp, wrench, wrest. ***Idiom:*** give a false coloring to. *See* TRUE.

pervert *noun* One whose sexual behavior differs from the accepted norm : deviant, deviate. *See* USUAL, SEX.

pesky *adjective*
Informal. Hard to treat, manage, or cope with : troublesome, wicked. *Slang:* mean[2]. *See* EASY.

pessimist *noun*
A prophet of misfortune or disaster : Cassandra, doomsayer, worrywart. *See* HOPE.

pessimistic *adjective*
Marked by little hopefulness : dark, dismal, gloomy. *See* HAPPY, HOPE.

pester *verb*
1. To disturb by repeated attacks : annoy, bait, bedevil, beleaguer, beset, harass, harry, plague, tease, torment, worry. *See* FEELINGS, PAIN.
2. To trouble persistently from or as if from all sides : badger, bedevil, beleaguer, beset, besiege, harass, harry, hound, importune, plague, solicit. *See* ATTACK.

pestering *noun*
The act of annoying : annoyance, botheration, bothering, exasperation, harassment, irritation, provocation, vexation. *See* FEELINGS, PAIN.

pestilent *adjective*
Extremely destructive or harmful : baneful, deadly, malignant, noxious, pernicious, pestilential, virulent. *See* HELP.

pestilential *adjective*
Extremely destructive or harmful : baneful, deadly, malignant, noxious, pernicious, pestilent, virulent. *See* HELP.

pet[1] *noun*
One liked or preferred above all others : darling, favorite. ***Idiom:*** apple of one's eye. *See* LIKE.

pet *adjective* Given special, usually doting treatment : darling, fair-haired, favored, favorite. *See* TREAT WELL.

pet *verb* **1.** To touch or stroke affectionately : caress, cuddle, fondle, pat. *See* TOUCH.
2. *Informal.* To engage in kissing and other amorous behavior : *Informal:* fool around, neck, spoon. *Slang:* make out. *See* SEX.

pet[2] *verb*
To be sullenly aloof or withdrawn, as in silent resentment or protest : mope, pout, sulk. *See* HAPPY.

petechia *noun*
A mark on the skin indicative of a disease, as typhus : stigma. *See* MARKS.

peter *verb*
To grow or cause to grow gradually less. Also used with *out* : abate, decrease, diminish, drain, dwindle, ebb, lessen, let up, rebate, reduce, tail away (*or* off), taper (off). *See* INCREASE.

petite *adjective*
Notably below average in amount, size, or scope : bantam, little, small, smallish. *See* BIG.

petition *noun*
An application to a higher authority, as for sanction or a decision : appeal. *Law:* prayer[1]. *See* ASK, LAW.

petition *verb* **1.** To bring an appeal or request, for example, to the attention of : address, appeal, apply, approach. *Obsolete:* sue. *See* REQUEST. **2.** To make application to a higher authority, as to a court of law : *Law:* appeal, sue. *See* LAW. **3.** To ask for employment, acceptance, or admission : apply, put in. *See* SEEK.

petitioner *noun*
1. One that asks a higher authority for something, as a favor or redress : appealer, appellant, suitor. *See* ASK, LAW. **2.** A person who applies for or seeks something, such as a job or position : applicant, aspirant, candidate, hopeful, seeker. *See* SEEK.

petrify *verb*
1. To make or become physically hard : cake, concrete, congeal, dry, harden, indurate, set[1], solidify. *See* SOLID. **2.** To render helpless, as by emotion : benumb, numb, paralyze, stun, stupefy, wither. *See* AFFECT.

pettifog *verb*
To raise unnecessary or trivial objections : carp, cavil, niggle, nitpick, quibble. ***Idiom:*** pick to pieces. *See* SUPPORT.

pettiness *noun*
Contemptible unimportance : inconsiderableness, negligibility, negligibleness, paltriness, smallness, triviality, trivialness. *See* IMPORTANT.

petty *adjective*
1. Contemptibly unimportant : inconsiderable, negligible, niggling, nugatory, paltry, picayune, piddling, small, small-minded, trifling. *Slang:* measly. ***Idiom:*** of no account. *See* IMPORTANT. **2.** Not broad or elevated in scope or understanding : limited, little, narrow, narrow-minded, small, small-minded. *See* LIMITED, WIDE. **3.** Ungenerously or pettily reluctant to spend money : cheap, close, close-fisted, costive, hard-fisted, mean[2], miserly, niggard, niggardly, parsimonious, penny-pinching, penurious, pinching, stingy, tight, tightfisted. *See* GIVE. **4.** Below another in standing or importance : inferior, junior, lesser, low, lower[2], minor, minor-league, secondary, small, subaltern, subordinate, under. *Informal:* smalltime. *See* OVER.

petulant *adjective*
Having or showing a bad temper : bad-tempered, cantankerous, crabbed, cranky, cross, disagreeable, fretful, grouchy, grumpy, ill-tempered, irascible, irritable, nasty, peevish, querulous, snappish, snappy, surly, testy, ugly, waspish. *Informal:* crabby, mean[2]. ***Idiom:*** out of sorts. *See* ATTITUDE.

phantasm *noun*
1. A supernatural being, such as a ghost : apparition, bogey, bogeyman, bogle, eidolon, ghost, phantasma, phantom, revenant, shade, shadow, specter, spirit, visitant, wraith. *Informal:* spook. *Regional:* haunt. *See* BEINGS, SUPERNATURAL. **2.** An illusory mental image : daydream, dream, fancy, fantasy, fiction, figment, illusion, phantasma, reverie, vision. *See* REAL. **3.** An erroneous perception of reality : delusion, hallucination, ignis fatuus, illusion, mirage, phantasma, will-o'-the-wisp. *See* REAL.

phantasma *noun*
1. A supernatural being, such as a ghost : apparition, bogey, bogeyman, bogle, eidolon, ghost, phantasm, phantom, revenant, shade, shadow, specter, spirit, visitant, wraith. *Informal:* spook. *Regional:* haunt. *See* BEINGS, SUPERNATURAL. **2.** An illusory mental image : daydream, dream, fancy, fantasy, fiction, figment, illusion, phantasm, reverie, vision. *See* REAL. **3.** An erroneous perception of reality : delusion, hallucination, ignis fatuus, illusion, mirage, phantasm, will-o'-the-wisp. *See* REAL.

phantasmagoria *noun*
An illusion of perceiving something that does not really exist : hallucination, phantasmagory. *Slang:* trip. *See* REAL.

phantasmagoric *adjective*
Of, relating to, or in the nature of an illusion; lacking reality : chimeric, chimerical, delusive, delusory, dreamlike, hallucinatory, illusive, illusory, phantasmal, phantasmic, visionary. *See* REAL.

phantasmagory *noun*
An illusion of perceiving something that does not really exist : hallucination, phantasmagoria. *Slang:* trip. *See* REAL.

phantasmal *adjective*
Of, relating to, or in the nature of an illusion; lacking reality : chimeric, chimerical, delusive, delusory, dreamlike, hallucinatory, illusive, illusory, phantasmagoric, phantasmic, visionary. *See* REAL.

phantasmic *adjective*
Of, relating to, or in the nature of an illusion; lacking reality : chimeric, chimerical, delusive, delusory, dreamlike, hallucinatory, illusive, illusory, phantasmagoric, phantasmal, visionary. *See* REAL.

phantom *noun*
A supernatural being, such as a ghost : apparition, bogey, bogeyman, bogle, eidolon, ghost, phantasm, phantasma, revenant, shade, shadow, specter, spirit, visitant, wraith. *Informal:* spook. *Regional:* haunt. *See* BEINGS, SUPERNATURAL.

pharisaic *adjective*
Of or practicing hypocrisy : hypocritical, Pecksniffian, pharisaical, phony, sanctimonious, two-faced. *See* HONEST.

pharisaical *adjective*
Of or practicing hypocrisy : hypocritical, Pecksniffian, pharisaic, phony, sanctimonious, two-faced. *See* HONEST.

pharisaism *noun*
A show or expression of feelings or beliefs one does not actually hold or possess : hypocrisy,

phoniness, sanctimoniousness, sanctimony, tartuffery, two-facedness. *See* HONEST.

pharisee *noun*
A person who practices hypocrisy : hypocrite, phony, tartuffe. *See* HONEST.

pharmaceutical *noun*
A substance used in the treatment of disease : drug, medicament, medication, medicine. *See* DRUGS.

phase *noun*
1. An interval regarded as a distinct evolutionary or developmental unit : period, stage. *See* TIME. **2.** The particular angle from which something is considered : angle², aspect, facet, frame of reference, hand, light¹, regard, respect, side. *See* PERSPECTIVE.

phenomenal *adjective*
1. Composed of or relating to things that occupy space and can be perceived by the senses : concrete, corporeal, material, objective, physical, sensible, substantial, tangible. *See* BODY, MATTER. **2.** So remarkable as to elicit disbelief : amazing, astonishing, astounding, fabulous, fantastic, fantastical, incredible, marvelous, miraculous, prodigious, stupendous, unbelievable, wonderful, wondrous. *See* GOOD.

phenomenon *noun*
1. Something having real, demonstrable existence : actuality, event, fact, reality. *See* REAL. **2.** One that evokes great surprise and admiration : astonishment, marvel, miracle, prodigy, sensation, stunner, wonder, wonderment. ***Idioms:*** one for the books, the eighth wonder of the world. *See* GOOD.

philander *verb*
To be sexually unfaithful to another : womanize. *Informal:* cheat, fool around, mess around, play around. *See* SEX.

philanderer *noun*
A man who philanders : Casanova, Don Juan, lady's man, womanizer. *Slang:* lady-killer, wolf. ***Idioms:*** man on the make, skirt chaser. *See* SEX.

philanthropic *adjective*
Of or concerned with charity : altruistic, benevolent, charitable, eleemosynary, philanthropical. *See* GIVE, KIND.

philanthropical *adjective*
Of or concerned with charity : altruistic, benevolent, charitable, eleemosynary, philanthropic. *See* GIVE, KIND.

philanthropy *noun*
1. Kindly, charitable interest in others : altruism, beneficence, benevolence, benignancy, benignity, charitableness, charity, goodwill, grace, kindheartedness, kindliness, kindness. *See* ATTITUDE, KIND. **2.** A charitable deed : benefaction, beneficence, benevolence, benignity, favor, kindliness, kindness, oblation, office (often used in plural). *See* GIVE, KIND.

philippic *noun*
A long, violent, or blustering speech, usually of censure or denunciation : diatribe, fulmination, harangue, jeremiad, tirade. *See* PRAISE.

Philistine also **philistine** *noun*
An unrefined, rude person : barbarian, boor, chuff, churl, vulgarian, yahoo. *See* GOOD.
philistine also **Philistine** *adjective* Lacking in delicacy or refinement : barbarian, barbaric, boorish, churlish, coarse, crass, crude, gross, ill-bred, indelicate, rough, rude, tasteless, uncivilized, uncouth, uncultivated, uncultured, unpolished, unrefined, vulgar. *See* COURTESY, SMOOTH.

philosopher *noun*
A person who seeks reason and truth by thinking and meditation : thinker. *See* THOUGHTS.

phlegm *noun*
Lack of emotion or interest : apathy, disinterest, impassivity, incuriosity, incuriousness, indifference, insensibility, insensibleness, lassitude, lethargy, listlessness, stolidity, stolidness, unconcern, uninterest, unresponsiveness. *See* FEELINGS.

phlegmatic *adjective*
Without emotion or interest : apathetic, detached, impassive, incurious, indifferent, insensible, lethargic, listless, stolid, unconcerned, uninterested, unresponsive. *See* FEELINGS.

phoenix *noun*
A person or thing so excellent as to have no equal or match : nonesuch, nonpareil, paragon. *See* GOOD.

phone *verb*
Informal. To communicate with (someone) by telephone : buzz, call, ring², telephone. *Informal:* dial. ***Idioms:*** get someone on the horn, give someone a buzz (*or* call *or* ring). *See* WORDS.

phoney *adjective & noun* See **phony.**

phoniness *noun*
1. Lack of sincerity : ambidexterity, artificiality, disingenuousness, insincerity. *See* HONEST. **2.** A show or expression of feelings or beliefs one does not actually hold or possess : hypocrisy, pharisaism, sanctimoniousness, sanctimony, tartuffery, two-facedness. *See* HONEST.

phony also **phoney** *adjective*
1. Fraudulently or deceptively imitative : bogus, counterfeit, fake, false, fraudulent, sham, spurious, suppositious, supposititious. *See* TRUE. **2.** Not genuine or sincere : affected, artificial, feigned, insincere, pretended. *See* TRUE. **3.** Of or practicing hypocrisy : hypocritical, Pecksniffian, pharisaic, pharisaical, sanctimonious, two-faced. *See* HONEST.
phony also **phoney** *noun* **1.** A fraudulent imitation : counterfeit, fake, forgery, sham. *See* TRUE. **2.** One who fakes : charlatan, fake, faker, fraud, humbug, impostor, mountebank, pretender, quack. *See* TRUE. **3.** A person who practices hypocrisy : hypocrite, pharisee, tartuffe. *See* HONEST.

photographic *adjective*
1. Of or relating to representation by drawings or pictures : graphic, hieroglyphic, illustrative, pictographic, pictorial. *See* SEE. **2.** Described verbally in sharp and accurate detail : graphic, lifelike, pictorial, picturesque, realistic, vivid. *See* SPECIFIC, WORDS.

phrase *noun*
1. A word or group of words forming a unit and conveying meaning : expression, locution. *See* WORDS. **2.** Choice of words and the way in which they are used : diction, parlance, phraseology, phrasing, verbalism, wordage, wording. *See* WORDS.
phrase *verb* To convey in language or words of a particular form : couch, express, formulate, put, word. *See* WORDS.

phraseology *noun*
Choice of words and the way in which they are used : diction, parlance, phrase, phrasing, verbalism, wordage, wording. *See* WORDS.

phrasing *noun*
Choice of words and the way in which they are used : diction, parlance, phrase, phraseology, verbalism, wordage, wording. *See* WORDS.

phthisic *noun*
An infectious disease producing lesions especially of the lungs. No longer in scientific use : consumption (no longer in scientific use), phthisis (no longer in scientific use), tuberculosis, white plague. *See* HEALTH.
phthisic *adjective* Relating to or afflicted with tuberculosis. No longer in scientific use : consumptive (no longer in scientific use), phthisical (no longer in scientific use), tubercular, tuberculate, tuberculous. *See* HEALTH.

phthisical *adjective*
Relating to or afflicted with tuberculosis. No longer in scientific use : consumptive (no longer in scientific use), phthisic (no longer in scientific use), tubercular, tuberculate, tuberculous. *See* HEALTH.

phthisis *noun*
An infectious disease producing lesions especially of the lungs. No longer in scientific use : consumption (no longer in scientific use), phthisic (no longer in scientific use), tuberculosis, white plague. *See* HEALTH.

phylactery *noun*
A small object worn or kept for its supposed magical power : amulet, charm, fetish, juju, periapt, talisman. *See* SUPERNATURAL.

physic *noun*
An agent used to restore health : cure, elixir, medicament, medication, medicine, nostrum, remedy. *See* HEALTH.
physic *verb* To administer or add a drug to : dose, drug, medicate, narcotize, opiate. *Informal:* dope (up). *See* DRUGS.

physical *adjective*
1. Of or relating to the human body : bodily, corporal, corporeal, fleshly, personal, somatic. *See* BODY. **2.** Relating to the desires and appetites of the body : animal, carnal, fleshly, sensual. *See* BODY. **3.** Composed of or relating to things that occupy space and can be perceived by the senses : concrete, corporeal, material, objective, phenomenal, sensible, substantial, tangible. *See* BODY, MATTER.

physicality *noun*
A preoccupation with the body and satisfaction of its desires : animalism, animality, carnality, fleshliness, sensuality. *See* BODY.

physiognomy *noun*
An outward appearance : aspect, countenance, face, look, surface, visage. *See* SURFACE.

physique *noun*
The physical or constitutional characteristics of a person : build, constitution, habit, habitus. *See* BODY.

picayune *adjective*
Contemptibly unimportant : inconsiderable, negligible, niggling, nugatory, paltry, petty, piddling, small, small-minded, trifling. *Slang:* measly. ***Idiom:*** of no account. *See* IMPORTANT.

pick *verb*
1. To make a choice from a number of alternatives. Also used with *out* : choose, cull, elect, opt (for), select, single (out). *See* CHOICE. **2.** To collect ripe crops : crop, garner, gather, harvest, reap. *See* COLLECT.
pick off *verb* To wound or kill with a firearm : gun (down), shoot. *Slang:* plug. *See* HELP.

pick on *verb* To scold or find fault with constantly : carp at, fuss at, nag, peck at. *Informal:* henpeck. *See* PRAISE.

pick out *verb* To perceive and fix the identity of, especially with difficulty : descry, discern, distinguish, make out, spot. *See* SEE.

pick up *verb* **1.** To move (something) to a higher position : boost, elevate, heave, hoist, lift, raise, rear[2], take up, uphold, uplift, upraise, uprear. *See* RISE. **2.** To collect (something) bit by bit : cull, extract, garner, gather, glean. *See* COLLECT. **3.** *Informal.* To come into possession of : acquire, come by, gain, get, obtain, procure, secure, win. *Informal:* land. *See* GET. **4.** *Informal.* To gain knowledge or mastery of by study : get, learn, master. *See* TEACH. **5.** *Informal.* To take into custody as a prisoner : apprehend, arrest, seize. *Informal:* nab. *Slang:* bust, collar, pinch, run in. *See* LAW. **6.** To begin or go on after an interruption : continue, renew, reopen, restart, resume, take up. *See* CONTINUE.

pick *noun* **1.** The superlative or most preferable part of something : best, choice, cream, crème de la crème, elite, flower, prize[1], top. ***Idioms:*** cream of the crop, flower of the flock, pick of the bunch (*or* crop) . *See* BETTER. **2.** One that is selected : choice, chosen, elect, select. *See* CHOICE.

picket *noun*
A person or special body of persons assigned to provide protection or keep watch over, for example : guard, lookout, protector, sentinel, sentry, ward, watch. *See* AWARENESS, SAFETY.

pickle *noun*
Informal. A difficult, often embarrassing situation or condition : box[1], corner, deep water, difficulty, dilemma, Dutch, fix, hole, hot spot, hot water, jam, plight[1], predicament, quagmire, scrape, soup, trouble. *Informal:* bind, spot. *See* EASY.

pickled *adjective*
Slang. Stupefied, excited, or muddled with alcoholic liquor : besotted, crapulent, crapulous, drunk, drunken, inebriate, inebriated, intoxicated, sodden, tipsy. *Informal:* cock-eyed, stewed. *Slang:* blind, bombed, boozed, boozy, crocked, high, lit (up), loaded, looped, pixilated, plastered, potted, sloshed, smashed, soused, stinking, stinko, stoned, tight, zonked. ***Idioms:*** drunk as a skunk, half-seas over, high as a kite, in one's cups, three sheets in (*or* to) the wind. *See* DRUGS.

pick-me-up *noun*
Informal. A medicine that restores or increases vigor : restorative, roborant, tonic. *Informal:* bracer. *See* HELP.

pick off *verb* See **pick.**

pick on *verb* See **pick.**

pick out *verb* See **pick.**

pick up *verb* See **pick.**

pickup *noun*
Slang. A seizing and holding by law : apprehension, arrest, seizure. *Slang:* bust, collar, pinch. *See* LAW.

picky *adjective*
Informal. Very difficult to please : choosy, dainty, exacting, fastidious, finical, finicky, fussy, meticulous, nice, particular, persnickety, squeamish. *See* ACCEPT.

pictographic *adjective*
Of or relating to representation by drawings or pictures : graphic, hieroglyphic, illustrative, photographic, pictorial. *See* SEE.

pictorial *adjective*
1. Of or relating to representation by drawings or pictures : graphic, hieroglyphic, illustrative, photographic, pictographic. *See* SEE.
2. Described verbally in sharp and accurate detail : graphic, lifelike, photographic, picturesque, realistic, vivid. *See* SPECIFIC, WORDS.

picture *noun*
One exactly resembling another : double, duplicate, image, portrait, spitting image. *Slang:* ringer. *See* SAME.

picture *verb* **1.** To form mental images of : conceive, envisage, envision, fancy, fantasize, image, imagine, see, think, vision, visualize. *Informal:* feature. *See* THOUGHTS. **2.** To present a lifelike image of : delineate, depict, describe, express, image, limn, portray, render, represent, show. *See* SHOW.

picturesque *adjective*
1. Evoking strong mental images through distinctiveness : colorful, vivid. *See* STRONG.
2. Described verbally in sharp and accurate detail : graphic, lifelike, photographic, pictorial, realistic, vivid. *See* SPECIFIC, WORDS.

piddling *adjective*
Contemptibly unimportant : inconsiderable, negligible, niggling, nugatory, paltry, petty, picayune, small, small-minded, trifling. *Slang:* measly. ***Idiom:*** of no account. *See* IMPORTANT.

piece *noun*
1. One of the parts into which something is divided : division, member, part, portion, section, segment, subdivision. *See* PART. **2.** One's

proper or expected function in a common effort : part, role, share. *See* DO, PARTICIPATE. **3.** A part severed from a whole : cut, portion, section, segment, slice. *See* PART. **4.** A small portion of food : bit[1], crumb, morsel, mouthful. *Informal:* bite. *See* BIG. **5.** Something that is the result of creative effort : composition, opus, production, work. *See* MAKE. **6.** A usually brief detail of news or information : bit[1], item, paragraph, squib, story. *See* WORDS. **7.** *Informal.* An extent, measured or unmeasured, of linear space : distance, length, space, stretch. *Informal:* way. *See* BIG.

piecemeal *adjective*
Proceeding very slowly by degrees : gradational, gradual, step-by-step. *See* FAST.

pierce *verb*
1. To penetrate with a sharp edge : cut, gash, incise, slash, slit. *See* ENTER, HELP. **2.** To make a hole or other opening in : breach, break (through), gap, hole, perforate, puncture. *See* OPEN. **3.** To pass into or through by overcoming resistance : break (through), enter, penetrate, perforate, puncture. *See* ENTER.

piercing *adjective*
1. Marked by severity or intensity : acute, gnawing, knifelike, lancinating, sharp, shooting, stabbing. *See* BIG. **2.** Elevated in pitch : high, high-pitched, piping, shrieky, shrill, shrilly, treble. *Music:* acute. *See* HIGH, SOUNDS.

pietism *noun*
A state of often extreme religious ardour : devotion, devoutness, piety, piousness, religionism, religiosity, religiousness. *See* RELIGION.

pietistic *adjective*
Deeply concerned with God and the beliefs and practice of religion : devotional, devout, godly, holy, pietistical, pious, prayerful, religious, saintly. *See* RELIGION.

pietistical *adjective*
Deeply concerned with God and the beliefs and practice of religion : devotional, devout, godly, holy, pietistic, pious, prayerful, religious, saintly. *See* RELIGION.

piety *noun*
A state of often extreme religious ardour : devotion, devoutness, pietism, piousness, religionism, religiosity, religiousness. *See* RELIGION.

piffle *noun*
Something that does not have or make sense : balderdash, blather, bunkum, claptrap, drivel, garbage, idiocy, nonsense, poppycock, rigmarole, rubbish, tomfoolery, trash, twaddle. *Informal:* tommyrot. *Slang:* applesauce, baloney, bilge, bull[1], bunk[2], crap, hooey, malarkey. *See* KNOWLEDGE.

pigeon *noun*
Slang. A person who is easily deceived or victimized : butt[3], dupe, fool, gull, lamb, pushover, victim. *Informal:* sucker. *Slang:* fall guy, gudgeon, mark, monkey, patsy, sap[1]. *Chiefly British:* mug. *See* WISE.

pigeonhole *verb*
1. To distribute into groups according to kinds : assort, categorize, class, classify, group, separate, sort (out). *See* COLLECT. **2.** To assign to a class or classes : categorize, class, classify, distribute, grade, group, place, range, rank[1], rate[1]. *See* GROUP, VALUE.

piggish *adjective*
Wanting to eat or drink more than one can reasonably consume : edacious, gluttonous, greedy, hoggish, ravenous, voracious. *See* DESIRE, INGESTION.

pigheaded *adjective*
Tenaciously unwilling to yield : bullheaded, dogged, hardheaded, headstrong, mulish, obstinate, pertinacious, perverse, stiff-necked, tenacious, willful. *See* RESIST.

pigheadedness *noun*
The quality or state of being stubbornly unyielding : bullheadedness, doggedness, hardheadedness, mulishness, obstinacy, obstinateness, pertinaciousness, pertinacity, perverseness, perversity, tenaciousness, tenacity, willfulness. *See* RESIST.

pigment *noun*
Something that imparts color : color, colorant, coloring, dye, dyestuff, stain, tincture. *See* COLORS.

pigmy *adjective* See **pygmy.**

pile *noun*
1. A group of things gathered haphazardly : agglomeration, bank[1], cumulus, drift, heap, hill, mass, mess, mound, mountain, shock[2], stack, tumble. *See* ORDER. **2.** *Informal.* A great deal : abundance, mass, mountain, much, plenty, profusion, wealth, world. *Informal:* barrel, heap, lot, pack, peck[2]. *Regional:* power, sight. *See* BIG. **3.** *Slang.* A large sum of money : fortune, mint. *Informal:* bundle, pretty penny, tidy sum, wad. *See* RICH. **4.** A usually permanent construction, such as a house or store : building, edifice, structure. *See* MAKE.

pile *verb* **1.** To put into a disordered pile. Also used with *up* : bank[1], drift, heap, hill, lump[1], mound, stack. *See* ORDER. **2.** To make or become full; put as much into as can be held :

charge, fill, freight, heap, load, pack. *See* FULL. **3.** To fill to overflowing : heap, lade, load. *See* FULL. **4.** To leave one's bed : arise, get up, rise, roll out. *Informal:* turn out. ***Idiom:*** rise and shine. *See* RISE.

pile up *verb* **1.** To bring together so as to increase in mass or number : accrue, accumulate, agglomerate, aggregate, amass, collect[1], cumulate, garner, gather, hive, roll up. *See* COLLECT. **2.** *Informal.* To undergo wrecking : crash, smash. *Informal:* crack up. *See* HELP.

pileup or **pile-up** *noun*
Informal. A wrecking of a vehicle : crash, smash, smashup, wreck. *Informal:* crackup. *See* HELP.

pile up *verb* See **pile.**

pilfer *verb*
To take (another's property) without permission : filch, purloin, snatch, steal, thieve. *Informal:* lift, swipe. *Slang:* cop, heist, hook, nip[1], pinch, rip off, snitch. ***Idiom:*** make (*or* walk) off with. *See* CRIMES, GIVE.

pilferage *noun*
The crime of taking someone else's property without consent : larceny, steal, theft, thievery. *Slang:* rip-off. *See* CRIMES.

pilferer *noun*
A person who steals : bandit, burglar, highwayman, housebreaker, larcener, larcenist, purloiner, robber, stealer, thief. *See* CRIMES.

pilgrimage *noun*
A journey undertaken with a specific objective : expedition, safari, tour, trek, voyage. *See* MOVE.

pill *noun*
Slang. An unpleasant, tiresome person : bore. *Slang:* drip, dweeb, jerk, nerd, poop[2]. *See* LIKE.

pillage *verb*
To rob of goods by force, especially in time of war : depredate, despoil, havoc, loot, plunder, ransack, rape, ravage, sack[2], spoliate, strip[1]. *Archaic:* harrow, spoil. *See* CRIMES, GIVE.

pillage *noun* Goods or property seized unlawfully, especially by a victor in wartime : booty, loot, plunder, spoil (used in plural). *Slang:* boodle. *Nautical:* prize[2]. *See* CRIMES, GIVE.

pilose *adjective*
Covered with hair : fleecy, furry, fuzzy, hairy, hirsute, woolly. *See* SMOOTH.

pilot *noun*
Something or someone that shows the way : conductor, director, escort, guide, lead, leader, shepherd, usher. *See* SHOW.

pilot *verb* **1.** To run and control (a motor vehicle) : drive, motor, wheel. *Slang:* tool. *See* MOVE. **2.** To direct the course of carefully : guide, jockey, maneuver, navigate, steer. ***Idiom:*** back and fill. *See* CONTROL, MOVE. **3.** To show the way to : conduct, direct, escort, guide, lead, route, shepherd, show, steer, usher. *See* SHOW.

pilot *adjective* Constituting a tentative model for future experiment or development : experimental, test, trial. *See* START.

pinch *verb*
1. To be severely sparing in order to economize : scrape, scrimp, skimp, stint. ***Idioms:*** pinch pennies, tighten (one's) belt. *See* SAVE. **2.** *Slang.* To take (another's property) without permission : filch, pilfer, purloin, snatch, steal, thieve. *Informal:* lift, swipe. *Slang:* cop, heist, hook, nip[1], rip off, snitch. ***Idiom:*** make (*or* walk) off with. *See* CRIMES, GIVE. **3.** *Slang.* To take into custody as a prisoner : apprehend, arrest, seize. *Informal:* nab, pick up. *Slang:* bust, collar, run in. *See* LAW.

pinch *noun* *Slang.* A seizing and holding by law : apprehension, arrest, seizure. *Slang:* bust, collar, pickup. *See* LAW.

pinchbeck *noun*
An inferior substitute imitating an original : copy, ersatz, imitation, simulation. *See* SUBSTITUTE.

pinch-hit *verb*
Informal. To act as a substitute : fill in, stand in, substitute, supply. *Informal:* sub. *See* SUBSTITUTE.

pinch hitter *noun*
Informal. One that takes the place of another : alternate, replacement, stand-in, substitute, surrogate. *Informal:* fill-in, sub. *See* SUBSTITUTE.

pinching *adjective*
Ungenerously or pettily reluctant to spend money : cheap, close, close-fisted, costive, hard-fisted, mean[2], miserly, niggard, niggardly, parsimonious, penny-pinching, penurious, petty, stingy, tight, tightfisted. *See* GIVE.

pine *verb*
1. To have a strong longing for : ache, covet, desire, hanker, long[2], pant, want, wish, yearn. *Informal:* hone[2]. *See* DESIRE. **2.** To waste away from longing or grief. Also used with *away* : languish, wither. *See* HEALTH.

pink-slip *verb*
Informal. To end the employment or service of : cashier, discharge, dismiss, drop, release, terminate. *Informal:* ax, fire. *Slang:* boot[1], bounce, can, sack[1]. ***Idioms:*** give someone his or

her walking papers, give someone the ax, give someone the gate, give someone the pink slip, let go, show someone the door. *See* KEEP.

pinnacle *noun*
The highest point or state : acme, apex, apogee, climax, crest, crown, culmination, height, meridian, peak, summit, top, zenith. *Informal:* payoff. *Medicine:* fastigium. *See* HIGH.

pin on *verb*
To ascribe (a misdeed or an error, for example) to : affix, assign, blame, fasten, fix, impute, place. *See* GIVE.

pinpoint *noun*
A very small mark : dash, dot, fleck, point, speck, spot. *See* MARKS.
pinpoint *verb* **1.** To look for and discover : find, locate, spot. *See* GET. **2.** To establish the identification of : identify, place, recognize. *Slang:* finger. ***Idiom:*** put one's finger on. *See* KNOWLEDGE.

pintsize *adjective*
Informal. Extremely small : diminutive, dwarf, Lilliputian, midget, miniature, minuscule, minute[2], pygmy, tiny, wee. *Informal:* peewee, pintsized, teensy, teensy-weensy, teeny, teeny-weeny, weeny. *See* BIG.

pintsized *adjective*
Informal. Extremely small : diminutive, dwarf, Lilliputian, midget, miniature, minuscule, minute[2], pygmy, tiny, wee. *Informal:* peewee, pintsize, teensy, teensy-weensy, teeny, teeny-weeny, weeny. *See* BIG.

pioneer *noun*
A person instrumental in the growth of something, especially in its early stages : builder, contributor, creator, developer. *See* MAKE.
pioneer *adjective* Preceding all others in time : earliest, first, initial, maiden, original, primary, prime, primordial. *See* START.

pious *adjective*
Deeply concerned with God and the beliefs and practice of religion : devotional, devout, godly, holy, pietistic, pietistical, prayerful, religious, saintly. *See* RELIGION.

piousness *noun*
A state of often extreme religious ardour : devotion, devoutness, pietism, piety, religionism, religiosity, religiousness. *See* RELIGION.

pip *noun*
A fertilized plant ovule capable of germinating : kernel, pit[2], seed. *See* START.

pipe dream *noun*
A fantastic, impracticable plan or desire : bubble, castle in the air, chimera, dream, fantasy, illusion, rainbow. *See* REAL.

piping *adjective*
Elevated in pitch : high, high-pitched, piercing, shrieky, shrill, shrilly, treble. *Music:* acute. *See* HIGH, SOUNDS.

pip-squeak *noun*
Informal. A totally insignificant person : cipher, nebbish, nobody, nonentity, nothing. *Informal:* zero. *Slang:* shrimp, zilch. *See* IMPORTANT.

piquant *adjective*
Affecting the organs of taste or smell with a strong and often harsh sensation : pungent, sharp, spicy, zesty. *Archaic:* poignant. *See* SMELLS, TASTE.

pique *noun*
Extreme displeasure caused by an insult or slight : dudgeon, huff, miff, offense, resentment, ruffled feathers, umbrage. *See* LIKE, PAIN.
pique *verb* **1.** To cause resentment or hurt by callous, rude behavior : affront, huff, insult, miff, offend, outrage. ***Idioms:*** add insult to injury, give offense to. *See* ATTACK, PAIN. **2.** To stir to action or feeling : egg on, excite, foment, galvanize, goad, impel, incite, inflame, inspire, instigate, motivate, move, prick, prod, prompt, propel, provoke, set off, spur, stimulate, touch off, trigger, work up. *See* CAUSE, EXCITE.

pirate *noun*
One who illicitly reproduces the artistic work, for example, of another : cribber, plagiarist, plagiarizer. *See* GIVE, WORDS.
pirate *verb* To reproduce (the artistic work of another, for example) illicitly : crib, plagiarize. *See* GIVE, WORDS.

pit[1] *noun*
1. An area sunk below its surroundings : basin, concavity, depression, dip, hollow, sag, sink, sinkhole. *See* CONVEX. **2.** A place known for its great filth or corruption : cesspit, cesspool, sink. *Slang:* armpit. *See* CLEAN, RIGHT.
pit *verb* To place in opposition or be in opposition to : counter, match, oppose, play off. ***Idioms:*** bump heads with, meet head-on, set (*or* be) at odds, set (*or* be) at someone's throat, trade blows (*or* punches). *See* SUPPORT.

pit[2] *noun*
A fertilized plant ovule capable of germinating : kernel, pip, seed. *See* START.

pitch *verb*
1. To send through the air with a motion of the hand or arm : cast, dart, dash, fling, heave, hurl, hurtle, launch, shoot, shy[2], sling, throw, toss. *Informal:* fire. *See* MOVE. **2.** To raise

upright : erect, put up, raise, rear[2], set up, upraise, uprear. *See* HORIZONTAL, RISE. **3.** To come to the ground suddenly and involuntarily : drop, fall, go down, nose-dive, plunge, spill, topple, tumble. ***Idiom:*** take a fall (*or* header *or* plunge *or* spill *or* tumble). *See* RISE. **4.** To lean suddenly, unsteadily, and erratically from the vertical axis : lurch, roll, seesaw, yaw. *See* MOVE, STRAIGHT. **5.** To move vigorously from side to side or up and down : heave, rock, roll, toss. *See* REPETITION. **6.** To slope downward : decline, descend, dip, drop, fall, sink. *See* RISE. **7.** *Informal.* To make known vigorously the positive features of (a product) : advertise, ballyhoo, build up, cry (up), popularize, promote, publicize, talk up. *Informal:* plug. *Slang:* push. *See* KNOWLEDGE.

pitch into *verb Informal.* To set upon with violent force : aggress, assail, assault, attack, beset, fall on (*or* upon), go at, have at, sail into, storm, strike. *Informal:* light into. *See* ATTACK.

pitch *noun* **1.** An act of throwing : cast, fling, heave, hurl, launch, shy[2], sling, throw, toss. *See* MOVE. **2.** A sudden involuntary drop to the ground : dive, fall, nosedive, plunge, spill, tumble. *Informal:* header. *See* RISE. **3.** A downward slope or distance : decline, declivity, descent, drop, fall. *See* RISE. **4.** Exceptionally great concentration, power, or force, especially in activity : depth (often used in plural), ferociousness, ferocity, fierceness, fury, intensity, severity, vehemence, vehemency, violence. *See* BIG, STRONG. **5.** *Informal.* A systematic effort or part of this effort to increase the importance or reputation of by favorable publicity : advertisement, ballyhoo, buildup, promotion, publicity, puffery. *Informal:* plug. *Slang:* hype. *See* KNOWLEDGE.

pitch-black *adjective*
Of the darkest achromatic visual value : black, ebon, ebony, inky, jet[1], jetty, onyx, pitchy, sable, sooty. *See* COLORS.

pitch-dark *adjective*
Having little or no light : black, dark. *See* LIGHT.

pitch into *verb* See **pitch.**

pitchy *adjective*
Of the darkest achromatic visual value : black, ebon, ebony, inky, jet[1], jetty, onyx, pitch-black, sable, sooty. *See* COLORS.

piteous *adjective*
1. Arousing or deserving pity : pathetic, pitiable, pitiful, poor, rueful, ruthful. *See* PITY. **2.** *Archaic.* Feeling or expressing pity : commiserative, compassionate, condolatory, pitying, sympathetic. *Archaic:* pitiful. *See* FEELINGS, PITY.

pitfall *noun*
A source of danger or difficulty not easily foreseen and avoided : booby trap, trap. *See* SAFETY.

pith *noun*
The most central and material part : core, essence, gist, heart, kernel, marrow, meat, nub, quintessence, root[1], soul, spirit, stuff, substance. *Law:* gravamen. *See* BE.

pithy *adjective*
Precisely meaningful and tersely cogent : aphoristic, compact[1], epigrammatic, epigrammatical, marrowy. *Informal:* brass-tacks. ***Idioms:*** down to brass tacks, to the point. *See* MEANING, STYLE.

pitiable *adjective*
Arousing or deserving pity : pathetic, piteous, pitiful, poor, rueful, ruthful. *See* PITY.

pitiful *adjective*
1. Arousing or deserving pity : pathetic, piteous, pitiable, poor, rueful, ruthful. *See* PITY. **2.** *Archaic.* Feeling or expressing pity : commiserative, compassionate, condolatory, pitying, sympathetic. *Archaic:* piteous. *See* FEELINGS, PITY.

pitiless *adjective*
Having or showing no mercy : merciless, remorseless, unmerciful. *See* KIND.

pity *noun*
1. Sympathetic, sad concern for someone in misfortune : commiseration, compassion, condolence, empathy, sympathy. *See* PITY. **2.** A great disappointment or regrettable fact : crime, shame. *Slang:* bummer. ***Idiom:*** a crying shame. *See* GOOD.

pity *verb* To experience or express compassion : ache, commiserate, compassionate, feel, sympathize, yearn. ***Idioms:*** be sorry, have (*or* take) pity. *See* PITY.

pitying *adjective*
Feeling or expressing pity : commiserative, compassionate, condolatory, sympathetic. *Archaic:* piteous, pitiful. *See* FEELINGS, PITY.

pivot *verb*
1. To turn or cause to turn in place, as on a hinge or fixed point, tracing an arclike path : swing, wheel. *See* MOVE. **2.** To move, as a gun, laterally : swivel, traverse. *See* MOVE. **3.** To change the direction or course of : avert, deflect, deviate, divert, shift, swing, turn, veer. *See* CHANGE.

pivotal *adjective*
Dominant in importance or influence : central, key. *See* IMPORTANT.

pixilated *adjective*
Slang. Stupefied, excited, or muddled with alcoholic liquor : besotted, crapulent, crapulous, drunk, drunken, inebriate, inebriated, intoxicated, sodden, tipsy. *Informal:* cock-eyed, stewed. *Slang:* blind, bombed, boozed, boozy, crocked, high, lit (up), loaded, looped, pickled, plastered, potted, sloshed, smashed, soused, stinking, stinko, stoned, tight, zonked. ***Idioms:*** drunk as a skunk, half-seas over, high as a kite, in one's cups, three sheets in (*or* to) the wind. *See* DRUGS.

placard *noun*
A usually public posting that conveys a message : bill[1], billboard, notice, poster, sign. *See* SHOW.

placate *verb*
To ease the anger or agitation of : appease, assuage, calm (down), conciliate, dulcify, gentle, mollify, pacify, propitiate, soften, soothe, sweeten. ***Idiom:*** pour oil on troubled water. *See* CALM.

place *noun*
1. A particular portion of space chosen for something : location, locus, point, spot. *See* PLACE. **2.** A building or shelter where one lives : abode, domicile, dwelling, habitation, home, house, lodging (often used in plural), residence. *Chiefly British:* dig (used in plural). *See* PROTECTION. **3.** A particular geographic area : locale, locality, location. *See* PLACE. **4.** The function or position customarily occupied by another : stead. *Archaic:* lieu. *See* PLACE, SUBSTITUTE. **5.** The proper or designated location : niche. *See* PLACE. **6.** A post of employment : appointment, berth, billet, job, office, position, situation, slot, spot. *Slang:* gig. *See* PLACE. **7.** Positioning of one individual vis-à-vis others : footing, position, rank[1], situation, standing, station, status. *See* PLACE.
place *verb* **1.** To deposit in a specified place : lay[1], put, set[1], stick. *See* PLACE, RISE. **2.** To put in or assign to a certain position or location : emplace, install, locate, position, set[1], site, situate, spot. *See* PLACE. **3.** To assign to a class or classes : categorize, class, classify, distribute, grade, group, pigeonhole, range, rank[1], rate[1]. *See* GROUP, VALUE. **4.** To calculate approximately : approximate, estimate, put, reckon, set[1]. *See* PRECISE. **5.** To establish the identification of : identify, pinpoint, recognize. *Slang:* finger. ***Idiom:*** put one's finger on. *See* KNOWLEDGE. **6.** To ascribe (a misdeed or an error, for example) to : affix, assign, blame, fasten, fix, impute, pin on. *See* GIVE. **7.** To complete a race or competition in a specified position : come in, finish, run. *See* BE.

placement *noun*
1. A way or condition of being arranged : arrangement, categorization, classification, deployment, disposal, disposition, distribution, formation, grouping, layout, lineup, order, organization, sequence. *See* ORDER. **2.** The place where a person or thing is located : emplacement, location, locus, position, site, situation. *See* PLACE.

placid *adjective*
1. Not excited or emotionally agitated : calm, peaceful, serene, tranquil. *See* CALM.
2. Motionless and undisturbed : calm, halcyon, peaceful, quiet, serene, still, stilly, tranquil, untroubled. *See* CALM.

placidity *noun*
1. Lack of emotional agitation : calm, calmness, peace, peacefulness, placidness, quietude, serenity, tranquillity. *See* CALM. **2.** An absence of motion or disturbance : calm, calmness, hush, lull, peace, peacefulness, placidness, quiet, quietness, serenity, stillness, tranquillity, untroubledness. *See* CALM.

placidness *noun*
1. Lack of emotional agitation : calm, calmness, peace, peacefulness, placidity, quietude, serenity, tranquillity. *See* CALM. **2.** An absence of motion or disturbance : calm, calmness, hush, lull, peace, peacefulness, placidity, quiet, quietness, serenity, stillness, tranquillity, untroubledness. *See* CALM.

plagiarist *noun*
One who illicitly reproduces the artistic work, for example, of another : cribber, pirate, plagiarizer. *See* GIVE, WORDS.

plagiarize *verb*
To reproduce (the artistic work of another, for example) illicitly : crib, pirate. *See* GIVE, WORDS.

plagiarizer *noun*
One who illicitly reproduces the artistic work, for example, of another : cribber, pirate, plagiarist. *See* GIVE, WORDS.

plague *noun*
1. A cause of suffering or harm : affliction, bane, curse, evil, ill, scourge, woe. *See* HELP.
2. A sudden increase in something, as the occurrence of a disease : epidemic, outbreak, rash[2]. *See* INCREASE. **3.** Something that annoys : aggravation, annoyance, besetment, bother,

irritant, irritation, nuisance, peeve, torment, vexation. *See* FEELINGS, PAIN.

plague *verb* **1.** To disturb by repeated attacks : annoy, bait, bedevil, beleaguer, beset, harass, harry, pester, tease, torment, worry. *See* FEELINGS, PAIN. **2.** To trouble persistently from or as if from all sides : badger, bedevil, beleaguer, beset, besiege, harass, harry, hound, importune, pester, solicit. *See* ATTACK. **3.** To bring great harm or suffering to : afflict, agonize, anguish, curse, excruciate, rack, scourge, smite, strike, torment, torture. *See* ATTACK, HELP.

plaguey *adjective* See **plaguy.**

plaguy also **plaguey** *adjective*
Troubling the nerves or peace of mind, as by repeated vexations : annoying, bothersome, galling, irksome, irritating, nettlesome, provoking, troublesome, vexatious. *See* PAIN.

plain *adjective*
1. Readily seen, perceived, or understood : apparent, clear, clear-cut, crystal clear, distinct, evident, manifest, noticeable, observable, obvious, patent, pronounced, visible. *See* SEE.
2. Easily seen through due to a lack of subtlety : broad, clear, obvious, patent, unmistakable, unsubtle. *See* CLEAR, SEE. **3.** Not elaborate or showy, as in appearance or style : modest, simple, unassuming, unostentatious, unpretentious. *See* PLAIN. **4.** Without addition, decoration, or qualification : bald, bare, dry, simple, unadorned, unvarnished. *See* PLAIN. **5.** Free from extraneous elements : absolute, perfect, pure, sheer[2], simple, unadulterated, undiluted, unmixed. *See* CLEAN. **6.** Not diluted or mixed with other substances : full-strength, neat, pure, straight, unblended, undiluted, unmixed. *See* CLEAN, STRONG. **7.** Being of no special quality or type : average, common, commonplace, cut-and-dried, formulaic, garden, garden-variety, indifferent, mediocre, ordinary, routine, run-of-the-mill, standard, stock, undistinguished, unexceptional, unremarkable. *See* GOOD, USUAL. **8.** Not handsome or beautiful : homely, unattractive, uncomely, unlovely. ***Idioms:*** not much for looks, not much to look at, short on looks. *See* BEAUTIFUL.
9. Completely such, without qualification or exception : absolute, all-out, arrant, complete, consummate, crashing, damned, dead, downright, flat, out-and-out, outright, perfect, pure, sheer[2], thorough, thoroughgoing, total, unbounded, unequivocal, unlimited, unmitigated, unqualified, unrelieved, unreserved, utter[2]. *Informal:* flat-out, positive. *Chiefly British:* blooming. *See* BIG, LIMITED.

plainness *noun*
1. The quality of being clear and easy to perceive or understand : clarity, clearness, distinctness, limpidity, limpidness, lucidity, lucidness, pellucidity, pellucidness, perspicuity, perspicuousness. *See* CLEAR. **2.** Lack of ostentation or pretension : modesty, simpleness, simplicity, unassumingness, unostentatiousness, unpretentiousness. *See* PLAIN.

plainspoken *adjective*
Manifesting honesty and directness, especially in speech : candid, direct, downright, forthright, frank, honest, ingenuous, man-to-man, open, straight, straightforward, straight-out, unreserved. *Informal:* straight-from-the-shoulder, straight-shooting. *See* CLEAR, SHOW.

plaintiff *noun*
One that makes a formal complaint, especially in court : accuser, claimant, complainant. *See* LAW.

plaintive *adjective*
Full of or expressive of sorrow : doleful, dolorous, lugubrious, mournful, rueful, sad, sorrowful, woebegone, woeful. *See* HAPPY.

plan *noun*
1. A method for making, doing, or accomplishing something : blueprint, design, game plan, idea, layout, project, schema, scheme, strategy. *See* PLANNED. **2.** A method used in dealing with something : approach, attack, course, line, modus operandi, procedure, tack, technique. *See* MEANS. **3.** Systematic arrangement and design : method, order, orderliness, organization, pattern, system, systematization, systemization. *See* ORDER.

plan *verb* **1.** To form a strategy for : blueprint, cast, chart, conceive, contrive, design, devise, formulate, frame, lay[1], project, scheme, strategize, work out. *Informal:* dope out. ***Idiom:*** lay plans. *See* PLANNED. **2.** To have in mind as a goal or purpose : aim, contemplate, design, intend, mean[1], project, propose, purpose, target. *Regional:* mind. *See* PLANNED, PURPOSE. **3.** To set the time for (an event or occasion) : schedule, time. *See* TIME. **4.** To work out and arrange the parts or details of : blueprint, design, lay out, map (out), set out. *See* PLANNED.

planar *adjective*
Having no irregularities, roughness, or indentations : even[1], flat, flush, level, plane[1], smooth, straight. *See* SMOOTH.

plane[1] *adjective*
Having no irregularities, roughness, or indentations : even[1], flat, flush, level, planar, smooth, straight. *See* SMOOTH.

plane[2] *verb*
To make even, smooth, or level : even[1], flat, flatten, level, smooth, straighten. *See* SMOOTH.

planetary *adjective*
So pervasive and all-inclusive as to exist in or affect the whole world : catholic, cosmic, cosmopolitan, ecumenical, global, pandemic, universal, worldwide. *See* LIMITED, SPECIFIC.

plangent *adjective*
Having a full sound : mellow, orotund, resonant, resounding, ringing, rotund, round, sonorous, vibrant. *See* SOUNDS.

plant *noun*
A building or complex in which an industry is located : factory, mill, work (used in plural). *See* MAKE, PLACE.
plant *verb* **1.** To put (seeds) into the ground for growth : seed, sow. *See* START. **2.** *Slang.* To put or keep out of sight : bury, cache, conceal, ensconce, hide[1], occult, secrete. *Slang:* stash. *See* SHOW.

plaster *verb*
To spread with a greasy, sticky, or dirty substance : bedaub, besmear, dab[1], daub, smear, smirch, smudge. *See* PUT ON.

plastered *adjective*
Slang. Stupefied with liquor : besotted, crapulent, crapulous, drunk, drunken, inebriate, inebriated, intoxicated, sodden, tipsy. *Informal:* cock-eyed, stewed. *Slang:* blind, bombed, boozed, boozy, crocked, high, lit (up), loaded, looped, pickled, pixilated, potted, sloshed, smashed, soused, stinking, stinko, stoned, tight, zonked. ***Idioms:*** drunk as a skunk, half-seas over, high as a kite, in one's cups, three sheets in (*or* to) the wind. *See* DRUGS.

plastic *adjective*
1. Capable of being shaped, bent, or drawn out, as by hammering or pressure : ductile, flexible, flexile, flexuous, malleable, moldable, pliable, pliant, supple, workable. *See* FLEXIBLE.
2. Changing easily, as in expression : changeable, fluid, mobile. *See* CHANGE. **3.** Easily altered or influenced : ductile, elastic, flexible, flexile, impressionable, malleable, pliable, pliant, suggestible, supple. *See* FLEXIBLE.
4. *Physics.* Capable of withstanding stress without injury : elastic, flexible, flexile, resilient, springy, supple. *See* FLEXIBLE.
5. Marked by unnaturalness, pretension, and often a slavish love of fads : artificial, factitious, synthetic, unnatural. *See* HONEST.

plasticity *noun*
The quality or state of being flexible : bounce, ductility, elasticity, flexibility, flexibleness, give, malleability, malleableness, pliability, pliableness, pliancy, pliantness, resilience, resiliency, spring, springiness, suppleness. *Obsolete:* flexure. *See* FLEXIBLE.

platform *noun*
A temporary framework with a floor : scaffold, scaffolding, stage. *See* MACHINE.

platitude *noun* A trite expression or idea : banality, bromide, cliché, commonplace, stereotype, truism. *See* SURPRISE.

platitudinal *adjective*
Without freshness or appeal because of overuse : banal, bromidic, clichéd, commonplace, corny, hackneyed, musty, overused, overworked, platitudinous, shopworn, stale, stereotyped, stereotypic, stereotypical, threadbare, timeworn, tired, trite, warmed-over, well-worn, worn-out. *See* EXCITE, USUAL.

platitudinous *adjective*
Without freshness or appeal because of overuse : banal, bromidic, clichéd, commonplace, corny, hackneyed, musty, overused, overworked, platitudinal, shopworn, stale, stereotyped, stereotypic, stereotypical, threadbare, timeworn, tired, trite, warmed-over, well-worn, worn-out. *See* EXCITE, USUAL.

plaudit *noun*
1. An expression of warm approval : acclaim, acclamation, applause, celebration, commendation, compliment, encomium, eulogy, kudos, laudation, panegyric, praise. *See* PRAISE.
2. Approval expressed by clapping : applause, hand, ovation. *See* PRAISE.

plausibility *noun*
Appearance of truth or authenticity : believability, color, credibility, credibleness, creditability, creditableness, plausibleness, verisimilitude. *See* LIKELY.

plausible *adjective*
Worthy of being believed : believable, colorable, credible, creditable. *See* TRUE.

plausibleness *noun*
Appearance of truth : believability, color, credibility, credibleness, creditability, creditableness, plausibility, verisimilitude. *See* LIKELY.

play *verb*
1. To occupy oneself with amusement or diversion : disport, recreate, sport. *See* WORK. **2.** To move one's fingers or hands in a nervous or aimless fashion : fiddle, fidget, fool, monkey,

putter, tinker, toy, trifle, twiddle. *See* TOUCH. **3.** To make a bet : bet, gamble, game, lay[1], wager. ***Idiom:*** put one's money on something. *See* GAMBLING. **4.** To treat lightly or flippantly : dally, flirt, toy, trifle. *See* WORK. **5.** To play the part of : act, do, enact, impersonate, perform, play-act, portray, represent. *See* ACTION, PERFORMING ARTS, SUBSTITUTE. **6.** To make music : perform. *See* PERFORMING ARTS. **7.** To perform according to one's artistic conception : execute, interpret, render. *See* PERFORMING ARTS. **8.** To be performed : run, show. *See* PERFORMING ARTS. **9.** To control to one's own advantage by artful or indirect means : exploit, maneuver, manipulate. *See* CONTROL, STRAIGHT. **10.** To cause to undergo or bear (something unwelcome or damaging, for example) : impose, inflict, visit, wreak. *See* GIVE, OVER, WILLING.

play along *verb Informal.* To agree to cooperate or participate : go along. *See* PARTICIPATE.

play around *verb Informal.* To be sexually unfaithful to another : philander, womanize. *Informal:* cheat, fool around, mess around. *See* SEX.

play down *verb* To make less emphatic or obvious : de-emphasize, tone down. *Informal:* soft-pedal. *See* SHOW.

play off *verb* To place in opposition or be in opposition to : counter, match, oppose, pit[1]. ***Idioms:*** bump heads with, meet head-on, set (*or* be) at odds, set (*or* be) at someone's throat, trade blows (*or* punches). *See* SUPPORT.

play out *verb* **1.** To cause (a line) to become longer and less taut : unreel, unroll, unwind. *See* GIVE. **2.** To use all of : consume, drain, draw down, eat up, exhaust, expend, finish, run through, spend, use up. *Informal:* polish off. *See* INCREASE. **3.** To make or become no longer active or productive : deplete, desiccate, dry up, give out, run out. *See* CONTINUE.

play up *verb* To accord emphasis to : accent, accentuate, emphasize, feature, highlight, italicize, point up, stress, underline, underscore. *See* IMPORTANT.

play *noun* **1.** Activity engaged in for relaxation and amusement : disport, diversion, fun, recreation, sport. *See* WORK. **2.** Actions taken as a joke : fun, game, sport. *See* WORK. **3.** The act of putting into play : application, employment, exercise, exertion, implementation, operation, usage, use, utilization. *See* USED. **4.** Suitable opportunity to accept or allow something : elbowroom, latitude, leeway, margin, room, scope. *See* PLACE, RESTRAINT. **5.** Ease of or space for movement : elbowroom, freedom. *See* TIGHTEN.

play-act *verb*
1. To play the part of : act, do, enact, impersonate, perform, play, portray, represent. *See* ACTION, PERFORMING ARTS, SUBSTITUTE. **2.** To behave affectedly or insincerely or take on a false or misleading appearance of : act, counterfeit, dissemble, fake, feign, pose, pretend, put on, sham, simulate. *See* HONEST, TRUE.

play along *verb* See **play.**

play around *verb* See **play.**

play down *verb* See **play.**

player *noun*
1. One who bets : bettor, gambler, gamester. *See* GAMBLING. **2.** A theatrical performer : actor, actress, thespian. *See* ACTION, PERFORMING ARTS, SUBSTITUTE. **3.** One who plays a musical instrument : musician, performer. *See* PERFORMING ARTS. **4.** One who participates : actor, participant, party. *See* PARTICIPATE.

playful *adjective*
Full of high-spirited fun : frisky, frolicsome, impish, mischievous, sportive, waggish. *See* WORK.

playfulness *noun*
The state of being full of high-spirited fun : friskiness, frolicsomeness, sportiveness, waggishness. *See* WORK.

play off *verb* See **play.**

play out *verb* See **play.**

plaything *noun*
An object for children to play with : toy. *See* WORK.

play up *verb* See **play.**

plea *noun*
1. An earnest or urgent request : appeal, entreaty, imploration, prayer[1], supplication. *See* ASK. **2.** An explanation offered to justify an action or make it better understood : excuse, pretext. *See* EXPLAIN.

plead *verb*
To make an earnest or urgent request : appeal, beg, beseech, crave, entreat, implore, pray, sue, supplicate. *Archaic:* conjure. *See* ASK.

pleasant *adjective*
1. To one's liking : agreeable, congenial, favorable, good, grateful, gratifying, nice, pleasing, pleasurable, satisfying, welcome. *See* LIKE. **2.** Affording enjoyment : enjoyable, gratifying, pleasing, pleasurable. *See* PAIN. **3.** Pleasant and friendly in disposition : affable, agreeable,

amiable, congenial, cordial, genial, good-natured, good-tempered, sociable, warm. *See* ATTITUDE, GOOD.

pleasantness *noun*
The quality of being pleasant and friendly : affability, agreeability, agreeableness, amenity, amiability, amiableness, congeniality, congenialness, cordiality, cordialness, friendliness, geniality, genialness, sociability, sociableness, warmth. *See* ATTITUDE, GOOD.

pleasantry *noun*
A courteous act or courteous acts that contribute to smoothness and ease in dealings and social relationships : amenity (used in plural), civility, courtesy, politeness, propriety (used in plural). *See* COURTESY.

please *verb*
1. To give great or keen pleasure to : cheer, delight, enchant, gladden, gratify, overjoy, pleasure, tickle. *Archaic:* joy. *See* HAPPY, LIKE.
2. To be satisfactory to : satisfy, suit. *See* PAIN. **3.** To have the desire or inclination to : choose, desire, like[1], want, will, wish. ***Idioms:*** have a mind, see fit. *See* DESIRE.

pleased *adjective*
Eagerly compliant : delighted, glad, happy, tickled. *See* HAPPY.

pleasing *adjective*
1. Affording enjoyment : enjoyable, gratifying, pleasant, pleasurable. *See* PAIN. **2.** To one's liking : agreeable, congenial, favorable, good, grateful, gratifying, nice, pleasant, pleasurable, satisfying, welcome. *See* LIKE. **3.** Providing joy and pleasure : cheerful, cheery, festive, glad, happy, joyful, joyous. *See* HAPPY.

pleasurable *adjective*
1. To one's liking : agreeable, congenial, favorable, good, grateful, gratifying, nice, pleasant, pleasing, satisfying, welcome. *See* LIKE.
2. Affording enjoyment : enjoyable, gratifying, pleasant, pleasing. *See* PAIN.

pleasure *noun*
1. A feeling of extreme gratification aroused by something good or desired : delectation, delight, enjoyment, joy. *See* HAPPY, LIKE.
2. The condition of responding pleasurably to something : delectation, enjoyment. *See* PAIN.
3. A desire for a particular thing or activity : fancy, liking, mind, will. *See* LIKE. **4.** Unrestricted freedom to choose : discretion, will. *See* FREE.
pleasure *verb* **1.** To give great or keen pleasure to : cheer, delight, enchant, gladden, gratify, overjoy, please, tickle. *Archaic:* joy. *See* HAPPY, LIKE. **2.** To feel or take joy or pleasure : delight, exult, joy, rejoice. *See* HAPPY.

pleat *noun*
A line or an arrangement made by the doubling of one part over another : crease, crimp, crinkle, crumple, fold, plica, plication, pucker, rimple, ruck[2], rumple, wrinkle. *See* SMOOTH.
pleat *verb* To bend together or make a crease in so that one part lies over another : crease, double, fold, ply[1], ruck[2]. *See* ORDER, SMOOTH.

pleb *noun*
The common people. Used in plural : common (used in plural), commonality, commonalty, commoner (used in plural), crowd, hoi polloi, mass (used in plural), mob, plebeian (used in plural), populace, public, ruck[1], third estate. *See* OVER.

plebeian *adjective*
Lacking high station or birth : baseborn, common, déclassé, declassed, humble, ignoble, lowly, mean[2], unwashed, vulgar. *Archaic:* base[2]. *See* OVER.
plebeian *noun* The common people. Used in plural : common (used in plural), commonality, commonalty, commoner (used in plural), crowd, hoi polloi, mass (used in plural), mob, pleb (used in plural), populace, public, ruck[1], third estate. *See* OVER.

pledge *noun*
1. A declaration that one will or will not do a certain thing : assurance, covenant, engagement, guarantee, guaranty, plight[2], promise, solemn word, vow, warrant, word, word of honor. *See* OBLIGATION. **2.** Something given to guarantee the repayment of a loan or the fulfillment of an obligation : earnest[2], guaranty, pawn[1], security, token, warrant. *See* TRANSACTIONS. **3.** The act of drinking to someone : toast. *See* DESIRE, REMEMBER.
pledge *verb* **1.** To guarantee by a solemn promise : covenant, plight[2], promise, swear, vow. ***Idiom:*** give one's word of honor. *See* AGREE, OBLIGATION. **2.** To assume an obligation : contract, engage, promise, undertake. *See* AGREE, OBLIGATION. **3.** To be morally bound to do : bind, charge, commit, obligate. *See* OBLIGATION. **4.** To give or deposit as a pawn : hypothecate, mortgage, pawn[1]. *Slang:* hock. *See* TRANSACTIONS. **5.** To salute by raising and drinking from a glass : drink, toast. *See* DESIRE, REMEMBER.

plenitude *noun*
Prosperity and a sufficiency of life's necessities : abundance, bounteousness, bountifulness, plenteousness, plenty. *See* RICH.

plenitudinous *adjective*
Characterized by abundance : abundant, ample, bounteous, bountiful, copious, generous, heavy, plenteous, plentiful, substantial, voluminous. *See* BIG, GIVE, RICH.

plenteous *adjective*
Characterized by abundance : abundant, ample, bounteous, bountiful, copious, generous, heavy, plenitudinous, plentiful, substantial, voluminous. *See* BIG, GIVE, RICH.

plenteousness *noun*
Prosperity and a sufficiency of life's necessities : abundance, bounteousness, bountifulness, plenitude, plenty. *See* RICH.

plentiful *adjective*
Characterized by abundance : abundant, ample, bounteous, bountiful, copious, generous, heavy, plenitudinous, plenteous, substantial, voluminous. *See* BIG, GIVE, RICH.

plenty *noun*
1. A great deal : abundance, mass, mountain, much, profusion, wealth, world. *Informal:* barrel, heap, lot, pack, peck[2], pile. *Regional:* power, sight. *See* BIG. **2.** Prosperity and a sufficiency of life's necessities : abundance, bounteousness, bountifulness, plenitude, plenteousness. *See* RICH.

pleonasm *noun*
Words or the use of words in excess of those needed for clarity or precision : diffuseness, diffusion, long-windedness, prolixity, redundancy, verbiage, verboseness, verbosity, windiness, wordage, wordiness. *See* EXCESS, STYLE, WORDS.

pleonastic *adjective*
Using or containing an excessive number of words : diffuse, long-winded, periphrastic, prolix, redundant, verbose, wordy. *See* EXCESS, STYLE, WORDS.

plethora *noun*
A condition of going or being beyond what is needed, desired, or appropriate : embarrassment, excess, excessiveness, exorbitance, extravagance, extravagancy, extravagantness, overabundance, superabundance, superfluity, superfluousness, surfeit. *See* EXCESS.

pliability *noun*
The quality or state of being flexible : bounce, ductility, elasticity, flexibility, flexibleness, give, malleability, malleableness, plasticity, pliableness, pliancy, pliantness, resilience, resiliency, spring, springiness, suppleness. *Obsolete:* flexure. *See* FLEXIBLE.

pliable *adjective*
1. Capable of being shaped, bent, or drawn out, as by hammering or pressure : ductile, flexible, flexile, flexuous, malleable, moldable, plastic, pliant, supple, workable. *See* FLEXIBLE. **2.** Capable of adapting or being adapted : adaptable, adaptive, adjustable, elastic, flexible, malleable, pliant, supple. *See* CHANGE. **3.** Easily altered or influenced : ductile, elastic, flexible, flexile, impressionable, malleable, plastic, pliant, suggestible, supple. *See* FLEXIBLE.

pliableness *noun*
The quality or state of being flexible : bounce, ductility, elasticity, flexibility, flexibleness, give, malleability, malleableness, plasticity, pliability, pliancy, pliantness, resilience, resiliency, spring, springiness, suppleness. *Obsolete:* flexure. *See* FLEXIBLE.

pliancy *noun*
The quality or state of being flexible : bounce, ductility, elasticity, flexibility, flexibleness, give, malleability, malleableness, plasticity, pliability, pliableness, pliantness, resilience, resiliency, spring, springiness, suppleness. *Obsolete:* flexure. *See* FLEXIBLE.

pliant *adjective*
1. Capable of being shaped, bent, or drawn out, as by hammering or pressure : ductile, flexible, flexile, flexuous, malleable, moldable, plastic, pliable, supple, workable. *See* FLEXIBLE. **2.** Capable of adapting or being adapted : adaptable, adaptive, adjustable, elastic, flexible, malleable, pliable, supple. *See* CHANGE. **3.** Easily altered or influenced : ductile, elastic, flexible, flexile, impressionable, malleable, plastic, pliable, suggestible, supple. *See* FLEXIBLE.

pliantness *noun*
The quality or state of being flexible : bounce, ductility, elasticity, flexibility, flexibleness, give, malleability, malleableness, plasticity, pliability, pliableness, pliancy, resilience, resiliency, spring, springiness, suppleness. *Obsolete:* flexure. *See* FLEXIBLE.

plica *noun*
A line or an arrangement made by the doubling of one part over another : crease, crimp, crinkle, crumple, fold, pleat, plication, pucker, rimple, ruck[2], rumple, wrinkle. *See* SMOOTH.

plication *noun*
A line or an arrangement made by the doubling of one part over another : crease, crimp, crinkle, crumple, fold, pleat, plica, pucker, rimple, ruck[2], rumple, wrinkle. *See* SMOOTH.

plight[1] *noun*
A difficult, often embarrassing situation or condition : box[1], corner, deep water, difficulty, dilemma, Dutch, fix, hole, hot spot, hot water,

jam, predicament, quagmire, scrape, soup, trouble. *Informal:* bind, pickle, spot. *See* EASY.

plight² *verb*
To guarantee by a solemn promise : covenant, pledge, promise, swear, vow. ***Idiom:*** give one's word of honor. *See* AGREE, OBLIGATION.
plight *noun* A declaration that one will or will not do a certain thing : assurance, covenant, engagement, guarantee, guaranty, pledge, promise, solemn word, vow, warrant, word, word of honor. *See* OBLIGATION.

plighted *adjective*
Pledged to marry : affianced, betrothed, engaged, intended. *See* MARRIAGE.

plod *verb*
1. To walk heavily, slowly, and with difficulty : slog, slop, toil, trudge, wade. *See* MOVE. **2.** To do tedious, laborious, and sometimes menial work : drudge, grub, slave, slog. *Informal:* grind. *See* WORK.

plodder *noun*
One who works or toils tirelessly : drudge, fag, grub, slave. *Informal:* grind, workhorse. *See* WORK.

plop *verb*
To drop or sink heavily and noisily : flop, plump², plunk. *See* RISE.

plot *noun*
1. A piece of land : lot, parcel, tract. *See* TERRITORY. **2.** The series of events and relationships forming the basis of a composition : story, story line. *See* HAPPEN, WORDS. **3.** A secret plan to achieve an evil or illegal end : cabal, collusion, connivance, conspiracy, intrigue, machination, scheme. *See* CRIMES, PLANNED.
plot *verb* **1.** To show graphically the direction or location of, as by using coordinates : chart, lay out, map (out). *See* SHOW. **2.** To work out a secret plan to achieve an evil or illegal end : collude, connive, conspire, intrigue, machinate, scheme. *See* CRIMES, PLANNED.

plow *verb*
To spade or dig (soil) to bring the undersoil to the surface : turn, turn over. *See* MOVE.

ploy *noun*
An indirect, usually cunning means of gaining an end : artifice, deception, device, dodge, feint, gimmick, imposture, jig, maneuver, ruse, sleight, stratagem, subterfuge, trick, wile. *Informal:* shenanigan, take-in. *See* HONEST, MEANS.

pluck *verb*
To remove from a fixed position : extract, pull, tear¹. *See* PUT IN.
pluck *noun* The quality of mind enabling one to face danger or hardship resolutely : braveness, bravery, courage, courageousness, dauntlessness, doughtiness, fearlessness, fortitude, gallantry, gameness, heart, intrepidity, intrepidness, mettle, nerve, pluckiness, spirit, stoutheartedness, undauntedness, valiance, valiancy, valiantness, valor. *Informal:* spunk, spunkiness. *Slang:* gut (used in plural), gutsiness, moxie. *See* FEAR.

pluckiness *noun*
The quality of mind enabling one to face danger or hardship resolutely : braveness, bravery, courage, courageousness, dauntlessness, doughtiness, fearlessness, fortitude, gallantry, gameness, heart, intrepidity, intrepidness, mettle, nerve, pluck, spirit, stoutheartedness, undauntedness, valiance, valiancy, valiantness, valor. *Informal:* spunk, spunkiness. *Slang:* gut (used in plural), gutsiness, moxie. *See* FEAR.

plucky *adjective*
Having or showing courage : audacious, bold, brave, courageous, dauntless, doughty, fearless, fortitudinous, gallant, game, hardy, heroic, intrepid, mettlesome, stout, stouthearted, unafraid, undaunted, valiant, valorous. *Informal:* spunky. *Slang:* gutsy, gutty. *See* FEAR.

plug *noun*
1. Something used to fill a hole, space, or container : choke, cork, fill, stop, stopper. *See* FULL. **2.** *Informal.* A systematic effort or part of this effort to increase the importance or reputation of by favorable publicity : advertisement, ballyhoo, buildup, promotion, publicity, puffery. *Informal:* pitch. *Slang:* hype. *See* KNOWLEDGE.
plug *verb* **1.** To plug up something, as a hole, space, or container : block, choke, clog, close, congest, cork, fill, stop. *See* FULL. **2.** *Slang.* To wound or kill with a firearm : gun (down), pick off, shoot. *See* HELP. **3.** *Informal.* To make known vigorously the positive features of (a product) : advertise, ballyhoo, build up, cry (up), popularize, promote, publicize, talk up. *Informal:* pitch. *Slang:* push. *See* KNOWLEDGE. **4.** *Informal.* To increase or seek to increase the importance or reputation of by favorable publicity : ballyhoo, boost, build up, enhance, promote, publicize, puff, talk up, tout. *Slang:* hype. *See* KNOWLEDGE.

plum *noun*
1. Something given in return for a service or accomplishment : accolade, award, guerdon, honorarium, premium, prize¹, reward. ***Idiom:***

token of appreciation (*or* esteem). *See* REWARD. **2.** A person or thing worth catching : prize[1]. *Informal:* catch. *Slang:* brass ring. *See* DESIRE.

plumb *adjective*
At right angles to the horizon or to level ground : perpendicular, upright, vertical. *See* HORIZONTAL.

plume *verb*
To be proud of (oneself), as for an accomplishment or achievement : congratulate, preen, pride. *See* RESPECT.

plummet *verb*
To undergo a sharp, rapid descent in value or price : dive, drop, fall, nose-dive, plunge, sink, skid, slump, tumble. ***Idiom:*** take a sudden downtrend (*or* downturn). *See* INCREASE.

plump[1] *adjective*
Well-rounded and full in form : chubby, plumpish, pudgy, roly-poly, rotund, round, tubby, zaftig. *See* FAT.

plump[2] *verb*
To drop or sink heavily and noisily : flop, plop, plunk. *See* RISE.
plump for *verb* To aid the cause of by approving or favoring : advocate, back, champion, endorse, get behind, recommend, side with, stand behind, stand by, support, uphold. ***Idioms:*** align oneself with, go to bat for, take the part of. *See* SUPPORT.

plump for *verb* See **plump.**

plumpish[2] *adjective*
Well-rounded and full in form : chubby, plump[1], pudgy, roly-poly, rotund, round, tubby, zaftig. *See* FAT.

plunder *verb*
To rob of goods by force, especially in time of war : depredate, despoil, havoc, loot, pillage, ransack, rape, ravage, sack[2], spoliate, strip[1]. *Archaic:* harrow, spoil. *See* CRIMES, GIVE.
plunder *noun* Goods or property seized unlawfully, especially by a victor in wartime : booty, loot, pillage, spoil (used in plural). *Slang:* boodle. *Nautical:* prize[2]. *See* CRIMES, GIVE.

plunge *verb*
1. To move or thrust at, under, or into the midst of with sudden force : dive, lunge, wade in (*or* into). *See* ENTER. **2.** To cause to penetrate with force : dig, drive, ram, run, sink, stab, stick, thrust. *See* PUT IN. **3.** To come to the ground suddenly and involuntarily : drop, fall, go down, nose-dive, pitch, spill, topple, tumble. ***Idiom:*** take a fall (*or* header *or* plunge *or* spill *or* tumble). *See* RISE. **4.** To move or advance against strong resistance : drive, forge[2], lunge. *See* MOVE. **5.** To undergo a sharp, rapid descent in value or price : dive, drop, fall, nose-dive, plummet, sink, skid, slump, tumble. ***Idiom:*** take a sudden downtrend (*or* downturn). *See* INCREASE.
plunge *noun* **1.** The act of plunging suddenly downward into or as if into water : dive, nosedive, swoop. *Informal:* header. *See* ENTER. **2.** A sudden involuntary drop to the ground : dive, fall, nosedive, pitch, spill, tumble. *Informal:* header. *See* RISE. **3.** A usually swift downward trend, as in prices : decline, descent, dip, dive, downslide, downswing, downtrend, downturn, drop, drop-off, fall, nosedive, skid, slide, slump, tumble. *See* INCREASE. **4.** The act of swimming : dip, duck, dunk, swim. *See* WORK.

plunging *adjective*
Cut to reveal the wearer's neck, chest, and back : décolleté, low, low-cut, low-neck, low-necked. *See* HIGH.

plunk *verb*
To drop or sink heavily and noisily : flop, plop, plump[2]. *See* RISE.

plush *adjective*
Characterized by extravagant, ostentatious magnificence : lavish, lush[1], luxuriant, luxurious, opulent, palatial, rich, sumptuous. *Informal:* plushy. *See* RICH.

plushy *adjective*
Informal. Characterized by extravagant, ostentatious magnificence : lavish, lush[1], luxuriant, luxurious, opulent, palatial, plush, rich, sumptuous. *See* RICH.

ply[1] *verb*
To bend together or make a crease in so that one part lies over another : crease, double, fold, pleat, ruck[2]. *See* ORDER, SMOOTH.

ply[2] *verb*
1. To use with or as if with the hands : handle, manipulate, wield. *See* CONTROL, USED. **2.** To bring to bear steadily or forcefully : exercise, exert, put out, throw, wield. *See* CAUSE.

pneumatic *adjective*
Of or relating to air : aerial, airy, atmospheric. *See* BREATH, HIGH.

pocket *noun*
A space in an otherwise solid mass : cavity, hole, hollow, vacuity, void. *See* CONVEX.

poem *noun*
1. A poetic work or poetic works : poesy, poetry, rhyme, verse. *See* WORDS. **2.** Something likened to poetry, as in form or style : lyricism, poetry. *See* STYLE, WORDS.

poesy *noun*
A poetic work or poetic works : poem, poetry, rhyme, verse. *See* WORDS.

poet *noun*
One who writes poetry : bard, muse[2], poetaster, poetess, rhymer, rhymester, versifier. *See* WORDS.

poetaster *noun*
One who writes poetry : bard, muse[2], poet, poetess, rhymer, rhymester, versifier. *See* WORDS.

poetess *noun*
One who writes poetry : bard, muse[2], poet, poetaster, rhymer, rhymester, versifier. *See* WORDS.

poetic *adjective*
Of, relating to, or having the characteristics of poetry : lyric, poetical. *See* WORDS.

poetical *adjective*
Of, relating to, or having the characteristics of poetry : lyric, poetic. *See* WORDS.

poetry *noun*
1. A poetic work or poetic works : poem, poesy, rhyme, verse. *See* WORDS. **2.** Something likened to poetry, as in form or style : lyricism, poem. *See* STYLE, WORDS.

pogrom *noun*
The savage killing of many victims : bloodbath, bloodletting, bloodshed, butchery, carnage, massacre, slaughter. *See* HELP.

poignant *adjective*
1. Exciting a deep, usually somber response : affecting, impressive, moving, stirring, touching. *See* TOUCH. **2.** *Archaic.* Affecting the organs of taste or smell with a strong and often harsh sensation : piquant, pungent, sharp, spicy, zesty. *See* SMELLS, TASTE.

point *noun*
1. A sharp or tapered end : acicula, acumination, apex, cusp, mucro, mucronation, tip[1]. *See* SHARP. **2.** A very small mark : dash, dot, fleck, pinpoint, speck, spot. *See* MARKS. **3.** A particular portion of space chosen for something : location, locus, place, spot. *See* PLACE. **4.** One of the units in a course, as on an ascending or descending scale : degree, grade, level, peg, rung, stage, step. *Informal:* notch. *See* BIG. **5.** A transitional interval beyond which some new action or different state of affairs is likely to begin or occur : borderline, brink, edge, threshold, verge. *See* EDGE. **6.** A particular interval of time that is limited and often crucial : instant, juncture, moment. *See* TIME. **7.** What one intends to do or achieve : aim, ambition, design, end, goal, intent, intention, mark, meaning, object, objective, purpose, target, view, why. ***Idioms:*** end in view, why and wherefore. *See* PLANNED, PURPOSE. **8.** What a speech, piece of writing, or artistic work is about : argument, matter, subject, subject matter, text, theme, topic. *See* MEANING. **9.** The gist of a specific action or situation : idea, import, meaning, purport, significance, significancy. *See* MEANING. **10.** A course of reasoning : argument, case. *See* REASON. **11.** An individually considered portion of a whole : article, detail, element, item, particular. *See* PART.

point *verb* **1.** To move (a weapon or blow, for example) in the direction of someone or something : aim, cast, direct, head, level, set[1], train, turn, zero in. *Military:* lay[1]. *See* SEEK. **2.** To call or direct attention to something : advert, bring up, mention, point out, refer, touch (on *or* upon). *See* WORDS. **3.** To mark with punctuation : punctuate. *See* MARKS.

point out *verb* **1.** To make known or identify, as by signs : denote, designate, indicate, mark, show, specify. *See* SHOW. **2.** To call or direct attention to something : advert, bring up, mention, point, refer, touch (on *or* upon). *See* WORDS.

point to *verb* **1.** To give grounds for believing in the existence or presence of : argue, attest, bespeak, betoken, indicate, mark, testify, witness. *See* SHOW. **2.** To lead to by logical inference : imply, indicate, suggest. *See* MEANING.

point up *verb* To accord emphasis to : accent, accentuate, emphasize, feature, highlight, italicize, play up, stress, underline, underscore. *See* IMPORTANT.

pointed *adjective*
1. Having an end that tapers to a point : acicular, aciculate, aciculated, acuminate, acute, cuspate, cuspated, cuspidate, cuspidated, mucronate, pointy, sharp. *See* SHARP. **2.** Readily attracting notice : arresting, bold, conspicuous, eye-catching, marked, noticeable, observable, outstanding, prominent, pronounced, remarkable, salient, signal, striking. ***Idiom:*** sticking out like a sore thumb. *See* SEE.

pointer *noun*
An item of advance or inside information given as a guide to action : steer, tip[3]. *Informal:* tip-off. *See* KNOWLEDGE.

pointless *adjective*
1. Without aim, purpose, or intent : aimless, desultory, purposeless. *See* PURPOSE. **2.** Lacking rational direction or purpose : meaning-

less, mindless, purposeless, senseless. ***Idiom:*** without rhyme or reason. *See* PURPOSE.

point of view *noun*
The position from which something is observed or considered : angle[2], eye, outlook, slant, standpoint, vantage, viewpoint. *See* PERSPECTIVE.

point out *verb* See **point.**

point to *verb* See **point.**

point up *verb* See **point.**

pointy *adjective*
Having an end that tapers to a point : acicular, aciculate, aciculated, acuminate, acute, cuspate, cuspated, cuspidate, cuspidated, mucronate, pointed, sharp. *See* SHARP.

poise *verb*
1. To place or be placed on a narrow or insecure surface : balance, perch. *See* POSTURE. **2.** To remain stationary over a place or object : hang, hover. *See* HANG.

poise *noun* **1.** A stable, calm state of the emotions : aplomb, balance, collectedness, composure, coolness, equanimity, imperturbability, imperturbableness, nonchalance, sang-froid, self-possession, unflappability. *Slang:* cool. *See* CALM, FEELINGS. **2.** Freedom from constraint, formality, embarrassment, or awkwardness : casualness, ease, easiness, informality, naturalness, spontaneity, unceremoniousness, unrestraint. *See* RESTRAINT, TIGHTEN.

poison *noun*
1. Anything that is injurious, destructive, or fatal : bane, canker, contagion, toxin, venom, virus. *See* HELP. **2.** One that contaminates : adulterant, adulterator, contaminant, contamination, contaminator, impurity, pollutant. *See* CLEAN.

poison *verb* **1.** To make physically impure : contaminate, defile, foul, pollute. *See* CLEAN. **2.** To have a destructive effect on : canker, envenom, infect. *Archaic:* empoison. *See* HELP.

poison *adjective* Capable of injuring or killing by poison : mephitic, mephitical, poisonous, toxic, toxicant, venomous, virulent. *See* HELP.

poisonous *adjective*
1. Capable of injuring or killing by poison : mephitic, mephitical, poison, toxic, toxicant, venomous, virulent. *See* HELP. **2.** Characterized by intense ill will or spite : black, despiteful, evil, hateful, malevolent, malicious, malign, malignant, mean[2], nasty, spiteful, venomous, vicious, wicked. *Slang:* bitchy. *See* ATTITUDE.

poisonousness *noun*
A desire to harm others or to see others suffer : despitefulness, ill will, malevolence, malice, maliciousness, malignancy, malignity, meanness, nastiness, spite, spitefulness, venomousness, viciousness. *See* ATTITUDE.

poke *verb*
1. To thrust against or into : dig, jab, jog, nudge, prod. *See* TOUCH. **2.** To cause to stick out : push, shove, thrust. *See* CONVEX. **3.** To look into or inquire about curiously, inquisitively, or in a meddlesome fashion : pry, snoop. *Informal:* nose (around). ***Idiom:*** stick one's nose into. *See* INVESTIGATE, PARTICIPATE. **4.** To reach about or search blindly or uncertainly : feel, fumble, grabble, grope. *See* SEEK, TOUCH. **5.** To go or move slowly so that progress is hindered : dally, dawdle, delay, dilly-dally, drag, lag, linger, loiter, procrastinate, tarry, trail. ***Idioms:*** drag one's feet (*or* heels), mark time, take one's time. *See* FAST.

poke *noun* **1.** An act of thrusting into or against, as to attract attention : dig, jab, jog, nudge. *See* TOUCH. **2.** One that lags : dawdler, dilly-dallier, lag, laggard, lagger, lingerer, loiterer, procrastinator, straggler, tarrier. *Informal:* slowpoke. *See* FAST.

pokerfaced *adjective*
Lacking expression : blank, deadpan, expressionless, inexpressive. *See* SHOW.

pokey[1] also **poky** *noun*
Slang. A place for the confinement of persons in lawful detention : brig, house of correction, jail, keep, penitentiary, prison. *Informal:* lockup, pen[3]. *Slang:* big house, can, clink, cooler, coop, hoosegow, joint, jug, slammer, stir[2]. *Chiefly Regional:* calaboose. *See* FREE.

pokey[2] *adjective* See **poky[1].**

poky[1] also **pokey** *adjective*
Informal. Proceeding at a rate less than usual or desired : dilatory, laggard, slow, slow-footed, slow-going, slow-paced, tardy. ***Idiom:*** slow as molasses in January. *See* FAST.

poky[2] *noun* See **pokey[1].**

polar *adjective*
1. Very cold : arctic, boreal, freezing, frigid, frosty, gelid, glacial, icy, wintry. *Archaic:* frore. ***Idiom:*** bitter (*or* bitterly) cold. *See* HOT. **2.** Diametrically opposed : antipodal, antipodean, antithetical, antonymic, antonymous, contradictory, contrary, converse[2], counter, diametric, diametrical, opposing, opposite, reverse. *See* SUPPORT.

polarity *noun*
The condition of being in conflict : antagonism, antithesis, contradiction, contradistinction, contraposition, contrariety, contrariness, opposition. *See* SUPPORT.

polemic *noun*
A discussion, often heated, in which a difference of opinion is expressed : altercation, argument, bicker, clash, contention, controversy, debate, difficulty, disagreement, dispute, fight, quarrel, run-in, spat, squabble, tiff, word (used in plural), wrangle. *Informal:* hassle, rhubarb, tangle. *See* CONFLICT.
polemic *adjective* Given to arguing : argumentative, combative, contentious, disputatious, eristic, litigious, polemical, quarrelsome, scrappy. *See* CONFLICT.

polemical *adjective*
Given to arguing : argumentative, combative, contentious, disputatious, eristic, litigious, polemic, quarrelsome, scrappy. *See* CONFLICT.

police *noun*
A member of a law-enforcement agency : bluecoat, finest, officer, patrolman, patrolwoman, peace officer, policeman, police officer, policewoman. *Informal:* cop, law. *Slang:* bull[1], copper, flatfoot, fuzz, gendarme, heat, man (often uppercase). *Chiefly British:* bobby, constable, peeler. *See* LAW.
police *verb* **1.** To maintain or keep in order with or as if with police : patrol. *See* LAW. **2.** To make or keep (an area) clean and orderly : clean (up), clear (up), neaten (up), spruce (up), straighten (up), tidy (up). *See* ORDER.

policeman *noun*
A member of a law-enforcement agency : bluecoat, finest, officer, patrolman, patrolwoman, peace officer, police, police officer, policewoman. *Informal:* cop, law. *Slang:* bull[1], copper, flatfoot, fuzz, gendarme, heat, man (often uppercase). *Chiefly British:* bobby, constable, peeler. *See* LAW.

police officer *noun*
A member of a law-enforcement agency : bluecoat, finest, officer, patrolman, patrolwoman, peace officer, police, policeman, policewoman. *Informal:* cop, law. *Slang:* bull[1], copper, flatfoot, fuzz, gendarme, heat, man (often uppercase). *Chiefly British:* bobby, constable, peeler. *See* LAW.

policewoman *noun*
A member of a law-enforcement agency : bluecoat, finest, officer, patrolman, patrolwoman, peace officer, police, policeman, police officer. *Informal:* cop, law. *Slang:* bull[1], copper, flatfoot, fuzz, gendarme, heat, man (often uppercase). *Chiefly British:* bobby, constable, peeler. *See* LAW.

policy *noun*
An official or prescribed plan or course of action : line, procedure, program. *See* PLANNED.

polish *verb*
1. To give a gleaming luster to, usually through friction : buff[1], burnish, furbish, glaze, gloss, shine, sleek. *See* LIGHT. **2.** To bring to perfection or completion : perfect, refine, smooth. *Idiom:* smooth off the rough edges. *See* BETTER. **3.** To improve by making minor changes or additions : retouch, touch up. *See* BETTER.
polish off *verb* **1.** *Informal.* To use all of : consume, drain, draw down, eat up, exhaust, expend, finish, play out, run through, spend, use up. *See* INCREASE. **2.** *Informal.* To eat completely or entirely : consume, devour, dispatch, eat up. *Informal:* put away. *See* INGESTION.
polish *noun* **1.** A radiant brightness or glow, usually due to light reflected from a smooth surface : burnish, glaze, gloss, luster, sheen, shine, sleekness. *See* LIGHT. **2.** Refined, effortless beauty of manner, form, and style : elegance, elegancy, grace, urbanity. *See* BEAUTIFUL, STYLE.

polished *adjective*
1. Having a high, radiant sheen : glassy, gleaming, glistening, glossy, lustrous, shining, shiny. *See* LIGHT. **2.** Characterized by discriminating taste and broad knowledge as a result of development or education : civilized, cultivated, cultured, educated, refined, urbane, well-bred. *See* CULTURE.

polish off *verb* See **polish.**

polite *adjective*
1. Full of polite concern for the well-being of others : attentive, considerate, courteous, gallant, solicitous, thoughtful. *See* CAREFUL, TREAT WELL. **2.** Characterized by good manners : civil, courteous, genteel, mannerly, well-bred, well-mannered. *See* COURTESY.

politeness *noun*
1. Well-mannered behavior toward others : civility, courteousness, courtesy, genteelness, gentility, mannerliness, politesse. *See* COURTESY. **2.** A courteous act or courteous acts that contribute to smoothness and ease in dealings and social relationships : amenity (used in plural), civility, courtesy, pleasantry, propriety (used in plural). *See* COURTESY.

politesse *noun*
Well-mannered behavior toward others : civility, courteousness, courtesy, genteelness, gentility, mannerliness, politeness. *See* COURTESY.

politic *adjective*
Showing sensitivity and skill in dealing with others : delicate, diplomatic, discreet, sensitive, tactful. *See* ABILITY.

polity *noun*
An organized geopolitical unit : body politic, country, land, nation, state. *See* POLITICS, TERRITORY.

poll *noun*
The uppermost part of the body : head, noddle, pate. *Slang:* bean, block, conk, dome, noggin, noodle, nut. *See* BODY.

pollutant *noun*
One that contaminates : adulterant, adulterator, contaminant, contamination, contaminator, impurity, poison. *See* CLEAN.

pollute *verb*
1. To make physically impure : contaminate, defile, foul, poison. *See* CLEAN. **2.** To make morally impure : contaminate, corrupt, defile, infect, soil, taint. *See* CLEAN. **3.** To spoil or mar the sanctity of : defile, desecrate, profane, violate. *See* CLEAN, RELIGION, SACRED.

pollution *noun*
1. The state of being contaminated : adulteration, contamination, sophistication. *See* CLEAN. **2.** Impure condition : defilement, dirtiness, foulness, impurity, uncleanness, unwholesomeness. *See* CLEAN.

Pollyanna *noun*
One who expects a favorable outcome or dwells on hopeful aspects : optimist. *See* HOPE.

poltroon *noun*
An ignoble, uncourageous person : coward, craven, dastard, funk. *Slang:* chicken, yellowbelly. *See* FEAR.

polychromatic *adjective*
Having many different colors : motley, multicolor, multicolored, polychrome, polychromic, polychromous, varicolored, variegated, versicolor, versicolored. *See* COLORS.

polychrome *adjective*
Having many different colors : motley, multicolor, multicolored, polychromatic, polychromic, polychromous, varicolored, variegated, versicolor, versicolored. *See* COLORS.

polychromic *adjective*
Having many different colors : motley, multicolor, multicolored, polychromatic, polychrome, polychromous, varicolored, variegated, versicolor, versicolored. *See* COLORS.

polychromous *adjective*
Having many different colors : motley, multicolor, multicolored, polychromatic, polychrome, polychromic, varicolored, variegated, versicolor, versicolored. *See* COLORS.

polymorphic *adjective*
Biology. Consisting of a number of different kinds : assorted, divers, diverse, diversified, heterogeneous, miscellaneous, mixed, motley, multifarious, multiform, sundry, varied, variegated, various. *Biology:* polymorphous. *See* SAME.

polymorphism *noun*
Biology. The quality of being made of many different elements, forms, kinds, or individuals : diverseness, diversification, diversity, heterogeneity, heterogeneousness, miscellaneousness, multifariousness, multiformity, multiplicity, variegation, variety, variousness. *See* SAME.

polymorphous *adjective*
Biology. Consisting of a number of different kinds : assorted, divers, diverse, diversified, heterogeneous, miscellaneous, mixed, motley, multifarious, multiform, sundry, varied, variegated, various. *Biology:* polymorphic. *See* SAME.

polysyllabic *adjective*
Having many syllables : long[1], sesquipedal, sesquipedalian. *See* LONG.

pomp *noun*
An impressive or ostentatious exhibition : array, display, panoply, parade, show, spectacle. *See* SHOW.

pomposity *noun*
Boastful self-importance or display : grandioseness, grandiosity, ostentation, pompousness, pretension, pretentiousness. *See* PLAIN.

pompous *adjective*
Characterized by an exaggerated show of dignity or self-importance : grandiose, hoity-toity, pretentious, puffed-up, puffy, self-important. *Informal:* highfalutin. *See* PLAIN.

pompousness *noun*
Boastful self-importance or display : grandioseness, grandiosity, ostentation, pomposity, pretension, pretentiousness. *See* PLAIN.

ponder *verb*
To think or think about carefully and at length : chew on (*or* over), cogitate, consider, contemplate, deliberate, entertain, excogitate, meditate, mull, muse[1], reflect, revolve, ruminate, study, think, think out, think over, think through, turn over, weigh. ***Idioms:*** cudgel one's brains, put on one's thinking cap, rack one's brain. *See* THOUGHTS.

ponderable *adjective*
Capable of being noticed or apprehended mentally : appreciable, detectable, discernible,

distinguishable, noticeable, observable, palpable, perceivable, perceptible, sensible. *See* KNOWLEDGE.

ponderosity *noun*
The state or quality of being physically heavy : heaviness, heftiness, massiveness, ponderousness, weight, weightiness. *Informal:* avoirdupois. *See* HEAVY.

ponderous *adjective*
1. Having a relatively great weight : heavy, heavyweight, hefty, massive, weighty. *See* HEAVY. **2.** Unwieldy or clumsy, especially due to excess weight : cumbersome, cumbrous, heavy, lumpish, lumpy. *See* EASY, HEAVY. **3.** Lacking fluency or gracefulness : elephantine, heavy-handed, labored. *See* GOOD.

ponderousness *noun*
The state or quality of being physically heavy : heaviness, heftiness, massiveness, ponderosity, weight, weightiness. *Informal:* avoirdupois. *See* HEAVY.

pool *noun*
A combination of businesses closely interconnected for common profit : cartel, combine, syndicate, trust. *See* GROUP, MONEY.

poop[1] *verb*
Slang. To make extremely tired. Also used with *out* : exhaust, fag (out), tire out, wear out. *Informal:* knock out, tucker (out). *Slang:* do in. ***Idioms:*** run ragged, take it out of. *See* TIRED.
poop out *verb* *Slang.* To lose so much strength and power as to become ineffective or motionless : burn out, give out, run down. *See* TIRED.

poop[2] *noun*
Slang. An unpleasant, tiresome person : bore. *Slang:* drip, dweeb, jerk, nerd, pill. *See* LIKE.

pooped *adjective*
Slang. Extremely tired. Also used with *out* : bleary, dead, drained, exhausted, fatigued, rundown, spent, tired out, wearied, weariful, weary, worn-down, worn-out. *Informal:* beat, bushed, tuckered (out). *Slang:* done in, fagged (out). ***Idioms:*** all in, ready to drop. *See* HEALTH, TIRED.

poop out *verb* See **poop**.

poor *adjective*
1. Having little or no money or wealth : beggarly, destitute, down-and-out, impecunious, impoverished, indigent, necessitous, needy, penniless, penurious, poverty-stricken. *Informal:* broke, strapped. ***Idioms:*** hard up, on one's uppers. *See* RICH. **2.** Below a standard of quality : bad, bum[1], unsatisfactory. ***Idioms:*** below par, not up to scratch (*or* snuff). *See* GOOD. **3.** Of decidedly inferior quality : base[2], cheap, lousy, miserable, paltry, rotten, shoddy, sleazy, trashy. *Informal:* cheesy. *Slang:* crummy, schlocky. *See* GOOD. **4.** Conspicuously deficient in quantity, fullness, or extent : exiguous, meager, puny, scant, scanty, skimpy, spare, sparse, stingy, thin. *Slang:* measly. *See* BIG, EXCESS. **5.** Arousing or deserving pity : pathetic, piteous, pitiable, pitiful, rueful, ruthful. *See* PITY.

poorly *adjective*
Chiefly Regional. Suffering from or affected with an illness : down, ill, sick, unwell. *Informal:* laid up. *See* HEALTH.

pop[1] *verb*
1. To make a sudden sharp, explosive noise : bang, bark, clap, crack, snap. *See* SOUNDS. **2.** To come open or fly apart suddenly and violently, as from internal pressure : blow[1] (out), burst, explode. *Slang:* bust. *See* EXPLOSION. **3.** To deliver a powerful blow to suddenly and sharply : bash, catch, clout, hit, knock, slam, slog, slug[3], smash, smite, sock, strike, swat, thwack, whack, wham, whop. *Informal:* biff, bop, clip[1], wallop. *Slang:* belt, conk, paste. ***Idioms:*** let someone have it, sock it to someone. *See* ATTACK, STRIKE.
pop in *verb* To go to or seek out the company of in order to socialize : call, come by, come over, drop by, drop in, look in, look up, run in, see, stop (by *or* in), visit. ***Idiom:*** pay a visit. *See* SEEK.
pop off *verb* *Informal.* To cease living : decease, demise, depart, die, drop, expire, go, pass away, pass (on), perish, succumb. *Slang:* check out, croak, kick in, kick off. ***Idioms:*** bite the dust, breathe one's last, cash in, give up the ghost, go to one's grave, kick the bucket, meet one's end (*or* Maker), pass on to the Great Beyond, turn up one's toes. *See* LIVE.
pop *noun* A sudden sharp, explosive noise : bang, bark, clap, crack, explosion, rat-a-tat-tat, report, snap. *See* SOUNDS.

pop[2] *noun*
Informal. A male parent : father, sire. *Informal:* dad, daddy, pa, papa, pappy[2]. *Slang:* old man. *See* KIN.

pop in *verb* See **pop[1]**.

pop off *verb* See **pop[1]**.

poppycock *noun*
Something that does not have or make sense : balderdash, blather, bunkum, claptrap, drivel, garbage, idiocy, nonsense, piffle, rigmarole, rubbish, tomfoolery, trash, twaddle. *Informal:* tommyrot. *Slang:* applesauce, baloney, bilge,

bull[1], bunk[2], crap, hooey, malarkey. *See* KNOWLEDGE.

populace *noun*
The common people : common (used in plural), commonality, commonalty, commoner (used in plural), crowd, hoi polloi, mass (used in plural), mob, pleb (used in plural), plebeian (used in plural), public, ruck[1], third estate. *See* OVER.

popular *adjective*
1. Widely known and discussed : famed, famous, leading, notorious, well-known. *See* KNOWLEDGE. **2.** Being a favorite : favored, favorite, preferred, well-liked. *See* LIKE. **3.** Of, representing, or carried on by people at large : democratic, general, public. *See* POLITICS, SPECIFIC. **4.** Suited to or within the means of ordinary people : moderate, modest, reasonable. *See* MONEY.

popularize *verb*
To make known vigorously the positive features of (a product) : advertise, ballyhoo, build up, cry (up), promote, publicize, talk up. *Informal:* pitch, plug. *Slang:* push. *See* KNOWLEDGE.

popularity *noun*
Wide recognition for one's deeds : celebrity, fame, famousness, notoriety, renown, reputation, repute. *See* KNOWLEDGE.

populate *verb*
To live in (a place), as does a people : inhabit, occupy, people. *See* PLACE.

porcine *adjective*
Having too much flesh : corpulent, fat, fatty, fleshy, gross, obese, overblown, overweight, portly, stout, weighty. *See* FAT.

pork *noun*
Slang. The political appointments or jobs that are at the disposal of those in power : patronage, spoil (used in plural). *See* POLITICS.

port *noun*
Archaic. Behavior through which one reveals one's personality : address, air, bearing, demeanor, manner, mien, presence, style. *See* BE, STYLE.

portend *verb*
To give an indication of something in advance : adumbrate, augur, bode, forecast, forerun, foreshadow, foretell, foretoken, prefigure, presage, prognosticate. *See* FORESIGHT, SHOW.

portent *noun*
A phenomenon that serves as a sign or warning of some future good or evil : augury, forerunner, foretoken, omen, prefigurement, presage, prognostic, prognostication, sign. ***Idiom:*** writing (*or* handwriting) on the wall. *See* FORESIGHT, WARN.

portentous *adjective*
Portending future disaster : apocalyptic, apocalyptical, baneful, dire, direful, fateful, fire-and-brimstone, grave[2], hellfire, ominous, unlucky. *See* LUCK, WARN.

portion *noun*
1. One of the parts into which something is divided : division, member, part, piece, section, segment, subdivision. *See* PART. **2.** A part severed from a whole : cut, piece, section, segment, slice. *See* PART. **3.** That which is allotted : allocation, allotment, allowance, dole, lot, measure, part, quantum, quota, ration, share, split. *Informal:* cut. *Slang:* divvy. *See* COLLECT. **4.** An individual quantity of food : helping, mess, serving. *See* INGESTION. **5.** A right or legal share in something : claim, interest, stake, title. *See* PART. **6.** That which is inevitably destined : destiny, fate, fortune, kismet, lot, predestination. *See* CERTAIN.

portion *verb* To give out in portions or shares. Also used with *out* : deal (out), dispense, distribute, divide, dole out, parcel out, ration (out), share. *Slang:* divvy. *See* COLLECT.

portly *adjective*
Having too much flesh : corpulent, fat, fatty, fleshy, gross, obese, overblown, overweight, porcine, stout, weighty. *See* FAT.

portrait *noun*
One exactly resembling another : double, duplicate, image, picture, spitting image. *Slang:* ringer. *See* SAME.

portray *verb*
1. To present a lifelike image of : delineate, depict, describe, express, image, limn, picture, render, represent, show. *See* SHOW. **2.** To play the part of : act, do, enact, impersonate, perform, play, play-act, represent. *See* ACTION, PERFORMING ARTS, SUBSTITUTE.

portrayal *noun*
The act or process of describing in lifelike imagery : delineation, depiction, description, expression, representation. *See* SHOW.

pose *verb*
1. To assume a particular position, as for a portrait : posture, sit. *See* POSTURE. **2.** To assume an exaggerated or unnatural attitude or pose : attitudinize, posture. ***Idiom:*** strike an attitude. *See* POSTURE. **3.** To represent oneself in a given character or as other than what one is : attitudinize, impersonate, masquerade, pass, posture. ***Idiom:*** pass oneself off as. *See* HONEST. **4.** To behave affectedly or insincerely or take on a

false or misleading appearance of : act, counterfeit, dissemble, fake, feign, play-act, pretend, put on, sham, simulate. *See* HONEST, TRUE. **5.** To state, as an idea, for consideration : advance, offer, propose, propound, put forward, set forth, submit, suggest. *See* OFFER. **6.** To seek an answer to (a question) : ask, put, raise. *See* ASK.

pose *noun* **1.** The way in which one is placed or arranged : attitude, position, posture. *See* POSTURE. **2.** The way in which a person holds or carries his or her body : attitude, carriage, posture, stance. *See* POSTURE. **3.** Artificial behavior adopted to impress others : affectation, affectedness, air (used in plural), mannerism, pretense. *See* HONEST, TRUE.

posh *adjective*

1. Being or in accordance with the current fashion : à la mode, chic, dashing, fashionable, mod, modish, smart, stylish, swank, swanky, trig. *Informal:* classy, in, sharp, snappy, swish, tony, trendy. *Slang:* with-it. ***Idioms:*** all the rage, up to the minute. *See* STYLE, USUAL. **2.** Catering to, used by, or admitting only the wealthy or socially superior : exclusive, fancy, swank, swanky. *Informal:* ritzy. *See* PLAIN.

posit *verb*

To take for granted without proof : assume, postulate, premise, presume, presuppose, suppose. *Informal:* reckon. *See* BELIEF.

position *noun*

1. The place where a person or thing is located : emplacement, location, locus, placement, site, situation. *See* PLACE. **2.** The way in which one is placed or arranged : attitude, pose, posture. *See* POSTURE. **3.** One's place and direction relative to one's surroundings : bearing (often used in plural), location, orientation, situation. *See* PLACE. **4.** A frame of mind affecting one's thoughts or behavior : attitude, outlook, posture, stance. *See* ATTITUDE. **5.** Something believed or accepted as true by a person : belief, conviction, feeling, idea, mind, notion, opinion, persuasion, sentiment, view. *See* OPINION. **6.** Positioning of one individual vis-à-vis others : footing, place, rank[1], situation, standing, station, status. *See* PLACE. **7.** A post of employment : appointment, berth, billet, job, office, place, situation, slot, spot. *Slang:* gig. *See* PLACE.

position *verb* To put in or assign to a certain position or location : emplace, install, locate, place, set[1], site, situate, spot. *See* PLACE.

positive *adjective*

1. Of a constructive nature : affirmative. *Informal:* upbeat. *See* HELP. **2.** Giving assent : affirmative, favorable. *See* AFFIRM. **3.** Clearly, fully, and sometimes emphatically expressed : categorical, clear, clear-cut, decided, definite, explicit, express, precise, specific, unambiguous, unequivocal. *See* CLEAR. **4.** Established beyond a doubt : certain, hard, inarguable, incontestable, incontrovertible, indisputable, indubitable, irrefutable, sure, unassailable, undeniable, undisputable, unquestionable. *See* CERTAIN, TRUE. **5.** Known positively : certain, definite, sure. ***Idiom:*** for certain. *See* CERTAIN. **6.** Having no doubt : assured, certain, confident, sure, undoubting. *See* CERTAIN. **7.** *Informal.* Completely such, without qualification or exception : absolute, all-out, arrant, complete, consummate, crashing, damned, dead, downright, flat, out-and-out, outright, perfect, plain, pure, sheer[2], thorough, thoroughgoing, total, unbounded, unequivocal, unlimited, unmitigated, unqualified, unrelieved, unreserved, utter[2]. *Informal:* flat-out. *Chiefly British:* blooming. *See* BIG, LIMITED.

positiveness *noun*

The fact or condition of being without doubt : assurance, assuredness, certainty, certitude, confidence, conviction, sureness, surety. *See* CERTAIN.

positively *adverb*

1. In a direct, positive manner : emphatically, flat, flatly. *Informal:* flat out. *See* STRONG. **2.** Without question : absolutely, certainly, doubtless, doubtlessly, undoubtedly. *See* CERTAIN, LIMITED. **3.** In truth : actually, fairly, genuinely, indeed, really, truly, truthfully, verily. ***Idiom:*** for fair. *See* REAL, TRUE.

possess *verb*

1. To keep at one's disposal : have, hold, own, retain. *See* KEEP. **2.** To hold on one's person : bear, carry, have. *Informal:* pack. *See* OWNED. **3.** To have the use or benefit of : enjoy, have, hold. *See* OWNED. **4.** To have at one's disposal : boast, command, enjoy, have, hold. *See* OWNED. **5.** To be endowed with as a visible characteristic or form : bear, carry, display, exhibit, have. *See* SHOW. **6.** To dominate the mind or thoughts of : obsess. *See* CONTROL.

possessed *adjective*

Not easily excited, even under pressure : calm, collected, composed, cool, cool-headed, detached, even[1], even-tempered, imperturbable, nonchalant, unflappable, unruffled. *See* CALM.

possession *noun*

1. The fact of possessing or the legal right to possess something : dominion, ownership, proprietorship, title. *See* OWNED. **2.** One's portable property. Used in plural : belonging (often used in plural), effect (used in plural), good (used in plural), lares and penates, personal effects, personal property, property, thing (often used in plural). *Informal:* stuff. *Law:* chattel, movable (often used in plural). *See* OWNED. **3.** Something, as land and assets, legally possessed. Used in plural : estate, holding (often used in plural), property. *See* LAW, OWNED. **4.** An area subject to rule by an outside power : colony, dependency, province, territory. *See* POLITICS.

possessive *adjective*
Fearful of the loss of position or affection : clutching, jealous. *See* OWNED.

possessor *noun*
A person who has legal title to property : holder, master, owner, proprietor. *See* OWNED.

possibility *noun*
1. The likeliness of a given event occurring : chance, likelihood, odds, probability, prospect (used in plural). *See* LIKELY. **2.** Something that may occur or be done : contingency, eventuality. *See* POSSIBLE.

possible *adjective*
1. Capable of occurring or being done : feasible, practicable, viable, workable. ***Idiom:*** within reach. *See* POSSIBLE. **2.** Capable of being but not yet in existence : eventual, latent, potential. *See* POSSIBLE. **3.** Having a chance of happening or being true : contingent, likely, probable. *See* LIKELY. **4.** Capable of being anticipated, considered, or imagined : conceivable, earthly, imaginable, likely, mortal, thinkable. ***Idioms:*** humanly possible, within the bounds (*or* range *or* realm) of possibility. *See* POSSIBLE. **5.** Capable of favorable development : potential. *See* POSSIBLE.

post[1] *verb*
To gain (a point or points) in a game or contest : score, tally. *Informal:* notch. *See* DO.

post[2] *noun*
An assigned position : station. *See* PLACE.
post *verb* **1.** To appoint and send to a particular place : assign, set[1], station. *See* PLACE. **2.** To put up as a stake in a game or speculation : bet, gamble, lay[1] (down), put, risk, stake, venture, wager. *Informal:* go. *See* GAMBLING.

post[3] *verb*
To place on a list or in a record : enter, insert, record, register. *See* REMEMBER.

poster *noun*
A usually public posting that conveys a message : bill[1], billboard, notice, placard, sign. *See* SHOW.

posterior *adjective*
1. Located in the rear : back, hind, hindmost, postern, rear[1]. *Nautical:* after. *See* PRECEDE. **2.** Following something else in time : after, later, subsequent, ulterior. *See* PRECEDE.
posterior *noun* The part of one's back on which one rests in sitting : buttock (used in plural), derrière, rump, seat. *Informal:* backside, behind, bottom, rear[1]. *Slang:* bun (used in plural), fanny, tush. *Chiefly British:* bum[2]. *See* OVER.

posterity *noun*
A group consisting of those descended directly from the same parents or ancestors : brood, get, issue, offspring, progeny, seed. *See* KIN.

postern *adjective*
Located in the rear : back, hind, hindmost, posterior, rear[1]. *Nautical:* after. *See* PRECEDE.

posthaste *adverb*
In a rapid way : apace, fast, quick, quickly. *Informal:* flat out, hell-for-leather, lickety-split, pronto. ***Idioms:*** full tilt, in a flash, in nothing flat, like a bat out of hell, like a blue streak, like a flash, like a house on fire, like a shot, like a streak, like greased lightning, like the wind, like wildfire. *See* FAST.

posthumous *adjective*
Occurring or done after death : postmortem. *See* TIME.

posting *noun*
An item inserted, as in a diary, register, or reference book : entry, insertion. *See* WORDS.

postmortem *adjective*
Occurring or done after death : posthumous. *See* TIME.

postpone *verb*
To put off until a later time : adjourn, defer[1], delay, hold off, hold up, remit, shelve, stay[1], suspend, table, waive. *Informal:* wait. ***Idiom:*** put on ice. *See* DO.

postponement *noun*
The act of putting off or the condition of being put off : adjournment, deferment, deferral, delay, stay[1], suspension, waiver. *See* TIME.

postulate *verb*
To take for granted without proof : assume, posit, premise, presume, presuppose, suppose. *Informal:* reckon. *See* BELIEF.
postulate *noun* Something taken to be true without proof : assumption, postulation, premise, presupposition, supposition, theory, thesis. *See* REASON.

postulation *noun*
Something taken to be true without proof : assumption, postulate, premise, presupposition, supposition, theory, thesis. *See* REASON.

posture *noun*
1. The way in which one is placed or arranged : attitude, pose, position. *See* POSTURE. **2.** The way in which a person holds or carries his or her body : attitude, carriage, pose, stance. *See* POSTURE. **3.** A frame of mind affecting one's thoughts or behavior : attitude, outlook, position, stance. *See* ATTITUDE.

posture *verb* **1.** To assume an exaggerated or unnatural attitude or pose : attitudinize, pose. ***Idiom:*** strike an attitude. *See* POSTURE. **2.** To represent oneself in a given character or as other than what one is : attitudinize, impersonate, masquerade, pass, pose. ***Idiom:*** pass oneself off as. *See* HONEST. **3.** To assume a particular position, as for a portrait : pose, sit. *See* POSTURE.

posy *noun*
Cut flowers that have been arranged in a usually small bunch : bouquet, nosegay. *See* THING.

pot *noun*
Something risked on an uncertain outcome : ante, bet, stake (often used in plural), wager. *See* GAMBLING.

potable *noun*
Any liquid that is fit for drinking : beverage, drink, drinkable, liquor. *See* DRY.

potation *noun*
An act of drinking or the amount swallowed : draft, drink, pull, quaff, sip, sup, swill. *Informal:* swig. *Slang:* belt. *See* MOUTH.

potence *noun*
The state or quality of being physically strong : brawn, might, muscle, potency, power, powerfulness, puissance, sinew, strength, thew (often used in plural). *See* STRONG.

potency *noun*
1. The state or quality of being physically strong : brawn, might, muscle, potence, power, powerfulness, puissance, sinew, strength, thew (often used in plural). *See* STRONG. **2.** Capacity or power for work or vigorous activity : animation, energy, force, might, power, puissance, sprightliness, steam, strength. *Informal:* get-up-and-go, go, pep, peppiness, zip. *See* ACTION. **3.** The power or capacity to produce a desired result : effect, effectiveness, effectuality, effectualness, efficaciousness, efficacy, efficiency, influence. *See* AFFECT.

potent *adjective*
1. Having great physical strength : mighty, powerful, puissant, strong. *See* STRONG.
2. Having a high concentration of the distinguishing ingredient : concentrated, stiff, strong. *See* STRONG. **3.** Having or able to exert great power : mighty, powerful, puissant. *See* STRONG.

potential *adjective*
1. Capable of being but not yet in existence : eventual, latent, possible. *See* POSSIBLE.
2. Capable of favorable development : possible. *See* POSSIBLE.

potential *noun* The inherent capacity for growth or development : potentiality. *See* POSSIBLE.

potentiality *noun*
The inherent capacity for growth or development : potential. *See* POSSIBLE.

pother *noun*
Needless trouble : bother, botheration, fuss. *See* EASY.

pother *verb* To worry over trifles : chafe, fuss. *Informal:* take on. *See* CALM.

potpourri *noun*
A collection of various things : assortment, conglomeration, gallimaufry, hodgepodge, jumble, medley, mélange, miscellany, mishmash, mixed bag, mixture, olio, patchwork, salmagundi, variety. *Slang:* grab bag. *See* COLLECT.

potted *adjective*
1. *Slang.* Stupefied, excited, or muddled with alcoholic liquor : besotted, crapulent, crapulous, drunk, drunken, inebriate, inebriated, intoxicated, sodden, tipsy. *Informal:* cock-eyed, stewed. *Slang:* blind, bombed, boozed, boozy, crocked, high, lit (up), loaded, looped, pickled, pixilated, plastered, sloshed, smashed, soused, stinking, stinko, stoned, tight, zonked. ***Idioms:*** drunk as a skunk, half-seas over, high as a kite, in one's cups, three sheets in (*or* to) the wind. *See* DRUGS. **2.** *Slang.* Stupefied, intoxicated, or otherwise influenced by the taking of drugs : drugged. *Informal:* doped. *Slang:* high, hopped-up, lit (up), spaced-out, stoned, turned-on, wiped-out, zonked. *See* DRUGS.

pouch *verb*
To curve outward past the normal or usual limit : bag, balloon, beetle, belly, bulge, jut, overhang, project, protrude, protuberate, stand out, stick out. *See* CONVEX.

pound *verb*
1. To hit heavily and repeatedly with violent blows : assail, assault, baste, batter, beat, belabor, buffet, drub, hammer, pummel, smash,

thrash, thresh. *Informal:* lambaste. *Slang:* clobber. ***Idiom:*** rain blows on. *See* ATTACK, STRIKE. **2.** To shape, break, or flatten with repeated blows : beat, forge[1], hammer. *See* REPETITION, STRIKE. **3.** To make rhythmic contractions, sounds, or movements : beat, palpitate, pulsate, pulse, throb. *See* REPETITION, SOUNDS. **4.** To fix (an idea, for example) in someone's mind by reemphasis and repetition : drill, drive, implant, impress, inculcate, instill. *See* TEACH.

pound *noun* **1.** A sudden sharp, powerful stroke : bang, blow[2], clout, crack, hit, lick, slug[3], sock, swat, thwack, welt, whack, wham, whop. *Informal:* bash, biff, bop, clip[1], wallop. *Slang:* belt, conk, paste. *See* ATTACK, STRIKE. **2.** A stroke or blow, especially one that produces a sound : beat, clunk, thud, thump. *See* ATTACK, SOUNDS, STRIKE.

pour *verb*

1. To cause (a liquid) to flow in a steady stream : decant, draw (off), effuse. *See* MOVE. **2.** To come forth or emit in abundance : flow, gush, run, rush, stream, surge, well[1]. *See* MOVE. **3.** To rain heavily. ***Idioms:*** come down in buckets (*or* sheets *or* torrents), rain cats and dogs. *See* DRY. **4.** To come or go in large numbers : flood, swarm, throng, troop. *See* BIG, MOVE.

pout *verb*

To be sullenly aloof or withdrawn, as in silent resentment or protest : mope, pet[2], sulk. *See* HAPPY.

pout *noun* A facial contortion indicating displeasure, disgust, or pain : face, grimace, moue, mouth. *Informal:* mug. *See* EXPRESS.

poverty *noun*

1. The condition of being extremely poor : beggary, destitution, impecuniosity, impecuniousness, impoverishment, indigence, need, neediness, pennilessness, penuriousness, penury, privation, want. *See* RICH. **2.** The condition or fact of being deficient : defect, deficiency, deficit, inadequacy, insufficiency, lack, paucity, scantiness, scantness, scarceness, scarcity, shortage, shortcoming, shortfall, underage[1]. *See* EXCESS.

poverty-stricken *adjective*

Having little or no money or wealth : beggarly, destitute, down-and-out, impecunious, impoverished, indigent, necessitous, needy, penniless, penurious, poor. *Informal:* broke, strapped. ***Idioms:*** hard up, on one's uppers. *See* RICH.

powder *verb*

1. To break up into tiny particles : bray, crush, granulate, grind, mill, pulverize, triturate. *See* HELP. **2.** To scatter or release in drops or small particles : besprinkle, dust, sprinkle. *See* STRIKE.

powdery *adjective*

Consisting of small particles : dusty, fine[1], pulverous, pulverulent. *See* BIG.

power *noun*

1. Capacity or power for work or vigorous activity : animation, energy, force, might, potency, puissance, sprightliness, steam, strength. *Informal:* get-up-and-go, go, pep, peppiness, zip. *See* ACTION. **2.** The state or quality of being physically strong : brawn, might, muscle, potence, potency, powerfulness, puissance, sinew, strength, thew (often used in plural). *See* STRONG. **3.** The right and power to command, decide, rule, or judge : authority, command, control, domination, dominion, jurisdiction, mastery, might, prerogative, sovereignty, sway. *Informal:* say-so. *See* OVER. **4.** Effective means of influencing, compelling, or punishing : force, weight. *Informal:* clout, muscle. *See* OVER, STRONG. **5.** The capacity to exert an influence : force, forcefulness, magnetism. *See* STRONG. **6.** *Regional.* A great deal : abundance, mass, mountain, much, plenty, profusion, wealth, world. *Informal:* barrel, heap, lot, pack, peck[2], pile. *Regional:* sight. *See* BIG.

powerful *adjective*

1. Having great physical strength : mighty, potent, puissant, strong. *See* STRONG. **2.** Conveying great physical force : hard, heavy, hefty, severe. *See* BIG. **3.** Having or able to exert great power : mighty, potent, puissant. *See* STRONG. **4.** Full of or displaying force : dynamic, dynamical, effective, forceful, forcible, hard-hitting, strong, vigorous. *See* STRONG. **5.** Having or exercising influence : consequential, important, influential, weighty. *See* AFFECT, IMPORTANT, STRONG.

powerfully *adverb*

With intense energy and force : energetically, forcefully, forcibly, hard, vigorously. ***Idioms:*** hammer and tongs, tooth and nail, with might and main. *See* STRONG.

powerfulness *noun*

The state or quality of being physically strong : brawn, might, muscle, potence, potency, power, puissance, sinew, strength, thew (often used in plural). *See* STRONG.

powerless *adjective*

1. Lacking power or strength : helpless, impotent. *See* ABILITY, HELP. **2.** Not capable of accomplishing anything : helpless, impotent, inadequate, incapable, ineffectual, weak. *See* ABILITY, STRONG.

powerlessness *noun*

1. Lack of ability or capacity : inability, incapability, incapacity, incompetence, incompetency. *See* ABILITY. **2.** The condition or state of being incapable of accomplishing or effecting anything : helplessness, impotence, inadequacy, incapability, ineffectiveness, ineffectuality, ineffectualness, inefficacy, uselessness. *See* AFFECT, STRONG.

powwow *noun*

Informal. A meeting for the exchange of views : colloquium, conference, discussion, parley, seminar. *Slang:* rap session. *See* MEET, WORDS.

powwow *verb Informal.* To meet and exchange views to reach a decision : advise, confer, consult, deliberate, parley, talk. *See* COLLECT, MEET, WORDS.

practicable *adjective*

1. Capable of occurring or being done : feasible, possible, viable, workable. ***Idiom:*** within reach. *See* POSSIBLE. **2.** Serving or capable of serving a useful purpose : functional, handy, practical, serviceable, useful, utilitarian. *See* USED. **3.** Available for use : accessible, employable, open, operable, operative, usable, utilizable. *See* POSSIBLE.

practical *adjective*

1. Resulting from experience or practice : practiced. *See* KNOWLEDGE. **2.** Serving or capable of serving a useful purpose : functional, handy, practicable, serviceable, useful, utilitarian. *See* USED. **3.** Having or indicating an awareness of things as they really are : down-to-earth, hard, hardheaded, matter-of-fact, objective, pragmatic, pragmatical, prosaic, realistic, sober, tough-minded, unromantic. *See* EXCITE, REAL. **4.** Involved in the essential nature of something but not shown or developed : implicit, virtual. *See* BE, SHOW.

practice *verb*

1. To do or perform repeatedly so as to master : rehearse. *See* WORK. **2.** To subject to or engage in forms of exertion in order to train, strengthen, or condition : drill, exercise, train, work out. *See* WORK. **3.** To work at, especially as a profession : pursue. *See* DO, WORK. **4.** To put into action or use : actuate, apply, employ, exercise, exploit, implement, use, utilize. ***Idioms:*** avail oneself of, bring into play, bring to bear, make use of, put into practice, put to use. *See* USED.

practice *noun* **1.** A habitual way of behaving : consuetude, custom, habit, habitude, manner, praxis, usage, usance, use, way, wont. *See* USUAL. **2.** Repetition of an action so as to develop or maintain one's skill : drill, exercise, rehearsal, study, training. *See* WORK. **3.** A working at a profession or occupation : pursuit. *See* DO, WORK.

practiced *adjective*

1. Proficient as a result of practice and study : accomplished, finished. *See* ABILITY. **2.** Skilled or knowledgeable through long practice : experienced, old, seasoned, versed, veteran. ***Idiom:*** knowing the ropes. *See* ABILITY. **3.** Resulting from experience or practice : practical. *See* KNOWLEDGE.

praetorian *adjective*

Ruthlessly seeking personal advantage : corrupt, mercenary, venal. *Informal:* crooked. *See* SELF.

pragmatic *adjective*

Having or indicating an awareness of things as they really are : down-to-earth, hard, hardheaded, matter-of-fact, objective, practical, pragmatical, prosaic, realistic, sober, tough-minded, unromantic. *See* EXCITE, REAL.

pragmatic *noun Archaic.* A person given to intruding in other people's affairs : busybody, interloper, meddler, quidnunc. *Informal:* kibitzer. *Slang:* buttinsky. *See* PARTICIPATE.

pragmatical *adjective*

Having or indicating an awareness of things as they really are : down-to-earth, hard, hardheaded, matter-of-fact, objective, practical, pragmatic, prosaic, realistic, sober, tough-minded, unromantic. *See* EXCITE, REAL.

praise *noun*

1. An expression of warm approval : acclaim, acclamation, applause, celebration, commendation, compliment, encomium, eulogy, kudos, laudation, panegyric, plaudit. *See* PRAISE. **2.** An expression of admiration or congratulation : commendation, compliment, congratulation (often used in plural), tribute. *See* PRAISE. **3.** The honoring of a deity, as in worship : exaltation, extolment, glorification, laudation, magnification. *See* RELIGION.

praise *verb* **1.** To express warm approval of : acclaim, applaud, commend, compliment, laud. *See* PRAISE. **2.** To pay a compliment to : commend, compliment, congratulate. ***Idiom:*** take off one's hat to. *See* PRAISE. **3.** To pay tribute or homage to : acclaim, celebrate, eulogize, exalt, extol, glorify, hail[2], honor, laud, magnify, panegyrize. ***Idiom:*** sing someone's praises.

See PRAISE. **4.** To honor (a deity) in religious worship : exalt, extol, glorify, laud, magnify. *See* RELIGION.

praiseworthy *adjective*
Deserving honor, respect, or admiration : admirable, commendable, creditable, deserving, estimable, exemplary, honorable, laudable, meritorious, reputable, respectable, worthy. *See* GOOD, PRAISE, RESPECT, VALUE.

prance *verb*
To walk with exaggerated or unnatural motions expressive of self-importance or self-display : flounce, peacock, strut, swagger, swank, swash. *Informal:* sashay. *See* MOVE, SELF-LOVE.

prank[1] *noun*
A mischievous act : antic, caper, frolic, joke, lark, trick. *Informal:* shenanigan. *Slang:* monkeyshine (often used in plural). *See* GOOD, WORK.

prank[2] *verb*
To dress in formal or special clothing : array, attire, deck[2] (out), dress up. *Informal:* trick out (*or* up). *Slang:* doll up. *See* ORDER, PLAIN, PUT ON.

prankishness *noun*
Annoying yet harmless, usually playful acts : devilry, deviltry, diablerie, high jinks, impishness, mischief, mischievousness, rascality, roguery, roguishness, tomfoolery. *Informal:* shenanigan (often used in plural). *See* GOOD.

prankster *noun*
One who causes minor trouble or damage : devil, imp, mischief, rascal, rogue, scamp. *Informal:* cutup. *See* GOOD.

prate *verb*
1. To talk rapidly, incoherently, or indistinctly : babble, blather, chatter, gabble, gibber, jabber, prattle. *See* WORDS. **2.** To talk volubly, persistently, and usually inconsequentially : babble, blabber, chatter, chitchat, clack, jabber, palaver, prattle, rattle (on), run on. *Informal:* go on, spiel. *Slang:* gab, gas, jaw, yak. ***Idioms:*** run off at the mouth, shoot the breeze (*or* bull). *See* WORDS.

prate *noun* **1.** Unintelligible or foolish talk : babble, blather, blatherskite, double talk, gabble, gibberish, jabber, jabberwocky, jargon, nonsense, prattle, twaddle. *See* WORDS. **2.** Incessant and usually inconsequential talk : babble, blab, blabber, chat, chatter, chitchat, jabber, palaver, prattle, small talk. *Slang:* gab, gas, yak. *See* WORDS.

prattle *verb*
1. To talk rapidly, incoherently, or indistinctly : babble, blather, chatter, gabble, gibber, jabber, prate. *See* WORDS. **2.** To talk volubly, persistently, and usually inconsequentially : babble, blabber, chatter, chitchat, clack, jabber, palaver, prate, rattle (on), run on. *Informal:* go on, spiel. *Slang:* gab, gas, jaw, yak. ***Idioms:*** run off at the mouth, shoot the breeze (*or* bull). *See* WORDS.

prattle *noun* **1.** Unintelligible or foolish talk : babble, blather, blatherskite, double talk, gabble, gibberish, jabber, jabberwocky, jargon, nonsense, prate, twaddle. *See* WORDS. **2.** Incessant and usually inconsequential talk : babble, blab, blabber, chat, chatter, chitchat, jabber, palaver, prate, small talk. *Slang:* gab, gas, yak. *See* WORDS.

praxis *noun*
A habitual way of behaving : consuetude, custom, habit, habitude, manner, practice, usage, usance, use, way, wont. *See* USUAL.

pray *verb*
1. To offer a reverent petition to God or a god : supplicate. *See* RELIGION. **2.** To make an earnest or urgent request : appeal, beg, beseech, crave, entreat, implore, plead, sue, supplicate. *Archaic:* conjure. *See* ASK.

prayer[1] *noun*
1. The act of praying : invocation, supplication. *See* RELIGION. **2.** A formula of words used in praying : collect[2], litany, orison, rogation (often used in plural). *See* RELIGION. **3.** An earnest or urgent request : appeal, entreaty, imploration, plea, supplication. *See* ASK. **4.** *Law.* An application to a higher authority, as for sanction or a decision : appeal, petition. *See* ASK, LAW.

prayer[2] *noun*
One who humbly entreats : beggar, suitor, suppliant, supplicant. *See* REQUEST.

prayerful *adjective*
Deeply concerned with God and the beliefs and practice of religion : devotional, devout, godly, holy, pietistic, pietistical, pious, religious, saintly. *See* RELIGION.

preach *verb*
1. To deliver a sermon, especially as a vocation : evangelize, sermonize. *See* RELIGION. **2.** To indulge in moral reflection, usually pompously : moralize, sermonize. *See* TEACH.

preacher *noun*
A person ordained for service in a Christian church : churchman, churchwoman, clergyman, clergywoman, cleric, clerical, clerk, divine, ecclesiastic, minister, parson. *Informal:* reverend. *See* RELIGION.

preachy *adjective*
Inclined to teach or moralize excessively : didactic, didactical. *See* TEACH.

preamble *noun*
A short section of preliminary remarks : foreword, induction, introduction, lead-in, overture, preface, prelude, prolegomenon, prologue. *See* START, WORDS.

precarious *adjective*
1. Not physically steady or firm : rickety, shaky, tottering, tottery, unstable, unsteady, wobbly. *See* FLEXIBLE. **2.** Lacking stability : infirm, insecure, shaky, tottering, tottery, unstable, unsteady, unsure, weak, wobbly. *See* CHANGE, STRONG.

precariousness *noun*
1. The quality or condition of being physically unsteady : instability, ricketiness, shakiness, unstableness, unsteadiness, wobbliness. *See* FLEXIBLE. **2.** The quality or condition of being erratic and undependable : insecureness, insecurity, instability, shakiness, unstableness, unsteadiness, unsureness. *See* CHANGE, STRONG.

precaution *noun*
1. Careful forethought to avoid harm or risk : calculation, care, carefulness, caution, chariness, gingerliness, wariness. *See* FEAR. **2.** The exercise of good judgment or common sense in practical matters : caution, circumspection, discretion, forehandedness, foresight, foresightedness, forethought, forethoughtfulness, prudence. *See* CAREFUL.

precede *verb*
1. To come, exist, or occur before in time : antecede, antedate, predate. *See* PRECEDE.
2. To begin (something) with preliminary or prefatory material : introduce, lead, preface, usher in. *See* START, WORDS.

precedence *noun*
The act, condition, or right of preceding : antecedence, precedency, priority, right of way. *See* PRECEDE.

precedency *noun*
The act, condition, or right of preceding : antecedence, precedence, priority, right of way. *See* PRECEDE.

precedent *noun*
A closely similar case in existence or in the past : example. *See* SAME.
precedent *adjective* **1.** Going before : advance, antecedent, anterior, earlier, preceding, previous, prior. *See* PRECEDE. **2.** Just gone by or elapsed : antecedent, anterior, earlier, foregoing, former, past, preceding, previous, prior. *See* TIME.

preceding *adjective*
1. Going before : advance, antecedent, anterior, earlier, precedent, previous, prior. *See* PRECEDE. **2.** Next before the present one : foregoing, last[1], latter, previous. *See* NEAR, PRECEDE. **3.** Just gone by or elapsed : antecedent, anterior, earlier, foregoing, former, past, precedent, previous, prior. *See* TIME.

precept *noun*
A principle governing affairs within or among political units : canon, decree, edict, institute, law, ordinance, prescription, regulation, rule. *See* LAW.

precinct *noun*
1. The boundary surrounding a certain area. Often used in plural : bound[2] (used in plural), confine (used in plural), limit (used in plural). *See* LIMITED. **2.** A surrounding area. Used in plural : environment, environs, locale, locality, neighborhood, surroundings, vicinity. *See* NEAR, PLACE.

precious *adjective*
1. Of great value : costly, inestimable, invaluable, priceless, valuable, worthy. ***Idioms:*** beyond price, of great price. *See* VALUE. **2.** Regarded with much love and tenderness : beloved, darling, dear, loved. *See* LOVE. **3.** Artificially genteel : affected, artificial, mannered. ***Informal:*** la-di-da. *See* GOOD, HONEST, PLAIN, TRUE.
precious *noun* A person who is much loved : beloved, darling, dear, honey, love, minion, sweet, sweetheart, truelove. ***Informal:*** sweetie. ***Idiom:*** light of one's life. *See* LOVE.

precipitance *noun*
Careless headlong action : haste, hastiness, hurriedness, precipitancy, precipitateness, precipitation, rashness, rush. *See* CAREFUL.

precipitancy *noun*
Careless headlong action : haste, hastiness, hurriedness, precipitance, precipitateness, precipitation, rashness, rush. *See* CAREFUL.

precipitant *adjective*
1. Characterized by unthinking boldness and haste : brash, foolhardy, harum-scarum, hasty, headlong, hotheaded, ill-considered, impetuous, improvident, impulsive, incautious, madcap, precipitate, rash[1], reckless, slapdash, temerarious, unconsidered. *See* CAREFUL. **2.** Happening quickly and without warning : abrupt, hurried, precipitate, sudden. *See* FAST, SURPRISE.

precipitate *verb*
To put down, especially in layers, by a natural process : deposit. *See* INCREASE.

precipitate *adjective* **1.** Characterized by unthinking boldness and haste : brash, foolhardy, harum-scarum, hasty, headlong, hotheaded, ill-considered, impetuous, improvident, impulsive, incautious, madcap, precipitant, rash[1], reckless, slapdash, temerarious, unconsidered. *See* CAREFUL. **2.** Happening quickly and without warning : abrupt, hurried, precipitant, sudden. *See* FAST, SURPRISE.

precipitate *noun* **1.** Matter that settles on a bottom or collects on a surface by a natural process : deposit, dreg (often used in plural), lees, precipitation, sediment. *See* LEFTOVER. **2.** Something brought about by a cause : aftermath, consequence, corollary, effect, end product, event, fruit, harvest, issue, outcome, ramification, result, resultant, sequel, sequence, sequent, upshot. *See* CAUSE.

precipitateness *noun*
Careless headlong action : haste, hastiness, hurriedness, precipitance, precipitancy, precipitation, rashness, rush. *See* CAREFUL.

precipitation *noun*
1. Careless headlong action : haste, hastiness, hurriedness, precipitance, precipitancy, precipitateness, rashness, rush. *See* CAREFUL. **2.** Matter that settles on a bottom or collects on a surface by a natural process : deposit, dreg (often used in plural), lees, precipitate, sediment. *See* LEFTOVER.

precipitous *adjective*
So sharply inclined as to be almost perpendicular : abrupt, bold, sheer[2], steep[1]. *See* HORIZONTAL.

precise *adjective*
1. Clearly, fully, and sometimes emphatically expressed : categorical, clear, clear-cut, decided, definite, explicit, express, positive, specific, unambiguous, unequivocal. *See* CLEAR. **2.** Having no errors : accurate, correct, errorless, exact, right, rigorous. *See* CORRECT, TRUE. **3.** Conforming to fact : accurate, correct, exact, faithful, right, rigorous, true, veracious, veridical. *See* CORRECT, HONEST, REAL, TRUE. **4.** Strictly distinguished from others : exact, very. *See* PRECISE. **5.** Marked by excessive concern for propriety and good form : bluenosed, genteel, old-maidish, priggish, prim, prissy, proper, prudish, puritanical, strait-laced, stuffy, Victorian. ***Idiom:*** prim and proper. *See* PLAIN.

precisely *adverb*
1. In an exact manner : even[1], exactly, just. *See* PRECISE, SAME. **2.** With precision or absolute conformity : bang, dead, direct, directly, exactly, fair, flush, just, right, smack[1], square, squarely, straight. *Slang:* smack-dab. *See* PRECISE.

preciseness *noun*
Freedom from error : accuracy, accurateness, correctness, exactitude, exactness, precision, rightness. *See* CORRECT.

precision *noun*
Freedom from error : accuracy, accurateness, correctness, exactitude, exactness, preciseness, rightness. *See* CORRECT.

preclude *verb*
To prohibit from occurring by advance planning or action : avert, forestall, forfend, obviate, prevent, rule out, stave off, ward (off). ***Idiom:*** nip in the bud. *See* ALLOW.

preclusion *noun*
The act of preventing : determent, deterrence, forestallment, obviation, prevention. *See* ALLOW.

preclusive *adjective*
Intended to prevent : deterrent, preventative, preventive. *See* ALLOW.

precocious *adjective*
1. Developing, occurring, or appearing before the expected time : early, premature, untimely. *See* TIME. **2.** Ahead of current trends or customs : advanced, forward, progressive. *See* PRECEDE.

precondition *noun*
Something indispensable : condition, essential, must, necessity, need, prerequisite, requirement, requisite, sine qua non. *See* NECESSARY.

precursor *noun*
1. One that indicates or announces someone or something to come : forerunner, foreshadower, harbinger, herald, presager. *See* FORESIGHT, SHOW. **2.** One that precedes, as in time : ancestor, antecedent, forerunner, predecessor, progenitor. *See* PRECEDE.

predate *verb*
To come, exist, or occur before in time : antecede, antedate, precede. *See* PRECEDE.

predecessor *noun*
1. One that precedes, as in time : ancestor, antecedent, forerunner, precursor, progenitor. *See* PRECEDE. **2.** *Archaic.* A person from whom one is descended : ancestor, antecedent, ascendant, father, forebear, forefather, foremother, mother, parent, progenitor. *See* KIN, PRECEDE.

predestinate *verb*
To determine the future of in advance : destine, fate, foreordain, predestine, predetermine, preordain. *See* CERTAIN.

predestination *noun*
That which is inevitably destined : destiny, fate, fortune, kismet, lot, portion. *See* CERTAIN.

predestine *verb*
To determine the future of in advance : destine, fate, foreordain, predestinate, predetermine, preordain. *See* CERTAIN.

predetermine *verb*
1. To determine the future of in advance : destine, fate, foreordain, predestinate, predestine, preordain. *See* CERTAIN. **2.** To consider and plan in advance : premeditate. *See* PLANNED.

predicament *noun*
A difficult, often embarrassing situation or condition : box[1], corner, deep water, difficulty, dilemma, Dutch, fix, hole, hot spot, hot water, jam, plight[1], quagmire, scrape, soup, trouble. *Informal:* bind, pickle, spot. *See* EASY.

predicate *verb*
To provide a basis for : base[1], build, establish, found, ground, rest[1], root[1], underpin. *See* OVER.

predict *verb*
To tell about or make known (future events) in advance, especially by means of special knowledge or inference : call, forecast, foretell, prognosticate, project. *See* FORESIGHT.

prediction *noun*
The act of predicting : forecast, outlook, prognosis, prognostication, projection. *See* FORESIGHT.

predictive *adjective*
Of or relating to prediction : prognostic, prognosticative. *See* FORESIGHT.

predilection *noun*
An inclination to something : bent, bias, cast, disposition, leaning, partiality, penchant, predisposition, proclivity, proneness, propensity, squint, tendency, trend, turn. *See* APPROACH, LIKE.

predispose *verb*
To have an impact on in a certain way : dispose, incline, influence, sway. *See* AFFECT, LIKE.

predisposition *noun*
An inclination to something : bent, bias, cast, disposition, leaning, partiality, penchant, predilection, proclivity, proneness, propensity, squint, tendency, trend, turn. *See* APPROACH, LIKE.

predominance *noun*
The condition or fact of being dominant : ascendance, ascendancy, dominance, domination, paramountcy, preeminence, preponderance, preponderancy, prepotency, supremacy. *See* OVER.

predominant *adjective*
1. Having preeminent significance : ascendant, dominant, prepotent, prevailing, regnant, ruling, supreme. *See* IMPORTANT. **2.** Most generally existing or encountered at a given time : current, prevailing, prevalent, regnant, rife, widespread. *See* SPECIFIC.

predominate *verb*
To occupy the preeminent position in : dominate, preponderate, prevail, reign, rule. ***Idioms:*** have the ascendancy, reign supreme. *See* OVER.

preeminence or **pre-eminence** *noun*
1. The condition or fact of being dominant : ascendance, ascendancy, dominance, domination, paramountcy, predominance, preponderance, preponderancy, prepotency, supremacy. *See* OVER. **2.** A position of exalted widely recognized importance : distinction, eminence, eminency, fame, glory, illustriousness, luster, mark, notability, note, prestige, prominence, prominency, renown. *See* IMPORTANT, KNOWLEDGE, RESPECT.

preeminent or **pre-eminent** *adjective*
1. Far beyond what is usual, normal, or customary : exceptional, extraordinary, magnificent, outstanding, rare, remarkable, singular, towering, uncommon, unusual. *Informal:* standout. *Slang:* awesome, out of sight. *See* BETTER, USUAL. **2.** Widely known and esteemed : celebrated, distinguished, eminent, famed, famous, great, illustrious, notable, noted, prestigious, prominent, redoubtable, renowned. *See* KNOWLEDGE, RESPECT.

preempt or **pre-empt** *verb*
1. To lay claim to for oneself or as one's right : appropriate, arrogate, assume, commandeer, seize, take, usurp. *See* GIVE. **2.** To cause to be busy or in use : engage, monopolize, occupy, tie up. *See* ACTION, USED.

preemption or **pre-emption** *noun*
The act of taking something for oneself : appropriation, arrogation, assumption, seizure, usurpation. *See* GIVE.

preen *verb*
To be proud of (oneself), as for an accomplishment or achievement : congratulate, plume, pride. *See* RESPECT.

preface *noun*
A short section of preliminary remarks : foreword, induction, introduction, lead-in, overture, preamble, prelude, prolegomenon, prologue. *See* START, WORDS.

preface *verb* To begin (something) with preliminary or prefatory material : introduce, lead, precede, usher in. *See* START, WORDS.

prefatory *adjective*
1. Before or in preparation for the main matter, action, or business : inductive, introductory, preliminary, preparatory, prolegomenous. *See* START. 2. Serving to introduce a subject or person, for example : introductory, preliminary, preparatory, prolegomenous. *See* START, WORDS.

prefer *verb*
To show partiality toward (someone) : favor. *Idiom:* play favorites. *See* FAIR.

preferable *adjective*
Of greater excellence than another : better[1], superior. *See* BETTER.

preference *noun*
1. The act of choosing : choice, election, option, selection. *See* CHOICE. 2. Favorable or preferential bias : favor, favoritism, partiality, partialness. *See* FAIR. 3. A liking for something : appetite, fondness, partiality, relish, taste, weakness. *See* LIKE.

preferential *adjective*
Disposed to favor one over another : favorable, partial. *See* FAIR.

preferred *adjective*
Being a favorite : favored, favorite, popular, well-liked. *See* LIKE.

prefigure *verb*
To give an indication of something in advance : adumbrate, augur, bode, forecast, forerun, foreshadow, foretell, foretoken, portend, presage, prognosticate. *See* FORESIGHT, SHOW.

prefigurement *noun*
A phenomenon that serves as a sign or warning of some future good or evil : augury, forerunner, foretoken, omen, portent, presage, prognostic, prognostication, sign. *Idiom:* writing (*or* handwriting) on the wall. *See* FORESIGHT, WARN.

pregnable *adjective*
Open to attack and capture because of a lack of protection : assailable, attackable, vincible, vulnerable. *See* STRONG.

pregnancy *noun*
The condition of carrying a developing fetus within the uterus : gestation, gravidity, gravidness, parturiency. *See* REPRODUCTION.

pregnant *adjective*
1. Carrying a developing fetus within the uterus : big, enceinte, expectant, expecting, gravid, parturient. *Slang:* gone. *Archaic:* great. *Idioms:* in a family way, with child. *See* REPRODUCTION. 2. Conveying hidden or unexpressed meaning : meaningful, significant, suggestive. *See* MEANING.

prejudice *noun*
1. An inclination for or against that inhibits impartial judgment : bias, one-sidedness, partiality, partisanship, prepossession, tendentiousness. *See* AFFECT, LIKE, STRAIGHT. 2. Irrational suspicion or hatred of a particular group, race, or religion : bigotry, intolerance. *See* LIKE.

prejudice *verb* 1. To cause to have a prejudiced view : bias, jaundice, prepossess, warp. *See* AFFECT, STRAIGHT. 2. To spoil the soundness or perfection of : blemish, damage, detract from, disserve, flaw, harm, hurt, impair, injure, mar, tarnish, vitiate. *See* BETTER, HELP.

prejudiced *adjective*
Exhibiting bias : biased, one-sided, partial, partisan, prejudicial, prepossessed, tendentious. *See* LIKE, STRAIGHT.

prejudicial *adjective*
Exhibiting bias : biased, one-sided, partial, partisan, prejudiced, prepossessed, tendentious. *See* LIKE, STRAIGHT.

prelect *verb*
To talk to an audience formally : address, lecture, speak. *Archaic:* bespeak. *See* WORDS.

prelection *noun*
A usually formal oral communication to an audience : address, allocution, declamation, lecture, oration, speech, talk. *See* WORDS.

preliminary *adjective*
1. Before or in preparation for the main matter, action, or business : inductive, introductory, prefatory, preparatory, prolegomenous. *See* START. 2. Serving to introduce a subject or person, for example : introductory, prefatory, preparatory, prolegomenous. *See* START, WORDS. 3. Not perfected, elaborated, or completed : rough, sketchy, tentative, unfinished, unperfected, unpolished. *See* START.

prelude *noun*
A short section of preliminary remarks : foreword, induction, introduction, lead-in, overture, preamble, preface, prolegomenon, prologue. *See* START, WORDS.

premature *adjective*
Developing, occurring, or appearing before the expected time : early, precocious, untimely. *See* TIME.

premeditate *verb*
To consider and plan in advance : predetermine. *See* PLANNED.

premeditated *adjective*
Planned, weighed, or estimated in advance : calculated, considered, deliberate, intentional. *See* PURPOSE.

premier *adjective*
Most important, influential, or significant : capital, cardinal, chief, first, foremost, key, leading, main, major, number one, paramount, primary, prime, principal, top. *See* IMPORTANT.

premise *noun*
Something taken to be true without proof : assumption, postulate, postulation, presupposition, supposition, theory, thesis. *See* REASON.
premise *verb* To take for granted without proof : assume, posit, postulate, presume, presuppose, suppose. *Informal:* reckon. *See* BELIEF.

premium *noun*
Something given in return for a service or accomplishment : accolade, award, guerdon, honorarium, plum, prize[1], reward. ***Idiom:*** token of appreciation (*or* esteem). *See* REWARD.

preoccupation *noun*
Total occupation of the attention or of the mind : absorption, engrossment, enthrallment, immersion, prepossession. *See* EXCITE.

preoccupied *adjective*
1. Having one's thoughts fully occupied : absorbed, deep, intent, rapt. ***Idiom:*** wrapped up in. *See* AWARENESS, EXCITE. **2.** So lost in thought as to be unaware of one's surroundings : absent, absent-minded, abstracted, bemused, distrait, faraway, inattentive. ***Idiom:*** a million miles away. *See* ABILITY, AWARENESS.

preoccupy *verb*
To occupy the full attention of : absorb, consume, engross, immerse, monopolize. *See* AWARENESS, EXCITE.

preordain *verb*
To determine the future of in advance : destine, fate, foreordain, predestinate, predestine, predetermine. *See* CERTAIN.

preparation *noun*
1. The condition of being made ready beforehand : preparedness, readiness. *See* PREPARED. **2.** A plan made in preparation for an undertaking. Often used in plural : arrangement (often used in plural), provision (often used in plural). *See* PLANNED.

preparatory *adjective*
1. Before or in preparation for the main matter, action, or business : inductive, introductory, prefatory, preliminary, prolegomenous. *See* START. **2.** Serving to introduce a subject or person, for example : introductory, prefatory, preliminary, prolegomenous. *See* START, WORDS.

prepare *verb*
1. To cause to be ready, as for use, consumption, or a special purpose : fit[1], fix, make, prime, ready. *See* PREPARED. **2.** To plan the details or arrangements of : arrange, lay out, schedule, work out. *See* PLANNED.

preparedness *noun*
The condition of being made ready beforehand : preparation, readiness. *See* PREPARED.

preponderance *noun*
1. The condition or fact of being dominant : ascendance, ascendancy, dominance, domination, paramountcy, predominance, preeminence, preponderancy, prepotency, supremacy. *See* OVER. **2.** The greatest part or portion : bulk, mass, preponderancy, weight. *See* BIG.

preponderancy *noun*
1. The condition or fact of being dominant : ascendance, ascendancy, dominance, domination, paramountcy, predominance, preeminence, preponderance, prepotency, supremacy. *See* OVER. **2.** The greatest part or portion : bulk, mass, preponderance, weight. *See* BIG.

preponderant *adjective*
Exercising controlling power or influence : commanding, controlling, dominant, dominating, dominative, governing, paramount, regnant, reigning, ruling. *See* OVER.

preponderate *verb*
To occupy the preeminent position in : dominate, predominate, prevail, reign, rule. ***Idioms:*** have the ascendancy, reign supreme. *See* OVER.

prepossess *verb*
To cause to have a prejudiced view : bias, jaundice, prejudice, warp. *See* AFFECT, STRAIGHT.

prepossessed *adjective*
Exhibiting bias : biased, one-sided, partial, partisan, prejudiced, prejudicial, tendentious. *See* LIKE, STRAIGHT.

prepossessing *adjective*
Pleasing to the eye or mind : attractive, bewitching, enchanting, engaging, enticing, fascinating, fetching, glamorous, lovely, pretty, sweet, taking, tempting, winning, winsome. *See* LIKE.

prepossession *noun*
1. An inclination for or against that inhibits impartial judgment : bias, one-sidedness, partiality, partisanship, prejudice, tendentiousness.

See AFFECT, LIKE, STRAIGHT. **2.** Total occupation of the attention or of the mind : absorption, engrossment, enthrallment, immersion, preoccupation. *See* EXCITE.

preposterous *adjective*
1. So senseless as to be laughable : absurd, foolish, harebrained, idiotic, imbecilic, insane, lunatic, mad, moronic, nonsensical, silly, softheaded, tomfool, unearthly, zany. *Informal:* cockeyed, crazy, loony, loopy. *Slang:* balmy[2], dippy, dopey, jerky, sappy, wacky. *See* ABILITY, KNOWLEDGE. **2.** Beyond all reason : obscene, outrageous, ridiculous, shocking, unconscionable, unreasonable. ***Idioms:*** out of bounds, out of sight. *See* USUAL.

preposterousness *noun*
Foolish behavior : absurdity, folly, foolery, foolishness, idiocy, imbecility, insanity, lunacy, madness, nonsense, senselessness, silliness, tomfoolery, zaniness. *Informal:* craziness. *See* ABILITY.

prepotency *noun*
The condition or fact of being dominant : ascendance, ascendancy, dominance, domination, paramountcy, predominance, preeminence, preponderance, preponderancy, supremacy. *See* OVER.

prepotent *adjective*
Having preeminent significance : ascendant, dominant, predominant, prevailing, regnant, ruling, supreme. *See* IMPORTANT.

prerequisite *noun*
Something indispensable : condition, essential, must, necessity, need, precondition, requirement, requisite, sine qua non. *See* NECESSARY.

prerogative *noun*
1. A privilege granted a person, as by virtue of birth : appanage, birthright, perquisite, right. *Law:* droit. *See* OWNED. **2.** The right and power to command, decide, rule, or judge : authority, command, control, domination, dominion, jurisdiction, mastery, might, power, sovereignty, sway. *Informal:* say-so. *See* OVER.

presage *noun*
A phenomenon that serves as a sign or warning of some future good or evil : augury, forerunner, foretoken, omen, portent, prefigurement, prognostic, prognostication, sign. ***Idiom:*** writing (*or* handwriting) on the wall. *See* FORESIGHT, WARN.

presage *verb* To give an indication of something in advance : adumbrate, augur, bode, forecast, forerun, foreshadow, foretell, foretoken, portend, prefigure, prognosticate. *See* FORESIGHT, SHOW.

presager *noun*
One that indicates or announces someone or something to come : forerunner, foreshadower, harbinger, herald, precursor. *See* FORESIGHT, SHOW.

prescience *noun*
Unusual or creative discernment or perception : farsightedness, foresight, vision. *See* FORESIGHT.

prescient *adjective*
Characterized by foresight : farsighted, foresighted, visionary. *See* FORESIGHT.

prescribe *verb*
To set forth expressly and authoritatively : decree, dictate, fix, impose, lay down, ordain. ***Idioms:*** call the shots (*or* tune), lay it on the line. *See* OVER.

prescript *noun*
A code or set of codes governing action or procedure, for example : dictate, regulation, rubric, rule. *See* ORDER.

prescription *noun*
A principle governing affairs within or among political units : canon, decree, edict, institute, law, ordinance, precept, regulation, rule. *See* LAW.

presence *noun*
1. The condition or fact of being present : occurrence. *See* BE. **2.** Behavior through which one reveals one's personality : address, air, bearing, demeanor, manner, mien, style. *Archaic:* port. *See* BE, STYLE.

present[1] *noun*
The current time : now, nowadays, today. *See* TIME.

present *adjective* In existence now : contemporary, current, existent, existing, new, now, present-day. *See* TIME.

present[2] *verb*
1. To make known socially : acquaint, introduce. *See* KNOWLEDGE. **2.** To produce on the stage : act (out), do, dramatize, enact, give, perform, put on, stage. *See* PERFORMING ARTS. **3.** To make a gift of : bestow, give (away), hand out. *See* GIVE. **4.** To give formally or officially : accord, award, bestow, confer, grant. *See* GIVE. **5.** To bring forward for formal consideration : adduce, cite, lay[1]. *Archaic:* allege. *See* LAW, WORDS. **6.** To put before another for acceptance : extend, offer, proffer, tender[2], volunteer. ***Idioms:*** come forward with, lay at someone's feet, lay before. *See* OFFER.

present *noun* Something bestowed freely : gift, presentation. *Chiefly British:* handsel. *See* GIVE.

presentable *adjective*
Proper in appearance : respectable. *Informal:* decent. *See* GOOD, USUAL.

presentation *noun*
1. The act of conferring, as of an honor : accordance, bestowal, bestowment, conference, conferment, conferral, grant. *See* GIVE. **2.** Something bestowed freely : gift, present[2]. *Chiefly British:* handsel. *See* GIVE. **3.** The instance or occasion of being presented for the first time to society : coming-out, debut. *See* KNOWLEDGE.

present-day *adjective*
In existence now : contemporary, current, existent, existing, new, now, present[1]. *See* TIME.

preservation *noun*
1. The careful guarding of an asset : conservancy, conservation, husbandry, management. *See* KEEP. **2.** The act or a means of defending : defense, guard, protection, protector, safeguard, security, shield, ward. *See* ATTACK.

preservative *adjective*
Able to preserve : conservative, protective. *See* HELP.

preserve *verb*
1. To protect (an asset) from loss or destruction : conserve, husband, save. *See* KEEP. **2.** To keep safe from danger, attack, or harm : defend, guard, protect, safeguard, secure, shield, ward. *Archaic:* fend. *See* ATTACK. **3.** To keep in a condition of good repair, efficiency, or use : keep up, maintain, sustain. *See* KEEP. **4.** To prepare (food) for storage and future use : can, conserve, put up. *See* KEEP.
preserve *noun* Public land kept for a special purpose : reservation, reserve. *See* TERRITORY.

press *verb*
1. To act on with a steady pushing force : crowd, crush. *See* PUSH. **2.** To exert pressure : bear, push. *See* OVER. **3.** To extract from by applying pressure : crush, express, squeeze. *See* TIGHTEN. **4.** To smooth by applying heat and pressure : iron, mangle[2]. *See* SMOOTH. **5.** To congregate, as around a person : crowd, flock, mob, throng. *See* COLLECT, TIGHTEN. **6.** To put one's arms around affectionately : clasp, embrace, enfold, hold, hug, squeeze. *Slang:* clinch. *Archaic:* bosom, clip[2], embosom. *See* TOUCH. **7.** To impel to action : exhort, urge. *See* CAUSE, PUSH. **8.** To do or achieve by forcing obstacles out of one's way : push, ram, shove. *See* PUSH. **9.** To solicit (something) insistently : insist, urge. *See* CONTINUE, SEEK.
press *noun* **1.** Journalists and journalism in general : fourth estate, medium (used in plural **media**). *British:* Fleet Street. *See* WORDS. **2.** An enormous number of persons gathered together : crowd, crush, drove, flock, horde, mass, mob, multitude, ruck[1], swarm, throng. *See* BIG, GROUP.

pressing *adjective*
Compelling immediate attention : burning, crying, dire, emergent, exigent, imperative, instant, urgent. *See* BIG.
pressing *noun* Urgent solicitation : insistence, insistency. *Archaic:* instance. *See* CONTINUE, SEEK.

pressure *noun*
1. The act, condition, or effect of exerting force on someone or something : strain[1], stress, tension. *See* PUSH. **2.** Power used to overcome resistance : coercion, compulsion, constraint, duress, force, strength, violence. *See* ATTACK.
pressure *verb* **1.** To cause (a person or thing) to act or move in spite of resistance : coerce, compel, constrain, force, make, obligate, oblige. *See* ATTACK. **2.** To maintain normal air pressure in : pressurize. *See* PUSH.

pressurize *verb*
To maintain normal air pressure in : pressure. *See* PUSH.

prestidigitation *noun*
The use of skillful tricks and deceptions to produce entertainingly baffling effects : conjuration, legerdemain, magic, sleight of hand. *See* PERFORMING ARTS.

prestige *noun*
1. The level of credit or respect at which one is regarded by others : face, standing, status. *See* RESPECT. **2.** A person's high standing among others : dignity, good name, good report, honor, reputation, repute, respect, status. *See* RESPECT. **3.** A position of exalted widely recognized importance : distinction, eminence, eminency, fame, glory, illustriousness, luster, mark, notability, note, preeminence, prominence, prominency, renown. *See* IMPORTANT, KNOWLEDGE, RESPECT.

prestigious *adjective*
Widely known and esteemed : celebrated, distinguished, eminent, famed, famous, great, illustrious, notable, noted, preeminent, prominent, redoubtable, renowned. *See* KNOWLEDGE, RESPECT.

presumable *adjective*
Based on probability or presumption : assumptive, likely, presumptive, probable, prospective. *Idiom:* taken for granted. *See* BELIEF, LIKELY.

presume *verb*
1. To take for granted without proof : assume, posit, postulate, premise, presuppose, suppose. *Informal:* reckon. *See* BELIEF. **2.** To have the courage to put forward, as an idea, especially when rebuff or criticism is likely : dare, hazard, pretend, venture. *See* TRY. **3.** To take advantage of unfairly : abuse, exploit, impose, use. *See* TREAT WELL.

presuming *adjective*
Rude and disrespectful : assuming, assumptive, audacious, bold, boldfaced, brash, brazen, cheeky, contumelious, familiar, forward, impertinent, impudent, insolent, malapert, nervy, overconfident, pert, presumptuous, pushy, sassy, saucy, smart. *Informal:* brassy, flip, fresh, smart-alecky, snippety, snippy, uppish, uppity. *Slang:* wise[1]. *See* ATTITUDE, COURTESY.

presumption *noun*
The quality of being arrogant : arrogance, haughtiness, hauteur, insolence, loftiness, lordliness, overbearingness, pride, pridefulness, proudness, superciliousness, superiority. *See* ATTITUDE.

presumptive *adjective*
1. Based on probability or presumption : assumptive, likely, presumable, probable, prospective. ***Idiom:*** taken for granted. *See* BELIEF, LIKELY. **2.** Presumed to be true, real, or genuine, especially on inconclusive grounds : conjectural, hypothetic, hypothetical, inferential, supposed, suppositional, suppositious, supposititious, suppositive. *See* BELIEF.

presumptuous *adjective*
Rude and disrespectful : assuming, assumptive, audacious, bold, boldfaced, brash, brazen, cheeky, contumelious, familiar, forward, impertinent, impudent, insolent, malapert, nervy, overconfident, pert, presuming, pushy, sassy, saucy, smart. *Informal:* brassy, flip, fresh, smart-alecky, snippety, snippy, uppish, uppity. *Slang:* wise[1]. *See* ATTITUDE, COURTESY.

presumptuousness *noun*
The state or quality of being impudent or arrogantly self-confident : assumption, audaciousness, audacity, boldness, brashness, brazenness, cheek, cheekiness, chutzpah, discourtesy, disrespect, effrontery, face, familiarity, forwardness, gall[1], impertinence, impudence, impudency, incivility, insolence, nerve, nerviness, overconfidence, pertness, pushiness, rudeness, sassiness, sauciness. *Informal:* brass, crust, sauce, uppishness, uppityness. *See* ATTITUDE, COURTESY.

presuppose *verb*
To take for granted without proof : assume, posit, postulate, premise, presume, suppose. *Informal:* reckon. *See* BELIEF.

presupposition *noun*
Something taken to be true without proof : assumption, postulate, postulation, premise, supposition, theory, thesis. *See* REASON.

pretend *verb*
1. To take on or give a false appearance of : affect[2], assume, counterfeit, fake, feign, put on, sham, simulate. ***Idiom:*** make believe. *See* TRUE. **2.** To behave affectedly or insincerely or take on a false or misleading appearance of : act, counterfeit, dissemble, fake, feign, play-act, pose, put on, sham, simulate. *See* HONEST, TRUE. **3.** To claim or allege insincerely or falsely : feign, profess. *See* TRUE. **4.** To contrive and present as genuine : counterfeit, fake, feign, simulate. ***Idioms:*** make believe, put on an act. *See* TRUE. **5.** To have the courage to put forward, as an idea, especially when rebuff or criticism is likely : dare, hazard, presume, venture. *See* TRY.

pretend *adjective Informal.* Made to imitate something else : artificial, imitation, manmade, mock, simulated, synthetic. *See* REAL.

pretended *adjective*
Not genuine or sincere : affected, artificial, feigned, insincere, phony. *See* TRUE.

pretender *noun*
1. One who fakes : charlatan, fake, faker, fraud, humbug, impostor, mountebank, phony, quack. *See* TRUE. **2.** One who sets forth a claim to a royal title : claimant, claimer. *See* OWNED.

pretense *noun*
1. The presentation of something false as true : charade, make-believe. *See* HONEST, TRUE. **2.** A display of insincere behavior : act, acting, disguise, dissemblance, masquerade, sham, show, simulation. *See* HONEST, TRUE. **3.** Artificial behavior adopted to impress others : affectation, affectedness, air (used in plural), mannerism, pose. *See* HONEST, TRUE. **4.** A professed rather than a real reason : pretension, pretext. *See* HONEST. **5.** A deceptive outward appearance : cloak, color, coloring, cover, disguise, disguisement, façade, face, false colors, front, gloss, guise, mask, masquerade, pretext, semblance, show, veil, veneer, window-dressing. *Slang:* put-on. *See* SHOW. **6.** A legitimate or supposed right to demand something as one's rightful due : claim, pretension, title. *Slang:* dibs. *See* OWNED, REQUEST.

pretension *noun*
1. A professed rather than a real reason :

pretense, pretext. *See* HONEST. **2.** A legitimate or supposed right to demand something as one's rightful due : claim, pretense, title. *Slang:* dibs. *See* OWNED, REQUEST. **3.** Boastful self-importance or display : grandioseness, grandiosity, ostentation, pomposity, pompousness, pretentiousness. *See* PLAIN.

pretentious *adjective*
1. Characterized by an exaggerated show of dignity or self-importance : grandiose, hoity-toity, pompous, puffed-up, puffy, self-important. *Informal:* highfalutin. *See* PLAIN. **2.** Marked by outward, often extravagant display : flamboyant, ostentatious, showy, splashy, splurgy. *See* PLAIN.

pretentiousness *noun*
Boastful self-importance or display : grandioseness, grandiosity, ostentation, pomposity, pompousness, pretension. *See* PLAIN.

preternatural *adjective*
1. Departing from the normal : aberrant, abnormal, anomalistic, anomalous, atypic, atypical, deviant, divergent, irregular, unnatural. *See* GOOD, USUAL. **2.** Greatly exceeding or departing from the normal course of nature : supernatural, unnatural. *See* USUAL. **3.** Of, coming from, or relating to forces or beings that exist outside the natural world : extramundane, extrasensory, metaphysical, miraculous, superhuman, supernatural, superphysical, supersensible, transcendental, unearthly. *See* SUPERNATURAL.

preternaturalness *noun*
The condition of being abnormal : aberrance, aberrancy, aberration, abnormality, anomaly, deviance, deviancy, deviation, irregularity, unnaturalness. *See* GOOD, USUAL.

pretext *noun*
1. A professed rather than a real reason : pretense, pretension. *See* HONEST. **2.** An explanation offered to justify an action or make it better understood : excuse, plea. *See* EXPLAIN. **3.** A deceptive outward appearance : cloak, color, coloring, cover, disguise, disguisement, façade, face, false colors, front, gloss, guise, mask, masquerade, pretense, semblance, show, veil, veneer, window-dressing. *Slang:* put-on. *See* SHOW.

pretty *adjective*
1. Pleasing to the eye or mind : attractive, bewitching, enchanting, engaging, enticing, fascinating, fetching, glamorous, lovely, prepossessing, sweet, taking, tempting, winning, winsome. *See* LIKE. **2.** Having qualities that delight the eye : attractive, beauteous, beautiful, comely, fair, good-looking, gorgeous, handsome, lovely, pulchritudinous, ravishing, sightly, stunning. *Scots:* bonny. ***Idiom:*** easy on the eyes. *See* BEAUTIFUL.

pretty *adverb* To some extent : fairly, rather. ***Idiom:*** more or less. *See* BIG.

pretty penny *noun*
Informal. A large sum of money : fortune, mint. *Informal:* bundle, tidy sum, wad. *Slang:* pile. *See* RICH.

prevail *verb*
To occupy the preeminent position in : dominate, predominate, preponderate, reign, rule. ***Idioms:*** have the ascendancy, reign supreme. *See* OVER.

prevail against (or **over**) *verb* To win a victory over, as in battle or a competition : beat, best, conquer, defeat, master, overcome, rout, subdue, subjugate, surmount, triumph over, vanquish, worst. *Informal:* trim, whip. *Slang:* ace, lick. ***Idioms:*** carry (*or* win) the day, get (*or* have) the best of, get (*or* have) the better of, go someone one better. *See* WIN.

prevail on (or **upon**) *verb* To succeed in causing (a person) to act in a certain way : argue into, bring, bring around (*or* round), convince, get, induce, persuade, sell (on), talk into. *See* PERSUASION.

prevail against or **over** *verb* See **prevail.**

prevailing *adjective*
1. Most generally existing or encountered at a given time : current, predominant, prevalent, regnant, rife, widespread. *See* SPECIFIC. **2.** Having preeminent significance : ascendant, dominant, predominant, prepotent, regnant, ruling, supreme. *See* IMPORTANT.

prevail on or **upon** *verb* See **prevail.**

prevalence *noun*
The quality or condition of being usual : customariness, habitualness, normalcy, normality, ordinariness, regularity, routineness, usualness. *See* USUAL.

prevalent *adjective*
Most generally existing or encountered at a given time : current, predominant, prevailing, regnant, rife, widespread. *See* SPECIFIC.

prevaricate *verb*
1. To stray from truthfulness or sincerity : equivocate, palter, shuffle. *See* TRUE. **2.** To make untrue declarations : falsify, fib, forswear, lie[2]. *Law:* perjure. *See* TRUE.

prevarication *noun*
1. The use or an instance of equivocal language : ambiguity, equivocation, equivoque,

euphemism, hedge, shuffle, tergiversation, weasel word. *Informal:* waffle. *See* CLEAR. **2.** An untrue declaration : canard, cock-and-bull story, falsehood, falsity, fib, fiction, inveracity, lie[2], misrepresentation, misstatement, story, tale, untruth. *Informal:* fish story, tall tale. *Slang:* whopper. *See* TRUE.

prevaricator *noun*
One who tells lies : fabricator, fabulist, falsifier, fibber, liar. *Informal:* storyteller. *Law:* perjurer. *See* TRUE.

prevent *verb*
To prohibit from occurring by advance planning or action : avert, forestall, forfend, obviate, preclude, rule out, stave off, ward (off). *Idiom:* nip in the bud. *See* ALLOW.

preventative *adjective*
1. Intended to prevent : deterrent, preclusive, preventive. *See* ALLOW. **2.** Defending against disease : preventive, prophylactic, protective. *See* ALLOW.

prevention *noun*
The act of preventing : determent, deterrence, forestallment, obviation, preclusion. *See* ALLOW.

preventive *adjective*
1. Intended to prevent : deterrent, preclusive, preventative. *See* ALLOW. **2.** Defending against disease : preventative, prophylactic, protective. *See* ALLOW.

previous *adjective*
1. Going before : advance, antecedent, anterior, earlier, precedent, preceding, prior. *See* PRECEDE. **2.** Next before the present one : foregoing, last[1], latter, preceding. *See* NEAR, PRECEDE. **3.** Just gone by or elapsed : antecedent, anterior, earlier, foregoing, former, past, precedent, preceding, prior. *See* TIME. **4.** Having been such previously : erstwhile, former, late, old, once, onetime, past, quondam, sometime, whilom. *See* PRECEDE.

previously *adverb*
1. At a time in the past : already, before, earlier, erstwhile, formerly, once. *Archaic:* aforetime, beforetime. *See* PRECEDE. **2.** Up to this time : before, earlier, heretofore, yet. *See* PRECEDE.

prey *noun*
One that is made to suffer injury, loss, or death : casualty, victim. *See* HELP.

price *noun*
1. An amount paid or to be paid for a purchase : charge, cost. *Informal:* tab. *See* TRANSACTIONS. **2.** A loss sustained in the accomplishment of or as the result of something : cost, expense, sacrifice, toll[1]. *See* TRANSACTIONS.

priceless *adjective*
1. Of great value : costly, inestimable, invaluable, precious, valuable, worthy. ***Idioms:*** beyond price, of great price. *See* VALUE. **2.** Extremely funny : hilarious, sidesplitting. *Informal:* killing, rich. *See* LAUGHTER.

prick *noun*
1. A sensation of physical discomfort occurring as the result of disease or injury : ache, pain, pang, prickle, smart, soreness, stab, sting, stitch, throe, twinge. *Informal:* misery. *See* PAIN. **2.** A small mark or hole made by a sharp, pointed object : perforation, puncture, stab. *See* MARKS, OPEN. **3.** A sharp, pointed object : needle, prickle, spine, thorn. *See* SHARP.

prick *verb* To stir to action or feeling : egg on, excite, foment, galvanize, goad, impel, incite, inflame, inspire, instigate, motivate, move, pique, prod, prompt, propel, provoke, set off, spur, stimulate, touch off, trigger, work up. *See* CAUSE, EXCITE.

prickle *noun*
1. A sharp, pointed object : needle, prick, spine, thorn. *See* SHARP. **2.** A sensation of physical discomfort occurring as the result of disease or injury : ache, pain, pang, prick, smart, soreness, stab, sting, stitch, throe, twinge. *Informal:* misery. *See* PAIN.

prickly *adjective*
1. Full of sharp needlelike protuberances : briery, echinate, pricky, spiny, thistly, thorny. *See* SHARP. **2.** So replete with interlocking points and complications as to be painfully irritating : nettlesome, spiny, thorny. *See* EASY, PAIN.

pricky *adjective*
Full of sharp needlelike protuberances : briery, echinate, prickly, spiny, thistly, thorny. *See* SHARP.

pride *noun*
1. A sense of one's own dignity or worth : amour-propre, ego, self-esteem, self-regard, self-respect. *See* RESPECT. **2.** The quality of being arrogant : arrogance, haughtiness, hauteur, insolence, loftiness, lordliness, overbearingness, presumption, pridefulness, proudness, superciliousness, superiority. *See* ATTITUDE. **3.** A regarding of oneself with undue favor : amour-propre, conceit, ego, egoism, egotism, narcissism, vainglory, vainness, vanity. *Slang:* ego trip. *See* SELF-LOVE.

pride *verb* To be proud of (oneself), as for an

accomplishment or achievement : congratulate, plume, preen. *See* RESPECT.

prideful *adjective*
1. Overly convinced of one's own superiority and importance : arrogant, haughty, high-and-mighty, insolent, lofty, lordly, overbearing, overweening, proud, supercilious, superior. ***Idiom:*** on one's high horse. *See* ATTITUDE. **2.** Properly valuing oneself, one's honor, or one's dignity : proud, self-respecting. *See* RESPECT.

pridefulness *noun*
The quality of being arrogant : arrogance, haughtiness, hauteur, insolence, loftiness, lordliness, overbearingness, presumption, pride, proudness, superciliousness, superiority. *See* ATTITUDE.

prier also **pryer** *noun*
A person who snoops : pry, snoop, snooper. *See* INVESTIGATE, PARTICIPATE.

priggish *adjective*
Marked by excessive concern for propriety and good form : bluenosed, genteel, old-maidish, precise, prim, prissy, proper, prudish, puritanical, strait-laced, stuffy, Victorian. ***Idiom:*** prim and proper. *See* PLAIN.

prim *adjective*
Marked by excessive concern for propriety and good form : bluenosed, genteel, old-maidish, precise, priggish, prissy, proper, prudish, puritanical, strait-laced, stuffy, Victorian. ***Idiom:*** prim and proper. *See* PLAIN.

primary *adjective*
1. Most important, influential, or significant : capital, cardinal, chief, first, foremost, key, leading, main, major, number one, paramount, premier, prime, principal, top. *See* IMPORTANT. **2.** Preceding all others in time : earliest, first, initial, maiden, original, pioneer, prime, primordial. *See* START. **3.** Not derived from something else : original, prime, primitive. *See* START. **4.** Arising from or going to the root or source : basal, basic, foundational, fundamental, original, radical, underlying. *See* SURFACE. **5.** Marked by the absence of any intervention : direct, firsthand, immediate. *See* CLEAR, NEAR.

prime *adjective*
1. Of fine quality : choice, fine[1], first-class, select, superior. *See* BETTER. **2.** Exceptionally good of its kind : ace, banner, blue-ribbon, brag, capital, champion, excellent, fine[1], first-class, first-rate, quality, splendid, superb, superior, terrific, tiptop, top. *Informal:* A-one, bully, dandy, great, swell, topflight, topnotch. *Slang:* boss. *Chiefly British:* tophole. *See* GOOD. **3.** Most important, influential, or significant : capital, cardinal, chief, first, foremost, key, leading, main, major, number one, paramount, premier, primary, principal, top. *See* IMPORTANT. **4.** Preceding all others in time : earliest, first, initial, maiden, original, pioneer, primary, primordial. *See* START. **5.** Not derived from something else : original, primary, primitive. *See* START.

prime *noun* A condition or time of vigor and freshness : bloom[1], blossom, efflorescence, florescence, flower, flush. *See* BETTER.

prime *verb* To cause to be ready, as for use, consumption, or a special purpose : fit[1], fix, make, prepare, ready. *See* PREPARED.

primeval *adjective*
Of or relating to early stages in the evolution of human culture : primitive. *See* START.

primitive *adjective*
1. Not derived from something else : original, primary, prime. *See* START. **2.** Of or being an irreducible element : basic, elemental, elementary, essential, fundamental, ultimate, underlying. *See* SURFACE. **3.** Of, existing, or occurring in a distant period : ancient, antediluvian, early. *See* START. **4.** Exhibiting lack of education or knowledge : backward, benighted, ignorant, unenlightened. *See* KNOWLEDGE. **5.** Lacking expert, careful craftsmanship : crude, raw, rough, rude, unpolished. *See* GOOD. **6.** Of or relating to early stages in the evolution of human culture : primeval. *See* START. **7.** Not civilized : barbarian, barbaric, barbarous, rude, savage, uncivilized, uncultivated, uncultured, wild. *Archaic:* uncivil. *See* CULTURE, WILD.

primordial *adjective*
Preceding all others in time : earliest, first, initial, maiden, original, pioneer, primary, prime. *See* START.

princely *adjective*
Large and impressive in size, scope, or extent : august, baronial, grand, grandiose, imposing, lordly, magnific, magnificent, majestic, noble, regal, royal, splendid, stately, sublime, superb. *See* BIG, GOOD.

principal *adjective*
1. Most important, influential, or significant : capital, cardinal, chief, first, foremost, key, leading, main, major, number one, paramount, premier, primary, prime, top. *See* IMPORTANT. **2.** Having or exercising authority : chief, head. *See* OVER.

principal *noun* The main performer in a theatrical production : lead, protagonist, star. *See* PERFORMING ARTS.

principle *noun*
1. A broad and basic rule or truth : axiom, fundamental, law, theorem, universal. *See* ORDER. **2.** Moral or ethical strength : character, fiber, honesty, integrity. *See* STRONG.

principled *adjective*
In accordance with principles of right or good conduct : ethical, moral, proper, right, righteous, rightful, right-minded, virtuous. *See* RIGHT.

print *noun*
1. The visible effect made on a surface by pressure : impress, impression, imprint, indent, indentation, mark, stamp. *See* MARKS. **2.** A visible sign or mark of the passage of someone or something : trace, track, trail. *See* MARKS.

printing *noun*
1. The act or process of publishing printed matter : issue, publication, publishing. *See* WORDS. **2.** The entire number of copies of a publication printed from a single typesetting : impression. *See* WORDS.

prior *adjective*
1. Going before : advance, antecedent, anterior, earlier, precedent, preceding, previous. *See* PRECEDE. **2.** Just gone by or elapsed : antecedent, anterior, earlier, foregoing, former, past, precedent, preceding, previous. *See* TIME.

priority *noun*
The act, condition, or right of preceding : antecedence, precedence, precedency, right of way. *See* PRECEDE.

prison *noun*
A place for the confinement of persons in lawful detention : brig, house of correction, jail, keep, penitentiary. *Informal:* lockup, pen[3]. *Slang:* big house, can, clink, cooler, coop, hoosegow, joint, jug, pokey[1], slammer, stir[2]. *Chiefly Regional:* calaboose. *See* FREE.

prissy *adjective*
Marked by excessive concern for propriety and good form : bluenosed, genteel, old-maidish, precise, priggish, prim, proper, prudish, puritanical, strait-laced, stuffy, Victorian. ***Idiom:*** prim and proper. *See* PLAIN.

private *adjective*
1. Belonging to, relating to, or affecting a particular person : individual, personal. *See* SPECIFIC. **2.** Belonging or confined to a particular person or group as opposed to the public or the government : personal, privy. *See* SPECIFIC. **3.** Known about by very few : auricular, confidential, inside, secret. *Informal:* hush-hush. *See* SHOW.

privation *noun*
1. The condition of being extremely poor : beggary, destitution, impecuniosity, impecuniousness, impoverishment, indigence, need, neediness, pennilessness, penuriousness, penury, poverty, want. *See* RICH. **2.** The condition of being deprived of what one once had or ought to have : deprival, deprivation, dispossession, divestiture, loss. *See* GIVE, RICH.

privileged *adjective*
Of or being information available only to authorized persons : classified, confidential, restricted. *See* SHOW.

privy *adjective*
Belonging or confined to a particular person or group as opposed to the public or the government : personal, private. *See* SPECIFIC.

prize[1] *noun*
1. Something given in return for a service or accomplishment : accolade, award, guerdon, honorarium, plum, premium, reward. ***Idiom:*** token of appreciation (*or* esteem). *See* REWARD. **2.** A memento received as a symbol of excellence or victory : accolade, award, trophy. *See* RESPECT. **3.** A person or thing worth catching : plum. *Informal:* catch. *Slang:* brass ring. *See* DESIRE. **4.** Someone or something considered exceptionally precious : gem, pearl, treasure. *See* VALUE. **5.** The superlative or most preferable part of something : best, choice, cream, crème de la crème, elite, flower, pick, top. ***Idioms:*** cream of the crop, flower of the flock, pick of the bunch (*or* crop). *See* BETTER.

prize *verb* **1.** To recognize the worth, quality, importance, or magnitude of : appreciate, cherish, esteem, respect, treasure, value. ***Idiom:*** set store by. *See* PRAISE. **2.** To have the highest regard for : cherish, treasure. ***Idiom:*** hold dear. *See* VALUE.

prize[2] *noun*
Nautical. Goods or property seized unlawfully, especially by a victor in wartime : booty, loot, pillage, plunder, spoil (used in plural). *Slang:* boodle. *See* CRIMES, GIVE.

probability *noun*
The likeliness of a given event occurring : chance, likelihood, odds, possibility, prospect (used in plural). *See* LIKELY.

probable *adjective*
1. Having a chance of happening or being true : contingent, likely, possible. *See* LIKELY.
2. Based on probability or presumption : assumptive, likely, presumable, presumptive,

prospective. *Idiom:* taken for granted. *See* BELIEF, LIKELY.

probe *noun*

1. The act or an instance of exploring or investigating : exploration, investigation, reconnaissance. *See* INVESTIGATE. **2.** Something, as a remark, used to determine the attitude of another : feeler. *Idiom:* trial balloon. *See* INVESTIGATE. **3.** A seeking of knowledge, data, or the truth about something : inquest, inquiry, inquisition, investigation, research. *See* INVESTIGATE.

probe *verb* **1.** To go into or through for the purpose of making discoveries or acquiring information : delve, dig, explore, inquire, investigate, look into, reconnoiter, scout[1]. *See* INVESTIGATE. **2.** To test the attitude of : feel out, sound[3] (out). ***Idioms:*** put out feelers, send up a trial balloon. *See* INVESTIGATE.

prober *noun*

One who inquires : inquirer, inquisitor, investigator, querier, quester, questioner, researcher. *See* ASK, INVESTIGATE.

probing *adjective*

Possessing or displaying perceptions of great accuracy and sensitivity : acute, incisive, keen[1], penetrating, perceptive, sensitive, sharp, trenchant. *See* CAREFUL, SHARP.

probity *noun*

The quality or state of being morally sound : good, goodness, morality, rectitude, righteousness, rightness, uprightness, virtue, virtuousness. *See* RIGHT.

problem *noun*

A situation that presents difficulty, uncertainty, or perplexity : hornets' nest, issue, question. *Informal:* can of worms. *See* EASY.

problematic *adjective*

1. In doubt or dispute : arguable, contested, debatable, disputable, doubtful, exceptionable, moot, mootable, problematical, questionable, uncertain. *See* CERTAIN. **2.** Not affording certainty : ambiguous, borderline, chancy, clouded, doubtful, dubious, dubitable, equivocal, inconclusive, indecisive, indeterminate, problematical, questionable, uncertain, unclear, unsure. *Informal:* iffy. ***Idioms:*** at issue, in doubt, in question. *See* CERTAIN, CLEAR.

problematical *adjective*

1. In doubt or dispute : arguable, contested, debatable, disputable, doubtful, exceptionable, moot, mootable, problematic, questionable, uncertain. *See* CERTAIN. **2.** Not affording certainty : ambiguous, borderline, chancy, clouded, doubtful, dubious, dubitable, equivocal, inconclusive, indecisive, indeterminate, problematic, questionable, uncertain, unclear, unsure. *Informal:* iffy. ***Idioms:*** at issue, in doubt, in question. *See* CERTAIN, CLEAR.

proboscis *noun*

The structure on the human face that contains the nostrils and organs of smell and forms the beginning of the respiratory tract : nose. *Informal:* beak, snoot. *Slang:* nozzle, schnoz, schnozzle, snout. *See* BODY, CONVEX.

procedure *noun*

1. A method used in dealing with something : approach, attack, course, line, modus operandi, plan, tack, technique. *See* MEANS. **2.** An action calculated to achieve an end : maneuver, measure (often used in plural), move, step, tactic. *See* ACTION. **3.** An official or prescribed plan or course of action : line, policy, program. *See* PLANNED.

proceed *verb*

1. To move along a particular course : fare, go, journey, pass, push on, remove, travel, wend. *Idiom:* make one's way. *See* MOVE. **2.** To go forward, especially toward a conclusion : advance, come (along), get along, march[1], move, progress. *See* APPROACH. **3.** To have as a source : arise, come, derive, emanate, flow, issue, originate, rise, spring, stem, upspring. *See* START.

procession *noun*

1. A number of things placed or occurring one after the other : chain, consecution, course, order, progression, round, run, sequence, series, string, succession, suite, train. *Informal:* streak. *See* ORDER. **2.** A way in which things follow each other in space or time : consecution, order, sequence, succession. *See* ORDER, PRECEDE.

proclaim *verb*

1. To bring to public notice or make known publicly : advertise, announce, annunciate, broadcast, declare, promulgate, publish. *See* KNOWLEDGE, WORDS. **2.** To make known the presence or arrival of : announce, herald, introduce, usher in. *See* KNOWLEDGE, START. **3.** To make manifest or apparent : demonstrate, display, evidence, evince, exhibit, manifest, reveal, show. *See* SHOW.

proclamation *noun*

1. The act of announcing : announcement, annunciation, declaration, promulgation, publication. *See* KNOWLEDGE. **2.** A public statement : announcement, annunciation, declaration, edict, manifesto, notice, pronouncement. *See* KNOWLEDGE.

proclivity *noun*
An inclination to something : bent, bias, cast, disposition, leaning, partiality, penchant, predilection, predisposition, proneness, propensity, squint, tendency, trend, turn. *See* APPROACH, LIKE.

procrastinate *verb*
To go or move slowly so that progress is hindered : dally, dawdle, delay, dilly-dally, drag, lag, linger, loiter, poke, tarry, trail. ***Idioms:*** drag one's feet (*or* heels), mark time, take one's time. *See* FAST.

procrastinator *noun*
One that lags : dawdler, dilly-dallier, lag, laggard, lagger, lingerer, loiterer, poke, straggler, tarrier. *Informal:* slowpoke. *See* FAST.

procreant *adjective*
Of or relating to reproduction : procreative, reproductive. *See* REPRODUCTION.

procreate *verb*
1. To be the biological father of : beget, breed, father, get, sire. *See* KIN. **2.** To produce sexually or asexually others of one's kind : breed, increase, multiply, proliferate, propagate, reproduce, spawn. *See* REPRODUCTION. **3.** To cause to come into existence : beget, breed, create, engender, father, hatch, make, originate, parent, produce, sire, spawn. ***Idiom:*** give birth (*or* rise) to. *See* MAKE.

procreation *noun*
The process by which an organism produces others of its kind : breeding, multiplication, proliferation, propagation, reproduction, spawning. *Obsolete:* increase. *See* REPRODUCTION.

procreative *adjective*
Of or relating to reproduction : procreant, reproductive. *See* REPRODUCTION.

procumbent *adjective*
Lying down : decumbent, flat, horizontal, prone, prostrate, recumbent. *See* HORIZONTAL.

procurable *adjective*
Capable of being obtained or used : acquirable, attainable, available, gettable, obtainable. *Idioms:* on hand, to be had. *See* GET.

procure *verb*
To come into possession of : acquire, come by, gain, get, obtain, secure, win. *Informal:* land, pick up. *See* GET.

prod *verb*
1. To thrust against or into : dig, jab, jog, nudge, poke. *See* TOUCH. **2.** To stir to action or feeling : egg on, excite, foment, galvanize, goad, impel, incite, inflame, inspire, instigate, motivate, move, pique, prick, prompt, propel, provoke, set off, spur, stimulate, touch off, trigger, work up. *See* CAUSE, EXCITE.

prod *noun* Something that causes and encourages a given response : encouragement, fillip, impetus, impulse, incentive, inducement, motivation, push, spur, stimulant, stimulation, stimulator, stimulus. *See* CAUSE.

prodigal *adjective*
1. Characterized by excessive or imprudent spending : extravagant, lavish, profligate, profuse, spendthrift, wasteful. *See* CAREFUL, EXCESS, SAVE. **2.** Given to or marked by unrestrained abundance : extravagant, exuberant, lavish, lush[1], luxuriant, opulent, profuse, riotous, superabundant. *See* BIG, EXCESS.

prodigal *noun* A person who spends money or resources wastefully : profligate, scattergood, spendthrift, waster, wastrel. *See* SAVE.

prodigality *noun*
Excessive or imprudent expenditure : extravagance, extravagancy, lavishness, profligacy, profuseness, profusion, squander, waste, wastefulness. *See* CAREFUL, SAVE.

prodigious *adjective*
1. Of extraordinary size and power : behemoth, Brobdingnagian, Bunyanesque, colossal, cyclopean, elephantine, enormous, gargantuan, giant, gigantesque, gigantic, herculean, heroic, huge, immense, jumbo, mammoth, massive, massy, mastodonic, mighty, monster, monstrous, monumental, mountainous, pythonic, stupendous, titanic, tremendous, vast. *Informal:* walloping. *Slang:* whopping. *See* BIG. **2.** So remarkable as to elicit disbelief : amazing, astonishing, astounding, fabulous, fantastic, fantastical, incredible, marvelous, miraculous, phenomenal, stupendous, unbelievable, wonderful, wondrous. *See* GOOD.

prodigiousness *noun*
The quality of being enormous : enormousness, hugeness, immenseness, immensity, stupendousness, tremendousness, vastness. *See* BIG.

prodigy *noun*
One that evokes great surprise and admiration : astonishment, marvel, miracle, phenomenon, sensation, stunner, wonder, wonderment. ***Idioms:*** one for the books, the eighth wonder of the world. *See* GOOD.

produce *verb*
1. To bring forth (a product) : bear, give, yield. *See* RICH. **2.** To bring (a product or idea, for example) into being : develop, generate. *See* KIN. **3.** To make as income or profit : bring in,

clear, draw, earn, gain, gross, net², pay, realize, repay, return, yield. *See* MONEY. **4.** To form by artistic effort : compose, create, indite, write. *See* MAKE. **5.** To create by forming, combining, or altering materials : assemble, build, construct, fabricate, fashion, forge¹, frame, make, manufacture, mold, put together, shape. *See* MAKE. **6.** To cause to come into existence : beget, breed, create, engender, father, hatch, make, originate, parent, procreate, sire, spawn. *Idiom:* give birth (*or* rise) to. *See* MAKE.
7. *Mathematics.* To make or become longer : draw out, elongate, extend, lengthen, prolong, prolongate, protract, spin (out), stretch (out). *See* INCREASE, LONG.

producer *noun*
A person or business that makes or builds something : assembler, builder, constructor, erector, maker, manufacturer. *See* MAKE.

product *noun*
Something produced by human effort : production. *See* MAKE.

production *noun*
1. Something produced by human effort : product. *See* MAKE. **2.** The amount or quantity produced : output, yield. *See* BIG. **3.** Something that is the result of creative effort : composition, opus, piece, work. *See* MAKE.

productive *adjective*
1. Producing or able to produce a desired effect : effective, effectual, efficacious, efficient. *See* THRIVE. **2.** Capable of reproducing : fecund, fertile, fruitful, prolific. *Biology:* proliferous. *See* RICH. **3.** Characterized by great productivity : fecund, fertile, fruitful, prolific, rich. *See* RICH. **4.** Acting effectively with minimal waste : efficient. *See* INDUSTRIOUS, THRIVE.

productiveness *noun*
The quality or state of being fertile : fecundity, fertility, fruitfulness, productivity, prolificacy, prolificness, richness. *See* RICH.

productivity *noun*
1. The quality or state of being fertile : fecundity, fertility, fruitfulness, productiveness, prolificacy, prolificness, richness. *See* RICH. **2.** The quality of being efficient : efficiency. *See* INDUSTRIOUS, THRIVE.

profanation *noun*
An act of disrespect or impiety toward something regarded as sacred : blasphemy, desecration, sacrilege, violation. *See* SACRED.

profane *adjective*
1. Showing irreverence and contempt for something sacred : blasphemous, sacrilegious. *See* SACRED. **2.** Not religious in subject matter, form, or use : lay², secular, temporal, worldly. *See* SACRED. **3.** Offensive to accepted standards of decency : barnyard, bawdy, broad, coarse, dirty, Fescennine, filthy, foul, gross, lewd, nasty, obscene, ribald, scatologic, scatological, scurrilous, smutty, vulgar. *Slang:* raunchy. *See* DECENT.
profane *verb* To spoil or mar the sanctity of : defile, desecrate, pollute, violate. *See* CLEAN, RELIGION, SACRED.

profaneness *noun*
The quality or state of being obscene : bawdiness, coarseness, dirtiness, filthiness, foulness, grossness, lewdness, obscenity, profanity, scurrility, scurrilousness, smuttiness, vulgarity, vulgarness. *Slang:* raunch, raunchiness. *See* DECENT.

profanity *noun*
1. The quality or state of being obscene : bawdiness, coarseness, dirtiness, filthiness, foulness, grossness, lewdness, obscenity, profaneness, scurrility, scurrilousness, smuttiness, vulgarity, vulgarness. *Slang:* raunch, raunchiness. *See* DECENT. **2.** Something that is offensive to accepted standards of decency : bawdry, dirt, filth, obscenity, ribaldry, scatology, smut, vulgarity. *Slang:* raunch. *See* DECENT.

profess *verb*
To claim or allege insincerely or falsely : feign, pretend. *See* TRUE.

profession *noun*
Activity pursued as a livelihood : art, business, calling, career, craft, employment, job, line, métier, occupation, pursuit, trade, vocation, work. *Slang:* racket. *Archaic:* employ. *See* ACTION.

professional *adjective*
Having or demonstrating a high degree of knowledge or skill : adept, crack, expert, master, masterful, masterly, proficient, skilled, skillful. *Slang:* crackerjack. *See* ABILITY.
professional *noun* A person with a high degree of knowledge or skill in a particular field : ace, adept, authority, dab hand, expert, master, past master, proficient, wizard. *Informal:* whiz. *Slang:* crackerjack. *Chiefly British:* dab². *See* ABILITY.

proffer *verb*
To put before another for acceptance : extend, offer, present², tender², volunteer. ***Idioms:*** come forward with, lay at someone's feet, lay before. *See* OFFER.

proffer *noun* Something offered : bid, offer, proposal, tender[2]. *See* OFFER.

proficiency *noun*
Natural or acquired facility in a specific activity : ability, adeptness, art, command, craft, expertise, expertness, knack, mastery, skill, technique. *Informal:* know-how. *See* ABILITY, KNOWLEDGE.

proficient *adjective*
Having or demonstrating a high degree of knowledge or skill : adept, crack, expert, master, masterful, masterly, professional, skilled, skillful. *Slang:* crackerjack. *See* ABILITY.
proficient *noun* A person with a high degree of knowledge or skill in a particular field : ace, adept, authority, dab hand, expert, master, past master, professional, wizard. *Informal:* whiz. *Slang:* crackerjack. *Chiefly British:* dab[2]. *See* ABILITY.

profile *noun*
A line marking and shaping the outer form of an object : contour, delineation, outline, silhouette. *See* EDGE, SURFACE.

profit *noun*
1. Something beneficial : advantage, avail, benefit, blessing, boon[1], favor, gain. *See* HELP. **2.** Something that contributes to or increases one's well-being : advantage, benefit, good, interest (often used in plural). *See* HELP. **3.** Something earned, won, or otherwise acquired : earnings, gain, return. *See* GET, MONEY. **4.** The quality of being suitable or adaptable to an end : account, advantage, avail, benefit, use, usefulness, utility. *See* USED.
profit *verb* **1.** To make a large profit : batten. *Slang:* clean up. ***Idiom:*** make a killing. *See* MONEY. **2.** To derive advantage : benefit, capitalize, gain. *See* HELP. **3.** To be an advantage to : advantage, avail, benefit, serve. *Archaic:* boot[2]. ***Idiom:*** stand someone in good stead. *See* HELP.

profitable *adjective*
1. Affording profit : advantageous, fat, lucrative, moneymaking, remunerative, rewarding. *See* GET. **2.** Affording benefit : advantageous, benefic, beneficent, beneficial, benignant, favorable, good, helpful, propitious, salutary, toward, useful. *See* HELP.

profligacy *noun*
1. Excessive freedom; lack of restraint : dissoluteness, dissolution, libertinism, license, licentiousness. *See* RESTRAINT. **2.** Excessive or imprudent expenditure : extravagance, extravagancy, lavishness, prodigality, profuseness, profusion, squander, waste, wastefulness. *See* CAREFUL, SAVE.

profligate *adjective*
1. Lacking in moral restraint : abandoned, dissipated, dissolute, fast, gay, incontinent, licentious, rakish, unbridled, unconstrained, uncontrolled, ungoverned, uninhibited, unrestrained, wanton, wild. *See* RESTRAINT. **2.** Characterized by excessive or imprudent spending : extravagant, lavish, prodigal, profuse, spendthrift, wasteful. *See* CAREFUL, EXCESS, SAVE.
profligate *noun* **1.** An immoral or licentious person : libertine, rake[1], wanton. *See* SEX. **2.** A person who spends money or resources wastefully : prodigal, scattergood, spendthrift, waster, wastrel. *See* SAVE.

profound *adjective*
1. Extending far downward or inward from a surface : abysmal, deep. *See* SURFACE. **2.** Resulting from or affecting one's innermost feelings : deep, intense, strong. *See* STRONG, SURFACE. **3.** Beyond the understanding of an average mind : abstruse, deep, esoteric, recondite. *Slang:* heavy. *See* EASY, SURFACE.

profoundness *noun*
Intellectual penetration or range : deepness, depth, profundity. *See* THOUGHTS.

profundity *noun*
1. Intellectual penetration or range : deepness, depth, profoundness. *See* THOUGHTS. **2.** Deep, thorough, or mature understanding : insight, sagaciousness, sagacity, sageness, sapience, wisdom. *See* WISE.

profuse *adjective*
1. Growing profusely : dense, heavy, lush[1], luxuriant, rank[2], thick. *See* BIG. **2.** Given to or marked by unrestrained abundance : extravagant, exuberant, lavish, lush[1], luxuriant, opulent, prodigal, riotous, superabundant. *See* BIG, EXCESS. **3.** Characterized by excessive or imprudent spending : extravagant, lavish, prodigal, profligate, spendthrift, wasteful. *See* CAREFUL, EXCESS, SAVE.

profuseness *noun*
Excessive or imprudent expenditure : extravagance, extravagancy, lavishness, prodigality, profligacy, profusion, squander, waste, wastefulness. *See* CAREFUL, SAVE.

profusion *noun*
1. Excessive or imprudent expenditure : extravagance, extravagancy, lavishness, prodigality, profligacy, profuseness, squander, waste, wastefulness. *See* CAREFUL, SAVE. **2.** A great deal : abundance, mass, mountain, much, plenty, wealth, world. *Informal:* barrel, heap, lot, pack, peck[2], pile. *Regional:* power, sight. *See* BIG.

progenitor *noun*
1. A person from whom one is descended : ancestor, antecedent, ascendant, father, forebear, forefather, foremother, mother, parent. *Archaic:* predecessor. *See* KIN, PRECEDE.
2. One that precedes, as in time : ancestor, antecedent, forerunner, precursor, predecessor. *See* PRECEDE.

progeny *noun*
1. One descended directly from the same parents or ancestors : child, descendant, offspring, scion. *See* KIN. **2.** A group consisting of those descended directly from the same parents or ancestors : brood, get, issue, offspring, posterity, seed. *See* KIN.

prognosis *noun*
The act of predicting : forecast, outlook, prediction, prognostication, projection. *See* FORESIGHT.

prognostic *adjective*
Of or relating to prediction : predictive, prognosticative. *See* FORESIGHT.
prognostic *noun* A phenomenon that serves as a sign or warning of some future good or evil : augury, forerunner, foretoken, omen, portent, prefigurement, presage, prognostication, sign. ***Idiom:*** writing (*or* handwriting) on the wall. *See* FORESIGHT, WARN.

prognosticate *verb*
1. To tell about or make known (future events) in advance, especially by means of special knowledge or inference : call, forecast, foretell, predict, project. *See* FORESIGHT. **2.** To give an indication of something in advance : adumbrate, augur, bode, forecast, forerun, foreshadow, foretell, foretoken, portend, prefigure, presage. *See* FORESIGHT, SHOW.

prognostication *noun*
1. The act of predicting : forecast, outlook, prediction, prognosis, projection. *See* FORESIGHT. **2.** A phenomenon that serves as a sign or warning of some future good or evil : augury, forerunner, foretoken, omen, portent, prefigurement, presage, prognostic, sign. ***Idiom:*** writing (*or* handwriting) on the wall. *See* FORESIGHT, WARN.

prognosticative *adjective*
Of or relating to prediction : predictive, prognostic. *See* FORESIGHT.

program *noun*
1. An organized list, as of procedures, activities, or events : agenda, calendar, docket, lineup, order of the day (often used in plural), schedule, timetable. *See* PLANNED. **2.** A document, such as a list or an outline, that gives, for example, the order of events in a public performance or the chief features of a stock offering : bill[1], prospectus, syllabus. *See* PLANNED, WORDS.
3. An official or prescribed plan or course of action : line, policy, procedure. *See* PLANNED.
program *verb* To enter on a schedule : schedule, slate. *See* REMEMBER.

progress *noun*
1. Forward movement : advance, advancement, furtherance, headway, march[1], progression. *See* BETTER, FORWARD. **2.** A progression from a simple form to a more complex one : development, evolution, evolvement, growth, unfolding. *See* CHANGE. **3.** Steady improvement, as of an individual or a society : amelioration, betterment, development, improvement, melioration. *See* BETTER.
progress *verb* To go forward, especially toward a conclusion : advance, come (along), get along, march[1], move, proceed. *See* APPROACH.

progression *noun*
1. Forward movement : advance, advancement, furtherance, headway, march[1], progress. *See* BETTER, FORWARD. **2.** A number of things placed or occurring one after the other : chain, consecution, course, order, procession, round, run, sequence, series, string, succession, suite, train. *Informal:* streak. *See* ORDER.

progressive *adjective*
1. Ahead of current trends or customs : advanced, forward, precocious. *See* PRECEDE.
2. Not narrow or conservative in thought, expression, or conduct : broad, broad-minded, liberal, open-minded, tolerant. *See* ATTITUDE, WIDE. **3.** Favoring civil liberties and social progress : liberal, liberalistic. *See* POLITICS.
progressive *noun* A person with liberal political opinions : liberal, liberalist. *See* POLITICS.

prohibit *verb*
To refuse to allow : ban, debar, disallow, enjoin, forbid, inhibit, interdict, outlaw, proscribe, taboo. *See* ALLOW.

prohibition *noun*
A refusal to allow : ban, disallowance, forbiddance, inhibition, interdiction, proscription, taboo. *See* ALLOW.

project *noun*
1. A method for making, doing, or accomplishing something : blueprint, design, game plan, idea, layout, plan, schema, scheme, strategy. *See* PLANNED. **2.** Something undertaken, especially something requiring extensive planning and work : enterprise, undertaking, venture. *See* WORK.

project *verb* **1.** To curve outward past the normal or usual limit : bag, balloon, beetle, belly, bulge, jut, overhang, pouch, protrude, protuberate, stand out, stick out. *See* CONVEX. **2.** To launch with great force : fire, hurtle, loose, propel, shoot. ***Idiom:*** let fly. *See* MOVE. **3.** To send out heat, light, or energy : cast, emit, irradiate, radiate, shed, throw. *See* MOVE. **4.** To form a strategy for : blueprint, cast, chart, conceive, contrive, design, devise, formulate, frame, lay[1], plan, scheme, strategize, work out. *Informal:* dope out. ***Idiom:*** lay plans. *See* PLANNED. **5.** To have in mind as a goal or purpose : aim, contemplate, design, intend, mean[1], plan, propose, purpose, target. *Regional:* mind. *See* PLANNED, PURPOSE. **6.** To tell about or make known (future events) in advance, especially by means of special knowledge or inference : call, forecast, foretell, predict, prognosticate. *See* FORESIGHT.

projection *noun*
1. A part that protrudes or extends outward : bulge, jut, knob, knot, overhang, protrusion, protuberance. *See* CONVEX. **2.** The act of predicting : forecast, outlook, prediction, prognosis, prognostication. *See* FORESIGHT.

prolegomenon *noun*
A short section of preliminary remarks : foreword, induction, introduction, lead-in, overture, preamble, preface, prelude, prologue. *See* START, WORDS.

prolegomenous *adjective*
1. Before or in preparation for the main matter, action, or business : inductive, introductory, prefatory, preliminary, preparatory. *See* START. **2.** Serving to introduce a subject or person, for example : introductory, prefatory, preliminary, preparatory. *See* START, WORDS.

proliferate *verb*
1. To produce sexually or asexually others of one's kind : breed, increase, multiply, procreate, propagate, reproduce, spawn. *See* REPRODUCTION. **2.** To make or become greater or larger : aggrandize, amplify, augment, boost, build, build up, burgeon, enlarge, escalate, expand, extend, grow, increase, magnify, mount, multiply, rise, run up, snowball, soar, swell, upsurge, wax. *Informal:* beef up. *See* INCREASE.

proliferation *noun*
1. The process by which an organism produces others of its kind : breeding, multiplication, procreation, propagation, reproduction, spawning. *Obsolete:* increase. *See* REPRODUCTION. **2.** The act of increasing or rising : aggrandizement, amplification, augment, augmentation, boost, buildup, enlargement, escalation, growth, hike, increase, jump, multiplication, raise, rise, swell, upsurge, upswing, upturn. *See* INCREASE. **3.** The result or product of building up : accretion, buildup, development, enlargement, multiplication. *See* INCREASE.

proliferous *adjective*
Biology. Capable of reproducing : fecund, fertile, fruitful, productive, prolific. *See* RICH.

prolific *adjective*
1. Capable of reproducing : fecund, fertile, fruitful, productive. *Biology:* proliferous. *See* RICH. **2.** Characterized by great productivity : fecund, fertile, fruitful, productive, rich. *See* RICH.

prolificacy *noun*
The quality or state of being fertile : fecundity, fertility, fruitfulness, productiveness, productivity, prolificness, richness. *See* RICH.

prolificness *noun*
The quality or state of being fertile : fecundity, fertility, fruitfulness, productiveness, productivity, prolificacy, richness. *See* RICH.

prolix *adjective*
Using or containing an excessive number of words : diffuse, long-winded, periphrastic, pleonastic, redundant, verbose, wordy. *See* EXCESS, STYLE, WORDS.

prolixity *noun*
Words or the use of words in excess of those needed for clarity or precision : diffuseness, diffusion, long-windedness, pleonasm, redundancy, verbiage, verboseness, verbosity, windiness, wordage, wordiness. *See* EXCESS, STYLE, WORDS.

prologue *noun*
A short section of preliminary remarks : foreword, induction, introduction, lead-in, overture, preamble, preface, prelude, prolegomenon. *See* START, WORDS.

prolong *verb*
To make or become longer : draw out, elongate, extend, lengthen, prolongate, protract, spin (out), stretch (out). *Mathematics:* produce. *See* INCREASE, LONG.

prolongate *verb*
To make or become longer : draw out, elongate, extend, lengthen, prolong, protract, spin (out), stretch (out). *Mathematics:* produce. *See* INCREASE, LONG.

prolongation *noun*
The act of making something longer or the condition of being made longer : elongation, extension, protraction. *See* LONG.

prolonged *adjective*
1. Of long duration : chronic, continuing, lingering, persistent, protracted. *See* CONTINUE. **2.** Extending tediously beyond a standard duration : dragging, drawn-out, lengthy, long[1], long-drawn-out, overlong, protracted. *See* EXCITE, LONG. **3.** Having great physical length : elongate, elongated, extended, lengthy, long[1]. *See* LONG.

promenade *noun*
An act of walking, especially for pleasure : amble, meander (often used in plural), perambulation, ramble, saunter, stroll, walk, wander. *See* MOVE.

promenade *verb* To walk at a leisurely pace : amble, meander, perambulate, ramble, saunter, stroll, wander. *Informal:* mosey. *See* MOVE.

prominence *noun*
1. A position of exalted widely recognized importance : distinction, eminence, eminency, fame, glory, illustriousness, luster, mark, notability, note, preeminence, prestige, prominency, renown. *See* IMPORTANT, KNOWLEDGE, RESPECT. **2.** A natural land elevation : eminence, hill, rise. *See* HIGH.

prominency *noun*
A position of exalted widely recognized importance : distinction, eminence, eminency, fame, glory, illustriousness, luster, mark, notability, note, preeminence, prestige, prominence, renown. *See* IMPORTANT, KNOWLEDGE, RESPECT.

prominent *adjective*
1. Readily attracting notice : arresting, bold, conspicuous, eye-catching, marked, noticeable, observable, outstanding, pointed, pronounced, remarkable, salient, signal, striking. ***Idiom:*** sticking out like a sore thumb. *See* SEE. **2.** Widely known and esteemed : celebrated, distinguished, eminent, famed, famous, great, illustrious, notable, noted, preeminent, prestigious, redoubtable, renowned. *See* KNOWLEDGE, RESPECT.

promise *noun*
A declaration that one will or will not do a certain thing : assurance, covenant, engagement, guarantee, guaranty, pledge, plight[2], solemn word, vow, warrant, word, word of honor. *See* OBLIGATION.

promise *verb* **1.** To assume an obligation : contract, engage, pledge, undertake. *See* AGREE, OBLIGATION. **2.** To guarantee by a solemn promise : covenant, pledge, plight[2], swear, vow. ***Idiom:*** give one's word of honor. *See* AGREE, OBLIGATION.

promising *adjective*
1. Showing great promise : coming, up-and-coming. ***Idiom:*** on the way up. *See* INCREASE. **2.** Inspiring confidence or hope : cheering, encouraging, heartening, hopeful, likely. *See* HELP.

promote *verb*
1. To raise in rank : advance, elevate, jump, raise, upgrade. *See* RISE. **2.** To help bring about : encourage, feed, foster. *See* HELP. **3.** To cause to move forward or upward, as toward a goal : advance, forward, further. *See* FORWARD, HELP. **4.** To make known vigorously the positive features of (a product) : advertise, ballyhoo, build up, cry (up), popularize, publicize, talk up. *Informal:* pitch, plug. *Slang:* push. *See* KNOWLEDGE. **5.** To increase or seek to increase the importance or reputation of by favorable publicity : ballyhoo, boost, build up, enhance, publicize, puff, talk up, tout. *Informal:* plug. *Slang:* hype. *See* KNOWLEDGE.

promotion *noun*
1. A progression upward in rank : advancement, elevation, jump, rise, upgrade. *See* RISE. **2.** A systematic effort or part of this effort to increase the importance or reputation of by favorable publicity : advertisement, ballyhoo, buildup, publicity, puffery. *Informal:* pitch, plug. *Slang:* hype. *See* KNOWLEDGE. **3.** The act or profession of promoting something, as a product : advertising, publicity. *See* KNOWLEDGE.

prompt *adjective*
Occurring, acting, or performed exactly at the time appointed : punctual, timely. ***Idioms:*** at (*or* on) the dot, on time. *See* TIME.

prompt *verb* To stir to action or feeling : egg on, excite, foment, galvanize, goad, impel, incite, inflame, inspire, instigate, motivate, move, pique, prick, prod, propel, provoke, set off, spur, stimulate, touch off, trigger, work up. *See* CAUSE, EXCITE.

promulgate *verb*
1. To bring to public notice or make known publicly : advertise, announce, annunciate, broadcast, declare, proclaim, publish. *See* KNOWLEDGE, WORDS. **2.** To make (information) generally known : advertise, blaze[2], blazon, broadcast, bruit, circulate, disseminate, noise, propagate, spread. ***Idioms:*** spread far and wide, spread the word. *See* KNOWLEDGE. **3.** To put in force or cause to be by legal authority : constitute, enact, establish, legislate, make. *See* ACTION, MAKE, POLITICS.

promulgation *noun*
The act of announcing : announcement, annunciation, declaration, proclamation, publication. *See* KNOWLEDGE.

prone *adjective*
1. Lying down : decumbent, flat, horizontal, procumbent, prostrate, recumbent. *See* HORIZONTAL. **2.** Having or showing a tendency or likelihood : apt, disposed, given, inclined, liable, likely. *See* LIKELY. **3.** Tending to incur : liable, open, subject, susceptible, susceptive, vulnerable. *See* LIKELY.

proneness *noun*
An inclination to something : bent, bias, cast, disposition, leaning, partiality, penchant, predilection, predisposition, proclivity, propensity, squint, tendency, trend, turn. *See* APPROACH, LIKE.

pronounce *verb*
To produce or make (speech sounds) : articulate, enunciate, say, utter[1], vocalize. *See* WORDS.

pronounced *adjective*
1. Readily seen, perceived, or understood : apparent, clear, clear-cut, crystal clear, distinct, evident, manifest, noticeable, observable, obvious, patent, plain, visible. *See* SEE. **2.** Readily attracting notice : arresting, bold, conspicuous, eye-catching, marked, noticeable, observable, outstanding, pointed, prominent, remarkable, salient, signal, striking. ***Idiom:*** sticking out like a sore thumb. *See* SEE. **3.** Without any doubt : clear, clear-cut, decided, definite, distinct, unquestionable. *See* CERTAIN.

pronouncement *noun*
1. An authoritative or official decision, especially one made by a court : decree, determination, edict, judgment, ruling. *See* LAW. **2.** A public statement : announcement, annunciation, declaration, edict, manifesto, notice, proclamation. *See* KNOWLEDGE.

pronto *adverb*
Informal. In a rapid way : apace, fast, posthaste, quick, quickly. *Informal:* flat out, hell-for-leather, lickety-split. ***Idioms:*** full tilt, in a flash, in nothing flat, like a bat out of hell, like a blue streak, like a flash, like a house on fire, like a shot, like a streak, like greased lightning, like the wind, like wildfire. *See* FAST.

proof *noun*
1. That which confirms : attestation, authentication, confirmation, corroboration, demonstration, evidence, substantiation, testament, testimonial, testimony, validation, verification, warrant. *See* TRUE. **2.** A fact or circumstance that gives logical support to an assertion, claim, or proposal : argument, ground (often used in plural), reason, wherefore, why. ***Idiom:*** why and wherefore. *See* REASON. **3.** A procedure that ascertains effectiveness, value, proper function, or other quality : assay, essay, test, trial, tryout. *See* INVESTIGATE.

proof *adjective* Having the capacity to withstand : immune, impervious, insusceptible, resistant, resistive, unsusceptible. *See* RESIST.

prop *noun*
A means or device that keeps something erect, stable, or secure : brace, buttress, crutch, shore, stay[2], support, underpinning. *See* SUPPORT.

prop *verb* To keep from yielding or failing during stress or difficulty : bolster, buoy (up), support, sustain, uphold. *See* HELP.

propagandize *verb*
To teach to accept a system of thought uncritically : brainwash, indoctrinate. *See* TEACH.

propagate *verb*
1. To bring into existence and foster the development of : breed, cultivate, grow, raise. *See* CARE FOR, REPRODUCTION. **2.** To produce sexually or asexually others of one's kind : breed, increase, multiply, procreate, proliferate, reproduce, spawn. *See* REPRODUCTION. **3.** To make (information) generally known : advertise, blaze[2], blazon, broadcast, bruit, circulate, disseminate, noise, promulgate, spread. ***Idioms:*** spread far and wide, spread the word. *See* KNOWLEDGE.

propagation *noun*
The process by which an organism produces others of its kind : breeding, multiplication, procreation, proliferation, reproduction, spawning. *Obsolete:* increase. *See* REPRODUCTION.

propel *verb*
1. To set or keep going : actuate, drive, impel, mobilize, move, run. *See* MOVE. **2.** To launch with great force : fire, hurtle, loose, project, shoot. ***Idiom:*** let fly. *See* MOVE. **3.** To force to move or advance with or as if with blows or pressure : drive, push, ram, shove, thrust. *See* MOVE. **4.** To stir to action or feeling : egg on, excite, foment, galvanize, goad, impel, incite, inflame, inspire, instigate, motivate, move, pique, prick, prod, prompt, provoke, set off, spur, stimulate, touch off, trigger, work up. *See* CAUSE, EXCITE.

propensity *noun*
An inclination to something : bent, bias, cast, disposition, leaning, partiality, penchant,

predilection, predisposition, proclivity, proneness, squint, tendency, trend, turn. *See* APPROACH, LIKE.

proper *adjective*
1. Suitable for a particular person, condition, occasion, or place : appropriate, apt, becoming, befitting, correct, felicitous, fit[1], fitting, happy, meet[2], right, tailor-made. *See* RIGHT. **2.** Suited to one's end or purpose : appropriate, befitting, convenient, expedient, fit[1], good, meet[2], suitable, tailor-made, useful. *See* AGREE, GOOD. **3.** Consistent with prevailing or accepted standards or circumstances : appropriate, deserved, due, fit[1], fitting, just, merited, right, rightful, suitable. *See* RIGHT. **4.** Conforming to accepted standards : becoming, befitting, comely, comme il faut, correct, decent, decorous, de rigueur, nice, respectable, right, seemly. *See* COURTESY. **5.** In accordance with principles of right or good conduct : ethical, moral, principled, right, righteous, rightful, right-minded, virtuous. *See* RIGHT. **6.** Marked by excessive concern for propriety and good form : bluenosed, genteel, old-maidish, precise, priggish, prim, prissy, prudish, puritanical, strait-laced, stuffy, Victorian. ***Idiom:*** prim and proper. *See* PLAIN.

properly *adverb*
In a fair, sporting manner : cleanly, correctly, fair, fairly. *See* FAIR.

properness *noun*
Conformity to recognized standards, as of conduct or appearance : comeliness, correctness, decency, decentness, decorousness, decorum, propriety, respectability, respectableness, seemliness. *See* USUAL.

property *noun*
1. One's portable property : belonging (often used in plural), effect (used in plural), good (used in plural), lares and penates, personal effects, personal property, possession (used in plural), thing (often used in plural). *Informal:* stuff. *Law:* chattel, movable (often used in plural). *See* OWNED. **2.** Something, as land and assets, legally possessed : estate, holding (often used in plural), possession (used in plural). *See* LAW, OWNED. **3.** Usually extensive real estate : acre (often used in plural), estate, land. *See* OWNED. **4.** A distinctive element : attribute, character, characteristic, feature, mark, peculiarity, quality, savor, trait. *See* BE.

prophecy *noun*
Something that is foretold by or as if by supernatural means : divination, oracle, soothsaying, vaticination, vision. *See* FORESIGHT.

prophesier *noun*
A person who foretells future events by or as if by supernatural means : augur, auspex, diviner, foreteller, haruspex, prophet, prophetess, seer, sibyl, soothsayer, vaticinator. *See* FORESIGHT.

prophesy *verb*
To tell about or make known (future events) by or as if by supernatural means : augur, divine, foretell, soothsay, vaticinate. *See* FORESIGHT.

prophet *noun*
A person who foretells future events by or as if by supernatural means : augur, auspex, diviner, foreteller, haruspex, prophesier, prophetess, seer, sibyl, soothsayer, vaticinator. *See* FORESIGHT.

prophetess *noun*
A person who foretells future events by or as if by supernatural means : augur, auspex, diviner, foreteller, haruspex, prophesier, prophet, seer, sibyl, soothsayer, vaticinator. *See* FORESIGHT.

prophetic also **prophetical** *adjective*
Of or relating to the foretelling of events by or as if by supernatural means : augural, divinitory, fatidic, fatidical, mantic, oracular, sibylline, vatic, vatical, vaticinal, visionary. *See* FORESIGHT.

prophylactic *adjective*
Defending against disease : preventative, preventive, protective. *See* ALLOW.

propitiate *verb*
To ease the anger or agitation of : appease, assuage, calm (down), conciliate, dulcify, gentle, mollify, pacify, placate, soften, soothe, sweeten. ***Idiom:*** pour oil on troubled water. *See* CALM.

propitious *adjective*
1. Affording benefit : advantageous, benefic, beneficent, beneficial, benignant, favorable, good, helpful, profitable, salutary, toward, useful. *See* HELP. **2.** Occurring at a fitting or advantageous time : auspicious, favorable, opportune, prosperous, seasonable, timely, well-timed. *See* LUCK. **3.** Indicative of future success or full of promise : auspicious, benign, bright, brilliant, fair, favorable, fortunate, good. *See* LUCK.

proportion *noun*
1. Relative intensity or amount, as of a quality or attribute : degree, extent, magnitude, measure. *See* BIG. **2.** Satisfying arrangement marked by even distribution of elements, as in a design : balance, harmony, symmetry. *See* BEAUTIFUL. **3.** The amount of space occupied

by something. Often used in plural : dimension, extent, magnitude, measure, size. *See* BIG.

proportion *verb* To bring into accord : accommodate, attune, conform, coordinate, harmonize, integrate, reconcile, tune. *See* AGREE.

proportional *adjective*
1. Properly or correspondingly related in size, amount, or scale : commensurable, commensurate, proportionate. ***Idiom:*** in proportion. *See* BIG. **2.** Characterized by or displaying symmetry, especially correspondence in scale or measure : balanced, proportionate, regular, symmetric, symmetrical. *See* SAME.

proportionate *adjective*
1. Properly or correspondingly related in size, amount, or scale : commensurable, commensurate, proportional. ***Idiom:*** in proportion. *See* BIG. **2.** Characterized by or displaying symmetry, especially correspondence in scale or measure : balanced, proportional, regular, symmetric, symmetrical. *See* SAME.

proposal *noun*
1. Something that is put forward for consideration : proposition, submission, suggestion. *See* OFFER. **2.** Something offered : bid, offer, proffer, tender[2]. *See* OFFER.

propose *verb*
1. To state, as an idea, for consideration : advance, offer, pose, propound, put forward, set forth, submit, suggest. *See* OFFER. **2.** To have in mind as a goal or purpose : aim, contemplate, design, intend, mean[1], plan, project, purpose, target. *Regional:* mind. *See* PLANNED, PURPOSE.

proposition *noun*
Something that is put forward for consideration : proposal, submission, suggestion. *See* OFFER.

propound *verb*
To state, as an idea, for consideration : advance, offer, pose, propose, put forward, set forth, submit, suggest. *See* OFFER.

proprietor *noun*
A person who has legal title to property : holder, master, owner, possessor. *See* OWNED.

proprietorship *noun*
The fact of possessing or the legal right to possess something : dominion, ownership, possession, title. *See* OWNED.

propriety *noun*
1. Conformity to recognized standards, as of conduct or appearance : comeliness, correctness, decency, decentness, decorousness, decorum, properness, respectability, respectableness, seemliness. *See* USUAL. **2.** The moral quality of a course of action : ethic (used in plural), ethicality, ethicalness, morality, righteousness, rightfulness, rightness. *See* RIGHT. **3.** Socially correct behavior. Also used in plural : decorum, etiquette, good form, manner (used in plural), mores, p's and q's. *See* USUAL. **4.** A courteous act or courteous acts that contribute to smoothness and ease in dealings and social relationships. Used in plural : amenity (used in plural), civility, courtesy, pleasantry, politeness. *See* COURTESY.

prosaic *adjective*
1. Having or indicating an awareness of things as they really are : down-to-earth, hard, hardheaded, matter-of-fact, objective, practical, pragmatic, pragmatical, realistic, sober, toughminded, unromantic. *See* EXCITE, REAL.
2. Lacking liveliness, charm, or surprise : arid, aseptic, colorless, drab, dry, dull, earthbound, flat, flavorless, lackluster, lifeless, lusterless, matter-of-fact, pedestrian, spiritless, sterile, stodgy, unimaginative, uninspired. *See* EXCITE.

proscenium *noun*
A raised platform on which theatrical performances are given : board (used in plural), stage. *See* PERFORMING ARTS.

proscribe *verb*
To refuse to allow : ban, debar, disallow, enjoin, forbid, inhibit, interdict, outlaw, prohibit, taboo. *See* ALLOW.

proscription *noun*
A refusal to allow : ban, disallowance, forbiddance, inhibition, interdiction, prohibition, taboo. *See* ALLOW.

prosecutable *adjective*
Subject to legal proceedings : *Law:* actionable, litigable, triable. *See* LAW.

prosecute *verb*
1. To institute or subject to legal proceedings : law, litigate, sue. ***Idiom:*** bring suit. *See* LAW.
2. To begin and carry through to completion : do, execute, perform. *Informal:* pull off. *See* DO.

prosecution *noun*
The act of beginning and carrying through to completion : discharge, effectuation, execution, performance. *See* DO.

prosopopeia also **prosopopoeia** *noun*
Rhetoric. A physical entity typifying an abstraction : embodiment, exteriorization, externalization, incarnation, manifestation, materialization, objectification, personalization, personification, substantiation, type. *See* SUBSTITUTE.

prosopopoeia *noun* See **prosopopeia.**

prospect *noun*
1. Something expected : anticipation, expectancy, expectation. *See* SURPRISE. **2.** The likeliness of a given event occurring. Used in plural : chance, likelihood, odds, possibility, probability. *See* LIKELY. **3.** Chance of success or advancement. Used in plural : future, outlook. *See* HOPE. **4.** That which is or can be seen : lookout, outlook, panorama, perspective, scene, sight, view, vista. *See* SEE.

prospective *adjective*
Based on probability or presumption : assumptive, likely, presumable, presumptive, probable. *Idiom:* taken for granted. *See* BELIEF, LIKELY.

prospectus *noun*
A document, such as a list or an outline, that gives, for example, the order of events in a public performance or the chief features of a stock offering : bill[1], program, syllabus. *See* PLANNED, WORDS.

prosper *verb*
To do or fare well : boom, flourish, go, thrive. *Slang:* score. ***Idioms:*** get (*or* go) somewhere, go great guns, go strong. *See* THRIVE.

prospering *adjective*
Improving, growing, or succeeding steadily : booming, boomy, flourishing, prosperous, roaring, thrifty, thriving. *See* THRIVE.

prosperity *noun*
1. A state of health, happiness, and prospering : weal[1], welfare, well-being. *See* BETTER.
2. Steady good fortune or financial security : comfort, ease, prosperousness. *Informal:* easy street. ***Idioms:*** comfortable (*or* easy) circumstances, the good life. *See* RICH, THRIVE.

prosperous *adjective*
1. Improving, growing, or succeeding steadily : booming, boomy, flourishing, prospering, roaring, thrifty, thriving. *See* THRIVE. **2.** Enjoying steady good fortune or financial security : comfortable, easy, well-heeled, well-off, well-to-do. *Informal:* well-fixed. ***Idioms:*** comfortably off, in clover, on easy street. *See* RICH, THRIVE. **3.** Occurring at a fitting or advantageous time : auspicious, favorable, opportune, propitious, seasonable, timely, well-timed. *See* LUCK.

prosperousness *noun*
Steady good fortune or financial security : comfort, ease, prosperity. *Informal:* easy street. ***Idioms:*** comfortable (*or* easy) circumstances, the good life. *See* RICH, THRIVE.

prostitute *noun*
A woman who engages in sexual intercourse for payment : bawd, call girl, camp follower, courtesan, harlot, scarlet woman, streetwalker, strumpet, tart[2], whore. *Slang:* hooker, moll. ***Idioms:*** lady of easy virtue, lady of pleasure, lady of the night. *See* SEX.

prostrate *verb*
1. To cause to fall, as from a shot or blow : bring down, cut down, down, drop, fell[1], flatten, floor, ground, knock down, level, strike down, throw. *Slang:* deck[1]. ***Idiom:*** lay low. *See* RISE. **2.** To affect deeply or completely, as with emotion : crush, engulf, overcome, overpower, overwhelm. *See* AFFECT.

prostrate *adjective* Lying down : decumbent, flat, horizontal, procumbent, prone, recumbent. *See* HORIZONTAL.

protagonist *noun*
The main performer in a theatrical production : lead, principal, star. *See* PERFORMING ARTS.

protean *adjective*
Having many aspects, uses, or abilities : all-around, all-round, many-sided, multifaceted, various, versatile. *See* ABILITY, SAME.

protect *verb*
To keep safe from danger, attack, or harm : defend, guard, preserve, safeguard, secure, shield, ward. *Archaic:* fend. *See* ATTACK.

protection *noun*
1. The act or a means of defending : defense, guard, preservation, protector, safeguard, security, shield, ward. *See* ATTACK. **2.** Something that physically protects, especially from danger : asylum, cover, covert, harbor, haven, refuge, retreat, sanctuary, shelter. *See* ATTACK, SAFETY.

protective *adjective*
1. Able to preserve : conservative, preservative. *See* HELP. **2.** Defending against disease : preventative, preventive, prophylactic. *See* ALLOW.

protector *noun*
1. A person or special body of persons assigned to provide protection or keep watch over, for example : guard, lookout, picket, sentinel, sentry, ward, watch. *See* AWARENESS, SAFETY.
2. The act or a means of defending : defense, guard, preservation, protection, safeguard, security, shield, ward. *See* ATTACK.

pro tem *adjective*
Temporarily assuming the duties of another : acting, ad interim, interim, provisional, temporary. *See* CONTINUE, SUBSTITUTE.

protest *verb*
To express opposition, often by argument : challenge, demur, except, expostulate, inveigh,

object, remonstrate. *Informal:* kick, squawk. *Idioms:* set up a squawk, take exception. *See* SUPPORT.

protest *noun* The act of expressing strong or reasoned opposition : challenge, demur, exception, expostulation, objection, protestation, remonstrance, remonstration, squawk. *Slang:* kick. *See* SUPPORT.

protestation *noun*
The act of expressing strong or reasoned opposition : challenge, demur, exception, expostulation, objection, protest, remonstrance, remonstration, squawk. *Slang:* kick. *See* SUPPORT.

protocol *noun*
Strict observance of social conventions : ceremoniousness, ceremony, formality, punctiliousness. *See* COURTESY.

protoplast *noun*
A first form from which varieties arise or imitations are made : archetype, father, master, original, prototype. *See* START.

prototypal *adjective*
Having the nature of, constituting, or serving as a type : archetypal, archetypic, archetypical, classic, classical, model, paradigmatic, prototypic, prototypical, quintessential, representative, typic, typical. *See* SAME, USUAL.

prototype *noun*
A first form from which varieties arise or imitations are made : archetype, father, master, original, protoplast. *See* START.

prototypic *adjective*
Having the nature of, constituting, or serving as a type : archetypal, archetypic, archetypical, classic, classical, model, paradigmatic, prototypal, prototypical, quintessential, representative, typic, typical. *See* SAME, USUAL.

prototypical *adjective*
Having the nature of, constituting, or serving as a type : archetypal, archetypic, archetypical, classic, classical, model, paradigmatic, prototypal, prototypic, quintessential, representative, typic, typical. *See* SAME, USUAL.

protract *verb*
To make or become longer : draw out, elongate, extend, lengthen, prolong, prolongate, spin (out), stretch (out). *Mathematics:* produce. *See* INCREASE, LONG.

protracted *adjective*
1. Of long duration : chronic, continuing, lingering, persistent, prolonged. *See* CONTINUE. **2.** Extending tediously beyond a standard duration : dragging, drawn-out, lengthy, long[1], long-drawn-out, overlong, prolonged. *See* EXCITE, LONG.

protractile *adjective*
Capable of being extended or expanded : expansible, expansile, extendible, extensible, extensile, stretch, stretchable. *See* INCREASE.

protraction *noun*
The act of making something longer or the condition of being made longer : elongation, extension, prolongation. *See* LONG.

protrude *verb*
To curve outward past the normal or usual limit : bag, balloon, beetle, belly, bulge, jut, overhang, pouch, project, protuberate, stand out, stick out. *See* CONVEX.

protrusion *noun*
A part that protrudes or extends outward : bulge, jut, knob, knot, overhang, projection, protuberance. *See* CONVEX.

protuberance *noun*
1. A part that protrudes or extends outward : bulge, jut, knob, knot, overhang, projection, protrusion. *See* CONVEX. **2.** An unevenness or elevation on a surface : bump, hump, knob, knot, lump[1], nub. *See* CONVEX.

protuberate *verb*
To curve outward past the normal or usual limit : bag, balloon, beetle, belly, bulge, jut, overhang, pouch, project, protrude, stand out, stick out. *See* CONVEX.

proud *adjective*
1. Properly valuing oneself, one's honor, or one's dignity : prideful, self-respecting. *See* RESPECT. **2.** Overly convinced of one's own superiority and importance : arrogant, haughty, high-and-mighty, insolent, lofty, lordly, overbearing, overweening, prideful, supercilious, superior. ***Idiom:*** on one's high horse. *See* ATTITUDE. **3.** Marked by extraordinary elegance, beauty, and splendor : brilliant, glorious, gorgeous, magnificent, resplendent, splendid, splendorous. *See* BEAUTIFUL.

proudness *noun*
The quality of being arrogant : arrogance, haughtiness, hauteur, insolence, loftiness, lordliness, overbearingness, presumption, pride, pridefulness, superciliousness, superiority. *See* ATTITUDE.

prove *verb*
1. To establish as true or genuine : authenticate, bear out, confirm, corroborate, demonstrate, endorse, establish, evidence, show, substantiate, validate, verify. *See* SHOW, SUPPORT. **2.** To subject to a procedure that ascertains effectiveness, value, proper function, or other quality : assay, check, essay, examine, test, try, try out. ***Idioms:*** bring to the test, make

trial of, put to the proof (*or* test). *See* INVESTIGATE. **3.** *Archaic.* To participate in or partake of personally : experience, feel, go through, have, know, meet[1] (with), see, suffer, taste (of), undergo. ***Idiom:*** run up against. *See* PARTICIPATE.

prove out *verb* To prove valid under scrutiny : hold (up), stand up. *Informal:* wash. ***Idioms:*** hold water, pass muster, ring true. *See* TRUE.

provenance *noun*
A point of origination : beginning, derivation, fount, fountain, fountainhead, mother, origin, parent, provenience, root[1], rootstock, source, spring, well[1]. *See* START.

provender *noun*
Something fit to be eaten : aliment, bread, comestible, diet, edible, esculent, fare, food, foodstuff, meat, nourishment, nurture, nutriment, nutrition, pabulum, pap, provision (used in plural), sustenance, victual. *Slang:* chow, eats, grub. *See* INGESTION.

provenience *noun*
A point of origination : beginning, derivation, fount, fountain, fountainhead, mother, origin, parent, provenance, root[1], rootstock, source, spring, well[1]. *See* START.

prove out *verb* See **prove.**

proverb *noun*
A usually pithy and familiar statement of an observation or principle generally accepted as wise or true : adage, aphorism, byword, maxim, motto, saw, saying. *See* WORDS.

provide *verb* **1.** To make (something) readily available :
afford, extend, offer. ***Idiom:*** place (*or* put) at one's disposal. *See* OFFER. **2.** To relinquish to the possession or control of another : deliver, furnish, give, hand, hand over, supply, transfer, turn over. *See* GIVE.

provide for *verb* To supply with the necessities of life : keep, maintain, support. ***Idiom:*** take care of. *See* CARE FOR.

provide for *verb* See **provide.**

providence *noun*
Careful use of material resources : economy, frugality, prudence, thrift, thriftiness. *See* SAVE.

provident *adjective*
Careful in the use of material resources : canny, chary, economical, frugal, prudent, saving, Scotch, sparing, thrifty. *See* CAREFUL, SAVE.

providential *adjective*
Characterized by luck or good fortune : fortunate, happy, lucky. *See* LUCK.

province *noun*
1. An area subject to rule by an outside power : colony, dependency, possession, territory. *See* POLITICS. **2.** A sphere of activity, experience, study, or interest : area, arena, bailiwick, circle, department, domain, field, orbit, realm, scene, subject, terrain, territory, world. *Slang:* bag. *See* TERRITORY.

provincial *adjective*
1. Of or relating to the countryside : arcadian, bucolic, campestral, country, pastoral, rural, rustic. *Informal:* hick. *See* URBAN. **2.** Having the restricted outlook often characteristic of geographic isolation : insular, limited, local, narrow, narrow-minded, parochial, small-town. *See* LIMITED.

provision *noun*
1. A plan made in preparation for an undertaking. Often used in plural : arrangement (often used in plural), preparation (often used in plural). *See* PLANNED. **2.** Something fit to be eaten. Used in plural : aliment, bread, comestible, diet, edible, esculent, fare, food, foodstuff, meat, nourishment, nurture, nutriment, nutrition, pabulum, pap, provender, sustenance, victual. *Slang:* chow, eats, grub. *See* INGESTION. **3.** A restricting or modifying element : condition, proviso, qualification, reservation, specification, stipulation, term (often used in plural). *Informal:* string (often used in plural). *See* LIMITED.

provisional *adjective*
1. Intended, used, or present for a limited time : impermanent, interim, short-range, short-term, temporary. *See* CONTINUE. **2.** Temporarily assuming the duties of another : acting, ad interim, interim, pro tem, temporary. *See* CONTINUE, SUBSTITUTE. **3.** Depending on or containing a condition or conditions : conditional, provisory, tentative. *See* LIMITED.

proviso *noun*
A restricting or modifying element : condition, provision, qualification, reservation, specification, stipulation, term (often used in plural). *Informal:* string (often used in plural). *See* LIMITED.

provisory *adjective*
Depending on or containing a condition or conditions : conditional, provisional, tentative. *See* LIMITED.

provocation *noun*
1. The act of annoying : annoyance, botheration, bothering, exasperation, harassment, irritation, pestering, vexation. *See* FEELINGS, PAIN. **2.** Behavior or an act that is intentionally

provocative : challenge, defiance. *See* ATTACK. **3.** Something that incites especially a violent response : goad, incitation, incitement, instigation, stimulus, trigger. *See* CAUSE.

provocative *adjective*
Bordering on indelicacy or impropriety : blue, earthy, off-color, racy, risqué, salty, scabrous, spicy, suggestive. *See* DECENT.

provoke *verb*
1. To cause to feel or show anger : anger, burn (up), enrage, incense[1], infuriate, madden. ***Idioms:*** make one hot under the collar, make one's blood boil, put one's back up. *See* FEELINGS. **2.** To trouble the nerves or peace of mind of, especially by repeated vexations : aggravate, annoy, bother, bug, chafe, disturb, exasperate, fret, gall[2], get, irk, irritate, nettle, peeve, put out, rile, ruffle, vex. ***Idioms:*** get in one's hair, get on one's nerves, get under one's skin. *See* FEELINGS, PAIN. **3.** To stir to action or feeling : egg on, excite, foment, galvanize, goad, impel, incite, inflame, inspire, instigate, motivate, move, pique, prick, prod, prompt, propel, set off, spur, stimulate, touch off, trigger, work up. *See* CAUSE, EXCITE. **4.** To behave so as to bring on (danger, for example) : court, invite, tempt. *See* SEEK.

provoking *adjective*
Troubling the nerves or peace of mind, as by repeated vexations : annoying, bothersome, galling, irksome, irritating, nettlesome, plaguy, troublesome, vexatious. *See* PAIN.

prowess *noun*
1. Skillfulness in the use of the hands or body : adroitness, deftness, dexterity, dexterousness, skill, sleight. *See* ABILITY. **2.** The quality or state of being heroic : gallantry, heroism, valiance, valiancy, valor. *See* FEAR.

prowl *verb*
To move silently and furtively : creep, glide, lurk, mouse, pussyfoot, skulk, slide, slink, slip, snake, sneak, steal. *Slang:* gumshoe. *See* MOVE.

prowler *noun*
One who behaves in a stealthy, furtive way : sneak, sneaker, weasel. *See* MOVE.

proximate *adjective*
1. Not far from another in space, time, or relation : adjacent, close, contiguous, immediate, near, nearby, nigh. ***Idioms:*** at hand, under one's nose, within a stone's throw, within hailing distance. *See* NEAR. **2.** About to occur at any moment : imminent, impending, momentary. *See* NEAR.

prude *noun*
A person who is too much concerned with being proper, modest, or righteous : bluenose, Mrs. Grundy, puritan, Victorian. *Informal:* old maid. *See* SEX.

prudence *noun*
1. The exercise of good judgment or common sense in practical matters : caution, circumspection, discretion, forehandedness, foresight, foresightedness, forethought, forethoughtfulness, precaution. *See* CAREFUL. **2.** Careful use of material resources : economy, frugality, providence, thrift, thriftiness. *See* SAVE.

prudent *adjective*
1. Possessing, proceeding from, or exhibiting good judgment and prudence : balanced, commonsensible, commonsensical, judicious, levelheaded, rational, reasonable, sagacious, sage, sane, sapient, sensible, sound[2], well-founded, well-grounded, wise[1]. *See* REASON, SANE. **2.** Careful in the use of material resources : canny, chary, economical, frugal, provident, saving, Scotch, sparing, thrifty. *See* CAREFUL, SAVE. **3.** Trying attentively to avoid danger, risk, or error : careful, cautious, chary, circumspect, forehanded, gingerly, wary. *See* CAREFUL.

prudish *adjective*
Marked by excessive concern for propriety and good form : bluenosed, genteel, old-maidish, precise, priggish, prim, prissy, proper, puritanical, strait-laced, stuffy, Victorian. ***Idiom:*** prim and proper. *See* PLAIN.

prune *verb*
To decrease, as in length or amount, by or as if by severing or excising : chop[1], clip[1], crop, cut, cut back, cut down, lop[1], lower[2], pare, shear, slash, trim, truncate. *See* INCREASE.

prurience *noun*
Sexual hunger : amativeness, concupiscence, desire, eroticism, erotism, itch, libidinousness, lust, lustfulness, passion, pruriency. *See* DESIRE, SEX.

pruriency *noun*
Sexual hunger : amativeness, concupiscence, desire, eroticism, erotism, itch, libidinousness, lust, lustfulness, passion, prurience. *See* DESIRE, SEX.

prurient *adjective*
Feeling or devoted to sexual love or desire : amative, amorous, concupiscent, erotic, lascivious, lecherous, lewd, libidinous, lustful, lusty, passionate, sexy. *See* SEX.

pry *verb*
To look into or inquire about curiously, inquisitively, or in a meddlesome fashion : poke, snoop. *Informal:* nose (around). ***Idiom:*** stick

one's nose into. *See* INVESTIGATE, PARTICIPATE.

pry *noun* A person who snoops : prier, snoop, snooper. *See* INVESTIGATE, PARTICIPATE.

pryer *noun* See **prier.**

p's and q's *noun*
Socially correct behavior : decorum, etiquette, good form, manner (used in plural), mores, propriety (also used in plural). *See* USUAL.

pseudonymous *adjective*
Being fictitious and not real, as a name : assumed, made-up. *See* TRUE.

psyche *noun*
1. The vital principle or animating force within living beings : breath, divine spark, élan vital, life force, soul, spirit, vital force, vitality. *See* BODY. **2.** The thought processes characteristic of an individual or group : ethos, mentality, mind, mindset, psychology. ***Idiom:*** what makes someone tick. *See* THOUGHTS.

psyched *adjective*
Informal. Feeling a very strong emotion : atingle, excited, fired up, thrilled, worked up. *Slang:* stoked, turned-on. *See* EXCITE.

psychic *adjective*
Relating to or performed by the mind : cerebral, intellective, intellectual, mental, psychical, psychological. *See* THOUGHTS.

psychical *adjective*
Relating to or performed by the mind : cerebral, intellective, intellectual, mental, psychic, psychological. *See* THOUGHTS.

psychological *adjective*
Relating to or performed by the mind : cerebral, intellective, intellectual, mental, psychic, psychical. *See* THOUGHTS.

psychology *noun*
The thought processes characteristic of an individual or group : ethos, mentality, mind, mindset, psyche. ***Idiom:*** what makes someone tick. *See* THOUGHTS.

psychopathy *noun*
Serious mental illness or disorder impairing a person's capacity to function normally and safely : brainsickness, craziness, dementia, derangement, disturbance, insaneness, insanity, lunacy, madness, mental illness, unbalance. *Psychiatry:* mania. *Psychology:* aberration, alienation. *See* SANE.

puberty *noun*
The time of life between childhood and maturity : adolescence, greenness, juvenescence, juvenility, salad days, spring, youth, youthfulness. *See* YOUTH.

public *adjective*
1. Of, concerning, or affecting the community or the people : civic, civil, national. *See* SPECIFIC. **2.** Belonging to, shared by, or applicable to all alike : common, communal, conjoint, general, joint, mutual. *See* GROUP. **3.** Of, representing, or carried on by people at large : democratic, general, popular. *See* POLITICS, SPECIFIC. **4.** Not restricted or confined to few : open, open-door, unrestricted. *See* OPEN.

public *noun* **1.** The common people : common (used in plural), commonality, commonalty, commoner (used in plural), crowd, hoi polloi, mass (used in plural), mob, pleb (used in plural), plebeian (used in plural), populace, ruck[1], third estate. *See* OVER. **2.** Persons as an organized body : community, people, society. *See* SPECIFIC. **3.** The body of persons who admire a public personality, especially an entertainer : audience, following. *See* LIKE.

public assistance *noun*
Assistance, especially money, food, and other necessities, given to the needy or dispossessed : aid, dole, handout, relief, welfare. *See* HELP.

publication *noun*
1. The act or process of publishing printed matter : issue, printing, publishing. *See* WORDS. **2.** An issue of printed material offered for sale or distribution : opus, title, volume, work. *See* WORDS. **3.** The act of announcing : announcement, annunciation, declaration, proclamation, promulgation. *See* KNOWLEDGE.

publicity *noun*
1. A systematic effort or part of this effort to increase the importance or reputation of by favorable publicity : advertisement, ballyhoo, buildup, promotion, puffery. *Informal:* pitch, plug. *Slang:* hype. *See* KNOWLEDGE. **2.** The act or profession of promoting something, as a product : advertising, promotion. *See* KNOWLEDGE.

publicize *verb*
1. To increase or seek to increase the importance or reputation of by favorable publicity : ballyhoo, boost, build up, enhance, promote, puff, talk up, tout. *Informal:* plug. *Slang:* hype. *See* KNOWLEDGE. **2.** To make known vigorously the positive features of (a product) : advertise, ballyhoo, build up, cry (up), popularize, promote, talk up. *Informal:* pitch, plug. *Slang:* push. *See* KNOWLEDGE.

publish *verb*
1. To present for circulation, exhibit, or sale : bring out, issue, put out. *See* WORDS. **2.** To be the author of (a published work or works) :

pen[1], write. *See* WORDS. **3.** To bring to public notice or make known publicly : advertise, announce, annunciate, broadcast, declare, proclaim, promulgate. *See* KNOWLEDGE, WORDS.

publishing *noun*
The act or process of publishing printed matter : issue, printing, publication. *See* WORDS.

pucker *noun*
A line or an arrangement made by the doubling of one part over another : crease, crimp, crinkle, crumple, fold, pleat, plica, plication, rimple, ruck[2], rumple, wrinkle. *See* SMOOTH.

pudgy *adjective*
Well-rounded and full in form : chubby, plump[1], plumpish, roly-poly, rotund, round, tubby, zaftig. *See* FAT.

puerile *adjective*
Of or characteristic of a child, especially in immaturity : babyish, childish, immature, infantile, juvenile. *See* YOUTH.

puff *noun*
An inhalation, as of a cigar, pipe, or cigarette : drag, draw, pull. *Slang:* hit. *See* BREATH.
puff *verb* **1.** To be in a state of motion, as air : blow[1], winnow. *See* BREATH. **2.** To breathe hard : blow[1], gasp, huff, pant. *See* BREATH. **3.** To increase or seek to increase the importance or reputation of by favorable publicity : ballyhoo, boost, build up, enhance, promote, publicize, talk up, tout. *Informal:* plug. *Slang:* hype. *See* KNOWLEDGE.

puffed-up *adjective*
Characterized by an exaggerated show of dignity or self-importance : grandiose, hoity-toity, pompous, pretentious, puffy, self-important. *Informal:* highfalutin. *See* PLAIN.

puffery *noun*
A systematic effort or part of this effort to increase the importance or reputation of by favorable publicity : advertisement, ballyhoo, buildup, promotion, publicity. *Informal:* pitch, plug. *Slang:* hype. *See* KNOWLEDGE.

puffy *adjective*
Characterized by an exaggerated show of dignity or self-importance : grandiose, hoity-toity, pompous, pretentious, puffed-up, self-important. *Informal:* highfalutin. *See* PLAIN.

pugnacious *adjective*
Having or showing an eagerness to fight : bellicose, belligerent, combative, contentious, hostile, militant, quarrelsome, scrappy, truculent, warlike. *See* ATTACK.

pugnaciousness *noun*
1. Warlike or hostile attitude or nature : bellicoseness, bellicosity, belligerence, belligerency, combativeness, contentiousness, hostility, militance, militancy, pugnacity, truculence, truculency. *See* ATTACK. **2.** The power or will to fight : bellicoseness, bellicosity, belligerence, belligerency, combativeness, contentiousness, fight, pugnacity, truculence, truculency. *See* CONFLICT.

pugnacity *noun*
1. Warlike or hostile attitude or nature : bellicoseness, bellicosity, belligerence, belligerency, combativeness, contentiousness, hostility, militance, militancy, pugnaciousness, truculence, truculency. *See* ATTACK. **2.** The power or will to fight : bellicoseness, bellicosity, belligerence, belligerency, combativeness, contentiousness, fight, pugnaciousness, truculence, truculency. *See* CONFLICT.

puissance *noun*
1. Capacity or power for work or vigorous activity : animation, energy, force, might, potency, power, sprightliness, steam, strength. *Informal:* get-up-and-go, go, pep, peppiness, zip. *See* ACTION. **2.** The state or quality of being physically strong : brawn, might, muscle, potence, potency, power, powerfulness, sinew, strength, thew (often used in plural). *See* STRONG.

puissant *adjective*
1. Having or able to exert great power : mighty, potent, powerful. *See* STRONG. **2.** Having great physical strength : mighty, potent, powerful, strong. *See* STRONG.

puke *verb*
Slang. To eject the contents of the stomach through the mouth : heave, throw up, vomit. *See* MOUTH.

pulchritudinous *adjective*
Having qualities that delight the eye : attractive, beauteous, beautiful, comely, fair, good-looking, gorgeous, handsome, lovely, pretty, ravishing, sightly, stunning. *Scots:* bonny. ***Idiom:*** easy on the eyes. *See* BEAUTIFUL.

pule *verb*
To cry with soft, intermittent, often plaintive sounds : whimper, whine. *See* SOUNDS.

pull *verb*
1. To exert force so as to move (something) toward the source of the force : drag, draw, haul, tow, tug. *See* PUSH. **2.** To remove from a fixed position : extract, pluck, tear[1]. *See* PUT IN. **3.** *Informal.* To direct or impel to oneself by some quality or action : allure, appeal, attract, draw, entice, lure, magnetize, take. *See* LIKE.

pull back *verb* To move back in the face of enemy attack or after a defeat : draw back, fall back, pull out, retire, retreat, withdraw. *Idioms:* beat a retreat, give ground (*or* way). *See* FORWARD.

pull down *verb* **1.** To pull down or break up so that reconstruction is impossible : demolish, destroy, dismantle, dynamite, knock down, level, pulverize, raze, tear down, wreck. *Aerospace:* destruct. *See* HELP. **2.** *Informal.* To receive, as wages, for one's labor : earn, gain, get, make, win. *Idioms:* earn (*or* make) a living, earn one's keep. *See* GIVE, MONEY.

pull in *verb* **1.** To come to a particular place : arrive, check in, get in, reach, show up, turn up. *Slang:* blow in. *Idiom:* make (*or* put in) an appearance. *See* START. **2.** To control, restrict, or arrest : bit[2], brake, bridle, check, constrain, curb, hold, hold back, hold down, hold in, inhibit, keep, keep back, rein (back, in, *or* up), restrain. *See* RESTRAINT.

pull off *verb* **1.** *Informal.* To begin and carry through to completion : do, execute, perform, prosecute. *See* DO. **2.** *Informal.* To be responsible for or guilty of (an error or crime) : commit, perpetrate. *See* DO, LAW.

pull on *verb* **1.** To put (an article of clothing) on one's person : assume, don, get on, put on, slip into, slip on. *See* PUT ON. **2.** To take into the mouth and swallow (a liquid) : drink, imbibe, quaff, sip, sup. *Informal:* swig, toss down (*or* off). *Slang:* belt. *Idiom:* wet one's whistle. *See* MOUTH.

pull out *verb* **1.** To move or proceed away from a place : depart, exit, get away, get off, go, go away, leave[1], quit, retire, run (along), withdraw. *Informal:* cut out, push off, shove off. *Slang:* blow[1], split, take off. *Idioms:* hit the road, take leave. *See* APPROACH. **2.** To move back in the face of enemy attack or after a defeat : draw back, fall back, pull back, retire, retreat, withdraw. *Idioms:* beat a retreat, give ground (*or* way). *See* FORWARD.

pull through *verb* To exist in spite of adversity : come through, last[2], persist, ride out, survive, weather. *See* LIVE.

pull *noun* **1.** The act of drawing or pulling a load : draft, drag, draw, haul, traction. *See* PUSH. **2.** An inhalation, as of a cigar, pipe, or cigarette : drag, draw, puff. *Slang:* hit. *See* BREATH. **3.** An act of drinking or the amount swallowed : draft, drink, potation, quaff, sip, sup, swill. *Informal:* swig. *Slang:* belt. *See* MOUTH. **4.** *Slang.* The power to produce an effect by indirect means : influence, leverage, sway, weight. *Informal:* clout. *See* AFFECT. **5.** *Informal.* The power or quality of attracting : allure, allurement, appeal, attraction, attractiveness, call, charisma, charm, draw, enchantment, enticement, fascination, glamour, lure, magnetism, witchery. *See* LIKE.

pullback *noun*
The moving back of a military force in the face of enemy attack or after a defeat : fallback, pullout, retirement, retreat, withdrawal. *See* FORWARD.

pull back *verb* See **pull.**

pull down *verb* See **pull.**

pull in *verb* See **pull.**

pull off *verb* See **pull.**

pull on *verb* See **pull.**

pullout *noun*
The moving back of a military force in the face of enemy attack or after a defeat : fallback, pullback, retirement, retreat, withdrawal. *See* FORWARD.

pull out *verb* See **pull.**

pull through *verb* See **pull.**

pullulate *verb*
To be abundantly filled or richly supplied : abound, bristle, crawl, flow, overflow, swarm, teem. *See* BIG, RICH.

pulp *verb*
To press forcefully so as to break up into a pulpy mass : crush, mash, mush, squash. *See* HELP.

pulpous *adjective*
Yielding easily to pressure or weight; not firm : mushy, pappy[1], pulpy, quaggy, soft, spongy, squashy, squishy, yielding. *See* RESIST.

pulpy *adjective*
Yielding easily to pressure or weight; not firm : mushy, pappy[1], pulpous, quaggy, soft, spongy, squashy, squishy, yielding. *See* RESIST.

pulsate *verb*
To make rhythmic contractions, sounds, or movements : beat, palpitate, pound, pulse, throb. *See* REPETITION, SOUNDS.

pulsation *noun*
A periodic contraction or sound of something coursing : beat, palpitation, pulse, throb. *See* REPETITION, SOUNDS.

pulse *noun*
A periodic contraction or sound of something coursing : beat, palpitation, pulsation, throb. *See* REPETITION, SOUNDS.

pulse *verb* To make rhythmic contractions, sounds, or movements : beat, palpitate, pound, pulsate, throb. *See* REPETITION, SOUNDS.

pulverize *verb*
1. To break up into tiny particles : bray, crush, granulate, grind, mill, powder, triturate. *See* HELP. **2.** To pull down or break up so that reconstruction is impossible : demolish, destroy, dismantle, dynamite, knock down, level, pull down, raze, tear down, wreck. *Aerospace:* destruct. *See* HELP.

pulverous *adjective*
Consisting of small particles : dusty, fine[1], powdery, pulverulent. *See* BIG.

pulverulent *adjective*
Consisting of small particles : dusty, fine[1], powdery, pulverous. *See* BIG.

pummel *verb*
To hit heavily and repeatedly with violent blows : assail, assault, baste, batter, beat, belabor, buffet, drub, hammer, pound, smash, thrash, thresh. *Informal:* lambaste. *Slang:* clobber. ***Idiom:*** rain blows on. *See* ATTACK, STRIKE.

pump *verb*
To remove (a liquid) by a steady, gradual process : drain, draw (off), let out, tap[2]. *See* INCREASE.

punch *verb*
To hit with a quick, sharp blow of the hand : box[2], buffet, bust, cuff, slap, smack[1], spank, swat, whack. *Informal:* clip[1], spat. *See* ATTACK, STRIKE.

punch *noun* **1.** A quick, sharp blow, especially with the hand : box[2], buffet, bust, chop[1], cuff, slap, smack[1], smacker, spank, swat, whack. *Informal:* clip[1], spat. *See* ATTACK, STRIKE. **2.** A quality of active mental and physical forcefulness : dash, starch, verve, vigor, vigorousness, vim, vitality. *Informal:* snap. ***Idiom:*** vim and vigor. *See* ACTION, TIRED. **3.** An aggressive readiness along with energy to undertake taxing efforts : drive, enterprise, hustle, initiative. *Informal:* get-up-and-go, gumption, push. *See* ACTION, TIRED, TRY. **4.** *Informal.* A stimulating or intoxicating effect : *Informal:* sting, wallop. *Slang:* kick. *See* DRUGS. **5.** *Informal.* The capacity to create a powerful effect : impact. *Informal:* wallop. *See* AFFECT.

punctilious *adjective*
1. Showing or marked by attentiveness to all aspects or details : careful, fastidious, meticulous, painstaking, scrupulous. *See* CAREFUL. **2.** Fond of or given to ceremony : ceremonious, conventional, courtly, formal. *See* COURTESY.

punctiliousness *noun*
1. Attentiveness to detail : care, carefulness, fastidiousness, meticulousness, pain (used in plural), painstaking, scrupulousness, thoroughness. *See* CAREFUL. **2.** Strict observance of social conventions : ceremoniousness, ceremony, formality, protocol. *See* COURTESY.

punctual *adjective*
Occurring, acting, or performed exactly at the time appointed : prompt, timely. ***Idioms:*** at (*or* on) the dot, on time. *See* TIME.

punctuate *verb*
To mark with punctuation : point. *See* MARKS.

puncture *verb*
1. To make a hole or other opening in : breach, break (through), gap, hole, perforate, pierce. *See* OPEN. **2.** To pass into or through by overcoming resistance : break (through), enter, penetrate, perforate, pierce. *See* ENTER. **3.** To cause to be no longer believed or valued : debunk, deflate, discredit, explode. *Informal:* shoot down. ***Idioms:*** knock the bottom out of, shoot full of holes. *See* VALUE.

puncture *noun* A small mark or hole made by a sharp, pointed object : perforation, prick, stab. *See* MARKS, OPEN.

pundit *noun*
A usually elderly person noted for wisdom, knowledge, and judgment : sage, savant, scholar. *See* WISE.

pungent *adjective*
1. Affecting the organs of taste or smell with a strong and often harsh sensation : piquant, sharp, spicy, zesty. *Archaic:* poignant. *See* SMELLS, TASTE. **2.** So sharp as to cause mental pain : acerbic, acid, acidic, acrid, astringent, biting, caustic, corrosive, cutting, mordacious, mordant, scathing, sharp, slashing, stinging, trenchant, truculent, vitriolic. *See* ATTACK, RESPECT.

puniness *noun*
The condition of being infirm or physically weak : debility, decrepitude, delicacy, delicateness, feebleness, flimsiness, fragileness, fragility, frailness, frailty, infirmity, insubstantiality, unsoundness, unsubstantiality, weakliness, weakness. *See* STRONG.

punish *verb*
To subject (one) to a penalty for a wrong : castigate, chastise, correct, discipline, penalize. *See* REWARD.

punishing *adjective*
Inflicting or aiming to inflict punishment : disciplinary, punitive, punitory. *See* REWARD.

punishment *noun*
Something, such as loss, pain, or confinement, imposed for wrongdoing : castigation,

chastisement, correction, discipline, penalty. *See* REWARD.

punitive *adjective*
Inflicting or aiming to inflict punishment : disciplinary, punishing, punitory. *See* REWARD.

punitory *adjective*
Inflicting or aiming to inflict punishment : disciplinary, punishing, punitive. *See* REWARD.

punk *noun*
Slang. A rough, violent person who engages in destructive actions : hoodlum, mug, roughneck, rowdy, ruffian, tough. *Informal:* toughie. *Slang:* hood. *See* ATTACK, CRIMES.

puny *adjective*
1. Not physically strong : decrepit, delicate, feeble, flimsy, fragile, frail, infirm, insubstantial, unsound, unsubstantial, weak, weakly. *See* STRONG. **2.** Conspicuously deficient in quantity, fullness, or extent : exiguous, meager, poor, scant, scanty, skimpy, spare, sparse, stingy, thin. *Slang:* measly. *See* BIG, EXCESS.

pup *noun*
An insignificant but arrogant and obnoxious young person : puppy. *Informal:* squirt. *Slang:* twerp. *See* YOUTH.

pupil *noun*
One who is being educated : learner, scholar, student. *See* TEACH.

puppet *noun*
A person used or controlled by others : cat's-paw, dupe, instrument, pawn[2], stooge, tool. *See* OVER.

puppy *noun*
An insignificant but arrogant and obnoxious young person : pup. *Informal:* squirt. *Slang:* twerp. *See* YOUTH.

purblind *adjective*
Unwilling or unable to perceive : blind, dull, uncomprehending, unperceptive. *See* SEE.

purchasable *adjective*
Capable of being bribed : buyable, corruptible, venal. *See* CRIMES, PERSUASION.

purchase *verb*
To acquire in exchange for money or something of equal value : buy. *See* GET, MONEY.
purchase *noun* Something bought or capable of being bought : buy. *See* GET, MONEY.

purchaser *noun*
One who buys goods or services : buyer, client, customer, patron. *See* TRANSACTIONS.

pure *adjective*
1. Not diluted or mixed with other substances : full-strength, neat, plain, straight, unblended, undiluted, unmixed. *See* CLEAN, STRONG. **2.** Free from extraneous elements : absolute, perfect, plain, sheer[2], simple, unadulterated, undiluted, unmixed. *See* CLEAN. **3.** Completely such, without qualification or exception : absolute, all-out, arrant, complete, consummate, crashing, damned, dead, downright, flat, out-and-out, outright, perfect, plain, sheer[2], thorough, thoroughgoing, total, unbounded, unequivocal, unlimited, unmitigated, unqualified, unrelieved, unreserved, utter[2]. *Informal:* flat-out, positive. *Chiefly British:* blooming. *See* BIG, LIMITED. **4.** Free from evil and corruption : angelic, angelical, clean, innocent, lily-white, sinless, unblemished, uncorrupted, undefiled, unstained, unsullied, untainted, virginal. ***Idiom:*** pure as the driven snow. *See* CLEAN, RIGHT, SEX. **5.** Morally beyond reproach, especially in sexual conduct : chaste, decent, modest, nice, virgin, virginal, virtuous. *See* GOOD, RESTRAINT, SEX.

pureblood *adjective*
Of pure breeding stock : full-blooded, high-bred, pureblooded, purebred, thoroughbred. *See* CLEAN.

pureblooded *adjective*
Of pure breeding stock : full-blooded, high-bred, pureblood, purebred, thoroughbred. *See* CLEAN.

purebred *adjective*
Of pure breeding stock : full-blooded, high-bred, pureblood, pureblooded, thoroughbred. *See* CLEAN.

pureness *noun*
The condition of being clean and free of contaminants : clarity, cleanliness, cleanness, purity, taintlessness. *See* CLEAN.

purgation *noun*
1. A freeing from sin, guilt, or defilement : lustration, purification. *See* CLEAN, RELIGION. **2.** The act or process of discharging bodily wastes or foreign substances : elimination, evacuation, excretion. *Medicine:* catharsis. *See* KEEP.

purgative *adjective*
1. Of, relating to, or tending to eliminate : cathartic, eliminative, eliminatory, evacuant, evacuative, excretory. *See* KEEP. **2.** Serving to purify of sin : expiatory, lustral, lustrative, purgatorial, purificatory. *See* CLEAN, RELIGION.

purgatorial *adjective*
Serving to purify of sin : expiatory, lustral, lustrative, purgative, purificatory. *See* CLEAN, RELIGION.

purge *verb*
1. To free from sin, guilt, or defilement :

cleanse, lustrate, purify. *See* CLEAN, RELIGION. **2.** *Law.* To free from a charge or imputation of guilt : absolve, clear, exculpate, exonerate, vindicate. *Law:* acquit. *See* LAW. **3.** To get rid of, especially by banishment or execution : eliminate, eradicate, liquidate, remove, wipe out. ***Idioms:*** do away with, put an end to. *See* HELP, KEEP. **4.** *Medicine.* To discharge (wastes or foreign substances) from the body : eliminate, evacuate, excrete. *See* KEEP.

purge *noun* The act or process of eliminating : clearance, elimination, eradication, liquidation, removal, riddance. *See* KEEP.

purification *noun*
1. The act or process of removing physical impurities : clarification, refinement. *See* CLEAN. **2.** A freeing from sin, guilt, or defilement : lustration, purgation. *See* CLEAN, RELIGION.

purificatory *adjective*
Serving to purify of sin : expiatory, lustral, lustrative, purgative, purgatorial. *See* CLEAN, RELIGION.

purifier *noun*
Something that purifies or cleans : clarifier, cleaner, cleanser, refiner, refinery. *See* CLEAN.

purify *verb*
1. To make or become clear by the removal of impurities : clarify, clean, cleanse, refine. *See* CLEAN. **2.** To free from sin, guilt, or defilement : cleanse, lustrate, purge. *See* CLEAN, RELIGION.

puritan *noun*
A person who is too much concerned with being proper, modest, or righteous : bluenose, Mrs. Grundy, prude, Victorian. *Informal:* old maid. *See* SEX.

puritanical *adjective*
Marked by excessive concern for propriety and good form : bluenosed, genteel, old-maidish, precise, priggish, prim, prissy, proper, prudish, strait-laced, stuffy, Victorian. ***Idiom:*** prim and proper. *See* PLAIN.

purity *noun*
1. The condition of being clean and free of contaminants : clarity, cleanliness, cleanness, pureness, taintlessness. *See* CLEAN. **2.** The condition of being chaste : chastity, decency, innocence, modesty, virginity, virtue, virtuousness. *See* GOOD, RESTRAINT, SEX.

purloin *verb*
To take (another's property) without permission : filch, pilfer, snatch, steal, thieve. *Informal:* lift, swipe. *Slang:* cop, heist, hook, nip[1], pinch, rip off, snitch. ***Idiom:*** make (*or* walk) off with. *See* CRIMES, GIVE.

purloiner *noun*
A person who steals : bandit, burglar, highwayman, housebreaker, larcener, larcenist, pilferer, robber, stealer, thief. *See* CRIMES.

purport *noun*
1. That which is signified by a word or expression : acceptation, connotation, denotation, import, intent, meaning, message, sense, significance, significancy, signification, value. *See* MEANING. **2.** The gist of a specific action or situation : idea, import, meaning, point, significance, significancy. *See* MEANING. **3.** The general sense or significance, as of an action or statement : amount, burden[2], drift, import, substance, tenor. ***Idioms:*** sum and substance, sum total. *See* MEANING. **4.** The thread or current of thought uniting or occurring in all the elements of a text or discourse : aim, burden[2], drift, intent, meaning, substance, tendency, tenor, thrust. *See* MEANING.

purpose *noun*
1. The proper activity of a person or thing : function, job, role, task. *See* DO. **2.** What one intends to do or achieve : aim, ambition, design, end, goal, intent, intention, mark, meaning, object, objective, point, target, view, why. ***Idioms:*** end in view, why and wherefore. *See* PLANNED, PURPOSE. **3.** Unwavering firmness of character, action, or will : decidedness, decision, decisiveness, determination, firmness, purposefulness, resoluteness, resolution, resolve, toughness, will, willpower. *See* CERTAIN, STRONG.

purpose *verb* To have in mind as a goal or purpose : aim, contemplate, design, intend, mean[1], plan, project, propose, target. *Regional:* mind. *See* PLANNED, PURPOSE.

purposeful *adjective*
Done or said on purpose : deliberate, intended, intentional, voluntary, willful, witting. *See* PURPOSE.

purposefulness *noun*
Unwavering firmness of character, action, or will : decidedness, decision, decisiveness, determination, firmness, purpose, resoluteness, resolution, resolve, toughness, will, willpower. *See* CERTAIN, STRONG.

purposeless *adjective*
1. Without aim, purpose, or intent : aimless, desultory, pointless. *See* PURPOSE. **2.** Lacking rational direction or purpose : meaningless, mindless, pointless, senseless. ***Idiom:*** without rhyme or reason. *See* PURPOSE.

pursue *verb*
1. To follow (another) with the intent of overtaking and capturing : chase, run after. ***Idioms:*** be (*or* go) in pursuit, give chase. *See* SEEK. **2.** To strengthen the effect of (an action) by further action : follow through, follow up. *See* CONTINUE. **3.** To work at, especially as a profession : practice. *See* DO, WORK. **4.** To go through (life) in a certain way : lead, live[1], pass. *See* BE. **5.** To attempt to gain the affection of : court, spark[2], woo. *Informal:* romance. *See* SEEK, SEX.

pursuing *noun*
An attempting to accomplish or attain : pursuit, quest, search. *See* SEEK.

pursuit *noun*
1. The following of another in an attempt to overtake and capture : chase, hot pursuit. *See* SEEK. **2.** An attempting to accomplish or attain : pursuing, quest, search. *See* SEEK. **3.** Activity pursued as a livelihood : art, business, calling, career, craft, employment, job, line, métier, occupation, profession, trade, vocation, work. *Slang:* racket. *Archaic:* employ. *See* ACTION. **4.** A working at a profession or occupation : practice. *See* DO, WORK.

purview *noun*
1. An area within which something or someone exists, acts, or has influence or power : ambit, compass, extension, extent, orbit, range, reach, realm, scope, sphere, sweep, swing. *See* TERRITORY. **2.** The extent of one's perception, understanding, knowledge, or vision : horizon, ken, range, reach, scope. *See* ABILITY, KNOWLEDGE, SEE.

push *verb*
1. To exert pressure : bear, press. *See* OVER. **2.** To force to move or advance with or as if with blows or pressure : drive, propel, ram, shove, thrust. *See* MOVE. **3.** To cause to stick out : poke, shove, thrust. *See* CONVEX. **4.** To force one's way into a place or situation : shove. *Informal:* muscle. *See* ENTER, PUSH. **5.** To do or achieve by forcing obstacles out of one's way : press, ram, shove. *See* PUSH. **6.** *Slang.* To make known vigorously the positive features of (a product) : advertise, ballyhoo, build up, cry (up), popularize, promote, publicize, talk up. *Informal:* pitch, plug. *See* KNOWLEDGE. **7.** *Slang.* To engage in the illicit sale of (narcotics) : deal, peddle. *See* TRANSACTIONS.

push off *verb Informal.* To move or proceed away from a place : depart, exit, get away, get off, go, go away, leave[1], pull out, quit, retire, run (along), withdraw. *Informal:* cut out, shove off. *Slang:* blow[1], split, take off. ***Idioms:*** hit the road, take leave. *See* APPROACH.

push on *verb* To move along a particular course : fare, go, journey, pass, proceed, remove, travel, wend. ***Idiom:*** make one's way. *See* MOVE.

push *noun* **1.** An act or instance of using force so as to propel ahead : butt[1], shove, thrust. *See* PUSH. **2.** An organized effort to accomplish a purpose : campaign, crusade, drive, movement. *See* ACTION, SEEK. **3.** Something that causes and encourages a given response : encouragement, fillip, impetus, impulse, incentive, inducement, motivation, prod, spur, stimulant, stimulation, stimulator, stimulus. *See* CAUSE. **4.** *Informal.* An aggressive readiness along with energy to undertake taxing efforts : drive, enterprise, hustle, initiative, punch. *Informal:* get-up-and-go, gumption. *See* ACTION, TIRED, TRY.

pusher *noun*
Slang. A person who sells narcotics illegally : dealer, peddler. *See* TRANSACTIONS.

pushiness *noun*
The state or quality of being impudent or arrogantly self-confident : assumption, audaciousness, audacity, boldness, brashness, brazenness, cheek, cheekiness, chutzpah, discourtesy, disrespect, effrontery, face, familiarity, forwardness, gall[1], impertinence, impudence, impudency, incivility, insolence, nerve, nerviness, overconfidence, pertness, presumptuousness, rudeness, sassiness, sauciness. *Informal:* brass, crust, sauce, uppishness, uppityness. *See* ATTITUDE, COURTESY.

push off *verb* See **push.**

push on *verb* See **push.**

pushover *noun*
1. A person who is easily deceived or victimized : butt[3], dupe, fool, gull, lamb, victim. *Informal:* sucker. *Slang:* fall guy, gudgeon, mark, monkey, patsy, pigeon, sap[1]. *Chiefly British:* mug. *See* WISE. **2.** An easily accomplished task : child's play, cinch, snap, walkaway, walkover. *Informal:* breeze. *Slang:* duck soup. *See* EASY.

pushy *adjective*
Rude and disrespectful : assuming, assumptive, audacious, bold, boldfaced, brash, brazen, cheeky, contumelious, familiar, forward, impertinent, impudent, insolent, malapert, nervy, overconfident, pert, presuming, presumptuous, sassy, saucy, smart. *Informal:* brassy, flip, fresh, smart-alecky, snippety, snippy, uppish, uppity.

Slang: wise[1]. *See* ATTITUDE, COURTESY.

pusillanimity *noun*
Ignoble lack of courage : chickenheartedness, cowardice, cowardliness, cravenness, dastardliness, faint-heartedness, funk, unmanliness. *Slang:* gutlessness, yellowness, yellow streak. *See* FEAR.

pusillanimous *adjective*
Ignobly lacking in courage : chickenhearted, cowardly, craven, dastardly, faint-hearted, lily-livered, unmanly. *Slang:* chicken, gutless, yellow, yellow-bellied. *See* FEAR.

puss *noun*
1. *Slang.* The opening in the body through which food is ingested : mouth. *Slang:* gob[2], trap. *See* MOUTH. **2.** *Slang.* The front surface of the head : countenance, face, feature (often used in plural), muzzle, visage. *Informal:* mug. *Slang:* kisser, map, pan. *See* PRECEDE.

pussyfoot *verb*
1. To move silently and furtively : creep, glide, lurk, mouse, prowl, skulk, slide, slink, slip, snake, sneak, steal. *Slang:* gumshoe. *See* MOVE. **2.** *Informal.* To use evasive or deliberately vague language : equivocate, euphemize, hedge, shuffle, tergiversate, weasel. *Informal:* waffle. ***Idioms:*** beat about (*or* around) the bush, mince words. *See* CLEAR.

put *verb*
1. To deposit in a specified place : lay[1], place, set[1], stick. *See* PLACE, RISE. **2.** To calculate approximately : approximate, estimate, place, reckon, set[1]. *See* PRECISE. **3.** To establish and apply as compulsory : assess, exact, impose, levy. *See* OBLIGATION, OVER, WILLING. **4.** To put up as a stake in a game or speculation : bet, gamble, lay[1] (down), post[2], risk, stake, venture, wager. *Informal:* go. *See* GAMBLING. **5.** To seek an answer to (a question) : ask, pose, raise. *See* ASK. **6.** To utter publicly : air, express, state, vent, ventilate. ***Idiom:*** come out with. *See* SHOW, WORDS. **7.** To express in another language, while systematically retaining the original sense : construe, render, translate. *See* WORDS. **8.** To convey in language or words of a particular form : couch, express, formulate, phrase, word. *See* WORDS.

put away *verb* **1.** *Informal.* To eat completely or entirely : consume, devour, dispatch, eat up. *Informal:* polish off. *See* INGESTION. **2.** *Informal.* To take the life of (a person or persons) unlawfully : destroy, finish (off), kill[1], liquidate, murder, slay. *Slang:* bump off, do in, knock off, off, rub out, waste, wipe out, zap. *See* HELP.

put by *verb* To reserve for the future : keep, lay aside, lay away, lay by, lay in, lay up, salt away, save (up), set by. *See* KEEP, SAVE.

put down *verb* To bring to an end forcibly as if by imposing a heavy weight : choke off, crush, extinguish, quash, quell, quench, squash, squelch, suppress. ***Idiom:*** put the lid on. *See* CONTINUE, WIN.

put forth *verb* To put forward (a topic) for discussion : bring up, broach, introduce, moot, raise. *See* START.

put forward *verb* To state, as an idea, for consideration : advance, offer, pose, propose, propound, set forth, submit, suggest. *See* OFFER.

put in *verb* **1.** To ask for employment, acceptance, or admission : apply, petition. *See* SEEK. **2.** To spend or complete (time), as a prison term : serve. *Informal:* do. *See* TIME. **3.** To use time in a particular way : pass, spend. *See* TIME. **4.** *Nautical.* To come or go into (a place) : come in, enter, go in, penetrate. ***Idioms:*** gain entrance (*or* entry), set foot in. *See* ENTER.

put off *verb* To offer or put into circulation (an inferior or spurious item) : fob off, foist, palm off, pass off. *See* HONEST.

put on *verb* **1.** To put (an article of clothing) on one's person : assume, don, get on, pull on, slip into, slip on. *See* PUT ON. **2.** To behave affectedly or insincerely or take on a false or misleading appearance of : act, counterfeit, dissemble, fake, feign, play-act, pose, pretend, sham, simulate. *See* HONEST, TRUE. **3.** To take on or give a false appearance of : affect[2], assume, counterfeit, fake, feign, pretend, sham, simulate. ***Idiom:*** make believe. *See* TRUE. **4.** To produce on the stage : act (out), do, dramatize, enact, give, perform, present[2], stage. *See* PERFORMING ARTS.

put out *verb* **1.** To cause to stop burning or giving light : douse, extinguish, quench, snuff out. *See* CONTINUE. **2.** To bring to bear steadily or forcefully : exercise, exert, ply[2], throw, wield. *See* CAUSE. **3.** To present for circulation, exhibit, or sale : bring out, issue, publish. *See* WORDS. **4.** To cause inconvenience for : discomfort, discommode, incommode, inconvenience, trouble. *See* COMFORT. **5.** To trouble the nerves or peace of mind of, especially by repeated vexations : aggravate, annoy, bother, bug, chafe, disturb, exasperate, fret, gall[2], get, irk, irritate, nettle, peeve, provoke, rile, ruffle, vex. ***Idioms:*** get in one's hair, get on one's nerves, get under one's skin. *See* FEELINGS, PAIN.

put through *verb* To bring about and carry to a successful conclusion : bring off, carry out, carry through, effect, effectuate, execute. *Informal:* swing. *See* DO.
put together *verb* To create by forming, combining, or altering materials : assemble, build, construct, fabricate, fashion, forge[1], frame, make, manufacture, mold, produce, shape. *See* MAKE.
put up *verb* **1.** To raise upright : erect, pitch, raise, rear[2], set up, upraise, uprear. *See* HORIZONTAL, RISE. **2.** To make or form (a structure) : build, construct, erect, raise, rear[2]. *See* MAKE. **3.** To prepare (food) for storage and future use : can, conserve, preserve. *See* KEEP. **4.** To provide with often temporary lodging : accommodate, bed (down), berth, bestow, billet, board, bunk[1], domicile, harbor, house, lodge, quarter, room. *See* PROTECTION.

putative *adjective*
Assumed to be such : reputed, supposed. *See* BELIEF.

put away *verb* See **put.**
put by *verb* See **put.**
put down *verb* See **put.**
put forth *verb* See **put.**
put forward *verb* See **put.**
put in *verb* See **put.**
put off *verb* See **put.**

put-on *noun*
Slang. A deceptive outward appearance : cloak, color, coloring, cover, disguise, disguisement, façade, face, false colors, front, gloss, guise, mask, masquerade, pretense, pretext, semblance, show, veil, veneer, window-dressing. *See* SHOW.

put on *verb* See **put.**
put out *verb* See **put.**

putrefaction *noun*
The condition of being decayed : breakdown, decay, decomposition, deterioration, disintegration, putrescence, putridness, rot, rottenness, spoilage. *See* BETTER, THRIVE.

putrefy *verb*
To become or cause to become rotten or unsound : break down, decay, decompose, deteriorate, disintegrate, molder, rot, spoil, taint, turn. ***Idioms:*** go bad, go to pot, go to seed. *See* BETTER, THRIVE.

putrescence *noun*
The condition of being decayed : breakdown, decay, decomposition, deterioration, disintegration, putrefaction, putridness, rot, rottenness, spoilage. *See* BETTER, THRIVE.

putrid *adjective*
1. Impaired because of decay : bad, rotten. *See* BETTER, TASTE, THRIVE. **2.** Smelling of mildew or decay : frowzy, fusty, moldy, musty, rancid, rank[2], rotten. *See* SMELLS.

putridness *noun*
The condition of being decayed : breakdown, decay, decomposition, deterioration, disintegration, putrefaction, putrescence, rot, rottenness, spoilage. *See* BETTER, THRIVE.

putter *verb*
1. To waste time by engaging in aimless activity : doodle, fool. *Informal:* fool around, mess around. *See* THRIVE. **2.** To be nervously or uselessly active : bustle, fuss. *Informal:* mess around. *See* ACTION, CALM. **3.** To move one's fingers or hands in a nervous or aimless fashion : fiddle, fidget, fool, monkey, play, tinker, toy, trifle, twiddle. *See* TOUCH.

put through *verb* See **put.**
put together *verb* See **put.**
put up *verb* See **put.**

puzzle *verb*
To cause to be unclear in mind or intent : addle, befuddle, bewilder, confound, confuse, discombobulate, dizzy, fuddle, jumble, mix up, muddle, mystify, perplex. *Informal:* throw. ***Idiom:*** make one's head reel (*or* swim *or* whirl). *See* CLEAR, FEELINGS.
puzzle out *verb* To find the key to (a code, for example) : break, crack, decipher, decrypt. *See* KNOWLEDGE.
puzzle *noun* Anything that arouses curiosity or perplexes because it is unexplained, inexplicable, or secret : conundrum, enigma, mystery, perplexity, puzzler, riddle. *See* SHOW.

puzzlement *noun*
A stunned or bewildered condition : befuddlement, bewilderedness, bewilderment, daze, discombobulation, fog, muddle, mystification, perplexity, stupefaction, stupor, trance. *See* AWARENESS.

puzzle out *verb* See **puzzle.**

puzzler *noun*
Anything that arouses curiosity or perplexes because it is unexplained, inexplicable, or secret : conundrum, enigma, mystery, perplexity, puzzle, riddle. *See* SHOW.

puzzling *adjective*
Difficult to explain or understand : arcane, cabalistic, cryptic, enigmatic, mysterious, mystic, mystical, mystifying, occult. *See* EXPLAIN, KNOWLEDGE.

pygmy also **pigmy** *adjective*
Extremely small : diminutive, dwarf, Lillipu-

tian, midget, miniature, minuscule, minute[2], tiny, wee. *Informal:* peewee, pintsize, pintsized, teensy, teensy-weensy, teeny, teeny-weeny, weeny. *See* BIG.

pyretic *adjective*
Being at a higher temperature than desirable : febrific, febrile, feverish, hectic, hot. *See* HOT.

pythonic *adjective*
Of extraordinary size and power : behemoth, Brobdingnagian, Bunyanesque, colossal, cyclopean, elephantine, enormous, gargantuan, giant, gigantesque, gigantic, herculean, heroic, huge, immense, jumbo, mammoth, massive, massy, mastodonic, mighty, monster, monstrous, monumental, mountainous, prodigious, stupendous, titanic, tremendous, vast. *Informal:* walloping. *Slang:* whopping. *See* BIG.

quack *noun*
One who fakes : charlatan, fake, faker, fraud, humbug, impostor, mountebank, phony, pretender. *See* TRUE.

quad *noun*
An area partially or entirely enclosed by walls or buildings : atrium, close, court, courtyard, enclosure, quadrangle, yard. *See* PLACE.

quadrangle *noun*
An area partially or entirely enclosed by walls or buildings : atrium, close, court, courtyard, enclosure, quad, yard. *See* PLACE.

quadrate *adjective*
Having four equal sides and four right angles : square. *See* GEOMETRY.
quadrate *verb Archaic.* To be compatible or in correspondence : accord, agree, check, chime, comport with, conform, consist, correspond, fit[1], harmonize, match, square, tally. *Informal:* jibe[1]. *See* AGREE.

quaff *verb*
To take into the mouth and swallow (a liquid) : drink, imbibe, pull on, sip, sup. *Informal:* swig, toss down (*or* off). *Slang:* belt. ***Idiom:*** wet one's whistle. *See* MOUTH.
quaff *noun* An act of drinking or the amount swallowed : draft, drink, potation, pull, sip, sup, swill. *Informal:* swig. *Slang:* belt. *See* MOUTH.

quag *noun*
A usually low-lying area of soft waterlogged ground and standing water : bog, fen, marsh, marshland, mire, morass, muskeg, quagmire, slough[1], swamp, swampland, wetland. *See* DRY.

quaggy *adjective*
Yielding easily to pressure or weight; not firm : mushy, pappy[1], pulpous, pulpy, soft, spongy, squashy, squishy, yielding. *See* RESIST.

quagmire *noun*
1. A usually low-lying area of soft waterlogged ground and standing water : bog, fen, marsh, marshland, mire, morass, muskeg, quag, slough[1], swamp, swampland, wetland. *See* DRY. **2.** A difficult, often embarrassing situation or condition : box[1], corner, deep water, difficulty, dilemma, Dutch, fix, hole, hot spot, hot water, jam, plight[1], predicament, scrape, soup, trouble. *Informal:* bind, pickle, spot. *See* EASY.

quail *verb*
To draw away involuntarily, usually out of fear or disgust : blench[1], cringe, flinch, recoil, shrink, shy[1], start, wince. *See* APPROACH, SEEK.

quaint *adjective*
1. Agreeably curious, especially in an old-fashioned or unusual way : funny, odd. *See* USUAL. **2.** Deviating from the customary : bizarre, cranky, curious, eccentric, erratic, freakish, idiosyncratic, odd, outlandish, peculiar, queer, quirky, singular, strange, unnatural, unusual, weird. *Slang:* kooky, screwball. *British Slang:* rum, rummy[2]. *See* USUAL.

quake *verb*
1. To move to and fro violently : rock, shake, tremble, vibrate. *See* REPETITION. **2.** To move to and fro in short, jerky movements : quaver, quiver, shake, shiver[1], shudder, tremble, twitter, vibrate. *See* REPETITION.

quake *noun* **1.** A nervous shaking of the body : quiver, shake, shiver[1], shudder, thrill, tic, tremor, twitch. *See* REPETITION. **2.** A shaking of the earth : earthquake, seism, temblor, tremblor, tremor. *Informal:* shake. *See* MOVE, REPETITION.

quaky *adjective*
Marked by or affected with tremors : aquiver, quivery, shaky, shivery, tremulant, tremulous, twittery. *See* REPETITION.

qualification *noun*
1. The quality or state of being eligible : eligibility, fitness, suitability, suitableness, worthiness. *See* ABILITY. **2.** A restricting or modifying element : condition, provision, proviso, reservation, specification, stipulation, term (often used in plural). *Informal:* string (often used in plural). *See* LIMITED.

qualified *adjective*
1. Satisfying certain requirements, as for selection : eligible, fit[1], fitted, suitable, worthy. *See* ABILITY. **2.** Not total, unlimited, or wholehearted : limited, modified, reserved, restricted. *See* BIG, LIMITED.

qualify *verb*
1. To give authority to : accredit, authorize, commission, empower, enable, entitle, license. *See* ALLOW. **2.** To make or become less severe or extreme : moderate, mute, soften, subdue, tame, temper, tone down. *See* INCREASE.

quality *noun*
1. A distinctive element : attribute, character, characteristic, feature, mark, peculiarity, property, savor, trait. *See* BE. **2.** A level of superiority that is usually high : caliber, merit, stature, value, virtue, worth. *See* GOOD, VALUE.
3. High style in quality, manner, or dress : refinement. *Informal:* class. *See* STYLE.
4. Degree of excellence : caliber, class, grade. *See* BE, VALUE. **5.** People of the highest social level : aristocracy, blue blood, crème de la crème, elite, flower, gentility, gentry, nobility, patriciate, society, upper class, who's who. *Informal:* upper crust. *See* OVER.

quality *adjective* Exceptionally good of its kind : ace, banner, blue-ribbon, brag, capital, champion, excellent, fine[1], first-class, first-rate, prime, splendid, superb, superior, terrific, tiptop, top. *Informal:* A-one, bully, dandy, great, swell, topflight, topnotch. *Slang:* boss. *Chiefly British:* tophole. *See* GOOD.

qualm *noun*
A feeling of uncertainty about the fitness or correctness of an action : compunction, misgiving, reservation, scruple. *See* CERTAIN.

quantity *noun*
1. An indefinite amount or extent : deal. *Informal:* lot. *See* BIG. **2.** A measurable whole : amount, body, budget, bulk, corpus, quantum. *See* BIG.

quantum *noun*
1. That which is allotted : allocation, allotment, allowance, dole, lot, measure, part, portion, quota, ration, share, split. *Informal:* cut. *Slang:* divvy. *See* COLLECT. **2.** A measurable whole : amount, body, budget, bulk, corpus, quantity. *See* BIG.

quarrel *noun*
A discussion, often heated, in which a difference of opinion is expressed : altercation, argument, bicker, clash, contention, controversy, debate, difficulty, disagreement, dispute, fight, polemic, run-in, spat, squabble, tiff, word (used in plural), wrangle. *Informal:* hassle, rhubarb, tangle. *See* CONFLICT.

quarrel *verb* To engage in a quarrel : argue, bicker, contend, dispute, fight, quibble, spat, squabble, tiff, wrangle. *Informal:* hassle, tangle. *Idioms:* cross swords, have it out, have words, lock horns. *See* CONFLICT.

quarrelsome *adjective*
1. Given to arguing : argumentative, combative, contentious, disputatious, eristic, litigious, polemic, polemical, scrappy. *See* CONFLICT.
2. Having or showing an eagerness to fight : bellicose, belligerent, combative, contentious, hostile, militant, pugnacious, scrappy, truculent, warlike. *See* ATTACK.

quarter *noun*
1. One of four equal parts of something : quartern. *See* PART. **2.** A part of the earth's surface : area, belt, district, locality, neighborhood, region, tract, zone. *Informal:* neck of the woods. *See* TERRITORY. **3.** A rather small part of a geographic unit considered in regard to its inhabitants or distinctive characteristics. Often uppercase : area, district, neighborhood. *See* TERRITORY.

quarter *verb* To provide with often temporary lodging : accommodate, bed (down), berth, bestow, billet, board, bunk[1], domicile, harbor, house, lodge, put up, room. *See* PROTECTION.

quartern *noun*
One of four equal parts of something : quarter. *See* PART.

quash *verb*
To bring to an end forcibly as if by imposing a heavy weight : choke off, crush, extinguish, put down, quell, quench, squash, squelch, sup-

press. ***Idiom:*** put the lid on. *See* CONTINUE, WIN.

quaver *verb*

To move to and fro in short, jerky movements : quake, quiver, shake, shiver[1], shudder, tremble, twitter, vibrate. *See* REPETITION.

queer *adjective*

1. Deviating from the customary : bizarre, cranky, curious, eccentric, erratic, freakish, idiosyncratic, odd, outlandish, peculiar, quaint, quirky, singular, strange, unnatural, unusual, weird. *Slang:* kooky, screwball. *British Slang:* rum, rummy[2]. *See* USUAL. **2.** Causing puzzlement; perplexing : curious, funny, odd, peculiar, strange, weird. *See* USUAL.

quell *verb*

To bring to an end forcibly as if by imposing a heavy weight : choke off, crush, extinguish, put down, quash, quench, squash, squelch, suppress. ***Idiom:*** put the lid on. *See* CONTINUE, WIN.

quench *verb*

1. To cause to stop burning or giving light : douse, extinguish, put out, snuff out. *See* CONTINUE. **2.** To hold (something requiring an outlet) in check : burke, choke (back), gag, hold back, hold down, hush (up), muffle, repress, smother, squelch, stifle, strangle, suppress, throttle. *Informal:* sit on (*or* upon). *See* RESTRAINT. **3.** To bring to an end forcibly as if by imposing a heavy weight : choke off, crush, extinguish, put down, quash, quell, squash, squelch, suppress. ***Idiom:*** put the lid on. *See* CONTINUE, WIN.

querier *noun*

One who inquires : inquirer, inquisitor, investigator, prober, quester, questioner, researcher. *See* ASK, INVESTIGATE.

querulous *adjective*

Having or showing a bad temper : bad-tempered, cantankerous, crabbed, cranky, cross, disagreeable, fretful, grouchy, grumpy, ill-tempered, irascible, irritable, nasty, peevish, petulant, snappish, snappy, surly, testy, ugly, waspish. *Informal:* crabby, mean[2]. ***Idiom:*** out of sorts. *See* ATTITUDE.

query *noun*

A request for data : inquiry, interrogation, question. *Law:* interrogatory. *See* ASK, INVESTIGATE.

query *verb* To put a question to (someone) : ask, examine, inquire, question, quiz. *See* ASK.

quest *noun*

An attempting to accomplish or attain : pursuing, pursuit, search. *See* SEEK.

quest *verb* To try to find something : cast about, hunt, look, search, seek. *See* SEEK.

question *noun*

1. A request for data : inquiry, interrogation, query. *Law:* interrogatory. *See* ASK, INVESTIGATE. **2.** A situation that presents difficulty, uncertainty, or perplexity : hornets' nest, issue, problem. *Informal:* can of worms. *See* EASY. **3.** A lack of conviction or certainty : doubt, doubtfulness, dubiety, dubiousness, incertitude, mistrust, skepticism, suspicion, uncertainty, wonder. *See* CERTAIN.

question *verb* **1.** To put a question to (someone) : ask, examine, inquire, query, quiz. *See* ASK. **2.** To be uncertain, disbelieving, or skeptical about : distrust, doubt, misdoubt, mistrust, wonder. ***Idiom:*** have one's doubts. *See* CERTAIN.

questionable *adjective*

1. In doubt or dispute : arguable, contested, debatable, disputable, doubtful, exceptionable, moot, mootable, problematic, problematical, uncertain. *See* CERTAIN. **2.** Not affording certainty : ambiguous, borderline, chancy, clouded, doubtful, dubious, dubitable, equivocal, inconclusive, indecisive, indeterminate, problematic, problematical, uncertain, unclear, unsure. *Informal:* iffy. ***Idioms:*** at issue, in doubt, in question. *See* CERTAIN, CLEAR. **3.** Not likely : doubtful, improbable, unapt, unlikely. *See* LIKELY. **4.** Of dubious character : doubtful, equivocal, shady, suspect, suspicious, uncertain. *Informal:* fishy. *See* HONEST.

questioner *noun*

1. One who inquires : inquirer, inquisitor, investigator, prober, querier, quester, researcher. *See* ASK, INVESTIGATE. **2.** One who conducts an official inquiry, usually with no regard for human rights : inquisitor, interrogator. *See* ASK, INVESTIGATE.

questioning *adjective*

1. Eager to acquire knowledge : curious, inquiring, inquisitive, investigative. *See* INVESTIGATE. **2.** Refusing or reluctant to believe : disbelieving, incredulous, skeptical, unbelieving. *See* BELIEF.

questioningly *adverb*

With skepticism : askance, doubtfully, dubiously, skeptically. ***Idiom:*** with a grain of salt. *See* BELIEF.

quester *noun*

One who inquires : inquirer, inquisitor, investigator, prober, querier, questioner, researcher. *See* ASK, INVESTIGATE.

queue *noun*
A group of people or things arranged in a row : column, file, line, rank[1], row[1], string, tier. *See* GROUP.

quibble *verb*
1. To raise unnecessary or trivial objections : carp, cavil, niggle, nitpick, pettifog. ***Idiom:*** pick to pieces. *See* SUPPORT. **2.** To engage in a quarrel : argue, bicker, contend, dispute, fight, quarrel, spat, squabble, tiff, wrangle. *Informal:* hassle, tangle. ***Idioms:*** cross swords, have it out, have words, lock horns. *See* CONFLICT.

quibbler *noun*
A person who finds fault, often severely and willfully : carper, caviler, critic, criticizer, faultfinder, hypercritic, niggler, nitpicker. *See* PRAISE.

quick *adjective*
1. Characterized by great celerity : breakneck, expeditious, fast, fleet, rapid, speedy, swift. *Informal:* hell-for-leather. ***Idiom:*** quick as a bunny (*or* wink). *See* FAST. **2.** Moving or performing quickly, lightly, and easily : agile, brisk, facile, nimble, spry. *See* ABILITY. **3.** Mentally quick and original : alert, bright, clever, intelligent, keen[1], quick-witted, sharp, sharp-witted, smart. ***Idiom:*** smart as a whip. *See* ABILITY. **4.** Accomplished in very little time : brief, expeditious, fast, flying, hasty, hurried, rapid, short, speedy, swift. *See* FAST.
quick *noun* A point of origin : bottom, center, core, focus, heart, hub, root[1]. *See* START.
quick *adverb* In a rapid way : apace, fast, posthaste, quickly. *Informal:* flat out, hell-for-leather, lickety-split, pronto. ***Idioms:*** full tilt, in a flash, in nothing flat, like a bat out of hell, like a blue streak, like a flash, like a house on fire, like a shot, like a streak, like greased lightning, like the wind, like wildfire. *See* FAST.

quicken *verb*
1. To increase the speed of : accelerate, expedite, hasten, hurry, hustle, speed (up), step up. *See* FAST. **2.** To make alive : animate, vitalize, vivify. *See* LIVE.

quickening *adjective*
Serving to enliven : animating, enlivening, rousing, stimulating, vitalizing, vivifying. *See* EXCITE.

quickly *adverb*
In a rapid way : apace, fast, posthaste, quick. *Informal:* flat out, hell-for-leather, lickety-split, pronto. ***Idioms:*** full tilt, in a flash, in nothing flat, like a bat out of hell, like a blue streak, like a flash, like a house on fire, like a shot, like a streak, like greased lightning, like the wind, like wildfire. *See* FAST.

quickness *noun*
1. Rapidness of movement or activity : celerity, dispatch, expedition, expeditiousness, fleetness, haste, hurry, hustle, rapidity, rapidness, speed, speediness, swiftness. *See* FAST. **2.** The quality or state of being mentally agile : agileness, agility, dexterity, dexterousness, nimbleness. *See* ABILITY.

quick-tempered *adjective*
Easily annoyed : choleric, irascible, peppery, testy, tetchy, touchy. *See* FEELINGS.

quick-witted *adjective*
Mentally quick and original : alert, bright, clever, intelligent, keen[1], quick, sharp, sharp-witted, smart. ***Idiom:*** smart as a whip. *See* ABILITY.

quidnunc *noun*
A person given to intruding in other people's affairs : busybody, interloper, meddler. *Informal:* kibitzer. *Slang:* buttinsky. *Archaic:* pragmatic. *See* PARTICIPATE.

quiescence *noun*
The condition of being temporarily inactive : abeyance, abeyancy, dormancy, intermission, latency, suspension. *See* ACTION.

quiescent *adjective*
Existing in a temporarily inactive form or state : abeyant, dormant, inactive, latent, sleeping. *See* ACTION, SHOW.

quiet *adjective*
1. Marked by, done with, or making no sound or noise : hushed, noiseless, silent, soundless, still, stilly. *Archaic:* hush. *See* SOUNDS. **2.** Not irritating, strident, or loud : hushed, low, low-key, low-keyed, small, soft, subdued, whispery. *See* SOUNDS. **3.** Motionless and undisturbed : calm, halcyon, peaceful, placid, serene, still, stilly, tranquil, untroubled. *See* CALM. **4.** Not showy or obtrusive : inobtrusive, restrained, subdued, tasteful, unobtrusive. *See* PLAIN.
quiet *noun* **1.** The absence of sound or noise : hush, noiselessness, quietness, silence, soundlessness, still, stillness. *See* SOUNDS. **2.** An absence of motion or disturbance : calm, calmness, hush, lull, peace, peacefulness, placidity, placidness, quietness, serenity, stillness, tranquillity, untroubledness. *See* CALM.
quiet *verb* **1.** To cause to become silent : hush, quieten, shush, shut up, silence, still. *See* SOUNDS. **2.** To make or become calm : allay, balm, becalm, calm (down), lull, settle, still, tranquilize. *See* CALM.

quieten *verb*
To cause to become silent : hush, quiet, shush, shut up, silence, still. *See* SOUNDS.

quietness *noun*
1. The absence of sound or noise : hush, noiselessness, quiet, silence, soundlessness, still, stillness. *See* SOUNDS. **2.** An absence of motion or disturbance : calm, calmness, hush, lull, peace, peacefulness, placidity, placidness, quiet, serenity, stillness, tranquillity, untroubledness. *See* CALM.

quietude *noun*
Lack of emotional agitation : calm, calmness, peace, peacefulness, placidity, placidness, serenity, tranquillity. *See* CALM.

quietus *noun*
The act or fact of dying : death, decease, demise, dissolution, extinction, passing, rest[1]. *Slang:* curtain (used in plural). *See* LIVE.

quintessence *noun*
1. The most central and material part : core, essence, gist, heart, kernel, marrow, meat, nub, pith, root[1], soul, spirit, stuff, substance. *Law:* gravamen. *See* BE. **2.** A basic trait or set of traits that define and establish the character of something : being, essence, essentiality, nature, substance, texture. *See* SURFACE.

quintessential *adjective*
Having the nature of, constituting, or serving as a type : archetypal, archetypic, archetypical, classic, classical, model, paradigmatic, prototypal, prototypic, prototypical, representative, typic, typical. *See* SAME, USUAL.

quip *noun*
1. Words or actions intended to excite laughter or amusement : gag, jape, jest, joke, witticism. *Informal:* funny, gag. *Slang:* ha-ha. *See* LAUGHTER. **2.** A flippant or sarcastic remark : crack, dig. *Slang:* wisecrack. *See* RESPECT, WORDS.

quipster *noun*
A person whose words or actions provoke or are intended to provoke amusement or laughter : clown, comedian, comic, farceur, funnyman, humorist, jester, joker, jokester, wag[2], wit, zany. *Informal:* card. *See* LAUGHTER.

quirk *noun*
Peculiar behavior : eccentricity, idiosyncrasy, peculiarity, quirkiness, singularity. *See* USUAL.

quirkiness *noun*
Peculiar behavior : eccentricity, idiosyncrasy, peculiarity, quirk, singularity. *See* USUAL.

quirky *adjective*
Deviating from the customary : bizarre, cranky, curious, eccentric, erratic, freakish, idiosyncratic, odd, outlandish, peculiar, quaint, queer, singular, strange, unnatural, unusual, weird. *Slang:* kooky, screwball. *British Slang:* rum, rummy[2]. *See* USUAL.

quit *verb*
1. To move or proceed away from a place : depart, exit, get away, get off, go, go away, leave[1], pull out, retire, run (along), withdraw. *Informal:* cut out, push off, shove off. *Slang:* blow[1], split, take off. ***Idioms:*** hit the road, take leave. *See* APPROACH. **2.** To relinquish one's engagement in or occupation with : demit, leave[1], resign, terminate. *See* CONTINUE. **3.** To give up or leave without intending to return or claim again : abandon, desert[3], forsake, leave[1], throw over. ***Idioms:*** run out on, walk out on. *See* KEEP. **4.** To cease trying to accomplish or continue : abandon, break off, desist, discontinue, give up, leave off, relinquish, remit, stop. *Informal:* swear off. *Slang:* lay off. ***Idioms:*** call it a day, call it quits, hang up one's fiddle, have done with, throw in the towel. *See* CONTINUE. **5.** To come to a cessation : arrest, belay, cease, check, discontinue, halt[1], leave off, stall[1], stop, surcease. ***Idiom:*** come to a halt (*or* standstill *or* stop). *See* CONTINUE. **6.** To conduct oneself in a specified way : acquit, act, bear, behave, carry, comport, demean[1], deport, do. *See* BE.

quit *adjective* Owing or being owed nothing : even[1], quits, square. *See* PAY.

quitclaim *noun*
A giving up of a possession, claim, or right : abandonment, abdication, demission, relinquishment, renunciation, resignation, surrender, waiver. *See* KEEP.

quitclaim *verb* To give up a possession, claim, or right : abandon, abdicate, cede, demit, forswear, hand over, relinquish, render, renounce, resign, surrender, waive, yield. *See* KEEP.

quite *adverb*
1. To the fullest extent : absolutely, all, altogether, completely, dead, entirely, flat, fully, just, perfectly, thoroughly, totally, utterly, well[2], wholly. *Informal:* clean, clear. ***Idioms:*** in toto, through and through. *See* BIG, LIMITED. **2.** To a considerable extent : considerably, far, much, well[2]. ***Idioms:*** by a long shot (*or* way), by a wide margin, by far. *See* BIG.

quits *adjective*
Owing or being owed nothing : even[1], quit, square. *See* PAY.

quittance *noun*
Something to make up for loss or damage : amends, compensation, indemnification, indemnity, offset, recompense, redress,

reimbursement, remuneration, reparation, repayment, requital, restitution, satisfaction, setoff. *See* SUBSTITUTE.

quiver *verb*
To move to and fro in short, jerky movements : quake, quaver, shake, shiver[1], shudder, tremble, twitter, vibrate. *See* REPETITION.
quiver *noun* A nervous shaking of the body : quake, shake, shiver[1], shudder, thrill, tic, tremor, twitch. *See* REPETITION.

quivery *adjective*
Marked by or affected with tremors : aquiver, quaky, shaky, shivery, tremulant, tremulous, twittery. *See* REPETITION.

quixotic *adjective*
Not compatible with reality : idealistic, romantic, starry-eyed, unrealistic, utopian, visionary. *See* HOPE, REAL.

quiz *verb*
1. To put a question to (someone) : ask, examine, inquire, query, question. *See* ASK. **2.** To subject to a test of knowledge or skill : check, examine, test. *See* INVESTIGATE. **3.** *Chiefly British.* To make fun or make fun of : deride, gibe, jeer, jest, laugh, mock, ridicule, scoff, scout[2], twit. ***Idiom:*** poke fun at. *See* LAUGHTER, RESPECT.
quiz *noun* A set of questions or exercises designed to determine knowledge or skill : catechism, catechization, exam, examination, test. *See* INVESTIGATE.

quondam *adjective*
Having been such previously : erstwhile, former, late, old, once, onetime, past, previous, sometime, whilom. *See* PRECEDE.

quota *noun*
That which is allotted : allocation, allotment, allowance, dole, lot, measure, part, portion, quantum, ration, share, split. *Informal:* cut. *Slang:* divvy. *See* COLLECT.

quotidian *adjective*
Of or suitable for ordinary days or routine occasions : everyday, workaday, workday. *See* GOOD, USUAL.

·R·

rabble *noun*
A group of persons regarded as the lowest class : dreg (often used in plural), lumpenproletariat, ragtag and bobtail, riffraff, trash. *Slang:* scum. ***Idioms:*** scum of the earth, tag and rag, the great unwashed. *See* OVER, RICH.

rabid *adjective*
1. Showing or having enthusiasm : ardent, enthusiastic, fervent, keen[1], mad, warm, zealous. *Informal:* crazy. *Slang:* gung ho, nuts. *See* CONCERN. **2.** Holding especially political views that deviate drastically and fundamentally from conventional or traditional beliefs : extreme, extremist, fanatic, fanatical, radical, revolutionary, ultra. *Slang:* far-out. *See* CONCERN, EDGE, POLITICS. **3.** Full of or marked by extreme anger : furious, irate, ireful, wrathful. ***Idioms:*** fit to be tied, foaming at the mouth, in a rage (*or* temper), in a towering rage. *See* FEELINGS.

race *noun*
A vying with others for victory or supremacy : battle, competition, contest, corrivalry, rivalry, strife, striving, struggle, tug of war, war, warfare. *See* CONFLICT.
race *verb* To move swiftly : bolt, bucket, bustle, dart, dash, festinate, flash, fleet, flit, fly, haste, hasten, hurry, hustle, pelt[2], rocket, run, rush, sail, scoot, scour[2], shoot, speed, sprint, tear[1], trot, whirl, whisk, whiz, wing, zip, zoom. *Informal:* hotfoot, rip. *Slang:* barrel, highball. *Chiefly British:* nip[1]. ***Idioms:*** get a move on, get cracking, go like lightning, go like the wind, hotfoot it, make haste, make time, make tracks, run like the wind, shake a leg, step (*or* jump) on it. *See* MOVE.

rack *verb*
1. To bring great harm or suffering to : afflict, agonize, anguish, curse, excruciate, plague, scourge, smite, strike, torment, torture. *See* ATTACK, HELP. **2.** To subject (another) to extreme physical cruelty, as in punishing : crucify, torment, torture. ***Idiom:*** put on the rack (*or* wheel). *See* PAIN, REWARD.

racket *noun*
1. Sounds or a sound, especially when loud, confused, or disagreeable : babel, clamor,

din, hubbub, hullabaloo, noise, pandemonium, rumpus, tumult, uproar. *See* SOUNDS. **2.** *Slang.* Activity pursued as a livelihood : art, business, calling, career, craft, employment, job, line, métier, occupation, profession, pursuit, trade, vocation, work. *Archaic:* employ. *See* ACTION.

racy *adjective*
Bordering on indelicacy or impropriety : blue, earthy, off-color, provocative, risqué, salty, scabrous, spicy, suggestive. *See* DECENT.

radiance *noun*
Exceptional brightness and clarity, as of a cut and polished stone : brilliance, brilliancy, fire, luminosity. *See* LIGHT.

radiant *adjective*
Giving off or reflecting light readily or in large amounts : beamy, bright, brilliant, effulgent, incandescent, irradiant, lambent, lucent, luminous, lustrous, refulgent, shiny. *See* LIGHT.

radiate *verb*
1. To emit a bright light : beam, blaze[1], burn, gleam, glow, incandesce, shine. *See* LIGHT.
2. To send out heat, light, or energy : cast, emit, irradiate, project, shed, throw. *See* MOVE.
3. To extend over a wide area : circulate, diffuse, disperse, disseminate, distribute, scatter, spread, strew. *See* MOVE, WIDE.

radical *adjective*
1. Arising from or going to the root or source : basal, basic, foundational, fundamental, original, primary, underlying. *See* SURFACE.
2. Holding especially political views that deviate drastically and fundamentally from conventional or traditional beliefs : extreme, extremist, fanatic, fanatical, rabid, revolutionary, ultra. *Slang:* far-out. *See* CONCERN, EDGE, POLITICS.
radical *noun* One who holds extreme views or advocates extreme measures : extremist, fanatic, revolutionary, revolutionist, ultra, zealot. *See* EDGE, CONCERN, POLITICS.

rafter *noun*
A large, oblong piece of wood or other material, used especially for construction : balk, beam, timber. *See* MATTER.

rag[1] *noun*
Torn and ragged clothing. Used in plural : tatter (used in plural). *See* BETTER, PUT ON.

rag[2] *verb*
Slang. To tease or mock good-humoredly : banter, chaff, joke, josh. *Informal:* kid, rib, ride. *Slang:* jive, razz. *See* LAUGHTER.

ragamuffin *noun*
A person wearing ragged or tattered clothing : scarecrow, tatterdemalion. *See* BETTER, RICH.

rage *noun*
1. Violent or unrestrained anger : furor, fury, irateness, ire, wrath, wrathfulness. *See* FEELINGS. **2.** A subject or activity that inspires lively interest : craze, enthusiasm, mania, passion. *See* CONCERN. **3.** The current custom : craze, fad, fashion, furor, mode, style, trend, vogue. *Informal:* thing. ***Idioms:*** the in thing, the last word, the latest thing. *See* STYLE, USUAL.
rage *verb* To be or become angry : anger, blow up, boil over, bristle, burn, explode, flare up, foam, fume, seethe. *Informal:* steam. ***Idioms:*** blow a fuse, blow a gasket, blow one's stack (*or* top), breathe fire, fly off the handle, get hot under the collar, hit the ceiling (*or* roof), lose one's temper, see red. *See* FEELINGS.

ragged *adjective*
1. Torn into or marked by shreds or tatters : raggedy, tatterdemalion, tattered. *See* BETTER.
2. Having a surface that is not smooth : coarse, cragged, craggy, harsh, ironbound, jagged, rough, rugged, scabrous, uneven. *See* SMOOTH.

raggedy *adjective*
Torn into or marked by shreds or tatters : ragged, tatterdemalion, tattered. *See* BETTER.

raging *adjective*
Violently disturbed or agitated, as by storms : dirty, heavy, roiled, roily, rough, rugged, stormy, tempestuous, tumultuous, turbulent, ugly, violent, wild. *See* CALM.

ragtag and bobtail *noun*
A group of persons regarded as the lowest class : dreg (often used in plural), lumpenproletariat, rabble, riffraff, trash. *Slang:* scum. ***Idioms:*** scum of the earth, tag and rag, the great unwashed. *See* OVER, RICH.

raid *noun*
An act of invading, especially by military forces : foray, incursion, inroad, invasion. *See* ATTACK, ENTER.
raid *verb* **1.** To make a surprise attack on : harry, maraud. *See* ATTACK. **2.** To enter so as to attack, plunder, destroy, or conquer : foray, invade, overrun. *See* ATTACK, ENTER.

rail against or **at** *verb*
To attack with harsh, often insulting language : abuse, assail, revile, vituperate. *See* PRAISE.

railing *noun*
Harsh, often insulting language : abuse, billingsgate, contumely, invective, obloquy, revilement, reviling, scurrility, scurrilousness, vituperation. *See* PRAISE.

raillery *noun*
Good-natured teasing : badinage, banter,

chaff, taunt. *Informal:* ribbing. *See* LAUGHTER.

raiment *noun*
Articles worn to cover the body : apparel, attire, clothes, clothing, dress, garment (used in plural), habiliment (often used in plural). *Informal:* dud (used in plural), tog (used in plural). *Slang:* thread (used in plural). *See* PUT ON.

rain *verb*
To give in great abundance : heap, lavish, shower. *See* BIG, GIVE.

rainbow *noun*
A fantastic, impracticable plan or desire : bubble, castle in the air, chimera, dream, fantasy, illusion, pipe dream. *See* REAL.

rainless *adjective*
Having little or no precipitation : arid, droughty, dry, thirsty. *See* DRY.

raise *verb*
1. To move (something) to a higher position : boost, elevate, heave, hoist, lift, pick up, rear², take up, uphold, uplift, upraise, uprear. *See* RISE. **2.** To raise upright : erect, pitch, put up, rear², set up, upraise, uprear. *See* HORIZONTAL, RISE. **3.** To make or form (a structure) : build, construct, erect, put up, rear². *See* MAKE. **4.** To increase in amount : boost, hike, jack (up), jump, up. *See* INCREASE. **5.** To increase markedly in level or intensity, especially of sound : amplify, elevate, heighten. *See* INCREASE. **6.** To raise in rank : advance, elevate, jump, promote, upgrade. *See* RISE. **7.** To bring into existence and foster the development of : breed, cultivate, grow, propagate. *See* CARE FOR, REPRODUCTION. **8.** To take care of and educate (a child) : bring up, rear². *See* CARE FOR. **9.** To seek an answer to (a question) : ask, pose, put. *See* ASK. **10.** To put forward (a topic) for discussion : bring up, broach, introduce, moot, put forth. *See* START. **11.** To induce or elicit (a reaction or emotion) : arouse, awake, awaken, kindle, rouse, stir¹ (up), waken. *See* EXCITE.
raise *noun* **1.** The act of increasing or rising : aggrandizement, amplification, augment, augmentation, boost, buildup, enlargement, escalation, growth, hike, increase, jump, multiplication, proliferation, rise, swell, upsurge, upswing, upturn. *See* INCREASE. **2.** The amount by which something is increased : advance, boost, hike, increase, increment, jump, rise. *See* INCREASE.

raised *adjective*
1. Being positioned above a given level : elevated. *See* RISE. **2.** Directed or pointed upward : erect, upright, upstanding. *See* HORIZONTAL. **3.** Abnormally increased, especially in intensity : elevated, heightened, high. *See* INCREASE.

rake¹ *noun*
An immoral or licentious person : libertine, profligate, wanton. *See* SEX.

rake² *verb*
To depart or cause to depart from true vertical or horizontal : cant¹, heel², incline, lean¹, list², slant, slope, tilt, tip². *See* STRAIGHT.
rake *noun* Deviation from a particular direction : cant¹, grade, gradient, heel², inclination, incline, lean¹, list², slant, slope, tilt, tip². *See* RISE, STRAIGHT.

rakish *adjective*
Lacking in moral restraint : abandoned, dissipated, dissolute, fast, gay, incontinent, licentious, profligate, unbridled, unconstrained, uncontrolled, ungoverned, uninhibited, unrestrained, wanton, wild. *See* RESTRAINT.

rally *verb*
1. To assemble, prepare, or put into operation, as for war or a similar emergency : marshal, mobilize, muster, organize. *See* MOVE. **2.** To regain one's health : come around (*or* round), convalesce, gain, improve, mend, perk up, recover, recuperate. *See* HEALTH.
rally *noun* A return to normal health : recovery, recuperation. *See* HEALTH.

rallying cry *noun*
A rallying term used by proponents of a cause : battle cry, call to arms, call to battle, cry, motto, war cry. *See* WORDS.

ram *verb*
1. To cause to penetrate with force : dig, drive, plunge, run, sink, stab, stick, thrust. *See* PUT IN. **2.** To force to move or advance with or as if with blows or pressure : drive, propel, push, shove, thrust. *See* MOVE. **3.** To do or achieve by forcing obstacles out of one's way : press, push, shove. *See* PUSH.

ramble *verb*
1. To move about at random, especially over a wide area : drift, gad, gallivant, meander, peregrinate, range, roam, rove, stray, traipse, wander. *See* MOVE. **2.** To walk at a leisurely pace : amble, meander, perambulate, promenade, saunter, stroll, wander. *Informal:* mosey. *See* MOVE. **3.** To turn aside, especially from the main subject in writing or speaking : deviate, digress, divagate, diverge, stray, wander. ***Idiom:*** go off at (*or* on) a tangent. *See* APPROACH.
ramble *noun* An act of walking, especially for pleasure : amble, meander (often used in plu-

ral), perambulation, promenade, saunter, stroll, walk, wander. *See* MOVE.

rambling *adjective*
Marked by or given to digression : digressive, discursive, excursive, parenthetic, parenthetical, tangential. *See* APPROACH.

ramification *noun*
Something brought about by a cause : aftermath, consequence, corollary, effect, end product, event, fruit, harvest, issue, outcome, precipitate, result, resultant, sequel, sequence, sequent, upshot. *See* CAUSE.

ramify *verb*
To separate into branches or branchlike parts : bifurcate, branch (out), diverge, divide, fork, subdivide. *See* PART.

rampage *noun*
A period of uncontrolled self-indulgence : binge, fling, orgy, spree. *Slang:* jag. *See* RESTRAINT.

ramshackle *adjective*
Falling to ruin : dilapidated, ruinous, rundown, tumbledown. *See* BETTER.

rancid *adjective*
Smelling of mildew or decay : frowzy, fusty, moldy, musty, putrid, rank[2], rotten. *See* SMELLS.

rancor *noun*
The quality or state of feeling bitter : acrimony, bitterness, embitterment, gall[1], rancorousness, resentfulness, resentment, virulence, virulency. *See* FEELINGS.

rancorous *adjective*
Bitingly hostile : acrimonious, bitter, embittered, hard, resentful, virulent. *See* ATTITUDE, LOVE.

rancorousness *noun*
The quality or state of feeling bitter : acrimony, bitterness, embitterment, gall[1], rancor, resentfulness, resentment, virulence, virulency. *See* FEELINGS.

random *adjective*
Having no particular pattern, purpose, organization, or structure : chance, desultory, haphazard, hit-or-miss, indiscriminate, spot, unplanned. *See* PLANNED.

range *noun*
1. The extent of one's perception, understanding, knowledge, or vision : horizon, ken, purview, reach, scope. *See* ABILITY, KNOWLEDGE, SEE. **2.** The ability or power to seize or attain : capacity, compass, grasp, reach, scope. *See* ABILITY. **3.** An area within which something or someone exists, acts, or has influence or power : ambit, compass, extension, extent, orbit, purview, reach, realm, scope, sphere, sweep, swing. *See* TERRITORY. **4.** Approximate size or amount : vicinity. *Informal:* neighborhood. *See* NEAR.

range *verb* **1.** To put into a deliberate order : arrange, array, deploy, dispose, marshal, order, organize, sort, systematize. *See* ORDER. **2.** To place in or form a line or lines : align, line (up). *See* ORDER. **3.** To assign to a class or classes : categorize, class, classify, distribute, grade, group, pigeonhole, place, rank[1], rate[1]. *See* GROUP, VALUE. **4.** To change or fluctuate within limits : extend, go, run, vary. *See* CHANGE. **5.** To move about at random, especially over a wide area : drift, gad, gallivant, meander, peregrinate, ramble, roam, rove, stray, traipse, wander. *See* MOVE.

rangy *adjective*
Tall, thin, and awkwardly built : gangling, gangly, lanky, spindling, spindly. *See* FAT.

rank[1] *noun*
1. Positioning of one individual vis-à-vis others : footing, place, position, situation, standing, station, status. *See* PLACE. **2.** A division of persons or things by quality, rank, or grade : bracket, class, grade, league, order, tier. *See* GROUP, VALUE. **3.** A group of people or things arranged in a row : column, file, line, queue, row[1], string, tier. *See* GROUP.

rank *verb* To assign to a class or classes : categorize, class, classify, distribute, grade, group, pigeonhole, place, range, rate[1]. *See* GROUP, VALUE.

rank[2] *adjective*
1. Growing profusely : dense, heavy, lush[1], luxuriant, profuse, thick. *See* BIG. **2.** Smelling of mildew or decay : frowzy, fusty, moldy, musty, putrid, rancid, rotten. *See* SMELLS. **3.** Conspicuously bad or offensive : arrant, capital, egregious, flagrant, glaring, gross. *See* GOOD.

rankness *noun*
The quality or state of being flagrant : atrociousness, atrocity, egregiousness, enormity, flagrance, flagrancy, flagrantness, glaringness, grossness, outrageousness. *See* GOOD.

ransack *verb*
1. To make a thorough search of : comb, forage, rummage, scour[2]. *Slang:* shake down. ***Idioms:*** beat the bushes, leave no stone unturned, look (*or* search) high and low, look (*or* search) up and down, turn inside out, turn upside down. *See* INVESTIGATE. **2.** To rob of goods by force, especially in time of war : depredate, despoil, havoc, loot, pillage, plunder,

rape, ravage, sack[2], spoliate, strip[1]. *Archaic:* harrow, spoil. *See* CRIMES, GIVE.

rant *verb*
To speak in a loud, pompous, or prolonged manner : declaim, harangue, mouth, perorate, rave. *See* WORDS.
rant *noun* Pretentious, pompous speech or writing : bombast, claptrap, fustian, grandiloquence, magniloquence, orotundity, turgidity. *See* PLAIN, STYLE, WORDS.

rap[1] *verb*
1. To make a noise by striking : knock, tap[1]. *See* SOUNDS. **2.** To criticize for a fault or an offense : admonish, call down, castigate, chastise, chide, dress down, rebuke, reprimand, reproach, reprove, scold, tax, upbraid. *Informal:* bawl out, lambaste. *Slang:* chew out. ***Idioms:*** bring (*or* call *or* take) to task, call on the carpet, haul (*or* rake) over the coals, let someone have it. *See* ATTACK, PRAISE. **3.** To find fault with : blame, censure, criticize, fault. *Informal:* cut up, pan. *Slang:* knock. *See* PRAISE.
rap out *verb* To speak suddenly or sharply, as from surprise or emotion : blurt (out), burst out, cry (out), ejaculate, exclaim. *See* WORDS.
rap *noun* **1.** The sound made by a light blow : knock, tap[1]. *See* SOUNDS. **2.** *Slang.* Words expressive of strong disapproval : admonishment, admonition, rebuke, reprimand, reproach, reproof, scolding. *See* PRAISE.
3. *Slang.* A judicial decision, especially one setting the punishment to be inflicted on a convicted person : judgment, sentence. *See* LAW.

rap[2] *noun*
Informal. The least bit : hoot, iota, jot, ounce, shred, whit. *Informal:* damn. *Slang:* diddly. *See* BIG.

rap[3] *noun*
Slang. An exchanging of views : conference, discussion, ventilation. *See* WORDS.
rap *verb* *Slang.* To speak together and exchange ideas and opinions about : bandy (about), discuss, moot, talk over, thrash out (*or* over), thresh out (*or* over), toss around. *Informal:* hash (over), kick around, knock about (*or* around). ***Idiom:*** go into a huddle. *See* WORDS.

rapacious *adjective*
Having an insatiable appetite for an activity or pursuit : avid, edacious, gluttonous, greedy, omnivorous, ravenous, unappeasable, voracious. *See* DESIRE.

rapaciousness *noun*
The quality or condition of being voracious : avidity, edacity, omnivorousness, rapacity, ravenousness, voracity. *See* DESIRE.

rapacity *noun*
The quality or condition of being voracious : avidity, edacity, omnivorousness, rapaciousness, ravenousness, voracity. *See* DESIRE.

rape *verb*
1. To compel (another) to participate in or submit to a sexual act : assault, force, ravish, violate. *See* SEX. **2.** To rob of goods by force, especially in time of war : depredate, despoil, havoc, loot, pillage, plunder, ransack, ravage, sack[2], spoliate, strip[1]. *Archaic:* harrow, spoil. *See* CRIMES, GIVE.

rapid *adjective*
1. Characterized by great celerity : breakneck, expeditious, fast, fleet, quick, speedy, swift. *Informal:* hell-for-leather. ***Idiom:*** quick as a bunny (*or* wink). *See* FAST. **2.** Accomplished in very little time : brief, expeditious, fast, flying, hasty, hurried, quick, short, speedy, swift. *See* FAST.

rapidity *noun*
Rapidness of movement or activity : celerity, dispatch, expedition, expeditiousness, fleetness, haste, hurry, hustle, quickness, rapidness, speed, speediness, swiftness. *See* FAST.

rapidness *noun*
Rapidness of movement or activity : celerity, dispatch, expedition, expeditiousness, fleetness, haste, hurry, hustle, quickness, rapidity, speed, speediness, swiftness. *See* FAST.

rap out *verb* See **rap[1]**.

rapport *noun*
Harmonious mutual understanding : accord, agreement, concord, concordance, concurrence, consonance, harmony, tune, unity. ***Idiom:*** meeting of the minds. *See* AGREE.

rapprochement *noun*
A reestablishment of friendship or harmony : conciliation, reconcilement, reconciliation. *See* LOVE.

rap session *noun*
Slang. A meeting for the exchange of views : colloquium, conference, discussion, parley, seminar. *Informal:* powwow. *See* MEET, WORDS.

rapt *adjective*
Having one's thoughts fully occupied : absorbed, deep, intent, preoccupied. ***Idiom:*** wrapped up in. *See* AWARENESS, EXCITE.

rapture *noun*
A state of elated bliss : ecstasy, heaven, paradise, seventh heaven, transport. *Informal:* cloud nine. *See* HAPPY.

rare *adjective*
1. Rarely occurring or appearing : infrequent, occasional, scarce, sporadic, uncommon, unusual. ***Idiom:*** few and far between. *See* USUAL. **2.** Far beyond what is usual, normal, or customary : exceptional, extraordinary, magnificent, outstanding, preeminent, remarkable, singular, standout, towering, uncommon, unusual. *Informal:* standout. *Slang:* awesome, out of sight. *See* BETTER, USUAL. **3.** Marked by great diffusion of component particles : rarefied, thin. *See* TIGHTEN.

rarefied *adjective*
Marked by great diffusion of component particles : rare, thin. *See* TIGHTEN.

rarefy *verb*
To become diffuse : attenuate, thin. *See* TIGHTEN.

rarely *adverb*
At rare intervals : infrequently, little, occasionally, seldom, sporadically. ***Idioms:*** hardly (*or* scarcely) ever, once in a blue moon. *See* USUAL.

raring *adjective*
Informal. Intensely desirous or interested : agog, ardent, athirst, avid, bursting, eager, impatient, keen[1], solicitous, thirsting, thirsty. ***Idioms:*** champing at the bit, ready and willing. *See* CONCERN.

rascal *noun*
One who causes minor trouble or damage : devil, imp, mischief, prankster, rogue, scamp. *Informal:* cutup. *See* GOOD.

rascality *noun*
Annoying yet harmless, usually playful acts : devilry, deviltry, diablerie, high jinks, impishness, mischief, mischievousness, prankishness, roguery, roguishness, tomfoolery. *Informal:* shenanigan (often used in plural). *See* GOOD.

rash[1] *adjective*
Characterized by unthinking boldness and haste : brash, foolhardy, harum-scarum, hasty, headlong, hotheaded, ill-considered, impetuous, improvident, impulsive, incautious, madcap, precipitant, precipitate, reckless, slapdash, temerarious, unconsidered. *See* CAREFUL.

rash[2] *noun*
A sudden increase in something, as the occurrence of a disease : epidemic, outbreak, plague. *See* INCREASE.

rashness *noun*
1. Careless headlong action : haste, hastiness, hurriedness, precipitance, precipitancy, precipitateness, precipitation, rush. *See* CAREFUL. **2.** Foolhardy boldness or disregard of danger : brashness, foolhardiness, incautiousness, recklessness, temerariousness, temerity. *See* CAREFUL.

rasp *verb*
To bring or come into abrasive contact, often with a harsh grating sound : grate, scrape, scratch. *See* SOUNDS.

raspberry *noun*
Slang. Any of various derisive sounds of disapproval : boo, catcall, hiss, hoot. *Slang:* bird, Bronx cheer, razz. *See* SOUNDS.

rasping *adjective*
Disagreeable to the sense of hearing : dry, grating, harsh, hoarse, jarring, raspy, raucous, rough, scratchy, squawky, strident. *See* SOUNDS.

raspy *adjective*
Disagreeable to the sense of hearing : dry, grating, harsh, hoarse, jarring, rasping, raucous, rough, scratchy, squawky, strident. *See* SOUNDS.

rat *noun*
1. *Informal.* One who betrays : betrayer, double-crosser, Judas, traitor. *See* TRUST. **2.** *Informal.* One who gives incriminating information about others : informant, informer, tattler, tattletale. *Informal:* tipster. *Slang:* fink, snitch, snitcher, squealer, stoolie, stool pigeon. *See* KNOWLEDGE, LAW. **3.** *Informal.* A person who has defected : apostate, defector, deserter, recreant, renegade, runagate, tergiversator, turncoat. *See* APPROACH.

rat *verb* **1.** *Slang.* To abandon one's cause or party usually to join another : apostatize, defect, desert[3], renegade, tergiversate, turn. ***Idioms:*** change sides, turn one's coat. *See* APPROACH, TRUST. **2.** *Slang.* To be treacherous to. Also used with *on* : betray, double-cross. *Slang:* sell out. ***Idiom:*** sell down the river. *See* TRUST. **3.** *Slang.* To give incriminating information about others, especially to the authorities : inform, talk, tattle, tip[3] (off). *Slang:* fink, sing, snitch, squeal, stool. ***Idiom:*** blow the whistle. *See* KNOWLEDGE, LAW.

rat-a-tat-tat *noun*
A sudden sharp, explosive noise : bang, bark, clap, crack, explosion, pop[1], report, snap. *See* SOUNDS.

rate[1] *verb*
1. To make a judgment as to the worth or value of : appraise, assay, assess, calculate, estimate, evaluate, gauge, judge, size up, valuate, value. ***Idiom:*** take the measure of. *See* VALUE. **2.** To assign to a class or classes : categorize, class, classify, distribute, grade, group, pigeonhole, place, range, rank[1]. *See* GROUP, VALUE.

3. *Informal.* To acquire as a result of one's behavior or effort : deserve, earn, gain, get, merit, win. *See* GET.

rate² *verb*
To reprimand loudly or harshly : bawl out, berate. *Informal:* tell off. ***Idioms:*** give hell to, give it to. *See* ATTACK.

rather *adverb*
To some extent : fairly, pretty. ***Idiom:*** more or less. *See* BIG.

ratification *noun*
An act of confirming officially : affirmation, approval, confirmation, sanction. *See* LAW.

ratify *verb*
To accept officially : adopt, affirm, approve, confirm, pass, sanction. *See* ACCEPT, LAW.

ratiocinate *verb*
To use the powers of the mind : cerebrate, cogitate, deliberate, reflect, speculate, think. ***Idioms:*** put on one's thinking cap, use one's head. *See* THOUGHTS.

ratiocination *noun*
Exact, valid, and rational reasoning : logic, rationality, reason. *See* REASON.

ratiocinative *adjective*
Able to reason validly : analytic, analytical, logical, rational. *See* REASON.

ration *noun*
That which is allotted : allocation, allotment, allowance, dole, lot, measure, part, portion, quantum, quota, share, split. *Informal:* cut. *Slang:* divvy. *See* COLLECT.
ration *verb* To give out in portions or shares. Also used with *out* : deal (out), dispense, distribute, divide, dole out, parcel out, portion (out), share. *Slang:* divvy. *See* COLLECT.

rational *adjective*
1. Able to reason validly : analytic, analytical, logical, ratiocinative. *See* REASON. 2. Possessing, proceeding from, or exhibiting good judgment and prudence : balanced, commonsensible, commonsensical, judicious, levelheaded, prudent, reasonable, sagacious, sage, sane, sapient, sensible, sound², well-founded, well-grounded, wise¹. *See* REASON, SANE. 3. Mentally healthy : compos mentis, lucid, sane. ***Idioms:*** all there, in one's right mind, of sound mind. *See* SANE. 4. Consistent with reason and intellect : consequent, intelligent, logical, reasonable. *See* REASON.

rationale *noun*
1. What is sound or reasonable : logic, rationality, rationalness, reason, sense. ***Idiom:*** rhyme or reason. *See* REASON. 2. A statement of causes or motives : account, explanation, justification, rationalization, reason. *See* EXPLAIN.

rationality *noun*
1. What is sound or reasonable : logic, rationale, rationalness, reason, sense. ***Idiom:*** rhyme or reason. *See* REASON. 2. Exact, valid, and rational reasoning : logic, ratiocination, reason. *See* REASON.

rationalization *noun*
A statement of causes or motives : account, explanation, justification, rationale, reason. *See* EXPLAIN.

rationalize *verb*
1. To show to be just, right, or valid : excuse, justify, vindicate. ***Idiom:*** make a case for. *See* RIGHT. 2. To offer reasons for or a cause of : account for, explain, justify. *See* EXPLAIN.

rationalness *noun*
What is sound or reasonable : logic, rationale, rationality, reason, sense. ***Idiom:*** rhyme or reason. *See* REASON.

rattle *verb*
1. To make or cause to make a succession of short, sharp sounds : brattle, chatter, clack, clatter. *See* SOUNDS. 2. To talk volubly, persistently, and usually inconsequentially. Also used with *on* : babble, blabber, chatter, chitchat, clack, jabber, palaver, prate, prattle, run on. *Informal:* go on, spiel. *Slang:* gab, gas, jaw, yak. ***Idioms:*** run off at the mouth, shoot the breeze (*or* bull). *See* WORDS. 3. *Informal.* To impair or destroy the composure of : agitate, bother, discompose, disquiet, distract, disturb, flurry, fluster, perturb, rock, ruffle, shake (up), toss, unsettle, upset. *See* CALM.

ratty *adjective*
Slang. Showing signs of wear and tear or neglect : bedraggled, broken-down, decaying, decrepit, dilapidated, dingy, down-at-heel, faded, mangy, rundown, scrubby, scruffy, seedy, shabby, shoddy, sleazy, tattered, tatty, threadbare. *Informal:* tacky². ***Idioms:*** all the worse for wear, gone to pot (*or* seed), past cure (*or* hope). *See* BETTER.

raucous *adjective*
Disagreeable to the sense of hearing : dry, grating, harsh, hoarse, jarring, rasping, raspy, rough, scratchy, squawky, strident. *See* SOUNDS.

raunch *noun*
1. *Slang.* The quality or state of being obscene : bawdiness, coarseness, dirtiness, filthiness, foulness, grossness, lewdness, obscenity, profaneness, profanity, scurrility, scurrilousness, smuttiness, vulgarity, vulgarness. *Slang:* raunchiness.

See DECENT. **2.** *Slang.* Something that is offensive to accepted standards of decency : bawdry, dirt, filth, obscenity, profanity, ribaldry, scatology, smut, vulgarity. *See* DECENT.

raunchiness *noun*
Slang. The quality or state of being obscene : bawdiness, coarseness, dirtiness, filthiness, foulness, grossness, lewdness, obscenity, profaneness, profanity, scurrility, scurrilousness, smuttiness, vulgarity, vulgarness. *Slang:* raunch. *See* DECENT.

raunchy *adjective*
Slang. Offensive to accepted standards of decency : barnyard, bawdy, broad, coarse, dirty, Fescennine, filthy, foul, gross, lewd, nasty, obscene, profane, ribald, scatologic, scatological, scurrilous, smutty, vulgar. *See* DECENT.

ravage *verb*
1. To destroy completely as or as if by conquering : desolate, devastate, waste. ***Idiom:*** lay waste. *See* HELP. **2.** To rob of goods by force, especially in time of war : depredate, despoil, havoc, loot, pillage, plunder, ransack, rape, sack[2], spoliate, strip[1]. *Archaic:* harrow, spoil. *See* CRIMES, GIVE.

rave *verb*
1. To speak in a loud, pompous, or prolonged manner : declaim, harangue, mouth, perorate, rant. *See* WORDS. **2.** To show enthusism : carry on, rhapsodize. *See* FEELINGS.

ravel *verb*
To make complex, intricate, or perplexing : complicate, embarrass, entangle, involve, perplex, snarl[2], tangle. *See* SIMPLE.

ravenous *adjective*
1. Desiring or craving food : famished, hungry, starving, voracious. *See* INGESTION. **2.** Wanting to eat or drink more than one can reasonably consume : edacious, gluttonous, greedy, hoggish, piggish, voracious. *See* DESIRE, INGESTION. **3.** Having an insatiable appetite for an activity or pursuit : avid, edacious, gluttonous, greedy, omnivorous, rapacious, unappeasable, voracious. *See* DESIRE.

ravenousness *noun*
The quality or condition of being voracious : avidity, edacity, omnivorousness, rapaciousness, rapacity, voracity. *See* DESIRE.

ravish *verb*
To compel (another) to participate in or submit to a sexual act : assault, force, rape, violate. *See* SEX.

ravishing *adjective*
Having qualities that delight the eye : attractive, beauteous, beautiful, comely, fair, good-looking, gorgeous, handsome, lovely, pretty, pulchritudinous, sightly, stunning. *Scots:* bonny. ***Idiom:*** easy on the eyes. *See* BEAUTIFUL.

raw *adjective*
1. Not cooked : uncooked. *See* INGESTION. **2.** In a natural state and still not prepared for use : crude, native, unprocessed, unrefined. *See* CLEAN. **3.** Lacking expert, careful craftsmanship : crude, primitive, rough, rude, unpolished. *See* GOOD. **4.** Lacking experience and the knowledge gained from it : green, inexperienced, inexpert, uninitiate, uninitiated, unpracticed, unseasoned, untried, unversed. *See* ABILITY.

rawboned *adjective*
Having little flesh or fat on the body : angular, bony, fleshless, gaunt, lank, lanky, lean[2], meager, scrawny, skinny, slender, slim, spare, thin, twiggy, weedy. ***Idioms:*** all skin and bones, thin as a rail. *See* FAT.

raw deal *noun*
An act that is not just : disservice, inequity, injustice, wrong. *Law:* injury. *See* LAW, RIGHT.

rawness *noun*
Lack of experience and the knowledge gained from it : greenness, inexperience, inexpertness. *See* ABILITY.

ray *noun*
A series of particles or waves traveling close together in parallel paths : beam, shaft. *See* LIGHT.

raze *verb*
To pull down or break up so that reconstruction is impossible : demolish, destroy, dismantle, dynamite, knock down, level, pull down, pulverize, tear down, wreck. *Aerospace:* destruct. *See* HELP.

razz *noun*
Slang. Any of various derisive sounds of disapproval : boo, catcall, hiss, hoot. *Slang:* bird, Bronx cheer, raspberry. *See* SOUNDS.
razz *verb Slang.* To tease or mock good-humoredly : banter, chaff, joke, josh. *Informal:* kid, rib, ride. *Slang:* jive, rag[2]. *See* LAUGHTER.

reach *verb*
1. To extend, especially an appendage : outstretch, stretch (out). *See* REACH. **2.** To succeed in doing : accomplish, achieve, attain, gain, realize. *Slang:* score. *See* DO. **3.** To succeed in communicating with : contact, get. ***Idioms:*** catch up with, get hold of, get in touch with, get

through to, get to. *See* REACH. **4.** To proceed on a certain course or for a certain distance : carry, extend, go, lead, run, stretch. *See* REACH. **5.** To come to a particular place : arrive, check in, get in, pull in, show up, turn up. *Slang:* blow in. ***Idiom:*** make (*or* put in) an appearance. *See* START. **6.** To come to in number or quantity : aggregate, amount, number, run into, total. ***Idiom:*** add up to. *See* INCREASE.

reach *noun* **1.** The measure of how far or long something goes in space, time, or degree : extent, length, span, stretch. *See* BIG. **2.** The ability or power to seize or attain : capacity, compass, grasp, range, scope. *See* ABILITY. **3.** The extent of one's perception, understanding, knowledge, or vision : horizon, ken, purview, range, scope. *See* ABILITY, KNOWLEDGE, SEE. **4.** An area within which something or someone exists, acts, or has power : ambit, compass, extension, extent, orbit, purview, range, realm, scope, sphere, sweep, swing. *See* TERRITORY. **5.** A wide and open area : distance, expanse, expansion, extent, space, spread, stretch, sweep. *See* PLACE.

react *verb*
1. To act in return to something, as a stimulus : respond. *See* ACTION. **2.** To present with a specified reaction : greet, meet[1], respond. *See* FEELINGS, GREETING.

reaction *noun*
1. An action elicited by a stimulus : response, retroaction. *See* ACTION. **2.** The way in which a machine or other thing performs or functions : behavior, functioning, operation, performance, working (often used in plural). *See* ACTION, MACHINE.

reactionary *adjective*
1. Vehemently, often fanatically opposing progress or reform : die-hard, mossbacked, ultraconservative. *See* POLITICS. **2.** Clinging to obsolete ideas : backward, conservative, unprogressive. *See* POLITICS.

reactionary *noun* A person who vehemently, often fanatically opposes progress and favors return to a previous condition : die-hard, mossback, ultraconservative. *See* POLITICS.

reactivate *verb*
To rouse from a state of inactivity or quiescence : reanimate, reawaken, rekindle, renew, resurrect, resuscitate, revitalize, revive, revivify. *See* AWARENESS.

reactivation *noun*
The act of reviving or condition of being revived : rebirth, renaissance, renascence, renewal, resurgence, resurrection, resuscitation, revitalization, revival, revivification. *See* AWARENESS.

read *verb*
1. To perceive and recognize the meaning of : accept, apprehend, catch (on), compass, comprehend, conceive, fathom, follow, get, grasp, make out, see, sense, take, take in, understand. *Informal:* savvy. *Slang:* dig. *Chiefly British:* twig. *Scots:* ken. ***Idioms:*** get (*or* have) a handle on, get the picture. *See* UNDERSTAND. **2.** To understand in a particular way : construe, interpret, take. *See* UNDERSTAND. **3.** To give a precise indication of, as on a register or scale : indicate, mark, record, register, show. *See* SHOW.

readiness *noun*
1. The condition of being made ready beforehand : preparation, preparedness. *See* PREPARED. **2.** The ability to perform without apparent effort : ease, easiness, effortlessness, facileness, facility. *See* EASY.

reading *noun*
One's artistic conception as shown by the way in which something such as a dramatic role or musical composition is rendered : execution, interpretation, performance, realization, rendering, rendition. *See* PERFORMING ARTS.

ready *adjective*
1. In a state of preparedness : set[1]. *Informal:* go. *Slang:* together. ***Idioms:*** all set, in working order. *See* PREPARED. **2.** Disposed to accept or agree : acquiescent, agreeable, game, minded, willing. *Archaic:* fain. *See* WILLING.

ready *verb* **1.** To prepare (oneself) for action : brace, forearm, fortify, gird, steel, strengthen. ***Idiom:*** gird (*or* gird up) one's loins. *See* PREPARED. **2.** To cause to be ready, as for use, consumption, or a special purpose : fit[1], fix, make, prepare, prime. *See* PREPARED.

real *adjective*
1. Having verifiable existence : concrete, objective, substantial, substantive, tangible. *See* REAL. **2.** In agreement or correspondence with fact : actual, true. *See* REAL. **3.** Not counterfeit or copied : actual, authentic, bona fide, genuine, good, indubitable, original, true, undoubted, unquestionable. *See* TRUE. **4.** Devoid of any hypocrisy or pretense : genuine, heartfelt, hearty, honest, natural, sincere, true, unaffected, unfeigned, unmannered. *See* TRUE.

realistic *adjective*
1. Having or indicating an awareness of things as they really are : down-to-earth, hard, hard-

headed, matter-of-fact, objective, practical, pragmatic, pragmatical, prosaic, sober, tough-minded, unromantic. *See* EXCITE, REAL. **2.** Accurately representing what is depicted or described : lifelike, natural, naturalistic, true, true-life, truthful. *See* REAL. **3.** Described verbally in sharp and accurate detail : graphic, lifelike, photographic, pictorial, picturesque, vivid. *See* SPECIFIC, WORDS.

reality *noun*
1. The fact or state of existing or of being actual : actuality, being, entity, existence. *See* BE, REAL. **2.** The quality of being actual or factual : actuality, fact, factuality, factualness, truth. *See* REAL. **3.** Something having real, demonstrable existence : actuality, event, fact, phenomenon. *See* REAL.

realization *noun*
1. The condition of being fulfilled : consummation, culmination, fruition, fulfillment, materialization. *See* DO, HAPPY. **2.** The condition of being in full force or operation : actualization, being, effect, materialization. *See* BE. **3.** One's artistic conception as shown by the way in which something such as a dramatic role or musical composition is rendered : execution, interpretation, performance, reading, rendering, rendition. *See* PERFORMING ARTS.

realize *verb*
1. To make real or actual : actualize, materialize. ***Idioms:*** bring to pass, carry into effect. *See* DO. **2.** To succeed in doing : accomplish, achieve, attain, gain, reach. *Slang:* score. *See* DO. **3.** To make as income or profit : bring in, clear, draw, earn, gain, gross, net[2], pay, produce, repay, return, yield. *See* MONEY. **4.** To achieve (a certain price) : bring (in), fetch, sell for. *See* GET.

really *adverb*
1. In point of fact : actually, indeed. *See* REAL, TRUE. **2.** In truth : actually, fairly, genuinely, indeed, positively, truly, truthfully, verily. ***Idiom:*** for fair. *See* REAL, TRUE.

realm *noun*
1. An area within which something or someone exists, acts, or has influence or power : ambit, compass, extension, extent, orbit, purview, range, reach, scope, sphere, sweep, swing. *See* TERRITORY. **2.** A sphere of activity, experience, study, or interest : area, arena, bailiwick, circle, department, domain, field, orbit, province, scene, subject, terrain, territory, world. *Slang:* bag. *See* TERRITORY.

realness *noun*
The quality of being authentic : authenticity, genuineness, truthfulness, validity. *See* TRUE.

ream *noun*
An indeterminately great amount or number : jillion, million (often used in plural), multiplicity, trillion. *Informal:* bushel, gob[1] (often used in plural), heap (often used in plural), load (often used in plural), lot, oodles, passel, peck[2], scad (often used in plural), slew, wad, zillion. *See* BIG.

reanimate *verb*
To rouse from a state of inactivity or quiescence : reactivate, reawaken, rekindle, renew, resurrect, resuscitate, revitalize, revive, revivify. *See* AWARENESS.

reap *verb*
To collect ripe crops : crop, garner, gather, harvest, pick. *See* COLLECT.

reappear *verb*
To happen again or repeatedly : recur, reoccur. *See* REPETITION.

reappearance *noun*
A repeated occurrence : recurrence, reoccurrence, return. *See* REPETITION.

rear[1] *noun*
1. The hindmost part of something : end, tag end, tail, tail end. *See* PRECEDE. **2.** The part or area farthest from the front : back, rearward. *See* PRECEDE. **3.** *Informal.* The part of one's back on which one rests in sitting : buttock (used in plural), derrière, posterior, rump, seat. *Informal:* backside, behind, bottom. *Slang:* bun (used in plural), fanny, tush. *Chiefly British:* bum[2]. *See* OVER.

rear *adjective* Located in the rear : back, hind, hindmost, posterior, postern. *Nautical:* after. *See* PRECEDE.

rear[2] *verb*
1. To take care of and educate (a child) : bring up, raise. *See* CARE FOR. **2.** To raise upright : erect, pitch, put up, raise, set up, upraise, uprear. *See* HORIZONTAL, RISE. **3.** To move (something) to a higher position : boost, elevate, heave, hoist, lift, pick up, raise, take up, uphold, uplift, upraise, uprear. *See* RISE. **4.** To make or form (a structure) : build, construct, erect, put up, raise. *See* MAKE.

rearmost *adjective*
Bringing up the rear : endmost, hindermost, hindmost, last[1], lattermost. *See* START.

rearrangement *noun*
A change in normal place or position : dislocation, displacement, disturbance, move, movement, shift. *See* MOVE.

rearward *adverb*
1. Toward the back : about, around, back,

backward, backwards. *See* PRECEDE. **2.** In or toward a former location or condition : about, around, back, backward, backwards, round. *See* APPROACH.

rearward *noun* The part or area farthest from the front : back, rear[1]. *See* PRECEDE.

reason *noun*

1. A basis for an action or a decision : cause, ground (often used in plural), motivation, motive, spring. *See* START. **2.** A justifying fact or consideration : basis, foundation, justification, warrant. *See* TRUE. **3.** A statement of causes or motives : account, explanation, justification, rationale, rationalization. *See* EXPLAIN. **4.** A fact or circumstance that gives logical support to an assertion, claim, or proposal : argument, ground (often used in plural), proof, wherefore, why. *Idiom:* why and wherefore. *See* REASON. **5.** That which provides a reason or justification : call, cause, ground (often used in plural), justification, necessity, occasion, wherefore, why. *Idiom:* why and wherefore. *See* START. **6.** Exact, valid, and rational reasoning : logic, ratiocination, rationality. *See* REASON. **7.** What is sound or reasonable : logic, rationale, rationality, rationalness, sense. *Idiom:* rhyme or reason. *See* REASON. **8.** A healthy mental state : lucidity, lucidness, mind, saneness, sanity, sense (often used in plural), soundness, wit (used in plural). *Slang:* marble (used in plural). *See* SANE.

reasonable *adjective*

1. Consistent with reason and intellect : consequent, intelligent, logical, rational. *See* REASON. **2.** Possessing, proceeding from, or exhibiting good judgment and prudence : balanced, commonsensible, commonsensical, judicious, levelheaded, prudent, rational, sagacious, sage, sane, sapient, sensible, sound[2], well-founded, well-grounded, wise[1]. *See* REASON, SANE. **3.** Kept within sensible limits : conservative, discreet, moderate, restrained, temperate. *See* PLAIN, RESTRAINT. **4.** Not excessive or extreme in amount, degree, or force : moderate, modest, temperate. *See* BIG, EDGE. **5.** Suited to or within the means of ordinary people : moderate, modest, popular. *See* MONEY.

reassume *verb*

To occupy or take again : re-claim, reoccupy, repossess, resume, retake, take back. *See* GIVE.

reawaken *verb*

To rouse from a state of inactivity or quiescence : reactivate, reanimate, rekindle, renew, resurrect, resuscitate, revitalize, revive, revivify. *See* AWARENESS.

rebate *noun*

An amount deducted : abatement, deduction, discount, reduction. *See* INCREASE.

rebate *verb* **1.** To take away (a quantity) from another quantity : abate, deduct, discount, subtract, take (off). *Informal:* knock off. *See* INCREASE. **2.** To grow or cause to grow gradually less : abate, decrease, diminish, drain, dwindle, ebb, lessen, let up, peter (out), reduce, tail away (*or* off), taper (off). *See* INCREASE.

rebel *verb*

To refuse allegiance to and oppose by force a government or ruling authority : mutiny, revolt, rise (up). *See* RESIST.

rebel *noun* A person who rebels : insurgent, insurrectionary, insurrectionist, mutineer, revolutionary, revolutionist. *See* RESIST.

rebellion *noun*

Organized opposition intended to change or overthrow existing authority : insurgence, insurgency, insurrection, mutiny, revolt, revolution, sedition, uprising. *See* RESIST.

rebellious *adjective*

Participating in open revolt against a government or ruling authority : insurgent, mutinous, revolutionary. *See* RESIST.

rebirth *noun*

1. A fundamental change in one's beliefs : conversion, metanoia, regeneration. *See* CHANGE. **2.** The act of reviving or condition of being revived : reactivation, renaissance, renascence, renewal, resurgence, resurrection, resuscitation, revitalization, revival, revivification. *See* AWARENESS.

rebound *verb*

1. To spring back after colliding with something : bounce. *See* APPROACH, MOVE. **2.** To jerk backward, as a gun upon firing : recoil. *See* FORWARD. **3.** To send back the sound of : echo, reecho, reflect, repeat, resound, reverberate. *See* SOUNDS.

rebound *noun* An act of bouncing or a bouncing movement : bounce, bound[1]. *See* APPROACH, MOVE.

rebuff *noun*

A deliberate slight : cut, snub, spurn. *Informal:* cold shoulder, go-by. *See* ACCEPT.

rebuff *verb* To slight (someone) deliberately : cut, shun, snub, spurn. *Informal:* coldshoulder. *Idioms:* close (*or* shut) the door on, give someone the cold shoulder, give someone the go-by, turn one's back on. *See* ACCEPT.

rebuild *verb*
To bring back to a previous normal condition : reclaim, recondition, reconstruct, rehabilitate, reinstate, rejuvenate, renovate, restitute, restore. *See* HELP.

rebuke *verb*
To criticize for a fault or an offense : admonish, call down, castigate, chastise, chide, dress down, rap[1], reprimand, reproach, reprove, scold, tax, upbraid. *Informal:* bawl out, lambaste. *Slang:* chew out. ***Idioms:*** bring (*or* call *or* take) to task, call on the carpet, haul (*or* rake) over the coals, let someone have it. *See* ATTACK, PRAISE.
rebuke *noun* Words expressive of strong disapproval : admonishment, admonition, reprimand, reproach, reproof, scolding. *Slang:* rap[1]. *See* PRAISE.

rebut *verb*
To prove or show to be false : belie, confute, discredit, disprove, refute. *See* AFFIRM.

recalcitrance *noun*
1. The disposition boldly to defy or resist authority or an opposing force : contempt, contumacy, defiance, despite, recalcitrancy. *See* RESIST. **2.** The quality or condition of being unruly : disorderliness, fractiousness, indocility, intractability, intractableness, obstinacy, obstinateness, obstreperousness, recalcitrancy, refractoriness, uncontrollability, uncontrollableness, ungovernableness, unmanageability, unruliness, untowardness, wildness. *See* CONTROL, ORDER, PEACE, RESIST.

recalcitrancy *noun*
1. The disposition boldly to defy or resist authority or an opposing force : contempt, contumacy, defiance, despite, recalcitrance. *See* RESIST. **2.** The quality or condition of being unruly : disorderliness, fractiousness, indocility, intractability, intractableness, obstinacy, obstinateness, obstreperousness, recalcitrance, refractoriness, uncontrollability, uncontrollableness, ungovernableness, unmanageability, unruliness, untowardness, wildness. *See* CONTROL, ORDER, PEACE, RESIST.

recalcitrant *adjective*
1. Marked by defiance : contumacious, defiant. *See* RESIST. **2.** Not submitting to discipline or control : disorderly, fractious, indocile, intractable, lawless, obstinate, obstreperous, refractory, uncontrollable, undisciplined, ungovernable, unmanageable, unruly, untoward, wild. ***Idiom:*** out of line. *See* CONTROL, ORDER, PEACE, RESIST.

recall *verb*
1. To renew an image or thought in the mind : bethink, mind, recollect, remember, reminisce, retain, revive, think. ***Idiom:*** bring to mind. *See* REMEMBER. **2.** To take back or remove : lift, repeal, rescind, reverse, revoke. *See* CONTINUE, LAW, MAKE. **3.** To disavow (something previously written or said) irrevocably and usually formally : abjure, recant, retract, take back, withdraw. *See* ACCEPT.
recall *noun* **1.** The power of retaining and recalling past experience : memory, recollection, remembrance, reminiscence. *See* REMEMBER. **2.** The act of reversing or annulling : repeal, rescission, reversal, revocation. *See* CONTINUE, LAW.

recant *verb*
To disavow (something previously written or said) irrevocably and usually formally : abjure, recall, retract, take back, withdraw. *See* ACCEPT.

recantation *noun*
A formal statement of disavowal : abjuration, palinode, retractation, retraction, withdrawal. *See* ACCEPT.

recap *verb*
Informal. To give a recapitulation of the salient facts of : abstract, epitomize, go over, recapitulate, review, run down, run through, summarize, sum up, synopsize, wrap up. *See* THOUGHTS.
recap *noun* *Informal.* A condensation of the essential or main points of something : recapitulation, rundown, run-through, sum, summary, summation, summing-up, wrap-up. *See* WORDS.

recapitulate *verb*
To give a recapitulation of the salient facts of : abstract, epitomize, go over, review, run down, run through, summarize, sum up, synopsize, wrap up. *Informal:* recap. *See* THOUGHTS.

recapitulation *noun*
A condensation of the essential or main points of something : rundown, run-through, sum, summary, summation, summing-up, wrap-up. *Informal:* recap. *See* WORDS.

recede *verb*
To move back or away from a point, limit, or mark : ebb, retract, retreat, retrocede, retrograde, retrogress. *See* APPROACH.

receivable *adjective*
Owed as a debt : due, outstanding, owed, owing, payable, unpaid, unsettled. *See* PAY.

receive *verb*
1. To admit to one's possession, presence, or awareness : accept, have, take. *See* ACCEPT.
2. To allow admittance, as to a group : accept, admit, take in. *See* ACCEPT.

received *adjective*
1. Generally approved or agreed upon : accepted, conventional, orthodox, recognized, sanctioned. *See* ACCEPT, AGREE, STRAIGHT, USUAL. **2.** Adhering to beliefs or practices approved by authority or tradition : canonical, orthodox, sanctioned, time-honored. *See* USUAL.

recent *adjective*
Of or relating to the present or times close to the present : latter-day, modern. *See* NEW, TIME.

recently *adverb*
1. Only a moment ago : just, newly. *See* TIME.
2. Not long ago : late, lately, latterly. ***Idiom:*** of late. *See* NEAR, PRECEDE, TIME.

receptive *adjective*
Ready and willing to receive favorably, as new ideas : acceptant, amenable, open, open-minded, responsive. *See* ACCEPT.

receptiveness *noun*
Ready acceptance of often new suggestions, ideas, influences, or opinions : open-mindedness, openness, receptivity, responsiveness. *See* ACCEPT.

receptivity *noun*
Ready acceptance of often new suggestions, ideas, influences, or opinions : open-mindedness, openness, receptiveness, responsiveness. *See* ACCEPT.

recess *noun*
A pause or interval, as from work or duty : break, intermission, respite, rest[1], time-out. *Informal:* breather. *See* CONTINUE.
recess *verb* To interrupt regular activity for a short period : break. ***Idioms:*** take a break, take a breather, take five (*or* ten). *See* CONTINUE.

recession *noun*
A period of decreased business activity and high unemployment : depression, slump. *See* RICH.

recidivation *noun*
A slipping from a higher or better condition to a lower or poorer one : backslide, backsliding, lapse, recidivism, relapse. *See* BETTER, REPETITION.

recidivism *noun*
A slipping from a higher or better condition to a lower or poorer one : backslide, backsliding, lapse, recidivation, relapse. *See* BETTER, REPETITION.

reciprocal *adjective*
Having the same relationship each to the other : mutual, reciprocative. *See* CONNECT.

reciprocate *verb*
1. To give or take mutually : requite, return. *See* CONNECT. **2.** To return like for like, especially to return an unfriendly or hostile action with a similar one : counter, hit back, retaliate, retort, strike back. *See* ATTACK, FORGIVENESS.

reciprocation *noun*
The act of retaliating : counteraction, counterattack, counterblow, reprisal, requital, retaliation, retribution, revenge, tit for tat, vengeance. ***Idioms:*** an eye for an eye, a tooth for a tooth, like for like, measure for measure. *See* ATTACK, FORGIVENESS.

reciprocative *adjective*
Having the same relationship each to the other : mutual, reciprocal. *See* CONNECT.

recite *verb*
To give a verbal account of : describe, narrate, recount, rehearse, relate, report, tell. *See* WORDS.

reckless *adjective*
1. Lacking or marked by a lack of care : careless, feckless, heedless, inattentive, irresponsible, thoughtless, unconcerned, unmindful, unthinking. *See* CAREFUL. **2.** Characterized by unthinking boldness and haste : brash, foolhardy, harum-scarum, hasty, headlong, hotheaded, ill-considered, impetuous, improvident, impulsive, incautious, madcap, precipitant, precipitate, rash[1], slapdash, temerarious, unconsidered. *See* CAREFUL.

recklessness *noun*
Foolhardy boldness or disregard of danger : brashness, foolhardiness, incautiousness, rashness, temerariousness, temerity. *See* CAREFUL.

reckon *verb*
1. To note (items) one by one so as to get a total : count, enumerate, number, numerate, tally, tell. *See* COUNT. **2.** To ascertain by mathematics : calculate, cast, cipher, compute, figure. *See* REASON. **3.** To calculate approximately : approximate, estimate, place, put, set[1]. *See* PRECISE. **4.** To look upon in a particular way : account, consider, deem, esteem, regard, see, view. *See* PERSPECTIVE.
5. *Informal.* To take for granted without proof : assume, posit, postulate, premise, presume, presuppose, suppose. *See* BELIEF.

reckon on (or **upon**) *verb* To place trust or confidence in : bank on (*or* upon), believe in, count on (*or* upon), depend on (*or* upon), rely on (*or* upon), trust (in). *See* TRUST.

reckoning *noun*
1. A noting of items one by one : count, enumeration, numeration, tally. *Archaic:* tale. *See* COUNT. **2.** The act, process, or result of calculating : calculation, computation, figuring. *See* REASON. **3.** A precise list of fees or charges : account, bill[1], check, invoice, statement. *Informal:* tab. *See* PAY.

reckon on or **upon** *verb* See **reckon.**

reclaim *verb*
1. To bring back to a previous normal condition : rebuild, recondition, reconstruct, rehabilitate, reinstate, rejuvenate, renovate, restitute, restore. *See* HELP. **2.** To extricate from an undesirable state : recover, redeem, rescue, salvage. *See* HELP.

re-claim *verb*
To occupy or take again : reassume, reoccupy, repossess, resume, retake, take back. *See* GIVE.

recline *verb*
1. To be or place oneself in a prostrate or recumbent position : lie[1] (down), repose, stretch (out). *See* HORIZONTAL. **2.** To take repose, as by sleeping or lying quietly : lie[1] (down), repose, rest[1], stretch (out). *See* CONTINUE.

recluse *adjective*
Solitary and shut off from society : secluded. *See* INCLUDE.

reclusion *noun*
The act of secluding or the state of being secluded : retirement, seclusion, sequestration. *See* INCLUDE.

recognition *noun*
Favorable notice, as of an achievement : acknowledgment, credit. *See* KNOWLEDGE.

recognize *verb*
1. To perceive to be identical with something held in the memory : know. *See* KNOWLEDGE, REMEMBER. **2.** To establish the identification of : identify, pinpoint, place. *Slang:* finger. ***Idiom:*** put one's finger on. *See* KNOWLEDGE. **3.** To express recognition of : acknowledge, admit. *See* AFFIRM, KNOWLEDGE.

recognized *adjective*
Generally approved or agreed upon : accepted, conventional, orthodox, received, sanctioned. *See* ACCEPT, AGREE, STRAIGHT, USUAL.

recoil *verb*
1. To jerk backward, as a gun upon firing : rebound. *See* FORWARD. **2.** To draw away involuntarily, usually out of fear or disgust : blench[1], cringe, flinch, quail, shrink, shy[1], start, wince. *See* APPROACH, SEEK.

recoil *noun* An act of drawing back in an involuntary or instinctive fashion : cringe, flinch, shrink, wince. *See* APPROACH, SEEK.

recollect *verb*
To renew an image or thought in the mind : bethink, mind, recall, remember, reminisce, retain, revive, think. ***Idiom:*** bring to mind. *See* REMEMBER.

recollection *noun*
1. The power of retaining and recalling past experience : memory, recall, remembrance, reminiscence. *See* REMEMBER. **2.** An act or instance of remembering : memory, remembrance, reminiscence. *See* REMEMBER.

recommend *verb*
1. To aid the cause of by approving or favoring : advocate, back, champion, endorse, get behind, plump for, side with, stand behind, stand by, support, uphold. ***Idioms:*** align oneself with, go to bat for, take the part of. *See* SUPPORT. **2.** To give recommendations to (someone) about a decision or course of action : advise, counsel. *Informal:* mentor. *See* OPINION.

recommendable *adjective*
Worth doing, especially for practical reasons : advisable, expedient, well[2]. *See* WISE.

recommendation *noun*
1. An indication of commendation or approval : backing, endorsement, support. *See* SUPPORT. **2.** A statement attesting to personal qualifications, character, and dependability : character, reference, testimonial. *See* SUPPORT. **3.** An opinion as to a decision or course of action : advice, counsel. *See* OPINION.

recompense *verb*
1. To give compensation to : compensate, indemnify, pay, redress, reimburse, remunerate, repay, requite. *See* PAY. **2.** To give payment to in return for goods or services rendered : compensate, pay, remunerate. *See* PAY. **3.** To give a satisfactory return to : compensate, indemnify, pay, remunerate, repay, requite, reward. *See* PAY.

recompense *noun* **1.** Something to make up for loss or damage : amends, compensation, indemnification, indemnity, offset, quittance, redress, reimbursement, remuneration, reparation, repayment, requital, restitution, satisfaction, setoff. *See* SUBSTITUTE. **2.** Something justly deserved : comeuppance, desert[2] (often used in plural), due, guerdon, reward, wage (often used in plural). *Informal:* lump[1] (used in plural). ***Idioms:*** what is coming to one, what one has coming. *See* REWARD. **3.** Something given in exchange for goods or services rendered : compensation, consideration, payment, remuneration. *See* PAY.

reconcile *verb*
1. To reestablish friendship between : conciliate, make up, reunite. *See* LOVE. **2.** To bring (something) into a state of agreement or accord : rectify, resolve, settle, smooth over, straighten out. *See* AGREE. **3.** To bring (oneself) to accept : resign. *See* ACCEPT. **4.** To make or become suitable to a particular situation or use : acclimate, acclimatize, accommodate, adapt, adjust, conform, fashion, fit[1], square, suit, tailor. *See* CHANGE. **5.** To bring into accord : accommodate, attune, conform, coordinate, harmonize, integrate, proportion, tune. *See* AGREE.

reconcilement *noun*
A reestablishment of friendship or harmony : conciliation, rapprochement, reconciliation. *See* LOVE.

reconciliation *noun*
A reestablishment of friendship or harmony : conciliation, rapprochement, reconcilement. *See* LOVE.

recondite *adjective*
Beyond the understanding of an average mind : abstruse, deep, esoteric, profound. *Slang:* heavy. *See* EASY, SURFACE.

recondition *verb*
1. To bring back to a previous normal condition : rebuild, reclaim, reconstruct, rehabilitate, reinstate, rejuvenate, renovate, restitute, restore. *See* HELP. **2.** To make new or as if new again : furbish, re-create, refresh, refurbish, rejuvenate, renew, renovate, restore, revamp. ***Idiom:*** give a new look to. *See* HELP, NEW.

reconnaissance *noun*
The act or an instance of exploring or investigating : exploration, investigation, probe. *See* INVESTIGATE.

reconnoiter *verb*
To go into or through for the purpose of making discoveries or acquiring information : delve, dig, explore, inquire, investigate, look into, probe, scout[1]. *See* INVESTIGATE.

reconsider *verb*
To consider again, especially with the possibility of change : reevaluate, reexamine, rethink, review. *See* THOUGHTS.

reconstruct *verb*
To bring back to a previous normal condition : rebuild, reclaim, recondition, rehabilitate, reinstate, rejuvenate, renovate, restitute, restore. *See* HELP.

record *verb*
1. To place on a list or in a record : enter, insert, post[3], register. *See* REMEMBER. **2.** To give a precise indication of, as on a register or scale : indicate, mark, read, register, show. *See* SHOW.

recount *verb*
To give a verbal account of : describe, narrate, recite, rehearse, relate, report, tell. *See* WORDS.

recoup *verb*
To get back : recover, regain, repossess, retrieve. *See* GET.
recoup *noun* The act of getting back or regaining : recovery, repossession, retrieval. *See* GET.

recourse *noun*
That to which one turns for help when in desperation : refuge, resort, resource. *See* HELP.

recover *verb*
1. To get back : recoup, regain, repossess, retrieve. *See* GET. **2.** To extricate from an undesirable state : reclaim, redeem, rescue, salvage. *See* HELP. **3.** To regain one's health : come around (*or* round), convalesce, gain, improve, mend, perk up, rally, recuperate. *See* HEALTH.

recovery *noun*
1. The act of getting back or regaining : recoup, repossession, retrieval. *See* GET. **2.** A return to normal health : rally, recuperation. *See* HEALTH. **3.** A return to former prosperity or status : comeback. *See* APPROACH, WIN.

recreance *noun*
An instance of defecting from or abandoning a cause : apostasy, defection, recreancy, tergiversation. *See* APPROACH, TRUST.

recreancy *noun*
An instance of defecting from or abandoning a cause : apostasy, defection, recreance, tergiversation. *See* APPROACH, TRUST.

recreant *adjective*
Not true to duty or obligation : disloyal, faithless, false, false-hearted, perfidious, traitorous, treacherous, unfaithful, untrue. *See* CONTINUE, TRUST.
recreant *noun* A person who has defected : apostate, defector, deserter, renegade, runagate, tergiversator, turncoat. *Informal:* rat. *See* APPROACH.

recreate *verb*
1. To occupy in an agreeable or pleasing way : amuse, divert, entertain, regale. *See* EXCITE.

2. To occupy oneself with amusement or diversion : disport, play, sport. *See* WORK.

re-create *verb*

To make new or as if new again : furbish, recondition, refresh, refurbish, rejuvenate, renew, renovate, restore, revamp. ***Idiom:*** give a new look to. *See* HELP, NEW.

recreation *noun*

1. Activity engaged in for relaxation and amusement : disport, diversion, fun, play, sport. *See* WORK. **2.** The condition of being amused : amusement, entertainment. *See* EXCITE.

3. Something, especially a performance or show, designed to entertain : amusement, distraction, diversion, entertainment. *See* EXCITE.

recrudesce *verb*

To come back to a former condition : recur, reoccur, return, revert. *See* REPETITION.

rectify *verb*

1. To make right what is wrong : amend, correct, emend, mend, redress, reform, remedy, right. *See* CORRECT. **2.** To bring (something) into a state of agreement or accord : reconcile, resolve, settle, smooth over, straighten out. *See* AGREE.

rectitude *noun*

The quality or state of being morally sound : good, goodness, morality, probity, righteousness, rightness, uprightness, virtue, virtuousness. *See* RIGHT.

recumbent *adjective*

Lying down : decumbent, flat, horizontal, procumbent, prone, prostrate. *See* HORIZONTAL.

recuperate *verb*

To regain one's health : come around (*or* round), convalesce, gain, improve, mend, perk up, rally, recover. *See* HEALTH.

recuperation *noun*

A return to normal health : rally, recovery. *See* HEALTH.

recur *verb*

1. To happen again or repeatedly : reappear, reoccur. *See* REPETITION. **2.** To come back to a former condition : recrudesce, reoccur, return, revert. *See* REPETITION.

recurrence *noun*

A repeated occurrence : reappearance, reoccurrence, return. *See* REPETITION.

recurrent *adjective*

Happening or appearing at regular intervals : cyclic, cyclical, isochronal, isochronous, periodic, periodical. ***Idiom:*** like clockwork. *See* REPETITION.

red-blooded *adjective*

Full of vigor : able-bodied, iron, lusty, robust, strapping, sturdy, vigorous, vital. *See* STRONG.

redden *verb*

To become red in the face : blush, color, crimson, flush, glow, mantle. *See* EXPRESS.

redeem *verb*

1. To extricate from an undesirable state : reclaim, recover, rescue, salvage. *See* HELP.

2. To make up for : balance, compensate, counterbalance, counterpoise, countervail, neutralize, offset, outweigh, set off. *See* SUBSTITUTE.

red-hot *adjective*

1. Marked by much heat : ardent, baking, blistering, boiling, broiling, burning, fiery, heated, hot, roasting, scalding, scorching, searing, sizzling, sultry, sweltering, torrid. *See* HOT.

2. Fired with intense feeling : ardent, blazing, burning, dithyrambic, fervent, fervid, fiery, flaming, glowing, heated, hot-blooded, impassioned, passionate, perfervid, scorching, torrid. *See* FEELINGS. **3.** Of great current interest : live[2]. *Informal:* hot. *See* EXCITE.

redo *verb*

To do or perform (an act) again : duplicate, repeat. *See* REPETITION.

redolence *noun*

A sweet or pleasant odor : aroma, bouquet, fragrance, perfume, scent. *See* SMELLS.

redolent *adjective*

Having a pleasant odor : aromatic, fragrant. *See* SMELLS.

redouble *verb*

1. To make or become twice as great : double, duplicate, geminate, twin. *See* BIG, INCREASE.

2. To make greater in intensity or severity : aggravate, deepen, enhance, heighten, intensify. *See* INCREASE.

redoubtable *adjective*

1. Causing or able to cause fear : appalling, dire, direful, dreadful, fearful, fearsome, formidable, frightful, ghastly, scary, terrible, tremendous. *See* FEAR. **2.** Widely known and esteemed : celebrated, distinguished, eminent, famed, famous, great, illustrious, notable, noted, preeminent, prestigious, prominent, renowned. *See* KNOWLEDGE, RESPECT.

redress *verb*

1. To make right what is wrong : amend, correct, emend, mend, rectify, reform, remedy, right. *See* CORRECT. **2.** To exact revenge for or from : avenge, pay back, pay off, repay, requite, vindicate. *Informal:* fix. *Archaic:* wreak. ***Idioms:*** even the score, get back at, get even with, pay back in kind (*or* in one's own coin), settle (*or* square) accounts, take an eye for an eye. *See* FORGIVENESS. **3.** To give compensation to : compensate, indemnify, pay, recompense, reimburse, remunerate, repay, requite. *See* PAY.

redress *noun* Something to make up for loss or damage : amends, compensation, indemnification, indemnity, offset, quittance, recompense, reimbursement, remuneration, reparation, repayment, requital, restitution, satisfaction, setoff. *See* SUBSTITUTE.

reduce *verb*
1. To grow or cause to grow gradually less : abate, decrease, diminish, drain, dwindle, ebb, lessen, let up, peter (out), rebate, tail away (*or* off), taper (off). *See* INCREASE. **2.** To make short or shorter the duration or extent of : abbreviate, abridge, condense, curtail, shorten. *See* INCREASE, LONG. **3.** To lower in rank or grade : break, bump, degrade, demote, downgrade. *Slang:* bust. *See* RISE. **4.** To become or make less in price or value : cheapen, depreciate, depress, devaluate, devalue, downgrade, lower[2], mark down, write down. *See* INCREASE, MONEY. **5.** To lose body weight, as by dieting : slim (down), trim down. *See* FAT, INCREASE.

reduction *noun*
1. The act or process of decreasing : abatement, curtailment, cut, cutback, decrease, decrement, diminishment, diminution, drain, slash, slowdown, taper. *See* INCREASE. **2.** The act or an instance of demoting : degradation, demotion. *See* RISE. **3.** A lowering in price or value : depreciation, devaluation, markdown, write-down. *See* INCREASE, MONEY. **4.** An amount deducted : abatement, deduction, discount, rebate. *See* INCREASE.

redundancy *noun*
Words or the use of words in excess of those needed for clarity or precision : diffuseness, diffusion, long-windedness, pleonasm, prolixity, verbiage, verboseness, verbosity, windiness, wordage, wordiness. *See* EXCESS, STYLE, WORDS.

redundant *adjective*
Using or containing an excessive number of words : diffuse, long-winded, periphrastic, pleonastic, prolix, verbose, wordy. *See* EXCESS, STYLE, WORDS.

reduplication *noun*
Something closely resembling another : carbon copy, copy, duplicate, facsimile, image, likeness, replica, replication, reproduction, simulacrum. *Archaic:* simulacre. *Law:* counterpart. *See* SAME.

reecho *verb*
To send back the sound of : echo, rebound, reflect, repeat, resound, reverberate. *See* SOUNDS.

reek *verb*
To have or give off a foul odor : smell, stink. *Idiom:* smell to high heaven. *See* SMELLS.

reeky *adjective*
Having an unpleasant odor : fetid, foul, foul-smelling, malodorous, mephitic, noisome, stinking. *Informal:* smelly. *See* SMELLS.

reel *verb*
1. To walk unsteadily : falter, lurch, stagger, stumble, teeter, totter, weave, wobble. *See* MOVE. **2.** To have the sensation of turning in circles : spin, swim, swirl, whirl. *See* REPETITION.

reeling *adjective*
Having a sensation of whirling or falling : dizzy, giddy, lightheaded, vertiginous, woozy. *See* AWARENESS.

reestablish *verb*
To bring back into existence or use : reinstate, reintroduce, renew, restore, return, revive. *See* INCREASE, KEEP.

reevaluate *verb*
To consider again, especially with the possibility of change : reconsider, reexamine, rethink, review. *See* THOUGHTS.

reexamine *verb*
To consider again, especially with the possibility of change : reconsider, reevaluate, rethink, review. *See* THOUGHTS.

ref *noun*
Sports. A person, usually appointed, who decides the issues or results, or supervises the conduct, of a competition or conflict : arbiter, arbitrator, judge, referee, umpire. *Sports:* ump. *See* DECIDE.

refer *verb*
1. To direct (a person) elsewhere for help or information : send, transfer, turn over. *See* MOVE. **2.** To regard as belonging to or resulting from another : accredit, ascribe, assign, attribute, charge, credit, impute, lay[1]. *See* GIVE. **3.** To call or direct attention to something : advert, bring up, mention, point, point out, touch (on *or* upon). *See* WORDS. **4.** To be pertinent : appertain, apply, bear on (*or* upon), concern, pertain, relate. *Idioms:* have a bearing on, have to do with. *See* RELEVANT. **5.** To look to when in need : apply, go, repair[2], resort, run, turn. *Idioms:* fall back on (*or* upon), have recourse to. *See* USED.

referee *noun*
A person, usually appointed, who decides the issues or results, or supervises the conduct, of a competition or conflict : arbiter, arbitrator, judge, umpire. *Sports:* ref, ump. *See* DECIDE.
referee *verb* To make a decision about (a controversy or dispute, for example) after deliberation, as in a court of law : adjudge, adjudicate, arbitrate, decide, decree, determine, judge, rule, umpire. *See* DECIDE, LAW.

reference *noun*
A statement attesting to personal qualifications, character, and dependability : character, recommendation, testimonial. *See* SUPPORT.

refine *verb*
1. To make or become clear by the removal of impurities : clarify, clean, cleanse, purify. *See* CLEAN. **2.** To bring to perfection or completion : perfect, polish, smooth. ***Idiom:*** smooth off the rough edges. *See* BETTER.

refined *adjective*
1. Characterized by discriminating taste and broad knowledge as a result of development or education : civilized, cultivated, cultured, educated, polished, urbane, well-bred. *See* CULTURE. **2.** So slight as to be difficult to notice or appreciate : delicate, fine[1], finespun, nice, subtle. *See* BIG.

refinement *noun*
1. The act or process of removing physical impurities : clarification, purification. *See* CLEAN. **2.** High style in quality, manner, or dress : quality. *Informal:* class. *See* STYLE. **3.** Enlightenment and excellent taste resulting from intellectual development : civilization, cultivation, culture. *See* CULTURE. **4.** The ability to distinguish, especially to recognize small differences or draw fine distinctions : discrimination, selectiveness, selectivity. *See* PRECISE.

refiner *noun*
Something that purifies or cleans : clarifier, cleaner, cleanser, purifier, refinery. *See* CLEAN.

refinery *noun*
Something that purifies or cleans : clarifier, cleaner, cleanser, purifier, refiner. *See* CLEAN.

refining *adjective*
Promoting culture : civilizing, cultural, edifying, enlightening, humanizing. *See* CULTURE.

reflect *verb*
1. To send back the sound of : echo, rebound, reecho, repeat, resound, reverberate. *See* SOUNDS. **2.** To send back or form an image of : image, mirror. *See* SHOW. **3.** To copy (another) slavishly : echo, image, imitate, mimic, mirror, parrot, repeat. *See* SAME. **4.** To think or think about carefully and at length : chew on (*or* over), cogitate, consider, contemplate, deliberate, entertain, excogitate, meditate, mull, muse[1], ponder, revolve, ruminate, study, think, think out, think over, think through, turn over, weigh. ***Idioms:*** cudgel one's brains, put on one's thinking cap, rack one's brain. *See* THOUGHTS. **5.** To use the powers of the mind, as in conceiving ideas, drawing inferences, and making judgments : cerebrate, cogitate, deliberate, ratiocinate, speculate, think. ***Idioms:*** put on one's thinking cap, use one's head. *See* THOUGHTS.

reflection *noun*
1. Something that is reflected : image. *See* SHOW. **2.** Imitative reproduction, as of the style of another : echo, imitation, reflex, repetition. *See* SAME. **3.** The act or process of thinking : brainwork, cerebration, cogitation, contemplation, deliberation, excogitation, meditation, rumination, speculation, thought. *See* THOUGHTS. **4.** An implied criticism : reproach, slur. *See* PRAISE.

reflective *adjective*
Of, characterized by, or disposed to thought : cogitative, contemplative, deliberative, excogitative, meditative, pensive, ruminative, speculative, thinking, thoughtful. ***Idiom:*** in a brown study. *See* THOUGHTS.

reflex *adjective*
Acting or happening without apparent forethought, prompting, or planning : automatic, impulsive, instinctive, involuntary, spontaneous, unpremeditated. *See* PLANNED.
reflex *noun* Imitative reproduction, as of the style of another : echo, imitation, reflection, repetition. *See* SAME.

reform *verb*
To make right what is wrong : amend, correct, emend, mend, rectify, redress, remedy, right. *See* CORRECT.

reformative *adjective*
Tending to correct : amendatory, corrective, emendatory, reformatory, remedial. *See* CORRECT.

reformatory *adjective*
Tending to correct : amendatory, corrective, emendatory, reformative, remedial. *See* CORRECT.

refract *verb*
To cause to move, especially at an angle : angle[2], bend, deflect, turn. *See* STRAIGHT.

refractoriness *noun*
The quality or condition of being unruly : disorderliness, fractiousness, indocility,

intractability, intractableness, obstinacy, obstinateness, obstreperousness, recalcitrance, recalcitrancy, uncontrollability, uncontrollableness, ungovernableness, unmanageability, unruliness, untowardness, wildness. *See* CONTROL, ORDER, PEACE, RESIST.

refractory *adjective*
Not submitting to discipline or control : disorderly, fractious, indocile, intractable, lawless, obstinate, obstreperous, recalcitrant, uncontrollable, undisciplined, ungovernable, unmanageable, unruly, untoward, wild. ***Idiom:*** out of line. *See* CONTROL, ORDER, PEACE, RESIST.

refrain *verb*
To hold oneself back : abstain, forbear, hold off, keep, withhold. *See* RESTRAINT.

refresh *verb*
1. To impart renewed energy and strength to (a person) : freshen, reinvigorate, rejuvenate, renew, restore, revitalize, revivify. *See* HELP, STRONG. **2.** To make new or as if new again : furbish, recondition, re-create, refurbish, rejuvenate, renew, renovate, restore, revamp. ***Idiom:*** give a new look to. *See* HELP, NEW.

refreshing *adjective*
Producing or stimulating physical, mental, or emotional vigor : bracing, energizing, exhilarant, exhilarating, innerving, intoxicating, invigorating, reinvigorating, renewing, restorative, roborant, stimulating, tonic. *See* HELP.

refuge *noun*
1. The state of being protected or safeguarded, as from danger or hardship : asylum, harborage, sanctuary, shelter. *See* SAFETY. **2.** Something that physically protects, especially from danger : asylum, cover, covert, harbor, haven, protection, retreat, sanctuary, shelter. *See* ATTACK, SAFETY. **3.** That to which one turns for help when in desperation : recourse, resort, resource. *See* HELP.

refugee *noun*
One who flees, as from home, confinement, captivity, or justice : escapee, fugitive, runaway. *See* SEEK.

refulgent *adjective*
Giving off or reflecting light readily or in large amounts : beamy, bright, brilliant, effulgent, incandescent, irradiant, lambent, lucent, luminous, lustrous, radiant, shiny. *See* LIGHT.

refund *verb*
To give back, especially money : reimburse, repay, restitute. *See* PAY.

refurbish *verb*
To make new or as if new again : furbish, recondition, re-create, refresh, rejuvenate, renew, renovate, restore, revamp. ***Idiom:*** give a new look to. *See* HELP, NEW.

refurbishment *noun*
The act of making new or as if new again : face-lift, facelifting, rejuvenation, renewal, renovation, restoration, revampment. *See* HELP, NEW.

refusal *noun*
1. A negative response : nay, no, rejection. *See* AFFIRM. **2.** A turning down of a request : denial, disallowance, rejection, turndown. *See* ACCEPT.

refuse *verb*
1. To be unwilling to accept, consider, or receive : decline, dismiss, reject, spurn, turn down. *Slang:* nix. ***Idiom:*** turn thumbs down on. *See* ACCEPT. **2.** To be unwilling to grant : deny, disallow, turn down, withhold. *See* ACCEPT.

refute *verb*
To prove or show to be false : belie, confute, discredit, disprove, rebut. *See* AFFIRM.

regain *verb*
To get back : recoup, recover, repossess, retrieve. *See* GET.

regal *adjective*
Large and impressive in size, scope, or extent : august, baronial, grand, grandiose, imposing, lordly, magnific, magnificent, majestic, noble, princely, royal, splendid, stately, sublime, superb. *See* BIG, GOOD.

regale *verb*
To occupy in an agreeable or pleasing way : amuse, divert, entertain, recreate. *See* EXCITE.

regalia *noun*
Showy and elaborate clothing or apparel : array, attire, finery, frippery. *See* PUT ON.

regard *verb*
1. To look at or on attentively or carefully : eye, observe, scrutinize, survey, watch. ***Idioms:*** have one's (*or* keep an) eye on, keep tabs on. *See* AWARENESS, SEE. **2.** To look upon in a particular way : account, consider, deem, esteem, reckon, see, view. *See* PERSPECTIVE. **3.** To have a high opinion of : admire, consider, esteem, honor, respect, value. ***Idioms:*** look up to, think highly (*or* much *or* well) of. *See* PRAISE.

regard *noun* **1.** An act of directing the eyes on an object : contemplation, look, sight, view. *See* SEE. **2.** Thoughtful attention : attentiveness, concern, consideration, solicitude, thoughtfulness. *See* ATTITUDE, CONCERN, KIND, TREAT WELL. **3.** Cautious attentiveness : care, carefulness, caution, gingerliness, heed, heedfulness, mindfulness. *See* CAREFUL. **4.** Curiosity about or attention to someone or something : concern, concernment, interest, interestedness. *See* CONCERN. **5.** The act of noting, observing, or taking into account : attention, cognizance, espial, heed, mark, note, notice, observance, observation, remark. *See* KNOWLEDGE, SEE. **6.** A feeling of deference, approval, and liking : account, admiration, appreciation, consideration, esteem, estimation, favor, honor, respect. *See* RESPECT. **7.** Friendly greetings. Used in plural : best, respect (used in plural). *See* GREETING. **8.** The particular angle from which something is considered : angle[2], aspect, facet, frame of reference, hand, light[1], phase, respect, side. *See* PERSPECTIVE.

regardful *adjective*
Concentrating the mental powers on something : attentive, heedful, intent. ***Idiom:*** all ears (*or* eyes). *See* EXCITE.

regardfulness *noun*
Concentration of the mental powers on something : attention, attentiveness, concentration, consideration, heedfulness. *See* EXCITE.

regeneration *noun*
A fundamental change in one's beliefs : conversion, metanoia, rebirth. *See* CHANGE.

regime *noun*
A system by which a political unit is controlled : governance, government, rule. *See* POLITICS.

regimen *noun*
The systematic application of remedies to effect a cure : care, rehabilitation, therapy, treatment. *Informal:* rehab. *See* HEALTH, HELP.

region *noun*
1. A part of the earth's surface : area, belt, district, locality, neighborhood, quarter, tract, zone. *Informal:* neck of the woods. *See* TERRITORY. **2.** A particular area used for or associated with a specific individual or activity : country, district, terrain, territory. *Slang:* turf. *See* TERRITORY.

regional *adjective*
Relating to or restricted to a particular territory : sectional, territorial. *See* TERRITORY.

register *noun*
A series, as of names or words, printed or written down : catalog, list[1], roll, roster, schedule. *See* REMEMBER.

register *verb* **1.** To place on a list or in a record : enter, insert, post[3], record. *See* REMEMBER. **2.** To give a precise indication of, as on a register or scale : indicate, mark, read, record, show. *See* SHOW. **3.** To come as a realization : dawn on (*or* upon), sink in, soak in. *See* KNOWLEDGE.

regnant *adjective*
1. Exercising controlling power or influence : commanding, controlling, dominant, dominating, dominative, governing, paramount, preponderant, reigning, ruling. *See* OVER. **2.** Having preeminent significance : ascendant, dominant, predominant, prepotent, prevailing, ruling, supreme. *See* IMPORTANT. **3.** Most generally existing or encountered at a given time : current, predominant, prevailing, prevalent, rife, widespread. *See* SPECIFIC.

regress *verb*
To slip from a higher or better condition to a former, usually lower or poorer one : backslide, lapse, relapse, retrogress, revert. *See* BETTER, REPETITION.

regression *noun*
A return to a former, usually worse condition : retrogradation, retrogression, reversion. *See* FORWARD, REPETITION.

regret *verb*
To feel or express sorrow for : deplore, repent, rue. *See* REGRET.

regret *noun* **1.** Unhappiness caused by the failure of one's hopes, desires, or expectations : disappointment, discontent, discontentment, disgruntlement, dissatisfaction, letdown. *See* HAPPY. **2.** A statement of acknowledgment expressing regret or asking pardon. Used in plural : apology, excuse, mea culpa. *See* REGRET.

regretful *adjective*
1. Expressing or inclined to express an apology : apologetic, contrite, penitent, repentant, sorry. *See* REGRET. **2.** Feeling or expressing regret for one's sins or misdeeds : compunctious, contrite, penitent, penitential, remorseful, repentant, sorry. *See* REGRET.

regrettable *adjective*
Causing sorrow or regret : deplorable, doleful, dolorous, grievous, lamentable, mournful, rueful, sad, sorrowful, woeful. *See* HAPPY.

regular *adjective*
1. Commonly practiced or used : accustomed, customary, habitual, usual, wonted. *See* USUAL. **2.** Occurring quite often : common, everyday, familiar, frequent, routine, widespread. *See* USUAL. **3.** Characterized by or displaying symmetry, especially correspondence in scale or measure : balanced, proportional, proportionate, symmetric, symmetrical. *See* SAME. **4.** Without imperfections or blemishes, as a line or contour : clean, perfect. *See* BEAUTIFUL. **5.** Arranged or proceeding in a set, systematized

pattern : methodic, methodical, orderly, systematic, systematical. *See* ABILITY, ORDER. **6.** Having no change or variation : changeless, constant, equable, even[1], invariable, invariant, same, steady, unchanging, uniform, unvarying. *See* SAME.

regularity *noun*
The quality or condition of being usual : customariness, habitualness, normalcy, normality, ordinariness, prevalence, routineness, usualness. *See* USUAL.

regularly *adverb*
In an expected or customary manner : commonly, consistently, customarily, frequently, generally, habitually, naturally, normally, often, routinely, typically, usually. ***Idioms:*** as usual, per usual. *See* BIG, USUAL.

regulate *verb*
1. To keep the mechanical operation of (a device) within proper parameters : control, govern. *See* CONTROL, MACHINE. **2.** To alter for proper functioning : adjust, fix, set[1], tune (up). *Music:* attune. *See* CHANGE, HELP.

regulation *noun*
1. A principle governing affairs within or among political units : canon, decree, edict, institute, law, ordinance, precept, prescription, rule. *See* LAW. **2.** A code or set of codes governing action or procedure, for example : dictate, prescript, rubric, rule. *See* ORDER.

regulatory *adjective*
Of or relating to government : governmental, gubernatorial. *See* POLITICS.

rehab *noun*
Informal. The systematic application of remedies to effect a cure : care, regimen, rehabilitation, therapy, treatment. *See* HEALTH, HELP.

rehabilitate *verb*
To bring back to a previous normal condition : rebuild, reclaim, recondition, reconstruct, reinstate, rejuvenate, renovate, restitute, restore. *See* HELP.

rehabilitation *noun*
The systematic application of remedies to effect a cure : care, regimen, therapy, treatment. *Informal:* rehab. *See* HEALTH, HELP.

rehearsal *noun*
Repetition of an action so as to develop or maintain one's skill : drill, exercise, practice, study, training. *See* WORK.

rehearse *verb*
1. To do or perform repeatedly so as to master : practice. *See* WORK. **2.** To give a verbal account of : describe, narrate, recite, recount, relate, report, tell. *See* WORDS.

reign *noun*
The act of exercising controlling power or the condition of being so controlled : command, control, dominance, domination, dominion, mastery, rule, sway. *See* OVER.

reign *verb* **1.** To exercise the authority of a sovereign : govern, rule. *Archaic:* sway. ***Idiom:*** wear the crown (*or* purple). *See* OVER. **2.** To occupy the preeminent position in : dominate, predominate, preponderate, prevail, rule. ***Idioms:*** have the ascendancy, reign supreme. *See* OVER.

reigning *adjective*
Exercising controlling power or influence : commanding, controlling, dominant, dominating, dominative, governing, paramount, preponderant, regnant, ruling. *See* OVER.

reimburse *verb*
1. To give back, especially money : refund, repay, restitute. *See* PAY. **2.** To give compensation to : compensate, indemnify, pay, recompense, redress, remunerate, repay, requite. *See* PAY.

reimbursement *noun*
Something to make up for loss or damage : amends, compensation, indemnification, indemnity, offset, quittance, recompense, redress, remuneration, reparation, repayment, requital, restitution, satisfaction, setoff. *See* SUBSTITUTE.

rein *verb*
To control, restrict, or arrest. Also used with *back*, *in*, or *up* : bit[2], brake, bridle, check, constrain, curb, hold, hold back, hold down, hold in, inhibit, keep, keep back, pull in, restrain. *See* RESTRAINT.

reinforce *verb*
To make or become tight or tighter : strengthen, tighten. *See* TIGHTEN.

reinstate *verb*
1. To bring back into existence or use : reestablish, reintroduce, renew, restore, return, revive. *See* INCREASE, KEEP. **2.** To put (someone) in the possession of a prior position or office : give back, replace, restore, return. *See* INCREASE, KEEP. **3.** To bring back to a previous normal condition : rebuild, reclaim, recondition, reconstruct, rehabilitate, rejuvenate, renovate, restitute, restore. *See* HELP.

reintroduce *verb*
To bring back into existence or use : reestablish, reinstate, renew, restore, return, revive. *See* INCREASE, KEEP.

reinvigorate *verb*
To impart renewed energy and strength to (a

person) : freshen, refresh, rejuvenate, renew, restore, revitalize, revivify. *See* HELP, STRONG.

reinvigorating *adjective*
Producing or stimulating physical, mental, or emotional vigor : bracing, energizing, exhilarant, exhilarating, innerving, intoxicating, invigorating, refreshing, renewing, restorative, roborant, stimulating, tonic. *See* HELP.

reiterate *verb*
To state again : iterate, repeat, restate. *See* REPETITION.

reiteration *noun*
The act or process of repeating : iteration, repetition, restatement. *See* REPETITION.

reiterative *adjective*
Characterized by repetition : iterative, repetitious, repetitive. *See* REPETITION.

reject *verb*
1. To be unwilling to accept, consider, or receive : decline, dismiss, refuse, spurn, turn down. *Slang:* nix. ***Idiom:*** turn thumbs down on. *See* ACCEPT. **2.** To refuse to recognize or acknowledge : deny, disacknowledge, disavow, disclaim, disown, renounce, repudiate. ***Idiom:*** turn one's back on. *See* ACCEPT.

rejection *noun*
1. A negative response : nay, no, refusal. *See* AFFIRM. **2.** A refusal to grant the truth of a statement or charge : contradiction, denial, disaffirmance, disaffirmation, disclaimer, negation. *Law:* traversal. *See* AFFIRM. **3.** A turning down of a request : denial, disallowance, refusal, turndown. *See* ACCEPT.

rejoice *verb*
1. To feel or take joy or pleasure : delight, exult, joy, pleasure. *See* HAPPY. **2.** To show joyful satisfaction in an event, especially by merrymaking : celebrate, revel. ***Idioms:*** kill the fatted calf, make merry. *See* LAUGHTER.

rejoicing *noun*
The act of showing joyful satisfaction in an event : celebration, festivity, merrymaking, revel (often used in plural), revelry. *See* LAUGHTER.

rejoin *verb*
To speak or act in response, as to a question : answer, reply, respond, retort, return, riposte. *See* ASK.

rejoinder *noun*
Something spoken or written in return, as to a question or demand : answer, reply, response. *See* ASK.

rejuvenate *verb*
1. To impart renewed energy and strength to (a person) : freshen, refresh, reinvigorate, renew, restore, revitalize, revivify. *See* HELP, STRONG. **2.** To bring back to a previous normal condition : rebuild, reclaim, recondition, reconstruct, rehabilitate, reinstate, renovate, restitute, restore. *See* HELP. **3.** To make new or as if new again : furbish, recondition, re-create, refresh, refurbish, renew, renovate, restore, revamp. ***Idiom:*** give a new look to. *See* HELP, NEW.

rejuvenation *noun*
The act of making new or as if new again : face-lift, facelifting, refurbishment, renewal, renovation, restoration, revampment. *See* HELP, NEW.

rekindle *verb*
To rouse from a state of inactivity or quiescence : reactivate, reanimate, reawaken, renew, resurrect, resuscitate, revitalize, revive, revivify. *See* AWARENESS.

relapse *verb*
To slip from a higher or better condition to a former, usually lower or poorer one : backslide, lapse, regress, retrogress, revert. *See* BETTER, REPETITION.

relapse *noun* A slipping from a higher or better condition to a lower or poorer one : backslide, backsliding, lapse, recidivation, recidivism. *See* BETTER, REPETITION.

relate *verb*
1. To give a verbal account of : describe, narrate, recite, recount, rehearse, report, tell. *See* WORDS. **2.** To be pertinent : appertain, apply, bear on (*or* upon), concern, pertain, refer. ***Idioms:*** have a bearing on, have to do with. *See* RELEVANT. **3.** To unite or be united in a relationship : affiliate, ally, associate, bind, combine, conjoin, connect, join, link. *See* CONNECT. **4.** To associate or affiliate oneself closely with a person or group : empathize, identify, sympathize. *See* SAME. **5.** To interact with another or others in a meaningful fashion : communicate, connect. *Slang:* click. ***Idioms:*** be on the same wavelength, hit it off. *See* CONNECT.

related *adjective*
Connected by or as if by kinship or common origin : agnate, akin, allied, cognate, connate, connatural, consanguine, consanguineous, kindred. *See* KIN.

relation *noun*
1. A logical or natural association between two or more things : connection, correlation, interconnection, interdependence, interrelationship, link, linkage, relationship, tie-in. *Informal:* hookup. *See* CONNECT. **2.** A person connected

to another person by blood or marriage : kin, kinsman, kinswoman, relative. *See* KIN.

relationship *noun*
A logical or natural association between two or more things : connection, correlation, interconnection, interdependence, interrelationship, link, linkage, relation, tie-in. *Informal:* hookup. *See* CONNECT.

relative *adjective*
1. Estimated by comparison : comparative. *See* SAME. **2.** Determined or to be determined by someone or something else : conditional, conditioned, contingent, dependent, reliant, subject. *See* START.
relative *noun* A person connected to another person by blood or marriage : kin, kinsman, kinswoman, relation. *See* KIN.

relax *verb*
1. To reduce in tension, pressure, or rigidity : ease, let up, loose, loosen, slack, slacken, untighten. *See* TIGHTEN. **2.** To take repose by ceasing work or other effort for an interval of time : rest[1], unbend, unwind. ***Idioms:*** lead (*or* live) the life of Riley, take it easy. *See* CONTINUE.

relaxation *noun*
Freedom from labor, responsibility, or strain : ease, leisure, repose, rest[1]. *See* CONTINUE.

relaxed *adjective*
1. Not tautly bound, held, or fastened : lax, loose, slack. *See* TIGHTEN. **2.** Unconstrained by rigid standards or ceremony : casual, easy, easygoing, informal, natural, spontaneous, unceremonious, unrestrained. *Informal:* laid-back. *See* PLAIN, TIGHTEN.

release *verb*
1. To set at liberty : discharge, emancipate, free, liberate, loose, manumit. *Slang:* spring. ***Idiom:*** let loose. *See* FREE. **2.** To discharge material, as vapor or fumes, usually suddenly and violently : emit, give, give forth, give off, give out, issue, let off, let out, send forth, throw off, vent. *See* FREE, MOVE. **3.** To free from or cast out something objectionable or undesirable : clear, disburden, disembarrass, disencumber, relieve, rid, shake off, throw off, unburden. *Slang:* shake. *See* KEEP. **4.** To end the employment or service of : cashier, discharge, dismiss, drop, terminate. *Informal:* ax, fire, pink-slip. *Slang:* boot[1], bounce, can, sack[1]. ***Idioms:*** give someone his or her walking papers, give someone the ax, give someone the gate, give someone the pink slip, let go, show someone the door. *See* KEEP.

relegate *verb*
To put in the charge of another for care, use, or performance : commend, commit, confide, consign, entrust, give (over), hand over, trust, turn over. ***Idiom:*** give in trust (*or* charge). *See* GIVE.

relent *verb*
To moderate or change a position or course of action as a result of pressure : ease off, slacken, soften, weaken, yield. ***Idiom:*** give way (*or* ground). *See* STRONG.

relentless *adjective*
1. Firmly, often unreasonably immovable in purpose or will : adamant, adamantine, brassbound, die-hard, grim, implacable, incompliant, inexorable, inflexible, intransigent, iron, obdurate, remorseless, rigid, stubborn, unbendable, unbending, uncompliant, uncompromising, unrelenting, unyielding. ***Idiom:*** stubborn as a mule (*or* ox). *See* RESIST. **2.** Existing or occurring without interruption or end : around-the-clock, ceaseless, constant, continual, continuous, endless, eternal, everlasting, incessant, interminable, nonstop, ongoing, perpetual, persistent, round-the-clock, timeless, unceasing, unending, unfailing, uninterrupted, unremitting. *See* CONTINUE.

relentlessness *noun*
The quality or state of being stubbornly inflexible : die-hardism, grimness, implacability, implacableness, incompliance, incompliancy, inexorability, inexorableness, inflexibility, inflexibleness, intransigence, intransigency, obduracy, obdurateness, remorselessness, rigidity, rigidness, stubbornness. *See* RESIST.

relevance *noun*
The fact of being related to the matter at hand : applicability, application, appositeness, bearing, concernment, germaneness, materiality, pertinence, pertinency, relevancy. *See* RELEVANT.

relevancy *noun*
The fact of being related to the matter at hand : applicability, application, appositeness, bearing, concernment, germaneness, materiality, pertinence, pertinency, relevance. *See* RELEVANT.

relevant *adjective*
Related to the matter at hand : applicable, apposite, apropos, germane, material, pertinent. ***Idiom:*** to the point. *See* RELEVANT.

reliable *adjective*
Capable of being depended upon : dependable, responsible, solid, sound[2], trustworthy, trusty. *See* TRUST.

reliance *noun*
Absolute certainty in the trustworthiness of another : belief, confidence, dependence, faith, trust. *See* BELIEF.

reliant *adjective*
Determined or to be determined by someone or something else : conditional, conditioned, contingent, dependent, relative, subject. *See* START.

relic *noun*
A mark or remnant that indicates the former presence of something : remains, trace, vestige. *See* LEFTOVER, MARKS.

relief *noun*
1. The act or an instance of helping : abetment, aid, assist, assistance, hand, help, succor, support. *See* HELP. **2.** Freedom, especially from pain : alleviation, assuagement, ease, mitigation, palliation. *See* INCREASE. **3.** Assistance, especially money, food, and other necessities, given to the needy or dispossessed : aid, dole, handout, public assistance, welfare. *See* HELP. **4.** A person or persons taking over the duties of another : replacement. *See* SUBSTITUTE.

relieve *verb*
1. To make less severe or more bearable : allay, alleviate, assuage, comfort, ease, lessen, lighten[2], mitigate, palliate. *See* INCREASE. **2.** To free from or cast out something objectionable or undesirable : clear, disburden, disembarrass, disencumber, release, rid, shake off, throw off, unburden. *Slang:* shake. *See* KEEP. **3.** To give support or assistance : abet, aid, assist, boost, help (out), succor. ***Idioms:*** give (*or* lend) a hand, give a leg up. *See* HELP. **4.** To free from an obligation or duty : absolve, discharge, dispense, excuse, exempt, let off, spare. *See* FREE. **5.** To free from a specific duty by acting as a substitute : spell[3], take over. *See* SUBSTITUTE.

reliever *noun*
A person who helps : abettor, aid, attendant, help, helper, succorer. *See* HELP.

religion *noun*
A system of religious belief : confession, creed, denomination, faith, persuasion, sect. *See* RELIGION.

religionism *noun*
A state of often extreme religious ardour : devotion, devoutness, pietism, piety, piousness, religiosity, religiousness. *See* RELIGION.

religiosity *noun*
A state of often extreme religious ardour : devotion, devoutness, pietism, piety, piousness, religionism, religiousness. *See* RELIGION.

religious *adjective*
1. Deeply concerned with God and the beliefs and practice of religion : devotional, devout, godly, holy, pietistic, pietistical, pious, prayerful, saintly. *See* RELIGION. **2.** In the service or worship of God or a god : divine, holy, sacred. *See* RELIGION. **3.** Of or relating to a church or to an established religion : church, churchly, ecclesiastical, spiritual. *See* RELIGION.

religiousness *noun*
A state of often extreme religious ardour : devotion, devoutness, pietism, piety, piousness, religionism, religiosity. *See* RELIGION.

relinquish *verb*
1. To give up a possession, claim, or right : abandon, abdicate, cede, demit, forswear, hand over, quitclaim, render, renounce, resign, surrender, waive, yield. *See* KEEP. **2.** To cease trying to accomplish or continue : abandon, break off, desist, discontinue, give up, leave off, quit, remit, stop. *Informal:* swear off. *Slang:* lay off. ***Idioms:*** call it a day, call it quits, hang up one's fiddle, have done with, throw in the towel. *See* CONTINUE. **3.** To let (something) go : abandon, cede, forgo, lay down, surrender, yield. *See* KEEP.

relinquishment *noun*
A giving up of a possession, claim, or right : abandonment, abdication, demission, quitclaim, renunciation, resignation, surrender, waiver. *See* KEEP.

relish *noun*
1. A liking for something : appetite, fondness, partiality, preference, taste, weakness. *See* LIKE. **2.** Spirited enjoyment : gusto, zest. *See* PAIN. **3.** A distinctive property of a substance affecting the gustatory sense : flavor, sapor, savor, smack[2], tang, taste, zest. *See* TASTE.
relish *verb* **1.** To receive pleasure from : enjoy, like[1], savor. *Informal:* go for. *Slang:* dig. *See* LIKE. **2.** To be avidly interested in : devour, feast on. *Slang:* eat up. *See* CONCERN.

relocate *verb*
To change one's residence or place of business, for example : move, remove, transfer. *See* MOVE.

relocation *noun*
The act or process of moving from one place to another : move, remotion, removal. *See* MOVE.

reluctance *noun*
The state of not being disposed or inclined : averseness, disinclination, indisposition, unwillingness. *See* WILLING.

reluctant *adjective*
Not inclined or willing to do or undertake : averse, disinclined, indisposed, loath, unwilling. *See* WILLING.

rely on or **upon** *verb*
To place trust or confidence in : bank on (*or* upon), believe in, count on (*or* upon), depend on (*or* upon), reckon on (*or* upon), trust (in). *See* TRUST.

remain *verb*
1. To continue to be in a place : abide, bide, linger, stay[1], tarry, wait. *Informal:* stick around. ***Idiom:*** stay put. *See* CONTINUE. **2.** To be in existence or in a certain state for an indefinitely long time : abide, continue, endure, go on, hold out, last[2], persist, stay[1]. *See* CONTINUE.

remainder *noun*
What remains after a part has been used or subtracted : balance, leavings, leftover, remains, remnant, residue, rest[2]. *See* LEFTOVER.

remaining *adjective*
Being what remains, especially after a part has been removed : leftover. *See* LEFTOVER.

remains *noun*
1. What remains after a part has been used or subtracted : balance, leavings, leftover, remainder, remnant, residue, rest[2]. *See* LEFTOVER. **2.** A mark or remnant that indicates the former presence of something : relic, trace, vestige. *See* LEFTOVER, MARKS. **3.** The physical frame of a dead person or animal : body, cadaver, carcass, corpse. *Slang:* stiff. *See* BODY.

remark *verb*
1. To state facts, opinions, or explanations : comment, note, observe. *See* WORDS. **2.** To perceive with a special effort of the senses or the mind : descry, detect, discern, distinguish, mark, mind, note, notice, observe, see. *See* KNOWLEDGE, SEE.

remark *noun* **1.** The act of noting, observing, or taking into account : attention, cognizance, espial, heed, mark, note, notice, observance, observation, regard. *See* KNOWLEDGE, SEE. **2.** An expression of fact or opinion : comment, note, obiter dictum, observation. *See* WORDS.

remarkable *adjective*
1. Readily attracting notice : arresting, bold, conspicuous, eye-catching, marked, noticeable, observable, outstanding, pointed, prominent, pronounced, salient, signal, striking. ***Idiom:*** sticking out like a sore thumb. *See* SEE. **2.** Far beyond what is usual, normal, or customary : exceptional, extraordinary, magnificent, outstanding, preeminent, rare, singular, towering, uncommon, unusual. *Informal:* standout. *Slang:* awesome, out of sight. *See* BETTER, USUAL.

remarkably *adverb*
In a manner or to a degree that is unusual : exceptionally, extraordinarily, singularly, uncommonly, unusually. *See* USUAL.

remedial *adjective*
1. Serving to cure : curative, restorative, therapeutic. *See* HEALTH. **2.** Tending to correct : amendatory, corrective, emendatory, reformative, reformatory. *See* CORRECT.

remedy *noun*
1. An agent used to restore health : cure, elixir, medicament, medication, medicine, nostrum, physic. *See* HEALTH. **2.** Something that corrects or counteracts : antidote, corrective, countermeasure, curative, cure. *See* BETTER.

remedy *verb* **1.** To rectify (an undesirable or unhealthy condition) : cure, heal. *See* HEALTH. **2.** To make right what is wrong : amend, correct, emend, mend, rectify, redress, reform, right. *See* CORRECT.

remember *verb*
1. To renew an image or thought in the mind : bethink, mind, recall, recollect, reminisce, retain, revive, think. ***Idiom:*** bring to mind. *See* REMEMBER. **2.** To care enough to keep (someone) in mind : think about, think of. *See* REMEMBER.

remembrance *noun*
1. An act or instance of remembering : memory, recollection, reminiscence. *See* REMEMBER. **2.** The power of retaining and recalling past experience : memory, recall, recollection, reminiscence. *See* REMEMBER. **3.** Something, as a structure or custom, serving to honor or keep alive a memory : commemoration, memorial, monument. *See* REMEMBER. **4.** Something that causes one to remember : keepsake, memento, reminder, souvenir, token, trophy. *See* REMEMBER.

reminder *noun*
Something that causes one to remember : keepsake, memento, remembrance, souvenir, token, trophy. *See* REMEMBER.

reminisce *verb*
To renew an image or thought in the mind : bethink, mind, recall, recollect, remember, retain, revive, think. ***Idiom:*** bring to mind. *See* REMEMBER.

reminiscence *noun*
1. An act or instance of remembering : memory, recollection, remembrance. *See* REMEMBER. **2.** The power of retaining and recalling

past experience : memory, recall, recollection, remembrance. *See* REMEMBER. **3.** A narrative of experiences undergone by the writer. Often used in plural : commentary (often used in plural), memoir. *See* WORDS.

reminiscent *adjective*
Tending to bring a memory, mood, or image, for example, subtly or indirectly to mind : allusive, connotative, evocative, impressionistic, suggestive. *See* SUGGEST.

remiss *adjective*
Guilty of neglect; lacking due care or concern : derelict, lax, neglectful, negligent, slack. *See* CAREFUL.

remission *noun*
1. The act or process of becoming less active or intense : abatement, ebb, letup, slackening, subsidence, wane. *See* INCREASE. **2.** The act or an instance of forgiving : absolution, amnesty, condonation, excuse, forgiveness, pardon. *See* FORGIVENESS.

remissness *noun*
The state or quality of being negligent : laxity, laxness, negligence, slackness. *See* CAREFUL.

remit *verb*
1. To grant forgiveness to or for : condone, excuse, forgive, pardon. ***Idiom:*** forgive and forget. *See* FORGIVENESS. **2.** To become or cause to become less active or intense : abate, bate, die (away, down, off, *or* out), ease (off *or* up), ebb, fall, fall off, lapse, let up, moderate, slacken, slack off, subside, wane. *See* INCREASE. **3.** To cease trying to accomplish or continue : abandon, break off, desist, discontinue, give up, leave off, quit, relinquish, stop. *Informal:* swear off. *Slang:* lay off. ***Idioms:*** call it a day, call it quits, hang up one's fiddle, have done with, throw in the towel. *See* CONTINUE. **4.** To put off until a later time : adjourn, defer[1], delay, hold off, hold up, postpone, shelve, stay[1], suspend, table, waive. *Informal:* wait. ***Idiom:*** put on ice. *See* DO.

remnant *noun*
What remains after a part has been used or subtracted : balance, leavings, leftover, remainder, remains, residue, rest[2]. *See* LEFTOVER.

remonstrance *noun*
The act of expressing strong or reasoned opposition : challenge, demur, exception, expostulation, objection, protest, protestation, remonstration, squawk. *Slang:* kick. *See* SUPPORT.

remonstrate *verb*
To express opposition, often by argument : challenge, demur, except, expostulate, inveigh, object, protest. *Informal:* kick, squawk. ***Idioms:*** set up a squawk, take exception. *See* SUPPORT.

remonstration *noun*
The act of expressing strong or reasoned opposition : challenge, demur, exception, expostulation, objection, protest, protestation, remonstrance, squawk. *Slang:* kick. *See* SUPPORT.

remorse *noun*
A feeling of regret for one's sins or misdeeds : compunction, contriteness, contrition, penitence, penitency, remorsefulness, repentance, rue. *Theology:* attrition. *See* REGRET.

remorseful *adjective*
Feeling or expressing regret for one's sins or misdeeds : compunctious, contrite, penitent, penitential, regretful, repentant, sorry. *See* REGRET.

remorsefulness *noun*
A feeling of regret for one's sins or misdeeds : compunction, contriteness, contrition, penitence, penitency, remorse, repentance, rue. *Theology:* attrition. *See* REGRET.

remorseless *adjective*
1. Having or showing no mercy : merciless, pitiless, unmerciful. *See* KIND. **2.** Firmly, often unreasonably immovable in purpose or will : adamant, adamantine, brassbound, die-hard, grim, implacable, incompliant, inexorable, inflexible, intransigent, iron, obdurate, relentless, rigid, stubborn, unbendable, unbending, uncompliant, uncompromising, unrelenting, unyielding. ***Idiom:*** stubborn as a mule (*or* ox). *See* RESIST. **3.** Devoid of remorse : impenitent, unrepentant. *See* REGRET.

remorselessness *noun*
The quality or state of being stubbornly inflexible : die-hardism, grimness, implacability, implacableness, incompliance, incompliancy, inexorability, inexorableness, inflexibility, inflexibleness, intransigence, intransigency, obduracy, obdurateness, relentlessness, rigidity, rigidness, stubbornness. *See* RESIST.

remote *adjective*
1. Far from others in space, time, or relationship : distant, far, faraway, far-flung, far-off, removed. ***Idiom:*** at a distance. *See* NEAR, TIME. **2.** Far from centers of human population : back, insular, isolated, lonely, lonesome, obscure, outlying, out-of-the-way, removed, secluded, solitary. ***Idiom:*** off the beaten path (*or* track). *See* NEAR. **3.** Small in degree, especially of probability : faint, negligible, outside, slender, slight, slim. *See* BIG. **4.** Not friendly, sociable, or warm in manner : aloof, chill, chilly, cool, distant, offish, reserved, reticent, solitary, standoffish, unapproachable,

uncommunicative, undemonstrative, withdrawn. *See* ATTITUDE, HOT.

remoteness *noun*
1. The fact or condition of being far removed or apart : distance, farness. *See* BIG, NEAR.
2. Dissociation from one's surroundings or worldly affairs : aloofness, detachment, distance. *See* ATTITUDE, CONCERN, INCLUDE, NEAR.

remotion *noun*
The act or process of moving from one place to another : move, relocation, removal. *See* MOVE.

removal *noun*
1. The act or process of moving from one place to another : move, relocation, remotion. *See* MOVE. **2.** The act or process of eliminating : clearance, elimination, eradication, liquidation, purge, riddance. *See* KEEP.

remove *verb*
1. To move (something) from a position occupied : take, take away, take off, take out, withdraw. *See* MOVE. **2.** To go or cause to go from one place to another : maneuver, move, shift, transfer. *See* MOVE. **3.** To move along a particular course : fare, go, journey, pass, proceed, push on, travel, wend. ***Idiom:*** make one's way. *See* MOVE. **4.** To change one's residence or place of business, for example : move, relocate, transfer. *See* MOVE. **5.** To take from one's own person : doff, take off. *See* PUT ON. **6.** To take or leave out : drop, eliminate, omit. *See* INCLUDE. **7.** To destroy all traces of : abolish, annihilate, blot out, clear, eradicate, erase, exterminate, extinguish, extirpate, kill[1], liquidate, obliterate, root[1] (out *or* up), rub out, snuff out, stamp out, uproot, wipe out. ***Idioms:*** do away with, make an end of, put an end to. *See* HELP, MAKE. **8.** To get rid of, especially by banishment or execution : eliminate, eradicate, liquidate, purge, wipe out. ***Idioms:*** do away with, put an end to. *See* HELP, KEEP.
remove *noun* Degree of separation, especially in time : distance. *See* NEAR.

removed *adjective*
1. Far from others in space, time, or relationship : distant, far, faraway, far-flung, far-off, remote. ***Idiom:*** at a distance. *See* NEAR, TIME.
2. Far from centers of human population : back, insular, isolated, lonely, lonesome, obscure, outlying, out-of-the-way, remote, secluded, solitary. ***Idiom:*** off the beaten path (*or* track). *See* NEAR. **3.** Set away from all others : alone, apart, detached, isolate, isolated, lone, solitary. *See* INCLUDE.

remunerate *verb*
1. To give payment to in return for goods or services rendered : compensate, pay, recompense. *See* PAY. **2.** To give compensation to : compensate, indemnify, pay, recompense, redress, reimburse, repay, requite. *See* PAY.
3. To give a satisfactory return to : compensate, indemnify, pay, recompense, repay, requite, reward. *See* PAY.

remuneration *noun*
1. Something given in exchange for goods or services rendered : compensation, consideration, payment, recompense. *See* PAY. **2.** Payment for work done : compensation, earnings, emolument, fee, hire, pay, salary, stipend, wage. *See* PAY. **3.** Something to make up for loss or damage : amends, compensation, indemnification, indemnity, offset, quittance, recompense, redress, reimbursement, reparation, repayment, requital, restitution, satisfaction, setoff. *See* SUBSTITUTE.

remunerative *adjective*
1. Affording compensation : compensative, compensatory. *See* SUBSTITUTE. **2.** Affording profit : advantageous, fat, lucrative, moneymaking, profitable, rewarding. *See* GET.

renaissance *noun*
The act of reviving or condition of being revived : reactivation, rebirth, renascence, renewal, resurgence, resurrection, resuscitation, revitalization, revival, revivification. *See* AWARENESS.

renascence *noun*
The act of reviving or condition of being revived : reactivation, rebirth, renaissance, renewal, resurgence, resurrection, resuscitation, revitalization, revival, revivification. *See* AWARENESS.

rend *verb*
To separate or pull apart by force : rip, rive, run, split, tear[1]. *See* ASSEMBLE, HELP.

render *verb*
1. To give up a possession, claim, or right : abandon, abdicate, cede, demit, forswear, hand over, quitclaim, relinquish, renounce, resign, surrender, waive, yield. *See* KEEP. **2.** To present a lifelike image of : delineate, depict, describe, express, image, limn, picture, portray, represent, show. *See* SHOW. **3.** To perform according to one's artistic conception : execute, interpret, play. *See* PERFORMING ARTS. **4.** To express in another language, while systematically retaining the original sense : construe, put, translate. *See* WORDS. **5.** To express the meaning of in other, especially simpler, words : paraphrase,

rephrase, restate, reword, translate. *See* WORDS. **6.** To deliver (an indictment or verdict, for example) : hand down, return. *See* LAW.

rendering *noun*

1. One's artistic conception as shown by the way in which something such as a dramatic role or musical composition is rendered : execution, interpretation, performance, reading, realization, rendition. *See* PERFORMING ARTS. **2.** A restating of something in other, especially simpler, words : paraphrase, restatement, translation, version. *See* WORDS.

rendezvous *noun*

1. A commitment to appear at a certain time and place : appointment, assignation, date, engagement, tryst. *See* AGREE. **2.** A frequently visited place : haunt, resort, stamping ground. *Slang:* hangout. *See* PLACE, REPETITION.

rendezvous *verb* To come together by arrangement : get together, meet[1]. *See* MEET.

rendition *noun*

One's artistic conception as shown by the way in which something such as a dramatic role or musical composition is rendered : execution, interpretation, performance, reading, realization, rendering. *See* PERFORMING ARTS.

renege *verb*

To abandon a former position or commitment : back down (*or* out), retreat. *Slang:* cop out, fink out. *See* RESIST.

renegade *noun*

A person who has defected : apostate, defector, deserter, recreant, runagate, tergiversator, turncoat. *Informal:* rat. *See* APPROACH.

renegade *verb* To abandon one's cause or party usually to join another : apostatize, defect, desert[3], tergiversate, turn. *Slang:* rat. ***Idioms:*** change sides, turn one's coat. *See* APPROACH, TRUST.

renew *verb*

1. To make new or as if new again : furbish, recondition, re-create, refresh, refurbish, rejuvenate, renovate, restore, revamp. ***Idiom:*** give a new look to. *See* HELP, NEW. **2.** To begin or go on after an interruption : continue, pick up, reopen, restart, resume, take up. *See* CONTINUE. **3.** To impart renewed energy and strength to (a person) : freshen, refresh, reinvigorate, rejuvenate, restore, revitalize, revivify. *See* HELP, STRONG. **4.** To rouse from a state of inactivity or quiescence : reactivate, reanimate, reawaken, rekindle, resurrect, resuscitate, revitalize, revive, revivify. *See* AWARENESS. **5.** To arrange for the extension of : extend. *See* CONTINUE. **6.** To bring back into existence or use : reestablish, reinstate, reintroduce, restore, return, revive. *See* INCREASE, KEEP.

renewal *noun*

1. The act of making new or as if new again : face-lift, facelifting, refurbishment, rejuvenation, renovation, restoration, revampment. *See* HELP, NEW. **2.** A continuing after interruption : continuation, resumption, resurgence, revival. *See* CONTINUE. **3.** The act of reviving or condition of being revived : reactivation, rebirth, renaissance, renascence, resurgence, resurrection, resuscitation, revitalization, revival, revivification. *See* AWARENESS.

renewing *adjective*

Producing or stimulating physical, mental, or emotional vigor : bracing, energizing, exhilarant, exhilarating, innerving, intoxicating, invigorating, refreshing, reinvigorating, restorative, roborant, stimulating, tonic. *See* HELP.

renitence *noun*

The act of resisting : opposition, renitency, resistance. *See* RESIST.

renitency *noun*

The act of resisting : opposition, renitence, resistance. *See* RESIST.

renitent *adjective*

Tending to resist, as an influence or idea : resistant, resisting, resistive. *See* RESIST.

renounce *verb*

1. To give up a possession, claim, or right : abandon, abdicate, cede, demit, forswear, hand over, quitclaim, relinquish, render, resign, surrender, waive, yield. *See* KEEP. **2.** To refuse to recognize or acknowledge : deny, disacknowledge, disavow, disclaim, disown, reject, repudiate. ***Idiom:*** turn one's back on. *See* ACCEPT.

renovate *verb*

1. To bring back to a previous normal condition : rebuild, reclaim, recondition, reconstruct, rehabilitate, reinstate, rejuvenate, restitute, restore. *See* HELP. **2.** To make new or as if new again : furbish, recondition, re-create, refresh, refurbish, rejuvenate, renew, restore, revamp. ***Idiom:*** give a new look to. *See* HELP, NEW.

renovation *noun*

The act of making new or as if new again : face-lift, facelifting, refurbishment, rejuvenation, renewal, restoration, revampment. *See* HELP, NEW.

renown *noun*

1. A position of widely recognized importance : distinction, eminence, eminency, fame, glory, illustriousness, luster, mark, notability, note, preeminence, prestige, prominence, prominency. *See* IMPORTANT, KNOWLEDGE, RESPECT. **2.** Wide recognition for one's deeds : celebrity, fame, famousness, notoriety, popularity, reputation, repute. *See* KNOWLEDGE.

renowned *adjective*
Widely known and esteemed : celebrated, distinguished, eminent, famed, famous, great, illustrious, notable, noted, preeminent, prestigious, prominent, redoubtable. *See* KNOWLEDGE, RESPECT.

rent[1] *verb*
1. To engage the temporary use of (something) for a fee : charter, hire, lease. *See* GET, TRANSACTIONS. **2.** To give temporary use of in return for payment : hire (out), lease, let. *See* TRANSACTIONS.

rent[2] *noun*
1. A hole made by tearing : rip, run, tear[1]. *See* HELP. **2.** An interruption in friendly relations : alienation, breach, break, disaffection, estrangement, fissure, rift, rupture, schism, split. *See* ASSEMBLE, HELP.

renunciation *noun*
A giving up of a possession, claim, or right : abandonment, abdication, demission, quitclaim, relinquishment, resignation, surrender, waiver. *See* KEEP.

reoccupy *verb*
To occupy or take again : reassume, re-claim, repossess, resume, retake, take back. *See* GIVE.

reoccur *verb*
1. To happen again or repeatedly : reappear, recur. *See* REPETITION. **2.** To come back to a former condition : recrudesce, recur, return, revert. *See* REPETITION.

reoccurrence *noun*
A repeated occurrence : reappearance, recurrence, return. *See* REPETITION.

reopen *verb*
To begin or go on after an interruption : continue, pick up, renew, restart, resume, take up. *See* CONTINUE.

rep *noun*
Informal. Public estimation of someone : character, name, report, reputation, repute. *See* RESPECT.

repair[1] *verb*
To restore to proper condition or functioning : doctor, fix, fix up, mend, overhaul, patch, revamp, right. ***Idiom:*** set right. *See* HELP.

repair[2] *verb*
1. To look to when in need : apply, go, refer, resort, run, turn. ***Idioms:*** fall back on (*or* upon), have recourse to. *See* USED. **2.** To visit regularly : frequent, hang around, haunt, resort. *Slang:* hang out. *See* PLACE.

reparation *noun*
Something to make up for loss or damage : amends, compensation, indemnification, indemnity, offset, quittance, recompense, redress, reimbursement, remuneration, repayment, requital, restitution, satisfaction, setoff. *See* SUBSTITUTE.

repartee *noun*
A spirited, incisive reply : comeback, retort, riposte. *See* ASK.

repay *verb*
1. To exact revenge for or from : avenge, pay back, pay off, redress, requite, vindicate. *Informal:* fix. *Archaic:* wreak. ***Idioms:*** even the score, get back at, get even with, pay back in kind (*or* in one's own coin), settle (*or* square) accounts, take an eye for an eye. *See* FORGIVENESS. **2.** To give back, especially money : refund, reimburse, restitute. *See* PAY. **3.** To give compensation to : compensate, indemnify, pay, recompense, redress, reimburse, remunerate, requite. *See* PAY. **4.** To make as income or profit : bring in, clear, draw, earn, gain, gross, net[2], pay, produce, realize, return, yield. *See* MONEY. **5.** To give a satisfactory return to : compensate, indemnify, pay, recompense, remunerate, requite, reward. *See* PAY.

repayment *noun*
Something to make up for loss or damage : amends, compensation, indemnification, indemnity, offset, quittance, recompense, redress, reimbursement, remuneration, reparation, requital, restitution, satisfaction, setoff. *See* SUBSTITUTE.

repeal *verb*
To take back or remove : lift, recall, rescind, reverse, revoke. *See* CONTINUE, LAW, MAKE.
repeal *noun* The act of reversing or annulling : recall, rescission, reversal, revocation. *See* CONTINUE, LAW.

repeat *verb*
1. To state again : iterate, reiterate, restate. *See* REPETITION. **2.** To send back the sound of : echo, rebound, reecho, reflect, resound, reverberate. *See* SOUNDS. **3.** To copy (another) slavishly : echo, image, imitate, mimic, mirror, parrot, reflect. *See* SAME. **4.** To do or perform (an act) again : duplicate, redo. *See* REPETITION.

repel *verb*
1. To turn or drive away : beat off, fend (off), keep off, parry, repulse, ward off. *See* ALLOW, STRIKE. **2.** To offend the senses or feelings of :

disgust, nauseate, revolt, sicken. *Idiom:* turn one's stomach. *See* LIKE.

repellence *noun*
Extreme hostility and dislike : abhorrence, abomination, antipathy, aversion, detestation, hate, hatred, horror, loathing, repellency, repugnance, repugnancy, repulsion, revulsion. *See* LOVE.

repellency *noun*
Extreme hostility and dislike : abhorrence, abomination, antipathy, aversion, detestation, hate, hatred, horror, loathing, repellence, repugnance, repugnancy, repulsion, revulsion. *See* LOVE.

repellent *adjective*
Extremely unpleasant to the senses or feelings : atrocious, disgusting, foul, horrid, nasty, nauseating, offensive, repulsive, revolting, sickening, ugly, unwholesome, vile. *See* LIKE, PAIN.

repent *verb*
To feel or express sorrow for : deplore, regret, rue. *See* REGRET.

repentance *noun*
A feeling of regret for one's sins or misdeeds : compunction, contriteness, contrition, penitence, penitency, remorse, remorsefulness, rue. *Theology:* attrition. *See* REGRET.

repentant *adjective*
1. Feeling or expressing regret for one's sins or misdeeds : compunctious, contrite, penitent, penitential, regretful, remorseful, sorry. *See* REGRET. **2.** Expressing or inclined to express an apology : apologetic, contrite, penitent, regretful, sorry. *See* REGRET.

repercussion *noun*
1. The strong effect exerted by one person or thing on another : force, impact, impression, influence. *See* AFFECT. **2.** Repetition of sound via reflection from a surface : echo, reverberation. *See* SOUNDS.

repetition *noun*
1. The act or process of repeating : iteration, reiteration, restatement. *See* REPETITION.
2. Imitative reproduction, as of the style of another : echo, imitation, reflection, reflex. *See* SAME.

repetitious *adjective*
Characterized by repetition : iterative, reiterative, repetitive. *See* REPETITION.

repetitive *adjective*
Characterized by repetition : iterative, reiterative, repetitious. *See* REPETITION.

rephrase *verb*
To express the meaning of in other, especially simpler, words : paraphrase, render, restate, reword, translate. *See* WORDS.

replace *verb*
1. To put (someone) in the possession of a prior position or office : give back, reinstate, restore, return. *See* INCREASE, KEEP. **2.** To substitute for or fill the place of : supersede, supplant, surrogate. *See* SUBSTITUTE.

replacement *noun*
1. One that takes the place of another : alternate, stand-in, substitute, surrogate. *Informal:* fill-in, pinch hitter, sub. *See* SUBSTITUTE. **2.** A person or persons taking over the duties of another : relief. *See* SUBSTITUTE.

replete *adjective*
1. Full of animation and activity : alive, rife. *See* BIG, RICH. **2.** Completely filled : brimful, brimming, bursting, chockablock, full, packed. *See* FULL.

repletion *noun*
The condition of being full to or beyond satisfaction : engorgement, satiation, satiety, surfeit. *See* EXCESS, FULL.

replica *noun*
Something closely resembling another : carbon copy, copy, duplicate, facsimile, image, likeness, reduplication, replication, reproduction, simulacrum. *Archaic:* simulacre. *Law:* counterpart. *See* SAME.

replicate *verb*
To make a copy of : copy, duplicate, imitate, reproduce, simulate. *See* SAME.

replication *noun*
Something closely resembling another : carbon copy, copy, duplicate, facsimile, image, likeness, reduplication, replica, reproduction, simulacrum. *Archaic:* simulacre. *Law:* counterpart. *See* SAME.

reply *verb*
To speak or act in response, as to a question : answer, rejoin, respond, retort, return, riposte. *See* ASK.
reply *noun* Something spoken or written in return, as to a question or demand : answer, rejoinder, response. *See* ASK.

report *noun*
1. A recounting of past events : account, chronicle, description, history, narration, narrative, statement, story, version. *See* WORDS.
2. Idle, often sensational and groundless talk about others : gossip, gossipry, hearsay, rumor, talebearing, tattle, tittle-tattle, word. *Slang:* scuttlebutt. *See* WORDS. **3.** Public estimation of someone : character, name, reputation, repute. *Informal:* rep. *See* RESPECT. **4.** A

sudden sharp, explosive noise : bang, bark, clap, crack, explosion, pop[1], rat-a-tat-tat, snap. *See* SOUNDS.

report *verb* **1.** To give a verbal account of : describe, narrate, recite, recount, rehearse, relate, tell. *See* WORDS. **2.** To observe, analyze, and relate the details of (an event) : cover. *See* WORDS. **3.** To make known : break, carry, communicate, convey, disclose, get across, impart, pass, tell, transmit. *See* KNOWLEDGE.

reportage *noun*
The reporting of news : coverage. *See* WORDS.

repose *noun*
Freedom from labor, responsibility, or strain : ease, leisure, relaxation, rest[1]. *See* CONTINUE.

repose *verb* **1.** To be or place oneself in a prostrate or recumbent position : lie[1] (down), recline, stretch (out). *See* HORIZONTAL. **2.** To take repose, as by sleeping or lying quietly : lie[1] (down), recline, rest[1], stretch (out). *See* CONTINUE. **3.** To have an inherent basis : consist, dwell, exist, inhere, lie[1], reside, rest[1]. *See* START.

repository *noun*
1. A place where something is deposited for safekeeping : archive, depository, magazine, store, storehouse, warehouse. *See* KEEP. **2.** One in whom secrets are confided : confessor, confidant, confidante. *See* SHOW, WORDS.

repossess *verb*
1. To get back : recoup, recover, regain, retrieve. *See* GET. **2.** To occupy or take again : reassume, re-claim, reoccupy, resume, retake, take back. *See* GIVE.

repossession *noun*
The act of getting back or regaining : recoup, recovery, retrieval. *See* GET.

reprehend *verb*
To feel or express strong disapproval of : censure, condemn, denounce, deplore, reprobate. *See* PRAISE.

reprehensible *adjective*
Deserving blame : blamable, blameful, blameworthy, censurable, culpable, guilty. ***Idiom:*** at fault. *See* PRAISE.

reprehension *noun*
A comment expressing fault : blame, censure, condemnation, criticism, denunciation, reprobation. *Informal:* pan. *Slang:* knock. *See* PRAISE.

represent *verb*
1. To serve as an example, image, or symbol of : epitomize, exemplify, illustrate, stand for, symbol, symbolize, typify. *See* SUBSTITUTE. **2.** To present a lifelike image of : delineate, depict, describe, express, image, limn, picture, portray, render, show. *See* SHOW. **3.** To serve as an official delegate of : speak for, stand for. *See* SUBSTITUTE. **4.** To play the part of : act, do, enact, impersonate, perform, play, play-act, portray. *See* ACTION, PERFORMING ARTS, SUBSTITUTE.

representation *noun*
The act or process of describing in lifelike imagery : delineation, depiction, description, expression, portrayal. *See* SHOW.

representative *noun*
1. One that is representative of a group or class : case, example, illustration, instance, sample, specimen. *See* SUBSTITUTE. **2.** One who stands for another : delegate, deputy. *See* SUBSTITUTE.

representative *adjective* **1.** Serving as a symbol : emblematic, emblematical, symbolic, symbolical. *See* SUBSTITUTE. **2.** Serving to describe : delineative, descriptive, graphic. *See* WORDS. **3.** Having the nature of, constituting, or serving as a type : archetypal, archetypic, archetypical, classic, classical, model, paradigmatic, prototypal, prototypic, prototypical, quintessential, typic, typical. *See* SAME, USUAL.

repress *verb*
To hold (something requiring an outlet) in check : burke, choke (back), gag, hold back, hold down, hush (up), muffle, quench, smother, squelch, stifle, strangle, suppress, throttle. *Informal:* sit on (*or* upon). *See* RESTRAINT.

repression *noun*
Sudden punitive action : clampdown, crackdown, suppression. *See* CONTINUE, WIN.

repressive *adjective*
Serving to restrain forcefully : suppressive. *See* ATTACK, RESTRAINT.

reprieve *noun*
Temporary immunity from penalties : grace, respite. *See* CONTINUE.

reprimand *verb*
To criticize for a fault or an offense : admonish, call down, castigate, chastise, chide, dress down, rap[1], rebuke, reproach, reprove, scold, tax, upbraid. *Informal:* bawl out, lambaste. *Slang:* chew out. ***Idioms:*** bring (*or* call *or* take) to task, call on the carpet, haul (*or* rake) over the coals, let someone have it. *See* ATTACK, PRAISE.

reprimand *noun* Words expressive of strong disapproval : admonishment, admonition, rebuke, reproach, reproof, scolding. *Slang:* rap[1]. *See* PRAISE.

reprisal *noun*
The act of retaliating : counteraction, counterattack, counterblow, reciprocation, requital, retaliation, retribution, revenge, tit for tat, vengeance. ***Idioms:*** an eye for an eye, a tooth for a tooth, like for like, measure for measure. *See* ATTACK, FORGIVENESS.

reproach *verb*
1. To criticize for a fault or an offense : admonish, call down, castigate, chastise, chide, dress down, rap[1], rebuke, reprimand, reprove, scold, tax, upbraid. *Informal:* bawl out, lambaste. *Slang:* chew out. ***Idioms:*** bring (*or* call *or* take) to task, call on the carpet, haul (*or* rake) over the coals, let someone have it. *See* ATTACK, PRAISE. **2.** To cause to feel embarrassment, dishonor, and often guilt : shame. ***Idioms:*** put to shame, put to the blush. *See* RESPECT.
reproach *noun* **1.** Words expressive of strong disapproval : admonishment, admonition, rebuke, reprimand, reproof, scolding. *Slang:* rap[1]. *See* PRAISE. **2.** An implied criticism : reflection, slur. *See* PRAISE.

reprobate *adjective*
Morally objectionable : bad, black, evil, immoral, iniquitous, peccant, sinful, vicious, wicked, wrong. *See* RIGHT.
reprobate *verb* To feel or express strong disapproval of : censure, condemn, denounce, deplore, reprehend. *See* PRAISE.

reprobation *noun*
A comment expressing fault : blame, censure, condemnation, criticism, denunciation, reprehension. *Informal:* pan. *Slang:* knock. *See* PRAISE.

reproduce *verb*
1. To make a copy of : copy, duplicate, imitate, replicate, simulate. *See* SAME. **2.** To produce sexually or asexually others of one's kind : breed, increase, multiply, procreate, proliferate, propagate, spawn. *See* REPRODUCTION.

reproduction *noun*
1. Something closely resembling another : carbon copy, copy, duplicate, facsimile, image, likeness, reduplication, replica, replication, simulacrum. *Archaic:* simulacre. *Law:* counterpart. *See* SAME. **2.** The process by which an organism produces others of its kind : breeding, multiplication, procreation, proliferation, propagation, spawning. *Obsolete:* increase. *See* REPRODUCTION.

reproductive *adjective*
1. Of or relating to reproduction : procreant, procreative. *See* REPRODUCTION. **2.** Employed in reproduction : sexual. *See* REPRODUCTION.

reproof *noun*
Words expressive of strong disapproval : admonishment, admonition, rebuke, reprimand, reproach, scolding. *Slang:* rap[1]. *See* PRAISE.

reprove *verb*
To criticize for a fault or an offense : admonish, call down, castigate, chastise, chide, dress down, rap[1], rebuke, reprimand, reproach, scold, tax, upbraid. *Informal:* bawl out, lambaste. *Slang:* chew out. ***Idioms:*** bring (*or* call *or* take) to task, call on the carpet, haul (*or* rake) over the coals, let someone have it. *See* ATTACK, PRAISE.

repudiate *verb*
To refuse to recognize or acknowledge : deny, disacknowledge, disavow, disclaim, disown, reject, renounce. ***Idiom:*** turn one's back on. *See* ACCEPT.

repugnance *noun*
Extreme hostility and dislike : abhorrence, abomination, antipathy, aversion, detestation, hate, hatred, horror, loathing, repellence, repellency, repugnancy, repulsion, revulsion. *See* LOVE.

repugnancy *noun*
Extreme hostility and dislike : abhorrence, abomination, antipathy, aversion, detestation, hate, hatred, horror, loathing, repellence, repellency, repugnance, repulsion, revulsion. *See* LOVE.

repugnant *adjective*
1. So objectionable as to elicit despisal or deserve condemnation : abhorrent, abominable, antipathetic, contemptible, despicable, despisable, detestable, disgusting, filthy, foul, infamous, loathsome, lousy, low, mean[2], nasty, nefarious, obnoxious, odious, rotten, shabby, vile, wretched. *See* GOOD. **2.** *Logic.* In sharp opposition : discrepant, incompatible, incongruent, incongruous, inconsistent. *See* AGREE.

repulse *verb*
To turn or drive away : beat off, fend (off), keep off, parry, repel, ward off. *See* ALLOW, STRIKE.

repulsion *noun*
Extreme hostility and dislike : abhorrence, abomination, antipathy, aversion, detestation, hate, hatred, horror, loathing, repellence, repellency, repugnance, repugnancy, revulsion. *See* LOVE.

repulsive *adjective*
Extremely unpleasant to the senses or feelings :

atrocious, disgusting, foul, horrid, nasty, nauseating, offensive, repellent, revolting, sickening, ugly, unwholesome, vile. *See* LIKE, PAIN.

reputable *adjective*
Deserving honor, respect, or admiration : admirable, commendable, creditable, deserving, estimable, exemplary, honorable, laudable, meritorious, praiseworthy, respectable, worthy. *See* GOOD, PRAISE, RESPECT, VALUE.

reputation *noun*
1. Public estimation of someone : character, name, report, repute. *Informal:* rep. *See* RESPECT. **2.** Wide recognition for one's deeds : celebrity, fame, famousness, notoriety, popularity, renown, repute. *See* KNOWLEDGE. **3.** A person's high standing among others : dignity, good name, good report, honor, prestige, repute, respect, status. *See* RESPECT.

repute *verb*
To regard in an appraising way : believe, suppose, think. *See* BELIEF.
repute *noun* **1.** Public estimation of someone : character, name, report, reputation. *Informal:* rep. *See* RESPECT. **2.** Wide recognition for one's deeds : celebrity, fame, famousness, notoriety, popularity, renown, reputation. *See* KNOWLEDGE. **3.** A person's high standing among others : dignity, good name, good report, honor, prestige, reputation, respect, status. *See* RESPECT.

reputed *adjective*
Assumed to be such : putative, supposed. *See* BELIEF.

request *verb*
To endeavor to obtain (something) by expressing one's needs or desires : ask (for), seek, solicit. *See* REQUEST.

require *verb*
1. To have as a need or prerequisite : ask, call for, demand, entail, involve, necessitate, take. *See* NECESSARY, OVER. **2.** To be without what is needed, required, or essential : lack, need, want. *See* OWNED. **3.** To ask for urgently or insistently : call for, claim, demand, exact, insist on (*or* upon), requisition. ***Idiom:*** cry out for. *See* REQUEST. **4.** To oblige to do or not do by force of authority, propriety, or custom : expect, suppose. *See* OBLIGATION.

required *adjective*
1. Incapable of being dispensed with : essential, indispensable, necessary, needful, requisite. *See* IMPORTANT, NECESSARY. **2.** Imposed on one by authority, command, or convention : compulsory, imperative, mandatory, necessary, obligatory, requisite. *See* OBLIGATION.

requirement *noun*
Something indispensable : condition, essential, must, necessity, need, precondition, prerequisite, requisite, sine qua non. *See* NECESSARY.

requisite *adjective*
1. Incapable of being dispensed with : essential, indispensable, necessary, needful, required. *See* IMPORTANT, NECESSARY. **2.** Imposed on one by authority, command, or convention : compulsory, imperative, mandatory, necessary, obligatory, required. *See* OBLIGATION.
requisite *noun* Something indispensable : condition, essential, must, necessity, need, precondition, prerequisite, requirement, sine qua non. *See* NECESSARY.

requisition *noun*
The act of demanding : call, claim, cry, demand, exaction. *See* REQUEST.
requisition *verb* To ask for urgently or insistently : call for, claim, demand, exact, insist on (*or* upon), require. ***Idiom:*** cry out for. *See* REQUEST.

requital *noun*
1. Something to make up for loss or damage : amends, compensation, indemnification, indemnity, offset, quittance, recompense, redress, reimbursement, remuneration, reparation, repayment, restitution, satisfaction, setoff. *See* SUBSTITUTE. **2.** The act of retaliating : counteraction, counterattack, counterblow, reciprocation, reprisal, retaliation, retribution, revenge, tit for tat, vengeance. ***Idioms:*** an eye for an eye, a tooth for a tooth, like for like, measure for measure. *See* ATTACK, FORGIVENESS.

requite *verb*
1. To give compensation to : compensate, indemnify, pay, recompense, redress, reimburse, remunerate, repay. *See* PAY. **2.** To give a satisfactory return to : compensate, indemnify, pay, recompense, remunerate, repay, reward. *See* PAY. **3.** To give or take mutually : reciprocate, return. *See* CONNECT. **4.** To exact revenge for or from : avenge, pay back, pay off, redress, repay, vindicate. *Informal:* fix. *Archaic:* wreak. ***Idioms:*** even the score, get back at, get even with, pay back in kind (*or* in one's own coin), settle (*or* square) accounts, take an eye for an eye. *See* FORGIVENESS.

rescind *verb*
To take back or remove : lift, recall, repeal, reverse, revoke. *See* CONTINUE, LAW, MAKE.

rescission *noun*
Reversing or annulling : recall, repeal, reversal, revocation. *See* CONTINUE, LAW.

rescue *verb*
1. To extricate, as from danger or confinement : deliver, save. ***Idiom:*** come to the rescue of. *See* HELP. 2. To extricate from an undesirable state : reclaim, recover, redeem, salvage. *See* HELP.
rescue *noun* Extrication from danger or confinement : deliverance, delivery, salvage, salvation. *See* HELP.

research *noun*
A seeking of knowledge, data, or the truth about something : inquest, inquiry, inquisition, investigation, probe. *See* INVESTIGATE.

researcher *noun*
One who inquires : inquirer, inquisitor, investigator, prober, querier, quester, questioner. *See* ASK, INVESTIGATE.

resemblance *noun*
The quality or state of being alike : affinity, alikeness, analogy, comparison, correspondence, likeness, parallelism, similarity, similitude, uniformity, uniformness. *See* SAME.

resemble *verb*
To be similar to, as in appearance : take after. *Chiefly Regional:* favor. *See* SAME.

resentful *adjective*
Bitingly hostile : acrimonious, bitter, embittered, hard, rancorous, virulent. *See* ATTITUDE, LOVE.

resentfulness *noun*
The quality or state of feeling bitter : acrimony, bitterness, embitterment, gall[1], rancor, rancorousness, resentment, virulence, virulency. *See* FEELINGS.

resentment *noun*
1. Extreme displeasure caused by an insult or slight : dudgeon, huff, miff, offense, pique, ruffled feathers, umbrage. *See* LIKE, PAIN. 2. The quality or state of feeling bitter : acrimony, bitterness, embitterment, gall[1], rancor, rancorousness, resentfulness, virulence, virulency. *See* FEELINGS.

reservation *noun*
1. A restricting or modifying element : condition, provision, proviso, qualification, specification, stipulation, term (often used in plural). *Informal:* string (often used in plural). *See* LIMITED. 2. A feeling of uncertainty about the fitness or correctness of an action : compunction, misgiving, qualm, scruple. *See* CERTAIN.
3. Public land kept for a special purpose : preserve, reserve. *See* TERRITORY.

reserve *verb*
1. To have and maintain in one's possession : hold, hold back, keep, keep back, retain, withhold. *See* KEEP. 2. To cause to be set aside, as for one's use, in advance : bespeak, book, engage. *See* GET.
reserve *noun* 1. A supply stored or hidden for future use : backlog, cache, hoard, inventory, nest egg, reservoir, stock, stockpile, store, treasure. *Slang:* stash. *See* COLLECT. 2. The keeping of one's thoughts and emotions to oneself : control, restraint, reticence, self-control, self-restraint, taciturnity, uncommunicativeness. *See* RESTRAINT. 3. Public land kept for a special purpose : preserve, reservation. *See* TERRITORY.
reserve *adjective* Used or held in reserve : auxiliary, backup, emergency, secondary, standby, supplemental, supplementary. *See* INCREASE.

reserved *adjective*
1. Not total, unlimited, or wholehearted : limited, modified, qualified, restricted. *See* BIG, LIMITED. 2. Tending to keep one's thoughts and emotions to oneself : controlled, inhibited, noncommittal, restrained, self-controlled, self-restrained. *See* RESTRAINT. 3. Not friendly, sociable, or warm in manner : aloof, chill, chilly, cool, distant, offish, remote, reticent, solitary, standoffish, unapproachable, uncommunicative, undemonstrative, withdrawn. *See* ATTITUDE, HOT. 4. Not speaking freely or openly : close, close-mouthed, incommunicable, incommunicative, reticent, silent, taciturn, tightlipped, uncommunicable, uncommunicative. *See* RESTRAINT, SOUNDS.

reservoir *noun*
A supply stored or hidden for future use : backlog, cache, hoard, inventory, nest egg, reserve, stock, stockpile, store, treasure. *Slang:* stash. *See* COLLECT.

reside *verb*
1. To have as one's domicile, usually for an extended period : abide, domicile, dwell, house, live[1]. *See* PLACE. 2. To have an inherent basis : consist, dwell, exist, inhere, lie[1], repose, rest[1]. *See* START.

residence *noun*
A building or shelter where one lives : abode, domicile, dwelling, habitation, home, house, lodging (often used in plural), place. *Chiefly British:* dig (used in plural). *See* PROTECTION.

residue *noun*
What remains after a part has been used or subtracted : balance, leavings, leftover, remainder, remains, remnant, rest[2]. *See* LEFTOVER.

resign *verb*
1. To bring (oneself) to accept : reconcile. *See* ACCEPT. **2.** To relinquish one's engagement in or occupation with : demit, leave[1], quit, terminate. *See* CONTINUE. **3.** To give up a possession, claim, or right : abandon, abdicate, cede, demit, forswear, hand over, quitclaim, relinquish, render, renounce, surrender, waive, yield. *See* KEEP.

resignation *noun*
1. A giving up of a possession, claim, or right : abandonment, abdication, demission, quitclaim, relinquishment, renunciation, surrender, waiver. *See* KEEP. **2.** The capacity of enduring hardship or inconvenience without complaint : forbearance, long-suffering, patience, tolerance. *See* ACCEPT.

resigned *adjective*
1. Submitting without objection or resistance : acquiescent, nonresistant, passive, submissive. *See* RESIST. **2.** Enduring or capable of enduring hardship or inconvenience without complaint : forbearing, long-suffering, patient. *See* ACCEPT.

resilience *noun*
1. The ability to recover quickly from depression or discouragement : bounce, buoyancy, elasticity, resiliency. *See* ABILITY. **2.** The quality or state of being flexible : bounce, ductility, elasticity, flexibility, flexibleness, give, malleability, malleableness, plasticity, pliability, pliableness, pliancy, pliantness, resiliency, spring, springiness, suppleness. *Obsolete:* flexure. *See* FLEXIBLE.

resiliency *noun*
1. The ability to recover quickly from depression or discouragement : bounce, buoyancy, elasticity, resilience. *See* ABILITY. **2.** The quality or state of being flexible : bounce, ductility, elasticity, flexibility, flexibleness, give, malleability, malleableness, plasticity, pliability, pliableness, pliancy, pliantness, resilience, spring, springiness, suppleness. *Obsolete:* flexure. *See* FLEXIBLE.

resilient *adjective*
Capable of withstanding stress without injury : elastic, flexible, flexile, springy, supple. *Physics:* plastic. *See* FLEXIBLE.

resist *verb*
1. To oppose actively and with force : withstand. ***Idioms:*** mount (*or* offer) resistance, put up a fight, stand up to (*or* against). *See* RESIST. **2.** To take a stand against : buck, challenge, contest, dispute, oppose, traverse. *See* SUPPORT.

resistance *noun*
1. The act of resisting : opposition, renitence, renitency. *See* RESIST. **2.** The capacity to withstand : immunity, imperviousness, insusceptibility, unsusceptibility. *See* RESIST. **3.** A clandestine organization of freedom fighters in an oppressed land : underground. *See* RESIST.

resistant *adjective*
1. Having the capacity to withstand : immune, impervious, insusceptible, proof, resistive, unsusceptible. *See* RESIST. **2.** Tending to resist, as an influence or idea : renitent, resisting, resistive. *See* RESIST.

resister *noun*
One that opposes another in a battle, contest, controversy, or debate : adversary, antagonist, opponent, opposer, opposition, oppositionist. *See* RESIST, SUPPORT.

resisting *adjective*
Tending to resist, as an influence or idea : renitent, resistant, resistive. *See* RESIST.

resistive *adjective*
1. Having the capacity to withstand : immune, impervious, insusceptible, proof, resistant, unsusceptible. *See* RESIST. **2.** Tending to resist, as an influence or idea : renitent, resistant, resisting. *See* RESIST.

resolute *adjective*
1. Not hesitating or wavering : decided, decisive, determined, firm[1]. *See* DECIDE. **2.** Indicating or possessing determination, resolution, or persistence : constant, determined, firm[1], steadfast, steady, stiff, tough, unbending, uncompromising, unflinching, unwavering, unyielding. *See* PURPOSE. **3.** On an unwavering course of action : bent, decided, determined, fixed, intent, set[1]. *See* DECIDE.

resoluteness *noun*
Unwavering firmness of character, action, or will : decidedness, decision, decisiveness, determination, firmness, purpose, purposefulness, resolution, resolve, toughness, will, willpower. *See* CERTAIN, STRONG.

resolution *noun*
1. Unwavering firmness of character, action, or will : decidedness, decision, decisiveness, determination, firmness, purpose, purposefulness, resoluteness, resolve, toughness, will, willpower. *See* CERTAIN, STRONG. **2.** A position reached after consideration : conclusion, decision, determination. *See* DECIDE.

resolve *verb*
1. To make up or cause to make up one's mind : conclude, decide, determine, settle. *See* DECIDE. **2.** To separate into parts for study :

analyze, anatomize, break down, dissect. *See* ASSEMBLE, INVESTIGATE. **3.** To find a solution for : clear up, decipher, explain, solve, unravel. *Informal:* dope out, figure out. ***Idiom:*** get to the bottom of. *See* ASK, REASON. **4.** To bring (something) into a state of agreement or accord : reconcile, rectify, settle, smooth over, straighten out. *See* AGREE.

resolve *noun* Unwavering firmness of character, action, or will : decidedness, decision, decisiveness, determination, firmness, purpose, purposefulness, resoluteness, resolution, toughness, will, willpower. *See* CERTAIN, STRONG.

resonant *adjective*
Having or producing a full, deep, or rich sound : mellow, orotund, plangent, resounding, ringing, rotund, round, sonorous, vibrant. *See* SOUNDS.

resort *verb*
1. To look to when in need : apply, go, refer, repair[2], run, turn. ***Idioms:*** fall back on (*or* upon), have recourse to. *See* USED. **2.** To visit regularly : frequent, hang around, haunt, repair[2]. *Slang:* hang out. *See* PLACE.

resort *noun* **1.** A frequently visited place : haunt, rendezvous, stamping ground. *Slang:* hangout. *See* PLACE, REPETITION. **2.** That to which one turns for help when in desperation : recourse, refuge, resource. *See* HELP.

resound *verb*
To send back the sound of : echo, rebound, reecho, reflect, repeat, reverberate. *See* SOUNDS.

resounding *adjective*
1. Having or producing a full, deep, or rich sound : mellow, orotund, plangent, resonant, ringing, rotund, round, sonorous, vibrant. *See* SOUNDS. **2.** Expressed or performed with emphasis : emphatic, forceful. *See* STRONG.

resource *noun*
1. That to which one turns for help when in desperation : recourse, refuge, resort. *See* HELP. **2.** The ability and the means to meet situations effectively. Often used in plural : resourcefulness, wherewithal. *See* ABILITY. **3.** All things, such as money, property, or goods, having economic value. Used in plural : asset (used in plural), capital, fortune, mean[3] (used in plural), wealth, wherewithal. *See* OWNED.

resourceful *adjective*
Able to use the means at one's disposal to meet situations effectively : ingenious, inventive. *See* ABILITY.

resourcefulness *noun*
The ability and the means to meet situations effectively : resource (often used in plural), wherewithal. *See* ABILITY.

respect *verb*
1. To have a high opinion of : admire, consider, esteem, honor, regard, value. ***Idioms:*** look up to, think highly (*or* much *or* well) of. *See* PRAISE. **2.** To recognize the worth, quality, importance, or magnitude of : appreciate, cherish, esteem, prize[1], treasure, value. ***Idiom:*** set store by. *See* PRAISE.

respect *noun* **1.** A feeling of deference, approval, and liking : account, admiration, appreciation, consideration, esteem, estimation, favor, honor, regard. *See* RESPECT. **2.** A person's high standing among others : dignity, good name, good report, honor, prestige, reputation, repute, status. *See* RESPECT. **3.** Friendly greetings. Used in plural : best, regard (used in plural). *See* GREETING. **4.** The particular angle from which something is considered : angle[2], aspect, facet, frame of reference, hand, light[1], phase, regard, side. *See* PERSPECTIVE.

respectability *noun*
Conformity to recognized standards, as of conduct or appearance : comeliness, correctness, decency, decentness, decorousness, decorum, properness, propriety, respectableness, seemliness. *See* USUAL.

respectable *adjective*
1. Deserving honor, respect, or admiration : admirable, commendable, creditable, deserving, estimable, exemplary, honorable, laudable, meritorious, praiseworthy, reputable, worthy. *See* GOOD, PRAISE, RESPECT, VALUE. **2.** Conforming to accepted standards : becoming, befitting, comely, comme il faut, correct, decent, decorous, de rigueur, nice, proper, right, seemly. *See* COURTESY. **3.** Of moderately good quality but less than excellent : acceptable, adequate, all right, average, common, decent, fair, fairish, goodish, moderate, passable, satisfactory, sufficient, tolerable. *Informal:* OK, tidy. *See* GOOD. **4.** Somewhat big : biggish, goodly, largish, sizable. *See* BIG. **5.** Proper in appearance : presentable. *Informal:* decent. *See* GOOD, USUAL.

respectableness *noun*
Conformity to recognized standards, as of conduct or appearance : comeliness, correctness, decency, decentness, decorousness, decorum, properness, propriety, respectability, seemliness. *See* USUAL.

respectful *adjective*
Marked by courteous submission or respect :

deferential, duteous, dutiful, obeisant. *See* RESIST.

respiration *noun*
The act or process of breathing : breath. *See* BREATH.

respire *verb*
To breathe in and out : breathe. *See* BREATH.

respite *noun*
1. A pause or interval, as from work or duty : break, intermission, recess, rest[1], time-out. *Informal:* breather. *See* CONTINUE. **2.** Temporary immunity from penalties : grace, reprieve. *See* CONTINUE.

resplendence *noun*
Brilliant, showy splendor : brilliance, brilliancy, glitter, glory, gorgeousness, magnificence, resplendency, sparkle, sumptuousness. *Informal:* glitz. *See* BEAUTIFUL.

resplendency *noun*
Brilliant, showy splendor : brilliance, brilliancy, glitter, glory, gorgeousness, magnificence, resplendence, sparkle, sumptuousness. *Informal:* glitz. *See* BEAUTIFUL.

resplendent *adjective*
Marked by extraordinary elegance, beauty, and splendor : brilliant, glorious, gorgeous, magnificent, proud, splendid, splendorous. *See* BEAUTIFUL.

respond *verb*
1. To speak or act in response, as to a question : answer, rejoin, reply, retort, return, riposte. *See* ASK. **2.** To act in return to something, as a stimulus : react. *See* ACTION. **3.** To present with a specified reaction : greet, meet[1], react. *See* FEELINGS, GREETING.

respondent *noun*
A person against whom an action is brought : *Law:* accused, defendant. *See* LAW.

response *noun*
1. Something spoken or written in return, as to a question or demand : answer, rejoinder, reply. *See* ASK. **2.** An action elicited by a stimulus : reaction, retroaction. *See* ACTION.

responsibility *noun*
An act or course of action that is demanded of one, as by position, custom, law, or religion : burden[1], charge, commitment, duty, imperative, must, need, obligation. *See* OBLIGATION.

responsible *adjective*
1. Legally obligated : accountable, amenable, answerable, liable. *See* LAW. **2.** Capable of being depended upon : dependable, reliable, solid, sound[2], trustworthy, trusty. *See* TRUST.

responsive *adjective*
1. Able to receive and respond to external stimuli : impressible, impressionable, sensible, sensitive, sentient, susceptible, susceptive. *See* AWARENESS. **2.** Ready and willing to receive favorably, as new ideas : acceptant, amenable, open, open-minded, receptive. *See* ACCEPT. **3.** Easily approached : accessible, approachable, welcoming. *See* APPROACH, ATTITUDE.

responsiveness *noun*
Ready acceptance of often new suggestions, ideas, influences, or opinions : open-mindedness, openness, receptiveness, receptivity. *See* ACCEPT.

rest[1] *noun*
1. A pause or interval, as from work or duty : break, intermission, recess, respite, time-out. *Informal:* breather. *See* CONTINUE. **2.** Freedom from labor, responsibility, or strain : ease, leisure, relaxation, repose. *See* CONTINUE. **3.** The act or fact of dying : death, decease, demise, dissolution, extinction, passing, quietus. *Slang:* curtain (used in plural). *See* LIVE.

rest *verb* **1.** To take repose by ceasing work or other effort for an interval of time : relax, unbend, unwind. ***Idioms:*** lead (*or* live) the life of Riley, take it easy. *See* CONTINUE. **2.** To take repose, as by sleeping or lying quietly : lie[1] (down), recline, repose, stretch (out). *See* CONTINUE. **3.** To have an inherent basis : consist, dwell, exist, inhere, lie[1], repose, reside. *See* START. **4.** To provide a basis for : base[1], build, establish, found, ground, predicate, root[1], underpin. *See* OVER.

rest on (or **upon**) *verb* To be determined by or contingent on something unknown, uncertain, or changeable : depend on (*or* upon), hang on, hang upon, hinge on (*or* upon), turn on, turn upon. *See* START.

rest[2] *noun*
What remains after a part has been used or subtracted : balance, leavings, leftover, remainder, remains, remnant, residue. *See* LEFTOVER.

restart *verb*
To begin or go on after an interruption : continue, pick up, renew, reopen, resume, take up. *See* CONTINUE.

restate *verb*
1. To state again : iterate, reiterate, repeat. *See* REPETITION. **2.** To express the meaning of in other, especially simpler, words : paraphrase, render, rephrase, reword, translate. *See* WORDS.

restatement *noun*
1. The act or process of repeating : iteration, reiteration, repetition. *See* REPETITION. **2.** A restating of something in other, especially

simpler, words : paraphrase, rendering, translation, version. *See* WORDS.

restitute *verb*
1. To bring back to a previous normal condition : rebuild, reclaim, recondition, reconstruct, rehabilitate, reinstate, rejuvenate, renovate, restore. *See* HELP. **2.** To give back, especially money : refund, reimburse, repay. *See* PAY.

restitution *noun*
Something to make up for loss or damage : amends, compensation, indemnification, indemnity, offset, quittance, recompense, redress, reimbursement, remuneration, reparation, repayment, requital, satisfaction, setoff. *See* SUBSTITUTE.

restive *adjective*
Feeling or exhibiting nervous tension : edgy, fidgety, jittery, jumpy, nervous, restless, skittish, tense, twitchy. *Slang:* uptight. ***Idioms:*** a bundle of nerves, all wound up, on edge. *See* TIGHTEN.

restiveness *noun*
An uneasy or nervous state : disquiet, disquietude, inquietude, restlessness, unease, uneasiness, unrest. *See* CALM.

restless *adjective*
1. Affording no quiet, repose, or rest : uneasy, unquiet, unsettled. *See* CALM, TIRED. **2.** Feeling or exhibiting nervous tension : edgy, fidgety, jittery, jumpy, nervous, restive, skittish, tense, twitchy. *Slang:* uptight. ***Idioms:*** a bundle of nerves, all wound up, on edge. *See* TIGHTEN.

restlessness *noun*
An uneasy or nervous state : disquiet, disquietude, inquietude, restiveness, unease, uneasiness, unrest. *See* CALM.

rest on or **upon** *verb* See **rest[1]**.

restoration *noun*
The act of making new or as if new again : face-lift, facelifting, refurbishment, rejuvenation, renewal, renovation, revampment. *See* HELP, NEW.

restorative *adjective*
1. Serving to cure : curative, remedial, therapeutic. *See* HEALTH. **2.** Producing or stimulating physical, mental, or emotional vigor : bracing, energizing, exhilarant, exhilarating, innerving, intoxicating, invigorating, refreshing, reinvigorating, renewing, roborant, stimulating, tonic. *See* HELP.

restorative *noun* A medicine that restores or increases vigor : roborant, tonic. *Informal:* bracer, pick-me-up. *See* HELP.

restore *verb*
1. To bring back into existence or use : reestablish, reinstate, reintroduce, renew, return, revive. *See* INCREASE, KEEP. **2.** To cause to come back to life or consciousness : bring around (*or* round), resuscitate, revive, revivify. *See* LIVE. **3.** To bring back to a previous normal condition : rebuild, reclaim, recondition, reconstruct, rehabilitate, reinstate, rejuvenate, renovate, restitute. *See* HELP. **4.** To make new or as if new again : furbish, recondition, re-create, refresh, refurbish, rejuvenate, renew, renovate, revamp. ***Idiom:*** give a new look to. *See* HELP, NEW. **5.** To impart renewed energy and strength to (a person) : freshen, refresh, reinvigorate, rejuvenate, renew, revitalize, revivify. *See* HELP, STRONG. **6.** To put (someone) in the possession of a prior position or office : give back, reinstate, replace, return. *See* INCREASE, KEEP. **7.** To send, put, or carry back to a former location : give back, return, take back. *See* INCREASE, KEEP.

restrain *verb*
To control, restrict, or arrest : bit[2], brake, bridle, check, constrain, curb, hold, hold back, hold down, hold in, inhibit, keep, keep back, pull in, rein (back, in, *or* up). *See* RESTRAINT.

restrained *adjective*
1. Kept within sensible limits : conservative, discreet, moderate, reasonable, temperate. *See* PLAIN, RESTRAINT. **2.** Not showy or obtrusive : inobtrusive, quiet, subdued, tasteful, unobtrusive. *See* PLAIN. **3.** Tending to keep one's thoughts and emotions to oneself : controlled, inhibited, noncommittal, reserved, self-controlled, self-restrained. *See* RESTRAINT.

restraint *noun*
1. The act of limiting or condition of being limited : circumscription, confinement, constraint, limitation, restriction. *See* LIMITED. **2.** Something that limits or restricts : check, circumscription, constraint, cramp[2], curb, inhibition, limit, limitation, restriction, stricture, trammel. *See* LIMITED. **3.** An instrument or means of restraining : bit[2], brake, bridle, leash, snaffle. *See* RESTRAINT. **4.** Something that physically confines the legs or arms : bond, chain (used in plural), fetter, handcuff (often used in plural), hobble, iron (used in plural), manacle, shackle. *Archaic:* gyve. *See* FREE. **5.** The keeping of one's thoughts and emotions to oneself : control, reserve, reticence, self-control, self-restraint, taciturnity, uncommunicativeness. *See* RESTRAINT.

restrict *verb*
To place a limit on : circumscribe, confine, limit. *See* LIMITED.

restricted *adjective*
1. Kept within certain limits : limited. *See* LIMITED. **2.** Not total, unlimited, or wholehearted : limited, modified, qualified, reserved. *See* BIG, LIMITED. **3.** Excluding or unavailable to certain minorities : segregated. *See* INCLUDE, LIMITED. **4.** Of or being information available only to authorized persons : classified, confidential, privileged. *See* SHOW.

restriction *noun*
1. The act of limiting or condition of being limited : circumscription, confinement, constraint, limitation, restraint. *See* LIMITED. **2.** Something that limits or restricts : check, circumscription, constraint, cramp[2], curb, inhibition, limit, limitation, restraint, stricture, trammel. *See* LIMITED.

result *verb*
To occur as a consequence : attend, ensue, follow. *See* CAUSE, PRECEDE.
result in *verb* To be the cause of : bring, bring about, bring on, cause, effect, effectuate, generate, induce, ingenerate, lead to, make, occasion, secure, set off, stir[1] (up), touch off, trigger. ***Idioms:*** bring to pass (*or* effect), give rise to. *See* START.
result *noun* **1.** Something brought about by a cause : aftermath, consequence, corollary, effect, end product, event, fruit, harvest, issue, outcome, precipitate, ramification, resultant, sequel, sequence, sequent, upshot. *See* CAUSE. **2.** *Mathematics.* Something worked out to explain, resolve, or provide a method for dealing with and settling a problem : answer, determination, solution. *See* ASK.

resultant *noun*
Something brought about by a cause : aftermath, consequence, corollary, effect, end product, event, fruit, harvest, issue, outcome, precipitate, ramification, result, sequel, sequence, sequent, upshot. *See* CAUSE.

result in *verb* See **result.**

resume *verb*
1. To begin or go on after an interruption : continue, pick up, renew, reopen, restart, take up. *See* CONTINUE. **2.** To occupy or take again : reassume, re-claim, reoccupy, repossess, retake, take back. *See* GIVE.

resumption *noun*
A continuing after interruption : continuation, renewal, resurgence, revival. *See* CONTINUE.

resurgence *noun*
1. A continuing after interruption : continuation, renewal, resumption, revival. *See* CONTINUE. **2.** The act of reviving or condition of being revived : reactivation, rebirth, renaissance, renascence, renewal, resurrection, resuscitation, revitalization, revival, revivification. *See* AWARENESS.

resurrect *verb*
To rouse from a state of inactivity or quiescence : reactivate, reanimate, reawaken, rekindle, renew, resuscitate, revitalize, revive, revivify. *See* AWARENESS.

resurrection *noun*
The act of reviving or condition of being revived : reactivation, rebirth, renaissance, renascence, renewal, resurgence, resuscitation, revitalization, revival, revivification. *See* AWARENESS.

resuscitate *verb*
1. To cause to come back to life or consciousness : bring around (*or* round), restore, revive, revivify. *See* LIVE. **2.** To rouse from a state of inactivity or quiescence : reactivate, reanimate, reawaken, rekindle, renew, resurrect, revitalize, revive, revivify. *See* AWARENESS.

resuscitation *noun*
The act of reviving or condition of being revived : reactivation, rebirth, renaissance, renascence, renewal, resurgence, resurrection, revitalization, revival, revivification. *See* AWARENESS.

retail *verb*
To offer for sale : deal (in), handle, market, merchandise, merchant, peddle, sell, trade (in), vend. *See* TRANSACTIONS.

retain *verb*
1. To keep at one's disposal : have, hold, own, possess. *See* KEEP. **2.** To have and maintain in one's possession : hold, hold back, keep, keep back, reserve, withhold. *See* KEEP. **3.** To persevere in some condition, action, or belief : keep, maintain, stay with. *See* CONTINUE. **4.** To renew an image or thought in the mind : bethink, mind, recall, recollect, remember, reminisce, revive, think. ***Idiom:*** bring to mind. *See* REMEMBER. **5.** To obtain the use or services of : employ, engage, hire, take on. ***Idiom:*** put on the payroll. *See* GET, WORK.

retained *adjective*
Having a job : employed, hired, jobholding, working. *See* WORK.

retake *verb*
To occupy or take again : reassume, re-claim,

reoccupy, repossess, resume, take back. *See* GIVE.

retaliate *verb*
To return like for like, especially to return an unfriendly or hostile action with a similar one : counter, hit back, reciprocate, retort, strike back. *See* ATTACK, FORGIVENESS.

retaliation *noun*
The act of retaliating : counteraction, counterattack, counterblow, reciprocation, reprisal, requital, retribution, revenge, tit for tat, vengeance. ***Idioms:*** an eye for an eye, a tooth for a tooth, like for like, measure for measure. *See* ATTACK, FORGIVENESS.

retard *verb*
To cause to be later or slower than expected or desired : delay, detain, hang up, hold up, lag, set back, slow (down *or* up), stall[2]. *See* HELP, TIME.

retardation *noun*
The condition or fact of being made late or slow : delay, detainment, holdup, lag. *See* HELP, TIME.

retarded *adjective*
Offensive. Having only a limited ability to learn and understand : backward, dull, simple, simple-minded, slow, slow-witted. *Informal:* soft. *Offensive:* feeble-minded, half-witted, weak-minded. *See* ABILITY.

rethink *verb*
To consider again, especially with the possibility of change : reconsider, reevaluate, reexamine, review. *See* THOUGHTS.

reticence *noun*
1. The keeping of one's thoughts and emotions to oneself : control, reserve, restraint, self-control, self-restraint, taciturnity, uncommunicativeness. *See* RESTRAINT. **2.** Reserve in speech, behavior, or dress : demureness, diffidence, modesty, self-effacement. *See* RESTRAINT.

reticent *adjective*
1. Not speaking freely or openly : close, close-mouthed, incommunicable, incommunicative, reserved, silent, taciturn, tightlipped, uncommunicable, uncommunicative. *See* RESTRAINT, SOUNDS. **2.** Not friendly, sociable, or warm in manner : aloof, chill, chilly, cool, distant, offish, remote, reserved, solitary, standoffish, unapproachable, uncommunicative, undemonstrative, withdrawn. *See* ATTITUDE, HOT.

retinue *noun*
A group of attendants or followers : entourage, following, suite, train. *See* OVER.

retire *verb*
1. To move or proceed away from a place : depart, exit, get away, get off, go, go away, leave[1], pull out, quit, run (along), withdraw. *Informal:* cut out, push off, shove off. *Slang:* blow[1], split, take off. ***Idioms:*** hit the road, take leave. *See* APPROACH. **2.** To go to bed : bed (down). *Informal:* turn in. *Slang:* crash, flop. ***Idioms:*** call it a night, hit the hay (*or* sack). *See* AWARENESS. **3.** To withdraw from business or active life : step down. ***Idioms:*** call it quits, hang up one's spurs, turn in one's badge. *See* CONTINUE. **4.** To remove from active service : pension (off), superannuate. ***Idiom:*** put out to pasture. *See* KEEP. **5.** To move back in the face of enemy attack or after a defeat : draw back, fall back, pull back, pull out, retreat, withdraw. ***Idioms:*** beat a retreat, give ground (*or* way). *See* FORWARD.

retirement *noun*
1. The act of secluding or the state of being secluded : reclusion, seclusion, sequestration. *See* INCLUDE. **2.** The moving back of a military force in the face of enemy attack or after a defeat : fallback, pullback, pullout, retreat, withdrawal. *See* FORWARD.

retiring *adjective*
Not forward but reticent or reserved in manner : backward, bashful, coy, demure, diffident, modest, self-effacing, shy[1], timid. *See* RESTRAINT.

retiringness *noun*
An awkwardness or lack of self-confidence in the presence of others : backwardness, bashfulness, coyness, shyness, timidity, timidness. *See* RESTRAINT.

retort *verb*
1. To speak or act in response, as to a question : answer, rejoin, reply, respond, return, riposte. *See* ASK. **2.** To return like for like, especially to return an unfriendly or hostile action with a similar one : counter, hit back, reciprocate, retaliate, strike back. *See* ATTACK, FORGIVENESS.

retort *noun* A spirited, incisive reply : comeback, repartee, riposte. *See* ASK.

retouch *verb*
To improve by making minor changes or additions : polish, touch up. *See* BETTER.

retract *verb*
1. To disavow (something previously written or said) irrevocably and usually formally : abjure, recall, recant, take back, withdraw. *See* ACCEPT. **2.** To pull back in : draw in, withdraw. *See* SHOW. **3.** To move back or away

from a point, limit, or mark : ebb, recede, retreat, retrocede, retrograde, retrogress. *See* APPROACH.

retractation *noun*
A formal statement of disavowal : abjuration, palinode, recantation, retraction, withdrawal. *See* ACCEPT.

retraction *noun*
A formal statement of disavowal : abjuration, palinode, recantation, retractation, withdrawal. *See* ACCEPT.

retreat *noun*
1. Something that physically protects, especially from danger : asylum, cover, covert, harbor, haven, protection, refuge, sanctuary, shelter. *See* ATTACK, SAFETY. **2.** The moving back of a military force in the face of enemy attack or after a defeat : fallback, pullback, pullout, retirement, withdrawal. *See* FORWARD.
retreat *verb* **1.** To move back or away from a point, limit, or mark : ebb, recede, retract, retrocede, retrograde, retrogress. *See* APPROACH. **2.** To move in a reverse direction : back, backpedal, backtrack, fall back, retrocede, retrograde, retrogress. ***Idiom:*** retrace one's steps. *See* FORWARD. **3.** To abandon a former position or commitment : back down (*or* out), renege. *Slang:* cop out, fink out. *See* RESIST. **4.** To move back in the face of enemy attack or after a defeat : draw back, fall back, pull back, pull out, retire, withdraw. ***Idioms:*** beat a retreat, give ground (*or* way). *See* FORWARD.

retribution *noun*
The act of retaliating : counteraction, counterattack, counterblow, reciprocation, reprisal, requital, retaliation, revenge, tit for tat, vengeance. ***Idioms:*** an eye for an eye, a tooth for a tooth, like for like, measure for measure. *See* ATTACK, FORGIVENESS.

retrieval *noun*
The act of getting back or regaining : recoup, recovery, repossession. *See* GET.

retrieve *verb*
To get back : recoup, recover, regain, repossess. *See* GET.

retroaction *noun*
An action elicited by a stimulus : reaction, response. *See* ACTION.

retrocede *verb*
1. To move back or away from a point, limit, or mark : ebb, recede, retract, retreat, retrograde, retrogress. *See* APPROACH. **2.** To move in a reverse direction : back, backpedal, backtrack, fall back, retreat, retrograde, retrogress. ***Idiom:*** retrace one's steps. *See* FORWARD.

retrogradation *noun*
A return to a former, usually worse condition : regression, retrogression, reversion. *See* FORWARD, REPETITION.

retrograde *adjective*
Directed or facing toward the back or rear : backward, retrogressive. *See* PRECEDE.
retrograde *verb* **1.** To move in a reverse direction : back, backpedal, backtrack, fall back, retreat, retrocede, retrogress. ***Idiom:*** retrace one's steps. *See* FORWARD. **2.** To move back or away from a point, limit, or mark : ebb, recede, retract, retreat, retrocede, retrogress. *See* APPROACH. **3.** To become lower in quality, character, or condition : atrophy, decline, degenerate, descend, deteriorate, sink, worsen. ***Idioms:*** go bad, go to pot, go to seed, go to the dogs. *See* BETTER.

retrogress *verb*
1. To slip from a higher or better condition to a former, usually lower or poorer one : backslide, lapse, regress, relapse, revert. *See* BETTER, REPETITION. **2.** To move in a reverse direction : back, backpedal, backtrack, fall back, retreat, retrocede, retrograde. ***Idiom:*** retrace one's steps. *See* FORWARD. **3.** To move back or away from a point, limit, or mark : ebb, recede, retract, retreat, retrocede, retrograde. *See* APPROACH.

retrogression *noun*
A return to a former, usually worse condition : regression, retrogradation, reversion. *See* FORWARD, REPETITION.

retrogressive *adjective*
Directed or facing toward the back or rear : backward, retrograde. *See* PRECEDE.

return *verb*
1. To come back to a former condition : recrudesce, recur, reoccur, revert. *See* REPETITION. **2.** To go again to a former place : come back, go back, revisit. *See* APPROACH. **3.** To send, put, or carry back to a former location : give back, restore, take back. *See* INCREASE, KEEP. **4.** To bring back into existence or use : reestablish, reinstate, reintroduce, renew, restore, revive. *See* INCREASE, KEEP. **5.** To speak or act in response, as to a question : answer, rejoin, reply, respond, retort, riposte. *See* ASK. **6.** To give or take mutually : reciprocate, requite. *See* CONNECT. **7.** To make as income or profit : bring in, clear, draw, earn, gain, gross, net[2], pay, produce, realize, repay, yield. *See* MONEY. **8.** To deliver (an indictment or verdict, for example) : hand down, render. *See* LAW. **9.** To put (someone) in the possession of a prior

position or office : give back, reinstate, replace, restore. *See* INCREASE, KEEP.

return *noun* **1.** A repeated occurrence : reappearance, recurrence, reoccurrence. *See* REPETITION. **2.** Something earned, won, or otherwise acquired : earnings, gain, profit. *See* GET, MONEY.

reunite *verb*
To reestablish friendship between : conciliate, make up, reconcile. *See* LOVE.

revamp *verb*
1. To restore to proper condition or functioning : doctor, fix, fix up, mend, overhaul, patch, repair[1], right. ***Idiom:*** set right. *See* HELP. **2.** To make new or as if new again : furbish, recondition, re-create, refresh, refurbish, rejuvenate, renew, renovate, restore. ***Idiom:*** give a new look to. *See* HELP, NEW. **3.** To prepare a new version of : amend, emend, emendate, revise, rework, rewrite. *See* CHANGE.

revampment *noun*
The act of making new or as if new again : face-lift, facelifting, refurbishment, rejuvenation, renewal, renovation, restoration. *See* HELP, NEW.

reveal *verb*
1. To disclose in a breach of confidence : betray, blab, divulge, expose, give away, let out, tell, uncover, unveil. *Informal:* spill. *Archaic:* discover. ***Idioms:*** let slip, let the cat out of the bag, spill the beans, tell all. *See* SHOW. **2.** To make visible; bring to view : bare, disclose, display, expose, show, unclothe, uncover, unmask, unveil. *Archaic:* discover. ***Idioms:*** bring to light, lay open, make plain. *See* SHOW. **3.** To make manifest or apparent : demonstrate, display, evidence, evince, exhibit, manifest, proclaim, show. *See* SHOW.

revel *verb*
1. To take extravagant pleasure : bask, indulge, luxuriate, roll, rollick, wallow. *See* LIKE. **2.** To show joyful satisfaction in an event, especially by merrymaking : celebrate, rejoice. ***Idioms:*** kill the fatted calf, make merry. *See* LAUGHTER. **3.** To behave riotously : carouse, frolic, riot, roister. *Informal:* hell (around). ***Idioms:*** blow off steam, cut loose, kick over the traces, kick up one's heels, let go, let loose, make merry, make whoopee, paint the town red, raise Cain (*or* the devil *or* hell), whoop it up. *See* RESTRAINT.

revel *noun* **1.** The act of showing joyful satisfaction in an event. Often used in plural : celebration, festivity, merrymaking, rejoicing, revelry. *See* LAUGHTER. **2.** Joyful, exuberant activity. Often used in plural : conviviality, festival, festiveness, festivity, fun, gaiety, jollity, merriment, merrymaking, revelry. *See* LAUGHTER.

revelation *noun*
Something disclosed : apocalypse, disclosure, exposé, exposure. *Informal:* eye opener. *See* SHOW.

revelry *noun*
1. The act of showing joyful satisfaction in an event : celebration, festivity, merrymaking, rejoicing, revel (often used in plural). *See* LAUGHTER. **2.** Joyful, exuberant activity : conviviality, festival, festiveness, festivity, fun, gaiety, jollity, merriment, merrymaking, revel (often used in plural). *See* LAUGHTER.

revenant *noun*
A supernatural being, such as a ghost : apparition, bogey, bogeyman, bogle, eidolon, ghost, phantasm, phantasma, phantom, shade, shadow, specter, spirit, visitant, wraith. *Informal:* spook. *Regional:* haunt. *See* BEINGS, SUPERNATURAL.

revenge *noun*
1. The act of retaliating : counteraction, counterattack, counterblow, reciprocation, reprisal, requital, retaliation, retribution, tit for tat, vengeance. ***Idioms:*** an eye for an eye, a tooth for a tooth, like for like, measure for measure. *See* ATTACK, FORGIVENESS. **2.** The quality or condition of being vindictive : spite, spitefulness, vengefulness, vindictiveness. *See* FORGIVENESS.

revengeful *adjective*
Disposed to seek revenge : spiteful, vengeful, vindictive. *See* FORGIVENESS.

reverberate *verb*
To send back the sound of : echo, rebound, reecho, reflect, repeat, resound. *See* SOUNDS.

reverberation *noun*
Repetition of sound via reflection from a surface : echo, repercussion. *See* SOUNDS.

revere *verb*
To regard with great awe and devotion : adore, idolize, reverence, venerate, worship. *See* SACRED.

reverence *noun*
The act of adoring, especially reverently : adoration, idolization, veneration, worship. *See* LIKE, LOVE, SACRED.

reverence *verb* To regard with great awe and devotion : adore, idolize, revere, venerate, worship. *See* SACRED.

reverend *noun*
Informal. A person ordained for service in a

Christian church : churchman, churchwoman, clergyman, clergywoman, cleric, clerical, clerk, divine, ecclesiastic, minister, parson, preacher. *See* RELIGION.

reverent *adjective*
Feeling or showing reverence : reverential, venerational, worshipful. *See* RESPECT.

reverential *adjective*
Feeling or showing reverence : reverent, venerational, worshipful. *See* RESPECT.

reverie *noun*
1. The condition of being so lost in solitary thought as to be unaware of one's surroundings : absent-mindedness, abstraction, bemusement, brown study, daydreaming, muse[2], study, trance. *See* AWARENESS. **2.** An illusory mental image : daydream, dream, fancy, fantasy, fiction, figment, illusion, phantasm, phantasma, vision. *See* REAL.

reversal *noun*
1. The act of changing or being changed, as from one course to the opposite : inversion, transposition, turnabout, turnaround. *See* CHANGE. **2.** A change for the worse : backset, reverse, setback. *See* BETTER. **3.** Reversing or annulling : recall, repeal, rescission, revocation. *See* CONTINUE, LAW.

reverse *adjective*
Diametrically opposed : antipodal, antipodean, antithetical, antonymic, antonymous, contradictory, contrary, converse[2], counter, diametric, diametrical, opposing, opposite, polar. *See* SUPPORT.
reverse *noun* **1.** That which is diametrically opposed to another : antipode, antipodes, antithesis, antonym, contrary, converse[2], counter, opposite. *Logic:* contradictory, contrapositive. *See* SUPPORT. **2.** A change from better to worse : backset, reversal, setback. *See* BETTER.
reverse *verb* **1.** To change to the opposite position, direction, or course : invert, transpose, turn (about, around, over, *or* round). *See* CHANGE. **2.** To turn sharply around : about-face, double (back). *See* APPROACH. **3.** To take back or remove : lift, recall, repeal, rescind, revoke. *See* CONTINUE, LAW, MAKE.

reversion *noun*
A return to a former, usually worse condition : regression, retrogradation, retrogression. *See* FORWARD, REPETITION.

revert *verb*
1. To come back to a former condition : recrudesce, recur, reoccur, return. *See* REPETITION. **2.** To slip from a higher or better condition to a former, usually lower or poorer one : backslide, lapse, regress, relapse, retrogress. *See* BETTER, REPETITION.

review *verb*
1. To give a recapitulation of the salient facts of : abstract, epitomize, go over, recapitulate, run down, run through, summarize, sum up, synopsize, wrap up. *Informal:* recap. *See* THOUGHTS. **2.** To consider again, especially with the possibility of change : reconsider, reevaluate, reexamine, rethink. *See* THOUGHTS. **3.** To write a critical report on : criticize. *See* OPINION, WORDS.
review *noun* **1.** A close or systematic study : analysis, examination, inspection, investigation, survey. *See* INVESTIGATE. **2.** Evaluative and critical discourse : criticism, critique, notice. *See* OPINION, WORDS. **3.** A formal military inspection : parade. *See* INVESTIGATE.

reviewer *noun*
A person who evaluates and reports on the worth of something : commentator, critic, judge. *See* VALUE.

revile *verb*
To attack with harsh, often insulting language : abuse, assail, rail against (*or* at), vituperate. *See* PRAISE.

revilement *noun*
Harsh, often insulting language : abuse, billingsgate, contumely, invective, obloquy, railing, reviling, scurrility, scurrilousness, vituperation. *See* PRAISE.

reviling *noun*
Harsh, often insulting language : abuse, billingsgate, contumely, invective, obloquy, railing, revilement, scurrility, scurrilousness, vituperation. *See* PRAISE.

revise *verb*
To prepare a new version of : amend, emend, emendate, revamp, rework, rewrite. *See* CHANGE.

revision *noun*
The act or process of revising : amendment, emendation, rewrite. *See* CHANGE.

revisit *verb*
To go again to a former place : come back, go back, return. *See* APPROACH.

revitalization *noun*
The act of reviving or condition of being revived : reactivation, rebirth, renaissance, renascence, renewal, resurgence, resurrection, resuscitation, revival, revivification. *See* AWARENESS.

revitalize *verb*
1. To impart renewed energy and strength to (a

person) : freshen, refresh, reinvigorate, rejuvenate, renew, restore, revivify. *See* HELP, STRONG. **2.** To rouse from a state of inactivity or quiescence : reactivate, reanimate, reawaken, rekindle, renew, resurrect, resuscitate, revive, revivify. *See* AWARENESS.

revival *noun*
1. The act of reviving or condition of being revived : reactivation, rebirth, renaissance, renascence, renewal, resurgence, resurrection, resuscitation, revitalization, revivification. *See* AWARENESS. **2.** A continuing after interruption : continuation, renewal, resumption, resurgence. *See* CONTINUE.

revive *verb*
1. To cause to come back to life or consciousness : bring around (*or* round), restore, resuscitate, revivify. *See* LIVE. **2.** To rouse from a state of inactivity or quiescence : reactivate, reanimate, reawaken, rekindle, renew, resurrect, resuscitate, revitalize, revivify. *See* AWARENESS. **3.** To bring back into existence or use : reestablish, reinstate, reintroduce, renew, restore, return. *See* INCREASE, KEEP. **4.** To renew an image or thought in the mind : bethink, mind, recall, recollect, remember, reminisce, retain, think. ***Idiom:*** bring to mind. *See* REMEMBER.

revivification *noun*
The act of reviving or condition of being revived : reactivation, rebirth, renaissance, renascence, renewal, resurgence, resurrection, resuscitation, revitalization, revival. *See* AWARENESS.

revivify *verb*
1. To cause to come back to life or consciousness : bring around (*or* round), restore, resuscitate, revive. *See* LIVE. **2.** To impart renewed energy and strength to (a person) : freshen, refresh, reinvigorate, rejuvenate, renew, restore, revitalize. *See* HELP, STRONG. **3.** To rouse from a state of inactivity or quiescence : reactivate, reanimate, reawaken, rekindle, renew, resurrect, resuscitate, revitalize, revive. *See* AWARENESS.

revocation *noun*
The act of reversing or annulling : recall, repeal, rescission, reversal. *See* CONTINUE, LAW.

revoke *verb*
To take back or remove : lift, recall, repeal, rescind, reverse. *See* CONTINUE, LAW, MAKE.

revolt *verb*
1. To refuse allegiance to and oppose by force a government or ruling authority : mutiny, rebel, rise (up). *See* RESIST. **2.** To offend the senses or feelings of : disgust, nauseate, repel, sicken. ***Idiom:*** turn one's stomach. *See* LIKE.
revolt *noun* Organized opposition intended to change or overthrow existing authority : insurgence, insurgency, insurrection, mutiny, rebellion, revolution, sedition, uprising. *See* RESIST.

revolting *adjective*
Extremely unpleasant to the senses or feelings : atrocious, disgusting, foul, horrid, nasty, nauseating, offensive, repellent, repulsive, sickening, ugly, unwholesome, vile. *See* LIKE, PAIN.

revolution *noun*
1. Circular movement around a point or about an axis : circuit, circulation, circumvolution, gyration, rotation, turn, wheel, whirl. *See* GEOMETRY, REPETITION. **2.** Organized opposition intended to change or overthrow existing authority : insurgence, insurgency, insurrection, mutiny, rebellion, revolt, sedition, uprising. *See* RESIST. **3.** A momentous or sweeping change : cataclysm, convulsion, upheaval. *See* CHANGE.

revolutionary *adjective*
1. Participating in open revolt against a government or ruling authority : insurgent, mutinous, rebellious. *See* RESIST. **2.** Holding especially political views that deviate drastically and fundamentally from conventional or traditional beliefs : extreme, extremist, fanatic, fanatical, rabid, radical, ultra. *Slang:* far-out. *See* CONCERN, EDGE, POLITICS.
revolutionary *noun* **1.** A person who rebels : insurgent, insurrectionary, insurrectionist, mutineer, rebel, revolutionist. *See* RESIST. **2.** One who holds extreme views or advocates extreme measures : extremist, fanatic, radical, revolutionist, ultra, zealot. *See* EDGE, CONCERN, POLITICS.

revolutionist *noun*
1. One who holds extreme views or advocates extreme measures : extremist, fanatic, radical, revolutionary, ultra, zealot. *See* EDGE, CONCERN, POLITICS. **2.** A person who rebels : insurgent, insurrectionary, insurrectionist, mutineer, rebel, revolutionary. *See* RESIST.

revolutionize *verb*
To bring about a radical change in : metamorphose, transform. *See* CHANGE.

revolve *verb*
1. To move or cause to move in circles or around an axis : circle, circumvolve, gyrate, orbit, rotate, turn, wheel. *See* MOVE, REPETITION. **2.** To think or think about carefully and at length : chew on (*or* over), cogitate,

consider, contemplate, deliberate, entertain, excogitate, meditate, mull, muse[1], ponder, reflect, ruminate, study, think, think out, think over, think through, turn over, weigh. ***Idioms:*** cudgel one's brains, put on one's thinking cap, rack one's brain. *See* THOUGHTS.

revulsion *noun*
Extreme hostility and dislike : abhorrence, abomination, antipathy, aversion, detestation, hate, hatred, horror, loathing, repellence, repellency, repugnance, repugnancy, repulsion. *See* LOVE.

reward *noun*
1. Something given in return for a service or accomplishment : accolade, award, guerdon, honorarium, plum, premium, prize[1]. ***Idiom:*** token of appreciation (*or* esteem). *See* REWARD. **2.** Something justly deserved : comeuppance, desert[2] (often used in plural), due, guerdon, recompense, wage (often used in plural). *Informal:* lump[1] (used in plural). ***Idioms:*** what is coming to one, what one has coming. *See* REWARD. **3.** A sum of money offered for a special service, such as the apprehension of a criminal : bonus, bounty. *See* LAW, REWARD.
reward *verb* **1.** To bestow a reward on : guerdon. *See* REWARD. **2.** To give a satisfactory return to : compensate, indemnify, pay, recompense, remunerate, repay, requite. *See* PAY.

rewarding *adjective*
Affording profit : advantageous, fat, lucrative, moneymaking, profitable, remunerative. *See* GET.

reword *verb*
To express the meaning of in other, especially simpler, words : paraphrase, render, rephrase, restate, translate. *See* WORDS.

rework *verb*
To prepare a new version of : amend, emend, emendate, revamp, revise, rewrite. *See* CHANGE.

rewrite *verb*
To prepare a new version of : amend, emend, emendate, revamp, revise, rework. *See* CHANGE.
rewrite *noun* The act or process of revising : amendment, emendation, revision. *See* CHANGE.

rhapsodize *verb*
To show enthusism : carry on, rave. *See* FEELINGS.

rhetoric *noun*
The art of public speaking : declamation, elocution, oratory. *See* WORDS.

rhetorical *adjective*
1. Of or relating to the art of public speaking : declamatory, elocutionary, oratorical. *See* WORDS. **2.** Characterized by language that is elevated and sometimes pompous in style : aureate, bombastic, declamatory, flowery, fustian, grandiloquent, high-flown, high-sounding, magniloquent, orotund, overblown, sonorous, swollen. *See* PLAIN, STYLE, WORDS.

rhetorician *noun*
A public speaker : orator. *See* WORDS.

rhodomontade *noun & adjective & verb* See **rodomontade.**

rhubarb *noun*
Informal. A discussion, often heated, in which a difference of opinion is expressed : altercation, argument, bicker, clash, contention, controversy, debate, difficulty, disagreement, dispute, fight, polemic, quarrel, run-in, spat, squabble, tiff, word (used in plural), wrangle. *Informal:* hassle, tangle. *See* CONFLICT.

rhyme *noun*
A poetic work or poetic works : poem, poesy, poetry, verse. *See* WORDS.

rhymer also **rimer** *noun*
One who writes poetry : bard, muse[2], poet, poetaster, poetess, rhymester, versifier. *See* WORDS.

rhymester also **rimester** *noun*
One who writes poetry : bard, muse[2], poet, poetaster, poetess, rhymer, versifier. *See* WORDS.

rhythm *noun*
The patterned, recurring alternation of contrasting elements, such as stressed and unstressed notes in music : beat, cadence, cadency, measure, meter, swing. *See* REPETITION.

rhythmic *adjective*
Marked by a regular rhythm : cadenced, measured, metrical, rhythmical. *See* REPETITION.

rhythmical *adjective*
Marked by a regular rhythm : cadenced, measured, metrical, rhythmic. *See* REPETITION.

rib *verb*
Informal. To tease or mock good-humoredly : banter, chaff, joke, josh. *Informal:* kid, ride. *Slang:* jive, rag[2], razz. *See* LAUGHTER.

ribald *adjective*
Offensive to accepted standards of decency : barnyard, bawdy, broad, coarse, dirty, Fescennine, filthy, foul, gross, lewd, nasty, obscene, profane, scatologic, scatological, scurrilous, smutty, vulgar. *Slang:* raunchy. *See* DECENT.

ribaldry *noun*
Something that is offensive to accepted standards of decency : bawdry, dirt, filth, obscenity, profanity, scatology, smut, vulgarity. *Slang:* raunch. *See* DECENT.

ribbing *noun*
Informal. Good-natured teasing : badinage, banter, chaff, raillery, taunt. *See* LAUGHTER.

rich *adjective*
1. Possessing a large amount of money, land, or other material possessions : affluent, flush, moneyed, wealthy. *Slang:* loaded. ***Idioms:*** having money to burn, in the money, made of money, rolling in money. *See* RICH. **2.** Characterized by extravagant, ostentatious magnificence : lavish, lush[1], luxuriant, luxurious, opulent, palatial, plush, sumptuous. *Informal:* plushy. *See* RICH. **3.** Characterized by great productivity : fecund, fertile, fruitful, productive, prolific. *See* RICH. **4.** Not readily digested because of richness : heavy. *See* INGESTION. **5.** Full of color : bright, colorful, gay, vivid. *See* COLORS. **6.** *Informal.* Extremely funny : hilarious, priceless, sidesplitting. *Informal:* killing. *See* LAUGHTER.

riches *noun*
A great amount of accumulated money and precious possessions : affluence, fortune, pelf, treasure, wealth. *See* OWNED, RICH.

richness *noun*
The quality or state of being fertile : fecundity, fertility, fruitfulness, productiveness, productivity, prolificacy, prolificness. *See* RICH.

ricketiness *noun*
The quality or condition of being physically unsteady : instability, precariousness, shakiness, unstableness, unsteadiness, wobbliness. *See* FLEXIBLE.

rickety *adjective*
Not physically steady or firm : precarious, shaky, tottering, tottery, unstable, unsteady, wobbly. *See* FLEXIBLE.

ricochet *verb*
To strike a surface at such an angle as to be deflected : carom, dap, glance, graze, skim, skip. *See* STRIKE.

rid *verb*
To free from or cast out something objectionable or undesirable : clear, disburden, disembarrass, disencumber, release, relieve, shake off, throw off, unburden. *Slang:* shake. *See* KEEP.

riddance *noun*
1. The act of getting rid of something useless or used up : disposal, dumping, elimination, jettison. *See* KEEP. **2.** The act or process of eliminating : clearance, elimination, eradication, liquidation, purge, removal. *See* KEEP.

riddle *noun*
Anything that arouses curiosity or perplexes because it is unexplained, inexplicable, or secret : conundrum, enigma, mystery, perplexity, puzzle, puzzler. *See* SHOW.

ride *verb*
1. *Informal.* To tease or mock good-humoredly : banter, chaff, joke, josh. *Informal:* kid, rib. *Slang:* jive, rag[2], razz. *See* LAUGHTER. **2.** *Informal.* To torment with persistent insult or ridicule : badger, bait, bullyrag, heckle, hector, hound, taunt. *Informal:* needle. ***Idiom:*** wave the red flag in front of the bull. *See* TREAT WELL.
ride out *verb* To exist in spite of adversity : come through, last[2], persist, pull through, survive, weather. *See* LIVE.
ride *noun* A trip in a motor vehicle : drive, run. *Informal:* spin, whirl. *See* MOVE.

ride out *verb* See **ride**.

ridicule *noun*
Words or actions intended to evoke contemptuous laughter : derision, mockery. *See* LAUGHTER, RESPECT.
ridicule *verb* To make fun or make fun of : deride, gibe, jeer, jest, laugh, mock, scoff, scout[2], twit. *Chiefly British:* quiz. ***Idiom:*** poke fun at. *See* LAUGHTER, RESPECT.

ridiculous *adjective*
1. Deserving laughter : comic, comical, farcical, funny, laughable, laughing, ludicrous, risible. *See* LAUGHTER. **2.** Beyond all reason : obscene, outrageous, preposterous, shocking, unconscionable, unreasonable. ***Idioms:*** out of bounds, out of sight. *See* USUAL.

ridiculousness *noun*
The quality of being laughable or comical : comedy, comicality, comicalness, drollery, drollness, farcicality, funniness, humor, humorousness, jocoseness, jocosity, jocularity, ludicrousness, wit, wittiness, zaniness. *See* LAUGHTER.

rife *adjective*
1. Most generally existing or encountered at a given time : current, predominant, prevailing, prevalent, regnant, widespread. *See* SPECIFIC. **2.** Full of animation and activity : alive, replete. *See* BIG, RICH.

riffle *verb*
1. *Games.* To mix together so as to change the order of arrangement : jumble, scramble, shuffle. *See* CHANGE, ORDER. **2.** To look through reading matter casually. Also used with

through : browse, dip into, flip through, glance at (*or* over *or* through), leaf (through), run through, scan, skim, thumb (through). *See* INVESTIGATE, WORDS.

riffraff *noun*
A group of persons regarded as the lowest class : dreg (often used in plural), lumpenproletariat, rabble, ragtag and bobtail, trash. *Slang:* scum. ***Idioms:*** scum of the earth, tag and rag, the great unwashed. *See* OVER, RICH.

rift *noun*
1. A usually narrow partial opening caused by splitting and rupture : break, chink, cleavage, cleft, crack, crevice, fissure, split. *See* OPEN. **2.** An interruption in friendly relations : alienation, breach, break, disaffection, estrangement, fissure, rent[2], rupture, schism, split. *See* ASSEMBLE, HELP.

rift *verb* To crack or split into two or more fragments by means of or as a result of force, a blow, or strain : break, fracture, rive, shatter, shiver[2], smash, splinter, sunder. *See* HELP.

rig *verb*
To supply what is needed for some activity or purpose : accouter, appoint, equip, fit[1], fit out (*or* up), furnish, gear, outfit, turn out. *See* GIVE.

rig *noun* **1.** Things needed for a task, journey, or other purpose : accouterment (often used in plural), apparatus, equipment, gear, material (used in plural), materiel, outfit, paraphernalia, tackle, thing (used in plural), turnout. *See* MEANS. **2.** *Informal.* A set or style of clothing : costume, dress, garb, guise, habiliment (often used in plural), outfit, turnout. *Informal:* getup. *See* PUT ON.

rigamarole *noun* See **rigmarole.**

right *adjective*
1. In accordance with principles of right or good conduct : ethical, moral, principled, proper, righteous, rightful, right-minded, virtuous. *See* RIGHT. **2.** Consistent with prevailing or accepted standards or circumstances : appropriate, deserved, due, fit[1], fitting, just, merited, proper, rightful, suitable. *See* RIGHT. **3.** Conforming to fact : accurate, correct, exact, faithful, precise, rigorous, true, veracious, veridical. *See* CORRECT, HONEST, REAL, TRUE. **4.** Having no errors : accurate, correct, errorless, exact, precise, rigorous. *See* CORRECT, TRUE. **5.** Conforming to accepted standards : becoming, befitting, comely, comme il faut, correct, decent, decorous, de rigueur, nice, proper, respectable, seemly. *See* COURTESY. **6.** Suitable for a particular person, condition, occasion, or place : appropriate, apt, becoming, befitting, correct, felicitous, fit[1], fitting, happy, meet[2], proper, tailor-made. *See* RIGHT. **7.** Having good health : fit[1], hale, healthful, healthy, hearty, sound[2], well[2], whole, wholesome. ***Idioms:*** fit as a fiddle, hale and hearty, in fine fettle. *See* HEALTH. **8.** Strongly favoring retention of the existing order : conservative, orthodox, rightist, right-wing, Tory, traditionalist, traditionalistic. *See* KEEP.

right *noun* **1.** A privilege granted a person, as by virtue of birth : appanage, birthright, perquisite, prerogative. *Law:* droit. *See* OWNED. **2.** Conferred power : authority, faculty, mandate. *Law:* competence, competency. *See* ABILITY.

right *adverb* **1.** In a direct line : dead, direct, directly, due, straight, straightaway. *See* STRAIGHT. **2.** With precision or absolute conformity : bang, dead, direct, directly, exactly, fair, flush, just, precisely, smack[1], square, squarely, straight. *Slang:* smack-dab. *See* PRECISE.

right *verb* **1.** To restore to or place in an upright or proper position : stand (up). *See* HORIZONTAL. **2.** To restore to proper condition or functioning : doctor, fix, fix up, mend, overhaul, patch, repair[1], revamp. ***Idiom:*** set right. *See* HELP. **3.** To make right what is wrong : amend, correct, emend, mend, rectify, redress, reform, remedy. *See* CORRECT.

right away *adverb*
Without delay : directly, forthwith, immediately, instant, instantly, now, right off, straightaway, straight off. ***Idioms:*** at once, first off. *See* TIME.

righteous *adjective*
1. Having or marked by uprightness in principle and action : good, honest, honorable, incorruptible, true, upright, upstanding. *Informal:* straight-shooting. ***Idiom:*** on the up-and-up (*or* up and up). *See* HONEST. **2.** In accordance with principles of right or good conduct : ethical, moral, principled, proper, right, rightful, right-minded, virtuous. *See* RIGHT.

righteousness *noun*
1. The quality or state of being morally sound : good, goodness, morality, probity, rectitude, rightness, uprightness, virtue, virtuousness. *See* RIGHT. **2.** The moral quality of a course of action : ethic (used in plural), ethicality, ethicalness, morality, propriety, rightfulness, rightness. *See* RIGHT.

rightful *adjective*
1. In accordance with principles of right or good conduct : ethical, moral, principled, proper, right, righteous, right-minded, virtuous. *See* RIGHT. **2.** Consistent with prevailing or accepted standards or circumstances : appropriate, deserved, due, fit[1], fitting, just, merited, proper, right, suitable. *See* RIGHT. **3.** Being so legitimately : legitimate, true. *See* TRUE.

rightfulness *noun*
The moral quality of a course of action : ethic (used in plural), ethicality, ethicalness, morality, propriety, righteousness, rightness. *See* RIGHT.

rightist *noun*
One who strongly favors retention of the existing order : conservative, orthodox, right-winger, Tory, traditionalist. *See* KEEP.
rightist *adjective* Strongly favoring retention of the existing order : conservative, orthodox, right, right-wing, Tory, traditionalist, traditionalistic. *See* KEEP.

right-minded *adjective*
In accordance with principles of right or good conduct : ethical, moral, principled, proper, right, righteous, rightful, virtuous. *See* RIGHT.

rightness *noun*
1. The quality or state of being morally sound : good, goodness, morality, probity, rectitude, righteousness, uprightness, virtue, virtuousness. *See* RIGHT. **2.** The moral quality of a course of action : ethic (used in plural), ethicality, ethicalness, morality, propriety, righteousness, rightfulness. *See* RIGHT. **3.** Freedom from error : accuracy, accurateness, correctness, exactitude, exactness, preciseness, precision. *See* CORRECT.

right off *adverb*
Without delay : directly, forthwith, immediately, instant, instantly, now, right away, straightaway, straight off. ***Idioms:*** at once, first off. *See* TIME.

right of way *noun*
The act, condition, or right of preceding : antecedence, precedence, precedency, priority. *See* PRECEDE.

right on *adverb*
Slang. It is so; as you say or ask : absolutely, agreed, all right, assuredly, aye, gladly, indubitably, roger, undoubtedly, unquestionably, willingly, yea, yes. *Informal:* OK, uh-huh, yeah, yep. *See* AFFIRM.

right-wing *adjective*
Strongly favoring retention of the existing order : conservative, orthodox, right, rightist, Tory, traditionalist, traditionalistic. *See* KEEP.

right-winger *noun*
One who strongly favors retention of the existing order : conservative, orthodox, rightist, Tory, traditionalist. *See* KEEP.

rigid *adjective*
1. Not changing shape or bending : inelastic, inflexible, stiff, unbending, unyielding. *See* FLEXIBLE. **2.** Incapable of changing or being modified : immutable, inalterable, inflexible, invariable, ironclad, unalterable, unchangeable. *See* FLEXIBLE. **3.** Firmly, often unreasonably immovable in purpose or will : adamant, adamantine, brassbound, die-hard, grim, implacable, incompliant, inexorable, inflexible, intransigent, iron, obdurate, relentless, remorseless, stubborn, unbendable, unbending, uncompliant, uncompromising, unrelenting, unyielding. ***Idiom:*** stubborn as a mule (*or* ox). *See* RESIST. **4.** Rigorous and unsparing in treating others : demanding, exacting, hard, harsh, severe, stern, strict, tough, unyielding. *See* EASY.

rigidity *noun*
1. The quality or state of being stubbornly inflexible : die-hardism, grimness, implacability, implacableness, incompliance, incompliancy, inexorability, inexorableness, inflexibility, inflexibleness, intransigence, intransigency, obduracy, obdurateness, relentlessness, remorselessness, rigidness, stubbornness. *See* RESIST. **2.** The fact or condition of being rigorous and unsparing : austerity, hardness, harshness, rigor, rigorousness, severity, sternness, strictness, stringency, toughness. *See* EASY.

rigidness *noun*
The quality or state of being stubbornly inflexible : die-hardism, grimness, implacability, implacableness, incompliance, incompliancy, inexorability, inexorableness, inflexibility, inflexibleness, intransigence, intransigency, obduracy, obdurateness, relentlessness, remorselessness, rigidity, stubbornness. *See* RESIST.

rigmarole also **rigamarole** *noun*
Something that does not have or make sense : balderdash, blather, bunkum, claptrap, drivel, garbage, idiocy, nonsense, piffle, poppycock, rubbish, tomfoolery, trash, twaddle. *Informal:* tommyrot. *Slang:* applesauce, baloney, bilge, bull[1], bunk[2], crap, hooey, malarkey. *See* KNOWLEDGE.

rigor *noun*
1. The fact or state of being rigorous : austerity, hardness, harshness, rigidity, rigorousness, severity, sternness, strictness, stringency, toughness. *See* EASY. **2.** Something

that obstructs progress and requires great effort to overcome : asperity, difficulty, hardship, vicissitude (often used in plural). ***Idioms:*** a hard (*or* tough) nut to crack, a hard (*or* tough) row to hoe, heavy sledding. *See* EASY.

rigorous *adjective*
1. Conforming completely to established rule : exact, strict, uncompromising. *See* USUAL.
2. Requiring great or extreme bodily, mental, or spiritual strength : arduous, backbreaking, burdensome, demanding, difficult, effortful, exacting, exigent, formidable, hard, heavy, laborious, onerous, oppressive, rough, severe, taxing, tough, trying, weighty. *See* HEAVY.
3. Not deviating from correctness, accuracy, or completeness : close, exact, faithful, full, strict. *See* CAREFUL. **4.** Having no errors : accurate, correct, errorless, exact, precise, right. *See* CORRECT, TRUE. **5.** Conforming to fact : accurate, correct, exact, faithful, precise, right, true, veracious, veridical. *See* CORRECT, HONEST, REAL, TRUE.

rigorousness *noun*
The fact or condition of being rigorous and unsparing : austerity, hardness, harshness, rigidity, rigor, severity, sternness, strictness, stringency, toughness. *See* EASY.

rile *verb*
To trouble the nerves or peace of mind of, especially by repeated vexations : aggravate, annoy, bother, bug, chafe, disturb, exasperate, fret, gall[2], get, irk, irritate, nettle, peeve, provoke, put out, ruffle, vex. ***Idioms:*** get in one's hair, get on one's nerves, get under one's skin. *See* FEELINGS, PAIN.

rim *noun*
A fairly narrow line or space forming a boundary : border, borderline, brim, brink, edge, edging, fringe, margin, periphery, verge. *Chiefly Military:* perimeter. *See* EDGE.
rim *verb* To put or form a border on : border, bound[2], edge, fringe, margin, skirt, verge. *See* EDGE.

rimer *noun* See **rhymer.**

rimester *noun* See **rhymester.**

rimple *noun*
A line or an arrangement made by the doubling of one part over another : crease, crimp, crinkle, crumple, fold, pleat, plica, plication, pucker, ruck[2], rumple, wrinkle. *See* SMOOTH.
rimple *verb* To make irregular folds in, especially by pressing or twisting : crease, crimp, crinkle, crumple, rumple, wrinkle. *See* SMOOTH.

rind *noun*
The outer covering of a fruit : peel, skin. *See* SURFACE.

ring[1] *noun*
1. A closed plane curve everywhere equidistant from a fixed point or something shaped like this : band[1], circle, circuit, disk, gyre, wheel. *Archaic:* orb. *See* GEOMETRY. **2.** A length of line folded over and joined at the ends so as to form a curve or circle : eye, loop. *See* STRAIGHT. **3.** A group of individuals united in a common cause : bloc, cartel, coalition, combination, combine, faction, party. *See* GROUP.
4. An organized group of criminals, hoodlums, or wrongdoers : band[2], gang, pack. *Informal:* mob. *See* GROUP.
ring *verb* **1.** To encircle with or as if with a band : band[1], begird, belt, cincture, compass, encompass, engirdle, gird, girdle, girt. *Archaic:* engird. *See* EDGE. **2.** To shut in on all sides : begird, beset, circle, compass, encircle, encompass, environ, gird, girdle, hedge, hem, surround. *See* OPEN.

ring[2] *verb*
1. To give forth or cause to give forth a clear, resonant sound : bong, chime, knell, peal, strike, toll[2]. *See* SOUNDS. **2.** To communicate with (someone) by telephone : buzz, call, telephone. *Informal:* dial, phone. ***Idioms:*** get someone on the horn, give someone a buzz (*or* call *or* ring). *See* WORDS.
ring *noun* A telephone communication : buzz, call. *See* WORDS.

ringer *noun*
Slang. One exactly resembling another : double, duplicate, image, picture, portrait, spitting image. *See* SAME.

ringing *adjective*
Having or producing a full, deep, or rich sound : mellow, orotund, plangent, resonant, resounding, rotund, round, sonorous, vibrant. *See* SOUNDS.

riot *noun*
1. A quarrel, fight, or disturbance marked by very noisy, disorderly, and often violent behavior : affray, brawl, broil[2], donnybrook, fray, free-for-all, melee, row[2], ruction, tumult. *Informal:* fracas. *Slang:* rumble. *See* ATTACK.
2. *Slang.* Something or someone uproariously funny or absurd : absurdity. *Informal:* hoot, joke, laugh, scream. *Slang:* gas, howl, panic. ***Idiom:*** a laugh a minute. *See* LAUGHTER.
riot *verb* To behave riotously : carouse, frolic, revel, roister. *Informal:* hell (around). ***Idioms:*** blow off steam, cut loose, kick over the traces,

kick up one's heels, let go, let loose, make merry, make whoopee, paint the town red, raise Cain (*or* the devil *or* hell), whoop it up. *See* RESTRAINT.

riot away *verb* To spend (money) excessively and usually foolishly : consume, dissipate, fool away, fritter away, squander, throw away, trifle away, waste. *Slang:* blow[1]. *See* SAVE.

riot away *verb* See **riot.**

riotous *adjective*

1. Upsetting civil order or peace : rowdy. *Law:* disorderly. *See* PEACE. **2.** Given to or marked by unrestrained abundance : extravagant, exuberant, lavish, lush[1], luxuriant, opulent, prodigal, profuse, superabundant. *See* BIG, EXCESS.

rip *verb*

1. To separate or pull apart by force : rend, rive, run, split, tear[1]. *See* ASSEMBLE, HELP. **2.** *Informal.* To move swiftly : bolt, bucket, bustle, dart, dash, festinate, flash, fleet, flit, fly, haste, hasten, hurry, hustle, pelt[2], race, rocket, run, rush, sail, scoot, scour[2], shoot, speed, sprint, tear[1], trot, whirl, whisk, whiz, wing, zip, zoom. *Informal:* hotfoot. *Slang:* barrel, highball. *Chiefly British:* nip[1]. ***Idioms:*** get a move on, get cracking, go like lightning, go like the wind, hotfoot it, make haste, make time, make tracks, run like the wind, shake a leg, step (*or* jump) on it. *See* MOVE.

rip into *verb* To criticize harshly and devastatingly : blister, drub, excoriate, flay, lash, scarify[1], scathe, scorch, score, scourge, slap, slash. *Informal:* roast. *Slang:* slam. ***Idioms:*** burn someone's ears, crawl all over, pin someone's ears back, put someone on the griddle, put someone on the hot seat, rake over the coals, read the riot act to. *See* PRAISE.

rip off *verb* **1.** *Slang.* To take (another's property) without permission : filch, pilfer, purloin, snatch, steal, thieve. *Informal:* lift, swipe. *Slang:* cop, heist, hook, nip[1], pinch, snitch. ***Idiom:*** make (*or* walk) off with. *See* CRIMES, GIVE. **2.** *Slang.* To exploit (another) by charging too much for something : fleece, overcharge. *Slang:* clip[1], gouge, nick, scalp, skin, soak. ***Idioms:*** make someone pay through the nose, take someone for a ride, take someone to the cleaners. *See* HONEST.

rip *noun* A hole made by tearing : rent[2], run, tear[1]. *See* HELP.

ripe *adjective*

1. Having reached full growth and development : adult, big, developed, full-blown, full-fledged, full-grown, grown, grown-up, mature. ***Idiom:*** of age. *See* YOUTH. **2.** Brought to full flavor and richness by aging : aged, mellow. *See* YOUTH.

ripen *verb*

To bring or come to full development : age, develop, grow, maturate, mature, mellow. *See* YOUTH.

rip into *verb* See **rip.**

rip-off *noun*

Slang. The crime of taking someone else's property without consent : larceny, pilferage, steal, theft, thievery. *See* CRIMES.

rip off *verb* See **rip.**

riposte *noun*

A spirited, incisive reply : comeback, repartee, retort. *See* ASK.

riposte *verb* To speak or act in response, as to a question : answer, rejoin, reply, respond, retort, return. *See* ASK.

ripping *adjective*

Informal. Particularly excellent : divine, fabulous, fantastic, fantastical, glorious, marvelous, sensational, splendid, superb, terrific, wonderful. *Informal:* dandy, dreamy, great, super, swell, tremendous. *Slang:* cool, groovy, hot, keen[1], neat, nifty. ***Idiom:*** out of this world. *See* GOOD.

rippling *adjective*

Emitting a murmuring sound felt to resemble a laugh : babbling, bubbling, burbling, gurgling, laughing. *See* LAUGHTER, SOUNDS.

rise *verb*

1. To adopt a standing posture : arise, get up, stand (up), uprise, upspring. ***Idiom:*** get to one's feet. *See* RISE. **2.** To leave one's bed : arise, get up, pile, roll out. *Informal:* turn out. ***Idiom:*** rise and shine. *See* RISE. **3.** To move from a lower to a higher position : arise, ascend, climb, lift, mount, soar. *See* RISE. **4.** To make or become greater or larger : aggrandize, amplify, augment, boost, build, build up, burgeon, enlarge, escalate, expand, extend, grow, increase, magnify, mount, multiply, proliferate, run up, snowball, soar, swell, upsurge, wax. *Informal:* beef up. *See* INCREASE. **5.** To have as a source : arise, come, derive, emanate, flow, issue, originate, proceed, spring, stem, upspring. *See* START. **6.** To attain a higher status, rank, or condition : advance, ascend, climb, mount. ***Idiom:*** go up the ladder. *See* INCREASE, RISE. **7.** To gain success : arrive, get ahead, get on, go far, succeed. ***Idioms:*** go places, make good, make it. *See* THRIVE. **8.** To refuse allegiance to and oppose by force a government or ruling authority. Also used with *up* : mutiny, rebel, revolt. *See* RESIST.

rise *noun* **1.** The act of rising or moving upward : ascension, ascent, rising. *See* RISE. **2.** An upward slope : acclivity, ascent. *See* RISE. **3.** A natural land elevation : eminence, hill, prominence. *See* HIGH. **4.** The act of increasing or rising : aggrandizement, amplification, augment, augmentation, boost, buildup, enlargement, escalation, growth, hike, increase, jump, multiplication, proliferation, raise, swell, upsurge, upswing, upturn. *See* INCREASE. **5.** The amount by which something is increased : advance, boost, hike, increase, increment, jump, raise. *See* INCREASE. **6.** A progression upward in rank : advancement, elevation, jump, promotion, upgrade. *See* RISE.

risible *adjective*
1. Arousing laughter : amusing, comic, comical, droll, funny, humorous, laughable, zany. *See* LAUGHTER. **2.** Deserving laughter : comic, comical, farcical, funny, laughable, laughing, ludicrous, ridiculous. *See* LAUGHTER.

rising *noun*
The act of rising or moving upward : ascension, ascent, rise. *See* RISE.

rising star *noun*
One showing much promise : comer, up-and-comer. *See* ABILITY.

risk *noun*
1. A possibility of danger or harm : chance, gamble, hazard. *See* SAFETY. **2.** Exposure to possible harm, loss, or injury : danger, endangerment, hazard, imperilment, jeopardy, peril. *See* SAFETY. **3.** A venture depending on chance : bet, gamble, speculation, wager. *See* GAMBLING.

risk *verb* **1.** To expose to possible loss or damage : adventure, compromise, hazard, venture. *See* SAFETY. **2.** To subject to danger or destruction : endanger, imperil, jeopardize, menace, peril, threaten. *See* SAFETY. **3.** To put up as a stake in a game or speculation : bet, gamble, lay[1] (down), post[2], put, stake, venture, wager. *Informal:* go. *See* GAMBLING. **4.** To run the risk of : adventure, chance, hazard, venture. *See* SAFETY.

risky *adjective*
Involving possible risk, loss, or injury : adventurous, chancy, dangerous, hazardous, jeopardous, parlous, perilous, treacherous, unsafe, venturesome, venturous. *Slang:* hairy. *See* SAFETY.

risqué *adjective*
Bordering on indelicacy or impropriety : blue, earthy, off-color, provocative, racy, salty, scabrous, spicy, suggestive. *See* DECENT.

rite *noun*
A formal act or set of acts prescribed by ritual : ceremonial, ceremony, liturgy, observance, office, ritual, service. *See* RITUAL.

ritual *noun*
1. A formal act or set of acts prescribed by ritual : ceremonial, ceremony, liturgy, observance, office, rite, service. *See* RITUAL. **2.** A conventional social gesture or act without intrinsic purpose : ceremony, form, formality. *See* RITUAL, USUAL.

ritual *adjective* Of or characterized by ceremony : ceremonial, ceremonious, formal, liturgical, ritualistic. *See* RITUAL.

ritualistic *adjective*
Of or characterized by ceremony : ceremonial, ceremonious, formal, liturgical, ritual. *See* RITUAL.

ritzy *adjective*
Informal. Catering to, used by, or admitting only the wealthy or socially superior : exclusive, fancy, posh, swank, swanky. *See* PLAIN.

rival *noun*
One that competes : competition, competitor, contender, contestant, corrival, opponent. *See* CONFLICT.

rival *verb* **1.** To come near, as in quality or amount : approach, approximate, border on (*or* upon), challenge, verge on. *See* SAME. **2.** To strive against (others) for victory : compete, contend, contest, emulate, vie. *See* CONFLICT.

rivalry *noun*
A vying with others for victory or supremacy : battle, competition, contest, corrivalry, race, strife, striving, struggle, tug of war, war, warfare. *See* CONFLICT.

rive *verb*
1. To separate or pull apart by force : rend, rip, run, split, tear[1]. *See* ASSEMBLE, HELP. **2.** To crack or split into two or more fragments by means of or as a result of force, a blow, or strain : break, fracture, rift, shatter, shiver[2], smash, splinter, sunder. *See* HELP.

rivet *verb*
To compel, as the attention, interest, or imagination, of : arrest, catch up, enthrall, fascinate, grip, hold, mesmerize, spellbind, transfix. *Slang:* grab. *See* EXCITE.

road *noun*
A course affording passage from one place to another : avenue, boulevard, drive, expressway, freeway, highway, path, roadway, route, street, superhighway, thoroughfare, thruway, turnpike, way. *See* MOVE, OPEN.

roadway *noun*
A course affording passage from one place to another : avenue, boulevard, drive, expressway, freeway, highway, path, road, route, street, superhighway, thoroughfare, thruway, turnpike, way. *See* MOVE, OPEN.

roam *verb*
To move about at random, especially over a wide area : drift, gad, gallivant, meander, peregrinate, ramble, range, rove, stray, traipse, wander. *See* MOVE.

roaming *adjective*
Traveling about, especially in search of adventure : errant, roving, wandering. *See* MOVE.

roar *verb*
1. To speak or say very loudly or with a shout : bawl, bellow, bluster, call, clamor, cry, halloo, holler, shout, vociferate, whoop, yawp, yell. *See* SOUNDS. **2.** To express great amusement or mirth : guffaw. *Informal:* break up. *Slang:* howl. *See* LAUGHTER. **3.** To make an earsplitting explosive noise : bang, blast, boom, thunder. *See* SOUNDS.
roar *noun* **1.** A loud, deep, prolonged sound : bawl, bellow, clamor. *See* SOUNDS. **2.** An earsplitting, explosive noise : bang, blast, boom, thunder. *See* SOUNDS.

roaring *adjective*
1. Marked by extremely high volume and intensity of sound : blaring, deafening, earsplitting, loud, stentorian. *See* SOUNDS. **2.** Improving, growing, or succeeding steadily : booming, boomy, flourishing, prospering, prosperous, thrifty, thriving. *See* THRIVE.

roast *verb*
1. To feel or look hot : bake, broil[1], burn, swelter. *See* HOT. **2.** *Informal.* To criticize harshly and devastatingly : blister, drub, excoriate, flay, lash, rip into, scarify[1], scathe, scorch, score, scourge, slap, slash. *Slang:* slam. ***Idioms:*** burn someone's ears, crawl all over, pin someone's ears back, put someone on the griddle, put someone on the hot seat, rake over the coals, read the riot act to. *See* PRAISE.

roasting *adjective*
Marked by much heat : ardent, baking, blistering, boiling, broiling, burning, fiery, heated, hot, red-hot, scalding, scorching, searing, sizzling, sultry, sweltering, torrid. *See* HOT.

rob *verb*
1. To take property or possessions from (a person or company, for example) unlawfully and usually forcibly : hold up, stick up. *Slang:* heist, knock off. *See* CRIMES, GIVE. **2.** To take or keep something away from : deprive, dispossess, divest, strip[1]. *See* GIVE.

robber *noun*
A person who steals : bandit, burglar, highwayman, housebreaker, larcener, larcenist, pilferer, purloiner, stealer, thief. *See* CRIMES.

robbery *noun*
The act or crime of taking another's property unlawfully and by force : holdup. *Slang:* heist, stickup. *See* CRIMES, GIVE.

robe *noun*
Clothing worn by members of a religious order : habit, vestment. *See* PUT ON.
robe *verb* To cover as if with clothes : cloak, clothe, drape, mantle. *See* PUT ON.

roborant *adjective*
Producing or stimulating physical, mental, or emotional vigor : bracing, energizing, exhilarant, exhilarating, innerving, intoxicating, invigorating, refreshing, reinvigorating, renewing, restorative, stimulating, tonic. *See* HELP.
roborant *noun* A medicine that restores or increases vigor : restorative, tonic. *Informal:* bracer, pick-me-up. *See* HELP.

robust *adjective*
1. Full of vigor : able-bodied, iron, lusty, red-blooded, strapping, sturdy, vigorous, vital. *See* STRONG. **2.** Characterized by marked muscular development; powerfully built : athletic, brawny, burly, husky[2], muscular, sinewy, sturdy. *See* STRONG.

rock *verb*
1. To move vigorously from side to side or up and down : heave, pitch, roll, toss. *See* REPETITION. **2.** To move to and fro violently : quake, shake, tremble, vibrate. *See* REPETITION. **3.** To cause to move to and fro violently : agitate, churn, convulse, shake. *See* CALM, REPETITION. **4.** To impair or destroy the composure of : agitate, bother, discompose, disquiet, distract, disturb, flurry, fluster, perturb, ruffle, shake (up), toss, unsettle, upset. *Informal:* rattle. *See* CALM.

rock bottom *noun*
A very low level, position, or degree : bottom, low. *See* HIGH.

rocket *verb*
1. To move swiftly : bolt, bucket, bustle, dart, dash, festinate, flash, fleet, flit, fly, haste, hasten, hurry, hustle, pelt[2], race, run, rush, sail, scoot, scour[2], shoot, speed, sprint, tear[1], trot, whirl, whisk, whiz, wing, zip, zoom. *Informal:* hotfoot, rip. *Slang:* barrel, highball. *Chiefly British:* nip[1]. ***Idioms:*** get a move on, get

cracking, go like lightning, go like the wind, hotfoot it, make haste, make time, make tracks, run like the wind, shake a leg, step (*or* jump) on it. *See* MOVE. **2.** To rise abruptly and precipitously : sky, skyrocket, soar. *Informal:* shoot up. *See* INCREASE.

rocky *adjective*
Affected or tending to be affected with minor health problems : ailing, indisposed, low, mean[2], off-color, sickly. ***Idiom:*** under the weather. *See* HEALTH.

rococo *adjective*
Elaborately and heavily ornamented : baroque, flamboyant, florid, ornate. *See* PLAIN.

rod *noun*
A relatively long, straight, rigid piece of metal or other solid material : bar, bloom[2], shaft, slab, stick. *See* THING.

rodomontade also **rhodomontade** *noun*
An act of boasting : boast, brag, braggadocio, fanfaronade, gasconade, vaunt. *Informal:* blow[1]. *See* PRAISE.
rodomontade also **rhodomontade** *adjective*
Characterized by or given to boasting : boastful, braggart. *See* ATTITUDE, PRAISE.
rodomontade also **rhodomontade** *verb* To talk with excessive pride : boast, brag, crow, gasconade, vaunt. *Informal:* blow[1]. *See* PRAISE.

rogation *noun*
A formula of words used in praying. Often used in plural : collect[2], litany, orison, prayer[1]. *See* RELIGION.

roger *adverb*
It is so; as you say or ask : absolutely, agreed, all right, assuredly, aye, gladly, indubitably, undoubtedly, unquestionably, willingly, yea, yes. *Informal:* OK, uh-huh, yeah, yep. *Slang:* right on. *See* AFFIRM.

rogue *noun*
One who causes minor trouble or damage : devil, imp, mischief, prankster, rascal, scamp. *Informal:* cutup. *See* GOOD.

roguery *noun*
Annoying yet harmless, usually playful acts : devilry, deviltry, diablerie, high jinks, impishness, mischief, mischievousness, prankishness, rascality, roguishness, tomfoolery. *Informal:* shenanigan (often used in plural). *See* GOOD.

roguishness *noun*
Annoying yet harmless, usually playful acts : devilry, deviltry, diablerie, high jinks, impishness, mischief, mischievousness, prankishness, rascality, roguery, tomfoolery. *Informal:* shenanigan (often used in plural). *See* GOOD.

roiled *adjective*
1. Having sediment or foreign particles stirred up or suspended : cloudy, muddy, murky, roily, turbid. *See* CLEAR. **2.** Violently disturbed or agitated, as by storms : dirty, heavy, raging, roily, rough, rugged, stormy, tempestuous, tumultuous, turbulent, ugly, violent, wild. *See* CALM.

roily *adjective*
1. Having sediment or foreign particles stirred up or suspended : cloudy, muddy, murky, roiled, turbid. *See* CLEAR. **2.** Violently disturbed or agitated, as by storms : dirty, heavy, raging, roiled, rough, rugged, stormy, tempestuous, tumultuous, turbulent, ugly, violent, wild. *See* CALM.

roister *verb*
To behave riotously : carouse, frolic, revel, riot. *Informal:* hell (around). ***Idioms:*** blow off steam, cut loose, kick over the traces, kick up one's heels, let go, let loose, make merry, make whoopee, paint the town red, raise Cain (*or* the devil *or* hell), whoop it up. *See* RESTRAINT.

role also **rôle** *noun*
1. One's proper or expected function in a common effort : part, piece, share. *See* DO, PARTICIPATE. **2.** The proper activity of a person or thing : function, job, purpose, task. *See* DO.

roll *verb*
1. To cover completely and closely, as with clothing or bandages : enfold, envelop, enwrap, infold, invest, swaddle, swathe, wrap, wrap up. *See* PUT ON. **2.** To move vigorously from side to side or up and down : heave, pitch, rock, toss. *See* REPETITION. **3.** To lean suddenly, unsteadily, and erratically from the vertical axis : lurch, pitch, seesaw, yaw. *See* MOVE, STRAIGHT. **4.** To make a continuous deep reverberating sound : boom, growl, grumble, rumble. *See* SOUNDS. **5.** To proceed with ease, especially of expression : flow, glide, sail. *See* MOVE. **6.** To take extravagant pleasure : bask, indulge, luxuriate, revel, rollick, wallow. *See* LIKE.
roll out *verb* To leave one's bed : arise, get up, pile, rise. *Informal:* turn out. ***Idiom:*** rise and shine. *See* RISE.
roll up *verb* To bring together so as to increase in mass or number : accrue, accumulate, agglomerate, aggregate, amass, collect[1], cumulate, garner, gather, hive, pile up. *See* COLLECT.
roll *noun* A series, as of names or words, printed or written down : catalog, list[1], register, roster, schedule. *See* REMEMBER.

rollick *verb*
1. To leap and skip about playfully : caper, cavort, dance, frisk, frolic, gambol, romp. *See* WORK. 2. To take extravagant pleasure : bask, indulge, luxuriate, revel, roll, wallow. *See* LIKE.

roll out *verb* See **roll.**

roll up *verb* See **roll.**

roly-poly *adjective*
Well-rounded and full in form : chubby, plump¹, plumpish, pudgy, rotund, round, tubby, zaftig. *See* FAT.

romance *noun*
1. An intimate sexual relationship between two people : affair, amour, love, love affair. *See* LOVE, SEX. 2. The passionate affection and desire felt by lovers for each other : amorousness, fancy, love, passion. *See* LOVE, SEX. 3. A strong, enthusiastic liking for something : love, love affair, passion. *See* LOVE.
romance *verb Informal.* To attempt to gain the affection of : court, pursue, spark², woo. *See* SEEK, SEX.

romantic *adjective*
1. Affectedly or extravagantly emotional : bathetic, gushy, maudlin, mawkish, sentimental, slushy, sobby, soft, soppy. *Informal:* gooey, mushy, schmaltzy, sloppy, soupy. *Slang:* drippy, sappy, tear-jerking. *See* FEELINGS. 2. Not compatible with reality : idealistic, quixotic, starry-eyed, unrealistic, utopian, visionary. *See* HOPE, REAL.

romanticize *verb*
To regard or imbue with affected or exaggerated emotion : sentimentalize. *See* FEELINGS, REAL.

Romeo *noun*
A man amorously attentive to women : amorist, Casanova, Don Juan, gallant, lady's man, Lothario. *See* SEX.

romp *verb*
To leap and skip about playfully : caper, cavort, dance, frisk, frolic, gambol, rollick. *See* WORK.
romp *noun Slang.* An easy victory : walkaway, walkover. *Informal:* runaway. *See* EASY, WIN.

roof *noun*
The highest point : apex, cap, crest, crown, height, peak, summit, top, vertex. *See* HIGH.

rook *noun*
A person who cheats : bilk, cheat, cheater, cozener, defrauder, sharper, swindler, trickster, victimizer. *Informal:* chiseler, crook, flimflammer. *Slang:* diddler, gyp, gypper. *See* HONEST.
rook *verb* To get money or something else from by deceitful trickery : bilk, cheat, cozen, defraud, gull, mulct, swindle, victimize. *Informal:* chisel, flimflam, take, trim. *Slang:* diddle¹, do, gyp, stick, sting. *See* HONEST.

rookie *noun*
Slang. One who is just starting to learn or do something : abecedarian, beginner, fledgling, freshman, greenhorn, initiate, neophyte, novice, novitiate, tenderfoot, tyro. *See* START.

room *noun*
Suitable opportunity to accept or allow something : elbowroom, latitude, leeway, margin, play, scope. *See* PLACE, RESTRAINT.
room *verb* To provide with often temporary lodging : accommodate, bed (down), berth, bestow, billet, board, bunk¹, domicile, harbor, house, lodge, put up, quarter. *See* PROTECTION.

roomy *adjective*
Having plenty of room : ample, capacious, commodious, spacious. *See* BIG.

root¹ *noun*
1. The most central and material part : core, essence, gist, heart, kernel, marrow, meat, nub, pith, quintessence, soul, spirit, stuff, substance. *Law:* gravamen. *See* BE. 2. A fundamental principle or underlying concept : base¹, basis, cornerstone, foundation, fundament, fundamental, rudiment (often used in plural). *See* OVER. 3. A point of origination : beginning, derivation, fount, fountain, fountainhead, mother, origin, parent, provenance, provenience, rootstock, source, spring, well¹. *See* START. 4. A point of origin from which ideas or influences, for example, originate : bottom, center, core, focus, heart, hub, quick. *See* START. 5. The main part of a word to which affixes are attached : base¹, stem, theme. *See* WORDS.
root *verb* 1. To implant so deeply as to make change nearly impossible : embed, entrench, fasten, fix, infix, ingrain, lodge. *See* MOVE. 2. To provide a basis for : base¹, build, establish, found, ground, predicate, rest¹, underpin. *See* OVER. 3. To destroy all traces of. Also used with *out* or *up* : abolish, annihilate, blot out, clear, eradicate, erase, exterminate, extinguish, extirpate, kill¹, liquidate, obliterate, remove, rub out, snuff out, stamp out, uproot, wipe out. ***Idioms:*** do away with, make an end of, put an end to. *See* HELP, MAKE.

root² *verb*
To express approval, especially by clapping : applaud, cheer, clap. ***Idiom:*** give someone a hand. *See* PRAISE.

rootstock *noun*
A point of origination : beginning, derivation, fount, fountain, fountainhead, mother, origin, parent, provenance, provenience, root[1], source, spring, well[1]. *See* START.

roseate *adjective*
Expecting a favorable outcome or dwelling on hopeful aspects : optimistic, Panglossian, rose-colored, rosy, sanguine. *Informal:* upbeat. ***Idioms:*** looking on the bright side, looking through rose-colored glasses. *See* HOPE.

rose-colored *adjective*
Expecting a favorable outcome or dwelling on hopeful aspects : optimistic, Panglossian, roseate, rosy, sanguine. *Informal:* upbeat. ***Idioms:*** looking on the bright side, looking through rose-colored glasses. *See* HOPE.

roster *noun*
A series, as of names or words, printed or written down : catalog, list[1], register, roll, schedule. *See* REMEMBER.

rosy *adjective*
1. Of a healthy reddish color : blooming, florid, flush, flushed, full-blooded, glowing, rubicund, ruddy, sanguine. *See* COLORS.
2. Expecting a favorable outcome or dwelling on hopeful aspects : optimistic, Panglossian, roseate, rose-colored, sanguine. *Informal:* upbeat. ***Idioms:*** looking on the bright side, looking through rose-colored glasses. *See* HOPE.

rot *verb*
To become or cause to become rotten or unsound : break down, decay, decompose, deteriorate, disintegrate, molder, putrefy, spoil, taint, turn. ***Idioms:*** go bad, go to pot, go to seed. *See* BETTER, THRIVE.
rot *noun* The condition of being decayed : breakdown, decay, decomposition, deterioration, disintegration, putrefaction, putrescence, putridness, rottenness, spoilage. *See* BETTER, THRIVE.

rotate *verb*
1. To move or cause to move in circles or around an axis : circle, circumvolve, gyrate, orbit, revolve, turn, wheel. *See* MOVE, REPETITION. **2.** To do, use, or occur in successive turns : alternate, interchange. *See* CHANGE.

rotation *noun*
1. Circular movement around a point or about an axis : circuit, circulation, circumvolution, gyration, revolution, turn, wheel, whirl. *See* GEOMETRY, REPETITION. **2.** Occurrence in successive turns : alternation, interchange. *See* CHANGE.

rotten *adjective*
1. Smelling of mildew or decay : frowzy, fusty, moldy, musty, putrid, rancid, rank[2]. *See* SMELLS. **2.** Impaired because of decay : bad, putrid. *See* BETTER, TASTE, THRIVE.
3. Utterly reprehensible in nature or behavior : corrupt, degenerate, depraved, flagitious, miscreant, perverse, unhealthy, villainous. *See* CLEAN, GOOD. **4.** So objectionable as to elicit despisal or deserve condemnation : abhorrent, abominable, antipathetic, contemptible, despicable, despisable, detestable, disgusting, filthy, foul, infamous, loathsome, lousy, low, mean[2], nasty, nefarious, obnoxious, odious, repugnant, shabby, vile, wretched. *See* GOOD. **5.** Of decidedly inferior quality : base[2], cheap, lousy, miserable, paltry, poor, shoddy, sleazy, trashy. *Informal:* cheesy. *Slang:* crummy, schlocky. *See* GOOD.

rottenness *noun*
The condition of being decayed : breakdown, decay, decomposition, deterioration, disintegration, putrefaction, putrescence, putridness, rot, spoilage. *See* BETTER, THRIVE.

rotund *adjective*
1. Well-rounded and full in form : chubby, plump[1], plumpish, pudgy, roly-poly, round, tubby, zaftig. *See* FAT. **2.** Having or producing a full, deep, or rich sound : mellow, orotund, plangent, resonant, resounding, ringing, round, sonorous, vibrant. *See* SOUNDS.

roué *noun*
An immoral or licentious man : lecher, satyr. *Informal:* dirty old man. *Slang:* lech. *See* SEX.

rough *adjective*
1. Having a surface that is not smooth : coarse, cragged, craggy, harsh, ironbound, jagged, ragged, rugged, scabrous, uneven. *See* SMOOTH.
2. Consisting of or covered with large particles : coarse, grainy, granular, gritty. *See* SMOOTH. **3.** Violently disturbed or agitated, as by storms : dirty, heavy, raging, roiled, roily, rugged, stormy, tempestuous, tumultuous, turbulent, ugly, violent, wild. *See* CALM.
4. Requiring great or extreme bodily, mental, or spiritual strength : arduous, backbreaking, burdensome, demanding, difficult, effortful, exacting, exigent, formidable, hard, heavy, laborious, onerous, oppressive, rigorous, severe, taxing, tough, trying, weighty. *See* HEAVY. **5.** Causing sharp, often prolonged discomfort : bitter, brutal, hard, harsh, severe. *See* COMFORT. **6.** Hard to deal with or get out of : tight, tricky. *Informal:* sticky. *See* EASY.
7. Lacking in delicacy or refinement : barbar-

ian, barbaric, boorish, churlish, coarse, crass, crude, gross, ill-bred, indelicate, philistine, rude, tasteless, uncivilized, uncouth, uncultivated, uncultured, unpolished, unrefined, vulgar. *See* COURTESY, SMOOTH. **8.** Marked by vigorous physical exertion : knockabout, rough-and-tumble, rugged, strenuous, tough. *See* ACTION. **9.** Disagreeable to the sense of hearing : dry, grating, harsh, hoarse, jarring, rasping, raspy, raucous, scratchy, squawky, strident. *See* SOUNDS. **10.** In a primitive state; not domesticated or cultivated; produced by nature : native, natural, uncultivated, undomesticated, untamed, wild. *See* WILD. **11.** Not perfected, elaborated, or completed : preliminary, sketchy, tentative, unfinished, unperfected, unpolished. *See* START. **12.** Lacking expert, careful craftsmanship : crude, primitive, raw, rude, unpolished. *See* GOOD.

rough *verb* To be rough or brutal with. Also used with *up* : knock about (*or* around), manhandle, slap around. *Slang:* mess up. *See* ATTACK, STRIKE.

rough in (or **out)** *verb* To draw up a preliminary plan or version of : adumbrate, block in (*or* out), draft, outline, sketch. *See* PLANNED.

rough up *verb* To injure or damage, as by abuse or heavy wear : batter, knock about (*or* around), mangle[1], maul. *See* ATTACK, HELP, STRIKE.

rough *noun* A preliminary plan or version, as of a written work : draft, outline, skeleton, sketch. *See* PLANNED, WORDS.

rough-and-tumble *adjective*
Marked by vigorous physical exertion : knockabout, rough, rugged, strenuous, tough. *See* ACTION.

rough in or **out** *verb* See **rough.**

roughly *adverb*
Near to in quantity or amount : about, almost, approximately, nearly. ***Idiom:*** on the order of. *See* NEAR.

roughneck *noun*
A rough, violent person who engages in destructive actions : hoodlum, mug, rowdy, ruffian, tough. *Informal:* toughie. *Slang:* hood, punk. *See* ATTACK, CRIMES.

roughness *noun*
Lack of smoothness or regularity : asymmetry, crookedness, inequality, irregularity, jaggedness, unevenness. *See* SMOOTH, STRAIGHT.

rough up *verb* See **rough.**

round *adjective*
1. Having the shape of a curve everywhere equidistant from a fixed point : annular, circular, globoid, globular, spheric, spherical. *See* GEOMETRY. **2.** Well-rounded and full in form : chubby, plump[1], plumpish, pudgy, roly-poly, rotund, tubby, zaftig. *See* FAT. **3.** Having or producing a full, deep, or rich sound : mellow, orotund, plangent, resonant, resounding, ringing, rotund, sonorous, vibrant. *See* SOUNDS. **4.** Not more or less : complete, entire, full, good, perfect, whole. *See* PART, PRECISE.

round *noun* **1.** Something bent : bend, bow[2], crook, curvature, curve, turn. *See* STRAIGHT. **2.** A course, process, or journey that ends where it began or repeats itself : circle, circuit, cycle, orbit, tour, turn. *See* REPETITION. **3.** A number of things placed or occurring one after the other : chain, consecution, course, order, procession, progression, run, sequence, series, string, succession, suite, train. *Informal:* streak. *See* ORDER. **4.** A course of action to be followed regularly. Often used in plural : routine, track. *See* USUAL. **5.** An area regularly covered, as by a policeman or reporter : beat, circuit, route. *See* TERRITORY.

round *verb* **1.** To swerve from a straight line : angle[2], arc, arch, bend, bow[2], crook, curve, turn. *See* STRAIGHT. **2.** To supply what is lacking. Also used with *off* or *out* : complement, complete, fill in (*or* out), supplement. *See* AGREE, PART.

round up *verb* To bring together : assemble, call, cluster, collect[1], congregate, convene, convoke, gather, get together, group, muster, summon. *See* COLLECT.

round *adverb* **1.** In or toward a former location or condition : about, around, back, backward, backwards, rearward. *See* APPROACH. **2.** From one end to the other : around, over, through, throughout. *See* PART.

roundabout *adjective*
1. Not taking a direct or straight line or course : anfractuous, circuitous, circular, devious, indirect, oblique, tortuous. *See* STRAIGHT. **2.** Characterized by repetition and excessive wordiness : circumlocutionary, tautological. *See* REPETITION, WORDS.

rounded *adjective*
Deviating from a straight line : arced, arched, arciform, bent, bowed, curved, curvilinear. *See* STRAIGHT.

round-the-clock *adjective*
Existing or occurring without interruption or end : around-the-clock, ceaseless, constant, continual, continuous, endless, eternal, everlasting, incessant, interminable, nonstop, ongoing, perpetual, persistent, relentless, timeless,

unceasing, unending, unfailing, uninterrupted, unremitting. *See* CONTINUE.

round up *verb* See **round.**

rouse *verb*

1. To cease sleeping : arouse, awake, awaken, stir[1], wake[1], waken. *See* AWARENESS. **2.** To induce or elicit (a reaction or emotion) : arouse, awake, awaken, kindle, raise, stir[1] (up), waken. *See* EXCITE.

rousing *adjective*

Serving to enliven : animating, enlivening, quickening, stimulating, vitalizing, vivifying. *See* EXCITE.

roustabout *noun*

One who labors : hand, laborer, operative, worker, working girl, workingman, workingwoman, workman, workwoman. *See* WORK.

rout *noun*

The act of defeating or the condition of being defeated : beating, defeat, drubbing, overthrow, thrashing, vanquishment. *Informal:* massacre, trimming, whipping. *Slang:* dusting, licking. *See* WIN.

rout *verb* To win a victory over, as in battle or a competition : beat, best, conquer, defeat, master, overcome, prevail against (*or* over), subdue, subjugate, surmount, triumph over, vanquish, worst. *Informal:* trim, whip. *Slang:* ace, lick. ***Idioms:*** carry (*or* win) the day, get (*or* have) the best of, get (*or* have) the better of, go someone one better. *See* WIN.

route *noun*

1. A course affording passage from one place to another : avenue, boulevard, drive, expressway, freeway, highway, path, road, roadway, street, superhighway, thoroughfare, thruway, turnpike, way. *See* MOVE, OPEN. **2.** An area regularly covered, as by a policeman or reporter : beat, circuit, round. *See* TERRITORY. **3.** A means or method of entering into or achieving something desirable : formula, key, secret. *Informal:* ticket. *See* MEANS.

route *verb* **1.** To cause (something) to be conveyed to a destination : address, consign, dispatch, forward, send, ship, transmit. *See* MOVE. **2.** To show the way to : conduct, direct, escort, guide, lead, pilot, shepherd, show, steer, usher. *See* SHOW.

routine *noun*

1. A course of action to be followed regularly : round (often used in plural), track. *See* USUAL. **2.** A habitual, laborious, often tiresome course of action : rut[1], treadmill. *Informal:* grind. *Slang:* groove. *See* USUAL. **3.** *Slang.* A particular kind of activity : *Informal:* bit[1]. *See* ACTION.

routine *adjective* **1.** Familiar through repetition : accustomed, chronic, habitual. *See* USUAL. **2.** Occurring quite often : common, everyday, familiar, frequent, regular, widespread. *See* USUAL. **3.** Being of no special quality or type : average, common, commonplace, cut-and-dried, formulaic, garden, garden-variety, indifferent, mediocre, ordinary, plain, run-of-the-mill, standard, stock, undistinguished, unexceptional, unremarkable. *See* GOOD, USUAL.

routinely *adverb*

In an expected or customary manner; for the most part : commonly, consistently, customarily, frequently, generally, habitually, naturally, normally, often, regularly, typically, usually. ***Idioms:*** as usual, per usual. *See* BIG, USUAL.

routineness *noun*

The quality or condition of being usual : customariness, habitualness, normalcy, normality, ordinariness, prevalence, regularity, usualness. *See* USUAL.

rove *verb*

To move about at random, especially over a wide area : drift, gad, gallivant, meander, peregrinate, ramble, range, roam, stray, traipse, wander. *See* MOVE.

roving *adjective*

Traveling about, especially in search of adventure : errant, roaming, wandering. *See* MOVE.

row[1] *noun*

A group of people or things arranged in a row : column, file, line, queue, rank[1], string, tier. *See* GROUP.

row[2] *noun*

A quarrel, fight, or disturbance marked by very noisy, disorderly, and often violent behavior : affray, brawl, broil[2], donnybrook, fray, free-for-all, melee, riot, ruction, tumult. *Informal:* fracas. *Slang:* rumble. *See* ATTACK.

row *verb* To quarrel noisily : brawl, broil[2], caterwaul, wrangle. *See* ATTACK.

rowdy *noun*

A rough, violent person who engages in destructive actions : hoodlum, mug, roughneck, ruffian, tough. *Informal:* toughie. *Slang:* hood, punk. *See* ATTACK, CRIMES.

rowdy *adjective* Upsetting civil order or peace : riotous. *Law:* disorderly. *See* PEACE.

royal *adjective*

Large and impressive in size, scope, or extent : august, baronial, grand, grandiose, imposing, lordly, magnific, magnificent, majestic, noble, princely, regal, splendid, stately, sublime, superb. *See* BIG, GOOD.

rub *verb*
To remove or invalidate by or as if by running a line through or wiping clean. Also used with *out* : annul, blot (out), cancel, cross (off *or* out), delete, efface, erase, expunge, obliterate, scratch (out), strike (out), undo, wipe (out), x (out). *Law:* vacate. *See* CONTINUE.
rub out *verb* **1.** To destroy all traces of : abolish, annihilate, blot out, clear, eradicate, erase, exterminate, extinguish, extirpate, kill[1], liquidate, obliterate, remove, root[1] (out *or* up), snuff out, stamp out, uproot, wipe out. ***Idioms:*** do away with, make an end of, put an end to. *See* HELP, MAKE. **2.** *Slang.* To take the life of (a person or persons) unlawfully : destroy, finish (off), kill[1], liquidate, murder, slay. *Informal:* put away. *Slang:* bump off, do in, knock off, off, waste, wipe out, zap. *See* HELP.
rub *noun* A tricky or unsuspected condition : snag. *Informal:* catch. *See* LIMITED.

rubbish *noun*
Something that does not have or make sense : balderdash, blather, bunkum, claptrap, drivel, garbage, idiocy, nonsense, piffle, poppycock, rigmarole, tomfoolery, trash, twaddle. *Informal:* tommyrot. *Slang:* applesauce, baloney, bilge, bull[1], bunk[2], crap, hooey, malarkey. *See* KNOWLEDGE.

rubble *noun*
The remains of something destroyed, disintegrated, or decayed : debris, ruin, wrack[2], wreck, wreckage. *See* LEFTOVER.

rubicund *adjective*
Of a healthy reddish color : blooming, florid, flush, flushed, full-blooded, glowing, rosy, ruddy, sanguine. *See* COLORS.

rub out *verb* See **rub.**

rubric *noun*
A code or set of codes governing action or procedure, for example : dictate, prescript, regulation, rule. *See* ORDER.

ruck[1] *noun*
1. An enormous number of persons gathered together : crowd, crush, drove, flock, horde, mass, mob, multitude, press, swarm, throng. *See* BIG, GROUP. **2.** A very large number of things grouped together : army, cloud, crowd, drove, flock, horde, host, legion, mass, mob, multitude, score (used in plural), swarm, throng. *See* BIG, GROUP. **3.** The common people : common (used in plural), commonality, commonalty, commoner (used in plural), crowd, hoi polloi, mass (used in plural), mob, pleb (used in plural), plebeian (used in plural), populace, public, third estate. *See* OVER.

ruck[2] *verb*
To bend together or make a crease in so that one part lies over another : crease, double, fold, pleat, ply[1]. *See* ORDER, SMOOTH.
ruck *noun* A line or an arrangement made by the doubling of one part over another : crease, crimp, crinkle, crumple, fold, pleat, plica, plication, pucker, rimple, rumple, wrinkle. *See* SMOOTH.

ruction *noun*
A quarrel, fight, or disturbance marked by very noisy, disorderly, and often violent behavior : affray, brawl, broil[2], donnybrook, fray, free-for-all, melee, riot, row[2], tumult. *Informal:* fracas. *Slang:* rumble. *See* ATTACK.

ruddy *adjective*
1. Of a healthy reddish color : blooming, florid, flush, flushed, full-blooded, glowing, rosy, rubicund, sanguine. *See* COLORS.
2. *Chiefly British.* So annoying or detestable as to deserve condemnation : accursed, blasted, blessed, bloody, confounded, cursed, damn, darn, execrable, infernal. *Informal:* blamed, damned. *Chiefly British:* blooming. *See* LIKE.

rude *adjective*
1. Not civilized : barbarian, barbaric, barbarous, primitive, savage, uncivilized, uncultivated, uncultured, wild. *Archaic:* uncivil. *See* CULTURE, WILD. **2.** Lacking expert, careful craftsmanship : crude, primitive, raw, rough, unpolished. *See* GOOD. **3.** Lacking in delicacy or refinement : barbarian, barbaric, boorish, churlish, coarse, crass, crude, gross, ill-bred, indelicate, philistine, rough, tasteless, uncivilized, uncouth, uncultivated, uncultured, unpolished, unrefined, vulgar. *See* COURTESY, SMOOTH. **4.** Lacking good manners : discourteous, disrespectful, ill-bred, ill-mannered, impolite, uncivil, ungracious, unmannerly, unpolished. *See* COURTESY. **5.** Characterized by unpleasant discordance of sound : cacophonous, discordant, disharmonious, dissonant, inharmonic, inharmonious, unharmonious, unmusical. *See* AGREE, SOUNDS.

rudeness *noun*
The state or quality of being impudent or arrogantly self-confident : assumption, audaciousness, audacity, boldness, brashness, brazenness, cheek, cheekiness, chutzpah, discourtesy, disrespect, effrontery, face, familiarity, forwardness, gall[1], impertinence, impudence, impudency, incivility, insolence, nerve, nerviness,

overconfidence, pertness, presumptuousness, pushiness, sassiness, sauciness. *Informal:* brass, crust, sauce, uppishness, uppityness. *See* ATTITUDE, COURTESY.

rudiment *noun*

1. A fundamental principle or underlying concept. Often used in plural : base[1], basis, cornerstone, foundation, fundament, fundamental, root[1]. *See* OVER. **2.** A fundamental irreducible constituent of a whole. Often used in plural : basic, element, essential, fundamental. ***Idiom:*** part and parcel. *See* PART.

rudimental *adjective*

Of or treating the most basic aspects : basal, basic, beginning, elementary, rudimentary. *See* SIMPLE, START.

rudimentary *adjective*

Of or treating the most basic aspects : basal, basic, beginning, elementary, rudimental. *See* SIMPLE, START.

rue *verb*

To feel or express sorrow for : deplore, regret, repent. *See* REGRET.

rue *noun* A feeling of regret for one's sins or misdeeds : compunction, contriteness, contrition, penitence, penitency, remorse, remorsefulness, repentance. *Theology:* attrition. *See* REGRET.

rueful *adjective*

1. Arousing or deserving pity : pathetic, piteous, pitiable, pitiful, poor, ruthful. *See* PITY. **2.** Causing sorrow or regret : deplorable, doleful, dolorous, grievous, lamentable, mournful, regrettable, sad, sorrowful, woeful. *See* HAPPY. **3.** Full of or expressive of sorrow : doleful, dolorous, lugubrious, mournful, plaintive, sad, sorrowful, woebegone, woeful. *See* HAPPY.

ruffian *noun*

1. A rough, violent person who engages in destructive actions : hoodlum, mug, roughneck, rowdy, tough. *Informal:* toughie. *Slang:* hood, punk. *See* ATTACK, CRIMES. **2.** A person who treats others violently and roughly, especially for hire : hoodlum, thug, tough. *Informal:* hooligan. *Slang:* goon, gorilla, hood. *See* ATTACK, CRIMES.

ruffle *verb*

1. To impair or destroy the composure of : agitate, bother, discompose, disquiet, distract, disturb, flurry, fluster, perturb, rock, shake (up), toss, unsettle, upset. *Informal:* rattle. *See* CALM. **2.** To trouble the nerves or peace of mind of, especially by repeated vexations : aggravate, annoy, bother, bug, chafe, disturb, exasperate, fret, gall[2], get, irk, irritate, nettle, peeve, provoke, put out, rile, vex. *Idioms:* get in one's hair, get on one's nerves, get under one's skin. *See* FEELINGS, PAIN.

ruffled feathers *noun*

Extreme displeasure caused by an insult or slight : dudgeon, huff, miff, offense, pique, resentment, umbrage. *See* LIKE, PAIN.

rugged *adjective*

1. Having a surface that is not smooth : coarse, cragged, craggy, harsh, ironbound, jagged, ragged, rough, scabrous, uneven. *See* SMOOTH. **2.** Physically toughened so as to have great endurance : hard, hard-bitten, hard-handed, hardy, tough. ***Idiom:*** hard as nails. *See* CONTINUE, STRONG. **3.** Violently disturbed or agitated, as by storms : dirty, heavy, raging, roiled, roily, rough, stormy, tempestuous, tumultuous, turbulent, ugly, violent, wild. *See* CALM. **4.** Marked by vigorous physical exertion : knockabout, rough, rough-and-tumble, strenuous, tough. *See* ACTION.

ruin *noun*

1. The act of destroying or state of being destroyed : bane, destruction, devastation, havoc, ruination, undoing, wrack[1], wreck, wreckage. *See* HELP, LEFTOVER. **2.** Something that causes total loss or severe impairment, as of one's health, fortune, honor, or hopes : bane, destroyer, destruction, downfall, ruination, undoing, wrecker. *See* HELP. **3.** The remains of something destroyed, disintegrated, or decayed : debris, rubble, wrack[2], wreck, wreckage. *See* LEFTOVER.

ruin *verb* **1.** To cause the complete ruin or wreckage of : bankrupt, break down, cross up, demolish, destroy, finish, shatter, sink, smash, spoil, torpedo, undo, wash up, wrack[2], wreck. *Slang:* total. ***Idiom:*** put the kibosh on. *See* HELP. **2.** To make or become unusable or inoperative : break, fail. *Slang:* bust. *See* HELP. **3.** To impair severely something such as the spirit, health, or effectiveness of : break, crush, destroy, overwhelm. *See* HELP. **4.** To reduce to financial insolvency : bankrupt, break, bust, impoverish, pauperize. *Slang:* clean out. *See* MONEY.

ruination *noun*

1. The act of destroying or state of being destroyed : bane, destruction, devastation, havoc, ruin, undoing, wrack[1], wreck, wreckage. *See* HELP, LEFTOVER. **2.** Something that causes total loss or severe impairment, as of one's health, fortune, honor, or hopes : bane, destroyer, destruction, downfall, ruin, undoing, wrecker. *See* HELP.

ruinous *adjective*
1. Causing ruin or destruction : calamitous, cataclysmal, cataclysmic, catastrophic, destructive, disastrous, fatal, fateful. *See* HELP. **2.** Having the capability or effect of damaging irreparably : destructive, pernicious. *See* HELP. **3.** Falling to ruin : dilapidated, ramshackle, rundown, tumbledown. *See* BETTER.

rulable *adjective*
Capable of being governed : administrable, controllable, governable, manageable. *See* CONTROL.

rule *noun*
1. The act of exercising controlling power or the condition of being so controlled : command, control, dominance, domination, dominion, mastery, reign, sway. *See* OVER. **2.** The continuous exercise of authority over a political unit : administration, control, direction, governance, government. *See* CONTROL, POLITICS. **3.** A system by which a political unit is controlled : governance, government, regime. *See* POLITICS. **4.** A principle governing affairs within or among political units : canon, decree, edict, institute, law, ordinance, precept, prescription, regulation. *See* LAW. **5.** A code or set of codes governing action or procedure, for example : dictate, prescript, regulation, rubric. *See* ORDER. **6.** A regular or customary matter, condition, or course of events : commonplace, norm, ordinary, usual. *See* USUAL.

rule *verb* **1.** To exercise authority or influence over : control, direct, dominate, govern. ***Idioms:*** be at the helm, be in the driver's seat, hold sway over, hold the reins. *See* OVER. **2.** To exercise the authority of a sovereign : govern, reign. *Archaic:* sway. ***Idiom:*** wear the crown (*or* purple). *See* OVER. **3.** To command or issue commands in an arrogant manner : boss, dictate, dominate, domineer, order, tyrannize. *See* OVER. **4.** To occupy the preeminent position in : dominate, predominate, preponderate, prevail, reign. ***Idioms:*** have the ascendancy, reign supreme. *See* OVER. **5.** To make a decision about (a controversy or dispute, for example) after deliberation, as in a court of law : adjudge, adjudicate, arbitrate, decide, decree, determine, judge, referee, umpire. *See* DECIDE, LAW.

rule out *verb* **1.** To prohibit from occurring by advance planning or action : avert, forestall, forfend, obviate, preclude, prevent, stave off, ward (off). ***Idiom:*** nip in the bud. *See* ALLOW. **2.** To keep from being admitted, included, or considered : bar, count out, debar, eliminate, except, exclude, keep out, shut out. *See* INCLUDE.

rule out *verb* See **rule.**

ruling *adjective*
1. Exercising controlling power or influence : commanding, controlling, dominant, dominating, dominative, governing, paramount, preponderant, regnant, reigning. *See* OVER. **2.** Having preeminent significance : ascendant, dominant, predominant, prepotent, prevailing, regnant, supreme. *See* IMPORTANT.

ruling *noun* An authoritative or official decision, especially one made by a court : decree, determination, edict, judgment, pronouncement. *See* LAW.

rum *adjective*
British Slang. Deviating from the customary : bizarre, cranky, curious, eccentric, erratic, freakish, idiosyncratic, odd, outlandish, peculiar, quaint, queer, quirky, singular, strange, unnatural, unusual, weird. *Slang:* kooky, screwball. *British Slang:* rummy[2]. *See* USUAL.

rumble *verb*
To make a continuous deep reverberating sound : boom, growl, grumble, roll. *See* SOUNDS.

rumble *noun* **1.** *Slang.* A physical conflict involving two or more : fight, fistfight, fisticuffs, scrap[2], scuffle, tussle. *See* CONFLICT. **2.** *Slang.* A quarrel, fight, or disturbance marked by very noisy, disorderly, and often violent behavior : affray, brawl, broil[2], donnybrook, fray, free-for-all, melee, riot, row[2], ruction, tumult. *Informal:* fracas. *See* ATTACK.

ruminate *verb*
To think or think about carefully and at length : chew on (*or* over), cogitate, consider, contemplate, deliberate, entertain, excogitate, meditate, mull, muse[1], ponder, reflect, revolve, study, think, think out, think over, think through, turn over, weigh. ***Idioms:*** cudgel one's brains, put on one's thinking cap, rack one's brain. *See* THOUGHTS.

rumination *noun*
The act or process of thinking : brainwork, cerebration, cogitation, contemplation, deliberation, excogitation, meditation, reflection, speculation, thought. *See* THOUGHTS.

ruminative *adjective*
Of, characterized by, or disposed to thought : cogitative, contemplative, deliberative, excogitative, meditative, pensive, reflective, speculative, thinking, thoughtful. ***Idiom:*** in a brown study. *See* THOUGHTS.

rummage *verb*
To make a thorough search of : comb, forage, ransack, scour[2]. *Slang:* shake down. ***Idioms:*** beat the bushes, leave no stone unturned, look (*or* search) high and low, look (*or* search) up and down, turn inside out, turn upside down. *See* INVESTIGATE.

rummy[1] *noun*
Slang. A person who is habitually drunk : drunk, drunkard, inebriate, sot, tippler. *Slang:* boozehound, boozer, lush[2], soak, souse, sponge, stiff. *See* DRUGS.

rummy[2] *adjective*
British Slang. Deviating from the customary : bizarre, cranky, curious, eccentric, erratic, freakish, idiosyncratic, odd, outlandish, peculiar, quaint, queer, quirky, singular, strange, unnatural, unusual, weird. *Slang:* kooky, screwball. *British Slang:* rum. *See* USUAL.

rumor *noun*
Idle, often sensational and groundless talk about others : gossip, gossipry, hearsay, report, talebearing, tattle, tittle-tattle, word. *Slang:* scuttlebutt. *See* WORDS.

rumor *verb* To engage in or spread gossip : blab, gossip, noise, talk, tattle, tittle-tattle, whisper. ***Idioms:*** tell tales, tell tales out of school. *See* WORDS.

rumormonger *noun*
A person habitually engaged in idle talk about others : blab, gossip, gossiper, gossipmonger, newsmonger, scandalmonger, tabby, talebearer, taleteller, tattle, tattler, tattletale, telltale, whisperer. *Slang:* yenta. *See* WORDS.

rump *noun*
The part of one's back on which one rests in sitting : buttock (used in plural), derrière, posterior, seat. *Informal:* backside, behind, bottom, rear[1]. *Slang:* bun (used in plural), fanny, tush. *Chiefly British:* bum[2]. *See* OVER.

rumple *verb*
1. To make irregular folds in, especially by pressing or twisting : crease, crimp, crinkle, crumple, rimple, wrinkle. *See* SMOOTH. **2.** To put (the hair or clothes) into a state of disarray : disarrange, dishevel, disorder, mess (up), muss (up), tousle. *See* ORDER.

rumple *noun* A line or an arrangement made by the doubling of one part over another : crease, crimp, crinkle, crumple, fold, pleat, plica, plication, pucker, rimple, ruck[2], wrinkle. *See* SMOOTH.

rumpus *noun*
1. Sounds or a sound, especially when loud, confused, or disagreeable : babel, clamor, din, hubbub, hullabaloo, noise, pandemonium, racket, tumult, uproar. *See* SOUNDS. **2.** Offensively loud and insistent utterances, especially of disapproval : clamor, hullabaloo, outcry, uproar, vociferation. ***Idiom:*** hue and cry. *See* LIKE, SOUNDS.

run *verb*
1. To move swiftly on foot so that both feet leave the ground during each stride : scamper, scurry, sprint. *See* MOVE. **2.** To move swiftly : bolt, bucket, bustle, dart, dash, festinate, flash, fleet, flit, fly, haste, hasten, hurry, hustle, pelt[2], race, rocket, rush, sail, scoot, scour[2], shoot, speed, sprint, tear[1], trot, whirl, whisk, whiz, wing, zip, zoom. *Informal:* hotfoot, rip. *Slang:* barrel, highball. *Chiefly British:* nip[1]. ***Idioms:*** get a move on, get cracking, go like lightning, go like the wind, hotfoot it, make haste, make time, make tracks, run like the wind, shake a leg, step (*or* jump) on it. *See* MOVE. **3.** To leave hastily : bolt, get out. *Informal:* clear out, get, hotfoot, skedaddle. *Slang:* hightail, scram, vamoose. ***Idioms:*** beat it, hightail it, hotfoot it, make tracks. *See* APPROACH. **4.** To move or proceed away from a place. Also used with *along* : depart, exit, get away, get off, go, go away, leave[1], pull out, quit, retire, withdraw. *Informal:* cut out, push off, shove off. *Slang:* blow[1], split, take off. ***Idioms:*** hit the road, take leave. *See* APPROACH. **5.** To be with as a companion. Also used with *around* : associate, consort, fraternize, hang around, hobnob, troop. *Slang:* hang out. ***Idiom:*** rub elbows (*or* shoulders) . *See* NEAR. **6.** To look to when in need : apply, go, refer, repair[2], resort, turn. ***Idioms:*** fall back on (*or* upon), have recourse to. *See* USED. **7.** To complete a race or competition in a specified position : come in, finish, place. *See* BE. **8.** To move freely as a liquid : circulate, course, flow, stream. *See* MOVE. **9.** To come forth or emit in abundance : flow, gush, pour, rush, stream, surge, well[1]. *See* MOVE. **10.** To change from a solid to a liquid : deliquesce, dissolve, flux, fuse, liquefy, melt, thaw. *See* SOLID. **11.** To proceed on a certain course or for a certain distance : carry, extend, go, lead, reach, stretch. *See* REACH. **12.** To change or fluctuate within limits : extend, go, range, vary. *See* CHANGE. **13.** To be performed : play, show. *See* PERFORMING ARTS. **14.** To urge to move along : drive, herd. *See* MOVE. **15.** To look for and pursue (game) in order to capture or kill it : chase, drive, hunt, stalk. *See* SEEK. **16.** To perform a function effectively : function, go, operate, take, work.

See THRIVE. **17.** To set or keep going : actuate, drive, impel, mobilize, move, propel. *See* MOVE. **18.** To control or direct the functioning of : manage, operate, use, work. *See* CONTROL. **19.** To import or export secretly and illegally : bootleg, smuggle. ***Idiom:*** run contraband. *See* CRIMES, MOVE. **20.** To separate or pull apart by force : rend, rip, rive, split, tear[1]. *See* ASSEMBLE, HELP. **21.** To cause to penetrate with force : dig, drive, plunge, ram, sink, stab, stick, thrust. *See* PUT IN. **22.** To control the course of (an activity) : carry on, conduct, direct, manage, operate, steer. *See* OVER. **23.** To have charge of (the affairs of others) : administer, administrate, direct, govern, head, manage, superintend, supervise. *See* OVER.

run across *verb* To find or meet by chance : bump into, chance on (*or* upon), come across, come on (*or* upon), find, happen on (*or* upon), light on (*or* upon), run into, stumble on (*or* upon), tumble on. *Archaic:* alight on (*or* upon). ***Idiom:*** meet up with. *See* MEET.

run after *verb* To follow (another) with the intent of overtaking and capturing : chase, pursue. ***Idioms:*** be (*or* go) in pursuit, give chase. *See* SEEK.

run away *verb* To break loose and leave suddenly, as from confinement or from a difficult or threatening situation : abscond, break out, decamp, escape, flee, fly, get away. *Informal:* skip (out). *Slang:* lam. *Regional:* absquatulate. ***Idioms:*** blow (*or* fly) the coop, cut and run, give someone the slip, make a getaway, take flight, take it on the lam. *See* FREE.

run down *verb* **1.** To lose so much strength and power as to become ineffective or motionless : burn out, give out. *Slang:* poop out[1]. *See* TIRED. **2.** To pursue and locate : hunt down, nose out, trace, track down. ***Idiom:*** run to earth (*or* ground). *See* GET. **3.** To think, represent, or speak of as small or unimportant : belittle, decry, denigrate, deprecate, depreciate, derogate, detract, discount, disparage, downgrade, minimize, slight, talk down. ***Idiom:*** make light (*or* little) of. *See* ATTACK, SHOW. **4.** To give a recapitulation of the salient facts of : abstract, epitomize, go over, recapitulate, review, run through, summarize, sum up, synopsize, wrap up. *Informal:* recap. *See* THOUGHTS.

run in *verb* **1.** *Slang.* To take into custody as a prisoner : apprehend, arrest, seize. *Informal:* nab, pick up. *Slang:* bust, collar, pinch. *See* LAW. **2.** To go to or seek out the company of in order to socialize : call, come by, come over, drop by, drop in, look in, look up, pop in, see, stop (by *or* in), visit. ***Idiom:*** pay a visit. *See* SEEK.

run into *verb* **1.** To find or meet by chance : bump into, chance on (*or* upon), come across, come on (*or* upon), find, happen on (*or* upon), light on (*or* upon), run across, stumble on (*or* upon), tumble on. *Archaic:* alight on (*or* upon). ***Idiom:*** meet up with. *See* MEET. **2.** To come up against : confront, encounter, face, meet[1]. *See* MEET. **3.** To come to in number or quantity : aggregate, amount, number, reach, total. ***Idiom:*** add up to. *See* INCREASE.

run on *verb* To talk volubly, persistently, and usually inconsequentially : babble, blabber, chatter, chitchat, clack, jabber, palaver, prate, prattle, rattle (on). *Informal:* go on, spiel. *Slang:* gab, gas, jaw, yak. ***Idioms:*** run off at the mouth, shoot the breeze (*or* bull). *See* WORDS.

run out *verb* **1.** To make or become no longer active or productive : deplete, desiccate, dry up, give out, play out. *See* CONTINUE. **2.** To prove deficient or insufficient : fail, give out. ***Idioms:*** fall short, run dry, run short. *See* EXCESS. **3.** To become void, especially through passage of time or an omission : expire, lapse. *See* CONTINUE, LAW.

run through *verb* **1.** To use all of : consume, drain, draw down, eat up, exhaust, expend, finish, play out, spend, use up. *Informal:* polish off. *See* INCREASE. **2.** To give a recapitulation of the salient facts of : abstract, epitomize, go over, recapitulate, review, run down, summarize, sum up, synopsize, wrap up. *Informal:* recap. *See* THOUGHTS. **3.** To look through reading matter casually : browse, dip into, flip through, glance at (*or* over *or* through), leaf (through), riffle (through), scan, skim, thumb (through). *See* INVESTIGATE, WORDS.

run up *verb* To make or become greater or larger : aggrandize, amplify, augment, boost, build, build up, burgeon, enlarge, escalate, expand, extend, grow, increase, magnify, mount, multiply, proliferate, rise, snowball, soar, swell, upsurge, wax. *Informal:* beef up. *See* INCREASE.

run *noun* **1.** A trip in a motor vehicle : drive, ride. *Informal:* spin, whirl. *See* MOVE. **2.** *Chiefly Regional.* A small stream : brook[1], creek. *Chiefly Regional:* branch, kill[2]. *See* DRY. **3.** A hole made by tearing : rent[2], rip, tear[1]. *See* HELP. **4.** A number of things placed or occurring one after the other : chain, consecution, course, order, procession, progression, round, sequence, series, string, succession, suite, train. *Informal:* streak. *See* ORDER.

run across *verb* See **run.**

run after *verb* See **run.**

runagate *noun*
A person who has defected : apostate, defector, deserter, recreant, renegade, tergiversator, turncoat. *Informal:* rat. *See* APPROACH.

runaway *noun*
1. One who flees, as from home, confinement, captivity, or justice : escapee, fugitive, refugee. *See* SEEK. **2.** *Informal.* An easy victory : walkaway, walkover. *Slang:* romp. *See* EASY, WIN.
runaway *adjective* **1.** Fleeing or having fled, as from home, confinement, captivity, or justice : escaped, fugitive. *See* SEEK. **2.** Out of control : amuck, uncontrolled. ***Idioms:*** out of hand, running wild. *See* CONTROL.

run away *verb* See **run.**

rundown *noun*
A condensation of the essential or main points of something : recapitulation, run-through, sum, summary, summation, summing-up, wrap-up. *Informal:* recap. *See* WORDS.
rundown also **run-down** *adjective* **1.** Extremely tired : bleary, dead, drained, exhausted, fatigued, spent, tired out, wearied, weariful, weary, worn-down, worn-out. *Informal:* beat, bushed, tuckered (out). *Slang:* done in, fagged (out), pooped (out). ***Idioms:*** all in, ready to drop. *See* HEALTH, TIRED. **2.** Falling to ruin : dilapidated, ramshackle, ruinous, tumbledown. *See* BETTER. **3.** Showing signs of wear and tear or neglect : bedraggled, broken-down, decaying, decrepit, dilapidated, dingy, down-at-heel, faded, mangy, scrubby, scruffy, seedy, shabby, shoddy, sleazy, tattered, tatty, threadbare. *Informal:* tacky[2]. *Slang:* ratty. ***Idioms:*** all the worse for wear, gone to pot (*or* seed), past cure (*or* hope). *See* BETTER.

run down *verb* See **run.**

rung *noun*
One of the units in a course, as on an ascending or descending scale : degree, grade, level, peg, point, stage, step. *Informal:* notch. *See* BIG.

run-in *noun*
1. A discussion, often heated, in which a difference of opinion is expressed : altercation, argument, bicker, clash, contention, controversy, debate, difficulty, disagreement, dispute, fight, polemic, quarrel, spat, squabble, tiff, word (used in plural), wrangle. *Informal:* hassle, rhubarb, tangle. *See* CONFLICT. **2.** A brief, hostile exposure to or contact with something such as danger or opposition : brush[2], clash, encounter, skirmish. *See* TOUCH.

run in *verb* See **run.**

run into *verb* See **run.**

runner *noun*
1. A person who carries messages or is sent on errands : bearer, carrier, conveyer, courier, envoy, messenger, transporter. *See* OVER. **2.** A person who engages in smuggling : bootlegger, contrabandist, smuggler. *See* CRIMES, MOVE. **3.** A young stemlike growth arising from a plant : bine, offshoot, shoot, sprig, sprout, tendril. *See* KIN.

running *adjective*
In action or full operation : active, alive, functioning, going, operating, operative, working. *See* ACTION, AWARENESS.

run-of-the-mill *adjective*
Being of no special quality or type : average, common, commonplace, cut-and-dried, formulaic, garden, garden-variety, indifferent, mediocre, ordinary, plain, routine, standard, stock, undistinguished, unexceptional, unremarkable. *See* GOOD, USUAL.

run on *verb* See **run.**

run out *verb* See **run.**

run-through *noun*
A condensation of the essential or main points of something : recapitulation, rundown, sum, summary, summation, summing-up, wrap-up. *Informal:* recap. *See* WORDS.

run through *verb* See **run.**

run up *verb* See **run.**

rupture *noun*
1. An opening, especially in a solid structure : breach, break, gap, hole, perforation. *See* OPEN. **2.** An interruption in friendly relations : alienation, breach, break, disaffection, estrangement, fissure, rent[2], rift, schism, split. *See* ASSEMBLE, HELP.
rupture *verb* To undergo partial breaking : crack, fissure, fracture, split. *See* HELP.

rural *adjective*
Of or relating to the countryside : arcadian, bucolic, campestral, country, pastoral, provincial, rustic. *Informal:* hick. *See* URBAN.

ruse *noun*
An indirect, usually cunning means of gaining an end : artifice, deception, device, dodge, feint, gimmick, imposture, jig, maneuver, ploy, sleight, stratagem, subterfuge, trick, wile. *Informal:* shenanigan, take-in. *See* HONEST, MEANS.

rush *verb*
1. To move swiftly : bolt, bucket, bustle, dart,

dash, festinate, flash, fleet, flit, fly, haste, hasten, hurry, hustle, pelt[2], race, rocket, run, sail, scoot, scour[2], shoot, speed, sprint, tear[1], trot, whirl, whisk, whiz, wing, zip, zoom. *Informal:* hotfoot, rip. *Slang:* barrel, highball. *Chiefly British:* nip[1]. ***Idioms:*** get a move on, get cracking, go like lightning, go like the wind, hotfoot it, make haste, make time, make tracks, run like the wind, shake a leg, step (*or* jump) on it. *See* MOVE. **2.** To come forth or emit in abundance : flow, gush, pour, run, stream, surge, well[1]. *See* MOVE.

rush *noun* **1.** Careless headlong action : haste, hastiness, hurriedness, precipitance, precipitancy, precipitateness, precipitation, rashness. *See* CAREFUL. **2.** A swift advance or attack : blitzkrieg, charge. *See* APPROACH. **3.** Something suggestive of running water : current, drift, flood, flow, flux, spate, stream, surge, tide. *See* MOVE.

rush *adjective* Designed to meet emergency needs as quickly as possible : *Informal:* crash, hurry-up. *See* FAST.

rustic *adjective*
1. Of or relating to the countryside : arcadian, bucolic, campestral, country, pastoral, provincial, rural. *Informal:* hick. *See* URBAN. **2.** Of a plain and unsophisticated nature : artless, homely, homespun, natural, unadorned, unpolished. *See* PLAIN.

rustic *noun* A clumsy, unsophisticated person : bumpkin, clodhopper, yokel. *See* ABILITY.

rut[1] *noun*
A habitual, laborious, often tiresome course of action : routine, treadmill. *Informal:* grind. *Slang:* groove. *See* USUAL.

rut[2] *noun*
A regular period of sexual excitement in female mammals : estrus, heat, season. *See* SEX.

ruthful *adjective*
Arousing or deserving pity : pathetic, piteous, pitiable, pitiful, poor, rueful. *See* PITY.

ruthless *adjective*
Lacking scruples or principles : conscienceless, unconscionable, unethical, unprincipled, unscrupulous. *See* HONEST.

·S·

sable *adjective*
Of the darkest achromatic visual value : black, ebon, ebony, inky, jet[1], jetty, onyx, pitch-black, pitchy, sooty. *See* COLORS.

sabotage *noun*
A deliberate and underhanded effort to defeat or do harm to an endeavor : subversion, undermining. *See* ATTACK.

sabotage *verb* To damage, destroy, or defeat by sabotage : subvert, undermine. *See* ATTACK.

saccharine *adjective*
1. Having or suggesting the taste of sugar : sugary, sweet. *See* TASTE. **2.** Purposefully contrived to gain favor : ingratiating, ingratiatory, insinuating, sugary. *See* PAIN.

sack[1] *noun*
Slang. The act of dismissing or the condition of being dismissed from employment : discharge, dismissal, termination. *Informal:* ax. *Slang:* boot[1], bounce. *See* KEEP.

sack *verb* *Slang.* To end the employment or service of : cashier, discharge, dismiss, drop, release, terminate. *Informal:* ax, fire, pink-slip. *Slang:* boot[1], bounce, can. ***Idioms:*** give someone his or her walking papers, give someone the ax, give someone the gate, give someone the pink slip, let go, show someone the door. *See* KEEP.

sack[2] *verb*
To rob of goods by force, especially in time of war : depredate, despoil, havoc, loot, pillage, plunder, ransack, rape, ravage, spoliate, strip[1]. *Archaic:* harrow, spoil. *See* CRIMES, GIVE.

sacrarium *noun*
A sacred or holy place : sanctorium, sanctuary, sanctum, shrine. *See* SACRED.

sacred *adjective*
1. In the service or worship of God or a god : divine, holy, religious. *See* RELIGION. **2.** Protected from violation or abuse by custom, law, or feelings of reverence : inviolable, sacrosanct. *See* SACRED. **3.** Regarded with particular reverence or respect : blessed, hallowed, holy, sacrosanct. *See* RELIGION, RESPECT. **4.** Given over exclusively to a single use or purpose :

consecrated, dedicated, devoted, hallowed. *See* GIVE, INCLUDE.

sacredness *noun*
1. The quality of being holy or sacred : blessedness, holiness, sacrosanctity, sanctity. *See* RELIGION. **2.** The quality or condition of being safe from assault, trespass, or violation : inviolability, sacrosanctity, sanctity. *See* SAFETY.

sacrifice *noun*
1. One or more living creatures slain and offered to a deity as part of a religious rite : hecatomb, immolation, offering, victim. *See* RELIGION. **2.** A loss sustained in the accomplishment of or as the result of something : cost, expense, price, toll[1]. *See* TRANSACTIONS.
sacrifice *verb* To offer as a sacrifice : immolate, victimize. *See* GIVE, RELIGION.

sacrilege *noun*
An act of disrespect or impiety toward something regarded as sacred : blasphemy, desecration, profanation, violation. *See* SACRED.

sacrilegious *adjective*
Showing irreverence and contempt for something sacred : blasphemous, profane. *See* SACRED.

sacrosanct *adjective*
1. Regarded with particular reverence or respect : blessed, hallowed, holy, sacred. *See* RELIGION, RESPECT. **2.** Protected from violation or abuse by custom, law, or feelings of reverence : inviolable, sacred. *See* SACRED.

sacrosanctity *noun*
1. The quality of being holy or sacred : blessedness, holiness, sacredness, sanctity. *See* RELIGION. **2.** The quality or condition of being safe from assault, trespass, or violation : inviolability, sacredness, sanctity. *See* SAFETY.

sad *adjective*
1. In low spirits : blue, dejected, depressed, desolate, dispirited, down, downcast, downhearted, dull, dysphoric, gloomy, heavy-hearted, low, melancholic, melancholy, spiritless, tristful, unhappy, wistful. ***Idiom:*** down at (*or* in) the mouth. *See* HAPPY. **2.** Full of or expressive of sorrow : doleful, dolorous, lugubrious, mournful, plaintive, rueful, sorrowful, woebegone, woeful. *See* HAPPY. **3.** Tending to cause sadness or low spirits : blue, cheerless, depressing, dismal, dispiriting, gloomy, joyless, melancholy. *See* HAPPY. **4.** Causing sorrow or regret : deplorable, doleful, dolorous, grievous, lamentable, mournful, regrettable, rueful, sorrowful, woeful. *See* HAPPY.

sadden *verb*
To make sad or gloomy : deject, depress, dispirit, oppress, weigh down. *See* HAPPY.

saddle *verb*
1. To place a burden or heavy load on : burden[1], charge, cumber, encumber, freight, lade, load, tax, weight. *See* OVER. **2.** To force (another) to accept a burden : foist, impose, inflict. *Informal:* stick. *See* GIVE, OVER, WILLING.

sadness *noun*
A feeling or spell of dismally low spirits : blues, dejection, depression, despondence, despondency, doldrums, dolefulness, downheartedness, dumps, dysphoria, funk, gloom, glumness, heavy-heartedness, melancholy, mope (used in plural), mournfulness, unhappiness. *See* FEELINGS, HAPPY.

safari *noun*
A journey undertaken with a specific objective : expedition, pilgrimage, tour, trek, voyage. *See* MOVE.

safe *adjective*
1. Free from danger, injury, or the threat of harm : unharmed, unhurt, uninjured, unscathed. ***Idiom:*** safe and sound. *See* SAFETY. **2.** Affording protection : secure. *See* SAFETY.

safeguard *noun*
The act or a means of defending : defense, guard, preservation, protection, protector, security, shield, ward. *See* ATTACK.
safeguard *verb* To keep safe from danger, attack, or harm : defend, guard, preserve, protect, secure, shield, ward. *Archaic:* fend. *See* ATTACK.

safeness *noun*
The quality or state of being safe : assurance, safety, security. *See* SAFETY.

safety *noun*
The quality or state of being safe : assurance, safeness, security. *See* SAFETY.

sag *verb*
1. To hang limply, loosely, and carelessly : droop, flop, loll, lop[2], slouch, wilt. *See* HANG. **2.** To become limp, as from loss of freshness : droop, flag[2], wilt. *See* BETTER. **3.** To decline, as in value or quantity, very gradually : drop off, fall off, slip. *See* INCREASE.
sag *noun* An area sunk below its surroundings : basin, concavity, depression, dip, hollow, pit[1], sink, sinkhole. *See* CONVEX.

sagacious *adjective*
1. Possessing or showing sound judgment and keen perception : knowing, sage, sapient, wise[1]. *See* WISE. **2.** Possessing, proceeding

from, or exhibiting good judgment and prudence : balanced, commonsensible, commonsensical, judicious, levelheaded, prudent, rational, reasonable, sage, sane, sapient, sensible, sound[2], well-founded, well-grounded, wise[1]. *See* REASON, SANE.

sagaciousness *noun*
Deep, thorough, or mature understanding : insight, profundity, sagacity, sageness, sapience, wisdom. *See* WISE.

sagacity *noun*
1. Skill in perceiving, discriminating, or judging : acumen, astuteness, clear-sightedness, discernment, discrimination, eye, keenness, nose, penetration, perceptiveness, percipience, percipiency, perspicacity, sageness, shrewdness, wit. *See* ABILITY, CAREFUL. **2.** Deep, thorough, or mature understanding : insight, profundity, sagaciousness, sageness, sapience, wisdom. *See* WISE.

sage *noun*
A usually elderly person noted for wisdom, knowledge, and judgment : pundit, savant, scholar. *See* WISE.
sage *adjective* **1.** Possessing or showing sound judgment and keen perception : knowing, sagacious, sapient, wise[1]. *See* WISE. **2.** Possessing, proceeding from, or exhibiting good judgment and prudence : balanced, commonsensible, commonsensical, judicious, levelheaded, prudent, rational, reasonable, sagacious, sane, sapient, sensible, sound[2], well-founded, well-grounded, wise[1]. *See* REASON, SANE.

sageness *noun*
1. Skill in perceiving, discriminating, or judging : acumen, astuteness, clear-sightedness, discernment, discrimination, eye, keenness, nose, penetration, perceptiveness, percipience, percipiency, perspicacity, sagacity, shrewdness, wit. *See* ABILITY, CAREFUL. **2.** Deep, thorough, or mature understanding : insight, profundity, sagaciousness, sagacity, sapience, wisdom. *See* WISE.

sail *verb*
1. To move swiftly : bolt, bucket, bustle, dart, dash, festinate, flash, fleet, flit, fly, haste, hasten, hurry, hustle, pelt[2], race, rocket, run, rush, scoot, scour[2], shoot, speed, sprint, tear[1], trot, whirl, whisk, whiz, wing, zip, zoom. *Informal:* hotfoot, rip. *Slang:* barrel, highball. *Chiefly British:* nip[1]. ***Idioms:*** get a move on, get cracking, go like lightning, go like the wind, hotfoot it, make haste, make time, make tracks, run like the wind, shake a leg, step (*or* jump) on it. *See* MOVE. **2.** To pass quickly and lightly through the air : dart, float, fly, shoot, skim. *See* MOVE. **3.** To move through the air with or as if with wings : flap, flit, flitter, flutter, fly, wing. *See* MOVE. **4.** To proceed with ease, especially of expression : flow, glide, roll. *See* MOVE.
sail in *verb* To start work on vigorously : attack, go at, tackle, wade in (*or* into). ***Idiom:*** hop to it. *See* WORK.
sail into *verb* To set upon with violent force : aggress, assail, assault, attack, beset, fall on (*or* upon), go at, have at, storm, strike. *Informal:* light into, pitch into. *See* ATTACK.

sail in *verb* See **sail.**

sail into *verb* See **sail.**

sailor *noun*
A person engaged in sailing or working on a ship : jack (uppercase), jack-tar, mariner, navigator, sea dog, seafarer, seaman. *Informal:* salt, tar. *Slang:* gob[3]. *See* SEA.

saintly *adjective*
Deeply concerned with God and the beliefs and practice of religion : devotional, devout, godly, holy, pietistic, pietistical, pious, prayerful, religious. *See* RELIGION.

salability *noun*
Market appeal : marketability, marketableness, salableness. *Slang:* sell. *See* DESIRE.

salableness *noun*
Market appeal : marketability, marketableness, salability. *Slang:* sell. *See* DESIRE.

salacious *adjective*
Of, concerning, or promoting sexual love or desire : amatory, amorous, aphrodisiac, erotic, lascivious, sexual, sexy. *See* SEX.

salad days *noun*
The time of life between childhood and maturity : adolescence, greenness, juvenescence, juvenility, puberty, spring, youth, youthfulness. *See* YOUTH.

salary *noun*
Payment for work done : compensation, earnings, emolument, fee, hire, pay, remuneration, stipend, wage. *See* PAY.

salesclerk *noun*
One who sells : clerk, salesgirl, salesman, salesperson, saleswoman, seller, vender. *See* TRANSACTIONS.

salesgirl *noun*
One who sells : clerk, salesclerk, salesman, salesperson, saleswoman, seller, vender. *See* TRANSACTIONS.

salesman *noun*
One who sells : clerk, salesclerk, salesgirl, salesperson, saleswoman, seller, vender. *See* TRANSACTIONS.

salesperson *noun*
One who sells : clerk, salesclerk, salesgirl, salesman, saleswoman, seller, vender. *See* TRANSACTIONS.

saleswoman *noun*
One who sells : clerk, salesclerk, salesgirl, salesman, salesperson, seller, vender. *See* TRANSACTIONS.

salient *adjective*
Readily attracting notice : arresting, bold, conspicuous, eye-catching, marked, noticeable, observable, outstanding, pointed, prominent, pronounced, remarkable, signal, striking. *Idiom:* sticking out like a sore thumb. *See* SEE.

salivate *verb*
To let saliva run from the mouth : dribble, drivel, drool, slaver, slobber. *See* DRY, MOUTH.

salivation *noun*
Saliva running from the mouth : drivel, drool, slaver, slobber. *See* DRY, MOUTH.

sallow *adjective*
Lacking color : ashen, ashy, bloodless, cadaverous, colorless, livid, lurid, pale, pallid, pasty, wan, waxen. *See* COLORS.

salmagundi *noun*
A collection of various things : assortment, conglomeration, gallimaufry, hodgepodge, jumble, medley, mélange, miscellany, mishmash, mixed bag, mixture, olio, patchwork, potpourri, variety. *Slang:* grab bag. *See* COLLECT.

salt *noun*
Informal. A person engaged in sailing or working on a ship : jack (uppercase), jack-tar, mariner, navigator, sailor, sea dog, seafarer, seaman. *Informal:* tar. *Slang:* gob[3]. *See* SEA.

salt away *verb* **1.** To reserve for the future : keep, lay aside, lay away, lay by, lay in, lay up, put by, save (up), set by. *See* KEEP, SAVE. **2.** To place (money) in a bank : bank[2], deposit, lay away. *Informal:* sock away. *See* KEEP, MONEY.

salt away *verb* See **salt.**

salty *adjective*
Bordering on indelicacy or impropriety : blue, earthy, off-color, provocative, racy, risqué, scabrous, spicy, suggestive. *See* DECENT.

salubrious *adjective*
Promoting good health : healthful, healthsome, healthy, hygienic, salutary, wholesome. *See* HEALTH.

salutary *adjective*
1. Affording benefit : advantageous, benefic, beneficent, beneficial, benignant, favorable, good, helpful, profitable, propitious, toward, useful. *See* HELP. **2.** Promoting good health : healthful, healthsome, healthy, hygienic, salubrious, wholesome. *See* HEALTH.

salutation *noun*
An expression, in words or gestures, marking a meeting of persons : greeting, hail[2], salute, welcome. *See* GREETING.

salute *verb*
1. To address in a friendly and respectful way : greet, hail[2], welcome. *See* GREETING. **2.** To approach for the purpose of speech : accost, greet, hail[2]. *See* APPROACH, GREETING, SEEK.

salute *noun* **1.** An expression, in words or gestures, marking a meeting of persons : greeting, hail[2], salutation, welcome. *See* GREETING. **2.** A formal token of appreciation and admiration for a person's high achievements : salvo, testimonial, tribute. *See* PRAISE.

salvage *noun*
Extrication from danger or confinement : deliverance, delivery, rescue, salvation. *See* HELP.

salvage *verb* To extricate from an undesirable state : reclaim, recover, redeem, rescue. *See* HELP.

salvation *noun*
Extrication from danger or confinement : deliverance, delivery, rescue, salvage. *See* HELP.

salvo *noun*
1. A concentrated outpouring, as of missiles, words, or blows : barrage, bombardment, burst, cannonade, fusillade, hail[1], shower, storm, volley. *See* ATTACK. **2.** A formal token of appreciation and admiration for a person's high achievements : salute, testimonial, tribute. *See* PRAISE.

same *adjective*
1. Being one and not another or others; not different in nature or identity : identic, identical, selfsame, very. *See* SAME. **2.** Agreeing exactly in value, quantity, or effect : equal, equivalent, even[1], identical, tantamount. ***Idioms:*** on a par, one and the same. *See* SAME. **3.** Remaining continually unchanged : changeless, consistent, constant, invariable, unchanging, unfailing. *See* CHANGE. **4.** Having no change or variation : changeless, constant, equable, even[1], invariable, invariant, regular, steady, unchanging, uniform, unvarying. *See* SAME.

sameness *noun*
1. The quality or condition of being exactly the same as something else : identicalness, identity, oneness, selfsameness. *See* SAME. **2.** The state of being equivalent : equality, equation, equiv-

alence, equivalency, par, parity. *See* SAME. **3.** A tiresome lack of variety : humdrum, monotone, monotonousness, monotony. *See* CHANGE, EXCITE.

sample *noun*
1. One that is representative of a group or class : case, example, illustration, instance, representative, specimen. *See* SUBSTITUTE. **2.** A limited or anticipatory experience : foretaste, taste. *See* FORESIGHT.

sanctify *verb*
To make sacred by a religious rite : bless, consecrate, hallow. *See* RELIGION.

sanctimonious *adjective*
Of or practicing hypocrisy : hypocritical, Pecksniffian, pharisaic, pharisaical, phony, two-faced. *See* HONEST.

sanctimoniousness *noun*
A show or expression of feelings or beliefs one does not actually hold or possess : hypocrisy, pharisaism, phoniness, sanctimony, tartuffery, two-facedness. *See* HONEST.

sanctimony *noun*
A show or expression of feelings or beliefs one does not actually hold or possess : hypocrisy, pharisaism, phoniness, sanctimoniousness, tartuffery, two-facedness. *See* HONEST.

sanction *noun*
1. The approving of an action, especially when done by one in authority : allowance, approbation, approval, authorization, consent, endorsement, leave[2], license, permission, permit. *Informal:* OK. *See* ALLOW. **2.** An act of confirming officially : affirmation, approval, confirmation, ratification. *See* LAW. **3.** A coercive measure intended to ensure compliance or conformity : interdict, interdiction, penalty. *See* REWARD.

sanction *verb* **1.** To give one's consent to : allow, approbate, approve, authorize, consent, endorse, let, permit. *Informal:* OK. *See* ALLOW. **2.** To accept officially : adopt, affirm, approve, confirm, pass, ratify. *See* ACCEPT, LAW.

sanctioned *adjective*
1. Generally approved or agreed upon : accepted, conventional, orthodox, received, recognized. *See* ACCEPT, AGREE, STRAIGHT, USUAL. **2.** Having or arising from authority : authoritative, conclusive, official, standard. *See* TRUE. **3.** Adhering to beliefs or practices approved by authority or tradition : canonical, orthodox, received, time-honored. *See* USUAL.

sanctity *noun*
1. The quality of being holy or sacred : blessedness, holiness, sacredness, sacrosanctity. *See* RELIGION. **2.** The quality or condition of being safe from assault, trespass, or violation : inviolability, sacredness, sacrosanctity. *See* SAFETY.

sanctorium *noun*
A sacred or holy place : sacrarium, sanctuary, sanctum, shrine. *See* SACRED.

sanctuary *noun*
1. A sacred or holy place : sacrarium, sanctorium, sanctum, shrine. *See* SACRED. **2.** Something that physically protects, especially from danger : asylum, cover, covert, harbor, haven, protection, refuge, retreat, shelter. *See* ATTACK, SAFETY. **3.** The state of being protected or safeguarded, as from danger or hardship : asylum, harborage, refuge, shelter. *See* SAFETY.

sanctum *noun*
A sacred or holy place : sacrarium, sanctorium, sanctuary, shrine. *See* SACRED.

sane *adjective*
1. Mentally healthy : compos mentis, lucid, rational. ***Idioms:*** all there, in one's right mind, of sound mind. *See* SANE. **2.** Possessing, proceeding from, or exhibiting good judgment and prudence : balanced, commonsensible, commonsensical, judicious, levelheaded, prudent, rational, reasonable, sagacious, sage, sapient, sensible, sound[2], well-founded, well-grounded, wise[1]. *See* REASON, SANE.

saneness *noun*
A healthy mental state : lucidity, lucidness, mind, reason, sanity, sense (often used in plural), soundness, wit (used in plural). *Slang:* marble (used in plural). *See* SANE.

sang-froid *noun*
A stable, calm state of the emotions : aplomb, balance, collectedness, composure, coolness, equanimity, imperturbability, imperturbableness, nonchalance, poise, self-possession, unflappability. *Slang:* cool. *See* CALM, FEELINGS.

sanguinary *adjective*
1. Attended by or causing bloodshed : bloody, gory, sanguineous. *See* BLOOD. **2.** Eager for bloodshed : bloodthirsty, bloody, bloody-minded, cutthroat, homicidal, murderous, sanguineous, slaughterous. *See* HELP.

sanguine *adjective*
1. Of a healthy reddish color : blooming, florid, flush, flushed, full-blooded, glowing, rosy, rubicund, ruddy. *See* COLORS. **2.** Expecting a favorable outcome or dwelling on hopeful aspects : optimistic, Panglossian, roseate, rose-colored, rosy. *Informal:* upbeat. ***Idioms:***

looking on the bright side, looking through rose-colored glasses. *See* HOPE.

sanguineness *noun*
A tendency to expect a favorable outcome or to dwell on hopeful aspects : optimism, sanguinity. *See* HOPE.

sanguineous *adjective*
1. Attended by or causing bloodshed : bloody, gory, sanguinary. *See* BLOOD. **2.** Eager for bloodshed : bloodthirsty, bloody, bloody-minded, cutthroat, homicidal, murderous, sanguinary, slaughterous. *See* HELP.

sanguinity *noun*
A tendency to expect a favorable outcome or to dwell on hopeful aspects : optimism, sanguineness. *See* HOPE.

sanitize *verb*
To render free of microorganisms : decontaminate, disinfect, sterilize. *See* CLEAN.

sanitized *adjective*
Free or freed from microorganisms : sterile, sterilized. *See* CLEAN.

sanity *noun*
A healthy mental state : lucidity, lucidness, mind, reason, saneness, sense (often used in plural), soundness, wit (used in plural). *Slang:* marble (used in plural). *See* SANE.

sap[1] *noun*
Slang. A person who is easily deceived or victimized : butt[3], dupe, fool, gull, lamb, pushover, victim. *Informal:* sucker. *Slang:* fall guy, gudgeon, mark, monkey, patsy, pigeon. *Chiefly British:* mug. *See* WISE.

sap[2] *verb*
1. To lessen or deplete the nerve, energy, or strength of : attenuate, debilitate, devitalize, enervate, enfeeble, undermine, undo, unnerve, weaken. *See* STRONG. **2.** To lessen or weaken severely, as by removing something essential : deplete, drain, exhaust, impoverish, use up. *See* GIVE, INCREASE, RICH.

sapience *noun*
Deep, thorough, or mature understanding : insight, profundity, sagaciousness, sagacity, sageness, wisdom. *See* WISE.

sapient *adjective*
1. Possessing or showing sound judgment and keen perception : knowing, sagacious, sage, wise[1]. *See* WISE. **2.** Possessing, proceeding from, or exhibiting good judgment and prudence : balanced, commonsensible, commonsensical, judicious, levelheaded, prudent, rational, reasonable, sagacious, sage, sane, sensible, sound[2], well-founded, well-grounded, wise[1]. *See* REASON, SANE.

sapor *noun*
A distinctive property of a substance affecting the gustatory sense : flavor, relish, savor, smack[2], tang, taste, zest. *See* TASTE.

sappiness *noun*
Slang. The quality or condition of being affectedly or overly emotional : bathos, maudlinism, mawkishness, sentimentalism, sentimentality. *Informal:* mush, mushiness, schmaltz, schmaltziness, sloppiness. *See* FEELINGS.

sappy *adjective*
1. *Slang.* Affectedly or extravagantly emotional : bathetic, gushy, maudlin, mawkish, romantic, sentimental, slushy, sobby, soft, soppy. *Informal:* gooey, mushy, schmaltzy, sloppy, soupy. *Slang:* drippy, tear-jerking. *See* FEELINGS. **2.** *Slang.* So senseless as to be laughable : absurd, foolish, harebrained, idiotic, imbecilic, insane, lunatic, mad, moronic, nonsensical, preposterous, silly, softheaded, tomfool, unearthly, zany. *Informal:* cockeyed, crazy, loony, loopy. *Slang:* balmy[2], dippy, dopey, jerky, wacky. *See* ABILITY, KNOWLEDGE.

sarcasm *noun*
Irony or bitterness, as of tone : acerbity, acidity, acridity, causticity, corrosiveness, mordacity, mordancy, trenchancy. *See* LAUGHTER, RESPECT.

sarcastic *adjective*
Contemptuous or ironic in manner or wit : derisive, jeering, mocking, satiric, satirical, scoffing, sneering. *See* LAUGHTER, RESPECT.

sardonic *adjective*
Marked by or displaying contemptuous mockery of the motives or virtues of others : cynic, cynical, ironic, ironical, wry. *See* ATTITUDE, RESPECT.

sashay *verb*
Informal. To walk with exaggerated or unnatural motions expressive of self-importance or self-display : flounce, peacock, prance, strut, swagger, swank, swash. *See* MOVE, SELF-LOVE.

sass *verb*
Informal. To utter an impertinent rejoinder : talk back, talk up. *Informal:* sauce. ***Idiom:*** give someone lip. *See* RESIST, WORDS.

sassiness *noun*
The state or quality of being impudent or arrogantly self-confident : assumption, audaciousness, audacity, boldness, brashness, brazenness, cheek, cheekiness, chutzpah, discourtesy, disrespect, effrontery, face, familiarity, forwardness, gall[1], impertinence, impudence, impudency,

incivility, insolence, nerve, nerviness, overconfidence, pertness, presumptuousness, pushiness, rudeness, sauciness. *Informal:* brass, crust, sauce, uppishness, uppityness. *See* ATTITUDE, COURTESY.

sassy *adjective*
Rude and disrespectful : assuming, assumptive, audacious, bold, boldfaced, brash, brazen, cheeky, contumelious, familiar, forward, impertinent, impudent, insolent, malapert, nervy, overconfident, pert, presuming, presumptuous, pushy, saucy, smart. *Informal:* brassy, flip, fresh, smart-alecky, snippety, snippy, uppish, uppity. *Slang:* wise[1]. *See* ATTITUDE, COURTESY.

satanic *adjective*
Perversely bad, cruel, or wicked : devilish, diabolic, diabolical, fiendish, ghoulish, hellish, infernal, ogreish, satanical. *See* KIND.

satanical *adjective*
Perversely bad, cruel, or wicked : devilish, diabolic, diabolical, fiendish, ghoulish, hellish, infernal, ogreish, satanic. *See* KIND.

sate *verb*
To satisfy to the full or to excess : cloy, engorge, glut, gorge, pall, satiate, surfeit. *See* EXCESS, FULL.

satellite *noun*
One who supports and adheres to another : adherent, cohort, disciple, follower, henchman, minion, partisan, supporter. *See* OVER, PRECEDE.

satiate *verb*
To satisfy to the full or to excess : cloy, engorge, glut, gorge, pall, sate, surfeit. *See* EXCESS, FULL.

satiation *noun*
The condition of being full to or beyond satisfaction : engorgement, repletion, satiety, surfeit. *See* EXCESS, FULL.

satiety *noun*
The condition of being full to or beyond satisfaction : engorgement, repletion, satiation, surfeit. *See* EXCESS, FULL.

satiny *adjective*
Smooth and lustrous as if polished : silken, silky, sleek. *See* SMOOTH.

satire *noun*
A work, as a novel or play, that exposes folly by the use of humor or irony : lampoon, lampoonery. *See* LAUGHTER, RESPECT.

satiric *adjective*
Contemptuous or ironic in manner or wit : derisive, jeering, mocking, sarcastic, satirical, scoffing, sneering. *See* LAUGHTER, RESPECT.

satirical *adjective*
Contemptuous or ironic in manner or wit : derisive, jeering, mocking, sarcastic, satiric, scoffing, sneering. *See* LAUGHTER, RESPECT.

satisfaction *noun*
Something to make up for loss or damage : amends, compensation, indemnification, indemnity, offset, quittance, recompense, redress, reimbursement, remuneration, reparation, repayment, requital, restitution, setoff. *See* SUBSTITUTE.

satisfactory *adjective*
1. Being what is needed without being in excess : adequate, comfortable, competent, decent, enough, sufficient. *See* EXCESS. **2.** Of moderately good quality but less than excellent : acceptable, adequate, all right, average, common, decent, fair, fairish, goodish, moderate, passable, respectable, sufficient, tolerable. *Informal:* OK, tidy. *See* GOOD. **3.** Serving to convince : cogent, convincing, persuasive, telling. *See* PERSUASION.

satisfied *adjective*
Having achieved satisfaction, as of one's goal : content, fulfilled, gratified, happy. *See* HAPPY.

satisfy *verb*
1. To be satisfactory to : please, suit. *See* PAIN. **2.** To grant or have what is demanded by (a need or desire) : appease, content, fulfill, gratify, indulge. *See* GIVE. **3.** To cause (another) to believe or feel sure about something : assure, convince, persuade, win over. *See* PERSUASION. **4.** To set right by giving what is due : clear, discharge, liquidate, pay (off *or* up), settle, square. *See* PAY. **5.** To supply fully or completely : answer, fill, fulfill, meet[1]. *See* DO.

satisfying *adjective*
To one's liking : agreeable, congenial, favorable, good, grateful, gratifying, nice, pleasant, pleasing, pleasurable, welcome. *See* LIKE.

saturate *verb*
1. To cause to be filled, as with a particular mood or tone : charge, freight, imbue, impregnate, permeate, pervade, suffuse, transfuse. *See* FULL. **2.** To make thoroughly wet : douse, drench, soak, sodden, sop, souse, wet. *See* DRY.

saturnine *adjective*
Broodingly and sullenly unhappy : dour, gloomy, glum, moody, morose, sour, sulky, sullen, surly. *See* HAPPY.

satyr *noun*
An immoral or licentious man : lecher, roué. *Informal:* dirty old man. *Slang:* lech. *See* SEX.

sauce *noun*
Informal. The state or quality of being

impudent or arrogantly self-confident : assumption, audaciousness, audacity, boldness, brashness, brazenness, cheek, cheekiness, chutzpah, discourtesy, disrespect, effrontery, face, familiarity, forwardness, gall[1], impertinence, impudence, impudency, incivility, insolence, nerve, nerviness, overconfidence, pertness, presumptuousness, pushiness, rudeness, sassiness, sauciness. *Informal:* brass, crust, uppishness, uppityness. *See* ATTITUDE, COURTESY.

sauce *verb Informal.* To utter an impertinent rejoinder : talk back, talk up. *Informal:* sass. ***Idiom:*** give someone lip. *See* RESIST, WORDS.

saucebox *noun*
Informal. One who is obnoxiously self-assertive and arrogant : malapert, witling. *Informal:* know-it-all, smart aleck, smarty, smarty-pants, wisenheimer. *Slang:* wiseacre, wisecracker, wise guy. *See* GOOD.

sauciness *noun*
The state or quality of being impudent or arrogantly self-confident : assumption, audaciousness, audacity, boldness, brashness, brazenness, cheek, cheekiness, chutzpah, discourtesy, disrespect, effrontery, face, familiarity, forwardness, gall[1], impertinence, impudence, impudency, incivility, insolence, nerve, nerviness, overconfidence, pertness, presumptuousness, pushiness, rudeness, sassiness. *Informal:* brass, crust, sauce, uppishness, uppityness. *See* ATTITUDE, COURTESY.

saucy *adjective*
Rude and disrespectful : assuming, assumptive, audacious, bold, boldfaced, brash, brazen, cheeky, contumelious, familiar, forward, impertinent, impudent, insolent, malapert, nervy, overconfident, pert, presuming, presumptuous, pushy, sassy, smart. *Informal:* brassy, flip, fresh, smart-alecky, snippety, snippy, uppish, uppity. *Slang:* wise[1]. *See* ATTITUDE, COURTESY.

saunter *verb*
To walk at a leisurely pace : amble, meander, perambulate, promenade, ramble, stroll, wander. *Informal:* mosey. *See* MOVE.

saunter *noun* An act of walking, especially for pleasure : amble, meander (often used in plural), perambulation, promenade, ramble, stroll, walk, wander. *See* MOVE.

savage *adjective*
1. Of or relating to wild animals : feral, wild. *See* WILD. **2.** Not civilized : barbarian, barbaric, barbarous, primitive, rude, uncivilized, uncultivated, uncultured, wild. *Archaic:* uncivil. *See* CULTURE, WILD. **3.** Showing or suggesting a disposition to be violently destructive without scruple or restraint : barbarous, bestial, cruel, fell[2], feral, ferocious, fierce, inhuman, truculent, vicious, wolfish. *See* KIND. **4.** So intense as to cause extreme suffering : cruel, ferocious, fierce, vicious. *See* HELP, KIND.

savagery *noun*
A cruel act or an instance of cruel behavior : barbarity, bestiality, brutality, cruelty, inhumanity, truculence, truculency. *See* ATTITUDE, KIND.

savant *noun*
A usually elderly person noted for wisdom, knowledge, and judgment : pundit, sage, scholar. *See* WISE.

save *verb*
1. To extricate, as from danger or confinement : deliver, rescue. ***Idiom:*** come to the rescue of. *See* HELP. **2.** To protect (an asset) from loss or destruction : conserve, husband, preserve. *See* KEEP. **3.** To use without wasting : conserve, economize, spare. *See* SAVE. **4.** To reserve for the future. Also used with *up* : keep, lay aside, lay away, lay by, lay in, lay up, put by, salt away, set by. *See* KEEP, SAVE. **5.** To accumulate and set aside for future use. Also used with *up* : lay in, lay up, stockpile, store (up). *See* KEEP.

saving *adjective*
Careful in the use of material resources : canny, chary, economical, frugal, provident, prudent, Scotch, sparing, thrifty. *See* CAREFUL, SAVE.

savoir-faire *noun*
The ability to say and do the right thing at the right time : address, diplomacy, tact, tactfulness. *See* ABILITY, COURTESY.

savor *noun*
1. A distinctive property of a substance affecting the gustatory sense : flavor, relish, sapor, smack[2], tang, taste, zest. *See* TASTE. **2.** A distinctive yet intangible quality deemed typical of a given thing : aroma, atmosphere, flavor, smack[2]. *See* TASTE. **3.** A distinctive element : attribute, character, characteristic, feature, mark, peculiarity, property, quality, trait. *See* BE.

savor *verb* **1.** To have a particular flavor or suggestion of something : smack[2], smell, suggest, taste. *See* SUGGEST. **2.** To receive pleasure from : enjoy, like[1], relish. *Informal:* go for. *Slang:* dig. *See* LIKE. **3.** To undergo an emotional reaction : experience, feel, have, know, taste. *See* FEELINGS.

savory *adjective*
Highly pleasing, especially to the sense of taste : ambrosial, appetizing, delectable, delicious, heavenly, luscious, scrumptious, tasteful, tasty, toothsome. *Slang:* yummy. *See* GOOD, INGESTION.

savvy *adjective*
Informal. Having or showing a clever awareness and resourcefulness in practical matters : astute, cagey, canny, knowing, perspicacious, shrewd, slick, smart, wise[1]. *See* ABILITY, CAREFUL.

savvy *noun Informal.* Intellectual hold : apprehension, comprehension, grasp, grip, hold, understanding. *See* KNOWLEDGE.

savvy *verb Informal.* To perceive and recognize the meaning of : accept, apprehend, catch (on), compass, comprehend, conceive, fathom, follow, get, grasp, make out, read, see, sense, take, take in, understand. *Slang:* dig. *Chiefly British:* twig. *Scots:* ken. ***Idioms:*** get (*or* have) a handle on, get the picture. *See* UNDERSTAND.

saw *noun*
A usually pithy and familiar statement expressing an observation or principle generally accepted as wise or true : adage, aphorism, byword, maxim, motto, proverb, saying. *See* WORDS.

say *verb*
1. To produce or make (speech sounds) : articulate, enunciate, pronounce, utter[1], vocalize. *See* WORDS. **2.** To put into words : articulate, communicate, convey, declare, express, state, talk, tell, utter[1], vent, verbalize, vocalize, voice. ***Idiom:*** give tongue (*or* vent *or* voice) to. *See* WORDS. **3.** To put into words positively and with conviction : affirm, allege, argue, assert, asseverate, aver, avouch, avow, claim, contend, declare, hold, maintain, state. ***Idiom:*** have it. *See* AFFIRM.

say *noun* The right or chance to express an opinion or participate in a decision : suffrage, voice, vote. *Informal:* say-so. *See* PARTICIPATE.

saying *noun*
1. Something said : statement, utterance, word. *See* WORDS. **2.** A usually pithy and familiar statement expressing an observation or principle generally accepted as wise or true : adage, aphorism, byword, maxim, motto, proverb, saw. *See* WORDS.

say-so *noun*
1. *Informal.* The right and power to command, decide, rule, or judge : authority, command, control, domination, dominion, jurisdiction, mastery, might, power, prerogative, sovereignty, sway. *See* OVER. **2.** *Informal.* The right or chance to express an opinion or participate in a decision : say, suffrage, voice, vote. *See* PARTICIPATE.

scabrous *adjective*
1. Having a surface that is not smooth : coarse, cragged, craggy, harsh, ironbound, jagged, ragged, rough, rugged, uneven. *See* SMOOTH.
2. Bordering on indelicacy or impropriety : blue, earthy, off-color, provocative, racy, risqué, salty, spicy, suggestive. *See* DECENT.

scad *noun*
Informal. An indeterminately great amount or number. Often used in plural : jillion, million (often used in plural), multiplicity, ream, trillion. *Informal:* bushel, gob[1] (often used in plural), heap (often used in plural), load (often used in plural), lot, oodles, passel, peck[2], slew, wad, zillion. *See* BIG.

scaffold *noun*
A temporary framework with a floor, used by workmen : platform, scaffolding, stage. *See* MACHINE.

scaffolding *noun*
A temporary framework with a floor, used by workmen : platform, scaffold, stage. *See* MACHINE.

scalding *adjective*
Marked by much heat : ardent, baking, blistering, boiling, broiling, burning, fiery, heated, hot, red-hot, roasting, scorching, searing, sizzling, sultry, sweltering, torrid. *See* HOT.

scale[1] *verb*
To remove the skin of : decorticate, pare, peel, skin, strip[1]. *See* PUT ON.

scale[2] *verb*
To move upward on or along : ascend, climb, go up, mount. *See* RISE.

scalp *verb*
Slang. To exploit (another) by charging too much for something : fleece, overcharge. *Slang:* clip[1], gouge, nick, rip off, skin, soak. ***Idioms:*** make someone pay through the nose, take someone for a ride, take someone to the cleaners. *See* HONEST.

scamp *noun*
One who causes minor trouble or damage : devil, imp, mischief, prankster, rascal, rogue. *Informal:* cutup. *See* GOOD.

scamper *verb*
To move swiftly on foot so that both feet leave the ground during each stride : run, scurry, sprint. *See* MOVE.

scan *verb*
1. To view broadly or from a height : look over, overlook, survey. *See* SEE. 2. To look through reading matter casually : browse, dip into, flip through, glance at (*or* over *or* through), leaf (through), riffle (through), run through, skim, thumb (through). *See* INVESTIGATE, WORDS.

scandal *noun*
The expression of injurious, malicious statements about someone : aspersion, calumniation, calumny, character assassination, defamation, denigration, detraction, slander, traducement, vilification. *Law:* libel. *See* ATTACK, CRIMES, LAW.

scandalize *verb*
To affect with a strong feeling of moral aversion : shock[1]. *See* RIGHT.

scandalmonger *noun*
A person habitually engaged in idle talk about others : blab, gossip, gossiper, gossipmonger, newsmonger, rumormonger, tabby, talebearer, taleteller, tattle, tattler, tattletale, telltale, whisperer. *Slang:* yenta. *See* WORDS.

scandalous *adjective*
1. Disgracefully and grossly offensive : atrocious, heinous, monstrous, outrageous, shocking. *Archaic:* enormous. *See* RIGHT. 2. Damaging to the reputation : calumnious, defamatory, detractive, injurious, invidious, slanderous. *Law:* libelous. *See* ATTACK, CRIMES, LAW.

scant *adjective*
1. Just sufficient : bare. *See* EXCESS. 2. Conspicuously deficient in quantity, fullness, or extent : exiguous, meager, poor, puny, scanty, skimpy, spare, sparse, stingy, thin. *Slang:* measly. *See* BIG, EXCESS.

scantiness *noun*
The condition or fact of being deficient : defect, deficiency, deficit, inadequacy, insufficiency, lack, paucity, poverty, scantness, scarceness, scarcity, shortage, shortcoming, shortfall, underage[1]. *See* EXCESS.

scantness *noun*
The condition or fact of being deficient : defect, deficiency, deficit, inadequacy, insufficiency, lack, paucity, poverty, scantiness, scarceness, scarcity, shortage, shortcoming, shortfall, underage[1]. *See* EXCESS.

scanty *adjective*
Conspicuously deficient in quantity, fullness, or extent : exiguous, meager, poor, puny, scant, skimpy, spare, sparse, stingy, thin. *Slang:* measly. *See* BIG, EXCESS.

scapegoat *noun*
One who is made an object of blame : goat, whipping boy. *Slang:* fall guy, patsy. *See* PRAISE.

scarce *adjective*
1. Not enough to meet a demand or requirement : deficient, inadequate, insufficient, short, shy[1], under, wanting. *See* BIG, EXCESS. 2. Rarely occurring or appearing : infrequent, occasional, rare, sporadic, uncommon, unusual. ***Idiom:*** few and far between. *See* USUAL.
scarce *adverb* By a very little; almost not : barely, hardly, just, scarcely. *See* NEAR.

scarcely *adverb*
By a very little; almost not : barely, hardly, just, scarce. *See* NEAR.

scarceness *noun*
The condition or fact of being deficient : defect, deficiency, deficit, inadequacy, insufficiency, lack, paucity, poverty, scantiness, scantness, scarcity, shortage, shortcoming, shortfall, underage[1]. *See* EXCESS.

scarcity *noun*
The condition or fact of being deficient : defect, deficiency, deficit, inadequacy, insufficiency, lack, paucity, poverty, scantiness, scantness, scarceness, shortage, shortcoming, shortfall, underage[1]. *See* EXCESS.

scare *verb*
To fill with fear : affright, alarm, frighten, panic, scarify², startle, terrify, terrorize. *Archaic:* fright. ***Idioms:*** make one's blood run cold, make one's hair stand on end, scare silly (*or* stiff), scare the daylights out of. *See* FEAR.

scarecrow *noun*
A person wearing ragged or tattered clothing : ragamuffin, tatterdemalion. *See* BETTER, RICH.

scaremonger *noun*
One who needlessly alarms others : alarmist. *See* POLITICS, WARN.

scarify¹ *verb*
To criticize harshly and devastatingly : blister, drub, excoriate, flay, lash, rip into, scathe, scorch, score, scourge, slap, slash. *Informal:* roast. *Slang:* slam. ***Idioms:*** burn someone's ears, crawl all over, pin someone's ears back, put someone on the griddle, put someone on the hot seat, rake over the coals, read the riot act to. *See* PRAISE.

scarify² *verb*
To fill with fear : affright, alarm, frighten, panic, scare, startle, terrify, terrorize. *Archaic:* fright. ***Idioms:*** make one's blood run cold, make one's hair stand on end, scare silly (*or*

stiff), scare the daylights out of. *See* FEAR.

scarlet woman *noun*
A woman who engages in sexual intercourse for payment : bawd, call girl, camp follower, courtesan, harlot, prostitute, streetwalker, strumpet, tart[2], whore. *Slang:* hooker, moll. ***Idioms:*** lady of easy virtue, lady of pleasure, lady of the night. *See* SEX.

scary *adjective*
Causing or able to cause fear : appalling, dire, direful, dreadful, fearful, fearsome, formidable, frightful, ghastly, redoubtable, terrible, tremendous. *See* FEAR.

scathe *verb*
To criticize harshly and devastatingly : blister, drub, excoriate, flay, lash, rip into, scarify[1], scorch, score, scourge, slap, slash. *Informal:* roast. *Slang:* slam. ***Idioms:*** burn someone's ears, crawl all over, pin someone's ears back, put someone on the griddle, put someone on the hot seat, rake over the coals, read the riot act to. *See* PRAISE.

scathing *adjective*
So sharp as to cause mental pain : acerbic, acid, acidic, acrid, astringent, biting, caustic, corrosive, cutting, mordacious, mordant, pungent, sharp, slashing, stinging, trenchant, truculent, vitriolic. *See* ATTACK, RESPECT.

scatologic *adjective*
Offensive to accepted standards of decency : barnyard, bawdy, broad, coarse, dirty, Fescennine, filthy, foul, gross, lewd, nasty, obscene, profane, ribald, scatological, scurrilous, smutty, vulgar. *Slang:* raunchy. *See* DECENT.

scatological *adjective*
Offensive to accepted standards of decency : barnyard, bawdy, broad, coarse, dirty, Fescennine, filthy, foul, gross, lewd, nasty, obscene, profane, ribald, scatologic, scurrilous, smutty, vulgar. *Slang:* raunchy. *See* DECENT.

scatology *noun*
Something that is offensive to accepted standards of decency : bawdry, dirt, filth, obscenity, profanity, ribaldry, smut, vulgarity. *Slang:* raunch. *See* DECENT.

scatter *verb*
1. To cause to separate and go in various directions : dispel, disperse, dissipate. *See* COLLECT. **2.** To disappear by or as if by rising : disperse, dissipate, lift. *See* COLLECT, RISE. **3.** To extend over a wide area : circulate, diffuse, disperse, disseminate, distribute, radiate, spread, strew. *See* MOVE, WIDE.

scatterbrained *adjective*
Given to lighthearted silliness : empty-headed, featherbrained, flighty, frivolous, frothy, giddy, harebrained, lighthearted, silly. *Informal:* gaga. *Slang:* birdbrained, dizzy. *See* ABILITY.

scattergood *noun*
A person who spends money or resources wastefully : prodigal, profligate, spendthrift, waster, wastrel. *See* SAVE.

scene *noun*
1. That which is or can be seen : lookout, outlook, panorama, perspective, prospect, sight, view, vista. *See* SEE. **2.** The place where an action or event occurs : locale, setting, site, stage. *See* PLACE. **3.** The properties, backdrops, and other objects arranged for a dramatic presentation : mise en scène, scenery, set[2], setting. *See* PERFORMING ARTS. **4.** A sphere of activity, experience, study, or interest : area, arena, bailiwick, circle, department, domain, field, orbit, province, realm, subject, terrain, territory, world. *Slang:* bag. *See* TERRITORY. **5.** *Slang.* Existing surroundings that affect an activity : circumstance (often used in plural), condition (used in plural), environment. *See* BE.

scenery *noun*
The properties, backdrops, and other objects arranged for a dramatic presentation : mise en scène, scene, set[2], setting. *See* PERFORMING ARTS.

scent *noun*
1. The quality of something that may be perceived by the olfactory sense : aroma, odor, smell. *See* SMELLS. **2.** A sweet or pleasant odor : aroma, bouquet, fragrance, perfume, redolence. *See* SMELLS. **3.** Evidence of passage left along a course followed by a hunted animal or fugitive : spoor, track, trail. *See* MARKS, SMELLS. **4.** The sense by which odors are perceived : nose, olfaction, smell. *See* SMELLS. **5.** A piece of information useful in a search : clue, lead. *See* SHOW.

scent *verb* **1.** To perceive with the olfactory sense : nose, smell, sniff, snuff, whiff. ***Idiom:*** catch (*or* get) a whiff of. *See* SMELLS. **2.** To fill with a pleasant odor : aromatize, perfume. *See* SMELLS.

sceptic *noun* See **skeptic.**

sceptical *adjective* See **skeptical.**

sceptically *adverb* See **skeptically.**

scepticism *noun* See **skepticism.**

schedule *noun*
1. A series, as of names or words, printed or written down : catalog, list[1], register, roll, roster. *See* REMEMBER. **2.** An organized list, as of procedures, activities, or events : agenda, calendar, docket, lineup, order of the day (often

used in plural), program, timetable. *See* PLANNED.

schedule *verb* **1.** To enter on a schedule : program, slate. *See* REMEMBER. **2.** To plan the details or arrangements of : arrange, lay out, prepare, work out. *See* PLANNED. **3.** To set the time for (an event or occasion) : plan, time. *See* TIME.

scheduled *adjective*
Known to be about to arrive : anticipated, due, expected. *See* SURPRISE.

schema *noun*
A method for making, doing, or accomplishing something : blueprint, design, game plan, idea, layout, plan, project, scheme, strategy. *See* PLANNED.

scheme *noun*
1. A method for making, doing, or accomplishing something : blueprint, design, game plan, idea, layout, plan, project, schema, strategy. *See* PLANNED. **2.** A secret plan to achieve an evil or illegal end : cabal, collusion, connivance, conspiracy, intrigue, machination, plot. *See* CRIMES, PLANNED.

scheme *verb* **1.** To work out a secret plan to achieve an evil or illegal end : collude, connive, conspire, intrigue, machinate, plot. *See* CRIMES, PLANNED. **2.** To form a strategy for : blueprint, cast, chart, conceive, contrive, design, devise, formulate, frame, lay[1], plan, project, strategize, work out. *Informal:* dope out. ***Idiom:*** lay plans. *See* PLANNED.

scheming *adjective*
1. Deceitfully clever : artful, crafty, cunning, foxy, guileful, sharp, sly, tricky, wily. *See* ABILITY, HONEST, MEANS. **2.** Coldly planning to achieve selfish aims : calculating, designing. *See* ATTITUDE.

schism *noun*
1. An interruption in friendly relations : alienation, breach, break, disaffection, estrangement, fissure, rent[2], rift, rupture, split. *See* ASSEMBLE, HELP. **2.** A state of disagreement and disharmony : clash, conflict, confrontation, contention, difference, difficulty, disaccord, discord, discordance, dissension, dissent, dissentience, dissidence, dissonance, faction, friction, inharmony, strife, variance, war, warfare. *See* CONFLICT. **3.** The condition of being divided, as in opinion : disunion, disunity, divergence, divergency, division. *See* ASSEMBLE.

schismatic *noun*
A person who dissents from the doctrine of an established church : dissenter, dissident, heretic, nonconformist, sectarian, sectary, separationist, separatist. *See* RELIGION.

schlep *verb*
Slang. To move while supporting : bear, carry, convey, lug[2], transport. *Informal:* tote. *See* OVER.

schlocky *adjective*
Slang. Of decidedly inferior quality : base[2], cheap, lousy, miserable, paltry, poor, rotten, shoddy, sleazy, trashy. *Informal:* cheesy. *Slang:* crummy. *See* GOOD.

schmaltz also **schmalz** *noun*
Informal. The quality or condition of being affectedly or overly emotional : bathos, maudlinism, mawkishness, sentimentalism, sentimentality. *Informal:* mush, mushiness, schmaltziness, sloppiness. *Slang:* sappiness. *See* FEELINGS.

schmaltziness also **schmalziness** *noun*
Informal. The quality or condition of being affectedly or overly emotional : bathos, maudlinism, mawkishness, sentimentalism, sentimentality. *Informal:* mush, mushiness, schmaltz, sloppiness. *Slang:* sappiness. *See* FEELINGS.

schmaltzy also **schmalzy** *adjective*
Informal. Affectedly or extravagantly emotional : bathetic, gushy, maudlin, mawkish, romantic, sentimental, slushy, sobby, soft, soppy. *Informal:* gooey, mushy, sloppy, soupy. *Slang:* drippy, sappy, tear-jerking. *See* FEELINGS.

schmalz *noun* See **schmaltz.**

schmalziness *noun* See **schmaltziness.**

schmalzy *adjective* See **schmaltzy.**

schmo *noun*
Slang. One deficient in judgment and good sense : ass, fool, idiot, imbecile, jackass, mooncalf, moron, nincompoop, ninny, nitwit, simple, simpleton, softhead, tomfool. *Informal:* dope, gander, goose. *Slang:* cretin, ding-dong, dip, goof, jerk, nerd, schmuck, turkey. *See* ABILITY.

schmuck *noun*
Slang. One deficient in judgment and good sense : ass, fool, idiot, imbecile, jackass, mooncalf, moron, nincompoop, ninny, nitwit, simple, simpleton, softhead, tomfool. *Informal:* dope, gander, goose. *Slang:* cretin, ding-dong, dip, goof, jerk, nerd, schmo, turkey. *See* ABILITY.

schnoz *noun*
Slang. The structure on the human face that contains the nostrils and organs of smell and forms the beginning of the respiratory tract : nose, proboscis. *Informal:* beak, snoot. *Slang:* nozzle, schnozzle, snout. *See* BODY, CONVEX.

schnozzle *noun*
Slang. The structure on the human face that

contains the nostrils and organs of smell and forms the beginning of the respiratory tract : nose, proboscis. *Informal:* beak, snoot. *Slang:* nozzle, schnoz, snout. *See* BODY, CONVEX.

scholar *noun*
1. A usually elderly person noted for wisdom, knowledge, and judgment : pundit, sage, savant. *See* WISE. **2.** One who is being educated : learner, pupil, student. *See* TEACH.

scholarly *adjective*
1. Having or showing profound knowledge and scholarship : erudite, learned, lettered, wise[1]. *See* KNOWLEDGE. **2.** Devoted to study or reading : bookish, studious. *See* TEACH.

scholarship *noun*
Known facts, ideas, and skill that have been imparted : education, erudition, instruction, knowledge, learning, science. *See* KNOWLEDGE.

scholastic *adjective*
Characterized by a narrow concern for book learning and formal rules, without knowledge or experience of practical matters : academic, bookish, donnish, formalistic, inkhorn, literary, pedantic, pedantical. *See* ATTITUDE, FLEXIBLE, TEACH.

school *verb*
To impart knowledge and skill to : coach, discipline, educate, instruct, teach, train, tutor. *See* TEACH.

schooling *noun*
The act, process, or art of imparting knowledge and skill : education, instruction, pedagogics, pedagogy, teaching, training, tuition, tutelage, tutoring. *See* TEACH.

science *noun*
Known facts, ideas, and skill that have been imparted : education, erudition, instruction, knowledge, learning, scholarship. *See* KNOWLEDGE.

scilicet *adverb*
That is to say : namely, specifically, videlicet. *Idiom:* to wit. *See* SPECIFIC.

scintillate *verb*
To emit light suddenly in rays or sparks : coruscate, flash, glance, gleam, glimmer, glint, glisten, glister, glitter, shimmer, spangle, sparkle, twinkle, wink. *See* LIGHT.

scintillating *adjective*
Amusing or pleasing because of wit or originality : clever, smart, sparkling, witty. *See* LAUGHTER.

scintillation *noun*
Sparkling, brilliant light : flash, glint, glisten, glister, glitter, shimmer, sparkle. *See* BEAUTIFUL, LIGHT.

scion *noun*
One descended directly from the same parents or ancestors : child, descendant, offspring, progeny. *See* KIN.

scoff *verb*
To make fun or make fun of : deride, gibe, jeer, jest, laugh, mock, ridicule, scout[2], twit. *Chiefly British:* quiz. ***Idiom:*** poke fun at. *See* LAUGHTER, RESPECT.

scoff *noun* An instance of mockery or derision : gibe, insult, jeer, taunt, twit. *See* LAUGHTER, RESPECT.

scoffing *adjective*
Contemptuous or ironic in manner or wit : derisive, jeering, mocking, sarcastic, satiric, satirical, sneering. *See* LAUGHTER, RESPECT.

scold *verb*
To criticize for a fault or an offense : admonish, call down, castigate, chastise, chide, dress down, rap[1], rebuke, reprimand, reproach, reprove, tax, upbraid. *Informal:* bawl out, lambaste. *Slang:* chew out. ***Idioms:*** bring (*or* call *or* take) to task, call on the carpet, haul (*or* rake) over the coals, let someone have it. *See* ATTACK, PRAISE.

scold *noun* A person, traditionally a woman, who persistently nags or criticizes : fishwife, fury, harpy, shrew, termagant, virago, vixen. *Informal:* battle-ax. *See* PRAISE.

scolding *noun*
Words expressive of strong disapproval : admonishment, admonition, rebuke, reprimand, reproach, reproof. *Slang:* rap[1]. *See* PRAISE.

scoop *noun*
Informal. New information, especially about recent events and happenings : advice (often used in plural), intelligence, news, tiding (often used in plural), word. *See* KNOWLEDGE, WORDS.

scoop *verb* **1.** To break, turn over, or remove (earth or sand, for example) with or as if with a tool : delve, dig, excavate, grub, shovel, spade. *See* ENTER. **2.** To take a substance, as liquid, from a container by plunging the hand or a utensil into it. Also used with *up* : bail[2], dip, lade, ladle. *See* GIVE. **3.** To make by digging : dig, excavate, shovel. *See* MAKE.

scoot *verb*
To move swiftly : bolt, bucket, bustle, dart, dash, festinate, flash, fleet, flit, fly, haste, hasten, hurry, hustle, pelt[2], race, rocket, run, rush, sail, scour[2], shoot, speed, sprint, tear[1], trot,

whirl, whisk, whiz, wing, zip, zoom. *Informal:* hotfoot, rip. *Slang:* barrel, highball. *Chiefly British:* nip[1]. ***Idioms:*** get a move on, get cracking, go like lightning, go like the wind, hotfoot it, make haste, make time, make tracks, run like the wind, shake a leg, step (*or* jump) on it. *See* MOVE.

scope *noun*
1. The extent of one's perception, understanding, knowledge, or vision : horizon, ken, purview, range, reach. *See* ABILITY, KNOWLEDGE, SEE. **2.** The ability or power to seize or attain : capacity, compass, grasp, range, reach. *See* ABILITY. **3.** Suitable opportunity to accept or allow something : elbowroom, latitude, leeway, margin, play, room. *See* PLACE, RESTRAINT. **4.** An area within which something or someone exists, acts, or has influence or power : ambit, compass, extension, extent, orbit, purview, range, reach, realm, sphere, sweep, swing. *See* TERRITORY.

scorch *verb*
1. To undergo or cause to undergo damage by or as if by fire : burn, char, sear, singe. *See* HOT. **2.** To criticize harshly and devastatingly : blister, drub, excoriate, flay, lash, rip into, scarify[1], scathe, score, scourge, slap, slash. *Informal:* roast. *Slang:* slam. ***Idioms:*** burn someone's ears, crawl all over, pin someone's ears back, put someone on the griddle, put someone on the hot seat, rake over the coals, read the riot act to. *See* PRAISE.

scorch *noun* Damage or a damaged substance that results from burning : burn, char, sear, singe. *See* HOT.

scorching *adjective*
1. Marked by much heat : ardent, baking, blistering, boiling, broiling, burning, fiery, heated, hot, red-hot, roasting, scalding, searing, sizzling, sultry, sweltering, torrid. *See* HOT. **2.** Fired with intense feeling : ardent, blazing, burning, dithyrambic, fervent, fervid, fiery, flaming, glowing, heated, hot-blooded, impassioned, passionate, perfervid, red-hot, torrid. *See* FEELINGS.

score *noun*
1. An incision, a notch, or a slight cut made with or as if with a knife : scotch, scratch, slash. *See* MARKS. **2.** The total number of points made by a contestant, side, or team in a game or contest : tally. *See* COUNT. **3.** A very large number of things grouped together. Used in plural : army, cloud, crowd, drove, flock, horde, host, legion, mass, mob, multitude, ruck[1], swarm, throng. *See* BIG, GROUP.

score *verb* **1.** To gain (a point or points) in a game or contest : post[1], tally. *Informal:* notch. *See* DO. **2.** To evaluate and assign a grade to : grade, mark. *See* VALUE. **3.** To criticize harshly and devastatingly : blister, drub, excoriate, flay, lash, rip into, scarify[1], scathe, scorch, scourge, slap, slash. *Informal:* roast. *Slang:* slam. ***Idioms:*** burn someone's ears, crawl all over, pin someone's ears back, put someone on the griddle, put someone on the hot seat, rake over the coals, read the riot act to. *See* PRAISE. **4.** *Slang.* To succeed in doing : accomplish, achieve, attain, gain, reach, realize. *See* DO. **5.** *Slang.* To do or fare well : boom, flourish, go, prosper, thrive. ***Idioms:*** get (*or* go) somewhere, go great guns, go strong. *See* THRIVE.

scorn *noun*
The feeling of despising : contempt, despisal, despite, disdain. *See* RESPECT.

scorn *verb* To regard with utter contempt and disdain : contemn, despise, disdain, scout[2]. ***Idioms:*** have no use for, look down on (*or* upon). *See* RESPECT.

scornful *adjective*
Showing scorn and disrespect toward (someone or something) : contemptuous, disdainful. ***Idiom:*** on one's high horse. *See* RESPECT.

scotch *noun*
An incision, a notch, or a slight cut made with or as if with a knife : score, scratch, slash. *See* MARKS.

Scotch *adjective*
Careful in the use of material resources : canny, chary, economical, frugal, provident, prudent, saving, sparing, thrifty. *See* CAREFUL, SAVE.

scour[1] *verb*
1. To rub hard in order to clean : scrub. *See* CLEAN, PUT ON. **2.** To remove (an outer layer or adherent matter) by rubbing a surface with considerable pressure : scrape, scrub. *See* PUT ON.

scour[2] *verb*
1. To make a thorough search of : comb, forage, ransack, rummage. *Slang:* shake down. ***Idioms:*** beat the bushes, leave no stone unturned, look (*or* search) high and low, look (*or* search) up and down, turn inside out, turn upside down. *See* INVESTIGATE. **2.** To move swiftly : bolt, bucket, bustle, dart, dash, festinate, flash, fleet, flit, fly, haste, hasten, hurry, hustle, pelt[2], race, rocket, run, rush, sail, scoot, shoot, speed, sprint, tear[1], trot, whirl, whisk, whiz, wing, zip, zoom. *Informal:* hotfoot, rip. *Slang:* barrel, highball. *Chiefly British:* nip[1].

Idioms: get a move on, get cracking, go like lightning, go like the wind, hotfoot it, make haste, make time, make tracks, run like the wind, shake a leg, step (*or* jump) on it. *See* MOVE.

scourge *noun*
A cause of suffering or harm : affliction, bane, curse, evil, ill, plague, woe. *See* HELP.
scourge *verb* **1.** To bring great harm or suffering to : afflict, agonize, anguish, curse, excruciate, plague, rack, smite, strike, torment, torture. *See* ATTACK, HELP. **2.** To criticize harshly and devastatingly : blister, drub, excoriate, flay, lash, rip into, scarify[1], scathe, scorch, score, slap, slash. *Informal:* roast. *Slang:* slam. *Idioms:* burn someone's ears, crawl all over, pin someone's ears back, put someone on the griddle, put someone on the hot seat, rake over the coals, read the riot act to. *See* PRAISE.

scout[1] *verb*
To go into or through for the purpose of making discoveries or acquiring information : delve, dig, explore, inquire, investigate, look into, probe, reconnoiter. *See* INVESTIGATE.

scout[2] *verb*
1. To regard with utter contempt and disdain : contemn, despise, disdain, scorn. *Idioms:* have no use for, look down on (*or* upon). *See* RESPECT. **2.** To make fun or make fun of : deride, gibe, jeer, jest, laugh, mock, ridicule, scoff, twit. *Chiefly British:* quiz. *Idiom:* poke fun at. *See* LAUGHTER, RESPECT.

scowl *verb*
1. To wrinkle one's brow, as in thought, puzzlement, or displeasure : frown, glower, lower[1]. *Idiom:* look black. *See* EXPRESS. **2.** To stare fixedly and angrily : glare, glower, lower[1]. *Idiom:* look daggers at. *See* EXPRESS, SEE.
scowl *noun* **1.** The act of wrinkling the brow, as in thought, puzzlement, or displeasure : black look, frown, glower, lower[1]. *See* EXPRESS. **2.** A fixed angry stare : glare, glower, lower. *See* EXPRESS, SEE.

scram *verb*
Slang. To leave hastily : bolt, get out, run. *Informal:* clear out, get, hotfoot, skedaddle. *Slang:* hightail, vamoose. *Idioms:* beat it, hightail it, hotfoot it, make tracks. *See* APPROACH.

scramble *verb*
1. To move or climb hurriedly, especially on all fours : clamber. *See* MOVE. **2.** To put into total disorder : ball up, confuse, disorder, jumble, mess up, muddle, snarl[2]. *Slang:* snafu. *Idiom:* play havoc with. *See* ORDER. **3.** To mix together so as to change the order of arrangement : jumble, shuffle. *Games:* riffle. *See* CHANGE, ORDER.
scramble *noun* A lack of order or regular arrangement : chaos, clutter, confusedness, confusion, derangement, disarrangement, disarray, disorder, disorderedness, disorderliness, disorganization, jumble, mess, mix-up, muddle, muss, topsy-turviness, tumble. *Slang:* snafu. *See* ORDER.

scrap[1] *noun*
1. A tiny amount : bit[1], crumb, dab[1], dash, dot, dram, drop, fragment, grain, iota, jot, minim, mite, modicum, molecule, ort, ounce, particle, scruple, shred, smidgen, speck, tittle, trifle, whit. *Chiefly British:* spot. *See* BIG. **2.** Residual matter : butt[4], end, fragment, ort (often used in plural), shard, stub. *See* LEFTOVER.
scrap *verb* To let go or get rid of as being useless or defective, for example : discard, dispose of, dump, junk, throw away, throw out. *Informal:* chuck, jettison, shuck (off). *Slang:* ditch. *See* KEEP.

scrap[2] *noun*
A physical conflict involving two or more : fight, fistfight, fisticuffs, scuffle, tussle. *Slang:* rumble. *See* CONFLICT.

scrape *verb*
1. To remove (an outer layer or adherent matter) by rubbing a surface with considerable pressure : scour[1], scrub. *See* PUT ON. **2.** To bring or come into abrasive contact, often with a harsh grating sound : grate, rasp, scratch. *See* SOUNDS. **3.** To be severely sparing in order to economize : pinch, scrimp, skimp, stint. *Idioms:* pinch pennies, tighten (one's) belt. *See* SAVE.
scrape *noun* A difficult, often embarrassing situation or condition : box[1], corner, deep water, difficulty, dilemma, Dutch, fix, hole, hot spot, hot water, jam, plight[1], predicament, quagmire, soup, trouble. *Informal:* bind, pickle, spot. *See* EASY.

scrappiness *noun*
The quality or state of being argumentative : argumentativeness, combativeness, contentiousness, disputatiousness, litigiousness. *See* CONFLICT.

scrappy *adjective*
1. Given to arguing : argumentative, combative, contentious, disputatious, eristic, litigious, polemic, polemical, quarrelsome. *See* CONFLICT. **2.** Having or showing an eagerness to fight : bellicose, belligerent, combative,

contentious, hostile, militant, pugnacious, quarrelsome, truculent, warlike. *See* ATTACK.

scratch *verb*
1. To bring or come into abrasive contact, often with a harsh grating sound : grate, rasp, scrape. *See* SOUNDS. **2.** To remove or invalidate by or as if by running a line through or wiping clean. Also used with *out* : annul, blot (out), cancel, cross (off *or* out), delete, efface, erase, expunge, obliterate, rub (out), strike (out), undo, wipe (out), x (out). *Law:* vacate. *See* CONTINUE. **3.** *Slang.* To decide not to go ahead with (something previously arranged) : call off, cancel. *Slang:* scrub. *See* CONTINUE.
scratch *noun* **1.** An incision, a notch, or a slight cut made with or as if with a knife : score, scotch, slash. *See* MARKS. **2.** *Slang.* Something, such as coins or printed bills, used as a medium of exchange : cash, currency, lucre, money. *Informal:* wampum. *Slang:* bread, cabbage, dough, gelt, green, jack, lettuce, long green, mazuma, moola. *Chiefly British:* brass. *See* MONEY.

scratchy *adjective*
Disagreeable to the sense of hearing : dry, grating, harsh, hoarse, jarring, rasping, raspy, raucous, rough, squawky, strident. *See* SOUNDS.

scrawny *adjective*
Having little flesh or fat on the body : angular, bony, fleshless, gaunt, lank, lanky, lean[2], meager, rawboned, skinny, slender, slim, spare, thin, twiggy, weedy. ***Idioms:*** all skin and bones, thin as a rail. *See* FAT.

screak *noun*
A long, loud, piercing cry or sound : scream, screech, shriek. *See* SOUNDS.
screak *verb* To utter a long, loud, piercing cry, as of pain or fright : scream, screech, shriek, shrill. *See* SOUNDS.

scream *verb*
1. To utter a long, loud, piercing cry, as of pain or fright : screak, screech, shriek, shrill. *See* SOUNDS. **2.** To proclaim in a blatantly startling way : blare, shout, shriek. *See* SHOW.
scream *noun* **1.** A long, loud, piercing cry or sound : screak, screech, shriek. *See* SOUNDS. **2.** *Informal.* Something or someone uproariously funny or absurd : absurdity. *Informal:* hoot, joke, laugh. *Slang:* gas, howl, panic, riot. ***Idiom:*** a laugh a minute. *See* LAUGHTER.

screech *noun*
A long, loud, piercing cry or sound : screak, scream, shriek. *See* SOUNDS.
screech *verb* To utter a long, loud, piercing cry, as of pain or fright : screak, scream, shriek, shrill. *See* SOUNDS.

screen *verb*
1. To cut off from sight : block (out), conceal, hide[1], obscure, obstruct, shroud, shut off (*or* out). *See* SHOW. **2.** To shelter, especially from light : shade, shadow. *See* PROTECTION. **3.** To examine (material) and remove parts considered harmful or improper for publication or transmission : bowdlerize, censor, expurgate. *See* INCLUDE, SHOW.

screened *adjective*
Concealed from view : hidden, secluded, secret. *See* SHOW.

screwball *noun*
Slang. A person regarded as strange, eccentric, or crazy : crackpot, crazy, eccentric, lunatic. *Informal:* crank, loon, loony. *Slang:* cuckoo, ding-a-ling, dingbat, kook, nut, weirdie, weirdo. *See* WISE.
screwball *adjective Slang.* Deviating from the customary : bizarre, cranky, curious, eccentric, erratic, freakish, idiosyncratic, odd, outlandish, peculiar, quaint, queer, quirky, singular, strange, unnatural, unusual, weird. *Slang:* kooky. *British Slang:* rum, rummy[2]. *See* USUAL.

screwup also **screw-up** *noun*
1. *Slang.* A clumsy person : blunderer, botcher, bungler, dub, foozler. ***Idiom:*** bull in a china shop. *See* ABILITY. **2.** *Slang.* A ruinous state of disorder : botch, foul-up, mess, muddle, shambles. *Informal:* hash. *Slang:* snafu. *See* CORRECT, ORDER.

screw up *verb*
Slang. To harm irreparably through inept handling; make a mess : ball up, blunder, boggle, botch, bungle, foul up, fumble, gum up, mess up, mishandle, mismanage, muddle, muff, spoil. *Informal:* bollix up, muck up. *Slang:* blow[1], goof up, louse up, snafu. ***Idiom:*** make a muck of. *See* CORRECT, HELP.

screwy *adjective*
Slang. Afflicted with or exhibiting irrationality and mental unsoundness : brainsick, crazy, daft, demented, disordered, distraught, dotty, insane, lunatic, mad, maniac, maniacal, mentally ill, moonstruck, off, touched, unbalanced, unsound, wrong. *Informal:* bonkers, cracked, daffy, gaga, loony. *Slang:* bananas, batty, buggy, cuckoo, fruity, loco, nuts, nutty, wacky. *Chiefly British:* crackers. *Law:* non compos mentis. ***Idioms:*** around the bend, crazy as a loon, mad as a hatter, not all there, nutty as a

fruitcake, off (*or* out of) one's head, off one's rocker, of unsound mind, out of one's mind, sick in the head, stark raving mad. *See* SANE.

scribe *verb*
To form letters, characters, or words on a surface with an instrument : engross, indite, inscribe, write. *See* REMEMBER.

scrimp *verb*
To be severely sparing in order to economize : pinch, scrape, skimp, stint. ***Idioms:*** pinch pennies, tighten (one's) belt. *See* SAVE.

scriptural *adjective*
Of or relating to representation by means of writing : calligraphic, graphic, written. *See* WORDS.

Scrooge also **scrooge** *noun*
A stingy person : miser, niggard, skinflint. *Informal:* penny pincher. *Slang:* cheapskate, stiff, tightwad. *See* GIVE.

scrub *verb*
1. To rub hard in order to clean : scour[1]. *See* CLEAN, PUT ON. **2.** To remove (an outer layer or adherent matter) by rubbing a surface with considerable pressure : scour[1], scrape. *See* PUT ON. **3.** *Slang.* To decide not to go ahead with (something previously arranged) : call off, cancel. *Slang:* scratch. *See* CONTINUE.

scrubby *adjective*
Showing signs of wear and tear or neglect : bedraggled, broken-down, decaying, decrepit, dilapidated, dingy, down-at-heel, faded, mangy, rundown, scruffy, seedy, shabby, shoddy, sleazy, tattered, tatty, threadbare. *Informal:* tacky[2]. *Slang:* ratty. ***Idioms:*** all the worse for wear, gone to pot (*or* seed), past cure (*or* hope). *See* BETTER.

scruffy *adjective*
Showing signs of wear and tear or neglect : bedraggled, broken-down, decaying, decrepit, dilapidated, dingy, down-at-heel, faded, mangy, rundown, scrubby, seedy, shabby, shoddy, sleazy, tattered, tatty, threadbare. *Informal:* tacky[2]. *Slang:* ratty. ***Idioms:*** all the worse for wear, gone to pot (*or* seed), past cure (*or* hope). *See* BETTER.

scrumptious *adjective*
Highly pleasing, especially to the sense of taste : ambrosial, appetizing, delectable, delicious, heavenly, luscious, savory, tasteful, tasty, toothsome. *Slang:* yummy. *See* GOOD, INGESTION.

scrunch *verb*
To incline the body : arch, bend, bow[1], hump, hunch, stoop. *See* POSTURE.

scruple *noun*
1. A feeling of uncertainty about the fitness or correctness of an action : compunction, misgiving, qualm, reservation. *See* CERTAIN. **2.** A tiny amount : bit[1], crumb, dab[1], dash, dot, dram, drop, fragment, grain, iota, jot, minim, mite, modicum, molecule, ort, ounce, particle, scrap[1], shred, smidgen, speck, tittle, trifle, whit. *Chiefly British:* spot. *See* BIG.

scrupulous *adjective*
Showing or marked by attentiveness to all aspects or details : careful, fastidious, meticulous, painstaking, punctilious. *See* CAREFUL.

scrupulousness *noun*
Attentiveness to detail : care, carefulness, fastidiousness, meticulousness, pain (used in plural), painstaking, punctiliousness, thoroughness. *See* CAREFUL.

scrutinize *verb*
1. To look at carefully or critically : check (out), con, examine, go over, inspect, peruse, study, survey, traverse, view. *Informal:* case. ***Idiom:*** give a going-over. *See* INVESTIGATE. **2.** To look at or on attentively or carefully : eye, observe, regard, survey, watch. ***Idioms:*** have one's (*or* keep an) eye on, keep tabs on. *See* AWARENESS, SEE.

scrutiny *noun*
1. The act of examining carefully : check, checkup, examination, inspection, perusal, study, view. *Informal:* going-over. *See* INVESTIGATE. **2.** The act of observing, often for an extended time : observance, observation, watch. *See* AWARENESS, SEE.

scuff *verb*
To drag (the feet) along the floor or ground while walking : scuffle, shamble, shuffle. *See* MOVE.

scuffle *verb*
1. To contend with an opponent at close quarters, as by attempting to throw him or her : grapple, tussle, wrestle. ***Idiom:*** go to the mat with. *See* CONFLICT, TOUCH. **2.** To drag (the feet) along the floor or ground while walking : scuff, shamble, shuffle. *See* MOVE.
scuffle *noun* A physical conflict involving two or more : fight, fistfight, fisticuffs, scrap[2], tussle. *Slang:* rumble. *See* CONFLICT.

scum *noun*
Slang. A group of persons regarded as the lowest class : dreg (often used in plural), lumpenproletariat, rabble, ragtag and bobtail, riffraff, trash. ***Idioms:*** scum of the earth, tag and rag, the great unwashed. *See* OVER, RICH.

scurrility *noun*
1. The quality or state of being obscene : bawdiness, coarseness, dirtiness, filthiness, foulness, grossness, lewdness, obscenity, profaneness, profanity, scurrilousness, smuttiness, vulgarity, vulgarness. *Slang:* raunch, raunchiness. *See* DECENT. **2.** Harsh, often insulting language : abuse, billingsgate, contumely, invective, obloquy, railing, revilement, reviling, scurrilousness, vituperation. *See* PRAISE.

scurrilous *adjective*
1. Of, relating to, or characterized by verbal abuse : abusive, contumelious, invective, opprobrious, vituperative. *See* ATTACK, ATTITUDE. **2.** Offensive to accepted standards of decency : barnyard, bawdy, broad, coarse, dirty, Fescennine, filthy, foul, gross, lewd, nasty, obscene, profane, ribald, scatologic, scatological, smutty, vulgar. *Slang:* raunchy. *See* DECENT.

scurrilousness *noun*
1. Harsh, often insulting language : abuse, billingsgate, contumely, invective, obloquy, railing, revilement, reviling, scurrility, vituperation. *See* PRAISE. **2.** The quality or state of being obscene : bawdiness, coarseness, dirtiness, filthiness, foulness, grossness, lewdness, obscenity, profaneness, profanity, scurrility, smuttiness, vulgarity, vulgarness. *Slang:* raunch, raunchiness. *See* DECENT.

scurry *verb*
To move swiftly on foot so that both feet leave the ground during each stride : run, scamper, sprint. *See* MOVE.

scuttlebutt *noun*
Slang. Idle, often sensational and groundless talk about others : gossip, gossipry, hearsay, report, rumor, talebearing, tattle, tittle-tattle, word. *See* WORDS.

sea dog *noun*
A person engaged in sailing or working on a ship : jack (uppercase), jack-tar, mariner, navigator, sailor, seafarer, seaman. *Informal:* salt, tar. *Slang:* gob[3]. *See* SEA.

seafarer *noun*
A person engaged in sailing or working on a ship : jack (uppercase), jack-tar, mariner, navigator, sailor, sea dog, seaman. *Informal:* salt, tar. *Slang:* gob[3]. *See* SEA.

seam *noun*
A point or position at which two or more things are joined : connection, coupling, joint, junction, juncture, union. *See* CONNECT.

seaman *noun*
A person engaged in sailing or working on a ship : jack (uppercase), jack-tar, mariner, navigator, sailor, sea dog, seafarer. *Informal:* salt, tar. *Slang:* gob[3]. *See* SEA.

sear *verb*
1. To undergo or cause to undergo damage by or as if by fire : burn, char, scorch, singe. *See* HOT. **2.** To make or become no longer fresh or shapely because of loss of moisture : dry up, mummify, shrivel, wither, wizen. *See* DRY.
sear *noun* Damage or a damaged substance that results from burning : burn, char, scorch, singe. *See* HOT.

search *verb*
1. To try to find something : cast about, hunt, look, quest, seek. *See* SEEK. **2.** To examine the person or personal effects of in order to find something lost or concealed : frisk, inspect. *Slang:* shake down. *See* INVESTIGATE.
search *noun* **1.** A thorough search of a place or persons : frisk. *Slang:* shakedown. *See* INVESTIGATE. **2.** An attempting to accomplish or attain : pursuing, pursuit, quest. *See* SEEK.

searing *adjective*
Marked by much heat : ardent, baking, blistering, boiling, broiling, burning, fiery, heated, hot, red-hot, roasting, scalding, scorching, sizzling, sultry, sweltering, torrid. *See* HOT.

season *noun*
1. A specific length of time characterized by the occurrence of certain conditions or events : period, span, stretch, term. *See* TIME. **2.** A regular period of sexual excitement in female mammals : estrus, heat, rut[2]. *See* SEX. **3.** A span designated for a given activity : period, time. *See* TIME.
season *verb* **1.** To impart flavor to : flavor. *See* TASTE. **2.** To make resistant to hardship, especially through continued exposure : acclimate, acclimatize, caseharden, harden, indurate, toughen. *See* CONTINUE, RESIST.

seasonable *adjective*
Occurring at a fitting or advantageous time : auspicious, favorable, opportune, propitious, prosperous, timely, well-timed. *See* LUCK.

seasoned *adjective*
Skilled or knowledgeable through long practice : experienced, old, practiced, versed, veteran. *Idiom:* knowing the ropes. *See* ABILITY.

seasoner *noun*
A substance that imparts taste : condiment, flavor, flavoring, seasoning, spice. *See* TASTE.

seasoning *noun*
A substance that imparts taste : condiment, flavor, flavoring, seasoner, spice. *See* TASTE.

seat *noun*
1. The part of one's back on which one rests in sitting : buttock (used in plural), derrière, posterior, rump. *Informal:* backside, behind, bottom, rear[1]. *Slang:* bun (used in plural), fanny, tush. *Chiefly British:* bum[2]. *See* OVER. **2.** The lowest or supporting part or structure : base[1], basis, bed, bottom, foot, footing, foundation, fundament, ground, groundwork, substratum, underpinning (often used in plural). *See* OVER. **3.** A place of concentrated activity, influence, or importance : center, focus, headquarters, heart, hub. *See* EDGE.
seat *verb* **1.** To cause to take a sitting position : sit (down). *See* RISE. **2.** To place securely in a position or condition : ensconce, establish, fix, install, settle. *See* PUT IN.

secede *verb*
To break away or withdraw from membership in an association or a federation : splinter (off). *Informal:* split. *See* PARTICIPATE, POLITICS.

seclude *verb*
1. To set apart from a group : close off, cut off, insulate, isolate, segregate, separate, sequester. *See* INCLUDE. **2.** To put into solitude : cloister, sequester, sequestrate. *See* INCLUDE.

secluded *adjective*
1. Solitary and shut off from society : recluse. *See* INCLUDE. **2.** Far from centers of human population : back, insular, isolated, lonely, lonesome, obscure, outlying, out-of-the-way, remote, removed, solitary. ***Idiom:*** off the beaten path (*or* track). *See* NEAR. **3.** Concealed from view : hidden, screened, secret. *See* SHOW.

seclusion *noun*
The act of secluding or the state of being secluded : reclusion, retirement, sequestration. *See* INCLUDE.

second[1] *noun*
A very brief time : crack, flash, instant, minute[1], moment, trice, twinkle, twinkling, wink. *Informal:* jiff, jiffy. *Chiefly British:* tick. *See* BIG, TIME.

second[2] *noun*
A person who holds a position auxiliary to another and assumes some of the superior's responsibilities : adjutant, aide, assistant, auxiliary, coadjutant, coadjutor, deputy, helper, lieutenant. *See* HELP.

secondary *adjective*
1. Below another in standing or importance : inferior, junior, lesser, low, lower[2], minor, minor-league, petty, small, subaltern, subordinate, under. *Informal:* smalltime. *See* OVER. **2.** Used or held in reserve : auxiliary, backup, emergency, reserve, standby, supplemental, supplementary. *See* INCREASE. **3.** Stemming from an original source : derivational, derivative, derived. *See* KIN.
secondary *noun* One belonging to a lower class or rank : inferior, junior, subaltern, subordinate, underling. *See* OVER.

second-class *adjective*
Of low or lower quality : common, inferior, low-grade, low-quality, mean[2], mediocre, second-rate, shabby, substandard. *See* BETTER.

second-rate *adjective*
Of low or lower quality : common, inferior, low-grade, low-quality, mean[2], mediocre, second-class, shabby, substandard. *See* BETTER.

secrecy *noun*
The habit, practice, or policy of keeping secrets : clandestineness, clandestinity, concealment, covertness, huggermugger, huggermuggery, secretiveness, secretness. *See* SHOW.

secret *adjective*
1. Concealed from view : hidden, screened, secluded. *See* SHOW. **2.** Existing or operating in a way so as to ensure complete concealment and confidentiality : clandestine, cloak-and-dagger, covert, huggermugger, sub-rosa, undercover. *Informal:* hush-hush. ***Idiom:*** under wraps. *See* SHOW. **3.** Known about by very few : auricular, confidential, inside, private. *Informal:* hush-hush. *See* SHOW.
secret *noun* A means or method of entering into or achieving something desirable : formula, key, route. *Informal:* ticket. *See* MEANS.

secrete *verb*
To put or keep out of sight : bury, cache, conceal, ensconce, hide[1], occult. *Slang:* plant, stash. *See* SHOW.

secretive *adjective*
Trickily secret : furtive, sly, sneaking, sneaky, surreptitious. *See* HONEST.

secretiveness *noun*
The habit, practice, or policy of keeping secrets : clandestineness, clandestinity, concealment, covertness, huggermugger, huggermuggery, secrecy, secretness. *See* SHOW.

secretly *adverb*
In a secret way : clandestinely, covertly, huggermugger, sub rosa. ***Idioms:*** by stealth, on the sly, under cover. *See* SHOW.

secretness *noun*
The habit, practice, or policy of keeping secrets : clandestineness, clandestinity, concealment, covertness, huggermugger, huggermuggery, secrecy, secretiveness. *See* SHOW.

sect *noun*
1. Those who accept and practice a particular religious belief : church, communion, denomination, faith, persuasion. *See* RELIGION. **2.** A system of religious belief : confession, creed, denomination, faith, persuasion, religion. *See* RELIGION.

sectarian *noun*
A person who dissents from the doctrine of an established church : dissenter, dissident, heretic, nonconformist, schismatic, sectary, separationist, separatist. *See* RELIGION.

sectary *noun*
1. One zealously devoted to a religion : devotee, enthusiast, fanatic, votary, zealot. *See* BELIEF, LOVE, RELIGION. **2.** A person who dissents from the doctrine of an established church : dissenter, dissident, heretic, nonconformist, schismatic, sectarian, separationist, separatist. *See* RELIGION.

section *noun*
1. One of the parts into which something is divided : division, member, part, piece, portion, segment, subdivision. *See* PART. **2.** A part severed from a whole : cut, piece, portion, segment, slice. *See* PART. **3.** A particular subdivision of a written work : part, passage, segment. *See* PART. **4.** A thin piece, especially of tissue, suitable for microscopic examination : slice. *See* PART.
section *verb* To make a division into parts, sections, or branches : break up, dissever, divide, part, partition, segment, separate. *See* ASSEMBLE, PART.

sectional *adjective*
Relating to or restricted to a particular territory : regional, territorial. *See* TERRITORY.

secular *adjective*
1. Relating to or characteristic of the earth or of human life on earth : earthbound, earthen, earthly, earthy, mundane, tellurian, telluric, temporal, terrene, terrestrial, worldly. *See* BODY, CULTURE, PLACE. **2.** Not religious in subject matter, form, or use : lay[2], profane, temporal, worldly. *See* SACRED.

secure *adjective*
1. Affording protection : safe. *See* SAFETY. **2.** Having a firm belief in one's own powers : assured, confident, self-assured, self-confident, self-possessed. *See* ATTITUDE, BELIEF. **3.** Not easily moved or shaken : firm[1], solid, sound[2], stable, strong, sturdy, substantial, sure, unshakable. *See* CONTINUE, STRONG. **4.** Firmly settled or positioned : fast, firm[1], stable, steady, strong, sure. *See* CONTINUE. **5.** Persistently holding to something : clinging, fast, firm[1], tenacious, tight. *See* FREE, TIGHTEN. **6.** Such as could not possibly fail or disappoint : certain, infallible, sure, unerring, unfailing. *Informal:* sure-fire. *See* CERTAIN.

secure *verb* **1.** To keep safe from danger, attack, or harm : defend, guard, preserve, protect, safeguard, shield, ward. *Archaic:* fend. *See* ATTACK. **2.** To make secure : anchor, catch, fasten, fix, moor. ***Idiom:*** make fast. *See* MOVE. **3.** To join one thing to another : affix, attach, clip[2], connect, couple, fasten, fix, moor. *See* ASSEMBLE. **4.** To make fast or firmly fixed, as by means of a cord or rope : bind, fasten, knot, tie, tie up. *See* KEEP, TIGHTEN. **5.** To render certain : assure, ensure, guarantee, insure, warrant. *Informal:* cinch. *See* CERTAIN. **6.** To give a promise of payment of : guarantee. *See* MONEY, OBLIGATION. **7.** To come into possession of : acquire, come by, gain, get, obtain, procure, win. *Informal:* land, pick up. *See* GET. **8.** To gain possession of, especially after a struggle or chase : capture, catch, get, net[1], take. *Informal:* bag. *Slang:* nail. *See* GET. **9.** To be the cause of : bring, bring about, bring on, cause, effect, effectuate, generate, induce, ingenerate, lead to, make, occasion, result in, set off, stir[1] (up), touch off, trigger. ***Idioms:*** bring to pass (*or* effect), give rise to. *See* START.

security *noun*
1. The quality or state of being safe : assurance, safeness, safety. *See* SAFETY. **2.** Reliability in withstanding pressure, force, or stress : fastness, firmness, hardness, soundness, stability, stableness, steadiness, strength, sturdiness, sureness. *See* BETTER, CHANGE, CONTINUE. **3.** The act or a means of defending : defense, guard, preservation, protection, protector, safeguard, shield, ward. *See* ATTACK. **4.** Something given to guarantee the repayment of a loan or the fulfillment of an obligation : earnest[2], guaranty, pawn[1], pledge, token, warrant. *See* TRANSACTIONS.

sedate *adjective*
Full of or marked by dignity and seriousness : earnest[1], grave[2], serious, sober, solemn, somber, staid. *See* ATTITUDE, HEAVY.

sedateness *noun*
High seriousness of manner or bearing : graveness, gravity, sobriety, solemnity, solemnness, staidness. *See* ATTITUDE, HEAVY, STYLE.

sedative *adjective*
Inducing sleep or sedation : hypnotic, narcotic, opiate, sleepy, slumberous, somnifacient, som-

niferous, somnific, somnolent, soporific. *See* AWARENESS.

sedative *noun* Something that induces sleep or sedation : hypnotic, narcotic, opiate, somnifacient, soporific. *See* AWARENESS.

sediment *noun*
Matter that settles on a bottom or collects on a surface by a natural process : deposit, dreg (often used in plural), lees, precipitate, precipitation. *See* LEFTOVER.

sedition *noun*
1. Organized opposition intended to change or overthrow existing authority : insurgence, insurgency, insurrection, mutiny, rebellion, revolt, revolution, uprising. *See* RESIST.
2. Willful violation of allegiance to one's country : seditiousness, traitorousness, treason. *See* TRUST.

seditious *adjective*
Involving or constituting treason : traitorous, treasonable, treasonous. *See* TRUST.

seditiousness *noun*
Willful violation of allegiance to one's country : sedition, traitorousness, treason. *See* TRUST.

seduce *verb*
1. To beguile or draw into a wrong or foolish course of action : allure, entice, inveigle, lure, tempt. ***Idiom:*** lead astray. *See* PERSUASION.
2. To lure or persuade into a sexual relationship or a sexual act : debauch, undo. *See* SEX.

seducer *noun*
1. One that seduces : allurer, charmer, enticer, inveigler, lurer, tempter. *See* PERSUASION. **2.** A man who seduces women : debaucher, Don Juan, Lothario. *See* SEX.

seduction *noun*
Something that attracts, especially with the promise of pleasure or reward : allurement, bait, come-on, enticement, inducement, inveiglement, invitation, lure, temptation. *See* LIKE.

seductive *adjective*
Tending to seduce : alluring, bewitching, come-hither, enticing, inveigling, inviting, luring, siren, tempting, witching. *See* LIKE, PERSUASION, SEX.

seductress *noun*
A usually unscrupulous woman who seduces or exploits men : enchantress, femme fatale, siren, temptress. *Informal:* vamp, witch. *See* SEX.

sedulous *adjective*
Characterized by steady attention and effort : assiduous, diligent, industrious, studious. *See* INDUSTRIOUS.

sedulousness *noun*
Steady attention and effort, as to one's occupation : application, assiduity, assiduousness, diligence, industriousness, industry. *See* INDUSTRIOUS.

see *verb*
1. To apprehend (images) by use of the eyes : behold, perceive. *Scots:* ken. *See* SEE. **2.** To perceive with a special effort of the senses or the mind : descry, detect, discern, distinguish, mark, mind, note, notice, observe, remark. *See* KNOWLEDGE, SEE. **3.** To form mental images of : conceive, envisage, envision, fancy, fantasize, image, imagine, picture, think, vision, visualize. *Informal:* feature. *See* THOUGHTS. **4.** To perceive and recognize the meaning of : accept, apprehend, catch (on), compass, comprehend, conceive, fathom, follow, get, grasp, make out, read, sense, take, take in, understand. *Informal:* savvy. *Slang:* dig. *Chiefly British:* twig. *Scots:* ken. ***Idioms:*** get (*or* have) a handle on, get the picture. *See* UNDERSTAND. **5.** To look upon in a particular way : account, consider, deem, esteem, reckon, regard, view. *See* PERSPECTIVE. **6.** To know in advance : anticipate, divine, envision, foreknow, foresee. *See* FORESIGHT, SEE. **7.** To participate in or partake of personally : experience, feel, go through, have, know, meet[1] (with), suffer, taste (of), undergo. *Archaic:* prove. ***Idiom:*** run up against. *See* PARTICIPATE. **8.** To be with another person socially on a regular basis : date, go out. *Informal:* take out. *See* CONNECT. **9.** To go to or seek out the company of in order to socialize : call, come by, come over, drop by, drop in, look in, look up, pop in, run in, stop (by *or* in), visit. ***Idiom:*** pay a visit. *See* SEEK.

see to *verb* To have the care and supervision of : attend, care for, look after, mind, minister to, tend[2], watch. ***Idioms:*** keep an eye on, look out for, take care (*or* charge) of, take under one's wing. *See* CARE FOR.

seeable *adjective*
Capable of being seen : discernible, perceivable, perceptible, viewable, visible, visual. *See* SEE.

seed *noun*
1. A fertilized plant ovule capable of germinating : kernel, pip, pit[2]. *See* START. **2.** A propagative part of a plant : spore, tuber. *See* START. **3.** A source of further growth and development : bud[1], embryo, germ, kernel, nucleus, spark[1]. *See* START. **4.** A group consisting of those descended directly from the same parents or ancestors : brood, get, issue,

offspring, posterity, progeny. *See* KIN. **5.** One's ancestors or their character or one's ancestral derivation : ancestry, birth, blood, bloodline, descent, extraction, family, genealogy, line, lineage, origin, parentage, pedigree, stock. *See* KIN, PRECEDE. **6.** The male fluid of fertilization : semen, sperm. *See* START.

seed *verb* To put (seeds) into the ground for growth : plant, sow. *See* START.

seedtime *noun*
The season of the year during which the weather becomes warmer and plants revive : spring, springtide, springtime. *See* TIME.

seedy *adjective*
Showing signs of wear and tear or neglect : bedraggled, broken-down, decaying, decrepit, dilapidated, dingy, down-at-heel, faded, mangy, rundown, scrubby, scruffy, shabby, shoddy, sleazy, tattered, tatty, threadbare. *Informal:* tacky[2]. *Slang:* ratty. ***Idioms:*** all the worse for wear, gone to pot (*or* seed), past cure (*or* hope). *See* BETTER.

seeing *noun*
The faculty of seeing : eye, eyesight, sight, vision. *Archaic:* light[1]. *See* SEE.

seek *verb*
1. To try to find something : cast about, hunt, look, quest, search. *See* SEEK. **2.** To strive toward a goal : aim, aspire. ***Idiom:*** set one's sights on. *See* SEEK, START. **3.** To endeavor to obtain (something) by expressing one's needs or desires : ask (for), request, solicit. *See* REQUEST. **4.** To make an attempt to do or make : assay, attempt, endeavor, essay, strive, try. ***Idioms:*** have a go at, have (*or* make *or* take) a shot at, have (*or* take) a whack at, make a stab at, take a crack at. *See* TRY.

seeker *noun*
A person who applies for or seeks something, such as a job or position : applicant, aspirant, candidate, hopeful, petitioner. *See* SEEK.

seem *verb*
To have the appearance of : appear, look, sound[1]. ***Idiom:*** strike one as (being). *See* SURFACE.

seeming *adjective*
Appearing as such but not necessarily so : apparent, external, ostensible, ostensive, outward, superficial. *See* SURFACE.

seemingly *adverb*
On the surface : apparently, evidently, externally, ostensibly, ostensively, outwardly, superficially. ***Idioms:*** on the face of it, to all appearances. *See* SURFACE.

seemliness *noun*
Conformity to recognized standards, as of conduct or appearance : comeliness, correctness, decency, decentness, decorousness, decorum, properness, propriety, respectability, respectableness. *See* USUAL.

seemly *adjective*
Conforming to accepted standards : becoming, befitting, comely, comme il faut, correct, decent, decorous, de rigueur, nice, proper, respectable, right. *See* COURTESY.

seep *verb*
To flow or leak out or emit something slowly : bleed, exude, leach, ooze, percolate, transpire, transude, weep. *See* MOVE, SOLID.

seer *noun*
1. Someone who sees something occur : eyewitness, viewer, witness. *See* SEE. **2.** A person who foretells future events by or as if by supernatural means : augur, auspex, diviner, foreteller, haruspex, prophesier, prophet, prophetess, sibyl, soothsayer, vaticinator. *See* FORESIGHT.

seesaw *verb*
To lean suddenly, unsteadily, and erratically from the vertical axis : lurch, pitch, roll, yaw. *See* MOVE, STRAIGHT.

seethe *verb*
1. To be in a state of emotional or mental turmoil : boil, bubble, burn, churn, ferment, simmer, smolder. *See* CALM. **2.** To be or become angry : anger, blow up, boil over, bristle, burn, explode, flare up, foam, fume, rage. *Informal:* steam. ***Idioms:*** blow a fuse, blow a gasket, blow one's stack (*or* top), breathe fire, fly off the handle, get hot under the collar, hit the ceiling (*or* roof), lose one's temper, see red. *See* FEELINGS.

see-through *adjective*
1. Free from what obscures or dims : clear, crystal clear, crystalline, limpid, lucid, pellucid, transparent. *See* CLEAR. **2.** Admitting light so that objects beyond can be seen : clear, crystal clear, crystalline, limpid, lucid, pellucid, translucent, transparent. *See* CLEAR.

see to *verb* See **see.**

segment *noun*
1. One of the parts into which something is divided : division, member, part, piece, portion, section, subdivision. *See* PART. **2.** A part severed from a whole : cut, piece, portion, section, slice. *See* PART. **3.** A particular subdivision of a written work : part, passage, section. *See* PART.

segment *verb* To make a division into parts, sections, or branches : break up, dissever, divide, part, partition, section, separate. *See* ASSEMBLE, PART.

segregate *verb*
To set apart from a group : close off, cut off, insulate, isolate, seclude, separate, sequester. *See* INCLUDE.

segregated *adjective*
Excluding or unavailable to certain minorities : restricted. *See* INCLUDE, LIMITED.

segregation *noun*
1. The act or process of isolating : insulation, isolation, separation, sequestration. *See* INCLUDE. **2.** The policy or practice of political, legal, economic, or social discrimination, as against the members of a minority group : apartheid, separatism. *See* INCLUDE.

seism *noun*
A shaking of the earth : earthquake, quake, temblor, tremblor, tremor. *Informal:* shake. *See* MOVE, REPETITION.

seize *verb*
1. To take firmly with the hand and maintain a hold on : clasp, clench, clutch[1], grab, grapple, grasp, grip. *See* KEEP. **2.** To get hold of (something moving) : catch, clutch[1], grab, snatch. *Informal:* nab. ***Idiom:*** lay hands on. *See* GET. **3.** To lay claim to for oneself or as one's right : appropriate, arrogate, assume, commandeer, preempt, take, usurp. *See* GIVE. **4.** To have a sudden overwhelming effect on : catch, strike, take. *See* ATTACK, OVER. **5.** To take into custody as a prisoner : apprehend, arrest. *Informal:* nab, pick up. *Slang:* bust, collar, pinch, run in. *See* LAW. **6.** To take quick and forcible possession of : commandeer, confiscate, expropriate, grab, snatch. ***Idiom:*** help oneself to. *See* GIVE.

seizure *noun*
1. The act of catching, especially a sudden taking and holding : catch, clutch[1], grab, snatch. *See* GET. **2.** The act of taking something for oneself : appropriation, arrogation, assumption, preemption, usurpation. *See* GIVE. **3.** A seizing and holding by law : apprehension, arrest. *Slang:* bust, collar, pickup, pinch. *See* LAW. **4.** The act of taking quick and forcible possession of : confiscation, expropriation. *See* GIVE. **5.** A sudden and often acute manifestation of a disease : access, attack, fit[2]. *Informal:* spell[3]. *See* HEALTH.

seldom *adverb*
At rare intervals : infrequently, little, occasionally, rarely, sporadically. ***Idioms:*** hardly (*or* scarcely) ever, once in a blue moon. *See* USUAL.

select *verb*
To make a choice from a number of alternatives : choose, cull, elect, opt (for), pick (out), single (out). *See* CHOICE.

select *adjective* **1.** Singled out in preference : choice, chosen, elect, exclusive. *See* CHOICE, INCLUDE. **2.** Of fine quality : choice, fine[1], first-class, prime, superior. *See* BETTER. **3.** Able to recognize small differences or draw fine distinctions : discriminate, discriminating, discriminative, discriminatory, selective. *See* PRECISE.

select *noun* One that is selected : choice, chosen, elect, pick. *See* CHOICE.

selection *noun*
The act of choosing : choice, election, option, preference. *See* CHOICE.

selective *adjective*
Able to recognize small differences or draw fine distinctions : discriminate, discriminating, discriminative, discriminatory, select. *See* PRECISE.

selectiveness *noun*
The ability to distinguish, especially to recognize small differences or draw fine distinctions : discrimination, refinement, selectivity. *See* PRECISE.

selectivity *noun*
The ability to distinguish, especially to recognize small differences or draw fine distinctions : discrimination, refinement, selectiveness. *See* PRECISE.

self *noun*
An individual's awareness of what constitutes his or her essential nature and distinguishes him or her from all others : ego. *See* BE, SELF.

self-absorbed *adjective*
Concerned only with oneself : egocentric, egoistic, egoistical, egomaniacal, egotistic, egotistical, self-centered, self-involved, selfish, self-seeking, self-serving. ***Idiom:*** wrapped up in oneself. *See* SELF.

self-absorption *noun*
Concern only for oneself : egocentricity, egocentrism, egoism, egomania, self-centeredness, self-involvement, selfishness. *See* SELF.

self-assurance *noun*
A firm belief in one's own powers : aplomb, assurance, confidence, self-confidence, self-possession. *See* ATTITUDE, BELIEF.

self-assured *adjective*
Having a firm belief in one's own powers :

assured, confident, secure, self-confident, self-possessed. *See* ATTITUDE, BELIEF.

self-centered *adjective*
Concerned only with oneself : egocentric, egoistic, egoistical, egomaniacal, egotistic, egotistical, self-absorbed, self-involved, selfish, self-seeking, self-serving. ***Idiom:*** wrapped up in oneself. *See* SELF.

self-centeredness *noun*
Concern only for oneself : egocentricity, egocentrism, egoism, egomania, self-absorption, self-involvement, selfishness. *See* SELF.

self-confidence *noun*
A firm belief in one's own powers : aplomb, assurance, confidence, self-assurance, self-possession. *See* ATTITUDE, BELIEF.

self-confident *adjective*
Having a firm belief in one's own powers : assured, confident, secure, self-assured, self-possessed. *See* ATTITUDE, BELIEF.

self-contained *adjective*
Free from the influence, guidance, or control of others : independent, self-reliant, self-sufficient. *See* DEPENDENCE.

self-control *noun*
The keeping of one's thoughts and emotions to oneself : control, reserve, restraint, reticence, self-restraint, taciturnity, uncommunicativeness. *See* RESTRAINT.

self-controlled *adjective*
Tending to keep one's thoughts and emotions to oneself : controlled, inhibited, noncommittal, reserved, restrained, self-restrained. *See* RESTRAINT.

self-denying *adjective*
Without concern for oneself : self-forgetful, self-forgetting, selfless, unselfish. *See* SELF.

self-determination *noun*
The capacity to manage one's own affairs, make one's own judgments, and provide for oneself : independence, self-reliance, self-sufficiency. *See* DEPENDENCE.

self-effacement *noun*
Reserve in speech, behavior, or dress : demureness, diffidence, modesty, reticence. *See* RESTRAINT.

self-effacing *adjective*
Not forward but reticent or reserved in manner : backward, bashful, coy, demure, diffident, modest, retiring, shy[1], timid. *See* RESTRAINT.

self-esteem *noun*
A sense of one's own dignity or worth : amour-propre, ego, pride, self-regard, self-respect. *See* RESPECT.

self-forgetful *adjective*
Without concern for oneself : self-denying, self-forgetting, selfless, unselfish. *See* SELF.

self-forgetting *adjective*
Without concern for oneself : self-denying, self-forgetful, selfless, unselfish. *See* SELF.

self-governing *adjective*
Having political independence : autonomous, free, independent, sovereign. *See* DEPENDENCE, FREE.

self-government *noun*
The condition of being politically free : autonomy, freedom, independence, independency, liberty, sovereignty. *See* DEPENDENCE, FREE.

selfhood *noun*
The set of behavioral or personal characteristics by which an individual is recognizable : identity, individualism, individuality. *See* BE.

self-importance *noun*
An exaggerated belief in one's own importance : egoism, egotism. *Informal:* bighead, bigheadedness, swelled head. *See* SELF-LOVE.

self-important *adjective*
Characterized by an exaggerated show of dignity or self-importance : grandiose, hoity-toity, pompous, pretentious, puffed-up, puffy. *Informal:* highfalutin. *See* PLAIN.

self-involved *adjective*
Concerned only with oneself : egocentric, egoistic, egoistical, egomaniacal, egotistic, egotistical, self-absorbed, self-centered, selfish, self-seeking, self-serving. ***Idiom:*** wrapped up in oneself. *See* SELF.

self-involvement *noun*
Concern only for oneself : egocentricity, egocentrism, egoism, egomania, self-absorption, self-centeredness, selfishness. *See* SELF.

selfish *adjective*
Concerned only with oneself : egocentric, egoistic, egoistical, egomaniacal, egotistic, egotistical, self-absorbed, self-centered, self-involved, self-seeking, self-serving. ***Idiom:*** wrapped up in oneself. *See* SELF.

selfishness *noun*
Concern only for oneself : egocentricity, egocentrism, egoism, egomania, self-absorption, self-centeredness, self-involvement. *See* SELF.

selfless *adjective*
Without concern for oneself : self-denying, self-forgetful, self-forgetting, unselfish. *See* SELF.

self-possessed *adjective*
Having a firm belief in one's own powers : assured, confident, secure, self-assured, self-confident. *See* ATTITUDE, BELIEF.

self-possession *noun*
1. A firm belief in one's own powers : aplomb, assurance, confidence, self-assurance, self-confidence. *See* ATTITUDE, BELIEF. **2.** A stable, calm state of the emotions : aplomb, balance, collectedness, composure, coolness, equanimity, imperturbability, imperturbableness, nonchalance, poise, sang-froid, unflappability. *Slang:* cool. *See* CALM, FEELINGS.

self-regard *noun*
A sense of one's own dignity or worth : amour-propre, ego, pride, self-esteem, self-respect. *See* RESPECT.

self-reliance *noun*
The capacity to manage one's own affairs, make one's own judgments, and provide for oneself : independence, self-determination, self-sufficiency. *See* DEPENDENCE.

self-reliant *adjective*
Free from the influence, guidance, or control of others : independent, self-contained, self-sufficient. *See* DEPENDENCE.

self-respect *noun*
A sense of one's own dignity or worth : amour-propre, ego, pride, self-esteem, self-regard. *See* RESPECT.

self-respecting *adjective*
Properly valuing oneself, one's honor, or one's dignity : prideful, proud. *See* RESPECT.

self-restrained *adjective*
Tending to keep one's thoughts and emotions to oneself : controlled, inhibited, noncommittal, reserved, restrained, self-controlled. *See* RESTRAINT.

self-restraint *noun*
The keeping of one's thoughts and emotions to oneself : control, reserve, restraint, reticence, self-control, taciturnity, uncommunicativeness. *See* RESTRAINT.

selfsame *adjective*
Being one and not another or others; not different in nature or identity : identic, identical, same, very. *See* SAME.

selfsameness *noun*
The quality or condition of being exactly the same as something else : identicalness, identity, oneness, sameness. *See* SAME.

self-seeking *adjective*
Concerned only with oneself : egocentric, egoistic, egoistical, egomaniacal, egotistic, egotistical, self-absorbed, self-centered, self-involved, selfish, self-serving. ***Idiom:*** wrapped up in oneself. *See* SELF.

self-serving *adjective*
Concerned only with oneself : egocentric, egoistic, egoistical, egomaniacal, egotistic, egotistical, self-absorbed, self-centered, self-involved, selfish, self-seeking. ***Idiom:*** wrapped up in oneself. *See* SELF.

self-sufficiency *noun*
The capacity to manage one's own affairs, make one's own judgments, and provide for oneself : independence, self-determination, self-reliance. *See* DEPENDENCE.

self-sufficient *adjective*
1. Free from the influence, guidance, or control of others : independent, self-contained, self-reliant. *See* DEPENDENCE. **2.** Able to support oneself financially : independent, self-supporting. *See* DEPENDENCE, MONEY.

self-supporting *adjective*
Able to support oneself financially : independent, self-sufficient. *See* DEPENDENCE, MONEY.

sell *verb*
1. To offer for sale : deal (in), handle, market, merchandise, merchant, peddle, retail, trade (in), vend. *See* TRANSACTIONS. **2.** To succeed in causing (a person) to act in a certain way. Also used with *on* : argue into, bring, bring around (*or* round), convince, get, induce, persuade, prevail on (*or* upon), talk into. *See* PERSUASION.

sell for *verb* **1.** To achieve (a certain price) : bring (in), fetch, realize. *See* GET. **2.** To require a specified price : cost, go for. *See* TRANSACTIONS.

sell off *verb* To get rid of completely by selling, especially in quantity or at a discount : close out, dump, sell out, unload. *See* TRANSACTIONS.

sell out *verb* **1.** To get rid of completely by selling, especially in quantity or at a discount : close out, dump, sell off, unload. *See* TRANSACTIONS. **2.** *Slang.* To be treacherous to : betray, double-cross. *Slang:* rat (on). ***Idiom:*** sell down the river. *See* TRUST.

sell *noun Slang.* Market appeal : marketability, marketableness, salability, salableness. *See* DESIRE.

seller *noun*
One who sells : clerk, salesclerk, salesgirl, salesman, salesperson, saleswoman, vender. *See* TRANSACTIONS.

sell for *verb* See **sell.**

sell off *verb* See **sell.**

sellout *noun*
Slang. An act of betraying : betrayal, double cross, treachery. *See* TRUST.

sell out *verb* See **sell.**

semaphore *verb*
To communicate by means of such devices as lights or signs : flag[1], signal. *See* EXPRESS, WORDS.

semblance *noun*
1. A deceptive outward appearance : cloak, color, coloring, cover, disguise, disguisement, façade, face, false colors, front, gloss, guise, mask, masquerade, pretense, pretext, show, veil, veneer, window-dressing. *Slang:* put-on. *See* SHOW. **2.** A slight amount or indication : breath, dash, ghost, hair, hint, intimation, shade, shadow, soupçon, streak, suggestion, suspicion, taste, tinge, touch, trace, whiff, whisper. *Informal:* whisker. *See* BIG, SHOW.

semen *noun*
The male fluid of fertilization : seed, sperm. *See* START.

seminar *noun*
A meeting for the exchange of views : colloquium, conference, discussion, parley. *Informal:* powwow. *Slang:* rap session. *See* MEET, WORDS.

sempiternal *adjective*
Without beginning or end : eternal, infinite. *See* LIMITED.

sempiternity *noun*
The totality of time without beginning or end : eternality, eternalness, eternity, infinity, perpetuity. *See* LIMITED.

send *verb*
1. To cause (something) to be conveyed to a destination : address, consign, dispatch, forward, route, ship, transmit. *See* MOVE. **2.** To direct or allow to leave. Also used with *away* : dismiss. ***Idioms:*** send about one's business, send packing, show someone the door. *See* KEEP. **3.** To direct (a person) elsewhere for help or information : refer, transfer, turn over. *See* MOVE. **4.** *Slang.* To move or excite greatly : carry away, electrify, enrapture, thrill, transport. *See* EXCITE.

send for *verb* To demand to appear, come, or assemble : call, convene, convoke, muster, summon. *See* REQUEST.

send forth *verb* To discharge material, as vapor or fumes, usually suddenly and violently : emit, give, give forth, give off, give out, issue, let off, let out, release, throw off, vent. *See* FREE, MOVE.

send up *verb* *Informal.* To place officially in confinement : commit, consign, institutionalize. *See* FREE.

send for *verb* See **send.**

send forth *verb* See **send.**

send up *verb* See **send.**

senectitude *noun*
Old age : age, agedness, elderliness, senescence, year (used in plural). *See* YOUTH.

senescence *noun*
Old age : age, agedness, elderliness, senectitude, year (used in plural). *See* YOUTH.

senile *adjective*
Exhibiting the mental and physical deterioration often accompanying old age : doddering, doting. *See* YOUTH.

senility *noun*
The condition of being senile : caducity, dotage. *See* YOUTH.

senior *adjective*
1. Of greater age than another : elder, older. *See* YOUTH. **2.** Far along in life or time : advanced, aged, elderly, old. ***Idiom:*** getting along (*or* on) in years. *See* NEW. **3.** Being at a rank above another : higher, superior. *See* OVER.

senior *noun* **1.** A person who is older than another : elder. *See* YOUTH. **2.** An elderly person : ancient, elder, golden ager, senior citizen. *Informal:* oldster, old-timer. *See* YOUTH. **3.** One who stands above another in rank : better[1], elder, superior. *Informal:* higher-up. *See* OVER.

senior citizen *noun*
An elderly person : ancient, elder, golden ager, senior. *Informal:* oldster, old-timer. *See* YOUTH.

sensation *noun*
1. The capacity for or an act of responding to a stimulus : feeling, sense, sensibility, sensitiveness, sensitivity, sentiment. *See* AWARENESS. **2.** A condition of intense public interest or excitement : brouhaha, stir[1], uproar. *Informal:* to-do. *Slang:* hoo-hah. *See* EXCITE. **3.** One that evokes great surprise and admiration : astonishment, marvel, miracle, phenomenon, prodigy, stunner, wonder, wonderment. ***Idioms:*** one for the books, the eighth wonder of the world. *See* GOOD.

sensational *adjective*
1. Of or relating to sensation or the senses : sensitive, sensorial, sensory, sensual, sensuous. *See* AWARENESS, BODY. **2.** Suggesting drama or a stage performance, as in emotionality or suspense : dramatic, histrionic, histrionical, melodramatic, spectacular, theatric, theatrical. *See* EXCITE, STYLE, SURPRISE. **3.** Particularly excellent : divine, fabulous, fantastic, fantastical, glorious, marvelous, splendid, superb, terrific, wonderful. *Informal:* dandy, dreamy, great,

ripping, super, swell, tremendous. *Slang:* cool, groovy, hot, keen[1], neat, nifty. ***Idiom:*** out of this world. *See* GOOD.

sense *noun*

1. The capacity for or an act of responding to a stimulus : feeling, sensation, sensibility, sensitiveness, sensitivity, sentiment. *See* AWARENESS. **2.** The condition of being aware : awareness, cognizance, consciousness, perception. *See* KNOWLEDGE. **3.** The faculty of thinking, reasoning, and acquiring and applying knowledge : brain (often used in plural), brainpower, intellect, intelligence, mentality, mind, understanding, wit. *Slang:* smart (used in plural). *See* ABILITY, THOUGHTS. **4.** The ability to make sensible decisions : common sense, judgment, wisdom. *Informal:* gumption, horse sense. *See* ABILITY. **5.** A healthy mental state. Often used in plural : lucidity, lucidness, mind, reason, saneness, sanity, soundness, wit (used in plural). *Slang:* marble (used in plural). *See* SANE. **6.** What is sound or reasonable : logic, rationale, rationality, rationalness, reason. ***Idiom:*** rhyme or reason. *See* REASON. **7.** That which is signified by a word or expression : acceptation, connotation, denotation, import, intent, meaning, message, purport, significance, significancy, signification, value. *See* MEANING.

sense *verb* **1.** To be intuitively aware of : apprehend, feel, intuit, perceive. ***Idioms:*** feel in one's bones, get vibrations. *See* KNOWLEDGE. **2.** To view in a certain way : believe, feel, hold, think. *See* OPINION. **3.** To perceive and recognize the meaning of : accept, apprehend, catch (on), compass, comprehend, conceive, fathom, follow, get, grasp, make out, read, see, take, take in, understand. *Informal:* savvy. *Slang:* dig. *Chiefly British:* twig. *Scots:* ken. ***Idioms:*** get (*or* have) a handle on, get the picture. *See* UNDERSTAND.

senseless *adjective*

1. Lacking rational direction or purpose : meaningless, mindless, pointless, purposeless. ***Idiom:*** without rhyme or reason. *See* PURPOSE. **2.** Displaying a complete lack of forethought and good sense : brainless, fatuous, foolish, insensate, mindless, silly, unintelligent, weak-minded, witless. *See* ABILITY, PLANNED. **3.** Lacking consciousness : cold, insensible, unconscious. ***Idioms:*** out cold, out like a light. *See* AWARENESS.

senselessness *noun*

Foolish behavior : absurdity, folly, foolery, foolishness, idiocy, imbecility, insanity, lunacy, madness, nonsense, preposterousness, silliness, tomfoolery, zaniness. *Informal:* craziness. *See* ABILITY.

sensibility *noun*

1. The capacity for or an act of responding to a stimulus : feeling, sensation, sense, sensitiveness, sensitivity, sentiment. *See* AWARENESS. **2.** The quality or condition of being emotionally and intuitively sensitive : feeling, sensitiveness, sensitivity. *See* AWARENESS.

sensible *adjective*

1. Composed of or relating to things that occupy space and can be perceived by the senses : concrete, corporeal, material, objective, phenomenal, physical, substantial, tangible. *See* BODY, MATTER. **2.** Capable of being noticed or apprehended mentally : appreciable, detectable, discernible, distinguishable, noticeable, observable, palpable, perceivable, perceptible, ponderable. *See* KNOWLEDGE. **3.** Able to receive and respond to external stimuli : impressible, impressionable, responsive, sensitive, sentient, susceptible, susceptive. *See* AWARENESS. **4.** Marked by comprehension, cognizance, and perception : alive, awake, aware, cognizant, sentient, wise[1]. *Slang:* hip. ***Idiom:*** on to. *See* KNOWLEDGE. **5.** Possessing, proceeding from, or exhibiting good judgment and prudence : balanced, commonsensible, commonsensical, judicious, levelheaded, prudent, rational, reasonable, sagacious, sage, sane, sapient, sound[2], well-founded, well-grounded, wise[1]. *See* REASON, SANE.

sensitive *adjective*

1. Able to receive and respond to external stimuli : impressible, impressionable, responsive, sensible, sentient, susceptible, susceptive. *See* AWARENESS. **2.** Of or relating to sensation or the senses : sensational, sensorial, sensory, sensual, sensuous. *See* AWARENESS, BODY. **3.** Possessing or displaying perceptions of great accuracy and sensitivity : acute, incisive, keen[1], penetrating, perceptive, probing, sharp, trenchant. *See* CAREFUL, SHARP. **4.** Readily stirred by emotion : emotional, feeling. *See* FEELINGS. **5.** Showing sensitivity and skill in dealing with others : delicate, diplomatic, discreet, politic, tactful. *See* ABILITY. **6.** Requiring great tact or skill : delicate, ticklish, touch-and-go, touchy, tricky. *See* EASY.

sensitiveness *noun*

1. The capacity for or an act of responding to a stimulus : feeling, sensation, sense, sensibility, sensitivity, sentiment. *See* AWARENESS. **2.** The quality or condition of being emotionally and intuitively sensitive : feeling, sensibility, sensitivity. *See* AWARENESS.

sensitivity *noun*

1. The capacity for or an act of responding to a stimulus : feeling, sensation, sense, sensibility, sensitiveness, sentiment. *See* AWARENESS.
2. The quality or condition of being emotionally and intuitively sensitive : feeling, sensibility, sensitiveness. *See* AWARENESS.

sensorial *adjective*

Of or relating to sensation or the senses : sensational, sensitive, sensory, sensual, sensuous. *See* AWARENESS, BODY.

sensory *adjective*

1. Of or relating to sensation or the senses : sensational, sensitive, sensorial, sensual, sensuous. *See* AWARENESS, BODY. **2.** Transmitting impulses from sense organs to nerve centers : afferent. *See* BODY.

sensual *adjective*

1. Of or relating to sensation or the senses : sensational, sensitive, sensorial, sensory, sensuous. *See* AWARENESS, BODY. **2.** Relating to, suggestive of, or appealing to sense gratification : epicurean, sensualistic, sensuous, voluptuous. *See* PAIN. **3.** Relating to the desires and appetites of the body : animal, carnal, fleshly, physical. *See* BODY. **4.** Suggesting sexuality : sexual, sexy, suggestive, voluptuous. *See* SEX.
5. Of or preoccupied with material rather than spiritual or intellectual things : material, materialistic. *See* BODY.

sensualism *noun*

The quality or condition of being sensuous : sensuality, sensuousness, voluptuousness. *See* PAIN.

sensualist *noun*

A person devoted to pleasure and luxury : epicure, epicurean, hedonist, sybarite, voluptuary. *See* PAIN.

sensualistic *adjective*

Relating to, suggestive of, or appealing to sense gratification : epicurean, sensual, sensuous, voluptuous. *See* PAIN.

sensuality *noun*

1. The quality or condition of being sensual : sexiness, sexuality, suggestiveness, voluptuousness. *See* SEX. **2.** The quality or condition of being sensuous : sensualism, sensuousness, voluptuousness. *See* PAIN. **3.** A preoccupation with the body and satisfaction of its desires : animalism, animality, carnality, fleshliness, physicality. *See* BODY.

sensuous *adjective*

1. Of or relating to sensation or the senses : sensational, sensitive, sensorial, sensory, sensual. *See* AWARENESS, BODY. **2.** Relating to, suggestive of, or appealing to sense gratification : epicurean, sensual, sensualistic, voluptuous. *See* PAIN.

sensuousness *noun*

The quality or condition of being sensuous : sensualism, sensuality, voluptuousness. *See* PAIN.

sentence *noun*

A judicial decision, especially one setting the punishment to be inflicted on a convicted person : judgment. *Slang:* rap[1]. *See* LAW.
sentence *verb* To pronounce judgment against : condemn, damn, doom. *See* LAW.

sentient *adjective*

1. Marked by comprehension, cognizance, and perception : alive, awake, aware, cognizant, sensible, wise[1]. *Slang:* hip. ***Idiom:*** on to. *See* KNOWLEDGE. **2.** Able to receive and respond to external stimuli : impressible, impressionable, responsive, sensible, sensitive, susceptible, susceptive. *See* AWARENESS.

sentiment *noun*

1. A general cast of mind with regard to something : attitude, feeling. *See* ATTITUDE.
2. Something believed or accepted as true by a person : belief, conviction, feeling, idea, mind, notion, opinion, persuasion, position, view. *See* OPINION. **3.** A complex and usually strong subjective response, such as love or hate : affection, affectivity, emotion, feeling. *See* FEELINGS. **4.** The capacity for or an act of responding to a stimulus : feeling, sensation, sense, sensibility, sensitiveness, sensitivity. *See* AWARENESS.

sentimental *adjective*

Affectedly or extravagantly emotional : bathetic, gushy, maudlin, mawkish, romantic, slushy, sobby, soft, soppy. *Informal:* gooey, mushy, schmaltzy, sloppy, soupy. *Slang:* drippy, sappy, tear-jerking. *See* FEELINGS.

sentimentalism *noun*

The quality or condition of being affectedly or overly emotional : bathos, maudlinism, mawkishness, sentimentality. *Informal:* mush, mushiness, schmaltz, schmaltziness, sloppiness. *Slang:* sappiness. *See* FEELINGS.

sentimentality *noun*

The quality or condition of being affectedly or overly emotional : bathos, maudlinism, mawkishness, sentimentalism. *Informal:* mush, mushiness, schmaltz, schmaltziness, sloppiness. *Slang:* sappiness. *See* FEELINGS.

sentimentalize *verb*
To regard or imbue with affected or exaggerated emotion : romanticize. *See* FEELINGS, REAL.

sentinel *noun*
A person or special body of persons assigned to provide protection or keep watch over, for example : guard, lookout, picket, protector, sentry, ward, watch. *See* AWARENESS, SAFETY.

sentry *noun*
A person or special body of persons assigned to provide protection or keep watch over, for example : guard, lookout, picket, protector, sentinel, ward, watch. *See* AWARENESS, SAFETY.

separate *verb*
1. To become or cause to become apart one from another : break, detach, disjoin, disjoint, disunite, divide, divorce, part, split (up). ***Idioms:*** part company, set at odds. *See* ASSEMBLE. **2.** To make a division into parts, sections, or branches : break up, dissever, divide, part, partition, section, segment. *See* ASSEMBLE, PART. **3.** To set apart (one kind or type) from others : sift, sort, winnow. *See* INCLUDE. **4.** To distribute into groups according to kinds : assort, categorize, class, classify, group, pigeonhole, sort (out). *See* COLLECT. **5.** To recognize as being different : differentiate, discern, discriminate, distinguish, know, tell. *See* SAME. **6.** To set apart from a group : close off, cut off, insulate, isolate, seclude, segregate, sequester. *See* INCLUDE. **7.** To terminate a relationship or an association by or as if by leaving one another : break off, break up, part. *Informal:* split (up). ***Idioms:*** call it quits, come to a parting of the ways, part company. *See* ASSEMBLE, CONTINUE. **8.** To release from military duty : demobilize, discharge, muster out. *See* FREE, KEEP.

separate *adjective* **1.** Being or related to a distinct entity : discrete, individual, particular, single, singular. *See* INCLUDE. **2.** Alone in a given category : lone, one, only, particular, single, singular, sole, solitary, unique. ***Idioms:*** first and last, one and only. *See* INCLUDE. **3.** Distinguished from others by nature or qualities : discrete, distinct, several, various. *See* SAME.

separately *adverb*
As a separate unit : apart, discretely, independently, individually, singly. ***Idioms:*** one at a time, one by one. *See* INCLUDE.

separateness *noun*
The quality of being individual : discreteness, distinctiveness, individuality, particularity, singularity. *See* INCLUDE.

separation *noun*
1. The act or an instance of separating one thing from another : detachment, disjunction, disjuncture, disseverance, disseverment, disunion, division, divorce, divorcement, parting, partition, severance, split. *See* ASSEMBLE, PART. **2.** The act or process of detaching : detachment, disconnection, disengagement, uncoupling. *See* ASSEMBLE. **3.** The act or an instance of distinguishing : differentiation, discrimination, distinction. *See* SAME. **4.** The act or process of isolating : insulation, isolation, segregation, sequestration. *See* INCLUDE. **5.** A space or interval between objects or points : gap, interspace, interstice, interval. *See* OPEN.

separationist *noun*
A person who dissents from the doctrine of an established church : dissenter, dissident, heretic, nonconformist, schismatic, sectarian, sectary, separatist. *See* RELIGION.

separatism *noun*
The policy or practice of political, legal, economic, or social discrimination, as against the members of a minority group : apartheid, segregation. *See* INCLUDE.

separatist *noun*
A person who dissents from the doctrine of an established church : dissenter, dissident, heretic, nonconformist, schismatic, sectarian, sectary, separationist. *See* RELIGION.

sepulcher *noun*
A burial place or receptacle for human remains : catacomb, cinerarium, crypt, grave[1], mausoleum, ossuary, sepulture, tomb, vault[1]. *See* KEEP, PLACE.

sepulture *noun*
A burial place or receptacle for human remains : catacomb, cinerarium, crypt, grave[1], mausoleum, ossuary, sepulcher, tomb, vault[1]. *See* KEEP, PLACE.

sequel *noun*
Something brought about by a cause : aftermath, consequence, corollary, effect, end product, event, fruit, harvest, issue, outcome, precipitate, ramification, result, resultant, sequence, sequent, upshot. *See* CAUSE.

sequence *noun*
1. Something brought about by a cause : aftermath, consequence, corollary, effect, end product, event, fruit, harvest, issue, outcome, precipitate, ramification, result, resultant, sequel, sequent, upshot. *See* CAUSE. **2.** A way in which things follow each other in space or time :

consecution, order, procession, succession. *See* ORDER, PRECEDE. **3.** A way or condition of being arranged : arrangement, categorization, classification, deployment, disposal, disposition, distribution, formation, grouping, layout, lineup, order, organization, placement. *See* ORDER. **4.** A number of things placed or occurring one after the other : chain, consecution, course, order, procession, progression, round, run, series, string, succession, suite, train. *Informal:* streak. *See* ORDER.

sequent *adjective*
Following one after another in an orderly pattern : consecutive, sequential, serial, subsequent, successional, successive. *See* PRECEDE, TIME.
sequent *noun* Something brought about by a cause : aftermath, consequence, corollary, effect, end product, event, fruit, harvest, issue, outcome, precipitate, ramification, result, resultant, sequel, sequence, upshot. *See* CAUSE.

sequential *adjective*
Following one after another in an orderly pattern : consecutive, sequent, serial, subsequent, successional, successive. *See* PRECEDE, TIME.

sequester *verb*
1. To put into solitude : cloister, seclude, sequestrate. *See* INCLUDE. **2.** To set apart from a group : close off, cut off, insulate, isolate, seclude, segregate, separate. *See* INCLUDE.

sequestrate *verb*
To put into solitude : cloister, seclude, sequester. *See* INCLUDE.

sequestration *noun*
1. The act or process of isolating : insulation, isolation, segregation, separation. *See* INCLUDE. **2.** The act of secluding or the state of being secluded : reclusion, retirement, seclusion. *See* INCLUDE.

sequin *noun*
A small sparkling decoration : glitter, spangle. *See* BEAUTIFUL.

sere *adjective*
Having little or no liquid or moisture : anhydrous, arid, bone-dry, dry, moistureless, waterless. *See* DRY.

serene *adjective*
1. Not excited or emotionally agitated : calm, peaceful, placid, tranquil. *See* CALM.
2. Motionless and undisturbed : calm, halcyon, peaceful, placid, quiet, still, stilly, tranquil, untroubled. *See* CALM.

serenity *noun*
1. Lack of emotional agitation : calm, calmness, peace, peacefulness, placidity, placidness, quietude, tranquillity. *See* CALM. **2.** An absence of motion or disturbance : calm, calmness, hush, lull, peace, peacefulness, placidity, placidness, quiet, quietness, stillness, tranquillity, untroubledness. *See* CALM.

serfdom *noun*
A state of subjugation to an owner or master : bondage, enslavement, helotry, servileness, servility, servitude, slavery, thrall, thralldom, villeinage, yoke. *See* OVER.

serial *adjective*
Following one after another in an orderly pattern : consecutive, sequent, sequential, subsequent, successional, successive. *See* PRECEDE, TIME.

series *noun*
A number of things placed or occurring one after the other : chain, consecution, course, order, procession, progression, round, run, sequence, string, succession, suite, train. *Informal:* streak. *See* ORDER.

serious *adjective*
1. Full of or marked by dignity and seriousness : earnest[1], grave[2], sedate, sober, solemn, somber, staid. *See* ATTITUDE, HEAVY.
2. Marked by sober sincerity : businesslike, earnest[1], no-nonsense, sobersided. ***Idiom:*** in earnest. *See* HEAVY, WORK. **3.** Having great consequence or weight : earnest[1], grave[2], heavy, momentous, severe, weighty. *See* IMPORTANT. **4.** Causing or marked by danger or pain, for example : dangerous, grave[2], grievous, severe. *See* HELP. **5.** Not easy to do, achieve, or master : arduous, difficult, hard, laborious, tall, tough, uphill. *See* EASY.

seriousness *noun*
1. Sober sincerity : earnestness, sobersidedness. *See* HEAVY, WORK. **2.** The condition of being grave and of involving serious consequences : graveness, gravity, momentousness, weightiness. *See* IMPORTANT.

sermonize *verb*
1. To deliver a sermon, especially as a vocation : evangelize, preach. *See* RELIGION. **2.** To indulge in moral reflection, usually pompously : moralize, preach. *See* TEACH.

serpentine *adjective*
Repeatedly curving in alternate directions : anfractuous, flexuous, meandrous, sinuous, snaky, tortuous, winding. *See* REPETITION, STRAIGHT.

serve *verb*
1. To work and care for : attend, do for, minister to, wait on (*or* upon). *See* CARE FOR. **2.** To place food before (someone) : wait on (*or*

upon). *See* INGESTION. **3.** To spend or complete (time), as a prison term : put in. *Informal:* do. *See* TIME. **4.** To perform the duties of another : act, function, officiate. *See* DO, SUBSTITUTE. **5.** To meet a need or requirement : answer, do, suffice, suit. *See* EXCESS, HELP. **6.** To be an advantage to : advantage, avail, benefit, profit. *Archaic:* boot[2]. ***Idiom:*** stand someone in good stead. *See* HELP.

service *noun*
1. The condition of being put to use : application, duty, employment, use, utilization. *See* USED. **2.** A formal act or set of acts prescribed by ritual : ceremonial, ceremony, liturgy, observance, office, rite, ritual. *See* RITUAL. **3.** A kindly act : favor, good turn, grace, indulgence, kindness. *Archaic:* benefit. *See* HELP.

serviceable *adjective*
1. In a condition to be used : employable, usable, utilizable. *See* USED. **2.** Serving or capable of serving a useful purpose : functional, handy, practicable, practical, useful, utilitarian. *See* USED.

servile *adjective*
Excessively eager to serve or obey : menial, obsequious, slavish, subservient. *See* OVER.

servileness *noun*
A state of subjugation to an owner or master : bondage, enslavement, helotry, serfdom, servility, servitude, slavery, thrall, thralldom, villeinage, yoke. *See* OVER.

servility *noun*
A state of subjugation to an owner or master : bondage, enslavement, helotry, serfdom, servileness, servitude, slavery, thrall, thralldom, villeinage, yoke. *See* OVER.

serving *noun*
An individual quantity of food : helping, mess, portion. *See* INGESTION.

servitude *noun*
A state of subjugation to an owner or master : bondage, enslavement, helotry, serfdom, servileness, servility, slavery, thrall, thralldom, villeinage, yoke. *See* OVER.

sesquipedal *adjective*
Having many syllables : long[1], polysyllabic, sesquipedalian. *See* LONG.

sesquipedalian *adjective*
Having many syllables : long[1], polysyllabic, sesquipedal. *See* LONG.

set[1] *verb*
1. To deposit in a specified place : lay[1], place, put, stick. *See* PLACE, RISE. **2.** To put in or assign to a certain position or location : emplace, install, locate, place, position, site, situate, spot. *See* PLACE. **3.** To alter for proper functioning : adjust, fix, regulate, tune (up). *Music:* attune. *See* CHANGE, HELP. **4.** To arrange tableware upon (a table) in preparation for a meal : lay[1], spread. *See* ORDER. **5.** To place (a story, for example) in a designated setting : lay[1]. *See* PLACE. **6.** To bring about or come to an agreement concerning : arrange, conclude, fix, negotiate, settle. *See* AGREE. **7.** To appoint and send to a particular place : assign, post[2], station. *See* PLACE. **8.** To calculate approximately : approximate, estimate, place, put, reckon. *See* PRECISE. **9.** To move (a weapon or blow, for example) in the direction of someone or something : aim, cast, direct, head, level, point, train, turn, zero in. *Military:* lay[1]. *See* SEEK. **10.** To change or be changed from a liquid into a soft, semisolid, or solid mass : clot, coagulate, congeal, curdle, gelatinize, jell, jelly. *See* SOLID. **11.** To make or become physically hard : cake, concrete, congeal, dry, harden, indurate, petrify, solidify. *See* SOLID.

set about *verb* To go about the initial step in doing (something) : approach, begin, commence, embark, enter, get off, inaugurate, initiate, institute, launch, lead off, open, set out, set to, start, take on, take up, undertake. *Informal:* kick off. ***Idioms:*** get cracking, get going, get the show on the road. *See* START.

set apart *verb* To make noticeable or different : characterize, differentiate, discriminate, distinguish, individualize, mark, signalize, singularize. *See* SAME.

set aside *verb* To put an end to, especially formally and with authority : abolish, abrogate, annihilate, annul, cancel, invalidate, negate, nullify, vitiate, void. *Law:* extinguish. *See* CONTINUE.

set back *verb* To cause to be later or slower than expected or desired : delay, detain, hang up, hold up, lag, retard, slow (down *or* up), stall[2]. *See* HELP, TIME.

set by *verb* To reserve for the future : keep, lay aside, lay away, lay by, lay in, lay up, put by, salt away, save (up). *See* KEEP, SAVE.

set down *verb* **1.** To register in or as if in a book : book, catalog, enroll, inscribe, list[1], write down. *See* REMEMBER. **2.** To come to rest on the ground : alight[1], land, light[2], settle, touch down. *See* MOVE.

set forth *verb* To state, as an idea, for consideration : advance, offer, pose, propose, propound, put forward, submit, suggest. *See* OFFER.

set off *verb* **1.** To be the cause of : bring, bring about, bring on, cause, effect, effectuate, generate, induce, ingenerate, lead to, make, occasion, result in, secure, stir¹ (up), touch off, trigger. ***Idioms:*** bring to pass (*or* effect), give rise to. *See* START. **2.** To stir to action or feeling : egg on, excite, foment, galvanize, goad, impel, incite, inflame, inspire, instigate, motivate, move, pique, prick, prod, prompt, propel, provoke, spur, stimulate, touch off, trigger, work up. *See* CAUSE, EXCITE. **3.** To endow with beauty and elegance by way of a notable addition : adorn, beautify, embellish, enhance, grace. *See* BEAUTIFUL. **4.** To act as an equalizing weight or force to : balance, compensate, counteract, counterbalance, counterpoise, countervail, make up, offset. *See* ORDER. **5.** To make up for : balance, compensate, counterbalance, counterpoise, countervail, neutralize, offset, outweigh, redeem. *See* SUBSTITUTE.

set out *verb* **1.** To go about the initial step in doing (something) : approach, begin, commence, embark, enter, get off, inaugurate, initiate, institute, launch, lead off, open, set about, set to, start, take on, take up, undertake. *Informal:* kick off. ***Idioms:*** get cracking, get going, get the show on the road. *See* START. **2.** To work out and arrange the parts or details of : blueprint, design, lay out, map (out), plan. *See* PLANNED. **3.** To proceed in a specified direction : bear, go, head, make, strike out. *See* APPROACH.

set to *verb* To go about the initial step in doing (something) : approach, begin, commence, embark, enter, get off, inaugurate, initiate, institute, launch, lead off, open, set about, set out, start, take on, take up, undertake. *Informal:* kick off. ***Idioms:*** get cracking, get going, get the show on the road. *See* START.

set up *verb* **1.** To raise upright : erect, pitch, put up, raise, rear², upraise, uprear. *See* HORIZONTAL, RISE. **2.** To bring into existence formally : constitute, create, establish, found, institute, organize, originate, start. *See* START. **3.** *Informal.* To pay for the food, drink, or entertainment of (another) : treat. *Informal:* stand. *Slang:* blow¹. ***Idiom:*** stand treat. *See* PAY.

set *adjective* **1.** Firmly established by long standing : confirmed, deep-rooted, deep-seated, entrenched, hard-shell, ineradicable, ingrained, inveterate, irradicable, settled. *See* CONTINUE. **2.** In a definite and final form; not likely to change : certain, firm¹, fixed, flat. *See* CHANGE. **3.** Fixed and distinct from others : express, particular, special, specific. *See* SPECIFIC. **4.** On an unwavering course of action : bent, decided, determined, fixed, intent, resolute. *See* DECIDE. **5.** In a state of preparedness : ready. *Informal:* go. *Slang:* together. ***Idioms:*** all set, in working order. *See* PREPARED.

set² *noun*

1. A number of individuals making up or considered a unit : array, band², batch, bevy, body, bunch, bundle, clump, cluster, clutch², collection, group, knot, lot, party. *See* GROUP. **2.** A subdivision of a larger group : category, class, classification, order. *See* GROUP. **3.** A group of people sharing an interest, activity, or achievement : circle, crowd, group. *See* GROUP. **4.** A particular social group : circle, clique, coterie, crowd. *Informal:* bunch, gang. *See* GROUP. **5.** The properties, backdrops, and other objects arranged for a dramatic presentation : mise en scène, scene, scenery, setting. *See* PERFORMING ARTS.

set about *verb* See **set¹**.

set apart *verb* See **set¹**.

set aside *verb* See **set¹**.

setback *noun*

A change from better to worse : backset, reversal, reverse. *See* BETTER.

set back *verb* See **set¹**.

set by *verb* See **set¹**.

set down *verb* See **set¹**.

set forth *verb* See **set¹**.

setoff *noun*

Something to make up for loss or damage : amends, compensation, indemnification, indemnity, offset, quittance, recompense, redress, reimbursement, remuneration, reparation, repayment, requital, restitution, satisfaction. *See* SUBSTITUTE.

set off *verb* See **set¹**.

set out *verb* See **set¹**.

setting *noun*

1. The place where an action or event occurs : locale, scene, site, stage. *See* PLACE. **2.** The properties, backdrops, and other objects arranged for a dramatic presentation : mise en scène, scene, scenery, set². *See* PERFORMING ARTS.

settle *verb*

1. To put into correct or conclusive form : arrange, conclude, dispose of, fix. *See* DO. **2.** To place securely in a position or condition : ensconce, establish, fix, install, seat. *See* PUT

IN. **3.** To make or become calm : allay, balm, becalm, calm (down), lull, quiet, still, tranquilize. *See* CALM. **4.** To fall or drift down to the bottom : gravitate, sink. *See* RISE. **5.** To come to rest on the ground : alight[1], land, light[2], set down, touch down. *See* MOVE. **6.** To set right by giving what is due : clear, discharge, liquidate, pay (off *or* up), satisfy, square. *See* PAY. **7.** To bring (something) into a state of agreement or accord : reconcile, rectify, resolve, smooth over, straighten out. *See* AGREE. **8.** To bring about or come to an agreement concerning : arrange, conclude, fix, negotiate, set[1]. *See* AGREE. **9.** To make up or cause to make up one's mind : conclude, decide, determine, resolve. *See* DECIDE.

settled *adjective*
Firmly established by long standing : confirmed, deep-rooted, deep-seated, entrenched, hard-shell, ineradicable, ingrained, inveterate, irradicable, set[1]. *See* CONTINUE.

settlement *noun*
A settlement of differences through mutual concession : accommodation, arrangement, compromise, give-and-take, medium. *Law:* composition. *See* AGREE.

set to *verb* See **set[1]**.

set up *verb* See **set[1]**.

seventh heaven *noun*
A state of elated bliss : ecstasy, heaven, paradise, rapture, transport. *Informal:* cloud nine. *See* HAPPY.

sever *verb*
To separate into parts with or as if with a sharp-edged instrument : carve, cleave[1], cut, dissever, slice, slit, split. *See* ASSEMBLE.

several *adjective*
1. Consisting of a number more than two or three but less than many : divers, some, sundry, various. *See* BIG. **2.** Distinguished from others by nature or qualities : discrete, distinct, separate, various. *See* SAME.

severance *noun*
The act or an instance of separating one thing from another : detachment, disjunction, disjuncture, disseverance, disseverment, disunion, division, divorce, divorcement, parting, partition, separation, split. *See* ASSEMBLE, PART.

severe *adjective*
1. Rigorous and unsparing in treating others : demanding, exacting, hard, harsh, rigid, stern, strict, tough, unyielding. *See* EASY. **2.** Cold and forbidding : austere, bleak, dour, grim, hard, harsh, stark. *See* ATTITUDE, HOT. **3.** Causing sharp, often prolonged discomfort : bitter, brutal, hard, harsh, rough. *See* COMFORT. **4.** Conveying great physical force : hard, heavy, hefty, powerful. *See* BIG. **5.** Having great consequence or weight : earnest[1], grave[2], heavy, momentous, serious, weighty. *See* IMPORTANT. **6.** Causing or marked by danger or pain, for example : dangerous, grave[2], grievous, serious. *See* HELP. **7.** Requiring great or extreme bodily, mental, or spiritual strength : arduous, backbreaking, burdensome, demanding, difficult, effortful, exacting, exigent, formidable, hard, heavy, laborious, onerous, oppressive, rigorous, rough, taxing, tough, trying, weighty. *See* HEAVY.

severity *noun*
1. The fact or condition of being rigorous and unsparing : austerity, hardness, harshness, rigidity, rigor, rigorousness, sternness, strictness, stringency, toughness. *See* EASY. **2.** Exceptionally great concentration, power, or force, especially in activity : depth (often used in plural), ferociousness, ferocity, fierceness, fury, intensity, pitch, vehemence, vehemency, violence. *See* BIG, STRONG.

sexiness *noun*
The quality or condition of being sensual : sensuality, sexuality, suggestiveness, voluptuousness. *See* SEX.

sexual *adjective*
1. Of, concerning, or promoting sexual love or desire : amatory, amorous, aphrodisiac, erotic, lascivious, salacious, sexy. *See* SEX. **2.** Suggesting sexuality : sensual, sexy, suggestive, voluptuous. *See* SEX. **3.** Employed in reproduction : reproductive. *See* REPRODUCTION.

sexuality *noun*
The quality or condition of being sensual : sensuality, sexiness, suggestiveness, voluptuousness. *See* SEX.

sexy *adjective*
1. Arousing erotic desire : desirable. *See* DESIRE, SEX. **2.** Suggesting sexuality : sensual, sexual, suggestive, voluptuous. *See* SEX. **3.** Of, concerning, or promoting sexual love or desire : amatory, amorous, aphrodisiac, erotic, lascivious, salacious, sexual. *See* SEX. **4.** Feeling or devoted to sexual love or desire : amative, amorous, concupiscent, erotic, lascivious, lecherous, lewd, libidinous, lustful, lusty, passionate, prurient. *See* SEX.

shabby *adjective*
1. Showing signs of wear and tear or neglect : bedraggled, broken-down, decaying, decrepit, dilapidated, dingy, down-at-heel, faded, mangy,

rundown, scrubby, scruffy, seedy, shoddy, sleazy, tattered, tatty, threadbare. *Informal:* tacky². *Slang:* ratty. ***Idioms:*** all the worse for wear, gone to pot (*or* seed), past cure (*or* hope). *See* BETTER. **2.** So objectionable as to elicit despisal or deserve condemnation : abhorrent, abominable, antipathetic, contemptible, despicable, despisable, detestable, disgusting, filthy, foul, infamous, loathsome, lousy, low, mean², nasty, nefarious, obnoxious, odious, repugnant, rotten, vile, wretched. *See* GOOD. **3.** Of low or lower quality : common, inferior, low-grade, low-quality, mean², mediocre, second-class, second-rate, substandard. *See* BETTER.

shack *noun*
An ugly, squalid dwelling : hole, hovel, hut, shanty. *See* GOOD, RICH.

shackle *noun*
Something that physically confines the legs or arms : bond, chain (used in plural), fetter, handcuff (often used in plural), hobble, iron (used in plural), manacle, restraint. *Archaic:* gyve. *See* FREE.
shackle *verb* To restrict the activity or free movement of : chain, fetter, hamper, hamstring, handcuff, hobble, leash, manacle, tie, trammel. *Informal:* hog-tie. *See* FREE, HELP.

shade *noun*
1. Comparative darkness that results from the blocking of light rays : penumbra, shadow, umbra, umbrage. *See* LIGHT. **2.** The degree of vividness of a color, as when modified by the addition of black or white pigment : gradation, hue, tinge, tint. *See* COLORS. **3.** The property by which the sense of vision can distinguish between objects, as a red apple and a green apple, that are very similar or identical in form and size : color, hue, tint, tone. *See* COLORS. **4.** A slight variation between nearly identical entities : gradation, nuance. *See* BIG. **5.** A slight amount or indication : breath, dash, ghost, hair, hint, intimation, semblance, shadow, soupçon, streak, suggestion, suspicion, taste, tinge, touch, trace, whiff, whisper. *Informal:* whisker. *See* BIG, SHOW. **6.** A supernatural being, such as a ghost : apparition, bogey, bogeyman, bogle, eidolon, ghost, phantasm, phantasma, phantom, revenant, shadow, specter, spirit, visitant, wraith. *Informal:* spook. *Regional:* haunt. *See* BEINGS, SUPERNATURAL.
shade *verb* **1.** To shelter, especially from light : screen, shadow. *See* PROTECTION. **2.** To make dark or darker : adumbrate, darken, shadow. *See* LIGHT. **3.** To make a slight reduction in (a price) : shave, trim. *See* INCREASE.

shaded *adjective*
Full of shade : shadowy, shady. *See* LIGHT.

shadiness *noun*
Lack of straightforwardness and honesty in action : chicanery, craft, craftiness, deviousness, dishonesty, indirection, shiftiness, slyness, sneakiness, trickery, trickiness, underhandedness. *See* HONEST.

shadow *noun*
1. Comparative darkness that results from the blocking of light rays : penumbra, shade, umbra, umbrage. *See* LIGHT. **2.** A supernatural being, such as a ghost : apparition, bogey, bogeyman, bogle, eidolon, ghost, phantasm, phantasma, phantom, revenant, shade, specter, spirit, visitant, wraith. *Informal:* spook. *Regional:* haunt. *See* BEINGS, SUPERNATURAL. **3.** An agent assigned to observe and report on another : watcher. *Informal:* tail. *See* INVESTIGATE. **4.** A slight amount or indication : breath, dash, ghost, hair, hint, intimation, semblance, shade, soupçon, streak, suggestion, suspicion, taste, tinge, touch, trace, whiff, whisper. *Informal:* whisker. *See* BIG, SHOW.
shadow *verb* **1.** To shelter, especially from light : screen, shade. *See* PROTECTION. **2.** To make dim or indistinct : becloud, bedim, befog, blear, blur, cloud, dim, dull, eclipse, fog, gloom, mist, obfuscate, obscure, overcast, overshadow. *See* CLEAR. **3.** To make dark or darker : adumbrate, darken, shade. *See* LIGHT. **4.** To keep (another) under surveillance by moving along behind : dog, follow, track, trail. *Informal:* bird-dog, tail. *See* PRECEDE.

shadowy *adjective*
1. Full of shade : shaded, shady. *See* LIGHT. **2.** Not clearly perceived or perceptible : blear, bleary, cloudy, dim, faint, foggy, fuzzy, hazy, indefinite, indistinct, misty, obscure, unclear, undistinct, vague. *See* CLEAR.

shady *adjective*
1. Full of shade : shaded, shadowy. *See* LIGHT. **2.** Casting shade : umbrageous. *See* LIGHT. **3.** Of dubious character : doubtful, equivocal, questionable, suspect, suspicious, uncertain. *Informal:* fishy. *See* HONEST.

shaft *noun*
1. A series of particles or waves traveling close together in parallel paths : beam, ray. *See* LIGHT. **2.** A relatively long, straight, rigid piece of metal or other solid material : bar, bloom², rod, slab, stick. *See* THING.

shake *verb*
1. To cause to move to and fro with short, jerky movements : jiggle, joggle. *See* REPETITION. **2.** To move to and fro in short, jerky movements : quake, quaver, quiver, shiver[1], shudder, tremble, twitter, vibrate. *See* REPETITION. **3.** To cause to move to and fro violently : agitate, churn, convulse, rock. *See* CALM, REPETITION. **4.** To move to and fro violently : quake, rock, tremble, vibrate. *See* REPETITION. **5.** To alter the settled state or position of : dislocate, displace, disturb, move, shift. *See* MOVE. **6.** *Slang.* To free from or cast out something objectionable or undesirable : clear, disburden, disembarrass, disencumber, release, relieve, rid, shake off, throw off, unburden. *See* KEEP. **7.** *Slang.* To get away from (a pursuer) : elude, evade, lose, shake off, slip, throw off. ***Idiom:*** give someone the shake (*or* slip). *See* SEEK. **8.** To impair or destroy the composure of. Also used with *up* : agitate, bother, discompose, disquiet, distract, disturb, flurry, fluster, perturb, rock, ruffle, toss, unsettle, upset. *Informal:* rattle. *See* CALM. **9.** To deprive of courage or the power to act as a result of fear, anxiety, or disgust : appall, consternate, daunt, dismay, horrify, shock[1]. *See* FEAR.

shake down *verb* **1.** *Slang.* To obtain by coercion or intimidation : exact, extort, squeeze, wrench, wrest, wring. *See* GET. **2.** *Slang.* To make a thorough search of : comb, forage, ransack, rummage, scour[2]. ***Idioms:*** beat the bushes, leave no stone unturned, look (*or* search) high and low, look (*or* search) up and down, turn inside out, turn upside down. *See* INVESTIGATE. **3.** *Slang.* To examine the person or personal effects of in order to find something lost or concealed : frisk, inspect, search. *See* INVESTIGATE.

shake off *verb* **1.** To free from or cast out something objectionable or undesirable : clear, disburden, disembarrass, disencumber, release, relieve, rid, throw off, unburden. *Slang:* shake. *See* KEEP. **2.** To get away from (a pursuer) : elude, evade, lose, slip, throw off. *Slang:* shake. ***Idiom:*** give someone the shake (*or* slip). *See* SEEK.

shake *noun* **1.** A nervous shaking of the body : quake, quiver, shiver[1], shudder, thrill, tic, tremor, twitch. *See* REPETITION. **2.** *Informal.* A shaking of the earth : earthquake, quake, seism, temblor, tremblor, tremor. *See* MOVE, REPETITION. **3.** *Informal.* A state of nervous restlessness or agitation. Used in plural : fidget (often used in plural), jitter (used in plural), jump (used in plural), shiver[1] (used in plural), tremble (often used in plural). *Informal:* all-overs. *Slang:* heebie-jeebies, jim-jams, willies. *See* CALM, FEAR.

shakedown *noun*
Slang. A thorough search of a place or persons : frisk, search. *See* INVESTIGATE.

shake down *verb* See **shake.**

shake off *verb* See **shake.**

shakeup *noun*
A thorough or drastic reorganization : overhaul. *Informal:* housecleaning. *See* CHANGE.

shakiness *noun*
1. The quality or condition of being physically unsteady : instability, precariousness, ricketiness, unstableness, unsteadiness, wobbliness. *See* FLEXIBLE. **2.** The quality or condition of being erratic and undependable : insecureness, insecurity, instability, precariousness, unstableness, unsteadiness, unsureness. *See* CHANGE, STRONG.

shaky *adjective*
1. Marked by or affected with tremors : aquiver, quaky, quivery, shivery, tremulant, tremulous, twittery. *See* REPETITION. **2.** Not physically steady or firm : precarious, rickety, tottering, tottery, unstable, unsteady, wobbly. *See* FLEXIBLE. **3.** Lacking stability : infirm, insecure, precarious, tottering, tottery, unstable, unsteady, unsure, weak, wobbly. *See* CHANGE, STRONG. **4.** Not plausible or believable : flimsy, implausible, improbable, inconceivable, incredible, thin, unbelievable, unconceivable, unconvincing, unsubstantial, weak. *See* LIKELY.

shallow *adjective*
1. Measuring little from bottom to top or surface : shoal. *See* SURFACE. **2.** Lacking in intellectual depth or thoroughness : cursory, one-dimensional, sketchy, skin-deep, superficial, uncritical. *See* SURFACE.

shallow *noun* A shallow part of a body of water. Often used in plural : shoal. *See* SURFACE.

sham *noun*
1. A fraudulent imitation : counterfeit, fake, forgery, phony. *See* TRUE. **2.** A false, derisive, or impudent imitation of something : burlesque, caricature, farce, mock, mockery, parody, travesty. *See* RESPECT, SAME. **3.** A display of insincere behavior : act, acting, disguise, dissemblance, masquerade, pretense, show, simulation. *See* HONEST, TRUE.

sham *adjective* Fraudulently or deceptively imitative : bogus, counterfeit, fake, false, fraudulent, phony, spurious, suppositious, supposititious. *See* TRUE.

sham *verb* **1.** To behave affectedly or insincerely or take on a false or misleading appearance of : act, counterfeit, dissemble, fake, feign, play-act, pose, pretend, put on, simulate. *See* HONEST, TRUE. **2.** To take on or give a false appearance of : affect[2], assume, counterfeit, fake, feign, pretend, put on, simulate. ***Idiom:*** make believe. *See* TRUE.

shamble *verb*
To drag (the feet) along the floor or ground while walking : scuff, scuffle, shuffle. *See* MOVE.

shambles *noun*
A ruinous state of disorder : botch, foul-up, mess, muddle. *Informal:* hash. *Slang:* screwup, snafu. *See* CORRECT, ORDER.

shame *noun*
1. Loss of or damage to one's reputation : bad name, bad odor, discredit, disgrace, dishonor, disrepute, humiliation, ignominy, ill repute, obloquy, odium, opprobrium. *See* RESPECT.
2. A great disappointment or regrettable fact : crime, pity. *Slang:* bummer. ***Idiom:*** a crying shame. *See* GOOD.

shame *verb* **1.** To cause to feel embarrassment, dishonor, and often guilt : reproach. ***Idioms:*** put to shame, put to the blush. *See* RESPECT.
2. To damage in reputation : discredit, disgrace, dishonor. ***Idiom:*** be a reproach to. *See* RESPECT.

shameful *adjective*
1. Meriting or causing shame or dishonor : discreditable, disgraceful, dishonorable, disreputable, ignominious, opprobrious. *See* RESPECT.
2. Worthy of severe disapproval : condemnable, deplorable, disgraceful, unfortunate. *See* GOOD.

shamefulness *noun*
The condition of being infamous : disgracefulness, dishonorableness, disreputability, disreputableness, ignominiousness, infamy. *See* GOOD, RESPECT, RIGHT.

shameless *adjective*
Characterized by or done without shame : bald-faced, barefaced, blatant, brazen, brazen-faced, unabashed, unblushing. *Informal:* brassy. *See* COURTESY, RESPECT, RIGHT.

shanty *noun*
An ugly, squalid dwelling : hole, hovel, hut, shack. *See* GOOD, RICH.

shape *noun*
1. The external outline of a thing : cast, configuration, figure, form, pattern. *See* SURFACE.
2. A state of sound readiness : condition, fettle, fitness, form, kilter, order, trim. *See* BETTER.

shape *verb* **1.** To give form to by or as if by pressing and kneading : form, model, mold. *See* SURFACE. **2.** To create by forming, combining, or altering materials : assemble, build, construct, fabricate, fashion, forge[1], frame, make, manufacture, mold, produce, put together. *See* MAKE. **3.** To create by combining parts or elements : build, compose, configure, form, pattern, structure. *See* MAKE.

shapeless *adjective*
Having no distinct shape : amorphous, formless, inchoate, unformed, unshaped. *See* ORDER.

shapely *adjective*
Having a full, voluptuous figure : buxom, curvaceous, curvy, well-developed. *Informal:* built. *Slang:* stacked. *See* BEAUTIFUL.

shard *noun*
Residual matter : butt[4], end, fragment, ort (often used in plural), scrap[1], stub. *See* LEFTOVER.

share *noun*
1. That which is allotted : allocation, allotment, allowance, dole, lot, measure, part, portion, quantum, quota, ration, split. *Informal:* cut. *Slang:* divvy. *See* COLLECT. **2.** One's proper or expected function in a common effort : part, piece, role. *See* DO, PARTICIPATE.

share *verb* **1.** To give out in portions or shares : deal (out), dispense, distribute, divide, dole out, parcel out, portion (out), ration (out). *Slang:* divvy. *See* COLLECT. **2.** To have a share, as in an act or result; have a hand in : conduce, contribute, partake, participate. ***Idiom:*** take part. *See* PARTICIPATE, START.

sharing *noun*
The act or fact of participating : involvement, participation. *See* PARTICIPATE.

sharp *adjective*
1. Having a fine edge, as for cutting : keen[1]. *See* SHARP. **2.** Having an end that tapers to a point : acicular, aciculate, aciculated, acuminate, acute, cuspate, cuspated, cuspidate, cuspidated, mucronate, pointed, pointy. *See* SHARP. **3.** Clearly defined; not ambiguous : clear, distinct, unambiguous, unequivocal, unmistakable. *See* CLEAR. **4.** Mentally quick and original : alert, bright, clever, intelligent, keen[1], quick, quick-witted, sharp-witted, smart. ***Idiom:*** smart as a whip. *See* ABILITY.
5. Possessing or displaying perceptions of great

accuracy and sensitivity : acute, incisive, keen[1], penetrating, perceptive, probing, sensitive, trenchant. *See* CAREFUL, SHARP. **6.** Deceitfully clever : artful, crafty, cunning, foxy, guileful, scheming, sly, tricky, wily. *See* ABILITY, HONEST, MEANS. **7.** So sharp as to cause mental pain : acerbic, acid, acidic, acrid, astringent, biting, caustic, corrosive, cutting, mordacious, mordant, pungent, scathing, slashing, stinging, trenchant, truculent, vitriolic. *See* ATTACK, RESPECT. **8.** Marked by severity or intensity : acute, gnawing, knifelike, lancinating, piercing, shooting, stabbing. *See* BIG. **9.** Affecting the organs of taste or smell with a strong and often harsh sensation : piquant, pungent, spicy, zesty. *Archaic:* poignant. *See* SMELLS, TASTE. **10.** *Informal.* Being or in accordance with the current fashion : à la mode, chic, dashing, fashionable, mod, modish, posh, smart, stylish, swank, swanky, trig. *Informal:* classy, in, snappy, swish, tony, trendy. *Slang:* with-it. ***Idioms:*** all the rage, up to the minute. *See* STYLE, USUAL.

sharpen *verb*
To give a sharp edge to : acuminate, edge, hone[1], whet. *See* SHARP.

sharper *noun*
A person who cheats : bilk, cheat, cheater, cozener, defrauder, rook, swindler, trickster, victimizer. *Informal:* chiseler, crook, flimflammer. *Slang:* diddler, gyp, gypper. *See* HONEST.

sharpness *noun*
A cutting quality : bite, edge, incisiveness, keenness, sting. *See* SHARP.

sharp-witted *adjective*
Mentally quick and original : alert, bright, clever, intelligent, keen[1], quick, quick-witted, sharp, smart. ***Idiom:*** smart as a whip. *See* ABILITY.

shatter *verb*
1. To crack or split into two or more fragments by means of or as a result of force, a blow, or strain : break, fracture, rift, rive, shiver[2], smash, splinter, sunder. *See* HELP. **2.** To cause the complete ruin or wreckage of : bankrupt, break down, cross up, demolish, destroy, finish, ruin, sink, smash, spoil, torpedo, undo, wash up, wrack[2], wreck. *Slang:* total. ***Idiom:*** put the kibosh on. *See* HELP.

shave *verb*
1. To make light and momentary contact with, as in passing : brush[1], flick, graze, kiss, skim. *See* TOUCH. **2.** To make a slight reduction in (a price) : shade, trim. *See* INCREASE.

shawl *noun*
A garment wrapped about a person : cloak, stole, wrap. *See* PUT ON.

shear *verb*
To decrease, as in length or amount, by or as if by severing or excising : chop[1], clip[1], crop, cut, cut back, cut down, lop[1], lower[2], pare, prune, slash, trim, truncate. *See* INCREASE.

sheath *noun*
A thin outer covering of an object : lamina, membrane, sheathing, skin. *See* SURFACE.

sheathe *verb*
To furnish with a covering of a different material : clad, cover, face, side, skin. *See* SURFACE.

sheathing *noun*
A thin outer covering of an object : lamina, membrane, sheath, skin. *See* SURFACE.

shed *verb*
1. To send out heat, light, or energy : cast, emit, irradiate, project, radiate, throw. *See* MOVE. **2.** To cast off by a natural process : exuviate, molt, slough[2], throw off. *See* PUT ON.

sheen *noun*
A radiant brightness or glow, usually due to light reflected from a smooth surface : burnish, glaze, gloss, luster, polish, shine, sleekness. *See* LIGHT.

sheer[1] *verb*
To turn aside sharply from a straight course : chop[2], cut, skew, slue[1], swerve, veer. *Nautical:* yaw. *See* CHANGE.

sheer[2] *adjective*
1. So light and insubstantial as to resemble air or a thin film : aerial, aery, airy, diaphanous, ethereal, filmy, gauzy, gossamer, gossamery, transparent, vaporous, vapory. *See* THICK. **2.** Completely such, without qualification or exception : absolute, all-out, arrant, complete, consummate, crashing, damned, dead, downright, flat, out-and-out, outright, perfect, plain, pure, thorough, thoroughgoing, total, unbounded, unequivocal, unlimited, unmitigated, unqualified, unrelieved, unreserved, utter[2]. *Informal:* flat-out, positive. *Chiefly British:* blooming. *See* BIG, LIMITED. **3.** Free from extraneous elements : absolute, perfect, plain, pure, simple, unadulterated, undiluted, unmixed. *See* CLEAN. **4.** So sharply inclined as to be almost perpendicular : abrupt, bold, precipitous, steep[1]. *See* HORIZONTAL.

shellac *verb*
Slang. To render totally ineffective by decisive defeat : annihilate, crush, drub, overpower,

overwhelm, smash, steamroller, thrash, trounce, vanquish. *Informal:* massacre, wallop. *Slang:* clobber, cream, smear. *See* WIN.

shell out *verb*
Informal. To distribute (money) as payment : disburse, expend, give, lay out, outlay, pay (out), spend. *Informal:* fork out (*or* over *or* up). *See* SAVE.

shelter *noun*
1. Dwellings in general : housing, lodging. ***Idiom:*** a roof over one's head. *See* PROTECTION. **2.** Something that physically protects, especially from danger : asylum, cover, covert, harbor, haven, protection, refuge, retreat, sanctuary. *See* ATTACK, SAFETY. **3.** An institution that provides care and shelter : asylum, home, hospice, hospital. *See* PROTECTION. **4.** The state of being protected or safeguarded, as from danger or hardship : asylum, harborage, refuge, sanctuary. *See* SAFETY.
shelter *verb* To give refuge to : harbor, haven, house. *See* PROTECTION.

shelve *verb*
To put off until a later time : adjourn, defer[1], delay, hold off, hold up, postpone, remit, stay[1], suspend, table, waive. *Informal:* wait. ***Idiom:*** put on ice. *See* DO.

shenanigan *noun*
1. *Informal.* An indirect, usually cunning means of gaining an end : artifice, deception, device, dodge, feint, gimmick, imposture, jig, maneuver, ploy, ruse, sleight, stratagem, subterfuge, trick, wile. *Informal:* take-in. *See* HONEST, MEANS. **2.** *Informal.* A mischievous act : antic, caper, frolic, joke, lark, prank[1], trick. *Slang:* monkeyshine (often used in plural). *See* GOOD, WORK. **3.** *Informal.* Annoying yet harmless, usually playful acts. Often used in plural : devilry, deviltry, diablerie, high jinks, impishness, mischief, mischievousness, prankishness, rascality, roguery, roguishness, tomfoolery. *See* GOOD.

shepherd *noun*
Something or someone that shows the way : conductor, director, escort, guide, lead, leader, pilot, usher. *See* SHOW.
shepherd *verb* To show the way to : conduct, direct, escort, guide, lead, pilot, route, show, steer, usher. *See* SHOW.

shield *noun*
The act or a means of defending : defense, guard, preservation, protection, protector, safeguard, security, ward. *See* ATTACK.
shield *verb* To keep safe from danger, attack, or harm : defend, guard, preserve, protect, safeguard, secure, ward. *Archaic:* fend. *See* ATTACK.

shift *verb*
1. To give up in return for something else : change, commute, exchange, interchange, substitute, switch, trade. *Informal:* swap. *See* CHANGE, SUBSTITUTE. **2.** To leave or discard for another : change, switch. *See* CHANGE, SUBSTITUTE. **3.** To alter the settled state or position of : dislocate, displace, disturb, move, shake. *See* MOVE. **4.** To go or cause to go from one place to another : maneuver, move, remove, transfer. *See* MOVE. **5.** To change the direction or course of : avert, deflect, deviate, divert, pivot, swing, turn, veer. *See* CHANGE. **6.** To progress or perform adequately, especially in difficult circumstances : do, fare, fend, get along, get by, manage, muddle through. *Informal:* make out. ***Idioms:*** make do, make shift. *See* THRIVE.
shift *noun* **1.** The act of exchanging or substituting : change, commutation, exchange, interchange, substitution, switch, trade, transposition. *Informal:* swap. *See* CHANGE, SUBSTITUTE. **2.** A limited, often assigned period of activity, duty, or opportunity : bout, go, hitch, inning (often used in plural), spell[3], stint, stretch, time, tour, trick, turn, watch. *See* TIME. **3.** Something used temporarily or reluctantly when other means are not available : expediency, expedient, makeshift, stopgap. *See* HELP, SUBSTITUTE. **4.** An often sudden change or departure, as in a trend : tack, turn, twist. *See* CHANGE. **5.** A change in normal place or position : dislocation, displacement, disturbance, move, movement, rearrangement. *See* MOVE. **6.** The process or result of changing from one appearance, state, or phase to another : change, changeover, conversion, metamorphosis, mutation, transfiguration, transformation, translation, transmogrification, transmutation, transubstantiation. *See* CHANGE. **7.** The process or an instance of passing from one form, state, or stage to another : change, passage, transit, transition. *See* CHANGE.

shiftiness *noun*
1. The act or practice of deceiving : cunning, deceit, deceitfulness, deception, double-dealing, duplicity, guile. *See* HONEST. **2.** Lack of straightforwardness and honesty in action : chicanery, craft, craftiness, deviousness, dishonesty, indirection, shadiness, slyness, sneakiness, trickery, trickiness, underhandedness. *See* HONEST.

shiftless *adjective*
Resistant to exertion and activity : fainéant, idle, indolent, lazy, slothful, sluggard, sluggish. *Informal:* do-nothing. ***Idiom:*** bone lazy. *See* ACTION, INDUSTRIOUS.

shiftlessness *noun*
The quality or state of being lazy : idleness, indolence, laziness, sloth, slothfulness, sluggardness, sluggishness. *Informal:* do-nothingism. *See* INDUSTRIOUS.

shifty *adjective*
Marked by treachery or deceit : devious, disingenuous, duplicitous, guileful, indirect, lubricious, sneaky, underhand, underhanded. *See* HONEST.

shilly-shally *verb*
To be irresolute in acting or doing : dither, falter, halt[2], hesitate, pause, stagger, vacillate, waver, wobble. *See* DECIDE.

shilly-shally *adjective* Given to or exhibiting hesitation : halting, hesitant, indecisive, irresolute, pendulous, tentative, timid, vacillant, vacillatory. *See* DECIDE.

shilly-shally *noun* The act of hesitating or state of being hesitant : hesitancy, hesitation, indecision, indecisiveness, irresoluteness, irresolution, pause, tentativeness, timidity, timidness, to-and-fro, vacillation. *See* DECIDE.

shimmer *verb*
To emit light suddenly in rays or sparks : coruscate, flash, glance, gleam, glimmer, glint, glisten, glister, glitter, scintillate, spangle, sparkle, twinkle, wink. *See* LIGHT.

shimmer *noun* Sparkling, brilliant light : flash, glint, glisten, glister, glitter, scintillation, sparkle. *See* BEAUTIFUL, LIGHT.

shindig *noun*
A big, exuberant party : celebration, shindy. *Slang:* bash, blast, blowout. *See* GROUP, RESTRAINT, WORK.

shindy *noun*
A big, exuberant party : celebration, shindig. *Slang:* bash, blast, blowout. *See* GROUP, RESTRAINT, WORK.

shine *verb*
1. To emit a bright light : beam, blaze[1], burn, gleam, glow, incandesce, radiate. *See* LIGHT. **2.** To give a gleaming luster to, usually through friction : buff[1], burnish, furbish, glaze, gloss, polish, sleek. *See* LIGHT. **3.** To be in one's prime : flourish, flower. ***Idioms:*** cut a figure, make a splash. *See* THRIVE.

shine *noun* A radiant brightness or glow, usually due to light reflected from a smooth surface : burnish, glaze, gloss, luster, polish, sheen, sleekness. *See* LIGHT.

shiner *noun*
Slang. A bruise surrounding the eye : black eye. *Informal:* mouse. *See* HEALTH, HELP.

shining *adjective*
Having a high, radiant sheen : glassy, gleaming, glistening, glossy, lustrous, polished, shiny. *See* LIGHT.

shiny *adjective*
1. Giving off or reflecting light readily or in large amounts : beamy, bright, brilliant, effulgent, incandescent, irradiant, lambent, lucent, luminous, lustrous, radiant, refulgent. *See* LIGHT. **2.** Having a high, radiant sheen : glassy, gleaming, glistening, glossy, lustrous, polished, shining. *See* LIGHT.

ship *verb*
To cause (something) to be conveyed to a destination : address, consign, dispatch, forward, route, send, transmit. *See* MOVE.

shipshape *adjective*
In good order or clean condition : neat, orderly, snug, spick-and-span, spruce, taut, tidy, trig, trim, well-groomed. *Chiefly British:* tight. ***Idiom:*** neat as a pin. *See* CLEAN, ORDER.

shipwreck *verb*
To damage, disable, or destroy (a seacraft) : wreck. *See* HELP.

shirk *verb*
1. To avoid the fulfillment of : disregard, neglect, slack. ***Idiom:*** let slide. *See* DO. **2.** To pass time without working or in avoiding work : bum[1] (around), idle, laze, loaf, loiter, lounge. *Slang:* diddle[2], goldbrick, goof (off). *See* INDUSTRIOUS.

shiver[1] *verb*
To move to and fro in short, jerky movements : quake, quaver, quiver, shake, shudder, tremble, twitter, vibrate. *See* REPETITION.

shiver *noun* **1.** A nervous shaking of the body : quake, quiver, shake, shudder, thrill, tic, tremor, twitch. *See* REPETITION. **2.** A state of nervous restlessness or agitation. Used in plural : fidget (often used in plural), jitter (used in plural), jump (used in plural), tremble (often used in plural). *Informal:* all-overs, shake (used in plural). *Slang:* heebie-jeebies, jim-jams, willies. *See* CALM, FEAR.

shiver[2] *verb*
To crack or split into two or more fragments by means of or as a result of force, a blow, or strain : break, fracture, rift, rive, shatter, smash, splinter, sunder. *See* HELP.

shivery *adjective*
1. Marked by or affected with tremors : aquiver, quaky, quivery, shaky, tremulant, tremulous, twittery. *See* REPETITION.
2. Marked by a low temperature : chill, chilly, cold, cool, nippy. *See* HOT.

shoal *noun*
A shallow part of a body of water : shallow (often used in plural). *See* SURFACE.
shoal *adjective* Measuring little from bottom to top or surface : shallow. *See* SURFACE.

shock[1] *noun*
1. Violent forcible contact between two or more things : bump, collision, concussion, crash, impact, jar, jolt, percussion, smash. *See* CONFLICT. **2.** Something that jars the mind or emotions : blow[2], jolt. *Psychiatry:* trauma. *See* STRIKE.
shock *verb* **1.** To deprive of courage or the power to act as a result of fear, anxiety, or disgust : appall, consternate, daunt, dismay, horrify, shake. *See* FEAR. **2.** To affect with a strong feeling of moral aversion : scandalize. *See* RIGHT. **3.** To inflict physical or mental injury or distress on : traumatize, wound. *See* HELP. **4.** To cause to experience a sudden momentary shock : electrify, jolt, startle. *See* EXCITE, SURPRISE.

shock[2] *noun*
A group of things gathered haphazardly : agglomeration, bank[1], cumulus, drift, heap, hill, mass, mess, mound, mountain, pile, stack, tumble. *See* ORDER.

shocking *adjective*
1. Disgracefully and grossly offensive : atrocious, heinous, monstrous, outrageous, scandalous. *Archaic:* enormous. *See* RIGHT. **2.** Very bad : appalling, awful, dreadful, fearful, frightful, ghastly, horrendous, horrible, terrible. *See* GOOD. **3.** Beyond all reason : obscene, outrageous, preposterous, ridiculous, unconscionable, unreasonable. ***Idioms:*** out of bounds, out of sight. *See* USUAL.

shoddy *adjective*
1. Of decidedly inferior quality : base[2], cheap, lousy, miserable, paltry, poor, rotten, sleazy, trashy. *Informal:* cheesy. *Slang:* crummy, schlocky. *See* GOOD. **2.** Showing signs of wear and tear or neglect : bedraggled, broken-down, decaying, decrepit, dilapidated, dingy, down-at-heel, faded, mangy, rundown, scrubby, scruffy, seedy, shabby, sleazy, tattered, tatty, threadbare. *Informal:* tacky[2]. *Slang:* ratty. ***Idioms:*** all the worse for wear, gone to pot (*or* seed), past cure (*or* hope). *See* BETTER.

shoo-in *noun*
Informal. A competitor regarded as the most likely winner : favorite. *See* WIN.

shoot *verb*
1. To wound or kill with a firearm : gun (down), pick off. *Slang:* plug. *See* HELP. **2.** To launch with great force : fire, hurtle, loose, project, propel. ***Idiom:*** let fly. *See* MOVE. **3.** To discharge a gun or firearm : fire. ***Idiom:*** take a shot at. *See* ACTION. **4.** To move swiftly : bolt, bucket, bustle, dart, dash, festinate, flash, fleet, flit, fly, haste, hasten, hurry, hustle, pelt[2], race, rocket, run, rush, sail, scoot, scour[2], speed, sprint, tear[1], trot, whirl, whisk, whiz, wing, zip, zoom. *Informal:* hotfoot, rip. *Slang:* barrel, highball. *Chiefly British:* nip[1]. ***Idioms:*** get a move on, get cracking, go like lightning, go like the wind, hotfoot it, make haste, make time, make tracks, run like the wind, shake a leg, step (*or* jump) on it. *See* MOVE. **5.** To pass quickly and lightly through the air : dart, float, fly, sail, skim. *See* MOVE. **6.** To send through the air with a motion of the hand or arm : cast, dart, dash, fling, heave, hurl, hurtle, launch, pitch, shy[2], sling, throw, toss. *Informal:* fire. *See* MOVE.
shoot down *verb Informal.* To cause to be no longer believed or valued : debunk, deflate, discredit, explode, puncture. ***Idioms:*** knock the bottom out of, shoot full of holes. *See* VALUE.
shoot up *verb Informal.* To rise abruptly and precipitously : rocket, sky, skyrocket, soar. *See* INCREASE.
shoot *noun* **1.** A young stemlike growth arising from a plant : bine, offshoot, runner, sprig, sprout, tendril. *See* KIN. **2.** A violent, excruciating seizure of pain : cramp[1], paroxysm, spasm, throe. *See* PAIN.

shoot down *verb* See **shoot.**

shooting *adjective*
Marked by severity or intensity : acute, gnawing, knifelike, lancinating, piercing, sharp, stabbing. *See* BIG.

shoot up *verb* See **shoot.**

shop *noun*
A retail establishment where merchandise is sold : boutique, emporium, outlet, store. *See* TRANSACTIONS.

shopworn *adjective*
Without freshness or appeal because of overuse : banal, bromidic, clichéd, commonplace, corny, hackneyed, musty, overused, overworked, platitudinal, platitudinous, stale, stereotyped, stereotypic, stereotypical, threadbare, timeworn, tired, trite, warmed-over, well-worn, worn-out. *See* EXCITE, USUAL.

shore *noun*
A means or device that keeps something erect, stable, or secure : brace, buttress, crutch, prop, stay[2], support, underpinning. *See* SUPPORT.

short *adjective*
1. Not long in time or duration : brief. *See* BIG, FAST. **2.** Accomplished in very little time : brief, expeditious, fast, flying, hasty, hurried, quick, rapid, speedy, swift. *See* FAST. **3.** Marked by or consisting of few words that are carefully chosen : brief, compendious, concise, laconic, lean[2], succinct, summary, terse. *See* BIG, STYLE, WORDS. **4.** Rudely unceremonious : abrupt, blunt, brief, brusque, crusty, curt, gruff, short-spoken. *See* ATTITUDE. **5.** Not enough to meet a demand or requirement : deficient, inadequate, insufficient, scarce, shy[1], under, wanting. *See* BIG, EXCESS.

short *adverb* **1.** Without any warning : abruptly, suddenly. ***Idiom:*** all of a sudden. *See* FAST. **2.** Without adequate preparation : aback, unawarely, unawares. ***Idiom:*** by surprise. *See* PREPARED.

shortage *noun*
The condition or fact of being deficient : defect, deficiency, deficit, inadequacy, insufficiency, lack, paucity, poverty, scantiness, scantness, scarceness, scarcity, shortcoming, shortfall, underage[1]. *See* EXCESS.

shortcoming *noun*
1. The condition or fact of being deficient : defect, deficiency, deficit, inadequacy, insufficiency, lack, paucity, poverty, scantiness, scantness, scarceness, scarcity, shortage, shortfall, underage[1]. *See* EXCESS. **2.** Something that mars the appearance or causes inadequacy or failure : blemish, bug, defect, fault, flaw, imperfection. *See* BEAUTIFUL, BETTER, HELP. **3.** An imperfection of character : failing, fault, foible, frailty, infirmity, weakness, weak point. *See* BETTER, HELP.

shorten *verb*
To make short or shorter the duration or extent of : abbreviate, abridge, condense, curtail, reduce. *See* INCREASE, LONG.

shortfall *noun*
The condition or fact of being deficient : defect, deficiency, deficit, inadequacy, insufficiency, lack, paucity, poverty, scantiness, scantness, scarceness, scarcity, shortage, shortcoming, underage[1]. *See* EXCESS.

short fuse *noun*
Slang. A tendency to become angry or irritable : irascibility, irascibleness, spleen, temper, temperament, tetchiness. *Informal:* dander. ***Idiom:*** low boiling point. *See* FEELINGS.

shorthanded *adjective*
Lacking the requisite workers or players : undermanned. *See* EXCESS.

short-lived *adjective*
Lasting or existing only for a short time : ephemeral, evanescent, fleet, fleeting, fugacious, fugitive, momentary, passing, temporal, temporary, transient, transitory. *See* CONTINUE, TIME.

short-range *adjective*
1. Intended, used, or present for a limited time : impermanent, interim, provisional, short-term, temporary. *See* CONTINUE. **2.** Designed or implemented so as to gain a temporary limited advantage : tactical. *See* NEAR.

short-spoken *adjective*
Rudely unceremonious : abrupt, blunt, brief, brusque, crusty, curt, gruff, short. *See* ATTITUDE.

short-term *adjective*
Intended, used, or present for a limited time : impermanent, interim, provisional, short-range, temporary. *See* CONTINUE.

shot *noun*
1. *Informal.* A trying to do or make something : attempt, crack, effort, endeavor, essay, go, offer, stab, trial, try. *Slang:* take. *Archaic:* assay. *See* TRY. **2.** *Informal.* A brief trial : crack, go, stab, try. *Informal:* fling, whack, whirl. *See* TRY. **3.** *Informal.* A favorable or advantageous combination of circumstances : break, chance, occasion, opening, opportunity. *See* LUCK. **4.** A small amount of liquor : dram, drop, jigger, sip, tot[1]. *Informal:* nip[2], slug[1]. *Slang:* snort. *See* BIG, INGESTION.

shoulder *verb*
To take upon oneself : assume, incur, tackle, take on, take over, undertake. *See* ACCEPT.

shout *noun*
A loud cry : call, halloo, holler, yell. *See* SOUNDS.

shout *verb* **1.** To speak or say very loudly or with a shout : bawl, bellow, bluster, call, clamor, cry, halloo, holler, roar, vociferate, whoop, yawp, yell. *See* SOUNDS. **2.** To proclaim in a blatantly startling way : blare, scream, shriek. *See* SHOW.

shove *verb*
1. To force to move or advance with or as if with blows or pressure : drive, propel, push, ram, thrust. *See* MOVE. **2.** To cause to stick out : poke, push, thrust. *See* CONVEX. **3.** To do or achieve by forcing obstacles out of one's

way : press, push, ram. *See* PUSH. **4.** To force one's way into a place or situation : push. *Informal:* muscle. *See* ENTER, PUSH.

shove off *verb Informal.* To move or proceed away from a place : depart, exit, get away, get off, go, go away, leave[1], pull out, quit, retire, run (along), withdraw. *Informal:* cut out, push off. *Slang:* blow[1], split, take off. ***Idioms:*** hit the road, take leave. *See* APPROACH.

shove *noun* An act or instance of using force so as to propel ahead : butt[1], push, thrust. *See* PUSH.

shovel *verb*

1. To break, turn over, or remove (earth or sand, for example) with or as if with a tool : delve, dig, excavate, grub, scoop, spade. *See* ENTER. **2.** To make by digging : dig, excavate, scoop. *See* MAKE.

shove off *verb* See **shove.**

show *verb*

1. To make visible; bring to view : bare, disclose, display, expose, reveal, unclothe, uncover, unmask, unveil. *Archaic:* discover. ***Idioms:*** bring to light, lay open, make plain. *See* SHOW. **2.** To come into view : appear, emerge, issue, loom, materialize. ***Idioms:*** make (*or* put in) an appearance, meet the eye. *See* SEE. **3.** To present a lifelike image of : delineate, depict, describe, express, image, limn, picture, portray, render, represent. *See* SHOW. **4.** To make a public and usually ostentatious show of. Also used with *off* : brandish, display, disport, exhibit, expose, flash, flaunt, parade, sport. *See* SHOW. **5.** To show the way to : conduct, direct, escort, guide, lead, pilot, route, shepherd, steer, usher. *See* SHOW. **6.** To make known or identify, as by signs : denote, designate, indicate, mark, point out, specify. *See* SHOW. **7.** To make manifest or apparent : demonstrate, display, evidence, evince, exhibit, manifest, proclaim, reveal. *See* SHOW. **8.** To give a precise indication of, as on a register or scale : indicate, mark, read, record, register. *See* SHOW. **9.** To be performed : play, run. *See* PERFORMING ARTS. **10.** To establish as true or genuine : authenticate, bear out, confirm, corroborate, demonstrate, endorse, establish, evidence, prove, substantiate, validate, verify. *See* SHOW, SUPPORT.

show up *verb* To come to a particular place : arrive, check in, get in, pull in, reach, turn up. *Slang:* blow in. ***Idiom:*** make (*or* put in) an appearance. *See* START.

show *noun* **1.** An act of showing or displaying : demonstration, display, exhibit, exhibition, manifestation. *See* SHOW. **2.** A deceptive outward appearance : cloak, color, coloring, cover, disguise, disguisement, façade, face, false colors, front, gloss, guise, mask, masquerade, pretense, pretext, semblance, veil, veneer, window-dressing. *Slang:* put-on. *See* SHOW. **3.** A display of insincere behavior : act, acting, disguise, dissemblance, masquerade, pretense, sham, simulation. *See* HONEST, TRUE. **4.** An impressive or ostentatious exhibition : array, display, panoply, parade, pomp, spectacle. *See* SHOW. **5.** A large public display, as of goods or works of art : exhibit, exhibition, exposition. *See* SHOW.

shower *noun*

A concentrated outpouring, as of missiles, words, or blows : barrage, bombardment, burst, cannonade, fusillade, hail[1], salvo, storm, volley. *See* ATTACK.

shower *verb* **1.** To direct a barrage at : barrage, bombard, cannonade, fusillade, pepper. *See* ATTACK. **2.** To give in great abundance : heap, lavish, rain. *See* BIG, GIVE.

show up *verb* See **show.**

showy *adjective*

Marked by outward, often extravagant display : flamboyant, ostentatious, pretentious, splashy, splurgy. *See* PLAIN.

shred *noun*

1. A tiny amount : bit[1], crumb, dab[1], dash, dot, dram, drop, fragment, grain, iota, jot, minim, mite, modicum, molecule, ort, ounce, particle, scrap[1], scruple, smidgen, speck, tittle, trifle, whit. *Chiefly British:* spot. *See* BIG.
2. The least bit : hoot, iota, jot, ounce, whit. *Informal:* damn, rap[2]. *Slang:* diddly. *See* BIG.

shrew *noun*

A person, traditionally a woman, who persistently nags or criticizes : fishwife, fury, harpy, scold, termagant, virago, vixen. *Informal:* battle-ax. *See* PRAISE.

shrewd *adjective*

Having or showing a clever awareness and resourcefulness in practical matters : astute, cagey, canny, knowing, perspicacious, slick, smart, wise[1]. *Informal:* savvy. *See* ABILITY, CAREFUL.

shrewdness *noun*

Skill in perceiving, discriminating, or judging : acumen, astuteness, clear-sightedness, discernment, discrimination, eye, keenness, nose, penetration, perceptiveness, percipience, percipiency, perspicacity, sagacity, sageness, wit. *See* ABILITY, CAREFUL.

shriek *noun*
A long, loud, piercing cry or sound : screak, scream, screech. *See* SOUNDS.
shriek *verb* **1.** To utter a long, loud, piercing cry, as of pain or fright : screak, scream, screech, shrill. *See* SOUNDS. **2.** To proclaim in a blatantly startling way : blare, scream, shout. *See* SHOW.

shrieky *adjective*
Elevated in pitch : high, high-pitched, piercing, piping, shrill, shrilly, treble. *Music:* acute. *See* HIGH, SOUNDS.

shrill *adjective*
Elevated in pitch : high, high-pitched, piercing, piping, shrieky, shrilly, treble. *Music:* acute. *See* HIGH, SOUNDS.
shrill *verb* To utter a long, loud, piercing cry, as of pain or fright : screak, scream, screech, shriek. *See* SOUNDS.

shrilly *adjective*
Elevated in pitch : high, high-pitched, piercing, piping, shrieky, shrill, treble. *Music:* acute. *See* HIGH, SOUNDS.

shrimp *noun*
Slang. A totally insignificant person : cipher, nebbish, nobody, nonentity, nothing. *Informal:* pip-squeak, zero. *Slang:* zilch. *See* IMPORTANT.

shrine *noun*
A sacred or holy place : sacrarium, sanctorium, sanctuary, sanctum. *See* SACRED.

shrink *verb*
1. To reduce in size, as by drawing together : compact[1], compress, constrict, constringe, contract. *See* INCREASE. **2.** To draw away involuntarily, usually out of fear or disgust : blench[1], cringe, flinch, quail, recoil, shy[1], start, wince. *See* APPROACH, SEEK.
shrink *noun* An act of drawing back in an involuntary or instinctive fashion : cringe, flinch, recoil, wince. *See* APPROACH, SEEK.

shrivel *verb*
To make or become no longer fresh or shapely because of loss of moisture : dry up, mummify, sear, wither, wizen. *See* DRY.

shroud *verb*
1. To cut off from sight : block (out), conceal, hide[1], obscure, obstruct, screen, shut off (*or* out). *See* SHOW. **2.** To surround and cover completely so as to obscure : cloak, clothe, enfold, enshroud, envelop, enwrap, infold, invest, veil, wrap. *See* SHOW. **3.** To prevent (something) from being known : cloak, conceal, cover (up), enshroud, hide[1], hush (up), mask, veil. ***Idioms:*** keep under cover, keep under wraps. *See* SHOW.

shrunken *adjective*
Physically haggard : cadaverous, drawn, emaciated, gaunt, skeletal, wasted. ***Idiom:*** skin and bones. *See* BETTER, TIRED.

shuck *verb*
Informal. To let go or get rid of as being useless or defective, for example. Also used with *off* : discard, dispose of, dump, junk, scrap[1], throw away, throw out. *Informal:* chuck, jettison. *Slang:* ditch. *See* KEEP.

shudder *verb*
To move to and fro in short, jerky movements : quake, quaver, quiver, shake, shiver[1], tremble, twitter, vibrate. *See* REPETITION.
shudder *noun* A nervous shaking of the body : quake, quiver, shake, shiver[1], thrill, tic, tremor, twitch. *See* REPETITION.

shuffle *verb*
1. To drag (the feet) along the floor or ground while walking : scuff, scuffle, shamble. *See* MOVE. **2.** To mix together so as to change the order of arrangement : jumble, scramble. *Games:* riffle. *See* CHANGE, ORDER. **3.** To proceed or perform in an unsteady, faltering manner : blunder, bumble[1], bungle, flounder, fudge, fumble, limp, muddle, stagger, stumble. *See* THRIVE. **4.** To use evasive or deliberately vague language : equivocate, euphemize, hedge, tergiversate, weasel. *Informal:* pussyfoot, waffle. ***Idioms:*** beat about (*or* around) the bush, mince words. *See* CLEAR. **5.** To stray from truthfulness or sincerity : equivocate, palter, prevaricate. *See* TRUE.
shuffle *noun* The use or an instance of equivocal language : ambiguity, equivocation, equivoque, euphemism, hedge, prevarication, tergiversation, weasel word. *Informal:* waffle. *See* CLEAR.

shun *verb*
1. To keep away from : avoid, burke, bypass, circumvent, dodge, duck, elude, escape, eschew, evade, get around. ***Idioms:*** fight shy of, give a wide berth to, have no truck with, keep (*or* stay *or* steer) clear of. *See* SEEK. **2.** To slight (someone) deliberately : cut, rebuff, snub, spurn. *Informal:* coldshoulder. ***Idioms:*** close (*or* shut) the door on, give someone the cold shoulder, give someone the go-by, turn one's back on. *See* ACCEPT, IGNORE.

shush *verb*
To cause to become silent : hush, quiet, quieten, shut up, silence, still. *See* SOUNDS.

shut *verb*
To move (a door, for example) in order to cover an opening : close. *See* OPEN.
shut in *verb* To confine within a limited area : cage, coop (in *or* up), enclose, fence (in), immure, mew (up), pen[2], shut up, wall (in *or* up). *See* FREE.
shut off (or **out)** *verb* To cut off from sight : block (out), conceal, hide[1], obscure, obstruct, screen, shroud. *See* SHOW.
shut out *verb* **1.** To exclude from normal social or professional activities : blackball, blacklist, boycott, ostracize. *See* ACCEPT. **2.** To keep from being admitted, included, or considered : bar, count out, debar, eliminate, except, exclude, keep out, rule out. *See* INCLUDE. **3.** To rid one's mind of : banish, cast out, dismiss, dispel. *See* KEEP.
shut up *verb* **1.** To confine within a limited area : cage, coop (in *or* up), enclose, fence (in), immure, mew (up), pen[2], shut in, wall (in *or* up). *See* FREE. **2.** To enclose so as to hinder or prohibit escape : closet, confine, imprison. *See* FREE. **3.** To cause to become silent : hush, quiet, quieten, shush, silence, still. *See* SOUNDS.

shuteye *noun*
Slang. The natural recurring condition of suspended consciousness by which the body rests : sleep, slumber. ***Idioms:*** land of Nod, the arms of Morpheus. *See* AWARENESS.

shut in *verb* See **shut.**
shut off or **out** *verb* See **shut.**
shut out *verb* See **shut.**
shut up *verb* See **shut.**

shy[1] *adjective*
1. Not forward but reticent or reserved in manner : backward, bashful, coy, demure, diffident, modest, retiring, self-effacing, timid. *See* RESTRAINT. **2.** Not enough to meet a demand or requirement : deficient, inadequate, insufficient, scarce, short, under, wanting. *See* BIG, EXCESS.
shy *verb* To draw away involuntarily, usually out of fear or disgust : blench[1], cringe, flinch, quail, recoil, shrink, start, wince. *See* APPROACH, SEEK.

shy[2] *verb*
To send through the air with a motion of the hand or arm : cast, dart, dash, fling, heave, hurl, hurtle, launch, pitch, shoot, sling, throw, toss. *Informal:* fire. *See* MOVE.
shy *noun* An act of throwing : cast, fling, heave, hurl, launch, pitch, sling, throw, toss. *See* MOVE.

shyness *noun*
An awkwardness or lack of self-confidence in the presence of others : backwardness, bashfulness, coyness, retiringness, timidity, timidness. *See* RESTRAINT.

sibilate *verb*
To make a sharp sibilant sound : fizz, fizzle, hiss, sizzle, swish, whiz, whoosh. *See* SOUNDS.

sibyl *noun*
A person who foretells future events by or as if by supernatural means : augur, auspex, diviner, foreteller, haruspex, prophesier, prophet, prophetess, seer, soothsayer, vaticinator. *See* FORESIGHT.

sibylline *adjective*
Of or relating to the foretelling of events by or as if by supernatural means : augural, divinitory, fatidic, fatidical, mantic, oracular, prophetic, vatic, vatical, vaticinal, visionary. *See* FORESIGHT.

sick *adjective*
1. Suffering from or affected with an illness : down, ill, unwell. *Informal:* laid up. *Chiefly Regional:* poorly. *See* HEALTH. **2.** Of or associated with sickness : anemic, peaked, sickly. *See* HEALTH. **3.** Susceptible to or marked by preoccupation with unwholesome matters : macabre, morbid, unhealthy, unwholesome. *See* GOOD. **4.** Out of patience with : disgusted, fed up, tired, weary. ***Idiom:*** sick and tired. *See* TIRED.

sicken *verb*
1. To become affected with a disease : catch, contract, develop, get, take. ***Idiom:*** come down with. *See* GET. **2.** To offend the senses or feelings of : disgust, nauseate, repel, revolt. ***Idiom:*** turn one's stomach. *See* LIKE.

sickening *adjective*
Extremely unpleasant to the senses or feelings : atrocious, disgusting, foul, horrid, nasty, nauseating, offensive, repellent, repulsive, revolting, ugly, unwholesome, vile. *See* LIKE, PAIN.

sickly *adjective*
1. Affected or tending to be affected with minor health problems : ailing, indisposed, low, mean[2], off-color, rocky. ***Idiom:*** under the weather. *See* HEALTH. **2.** Of or associated with sickness : anemic, peaked, sick. *See* HEALTH.

sickness *noun*
1. The condition of being sick : affliction, disorder, illness, indisposition, infirmity. *See* HEALTH. **2.** A pathological condition of mind or body : ailment, complaint, disease, disorder, ill, illness, infirmity, malady. *See* HEALTH.

side *noun*
1. One of two or more contrasted parts or places identified by its location with respect to a center : flank, hand. *See* PLACE. **2.** One of two or more opposing opinions, actions, or attitudes, as in a disagreement : part. *See* PERSPECTIVE. **3.** The particular angle from which something is considered : angle², aspect, facet, frame of reference, hand, light¹, phase, regard, respect. *See* PERSPECTIVE.
side *verb* To furnish with a covering of a different material : clad, cover, face, sheathe, skin. *See* SURFACE.
side with *verb* To aid the cause of by approving or favoring : advocate, back, champion, endorse, get behind, plump for, recommend, stand behind, stand by, support, uphold. *Idioms:* align oneself with, go to bat for, take the part of. *See* SUPPORT.

sidekick *noun*
Slang. A person whom one knows well, likes, and trusts : amigo, brother, chum, confidant, confidante, familiar, friend, intimate¹, mate. *Informal:* bud², buddy, pal. *See* LOVE.

sidesplitting *adjective*
Extremely funny : hilarious, priceless. *Informal:* killing, rich. *See* LAUGHTER.

sidestep *verb*
To avoid fulfilling or answering completely : dodge, duck, evade, hedge, skirt. *See* SEEK.

side with *verb* See **side.**

sidle *verb*
To advance carefully and gradually : ease, edge. *See* CAREFUL, MOVE.

siege *noun*
1. A prolonged surrounding of an objective by hostile troops : beleaguerment, besiegement, blockade, investment. *See* ATTACK. **2.** An often prolonged period, as of illness : bout. *See* TIME.
siege *verb* To surround with hostile troops : beleaguer, beset, besiege, blockade, invest. *Idiom:* lay siege to. *See* ATTACK.

siesta *noun*
A brief sleep : catnap, doze, nap, snooze. *See* AWARENESS.
siesta *verb* To sleep for a brief period : catnap, doze (off), nap, nod (off), snooze. *Idiom:* catch (*or* grab *or* take) forty winks. *See* AWARENESS.

sift *verb*
To set apart (one kind or type) from others : separate, sort, winnow. *See* INCLUDE.

sigh *verb*
To make a low, continuous, and indistinct sound : murmur, sough, whisper. *See* SOUNDS.
sigh *noun* A low, indistinct, and often continuous sound : mumble, murmur, sough, susurration, susurrus, whisper. *See* SOUNDS.

sight *noun*
1. An act of directing the eyes on an object : contemplation, look, regard, view. *See* SEE. **2.** The faculty of seeing : eye, eyesight, seeing, vision. *Archaic:* light¹. *See* SEE. **3.** That which is or can be seen : lookout, outlook, panorama, perspective, prospect, scene, view, vista. *See* SEE. **4.** *Informal.* An unsightly object : mess, monstrosity, ugliness. *Informal:* fright, ugly. *See* BEAUTIFUL. **5.** *Regional.* A great deal : abundance, mass, mountain, much, plenty, profusion, wealth, world. *Informal:* barrel, heap, lot, pack, peck², pile. *Regional:* power. *See* BIG.

sightless *adjective*
Without the sense of sight : blind, eyeless, unseeing. *See* SEE.

sightlessness *noun*
The condition of not being able to see : blindness. *See* SEE.

sightly *adjective*
Having qualities that delight the eye : attractive, beauteous, beautiful, comely, fair, good-looking, gorgeous, handsome, lovely, pretty, pulchritudinous, ravishing, stunning. *Scots:* bonny. *Idiom:* easy on the eyes. *See* BEAUTIFUL.

sightseer *noun*
One who travels for pleasure : excursionist, tourist. *Chiefly British:* tripper. *See* MOVE.

sign *noun*
1. Something visible or evident that gives grounds for believing in the existence or presence of something else : badge, evidence, index, indication, indicator, manifestation, mark, note, signification, stamp, symptom, token, witness. *See* SHOW. **2.** Something that takes the place of words in communicating a thought or feeling : expression, gesture, indication, token. *See* SHOW. **3.** An expressive, meaningful bodily movement : gesticulation, gesture, indication, motion, signal. *Informal:* high sign. *See* EXPRESS. **4.** A usually public posting that conveys a message : bill¹, billboard, notice, placard, poster. *See* SHOW. **5.** A conventional mark used in a writing system : character, symbol. *See* MARKS. **6.** A phenomenon that

serves as a sign or warning of some future good or evil : augury, forerunner, foretoken, omen, portent, prefigurement, presage, prognostic, prognostication. ***Idiom:*** writing (*or* handwriting) on the wall. *See* FORESIGHT, WARN.

sign *verb* **1.** To affix one's signature to : autograph, endorse, inscribe, subscribe, undersign. ***Idioms:*** put one's John Hancock on, set one's hand to. *See* LAW. **2.** To make bodily motions so as to convey an idea or complement speech : gesticulate, gesture, motion, signal, signalize. ***Idiom:*** give the high sign. *See* EXPRESS.

sign on *verb Informal.* To become a member of : enlist, enroll, enter, join, muster in, sign up. *See* PARTICIPATE.

sign over *verb* To change the ownership of (property) by means of a legal document : cede, deed, grant, make over. *Law:* alien, alienate, assign, convey, transfer. *See* GIVE, LAW.

sign up *verb* To become a member of : enlist, enroll, enter, join, muster in. *Informal:* sign on. *See* PARTICIPATE.

signal *noun*

An expressive, meaningful bodily movement : gesticulation, gesture, indication, motion, sign. *Informal:* high sign. *See* EXPRESS.

signal *adjective* Readily attracting notice : arresting, bold, conspicuous, eye-catching, marked, noticeable, observable, outstanding, pointed, prominent, pronounced, remarkable, salient, striking. ***Idiom:*** sticking out like a sore thumb. *See* SEE.

signal *verb* **1.** To communicate by means of such devices as lights or signs : flag[1], semaphore. *See* EXPRESS, WORDS. **2.** To make bodily motions so as to convey an idea or complement speech : gesticulate, gesture, motion, sign, signalize. ***Idiom:*** give the high sign. *See* EXPRESS.

signalize *verb*

1. To make noticeable or different : characterize, differentiate, discriminate, distinguish, individualize, mark, set apart, singularize. *See* SAME. **2.** To cause to be eminent or recognized : distinguish, elevate, ennoble, exalt, honor. *See* RESPECT. **3.** To make bodily motions so as to convey an idea or complement speech : gesticulate, gesture, motion, sign, signal. ***Idiom:*** give the high sign. *See* EXPRESS.

significance *noun*

1. The quality or state of being important : concern, concernment, consequence, import, importance, moment, significancy, weight, weightiness. *See* IMPORTANT. **2.** That which is signified by a word or expression : acceptation, connotation, denotation, import, intent, meaning, message, purport, sense, significancy, signification, value. *See* MEANING. **3.** The gist of a specific action or situation : idea, import, meaning, point, purport, significancy. *See* MEANING.

significancy *noun*

1. The quality or state of being important : concern, concernment, consequence, import, importance, moment, significance, weight, weightiness. *See* IMPORTANT. **2.** That which is signified by a word or expression : acceptation, connotation, denotation, import, intent, meaning, message, purport, sense, significance, signification, value. *See* MEANING. **3.** The gist of a specific action or situation : idea, import, meaning, point, purport, significance. *See* MEANING.

significant *adjective*

1. Effectively conveying meaning, feeling, or mood : eloquent, expressive, meaning, meaningful. *See* EXPRESS, SHOW. **2.** Conveying hidden or unexpressed meaning : meaningful, pregnant, suggestive. *See* MEANING. **3.** Having great significance : big, consequential, considerable, historic, important, large, material, meaningful, monumental, substantial. *See* IMPORTANT.

signification *noun*

1. That which is signified by a word or expression : acceptation, connotation, denotation, import, intent, meaning, message, purport, sense, significance, significancy, value. *See* MEANING. **2.** Something visible or evident that gives grounds for believing in the existence or presence of something else : badge, evidence, index, indication, indicator, manifestation, mark, note, sign, stamp, symptom, token, witness. *See* SHOW.

signify *verb*

1. To have or convey a particular idea : connote, denote, import, intend, mean[1], spell[1]. ***Idiom:*** add up to. *See* MEANING. **2.** To be of significance or importance : count, import, matter, weigh. *See* IMPORTANT.

sign on *verb* See **sign.**

sign over *verb* See **sign.**

sign up *verb* See **sign.**

silence *noun*

1. The avoidance of speech : dumbness, muteness, speechlessness, wordlessness. *See* WORDS. **2.** The absence of sound or noise : hush, noiselessness, quiet, quietness, soundlessness, still, stillness. *See* SOUNDS.

silence *verb* To cause to become silent : hush, quiet, quieten, shush, shut up, still. *See* SOUNDS.

silent *adjective*
1. Marked by, done with, or making no sound or noise : hushed, noiseless, quiet, soundless, still, stilly. *Archaic:* hush. *See* SOUNDS. **2.** Not speaking freely or openly : close, close-mouthed, incommunicable, incommunicative, reserved, reticent, taciturn, tightlipped, uncommunicable, uncommunicative. *See* RESTRAINT, SOUNDS. **3.** Temporarily unable or unwilling to speak, as from shock or fear : dumb, inarticulate, mum, mute, speechless, voiceless, wordless. *See* WORDS. **4.** Not voiced or expressed : tacit, undeclared, unexpressed, unsaid, unspoken, unuttered, unvoiced, wordless. *See* WORDS.

silhouette *noun*
A line marking and shaping the outer form of an object : contour, delineation, outline, profile. *See* EDGE, SURFACE.

silken *adjective*
Smooth and lustrous as if polished : satiny, silky, sleek. *See* SMOOTH.

silky *adjective*
Smooth and lustrous as if polished : satiny, silken, sleek. *See* SMOOTH.

silliness *noun*
Foolish behavior : absurdity, folly, foolery, foolishness, idiocy, imbecility, insanity, lunacy, madness, nonsense, preposterousness, senselessness, tomfoolery, zaniness. *Informal:* craziness. *See* ABILITY.

silly *adjective*
1. Displaying a complete lack of forethought and good sense : brainless, fatuous, foolish, insensate, mindless, senseless, unintelligent, weak-minded, witless. *See* ABILITY, PLANNED. **2.** So senseless as to be laughable : absurd, foolish, harebrained, idiotic, imbecilic, insane, lunatic, mad, moronic, nonsensical, preposterous, softheaded, tomfool, unearthly, zany. *Informal:* cockeyed, crazy, loony, loopy. *Slang:* balmy[2], dippy, dopey, jerky, sappy, wacky. *See* ABILITY, KNOWLEDGE. **3.** Given to lighthearted silliness : empty-headed, featherbrained, flighty, frivolous, frothy, giddy, harebrained, lighthearted, scatterbrained. *Informal:* gaga. *Slang:* birdbrained, dizzy. *See* ABILITY.

silver-tongued *adjective*
Fluently persuasive and forceful : articulate, eloquent, facund, smooth-spoken. *See* WORDS.

similar *adjective*
Possessing the same or almost the same characteristics : alike, analogous, comparable, corresponding, equivalent, like[2], parallel, uniform. *See* SAME.

similarity *noun*
The quality or state of being alike : affinity, alikeness, analogy, comparison, correspondence, likeness, parallelism, resemblance, similitude, uniformity, uniformness. *See* SAME.

similitude *noun*
The quality or state of being alike : affinity, alikeness, analogy, comparison, correspondence, likeness, parallelism, resemblance, similarity, uniformity, uniformness. *See* SAME.

simmer *verb*
1. To cook (food) in liquid heated to the point of steaming : boil, parboil, stew. *See* INGESTION. **2.** To be in a state of emotional or mental turmoil : boil, bubble, burn, churn, ferment, seethe, smolder. *See* CALM.
simmer down *verb* To bring one's emotions under control : collect[1], compose, contain, control, cool. ***Idiom:*** cool it. *See* RESTRAINT.

simmer down *verb* See **simmer.**

simper *verb*
To smile in an affected, knowing way : smirk. *See* EXPRESS.
simper *noun* An affected, knowing smile : smirk. *See* EXPRESS.

simple *adjective*
1. Free from extraneous elements : absolute, perfect, plain, pure, sheer[2], unadulterated, undiluted, unmixed. *See* CLEAN. **2.** Posing no difficulty : easy, effortless, facile, smooth. *Informal:* snap. ***Idioms:*** easy as ABC, easy as falling off a log, easy as one-two-three, easy as pie, like taking candy from a baby, nothing to it. *See* EASY. **3.** Without addition, decoration, or qualification : bald, bare, dry, plain, unadorned, unvarnished. *See* PLAIN. **4.** Not elaborate or showy, as in appearance or style : modest, plain, unassuming, unostentatious, unpretentious. *See* PLAIN. **5.** Having only a limited ability to learn and understand : backward, dull, simple-minded, slow, slow-witted. *Informal:* soft. *Offensive:* feeble-minded, half-witted, retarded, weak-minded. *See* ABILITY. **6.** Free from guile, cunning, or deceit : artless, guileless, ingenuous, innocent, naive, natural, unaffected, unsophisticated, unstudied, unworldly. *See* HONEST. **7.** Of little distinction : humble, lowly, mean[2]. *See* PLAIN.
simple *noun* One deficient in judgment and good sense : ass, fool, idiot, imbecile, jackass,

mooncalf, moron, nincompoop, ninny, nitwit, simpleton, softhead, tomfool. *Informal:* dope, gander, goose. *Slang:* cretin, ding-dong, dip, goof, jerk, nerd, schmo, schmuck, turkey. *See* ABILITY.

simple-minded or **simpleminded** *adjective*
Having only a limited ability to learn and understand : backward, dull, simple, slow, slow-witted. *Informal:* soft. *Offensive:* feeble-minded, half-witted, retarded, weak-minded. *See* ABILITY.

simpleness *noun*
Lack of ostentation or pretension : modesty, plainness, simplicity, unassumingness, unostentatiousness, unpretentiousness. *See* PLAIN.

simpleton *noun*
One deficient in judgment and good sense : ass, fool, idiot, imbecile, jackass, mooncalf, moron, nincompoop, ninny, nitwit, simple, softhead, tomfool. *Informal:* dope, gander, goose. *Slang:* cretin, ding-dong, dip, goof, jerk, nerd, schmo, schmuck, turkey. *See* ABILITY.

simplicity *noun*
Lack of ostentation or pretension : modesty, plainness, simpleness, unassumingness, unostentatiousness, unpretentiousness. *See* PLAIN.

simplify *verb*
To reduce in complexity or scope : boil down. *See* INCREASE, SIMPLE.

simulacre *noun*
Archaic. Something closely resembling another : carbon copy, copy, duplicate, facsimile, image, likeness, reduplication, replica, replication, reproduction, simulacrum. *Law:* counterpart. *See* SAME.

simulacrum *noun*
Something closely resembling another : carbon copy, copy, duplicate, facsimile, image, likeness, reduplication, replica, replication, reproduction. *Archaic:* simulacre. *Law:* counterpart. *See* SAME.

simulate *verb*
1. To make a copy of : copy, duplicate, imitate, replicate, reproduce. *See* SAME. **2.** To contrive and present as genuine : counterfeit, fake, feign, pretend. ***Idioms:*** make believe, put on an act. *See* TRUE. **3.** To behave affectedly or insincerely or take on a false or misleading appearance of : act, counterfeit, dissemble, fake, feign, play-act, pose, pretend, put on, sham. *See* HONEST, TRUE. **4.** To take on or give a false appearance of : affect[2], assume, counterfeit, fake, feign, pretend, put on, sham. ***Idiom:*** make believe. *See* TRUE.

simulated *adjective*
Made to imitate something else : artificial, imitation, manmade, mock, synthetic. *Informal:* pretend. *See* REAL.

simulation *noun*
1. An inferior substitute imitating an original : copy, ersatz, imitation, pinchbeck. *See* SUBSTITUTE. **2.** A display of insincere behavior : act, acting, disguise, dissemblance, masquerade, pretense, sham, show. *See* HONEST, TRUE.

simultaneous *adjective*
Existing or occurring at the same moment : coincident, contemporary. *See* TIME.

simultaneously *adverb*
At the same time : concurrently, synchronously, together. ***Idioms:*** all at once, all together. *See* ACCOMPANIED, TIME.

sin *noun*
1. A wicked act or wicked behavior : crime, deviltry, diablerie, evil, evildoing, immorality, iniquity, misdeed, offense, peccancy, wickedness, wrong, wrongdoing. *See* RIGHT. **2.** That which is morally bad or objectionable : evil, iniquity, peccancy, wickedness, wrong. *See* RIGHT. **3.** Something that offends one's sense of propriety, fairness, or justice : crime, offense, outrage. *See* RIGHT.
sin *verb* To violate a moral or divine law : err, offend, transgress, trespass. *See* RIGHT.

sincere *adjective*
Devoid of any hypocrisy or pretense : genuine, heartfelt, hearty, honest, natural, real, true, unaffected, unfeigned, unmannered. *See* TRUE.

sine qua non *noun*
Something indispensable : condition, essential, must, necessity, need, precondition, prerequisite, requirement, requisite. *See* NECESSARY.

sinew *noun*
The state or quality of being physically strong : brawn, might, muscle, potence, potency, power, powerfulness, puissance, strength, thew (often used in plural). *See* STRONG.

sinewy *adjective*
Characterized by marked muscular development; powerfully built : athletic, brawny, burly, husky[2], muscular, robust, sturdy. *See* STRONG.

sinful *adjective*
Morally objectionable : bad, black, evil, immoral, iniquitous, peccant, reprobate, vicious, wicked, wrong. *See* RIGHT.

sing *verb*
1. To utter words or sounds in musical tones : carol, chant, vocalize. *Archaic:* tune. *See* SOUNDS. **2.** *Slang.* To give incriminating infor-

mation about others, especially to the authorities : inform, talk, tattle, tip[3] (off). *Slang:* fink, rat, snitch, squeal, stool. ***Idiom:*** blow the whistle. *See* KNOWLEDGE, LAW.

singe *verb*
To undergo or cause to undergo damage by or as if by fire : burn, char, scorch, sear. *See* HOT.
singe *noun* Damage or a damaged substance that results from burning : burn, char, scorch, sear. *See* HOT.

singer *noun*
A person who sings : songster, songstress, vocalist, voice. *See* PERFORMING ARTS.

single *adjective*
1. Lacking the company of others : alone, companionless, lone, lonely, lonesome, solitary, unaccompanied. *See* INCLUDE. **2.** Alone in a given category : lone, one, only, particular, separate, singular, sole, solitary, unique. ***Idioms:*** first and last, one and only. *See* INCLUDE. **3.** Being or related to a distinct entity : discrete, individual, particular, separate, singular. *See* INCLUDE. **4.** Not divided among or shared with others : exclusive, sole. *See* INCLUDE. **5.** Without a spouse : fancy-free, footloose, lone, sole, spouseless, unattached, unmarried, unwed. ***Idiom:*** footloose and fancy-free. *See* MARRIAGE.
single *verb* To make a choice from a number of alternatives. Also used with *out* : choose, cull, elect, opt (for), pick (out), select. *See* CHOICE.

single-handedly *adverb*
Without the presence or aid of another : alone, singly, solely, solitarily, solo. ***Idioms:*** all by one's lonesome, by oneself. *See* INCLUDE.

singleness *noun*
1. The quality or state of being alone : aloneness, isolation, loneliness, solitariness, solitude. *See* INCLUDE. **2.** The condition of being one : oneness, singularity, unity. *See* PART. **3.** The quality or condition of being unique : oneness, singularity, uniqueness. *See* SAME.

singly *adverb*
1. Without the presence or aid of another : alone, single-handedly, solely, solitarily, solo. ***Idioms:*** all by one's lonesome, by oneself. *See* INCLUDE. **2.** As a separate unit : apart, discretely, independently, individually, separately. ***Idioms:*** one at a time, one by one. *See* INCLUDE.

singular *adjective*
1. Being or related to a distinct entity : discrete, individual, particular, separate, single. *See* INCLUDE. **2.** Alone in a given category : lone, one, only, particular, separate, single, sole, solitary, unique. ***Idioms:*** first and last, one and only. *See* INCLUDE. **3.** Without equal or rival : alone, incomparable, matchless, nonpareil, only, peerless, unequaled, unexampled, unique, unmatched, unparalleled, unrivaled. *See* SAME. **4.** Far beyond what is usual, normal, or customary : exceptional, extraordinary, magnificent, outstanding, preeminent, rare, remarkable, towering, uncommon, unusual. *Informal:* standout. *Slang:* awesome, out of sight. *See* BETTER, USUAL. **5.** Deviating from the customary : bizarre, cranky, curious, eccentric, erratic, freakish, idiosyncratic, odd, outlandish, peculiar, quaint, queer, quirky, strange, unnatural, unusual, weird. *Slang:* kooky, screwball. *British Slang:* rum, rummy[2]. *See* USUAL.

singularity *noun*
1. The condition of being one : oneness, singleness, unity. *See* PART. **2.** The quality of being individual : discreteness, distinctiveness, individuality, particularity, separateness. *See* INCLUDE. **3.** The quality or condition of being unique : oneness, singleness, uniqueness. *See* SAME. **4.** Peculiar behavior : eccentricity, idiosyncrasy, peculiarity, quirk, quirkiness. *See* USUAL.

singularize *verb*
To make noticeable or different : characterize, differentiate, discriminate, distinguish, individualize, mark, set apart, signalize. *See* SAME.

singularly *adverb*
In a manner or to a degree that is unusual : exceptionally, extraordinarily, remarkably, uncommonly, unusually. *See* USUAL.

sinister *adjective*
Strongly suggestive of great harm, menace, or evil : baleful, malign. *See* WARN.

sink *verb*
1. To fall or drift down to the bottom : gravitate, settle. *See* RISE. **2.** To go beneath the surface or to the bottom of a liquid : founder[1], submerge, submerse. *See* RISE. **3.** To go from a more erect posture to a less erect posture : drop, fall, slump. *See* RISE. **4.** To slope downward : decline, descend, dip, drop, fall, pitch. *See* RISE. **5.** To become lower in quality, character, or condition : atrophy, decline, degenerate, descend, deteriorate, retrograde, worsen. ***Idioms:*** go bad, go to pot, go to seed, go to the dogs. *See* BETTER. **6.** To bring oneself down to a lower level of behavior : descend, lower[2], stoop. *See* RISE. **7.** To undergo moral deterioration : fall, slip. ***Idiom:*** go bad (*or* wrong). *See* RIGHT. **8.** To cause the complete ruin or

wreckage of : bankrupt, break down, cross up, demolish, destroy, finish, ruin, shatter, smash, spoil, torpedo, undo, wash up, wrack[2], wreck. *Slang:* total. ***Idiom:*** put the kibosh on. *See* HELP. **9.** To undergo a sharp, rapid descent in value or price : dive, drop, fall, nose-dive, plummet, plunge, skid, slump, tumble. ***Idiom:*** take a sudden downtrend (*or* downturn). *See* INCREASE. **10.** To lose strength or power : decline, degenerate, deteriorate, fade, fail, flag[2], languish, wane, waste (away), weaken. *Informal:* fizzle (out). ***Idioms:*** go downhill, hit the skids. *See* INCREASE, STRONG. **11.** To cause to penetrate with force : dig, drive, plunge, ram, run, stab, stick, thrust. *See* PUT IN.

sink in *verb* To come as a realization : dawn on (*or* upon), register, soak in. *See* KNOWLEDGE.

sink *noun* **1.** An area sunk below its surroundings : basin, concavity, depression, dip, hollow, pit[1], sag, sinkhole. *See* CONVEX. **2.** A place known for its great filth or corruption : cesspit, cesspool, pit[1]. *Slang:* armpit. *See* CLEAN, RIGHT.

sinkhole *noun*
An area sunk below its surroundings : basin, concavity, depression, dip, hollow, pit[1], sag, sink. *See* CONVEX.

sink in *verb* See **sink.**

sinless *adjective*
Free from evil and corruption : angelic, angelical, clean, innocent, lily-white, pure, unblemished, uncorrupted, undefiled, unstained, unsullied, untainted, virginal. ***Idiom:*** pure as the driven snow. *See* CLEAN, RIGHT, SEX.

sinuate *verb*
To move sinuously : slither, snake, undulate. *See* MOVE.

sinuous *adjective*
Repeatedly curving in alternate directions : anfractuous, flexuous, meandrous, serpentine, snaky, tortuous, winding. *See* REPETITION, STRAIGHT.

sip *verb*
To take into the mouth and swallow (a liquid) : drink, imbibe, pull on, quaff, sup. *Informal:* swig, toss down (*or* off). *Slang:* belt. ***Idiom:*** wet one's whistle. *See* MOUTH.

sip *noun* **1.** An act of drinking or the amount swallowed : draft, drink, potation, pull, quaff, sup, swill. *Informal:* swig. *Slang:* belt. *See* MOUTH. **2.** A small amount of liquor : dram, drop, jigger, shot, tot[1]. *Informal:* nip[2], slug[1]. *Slang:* snort. *See* BIG, INGESTION.

sire *noun*
A male parent : father. *Informal:* dad, daddy, pa, papa, pappy[2], pop[2]. *Slang:* old man. *See* KIN.

sire *verb* **1.** To be the biological father of : beget, breed, father, get, procreate. *See* KIN. **2.** To cause to come into existence : beget, breed, create, engender, father, hatch, make, originate, parent, procreate, produce, spawn. ***Idiom:*** give birth (*or* rise) to. *See* MAKE.

siren *noun*
A usually unscrupulous woman who seduces or exploits men : enchantress, femme fatale, seductress, temptress. *Informal:* vamp, witch. *See* SEX.

siren *adjective* Tending to seduce : alluring, bewitching, come-hither, enticing, inveigling, inviting, luring, seductive, tempting, witching. *See* LIKE, PERSUASION, SEX.

sissified *adjective*
Having qualities more appropriate to women than to men : effeminate, epicene, feminine, sissyish, unmanly, womanish. *See* GENDER.

sissiness or **sissyness** *noun*
The quality of being effeminate : effeminacy, effeminateness, femininity, unmanliness, womanishness. *See* GENDER.

sissyish *adjective*
Having qualities more appropriate to women than to men : effeminate, epicene, feminine, sissified, unmanly, womanish. *See* GENDER.

sissyness *noun* See **sissiness.**

sit *verb*
1. To assume a particular position, as for a portrait : pose, posture. *See* POSTURE. **2.** To cause to take a sitting position. Also used with *down* : seat. *See* RISE.

sit on (or **upon**) *verb Informal.* To hold (something requiring an outlet) in check : burke, choke (back), gag, hold back, hold down, hush (up), muffle, quench, repress, smother, squelch, stifle, strangle, suppress, throttle. *See* RESTRAINT.

site *noun*
1. The place where a person or thing is located : emplacement, location, locus, placement, position, situation. *See* PLACE. **2.** The place where an action or event occurs : locale, scene, setting, stage. *See* PLACE.

site *verb* To put in or assign to a certain position or location : emplace, install, locate, place, position, set[1], situate, spot. *See* PLACE.

sit on or **upon** *verb* See **sit.**

situate *verb*
To put in or assign to a certain position or loca-

tion : emplace, install, locate, place, position, set[1], site, spot. *See* PLACE.

situation *noun*
1. One's place and direction relative to one's surroundings : bearing (often used in plural), location, orientation, position. *See* PLACE. **2.** The place where a person or thing is located : emplacement, location, locus, placement, position, site. *See* PLACE. **3.** Positioning of one individual vis-à-vis others : footing, place, position, rank[1], standing, station, status. *See* PLACE. **4.** Manner of being or form of existence : condition, mode, state, status. *See* BE. **5.** A post of employment : appointment, berth, billet, job, office, place, position, slot, spot. *Slang:* gig. *See* PLACE.

sixth sense *noun*
The power to discern the true nature of a person or situation : insight, instinct, intuition, intuitiveness, penetration. *See* THOUGHTS.

sizable also **sizeable** *adjective*
1. Notably above average in amount, size, or scope : big, considerable, extensive, good, great, healthy, large, large-scale. *Informal:* tidy. *See* BIG. **2.** Somewhat big : biggish, goodly, largish, respectable. *See* BIG.

sizableness also **sizeableness** *noun*
The quality or state of being large in amount, extent, or importance : amplitude, bigness, greatness, largeness, magnitude, size. *See* BIG.

size *noun*
1. The amount of space occupied by something : dimension, extent, magnitude, measure, proportion (often used in plural). *See* BIG. **2.** The quality or state of being large in amount, extent, or importance : amplitude, bigness, greatness, largeness, magnitude, sizableness. *See* BIG. **3.** Great extent, amount, or dimension : amplitude, bulk, magnitude, mass, volume (often used in plural). *See* BIG.
size up *verb* To make a judgment as to the worth or value of : appraise, assay, assess, calculate, estimate, evaluate, gauge, judge, rate[1], valuate, value. ***Idiom:*** take the measure of. *See* VALUE.

sizeable *adjective* See **sizable.**

sizeableness *noun* See **sizableness.**

size up *verb* See **size.**

sizzle *verb*
To make a sharp sibilant sound : fizz, fizzle, hiss, sibilate, swish, whiz, whoosh. *See* SOUNDS.

sizzling *adjective*
Marked by much heat : ardent, baking, blistering, boiling, broiling, burning, fiery, heated, hot, red-hot, roasting, scalding, scorching, searing, sultry, sweltering, torrid. *See* HOT.

skedaddle *verb*
Informal. To leave hastily : bolt, get out, run. *Informal:* clear out, get, hotfoot. *Slang:* hightail, scram, vamoose. ***Idioms:*** beat it, hightail it, hotfoot it, make tracks. *See* APPROACH.

skein *noun*
1. Something that is intricately and often bewilderingly complex : cat's cradle, entanglement, jungle, knot, labyrinth, maze, mesh (often used in plural), morass, snarl[2], tangle, web. *See* SIMPLE. **2.** Something that suggests the continuousness of a fine continuous filament : strand, thread. *See* CONTINUE.

skeletal *adjective*
Physically haggard : cadaverous, drawn, emaciated, gaunt, shrunken, wasted. ***Idiom:*** skin and bones. *See* BETTER, TIRED.

skeleton *noun*
A preliminary plan or version, as of a written work : draft, outline, rough, sketch. *See* PLANNED, WORDS.

skeptic also **sceptic** *noun*
One who habitually or instinctively doubts or questions : doubter, doubting Thomas, nonbeliever, unbeliever. *See* BELIEF.

skeptical also **sceptical** *adjective*
1. Experiencing doubt : doubtful, dubious, uncertain, undecided, unsure. ***Idiom:*** in doubt. *See* CERTAIN. **2.** Refusing or reluctant to believe : disbelieving, incredulous, questioning, unbelieving. *See* BELIEF.

skeptically also **sceptically** *adverb*
With skepticism : askance, doubtfully, dubiously, questioningly. ***Idiom:*** with a grain of salt. *See* BELIEF.

skepticism also **scepticism** *noun*
A lack of conviction or certainty : doubt, doubtfulness, dubiety, dubiousness, incertitude, mistrust, question, suspicion, uncertainty, wonder. *See* CERTAIN.

sketch *noun*
1. A preliminary plan or version, as of a written work : draft, outline, rough, skeleton. *See* PLANNED, WORDS. **2.** A short theatrical piece within a larger production : act, skit. *See* PERFORMING ARTS.
sketch *verb* To draw up a preliminary plan or version of : adumbrate, block in (*or* out), draft, outline, rough in (*or* out). *See* PLANNED.

sketchy *adjective*
1. Not perfected, elaborated, or completed : preliminary, rough, tentative, unfinished, unperfected, unpolished. *See* START. **2.** Lacking

in intellectual depth or thoroughness : cursory, one-dimensional, shallow, skin-deep, superficial, uncritical. *See* SURFACE.

skew *verb*
1. To turn aside sharply from a straight course : chop[2], cut, sheer[1], slue[1], swerve, veer. *Nautical:* yaw. *See* CHANGE. **2.** To direct (material) to the interests of a particular group : bias, slant. *Informal:* angle[2]. *See* STRAIGHT.

skid *noun*
A usually swift downward trend, as in prices : decline, descent, dip, dive, downslide, downswing, downtrend, downturn, drop, drop-off, fall, nosedive, plunge, slide, slump, tumble. *See* INCREASE.
skid *verb* **1.** To lose one's balance and fall or almost fall : slide, slip, slither. ***Idiom:*** take a skid (*or* slide). *See* MOVE. **2.** To undergo a sharp, rapid descent in value or price : dive, drop, fall, nose-dive, plummet, plunge, sink, slump, tumble. ***Idiom:*** take a sudden downtrend (*or* downturn). *See* INCREASE.

skill *noun*
1. Natural or acquired facility in a specific activity : ability, adeptness, art, command, craft, expertise, expertness, knack, mastery, proficiency, technique. *Informal:* know-how. *See* ABILITY, KNOWLEDGE. **2.** Skillfulness in the use of the hands or body : adroitness, deftness, dexterity, dexterousness, prowess, sleight. *See* ABILITY.

skilled *adjective*
1. Having the ability to perform well : able, capable, competent, good, skillful. *See* ABILITY. **2.** Having or demonstrating a high degree of knowledge or skill : adept, crack, expert, master, masterful, masterly, professional, proficient, skillful. *Slang:* crackerjack. *See* ABILITY.

skillful also **skilful** *adjective*
1. Having the ability to perform well : able, capable, competent, good, skilled. *See* ABILITY. **2.** Having or demonstrating a high degree of knowledge or skill : adept, crack, expert, master, masterful, masterly, professional, proficient, skilled. *Slang:* crackerjack. *See* ABILITY. **3.** Showing art or skill in performing or doing : adroit, artful, deft, dexterous. *See* ABILITY, KNOWLEDGE. **4.** Well done or executed : adroit, clean, deft, neat. *See* ABILITY, GOOD.

skim *verb*
1. To strike a surface at such an angle as to be deflected : carom, dap, glance, graze, ricochet, skip. *See* STRIKE. **2.** To make light and momentary contact with, as in passing : brush[1], flick, graze, kiss, shave. *See* TOUCH. **3.** To pass quickly and lightly through the air : dart, float, fly, sail, shoot. *See* MOVE. **4.** To look through reading matter casually : browse, dip into, flip through, glance at (*or* over *or* through), leaf (through), riffle (through), run through, scan, thumb (through). *See* INVESTIGATE, WORDS.
skim *noun* Light and momentary contact with another person or thing : brush[1], flick, graze. *See* TOUCH.

skimp *verb*
To be severely sparing in order to economize : pinch, scrape, scrimp, stint. ***Idioms:*** pinch pennies, tighten (one's) belt. *See* SAVE.

skimpy *adjective*
Conspicuously deficient in quantity, fullness, or extent : exiguous, meager, poor, puny, scant, scanty, spare, sparse, stingy, thin. *Slang:* measly. *See* BIG, EXCESS.

skin *noun*
1. The tissue forming the external covering of the body : epidermis, integument. *See* SURFACE. **2.** A thin outer covering of an object : lamina, membrane, sheath, sheathing. *See* SURFACE. **3.** The outer covering of a fruit : peel, rind. *See* SURFACE.
skin *verb* **1.** To remove the skin of : decorticate, pare, peel, scale[1], strip[1]. *See* PUT ON. **2.** To furnish with a covering of a different material : clad, cover, face, sheathe, side. *See* SURFACE. **3.** *Slang.* To exploit (another) by charging too much for something : fleece, overcharge. *Slang:* clip[1], gouge, nick, rip off, scalp, soak. ***Idioms:*** make someone pay through the nose, take someone for a ride, take someone to the cleaners. *See* HONEST.

skin-deep *adjective*
Lacking in intellectual depth or thoroughness : cursory, one-dimensional, shallow, sketchy, superficial, uncritical. *See* SURFACE.

skinflint *noun*
A stingy person : miser, niggard, Scrooge. *Informal:* penny pincher. *Slang:* cheapskate, stiff, tightwad. *See* GIVE.

skinny *adjective*
Having little flesh or fat on the body : angular, bony, fleshless, gaunt, lank, lanky, lean[2], meager, rawboned, scrawny, slender, slim, spare, thin, twiggy, weedy. ***Idioms:*** all skin and bones, thin as a rail. *See* FAT.

skip *verb*
1. To bound lightly : hop, skitter, spring, trip. *See* MOVE. **2.** To strike a surface at such an angle as to be deflected : carom, dap, glance, graze, ricochet, skim. *See* STRIKE. **3.** To cease

consideration or treatment of : dismiss, drop, give over, give up. ***Idioms:*** have done with, wash one's hands of. *See* KEEP. **4.** *Informal.* To break loose and leave suddenly, as from confinement or from a difficult or threatening situation. Also used with *out* : abscond, break out, decamp, escape, flee, fly, get away, run away. *Slang:* lam. *Regional:* absquatulate. ***Idioms:*** blow (*or* fly) the coop, cut and run, give someone the slip, make a getaway, take flight, take it on the lam. *See* FREE. **5.** *Informal.* To fail to attend on purpose : cut, truant. ***Idioms:*** go AWOL, play hooky (*or* truant). *See* SEEK.

skip *noun* A light bounding movement : hop, spring. *See* MOVE.

skirmish *noun*
A brief, hostile exposure to or contact with something such as danger or opposition : brush[2], clash, encounter, run-in. *See* TOUCH.

skirt *noun*
The periphery of a city or town. Used in plural : edge, environs, fringe, outskirt (often used in plural), suburb (used in plural). *See* EDGE.

skirt *verb* **1.** To put or form a border on : border, bound[2], edge, fringe, margin, rim, verge. *See* EDGE. **2.** To pass around but not through : bypass, circumnavigate, circumvent, detour, go around. *See* SEEK. **3.** To avoid fulfilling or answering completely : dodge, duck, evade, hedge, sidestep. *See* SEEK.

skit *noun*
A short theatrical piece within a larger production : act, sketch. *See* PERFORMING ARTS.

skitter *verb*
To bound lightly : hop, skip, spring, trip. *See* MOVE.

skittish *adjective*
Feeling or exhibiting nervous tension : edgy, fidgety, jittery, jumpy, nervous, restive, restless, tense, twitchy. *Slang:* uptight. ***Idioms:*** a bundle of nerves, all wound up, on edge. *See* TIGHTEN.

skulk *verb*
To move silently and furtively : creep, glide, lurk, mouse, prowl, pussyfoot, slide, slink, slip, snake, sneak, steal. *Slang:* gumshoe. *See* MOVE.

sky *noun*
The celestial regions as seen from the earth : air, firmament, heaven (often used in plural). *Archaic:* welkin. *See* HIGH.

sky *verb* To rise abruptly and precipitously : rocket, skyrocket, soar. *Informal:* shoot up. *See* INCREASE.

sky-high *adjective*
1. Imposingly high : aerial, airy, lofty, soaring, towering. *See* HIGH. **2.** Vastly exceeding a normal limit, as in cost : steep[1], stiff, stratospheric, unconscionable. *See* BIG, USUAL.

skyrocket *verb*
To rise abruptly and precipitously : rocket, sky, soar. *Informal:* shoot up. *See* INCREASE.

slab *noun*
A relatively long, straight, rigid piece of metal or other solid material : bar, bloom[2], rod, shaft, stick. *See* THING.

slack *adjective*
1. Characterized by reduced economic activity : down, dull, off, slow, sluggish, soft. *See* INCREASE. **2.** Not tautly bound, held, or fastened : lax, loose, relaxed. *See* TIGHTEN. **3.** Guilty of neglect; lacking due care or concern : derelict, lax, neglectful, negligent, remiss. *See* CAREFUL.

slack *verb* **1.** To reduce in tension, pressure, or rigidity : ease, let up, loose, loosen, relax, slacken, untighten. *See* TIGHTEN. **2.** To avoid the fulfillment of : disregard, neglect, shirk. ***Idiom:*** let slide. *See* DO.

slack off *verb* To become or cause to become less active or intense : abate, bate, die (away, down, off, *or* out), ease (off *or* up), ebb, fall, fall off, lapse, let up, moderate, remit, slacken, subside, wane. *See* INCREASE.

slacken *verb*
1. To reduce in tension, pressure, or rigidity : ease, let up, loose, loosen, relax, slack, untighten. *See* TIGHTEN. **2.** To become or cause to become less active or intense : abate, bate, die (away, down, off, *or* out), ease (off *or* up), ebb, fall, fall off, lapse, let up, moderate, remit, slack off, subside, wane. *See* INCREASE. **3.** To moderate or change a position or course of action as a result of pressure : ease off, relent, soften, weaken, yield. ***Idiom:*** give way (*or* ground). *See* STRONG.

slackening *noun*
The act or process of becoming less active or intense : abatement, ebb, letup, remission, subsidence, wane. *See* INCREASE.

slackness *noun*
The state or quality of being negligent : laxity, laxness, negligence, remissness. *See* CAREFUL.

slack off *verb* See **slack.**

slam *verb*
1. To strike, set down, or close in such a way as to make a loud noise : bang[1], clap, crash, whack. *See* SOUNDS. **2.** To deliver a powerful blow to suddenly and sharply : bash, catch, clout, hit, knock, pop[1], slog, slug[3], smash, smite, sock, strike, swat, thwack, whack,

wham, whop. *Informal:* biff, bop, clip[1], wallop. *Slang:* belt, conk, paste. ***Idioms:*** let someone have it, sock it to someone. *See* ATTACK, STRIKE. **3.** *Slang.* To criticize harshly and devastatingly : blister, drub, excoriate, flay, lash, rip into, scarify[1], scathe, scorch, score, scourge, slap, slash. *Informal:* roast. ***Idioms:*** burn someone's ears, crawl all over, pin someone's ears back, put someone on the griddle, put someone on the hot seat, rake over the coals, read the riot act to. *See* PRAISE.

slam *noun* A forceful movement causing a loud noise : bang, crash, smash, wham. *See* STRIKE.

slammer *noun*
Slang. A place for the confinement of persons in lawful detention : brig, house of correction, jail, keep, penitentiary, prison. *Informal:* lockup, pen[3]. *Slang:* big house, can, clink, cooler, coop, hoosegow, joint, jug, pokey[1], stir[2]. *Chiefly Regional:* calaboose. *See* FREE.

slander *noun*
The expression of injurious, malicious statements about someone : aspersion, calumniation, calumny, character assassination, defamation, denigration, detraction, scandal, traducement, vilification. *Law:* libel. *See* ATTACK, CRIMES, LAW.

slander *verb* To make defamatory statements about : asperse, backbite, calumniate, defame, malign, slur, tear down, traduce, vilify. *Law:* libel. ***Idiom:*** cast aspersions on. *See* ATTACK, CRIMES, LAW.

slanderous *adjective*
Damaging to the reputation : calumnious, defamatory, detractive, injurious, invidious, scandalous. *Law:* libelous. *See* ATTACK, CRIMES, LAW.

slant *verb*
1. To depart or cause to depart from true vertical or horizontal : cant[1], heel[2], incline, lean[1], list[2], rake[2], slope, tilt, tip[2]. *See* STRAIGHT. **2.** To have a tendency or inclination : incline, lean[1], squint, tend[1], trend. *See* LIKELY. **3.** To direct (material) to the interests of a particular group : bias, skew. *Informal:* angle[2]. *See* STRAIGHT.

slant *noun* **1.** Deviation from a particular direction : cant[1], grade, gradient, heel[2], inclination, incline, lean[1], list[2], rake[2], slope, tilt, tip[2]. *See* RISE, STRAIGHT. **2.** The position from which something is observed or considered : angle[2], eye, outlook, point of view, standpoint, vantage, viewpoint. *See* PERSPECTIVE.

slanted *adjective*
Angled at a slant : beveled, bias, biased, diagonal, oblique, slanting. *See* STRAIGHT.

slanting *adjective*
Angled at a slant : beveled, bias, biased, diagonal, oblique, slanted. *See* STRAIGHT.

slap *noun*
A quick, sharp blow, especially with the hand : box[2], buffet, bust, chop[1], cuff, punch, smack[1], smacker, spank, swat, whack. *Informal:* clip[1], spat. *See* ATTACK, STRIKE.

slap *verb* **1.** To hit with a quick, sharp blow of the hand : box[2], buffet, bust, cuff, punch, smack[1], spank, swat, whack. *Informal:* clip[1], spat. *See* ATTACK, STRIKE. **2.** To criticize harshly and devastatingly : blister, drub, excoriate, flay, lash, rip into, scarify[1], scathe, scorch, score, scourge, slash. *Informal:* roast. *Slang:* slam. ***Idioms:*** burn someone's ears, crawl all over, pin someone's ears back, put someone on the griddle, put someone on the hot seat, rake over the coals, read the riot act to. *See* PRAISE.

slap around *verb* To be rough or brutal with : knock about (*or* around), manhandle, rough (up). *Slang:* mess up. *See* ATTACK, STRIKE.

slap around *verb* See **slap.**

slapdash *adjective*
1. Indifferent to correctness, accuracy, or neatness : careless, messy, slipshod, sloppy, slovenly, untidy. *See* CAREFUL. **2.** Characterized by unthinking boldness and haste : brash, foolhardy, harum-scarum, hasty, headlong, hotheaded, ill-considered, impetuous, improvident, impulsive, incautious, madcap, precipitant, precipitate, rash[1], reckless, temerarious, unconsidered. *See* CAREFUL.

slash *verb*
1. To penetrate with a sharp edge : cut, gash, incise, pierce, slit. *See* ENTER, HELP. **2.** To criticize harshly and devastatingly : blister, drub, excoriate, flay, lash, rip into, scarify[1], scathe, scorch, score, scourge, slap. *Informal:* roast. *Slang:* slam. ***Idioms:*** burn someone's ears, crawl all over, pin someone's ears back, put someone on the griddle, put someone on the hot seat, rake over the coals, read the riot act to. *See* PRAISE. **3.** To decrease, as in length or amount, by or as if by severing or excising : chop[1], clip[1], crop, cut, cut back, cut down, lop[1], lower[2], pare, prune, shear, trim, truncate. *See* INCREASE.

slash *noun* **1.** The result of cutting : cut, gash, incision, slice, slit, split. *See* ENTER, HELP. **2.** An incision, a notch, or a slight cut made with or as if with a knife : score, scotch, scratch. *See* MARKS. **3.** The act or process of decreasing : abatement, curtailment, cut, cutback, decrease, decrement, diminishment, diminution, drain, reduction, slowdown, taper. *See* INCREASE.

slashing *adjective*
So sharp as to cause mental pain : acerbic, acid, acidic, acrid, astringent, biting, caustic, corrosive, cutting, mordacious, mordant, pungent, scathing, sharp, stinging, trenchant, truculent, vitriolic. *See* ATTACK, RESPECT.

slate *noun*
A list of candidates proposed or endorsed by a political party : lineup, ticket. *See* POLITICS.
slate *verb* To enter on a schedule : program, schedule. *See* REMEMBER.

slattern *noun*
A vulgar promiscuous woman who flouts propriety : baggage, hussy, jade, slut, tart[2], tramp, wanton, wench, whore. *Slang:* floozy. *See* SEX.

slaughter *noun*
The savage killing of many victims : bloodbath, bloodletting, bloodshed, butchery, carnage, massacre, pogrom. *See* HELP.
slaughter *verb* To kill savagely and indiscriminately : annihilate, butcher, decimate, massacre. *See* CRIMES, HELP, MAKE.

slaughterer *noun*
One who murders another : butcher, cutthroat, homicide, killer, manslayer, massacrer, murderer, murderess, slayer, triggerman. *See* HELP.

slaughterous *adjective*
Eager for bloodshed : bloodthirsty, bloody, bloody-minded, cutthroat, homicidal, murderous, sanguinary, sanguineous. *See* HELP.

slave *noun*
One who works or toils tirelessly : drudge, fag, grub, plodder. *Informal:* grind, workhorse. *See* WORK.
slave *verb* To do tedious, laborious, and sometimes menial work : drudge, grub, plod, slog. *Informal:* grind. *See* WORK.

slaver *verb*
1. To let saliva run from the mouth : dribble, drivel, drool, salivate, slobber. *See* DRY, MOUTH. **2.** To support slavishly every opinion or suggestion of a superior : bootlick, cringe, fawn, grovel, kowtow, toady, truckle. *Informal:* apple-polish, brownnose, cotton. *Slang:* suck up. ***Idioms:*** curry favor, dance attendance, kiss someone's feet, lick someone's boots. *See* OVER. **3.** To compliment excessively and ingratiatingly : adulate, blandish, butter up, flatter, honey. *Informal:* soft-soap, sweet-talk. *See* PRAISE.
slaver *noun* **1.** Saliva running from the mouth : drivel, drool, salivation, slobber. *See* DRY, MOUTH. **2.** Excessive, ingratiating praise : adulation, blandishment, blarney, flattery, incense[2], oil. *Informal:* soft soap. ***Idiom:*** honeyed words. *See* PRAISE.

slavery *noun*
A state of subjugation to an owner or master : bondage, enslavement, helotry, serfdom, servileness, servility, servitude, thrall, thralldom, villeinage, yoke. *See* OVER.

slavish *adjective*
1. Excessively eager to serve or obey : menial, obsequious, servile, subservient. *See* OVER.
2. Copying another in an inferior or obsequious way : apish, emulative, imitative. *See* SAME.

slay *verb*
1. To cause the death of : carry off, cut down, cut off, destroy, dispatch, finish (off), kill[1]. *Slang:* waste, zap. ***Idioms:*** put an end to, put to sleep. *See* HELP. **2.** To take the life of (a person or persons) unlawfully : destroy, finish (off), kill[1], liquidate, murder. *Informal:* put away. *Slang:* bump off, do in, knock off, off, rub out, waste, wipe out, zap. *See* HELP.

slayer *noun*
One who murders another : butcher, cutthroat, homicide, killer, manslayer, massacrer, murderer, murderess, slaughterer, triggerman. *See* HELP.

sleazy *adjective*
1. Showing signs of wear and tear or neglect : bedraggled, broken-down, decaying, decrepit, dilapidated, dingy, down-at-heel, faded, mangy, rundown, scrubby, scruffy, seedy, shabby, shoddy, tattered, tatty, threadbare. *Informal:* tacky[2]. *Slang:* ratty. ***Idioms:*** all the worse for wear, gone to pot (*or* seed), past cure (*or* hope). *See* BETTER. **2.** Of decidedly inferior quality : base[2], cheap, lousy, miserable, paltry, poor, rotten, shoddy, trashy. *Informal:* cheesy. *Slang:* crummy, schlocky. *See* GOOD.

sled *verb*
To ride on a sled in the snow : sledge, slide. *See* MOVE.

sledge *verb*
To ride on a sled in the snow : sled, slide. *See* MOVE.

sleek *adjective*
1. Smooth and lustrous as if polished : satiny, silken, silky. *See* SMOOTH. **2.** Having slender and graceful lines : streamlined, trim. *See* BEAUTIFUL. **3.** Affectedly and self-servingly

earnest : fulsome, oily, oleaginous, smarmy, unctuous. *See* ATTITUDE, HONEST.

sleek *verb* To give a gleaming luster to, usually through friction : buff[1], burnish, furbish, glaze, gloss, polish, shine. *See* LIGHT.

sleek over *verb* To conceal or make light of a fault or offense : explain away, extenuate, gloss over, gloze (over), palliate, whitewash. *See* SHOW.

sleekness *noun*
A radiant brightness or glow, usually due to light reflected from a smooth surface : burnish, glaze, gloss, luster, polish, sheen, shine. *See* LIGHT.

sleek over *verb* See **sleek.**

sleep *noun*
The natural recurring condition of suspended consciousness by which the body rests : slumber. *Slang:* shuteye. ***Idioms:*** land of Nod, the arms of Morpheus. *See* AWARENESS.

sleep *verb* To be asleep : slumber. ***Idioms:*** be in the land of Nod, catch some shuteye, sleep like a log (*or* rock *or* top), sleep tight. *See* AWARENESS.

sleep in *verb* To sleep longer than intended : oversleep. *See* AWARENESS.

sleep with *verb* To engage in sexual relations with : bed, copulate, couple, have, mate, take. ***Idioms:*** go to bed with, make love, make whoopee, roll in the hay. *See* SEX.

sleeper *noun*
A dazzling, often sudden instance of success : hit. *Informal:* smash, smash hit, ten-strike, wow. *Slang:* boff, boffo, boffola. *See* THRIVE.

sleep in *verb* See **sleep.**

sleeping *adjective*
1. In a state of sleep : asleep, unawake. ***Idioms:*** dead to the world, fast (*or* sound) asleep, in a sound (*or* wakeless) sleep, out like a light. *See* AWARENESS. **2.** Existing in a temporarily inactive form or state : abeyant, dormant, inactive, latent, quiescent. *See* ACTION, SHOW.

sleepless *adjective*
Marked by an absence of sleep : slumberless, wakeful. *See* AWARENESS.

sleep with *verb* See **sleep.**

sleepy *adjective*
1. Ready for or needing sleep : dozy, drowsy, nodding, slumberous, slumbery, somnolent, soporific. *See* AWARENESS. **2.** Inducing sleep or sedation : hypnotic, narcotic, opiate, sedative, slumberous, somnifacient, somniferous, somnific, somnolent, soporific. *See* AWARENESS.

sleight *noun*
1. Skillfulness in the use of the hands or body : adroitness, deftness, dexterity, dexterousness, prowess, skill. *See* ABILITY. **2.** An indirect, usually cunning means of gaining an end : artifice, deception, device, dodge, feint, gimmick, imposture, jig, maneuver, ploy, ruse, stratagem, subterfuge, trick, wile. *Informal:* shenanigan, take-in. *See* HONEST, MEANS.

sleight of hand *noun*
The use of skillful tricks and deceptions to produce entertainingly baffling effects : conjuration, legerdemain, magic, prestidigitation. *See* PERFORMING ARTS.

slender *adjective*
1. Having little flesh or fat on the body : angular, bony, fleshless, gaunt, lank, lanky, lean[2], meager, rawboned, scrawny, skinny, slim, spare, thin, twiggy, weedy. ***Idioms:*** all skin and bones, thin as a rail. *See* FAT. **2.** Small in degree, especially of probability : faint, negligible, outside, remote, slight, slim. *See* BIG.

sleuth *noun*
A person whose work is investigating crimes or obtaining hidden evidence or information : detective, investigator. *Informal:* eye. *Slang:* dick, gumshoe. *See* INVESTIGATE.

slew also **slue** *noun*
Informal. An indeterminately great amount or number : jillion, million (often used in plural), multiplicity, ream, trillion. *Informal:* bushel, gob[1] (often used in plural), heap (often used in plural), load (often used in plural), lot, oodles, passel, peck[2], scad (often used in plural), wad, zillion. *See* BIG.

slice *noun*
1. The result of cutting : cut, gash, incision, slash, slit, split. *See* ENTER, HELP. **2.** A part severed from a whole : cut, piece, portion, section, segment. *See* PART. **3.** A thin piece, especially of tissue, suitable for microscopic examination : section. *See* PART.

slice *verb* To separate into parts with or as if with a sharp-edged instrument : carve, cleave[1], cut, dissever, sever, slit, split. *See* ASSEMBLE.

slick *adjective*
1. So smooth and glassy as to offer insecure hold or footing : lubricious, slippery, slithery. ***Idiom:*** slippery as an eel. *See* SMOOTH. **2.** Exhibiting or possessing skill and ease in performance : adroit, clever, deft, dexterous, facile, handy, nimble. *See* ABILITY. **3.** Having or showing a clever awareness and resourcefulness in practical matters : astute, cagey, canny, knowing, perspicacious, shrewd, smart, wise[1]. *Informal:* savvy. *See* ABILITY, CAREFUL. **4.** Characterized by ready but often insincere or

superficial discourse : facile, glib, smooth-tongued. *See* SURFACE, WORDS.

slick up *verb* To make neat and trim; make presentable : clean (up), freshen (up), groom, neaten (up), spruce (up), tidy (up), trig (out), trim. *See* ORDER.

slick up *verb* See **slick.**

slide *verb*

1. To pass smoothly, quietly, and undisturbed on or as if on a slippery surface : coast, drift. *See* MOVE. **2.** To ride on a sled in the snow : sled, sledge. *See* MOVE. **3.** To move smoothly, continuously, and effortlessly : glide, glissade, lapse, slip, slither. *See* MOVE. **4.** To move silently and furtively : creep, glide, lurk, mouse, prowl, pussyfoot, skulk, slink, slip, snake, sneak, steal. *Slang:* gumshoe. *See* MOVE. **5.** To move along in a crouching or prone position : crawl, creep, snake, worm. *See* MOVE. **6.** To maneuver gently and slowly into place : ease, glide, slip. *See* CAREFUL, EASY. **7.** To lose one's balance and fall or almost fall : skid, slip, slither. ***Idiom:*** take a skid (*or* slide). *See* MOVE. **8.** To shift or be shifted out of place : slip. *See* MOVE.

slide *noun* A usually swift downward trend, as in prices : decline, descent, dip, dive, downslide, downswing, downtrend, downturn, drop, drop-off, fall, nosedive, plunge, skid, slump, tumble. *See* INCREASE.

slight *adjective*

1. Of small intensity : gentle, light[2], moderate, soft. *See* STRONG. **2.** Small in degree, especially of probability : faint, negligible, outside, remote, slender, slim. *See* BIG.

slight *verb* **1.** To think, represent, or speak of as small or unimportant : belittle, decry, denigrate, deprecate, depreciate, derogate, detract, discount, disparage, downgrade, minimize, run down, talk down. ***Idiom:*** make light (*or* little) of. *See* ATTACK, SHOW. **2.** To refuse to pay attention to (a person); treat with contempt : disregard, ignore, neglect. *Regional:* igg. *See* CONCERN, THOUGHTS. **3.** To fail to care for or give proper attention to : disregard, ignore, neglect. *See* CARE FOR, CONCERN.

slight *noun* **1.** An act or instance of neglecting : disregard, neglect, oversight. *See* CARE FOR, CONCERN. **2.** An act that offends a person's sense of pride or dignity : affront, contumely, despite, indignity, insult, offense, outrage. ***Idiom:*** slap in the face. *See* ATTACK.

slighting *adjective*

Tending or intending to belittle : deprecative, deprecatory, depreciative, depreciatory, derogative, derogatory, detractive, disparaging, low, pejorative, uncomplimentary. *See* PRAISE.

slim *adjective*

1. Having little flesh or fat on the body : angular, bony, fleshless, gaunt, lank, lanky, lean[2], meager, rawboned, scrawny, skinny, slender, spare, thin, twiggy, weedy. ***Idioms:*** all skin and bones, thin as a rail. *See* FAT. **2.** Small in degree, especially of probability : faint, negligible, outside, remote, slender, slight. *See* BIG.

slim *verb* **1.** To make physically thin or thinner : thin. *Archaic:* extenuate. *See* FAT, INCREASE. **2.** To lose body weight, as by dieting. Also used with *down* : reduce, trim down. *See* FAT, INCREASE.

slime *noun*

A viscous, usually offensively dirty substance : mire, muck, ooze, slop, sludge, slush. *See* CLEAN.

slimy *adjective*

Of, relating to, or covered with slime : miry, mucky, oozy, sludgy, slushy. *See* CLEAN.

sling *noun*

An act of throwing : cast, fling, heave, hurl, launch, pitch, shy[2], throw, toss. *See* MOVE.

sling *verb* **1.** To send through the air with a motion of the hand or arm : cast, dart, dash, fling, heave, hurl, hurtle, launch, pitch, shoot, shy[2], throw, toss. *Informal:* fire. *See* MOVE. **2.** To fasten or be fastened at one point with no support from below : dangle, depend, hang, suspend, swing. *See* HANG.

slink *verb*

To move silently and furtively : creep, glide, lurk, mouse, prowl, pussyfoot, skulk, slide, slip, snake, sneak, steal. *Slang:* gumshoe. *See* MOVE.

slinkiness *noun*

The act of proceeding slowly, deliberately, and secretly to escape observation : furtiveness, sneakiness, stealth, stealthiness. *See* MOVE.

slinky *adjective*

So slow, deliberate, and secret as to escape observation : catlike, feline, furtive, sneaking, sneaky, stealthy. *See* MOVE.

slip *verb*

1. To move smoothly, continuously, and effortlessly : glide, glissade, lapse, slide, slither. *See* MOVE. **2.** To move silently and furtively : creep, glide, lurk, mouse, prowl, pussyfoot, skulk, slide, slink, snake, sneak, steal. *Slang:* gumshoe. *See* MOVE. **3.** To lose one's balance and fall or almost fall : skid, slide, slither. ***Idiom:*** take a skid (*or* slide). *See* MOVE. **4.** To shift or be shifted out of place : slide. *See* MOVE. **5.** To maneuver gently and slowly into place : ease, glide, slide. *See* CAREFUL, EASY. **6.** To free from ties or fasteners : disengage, loose, loosen, unbind, unclasp, undo, unfasten, unloose, unloosen, untie. *See* TIGHTEN. **7.** To get away from (a pursuer) : elude, evade, lose, shake off, throw off. *Slang:* shake. ***Idiom:*** give someone the shake (*or* slip). *See* SEEK. **8.** To bring forth a nonviable fetus prematurely : abort, miscarry. *See* REPRODUCTION. **9.** To displace (a bone) from a socket or joint : dislocate, throw out. ***Idiom:*** throw out of joint. *See* HELP. **10.** To decline, as in value or quantity, very gradually : drop off, fall off, sag. *See* INCREASE. **11.** To make an error or mistake : err, miscue, mistake, slip up, stumble, trip up. *See* CORRECT. **12.** To undergo moral deterioration : fall, sink. ***Idiom:*** go bad (*or* wrong). *See* RIGHT.

slip into *verb* To put (an article of clothing) on one's person : assume, don, get on, pull on, put on, slip on. *See* PUT ON.

slip on *verb* To put (an article of clothing) on one's person : assume, don, get on, pull on, put on, slip into. *See* PUT ON.

slip up *verb* To make an error or mistake : err, miscue, mistake, slip, stumble, trip up. *See* CORRECT.

slip *noun* **1.** An act or thought that unintentionally deviates from what is correct, right, or true : erratum, error, inaccuracy, incorrectness, lapse, miscue, misstep, mistake, slip-up, trip. *See* CORRECT. **2.** A minor mistake : lapse, slip-up. *Informal:* fluff. *See* CORRECT.

slip into *verb* See **slip.**

slip on *verb* See **slip.**

slippery *adjective*

1. So smooth and glassy as to offer insecure hold or footing : lubricious, slick, slithery. ***Idiom:*** slippery as an eel. *See* SMOOTH. **2.** Characterized by or exhibiting evasion : elusive, evasive. *See* SEEK.

slipshod *adjective*

1. Indifferent to correctness, accuracy, or neatness : careless, messy, slapdash, sloppy, slovenly, untidy. *See* CAREFUL. **2.** Marked by an absence of cleanliness and order : disheveled, messy, mussy, sloppy, slovenly, unkempt, untidy. *See* ORDER.

slip-up *noun*

1. An act or thought that unintentionally deviates from what is correct, right, or true : erratum, error, inaccuracy, incorrectness, lapse, miscue, misstep, mistake, slip, trip. *See* CORRECT. **2.** A minor mistake : lapse, slip. *Informal:* fluff. *See* CORRECT.

slip up *verb* See **slip.**

slit *noun*

The result of cutting : cut, gash, incision, slash, slice, split. *See* ENTER, HELP.

slit *verb* **1.** To penetrate with a sharp edge : cut, gash, incise, pierce, slash. *See* ENTER, HELP. **2.** To separate into parts with or as if with a sharp-edged instrument : carve, cleave[1], cut, dissever, sever, slice, split. *See* ASSEMBLE.

slither *verb*

1. To lose one's balance and fall or almost fall : skid, slide, slip. ***Idiom:*** take a skid (*or* slide). *See* MOVE. **2.** To move sinuously : sinuate, snake, undulate. *See* MOVE. **3.** To move smoothly, continuously, and effortlessly : glide, glissade, lapse, slide, slip. *See* MOVE.

slithery *adjective*

So smooth and glassy as to offer insecure hold or footing : lubricious, slick, slippery. ***Idiom:*** slippery as an eel. *See* SMOOTH.

slobber *verb*

To let saliva run from the mouth : dribble, drivel, drool, salivate, slaver. *See* DRY, MOUTH.

slobber *noun* Saliva running from the mouth : drivel, drool, salivation, slaver. *See* DRY, MOUTH.

slog *verb*

1. To walk heavily, slowly, and with difficulty : plod, slop, toil, trudge, wade. *See* MOVE. **2.** To do tedious, laborious, and sometimes menial work : drudge, grub, plod, slave. *Informal:* grind. *See* WORK. **3.** To deliver a powerful blow to suddenly and sharply : bash, catch, clout, hit, knock, pop[1], slam, slug[3], smash, smite, sock, strike, swat, thwack, whack, wham, whop. *Informal:* biff, bop, clip[1], wallop. *Slang:* belt, conk, paste. ***Idioms:*** let someone have it, sock it to someone. *See* ATTACK, STRIKE.

slop *noun*

A viscous, usually offensively dirty substance : mire, muck, ooze, slime, sludge, slush. *See* CLEAN.

slop *verb* **1.** To hurl or scatter liquid upon : bespatter, dash, slosh, spatter, splash, splatter, spray, swash. *See* STRIKE. **2.** To walk heavily, slowly, and with difficulty : plod, slog, toil, trudge, wade. *See* MOVE.

slope *verb*

To depart or cause to depart from true vertical or horizontal : cant[1], heel[2], incline, lean[1], list[2], rake[2], slant, tilt, tip[2]. *See* STRAIGHT.

slope *noun* Deviation from a particular direction : cant[1], grade, gradient, heel[2], inclination, incline, lean[1], list[2], rake[2], slant, tilt, tip[2]. *See* RISE, STRAIGHT.

sloppiness *noun*

1. The state of being messy or unkempt : disorderliness, messiness, slovenliness, untidiness. *See* ORDER. **2.** *Informal.* The quality or condition of being affectedly or overly emotional : bathos, maudlinism, mawkishness, sentimentalism, sentimentality. *Informal:* mush, mushiness, schmaltz, schmaltziness. *Slang:* sappiness. *See* FEELINGS.

sloppy *adjective*

1. Marked by an absence of cleanliness and order : disheveled, messy, mussy, slipshod, slovenly, unkempt, untidy. *See* ORDER.
2. Indifferent to correctness, accuracy, or neatness : careless, messy, slapdash, slipshod, slovenly, untidy. *See* CAREFUL. **3.** *Informal.* Affectedly or extravagantly emotional : bathetic, gushy, maudlin, mawkish, romantic, sentimental, slushy, sobby, soft, soppy. *Informal:* gooey, mushy, schmaltzy, soupy. *Slang:* drippy, sappy, tear-jerking. *See* FEELINGS.

slosh *verb*

To hurl or scatter liquid upon : bespatter, dash, slop, spatter, splash, splatter, spray, swash. *See* STRIKE.

sloshed *adjective*

Slang. Stupefied, excited, or muddled with alcoholic liquor : besotted, crapulent, crapulous, drunk, drunken, inebriate, inebriated, intoxicated, sodden, tipsy. *Informal:* cock-eyed, stewed. *Slang:* blind, bombed, boozed, boozy, crocked, high, lit (up), loaded, looped, pickled, pixilated, plastered, potted, smashed, soused, stinking, stinko, stoned, tight, zonked. ***Idioms:*** drunk as a skunk, half-seas over, high as a kite, in one's cups, three sheets in (*or* to) the wind. *See* DRUGS.

slot *noun*

A post of employment : appointment, berth, billet, job, office, place, position, situation, spot. *Slang:* gig. *See* PLACE.

sloth *noun*

The quality or state of being lazy : idleness, indolence, laziness, shiftlessness, slothfulness, sluggardness, sluggishness. *Informal:* do-nothingism. *See* INDUSTRIOUS.

slothful *adjective*

Resistant to exertion and activity : fainéant, idle, indolent, lazy, shiftless, sluggard, sluggish. *Informal:* do-nothing. ***Idiom:*** bone lazy. *See* ACTION, INDUSTRIOUS.

slothfulness *noun*

The quality or state of being lazy : idleness, indolence, laziness, shiftlessness, sloth, sluggardness, sluggishness. *Informal:* do-nothingism. *See* INDUSTRIOUS.

slouch *verb*

1. To take on or move with an awkward, slovenly posture : loll, slump. *See* MOVE, POSTURE. **2.** To hang limply, loosely, and carelessly : droop, flop, loll, lop[2], sag, wilt. *See* HANG.

slouch *noun Slang.* A self-indulgent person who spends time avoiding work or other useful activity : bum[1], drone[1], fainéant, good-for-nothing, idler, layabout, loafer, ne'er-do-well, no-good, slugabed, sluggard, wastrel. *Informal:* do-little, do-nothing, lazybones, slug[2]. *See* INDUSTRIOUS.

slough[1] *noun*

A usually low-lying area of soft waterlogged ground and standing water : bog, fen, marsh, marshland, mire, morass, muskeg, quag, quagmire, swamp, swampland, wetland. *See* DRY.

slough[2] *verb*

To cast off by a natural process : exuviate, molt, shed, throw off. *See* PUT ON.

slovenliness *noun*

The state of being messy or unkempt : disorderliness, messiness, sloppiness, untidiness. *See* ORDER.

slovenly *adjective*

1. Marked by an absence of cleanliness and order : disheveled, messy, mussy, slipshod, sloppy, unkempt, untidy. *See* ORDER. **2.** Indifferent to correctness, accuracy, or neatness : careless, messy, slapdash, slipshod, sloppy, untidy. *See* CAREFUL.

slow *adjective*

1. Proceeding at a rate less than usual or desired : dilatory, laggard, slow-footed, slow-going, slow-paced, tardy. *Informal:* poky[1]. ***Idiom:*** slow as molasses in January. *See* FAST.
2. Characterized by reduced economic activity : down, dull, off, slack, sluggish, soft. *See* INCREASE. **3.** Having only a limited ability to learn and understand : backward, dull, simple, simple-minded, slow-witted. *Informal:* soft. *Offensive:* feeble-minded, half-witted, retarded, weak-minded. *See* ABILITY.

slow *adverb* So as to fall behind schedule : behind, behindhand, late. ***Idiom:*** behind time. *See* TIME.

slow *verb* To cause to be later or slower than expected or desired. Also used with *down* or *up* : delay, detain, hang up, hold up, lag, retard, set back, stall[2]. *See* HELP, TIME.

slowdown *noun*
The act or process of decreasing : abatement, curtailment, cut, cutback, decrease, decrement, diminishment, diminution, drain, reduction, slash, taper. *See* INCREASE.

slow-footed *adjective*
Proceeding at a rate less than usual or desired : dilatory, laggard, slow, slow-going, slow-paced, tardy. *Informal:* poky[1]. ***Idiom:*** slow as molasses in January. *See* FAST.

slow-going *adjective*
Proceeding at a rate less than usual or desired : dilatory, laggard, slow, slow-footed, slow-paced, tardy. *Informal:* poky[1]. ***Idiom:*** slow as molasses in January. *See* FAST.

slow-paced *adjective*
Proceeding at a rate less than usual or desired : dilatory, laggard, slow, slow-footed, slow-going, tardy. *Informal:* poky[1]. ***Idiom:*** slow as molasses in January. *See* FAST.

slowpoke *noun*
Informal. One that lags : dawdler, dilly-dallier, lag, laggard, lagger, lingerer, loiterer, poke, procrastinator, straggler, tarrier. *See* FAST.

slow-witted or **slowwitted** *adjective*
Having only a limited ability to learn and understand : backward, dull, simple, simple-minded, slow. *Informal:* soft. *Offensive:* feeble-minded, half-witted, retarded, weak-minded. *See* ABILITY.

sludge *noun*
A viscous, usually offensively dirty substance : mire, muck, ooze, slime, slop, slush. *See* CLEAN.

sludgy *adjective*
Of, relating to, or covered with slime : miry, mucky, oozy, slimy, slushy. *See* CLEAN.

slue[1] *verb*
To turn aside sharply from a straight course : chop[2], cut, sheer[1], skew, swerve, veer. *Nautical:* yaw. *See* CHANGE.

slue[2] *noun* See **slew.**

slug[1] *noun*
Informal. A small amount of liquor : dram, drop, jigger, shot, sip, tot[1]. *Informal:* nip[2]. *Slang:* snort. *See* BIG, INGESTION.

slug[2] *noun*
Informal. A self-indulgent person who spends time avoiding work or other useful activity : bum[1], drone[1], fainéant, good-for-nothing, idler, layabout, loafer, ne'er-do-well, no-good, slugabed, sluggard, wastrel. *Informal:* do-little, do-nothing, lazybones. *Slang:* slouch. *See* INDUSTRIOUS.

slug[3] *verb*
To deliver a powerful blow to suddenly and sharply : bash, catch, clout, hit, knock, pop[1], slam, slog, smash, smite, sock, strike, swat, thwack, whack, wham, whop. *Informal:* biff, bop, clip[1], wallop. *Slang:* belt, conk, paste. ***Idioms:*** let someone have it, sock it to someone. *See* ATTACK, STRIKE.

slug *noun* A sudden sharp, powerful stroke : bang, blow[2], clout, crack, hit, lick, pound, sock, swat, thwack, welt, whack, wham, whop. *Informal:* bash, biff, bop, clip[1], wallop. *Slang:* belt, conk, paste. *See* ATTACK, STRIKE.

slugabed *noun*
A self-indulgent person who spends time avoiding work or other useful activity : bum[1], drone[1], fainéant, good-for-nothing, idler, layabout, loafer, ne'er-do-well, no-good, sluggard, wastrel. *Informal:* do-little, do-nothing, lazybones, slug[2]. *Slang:* slouch. *See* INDUSTRIOUS.

sluggard *noun*
A self-indulgent person who spends time avoiding work or other useful activity : bum[1], drone[1], fainéant, good-for-nothing, idler, layabout, loafer, ne'er-do-well, no-good, slugabed, wastrel. *Informal:* do-little, do-nothing, lazybones, slug[2]. *Slang:* slouch. *See* INDUSTRIOUS.

sluggard *adjective* Resistant to exertion and activity : fainéant, idle, indolent, lazy, shiftless, slothful, sluggish. *Informal:* do-nothing. ***Idiom:*** bone lazy. *See* ACTION, INDUSTRIOUS.

sluggardness *noun*
The quality or state of being lazy : idleness, indolence, laziness, shiftlessness, sloth, slothfulness, sluggishness. *Informal:* do-nothingism. *See* INDUSTRIOUS.

sluggish *adjective*
1. Characterized by reduced economic activity : down, dull, off, slack, slow, soft. *See* INCREASE. **2.** Lacking mental and physical alertness and activity : hebetudinous, lethargic, stupid, stuporous, torpid. *Slang:* dopey. *See* ACTION. **3.** Resistant to exertion and activity : fainéant, idle, indolent, lazy, shiftless, slothful, sluggard. *Informal:* do-nothing. ***Idiom:*** bone lazy. *See* ACTION, INDUSTRIOUS.

sluggishness *noun*
1. A deficiency in mental and physical alertness and activity : dullness, hebetude, languidness, languor, lassitude, leadenness, lethargy, listlessness, stupor, torpidity, torpor. *See* ACTION.

2. The quality or state of being lazy : idleness, indolence, laziness, shiftlessness, sloth, slothfulness, sluggardness. *Informal:* do-nothingism. *See* INDUSTRIOUS.

slumber *verb*
To be asleep : sleep. ***Idioms:*** be in the land of Nod, catch some shuteye, sleep like a log (*or* rock *or* top), sleep tight. *See* AWARENESS.
slumber *noun* The natural recurring condition of suspended consciousness by which the body rests : sleep. *Slang:* shuteye. ***Idioms:*** land of Nod, the arms of Morpheus. *See* AWARENESS.

slumberless *adjective*
Marked by an absence of sleep : sleepless, wakeful. *See* AWARENESS.

slumberous or **slumbrous** *adjective*
1. Ready for or needing sleep : dozy, drowsy, nodding, sleepy, slumbery, somnolent, soporific. *See* AWARENESS. **2.** Inducing sleep or sedation : hypnotic, narcotic, opiate, sedative, sleepy, somnifacient, somniferous, somnific, somnolent, soporific. *See* AWARENESS.

slumbery *adjective*
Ready for or needing sleep : dozy, drowsy, nodding, sleepy, slumberous, somnolent, soporific. *See* AWARENESS.

slumbrous *adjective* See **slumberous.**

slump *verb*
1. To go from a more erect posture to a less erect posture : drop, fall, sink. *See* RISE. **2.** To take on or move with an awkward, slovenly posture : loll, slouch. *See* MOVE, POSTURE.
3. To undergo a sharp, rapid descent in value or price : dive, drop, fall, nose-dive, plummet, plunge, sink, skid, tumble. ***Idiom:*** take a sudden downtrend (*or* downturn). *See* INCREASE.
slump *noun* **1.** A usually swift downward trend, as in prices : decline, descent, dip, dive, downslide, downswing, downtrend, downturn, drop, drop-off, fall, nosedive, plunge, skid, slide, tumble. *See* INCREASE. **2.** A period of decreased business activity and high unemployment : depression, recession. *See* RICH.

slur *verb*
To make defamatory statements about : asperse, backbite, calumniate, defame, malign, slander, tear down, traduce, vilify. *Law:* libel. ***Idiom:*** cast aspersions on. *See* ATTACK, CRIMES, LAW.
slur *noun* An implied criticism : reflection, reproach. *See* PRAISE.

slush *noun*
A viscous, usually offensively dirty substance : mire, muck, ooze, slime, slop, sludge. *See* CLEAN.
slush *verb* To soil with mud : bemire, mire, muck (up), mud, muddy. *See* CLEAN.

slushy *adjective*
1. Of, relating to, or covered with slime : miry, mucky, oozy, slimy, sludgy. *See* CLEAN.
2. Affectedly or extravagantly emotional : bathetic, gushy, maudlin, mawkish, romantic, sentimental, sobby, soft, soppy. *Informal:* gooey, mushy, schmaltzy, sloppy, soupy. *Slang:* drippy, sappy, tear-jerking. *See* FEELINGS.

slut *noun*
A vulgar promiscuous woman who flouts propriety : baggage, hussy, jade, slattern, tart², tramp, wanton, wench, whore. *Slang:* floozy. *See* SEX.

sly *adjective*
1. Deceitfully clever : artful, crafty, cunning, foxy, guileful, scheming, sharp, tricky, wily. *See* ABILITY, HONEST, MEANS. **2.** Trickily secret : furtive, secretive, sneaking, sneaky, surreptitious. *See* HONEST.

slyness *noun*
1. Deceitful cleverness : art, artfulness, artifice, craft, craftiness, cunning, foxiness, guile, wiliness. *See* HONEST, MEANS. **2.** Lack of straightforwardness and honesty in action : chicanery, craft, craftiness, deviousness, dishonesty, indirection, shadiness, shiftiness, sneakiness, trickery, trickiness, underhandedness. *See* HONEST.

smack¹ *verb*
1. To touch or caress with the lips, especially as a sign of passion or affection : buss, kiss, osculate. *Informal:* peck¹. *Slang:* smooch. *See* TOUCH. **2.** To hit with a quick, sharp blow of the hand : box², buffet, bust, cuff, punch, slap, spank, swat, whack. *Informal:* clip¹, spat. *See* ATTACK, STRIKE.
smack *noun* **1.** The act or an instance of kissing : buss, kiss, osculation, smacker. *Informal:* peck¹. *Slang:* smooch. *See* TOUCH. **2.** A quick, sharp blow, especially with the hand : box², buffet, bust, chop¹, cuff, punch, slap, smacker, spank, swat, whack. *Informal:* clip¹, spat. *See* ATTACK, STRIKE.
smack *adverb* With precision or absolute conformity : bang, dead, direct, directly, exactly, fair, flush, just, precisely, right, square, squarely, straight. *Slang:* smack-dab. *See* PRECISE.

smack² *noun*
1. A distinctive property of a substance affecting the gustatory sense : flavor, relish, sapor, savor, tang, taste, zest. *See* TASTE. **2.** A distinctive yet intangible quality deemed typical of a

given thing : aroma, atmosphere, flavor, savor. *See* TASTE.

smack *verb* To have a particular flavor or suggestion of something : savor, smell, suggest, taste. *See* SUGGEST.

smack-dab *adverb*
Slang. With precision or absolute conformity : bang, dead, direct, directly, exactly, fair, flush, just, precisely, right, smack[1], square, squarely, straight. *See* PRECISE.

smacker *noun*
1. The act or an instance of kissing : buss, kiss, osculation, smack[1]. *Informal:* peck[1]. *Slang:* smooch. *See* TOUCH. **2.** A quick, sharp blow, especially with the hand : box[2], buffet, bust, chop[1], cuff, punch, slap, smack[1], spank, swat, whack. *Informal:* clip[1], spat. *See* ATTACK, STRIKE.

small *adjective*
1. Notably below average in amount, size, or scope : bantam, little, petite, smallish. *See* BIG. **2.** Contemptibly unimportant : inconsiderable, negligible, niggling, nugatory, paltry, petty, picayune, piddling, small-minded, trifling. *Slang:* measly. ***Idiom:*** of no account. *See* IMPORTANT. **3.** Below another in standing or importance : inferior, junior, lesser, low, lower[2], minor, minor-league, petty, secondary, subaltern, subordinate, under. *Informal:* smalltime. *See* OVER. **4.** Not yet large in size because of incomplete growth : little. *See* YOUTH. **5.** Not broad or elevated in scope or understanding : limited, little, narrow, narrow-minded, petty, small-minded. *See* LIMITED, WIDE. **6.** Not irritating, strident, or loud : hushed, low, low-key, low-keyed, quiet, soft, subdued, whispery. *See* SOUNDS.

small change *noun*
1. A small or trifling amount of money : *Informal:* peanut (used in plural). *Slang:* chicken feed, two bits. *See* BIG, MONEY. **2.** Something or things that are unimportant : fiddle-faddle, frippery, frivolity, froth, minutia, nonsense, small potatoes, trifle, trivia, triviality. *See* IMPORTANT, SURFACE.

smallest *adjective*
Comprising the least possible : littlest, minimal, minimum. *See* BIG.

smallish *adjective*
Notably below average in amount, size, or scope : bantam, little, petite, small. *See* BIG.

small-minded *adjective*
1. Not broad or elevated in scope or understanding : limited, little, narrow, narrow-minded, petty, small. *See* LIMITED, WIDE. **2.** Contemptibly unimportant : inconsiderable, negligible, niggling, nugatory, paltry, petty, picayune, piddling, small, trifling. *Slang:* measly. ***Idiom:*** of no account. *See* IMPORTANT.

smallness *noun*
Contemptible unimportance : inconsiderableness, negligibility, negligibleness, paltriness, pettiness, triviality, trivialness. *See* IMPORTANT.

small potatoes *noun*
Something or things that are unimportant : fiddle-faddle, frippery, frivolity, froth, minutia, nonsense, small change, trifle, trivia, triviality. *See* IMPORTANT, SURFACE.

small talk *noun*
Incessant and usually inconsequential talk : babble, blab, blabber, chat, chatter, chitchat, jabber, palaver, prate, prattle. *Slang:* gab, gas, yak. *See* WORDS.

smalltime or **small-time** *adjective*
Informal. Below another in standing or importance : inferior, junior, lesser, low, lower[2], minor, minor-league, petty, secondary, small, subaltern, subordinate, under. *See* OVER.

small-town *adjective*
Having the restricted outlook often characteristic of geographic isolation : insular, limited, local, narrow, narrow-minded, parochial, provincial. *See* LIMITED.

smarmy *adjective*
Affectedly and self-servingly earnest : fulsome, oily, oleaginous, sleek, unctuous. *See* ATTITUDE, HONEST.

smart *adjective*
1. Mentally quick and original : alert, bright, clever, intelligent, keen[1], quick, quick-witted, sharp, sharp-witted. ***Idiom:*** smart as a whip. *See* ABILITY. **2.** Amusing or pleasing because of wit or originality : clever, scintillating, sparkling, witty. *See* LAUGHTER. **3.** Rude and disrespectful : assuming, assumptive, audacious, bold, bold-faced, brash, brazen, cheeky, contumelious, familiar, forward, impertinent, impudent, insolent, malapert, nervy, overconfident, pert, presuming, presumptuous, pushy, sassy, saucy. *Informal:* brassy, flip, fresh, smart-alecky, snippety, snippy, uppish, uppity. *Slang:* wise[1]. *See* ATTITUDE, COURTESY. **4.** Having or showing a clever awareness and resourcefulness in practical matters : astute, cagey, canny, knowing, perspicacious, shrewd, slick, wise[1]. *Informal:* savvy. *See* ABILITY, CAREFUL. **5.** Being or in accordance with the current fashion : à la mode, chic, dashing, fashionable, mod, modish, posh, stylish, swank, swanky,

trig. *Informal:* classy, in, sharp, snappy, swish, tony, trendy. *Slang:* with-it. ***Idioms:*** all the rage, up to the minute. *See* STYLE, USUAL.

smart *verb* To feel or cause to feel heat or discomfort : bite, burn, sting. *See* PAIN.

smart *noun* **1.** A sensation of physical discomfort occurring as the result of disease or injury : ache, pain, pang, prick, prickle, soreness, stab, sting, stitch, throe, twinge. *Informal:* misery. *See* PAIN. **2.** *Slang.* The faculty of thinking, reasoning, and acquiring and applying knowledge. Used in plural : brain (often used in plural), brainpower, intellect, intelligence, mentality, mind, sense, understanding, wit. *See* ABILITY, THOUGHTS.

smart aleck *noun*
Informal. One who is obnoxiously self-assertive and arrogant : malapert, witling. *Informal:* know-it-all, saucebox, smarty, smarty-pants, wisenheimer. *Slang:* wiseacre, wisecracker, wise guy. *See* GOOD.

smart-alecky *adjective*
Informal. Rude and disrespectful : assuming, assumptive, audacious, bold, boldfaced, brash, brazen, cheeky, contumelious, familiar, forward, impertinent, impudent, insolent, malapert, nervy, overconfident, pert, presuming, presumptuous, pushy, sassy, saucy, smart. *Informal:* brassy, flip, fresh, snippety, snippy, uppish, uppity. *Slang:* wise[1]. *See* ATTITUDE, COURTESY.

smarten *verb*
To improve in appearance, especially by refurbishing. Also used with *up* : fix up, spruce (up). *See* BETTER.

smarting *adjective*
Marked by, causing, or experiencing physical pain : aching, achy, afflictive, hurtful, nagging, painful, sore. *See* PAIN.

smarty *noun*
Informal. One who is obnoxiously self-assertive and arrogant : malapert, witling. *Informal:* know-it-all, saucebox, smart aleck, smarty-pants, wisenheimer. *Slang:* wiseacre, wisecracker, wise guy. *See* GOOD.

smarty-pants *noun*
Informal. One who is obnoxiously self-assertive and arrogant : malapert, witling. *Informal:* know-it-all, saucebox, smart aleck, smarty, wisenheimer. *Slang:* wiseacre, wisecracker, wise guy. *See* GOOD.

smash *verb*
1. To crack or split into two or more fragments by means of or as a result of force, a blow, or strain : break, fracture, rift, rive, shatter, shiver[2], splinter, sunder. *See* HELP. **2.** To strike together with a loud, harsh noise : clash, crash. *See* SOUNDS. **3.** To undergo wrecking : crash. *Informal:* crack up, pile up. *See* HELP. **4.** To deliver a powerful blow to suddenly and sharply : bash, catch, clout, hit, knock, pop[1], slam, slog, slug[3], smite, sock, strike, swat, thwack, whack, wham, whop. *Informal:* biff, bop, clip[1], wallop. *Slang:* belt, conk, paste. ***Idioms:*** let someone have it, sock it to someone. *See* ATTACK, STRIKE. **5.** To hit heavily and repeatedly with violent blows : assail, assault, baste, batter, beat, belabor, buffet, drub, hammer, pound, pummel, thrash, thresh. *Informal:* lambaste. *Slang:* clobber. ***Idiom:*** rain blows on. *See* ATTACK, STRIKE. **6.** To cause the complete ruin or wreckage of : bankrupt, break down, cross up, demolish, destroy, finish, ruin, shatter, sink, spoil, torpedo, undo, wash up, wrack[2], wreck. *Slang:* total. ***Idiom:*** put the kibosh on. *See* HELP. **7.** To render totally ineffective by decisive defeat : annihilate, crush, drub, overpower, overwhelm, steamroller, thrash, trounce, vanquish. *Informal:* massacre, wallop. *Slang:* clobber, cream, shellac, smear. *See* WIN.

smash *noun* **1.** A loud striking together : clash, crash. *See* SOUNDS. **2.** A forceful movement causing a loud noise : bang, crash, slam, wham. *See* STRIKE. **3.** An abrupt disastrous failure : breakdown, collapse, crash, debacle, smashup, wreck. *See* MONEY. **4.** Violent forcible contact between two or more things : bump, collision, concussion, crash, impact, jar, jolt, percussion, shock[1]. *See* CONFLICT. **5.** A wrecking of a vehicle : crash, smashup, wreck. *Informal:* crackup, pileup. *See* HELP. **6.** *Informal.* A dazzling, often sudden instance of success : hit, sleeper. *Informal:* smash hit, tenstrike, wow. *Slang:* boff, boffo, boffola. *See* THRIVE.

smashed *adjective*
Slang. Stupefied, excited, or muddled with alcoholic liquor : besotted, crapulent, crapulous, drunk, drunken, inebriate, inebriated, intoxicated, sodden, tipsy. *Informal:* cock-eyed, stewed. *Slang:* blind, bombed, boozed, boozy, crocked, high, lit (up), loaded, looped, pickled, pixilated, plastered, potted, sloshed, soused, stinking, stinko, stoned, tight, zonked. ***Idioms:*** drunk as a skunk, half-seas over, high as a kite, in one's cups, three sheets in (*or* to) the wind. *See* DRUGS.

smash hit *noun*
Informal. A dazzling, often sudden instance of

success : hit, sleeper. *Informal:* smash, tenstrike, wow. *Slang:* boff, boffo, boffola. *See* THRIVE.

smashup *noun*
1. An abrupt disastrous failure : breakdown, collapse, crash, debacle, smash, wreck. *See* MONEY. **2.** A wrecking of a vehicle : crash, smash, wreck. *Informal:* crackup, pileup. *See* HELP.

smatterer *noun*
One lacking professional skill and ease in a particular pursuit : amateur, dabbler, dilettante, nonprofessional, uninitiate. *See* ABILITY.

smaze *noun*
A thick, heavy atmospheric condition offering reduced visibility because of the presence of suspended particles : brume, fog, haze, mist, murk. *See* CLEAR.

smear *verb*
1. To spread with a greasy, sticky, or dirty substance : bedaub, besmear, dab[1], daub, plaster, smirch, smudge. *See* PUT ON. **2.** To contaminate the reputation of : befoul, besmear, besmirch, bespatter, blacken, cloud, denigrate, dirty, smudge, smut, soil, spatter, stain, sully, taint, tarnish. ***Idioms:*** give a black eye to, sling (*or* throw) mud on. *See* ATTACK, CLEAN. **3.** *Slang.* To render totally ineffective by decisive defeat : annihilate, crush, drub, overpower, overwhelm, smash, steamroller, thrash, trounce, vanquish. *Informal:* massacre, wallop. *Slang:* clobber, cream, shellac. *See* WIN.
smear *noun* **1.** A discolored mark made by smearing : blot, blotch, daub, smirch, smudge, smutch, splotch, stain. *See* MARKS. **2.** An attempt to destroy someone's reputation : mudslinging, smear campaign. *See* PRAISE.

smear campaign *noun*
An attempt to destroy someone's reputation : mudslinging, smear. *See* PRAISE.

smell *verb*
1. To perceive with the olfactory sense : nose, scent, sniff, snuff, whiff. ***Idiom:*** catch (*or* get) a whiff of. *See* SMELLS. **2.** To have or give off a foul odor : reek, stink. ***Idiom:*** smell to high heaven. *See* SMELLS. **3.** To have a particular flavor or suggestion of something : savor, smack[2], suggest, taste. *See* SUGGEST.
smell *noun* **1.** The sense by which odors are perceived : nose, olfaction, scent. *See* SMELLS. **2.** The quality of something that may be perceived by the olfactory sense : aroma, odor, scent. *See* SMELLS. **3.** A general impression produced by a predominant quality or characteristic : air, ambiance, atmosphere, aura, feel, feeling, mood, tone. *See* BE.

smelly *adjective*
Informal. Having an unpleasant odor : fetid, foul, foul-smelling, malodorous, mephitic, noisome, reeky, stinking. *See* SMELLS.

smidgen also **smidgeon** or **smidgin** *noun*
A tiny amount : bit[1], crumb, dab[1], dash, dot, dram, drop, fragment, grain, iota, jot, minim, mite, modicum, molecule, ort, ounce, particle, scrap[1], scruple, shred, speck, tittle, trifle, whit. *Chiefly British:* spot. *See* BIG.

smidgeon *noun* See **smidgen.**

smidgin *noun* See **smidgen.**

smile *noun*
A facial expression marked by an upward curving of the lips : grin. *See* EXPRESS.
smile *verb* To curve the lips upward in expressing amusement, pleasure, or happiness : beam, grin. ***Idioms:*** break into a smile, crack a smile. *See* EXPRESS.
smile on (or **upon**) *verb* To lend supportive approval to : countenance, encourage, favor. *See* SUPPORT.

smile on or **upon** *verb* See **smile.**

smirch *verb*
To spread with a greasy, sticky, or dirty substance : bedaub, besmear, dab[1], daub, plaster, smear, smudge. *See* PUT ON.
smirch *noun* A discolored mark made by smearing : blot, blotch, daub, smear, smudge, smutch, splotch, stain. *See* MARKS.

smirk *verb*
To smile in an affected, knowing way : simper. *See* EXPRESS.
smirk *noun* An affected, knowing smile : simper. *See* EXPRESS.

smite *verb*
1. To deliver a powerful blow to suddenly and sharply : bash, catch, clout, hit, knock, pop[1], slam, slog, slug[3], smash, sock, strike, swat, thwack, whack, wham, whop. *Informal:* biff, bop, clip[1], wallop. *Slang:* belt, conk, paste. ***Idioms:*** let someone have it, sock it to someone. *See* ATTACK, STRIKE. **2.** To bring great harm or suffering to : afflict, agonize, anguish, curse, excruciate, plague, rack, scourge, strike, torment, torture. *See* ATTACK, HELP.

smitten *adjective*
Affected with intense romantic attraction : enamored, infatuate, infatuated. *Slang:* gone. *See* EXCITE, SEX.

smoggy *adjective*
Heavy, dark, or dense, especially with impurities : hazy, murky, turbid. *See* CLEAR.

smolder *verb*
To be in a state of emotional or mental turmoil : boil, bubble, burn, churn, ferment, seethe, simmer. *See* CALM.

smooch *noun*
Slang. The act or an instance of kissing : buss, kiss, osculation, smack[1], smacker. *Informal:* peck[1]. *See* TOUCH.
smooch *verb Slang.* To touch or caress with the lips, especially as a sign of passion or affection : buss, kiss, osculate, smack[1]. *Informal:* peck[1]. *See* TOUCH.

smooth *adjective*
1. Having no irregularities, roughness, or indentations : even[1], flat, flush, level, planar, plane[1], straight. *See* SMOOTH. **2.** Free from severity or violence, as in movement : balmy[1], delicate, faint, gentle, mild, soft. *See* CALM, STRONG. **3.** Posing no difficulty : easy, effortless, facile, simple. *Informal:* snap. ***Idioms:*** easy as ABC, easy as falling off a log, easy as one-two-three, easy as pie, like taking candy from a baby, nothing to it. *See* EASY. **4.** Effortlessly gracious and tactful in social manner : bland, suave, urbane. *See* STYLE. **5.** Marked by facility, especially of expression : easy, effortless, flowing, fluent, fluid, graceful. *See* STYLE.
smooth *verb* **1.** To make even, smooth, or level : even[1], flat, flatten, level, plane[2], straighten. *See* SMOOTH. **2.** To bring to perfection or completion : perfect, polish, refine. ***Idiom:*** smooth off the rough edges. *See* BETTER.
smooth over *verb* To bring (something) into a state of agreement or accord : reconcile, rectify, resolve, settle, straighten out. *See* AGREE.

smooth over *verb* See **smooth.**

smooth-spoken *adjective*
Fluently persuasive and forceful : articulate, eloquent, facund, silver-tongued. *See* WORDS.

smooth-tongued *adjective*
Characterized by ready but often insincere or superficial discourse : facile, glib, slick. *See* SURFACE, WORDS.

smother *verb*
1. To stop the breathing of : asphyxiate, choke, stifle, suffocate. *See* BREATH. **2.** To hold (something requiring an outlet) in check : burke, choke (back), gag, hold back, hold down, hush (up), muffle, quench, repress, squelch, stifle, strangle, suppress, throttle. *Informal:* sit on (*or* upon). *See* RESTRAINT.

smudge *verb*
1. To make dirty : befoul, begrime, besmirch, besoil, black, blacken, defile, dirty, smutch, soil, sully. *See* CLEAN. **2.** To spread with a greasy, sticky, or dirty substance : bedaub, besmear, dab[1], daub, plaster, smear, smirch. *See* PUT ON. **3.** To contaminate the reputation of : befoul, besmear, besmirch, bespatter, blacken, cloud, denigrate, dirty, smear, smut, soil, spatter, stain, sully, taint, tarnish. ***Idioms:*** give a black eye to, sling (*or* throw) mud on. *See* ATTACK, CLEAN.
smudge *noun* A discolored mark made by smearing : blot, blotch, daub, smear, smirch, smutch, splotch, stain. *See* MARKS.

smuggle *verb*
1. To import or export secretly and illegally : bootleg, run. ***Idiom:*** run contraband. *See* CRIMES, MOVE. **2.** To bring in or take out secretly : sneak, spirit. *See* MOVE.

smuggler *noun*
A person who engages in smuggling : bootlegger, contrabandist, runner. *See* CRIMES, MOVE.

smut *noun*
Something that is offensive to accepted standards of decency : bawdry, dirt, filth, obscenity, profanity, ribaldry, scatology, vulgarity. *Slang:* raunch. *See* DECENT.
smut *verb* **1.** To soil with foreign matter : bestain, discolor, stain. *See* CLEAN, MARKS. **2.** To contaminate the reputation of : befoul, besmear, besmirch, bespatter, blacken, cloud, denigrate, dirty, smear, smudge, soil, spatter, stain, sully, taint, tarnish. ***Idioms:*** give a black eye to, sling (*or* throw) mud on. *See* ATTACK, CLEAN.

smutch *verb*
To make dirty : befoul, begrime, besmirch, besoil, black, blacken, defile, dirty, smudge, soil, sully. *See* CLEAN.
smutch *noun* A discolored mark made by smearing : blot, blotch, daub, smear, smirch, smudge, splotch, stain. *See* MARKS.

smuttiness *noun*
1. The condition or state of being dirty : dirtiness, filth, filthiness, foulness, griminess, grubbiness, squalor, uncleanliness, uncleanness. *See* CLEAN. **2.** The quality or state of being obscene : bawdiness, coarseness, dirtiness, filthiness, foulness, grossness, lewdness, obscenity, profaneness, profanity, scurrility, scurrilousness, vulgarity, vulgarness. *Slang:* raunch, raunchiness. *See* DECENT.

smutty *adjective*
1. Covered or stained with or as if with dirt or other impurities : black, dirty, filthy, grimy, grubby, soiled, unclean, uncleanly. *See* CLEAN.

2. Offensive to accepted standards of decency : barnyard, bawdy, broad, coarse, dirty, Fescennine, filthy, foul, gross, lewd, nasty, obscene, profane, ribald, scatologic, scatological, scurrilous, vulgar. *Slang:* raunchy. *See* DECENT.

snack *noun*
A light meal : bite, morsel. *See* INGESTION.

snaffle *noun*
An instrument or means of restraining : bit[2], brake, bridle, leash, restraint. *See* RESTRAINT.

snafu *noun*
1. *Slang.* A ruinous state of disorder : botch, foul-up, mess, muddle, shambles. *Informal:* hash. *Slang:* screwup. *See* CORRECT, ORDER.
2. *Slang.* A lack of order or regular arrangement : chaos, clutter, confusedness, confusion, derangement, disarrangement, disarray, disorder, disorderedness, disorderliness, disorganization, jumble, mess, mix-up, muddle, muss, scramble, topsy-turviness, tumble. *See* ORDER.
snafu *verb* **1.** *Slang.* To put into total disorder : ball up, confuse, disorder, jumble, mess up, muddle, scramble, snarl[2]. ***Idiom:*** play havoc with. *See* ORDER. **2.** *Slang.* To harm irreparably through inept handling; make a mess : ball up, blunder, boggle, botch, bungle, foul up, fumble, gum up, mess up, mishandle, mismanage, muddle, muff, spoil. *Informal:* bollix up, muck up. *Slang:* blow[1], goof up, louse up, screw up. ***Idiom:*** make a muck of. *See* CORRECT, HELP.

snag *noun*
1. Something that impedes or prevents entry or passage : bar, barricade, barrier, block, blockage, clog, hamper, hindrance, hurdle, impediment, obstacle, obstruction, stop, traverse, wall. *See* HELP, OPEN. **2.** A tricky or unsuspected condition : rub. *Informal:* catch. *See* LIMITED.

snail's pace *noun*
A very slow rate of speed : crawl, creep. *See* FAST.

snake *verb*
1. To move sinuously : sinuate, slither, undulate. *See* MOVE. **2.** To move or proceed on a repeatedly curving course : coil, corkscrew, curl, entwine, meander, spiral, twine, twist, weave, wind[2], wreathe. *See* REPETITION, STRAIGHT. **3.** To move along in a crouching or prone position : crawl, creep, slide, worm. *See* MOVE. **4.** To move silently and furtively : creep, glide, lurk, mouse, prowl, pussyfoot, skulk, slide, slink, slip, sneak, steal. *Slang:* gumshoe. *See* MOVE.

snaky *adjective*
Repeatedly curving in alternate directions : anfractuous, flexuous, meandrous, serpentine, sinuous, tortuous, winding. *See* REPETITION, STRAIGHT.

snap *verb*
1. To make a light, sharp noise : clack, click. *See* SOUNDS. **2.** To make a sudden sharp, explosive noise : bang, bark, clap, crack, pop[1]. *See* SOUNDS. **3.** To give way mentally and emotionally : break (down), collapse, crack. *Informal:* crack up, fold. *See* EXPLOSION.
4. To grasp at (something) eagerly, forcibly, and abruptly with the jaws : catch, nip[1], snatch, strike. *See* REACH. **5.** To speak abruptly and sharply : bark, snarl[1]. ***Idioms:*** bite someone's head off, snap someone's head (*or* nose) off. *See* WORDS. **6.** To move or cause to move with a sudden abrupt motion : jerk, lurch, twitch, wrench, yank. *See* MOVE, PUSH.
snap *noun* **1.** A light, sharp noise : clack, click. *See* SOUNDS. **2.** A sudden sharp, explosive noise : bang, bark, clap, crack, explosion, pop[1], rat-a-tat-tat, report. *See* SOUNDS. **3.** A sudden motion, such as a pull : jerk, lurch, tug, twitch, wrench, yank. *See* MOVE, PUSH.
4. *Informal.* A quality of active mental and physical forcefulness : dash, punch, starch, verve, vigor, vigorousness, vim, vitality. ***Idiom:*** vim and vigor. *See* ACTION, TIRED. **5.** An easily accomplished task : child's play, cinch, pushover, walkaway, walkover. *Informal:* breeze. *Slang:* duck soup. *See* EASY.
snap *adjective* **1.** Spoken, performed, or composed with little or no preparation or forethought : ad-lib, extemporaneous, extemporary, extempore, impromptu, improvised, offhand, spur-of-the-moment, unrehearsed. *Informal:* off-the-cuff. *See* PREPARED.
2. *Informal.* Posing no difficulty : easy, effortless, facile, simple, smooth. ***Idioms:*** easy as ABC, easy as falling off a log, easy as one-two-three, easy as pie, like taking candy from a baby, nothing to it. *See* EASY.

snappish *adjective*
Having or showing a bad temper : bad-tempered, cantankerous, crabbed, cranky, cross, disagreeable, fretful, grouchy, grumpy, ill-tempered, irascible, irritable, nasty, peevish, petulant, querulous, snappy, surly, testy, ugly, waspish. *Informal:* crabby, mean[2]. ***Idiom:*** out of sorts. *See* ATTITUDE.

snappy *adjective*
1. *Informal.* Full of or characterized by a lively, emphatic, eager quality : fiery, high-spirited,

mettlesome, peppery, spirited, vibrant. *See* ACTION, FEELINGS. **2.** *Informal.* Disposed to action : active, brisk, driving, dynamic, dynamical, energetic, enterprising, lively, sprightly, spry, vigorous, zippy. *Informal:* peppy. *See* ACTION. **3.** *Informal.* Being or in accordance with the current fashion : à la mode, chic, dashing, fashionable, mod, modish, posh, smart, stylish, swank, swanky, trig. *Informal:* classy, in, sharp, swish, tony, trendy. *Slang:* with-it. ***Idioms:*** all the rage, up to the minute. *See* STYLE, USUAL. **4.** Having or showing a bad temper : bad-tempered, cantankerous, crabbed, cranky, cross, disagreeable, fretful, grouchy, grumpy, ill-tempered, irascible, irritable, nasty, peevish, petulant, querulous, snappish, surly, testy, ugly, waspish. *Informal:* crabby, mean[2]. ***Idiom:*** out of sorts. *See* ATTITUDE.

snare *noun*
Something that leads one into a place or situation from which escape is difficult : bait, lure, trap. *See* LIKE, SAFETY.
snare *verb* To gain control of or an advantage over by or as if by trapping : catch, enmesh, ensnare, ensnarl, entrap, tangle, trammel, trap, web. *See* FREE.

snarl[1] *verb*
To speak abruptly and sharply : bark, snap. ***Idioms:*** bite someone's head off, snap someone's head (*or* nose) off. *See* WORDS.

snarl[2] *noun*
Something that is intricately and often bewilderingly complex : cat's cradle, entanglement, jungle, knot, labyrinth, maze, mesh (often used in plural), morass, skein, tangle, web. *See* SIMPLE.
snarl *verb* **1.** To twist together so that separation is difficult : ensnarl, entangle, foul, tangle. *See* ORDER. **2.** To make complex, intricate, or perplexing : complicate, embarrass, entangle, involve, perplex, ravel, tangle. *See* SIMPLE. **3.** To put into total disorder : ball up, confuse, disorder, jumble, mess up, muddle, scramble. *Slang:* snafu. ***Idiom:*** play havoc with. *See* ORDER.

snatch *verb*
1. To grasp at (something) eagerly, forcibly, and abruptly with the jaws : catch, nip[1], snap, strike. *See* REACH. **2.** To get hold of (something moving) : catch, clutch[1], grab, seize. *Informal:* nab. ***Idiom:*** lay hands on. *See* GET. **3.** To take quick and forcible possession of : commandeer, confiscate, expropriate, grab, seize. ***Idiom:*** help oneself to. *See* GIVE. **4.** To take (another's property) without permission : filch, pilfer, purloin, steal, thieve. *Informal:* lift, swipe. *Slang:* cop, heist, hook, nip[1], pinch, rip off, snitch. ***Idiom:*** make (*or* walk) off with. *See* CRIMES, GIVE. **5.** To seize and detain (a person) unlawfully : abduct, kidnap, spirit away. *See* CRIMES, FREE.
snatch *noun* The act of catching, especially a sudden taking and holding : catch, clutch[1], grab, seizure. *See* GET.

sneak *verb*
1. To move silently and furtively : creep, glide, lurk, mouse, prowl, pussyfoot, skulk, slide, slink, slip, snake, steal. *Slang:* gumshoe. *See* MOVE. **2.** To bring in or take out secretly : smuggle, spirit. *See* MOVE.
sneak *noun* One who behaves in a stealthy, furtive way : prowler, sneaker, weasel. *See* MOVE.

sneaker *noun*
One who behaves in a stealthy, furtive way : prowler, sneak, weasel. *See* MOVE.

sneakiness *noun*
1. The act of proceeding slowly, deliberately, and secretly to escape observation : furtiveness, slinkiness, stealth, stealthiness. *See* MOVE. **2.** Lack of straightforwardness and honesty in action : chicanery, craft, craftiness, deviousness, dishonesty, indirection, shadiness, shiftiness, slyness, trickery, trickiness, underhandedness. *See* HONEST.

sneaking *adjective*
1. So slow, deliberate, and secret as to escape observation : catlike, feline, furtive, slinky, sneaky, stealthy. *See* MOVE. **2.** Trickily secret : furtive, secretive, sly, sneaky, surreptitious. *See* HONEST.

sneaky *adjective*
1. So slow, deliberate, and secret as to escape observation : catlike, feline, furtive, slinky, sneaking, stealthy. *See* MOVE. **2.** Trickily secret : furtive, secretive, sly, sneaking, surreptitious. *See* HONEST. **3.** Marked by treachery or deceit : devious, disingenuous, duplicitous, guileful, indirect, lubricious, shifty, underhand, underhanded. *See* HONEST.

sneer *noun*
A facial expression or laugh conveying scorn or derision : fleer, snicker, snigger. *See* EXPRESS, LAUGHTER, RESPECT.
sneer *verb* To smile or laugh scornfully or derisively : fleer, snicker, snigger. ***Idiom:*** curl one's lip. *See* EXPRESS, LAUGHTER, RESPECT.

sneering *adjective*
Contemptuous or ironic in manner or wit :

derisive, jeering, mocking, sarcastic, satiric, satirical, scoffing. *See* LAUGHTER, RESPECT.

snicker *verb*
1. To laugh in a stifled way : giggle, snigger, titter. *See* LAUGHTER. **2.** To smile or laugh scornfully or derisively : fleer, sneer, snigger. ***Idiom:*** curl one's lip. *See* EXPRESS, LAUGHTER, RESPECT.
snicker *noun* **1.** A stifled laugh : giggle, snigger, titter. *See* LAUGHTER. **2.** A facial expression or laugh conveying scorn or derision : fleer, sneer, snigger. *See* EXPRESS, LAUGHTER, RESPECT.

sniff *verb*
To perceive with the olfactory sense : nose, scent, smell, snuff, whiff. ***Idiom:*** catch (*or* get) a whiff of. *See* SMELLS.

snigger *noun*
1. A stifled laugh : giggle, snicker, titter. *See* LAUGHTER. **2.** A facial expression or laugh conveying scorn or derision : fleer, sneer, snicker. *See* EXPRESS, LAUGHTER, RESPECT.
snigger *verb* **1.** To laugh in a stifled way : giggle, snicker, titter. *See* LAUGHTER. **2.** To smile or laugh scornfully or derisively : fleer, sneer, snicker. ***Idiom:*** curl one's lip. *See* EXPRESS, LAUGHTER, RESPECT.

snippety *adjective*
Informal. Rude and disrespectful : assuming, assumptive, audacious, bold, boldfaced, brash, brazen, cheeky, contumelious, familiar, forward, impertinent, impudent, insolent, malapert, nervy, overconfident, pert, presuming, presumptuous, pushy, sassy, saucy, smart. *Informal:* brassy, flip, fresh, smart-alecky, snippy, uppish, uppity. *Slang:* wise[1]. *See* ATTITUDE, COURTESY.

snippy *adjective*
Informal. Rude and disrespectful : assuming, assumptive, audacious, bold, boldfaced, brash, brazen, cheeky, contumelious, familiar, forward, impertinent, impudent, insolent, malapert, nervy, overconfident, pert, presuming, presumptuous, pushy, sassy, saucy, smart. *Informal:* brassy, flip, fresh, smart-alecky, snippety, uppish, uppity. *Slang:* wise[1]. *See* ATTITUDE, COURTESY.

snit *noun*
Informal. A condition of excited distress : fume. *Informal:* state, sweat, swivet. *Slang:* tizzy. *See* CALM.

snitch *verb*
1. *Slang.* To take (another's property) without permission : filch, pilfer, purloin, snatch, steal, thieve. *Informal:* lift, swipe. *Slang:* cop, heist, hook, nip[1], pinch, rip off. ***Idiom:*** make (*or* walk) off with. *See* CRIMES, GIVE. **2.** *Slang.* To give incriminating information about others, especially to the authorities : inform, talk, tattle, tip[3] (off). *Slang:* fink, rat, sing, squeal, stool. ***Idiom:*** blow the whistle. *See* KNOWLEDGE, LAW.
snitch *noun Slang.* One who gives incriminating information about others : informant, informer, tattler, tattletale. *Informal:* rat, tipster. *Slang:* fink, snitcher, squealer, stoolie, stool pigeon. *See* KNOWLEDGE, LAW.

snitcher *noun*
Slang. One who gives incriminating information about others : informant, informer, tattler, tattletale. *Informal:* rat, tipster. *Slang:* fink, snitch, squealer, stoolie, stool pigeon. *See* KNOWLEDGE, LAW.

snob *noun*
One who despises people or things regarded as inferior, especially because of social or intellectual pretension : elitist. *Informal:* snoot. *See* ATTITUDE, SELF-LOVE.

snobbish *adjective*
Characteristic of or resembling a snob : elitist, snobby. *Informal:* high-hat, snooty, stuck-up, uppish, uppity. *See* ATTITUDE, SELF-LOVE.

snobby *adjective*
Characteristic of or resembling a snob : elitist, snobbish. *Informal:* high-hat, snooty, stuck-up, uppish, uppity. *See* ATTITUDE, SELF-LOVE.

snoop *verb*
To look into or inquire about curiously, inquisitively, or in a meddlesome fashion : poke, pry. *Informal:* nose (around). ***Idiom:*** stick one's nose into. *See* INVESTIGATE, PARTICIPATE.
snoop *noun* A person who snoops : prier, pry, snooper. *See* INVESTIGATE, PARTICIPATE.

snooper *noun*
A person who snoops : prier, pry, snoop. *See* INVESTIGATE, PARTICIPATE.

snoopiness *noun*
Informal. Undue interest in the affairs of others : curiosity, curiousness, inquisitiveness. *Informal:* nosiness. *See* INVESTIGATE.

snoopy *adjective*
Informal. Unduly interested in the affairs of others : curious, inquisitive, inquisitorial. *Informal:* nosy. *See* INVESTIGATE.

snoot *noun*
1. *Informal.* The structure on the human face that contains the nostrils and organs of smell and forms the beginning of the respiratory tract : nose, proboscis. *Informal:* beak. *Slang:*

nozzle, schnoz, schnozzle, snout. *See* BODY, CONVEX. **2.** *Informal.* One who despises people or things regarded as inferior, especially because of social or intellectual pretension : elitist, snob. *See* ATTITUDE, SELF-LOVE.

snooty *adjective*
Informal. Characteristic of or resembling a snob : elitist, snobbish, snobby. *Informal:* high-hat, stuck-up, uppish, uppity. *See* ATTITUDE, SELF-LOVE.

snooze *verb*
To sleep for a brief period : catnap, doze (off), nap, nod (off), siesta. ***Idiom:*** catch (*or* grab *or* take) forty winks. *See* AWARENESS.
snooze *noun* A brief sleep : catnap, doze, nap, siesta. *See* AWARENESS.

snort *noun*
Slang. A small amount of liquor : dram, drop, jigger, shot, sip, tot[1]. *Informal:* nip[2], slug[1]. *See* BIG, INGESTION.

snout *noun*
Slang. The structure on the human face that contains the nostrils and organs of smell and forms the beginning of the respiratory tract : nose, proboscis. *Informal:* beak, snoot. *Slang:* nozzle, schnoz, schnozzle. *See* BODY, CONVEX.

snowball *verb*
1. To increase or expand suddenly, rapidly, or without control : explode, mushroom. *See* INCREASE. **2.** To make or become greater or larger : aggrandize, amplify, augment, boost, build, build up, burgeon, enlarge, escalate, expand, extend, grow, increase, magnify, mount, multiply, proliferate, rise, run up, soar, swell, upsurge, wax. *Informal:* beef up. *See* INCREASE.

snub *verb*
To slight (someone) deliberately : cut, rebuff, shun, spurn. *Informal:* coldshoulder. ***Idioms:*** close (*or* shut) the door on, give someone the cold shoulder, give someone the go-by, turn one's back on. *See* ACCEPT.
snub *noun* A deliberate slight : cut, rebuff, spurn. *Informal:* cold shoulder, go-by. *See* ACCEPT.

snuff *verb*
To perceive with the olfactory sense : nose, scent, smell, sniff, whiff. ***Idiom:*** catch (*or* get) a whiff of. *See* SMELLS.

snuff out *verb*
1. To cause to stop burning or giving light : douse, extinguish, put out, quench. *See* CONTINUE. **2.** To destroy all traces of : abolish, annihilate, blot out, clear, eradicate, erase, exterminate, extinguish, extirpate, kill[1], liquidate, obliterate, remove, root[1] (out *or* up), rub out, stamp out, uproot, wipe out. ***Idioms:*** do away with, make an end of, put an end to. *See* HELP, MAKE.

snug *adjective*
1. Affording pleasurable ease : comfortable, cozy, easeful, easy. *Informal:* comfy, soft. *See* GOOD. **2.** In good order or clean condition : neat, orderly, shipshape, spick-and-span, spruce, taut, tidy, trig, trim, well-groomed. *Chiefly British:* tight. ***Idiom:*** neat as a pin. *See* CLEAN, ORDER. **3.** Affording little room for movement : close, confining, cramped, crowded, narrow, tight. *See* TIGHTEN.
snug *verb* To lie or press close together, usually with another person or thing : cuddle, nestle, nuzzle, snuggle. *See* NEAR.

snuggle *verb*
To lie or press close together, usually with another person or thing : cuddle, nestle, nuzzle, snug. *See* NEAR.

soak *verb*
1. To make thoroughly wet : douse, drench, saturate, sodden, sop, souse, wet. *See* DRY. **2.** To saturate (something) with a liquid : steep[2]. *Chemistry:* infuse. *See* DRY. **3.** To take in (moisture or liquid). Also used with *up* : absorb, drink, imbibe, sop up, take up. *See* GIVE. **4.** *Informal.* To take in and incorporate, especially mentally. Also used with *up* : absorb, assimilate, digest, imbibe, take up. *See* ACCEPT. **5.** *Informal.* To take alcoholic liquor, especially excessively or habitually : drink, guzzle, imbibe, tipple. *Informal:* nip[2]. *Slang:* booze, lush[2], tank up. ***Idioms:*** bend the elbow, hit the bottle. *See* DRUGS. **6.** *Slang.* To exploit (another) by charging too much for something : fleece, overcharge. *Slang:* clip[1], gouge, nick, rip off, scalp, skin. ***Idioms:*** make someone pay through the nose, take someone for a ride, take someone to the cleaners. *See* HONEST.
soak in *verb* To come as a realization : dawn on (*or* upon), register, sink in. *See* KNOWLEDGE.
soak *noun Slang.* A person who is habitually drunk : drunk, drunkard, inebriate, sot, tippler. *Slang:* boozehound, boozer, lush[2], rummy[1], souse, sponge, stiff. *See* DRUGS.

soak in *verb* See **soak**.

soar *verb*
1. To move from a lower to a higher position : arise, ascend, climb, lift, mount, rise. *See* RISE. **2.** To make or become greater or larger : aggrandize, amplify, augment, boost, build,

build up, burgeon, enlarge, escalate, expand, extend, grow, increase, magnify, mount, multiply, proliferate, rise, run up, snowball, swell, upsurge, wax. *Informal:* beef up. *See* INCREASE. **3.** To rise abruptly and precipitously : rocket, sky, skyrocket. *Informal:* shoot up. *See* INCREASE.

soaring *adjective*
Imposingly high : aerial, airy, lofty, sky-high, towering. *See* HIGH.

sob *verb*
To make inarticulate sounds of grief or pain, usually accompanied by tears : bawl, blubber, cry, howl, keen[2], wail, weep, yowl. *See* HAPPY, SOUNDS.

sobbing *noun*
A fit of crying : bawling, blubbering, cry, tear[2] (used in plural), wailing, weeping. *See* SOUNDS.

sobby *adjective*
Affectedly or extravagantly emotional : bathetic, gushy, maudlin, mawkish, romantic, sentimental, slushy, soft, soppy. *Informal:* gooey, mushy, schmaltzy, sloppy, soupy. *Slang:* drippy, sappy, tear-jerking. *See* FEELINGS.

sober *adjective*
1. Exercising moderation and self-restraint in appetites and behavior : abstemious, continent, temperate. *See* RESTRAINT. **2.** Having or indicating an awareness of things as they really are : down-to-earth, hard, hardheaded, matter-of-fact, objective, practical, pragmatic, pragmatical, prosaic, realistic, tough-minded, unromantic. *See* EXCITE, REAL. **3.** Full of or marked by dignity and seriousness : earnest[1], grave[2], sedate, serious, solemn, somber, staid. *See* ATTITUDE, HEAVY.

soberness *noun*
The practice of refraining from use of alcoholic liquors : abstinence, dryness, sobriety, teetotalism, temperance. *See* DRUGS, RESTRAINT, USED.

sobersided *adjective*
Marked by sober sincerity : businesslike, earnest[1], no-nonsense, serious. *Idiom:* in earnest. *See* HEAVY, WORK.

sobersidedness *noun*
Sober sincerity : earnestness, seriousness. *See* HEAVY, WORK.

sobriety *noun*
1. High seriousness of manner or bearing : graveness, gravity, sedateness, solemnity, solemnness, staidness. *See* ATTITUDE, HEAVY, STYLE. **2.** The practice of refraining from use of alcoholic liquors : abstinence, dryness, soberness, teetotalism, temperance. *See* DRUGS, RESTRAINT, USED.

sociability *noun*
The quality of being pleasant and friendly : affability, agreeability, agreeableness, amenity, amiability, amiableness, congeniality, congenialness, cordiality, cordialness, friendliness, geniality, genialness, pleasantness, sociableness, warmth. *See* ATTITUDE, GOOD.

sociable *adjective*
1. Liking company : companionable, convivial, social. *Chiefly British:* matey. *See* ATTITUDE. **2.** Spent, marked by, or enjoyed in the company of others : companionable, convivial, social. *See* ATTITUDE, PARTICIPATE. **3.** Pleasant and friendly in disposition : affable, agreeable, amiable, congenial, cordial, genial, good-natured, good-tempered, pleasant, warm. *See* ATTITUDE, GOOD.

sociableness *noun*
The quality of being pleasant and friendly : affability, agreeability, agreeableness, amenity, amiability, amiableness, congeniality, congenialness, cordiality, cordialness, friendliness, geniality, genialness, pleasantness, sociability, warmth. *See* ATTITUDE, GOOD.

social *adjective*
1. Of, characterized by, or inclined to living together in communities : gregarious. *See* CONNECT, GROUP. **2.** Of or relating to the structure, organization, or functioning of society : societal. *See* GROUP. **3.** Liking company : companionable, convivial, sociable. *Chiefly British:* matey. *See* ATTITUDE. **4.** Spent, marked by, or enjoyed in the company of others : companionable, convivial, sociable. *See* ATTITUDE, PARTICIPATE.

socialize *verb*
1. To place under government or group ownership or control : communalize, nationalize. *See* POLITICS, SPECIFIC. **2.** To fit for companionship with others, especially in attitude or manners : acculturate, civilize, humanize. *See* TEACH. **3.** To take part in social activities : mingle, mix. *See* GROUP.

societal *adjective*
Of or relating to the structure, organization, or functioning of society : social. *See* GROUP.

society *noun*
1. Persons as an organized body : community, people, public. *See* SPECIFIC. **2.** A group of people united in a relationship and having some interest, activity, or purpose in common : association, club, confederation, congress, federation, fellowship, fraternity, guild, league, order,

organization, sorority, union. *See* GROUP. **3.** People of the highest social level : aristocracy, blue blood, crème de la crème, elite, flower, gentility, gentry, nobility, patriciate, quality, upper class, who's who. *Informal:* upper crust. *See* OVER. **4.** A pleasant association among people : companionship, company, fellowship. *See* CONNECT, GROUP.

sock *verb*
To deliver a powerful blow to suddenly and sharply : bash, catch, clout, hit, knock, pop[1], slam, slog, slug[3], smash, smite, strike, swat, thwack, whack, wham, whop. *Informal:* biff, bop, clip[1], wallop. *Slang:* belt, conk, paste. ***Idioms:*** let someone have it, sock it to someone. *See* ATTACK, STRIKE.

sock *noun* A sudden sharp, powerful stroke : bang, blow[2], clout, crack, hit, lick, pound, slug[3], swat, thwack, welt, whack, wham, whop. *Informal:* bash, biff, bop, clip[1], wallop. *Slang:* belt, conk, paste. *See* ATTACK, STRIKE.

sock away *verb*
Informal. To place (money) in a bank : bank[2], deposit, lay away. *Informal:* salt away. *See* KEEP, MONEY.

sodden *adjective*
1. Covered with or full of liquid : soggy, sopping, soppy, wet. *See* DRY. **2.** Stupefied, excited, or muddled with alcoholic liquor : besotted, crapulent, crapulous, drunk, drunken, inebriate, inebriated, intoxicated, tipsy. *Informal:* cock-eyed, stewed. *Slang:* blind, bombed, boozed, boozy, crocked, high, lit (up), loaded, looped, pickled, pixilated, plastered, potted, sloshed, smashed, soused, stinking, stinko, stoned, tight, zonked. ***Idioms:*** drunk as a skunk, half-seas over, high as a kite, in one's cups, three sheets in (*or* to) the wind. *See* DRUGS.

sodden *verb* To make thoroughly wet : douse, drench, saturate, soak, sop, souse, wet. *See* DRY.

soft *adjective*
1. Yielding easily to pressure or weight; not firm : mushy, pappy[1], pulpous, pulpy, quaggy, spongy, squashy, squishy, yielding. *See* RESIST. **2.** Not irritating, strident, or loud : hushed, low, low-key, low-keyed, quiet, small, subdued, whispery. *See* SOUNDS. **3.** Free from severity or violence, as in movement : balmy[1], delicate, faint, gentle, mild, smooth. *See* CALM, STRONG. **4.** Of small intensity : gentle, light[2], moderate, slight. *See* STRONG. **5.** Of a kindly, considerate character : gentle, mild, softhearted, tender[1], tenderhearted. *See* KIND. **6.** Not strict or severe : charitable, clement, easy, forbearing, indulgent, lax, lenient, merciful, tolerant. *See* ACCEPT. **7.** Affectedly or extravagantly emotional : bathetic, gushy, maudlin, mawkish, romantic, sentimental, slushy, sobby, soppy. *Informal:* gooey, mushy, schmaltzy, sloppy, soupy. *Slang:* drippy, sappy, tear-jerking. *See* FEELINGS. **8.** *Informal.* Having only a limited ability to learn and understand : backward, dull, simple, simple-minded, slow, slow-witted. *Offensive:* feeble-minded, half-witted, retarded, weak-minded. *See* ABILITY. **9.** Characterized by reduced economic activity : down, dull, off, slack, slow, sluggish. *See* INCREASE. **10.** *Informal.* Affording pleasurable ease : comfortable, cozy, easeful, easy, snug. *Informal:* comfy. *See* GOOD.

soften *verb*
1. To moderate or change a position or course of action as a result of pressure : ease off, relent, slacken, weaken, yield. ***Idiom:*** give way (*or* ground). *See* STRONG. **2.** To make or become less severe or extreme : moderate, mute, qualify, subdue, tame, temper, tone down. *See* INCREASE. **3.** To ease the anger or agitation of : appease, assuage, calm (down), conciliate, dulcify, gentle, mollify, pacify, placate, propitiate, soothe, sweeten. ***Idiom:*** pour oil on troubled water. *See* CALM.

softhead *noun*
One deficient in judgment and good sense : ass, fool, idiot, imbecile, jackass, mooncalf, moron, nincompoop, ninny, nitwit, simple, simpleton, tomfool. *Informal:* dope, gander, goose. *Slang:* cretin, ding-dong, dip, goof, jerk, nerd, schmo, schmuck, turkey. *See* ABILITY.

softheaded *adjective*
So senseless as to be laughable : absurd, foolish, harebrained, idiotic, imbecilic, insane, lunatic, mad, moronic, nonsensical, preposterous, silly, tomfool, unearthly, zany. *Informal:* cockeyed, crazy, loony, loopy. *Slang:* balmy[2], dippy, dopey, jerky, sappy, wacky. *See* ABILITY, KNOWLEDGE.

softhearted *adjective*
Of a kindly, considerate character : gentle, mild, soft, tender[1], tenderhearted. *See* KIND.

soft-pedal *verb*
Informal. To make less emphatic or obvious : de-emphasize, play down, tone down. *See* SHOW.

soft soap *noun*
Informal. Excessive, ingratiating praise :

adulation, blandishment, blarney, flattery, incense[2], oil, slaver. ***Idiom:*** honeyed words. *See* PRAISE.

soft-soap *verb* **1.** *Informal.* To persuade or try to persuade by gentle persistent urging or flattery : blandish, cajole, coax, honey, wheedle. *Informal:* sweet-talk. *See* PERSUASION. **2.** *Informal.* To compliment excessively and ingratiatingly : adulate, blandish, butter up, flatter, honey, slaver. *Informal:* sweet-talk. *See* PRAISE.

soggy *adjective*
1. Covered with or full of liquid : sodden, sopping, soppy, wet. *See* DRY. **2.** Damp and warm : humid, muggy, sticky, sultry. *See* DRY, HOT.

soil *verb*
1. To make dirty : befoul, begrime, besmirch, besoil, black, blacken, defile, dirty, smudge, smutch, sully. *See* CLEAN. **2.** To contaminate the reputation of : befoul, besmear, besmirch, bespatter, blacken, cloud, denigrate, dirty, smear, smudge, smut, spatter, stain, sully, taint, tarnish. ***Idioms:*** give a black eye to, sling (*or* throw) mud on. *See* ATTACK, CLEAN. **3.** To make morally impure : contaminate, corrupt, defile, infect, pollute, taint. *See* CLEAN.

soiled *adjective*
Covered or stained with or as if with dirt or other impurities : black, dirty, filthy, grimy, grubby, smutty, unclean, uncleanly. *See* CLEAN.

soiree also **soirée** *noun*
A large or important social gathering : affair, celebration, festivity, fete, function, gala, occasion, party. *Informal:* do. *Slang:* bash. *See* GROUP, WORK.

sojourn *verb*
To remain as a guest or lodger : lodge, stay[1], visit. *See* PLACE.
sojourn *noun* A remaining in a place as a guest or lodger : stay[1], visit. *See* PLACE.

solace *noun*
A consoling in time of grief or pain : comfort, consolation. *See* HELP.
solace *verb* To give hope to in time of grief or pain : comfort, console, soothe. *See* HELP.

soldier *noun*
One who engages in a combat or struggle : belligerent, combatant, fighter, warrior. *See* CONFLICT.

soldierly *adjective*
Relating to, characteristic of, or performed by troops : martial, military. *See* PEACE.

soldier of fortune *noun*
A freelance fighter : adventurer, Hessian, mercenary. *See* GET.

sole *adjective*
1. Alone in a given category : lone, one, only, particular, separate, single, singular, solitary, unique. ***Idioms:*** first and last, one and only. *See* INCLUDE. **2.** Not divided among or shared with others : exclusive, single. *See* INCLUDE. **3.** Without a spouse : fancy-free, footloose, lone, single, spouseless, unattached, unmarried, unwed. ***Idiom:*** footloose and fancy-free. *See* MARRIAGE.

solecism *noun*
A term that offends against established usage standards : barbarism, corruption, vulgarism. *See* STYLE.

solely *adverb*
1. Without the presence or aid of another : alone, single-handedly, singly, solitarily, solo. ***Idioms:*** all by one's lonesome, by oneself. *See* INCLUDE. **2.** To the exclusion of anyone or anything else : alone, but, entirely, exclusively, only. *See* INCLUDE.

solemn *adjective*
Full of or marked by dignity and seriousness : earnest[1], grave[2], sedate, serious, sober, somber, staid. *See* ATTITUDE, HEAVY.

solemnity *noun*
High seriousness of manner or bearing : graveness, gravity, sedateness, sobriety, solemnness, staidness. *See* ATTITUDE, HEAVY, STYLE.

solemnize *verb*
To mark (a day or an event) with ceremonies of respect, festivity, or rejoicing : celebrate, commemorate, keep, observe. *See* REMEMBER.

solemnness *noun*
High seriousness of manner or bearing : graveness, gravity, sedateness, sobriety, solemnity, staidness. *See* ATTITUDE, HEAVY, STYLE.

solemn word *noun*
A declaration that one will or will not do a certain thing : assurance, covenant, engagement, guarantee, guaranty, pledge, plight[2], promise, vow, warrant, word, word of honor. *See* OBLIGATION.

solicit *verb*
1. To endeavor to obtain (something) by expressing one's needs or desires : ask (for), request, seek. *See* REQUEST. **2.** To trouble persistently from or as if from all sides : badger, bedevil, beleaguer, beset, besiege, harass, harry, hound, importune, pester, plague. *See* ATTACK.

solicitous *adjective*
1. In a state of anxiety or uneasiness : agitated,

anxious, concerned, distressed, nervous, uneasy, unsettled. *See* FEELINGS. **2.** Intensely desirous or interested : agog, ardent, athirst, avid, bursting, eager, impatient, keen[1], thirsting, thirsty. *Informal:* raring. ***Idioms:*** champing at the bit, ready and willing. *See* CONCERN. **3.** Full of polite concern for the well-being of others : attentive, considerate, courteous, gallant, polite, thoughtful. *See* CAREFUL, TREAT WELL.

solicitude *noun*
1. A troubled or anxious state of mind : angst, anxiety, anxiousness, care, concern, disquiet, disquietude, distress, nervousness, unease, uneasiness, worry. *See* FEELINGS. **2.** Thoughtful attention : attentiveness, concern, consideration, regard, thoughtfulness. *See* ATTITUDE, CONCERN, KIND, TREAT WELL.

solid *adjective*
1. Unyielding to pressure or force : firm[1], hard, incompressible. *See* RESIST, STRONG. **2.** Not easily moved or shaken : firm[1], secure, sound[2], stable, strong, sturdy, substantial, sure, unshakable. *See* CONTINUE, STRONG. **3.** Based on good judgment, reasoning, or evidence : cogent, just, sound[2], tight, valid, well-founded, well-grounded. *See* GOOD, REASON. **4.** Capable of being depended upon : dependable, reliable, responsible, sound[2], trustworthy, trusty. *See* TRUST. **5.** Being in or characterized by complete agreement : unanimous. ***Idioms:*** as one, at one, of one mind, with one voice. *See* AGREE.

solidarity *noun*
An identity or coincidence of interests, purposes, or sympathies among the members of a group : oneness, union, unity. *See* AGREE.

solidify *verb*
To make or become physically hard : cake, concrete, congeal, dry, harden, indurate, petrify, set[1]. *See* SOLID.

solidity *noun*
1. The quality, condition, or degree of being thick : compactness, density, thickness. *See* THICK. **2.** The condition of being free from defects or flaws : durability, firmness, integrity, soundness, stability, strength, wholeness. *See* BETTER.

solitarily *adverb*
Without the presence or aid of another : alone, single-handedly, singly, solely, solo. ***Idioms:*** all by one's lonesome, by oneself. *See* INCLUDE.

solitariness *noun*
The quality or state of being alone : aloneness, isolation, loneliness, singleness, solitude. *See* INCLUDE.

solitary *adjective*
1. Set away from all others : alone, apart, detached, isolate, isolated, lone, removed. *See* INCLUDE. **2.** Lacking the company of others : alone, companionless, lone, lonely, lonesome, single, unaccompanied. *See* INCLUDE. **3.** Far from centers of human population : back, insular, isolated, lonely, lonesome, obscure, outlying, out-of-the-way, remote, removed, secluded. ***Idiom:*** off the beaten path (*or* track). *See* NEAR. **4.** Not friendly, sociable, or warm in manner : aloof, chill, chilly, cool, distant, offish, remote, reserved, reticent, standoffish, unapproachable, uncommunicative, undemonstrative, withdrawn. *See* ATTITUDE, HOT. **5.** Alone in a given category : lone, one, only, particular, separate, single, singular, sole, unique. ***Idioms:*** first and last, one and only. *See* INCLUDE.

solitude *noun*
The quality or state of being alone : aloneness, isolation, loneliness, singleness, solitariness. *See* INCLUDE.

solo *adverb*
Without the presence or aid of another : alone, single-handedly, singly, solely, solitarily. ***Idioms:*** all by one's lonesome, by oneself. *See* INCLUDE.

solution *noun*
Something worked out to explain, resolve, or provide a method for dealing with and settling a problem : answer, determination. *Mathematics:* result. *See* ASK.

solve *verb*
1. To find a solution for : clear up, decipher, explain, resolve, unravel. *Informal:* dope out, figure out. ***Idiom:*** get to the bottom of. *See* ASK, REASON. **2.** To arrive at an answer to (a mathematical problem) : work, work out. *Informal:* figure out. *See* REASON.

somatic *adjective*
Of or relating to the human body : bodily, corporal, corporeal, fleshly, personal, physical. *See* BODY.

somber *adjective*
1. Dark and depressing : black, bleak, blue, cheerless, dark, desolate, dismal, dreary, gloomy, glum, joyless, tenebrific. *See* HAPPY, LIGHT. **2.** Full of or marked by dignity and seriousness : earnest[1], grave[2], sedate, serious, sober, solemn, staid. *See* ATTITUDE, HEAVY.

some *adjective*
Consisting of a number more than two or three

but less than many : divers, several, sundry, various. *See* BIG.

somebody *noun*
Informal. An important, influential person : character, dignitary, eminence, leader, lion, nabob, notability, notable, personage. *Informal:* big-timer, heavyweight, someone, VIP. *Slang:* big shot, big wheel, bigwig, muckamuck. *See* IMPORTANT.

someone *noun*
Informal. An important, influential person : character, dignitary, eminence, leader, lion, nabob, notability, notable, personage. *Informal:* big-timer, heavyweight, somebody, VIP. *Slang:* big shot, big wheel, bigwig, muckamuck. *See* IMPORTANT.

something *noun*
One that exists independently : being, entity, existence, existent, individual, object, thing. *See* BE, THING.

sometime *adjective*
Having been such previously : erstwhile, former, late, old, once, onetime, past, previous, quondam, whilom. *See* PRECEDE.

sometimes *adverb*
1. Once in a while; at times : betimes, intermittently, occasionally, periodically, sporadically. ***Idioms:*** ever and again (*or* anon), now and again (*or* then). *See* CONTINUE. **2.** At times : now. *See* TIME.

somnifacient *adjective*
Inducing sleep or sedation : hypnotic, narcotic, opiate, sedative, sleepy, slumberous, somniferous, somnific, somnolent, soporific. *See* AWARENESS.
somnifacient *noun* Something that induces sleep or sedation : hypnotic, narcotic, opiate, sedative, soporific. *See* AWARENESS.

somniferous *adjective*
Inducing sleep or sedation : hypnotic, narcotic, opiate, sedative, sleepy, slumberous, somnifacient, somnific, somnolent, soporific. *See* AWARENESS.

somnific *adjective*
Inducing sleep or sedation : hypnotic, narcotic, opiate, sedative, sleepy, slumberous, somnifacient, somniferous, somnolent, soporific. *See* AWARENESS.

somnolent *adjective*
1. Ready for or needing sleep : dozy, drowsy, nodding, sleepy, slumberous, slumbery, soporific. *See* AWARENESS. **2.** Inducing sleep or sedation : hypnotic, narcotic, opiate, sedative, sleepy, slumberous, somnifacient, somniferous, somnific, soporific. *See* AWARENESS.

sonance *noun*
The sensation caused by vibrating wave motion that is perceived by the organs of hearing : noise, sound[1]. *See* SOUNDS.

sonant *adjective*
Produced by the voice : articulate, oral, spoken, uttered, vocal, voiced. *See* SOUNDS.

songster *noun*
A person who sings : singer, songstress, vocalist, voice. *See* PERFORMING ARTS.

songstress *noun*
A person who sings : singer, songster, vocalist, voice. *See* PERFORMING ARTS.

sonorous *adjective*
1. Having or producing a full, deep, or rich sound : mellow, orotund, plangent, resonant, resounding, ringing, rotund, round, vibrant. *See* SOUNDS. **2.** Characterized by language that is elevated and sometimes pompous in style : aureate, bombastic, declamatory, flowery, fustian, grandiloquent, high-flown, high-sounding, magniloquent, orotund, overblown, rhetorical, swollen. *See* PLAIN, STYLE, WORDS.

soothe *verb*
1. To ease the anger or agitation of : appease, assuage, calm (down), conciliate, dulcify, gentle, mollify, pacify, placate, propitiate, soften, sweeten. ***Idiom:*** pour oil on troubled water. *See* CALM. **2.** To give hope to in time of grief or pain : comfort, console, solace. *See* HELP.

soothsay *verb*
To tell about or make known (future events) by or as if by supernatural means : augur, divine, foretell, prophesy, vaticinate. *See* FORESIGHT.

soothsayer *noun*
A person who foretells future events by or as if by supernatural means : augur, auspex, diviner, foreteller, haruspex, prophesier, prophet, prophetess, seer, sibyl, vaticinator. *See* FORESIGHT.

soothsaying *noun*
Something that is foretold by or as if by supernatural means : divination, oracle, prophecy, vaticination, vision. *See* FORESIGHT.

sooty *adjective*
Of the darkest achromatic visual value : black, ebon, ebony, inky, jet[1], jetty, onyx, pitch-black, pitchy, sable. *See* COLORS.

sop *verb*
To make thoroughly wet : douse, drench, saturate, soak, sodden, souse, wet. *See* DRY.
sop up *verb* To take in (moisture or liquid) : absorb, drink, imbibe, soak (up), take up. *See* GIVE.

sophism *noun*
Plausible but invalid reasoning : casuistry, fallacy, sophistry, speciousness, spuriousness. *See* CORRECT, TRUE.

sophistic *adjective*
Containing fundamental errors in reasoning : fallacious, false, illogical, invalid, specious, spurious, unsound. *See* CORRECT, TRUE.

sophisticate *verb*
To make impure or inferior by deceptively adding foreign substances : adulterate, debase, doctor, load. *See* CLEAN.

sophisticated *adjective*
1. Experienced in the ways of the world; lacking natural simplicity : cosmopolitan, worldly, worldly-wise. *See* KNOWLEDGE. **2.** Mixed with other substances : adulterated, alloyed, doctored, impure, loaded. *See* CLEAN. **3.** Appealing to or engaging the intellect : cerebral, intellectual, thoughtful. *Informal:* highbrow. *See* THOUGHTS.

sophistication *noun*
The state of being contaminated : adulteration, contamination, pollution. *See* CLEAN.

sophistry *noun*
Plausible but invalid reasoning : casuistry, fallacy, sophism, speciousness, spuriousness. *See* CORRECT, TRUE.

soporific *adjective*
1. Inducing sleep or sedation : hypnotic, narcotic, opiate, sedative, sleepy, slumberous, somnifacient, somniferous, somnific, somnolent. *See* AWARENESS. **2.** Ready for or needing sleep : dozy, drowsy, nodding, sleepy, slumberous, slumbery, somnolent. *See* AWARENESS.
soporific *noun* Something that induces sleep or sedation : hypnotic, narcotic, opiate, sedative, somnifacient. *See* AWARENESS.

sopping *adjective*
Covered with or full of liquid : sodden, soggy, soppy, wet. *See* DRY.

soppy *adjective*
1. Covered with or full of liquid : sodden, soggy, sopping, wet. *See* DRY. **2.** Affectedly or extravagantly emotional : bathetic, gushy, maudlin, mawkish, romantic, sentimental, slushy, sobby, soft. *Informal:* gooey, mushy, schmaltzy, sloppy, soupy. *Slang:* drippy, sappy, tear-jerking. *See* FEELINGS.

sop up *verb* See **sop**.

sorceress *noun*
A woman who practices magic : enchantress, hag, lamia, witch. *See* SUPERNATURAL.

sorcery *noun*
The use of supernatural powers to influence or predict events : conjuration, magic, sortilege, thaumaturgy, theurgy, witchcraft, witchery, witching, wizardry. *See* SUPERNATURAL.

sordid *adjective*
Having or proceeding from low moral standards : base², ignoble, low, low-down, mean², squalid, vile. *See* RIGHT.

sore *adjective*
1. Marked by, causing, or experiencing physical pain : aching, achy, afflictive, hurtful, nagging, painful, smarting. *See* PAIN. **2.** *Informal.* Feeling or showing anger : angry, choleric, indignant, mad. ***Idiom:*** hot under the collar. *See* FEELINGS.

sorehead *noun*
Slang. A person who habitually complains or grumbles : complainer, crab, faultfinder, grouch, growler, grumbler, grump, murmurer, mutterer, whiner. *Informal:* crank, griper, grouser. *Slang:* bellyacher, sourpuss. *See* HAPPY.

soreness *noun*
1. A sensation of physical discomfort occurring as the result of disease or injury : ache, pain, pang, prick, prickle, smart, stab, sting, stitch, throe, twinge. *Informal:* misery. *See* PAIN.
2. An instance of being irritated, as in a part of the body : inflammation, irritation. *See* HELP.

sorority *noun*
A group of people united in a relationship and having some interest, activity, or purpose in common : association, club, confederation, congress, federation, fellowship, fraternity, guild, league, order, organization, society, union. *See* GROUP.

sorrow *noun*
Mental anguish or pain caused by loss or despair : grief, heartache, heartbreak. *See* HAPPY.
sorrow *verb* To feel, show, or express grief : grieve, lament, mourn, suffer. *See* HAPPY.

sorrowful *adjective*
1. Full of or expressive of sorrow : doleful, dolorous, lugubrious, mournful, plaintive, rueful, sad, woebegone, woeful. *See* HAPPY.
2. Causing sorrow or regret : deplorable, doleful, dolorous, grievous, lamentable, mournful, regrettable, rueful, sad, woeful. *See* HAPPY.

sorry *adjective*
1. Expressing or inclined to express an apology : apologetic, contrite, penitent, regretful, repentant. *See* REGRET. **2.** Feeling or expressing regret for one's sins or misdeeds : compunctious, contrite, penitent, penitential, regretful,

remorseful, repentant. *See* REGRET. **3.** Disturbing because of failure to measure up to a standard or produce the desired results : disappointing, unlucky. *See* HAPPY.

sort *noun*
A class that is defined by the common attribute or attributes possessed by all its members : breed, cast, description, feather, ilk, kind[2], lot, manner, mold, nature, order, species, stamp, stripe, type, variety. *Informal:* persuasion. *See* GROUP.

sort *verb* **1.** To distribute into groups according to kinds. Also used with *out* : assort, categorize, class, classify, group, pigeonhole, separate. *See* COLLECT. **2.** To put into a deliberate order : arrange, array, deploy, dispose, marshal, order, organize, range, systematize. *See* ORDER. **3.** To set apart (one kind or type) from others : separate, sift, winnow. *See* INCLUDE.

sortilege *noun*
The use of supernatural powers to influence or predict events : conjuration, magic, sorcery, thaumaturgy, theurgy, witchcraft, witchery, witching, wizardry. *See* SUPERNATURAL.

sot *noun*
A person who is habitually drunk : drunk, drunkard, inebriate, tippler. *Slang:* boozehound, boozer, lush[2], rummy[1], soak, souse, sponge, stiff. *See* DRUGS.

sough *noun*
A low, indistinct, and often continuous sound : mumble, murmur, sigh, susurration, susurrus, whisper. *See* SOUNDS.

sough *verb* To make a low, continuous, and indistinct sound : murmur, sigh, whisper. *See* SOUNDS.

soul *noun*
1. The vital principle or animating force within living beings : breath, divine spark, élan vital, life force, psyche, spirit, vital force, vitality. *See* BODY. **2.** The essential being of a person, regarded as immaterial and immortal : spirit. *See* BE. **3.** A member of the human race : being, body, creature, homo, human, human being, individual, life, man, mortal, party, person, personage. *See* BEINGS. **4.** The most central and material part : core, essence, gist, heart, kernel, marrow, meat, nub, pith, quintessence, root[1], spirit, stuff, substance. *Law:* gravamen. *See* BE. **5.** The seat of a person's innermost emotions and feelings : bosom, breast, heart. ***Idioms:*** bottom of one's heart, cockles of one's heart, one's heart of hearts. *See* FEELINGS.

sound[1] *noun*
1. The sensation caused by vibrating wave motion that is perceived by the organs of hearing : noise, sonance. *See* SOUNDS. **2.** Range of audibility : earshot, hearing. *See* SOUNDS.

sound *verb* To have the appearance of : appear, look, seem. ***Idiom:*** strike one as (being). *See* SURFACE.

sound[2] *adjective*
1. In excellent condition : entire, flawless, good, intact, perfect, unblemished, unbroken, undamaged, unharmed, unhurt, unimpaired, uninjured, unmarred, whole. *See* THRIVE. **2.** Having good health : fit[1], hale, healthful, healthy, hearty, right, well[2], whole, wholesome. ***Idioms:*** fit as a fiddle, hale and hearty, in fine fettle. *See* HEALTH. **3.** Not easily moved or shaken : firm[1], secure, solid, stable, strong, sturdy, substantial, sure, unshakable. *See* CONTINUE, STRONG. **4.** Based on good judgment, reasoning, or evidence : cogent, just, solid, tight, valid, well-founded, well-grounded. *See* GOOD, REASON. **5.** Capable of being depended upon : dependable, reliable, responsible, solid, trustworthy, trusty. *See* TRUST. **6.** Possessing, proceeding from, or exhibiting good judgment and prudence : balanced, commonsensible, commonsensical, judicious, levelheaded, prudent, rational, reasonable, sagacious, sage, sane, sapient, sensible, well-founded, well-grounded, wise[1]. *See* REASON, SANE.

sound[3] *verb*
To test the attitude of. Also used with *out* : feel out, probe. ***Idioms:*** put out feelers, send up a trial balloon. *See* INVESTIGATE.

soundless *adjective*
Marked by, done with, or making no sound or noise : hushed, noiseless, quiet, silent, still, stilly. *Archaic:* hush. *See* SOUNDS.

soundlessness *noun*
The absence of sound or noise : hush, noiselessness, quiet, quietness, silence, still, stillness. *See* SOUNDS.

soundness *noun*
1. The condition of being free from defects or flaws : durability, firmness, integrity, solidity, stability, strength, wholeness. *See* BETTER. **2.** The condition of being physically and mentally sound : haleness, health, healthiness, heartiness, wholeness. *See* HEALTH. **3.** A healthy mental state : lucidity, lucidness, mind, reason, saneness, sanity, sense (often used in plural), wit (used in plural). *Slang:* marble (used in plural). *See* SANE. **4.** Reliability in withstanding pressure, force, or stress : fastness, firm-

ness, hardness, security, stability, stableness, steadiness, strength, sturdiness, sureness. *See* BETTER, CHANGE, CONTINUE.

soup *noun*
A difficult, often embarrassing situation or condition : box[1], corner, deep water, difficulty, dilemma, Dutch, fix, hole, hot spot, hot water, jam, plight[1], predicament, quagmire, scrape, trouble. *Informal:* bind, pickle, spot. *See* EASY.

soupçon *noun*
A slight amount or indication : breath, dash, ghost, hair, hint, intimation, semblance, shade, shadow, streak, suggestion, suspicion, taste, tinge, touch, trace, whiff, whisper. *Informal:* whisker. *See* BIG, SHOW.

soupy *adjective*
Informal. Affectedly or extravagantly emotional : bathetic, gushy, maudlin, mawkish, romantic, sentimental, slushy, sobby, soft, soppy. *Informal:* gooey, mushy, schmaltzy, sloppy. *Slang:* drippy, sappy, tear-jerking. *See* FEELINGS.

sour *adjective*
1. Having a taste characteristic of that produced by acids : acerb, acerbic, acetous, acid, acidulous, dry, tangy, tart[1]. *See* TASTE. **2.** Having a noticeably sharp pungent taste or smell : acerbic, acrid, bitter, harsh. *See* TASTE. **3.** Broodingly and sullenly unhappy : dour, gloomy, glum, moody, morose, saturnine, sulky, sullen, surly. *See* HAPPY. **4.** Not in accordance with what is usual or expected : amiss, astray, awry, wrong. *See* SURPRISE, THRIVE.

sour *verb* To make or become bitter : embitter. *See* HAPPY.

source *noun*
1. A point of origination : beginning, derivation, fount, fountain, fountainhead, mother, origin, parent, provenance, provenience, root[1], rootstock, spring, well[1]. *See* START. **2.** An acquaintance who is in a position to help : connection, contact. *See* CONNECT.

sourpuss *noun*
Slang. A person who habitually complains or grumbles : complainer, crab, faultfinder, grouch, growler, grumbler, grump, murmurer, mutterer, whiner. *Informal:* crank, griper, grouser. *Slang:* bellyacher, sorehead. *See* HAPPY.

souse *verb*
1. To plunge briefly in or into a liquid : dip, douse, duck, dunk, immerge, immerse, submerge, submerse. *See* ENTER. **2.** To make thoroughly wet : douse, drench, saturate, soak, sodden, sop, wet. *See* DRY.

souse *noun* *Slang.* A person who is habitually drunk : drunk, drunkard, inebriate, sot, tippler. *Slang:* boozehound, boozer, lush[2], rummy[1], soak, sponge, stiff. *See* DRUGS.

soused *adjective*
Slang. Stupefied, excited, or muddled with alcoholic liquor : besotted, crapulent, crapulous, drunk, drunken, inebriate, inebriated, intoxicated, sodden, tipsy. *Informal:* cock-eyed, stewed. *Slang:* blind, bombed, boozed, boozy, crocked, high, lit (up), loaded, looped, pickled, pixilated, plastered, potted, sloshed, smashed, stinking, stinko, stoned, tight, zonked. ***Idioms:*** drunk as a skunk, half-seas over, high as a kite, in one's cups, three sheets in (*or* to) the wind. *See* DRUGS.

souvenir *noun*
Something that causes one to remember : keepsake, memento, remembrance, reminder, token, trophy. *See* REMEMBER.

sovereign *adjective*
Having political independence : autonomous, free, independent, self-governing. *See* DEPENDENCE, FREE.

sovereignty *noun*
1. The right and power to command, decide, rule, or judge : authority, command, control, domination, dominion, jurisdiction, mastery, might, power, prerogative, sway. *Informal:* say-so. *See* OVER. **2.** The condition of being politically free : autonomy, freedom, independence, independency, liberty, self-government. *See* DEPENDENCE, FREE.

sow *verb*
To put (seeds) into the ground for growth : plant, seed. *See* START.

space *noun*
1. An extent, measured or unmeasured, of linear space : distance, length, stretch. *Informal:* piece, way. *See* BIG. **2.** A wide and open area, as of land, sky, or water : distance, expanse, expansion, extent, reach, spread, stretch, sweep. *See* PLACE. **3.** A rather short period : bit[1], spell[3], time, while. *See* BIG.

spaced-out *adjective*
Slang. Stupefied, intoxicated, or otherwise influenced by the taking of drugs : drugged. *Informal:* doped. *Slang:* high, hopped-up, lit (up), potted, stoned, turned-on, wiped-out, zonked. *See* DRUGS.

spacious *adjective*
1. Having plenty of room : ample, capacious, commodious, roomy. *See* BIG. **2.** Large in expanse : ample, broad, expansive, extensive. *See* WIDE.

spade *verb*
To break, turn over, or remove (earth or sand, for example) with or as if with a tool : delve, dig, excavate, grub, scoop, shovel. *See* ENTER.

span *noun*
1. The measure of how far or long something goes in space, time, or degree : extent, length, reach, stretch. *See* BIG. **2.** The period during which someone or something exists : day (often used in plural), duration, existence, life, lifetime, term. *See* LIVE, TIME. **3.** A specific length of time characterized by the occurrence of certain conditions or events : period, season, stretch, term. *See* TIME. **4.** A limited or specific period of time during which something happens, lasts, or extends : duration, stretch, term, time. *See* TIME.

spangle *noun*
A small sparkling decoration : glitter, sequin. *See* BEAUTIFUL.
spangle *verb* To emit light suddenly in rays or sparks : coruscate, flash, glance, gleam, glimmer, glint, glisten, glister, glitter, scintillate, shimmer, sparkle, twinkle, wink. *See* LIGHT.

spank *verb*
To hit with a quick, sharp blow of the hand : box[2], buffet, bust, cuff, punch, slap, smack[1], swat, whack. *Informal:* clip[1], spat. *See* ATTACK, STRIKE.
spank *noun* A quick, sharp blow, especially with the hand : box[2], buffet, bust, chop[1], cuff, punch, slap, smack[1], smacker, swat, whack. *Informal:* clip[1], spat. *See* ATTACK, STRIKE.

spanner *noun*
Chiefly British. A tool with jaws for gripping and twisting : wrench. *See* MACHINE.

spare *verb*
1. To treat with inordinate gentleness and care : favor. ***Idiom:*** handle (*or* treat) with kid gloves. *See* TREAT WELL. **2.** To free from an obligation or duty : absolve, discharge, dispense, excuse, exempt, let off, relieve. *See* FREE. **3.** To use without wasting : conserve, economize, save. *See* SAVE.
spare *adjective* **1.** Being more than is needed, desired, or appropriate : de trop, excess, extra, supererogatory, superfluous, supernumerary, surplus. *See* EXCESS. **2.** Conspicuously deficient in quantity, fullness, or extent : exiguous, meager, poor, puny, scant, scanty, skimpy, sparse, stingy, thin. *Slang:* measly. *See* BIG, EXCESS. **3.** Having little flesh or fat on the body : angular, bony, fleshless, gaunt, lank, lanky, lean[2], meager, rawboned, scrawny, skinny, slender, slim, thin, twiggy, weedy. ***Idioms:*** all skin and bones, thin as a rail. *See* FAT. **4.** Characterized by an economy of artistic expression : lean[2], tight. *See* STYLE.

sparing *adjective*
Careful in the use of material resources : canny, chary, economical, frugal, provident, prudent, saving, Scotch, thrifty. *See* CAREFUL, SAVE.

spark[1] *noun*
1. A sudden quick light : blink, coruscation, flash, flicker, glance, gleam, glimmer, glint, twinkle, wink. *See* LIGHT. **2.** A source of further growth and development : bud[1], embryo, germ, kernel, nucleus, seed. *See* START.

spark[2] *verb*
To attempt to gain the affection of : court, pursue, woo. *Informal:* romance. *See* SEEK, SEX.

sparkle *verb*
To emit light suddenly in rays or sparks : coruscate, flash, glance, gleam, glimmer, glint, glisten, glister, glitter, scintillate, shimmer, spangle, twinkle, wink. *See* LIGHT.
sparkle *noun* **1.** A lively, emphatic, eager quality or manner : animation, bounce, brio, dash, élan, esprit, life, liveliness, pertness, spirit, verve, vigor, vim, vivaciousness, vivacity, zip. *Informal:* ginger, pep, peppiness. *Slang:* oomph. *See* ACTION. **2.** Sparkling, brilliant light : flash, glint, glisten, glister, glitter, scintillation, shimmer. *See* BEAUTIFUL, LIGHT. **3.** Brilliant, showy splendor : brilliance, brilliancy, glitter, glory, gorgeousness, magnificence, resplendence, resplendency, sumptuousness. *Informal:* glitz. *See* BEAUTIFUL.

sparkling *adjective*
1. Full of joyful, unrestrained high spirits : ebullient, effervescent, exuberant. *See* HAPPY. **2.** Amusing or pleasing because of wit or originality : clever, scintillating, smart, witty. *See* LAUGHTER.

sparse *adjective*
Conspicuously deficient in quantity, fullness, or extent : exiguous, meager, poor, puny, scant, scanty, skimpy, spare, stingy, thin. *Slang:* measly. *See* BIG, EXCESS.

spasm *noun*
A violent, excruciating seizure of pain : cramp[1], paroxysm, shoot, throe. *See* PAIN.

spat *noun*
1. A discussion, often heated, in which a difference of opinion is expressed : altercation, argument, bicker, clash, contention, controversy, debate, difficulty, disagreement, dispute, fight, polemic, quarrel, run-in, squabble, tiff, word

(used in plural), wrangle. *Informal:* hassle, rhubarb, tangle. *See* CONFLICT. **2.** *Informal.* A quick, sharp blow, especially with the hand : box[2], buffet, bust, chop[1], cuff, punch, slap, smack[1], smacker, spank, swat, whack. *Informal:* clip[1]. *See* ATTACK, STRIKE.

spat *verb* **1.** To engage in a quarrel : argue, bicker, contend, dispute, fight, quarrel, quibble, squabble, tiff, wrangle. *Informal:* hassle, tangle. ***Idioms:*** cross swords, have it out, have words, lock horns. *See* CONFLICT. **2.** *Informal.* To hit with a quick, sharp blow of the hand : box[2], buffet, bust, cuff, punch, slap, smack[1], spank, swat, whack. *Informal:* clip[1]. *See* ATTACK, STRIKE.

spate *noun*

1. A sudden or rapid flowing outward : efflux, gush, outflow, outpour, outpouring. *See* MOVE. **2.** Something suggestive of running water : current, drift, flood, flow, flux, rush, stream, surge, tide. *See* MOVE. **3.** *Chiefly British.* An abundant, usually overwhelming flow or fall, as of a river or rain : alluvion, cataclysm, cataract, deluge, downpour, flood, freshet, inundation, Niagara, overflow, torrent. *See* BIG.

spatter *verb*

1. To hurl or scatter liquid upon : bespatter, dash, slop, slosh, splash, splatter, spray, swash. *See* STRIKE. **2.** To mark or soil with spots : bespatter, blotch, splatter, splotch, spot. *See* MARKS. **3.** To contaminate the reputation of : befoul, besmear, besmirch, bespatter, blacken, cloud, denigrate, dirty, smear, smudge, smut, soil, stain, sully, taint, tarnish. ***Idioms:*** give a black eye to, sling (*or* throw) mud on. *See* ATTACK, CLEAN.

spawn *verb*

1. To produce sexually or asexually others of one's kind : breed, increase, multiply, procreate, proliferate, propagate, reproduce. *See* REPRODUCTION. **2.** To cause to come into existence : beget, breed, create, engender, father, hatch, make, originate, parent, procreate, produce, sire. ***Idiom:*** give birth (*or* rise) to. *See* MAKE.

spawning *noun*

The process by which an organism produces others of its kind : breeding, multiplication, procreation, proliferation, propagation, reproduction. *Obsolete:* increase. *See* REPRODUCTION.

spay *verb*

To render incapable of reproducing sexually : alter, castrate, fix, geld, neuter, sterilize, unsex. *See* REPRODUCTION, RICH.

speak *verb*

1. To engage in spoken exchange : chat, confabulate, converse[1], discourse, talk. *Informal:* confab, visit. *See* WORDS. **2.** To direct speech to : address, talk. *See* WORDS. **3.** To express oneself in speech : talk, verbalize, vocalize. ***Idioms:*** open one's mouth (*or* lips), put in (*or* into) words, wag one's tongue. *See* WORDS. **4.** To talk to an audience formally : address, lecture, prelect. *Archaic:* bespeak. *See* WORDS.

speak for *verb* To serve as an official delegate of : represent, stand for. *See* SUBSTITUTE.

speaker *noun*

1. A person who speaks on behalf of another or others : mouth, spokesman, spokesperson, spokeswoman. *Informal:* mouthpiece. *See* SUBSTITUTE. **2.** One who delivers a public speech : declaimer, lecturer, speechifier, speechmaker. *See* WORDS.

speak for *verb* See **speak.**

special *adjective*

1. Fixed and distinct from others : express, particular, set[1], specific. *See* SPECIFIC. **2.** Of, relating to, or intended for a distinctive thing or group : especial, individual, particular, specific. *See* SPECIFIC.

specialty *noun*

1. Something at which a person excels : forte, long suit, métier, strong point, strong suit. *Slang:* bag, thing. *See* ABILITY. **2.** An area of academic study that is part of a larger body of learning : branch, discipline. *See* PART.

species *noun*

A class that is defined by the common attribute or attributes possessed by all its members : breed, cast, description, feather, ilk, kind[2], lot, manner, mold, nature, order, sort, stamp, stripe, type, variety. *Informal:* persuasion. *See* GROUP.

specific *adjective*

1. Clearly, fully, and sometimes emphatically expressed : categorical, clear, clear-cut, decided, definite, explicit, express, positive, precise, unambiguous, unequivocal. *See* CLEAR. **2.** Fixed and distinct from others : express, particular, set[1], special. *See* SPECIFIC. **3.** Of, relating to, or intended for a distinctive thing or group : especial, individual, particular, special. *See* SPECIFIC.

specifically *adverb*

That is to say : namely, scilicet, videlicet. ***Idiom:*** to wit. *See* SPECIFIC.

specification *noun*
A restricting or modifying element : condition, provision, proviso, qualification, reservation, stipulation, term (often used in plural). *Informal:* string (often used in plural). *See* LIMITED.

specify *verb*
1. To make known or identify, as by signs : denote, designate, indicate, mark, point out, show. *See* SHOW. **2.** To refer to by name : cite, instance, mention, name. *See* SPECIFIC. **3.** To make specific : detail, particularize, stipulate. *See* SPECIFIC.

specimen *noun*
One that is representative of a group or class : case, example, illustration, instance, representative, sample. *See* SUBSTITUTE.

specious *adjective*
1. Containing fundamental errors in reasoning : fallacious, false, illogical, invalid, sophistic, spurious, unsound. *See* CORRECT, TRUE. **2.** Devoid of truth : counterfactual, false, spurious, truthless, untrue, untruthful, wrong. *See* TRUE.

speciousness *noun*
Plausible but invalid reasoning : casuistry, fallacy, sophism, sophistry, spuriousness. *See* CORRECT, TRUE.

speck *noun*
1. A very small mark : dash, dot, fleck, pinpoint, point, spot. *See* MARKS. **2.** A tiny amount : bit[1], crumb, dab[1], dash, dot, dram, drop, fragment, grain, iota, jot, minim, mite, modicum, molecule, ort, ounce, particle, scrap[1], scruple, shred, smidgen, tittle, trifle, whit. *Chiefly British:* spot. *See* BIG.

speck *verb* To mark with many small spots : bespeckle, besprinkle, dapple, dot, fleck, freckle, mottle, pepper, speckle, sprinkle, stipple. *See* MARKS.

speckle *verb*
To mark with many small spots : bespeckle, besprinkle, dapple, dot, fleck, freckle, mottle, pepper, speck, sprinkle, stipple. *See* MARKS.

spectacle *noun*
An impressive or ostentatious exhibition : array, display, panoply, parade, pomp, show. *See* SHOW.

spectacular *adjective*
Suggesting drama or a stage performance, as in emotionality or suspense : dramatic, histrionic, histrionical, melodramatic, sensational, theatric, theatrical. *See* EXCITE, STYLE, SURPRISE.

spectator *noun*
Someone who observes : beholder, bystander, looker-on, observer, onlooker, watcher. *See* AWARENESS, SEE.

specter *noun*
A supernatural being, such as a ghost : apparition, bogey, bogeyman, bogle, eidolon, ghost, phantasm, phantasma, phantom, revenant, shade, shadow, spirit, visitant, wraith. *Informal:* spook. *Regional:* haunt. *See* BEINGS, SUPERNATURAL.

spectral *adjective*
Gruesomely suggestive of ghosts or death : cadaverous, deadly, deathlike, deathly, ghastly, ghostlike, ghostly. *See* LIVE.

speculate *verb*
1. To use the powers of the mind, as in conceiving ideas, drawing inferences, and making judgments : cerebrate, cogitate, deliberate, ratiocinate, reflect, think. ***Idioms:*** put on one's thinking cap, use one's head. *See* THOUGHTS. **2.** To draw an inference on the basis of inconclusive evidence or insufficient information : conjecture, guess, infer, suppose, surmise. *See* OPINION. **3.** To formulate or assert as a tentative explanation : hypothesize, theorize. *See* BELIEF, THOUGHTS. **4.** To take a risk in the hope of gaining advantage : gamble, venture. ***Idiom:*** take a flyer. *See* GAMBLING.

speculation *noun*
1. The act or process of thinking : brainwork, cerebration, cogitation, contemplation, deliberation, excogitation, meditation, reflection, rumination, thought. *See* THOUGHTS. **2.** A judgment, estimate, or opinion arrived at by guessing : conjecture, guess, guesswork, supposition, surmise. *See* OPINION. **3.** Abstract reasoning : conjecture, theory. *See* BELIEF, THOUGHTS. **4.** A venture depending on chance : bet, gamble, risk, wager. *See* GAMBLING.

speculative *adjective*
1. Of, characterized by, or disposed to thought : cogitative, contemplative, deliberative, excogitative, meditative, pensive, reflective, ruminative, thinking, thoughtful. ***Idiom:*** in a brown study. *See* THOUGHTS. **2.** Concerned primarily with theories rather than practical matters : abstract, academic, theoretic, theoretical. *See* THOUGHTS.

speculator *noun*
1. One who speculates for quick profits : adventurer, gambler, operator. *See* GAMBLING, MONEY. **2.** A person engaged in buying and selling : businessperson, dealer, merchandiser, merchant, trader, tradesman, trafficker. *See* TRANSACTIONS.

speech *noun*
1. The faculty, act, or product of speaking : discourse, talk, utterance, verbalization, vocalization. *See* WORDS. **2.** Spoken exchange : chat, colloquy, confabulation, conversation, converse[1], dialogue, discourse, talk. *Informal:* confab. *Slang:* jaw. *See* WORDS. **3.** A usually formal oral communication to an audience : address, allocution, declamation, lecture, oration, prelection, talk. *See* WORDS. **4.** A system of terms used by a people sharing a history and culture : dialect, language, tongue, vernacular. *Linguistics:* langue. *See* WORDS.

speechifier *noun*
One who delivers a public speech : declaimer, lecturer, speaker, speechmaker. *See* WORDS.

speechless *adjective*
1. Lacking the power or faculty of speech : aphonic, dumb, inarticulate, mute, voiceless. *See* WORDS. **2.** Temporarily unable or unwilling to speak, as from shock or fear : dumb, inarticulate, mum, mute, silent, voiceless, wordless. *See* WORDS.

speechlessness *noun*
The avoidance of speech : dumbness, muteness, silence, wordlessness. *See* WORDS.

speechmaker *noun*
One who delivers a public speech : declaimer, lecturer, speaker, speechifier. *See* WORDS.

speed *noun*
1. Rate of motion or performance : pace, tempo, velocity. *Informal:* clip[1]. *See* FAST.
2. Rapidness of movement or activity : celerity, dispatch, expedition, expeditiousness, fleetness, haste, hurry, hustle, quickness, rapidity, rapidness, speediness, swiftness. *See* FAST.
speed *verb* **1.** To increase the speed of. Also used with *up* : accelerate, expedite, hasten, hurry, hustle, quicken, step up. *See* FAST. **2.** To move swiftly : bolt, bucket, bustle, dart, dash, festinate, flash, fleet, flit, fly, haste, hasten, hurry, hustle, pelt[2], race, rocket, run, rush, sail, scoot, scour[2], shoot, sprint, tear[1], trot, whirl, whisk, whiz, wing, zip, zoom. *Informal:* hotfoot, rip. *Slang:* barrel, highball. *Chiefly British:* nip[1]. *Idioms:* get a move on, get cracking, go like lightning, go like the wind, hotfoot it, make haste, make time, make tracks, run like the wind, shake a leg, step (*or* jump) on it. *See* MOVE.

speediness *noun*
Rapidness of movement or activity : celerity, dispatch, expedition, expeditiousness, fleetness, haste, hurry, hustle, quickness, rapidity, rapidness, speed, swiftness. *See* FAST.

speedy *adjective*
1. Characterized by great celerity : breakneck, expeditious, fast, fleet, quick, rapid, swift. *Informal:* hell-for-leather. *Idiom:* quick as a bunny (*or* wink). *See* FAST. **2.** Accomplished in very little time : brief, expeditious, fast, flying, hasty, hurried, quick, rapid, short, swift. *See* FAST.

spell[1] *verb*
To have or convey a particular idea : connote, denote, import, intend, mean[1], signify. *Idiom:* add up to. *See* MEANING.
spell out *verb* To make understandable : construe, decipher, explain, explicate, expound, interpret. *Archaic:* enucleate. *Idiom:* put into plain English. *See* EXPLAIN.

spell[2] *noun*
An object or power that one uses to cause often evil events : charm, evil eye, magic. *Slang:* whammy. *See* SUPERNATURAL.
spell *verb* To act upon with or as if with magic : bewitch, charm, enchant, enthrall, entrance[2], spellbind, voodoo, witch. *See* PERSUASION.

spell[3] *noun*
1. A rather short period : bit[1], space, time, while. *See* BIG. **2.** A limited, often assigned period of activity, duty, or opportunity : bout, go, hitch, inning (often used in plural), shift, stint, stretch, time, tour, trick, turn, watch. *See* TIME. **3.** *Informal.* A sudden and often acute manifestation of a disease : access, attack, fit[2], seizure. *See* HEALTH.
spell *verb* To free from a specific duty by acting as a substitute : relieve, take over. *See* SUBSTITUTE.

spellbind *verb*
1. To act upon with or as if with magic : bewitch, charm, enchant, enthrall, entrance[2], spell[2], voodoo, witch. *See* PERSUASION. **2.** To compel, as the attention, interest, or imagination, of : arrest, catch up, enthrall, fascinate, grip, hold, mesmerize, rivet, transfix. *Slang:* grab. *See* EXCITE.

spell out *verb* See **spell[1]**.

spend *verb*
1. To use all of : consume, drain, draw down, eat up, exhaust, expend, finish, play out, run through, use up. *Informal:* polish off. *See* INCREASE. **2.** To be depleted : consume, go. *Idiom:* go down the drain. *See* INCREASE.
3. To distribute (money) as payment : disburse, expend, give, lay out, outlay, pay (out). *Informal:* fork out (*or* over *or* up), shell out. *See*

SAVE. **4.** To use time in a particular way : pass, put in. *See* TIME.

spendthrift *noun*
A wasteful person : prodigal, profligate, scattergood, waster, wastrel. *See* SAVE.
spendthrift *adjective* Characterized by excessive or imprudent spending : extravagant, lavish, prodigal, profligate, profuse, wasteful. *See* CAREFUL, EXCESS, SAVE.

spent *adjective*
Extremely tired : bleary, dead, drained, exhausted, fatigued, rundown, tired out, wearied, weariful, weary, worn-down, worn-out. *Informal:* beat, bushed, tuckered (out). *Slang:* done in, fagged (out), pooped (out). ***Idioms:*** all in, ready to drop. *See* HEALTH, TIRED.

sperm *noun*
The male fluid of fertilization : seed, semen. *See* START.

spew *verb*
To send forth (confined matter) violently : belch, disgorge, eject, eruct, erupt, expel. *Geology:* extravasate. *See* EXPLOSION.

sphere *noun*
An area within which something or someone exists, acts, or has influence or power : ambit, compass, extension, extent, orbit, purview, range, reach, realm, scope, sweep, swing. *See* TERRITORY.

spheric *adjective*
Having the shape of a curve everywhere equidistant from a fixed point : annular, circular, globoid, globular, round, spherical. *See* GEOMETRY.

spherical *adjective*
Having the shape of a curve everywhere equidistant from a fixed point : annular, circular, globoid, globular, round, spheric. *See* GEOMETRY.

spic-and-span *adjective* See **spick-and-span.**

spice *noun*
A substance that imparts taste : condiment, flavor, flavoring, seasoner, seasoning. *See* TASTE.

spick-and-span also **spic-and-span** *adjective*
In good order or clean condition : neat, orderly, shipshape, snug, spruce, taut, tidy, trig, trim, well-groomed. *Chiefly British:* tight. ***Idiom:*** neat as a pin. *See* CLEAN, ORDER.

spicy *adjective*
1. Affecting the organs of taste or smell with a strong and often harsh sensation : piquant, pungent, sharp, zesty. *Archaic:* poignant. *See* SMELLS, TASTE. **2.** Bordering on indelicacy or impropriety : blue, earthy, off-color, provocative, racy, risqué, salty, scabrous, suggestive. *See* DECENT.

spiel *verb*
Informal. To talk volubly, persistently, and usually inconsequentially : babble, blabber, chatter, chitchat, clack, jabber, palaver, prate, prattle, rattle (on), run on. *Informal:* go on. *Slang:* gab, gas, jaw, yak. ***Idioms:*** run off at the mouth, shoot the breeze (*or* bull). *See* WORDS.

spill *verb*
1. To grow or spread in a disorderly or planless fashion : sprawl, straggle. *See* ORDER. **2.** To come to the ground suddenly and involuntarily : drop, fall, go down, nose-dive, pitch, plunge, topple, tumble. ***Idiom:*** take a fall (*or* header *or* plunge *or* spill *or* tumble). *See* RISE. **3.** *Informal.* To disclose in a breach of confidence : betray, blab, divulge, expose, give away, let out, reveal, tell, uncover, unveil. *Archaic:* discover. ***Idioms:*** let slip, let the cat out of the bag, spill the beans, tell all. *See* SHOW.
spill *noun* A sudden involuntary drop to the ground : dive, fall, nosedive, pitch, plunge, tumble. *Informal:* header. *See* RISE.

spin *verb*
1. To make or become longer. Also used with *out* : draw out, elongate, extend, lengthen, prolong, prolongate, protract, stretch (out). *Mathematics:* produce. *See* INCREASE, LONG. **2.** To rotate rapidly : swirl, twirl, whirl. *See* REPETITION. **3.** To have the sensation of turning in circles : reel, swim, swirl, whirl. *See* REPETITION.
spin *noun Informal.* A trip in a motor vehicle : drive, ride, run. *Informal:* whirl. *See* MOVE.

spindling *adjective*
Tall, thin, and awkwardly built : gangling, gangly, lanky, rangy, spindly. *See* FAT.

spindly *adjective*
Tall, thin, and awkwardly built : gangling, gangly, lanky, rangy, spindling. *See* FAT.

spine *noun*
A sharp, pointed object : needle, prick, prickle, thorn. *See* SHARP.

spinoff or **spin-off** *noun*
Something derived from another : byproduct, derivation, derivative, descendant, offshoot, outgrowth. *See* KIN.

spiny *adjective*
1. Full of sharp needlelike protuberances : briery, echinate, prickly, pricky, thistly, thorny. *See* SHARP. **2.** So replete with interlocking points and complications as to be painfully

irritating : nettlesome, prickly, thorny. *See* EASY, PAIN.

spiral *verb*
To move or proceed on a repeatedly curving course : coil, corkscrew, curl, entwine, meander, snake, twine, twist, weave, wind[2], wreathe. *See* REPETITION, STRAIGHT.

spirit *noun*
1. The vital principle or animating force within living beings : breath, divine spark, élan vital, life force, psyche, soul, vital force, vitality. *See* BODY. **2.** The essential being of a person, regarded as immaterial and immortal : soul. *See* BE. **3.** A supernatural being, such as a ghost : apparition, bogey, bogeyman, bogle, eidolon, ghost, phantasm, phantasma, phantom, revenant, shade, shadow, specter, visitant, wraith. *Informal:* spook. *Regional:* haunt. *See* BEINGS, SUPERNATURAL. **4.** The most central and material part : core, essence, gist, heart, kernel, marrow, meat, nub, pith, quintessence, root[1], soul, stuff, substance. *Law:* gravamen. *See* BE. **5.** A temporary state of mind or feeling. Used in plural : frame of mind, humor, mood, temper, vein. *See* FEELINGS. **6.** A lively, emphatic, eager quality or manner : animation, bounce, brio, dash, élan, esprit, life, liveliness, pertness, sparkle, verve, vigor, vim, vivaciousness, vivacity, zip. *Informal:* ginger, pep, peppiness. *Slang:* oomph. *See* ACTION. **7.** The quality of mind enabling one to face danger or hardship resolutely : braveness, bravery, courage, courageousness, dauntlessness, doughtiness, fearlessness, fortitude, gallantry, gameness, heart, intrepidity, intrepidness, mettle, nerve, pluck, pluckiness, stoutheartedness, undauntedness, valiance, valiancy, valiantness, valor. *Informal:* spunk, spunkiness. *Slang:* gut (used in plural), gutsiness, moxie. *See* FEAR. **8.** A prevailing quality, as of thought, behavior, or attitude : climate, mood, temper, tone. *See* ATTITUDE.

spirit *verb* To bring in or take out secretly : smuggle, sneak. *See* MOVE.

spirit away *verb* To seize and detain (a person) unlawfully : abduct, kidnap, snatch. *See* CRIME, FREE.

spirit away *verb* See **spirit.**

spirited *adjective*
1. Very brisk, alert, and full of high spirits : animated, bouncy, chipper, dashing, high-spirited, lively, pert, vivacious. *Informal:* peppy. ***Idioms:*** bright-eyed and bushy-tailed, full of life. *See* ACTION. **2.** Full of or characterized by a lively, emphatic, eager quality : fiery, high-spirited, mettlesome, peppery, vibrant. *Informal:* snappy. *See* ACTION, FEELINGS.

spiritless *adjective*
1. Lacking energy and vitality or showing such a lack : flagging, lackadaisical, languid, languorous, leaden, limp, listless, lymphatic. *See* ACTION, TIRED. **2.** In low spirits : blue, dejected, depressed, desolate, dispirited, down, downcast, downhearted, dull, dysphoric, gloomy, heavy-hearted, low, melancholic, melancholy, sad, tristful, unhappy, wistful. ***Idiom:*** down at (*or* in) the mouth. *See* HAPPY. **3.** Lacking liveliness, charm, or surprise : arid, aseptic, colorless, drab, dry, dull, earthbound, flat, flavorless, lackluster, lifeless, lusterless, matter-of-fact, pedestrian, prosaic, sterile, stodgy, unimaginative, uninspired. *See* EXCITE.

spiritual *adjective*
1. Having no body, form, or substance : bodiless, discarnate, disembodied, immaterial, incorporeal, insubstantial, metaphysical, nonphysical, unbodied, uncorporal, unsubstantial. *See* BODY. **2.** Of or concerned with the spirit rather than the body or material things : numinous, otherworldly, unworldly. *See* BODY. **3.** Of or relating to a church or to an established religion : church, churchly, ecclesiastical, religious. *See* RELIGION.

spirituous *adjective*
Containing alcohol : alcoholic, hard, intoxicative, strong. *See* INGESTION.

spite *noun*
1. A desire to harm others or to see others suffer : despitefulness, ill will, malevolence, malice, maliciousness, malignancy, malignity, meanness, nastiness, poisonousness, spitefulness, venomousness, viciousness. *See* ATTITUDE. **2.** The quality or condition of being vindictive : revenge, spitefulness, vengefulness, vindictiveness. *See* FORGIVENESS.

spiteful *adjective*
1. Characterized by intense ill will or spite : black, despiteful, evil, hateful, malevolent, malicious, malign, malignant, mean[2], nasty, poisonous, venomous, vicious, wicked. *Slang:* bitchy. *See* ATTITUDE. **2.** Disposed to seek revenge : revengeful, vengeful, vindictive. *See* FORGIVENESS.

spitefulness *noun*
1. A desire to harm others or to see others suffer : despitefulness, ill will, malevolence, malice, maliciousness, malignancy, malignity, meanness, nastiness, poisonousness, spite, venomousness, viciousness. *See* ATTITUDE. **2.** The quality or condition of being vindictive :

revenge, spite, vengefulness, vindictiveness. *See* FORGIVENESS.

spitting image *noun*
One exactly resembling another : double, duplicate, image, picture, portrait. *Slang:* ringer. *See* SAME.

splash *verb*
1. To hurl or scatter liquid upon : bespatter, dash, slop, slosh, spatter, splatter, spray, swash. *See* STRIKE. **2.** To flow or move with a low slapping sound : bubble, burble, gurgle, lap, swash, wash. *See* MOVE, SOUNDS.

splashy *adjective*
Marked by outward, often extravagant display : flamboyant, ostentatious, pretentious, showy, splurgy. *See* PLAIN.

splatter *verb*
1. To hurl or scatter liquid upon : bespatter, dash, slop, slosh, spatter, splash, spray, swash. *See* STRIKE. **2.** To mark or soil with spots : bespatter, blotch, spatter, splotch, spot. *See* MARKS.

spleen *noun*
A tendency to become angry or irritable : irascibility, irascibleness, temper, temperament, tetchiness. *Informal:* dander. *Slang:* short fuse. ***Idiom:*** low boiling point. *See* FEELINGS.

splendid *adjective*
1. Marked by extraordinary elegance, beauty, and splendor : brilliant, glorious, gorgeous, magnificent, proud, resplendent, splendorous. *See* BEAUTIFUL. **2.** Large and impressive in size, scope, or extent : august, baronial, grand, grandiose, imposing, lordly, magnific, magnificent, majestic, noble, princely, regal, royal, stately, sublime, superb. *See* BIG, GOOD.
3. Exceptionally good of its kind : ace, banner, blue-ribbon, brag, capital, champion, excellent, fine[1], first-class, first-rate, prime, quality, superb, superior, terrific, tiptop, top. *Informal:* A-one, bully, dandy, great, swell, topflight, topnotch. *Slang:* boss. *Chiefly British:* tophole. *See* GOOD. **4.** Particularly excellent : divine, fabulous, fantastic, fantastical, glorious, marvelous, sensational, superb, terrific, wonderful. *Informal:* dandy, dreamy, great, ripping, super, swell, tremendous. *Slang:* cool, groovy, hot, keen[1], neat, nifty. ***Idiom:*** out of this world. *See* GOOD.

splendor *noun*
Something meriting the highest praise or regard : glory, grandeur, grandiosity, grandness, greatness, majesty. *See* PRAISE.

splendorous or **splendrous** *adjective*
Marked by extraordinary elegance, beauty, and splendor : brilliant, glorious, gorgeous, magnificent, proud, resplendent, splendid. *See* BEAUTIFUL.

splendrous *adjective* See **splendorous.**

splinter *verb*
1. To crack or split into two or more fragments by means of or as a result of force, a blow, or strain : break, fracture, rift, rive, shatter, shiver[2], smash, sunder. *See* HELP. **2.** To break away or withdraw from membership in an association or a federation. Also used with *off* : secede. *Informal:* split. *See* PARTICIPATE, POLITICS.

split *verb*
1. To separate into parts with or as if with a sharp-edged instrument : carve, cleave[1], cut, dissever, sever, slice, slit. *See* ASSEMBLE. **2.** To undergo partial breaking : crack, fissure, fracture, rupture. *See* HELP. **3.** To separate or pull apart by force : rend, rip, rive, run, tear[1]. *See* ASSEMBLE, HELP. **4.** To become or cause to become apart one from another. Also used with *up* : break, detach, disjoin, disjoint, disunite, divide, divorce, part, separate. ***Idioms:*** part company, set at odds. *See* ASSEMBLE.
5. *Informal.* To break away or withdraw from membership in an association or a federation : secede, splinter (off). *See* PARTICIPATE, POLITICS. **6.** *Informal.* To terminate a relationship or an association by or as if by leaving one another. Also used with *up* : break off, break up, part, separate. ***Idioms:*** call it quits, come to a parting of the ways, part company. *See* ASSEMBLE, CONTINUE. **7.** *Slang.* To move or proceed away from a place : depart, exit, get away, get off, go, go away, leave[1], pull out, quit, retire, run (along), withdraw. *Informal:* cut out, push off, shove off. *Slang:* blow[1], take off. ***Idioms:*** hit the road, take leave. *See* APPROACH.

split *noun* **1.** The act or an instance of separating one thing from another : detachment, disjunction, disjuncture, disseverance, disseverment, disunion, division, divorce, divorcement, parting, partition, separation, severance. *See* ASSEMBLE, PART. **2.** The result of cutting : cut, gash, incision, slash, slice, slit. *See* ENTER, HELP. **3.** A usually narrow partial opening caused by splitting and rupture : break, chink, cleavage, cleft, crack, crevice, fissure, rift. *See* OPEN. **4.** An interruption in friendly relations : alienation, breach, break, disaffection, estrangement, fissure, rent[2], rift, rupture, schism. *See* ASSEMBLE, HELP. **5.** That which is allotted : allocation, allotment, allowance, dole, lot, measure, part, portion, quantum, quota, ration, share. *Informal:* cut. *Slang:* divvy. *See* COLLECT.

splotch *noun*
A discolored mark made by smearing : blot, blotch, daub, smear, smirch, smudge, smutch, stain. *See* MARKS.
splotch *verb* To mark or soil with spots : bespatter, blotch, spatter, splatter, spot. *See* MARKS.

splurgy *adjective*
Marked by outward, often extravagant display : flamboyant, ostentatious, pretentious, showy, splashy. *See* PLAIN.

splutter *verb*
To make a series of short, sharp noises : crackle, crepitate, sputter. *See* SOUNDS.

spoil *verb*
1. To become or cause to become rotten or unsound : break down, decay, decompose, deteriorate, disintegrate, molder, putrefy, rot, taint, turn. ***Idioms:*** go bad, go to pot, go to seed. *See* BETTER, THRIVE. **2.** To cause the complete ruin or wreckage of : bankrupt, break down, cross up, demolish, destroy, finish, ruin, shatter, sink, smash, torpedo, undo, wash up, wrack^2, wreck. *Slang:* total. ***Idiom:*** put the kibosh on. *See* HELP. **3.** To harm irreparably through inept handling; make a mess : ball up, blunder, boggle, botch, bungle, foul up, fumble, gum up, mess up, mishandle, mismanage, muddle, muff. *Informal:* bollix up, muck up. *Slang:* blow^1, goof up, louse up, screw up, snafu. ***Idiom:*** make a muck of. *See* CORRECT, HELP. **4.** To treat with indulgence and often overtender care : baby, cater, coddle, cosset, indulge, mollycoddle, overindulge, pamper. *See* TREAT WELL. **5.** *Archaic.* To rob of goods by force, especially in time of war : depredate, despoil, havoc, loot, pillage, plunder, ransack, rape, ravage, sack^2, spoliate, strip^1. *Archaic:* harrow. *See* CRIMES, GIVE.
spoil *noun* **1.** Goods or property seized unlawfully, especially by a victor in wartime. Used in plural : booty, loot, pillage, plunder. *Slang:* boodle. *Nautical:* prize^2. *See* CRIMES, GIVE. **2.** The political appointments or jobs that are at the disposal of those in power. Used in plural : patronage. *Slang:* pork. *See* POLITICS.

spoilage *noun*
The condition of being decayed : breakdown, decay, decomposition, deterioration, disintegration, putrefaction, putrescence, putridness, rot, rottenness. *See* BETTER, THRIVE.

spoken *adjective*
1. Expressed or transmitted in speech : oral, unwritten, verbal, word-of-mouth. *See* WORDS. **2.** Produced by the voice : articulate, oral, sonant, uttered, vocal, voiced. *See* SOUNDS.

spokesman *noun*
A person who speaks on behalf of another or others : mouth, speaker, spokesperson, spokeswoman. *Informal:* mouthpiece. *See* SUBSTITUTE.

spokesperson *noun*
A person who speaks on behalf of another or others : mouth, speaker, spokesman, spokeswoman. *Informal:* mouthpiece. *See* SUBSTITUTE.

spokeswoman *noun*
A person who speaks on behalf of another or others : mouth, speaker, spokesman, spokesperson. *Informal:* mouthpiece. *See* SUBSTITUTE.

spoliate *verb*
To rob of goods by force, especially in time of war : depredate, despoil, havoc, loot, pillage, plunder, ransack, rape, ravage, sack^2, strip^1. *Archaic:* harrow, spoil. *See* CRIMES, GIVE.

sponge *noun*
1. One who depends on another for support without reciprocating : bloodsucker, hanger-on, leech, parasite. *Slang:* freeloader. *See* DEPENDENCE. **2.** *Slang.* A person who is habitually drunk : drunk, drunkard, inebriate, sot, tippler. *Slang:* boozehound, boozer, lush^2, rummy^1, soak, souse, stiff. *See* DRUGS.
sponge *verb Informal.* To take advantage of the generosity of others : leech. *Slang:* freeload. *See* DEPENDENCE.

spongy *adjective*
Yielding easily to pressure or weight; not firm : mushy, pappy^1, pulpous, pulpy, quaggy, soft, squashy, squishy, yielding. *See* RESIST.

sponsor *noun*
1. One who assumes financial responsibility for another : backer, guarantor, guaranty, surety, underwriter. *Informal:* angel. *See* LAW, SUPPORT. **2.** A person who supports or champions an activity, cause, or institution, for example : backer, benefactor, contributor, friend, patron, supporter. *Informal:* angel. *See* HELP.
sponsor *verb* To act as a patron to : patronize, support. *See* HELP.

sponsorship *noun*
Aid or support given by a patron : aegis, auspice (often used in plural), backing, patronage, patronization. *See* HELP.

spontaneity *noun*
Freedom from constraint, formality, embarrassment, or awkwardness : casualness, ease, easiness, informality, naturalness, poise, unceremoniousness, unrestraint. *See* RESTRAINT, TIGHTEN.

spontaneous *adjective*
1. Acting or happening without apparent forethought, prompting, or planning : automatic, impulsive, instinctive, involuntary, reflex, unpremeditated. *See* PLANNED. **2.** Done by one's own choice : free, uncompelled, unforced, volitional, voluntary, willful. *See* WILLING. **3.** Unconstrained by rigid standards or ceremony : casual, easy, easygoing, informal, natural, relaxed, unceremonious, unrestrained. *Informal:* laid-back. *See* PLAIN, TIGHTEN.

spontaneously *adverb*
Of one's own free will : freely, voluntarily, willfully, willingly. ***Idioms:*** of one's own accord, on one's own volition. *See* WILLING.

spook *noun*
1. *Informal.* A supernatural being, such as a ghost : apparition, bogey, bogeyman, bogle, eidolon, ghost, phantasm, phantasma, phantom, revenant, shade, shadow, specter, spirit, visitant, wraith. *Regional:* haunt. *See* BEINGS, SUPERNATURAL. **2.** *Informal.* A person who secretly observes others to obtain information : agent, operative, spy. ***Idiom:*** secret (*or* undercover) agent. *See* INVESTIGATE.

spooky *adjective*
Informal. Of a mysteriously strange and usually frightening nature : eerie, uncanny, unearthly, weird. *See* FEAR, USUAL.

spoon *verb*
Informal. To engage in kissing, caressing, and other amorous behavior : *Informal:* fool around, neck, pet[1]. *Slang:* make out. *See* SEX.

spoor *noun*
Evidence of passage left along a course followed by a hunted animal or fugitive : scent, track, trail. *See* MARKS, SMELLS.

sporadic *adjective*
1. Happening or appearing now and then : fitful, intermittent, occasional, periodic, periodical. *Informal:* on-again, off-again. *See* CONTINUE. **2.** Rarely occurring or appearing : infrequent, occasional, rare, scarce, uncommon, unusual. ***Idiom:*** few and far between. *See* USUAL.

sporadically *adverb*
1. Once in a while; at times : betimes, intermittently, occasionally, periodically, sometimes. ***Idioms:*** ever and again (*or* anon), now and again (*or* then). *See* CONTINUE. **2.** At rare intervals : infrequently, little, occasionally, rarely, seldom. ***Idioms:*** hardly (*or* scarcely) ever, once in a blue moon. *See* USUAL.

spore *noun*
A propagative part of a plant : seed, tuber. *See* START.

sport *noun*
1. Activity engaged in for relaxation and amusement : disport, diversion, fun, play, recreation. *See* WORK. **2.** Actions taken as a joke : fun, game, play. *See* WORK.

sport *verb* **1.** To occupy oneself with amusement or diversion : disport, play, recreate. *See* WORK. **2.** To make a public and usually ostentatious show of : brandish, display, disport, exhibit, expose, flash, flaunt, parade, show (off). *See* SHOW.

sporting *adjective*
According to the rules : clean, fair, sportsmanlike, sportsmanly. *See* FAIR.

sportive *adjective*
Full of high-spirited fun : frisky, frolicsome, impish, mischievous, playful, waggish. *See* WORK.

sportiveness *noun*
The state of being full of high-spirited fun : friskiness, frolicsomeness, playfulness, waggishness. *See* WORK.

sportsmanlike *adjective*
According to the rules : clean, fair, sporting, sportsmanly. *See* FAIR.

sportsmanly *adjective*
According to the rules : clean, fair, sporting, sportsmanlike. *See* FAIR.

spot *noun*
1. A very small mark : dash, dot, fleck, pinpoint, point, speck. *See* MARKS. **2.** A mark of discredit or disgrace : black eye, blemish, blot, onus, stain, stigma, taint, tarnish. *Archaic:* attaint. ***Idiom:*** a blot on one's escutcheon. *See* MARKS, RESPECT. **3.** A particular portion of space chosen for something : location, locus, place, point. *See* PLACE. **4.** A post of employment : appointment, berth, billet, job, office, place, position, situation, slot. *Slang:* gig. *See* PLACE. **5.** *Informal.* A difficult, often embarrassing situation or condition : box[1], corner, deep water, difficulty, dilemma, Dutch, fix, hole, hot spot, hot water, jam, plight[1], predicament, quagmire, scrape, soup, trouble. *Informal:* bind, pickle. *See* EASY. **6.** *Chiefly British.* A tiny amount : bit[1], crumb, dab[1], dash, dot, dram, drop, fragment, grain, iota,

jot, minim, mite, modicum, molecule, ort, ounce, particle, scrap[1], scruple, shred, smidgen, speck, tittle, trifle, whit. *See* BIG.

spot *verb* **1.** To mark or soil with spots : bespatter, blotch, spatter, splatter, splotch. *See* MARKS. **2.** To put in or assign to a certain position or location : emplace, install, locate, place, position, set[1], site, situate. *See* PLACE. **3.** To perceive, especially barely or fleetingly : catch, descry, detect, discern, espy, glimpse, spy. *See* SEE. **4.** To perceive and fix the identity of, especially with difficulty : descry, discern, distinguish, make out, pick out. *See* SEE. **5.** To look for and discover : find, locate, pinpoint. *See* GET.

spot *adjective* Having no particular pattern, purpose, organization, or structure : chance, desultory, haphazard, hit-or-miss, indiscriminate, random, unplanned. *See* PLANNED.

spotless *adjective*
Free from dirt, stain, or impurities : antiseptic, clean, cleanly, immaculate, stainless, unsoiled, unsullied. *See* CLEAN.

spotty *adjective*
Lacking consistency or regularity in quality or performance : erratic, inconsistent, patchy, uneven, unsteady, variable. *See* CONTINUE, SAME.

spousal *adjective*
Of, relating to, or typical of marriage : conjugal, connubial, hymeneal, marital, married, matrimonial, nuptial, wedded. *See* MARRIAGE.

spousal *noun* The act or ceremony by which two people become husband and wife. Often used in plural : bridal, espousal, marriage, nuptial (often used in plural), wedding. *See* MARRIAGE.

spouse *noun*
A husband or wife : consort, mate, partner. *Informal:* better half. *See* MARRIAGE.

spouseless *adjective*
Without a spouse : fancy-free, footloose, lone, single, sole, unattached, unmarried, unwed. ***Idiom:*** footloose and fancy-free. *See* MARRIAGE.

spout *verb*
To eject or be ejected in a sudden thin, swift stream : jet[2], spray, spurt, squirt. *See* MOVE.

spout *noun* A sudden swift stream of ejected liquid : jet[2], spray, spurt, squirt. *See* MOVE.

sprain *verb*
To injure a (bodily part) by twisting : turn, wrench. *See* HEALTH.

sprawl *verb*
1. To sit or lie with the limbs spread out awkwardly : drape, loll, spread-eagle, straddle. *See* POSTURE. **2.** To grow or spread in a disorderly or planless fashion : spill, straggle. *See* ORDER.

spray *noun*
A sudden swift stream of ejected liquid : jet[2], spout, spurt, squirt. *See* MOVE.

spray *verb* **1.** To eject or be ejected in a sudden thin, swift stream : jet[2], spout, spurt, squirt. *See* MOVE. **2.** To hurl or scatter liquid upon : bespatter, dash, slop, slosh, spatter, splash, splatter, swash. *See* STRIKE.

spread *verb*
1. To move or arrange so as to cover a larger area : expand, extend, fan[1] (out), open (out *or* up), outstretch, stretch, unfold, unroll. *See* MOVE. **2.** To extend over a wide area : circulate, diffuse, disperse, disseminate, distribute, radiate, scatter, strew. *See* MOVE, WIDE. **3.** To extend over the surface of : blanket, cap, cover, overlay. *See* PUT ON. **4.** To cause (a disease) to pass to another or others : carry, communicate, convey, give, pass, transmit. *See* MOVE. **5.** To make (information) generally known : advertise, blaze[2], blazon, broadcast, bruit, circulate, disseminate, noise, promulgate, propagate. ***Idioms:*** spread far and wide, spread the word. *See* KNOWLEDGE. **6.** To become known far and wide : circulate, get around, go around, travel. ***Idiom:*** go (*or* make) the rounds. *See* KNOWLEDGE. **7.** To arrange tableware upon (a table) in preparation for a meal : lay[1], set[1]. *See* ORDER.

spread *noun* **1.** The act of increasing in dimensions, scope, or inclusiveness : enlargement, expansion, extension. *See* INCREASE. **2.** A wide and open area, as of land, sky, or water : distance, expanse, expansion, extent, reach, space, stretch, sweep. *See* PLACE. **3.** *Informal.* A large meal elaborately prepared or served : banquet, feast, junket. *Informal:* feed. *See* INGESTION.

spread-eagle *verb*
To sit or lie with the limbs spread out awkwardly : drape, loll, sprawl, straddle. *See* POSTURE.

spree *noun*
1. A drinking bout : binge, brannigan, carousal, carouse, drunk. *Slang:* bat[2], bender, booze, jag, tear[1]. *See* DRUGS, RESTRAINT. **2.** A period of uncontrolled self-indulgence : binge, fling, orgy, rampage. *Slang:* jag. *See* RESTRAINT.

sprig *noun*
A young stemlike growth arising from a plant :

bine, offshoot, runner, shoot, sprout, tendril. *See* KIN.

sprightliness *noun*
Capacity or power for work or vigorous activity : animation, energy, force, might, potency, power, puissance, steam, strength. *Informal:* get-up-and-go, go, pep, peppiness, zip. *See* ACTION.

sprightly *adjective*
1. Possessing, exerting, or displaying energy : active, brisk, dynamic, dynamical, energetic, forceful, kinetic, lively, strenuous, vigorous. *Informal:* peppy. *See* ACTION. **2.** Disposed to action : active, brisk, driving, dynamic, dynamical, energetic, enterprising, lively, spry, vigorous, zippy. *Informal:* peppy, snappy. *See* ACTION.

spring *verb*
1. To move off the ground by a muscular effort of the legs and feet : hurdle, jump, leap, vault[2]. *See* MOVE, RISE. **2.** To bound lightly : hop, skip, skitter, trip. *See* MOVE. **3.** To move in a lively way : bounce, bound[1], jump, leap. *See* MOVE. **4.** To have as a source : arise, come, derive, emanate, flow, issue, originate, proceed, rise, stem, upspring. *See* START. **5.** To have hereditary derivation : derive, descend, issue. ***Idiom:*** trace one's descent. *See* KIN. **6.** *Slang.* To set at liberty : discharge, emancipate, free, liberate, loose, manumit, release. ***Idiom:*** let loose. *See* FREE.

spring *noun* **1.** The quality or state of being flexible : bounce, ductility, elasticity, flexibility, flexibleness, give, malleability, malleableness, plasticity, pliability, pliableness, pliancy, pliantness, resilience, resiliency, springiness, suppleness. *Obsolete:* flexure. *See* FLEXIBLE. **2.** The act of jumping : jump, leap, vault[2]. *See* MOVE, RISE. **3.** A light bounding movement : hop, skip. *See* MOVE. **4.** A sudden lively movement : bounce, bound[1], jump, leap. *See* MOVE. **5.** A point of origination : beginning, derivation, fount, fountain, fountainhead, mother, origin, parent, provenance, provenience, root[1], rootstock, source, well[1]. *See* START. **6.** A basis for an action or a decision : cause, ground (often used in plural), motivation, motive, reason. *See* START. **7.** The initial stage of a developmental process : beginning, birth, commencement, dawn, genesis, inception, nascence, nascency, onset, opening, origin, outset, start. *See* START. **8.** The season of the year during which the weather becomes warmer and plants revive : seedtime, springtide, springtime. *See* TIME. **9.** The time of life between childhood and maturity : adolescence, greenness, juvenescence, juvenility, puberty, salad days, youth, youthfulness. *See* YOUTH.

spring *adjective* Of, occurring in, or characteristic of the season of spring : vernal. *See* TIME.

springiness *noun*
The quality or state of being flexible : bounce, ductility, elasticity, flexibility, flexibleness, give, malleability, malleableness, plasticity, pliability, pliableness, pliancy, pliantness, resilience, resiliency, spring, suppleness. *Obsolete:* flexure. *See* FLEXIBLE.

springtide *noun*
The season of the year during which the weather becomes warmer and plants revive : seedtime, spring, springtime. *See* TIME.

springtime *noun*
The season of the year during which the weather becomes warmer and plants revive : seedtime, spring, springtide. *See* TIME.

springy *adjective*
Capable of withstanding stress without injury : elastic, flexible, flexile, resilient, supple. *Physics:* plastic. *See* FLEXIBLE.

sprinkle *verb*
1. To scatter or release in drops or small particles : besprinkle, dust, powder. *See* STRIKE. **2.** To mark with many small spots : bespeckle, besprinkle, dapple, dot, fleck, freckle, mottle, pepper, speck, speckle, stipple. *See* MARKS.

sprint *verb*
1. To move swiftly on foot so that both feet leave the ground during each stride : run, scamper, scurry. *See* MOVE. **2.** To move swiftly : bolt, bucket, bustle, dart, dash, festinate, flash, fleet, flit, fly, haste, hasten, hurry, hustle, pelt[2], race, rocket, run, rush, sail, scoot, scour[2], shoot, speed, tear[1], trot, whirl, whisk, whiz, wing, zip, zoom. *Informal:* hotfoot, rip. *Slang:* barrel, highball. *Chiefly British:* nip[1]. ***Idioms:*** get a move on, get cracking, go like lightning, go like the wind, hotfoot it, make haste, make time, make tracks, run like the wind, shake a leg, step (*or* jump) on it. *See* MOVE.

sprout *noun*
A young stemlike growth arising from a plant : bine, offshoot, runner, shoot, sprig, tendril. *See* KIN.

spruce *adjective*
In good order or clean condition : neat, orderly, shipshape, snug, spick-and-span, taut, tidy, trig, trim, well-groomed. *Chiefly British:* tight. ***Idiom:*** neat as a pin. *See* CLEAN, ORDER.

spruce *verb* **1.** To improve in appearance, especially by refurbishing. Also used with *up* : fix up, smarten (up). *See* BETTER. **2.** To make or keep (an area) clean and orderly. Also used with *up* : clean (up), clear (up), neaten (up), police, straighten (up), tidy (up). *See* ORDER. **3.** To make neat and trim; make presentable. Also used with *up* : clean (up), freshen (up), groom, neaten (up), slick up, tidy (up), trig (out), trim. *See* ORDER.

spry *adjective*
1. Moving or performing quickly, lightly, and easily : agile, brisk, facile, nimble, quick. *See* ABILITY. **2.** Disposed to action : active, brisk, driving, dynamic, dynamical, energetic, enterprising, lively, sprightly, vigorous, zippy. *Informal:* peppy, snappy. *See* ACTION.

spume *noun*
A mass of bubbles in or on the surface of a liquid : foam, froth, head, lather, suds, yeast. *See* SOLID.

spume *verb* To form or cause to form foam : bubble, cream, effervesce, fizz, foam, froth, lather, suds, yeast. *See* SOLID.

spumous *adjective*
Consisting of or resembling foam : foamy, frothy, lathery, spumy, sudsy, yeasty. *See* SOLID.

spumy *adjective*
Consisting of or resembling foam : foamy, frothy, lathery, spumous, sudsy, yeasty. *See* SOLID.

spunk *noun*
Informal. The quality of mind enabling one to face danger or hardship resolutely : braveness, bravery, courage, courageousness, dauntlessness, doughtiness, fearlessness, fortitude, gallantry, gameness, heart, intrepidity, intrepidness, mettle, nerve, pluck, pluckiness, spirit, stoutheartedness, undauntedness, valiance, valiancy, valiantness, valor. *Informal:* spunkiness. *Slang:* gut (used in plural), gutsiness, moxie. *See* FEAR.

spunkiness *noun*
Informal. The quality of mind enabling one to face danger or hardship resolutely : braveness, bravery, courage, courageousness, dauntlessness, doughtiness, fearlessness, fortitude, gallantry, gameness, heart, intrepidity, intrepidness, mettle, nerve, pluck, pluckiness, spirit, stoutheartedness, undauntedness, valiance, valiancy, valiantness, valor. *Informal:* spunk. *Slang:* gut (used in plural), gutsiness, moxie. *See* FEAR.

spunky *adjective*
Informal. Having or showing courage : audacious, bold, brave, courageous, dauntless, doughty, fearless, fortitudinous, gallant, game, hardy, heroic, intrepid, mettlesome, plucky, stout, stouthearted, unafraid, undaunted, valiant, valorous. *Slang:* gutsy, gutty. *See* FEAR.

spur *noun*
Something that causes and encourages a given response : encouragement, fillip, impetus, impulse, incentive, inducement, motivation, prod, push, stimulant, stimulation, stimulator, stimulus. *See* CAUSE.

spur *verb* To stir to action or feeling : egg on, excite, foment, galvanize, goad, impel, incite, inflame, inspire, instigate, motivate, move, pique, prick, prod, prompt, propel, provoke, set off, stimulate, touch off, trigger, work up. *See* CAUSE, EXCITE.

spurious *adjective*
1. Fraudulently or deceptively imitative : bogus, counterfeit, fake, false, fraudulent, phony, sham, suppositious, supposititious. *See* TRUE. **2.** Containing fundamental errors in reasoning : fallacious, false, illogical, invalid, sophistic, specious, unsound. *See* CORRECT, TRUE. **3.** Devoid of truth : counterfactual, false, specious, truthless, untrue, untruthful, wrong. *See* TRUE. **4.** Born to parents who are not married to each other : baseborn, bastard, illegitimate, misbegotten, natural, unlawful. *See* KIN, LAW.

spuriousness *noun*
Plausible but invalid reasoning : casuistry, fallacy, sophism, sophistry, speciousness. *See* CORRECT, TRUE.

spurn *verb*
1. To be unwilling to accept, consider, or receive : decline, dismiss, refuse, reject, turn down. *Slang:* nix. ***Idiom:*** turn thumbs down on. *See* ACCEPT. **2.** To slight (someone) deliberately : cut, rebuff, shun, snub. *Informal:* cold-shoulder. ***Idioms:*** close (*or* shut) the door on, give someone the cold shoulder, give someone the go-by, turn one's back on. *See* ACCEPT.

spurn *noun* A deliberate slight : cut, rebuff, snub. *Informal:* cold shoulder, go-by. *See* ACCEPT.

spur-of-the-moment *adjective*
Spoken, performed, or composed with little or no preparation or forethought : ad-lib, extemporaneous, extemporary, extempore, impromptu, improvised, offhand, snap, unrehearsed. *Informal:* off-the-cuff. *See* PREPARED.

spurt *noun*
A sudden swift stream of ejected liquid : jet[2], spout, spray, squirt. *See* MOVE.

spurt *verb* To eject or be ejected in a sudden thin, swift stream : jet[2], spout, spray, squirt. *See* MOVE.

sputter *verb*
To make a series of short, sharp noises : crackle, crepitate, splutter. *See* SOUNDS.

spy *noun*
A person who secretly observes others to obtain information : agent, operative. *Informal:* spook. ***Idiom:*** secret (*or* undercover) agent. *See* INVESTIGATE.

spy *verb* **1.** To observe or listen in secret to obtain information : eavesdrop. *See* INVESTIGATE. **2.** To perceive, especially barely or fleetingly : catch, descry, detect, discern, espy, glimpse, spot. *See* SEE.

squabble *verb*
To engage in a quarrel : argue, bicker, contend, dispute, fight, quarrel, quibble, spat, tiff, wrangle. *Informal:* hassle, tangle. ***Idioms:*** cross swords, have it out, have words, lock horns. *See* CONFLICT.

squabble *noun* A discussion, often heated, in which a difference of opinion is expressed : altercation, argument, bicker, clash, contention, controversy, debate, difficulty, disagreement, dispute, fight, polemic, quarrel, run-in, spat, tiff, word (used in plural), wrangle. *Informal:* hassle, rhubarb, tangle. *See* CONFLICT.

squalid *adjective*
1. Heavily soiled; very dirty or unclean : filthy, foul, nasty, vile. *See* CLEAN. **2.** Having or proceeding from low moral standards : base[2], ignoble, low, low-down, mean[2], sordid, vile. *See* RIGHT.

squalor *noun*
The condition or state of being dirty : dirtiness, filth, filthiness, foulness, griminess, grubbiness, smuttiness, uncleanliness, uncleanness. *See* CLEAN.

squander *verb*
1. To use up foolishly or needlessly : consume, devour, dissipate, waste. *See* SAVE. **2.** To spend (money) excessively and usually foolishly : consume, dissipate, fool away, fritter away, riot away, throw away, trifle away, waste. *Slang:* blow[1]. *See* SAVE.

squander *noun* Excessive or imprudent expenditure : extravagance, extravagancy, lavishness, prodigality, profligacy, profuseness, profusion, waste, wastefulness. *See* CAREFUL, SAVE.

square *noun*
Slang. An old-fashioned person who is reluctant to change or innovate : fogy, fossil, fuddy-duddy, mossback. *Informal:* stick-in-the-mud. *See* NEW.

square *adjective* **1.** Having four equal sides and four right angles : quadrate. *See* GEOMETRY. **2.** Free from bias in judgment : disinterested, dispassionate, equitable, fair, fair-minded, impartial, indifferent, just, nonpartisan, objective, unbiased, unprejudiced. ***Idiom:*** fair and square. *See* FAIR. **3.** Owing or being owed nothing : even[1], quit, quits. *See* PAY. **4.** *Slang.* Conforming to established practice or standards : button-down, conformist, conventional, establishmentarian, orthodox, straight, traditional. *See* USUAL.

square *verb* **1.** To make equal : equalize, equate, even[1], level. *See* SAME. **2.** To make or become suitable to a particular situation or use : acclimate, acclimatize, accommodate, adapt, adjust, conform, fashion, fit[1], reconcile, suit, tailor. *See* CHANGE. **3.** To be compatible or in correspondence : accord, agree, check, chime, comport with, conform, consist, correspond, fit[1], harmonize, match, tally. *Informal:* jibe[1]. *Archaic:* quadrate. *See* AGREE. **4.** To set right by giving what is due : clear, discharge, liquidate, pay (off *or* up), satisfy, settle. *See* PAY.

square *adverb* With precision or absolute conformity : bang, dead, direct, directly, exactly, fair, flush, just, precisely, right, smack[1], squarely, straight. *Slang:* smack-dab. *See* PRECISE.

squarely *adverb*
With precision or absolute conformity : bang, dead, direct, directly, exactly, fair, flush, just, precisely, right, smack[1], square, straight. *Slang:* smack-dab. *See* PRECISE.

squash *verb*
1. To press forcefully so as to break up into a pulpy mass : crush, mash, mush, pulp. *See* HELP. **2.** To bring to an end forcibly as if by imposing a heavy weight : choke off, crush, extinguish, put down, quash, quell, quench, squelch, suppress. ***Idiom:*** put the lid on. *See* CONTINUE, WIN.

squashy *adjective*
Yielding easily to pressure or weight; not firm : mushy, pappy[1], pulpous, pulpy, quaggy, soft, spongy, squishy, yielding. *See* RESIST.

squat *verb*
1. To sit on one's heels : hunker (down). *See* POSTURE. **2.** To stoop low with the limbs pulled in close to the body : crouch, huddle, hunch, hunker (down). *See* HIGH.

squat *adjective* Short, heavy, and solidly built : blocky, chunky, compact[1], dumpy, heavyset, stocky, stodgy, stubby, stumpy, thick, thickset. *See* FAT.

squawk *verb*
Informal. To express opposition, often by argument : challenge, demur, except, expostulate, inveigh, object, protest, remonstrate. *Informal:* kick. ***Idioms:*** set up a squawk, take exception. *See* SUPPORT.
squawk *noun* The act of expressing strong or reasoned opposition : challenge, demur, exception, expostulation, objection, protest, protestation, remonstrance, remonstration. *Slang:* kick. *See* SUPPORT.

squawky *adjective*
Disagreeable to the sense of hearing : dry, grating, harsh, hoarse, jarring, rasping, raspy, raucous, rough, scratchy, strident. *See* SOUNDS.

squeal *verb*
1. To utter a shrill, short cry : yap, yawp, yelp, yip. *See* SOUNDS. **2.** *Slang.* To give incriminating information about others, especially to the authorities : inform, talk, tattle, tip[3] (off). *Slang:* fink, rat, sing, snitch, stool. ***Idiom:*** blow the whistle. *See* KNOWLEDGE, LAW.
squeal *noun* A shrill, short cry : yap, yawp, yelp, yip. *See* SOUNDS.

squealer *noun*
Slang. One who gives incriminating information about others : informant, informer, tattler, tattletale. *Informal:* rat, tipster. *Slang:* fink, snitch, snitcher, stoolie, stool pigeon. *See* KNOWLEDGE, LAW.

squeamish *adjective*
Very difficult to please : choosy, dainty, exacting, fastidious, finical, finicky, fussy, meticulous, nice, particular, persnickety. *Informal:* picky. *See* ACCEPT.

squeeze *verb*
1. To subject to compression : compact[1], compress, constrict, constringe. *See* TIGHTEN. **2.** To put one's arms around affectionately : clasp, embrace, enfold, hold, hug, press. *Slang:* clinch. *Archaic:* bosom, clip[2], embosom. *See* TOUCH. **3.** To extract from by applying pressure : crush, express, press. *See* TIGHTEN. **4.** To obtain by coercion or intimidation : exact, extort, wrench, wrest, wring. *Slang:* shake down. *See* GET.
squeeze *noun* **1.** A compressing of something : compression, constriction. *See* TIGHTEN. **2.** The act of embracing : clasp, embrace, hug. *Slang:* clinch. *See* TOUCH.

squelch *verb*
1. To bring to an end forcibly as if by imposing a heavy weight : choke off, crush, extinguish, put down, quash, quell, quench, squash, suppress. ***Idiom:*** put the lid on. *See* CONTINUE, WIN. **2.** To hold (something requiring an outlet) in check : burke, choke (back), gag, hold back, hold down, hush (up), muffle, quench, repress, smother, stifle, strangle, suppress, throttle. *Informal:* sit on (*or* upon). *See* RESTRAINT.

squib *noun*
A usually brief detail of news or information : bit[1], item, paragraph, piece, story. *See* WORDS.

squiggle *verb*
To move or proceed with short irregular motions up and down or from side to side : squirm, waggle, wiggle, worm, wriggle, writhe. *See* MOVE, REPETITION.

squinch *verb*
To peer with the eyes partly closed : squint. ***Idiom:*** screw up one's eyes. *See* SEE.

squint *verb*
1. To peer with the eyes partly closed : squinch. ***Idiom:*** screw up one's eyes. *See* SEE. **2.** To have a tendency or inclination : incline, lean[1], slant, tend[1], trend. *See* LIKELY.
squint *noun* **1.** An inclination to something : bent, bias, cast, disposition, leaning, partiality, penchant, predilection, predisposition, proclivity, proneness, propensity, tendency, trend, turn. *See* APPROACH, LIKE. **2.** The condition of not having the visual axes parallel : cross-eye, strabismus. *See* SEE.

squint-eyed *adjective*
Marked by or affected with a squint : cross-eyed, squinty, strabismal, strabismic. *See* SEE.

squinty *adjective*
Marked by or affected with a squint : cross-eyed, squint-eyed, strabismal, strabismic. *See* SEE.

squirm *verb*
1. To move or proceed with short irregular motions up and down or from side to side : squiggle, waggle, wiggle, worm, wriggle, writhe. *See* MOVE, REPETITION. **2.** To twist and turn, as in pain, struggle, or embarrassment : agonize, toss, turn, writhe. *See* REPETITION.

squirrel *verb*
To store up (supplies or money), usually well beyond one's needs. Also used with *away* : hoard, stockpile, treasure. *Slang:* stash. *See* COLLECT, GIVE.

squirt *verb*
To eject or be ejected in a sudden thin, swift stream : jet[2], spout, spray, spurt. *See* MOVE.
squirt *noun* **1.** A sudden swift stream of ejected liquid : jet[2], spout, spray, spurt. *See* MOVE. **2.** *Informal.* An insignificant but arrogant and obnoxious young person : pup, puppy. *Slang:* twerp. *See* YOUTH.

squishy *adjective*
Yielding easily to pressure or weight; not firm : mushy, pappy[1], pulpous, pulpy, quaggy, soft, spongy, squashy, yielding. *See* RESIST.

stab *verb*
To cause to penetrate with force : dig, drive, plunge, ram, run, sink, stick, thrust. *See* PUT IN.
stab *noun* **1.** A small mark or hole made by a sharp, pointed object : perforation, prick, puncture. *See* MARKS, OPEN. **2.** A sensation of physical discomfort occurring as the result of disease or injury : ache, pain, pang, prick, prickle, smart, soreness, sting, stitch, throe, twinge. *Informal:* misery. *See* PAIN. **3.** A trying to do or make something : attempt, crack, effort, endeavor, essay, go, offer, trial, try. *Informal:* shot. *Slang:* take. *Archaic:* assay. *See* TRY. **4.** A brief trial : crack, go, try. *Informal:* fling, shot, whack, whirl. *See* TRY.

stabbing *adjective*
Marked by severity or intensity : acute, gnawing, knifelike, lancinating, piercing, sharp, shooting. *See* BIG.

stability *noun*
1. The condition of being free from defects or flaws : durability, firmness, integrity, solidity, soundness, strength, wholeness. *See* BETTER. **2.** Reliability in withstanding pressure, force, or stress : fastness, firmness, hardness, security, soundness, stableness, steadiness, strength, sturdiness, sureness. *See* BETTER, CHANGE, CONTINUE.

stabilize *verb*
1. To make stable : steady. *See* CHANGE. **2.** To put in balance : balance, counterbalance, equalize, steady. *See* ORDER.

stable *adjective*
1. Not easily moved or shaken : firm[1], secure, solid, sound[2], strong, sturdy, substantial, sure, unshakable. *See* CONTINUE, STRONG. **2.** Firmly settled or positioned : fast, firm[1], secure, steady, strong, sure. *See* CONTINUE. **3.** Consistently reliable, especially because of resistance to outside pressures : steadfast, steady, steady-going. *See* CONTINUE.

stableness *noun*
Reliability in withstanding pressure, force, or stress : fastness, firmness, hardness, security, soundness, stability, steadiness, strength, sturdiness, sureness. *See* BETTER, CHANGE, CONTINUE.

stack *noun*
A group of things gathered haphazardly : agglomeration, bank[1], cumulus, drift, heap, hill, mass, mess, mound, mountain, pile, shock[2], tumble. *See* ORDER.
stack *verb* To put into a disordered pile : bank[1], drift, heap, hill, lump[1], mound, pile (up). *See* ORDER.
stack up *verb Informal.* To be equal or alike : compare, correspond, equal, match, measure up, parallel, touch. *See* SAME.

stacked *adjective*
Slang. Having a full, voluptuous figure : buxom, curvaceous, curvy, shapely, well-developed. *Informal:* built. *See* BEAUTIFUL.

stack up *verb* See **stack.**

staff *noun*
A fairly long straight piece of solid material used especially as a support in walking : cane, stave, stick, walking stick. *See* MACHINE.

stage *noun*
1. A raised platform on which theatrical performances are given : board (used in plural), proscenium. *See* PERFORMING ARTS. **2.** The art and occupation of an actor : acting, dramatics. *See* ACTION, PERFORMING ARTS, SUBSTITUTE. **3.** A temporary framework with a floor, used by workmen : platform, scaffold, scaffolding. *See* MACHINE. **4.** The place where an action or event occurs : locale, scene, setting, site. *See* PLACE. **5.** One of the units in a course, as on an ascending or descending scale : degree, grade, level, peg, point, rung, step. *Informal:* notch. *See* BIG. **6.** An interval regarded as a distinct evolutionary or developmental unit : period, phase. *See* TIME.
stage *verb* **1.** To produce on the stage : act (out), do, dramatize, enact, give, perform, present[2], put on. *See* PERFORMING ARTS. **2.** To organize and carry out (an activity) : give, have, hold. *See* CONTROL, PLANNED.

stagger *verb*
1. To walk unsteadily : falter, lurch, reel, stumble, teeter, totter, weave, wobble. *See* MOVE. **2.** To proceed or perform in an unsteady, faltering manner : blunder, bumble[1], bungle, flounder, fudge, fumble, limp, muddle, shuffle, stumble. *See* THRIVE. **3.** To be irresolute in acting or doing : dither, falter, halt[2], hesitate, pause,

shilly-shally, vacillate, waver, wobble. *See* DECIDE. **4.** To overwhelm with surprise, wonder, or bewilderment : boggle, bowl over, dumbfound, flabbergast, floor. *See* EXCITE, SURPRISE.

staggering *adjective*
1. Of such a character as to overwhelm : *Informal:* mind-blowing, mind-boggling. *See* BIG, EXCITE, SURPRISE. **2.** Awesomely or forbiddingly intense : overpowering, overwhelming, towering. *See* BIG.

staginess *noun*
Showy mannerisms and behavior : exhibitionism, theatricalism, theatricality, theatricalness. *See* PLAIN, STYLE.

stagnation *noun*
A lack of action or activity : idleness, inaction, inactivity, inertness, inoperativeness. *See* ACTION.

staid *adjective*
Full of or marked by dignity and seriousness : earnest[1], grave[2], sedate, serious, sober, solemn, somber. *See* ATTITUDE, HEAVY.

staidness *noun*
High seriousness of manner or bearing : graveness, gravity, sedateness, sobriety, solemnity, solemnness. *See* ATTITUDE, HEAVY, STYLE.

stain *verb*
1. To soil with foreign matter : bestain, discolor, smut. *See* CLEAN, MARKS. **2.** To contaminate the reputation of : befoul, besmear, besmirch, bespatter, blacken, cloud, denigrate, dirty, smear, smudge, smut, soil, spatter, sully, taint, tarnish. ***Idioms:*** give a black eye to, sling (*or* throw) mud on. *See* ATTACK, CLEAN. **3.** To ruin utterly in character or quality : animalize, bastardize, bestialize, brutalize, canker, corrupt, debase, debauch, demoralize, deprave, pervert, vitiate, warp. *See* CLEAN, HELP. **4.** To impart color to : color, dye, tincture, tint. *See* COLORS.

stain *noun* **1.** A discolored mark made by smearing : blot, blotch, daub, smear, smirch, smudge, smutch, splotch. *See* MARKS. **2.** A mark of discredit or disgrace : black eye, blemish, blot, onus, spot, stigma, taint, tarnish. *Archaic:* attaint. ***Idiom:*** a blot on one's escutcheon. *See* MARKS, RESPECT. **3.** Something that imparts color : color, colorant, coloring, dye, dyestuff, pigment, tincture. *See* COLORS.

stainless *adjective*
Free from dirt, stain, or impurities : antiseptic, clean, cleanly, immaculate, spotless, unsoiled, unsullied. *See* CLEAN.

stake *noun*
1. Something risked on an uncertain outcome. Often used in plural : ante, bet, pot, wager. *See* GAMBLING. **2.** A right or legal share in something : claim, interest, portion, title. *See* PART. **3.** Money or property used to produce more wealth : backing, capital, capitalization, financing, funding, grubstake, subsidization. *See* HELP, MONEY.

stake *verb* **1.** To put up as a stake in a game or speculation : bet, gamble, lay[1] (down), post[2], put, risk, venture, wager. *Informal:* go. *See* GAMBLING. **2.** To supply capital to or for : back, capitalize, finance, fund, grubstake, subsidize. *Informal:* bankroll. ***Idiom:*** put up money for. *See* HELP, MONEY.

stale *adjective*
1. Having lost tang or effervescence : flat. *See* SOLID, TASTE. **2.** Without freshness or appeal because of overuse : banal, bromidic, clichéd, commonplace, corny, hackneyed, musty, overused, overworked, platitudinal, platitudinous, shopworn, stereotyped, stereotypic, stereotypical, threadbare, timeworn, tired, trite, warmed-over, well-worn, worn-out. *See* EXCITE, USUAL.

stalemate *noun*
An equality of scores, votes, or performances in a contest : dead heat, deadlock, draw, standoff, tie. *See* SAME.

stalk *verb*
1. To walk with long steps, especially in a vigorous manner : march[1], stride. *See* MOVE. **2.** To look for and pursue (game) in order to capture or kill it : chase, drive, hunt, run. *See* SEEK.

stall[1] *verb*
1. To prevent the occurrence or continuation of a movement, action, or operation : arrest, belay, cease, check, discontinue, halt[1], stay[1], stop, surcease. ***Idioms:*** bring to a standstill, call a halt to, put a stop to. *See* CONTINUE. **2.** To come to a cessation : arrest, belay, cease, check, discontinue, halt[1], leave off, quit, stop, surcease. ***Idiom:*** come to a halt (*or* standstill *or* stop). *See* CONTINUE.

stall[2] *verb*
To cause to be later or slower than expected or desired : delay, detain, hang up, hold up, lag, retard, set back, slow (down *or* up). *See* HELP, TIME.

stalwart *adjective*
Capable of exerting considerable effort or of withstanding considerable stress or hardship : hardy, stout, strong, sturdy, tough. *See* STRONG.

stamina *noun*
The quality or power of withstanding hardship or stress : endurance, staying power. *See* CONTINUE.

stammer *verb*
To introduce involuntary repetitions and pauses into one's speech : stutter. *See* WORDS.
stammer *noun* A speech impediment marked by involuntary repetitions and pauses : stammering, stutter, stuttering. *See* WORDS.

stammering *noun*
A speech impediment marked by involuntary repetitions and pauses : stammer, stutter, stuttering. *See* WORDS.

stamp *verb*
1. To step on heavily and repeatedly so as to crush, injure, or destroy : stomp, tramp, trample, tread, tromp. *See* HELP. **2.** To walk with loud, heavy steps : stomp, tramp, trample. *Informal:* tromp. *See* MOVE, SOUNDS. **3.** To produce a deep impression of : engrave, etch, fix, grave[3], impress, imprint, inscribe. *See* MARKS.
stamp out *verb* To destroy all traces of : abolish, annihilate, blot out, clear, eradicate, erase, exterminate, extinguish, extirpate, kill[1], liquidate, obliterate, remove, root[1] (out *or* up), rub out, snuff out, uproot, wipe out. ***Idioms:*** do away with, make an end of, put an end to. *See* HELP, MAKE.
stamp *noun* **1.** The visible effect made on a surface by pressure : impress, impression, imprint, indent, indentation, mark, print. *See* MARKS. **2.** Something visible or evident that gives grounds for believing in the existence or presence of something else : badge, evidence, index, indication, indicator, manifestation, mark, note, sign, signification, symptom, token, witness. *See* SHOW. **3.** A class that is defined by the common attribute or attributes possessed by all its members : breed, cast, description, feather, ilk, kind[2], lot, manner, mold, nature, order, sort, species, stripe, type, variety. *Informal:* persuasion. *See* GROUP.

stamping ground *noun*
1. A frequently visited place : haunt, rendezvous, resort. *Slang:* hangout. *See* PLACE, REPETITION. **2.** The natural environment of an animal or plant : habitat, haunt, home. *See* TERRITORY.

stamp out *verb* See **stamp.**

stance *noun*
1. The way in which a person holds or carries his or her body : attitude, carriage, pose, posture. *See* POSTURE. **2.** A frame of mind affecting one's thoughts or behavior : attitude, outlook, position, posture. *See* ATTITUDE.

stand *verb*
1. To adopt a standing posture. Also used with *up* : arise, get up, rise, uprise, upspring. ***Idiom:*** get to one's feet. *See* RISE. **2.** To restore to or place in an upright or proper position. Also used with *up* : right. *See* HORIZONTAL. **3.** To put up with. Also used with *for* : abide, accept, bear, brook[2], endure, go, stomach, suffer, support, sustain, swallow, take, tolerate, withstand. *Informal:* lump[2]. ***Idioms:*** take it, take it lying down. *See* ACCEPT. **4.** *Informal.* To pay for the food, drink, or entertainment of (another) : treat. *Informal:* set up. *Slang:* blow[1]. ***Idiom:*** stand treat. *See* PAY.
stand behind *verb* To aid the cause of by approving or favoring : advocate, back, champion, endorse, get behind, plump for, recommend, side with, stand by, support, uphold. ***Idioms:*** align oneself with, go to bat for, take the part of. *See* SUPPORT.
stand by *verb* To aid the cause of by approving or favoring : advocate, back, champion, endorse, get behind, plump for, recommend, side with, stand behind, support, uphold. ***Idioms:*** align oneself with, go to bat for, take the part of. *See* SUPPORT.
stand for *verb* **1.** To serve as an example, image, or symbol of : epitomize, exemplify, illustrate, represent, symbol, symbolize, typify. *See* SUBSTITUTE. **2.** To serve as an official delegate of : represent, speak for. *See* SUBSTITUTE.
stand in *verb* To act as a substitute : fill in, substitute, supply. *Informal:* pinch-hit, sub. *See* SUBSTITUTE.
stand out *verb* **1.** To curve outward past the normal or usual limit : bag, balloon, beetle, belly, bulge, jut, overhang, pouch, project, protrude, protuberate, stick out. *See* CONVEX. **2.** To be obtrusively conspicuous : glare, stick out. ***Idioms:*** stare someone in the face, stick out like a sore thumb. *See* SEE.
stand up *verb* **1.** To prove valid under scrutiny : hold (up), prove out. *Informal:* wash. ***Idioms:*** hold water, pass muster, ring true. *See* TRUE. **2.** To withstand stress or difficulty : bear up, endure, hold up. *See* CONTINUE.

standard *noun*
1. Fabric used especially as a symbol : banderole, banner, banneret, color (used in plural), ensign, flag[1], jack, oriflamme, pennant, pennon, streamer. *See* SUBSTITUTE. **2.** A means by which individuals are compared and judged :

benchmark, criterion, gauge, mark, measure, test, touchstone, yardstick. *See* USUAL. **3.** One that is worthy of imitation or duplication : beau ideal, example, exemplar, ideal, mirror, model, paradigm, pattern. *See* GOOD.

standard *adjective* **1.** Having or arising from authority : authoritative, conclusive, official, sanctioned. *See* TRUE. **2.** Being of no special quality or type : average, common, commonplace, cut-and-dried, formulaic, garden, garden-variety, indifferent, mediocre, ordinary, plain, routine, run-of-the-mill, stock, undistinguished, unexceptional, unremarkable. *See* GOOD, USUAL.

stand behind *verb* See **stand.**

standby *adjective*
Used or held in reserve : auxiliary, backup, emergency, reserve, secondary, supplemental, supplementary. *See* INCREASE.

stand by *verb* See **stand.**

stand for *verb* See **stand.**

stand-in *noun*
One that takes the place of another : alternate, replacement, substitute, surrogate. *Informal:* fill-in, pinch hitter, sub. *See* SUBSTITUTE.

stand in *verb* See **stand.**

standing *noun*
1. Positioning of one individual vis-à-vis others : footing, place, position, rank[1], situation, station, status. *See* PLACE. **2.** The level of credit or respect at which one is regarded by others : face, prestige, status. *See* RESPECT.

standoff *noun*
An equality of scores, votes, or performances in a contest : dead heat, deadlock, draw, stalemate, tie. *See* SAME.

standoffish *adjective*
Not friendly, sociable, or warm in manner : aloof, chill, chilly, cool, distant, offish, remote, reserved, reticent, solitary, unapproachable, uncommunicative, undemonstrative, withdrawn. *See* ATTITUDE, HOT.

standout *adjective*
Informal. Far beyond what is usual, normal, or customary : exceptional, extraordinary, magnificent, outstanding, preeminent, rare, remarkable, singular, towering, uncommon, unusual. *Slang:* awesome, out of sight. *See* BETTER, USUAL.

stand out *verb* See **stand.**

standpoint *noun*
The position from which something is observed or considered : angle[2], eye, outlook, point of view, slant, vantage, viewpoint. *See* PERSPECTIVE.

standstill *noun*
The condition of being stopped : cessation, discontinuance, discontinuation, halt[1], stop, stoppage, surcease. *See* CONTINUE.

stand up *verb* See **stand.**

star *noun*
The main performer in a theatrical production : lead, principal, protagonist. *See* PERFORMING ARTS.

starch *noun*
A quality of active mental and physical forcefulness : dash, punch, verve, vigor, vigorousness, vim, vitality. *Informal:* snap. ***Idiom:*** vim and vigor. *See* ACTION, TIRED.

starch *verb* To make stiff or stiffer : stiffen. *See* FLEXIBLE.

starchy *adjective*
So rigidly constrained, formal, or awkward as to lack all grace and spontaneity : buckram, stiff, stilted, wooden. *See* FLEXIBLE.

star-crossed *adjective*
Involving or undergoing chance misfortune : hapless, ill-fated, ill-starred, luckless, unfortunate, unhappy, unlucky, untoward. *See* LUCK.

stare *verb*
To look intently and fixedly : eye, gape, gawk, gaze, goggle, ogle, peer[1]. ***Idioms:*** gaze openmouthed, rivet the eyes on. *See* SEE.

stare *noun* An intent fixed look : gape, gaze. *See* SEE.

stark *adjective*
Cold and forbidding : austere, bleak, dour, grim, hard, harsh, severe. *See* ATTITUDE, HOT.

starkers *adjective*
Chiefly British. Not wearing any clothes : au naturel, bare, naked, nude, unclad. ***Idioms:*** in one's birthday suit, in the altogether (*or* buff *or* raw), naked as a jaybird, stark naked, without a stitch. *See* PUT ON, SHOW.

starry-eyed *adjective*
Not compatible with reality : idealistic, quixotic, romantic, unrealistic, utopian, visionary. *See* HOPE, REAL.

start *verb*
1. To go about the initial step in doing (something) : approach, begin, commence, embark, enter, get off, inaugurate, initiate, institute, launch, lead off, open, set about, set out, set to, take on, take up, undertake. *Informal:* kick off. ***Idioms:*** get cracking, get going, get the show on the road. *See* START. **2.** To come into being : arise, begin, commence, originate. *See* START. **3.** To bring into existence formally : constitute, create, establish, found, institute, organize, originate, set up. *See* START. **4.** To move

suddenly and involuntarily : bolt, jump. *See* MOVE. **5.** To draw away involuntarily, usually out of fear or disgust : blench[1], cringe, flinch, quail, recoil, shrink, shy[1], wince. *See* APPROACH, SEEK.

start *noun* **1.** The act or process of bringing or being brought into existence : beginning, commencement, inauguration, inception, incipience, incipiency, initiation, launch, leadoff, opening, origination. *Informal:* kickoff. *See* START. **2.** The initial stage of a developmental process : beginning, birth, commencement, dawn, genesis, inception, nascence, nascency, onset, opening, origin, outset, spring. *See* START. **3.** A sudden and involuntary movement : bolt, jump, startle. *See* MOVE. **4.** A factor conducive to superiority and success : advantage, handicap, head start, odds, vantage. *See* HELP.

startle *verb*
1. To cause to experience a sudden momentary shock : electrify, jolt, shock[1]. *See* EXCITE, SURPRISE. **2.** To fill with fear : affright, alarm, frighten, panic, scare, scarify[2], terrify, terrorize. *Archaic:* fright. ***Idioms:*** make one's blood run cold, make one's hair stand on end, scare silly (*or* stiff), scare the daylights out of. *See* FEAR. **3.** To impress strongly by what is unexpected or unusual : amaze, astonish, astound, awe, surprise. ***Idioms:*** catch (*or* take) unawares, take aback. *See* SURPRISE.

startle *noun* A sudden and involuntary movement : bolt, jump, start. *See* MOVE.

start-up or **startup** *noun*
The act of founding or establishing : constitution, creation, establishment, foundation, institution, organization, origination. *See* START.

starving *adjective*
Desiring or craving food : famished, hungry, ravenous, voracious. *See* INGESTION.

stash *verb*
1. *Slang.* To put or keep out of sight : bury, cache, conceal, ensconce, hide[1], occult, secrete. *Slang:* plant. *See* SHOW. **2.** *Slang.* To store up (supplies or money), usually well beyond one's needs : hoard, squirrel (away), stockpile, treasure. *See* COLLECT, GIVE.

stash *noun Slang.* A supply stored or hidden for future use : backlog, cache, hoard, inventory, nest egg, reserve, reservoir, stock, stockpile, store, treasure. *See* COLLECT.

stasis *noun*
A stable state characterized by the cancellation of all forces by equal opposing forces : balance, counterpoise, equilibrium, equipoise. *See* ORDER.

state *noun*
1. Manner of being or form of existence : condition, mode, situation, status. *See* BE. **2.** *Informal.* A condition of excited distress : fume. *Informal:* snit, sweat, swivet. *Slang:* tizzy. *See* CALM. **3.** An organized geopolitical unit : body politic, country, land, nation, polity. *See* POLITICS, TERRITORY.

state *verb* **1.** To put into words : articulate, communicate, convey, declare, express, say, talk, tell, utter[1], vent, verbalize, vocalize, voice. ***Idiom:*** give tongue (*or* vent *or* voice) to. *See* WORDS. **2.** To utter publicly : air, express, put, vent, ventilate. ***Idiom:*** come out with. *See* SHOW, WORDS. **3.** To declare by way of a systematic statement : enounce, enunciate. *See* WORDS. **4.** To put into words positively and with conviction : affirm, allege, argue, assert, asseverate, aver, avouch, avow, claim, contend, declare, hold, maintain, say. ***Idiom:*** have it. *See* AFFIRM.

stately *adjective*
1. Large and impressive in size, scope, or extent : august, baronial, grand, grandiose, imposing, lordly, magnific, magnificent, majestic, noble, princely, regal, royal, splendid, sublime, superb. *See* BIG, GOOD. **2.** Characterized by elaborate but usually formal courtesy : chivalrous, courtly, gallant, gracious, knightly. *See* ATTITUDE, COURTESY.

statement *noun*
1. The act or an instance of expressing in words : articulation, expression, utterance, verbalization, vocalization, voice. *See* WORDS. **2.** The act of asserting positively : affirmation, allegation, assertion, asseveration, averment, claim, declaration. *See* AFFIRM. **3.** A recounting of past events : account, chronicle, description, history, narration, narrative, report, story, version. *See* WORDS. **4.** Something said : saying, utterance, word. *See* WORDS. **5.** A precise list of fees or charges : account, bill[1], check, invoice, reckoning. *Informal:* tab. *See* PAY.

station *noun*
1. An assigned position : post[2]. *See* PLACE. **2.** A center of organization, supply, or activity : base[1], complex, headquarters. *Military:* installation. *See* PLACE. **3.** Positioning of one individual vis-à-vis others : footing, place, position, rank[1], situation, standing, status. *See* PLACE.

station *verb* To appoint and send to a particular place : assign, post[2], set[1]. *See* PLACE.

stationary *adjective*
1. Not moving : immobile, motionless, still, stock-still, unmoving. *See* MOVE. **2.** Firmly in

position : fixed, immobile, immovable, steadfast, steady, unmovable, unmoving. *See* MOVE.

stature *noun*
A level of superiority that is usually high : caliber, merit, quality, value, virtue, worth. *See* GOOD, VALUE.

status *noun*
1. Positioning of one individual vis-à-vis others : footing, place, position, rank[1], situation, standing, station. *See* PLACE. **2.** The level of credit or respect at which one is regarded by others : face, prestige, standing. *See* RESPECT. **3.** An established position from which to operate or deal with others : basis, footing, term (often used in plural). *See* CONNECT. **4.** A person's high standing among others : dignity, good name, good report, honor, prestige, reputation, repute, respect. *See* RESPECT. **5.** Manner of being or form of existence : condition, mode, situation, state. *See* BE.

statute *noun*
The formal product of a legislative or judicial body : act, assize, bill[1], enactment, law, legislation, lex, measure. *See* LAW.

staunch *adjective*
Adhering firmly and devotedly, as to a person, a cause, or a duty : allegiant, constant, faithful, fast, firm[1], liege, loyal, steadfast, true. *See* CONTINUE, TRUST.

stave *noun*
A fairly long straight piece of solid material used especially as a support in walking : cane, staff, stick, walking stick. *See* MACHINE.
stave off *verb* To prohibit from occurring by advance planning or action : avert, forestall, forfend, obviate, preclude, prevent, rule out, ward (off). ***Idiom:*** nip in the bud. *See* ALLOW.

stave off *verb* See **stave.**

stay[1] *verb*
1. To continue to be in a place : abide, bide, linger, remain, tarry, wait. *Informal:* stick around. ***Idiom:*** stay put. *See* CONTINUE. **2.** To be in existence or in a certain state for an indefinitely long time : abide, continue, endure, go on, hold out, last[2], persist, remain. *See* CONTINUE. **3.** To remain as a guest or lodger : lodge, sojourn, visit. *See* PLACE. **4.** To stop temporarily and remain, as if reluctant to leave : abide, bide, linger, pause, tarry, wait. *See* CONTINUE. **5.** To prevent the occurrence or continuation of a movement, action, or operation : arrest, belay, cease, check, discontinue, halt[1], stall[1], stop, surcease. ***Idioms:*** bring to a standstill, call a halt to, put a stop to. *See* CONTINUE. **6.** To put off until a later time : adjourn, defer[1], delay, hold off, hold up, postpone, remit, shelve, suspend, table, waive. *Informal:* wait. ***Idiom:*** put on ice. *See* DO.
stay with *verb* To persevere in some condition, action, or belief : keep, maintain, retain. *See* CONTINUE.
stay *noun* **1.** The act of stopping : cessation, check, cut-off, discontinuance, discontinuation, halt[1], stop, stoppage, surcease. *See* CONTINUE. **2.** A remaining in a place as a guest or lodger : sojourn, visit. *See* PLACE. **3.** The act of putting off or the condition of being put off : adjournment, deferment, deferral, delay, postponement, suspension, waiver. *See* TIME.

stay[2] *noun*
A means or device that keeps something erect, stable, or secure : brace, buttress, crutch, prop, shore, support, underpinning. *See* SUPPORT.

staying power *noun*
The quality or power of withstanding hardship or stress : endurance, stamina. *See* CONTINUE.

stay with *verb* See **stay[1].**

stead *noun*
The function or position customarily occupied by another : place. *Archaic:* lieu. *See* PLACE, SUBSTITUTE.

steadfast *adjective*
1. Firmly in position : fixed, immobile, immovable, stationary, steady, unmovable, unmoving. *See* MOVE. **2.** Consistently reliable, especially because of resistance to outside pressures : stable, steady, steady-going. *See* CONTINUE. **3.** Indicating or possessing determination, resolution, or persistence : constant, determined, firm[1], resolute, steady, stiff, tough, unbending, uncompromising, unflinching, unwavering, unyielding. *See* PURPOSE. **4.** Adhering firmly and devotedly, as to a person, a cause, or a duty : allegiant, constant, faithful, fast, firm[1], liege, loyal, staunch, true. *See* CONTINUE, TRUST.

steadfastness *noun*
Faithfulness or devotion to a person, a cause, obligations, or duties : allegiance, constancy, faithfulness, fealty, fidelity, loyalty. *See* CONTINUE, OBLIGATION.

steadiness *noun*
Reliability in withstanding pressure, force, or stress : fastness, firmness, hardness, security, soundness, stability, stableness, strength, sturdiness, sureness. *See* BETTER, CHANGE, CONTINUE.

steady *adjective*
1. Firmly in position : fixed, immobile,

immovable, stationary, steadfast, unmovable, unmoving. *See* MOVE. **2.** Firmly settled or positioned : fast, firm[1], secure, stable, strong, sure. *See* CONTINUE. **3.** Having no change or variation : changeless, constant, equable, even[1], invariable, invariant, regular, same, unchanging, uniform, unvarying. *See* SAME. **4.** Indicating or possessing determination, resolution, or persistence : constant, determined, firm[1], resolute, steadfast, stiff, tough, unbending, uncompromising, unflinching, unwavering, unyielding. *See* PURPOSE. **5.** Consistently reliable, especially because of resistance to outside pressures : stable, steadfast, steady-going. *See* CONTINUE.

steady *verb* **1.** To make stable : stabilize. *See* CHANGE. **2.** To put in balance : balance, counterbalance, equalize, stabilize. *See* ORDER.

steady-going *adjective*
Consistently reliable, especially because of resistance to outside pressures : stable, steadfast, steady. *See* CONTINUE.

steal *verb*
1. To take (another's property) without permission : filch, pilfer, purloin, snatch, thieve. *Informal:* lift, swipe. *Slang:* cop, heist, hook, nip[1], pinch, rip off, snitch. ***Idiom:*** make (*or* walk) off with. *See* CRIMES, GIVE. **2.** To move silently and furtively : creep, glide, lurk, mouse, prowl, pussyfoot, skulk, slide, slink, slip, snake, sneak. *Slang:* gumshoe. *See* MOVE.

steal *noun* **1.** The crime of taking someone else's property without consent : larceny, pilferage, theft, thievery. *Slang:* rip-off. *See* CRIMES. **2.** *Slang.* Something offered or bought at a low price : bargain. *Informal:* buy, deal. *See* MONEY, TRANSACTIONS.

stealer *noun*
A person who steals : bandit, burglar, highwayman, housebreaker, larcener, larcenist, pilferer, purloiner, robber, thief. *See* CRIMES.

stealth *noun*
The act of proceeding slowly, deliberately, and secretly to escape observation : furtiveness, slinkiness, sneakiness, stealthiness. *See* MOVE.

stealthiness *noun*
The act of proceeding slowly, deliberately, and secretly to escape observation : furtiveness, slinkiness, sneakiness, stealth. *See* MOVE.

stealthy *adjective*
So slow, deliberate, and secret as to escape observation : catlike, feline, furtive, slinky, sneaking, sneaky. *See* MOVE.

steam *noun*
Capacity or power for work or vigorous activity : animation, energy, force, might, potency, power, puissance, sprightliness, strength. *Informal:* get-up-and-go, go, pep, peppiness, zip. *See* ACTION.

steam *verb Informal.* To be or become angry : anger, blow up, boil over, bristle, burn, explode, flare up, foam, fume, rage, seethe. ***Idioms:*** blow a fuse, blow a gasket, blow one's stack (*or* top), breathe fire, fly off the handle, get hot under the collar, hit the ceiling (*or* roof), lose one's temper, see red. *See* FEELINGS.

steamroller *verb*
To render totally ineffective by decisive defeat : annihilate, crush, drub, overpower, overwhelm, smash, thrash, trounce, vanquish. *Informal:* massacre, wallop. *Slang:* clobber, cream, shellac, smear. *See* WIN.

steel *verb*
To prepare (oneself) for action : brace, forearm, fortify, gird, ready, strengthen. ***Idiom:*** gird (*or* gird up) one's loins. *See* PREPARED.

steep[1] *adjective*
1. So sharply inclined as to be almost perpendicular : abrupt, bold, precipitous, sheer[2]. *See* HORIZONTAL. **2.** Vastly exceeding a normal limit, as in cost : sky-high, stiff, stratospheric, unconscionable. *See* BIG, USUAL.

steep[2] *verb*
To saturate (something) with a liquid : soak. *Chemistry:* infuse. *See* DRY.

steer *verb*
1. To direct the course of carefully : guide, jockey, maneuver, navigate, pilot. ***Idiom:*** back and fill. *See* CONTROL, MOVE. **2.** To show the way to : conduct, direct, escort, guide, lead, pilot, route, shepherd, show, usher. *See* SHOW. **3.** To control the course of (an activity) : carry on, conduct, direct, manage, operate, run. *See* OVER.

steer *noun* An item of advance or inside information given as a guide to action : pointer, tip[3]. *Informal:* tip-off. *See* KNOWLEDGE.

stem *noun*
The main part of a word to which affixes are attached : base[1], root[1], theme. *See* WORDS.

stem *verb* To have as a source : arise, come, derive, emanate, flow, issue, originate, proceed, rise, spring, upspring. *See* START.

stentorian *adjective*
Marked by extremely high volume and intensity of sound : blaring, deafening, earsplitting, loud, roaring. *See* SOUNDS.

step *noun*
1. The act or manner of going on foot : footfall, footstep, tread. *See* MOVE, SOUNDS. **2.** An

action calculated to achieve an end : maneuver, measure (often used in plural), move, procedure, tactic. *See* ACTION. **3.** One of the units in a course, as on an ascending or descending scale : degree, grade, level, peg, point, rung, stage. *Informal:* notch. *See* BIG.

step *verb* **1.** To go on foot : ambulate, foot, pace, tread, walk. *Slang:* hoof. ***Idiom:*** foot it. *See* MOVE. **2.** To move rhythmically to music, using patterns of steps or gestures : dance, foot. *Slang:* hoof. ***Idioms:*** cut a rug, foot it, trip the light fantastic. *See* REPETITION, WORK.

step down *verb* To withdraw from business or active life : retire. ***Idioms:*** call it quits, hang up one's spurs, turn in one's badge. *See* CONTINUE.

step up *verb* To increase the speed of : accelerate, expedite, hasten, hurry, hustle, quicken, speed (up). *See* FAST.

step-by-step *adjective*
Proceeding very slowly by degrees : gradational, gradual, piecemeal. *See* FAST.

step down *verb* See **step.**

step up *verb* See **step.**

stereotype *noun*
A trite expression or idea : banality, bromide, cliché, commonplace, platitude, truism. *See* SURPRISE.

stereotyped *adjective*
Without freshness or appeal because of overuse : banal, bromidic, clichéd, commonplace, corny, hackneyed, musty, overused, overworked, platitudinal, platitudinous, shopworn, stale, stereotypic, stereotypical, threadbare, timeworn, tired, trite, warmed-over, well-worn, worn-out. *See* EXCITE, USUAL.

stereotypic *adjective*
Without freshness or appeal because of overuse : banal, bromidic, clichéd, commonplace, corny, hackneyed, musty, overused, overworked, platitudinal, platitudinous, shopworn, stale, stereotyped, stereotypical, threadbare, timeworn, tired, trite, warmed-over, well-worn, worn-out. *See* EXCITE, USUAL.

stereotypical *adjective*
Without freshness or appeal because of overuse : banal, bromidic, clichéd, commonplace, corny, hackneyed, musty, overused, overworked, platitudinal, platitudinous, shopworn, stale, stereotyped, stereotypic, threadbare, timeworn, tired, trite, warmed-over, well-worn, worn-out. *See* EXCITE, USUAL.

sterile *adjective*
1. Unable to produce offspring : barren, childless, impotent, infertile, unfruitful. *See* RICH. **2.** Lacking or unable to produce growing plants or crops : barren, infertile, unfruitful, unproductive. *See* RICH. **3.** Free or freed from microorganisms : sanitized, sterilized. *See* CLEAN. **4.** Lacking originality : uncreative, unimaginative, uninspired, uninventive, unoriginal. *See* RICH. **5.** Lacking liveliness, charm, or surprise : arid, aseptic, colorless, drab, dry, dull, earthbound, flat, flavorless, lackluster, lifeless, lusterless, matter-of-fact, pedestrian, prosaic, spiritless, stodgy, unimaginative, uninspired. *See* EXCITE.

sterileness *noun*
A lack of excitement, liveliness, or interest : asepticism, blandness, colorlessness, drabness, dreariness, dryness, dullness, flatness, flavorlessness, insipidity, insipidness, jejuneness, lifelessness, sterility, stodginess, vapidity, vapidness, weariness. *See* EXCITE.

sterility *noun*
1. The state or condition of being unable to reproduce sexually : barrenness, infertility, sterilization. *See* REPRODUCTION, RICH. **2.** The state or condition of being free from microorganisms : sterilization. *See* CLEAN. **3.** A lack of excitement, liveliness, or interest : asepticism, blandness, colorlessness, drabness, dreariness, dryness, dullness, flatness, flavorlessness, insipidity, insipidness, jejuneness, lifelessness, sterileness, stodginess, vapidity, vapidness, weariness. *See* EXCITE.

sterilization *noun*
1. The act or an instance of making one incapable of reproducing sexually : castration. *See* REPRODUCTION, RICH. **2.** The state or condition of being unable to reproduce sexually : barrenness, infertility, sterility. *See* REPRODUCTION, RICH. **3.** The state or condition of being free from microorganisms : sterility. *See* CLEAN.

sterilize *verb*
1. To render free of microorganisms : decontaminate, disinfect, sanitize. *See* CLEAN. **2.** To render incapable of reproducing sexually : alter, castrate, fix, geld, neuter, spay, unsex. *See* REPRODUCTION, RICH.

sterilized *adjective*
Free or freed from microorganisms : sanitized, sterile. *See* CLEAN.

stern *adjective*
Rigorous and unsparing in treating others : demanding, exacting, hard, harsh, rigid, severe, strict, tough, unyielding. *See* EASY.

sternness *noun*
The fact or condition of being rigorous and

unsparing : austerity, hardness, harshness, rigidity, rigor, rigorousness, severity, strictness, stringency, toughness. *See* EASY.

stew *verb*
1. To cook (food) in liquid heated to the point of steaming : boil, parboil, simmer. *See* INGESTION. **2.** *Informal.* To focus the attention on something moodily and at length : brood, cark, dwell, fret, mope, worry. *See* CONCERN, THOUGHTS.
stew *noun Informal.* A state of discomposure : agitation, dither, fluster, flutter, perturbation, tumult, turmoil, upset. *Informal:* lather. *See* CALM.

stewed *adjective*
Informal. Stupefied, excited, or muddled with alcoholic liquor : besotted, crapulent, crapulous, drunk, drunken, inebriate, inebriated, intoxicated, sodden, tipsy. *Informal:* cock-eyed. *Slang:* blind, bombed, boozed, boozy, crocked, high, lit (up), loaded, looped, pickled, pixilated, plastered, potted, sloshed, smashed, soused, stinking, stinko, stoned, tight, zonked. ***Idioms:*** drunk as a skunk, half-seas over, high as a kite, in one's cups, three sheets in (*or* to) the wind. *See* DRUGS.

stick *noun*
1. A fairly long straight piece of solid material used especially as a support in walking : cane, staff, stave, walking stick. *See* MACHINE. **2.** A relatively long, straight, rigid piece of metal or other solid material : bar, bloom[2], rod, shaft, slab. *See* THING.
stick *verb* **1.** To cause to penetrate with force : dig, drive, plunge, ram, run, sink, stab, thrust. *See* PUT IN. **2.** To become or cause to become stuck or lodged : catch, fix, lodge. *See* MOVE. **3.** To hold fast : adhere, bond, cleave[2], cling, cohere. *See* CONNECT. **4.** To deposit in a specified place : lay[1], place, put, set[1]. *See* PLACE, RISE. **5.** *Informal.* To make incapable of finding something to think, do, or say : confound, nonplus. *Informal:* flummox, stump, throw. *Slang:* beat. ***Idiom:*** put someone at a loss. *See* AFFECT, KNOWLEDGE. **6.** *Informal.* To force (another) to accept a burden : foist, impose, inflict, saddle. *See* GIVE, OVER, WILLING. **7.** *Slang.* To get money or something else from by deceitful trickery : bilk, cheat, cozen, defraud, gull, mulct, rook, swindle, victimize. *Informal:* chisel, flimflam, take, trim. *Slang:* diddle[1], do, gyp, sting. *See* HONEST.
stick around *verb Informal.* To continue to be in a place : abide, bide, linger, remain, stay[1], tarry, wait. ***Idiom:*** stay put. *See* CONTINUE.
stick out *verb* **1.** To curve outward past the normal or usual limit : bag, balloon, beetle, belly, bulge, jut, overhang, pouch, project, protrude, protuberate, stand out. *See* CONVEX. **2.** To be obtrusively conspicuous : glare, stand out. ***Idioms:*** stare someone in the face, stick out like a sore thumb. *See* SEE.
stick up *verb* To take property or possessions from (a person or company, for example) unlawfully and usually forcibly : hold up, rob. *Slang:* heist, knock off. *See* CRIMES, GIVE.

stick around *verb* See **stick.**

stick-in-the-mud *noun*
Informal. An old-fashioned person who is reluctant to change or innovate : fogy, fossil, fuddy-duddy, mossback. *Slang:* square. *See* NEW.

stick out *verb* See **stick.**

stickup *noun*
Slang. The act or crime of taking another's property unlawfully and by force : holdup, robbery. *Slang:* heist. *See* CRIMES, GIVE.

stick up *verb* See **stick.**

sticky *adjective*
1. Having the property of adhering : adhesive, gluey, gooey, gummy, tacky[1]. *See* CLEAN, KEEP. **2.** Damp and warm : humid, muggy, soggy, sultry. *See* DRY, HOT. **3.** *Informal.* Hard to deal with or get out of : rough, tight, tricky. *See* EASY.

stiff *adjective*
1. Not changing shape or bending : inelastic, inflexible, rigid, unbending, unyielding. *See* FLEXIBLE. **2.** Stretched tightly : taut, tense, tight. *See* TIGHTEN. **3.** So rigidly constrained, formal, or awkward as to lack all grace and spontaneity : buckram, starchy, stilted, wooden. *See* FLEXIBLE. **4.** Indicating or possessing determination, resolution, or persistence : constant, determined, firm[1], resolute, steadfast, steady, tough, unbending, uncompromising, unflinching, unwavering, unyielding. *See* PURPOSE. **5.** Having a high concentration of the distinguishing ingredient : concentrated, potent, strong. *See* STRONG. **6.** Vastly exceeding a normal limit, as in cost : sky-high, steep[1], stratospheric, unconscionable. *See* BIG, USUAL.
stiff *noun* **1.** *Slang.* The physical frame of a dead person or animal : body, cadaver, carcass, corpse, remains. *See* BODY. **2.** *Slang.* A person who is habitually drunk : drunk, drunkard, inebriate, sot, tippler. *Slang:* boozehound, boozer, lush[2], rummy[1], soak, souse, sponge. *See* DRUGS. **3.** *Slang.* A stingy person :

miser, niggard, Scrooge, skinflint. *Informal:* penny pincher. *Slang:* cheapskate, tightwad. *See* GIVE.

stiffen *verb*
1. To make stiff or stiffer : starch. *See* FLEXIBLE. 2. To make or become tense : tauten, tense, tighten. *See* TIGHTEN.

stiff-necked *adjective*
Tenaciously unwilling to yield : bullheaded, dogged, hardheaded, headstrong, mulish, obstinate, pertinacious, perverse, pigheaded, tenacious, willful. *See* RESIST.

stifle *verb*
1. To hold (something requiring an outlet) in check : burke, choke (back), gag, hold back, hold down, hush (up), muffle, quench, repress, smother, squelch, strangle, suppress, throttle. *Informal:* sit on (*or* upon). *See* RESTRAINT. 2. To decrease or dull the sound of : dampen, deaden, muffle, mute. *See* INCREASE, SOUNDS. 3. To keep from being published or transmitted : ban, black out, censor, hush (up), suppress. ***Idiom:*** keep (*or* put) a lid on. *See* SHOW. 4. To stop the breathing of : asphyxiate, choke, smother, suffocate. *See* BREATH.

stifling *adjective*
Oppressive due to a lack of fresh air : airless, close, stuffy. *See* BREATH, OPEN.

stigma *noun*
1. A mark of discredit or disgrace : black eye, blemish, blot, onus, spot, stain, taint, tarnish. *Archaic:* attaint. ***Idiom:*** a blot on one's escutcheon. *See* MARKS, RESPECT. 2. A mark on the skin indicative of a disease, as typhus : petechia. *See* MARKS.

stigmatize *verb*
To mark with disgrace or infamy : brand. ***Idiom:*** give someone a bad name. *See* MARKS, RESPECT.

still *adjective*
1. Marked by, done with, or making no sound or noise : hushed, noiseless, quiet, silent, soundless, stilly. *Archaic:* hush. *See* SOUNDS. 2. Not moving : immobile, motionless, stationary, stock-still, unmoving. *See* MOVE. 3. Motionless and undisturbed : calm, halcyon, peaceful, placid, quiet, serene, stilly, tranquil, untroubled. *See* CALM. 4. Marked by an absence of circulating air : airless, breathless, breezeless, windless. *See* BREATH.

still *noun* The absence of sound or noise : hush, noiselessness, quiet, quietness, silence, soundlessness, stillness. *See* SOUNDS.

still *adverb* 1. In addition : additionally, also, besides, further, furthermore, item, likewise, more, moreover, too, yet. ***Idioms:*** as well, to boot. *See* INCREASE. 2. To a more extreme degree : even[1], yet. *See* BIG. 3. In spite of a preceding event or consideration : all the same, however, nevertheless, nonetheless, yet. *Informal:* still and all. ***Idiom:*** be that as it may. *See* AFFIRM.

still *verb* 1. To cause to become silent : hush, quiet, quieten, shush, shut up, silence. *See* SOUNDS. 2. To make or become calm : allay, balm, becalm, calm (down), lull, quiet, settle, tranquilize. *See* CALM.

still and all *adverb*
Informal. In spite of a preceding event or consideration : all the same, however, nevertheless, nonetheless, still, yet. ***Idiom:*** be that as it may. *See* AFFIRM.

stillness *noun*
1. The absence of sound or noise : hush, noiselessness, quiet, quietness, silence, soundlessness, still. *See* SOUNDS. 2. An absence of motion or disturbance : calm, calmness, hush, lull, peace, peacefulness, placidity, placidness, quiet, quietness, serenity, tranquillity, untroubledness. *See* CALM.

stilly *adjective*
1. Marked by, done with, or making no sound or noise : hushed, noiseless, quiet, silent, soundless, still. *Archaic:* hush. *See* SOUNDS. 2. Motionless and undisturbed : calm, halcyon, peaceful, placid, quiet, serene, still, tranquil, untroubled. *See* CALM.

stilted *adjective*
So rigidly constrained, formal, or awkward as to lack all grace and spontaneity : buckram, starchy, stiff, wooden. *See* FLEXIBLE.

stimulant *noun*
Something that causes and encourages a given response : encouragement, fillip, impetus, impulse, incentive, inducement, motivation, prod, push, spur, stimulation, stimulator, stimulus. *See* CAUSE.

stimulate *verb*
1. To stir to action or feeling : egg on, excite, foment, galvanize, goad, impel, incite, inflame, inspire, instigate, motivate, move, pique, prick, prod, prompt, propel, provoke, set off, spur, touch off, trigger, work up. *See* CAUSE, EXCITE. 2. To give or impart vitality and energy to (someone or something) : energize, exhilarate, invigorate, vitalize. *See* HELP.

stimulating *adjective*
1. Serving to enliven : animating, enlivening, quickening, rousing, vitalizing, vivifying. *See* EXCITE. 2. Producing or stimulating physical,

mental, or emotional vigor : bracing, energizing, exhilarant, exhilarating, innerving, intoxicating, invigorating, refreshing, reinvigorating, renewing, restorative, roborant, tonic. *See* HELP.

stimulation *noun*
1. Something that encourages : encouragement, inspiration, motivation. *See* HELP.
2. Something that causes and encourages a given response : encouragement, fillip, impetus, impulse, incentive, inducement, motivation, prod, push, spur, stimulant, stimulator, stimulus. *See* CAUSE.

stimulator *noun*
Something that causes and encourages a given response : encouragement, fillip, impetus, impulse, incentive, inducement, motivation, prod, push, spur, stimulant, stimulation, stimulus. *See* CAUSE.

stimulus *noun*
1. Something that causes and encourages a given response : encouragement, fillip, impetus, impulse, incentive, inducement, motivation, prod, push, spur, stimulant, stimulation, stimulator. *See* CAUSE. **2.** Something that incites especially a violent response : goad, incitation, incitement, instigation, provocation, trigger. *See* CAUSE.

sting *verb*
1. To cause to become sore or inflamed : burn, inflame, irritate. *See* HELP. **2.** To feel or cause to feel a sensation of heat or discomfort : bite, burn, smart. *See* PAIN. **3.** *Slang.* To get money or something else from by deceitful trickery : bilk, cheat, cozen, defraud, gull, mulct, rook, swindle, victimize. *Informal:* chisel, flimflam, take, trim. *Slang:* diddle[1], do, gyp, stick. *See* HONEST.

sting *noun* **1.** A sensation of physical discomfort occurring as the result of disease or injury : ache, pain, pang, prick, prickle, smart, soreness, stab, stitch, throe, twinge. *Informal:* misery. *See* PAIN. **2.** A cutting quality : bite, edge, incisiveness, keenness, sharpness. *See* SHARP.
3. *Informal.* A stimulating or intoxicating effect : *Informal:* punch, wallop. *Slang:* kick. *See* DRUGS.

stinging *adjective*
So sharp as to cause mental pain : acerbic, acid, acidic, acrid, astringent, biting, caustic, corrosive, cutting, mordacious, mordant, pungent, scathing, sharp, slashing, trenchant, truculent, vitriolic. *See* ATTACK, RESPECT.

stingy *adjective*
1. Ungenerously or pettily reluctant to spend money : cheap, close, close-fisted, costive, hard-fisted, mean[2], miserly, niggard, niggardly, parsimonious, penny-pinching, penurious, petty, pinching, tight, tightfisted. *See* GIVE.
2. Conspicuously deficient in quantity, fullness, or extent : exiguous, meager, poor, puny, scant, scanty, skimpy, spare, sparse, thin. *Slang:* measly. *See* BIG, EXCESS.

stink *verb*
To have or give off a foul odor : reek, smell. ***Idiom:*** smell to high heaven. *See* SMELLS.

stinking *adjective*
1. Having an unpleasant odor : fetid, foul, foul-smelling, malodorous, mephitic, noisome, reeky. *Informal:* smelly. *See* SMELLS. **2.** *Slang.* Stupefied, excited, or muddled with alcoholic liquor : besotted, crapulent, crapulous, drunk, drunken, inebriate, inebriated, intoxicated, sodden, tipsy. *Informal:* cock-eyed, stewed. *Slang:* blind, bombed, boozed, boozy, crocked, high, lit (up), loaded, looped, pickled, pixilated, plastered, potted, sloshed, smashed, soused, stinko, stoned, tight, zonked. ***Idioms:*** drunk as a skunk, half-seas over, high as a kite, in one's cups, three sheets in (*or* to) the wind. *See* DRUGS.

stinko *adjective*
Slang. Stupefied, excited, or muddled with alcoholic liquor : besotted, crapulent, crapulous, drunk, drunken, inebriate, inebriated, intoxicated, sodden, tipsy. *Informal:* cock-eyed, stewed. *Slang:* blind, bombed, boozed, boozy, crocked, high, lit (up), loaded, looped, pickled, pixilated, plastered, potted, sloshed, smashed, soused, stinking, stoned, tight, zonked. ***Idioms:*** drunk as a skunk, half-seas over, high as a kite, in one's cups, three sheets in (*or* to) the wind. *See* DRUGS.

stint *verb*
To be severely sparing in order to economize : pinch, scrape, scrimp, skimp. ***Idioms:*** pinch pennies, tighten (one's) belt. *See* SAVE.

stint *noun* **1.** A piece of work that has been assigned : assignment, chore, duty, job, office, task. *See* WORK. **2.** A limited, often assigned period of activity, duty, or opportunity : bout, go, hitch, inning (often used in plural), shift, spell[3], stretch, time, tour, trick, turn, watch. *See* TIME.

stipend *noun*
Payment for work done : compensation, earnings, emolument, fee, hire, pay, remuneration, salary, wage. *See* PAY.

stipple *verb*
To mark with many small spots : bespeckle,

besprinkle, dapple, dot, fleck, freckle, mottle, pepper, speck, speckle, sprinkle. *See* MARKS.

stipulate *verb*
To make specific : detail, particularize, specify. *See* SPECIFIC.

stipulation *noun*
A restricting or modifying element : condition, provision, proviso, qualification, reservation, specification, term (often used in plural). *Informal:* string (often used in plural). *See* LIMITED.

stir[1] *verb*
1. To put together into one mass so that the constituent parts are more or less homogeneous : admix, amalgamate, blend, commingle, commix, fuse, intermingle, intermix, merge, mingle, mix. *See* ASSEMBLE. **2.** To impart slight movement to : budge, move. *See* MOVE. **3.** To make a slight movement : budge, move. *See* MOVE. **4.** To cease sleeping : arouse, awake, awaken, rouse, wake[1], waken. *See* AWARENESS. **5.** To induce or elicit (a reaction or emotion). Also used with *up* : arouse, awake, awaken, kindle, raise, rouse, waken. *See* EXCITE. **6.** To be the cause of. Also used with *up* : bring, bring about, bring on, cause, effect, effectuate, generate, induce, ingenerate, lead to, make, occasion, result in, secure, set off, touch off, trigger. ***Idioms:*** bring to pass (*or* effect), give rise to. *See* START. **7.** To arouse the emotions of; make ardent : animate, enkindle, fire, impassion, inspire, kindle. *See* EXCITE.

stir *noun* **1.** The act or process of moving : motion, move, movement. *See* MOVE. **2.** An interruption of regular procedure or of public peace : agitation, commotion, disorder, disturbance, helter-skelter, tumult, turbulence, turmoil, uproar. *Informal:* flap, to-do. *See* CALM, ORDER. **3.** Agitated, excited movement and activity : bustle, flurry, whirl, whirlpool. *See* CALM. **4.** A condition of intense public interest or excitement : brouhaha, sensation, uproar. *Informal:* to-do. *Slang:* hoo-hah. *See* EXCITE.

stir[2] *noun*
Slang. A place for the confinement of persons in lawful detention : brig, house of correction, jail, keep, penitentiary, prison. *Informal:* lockup, pen[3]. *Slang:* big house, can, clink, cooler, coop, hoosegow, joint, jug, pokey[1], slammer. *Chiefly Regional:* calaboose. *See* FREE.

stirring *adjective*
Exciting a deep, usually somber response : affecting, impressive, moving, poignant, touching. *See* TOUCH.

stitch *noun*
A sensation of physical discomfort occurring as the result of disease or injury : ache, pain, pang, prick, prickle, smart, soreness, stab, sting, throe, twinge. *Informal:* misery. *See* PAIN.

stock *noun*
1. A supply stored or hidden for future use : backlog, cache, hoard, inventory, nest egg, reserve, reservoir, stockpile, store, treasure. *Slang:* stash. *See* COLLECT. **2.** A group of people sharing common ancestry : clan, family, house, kindred, lineage, tribe. ***Idioms:*** flesh and blood, kith and kin. *See* KIN. **3.** One's ancestors or their character or one's ancestral derivation : ancestry, birth, blood, bloodline, descent, extraction, family, genealogy, line, lineage, origin, parentage, pedigree, seed. *See* KIN, PRECEDE.

stock *verb* To have for sale : carry, keep. *See* KEEP.

stock *adjective* Being of no special quality or type : average, common, commonplace, cut-and-dried, formulaic, garden, garden-variety, indifferent, mediocre, ordinary, plain, routine, run-of-the-mill, standard, undistinguished, unexceptional, unremarkable. *See* GOOD, USUAL.

stockpile *noun*
A supply stored or hidden for future use : backlog, cache, hoard, inventory, nest egg, reserve, reservoir, stock, store, treasure. *Slang:* stash. *See* COLLECT.

stockpile *verb* **1.** To accumulate and set aside for future use : lay in, lay up, save (up), store (up). *See* KEEP. **2.** To store up (supplies or money), usually well beyond one's needs : hoard, squirrel (away), treasure. *Slang:* stash. *See* COLLECT, GIVE.

stock-still *adjective*
Not moving : immobile, motionless, stationary, still, unmoving. *See* MOVE.

stocky *adjective*
Short, heavy, and solidly built : blocky, chunky, compact[1], dumpy, heavyset, squat, stodgy, stubby, stumpy, thick, thickset. *See* FAT.

stodginess *noun*
A lack of excitement, liveliness, or interest : asepticism, blandness, colorlessness, drabness, dreariness, dryness, dullness, flatness, flavorlessness, insipidity, insipidness, jejuneness, lifelessness, sterileness, sterility, vapidity, vapidness, weariness. *See* EXCITE.

stodgy *adjective*
1. Lacking liveliness, charm, or surprise : arid,

aseptic, colorless, drab, dry, dull, earthbound, flat, flavorless, lackluster, lifeless, lusterless, matter-of-fact, pedestrian, prosaic, spiritless, sterile, unimaginative, uninspired. *See* EXCITE. **2.** Having a dense or viscous consistency : gelatinous, heavy, thick. *See* SOLID. **3.** Short, heavy, and solidly built : blocky, chunky, compact[1], dumpy, heavyset, squat, stocky, stubby, stumpy, thick, thickset. *See* FAT.

stoked *adjective*
Slang. Feeling a very strong emotion : atingle, excited, fired up, thrilled, worked up. *Informal:* psyched. *Slang:* turned-on. *See* EXCITE.

stole *noun*
A garment wrapped about a person : cloak, shawl, wrap. *See* PUT ON.

stolid *adjective*
Without emotion or interest : apathetic, detached, impassive, incurious, indifferent, insensible, lethargic, listless, phlegmatic, unconcerned, uninterested, unresponsive. *See* FEELINGS.

stolidity *noun*
Lack of emotion or interest : apathy, disinterest, impassivity, incuriosity, incuriousness, indifference, insensibility, insensibleness, lassitude, lethargy, listlessness, phlegm, stolidness, unconcern, uninterest, unresponsiveness. *See* FEELINGS.

stolidness *noun*
Lack of emotion or interest : apathy, disinterest, impassivity, incuriosity, incuriousness, indifference, insensibility, insensibleness, lassitude, lethargy, listlessness, phlegm, stolidity, unconcern, uninterest, unresponsiveness. *See* FEELINGS.

stomach *noun*
A desire for food or drink : appetite, hunger, taste, thirst. *See* DESIRE.
stomach *verb* To put up with : abide, accept, bear, brook[2], endure, go, stand (for), suffer, support, sustain, swallow, take, tolerate, withstand. *Informal:* lump[2]. ***Idioms:*** take it, take it lying down. *See* ACCEPT.

stomp *verb*
1. To step on heavily and repeatedly so as to crush, injure, or destroy : stamp, tramp, trample, tread, tromp. *See* HELP. **2.** To walk with loud, heavy steps : stamp, tramp, trample. *Informal:* tromp. *See* MOVE, SOUNDS.

stoned *adjective*
1. *Slang.* Stupefied, excited, or muddled with alcoholic liquor : besotted, crapulent, crapulous, drunk, drunken, inebriate, inebriated, intoxicated, sodden, tipsy. *Informal:* cock-eyed, stewed. *Slang:* blind, bombed, boozed, boozy, crocked, high, lit (up), loaded, looped, pickled, pixilated, plastered, potted, sloshed, smashed, soused, stinking, stinko, tight, zonked. ***Idioms:*** drunk as a skunk, half-seas over, high as a kite, in one's cups, three sheets in (*or* to) the wind. *See* DRUGS. **2.** *Slang.* Stupefied, intoxicated, or otherwise influenced by the taking of drugs : drugged. *Informal:* doped. *Slang:* high, hopped-up, lit (up), potted, spaced-out, turned-on, wiped-out, zonked. *See* DRUGS.

stonyhearted *adjective*
Completely lacking in compassion : callous, cold-blooded, cold-hearted, compassionless, hard, hard-boiled, hardened, hardhearted, heartless, obdurate, unfeeling. *See* ATTITUDE.

stooge *noun*
A person used or controlled by others : cat's-paw, dupe, instrument, pawn[2], puppet, tool. *See* OVER.

stool *verb*
Slang. To give incriminating information about others, especially to the authorities : inform, talk, tattle, tip[3] (off). *Slang:* fink, rat, sing, snitch, squeal. ***Idiom:*** blow the whistle. *See* KNOWLEDGE, LAW.

stoolie *noun*
Slang. One who gives incriminating information about others : informant, informer, tattler, tattletale. *Informal:* rat, tipster. *Slang:* fink, snitch, snitcher, squealer, stool pigeon. *See* KNOWLEDGE, LAW.

stool pigeon *noun*
Slang. One who gives incriminating information about others : informant, informer, tattler, tattletale. *Informal:* rat, tipster. *Slang:* fink, snitch, snitcher, squealer, stoolie. *See* KNOWLEDGE, LAW.

stoop *verb*
1. To incline the body : arch, bend, bow[1], hump, hunch, scrunch. *See* POSTURE. **2.** To bring oneself down to a lower level of behavior : descend, lower[2], sink. *See* RISE. **3.** To descend to a level considered inappropriate to one's dignity : condescend, deign, vouchsafe. *See* OVER, RISE.

stop *verb*
1. To plug up something, as a hole, space, or container : block, choke, clog, close, congest, cork, fill, plug. *See* FULL. **2.** To come to a cessation : arrest, belay, cease, check, discontinue, halt[1], leave off, quit, stall[1], surcease. ***Idiom:*** come to a halt (*or* standstill *or* stop). *See* CONTINUE. **3.** To prevent the occurrence or continuation of a movement, action, or operation :

arrest, belay, cease, check, discontinue, halt[1], stall[1], stay[1], surcease. ***Idioms:*** bring to a standstill, call a halt to, put a stop to. *See* CONTINUE. **4.** To cause to cease regular activity : idle, immobilize, tie up. ***Idiom:*** bring to a screeching halt. *See* CONTINUE. **5.** To cease trying to accomplish or continue : abandon, break off, desist, discontinue, give up, leave off, quit, relinquish, remit. *Informal:* swear off. *Slang:* lay off. ***Idioms:*** call it a day, call it quits, hang up one's fiddle, have done with, throw in the towel. *See* CONTINUE. **6.** To desist from, cease, or discontinue (a habit, for example) : break, cut out, give up, leave off. *Slang:* kick. *See* CONTINUE. **7.** To go to or seek out the company of in order to socialize. Also used with *by* or *in* : call, come by, come over, drop by, drop in, look in, look up, pop in, run in, see, visit. ***Idiom:*** pay a visit. *See* SEEK.

stop *noun* **1.** The act of stopping : cessation, check, cut-off, discontinuance, discontinuation, halt[1], stay[1], stoppage, surcease. *See* CONTINUE. **2.** The condition of being stopped : cessation, discontinuance, discontinuation, halt[1], standstill, stoppage, surcease. *See* CONTINUE. **3.** A concluding or terminating : cease, cessation, close, closing, closure, completion, conclusion, consummation, end, ending, end of the line, finish, period, stopping point, termination, terminus, wind-up, wrap-up. *See* CONTINUE. **4.** Something that impedes or prevents entry or passage : bar, barricade, barrier, block, blockage, clog, hamper, hindrance, hurdle, impediment, obstacle, obstruction, snag, traverse, wall. *See* HELP, OPEN. **5.** Something used to fill a hole, space, or container : choke, cork, fill, plug, stopper. *See* FULL.

stopgap *noun*
Something used temporarily or reluctantly when other means are not available : expediency, expedient, makeshift, shift. *See* HELP, SUBSTITUTE.

stoppage *noun*
1. The act of stopping : cessation, check, cut-off, discontinuance, discontinuation, halt[1], stay[1], stop, surcease. *See* CONTINUE. **2.** The condition of being stopped : cessation, discontinuance, discontinuation, halt[1], standstill, stop, surcease. *See* CONTINUE. **3.** A cessation of normal activity, caused by an accident or strike, for example : gridlock, immobilization, jam, tie-up. *See* CONTINUE.

stopper *noun*
Something used to fill a hole, space, or container : choke, cork, fill, plug, stop. *See* FULL.

stopping point *noun*
A concluding or terminating : cease, cessation, close, closing, closure, completion, conclusion, consummation, end, ending, end of the line, finish, period, stop, termination, terminus, wind-up, wrap-up. *See* CONTINUE.

store *noun*
1. A retail establishment where merchandise is sold : boutique, emporium, outlet, shop. *See* TRANSACTIONS. **2.** A supply stored or hidden for future use : backlog, cache, hoard, inventory, nest egg, reserve, reservoir, stock, stockpile, treasure. *Slang:* stash. *See* COLLECT. **3.** A place where something is deposited for safekeeping : archive, depository, magazine, repository, storehouse, warehouse. *See* KEEP.

store *verb* **1.** To accumulate and set aside for future use. Also used with *up* : lay in, lay up, save (up), stockpile. *See* KEEP. **2.** To have or put in a customary place : keep. *See* PLACE.

storehouse *noun*
A place where something is deposited for safekeeping : archive, depository, magazine, repository, store, warehouse. *See* KEEP.

storm *noun*
A concentrated outpouring, as of missiles, words, or blows : barrage, bombardment, burst, cannonade, fusillade, hail[1], salvo, shower, volley. *See* ATTACK.

storm *verb* To set upon with violent force : aggress, assail, assault, attack, beset, fall on (*or* upon), go at, have at, sail into, strike. *Informal:* light into, pitch into. *See* ATTACK.

stormy *adjective*
1. Violently disturbed or agitated, as by storms : dirty, heavy, raging, roiled, roily, rough, rugged, tempestuous, tumultuous, turbulent, ugly, violent, wild. *See* CALM.
2. Marked by unrest or disturbance : tempestuous, tumultuous, turbulent. *See* CALM.

story *noun*
1. A recounting of past events : account, chronicle, description, history, narration, narrative, report, statement, version. *See* WORDS.
2. A narrative not based on fact : fable, fiction. *See* REAL. **3.** The series of events and relationships forming the basis of a composition : plot, story line. *See* HAPPEN, WORDS. **4.** A usually brief detail of news or information : bit[1], item, paragraph, piece, squib. *See* WORDS. **5.** An entertaining and often oral account of a real or fictitious occurrence : anecdote, fable, tale. *Informal:* tall tale, yarn. *See* WORDS. **6.** An untrue declaration : canard, cock-and-bull story, falsehood, falsity, fib, fiction, inveracity,

lie[2], misrepresentation, misstatement, prevarication, tale, untruth. *Informal:* fish story, tall tale. *Slang:* whopper. *See* TRUE.

story line *noun*
The series of events and relationships forming the basis of a composition : plot, story. *See* HAPPEN, WORDS.

storyteller *noun*
Informal. One who tells lies : fabricator, fabulist, falsifier, fibber, liar, prevaricator. *Law:* perjurer. *See* TRUE.

stout *adjective*
1. Having or showing courage : audacious, bold, brave, courageous, dauntless, doughty, fearless, fortitudinous, gallant, game, hardy, heroic, intrepid, mettlesome, plucky, stouthearted, unafraid, undaunted, valiant, valorous. *Informal:* spunky. *Slang:* gutsy, gutty. *See* FEAR. **2.** Capable of exerting considerable effort or of withstanding considerable stress or hardship : hardy, stalwart, strong, sturdy, tough. *See* STRONG. **3.** Having a large body, especially in girth : bulky, heavy, hefty, hulking, hulky, husky[2]. *See* BIG. **4.** Having too much flesh : corpulent, fat, fatty, fleshy, gross, obese, overblown, overweight, porcine, portly, weighty. *See* FAT.

stouthearted *adjective*
Having or showing courage : audacious, bold, brave, courageous, dauntless, doughty, fearless, fortitudinous, gallant, game, hardy, heroic, intrepid, mettlesome, plucky, stout, unafraid, undaunted, valiant, valorous. *Informal:* spunky. *Slang:* gutsy, gutty. *See* FEAR.

stoutheartedness *noun*
The quality of mind enabling one to face danger or hardship resolutely : braveness, bravery, courage, courageousness, dauntlessness, doughtiness, fearlessness, fortitude, gallantry, gameness, heart, intrepidity, intrepidness, mettle, nerve, pluck, pluckiness, spirit, undauntedness, valiance, valiancy, valiantness, valor. *Informal:* spunk, spunkiness. *Slang:* gut (used in plural), gutsiness, moxie. *See* FEAR.

strabismal *adjective*
Marked by or affected with a squint : cross-eyed, squint-eyed, squinty, strabismic. *See* SEE.

strabismic *adjective*
Marked by or affected with a squint : cross-eyed, squint-eyed, squinty, strabismal. *See* SEE.

strabismus *noun*
The condition of not having the visual axes parallel : cross-eye, squint. *See* SEE.

straddle *verb*
1. To sit or stand with a leg on each side of : bestride, stride. *See* POSTURE. **2.** To sit or lie with the limbs spread out awkwardly : drape, loll, sprawl, spread-eagle. *See* POSTURE.

straggle *verb*
To grow or spread in a disorderly or planless fashion : spill, sprawl. *See* ORDER.

straggler *noun*
One that lags : dawdler, dilly-dallier, lag, laggard, lagger, lingerer, loiterer, poke, procrastinator, tarrier. *Informal:* slowpoke. *See* FAST.

straight *adjective*
1. Proceeding or lying in an uninterrupted line or course : direct, straightforward, through. *See* STRAIGHT. **2.** Having no irregularities, roughness, or indentations : even[1], flat, flush, level, planar, plane[1], smooth. *See* SMOOTH. **3.** Manifesting honesty and directness, especially in speech : candid, direct, downright, forthright, frank, honest, ingenuous, man-to-man, open, plainspoken, straightforward, straight-out, unreserved. *Informal:* straight-from-the-shoulder, straight-shooting. *See* CLEAR, SHOW. **4.** Conforming to established practice or standards : button-down, conformist, conventional, establishmentarian, orthodox, traditional. *Slang:* square. *See* USUAL. **5.** Not diluted or mixed with other substances : full-strength, neat, plain, pure, unblended, undiluted, unmixed. *See* CLEAN, STRONG.

straight *adverb* **1.** In a direct line : dead, direct, directly, due, right, straightaway. *See* STRAIGHT. **2.** With precision or absolute conformity : bang, dead, direct, directly, exactly, fair, flush, just, precisely, right, smack[1], square, squarely. *Slang:* smack-dab. *See* PRECISE.

straightaway *adverb*
1. In a direct line : dead, direct, directly, due, right, straight. *See* STRAIGHT. **2.** Without delay : directly, forthwith, immediately, instant, instantly, now, right away, right off, straight off. ***Idioms:*** at once, first off. *See* TIME.

straighten *verb*
1. To make even, smooth, or level : even[1], flat, flatten, level, plane[2], smooth. *See* SMOOTH. **2.** To make or keep (an area) clean and orderly. Also used with *up* : clean (up), clear (up), neaten (up), police, spruce (up), tidy (up). *See* ORDER.

straighten out *verb* To bring (something) into a state of agreement or accord : reconcile, rectify, resolve, settle, smooth over. *See* AGREE.

straighten out *verb* See **straighten.**

straightforward *adjective*
1. Proceeding or lying in an uninterrupted line or course : direct, straight, through. *See*

STRAIGHT. **2.** Manifesting honesty and directness, especially in speech : candid, direct, downright, forthright, frank, honest, ingenuous, man-to-man, open, plainspoken, straight, straight-out, unreserved. *Informal:* straight-from-the-shoulder, straight-shooting. *See* CLEAR, SHOW.

straight-from-the-shoulder *adjective*
Informal. Manifesting honesty and directness, especially in speech : candid, direct, downright, forthright, frank, honest, ingenuous, man-to-man, open, plainspoken, straight, straightforward, straight-out, unreserved. *Informal:* straight-shooting. *See* CLEAR, SHOW.

straight off *adverb*
Without delay : directly, forthwith, immediately, instant, instantly, now, right away, right off, straightaway. ***Idioms:*** at once, first off. *See* TIME.

straight-out *adjective*
Manifesting honesty and directness, especially in speech : candid, direct, downright, forthright, frank, honest, ingenuous, man-to-man, open, plainspoken, straight, straightforward, unreserved. *Informal:* straight-from-the-shoulder, straight-shooting. *See* CLEAR, SHOW.

straight-shooting *adjective*
1. *Informal.* Having or marked by uprightness in principle and action : good, honest, honorable, incorruptible, righteous, true, upright, upstanding. ***Idiom:*** on the up-and-up (*or* up and up). *See* HONEST. **2.** *Informal.* Manifesting honesty and directness, especially in speech : candid, direct, downright, forthright, frank, honest, ingenuous, man-to-man, open, plainspoken, straight, straightforward, straight-out, unreserved. *Informal:* straight-from-the-shoulder. *See* CLEAR, SHOW.

strain[1] *verb*
To exert one's mental or physical powers, usually under difficulty and to the point of exhaustion : drive, fag, labor, moil, strive, sweat, toil, travail, tug, work. ***Idiom:*** break one's back (*or* neck). *See* WORK.

strain *noun* **1.** The use of energy to do something : effort, endeavor, exertion, pain (used in plural), striving, struggle, trouble, while. *Informal:* elbow grease. *See* WORK. **2.** The act, condition, or effect of exerting force on someone or something : pressure, stress, tension. *See* PUSH.

strain[2] *noun*
1. An intermixture of a contrasting or unexpected quality, especially in a person's character : streak, vein. *See* BE. **2.** A pleasing succession of musical tones forming a usually brief aesthetic unit : air, aria, melody, tune. *Obsolete:* note. *See* SOUNDS.

strained *adjective*
Not natural or spontaneous : contrived, effortful, forced, labored. *See* TRUE.

strait-laced *adjective*
Marked by excessive concern for propriety and good form : bluenosed, genteel, old-maidish, precise, priggish, prim, prissy, proper, prudish, puritanical, stuffy, Victorian. ***Idiom:*** prim and proper. *See* PLAIN.

strand *noun*
Something that suggests the continuousness of a fine continuous filament : skein, thread. *See* CONTINUE.

strange *adjective*
1. Deviating from the customary : bizarre, cranky, curious, eccentric, erratic, freakish, idiosyncratic, odd, outlandish, peculiar, quaint, queer, quirky, singular, unnatural, unusual, weird. *Slang:* kooky, screwball. *British Slang:* rum, rummy[2]. *See* USUAL. **2.** Causing puzzlement; perplexing : curious, funny, odd, peculiar, queer, weird. *See* USUAL. **3.** Of, from, or characteristic of another place or part of the world : alien, exotic, foreign. *Archaic:* outlandish. *See* NATIVE.

stranger *noun*
A person coming from another country or into a new community : alien, émigré, foreigner, newcomer, outlander, outsider. *See* NATIVE.

strangle *verb*
1. To interfere with or stop the normal breathing of, especially by constricting the windpipe : choke, throttle. *See* BREATH. **2.** To hold (something requiring an outlet) in check : burke, choke (back), gag, hold back, hold down, hush (up), muffle, quench, repress, smother, squelch, stifle, suppress, throttle. *Informal:* sit on (*or* upon). *See* RESTRAINT.

strapped *adjective*
Informal. Having little or no money or wealth : beggarly, destitute, down-and-out, impecunious, impoverished, indigent, necessitous, needy, penniless, penurious, poor, poverty-stricken. *Informal:* broke. ***Idioms:*** hard up, on one's uppers. *See* RICH.

strapping *adjective*
Full of vigor : able-bodied, iron, lusty, red-blooded, robust, sturdy, vigorous, vital. *See* STRONG.

stratagem *noun*
1. A method of deploying troops and equipment

in combat : maneuver, tactic. *See* MEANS. **2.** An indirect, usually cunning means of gaining an end : artifice, deception, device, dodge, feint, gimmick, imposture, jig, maneuver, ploy, ruse, sleight, subterfuge, trick, wile. *Informal:* shenanigan, take-in. *See* HONEST, MEANS.

strategize *verb*
To form a strategy for : blueprint, cast, chart, conceive, contrive, design, devise, formulate, frame, lay[1], plan, project, scheme, work out. *Informal:* dope out. ***Idiom:*** lay plans. *See* PLANNED.

strategy *noun*
A method for making, doing, or accomplishing something : blueprint, design, game plan, idea, layout, plan, project, schema, scheme. *See* PLANNED.

stratospheric *adjective*
Vastly exceeding a normal limit, as in cost : sky-high, steep[1], stiff, unconscionable. *See* BIG, USUAL.

straw boss *noun*
Informal. Someone who directs and supervises workers : boss, director, foreman, foreperson, forewoman, head, manager, overseer, superintendent, supervisor, taskmaster, taskmistress. *Slang:* chief. *See* OVER.

stray *verb*
1. To move about at random, especially over a wide area : drift, gad, gallivant, meander, peregrinate, ramble, range, roam, rove, traipse, wander. *See* MOVE. **2.** To turn away from a prescribed course of action or conduct : depart, deviate, digress, diverge, swerve, veer. *Archaic:* err. *See* APPROACH, CORRECT. **3.** To turn aside, especially from the main subject in writing or speaking : deviate, digress, divagate, diverge, ramble, wander. ***Idiom:*** go off at (*or* on) a tangent. *See* APPROACH.

stray *adjective* **1.** Unable to find the correct way or place to go : astray, disoriented, lost. *See* SEEK. **2.** Without a fixed or regular course : devious, erratic, wandering. *See* PURPOSE.

streak *noun*
1. A slight amount or indication : breath, dash, ghost, hair, hint, intimation, semblance, shade, shadow, soupçon, suggestion, suspicion, taste, tinge, touch, trace, whiff, whisper. *Informal:* whisker. *See* BIG, SHOW. **2.** An intermixture of a contrasting or unexpected quality, especially in a person's character : strain[2], vein. *See* BE. **3.** *Informal.* A number of things placed or occurring one after the other : chain, consecution, course, order, procession, progression, round, run, sequence, series, string, succession, suite, train. *See* ORDER.

streak *verb* To mark with a line or band, as of different color or texture : striate, stripe, variegate. *See* MARKS.

stream *noun*
Something suggestive of running water : current, drift, flood, flow, flux, rush, spate, surge, tide. *See* MOVE.

stream *verb* **1.** To move freely as a liquid : circulate, course, flow, run. *See* MOVE. **2.** To come forth or emit in abundance : flow, gush, pour, run, rush, surge, well[1]. *See* MOVE.

streamer *noun*
Fabric used especially as a symbol : banderole, banner, banneret, color (used in plural), ensign, flag[1], jack, oriflamme, pennant, pennon, standard. *See* SUBSTITUTE.

streamlined *adjective*
Having slender and graceful lines : sleek, trim. *See* BEAUTIFUL.

street *noun*
A course affording passage from one place to another : avenue, boulevard, drive, expressway, freeway, highway, path, road, roadway, route, superhighway, thoroughfare, thruway, turnpike, way. *See* MOVE, OPEN.

streetwalker *noun*
A woman who engages in sexual intercourse for payment : bawd, call girl, camp follower, courtesan, harlot, prostitute, scarlet woman, strumpet, tart[2], whore. *Slang:* hooker, moll. ***Idioms:*** lady of easy virtue, lady of pleasure, lady of the night. *See* SEX.

strength *noun*
1. The state or quality of being physically strong : brawn, might, muscle, potence, potency, power, powerfulness, puissance, sinew, thew (often used in plural). *See* STRONG. **2.** Power used to overcome resistance : coercion, compulsion, constraint, duress, force, pressure, violence. *See* ATTACK. **3.** The condition of being free from defects or flaws : durability, firmness, integrity, solidity, soundness, stability, wholeness. *See* BETTER. **4.** Reliability in withstanding pressure, force, or stress : fastness, firmness, hardness, security, soundness, stability, stableness, steadiness, sturdiness, sureness. *See* BETTER, CHANGE, CONTINUE. **5.** Capacity or power for work or vigorous activity : animation, energy, force, might, potency, power, puissance, sprightliness, steam. *Informal:* get-up-and-go, go, pep, peppiness, zip. *See* ACTION.

strengthen *verb*
1. To become or cause to become tough or strong : toughen. *See* STRONG. **2.** To prepare (oneself) for action : brace, forearm, fortify, gird, ready, steel. ***Idiom:*** gird (*or* gird up) one's loins. *See* PREPARED. **3.** To make or become tight or tighter : reinforce, tighten. *See* TIGHTEN. **4.** To make firmer in a particular conviction or habit : confirm, fortify, harden. *See* STRONG.

strenuous *adjective*
1. Marked by vigorous physical exertion : knockabout, rough, rough-and-tumble, rugged, tough. *See* ACTION. **2.** Possessing, exerting, or displaying energy : active, brisk, dynamic, dynamical, energetic, forceful, kinetic, lively, sprightly, vigorous. *Informal:* peppy. *See* ACTION.

strenuously *adverb*
In a violent, strenuous way : fiercely, frantically, frenziedly, furiously, hard. *See* STRONG.

stress *noun*
1. Special weight placed upon something considered important : accent, accentuation, emphasis. *See* IMPORTANT. **2.** The act, condition, or effect of exerting force on someone or something : pressure, strain[1], tension. *See* PUSH.

stress *verb* To accord emphasis to : accent, accentuate, emphasize, feature, highlight, italicize, play up, point up, underline, underscore. *See* IMPORTANT.

stretch *verb*
1. To make or become longer. Also used with *out* : draw out, elongate, extend, lengthen, prolong, prolongate, protract, spin (out). *Mathematics:* produce. *See* INCREASE, LONG. **2.** To move or arrange so as to cover a larger area : expand, extend, fan[1] (out), open (out *or* up), outstretch, spread, unfold, unroll. *See* MOVE. **3.** To proceed on a certain course or for a certain distance : carry, extend, go, lead, reach, run. *See* REACH. **4.** To extend, especially an appendage. Also used with *out* : outstretch, reach. *See* REACH. **5.** To be or place oneself in a prostrate or recumbent position. Also used with *out* : lie[1] (down), recline, repose. *See* HORIZONTAL. **6.** To take repose, as by sleeping or lying quietly. Also used with *out* : lie[1] (down), recline, repose, rest[1]. *See* CONTINUE.

stretch *noun* **1.** The measure of how far or long something goes in space, time, or degree : extent, length, reach, span. *See* BIG. **2.** An extent, measured or unmeasured, of linear space : distance, length, space. *Informal:* piece, way. *See* BIG. **3.** A wide and open area, as of land, sky, or water : distance, expanse, expansion, extent, reach, space, spread, sweep. *See* PLACE. **4.** A specific length of time characterized by the occurrence of certain conditions or events : period, season, span, term. *See* TIME. **5.** A limited or specific period of time during which something happens, lasts, or extends : duration, span, term, time. *See* TIME. **6.** A term of service, as in the military or in prison : hitch, time, tour. *See* TIME. **7.** A limited, often assigned period of activity, duty, or opportunity : bout, go, hitch, inning (often used in plural), shift, spell[3], stint, time, tour, trick, turn, watch. *See* TIME.

stretch *adjective* Capable of being extended or expanded : expansible, expansile, extendible, extensible, extensile, protractile, stretchable. *See* INCREASE.

stretchable *adjective*
Capable of being extended or expanded : expansible, expansile, extendible, extensible, extensile, protractile, stretch. *See* INCREASE.

strew *verb*
To extend over a wide area : circulate, diffuse, disperse, disseminate, distribute, radiate, scatter, spread. *See* MOVE, WIDE.

striate *verb*
To mark with a line or band, as of different color or texture : streak, stripe, variegate. *See* MARKS.

strict *adjective*
1. Not deviating from correctness, accuracy, or completeness : close, exact, faithful, full, rigorous. *See* CAREFUL. **2.** Rigorous and unsparing in treating others : demanding, exacting, hard, harsh, rigid, severe, stern, tough, unyielding. *See* EASY. **3.** Conforming completely to established rule : exact, rigorous, uncompromising. *See* USUAL.

strictness *noun*
The fact or condition of being rigorous and unsparing : austerity, hardness, harshness, rigidity, rigor, rigorousness, severity, sternness, stringency, toughness. *See* EASY.

stricture *noun*
1. Something that limits or restricts : check, circumscription, constraint, cramp[2], curb, inhibition, limit, limitation, restraint, restriction, trammel. *See* LIMITED. **2.** *Pathology.* A becoming narrow or narrower : constriction. *See* WIDE.

stride *verb*
1. To walk with long steps, especially in a

vigorous manner : march[1], stalk. *See* MOVE. **2.** To sit or stand with a leg on each side of : bestride, straddle. *See* POSTURE.

strident *adjective*

1. Disagreeable to the sense of hearing : dry, grating, harsh, hoarse, jarring, rasping, raspy, raucous, rough, scratchy, squawky. *See* SOUNDS. **2.** Offensively loud and insistent : blatant, boisterous, clamorous, obstreperous, vociferous. *Informal:* loudmouthed. *See* SOUNDS.

strife *noun*

1. A state of disagreement and disharmony : clash, conflict, confrontation, contention, difference, difficulty, disaccord, discord, discordance, dissension, dissent, dissentience, dissidence, dissonance, faction, friction, inharmony, schism, variance, war, warfare. *See* CONFLICT. **2.** A state of open, prolonged fighting : belligerency, conflict, confrontation, hostility (used in plural), struggle, war, warfare. *See* CONFLICT. **3.** A vying with others for victory or supremacy : battle, competition, contest, corrivalry, race, rivalry, striving, struggle, tug of war, war, warfare. *See* CONFLICT.

strike *verb*

1. To deliver a powerful blow to suddenly and sharply : bash, catch, clout, hit, knock, pop[1], slam, slog, slug[3], smash, smite, sock, swat, thwack, whack, wham, whop. *Informal:* biff, bop, clip[1], wallop. *Slang:* belt, conk, paste. ***Idioms:*** let someone have it, sock it to someone. *See* ATTACK, STRIKE. **2.** To set upon with violent force : aggress, assail, assault, attack, beset, fall on (*or* upon), go at, have at, sail into, storm. *Informal:* light into, pitch into. *See* ATTACK. **3.** To bring great harm or suffering to : afflict, agonize, anguish, curse, excruciate, plague, rack, scourge, smite, torment, torture. *See* ATTACK, HELP. **4.** To grasp at (something) eagerly, forcibly, and abruptly with the jaws : catch, nip[1], snap, snatch. *See* REACH. **5.** To give forth or cause to give forth a clear, resonant sound : bong, chime, knell, peal, ring[2], toll[2]. *See* SOUNDS. **6.** To remove or invalidate by or as if by running a line through or wiping clean. Also used with *out* : annul, blot (out), cancel, cross (off *or* out), delete, efface, erase, expunge, obliterate, rub (out), scratch (out), undo, wipe (out), x (out). *Law:* vacate. *See* CONTINUE. **7.** To evoke a usually strong mental or emotional response from : affect[1], get (to), impress, move, touch. *See* TOUCH. **8.** To enter a person's mind : hit, occur. ***Idiom:*** cross one's mind. *See* HAPPEN. **9.** To have a sudden overwhelming effect on : catch, seize, take. *See* ATTACK, OVER. **10.** To cease working in support of demands made upon an employer : walk out. ***Idiom:*** go on strike. *See* CONTINUE.

strike back *verb* To return like for like, especially to return an unfriendly or hostile action with a similar one : counter, hit back, reciprocate, retaliate, retort. *See* ATTACK, FORGIVENESS.

strike down *verb* To cause to fall, as from a shot or blow : bring down, cut down, down, drop, fell[1], flatten, floor, ground, knock down, level, prostrate, throw. *Slang:* deck[1]. ***Idiom:*** lay low. *See* RISE.

strike out *verb* To proceed in a specified direction : bear, go, head, make, set out. *See* APPROACH.

strike *noun* **1.** The act of attacking : aggression, assailment, assault, attack, attempt, offense, offensive, onrush, onset, onslaught. *See* ATTACK. **2.** Something that has been discovered : ascertainment, discovery, find, finding. *See* TEACH.

strike back *verb* See **strike.**

strike down *verb* See **strike.**

strike out *verb* See **strike.**

striking *adjective*

Readily attracting notice : arresting, bold, conspicuous, eye-catching, marked, noticeable, observable, outstanding, pointed, prominent, pronounced, remarkable, salient, signal. ***Idiom:*** sticking out like a sore thumb. *See* SEE.

string *noun*

1. A group of people or things arranged in a row : column, file, line, queue, rank[1], row[1], tier. *See* GROUP. **2.** A number of things placed or occurring one after the other : chain, consecution, course, order, procession, progression, round, run, sequence, series, succession, suite, train. *Informal:* streak. *See* ORDER. **3.** *Informal.* A restricting or modifying element. Often used in plural : condition, provision, proviso, qualification, reservation, specification, stipulation, term (often used in plural). *See* LIMITED.

string *verb* To put (objects) onto a fine continuous filament : thread. *See* ORDER.

string up *verb* *Informal.* To execute by suspending by the neck : gibbet, hang. *Slang:* swing. *See* HELP.

stringency *noun*

The fact or condition of being rigorous and unsparing : austerity, hardness, harshness, rigidity, rigor, rigorousness, severity, sternness, strictness, toughness. *See* EASY.

string up *verb* See **string.**

strip[1] *verb*

1. To remove all the clothing from : disrobe, unclothe, undress. *See* PUT ON, SHOW. **2.** To remove the skin of : decorticate, pare, peel, scale[1], skin. *See* PUT ON. **3.** To take or keep something away from : deprive, dispossess, divest, rob. *See* GIVE. **4.** To make bare : bare, denude, disrobe, divest, expose, uncover. *See* PUT ON. **5.** To rob of goods by force, especially in time of war : depredate, despoil, havoc, loot, pillage, plunder, ransack, rape, ravage, sack[2], spoliate. *Archaic:* harrow, spoil. *See* CRIMES, GIVE.

strip[2] *noun*

A long narrow piece, as of material : band[1], bandeau, fillet, stripe. *See* MATTER.

stripe *noun*

1. A long narrow piece, as of material : band[1], bandeau, fillet, strip[2]. *See* MATTER. **2.** A class that is defined by the common attribute or attributes possessed by all its members : breed, cast, description, feather, ilk, kind[2], lot, manner, mold, nature, order, sort, species, stamp, type, variety. *Informal:* persuasion. *See* GROUP.

stripe *verb* To mark with a line or band, as of different color or texture : streak, striate, variegate. *See* MARKS.

strive *verb*

1. To exert one's mental or physical powers, usually under difficulty and to the point of exhaustion : drive, fag, labor, moil, strain[1], sweat, toil, travail, tug, work. ***Idiom:*** break one's back (*or* neck). *See* WORK. **2.** To make an attempt to do or make : assay, attempt, endeavor, essay, seek, try. ***Idioms:*** have a go at, have (*or* make *or* take) a shot at, have (*or* take) a whack at, make a stab at, take a crack at. *See* TRY.

striving *noun*

1. The use of energy to do something : effort, endeavor, exertion, pain (used in plural), strain[1], struggle, trouble, while. *Informal:* elbow grease. *See* WORK. **2.** A vying with others for victory or supremacy : battle, competition, contest, corrivalry, race, rivalry, strife, struggle, tug of war, war, warfare. *See* CONFLICT.

stroll *verb*

To walk at a leisurely pace : amble, meander, perambulate, promenade, ramble, saunter, wander. *Informal:* mosey. *See* MOVE.

stroll *noun* An act of walking, especially for pleasure : amble, meander (often used in plural), perambulation, promenade, ramble, saunter, walk, wander. *See* MOVE.

strong *adjective*

1. Having great physical strength : mighty, potent, powerful, puissant. *See* STRONG. **2.** Capable of exerting considerable effort or of withstanding considerable stress or hardship : hardy, stalwart, stout, sturdy, tough. *See* STRONG. **3.** Full of or displaying force : dynamic, dynamical, effective, forceful, forcible, hard-hitting, powerful, vigorous. *See* STRONG. **4.** Not easily moved or shaken : firm[1], secure, solid, sound[2], stable, sturdy, substantial, sure, unshakable. *See* CONTINUE, STRONG. **5.** Firmly settled or positioned : fast, firm[1], secure, stable, steady, sure. *See* CONTINUE. **6.** Intensely violent in sustained velocity : fierce, furious, heavy, high. *See* STRONG. **7.** Resulting from or affecting one's innermost feelings : deep, intense, profound. *See* STRONG, SURFACE. **8.** Having a high concentration of the distinguishing ingredient : concentrated, potent, stiff. *See* STRONG. **9.** Containing alcohol : alcoholic, hard, intoxicative, spirituous. *See* INGESTION.

strong-arm *adjective*

Informal. Accomplished by force : coercive, forcible, violent. *See* ATTACK.

strong-arm *verb* **1.** *Informal.* To compel by pressure or threats : blackjack, coerce, dragoon, force. *Informal:* hijack. *See* PERSUASION. **2.** *Informal.* To domineer or drive into compliance by the use of as threats or force, for example : bludgeon, browbeat, bulldoze, bully, bullyrag, cow, hector, intimidate, menace, threaten. *See* OVER.

strongman *noun*

An absolute ruler, especially one who is harsh and oppressive : Big Brother, despot, dictator, führer, man on horseback, oppressor, totalitarian, tyrant. *See* OVER.

strong point *noun*

Something at which a person excels : forte, long suit, métier, specialty, strong suit. *Slang:* bag, thing. *See* ABILITY.

strong suit *noun*

Something at which a person excels : forte, long suit, métier, specialty, strong point. *Slang:* bag, thing. *See* ABILITY.

structure *noun*

A usually permanent construction, such as a house or store : building, edifice, pile. *See* MAKE.

structure *verb* To create by combining parts or elements : build, compose, configure, form, pattern, shape. *See* MAKE.

struggle *verb*
To strive in opposition : battle, combat, contend, duel, fight, tilt, war, wrestle. *See* CONFLICT.

struggle *noun* **1.** The use of energy to do something : effort, endeavor, exertion, pain (used in plural), strain[1], striving, trouble, while. *Informal:* elbow grease. *See* WORK. **2.** A vying with others for victory or supremacy : battle, competition, contest, corrivalry, race, rivalry, strife, striving, tug of war, war, warfare. *See* CONFLICT. **3.** A state of open, prolonged fighting : belligerency, conflict, confrontation, hostility (used in plural), strife, war, warfare. *See* CONFLICT.

strumpet *noun*
A woman who engages in sexual intercourse for payment : bawd, call girl, camp follower, courtesan, harlot, prostitute, scarlet woman, streetwalker, tart[2], whore. *Slang:* hooker, moll. ***Idioms:*** lady of easy virtue, lady of pleasure, lady of the night. *See* SEX.

strut *verb*
To walk with exaggerated or unnatural motions expressive of self-importance or self-display : flounce, peacock, prance, swagger, swank, swash. *Informal:* sashay. *See* MOVE, SELF-LOVE.

stub *noun*
Residual matter : butt[4], end, fragment, ort (often used in plural), scrap[1], shard. *See* LEFTOVER.

stubborn *adjective*
1. Firmly, often unreasonably immovable in purpose or will : adamant, adamantine, brassbound, die-hard, grim, implacable, incompliant, inexorable, inflexible, intransigent, iron, obdurate, relentless, remorseless, rigid, unbendable, unbending, uncompliant, uncompromising, unrelenting, unyielding. ***Idiom:*** stubborn as a mule (*or* ox). *See* RESIST. **2.** Difficult to alleviate or cure : obstinate, persistent, pertinacious. *See* CONTINUE.

stubbornness *noun*
The quality or state of being stubbornly inflexible : die-hardism, grimness, implacability, implacableness, incompliance, incompliancy, inexorability, inexorableness, inflexibility, inflexibleness, intransigence, intransigency, obduracy, obdurateness, relentlessness, remorselessness, rigidity, rigidness. *See* RESIST.

stubby *adjective*
Short, heavy, and solidly built : blocky, chunky, compact[1], dumpy, heavyset, squat, stocky, stodgy, stumpy, thick, thickset. *See* FAT.

stuck-up *adjective*
1. *Informal.* Thinking too highly of oneself : conceited, egoistic, egoistical, egotistic, egotistical, narcissistic, vain, vainglorious. *Informal:* bigheaded, swellheaded. *See* SELF-LOVE. **2.** *Informal.* Characteristic of or resembling a snob : elitist, snobbish, snobby. *Informal:* high-hat, snooty, uppish, uppity. *See* ATTITUDE, SELF-LOVE.

stud *noun*
Slang. A person regarded as physically attractive. Used of a man : beauty, belle (used of a woman), lovely, stunner. *Slang:* babe, doll, hunk (used of a man), knockout, looker. *See* BEAUTIFUL.

student *noun*
One who is being educated : learner, pupil, scholar. *See* TEACH.

studied *adjective*
Resulting from deliberation and careful thought : advised, calculated, considered, studious. *See* WISE.

studious *adjective*
1. Devoted to study or reading : bookish, scholarly. *See* TEACH. **2.** Characterized by steady attention and effort : assiduous, diligent, industrious, sedulous. *See* INDUSTRIOUS. **3.** Resulting from deliberation and careful thought : advised, calculated, considered, studied. *See* WISE.

study *noun*
1. A careful considering of a matter : advisement, calculation, consideration, deliberation, lucubration. *See* THOUGHTS. **2.** The act of examining carefully : check, checkup, examination, inspection, perusal, scrutiny, view. *Informal:* going-over. *See* INVESTIGATE. **3.** The condition of being so lost in solitary thought as to be unaware of one's surroundings : absent-mindedness, abstraction, bemusement, brown study, daydreaming, muse[2], reverie, trance. *See* AWARENESS. **4.** Repetition of an action so as to develop or maintain one's skill : drill, exercise, practice, rehearsal, training. *See* WORK.

study *verb* **1.** To apply one's mind to the acquisition or production of knowledge : con, lucubrate. *See* TEACH. **2.** To look at carefully or critically : check (out), con, examine, go over, inspect, peruse, scrutinize, survey, traverse, view. *Informal:* case. *Idiom:* give a going-over. *See* INVESTIGATE. **3.** To think or think about carefully and at length : chew on (*or* over), cogitate, consider, contemplate, deliberate, entertain, excogitate, meditate, mull, muse[1], ponder, reflect, revolve, ruminate, think, think out, think over, think through, turn over, weigh. *Idioms:* cudgel one's brains, put on one's thinking cap, rack one's brain. *See* THOUGHTS.

stuff *noun*

1. That from which things are or can be made : material, matter, substance. *Idiom:* grist for one's mill. *See* MATTER. **2.** The most central and material part : core, essence, gist, heart, kernel, marrow, meat, nub, pith, quintessence, root[1], soul, spirit, substance. *Law:* gravamen. *See* BE. **3.** *Informal.* One's portable property : belonging (often used in plural), effect (used in plural), good (used in plural), lares and penates, personal effects, personal property, possession (used in plural), property, thing (often used in plural). *Law:* chattel, movable (often used in plural). *See* OWNED. **4.** The basic substance or essential elements of character that qualify a person for a specified role : material, timber. *See* BE.

stuff *verb* To fill to excess by compressing or squeezing tightly : cram, crowd, jam, load, mob, pack. *Informal:* jam-pack. *See* FULL, TIGHTEN.

stuffy *adjective*

1. Oppressive due to a lack of fresh air : airless, close, stifling. *See* BREATH, OPEN. **2.** Arousing no interest or curiosity : boring, drear, dreary, dry, dull, humdrum, irksome, monotonous, tedious, tiresome, uninteresting, weariful, wearisome, weary. *See* EXCITE. **3.** Marked by excessive concern for propriety and good form : bluenosed, genteel, old-maidish, precise, priggish, prim, prissy, proper, prudish, puritanical, strait-laced, Victorian. *Idiom:* prim and proper. *See* PLAIN.

stumble *verb*

1. To catch the foot against something and lose one's balance : trip. *Idioms:* lose one's footing, make a false step. *See* MOVE. **2.** To walk unsteadily : falter, lurch, reel, stagger, teeter, totter, weave, wobble. *See* MOVE. **3.** To move awkwardly or clumsily : blunder[1], bumble[1]. *See* ABILITY, MOVE. **4.** To proceed or perform in an unsteady, faltering manner : blunder, bumble[1], bungle, flounder, fudge, fumble, limp, muddle, shuffle, stagger. *See* THRIVE. **5.** To make an error or mistake : err, miscue, mistake, slip, slip up, trip up. *See* CORRECT.

stumble on (or **upon)** *verb* To find or meet by chance : bump into, chance on (*or* upon), come across, come on (*or* upon), find, happen on (*or* upon), light on (*or* upon), run across, run into, tumble on. *Archaic:* alight on (*or* upon). *Idiom:* meet up with. *See* MEET.

stumble *noun* A stupid, clumsy mistake : blunder, bull[2], bungle, foozle, fumble, muff. *Informal:* blooper, boner. *Slang:* bloomer, goof. *See* CORRECT.

stumble on or **upon** *verb* See **stumble.**

stump *verb*

1. To move heavily : clump, galumph, hulk, lumber, lump[1]. *See* MOVE. **2.** *Informal.* To prevent from accomplishing a purpose : baffle, balk, check, checkmate, defeat, foil, frustrate, stymie, thwart. *Informal:* cross. *Idiom:* cut the ground from under. *See* ALLOW. **3.** *Informal.* To make incapable of finding something to think, do, or say : confound, nonplus. *Informal:* flummox, stick, throw. *Slang:* beat. *Idiom:* put someone at a loss. *See* AFFECT, KNOWLEDGE.

stumpy *adjective*

Short, heavy, and solidly built : blocky, chunky, compact[1], dumpy, heavyset, squat, stocky, stodgy, stubby, thick, thickset. *See* FAT.

stun *verb*

1. To dull the senses, as with a heavy blow, a shock, or fatigue : bedaze, bemuse, benumb, daze, stupefy. *Chiefly Regional:* maze. *See* AWARENESS. **2.** To render helpless, as by emotion : benumb, numb, paralyze, petrify, stupefy, wither. *See* AFFECT.

stunner *noun*

1. One that evokes great surprise and admiration : astonishment, marvel, miracle, phenomenon, prodigy, sensation, wonder, wonderment. *Idioms:* one for the books, the eighth wonder of the world. *See* GOOD. **2.** A person regarded as physically attractive : beauty, belle (used of a woman), lovely. *Slang:* babe, doll, hunk (used of a man), knockout, looker, stud (used of a man). *See* BEAUTIFUL.

stunning *adjective*

Having qualities that delight the eye : attractive, beauteous, beautiful, comely, fair, good-looking, gorgeous, handsome, lovely, pretty, pulchritudinous, ravishing, sightly. *Scots:* bonny. *Idiom:* easy on the eyes. *See* BEAUTIFUL.

stunt *noun*

1. A great or heroic deed : achievement,

exploit, feat, gest, masterstroke, tour de force. *See* ACTION. **2.** A clever, dexterous act : feat, trick. *See* ABILITY, EXCITE, GOOD.

stupefaction *noun*
A stunned or bewildered condition : befuddlement, bewilderedness, bewilderment, daze, discombobulation, fog, muddle, mystification, perplexity, puzzlement, stupor, trance. *See* AWARENESS.

stupefy *verb*
1. To dull the senses, as with a heavy blow, a shock, or fatigue : bedaze, bemuse, benumb, daze, stun. *Chiefly Regional:* maze. *See* AWARENESS. **2.** To make or become less keen or responsive : dim, dull, hebetate. *See* AWARENESS. **3.** To render helpless, as by emotion : benumb, numb, paralyze, petrify, stun, wither. *See* AFFECT.

stupendous *adjective*
1. So remarkable as to elicit disbelief : amazing, astonishing, astounding, fabulous, fantastic, fantastical, incredible, marvelous, miraculous, phenomenal, prodigious, unbelievable, wonderful, wondrous. *See* GOOD. **2.** Of extraordinary size and power : behemoth, Brobdingnagian, Bunyanesque, colossal, cyclopean, elephantine, enormous, gargantuan, giant, gigantesque, gigantic, herculean, heroic, huge, immense, jumbo, mammoth, massive, massy, mastodonic, mighty, monster, monstrous, monumental, mountainous, prodigious, pythonic, titanic, tremendous, vast. *Informal:* walloping. *Slang:* whopping. *See* BIG.

stupendousness *noun*
The quality of being enormous : enormousness, hugeness, immenseness, immensity, prodigiousness, tremendousness, vastness. *See* BIG.

stupid *adjective*
1. Lacking mental and physical alertness and activity : hebetudinous, lethargic, sluggish, stuporous, torpid. *Slang:* dopey. *See* ACTION. **2.** Lacking in intelligence : blockheaded, dense, doltish, dumb, hebetudinous, obtuse, thickheaded, thick-witted. *Informal:* thick. *Slang:* dimwitted, dopey. *See* ABILITY.

stupor *noun*
1. A deficiency in mental and physical alertness and activity : dullness, hebetude, languidness, languor, lassitude, leadenness, lethargy, listlessness, sluggishness, torpidity, torpor. *See* ACTION. **2.** A stunned or bewildered condition : befuddlement, bewilderedness, bewilderment, daze, discombobulation, fog, muddle, mystification, perplexity, puzzlement, stupefaction, trance. *See* AWARENESS.

stuporous *adjective*
1. Lacking responsiveness or alertness : benumbed, dull, insensible, insensitive, numb, torpid, unresponsive, wooden. *See* AWARENESS. **2.** Lacking mental and physical alertness and activity : hebetudinous, lethargic, sluggish, stupid, torpid. *Slang:* dopey. *See* ACTION.

sturdiness *noun*
Reliability in withstanding pressure, force, or stress : fastness, firmness, hardness, security, soundness, stability, stableness, steadiness, strength, sureness. *See* BETTER, CHANGE, CONTINUE.

sturdy *adjective*
1. Characterized by marked muscular development; powerfully built : athletic, brawny, burly, husky[2], muscular, robust, sinewy. *See* STRONG. **2.** Capable of exerting considerable effort or of withstanding considerable stress or hardship : hardy, stalwart, stout, strong, tough. *See* STRONG. **3.** Not easily moved or shaken : firm[1], secure, solid, sound[2], stable, strong, substantial, sure, unshakable. *See* CONTINUE, STRONG. **4.** Full of vigor : able-bodied, iron, lusty, red-blooded, robust, strapping, vigorous, vital. *See* STRONG.

Sturm und Drang *noun*
A state of uneasiness and usually resentment brewing to an eventual explosion : ferment, turmoil, unrest. *See* CALM, PEACE.

stutter *verb*
To introduce involuntary repetitions and pauses into one's speech : stammer. *See* WORDS.
stutter *noun* A speech impediment marked by involuntary repetitions and pauses : stammer, stammering, stuttering. *See* WORDS.

stuttering *noun*
A speech impediment marked by involuntary repetitions and pauses : stammer, stammering, stutter. *See* WORDS.

style *noun*
1. A distinctive way of expressing oneself : fashion, manner, mode, tone, vein. *See* STYLE. **2.** The approach used to do something : fashion, manner, method, mode, modus operandi, system, way, wise[2]. *See* MEANS. **3.** Behavior through which one reveals one's personality : address, air, bearing, demeanor, manner, mien, presence. *Archaic:* port. *See* BE, STYLE. **4.** The current custom : craze, fad, fashion, furor, mode, rage, trend, vogue. *Informal:* thing. *Idioms:* the in thing, the last word, the latest thing. *See* STYLE, USUAL. **5.** The word or words by which one is called and identified : appellation, appellative, cognomen, denomina-

tion, designation, epithet, name, nickname, tag, title. *Slang:* handle, moniker. *See* SPECIFIC, WORDS.

style *verb* **1.** To give a name or title to : baptize, call, christen, denominate, designate, dub, entitle, name, term, title. *See* SPECIFIC, WORDS. **2.** To describe with a word or term : call, characterize, designate, label, name, tag, term. *See* SPECIFIC, WORDS.

stylish *adjective*
Being or in accordance with the current fashion : à la mode, chic, dashing, fashionable, mod, modish, posh, smart, swank, swanky, trig. *Informal:* classy, in, sharp, snappy, swish, tony, trendy. *Slang:* with-it. ***Idioms:*** all the rage, up to the minute. *See* STYLE, USUAL.

stylize *verb*
To make conventional : conform, conventionalize. *See* USUAL.

stymie *verb*
To prevent from accomplishing a purpose : baffle, balk, check, checkmate, defeat, foil, frustrate, thwart. *Informal:* cross, stump. ***Idiom:*** cut the ground from under. *See* ALLOW.

suave *adjective*
Effortlessly gracious and tactful in social manner : bland, smooth, urbane. *See* STYLE.

sub *noun*
Informal. One that takes the place of another : alternate, replacement, stand-in, substitute, surrogate. *Informal:* fill-in, pinch hitter. *See* SUBSTITUTE.

sub *verb* *Informal.* To act as a substitute : fill in, stand in, substitute, supply. *Informal:* pinch-hit. *See* SUBSTITUTE.

subaltern *adjective*
Below another in standing or importance : inferior, junior, lesser, low, lower[2], minor, minor-league, petty, secondary, small, subordinate, under. *Informal:* smalltime. *See* OVER.

subaltern *noun* One belonging to a lower class or rank : inferior, junior, secondary, subordinate, underling. *See* OVER.

subdivide *verb*
To separate into branches or branchlike parts : bifurcate, branch (out), diverge, divide, fork, ramify. *See* PART.

subdivision *noun*
1. One of the parts into which something is divided : division, member, part, piece, portion, section, segment. *See* PART. **2.** A part of a family, tribe, or other group, or of such a group's language, that is believed to stem from a common ancestor : branch, division, offshoot. *See* PART.

subdue *verb*
1. To win a victory over, as in battle or a competition : beat, best, conquer, defeat, master, overcome, prevail against (*or* over), rout, subjugate, surmount, triumph over, vanquish, worst. *Informal:* trim, whip. *Slang:* ace, lick. ***Idioms:*** carry (*or* win) the day, get (*or* have) the best of, get (*or* have) the better of, go someone one better. *See* WIN. **2.** To make or become less severe or extreme : moderate, mute, qualify, soften, tame, temper, tone down. *See* INCREASE.

subdued *adjective*
1. Not irritating, strident, or loud : hushed, low, low-key, low-keyed, quiet, small, soft, whispery. *See* SOUNDS. **2.** Not showy or obtrusive : inobtrusive, quiet, restrained, tasteful, unobtrusive. *See* PLAIN.

subject *adjective*
1. In a position of subordination : collateral, dependent, subordinate, subservient. *See* OVER, PART. **2.** Tending to incur : liable, open, prone, susceptible, susceptive, vulnerable. *See* LIKELY. **3.** Determined or to be determined by someone or something else : conditional, conditioned, contingent, dependent, relative, reliant. *See* START.

subject *noun* **1.** A person owing loyalty to and entitled to the protection of a given state : citizen, national. *See* GROUP, POLITICS. **2.** What a speech, piece of writing, or artistic work is about : argument, matter, point, subject matter, text, theme, topic. *See* MEANING. **3.** A sphere of activity, experience, study, or interest : area, arena, bailiwick, circle, department, domain, field, orbit, province, realm, scene, terrain, territory, world. *Slang:* bag. *See* TERRITORY.

subject *verb* **1.** To lay open, as to something undesirable or injurious : expose. ***Idiom:*** open the door to. *See* PROTECTION. **2.** To make subservient or subordinate : enslave, enthrall, subjugate. *See* FREE.

subjective *adjective*
Based on individual judgment or discretion : arbitrary, discretionary, judgmental, personal. *See* OPINION, SURPRISE.

subject matter *noun*
What a speech, piece of writing, or artistic work is about : argument, matter, point, subject, text, theme, topic. *See* MEANING.

subjoin *verb*
To add as a supplement or an appendix : affix, annex, append, attach. *See* INCREASE.

subjugate *verb*
1. To win a victory over, as in battle or a com-

petition : beat, best, conquer, defeat, master, overcome, prevail against (*or* over), rout, subdue, surmount, triumph over, vanquish, worst. *Informal:* trim, whip. *Slang:* ace, lick. ***Idioms:*** carry (*or* win) the day, get (*or* have) the best of, get (*or* have) the better of, go someone one better. *See* WIN. **2.** To make subservient or subordinate : enslave, enthrall, subject. *See* FREE.

sublime *adjective*
Large and impressive in size, scope, or extent : august, baronial, grand, grandiose, imposing, lordly, magnific, magnificent, majestic, noble, princely, regal, royal, splendid, stately, superb. *See* BIG, GOOD.

submerge *verb*
1. To plunge briefly in or into a liquid : dip, douse, duck, dunk, immerge, immerse, souse, submerse. *See* ENTER. **2.** To go beneath the surface or to the bottom of a liquid : founder[1], sink, submerse. *See* RISE. **3.** To flow over completely : deluge, drown, engulf, flood, flush, inundate, overflow, overwhelm, whelm. *See* FULL. **4.** To conceal in obscurity : hide[1], obscure. *See* SHOW.

submerse *verb*
1. To plunge briefly in or into a liquid : dip, douse, duck, dunk, immerge, immerse, souse, submerge. *See* ENTER. **2.** To go beneath the surface or to the bottom of a liquid : founder[1], sink, submerge. *See* RISE.

submission *noun*
1. The act of submitting or surrendering to the power of another : capitulation, surrender. *See* RESIST, WIN. **2.** The quality or state of willingly carrying out the wishes of others : acquiescence, amenability, amenableness, compliance, compliancy, deference, obedience, submissiveness, tractability, tractableness. *See* RESIST. **3.** Something that is put forward for consideration : proposal, proposition, suggestion. *See* OFFER.

submissive *adjective*
1. Submitting without objection or resistance : acquiescent, nonresistant, passive, resigned. *See* RESIST. **2.** Willing to carry out the wishes of others : amenable, biddable, compliant, conformable, docile, obedient, supple, tractable. *See* RESIST.

submissiveness *noun*
The quality or state of willingly carrying out the wishes of others : acquiescence, amenability, amenableness, compliance, compliancy, deference, obedience, submission, tractability, tractableness. *See* RESIST.

submit *verb*
1. To conform to the will or judgment of another, especially out of respect or courtesy : bow[1], defer[2], yield. ***Idioms:*** give ground, give way. *See* PRECEDE, RESIST. **2.** To give in from or as if from a gradual loss of strength : bow[1], buckle, capitulate, succumb, surrender, yield. *Informal:* fold. *See* RESIST. **3.** To commit to the consideration or judgment of another : turn in. *See* GIVE. **4.** To state, as an idea, for consideration : advance, offer, pose, propose, propound, put forward, set forth, suggest. *See* OFFER.

subordinate *adjective*
1. Below another in standing or importance : inferior, junior, lesser, low, lower[2], minor, minor-league, petty, secondary, small, subaltern, under. *Informal:* smalltime. *See* OVER. **2.** In a position of subordination : collateral, dependent, subject, subservient. *See* OVER, PART.

subordinate *noun* One belonging to a lower class or rank : inferior, junior, secondary, subaltern, underling. *See* OVER.

sub rosa *adverb*
In a secret way : clandestinely, covertly, huggermugger, secretly. ***Idioms:*** by stealth, on the sly, under cover. *See* SHOW.

sub-rosa *adjective* Existing or operating in a way so as to ensure complete concealment and confidentiality : clandestine, cloak-and-dagger, covert, huggermugger, secret, undercover. *Informal:* hush-hush. ***Idiom:*** under wraps. *See* SHOW.

subscribe *verb*
1. To give in common with others : chip in, contribute, donate. *Informal:* kick in. *Slang:* come across. *See* GIVE. **2.** To respond affirmatively; receive with agreement or compliance : accede, accept, acquiesce, agree, assent, consent, nod, yes. *See* AGREE. **3.** To affix one's signature to : autograph, endorse, inscribe, sign, undersign. ***Idioms:*** put one's John Hancock on, set one's hand to. *See* LAW.

subscription *noun*
Something given to a charity or cause : alms, benefaction, beneficence, charity, contribution, donation, gift, handout, offering. *See* GIVE.

subsequent *adjective*
1. Following something else in time : after, later, posterior, ulterior. *See* PRECEDE. **2.** Being or occurring in the time ahead : coming, future, later. *See* PRECEDE, TIME. **3.** Following one after another in an orderly pattern : consecutive, sequent, sequential, serial, successional, successive. *See* PRECEDE, TIME.

subsequently *adverb*
At a subsequent time : after, afterward, afterwards, later, latterly, next, ulteriorly. ***Idioms:*** after a while, by and by, later on. *See* PRECEDE.

subservient *adjective*
1. In a position of subordination : collateral, dependent, subject, subordinate. *See* OVER, PART. **2.** Excessively eager to serve or obey : menial, obsequious, servile, slavish. *See* OVER.

subside *verb*
To become or cause to become less active or intense : abate, bate, die (away, down, off, *or* out), ease (off *or* up), ebb, fall, fall off, lapse, let up, moderate, remit, slacken, slack off, wane. *See* INCREASE.

subsidence *noun*
The act or process of becoming less active or intense : abatement, ebb, letup, remission, slackening, wane. *See* INCREASE.

subsidiary *adjective*
Giving or able to give help or support : accessory, ancillary, assistant, auxiliary, collateral, contributory, supportive. *See* HELP.
subsidiary *noun* A local unit of a business or an auxiliary controlled by such a business : affiliate, branch, division. *See* PART.

subsidization *noun*
Money or property used to produce more wealth : backing, capital, capitalization, financing, funding, grubstake, stake. *See* HELP, MONEY.

subsidize *verb*
To supply capital to or for : back, capitalize, finance, fund, grubstake, stake. *Informal:* bankroll. ***Idiom:*** put up money for. *See* HELP, MONEY.

subsidy *noun*
Something, as a gift, granted for a definite purpose : appropriation, grant, subvention. *See* GIVE.

subsist *verb*
1. To have being or actuality : be, exist. *See* BE. **2.** To have reality or life : be, breathe, exist, live[1]. *See* BE. **3.** To maintain existence in a certain way : feed, live[1]. *See* INGESTION.

subsistence *noun*
The means needed to support life : alimentation, alimony, bread, bread and butter, keep, livelihood, living, maintenance, support, sustenance, upkeep. *See* MONEY.

substance *noun*
1. That which occupies space and can be perceived by the senses : materiality, matter. *See* BODY. **2.** That from which things are or can be made : material, matter, stuff. ***Idiom:*** grist for one's mill. *See* MATTER. **3.** A basic trait or set of traits that define and establish the character of something : being, essence, essentiality, nature, quintessence, texture. *See* SURFACE. **4.** The most central and material part : core, essence, gist, heart, kernel, marrow, meat, nub, pith, quintessence, root[1], soul, spirit, stuff. *Law:* gravamen. *See* BE. **5.** The general sense or significance, as of an action or statement : amount, burden[2], drift, import, purport, tenor. ***Idioms:*** sum and substance, sum total. *See* MEANING. **6.** The thread or current of thought uniting or occurring in all the elements of a text or discourse : aim, burden[2], drift, intent, meaning, purport, tendency, tenor, thrust. *See* MEANING.

substandard *adjective*
Of low or lower quality : common, inferior, low-grade, low-quality, mean[2], mediocre, second-class, second-rate, shabby. *See* BETTER.

substantial *adjective*
1. Composed of or relating to things that occupy space and can be perceived by the senses : concrete, corporeal, material, objective, phenomenal, physical, sensible, tangible. *See* BODY, MATTER. **2.** Having verifiable existence : concrete, objective, real, substantive, tangible. *See* REAL. **3.** Not easily moved or shaken : firm[1], secure, solid, sound[2], stable, strong, sturdy, sure, unshakable. *See* CONTINUE, STRONG. **4.** Characterized by abundance : abundant, ample, bounteous, bountiful, copious, generous, heavy, plenitudinous, plenteous, plentiful, voluminous. *See* BIG, GIVE, RICH. **5.** Having great significance : big, consequential, considerable, historic, important, large, material, meaningful, monumental, significant. *See* IMPORTANT.

substantiate *verb*
1. To present evidence in support of : back (up), buttress, corroborate. *See* SUPPORT. **2.** To assure the certainty or validity of : attest, authenticate, back (up), bear out, confirm, corroborate, evidence, justify, testify (to), validate, verify, warrant. *See* SUPPORT, TRUE. **3.** To establish as true or genuine : authenticate, bear out, confirm, corroborate, demonstrate, endorse, establish, evidence, prove, show, validate, verify. *See* SHOW, SUPPORT. **4.** To represent (an abstraction, for example) in or as if in bodily form : body forth, embody, exteriorize, externalize, incarnate, manifest, materialize, objectify, personalize, personify. *See* SUBSTITUTE.

substantiation *noun*
1. That which confirms : attestation, authentication, confirmation, corroboration, demonstration, evidence, proof, testament, testimonial, testimony, validation, verification, warrant. *See* TRUE. **2.** A physical entity typifying an abstraction : embodiment, exteriorization, externalization, incarnation, manifestation, materialization, objectification, personalization, personification, type. *Rhetoric:* prosopopeia. *See* SUBSTITUTE.

substantive *adjective*
Having verifiable existence : concrete, objective, real, substantial, tangible. *See* REAL.

substitute *noun*
One that takes the place of another : alternate, replacement, stand-in, surrogate. *Informal:* fill-in, pinch hitter, sub. *See* SUBSTITUTE.
substitute *verb* **1.** To give up in return for something else : change, commute, exchange, interchange, shift, switch, trade. *Informal:* swap. *See* CHANGE, SUBSTITUTE. **2.** To act as a substitute : fill in, stand in, supply. *Informal:* pinch-hit, sub. *See* SUBSTITUTE.

substitution *noun*
The act of exchanging or substituting : change, commutation, exchange, interchange, shift, switch, trade, transposition. *Informal:* swap. *See* CHANGE, SUBSTITUTE.

substratum *noun*
The lowest or supporting part or structure : base[1], basis, bed, bottom, foot, footing, foundation, fundament, ground, groundwork, seat, underpinning (often used in plural). *See* OVER.

subsume *verb*
To have as a part : comprehend, comprise, contain, embody, embrace, encompass, have, include, involve, take in. *See* INCLUDE.

subterfuge *noun*
An indirect, usually cunning means of gaining an end : artifice, deception, device, dodge, feint, gimmick, imposture, jig, maneuver, ploy, ruse, sleight, stratagem, trick, wile. *Informal:* shenanigan, take-in. *See* HONEST, MEANS.

subterranean *adjective*
Located or operating beneath the earth's surface : hypogeal, hypogean, hypogeous, subterrestrial, underground. *See* SURFACE.

subterrestrial *adjective*
Located or operating beneath the earth's surface : hypogeal, hypogean, hypogeous, subterranean, underground. *See* SURFACE.

subtle *adjective*
1. So slight as to be difficult to notice or appreciate : delicate, fine[1], finespun, nice, refined. *See* BIG. **2.** Able to make or detect effects of great subtlety or precision : delicate, fine[1], nice. *See* PRECISE.

subtract *verb*
To take away (a quantity) from another quantity : abate, deduct, discount, rebate, take (off). *Informal:* knock off. *See* INCREASE.

suburb *noun*
The periphery of a city or town. Used in plural : edge, environs, fringe, outskirt (often used in plural), skirt (used in plural). *See* EDGE.

subvention *noun*
Something, as a gift, granted for a definite purpose : appropriation, grant, subsidy. *See* GIVE.

subversion *noun*
A deliberate and underhanded effort to defeat or do harm to an endeavor : sabotage, undermining. *See* ATTACK.

subvert *verb*
1. To bring about the downfall of : bring down, overthrow, overturn, topple, tumble, unhorse. *See* HELP. **2.** To damage, destroy, or defeat by sabotage : sabotage, undermine. *See* ATTACK.

succeed *verb*
1. To occur after in time : ensue, follow, supervene. ***Idiom:*** follow on (*or* upon) the heels of. *See* PRECEDE, TIME. **2.** To gain success : arrive, get ahead, get on, go far, rise. ***Idioms:*** go places, make good, make it. *See* THRIVE. **3.** To turn out well : come off, go, go over, pan out, work, work out. *Slang:* click. *See* THRIVE.

success *noun*
The achievement of something desired, planned, or attempted : arrival, successfulness. *See* THRIVE.

successfulness *noun*
The achievement of something desired, planned, or attempted : arrival, success. *See* THRIVE.

succession *noun*
1. A way in which things follow each other in space or time : consecution, order, procession, sequence. *See* ORDER, PRECEDE. **2.** A number of things placed or occurring one after the other : chain, consecution, course, order, procession, progression, round, run, sequence, series, string, suite, train. *Informal:* streak. *See* ORDER.

successional *adjective*
Following one after another in an orderly pattern : consecutive, sequent, sequential, serial, subsequent, successive. *See* PRECEDE, TIME.

successive *adjective*
Following one after another in an orderly pattern : consecutive, sequent, sequential, serial, subsequent, successional. *See* PRECEDE, TIME.

succinct *adjective*
Marked by or consisting of few words that are carefully chosen : brief, compendious, concise, laconic, lean[2], short, summary, terse. *See* BIG, STYLE, WORDS.

succor *noun*
The act or an instance of helping : abetment, aid, assist, assistance, hand, help, relief, support. *See* HELP.
succor *verb* To give support or assistance : abet, aid, assist, boost, help (out), relieve. ***Idioms:*** give (*or* lend) a hand, give a leg up. *See* HELP.

succorer *noun*
A person who helps : abettor, aid, attendant, help, helper, reliever. *See* HELP.

succumb *verb*
1. To give in from or as if from a gradual loss of strength : bow[1], buckle, capitulate, submit, surrender, yield. *Informal:* fold. *See* RESIST. **2.** To suddenly lose all health or strength : break (down), cave in, collapse, crack, drop, give out. *Informal:* crack up. *Slang:* conk out. ***Idiom:*** give way. *See* HEALTH. **3.** To cease living : decease, demise, depart, die, drop, expire, go, pass away, pass (on), perish. *Informal:* pop off. *Slang:* check out, croak, kick in, kick off. ***Idioms:*** bite the dust, breathe one's last, cash in, give up the ghost, go to one's grave, kick the bucket, meet one's end (*or* Maker), pass on to the Great Beyond, turn up one's toes. *See* LIVE.

suck *verb*
To draw in so that extrication is difficult : catch up, embrangle, embroil, implicate, involve, mix up. *See* FREE, PARTICIPATE.
suck up *verb* *Slang.* To support slavishly every opinion or suggestion of a superior : bootlick, cringe, fawn, grovel, kowtow, slaver, toady, truckle. *Informal:* apple-polish, brownnose, cotton. ***Idioms:*** curry favor, dance attendance, kiss someone's feet, lick someone's boots. *See* OVER.

sucker *noun*
Informal. A person who is easily deceived or victimized : butt[3], dupe, fool, gull, lamb, pushover, victim. *Slang:* fall guy, gudgeon, mark, monkey, patsy, pigeon, sap[1]. *Chiefly British:* mug. *See* WISE.

suck up *verb* See **suck.**

sudden *adjective*
Happening quickly and without warning : abrupt, hurried, precipitant, precipitate. *See* FAST, SURPRISE.

suddenly *adverb*
Without any warning : abruptly, short. ***Idiom:*** all of a sudden. *See* FAST.

sudoriferous *adjective*
Producing or covered with sweat : perspiring, sweating, sweaty. *See* DRY.

suds *noun*
A mass of bubbles in or on the surface of a liquid : foam, froth, head, lather, spume, yeast. *See* SOLID.
suds *verb* To form or cause to form foam : bubble, cream, effervesce, fizz, foam, froth, lather, spume, yeast. *See* SOLID.

sudsy *adjective*
Consisting of or resembling foam : foamy, frothy, lathery, spumous, spumy, yeasty. *See* SOLID.

sue *verb*
1. To institute or subject to legal proceedings : law, litigate, prosecute. ***Idiom:*** bring suit. *See* LAW. **2.** To make an earnest or urgent request : appeal, beg, beseech, crave, entreat, implore, plead, pray, supplicate. *Archaic:* conjure. *See* ASK. **3.** *Law.* To make application to a higher authority, as to a court of law : petition. *Law:* appeal. *See* LAW. **4.** *Obsolete.* To bring an appeal or request, for example, to the attention of : address, appeal, apply, approach, petition. *See* REQUEST.

suet *noun*
Adipose tissue : fat. *See* FAT.

suffer *verb*
1. To feel, show, or express grief : grieve, lament, mourn, sorrow. *See* HAPPY. **2.** To participate in or partake of personally : experience, feel, go through, have, know, meet[1] (with), see, taste (of), undergo. *Archaic:* prove. ***Idiom:*** run up against. *See* PARTICIPATE. **3.** To put up with : abide, accept, bear, brook[2], endure, go, stand (for), stomach, support, sustain, swallow, take, tolerate, withstand. *Informal:* lump[2]. ***Idioms:*** take it, take it lying down. *See* ACCEPT. **4.** To neither forbid nor prevent : allow, have, let, permit, tolerate. *See* ALLOW.

sufferable *adjective*
Capable of being tolerated : bearable, endurable, tolerable. *See* CONTINUE.

suffering *noun*
A state of prolonged anguish and privation : misery, woe, wretchedness. *See* HAPPY.
suffering *adjective* Having a painful ailment : afflicted, miserable, wretched. *See* HAPPY.

suffice *verb*
To meet a need or requirement : answer, do, serve, suit. *See* EXCESS, HELP.

sufficiency *noun*
An adequate quantity : adequacy, enough. *See* EXCESS.

sufficient *adjective*
1. Being what is needed without being in excess : adequate, comfortable, competent, decent, enough, satisfactory. *See* EXCESS. **2.** Of moderately good quality but less than excellent : acceptable, adequate, all right, average, common, decent, fair, fairish, goodish, moderate, passable, respectable, satisfactory, tolerable. *Informal:* OK, tidy. *See* GOOD.

suffocate *verb*
To stop the breathing of : asphyxiate, choke, smother, stifle. *See* BREATH.

suffrage *noun*
The right or chance to express an opinion or participate in a decision : say, voice, vote. *Informal:* say-so. *See* PARTICIPATE.

suffuse *verb*
To cause to be filled, as with a particular mood or tone : charge, freight, imbue, impregnate, permeate, pervade, saturate, transfuse. *See* FULL.

sugar *verb*
To make superficially more acceptable or appealing : candy, gild, honey, sugarcoat, sweeten. *See* LIKE.

sugarcoat *verb*
1. To make superficially more acceptable or appealing : candy, gild, honey, sugar, sweeten. *See* LIKE. **2.** To give a deceptively attractive appearance to : color, gild, gloss (over), gloze (over), varnish, veneer, whitewash. ***Idioms:*** paper over, put a good face on. *See* TRUE.

sugary *adjective*
1. Having or suggesting the taste of sugar : saccharine, sweet. *See* TASTE. **2.** Purposefully contrived to gain favor : ingratiating, ingratiatory, insinuating, saccharine. *See* PAIN.

suggest *verb*
1. To state, as an idea, for consideration : advance, offer, pose, propose, propound, put forward, set forth, submit. *See* OFFER. **2.** To lead to by logical inference : imply, indicate, point to. *See* MEANING. **3.** To convey an idea by indirect, subtle means : hint, imply, insinuate, intimate[2]. ***Idiom:*** drop a hint. *See* SHOW, SUGGEST. **4.** To have a particular flavor or suggestion of something : savor, smack[2], smell, taste. *See* SUGGEST.

suggestible *adjective*
Easily altered or influenced : ductile, elastic, flexible, flexile, impressionable, malleable, plastic, pliable, pliant, supple. *See* FLEXIBLE.

suggestion *noun*
1. Something that is put forward for consideration : proposal, proposition, submission. *See* OFFER. **2.** Something, such as a feeling, thought, or idea, associated in one's mind or imagination with a specific person or thing : association, connection, connotation. *See* SUGGEST. **3.** A subtle pointing out : clue, cue, hint, intimation. *See* KNOWLEDGE, SUGGEST. **4.** A slight amount or indication : breath, dash, ghost, hair, hint, intimation, semblance, shade, shadow, soupçon, streak, suspicion, taste, tinge, touch, trace, whiff, whisper. *Informal:* whisker. *See* BIG, SHOW.

suggestive *adjective*
1. Tending to bring a memory, mood, or image, for example, subtly or indirectly to mind : allusive, connotative, evocative, impressionistic, reminiscent. *See* SUGGEST. **2.** Provoking a change of outlook and especially gradual doubt and suspicion : insinuating, insinuative, insinuatory. *See* SUGGEST. **3.** Conveying hidden or unexpressed meaning : meaningful, pregnant, significant. *See* MEANING. **4.** Bordering on indelicacy or impropriety : blue, earthy, off-color, provocative, racy, risqué, salty, scabrous, spicy. *See* DECENT. **5.** Suggesting sexuality : sensual, sexual, sexy, voluptuous. *See* SEX.

suggestiveness *noun*
The quality or condition of being sensual : sensuality, sexiness, sexuality, voluptuousness. *See* SEX.

suit *noun*
1. A legal proceeding to demand justice or enforce a right : action, case, cause, instance, lawsuit. *See* LAW. **2.** Romantic attentions : address (often used in plural), courtship. *See* SEEK, SEX.
suit *verb* **1.** To meet a need or requirement : answer, do, serve, suffice. *See* EXCESS, HELP. **2.** To make or become suitable to a particular situation or use : acclimate, acclimatize, accommodate, adapt, adjust, conform, fashion, fit[1], reconcile, square, tailor. *See* CHANGE. **3.** To be in keeping with : become, befit, conform, correspond, fit[1], go with, match. *See* AGREE. **4.** To be appropriate or suitable to : become, befit, behoove. *Archaic:* beseem. *See* AGREE. **5.** To look good on or with : become, enhance, flatter. ***Idiom:*** put in the best light. *See*

AGREE, BEAUTIFUL. **6.** To be satisfactory to : please, satisfy. *See* PAIN.

suitability *noun*
The quality or state of being eligible : eligibility, fitness, qualification, suitableness, worthiness. *See* ABILITY.

suitable *adjective*
1. Suited to one's end or purpose : appropriate, befitting, convenient, expedient, fit[1], good, meet[2], proper, tailor-made, useful. *See* AGREE, GOOD. **2.** Consistent with prevailing or accepted standards or circumstances : appropriate, deserved, due, fit[1], fitting, just, merited, proper, right, rightful. *See* RIGHT. **3.** Satisfying certain requirements, as for selection : eligible, fit[1], fitted, qualified, worthy. *See* ABILITY.

suitableness *noun*
The quality or state of being eligible : eligibility, fitness, qualification, suitability, worthiness. *See* ABILITY.

suite *noun*
1. A group of attendants or followers : entourage, following, retinue, train. *See* OVER. **2.** A number of things placed or occurring one after the other : chain, consecution, course, order, procession, progression, round, run, sequence, series, string, succession, train. *Informal:* streak. *See* ORDER.

suitor *noun*
1. A man who courts a woman : admirer, beau, courter, swain, wooer. *See* SEX. **2.** One that asks a higher authority for something, as a favor or redress : appealer, appellant, petitioner. *See* ASK, LAW. **3.** One who humbly entreats : beggar, prayer[2], suppliant, supplicant. *See* REQUEST.

sulk *verb*
To be sullenly aloof or withdrawn, as in silent resentment or protest : mope, pet[2], pout. *See* HAPPY.

sulky *adjective*
Broodingly and sullenly unhappy : dour, gloomy, glum, moody, morose, saturnine, sour, sullen, surly. *See* HAPPY.

sullen *adjective*
1. Broodingly and sullenly unhappy : dour, gloomy, glum, moody, morose, saturnine, sour, sulky, surly. *See* HAPPY. **2.** Characterized by or expressive of a foreboding somberness : dark, lowery. *See* WARN.

sully *verb*
1. To make dirty : befoul, begrime, besmirch, besoil, black, blacken, defile, dirty, smudge, smutch, soil. *See* CLEAN. **2.** To contaminate the reputation of : befoul, besmear, besmirch, bespatter, blacken, cloud, denigrate, dirty, smear, smudge, smut, soil, spatter, stain, taint, tarnish. ***Idioms:*** give a black eye to, sling (*or* throw) mud on. *See* ATTACK, CLEAN.

sultry *adjective*
1. Damp and warm : humid, muggy, soggy, sticky. *See* DRY, HOT. **2.** Marked by much heat : ardent, baking, blistering, boiling, broiling, burning, fiery, heated, hot, red-hot, roasting, scalding, scorching, searing, sizzling, sweltering, torrid. *See* HOT.

sum *noun*
1. A number or quantity obtained as a result of addition : aggregate, amount, summation, sum total, total, totality. *Archaic:* tale. *See* COUNT. **2.** An amount or quantity from which nothing is left out or held back : aggregate, all, entirety, everything, gross, total, totality, whole. *Informal:* work (used in plural). ***Idioms:*** everything but (*or* except) the kitchen sink; lock, stock, and barrel; the whole ball of wax (*or* kit and caboodle *or* megillah *or* nine yards *or* shebang). *See* PART. **3.** An organized array of individual elements and parts forming and working as a unit : entity, integral, system, totality, whole. *See* PART. **4.** A condensation of the essential or main points of something : recapitulation, rundown, run-through, summary, summation, summing-up, wrap-up. *Informal:* recap. *See* WORDS.

sum *verb* To combine (figures) to form a sum. Also used with *up* : add (up), cast, foot (up), tot[2] (up), total, totalize. *See* INCREASE.

sum up *verb* To give a recapitulation of the salient facts of : abstract, epitomize, go over, recapitulate, review, run down, run through, summarize, synopsize, wrap up. *Informal:* recap. *See* THOUGHTS.

summarize *verb*
To give a recapitulation of the salient facts of : abstract, epitomize, go over, recapitulate, review, run down, run through, sum up, synopsize, wrap up. *Informal:* recap. *See* THOUGHTS.

summary *adjective*
Marked by or consisting of few words that are carefully chosen : brief, compendious, concise, laconic, lean[2], short, succinct, terse. *See* BIG, STYLE, WORDS.

summary *noun* A condensation of the essential or main points of something : recapitulation, rundown, run-through, sum, summation, summing-up, wrap-up. *Informal:* recap. *See* WORDS.

summation *noun*
1. The act or process of adding : addition, totalization. *See* INCREASE. 2. A number or quantity obtained as a result of addition : aggregate, amount, sum, sum total, total, totality. *Archaic:* tale. *See* COUNT. 3. A condensation of the essential or main points of something : recapitulation, rundown, run-through, sum, summary, summing-up, wrap-up. *Informal:* recap. *See* WORDS.

summer *noun*
The season occurring between spring and autumn : summertime. *See* TIME.

summertime *noun*
The season occurring between spring and autumn : summer. *See* TIME.

summing-up *noun*
A condensation of the essential or main points of something : recapitulation, rundown, run-through, sum, summary, summation, wrap-up. *Informal:* recap. *See* WORDS.

summit *noun*
1. The highest point : apex, cap, crest, crown, height, peak, roof, top, vertex. *See* HIGH.
2. The highest point or state : acme, apex, apogee, climax, crest, crown, culmination, height, meridian, peak, pinnacle, top, zenith. *Informal:* payoff. *Medicine:* fastigium. *See* HIGH.

summon *verb*
1. To bring together : assemble, call, cluster, collect[1], congregate, convene, convoke, gather, get together, group, muster, round up. *See* COLLECT. 2. To demand to appear, come, or assemble : call, convene, convoke, muster, send for. *See* REQUEST. 3. To call forth or bring out (something latent, hidden, or unexpressed) : draw (out), educe, elicit, evoke. *See* SHOW.

sumptuous *adjective*
Characterized by extravagant, ostentatious magnificence : lavish, lush[1], luxuriant, luxurious, opulent, palatial, plush, rich. *Informal:* plushy. *See* RICH.

sumptuousness *noun*
Brilliant, showy splendor : brilliance, brilliancy, glitter, glory, gorgeousness, magnificence, resplendence, resplendency, sparkle. *Informal:* glitz. *See* BEAUTIFUL.

sum total *noun*
A number or quantity obtained as a result of addition : aggregate, amount, sum, summation, total, totality. *Archaic:* tale. *See* COUNT.

sum up *verb* See **sum.**

sunder *verb*
To crack or split into two or more fragments by means of or as a result of force, a blow, or strain : break, fracture, rift, rive, shatter, shiver[2], smash, splinter. *See* HELP.

sundries *noun*
Articles too small or numerous to be specified : etcetera (used in plural), oddment (used in plural), odds and ends. *See* THING.

sundry *adjective*
1. Consisting of a number of different kinds : assorted, divers, diverse, diversified, heterogeneous, miscellaneous, mixed, motley, multifarious, multiform, varied, variegated, various. *Biology:* polymorphic, polymorphous. *See* SAME. 2. Consisting of a number more than two or three but less than many : divers, several, some, various. *See* BIG.

sunken *adjective*
Curving inward : cavernous, concave, hollow, indented. *See* CONVEX.

sunny *adjective*
1. Free from clouds or mist, for example : clear, cloudless, fair, fine[1], unclouded. *See* CLEAR. 2. Being in or showing good spirits : bright, cheerful, cheery, chipper, happy, lighthearted. *See* HAPPY.

sunrise *noun*
The first appearance of daylight in the morning : aurora, cockcrow, dawn, dawning, daybreak, morn, morning, sunup. *See* START.

sunup *noun*
The first appearance of daylight in the morning : aurora, cockcrow, dawn, dawning, daybreak, morn, morning, sunrise. *See* START.

sup *verb*
To take into the mouth and swallow (a liquid) : drink, imbibe, pull on, quaff, sip. *Informal:* swig, toss down (*or* off). *Slang:* belt. ***Idiom:*** wet one's whistle. *See* MOUTH.

sup *noun* An act of drinking or the amount swallowed : draft, drink, potation, pull, quaff, sip, swill. *Informal:* swig. *Slang:* belt. *See* MOUTH.

super *adjective*
Informal. Particularly excellent : divine, fabulous, fantastic, fantastical, glorious, marvelous, sensational, splendid, superb, terrific, wonderful. *Informal:* dandy, dreamy, great, ripping, swell, tremendous. *Slang:* cool, groovy, hot, keen[1], neat, nifty. ***Idiom:*** out of this world. *See* GOOD.

super *adverb* *Informal.* Too much : overly, overmuch, unduly. *See* EXCESS.

superabundance *noun*
A condition of going or being beyond what is needed, desired, or appropriate : embarrassment, excess, excessiveness, exorbitance, extravagance, extravagancy, extravagantness, overabundance, plethora, superfluity, superfluousness, surfeit. *See* EXCESS.

superabundant *adjective*
Given to or marked by unrestrained abundance : extravagant, exuberant, lavish, lush[1], luxuriant, opulent, prodigal, profuse, riotous. *See* BIG, EXCESS.

superannuate *verb*
1. To remove from active service : pension (off), retire. ***Idiom:*** put out to pasture. *See* KEEP. **2.** To make or become obsolete : obsolesce, obsolete, outdate. *See* NEW, USED.

superb *adjective*
1. Exceptionally good of its kind : ace, banner, blue-ribbon, brag, capital, champion, excellent, fine[1], first-class, first-rate, prime, quality, splendid, superior, terrific, tiptop, top. *Informal:* A-one, bully, dandy, great, swell, top-flight, topnotch. *Slang:* boss. *Chiefly British:* tophole. *See* GOOD. **2.** Particularly excellent : divine, fabulous, fantastic, fantastical, glorious, marvelous, sensational, splendid, terrific, wonderful. *Informal:* dandy, dreamy, great, ripping, super, swell, tremendous. *Slang:* cool, groovy, hot, keen[1], neat, nifty. ***Idiom:*** out of this world. *See* GOOD. **3.** Large and impressive in size, scope, or extent : august, baronial, grand, grandiose, imposing, lordly, magnific, magnificent, majestic, noble, princely, regal, royal, splendid, stately, sublime. *See* BIG, GOOD.

superbness *noun*
The quality of being exceptionally good of its kind : excellence, fineness, superiority. *See* GOOD.

supercilious *adjective*
Overly convinced of one's own superiority and importance : arrogant, haughty, high-and-mighty, insolent, lofty, lordly, overbearing, overweening, prideful, proud, superior. ***Idiom:*** on one's high horse. *See* ATTITUDE.

superciliousness *noun*
The quality of being arrogant : arrogance, haughtiness, hauteur, insolence, loftiness, lordliness, overbearingness, presumption, pride, pridefulness, proudness, superiority. *See* ATTITUDE.

supererogative *adjective*
Not required, necessary, or warranted by the circumstances of the case : gratuitous, supererogatory, uncalled-for, wanton. *See* NECESSARY.

supererogatory *adjective*
1. Being more than is needed, desired, or appropriate : de trop, excess, extra, spare, superfluous, supernumerary, surplus. *See* EXCESS.
2. Not required, necessary, or warranted by the circumstances of the case : gratuitous, supererogative, uncalled-for, wanton. *See* NECESSARY.

superficial *adjective*
1. Lacking in intellectual depth or thoroughness : cursory, one-dimensional, shallow, sketchy, skin-deep, uncritical. *See* SURFACE.
2. Appearing as such but not necessarily so : apparent, external, ostensible, ostensive, outward, seeming. *See* SURFACE.

superficially *adverb*
On the surface : apparently, evidently, externally, ostensibly, ostensively, outwardly, seemingly. ***Idioms:*** on the face of it, to all appearances. *See* SURFACE.

superfluity *noun*
1. A condition of going or being beyond what is needed, desired, or appropriate : embarrassment, excess, excessiveness, exorbitance, extravagance, extravagancy, extravagantness, overabundance, plethora, superabundance, superfluousness, surfeit. *See* EXCESS. **2.** An amount or quantity beyond what is needed, desired, or appropriate : excess, fat, glut, overage, overflow, overmuch, overrun, overstock, oversupply, surplus, surplusage. *See* EXCESS.

superfluous *adjective*
Being more than is needed, desired, or appropriate : de trop, excess, extra, spare, supererogatory, supernumerary, surplus. *See* EXCESS.

superfluousness *noun*
A condition of going or being beyond what is needed, desired, or appropriate : embarrassment, excess, excessiveness, exorbitance, extravagance, extravagancy, extravagantness, overabundance, plethora, superabundance, superfluity, surfeit. *See* EXCESS.

superhighway *noun*
A course affording passage from one place to another : avenue, boulevard, drive, expressway, freeway, highway, path, road, roadway, route, street, thoroughfare, thruway, turnpike, way. *See* MOVE, OPEN.

superhuman *adjective*
Of, coming from, or relating to forces or beings that exist outside the natural world : extramundane, extrasensory, metaphysical,

miraculous, preternatural, supernatural, superphysical, supersensible, transcendental, unearthly. *See* SUPERNATURAL.

superintend *verb*
1. To have charge of (the affairs of others) : administer, administrate, direct, govern, head, manage, run, supervise. *See* OVER. **2.** To direct and watch over the work and performance of others : boss, overlook, oversee, supervise, watch over. *See* OVER.

superintendence *noun*
1. Authoritative control over the affairs of others : administration, direction, government, management, supervision. *See* OVER. **2.** The function of watching, guarding, or overseeing : care, charge, custody, guardianship, keeping, supervision, trust. *See* CARE FOR.

superintendent *noun*
Someone who directs and supervises workers : boss, director, foreman, foreperson, forewoman, head, manager, overseer, supervisor, taskmaster, taskmistress. *Informal:* straw boss. *Slang:* chief. *See* OVER.

superior *adjective*
1. Being at a rank above another : higher, senior. *See* OVER. **2.** Of greater excellence than another : better[1], preferable. *See* BETTER. **3.** Of fine quality : choice, fine[1], first-class, prime, select. *See* BETTER. **4.** Exceptionally good of its kind : ace, banner, blue-ribbon, brag, capital, champion, excellent, fine[1], first-class, first-rate, prime, quality, splendid, superb, terrific, tiptop, top. *Informal:* A-one, bully, dandy, great, swell, topflight, topnotch. *Slang:* boss. *Chiefly British:* tophole. *See* GOOD. **5.** Overly convinced of one's own superiority and importance : arrogant, haughty, high-and-mighty, insolent, lofty, lordly, overbearing, overweening, prideful, proud, supercilious. ***Idiom:*** on one's high horse. *See* ATTITUDE. **6.** Being at a height or level above another : higher, upper. *See* HIGH.
superior *noun* One who stands above another in rank : better[1], elder, senior. *Informal:* higher-up. *See* OVER.

superiority *noun*
1. The quality of being exceptionally good of its kind : excellence, fineness, superbness. *See* GOOD. **2.** A dominating position, as in a conflict : advantage, better[1], bulge, draw, drop, edge, upper hand, vantage. *Informal:* inside track, jump. *See* OVER. **3.** The quality of being arrogant : arrogance, haughtiness, hauteur, insolence, loftiness, lordliness, overbearingness, presumption, pride, pridefulness, proudness, superciliousness. *See* ATTITUDE.

superlative *adjective*
Surpassing all others in quality : best, optimal, optimum, unsurpassed. *See* BETTER.

supernatural *adjective*
1. Of, coming from, or relating to forces or beings that exist outside the natural world : extramundane, extrasensory, metaphysical, miraculous, preternatural, superhuman, superphysical, supersensible, transcendental, unearthly. *See* SUPERNATURAL. **2.** Greatly exceeding or departing from the normal course of nature : preternatural, unnatural. *See* USUAL.

supernumerary *adjective*
Being more than is needed, desired, or appropriate : de trop, excess, extra, spare, supererogatory, superfluous, surplus. *See* EXCESS.

superphysical *adjective*
Of, coming from, or relating to forces or beings that exist outside the natural world : extramundane, extrasensory, metaphysical, miraculous, preternatural, superhuman, supernatural, supersensible, transcendental, unearthly. *See* SUPERNATURAL.

superscribe *verb*
To mark (a written communication) with its destination : address, direct. *See* START.

supersede *verb*
To substitute for or fill the place of : replace, supplant, surrogate. *See* SUBSTITUTE.

superseded *adjective*
No longer in use : obsolete. ***Idioms:*** in mothballs, on the shelf. *See* NEW, USED.

supersensible *adjective*
Of, coming from, or relating to forces or beings that exist outside the natural world : extramundane, extrasensory, metaphysical, miraculous, preternatural, superhuman, supernatural, superphysical, transcendental, unearthly. *See* SUPERNATURAL.

supervene *verb*
To occur after in time : ensue, follow, succeed. ***Idiom:*** follow on (*or* upon) the heels of. *See* PRECEDE, TIME.

supervenient *adjective*
Not part of the real or essential nature of a thing : adscititious, adventitious, incidental. *See* SURFACE.

supervise *verb*
1. To have charge of (the affairs of others) : administer, administrate, direct, govern, head, manage, run, superintend. *See* OVER. **2.** To direct and watch over the work and perform-

ance of others : boss, overlook, oversee, superintend, watch over. *See* OVER.

supervision *noun*

1. Authoritative control over the affairs of others : administration, direction, government, management, superintendence. *See* OVER.
2. The function of watching, guarding, or overseeing : care, charge, custody, guardianship, keeping, superintendence, trust. *See* CARE FOR.

supervisor *noun*

Someone who directs and supervises workers : boss, director, foreman, foreperson, forewoman, head, manager, overseer, superintendent, taskmaster, taskmistress. *Informal:* straw boss. *Slang:* chief. *See* OVER.

supervisory *adjective*

Of, for, or relating to administration or administrators : administrative, directorial, executive, managerial, ministerial. *See* OVER.

supplant *verb*

1. To take the place of (another) against the other's will : cut out, displace. *See* SUBSTITUTE. **2.** To substitute for or fill the place of : replace, supersede, surrogate. *See* SUBSTITUTE.

supple *adjective*

1. Capable of being shaped, bent, or drawn out, as by hammering or pressure : ductile, flexible, flexile, flexuous, malleable, moldable, plastic, pliable, pliant, workable. *See* FLEXIBLE.
2. Capable of withstanding stress without injury : elastic, flexible, flexile, resilient, springy. *Physics:* plastic. *See* FLEXIBLE. **3.** Easily altered or influenced : ductile, elastic, flexible, flexile, impressionable, malleable, plastic, pliable, pliant, suggestible. *See* FLEXIBLE.
4. Capable of adapting or being adapted : adaptable, adaptive, adjustable, elastic, flexible, malleable, pliable, pliant. *See* CHANGE. **5.** Willing to carry out the wishes of others : amenable, biddable, compliant, conformable, docile, obedient, submissive, tractable. *See* RESIST.

supplement *noun*

1. Something that completes another : complement. *See* AGREE, PART. **2.** A subordinate element added to another entity : accessory, adjunct, appendage, appurtenance, attachment. *See* INCREASE.

supplement *verb* To supply what is lacking : complement, complete, fill in (*or* out), round (off *or* out). *See* AGREE, PART.

supplemental *adjective*

1. Forming or serving as a complement : complemental, complementary. *See* AGREE, PART.
2. Used or held in reserve : auxiliary, backup, emergency, reserve, secondary, standby, supplementary. *See* INCREASE.

supplementary *adjective*

Used or held in reserve : auxiliary, backup, emergency, reserve, secondary, standby, supplemental. *See* INCREASE.

suppleness *noun*

The quality or state of being flexible : bounce, ductility, elasticity, flexibility, flexibleness, give, malleability, malleableness, plasticity, pliability, pliableness, pliancy, pliantness, resilience, resiliency, spring, springiness. *Obsolete:* flexure. *See* FLEXIBLE.

suppliant *noun*

One who humbly entreats : beggar, prayer[2], suitor, supplicant. *See* REQUEST.

supplicant *noun*

One who humbly entreats : beggar, prayer[2], suitor, suppliant. *See* REQUEST.

supplicate *verb*

1. To make an earnest or urgent request : appeal, beg, beseech, crave, entreat, implore, plead, pray, sue. *Archaic:* conjure. *See* ASK.
2. To offer a reverent petition to God or a god : pray. *See* RELIGION.

supplication *noun*

1. An earnest or urgent request : appeal, entreaty, imploration, plea, prayer[1]. *See* ASK.
2. The act of praying : invocation, prayer[1]. *See* RELIGION.

supply *verb*

1. To relinquish to the possession or control of another : deliver, furnish, give, hand, hand over, provide, transfer, turn over. *See* GIVE.
2. To act as a substitute : fill in, stand in, substitute. *Informal:* pinch-hit, sub. *See* SUBSTITUTE.

support *verb*

1. To sustain the weight of : bear, carry, hold, uphold. *See* SUPPORT. **2.** To hold up : bear, carry, sustain. *See* OVER. **3.** To keep from yielding or failing during stress or difficulty : bolster, buoy (up), prop, sustain, uphold. *See* HELP. **4.** To supply with the necessities of life : keep, maintain, provide for. ***Idiom:*** take care of. *See* CARE FOR. **5.** To aid the cause of by approving or favoring : advocate, back, champion, endorse, get behind, plump for, recommend, side with, stand behind, stand by, uphold. ***Idioms:*** align oneself with, go to bat for, take the part of. *See* SUPPORT. **6.** To act as a patron to : patronize, sponsor. *See* HELP.
7. To put up with : abide, accept, bear, brook[2], endure, go, stand (for), stomach, suffer, sustain, swallow, take, tolerate, withstand.

Informal: lump^2. ***Idioms:*** take it, take it lying down. *See* ACCEPT.

support *noun* **1.** The act or an instance of helping : abetment, aid, assist, assistance, hand, help, relief, succor. *See* HELP. **2.** An indication of commendation or approval : backing, endorsement, recommendation. *See* SUPPORT. **3.** A means or device that keeps something erect, stable, or secure : brace, buttress, crutch, prop, shore, stay^2, underpinning. *See* SUPPORT. **4.** The means needed to support life : alimentation, alimony, bread, bread and butter, keep, livelihood, living, maintenance, subsistence, sustenance, upkeep. *See* MONEY.

supporter *noun*
1. One who supports and adheres to another : adherent, cohort, disciple, follower, henchman, minion, partisan, satellite. *See* OVER, PRECEDE. **2.** A person who supports or champions an activity, cause, or institution, for example : backer, benefactor, contributor, friend, patron, sponsor. *Informal:* angel. *See* HELP.

supportive *adjective*
Giving or able to give help or support : accessory, ancillary, assistant, auxiliary, collateral, contributory, subsidiary. *See* HELP.

suppose *verb*
1. To take for granted without proof : assume, posit, postulate, premise, presume, presuppose. *Informal:* reckon. *See* BELIEF. **2.** To draw an inference on the basis of inconclusive evidence or insufficient information : conjecture, guess, infer, speculate, surmise. *See* OPINION. **3.** To regard in an appraising way : believe, repute, think. *See* BELIEF. **4.** To oblige to do or not do by force of authority, propriety, or custom : expect, require. *See* OBLIGATION.

supposed *adjective*
1. Presumed to be true, real, or genuine, especially on inconclusive grounds : conjectural, hypothetic, hypothetical, inferential, presumptive, suppositional, suppositious, supposititious, suppositive. *See* BELIEF. **2.** Assumed to be such : putative, reputed. *See* BELIEF.

supposition *noun*
1. A judgment, estimate, or opinion arrived at by guessing : conjecture, guess, guesswork, speculation, surmise. *See* OPINION. **2.** Something taken to be true without proof : assumption, postulate, postulation, premise, presupposition, theory, thesis. *See* REASON.

suppositional *adjective*
Presumed to be true, real, or genuine, especially on inconclusive grounds : conjectural, hypothetic, hypothetical, inferential, presumptive, supposed, suppositious, supposititious, suppositive. *See* BELIEF.

suppositious *adjective*
1. Fraudulently or deceptively imitative : bogus, counterfeit, fake, false, fraudulent, phony, sham, spurious, supposititious. *See* TRUE. **2.** Presumed to be true, real, or genuine, especially on inconclusive grounds : conjectural, hypothetic, hypothetical, inferential, presumptive, supposed, suppositional, supposititious, suppositive. *See* BELIEF.

supposititious *adjective*
1. Fraudulently or deceptively imitative : bogus, counterfeit, fake, false, fraudulent, phony, sham, spurious, suppositious. *See* TRUE. **2.** Presumed to be true, real, or genuine, especially on inconclusive grounds : conjectural, hypothetic, hypothetical, inferential, presumptive, supposed, suppositional, suppositious, suppositive. *See* BELIEF.

suppositive *adjective*
Presumed to be true, real, or genuine, especially on inconclusive grounds : conjectural, hypothetic, hypothetical, inferential, presumptive, supposed, suppositional, suppositious, supposititious. *See* BELIEF.

suppress *verb*
1. To bring to an end forcibly as if by imposing a heavy weight : choke off, crush, extinguish, put down, quash, quell, quench, squash, squelch. ***Idiom:*** put the lid on. *See* CONTINUE, WIN. **2.** To keep from being published or transmitted : ban, black out, censor, hush (up), stifle. ***Idiom:*** keep (*or* put) a lid on. *See* SHOW. **3.** To hold (something requiring an outlet) in check : burke, choke (back), gag, hold back, hold down, hush (up), muffle, quench, repress, smother, squelch, stifle, strangle, throttle. *Informal:* sit on (*or* upon). *See* RESTRAINT.

suppression *noun*
Sudden punitive action : clampdown, crackdown, repression. *See* CONTINUE, WIN.

suppressive *adjective*
Serving to restrain forcefully : repressive. *See* ATTACK, RESTRAINT.

supremacy *noun*
The condition or fact of being dominant : ascendance, ascendancy, dominance, domination, paramountcy, predominance, preeminence, preponderance, preponderancy, prepotency. *See* OVER.

supreme *adjective*
1. Having preeminent significance : ascendant, dominant, predominant, prepotent, prevailing, regnant, ruling. *See* IMPORTANT. **2.** Of the

greatest possible degree, quality, or intensity : extreme, transcendent, ultimate, unsurpassable, utmost, uttermost. *See* BETTER, BIG. **3.** Conforming to an ultimate form of perfection or excellence : exemplary, ideal, model, perfect. *See* GOOD.

surcease *verb*

1. To prevent the occurrence or continuation of a movement, action, or operation : arrest, belay, cease, check, discontinue, halt[1], stall[1], stay[1], stop. ***Idioms:*** bring to a standstill, call a halt to, put a stop to. *See* CONTINUE. **2.** To come to a cessation : arrest, belay, cease, check, discontinue, halt[1], leave off, quit, stall[1], stop. ***Idiom:*** come to a halt (*or* standstill *or* stop). *See* CONTINUE.

surcease *noun* **1.** The act of stopping : cessation, check, cut-off, discontinuance, discontinuation, halt[1], stay[1], stop, stoppage. *See* CONTINUE. **2.** The condition of being stopped : cessation, discontinuance, discontinuation, halt[1], standstill, stop, stoppage. *See* CONTINUE.

sure *adjective*

1. Established beyond a doubt : certain, hard, inarguable, incontestable, incontrovertible, indisputable, indubitable, irrefutable, positive, unassailable, undeniable, undisputable, unquestionable. *See* CERTAIN, TRUE. **2.** Known positively : certain, definite, positive. ***Idiom:*** for certain. *See* CERTAIN. **3.** Bound to happen : certain, inescapable, inevitable, unavoidable. *See* CERTAIN. **4.** Such as could not possibly fail or disappoint : certain, infallible, secure, unerring, unfailing. *Informal:* sure-fire. *See* CERTAIN. **5.** Not easily moved or shaken : firm[1], secure, solid, sound[2], stable, strong, sturdy, substantial, unshakable. *See* CONTINUE, STRONG. **6.** Firmly settled or positioned : fast, firm[1], secure, stable, steady, strong. *See* CONTINUE. **7.** Having no doubt : assured, certain, confident, positive, undoubting. *See* CERTAIN.

sure-fire *adjective*

Informal. Such as could not possibly fail or disappoint : certain, infallible, secure, sure, unerring, unfailing. *See* CERTAIN.

sureness *noun*

1. The fact or condition of being without doubt : assurance, assuredness, certainty, certitude, confidence, conviction, positiveness, surety. *See* CERTAIN. **2.** Reliability in withstanding pressure, force, or stress : fastness, firmness, hardness, security, soundness, stability, stableness, steadiness, strength, sturdiness. *See* BETTER, CHANGE, CONTINUE.

sure thing *noun*

A clearly established fact : certainty, cinch. *See* CERTAIN, TRUE.

surety *noun*

1. The fact or condition of being without doubt : assurance, assuredness, certainty, certitude, confidence, conviction, positiveness, sureness. *See* CERTAIN. **2.** An assumption of responsibility, as one given by a manufacturer, for the quality, worth, or durability of a product : guarantee, guaranty, warrant, warranty. *See* OBLIGATION. **3.** One who assumes financial responsibility for another : backer, guarantor, guaranty, sponsor, underwriter. *Informal:* angel. *See* LAW, SUPPORT.

surface *noun*

1. The outer layer of an object : face, top. *See* SURFACE. **2.** An outward appearance : aspect, countenance, face, look, physiognomy, visage. *See* SURFACE.

surfeit *verb*

To satisfy to the full or to excess : cloy, engorge, glut, gorge, pall, sate, satiate. *See* EXCESS, FULL.

surfeit *noun* **1.** Immoderate indulgence, as in food or drink : excess, intemperance, overindulgence. *See* EXCESS. **2.** The condition of being full to or beyond satisfaction : engorgement, repletion, satiation, satiety. *See* EXCESS, FULL. **3.** More than is needed, desired, or appropriate : embarrassment, excess, excessiveness, exorbitance, extravagance, extravagancy, extravagantness, overabundance, plethora, superabundance, superfluity, superfluousness. *See* EXCESS.

surge *verb*

To come forth or emit in abundance : flow, gush, pour, run, rush, stream, well[1]. *See* MOVE.

surge *noun* Something suggestive of running water : current, drift, flood, flow, flux, rush, spate, stream, tide. *See* MOVE.

surly *adjective*

1. Broodingly and sullenly unhappy : dour, gloomy, glum, moody, morose, saturnine, sour, sulky, sullen. *See* HAPPY. **2.** Having or showing a bad temper : bad-tempered, cantankerous, crabbed, cranky, cross, disagreeable, fretful, grouchy, grumpy, ill-tempered, irascible, irritable, nasty, peevish, petulant, querulous, snappish, snappy, testy, ugly, waspish. *Informal:* crabby, mean[2]. ***Idiom:*** out of sorts. *See* ATTITUDE.

surmise *verb*
To draw an inference on the basis of inconclusive evidence or insufficient information : conjecture, guess, infer, speculate, suppose. *See* OPINION.
surmise *noun* A judgment, estimate, or opinion arrived at by guessing : conjecture, guess, guesswork, speculation, supposition. *See* OPINION.

surmount *verb*
1. To win a victory over, as in battle or a competition : beat, best, conquer, defeat, master, overcome, prevail against (*or* over), rout, subdue, subjugate, triumph over, vanquish, worst. *Informal:* trim, whip. *Slang:* ace, lick. ***Idioms:*** carry (*or* win) the day, get (*or* have) the best of, get (*or* have) the better of, go someone one better. *See* WIN. **2.** To pass by or over safely or successfully : clear, hurdle, negotiate. *See* THRIVE.

surpass *verb*
1. To go beyond the limits of : exceed, overreach, overrun, overstep, transcend. *See* EXCESS. **2.** To be greater or better than : best, better[1], exceed, excel, outdo, outmatch, outrun, outshine, outstrip, pass, top, transcend. *Informal:* beat. ***Idioms:*** go beyond, go one better. *See* BIG.

surplus *adjective*
Being more than is needed, desired, or appropriate : de trop, excess, extra, spare, supererogatory, superfluous, supernumerary. *See* EXCESS.
surplus *noun* An amount or quantity beyond what is needed, desired, or appropriate : excess, fat, glut, overage, overflow, overmuch, overrun, overstock, oversupply, superfluity, surplusage. *See* EXCESS.

surplusage *noun*
An amount or quantity beyond what is needed, desired, or appropriate : excess, fat, glut, overage, overflow, overmuch, overrun, overstock, oversupply, superfluity, surplus. *See* EXCESS.

surprise *verb*
1. To come upon, especially suddenly or unexpectedly : catch, hit on (*or* upon), take. *Informal:* hit. *See* SURPRISE. **2.** To attack suddenly and without warning : ambuscade, ambush, bushwhack, waylay. *See* ATTACK. **3.** To impress strongly by what is unexpected or unusual : amaze, astonish, astound, awe, startle. ***Idioms:*** catch (*or* take) unawares, take aback. *See* SURPRISE.

surrender *verb*
1. To undergo capture, defeat, or ruin : collapse, fall, go down, go under, topple. *See* RESIST, WIN. **2.** To let (something) go : abandon, cede, forgo, lay down, relinquish, yield. *See* KEEP. **3.** To give up a possession, claim, or right : abandon, abdicate, cede, demit, forswear, hand over, quitclaim, relinquish, render, renounce, resign, waive, yield. *See* KEEP. **4.** To yield (oneself) unrestrainedly, as to a particular impulse : abandon, give over, give up. *See* RESIST. **5.** To give in from or as if from a gradual loss of strength : bow[1], buckle, capitulate, submit, succumb, yield. *Informal:* fold. *See* RESIST.
surrender *noun* **1.** The act of submitting or surrendering to the power of another : capitulation, submission. *See* RESIST, WIN. **2.** The act of delivering or the condition of being delivered : delivery, transfer. *See* GIVE. **3.** A giving up of a possession, claim, or right : abandonment, abdication, demission, quitclaim, relinquishment, renunciation, resignation, waiver. *See* KEEP.

surreptitious *adjective*
Trickily secret : furtive, secretive, sly, sneaking, sneaky. *See* HONEST.

surrogate *noun*
One that takes the place of another : alternate, replacement, stand-in, substitute. *Informal:* fill-in, pinch hitter, sub. *See* SUBSTITUTE.
surrogate *verb* To substitute for or fill the place of : replace, supersede, supplant. *See* SUBSTITUTE.

surround *verb*
To shut in on all sides : begird, beset, circle, compass, encircle, encompass, environ, gird, girdle, hedge, hem, ring[1]. *See* OPEN.

surroundings *noun*
1. A surrounding area : environment, environs, locale, locality, neighborhood, precinct (used in plural), vicinity. *See* NEAR, PLACE. **2.** The totality of surrounding conditions and circumstances affecting growth or development : ambiance, atmosphere, climate, environment, medium, milieu, mise en scène, world. *See* BE, LIMITED, PLACE.

surveillance *noun*
The act of carefully watching : lookout, vigil, vigilance, watch. ***Idiom:*** watch and ward. *See* AWARENESS.

survey *verb*
1. To look at carefully or critically : check (out), con, examine, go over, inspect, peruse, scrutinize, study, traverse, view. *Informal:* case. ***Idiom:*** give a going-over. *See* INVESTIGATE. **2.** To look at or on attentively or carefully :

eye, observe, regard, scrutinize, watch. *Idioms:* have one's (*or* keep an) eye on, keep tabs on. *See* AWARENESS, SEE. **3.** To view broadly or from a height : look over, overlook, scan. *See* SEE.

survey *noun* **1.** A close or systematic study : analysis, examination, inspection, investigation, review. *See* INVESTIGATE. **2.** A general or comprehensive view or treatment : overview. *See* THOUGHTS.

survive *verb*
1. To exist in spite of adversity : come through, last[2], persist, pull through, ride out, weather. *See* LIVE. **2.** To live, exist, or remain longer than : outlast, outlive, outwear. *See* CONTINUE.

susceptibility *noun*
The condition of being laid open to something undesirable or injurious : exposure, liability, openness, susceptibleness, vulnerability, vulnerableness. *See* PROTECTION.

susceptible *adjective*
1. Easily imposed on or tricked : credulous, dupable, easy, exploitable, gullible, naive. *See* WISE. **2.** Tending to incur : liable, open, prone, subject, susceptive, vulnerable. *See* LIKELY. **3.** Able to receive and respond to external stimuli : impressible, impressionable, responsive, sensible, sensitive, sentient, susceptive. *See* AWARENESS.

susceptibleness *noun*
The condition of being laid open to something undesirable or injurious : exposure, liability, openness, susceptibility, vulnerability, vulnerableness. *See* PROTECTION.

susceptive *adjective*
1. Able to receive and respond to external stimuli : impressible, impressionable, responsive, sensible, sensitive, sentient, susceptible. *See* AWARENESS. **2.** Tending to incur : liable, open, prone, subject, susceptible, vulnerable. *See* LIKELY.

suspect *verb*
To lack trust or confidence in : distrust, doubt, misdoubt, mistrust. *See* TRUST.

suspect *adjective* Of dubious character : doubtful, equivocal, questionable, shady, suspicious, uncertain. *Informal:* fishy. *See* HONEST.

suspend *verb*
1. To stop suddenly, as a conversation, activity, or relationship : break off, cease, discontinue, interrupt, terminate. *See* CONTINUE. **2.** To put off until a later time : adjourn, defer[1], delay, hold off, hold up, postpone, remit, shelve, stay[1], table, waive. *Informal:* wait. *Idiom:* put on ice. *See* DO. **3.** To fasten or be fastened at one point with no support from below : dangle, depend, hang, sling, swing. *See* HANG.

suspension *noun*
1. The condition of being temporarily inactive : abeyance, abeyancy, dormancy, intermission, latency, quiescence. *See* ACTION. **2.** A cessation of continuity or regularity : break, discontinuance, discontinuation, discontinuity, disruption, interruption, pause. *See* CONTINUE. **3.** The act of putting off or the condition of being put off : adjournment, deferment, deferral, delay, postponement, stay[1], waiver. *See* TIME.

suspicion *noun*
1. Intuitive cognition : feeling, hunch, idea, impression, intuition. *See* THOUGHTS. **2.** Lack of trust : distrust, doubt, leeriness, mistrust. *See* TRUST. **3.** A lack of conviction or certainty : doubt, doubtfulness, dubiety, dubiousness, incertitude, mistrust, question, skepticism, uncertainty, wonder. *See* CERTAIN. **4.** A subtle quality underlying or felt to underlie a situation, action, or person : hint, implication, inkling, undercurrent, undertone. *See* SHOW, SUGGEST. **5.** A slight amount or indication : breath, dash, ghost, hair, hint, intimation, semblance, shade, shadow, soupçon, streak, suggestion, taste, tinge, touch, trace, whiff, whisper. *Informal:* whisker. *See* BIG, SHOW.

suspicious *adjective*
1. Of dubious character : doubtful, equivocal, questionable, shady, suspect, uncertain. *Informal:* fishy. *See* HONEST. **2.** Lacking trust or confidence : distrustful, doubting, leery, mistrustful, untrusting. *See* TRUST.

sustain *verb*
1. To keep in a condition of good repair, efficiency, or use : keep up, maintain, preserve. *See* KEEP. **2.** To hold up : bear, carry, support. *See* OVER. **3.** To keep from yielding or failing during stress or difficulty : bolster, buoy (up), prop, support, uphold. *See* HELP. **4.** To put up with : abide, accept, bear, brook[2], endure, go, stand (for), stomach, suffer, support, swallow, take, tolerate, withstand. *Informal:* lump[2]. *Idioms:* take it, take it lying down. *See* ACCEPT.

sustenance *noun*
1. Something fit to be eaten : aliment, bread, comestible, diet, edible, esculent, fare, food, foodstuff, meat, nourishment, nurture, nutriment, nutrition, pabulum, pap, provender, provision (used in plural), victual. *Slang:* chow, eats, grub. *See* INGESTION. **2.** That which sustains the mind or spirit : aliment, bread, food,

nourishment, nutriment, pabulum, pap. *See* CARE FOR, INGESTION. **3.** The means needed to support life : alimentation, alimony, bread, bread and butter, keep, livelihood, living, maintenance, subsistence, support, upkeep. *See* MONEY.

susurration *noun*
A low, indistinct, and often continuous sound : mumble, murmur, sigh, sough, susurrus, whisper. *See* SOUNDS.

susurrus *noun*
A low, indistinct, and often continuous sound : mumble, murmur, sigh, sough, susurration, whisper. *See* SOUNDS.

swaddle *verb*
To cover completely and closely, as with clothing or bandages : enfold, envelop, enwrap, infold, invest, roll, swathe, wrap, wrap up. *See* PUT ON.

swagger *verb*
To walk with exaggerated or unnatural motions expressive of self-importance or self-display : flounce, peacock, prance, strut, swank, swash. *Informal:* sashay. *See* MOVE, SELF-LOVE.

swain *noun*
A man who courts a woman : admirer, beau, courter, suitor, wooer. *See* SEX.

swallow *verb*
1. To cause to pass from the mouth into the stomach : ingest, take. *See* MOUTH. **2.** To put up with : abide, accept, bear, brook[2], endure, go, stand (for), stomach, suffer, support, sustain, take, tolerate, withstand. *Informal:* lump[2]. ***Idioms:*** take it, take it lying down. *See* ACCEPT. **3.** To do away with completely and destructively. Also used with *up* : consume, devour, eat (up), waste. *See* HELP. **4.** *Slang.* To regard (something) as true or real : accept, believe. *Slang:* buy. *See* OPINION.
swallow *noun* An act of swallowing : gulp, ingestion. *See* MOUTH.

swamp *noun*
A usually low-lying area of soft waterlogged ground and standing water : bog, fen, marsh, marshland, mire, morass, muskeg, quag, quagmire, slough[1], swampland, wetland. *See* DRY.
swamp *verb* To affect as if by an outpouring of water : deluge, flood, inundate, overwhelm, whelm. *See* FULL.

swampland *noun*
A usually low-lying area of soft waterlogged ground and standing water : bog, fen, marsh, marshland, mire, morass, muskeg, quag, quagmire, slough[1], swamp, wetland. *See* DRY.

swank *adjective*
1. Being or in accordance with the current fashion : à la mode, chic, dashing, fashionable, mod, modish, posh, smart, stylish, swanky, trig. *Informal:* classy, in, sharp, snappy, swish, tony, trendy. *Slang:* with-it. ***Idioms:*** all the rage, up to the minute. *See* STYLE, USUAL. **2.** Catering to, used by, or admitting only the wealthy or socially superior : exclusive, fancy, posh, swanky. *Informal:* ritzy. *See* PLAIN.
swank *verb* To walk with exaggerated or unnatural motions expressive of self-display or self-importance : flounce, peacock, prance, strut, swagger, swash. *Informal:* sashay. *See* MOVE, SELF-LOVE.

swanky *adjective*
1. Being or in accordance with the current fashion : à la mode, chic, dashing, fashionable, mod, modish, posh, smart, stylish, swank, trig. *Informal:* classy, in, sharp, snappy, swish, tony, trendy. *Slang:* with-it. ***Idioms:*** all the rage, up to the minute. *See* STYLE, USUAL. **2.** Catering to, used by, or admitting only the wealthy or socially superior : exclusive, fancy, posh, swank. *Informal:* ritzy. *See* PLAIN.

swap also **swop** *verb*
Informal. To give up in return for something else : change, commute, exchange, interchange, shift, substitute, switch, trade. *See* CHANGE, SUBSTITUTE.
swap also **swop** *noun Informal.* The act of exchanging or substituting : change, commutation, exchange, interchange, shift, substitution, switch, trade, transposition. *See* CHANGE, SUBSTITUTE.

swarm *noun*
1. An enormous number of persons gathered together : crowd, crush, drove, flock, horde, mass, mob, multitude, press, ruck[1], throng. *See* BIG, GROUP. **2.** A very large number of things grouped together : army, cloud, crowd, drove, flock, horde, host, legion, mass, mob, multitude, ruck[1], score (used in plural), throng. *See* BIG, GROUP.
swarm *verb* **1.** To come or go in large numbers : flood, pour, throng, troop. *See* BIG, MOVE. **2.** To be abundantly filled or richly supplied : abound, bristle, crawl, flow, overflow, pullulate, teem. *See* BIG, RICH.

swarthy *adjective*
Of a complexion tending toward brown or black : bistered, black-a-vised, brunet, dark, dusky. *See* COLORS.

swash *verb*
1. To flow or move with a low slapping sound :

bubble, burble, gurgle, lap, splash, wash. *See* MOVE, SOUNDS. **2.** To hurl or scatter liquid upon : bespatter, dash, slop, slosh, spatter, splash, splatter, spray. *See* STRIKE. **3.** To walk with exaggerated or unnatural motions expressive of self-importance or self-display : flounce, peacock, prance, strut, swagger, swank. *Informal:* sashay. *See* MOVE, SELF-LOVE.

swat *verb*
1. To deliver a powerful blow to suddenly and sharply : bash, catch, clout, hit, knock, pop[1], slam, slog, slug[3], smash, smite, sock, strike, thwack, whack, wham, whop. *Informal:* biff, bop, clip[1], wallop. *Slang:* belt, conk, paste. ***Idioms:*** let someone have it, sock it to someone. *See* ATTACK, STRIKE. **2.** To hit with a quick, sharp blow of the hand : box[2], buffet, bust, cuff, punch, slap, smack[1], spank, whack. *Informal:* clip[1], spat. *See* ATTACK, STRIKE.
swat *noun* **1.** A sudden sharp, powerful stroke : bang, blow[2], clout, crack, hit, lick, pound, slug[3], sock, thwack, welt, whack, wham, whop. *Informal:* bash, biff, bop, clip[1], wallop. *Slang:* belt, conk, paste. *See* ATTACK, STRIKE. **2.** A quick, sharp blow, especially with the hand : box[2], buffet, bust, chop[1], cuff, punch, slap, smack[1], smacker, spank, whack. *Informal:* clip[1], spat. *See* ATTACK, STRIKE.

swathe *verb*
To cover completely and closely, as with clothing or bandages : enfold, envelop, enwrap, infold, invest, roll, swaddle, wrap, wrap up. *See* PUT ON.

sway *verb*
1. To move rhythmically back and forth suspended or as if suspended from above : oscillate, swing. *See* MOVE, REPETITION. **2.** To move back and forth or from side to side, as if about to fall : teeter, totter, vacillate, waver, weave, wobble. *See* REPETITION. **3.** To have an impact on in a certain way : dispose, incline, influence, predispose. *See* AFFECT, LIKE. **4.** *Archaic.* To exercise the authority of a sovereign : govern, reign, rule. ***Idiom:*** wear the crown (*or* purple). *See* OVER.
sway *noun* **1.** The right and power to command, decide, rule, or judge : authority, command, control, domination, dominion, jurisdiction, mastery, might, power, prerogative, sovereignty. *Informal:* say-so. *See* OVER. **2.** The power to produce an effect by indirect means : influence, leverage, weight. *Informal:* clout. *Slang:* pull. *See* AFFECT. **3.** The act of exercising controlling power or the condition of being so controlled : command, control, dominance, domination, dominion, mastery, reign, rule. *See* OVER.

swear *verb*
1. To guarantee by a solemn promise : covenant, pledge, plight[2], promise, vow. ***Idiom:*** give one's word of honor. *See* AGREE, OBLIGATION. **2.** To use profane or obscene language : blaspheme, curse, damn. *Informal:* cuss. *See* DECENT, SACRED, WORDS. **3.** To give evidence or testimony under oath : attest, testify, witness. *Law:* depone, depose. ***Idioms:*** bear witness, take the stand. *See* LAW.
swear off *verb Informal.* To cease trying to accomplish or continue : abandon, break off, desist, discontinue, give up, leave off, quit, relinquish, remit, stop. *Slang:* lay off. ***Idioms:*** call it a day, call it quits, hang up one's fiddle, have done with, throw in the towel. *See* CONTINUE.

swear off *verb* See **swear.**

swearword *noun*
A profane or obscene term : blasphemy, curse, epithet, expletive, oath. *Informal:* cuss. *See* DECENT, SACRED, WORDS.

sweat *verb*
1. To excrete moisture through the pores of the skin : lather, perspire. *See* DRY. **2.** To exert one's mental or physical powers, usually under difficulty and to the point of exhaustion : drive, fag, labor, moil, strain[1], strive, toil, travail, tug, work. ***Idiom:*** break one's back (*or* neck). *See* WORK.
sweat out *verb Slang.* To carry on through despite hardships : endure. *Slang:* tough out. *See* CONTINUE.
sweat *noun* **1.** Moisture excreted through the pores of the skin : lather, perspiration. *See* DRY. **2.** *Informal.* Physical exertion that is usually difficult and exhausting : drudgery, labor, moil, toil, travail, work. *Chiefly British:* fag. ***Idiom:*** sweat of one's brow. *See* WORK. **3.** *Informal.* A condition of excited distress : fume. *Informal:* snit, state, swivet. *Slang:* tizzy. *See* CALM.

sweating *adjective*
Producing or covered with sweat : perspiring, sudoriferous, sweaty. *See* DRY.

sweat out *verb* See **sweat.**

sweaty *adjective*
Producing or covered with sweat : perspiring, sudoriferous, sweating. *See* DRY.

sweep *verb*
To wield boldly and dramatically : brandish, flourish, wave. *See* EXPRESS.

sweep *noun* **1.** A wide and open area, as of land, sky, or water : distance, expanse, expansion, extent, reach, space, spread, stretch. *See* PLACE. **2.** An area within which something or someone exists, acts, or has influence or power : ambit, compass, extension, extent, orbit, purview, range, reach, realm, scope, sphere, swing. *See* TERRITORY.

sweeping *adjective*
Covering a wide scope : all-around, all-inclusive, all-round, broad, broad-spectrum, comprehensive, expansive, extended, extensive, far-ranging, far-reaching, general, global, inclusive, large, overall, wide-ranging, wide-reaching, widespread. *See* SPECIFIC.

sweet *adjective*
1. Having or suggesting the taste of sugar : saccharine, sugary. *See* TASTE. **2.** Pleasing to the eye or mind : attractive, bewitching, enchanting, engaging, enticing, fascinating, fetching, glamorous, lovely, prepossessing, pretty, taking, tempting, winning, winsome. *See* LIKE. **3.** Easy to love : adorable, lovable. *See* GOOD, LIKE, LOVE.

sweet *noun* A person who is much loved : beloved, darling, dear, honey, love, minion, precious, sweetheart, truelove. *Informal:* sweetie. ***Idiom:*** light of one's life. *See* LOVE.

sweeten *verb*
1. To make superficially more acceptable or appealing : candy, gild, honey, sugar, sugarcoat. *See* LIKE. **2.** To ease the anger or agitation of : appease, assuage, calm (down), conciliate, dulcify, gentle, mollify, pacify, placate, propitiate, soften, soothe. ***Idiom:*** pour oil on troubled water. *See* CALM.

sweetheart *noun*
A person who is much loved : beloved, darling, dear, honey, love, minion, precious, sweet, truelove. *Informal:* sweetie. ***Idiom:*** light of one's life. *See* LOVE.

sweetie *noun*
Informal. A person who is much loved : beloved, darling, dear, honey, love, minion, precious, sweet, sweetheart, truelove. ***Idiom:*** light of one's life. *See* LOVE.

sweet-talk *verb*
1. *Informal.* To persuade or try to persuade by gentle persistent urging or flattery : blandish, cajole, coax, honey, wheedle. *Informal:* soft-soap. *See* PERSUASION. **2.** *Informal.* To compliment excessively and ingratiatingly : adulate, blandish, butter up, flatter, honey, slaver. *Informal:* soft-soap. *See* PRAISE.

swell *verb*
To make or become greater or larger : aggrandize, amplify, augment, boost, build, build up, burgeon, enlarge, escalate, expand, extend, grow, increase, magnify, mount, multiply, proliferate, rise, run up, snowball, soar, upsurge, wax. *Informal:* beef up. *See* INCREASE.

swell *noun* The act of increasing or rising : aggrandizement, amplification, augment, augmentation, boost, buildup, enlargement, escalation, growth, hike, increase, jump, multiplication, proliferation, raise, rise, upsurge, upswing, upturn. *See* INCREASE.

swell *adjective* **1.** *Informal.* Exceptionally good of its kind : ace, banner, blue-ribbon, brag, capital, champion, excellent, fine[1], first-class, first-rate, prime, quality, splendid, superb, superior, terrific, tiptop, top. *Informal:* A-one, bully, dandy, great, topflight, topnotch. *Slang:* boss. *Chiefly British:* tophole. *See* GOOD. **2.** *Informal.* Particularly excellent : divine, fabulous, fantastic, fantastical, glorious, marvelous, sensational, splendid, superb, terrific, wonderful. *Informal:* dandy, dreamy, great, ripping, super, tremendous. *Slang:* cool, groovy, hot, keen[1], neat, nifty. ***Idiom:*** out of this world. *See* GOOD.

swelled head *noun*
Informal. An exaggerated belief in one's own importance : egoism, egotism, self-importance. *Informal:* bighead, bigheadedness. *See* SELF-LOVE.

swellhead *noun*
Informal. A conceited, self-centered person : egocentric, egoist, egomaniac, egotist, narcissist. *See* SELF, SELF-LOVE.

swellheaded *adjective*
Informal. Thinking too highly of oneself : conceited, egoistic, egoistical, egotistic, egotistical, narcissistic, vain, vainglorious. *Informal:* bigheaded, stuck-up. *See* SELF-LOVE.

swelling *noun*
A small raised area of skin resulting from a light blow or an insect sting, for example : bump, bunch, knot, lump[1]. *See* CONVEX.

swelter *verb*
To feel or look hot : bake, broil[1], burn, roast. *See* HOT.

sweltering *adjective*
Marked by much heat : ardent, baking, blistering, boiling, broiling, burning, fiery, heated, hot, red-hot, roasting, scalding, scorching, searing, sizzling, sultry, torrid. *See* HOT.

swerve *verb*
1. To turn aside sharply from a straight course :

chop[2], cut, sheer[1], skew, slue[1], veer. *Nautical:* yaw. *See* CHANGE. **2.** To turn away from a prescribed course of action or conduct : depart, deviate, digress, diverge, stray, veer. *Archaic:* err. *See* APPROACH, CORRECT.

swift *adjective*
1. Characterized by great celerity : breakneck, expeditious, fast, fleet, quick, rapid, speedy. *Informal:* hell-for-leather. ***Idiom:*** quick as a bunny (*or* wink). *See* FAST. **2.** Accomplished in very little time : brief, expeditious, fast, flying, hasty, hurried, quick, rapid, short, speedy. *See* FAST.

swiftness *noun*
Rapidness of movement or activity : celerity, dispatch, expedition, expeditiousness, fleetness, haste, hurry, hustle, quickness, rapidity, rapidness, speed, speediness. *See* FAST.

swig *noun*
Informal. An act of drinking or the amount swallowed : draft, drink, potation, pull, quaff, sip, sup, swill. *Slang:* belt. *See* MOUTH.
swig *verb Informal.* To take into the mouth and swallow (a liquid) : drink, imbibe, pull on, quaff, sip, sup. *Informal:* toss down (*or* off). *Slang:* belt. ***Idiom:*** wet one's whistle. *See* MOUTH.

swill *verb*
To swallow (food or drink) greedily or rapidly in large amounts : bolt, down, englut, engorge, gobble, gulp, guzzle, ingurgitate, wolf. *See* INGESTION.
swill *noun* An act of drinking or the amount swallowed : draft, drink, potation, pull, quaff, sip, sup. *Informal:* swig. *Slang:* belt. *See* MOUTH.

swim *verb*
To have the sensation of turning in circles : reel, spin, swirl, whirl. *See* REPETITION.
swim *noun* The act of swimming : dip, duck, dunk, plunge. *See* WORK.

swindle *verb*
To get money or something else from by deceitful trickery : bilk, cheat, cozen, defraud, gull, mulct, rook, victimize. *Informal:* chisel, flimflam, take, trim. *Slang:* diddle[1], do, gyp, stick, sting. *See* HONEST.
swindle *noun* An act of cheating : cheat, fraud, victimization. *Informal:* flimflam. *Slang:* gyp. *See* HONEST.

swindler *noun*
A person who cheats : bilk, cheat, cheater, cozener, defrauder, rook, sharper, trickster, victimizer. *Informal:* chiseler, crook, flimflammer. *Slang:* diddler, gyp, gypper. *See* HONEST.

swing *verb*
1. To move rhythmically back and forth suspended or as if suspended from above : oscillate, sway. *See* MOVE, REPETITION. **2.** To fasten or be fastened at one point with no support from below : dangle, depend, hang, sling, suspend. *See* HANG. **3.** To change the direction or course of : avert, deflect, deviate, divert, pivot, shift, turn, veer. *See* CHANGE. **4.** To turn or cause to turn in place, as on a hinge or fixed point, tracing an arclike path : pivot, wheel. *See* MOVE. **5.** To change one's attitudes or policies, for example : vacillate, waver. *See* CHANGE, DECIDE. **6.** *Slang.* To execute by suspending by the neck : gibbet, hang. *Informal:* string up. *See* HELP. **7.** *Informal.* To bring about and carry to a successful conclusion : bring off, carry out, carry through, effect, effectuate, execute, put through. *See* DO.
swing *noun* **1.** An area within which something or someone exists, acts, or has influence or power : ambit, compass, extension, extent, orbit, purview, range, reach, realm, scope, sphere, sweep. *See* TERRITORY. **2.** The patterned, recurring alternation of contrasting elements, such as stressed and unstressed notes in music : beat, cadence, cadency, measure, meter, rhythm. *See* REPETITION.

swipe *verb*
Informal. To take (another's property) without permission : filch, pilfer, purloin, snatch, steal, thieve. *Informal:* lift. *Slang:* cop, heist, hook, nip[1], pinch, rip off, snitch. ***Idiom:*** make (*or* walk) off with. *See* CRIMES, GIVE.

swirl *verb*
1. To move or cause to move like a rapid rotary current of liquid : eddy, whirl. *See* MOVE, REPETITION. **2.** To rotate rapidly : spin, twirl, whirl. *See* REPETITION. **3.** To have the sensation of turning in circles : reel, spin, swim, whirl. *See* REPETITION.

swish *verb*
To make a sharp sibilant sound : fizz, fizzle, hiss, sibilate, sizzle, whiz, whoosh. *See* SOUNDS.
swish *adjective Informal.* Being or in accordance with the current fashion : à la mode, chic, dashing, fashionable, mod, modish, posh, smart, stylish, swank, swanky, trig. *Informal:* classy, in, sharp, snappy, tony, trendy. *Slang:* with-it. ***Idioms:*** all the rage, up to the minute. *See* STYLE, USUAL.

switch *noun*
The act of exchanging or substituting : change, commutation, exchange, interchange, shift,

substitution, trade, transposition. *Informal:* swap. *See* CHANGE, SUBSTITUTE.

switch *verb* **1.** To move to and fro vigorously and usually repeatedly : wag[1], waggle, wave. *See* REPETITION. **2.** To leave or discard for another : change, shift. *See* CHANGE, SUBSTITUTE. **3.** To give up in return for something else : change, commute, exchange, interchange, shift, substitute, trade. *Informal:* swap. *See* CHANGE, SUBSTITUTE.

swivel *verb*
To move, as a gun, laterally : pivot, traverse. *See* MOVE.

swivet *noun*
Informal. A condition of excited distress : fume. *Informal:* snit, state, sweat. *Slang:* tizzy. *See* CALM.

swollen *adjective*
Characterized by language that is elevated and sometimes pompous in style : aureate, bombastic, declamatory, flowery, fustian, grandiloquent, high-flown, high-sounding, magniloquent, orotund, overblown, rhetorical, sonorous. *See* PLAIN, STYLE, WORDS.

swoon *verb*
To suffer temporary lack of consciousness : black out, faint, keel over, pass out. *See* AWARENESS.

swoon *noun* A temporary loss of consciousness : blackout, faint. *Pathology:* syncope. *See* AWARENESS.

swoop *noun*
The act of plunging suddenly downward into or as if into water : dive, nosedive, plunge. *Informal:* header. *See* ENTER.

swop *verb & noun* See **swap.**

sword of Damocles *noun*
One regarded as an imminent danger : menace, threat. *Idiom:* clear and present danger. *See* SAFETY.

sybarite also **Sybarite** *noun*
A person devoted to pleasure and luxury : epicure, epicurean, hedonist, sensualist, voluptuary. *See* PAIN.

sybaritic *adjective*
Characterized by or devoted to pleasure and luxury as a lifestyle : epicurean, hedonic, hedonistic, voluptuary, voluptuous. *See* PAIN.

sycophant *noun*
One who flatters another excessively : adulator, courtier, flatterer, toady. *Informal:* apple-polisher. *See* OVER, PRAISE.

syllabus *noun*
A document, such as a list or an outline, that gives, for example, the order of events in a public performance or the chief features of a stock offering : bill[1], program, prospectus. *See* PLANNED, WORDS.

symbol *noun*
1. An object associated with and serving to identify something else : attribute, emblem. *See* SUBSTITUTE. **2.** A conventional mark used in a writing system : character, sign. *See* MARKS.

symbol *verb* To serve as an example, image, or symbol of : epitomize, exemplify, illustrate, represent, stand for, symbolize, typify. *See* SUBSTITUTE.

symbolic *adjective*
Serving as a symbol : emblematic, emblematical, representative, symbolical. *See* SUBSTITUTE.

symbolical *adjective*
Serving as a symbol : emblematic, emblematical, representative, symbolic. *See* SUBSTITUTE.

symbolize *verb*
To serve as an example, image, or symbol of : epitomize, exemplify, illustrate, represent, stand for, symbol, typify. *See* SUBSTITUTE.

symmetric *adjective*
Characterized by or displaying symmetry, especially correspondence in scale or measure : balanced, proportional, proportionate, regular, symmetrical. *See* SAME.

symmetrical *adjective*
1. Characterized by or displaying symmetry, especially correspondence in scale or measure : balanced, proportional, proportionate, regular, symmetric. *See* SAME. **2.** Having components pleasingly combined : balanced, congruous, harmonious. *See* BEAUTIFUL.

symmetry *noun*
Satisfying arrangement marked by even distribution of elements, as in a design : balance, harmony, proportion. *See* BEAUTIFUL.

sympathetic *adjective*
1. Cognizant of and comprehending the needs, feelings, problems, and views of others : empathetic, empathic, feeling, understanding. *See* UNDERSTAND. **2.** Feeling or expressing pity : commiserative, compassionate, condolatory, pitying. *Archaic:* piteous, pitiful. *See* FEELINGS, PITY.

sympathize *verb*
1. To experience or express compassion : ache, commiserate, compassionate, feel, pity, yearn. *Idioms:* be sorry, have (*or* take) pity. *See* PITY. **2.** To understand or be sensitive to another's feelings or ideas : empathize. *See* UNDERSTAND. **3.** To associate or affiliate oneself

closely with a person or group : empathize, identify, relate. *See* SAME.

sympathy *noun*
1. A very close understanding between persons : empathy. *See* CONNECT, LOVE, UNDERSTAND. **2.** Sympathetic, sad concern for someone in misfortune : commiseration, compassion, condolence, empathy, pity. *See* PITY.

symphonic *adjective*
Characterized by harmony of sound : consonant, harmonic, harmonious, musical, symphonious. *See* BEAUTIFUL, SOUNDS.

symphonious *adjective*
Characterized by harmony of sound : consonant, harmonic, harmonious, musical, symphonic. *See* BEAUTIFUL, SOUNDS.

symphony *noun*
Pleasing agreement, as of musical sounds : accord, concert, concord, harmony, tune. *Music:* consonance. *See* BEAUTIFUL.

symptom *noun*
Something visible or evident that gives grounds for believing in the existence or presence of something else : badge, evidence, index, indication, indicator, manifestation, mark, note, sign, signification, stamp, token, witness. *See* SHOW.

synchronic *adjective*
Belonging to the same period of time as another : coetaneous, coeval, coexistent, concurrent, contemporaneous, contemporary, synchronous. *See* TIME.

synchronize *verb*
To occur at the same time : coincide, concur. *See* NEAR.

synchronous *adjective*
Belonging to the same period of time as another : coetaneous, coeval, coexistent, concurrent, contemporaneous, contemporary, synchronic. *See* TIME.

synchronously *adverb*
At the same time : concurrently, simultaneously, together. ***Idioms:*** all at once, all together. *See* ACCOMPANIED, TIME.

syncope *noun*
Pathology. A temporary loss of consciousness : blackout, faint, swoon. *See* AWARENESS.

syndicate *noun*
A combination of businesses closely interconnected for common profit : cartel, combine, pool, trust. *See* GROUP, MONEY.

synergetic *adjective*
Working together toward a common end : collaborative, cooperative, synergic, synergistic. *See* CONFLICT.

synergic *adjective*
Working together toward a common end : collaborative, cooperative, synergetic, synergistic. *See* CONFLICT.

synergistic *adjective*
Working together toward a common end : collaborative, cooperative, synergetic, synergic. *See* CONFLICT.

synergy *noun*
Joint work toward a common end : coaction, collaboration, cooperation, teamwork. *See* CONFLICT.

synopsis *noun*
A short summary or version prepared by cutting down a larger work : abridgment, abstract, brief, condensation, epitome. *See* WORDS.

synopsize *verb*
To give a recapitulation of the salient facts of : abstract, epitomize, go over, recapitulate, review, run down, run through, summarize, sum up, wrap up. *Informal:* recap. *See* THOUGHTS.

synthesize *verb*
To combine and adapt in order to attain a particular effect : arrange, blend, coordinate, harmonize, integrate, orchestrate, unify. *See* BEAUTIFUL.

synthetic *adjective*
1. Marked by unnaturalness, pretension, and often a slavish love of fads : artificial, factitious, plastic, unnatural. *See* HONEST. **2.** Made by human beings instead of nature : artificial, manmade, manufactured. *See* CULTURE. **3.** Made to imitate something else : artificial, imitation, manmade, mock, simulated. *Informal:* pretend. *See* REAL.

system *noun*
1. An organized array of individual elements and parts forming and working as a unit : entity, integral, sum, totality, whole. *See* PART. **2.** A usually large entity composed of interconnected parts : complex. *See* PART. **3.** Systematic arrangement and design : method, order, orderliness, organization, pattern, plan, systematization, systemization. *See* ORDER. **4.** The approach used to do something : fashion, manner, method, mode, modus operandi, style, way, wise[2]. *See* MEANS.

systematic *adjective*
Arranged or proceeding in a set, systematized pattern : methodic, methodical, orderly, regular, systematical. *See* ABILITY, ORDER.

systematical *adjective*
Arranged or proceeding in a set, systematized pattern : methodic, methodical, orderly, regular, systematic. *See* ABILITY, ORDER.

systematization *noun*
Systematic arrangement and design : method, order, orderliness, organization, pattern, plan, system, systemization. *See* ORDER.

systematize *verb*
1. To put into a deliberate order : arrange, array, deploy, dispose, marshal, order, organize, range, sort. *See* ORDER. **2.** To arrange in an orderly manner : methodize, order, organize, systemize. *See* ORDER.

systemization *noun*
Systematic arrangement and design : method, order, orderliness, organization, pattern, plan, system, systematization. *See* ORDER.

systemize *verb*
To arrange in an orderly manner : methodize, order, organize, systematize. *See* ORDER.

•T•

tab *noun*
1. *Informal.* A precise list of fees or charges : account, bill[1], check, invoice, reckoning, statement. *See* PAY. **2.** *Informal.* An amount paid or to be paid for a purchase : charge, cost, price. *See* TRANSACTIONS.

tabby *noun*
A person habitually engaged in idle talk about others : blab, gossip, gossiper, gossipmonger, newsmonger, rumormonger, scandalmonger, talebearer, taleteller, tattle, tattler, tattletale, telltale, whisperer. *Slang:* yenta. *See* WORDS.

table *noun*
An orderly columnar display of data : chart, tabulation. *See* KNOWLEDGE.
table *verb* To put off until a later time : adjourn, defer[1], delay, hold off, hold up, postpone, remit, shelve, stay[1], suspend, waive. *Informal:* wait. ***Idiom:*** put on ice. *See* DO.

taboo also **tabu** *noun*
A refusal to allow : ban, disallowance, forbiddance, inhibition, interdiction, prohibition, proscription. *See* ALLOW.
taboo also **tabu** *adjective* Not allowed : forbidden, impermissible, verboten. *See* ALLOW.
taboo also **tabu** *verb* To refuse to allow : ban, debar, disallow, enjoin, forbid, inhibit, interdict, outlaw, prohibit, proscribe. *See* ALLOW.

tabu *noun & adjective & verb* See **taboo.**

tabulation *noun*
An orderly columnar display of data : chart, table. *See* KNOWLEDGE.

tacit *adjective*
1. Not voiced or expressed : silent, undeclared, unexpressed, unsaid, unspoken, unuttered, unvoiced, wordless. *See* WORDS. **2.** Conveyed indirectly without words or speech : implicit, implied, inferred, understood, unsaid, unspoken, unuttered, wordless. ***Idiom:*** taken for granted. *See* SHOW.

taciturn *adjective*
Not speaking freely or openly : close, close-mouthed, incommunicable, incommunicative, reserved, reticent, silent, tightlipped, uncommunicable, uncommunicative. *See* RESTRAINT, SOUNDS.

taciturnity *noun*
The keeping of one's thoughts and emotions to oneself : control, reserve, restraint, reticence, self-control, self-restraint, uncommunicativeness. *See* RESTRAINT.

tack *noun*
1. A method used in dealing with something : approach, attack, course, line, modus operandi, plan, procedure, technique. *See* MEANS. **2.** An often sudden change or departure, as in a trend : shift, turn, twist. *See* CHANGE.

tackle *noun*
Things needed for a task, journey, or other purpose : accouterment (often used in plural), apparatus, equipment, gear, material (used in plural), materiel, outfit, paraphernalia, rig, thing (used in plural), turnout. *See* MEANS.
tackle *verb* **1.** To take upon oneself : assume, incur, shoulder, take on, take over, undertake. *See* ACCEPT. **2.** To start work on vigorously : attack, go at, sail in, wade in (*or* into). ***Idiom:*** hop to it. *See* WORK.

tacky[1] *adjective*
Having the property of adhering : adhesive, gluey, gooey, gummy, sticky. *See* CLEAN, KEEP.

tacky[2] *adjective*
1. *Informal.* Showing signs of wear and tear or neglect : bedraggled, broken-down, decaying, decrepit, dilapidated, dingy, down-at-heel, faded, mangy, rundown, scrubby, scruffy, seedy, shabby, shoddy, sleazy, tattered, tatty, threadbare. *Slang:* ratty. ***Idioms:*** all the worse for wear, gone to pot (*or* seed), past cure (*or* hope). *See* BETTER. **2.** *Informal.* Lacking style and good taste : inelegant, tasteless, unbecoming. *See* STYLE. **3.** *Informal.* Quite outmoded or unfashionable : dowdy, frumpish. *See* NEW. **4.** *Informal.* Tastelessly showy : brummagem, chintzy, flashy, garish, gaudy, glaring, loud, meretricious, tawdry, tinsel. *See* STYLE.

tact *noun*
The ability to say and do the right thing at the right time : address, diplomacy, savoir-faire, tactfulness. *See* ABILITY, COURTESY.

tactful *adjective*
Showing sensitivity and skill in dealing with others : delicate, diplomatic, discreet, politic, sensitive. *See* ABILITY.

tactfulness *noun*
The ability to say and do the right thing at the right time : address, diplomacy, savoir-faire, tact. *See* ABILITY, COURTESY.

tactic *noun*
1. An action calculated to achieve an end : maneuver, measure (often used in plural), move, procedure, step. *See* ACTION. **2.** A method of deploying troops and equipment in combat : maneuver, stratagem. *See* MEANS.

tactical *adjective*
Designed or implemented so as to gain a temporary limited advantage : short-range. *See* NEAR.

tactile *adjective*
1. Discernible by touch : palpable, tangible, touchable. *See* TOUCH. **2.** Of, relating to, or arising from the sense of touch : tactual. *See* TOUCH.

tactility *noun*
1. The quality or condition of being discernible by touch : palpability, tangibility, tangibleness, touchableness. *See* TOUCH. **2.** The faculty or ability to perceive tactile stimulation : feel, feeling, touch. *See* TOUCH.

tactless *adjective*
Lacking sensitivity and skill in dealing with others : brash, clumsy, gauche, impolitic, indelicate, maladroit, undiplomatic, unpolitic, untactful. *See* ABILITY, COURTESY.

tactual *adjective*
Of, relating to, or arising from the sense of touch : tactile. *See* TOUCH.

tag *noun*
1. An identifying or descriptive slip : label, ticket. *See* MARKS. **2.** The word or words by which one is called and identified : appellation, appellative, cognomen, denomination, designation, epithet, name, nickname, style, title. *Slang:* handle, moniker. *See* SPECIFIC, WORDS.
tag *verb* **1.** To set off by or as if by a mark indicating ownership or manufacture : brand, identify, label, mark, trademark. *See* MARKS. **2.** To attach a ticket to : label, mark, ticket. *See* MARKS. **3.** To describe with a word or term : call, characterize, designate, label, name, style, term. *See* SPECIFIC, WORDS. **4.** To follow closely or persistently : dog, heel[1], trail. *See* PRECEDE.

tag end *noun*
The hindmost part of something : end, rear[1], tail, tail end. *See* PRECEDE.

tail *noun*
1. The hindmost part of something : end, rear[1], tag end, tail end. *See* PRECEDE. **2.** Something that follows : trail, train, wake[2]. *See* PRECEDE. **3.** *Informal.* An agent assigned to observe and report on another : shadow, watcher. *See* INVESTIGATE.
tail *verb Informal.* To keep (another) under surveillance by moving along behind : dog, follow, shadow, track, trail. *Informal:* bird-dog. *See* PRECEDE.
tail away (or **off**) *verb* To grow or cause to grow gradually less : abate, decrease, diminish, drain, dwindle, ebb, lessen, let up, peter (out), rebate, reduce, taper (off). *See* INCREASE.

tail away or **off** *verb* See **tail.**

tail end *noun*
The hindmost part of something : end, rear[1], tag end, tail. *See* PRECEDE.

tailor *verb*
To make or become suitable to a particular situation or use : acclimate, acclimatize, accommodate, adapt, adjust, conform, fashion, fit[1], reconcile, square, suit. *See* CHANGE.

tailor-made *adjective*
1. Made according to the specifications of the buyer : custom, custom-built, customized, custom-made, made-to-order. *See* AGREE. **2.** Suitable for a particular person, condition, occasion, or place : appropriate, apt, becoming, befitting, correct, felicitous, fit[1], fitting,

happy, meet², proper, right. *See* RIGHT. **3.** Suited to one's end or purpose : appropriate, befitting, convenient, expedient, fit¹, good, meet², proper, suitable, useful. *See* AGREE, GOOD.

taint *verb*

1. To become or cause to become rotten or unsound : break down, decay, decompose, deteriorate, disintegrate, molder, putrefy, rot, spoil, turn. ***Idioms:*** go bad, go to pot, go to seed. *See* BETTER, THRIVE. **2.** To make morally impure : contaminate, corrupt, defile, infect, pollute, soil. *See* CLEAN. **3.** To contaminate the reputation of : befoul, besmear, besmirch, bespatter, blacken, cloud, denigrate, dirty, smear, smudge, smut, soil, spatter, stain, sully, tarnish. ***Idioms:*** give a black eye to, sling (*or* throw) mud on. *See* ATTACK, CLEAN.

taint *noun* A mark of discredit or disgrace : black eye, blemish, blot, onus, spot, stain, stigma, tarnish. *Archaic:* attaint. ***Idiom:*** a blot on one's escutcheon. *See* MARKS, RESPECT.

taintlessness *noun*

The condition of being clean and free of contaminants : clarity, cleanliness, cleanness, pureness, purity. *See* CLEAN.

take *verb*

1. To obtain possession or control of : capture, gain, get, win. *Slang:* cop. *See* GET. **2.** To gain possession of, especially after a struggle or chase : capture, catch, get, net¹, secure. *Informal:* bag. *Slang:* nail. *See* GET. **3.** To become affected with a disease : catch, contract, develop, get, sicken. ***Idiom:*** come down with. *See* GET. **4.** To come upon, especially suddenly or unexpectedly : catch, hit on (*or* upon), surprise. *Informal:* hit. *See* SURPRISE. **5.** To have a sudden overwhelming effect on : catch, seize, strike. *See* ATTACK, OVER. **6.** To direct or impel to oneself by some quality or action : allure, appeal, attract, draw, entice, lure, magnetize. *Informal:* pull. *See* LIKE. **7.** To cause to pass from the mouth into the stomach : ingest, swallow. *See* MOUTH. **8.** To admit to one's possession, presence, or awareness : accept, have, receive. *See* ACCEPT. **9.** To engage in sexual relations with : bed, copulate, couple, have, mate, sleep with. ***Idioms:*** go to bed with, make love, make whoopee, roll in the hay. *See* SEX. **10.** To receive (something given or offered) willingly and gladly. Also used with *up* : accept, embrace, welcome. *See* ACCEPT. **11.** To lay claim to for oneself or as one's right : appropriate, arrogate, assume, commandeer, preempt, seize, usurp. *See* GIVE. **12.** To go aboard (a means of transport) : board, catch. *See* USED. **13.** To have as a need or prerequisite : ask, call for, demand, entail, involve, necessitate, require. *See* NECESSARY, OVER. **14.** To obtain from another source : derive, draw, get. *See* KIN. **15.** To put up with : abide, accept, bear, brook², endure, go, stand (for), stomach, suffer, support, sustain, swallow, tolerate, withstand. *Informal:* lump². ***Idioms:*** take it, take it lying down. *See* ACCEPT. **16.** To perform a function effectively : function, go, operate, run, work. *See* THRIVE. **17.** To perceive and recognize the meaning of : accept, apprehend, catch (on), compass, comprehend, conceive, fathom, follow, get, grasp, make out, read, see, sense, take in, understand. *Informal:* savvy. *Slang:* dig. *Chiefly British:* twig. *Scots:* ken. ***Idioms:*** get (*or* have) a handle on, get the picture. *See* UNDERSTAND. **18.** To understand in a particular way : construe, interpret, read. *See* UNDERSTAND. **19.** To cause to come along with oneself : bear, bring, carry, convey, fetch, transport. *See* ACCOMPANIED. **20.** To move (something) from a position occupied : remove, take away, take off, take out, withdraw. *See* MOVE. **21.** To take away (a quantity) from another quantity. Also used with *off* : abate, deduct, discount, rebate, subtract. *Informal:* knock off. *See* INCREASE. **22.** *Informal:* To get money or something else from by deceitful trickery : bilk, cheat, cozen, defraud, gull, mulct, rook, swindle, victimize. *Informal:* chisel, flimflam, trim. *Slang:* diddle¹, do, gyp, stick, sting. *See* HONEST.

take after *verb* To be similar to, as in appearance : resemble. *Chiefly Regional:* favor. *See* SAME.

take away *verb* To move (something) from a position occupied : remove, take, take off, take out, withdraw. *See* MOVE.

take back *verb* **1.** To occupy or take again : reassume, re-claim, reoccupy, repossess, resume, retake. *See* GIVE. **2.** To send, put, or carry back to a former location : give back, restore, return. *See* INCREASE, KEEP. **3.** To disavow (something previously written or said) irrevocably and usually formally : abjure, recall, recant, retract, withdraw. *See* ACCEPT.

take down *verb* **1.** To cause to descend : depress, drop, let down, lower². *See* RISE. **2.** To take (something) apart : break down, disassemble, dismantle, dismount. *See* ASSEMBLE.

take in *verb* **1.** To allow admittance, as to a group : accept, admit, receive. *See* ACCEPT.

2. To have as a part : comprehend, comprise, contain, embody, embrace, encompass, have, include, involve, subsume. *See* INCLUDE. **3.** To perceive and recognize the meaning of : accept, apprehend, catch (on), compass, comprehend, conceive, fathom, follow, get, grasp, make out, read, see, sense, take, understand. *Informal:* savvy. *Slang:* dig. *Chiefly British:* twig. *Scots:* ken. ***Idioms:*** get (*or* have) a handle on, get the picture. *See* UNDERSTAND. **4.** To cause to accept what is false, especially by trickery or misrepresentation : beguile, betray, bluff, cozen, deceive, delude, double-cross, dupe, fool, four-flush, hoodwink, humbug, mislead, trick. *Informal:* bamboozle, have. ***Idioms:*** lead astray, play false, pull the wool over someone's eyes, put something over on, take for a ride. *See* HONEST.

take off *verb* **1.** To take from one's own person : doff, remove. *See* PUT ON. **2.** To move (something) from a position occupied : remove, take, take away, take out, withdraw. *See* MOVE. **3.** *Slang.* To move or proceed away from a place : depart, exit, get away, get off, go, go away, leave[1], pull out, quit, retire, run (along), withdraw. *Informal:* cut out, push off, shove off. *Slang:* blow[1], split. ***Idioms:*** hit the road, take leave. *See* APPROACH. **4.** To rise up in flight : lift (off). *See* RISE.

take on *verb* **1.** To take upon oneself : assume, incur, shoulder, tackle, take over, undertake. *See* ACCEPT. **2.** To go about the initial step in doing (something) : approach, begin, commence, embark, enter, get off, inaugurate, initiate, institute, launch, lead off, open, set about, set out, set to, start, take up, undertake. *Informal:* kick off. ***Idioms:*** get cracking, get going, get the show on the road. *See* START. **3.** To obtain the use or services of : employ, engage, hire, retain. ***Idiom:*** put on the payroll. *See* GET, WORK. **4.** To enter into conflict with : encounter, engage, meet[1]. ***Idiom:*** do (*or* join) battle with. *See* CONFLICT, MEET. **5.** To worry over trifles : chafe, pother. *Informal:* fuss. *See* CALM. **6.** To take, as another's idea, and make one's own : adopt, embrace, espouse, take up. *See* ACCEPT, GIVE.

take out *verb* **1.** To move (something) from a position occupied : remove, take, take away, take off, withdraw. *See* MOVE. **2.** *Informal.* To be with another person socially on a regular basis : date, go out, see. *See* CONNECT.

take over *verb* **1.** To seize and move into by force : occupy. *See* ATTACK. **2.** To take upon oneself : assume, incur, shoulder, tackle, take on, undertake. *See* ACCEPT. **3.** To free from a specific duty by acting as a substitute : relieve, spell[3]. *See* SUBSTITUTE.

take to *verb* To find agreeable : fancy, like[1]. *Chiefly British:* conceit. *See* LIKE.

take up *verb* **1.** To move (something) to a higher position : boost, elevate, heave, hoist, lift, pick up, raise, rear[2], uphold, uplift, upraise, uprear. *See* RISE. **2.** To begin or go on after an interruption : continue, pick up, renew, reopen, restart, resume. *See* CONTINUE. **3.** To be occupied or concerned with : consider, deal with, treat. ***Idiom:*** have to do with. *See* RELEVANT. **4.** To go about the initial step in doing (something) : approach, begin, commence, embark, enter, get off, inaugurate, initiate, institute, launch, lead off, open, set about, set out, set to, start, take on, undertake. *Informal:* kick off. ***Idioms:*** get cracking, get going, get the show on the road. *See* START. **5.** To take in (moisture or liquid) : absorb, drink, imbibe, soak (up), sop up. *See* GIVE. **6.** To take in and incorporate, especially mentally : absorb, assimilate, digest, imbibe. *Informal:* soak (up). *See* ACCEPT. **7.** To take, as another's idea, and make one's own : adopt, embrace, espouse, take on. *See* ACCEPT, GIVE.

take *noun* **1.** The amount of money collected as admission, especially to a sporting event : box office, gate. *See* MONEY. **2.** *Slang.* A trying to do or make something : attempt, crack, effort, endeavor, essay, go, offer, stab, trial, try. *Informal:* shot. *Archaic:* assay. *See* TRY.

take after *verb* See **take.**

take away *verb* See **take.**

take back *verb* See **take.**

take down *verb* See **take.**

take-in *noun*

Informal. An indirect, usually cunning means of gaining an end : artifice, deception, device, dodge, feint, gimmick, imposture, jig, maneuver, ploy, ruse, sleight, stratagem, subterfuge, trick, wile. *Informal:* shenanigan. *See* HONEST, MEANS.

take in *verb* See **take.**

takeoff *noun*

1. The act of rising in flight : liftoff. *See* RISE. **2.** *Informal.* A usually amusing caricature of another : imitation, parody. *See* LAUGHTER, RESPECT, SAME.

take off *verb* See **take.**

take on *verb* See **take.**

take out *verb* See **take.**

take over *verb* See **take.**

take to *verb* See **take.**

take up *verb* See **take.**

taking *adjective*

1. Pleasing to the eye or mind : attractive, bewitching, enchanting, engaging, enticing, fascinating, fetching, glamorous, lovely, prepossessing, pretty, sweet, tempting, winning, winsome. *See* LIKE. **2.** Capable of transmission by infection : catching, communicable, contagious, infectious. *See* MOVE.

tale *noun*

1. An untrue declaration : canard, cock-and-bull story, falsehood, falsity, fib, fiction, inveracity, lie[2], misrepresentation, misstatement, prevarication, story, untruth. *Informal:* fish story, tall tale. *Slang:* whopper. *See* TRUE. **2.** An entertaining and often oral account of a real or fictitious occurrence : anecdote, fable, story. *Informal:* tall tale, yarn. *See* WORDS. **3.** *Archaic.* A noting of items one by one : count, enumeration, numeration, reckoning, tally. *See* COUNT. **4.** *Archaic.* A number or quantity obtained as a result of addition : aggregate, amount, sum, summation, sum total, total, totality. *See* COUNT.

talebearer *noun*

A person habitually engaged in idle talk about others : blab, gossip, gossiper, gossipmonger, newsmonger, rumormonger, scandalmonger, tabby, taleteller, tattle, tattler, tattletale, telltale, whisperer. *Slang:* yenta. *See* WORDS.

talebearing *noun*

Idle, often sensational and groundless talk about others : gossip, gossipry, hearsay, report, rumor, tattle, tittle-tattle, word. *Slang:* scuttlebutt. *See* WORDS.

talebearing *adjective* Inclined to gossip : blabby, gossipy, taletelling. *See* WORDS.

talent *noun*

An innate capability : aptitude, aptness, bent, faculty, flair, genius, gift, head, instinct, knack, turn. *See* ABILITY, APPROACH.

talented *adjective*

Having talent : endowed, gifted. *See* ABILITY, GIVE.

taleteller *noun*

A person habitually engaged in idle talk about others : blab, gossip, gossiper, gossipmonger, newsmonger, rumormonger, scandalmonger, tabby, talebearer, tattle, tattler, tattletale, telltale, whisperer. *Slang:* yenta. *See* WORDS.

taletelling *adjective*

Inclined to gossip : blabby, gossipy, talebearing. *See* WORDS.

talisman *noun*

A small object worn or kept for its supposed magical power : amulet, charm, fetish, juju, periapt, phylactery. *See* SUPERNATURAL.

talismanic *adjective*

Having, brought about by, or relating to supernatural powers or magic : fey, magic, magical, thaumaturgic, thaumaturgical, theurgic, theurgical, witching, wizardly. *See* SUPERNATURAL.

talk *verb*

1. To engage in spoken exchange : chat, confabulate, converse[1], discourse, speak. *Informal:* confab, visit. *See* WORDS. **2.** To direct speech to : address, speak. *See* WORDS. **3.** To express oneself in speech : speak, verbalize, vocalize. ***Idioms:*** open one's mouth (*or* lips), put in (*or* into) words, wag one's tongue. *See* WORDS. **4.** To put into words : articulate, communicate, convey, declare, express, say, state, tell, utter[1], vent, verbalize, vocalize, voice. ***Idiom:*** give tongue (*or* vent *or* voice) to. *See* WORDS. **5.** To engage in or spread gossip : blab, gossip, noise, rumor, tattle, tittle-tattle, whisper. ***Idioms:*** tell tales, tell tales out of school. *See* WORDS. **6.** To meet and exchange views to reach a decision : advise, confer, consult, deliberate, parley. *Informal:* powwow. *See* COLLECT, MEET, WORDS. **7.** To give incriminating information about others, especially to the authorities : inform, tattle, tip[3] (off). *Slang:* fink, rat, sing, snitch, squeal, stool. ***Idiom:*** blow the whistle. *See* KNOWLEDGE, LAW.

talk back *verb* To utter an impertinent rejoinder : talk up. *Informal:* sass, sauce. ***Idiom:*** give someone lip. *See* RESIST, WORDS.

talk down *verb* To think, represent, or speak of as small or unimportant : belittle, decry, denigrate, deprecate, depreciate, derogate, detract, discount, disparage, downgrade, minimize, run down, slight. ***Idiom:*** make light (*or* little) of. *See* ATTACK, SHOW.

talk into *verb* To succeed in causing (a person) to act in a certain way : argue into, bring, bring around (*or* round), convince, get, induce, persuade, prevail on (*or* upon), sell (on). *See* PERSUASION.

talk over *verb* To speak together and exchange ideas and opinions about : bandy (about), discuss, moot, thrash out (*or* over), thresh out (*or* over), toss around. *Informal:* hash (over), kick around, knock about (*or* around). *Slang:* rap[3]. ***Idiom:*** go into a huddle. *See* WORDS.

talk up *verb* **1.** To increase or seek to increase the importance or reputation of by favorable publicity : ballyhoo, boost, build up, enhance, promote, publicize, puff, tout. *Informal:* plug. *Slang:* hype. *See* KNOWLEDGE. **2.** To make known vigorously the positive features of (a product) : advertise, ballyhoo, build up, cry (up), popularize, promote, publicize. *Informal:* pitch, plug. *Slang:* push. *See* KNOWLEDGE. **3.** To utter an impertinent rejoinder : talk back. *Informal:* sass, sauce. ***Idiom:*** give someone lip. *See* RESIST, WORDS.

talk *noun* **1.** Spoken exchange : chat, colloquy, confabulation, conversation, converse[1], dialogue, discourse, speech. *Informal:* confab. *Slang:* jaw. *See* WORDS. **2.** The faculty, act, or product of speaking : discourse, speech, utterance, verbalization, vocalization. *See* WORDS. **3.** A usually formal oral communication to an audience : address, allocution, declamation, lecture, oration, prelection, speech. *See* WORDS. **4.** The act or process of dealing with another to reach an agreement. Often used in plural : negotiation, parley. *See* WORDS.

talkative *adjective*
Given to conversation : chatty, conversational, garrulous, loquacious, talky, voluble. *Slang:* gabby. *See* WORDS.

talk back *verb* See **talk.**

talk down *verb* See **talk.**

talker *noun*
One given to conversation : confabulator, conversationalist, conversationist, discourser. *See* WORDS.

talk into *verb* See **talk.**

talk over *verb* See **talk.**

talk up *verb* See **talk.**

talky *adjective*
Given to conversation : chatty, conversational, garrulous, loquacious, talkative, voluble. *Slang:* gabby. *See* WORDS.

tall *adjective*
1. Extending to a great height : high. *See* HIGH. **2.** Having a rather great upward projection : high, long[1]. *See* HIGH. **3.** Not easy to do, achieve, or master : arduous, difficult, hard, laborious, serious, tough, uphill. *See* EASY.

tall tale *noun*
1. *Informal.* An entertaining and often oral account of a real or fictitious occurrence : anecdote, fable, story, tale. *Informal:* yarn. *See* WORDS. **2.** *Informal.* An untrue declaration : canard, cock-and-bull story, falsehood, falsity, fib, fiction, inveracity, lie[2], misrepresentation, misstatement, prevarication, story, tale, untruth. *Informal:* fish story. *Slang:* whopper. *See* TRUE.

tall talk *noun*
The act or an instance of exaggerating : exaggeration, hyperbole, hyperbolism, overstatement. *See* INCREASE.

tally *noun*
1. A noting of items one by one : count, enumeration, numeration, reckoning. *Archaic:* tale. *See* COUNT. **2.** The total number of points made by a contestant, side, or team in a game or contest : score. *See* COUNT.

tally *verb* **1.** To note (items) one by one so as to get a total : count, enumerate, number, numerate, reckon, tell. *See* COUNT. **2.** To gain (a point or points) in a game or contest : post[1], score. *Informal:* notch. *See* DO. **3.** To be compatible or in correspondence : accord, agree, check, chime, comport with, conform, consist, correspond, fit[1], harmonize, match, square. *Informal:* jibe[1]. *Archaic:* quadrate. *See* AGREE.

tame *adjective*
1. Trained or bred to live with and be of use to people : domestic. *See* WILD. **2.** Easily managed or handled : docile, gentle, meek, mild. *See* WILD.

tame *verb* **1.** To train to live with and be of use to people : domesticate, domesticize, gentle, master. *See* WILD. **2.** To make (an animal) docile : break, bust, gentle, master. *See* WILD. **3.** To make or become less severe or extreme : moderate, mute, qualify, soften, subdue, temper, tone down. *See* INCREASE.

tamper *verb*
1. To handle something idly, ignorantly, or destructively : fiddle, fool, meddle, mess, tinker. *Informal:* monkey. *See* HELP, TOUCH. **2.** To prearrange the outcome of (a contest) unlawfully : fix. ***Idiom:*** stack the deck. *See* CRIMES.

tang *noun*
A distinctive property of a substance affecting the gustatory sense : flavor, relish, sapor, savor, smack[2], taste, zest. *See* TASTE.

tangent *noun*
An instance of digressing : aside, deviation, digression, divagation, divergence, divergency, excursion, excursus, irrelevancy, parenthesis. *See* APPROACH.

tangential *adjective*
Marked by or given to digression : digressive, discursive, excursive, parenthetic, parenthetical, rambling. *See* APPROACH.

tangibility *noun*
The quality or condition of being discernible by touch : palpability, tactility, tangibleness, touchableness. *See* TOUCH.

tangible *adjective*
1. Discernible by touch : palpable, tactile,

touchable. *See* TOUCH. **2.** Composed of or relating to things that occupy space and can be perceived by the senses : concrete, corporeal, material, objective, phenomenal, physical, sensible, substantial. *See* BODY, MATTER. **3.** Having verifiable existence : concrete, objective, real, substantial, substantive. *See* REAL.

tangibleness *noun*
The quality or condition of being discernible by touch : palpability, tactility, tangibility, touchableness. *See* TOUCH.

tangle *verb*
1. To twist together so that separation is difficult : ensnarl, entangle, foul, snarl[2]. *See* ORDER. **2.** To make complex, intricate, or perplexing : complicate, embarrass, entangle, involve, perplex, ravel, snarl[2]. *See* SIMPLE. **3.** To gain control of or an advantage over by or as if by trapping : catch, enmesh, ensnare, ensnarl, entrap, snare, trammel, trap, web. *See* FREE. **4.** *Informal.* To engage in a quarrel : argue, bicker, contend, dispute, fight, quarrel, quibble, spat, squabble, tiff, wrangle. *Informal:* hassle. ***Idioms:*** cross swords, have it out, have words, lock horns. *See* CONFLICT.

tangle *noun* **1.** Something that is intricately and often bewilderingly complex : cat's cradle, entanglement, jungle, knot, labyrinth, maze, mesh (often used in plural), morass, skein, snarl[2], web. *See* SIMPLE. **2.** *Informal.* A discussion, often heated, in which a difference of opinion is expressed : altercation, argument, bicker, clash, contention, controversy, debate, difficulty, disagreement, dispute, fight, polemic, quarrel, run-in, spat, squabble, tiff, word (used in plural), wrangle. *Informal:* hassle, rhubarb. *See* CONFLICT.

tangled *adjective*
Difficult to understand because of intricacy : byzantine, complex, complicated, convoluted, daedal, Daedalian, elaborate, intricate, involute, involved, knotty, labyrinthine. *See* SIMPLE.

tangy *adjective*
Having a taste characteristic of that produced by acids : acerb, acerbic, acetous, acid, acidulous, dry, sour, tart[1]. *See* TASTE.

tank up *verb*
Slang. To take alcoholic liquor, especially excessively or habitually : drink, guzzle, imbibe, tipple. *Informal:* nip[2]. *Slang:* booze, lush[2], soak. ***Idioms:*** bend the elbow, hit the bottle. *See* DRUGS.

tantalize *verb*
To excite (another) by exposing something desirable while keeping it out of reach : bait, tease. *See* EXCITE.

tantamount *adjective*
Agreeing exactly in value, quantity, or effect : equal, equivalent, even[1], identical, same. ***Idioms:*** on a par, one and the same. *See* SAME.

tantrum *noun*
An angry outburst : fit[2], huff, passion, temper. *Informal:* conniption, conniption fit. *See* FEELINGS.

tap[1] *verb*
1. To make a noise by striking : knock, rap[1]. *See* SOUNDS. **2.** To select for an office or position : appoint, designate, make, name, nominate. *See* CHOICE.

tap *noun* The sound made by a light blow : knock, rap[1]. *See* SOUNDS.

tap[2] *verb*
1. To remove (a liquid) by a steady, gradual process : drain, draw (off), let out, pump. *See* INCREASE. **2.** To monitor (telephone calls) with a concealed listening device connected to the circuit : bug, wiretap. *See* INVESTIGATE.

taper *noun*
The act or process of decreasing : abatement, curtailment, cut, cutback, decrease, decrement, diminishment, diminution, drain, reduction, slash, slowdown. *See* INCREASE.

taper *verb* To grow or cause to grow gradually less. Also used with *off* : abate, decrease, diminish, drain, dwindle, ebb, lessen, let up, peter (out), rebate, reduce, tail away (*or* off). *See* INCREASE.

tar *noun*
Informal. A person engaged in sailing or working on a ship : jack (uppercase), jack-tar, mariner, navigator, sailor, sea dog, seafarer, seaman. *Informal:* salt. *Slang:* gob[3]. *See* SEA.

tardily *adverb*
Not on time : behind, behindhand, belatedly, late. *See* TIME.

tardiness *noun*
The quality or condition of not being on time : belatedness, lateness. *See* TIME.

tardy *adjective*
1. Not being on time : behindhand, belated, late, overdue. *See* TIME. **2.** Proceeding at a rate less than usual or desired : dilatory, laggard, slow, slow-footed, slow-going, slow-paced. *Informal:* poky[1]. ***Idiom:*** slow as molasses in January. *See* FAST.

target *noun*
1. One that is fired at, attacked, or abused : butt[3], mark. *See* SEEK. **2.** What one intends to do or achieve : aim, ambition, design, end,

goal, intent, intention, mark, meaning, object, objective, point, purpose, view, why. *Idioms:* end in view, why and wherefore. *See* PLANNED, PURPOSE.

target *verb* **1.** To make a target of : mark. *Idiom:* draw (*or* get) a bead on. *See* SEEK. **2.** To have in mind as a goal or purpose : aim, contemplate, design, intend, mean[1], plan, project, propose, purpose. *Regional:* mind. *See* PLANNED, PURPOSE.

tariff *noun*
A compulsory contribution, usually of money, that is required for the support of a government : assessment, duty, impost, levy, tax. *See* MONEY, PAY, POLITICS.

tarnish *verb*
1. To spoil the soundness or perfection of : blemish, damage, detract from, disserve, flaw, harm, hurt, impair, injure, mar, prejudice, vitiate. *See* BETTER, HELP. **2.** To contaminate the reputation of : befoul, besmear, besmirch, bespatter, blacken, cloud, denigrate, dirty, smear, smudge, smut, soil, spatter, stain, sully, taint. *Idioms:* give a black eye to, sling (*or* throw) mud on. *See* ATTACK, CLEAN.

tarnish *noun* A mark of discredit or disgrace : black eye, blemish, blot, onus, spot, stain, stigma, taint. *Archaic:* attaint. *Idiom:* a blot on one's escutcheon. *See* MARKS, RESPECT.

tarrier *noun*
One that lags : dawdler, dilly-dallier, lag, laggard, lagger, lingerer, loiterer, poke, procrastinator, straggler. *Informal:* slowpoke. *See* FAST.

tarry *verb*
1. To go or move slowly so that progress is hindered : dally, dawdle, delay, dilly-dally, drag, lag, linger, loiter, poke, procrastinate, trail. *Idioms:* drag one's feet (*or* heels), mark time, take one's time. *See* FAST. **2.** To stop temporarily and remain, as if reluctant to leave : abide, bide, linger, pause, stay[1], wait. *See* CONTINUE. **3.** To continue to be in a place : abide, bide, linger, remain, stay[1], wait. *Informal:* stick around. *Idiom:* stay put. *See* CONTINUE.

tart[1] *adjective*
Having a taste characteristic of that produced by acids : acerb, acerbic, acetous, acid, acidulous, dry, sour, tangy. *See* TASTE.

tart[2] *noun*
1. A woman who engages in sexual intercourse for payment : bawd, call girl, camp follower, courtesan, harlot, prostitute, scarlet woman, streetwalker, strumpet, whore. *Slang:* hooker, moll. *Idioms:* lady of easy virtue, lady of pleasure, lady of the night. *See* SEX. **2.** A vulgar promiscuous woman who flouts propriety : baggage, hussy, jade, slattern, slut, tramp, wanton, wench, whore. *Slang:* floozy. *See* SEX.

tartufe *noun* See **tartuffe.**

tartuffe also **tartufe** *noun*
A person who practices hypocrisy : hypocrite, pharisee, phony. *See* HONEST.

tartuffery *noun*
A show or expression of feelings or beliefs one does not actually hold or possess : hypocrisy, pharisaism, phoniness, sanctimoniousness, sanctimony, two-facedness. *See* HONEST.

task *noun*
1. A piece of work that has been assigned : assignment, chore, duty, job, office, stint. *See* WORK. **2.** A difficult or tedious undertaking : chore, effort. *Informal:* job. *See* HEAVY, WORK. **3.** The proper activity of a person or thing : function, job, purpose, role. *See* DO.

task *verb* To force to work : drive, tax, work. *Idiom:* crack the whip. *See* WORK.

taskmaster *noun*
Someone who directs and supervises workers : boss, director, foreman, foreperson, forewoman, head, manager, overseer, superintendent, supervisor, taskmistress. *Informal:* straw boss. *Slang:* chief. *See* OVER.

taskmistress *noun*
Someone who directs and supervises workers : boss, director, foreman, foreperson, forewoman, head, manager, overseer, superintendent, supervisor, taskmaster. *Informal:* straw boss. *Slang:* chief. *See* OVER.

taste *verb*
1. To have a particular flavor or suggestion of something : savor, smack[2], smell, suggest. *See* SUGGEST. **2.** To undergo an emotional reaction : experience, feel, have, know, savor. *See* FEELINGS. **3.** To participate in or partake of personally. Also used with *of* : experience, feel, go through, have, know, meet[1] (with), see, suffer, undergo. *Archaic:* prove. *Idiom:* run up against. *See* PARTICIPATE.

taste *noun* **1.** A desire for food or drink : appetite, hunger, stomach, thirst. *See* DESIRE. **2.** A distinctive property of a substance affecting the gustatory sense : flavor, relish, sapor, savor, smack[2], tang, zest. *See* TASTE. **3.** A limited or anticipatory experience : foretaste, sample. *See* FORESIGHT. **4.** A slight amount or indication : breath, dash, ghost, hair, hint, intimation, semblance, shade, shadow, soupçon, streak, suggestion, suspicion, tinge, touch, trace, whiff, whisper. *Informal:* whisker. *See* BIG, SHOW. **5.** A liking : appetite, fondness, partiality, preference, relish, weakness. *See* LIKE. **6.** The faculty or sense of discerning what is aesthetically pleasing or appropriate : tastefulness. *See* STYLE.

tasteful *adjective*
1. Showing good taste : artistic, tasty. *Informal:* aesthetic. *See* STYLE. **2.** Highly pleasing, especially to the sense of taste : ambrosial, appetizing, delectable, delicious, heavenly, luscious, savory, scrumptious, tasty, toothsome. *Slang:* yummy. *See* GOOD, INGESTION. **3.** Not showy or obtrusive : inobtrusive, quiet, restrained, subdued, unobtrusive. *See* PLAIN.

tastefulness *noun*
The faculty or sense of discerning what is aesthetically pleasing or appropriate : taste. *See* STYLE.

tasteless *adjective*
1. Lacking an appetizing flavor : bland, flat, flavorless, insipid, unsavory. *See* TASTE.
2. Lacking style and good taste : inelegant, unbecoming. *Informal:* tacky². *See* STYLE.
3. Lacking in delicacy or refinement : barbarian, barbaric, boorish, churlish, coarse, crass, crude, gross, ill-bred, indelicate, philistine, rough, rude, uncivilized, uncouth, uncultivated, uncultured, unpolished, unrefined, vulgar. *See* COURTESY, SMOOTH.

tasty *adjective*
1. Highly pleasing, especially to the sense of taste : ambrosial, appetizing, delectable, delicious, heavenly, luscious, savory, scrumptious, tasteful, toothsome. *Slang:* yummy. *See* GOOD, INGESTION. **2.** Showing good taste : artistic, tasteful. *Informal:* aesthetic. *See* STYLE.

tatter *noun*
Torn and ragged clothing. Used in plural : rag¹ (used in plural). *See* BETTER, PUT ON.

tatterdemalion *noun*
A person wearing ragged or tattered clothing : ragamuffin, scarecrow. *See* BETTER, RICH.
tatterdemalion *adjective* Torn into or marked by shreds or tatters : ragged, raggedy, tattered. *See* BETTER.

tattered *adjective*
1. Torn into or marked by shreds or tatters : ragged, raggedy, tatterdemalion. *See* BETTER.
2. Showing signs of wear and tear or neglect : bedraggled, broken-down, decaying, decrepit, dilapidated, dingy, down-at-heel, faded, mangy, rundown, scrubby, scruffy, seedy, shabby, shoddy, sleazy, tatty, threadbare. *Informal:* tacky². *Slang:* ratty. ***Idioms:*** all the worse for wear, gone to pot (*or* seed), past cure (*or* hope). *See* BETTER.

tattle *verb*
1. To engage in or spread gossip : blab, gossip, noise, rumor, talk, tittle-tattle, whisper. ***Idioms:*** tell tales, tell tales out of school. *See* WORDS.
2. To give incriminating information about others, especially to the authorities : inform, talk, tip³ (off). *Slang:* fink, rat, sing, snitch, squeal, stool. ***Idiom:*** blow the whistle. *See* KNOWLEDGE, LAW.
tattle *noun* **1.** Idle, often sensational and groundless talk about others : gossip, gossipry, hearsay, report, rumor, talebearing, tittle-tattle, word. *Slang:* scuttlebutt. *See* WORDS. **2.** A person habitually engaged in idle talk about others : blab, gossip, gossiper, gossipmonger, newsmonger, rumormonger, scandalmonger, tabby, talebearer, taleteller, tattler, tattletale, telltale, whisperer. *Slang:* yenta. *See* WORDS.

tattler *noun*
1. A person habitually engaged in idle talk about others : blab, gossip, gossiper, gossipmonger, newsmonger, rumormonger, scandalmonger, tabby, talebearer, taleteller, tattle, tattletale, telltale, whisperer. *Slang:* yenta. *See* WORDS. **2.** One who gives incriminating information about others : informant, informer, tattletale. *Informal:* rat, tipster. *Slang:* fink, snitch, snitcher, squealer, stoolie, stool pigeon. *See* KNOWLEDGE, LAW.

tattletale *noun*
1. A person habitually engaged in idle talk about others : blab, gossip, gossiper, gossipmonger, newsmonger, rumormonger, scandalmonger, tabby, talebearer, taleteller, tattle, tattler, telltale, whisperer. *Slang:* yenta. *See* WORDS. **2.** One who gives incriminating information about others : informant, informer, tattler. *Informal:* rat, tipster. *Slang:* fink, snitch, snitcher, squealer, stoolie, stool pigeon. *See* KNOWLEDGE, LAW.

tatty *adjective*
Showing signs of wear and tear or neglect : bedraggled, broken-down, decaying, decrepit, dilapidated, dingy, down-at-heel, faded, mangy, rundown, scrubby, scruffy, seedy, shabby, shoddy, sleazy, tattered, threadbare. *Informal:* tacky². *Slang:* ratty. ***Idioms:*** all the worse for wear, gone to pot (*or* seed), past cure (*or* hope). *See* BETTER.

taunt *verb*
To torment with persistent insult or ridicule : badger, bait, bullyrag, heckle, hector, hound. *Informal:* needle, ride. ***Idiom:*** wave the red flag in front of the bull. *See* TREAT WELL.

taunt *noun* **1.** An instance of mockery or derision : gibe, insult, jeer, scoff, twit. *See* LAUGHTER, RESPECT. **2.** Good-natured teasing : badinage, banter, chaff, raillery. *Informal:* ribbing. *See* LAUGHTER.

taut *adjective*
1. Stretched tightly : stiff, tense, tight. *See* TIGHTEN. **2.** In good order or clean condition : neat, orderly, shipshape, snug, spick-and-span, spruce, tidy, trig, trim, well-groomed. *Chiefly British:* tight. ***Idiom:*** neat as a pin. *See* CLEAN, ORDER.

tauten *verb*
To make or become tense : stiffen, tense, tighten. *See* TIGHTEN.

tautological *adjective*
Characterized by repetition and excessive wordiness : circumlocutionary, roundabout. *See* REPETITION, WORDS.

tawdry *adjective*
Tastelessly showy : brummagem, chintzy, flashy, garish, gaudy, glaring, loud, meretricious, tinsel. *Informal:* tacky[2]. *See* STYLE.

tax *noun*
1. A compulsory contribution, usually of money, that is required for the support of a government : assessment, duty, impost, levy, tariff. *See* MONEY, PAY, POLITICS. **2.** A duty or responsibility that is a source of anxiety, worry, or hardship : burden[1], millstone, onus, weight. *Informal:* headache. *See* HEAVY, OVER.

tax *verb* **1.** To place a burden or heavy load on : burden[1], charge, cumber, encumber, freight, lade, load, saddle, weight. *See* OVER. **2.** To force to work : drive, task, work. ***Idiom:*** crack the whip. *See* WORK. **3.** To make an accusation against : accuse, arraign, charge, denounce, incriminate, indict. *See* ATTACK, LAW, PRAISE. **4.** To criticize for a fault or an offense : admonish, call down, castigate, chastise, chide, dress down, rap[1], rebuke, reprimand, reproach, reprove, scold, upbraid. *Informal:* bawl out, lambaste. *Slang:* chew out. ***Idioms:*** bring (*or* call *or* take) to task, call on the carpet, haul (*or* rake) over the coals, let someone have it. *See* ATTACK, PRAISE.

taxing *adjective*
Requiring great or extreme bodily, mental, or spiritual strength : arduous, backbreaking, burdensome, demanding, difficult, effortful, exacting, exigent, formidable, hard, heavy, laborious, onerous, oppressive, rigorous, rough, severe, tough, trying, weighty. *See* HEAVY.

teach *verb*
To impart knowledge and skill to : coach, discipline, educate, instruct, school, train, tutor. *See* TEACH.

teachable *adjective*
Capable of being educated : educable, trainable. *See* TEACH.

teacher *noun*
One who educates : educator, instructor, pedagogue, trainer, tutor. *See* TEACH.

teaching *noun*
1. The act, process, or art of imparting knowledge and skill : education, instruction, pedagogics, pedagogy, schooling, training, tuition, tutelage, tutoring. *See* TEACH. **2.** A principle taught or advanced for belief, as by a religious or philosophical group : doctrine, dogma, tenet. *See* BELIEF.

team *noun*
A group of people organized for a particular purpose : body, corps, crew, detachment, force, gang, unit. *See* GROUP.

teamwork *noun*
Joint work toward a common end : coaction, collaboration, cooperation, synergy. *See* CONFLICT.

tear[1] *verb*
1. To separate or pull apart by force : rend, rip, rive, run, split. *See* ASSEMBLE, HELP. **2.** To remove from a fixed position : extract, pluck, pull. *See* PUT IN. **3.** To move swiftly : bolt, bucket, bustle, dart, dash, festinate, flash, fleet, flit, fly, haste, hasten, hurry, hustle, pelt[2], race, rocket, run, rush, sail, scoot, scour[2], shoot, speed, sprint, trot, whirl, whisk, whiz, wing, zip, zoom. *Informal:* hotfoot, rip. *Slang:* barrel, highball. *Chiefly British:* nip[1]. ***Idioms:*** get a move on, get cracking, go like lightning, go like the wind, hotfoot it, make haste, make time, make tracks, run like the wind, shake a leg, step (*or* jump) on it. *See* MOVE.

tear down *verb* **1.** To pull down or break up so that reconstruction is impossible : demolish, destroy, dismantle, dynamite, knock down, level, pull down, pulverize, raze, wreck. *Aerospace:* destruct. *See* HELP. **2.** To make defamatory statements about : asperse, backbite, calumniate, defame, malign, slander, slur, traduce, vilify. *Law:* libel. ***Idiom:*** cast aspersions on. *See* ATTACK, CRIMES, LAW.

tear *noun* **1.** A hole made by tearing : rent[2], rip, run. *See* HELP. **2.** *Slang.* A drinking bout : binge, brannigan, carousal, carouse, drunk, spree. *Slang:* bat[2], bender, booze, jag. *See* DRUGS, RESTRAINT.

tear[2] *noun*
1. A drop of the clear liquid secreted by the

glands of the eyes : teardrop. *See* DRY. **2.** A fit of crying. Used in plural : bawling, blubbering, cry, sobbing, wailing, weeping. *See* SOUNDS.

tear *verb* To fill with tears : water. *See* DRY.

tear down *verb* See **tear[1]**.

teardrop *noun*
A drop of the clear liquid secreted by the glands of the eyes : tear[2]. *See* DRY.

tearful *adjective*
Filled with or shedding tears : lachrymose, teary, weeping, weepy. ***Idiom:*** in tears. *See* HAPPY.

tear-jerking *adjective*
Slang. Affectedly or extravagantly emotional : bathetic, gushy, maudlin, mawkish, romantic, sentimental, slushy, sobby, soft, soppy. *Informal:* gooey, mushy, schmaltzy, sloppy, soupy. *Slang:* drippy, sappy. *See* FEELINGS.

teary *adjective*
Filled with or shedding tears : lachrymose, tearful, weeping, weepy. ***Idiom:*** in tears. *See* HAPPY.

tease *verb*
1. To disturb by repeated attacks : annoy, bait, bedevil, beleaguer, beset, harass, harry, pester, plague, torment, worry. *See* FEELINGS, PAIN. **2.** To excite (another) by exposing something desirable while keeping it out of reach : bait, tantalize. *See* EXCITE.

techiness *noun* See **tetchiness.**

technicality *noun*
A small, often specialized element of a whole : detail, fine print, item, particular. *See* GROUP.

technique *noun*
1. A method used in dealing with something : approach, attack, course, line, modus operandi, plan, procedure, tack. *See* MEANS. **2.** Natural or acquired facility in a specific activity : ability, adeptness, art, command, craft, expertise, expertness, knack, mastery, proficiency, skill. *Informal:* know-how. *See* ABILITY, KNOWLEDGE.

techy *adjective* See **tetchy.**

tedious *adjective*
Arousing no interest or curiosity : boring, drear, dreary, dry, dull, humdrum, irksome, monotonous, stuffy, tiresome, uninteresting, weariful, wearisome, weary. *See* EXCITE.

teem *verb*
To be abundantly filled or richly supplied : abound, bristle, crawl, flow, overflow, pullulate, swarm. *See* BIG, RICH.

teen *noun*
A young person, usually between the ages of 13 and 19 : adolescent, teenager, youth. *Informal:* teener. *See* YOUTH.

teenager *noun*
A young person, usually between the ages of 13 and 19 : adolescent, teen, youth. *Informal:* teener. *See* YOUTH.

teener *noun*
Informal. A young person, usually between the ages of 13 and 19 : adolescent, teen, teenager, youth. *See* YOUTH.

teensy *adjective*
Informal. Extremely small : diminutive, dwarf, Lilliputian, midget, miniature, minuscule, minute[2], pygmy, tiny, wee. *Informal:* peewee, pintsize, pintsized, teensy-weensy, teeny, teeny-weeny, weeny. *See* BIG.

teensy-weensy *adjective*
Informal. Extremely small : diminutive, dwarf, Lilliputian, midget, miniature, minuscule, minute[2], pygmy, tiny, wee. *Informal:* peewee, pintsize, pintsized, teensy, teeny, teeny-weeny, weeny. *See* BIG.

teeny *adjective*
Informal. Extremely small : diminutive, dwarf, Lilliputian, midget, miniature, minuscule, minute[2], pygmy, tiny, wee. *Informal:* peewee, pintsize, pintsized, teensy, teensy-weensy, teeny-weeny, weeny. *See* BIG.

teeny-weeny *adjective*
Informal. Extremely small : diminutive, dwarf, Lilliputian, midget, miniature, minuscule, minute[2], pygmy, tiny, wee. *Informal:* peewee, pintsize, pintsized, teensy, teensy-weensy, teeny, weeny. *See* BIG.

teeter *verb*
1. To walk unsteadily : falter, lurch, reel, stagger, stumble, totter, weave, wobble. *See* MOVE. **2.** To move back and forth or from side to side, as if about to fall : sway, totter, vacillate, waver, weave, wobble. *See* REPETITION.

teetotalism *noun*
The practice of refraining from use of alcoholic liquors : abstinence, dryness, soberness, sobriety, temperance. *See* DRUGS, RESTRAINT, USED.

telephone *verb*
To communicate with (someone) by telephone : buzz, call, ring[2]. *Informal:* dial, phone. ***Idioms:*** get someone on the horn, give someone a buzz (*or* call *or* ring). *See* WORDS.

tell *verb*
1. To give a verbal account of : describe, narrate, recite, recount, rehearse, relate, report. *See* WORDS. **2.** To put into words : articulate, communicate, convey, declare, express, say,

state, talk, utter[1], vent, verbalize, vocalize, voice. *Idiom:* give tongue (*or* vent *or* voice) to. *See* WORDS. **3.** To make known : break, carry, communicate, convey, disclose, get across, impart, pass, report, transmit. *See* KNOWLEDGE. **4.** To disclose in a breach of confidence : betray, blab, divulge, expose, give away, let out, reveal, uncover, unveil. *Informal:* spill. *Archaic:* discover. ***Idioms:*** let slip, let the cat out of the bag, spill the beans, tell all. *See* SHOW. **5.** To impart information to : acquaint, advise, apprise, educate, enlighten, inform, notify. *See* KNOWLEDGE, TEACH. **6.** To give orders to : bid, charge, command, direct, enjoin, instruct, order. *See* OVER, WORDS. **7.** To recognize as being different : differentiate, discern, discriminate, distinguish, know, separate. *See* SAME. **8.** To note (items) one by one so as to get a total : count, enumerate, number, numerate, reckon, tally. *See* COUNT.

tell off *verb Informal.* To reprimand loudly or harshly : bawl out, berate, rate[2]. ***Idioms:*** give hell to, give it to. *See* ATTACK.

telling *adjective*
Serving to convince : cogent, convincing, persuasive, satisfactory. *See* PERSUASION.

tell off *verb* See **tell.**

telltale *noun*
A person habitually engaged in idle talk about others : blab, gossip, gossiper, gossipmonger, newsmonger, rumormonger, scandalmonger, tabby, talebearer, taleteller, tattle, tattler, tattletale, whisperer. *Slang:* yenta. *See* WORDS.

tellurian *adjective*
Relating to or characteristic of the earth or of human life on earth : earthbound, earthen, earthly, earthy, mundane, secular, telluric, temporal, terrene, terrestrial, worldly. *See* BODY, CULTURE, PLACE.

telluric *adjective*
Relating to or characteristic of the earth or of human life on earth : earthbound, earthen, earthly, earthy, mundane, secular, tellurian, temporal, terrene, terrestrial, worldly. *See* BODY, CULTURE, PLACE.

temerarious *adjective*
Characterized by unthinking boldness and haste : brash, foolhardy, harum-scarum, hasty, headlong, hotheaded, ill-considered, impetuous, improvident, impulsive, incautious, madcap, precipitant, precipitate, rash[1], reckless, slapdash, unconsidered. *See* CAREFUL.

temerariousness *noun*
Foolhardy boldness or disregard of danger : brashness, foolhardiness, incautiousness, rashness, recklessness, temerity. *See* CAREFUL.

temblor *noun*
A shaking of the earth : earthquake, quake, seism, tremblor, tremor. *Informal:* shake. *See* MOVE, REPETITION.

temerity *noun*
Foolhardy boldness or disregard of danger : brashness, foolhardiness, incautiousness, rashness, recklessness, temerariousness. *See* CAREFUL.

temper *verb*
To make or become less severe or extreme : moderate, mute, qualify, soften, subdue, tame, tone down. *See* INCREASE.

temper *noun* **1.** A person's customary manner of emotional response : complexion, disposition, humor, nature, temperament. *See* BE. **2.** A temporary state of mind or feeling : frame of mind, humor, mood, spirit (used in plural), vein. *See* FEELINGS. **3.** A tendency to become angry or irritable : irascibility, irascibleness, spleen, temperament, tetchiness. *Informal:* dander. *Slang:* short fuse. ***Idiom:*** low boiling point. *See* FEELINGS. **4.** An angry outburst : fit[2], huff, passion, tantrum. *Informal:* conniption, conniption fit. *See* FEELINGS. **5.** A prevailing quality, as of thought, behavior, or attitude : climate, mood, spirit, tone. *See* ATTITUDE.

temperament *noun*
1. A person's customary manner of emotional response : complexion, disposition, humor, nature, temper. *See* BE. **2.** A tendency to become angry or irritable : irascibility, irascibleness, spleen, temper, tetchiness. *Informal:* dander. *Slang:* short fuse. ***Idiom:*** low boiling point. *See* FEELINGS.

temperamental *adjective*
1. Given to changeable emotional states, especially of anger or gloom : moody. *See* FEELINGS. **2.** Following no predictable pattern : capricious, changeable, erratic, fantastic, fantastical, fickle, freakish, inconsistent, inconstant, mercurial, ticklish, uncertain, unpredictable, unstable, unsteady, variable, volatile, whimsical. *See* CHANGE, CONTINUE.

temperance *noun*
1. Avoidance of extremes of opinion, feeling, or personal conduct : measure, moderateness, moderation. *See* EDGE. **2.** The practice of refraining from use of alcoholic liquors : abstinence, dryness, soberness, sobriety, teetotalism. *See* DRUGS, RESTRAINT, USED.

temperate *adjective*
1. Exercising moderation and self-restraint in

appetites and behavior : abstemious, continent, sober. *See* RESTRAINT. **2.** Not excessive or extreme in amount, degree, or force : moderate, modest, reasonable. *See* BIG, EDGE. **3.** Kept within sensible limits : conservative, discreet, moderate, reasonable, restrained. *See* PLAIN, RESTRAINT. **4.** Free from extremes in temperature : mild, moderate. *See* EDGE.

tempestuous *adjective*
1. Violently disturbed or agitated, as by storms : dirty, heavy, raging, roiled, roily, rough, rugged, stormy, tumultuous, turbulent, ugly, violent, wild. *See* CALM. **2.** Marked by unrest or disturbance : stormy, tumultuous, turbulent. *See* CALM.

tempo *noun*
Rate of motion or performance : pace, speed, velocity. *Informal:* clip[1]. *See* FAST.

temporal *adjective*
1. Relating to or characteristic of the earth or of human life on earth : earthbound, earthen, earthly, earthy, mundane, secular, tellurian, telluric, terrene, terrestrial, worldly. *See* BODY, CULTURE, PLACE. **2.** Lasting or existing only for a short time : ephemeral, evanescent, fleet, fleeting, fugacious, fugitive, momentary, passing, short-lived, temporary, transient, transitory. *See* CONTINUE, TIME. **3.** Not religious in subject matter, form, or use : lay[2], profane, secular, worldly. *See* SACRED.

temporary *adjective*
1. Lasting or existing only for a short time : ephemeral, evanescent, fleet, fleeting, fugacious, fugitive, momentary, passing, short-lived, temporal, transient, transitory. *See* CONTINUE, TIME. **2.** Intended, used, or present for a limited time : impermanent, interim, provisional, short-range, short-term. *See* CONTINUE. **3.** Temporarily assuming the duties of another : acting, ad interim, interim, pro tem, provisional. *See* CONTINUE, SUBSTITUTE.

tempt *verb*
1. To beguile or draw into a wrong or foolish course of action : allure, entice, inveigle, lure, seduce. ***Idiom:*** lead astray. *See* PERSUASION. **2.** To behave so as to bring on (danger, for example) : court, invite, provoke. *See* SEEK.

temptation *noun*
Something that attracts, especially with the promise of pleasure or reward : allurement, bait, come-on, enticement, inducement, inveiglement, invitation, lure, seduction. *See* LIKE.

tempter *noun*
One that seduces : allurer, charmer, enticer, inveigler, lurer, seducer. *See* PERSUASION.

tempting *adjective*
1. Pleasing to the eye or mind : attractive, bewitching, enchanting, engaging, enticing, fascinating, fetching, glamorous, lovely, prepossessing, pretty, sweet, taking, winning, winsome. *See* LIKE. **2.** Tending to seduce : alluring, bewitching, come-hither, enticing, inveigling, inviting, luring, seductive, siren, witching. *See* LIKE, PERSUASION, SEX.

temptress *noun*
A usually unscrupulous woman who seduces or exploits men : enchantress, femme fatale, seductress, siren. *Informal:* vamp, witch. *See* SEX.

tenable *adjective*
1. Capable of being justified : defensible, excusable, justifiable. *See* FORGIVENESS, RIGHT. **2.** Capable of being defended against armed attack : defendable, defensible. *See* ATTACK.

tenacious *adjective*
1. Tenaciously unwilling to yield : bullheaded, dogged, hardheaded, headstrong, mulish, obstinate, pertinacious, perverse, pigheaded, stiff-necked, willful. *See* RESIST. **2.** Persistently holding to something : clinging, fast, firm[1], secure, tight. *See* FREE, TIGHTEN.

tenaciousness *noun*
The quality or state of being stubbornly unyielding : bullheadedness, doggedness, hardheadedness, mulishness, obstinacy, obstinateness, pertinaciousness, pertinacity, perverseness, perversity, pigheadedness, tenacity, willfulness. *See* RESIST.

tenacity *noun*
The quality or state of being stubbornly unyielding : bullheadedness, doggedness, hardheadedness, mulishness, obstinacy, obstinateness, pertinaciousness, pertinacity, perverseness, perversity, pigheadedness, tenaciousness, willfulness. *See* RESIST.

tend[1] *verb*
To have a tendency or inclination : incline, lean[1], slant, squint, trend. *See* LIKELY.

tend[2] *verb*
1. To have the care and supervision of : attend, care for, look after, mind, minister to, see to, watch. ***Idioms:*** keep an eye on, look out for, take care (*or* charge) of, take under one's wing. *See* CARE FOR. **2.** To prepare (soil) for the planting and raising of crops : cultivate, culture, dress, till, work. *See* PREPARED, TOUCH.

tendency *noun*
1. An inclination to something : bent, bias, cast, disposition, leaning, partiality, penchant,

predilection, predisposition, proclivity, proneness, propensity, squint, trend, turn. *See* APPROACH, LIKE. **2.** The thread or current of thought uniting or occurring in all the elements of a text or discourse : aim, burden[2], drift, intent, meaning, purport, substance, tenor, thrust. *See* MEANING.

tendentious *adjective*
Exhibiting bias : biased, one-sided, partial, partisan, prejudiced, prejudicial, prepossessed. *See* LIKE, STRAIGHT.

tendentiousness *noun*
An inclination for or against that inhibits impartial judgment : bias, one-sidedness, partiality, partisanship, prejudice, prepossession. *See* AFFECT, LIKE, STRAIGHT.

tender[1] *adjective*
Of a kindly, considerate character : gentle, mild, soft, softhearted, tenderhearted. *See* KIND.

tender[2] *noun*
Something offered : bid, offer, proffer, proposal. *See* OFFER.
tender *verb* To put before another for acceptance : extend, offer, present[2], proffer, volunteer. ***Idioms:*** come forward with, lay at someone's feet, lay before. *See* OFFER.

tenderfoot *noun*
One who is just starting to learn or do something : abecedarian, beginner, fledgling, freshman, greenhorn, initiate, neophyte, novice, novitiate, tyro. *Slang:* rookie. *See* START.

tenderhearted *adjective*
Of a kindly, considerate character : gentle, mild, soft, softhearted, tender[1]. *See* KIND.

tendril *noun*
A young stemlike growth arising from a plant : bine, offshoot, runner, shoot, sprig, sprout. *See* KIN.

tenebrific *adjective*
Dark and depressing : black, bleak, blue, cheerless, dark, desolate, dismal, dreary, gloomy, glum, joyless, somber. *See* HAPPY, LIGHT.

tenet *noun*
A principle taught or advanced for belief, as by a religious or philosophical group : doctrine, dogma, teaching. *See* BELIEF.

tenor *noun*
1. The thread or current of thought uniting or occurring in all the elements of a text or discourse : aim, burden[2], drift, intent, meaning, purport, substance, tendency, thrust. *See* MEANING. **2.** The general sense or significance, as of an action or statement : amount, burden[2], drift, import, purport, substance. ***Idioms:*** sum and substance, sum total. *See* MEANING.

tense *adjective*
1. Stretched tightly : stiff, taut, tight. *See* TIGHTEN. **2.** Feeling or exhibiting nervous tension : edgy, fidgety, jittery, jumpy, nervous, restive, restless, skittish, twitchy. *Slang:* uptight. ***Idioms:*** a bundle of nerves, all wound up, on edge. *See* TIGHTEN.
tense *verb* To make or become tense : stiffen, tauten, tighten. *See* TIGHTEN.

tension *noun*
The act, condition, or effect of exerting force on someone or something : pressure, strain[1], stress. *See* PUSH.

ten-strike *noun*
Informal. A dazzling, often sudden instance of success : hit, sleeper. *Informal:* smash, smash hit, wow. *Slang:* boff, boffo, boffola. *See* THRIVE.

tentative *adjective*
1. Not perfected, elaborated, or completed : preliminary, rough, sketchy, unfinished, unperfected, unpolished. *See* START. **2.** Depending on or containing a condition or conditions : conditional, provisional, provisory. *See* LIMITED. **3.** Given to or exhibiting hesitation : halting, hesitant, indecisive, irresolute, pendulous, shilly-shally, timid, vacillant, vacillatory. *See* DECIDE.

tentativeness *noun*
The act of hesitating or state of being hesitant : hesitancy, hesitation, indecision, indecisiveness, irresoluteness, irresolution, pause, shilly-shally, timidity, timidness, to-and-fro, vacillation. *See* DECIDE.

tenuous *adjective*
Having little substance or significance; not solidly based : feeble, flimsy, insubstantial, unsubstantial. *See* STRONG.

tenure *noun*
The holding of something, such as a position : incumbency, occupancy, occupation. *See* PLACE.

tepid *adjective*
Lacking warmth, interest, enthusiasm, or involvement : halfhearted, lukewarm, unenthusiastic. *See* ATTITUDE, HOT.

tergiversate *verb*
1. To use evasive or deliberately vague language : equivocate, euphemize, hedge, shuffle, weasel. *Informal:* pussyfoot, waffle. ***Idioms:*** beat about (*or* around) the bush, mince words. *See* CLEAR. **2.** To abandon one's cause or party : apostatize, defect, desert[3], renegade,

turn. *Slang:* rat. ***Idioms:*** change sides, turn one's coat. *See* APPROACH, TRUST.

tergiversation *noun*

1. An instance of defecting from or abandoning a cause : apostasy, defection, recreance, recreancy. *See* APPROACH, TRUST. **2.** The use or an instance of equivocal language : ambiguity, equivocation, equivoque, euphemism, hedge, prevarication, shuffle, weasel word. *Informal:* waffle. *See* CLEAR. **3.** An expression or term liable to more than one interpretation : ambiguity, double-entendre, equivocality, equivocation, equivoque. *See* CLEAR.

tergiversator *noun*

A person who has defected : apostate, defector, deserter, recreant, renegade, runagate, turncoat. *Informal:* rat. *See* APPROACH.

term *noun*

1. A limited or specific period of time during which something happens, lasts, or extends : duration, span, stretch, time. *See* TIME. **2.** The period during which someone or something exists : day (often used in plural), duration, existence, life, lifetime, span. *See* LIVE, TIME. **3.** A specific length of time characterized by the occurrence of certain conditions or events : period, season, span, stretch. *See* TIME. **4.** A sound or combination of sounds that symbolizes and communicates a meaning : expression, locution, word. *See* WORDS. **5.** A restricting or modifying element. Often used in plural : condition, provision, proviso, qualification, reservation, specification, stipulation. *Informal:* string (often used in plural). *See* LIMITED. **6.** An established position from which to operate or deal with others. Often used in plural : basis, footing, status. *See* CONNECT.

term *verb* **1.** To describe with a word or term : call, characterize, designate, label, name, style, tag. *See* SPECIFIC, WORDS. **2.** To give a name or title to : baptize, call, christen, denominate, designate, dub, entitle, name, style, title. *See* SPECIFIC, WORDS.

termagant *noun*

A person, traditionally a woman, who persistently nags or criticizes : fishwife, fury, harpy, scold, shrew, virago, vixen. *Informal:* battle-ax. *See* PRAISE.

terminal *adjective*

1. Of or relating to a terminative condition, stage, or point : final, last[1], latter, ultimate. *See* START. **2.** Coming after all others : closing, concluding, final, last[1]. *See* START.

terminate *verb*

1. To bring or come to a natural or proper end : close, complete, conclude, consummate, end, finish, wind up, wrap up. *See* START. **2.** To relinquish one's engagement in or occupation with : demit, leave[1], quit, resign. *See* CONTINUE. **3.** To stop suddenly, as a conversation, activity, or relationship : break off, cease, discontinue, interrupt, suspend. *See* CONTINUE. **4.** To end the employment or service of : cashier, discharge, dismiss, drop, release. *Informal:* ax, fire, pink-slip. *Slang:* boot[1], bounce, can, sack[1]. ***Idioms:*** give someone his or her walking papers, give someone the ax, give someone the gate, give someone the pink slip, let go, show someone the door. *See* KEEP.

termination *noun*

1. A concluding or terminating : cease, cessation, close, closing, closure, completion, conclusion, consummation, end, ending, end of the line, finish, period, stop, stopping point, terminus, wind-up, wrap-up. *See* CONTINUE. **2.** The act of dismissing or the condition of being dismissed from employment : discharge, dismissal. *Informal:* ax. *Slang:* boot[1], bounce, sack[1]. *See* KEEP. **3.** The last part : close, conclusion, end, ending, finale, finish, last[1], wind-up, wrap-up. *See* START.

terminology *noun*

Specialized expressions indigenous to a particular field, subject, trade, or subculture : argot, cant[2], dialect, idiom, jargon, language, lexicon, lingo, patois, vernacular, vocabulary. *See* WORDS.

terminus *noun*

A concluding or terminating : cease, cessation, close, closing, closure, completion, conclusion, consummation, end, ending, end of the line, finish, period, stop, stopping point, termination, wind-up, wrap-up. *See* CONTINUE.

terpsichorean *noun*

A person who dances, especially professionally : dancer. *Slang:* hoofer. *See* REPETITION.

terrain *noun*

1. The character, natural features, and configuration of land : topography. ***Idiom:*** the lay of the land. *See* SURFACE. **2.** A sphere of activity, experience, study, or interest : area, arena, bailiwick, circle, department, domain, field, orbit, province, realm, scene, subject, territory, world. *Slang:* bag. *See* TERRITORY. **3.** A particular area used for or associated with a specific individual or activity : country, district, region, territory. *Slang:* turf. *See* TERRITORY.

terrene *adjective*

Relating to or characteristic of the earth or of human life on earth : earthbound, earthen, earthly, earthy, mundane, secular, tellurian, telluric, temporal, terrestrial, worldly. *See* BODY, CULTURE, PLACE.

terrestrial *adjective*

1. Relating to or characteristic of the earth or of human life on earth : earthbound, earthen, earthly, earthy, mundane, secular, tellurian, telluric, temporal, terrene, worldly. *See* BODY, CULTURE, PLACE. **2.** Consisting of or resembling soil : earthen, earthlike, earthy. *See* MATTER.

terrible *adjective*

1. Causing or able to cause fear : appalling, dire, direful, dreadful, fearful, fearsome, formidable, frightful, ghastly, redoubtable, scary, tremendous. *See* FEAR. **2.** Extreme in degree, strength, or effect : desperate, fierce, furious, intense, vehement, violent. *See* BIG, STRONG. **3.** Very bad : appalling, awful, dreadful, fearful, frightful, ghastly, horrendous, horrible, shocking. *See* GOOD.

terrific *adjective*

1. Causing great horror : bloodcurdling, hair-raising, horrible, horrid, horrific. *See* FEAR. **2.** Exceptionally good of its kind : ace, banner, blue-ribbon, brag, capital, champion, excellent, fine[1], first-class, first-rate, prime, quality, splendid, superb, superior, tiptop, top. *Informal:* A-one, bully, dandy, great, swell, top-flight, topnotch. *Slang:* boss. *Chiefly British:* tophole. *See* GOOD. **3.** Particularly excellent : divine, fabulous, fantastic, fantastical, glorious, marvelous, sensational, splendid, superb, wonderful. *Informal:* dandy, dreamy, great, ripping, super, swell, tremendous. *Slang:* cool, groovy, hot, keen[1], neat, nifty. ***Idiom:*** out of this world. *See* GOOD.

terrify *verb*

To fill with fear : affright, alarm, frighten, panic, scare, scarify[2], startle, terrorize. *Archaic:* fright. ***Idioms:*** make one's blood run cold, make one's hair stand on end, scare silly (*or* stiff), scare the daylights out of. *See* FEAR.

territorial *adjective*

Relating to or restricted to a particular territory : regional, sectional. *See* TERRITORY.

territory *noun*

1. An area subject to rule by an outside power : colony, dependency, possession, province. *See* POLITICS. **2.** A particular area used for or associated with a specific individual or activity : country, district, region, terrain. *Slang:* turf. *See* TERRITORY. **3.** A sphere of activity, experience, study, or interest : area, arena, bailiwick, circle, department, domain, field, orbit, province, realm, scene, subject, terrain, world. *Slang:* bag. *See* TERRITORY.

terror *noun*

Great agitation and anxiety caused by the expectation or the realization of danger : affright, alarm, apprehension, dread, fear, fearfulness, fright, funk, horror, panic, trepidation. *Slang:* cold feet. ***Idiom:*** fear and trembling. *See* FEAR.

terrorize *verb*

To fill with fear : affright, alarm, frighten, panic, scare, scarify[2], startle, terrify. *Archaic:* fright. ***Idioms:*** make one's blood run cold, make one's hair stand on end, scare silly (*or* stiff), scare the daylights out of. *See* FEAR.

terse *adjective*

Marked by or consisting of few words that are carefully chosen : brief, compendious, concise, laconic, lean[2], short, succinct, summary. *See* BIG, STYLE, WORDS.

test *noun*

1. A procedure that ascertains effectiveness, value, proper function, or other quality : assay, essay, proof, trial, tryout. *See* INVESTIGATE. **2.** An operation employed to resolve an uncertainty : experiment, experimentation, trial. *See* INVESTIGATE. **3.** A set of questions or exercises designed to determine knowledge or skill : catechism, catechization, exam, examination, quiz. *See* INVESTIGATE. **4.** A means by which individuals are compared and judged : benchmark, criterion, gauge, mark, measure, standard, touchstone, yardstick. *See* USUAL.

test *adjective* Constituting a tentative model for future experiment or development : experimental, pilot, trial. *See* START.

test *verb* **1.** To subject to a procedure that ascertains effectiveness, value, proper function, or other quality : assay, check, essay, examine, prove, try, try out. ***Idioms:*** bring to the test, make trial of, put to the proof (*or* test). *See* INVESTIGATE. **2.** To subject to a test of knowledge or skill : check, examine, quiz. *See* INVESTIGATE. **3.** To engage in experiments : experiment. *See* INVESTIGATE.

testament *noun*

That which confirms : attestation, authentication, confirmation, corroboration, demonstration, evidence, proof, substantiation, testimonial, testimony, validation, verification, warrant. *See* TRUE.

testifier *noun*

One who testifies, especially in court : attestant, attester, witness. *Law:* deponent. *See* LAW.

testify *verb*
1. To give evidence or testimony under oath : attest, swear, witness. *Law:* depone, depose. *Idioms:* bear witness, take the stand. *See* LAW. **2.** To confirm formally as true, accurate, or genuine : attest, certify, vouch (for), witness. *Idiom:* bear witness to. *See* AFFIRM. **3.** To assure the certainty or validity of. Also used with *to* : attest, authenticate, back (up), bear out, confirm, corroborate, evidence, justify, substantiate, validate, verify, warrant. *See* SUPPORT, TRUE. **4.** To give grounds for believing in the existence or presence of : argue, attest, bespeak, betoken, indicate, mark, point to, witness. *See* SHOW.

testimonial *noun*
1. That which confirms : attestation, authentication, confirmation, corroboration, demonstration, evidence, proof, substantiation, testament, testimony, validation, verification, warrant. *See* TRUE. **2.** A statement attesting to personal qualifications, character, and dependability : character, recommendation, reference. *See* SUPPORT. **3.** A formal token of appreciation and admiration for a person's high achievements : salute, salvo, tribute. *See* PRAISE.

testimony *noun*
1. A formal declaration of truth or fact given under oath : witness. *Law:* deposition. *See* LAW. **2.** That which confirms : attestation, authentication, confirmation, corroboration, demonstration, evidence, proof, substantiation, testament, testimonial, validation, verification, warrant. *See* TRUE.

testy *adjective*
1. Easily annoyed : choleric, irascible, peppery, quick-tempered, tetchy, touchy. *See* FEELINGS. **2.** Having or showing a bad temper : bad-tempered, cantankerous, crabbed, cranky, cross, disagreeable, fretful, grouchy, grumpy, ill-tempered, irascible, irritable, nasty, peevish, petulant, querulous, snappish, snappy, surly, ugly, waspish. *Informal:* crabby, mean[2]. *Idiom:* out of sorts. *See* ATTITUDE.

tetchiness also **techiness** *noun*
A tendency to become angry or irritable : irascibility, irascibleness, spleen, temper, temperament. *Informal:* dander. *Slang:* short fuse. *Idiom:* low boiling point. *See* FEELINGS.

tetchy also **techy** *adjective*
Easily annoyed : choleric, irascible, peppery, quick-tempered, testy, touchy. *See* FEELINGS.

text *noun*
What a speech, piece of writing, or artistic work is about : argument, matter, point, subject, subject matter, theme, topic. *See* MEANING.

texture *noun*
1. A distinctive, complex underlying pattern or structure : contexture, fabric, fiber, warp and woof, web. *See* BE. **2.** A basic trait or set of traits that define and establish the character of something : being, essence, essentiality, nature, quintessence, substance. *See* SURFACE.

thalassic *adjective*
Of or relating to the seas or oceans : marine, maritime, oceanic, pelagic. *See* SEA.

thankful *adjective*
Showing or feeling gratitude : appreciative, grateful. *See* GRATEFUL.

thankfulness *noun*
A being grateful : appreciation, gratefulness, gratitude, thanks. *See* GRATEFUL.

thankless *adjective*
1. Not showing or feeling gratitude : unappreciative, ungrateful, unthankful, unthanking. *See* GRATEFUL. **2.** Not apt to be appreciated : unappreciated, ungrateful, unthankful. *See* GRATEFUL.

thanks *noun*
1. A being grateful : appreciation, gratefulness, gratitude, thankfulness. *See* GRATEFUL. **2.** A short prayer said at meals : benediction, blessing, grace, thanksgiving. *See* GRATEFUL, RELIGION.

thanksgiving *noun*
A short prayer said at meals : benediction, blessing, grace, thanks. *See* GRATEFUL, RELIGION.

thaumaturgic *adjective*
Having, brought about by, or relating to supernatural powers or magic : fey, magic, magical, talismanic, thaumaturgical, theurgic, theurgical, witching, wizardly. *See* SUPERNATURAL.

thaumaturgical *adjective*
Having, brought about by, or relating to supernatural powers or magic : fey, magic, magical, talismanic, thaumaturgic, theurgic, theurgical, witching, wizardly. *See* SUPERNATURAL.

thaumaturgy *noun*
The use of supernatural powers to influence or predict events : conjuration, magic, sorcery, sortilege, theurgy, witchcraft, witchery, witching, wizardry. *See* SUPERNATURAL.

thaw *verb*
To change from a solid to a liquid : deliquesce, dissolve, flux, fuse, liquefy, melt, run. *See* SOLID.

theatric *adjective*
1. Of or relating to drama or the theater : dramatic, dramaturgic, dramaturgical, histrionic,

histrionical, theatrical, thespian. *See* PERFORMING ARTS. **2.** Suggesting drama or a stage performance, as in emotionality or suspense : dramatic, histrionic, histrionical, melodramatic, sensational, spectacular, theatrical. *See* EXCITE, STYLE, SURPRISE.

theatrical *adjective*
1. Of or relating to drama or the theater : dramatic, dramaturgic, dramaturgical, histrionic, histrionical, theatric, thespian. *See* PERFORMING ARTS. **2.** Suggesting drama or a stage performance, as in emotionality or suspense : dramatic, histrionic, histrionical, melodramatic, sensational, spectacular, theatric. *See* EXCITE, STYLE, SURPRISE.
theatrical *noun* Overemotional exaggerated behavior calculated for effect. Used in plural : dramatics, histrionics, melodramatics, theatrics. *See* FEELINGS, STYLE.

theatricalism *noun*
Showy mannerisms and behavior : exhibitionism, staginess, theatricality, theatricalness. *See* PLAIN, STYLE.

theatricality *noun*
Showy mannerisms and behavior : exhibitionism, staginess, theatricalism, theatricalness. *See* PLAIN, STYLE.

theatricalness *noun*
Showy mannerisms and behavior : exhibitionism, staginess, theatricalism, theatricality. *See* PLAIN, STYLE.

theatrics *noun*
Overemotional exaggerated behavior calculated for effect : dramatics, histrionics, melodramatics, theatrical (used in plural). *See* FEELINGS, STYLE.

theft *noun*
The crime of taking someone else's property without consent : larceny, pilferage, steal, thievery. *Slang:* rip-off. *See* CRIMES.

thematic *adjective*
Of, constituting, or relating to a theme or themes : topical. *See* MEANING.

theme *noun*
1. What a speech, piece of writing, or artistic work is about : argument, matter, point, subject, subject matter, text, topic. *See* MEANING. **2.** A relatively brief discourse written especially as an exercise : composition, essay, paper. *See* WORDS. **3.** The main part of a word to which affixes are attached : base[1], root[1], stem. *See* WORDS.

theorem *noun*
A broad and basic rule or truth : axiom, fundamental, law, principle, universal. *See* ORDER.

theoretic *adjective*
1. Existing only in concept and not in reality : abstract, hypothetic, hypothetical, ideal, theoretical, transcendent, transcendental. *See* REAL. **2.** Concerned primarily with theories rather than practical matters : abstract, academic, speculative, theoretical. *See* THOUGHTS.

theoretical *adjective*
1. Existing only in concept and not in reality : abstract, hypothetic, hypothetical, ideal, theoretic, transcendent, transcendental. *See* REAL. **2.** Concerned primarily with theories rather than practical matters : abstract, academic, speculative, theoretic. *See* THOUGHTS.

theorize *verb*
To formulate or assert as a tentative explanation : hypothesize, speculate. *See* BELIEF, THOUGHTS.

theory *noun*
1. Abstract reasoning : conjecture, speculation. *See* BELIEF, THOUGHTS. **2.** A belief used as the basis for action : hypothesis. *See* BELIEF, THOUGHTS. **3.** Something taken to be true without proof : assumption, postulate, postulation, premise, presupposition, supposition, thesis. *See* REASON.

therapeutic *adjective*
Serving to cure : curative, remedial, restorative. *See* HEALTH.

therapy *noun*
The systematic application of remedies to effect a cure : care, regimen, rehabilitation, treatment. *Informal:* rehab. *See* HEALTH, HELP.

thesis *noun*
1. A hypothetical controversial proposition : contention, contestation. *See* OPINION. **2.** A thorough, written presentation of an original point of view : dissertation. *See* WORDS. **3.** Something taken to be true without proof : assumption, postulate, postulation, premise, presupposition, supposition, theory. *See* REASON.

thespian *adjective*
Of or relaing to drama or the theater : dramatic, dramaturgic, dramaturgical, histrionic, histrionical, theatric, theatrical. *See* PERFORMING ARTS.
thespian *noun* A theatrical performer : actor, actress, player. *See* ACTION, PERFORMING ARTS, SUBSTITUTE.

theurgic *adjective*
Having, brought about by, or relating to supernatural powers or magic : fey, magic, magical,

talismanic, thaumaturgic, thaumaturgical, theurgical, witching, wizardly. *See* SUPERNATURAL.

theurgical *adjective*
Having, brought about by, or relating to supernatural powers or magic : fey, magic, magical, talismanic, thaumaturgic, thaumaturgical, theurgic, witching, wizardly. *See* SUPERNATURAL.

theurgy *noun*
The use of supernatural powers to influence or predict events : conjuration, magic, sorcery, sortilege, thaumaturgy, witchcraft, witchery, witching, wizardry. *See* SUPERNATURAL.

thew *noun*
The state or quality of being physically strong. Often used in plural : brawn, might, muscle, potence, potency, power, powerfulness, puissance, sinew, strength. *See* STRONG.

thick *adjective*
1. Relatively great in extent from one surface to the opposite : fat. *See* THICK. **2.** Short, heavy, and solidly built : blocky, chunky, compact[1], dumpy, heavyset, squat, stocky, stodgy, stubby, stumpy, thickset. *See* FAT. **3.** Having all parts near to each other : close, compact[1], crowded, dense, packed, tight. *See* TIGHTEN. **4.** Growing profusely : dense, heavy, lush[1], luxuriant, profuse, rank[2]. *See* BIG. **5.** Having a dense or viscous consistency : gelatinous, heavy, stodgy. *See* SOLID. **6.** *Informal.* Lacking in intelligence : blockheaded, dense, doltish, dumb, hebetudinous, obtuse, stupid, thickheaded, thick-witted. *Slang:* dimwitted, dopey. *See* ABILITY. **7.** *Informal.* Very closely associated : chummy, close, familiar, friendly, intimate[1]. *Slang:* tight. ***Idiom:*** hand in glove with. *See* LOVE.

thick *noun* The most intensely active central part : eye, midst. *See* EDGE.

thicken *verb*
To make thick or thicker, especially through evaporation or condensation : condense, inspissate. *See* SOLID.

thickhead *noun*
A mentally dull person : blockhead, chump[1], clod, dolt, dullard, dummkopf, dummy, dunce, numskull. *Slang:* dimwit, dumbbell, dumbo. *See* ABILITY.

thickheaded *adjective*
Lacking in intelligence : blockheaded, dense, doltish, dumb, hebetudinous, obtuse, stupid, thick-witted. *Informal:* thick. *Slang:* dimwitted, dopey. *See* ABILITY.

thickness *noun*
The quality, condition, or degree of being thick : compactness, density, solidity. *See* THICK.

thickset *adjective*
Short, heavy, and solidly built : blocky, chunky, compact[1], dumpy, heavyset, squat, stocky, stodgy, stubby, stumpy, thick. *See* FAT.

thick-witted *adjective*
Lacking in intelligence : blockheaded, dense, doltish, dumb, hebetudinous, obtuse, stupid, thickheaded. *Informal:* thick. *Slang:* dimwitted, dopey. *See* ABILITY.

thief *noun*
A person who steals : bandit, burglar, highwayman, housebreaker, larcener, larcenist, pilferer, purloiner, robber, stealer. *See* CRIMES.

thieve *verb*
To take (another's property) without permission : filch, pilfer, purloin, snatch, steal. *Informal:* lift, swipe. *Slang:* cop, heist, hook, nip[1], pinch, rip off, snitch. ***Idiom:*** make (*or* walk) off with. *See* CRIMES, GIVE.

thievery *noun*
The crime of taking someone else's property without consent : larceny, pilferage, steal, theft. *Slang:* rip-off. *See* CRIMES.

thievish *adjective*
Tending to larceny : larcenous. *See* CRIMES.

thin *adjective*
1. Having little flesh or fat on the body : angular, bony, fleshless, gaunt, lank, lanky, lean[2], meager, rawboned, scrawny, skinny, slender, slim, spare, twiggy, weedy. ***Idioms:*** all skin and bones, thin as a rail. *See* FAT. **2.** Marked by great diffusion of component particles : rare, rarefied. *See* TIGHTEN. **3.** Lower than normal in strength or concentration due to admixture : dilute, washy, watered-down, waterish, watery, weak. *See* STRONG. **4.** Conspicuously deficient in quantity, fullness, or extent : exiguous, meager, poor, puny, scant, scanty, skimpy, spare, sparse, stingy. *Slang:* measly. *See* BIG, EXCESS. **5.** Not plausible or believable : flimsy, implausible, improbable, inconceivable, incredible, shaky, unbelievable, unconceivable, unconvincing, unsubstantial, weak. *See* LIKELY.

thin *verb* **1.** To make physically thin or thinner : slim. *Archaic:* extenuate. *See* FAT, INCREASE. **2.** To become diffuse : attenuate, rarefy. *See* TIGHTEN. **3.** To lessen the strength of by or as if by admixture : attenuate, cut, dilute, water (down), weaken. *See* STRONG.

thing *noun*
1. One that exists independently : being, entity, existence, existent, individual, object, something. *See* BE, THING. **2.** Something having

material existence : article, item, object. *See* THING. **3.** A small specialized mechanical device : concern, contraption, contrivance, gadget, gimmick, jigger. *Informal:* doodad, doohickey, widget. *Slang:* gizmo. *See* MACHINE. **4.** One's portable property. Often used in plural : belonging (often used in plural), effect (used in plural), good (used in plural), lares and penates, personal effects, personal property, possession (used in plural), property. *Informal:* stuff. *Law:* chattel, movable (often used in plural). *See* OWNED. **5.** Things needed for a task, journey, or other purpose. Used in plural : accouterment (often used in plural), apparatus, equipment, gear, material (used in plural), materiel, outfit, paraphernalia, rig, tackle, turnout. *See* MEANS. **6.** Something done : act, action, deed, doing, work. *See* DO. **7.** Something to be done, considered, or dealt with : affair, business, matter. *See* THING. **8.** Something that happens : circumstance, event, happening, incident, occasion, occurrence. *See* HAPPEN. **9.** Something significant that happens : circumstance, development, episode, event, happening, incident, news, occasion, occurrence. *See* HAPPEN. **10.** *Informal.* An irrational preoccupation : fetish, fixation, mania, obsession. *See* CONCERN. **11.** *Informal.* The current custom : craze, fad, fashion, furor, mode, rage, style, trend, vogue. ***Idioms:*** the in thing, the last word, the latest thing. *See* STYLE, USUAL. **12.** *Slang.* Something at which a person excels : forte, long suit, métier, specialty, strong point, strong suit. *Slang:* bag. *See* ABILITY.

think *verb*

1. To think or think about carefully and at length : chew on (*or* over), cogitate, consider, contemplate, deliberate, entertain, excogitate, meditate, mull, muse[1], ponder, reflect, revolve, ruminate, study, think out, think over, think through, turn over, weigh. ***Idioms:*** cudgel one's brains, put on one's thinking cap, rack one's brain. *See* THOUGHTS. **2.** To use the powers of the mind, as in conceiving ideas, drawing inferences, and making judgments : cerebrate, cogitate, deliberate, ratiocinate, reflect, speculate. ***Idioms:*** put on one's thinking cap, use one's head. *See* THOUGHTS. **3.** To view in a certain way : believe, feel, hold, sense. *See* OPINION. **4.** To regard in an appraising way : believe, repute, suppose. *See* BELIEF. **5.** To have an opinion : believe, consider, deem, hold, opine. *Informal:* figure, judge. ***Idiom:*** be of the opinion. *See* OPINION. **6.** To renew an image or thought in the mind : bethink, mind, recall, recollect, remember, reminisce, retain, revive. ***Idiom:*** bring to mind. *See* REMEMBER. **7.** To form mental images of : conceive, envisage, envision, fancy, fantasize, image, imagine, picture, see, vision, visualize. *Informal:* feature. *See* THOUGHTS.

think about *verb* To care enough to keep (someone) in mind : remember, think of. *See* REMEMBER.

think of *verb* **1.** To receive (an idea) and take it into consideration : consider, entertain, hear of. *See* THOUGHTS. **2.** To care enough to keep (someone) in mind : remember, think about. *See* REMEMBER.

think out *verb* To think or think about carefully and at length : chew on (*or* over), cogitate, consider, contemplate, deliberate, entertain, excogitate, meditate, mull, muse[1], ponder, reflect, revolve, ruminate, study, think, think over, think through, turn over, weigh. ***Idioms:*** cudgel one's brains, put on one's thinking cap, rack one's brain. *See* THOUGHTS.

think over *verb* To think or think about carefully and at length : chew on (*or* over), cogitate, consider, contemplate, deliberate, entertain, excogitate, meditate, mull, muse[1], ponder, reflect, revolve, ruminate, study, think, think out, think through, turn over, weigh. ***Idioms:*** cudgel one's brains, put on one's thinking cap, rack one's brain. *See* THOUGHTS.

think through *verb* To think or think about carefully and at length : chew on (*or* over), cogitate, consider, contemplate, deliberate, entertain, excogitate, meditate, mull, muse[1], ponder, reflect, revolve, ruminate, study, think, think out, think over, turn over, weigh. ***Idioms:*** cudgel one's brains, put on one's thinking cap, rack one's brain. *See* THOUGHTS.

think up *verb* To use ingenuity in making, developing, or achieving : concoct, contrive, devise, dream up, fabricate, formulate, hatch, invent, make up. *Informal:* cook up. ***Idiom:*** come up with. *See* MAKE.

thinkable *adjective*

Capable of being anticipated, considered, or imagined : conceivable, earthly, imaginable, likely, mortal, possible. ***Idioms:*** humanly possible, within the bounds (*or* range *or* realm) of possibility. *See* POSSIBLE.

think about *verb* See **think.**

thinker *noun*

1. A person who seeks reason and truth by thinking and meditation : philosopher. *See* THOUGHTS. **2.** A person of great mental ability : brain, intellect, intellectual, mind. *See* ABILITY.

thinking *adjective*
Of, characterized by, or disposed to thought : cogitative, contemplative, deliberative, excogitative, meditative, pensive, reflective, ruminative, speculative, thoughtful. ***Idiom:*** in a brown study. *See* THOUGHTS.

think of *verb* See **think.**

think out *verb* See **think.**

think over *verb* See **think.**

think through *verb* See **think.**

think up *verb* See **think.**

third estate *noun*
The common people : common (used in plural), commonality, commonalty, commoner (used in plural), crowd, hoi polloi, mass (used in plural), mob, pleb (used in plural), plebeian (used in plural), populace, public, ruck[1]. *See* OVER.

thirst *noun*
1. A desire for food or drink : appetite, hunger, stomach, taste. *See* DESIRE. **2.** A strong wanting of what promises enjoyment or pleasure : appetence, appetency, appetite, craving, desire, hunger, itch, longing, lust, wish, yearning, yen. *See* DESIRE.
thirst *verb* To have a greedy, obsessive desire : crave, hunger, itch, lust. *See* DESIRE.

thirsting *adjective*
Intensely desirous or interested : agog, ardent, athirst, avid, bursting, eager, impatient, keen[1], solicitous, thirsty. *Informal:* raring. ***Idioms:*** champing at the bit, ready and willing. *See* CONCERN.

thirsty *adjective*
1. Needing or desiring drink : dry, parched. *Archaic:* athirst. *See* DRY. **2.** Having little or no precipitation : arid, droughty, dry, rainless. *See* DRY. **3.** Intensely desirous or interested : agog, ardent, athirst, avid, bursting, eager, impatient, keen[1], solicitous, thirsting. *Informal:* raring. ***Idioms:*** champing at the bit, ready and willing. *See* CONCERN.

thistly *adjective*
Full of sharp needlelike protuberances : briery, echinate, prickly, pricky, spiny, thorny. *See* SHARP.

thorn *noun*
1. A sharp, pointed object : needle, prick, prickle, spine. *See* SHARP. **2.** One that makes another totally miserable by causing sharp pain and irritation : trial. *Informal:* pain. ***Idioms:*** pain in the neck, thorn in the flesh (*or* side). *See* PAIN.

thorny *adjective*
1. Full of sharp needlelike protuberances : briery, echinate, prickly, pricky, spiny, thistly. *See* SHARP. **2.** So replete with interlocking points and complications as to be painfully irritating : nettlesome, prickly, spiny. *See* EASY, PAIN.

thorough *adjective*
1. Covering all aspects with painstaking accuracy : all-out, complete, exhaustive, full-dress, intensive, thoroughgoing, thoroughpaced. *See* BIG, CAREFUL. **2.** Characterized by attention to detail : blow-by-blow, circumstantial, detailed, full, minute[2], particular. *See* SPECIFIC. **3.** Completely such, without qualification or exception : absolute, all-out, arrant, complete, consummate, crashing, damned, dead, downright, flat, out-and-out, outright, perfect, plain, pure, sheer[2], thoroughgoing, total, unbounded, unequivocal, unlimited, unmitigated, unqualified, unrelieved, unreserved, utter[2]. *Informal:* flat-out, positive. *Chiefly British:* blooming. *See* BIG, LIMITED.

thoroughbred *adjective*
1. Of pure breeding stock : full-blooded, highbred, pureblood, pureblooded, purebred. *See* CLEAN. **2.** Of high birth or social position : aristocratic, blue-blooded, elite, highborn, highbred, noble, patrician, upper-class, wellborn. *Informal:* upper-crust. *See* OVER.

thoroughfare *noun*
A course affording passage from one place to another : avenue, boulevard, drive, expressway, freeway, highway, path, road, roadway, route, street, superhighway, thruway, turnpike, way. *See* MOVE, OPEN.

thoroughgoing *adjective*
1. Covering all aspects with painstaking accuracy : all-out, complete, exhaustive, full-dress, intensive, thorough, thoroughpaced. *See* BIG, CAREFUL. **2.** Completely such, without qualification or exception : absolute, all-out, arrant, complete, consummate, crashing, damned, dead, downright, flat, out-and-out, outright, perfect, plain, pure, sheer[2], thorough, total, unbounded, unequivocal, unlimited, unmitigated, unqualified, unrelieved, unreserved, utter[2]. *Informal:* flat-out, positive. *Chiefly British:* blooming. *See* BIG, LIMITED.

thoroughly *adverb*
1. To the fullest extent : absolutely, all, altogether, completely, dead, entirely, flat, fully, just, perfectly, quite, totally, utterly, well[2], wholly. *Informal:* clean, clear. ***Idioms:*** in toto, through and through. *See* BIG, LIMITED. **2.** In a complete manner : completely, exhaustively,

intensively. *Idioms:* in and out, inside out, up and down. *See* LIMITED, PART.

thoroughness *noun*
Attentiveness to detail : care, carefulness, fastidiousness, meticulousness, pain (used in plural), painstaking, punctiliousness, scrupulousness. *See* CAREFUL.

thoroughpaced *adjective*
Covering all aspects with painstaking accuracy : all-out, complete, exhaustive, full-dress, intensive, thorough, thoroughgoing. *See* BIG, CAREFUL.

thought *noun*
1. The act or process of thinking : brainwork, cerebration, cogitation, contemplation, deliberation, excogitation, meditation, reflection, rumination, speculation. *See* THOUGHTS.
2. That which exists in the mind as the product of careful mental activity : concept, conception, idea, image, notion, perception. *See* THOUGHTS.

thoughtful *adjective*
1. Of, characterized by, or disposed to thought : cogitative, contemplative, deliberative, excogitative, meditative, pensive, reflective, ruminative, speculative, thinking. *Idiom:* in a brown study. *See* THOUGHTS. **2.** Appealing to or engaging the intellect : cerebral, intellectual, sophisticated. *Informal:* highbrow. *See* THOUGHTS. **3.** Full of polite concern for the well-being of others : attentive, considerate, courteous, gallant, polite, solicitous. *See* CAREFUL, TREAT WELL.

thoughtfulness *noun*
Thoughtful attention : attentiveness, concern, consideration, regard, solicitude. *See* ATTITUDE, CONCERN, KIND, TREAT WELL.

thoughtless *adjective*
1. Lacking or marked by a lack of care : careless, feckless, heedless, inattentive, irresponsible, reckless, unconcerned, unmindful, unthinking. *See* CAREFUL. **2.** Devoid of consideration for others' feelings : disregardful, inconsiderate, unthinking, unthoughtful. *See* CAREFUL, COURTESY.

thoughtlessness *noun*
1. A careless, often reckless disregard for consequences : abandon, carelessness, heedlessness. *See* CAREFUL. **2.** A lack of consideration for others' feelings : disregard, inconsiderateness, inconsideration, unthoughtfulness. *See* COURTESY.

thraldom *noun* See **thralldom.**

thrall *noun*
A state of subjugation to an owner or master : bondage, enslavement, helotry, serfdom, servileness, servility, servitude, slavery, thralldom, villeinage, yoke. *See* OVER.

thralldom or **thraldom** *noun*
A state of subjugation to an owner or master : bondage, enslavement, helotry, serfdom, servileness, servility, servitude, slavery, thrall, villeinage, yoke. *See* OVER.

thrash *verb*
1. To beat (plants) with a machine or by hand to separate the grain from the straw : flail, thresh. *See* ATTACK, STRIKE. **2.** To hit heavily and repeatedly with violent blows : assail, assault, baste, batter, beat, belabor, buffet, drub, hammer, pound, pummel, smash, thresh. *Informal:* lambaste. *Slang:* clobber. *Idiom:* rain blows on. *See* ATTACK, STRIKE. **3.** To punish with blows or lashes : beat, flog, hide[2], lash, whip. *Informal:* trim. *Slang:* lay into, lick. *See* ATTACK, REWARD. **4.** To swing about or strike at wildly : flail, thresh, toss. *Idiom:* toss and turn. *See* ATTACK, MOVE, STRIKE. **5.** To render totally ineffective by decisive defeat : annihilate, crush, drub, overpower, overwhelm, smash, steamroller, trounce, vanquish. *Informal:* massacre, wallop. *Slang:* clobber, cream, shellac, smear. *See* WIN.
thrash out (or **over**) *verb* To speak together and exchange ideas and opinions about : bandy (about), discuss, moot, talk over, thresh out (*or* over), toss around. *Informal:* hash (over), kick around, knock about (*or* around). *Slang:* rap[3]. *Idiom:* go into a huddle. *See* WORDS.

thrashing *noun*
1. A punishment dealt with blows or lashes : beating, flogging, hiding, lashing, whipping. *Informal:* trimming. *Slang:* licking. *See* ATTACK, REWARD. **2.** The act of defeating or the condition of being defeated : beating, defeat, drubbing, overthrow, rout, vanquishment. *Informal:* massacre, trimming, whipping. *Slang:* dusting, licking. *See* WIN.

thrash out or **over** *verb* See **thrash.**

thread *noun*
1. A very fine continuous strand : fiber, fibril, filament. *See* THING. **2.** Something that suggests the continuousness of a fine continuous filament : skein, strand. *See* CONTINUE.
3. *Slang.* Articles worn to cover the body. Used in plural : apparel, attire, clothes, clothing, dress, garment (used in plural), habiliment (often used in plural), raiment. *Informal:* dud (used in plural), tog (used in plural). *See* PUT ON.

thread *verb* To put (objects) onto a fine continuous filament : string. *See* ORDER.

threadbare *adjective*
1. Showing signs of wear and tear or neglect : bedraggled, broken-down, decaying, decrepit, dilapidated, dingy, down-at-heel, faded, mangy, rundown, scrubby, scruffy, seedy, shabby, shoddy, sleazy, tattered, tatty. *Informal:* tacky[2]. *Slang:* ratty. ***Idioms:*** all the worse for wear, gone to pot (*or* seed), past cure (*or* hope). *See* BETTER. **2.** Without freshness or appeal because of overuse : banal, bromidic, clichéd, commonplace, corny, hackneyed, musty, overused, overworked, platitudinal, platitudinous, shopworn, stale, stereotyped, stereotypic, stereotypical, timeworn, tired, trite, warmed-over, well-worn, worn-out. *See* EXCITE, USUAL.

threat *noun*
1. An expression of the intent to hurt or punish another : intimidation, menace. *See* WARN. **2.** An indication of impending danger or harm : foreboding, forewarning, thundercloud. ***Idioms:*** gathering clouds, storm clouds. *See* FORESIGHT. **3.** One regarded as an imminent danger : menace, sword of Damocles. ***Idiom:*** clear and present danger. *See* SAFETY.

threaten *verb*
1. To domineer or drive into compliance by the use of as threats or force, for example : bludgeon, browbeat, bulldoze, bully, bullyrag, cow, hector, intimidate, menace. *Informal:* strong-arm. *See* OVER. **2.** To subject to danger or destruction : endanger, imperil, jeopardize, menace, peril, risk. *See* SAFETY. **3.** To give warning signs of (impending peril) : forebode, forewarn. *See* FORESIGHT. **4.** To be imminent : brew, hang over, impend, loom, lower[1], menace, overhang. *See* NEAR.

threatening *adjective*
Expressing, indicating, or warning of an impending danger or misfortune : minacious, minatory. *See* FORESIGHT, NEAR.

three *noun*
A group of three individuals : threesome, triad, trine, trinity, trio, triple, triumvirate, triune, triunity, troika. *See* GROUP.

threesome *noun*
A group of three individuals : three, triad, trine, trinity, trio, triple, triumvirate, triune, triunity, troika. *See* GROUP.

thresh *verb*
1. To beat (plants) with a machine or by hand to separate the grain from the straw : flail, thrash. *See* ATTACK, STRIKE. **2.** To hit heavily and repeatedly with violent blows : assail, assault, baste, batter, beat, belabor, buffet, drub, hammer, pound, pummel, smash, thrash. *Informal:* lambaste. *Slang:* clobber. ***Idiom:*** rain blows on. *See* ATTACK, STRIKE. **3.** To swing about or strike at wildly : flail, thrash, toss. ***Idiom:*** toss and turn. *See* ATTACK, MOVE, STRIKE.

thresh out (or **over**) *verb* To speak together and exchange ideas and opinions about : bandy (about), discuss, moot, talk over, thrash out (*or* over), toss around. *Informal:* hash (over), kick around, knock about (*or* around). *Slang:* rap[3]. ***Idiom:*** go into a huddle. *See* WORDS.

threshold *noun*
A transitional interval beyond which some new action or different state of affairs is likely to begin or occur : borderline, brink, edge, point, verge. *See* EDGE.

thresh out or **over** *verb* See **thresh**

thrift *noun*
Careful use of material resources : economy, frugality, providence, prudence, thriftiness. *See* SAVE.

thriftiness *noun*
Careful use of material resources : economy, frugality, providence, prudence, thrift. *See* SAVE.

thriftless *adjective*
Reckless, especially in the use of material resources : improvident, unthrifty. *See* CAREFUL.

thrifty *adjective*
1. Careful in the use of material resources : canny, chary, economical, frugal, provident, prudent, saving, Scotch, sparing. *See* CAREFUL, SAVE. **2.** Improving, growing, or succeeding steadily : booming, boomy, flourishing, prospering, prosperous, roaring, thriving. *See* THRIVE.

thrill *verb*
To move or excite greatly : carry away, electrify, enrapture, transport. *Slang:* send. *See* EXCITE.

thrill *noun* **1.** A strong, pleasant feeling of excitement or stimulation : lift. *Informal:* wallop. *Slang:* bang, boot[1], high, kick. *See* EXCITE. **2.** A nervous shaking of the body : quake, quiver, shake, shiver[1], shudder, tic, tremor, twitch. *See* REPETITION.

thrilled *adjective*
Feeling a very strong emotion : atingle, excited, fired up, worked up. *Informal:* psyched. *Slang:* stoked, turned-on. *See* EXCITE.

thrive *verb*
1. To do or fare well : boom, flourish, go, prosper. *Slang:* score. ***Idioms:*** get (*or* go) somewhere, go great guns, go strong. *See* THRIVE. **2.** To grow rapidly and luxuriantly : bloom[1], blossom, flourish. *See* THRIVE.

thriving *adjective*
Improving, growing, or succeeding steadily : booming, boomy, flourishing, prospering, prosperous, roaring, thrifty. *See* THRIVE.

throb *verb*
To make rhythmic contractions, sounds, or movements : beat, palpitate, pound, pulsate, pulse. *See* REPETITION, SOUNDS.
throb *noun* A periodic contraction or sound of something coursing : beat, palpitation, pulsation, pulse. *See* REPETITION, SOUNDS.

throe *noun*
1. A violent, excruciating seizure of pain : cramp[1], paroxysm, shoot, spasm. *See* PAIN. **2.** A sensation of physical discomfort occurring as the result of disease or injury : ache, pain, pang, prick, prickle, smart, soreness, stab, sting, stitch, twinge. *Informal:* misery. *See* PAIN. **3.** A condition of anguished struggle and disorder. Used in plural : convulsion, paroxysm. *See* CALM.

throng *noun*
1. An enormous number of persons gathered together : crowd, crush, drove, flock, horde, mass, mob, multitude, press, ruck[1], swarm. *See* BIG, GROUP. **2.** A very large number of things grouped together : army, cloud, crowd, drove, flock, horde, host, legion, mass, mob, multitude, ruck[1], score (used in plural), swarm. *See* BIG, GROUP.
throng *verb* **1.** To congregate, as around a person : crowd, flock, mob, press. *See* COLLECT, TIGHTEN. **2.** To come or go in large numbers : flood, pour, swarm, troop. *See* BIG, MOVE.

throttle *verb*
1. To hold (something requiring an outlet) in check : burke, choke (back), gag, hold back, hold down, hush (up), muffle, quench, repress, smother, squelch, stifle, strangle, suppress. *Informal:* sit on (*or* upon). *See* RESTRAINT. **2.** To interfere with or stop the normal breathing of, especially by constricting the windpipe : choke, strangle. *See* BREATH.

through *adverb*
1. From one end to the other : around, over, round, throughout. *See* PART. **2.** To an end or conclusion : over. *See* START.
through *adjective* **1.** Proceeding or lying in an uninterrupted line or course : direct, straight, straightforward. *See* STRAIGHT. **2.** Having reached completion : complete, done. *See* PART. **3.** Having no further relationship : done, finished. *See* START. **4.** No longer effective, capable, or valuable : done, done for, finished, washed-up. *Informal:* kaput. ***Idioms:*** at the end of the line (*or* road), over the hill, past one's prime. *See* ABILITY, START.

throughout *adverb*
From one end to the other : around, over, round, through. *See* PART.

throw *verb*
1. To send through the air with a motion of the hand or arm : cast, dart, dash, fling, heave, hurl, hurtle, launch, pitch, shoot, shy[2], sling, toss. *Informal:* fire. *See* MOVE. **2.** To cause to fall, as from a shot or blow : bring down, cut down, down, drop, fell[1], flatten, floor, ground, knock down, level, prostrate, strike down. *Slang:* deck[1]. ***Idiom:*** lay low. *See* RISE. **3.** *Informal.* To cause to be unclear in mind or intent : addle, befuddle, bewilder, confound, confuse, discombobulate, dizzy, fuddle, jumble, mix up, muddle, mystify, perplex, puzzle. ***Idiom:*** make one's head reel (*or* swim *or* whirl). *See* CLEAR, FEELINGS. **4.** *Informal.* To make incapable of finding something to think, do, or say : confound, nonplus. *Informal:* flummox, stick, stump. *Slang:* beat. ***Idiom:*** put someone at a loss. *See* AFFECT, KNOWLEDGE. **5.** To bring to bear steadily or forcefully : exercise, exert, ply[2], put out, wield. *See* CAUSE. **6.** To send out heat, light, or energy : cast, emit, irradiate, project, radiate, shed. *See* MOVE. **7.** To release or move (a switch, for example) in order to activate, deactivate, or control a device : trip. *See* MOVE.

throw away *verb* **1.** To let go or get rid of as being useless or defective, for example : discard, dispose of, dump, junk, scrap[1], throw out. *Informal:* chuck, jettison, shuck (off). *Slang:* ditch. *See* KEEP. **2.** To spend (money) excessively and usually foolishly : consume, dissipate, fool away, fritter away, riot away, squander, trifle away, waste. *Slang:* blow[1]. *See* SAVE.

throw off *verb* **1.** To free from or cast out something objectionable or undesirable : clear, disburden, disembarrass, disencumber, release, relieve, rid, shake off, unburden. *Slang:* shake. *See* KEEP. **2.** To cast off by a natural process : exuviate, molt, shed, slough[2]. *See* PUT ON. **3.** To discharge material, as vapor or fumes, usually suddenly and violently : emit, give, give forth, give off, give out, issue, let off, let out, release, send forth, vent. *See* FREE, MOVE. **4.** To get away from (a pursuer) : elude, evade, lose, shake off, slip. *Slang:* shake. ***Idiom:*** give someone the shake (*or* slip). *See* SEEK.

throw out *verb* **1.** To let go or get rid of as being useless or defective, for example : discard, dispose of, dump, junk, scrap[1], throw away. *Informal:* chuck, jettison, shuck (off). *Slang:* ditch. *See* KEEP. **2.** To put out by force : bump, dismiss, eject, evict, expel, oust. *Informal:* chuck. *Slang:* boot[1] (out), bounce, kick out. ***Idioms:*** give someone the boot, give someone the heave-ho (*or* old heave-ho), send packing, show someone the door, throw out on one's ear. *See* KEEP. **3.** To displace (a bone) from a socket or joint : dislocate, slip. ***Idiom:*** throw out of joint. *See* HELP.

throw over *verb* To give up or leave without intending to return or claim again : abandon, desert[3], forsake, leave[1], quit. ***Idioms:*** run out on, walk out on. *See* KEEP.

throw up *verb* To eject the contents of the stomach through the mouth : heave, vomit. *Slang:* puke. *See* MOUTH.

throw *noun* An act of throwing : cast, fling, heave, hurl, launch, pitch, shy[2], sling, toss. *See* MOVE.

throw away *verb* See **throw.**

throw off *verb* See **throw.**

throw out *verb* See **throw.**

throw over *verb* See **throw.**

throw up *verb* See **throw.**

thrust *verb*

1. To force to move or advance with or as if with blows or pressure : drive, propel, push, ram, shove. *See* MOVE. **2.** To cause to penetrate with force : dig, drive, plunge, ram, run, sink, stab, stick. *See* PUT IN. **3.** To cause to stick out : poke, push, shove. *See* CONVEX.

thrust *noun* **1.** An act or instance of using force so as to propel ahead : butt[1], push, shove. *See* PUSH. **2.** The thread or current of thought uniting or occurring in all the elements of a text or discourse : aim, burden[2], drift, intent, meaning, purport, substance, tendency, tenor. *See* MEANING.

thruway *noun*

A course affording passage from one place to another : avenue, boulevard, drive, expressway, freeway, highway, path, road, roadway, route, street, superhighway, thoroughfare, turnpike, way. *See* MOVE, OPEN.

thud *noun*

A stroke or blow, especially one that produces a sound : beat, clunk, pound, thump. *See* ATTACK, SOUNDS, STRIKE.

thud *verb* To make a dull sound by or as if by striking a surface with a heavy object : clomp, clump, clunk. *See* SOUNDS.

thug *noun*

A person who treats others violently and roughly, especially for hire : hoodlum, ruffian, tough. *Informal:* hooligan. *Slang:* goon, gorilla, hood. *See* ATTACK, CRIMES.

thumb *verb*

To look through reading matter casually. Also used with *through* : browse, dip into, flip through, glance at (*or* over *or* through), leaf (through), riffle (through), run through, scan, skim. *See* INVESTIGATE, WORDS.

thump *noun*

A stroke or blow, especially one that produces a sound : beat, clunk, pound, thud. *See* ATTACK, SOUNDS, STRIKE.

thunder *noun*

An earsplitting, explosive noise : bang, blast, boom, roar. *See* SOUNDS.

thunder *verb* To make an earsplitting explosive noise : bang, blast, boom, roar. *See* SOUNDS.

thundercloud *noun*

An indication of impending danger or harm : foreboding, forewarning, threat. ***Idioms:*** gathering clouds, storm clouds. *See* FORESIGHT.

thwack *verb*

To deliver a powerful blow to suddenly and sharply : bash, catch, clout, hit, knock, pop[1], slam, slog, slug[3], smash, smite, sock, strike, swat, whack, wham, whop. *Informal:* biff, bop, clip[1], wallop. *Slang:* belt, conk, paste. ***Idioms:*** let someone have it, sock it to someone. *See* ATTACK, STRIKE.

thwack *noun* A sudden sharp, powerful stroke : bang, blow[2], clout, crack, hit, lick, pound, slug[3], sock, swat, welt, whack, wham, whop. *Informal:* bash, biff, bop, clip[1], wallop. *Slang:* belt, conk, paste. *See* ATTACK, STRIKE.

thwart *verb*

To prevent from accomplishing a purpose : baffle, balk, check, checkmate, defeat, foil, frustrate, stymie. *Informal:* cross, stump. ***Idiom:*** cut the ground from under. *See* ALLOW.

thwart *adjective* Situated or lying across : crossing, crosswise, transversal, transverse, traverse. *See* HORIZONTAL.

tic *noun*

A nervous shaking of the body : quake, quiver, shake, shiver[1], shudder, thrill, tremor, twitch. *See* REPETITION.

tick *noun*
Chiefly British. A very brief time : crack, flash, instant, minute[1], moment, second[1], trice, twinkle, twinkling, wink. *Informal:* jiff, jiffy. *See* BIG, TIME.
tick off *verb* To name or specify one by one : enumerate, itemize, list[1], numerate. *See* COUNT, SPECIFIC.

ticker *noun*
Slang. The circulatory organ of the body : heart. *See* BODY.

ticket *noun*
1. An identifying or descriptive slip : label, tag. *See* MARKS. **2.** A list of candidates proposed or endorsed by a political party : lineup, slate. *See* POLITICS. **3.** *Informal.* A means or method of entering into or achieving something desirable : formula, key, route, secret. *See* MEANS.
ticket *verb* To attach a ticket to : label, mark, tag. *See* MARKS.

tickle *verb*
To give great or keen pleasure to : cheer, delight, enchant, gladden, gratify, overjoy, please, pleasure. *Archaic:* joy. *See* HAPPY, LIKE.

tickled *adjective*
Eagerly compliant : delighted, glad, happy, pleased. *See* HAPPY.

ticklish *adjective*
1. Following no predictable pattern : capricious, changeable, erratic, fantastic, fantastical, fickle, freakish, inconsistent, inconstant, mercurial, temperamental, uncertain, unpredictable, unstable, unsteady, variable, volatile, whimsical. *See* CHANGE, CONTINUE. **2.** Requiring great tact or skill : delicate, sensitive, touch-and-go, touchy, tricky. *See* EASY.

tick off *verb* See **tick.**

tidbit *noun*
Something fine and delicious, especially a food : dainty, delicacy, morsel, treat. *Informal:* goody. *See* GOOD, INGESTION.

tide *noun*
Something suggestive of running water : current, drift, flood, flow, flux, rush, spate, stream, surge. *See* MOVE.

tiding *noun*
New information, especially about recent events and happenings. Often used in plural : advice (often used in plural), intelligence, news, word. *Informal:* scoop. *See* KNOWLEDGE, WORDS.

tidy *adjective*
1. In good order or clean condition : neat, orderly, shipshape, snug, spick-and-span, spruce, taut, trig, trim, well-groomed. *Chiefly British:* tight. ***Idiom:*** neat as a pin. *See* CLEAN, ORDER. **2.** *Informal.* Of moderately good quality but less than excellent : acceptable, adequate, all right, average, common, decent, fair, fairish, goodish, moderate, passable, respectable, satisfactory, sufficient, tolerable. *Informal:* OK. *See* GOOD. **3.** *Informal.* Notably above average in amount, size, or scope : big, considerable, extensive, good, great, healthy, large, large-scale, sizable. *See* BIG.
tidy *verb* **1.** To make or keep (an area) clean and orderly. Also used with *up* : clean (up), clear (up), neaten (up), police, spruce (up), straighten (up). *See* ORDER. **2.** To make neat and trim; make presentable. Also used with *up* : clean (up), freshen (up), groom, neaten (up), slick up, spruce (up), trig (out), trim. *See* ORDER.

tidy sum *noun*
Informal. A large sum of money : fortune, mint. *Informal:* bundle, pretty penny, wad. *Slang:* pile. *See* RICH.

tie *verb*
1. To make fast or firmly fixed, as by means of a cord or rope : bind, fasten, knot, secure, tie up. *See* KEEP, TIGHTEN. **2.** To restrict the activity or free movement of : chain, fetter, hamper, hamstring, handcuff, hobble, leash, manacle, shackle, trammel. *Informal:* hog-tie. *See* FREE, HELP. **3.** To do or make something equal to : equal, match, meet[1]. *See* SAME.
tie up *verb* **1.** To make fast or firmly fixed, as by means of a cord or rope : bind, fasten, knot, secure, tie. *See* KEEP, TIGHTEN. **2.** To cause to cease regular activity : idle, immobilize, stop. ***Idiom:*** bring to a screeching halt. *See* CONTINUE. **3.** To cause to be busy or in use : engage, monopolize, occupy, preempt. *See* ACTION, USED.
tie *noun* **1.** That which unites or binds : bond, knot, ligament, ligature, link, nexus, vinculum, yoke. *See* CONNECT. **2.** An equality of scores, votes, or performances in a contest : dead heat, deadlock, draw, stalemate, standoff. *See* SAME.

tie-in *noun*
A logical or natural association between two or more things : connection, correlation, interconnection, interdependence, interrelationship, link, linkage, relation, relationship. *Informal:* hookup. *See* CONNECT.

tier *noun*
1. A group of people or things arranged in a row : column, file, line, queue, rank[1], row[1],

string. *See* GROUP. **2.** A division of persons or things by quality, rank, or grade : bracket, class, grade, league, order, rank[1]. *See* GROUP, VALUE.

tie-up *noun*
A cessation of normal activity, caused by an accident or strike, for example : gridlock, immobilization, jam, stoppage. *See* CONTINUE.

tie up *verb* See **tie.**

tiff *noun*
A discussion, often heated, in which a difference of opinion is expressed : altercation, argument, bicker, clash, contention, controversy, debate, difficulty, disagreement, dispute, fight, polemic, quarrel, run-in, spat, squabble, word (used in plural), wrangle. *Informal:* hassle, rhubarb, tangle. *See* CONFLICT.
tiff *verb* To engage in a quarrel : argue, bicker, contend, dispute, fight, quarrel, quibble, spat, squabble, wrangle. *Informal:* hassle, tangle. ***Idioms:*** cross swords, have it out, have words, lock horns. *See* CONFLICT.

tiger *noun*
A perversely bad, cruel, or wicked person : archfiend, beast, devil, fiend, ghoul, monster, ogre, vampire. *See* KIND.

tight *adjective*
1. Persistently holding to something : clinging, fast, firm[1], secure, tenacious. *See* FREE, TIGHTEN. **2.** Stretched tightly : stiff, taut, tense. *See* TIGHTEN. **3.** Having all parts near to each other : close, compact[1], crowded, dense, packed, thick. *See* TIGHTEN. **4.** Based on good judgment, reasoning, or evidence : cogent, just, solid, sound[2], valid, well-founded, well-grounded. *See* GOOD, REASON. **5.** Characterized by an economy of artistic expression : lean[2], spare. *See* STYLE. **6.** Affording little room for movement : close, confining, cramped, crowded, narrow, snug. *See* TIGHTEN. **7.** *Slang.* Very closely associated : chummy, close, familiar, friendly, intimate[1]. *Informal:* thick. ***Idiom:*** hand in glove with. *See* LOVE. **8.** Ungenerously or pettily reluctant to spend money : cheap, close, close-fisted, costive, hard-fisted, mean[2], miserly, niggard, niggardly, parsimonious, penny-pinching, penurious, petty, pinching, stingy, tightfisted. *See* GIVE. **9.** Hard to deal with or get out of : rough, tricky. *Informal:* sticky. *See* EASY. **10.** Nearly equivalent or even : close, neck and neck, nip and tuck. *See* NEAR. **11.** *Chiefly British.* In good order or clean condition : neat, orderly, shipshape, snug, spick-and-span, spruce, taut, tidy, trig, trim, well-groomed. ***Idiom:*** neat as a pin. *See* CLEAN, ORDER. **12.** *Slang.* Stupefied, excited, or muddled with alcoholic liquor : besotted, crapulent, crapulous, drunk, drunken, inebriate, inebriated, intoxicated, sodden, tipsy. *Informal:* cock-eyed, stewed. *Slang:* blind, bombed, boozed, boozy, crocked, high, lit (up), loaded, looped, pickled, pixilated, plastered, potted, sloshed, smashed, soused, stinking, stinko, stoned, zonked. ***Idioms:*** drunk as a skunk, half-seas over, high as a kite, in one's cups, three sheets in (*or* to) the wind. *See* DRUGS.

tighten *verb*
1. To make or become tight or tighter : reinforce, strengthen. *See* TIGHTEN. **2.** To make or become tense : stiffen, tauten, tense. *See* TIGHTEN.

tightfisted *adjective*
Ungenerously or pettily reluctant to spend money : cheap, close, close-fisted, costive, hard-fisted, mean[2], miserly, niggard, niggardly, parsimonious, penny-pinching, penurious, petty, pinching, stingy, tight. *See* GIVE.

tightlipped also **tight-lipped** *adjective*
Not speaking freely or openly : close, close-mouthed, incommunicable, incommunicative, reserved, reticent, silent, taciturn, uncommunicable, uncommunicative. *See* RESTRAINT, SOUNDS.

tightwad *noun*
Slang. A stingy person : miser, niggard, Scrooge, skinflint. *Informal:* penny pincher. *Slang:* cheapskate, stiff. *See* GIVE.

till *verb*
To prepare (soil) for the planting and raising of crops : cultivate, culture, dress, tend[2], work. *See* PREPARED, TOUCH.

tilt *verb*
1. To depart or cause to depart from true vertical or horizontal : cant[1], heel[2], incline, lean[1], list[2], rake[2], slant, slope, tip[2]. *See* STRAIGHT. **2.** To strive in opposition : battle, combat, contend, duel, fight, struggle, war, wrestle. *See* CONFLICT.
tilt *noun* **1.** Deviation from a particular direction : cant[1], grade, gradient, heel[2], inclination, incline, lean[1], list[2], rake[2], slant, slope, tip[2]. *See* RISE, STRAIGHT. **2.** Any competition or test of opposing wills likened to the sport in which knights fought with lances : joust, tournament, tourney. *See* CONFLICT.

timber *noun*
1. A large, oblong piece of wood or other material, used especially for construction : balk, beam, rafter. *See* MATTER. **2.** The basic sub-

stance or essential elements of character that qualify a person for a specified role : material, stuff. *See* BE.

timbre *noun*

A sound of distinct pitch and quality : tonality, tone, tone color. *See* SOUNDS.

time *noun*

1. A rather short period : bit[1], space, spell[3], while. *See* BIG. **2.** The general point at which an event occurs : occasion. ***Idiom:*** point in time. *See* TIME. **3.** A limited or specific period of time during which something happens, lasts, or extends : duration, span, stretch, term. *See* TIME. **4.** A particular time notable for its distinctive characteristics. Often used in plural : age, day, epoch, era, period. *See* TIME. **5.** A span designated for a given activity : period, season. *See* TIME. **6.** A term of service, as in the military or in prison : hitch, stretch, tour. *See* TIME. **7.** A limited, often assigned period of activity, duty, or opportunity : bout, go, hitch, inning (often used in plural), shift, spell[3], stint, stretch, tour, trick, turn, watch. *See* TIME.

time *verb* **1.** To set the time for (an event or occasion) : plan, schedule. *See* TIME. **2.** To record the speed or duration of : clock. *See* REMEMBER, TIME.

time-honored *adjective*

Adhering to beliefs or practices approved by authority or tradition : canonical, orthodox, received, sanctioned. *See* USUAL.

timeless *adjective*

1. Existing or occurring without interruption or end : around-the-clock, ceaseless, constant, continual, continuous, endless, eternal, everlasting, incessant, interminable, nonstop, ongoing, perpetual, persistent, relentless, round-the-clock, unceasing, unending, unfailing, uninterrupted, unremitting. *See* CONTINUE. **2.** Existing unchanged forever : ageless, dateless, eternal. *Archaic:* eterne. *See* CHANGE.

timely *adjective*

1. Occurring at a fitting or advantageous time : auspicious, favorable, opportune, propitious, prosperous, seasonable, well-timed. *See* LUCK. **2.** Occurring, acting, or performed exactly at the time appointed : prompt, punctual. *Idioms:* at (*or* on) the dot, on time. *See* TIME.

time-out *noun*

A pause or interval, as from work or duty : break, intermission, recess, respite, rest[1]. *Informal:* breather. *See* CONTINUE.

timetable *noun*

An organized list, as of procedures, activities, or events : agenda, calendar, docket, lineup, order of the day (often used in plural), program, schedule. *See* PLANNED.

timeworn *adjective*

1. Belonging to, existing, or occurring in times long past : age-old, ancient, antediluvian, antiquated, antique, archaic, hoary, old, olden, old-time, venerable. ***Idioms:*** old as Methuselah, old as the hills. *See* NEW. **2.** Without freshness or appeal because of overuse : banal, bromidic, clichéd, commonplace, corny, hackneyed, musty, overused, overworked, platitudinal, platitudinous, shopworn, stale, stereotyped, stereotypic, stereotypical, threadbare, tired, trite, warmed-over, well-worn, worn-out. *See* EXCITE, USUAL.

timid *adjective*

1. Not forward but reticent or reserved in manner : backward, bashful, coy, demure, diffident, modest, retiring, self-effacing, shy[1]. *See* RESTRAINT. **2.** Given to or exhibiting hesitation : halting, hesitant, indecisive, irresolute, pendulous, shilly-shally, tentative, vacillant, vacillatory. *See* DECIDE.

timidity *noun*

1. An awkwardness or lack of self-confidence in the presence of others : backwardness, bashfulness, coyness, retiringness, shyness, timidness. *See* RESTRAINT. **2.** The act of hesitating or state of being hesitant : hesitancy, hesitation, indecision, indecisiveness, irresoluteness, irresolution, pause, shilly-shally, tentativeness, timidness, to-and-fro, vacillation. *See* DECIDE.

timidness *noun*

1. An awkwardness or lack of self-confidence in the presence of others : backwardness, bashfulness, coyness, retiringness, shyness, timidity. *See* RESTRAINT. **2.** The act of hesitating or state of being hesitant : hesitancy, hesitation, indecision, indecisiveness, irresoluteness, irresolution, pause, shilly-shally, tentativeness, timidity, to-and-fro, vacillation. *See* DECIDE.

tincture *noun*

Something that imparts color : color, colorant, coloring, dye, dyestuff, pigment, stain. *See* COLORS.

tincture *verb* To impart color to : color, dye, stain, tint. *See* COLORS.

tinge *noun*

1. A shade of a color, especially a pale or delicate variation : cast, hue, tint, tone. *See* COLORS. **2.** The degree of vividness of a color, as when modified by the addition of black or white pigment : gradation, hue, shade, tint. *See* COLORS. **3.** A slight amount or indication :

breath, dash, ghost, hair, hint, intimation, semblance, shade, shadow, soupçon, streak, suggestion, suspicion, taste, touch, trace, whiff, whisper. *Informal:* whisker. *See* BIG, SHOW.

tinker *verb*

1. To handle something idly, ignorantly, or destructively : fiddle, fool, meddle, mess, tamper. *Informal:* monkey. *See* HELP, TOUCH.
2. To move one's fingers or hands in a nervous or aimless fashion : fiddle, fidget, fool, monkey, play, putter, toy, trifle, twiddle. *See* TOUCH.

tinsel *adjective*

Tastelessly showy : brummagem, chintzy, flashy, garish, gaudy, glaring, loud, meretricious, tawdry. *Informal:* tacky[2]. *See* STYLE.

tint *noun*

1. The property by which the sense of vision can distinguish between objects, as a red apple and a green apple, that are very similar or identical in form and size : color, hue, shade, tone. *See* COLORS. **2.** A shade of a color, especially a pale or delicate variation : cast, hue, tinge, tone. *See* COLORS. **3.** The degree of vividness of a color, as when modified by the addition of black or white pigment : gradation, hue, shade, tinge. *See* COLORS.

tint *verb* To impart color to : color, dye, stain, tincture. *See* COLORS.

tiny *adjective*

Extremely small : diminutive, dwarf, Lilliputian, midget, miniature, minuscule, minute[2], pygmy, wee. *Informal:* peewee, pint-size, pint-sized, teensy-weensy, teensy, teeny, teeny-weeny, weeny. *See* BIG.

tip¹ *noun*

A sharp or tapered end : acicula, acumination, apex, cusp, mucro, mucronation, point. *See* SHARP.

tip² *verb*

To depart or cause to depart from true vertical or horizontal : cant[1], heel[2], incline, lean[1], list[2], rake[2], slant, slope, tilt. *See* STRAIGHT.

tip *noun* Deviation from a particular direction : cant[1], grade, gradient, heel[2], inclination, incline, lean[1], list[2], rake[2], slant, slope, tilt. *See* RISE, STRAIGHT.

tip³ *noun*

1. A material favor or gift, usually money, given in return for service : cumshaw, gratuity, largess, perquisite. *See* GIVE, TRANSACTIONS.
2. An item of advance or inside information given as a guide to action : pointer, steer. *Informal:* tip-off. *See* KNOWLEDGE.

tip *verb* To give incriminating information about others, especially to the authorities. Also used with *off* : inform, talk, tattle. *Slang:* fink, rat, sing, snitch, squeal, stool. ***Idiom:*** blow the whistle. *See* KNOWLEDGE, LAW.

tip-off *noun*

Informal. An item of advance or inside information given as a guide to action : pointer, steer, tip[3]. *See* KNOWLEDGE.

tipple *verb*

To take alcoholic liquor, especially excessively or habitually : drink, guzzle, imbibe. *Informal:* nip[2]. *Slang:* booze, lush[2], soak, tank up. ***Idioms:*** bend the elbow, hit the bottle. *See* DRUGS.

tippler *noun*

A person who is habitually drunk : drunk, drunkard, inebriate, sot. *Slang:* boozehound, boozer, lush[2], rummy[1], soak, souse, sponge, stiff. *See* DRUGS.

tipsiness *noun*

The condition of being intoxicated with alcoholic liquor : crapulence, drunkenness, inebriation, inebriety, insobriety, intoxication. *See* DRUGS.

tipster *noun*

Informal. One who gives incriminating information about others : informant, informer, tattler, tattletale. *Informal:* rat. *Slang:* fink, snitch, snitcher, squealer, stoolie, stool pigeon. *See* KNOWLEDGE, LAW.

tipsy *adjective*

Stupefied, excited, or muddled with alcoholic liquor : besotted, crapulent, crapulous, drunk, drunken, inebriate, inebriated, intoxicated, sodden. *Informal:* cock-eyed, stewed. *Slang:* blind, bombed, boozed, boozy, crocked, high, lit (up), loaded, looped, pickled, pixilated, plastered, potted, sloshed, smashed, soused, stinking, stinko, stoned, tight, zonked. ***Idioms:*** drunk as a skunk, half-seas over, high as a kite, in one's cups, three sheets in (*or* to) the wind. *See* DRUGS.

tiptop *adjective*

Exceptionally good of its kind : ace, banner, blue-ribbon, brag, capital, champion, excellent, fine[1], first-class, first-rate, prime, quality, splendid, superb, superior, terrific, top. *Informal:* A-one, bully, dandy, great, swell, topflight, topnotch. *Slang:* boss. *Chiefly British:* tophole. *See* GOOD.

tirade *noun*

A long, violent, or blustering speech, usually of censure or denunciation : diatribe, fulmination, harangue, jeremiad, philippic. *See* PRAISE.

tire *verb*
1. To diminish the strength and energy of : drain, fatigue, jade, wear, wear down, wear out, weary. *See* TIRED. **2.** To fatigue with dullness or tedium : bore, weary. *See* EXCITE.

tired *adjective*
1. Out of patience with : disgusted, fed up, sick, weary. ***Idiom:*** sick and tired. *See* TIRED. **2.** Without freshness or appeal because of overuse : banal, bromidic, clichéd, commonplace, corny, hackneyed, musty, overused, overworked, platitudinal, platitudinous, shopworn, stale, stereotyped, stereotypic, stereotypical, threadbare, timeworn, trite, warmed-over, well-worn, worn-out. *See* EXCITE, USUAL.

tiredness *noun*
The condition of being extremely tired : exhaustion, fatigue, weariness. *See* TIRED.

tired out *adjective*
Extremely tired : bleary, dead, drained, exhausted, fatigued, rundown, spent, wearied, weariful, weary, worn-down, worn-out. *Informal:* beat, bushed, tuckered (out). *Slang:* done in, fagged (out), pooped (out). ***Idioms:*** all in, ready to drop. *See* HEALTH, TIRED.

tireless *adjective*
Having or showing a capacity for protracted effort, regardless of difficulty or frustration : indefatigable, inexhaustible, unfailing, unflagging, untiring, unwearied, weariless. *See* CONTINUE, TIRED.

tire out *verb*
To make extremely tired : exhaust, fag (out), wear out. *Informal:* knock out, tucker (out). *Slang:* do in, poop[1] (out). ***Idioms:*** run ragged, take it out of. *See* TIRED.

tiresome *adjective*
Arousing no interest or curiosity : boring, drear, dreary, dry, dull, humdrum, irksome, monotonous, stuffy, tedious, uninteresting, weariful, wearisome, weary. *See* EXCITE.

tiring *adjective*
Causing fatigue : draining, exhausting, fatiguing, wearing, wearying. *See* TIRED.

tiro *noun* See **tyro.**

tissue *noun*
An interwoven or interrelated number of things : network, web. *See* GROUP.

titan *noun*
One that is extraordinarily large and powerful : behemoth, giant, Goliath, jumbo, leviathan, mammoth, monster. *Slang:* whopper. *See* BEINGS, BIG.

titanic *adjective*
Of extraordinary size and power : behemoth, Brobdingnagian, Bunyanesque, colossal, cyclopean, elephantine, enormous, gargantuan, giant, gigantesque, gigantic, herculean, heroic, huge, immense, jumbo, mammoth, massive, massy, mastodonic, mighty, monster, monstrous, monumental, mountainous, prodigious, pythonic, stupendous, tremendous, vast. *Informal:* walloping. *Slang:* whopping. *See* BIG.

tit for tat *noun*
The act of retaliating : counteraction, counterattack, counterblow, reciprocation, reprisal, requital, retaliation, retribution, revenge, vengeance. ***Idioms:*** an eye for an eye, a tooth for a tooth, like for like, measure for measure. *See* ATTACK, FORGIVENESS.

title *noun*
1. An issue of printed material offered for sale or distribution : opus, publication, volume, work. *See* WORDS. **2.** The fact of possessing or the legal right to possess something : dominion, ownership, possession, proprietorship. *See* OWNED. **3.** A legitimate or supposed right to demand something as one's rightful due : claim, pretense, pretension. *Slang:* dibs. *See* OWNED, REQUEST. **4.** A right or legal share in something : claim, interest, portion, stake. *See* PART. **5.** The word or words by which one is called and identified : appellation, appellative, cognomen, denomination, designation, epithet, name, nickname, style, tag. *Slang:* handle, moniker. *See* SPECIFIC, WORDS.

title *verb* To give a name or title to : baptize, call, christen, denominate, designate, dub, entitle, name, style, term. *See* SPECIFIC, WORDS.

titter *verb*
To laugh in a stifled way : giggle, snicker, snigger. *See* LAUGHTER.

titter *noun* A stifled laugh : giggle, snicker, snigger. *See* LAUGHTER.

tittle *noun*
A tiny amount : bit[1], crumb, dab[1], dash, dot, dram, drop, fragment, grain, iota, jot, minim, mite, modicum, molecule, ort, ounce, particle, scrap[1], scruple, shred, smidgen, speck, trifle, whit. *Chiefly British:* spot. *See* BIG.

tittle-tattle *noun*
Idle, often sensational and groundless talk about others : gossip, gossipry, hearsay, report, rumor, talebearing, tattle, word. *Slang:* scuttlebutt. *See* WORDS.

tittle-tattle *verb* To engage in or spread gossip : blab, gossip, noise, rumor, talk, tattle, whisper. ***Idioms:*** tell tales, tell tales out of school. *See* WORDS.

tizzy *noun*
Slang. A condition of excited distress : fume. *Informal:* snit, state, sweat, swivet. *See* CALM.

toady *noun*
One who flatters another excessively : adulator, courtier, flatterer, sycophant. *Informal:* apple-polisher. *See* OVER, PRAISE.
toady *verb* To support slavishly every opinion or suggestion of a superior : bootlick, cringe, fawn, grovel, kowtow, slaver, truckle. *Informal:* apple-polish, brownnose, cotton. *Slang:* suck up. ***Idioms:*** curry favor, dance attendance, kiss someone's feet, lick someone's boots. *See* OVER.

to-and-fro *noun*
The act of hesitating or state of being hesitant : hesitancy, hesitation, indecision, indecisiveness, irresoluteness, irresolution, pause, shilly-shally, tentativeness, timidity, timidness, vacillation. *See* DECIDE.

toast *noun*
The act of drinking to someone : pledge. *See* DESIRE, REMEMBER.
toast *verb* To salute by raising and drinking from a glass : drink, pledge. *See* DESIRE, REMEMBER.

tocsin *noun*
A signal that warns of imminent danger : alarm, alarum, alert, warning. *See* WARN.

today *noun*
The current time : now, nowadays, present[1]. *See* TIME.
today *adverb* At the present; these days : now, nowadays. *See* TIME.

to-do *noun*
1. *Informal.* An interruption of regular procedure or of public peace : agitation, commotion, disorder, disturbance, helter-skelter, stir[1], tumult, turbulence, turmoil, uproar. *Informal:* flap. *See* CALM, ORDER. **2.** *Informal.* A condition of intense public interest or excitement : brouhaha, sensation, stir[1], uproar. *Slang:* hoo-hah. *See* EXCITE. **3.** *Informal.* Busy and useless activity : ado, fuss. *See* ACTION, CALM.

tog *noun*
Informal. Articles worn to cover the body. Used in plural : apparel, attire, clothes, clothing, dress, garment (used in plural), habiliment (often used in plural), raiment. *Informal:* dud (used in plural). *Slang:* thread (used in plural). *See* PUT ON.
tog *verb Informal.* To put clothes on : apparel, attire, clothe, dress, garb, garment, invest. *See* PUT ON.

together *adverb*
1. In, into, or as a single body : jointly. ***Idioms:*** as one, in one breath, in the same breath, in unison, with one accord, with one voice. *See* ACCOMPANIED. **2.** At the same time : concurrently, simultaneously, synchronously. ***Idioms:*** all at once, all together. *See* ACCOMPANIED, TIME.
together *adjective Slang.* In a state of preparedness : ready, set[1]. *Informal:* go. ***Idioms:*** all set, in working order. *See* PREPARED.

toil *verb*
1. To exert one's mental or physical powers, usually under difficulty and to the point of exhaustion : drive, fag, labor, moil, strain[1], strive, sweat, travail, tug, work. ***Idiom:*** break one's back (*or* neck). *See* WORK. **2.** To walk heavily, slowly, and with difficulty : plod, slog, slop, trudge, wade. *See* MOVE.
toil *noun* Physical exertion that is usually difficult and exhausting : drudgery, labor, moil, travail, work. *Informal:* sweat. *Chiefly British:* fag. ***Idiom:*** sweat of one's brow. *See* WORK.

token *noun*
1. Something visible or evident that gives grounds for believing in the existence or presence of something else : badge, evidence, index, indication, indicator, manifestation, mark, note, sign, signification, stamp, symptom, witness. *See* SHOW. **2.** Something that takes the place of words in communicating a thought or feeling : expression, gesture, indication, sign. *See* SHOW. **3.** Something given to guarantee the repayment of a loan or the fulfillment of an obligation : earnest[2], guaranty, pawn[1], pledge, security, warrant. *See* TRANSACTIONS. **4.** Something that causes one to remember : keepsake, memento, remembrance, reminder, souvenir, trophy. *See* REMEMBER.

tolerable *adjective*
1. Capable of being tolerated : bearable, endurable, sufferable. *See* CONTINUE. **2.** Of moderately good quality but less than excellent : acceptable, adequate, all right, average, common, decent, fair, fairish, goodish, moderate, passable, respectable, satisfactory, sufficient. *Informal:* OK, tidy. *See* GOOD.

tolerance *noun*
1. Forbearing or lenient treatment : charitableness, charity, forbearance, indulgence, lenience, leniency, lenity, toleration. *See* ACCEPT. **2.** The capacity of enduring hardship or inconvenience without complaint : forbearance, long-suffering, patience, resignation. *See* ACCEPT.

tolerant *adjective*
1. Not narrow or conservative in thought, expression, or conduct : broad, broad-minded, liberal, open-minded, progressive. *See* ATTITUDE, WIDE. **2.** Not strict or severe : charitable, clement, easy, forbearing, indulgent, lax, lenient, merciful, soft. *See* ACCEPT.

tolerate *verb*
1. To neither forbid nor prevent : allow, have, let, permit, suffer. *See* ALLOW. **2.** To put up with : abide, accept, bear, brook[2], endure, go, stand (for), stomach, suffer, support, sustain, swallow, take, withstand. *Informal:* lump[2]. ***Idioms:*** take it, take it lying down. *See* ACCEPT.

toleration *noun*
Forbearing or lenient treatment : charitableness, charity, forbearance, indulgence, lenience, leniency, lenity, tolerance. *See* ACCEPT.

toll[1] *noun*
1. A fixed amount of money charged for a privilege or service : charge, exaction, fee. *See* MONEY, PAY, TRANSACTIONS. **2.** A loss sustained in the accomplishment of or as the result of something : cost, expense, price, sacrifice. *See* TRANSACTIONS.

toll[2] *verb*
To give forth or cause to give forth a clear, resonant sound : bong, chime, knell, peal, ring[2], strike. *See* SOUNDS.

tomb *noun*
A burial place or receptacle for human remains : catacomb, cinerarium, crypt, grave[1], mausoleum, ossuary, sepulcher, sepulture, vault[1]. *See* KEEP, PLACE.

tome *noun*
A printed and bound work : book, volume. *See* WORDS.

tomfool *noun*
One deficient in judgment and good sense : ass, fool, idiot, imbecile, jackass, mooncalf, moron, nincompoop, ninny, nitwit, simple, simpleton, softhead. *Informal:* dope, gander, goose. *Slang:* cretin, ding-dong, dip, goof, jerk, nerd, schmo, schmuck, turkey. *See* ABILITY.

tomfool *adjective* So senseless as to be laughable : absurd, foolish, harebrained, idiotic, imbecilic, insane, lunatic, mad, moronic, nonsensical, preposterous, silly, softheaded, unearthly, zany. *Informal:* cockeyed, crazy, loony, loopy. *Slang:* balmy[2], dippy, dopey, jerky, sappy, wacky. *See* ABILITY, KNOWLEDGE.

tomfoolery *noun*
1. Foolish behavior : absurdity, folly, foolery, foolishness, idiocy, imbecility, insanity, lunacy, madness, nonsense, preposterousness, senselessness, silliness, zaniness. *Informal:* craziness. *See* ABILITY. **2.** Annoying yet harmless, usually playful acts : devilry, deviltry, diablerie, high jinks, impishness, mischief, mischievousness, prankishness, rascality, roguery, roguishness. *Informal:* shenanigan (often used in plural). *See* GOOD. **3.** Something that does not have or make sense : balderdash, blather, bunkum, claptrap, drivel, garbage, idiocy, nonsense, piffle, poppycock, rigmarole, rubbish, trash, twaddle. *Informal:* tommyrot. *Slang:* applesauce, baloney, bilge, bull[1], bunk[2], crap, hooey, malarkey. *See* KNOWLEDGE.

tommyrot *noun*
Informal. Something that does not have or make sense : balderdash, blather, bunkum, claptrap, drivel, garbage, idiocy, nonsense, piffle, poppycock, rigmarole, rubbish, tomfoolery, trash, twaddle. *Slang:* applesauce, baloney, bilge, bull[1], bunk[2], crap, hooey, malarkey. *See* KNOWLEDGE.

tonality *noun*
A sound of distinct pitch and quality : timbre, tone, tone color. *See* SOUNDS.

tone *noun*
1. A sound of distinct pitch and quality : timbre, tonality, tone color. *See* SOUNDS. **2.** A particular vocal quality that indicates some emotion or feeling : accent, inflection, intonation. ***Idiom:*** tone of voice. *See* SOUNDS. **3.** A distinctive way of expressing oneself : fashion, manner, mode, style, vein. *See* STYLE. **4.** A general impression produced by a predominant quality or characteristic : air, ambiance, atmosphere, aura, feel, feeling, mood, smell. *See* BE. **5.** A prevailing quality, as of thought, behavior, or attitude : climate, mood, spirit, temper. *See* ATTITUDE. **6.** The property by which the sense of vision can distinguish between objects, as a red apple and a green apple, that are very similar or identical in form and size : color, hue, shade, tint. *See* COLORS. **7.** A shade of a color, especially a pale or delicate variation : cast, hue, tinge, tint. *See* COLORS.

tone down *verb* **1.** To make less emphatic or obvious : de-emphasize, play down. *Informal:* soft-pedal. *See* SHOW. **2.** To make or become less severe or extreme : moderate, mute, qualify, soften, subdue, tame, temper. *See* INCREASE.

tone color *noun*
A sound of distinct pitch and quality : timbre, tonality, tone. *See* SOUNDS.
tone down *verb* See **tone.**
toney *adjective* See **tony.**
tongue *noun*
A system of terms used by a people sharing a history and culture : dialect, language, speech, vernacular. *Linguistics:* langue. *See* WORDS.
tonic *noun*
A medicine that restores or increases vigor : restorative, roborant. *Informal:* bracer, pick-me-up. *See* HELP.
tonic *adjective* Producing or stimulating physical, mental, or emotional vigor : bracing, energizing, exhilarant, exhilarating, innerving, intoxicating, invigorating, refreshing, reinvigorating, renewing, restorative, roborant, stimulating. *See* HELP.
tony also **toney** *adjective*
Informal. Being or in accordance with the current fashion : à la mode, chic, dashing, fashionable, mod, modish, posh, smart, stylish, swank, swanky, trig. *Informal:* classy, in, sharp, snappy, swish, trendy. *Slang:* with-it. ***Idioms:*** all the rage, up to the minute. *See* STYLE, USUAL.
too *adverb*
In addition : additionally, also, besides, further, furthermore, item, likewise, more, moreover, still, yet. *Idioms:* as well, to boot. *See* INCREASE.
tool *noun*
1. A device used to do work or perform a task : implement, instrument, utensil. *See* MACHINE, MEANS. **2.** A person used or controlled by others : cat's-paw, dupe, instrument, pawn[2], puppet, stooge. *See* OVER.
tool *verb Slang.* To run and control (a motor vehicle) : drive, motor, pilot, wheel. *See* MOVE.
toothsome *adjective*
Highly pleasing, especially to the sense of taste : ambrosial, appetizing, delectable, delicious, heavenly, luscious, savory, scrumptious, tasteful, tasty. *Slang:* yummy. *See* GOOD, INGESTION.
top *noun*
1. The highest point : apex, cap, crest, crown, height, peak, roof, summit, vertex. *See* HIGH. **2.** The outer layer of an object : face, surface. *See* SURFACE. **3.** The highest point or state : acme, apex, apogee, climax, crest, crown, culmination, height, meridian, peak, pinnacle, summit, zenith. *Informal:* payoff. *Medicine:* fastigium. *See* HIGH. **4.** The greatest quantity or highest degree attainable : maximum, outside, ultimate, utmost, uttermost. ***Idiom:*** ne plus ultra. *See* HIGH, LIMITED. **5.** The superlative or most preferable part of something : best, choice, cream, crème de la crème, elite, flower, pick, prize[1]. ***Idioms:*** cream of the crop, flower of the flock, pick of the bunch (*or* crop). *See* BETTER.
top *adjective* **1.** Of, being, located at, or forming the top : highest, loftiest, topmost, upmost, uppermost. *See* HIGH. **2.** Greatest in quantity or highest in degree that has been or can be attained : maximal, maximum, topmost, ultimate, utmost, uttermost. *See* HIGH, LIMITED. **3.** Exceptionally good of its kind : ace, banner, blue-ribbon, brag, capital, champion, excellent, fine[1], first-class, first-rate, prime, quality, splendid, superb, superior, terrific, tiptop. *Informal:* A-one, bully, dandy, great, swell, topflight, topnotch. *Slang:* boss. *Chiefly British:* tophole. *See* GOOD. **4.** Preeminent in rank or position : highest, top-drawer. *See* OVER. **5.** Most important, influential, or significant : capital, cardinal, chief, first, foremost, key, leading, main, major, number one, paramount, premier, primary, prime, principal. *See* IMPORTANT.
top *verb* **1.** To put a topping on : cap, crown, top off. *See* OVER, PUT ON. **2.** To be greater or better than : best, better[1], exceed, excel, outdo, outmatch, outrun, outshine, outstrip, pass, surpass, transcend. *Informal:* beat. ***Idioms:*** go beyond, go one better. *See* BIG. **3.** To reach or bring to a climax. Also used with *off* or *out* : cap, climax, crest, crown, culminate, peak. *See* EXCITE.
top off *verb* To put a topping on : cap, crown, top. *See* OVER, PUT ON.
top-drawer *adjective*
Preeminent in rank or position : highest, top. *See* OVER.
topflight *adjective*
Informal. Exceptionally good of its kind : ace, banner, blue-ribbon, brag, capital, champion, excellent, fine[1], first-class, first-rate, prime, quality, splendid, superb, superior, terrific, tiptop, top. *Informal:* A-one, bully, dandy, great, swell, topnotch. *Slang:* boss. *Chiefly British:* tophole. *See* GOOD.
tophole *adjective*
Chiefly British. Exceptionally good of its kind : ace, banner, blue-ribbon, brag, capital, champion, excellent, fine[1], first-class, first-rate, prime, quality, splendid, superb, superior, terri-

fic, tiptop, top. *Informal:* A-one, bully, dandy, great, swell, topflight, topnotch. *Slang:* boss. *See* GOOD.

topic *noun*
What a speech, piece of writing, or artistic work is about : argument, matter, point, subject, subject matter, text, theme. *See* MEANING.

topical *adjective*
Of, constituting, or relating to a theme or themes : thematic. *See* MEANING.

topmost *adjective*
1. Of, being, located at, or forming the top : highest, loftiest, top, upmost, uppermost. *See* HIGH. **2.** Greatest in quantity or highest in degree that has been or can be attained : maximal, maximum, top, ultimate, utmost, uttermost. *See* HIGH, LIMITED.

topnotch *adjective*
Informal. Exceptionally good of its kind : ace, banner, blue-ribbon, brag, capital, champion, excellent, fine[1], first-class, first-rate, prime, quality, splendid, superb, superior, terrific, tiptop, top. *Informal:* A-one, bully, dandy, great, swell, topflight. *Slang:* boss. *Chiefly British:* tophole. *See* GOOD.

top off *verb* See **top.**

topography *noun*
The character, natural features, and configuration of land : terrain. ***Idiom:*** the lay of the land. *See* SURFACE.

topple *verb*
1. To turn or cause to turn from a vertical or horizontal position : capsize, knock over, overthrow, overturn, turn over, upset. *See* CHANGE, HORIZONTAL, MOVE. **2.** To come to the ground suddenly and involuntarily : drop, fall, go down, nose-dive, pitch, plunge, spill, tumble. ***Idiom:*** take a fall (*or* header *or* plunge *or* spill *or* tumble). *See* RISE. **3.** To bring about the downfall of : bring down, overthrow, overturn, subvert, tumble, unhorse. *See* HELP. **4.** To undergo capture, defeat, or ruin : collapse, fall, go down, go under, surrender. *See* RESIST, WIN.

topsy-turviness *noun*
A lack of order or regular arrangement : chaos, clutter, confusedness, confusion, derangement, disarrangement, disarray, disorder, disorderedness, disorderliness, disorganization, jumble, mess, mix-up, muddle, muss, scramble, tumble. *Slang:* snafu. *See* ORDER.

topsy-turvy *adjective*
Characterized by physical confusion : chaotic, confused, disordered, helter-skelter, higgledy-piggledy, upside-down. *Informal:* mixed-up. *See* ORDER.

torch *verb*
Slang. To cause to burn or undergo combustion : enkindle, fire, ignite, kindle, light[1]. ***Idioms:*** set afire (*or* on fire), set fire to. *See* HOT, START.

torment *noun*
1. A state of physical or mental suffering : affliction, agony, anguish, distress, hurt, misery, pain, torture, woe, wound, wretchedness. *See* HAPPY. **2.** Excruciating punishment : hell, living hell, persecution, torture. ***Idiom:*** tortures of the damned. *See* REWARD. **3.** Something that annoys : aggravation, annoyance, besetment, bother, irritant, irritation, nuisance, peeve, plague, vexation. *See* FEELINGS, PAIN.

torment *verb* **1.** To subject (another) to extreme physical cruelty, as in punishing : crucify, rack, torture. ***Idiom:*** put on the rack (*or* wheel). *See* PAIN, REWARD. **2.** To bring great harm or suffering to : afflict, agonize, anguish, curse, excruciate, plague, rack, scourge, smite, strike, torture. *See* ATTACK, HELP. **3.** To come to mind continually : haunt, obsess, trouble, weigh on (*or* upon). *See* REPETITION. **4.** To disturb by repeated attacks : annoy, bait, bedevil, beleaguer, beset, harass, harry, pester, plague, tease, worry. *See* FEELINGS, PAIN.

tormenting *adjective*
Extraordinarily painful or distressing : agonizing, anguishing, excruciating, harrowing, torturous. *See* PAIN.

torpedo *verb*
To cause the complete ruin or wreckage of : bankrupt, break down, cross up, demolish, destroy, finish, ruin, shatter, sink, smash, spoil, undo, wash up, wrack[2], wreck. *Slang:* total. ***Idiom:*** put the kibosh on. *See* HELP.

torpid *adjective*
1. Lacking responsiveness or alertness : benumbed, dull, insensible, insensitive, numb, stuporous, unresponsive, wooden. *See* AWARENESS. **2.** Lacking mental and physical alertness and activity : hebetudinous, lethargic, sluggish, stupid, stuporous. *Slang:* dopey. *See* ACTION.

torpidity *noun*
A deficiency in mental and physical alertness and activity : dullness, hebetude, languidness, languor, lassitude, leadenness, lethargy, listlessness, sluggishness, stupor, torpor. *See* ACTION.

torpor *noun*
A deficiency in mental and physical alertness and activity : dullness, hebetude, languidness,

languor, lassitude, leadenness, lethargy, listlessness, sluggishness, stupor, torpidity. *See* ACTION.

torrent *noun*
An abundant, usually overwhelming flow or fall, as of a river or rain : alluvion, cataclysm, cataract, deluge, downpour, flood, freshet, inundation, Niagara, overflow. *Chiefly British:* spate. *See* BIG.

torrid *adjective*
1. Marked by much heat : ardent, baking, blistering, boiling, broiling, burning, fiery, heated, hot, red-hot, roasting, scalding, scorching, searing, sizzling, sultry, sweltering. *See* HOT.
2. Fired with intense feeling : ardent, blazing, burning, dithyrambic, fervent, fervid, fiery, flaming, glowing, heated, hot-blooded, impassioned, passionate, perfervid, red-hot, scorching. *See* FEELINGS.

torridity *noun*
Intense warmth : fervor, heat, hotness, torridness. *See* HOT.

torridness *noun*
Intense warmth : fervor, heat, hotness, torridity. *See* HOT.

tortuous *adjective*
1. Repeatedly curving in alternate directions : anfractuous, flexuous, meandrous, serpentine, sinuous, snaky, winding. *See* REPETITION, STRAIGHT. **2.** Not taking a direct or straight line or course : anfractuous, circuitous, circular, devious, indirect, oblique, roundabout. *See* STRAIGHT.

torture *noun*
1. Excruciating punishment : hell, living hell, persecution, torment. ***Idiom:*** tortures of the damned. *See* REWARD. **2.** A state of physical or mental suffering : affliction, agony, anguish, distress, hurt, misery, pain, torment, woe, wound, wretchedness. *See* HAPPY.
torture *verb* **1.** To subject (another) to extreme physical cruelty, as in punishing : crucify, rack, torment. ***Idiom:*** put on the rack (*or* wheel). *See* PAIN, REWARD. **2.** To bring great harm or suffering to : afflict, agonize, anguish, curse, excruciate, plague, rack, scourge, smite, strike, torment. *See* ATTACK, HELP.

torturous *adjective*
Extraordinarily painful or distressing : agonizing, anguishing, excruciating, harrowing, tormenting. *See* PAIN.

Tory *noun*
One who strongly favors retention of the existing order : conservative, orthodox, rightist, right-winger, traditionalist. *See* KEEP.
Tory *adjective* Strongly favoring retention of the existing order : conservative, orthodox, right, rightist, right-wing, traditionalist, traditionalistic. *See* KEEP.

toss *verb*
1. To send through the air with a motion of the hand or arm : cast, dart, dash, fling, heave, hurl, hurtle, launch, pitch, shoot, shy[2], sling, throw. *Informal:* fire. *See* MOVE. **2.** To move vigorously from side to side or up and down : heave, pitch, rock, roll. *See* REPETITION. **3.** To swing about or strike at wildly : flail, thrash, thresh. ***Idiom:*** toss and turn. *See* ATTACK, MOVE, STRIKE. **4.** To twist and turn, as in pain, struggle, or embarrassment : agonize, squirm, turn, writhe. *See* REPETITION. **5.** To impair or destroy the composure of : agitate, bother, discompose, disquiet, distract, disturb, flurry, fluster, perturb, rock, ruffle, shake (up), unsettle, upset. *Informal:* rattle. *See* CALM.
6. To throw (a coin) in order to decide something : flip. ***Idiom:*** call heads or tails. *See* LUCK, MOVE.
toss around *verb* To speak together and exchange ideas and opinions about : bandy (about), discuss, moot, talk over, thrash out (*or* over), thresh out (*or* over). *Informal:* hash (over), kick around, knock about (*or* around). *Slang:* rap[3]. ***Idiom:*** go into a huddle. *See* WORDS.
toss down (or **off**) *verb* *Informal.* To take into the mouth and swallow (a liquid) : drink, imbibe, pull on, quaff, sip, sup. *Informal:* swig. *Slang:* belt. ***Idiom:*** wet one's whistle. *See* MOUTH.
toss *noun* An act of throwing : cast, fling, heave, hurl, launch, pitch, shy[2], sling, throw. *See* MOVE.

toss around *verb* See **toss.**

toss down or **off** *verb* See **toss.**

tot[1] *noun*
1. A young person between birth and puberty : bud[1], child, innocent, juvenile, moppet, youngster. *Informal:* kid. *Scots:* bairn. *See* KIN, YOUTH. **2.** A small amount of liquor : dram, drop, jigger, shot, sip. *Informal:* nip[2], slug[1]. *Slang:* snort. *See* BIG, INGESTION.

tot[2] *verb*
To combine (figures) to form a sum. Also used with *up* : add (up), cast, foot (up), sum (up), total, totalize. *See* INCREASE.

total *noun*
1. A number or quantity obtained as a result of addition : aggregate, amount, sum, summa-

tion, sum total, totality. *Archaic:* tale. *See* COUNT. **2.** An amount or quantity from which nothing is left out or held back : aggregate, all, entirety, everything, gross, sum, totality, whole. *Informal:* work (used in plural). ***Idioms:*** everything but (*or* except) the kitchen sink; lock, stock, and barrel; the whole ball of wax (*or* kit and caboodle *or* megillah *or* nine yards *or* shebang). *See* PART.

total *adjective* **1.** Including every constituent or individual : all, complete, entire, gross, whole. *See* PART. **2.** Completely such, without qualification or exception : absolute, all-out, arrant, complete, consummate, crashing, damned, dead, downright, flat, out-and-out, outright, perfect, plain, pure, sheer[2], thorough, thoroughgoing, unbounded, unequivocal, unlimited, unmitigated, unqualified, unrelieved, unreserved, utter[2]. *Informal:* flat-out, positive. *Chiefly British:* blooming. *See* BIG, LIMITED.

total *verb* **1.** To combine (figures) to form a sum : add (up), cast, foot (up), sum (up), tot[2] (up), totalize. *See* INCREASE. **2.** To come to in number or quantity : aggregate, amount, number, reach, run into. ***Idiom:*** add up to. *See* INCREASE. **3.** *Slang.* To cause the complete ruin or wreckage of : bankrupt, break down, cross up, demolish, destroy, finish, ruin, shatter, sink, smash, spoil, torpedo, undo, wash up, wrack[2], wreck. ***Idiom:*** put the kibosh on. *See* HELP.

totalitarian *adjective*

1. Characterized by or favoring absolute obedience to authority : authoritarian, autocratic, despotic, dictatorial, tyrannic, tyrannical. *See* OVER. **2.** Having and exercising complete political power and control : absolute, absolutistic, arbitrary, autarchic, autarchical, autocratic, autocratical, despotic, dictatorial, monocratic, tyrannic, tyrannical, tyrannous. *See* OVER, POLITICS.

totalitarian *noun* **1.** One who imposes or favors absolute obedience to authority : authoritarian, autocrat, despot, dictator, martinet, tyrant. *See* OVER. **2.** An absolute ruler, especially one who is harsh and oppressive : Big Brother, despot, dictator, führer, man on horseback, oppressor, strongman, tyrant. *See* OVER.

totalitarianism *noun*

1. Absolute power, especially when exercised unjustly or cruelly : autocracy, despotism, dictatorship, tyranny. *See* OVER, POLITICS. **2.** A political doctrine advocating the principle of absolute rule : absolutism, authoritarianism, autocracy, despotism, dictatorship. *See* OVER, POLITICS.

totality *noun*

1. The state of being entirely whole : completeness, entirety, integrity, oneness, wholeness. *See* PART. **2.** An amount or quantity from which nothing is left out or held back : aggregate, all, entirety, everything, gross, sum, total, whole. *Informal:* work (used in plural). ***Idioms:*** everything but (*or* except) the kitchen sink; lock, stock, and barrel; the whole ball of wax (*or* kit and caboodle *or* megillah *or* nine yards *or* shebang). *See* PART. **3.** A number or quantity obtained as a result of addition : aggregate, amount, sum, summation, sum total, total. *Archaic:* tale. *See* COUNT. **4.** An organized array of individual elements and parts forming and working as a unit : entity, integral, sum, system, whole. *See* PART.

totalization *noun*

The act or process of adding : addition, summation. *See* INCREASE.

totalize *verb*

To combine (figures) to form a sum : add (up), cast, foot (up), sum (up), tot[2] (up), total. *See* INCREASE.

totally *adverb*

To the fullest extent : absolutely, all, altogether, completely, dead, entirely, flat, fully, just, perfectly, quite, thoroughly, utterly, well[2], wholly. *Informal:* clean, clear. ***Idioms:*** in toto, through and through. *See* BIG, LIMITED.

tote *verb*

Informal. To move while supporting : bear, carry, convey, lug[2], transport. *Slang:* schlep. *See* OVER.

totter *verb*

1. To move back and forth or from side to side, as if about to fall : sway, teeter, vacillate, waver, weave, wobble. *See* REPETITION. **2.** To walk unsteadily : falter, lurch, reel, stagger, stumble, teeter, weave, wobble. *See* MOVE.

tottering *adjective*

1. Not physically steady or firm : precarious, rickety, shaky, tottery, unstable, unsteady, wobbly. *See* FLEXIBLE. **2.** Lacking stability : infirm, insecure, precarious, shaky, tottery, unstable, unsteady, unsure, weak, wobbly. *See* CHANGE, STRONG.

tottery *adjective*

1. Not physically steady or firm : precarious, rickety, shaky, tottering, unstable, unsteady, wobbly. *See* FLEXIBLE. **2.** Lacking stability :

infirm, insecure, precarious, shaky, tottering, unstable, unsteady, unsure, weak, wobbly. *See* CHANGE, STRONG.

touch *verb*

1. To bring the hands or fingers, for example, into contact with so as to give or receive a physical sensation : feel, finger, handle, palpate. *See* TOUCH. **2.** To bring into or make contact with : contact. *See* TOUCH. **3.** To be contiguous or next to : abut, adjoin, border, bound[2], butt[2], join, meet[1], neighbor, verge. *See* NEAR. **4.** To be equal or alike : compare, correspond, equal, match, measure up, parallel. *Informal:* stack up. *See* SAME. **5.** To call or direct attention to something. Also used with *on* or *upon* : advert, bring up, mention, point, point out, refer. *See* WORDS. **6.** To evoke a usually strong mental or emotional response from : affect[1], get (to), impress, move, strike. *See* TOUCH.

touch down *verb* To come to rest on the ground : alight[1], land, light[2], set down, settle. *See* MOVE.

touch off *verb* **1.** To release or cause to release energy suddenly and violently, especially with a loud noise : blast, blow[1] (up), burst, detonate, explode, fire, fulminate, go off. *See* EXPLOSION. **2.** To be the cause of : bring, bring about, bring on, cause, effect, effectuate, generate, induce, ingenerate, lead to, make, occasion, result in, secure, set off, stir[1] (up), trigger. ***Idioms:*** bring to pass (*or* effect), give rise to. *See* START. **3.** To stir to action or feeling : egg on, excite, foment, galvanize, goad, impel, incite, inflame, inspire, instigate, motivate, move, pique, prick, prod, prompt, propel, provoke, set off, spur, stimulate, trigger, work up. *See* CAUSE, EXCITE.

touch up *verb* To improve by making minor changes or additions : polish, retouch. *See* BETTER.

touch *noun* **1.** An act of touching : feeling, palpation. *See* TOUCH. **2.** A coming together so as to be touching : contact, contingence. *See* TOUCH. **3.** The faculty or ability to perceive tactile stimulation : feel, feeling, tactility. *See* TOUCH. **4.** A particular sensation conveyed by means of physical contact : feel, feeling. *See* TOUCH. **5.** A slight amount or indication : breath, dash, ghost, hair, hint, intimation, semblance, shade, shadow, soupçon, streak, suggestion, suspicion, taste, tinge, trace, whiff, whisper. *Informal:* whisker. *See* BIG, SHOW. **6.** A situation allowing exchange of ideas or messages : communication, contact, intercommunication. *See* CONNECT, TOUCH.

touchable *adjective*

Discernible by touch : palpable, tactile, tangible. *See* TOUCH.

touchableness *noun*

The quality or condition of being discernible by touch : palpability, tactility, tangibility, tangibleness. *See* TOUCH.

touch-and-go *adjective*

Requiring great tact or skill : delicate, sensitive, ticklish, touchy, tricky. *See* EASY.

touch down *verb* See **touch.**

touched *adjective*

Afflicted with or exhibiting irrationality and mental unsoundness : brainsick, crazy, daft, demented, disordered, distraught, dotty, insane, lunatic, mad, maniac, maniacal, mentally ill, moonstruck, off, unbalanced, unsound, wrong. *Informal:* bonkers, cracked, daffy, gaga, loony. *Slang:* bananas, batty, buggy, cuckoo, fruity, loco, nuts, nutty, screwy, wacky. *Chiefly British:* crackers. *Law:* non compos mentis. ***Idioms:*** around the bend, crazy as a loon, mad as a hatter, not all there, nutty as a fruitcake, off (*or* out of) one's head, off one's rocker, of unsound mind, out of one's mind, sick in the head, stark raving mad. *See* SANE.

touching *adjective*

Exciting a deep, usually somber response : affecting, impressive, moving, poignant, stirring. *See* TOUCH.

touch off *verb* See **touch.**

touchstone *noun*

A means by which individuals are compared and judged : benchmark, criterion, gauge, mark, measure, standard, test, yardstick. *See* USUAL.

touch up *verb* See **touch.**

touchy *adjective*

1. Easily annoyed : choleric, irascible, peppery, quick-tempered, testy, tetchy. *See* FEELINGS. **2.** Requiring great tact or skill : delicate, sensitive, ticklish, touch-and-go, tricky. *See* EASY.

tough *adjective*

1. Physically toughened so as to have great endurance : hard, hard-bitten, hard-handed, hardy, rugged. ***Idiom:*** hard as nails. *See* CONTINUE, STRONG. **2.** Capable of exerting considerable effort or of withstanding considerable stress or hardship : hardy, stalwart, stout, strong, sturdy. *See* STRONG. **3.** Requiring great or extreme bodily, mental, or spiritual strength : arduous, backbreaking, burdensome, demanding, difficult, effortful, exacting, exigent, formidable, hard, heavy, laborious, onerous, oppressive, rigorous, rough, severe, taxing, trying, weighty. *See* HEAVY. **4.** Not easy to do, achieve, or master : arduous, difficult, hard, laborious, serious, tall, uphill. *See* EASY. **5.** Marked by vigorous physical exertion : knockabout, rough, rough-and-tumble, rugged, strenuous. *See* ACTION. **6.** Rigorous and unsparing in treating others : demanding, exacting, hard, harsh, rigid, severe, stern, strict, unyielding. *See* EASY. **7.** Indicating or possessing determination, resolution, or persistence : constant, determined, firm[1], resolute, steadfast, steady, stiff, unbending, uncompromising, unflinching, unwavering, unyielding. *See* PURPOSE.

tough *noun* **1.** A rough, violent person who engages in destructive actions : hoodlum, mug, roughneck, rowdy, ruffian. *Informal:* toughie. *Slang:* hood, punk. *See* ATTACK, CRIMES. **2.** A person who treats others violently and roughly, especially for hire : hoodlum, ruffian, thug. *Informal:* hooligan. *Slang:* goon, gorilla, hood. *See* ATTACK, CRIMES.

tough out *verb Slang.* To carry on through despite hardships : endure. *Slang:* sweat out. *See* CONTINUE.

toughen *verb*

1. To become or cause to become tough or strong : strengthen. *See* STRONG. **2.** To make resistant to hardship, especially through continued exposure : acclimate, acclimatize, caseharden, harden, indurate, season. *See* CONTINUE, RESIST.

toughie *noun*

Informal. A rough, violent person who engages in destructive actions : hoodlum, mug, roughneck, rowdy, ruffian, tough. *Slang:* hood, punk. *See* ATTACK, CRIMES.

tough-minded *adjective*

Having or indicating an awareness of things as they really are : down-to-earth, hard, hardheaded, matter-of-fact, objective, practical, pragmatic, pragmatical, prosaic, realistic, sober, unromantic. *See* EXCITE, REAL.

toughness *noun*

1. The fact or condition of being rigorous and unsparing : austerity, hardness, harshness, rigidity, rigor, rigorousness, severity, sternness, strictness, stringency. *See* EASY. **2.** Unwavering firmness of character, action, or will : decidedness, decision, decisiveness, determination, firmness, purpose, purposefulness, resoluteness, resolution, resolve, will, willpower. *See* CERTAIN, STRONG.

tough out *verb* See **tough.**

tour *noun*

1. A course, process, or journey that ends where it began or repeats itself : circle, circuit, cycle, orbit, round, turn. *See* REPETITION. **2.** A journey undertaken with a specific objective : expedition, pilgrimage, safari, trek, voyage. *See* MOVE. **3.** A limited, often assigned period of activity, duty, or opportunity : bout, go, hitch, inning (often used in plural), shift, spell[3], stint, stretch, time, trick, turn, watch. *See* TIME. **4.** A term of service, as in the military or in prison : hitch, stretch, time. *See* TIME.

tour de force *noun*

A great or heroic deed : achievement, exploit, feat, gest, masterstroke, stunt. *See* ACTION.

tourist *noun*

One who travels for pleasure : excursionist, sightseer. *Chiefly British:* tripper. *See* MOVE.

tournament *noun*

Any competition or test of opposing wills likened to the sport in which knights fought with lances : joust, tilt, tourney. *See* CONFLICT.

tourney *noun*

Any competition or test of opposing wills likened to the sport in which knights fought with lances : joust, tilt, tournament. *See* CONFLICT.

tousle *verb*

To put (the hair or clothes) into a state of disarray : disarrange, dishevel, disorder, mess (up), muss (up), rumple. *See* ORDER.

tout *verb*

To increase or seek to increase the importance or reputation of by favorable publicity : ballyhoo, boost, build up, enhance, promote, publicize, puff, talk up. *Informal:* plug. *Slang:* hype. *See* KNOWLEDGE.

touzle *verb* See **tousle.**

tow *verb*

To exert force so as to move (something) toward the source of the force : drag, draw, haul, pull, tug. *See* PUSH.

toward *adjective*

Affording benefit : advantageous, benefic, beneficent, beneficial, benignant, favorable, good, helpful, profitable, propitious, salutary, useful. *See* HELP.

tower above or **over** *verb*

To rise above, especially so as to afford a view of : command, dominate, overlook. *See* OVER.

towering *adjective*

1. Imposingly high : aerial, airy, lofty, sky-high, soaring. *See* HIGH. **2.** Far beyond what is usual, normal, or customary : exceptional, extraordinary, magnificent, outstanding, preeminent, rare, remarkable, singular, uncommon, unusual. *Informal:* standout. *Slang:* awesome, out of sight. *See* BETTER, USUAL. **3.** Awesomely or forbiddingly intense : overpowering, overwhelming, staggering. *See* BIG.

towheaded *adjective*
Having light hair : blond, fair, fair-haired. *See* COLORS.

town *noun*
Informal. A large and important town : city, metropolis, municipality. *Informal:* burg. *See* URBAN.

toxic *adjective*
Capable of injuring or killing by poison : mephitic, mephitical, poison, poisonous, toxicant, venomous, virulent. *See* HELP.

toxicant *adjective*
Capable of injuring or killing by poison : mephitic, mephitical, poison, poisonous, toxic, venomous, virulent. *See* HELP.

toxin *noun*
Anything that is injurious, destructive, or fatal : bane, canker, contagion, poison, venom, virus. *See* HELP.

toy *noun*
1. An object for children to play with : plaything. *See* WORK. **2.** A small showy article : bauble, bibelot, gewgaw, gimcrack, knickknack, novelty, trifle, trinket, whatnot. *See* THING.

toy *verb* **1.** To move one's fingers or hands in a nervous or aimless fashion : fiddle, fidget, fool, monkey, play, putter, tinker, trifle, twiddle. *See* TOUCH. **2.** To treat lightly or flippantly : dally, flirt, play, trifle. *See* WORK. **3.** To make amorous advances without serious intentions : coquet, dally, flirt, trifle. *See* SEX.

trace *noun*
1. A visible sign or mark of the passage of someone or something : print, track, trail. *See* MARKS. **2.** A mark or remnant that indicates the former presence of something : relic, remains, vestige. *See* LEFTOVER, MARKS. **3.** A slight amount or indication : breath, dash, ghost, hair, hint, intimation, semblance, shade, shadow, soupçon, streak, suggestion, suspicion, taste, tinge, touch, whiff, whisper. *Informal:* whisker. *See* BIG, SHOW.

trace *verb* **1.** To follow the traces or scent of, as in hunting : track, trail. *See* MARKS, SEEK. **2.** To pursue and locate : hunt down, nose out, run down, track down. ***Idiom:*** run to earth (*or* ground). *See* GET.

track *noun*
1. A visible sign or mark of the passage of someone or something : print, trace, trail. *See* MARKS. **2.** Evidence of passage left along a course followed by a hunted animal or fugitive : scent, spoor, trail. *See* MARKS, SMELLS. **3.** A course of action to be followed regularly : round (often used in plural), routine. *See* USUAL.

track *verb* **1.** To follow the traces or scent of, as in hunting : trace, trail. *See* MARKS, SEEK. **2.** To keep (another) under surveillance by moving along behind : dog, follow, shadow, trail. *Informal:* bird-dog, tail. *See* PRECEDE. **3.** To go across : cross, pass, transit, traverse. *See* MOVE.

track down *verb* To pursue and locate : hunt down, nose out, run down, trace. ***Idiom:*** run to earth (*or* ground). *See* GET.

track down *verb* See **track.**

tract *noun*
1. A part of the earth's surface : area, belt, district, locality, neighborhood, quarter, region, zone. *Informal:* neck of the woods. *See* TERRITORY. **2.** A piece of land : lot, parcel, plot. *See* TERRITORY.

tractability *noun*
The quality or state of willingly carrying out the wishes of others : acquiescence, amenability, amenableness, compliance, compliancy, deference, obedience, submission, submissiveness, tractableness. *See* RESIST.

tractable *adjective*
Willing to carry out the wishes of others : amenable, biddable, compliant, conformable, docile, obedient, submissive, supple. *See* RESIST.

tractableness *noun*
The quality or state of willingly carrying out the wishes of others : acquiescence, amenability, amenableness, compliance, compliancy, deference, obedience, submission, submissiveness, tractability. *See* RESIST.

traction *noun*
The act of drawing or pulling a load : draft, drag, draw, haul, pull. *See* PUSH.

trade *noun*
1. Commercial, industrial, or professional activity in general : business, commerce, industry, trading, traffic. *See* ACTION. **2.** The commercial transactions of customers with a supplier : business, custom, patronage, traffic. *See* TRANSACTIONS. **3.** The act of exchanging or substituting : change, commutation, exchange,

interchange, shift, substitution, switch, transposition. *Informal:* swap. *See* CHANGE, SUBSTITUTE. **4.** Activity pursued as a livelihood : art, business, calling, career, craft, employment, job, line, métier, occupation, profession, pursuit, vocation, work. *Slang:* racket. *Archaic:* employ. *See* ACTION.

trade *verb* **1.** To give up in return for something else : change, commute, exchange, interchange, shift, substitute, switch. *Informal:* swap. *See* CHANGE, SUBSTITUTE. **2.** To offer for sale. Also used with *in* : deal (in), handle, market, merchandise, merchant, peddle, retail, sell, vend. *See* TRANSACTIONS.

trademark *noun*
A name or other device placed on merchandise to signify its ownership or manufacture : brand, colophon, label, mark. *See* MARKS.

trademark *verb* To set off by or as if by a mark indicating ownership or manufacture : brand, identify, label, mark, tag. *See* MARKS.

trader *noun*
A person engaged in buying and selling : businessperson, dealer, merchandiser, merchant, speculator, tradesman, trafficker. *See* TRANSACTIONS.

tradesman *noun*
A person engaged in buying and selling : businessperson, dealer, merchandiser, merchant, speculator, trader, trafficker. *See* TRANSACTIONS.

trading *noun*
Commercial, industrial, or professional activity in general : business, commerce, industry, trade, traffic. *See* ACTION.

tradition *noun*
1. Something immaterial, as a style or philosophy, that is passed from one generation to another : heritage, inheritance, legacy. *See* AFFECT. **2.** A body of traditional beliefs and notions accumulated about a particular subject : folklore, legend, lore, myth, mythology, mythos. *See* KNOWLEDGE.

traditional *adjective*
Conforming to established practice or standards : button-down, conformist, conventional, establishmentarian, orthodox, straight. *Slang:* square. *See* USUAL.

traditionalist *adjective*
Strongly favoring retention of the existing order : conservative, orthodox, right, rightist, right-wing, Tory, traditionalistic. *See* KEEP.

traditionalist *noun* One who strongly favors retention of the existing order : conservative, orthodox, rightist, right-winger, Tory. *See* KEEP.

traditionalistic *adjective*
Strongly favoring retention of the existing order : conservative, orthodox, right, rightist, right-wing, Tory, traditionalist. *See* KEEP.

traduce *verb*
To make defamatory statements about : asperse, backbite, calumniate, defame, malign, slander, slur, tear down, vilify. *Law:* libel. *Idiom:* cast aspersions on. *See* ATTACK, CRIMES, LAW.

traducement *noun*
The expression of injurious, malicious statements about someone : aspersion, calumniation, calumny, character assassination, defamation, denigration, detraction, scandal, slander, vilification. *Law:* libel. *See* ATTACK, CRIMES, LAW.

traffic *noun*
1. Commercial, industrial, or professional activity in general : business, commerce, industry, trade, trading. *See* ACTION. **2.** The commercial transactions of customers with a supplier : business, custom, patronage, trade. *See* TRANSACTIONS.

trafficker *noun*
A person engaged in buying and selling : businessperson, dealer, merchandiser, merchant, speculator, trader, tradesman. *See* TRANSACTIONS.

tragedy *noun*
An occurrence inflicting widespread destruction and distress : calamity, cataclysm, catastrophe, disaster. *See* HELP.

trail *verb*
1. To hang or cause to hang down and be pulled along behind : drag, draggle, train. *See* HANG. **2.** To go or move slowly so that progress is hindered : dally, dawdle, delay, dilly-dally, drag, lag, linger, loiter, poke, procrastinate, tarry. *Idioms:* drag one's feet (*or* heels), mark time, take one's time. *See* FAST. **3.** To follow the traces or scent of, as in hunting : trace, track. *See* MARKS, SEEK. **4.** To keep (another) under surveillance by moving along behind : dog, follow, shadow, track. *Informal:* bird-dog, tail. *See* PRECEDE. **5.** To follow closely or persistently : dog, heel[1], tag. *See* PRECEDE.

trail *noun* **1.** Something that follows or is drawn along behind : tail, train, wake[2]. *See* PRECEDE. **2.** A visible sign or mark of the passage of someone or something : print, trace, track. *See* MARKS. **3.** Evidence of passage left along a course followed by a hunted animal or fugitive : scent, spoor, track. *See* MARKS, SMELLS.

train *noun*

1. Something that follows or is drawn along behind : tail, trail, wake[2]. *See* PRECEDE. 2. A group of attendants or followers : entourage, following, retinue, suite. *See* OVER. 3. A number of things placed or occurring one after the other : chain, consecution, course, order, procession, progression, round, run, sequence, series, string, succession, suite. *Informal:* streak. *See* ORDER.

train *verb* 1. To impart knowledge and skill to : coach, discipline, educate, instruct, school, teach, tutor. *See* TEACH. 2. To subject to or engage in forms of exertion in order to train, strengthen, or condition : drill, exercise, practice, work out. *See* WORK. 3. To move (a weapon or blow, for example) in the direction of someone or something : aim, cast, direct, head, level, point, set[1], turn, zero in. *Military:* lay[1]. *See* SEEK. 4. To hang or cause to hang down and be pulled along behind : drag, draggle, trail. *See* HANG.

trainable *adjective*

Capable of being educated : educable, teachable. *See* TEACH.

trainer *noun*

One who educates : educator, instructor, pedagogue, teacher, tutor. *See* TEACH.

training *noun*

1. The act, process, or art of imparting knowledge and skill : education, instruction, pedagogics, pedagogy, schooling, teaching, tuition, tutelage, tutoring. *See* TEACH. 2. Repetition of an action so as to develop or maintain one's skill : drill, exercise, practice, rehearsal, study. *See* WORK.

traipse *verb*

1. To travel about or journey on foot : backpack, hike, march[1], peregrinate, tramp, trek. *See* MOVE. 2. To move about at random, especially over a wide area : drift, gad, gallivant, meander, peregrinate, ramble, range, roam, rove, stray, wander. *See* MOVE.

trait *noun*

A distinctive element : attribute, character, characteristic, feature, mark, peculiarity, property, quality, savor. *See* BE.

traitor *noun*

One who betrays : betrayer, double-crosser, Judas. *Informal:* rat. *See* TRUST.

traitorous *adjective*

1. Not true to duty or obligation : disloyal, faithless, false, false-hearted, perfidious, recreant, treacherous, unfaithful, untrue. *See* CONTINUE, TRUST. 2. Involving or constituting treason : seditious, treasonable, treasonous. *See* TRUST.

traitorousness *noun*

1. Willful violation of allegiance to one's country : sedition, seditiousness, treason. *See* TRUST. 2. Betrayal, especially of a moral obligation : disloyalty, faithlessness, false-heartedness, falseness, falsity, infidelity, perfidiousness, perfidy, treacherousness, treachery, unfaithfulness. *See* CONTINUE, TRUST.

trammel *noun*

Something that limits or restricts : check, circumscription, constraint, cramp[2], curb, inhibition, limit, limitation, restraint, restriction, stricture. *See* LIMITED.

trammel *verb* 1. To gain control of or an advantage over by or as if by trapping : catch, enmesh, ensnare, ensnarl, entrap, snare, tangle, trap, web. *See* FREE. 2. To restrict the activity or free movement of : chain, fetter, hamper, hamstring, handcuff, hobble, leash, manacle, shackle, tie. *Informal:* hog-tie. *See* FREE, HELP.

tramp *verb*

1. To walk with loud, heavy steps : stamp, stomp, trample. *Informal:* tromp. *See* MOVE, SOUNDS. 2. To travel about or journey on foot : backpack, hike, march[1], peregrinate, traipse, trek. *See* MOVE. 3. To step on heavily and repeatedly so as to crush, injure, or destroy : stamp, stomp, trample, tread, tromp. *See* HELP.

tramp *noun* A vulgar promiscuous woman who flouts propriety : baggage, hussy, jade, slattern, slut, tart[2], wanton, wench, whore. *Slang:* floozy. *See* SEX.

trample *verb*

1. To step on heavily and repeatedly so as to crush, injure, or destroy : stamp, stomp, tramp, tread, tromp. *See* HELP. 2. To walk with loud, heavy steps : stamp, stomp, tramp. *Informal:* tromp. *See* MOVE, SOUNDS. 3. To treat arbitrarily or cruelly : grind, tyrannize. *See* OVER.

trance *noun*

1. The condition of being so lost in solitary thought as to be unaware of one's surroundings : absent-mindedness, abstraction, bemusement, brown study, daydreaming, muse[2], reverie, study. *See* AWARENESS. 2. A stunned or bewildered condition : befuddlement, bewilderedness, bewilderment, daze, discombobulation, fog, muddle, mystification, perplexity,

puzzlement, stupefaction, stupor. *See* AWARENESS.

tranquil *adjective*

1. Motionless and undisturbed : calm, halcyon, peaceful, placid, quiet, serene, still, stilly, untroubled. *See* CALM. **2.** Not excited or emotionally agitated : calm, peaceful, placid, serene. *See* CALM.

tranquility *noun* See **tranquillity.**

tranquilize also **tranquillize** *verb*

To make or become calm : allay, balm, becalm, calm (down), lull, quiet, settle, still. *See* CALM.

tranquillity or **tranquility** *noun*

1. An absence of motion or disturbance : calm, calmness, hush, lull, peace, peacefulness, placidity, placidness, quiet, quietness, serenity, stillness, untroubledness. *See* CALM. **2.** Lack of emotional agitation : calm, calmness, peace, peacefulness, placidity, placidness, quietude, serenity. *See* CALM.

tranquillize *verb* See **tranquilize.**

transaction *noun*

An agreement, especially one involving a sale or exchange : bargain, compact[2], contract, covenant, deal. *See* AGREE.

transcend *verb*

1. To go beyond the limits of : exceed, overreach, overrun, overstep, surpass. *See* EXCESS. **2.** To be greater or better than : best, better[1], exceed, excel, outdo, outmatch, outrun, outshine, outstrip, pass, surpass, top. *Informal:* beat. ***Idioms:*** go beyond, go one better. *See* BIG.

transcendent *adjective*

1. Of the greatest possible degree, quality, or intensity : extreme, supreme, ultimate, unsurpassable, utmost, uttermost. *See* BETTER, BIG. **2.** Existing only in concept and not in reality : abstract, hypothetic, hypothetical, ideal, theoretic, theoretical, transcendental. *See* REAL.

transcendental *adjective*

1. Existing only in concept and not in reality : abstract, hypothetic, hypothetical, ideal, theoretic, theoretical, transcendent. *See* REAL. **2.** Of, coming from, or relating to forces or beings that exist outside the natural world : extramundane, extrasensory, metaphysical, miraculous, preternatural, superhuman, supernatural, superphysical, supersensible, unearthly. *See* SUPERNATURAL.

transfer *verb*

1. To go or cause to go from one place to another : maneuver, move, remove, shift. *See* MOVE. **2.** To change one's residence or place of business, for example : move, relocate, remove. *See* MOVE. **3.** To relinquish to the possession or control of another : deliver, furnish, give, hand, hand over, provide, supply, turn over. *See* GIVE. **4.** To direct (a person) elsewhere for help or information : refer, send, turn over. *See* MOVE. **5.** *Law.* To change the ownership of (property) by means of a legal document : cede, deed, grant, make over, sign over. *Law:* alien, alienate, assign, convey. *See* GIVE, LAW.

transfer *noun* **1.** The act of delivering or the condition of being delivered : delivery, surrender. *See* GIVE. **2.** A making over of legal ownership or title : *Law:* alienation, assignment, conveyance, grant, transferal. *See* LAW.

transferal *noun*

A making over of legal ownership or title : *Law:* alienation, assignment, conveyance, grant, transfer. *See* LAW.

transfiguration *noun*

The process or result of changing from one appearance, state, or phase to another : change, changeover, conversion, metamorphosis, mutation, shift, transformation, translation, transmogrification, transmutation, transubstantiation. *See* CHANGE.

transfigure *verb*

To change into a different form, substance, or state : convert, metamorphose, mutate, transform, translate, transmogrify, transmute, transpose, transubstantiate. *See* CHANGE.

transfix *verb*

To compel, as the attention, interest, or imagination, of : arrest, catch up, enthrall, fascinate, grip, hold, mesmerize, rivet, spellbind. *Slang:* grab. *See* EXCITE.

transform *verb*

1. To change into a different form, substance, or state : convert, metamorphose, mutate, transfigure, translate, transmogrify, transmute, transpose, transubstantiate. *See* CHANGE. **2.** To bring about a radical change in : metamorphose, revolutionize. *See* CHANGE.

transformation *noun*

The process or result of changing from one appearance, state, or phase to another : change, changeover, conversion, metamorphosis, mutation, shift, transfiguration, translation, transmogrification, transmutation, transubstantiation. *See* CHANGE.

transfuse *verb*

To cause to be filled, as with a particular mood or tone : charge, freight, imbue, impregnate, permeate, pervade, saturate, suffuse. *See* FULL.

transgress *verb*
1. To refuse or fail to obey : break, defy, disobey, flout, violate. ***Idiom:*** pay no attention to. *See* RESIST. **2.** To violate a moral or divine law : err, offend, sin, trespass. *See* RIGHT. **3.** To fail to fulfill (a promise) or conform to (a regulation) : breach, break, contravene, infringe, violate. *See* DO.

transgression *noun*
An act or instance of breaking a law or regulation or of nonfulfillment of an obligation or promise, for example : breach, contravention, infraction, infringement, trespass, violation. *See* RIGHT.

transient *adjective*
Lasting or existing only for a short time : ephemeral, evanescent, fleet, fleeting, fugacious, fugitive, momentary, passing, short-lived, temporal, temporary, transitory. *See* CONTINUE, TIME.

transit *noun*
1. The moving of persons or goods from one place to another : carriage, conveyance, transport, transportation. *See* MOVE. **2.** The process or an instance of passing from one form, state, or stage to another : change, passage, shift, transition. *See* CHANGE.
transit *verb* To go across : cross, pass, track, traverse. *See* MOVE.

transition *noun*
The process or an instance of passing from one form, state, or stage to another : change, passage, shift, transit. *See* CHANGE.

transitory *adjective*
Lasting or existing only for a short time : ephemeral, evanescent, fleet, fleeting, fugacious, fugitive, momentary, passing, short-lived, temporal, temporary, transient. *See* CONTINUE, TIME.

translate *verb*
1. To express in another language, while systematically retaining the original sense : construe, put, render. *See* WORDS. **2.** To express the meaning of in other, especially simpler, words : paraphrase, render, rephrase, restate, reword. *See* WORDS. **3.** To change into a different form, substance, or state : convert, metamorphose, mutate, transfigure, transform, transmogrify, transmute, transpose, transubstantiate. *See* CHANGE.

translation *noun*
1. A restating of something in other, especially simpler, words : paraphrase, rendering, restatement, version. *See* WORDS. **2.** The process or result of changing from one appearance, state, or phase to another : change, changeover, conversion, metamorphosis, mutation, shift, transfiguration, transformation, transmogrification, transmutation, transubstantiation. *See* CHANGE.

translucent *adjective*
Admitting light so that objects beyond can be seen : clear, crystal clear, crystalline, limpid, lucid, pellucid, see-through, transparent. *See* CLEAR.

transmigrant *noun*
One who emigrates : emigrant, immigrant, migrant. *See* APPROACH.

transmigrate *verb*
1. To leave one's native land and settle in another : emigrate, immigrate, migrate. *See* APPROACH. **2.** To change habitat seasonally : migrate. *See* MOVE.

transmigration *noun*
Departure from one's native land to settle in another : emigration, exodus, immigration, migration. *See* APPROACH.

transmigratory *adjective*
Moving from one habitat to another on a seasonal basis : migrant, migrational, migratory. *See* MOVE.

transmit *verb*
1. To cause to be transferred from one to another : convey, hand (over), pass. *See* GIVE. **2.** To cause (something) to be conveyed to a destination : address, consign, dispatch, forward, route, send, ship. *See* MOVE. **3.** To cause (a disease) to pass to another or others : carry, communicate, convey, give, pass, spread. *See* MOVE. **4.** To convey (something) from one generation to the next : bequeath, hand down, hand on, pass (along *or* on). *See* GIVE. **5.** To make known : break, carry, communicate, convey, disclose, get across, impart, pass, report, tell. *See* KNOWLEDGE. **6.** To serve as a conduit : carry, channel, conduct, convey. *See* ALLOW.

transmogrification *noun*
The process or result of changing from one appearance, state, or phase to another : change, changeover, conversion, metamorphosis, mutation, shift, transfiguration, transformation, translation, transmutation, transubstantiation. *See* CHANGE.

transmogrify *verb*
To change into a different form, substance, or state : convert, metamorphose, mutate, transfigure, transform, translate, transmute, transpose, transubstantiate. *See* CHANGE.

transmutation *noun*
The process or result of changing from one appearance, state, or phase to another : change, changeover, conversion, metamorphosis, mutation, shift, transfiguration, transformation, translation, transmogrification, transubstantiation. *See* CHANGE.

transmute *verb*
To change into a different form, substance, or state : convert, metamorphose, mutate, transfigure, transform, translate, transmogrify, transpose, transubstantiate. *See* CHANGE.

transparent *adjective*
1. Free from what obscures or dims : clear, crystal clear, crystalline, limpid, lucid, pellucid, see-through. *See* CLEAR. **2.** Admitting light so that objects beyond can be seen : clear, crystal clear, crystalline, limpid, lucid, pellucid, see-through, translucent. *See* CLEAR. **3.** So light and insubstantial as to resemble air or a thin film : aerial, aery, airy, diaphanous, ethereal, filmy, gauzy, gossamer, gossamery, sheer[2], vaporous, vapory. *See* THICK.

transpire *verb*
1. To be made public : break, come out, get out, out. *Informal:* leak (out). ***Idiom:*** come to light. *See* KNOWLEDGE, SHOW. **2.** To take place : befall, betide, come, come about, come off, develop, hap, happen, occur, pass. ***Idiom:*** come to pass. *See* HAPPEN. **3.** To flow or leak out or emit something slowly : bleed, exude, leach, ooze, percolate, seep, transude, weep. *See* MOVE, SOLID.

transport *verb*
1. To move while supporting : bear, carry, convey, lug[2]. *Informal:* tote. *Slang:* schlep. *See* OVER. **2.** To cause to come along with oneself : bear, bring, carry, convey, fetch, take. *See* ACCOMPANIED. **3.** To move or excite greatly : carry away, electrify, enrapture, thrill. *Slang:* send. *See* EXCITE. **4.** To force to leave a country or place by official decree : banish, deport, exile, expatriate, expel, ostracize. *See* ACCEPT.
transport *noun* **1.** The moving of persons or goods from one place to another : carriage, conveyance, transit, transportation. *See* MOVE. **2.** A state of elated bliss : ecstasy, heaven, paradise, rapture, seventh heaven. *Informal:* cloud nine. *See* HAPPY.

transportable *adjective*
Capable of moving or being moved from place to place : mobile, movable, moving, traveling. *See* MOVE.

transportation *noun*
1. The moving of persons or goods from one place to another : carriage, conveyance, transit, transport. *See* MOVE. **2.** Enforced removal from one's native country by official decree : banishment, deportation, exile, expatriation, extradition, ostracism. *See* ACCEPT, REWARD.

transporter *noun*
A person who carries messages or is sent on errands : bearer, carrier, conveyer, courier, envoy, messenger, runner. *See* OVER.

transpose *verb*
1. To change to the opposite position, direction, or course : invert, reverse, turn (about, around, over, *or* round). *See* CHANGE. **2.** To change into a different form, substance, or state : convert, metamorphose, mutate, transfigure, transform, translate, transmogrify, transmute, transubstantiate. *See* CHANGE.

transposition *noun*
1. The act of exchanging or substituting : change, commutation, exchange, interchange, shift, substitution, switch, trade. *Informal:* swap. *See* CHANGE, SUBSTITUTE. **2.** The act of changing or being changed from one position, direction, or course to the opposite : inversion, reversal, turnabout, turnaround. *See* CHANGE.

transubstantiate *verb*
To change into a different form, substance, or state : convert, metamorphose, mutate, transfigure, transform, translate, transmogrify, transmute, transpose. *See* CHANGE.

transubstantiation *noun*
The process or result of changing from one appearance, state, or phase to another : change, changeover, conversion, metamorphosis, mutation, shift, transfiguration, transformation, translation, transmogrification, transmutation. *See* CHANGE.

transude *verb*
To flow or leak out or emit something slowly : bleed, exude, leach, ooze, percolate, seep, transpire, weep. *See* MOVE, SOLID.

transversal *adjective*
Situated or lying across : crossing, crosswise, thwart, transverse, traverse. *See* HORIZONTAL.

transverse *adjective*
Situated or lying across : crossing, crosswise, thwart, transversal, traverse. *See* HORIZONTAL.

trap *noun*
1. Something that leads one into a place or situation from which escape is difficult : bait, lure, snare. *See* LIKE, SAFETY. **2.** A source of danger or difficulty not easily foreseen and avoided : booby trap, pitfall. *See* SAFETY. **3.** An attack or stratagem for capturing or tricking an

unsuspecting person : ambuscade, ambush. *See* ATTACK. **4.** *Slang.* The opening in the body through which food is ingested : mouth. *Slang:* gob[2], puss. *See* MOUTH.

trap *verb* To gain control of or an advantage over by or as if by trapping : catch, enmesh, ensnare, ensnarl, entrap, snare, tangle, trammel, web. *See* FREE.

trash *noun*

1. Something that does not have or make sense : balderdash, blather, bunkum, claptrap, drivel, garbage, idiocy, nonsense, piffle, poppycock, rigmarole, rubbish, tomfoolery, twaddle. *Informal:* tommyrot. *Slang:* applesauce, baloney, bilge, bull[1], bunk[2], crap, hooey, malarkey. *See* KNOWLEDGE. **2.** A group of persons regarded as the lowest class : dreg (often used in plural), lumpenproletariat, rabble, ragtag and bobtail, riffraff. *Slang:* scum. ***Idioms:*** scum of the earth, tag and rag, the great unwashed. *See* OVER, RICH.

trash *verb* *Slang.* To injure or destroy (property) maliciously : vandalize. *See* HELP.

trashy *adjective*

Of decidedly inferior quality : base[2], cheap, lousy, miserable, paltry, poor, rotten, shoddy, sleazy. *Informal:* cheesy. *Slang:* crummy, schlocky. *See* GOOD.

trauma *noun*

1. Marked tissue damage, especially when produced by physical injury : traumatism, wound. *See* HELP. **2.** *Psychiatry.* Something that jars the mind or emotions : blow[2], jolt, shock[1]. *See* STRIKE.

traumatism *noun*

Marked tissue damage, especially when produced by physical injury : trauma, wound. *See* HELP.

traumatize *verb*

To inflict physical or mental injury or distress on : shock[1], wound. *See* HELP.

travail *noun*

1. Physical exertion that is usually difficult and exhausting : drudgery, labor, moil, toil, work. *Informal:* sweat. *Chiefly British:* fag. ***Idiom:*** sweat of one's brow. *See* WORK. **2.** The act or process of bringing forth young : accouchement, birth, birthing, childbearing, childbirth, delivery, labor, lying-in, parturition. *See* START.

travail *verb* To exert one's mental or physical powers, usually under difficulty and to the point of exhaustion : drive, fag, labor, moil, strain[1], strive, sweat, toil, tug, work. ***Idiom:*** break one's back (*or* neck). *See* WORK.

travel *verb*

1. To make or go on a journey : journey, pass, peregrinate, trek, trip. ***Idiom:*** hit the road. *See* MOVE. **2.** To move along a particular course : fare, go, journey, pass, proceed, push on, remove, wend. ***Idiom:*** make one's way. *See* MOVE. **3.** To become known far and wide : circulate, get around, go around, spread. ***Idiom:*** go (*or* make) the rounds. *See* KNOWLEDGE.

traveling *adjective*

Capable of moving or being moved from place to place : mobile, movable, moving, transportable. *See* MOVE.

traversal *noun*

Law. A refusal to grant the truth of a statement or charge : contradiction, denial, disaffirmance, disaffirmation, disclaimer, negation, rejection. *See* AFFIRM.

traverse *verb*

1. To go across : cross, pass, track, transit. *See* MOVE. **2.** To move in a zigzag manner, as on a ski slope : zigzag. *See* MOVE, RISE. **3.** To move, as a gun, laterally : pivot, swivel. *See* MOVE. **4.** To look at carefully or critically : check (out), con, examine, go over, inspect, peruse, scrutinize, study, survey, view. *Informal:* case. ***Idiom:*** give a going-over. *See* INVESTIGATE. **5.** To take a stand against : buck, challenge, contest, dispute, oppose, resist. *See* SUPPORT. **6.** *Law.* To refuse to admit the truth, reality, value, or worth of : contradict, contravene, controvert, deny, disaffirm, gainsay, negate, negative, oppugn. *See* AFFIRM.

traverse *noun* Something that impedes or prevents entry or passage : bar, barricade, barrier, block, blockage, clog, hamper, hindrance, hurdle, impediment, obstacle, obstruction, snag, stop, wall. *See* HELP, OPEN.

traverse *adjective* Situated or lying across : crossing, crosswise, thwart, transversal, transverse. *See* HORIZONTAL.

travesty *noun*

A false, derisive, or impudent imitation of something : burlesque, caricature, farce, mock, mockery, parody, sham. *See* RESPECT, SAME.

travesty *verb* To copy (the manner or expression of another), especially in an exaggerated or mocking way : ape, burlesque, caricature, imitate, mimic, mock, parody. ***Idiom:*** do a takeoff on. *See* SAME.

treacherous *adjective*

1. Not true to duty or obligation : disloyal, faithless, false, false-hearted, perfidious, recreant, traitorous, unfaithful, untrue. *See* CONTINUE, TRUST. **2.** Involving possible risk, loss, or injury : adventurous, chancy, dangerous, hazardous, jeopardous, parlous, perilous, risky, unsafe, venturesome, venturous. *Slang:* hairy. *See* SAFETY.

treacherousness *noun*
1. Willful betrayal of fidelity, confidence, or trust : perfidy, treachery, treason. *See* TRUST. **2.** Betrayal, especially of a moral obligation : disloyalty, faithlessness, false-heartedness, falseness, falsity, infidelity, perfidiousness, perfidy, traitorousness, treachery, unfaithfulness. *See* CONTINUE, TRUST.

treachery *noun*
1. Willful betrayal of fidelity, confidence, or trust : perfidy, treacherousness, treason. *See* TRUST. **2.** Betrayal, especially of a moral obligation : disloyalty, faithlessness, false-heartedness, falseness, falsity, infidelity, perfidiousness, perfidy, traitorousness, treacherousness, unfaithfulness. *See* CONTINUE, TRUST. **3.** An act of betraying : betrayal, double cross. *Slang:* sellout. *See* TRUST.

tread *verb*
1. To go on foot : ambulate, foot, pace, step, walk. *Slang:* hoof. ***Idiom:*** foot it. *See* MOVE. **2.** To step on heavily and repeatedly so as to crush, injure, or destroy : stamp, stomp, tramp, trample, tromp. *See* HELP.
tread *noun* The act or manner of going on foot : footfall, footstep, step. *See* MOVE, SOUNDS.

treadmill *noun*
A habitual, laborious, often tiresome course of action : routine, rut[1]. *Informal:* grind. *Slang:* groove. *See* USUAL.

treason *noun*
1. Willful violation of allegiance to one's country : sedition, seditiousness, traitorousness. *See* TRUST. **2.** Willful betrayal of fidelity, confidence, or trust : perfidy, treacherousness, treachery. *See* TRUST.

treasonable *adjective*
Involving or constituting treason : seditious, traitorous, treasonous. *See* TRUST.

treasonous *adjective*
Involving or constituting treason : seditious, traitorous, treasonable. *See* TRUST.

treasure *noun*
1. A supply stored or hidden for future use : backlog, cache, hoard, inventory, nest egg, reserve, reservoir, stock, stockpile, store. *Slang:* stash. *See* COLLECT. **2.** A great amount of accumulated money and precious possessions : affluence, fortune, pelf, riches, wealth. *See* OWNED, RICH. **3.** Someone or something considered exceptionally precious : gem, pearl, prize[1]. *See* VALUE.
treasure *verb* **1.** To recognize the worth, quality, importance, or magnitude of : appreciate, cherish, esteem, prize[1], respect, value. ***Idiom:*** set store by. *See* PRAISE. **2.** To have the highest regard for : cherish, prize[1]. ***Idiom:*** hold dear. *See* VALUE. **3.** To store up (supplies or money), usually well beyond one's needs : hoard, squirrel (away), stockpile. *Slang:* stash. *See* COLLECT, GIVE.

treasure house *noun*
A place where one keeps one's valuables : treasury. *See* KEEP.

treasury *noun*
A place where one keeps one's valuables : treasure house. *See* KEEP.

treat *verb*
1. To behave in a specified way toward : deal with, handle. *See* TREAT WELL. **2.** To be occupied or concerned with : consider, deal with, take up. ***Idiom:*** have to do with. *See* RELEVANT. **3.** To pay for the food, drink, or entertainment of (another) : *Informal:* set up, stand. *Slang:* blow[1]. ***Idiom:*** stand treat. *See* PAY. **4.** To give medical aid to : *Informal:* doctor. *See* HEALTH, HELP.
treat *noun* Something fine and delicious, especially a food : dainty, delicacy, morsel, tidbit. *Informal:* goody. *See* GOOD, INGESTION.

treatise *noun*
A formal, lengthy exposition of a topic : discourse, disquisition, dissertation. *See* WORDS.

treatment *noun*
The systematic application of remedies to effect a cure : care, regimen, rehabilitation, therapy. *Informal:* rehab. *See* HEALTH, HELP.

treaty *noun*
A formal, usually written settlement between nations : accord, agreement, concord, convention, pact. *See* AGREE, POLITICS.

treble *adjective*
Elevated in pitch : high, high-pitched, piercing, piping, shrieky, shrill, shrilly. *Music:* acute. *See* HIGH, SOUNDS.

trek *verb*
1. To make or go on a journey : journey, pass, peregrinate, travel, trip. ***Idiom:*** hit the road. *See* MOVE. **2.** To travel about or journey on foot : backpack, hike, march[1], peregrinate, traipse, tramp. *See* MOVE.
trek *noun* A journey undertaken with a specific objective : expedition, pilgrimage, safari, tour, voyage. *See* MOVE.

tremble *verb*
1. To move to and fro in short, jerky movements : quake, quaver, quiver, shake, shiver[1], shudder, twitter, vibrate. *See* REPETITION.
2. To move to and fro violently : quake, rock, shake, vibrate. *See* REPETITION.
tremble *noun* A state of nervous restlessness or agitation. Often used in the plural : fidget (often used in plural), jitter (used in plural), jump (used in plural), shiver[1] (used in plural). *Informal:* all-overs, shake (used in plural). *Slang:* heebie-jeebies, jim-jams, willies. *See* CALM, FEAR.

tremblor *noun*
A shaking of the earth : earthquake, quake, seism, temblor, tremor. *Informal:* shake. *See* MOVE, REPETITION.

tremendous *adjective*
1. Of extraordinary size and power : behemoth, Brobdingnagian, Bunyanesque, colossal, cyclopean, elephantine, enormous, gargantuan, giant, gigantesque, gigantic, herculean, heroic, huge, immense, jumbo, mammoth, massive, massy, mastodonic, mighty, monster, monstrous, monumental, mountainous, prodigious, pythonic, stupendous, titanic, vast. *Informal:* walloping. *Slang:* whopping. *See* BIG.
2. *Informal.* Particularly excellent : divine, fabulous, fantastic, fantastical, glorious, marvelous, sensational, splendid, superb, terrific, wonderful. *Informal:* dandy, dreamy, great, ripping, super, swell. *Slang:* cool, groovy, hot, keen[1], neat, nifty. ***Idiom:*** out of this world. *See* GOOD. **3.** Causing or able to cause fear : appalling, dire, direful, dreadful, fearful, fearsome, formidable, frightful, ghastly, redoubtable, scary, terrible. *See* FEAR.

tremendousness *noun*
The quality of being enormous : enormousness, hugeness, immenseness, immensity, prodigiousness, stupendousness, vastness. *See* BIG.

tremor *noun*
1. A shaking of the earth : earthquake, quake, seism, temblor, tremblor. *Informal:* shake. *See* MOVE, REPETITION. **2.** A nervous shaking of the body : quake, quiver, shake, shiver[1], shudder, thrill, tic, twitch. *See* REPETITION.

tremulant *adjective*
Marked by or affected with tremors : aquiver, quaky, quivery, shaky, shivery, tremulous, twittery. *See* REPETITION.

tremulous *adjective*
Marked by or affected with tremors : aquiver, quaky, quivery, shaky, shivery, tremulant, twittery. *See* REPETITION.

trenchancy *noun*
Irony or bitterness, as of tone : acerbity, acidity, acridity, causticity, corrosiveness, mordacity, mordancy, sarcasm. *See* LAUGHTER, RESPECT.

trenchant *adjective*
1. Possessing or displaying perceptions of great accuracy and sensitivity : acute, incisive, keen[1], penetrating, perceptive, probing, sensitive, sharp. *See* CAREFUL, SHARP. **2.** So sharp as to cause mental pain : acerbic, acid, acidic, acrid, astringent, biting, caustic, corrosive, cutting, mordacious, mordant, pungent, scathing, sharp, slashing, stinging, truculent, vitriolic. *See* ATTACK, RESPECT.

trend *noun*
1. An inclination to something : bent, bias, cast, disposition, leaning, partiality, penchant, predilection, predisposition, proclivity, proneness, propensity, squint, tendency, turn. *See* APPROACH, LIKE. **2.** The current custom : craze, fad, fashion, furor, mode, rage, style, vogue. *Informal:* thing. ***Idioms:*** the in thing, the last word, the latest thing. *See* STYLE, USUAL.
trend *verb* To have a tendency or inclination : incline, lean[1], slant, squint, tend[1]. *See* LIKELY.

trendy *adjective*
Informal. Being or in accordance with the current fashion : à la mode, chic, dashing, fashionable, mod, modish, posh, smart, stylish, swank, swanky, trig. *Informal:* classy, in, sharp, snappy, swish, tony. *Slang:* with-it. ***Idioms:*** all the rage, up to the minute. *See* STYLE, USUAL.

trepidation *noun*
Great agitation and anxiety caused by the expectation or the realization of danger : affright, alarm, apprehension, dread, fear, fearfulness, fright, funk, horror, panic, terror. *Slang:* cold feet. ***Idiom:*** fear and trembling. *See* FEAR.

trespass *verb*
1. To violate a moral or divine law : err, offend, sin, transgress. *See* RIGHT. **2.** *Law.* To enter forcibly or illegally : break in, burglarize. *See* CRIMES, ENTER.
trespass *noun* **1.** An act or instance of breaking a law or regulation or of nonfulfillment of an obligation or promise, for example : breach, contravention, infraction, infringement, transgression, violation. *See* RIGHT. **2.** The act of entering a building or room with the intent to commit theft : break-in, burglary. *See* CRIMES. **3.** An advance beyond proper or legal limits : encroachment, entrenchment, impinge-

ment, infringement, intrusion, obtrusion. *See* ENTER.

triable *adjective*
Subject to legal proceedings : *Law:* actionable, litigable, prosecutable. *See* LAW.

triad *noun*
A group of three individuals : three, threesome, trine, trinity, trio, triple, triumvirate, triune, triunity, troika. *See* GROUP.

trial *noun*
1. The examination and deciding upon evidence, charges, and claims in court : hearing. *See* LAW. **2.** A procedure that ascertains effectiveness, value, proper function, or other quality : assay, essay, proof, test, tryout. *See* INVESTIGATE. **3.** An operation employed to resolve an uncertainty : experiment, experimentation, test. *See* INVESTIGATE. **4.** A trying to do or make something : attempt, crack, effort, endeavor, essay, go, offer, stab, try. *Informal:* shot. *Slang:* take. *Archaic:* assay. *See* TRY. **5.** A state of pain or anguish that tests one's resiliency and character : crucible, ordeal, tribulation, visitation. *See* EASY. **6.** Something hard to bear physically or emotionally : affliction, burden[1], cross, tribulation. *See* HEAVY, OVER. **7.** One that makes another totally miserable by causing sharp pain and irritation : thorn. *Informal:* pain. ***Idioms:*** pain in the neck, thorn in the flesh (*or* side). *See* PAIN.
trial *adjective* Constituting a tentative model for future experiment or development : experimental, pilot, test. *See* START.

tribe *noun*
A group of people sharing common ancestry : clan, family, house, kindred, lineage, stock. ***Idioms:*** flesh and blood, kith and kin. *See* KIN.

tribulation *noun*
1. Something hard to bear physically or emotionally : affliction, burden[1], cross, trial. *See* HEAVY, OVER. **2.** A state of pain or anguish that tests one's resiliency and character : crucible, ordeal, trial, visitation. *See* EASY.

tribunal *noun*
A judicial assembly : bar, court. *See* LAW.

tribute *noun*
1. An expression of admiration or congratulation : commendation, compliment, congratulation (often used in plural), praise. *See* PRAISE. **2.** A formal token of appreciation and admiration for a person's high achievements : salute, salvo, testimonial. *See* PRAISE.

trice *noun*
A very brief time : crack, flash, instant, minute[1], moment, second[1], twinkle, twinkling, wink. *Informal:* jiff, jiffy. *Chiefly British:* tick. *See* BIG, TIME.

trick *noun*
1. An indirect, usually cunning means of gaining an end : artifice, deception, device, dodge, feint, gimmick, imposture, jig, maneuver, ploy, ruse, sleight, stratagem, subterfuge, wile. *Informal:* shenanigan, take-in. *See* HONEST, MEANS. **2.** A mischievous act : antic, caper, frolic, joke, lark, prank[1]. *Informal:* shenanigan. *Slang:* monkeyshine (often used in plural). *See* GOOD, WORK. **3.** The proper method for doing, using, or handling something : feel, knack. *Informal:* hang. *See* ABILITY. **4.** A clever, dexterous act : feat, stunt. *See* ABILITY, EXCITE, GOOD. **5.** A limited, often assigned period of activity, duty, or opportunity : bout, go, hitch, inning (often used in plural), shift, spell[3], stint, stretch, time, tour, turn, watch. *See* TIME.
trick *verb* To cause to accept what is false, especially by trickery or misrepresentation : beguile, betray, bluff, cozen, deceive, delude, double-cross, dupe, fool, hoodwink, humbug, mislead, take in. *Informal:* bamboozle, have. *Slang:* four-flush. ***Idioms:*** lead astray, play false, pull the wool over someone's eyes, put something over on, take for a ride. *See* HONEST.
trick out (or **up**) *verb Informal.* To dress in formal or special clothing : array, attire, deck[2] (out), dress up, prank[2]. *Slang:* doll up. *See* ORDER, PLAIN, PUT ON.
trick *adjective* So weak or defective as to be liable to fail : undependable, unreliable. *See* STRONG.

trickery *noun*
Lack of straightforwardness and honesty in action : chicanery, craft, craftiness, deviousness, dishonesty, indirection, shadiness, shiftiness, slyness, sneakiness, trickiness, underhandedness. *See* HONEST.

trickiness *noun*
Lack of straightforwardness and honesty in action : chicanery, craft, craftiness, deviousness, dishonesty, indirection, shadiness, shiftiness, slyness, sneakiness, trickery, underhandedness. *See* HONEST.

trickle *verb*
To fall or let fall in drops of liquid : distill, dribble, drip, drop, weep. *See* RISE.
trickle *noun* The process or sound of dripping : dribble, drip. *See* RISE, SOUNDS.

trick out or **up** *verb* See **trick.**

trickster *noun*
A person who cheats : bilk, cheat, cheater, cozener, defrauder, rook, sharper, swindler, victimizer. *Informal:* chiseler, crook, flimflammer. *Slang:* diddler, gyp, gypper. *See* HONEST.

tricky *adjective*
1. Deceitfully clever : artful, crafty, cunning, foxy, guileful, scheming, sharp, sly, wily. *See* ABILITY, HONEST, MEANS. **2.** Requiring great tact or skill : delicate, sensitive, ticklish, touch-and-go, touchy. *See* EASY. **3.** Hard to deal with or get out of : rough, tight. *Informal:* sticky. *See* EASY.

trifle *noun*
1. Something or things that are unimportant : fiddle-faddle, frippery, frivolity, froth, minutia, nonsense, small change, small potatoes, trivia, triviality. *See* IMPORTANT, SURFACE. **2.** A small showy article : bauble, bibelot, gewgaw, gimcrack, knickknack, novelty, toy, trinket, whatnot. *See* THING. **3.** A tiny amount : bit[1], crumb, dab[1], dash, dot, dram, drop, fragment, grain, iota, jot, minim, mite, modicum, molecule, ort, ounce, particle, scrap[1], scruple, shred, smidgen, speck, tittle, whit. *Chiefly British:* spot. *See* BIG.

trifle *verb* **1.** To treat lightly or flippantly : dally, flirt, play, toy. *See* WORK. **2.** To move one's fingers or hands in a nervous or aimless fashion : fiddle, fidget, fool, monkey, play, putter, tinker, toy, twiddle. *See* TOUCH. **3.** To make amorous advances without serious intentions : coquet, dally, flirt, toy. *See* SEX.

trifle away *verb* **1.** To pass (time) without working or in avoiding work : dawdle (away), fiddle away, idle (away), kill[1], waste, while (away), wile (away). *See* INDUSTRIOUS. **2.** To spend (money) excessively and usually foolishly : consume, dissipate, fool away, fritter away, riot away, squander, throw away, waste. *Slang:* blow[1]. *See* SAVE.

trifle away *verb* See **trifle.**

trifling *adjective*
Contemptibly unimportant : inconsiderable, negligible, niggling, nugatory, paltry, petty, picayune, piddling, small, small-minded. *Slang:* measly. ***Idiom:*** of no account. *See* IMPORTANT.

trig *adjective*
1. Being or in accordance with the current fashion : à la mode, chic, dashing, fashionable, mod, modish, posh, smart, stylish, swank, swanky. *Informal:* classy, in, sharp, snappy, swish, tony, trendy. *Slang:* with-it. ***Idioms:*** all the rage, up to the minute. *See* STYLE, USUAL. **2.** In good order or clean condition : neat, orderly, shipshape, snug, spick-and-span, spruce, taut, tidy, trim, well-groomed. *Chiefly British:* tight. ***Idiom:*** neat as a pin. *See* CLEAN, ORDER.

trig *verb* To make neat and trim; make presentable. Also used with *out* : clean (up), freshen (up), groom, neaten (up), slick up, spruce (up), tidy (up), trim. *See* ORDER.

trigger *noun*
Something that incites especially a violent response : goad, incitation, incitement, instigation, provocation, stimulus. *See* CAUSE.

trigger *verb* **1.** To be the cause of : bring, bring about, bring on, cause, effect, effectuate, generate, induce, ingenerate, lead to, make, occasion, result in, secure, set off, stir[1] (up), touch off. ***Idioms:*** bring to pass (*or* effect), give rise to. *See* START. **2.** To stir to action or feeling : egg on, excite, foment, galvanize, goad, impel, incite, inflame, inspire, instigate, motivate, move, pique, prick, prod, prompt, propel, provoke, set off, spur, stimulate, touch off, work up. *See* CAUSE, EXCITE.

triggerman *noun*
One who murders another : butcher, cutthroat, homicide, killer, manslayer, massacrer, murderer, murderess, slaughterer, slayer. *See* HELP.

trillion *noun*
An indeterminately great amount or number : jillion, million (often used in plural), multiplicity, ream. *Informal:* bushel, gob[1] (often used in plural), heap (often used in plural), load (often used in plural), lot, oodles, passel, peck[2], scad (often used in plural), slew, wad, zillion. *See* BIG.

trim *verb*
1. To make neat and trim; make presentable : clean (up), freshen (up), groom, neaten (up), slick up, spruce (up), tidy (up), trig (out). *See* ORDER. **2.** To decrease, as in length or amount, by or as if by severing or excising : chop[1], clip[1], crop, cut, cut back, cut down, lop[1], lower[2], pare, prune, shear, slash, truncate. *See* INCREASE. **3.** To make a slight reduction in (a price) : shade, shave. *See* INCREASE. **4.** To furnish with decorations : adorn, bedeck, deck[2] (out), decorate, dress (up), embellish, garnish, ornament. *See* BEAUTIFUL. **5.** *Informal.* To punish with blows or lashes : beat, flog, hide[2], lash, thrash, whip. *Slang:* lay into, lick. *See* ATTACK, REWARD. **6.** *Informal.* To win a victory over, as in battle or a competition : beat,

best, conquer, defeat, master, overcome, prevail against (*or* over), rout, subdue, subjugate, surmount, triumph over, vanquish, worst. *Informal:* whip. *Slang:* ace, lick. ***Idioms:*** carry (*or* win) the day, get (*or* have) the best of, get (*or* have) the better of, go someone one better. *See* WIN. **7.** *Informal.* To get money or something else from by deceitful trickery : bilk, cheat, cozen, defraud, gull, mulct, rook, swindle, victimize. *Informal:* chisel, flimflam, take. *Slang:* diddle[1], do, gyp, stick, sting. *See* HONEST.

trim down *verb* To lose body weight, as by dieting : reduce, slim (down). *See* FAT, INCREASE.

trim *noun* **1.** A state of sound readiness : condition, fettle, fitness, form, kilter, order, shape. *See* BETTER. **2.** Something that adorns : adornment, decoration, embellishment, garnishment, garniture, ornament, ornamentation, trimming. *See* BEAUTIFUL.

trim *adjective* **1.** In good order or clean condition : neat, orderly, shipshape, snug, spick-and-span, spruce, taut, tidy, trig, well-groomed. *Chiefly British:* tight. ***Idiom:*** neat as a pin. *See* CLEAN, ORDER. **2.** Having slender and graceful lines : sleek, streamlined. *See* BEAUTIFUL.

trim down *verb* See **trim**.

trimming *noun*
1. Something that adorns : adornment, decoration, embellishment, garnishment, garniture, ornament, ornamentation, trim. *See* BEAUTIFUL. **2.** *Informal.* The act of defeating or the condition of being defeated : beating, defeat, drubbing, overthrow, rout, thrashing, vanquishment. *Informal:* massacre, whipping. *Slang:* dusting, licking. *See* WIN. **3.** *Informal.* A punishment dealt with blows or lashes : beating, flogging, hiding, lashing, thrashing, whipping. *Slang:* licking. *See* ATTACK, REWARD.

trine *noun*
A group of three individuals : three, threesome, triad, trinity, trio, triple, triumvirate, triune, triunity, troika. *See* GROUP.

trinity *noun*
A group of three individuals : three, threesome, triad, trine, trio, triple, triumvirate, triune, triunity, troika. *See* GROUP.

trinket *noun*
A small showy article : bauble, bibelot, gewgaw, gimcrack, knickknack, novelty, toy, trifle, whatnot. *See* THING.

trio *noun*
A group of three individuals : three, threesome, triad, trine, trinity, triple, triumvirate, triune, triunity, troika. *See* GROUP.

trip *noun*
1. A usually short journey taken for pleasure : excursion, jaunt, junket, outing. *See* MOVE. **2.** An act or thought that unintentionally deviates from what is correct, right, or true : erratum, error, inaccuracy, incorrectness, lapse, miscue, misstep, mistake, slip, slip-up. *See* CORRECT. **3.** *Slang.* An illusion of perceiving something that does not really exist : hallucination, phantasmagoria, phantasmagory. *See* REAL. **4.** *Slang.* A temporary concentration of interest : *Slang:* kick. *See* EXCITE.

trip *verb* **1.** To catch the foot against something and lose one's balance : stumble. ***Idioms:*** lose one's footing, make a false step. *See* MOVE. **2.** To bound lightly : hop, skip, skitter, spring. *See* MOVE. **3.** To make or go on a journey : journey, pass, peregrinate, travel, trek. ***Idiom:*** hit the road. *See* MOVE. **4.** To release or move (a switch, for example) in order to control a device : throw. *See* MOVE.

trip up *verb* To make an error or mistake : err, miscue, mistake, slip, slip up, stumble. *See* CORRECT.

triple *noun*
A group of three individuals : three, threesome, triad, trine, trinity, trio, triumvirate, triune, triunity, troika. *See* GROUP.

tripper *noun*
Chiefly British. One who travels for pleasure : excursionist, sightseer, tourist. *See* MOVE.

trip up *verb* See **trip**.

tristful *adjective*
In low spirits : blue, dejected, depressed, desolate, dispirited, down, downcast, downhearted, dull, dysphoric, gloomy, heavy-hearted, low, melancholic, melancholy, sad, spiritless, unhappy, wistful. ***Idiom:*** down at (*or* in) the mouth. *See* HAPPY.

trite *adjective*
Without freshness or appeal because of overuse : banal, bromidic, clichéd, commonplace, corny, hackneyed, musty, overused, overworked, platitudinal, platitudinous, shopworn, stale, stereotyped, stereotypic, stereotypical, threadbare, timeworn, tired, warmed-over, well-worn, worn-out. *See* EXCITE, USUAL.

triturate *verb*
To break up into tiny particles : bray, crush, granulate, grind, mill, powder, pulverize. *See* HELP.

triumph *verb*
To feel or express an uplifting joy over a success

or victory : crow, exult, glory, jubilate. *See* HAPPY.

triumph over *verb* To win a victory over, as in battle or a competition : beat, best, conquer, defeat, master, overcome, prevail against (*or* over), rout, subdue, subjugate, surmount, vanquish, worst. *Informal:* trim, whip. *Slang:* ace, lick. ***Idioms:*** carry (*or* win) the day, get (*or* have) the best of, get (*or* have) the better of, go someone one better. *See* WIN.

triumph *noun* **1.** The act of conquering : conquest, victory, win. *See* WIN. **2.** The act or condition of feeling an uplifting joy over a success or victory : exultance, exultancy, exultation, jubilance, jubilation. *See* HAPPY.

triumphal *adjective*
Relating to, having the nature of, or experiencing triumph : conquering, triumphant, victorious, winning. *See* WIN.

triumphant *adjective*
1. Feeling or expressing an uplifting joy over a success or victory : exultant, jubilant. *See* HAPPY. **2.** Relating to, having the nature of, or experiencing triumph : conquering, triumphal, victorious, winning. *See* WIN.

triumvirate *noun*
A group of three individuals : three, threesome, triad, trine, trinity, trio, triple, triune, triunity, troika. *See* GROUP.

triune *noun*
A group of three individuals : three, threesome, triad, trine, trinity, trio, triple, triumvirate, triunity, troika. *See* GROUP.

triunity *noun*
A group of three individuals : three, threesome, triad, trine, trinity, trio, triple, triumvirate, triune, troika. *See* GROUP.

trivia *noun*
Something or things that are unimportant : fiddle-faddle, frippery, frivolity, froth, minutia, nonsense, small change, small potatoes, trifle, triviality. *See* IMPORTANT, SURFACE.

trivial *adjective*
Not of great importance : inconsequent, inconsequential, insignificant, little, unimportant. *See* BIG.

triviality *noun*
1. Contemptible unimportance : inconsiderableness, negligibility, negligibleness, paltriness, pettiness, smallness, trivialness. *See* IMPORTANT. **2.** Something or things that are unimportant : fiddle-faddle, frippery, frivolity, froth, minutia, nonsense, small change, small potatoes, trifle, trivia. *See* IMPORTANT, SURFACE.

trivialness *noun*
Contemptible unimportance : inconsiderableness, negligibility, negligibleness, paltriness, pettiness, smallness, triviality. *See* IMPORTANT.

troika *noun*
A group of three individuals : three, threesome, triad, trine, trinity, trio, triple, triumvirate, triune, triunity. *See* GROUP.

tromp *verb*
1. *Informal.* To walk with loud, heavy steps : stamp, stomp, tramp, trample. *See* MOVE, SOUNDS. **2.** To step on heavily and repeatedly so as to crush, injure, or destroy : stamp, stomp, tramp, trample, tread. *See* HELP.

troop *noun*
1. A number of persons who have come or been gathered together : assemblage, assembly, body, company, conclave, conference, congregation, congress, convention, convocation, crowd, gathering, group, meeting, muster. *Informal:* get-together. *See* COLLECT. **2.** A group of people acting together in a shared activity : band[2], company, corps, party, troupe. *See* PERFORMING ARTS.

troop *verb* **1.** To come or go in large numbers : flood, pour, swarm, throng. *See* BIG, MOVE. **2.** To be with as a companion : associate, consort, fraternize, hang around, hobnob, run (around). *Slang:* hang out. ***Idiom:*** rub elbows (*or* shoulders) . *See* NEAR.

trophy *noun*
1. A memento received as a symbol of excellence or victory : accolade, award, prize[1]. *See* RESPECT. **2.** Something that causes one to remember : keepsake, memento, remembrance, reminder, souvenir, token. *See* REMEMBER.

tropic *adjective*
Of or relating to the Tropics : tropical. *See* HOT.

tropical *adjective*
Of or relating to the Tropics : tropic. *See* HOT.

trot *noun*
1. A person's steady easy gait that is faster than a walk but slower than a run : jog, lope. *See* MOVE. **2.** *Archaic.* An ugly, frightening old woman : beldam, crone, hag, witch. *Slang:* biddy. *See* BEAUTIFUL.

trot *verb* **1.** To move with a steady easy gait faster than a walk but slower than a run : jog, lope. *See* MOVE. **2.** To move swiftly : bolt, bucket, bustle, dart, dash, festinate, flash, fleet, flit, fly, haste, hasten, hurry, hustle, pelt[2], race, rocket, run, rush, sail, scoot, scour[2], shoot, speed, sprint, tear[1], whirl, whisk, whiz, wing, zip, zoom. *Informal:* hotfoot, rip. *Slang:* barrel, highball. *Chiefly British:* nip[1]. ***Idioms:*** get a move on, get cracking, go like lightning, go like the wind, hotfoot it, make haste, make time, make tracks, run like the wind, shake a leg, step (*or* jump) on it. *See* MOVE.

troth *noun*
The act or condition of being pledged to marry : betrothal, engagement, espousal. *See* MARRIAGE.

trouble *noun*
1. The condition of being in need of immediate assistance : distress, exigence, exigency, hot water. *See* HELP. **2.** The state or quality of being inconvenient : discomfort, incommodiousness, incommodity, inconvenience. *See* COMFORT. **3.** A difficult, often embarrassing situation or condition : box[1], corner, deep water, difficulty, dilemma, Dutch, fix, hole, hot spot, hot water, jam, plight[1], predicament, quagmire, scrape, soup. *Informal:* bind, pickle, spot. *See* EASY. **4.** A cause of distress or anxiety : care, concern, worry. *See* CONCERN. **5.** The use of energy to do something : effort, endeavor, exertion, pain (used in plural), strain[1], striving, struggle, while. *Informal:* elbow grease. *See* WORK.

trouble *verb* **1.** To cause anxious uneasiness in : ail, cark, concern, distress, worry. *See* CONCERN. **2.** To come to mind continually : haunt, obsess, torment, weigh on (*or* upon). *See* REPETITION. **3.** To cause inconvenience for : discomfort, discommode, incommode, inconvenience, put out. *See* COMFORT.

troublesome *adjective*
1. Causing difficulty, trouble, or discomfort : difficult, incommodious, inconvenient. *See* COMFORT. **2.** Troubling to the mind or emotions : disquieting, disruptive, distressful, distressing, disturbing, intrusive, perturbing, troublous, unsettling, upsetting, worrisome. *See* HAPPY, PAIN. **3.** Troubling the nerves or peace of mind, as by repeated vexations : annoying, bothersome, galling, irksome, irritating, nettlesome, plaguy, provoking, vexatious. *See* PAIN. **4.** Hard to treat, manage, or cope with : wicked. *Informal:* pesky. *Slang:* mean[2]. *See* EASY.

troublous *adjective*
Troubling to the mind or emotions : disquieting, disruptive, distressful, distressing, disturbing, intrusive, perturbing, troublesome, unsettling, upsetting, worrisome. *See* HAPPY, PAIN.

trounce *verb*
To render totally ineffective by decisive defeat : annihilate, crush, drub, overpower, overwhelm, smash, steamroller, thrash, vanquish. *Informal:* massacre, wallop. *Slang:* clobber, cream, shellac, smear. *See* WIN.

troupe *noun*
A group of people acting together in a shared activity : band[2], company, corps, party, troop. *See* PERFORMING ARTS.

truancy *noun*
An unexcused absence : cut, truantry. *Informal:* hooky. *See* SEEK.

truant *verb*
To fail to attend on purpose : cut. *Informal:* skip. ***Idioms:*** go AWOL, play hooky (*or* truant). *See* SEEK.

truantry *noun*
An unexcused absence : cut, truancy. *Informal:* hooky. *See* SEEK.

truce *noun*
A temporary cessation of hostilities by mutual consent of the contending parties : armistice, cease-fire. *See* CONTINUE.

truckle *verb*
To support slavishly every opinion or suggestion of a superior : bootlick, cringe, fawn, grovel, kowtow, slaver, toady. *Informal:* apple-polish, brownnose, cotton. *Slang:* suck up. ***Idioms:*** curry favor, dance attendance, kiss someone's feet, lick someone's boots. *See* OVER.

truculence *noun*
1. Warlike or hostile attitude or nature : bellicoseness, bellicosity, belligerence, belligerency, combativeness, contentiousness, hostility, militance, militancy, pugnaciousness, pugnacity, truculency. *See* ATTACK. **2.** The power or will to fight : bellicoseness, bellicosity, belligerence, belligerency, combativeness, contentiousness, fight, pugnaciousness, pugnacity, truculency. *See* CONFLICT. **3.** A cruel act or an instance of cruel behavior : barbarity, bestiality, brutality, cruelty, inhumanity, savagery, truculency. *See* ATTITUDE, KIND.

truculency *noun*
1. Warlike or hostile attitude or nature : bellicoseness, bellicosity, belligerence, belligerency, combativeness, contentiousness, hostility, militance, militancy, pugnaciousness, pugnacity, truculence. *See* ATTACK. **2.** The power or will to fight : bellicoseness, bellicosity, belligerence, belligerency, combativeness, contentiousness, fight, pugnaciousness, pugnacity, truculence. *See* CONFLICT. **3.** A cruel act or an instance of

cruel behavior : barbarity, bestiality, brutality, cruelty, inhumanity, savagery, truculence. *See* ATTITUDE, KIND.

truculent *adjective*

1. Having or showing an eagerness to fight : bellicose, belligerent, combative, contentious, hostile, militant, pugnacious, quarrelsome, scrappy, warlike. *See* ATTACK. **2.** So sharp as to cause mental pain : acerbic, acid, acidic, acrid, astringent, biting, caustic, corrosive, cutting, mordacious, mordant, pungent, scathing, sharp, slashing, stinging, trenchant, vitriolic. *See* ATTACK, RESPECT. **3.** Showing or suggesting a disposition to be violently destructive without scruple or restraint : barbarous, bestial, cruel, fell[2], feral, ferocious, fierce, inhuman, savage, vicious, wolfish. *See* KIND.

trudge *verb*

To walk heavily, slowly, and with difficulty : plod, slog, slop, toil, wade. *See* MOVE.

true *adjective*

1. Conforming to fact : accurate, correct, exact, faithful, precise, right, rigorous, veracious, veridical. *See* CORRECT, HONEST, REAL, TRUE. **2.** In agreement or correspondence with fact : actual, real. *See* REAL. **3.** Having or marked by uprightness in principle and action : good, honest, honorable, incorruptible, righteous, upright, upstanding. *Informal:* straight-shooting. ***Idiom:*** on the up-and-up (*or* up and up). *See* HONEST. **4.** Not counterfeit or copied : actual, authentic, bona fide, genuine, good, indubitable, original, real, undoubted, unquestionable. *See* TRUE. **5.** Worthy of belief, as because of precision or faithfulness to an original : authentic, authoritative, convincing, credible, faithful, trustworthy, valid. *See* TRUE. **6.** Accurately representing what is depicted or described : lifelike, natural, naturalistic, realistic, true-life, truthful. *See* REAL. **7.** Adhering firmly and devotedly, as to a person, a cause, or a duty : allegiant, constant, faithful, fast, firm[1], liege, loyal, staunch, steadfast. *See* CONTINUE, TRUST. **8.** Devoid of any hypocrisy or pretense : genuine, heartfelt, hearty, honest, natural, real, sincere, unaffected, unfeigned, unmannered. *See* TRUE. **9.** Being so legitimately : legitimate, rightful. *See* TRUE.

true-life *adjective*

Accurately representing what is depicted or described : lifelike, natural, naturalistic, realistic, true, truthful. *See* REAL.

truelove *noun*

A person who is much loved : beloved, darling, dear, honey, love, minion, precious, sweet, sweetheart. *Informal:* sweetie. ***Idiom:*** light of one's life. *See* LOVE.

truism *noun*

A trite expression or idea : banality, bromide, cliché, commonplace, platitude, stereotype. *See* SURPRISE.

truly *adverb*

In truth : actually, fairly, genuinely, indeed, positively, really, truthfully, verily. ***Idiom:*** for fair. *See* REAL, TRUE.

trump *noun*

Something, especially something held in reserve, that gives one a decisive advantage : trump card. *Informal:* clincher. ***Idiom:*** ace in the hole. *See* HELP, WIN.

trump *verb* To outmaneuver (an opponent), especially with the aid of some extra resource : finesse. *Informal:* one-up. *See* WIN.

trump card *noun*

Something, especially something held in reserve, that gives one a decisive advantage : trump. *Informal:* clincher. ***Idiom:*** ace in the hole. *See* HELP, WIN.

truncate *verb*

To decrease, as in length or amount, by or as if by severing or excising : chop[1], clip[1], crop, cut, cut back, cut down, lop[1], lower[2], pare, prune, shear, slash, trim. *See* INCREASE.

trust *noun*

1. Absolute certainty in the trustworthiness of another : belief, confidence, dependence, faith, reliance. *See* BELIEF. **2.** The function of watching, guarding, or overseeing : care, charge, custody, guardianship, keeping, superintendence, supervision. *See* CARE FOR. **3.** A combination of businesses closely interconnected for common profit : cartel, combine, pool, syndicate. *See* GROUP, MONEY.

trust *verb* **1.** To place trust or confidence in. Also used with *in* : bank on (*or* upon), believe in, count on (*or* upon), depend on (*or* upon), reckon on (*or* upon), rely on (*or* upon). *See* TRUST. **2.** To have confidence in the truthfulness of : believe, credit. ***Idiom:*** take at one's word. *See* OPINION. **3.** To put in the charge of another for care, use, or performance : commend, commit, confide, consign, entrust, give (over), hand over, relegate, turn over. ***Idiom:*** give in trust (*or* charge). *See* GIVE. **4.** To place a trust upon : charge, entrust. *See* TRUST.

trustworthy *adjective*

1. Capable of being depended upon : dependable, reliable, responsible, solid, sound[2], trusty. *See* TRUST. **2.** Worthy of belief, as because of precision or faithfulness to an original : authentic, authoritative, convincing, credible, faithful, true, valid. *See* TRUE.

trusty *adjective*
Capable of being depended upon : dependable, reliable, responsible, solid, sound², trustworthy. *See* TRUST.

truth *noun*
1. Correspondence with fact or truth : accuracy, correctness, exactitude, exactness, fidelity, veraciousness, veracity, veridicality, verity. *See* TRUE. **2.** Freedom from deceit or falseness : truthfulness, veracity. *See* TRUE. **3.** The quality of being actual or factual : actuality, fact, factuality, factualness, reality. *See* REAL.

truthful *adjective*
1. Consistently telling the truth : veracious, veridical. *See* TRUE. **2.** Accurately representing what is depicted or described : lifelike, natural, naturalistic, realistic, true, true-life. *See* REAL.

truthfully *adverb*
In truth : actually, fairly, genuinely, indeed, positively, really, truly, verily. ***Idiom:*** for fair. *See* REAL, TRUE.

truthfulness *noun*
1. Freedom from deceit or falseness : truth, veracity. *See* TRUE. **2.** The quality of being authentic : authenticity, genuineness, realness, validity. *See* TRUE.

truthless *adjective*
Devoid of truth : counterfactual, false, specious, spurious, untrue, untruthful, wrong. *See* TRUE.

truthlessness *noun*
The practice of lying : falsehood, inveracity, mendacity, perjury, untruthfulness. *See* TRUE.

try *verb*
1. To make an attempt to do or make : assay, attempt, endeavor, essay, seek, strive. ***Idioms:*** have a go at, have (*or* make *or* take) a shot at, have (*or* take) a whack at, make a stab at, take a crack at. *See* TRY. **2.** To subject to a procedure that ascertains effectiveness, value, proper function, or other quality : assay, check, essay, examine, prove, test, try out. ***Idioms:*** bring to the test, make trial of, put to the proof (*or* test). *See* INVESTIGATE.

try out *verb* To subject to a procedure that ascertains effectiveness, value, proper function, or other quality : assay, check, essay, examine, prove, test, try. ***Idioms:*** bring to the test, make trial of, put to the proof (*or* test). *See* INVESTIGATE.

try *noun* **1.** A trying to do or make something : attempt, crack, effort, endeavor, essay, go, offer, stab, trial. *Informal:* shot. *Slang:* take. *Archaic:* assay. *See* TRY. **2.** A brief trial : crack, go, stab. *Informal:* fling, shot, whack, whirl. *See* TRY.

trying *adjective*
Requiring great or extreme bodily, mental, or spiritual strength : arduous, backbreaking, burdensome, demanding, difficult, effortful, exacting, exigent, formidable, hard, heavy, laborious, onerous, oppressive, rigorous, rough, severe, taxing, tough, weighty. *See* HEAVY.

tryout *noun*
A procedure that ascertains effectiveness, value, proper function, or other quality : assay, essay, proof, test, trial. *See* INVESTIGATE.

try out *verb* See **try.**

tryst *noun*
A commitment to appear at a certain time and place : appointment, assignation, date, engagement, rendezvous. *See* AGREE.

tubby *adjective*
Well-rounded and full in form : chubby, plump¹, plumpish, pudgy, roly-poly, rotund, round, zaftig. *See* FAT.

tuber *noun*
A propagative part of a plant : seed, spore. *See* START.

tubercular *adjective*
Relating to or afflicted with tuberculosis : consumptive (no longer in scientific use), phthisic (no longer in scientific use), phthisical (no longer in scientific use), tuberculate, tuberculous. *See* HEALTH.

tuberculate *adjective*
Relating to or afflicted with tuberculosis : consumptive (no longer in scientific use), phthisic (no longer in scientific use), phthisical (no longer in scientific use), tubercular, tuberculous. *See* HEALTH.

tuberculosis *noun*
An infectious disease producing lesions especially of the lungs : consumption (no longer in scientific use), phthisic (no longer in scientific use), phthisis (no longer in scientific use), white plague. *See* HEALTH.

tuberculous *adjective*
Relating to or afflicted with tuberculosis : consumptive (no longer in scientific use), phthisic (no longer in scientific use), phthisical (no longer in scientific use), tubercular, tuberculate. *See* HEALTH.

tucker *verb*
Informal. To make extremely tired. Also used with *out* : exhaust, fag (out), tire out, wear out. *Informal:* knock out. *Slang:* do in, poop¹

(out). *Idioms:* run ragged, take it out of. *See* TIRED.

tuckered *adjective*
Informal. Extremely tired. Also used with *out* : bleary, dead, drained, exhausted, fatigued, rundown, spent, tired out, wearied, weariful, weary, worn-down, worn-out. *Informal:* beat, bushed. *Slang:* done in, fagged (out), pooped (out). *Idioms:* all in, ready to drop. *See* HEALTH, TIRED.

tug *verb*
1. To exert force so as to move (something) toward the source of the force : drag, draw, haul, pull, tow. *See* PUSH. **2.** To exert one's mental or physical powers, usually under difficulty and to the point of exhaustion : drive, fag, labor, moil, strain[1], strive, sweat, toil, travail, work. *Idiom:* break one's back (*or* neck). *See* WORK.
tug *noun* A sudden motion, such as a pull : jerk, lurch, snap, twitch, wrench, yank. *See* MOVE, PUSH.

tug of war *noun*
A vying with others for victory or supremacy : battle, competition, contest, corrivalry, race, rivalry, strife, striving, struggle, war, warfare. *See* CONFLICT.

tuition *noun*
The act, process, or art of imparting knowledge and skill : education, instruction, pedagogics, pedagogy, schooling, teaching, training, tutelage, tutoring. *See* TEACH.

tumble *verb*
1. To come to the ground suddenly and involuntarily : drop, fall, go down, nose-dive, pitch, plunge, spill, topple. *Idiom:* take a fall (*or* header *or* plunge *or* spill *or* tumble). *See* RISE. **2.** To undergo a sharp, rapid descent in value or price : dive, drop, fall, nose-dive, plummet, plunge, sink, skid, slump. *Idiom:* take a sudden downtrend (*or* downturn). *See* INCREASE. **3.** To bring about the downfall of : bring down, overthrow, overturn, subvert, topple, unhorse. *See* HELP. **4.** To put out of proper order : derange, disarrange, disarray, disorder, disorganize, disrupt, disturb, jumble, mess up, mix up, muddle, unsettle, upset. *See* ORDER.
tumble on *verb* To find or meet by chance : bump into, chance on (*or* upon), come across, come on (*or* upon), find, happen on (*or* upon), light on (*or* upon), run across, run into, stumble on (*or* upon). *Archaic:* alight on (*or* upon). *Idiom:* meet up with. *See* MEET.
tumble *noun* **1.** A sudden involuntary drop to the ground : dive, fall, nosedive, pitch, plunge, spill. *Informal:* header. *See* RISE. **2.** A usually swift downward trend, as in prices : decline, descent, dip, dive, downslide, downswing, downtrend, downturn, drop, drop-off, fall, nosedive, plunge, skid, slide, slump. *See* INCREASE. **3.** A lack of order or regular arrangement : chaos, clutter, confusedness, confusion, derangement, disarrangement, disarray, disorder, disorderedness, disorderliness, disorganization, jumble, mess, mix-up, muddle, muss, scramble, topsy-turviness. *Slang:* snafu. *See* ORDER. **4.** A group of things gathered haphazardly : agglomeration, bank[1], cumulus, drift, heap, hill, mass, mess, mound, mountain, pile, shock[2], stack. *See* ORDER.

tumbledown *adjective*
Falling to ruin : dilapidated, ramshackle, ruinous, rundown. *See* BETTER.

tumble on *verb* See **tumble.**

tumescent *adjective*
Filled up with or as if with something insubstantial : flatulent, inflated, overblown, tumid, turgid, windy. *See* INCREASE, PLAIN.

tumid *adjective*
Filled up with or as if with something insubstantial : flatulent, inflated, overblown, tumescent, turgid, windy. *See* INCREASE, PLAIN.

tumult *noun*
1. Sounds or a sound, especially when loud, confused, or disagreeable : babel, clamor, din, hubbub, hullabaloo, noise, pandemonium, racket, rumpus, uproar. *See* SOUNDS. **2.** A quarrel, fight, or disturbance marked by very noisy, disorderly, and often violent behavior : affray, brawl, broil[2], donnybrook, fray, free-for-all, melee, riot, row[2], ruction. *Informal:* fracas. *Slang:* rumble. *See* ATTACK. **3.** An interruption of regular procedure or of public peace : agitation, commotion, disorder, disturbance, helter-skelter, stir[1], turbulence, turmoil, uproar. *Informal:* flap, to-do. *See* CALM, ORDER. **4.** A state of discomposure : agitation, dither, fluster, flutter, perturbation, turmoil, upset. *Informal:* lather, stew. *See* CALM.

tumultuous *adjective*
1. Marked by unrest or disturbance : stormy, tempestuous, turbulent. *See* CALM. **2.** Violently disturbed or agitated, as by storms : dirty, heavy, raging, roiled, roily, rough, rugged, stormy, tempestuous, turbulent, ugly, violent, wild. *See* CALM.

tune *noun*
1. A pleasing succession of musical tones forming a usually brief aesthetic unit : air, aria, melody, strain[2]. *Obsolete:* note. *See* SOUNDS.

2. Pleasing agreement, as of musical sounds : accord, concert, concord, harmony, symphony. *Music:* consonance. *See* BEAUTIFUL. **3.** Harmonious mutual understanding : accord, agreement, concord, concordance, concurrence, consonance, harmony, rapport, unity. *Idiom:* meeting of the minds. *See* AGREE.

tune *verb* **1.** *Archaic.* To utter words or sounds in musical tones : carol, chant, sing, vocalize. *See* SOUNDS. **2.** To bring into accord : accommodate, attune, conform, coordinate, harmonize, integrate, proportion, reconcile. *See* AGREE. **3.** To alter for proper functioning. Also used with *up* : adjust, fix, regulate, set[1]. *Music:* attune. *See* CHANGE, HELP.

tuneful *adjective*
1. Having or producing a pleasing melody : melodic, melodious, musical. *See* SOUNDS. **2.** Resembling or having the effect of music, especially pleasing music : dulcet, euphonic, euphonious, melodic, melodious, musical. *See* SOUNDS.

turbid *adjective*
1. Having sediment or foreign particles stirred up or suspended : cloudy, muddy, murky, roiled, roily. *See* CLEAR. **2.** Heavy, dark, or dense, especially with impurities : hazy, murky, smoggy. *See* CLEAR. **3.** Mentally uncertain : addled, addlepated, confused, confounded, confusional, muddle-headed, perplexed. *Informal:* mixed-up. *See* CLEAR.

turbulence *noun*
1. The condition of being physically agitated : agitation, commotion, convulsion. *See* CALM. **2.** An interruption of regular procedure or of public peace : agitation, commotion, disorder, disturbance, helter-skelter, stir[1], tumult, turmoil, uproar. *Informal:* flap, to-do. *See* CALM, ORDER.

turbulent *adjective*
1. Violently disturbed or agitated, as by storms : dirty, heavy, raging, roiled, roily, rough, rugged, stormy, tempestuous, tumultuous, ugly, violent, wild. *See* CALM. **2.** Marked by unrest or disturbance : stormy, tempestuous, tumultuous. *See* CALM.

turf *noun*
Slang. A particular area used for or associated with a specific individual or activity : country, district, region, terrain, territory. *See* TERRITORY.

turgid *adjective*
Filled up with or as if with something insubstantial : flatulent, inflated, overblown, tumescent, tumid, windy. *See* INCREASE, PLAIN.

turgidity *noun*
Pretentious, pompous speech or writing : bombast, claptrap, fustian, grandiloquence, magniloquence, orotundity, rant. *See* PLAIN, STYLE, WORDS.

turkey *noun*
Slang. One deficient in judgment and good sense : ass, fool, idiot, imbecile, jackass, mooncalf, moron, nincompoop, ninny, nitwit, simple, simpleton, softhead, tomfool. *Informal:* dope, gander, goose. *Slang:* cretin, ding-dong, dip, goof, jerk, nerd, schmo, schmuck. *See* ABILITY.

turmoil *noun*
1. A state of discomposure : agitation, dither, fluster, flutter, perturbation, tumult, upset. *Informal:* lather, stew. *See* CALM. **2.** An interruption of regular procedure or of public peace : agitation, commotion, disorder, disturbance, helter-skelter, stir[1], tumult, turbulence, uproar. *Informal:* flap, to-do. *See* CALM, ORDER. **3.** A state of uneasiness and usually resentment brewing to an eventual explosion : ferment, Sturm und Drang, unrest. *See* CALM, PEACE.

turn *verb*
1. To move or cause to move in circles or around an axis : circle, circumvolve, gyrate, orbit, revolve, rotate, wheel. *See* MOVE, REPETITION. **2.** To spade or dig (soil) to bring the undersoil to the surface : plow, turn over. *See* MOVE. **3.** To make or become less sharp-edged : blunt, dull. *Idiom:* take the edge off. *See* SHARP. **4.** To twist and turn, as in pain, struggle, or embarrassment : agonize, squirm, toss, writhe. *See* REPETITION. **5.** To injure a (bodily part) by twisting : sprain, wrench. *See* HEALTH. **6.** To disturb the health or physiological functioning of : derange, disorder, unsettle, upset. *See* HEALTH. **7.** To change the direction or course of : avert, deflect, deviate, divert, pivot, shift, swing, veer. *See* CHANGE. **8.** To cause to move, especially at an angle : angle[2], bend, deflect, refract. *See* STRAIGHT. **9.** To swerve from a straight line : angle[2], arc, arch, bend, bow[2], crook, curve, round. *See* STRAIGHT. **10.** To change to the opposite position, direction, or course. Also used with *about*, *around*, *over*, or *round* : invert, reverse, transpose. *See* CHANGE. **11.** To make or become different : alter, change, modify, mutate, vary. *See* CHANGE. **12.** To abandon one's cause or party usually to join another : apostatize, defect, desert[3], renegade, tergiversate. *Slang:* rat. *Idioms:* change sides, turn one's coat. *See* APPROACH, TRUST. **13.** To move (a weapon or

blow, for example) in the direction of someone or something : aim, cast, direct, head, level, point, set[1], train, zero in. *Military:* lay[1]. *See* SEEK. **14.** To devote (oneself or one's efforts) : address, apply, bend, buckle down, concentrate, dedicate, devote, direct, focus, give. *See* COLLECT, WORK. **15.** To become or cause to become rotten or unsound : break down, decay, decompose, deteriorate, disintegrate, molder, putrefy, rot, spoil, taint. *Idioms:* go bad, go to pot, go to seed. *See* BETTER, THRIVE. **16.** To look to when in need : apply, go, refer, repair[2], resort, run. *Idioms:* fall back on (*or* upon), have recourse to. *See* USED. **17.** To come to be. Also used with *out* : become, come, get, grow, wax. *See* CHANGE.

turn down *verb* **1.** To be unwilling to accept, consider, or receive : decline, dismiss, refuse, reject, spurn. *Slang:* nix. *Idiom:* turn thumbs down on. *See* ACCEPT. **2.** To be unwilling to grant : deny, disallow, refuse, withhold. *See* ACCEPT. **3.** To prevent or forbid authoritatively : blackball, negative, veto. *Slang:* nix. *Idiom:* turn thumbs down on. *See* ACCEPT.

turn in *verb* **1.** To commit to the consideration or judgment of another : submit. *See* GIVE. **2.** *Informal.* To go to bed : bed (down), retire. *Slang:* crash, flop. *Idioms:* call it a night, hit the hay (*or* sack). *See* AWARENESS.

turn off *verb Slang.* To be very disagreeable to : displease, offend. *Idioms:* give offense to, not set right (*or* well) with. *See* LIKE, PAIN.

turn on *verb* **1.** To be determined by or contingent on something unknown, uncertain, or changeable : depend on (*or* upon), hang on, hang upon, hinge on (*or* upon), rest on (*or* upon), turn upon. *See* START. **2.** *Slang.* To arouse the interest and attention of : attract, interest, intrigue. *See* EXCITE.

turn out *verb* **1.** To supply what is needed for some activity or purpose : accouter, appoint, equip, fit[1], fit out (*or* up), furnish, gear, outfit, rig. *See* GIVE. **2.** *Informal.* To leave one's bed : arise, get up, pile, rise, roll out. *Idiom:* rise and shine. *See* RISE.

turn over *verb* **1.** To spade or dig (soil) to bring the undersoil to the surface : plow, turn. *See* MOVE. **2.** To turn or cause to turn from a vertical or horizontal position : capsize, knock over, overthrow, overturn, topple, upset. *See* CHANGE, HORIZONTAL, MOVE. **3.** To think or think about carefully and at length : chew on (*or* over), cogitate, consider, contemplate, deliberate, entertain, excogitate, meditate, mull, muse[1], ponder, reflect, revolve, ruminate, study, think, think out, think over, think through, weigh. *Idioms:* cudgel one's brains, put on one's thinking cap, rack one's brain. *See* THOUGHTS. **4.** To relinquish to the possession or control of another : deliver, furnish, give, hand, hand over, provide, supply, transfer. *See* GIVE. **5.** To put in the charge of another for care, use, or performance : commend, commit, confide, consign, entrust, give (over), hand over, relegate, trust. *Idiom:* give in trust (*or* charge). *See* GIVE. **6.** To direct (a person) elsewhere for help or information : refer, send, transfer. *See* MOVE.

turn up *verb* **1.** To find by investigation : dig (out *or* up), uncover, unearth. *See* SHOW. **2.** To come to a particular place : arrive, check in, get in, pull in, reach, show up. *Slang:* blow in. *Idiom:* make (*or* put in) an appearance. *See* START.

turn upon *verb* To be determined by or contingent on something unknown, uncertain, or changeable : depend on (*or* upon), hang on, hang upon, hinge on (*or* upon), rest on (*or* upon), turn on. *See* START.

turn *noun* **1.** Circular movement around a point or about an axis : circuit, circulation, circumvolution, gyration, revolution, rotation, wheel, whirl. *See* GEOMETRY, REPETITION. **2.** A calculated change in position : evolution, maneuver, move, movement. *See* MOVE. **3.** Something bent : bend, bow[2], crook, curvature, curve, round. *See* STRAIGHT. **4.** An often sudden change or departure, as in a trend : shift, tack, twist. *See* CHANGE. **5.** A limited, often assigned period of activity, duty, or opportunity : bout, go, hitch, inning (often used in plural), shift, spell[3], stint, stretch, time, tour, trick, watch. *See* TIME. **6.** An inclination to something : bent, bias, cast, disposition, leaning, partiality, penchant, predilection, predisposition, proclivity, proneness, propensity, squint, tendency, trend. *See* APPROACH, LIKE. **7.** An innate capability : aptitude, aptness, bent, faculty, flair, genius, gift, head, instinct, knack, talent. *See* ABILITY, APPROACH. **8.** A course, process, or journey that ends where it began or repeats itself : circle, circuit, cycle, orbit, round, tour. *See* REPETITION. **9.** A usually brief and regular journey on foot, especially for exercise : constitutional, walk. *See* MOVE.

turnabout *noun*

The act of changing or being changed from one position, direction, or course to the opposite :

inversion, reversal, transposition, turnaround. *See* CHANGE.

turnaround *noun*
The act of changing or being changed from one position, direction, or course to the opposite : inversion, reversal, transposition, turnabout. *See* CHANGE.

turncoat *noun*
A person who has defected : apostate, defector, deserter, recreant, renegade, runagate, tergiversator. *Informal:* rat. *See* APPROACH.

turndown *noun*
A turning down of a request : denial, disallowance, refusal, rejection. *See* ACCEPT.

turn down *verb* See **turn.**

turned-on *adjective*
1. *Slang.* Feeling a very strong emotion : atingle, excited, fired up, thrilled, worked up. *Informal:* psyched. *Slang:* stoked. *See* EXCITE. **2.** *Slang.* Stupefied, intoxicated, or otherwise influenced by the taking of drugs : drugged. *Informal:* doped. *Slang:* high, hopped-up, lit (up), potted, spaced-out, stoned, wiped-out, zonked. *See* DRUGS.

turn in *verb* See **turn.**

turning point *noun*
A decisive point : climacteric, crisis, crossroad (used in plural), exigence, exigency, head, juncture, pass, zero hour. *See* DECIDE.

turnkey *noun*
A guard or keeper of a prison : jailer, warden. *British:* warder. *See* FREE.

turn off *verb* See **turn.**

turn on *verb* See **turn.**

turnout *noun*
1. Things needed for a task, journey, or other purpose : accouterment (often used in plural), apparatus, equipment, gear, material (used in plural), materiel, outfit, paraphernalia, rig, tackle, thing (used in plural). *See* MEANS. **2.** A set or style of clothing : costume, dress, garb, guise, habiliment (often used in plural), outfit. *Informal:* getup, rig. *See* PUT ON.

turn out *verb* See **turn.**

turn over *verb* See **turn.**

turnpike *noun*
A course affording passage from one place to another : avenue, boulevard, drive, expressway, freeway, highway, path, road, roadway, route, street, superhighway, thoroughfare, thruway, way. *See* MOVE, OPEN.

turn up *verb* See **turn.**

turpitude *noun*
Degrading, immoral acts or habits : bestiality, corruption, depravity, flagitiousness, immorality, perversion, vice, villainousness, villainy, wickedness. *See* CLEAN.

tush *noun*
Slang. The part of one's back on which one rests in sitting : buttock (used in plural), derrière, posterior, rump, seat. *Informal:* backside, behind, bottom, rear[1]. *Slang:* bun (used in plural), fanny. *Chiefly British:* bum[2]. *See* OVER.

tussle *verb*
To contend with an opponent at close quarters, as by attempting to throw him or her : grapple, scuffle, wrestle. ***Idiom:*** go to the mat with. *See* CONFLICT, TOUCH.
tussle *noun* A physical conflict involving two or more : fight, fistfight, fisticuffs, scrap[2], scuffle. *Slang:* rumble. *See* CONFLICT.

tutelage *noun*
The act, process, or art of imparting knowledge and skill : education, instruction, pedagogics, pedagogy, schooling, teaching, training, tuition, tutoring. *See* TEACH.

tutor *noun*
One who educates : educator, instructor, pedagogue, teacher, trainer. *See* TEACH.
tutor *verb* To impart knowledge and skill to : coach, discipline, educate, instruct, school, teach, train. *See* TEACH.

tutoring *noun*
The act, process, or art of imparting knowledge and skill : education, instruction, pedagogics, pedagogy, schooling, teaching, training, tuition, tutelage. *See* TEACH.

twaddle *noun*
1. Unintelligible or foolish talk : babble, blather, blatherskite, double talk, gabble, gibberish, jabber, jabberwocky, jargon, nonsense, prate, prattle. *See* WORDS. **2.** Something that does not have or make sense : balderdash, blather, bunkum, claptrap, drivel, garbage, idiocy, nonsense, piffle, poppycock, rigmarole, rubbish, tomfoolery, trash. *Informal:* tommyrot. *Slang:* applesauce, baloney, bilge, bull[1], bunk[2], crap, hooey, malarkey. *See* KNOWLEDGE.

twelvemonth *noun*
A period of time of approximately 12 months, especially that period during which the earth completes a single revolution around the sun : year. *See* TIME.

twerp also **twirp** *noun*
Slang. An insignificant but arrogant and obnoxious young person : pup, puppy. *Informal:* squirt. *See* YOUTH.

twiddle *verb*
To move one's fingers or hands in a nervous or

aimless fashion : fiddle, fidget, fool, monkey, play, putter, tinker, toy, trifle. *See* TOUCH.

twig *verb*
Chiefly British. To perceive and recognize the meaning of : accept, apprehend, catch (on), compass, comprehend, conceive, fathom, follow, get, grasp, make out, read, see, sense, take, take in, understand. *Informal:* savvy. *Slang:* dig. *Scots:* ken. ***Idioms:*** get (*or* have) a handle on, get the picture. *See* UNDERSTAND.

twiggy *adjective*
Having little flesh or fat on the body : angular, bony, fleshless, gaunt, lank, lanky, lean[2], meager, rawboned, scrawny, skinny, slender, slim, spare, thin, weedy. ***Idioms:*** all skin and bones, thin as a rail. *See* FAT.

twilight *noun*
The period between afternoon and nighttime : dusk, eve, evening, eventide, gloaming, nightfall. *Archaic:* even[2], vesper. *See* START.

twin *noun*
One of a matched pair of things : companion, counterpart, double, duplicate, fellow, match, mate. *See* SAME.
twin *adjective* Consisting of two identical or similar related things, parts, or elements : double, dual, paired. *See* SAME.
twin *verb* To make or become twice as great : double, duplicate, geminate, redouble. *See* BIG, INCREASE.

twine *verb*
To move or proceed on a repeatedly curving course : coil, corkscrew, curl, entwine, meander, snake, spiral, twist, weave, wind[2], wreathe. *See* REPETITION, STRAIGHT.

twinge *noun*
A sensation of physical discomfort occurring as the result of disease or injury : ache, pain, pang, prick, prickle, smart, soreness, stab, sting, stitch, throe. *Informal:* misery. *See* PAIN.
twinge *verb* To have or cause a feeling of physical pain or discomfort : ache, hurt, pain, pang. *See* PAIN.

twinkle *verb*
1. To shine with intermittent gleams : blink, flash, flicker, glimmer, wink. *See* CONTINUE, LIGHT. **2.** To emit light suddenly in rays or sparks : coruscate, flash, glance, gleam, glimmer, glint, glisten, glister, glitter, scintillate, shimmer, spangle, sparkle, wink. *See* LIGHT. **3.** To open and close the eyes rapidly : bat[1], blink, nictate, nictitate, wink. *See* REPETITION, SEE.
twinkle *noun* **1.** A sudden quick light : blink, coruscation, flash, flicker, glance, gleam, glimmer, glint, spark[1], wink. *See* LIGHT. **2.** A very brief time : crack, flash, instant, minute[1], moment, second[1], trice, twinkling, wink. *Informal:* jiff, jiffy. *Chiefly British:* tick. *See* BIG, TIME.

twinkling *noun*
A very brief time : crack, flash, instant, minute[1], moment, second[1], trice, twinkle, wink. *Informal:* jiff, jiffy. *Chiefly British:* tick. *See* BIG, TIME.

twirl *verb*
To rotate rapidly : spin, swirl, whirl. *See* REPETITION.

twirp *noun* See **twerp.**

twist *verb*
1. To move or proceed on a repeatedly curving course : coil, corkscrew, curl, entwine, meander, snake, spiral, twine, weave, wind[2], wreathe. *See* REPETITION, STRAIGHT. **2.** To alter and spoil the natural form or appearance of : contort, deform, disfigure, distort, misshape. *See* BEAUTIFUL. **3.** To give an inaccurate view of by representing falsely or misleadingly : belie, color, distort, falsify, load, misrepresent, misstate, pervert, warp, wrench, wrest. ***Idiom:*** give a false coloring to. *See* TRUE.
twist *noun* **1.** An often sudden change or departure, as in a trend : shift, tack, turn. *See* CHANGE. **2.** A clever, unexpected new trick or method : gimmick. *Informal:* kicker, wrinkle. *Slang:* angle[2], kick. *See* ABILITY, EXCITE, GOOD.

twit *verb*
To make fun or make fun of : deride, gibe, jeer, jest, laugh, mock, ridicule, scoff, scout[2]. *Chiefly British:* quiz. ***Idiom:*** poke fun at. *See* LAUGHTER, RESPECT.
twit *noun* An instance of mockery or derision : gibe, insult, jeer, scoff, taunt. *See* LAUGHTER, RESPECT.

twitch *verb*
To move or cause to move with a sudden abrupt motion : jerk, lurch, snap, wrench, yank. *See* MOVE, PUSH.
twitch *noun* **1.** A nervous shaking of the body : quake, quiver, shake, shiver[1], shudder, thrill, tic, tremor. *See* REPETITION. **2.** A sudden motion, such as a pull : jerk, lurch, snap, tug, wrench, yank. *See* MOVE, PUSH.

twitchy *adjective*
Feeling or exhibiting nervous tension : edgy, fidgety, jittery, jumpy, nervous, restive, restless, skittish, tense. *Slang:* uptight. ***Idioms:*** a bundle of nerves, all wound up, on edge. *See* TIGHTEN.

twitter *verb*
To move to and fro in short, jerky movements : quake, quaver, quiver, shake, shiver[1], shudder, tremble, vibrate. *See* REPETITION.

twittery *adjective*
Marked by or affected with tremors : aquiver, quaky, quivery, shaky, shivery, tremulant, tremulous. *See* REPETITION.

two *noun*
Two items of the same kind together : brace, couple, couplet, doublet, duet, duo, match, pair, twosome, yoke. *See* GROUP, SAME.

two bits *noun*
Slang. A small or trifling amount of money : small change. *Informal:* peanut (used in plural). *Slang:* chicken feed. *See* BIG, MONEY.

two-faced *adjective*
1. Of or practicing hypocrisy : hypocritical, Pecksniffian, pharisaic, pharisaical, phony, sanctimonious. *See* HONEST. **2.** Being or acting so as to conceal one's real intentions : double, double-dealing, double-faced. *See* HONEST.

two-facedness *noun*
A show or expression of feelings or beliefs one does not actually hold or possess : hypocrisy, pharisaism, phoniness, sanctimoniousness, sanctimony, tartuffery. *See* HONEST.

two-fisted *adjective*
Informal. Indulging in drink to an excessive degree : hard, heavy. *See* EXCESS.

twofold *adjective*
1. Composed of two parts or things : biform, binary, double, dual, duple, duplex, duplicate, geminate. *See* PART. **2.** Twice as much or as large : double. *See* BIG.

twosome *noun*
1. Two persons united, as by marriage : couple, duo, pair. *See* GROUP. **2.** Two items of the same kind together : brace, couple, couplet, doublet, duet, duo, match, pair, two, yoke. *See* GROUP, SAME.

type *noun*
1. A class that is defined by the common attribute or attributes possessed by all its members : breed, cast, description, feather, ilk, kind[2], lot, manner, mold, nature, order, sort, species, stamp, stripe, variety. *Informal:* persuasion. *See* GROUP. **2.** A physical entity typifying an abstraction : embodiment, exteriorization, externalization, incarnation, manifestation, materialization, objectification, personalization, personification, substantiation. *Rhetoric:* prosopopeia. *See* SUBSTITUTE.

typic *adjective*
Having the nature of, constituting, or serving as a type : archetypal, archetypic, archetypical, classic, classical, model, paradigmatic, prototypal, prototypic, prototypical, quintessential, representative, typical. *See* SAME, USUAL.

typical *adjective*
1. Commonly encountered : average, common, commonplace, general, normal, ordinary, usual. *See* SURPRISE. **2.** Serving to identify or set apart an individual or group : characteristic, distinctive, individual, peculiar, vintage. *See* SAME. **3.** Having the nature of, constituting, or serving as a type : archetypal, archetypic, archetypical, classic, classical, model, paradigmatic, prototypal, prototypic, prototypical, quintessential, representative, typic. *See* SAME, USUAL.

typically *adverb*
In an expected or customary manner; for the most part : commonly, consistently, customarily, frequently, generally, habitually, naturally, normally, often, regularly, routinely, usually. ***Idioms:*** as usual, per usual. *See* BIG, USUAL.

typify *verb*
To serve as an example, image, or symbol of : epitomize, exemplify, illustrate, represent, stand for, symbol, symbolize. *See* SUBSTITUTE.

tyrannic *adjective*
1. Having and exercising complete political power and control : absolute, absolutistic, arbitrary, autarchic, autarchical, autocratic, autocratical, despotic, dictatorial, monocratic, totalitarian, tyrannical, tyrannous. *See* OVER, POLITICS. **2.** Characterized by or favoring absolute obedience to authority : authoritarian, autocratic, despotic, dictatorial, totalitarian, tyrannical. *See* OVER.

tyrannical *adjective*
1. Characterized by or favoring absolute obedience to authority : authoritarian, autocratic, despotic, dictatorial, totalitarian, tyrannic. *See* OVER. **2.** Having and exercising complete political power and control : absolute, absolutistic, arbitrary, autarchic, autarchical, autocratic, autocratical, despotic, dictatorial, monocratic, totalitarian, tyrannic, tyrannous. *See* OVER, POLITICS.

tyrannize *verb*
1. To treat arbitrarily or cruelly : grind, trample. *See* OVER. **2.** To command or issue commands in an arrogant manner : boss, dictate, dominate, domineer, order, rule. *See* OVER.

tyrannous *adjective*
Having and exercising complete political power

and control : absolute, absolutistic, arbitrary, autarchic, autarchical, autocratic, autocratical, despotic, dictatorial, monocratic, totalitarian, tyrannic, tyrannical. *See* OVER, POLITICS.

tyranny *noun*
1. A government in which a single leader or party exercises absolute control over all citizens and every aspect of their lives : absolutism, autarchy, autocracy, despotism, dictatorship, monocracy. *See* OVER, POLITICS. **2.** Absolute power, especially when exercised unjustly or cruelly : autocracy, despotism, dictatorship, totalitarianism. *See* OVER, POLITICS.

tyrant *noun*
1. An absolute ruler, especially one who is harsh and oppressive : Big Brother, despot, dictator, führer, man on horseback, oppressor, strongman, totalitarian. *See* OVER. **2.** One who imposes or favors absolute obedience to authority : authoritarian, autocrat, despot, dictator, martinet, totalitarian. *See* OVER.

tyro also **tiro** *noun*
One who is just starting to learn or do something : abecedarian, beginner, fledgling, freshman, greenhorn, initiate, neophyte, novice, novitiate, tenderfoot. *Slang:* rookie. *See* START.

·U·

ubiquitous *adjective*
Ever present in all places : omnipresent, universal. *See* LIMITED, SPECIFIC.

ugliness *noun*
1. The quality or condition of being ugly : hideousness, unsightliness. *See* BEAUTIFUL. **2.** An unsightly object : mess, monstrosity. *Informal:* fright, sight, ugly. *See* BEAUTIFUL.

ugly *adjective*
1. Extremely displeasing to the eye : hideous, ill-favored, unsightly. ***Idiom:*** ugly as sin. *See* BEAUTIFUL. **2.** Extremely unpleasant to the senses or feelings : atrocious, disgusting, foul, horrid, nasty, nauseating, offensive, repellent, repulsive, revolting, sickening, unwholesome, vile. *See* LIKE, PAIN. **3.** Violently disturbed or agitated, as by storms : dirty, heavy, raging, roiled, roily, rough, rugged, stormy, tempestuous, tumultuous, turbulent, violent, wild. *See* CALM. **4.** Having or showing a bad temper : bad-tempered, cantankerous, crabbed, cranky, cross, disagreeable, fretful, grouchy, grumpy, ill-tempered, irascible, irritable, nasty, peevish, petulant, querulous, snappish, snappy, surly, testy, waspish. *Informal:* crabby, mean[2]. ***Idiom:*** out of sorts. *See* ATTITUDE.
ugly *noun Informal.* An unsightly object : mess, monstrosity, ugliness. *Informal:* fright, sight. *See* BEAUTIFUL.

uh-huh *adverb*
Informal. It is so; as you say or ask : absolutely, agreed, all right, assuredly, aye, gladly, indubitably, roger, undoubtedly, unquestionably, willingly, yea, yes. *Informal:* OK, yeah, yep. *Slang:* right on. *See* AFFIRM.

ulterior *adjective*
1. Lying beyond what is obvious or avowed : buried, concealed, covert, hidden, obscured. ***Idiom:*** under cover (*or* wraps). *See* SHOW. **2.** Following something else in time : after, later, posterior, subsequent. *See* PRECEDE.

ulteriorly *adverb*
At a subsequent time : after, afterward, afterwards, later, latterly, next, subsequently. ***Idioms:*** after a while, by and by, later on. *See* PRECEDE.

ultimate *adjective*
1. Of or relating to a terminative condition, stage, or point : final, last[1], latter, terminal. *See* START. **2.** Of or being an irreducible element : basic, elemental, elementary, essential, fundamental, primitive, underlying. *See* SURFACE. **3.** Greatest in quantity or highest in degree that has been or can be attained : maximal, maximum, top, topmost, utmost, uttermost. *See* HIGH, LIMITED. **4.** Of the greatest possible degree, quality, or intensity : extreme, supreme, transcendent, unsurpassable, utmost, uttermost. *See* BETTER, BIG. **5.** Most distant or remote, as from a center : extreme, farthermost, farthest, furthermost, furthest, outermost, outmost, utmost, uttermost. *See* BIG, EDGE.
ultimate *noun* The greatest quantity or highest degree attainable : maximum, outside, top,

utmost, uttermost. ***Idiom:*** ne plus ultra. *See* HIGH, LIMITED.

ultimately *adverb*
After a considerable length of time, usually after a delay : finally. ***Idioms:*** at last, at long last, in the end. *See* START, TIME.

ultra *adjective*
Holding especially political views that deviate drastically and fundamentally from conventional or traditional beliefs : extreme, extremist, fanatic, fanatical, rabid, radical, revolutionary. *Slang:* far-out. *See* CONCERN, EDGE, POLITICS.
ultra *noun* One who holds extreme views or advocates extreme measures : extremist, fanatic, radical, revolutionary, revolutionist, zealot. *See* EDGE, CONCERN, POLITICS.

ultraconservative *adjective*
Vehemently, often fanatically opposing progress or reform : die-hard, mossbacked, reactionary. *See* POLITICS.
ultraconservative *noun* A person who vehemently, often fanatically opposes progress and favors return to a previous condition : die-hard, mossback, reactionary. *See* POLITICS.

ululate *verb*
To utter or emit a long, mournful, plaintive sound : bay², howl, moan, wail, yowl. *See* SOUNDS.

ululation *noun*
A long, mournful cry : bay², howl, moan, wail, yowl. *See* SOUNDS.

umbra *noun*
Comparative darkness that results from the blocking of light rays : penumbra, shade, shadow, umbrage. *See* LIGHT.

umbrage *noun*
1. Extreme displeasure caused by an insult or slight : dudgeon, huff, miff, offense, pique, resentment, ruffled feathers. *See* LIKE, PAIN. **2.** Comparative darkness that results from the blocking of light rays : penumbra, shade, shadow, umbra. *See* LIGHT.

umbrageous *adjective*
Casting shade : shady. *See* LIGHT.

ump *noun*
Sports. A person, usually appointed, who decides the issues or results, or supervises the conduct, of a competition or conflict : arbiter, arbitrator, judge, referee, umpire. *Sports:* ref. *See* DECIDE.

umpire *noun*
A person, usually appointed, who decides the issues or results, or supervises the conduct, of a competition or conflict : arbiter, arbitrator, judge, referee. *Sports:* ref, ump. *See* DECIDE.
umpire *verb* To make a decision about (a controversy or dispute, for example) after deliberation, as in a court of law : adjudge, adjudicate, arbitrate, decide, decree, determine, judge, referee, rule. *See* DECIDE, LAW.

unabashed *adjective*
Characterized by or done without shame : bald-faced, barefaced, blatant, brazen, brazen-faced, shameless, unblushing. *Informal:* brassy. *See* COURTESY, RESPECT, RIGHT.

unabbreviated *adjective*
Not shortened by omissions : complete, unabridged, uncensored, uncut, unexpurgated. *See* PART.

unable *adjective*
Totally incapable of doing a job : incompetent, unfit, unqualified. *See* ABILITY.

unabridged *adjective*
Not shortened by omissions : complete, unabbreviated, uncensored, uncut, unexpurgated. *See* PART.

unacceptable *adjective*
Arousing disapproval : exceptionable, ill-favored, inadmissible, objectionable, undesirable, unwanted, unwelcome. *See* LIKE.

unaccompanied *adjective*
Lacking the company of others : alone, companionless, lone, lonely, lonesome, single, solitary. *See* INCLUDE.

unaccountable *adjective*
That cannot be explained : inexplicable, unexplainable. *See* EXPLAIN.

unacquainted *adjective*
Not aware or informed : ignorant, innocent, oblivious, unaware, unconscious, unenlightened, unfamiliar, uninformed, unknowing, unwitting. ***Idiom:*** in the dark. *See* KNOWLEDGE.

unadorned *adjective*
1. Without addition, decoration, or qualification : bald, bare, dry, plain, simple, unvarnished. *See* PLAIN. **2.** Of a plain and unsophisticated nature : artless, homely, homespun, natural, rustic, unpolished. *See* PLAIN.

unadulterated *adjective*
1. Free from extraneous elements : absolute, perfect, plain, pure, sheer², simple, undiluted, unmixed. *See* CLEAN. **2.** Produced by nature; not artificial or manmade : natural, organic. ***Idiom:*** pure as the driven snow. *See* CULTURE.

unadvantageous *adjective*
Tending to discourage, retard, or make more difficult : adverse, disadvantageous, negative,

unfavorable, unsatisfactory, untoward. *See* HELP.

unaffected *adjective*
1. Not affected by or showing emotion : cold, cold-blooded, emotionless, unemotional, unmoved. *See* ATTITUDE, HOT. **2.** Free from guile, cunning, or deceit : artless, guileless, ingenuous, innocent, naive, natural, simple, unsophisticated, unstudied, unworldly. *See* HONEST. **3.** Devoid of any hypocrisy or pretense : genuine, heartfelt, hearty, honest, natural, real, sincere, true, unfeigned, unmannered. *See* TRUE.

unafraid *adjective*
Having or showing courage : audacious, bold, brave, courageous, dauntless, doughty, fearless, fortitudinous, gallant, game, hardy, heroic, intrepid, mettlesome, plucky, stout, stouthearted, undaunted, valiant, valorous. *Informal:* spunky. *Slang:* gutsy, gutty. *See* FEAR.

unalterable *adjective*
1. Incapable of changing or being modified : immutable, inalterable, inflexible, invariable, ironclad, rigid, unchangeable. *See* FLEXIBLE. **2.** That cannot be revoked or undone : irreversible, irrevocable. ***Idiom:*** beyond recall. *See* CHANGE.

unambiguous *adjective*
1. Clearly defined; not ambiguous : clear, distinct, sharp, unequivocal, unmistakable. *See* CLEAR. **2.** Clearly, fully, and sometimes emphatically expressed : categorical, clear, clear-cut, decided, definite, explicit, express, positive, precise, specific, unequivocal. *See* CLEAR.

unanimity *noun*
The quality or condition of being in complete agreement or harmony : consensus, unanimousness. *See* AGREE.

unanimous *adjective*
Being in or characterized by complete agreement : solid. ***Idioms:*** as one, at one, of one mind, with one voice. *See* AGREE.

unanimousness *noun*
The quality or condition of being in complete agreement or harmony : consensus, unanimity. *See* AGREE.

unappeasable *adjective*
Having an insatiable appetite for an activity or pursuit : avid, edacious, gluttonous, greedy, omnivorous, rapacious, ravenous, voracious. *See* DESIRE.

unappetizing *adjective*
So unpleasant in flavor as to be inedible : distasteful, unpalatable, unsavory. *See* TASTE.

unappreciated *adjective*
Not apt to be appreciated : thankless, ungrateful, unthankful. *See* GRATEFUL.

unappreciative *adjective*
Not showing or feeling gratitude : thankless, ungrateful, unthankful, unthanking. *See* GRATEFUL.

unapproachable *adjective*
1. Not friendly, sociable, or warm in manner : aloof, chill, chilly, cool, distant, offish, remote, reserved, reticent, solitary, standoffish, uncommunicative, undemonstrative, withdrawn. *See* ATTITUDE, HOT. **2.** Unable to be reached : inaccessible, inapproachable, unattainable, unavailable, unreachable. ***Idioms:*** beyond reach, out of the way. *See* REACH.

unapt *adjective*
1. Not suited to circumstances : improper, inappropriate, inapt, incongruous, inept, malapropos, unbecoming, unbefitting, unfit, unseemly, unsuitable. ***Idiom:*** out of place. *See* AGREE, USUAL. **2.** Not likely : doubtful, improbable, questionable, unlikely. *See* LIKELY.

unassailable *adjective*
Established beyond a doubt : certain, hard, inarguable, incontestable, incontrovertible, indisputable, indubitable, irrefutable, positive, sure, undeniable, undisputable, unquestionable. *See* CERTAIN, TRUE.

unassuming *adjective*
Not elaborate or showy, as in appearance or style : modest, plain, simple, unostentatious, unpretentious. *See* PLAIN.

unassumingness *noun*
Lack of ostentation or pretension : modesty, plainness, simpleness, simplicity, unostentatiousness, unpretentiousness. *See* PLAIN.

unattached *adjective*
Without a spouse : fancy-free, footloose, lone, single, sole, spouseless, unmarried, unwed. ***Idiom:*** footloose and fancy-free. *See* MARRIAGE.

unattainable *adjective*
1. Not capable of happening or being done : impossible, impracticable, impractical, unrealizable, unthinkable, unworkable. ***Idiom:*** out of the question. *See* POSSIBLE. **2.** Unable to be reached : inaccessible, inapproachable, unapproachable, unavailable, unreachable. ***Idioms:*** beyond reach, out of the way. *See* REACH.

unattractive *adjective*
Not handsome or beautiful : homely, plain, uncomely, unlovely. ***Idioms:*** not much for

looks, not much to look at, short on looks. *See* BEAUTIFUL.

unavailable *adjective*
Unable to be reached : inaccessible, inapproachable, unapproachable, unattainable, unreachable. ***Idioms:*** beyond reach, out of the way. *See* REACH.

unavailing *adjective*
Having no useful result : barren, bootless, fruitless, futile, unprofitable, unsuccessful, useless, vain. ***Idiom:*** in vain. *See* THRIVE, USED.

unavailingness *noun*
The condition or quality of being useless or ineffective : bootlessness, fruitlessness, futility, unprofitableness, uselessness, vainness, vanity. *See* THRIVE, USED.

unavoidable *adjective*
Bound to happen : certain, inescapable, inevitable, sure. *See* CERTAIN.

unawake *adjective*
In a state of sleep : asleep, sleeping. ***Idioms:*** dead to the world, fast (*or* sound) asleep, in a sound (*or* wakeless) sleep, out like a light. *See* AWARENESS.

unaware *adjective*
Not aware or informed : ignorant, innocent, oblivious, unacquainted, unconscious, unenlightened, unfamiliar, uninformed, unknowing, unwitting. ***Idiom:*** in the dark. *See* KNOWLEDGE.

unawarely *adverb*
Without adequate preparation : aback, short, unawares. ***Idiom:*** by surprise. *See* PREPARED.

unawareness *noun*
The condition of being uninformed or unaware : ignorance, innocence, nescience, obliviousness, unconsciousness, unfamiliarity. *See* KNOWLEDGE.

unawares *adverb*
Without adequate preparation : aback, short, unawarely. ***Idiom:*** by surprise. *See* PREPARED.

unbalance *verb*
To make insane : craze, derange, madden, unhinge. *See* SANE.

unbalance *noun* Serious mental illness or disorder impairing a person's capacity to function normally and safely : brainsickness, craziness, dementia, derangement, disturbance, insaneness, insanity, lunacy, madness, mental illness, psychopathy. *Psychiatry:* mania. *Psychology:* aberration, alienation. *See* SANE.

unbalanced *adjective*
Afflicted with or exhibiting irrationality and mental unsoundness : brainsick, crazy, daft, demented, disordered, distraught, dotty, insane, lunatic, mad, maniac, maniacal, mentally ill, moonstruck, off, touched, unsound, wrong. *Informal:* bonkers, cracked, daffy, gaga, loony. *Slang:* bananas, batty, buggy, cuckoo, fruity, loco, nuts, nutty, screwy, wacky. *Chiefly British:* crackers. *Law:* non compos mentis. ***Idioms:*** around the bend, crazy as a loon, mad as a hatter, not all there, nutty as a fruitcake, off (*or* out of) one's head, off one's rocker, of unsound mind, out of one's mind, sick in the head, stark raving mad. *See* SANE.

unbearable *adjective*
So unpleasant or painful as not to be endured or tolerated : impossible, insufferable, insupportable, intolerable, unendurable, unsufferable, unsupportable. *See* PAIN.

unbecoming *adjective*
1. Not suited to circumstances : improper, inappropriate, inapt, incongruous, inept, malapropos, unapt, unbefitting, unfit, unseemly, unsuitable. ***Idiom:*** out of place. *See* AGREE, USUAL. **2.** Lacking style and good taste : inelegant, tasteless. *Informal:* tacky[2]. *See* STYLE. **3.** Not in keeping with conventional mores : immodest, improper, indecent, indecorous, indelicate, naughty, unbefitting, unseemly, untoward. ***Idiom:*** out of line. *See* USUAL.

unbecomingness *noun*
The condition of being improper : improperness, impropriety, inappropriateness, unfitness, unseemliness, unsuitability, unsuitableness. *See* AGREE, USUAL.

unbefitting *adjective*
1. Not suited to circumstances : improper, inappropriate, inapt, incongruous, inept, malapropos, unapt, unbecoming, unfit, unseemly, unsuitable. ***Idiom:*** out of place. *See* AGREE, USUAL. **2.** Not in keeping with conventional mores : immodest, improper, indecent, indecorous, indelicate, naughty, unbecoming, unseemly, untoward. ***Idiom:*** out of line. *See* USUAL.

unbelief *noun*
The refusal or reluctance to believe : disbelief, discredit, incredulity, incredulousness. *See* BELIEF.

unbelievable *adjective*
1. Not to be believed : inconceivable, incredible, unimaginable, unthinkable. ***Idioms:*** beyond belief, contrary to all reason. *See* BELIEF. **2.** Not plausible or believable : flimsy, implausible, improbable, inconceivable, incredible, shaky, thin, unconceivable, unconvincing, unsubstantial, weak. *See* LIKELY. **3.** So remarkable as to elicit disbelief : amazing,

astonishing, astounding, fabulous, fantastic, fantastical, incredible, marvelous, miraculous, phenomenal, prodigious, stupendous, wonderful, wondrous. *See* GOOD.

unbeliever *noun*
One who habitually or instinctively doubts or questions : doubter, doubting Thomas, nonbeliever, skeptic. *See* BELIEF.

unbelieving *adjective*
Refusing or reluctant to believe : disbelieving, incredulous, questioning, skeptical. *See* BELIEF.

unbend *verb*
To take repose by ceasing work or other effort for an interval of time : relax, rest[1], unwind. ***Idioms:*** lead (*or* live) the life of Riley, take it easy. *See* CONTINUE.

unbendable *adjective*
Firmly, often unreasonably immovable in purpose or will : adamant, adamantine, brassbound, die-hard, grim, implacable, incompliant, inexorable, inflexible, intransigent, iron, obdurate, relentless, remorseless, rigid, stubborn, unbending, uncompliant, uncompromising, unrelenting, unyielding. ***Idiom:*** stubborn as a mule (*or* ox). *See* RESIST.

unbending *adjective*
1. Not changing shape or bending : inelastic, inflexible, rigid, stiff, unyielding. *See* FLEXIBLE. **2.** Firmly, often unreasonably immovable in purpose or will : adamant, adamantine, brassbound, die-hard, grim, implacable, incompliant, inexorable, inflexible, intransigent, iron, obdurate, relentless, remorseless, rigid, stubborn, unbendable, uncompliant, uncompromising, unrelenting, unyielding. ***Idiom:*** stubborn as a mule (*or* ox). *See* RESIST. **3.** Indicating or possessing determination, resolution, or persistence : constant, determined, firm[1], resolute, steadfast, steady, stiff, tough, uncompromising, unflinching, unwavering, unyielding. *See* PURPOSE.

unbiased *adjective*
1. Free from bias in judgment : disinterested, dispassionate, equitable, fair, fair-minded, impartial, indifferent, just, nonpartisan, objective, square, unprejudiced. ***Idiom:*** fair and square. *See* FAIR. **2.** Not inclining toward or actively taking either side in a matter under dispute : impartial, neuter, neutral, nonaligned, nonpartisan, uncommitted, uninvolved, unprejudiced. ***Idiom:*** on the fence. *See* FAIR.

unbind *verb*
To free from ties or fasteners : disengage, loose, loosen, slip, unclasp, undo, unfasten, unloose, unloosen, untie. *See* TIGHTEN.

unblamable also **unblameable** *adjective*
1. Free from guilt or blame : blameless, faultless, guiltless, harmless, innocent, irreproachable, lily-white. *Slang:* clean. ***Idiom:*** in the clear. *See* RIGHT. **2.** Beyond reproach : blameless, exemplary, good, irreprehensible, irreproachable, lily-white. *See* RIGHT.

unblameable *adjective* See **unblamable.**

unblemished *adjective*
1. Free from flaws or blemishes : clear, flawless, unmarked. *See* BEAUTIFUL. **2.** In excellent condition : entire, flawless, good, intact, perfect, sound[2], unbroken, undamaged, unharmed, unhurt, unimpaired, uninjured, unmarred, whole. *See* THRIVE. **3.** Free from evil and corruption : angelic, angelical, clean, innocent, lily-white, pure, sinless, uncorrupted, undefiled, unstained, unsullied, untainted, virginal. ***Idiom:*** pure as the driven snow. *See* CLEAN, RIGHT, SEX.

unblended or **unblent** *adjective*
Not diluted or mixed with other substances : full-strength, neat, plain, pure, straight, undiluted, unmixed. *See* CLEAN, STRONG.

unblent *adjective* See **unblended.**

unblock *verb*
To rid of obstructions : clear, free, open. *See* OPEN.

unblocked *adjective*
Free from obstructions : clear, free, open, unimpeded, unobstructed. *See* OPEN.

unblushing *adjective*
Characterized by or done without shame : bald-faced, barefaced, blatant, brazen, brazen-faced, shameless, unabashed. *Informal:* brassy. *See* COURTESY, RESPECT, RIGHT.

unbodied *adjective*
Having no body, form, or substance : bodiless, discarnate, disembodied, immaterial, incorporeal, insubstantial, metaphysical, nonphysical, spiritual, uncorporal, unsubstantial. *See* BODY.

unbounded *adjective*
1. Having no ends or limits : boundless, endless, illimitable, immeasurable, infinite, limitless, measureless, unlimited. *See* LIMITED.
2. Completely such, without qualification or exception : absolute, all-out, arrant, complete, consummate, crashing, damned, dead, downright, flat, out-and-out, outright, perfect, plain, pure, sheer[2], thorough, thoroughgoing, total, unequivocal, unlimited, unmitigated, unqualified, unrelieved, unreserved, utter[2]. *Informal:*

flat-out, positive. *Chiefly British:* blooming. *See* BIG, LIMITED.

unboundedness *noun*
The state or quality of being infinite : boundlessness, immeasurability, immeasurableness, inexhaustibility, inexhaustibleness, infiniteness, infinity, limitlessness, measurelessness, unlimitedness. *See* LIMITED.

unbridled *adjective*
Lacking in moral restraint : abandoned, dissipated, dissolute, fast, gay, incontinent, licentious, profligate, rakish, unconstrained, uncontrolled, ungoverned, uninhibited, unrestrained, wanton, wild. *See* RESTRAINT.

unbroken *adjective*
In excellent condition : entire, flawless, good, intact, perfect, sound[2], unblemished, undamaged, unharmed, unhurt, unimpaired, uninjured, unmarred, whole. *See* THRIVE.

unburden *verb*
To free from or cast out something objectionable or undesirable : clear, disburden, disembarrass, disencumber, release, relieve, rid, shake off, throw off. *Slang:* shake. *See* KEEP.

uncalled-for *adjective*
1. Not necessary : dispensable, inessential, needless, nonessential, unessential, unnecessary, unneeded, unrequired. *See* NECESSARY. **2.** Not required, necessary, or warranted by the circumstances of the case : gratuitous, supererogative, supererogatory, wanton. *See* NECESSARY.

uncanny *adjective*
Of a mysteriously strange and usually frightening nature : eerie, unearthly, weird. *Informal:* spooky. *See* FEAR, USUAL.

uncaring *adjective*
Not sympathetic : uncharitable, uncompassionate, unmoved, unpitying, unstirred, unsympathetic, untouched. *See* FEELINGS.

unceasing *adjective*
Existing or occurring without interruption or end : around-the-clock, ceaseless, constant, continual, continuous, endless, eternal, everlasting, incessant, interminable, nonstop, ongoing, perpetual, persistent, relentless, round-the-clock, timeless, unending, unfailing, uninterrupted, unremitting. *See* CONTINUE.

uncensored *adjective*
Not shortened by omissions : complete, unabbreviated, unabridged, uncut, unexpurgated. *See* PART.

unceremonious *adjective*
Unconstrained by rigid standards or ceremony : casual, easy, easygoing, informal, natural, relaxed, spontaneous, unrestrained. *Informal:* laid-back. *See* PLAIN, TIGHTEN.

unceremoniousness *noun*
Freedom from constraint, formality, embarrassment, or awkwardness : casualness, ease, easiness, informality, naturalness, poise, spontaneity, unrestraint. *See* RESTRAINT, TIGHTEN.

uncertain *adjective*
1. Not affording certainty : ambiguous, borderline, chancy, clouded, doubtful, dubious, dubitable, equivocal, inconclusive, indecisive, indeterminate, problematic, problematical, questionable, unclear, unsure. *Informal:* iffy. ***Idioms:*** at issue, in doubt, in question. *See* CERTAIN, CLEAR. **2.** In doubt or dispute : arguable, contested, debatable, disputable, doubtful, exceptionable, moot, mootable, problematic, problematical, questionable. *See* CERTAIN. **3.** Liable to more than one interpretation : ambiguous, cloudy, equivocal, inexplicit, nebulous, obscure, unclear, vague. *See* CERTAIN, CLEAR. **4.** Of dubious character : doubtful, equivocal, questionable, shady, suspect, suspicious. *Informal:* fishy. *See* HONEST. **5.** Marked by lack of firm decision or commitment; of questionable outcome : indefinite, open, undecided, undetermined, unresolved, unsettled, unsure, vague. ***Idiom:*** up in the air. *See* CERTAIN. **6.** Experiencing doubt : doubtful, dubious, skeptical, undecided, unsure. ***Idiom:*** in doubt. *See* CERTAIN. **7.** Capable of or liable to change : alterable, changeable, fluid, inconstant, mutable, unsettled, unstable, unsteady, variable, variant. *Archaic:* various. *See* CHANGE. **8.** Following no predictable pattern : capricious, changeable, erratic, fantastic, fantastical, fickle, freakish, inconsistent, inconstant, mercurial, temperamental, ticklish, unpredictable, unstable, unsteady, variable, volatile, whimsical. *See* CHANGE, CONTINUE.

uncertainty *noun*
1. The quality or state of being ambiguous : ambiguity, ambiguousness, cloudiness, equivocalness, indefiniteness, nebulousness, obscureness, obscurity, unclearness, vagueness. *See* CLEAR. **2.** A lack of conviction or certainty : doubt, doubtfulness, dubiety, dubiousness, incertitude, mistrust, question, skepticism, suspicion, wonder. *See* CERTAIN.

unchangeable *adjective*
Incapable of changing or being modified : immutable, inalterable, inflexible, invariable, ironclad, rigid, unalterable. *See* FLEXIBLE.

unchanging *adjective*
1. Remaining continually unchanged : changeless, consistent, constant, invariable, same, unfailing. *See* CHANGE. **2.** Having no change or variation : changeless, constant, equable, even[1], invariable, invariant, regular, same, steady, uniform, unvarying. *See* SAME.

uncharitable *adjective*
Not sympathetic : uncaring, uncompassionate, unmoved, unpitying, unstirred, unsympathetic, untouched. *See* FEELINGS.

unchaste *adjective*
Not chaste or moral : immoral, impure, unclean, uncleanly. *See* GOOD, RESTRAINT, SEX.

uncivil *adjective*
1. Lacking good manners : discourteous, disrespectful, ill-bred, ill-mannered, impolite, rude, ungracious, unmannerly, unpolished. *See* COURTESY. **2.** *Archaic.* Not civilized : barbarian, barbaric, barbarous, primitive, rude, savage, uncivilized, uncultivated, uncultured, wild. *See* CULTURE, WILD.

uncivilized *adjective*
1. Not civilized : barbarian, barbaric, barbarous, primitive, rude, savage, uncultivated, uncultured, wild. *Archaic:* uncivil. *See* CULTURE, WILD. **2.** Lacking in delicacy or refinement : barbarian, barbaric, boorish, churlish, coarse, crass, crude, gross, ill-bred, indelicate, philistine, rough, rude, tasteless, uncouth, uncultivated, uncultured, unpolished, unrefined, vulgar. *See* COURTESY, SMOOTH.

unclad *adjective*
Not wearing any clothes : au naturel, bare, naked, nude. *Chiefly British:* starkers. ***Idioms:*** in one's birthday suit, in the altogether (*or* buff *or* raw), naked as a jaybird, stark naked, without a stitch. *See* PUT ON, SHOW.

unclasp *verb*
To free from ties or fasteners : disengage, loose, loosen, slip, unbind, undo, unfasten, unloose, unloosen, untie. *See* TIGHTEN.

unclean *adjective*
1. Covered or stained with or as if with dirt or other impurities : black, dirty, filthy, grimy, grubby, smutty, soiled, uncleanly. *See* CLEAN. **2.** Not chaste or moral : immoral, impure, unchaste, uncleanly. *See* GOOD, RESTRAINT, SEX. **3.** Ceremonially or religiously unfit : impure. *See* CLEAN, RELIGION, SACRED.

uncleanliness *noun*
The condition or state of being dirty : dirtiness, filth, filthiness, foulness, griminess, grubbiness, smuttiness, squalor, uncleanness. *See* CLEAN.

uncleanly *adjective*
1. Covered or stained with or as if with dirt or other impurities : black, dirty, filthy, grimy, grubby, smutty, soiled, unclean. *See* CLEAN. **2.** Not chaste or moral : immoral, impure, unchaste, unclean. *See* GOOD, RESTRAINT, SEX.

uncleanness *noun*
1. The condition or state of being dirty : dirtiness, filth, filthiness, foulness, griminess, grubbiness, smuttiness, squalor, uncleanliness. *See* CLEAN. **2.** Impure condition : defilement, dirtiness, foulness, impurity, pollution, unwholesomeness. *See* CLEAN.

unclear *adjective*
1. Liable to more than one interpretation : ambiguous, cloudy, equivocal, inexplicit, nebulous, obscure, uncertain, vague. *See* CERTAIN, CLEAR. **2.** Not affording certainty : ambiguous, borderline, chancy, clouded, doubtful, dubious, dubitable, equivocal, inconclusive, indecisive, indeterminate, problematic, problematical, questionable, uncertain, unsure. *Informal:* iffy. ***Idioms:*** at issue, in doubt, in question. *See* CERTAIN, CLEAR. **3.** Not clearly perceived or perceptible : blear, bleary, cloudy, dim, faint, foggy, fuzzy, hazy, indefinite, indistinct, misty, obscure, shadowy, undistinct, vague. *See* CLEAR.

unclearness *noun*
The quality or state of being ambiguous : ambiguity, ambiguousness, cloudiness, equivocalness, indefiniteness, nebulousness, obscureness, obscurity, uncertainty, vagueness. *See* CLEAR.

unclose *verb*
To become or cause to become open : open, undo. *See* OPEN.

unclothe *verb*
1. To remove all the clothing from : disrobe, strip[1], undress. *See* PUT ON, SHOW. **2.** To make visible; bring to view : bare, disclose, display, expose, reveal, show, uncover, unmask, unveil. *Archaic:* discover. ***Idioms:*** bring to light, lay open, make plain. *See* SHOW.

unclouded *adjective*
Free from clouds or mist, for example : clear, cloudless, fair, fine[1], sunny. *See* CLEAR.

uncomely *adjective*
Not handsome or beautiful : homely, plain, unattractive, unlovely. ***Idioms:*** not much for looks, not much to look at, short on looks. *See* BEAUTIFUL.

uncomfortable *adjective*
1. Characterized by embarrassment and dis-

comfort : awkward, constrained, uneasy. *See* FEELINGS. **2.** Causing discomfort : comfortless, uncomforting. *Informal:* uncomfy. *See* COMFORT.

uncomforting *adjective*
Causing discomfort : comfortless, uncomfortable. *Informal:* uncomfy. *See* COMFORT.

uncomfy *adjective*
Informal. Causing discomfort : comfortless, uncomfortable, uncomforting. *See* COMFORT.

uncommitted *adjective*
Not inclining toward or actively taking either side in a matter under dispute : impartial, neuter, neutral, nonaligned, nonpartisan, unbiased, uninvolved, unprejudiced. ***Idiom:*** on the fence. *See* FAIR.

uncommon *adjective*
1. Rarely occurring or appearing : infrequent, occasional, rare, scarce, sporadic, unusual. ***Idiom:*** few and far between. *See* USUAL. **2.** Far beyond what is usual, normal, or customary : exceptional, extraordinary, magnificent, outstanding, preeminent, rare, remarkable, singular, towering, unusual. *Informal:* standout. *Slang:* awesome, out of sight. *See* BETTER, USUAL.

uncommonly *adverb*
In a manner or to a degree that is unusual : exceptionally, extraordinarily, remarkably, singularly, unusually. *See* USUAL.

uncommunicable *adjective*
Not speaking freely or openly : close, closemouthed, incommunicable, incommunicative, reserved, reticent, silent, taciturn, tightlipped, uncommunicative. *See* RESTRAINT, SOUNDS.

uncommunicative *adjective*
1. Not speaking freely or openly : close, closemouthed, incommunicable, incommunicative, reserved, reticent, silent, taciturn, tightlipped, uncommunicable. *See* RESTRAINT, SOUNDS. **2.** Not friendly, sociable, or warm in manner : aloof, chill, chilly, cool, distant, offish, remote, reserved, reticent, solitary, standoffish, unapproachable, undemonstrative, withdrawn. *See* ATTITUDE, HOT.

uncommunicativeness *noun*
The keeping of one's thoughts and emotions to oneself : control, reserve, restraint, reticence, self-control, self-restraint, taciturnity. *See* RESTRAINT.

uncompassionate *adjective*
Not sympathetic : uncaring, uncharitable, unmoved, unpitying, unstirred, unsympathetic, untouched. *See* FEELINGS.

uncompelled *adjective*
Done by one's own choice : free, spontaneous, unforced, volitional, voluntary, willful. *See* WILLING.

uncompensated *adjective*
Contributing one's time without pay : unpaid, unrecompensed, unremunerated, unsalaried, voluntary. *See* PAY, WORK.

uncompliant *adjective*
Firmly, often unreasonably immovable in purpose or will : adamant, adamantine, brassbound, die-hard, grim, implacable, incompliant, inexorable, inflexible, intransigent, iron, obdurate, relentless, remorseless, rigid, stubborn, unbendable, unbending, uncompromising, unrelenting, unyielding. ***Idiom:*** stubborn as a mule (*or* ox). *See* RESIST.

uncomplimentary *adjective*
Tending or intending to belittle : deprecative, deprecatory, depreciative, depreciatory, derogative, derogatory, detractive, disparaging, low, pejorative, slighting. *See* PRAISE.

uncomprehending *adjective*
Unwilling or unable to perceive : blind, dull, purblind, unperceptive. *See* SEE.

uncomprehensible *adjective*
Incapable of being grasped by the intellect or understanding : impenetrable, incomprehensible, inscrutable, unfathomable, unintelligible. *See* KNOWLEDGE.

uncompromising *adjective*
1. Firmly, often unreasonably immovable in purpose or will : adamant, adamantine, brassbound, die-hard, grim, implacable, incompliant, inexorable, inflexible, intransigent, iron, obdurate, relentless, remorseless, rigid, stubborn, unbendable, unbending, uncompliant, unrelenting, unyielding. ***Idiom:*** stubborn as a mule (*or* ox). *See* RESIST. **2.** Indicating or possessing determination, resolution, or persistence : constant, determined, firm[1], resolute, steadfast, steady, stiff, tough, unbending, unflinching, unwavering, unyielding. *See* PURPOSE. **3.** Conforming completely to established rule : exact, rigorous, strict. *See* USUAL.

unconceivable *adjective*
Not plausible or believable : flimsy, implausible, improbable, inconceivable, incredible, shaky, thin, unbelievable, unconvincing, unsubstantial, weak. *See* LIKELY.

unconcern *noun*
Lack of emotion or interest : apathy, disinterest, impassivity, incuriosity, incuriousness, indifference, insensibility, insensibleness, lassitude, lethargy, listlessness, phlegm, stolidity,

stolidness, uninterest, unresponsiveness. *See* FEELINGS.

unconcerned *adjective*

1. Without emotion or interest : apathetic, detached, impassive, incurious, indifferent, insensible, lethargic, listless, phlegmatic, stolid, uninterested, unresponsive. *See* FEELINGS. **2.** Lacking interest in one's surroundings or worldly affairs : aloof, detached, disinterested, incurious, indifferent, uninterested, uninvolved. *See* ATTITUDE, CONCERN. **3.** Lacking or marked by a lack of care : careless, feckless, heedless, inattentive, irresponsible, reckless, thoughtless, unmindful, unthinking. *See* CAREFUL. **4.** Showing no concern, attention, or regard : careless, forgetful, heedless, mindless, unheeding, unmindful, unobservant, unthinking. *See* CAREFUL.

unconditional *adjective*

1. Without limitations or mitigating conditions : absolute, unconditioned, unqualified, unreserved. *See* LIMITED. **2.** Having no reservations : absolute, implicit, undoubting, unfaltering, unhesitating, unquestioning, unreserved, wholehearted. *See* BIG, LIMITED.

unconditioned *adjective*

Without limitations or mitigating conditions : absolute, unconditional, unqualified, unreserved. *See* LIMITED.

unconfined *adjective*

Able to move about at will without bounds or restraint : free, loose, unrestrained. ***Idioms:*** at large, at liberty, free as a bird, on the loose. *See* FREE.

uncongenial *adjective*

1. Devoid of harmony and accord : discordant, inconsonant, inharmonious, unharmonious. *See* AGREE. **2.** Not pleasant or agreeable : bad, disagreeable, displeasing, offensive, unpleasant, unsympathetic. *Informal:* icky. *Slang:* yucky. *See* GOOD, PAIN.

unconquerable *adjective*

Incapable of being conquered, overrun, or subjugated : impregnable, indomitable, invincible. *See* DO, WIN.

unconscionable *adjective*

1. Lacking scruples or principles : conscienceless, ruthless, unethical, unprincipled, unscrupulous. *See* HONEST. **2.** Beyond all reason : obscene, outrageous, preposterous, ridiculous, shocking, unreasonable. ***Idioms:*** out of bounds, out of sight. *See* USUAL. **3.** Vastly exceeding a normal limit, as in cost : sky-high, steep[1], stiff, stratospheric. *See* BIG, USUAL.

unconscious *adjective*

1. Lacking consciousness : cold, insensible, senseless. ***Idioms:*** out cold, out like a light. *See* AWARENESS. **2.** Not aware or informed : ignorant, innocent, oblivious, unacquainted, unaware, unenlightened, unfamiliar, uninformed, unknowing, unwitting. ***Idiom:*** in the dark. *See* KNOWLEDGE.

unconsciousness *noun*

The condition of being uninformed or unaware : ignorance, innocence, nescience, obliviousness, unawareness, unfamiliarity. *See* KNOWLEDGE.

unconsidered *adjective*

Characterized by unthinking boldness and haste : brash, foolhardy, harum-scarum, hasty, headlong, hotheaded, ill-considered, impetuous, improvident, impulsive, incautious, madcap, precipitant, precipitate, rash[1], reckless, slapdash, temerarious. *See* CAREFUL.

unconspicuous *adjective*

Not readily noticed or seen : inconspicuous, obscure, unnoticeable, unobtrusive. ***Idiom:*** having (*or* keeping) a low profile. *See* SEE.

unconstrained *adjective*

Lacking in moral restraint : abandoned, dissipated, dissolute, fast, gay, incontinent, licentious, profligate, rakish, unbridled, uncontrolled, ungoverned, uninhibited, unrestrained, wanton, wild. *See* RESTRAINT.

uncontrollability *noun*

The quality or condition of being unruly : disorderliness, fractiousness, indocility, intractability, intractableness, obstinacy, obstinateness, obstreperousness, recalcitrance, recalcitrancy, refractoriness, uncontrollableness, ungovernableness, unmanageability, unruliness, untowardness, wildness. *See* CONTROL, ORDER, PEACE, RESIST.

uncontrollable *adjective*

Not submitting to discipline or control : disorderly, fractious, indocile, intractable, lawless, obstinate, obstreperous, recalcitrant, refractory, undisciplined, ungovernable, unmanageable, unruly, untoward, wild. ***Idiom:*** out of line. *See* CONTROL, ORDER, PEACE, RESIST.

uncontrollableness *noun*

The quality or condition of being unruly : disorderliness, fractiousness, indocility, intractability, intractableness, obstinacy, obstinateness, obstreperousness, recalcitrance, recalcitrancy, refractoriness, uncontrollability, ungovernableness, unmanageability, unruliness, untowardness, wildness. *See* CONTROL, ORDER, PEACE, RESIST.

uncontrolled *adjective*
1. Out of control : amuck, runaway. ***Idioms:*** out of hand, running wild. *See* CONTROL. **2.** Lacking in moral restraint : abandoned, dissipated, dissolute, fast, gay, incontinent, licentious, profligate, rakish, unbridled, unconstrained, ungoverned, uninhibited, unrestrained, wanton, wild. *See* RESTRAINT.

unconventional *adjective*
Not usual or ordinary : atypic, atypical, novel, unordinary, unusual, unwonted. *Slang:* offbeat. *See* USUAL.

unconvincing *adjective*
Not plausible or believable : flimsy, implausible, improbable, inconceivable, incredible, shaky, thin, unbelievable, unconceivable, unsubstantial, weak. *See* LIKELY.

uncooked *adjective*
Not cooked : raw. *See* INGESTION.

uncorporal *adjective*
Having no body, form, or substance : bodiless, discarnate, disembodied, immaterial, incorporeal, insubstantial, metaphysical, nonphysical, spiritual, unbodied, unsubstantial. *See* BODY.

uncorrupted *adjective*
Free from evil and corruption : angelic, angelical, clean, innocent, lily-white, pure, sinless, unblemished, undefiled, unstained, unsullied, untainted, virginal. ***Idiom:*** pure as the driven snow. *See* CLEAN, RIGHT, SEX.

uncountable *adjective*
Too great to be calculated : countless, immeasurable, incalculable, incomputable, inestimable, infinite, innumerable, measureless. *See* BIG.

uncouple *verb*
To separate one thing from another thing : detach, disconnect, disengage. *See* ASSEMBLE.

uncoupling *noun*
The act or process of detaching : detachment, disconnection, disengagement, separation. *See* ASSEMBLE.

uncouth *adjective*
Lacking in delicacy or refinement : barbarian, barbaric, boorish, churlish, coarse, crass, crude, gross, ill-bred, indelicate, philistine, rough, rude, tasteless, uncivilized, uncultivated, uncultured, unpolished, unrefined, vulgar. *See* COURTESY, SMOOTH.

uncover *verb*
1. To make bare : bare, denude, disrobe, divest, expose, strip[1]. *See* PUT ON. **2.** To make visible; bring to view : bare, disclose, display, expose, reveal, show, unclothe, unmask, unveil. *Archaic:* discover. ***Idioms:*** bring to light, lay open, make plain. *See* SHOW. **3.** To find by investigation : dig (out *or* up), turn up, unearth. *See* SHOW. **4.** To disclose in a breach of confidence : betray, blab, divulge, expose, give away, let out, reveal, tell, unveil. *Informal:* spill. *Archaic:* discover. ***Idioms:*** let slip, let the cat out of the bag, spill the beans, tell all. *See* SHOW.

uncovered *adjective*
Having no protecting or concealing cover : exposed, open, unprotected. *See* PROTECTION.

uncreative *adjective*
Lacking originality : sterile, unimaginative, uninspired, uninventive, unoriginal. *See* RICH.

uncritical *adjective*
Lacking in intellectual depth or thoroughness : cursory, one-dimensional, shallow, sketchy, skin-deep, superficial. *See* SURFACE.

unctuous *adjective*
1. Affectedly and self-servingly earnest : fulsome, oily, oleaginous, sleek, smarmy. *See* ATTITUDE, HONEST. **2.** Having the qualities of fat : adipose, fat, fatty, greasy, oily, oleaginous. *See* FAT.

uncultivated *adjective*
1. In a primitive state; not domesticated or cultivated; produced by nature : native, natural, rough, undomesticated, untamed, wild. *See* WILD. **2.** Not civilized : barbarian, barbaric, barbarous, primitive, rude, savage, uncivilized, uncultured, wild. *Archaic:* uncivil. *See* CULTURE, WILD. **3.** Lacking in delicacy or refinement : barbarian, barbaric, boorish, churlish, coarse, crass, crude, gross, ill-bred, indelicate, philistine, rough, rude, tasteless, uncivilized, uncouth, uncultured, unpolished, unrefined, vulgar. *See* COURTESY, SMOOTH.

uncultured *adjective*
1. Not civilized : barbarian, barbaric, barbarous, primitive, rude, savage, uncivilized, uncultivated, wild. *Archaic:* uncivil. *See* CULTURE, WILD. **2.** Lacking in delicacy or refinement : barbarian, barbaric, boorish, churlish, coarse, crass, crude, gross, ill-bred, indelicate, philistine, rough, rude, tasteless, uncivilized, uncouth, uncultivated, unpolished, unrefined, vulgar. *See* COURTESY, SMOOTH.

uncut *adjective*
Not shortened by omissions : complete, unabbreviated, unabridged, uncensored, unexpurgated. *See* PART.

undamaged *adjective*
In excellent condition : entire, flawless, good, intact, perfect, sound[2], unblemished, unbroken, unharmed, unhurt, unimpaired, uninjured, unmarred, whole. *See* THRIVE.

undaunted *adjective*
Having or showing courage : audacious, bold, brave, courageous, dauntless, doughty, fearless, fortitudinous, gallant, game, hardy, heroic, intrepid, mettlesome, plucky, stout, stouthearted, unafraid, valiant, valorous. *Informal:* spunky. *Slang:* gutsy, gutty. *See* FEAR.

undauntedness *noun*
The quality of mind enabling one to face danger or hardship resolutely : braveness, bravery, courage, courageousness, dauntlessness, doughtiness, fearlessness, fortitude, gallantry, gameness, heart, intrepidity, intrepidness, mettle, nerve, pluck, pluckiness, spirit, stoutheartedness, valiance, valiancy, valiantness, valor. *Informal:* spunk, spunkiness. *Slang:* gut (used in plural), gutsiness, moxie. *See* FEAR.

undecided *adjective*
1. Marked by lack of firm decision or commitment; of questionable outcome : indefinite, open, uncertain, undetermined, unresolved, unsettled, unsure, vague. *Idiom:* up in the air. *See* CERTAIN. **2.** Experiencing doubt : doubtful, dubious, skeptical, uncertain, unsure. *Idiom:* in doubt. *See* CERTAIN.

undeclared *adjective*
Not voiced or expressed : silent, tacit, unexpressed, unsaid, unspoken, unuttered, unvoiced, wordless. *See* WORDS.

undefiled *adjective*
Free from evil and corruption : angelic, angelical, clean, innocent, lily-white, pure, sinless, unblemished, uncorrupted, unstained, unsullied, untainted, virginal. *Idiom:* pure as the driven snow. *See* CLEAN, RIGHT, SEX.

undemonstrated *adjective*
Not tested or proved : unpracticed, unproved, untested, untried. *See* ABILITY, KNOWLEDGE.

undemonstrative *adjective*
Not friendly, sociable, or warm in manner : aloof, chill, chilly, cool, distant, offish, remote, reserved, reticent, solitary, standoffish, unapproachable, uncommunicative, withdrawn. *See* ATTITUDE, HOT.

undeniable *adjective*
Established beyond a doubt : certain, hard, inarguable, incontestable, incontrovertible, indisputable, indubitable, irrefutable, positive, sure, unassailable, undisputable, unquestionable. *See* CERTAIN, TRUE.

undependable *adjective*
1. Not to be depended on : unreliable, untrustworthy. *See* TRUST. **2.** So weak or defective as to be liable to fail : trick, unreliable. *See* STRONG.

under *adjective*
1. Not enough to meet a demand or requirement : deficient, inadequate, insufficient, scarce, short, shy[1], wanting. *See* BIG, EXCESS. **2.** Below another in standing or importance : inferior, junior, lesser, low, lower[2], minor, minor-league, petty, secondary, small, subaltern, subordinate. *Informal:* smalltime. *See* OVER.

underage[1] *noun*
The condition or fact of being deficient : defect, deficiency, deficit, inadequacy, insufficiency, lack, paucity, poverty, scantiness, scantness, scarceness, scarcity, shortage, shortcoming, shortfall. *See* EXCESS.

underage[2] *adjective*
Not yet a legal adult : *Law:* minor. *See* LAW, YOUTH.

undercover *adjective*
Existing or operating in a way so as to ensure complete concealment and confidentiality : clandestine, cloak-and-dagger, covert, hugger-mugger, secret, sub-rosa. *Informal:* hush-hush. *Idiom:* under wraps. *See* SHOW.

undercurrent *noun*
A subtle quality underlying or felt to underlie a situation, action, or person : hint, implication, inkling, suspicion, undertone. *See* SHOW, SUGGEST.

underdeveloped *adjective*
Not progressing and developing as fast as others, as in economic and social aspects : backward, lagging, undeveloped. *See* PRECEDE.

underdog *noun*
A person living under very unhappy circumstances : loser, miserable, underprivileged, unfortunate, wretch. *See* RICH.

undergo *verb*
To participate in or partake of personally : experience, feel, go through, have, know, meet[1] (with), see, suffer, taste (of). *Archaic:* prove. *Idiom:* run up against. *See* PARTICIPATE.

underground *adjective*
Located or operating beneath the earth's surface : hypogeal, hypogean, hypogeous, subterranean, subterrestrial. *See* SURFACE.
underground *noun* A clandestine organization of freedom fighters in an oppressed land : resistance. *See* RESIST.

underhand *adjective*
Marked by treachery or deceit : devious, disingenuous, duplicitous, guileful, indirect, lubricious, shifty, sneaky, underhanded. *See* HONEST.

underhanded *adjective*
Marked by treachery or deceit : devious, disingenuous, duplicitous, guileful, indirect, lubricious, shifty, sneaky, underhand. *See* HONEST.

underhandedness *noun*
Lack of straightforwardness and honesty in action : chicanery, craft, craftiness, deviousness, dishonesty, indirection, shadiness, shiftiness, slyness, sneakiness, trickery, trickiness. *See* HONEST.

underline *verb*
To accord emphasis to : accent, accentuate, emphasize, feature, highlight, italicize, play up, point up, stress, underscore. *See* IMPORTANT.

underling *noun*
One belonging to a lower class or rank : inferior, junior, secondary, subaltern, subordinate. *See* OVER.

underlying *adjective*
1. Arising from or going to the root or source : basal, basic, foundational, fundamental, original, primary, radical. *See* SURFACE. **2.** Of or being an irreducible element : basic, elemental, elementary, essential, fundamental, primitive, ultimate. *See* SURFACE.

undermanned *adjective*
Lacking the requisite workers or players : shorthanded. *See* EXCESS.

undermine *verb*
1. To lessen or deplete the nerve, energy, or strength of : attenuate, debilitate, devitalize, enervate, enfeeble, sap[2], undo, unnerve, weaken. *See* STRONG. **2.** To damage, destroy, or defeat by sabotage : sabotage, subvert. *See* ATTACK.

undermining *noun*
A deliberate and underhanded effort to defeat or do harm to an endeavor : sabotage, subversion. *See* ATTACK.

undermost *adjective*
Opposite to or farthest from the top : bottom, lowermost, lowest, nethermost. *See* OVER.

underneath *noun*
A side or surface that is below or under : bottom, underside, undersurface. *See* OVER.

underpin *verb*
To provide a basis for : base[1], build, establish, found, ground, predicate, rest[1], root[1]. *See* OVER.

underpinning *noun*
1. A means or device that keeps something erect, stable, or secure : brace, buttress, crutch, prop, shore, stay[2], support. *See* SUPPORT.
2. The lowest or supporting part or structure. Often used in plural : base[1], basis, bed, bottom, foot, footing, foundation, fundament, ground, groundwork, seat, substratum. *See* OVER. **3.** That on which something immaterial, such as an argument or a charge, rests. Often used in plural : base[1], basis, footing, foundation, fundament, ground (often used in plural), groundwork. *See* OVER.

underprivileged *adjective*
Economically and socially below standard : backward, depressed, deprived, disadvantaged, impoverished. *See* RICH.
underprivileged *noun* A person living under very unhappy circumstances : loser, miserable, underdog, unfortunate, wretch. *See* RICH.

underscore *verb*
To accord emphasis to : accent, accentuate, emphasize, feature, highlight, italicize, play up, point up, stress, underline. *See* IMPORTANT.

underside *noun*
A side or surface that is below or under : bottom, underneath, undersurface. *See* OVER.

undersign *verb*
To affix one's signature to : autograph, endorse, inscribe, sign, subscribe. ***Idioms:*** put one's John Hancock on, set one's hand to. *See* LAW.

understand *verb*
1. To perceive directly with the intellect : apprehend, compass, comprehend, fathom, grasp, know. *Scots:* ken. *See* KNOWLEDGE.
2. To perceive and recognize the meaning of : accept, apprehend, catch (on), compass, comprehend, conceive, fathom, follow, get, grasp, make out, read, see, sense, take, take in. *Informal:* savvy. *Slang:* dig. *Chiefly British:* twig. *Scots:* ken. ***Idioms:*** get (*or* have) a handle on, get the picture. *See* UNDERSTAND. **3.** To arrive at (a conclusion) from evidence or reasoning : conclude, deduce, deduct, draw, gather, infer, judge. *See* REASON.

understandable *adjective*
Capable of being readily understood : comprehensible, fathomable, intelligible, knowable. *See* KNOWLEDGE.

understanding *noun*
1. Intellectual hold : apprehension, comprehension, grasp, grip, hold. *Informal:* savvy. *See* KNOWLEDGE. **2.** The faculty of thinking, reasoning, and acquiring and applying knowledge : brain (often used in plural), brainpower, intellect, intelligence, mentality, mind, sense, wit. *Slang:* smart (used in plural). *See* ABILITY, THOUGHTS. **3.** An act or state of agreeing between parties regarding a course of action :

accord, agreement, arrangement, bargain, compact[2], deal, pact. *See* AGREE.

understanding *adjective* Cognizant of and comprehending the needs, feelings, problems, and views of others : empathetic, empathic, feeling, sympathetic. *See* UNDERSTAND.

understood *adjective*
Conveyed indirectly without words or speech : implicit, implied, inferred, tacit, unsaid, unspoken, unuttered, wordless. ***Idiom:*** taken for granted. *See* SHOW.

undersurface *noun*
A side or surface that is below or under : bottom, underneath, underside. *See* OVER.

undertake *verb*
1. To take upon oneself : assume, incur, shoulder, tackle, take on, take over. *See* ACCEPT.
2. To assume an obligation : contract, engage, pledge, promise. *See* AGREE, OBLIGATION.
3. To go about the initial step in doing (something) : approach, begin, commence, embark, enter, get off, inaugurate, initiate, institute, launch, lead off, open, set about, set out, set to, start, take on, take up. *Informal:* kick off. ***Idioms:*** get cracking, get going, get the show on the road. *See* START.

undertaking *noun*
Something undertaken, especially something requiring extensive planning and work : enterprise, project, venture. *See* WORK.

undertone *noun*
A subtle quality underlying or felt to underlie a situation, action, or person : hint, implication, inkling, suspicion, undercurrent. *See* SHOW, SUGGEST.

underwriter *noun*
One who assumes financial responsibility for another : backer, guarantor, guaranty, sponsor, surety. *Informal:* angel. *See* LAW, SUPPORT.

undescribable *adjective*
That cannot be described : incommunicable, indefinable, indescribable, ineffable, inexpressible, unspeakable, unutterable. ***Idioms:*** beyond description (*or* words), defying description. *See* WORDS.

undesigned *adjective*
Not intended : inadvertent, undevised, unintended, unintentional, unmeant, unplanned, unwitting. *See* PLANNED.

undesirable *adjective*
1. Arousing disapproval : exceptionable, ill-favored, inadmissible, objectionable, unacceptable, unwanted, unwelcome. *See* LIKE. **2.** Not welcome or wanted : undesired, uninvited, unsought, unwanted, unwelcome, unwished-for. *See* LIKE.

undesired *adjective*
Not welcome or wanted : undesirable, uninvited, unsought, unwanted, unwelcome, unwished-for. *See* LIKE.

undetected *adjective*
Not found : undiscovered, unexposed, unfound. *See* KNOWLEDGE.

undetermined *adjective*
1. Marked by lack of firm decision or commitment; of questionable outcome : indefinite, open, uncertain, undecided, unresolved, unsettled, unsure, vague. ***Idiom:*** up in the air. *See* CERTAIN. **2.** Lacking precise limits : indefinite, indeterminate, inexact. *See* LIMITED.

undeveloped *adjective*
Not progressing and developing as fast as others, as in economic and social aspects : backward, lagging, underdeveloped. *See* PRECEDE.

undevised *adjective*
Not intended : inadvertent, undesigned, unintended, unintentional, unmeant, unplanned, unwitting. *See* PLANNED.

undiluted *adjective*
1. Free from extraneous elements : absolute, perfect, plain, pure, sheer[2], simple, unadulterated, unmixed. *See* CLEAN. **2.** Not diluted or mixed with other substances : full-strength, neat, plain, pure, straight, unblended, unmixed. *See* CLEAN, STRONG.

undiplomatic *adjective*
Lacking sensitivity and skill in dealing with others : brash, clumsy, gauche, impolitic, indelicate, maladroit, tactless, unpolitic, untactful. *See* ABILITY, COURTESY.

undisciplined *adjective*
Not submitting to discipline or control : disorderly, fractious, indocile, intractable, lawless, obstinate, obstreperous, recalcitrant, refractory, uncontrollable, ungovernable, unmanageable, unruly, untoward, wild. ***Idiom:*** out of line. *See* CONTROL, ORDER, PEACE, RESIST.

undiscovered *adjective*
Not found : undetected, unexposed, unfound. *See* KNOWLEDGE.

undisputable *adjective*
Established beyond a doubt : certain, hard, inarguable, incontestable, incontrovertible, indisputable, indubitable, irrefutable, positive, sure, unassailable, undeniable, unquestionable. *See* CERTAIN, TRUE.

undistinct *adjective*
Not clearly perceived or perceptible : blear, bleary, cloudy, dim, faint, foggy, fuzzy, hazy,

indefinite, indistinct, misty, obscure, shadowy, unclear, vague. *See* CLEAR.

undistinguished *adjective*
Being of no special quality or type : average, common, commonplace, cut-and-dried, formulaic, garden, garden-variety, indifferent, mediocre, ordinary, plain, routine, run-of-the-mill, standard, stock, unexceptional, unremarkable. *See* GOOD, USUAL.

undivided *adjective*
Not diffused or dispersed : concentrated, exclusive, intensive, unswerving, whole. *See* COLLECT, EDGE, PART.

undo *verb*
1. To remove or invalidate by or as if by running a line through or wiping clean : annul, blot (out), cancel, cross (off *or* out), delete, efface, erase, expunge, obliterate, rub (out), scratch (out), strike (out), wipe (out), x (out). *Law:* vacate. *See* CONTINUE. **2.** To free from ties or fasteners : disengage, loose, loosen, slip, unbind, unclasp, unfasten, unloose, unloosen, untie. *See* TIGHTEN. **3.** To become or cause to become open : open, unclose. *See* OPEN. **4.** To cause the complete ruin or wreckage of : bankrupt, break down, cross up, demolish, destroy, finish, ruin, shatter, sink, smash, spoil, torpedo, wash up, wrack[2], wreck. *Slang:* total. ***Idiom:*** put the kibosh on. *See* HELP. **5.** To lessen or deplete the nerve, energy, or strength of : attenuate, debilitate, devitalize, enervate, enfeeble, sap[2], undermine, unnerve, weaken. *See* STRONG. **6.** To lure or persuade into a sexual relationship or a sexual act : debauch, seduce. *See* SEX.

undoing *noun*
1. The act of destroying or state of being destroyed : bane, destruction, devastation, havoc, ruin, ruination, wrack[1], wreck, wreckage. *See* HELP, LEFTOVER. **2.** Something that causes total loss or severe impairment, as of one's health, fortune, honor, or hopes : bane, destroyer, destruction, downfall, ruin, ruination, wrecker. *See* HELP.

undomesticated *adjective*
In a primitive state; not domesticated or cultivated; produced by nature : native, natural, rough, uncultivated, untamed, wild. *See* WILD.

undoubted *adjective*
Not counterfeit or copied : actual, authentic, bona fide, genuine, good, indubitable, original, real, true, unquestionable. *See* TRUE.

undoubtedly *adverb*
1. Without question : absolutely, certainly, doubtless, doubtlessly, positively. *See* CERTAIN, LIMITED. **2.** It is so; as you say or ask : absolutely, agreed, all right, assuredly, aye, gladly, indubitably, roger, unquestionably, willingly, yea, yes. *Informal:* OK, uh-huh, yeah, yep. *Slang:* right on. *See* AFFIRM.

undoubting *adjective*
1. Having no doubt : assured, certain, confident, positive, sure. *See* CERTAIN. **2.** Having no reservations : absolute, implicit, unconditional, unfaltering, unhesitating, unquestioning, unreserved, wholehearted. *See* BIG, LIMITED.

undress *verb*
To remove all the clothing from : disrobe, strip[1], unclothe. *See* PUT ON, SHOW.
undress *noun* The state of being without clothes : bareness, nakedness, nudeness, nudity. *See* PUT ON, SHOW.

undue *adjective*
Exceeding a normal or reasonable limit : excessive, exorbitant, extravagant, extreme, immoderate, inordinate, overabundant, overmuch. *See* EXCESS.

undulate *verb*
1. To move sinuously : sinuate, slither, snake. *See* MOVE. **2.** To have or cause to have a curved or sinuous form or surface : curl, curve, wave. *See* STRAIGHT.

unduly *adverb*
Too much : overly, overmuch. *Informal:* super. *See* EXCESS.

undying *adjective*
Not being subject to death : deathless, immortal. *See* CONTINUE, LIVE.

unearth *verb*
To find by investigation : dig (out *or* up), turn up, uncover. *See* SHOW.

unearthly *adjective*
1. Of, coming from, or relating to forces or beings that exist outside the natural world : extramundane, extrasensory, metaphysical, miraculous, preternatural, superhuman, supernatural, superphysical, supersensible, transcendental. *See* SUPERNATURAL. **2.** Of a mysteriously strange and usually frightening nature : eerie, uncanny, weird. *Informal:* spooky. *See* FEAR, USUAL. **3.** So senseless as to be laughable : absurd, foolish, harebrained, idiotic, imbecilic, insane, lunatic, mad, moronic, nonsensical, preposterous, silly, softheaded, tomfool, zany. *Informal:* cockeyed, crazy, loony, loopy. *Slang:* balmy[2], dippy, dopey, jerky, sappy, wacky. *See* ABILITY, KNOWLEDGE.

unease *noun*
1. A troubled or anxious state of mind : angst, anxiety, anxiousness, care, concern, disquiet,

disquietude, distress, nervousness, solicitude, uneasiness, worry. *See* FEELINGS. **2.** An uneasy or nervous state : disquiet, disquietude, inquietude, restiveness, restlessness, uneasiness, unrest. *See* CALM.

uneasiness *noun*
1. A troubled or anxious state of mind : angst, anxiety, anxiousness, care, concern, disquiet, disquietude, distress, nervousness, solicitude, unease, worry. *See* FEELINGS. **2.** An uneasy or nervous state : disquiet, disquietude, inquietude, restiveness, restlessness, unease, unrest. *See* CALM.

uneasy *adjective*
1. In a state of anxiety or uneasiness : agitated, anxious, concerned, distressed, nervous, solicitous, unsettled. *See* FEELINGS. **2.** Affording no quiet, repose, or rest : restless, unquiet, unsettled. *See* CALM, TIRED. **3.** Characterized by embarrassment and discomfort : awkward, constrained, uncomfortable. *See* FEELINGS.

uneducated *adjective*
Without education or knowledge : ignorant, illiterate, nescient, uninstructed, unlearned, unschooled, untaught. *See* KNOWLEDGE.

unemotional *adjective*
1. Not affected by or showing emotion : cold, cold-blooded, emotionless, unaffected, unmoved. *See* ATTITUDE, HOT. **2.** With little or no emotion or expression : dry, impassive, matter-of-fact. *See* ATTITUDE, EXCITE.

unemployed *adjective*
1. Out of work : jobless, workless. *See* WORK. **2.** Not occupied or put to use : idle, inactive, unused, vacant. *See* USED.

unending *adjective*
1. Existing or occurring without interruption or end : around-the-clock, ceaseless, constant, continual, continuous, endless, eternal, everlasting, incessant, interminable, nonstop, ongoing, perpetual, persistent, relentless, round-the-clock, timeless, unceasing, unfailing, uninterrupted, unremitting. *See* CONTINUE. **2.** Enduring for all time : amaranthine, ceaseless, endless, eternal, everlasting, immortal, never-ending, perpetual, world without end. *Archaic:* eterne. *See* CONTINUE.

unendurable *adjective*
So unpleasant or painful as not to be endured or tolerated : impossible, insufferable, insupportable, intolerable, unbearable, unsufferable, unsupportable. *See* PAIN.

unenlightened *adjective*
1. Exhibiting lack of education or knowledge : backward, benighted, ignorant, primitive. *See* KNOWLEDGE. **2.** Not aware or informed : ignorant, innocent, oblivious, unacquainted, unaware, unconscious, unfamiliar, uninformed, unknowing, unwitting. ***Idiom:*** in the dark. *See* KNOWLEDGE.

unenthusiastic *adjective*
Lacking warmth, interest, enthusiasm, or involvement : halfhearted, lukewarm, tepid. *See* ATTITUDE, HOT.

unequal *adjective*
1. Lacking capability : inadequate, incapable, incompetent, unfit, unqualified. *See* ABILITY, EXCESS. **2.** Not fair, right, or just : inequitable, unfair, unjust. *See* FAIR.

unequaled also **unequalled** *adjective*
Without equal or rival : alone, incomparable, matchless, nonpareil, only, peerless, singular, unexampled, unique, unmatched, unparalleled, unrivaled. *See* SAME.

unequivocal *adjective*
1. Clearly defined; not ambiguous : clear, distinct, sharp, unambiguous, unmistakable. *See* CLEAR. **2.** Clearly, fully, and sometimes emphatically expressed : categorical, clear, clear-cut, decided, definite, explicit, express, positive, precise, specific, unambiguous. *See* CLEAR. **3.** Completely such, without qualification or exception : absolute, all-out, arrant, complete, consummate, crashing, damned, dead, downright, flat, out-and-out, outright, perfect, plain, pure, sheer[2], thorough, thoroughgoing, total, unbounded, unlimited, unmitigated, unqualified, unrelieved, unreserved, utter[2]. *Informal:* flat-out, positive. *Chiefly British:* blooming. *See* BIG, LIMITED.

unerring *adjective*
Such as could not possibly fail or disappoint : certain, infallible, secure, sure, unfailing. *Informal:* sure-fire. *See* CERTAIN.

unessential *adjective*
Not necessary : dispensable, inessential, needless, nonessential, uncalled-for, unnecessary, unneeded, unrequired. *See* NECESSARY.

unethical *adjective*
Lacking scruples or principles : conscienceless, ruthless, unconscionable, unprincipled, unscrupulous. *See* HONEST.

uneven *adjective*
1. Lacking consistency or regularity in quality or performance : erratic, inconsistent, patchy, spotty, unsteady, variable. *See* CONTINUE, SAME. **2.** Having a surface that is not smooth : coarse, cragged, craggy, harsh, ironbound, jagged, ragged, rough, rugged, scabrous. *See* SMOOTH.

unevenness *noun*
Lack of smoothness or regularity : asymmetry, crookedness, inequality, irregularity, jaggedness, roughness. *See* SMOOTH, STRAIGHT.

unexampled *adjective*
Without equal or rival : alone, incomparable, matchless, nonpareil, only, peerless, singular, unequaled, unique, unmatched, unparalleled, unrivaled. *See* SAME.

unexceptional *adjective*
Being of no special quality or type : average, common, commonplace, cut-and-dried, formulaic, garden, garden-variety, indifferent, mediocre, ordinary, plain, routine, run-of-the-mill, standard, stock, undistinguished, unremarkable. *See* GOOD, USUAL.

unexplainable *adjective*
That cannot be explained : inexplicable, unaccountable. *See* EXPLAIN.

unexposed *adjective*
Not found : undetected, undiscovered, unfound. *See* KNOWLEDGE.

unexpressed *adjective*
Not voiced or expressed : silent, tacit, undeclared, unsaid, unspoken, unuttered, unvoiced, wordless. *See* WORDS.

unexpurgated *adjective*
Not shortened by omissions : complete, unabbreviated, unabridged, uncensored, uncut. *See* PART.

unfailing *adjective*
1. Remaining continually unchanged : changeless, consistent, constant, invariable, same, unchanging. *See* CHANGE. **2.** Existing or occurring without interruption or end : around-the-clock, ceaseless, constant, continual, continuous, endless, eternal, everlasting, incessant, interminable, nonstop, ongoing, perpetual, persistent, relentless, round-the-clock, timeless, unceasing, unending, uninterrupted, unremitting. *See* CONTINUE. **3.** Having or showing a capacity for protracted effort, regardless of difficulty or frustration : indefatigable, inexhaustible, tireless, unflagging, untiring, unwearied, weariless. *See* CONTINUE, TIRED. **4.** Such as could not possibly fail or disappoint : certain, infallible, secure, sure, unerring. *Informal:* surefire. *See* CERTAIN.

unfair *adjective*
Not fair, right, or just : inequitable, unequal, unjust. *See* FAIR.

unfairness *noun*
Lack of justice : inequity, iniquity, injustice, unjustness, wrong. *See* LAW, RIGHT.

unfaithful *adjective*
Not true to duty or obligation : disloyal, faithless, false, false-hearted, perfidious, recreant, traitorous, treacherous, untrue. *See* CONTINUE, TRUST.

unfaithfulness *noun*
Betrayal, especially of a moral obligation : disloyalty, faithlessness, false-heartedness, falseness, falsity, infidelity, perfidiousness, perfidy, traitorousness, treacherousness, treachery. *See* CONTINUE, TRUST.

unfaltering *adjective*
Having no reservations : absolute, implicit, unconditional, undoubting, unhesitating, unquestioning, unreserved, wholehearted. *See* BIG, LIMITED.

unfamiliar *adjective*
1. Not aware or informed : ignorant, innocent, oblivious, unacquainted, unaware, unconscious, unenlightened, uninformed, unknowing, unwitting. ***Idiom:*** in the dark. *See* KNOWLEDGE. **2.** Not the same as what was previously known or done : different, fresh, innovative, inventive, new, newfangled, novel, original, unprecedented. *See* NEW.

unfamiliarity *noun*
The condition of being uninformed or unaware : ignorance, innocence, nescience, obliviousness, unawareness, unconsciousness. *See* KNOWLEDGE.

unfasten *verb*
To free from ties or fasteners : disengage, loose, loosen, slip, unbind, unclasp, undo, unloose, unloosen, untie. *See* TIGHTEN.

unfathomable *adjective*
Incapable of being grasped by the intellect or understanding : impenetrable, incomprehensible, inscrutable, uncomprehensible, unintelligible. *See* KNOWLEDGE.

unfavorable *adjective*
1. Tending to discourage, retard, or make more difficult : adverse, disadvantageous, negative, unadvantageous, unsatisfactory, untoward. *See* HELP. **2.** Bringing, predicting, or characterized by misfortune : bad, evil, ill, inauspicious, unpropitious. *See* LUCK.

unfeeling *adjective*
1. Lacking physical feeling or sensitivity : asleep, dead, insensible, insensitive, numb. *See* AWARENESS. **2.** Completely lacking in compassion : callous, cold-blooded, cold-hearted, compassionless, hard, hard-boiled, hardened, hardhearted, heartless, obdurate, stonyhearted. *See* ATTITUDE.

unfeigned *adjective*
Devoid of any hypocrisy or pretense : genuine, heartfelt, hearty, honest, natural, real, sincere, true, unaffected, unmannered. *See* TRUE.

unfinished *adjective*
Not perfected, elaborated, or completed : preliminary, rough, sketchy, tentative, unperfected, unpolished. *See* START.

unfit *adjective*
1. Not suited to a given purpose : ill-suited, inappropriate, inapt, unsuitable, unsuited. *See* ABILITY. **2.** Not suited to circumstances : improper, inappropriate, inapt, incongruous, inept, malapropos, unapt, unbecoming, unbefitting, unseemly, unsuitable. ***Idiom:*** out of place. *See* AGREE, USUAL. **3.** Lacking capability : inadequate, incapable, incompetent, unequal, unqualified. *See* ABILITY, EXCESS. **4.** Totally incapable of doing a job : incompetent, unable, unqualified. *See* ABILITY.
unfit *verb* To make incapable, as of doing a job : disable, disqualify. *See* ABILITY.

unfitness *noun*
The condition of being improper : improperness, impropriety, inappropriateness, unbecomingness, unseemliness, unsuitability, unsuitableness. *See* AGREE, USUAL.

unflagging *adjective*
Having or showing a capacity for protracted effort, regardless of difficulty or frustration : indefatigable, inexhaustible, tireless, unfailing, untiring, unwearied, weariless. *See* CONTINUE, TIRED.

unflappability *noun*
A stable, calm state of the emotions : aplomb, balance, collectedness, composure, coolness, equanimity, imperturbability, imperturbableness, nonchalance, poise, sang-froid, self-possession. *Slang:* cool. *See* CALM, FEELINGS.

unflappable *adjective*
Not easily excited, even under pressure : calm, collected, composed, cool, cool-headed, detached, even[1], even-tempered, imperturbable, nonchalant, possessed, unruffled. *See* CALM.

unflawed *adjective*
Supremely excellent in quality or nature : absolute, consummate, faultless, flawless, impeccable, indefectible, perfect. *See* GOOD.

unflinching *adjective*
Indicating or possessing determination, resolution, or persistence : constant, determined, firm[1], resolute, steadfast, steady, stiff, tough, unbending, uncompromising, unwavering, unyielding. *See* PURPOSE.

unfold *verb*
1. To move or arrange so as to cover a larger area : expand, extend, fan[1] (out), open (out *or* up), outstretch, spread, stretch, unroll. *See* MOVE. **2.** To be disclosed gradually : develop, evolve. *See* SHOW.

unfolding *noun*
A progression from a simple form to a more complex one : development, evolution, evolvement, growth, progress. *See* CHANGE.

unforbearing *adjective*
Being unable or unwilling to endure irritation or opposition, for example : fretful, impatient, intolerant. *See* ACCEPT, ATTITUDE, CALM.

unforced *adjective*
Done by one's own choice : free, spontaneous, uncompelled, volitional, voluntary, willful. *See* WILLING.

unforgivable *adjective*
Impossible to excuse, pardon, or justify : indefensible, inexcusable, unjustifiable, unpardonable. *See* FORGIVENESS.

unformed *adjective*
Having no distinct shape : amorphous, formless, inchoate, shapeless, unshaped. *See* ORDER.

unfortunate *adjective*
1. Involving or undergoing chance misfortune : hapless, ill-fated, ill-starred, luckless, star-crossed, unhappy, unlucky, untoward. *See* LUCK. **2.** Worthy of severe disapproval : condemnable, deplorable, disgraceful, shameful. *See* GOOD. **3.** Characterized by inappropriateness and gracelessness, especially in expression : awkward, ill-chosen, inappropriate, inept, infelicitous, unhappy. *See* ABILITY, GOOD.
unfortunate *noun* A person living under very unhappy circumstances : loser, miserable, underdog, underprivileged, wretch. *See* RICH.

unfortunateness *noun*
Bad fortune : adversity, haplessness, misfortune, unluckiness, untowardness. *See* LUCK.

unfound *adjective*
Not found : undetected, undiscovered, unexposed. *See* KNOWLEDGE.

unfounded *adjective*
Having no basis or foundation in fact : baseless, bottomless, groundless, idle, unwarranted. *See* TRUE.

unfoundedly *adverb*
Without basis or foundation in fact : groundlessly, unwarrantedly. *See* REASON.

unfrequented *adjective*
Empty of people : deserted, desolate, forlorn, godforsaken, lonely, lonesome. *See* FULL.

unfriendly *adjective*
Feeling or showing unfriendliness : hostile, inimical. *See* LOVE.

unfruitful *adjective*
1. Unable to produce offspring : barren, childless, impotent, infertile, sterile. *See* RICH.
2. Lacking or unable to produce growing plants or crops : barren, infertile, sterile, unproductive. *See* RICH.

ungainly *adjective*
1. Lacking dexterity and grace in physical movement : awkward, clumsy, gawky, graceless, inept, lumpish, maladroit, ungraceful. *Slang:* klutzy. ***Idiom:*** all thumbs. *See* ABILITY.
2. Difficult to handle or manage : awkward, bulky, clumsy, unhandy, unmanageable, unwieldy. *See* EASY.

ungovernable *adjective*
Not submitting to discipline or control : disorderly, fractious, indocile, intractable, lawless, obstinate, obstreperous, recalcitrant, refractory, uncontrollable, undisciplined, unmanageable, unruly, untoward, wild. ***Idiom:*** out of line. *See* CONTROL, ORDER, PEACE, RESIST.

ungovernableness *noun*
The quality or condition of being unruly : disorderliness, fractiousness, indocility, intractability, intractableness, obstinacy, obstinateness, obstreperousness, recalcitrance, recalcitrancy, refractoriness, uncontrollability, uncontrollableness, unmanageability, unruliness, untowardness, wildness. *See* CONTROL, ORDER, PEACE, RESIST.

ungoverned *adjective*
Lacking in moral restraint : abandoned, dissipated, dissolute, fast, gay, incontinent, licentious, profligate, rakish, unbridled, unconstrained, uncontrolled, uninhibited, unrestrained, wanton, wild. *See* RESTRAINT.

ungraceful *adjective*
Lacking dexterity and grace in physical movement : awkward, clumsy, gawky, graceless, inept, lumpish, maladroit, ungainly. *Slang:* klutzy. ***Idiom:*** all thumbs. *See* ABILITY.

ungracious *adjective*
Lacking good manners : discourteous, disrespectful, ill-bred, ill-mannered, impolite, rude, uncivil, unmannerly, unpolished. *See* COURTESY.

ungraciousness *noun*
Lack of cordiality and hospitableness : inhospitableness, inhospitality, unreceptiveness, unwelcome, unwelcomeness. *See* LIKE.

ungrateful *adjective*
1. Not showing or feeling gratitude : thankless, unappreciative, unthankful, unthanking. *See* GRATEFUL. **2.** Not apt to be appreciated : thankless, unappreciated, unthankful. *See* GRATEFUL.

unguarded *adjective*
Inadequately protected : insecure, unprotected, unsafe. *See* SAFETY.

unhandy *adjective*
Difficult to handle or manage : awkward, bulky, clumsy, ungainly, unmanageable, unwieldy. *See* EASY.

unhappiness *noun*
A feeling or spell of dismally low spirits : blues, dejection, depression, despondence, despondency, doldrums, dolefulness, downheartedness, dumps, dysphoria, funk, gloom, glumness, heavy-heartedness, melancholy, mope (used in plural), mournfulness, sadness. *See* FEELINGS, HAPPY.

unhappy *adjective*
1. In low spirits : blue, dejected, depressed, desolate, dispirited, down, downcast, downhearted, dull, dysphoric, gloomy, heavy-hearted, low, melancholic, melancholy, sad, spiritless, tristful, wistful. ***Idiom:*** down at (*or* in) the mouth. *See* HAPPY. **2.** Involving or undergoing chance misfortune : hapless, ill-fated, ill-starred, luckless, star-crossed, unfortunate, unlucky, untoward. *See* LUCK.
3. Characterized by inappropriateness and gracelessness, especially in expression : awkward, ill-chosen, inappropriate, inept, infelicitous, unfortunate. *See* ABILITY, GOOD.

unharmed *adjective*
1. Free from danger, injury, or the threat of harm : safe, unhurt, uninjured, unscathed. ***Idiom:*** safe and sound. *See* SAFETY. **2.** In excellent condition : entire, flawless, good, intact, perfect, sound[2], unblemished, unbroken, undamaged, unhurt, unimpaired, uninjured, unmarred, whole. *See* THRIVE.

unharmonious *adjective*
1. Characterized by unpleasant discordance of sound : cacophonous, discordant, disharmonious, dissonant, inharmonic, inharmonious, rude, unmusical. *See* AGREE, SOUNDS.
2. Devoid of harmony and accord : discordant, inconsonant, inharmonious, uncongenial. *See* AGREE.

unhealthy *adjective*
1. Not sustaining or promoting health : insalubrious, unsalutary, unwholesome. *See* HEALTH. **2.** Morally detrimental : contaminative, corruptive, demoralizing, unwholesome. *See* RIGHT. **3.** Utterly reprehensible in nature or behavior : corrupt, degenerate, depraved, flagitious, miscreant, perverse, rotten, villainous. *See* CLEAN, GOOD. **4.** Susceptible to or marked by preoccupation with unwholesome matters : macabre, morbid, sick, unwholesome. *See* GOOD.

unheard-of *adjective*
Not known or not widely known by name : nameless, obscure, unknown. *See* KNOWLEDGE.

unheeding *adjective*
Showing no concern, attention, or regard : careless, forgetful, heedless, mindless, unconcerned, unmindful, unobservant, unthinking. *See* CAREFUL.

unhesitating *adjective*
Having no reservations : absolute, implicit, unconditional, undoubting, unfaltering, unquestioning, unreserved, wholehearted. *See* BIG, LIMITED.

unhinge *verb*
To make insane : craze, derange, madden, unbalance. *See* SANE.

unhorse *verb*
To bring about the downfall of : bring down, overthrow, overturn, subvert, topple, tumble. *See* HELP.

unhospitable *adjective*
So disagreeable as to discourage approach : forbidding, inhospitable, uninviting. *See* WARN.

unhurried *adjective*
Careful and slow in acting, moving, or deciding : deliberate, leisurely, measured. *See* FAST.

unhurt *adjective*
1. Free from danger, injury, or the threat of harm : safe, unharmed, uninjured, unscathed. ***Idiom:*** safe and sound. *See* SAFETY. **2.** In excellent condition : entire, flawless, good, intact, perfect, sound[2], unblemished, unbroken, undamaged, unharmed, unimpaired, uninjured, unmarred, whole. *See* THRIVE.

unification *noun*
1. A bringing together into a whole : coalition, consolidation, union, unity. *See* PART. **2.** The result of combining : combination, composite, compound, conjugation, union, unity. *See* ASSEMBLE.

uniform *adjective*
1. Having no change or variation : changeless, constant, equable, even[1], invariable, invariant, regular, same, steady, unchanging, unvarying. *See* SAME. **2.** Possessing the same or almost the same characteristics : alike, analogous, comparable, corresponding, equivalent, like[2], parallel, similar. *See* SAME.

uniformity *noun*
The quality or state of being alike : affinity, alikeness, analogy, comparison, correspondence, likeness, parallelism, resemblance, similarity, similitude, uniformness. *See* SAME.

uniformness *noun*
The quality or state of being alike : affinity, alikeness, analogy, comparison, correspondence, likeness, parallelism, resemblance, similarity, similitude, uniformity. *See* SAME.

unify *verb*
1. To bring or come together into a united whole : coalesce, combine, compound, concrete, conjoin, conjugate, connect, consolidate, couple, join, link, marry, meld, unite, wed, yoke. *See* ASSEMBLE. **2.** To combine and adapt in order to attain a particular effect : arrange, blend, coordinate, harmonize, integrate, orchestrate, synthesize. *See* BEAUTIFUL.

unimaginable *adjective*
Not to be believed : inconceivable, incredible, unbelievable, unthinkable. ***Idioms:*** beyond belief, contrary to all reason. *See* BELIEF.

unimaginative *adjective*
1. Lacking originality : sterile, uncreative, uninspired, uninventive, unoriginal. *See* RICH. **2.** Lacking liveliness, charm, or surprise : arid, aseptic, colorless, drab, dry, dull, earthbound, flat, flavorless, lackluster, lifeless, lusterless, matter-of-fact, pedestrian, prosaic, spiritless, sterile, stodgy, uninspired. *See* EXCITE.

unimpaired *adjective*
In excellent condition : entire, flawless, good, intact, perfect, sound[2], unblemished, unbroken, undamaged, unharmed, unhurt, uninjured, unmarred, whole. *See* THRIVE.

unimpeded *adjective*
Free from obstructions : clear, free, open, unblocked, unobstructed. *See* OPEN.

unimportance *noun*
Lack of importance : inconsequence, inconsequentiality, inconsequentialness, indifference, insignificance, insignificancy. *See* CONCERN.

unimportant *adjective*
Not of great importance : inconsequent, inconsequential, insignificant, little, trivial. *See* BIG.

unimpressionable *adjective*
Not capable of being affected or impressed :

impassible, impassive, insensitive, insusceptible, unsusceptible. *See* AFFECT.

uninformed *adjective*
Not aware or informed : ignorant, innocent, oblivious, unacquainted, unaware, unconscious, unenlightened, unfamiliar, unknowing, unwitting. ***Idiom:*** in the dark. *See* KNOWLEDGE.

uninhabited *adjective*
Not spoken for or occupied : free, open, unoccupied, unreserved. *See* OWNED.

uninhibited *adjective*
Lacking in moral restraint : abandoned, dissipated, dissolute, fast, gay, incontinent, licentious, profligate, rakish, unbridled, unconstrained, uncontrolled, ungoverned, unrestrained, wanton, wild. *See* RESTRAINT.

uninitiate *adjective*
Lacking experience and the knowledge gained from it : green, inexperienced, inexpert, raw, uninitiated, unpracticed, unseasoned, untried, unversed. *See* ABILITY.
uninitiate *noun* One lacking professional skill and ease in a particular pursuit : amateur, dabbler, dilettante, nonprofessional, smatterer. *See* ABILITY.

uninitiated *adjective*
Lacking experience and the knowledge gained from it : green, inexperienced, inexpert, raw, uninitiate, unpracticed, unseasoned, untried, unversed. *See* ABILITY.

uninjured *adjective*
1. Free from danger, injury, or the threat of harm : safe, unharmed, unhurt, unscathed. ***Idiom:*** safe and sound. *See* SAFETY. **2.** In excellent condition : entire, flawless, good, intact, perfect, sound[2], unblemished, unbroken, undamaged, unharmed, unhurt, unimpaired, unmarred, whole. *See* THRIVE.

uninspired *adjective*
1. Lacking liveliness, charm, or surprise : arid, aseptic, colorless, drab, dry, dull, earthbound, flat, flavorless, lackluster, lifeless, lusterless, matter-of-fact, pedestrian, prosaic, spiritless, sterile, stodgy, unimaginative. *See* EXCITE.
2. Lacking originality : sterile, uncreative, unimaginative, uninventive, unoriginal. *See* RICH.

uninstructed *adjective*
Without education or knowledge : ignorant, illiterate, nescient, uneducated, unlearned, unschooled, untaught. *See* KNOWLEDGE.

unintelligent *adjective*
Displaying a complete lack of forethought and good sense : brainless, fatuous, foolish, insensate, mindless, senseless, silly, weak-minded, witless. *See* ABILITY, PLANNED.

unintelligible *adjective*
Incapable of being grasped by the intellect or understanding : impenetrable, incomprehensible, inscrutable, uncomprehensible, unfathomable. *See* KNOWLEDGE.

unintended *adjective*
Not intended : inadvertent, undesigned, undevised, unintentional, unmeant, unplanned, unwitting. *See* PLANNED.

unintentional *adjective*
Not intended : inadvertent, undesigned, undevised, unintended, unmeant, unplanned, unwitting. *See* PLANNED.

uninterest *noun*
Lack of emotion or interest : apathy, disinterest, impassivity, incuriosity, incuriousness, indifference, insensibility, insensibleness, lassitude, lethargy, listlessness, phlegm, stolidity, stolidness, unconcern, unresponsiveness. *See* FEELINGS.

uninterested *adjective*
1. Without emotion or interest : apathetic, detached, impassive, incurious, indifferent, insensible, lethargic, listless, phlegmatic, stolid, unconcerned, unresponsive. *See* FEELINGS.
2. Lacking interest in one's surroundings or worldly affairs : aloof, detached, disinterested, incurious, indifferent, unconcerned, uninvolved. *See* ATTITUDE, CONCERN.

uninteresting *adjective*
Arousing no interest or curiosity : boring, drear, dreary, dry, dull, humdrum, irksome, monotonous, stuffy, tedious, tiresome, weariful, wearisome, weary. *See* EXCITE.

uninterrupted *adjective*
Existing or occurring without interruption or end : around-the-clock, ceaseless, constant, continual, continuous, endless, eternal, everlasting, incessant, interminable, nonstop, ongoing, perpetual, persistent, relentless, round-the-clock, timeless, unceasing, unending, unfailing, unremitting. *See* CONTINUE.

uninventive *adjective*
Lacking originality : sterile, uncreative, unimaginative, uninspired, unoriginal. *See* RICH.

uninvited *adjective*
Not welcome or wanted : undesirable, undesired, unsought, unwanted, unwelcome, unwished-for. *See* LIKE.

uninviting *adjective*
So disagreeable as to discourage approach :

forbidding, inhospitable, unhospitable. *See* WARN.

uninvolved *adjective*
1. Lacking interest in one's surroundings or worldly affairs : aloof, detached, disinterested, incurious, indifferent, unconcerned, uninterested. *See* ATTITUDE, CONCERN. **2.** Not inclining toward or actively taking either side in a matter under dispute : impartial, neuter, neutral, nonaligned, nonpartisan, unbiased, uncommitted, unprejudiced. ***Idiom:*** on the fence. *See* FAIR.

union *noun*
1. A bringing together into a whole : coalition, consolidation, unification, unity. *See* PART.
2. The result of combining : combination, composite, compound, conjugation, unification, unity. *See* ASSEMBLE. **3.** A group of people united in a relationship and having some interest, activity, or purpose in common : association, club, confederation, congress, federation, fellowship, fraternity, guild, league, order, organization, society, sorority. *See* GROUP.
4. An association, especially of nations for a common cause : alliance, Anschluss, bloc, cartel, coalition, confederacy, confederation, federation, league, organization. *See* CONNECT, GROUP, POLITICS. **5.** An identity or coincidence of interests, purposes, or sympathies among the members of a group : oneness, solidarity, unity. *See* AGREE. **6.** A point or position at which two or more things are joined : connection, coupling, joint, junction, juncture, seam. *See* CONNECT.

unique *adjective*
1. Alone in a given category : lone, one, only, particular, separate, single, singular, sole, solitary. ***Idioms:*** first and last, one and only. *See* INCLUDE. **2.** Without equal or rival : alone, incomparable, matchless, nonpareil, only, peerless, singular, unequaled, unexampled, unmatched, unparalleled, unrivaled. *See* SAME.

uniqueness *noun*
The quality or condition of being unique : oneness, singleness, singularity. *See* SAME.

unit *noun*
A group of people organized for a particular purpose : body, corps, crew, detachment, force, gang, team. *See* GROUP.

unite *verb*
1. To bring or come together into a united whole : coalesce, combine, compound, concrete, conjoin, conjugate, connect, consolidate, couple, join, link, marry, meld, unify, wed, yoke. *See* ASSEMBLE. **2.** To assemble or join in a group : band[2], combine, gang up, league. *See* COLLECT.

unity *noun*
1. The condition of being one : oneness, singleness, singularity. *See* PART. **2.** Harmonious mutual understanding : accord, agreement, concord, concordance, concurrence, consonance, harmony, rapport, tune. ***Idiom:*** meeting of the minds. *See* AGREE. **3.** A bringing together into a whole : coalition, consolidation, unification, union. *See* PART. **4.** The result of combining : combination, composite, compound, conjugation, unification, union. *See* ASSEMBLE.
5. An identity or coincidence of interests, purposes, or sympathies among the members of a group : oneness, solidarity, union. *See* AGREE.

universal *adjective*
1. So pervasive and all-inclusive as to exist in or affect the whole world : catholic, cosmic, cosmopolitan, ecumenical, global, pandemic, planetary, worldwide. *See* LIMITED, SPECIFIC.
2. Ever present in all places : omnipresent, ubiquitous. *See* LIMITED, SPECIFIC.
3. Belonging or relating to the whole : common, general, generic. *See* SPECIFIC.
universal *noun* A broad and basic rule or truth : axiom, fundamental, law, principle, theorem. *See* ORDER.

universalize *verb*
To make universal : generalize. *See* SPECIFIC.

universe *noun*
1. The totality of all existing things : cosmos, creation, macrocosm, nature, world. *See* MATTER, PART. **2.** The human race : earth, flesh, Homo sapiens, humanity, humankind, man, mankind, world. *See* CULTURE.

unjust *adjective*
Not fair, right, or just : inequitable, unequal, unfair. *See* FAIR.

unjustifiable *adjective*
Impossible to excuse, pardon, or justify : indefensible, inexcusable, unforgivable, unpardonable. *See* FORGIVENESS.

unjustness *noun*
Lack of justice : inequity, iniquity, injustice, unfairness, wrong. *See* LAW, RIGHT.

unkempt *adjective*
Marked by an absence of cleanliness and order : disheveled, messy, mussy, slipshod, sloppy, slovenly, untidy. *See* ORDER.

unknowing *adjective*
Not aware or informed : ignorant, innocent, oblivious, unacquainted, unaware, unconscious, unenlightened, unfamiliar, uninformed,

unwitting. *Idiom:* in the dark. *See* KNOWLEDGE.

unknown *adjective*
Not known or not widely known by name : nameless, obscure, unheard-of. *See* KNOWLEDGE.

unlade *verb*
To remove the cargo or load from : disburden, discharge, dump, unload. *See* PUT IN.

unlawful *adjective*
1. Prohibited by law : illegal, illegitimate, illicit, lawless, outlawed, wrongful. *See* CRIMES, LAW. **2.** Of, involving, or being a crime : criminal, illegal, illegitimate, illicit, lawless, wrongful. *See* CRIMES. **3.** Contrary to accepted, especially moral conventions : illicit. *See* RIGHT. **4.** Born to parents who are not married to each other : baseborn, bastard, illegitimate, misbegotten, natural, spurious. *See* KIN, LAW.

unlawfulness *noun*
The state or quality of being illegal : illegality, illegitimacy, illicitness. *See* CRIMES, LAW.

unlearned *adjective*
1. Without education or knowledge : ignorant, illiterate, nescient, uneducated, uninstructed, unschooled, untaught. *See* KNOWLEDGE.
2. Lacking the requisite scholarship or instruction : unscholarly, unstudious. *See* KNOWLEDGE.

unlike *adjective*
Not like another in nature, quality, amount, or form : different, disparate, dissimilar, divergent, diverse, variant, various. *See* SAME.

unlikely *adjective*
Not likely : doubtful, improbable, questionable, unapt. *See* LIKELY.

unlikeness *noun*
The condition of being unlike or dissimilar : difference, discrepance, discrepancy, disparity, dissimilarity, dissimilitude, distinction, divarication, divergence, divergency. *See* SAME.

unlimited *adjective*
1. Having no ends or limits : boundless, endless, illimitable, immeasurable, infinite, limitless, measureless, unbounded. *See* LIMITED.
2. Completely such, without qualification or exception : absolute, all-out, arrant, complete, consummate, crashing, damned, dead, downright, flat, out-and-out, outright, perfect, plain, pure, sheer[2], thorough, thoroughgoing, total, unbounded, unequivocal, unmitigated, unqualified, unrelieved, unreserved, utter[2]. *Informal:* flat-out, positive. *Chiefly British:* blooming. *See* BIG, LIMITED.

unlimitedness *noun*
The state or quality of being infinite : boundlessness, immeasurability, immeasurableness, inexhaustibility, inexhaustibleness, infiniteness, infinity, limitlessness, measurelessness, unboundedness. *See* LIMITED.

unload *verb*
1. To remove the cargo or load from : disburden, discharge, dump, unlade. *See* PUT IN.
2. To get rid of completely by selling, especially in quantity or at a discount : close out, dump, sell off, sell out. *See* TRANSACTIONS.

unloose *verb*
To free from ties or fasteners : disengage, loose, loosen, slip, unbind, unclasp, undo, unfasten, unloosen, untie. *See* TIGHTEN.

unloosen *verb*
To free from ties or fasteners : disengage, loose, loosen, slip, unbind, unclasp, undo, unfasten, unloose, untie. *See* TIGHTEN.

unlovely *adjective*
Not handsome or beautiful : homely, plain, unattractive, uncomely. *Idioms:* not much for looks, not much to look at, short on looks. *See* BEAUTIFUL.

unluckiness *noun*
Bad fortune : adversity, haplessness, misfortune, unfortunateness, untowardness. *See* LUCK.

unlucky *adjective*
1. Involving or undergoing chance misfortune : hapless, ill-fated, ill-starred, luckless, star-crossed, unfortunate, unhappy, untoward. *See* LUCK. **2.** Portending future disaster : apocalyptic, apocalyptical, baneful, dire, direful, fateful, fire-and-brimstone, grave[2], hellfire, ominous, portentous. *See* LUCK, WARN. **3.** Disturbing because of failure to measure up to a standard or produce the desired results : disappointing, sorry. *See* HAPPY.

unmanageability *noun*
The quality or condition of being unruly : disorderliness, fractiousness, indocility, intractability, intractableness, obstinacy, obstinateness, obstreperousness, recalcitrance, recalcitrancy, refractoriness, uncontrollability, uncontrollableness, ungovernableness, unruliness, untowardness, wildness. *See* CONTROL, ORDER, PEACE, RESIST.

unmanageable *adjective*
1. Difficult to handle or manage : awkward, bulky, clumsy, ungainly, unhandy, unwieldy. *See* EASY. **2.** Not submitting to discipline or control : disorderly, fractious, indocile, intractable, lawless, obstinate, obstreperous,

recalcitrant, refractory, uncontrollable, undisciplined, ungovernable, unruly, untoward, wild. ***Idiom:*** out of line. *See* CONTROL, ORDER, PEACE, RESIST.

unmanliness *noun*

1. Ignoble lack of courage : chickenheartedness, cowardice, cowardliness, cravenness, dastardliness, faint-heartedness, funk, pusillanimity. *Slang:* gutlessness, yellowness, yellow streak. *See* FEAR. **2.** The quality of being effeminate : effeminacy, effeminateness, femininity, sissiness, womanishness. *See* GENDER.

unmanly *adjective*

1. Ignobly lacking in courage : chickenhearted, cowardly, craven, dastardly, faint-hearted, lily-livered, pusillanimous. *Slang:* chicken, gutless, yellow, yellow-bellied. *See* FEAR. **2.** Having qualities more appropriate to women than to men : effeminate, epicene, feminine, sissified, sissyish, womanish. *See* GENDER.

unmannered *adjective*

Devoid of any hypocrisy or pretense : genuine, heartfelt, hearty, honest, natural, real, sincere, true, unaffected, unfeigned. *See* TRUE.

unmannerly *adjective*

Lacking good manners : discourteous, disrespectful, ill-bred, ill-mannered, impolite, rude, uncivil, ungracious, unpolished. *See* COURTESY.

unmarked *adjective*

Free from flaws or blemishes : clear, flawless, unblemished. *See* BEAUTIFUL.

unmarred *adjective*

In excellent condition : entire, flawless, good, intact, perfect, sound[2], unblemished, unbroken, undamaged, unharmed, unhurt, unimpaired, uninjured, whole. *See* THRIVE.

unmarried *adjective*

Without a spouse : fancy-free, footloose, lone, single, sole, spouseless, unattached, unwed. ***Idiom:*** footloose and fancy-free. *See* MARRIAGE.

unmask *verb*

To make visible; bring to view : bare, disclose, display, expose, reveal, show, unclothe, uncover, unveil. *Archaic:* discover. ***Idioms:*** bring to light, lay open, make plain. *See* SHOW.

unmatched *adjective*

Without equal or rival : alone, incomparable, matchless, nonpareil, only, peerless, singular, unequaled, unexampled, unique, unparalleled, unrivaled. *See* SAME.

unmeant *adjective*

Not intended : inadvertent, undesigned, undevised, unintended, unintentional, unplanned, unwitting. *See* PLANNED.

unmentionable *adjective*

That may not be spoken of or uttered : unspeakable. *See* DECENT, GOOD, WORDS.

unmerciful *adjective*

Having or showing no mercy : merciless, pitiless, remorseless. *See* KIND.

unmindful *adjective*

1. Lacking or marked by a lack of care : careless, feckless, heedless, inattentive, irresponsible, reckless, thoughtless, unconcerned, unthinking. *See* CAREFUL. **2.** Showing no concern, attention, or regard : careless, forgetful, heedless, mindless, unconcerned, unheeding, unobservant, unthinking. *See* CAREFUL.

unmistakable *adjective*

1. Clearly defined; not ambiguous : clear, distinct, sharp, unambiguous, unequivocal. *See* CLEAR. **2.** Easily seen through due to a lack of subtlety : broad, clear, obvious, patent, plain, unsubtle. *See* CLEAR, SEE.

unmitigated *adjective*

Completely such, without qualification or exception : absolute, all-out, arrant, complete, consummate, crashing, damned, dead, downright, flat, out-and-out, outright, perfect, plain, pure, sheer[2], thorough, thoroughgoing, total, unbounded, unequivocal, unlimited, unqualified, unrelieved, unreserved, utter[2]. *Informal:* flat-out, positive. *Chiefly British:* blooming. *See* BIG, LIMITED.

unmixed *adjective*

1. Free from extraneous elements : absolute, perfect, plain, pure, sheer[2], simple, unadulterated, undiluted. *See* CLEAN. **2.** Not diluted or mixed with other substances : full-strength, neat, plain, pure, straight, unblended, undiluted. *See* CLEAN, STRONG.

unmovable *adjective*

Firmly in position : fixed, immobile, immovable, stationary, steadfast, steady, unmoving. *See* MOVE.

unmoved *adjective*

1. Not affected by or showing emotion : cold, cold-blooded, emotionless, unaffected, unemotional. *See* ATTITUDE, HOT. **2.** Not sympathetic : uncaring, uncharitable, uncompassionate, unpitying, unstirred, unsympathetic, untouched. *See* FEELINGS.

unmoving *adjective*

1. Not moving : immobile, motionless, stationary, still, stock-still. *See* MOVE. **2.** Firmly in position : fixed, immobile, immovable, stationary, steadfast, steady, unmovable. *See* MOVE.

unmusical *adjective*
Characterized by unpleasant discordance of sound : cacophonous, discordant, disharmonious, dissonant, inharmonic, inharmonious, rude, unharmonious. *See* AGREE, SOUNDS.

unnamed *adjective*
Having an unknown name or author : anonymous, nameless, unsigned. *See* KNOWLEDGE.

unnatural *adjective*
1. Greatly exceeding or departing from the normal course of nature : preternatural, supernatural. *See* USUAL. **2.** Deviating from the customary : bizarre, cranky, curious, eccentric, erratic, freakish, idiosyncratic, odd, outlandish, peculiar, quaint, queer, quirky, singular, strange, unusual, weird. *Slang:* kooky, screwball. *British Slang:* rum, rummy[2]. *See* USUAL. **3.** Departing from the normal : aberrant, abnormal, anomalistic, anomalous, atypic, atypical, deviant, divergent, irregular, preternatural. *See* GOOD, USUAL. **4.** Marked by unnaturalness, pretension, and often a slavish love of fads : artificial, factitious, plastic, synthetic. *See* HONEST.

unnaturalness *noun*
The condition of being abnormal : aberrance, aberrancy, aberration, abnormality, anomaly, deviance, deviancy, deviation, irregularity, preternaturalness. *See* GOOD, USUAL.

unnecessary *adjective*
Not necessary : dispensable, inessential, needless, nonessential, uncalled-for, unessential, unneeded, unrequired. *See* NECESSARY.

unneeded *adjective*
Not necessary : dispensable, inessential, needless, nonessential, uncalled-for, unessential, unnecessary, unrequired. *See* NECESSARY.

unnegotiable *adjective*
Incapable of being used or availed of to advantage : impracticable, impractical, unserviceable, unusable, unworkable, useless. *See* USED.

unnerve *verb*
To lessen or deplete the nerve, energy, or strength of : attenuate, debilitate, devitalize, enervate, enfeeble, sap[2], undermine, undo, weaken. *See* STRONG.

unnoticeable *adjective*
1. Not readily noticed or seen : inconspicuous, obscure, unconspicuous, unobtrusive. ***Idiom:*** having (*or* keeping) a low profile. *See* SEE.
2. Incapable of being apprehended by the mind or the senses : impalpable, imperceptible, imponderable, inappreciable, indiscernible, indistinguishable, insensible, intangible, invisible, unobservable. *See* KNOWLEDGE.

unobjectionable *adjective*
Capable of being accepted : acceptable, admissible. *See* ACCEPT.

unobservable *adjective*
Incapable of being apprehended by the mind or the senses : impalpable, imperceptible, imponderable, inappreciable, indiscernible, indistinguishable, insensible, intangible, invisible, unnoticeable. *See* KNOWLEDGE.

unobservant *adjective*
Showing no concern, attention, or regard : careless, forgetful, heedless, mindless, unconcerned, unheeding, unmindful, unthinking. *See* CAREFUL.

unobstructed *adjective*
Free from obstructions : clear, free, open, unblocked, unimpeded. *See* OPEN.

unobtrusive *adjective*
1. Not readily noticed or seen : inconspicuous, obscure, unconspicuous, unnoticeable. ***Idiom:*** having (*or* keeping) a low profile. *See* SEE.
2. Not showy or obtrusive : inobtrusive, quiet, restrained, subdued, tasteful. *See* PLAIN.

unoccupied *adjective*
Not spoken for or occupied : free, open, uninhabited, unreserved. *See* OWNED.

unoffensive *adjective*
Devoid of hurtful qualities : harmless, hurtless, innocent, innocuous, inoffensive. *See* HELP.

unordinary *adjective*
Not usual or ordinary : atypic, atypical, novel, unconventional, unusual, unwonted. *Slang:* offbeat. *See* USUAL.

unoriginal *adjective*
Lacking originality : sterile, uncreative, unimaginative, uninspired, uninventive. *See* RICH.

unostentatious *adjective*
Not elaborate or showy, as in appearance or style : modest, plain, simple, unassuming, unpretentious. *See* PLAIN.

unostentatiousness *noun*
Lack of ostentation or pretension : modesty, plainness, simpleness, simplicity, unassumingness, unpretentiousness. *See* PLAIN.

unpaid *adjective*
1. Owed as a debt : due, outstanding, owed, owing, payable, receivable, unsettled. *See* PAY.
2. Contributing one's time without pay : uncompensated, unrecompensed, unremunerated, unsalaried, voluntary. *See* PAY, WORK.

unpalatable *adjective*
1. So unpleasant in flavor as to be inedible : distasteful, unappetizing, unsavory. *See* TASTE.

2. Difficult to accept : bitter, distasteful, indigestible, painful. *See* LIKE.

unparalleled *adjective*
Without equal or rival : alone, incomparable, matchless, nonpareil, only, peerless, singular, unequaled, unexampled, unique, unmatched, unrivaled. *See* SAME.

unpardonable *adjective*
Impossible to excuse, pardon, or justify : indefensible, inexcusable, unforgivable, unjustifiable. *See* FORGIVENESS.

unperceptive *adjective*
Unwilling or unable to perceive : blind, dull, purblind, uncomprehending. *See* SEE.

unperfected *adjective*
Not perfected, elaborated, or completed : preliminary, rough, sketchy, tentative, unfinished, unpolished. *See* START.

unpitying *adjective*
Not sympathetic : uncaring, uncharitable, uncompassionate, unmoved, unstirred, unsympathetic, untouched. *See* FEELINGS.

unplanned *adjective*
1. Not intended : inadvertent, undesigned, undevised, unintended, unintentional, unmeant, unwitting. *See* PLANNED. **2.** Having no particular pattern, purpose, organization, or structure : chance, desultory, haphazard, hit-or-miss, indiscriminate, random, spot. *See* PLANNED.

unpleasant *adjective*
Not pleasant or agreeable : bad, disagreeable, displeasing, offensive, uncongenial, unsympathetic. *Informal:* icky. *Slang:* yucky. *See* GOOD, PAIN.

unpolished *adjective*
1. Not perfected, elaborated, or completed : preliminary, rough, sketchy, tentative, unfinished, unperfected. *See* START. **2.** Lacking expert, careful craftsmanship : crude, primitive, raw, rough, rude. *See* GOOD. **3.** Lacking good manners : discourteous, disrespectful, ill-bred, ill-mannered, impolite, rude, uncivil, ungracious, unmannerly. *See* COURTESY. **4.** Lacking in delicacy or refinement : barbarian, barbaric, boorish, churlish, coarse, crass, crude, gross, ill-bred, indelicate, philistine, rough, rude, tasteless, uncivilized, uncouth, uncultivated, uncultured, unrefined, vulgar. *See* COURTESY, SMOOTH. **5.** Of a plain and unsophisticated nature : artless, homely, homespun, natural, rustic, unadorned. *See* PLAIN.

unpolitic *adjective*
Lacking sensitivity and skill in dealing with others : brash, clumsy, gauche, impolitic, indelicate, maladroit, tactless, undiplomatic, untactful. *See* ABILITY, COURTESY.

unpracticed *adjective*
1. Not tested or proved : undemonstrated, unproved, untested, untried. *See* ABILITY, KNOWLEDGE. **2.** Lacking experience and the knowledge gained from it : green, inexperienced, inexpert, raw, uninitiate, uninitiated, unseasoned, untried, unversed. *See* ABILITY.

unprecedented *adjective*
Not the same as what was previously known or done : different, fresh, innovative, inventive, new, newfangled, novel, original, unfamiliar. *See* NEW.

unpredictable *adjective*
Following no predictable pattern : capricious, changeable, erratic, fantastic, fantastical, fickle, freakish, inconsistent, inconstant, mercurial, temperamental, ticklish, uncertain, unstable, unsteady, variable, volatile, whimsical. *See* CHANGE, CONTINUE.

unprejudiced *adjective*
1. Free from bias in judgment : disinterested, dispassionate, equitable, fair, fair-minded, impartial, indifferent, just, nonpartisan, objective, square, unbiased. ***Idiom:*** fair and square. *See* FAIR. **2.** Not inclining toward or actively taking either side in a matter under dispute : impartial, neuter, neutral, nonaligned, nonpartisan, unbiased, uncommitted, uninvolved. ***Idiom:*** on the fence. *See* FAIR.

unpremeditated *adjective*
Acting or happening without apparent forethought, prompting, or planning : automatic, impulsive, instinctive, involuntary, reflex, spontaneous. *See* PLANNED.

unpretentious *adjective*
Not elaborate or showy, as in appearance or style : modest, plain, simple, unassuming, unostentatious. *See* PLAIN.

unpretentiousness *noun*
Lack of ostentation or pretension : modesty, plainness, simpleness, simplicity, unassumingness, unostentatiousness. *See* PLAIN.

unprincipled *adjective*
Lacking scruples or principles : conscienceless, ruthless, unconscionable, unethical, unscrupulous. *See* HONEST.

unprocessed *adjective*
In a natural state and still not prepared for use : crude, native, raw, unrefined. *See* CLEAN.

unproductive *adjective*
Lacking or unable to produce growing plants or crops : barren, infertile, sterile, unfruitful. *See* RICH.

unprofessional *adjective*
Lacking the required professional skill : amateurish, dilettante, dilettantish, nonprofessional, unskilled, unskillful. *See* ABILITY.

unprofitable *adjective*
Having no useful result : barren, bootless, fruitless, futile, unavailing, unsuccessful, useless, vain. ***Idiom:*** in vain. *See* THRIVE, USED.

unprofitableness *noun*
The condition or quality of being useless or ineffective : bootlessness, fruitlessness, futility, unavailingness, uselessness, vainness, vanity. *See* THRIVE, USED.

unprogressive *adjective*
Clinging to obsolete ideas : backward, conservative, reactionary. *See* POLITICS.

unpropitious *adjective*
Bringing, predicting, or characterized by misfortune : bad, evil, ill, inauspicious, unfavorable. *See* LUCK.

unprotected *adjective*
1. Devoid of help or protection : defenseless, helpless. *See* SAFETY. **2.** Inadequately protected : insecure, unguarded, unsafe. *See* SAFETY. **3.** Having no protecting or concealing cover : exposed, open, uncovered. *See* PROTECTION.

unproved *adjective*
Not tested or proved : undemonstrated, unpracticed, untested, untried. *See* ABILITY, KNOWLEDGE.

unqualified *adjective*
1. Lacking capability : inadequate, incapable, incompetent, unequal, unfit. *See* ABILITY, EXCESS. **2.** Totally incapable of doing a job : incompetent, unable, unfit. *See* ABILITY. **3.** Without limitations or mitigating conditions : absolute, unconditional, unconditioned, unreserved. *See* LIMITED. **4.** Completely such, without qualification or exception : absolute, all-out, arrant, complete, consummate, crashing, damned, dead, downright, flat, out-and-out, outright, perfect, plain, pure, sheer[2], thorough, thoroughgoing, total, unbounded, unequivocal, unlimited, unmitigated, unrelieved, unreserved, utter[2]. *Informal:* flat-out, positive. *Chiefly British:* blooming. *See* BIG, LIMITED.

unquestionable *adjective*
1. Established beyond a doubt : certain, hard, inarguable, incontestable, incontrovertible, indisputable, indubitable, irrefutable, positive, sure, unassailable, undeniable, undisputable. *See* CERTAIN, TRUE. **2.** Without any doubt : clear, clear-cut, decided, definite, distinct, pronounced. *See* CERTAIN. **3.** Not counterfeit or copied : actual, authentic, bona fide, genuine, good, indubitable, original, real, true, undoubted. *See* TRUE.

unquestionably *adverb*
It is so; as you say or ask : absolutely, agreed, all right, assuredly, aye, gladly, indubitably, roger, undoubtedly, willingly, yea, yes. *Informal:* OK, uh-huh, yeah, yep. *Slang:* right on. *See* AFFIRM.

unquestioning *adjective*
Having no reservations : absolute, implicit, unconditional, undoubting, unfaltering, unhesitating, unreserved, wholehearted. *See* BIG, LIMITED.

unquiet *adjective*
Affording no quiet, repose, or rest : restless, uneasy, unsettled. *See* CALM, TIRED.

unravel *verb*
To find a solution for : clear up, decipher, explain, resolve, solve. *Informal:* dope out, figure out. ***Idiom:*** get to the bottom of. *See* ASK, REASON.

unreachable *adjective*
Unable to be reached : inaccessible, inapproachable, unapproachable, unattainable, unavailable. ***Idioms:*** beyond reach, out of the way. *See* REACH.

unreal *adjective*
Existing only in the imagination : chimeric, chimerical, conceptual, fanciful, fantastic, fantastical, imaginary, notional, visionary. *See* REAL.

unrealistic *adjective*
Not compatible with reality : idealistic, quixotic, romantic, starry-eyed, utopian, visionary. *See* HOPE, REAL.

unrealizable *adjective*
Not capable of happening or being done : impossible, impracticable, impractical, unattainable, unthinkable, unworkable. ***Idiom:*** out of the question. *See* POSSIBLE.

unreason *noun*
The absence of reason : illogicality, illogicalness, irrationality, unreasonableness. *See* REASON.

unreasonable *adjective*
1. Not governed by or predicated on reason : illogical, irrational, unreasoned. ***Idiom:*** out of bounds. *See* REASON. **2.** Beyond all reason : obscene, outrageous, preposterous, ridiculous, shocking, unconscionable. ***Idioms:*** out of bounds, out of sight. *See* USUAL.

unreasonableness *noun*
Absence of reason : illogicality, illogicalness,

irrationality, unreason. *See* REASON.

unreasoned *adjective*
Not governed by or predicated on reason : illogical, irrational, unreasonable. ***Idiom:*** out of bounds. *See* REASON.

unreceptiveness *noun*
Lack of cordiality and hospitableness : inhospitableness, inhospitality, ungraciousness, unwelcome, unwelcomeness. *See* LIKE.

unrecompensed *adjective*
Contributing one's time without pay : uncompensated, unpaid, unremunerated, unsalaried, voluntary. *See* PAY, WORK.

unreel *verb*
To cause (a line) to become longer and less taut : play out, unroll, unwind. *See* GIVE.

unrefined *adjective*
1. In a natural state and still not prepared for use : crude, native, raw, unprocessed. *See* CLEAN. **2.** Lacking in delicacy or refinement : barbarian, barbaric, boorish, churlish, coarse, crass, crude, gross, ill-bred, indelicate, philistine, rough, rude, tasteless, uncivilized, uncouth, uncultivated, uncultured, unpolished, vulgar. *See* COURTESY, SMOOTH.

unrehearsed *adjective*
Spoken, performed, or composed with little or no preparation or forethought : ad-lib, extemporaneous, extemporary, extempore, impromptu, improvised, offhand, snap, spur-of-the-moment. *Informal:* off-the-cuff. *See* PREPARED.

unrelenting *adjective*
Firmly, often unreasonably immovable in purpose or will : adamant, adamantine, brass-bound, die-hard, grim, implacable, incompliant, inexorable, inflexible, intransigent, iron, obdurate, relentless, remorseless, rigid, stubborn, unbendable, unbending, uncompliant, uncompromising, unyielding. ***Idiom:*** stubborn as a mule (*or* ox). *See* RESIST.

unreliable *adjective*
1. So weak or defective as to be liable to fail : trick, undependable. *See* STRONG. **2.** Not to be depended on : undependable, untrustworthy. *See* TRUST.

unrelieved *adjective*
Completely such, without qualification or exception : absolute, all-out, arrant, complete, consummate, crashing, damned, dead, downright, flat, out-and-out, outright, perfect, plain, pure, sheer[2], thorough, thoroughgoing, total, unbounded, unequivocal, unlimited, unmitigated, unqualified, unreserved, utter[2]. *Informal:* flat-out, positive. *Chiefly British:* blooming. *See* BIG, LIMITED.

unremarkable *adjective*
Being of no special quality or type : average, common, commonplace, cut-and-dried, formulaic, garden, garden-variety, indifferent, mediocre, ordinary, plain, routine, run-of-the-mill, standard, stock, undistinguished, unexceptional. *See* GOOD, USUAL.

unremitting *adjective*
Existing or occurring without interruption or end : around-the-clock, ceaseless, constant, continual, continuous, endless, eternal, everlasting, incessant, interminable, nonstop, ongoing, perpetual, persistent, relentless, round-the-clock, timeless, unceasing, unending, unfailing, uninterrupted. *See* CONTINUE.

unremunerated *adjective*
Contributing one's time without pay : uncompensated, unpaid, unrecompensed, unsalaried, voluntary. *See* PAY, WORK.

unrepentant *adjective*
Devoid of remorse : impenitent, remorseless. *See* REGRET.

unrequired *adjective*
Not necessary : dispensable, inessential, needless, nonessential, uncalled-for, unessential, unnecessary, unneeded. *See* NECESSARY.

unreserved *adjective*
1. Not spoken for or occupied : free, open, uninhabited, unoccupied. *See* OWNED. **2.** Without limitations or mitigating conditions : absolute, unconditional, unconditioned, unqualified. *See* LIMITED. **3.** Having no reservations : absolute, implicit, unconditional, undoubting, unfaltering, unhesitating, unquestioning, wholehearted. *See* BIG, LIMITED. **4.** Manifesting honesty and directness, especially in speech : candid, direct, downright, forthright, frank, honest, ingenuous, man-to-man, open, plainspoken, straight, straightforward, straight-out. *Informal:* straight-from-the-shoulder, straight-shooting. *See* CLEAR, SHOW. **5.** Disposed to be open, sociable, and talkative : communicable, communicative, expansive, extraverted, extroverted, gregarious, outgoing. *See* ATTITUDE. **6.** Completely such, without qualification or exception : absolute, all-out, arrant, complete, consummate, crashing, damned, dead, downright, flat, out-and-out, outright, perfect, plain, pure, sheer[2], thorough, thoroughgoing, total, unbounded, unequivocal, unlimited, unmitigated, unqualified, unrelieved, utter[2]. *Informal:* flat-out, positive. *Chiefly British:* blooming. *See* BIG, LIMITED.

unresolved *adjective*
Marked by lack of firm decision or commitment; of questionable outcome : indefinite, open, uncertain, undecided, undetermined, unsettled, unsure, vague. ***Idiom:*** up in the air. *See* CERTAIN.

unresponsive *adjective*
1. Lacking responsiveness or alertness : benumbed, dull, insensible, insensitive, numb, stuporous, torpid, wooden. *See* AWARENESS.
2. Without emotion or interest : apathetic, detached, impassive, incurious, indifferent, insensible, lethargic, listless, phlegmatic, stolid, unconcerned, uninterested. *See* FEELINGS.
3. Deficient in or lacking sexual desire : ardorless, cold, frigid, inhibited, passionless. *See* SEX.

unresponsiveness *noun*
Lack of emotion or interest : apathy, disinterest, impassivity, incuriosity, incuriousness, indifference, insensibility, insensibleness, lassitude, lethargy, listlessness, phlegm, stolidity, stolidness, unconcern, uninterest. *See* FEELINGS.

unrest *noun*
1. An uneasy or nervous state : disquiet, disquietude, inquietude, restiveness, restlessness, unease, uneasiness. *See* CALM. **2.** A state of uneasiness and usually resentment brewing to an eventual explosion : ferment, Sturm und Drang, turmoil. *See* CALM, PEACE.

unrestrained *adjective*
1. Able to move about at will without bounds or restraint : free, loose, unconfined. ***Idioms:*** at large, at liberty, free as a bird, on the loose. *See* FREE. **2.** Lacking in moral restraint : abandoned, dissipated, dissolute, fast, gay, incontinent, licentious, profligate, rakish, unbridled, unconstrained, uncontrolled, ungoverned, uninhibited, wanton, wild. *See* RESTRAINT.
3. Unconstrained by rigid standards or ceremony : casual, easy, easygoing, informal, natural, relaxed, spontaneous, unceremonious. *Informal:* laid-back. *See* PLAIN, TIGHTEN.

unrestraint *noun*
1. A complete surrender of inhibitions : abandon, abandonment, incontinence, wantonness, wildness. *See* RESTRAINT. **2.** Freedom from constraint, formality, embarrassment, or awkwardness : casualness, ease, easiness, informality, naturalness, poise, spontaneity, unceremoniousness. *See* RESTRAINT, TIGHTEN.

unrestricted *adjective*
Not restricted or confined to few : open, open-door, public. *See* OPEN.

unrivaled or **unrivalled** *adjective*
Without equal or rival : alone, incomparable, matchless, nonpareil, only, peerless, singular, unequaled, unexampled, unique, unmatched, unparalleled. *See* SAME.

unroll *verb*
1. To cause (a line) to become longer and less taut : play out, unreel, unwind. *See* GIVE.
2. To move or arrange so as to cover a larger area : expand, extend, fan[1] (out), open (out *or* up), outstretch, spread, stretch, unfold. *See* MOVE.

unromantic *adjective*
Having or indicating an awareness of things as they really are : down-to-earth, hard, hard-headed, matter-of-fact, objective, practical, pragmatic, pragmatical, prosaic, realistic, sober, tough-minded. *See* EXCITE, REAL.

unruffled *adjective*
Not easily excited, even under pressure : calm, collected, composed, cool, cool-headed, detached, even[1], even-tempered, imperturbable, nonchalant, possessed, unflappable. *See* CALM.

unruliness *noun*
The quality or condition of being unruly : disorderliness, fractiousness, indocility, intractability, intractableness, obstinacy, obstinateness, obstreperousness, recalcitrance, recalcitrancy, refractoriness, uncontrollability, uncontrollableness, ungovernableness, unmanageability, untowardness, wildness. *See* CONTROL, ORDER, PEACE, RESIST.

unruly *adjective*
Not submitting to discipline or control : disorderly, fractious, indocile, intractable, lawless, obstinate, obstreperous, recalcitrant, refractory, uncontrollable, undisciplined, ungovernable, unmanageable, untoward, wild. ***Idiom:*** out of line. *See* CONTROL, ORDER, PEACE, RESIST.

unsafe *adjective*
1. Inadequately protected : insecure, unguarded, unprotected. *See* SAFETY.
2. Involving possible risk, loss, or injury : adventurous, chancy, dangerous, hazardous, jeopardous, parlous, perilous, risky, treacherous, venturesome, venturous. *Slang:* hairy. *See* SAFETY.

unsaid *adjective*
1. Not voiced or expressed : silent, tacit, undeclared, unexpressed, unspoken, unuttered, unvoiced, wordless. *See* WORDS. **2.** Conveyed indirectly without words or speech : implicit, implied, inferred, tacit, understood, unspoken, unuttered, wordless. ***Idiom:*** taken for granted. *See* SHOW.

unsalaried *adjective*
Contributing one's time without pay : uncompensated, unpaid, unrecompensed, unremunerated, voluntary. *See* PAY, WORK.

unsalutary *adjective*
Not sustaining or promoting health : insalubrious, unhealthy, unwholesome. *See* HEALTH.

unsatisfactory *adjective*
1. Below a standard of quality : bad, bum[1], poor. ***Idioms:*** below par, not up to scratch (*or* snuff). *See* GOOD. **2.** Tending to discourage, retard, or make more difficult : adverse, disadvantageous, negative, unadvantageous, unfavorable, untoward. *See* HELP.

unsavory *adjective*
1. Lacking an appetizing flavor : bland, flat, flavorless, insipid, tasteless. *See* TASTE. **2.** So unpleasant in flavor as to be inedible : distasteful, unappetizing, unpalatable. *See* TASTE.

unscathed *adjective*
Free from danger, injury, or the threat of harm : safe, unharmed, unhurt, uninjured. ***Idiom:*** safe and sound. *See* SAFETY.

unscholarly *adjective*
Lacking the requisite scholarship or instruction : unlearned, unstudious. *See* KNOWLEDGE.

unschooled *adjective*
Without education or knowledge : ignorant, illiterate, nescient, uneducated, uninstructed, unlearned, untaught. *See* KNOWLEDGE.

unscrupulous *adjective*
Lacking scruples or principles : conscienceless, ruthless, unconscionable, unethical, unprincipled. *See* HONEST.

unseasonable *adjective*
Not suitable for or characteristic of the season : untimely. *See* USUAL.

unseasoned *adjective*
Lacking experience and the knowledge gained from it : green, inexperienced, inexpert, raw, uninitiate, uninitiated, unpracticed, untried, unversed. *See* ABILITY.

unseeing *adjective*
Without the sense of sight : blind, eyeless, sightless. *See* SEE.

unseemliness *noun*
The condition of being improper : improperness, impropriety, inappropriateness, unbecomingness, unfitness, unsuitability, unsuitableness. *See* AGREE, USUAL.

unseemly *adjective*
1. Not in keeping with conventional mores : immodest, improper, indecent, indecorous, indelicate, naughty, unbecoming, unbefitting, untoward. ***Idiom:*** out of line. *See* USUAL. **2.** Not suited to circumstances : improper, inappropriate, inapt, incongruous, inept, malapropos, unapt, unbecoming, unbefitting, unfit, unsuitable. ***Idiom:*** out of place. *See* AGREE, USUAL.

unselfish *adjective*
1. Willing to give of oneself and one's possessions : big, big-hearted, generous, great-hearted, large-hearted, magnanimous. *See* GIVE. **2.** Without concern for oneself : self-denying, self-forgetful, self-forgetting, selfless. *See* SELF.

unselfishness *noun*
The quality or state of being generous : big-heartedness, bounteousness, bountifulness, free-handedness, generosity, generousness, great-heartedness, large-heartedness, lavishness, liberality, magnanimity, magnanimousness, munificence, openhandedness, unsparingness. *See* GIVE.

unserviceable *adjective*
Incapable of being used or availed of to advantage : impracticable, impractical, unnegotiable, unusable, unworkable, useless. *See* USED.

unsettle *verb*
1. To put out of proper order : derange, disarrange, disarray, disorder, disorganize, disrupt, disturb, jumble, mess up, mix up, muddle, tumble, upset. *See* ORDER. **2.** To disturb the health or physiological functioning of : derange, disorder, turn, upset. *See* HEALTH. **3.** To impair or destroy the composure of : agitate, bother, discompose, disquiet, distract, disturb, flurry, fluster, perturb, rock, ruffle, shake (up), toss, upset. *Informal:* rattle. *See* CALM.

unsettled *adjective*
1. Affording no quiet, repose, or rest : restless, uneasy, unquiet. *See* CALM, TIRED. **2.** In a state of anxiety or uneasiness : agitated, anxious, concerned, distressed, nervous, solicitous, uneasy. *See* FEELINGS. **3.** Capable of or liable to change : alterable, changeable, fluid, inconstant, mutable, uncertain, unstable, unsteady, variable, variant. *Archaic:* various. *See* CHANGE. **4.** Marked by lack of firm decision or commitment; of questionable outcome : indefinite, open, uncertain, undecided, undetermined, unresolved, unsure, vague. ***Idiom:*** up in the air. *See* CERTAIN. **5.** Owed as a debt : due, outstanding, owed, owing, payable, receivable, unpaid. *See* PAY.

unsettling *adjective*
Troubling to the mind or emotions : disquieting, disruptive, distressful, distressing, disturb-

ing, intrusive, perturbing, troublesome, troublous, upsetting, worrisome. *See* HAPPY, PAIN.

unsex *verb*
To render incapable of reproducing sexually : alter, castrate, fix, geld, neuter, spay, sterilize. *See* REPRODUCTION, RICH.

unshakable *adjective*
Not easily moved or shaken : firm[1], secure, solid, sound[2], stable, strong, sturdy, substantial, sure. *See* CONTINUE, STRONG.

unshaped *adjective*
Having no distinct shape : amorphous, formless, inchoate, shapeless, unformed. *See* ORDER.

unsightliness *noun*
The quality or condition of being ugly : hideousness, ugliness. *See* BEAUTIFUL.

unsightly *adjective*
Extremely displeasing to the eye : hideous, ill-favored, ugly. *Idiom:* ugly as sin. *See* BEAUTIFUL.

unsigned *adjective*
Having an unknown name or author : anonymous, nameless, unnamed. *See* KNOWLEDGE.

unskilled *adjective*
1. Lacking the qualities, as efficiency or skill, required to produce desired results : inapt, incapable, incompetent, inefficient, inept, inexpert, unskillful, unworkmanlike. *See* ABILITY. **2.** Lacking the required professional skill : amateurish, dilettante, dilettantish, nonprofessional, unprofessional, unskillful. *See* ABILITY.

unskillful *adjective*
1. Lacking the qualities, as efficiency or skill, required to produce desired results : inapt, incapable, incompetent, inefficient, inept, inexpert, unskilled, unworkmanlike. *See* ABILITY. **2.** Lacking the required professional skill : amateurish, dilettante, dilettantish, nonprofessional, unprofessional, unskilled. *See* ABILITY. **3.** Clumsily lacking in the ability to do or perform : awkward, bumbling, clumsy, gauche, heavy-handed, inept, maladroit. *See* ABILITY.

unsleeping *adjective*
Not in a state of sleep : awake, wakeful, wide-awake. *See* AWARENESS.

unsoiled *adjective*
Free from dirt, stain, or impurities : antiseptic, clean, cleanly, immaculate, spotless, stainless, unsullied. *See* CLEAN.

unsophisticated *adjective*
Free from guile, cunning, or deceit : artless, guileless, ingenuous, innocent, naive, natural, simple, unaffected, unstudied, unworldly. *See* HONEST.

unsought *adjective*
Not welcome or wanted : undesirable, undesired, uninvited, unwanted, unwelcome, unwished-for. *See* LIKE.

unsound *adjective*
1. Not physically strong : decrepit, delicate, feeble, flimsy, fragile, frail, infirm, insubstantial, puny, unsubstantial, weak, weakly. *See* STRONG. **2.** Afflicted with or exhibiting irrationality and mental unsoundness : brainsick, crazy, daft, demented, disordered, distraught, dotty, insane, lunatic, mad, maniac, maniacal, mentally ill, moonstruck, off, touched, unbalanced, wrong. *Informal:* bonkers, cracked, daffy, gaga, loony. *Slang:* bananas, batty, buggy, cuckoo, fruity, loco, nuts, nutty, screwy, wacky. *Chiefly British:* crackers. *Law:* non compos mentis. ***Idioms:*** around the bend, crazy as a loon, mad as a hatter, not all there, nutty as a fruitcake, off (*or* out of) one's head, off one's rocker, of unsound mind, out of one's mind, sick in the head, stark raving mad. *See* SANE. **3.** Containing fundamental errors in reasoning : fallacious, false, illogical, invalid, sophistic, specious, spurious. *See* CORRECT, TRUE. **4.** Containing an error or errors : erroneous, fallacious, false, inaccurate, incorrect, mistaken, off, untrue, wrong. ***Idioms:*** all wet, in error, off base, off (*or* wide of) the mark. *See* CORRECT. **5.** Not wise : ill-advised, ill-considered, impolitic, imprudent, indiscreet, injudicious, unwise. *See* WISE.

unsoundness *noun*
The condition of being infirm or physically weak : debility, decrepitude, delicacy, delicateness, feebleness, flimsiness, fragileness, fragility, frailness, frailty, infirmity, insubstantiality, puniness, unsubstantiality, weakliness, weakness. *See* STRONG.

unsparing *adjective*
Characterized by bounteous giving : free, freehanded, generous, handsome, lavish, liberal, munificent, openhanded, unstinting. *See* GIVE.

unsparingness *noun*
The quality or state of being generous : bigheartedness, bounteousness, bountifulness, freehandedness, generosity, generousness, greatheartedness, large-heartedness, lavishness, liberality, magnanimity, magnanimousness, munificence, openhandedness, unselfishness. *See* GIVE.

unspeakable *adjective*
1. That cannot be described : incommunicable, indefinable, indescribable, ineffable, inexpressible, undescribable, unutterable. ***Idioms:*** beyond

description (*or* words), defying description. *See* WORDS. **2.** That may not be spoken of or uttered : unmentionable. *See* DECENT, GOOD, WORDS.

unspoken *adjective*
1. Not voiced or expressed : silent, tacit, undeclared, unexpressed, unsaid, unuttered, unvoiced, wordless. *See* WORDS. **2.** Conveyed indirectly without words or speech : implicit, implied, inferred, tacit, understood, unsaid, unuttered, wordless. ***Idiom:*** taken for granted. *See* SHOW.

unstable *adjective*
1. Capable of or liable to change : alterable, changeable, fluid, inconstant, mutable, uncertain, unsettled, unsteady, variable, variant. *Archaic:* various. *See* CHANGE. **2.** Following no predictable pattern : capricious, changeable, erratic, fantastic, fantastical, fickle, freakish, inconsistent, inconstant, mercurial, temperamental, ticklish, uncertain, unpredictable, unsteady, variable, volatile, whimsical. *See* CHANGE, CONTINUE. **3.** Lacking stability : infirm, insecure, precarious, shaky, tottering, tottery, unsteady, unsure, weak, wobbly. *See* CHANGE, STRONG. **4.** Not physically steady or firm : precarious, rickety, shaky, tottering, tottery, unsteady, wobbly. *See* FLEXIBLE.

unstableness *noun*
1. The quality or condition of being physically unsteady : instability, precariousness, ricketiness, shakiness, unsteadiness, wobbliness. *See* FLEXIBLE. **2.** The quality or condition of being erratic and undependable : insecureness, insecurity, instability, precariousness, shakiness, unsteadiness, unsureness. *See* CHANGE, STRONG.

unstained *adjective*
Free from evil and corruption : angelic, angelical, clean, innocent, lily-white, pure, sinless, unblemished, uncorrupted, undefiled, unsullied, untainted, virginal. ***Idiom:*** pure as the driven snow. *See* CLEAN, RIGHT, SEX.

unsteadiness *noun*
1. The quality or condition of being physically unsteady : instability, precariousness, ricketiness, shakiness, unstableness, wobbliness. *See* FLEXIBLE. **2.** The quality or condition of being erratic and undependable : insecureness, insecurity, instability, precariousness, shakiness, unstableness, unsureness. *See* CHANGE, STRONG.

unsteady *adjective*
1. Not physically steady or firm : precarious, rickety, shaky, tottering, tottery, unstable, wobbly. *See* FLEXIBLE. **2.** Lacking stability : infirm, insecure, precarious, shaky, tottering, tottery, unstable, unsure, weak, wobbly. *See* CHANGE, STRONG. **3.** Capable of or liable to change : alterable, changeable, fluid, inconstant, mutable, uncertain, unsettled, unstable, variable, variant. *Archaic:* various. *See* CHANGE. **4.** Following no predictable pattern : capricious, changeable, erratic, fantastic, fantastical, fickle, freakish, inconsistent, inconstant, mercurial, temperamental, ticklish, uncertain, unpredictable, unstable, variable, volatile, whimsical. *See* CHANGE, CONTINUE. **5.** Lacking consistency or regularity in quality or performance : erratic, inconsistent, patchy, spotty, uneven, variable. *See* CONTINUE, SAME.

unstinting *adjective*
Characterized by bounteous giving : free, freehanded, generous, handsome, lavish, liberal, munificent, openhanded, unsparing. *See* GIVE.

unstirred *adjective*
Not sympathetic : uncaring, uncharitable, uncompassionate, unmoved, unpitying, unsympathetic, untouched. *See* FEELINGS.

unstudied *adjective*
Free from guile, cunning, or deceit : artless, guileless, ingenuous, innocent, naive, natural, simple, unaffected, unsophisticated, unworldly. *See* HONEST.

unstudious *adjective*
Lacking the requisite scholarship or instruction : unlearned, unscholarly. *See* KNOWLEDGE.

unsubstantial *adjective*
1. Having no body, form, or substance : bodiless, discarnate, disembodied, immaterial, incorporeal, insubstantial, metaphysical, nonphysical, spiritual, unbodied, uncorporal. *See* BODY. **2.** Not physically strong : decrepit, delicate, feeble, flimsy, fragile, frail, infirm, insubstantial, puny, unsound, weak, weakly. *See* STRONG. **3.** Having little substance or significance; not solidly based : feeble, flimsy, insubstantial, tenuous. *See* STRONG. **4.** Not plausible or believable : flimsy, implausible, improbable, inconceivable, incredible, shaky, thin, unbelievable, unconceivable, unconvincing, weak. *See* LIKELY.

unsubstantiality *noun*
The condition of being infirm or physically weak : debility, decrepitude, delicacy, delicateness, feebleness, flimsiness, fragileness, fragility, frailness, frailty, infirmity, insubstantiality,

puniness, unsoundness, weakliness, weakness. *See* STRONG.

unsubtle *adjective*
Easily seen through due to a lack of subtlety : broad, clear, obvious, patent, plain, unmistakable. *See* CLEAR, SEE.

unsuccess *noun*
The condition of not achieving the desired end : failure, unsuccessfulness. *See* THRIVE.

unsuccessful *adjective*
Having no useful result : barren, bootless, fruitless, futile, unavailing, unprofitable, useless, vain. ***Idiom:*** in vain. *See* THRIVE, USED.

unsuccessfulness *noun*
The condition of not achieving the desired end : failure, unsuccess. *See* THRIVE.

unsufferable *adjective*
So unpleasant or painful as not to be endured or tolerated : impossible, insufferable, insupportable, intolerable, unbearable, unendurable, unsupportable. *See* PAIN.

unsuitability *noun*
The condition of being improper : improperness, impropriety, inappropriateness, unbecomingness, unfitness, unseemliness, unsuitableness. *See* AGREE, USUAL.

unsuitable *adjective*
1. Not suited to circumstances : improper, inappropriate, inapt, incongruous, inept, malapropos, unapt, unbecoming, unbefitting, unfit, unseemly. ***Idiom:*** out of place. *See* AGREE, USUAL. **2.** Not suited to a given purpose : ill-suited, inappropriate, inapt, unfit, unsuited. *See* ABILITY.

unsuitableness *noun*
The condition of being improper : improperness, impropriety, inappropriateness, unbecomingness, unfitness, unseemliness, unsuitability. *See* AGREE, USUAL.

unsuited *adjective*
Not suited to a given purpose : ill-suited, inappropriate, inapt, unfit, unsuitable. *See* ABILITY.

unsullied *adjective*
1. Free from dirt, stain, or impurities : antiseptic, clean, cleanly, immaculate, spotless, stainless, unsoiled. *See* CLEAN. **2.** Free from evil and corruption : angelic, angelical, clean, innocent, lily-white, pure, sinless, unblemished, uncorrupted, undefiled, unstained, untainted, virginal. ***Idiom:*** pure as the driven snow. *See* CLEAN, RIGHT, SEX.

unsupportable *adjective*
So unpleasant or painful as not to be endured or tolerated : impossible, insufferable, insupportable, intolerable, unbearable, unendurable, unsufferable. *See* PAIN.

unsure *adjective*
1. Not affording certainty : ambiguous, borderline, chancy, clouded, doubtful, dubious, dubitable, equivocal, inconclusive, indecisive, indeterminate, problematic, problematical, questionable, uncertain, unclear. *Informal:* iffy. ***Idioms:*** at issue, in doubt, in question. *See* CERTAIN, CLEAR. **2.** Marked by lack of firm decision or commitment; of questionable outcome : indefinite, open, uncertain, undecided, undetermined, unresolved, unsettled, vague. ***Idiom:*** up in the air. *See* CERTAIN. **3.** Lacking stability : infirm, insecure, precarious, shaky, tottering, tottery, unstable, unsteady, weak, wobbly. *See* CHANGE, STRONG. **4.** Experiencing doubt : doubtful, dubious, skeptical, uncertain, undecided. ***Idiom:*** in doubt. *See* CERTAIN.

unsureness *noun*
The quality or condition of being erratic and undependable : insecureness, insecurity, instability, precariousness, shakiness, unstableness, unsteadiness. *See* CHANGE, STRONG.

unsurpassable *adjective*
Of the greatest possible degree, quality, or intensity : extreme, supreme, transcendent, ultimate, utmost, uttermost. *See* BETTER, BIG.

unsurpassed *adjective*
Surpassing all others in quality : best, optimal, optimum, superlative. *See* BETTER.

unsusceptibility *noun*
The capacity to withstand : immunity, imperviousness, insusceptibility, resistance. *See* RESIST.

unsusceptible *adjective*
1. Having the capacity to withstand : immune, impervious, insusceptible, proof, resistant, resistive. *See* RESIST. **2.** Not capable of being affected or impressed : impassible, impassive, insensitive, insusceptible, unimpressionable. *See* AFFECT.

unswerving *adjective*
Not diffused or dispersed : concentrated, exclusive, intensive, undivided, whole. *See* COLLECT, EDGE, PART.

unsympathetic *adjective*
1. Not sympathetic : uncaring, uncharitable, uncompassionate, unmoved, unpitying, unstirred, untouched. *See* FEELINGS. **2.** Not pleasant or agreeable : bad, disagreeable, displeasing, offensive, uncongenial, unpleasant. *Informal:* icky. *Slang:* yucky. *See* GOOD, PAIN.

unsystematic *adjective*
Lacking regular or logical order : disorderly, messy. *See* ORDER.

untactful *adjective*
Lacking sensitivity and skill in dealing with others : brash, clumsy, gauche, impolitic, indelicate, maladroit, tactless, undiplomatic, unpolitic. *See* ABILITY, COURTESY.

untainted *adjective*
Free from evil and corruption : angelic, angelical, clean, innocent, lily-white, pure, sinless, unblemished, uncorrupted, undefiled, unstained, unsullied, virginal. ***Idiom:*** pure as the driven snow. *See* CLEAN, RIGHT, SEX.

untamed *adjective*
In a primitive state; not domesticated or cultivated; produced by nature : native, natural, rough, uncultivated, undomesticated, wild. *See* WILD.

untangle *verb*
To free from an entanglement : clear, disengage, disentangle, disinvolve, extricate. *See* FREE.

untaught *adjective*
Without education or knowledge : ignorant, illiterate, nescient, uneducated, uninstructed, unlearned, unschooled. *See* KNOWLEDGE.

untested *adjective*
Not tested or proved : undemonstrated, unpracticed, unproved, untried. *See* ABILITY, KNOWLEDGE.

unthankful *adjective*
1. Not showing or feeling gratitude : thankless, unappreciative, ungrateful, unthanking. *See* GRATEFUL. **2.** Not apt to be appreciated : thankless, unappreciated, ungrateful. *See* GRATEFUL.

unthanking *adjective*
Not showing or feeling gratitude : thankless, unappreciative, ungrateful, unthankful. *See* GRATEFUL.

unthinkable *adjective*
1. Not to be believed : inconceivable, incredible, unbelievable, unimaginable. ***Idioms:*** beyond belief, contrary to all reason. *See* BELIEF. **2.** Not capable of happening or being done : impossible, impracticable, impractical, unattainable, unrealizable, unworkable. ***Idiom:*** out of the question. *See* POSSIBLE.

unthinking *adjective*
1. Lacking or marked by a lack of care : careless, feckless, heedless, inattentive, irresponsible, reckless, thoughtless, unconcerned, unmindful. *See* CAREFUL. **2.** Showing no concern, attention, or regard : careless, forgetful, heedless, mindless, unconcerned, unheeding, unmindful, unobservant. *See* CAREFUL. **3.** Devoid of consideration for others' feelings : disregardful, inconsiderate, thoughtless, unthoughtful. *See* CAREFUL, COURTESY.

unthoughtful *adjective*
Devoid of consideration for others' feelings : disregardful, inconsiderate, thoughtless, unthinking. *See* CAREFUL, COURTESY.

unthoughtfulness *noun*
A lack of consideration for others' feelings : disregard, inconsiderateness, inconsideration, thoughtlessness. *See* COURTESY.

unthrifty *adjective*
Reckless, especially in the use of material resources : improvident, thriftless. *See* CAREFUL.

untidiness *noun*
The state of being messy or unkempt : disorderliness, messiness, sloppiness, slovenliness. *See* ORDER.

untidy *adjective*
1. Marked by an absence of cleanliness and order : disheveled, messy, mussy, slipshod, sloppy, slovenly, unkempt. *See* ORDER. **2.** Indifferent to correctness, accuracy, or neatness : careless, messy, slapdash, slipshod, sloppy, slovenly. *See* CAREFUL.

untie *verb*
To free from ties or fasteners : disengage, loose, loosen, slip, unbind, unclasp, undo, unfasten, unloose, unloosen. *See* TIGHTEN.

untighten *verb*
To reduce in tension, pressure, or rigidity : ease, let up, loose, loosen, relax, slack, slacken. *See* TIGHTEN.

untimely *adjective*
1. Not occurring at a favorable time : ill-timed, inconvenient, inopportune. *See* TIME. **2.** Not suitable for or characteristic of the season : unseasonable. *See* USUAL. **3.** Developing, occurring, or appearing before the expected time : early, precocious, premature. *See* TIME.

untiring *adjective*
Having or showing a capacity for protracted effort, regardless of difficulty or frustration : indefatigable, inexhaustible, tireless, unfailing, unflagging, unwearied, weariless. *See* CONTINUE, TIRED.

untouched *adjective*
Not sympathetic : uncaring, uncharitable, uncompassionate, unmoved, unpitying, unstirred, unsympathetic. *See* FEELINGS.

untoward *adjective*
1. Tending to discourage, retard, or make more

difficult : adverse, disadvantageous, negative, unadvantageous, unfavorable, unsatisfactory. *See* HELP. **2.** Involving or undergoing chance misfortune : hapless, ill-fated, ill-starred, luckless, star-crossed, unfortunate, unhappy, unlucky. *See* LUCK. **3.** Not submitting to discipline or control : disorderly, fractious, indocile, intractable, lawless, obstinate, obstreperous, recalcitrant, refractory, uncontrollable, undisciplined, ungovernable, unmanageable, unruly, wild. ***Idiom:*** out of line. *See* CONTROL, ORDER, PEACE, RESIST. **4.** Not in keeping with conventional mores : immodest, improper, indecent, indecorous, indelicate, naughty, unbecoming, unbefitting, unseemly. ***Idiom:*** out of line. *See* USUAL.

untowardness *noun*

1. Bad fortune : adversity, haplessness, misfortune, unfortunateness, unluckiness. *See* LUCK. **2.** The quality or condition of being unruly : disorderliness, fractiousness, indocility, intractability, intractableness, obstinacy, obstinateness, obstreperousness, recalcitrance, recalcitrancy, refractoriness, uncontrollability, uncontrollableness, ungovernableness, unmanageability, unruliness, wildness. *See* CONTROL, ORDER, PEACE, RESIST.

untried *adjective*

1. Not tested or proved : undemonstrated, unpracticed, unproved, untested. *See* ABILITY, KNOWLEDGE. **2.** Lacking experience and the knowledge gained from it : green, inexperienced, inexpert, raw, uninitiate, uninitiated, unpracticed, unseasoned, unversed. *See* ABILITY.

untroubled *adjective*

Motionless and undisturbed : calm, halcyon, peaceful, placid, quiet, serene, still, stilly, tranquil. *See* CALM.

untroubledness *noun*

An absence of motion or disturbance : calm, calmness, hush, lull, peace, peacefulness, placidity, placidness, quiet, quietness, serenity, stillness, tranquillity. *See* CALM.

untrue *adjective*

1. Devoid of truth : counterfactual, false, specious, spurious, truthless, untruthful, wrong. *See* TRUE. **2.** Containing an error or errors : erroneous, fallacious, false, inaccurate, incorrect, mistaken, off, unsound, wrong. ***Idioms:*** all wet, in error, off base, off (*or* wide of) the mark. *See* CORRECT. **3.** Not true to duty or obligation : disloyal, faithless, false, false-hearted, perfidious, recreant, traitorous, treacherous, unfaithful. *See* CONTINUE, TRUST.

untrusting *adjective*

Lacking trust or confidence : distrustful, doubting, leery, mistrustful, suspicious. *See* TRUST.

untrustworthy *adjective*

Not to be depended on : undependable, unreliable. *See* TRUST.

untruth *noun*

1. An untrue declaration : canard, cock-and-bull story, falsehood, falsity, fib, fiction, inveracity, lie[2], misrepresentation, misstatement, prevarication, story, tale. *Informal:* fish story, tall tale. *Slang:* whopper. *See* TRUE. **2.** An erroneous or false idea : erroneousness, error, fallacy, falsehood, falseness, falsity. *See* CORRECT, TRUE.

untruthful *adjective*

1. Devoid of truth : counterfactual, false, specious, spurious, truthless, untrue, wrong. *See* TRUE. **2.** Given to or marked by deliberate concealment or misrepresentation of the truth : deceitful, dishonest, lying, mendacious. *See* HONEST.

untruthfulness *noun*

The practice of lying : falsehood, inveracity, mendacity, perjury, truthlessness. *See* TRUE.

unusable *adjective*

1. Incapable of being used or availed of to advantage : impracticable, impractical, unnegotiable, unserviceable, unworkable, useless. *See* USED. **2.** Having no useful purpose : ineffectual, inutile, useless, worthless. *See* USED.

unused *adjective*

Not occupied or put to use : idle, inactive, unemployed, vacant. *See* USED.

unusual *adjective*

1. Rarely occurring or appearing : infrequent, occasional, rare, scarce, sporadic, uncommon. ***Idiom:*** few and far between. *See* USUAL. **2.** Not usual or ordinary : atypic, atypical, novel, unconventional, unordinary, unwonted. *Slang:* offbeat. *See* USUAL. **3.** Deviating from the customary : bizarre, cranky, curious, eccentric, erratic, freakish, idiosyncratic, odd, outlandish, peculiar, quaint, queer, quirky, singular, strange, unnatural, weird. *Slang:* kooky, screwball. *British Slang:* rum, rummy[2]. *See* USUAL. **4.** Far beyond what is usual, normal, or customary : exceptional, extraordinary, magnificent, outstanding, preeminent, rare, remarkable, singular, towering, uncommon. *Informal:* standout. *Slang:* awesome, out of sight. *See* BETTER, USUAL.

unusually *adverb*
In a manner or to a degree that is unusual : exceptionally, extraordinarily, remarkably, singularly, uncommonly. *See* USUAL.

unutterable *adjective*
That cannot be described : incommunicable, indefinable, indescribable, ineffable, inexpressible, undescribable, unspeakable. ***Idioms:*** beyond description (*or* words), defying description. *See* WORDS.

unuttered *adjective*
1. Not voiced or expressed : silent, tacit, undeclared, unexpressed, unsaid, unspoken, unvoiced, wordless. *See* WORDS. **2.** Conveyed indirectly without words or speech : implicit, implied, inferred, tacit, understood, unsaid, unspoken, wordless. ***Idiom:*** taken for granted. *See* SHOW.

unvarnished *adjective*
Without addition, decoration, or qualification : bald, bare, dry, plain, simple, unadorned. *See* PLAIN.

unvarying *adjective*
Having no change or variation : changeless, constant, equable, even[1], invariable, invariant, regular, same, steady, unchanging, uniform. *See* SAME.

unveil *verb*
1. To make visible; bring to view : bare, disclose, display, expose, reveal, show, unclothe, uncover, unmask. *Archaic:* discover. ***Idioms:*** bring to light, lay open, make plain. *See* SHOW. **2.** To disclose in a breach of confidence : betray, blab, divulge, expose, give away, let out, reveal, tell, uncover. *Informal:* spill. *Archaic:* discover. ***Idioms:*** let slip, let the cat out of the bag, spill the beans, tell all. *See* SHOW.

unversed *adjective*
Lacking experience and the knowledge gained from it : green, inexperienced, inexpert, raw, uninitiate, uninitiated, unpracticed, unseasoned, untried. *See* ABILITY.

unvoiced *adjective*
Not voiced or expressed : silent, tacit, undeclared, unexpressed, unsaid, unspoken, unuttered, wordless. *See* WORDS.

unwanted *adjective*
1. Not welcome or wanted : undesirable, undesired, uninvited, unsought, unwelcome, unwished-for. *See* LIKE. **2.** Arousing disapproval : exceptionable, ill-favored, inadmissible, objectionable, unacceptable, undesirable, unwelcome. *See* LIKE.

unwarranted *adjective*
Having no basis or foundation in fact : baseless, bottomless, groundless, idle, unfounded. *See* TRUE.

unwarrantedly *adverb*
Without basis or foundation in fact : groundlessly, unfoundedly. *See* REASON.

unwashed *adjective*
Lacking high station or birth : baseborn, common, déclassé, declassed, humble, ignoble, lowly, mean[2], plebeian, vulgar. *Archaic:* base[2]. *See* OVER.

unwavering *adjective*
Indicating or possessing determination, resolution, or persistence : constant, determined, firm[1], resolute, steadfast, steady, stiff, tough, unbending, uncompromising, unflinching, unyielding. *See* PURPOSE.

unwearied *adjective*
Having or showing a capacity for protracted effort, regardless of difficulty or frustration : indefatigable, inexhaustible, tireless, unfailing, unflagging, untiring, weariless. *See* CONTINUE, TIRED.

unwed *adjective*
Without a spouse : fancy-free, footloose, lone, single, sole, spouseless, unattached, unmarried. ***Idiom:*** footloose and fancy-free. *See* MARRIAGE.

unwelcome *adjective*
1. Not welcome or wanted : undesirable, undesired, uninvited, unsought, unwanted, unwished-for. *See* LIKE. **2.** Arousing disapproval : exceptionable, ill-favored, inadmissible, objectionable, unacceptable, undesirable, unwanted. *See* LIKE.
unwelcome *noun* Lack of cordiality and hospitableness : inhospitableness, inhospitality, ungraciousness, unreceptiveness, unwelcomeness. *See* LIKE.

unwelcomeness *noun*
Lack of cordiality and hospitableness : inhospitableness, inhospitality, ungraciousness, unreceptiveness, unwelcome. *See* LIKE.

unwell *adjective*
Suffering from or affected with an illness : down, ill, sick. *Informal:* laid up. *Chiefly Regional:* poorly. *See* HEALTH.

unwholesome *adjective*
1. Not sustaining or promoting health : insalubrious, unhealthy, unsalutary. *See* HEALTH. **2.** Morally detrimental : contaminative, corruptive, demoralizing, unhealthy. *See* RIGHT. **3.** Susceptible to or marked by preoccupation with unwholesome matters : macabre, morbid, sick, unhealthy. *See* GOOD. **4.** Extremely unpleasant to the senses or feelings : atrocious,

disgusting, foul, horrid, nasty, nauseating, offensive, repellent, repulsive, revolting, sickening, ugly, vile. *See* LIKE, PAIN.

unwholesomeness *noun*
Impure condition : defilement, dirtiness, foulness, impurity, pollution, uncleanness. *See* CLEAN.

unwieldy *adjective*
Difficult to handle or manage : awkward, bulky, clumsy, ungainly, unhandy, unmanageable. *See* EASY.

unwilling *adjective*
Not inclined or willing to do or undertake : averse, disinclined, indisposed, loath, reluctant. *See* WILLING.

unwillingness *noun*
The state of not being disposed or inclined : averseness, disinclination, indisposition, reluctance. *See* WILLING.

unwind *verb*
1. To cause (a line) to become longer and less taut : play out, unreel, unroll. *See* GIVE. **2.** To take repose by ceasing work or other effort for an interval of time : relax, rest[1], unbend. ***Idioms:*** lead (*or* live) the life of Riley, take it easy. *See* CONTINUE.

unwise *adjective*
Not wise : ill-advised, ill-considered, impolitic, imprudent, indiscreet, injudicious, unsound. *See* WISE.

unwished-for *adjective*
Not welcome or wanted : undesirable, undesired, uninvited, unsought, unwanted, unwelcome. *See* LIKE.

unwitting *adjective*
1. Not aware or informed : ignorant, innocent, oblivious, unacquainted, unaware, unconscious, unenlightened, unfamiliar, uninformed, unknowing. ***Idiom:*** in the dark. *See* KNOWLEDGE. **2.** Not intended : inadvertent, undesigned, undevised, unintended, unintentional, unmeant, unplanned. *See* PLANNED.

unwonted *adjective*
Not usual or ordinary : atypic, atypical, novel, unconventional, unordinary, unusual. *Slang:* offbeat. *See* USUAL.

unworkable *adjective*
1. Not capable of happening or being done : impossible, impracticable, impractical, unattainable, unrealizable, unthinkable. ***Idiom:*** out of the question. *See* POSSIBLE. **2.** Incapable of being used or availed of to advantage : impracticable, impractical, unnegotiable, unserviceable, unusable, useless. *See* USED.

unworkmanlike *adjective*
Lacking the qualities, as efficiency or skill, required to produce desired results : inapt, incapable, incompetent, inefficient, inept, inexpert, unskilled, unskillful. *See* ABILITY.

unworldly *adjective*
1. Of or concerned with the spirit rather than the body or material things : numinous, otherworldly, spiritual. *See* BODY. **2.** Free from guile, cunning, or deceit : artless, guileless, ingenuous, innocent, naive, natural, simple, unaffected, unsophisticated, unstudied. *See* HONEST.

unwritten *adjective*
Expressed or transmitted in speech : oral, spoken, verbal, word-of-mouth. *See* WORDS.

unyielding *adjective*
1. Not changing shape or bending : inelastic, inflexible, rigid, stiff, unbending. *See* FLEXIBLE. **2.** Indicating or possessing determination, resolution, or persistence : constant, determined, firm[1], resolute, steadfast, steady, stiff, tough, unbending, uncompromising, unflinching, unwavering. *See* PURPOSE. **3.** Rigorous and unsparing in treating others : demanding, exacting, hard, harsh, rigid, severe, stern, strict, tough. *See* EASY. **4.** Firmly, often unreasonably immovable in purpose or will : adamant, adamantine, brassbound, die-hard, grim, implacable, incompliant, inexorable, inflexible, intransigent, iron, obdurate, relentless, remorseless, rigid, stubborn, unbendable, unbending, uncompliant, uncompromising, unrelenting. ***Idiom:*** stubborn as a mule (*or* ox). *See* RESIST.

up *adjective*
Slang. Feeling great delight and joy : elate, elated, elevated, overjoyed. *See* HAPPY.
up *verb* To increase in amount : boost, hike, jack (up), jump, raise. *See* INCREASE.

up-and-comer *noun*
One showing much promise : comer, rising star. *See* ABILITY.

up-and-coming *adjective*
Showing great promise : coming, promising. ***Idiom:*** on the way up. *See* INCREASE.

upbeat *adjective*
1. *Informal.* Expecting a favorable outcome or dwelling on hopeful aspects : optimistic, Panglossian, roseate, rose-colored, rosy, sanguine. ***Idioms:*** looking on the bright side, looking through rose-colored glasses. *See* HOPE.
2. *Informal.* Of a constructive nature : affirmative, positive. *See* HELP.

upbraid *verb*
To criticize for a fault or offense : admonish,

call down, castigate, chastise, chide, dress down, rap[1], rebuke, reprimand, reproach, reprove, scold, tax. *Informal:* bawl out, lambaste. *Slang:* chew out. ***Idioms:*** bring (*or* call *or* take) to task, call on the carpet, haul (*or* rake) over the coals, let someone have it. *See* ATTACK, PRAISE.

upcoming *adjective*
In the relatively near future : approaching, coming, forthcoming. *See* NEAR.

update *verb*
To make modern in appearance or style : modernize. *See* NEW.

upgrade *verb*
1. To advance to a more desirable state : ameliorate, amend, better[1], help, improve, meliorate. *See* HELP. **2.** To raise in rank : advance, elevate, jump, promote, raise. *See* RISE.
upgrade *noun* **1.** The act of making better or the condition of being made better : amelioration, amendment, betterment, improvement, melioration. *See* BETTER. **2.** A progression upward in rank : advancement, elevation, jump, promotion, rise. *See* RISE.

upheaval *noun*
A momentous or sweeping change : cataclysm, convulsion, revolution. *See* CHANGE.

uphill *adjective*
Not easy to do, achieve, or master : arduous, difficult, hard, laborious, serious, tall, tough. *See* EASY.

uphold *verb*
1. To move (something) to a higher position : boost, elevate, heave, hoist, lift, pick up, raise, rear[2], take up, uplift, upraise, uprear. *See* RISE. **2.** To keep from yielding or failing during stress or difficulty : bolster, buoy (up), prop, support, sustain. *See* HELP. **3.** To sustain the weight of : bear, carry, hold, support. *See* SUPPORT. **4.** To aid the cause of by approving or favoring : advocate, back, champion, endorse, get behind, plump for, recommend, side with, stand behind, stand by, support. ***Idioms:*** align oneself with, go to bat for, take the part of. *See* SUPPORT.

upkeep *noun*
The means needed to support life : alimentation, alimony, bread, bread and butter, keep, livelihood, living, maintenance, subsistence, support, sustenance. *See* MONEY.

uplift *verb*
1. To move (something) to a higher position : boost, elevate, heave, hoist, lift, pick up, raise, rear[2], take up, uphold, upraise, uprear. *See* RISE. **2.** To raise to a high position or status : aggrandize, apotheosize, dignify, elevate, ennoble, exalt, glorify, magnify. ***Idiom:*** put on a pedestal. *See* RISE. **3.** To raise the spirits of : animate, buoy (up), elate, elevate, exhilarate, flush, inspire, inspirit, lift. *Obsolete:* exalt. *See* HAPPY.
uplift *noun* High spirits : animation, elatedness, elation, euphoria, exaltation, exhilaration, inspiration, lift. *See* HAPPY.

upmost *adjective*
Of, being, located at, or forming the top : highest, loftiest, top, topmost, uppermost. *See* HIGH.

upper *adjective*
Being at a height or level above another : higher, superior. *See* HIGH.

upper class *noun*
People of the highest social level : aristocracy, blue blood, crème de la crème, elite, flower, gentility, gentry, nobility, patriciate, quality, society, who's who. *Informal:* upper crust. *See* OVER.
upper-class *adjective* Of high birth or social position : aristocratic, blue-blooded, elite, highborn, highbred, noble, patrician, thoroughbred, wellborn. *Informal:* upper-crust. *See* OVER.

upper crust *noun*
Informal. People of the highest social level : aristocracy, blue blood, crème de la crème, elite, flower, gentility, gentry, nobility, patriciate, quality, society, upper class, who's who. *See* OVER.
upper-crust *adjective Informal.* Of high birth or social position : aristocratic, blue-blooded, elite, highborn, highbred, noble, patrician, thoroughbred, upper-class, wellborn. *See* OVER.

upper hand *noun*
A dominating position, as in a conflict : advantage, better[1], bulge, draw, drop, edge, superiority, vantage. *Informal:* inside track, jump. *See* OVER.

uppermost *adjective*
Of, being, located at, or forming the top : highest, loftiest, top, topmost, upmost. *See* HIGH.

uppish *adjective*
1. *Informal.* Characteristic of or resembling a snob : elitist, snobbish, snobby. *Informal:* high-hat, snooty, stuck-up, uppity. *See* ATTITUDE, SELF-LOVE. **2.** *Informal.* Rude and disrespectful : assuming, assumptive, audacious, bold, boldfaced, brash, brazen, cheeky, contumelious, familiar, forward, impertinent, impudent, insolent, malapert, nervy, overconfident,

pert, presuming, presumptuous, pushy, sassy, saucy, smart. *Informal:* brassy, flip, fresh, smart-alecky, snippety, snippy, uppity. *Slang:* wise[1]. *See* ATTITUDE, COURTESY.

uppishness *noun*
Informal. The state or quality of being impudent or arrogantly self-confident : assumption, audaciousness, audacity, boldness, brashness, brazenness, cheek, cheekiness, chutzpah, discourtesy, disrespect, effrontery, face, familiarity, forwardness, gall[1], impertinence, impudence, impudency, incivility, insolence, nerve, nerviness, overconfidence, pertness, presumptuousness, pushiness, rudeness, sassiness, sauciness. *Informal:* brass, crust, sauce, uppityness. *See* ATTITUDE, COURTESY.

uppity *adjective*
1. *Informal.* Characteristic of or resembling a snob : elitist, snobbish, snobby. *Informal:* high-hat, snooty, stuck-up, uppish. *See* ATTITUDE, SELF-LOVE. **2.** *Informal.* Rude and disrespectful : assuming, assumptive, audacious, bold, boldfaced, brash, brazen, cheeky, contumelious, familiar, forward, impertinent, impudent, insolent, malapert, nervy, overconfident, pert, presuming, presumptuous, pushy, sassy, saucy, smart, wise[1]. *Informal:* brassy, flip, fresh, smart-alecky, snippety, snippy, uppish. *See* ATTITUDE, COURTESY.

uppityness *noun*
Informal. The state or quality of being impudent or arrogantly self-confident : assumption, audaciousness, audacity, boldness, brashness, brazenness, cheek, cheekiness, chutzpah, discourtesy, disrespect, effrontery, face, familiarity, forwardness, gall[1], impertinence, impudence, impudency, incivility, insolence, nerve, nerviness, overconfidence, pertness, presumptuousness, pushiness, rudeness, sassiness, sauciness. *Informal:* brass, crust, sauce, uppishness. *See* ATTITUDE, COURTESY.

upraise *verb*
1. To raise upright : erect, pitch, put up, raise, rear[2], set up, uprear. *See* HORIZONTAL, RISE. **2.** To move (something) to a higher position : boost, elevate, heave, hoist, lift, pick up, raise, rear[2], take up, uphold, uplift, uprear. *See* RISE.

uprear *verb*
1. To raise upright : erect, pitch, put up, raise, rear[2], set up, upraise. *See* HORIZONTAL, RISE. **2.** To move (something) to a higher position : boost, elevate, heave, hoist, lift, pick up, raise, rear[2], take up, uphold, uplift, upraise. *See* RISE.

upright *adjective*
1. At right angles to the horizon or to level ground : perpendicular, plumb, vertical. *See* HORIZONTAL. **2.** Directed or pointed upward : erect, raised, upstanding. *See* HORIZONTAL. **3.** Having or marked by uprightness in principle and action : good, honest, honorable, incorruptible, righteous, true, upstanding. *Informal:* straight-shooting. ***Idiom:*** on the up-and-up (*or* up and up). *See* HONEST.

uprightness *noun*
The quality or state of being morally sound : good, goodness, morality, probity, rectitude, righteousness, rightness, virtue, virtuousness. *See* RIGHT.

uprise *verb*
To adopt a standing posture : arise, get up, rise, stand (up), upspring. ***Idiom:*** get to one's feet. *See* RISE.

uprising *noun*
Organized opposition intended to change or overthrow existing authority : insurgence, insurgency, insurrection, mutiny, rebellion, revolt, revolution, sedition. *See* RESIST.

uproar *noun*
1. A condition of intense public interest or excitement : brouhaha, sensation, stir[1]. *Informal:* to-do. *Slang:* hoo-hah. *See* EXCITE. **2.** An interruption of regular procedure or of public peace : agitation, commotion, disorder, disturbance, helter-skelter, stir[1], tumult, turbulence, turmoil. *Informal:* flap, to-do. *See* CALM, ORDER. **3.** Sounds or a sound, especially when loud, confused, or disagreeable : babel, clamor, din, hubbub, hullabaloo, noise, pandemonium, racket, rumpus, tumult. *See* SOUNDS. **4.** Offensively loud and insistent utterances, especially of disapproval : clamor, hullabaloo, outcry, rumpus, vociferation. ***Idiom:*** hue and cry. *See* LIKE, SOUNDS.

uproot *verb*
To destroy all traces of : abolish, annihilate, blot out, clear, eradicate, erase, exterminate, extinguish, extirpate, kill[1], liquidate, obliterate, remove, root[1] (out *or* up), rub out, snuff out, stamp out, wipe out. ***Idioms:*** do away with, make an end of, put an end to. *See* HELP, MAKE.

upset *verb*
1. To turn or cause to turn from a vertical or horizontal position : capsize, knock over, overthrow, overturn, topple, turn over. *See* CHANGE, HORIZONTAL, MOVE. **2.** To disturb the health or physiological functioning of : derange, disorder, turn, unsettle. *See* HEALTH.

3. To put out of proper order : derange, disarrange, disarray, disorder, disorganize, disrupt, disturb, jumble, mess up, mix up, muddle, tumble, unsettle. *See* ORDER. **4.** To break up the order or progress of : disrupt, disturb. *See* ORDER. **5.** To impair or destroy the composure of : agitate, bother, discompose, disquiet, distract, disturb, flurry, fluster, perturb, rock, ruffle, shake (up), toss, unsettle. *Informal:* rattle. *See* CALM.

upset *noun* **1.** The act or an example of upsetting : disordering, disorganization, disruption. *See* ORDER. **2.** A state of discomposure : agitation, dither, fluster, flutter, perturbation, tumult, turmoil. *Informal:* lather, stew. *See* CALM.

upset *adjective* Turned over completely : capsized, inverted, overturned, upside-down, upturned. *See* HORIZONTAL.

upsetting *adjective*
Troubling to the mind or emotions : disquieting, disruptive, distressful, distressing, disturbing, intrusive, perturbing, troublesome, troublous, unsettling, worrisome. *See* HAPPY, PAIN.

upshot *noun*
Something brought about by a cause : aftermath, consequence, corollary, effect, end product, event, fruit, harvest, issue, outcome, precipitate, ramification, result, resultant, sequel, sequence, sequent. *See* CAUSE.

upside-down *adjective*
1. Turned over completely : capsized, inverted, overturned, upset, upturned. *See* HORIZONTAL. **2.** Characterized by physical confusion : chaotic, confused, disordered, helter-skelter, higgledy-piggledy, topsy-turvy. *Informal:* mixed-up. *See* ORDER.

upspring *verb*
1. To adopt a standing posture : arise, get up, rise, stand (up), uprise. ***Idiom:*** get to one's feet. *See* RISE. **2.** To have as a source : arise, come, derive, emanate, flow, issue, originate, proceed, rise, spring, stem. *See* START.

upstanding *adjective*
1. Directed or pointed upward : erect, raised, upright. *See* HORIZONTAL. **2.** Having or marked by uprightness in principle and action : good, honest, honorable, incorruptible, righteous, true, upright. *Informal:* straight-shooting. ***Idiom:*** on the up-and-up (*or* up and up). *See* HONEST.

upstandingness *noun*
The quality of being honest : honesty, honor, honorableness, incorruptibility, integrity. *See* HONEST.

upsurge *verb*
To make or become greater or larger : aggrandize, amplify, augment, boost, build, build up, burgeon, enlarge, escalate, expand, extend, grow, increase, magnify, mount, multiply, proliferate, rise, run up, snowball, soar, swell, wax. *Informal:* beef up. *See* INCREASE.

upsurge *noun* The act of increasing or rising : aggrandizement, amplification, augment, augmentation, boost, buildup, enlargement, escalation, growth, hike, increase, jump, multiplication, proliferation, raise, rise, swell, upswing, upturn. *See* INCREASE.

upswing *noun*
The act of increasing or rising : aggrandizement, amplification, augment, augmentation, boost, buildup, enlargement, escalation, growth, hike, increase, jump, multiplication, proliferation, raise, rise, swell, upsurge, upturn. *See* INCREASE.

uptight *adjective*
Slang. Feeling or exhibiting nervous tension : edgy, fidgety, jittery, jumpy, nervous, restive, restless, skittish, tense, twitchy. ***Idioms:*** a bundle of nerves, all wound up, on edge. *See* TIGHTEN.

up to *adjective*
Having the necessary strength or ability : equal. *See* ABILITY.

up-to-date *adjective*
Characteristic of recent times or informed of what is current : au courant, contemporary, current, mod, modern, up-to-the-minute. *See* KNOWLEDGE, NEW.

up-to-the-minute *adjective*
Characteristic of recent times or informed of what is current : au courant, contemporary, current, mod, modern, up-to-date. *See* KNOWLEDGE, NEW.

upturn *noun*
The act of increasing or rising : aggrandizement, amplification, augment, augmentation, boost, buildup, enlargement, escalation, growth, hike, increase, jump, multiplication, proliferation, raise, rise, swell, upsurge, upswing. *See* INCREASE.

upturned *adjective*
Turned over completely : capsized, inverted, overturned, upset, upside-down. *See* HORIZONTAL.

urban *adjective*
Of, in, or belonging to a city : city, metropolitan, municipal. *See* URBAN.

urbane *adjective*
1. Effortlessly gracious and tactful in social manner : bland, smooth, suave. *See* STYLE. **2.** Characterized by discriminating taste and broad knowledge as a result of development or education : civilized, cultivated, cultured, educated, polished, refined, well-bred. *See* CULTURE.

urbanity *noun*
Refined, effortless beauty of manner, form, and style : elegance, elegancy, grace, polish. *See* BEAUTIFUL, STYLE.

urbanize *verb*
To imbue with city ways, manners, and customs : citify, metropolitanize. *See* URBAN.

urge *verb*
1. To solicit (something) insistently : insist, press. *See* CONTINUE, SEEK. **2.** To impel to action : exhort, press. *See* CAUSE, PUSH.

urgent *adjective*
1. Compelling immediate attention : burning, crying, dire, emergent, exigent, imperative, instant, pressing. *See* BIG. **2.** Firm or obstinate, as in making a demand or maintaining a stand : importunate, importune, insistent, persistent. *See* CONTINUE.

usable also **useable** *adjective*
1. Available for use : accessible, employable, open, operable, operative, practicable, utilizable. *See* POSSIBLE. **2.** In a condition to be used : employable, serviceable, utilizable. *See* USED.

usage *noun*
1. The act of putting into play : application, employment, exercise, exertion, implementation, operation, play, use, utilization. *See* USED. **2.** A quantity consumed : consumption, use. *See* GIVE, USED. **3.** A habitual way of behaving : consuetude, custom, habit, habitude, manner, practice, praxis, usance, use, way, wont. *See* USUAL.

usance *noun*
A habitual way of behaving : consuetude, custom, habit, habitude, manner, practice, praxis, usage, use, way, wont. *See* USUAL.

use *verb*
1. To put into action or use : actuate, apply, employ, exercise, exploit, implement, practice, utilize. ***Idioms:*** avail oneself of, bring into play, bring to bear, make use of, put into practice, put to use. *See* USED. **2.** To control or direct the functioning of : manage, operate, run, work. *See* CONTROL. **3.** To take advantage of unfairly : abuse, exploit, impose, presume. *See* TREAT WELL.

use up *verb* **1.** To use all of : consume, drain, draw down, eat up, exhaust, expend, finish, play out, run through, spend. *Informal:* polish off. *See* INCREASE. **2.** To lessen or weaken severely, as by removing something essential : deplete, drain, exhaust, impoverish, sap[2]. *See* GIVE, INCREASE, RICH.

use *noun* **1.** The act of putting into play : application, employment, exercise, exertion, implementation, operation, play, usage, utilization. *See* USED. **2.** The condition of being put to use : application, duty, employment, service, utilization. *See* USED. **3.** A quantity consumed : consumption, usage. *See* GIVE, USED. **4.** The quality of being suitable or adaptable to an end : account, advantage, avail, benefit, profit, usefulness, utility. *See* USED. **5.** A habitual way of behaving : consuetude, custom, habit, habitude, manner, practice, praxis, usage, usance, way, wont. *See* USUAL.

useable *adjective* See **usable.**

used *adjective*
In the habit : accustomed, habituated, wont. *See* USUAL.

useful *adjective*
1. Serving or capable of serving a useful purpose : functional, handy, practicable, practical, serviceable, utilitarian. *See* USED. **2.** Affording benefit : advantageous, benefic, beneficent, beneficial, benignant, favorable, good, helpful, profitable, propitious, salutary, toward. *See* HELP. **3.** Suited to one's end or purpose : appropriate, befitting, convenient, expedient, fit[1], good, meet[2], proper, suitable, tailor-made. *See* AGREE, GOOD.

usefulness *noun*
The quality of being suitable or adaptable to an end : account, advantage, avail, benefit, profit, use, utility. *See* USED.

useless *adjective*
1. Having no useful purpose : ineffectual, inutile, unusable, worthless. *See* USED. **2.** Incapable of being used or availed of to advantage : impracticable, impractical, unnegotiable, unserviceable, unusable, unworkable. *See* USED. **3.** Having no useful result : barren, bootless, fruitless, futile, unavailing, unprofitable, unsuccessful, vain. ***Idiom:*** in vain. *See* THRIVE, USED. **4.** Not having the desired effect : ineffective, ineffectual, inefficacious, inefficient. *See* AFFECT.

uselessness *noun*
1. The condition or quality of being useless or ineffective : bootlessness, fruitlessness, futility, unavailingness, unprofitableness, vainness,

vanity. *See* THRIVE, USED. **2.** The condition or state of being incapable of accomplishing or effecting anything : helplessness, impotence, inadequacy, incapability, ineffectiveness, ineffectuality, ineffectualness, inefficacy, powerlessness. *See* AFFECT, STRONG.

user *noun*
One who consumes goods and services : consumer, customer. *See* GIVE, USED.

use up *verb* See **use.**

usher *noun*
Something or someone that shows the way : conductor, director, escort, guide, lead, leader, pilot, shepherd. *See* SHOW.
usher *verb* To show the way to : conduct, direct, escort, guide, lead, pilot, route, shepherd, show, steer. *See* SHOW.
usher in *verb* **1.** To make known the presence or arrival of : announce, herald, introduce, proclaim. *See* KNOWLEDGE, START. **2.** To begin (something) with preliminary or prefatory material : introduce, lead, precede, preface. *See* START, WORDS.

usher in *verb* See **usher.**

usual *adjective*
1. Commonly encountered : average, common, commonplace, general, normal, ordinary, typical. *See* SURPRISE. **2.** Commonly practiced or used : accustomed, customary, habitual, regular, wonted. *See* USUAL.
usual *noun* A regular or customary matter, condition, or course of events : commonplace, norm, ordinary, rule. *See* USUAL.

usually *adverb*
In an expected or customary manner; for the most part : commonly, consistently, customarily, frequently, generally, habitually, naturally, normally, often, regularly, routinely, typically. ***Idioms:*** as usual, per usual. *See* BIG, USUAL.

usualness *noun*
The quality or condition of being usual : customariness, habitualness, normalcy, normality, ordinariness, prevalence, regularity, routineness. *See* USUAL.

usurp *verb*
To lay claim to for oneself or as one's right : appropriate, arrogate, assume, commandeer, preempt, seize, take. *See* GIVE.

usurpation *noun*
The act of taking something for oneself : appropriation, arrogation, assumption, preemption, seizure. *See* GIVE.

utensil *noun*
A device used to do work or perform a task : implement, instrument, tool. *See* MACHINE, MEANS.

utilitarian *adjective*
Serving or capable of serving a useful purpose : functional, handy, practicable, practical, serviceable, useful. *See* USED.

utility *noun*
The quality of being suitable or adaptable to an end : account, advantage, avail, benefit, profit, use, usefulness. *See* USED.

utilizable *adjective*
1. Available for use : accessible, employable, open, operable, operative, practicable, usable. *See* POSSIBLE. **2.** In a condition to be used : employable, serviceable, usable. *See* USED.

utilization *noun*
1. The act of putting into play : application, employment, exercise, exertion, implementation, operation, play, usage, use. *See* USED. **2.** The condition of being put to use : application, duty, employment, service, use. *See* USED.

utilize *verb*
To put into action or use : actuate, apply, employ, exercise, exploit, implement, practice, use. ***Idioms:*** avail oneself of, bring into play, bring to bear, make use of, put into practice, put to use. *See* USED.

utmost *adjective*
1. Most distant or remote, as from a center : extreme, farthermost, farthest, furthermost, furthest, outermost, outmost, ultimate, uttermost. *See* BIG, EDGE. **2.** Of the greatest possible degree, quality, or intensity : extreme, supreme, transcendent, ultimate, unsurpassable, uttermost. *See* BETTER, BIG. **3.** Greatest in quantity or highest in degree that has been or can be attained : maximal, maximum, top, topmost, ultimate, uttermost. *See* HIGH, LIMITED.
utmost *noun* The greatest quantity or highest degree attainable : maximum, outside, top, ultimate, uttermost. ***Idiom:*** ne plus ultra. *See* HIGH, LIMITED.

utopian *adjective*
1. Not compatible with reality : idealistic, quixotic, romantic, starry-eyed, unrealistic, visionary. *See* HOPE, REAL. **2.** Showing a tendency to envision things in perfect but unrealistic form : idealistic, visionary. *See* HOPE, REAL.
utopian *noun* A person inclined to be imaginative or idealistic but impractical : dreamer, idealist, visionary. *See* ABILITY, HOPE.

utter[1] *verb*
1. To produce or make (speech sounds) : artic-

ulate, enunciate, pronounce, say, vocalize. *See* WORDS. **2.** To put into words : articulate, communicate, convey, declare, express, say, state, talk, tell, vent, verbalize, vocalize, voice. ***Idiom:*** give tongue (*or* vent *or* voice) to. *See* WORDS.

utter² *adjective*
Completely such, without qualification or exception : absolute, all-out, arrant, complete, consummate, crashing, damned, dead, downright, flat, out-and-out, outright, perfect, plain, pure, sheer², thorough, thoroughgoing, total, unbounded, unequivocal, unlimited, unmitigated, unqualified, unrelieved, unreserved. *Informal:* flat-out, positive. *Chiefly British:* blooming. *See* BIG, LIMITED.

utterance *noun*
1. The act or an instance of expressing in words : articulation, expression, statement, verbalization, vocalization, voice. *See* WORDS. **2.** The use of the speech organs to produce sounds : articulation, enunciation, vocalism, vocalization, voicing. *See* SOUNDS, WORDS. **3.** The faculty, act, or product of speaking : discourse, speech, talk, verbalization, vocalization. *See* WORDS. **4.** Something said : saying, statement, word. *See* WORDS.

uttered *adjective*
Produced by the voice : articulate, oral, sonant, spoken, vocal, voiced. *See* SOUNDS.

utterly *adverb*
To the fullest extent : absolutely, all, altogether, completely, dead, entirely, flat, fully, just, perfectly, quite, thoroughly, totally, well², wholly. *Informal:* clean, clear. ***Idioms:*** in toto, through and through. *See* BIG, LIMITED.

uttermost *adjective*
1. Of the greatest possible degree, quality, or intensity : extreme, supreme, transcendent, ultimate, unsurpassable, utmost. *See* BETTER, BIG. **2.** Greatest in quantity or highest in degree that has been or can be attained : maximal, maximum, top, topmost, ultimate, utmost. *See* HIGH, LIMITED. **3.** Most distant or remote, as from a center : extreme, farthermost, farthest, furthermost, furthest, outermost, outmost, ultimate, utmost. *See* BIG, EDGE.
uttermost *noun* The greatest quantity or highest degree attainable : maximum, outside, top, ultimate, utmost. ***Idiom:*** ne plus ultra. *See* HIGH, LIMITED.

·V·

vacancy *noun*
1. Total absence of matter : emptiness, vacuity, vacuum, void. *See* FULL. **2.** Empty, unfilled space : barrenness, emptiness, nothingness, vacuity, vacuum, void. *See* FULL. **3.** Total lack of ideas, meaning, or substance : barrenness, blankness, emptiness, hollowness, inanity, vacuity, vacuousness. *See* FULL.

vacant *adjective*
1. Containing nothing : bare, blank, clear, empty, vacuous, void. *See* FULL. **2.** Not occupied or put to use : idle, inactive, unemployed, unused. *See* USED. **3.** Lacking intelligent thought or content : blank, empty, empty-headed, inane, vacuous. *See* FULL. **4.** Lacking value, use, or substance : empty, hollow, idle, otiose, vain. *See* FULL.

vacate *verb*
1. To remove the contents of : clean out, clear, empty (out), evacuate, void. *See* FULL. **2.** *Law.* To remove or invalidate by or as if by running a line through or wiping clean : annul, blot (out), cancel, cross (off *or* out), delete, efface, erase, expunge, obliterate, rub (out), scratch (out), strike (out), undo, wipe (out), x (out). *See* CONTINUE.

vacation *noun*
A regularly scheduled period spent away from work or duty, often in recreation : furlough, leave². *Chiefly British:* holiday. *See* WORK.

vacillant *adjective*
Given to or exhibiting hesitation : halting, hesitant, indecisive, irresolute, pendulous, shilly-shally, tentative, timid, vacillatory. *See* DECIDE.

vacillate *verb*
1. To move back and forth or from side to side, as if about to fall : sway, teeter, totter, waver, weave, wobble. *See* REPETITION. **2.** To be irresolute in acting or doing : dither, falter,

halt[2], hesitate, pause, shilly-shally, stagger, waver, wobble. *See* DECIDE. **3.** To change one's attitudes or policies, for example : swing, waver. *See* CHANGE, DECIDE.

vacillation *noun*
The act of hesitating or state of being hesitant : hesitancy, hesitation, indecision, indecisiveness, irresoluteness, irresolution, pause, shilly-shally, tentativeness, timidity, timidness, to-and-fro. *See* DECIDE.

vacillatory *adjective*
Given to or exhibiting hesitation : halting, hesitant, indecisive, irresolute, pendulous, shilly-shally, tentative, timid, vacillant. *See* DECIDE.

vacuity *noun*
1. Total absence of matter : emptiness, vacancy, vacuum, void. *See* FULL. **2.** Empty, unfilled space : barrenness, emptiness, nothingness, vacancy, vacuum, void. *See* FULL. **3.** A space in an otherwise solid mass : cavity, hole, hollow, pocket, void. *See* CONVEX. **4.** Total lack of ideas, meaning, or substance : barrenness, blankness, emptiness, hollowness, inanity, vacancy, vacuousness. *See* FULL.

vacuous *adjective*
1. Containing nothing : bare, blank, clear, empty, vacant, void. *See* FULL. **2.** Lacking intelligent thought or content : blank, empty, empty-headed, inane, vacant. *See* FULL.

vacuousness *noun*
Total lack of ideas, meaning, or substance : barrenness, blankness, emptiness, hollowness, inanity, vacancy, vacuity. *See* FULL.

vacuum *noun*
1. Total absence of matter : emptiness, vacancy, vacuity, void. *See* FULL. **2.** Empty, unfilled space : barrenness, emptiness, nothingness, vacancy, vacuity, void. *See* FULL. **3.** A desolate sense of loss : blankness, desolation, emptiness, hollowness, void. *See* FULL.

vagabond *adjective*
Leading the life of a person without a fixed domicile; moving from place to place : itinerant, nomadic, peripatetic, vagrant. *See* MOVE.

vagary *noun*
An impulsive, often illogical turn of mind : bee, boutade, caprice, conceit, fancy, freak, humor, impulse, megrim, notion, whim, whimsy. ***Idiom:*** bee in one's bonnet. *See* THOUGHTS.

vagrant *adjective*
Leading the life of a person without a fixed domicile; moving from place to place : itinerant, nomadic, peripatetic, vagabond. *See* MOVE.

vague *adjective*
1. Liable to more than one interpretation : ambiguous, cloudy, equivocal, inexplicit, nebulous, obscure, uncertain, unclear. *See* CERTAIN, CLEAR. **2.** Not clearly perceived or perceptible : blear, bleary, cloudy, dim, faint, foggy, fuzzy, hazy, indefinite, indistinct, misty, obscure, shadowy, unclear, undistinct. *See* CLEAR. **3.** Marked by lack of firm decision or commitment; of questionable outcome : indefinite, open, uncertain, undecided, undetermined, unresolved, unsettled, unsure. ***Idiom:*** up in the air. *See* CERTAIN.

vagueness *noun*
The quality or state of being ambiguous : ambiguity, ambiguousness, cloudiness, equivocalness, indefiniteness, nebulousness, obscureness, obscurity, uncertainty, unclearness. *See* CLEAR.

vain *adjective*
1. Having no useful result : barren, bootless, fruitless, futile, unavailing, unprofitable, unsuccessful, useless. ***Idiom:*** in vain. *See* THRIVE, USED. **2.** Lacking value, use, or substance : empty, hollow, idle, otiose, vacant. *See* FULL. **3.** Unduly preoccupied with one's own appearance : conceited, narcissistic. *See* SELF-LOVE. **4.** Thinking too highly of oneself : conceited, egoistic, egoistical, egotistic, egotistical, narcissistic, vainglorious. *Informal:* bigheaded, stuck-up, swellheaded. *See* SELF-LOVE.

vainglorious *adjective*
Thinking too highly of oneself : conceited, egoistic, egoistical, egotistic, egotistical, narcissistic, vain. *Informal:* bigheaded, stuck-up, swellheaded. *See* SELF-LOVE.

vainglory *noun*
A regarding of oneself with undue favor : amour-propre, conceit, ego, egoism, egotism, narcissism, pride, vainness, vanity. *Slang:* ego trip. *See* SELF-LOVE.

vainness *noun*
1. The condition or quality of being useless or ineffective : bootlessness, fruitlessness, futility, unavailingness, unprofitableness, uselessness, vanity. *See* THRIVE, USED. **2.** A regarding of oneself with undue favor : amour-propre, conceit, ego, egoism, egotism, narcissism, pride, vainglory, vanity. *Slang:* ego trip. *See* SELF-LOVE.

valediction *noun*
A separation of two or more people : adieu, farewell, good-bye, leave-taking, parting. *See* APPROACH.

valedictory *adjective*
Of, done, given, or said on departing : departing, farewell, good-bye, parting. *See* APPROACH.

valiance *noun*
1. The quality of mind enabling one to face danger or hardship resolutely : braveness, bravery, courage, courageousness, dauntlessness, doughtiness, fearlessness, fortitude, gallantry, gameness, heart, intrepidity, intrepidness, mettle, nerve, pluck, pluckiness, spirit, stouthearted-ness, undauntedness, valiancy, valiantness, valor. *Informal:* spunk, spunkiness. *Slang:* gut (used in plural), gutsiness, moxie. *See* FEAR.
2. The quality or state of being heroic : gallantry, heroism, prowess, valiancy, valor. *See* FEAR.

valiancy *noun*
1. The quality of mind enabling one to face danger or hardship resolutely : braveness, bravery, courage, courageousness, dauntlessness, doughtiness, fearlessness, fortitude, gallantry, gameness, heart, intrepidity, intrepidness, mettle, nerve, pluck, pluckiness, spirit, stouthearted-ness, undauntedness, valiance, valiantness, valor. *Informal:* spunk, spunkiness. *Slang:* gut (used in plural), gutsiness, moxie. *See* FEAR.
2. The quality or state of being heroic : gallantry, heroism, prowess, valiance, valor. *See* FEAR.

valiant *adjective*
Having or showing courage : audacious, bold, brave, courageous, dauntless, doughty, fearless, fortitudinous, gallant, game, hardy, heroic, intrepid, mettlesome, plucky, stout, stout-hearted, unafraid, undaunted, valorous. *Informal:* spunky. *Slang:* gutsy, gutty. *See* FEAR.

valiantness *noun*
The quality of mind enabling one to face danger or hardship resolutely : braveness, bravery, courage, courageousness, dauntlessness, doughtiness, fearlessness, fortitude, gallantry, gameness, heart, intrepidity, intrepidness, mettle, nerve, pluck, pluckiness, spirit, stouthearted-ness, undauntedness, valiance, valiancy, valor. *Informal:* spunk, spunkiness. *Slang:* gut (used in plural), gutsiness, moxie. *See* FEAR.

valid *adjective*
1. Based on good judgment, reasoning, or evidence : cogent, just, solid, sound[2], tight, well-founded, well-grounded. *See* GOOD, REASON.
2. Worthy of belief, as because of precision or faithfulness to an original : authentic, authoritative, convincing, credible, faithful, true, trustworthy. *See* TRUE.

validate *verb*
1. To assure the certainty or validity of : attest, authenticate, back (up), bear out, confirm, corroborate, evidence, justify, substantiate, testify (to), verify, warrant. *See* SUPPORT, TRUE.
2. To establish as true or genuine : authenticate, bear out, confirm, corroborate, demonstrate, endorse, establish, evidence, prove, show, substantiate, verify. *See* SHOW, SUPPORT.

validation *noun*
That which confirms : attestation, authentication, confirmation, corroboration, demonstration, evidence, proof, substantiation, testament, testimonial, testimony, verification, warrant. *See* TRUE.

validity *noun*
The quality of being authentic : authenticity, genuineness, realness, truthfulness. *See* TRUE.

valor *noun*
1. The quality of mind enabling one to face danger or hardship resolutely : braveness, bravery, courage, courageousness, dauntlessness, doughtiness, fearlessness, fortitude, gallantry, gameness, heart, intrepidity, intrepidness, mettle, nerve, pluck, pluckiness, spirit, stouthearted-ness, undauntedness, valiance, valiancy, valiantness. *Informal:* spunk, spunkiness. *Slang:* gut (used in plural), gutsiness, moxie. *See* FEAR.
2. The quality or state of being heroic : gallantry, heroism, prowess, valiance, valiancy. *See* FEAR.

valorous *adjective*
Having or showing courage : audacious, bold, brave, courageous, dauntless, doughty, fearless, fortitudinous, gallant, game, hardy, heroic, intrepid, mettlesome, plucky, stout, stout-hearted, unafraid, undaunted, valiant. *Informal:* spunky. *Slang:* gutsy, gutty. *See* FEAR.

valuable *adjective*
Of great value : costly, inestimable, invaluable, precious, priceless, worthy. ***Idioms:*** beyond price, of great price. *See* VALUE.

valuate *verb*
To make a judgment as to the worth or value of : appraise, assay, assess, calculate, estimate, evaluate, gauge, judge, rate[1], size up, value. *Idiom:* take the measure of. *See* VALUE.

valuation *noun*
1. The act or result of judging the worth or value of something or someone : appraisal,

appraisement, assessment, estimate, estimation, evaluation, judgment. *See* VALUE. **2.** A measure of those qualities that determine merit, desirability, usefulness, or importance : account, value, worth. *See* VALUE.

value *noun*

1. A measure of those qualities that determine merit, desirability, usefulness, or importance : account, valuation, worth. *See* VALUE. **2.** A level of superiority that is usually high : caliber, merit, quality, stature, virtue, worth. *See* GOOD, VALUE. **3.** That which is signified by a word or expression : acceptation, connotation, denotation, import, intent, meaning, message, purport, sense, significance, significancy, signification. *See* MEANING.

value *verb* **1.** To make a judgment as to the worth or value of : appraise, assay, assess, calculate, estimate, evaluate, gauge, judge, rate[1], size up, valuate. ***Idiom:*** take the measure of. *See* VALUE. **2.** To have a high opinion of : admire, consider, esteem, honor, regard, respect. ***Idioms:*** look up to, think highly (*or* much *or* well) of. *See* PRAISE. **3.** To recognize the worth, quality, importance, or magnitude of : appreciate, cherish, esteem, prize[1], respect, treasure. ***Idiom:*** set store by. *See* PRAISE.

valueless *adjective*

Lacking all worth and value : drossy, good-for-nothing, inutile, no-good, nothing, worthless. *Informal:* no-account. *See* VALUE.

vamoose *verb*

Slang. To leave hastily : bolt, get out, run. *Informal:* clear out, get, hotfoot, skedaddle. *Slang:* hightail, scram. ***Idioms:*** beat it, hightail it, hotfoot it, make tracks. *See* APPROACH.

vamp *noun*

1. *Informal.* A usually unscrupulous woman who seduces or exploits men : enchantress, femme fatale, seductress, siren, temptress. *Informal:* witch. *See* SEX. **2.** *Informal.* A woman who is given to flirting : coquette, flirt. *See* SEX.

vampire *noun*

A perversely bad, cruel, or wicked person : archfiend, beast, devil, fiend, ghoul, monster, ogre, tiger. *See* KIND.

vandalize *verb*

To injure or destroy (property) maliciously : *Slang:* trash. *See* HELP.

vanish *verb*

To pass out of sight either gradually or suddenly : disappear, evanesce, evaporate, fade, fade out. *See* SHOW.

vanished *adjective*

No longer in use, force, or operation : dead, defunct, extinct, lost. *See* LIVE, NEW.

vanishment *noun*

The act or an example of passing out of sight : disappearance, evanescence, evaporation, fade-out. *See* SHOW.

vanity *noun*

1. A regarding of oneself with undue favor : amour-propre, conceit, ego, egoism, egotism, narcissism, pride, vainglory, vainness. *Slang:* ego trip. *See* SELF-LOVE. **2.** The condition or quality of being useless or ineffective : bootlessness, fruitlessness, futility, unavailingness, unprofitableness, uselessness, vainness. *See* THRIVE, USED.

vanquish *verb*

1. To win a victory over, as in battle or a competition : beat, best, conquer, defeat, master, overcome, prevail against (*or* over), rout, subdue, subjugate, surmount, triumph over, worst. *Informal:* trim, whip. *Slang:* ace, lick. ***Idioms:*** carry (*or* win) the day, get (*or* have) the best of, get (*or* have) the better of, go someone one better. *See* WIN. **2.** To render totally ineffective by decisive defeat : annihilate, crush, drub, overpower, overwhelm, smash, steamroller, thrash, trounce. *Informal:* massacre, wallop. *Slang:* clobber, cream, shellac, smear. *See* WIN.

vanquishment *noun*

The act of defeating or the condition of being defeated : beating, defeat, drubbing, overthrow, rout, thrashing. *Informal:* massacre, trimming, whipping. *Slang:* dusting, licking. *See* WIN.

vantage *noun*

1. A factor conducive to superiority and success : advantage, handicap, head start, odds, start. *See* HELP. **2.** A dominating position, as in a conflict : advantage, better[1], bulge, draw, drop, edge, superiority, upper hand. *Informal:* inside track, jump. *See* OVER. **3.** The position from which something is observed or considered : angle[2], eye, outlook, point of view, slant, standpoint, viewpoint. *See* PERSPECTIVE.

vapid *adjective*

Lacking the qualities requisite for spiritedness and originality : bland, innocuous, insipid, jejune, namby-pamby, washy, waterish, watery. *Informal:* wishy-washy. *See* EXCITE, GOOD.

vapidity *noun*

1. A lack of excitement, liveliness, or interest : asepticism, blandness, colorlessness, drabness, dreariness, dryness, dullness, flatness, flavorlessness, insipidity, insipidness, jejuneness, lifelessness, sterileness, sterility, stodginess, vapidness, weariness. *See* EXCITE. **2.** The state or quality of being insipid : blandness, innocuousness, insipidity, insipidness, jejuneness, vapidness, washiness, wateriness. *Informal:* wishy-washiness. *See* EXCITE, TASTE.

vapidness *noun*
1. A lack of excitement, liveliness, or interest : asepticism, blandness, colorlessness, drabness, dreariness, dryness, dullness, flatness, flavorlessness, insipidity, insipidness, jejuneness, lifelessness, sterileness, sterility, stodginess, vapidity, weariness. *See* EXCITE. **2.** The state or quality of being insipid : blandness, innocuousness, insipidity, insipidness, jejuneness, vapidity, washiness, wateriness. *Informal:* wishy-washiness. *See* EXCITE, TASTE.

vaporize *verb*
To pass off as vapor, especially when heated : boil away, evaporate, volatilize. *See* SOLID.

vaporous *adjective*
So light and insubstantial as to resemble air or a thin film : aerial, aery, airy, diaphanous, ethereal, filmy, gauzy, gossamer, gossamery, sheer[2], transparent, vapory. *See* THICK.

vapory *adjective*
So light and insubstantial as to resemble air or a thin film : aerial, aery, airy, diaphanous, ethereal, filmy, gauzy, gossamer, gossamery, sheer[2], transparent, vaporous. *See* THICK.

variable *adjective*
1. Capable of or liable to change : alterable, changeable, fluid, inconstant, mutable, uncertain, unsettled, unstable, unsteady, variant. *Archaic:* various. *See* CHANGE. **2.** Following no predictable pattern : capricious, changeable, erratic, fantastic, fantastical, fickle, freakish, inconsistent, inconstant, mercurial, temperamental, ticklish, uncertain, unpredictable, unstable, unsteady, volatile, whimsical. *See* CHANGE, CONTINUE. **3.** Lacking consistency or regularity in quality or performance : erratic, inconsistent, patchy, spotty, uneven, unsteady. *See* CONTINUE, SAME.

variance *noun*
1. The condition or fact of varying : difference, variation. *See* CHANGE, SAME. **2.** A state of disagreement and disharmony : clash, conflict, confrontation, contention, difference, difficulty, disaccord, discord, discordance, dissension, dissent, dissentience, dissidence, dissonance, faction, friction, inharmony, schism, strife, war, warfare. *See* CONFLICT.

variant *adjective*
1. Not like another in nature, quality, amount, or form : different, disparate, dissimilar, divergent, diverse, unlike, various. *See* SAME. **2.** Capable of or liable to change : alterable, changeable, fluid, inconstant, mutable, uncertain, unsettled, unstable, unsteady, variable. *Archaic:* various. *See* CHANGE.

variant *noun* One that is slightly different from others of the same kind or designation : variation, variety, version. *See* SAME.

variation *noun*
1. The condition or fact of varying : difference, variance. *See* CHANGE, SAME. **2.** The process or result of making or becoming different : alteration, change, modification, mutation, permutation. *See* CHANGE. **3.** One that is slightly different from others of the same kind or designation : variant, variety, version. *See* SAME.

varicolored *adjective*
Having many different colors : motley, multicolor, multicolored, polychromatic, polychrome, polychromic, polychromous, variegated, versicolor, versicolored. *See* COLORS.

varied *adjective*
Consisting of a number of different kinds : assorted, divers, diverse, diversified, heterogeneous, miscellaneous, mixed, motley, multifarious, multiform, sundry, variegated, various. *Biology:* polymorphic, polymorphous. *See* SAME.

variegate *verb*
To mark with a line or band, as of different color or texture : streak, striate, stripe. *See* MARKS.

variegated *adjective*
1. Having many different colors : motley, multicolor, multicolored, polychromatic, polychrome, polychromic, polychromous, varicolored, versicolor, versicolored. *See* COLORS. **2.** Consisting of a number of different kinds : assorted, divers, diverse, diversified, heterogeneous, miscellaneous, mixed, motley, multifarious, multiform, sundry, varied, various. *Biology:* polymorphic, polymorphous. *See* SAME.

variegation *noun*
The quality of being made of many different elements, forms, kinds, or individuals : diverseness, diversification, diversity, heterogeneity, heterogeneousness, miscellaneousness, multifariousness, multiformity, multiplicity, variety, variousness. *Biology:* polymorphism. *See* SAME.

variety *noun*
1. The quality of being made of many different elements, forms, kinds, or individuals : diverseness, diversification, diversity, heterogeneity, heterogeneousness, miscellaneousness, multifariousness, multiformity, multiplicity, variegation, variousness. *Biology:* polymorphism. *See* SAME. **2.** A collection of various things : assortment, conglomeration, gallimaufry, hodgepodge, jumble, medley, mélange, miscellany, mishmash, mixed bag, mixture, olio, patchwork, potpourri, salmagundi. *Slang:* grab bag. *See* COLLECT. **3.** A class that is defined by the common attribute or attributes possessed by all its members : breed, cast, description, feather, ilk, kind[2], lot, manner, mold, nature, order, sort, species, stamp, stripe, type. *Informal:* persuasion. *See* GROUP. **4.** One that is slightly different from others of the same kind or designation : variant, variation, version. *See* SAME.

various *adjective*
1. Consisting of a number of different kinds : assorted, divers, diverse, diversified, heterogeneous, miscellaneous, mixed, motley, multifarious, multiform, sundry, varied, variegated. *Biology:* polymorphic, polymorphous. *See* SAME. **2.** Not like another in nature, quality, amount, or form : different, disparate, dissimilar, divergent, diverse, unlike, variant. *See* SAME. **3.** Consisting of a number more than two or three but less than many : divers, several, some, sundry. *See* BIG. **4.** Having many aspects, uses, or abilities : all-around, all-round, many-sided, multifaceted, protean, versatile. *See* ABILITY, SAME. **5.** Distinguished from others by nature or qualities : discrete, distinct, separate, several. *See* SAME. **6.** *Archaic.* Capable of or liable to change : alterable, changeable, fluid, inconstant, mutable, uncertain, unsettled, unstable, unsteady, variable, variant. *See* CHANGE.

variousness *noun*
The quality of being made of many different elements, forms, kinds, or individuals : diverseness, diversification, diversity, heterogeneity, heterogeneousness, miscellaneousness, multifariousness, multiformity, multiplicity, variegation, variety. *Biology:* polymorphism. *See* SAME.

varnish *verb*
To give a deceptively attractive appearance to : color, gild, gloss (over), gloze (over), sugarcoat, veneer, whitewash. ***Idioms:*** paper over, put a good face on. *See* TRUE.

vary *verb*
1. To make or become different : alter, change, modify, mutate, turn. *See* CHANGE. **2.** To change or fluctuate within limits : extend, go, range, run. *See* CHANGE. **3.** To be unlike or dissimilar : differ, disagree, diverge. ***Idiom:*** be at variance. *See* SAME. **4.** To be of different opinion : differ, disaccord, disagree, discord, dissent. ***Idiom:*** join (*or* take) issue. *See* AGREE.

vast *adjective*
Of extraordinary size and power : behemoth, Brobdingnagian, Bunyanesque, colossal, cyclopean, elephantine, enormous, gargantuan, giant, gigantesque, gigantic, herculean, heroic, huge, immense, jumbo, mammoth, massive, massy, mastodonic, mighty, monster, monstrous, monumental, mountainous, prodigious, pythonic, stupendous, titanic, tremendous. *Informal:* walloping. *Slang:* whopping. *See* BIG.

vastness *noun*
The quality of being enormous : enormousness, hugeness, immenseness, immensity, prodigiousness, stupendousness, tremendousness. *See* BIG.

vatic *adjective*
Of or relating to the foretelling of events by or as if by supernatural means : augural, divinitory, fatidic, fatidical, mantic, oracular, prophetic, sibylline, vatical, vaticinal, visionary. *See* FORESIGHT.

vatical *adjective*
Of or relating to the foretelling of events by or as if by supernatural means : augural, divinitory, fatidic, fatidical, mantic, oracular, prophetic, sibylline, vatic, vaticinal, visionary. *See* FORESIGHT.

vaticinal *adjective*
Of or relating to the foretelling of events by or as if by supernatural means : augural, divinitory, fatidic, fatidical, mantic, oracular, prophetic, sibylline, vatic, vatical, visionary. *See* FORESIGHT.

vaticinate *verb*
To tell about or make known (future events) by or as if by supernatural means : augur, divine, foretell, prophesy, soothsay. *See* FORESIGHT.

vaticination *noun*
Something that is foretold by or as if by supernatural means : divination, oracle, prophecy, soothsaying, vision. *See* FORESIGHT.

vaticinator *noun*
A person who foretells future events by or as if by supernatural means : augur, auspex, diviner, foreteller, haruspex, prophesier,

prophet, prophetess, seer, sibyl, soothsayer. *See* FORESIGHT.

vault[1] *noun*
A burial place or receptacle for human remains : catacomb, cinerarium, crypt, grave[1], mausoleum, ossuary, sepulcher, sepulture, tomb. *See* KEEP, PLACE.

vault[2] *verb*
To move off the ground by a muscular effort of the legs and feet : hurdle, jump, leap, spring. *See* MOVE, RISE.
vault *noun* The act of jumping : jump, leap, spring. *See* MOVE, RISE.

vaunt *verb*
To talk with excessive pride : boast, brag, crow, gasconade, rodomontade. *Informal:* blow[1]. *See* PRAISE.
vaunt *noun* An act of boasting : boast, brag, braggadocio, fanfaronade, gasconade, rodomontade. *Informal:* blow[1]. *See* PRAISE.

vaunter *noun*
One given to boasting : boaster, brag, braggadocio, braggart, bragger. *Informal:* blowhard. *Slang:* blower. *See* PRAISE.

vector *noun*
The compass direction in which a ship or an aircraft moves : bearing, course, heading. *See* APPROACH.

veer *verb*
1. To turn aside sharply from a straight course : chop[2], cut, sheer[1], skew, slue[1], swerve. *Nautical:* yaw. *See* CHANGE. **2.** To turn away from a prescribed course of action or conduct : depart, deviate, digress, diverge, stray, swerve. *Archaic:* err. *See* APPROACH, CORRECT. **3.** To change the direction or course of : avert, deflect, deviate, divert, pivot, shift, swing, turn. *See* CHANGE.

vehemence *noun*
Exceptionally great concentration, power, or force, especially in activity : depth (often used in plural), ferociousness, ferocity, fierceness, fury, intensity, pitch, severity, vehemency, violence. *See* BIG, STRONG.

vehemency *noun*
Exceptionally great concentration, power, or force, especially in activity : depth (often used in plural), ferociousness, ferocity, fierceness, fury, intensity, pitch, severity, vehemence, violence. *See* BIG, STRONG.

vehement *adjective*
Extreme in degree, strength, or effect : desperate, fierce, furious, intense, terrible, violent. *See* BIG, STRONG.

veil *noun*
A deceptive outward appearance : cloak, color, coloring, cover, disguise, disguisement, façade, face, false colors, front, gloss, guise, mask, masquerade, pretense, pretext, semblance, show, veneer, window-dressing. *Slang:* put-on. *See* SHOW.
veil *verb* **1.** To surround and cover completely so as to obscure : cloak, clothe, enfold, enshroud, envelop, enwrap, infold, invest, shroud, wrap. *See* SHOW. **2.** To prevent (something) from being known : cloak, conceal, cover (up), enshroud, hide[1], hush (up), mask, shroud. ***Idioms:*** keep under cover, keep under wraps. *See* SHOW.

vein *noun*
1. An intermixture of a contrasting or unexpected quality, especially in a person's character : strain[2], streak. *See* BE. **2.** A temporary state of mind or feeling : frame of mind, humor, mood, spirit (used in plural), temper. *See* FEELINGS. **3.** A distinctive way of expressing oneself : fashion, manner, mode, style, tone. *See* STYLE.

velocity *noun*
Rate of motion or performance : pace, speed, tempo. *Informal:* clip[1]. *See* FAST.

venal *adjective*
1. Capable of being bribed : buyable, corruptible, purchasable. *See* CRIMES, PERSUASION. **2.** Ruthlessly seeking personal advantage : corrupt, mercenary, praetorian. *Informal:* crooked. *See* SELF. **3.** Marked by dishonesty, especially in matters of public trust : corrupt, dishonest. *Informal:* crooked. *See* HONEST.

vend *verb*
1. To offer for sale : deal (in), handle, market, merchandise, merchant, peddle, retail, sell, trade (in). *See* TRANSACTIONS. **2.** To travel about selling goods : hawk, huckster, peddle. *See* TRANSACTIONS.

vender or **vendor** *noun*
One who sells : clerk, salesclerk, salesgirl, salesman, salesperson, saleswoman, seller. *See* TRANSACTIONS.

vendor *noun* See **vender.**

veneer *noun*
A deceptive outward appearance : cloak, color, coloring, cover, disguise, disguisement, façade, face, false colors, front, gloss, guise, mask, masquerade, pretense, pretext, semblance, show, veil, window-dressing. *Slang:* put-on. *See* SHOW.
veneer *verb* To give a deceptively attractive appearance to : color, gild, gloss (over), gloze

(over), sugarcoat, varnish, whitewash. ***Idioms:*** paper over, put a good face on. *See* TRUE.

venerable *adjective*
Belonging to, existing, or occurring in times long past : age-old, ancient, antediluvian, antiquated, antique, archaic, hoary, old, olden, old-time, timeworn. ***Idioms:*** old as Methuselah, old as the hills. *See* NEW.

venerate *verb*
To regard with great awe and devotion : adore, idolize, revere, reverence, worship. *See* SACRED.

veneration *noun*
The act of adoring, especially reverently : adoration, idolization, reverence, worship. *See* LIKE, LOVE, SACRED.

venerational *adjective*
Feeling or showing reverence : reverent, reverential, worshipful. *See* RESPECT.

vengeance *noun*
The act of retaliating : counteraction, counterattack, counterblow, reciprocation, reprisal, requital, retaliation, retribution, revenge, tit for tat. ***Idioms:*** an eye for an eye, a tooth for a tooth, like for like, measure for measure. *See* ATTACK, FORGIVENESS.

vengeful *adjective*
Disposed to seek revenge : revengeful, spiteful, vindictive. *See* FORGIVENESS.

vengefulness *noun*
The quality or condition of being vindictive : revenge, spite, spitefulness, vindictiveness. *See* FORGIVENESS.

venial *adjective*
Admitting of forgiveness or pardon : excusable, forgivable, pardonable. *See* FORGIVENESS.

venom *noun*
Anything that is injurious, destructive, or fatal : bane, canker, contagion, poison, toxin, virus. *See* HELP.

venomous *adjective*
1. Capable of injuring or killing by poison : mephitic, mephitical, poison, poisonous, toxic, toxicant, virulent. *See* HELP. **2.** Characterized by intense ill will or spite : black, despiteful, evil, hateful, malevolent, malicious, malign, malignant, mean[2], nasty, poisonous, spiteful, vicious, wicked. *Slang:* bitchy. *See* ATTITUDE.

venomousness *noun*
A desire to harm others or to see others suffer : despitefulness, ill will, malevolence, malice, maliciousness, malignancy, malignity, meanness, nastiness, poisonousness, spite, spitefulness, viciousness. *See* ATTITUDE.

vent *noun*
An open space allowing passage : aperture, hole, mouth, opening, orifice, outlet. *See* OPEN.
vent *verb* **1.** To utter publicly : air, express, put, state, ventilate. ***Idiom:*** come out with. *See* SHOW, WORDS. **2.** To put into words : articulate, communicate, convey, declare, express, say, state, talk, tell, utter[1], verbalize, vocalize, voice. ***Idiom:*** give tongue (*or* vent *or* voice) to. *See* WORDS. **3.** To discharge material, as vapor or fumes, usually suddenly and violently : emit, give, give forth, give off, give out, issue, let off, let out, release, send forth, throw off. *See* FREE, MOVE.

ventilate *verb*
1. To expose to circulating air : aerate, air, wind[1]. *See* BREATH, OPEN. **2.** To utter publicly : air, express, put, state, vent. ***Idiom:*** come out with. *See* SHOW, WORDS.

ventilation *noun*
An exchanging of views : conference, discussion. *Slang:* rap[3]. *See* WORDS.

venture *noun*
1. An exciting, often hazardous undertaking : adventure, emprise, enterprise. *See* SAFETY. **2.** Something undertaken, especially something requiring extensive planning and work : enterprise, project, undertaking. *See* WORK.
venture *verb* **1.** To expose to possible loss or damage : adventure, compromise, hazard, risk. *See* SAFETY. **2.** To put up as a stake in a game or speculation : bet, gamble, lay[1] (down), post[2], put, risk, stake, wager. *Informal:* go. *See* GAMBLING. **3.** To run the risk of : adventure, chance, hazard, risk. *See* SAFETY. **4.** To take a risk in the hope of gaining advantage : gamble, speculate. ***Idiom:*** take a flyer. *See* GAMBLING. **5.** To have the courage to put forward, as an idea, especially when rebuff or criticism is likely : dare, hazard, presume, pretend. *See* TRY.

venturer *noun*
One who engages in exciting, risky pursuits : adventurer, daredevil. *See* SAFETY.

venturesome *adjective*
1. Taking or willing to take risks : adventuresome, adventurous, audacious, bold, daredevil, daring, enterprising, venturous. *See* SAFETY. **2.** Involving possible risk, loss, or injury : adventurous, chancy, dangerous, hazardous, jeopardous, parlous, perilous, risky, treacherous, unsafe, venturous. *Slang:* hairy. *See* SAFETY.

venturesomeness *noun*
Willingness to take risks : adventuresomeness,

adventurousness, audaciousness, audacity, boldness, daredevilry, daredeviltry, daring, daringness, venturousness. *See* SAFETY.

venturous *adjective*
1. Taking or willing to take risks : adventuresome, adventurous, audacious, bold, daredevil, daring, enterprising, venturesome. *See* SAFETY. **2.** Involving possible risk, loss, or injury : adventurous, chancy, dangerous, hazardous, jeopardous, parlous, perilous, risky, treacherous, unsafe, venturesome. *Slang:* hairy. *See* SAFETY.

venturousness *noun*
Willingness to take risks : adventuresomeness, adventurousness, audaciousness, audacity, boldness, daredevilry, daredeviltry, daring, daringness, venturesomeness. *See* SAFETY.

veracious *adjective*
1. Consistently telling the truth : truthful, veridical. *See* TRUE. **2.** Conforming to fact : accurate, correct, exact, faithful, precise, right, rigorous, true, veridical. *See* CORRECT, HONEST, REAL, TRUE.

veraciousness *noun*
Correspondence with fact or truth : accuracy, correctness, exactitude, exactness, fidelity, truth, veracity, veridicality, verity. *See* TRUE.

veracity *noun*
1. Freedom from deceit or falseness : truth, truthfulness. *See* TRUE. **2.** Correspondence with fact or truth : accuracy, correctness, exactitude, exactness, fidelity, truth, veraciousness, veridicality, verity. *See* TRUE.

verbal *adjective*
1. Relating to, consisting of, or having the nature of words : wordy. *See* WORDS. **2.** Expressed or transmitted in speech : oral, spoken, unwritten, word-of-mouth. *See* WORDS. **3.** Employing the very same words as another : literal, verbatim, word-for-word. *See* SAME.

verbalism *noun*
Choice of words and the way in which they are used : diction, parlance, phrase, phraseology, phrasing, wordage, wording. *See* WORDS.

verbalization *noun*
1. The act or an instance of expressing in words : articulation, expression, statement, utterance, vocalization, voice. *See* WORDS. **2.** The faculty, act, or product of speaking : discourse, speech, talk, utterance, vocalization. *See* WORDS.

verbalize *verb*
1. To put into words : articulate, communicate, convey, declare, express, say, state, talk, tell, utter[1], vent, vocalize, voice. ***Idiom:*** give tongue (*or* vent *or* voice) to. *See* WORDS. **2.** To express oneself in speech : speak, talk, vocalize. ***Idioms:*** open one's mouth (*or* lips), put in (*or* into) words, wag one's tongue. *See* WORDS.

verbatim *adjective*
Employing the very same words as another : literal, verbal, word-for-word. *See* SAME.

verbiage *noun*
Words or the use of words in excess of those needed for clarity or precision : diffuseness, diffusion, long-windedness, pleonasm, prolixity, redundancy, verboseness, verbosity, windiness, wordage, wordiness. *See* EXCESS, STYLE, WORDS.

verbose *adjective*
Using or containing an excessive number of words : diffuse, long-winded, periphrastic, pleonastic, prolix, redundant, wordy. *See* EXCESS, STYLE, WORDS.

verboseness *noun*
Words or the use of words in excess of those needed for clarity or precision : diffuseness, diffusion, long-windedness, pleonasm, prolixity, redundancy, verbiage, verbosity, windiness, wordage, wordiness. *See* EXCESS, STYLE, WORDS.

verbosity *noun*
Words or the use of words in excess of those needed for clarity or precision : diffuseness, diffusion, long-windedness, pleonasm, prolixity, redundancy, verbiage, verboseness, windiness, wordage, wordiness. *See* EXCESS, STYLE, WORDS.

verboten *adjective*
Not allowed : forbidden, impermissible, taboo. *See* ALLOW.

verge *noun*
1. A fairly narrow line or space forming a boundary : border, borderline, brim, brink, edge, edging, fringe, margin, periphery, rim. *Chiefly Military:* perimeter. *See* EDGE. **2.** A transitional interval beyond which some new action or different state of affairs is likely to begin or occur : borderline, brink, edge, point, threshold. *See* EDGE.

verge *verb* **1.** To be contiguous or next to : abut, adjoin, border, bound[2], butt[2], join, meet[1], neighbor, touch. *See* NEAR. **2.** To put or form a border on : border, bound[2], edge, fringe, margin, rim, skirt. *See* EDGE.

verge on *verb* To come near, as in quality or amount : approach, approximate, border on (*or* upon), challenge, rival. *See* SAME.

verge on *verb* See **verge.**

veridical *adjective*
1. Consistently telling the truth : truthful, veracious. *See* TRUE. **2.** Conforming to fact : accurate, correct, exact, faithful, precise, right, rigorous, true, veracious. *See* CORRECT, HONEST, REAL, TRUE.

veridicality *noun*
Correspondence with fact or truth : accuracy, correctness, exactitude, exactness, fidelity, truth, veraciousness, veracity, verity. *See* TRUE.

verification *noun*
That which confirms : attestation, authentication, confirmation, corroboration, demonstration, evidence, proof, substantiation, testament, testimonial, testimony, validation, warrant. *See* TRUE.

verify *verb*
1. To assure the certainty or validity of : attest, authenticate, back (up), bear out, confirm, corroborate, evidence, justify, substantiate, testify (to), validate, warrant. *See* SUPPORT, TRUE. **2.** To establish as true or genuine : authenticate, bear out, confirm, corroborate, demonstrate, endorse, establish, evidence, prove, show, substantiate, validate. *See* SHOW, SUPPORT.

verily *adverb*
In truth : actually, fairly, genuinely, indeed, positively, really, truly, truthfully. ***Idiom:*** for fair. *See* REAL, TRUE.

verisimilitude *noun*
Appearance of truth or authenticity : believability, color, credibility, credibleness, creditability, creditableness, plausibility, plausibleness. *See* LIKELY.

verity *noun*
Correspondence with fact or truth : accuracy, correctness, exactitude, exactness, fidelity, truth, veraciousness, veracity, veridicality. *See* TRUE.

vernacular *noun*
1. A system of terms used by a people sharing a history and culture : dialect, language, speech, tongue. *Linguistics:* langue. *See* WORDS. **2.** A variety of a language that differs from the standard form : argot, cant[2], dialect, jargon, lingo, patois. *See* WORDS. **3.** Specialized expressions indigenous to a particular field, subject, trade, or subculture : argot, cant[2], dialect, idiom, jargon, language, lexicon, lingo, patois, terminology, vocabulary. *See* WORDS.

vernal *adjective*
Of, occurring in, or characteristic of the season of spring : spring. *See* TIME.

versant *adjective*
Having good knowledge of : acquainted, conversant, familiar, versed. ***Idiom:*** up on. *See* KNOWLEDGE.

versatile *adjective*
Having many aspects, uses, or abilities : all-around, all-round, many-sided, multifaceted, protean, various. *See* ABILITY, SAME.

verse *noun*
A poetic work or poetic works : poem, poesy, poetry, rhyme. *See* WORDS.

versed *adjective*
1. Skilled or knowledgeable through long practice : experienced, old, practiced, seasoned, veteran. ***Idiom:*** knowing the ropes. *See* ABILITY. **2.** Having good knowledge of : acquainted, conversant, familiar, versant. ***Idiom:*** up on. *See* KNOWLEDGE.

versicolor *adjective*
Having many different colors : motley, multicolor, multicolored, polychromatic, polychrome, polychromic, polychromous, varicolored, variegated, versicolored. *See* COLORS.

versicolored *adjective*
Having many different colors : motley, multicolor, multicolored, polychromatic, polychrome, polychromic, polychromous, varicolored, variegated, versicolor. *See* COLORS.

versifier *noun*
One who writes poetry : bard, muse[2], poet, poetaster, poetess, rhymer, rhymester. *See* WORDS.

version *noun*
1. A recounting of past events : account, chronicle, description, history, narration, narrative, report, statement, story. *See* WORDS. **2.** A restating of something in other, especially simpler, words : paraphrase, rendering, restatement, translation. *See* WORDS. **3.** One that is slightly different from others of the same kind or designation : variant, variation, variety. *See* SAME.

vertex *noun*
The highest point : apex, cap, crest, crown, height, peak, roof, summit, top. *See* HIGH.

vertical *adjective*
At right angles to the horizon or to level ground : perpendicular, plumb, upright. *See* HORIZONTAL.

vertiginous *adjective*
1. Having a sensation of whirling or falling : dizzy, giddy, lightheaded, reeling, woozy. *See* AWARENESS. **2.** Producing dizziness or vertigo : dizzy, dizzying, giddy. *See* AWARENESS.

vertiginousness *noun*
A sensation of whirling or falling : dizziness, giddiness, lightheadedness, vertigo, wooziness. *See* AWARENESS.

vertigo *noun*
A sensation of whirling or falling : dizziness, giddiness, lightheadedness, vertiginousness, wooziness. *See* AWARENESS.

verve *noun*
1. A lively, emphatic, eager quality or manner : animation, bounce, brio, dash, élan, esprit, life, liveliness, pertness, sparkle, spirit, vigor, vim, vivaciousness, vivacity, zip. *Informal:* ginger, pep, peppiness. *Slang:* oomph. *See* ACTION.
2. A quality of active mental and physical forcefulness : dash, punch, starch, vigor, vigorousness, vim, vitality. *Informal:* snap. ***Idiom:*** vim and vigor. *See* ACTION, TIRED.

very *adverb*
To a high degree : awfully, dreadfully, eminently, exceedingly, exceptionally, extra, extremely, greatly, highly, most, notably. *Informal:* awful. *Chiefly Regional:* mighty. *See* BIG.
very *adjective* **1.** Being one and not another or others; not different in nature or identity : identic, identical, same, selfsame. *See* SAME.
2. Strictly distinguished from others : exact, precise. *See* PRECISE. **3.** Considered apart from anything else : mere. *See* INCLUDE, SPECIFIC.

vesper *noun*
Archaic. The period between afternoon and nighttime : dusk, eve, evening, eventide, gloaming, nightfall, twilight. *Archaic:* even[2]. *See* START.

vestige *noun*
A mark or remnant that indicates the former presence of something : relic, remains, trace. *See* LEFTOVER, MARKS.

vestment *noun*
Clothing worn by members of a religious order : habit, robe. *See* PUT ON.

vet *noun*
Informal. One who has had long experience in a given activity or capacity : old hand, veteran. *Informal:* old-timer. *See* ABILITY, KNOWLEDGE.

veteran *noun*
One who has had long experience in a given activity or capacity : old hand. *Informal:* old-timer, vet. *See* ABILITY, KNOWLEDGE.
veteran *adjective* Skilled or knowledgeable through long practice : experienced, old, practiced, seasoned, versed. ***Idiom:*** knowing the ropes. *See* ABILITY.

veto *verb*
To prevent or forbid authoritatively : blackball, negative, turn down. *Slang:* nix. ***Idiom:*** turn thumbs down on. *See* ACCEPT.

vex *verb*
To trouble the nerves or peace of mind of, especially by repeated vexations : aggravate, annoy, bother, bug, chafe, disturb, exasperate, fret, gall[2], get, irk, irritate, nettle, peeve, provoke, put out, rile, ruffle. ***Idioms:*** get in one's hair, get on one's nerves, get under one's skin. *See* FEELINGS, PAIN.

vexation *noun*
1. The act of annoying : annoyance, botheration, bothering, exasperation, harassment, irritation, pestering, provocation. *See* FEELINGS, PAIN. **2.** The feeling of being annoyed : aggravation, annoyance, bother, botheration, exasperation, irritation. *See* FEELINGS, PAIN.
3. Something that annoys : aggravation, annoyance, besetment, bother, irritant, irritation, nuisance, peeve, plague, torment. *See* FEELINGS, PAIN.

vexatious *adjective*
Troubling the nerves or peace of mind, as by repeated vexations : annoying, bothersome, galling, irksome, irritating, nettlesome, plaguy, provoking, troublesome. *See* PAIN.

viable *adjective*
Capable of occurring or being done : feasible, possible, practicable, workable. ***Idiom:*** within reach. *See* POSSIBLE.

vibrant *adjective*
1. Full of or characterized by a lively, emphatic, eager quality : fiery, high-spirited, mettlesome, peppery, spirited. *Informal:* snappy. *See* ACTION, FEELINGS. **2.** Having or producing a full, deep, or rich sound : mellow, orotund, plangent, resonant, resounding, ringing, rotund, round, sonorous. *See* SOUNDS.

vibrate *verb*
1. To move to and fro in short, jerky movements : quake, quaver, quiver, shake, shiver[1], shudder, tremble, twitter. *See* REPETITION.
2. To move to and fro violently : quake, rock, shake, tremble. *See* REPETITION.

vice *noun*
Degrading, immoral acts or habits : bestiality, corruption, depravity, flagitiousness, immorality, perversion, turpitude, villainousness, villainy, wickedness. *See* CLEAN.

vicinity *noun*
1. A surrounding area : environment, environs, locale, locality, neighborhood, precinct (used in plural), surroundings. *See* NEAR, PLACE. **2.** A surrounding site : area, locality, neighborhood. *See* NEAR, PLACE. **3.** Approximate size or amount : range. *Informal:* neighborhood. *See* NEAR.

vicious *adjective*
1. Morally objectionable : bad, black, evil, immoral, iniquitous, peccant, reprobate, sinful, wicked, wrong. *See* RIGHT. **2.** Characterized by intense ill will or spite : black, despiteful, evil, hateful, malevolent, malicious, malign, malignant, mean[2], nasty, poisonous, spiteful, venomous, wicked. *Slang:* bitchy. *See* ATTITUDE. **3.** So intense as to cause extreme suffering : cruel, ferocious, fierce, savage. *See* HELP, KIND. **4.** Showing or suggesting a disposition to be violently destructive without scruple or restraint : barbarous, bestial, cruel, fell[2], feral, ferocious, fierce, inhuman, savage, truculent, wolfish. *See* KIND.

viciousness *noun*
A desire to harm others or to see others suffer : despitefulness, ill will, malevolence, malice, maliciousness, malignancy, malignity, meanness, nastiness, poisonousness, spite, spitefulness, venomousness. *See* ATTITUDE.

vicissitude *noun*
Something that obstructs progress and requires great effort to overcome. Often used in plural : asperity, difficulty, hardship, rigor. ***Idioms:*** a hard (*or* tough) nut to crack, a hard (*or* tough) row to hoe, heavy sledding. *See* EASY.

victim *noun*
1. One or more living creatures slain and offered to a deity as part of a religious rite : hecatomb, immolation, offering, sacrifice. *See* RELIGION. **2.** One that is made to suffer injury, loss, or death : casualty, prey. *See* HELP. **3.** A person who is easily deceived or victimized : butt[3], dupe, fool, gull, lamb, pushover. *Informal:* sucker. *Slang:* fall guy, gudgeon, mark, monkey, patsy, pigeon, sap[1]. *Chiefly British:* mug. *See* WISE.

victimization *noun*
An act of cheating : cheat, fraud, swindle. *Informal:* flimflam. *Slang:* gyp. *See* HONEST.

victimize *verb*
1. To get money or something else from by deceitful trickery : bilk, cheat, cozen, defraud, gull, mulct, rook, swindle. *Informal:* chisel, flimflam, take, trim. *Slang:* diddle[1], do, gyp, stick, sting. *See* HONEST. **2.** To offer as a sacrifice : immolate, sacrifice. *See* GIVE, RELIGION.

victimizer *noun*
A person who cheats : bilk, cheat, cheater, cozener, defrauder, rook, sharper, swindler, trickster. *Informal:* chiseler, crook, flimflammer. *Slang:* diddler, gyp, gypper. *See* HONEST.

victor *noun*
1. One that conquers : conqueror, conquistador, master, winner. *See* WIN. **2.** One that wins a contest or competition : winner. *See* WIN.

Victorian *adjective*
Marked by excessive concern for propriety and good form : bluenosed, genteel, old-maidish, precise, priggish, prim, prissy, proper, prudish, puritanical, strait-laced, stuffy. ***Idiom:*** prim and proper. *See* PLAIN.
Victorian *noun* A person who is too much concerned with being proper, modest, or righteous : bluenose, Mrs. Grundy, prude, puritan. *Informal:* old maid. *See* SEX.

victorious *adjective*
Relating to, having the nature of, or experiencing triumph : conquering, triumphal, triumphant, winning. *See* WIN.

victory *noun*
The act of conquering : conquest, triumph, win. *See* WIN.

victual *noun*
Something fit to be eaten : aliment, bread, comestible, diet, edible, esculent, fare, food, foodstuff, meat, nourishment, nurture, nutriment, nutrition, pabulum, pap, provender, provision (used in plural), sustenance. *Slang:* chow, eats, grub. *See* INGESTION.

videlicet *adverb*
That is to say : namely, scilicet, specifically. ***Idiom:*** to wit. *See* SPECIFIC.

vie *verb*
To strive against (others) for victory : compete, contend, contest, emulate, rival. *See* CONFLICT.

view *noun*
1. An act of directing the eyes on an object : contemplation, look, regard, sight. *See* SEE. **2.** The act of examining carefully : check, checkup, examination, inspection, perusal, scrutiny, study. *Informal:* going-over. *See* INVESTIGATE. **3.** Something believed or accepted as true by a person : belief, conviction, feeling, idea, mind, notion, opinion, persuasion, position, sentiment. *See* OPINION. **4.** That which is or can be seen : lookout, outlook, panorama, perspective, prospect, scene, sight, vista. *See* SEE. **5.** What one intends to do

or achieve : aim, ambition, design, end, goal, intent, intention, mark, meaning, object, objective, point, purpose, target, why. ***Idioms:*** end in view, why and wherefore. *See* PLANNED, PURPOSE.

view *verb* **1.** To direct the eyes on an object : consider, contemplate, eye, look. ***Idiom:*** clap (*or* lay *or* set) one's eyes on. *See* SEE. **2.** To look at carefully or critically : check (out), con, examine, go over, inspect, peruse, scrutinize, study, survey, traverse. *Informal:* case. ***Idiom:*** give a going-over. *See* INVESTIGATE. **3.** To look upon in a particular way : account, consider, deem, esteem, reckon, regard, see. *See* PERSPECTIVE.

viewable *adjective*
Capable of being seen : discernible, perceivable, perceptible, seeable, visible, visual. *See* SEE.

viewer *noun*
Someone who sees something occur : eyewitness, seer, witness. *See* SEE.

viewpoint *noun*
The position from which something is observed or considered : angle², eye, outlook, point of view, slant, standpoint, vantage. *See* PERSPECTIVE.

vigil *noun*
The act of carefully watching : lookout, surveillance, vigilance, watch. ***Idiom:*** watch and ward. *See* AWARENESS.

vigilance *noun*
1. The act of carefully watching : lookout, surveillance, vigil, watch. ***Idiom:*** watch and ward. *See* AWARENESS. **2.** The condition of being alert : alertness, wakefulness, wariness, watchfulness. *See* AWARENESS.

vigilant *adjective*
Vigilantly attentive : alert, observant, open-eyed, wakeful, wary, watchful, wide-awake. ***Idiom:*** on the ball. *See* AWARENESS.

vigor *noun*
1. A lively, emphatic, eager quality or manner : animation, bounce, brio, dash, élan, esprit, life, liveliness, pertness, sparkle, spirit, verve, vim, vivaciousness, vivacity, zip. *Informal:* ginger, pep, peppiness. *Slang:* oomph. *See* ACTION. **2.** A quality of active mental and physical forcefulness : dash, punch, starch, verve, vigorousness, vim, vitality. *Informal:* snap. ***Idiom:*** vim and vigor. *See* ACTION, TIRED.

vigorous *adjective*
1. Possessing, exerting, or displaying energy : active, brisk, dynamic, dynamical, energetic, forceful, kinetic, lively, sprightly, strenuous. *Informal:* peppy. *See* ACTION. **2.** Full of vigor : able-bodied, iron, lusty, red-blooded, robust, strapping, sturdy, vital. *See* STRONG. **3.** Disposed to action : active, brisk, driving, dynamic, dynamical, energetic, enterprising, lively, sprightly, spry, zippy. *Informal:* peppy, snappy. *See* ACTION. **4.** Full of or displaying force : dynamic, dynamical, effective, forceful, forcible, hard-hitting, powerful, strong. *See* STRONG.

vigorously *adverb*
With intense energy and force : energetically, forcefully, forcibly, hard, powerfully. ***Idioms:*** hammer and tongs, tooth and nail, with might and main. *See* STRONG.

vigorousness *noun*
A quality of active mental and physical forcefulness : dash, punch, starch, verve, vigor, vim, vitality. *Informal:* snap. ***Idiom:*** vim and vigor. *See* ACTION, TIRED.

vile *adjective*
1. So objectionable as to elicit despisal or deserve condemnation : abhorrent, abominable, antipathetic, contemptible, despicable, despisable, detestable, disgusting, filthy, foul, infamous, loathsome, lousy, low, mean², nasty, nefarious, obnoxious, odious, repugnant, rotten, shabby, wretched. *See* GOOD. **2.** Heavily soiled; very dirty or unclean : filthy, foul, nasty, squalid. *See* CLEAN. **3.** Extremely unpleasant to the senses or feelings : atrocious, disgusting, foul, horrid, nasty, nauseating, offensive, repellent, repulsive, revolting, sickening, ugly, unwholesome. *See* LIKE, PAIN. **4.** Having or proceeding from low moral standards : base², ignoble, low, low-down, mean², sordid, squalid. *See* RIGHT.

vilification *noun*
The expression of injurious, malicious statements about someone : aspersion, calumniation, calumny, character assassination, defamation, denigration, detraction, scandal, slander, traducement. *Law:* libel. *See* ATTACK, CRIMES, LAW.

vilify *verb*
To make defamatory statements about : asperse, backbite, calumniate, defame, malign, slander, slur, tear down, traduce. *Law:* libel. ***Idiom:*** cast aspersions on. *See* ATTACK, CRIMES, LAW.

villain *noun*
A mean, worthless character in a story or play : *Slang:* heavy. *See* RIGHT.

villainage *noun* See **villeinage.**

villainous *adjective*
Utterly reprehensible in nature or behavior :

corrupt, degenerate, depraved, flagitious, miscreant, perverse, rotten, unhealthy. *See* CLEAN, GOOD.

villainousness *noun*
Degrading, immoral acts or habits : bestiality, corruption, depravity, flagitiousness, immorality, perversion, turpitude, vice, villainy, wickedness. *See* CLEAN.

villainy *noun*
Degrading, immoral acts or habits : bestiality, corruption, depravity, flagitiousness, immorality, perversion, turpitude, vice, villainousness, wickedness. *See* CLEAN.

villeinage also **villainage** *noun*
A state of subjugation to an owner or master : bondage, enslavement, helotry, serfdom, servileness, servility, servitude, slavery, thrall, thralldom, yoke. *See* OVER.

vim *noun*
1. A lively, emphatic, eager quality or manner : animation, bounce, brio, dash, élan, esprit, life, liveliness, pertness, sparkle, spirit, verve, vigor, vivaciousness, vivacity, zip. *Informal:* ginger, pep, peppiness. *Slang:* oomph. *See* ACTION. **2.** A quality of active mental and physical forcefulness : dash, punch, starch, verve, vigor, vigorousness, vitality. *Informal:* snap. ***Idiom:*** vim and vigor. *See* ACTION, TIRED.

vincible *adjective*
Open to attack and capture because of a lack of protection : assailable, attackable, pregnable, vulnerable. *See* STRONG.

vinculum *noun*
That which unites or binds : bond, knot, ligament, ligature, link, nexus, tie, yoke. *See* CONNECT.

vindicate *verb*
1. To free from a charge or imputation of guilt : absolve, clear, exculpate, exonerate. *Law:* acquit, purge. *See* LAW. **2.** To support against arguments, attack, or criticism : apologize, defend, justify, maintain. ***Idioms:*** speak up for, stand up for, stick up for. *See* SUPPORT. **3.** To show to be just, right, or valid : excuse, justify, rationalize. ***Idiom:*** make a case for. *See* RIGHT. **4.** To defend, maintain, or insist on the recognition of (one's rights, for example) : assert, claim. *See* ATTACK. **5.** To exact revenge for or from : avenge, pay back, pay off, redress, repay, requite. *Informal:* fix. *Archaic:* wreak. ***Idioms:*** even the score, get back at, get even with, pay back in kind (*or* in one's own coin), settle (*or* square) accounts, take an eye for an eye. *See* FORGIVENESS.

vindication *noun*
1. A freeing or clearing from accusation or guilt : exculpation, exoneration. *Law:* acquittal. *See* LAW. **2.** A statement that justifies or defends something, such as a past action or policy : apologetic, apologia, apology, defense, justification. *See* ATTACK.

vindictive *adjective*
Disposed to seek revenge : revengeful, spiteful, vengeful. *See* FORGIVENESS.

vindictiveness *noun*
The quality or condition of being vindictive : revenge, spite, spitefulness, vengefulness. *See* FORGIVENESS.

vintage *noun*
Informal. A period of origin : year. *See* TIME.
vintage *adjective* **1.** Characterized by enduring excellence, appeal, and importance : classic, classical. *See* GOOD. **2.** Of a style or method formerly in vogue : antiquated, antique, archaic, bygone, dated, dowdy, fusty, old, old-fashioned, old-time, outdated, outmoded, out-of-date, passé. *See* NEW. **3.** Serving to identify or set apart an individual or group : characteristic, distinctive, individual, peculiar, typical. *See* SAME.

violate *verb*
1. To fail to fulfill (a promise) or conform to (a regulation) : breach, break, contravene, infringe, transgress. *See* DO. **2.** To refuse or fail to obey : break, defy, disobey, flout, transgress. ***Idiom:*** pay no attention to. *See* RESIST. **3.** To compel (another) to participate in or submit to a sexual act : assault, force, rape, ravish. *See* SEX. **4.** To deprive of virginity : defile, deflower. *See* SEX. **5.** To spoil or mar the sanctity of : defile, desecrate, pollute, profane. *See* CLEAN, RELIGION, SACRED.

violation *noun*
1. An act or instance of breaking a law or regulation or of nonfulfillment of an obligation or promise, for example : breach, contravention, infraction, infringement, transgression, trespass. *See* RIGHT. **2.** An act of disrespect or impiety toward something regarded as sacred : blasphemy, desecration, profanation, sacrilege. *See* SACRED.

violence *noun*
1. Power used to overcome resistance : coercion, compulsion, constraint, duress, force, pressure, strength. *See* ATTACK. **2.** Exceptionally great concentration, power, or force, especially in activity : depth (often used in plural), ferociousness, ferocity, fierceness, fury, inten-

sity, pitch, severity, vehemence, vehemency. *See* BIG, STRONG.

violent *adjective*

1. Accomplished by force : coercive, forcible. *Informal:* strong-arm. *See* ATTACK. 2. Extreme in degree, strength, or effect : desperate, fierce, furious, intense, terrible, vehement. *See* BIG, STRONG. 3. Violently disturbed or agitated, as by storms : dirty, heavy, raging, roiled, roily, rough, rugged, stormy, tempestuous, tumultuous, turbulent, ugly, wild. *See* CALM.

VIP *noun*

Informal. An important, influential person : character, dignitary, eminence, leader, lion, nabob, notability, notable, personage. *Informal:* big-timer, heavyweight, somebody, someone. *Slang:* big shot, big wheel, bigwig, muckamuck. *See* IMPORTANT.

virago *noun*

A person, traditionally a woman, who persistently nags or criticizes : fishwife, fury, harpy, scold, shrew, termagant, vixen. *Informal:* battle-ax. *See* PRAISE.

virgin *noun*

A pure, uncorrupted person : angel, innocent, lamb. *See* CLEAN, RIGHT.

virgin *adjective* Morally beyond reproach, especially in sexual conduct : chaste, decent, modest, nice, pure, virginal, virtuous. *See* GOOD, RESTRAINT, SEX.

virginal *adjective*

1. Morally beyond reproach, especially in sexual conduct : chaste, decent, modest, nice, pure, virgin, virtuous. *See* GOOD, RESTRAINT, SEX. 2. Free from evil and corruption : angelic, angelical, clean, innocent, lily-white, pure, sinless, unblemished, uncorrupted, undefiled, unstained, unsullied, untainted. ***Idiom:*** pure as the driven snow. *See* CLEAN, RIGHT, SEX.

virginity *noun*

The condition of being chaste : chastity, decency, innocence, modesty, purity, virtue, virtuousness. *See* GOOD, RESTRAINT, SEX.

virile *adjective*

Of, characteristic of, or befitting the male sex : macho, male, manful, manlike, manly, mannish, masculine. *See* GENDER.

virtual *adjective*

Involved in the essential nature of something but not shown or developed : implicit, practical. *See* BE, SHOW.

virtue *noun*

1. The quality or state of being morally sound : good, goodness, morality, probity, rectitude, righteousness, rightness, uprightness, virtuousness. *See* RIGHT. 2. The condition of being chaste : chastity, decency, innocence, modesty, purity, virginity, virtuousness. *See* GOOD, RESTRAINT, SEX. 3. A special feature or quality that confers superiority : beauty, distinction, excellence, merit, perfection. *See* GOOD. 4. A level of superiority that is usually high : caliber, merit, quality, stature, value, worth. *See* GOOD, VALUE.

virtuous *adjective*

1. In accordance with principles of right or good conduct : ethical, moral, principled, proper, right, righteous, rightful, right-minded. *See* RIGHT. 2. Morally beyond reproach, especially in sexual conduct : chaste, decent, modest, nice, pure, virgin, virginal. *See* GOOD, RESTRAINT, SEX.

virtuousness *noun*

1. The quality or state of being morally sound : good, goodness, morality, probity, rectitude, righteousness, rightness, uprightness, virtue. *See* RIGHT. 2. The condition of being chaste : chastity, decency, innocence, modesty, purity, virginity, virtue. *See* GOOD, RESTRAINT, SEX.

virulence *noun*

The quality or state of feeling bitter : acrimony, bitterness, embitterment, gall[1], rancor, rancorousness, resentfulness, resentment, virulency. *See* FEELINGS.

virulency *noun*

The quality or state of feeling bitter : acrimony, bitterness, embitterment, gall[1], rancor, rancorousness, resentfulness, resentment, virulence. *See* FEELINGS.

virulent *adjective*

1. Extremely destructive or harmful : baneful, deadly, malignant, noxious, pernicious, pestilent, pestilential. *See* HELP. 2. Capable of injuring or killing by poison : mephitic, mephitical, poison, poisonous, toxic, toxicant, venomous. *See* HELP. 3. Bitingly hostile : acrimonious, bitter, embittered, hard, rancorous, resentful. *See* ATTITUDE, LOVE.

virus *noun*

Anything that is injurious, destructive, or fatal : bane, canker, contagion, poison, toxin, venom. *See* HELP.

visage *noun*

1. The front surface of the head : countenance, face, feature (often used in plural), muzzle. *Informal:* mug. *Slang:* kisser, map, pan, puss. *See* PRECEDE. 2. A disposition of the facial features that conveys meaning, feeling, or mood :

aspect, cast, countenance, expression, face, look. *See* EXPRESS. **3.** An outward appearance : aspect, countenance, face, look, physiognomy, surface. *See* SURFACE.

vis-à-vis *noun*
One that has the same functions and characteristics as another : counterpart, opposite number. *See* SAME.

visceral *adjective*
1. Of, relating to, or arising from one's mental or spiritual being : inner, interior, internal, intimate[1], inward. *Slang:* gut. *See* BODY.
2. Derived from or prompted by a natural tendency or impulse : instinctive, instinctual, intuitive. *See* THOUGHTS.

viscid *adjective*
Having a heavy, gluey quality : glutinous, mucilaginous, viscose, viscous. *See* SOLID.

viscidity *noun*
The physical property of being viscous : glutinousness, viscosity. *See* SOLID.

viscose *adjective*
Having a heavy, gluey quality : glutinous, mucilaginous, viscid, viscous. *See* SOLID.

viscosity *noun*
The physical property of being viscous : glutinousness, viscidity. *See* SOLID.

viscous *adjective*
Having a heavy, gluey quality : glutinous, mucilaginous, viscid, viscose. *See* SOLID.

visibility *noun*
The quality, condition, or degree of being visible : perceptibility, visuality, visualness. *See* SEE.

visible *adjective*
1. Capable of being seen : discernible, perceivable, perceptible, seeable, viewable, visual. *See* SEE. **2.** Readily seen, perceived, or understood : apparent, clear, clear-cut, crystal clear, distinct, evident, manifest, noticeable, observable, obvious, patent, plain, pronounced. *See* SEE.

vision *noun*
1. The faculty of seeing : eye, eyesight, seeing, sight. *Archaic:* light[1]. *See* SEE. **2.** Unusual or creative discernment or perception : farsightedness, foresight, prescience. *See* FORESIGHT.
3. An illusory mental image : daydream, dream, fancy, fantasy, fiction, figment, illusion, phantasm, phantasma, reverie. *See* REAL.
4. Something that is foretold by or as if by supernatural means : divination, oracle, prophecy, soothsaying, vaticination. *See* FORESIGHT.

vision *verb* To form mental images of : conceive, envisage, envision, fancy, fantasize, image, imagine, picture, see, think, visualize. *Informal:* feature. *See* THOUGHTS.

visionary *adjective*
1. Characterized by foresight : farsighted, foresighted, prescient. *See* FORESIGHT. **2.** Of, relating to, or in the nature of an illusion; lacking reality : chimeric, chimerical, delusive, delusory, dreamlike, hallucinatory, illusive, illusory, phantasmagoric, phantasmal, phantasmic. *See* REAL. **3.** Existing only in the imagination : chimeric, chimerical, conceptual, fanciful, fantastic, fantastical, imaginary, notional, unreal. *See* REAL. **4.** Of or relating to the foretelling of events by or as if by supernatural means : augural, divinitory, fatidic, fatidical, mantic, oracular, prophetic, sibylline, vatic, vatical, vaticinal. *See* FORESIGHT. **5.** Given to daydreams or reverie : dreamy, moony, woolgathering. *See* REAL. **6.** Not compatible with reality : idealistic, quixotic, romantic, starry-eyed, unrealistic, utopian. *See* HOPE, REAL. **7.** Showing a tendency to envision things in perfect but unrealistic form : idealistic, utopian. *See* HOPE, REAL.

visionary *noun* A person inclined to be imaginative or idealistic but impractical : dreamer, idealist, utopian. *See* ABILITY, HOPE.

visit *verb*
1. To go to or seek out the company of in order to socialize : call, come by, come over, drop by, drop in, look in, look up, pop in, run in, see, stop (by *or* in). ***Idiom:*** pay a visit. *See* SEEK.
2. To remain as a guest or lodger : lodge, sojourn, stay[1]. *See* PLACE. **3.** *Informal.* To engage in spoken exchange : chat, confabulate, converse[1], discourse, speak, talk. *Informal:* confab. *See* WORDS. **4.** To cause to undergo or bear (something unwelcome or damaging, for example) : impose, inflict, play, wreak. *See* GIVE, OVER, WILLING.

visit *noun* **1.** An act or an instance of going or coming to see another : call, look-in, visitation. *See* SEEK. **2.** A remaining in a place as a guest or lodger : sojourn, stay[1]. *See* PLACE.

visitant *noun*
1. A person or persons visiting one : company, guest, visitor. *See* ACCOMPANIED. **2.** A supernatural being, such as a ghost : apparition, bogey, bogeyman, bogle, eidolon, ghost, phantasm, phantasma, phantom, revenant, shade, shadow, specter, spirit, wraith. *Informal:* spook. *Regional:* haunt. *See* BEINGS, SUPERNATURAL.

visitation *noun*
1. An act or an instance of going or coming to

see another : call, look-in, visit. *See* SEEK. **2.** A state of pain or anguish that tests one's resiliency and character : crucible, ordeal, trial, tribulation. *See* EASY.

visitor *noun*
1. A person or persons visiting one : company, guest, visitant. *See* ACCOMPANIED. **2.** One that arrives : arrival, comer. *See* ENTER.

visor *noun*
The projecting rim on the front of a cap : bill², brim, peak. *See* CONVEX, PROTECTION.

vista *noun*
That which is or can be seen : lookout, outlook, panorama, perspective, prospect, scene, sight, view. *See* SEE.

visual *adjective*
1. Serving, resulting from, or relating to the sense of sight : optic, optical. *See* SEE. **2.** Capable of being seen : discernible, perceivable, perceptible, seeable, viewable, visible. *See* SEE.

visuality *noun*
The quality, condition, or degree of being visible : perceptibility, visibility, visualness. *See* SEE.

visualize *verb*
To form mental images of : conceive, envisage, envision, fancy, fantasize, image, imagine, picture, see, think, vision. *Informal:* feature. *See* THOUGHTS.

visualness *noun*
The quality, condition, or degree of being visible : perceptibility, visibility, visuality. *See* SEE.

vital *adjective*
1. Marked by or exhibiting life : alive, animate, animated, live², living. *See* LIVE. **2.** Full of vigor : able-bodied, iron, lusty, red-blooded, robust, strapping, sturdy, vigorous. *See* STRONG. **3.** Constituting or forming part of the essence of something : basic, constitutional, constitutive, essential, fundamental, integral. *See* BE, SURFACE. **4.** Causing or tending to cause death : deadly, deathly, fatal, lethal, mortal. *See* LIVE.

vital force *noun*
The vital principle or animating force within living beings : breath, divine spark, élan vital, life force, psyche, soul, spirit, vitality. *See* BODY.

vitality *noun*
1. The vital principle or animating force within living beings : breath, divine spark, élan vital, life force, psyche, soul, spirit, vital force. *See* BODY. **2.** A quality of active mental and physical forcefulness : dash, punch, starch, verve, vigor, vigorousness, vim. *Informal:* snap. ***Idiom:*** vim and vigor. *See* ACTION, TIRED.

vitalize *verb*
1. To make alive : animate, quicken, vivify. *See* LIVE. **2.** To give or impart vitality and energy to (someone or something) : energize, exhilarate, invigorate, stimulate. *See* HELP.

vitalizing *adjective*
Serving to enliven : animating, enlivening, quickening, rousing, stimulating, vivifying. *See* EXCITE.

vitiate *verb*
1. To spoil the soundness or perfection of : blemish, damage, detract from, disserve, flaw, harm, hurt, impair, injure, mar, prejudice, tarnish. *See* BETTER, HELP. **2.** To ruin utterly in character or quality : animalize, bastardize, bestialize, brutalize, canker, corrupt, debase, debauch, demoralize, deprave, pervert, stain, warp. *See* CLEAN, HELP. **3.** To put an end to, especially formally and with authority : abolish, abrogate, annihilate, annul, cancel, invalidate, negate, nullify, set aside, void. *Law:* extinguish. *See* CONTINUE.

vitriolic *adjective*
So sharp as to cause mental pain : acerbic, acid, acidic, acrid, astringent, biting, caustic, corrosive, cutting, mordacious, mordant, pungent, scathing, sharp, slashing, stinging, trenchant, truculent. *See* ATTACK, RESPECT.

vituperate *verb*
To attack with harsh, often insulting language : abuse, assail, rail against (*or* at), revile. *See* PRAISE.

vituperation *noun*
Harsh, often insulting language : abuse, billingsgate, contumely, invective, obloquy, railing, revilement, reviling, scurrility, scurrilousness. *See* PRAISE.

vituperative *adjective*
Of, relating to, or characterized by verbal abuse : abusive, contumelious, invective, opprobrious, scurrilous. *See* ATTACK, ATTITUDE.

vivacious *adjective*
Very brisk, alert, and full of high spirits : animated, bouncy, chipper, dashing, high-spirited, lively, pert, spirited. *Informal:* peppy. ***Idioms:*** bright-eyed and bushy-tailed, full of life. *See* ACTION.

vivaciousness *noun*
A lively, emphatic, eager quality or manner : animation, bounce, brio, dash, élan, esprit, life, liveliness, pertness, sparkle, spirit, verve, vigor,

vim, vivacity, zip. *Informal:* ginger, pep, peppiness. *Slang:* oomph. *See* ACTION.

vivacity *noun*
A lively, emphatic, eager quality or manner : animation, bounce, brio, dash, élan, esprit, life, liveliness, pertness, sparkle, spirit, verve, vigor, vim, vivaciousness, zip. *Informal:* ginger, pep, peppiness. *Slang:* oomph. *See* ACTION.

vivid *adjective*
1. Full of color : bright, colorful, gay, rich. *See* COLORS. **2.** Evoking strong mental images through distinctiveness : colorful, picturesque. *See* STRONG. **3.** Described verbally in sharp and accurate detail : graphic, lifelike, photographic, pictorial, picturesque, realistic. *See* SPECIFIC, WORDS.

vivify *verb*
To make alive : animate, quicken, vitalize. *See* LIVE.

vivifying *adjective*
Serving to enliven : animating, enlivening, quickening, rousing, stimulating, vitalizing. *See* EXCITE.

vixen *noun*
A person, traditionally a woman, who persistently nags or criticizes : fishwife, fury, harpy, scold, shrew, termagant, virago. *Informal:* battle-ax. *See* PRAISE.

vocabulary *noun*
1. All the words of a language : lexicon, wordhoard. *See* WORDS. **2.** An alphabetical list of words often defined or translated : dictionary, glossary, lexicon, wordbook. *See* WORDS. **3.** Specialized expressions indigenous to a particular field, subject, trade, or subculture : argot, cant[2], dialect, idiom, jargon, language, lexicon, lingo, patois, terminology, vernacular. *See* WORDS.

vocal *adjective*
1. Produced by the voice : articulate, oral, sonant, spoken, uttered, voiced. *See* SOUNDS. **2.** Speaking or spoken without reserve : free, free-spoken, outspoken. *See* RESTRAINT. **3.** Characterized by, containing, or functioning as a vowel or vowels : vocalic, vowel. *See* SOUNDS.

vocalic *adjective*
Characterized by, containing, or functioning as a vowel or vowels : vocal, vowel. *See* SOUNDS.

vocalism *noun*
The use of the speech organs to produce sounds : articulation, enunciation, utterance, vocalization, voicing. *See* SOUNDS, WORDS.

vocalist *noun*
A person who sings : singer, songster, songstress, voice. *See* PERFORMING ARTS.

vocalization *noun*
1. The faculty, act, or product of speaking : discourse, speech, talk, utterance, verbalization. *See* WORDS. **2.** The use of the speech organs to produce sounds : articulation, enunciation, utterance, vocalism, voicing. *See* SOUNDS, WORDS. **3.** The act or an instance of expressing in words : articulation, expression, statement, utterance, verbalization, voice. *See* WORDS.

vocalize *verb*
1. To produce or make (speech sounds) : articulate, enunciate, pronounce, say, utter[1]. *See* WORDS. **2.** To put into words : articulate, communicate, convey, declare, express, say, state, talk, tell, utter[1], vent, verbalize, voice. ***Idiom:*** give tongue (*or* vent *or* voice) to. *See* WORDS. **3.** To express oneself in speech : speak, talk, verbalize. ***Idioms:*** open one's mouth (*or* lips), put in (*or* into) words, wag one's tongue. *See* WORDS. **4.** To utter words or sounds in musical tones : carol, chant, sing. *Archaic:* tune. *See* SOUNDS.

vocation *noun*
1. Activity pursued as a livelihood : art, business, calling, career, craft, employment, job, line, métier, occupation, profession, pursuit, trade, work. *Slang:* racket. *Archaic:* employ. *See* ACTION. **2.** An inner urge to pursue an activity or perform a service : calling, mission. *See* DESIRE.

vociferate *verb*
To speak or say very loudly or with a shout : bawl, bellow, bluster, call, clamor, cry, halloo, holler, roar, shout, whoop, yawp, yell. *See* SOUNDS.

vociferation *noun*
Offensively loud and insistent utterances, especially of disapproval : clamor, hullabaloo, outcry, rumpus, uproar. ***Idiom:*** hue and cry. *See* LIKE, SOUNDS.

vociferous *adjective*
Offensively loud and insistent : blatant, boisterous, clamorous, obstreperous, strident. *Informal:* loudmouthed. *See* SOUNDS.

vogue *noun*
The current custom : craze, fad, fashion, furor, mode, rage, style, trend. *Informal:* thing. *Idioms:* the in thing, the last word, the latest thing. *See* STYLE, USUAL.

voice *noun*
1. A person who sings : singer, songster, songstress, vocalist. *See* PERFORMING ARTS. **2.** The

act or an instance of expressing in words : articulation, expression, statement, utterance, verbalization, vocalization. *See* WORDS. **3.** The right or chance to express an opinion or participate in a decision : say, suffrage, vote. *Informal:* say-so. *See* PARTICIPATE.

voice *verb* To put into words : articulate, communicate, convey, declare, express, say, state, talk, tell, utter[1], vent, verbalize, vocalize. ***Idiom:*** give tongue (*or* vent *or* voice) to. *See* WORDS.

voiced *adjective*
Produced by the voice : articulate, oral, sonant, spoken, uttered, vocal. *See* SOUNDS.

voiceless *adjective*
1. Lacking the power or faculty of speech : aphonic, dumb, inarticulate, mute, speechless. *See* WORDS. **2.** Temporarily unable or unwilling to speak, as from shock or fear : dumb, inarticulate, mum, mute, silent, speechless, wordless. *See* WORDS.

voicing *noun*
The use of the speech organs to produce sounds : articulation, enunciation, utterance, vocalism, vocalization. *See* SOUNDS, WORDS.

void *adjective*
1. Containing nothing : bare, blank, clear, empty, vacant, vacuous. *See* FULL. **2.** Not having a desirable element : barren, destitute, devoid, empty, innocent, lacking, wanting. ***Idiom:*** in want of. *See* FULL.

void *noun* **1.** Empty, unfilled space : barrenness, emptiness, nothingness, vacancy, vacuity, vacuum. *See* FULL. **2.** A space in an otherwise solid mass : cavity, hole, hollow, pocket, vacuity. *See* CONVEX. **3.** Total absence of matter : emptiness, vacancy, vacuity, vacuum. *See* FULL. **4.** An interval during which continuity is suspended : break, gap, hiatus, interim, lacuna. *See* CONTINUE. **5.** A desolate sense of loss : blankness, desolation, emptiness, hollowness, vacuum. *See* FULL.

void *verb* **1.** To remove the contents of : clean out, clear, empty (out), evacuate, vacate. *See* FULL. **2.** To put an end to, especially formally and with authority : abolish, abrogate, annihilate, annul, cancel, invalidate, negate, nullify, set aside, vitiate. *Law:* extinguish. *See* CONTINUE.

voidance *noun*
An often formal act of putting an end to : abolishment, abolition, abrogation, annihilation, annulment, cancellation, defeasance, invalidation, negation, nullification. *Law:* avoidance, extinguishment. *See* CONTINUE.

volatile *adjective*
Following no predictable pattern : capricious, changeable, erratic, fantastic, fantastical, fickle, freakish, inconsistent, inconstant, mercurial, temperamental, ticklish, uncertain, unpredictable, unstable, unsteady, variable, whimsical. *See* CHANGE, CONTINUE.

volatilize *verb*
To pass off as vapor, especially when heated : boil away, evaporate, vaporize. *See* SOLID.

volition *noun*
The mental faculty by which one deliberately chooses or decides : will. *See* WILLING.

volitional *adjective*
1. Done by one's own choice : free, spontaneous, uncompelled, unforced, voluntary, willful. *See* WILLING. **2.** Of or relating to free exercise of the will : voluntary, willing. *See* WILLING.

volley *noun*
A concentrated outpouring, as of missiles, words, or blows : barrage, bombardment, burst, cannonade, fusillade, hail[1], salvo, shower, storm. *See* ATTACK.

voluble *adjective*
Given to conversation : chatty, conversational, garrulous, loquacious, talkative, talky. *Slang:* gabby. *See* WORDS.

volume *noun*
1. A printed and bound work : book, tome. *See* WORDS. **2.** An issue of printed material offered for sale or distribution : opus, publication, title, work. *See* WORDS. **3.** Great extent, amount, or dimension. Often used in plural : amplitude, bulk, magnitude, mass, size. *See* BIG.

voluminous *adjective*
1. Of full measure; not narrow or restricted : ample, capacious, full, wide. *See* TIGHTEN. **2.** Characterized by abundance : abundant, ample, bounteous, bountiful, copious, generous, heavy, plenitudinous, plenteous, plentiful, substantial. *See* BIG, GIVE, RICH.

voluntarily *adverb*
Of one's own free will : freely, spontaneously, willfully, willingly. ***Idioms:*** of one's own accord, on one's own volition. *See* WILLING.

voluntary *adjective*
1. Of or relating to free exercise of the will : volitional, willing. *See* WILLING. **2.** Done by one's own choice : free, spontaneous, uncompelled, unforced, volitional, willful. *See* WILLING. **3.** Contributing one's time without pay : uncompensated, unpaid, unrecompensed, unremunerated, unsalaried. *See* PAY, WORK. **4.** Done or said on purpose : deliberate,

intended, intentional, purposeful, willful, witting. *See* PURPOSE.

voluntary *noun* Someone who offers his or her services freely : volunteer. *See* WILLING, WORK.

volunteer *noun*
Someone who offers his or her services freely : voluntary. *See* WILLING, WORK.

volunteer *verb* To put before another for acceptance : extend, offer, present[2], proffer, tender[2]. ***Idioms:*** come forward with, lay at someone's feet, lay before. *See* OFFER.

voluptuary *noun*
A person devoted to pleasure and luxury : epicure, epicurean, hedonist, sensualist, sybarite. *See* PAIN.

voluptuary *adjective* Characterized by or devoted to pleasure and luxury as a lifestyle : epicurean, hedonic, hedonistic, sybaritic, voluptuous. *See* PAIN.

voluptuous *adjective*
1. Characterized by or devoted to pleasure and luxury as a lifestyle : epicurean, hedonic, hedonistic, sybaritic, voluptuary. *See* PAIN. **2.** Relating to, suggestive of, or appealing to sense gratification : epicurean, sensual, sensualistic, sensuous. *See* PAIN. **3.** Suggesting sexuality : sensual, sexual, sexy, suggestive. *See* SEX.

voluptuousness *noun*
1. The quality or condition of being sensuous : sensualism, sensuality, sensuousness. *See* PAIN. **2.** The quality or condition of being sensual : sensuality, sexiness, sexuality, suggestiveness. *See* SEX.

vomit *verb*
To eject the contents of the stomach through the mouth : heave, throw up. *Slang:* puke. *See* MOUTH.

voodoo *verb*
To act upon with or as if with magic : bewitch, charm, enchant, enthrall, entrance[2], spell[2], spellbind, witch. *See* PERSUASION.

voracious *adjective*
1. Wanting to eat or drink more than one can reasonably consume : edacious, gluttonous, greedy, hoggish, piggish, ravenous. *See* DESIRE, INGESTION. **2.** Desiring or craving food : famished, hungry, ravenous, starving. *See* INGESTION. **3.** Having an insatiable appetite for an activity or pursuit : avid, edacious, gluttonous, greedy, omnivorous, rapacious, ravenous, unappeasable. *See* DESIRE.

voracity *noun*
The quality or condition of being voracious : avidity, edacity, omnivorousness, rapaciousness, rapacity, ravenousness. *See* DESIRE.

votary *noun*
One zealously devoted to a religion : devotee, enthusiast, fanatic, sectary, zealot. *See* BELIEF, LOVE, RELIGION.

vote *noun*
The right or chance to express an opinion or participate in a decision : say, suffrage, voice. *Informal:* say-so. *See* PARTICIPATE.

vote *verb* To select by vote for an office. Also used with *in* : ballot, elect. *See* CHOICE, POLITICS.

voter *noun*
One who votes : balloter, elector. *See* CHOICE, POLITICS.

vouch *verb*
To confirm formally as true, accurate, or genuine. Also used with *for* : attest, certify, testify, witness. ***Idiom:*** bear witness to. *See* AFFIRM.

vouchsafe *verb*
1. To let have as a favor, prerogative, or privilege : accord, award, concede, give, grant. *See* GIVE. **2.** To descend to a level considered inappropriate to one's dignity : condescend, deign, stoop. *See* OVER, RISE.

vow *noun*
A declaration that one will or will not do a certain thing : assurance, covenant, engagement, guarantee, guaranty, pledge, plight[2], promise, solemn word, warrant, word, word of honor. *See* OBLIGATION.

vow *verb* To guarantee by a solemn promise : covenant, pledge, plight[2], promise, swear. ***Idiom:*** give one's word of honor. *See* AGREE, OBLIGATION.

vowel *adjective*
Characterized by, containing, or functioning as a vowel or vowels : vocal, vocalic. *See* SOUNDS.

voyage *noun*
A journey undertaken with a specific objective : expedition, pilgrimage, safari, tour, trek. *See* MOVE.

vulgar *adjective*
1. Lacking high station or birth : baseborn, common, déclassé, declassed, humble, ignoble, lowly, mean[2], plebeian, unwashed. *Archaic:* base[2]. *See* OVER. **2.** Lacking in delicacy or refinement : barbarian, barbaric, boorish, churlish, coarse, crass, crude, gross, ill-bred, indelicate, philistine, rough, rude, tasteless, uncivilized, uncouth, uncultivated, uncultured, unpolished, unrefined. *See* COURTESY,

SMOOTH. **3.** Offensive to accepted standards of decency : barnyard, bawdy, broad, coarse, dirty, Fescennine, filthy, foul, gross, lewd, nasty, obscene, profane, ribald, scatologic, scatological, scurrilous, smutty. *Slang:* raunchy. *See* DECENT.

vulgarian *noun*
An unrefined, rude person : barbarian, boor, chuff, churl, Philistine, yahoo. *See* GOOD.

vulgarism *noun*
A term that offends against established usage standards : barbarism, corruption, solecism. *See* STYLE.

vulgarity *noun*
1. The quality or state of being obscene : bawdiness, coarseness, dirtiness, filthiness, foulness, grossness, lewdness, obscenity, profaneness, profanity, scurrility, scurrilousness, smuttiness, vulgarness. *Slang:* raunch, raunchiness. *See* DECENT. **2.** Something that is offensive to accepted standards of decency : bawdry, dirt, filth, obscenity, profanity, ribaldry, scatology, smut. *Slang:* raunch. *See* DECENT.

vulgarness *noun*
The quality or state of being obscene : bawdiness, coarseness, dirtiness, filthiness, foulness, grossness, lewdness, obscenity, profaneness, profanity, scurrility, scurrilousness, smuttiness, vulgarity. *Slang:* raunch, raunchiness. *See* DECENT.

vulnerability *noun*
The condition of being laid open to something undesirable or injurious : exposure, liability, openness, susceptibility, susceptibleness, vulnerableness. *See* PROTECTION.

vulnerable *adjective*
1. Tending to incur : liable, open, prone, subject, susceptible, susceptive. *See* LIKELY.
2. Open to attack and capture because of a lack of protection : assailable, attackable, pregnable, vincible. *See* STRONG.

vulnerableness *noun*
The condition of being laid open to something undesirable or injurious : exposure, liability, openness, susceptibility, susceptibleness, vulnerability. *See* PROTECTION.

wacky also **whacky** *adjective*
1. *Slang.* So senseless as to be laughable : absurd, foolish, harebrained, idiotic, imbecilic, insane, lunatic, mad, moronic, nonsensical, preposterous, silly, softheaded, tomfool, unearthly, zany. *Informal:* cockeyed, crazy, loony, loopy. *Slang:* balmy[2], dippy, dopey, jerky, sappy. *See* ABILITY, KNOWLEDGE. **2.** *Slang.* Afflicted with or exhibiting irrationality and mental unsoundness : brainsick, crazy, daft, demented, disordered, distraught, dotty, insane, lunatic, mad, maniac, maniacal, mentally ill, moonstruck, off, touched, unbalanced, unsound, wrong. *Informal:* bonkers, cracked, daffy, gaga, loony. *Slang:* bananas, batty, buggy, cuckoo, fruity, loco, nuts, nutty, screwy. *Chiefly British:* crackers. *Law:* non compos mentis. ***Idioms:*** around the bend, crazy as a loon, mad as a hatter, not all there, nutty as a fruitcake, off (*or* out of) one's head, off one's rocker, of unsound mind, out of one's mind, sick in the head, stark raving mad. *See* SANE.

wad *noun*
1. An irregularly shaped mass of indefinite size : chunk, clod, clump, gob[1], hunch, lump[1], nugget. *Informal:* hunk. *See* PART. **2.** *Informal.* An indeterminately great amount or number : jillion, million (often used in plural), multiplicity, ream, trillion. *Informal:* bushel, gob[1] (often used in plural), heap (often used in plural), load (often used in plural), lot, oodles, passel, peck[2], scad (often used in plural), slew, zillion. *See* BIG. **3.** *Informal.* A large sum of money : fortune, mint. *Informal:* bundle, pretty penny, tidy sum. *Slang:* pile. *See* RICH.

wade *verb*
To walk heavily, slowly, and with difficulty : plod, slog, slop, toil, trudge. *See* MOVE.
wade in (or **into)** *verb* **1.** To move or thrust at, under, or into the midst of with sudden force : dive, lunge, plunge. *See* ENTER. **2.** To start work on vigorously : attack, go at, sail in, tackle. ***Idiom:*** hop to it. *See* WORK.

wade in or **into** *verb* See **wade**.

waffle *verb*
Informal. To use evasive or deliberately vague language : equivocate, euphemize, hedge, shuffle, tergiversate, weasel. *Informal:* pussyfoot. ***Idioms:*** beat about (*or* around) the bush, mince words. *See* CLEAR.
waffle *noun Informal.* The use or an instance of equivocal language : ambiguity, equivocation, equivoque, euphemism, hedge, prevarication, shuffle, tergiversation, weasel word. *See* CLEAR.

wag¹ *verb*
To move to and fro vigorously and usually repeatedly : switch, waggle, wave. *See* REPETITION.

wag² *noun*
A person whose words or actions provoke or are intended to provoke amusement or laughter : clown, comedian, comic, farceur, funnyman, humorist, jester, joker, jokester, quipster, wit, zany. *Informal:* card. *See* LAUGHTER.

wage *noun*
1. Payment for work done : compensation, earnings, emolument, fee, hire, pay, remuneration, salary, stipend. *See* PAY. **2.** Something justly deserved. Often used in plural : comeuppance, desert² (often used in plural), due, guerdon, recompense, reward. *Informal:* lump¹ (used in plural). ***Idioms:*** what is coming to one, what one has coming. *See* REWARD.
wage *verb* To engage in (a war or campaign, for example) : carry on, carry out, conduct. *See* DO.

wager *noun*
1. A venture depending on chance : bet, gamble, risk, speculation. *See* GAMBLING. **2.** Something risked on an uncertain outcome : ante, bet, pot, stake (often used in plural). *See* GAMBLING.
wager *verb* **1.** To put up as a stake in a game or speculation : bet, gamble, lay¹ (down), post², put, risk, stake, venture. *Informal:* go. *See* GAMBLING. **2.** To make a bet : bet, gamble, game, lay¹, play. ***Idiom:*** put one's money on something. *See* GAMBLING.

waggish *adjective*
Full of high-spirited fun : frisky, frolicsome, impish, mischievous, playful, sportive. *See* WORK.

waggishness *noun*
The state of being full of high-spirited fun : friskiness, frolicsomeness, playfulness, sportiveness. *See* WORK.

waggle *verb*
1. To move to and fro vigorously and usually repeatedly : switch, wag¹, wave. *See* REPETITION. **2.** To move (one's arms or wings, for example) up and down : beat, flap, flitter, flop, flutter, wave. *See* REPETITION. **3.** To move or proceed with short irregular motions up and down or from side to side : squiggle, squirm, wiggle, worm, wriggle, writhe. *See* MOVE, REPETITION.

wail *verb*
1. To make inarticulate sounds of grief or pain, usually accompanied by tears : bawl, blubber, cry, howl, keen², sob, weep, yowl. *See* HAPPY, SOUNDS. **2.** To cry loudly, as a healthy child does from pain or distress : bawl, howl, yowl. *See* SOUNDS. **3.** To utter or emit a long, mournful, plaintive sound : bay², howl, moan, ululate, yowl. *See* SOUNDS.
wail *noun* A long, mournful cry : bay², howl, moan, ululation, yowl. *See* SOUNDS.

wailing *noun*
A fit of crying : bawling, blubbering, cry, sobbing, tear² (used in plural), weeping. *See* SOUNDS.

wait *verb*
1. To look forward to confidently. Also used with *for* : anticipate, await, bargain for (*or* on), count on, depend on (*or* upon), expect, look for. *Informal:* figure on. *See* SURPRISE. **2.** To continue to be in a place : abide, bide, linger, remain, stay¹, tarry. *Informal:* stick around. ***Idiom:*** stay put. *See* CONTINUE. **3.** To stop temporarily and remain, as if reluctant to leave : abide, bide, linger, pause, stay¹, tarry. *See* CONTINUE. **4.** *Informal.* To put off until a later time : adjourn, defer¹, delay, hold off, hold up, postpone, remit, shelve, stay¹, suspend, table, waive. ***Idiom:*** put on ice. *See* DO.
wait on (or **upon)** *verb* **1.** To work and care for : attend, do for, minister to, serve. *See* CARE FOR. **2.** To place food before (someone) : serve. *See* INGESTION.
wait *noun* An act or the time of waiting : waiting. *See* CONTINUE.

waiting *noun*
An act or the time of waiting : wait. *See* CONTINUE.

wait on or **upon** *verb* See **wait.**

waive *verb*
1. To give up a possession, claim, or right : abandon, abdicate, cede, demit, forswear, hand over, quitclaim, relinquish, render, renounce, resign, surrender, yield. *See* KEEP. **2.** To put off until a later time : adjourn, defer¹, delay, hold off, hold up, postpone, remit, shelve, stay¹, sus-

pend, table. *Informal:* wait. ***Idiom:*** put on ice. *See* DO.

waiver *noun*
1. A giving up of a possession, claim, or right : abandonment, abdication, demission, quitclaim, relinquishment, renunciation, resignation, surrender. *See* KEEP. **2.** The act of putting off or the condition of being put off : adjournment, deferment, deferral, delay, postponement, stay[1], suspension. *See* TIME.

wake[1] *verb*
To cease sleeping : arouse, awake, awaken, rouse, stir[1], waken. *See* AWARENESS.
wake *noun* A watch over the body of a dead person before burial : watch. *See* RITUAL.

wake[2] *noun*
Something that follows or is drawn along behind : tail, trail, train. *See* PRECEDE.

wakeful *adjective*
1. Not in a state of sleep : awake, unsleeping, wide-awake. *See* AWARENESS. **2.** Marked by an absence of sleep : sleepless, slumberless. *See* AWARENESS. **3.** Vigilantly attentive : alert, observant, open-eyed, vigilant, wary, watchful, wide-awake. ***Idiom:*** on the ball. *See* AWARENESS.

wakefulness *noun*
The condition of being alert : alertness, vigilance, wariness, watchfulness. *See* AWARENESS.

waken *verb*
1. To cease sleeping : arouse, awake, awaken, rouse, stir[1], wake[1]. *See* AWARENESS. **2.** To induce or elicit (a reaction or emotion) : arouse, awake, awaken, kindle, raise, rouse, stir[1] (up). *See* EXCITE.

wale *noun*
A ridge or bump raised on the flesh, as by a lash or blow : weal[2], welt, wheal, whelk. *See* MARKS.

walk *verb*
To go on foot : ambulate, foot, pace, step, tread. *Slang:* hoof. ***Idiom:*** foot it. *See* MOVE.
walk out *verb* To cease working in support of demands made upon an employer : strike. *Idiom:* go on strike. *See* CONTINUE.
walk *noun* **1.** An act of walking, especially for pleasure : amble, meander (often used in plural), perambulation, promenade, ramble, saunter, stroll, wander. *See* MOVE. **2.** A usually brief and regular journey on foot, especially for exercise : constitutional, turn. *See* MOVE.

walkaway *noun*
1. An easy victory : walkover. *Informal:* runaway. *Slang:* romp. *See* EASY, WIN. **2.** An easily accomplished task : child's play, cinch, pushover, snap, walkover. *Informal:* breeze. *Slang:* duck soup. *See* EASY.

walking stick *noun*
A fairly long straight piece of solid material used especially as a support in walking : cane, staff, stave, stick. *See* MACHINE.

walk out *verb* See **walk.**

walkover *noun*
1. An easy victory : walkaway. *Informal:* runaway. *Slang:* romp. *See* EASY, WIN. **2.** An easily accomplished task : child's play, cinch, pushover, snap, walkaway. *Informal:* breeze. *Slang:* duck soup. *See* EASY.

wall *noun*
1. A solid structure that encloses an area or separates one area from another : barrier, partition. *See* INCLUDE, THING. **2.** Something that impedes or prevents entry or passage : bar, barricade, barrier, block, blockage, clog, hamper, hindrance, hurdle, impediment, obstacle, obstruction, snag, stop, traverse. *See* HELP, OPEN.
wall *verb* **1.** To separate with or as if with a wall : fence, partition. *See* INCLUDE. **2.** To confine within a limited area. Also used with *in* or *up* : cage, coop (in *or* up), enclose, fence (in), immure, mew (up), pen[2], shut in, shut up. *See* FREE. **3.** To shut in with or as if with bars : bar, confine, lock. *See* FREE.

wallop *verb*
1. *Informal.* To deliver a powerful blow to suddenly and sharply : bash, catch, clout, hit, knock, pop[1], slam, slog, slug[3], smash, smite, sock, strike, swat, thwack, whack, wham, whop. *Informal:* biff, bop, clip[1]. *Slang:* belt, conk, paste. ***Idioms:*** let someone have it, sock it to someone. *See* ATTACK, STRIKE.
2. *Informal.* To render totally ineffective by decisive defeat : annihilate, crush, drub, overpower, overwhelm, smash, steamroller, thrash, trounce, vanquish. *Informal:* massacre. *Slang:* clobber, cream, shellac, smear. *See* WIN.
wallop *noun* **1.** *Informal.* A sudden sharp, powerful stroke : bang, blow[2], clout, crack, hit, lick, pound, slug[3], sock, swat, thwack, welt, whack, wham, whop. *Informal:* bash, biff, bop, clip[1]. *Slang:* belt, conk, paste. *See* ATTACK, STRIKE. **2.** *Informal.* The capacity to create a powerful effect : impact. *Informal:* punch. *See* AFFECT. **3.** *Informal.* A stimulating or intoxicating effect : *Informal:* punch, sting. *Slang:* kick. *See* DRUGS. **4.** *Informal.* A strong, pleasant feeling of excitement or stimulation :

lift, thrill. *Slang:* bang, boot[1], high, kick. *See* EXCITE.

walloping *adjective*
Informal. Of extraordinary size and power : behemoth, Brobdingnagian, Bunyanesque, colossal, cyclopean, elephantine, enormous, gargantuan, giant, gigantesque, gigantic, herculean, heroic, huge, immense, jumbo, mammoth, massive, massy, mastodonic, mighty, monster, monstrous, monumental, mountainous, prodigious, pythonic, stupendous, titanic, tremendous, vast. *Slang:* whopping. *See* BIG.

wallow *verb*
1. To take extravagant pleasure : bask, indulge, luxuriate, revel, roll, rollick. *See* LIKE. **2.** To move about in an indolent or clumsy manner : flounder, welter. *See* MOVE.

waltz *verb*
Slang. To move swiftly and effortlessly : zip. *Informal:* breeze. *See* EASY.

wampum *noun*
Informal. Something, such as coins or printed bills, used as a medium of exchange : cash, currency, lucre, money. *Slang:* bread, cabbage, dough, gelt, green, jack, lettuce, long green, mazuma, moola, scratch. *Chiefly British:* brass. *See* MONEY.

wan *adjective*
1. Pale and exhausted, as because of worry or sleeplessness : careworn, drawn, gaunt, haggard, hollow-eyed, worn. *See* TIRED. **2.** Lacking color : ashen, ashy, bloodless, cadaverous, colorless, livid, lurid, pale, pallid, pasty, sallow, waxen. *See* COLORS.

wan *verb* To lose normal coloration; turn pale : blanch, bleach, etiolate, pale. *See* COLORS.

wander *verb*
1. To move about at random, especially over a wide area : drift, gad, gallivant, meander, peregrinate, ramble, range, roam, rove, stray, traipse. *See* MOVE. **2.** To walk at a leisurely pace : amble, meander, perambulate, promenade, ramble, saunter, stroll. *Informal:* mosey. *See* MOVE. **3.** To turn aside, especially from the main subject in writing or speaking : deviate, digress, divagate, diverge, ramble, stray. ***Idiom:*** go off at (*or* on) a tangent. *See* APPROACH.

wander *noun* An act of walking, especially for pleasure : amble, meander (often used in plural), perambulation, promenade, ramble, saunter, stroll, walk. *See* MOVE.

wandering *adjective*
1. Traveling about, especially in search of adventure : errant, roaming, roving. *See* MOVE. **2.** Without a fixed or regular course : devious, erratic, stray. *See* PURPOSE.

wane *verb*
1. To become or cause to become less active or intense : abate, bate, die (away, down, off, *or* out), ease (off *or* up), ebb, fall, fall off, lapse, let up, moderate, remit, slacken, slack off, subside. *See* INCREASE. **2.** To lose strength or power : decline, degenerate, deteriorate, fade, fail, flag[2], languish, sink, waste (away), weaken. *Informal:* fizzle (out). ***Idioms:*** go downhill, hit the skids. *See* INCREASE, STRONG.

wane *noun* The act or process of becoming less active or intense : abatement, ebb, letup, remission, slackening, subsidence. *See* INCREASE.

wangle *verb*
Informal. To make, achieve, or get through contrivance or guile : engineer, finesse, worm. *Informal:* finagle. *See* GET, MAKE.

want *verb*
1. To have a strong longing for : ache, covet, desire, hanker, long[2], pant, pine, wish, yearn. *Informal:* hone[2]. *See* DESIRE. **2.** To be without what is needed, required, or essential : lack, need, require. *See* OWNED. **3.** To have the desire or inclination to : choose, desire, like[1], please, will, wish. ***Idioms:*** have a mind, see fit. *See* DESIRE.

want *noun* **1.** The condition of lacking a needed or usual amount : absence, dearth, lack. *See* EXCESS. **2.** The condition of being extremely poor : beggary, destitution, impecuniosity, impecuniousness, impoverishment, indigence, need, neediness, pennilessness, penuriousness, penury, poverty, privation. *See* RICH. **3.** Something asked for or needed : demand, exigence, exigency (often used in plural), need. *See* NECESSARY, OVER.

wanting *adjective*
1. Not present : absent, away, gone, missing. *See* ABSENCE. **2.** Deficient in a usual or needed amount : absent, lacking. *See* EXCESS. **3.** Lacking an essential element : defective, deficient, incomplete, lacking. *See* BETTER, EXCESS. **4.** Not having a desirable element : barren, destitute, devoid, empty, innocent, lacking, void. ***Idiom:*** in want of. *See* FULL. **5.** Not enough to meet a demand or requirement : deficient, inadequate, insufficient, scarce, short, shy[1], under. *See* BIG, EXCESS.

wanton *adjective*
1. Lacking in moral restraint : abandoned, dissipated, dissolute, fast, gay, incontinent, licentious, profligate, rakish, unbridled,

unconstrained, uncontrolled, ungoverned, uninhibited, unrestrained, wild. *See* RESTRAINT. **2.** Marked by an absence of conventional restraint in sexual behavior; sexually unrestrained : easy, fast, libertine, light[2], loose, whorish. *See* SEX. **3.** Not required, necessary, or warranted by the circumstances of the case : gratuitous, supererogative, supererogatory, uncalled-for. *See* NECESSARY.

wanton *noun* **1.** An immoral or licentious person : libertine, profligate, rake[1]. *See* SEX. **2.** A vulgar promiscuous woman who flouts propriety : baggage, hussy, jade, slattern, slut, tart[2], tramp, wench, whore. *Slang:* floozy. *See* SEX.

wantonness *noun*
A complete surrender of inhibitions : abandon, abandonment, incontinence, unrestraint, wildness. *See* RESTRAINT.

war *noun*
1. A vying with others for victory or supremacy : battle, competition, contest, corrivalry, race, rivalry, strife, striving, struggle, tug of war, warfare. *See* CONFLICT. **2.** A state of open, prolonged fighting : belligerency, conflict, confrontation, hostility (used in plural), strife, struggle, warfare. *See* CONFLICT. **3.** A state of disagreement and disharmony : clash, conflict, confrontation, contention, difference, difficulty, disaccord, discord, discordance, dissension, dissent, dissentience, dissidence, dissonance, faction, friction, inharmony, schism, strife, variance, warfare. *See* CONFLICT.

war *verb* To strive in opposition : battle, combat, contend, duel, fight, struggle, tilt, wrestle. *See* CONFLICT.

war cry *noun*
A rallying term used by proponents of a cause : battle cry, call to arms, call to battle, cry, motto, rallying cry. *See* WORDS.

ward *noun*
1. A person who relies on another for support : charge, dependent. *See* GIVE. **2.** The state of being detained by legal authority : charge, confinement, custody, detention. *See* FREE. **3.** The act or a means of defending : defense, guard, preservation, protection, protector, safeguard, security, shield. *See* ATTACK. **4.** A person or special body of persons assigned to provide protection or keep watch over, for example : guard, lookout, picket, protector, sentinel, sentry, watch. *See* AWARENESS, SAFETY.

ward *verb* **1.** To keep safe from danger, attack, or harm : defend, guard, preserve, protect, safeguard, secure, shield. *Archaic:* fend. *See* ATTACK. **2.** To prohibit from occurring by advance planning or action. Also used with *off* : avert, forestall, forfend, obviate, preclude, prevent, rule out, stave off. ***Idiom:*** nip in the bud. *See* ALLOW.

ward off *verb* To turn or drive away : beat off, fend (off), keep off, parry, repel, repulse. *See* ALLOW, STRIKE.

warden *noun*
A guard or keeper of a prison : jailer, turnkey. *British:* warder. *See* FREE.

warder *noun*
British. A guard or keeper of a prison : jailer, turnkey, warden. *See* FREE.

ward off *verb* See **ward.**

ware *noun*
A product or products bought and sold in commerce : commodity, good (used in plural), line, merchandise. *See* MATTER, TRANSACTIONS.

warehouse *noun*
A place where something is deposited for safekeeping : archive, depository, magazine, repository, store, storehouse. *See* KEEP.

warfare *noun*
1. A vying with others for victory or supremacy : battle, competition, contest, corrivalry, race, rivalry, strife, striving, struggle, tug of war, war. *See* CONFLICT. **2.** A state of open, prolonged fighting : belligerency, conflict, confrontation, hostility (used in plural), strife, struggle, war. *See* CONFLICT. **3.** A state of disagreement and disharmony : clash, conflict, confrontation, contention, difference, difficulty, disaccord, discord, discordance, dissension, dissent, dissentience, dissidence, dissonance, faction, friction, inharmony, schism, strife, variance, war. *See* CONFLICT.

wariness *noun*
1. The condition of being alert : alertness, vigilance, wakefulness, watchfulness. *See* AWARENESS. **2.** Careful forethought to avoid harm or risk : calculation, care, carefulness, caution, chariness, gingerliness, precaution. *See* FEAR.

warlike *adjective*
1. Having or showing an eagerness to fight : bellicose, belligerent, combative, contentious, hostile, militant, pugnacious, quarrelsome, scrappy, truculent. *See* ATTACK. **2.** Of, relating to, or inclined toward war : bellicose, martial, militaristic, military. *See* PEACE.

warm *adjective*
1. Showing or having enthusiasm : ardent, enthusiastic, fervent, keen[1], mad, rabid, zealous. *Informal:* crazy. *Slang:* gung ho, nuts. *See* CONCERN. **2.** Pleasant and friendly in disposition : affable, agreeable, amiable, congenial,

cordial, genial, good-natured, good-tempered, pleasant, sociable. *See* ATTITUDE, GOOD.

warmed-over *adjective*
Without freshness or appeal because of overuse : banal, bromidic, clichéd, commonplace, corny, hackneyed, musty, overused, overworked, platitudinal, platitudinous, shopworn, stale, stereotyped, stereotypic, stereotypical, threadbare, timeworn, tired, trite, well-worn, worn-out. *See* EXCITE, USUAL.

warmhearted *adjective*
Of or befitting a friend or friends : amicable, friendly, neighborly. *See* ATTITUDE, LOVE.

warmth *noun*
1. The quality of being pleasant and friendly : affability, agreeability, agreeableness, amenity, amiability, amiableness, congeniality, congenialness, cordiality, cordialness, friendliness, geniality, genialness, pleasantness, sociability, sociableness. *See* ATTITUDE, GOOD. **2.** Intensity of feeling or reaction : excitation, excitement, heat. *See* EXCITE, FEELINGS, HOT.

warn *verb*
To notify (someone) of imminent danger or risk : admonish, alarm, alert, caution, forewarn. *See* WARN.

warning *noun*
1. Advice to beware, as of a person or thing : admonishment, admonition, caution, caveat, monition. *See* WARN. **2.** An instance that warns or discourages prospective imitators : example, lesson. *See* WARN. **3.** A signal that warns of imminent danger : alarm, alarum, alert, tocsin. *See* WARN.

warning *adjective* Giving warning : admonishing, admonitory, cautionary, monitory. *See* WARN.

warp *verb*
1. To ruin utterly in character or quality : animalize, bastardize, bestialize, brutalize, canker, corrupt, debase, debauch, demoralize, deprave, pervert, stain, vitiate. *See* CLEAN, HELP. **2.** To give an inaccurate view of by representing falsely or misleadingly : belie, color, distort, falsify, load, misrepresent, misstate, pervert, twist, wrench, wrest. ***Idiom:*** give a false coloring to. *See* TRUE. **3.** To cause to have a prejudiced view : bias, jaundice, prejudice, prepossess. *See* AFFECT, STRAIGHT.

warp and woof *noun*
A distinctive, complex underlying pattern or structure : contexture, fabric, fiber, texture, web. *See* BE.

warrant *noun*
1. A justifying fact or consideration : basis, foundation, justification, reason. *See* TRUE. **2.** That which confirms : attestation, authentication, confirmation, corroboration, demonstration, evidence, proof, substantiation, testament, testimonial, testimony, validation, verification. *See* TRUE. **3.** Something given to guarantee the repayment of a loan or the fulfillment of an obligation : earnest[2], guaranty, pawn[1], pledge, security, token. *See* TRANSACTIONS. **4.** An assumption of responsibility, as one given by a manufacturer, for the quality, worth, or durability of a product : guarantee, guaranty, surety, warranty. *See* OBLIGATION. **5.** A declaration that one will or will not do a certain thing : assurance, covenant, engagement, guarantee, guaranty, pledge, plight[2], promise, solemn word, vow, word, word of honor. *See* OBLIGATION. **6.** Proof of legal permission to do something : license, permit. ***Idiom:*** piece of paper. *See* ALLOW, LAW.

warrant *verb* **1.** To assure the certainty or validity of : attest, authenticate, back (up), bear out, confirm, corroborate, evidence, justify, substantiate, testify (to), validate, verify. *See* SUPPORT, TRUE. **2.** To render certain : assure, ensure, guarantee, insure, secure. *Informal:* cinch. *See* CERTAIN. **3.** To assume responsibility for the quality, worth, or durability of : certify, guarantee, guaranty. *See* OBLIGATION. **4.** To be a proper or sufficient occasion for : call for, justify, occasion. *See* RIGHT.

warranty *noun*
An assumption of responsibility, as one given by a manufacturer, for the quality, worth, or durability of a product : guarantee, guaranty, surety, warrant. *See* OBLIGATION.

warrior *noun*
One who engages in a combat or struggle : belligerent, combatant, fighter, soldier. *See* CONFLICT.

wary *adjective*
1. Vigilantly attentive : alert, observant, open-eyed, vigilant, wakeful, watchful, wide-awake. ***Idiom:*** on the ball. *See* AWARENESS. **2.** Trying attentively to avoid danger, risk, or error : careful, cautious, chary, circumspect, forehanded, gingerly, prudent. *See* CAREFUL.

wash *verb*
1. To make moist : bathe, dampen, moisten, wet. *See* DRY. **2.** To flow against or along : bathe, lap, lave, lip. *See* DRY. **3.** To flow or move with a low slapping sound : bubble, burble, gurgle, lap, splash, swash. *See* MOVE, SOUNDS. **4.** To move along with or be carried away by the action of water : drift, float. *See*

MOVE. **5.** *Informal.* To prove valid under scrutiny : hold (up), prove out, stand up. ***Idioms:*** hold water, pass muster, ring true. *See* TRUE.

wash up *verb* To cause the complete ruin or wreckage of : bankrupt, break down, cross up, demolish, destroy, finish, ruin, shatter, sink, smash, spoil, torpedo, undo, wrack[2], wreck. *Slang:* total. ***Idiom:*** put the kibosh on. *See* HELP.

washed-up *adjective*
No longer effective, capable, or valuable : done, done for, finished, through. *Informal:* kaput. ***Idioms:*** at the end of the line (*or* road), over the hill, past one's prime. *See* ABILITY, START.

washiness *noun*
The state or quality of being insipid : blandness, innocuousness, insipidity, insipidness, jejuneness, vapidity, vapidness, wateriness. *Informal:* wishy-washiness. *See* EXCITE, TASTE.

washout *noun*
One that fails completely : bust, failure, fiasco, loser. *Informal:* dud, flop, lemon. *Slang:* bomb. *See* THRIVE.

wash up *verb* See **wash.**

washy *adjective*
1. Lower than normal in strength or concentration due to admixture : dilute, thin, watered-down, waterish, watery, weak. *See* STRONG. **2.** Lacking the qualities requisite for spiritedness and originality : bland, innocuous, insipid, jejune, namby-pamby, vapid, waterish, watery. *Informal:* wishy-washy. *See* EXCITE, GOOD.

waspish *adjective*
Having or showing a bad temper : bad-tempered, cantankerous, crabbed, cranky, cross, disagreeable, fretful, grouchy, grumpy, ill-tempered, irascible, irritable, nasty, peevish, petulant, querulous, snappish, snappy, surly, testy, ugly. *Informal:* crabby, mean[2]. ***Idiom:*** out of sorts. *See* ATTITUDE.

waste *verb*
1. To use up foolishly or needlessly : consume, devour, dissipate, squander. *See* SAVE. **2.** To spend (money) excessively and usually foolishly : consume, dissipate, fool away, fritter away, riot away, squander, throw away, trifle away. *Slang:* blow[1]. *See* SAVE. **3.** To pass (time) without working or in avoiding work : dawdle (away), fiddle away, idle (away), kill[1], trifle away, while (away), wile (away). *See* INDUSTRIOUS. **4.** To lose strength or power. Also used with *away* : decline, degenerate, deteriorate, fade, fail, flag[2], languish, sink, wane, weaken. *Informal:* fizzle (out). ***Idioms:*** go downhill, hit the skids. *See* INCREASE, STRONG. **5.** To fail to take advantage of : lose, miss. ***Idioms:*** let slip, let slip through one's fingers, lose out on. *See* USED. **6.** To do away with completely and destructively : consume, devour, eat (up), swallow (up). *See* HELP. **7.** To destroy completely as or as if by conquering : desolate, devastate, ravage. ***Idiom:*** lay waste. *See* HELP. **8.** *Slang.* To cause the death of : carry off, cut down, cut off, destroy, dispatch, finish (off), kill[1], slay. *Slang:* zap. ***Idioms:*** put an end to, put to sleep. *See* HELP. **9.** *Slang.* To take the life of (a person or persons) unlawfully : destroy, finish (off), kill[1], liquidate, murder, slay. *Informal:* put away. *Slang:* bump off, do in, knock off, off, rub out, wipe out, zap. *See* HELP.

waste *noun* **1.** Excessive or imprudent expenditure : extravagance, extravagancy, lavishness, prodigality, profligacy, profuseness, profusion, squander, wastefulness. *See* CAREFUL, SAVE. **2.** A tract of unproductive land : badlands, barren (often used in plural), desert[1], wasteland, wilderness. *See* RICH.

wasted *adjective*
Physically haggard : cadaverous, drawn, emaciated, gaunt, shrunken, skeletal. ***Idiom:*** skin and bones. *See* BETTER, TIRED.

wasteful *adjective*
Characterized by excessive or imprudent spending : extravagant, lavish, prodigal, profligate, profuse, spendthrift. *See* CAREFUL, EXCESS, SAVE.

wastefulness *noun*
Excessive or imprudent expenditure : extravagance, extravagancy, lavishness, prodigality, profligacy, profuseness, profusion, squander, waste. *See* CAREFUL, SAVE.

wasteland *noun*
A tract of unproductive land : badlands, barren (often used in plural), desert[1], waste, wilderness. *See* RICH.

waster *noun*
A person who spends money or resources wastefully : prodigal, profligate, scattergood, spendthrift, wastrel. *See* SAVE.

wastrel *noun*
1. A person who spends money or resources wastefully : prodigal, profligate, scattergood, spendthrift, waster. *See* SAVE. **2.** A self-indulgent person who spends time avoiding work or other useful activity : bum[1], drone[1], fainéant, good-for-nothing, idler, layabout, loafer, ne'er-do-well, no-good, slugabed, sluggard. *Informal:* do-little, do-nothing,

lazybones, slug[2]. *Slang:* slouch. *See* INDUSTRIOUS.

watch *verb*
1. To look at or on attentively or carefully : eye, observe, regard, scrutinize, survey. ***Idioms:*** have one's (*or* keep an) eye on, keep tabs on. *See* AWARENESS, SEE. **2.** To have the care and supervision of : attend, care for, look after, mind, minister to, see to, tend[2]. ***Idioms:*** keep an eye on, look out for, take care (*or* charge) of, take under one's wing. *See* CARE FOR.
watch out *verb* To be careful : beware, look out, mind. ***Idioms:*** be on guard, be on the lookout, keep an eye peeled, take care (*or* heed). *See* AWARENESS, CAREFUL.
watch over *verb* To direct and watch over the work and performance of others : boss, overlook, oversee, superintend, supervise. *See* OVER.
watch *noun* **1.** The act of observing, often for an extended time : observance, observation, scrutiny. *See* AWARENESS, SEE. **2.** The act of carefully watching : lookout, surveillance, vigil, vigilance. ***Idiom:*** watch and ward. *See* AWARENESS. **3.** A person or special body of persons assigned to provide protection or keep watch over, for example : guard, lookout, picket, protector, sentinel, sentry, ward. *See* AWARENESS, SAFETY. **4.** A limited, often assigned period of activity, duty, or opportunity : bout, go, hitch, inning (often used in plural), shift, spell[3], stint, stretch, time, tour, trick, turn. *See* TIME. **5.** A watch over the body of a dead person before burial : wake[1]. *See* RITUAL.

watcher *noun*
1. Someone who observes : beholder, bystander, looker-on, observer, onlooker, spectator. *See* AWARENESS, SEE. **2.** An agent assigned to observe and report on another : shadow. *Informal:* tail. *See* INVESTIGATE.

watchful *adjective*
1. Vigilantly attentive : alert, observant, open-eyed, vigilant, wakeful, wary, wide-awake. ***Idiom:*** on the ball. *See* AWARENESS. **2.** Cautiously attentive : careful, heedful, mindful, observant. *See* CAREFUL.

watchfulness *noun*
The condition of being alert : alertness, vigilance, wakefulness, wariness. *See* AWARENESS.

watch out *verb* See **watch.**

watch over *verb* See **watch.**

water *verb*
1. To lessen the strength of by or as if by admixture. Also used with *down* : attenuate, cut, dilute, thin, weaken. *See* STRONG. **2.** To fill with tears : tear[2]. *See* DRY.

watered-down *adjective*
Lower than normal in strength or concentration due to admixture : dilute, thin, washy, waterish, watery, weak. *See* STRONG.

wateriness *noun*
The state or quality of being insipid : blandness, innocuousness, insipidity, insipidness, jejuneness, vapidity, vapidness, washiness. *Informal:* wishy-washiness. *See* EXCITE, TASTE.

waterish *adjective*
1. Lower than normal in strength or concentration due to admixture : dilute, thin, washy, watered-down, watery, weak. *See* STRONG. **2.** Being weak in quality or substance : anemic, bloodless, pale, pallid, watery. *See* STRONG. **3.** Lacking the qualities requisite for spiritedness and originality : bland, innocuous, insipid, jejune, namby-pamby, vapid, washy, watery. *Informal:* wishy-washy. *See* EXCITE, GOOD.

waterless *adjective*
Having little or no liquid or moisture : anhydrous, arid, bone-dry, dry, moistureless, sere. *See* DRY.

waterloo *noun*
A disastrous overwhelming defeat or ruin : collapse, downfall, fall. *See* THRIVE.

watershed *noun*
The region drained by a river system : basin. *See* TERRITORY.

watery *adjective*
1. Lower than normal in strength or concentration due to admixture : dilute, thin, washy, watered-down, waterish, weak. *See* STRONG. **2.** Being weak in quality or substance : anemic, bloodless, pale, pallid, waterish. *See* STRONG. **3.** Lacking the qualities requisite for spiritedness and originality : bland, innocuous, insipid, jejune, namby-pamby, vapid, washy, waterish. *Informal:* wishy-washy. *See* EXCITE, GOOD.

wave *verb*
1. To move to and fro vigorously and usually repeatedly : switch, wag[1], waggle. *See* REPETITION. **2.** To move or cause to move about while being fixed at one edge : flap, flutter, fly. *See* REPETITION. **3.** To move (one's arms or wings, for example) up and down : beat, flap, flitter, flop, flutter, waggle. *See* REPETITION. **4.** To wield boldly and dramatically : brandish, flourish, sweep. *See* EXPRESS. **5.** To have or cause to have a curved or sinuous form or surface : curl, curve, undulate. *See* STRAIGHT.

waver *verb*
1. To move back and forth or from side to side, as if about to fall : sway, teeter, totter, vacillate, weave, wobble. *See* REPETITION. **2.** To be irresolute in acting or doing : dither, falter, halt[2], hesitate, pause, shilly-shally, stagger, vacillate, wobble. *See* DECIDE. **3.** To change one's attitudes or policies, for example : swing, vacillate. *See* CHANGE, DECIDE.

wax *verb*
1. To make or become greater or larger : aggrandize, amplify, augment, boost, build, build up, burgeon, enlarge, escalate, expand, extend, grow, increase, magnify, mount, multiply, proliferate, rise, run up, snowball, soar, swell, upsurge. *Informal:* beef up. *See* INCREASE. **2.** To come to be : become, come, get, grow, turn (out). *See* CHANGE.

waxen *adjective*
Lacking color : ashen, ashy, bloodless, cadaverous, colorless, livid, lurid, pale, pallid, pasty, sallow, wan. *See* COLORS.

way *noun*
1. A course affording passage from one place to another : avenue, boulevard, drive, expressway, freeway, highway, path, road, roadway, route, street, superhighway, thoroughfare, thruway, turnpike. *See* MOVE, OPEN. **2.** The approach used to do something : fashion, manner, method, mode, modus operandi, style, system, wise[2]. *See* MEANS. **3.** A habitual way of behaving : consuetude, custom, habit, habitude, manner, practice, praxis, usage, usance, use, wont. *See* USUAL. **4.** The manner in which one behaves : action (often used in plural), behavior, comportment, conduct, deportment. *See* BE. **5.** *Informal.* An extent, measured or unmeasured, of linear space : distance, length, space, stretch. *Informal:* piece. *See* BIG.

waylay *verb*
To attack suddenly and without warning : ambuscade, ambush, bushwhack, surprise. *See* ATTACK.

wayward *adjective*
Given to acting in opposition to others : balky, contrarious, contrary, difficult, froward, impossible, ornery, perverse. *See* ATTITUDE, SUPPORT.

weak *adjective*
1. Not physically strong : decrepit, delicate, feeble, flimsy, fragile, frail, infirm, insubstantial, puny, unsound, unsubstantial, weakly. *See* STRONG. **2.** So lacking in strength as to be barely audible : faint, feeble. *See* STRONG. **3.** Lacking stability : infirm, insecure, precarious, shaky, tottering, tottery, unstable, unsteady, unsure, wobbly. *See* CHANGE, STRONG. **4.** Not capable of accomplishing anything : helpless, impotent, inadequate, incapable, ineffectual, powerless. *See* ABILITY, STRONG. **5.** Lower than normal in strength or concentration due to admixture : dilute, thin, washy, watered-down, waterish, watery. *See* STRONG. **6.** Not plausible or believable : flimsy, implausible, improbable, inconceivable, incredible, shaky, thin, unbelievable, unconceivable, unconvincing, unsubstantial. *See* LIKELY.

weaken *verb*
1. To lose strength or power : decline, degenerate, deteriorate, fade, fail, flag[2], languish, sink, wane, waste (away). *Informal:* fizzle (out). ***Idioms:*** go downhill, hit the skids. *See* INCREASE, STRONG. **2.** To lessen or deplete the nerve, energy, or strength of : attenuate, debilitate, devitalize, enervate, enfeeble, sap[2], undermine, undo, unnerve. *See* STRONG. **3.** To lessen the strength of by or as if by admixture : attenuate, cut, dilute, thin, water (down). *See* STRONG. **4.** To moderate or change a position or course of action as a result of pressure : ease off, relent, slacken, soften, yield. ***Idiom:*** give way (*or* ground). *See* STRONG.

weakliness *noun*
The condition of being infirm or physically weak : debility, decrepitude, delicacy, delicateness, feebleness, flimsiness, fragileness, fragility, frailness, frailty, infirmity, insubstantiality, puniness, unsoundness, unsubstantiality, weakness. *See* STRONG.

weakling *noun*
A person who behaves in a childish, weak, or spoiled way : baby, milksop, milquetoast, mollycoddle. ***Idiom:*** mama's boy (*or* girl). *See* YOUTH.

weakly *adjective*
Not physically strong : decrepit, delicate, feeble, flimsy, fragile, frail, infirm, insubstantial, puny, unsound, unsubstantial, weak. *See* STRONG.

weak-minded *adjective*
1. Displaying a complete lack of forethought and good sense : brainless, fatuous, foolish, insensate, mindless, senseless, silly, unintelligent, witless. *See* ABILITY, PLANNED.
2. *Offensive.* Having only a limited ability to learn and understand : backward, dull, simple, simple-minded, slow, slow-witted. *Informal:* soft. *Offensive:* feeble-minded, half-witted, retarded. *See* ABILITY.

weakness *noun*
1. The condition of being infirm or physically weak : debility, decrepitude, delicacy, delicateness, feebleness, flimsiness, fragileness, fragility, frailness, frailty, infirmity, insubstantiality, puniness, unsoundness, unsubstantiality, weakliness. *See* STRONG. **2.** An imperfection of character : failing, fault, foible, frailty, infirmity, shortcoming, weak point. *See* BETTER, HELP. **3.** A liking for something : appetite, fondness, partiality, preference, relish, taste. *See* LIKE.

weak point *noun*
An imperfection of character : failing, fault, foible, frailty, infirmity, shortcoming, weakness. *See* BETTER, HELP.

weal[1] *noun*
A state of health, happiness, and prospering : prosperity, welfare, well-being. *See* BETTER.

weal[2] *noun*
A ridge or bump raised on the flesh, as by a lash or blow : wale, welt, wheal, whelk. *See* MARKS.

wealth *noun*
1. A great amount of accumulated money and precious possessions : affluence, fortune, pelf, riches, treasure. *See* OWNED, RICH. **2.** All things, such as money, property, or goods, having economic value : asset (used in plural), capital, fortune, mean[3] (used in plural), resource (used in plural), wherewithal. *See* OWNED. **3.** A great deal : abundance, mass, mountain, much, plenty, profusion, world. *Informal:* barrel, heap, lot, pack, peck[2], pile. *Regional:* power, sight. *See* BIG.

wealthy *adjective*
Possessing a large amount of money, land, or other material possessions : affluent, flush, moneyed, rich. *Slang:* loaded. ***Idioms:*** having money to burn, in the money, made of money, rolling in money. *See* RICH.

wear *verb*
1. To consume gradually, as by chemical reaction or friction : bite, corrode, eat, erode, gnaw, wear away. *See* ATTACK. **2.** To diminish the strength and energy of : drain, fatigue, jade, tire, wear down, wear out, weary. *See* TIRED.
wear away *verb* To consume gradually, as by chemical reaction or friction : bite, corrode, eat, erode, gnaw, wear. *See* ATTACK.
wear down *verb* To diminish the strength and energy of : drain, fatigue, jade, tire, wear, wear out, weary. *See* TIRED.
wear out *verb* **1.** To make extremely tired : exhaust, fag (out), tire out. *Informal:* knock out, tucker (out). *Slang:* do in, poop[1] (out). *Idioms:* run ragged, take it out of. *See* TIRED. **2.** To diminish the strength and energy of : drain, fatigue, jade, tire, wear, wear down, weary. *See* TIRED.

wear away *verb* See **wear.**

wear down *verb* See **wear.**

wearied *adjective*
Extremely tired : bleary, dead, drained, exhausted, fatigued, rundown, spent, tired out, weariful, weary, worn-down, worn-out. *Informal:* beat, bushed, tuckered (out). *Slang:* done in, fagged (out), pooped (out). ***Idioms:*** all in, ready to drop. *See* HEALTH, TIRED.

weariful *adjective*
1. Arousing no interest or curiosity : boring, drear, dreary, dry, dull, humdrum, irksome, monotonous, stuffy, tedious, tiresome, uninteresting, wearisome, weary. *See* EXCITE. **2.** Extremely tired : bleary, dead, drained, exhausted, fatigued, rundown, spent, tired out, wearied, weary, worn-down, worn-out. *Informal:* beat, bushed, tuckered (out). *Slang:* done in, fagged (out), pooped (out). ***Idioms:*** all in, ready to drop. *See* HEALTH, TIRED.

weariless *adjective*
Having or showing a capacity for protracted effort, regardless of difficulty or frustration : indefatigable, inexhaustible, tireless, unfailing, unflagging, untiring, unwearied. *See* CONTINUE, TIRED.

weariness *noun*
1. The condition of being extremely tired : exhaustion, fatigue, tiredness. *See* TIRED. **2.** A lack of excitement, liveliness, or interest : asepticism, blandness, colorlessness, drabness, dreariness, dryness, dullness, flatness, flavorlessness, insipidity, insipidness, jejuneness, lifelessness, sterileness, sterility, stodginess, vapidity, vapidness. *See* EXCITE.

wearing *adjective*
Causing fatigue : draining, exhausting, fatiguing, tiring, wearying. *See* TIRED.

wearisome *adjective*
Arousing no interest or curiosity : boring, drear, dreary, dry, dull, humdrum, irksome, monotonous, stuffy, tedious, tiresome, uninteresting, weariful, weary. *See* EXCITE.

wear out *verb* See **wear.**

weary *adjective*
1. Extremely tired : bleary, dead, drained, exhausted, fatigued, rundown, spent, tired out, wearied, weariful, worn-down, worn-out. *Informal:* beat, bushed, tuckered (out). *Slang:* done in, fagged (out), pooped (out). ***Idioms:*** all in, ready to drop. *See* HEALTH, TIRED. **2.** Out

of patience with : disgusted, fed up, sick, tired. *Idiom:* sick and tired. *See* TIRED. **3.** Arousing no interest or curiosity : boring, drear, dreary, dry, dull, humdrum, irksome, monotonous, stuffy, tedious, tiresome, uninteresting, weariful, wearisome. *See* EXCITE.

weary *verb* **1.** To diminish the strength and energy of : drain, fatigue, jade, tire, wear, wear down, wear out. *See* TIRED. **2.** To fatigue with dullness or tedium : bore, tire. *See* EXCITE.

wearying *adjective*
Causing fatigue : draining, exhausting, fatiguing, tiring, wearing. *See* TIRED.

weasel *noun*
One who behaves in a stealthy, furtive way : prowler, sneak, sneaker. *See* MOVE.

weasel *verb* To use evasive or deliberately vague language : equivocate, euphemize, hedge, shuffle, tergiversate. *Informal:* pussyfoot, waffle. *Idioms:* beat about (*or* around) the bush, mince words. *See* CLEAR.

weasel word *noun*
The use or an instance of equivocal language : ambiguity, equivocation, equivoque, euphemism, hedge, prevarication, shuffle, tergiversation. *Informal:* waffle. *See* CLEAR.

weather *verb*
To exist in spite of adversity : come through, last[2], persist, pull through, ride out, survive. *See* LIVE.

weave *verb*
1. To move back and forth or from side to side, as if about to fall : sway, teeter, totter, vacillate, waver, wobble. *See* REPETITION. **2.** To walk unsteadily : falter, lurch, reel, stagger, stumble, teeter, totter, wobble. *See* MOVE.
3. To move or proceed on a repeatedly curving course : coil, corkscrew, curl, entwine, meander, snake, spiral, twine, twist, wind[2], wreathe. *See* REPETITION, STRAIGHT.

web *noun*
1. An open fabric woven of strands that are interlaced and knotted at usually regular intervals : mesh, net[1], netting, network. *See* THING. **2.** Something that is intricately and often bewilderingly complex : cat's cradle, entanglement, jungle, knot, labyrinth, maze, mesh (often used in plural), morass, skein, snarl[2], tangle. *See* SIMPLE. **3.** An interwoven or interrelated number of things : network, tissue. *See* GROUP. **4.** A distinctive, complex underlying pattern or structure : contexture, fabric, fiber, texture, warp and woof. *See* BE.

web *verb* To gain control of or an advantage over by or as if by trapping : catch, enmesh, ensnare, ensnarl, entrap, snare, tangle, trammel, trap. *See* FREE.

wed *verb*
1. To join or be joined in marriage : espouse, marry, mate. *Slang:* hitch. *Idiom:* tie the knot. *See* MARRIAGE. **2.** To bring or come together into a united whole : coalesce, combine, compound, concrete, conjoin, conjugate, connect, consolidate, couple, join, link, marry, meld, unify, unite, yoke. *See* ASSEMBLE.

wedded *adjective*
Of, relating to, or typical of marriage : conjugal, connubial, hymeneal, marital, married, matrimonial, nuptial, spousal. *See* MARRIAGE.

wedding *noun*
The act or ceremony by which two people become husband and wife : bridal, espousal, marriage, nuptial (often used in plural), spousal (often used in plural). *See* MARRIAGE.

wedlock *noun*
The state of being united as husband and wife : conjugality, connubiality, marriage, matrimony. *See* MARRIAGE.

wee *adjective*
Extremely small : diminutive, dwarf, Lilliputian, midget, miniature, minuscule, minute[2], pygmy, tiny. *Informal:* peewee, pintsize, pintsized, teensy, teensy-weensy, teeny, teeny-weeny, weeny. *See* BIG.

weedy *adjective*
Having little flesh or fat on the body : angular, bony, fleshless, gaunt, lank, lanky, lean[2], meager, rawboned, scrawny, skinny, slender, slim, spare, thin, twiggy. *Idioms:* all skin and bones, thin as a rail. *See* FAT.

weeny *adjective*
Informal. Extremely small : diminutive, dwarf, Lilliputian, midget, miniature, minuscule, minute[2], pygmy, tiny, wee. *Informal:* peewee, pintsize, pintsized, teensy, teensy-weensy, teeny, teeny-weeny. *See* BIG.

weep *verb*
1. To make inarticulate sounds of grief or pain, usually accompanied by tears : bawl, blubber, cry, howl, keen[2], sob, wail, yowl. *See* HAPPY, SOUNDS. **2.** To flow or leak out or emit something slowly : bleed, exude, leach, ooze, percolate, seep, transpire, transude. *See* MOVE, SOLID. **3.** To fall or let fall in drops of liquid : distill, dribble, drip, drop, trickle. *See* RISE.

weeping *adjective*
Filled with or shedding tears : lachrymose, tearful, teary, weepy. *Idiom:* in tears. *See* HAPPY.

weeping *noun* A fit of crying : bawling, blubbering, cry, sobbing, tear[2] (used in plural), wailing. *See* SOUNDS.

weepy *adjective*
Filled with or shedding tears : lachrymose, tearful, teary, weeping. ***Idiom:*** in tears. *See* HAPPY.

weigh *verb*
1. To be of significance or importance : count, import, matter, signify. *See* IMPORTANT. **2.** To think or think about carefully and at length : chew on (*or* over), cogitate, consider, contemplate, deliberate, entertain, excogitate, meditate, mull, muse[1], ponder, reflect, revolve, ruminate, study, think, think out, think over, think through, turn over. ***Idioms:*** cudgel one's brains, put on one's thinking cap, rack one's brain. *See* THOUGHTS.
weigh down *verb* To make sad or gloomy : deject, depress, dispirit, oppress, sadden. *See* HAPPY.
weigh on (or **upon**) *verb* To come to mind continually : haunt, obsess, torment, trouble. *See* REPETITION.

weigh down *verb* See **weigh.**

weigh on or **upon** *verb* See **weigh.**

weight *noun*
1. The state or quality of being physically heavy : heaviness, heftiness, massiveness, ponderosity, ponderousness, weightiness. *Informal:* avoirdupois. *See* HEAVY. **2.** A duty or responsibility that is a source of anxiety, worry, or hardship : burden[1], millstone, onus, tax. *Informal:* headache. *See* HEAVY, OVER. **3.** The greatest part or portion : bulk, mass, preponderance, preponderancy. *See* BIG. **4.** The power to produce an effect by indirect means : influence, leverage, sway. *Informal:* clout. *Slang:* pull. *See* AFFECT. **5.** Effective means of influencing, compelling, or punishing : force, power. *Informal:* clout, muscle. *See* OVER, STRONG. **6.** The quality or state of being important : concern, concernment, consequence, import, importance, moment, significance, significancy, weightiness. *See* IMPORTANT.
weight *verb* To place a burden or heavy load on : burden[1], charge, cumber, encumber, freight, lade, load, saddle, tax. *See* OVER.

weightiness *noun*
1. The state or quality of being physically heavy : heaviness, heftiness, massiveness, ponderosity, ponderousness, weight. *Informal:* avoirdupois. *See* HEAVY. **2.** The condition of being grave and of involving serious consequences : graveness, gravity, momentousness, seriousness. *See* IMPORTANT. **3.** The quality or state of being important : concern, concernment, consequence, import, importance, moment, significance, significancy, weight. *See* IMPORTANT.

weightless *adjective*
Having little weight; not heavy : light[2], lightweight. ***Idiom:*** light as a feather. *See* HEAVY.

weighty *adjective*
1. Having a relatively great weight : heavy, heavyweight, hefty, massive, ponderous. *See* HEAVY. **2.** Having too much flesh : corpulent, fat, fatty, fleshy, gross, obese, overblown, overweight, porcine, portly, stout. *See* FAT. **3.** Requiring great or extreme bodily, mental, or spiritual strength : arduous, backbreaking, burdensome, demanding, difficult, effortful, exacting, exigent, formidable, hard, heavy, laborious, onerous, oppressive, rigorous, rough, severe, taxing, tough, trying. *See* HEAVY. **4.** Having great consequence or weight : earnest[1], grave[2], heavy, momentous, serious, severe. *See* IMPORTANT. **5.** Having or exercising influence : consequential, important, influential, powerful. *See* AFFECT, IMPORTANT, STRONG.

weird *adjective*
1. Of a mysteriously strange and usually frightening nature : eerie, uncanny, unearthly. *Informal:* spooky. *See* FEAR, USUAL. **2.** Deviating from the customary : bizarre, cranky, curious, eccentric, erratic, freakish, idiosyncratic, odd, outlandish, peculiar, quaint, queer, quirky, singular, strange, unnatural, unusual. *Slang:* kooky, screwball. *British Slang:* rum, rummy[2]. *See* USUAL. **3.** Causing puzzlement; perplexing : curious, funny, odd, peculiar, queer, strange. *See* USUAL.

weirdie also **weirdy** *noun*
Slang. A person regarded as strange, eccentric, or crazy : crackpot, crazy, eccentric, lunatic. *Informal:* crank, loon, loony. *Slang:* cuckoo, ding-a-ling, dingbat, kook, nut, screwball, weirdo. *See* WISE.

weirdo *noun*
Slang. A person regarded as strange, eccentric, or crazy : crackpot, crazy, eccentric, lunatic. *Informal:* crank, loon, loony. *Slang:* cuckoo, ding-a-ling, dingbat, kook, nut, screwball, weirdie. *See* WISE.

weirdy *noun* See **weirdie.**

weisenheimer *noun* See **wisenheimer.**

welcome *adjective*
To one's liking : agreeable, congenial, favorable, good, grateful, gratifying, nice, pleasant,

pleasing, pleasurable, satisfying. *See* LIKE.

welcome *noun* An expression, in words or gestures, marking a meeting of persons : greeting, hail[2], salutation, salute. *See* GREETING.

welcome *verb* **1.** To address in a friendly and respectful way : greet, hail[2], salute. *See* GREETING. **2.** To receive (something given or offered) willingly and gladly : accept, embrace, take (up). *See* ACCEPT.

welcoming *adjective*
Easily approached : accessible, approachable, responsive. *See* APPROACH, ATTITUDE.

welfare *noun*
1. A state of health, happiness, and prospering : prosperity, weal[1], well-being. *See* BETTER.
2. Assistance, especially money, food, and other necessities, given to the needy or dispossessed : aid, dole, handout, public assistance, relief. *See* HELP.

welkin *noun*
Archaic. The celestial regions as seen from the earth : air, firmament, heaven (often used in plural), sky. *See* HIGH.

well[1] *noun*
A point of origination : beginning, derivation, fount, fountain, fountainhead, mother, origin, parent, provenance, provenience, root[1], rootstock, source, spring. *See* START.

well *verb* To come forth or emit in abundance : flow, gush, pour, run, rush, stream, surge. *See* MOVE.

well[2] *adverb*
1. To the fullest extent : absolutely, all, altogether, completely, dead, entirely, flat, fully, just, perfectly, quite, thoroughly, totally, utterly, wholly. *Informal:* clean, clear. ***Idioms:*** in toto, through and through. *See* BIG, LIMITED. **2.** To a considerable extent : considerably, far, much, quite. ***Idioms:*** by a long shot (*or* way), by a wide margin, by far. *See* BIG.

well *adjective* **1.** Having good health : fit[1], hale, healthful, healthy, hearty, right, sound[2], whole, wholesome. ***Idioms:*** fit as a fiddle, hale and hearty, in fine fettle. *See* HEALTH.
2. Worth doing, especially for practical reasons : advisable, expedient, recommendable. *See* WISE.

well-being *noun*
A state of health, happiness, and prospering : prosperity, weal[1], welfare. *See* BETTER.

wellborn *adjective*
Of high birth or social position : aristocratic, blue-blooded, elite, highborn, highbred, noble, patrician, thoroughbred, upper-class. *Informal:* upper-crust. *See* OVER.

well-bred *adjective*
1. Characterized by discriminating taste and broad knowledge as a result of development or education : civilized, cultivated, cultured, educated, polished, refined, urbane. *See* CULTURE.
2. Characterized by good manners : civil, courteous, genteel, mannerly, polite, well-mannered. *See* COURTESY.

well-developed *adjective*
Having a full, voluptuous figure : buxom, curvaceous, curvy, shapely. *Informal:* built. *Slang:* stacked. *See* BEAUTIFUL.

well-fixed *adjective*
Informal. Enjoying steady good fortune or financial security : comfortable, easy, prosperous, well-heeled, well-off, well-to-do. ***Idioms:*** comfortably off, in clover, on easy street. *See* RICH, THRIVE.

well-founded *adjective*
1. Possessing, proceeding from, or exhibiting good judgment and prudence : balanced, commonsensible, commonsensical, judicious, levelheaded, prudent, rational, reasonable, sagacious, sage, sane, sapient, sensible, sound[2], well-grounded, wise[1]. *See* REASON, SANE.
2. Based on good judgment, reasoning, or evidence : cogent, just, solid, sound[2], tight, valid, well-grounded. *See* GOOD, REASON.

well-groomed *adjective*
In good order or clean condition : neat, orderly, shipshape, snug, spick-and-span, spruce, taut, tidy, trig, trim. *Chiefly British:* tight. ***Idiom:*** neat as a pin. *See* CLEAN, ORDER.

well-grounded *adjective*
1. Possessing, proceeding from, or exhibiting good judgment and prudence : balanced, commonsensible, commonsensical, judicious, levelheaded, prudent, rational, reasonable, sagacious, sage, sane, sapient, sensible, sound[2], well-founded, wise[1]. *See* REASON, SANE.
2. Based on good judgment, reasoning, or evidence : cogent, just, solid, sound[2], tight, valid, well-founded. *See* GOOD, REASON.

well-heeled *adjective*
Enjoying steady good fortune or financial security : comfortable, easy, prosperous, well-off, well-to-do. *Informal:* well-fixed. ***Idioms:*** comfortably off, in clover, on easy street. *See* RICH, THRIVE.

well-known *adjective*
Widely known and discussed : famed, famous, leading, notorious, popular. *See* KNOWLEDGE.

well-liked *adjective*
Being a favorite : favored, favorite, popular, preferred. *See* LIKE.

well-mannered *adjective*
Characterized by good manners : civil, courteous, genteel, mannerly, polite, well-bred. *See* COURTESY.

well-off *adjective*
Enjoying steady good fortune or financial security : comfortable, easy, prosperous, well-heeled, well-to-do. *Informal:* well-fixed. ***Idioms:*** comfortably off, in clover, on easy street. *See* RICH, THRIVE.

well-timed *adjective*
Occurring at a fitting or advantageous time : auspicious, favorable, opportune, propitious, prosperous, seasonable, timely. *See* LUCK.

well-to-do *adjective*
Enjoying steady good fortune or financial security : comfortable, easy, prosperous, well-heeled, well-off. *Informal:* well-fixed. ***Idioms:*** comfortably off, in clover, on easy street. *See* RICH, THRIVE.

well-worn *adjective*
Without freshness or appeal because of overuse : banal, bromidic, clichéd, commonplace, corny, hackneyed, musty, overused, overworked, platitudinal, platitudinous, shopworn, stale, stereotyped, stereotypic, stereotypical, threadbare, timeworn, tired, trite, warmed-over, worn-out. *See* EXCITE, USUAL.

welt *noun*
1. A ridge or bump raised on the flesh, as by a lash or blow : wale, weal[2], wheal, whelk. *See* MARKS. **2.** A sudden sharp, powerful stroke : bang, blow[2], clout, crack, hit, lick, pound, slug[3], sock, swat, thwack, whack, wham, whop. *Informal:* bash, biff, bop, clip[1], wallop. *Slang:* belt, conk, paste. *See* ATTACK, STRIKE.

welter *verb*
To move about in an indolent or clumsy manner : flounder, wallow. *See* MOVE.

wench *noun*
A vulgar promiscuous woman who flouts propriety : baggage, hussy, jade, slattern, slut, tart[2], tramp, wanton, whore. *Slang:* floozy. *See* SEX.

wend *verb*
To move along a particular course : fare, go, journey, pass, proceed, push on, remove, travel. ***Idiom:*** make one's way. *See* MOVE.

wet *adjective*
Covered with or full of liquid : sodden, soggy, sopping, soppy. *See* DRY.
wet *verb* **1.** To make thoroughly wet : douse, drench, saturate, soak, sodden, sop, souse. *See* DRY. **2.** To make moist : bathe, dampen, moisten, wash. *See* DRY.

wetland *noun*
A usually low-lying area of soft waterlogged ground and standing water : bog, fen, marsh, marshland, mire, morass, muskeg, quag, quagmire, slough[1], swamp, swampland. *See* DRY.

whack *verb*
1. To deliver a powerful blow to suddenly and sharply : bash, catch, clout, hit, knock, pop[1], slam, slog, slug[3], smash, smite, sock, strike, swat, thwack, wham, whop. *Informal:* biff, bop, clip[1], wallop. *Slang:* belt, conk, paste. ***Idioms:*** let someone have it, sock it to someone. *See* ATTACK, STRIKE. **2.** To hit with a quick, sharp blow of the hand : box[2], buffet, bust, cuff, punch, slap, smack[1], spank, swat. *Informal:* clip[1], spat. *See* ATTACK, STRIKE. **3.** To strike, set down, or close in such a way as to make a loud noise : bang[1], clap, crash, slam. *See* SOUNDS.
whack *noun* **1.** A sudden sharp, powerful stroke : bang, blow[2], clout, crack, hit, lick, pound, slug[3], sock, swat, thwack, welt, wham, whop. *Informal:* bash, biff, bop, clip[1], wallop. *Slang:* belt, conk, paste. *See* ATTACK, STRIKE. **2.** A quick, sharp blow, especially with the hand : box[2], buffet, bust, chop[1], cuff, punch, slap, smack[1], smacker, spank, swat. *Informal:* clip[1], spat. *See* ATTACK, STRIKE. **3.** *Informal.* A brief trial : crack, go, stab, try. *Informal:* fling, shot, whirl. *See* TRY.

whacky *adjective* See **wacky.**

wham *noun*
1. A sudden sharp, powerful stroke : bang, blow[2], clout, crack, hit, lick, pound, slug[3], sock, swat, thwack, welt, whack, whop. *Informal:* bash, biff, bop, clip[1], wallop. *Slang:* belt, conk, paste. *See* ATTACK, STRIKE. **2.** A forceful movement causing a loud noise : bang, crash, slam, smash. *See* STRIKE.
wham *verb* To deliver a powerful blow to suddenly and sharply : bash, catch, clout, hit, knock, pop[1], slam, slog, slug[3], smash, smite, sock, strike, swat, thwack, whack, whop. *Informal:* biff, bop, clip[1], wallop. *Slang:* belt, conk, paste. ***Idioms:*** let someone have it, sock it to someone. *See* ATTACK, STRIKE.

whammy *noun*
Slang. An object or power that one uses to cause often evil events : charm, evil eye, magic, spell[2]. *See* SUPERNATURAL.

whatnot *noun*
A small showy article : bauble, bibelot, gewgaw, gimcrack, knickknack, novelty, toy, trifle, trinket. *See* THING.

wheal *noun*
A ridge or bump raised on the flesh, as by a lash or blow : wale, weal[2], welt, whelk. *See* MARKS.

wheedle *verb*
To persuade or try to persuade by gentle persistent urging or flattery : blandish, cajole, coax, honey. *Informal:* soft-soap, sweet-talk. *See* PERSUASION.

wheel *noun*
1. A closed plane curve everywhere equidistant from a fixed point or something shaped like this : band[1], circle, circuit, disk, gyre, ring[1]. *Archaic:* orb. *See* GEOMETRY. **2.** Circular movement around a point or about an axis : circuit, circulation, circumvolution, gyration, revolution, rotation, turn, whirl. *See* GEOMETRY, REPETITION.

wheel *verb* **1.** To move or cause to move in circles or around an axis : circle, circumvolve, gyrate, orbit, revolve, rotate, turn. *See* MOVE, REPETITION. **2.** To run and control (a motor vehicle) : drive, motor, pilot. *Slang:* tool. *See* MOVE. **3.** To turn or cause to turn in place, as on a hinge or fixed point, tracing an arclike path : pivot, swing. *See* MOVE.

whelk *noun*
A ridge or bump raised on the flesh, as by a lash or blow : wale, weal[2], welt, wheal. *See* MARKS.

whelm *verb*
1. To flow over completely : deluge, drown, engulf, flood, flush, inundate, overflow, overwhelm, submerge. *See* FULL. **2.** To affect as if by an outpouring of water : deluge, flood, inundate, overwhelm, swamp. *See* FULL.

wherefore *noun*
1. That which provides a reason or justification : call, cause, ground (often used in plural), justification, necessity, occasion, reason, why. ***Idiom:*** why and wherefore. *See* START. **2.** A fact or circumstance that gives logical support to an assertion, claim, or proposal : argument, ground (often used in plural), proof, reason, why. ***Idiom:*** why and wherefore. *See* REASON.

wherewithal *noun*
1. The ability and the means to meet situations effectively : resource (often used in plural), resourcefulness. *See* ABILITY. **2.** All things, such as money, property, or goods, having economic value : asset (used in plural), capital, fortune, mean[3] (used in plural), resource (used in plural), wealth. *See* OWNED.

whet *verb*
To give a sharp edge to : acuminate, edge, hone[1], sharpen. *See* SHARP.

whiff *noun*
A slight amount or indication : breath, dash, ghost, hair, hint, intimation, semblance, shade, shadow, soupçon, streak, suggestion, suspicion, taste, tinge, touch, trace, whisper. *Informal:* whisker. *See* BIG, SHOW.

whiff *verb* To perceive with the olfactory sense : nose, scent, smell, sniff, snuff. ***Idiom:*** catch (*or* get) a whiff of. *See* SMELLS.

while *noun*
1. A rather short period : bit[1], space, spell[3], time. *See* BIG. **2.** The use of energy to do something : effort, endeavor, exertion, pain (used in plural), strain[1], striving, struggle, trouble. *Informal:* elbow grease. *See* WORK.

while *verb* To pass (time) without working or in avoiding work. Also used with *away* : dawdle (away), fiddle away, idle (away), kill[1], trifle away, waste, wile (away). *See* INDUSTRIOUS.

whilom *adjective*
Having been such previously : erstwhile, former, late, old, once, onetime, past, previous, quondam, sometime. *See* PRECEDE.

whim *noun*
An impulsive, often illogical turn of mind : bee, boutade, caprice, conceit, fancy, freak, humor, impulse, megrim, notion, vagary, whimsy. ***Idiom:*** bee in one's bonnet. *See* THOUGHTS.

whimper *verb*
To cry with soft, intermittent, often plaintive sounds : pule, whine. *See* SOUNDS.

whimsey *noun* See **whimsy.**

whimsical *adjective*
1. Determined or marked by whim or caprice rather than reason : arbitrary, capricious. *See* SURPRISE. **2.** Following no predictable pattern : capricious, changeable, erratic, fantastic, fantastical, fickle, freakish, inconsistent, inconstant, mercurial, temperamental, ticklish, uncertain, unpredictable, unstable, unsteady, variable, volatile. *See* CHANGE, CONTINUE. **3.** Appealing to fancy : fanciful, fancy, fantastic, fantastical, imaginative. *See* PLAIN.

whimsy also **whimsey** *noun*
An impulsive, often illogical turn of mind : bee, boutade, caprice, conceit, fancy, freak, humor, impulse, megrim, notion, vagary, whim. ***Idiom:*** bee in one's bonnet. *See* THOUGHTS.

whine *verb*
1. To cry with soft, intermittent, often plaintive sounds : pule, whimper. *See* SOUNDS. **2.** To

express negative feelings, especially of dissatisfaction or resentment : complain, grouch, grump. *Informal:* crab, gripe, grouse, kick. *Slang:* beef, bellyache, bitch. *See* FEELINGS, HAPPY.

whiner *noun*
A person who habitually complains or grumbles : complainer, crab, faultfinder, grouch, growler, grumbler, grump, murmurer, mutterer. *Informal:* crank, griper, grouser. *Slang:* bellyacher, sorehead, sourpuss. *See* HAPPY.

whip *verb*
1. To punish with blows or lashes : beat, flog, hide[2], lash, thrash. *Informal:* trim. *Slang:* lay into, lick. *See* ATTACK, REWARD. **2.** To mix rapidly to a frothy consistency : beat, whisk. *See* ASSEMBLE, REPETITION. **3.** *Informal.* To win a victory over, as in battle or a competition : beat, best, conquer, defeat, master, overcome, prevail against (*or* over), rout, subdue, subjugate, surmount, triumph over, vanquish, worst. *Informal:* trim. *Slang:* ace, lick. ***Idioms:*** carry (*or* win) the day, get (*or* have) the best of, get (*or* have) the better of, go someone one better. *See* WIN.

whipping *noun*
1. A punishment dealt with blows or lashes : beating, flogging, hiding, lashing, thrashing. *Informal:* trimming. *Slang:* licking. *See* ATTACK, REWARD. **2.** *Informal.* The act of defeating or the condition of being defeated : beating, defeat, drubbing, overthrow, rout, thrashing, vanquishment. *Informal:* massacre, trimming. *Slang:* dusting, licking. *See* WIN.

whipping boy *noun*
One who is made an object of blame : goat, scapegoat. *Slang:* fall guy, patsy. *See* PRAISE.

whir *verb*
To make a continuous low-pitched droning sound : bumble[2], burr, buzz, drone[2], hum, whiz. *See* SOUNDS.
whir *noun* A continuous low-pitched droning sound : bumble[2], burr, buzz, drone[2], hum, whiz. *See* SOUNDS.

whirl *verb*
1. To rotate rapidly : spin, swirl, twirl. *See* REPETITION. **2.** To move or cause to move like a rapid rotary current of liquid : eddy, swirl. *See* MOVE, REPETITION. **3.** To have the sensation of turning in circles : reel, spin, swim, swirl. *See* REPETITION. **4.** To move swiftly : bolt, bucket, bustle, dart, dash, festinate, flash, fleet, flit, fly, haste, hasten, hurry, hustle, pelt[2], race, rocket, run, rush, sail, scoot, scour[2], shoot, speed, sprint, tear[1], trot, whisk, whiz, wing, zip, zoom. *Informal:* hotfoot, rip. *Slang:* barrel, highball. *Chiefly British:* nip[1]. ***Idioms:*** get a move on, get cracking, go like lightning, go like the wind, hotfoot it, make haste, make time, make tracks, run like the wind, shake a leg, step (*or* jump) on it. *See* MOVE.
whirl *noun* **1.** Circular movement around a point or about an axis : circuit, circulation, circumvolution, gyration, revolution, rotation, turn, wheel. *See* GEOMETRY, REPETITION. **2.** Agitated, excited movement and activity : bustle, flurry, stir[1], whirlpool. *See* CALM. **3.** *Informal.* A trip in a motor vehicle : drive, ride, run. *Informal:* spin. *See* MOVE. **4.** *Informal.* A brief trial : crack, go, stab, try. *Informal:* fling, shot, whack. *See* TRY.

whirlpool *noun*
Agitated, excited movement and activity : bustle, flurry, stir[1], whirl. *See* CALM.

whisk *verb*
1. To move swiftly : bolt, bucket, bustle, dart, dash, festinate, flash, fleet, flit, fly, haste, hasten, hurry, hustle, pelt[2], race, rocket, run, rush, sail, scoot, scour[2], shoot, speed, sprint, tear[1], trot, whirl, whiz, wing, zip, zoom. *Informal:* hotfoot, rip. *Slang:* barrel, highball. *Chiefly British:* nip[1]. ***Idioms:*** get a move on, get cracking, go like lightning, go like the wind, hotfoot it, make haste, make time, make tracks, run like the wind, shake a leg, step (*or* jump) on it. *See* MOVE. **2.** To mix rapidly to a frothy consistency : beat, whip. *See* ASSEMBLE, REPETITION.

whisker *noun*
Informal. A slight amount or indication : breath, dash, ghost, hair, hint, intimation, semblance, shade, shadow, soupçon, streak, suggestion, suspicion, taste, tinge, touch, trace, whiff, whisper. *See* BIG, SHOW.

whisper *noun*
1. A low, indistinct, and often continuous sound : mumble, murmur, sigh, sough, susurration, susurrus. *See* SOUNDS. **2.** A slight amount or indication : breath, dash, ghost, hair, hint, intimation, semblance, shade, shadow, soupçon, streak, suggestion, suspicion, taste, tinge, touch, trace, whiff. *Informal:* whisker. *See* BIG, SHOW.
whisper *verb* **1.** To speak or utter indistinctly, as by lowering the voice or partially closing the mouth : mumble, murmur, mutter. *See* SOUNDS. **2.** To engage in or spread gossip : blab, gossip, noise, rumor, talk, tattle, tittle-tattle. ***Idioms:*** tell tales, tell tales out of school. *See* WORDS. **3.** To tell in confidence : breathe,

confide. *See* SHOW, WORDS. **4.** To make a low, continuous, and indistinct sound : murmur, sigh, sough. *See* SOUNDS.

whisperer *noun*
A person habitually engaged in idle talk about others : blab, gossip, gossiper, gossipmonger, newsmonger, rumormonger, scandalmonger, tabby, talebearer, taleteller, tattle, tattler, tattletale, telltale. *Slang:* yenta. *See* WORDS.

whispery *adjective*
Not irritating, strident, or loud : hushed, low, low-key, low-keyed, quiet, small, soft, subdued. *See* SOUNDS.

whit *noun*
1. The least bit : hoot, iota, jot, ounce, shred. *Informal:* damn, rap[2]. *Slang:* diddly. *See* BIG. **2.** A tiny amount : bit[1], crumb, dab[1], dash, dot, dram, drop, fragment, grain, iota, jot, minim, mite, modicum, molecule, ort, ounce, particle, scrap[1], scruple, shred, smidgen, speck, tittle, trifle. *Chiefly British:* spot. *See* BIG.

white plague *noun*
An infectious disease producing lesions especially of the lungs : consumption (no longer in scientific use), phthisic (no longer in scientific use), phthisis (no longer in scientific use), tuberculosis. *See* HEALTH.

whitewash *verb*
1. To give a deceptively attractive appearance to : color, gild, gloss (over), gloze (over), sugarcoat, varnish, veneer. ***Idioms:*** paper over, put a good face on. *See* TRUE. **2.** To conceal or make light of a fault or offense : explain away, extenuate, gloss over, gloze (over), palliate, sleek over. *See* SHOW.

whiz also **whizz** *verb*
1. To make a continuous low-pitched droning sound : bumble[2], burr, buzz, drone[2], hum, whir. *See* SOUNDS. **2.** To make a sharp sibilant sound : fizz, fizzle, hiss, sibilate, sizzle, swish, whoosh. *See* SOUNDS. **3.** To move swiftly : bolt, bucket, bustle, dart, dash, festinate, flash, fleet, flit, fly, haste, hasten, hurry, hustle, pelt[2], race, rocket, run, rush, sail, scoot, scour[2], shoot, speed, sprint, tear[1], trot, whirl, whisk, wing, zip, zoom. *Informal:* hotfoot, rip. *Slang:* barrel, highball. *Chiefly British:* nip[1]. ***Idioms:*** get a move on, get cracking, go like lightning, go like the wind, hotfoot it, make haste, make time, make tracks, run like the wind, shake a leg, step (*or* jump) on it. *See* MOVE.

whiz also **whizz** *noun* **1.** A continuous low-pitched droning sound : bumble[2], burr, buzz, drone[2], hum, whir. *See* SOUNDS. **2.** *Informal.* A person with a high degree of knowledge or skill in a particular field : ace, adept, authority, dab hand, expert, master, past master, professional, proficient, wizard. *Slang:* crackerjack. *Chiefly British:* dab[2]. *See* ABILITY.

whizz *verb & noun* See **whiz.**

whole *adjective*
1. Including every constituent or individual : all, complete, entire, gross, total. *See* PART. **2.** Lacking nothing essential or normal : complete, entire, full, intact, integral, perfect. *See* PART. **3.** Not diffused or dispersed : concentrated, exclusive, intensive, undivided, unswerving. *See* COLLECT, EDGE, PART. **4.** Not more or less : complete, entire, full, good, perfect, round. *See* PART, PRECISE. **5.** In excellent condition : entire, flawless, good, intact, perfect, sound[2], unblemished, unbroken, undamaged, unharmed, unhurt, unimpaired, uninjured, unmarred. *See* THRIVE. **6.** Having good health : fit[1], hale, healthful, healthy, hearty, right, sound[2], well[2], wholesome. ***Idioms:*** fit as a fiddle, hale and hearty, in fine fettle. *See* HEALTH.

whole *noun* **1.** An amount or quantity from which nothing is left out or held back : aggregate, all, entirety, everything, gross, sum, total, totality. *Informal:* work (used in plural). ***Idioms:*** everything but (*or* except) the kitchen sink; lock, stock, and barrel; the whole ball of wax (*or* kit and caboodle *or* megillah *or* nine yards *or* shebang). *See* PART. **2.** An organized array of individual elements and parts forming and working as a unit : entity, integral, sum, system, totality. *See* PART.

wholehearted *adjective*
Having no reservations : absolute, implicit, unconditional, undoubting, unfaltering, unhesitating, unquestioning, unreserved. *See* BIG, LIMITED.

wholeness *noun*
1. The state of being entirely whole : completeness, entirety, integrity, oneness, totality. *See* PART. **2.** The condition of being free from defects or flaws : durability, firmness, integrity, solidity, soundness, stability, strength. *See* BETTER. **3.** The condition of being physically and mentally sound : haleness, health, healthiness, heartiness, soundness. *See* HEALTH.

wholesome *adjective*
1. Promoting good health : healthful, healthsome, healthy, hygienic, salubrious, salutary. *See* HEALTH. **2.** Not lewd or obscene : clean, decent, modest. *See* DECENT. **3.** Having good health : fit[1], hale, healthful, healthy, hearty, right, sound[2], well[2], whole. ***Idioms:*** fit as

a fiddle, hale and hearty, in fine fettle. *See* HEALTH.

wholly *adverb*
To the fullest extent : absolutely, all, altogether, completely, dead, entirely, flat, fully, just, perfectly, quite, thoroughly, totally, utterly, well[2]. *Informal:* clean, clear. ***Idioms:*** in toto, through and through. *See* BIG, LIMITED.

whoop *verb*
To speak or say very loudly or with a shout : bawl, bellow, bluster, call, clamor, cry, halloo, holler, roar, shout, vociferate, yawp, yell. *See* SOUNDS.

whoosh *verb*
To make a sharp sibilant sound : fizz, fizzle, hiss, sibilate, sizzle, swish, whiz. *See* SOUNDS.

whop *verb*
To deliver a powerful blow to suddenly and sharply : bash, catch, clout, hit, knock, pop[1], slam, slog, slug[3], smash, smite, sock, strike, swat, thwack, whack, wham. *Informal:* biff, bop, clip[1], wallop. *Slang:* belt, conk, paste. ***Idioms:*** let someone have it, sock it to someone. *See* ATTACK, STRIKE.
whop *noun* A sudden sharp, powerful stroke : bang, blow[2], clout, crack, hit, lick, pound, slug[3], sock, swat, thwack, welt, whack, wham. *Informal:* bash, biff, bop, clip[1], wallop. *Slang:* belt, conk, paste. *See* ATTACK, STRIKE.

whopper *noun*
1. *Slang.* One that is extraordinarily large and powerful : behemoth, giant, Goliath, jumbo, leviathan, mammoth, monster, titan. *See* BEINGS, BIG. **2.** *Slang.* An untrue declaration : canard, cock-and-bull story, falsehood, falsity, fib, fiction, inveracity, lie[2], misrepresentation, misstatement, prevarication, story, tale, untruth. *Informal:* fish story, tall tale. *See* TRUE.

whopping *adjective*
Slang. Of extraordinary size and power : behemoth, Brobdingnagian, Bunyanesque, colossal, cyclopean, elephantine, enormous, gargantuan, giant, gigantesque, gigantic, herculean, heroic, huge, immense, jumbo, mammoth, massive, massy, mastodonic, mighty, monster, monstrous, monumental, mountainous, prodigious, pythonic, stupendous, titanic, tremendous, vast. *Informal:* walloping. *See* BIG.

whore *noun*
1. A woman who engages in sexual intercourse for payment : bawd, call girl, camp follower, courtesan, harlot, prostitute, scarlet woman, streetwalker, strumpet, tart[2]. *Slang:* hooker, moll. ***Idioms:*** lady of easy virtue, lady of pleasure, lady of the night. *See* SEX. **2.** A vulgar promiscuous woman who flouts propriety : baggage, hussy, jade, slattern, slut, tart[2], tramp, wanton, wench. *Slang:* floozy. *See* SEX.

whorish *adjective*
Marked by an absence of conventional restraint in sexual behavior; sexually unrestrained : easy, fast, libertine, light[2], loose, wanton. *See* SEX.

who's who or **Who's Who** *noun*
People of the highest social level : aristocracy, blue blood, crème de la crème, elite, flower, gentility, gentry, nobility, patriciate, quality, society, upper class. *Informal:* upper crust. *See* OVER.

why *noun*
1. That which provides a reason or justification : call, cause, ground (often used in plural), justification, necessity, occasion, reason, wherefore. ***Idiom:*** why and wherefore. *See* START. **2.** A fact or circumstance that gives logical support to an assertion, claim, or proposal : argument, ground (often used in plural), proof, reason, wherefore. ***Idiom:*** why and wherefore. *See* REASON. **3.** What one intends to do or achieve : aim, ambition, design, end, goal, intent, intention, mark, meaning, object, objective, point, purpose, target, view. ***Idioms:*** end in view, why and wherefore. *See* PLANNED, PURPOSE.

wicked *adjective*
1. Morally objectionable : bad, black, evil, immoral, iniquitous, peccant, reprobate, sinful, vicious, wrong. *See* RIGHT. **2.** Characterized by intense ill will or spite : black, despiteful, evil, hateful, malevolent, malicious, malign, malignant, mean[2], nasty, poisonous, spiteful, venomous, vicious. *Slang:* bitchy. *See* ATTITUDE. **3.** Hard to treat, manage, or cope with : troublesome. *Informal:* pesky. *Slang:* mean[2]. *See* EASY.

wickedness *noun*
1. That which is morally bad or objectionable : evil, iniquity, peccancy, sin, wrong. *See* RIGHT. **2.** Degrading, immoral acts or habits : bestiality, corruption, depravity, flagitiousness, immorality, perversion, turpitude, vice, villainousness, villainy. *See* CLEAN. **3.** A wicked act or wicked behavior : crime, deviltry, diablerie, evil, evildoing, immorality, iniquity, misdeed, offense, peccancy, sin, wrong, wrongdoing. *See* RIGHT.

wide *adjective*
1. Extending over a large area from side to side : broad. *See* WIDE. **2.** Of full measure; not

narrow or restricted : ample, capacious, full, voluminous. *See* TIGHTEN.

wide-awake *adjective*

1. Not in a state of sleep : awake, unsleeping, wakeful. *See* AWARENESS. 2. Vigilantly attentive : alert, observant, open-eyed, vigilant, wakeful, wary, watchful. ***Idiom:*** on the ball. *See* AWARENESS.

widen *verb*

1. To make or become broad or broader : broaden. *See* WIDE. 2. To make or become more comprehensive or inclusive : broaden, expand, extend. *See* INCREASE.

wideness *noun*

The extent of something from side to side : breadth, broadness, width. *See* WIDE.

wide-ranging *adjective*

Covering a wide scope : all-around, all-inclusive, all-round, broad, broad-spectrum, comprehensive, expansive, extended, extensive, far-ranging, far-reaching, general, global, inclusive, large, overall, sweeping, wide-reaching, widespread. *See* SPECIFIC.

wide-reaching *adjective*

Covering a wide scope : all-around, all-inclusive, all-round, broad, broad-spectrum, comprehensive, expansive, extended, extensive, far-ranging, far-reaching, general, global, inclusive, large, overall, sweeping, wide-ranging, widespread. *See* SPECIFIC.

widespread *adjective*

1. Spread out over a large area : far-flung. *See* WIDE. 2. Covering a wide scope : all-around, all-inclusive, all-round, broad, broad-spectrum, comprehensive, expansive, extended, extensive, far-ranging, far-reaching, general, global, inclusive, large, overall, sweeping, wide-ranging, wide-reaching. *See* SPECIFIC. 3. Occurring quite often : common, everyday, familiar, frequent, regular, routine. *See* USUAL. 4. Most generally existing or encountered at a given time : current, predominant, prevailing, prevalent, regnant, rife. *See* SPECIFIC.

widget *noun*

Informal. A small specialized mechanical device : concern, contraption, contrivance, gadget, gimmick, jigger, thing. *Informal:* doodad, doohickey. *Slang:* gizmo. *See* MACHINE.

width *noun*

The extent of something from side to side : breadth, broadness, wideness. *See* WIDE.

wield *verb*

1. To use with or as if with the hands : handle, manipulate, ply[2]. *See* CONTROL, USED. 2. To bring to bear steadily or forcefully : exercise, exert, ply[2], put out, throw. *See* CAUSE.

wiggle *verb*

To move or proceed with short irregular motions up and down or from side to side : squiggle, squirm, waggle, worm, wriggle, writhe. *See* MOVE, REPETITION.

wild *adjective*

1. In a primitive state; not domesticated or cultivated; produced by nature : native, natural, rough, uncultivated, undomesticated, untamed. *See* WILD. 2. Of or relating to wild animals : feral, savage. *See* WILD. 3. Not civilized : barbarian, barbaric, barbarous, primitive, rude, savage, uncivilized, uncultivated, uncultured. *Archaic:* uncivil. *See* CULTURE, WILD. 4. Not submitting to discipline or control : disorderly, fractious, indocile, intractable, lawless, obstinate, obstreperous, recalcitrant, refractory, uncontrollable, undisciplined, ungovernable, unmanageable, unruly, untoward. ***Idiom:*** out of line. *See* CONTROL, ORDER, PEACE, RESIST. 5. Lacking in moral restraint : abandoned, dissipated, dissolute, fast, gay, incontinent, licentious, profligate, rakish, unbridled, unconstrained, uncontrolled, ungoverned, uninhibited, unrestrained, wanton. *See* RESTRAINT. 6. Marked by extreme excitement, confusion, or agitation : delirious, frantic, frenetic, frenzied, mad. *Archaic:* madding. *See* CALM. 7. Violently disturbed or agitated, as by storms : dirty, heavy, raging, roiled, roily, rough, rugged, stormy, tempestuous, tumultuous, turbulent, ugly, violent. *See* CALM.

wild *noun* An uninhabited region left in its natural state : bush, wilderness, wildness. *See* WILD.

wilderness *noun*

1. A tract of unproductive land : badlands, barren (often used in plural), desert[1], waste, wasteland. *See* RICH. 2. An uninhabited region left in its natural state : bush, wild, wildness. *See* WILD.

wildness *noun*

1. An uninhabited region left in its natural state : bush, wild, wilderness. *See* WILD.
2. The quality or condition of being unruly : disorderliness, fractiousness, indocility, intractability, intractableness, obstinacy, obstinateness, obstreperousness, recalcitrance, recalcitrancy, refractoriness, uncontrollability, uncontrollableness, ungovernableness, unmanageability, unruliness, untowardness. *See* CONTROL, ORDER, PEACE, RESIST. 3. A complete surrender of inhibitions : abandon,

abandonment, incontinence, unrestraint, wantonness. *See* RESTRAINT.

wile *noun*
An indirect, usually cunning means of gaining an end : artifice, deception, device, dodge, feint, gimmick, imposture, jig, maneuver, ploy, ruse, sleight, stratagem, subterfuge, trick. *Informal:* shenanigan, take-in. *See* HONEST, MEANS.
wile *verb* To pass (time) without working or in avoiding work. Also used with *away* : dawdle (away), fiddle away, idle (away), kill[1], trifle away, waste, while (away). *See* INDUSTRIOUS.

wilful *adjective* See **willful.**

wilfulness *noun* See **willfulness.**

wilfully *adverb* See **willfully.**

wiliness *noun*
Deceitful cleverness : art, artfulness, artifice, craft, craftiness, cunning, foxiness, guile, slyness. *See* HONEST, MEANS.

will *noun*
1. The mental faculty by which one deliberately chooses or decides : volition. *See* WILLING.
2. Unwavering firmness of character, action, or will : decidedness, decision, decisiveness, determination, firmness, purpose, purposefulness, resoluteness, resolution, resolve, toughness, willpower. *See* CERTAIN, STRONG. **3.** A desire for a particular thing or activity : fancy, liking, mind, pleasure. *See* LIKE. **4.** Unrestricted freedom to choose : discretion, pleasure. *See* FREE.
will *verb* **1.** To have the desire or inclination to : choose, desire, like[1], please, want, wish. ***Idioms:*** have a mind, see fit. *See* DESIRE. **2.** To give (property) to another person after one's death : leave[1]. *Law:* bequeath, devise. *See* GIVE, LAW.

willful also **wilfull** *adjective*
1. Done or said on purpose : deliberate, intended, intentional, purposeful, voluntary, witting. *See* PURPOSE. **2.** Done by one's own choice : free, spontaneous, uncompelled, unforced, volitional, voluntary. *See* WILLING.
3. Tenaciously unwilling to yield : bullheaded, dogged, hardheaded, headstrong, mulish, obstinate, pertinacious, perverse, pigheaded, stiff-necked, tenacious. *See* RESIST.

willfully also **wilfully** *adverb*
Of one's own free will : freely, spontaneously, voluntarily, willingly. ***Idioms:*** of one's own accord, on one's own volition. *See* WILLING.

willfulness also **wilfulness** *noun*
The quality or state of being stubbornly unyielding : bullheadedness, doggedness, hardheadedness, mulishness, obstinacy, obstinateness, pertinaciousness, pertinacity, perverseness, perversity, pigheadedness, tenaciousness, tenacity. *See* RESIST.

willies *noun*
Slang. A state of nervous restlessness or agitation : fidget (often used in plural), jitter (used in plural), jump (used in plural), shiver[1] (used in plural), tremble (often used in plural). *Informal:* all-overs, shake (used in plural). *Slang:* heebie-jeebies, jim-jams. *See* CALM, FEAR.

willing *adjective*
1. Disposed to accept or agree : acquiescent, agreeable, game, minded, ready. *Archaic:* fain. *See* WILLING. **2.** Of or relating to free exercise of the will : volitional, voluntary. *See* WILLING.

willingly *adverb*
1. Of one's own free will : freely, spontaneously, voluntarily, willfully. ***Idioms:*** of one's own accord, on one's own volition. *See* WILLING. **2.** It is so; as you say or ask : absolutely, agreed, all right, assuredly, aye, gladly, indubitably, roger, undoubtedly, unquestionably, yea, yes. *Informal:* OK, uh-huh, yeah, yep. *Slang:* right on. *See* AFFIRM.

will-o'-the-wisp *noun*
An erroneous perception of reality : delusion, hallucination, ignis fatuus, illusion, mirage, phantasm, phantasma. *See* REAL.

willpower or **will power** *noun*
Unwavering firmness of character, action, or will : decidedness, decision, decisiveness, determination, firmness, purpose, purposefulness, resoluteness, resolution, resolve, toughness, will. *See* CERTAIN, STRONG.

willy-nilly *adverb*
Without regard to desire or inclination : helplessly, involuntarily, perforce. *See* WILLING.

wilt *verb*
1. To become limp, as from loss of freshness : droop, flag[2], sag. *See* BETTER. **2.** To hang limply, loosely, and carelessly : droop, flop, loll, lop[2], sag, slouch. *See* HANG.

wily *adjective*
Deceitfully clever : artful, crafty, cunning, foxy, guileful, scheming, sharp, sly, tricky. *See* ABILITY, HONEST, MEANS.

win *verb*
1. To acquire as a result of one's behavior or effort : deserve, earn, gain, get, merit. *Informal:* rate[1]. *See* GET. **2.** To obtain possession or control of : capture, gain, get, take. *Slang:* cop. *See* GET. **3.** To come into possession

of : acquire, come by, gain, get, obtain, procure, secure. *Informal:* land, pick up. *See* GET. **4.** To receive, as wages, for one's labor : earn, gain, get, make. *Informal:* pull down. ***Idioms:*** earn (*or* make) a living, earn one's keep. *See* GIVE, MONEY.

win over *verb* To cause (another) to believe or feel sure about something : assure, convince, persuade, satisfy. *See* PERSUASION.

win *noun* The act of conquering : conquest, triumph, victory. *See* WIN.

wince *verb*

To draw away involuntarily, usually out of fear or disgust : blench[1], cringe, flinch, quail, recoil, shrink, shy[1], start. *See* APPROACH, SEEK.

wince *noun* An act of drawing back in an involuntary or instinctive fashion : cringe, flinch, recoil, shrink. *See* APPROACH, SEEK.

wind[1] *noun*

A natural movement or current of air : air, blast, blow[1], breeze, gust, zephyr. *Archaic:* gale. *See* BREATH.

wind *verb* To expose to circulating air : aerate, air, ventilate. *See* BREATH, OPEN.

wind[2] *verb*

1. To move or proceed on a repeatedly curving course : coil, corkscrew, curl, entwine, meander, snake, spiral, twine, twist, weave, wreathe. *See* REPETITION, STRAIGHT. **2.** To introduce gradually and slyly : edge, foist, infiltrate, insinuate, work, worm. *See* ENTER.

wind up *verb* To bring or come to a natural or proper end : close, complete, conclude, consummate, end, finish, terminate, wrap up. *See* START.

windiness *noun*

Words or the use of words in excess of those needed for clarity or precision : diffuseness, diffusion, long-windedness, pleonasm, prolixity, redundancy, verbiage, verboseness, verbosity, wordage, wordiness. *See* EXCESS, STYLE, WORDS.

winding *adjective*

Repeatedly curving in alternate directions : anfractuous, flexuous, meandrous, serpentine, sinuous, snaky, tortuous. *See* REPETITION, STRAIGHT.

windless *adjective*

Marked by an absence of circulating air : airless, breathless, breezeless, still. *See* BREATH.

window-dressing also **window dressing** *noun*

A deceptive outward appearance : cloak, color, coloring, cover, disguise, disguisement, façade, face, false colors, front, gloss, guise, mask, masquerade, pretense, pretext, semblance, show, veil, veneer. *Slang:* put-on. *See* SHOW.

wind-up or **windup** *noun*

1. A concluding or terminating : cease, cessation, close, closing, closure, completion, conclusion, consummation, end, ending, end of the line, finish, period, stop, stopping point, termination, terminus, wrap-up. *See* CONTINUE. **2.** The last part : close, conclusion, end, ending, finale, finish, last[1], termination, wrap-up. *See* START.

wind up *verb* See **wind[2]**.

windy *adjective*

1. Exposed to or characterized by the presence of freely circulating air or wind : airy, blowy, breezy, gusty. *See* BREATH. **2.** Filled up with or as if with something insubstantial : flatulent, inflated, overblown, tumescent, tumid, turgid. *See* INCREASE, PLAIN.

wing *noun*

1. A part added to a main structure : annex, arm, extension. *See* PART. **2.** A component of government that performs a given function : agency, arm, branch, department, division, organ. *See* PART.

wing *verb* **1.** To move through the air with or as if with wings : flap, flit, flitter, flutter, fly, sail. *See* MOVE. **2.** To move swiftly : bolt, bucket, bustle, dart, dash, festinate, flash, fleet, flit, fly, haste, hasten, hurry, hustle, pelt[2], race, rocket, run, rush, sail, scoot, scour[2], shoot, speed, sprint, tear[1], trot, whirl, whisk, whiz, zip, zoom. *Informal:* hotfoot, rip. *Slang:* barrel, highball. *Chiefly British:* nip[1]. ***Idioms:*** get a move on, get cracking, go like lightning, go like the wind, hotfoot it, make haste, make time, make tracks, run like the wind, shake a leg, step (*or* jump) on it. *See* MOVE.

wink *verb*

1. To open and close the eyes rapidly : bat[1], blink, nictate, nictitate, twinkle. *See* REPETITION, SEE. **2.** To shine with intermittent gleams : blink, flash, flicker, glimmer, twinkle. *See* CONTINUE, LIGHT. **3.** To emit light suddenly in rays or sparks : coruscate, flash, glance, gleam, glimmer, glint, glisten, glister, glitter, scintillate, shimmer, spangle, sparkle, twinkle. *See* LIGHT.

wink at *verb* To pretend not to see : blink (at), connive at, disregard, ignore, pass over. ***Idioms:*** be blind to, close (*or* shut) one's eyes to, look the other way, turn a blind eye to. *See* SEE.

wink *noun* **1.** A brief closing of the eyes : blink, nictation, nictitation. *See* SEE. **2.** A very brief time : crack, flash, instant, minute[1], moment, second[1], trice, twinkle, twinkling. *Informal:* jiff, jiffy. *Chiefly British:* tick. *See* BIG, TIME. **3.** A sudden quick light : blink, coruscation, flash, flicker, glance, gleam, glimmer, glint, spark[1], twinkle. *See* LIGHT.

wink at *verb* See **wink.**

winner *noun*
1. One that wins a contest or competition : victor. *See* WIN. **2.** One that conquers : conqueror, conquistador, master, victor. *See* WIN.

winning *adjective*
1. Relating to, having the nature of, or experiencing triumph : conquering, triumphal, triumphant, victorious. *See* WIN. **2.** Pleasing to the eye or mind : attractive, bewitching, enchanting, engaging, enticing, fascinating, fetching, glamorous, lovely, prepossessing, pretty, sweet, taking, tempting, winsome. *See* LIKE.

winnow *verb*
1. To set apart (one kind or type) from others : separate, sift, sort. *See* INCLUDE. **2.** To be in a state of motion, as air : blow[1], puff. *See* BREATH.

win over *verb* See **win.**

winsome *adjective*
Pleasing to the eye or mind : attractive, bewitching, enchanting, engaging, enticing, fascinating, fetching, glamorous, lovely, prepossessing, pretty, sweet, taking, tempting, winning. *See* LIKE.

wintriness *noun*
Extreme lack of warmth : frigidity, frigidness, frostiness, gelidity, gelidness, iciness. *See* HOT.

wintry *adjective*
Very cold : arctic, boreal, freezing, frigid, frosty, gelid, glacial, icy, polar. *Archaic:* frore. *Idiom:* bitter (*or* bitterly) cold. *See* HOT.

wipe *verb*
To remove or invalidate by or as if by running a line through or wiping clean. Also used with *out* : annul, blot (out), cancel, cross (off *or* out), delete, efface, erase, expunge, obliterate, rub (out), scratch (out), strike (out), undo, x (out). *Law:* vacate. *See* CONTINUE.

wipe out *verb* **1.** To destroy all traces of : abolish, annihilate, blot out, clear, eradicate, erase, exterminate, extinguish, extirpate, kill[1], liquidate, obliterate, remove, root[1] (out *or* up), rub out, snuff out, stamp out, uproot. *Idioms:* do away with, make an end of, put an end to. *See* HELP, MAKE. **2.** To get rid of, especially by banishment or execution : eliminate, eradicate, liquidate, purge, remove. *Idioms:* do away with, put an end to. *See* HELP, KEEP. **3.** *Slang.* To take the life of (a person or persons) unlawfully : destroy, finish (off), kill[1], liquidate, murder, slay. *Informal:* put away. *Slang:* bump off, do in, knock off, off, rub out, waste, zap. *See* HELP.

wiped-out *adjective*
Slang. Stupefied, intoxicated, or otherwise influenced by the taking of drugs : drugged. *Informal:* doped. *Slang:* high, hopped-up, lit (up), potted, spaced-out, stoned, turned-on, zonked. *See* DRUGS.

wipe out *verb* See **wipe.**

wiretap *verb*
To monitor (telephone calls) with a concealed listening device connected to the circuit : bug, tap[2]. *See* INVESTIGATE.

wisdom *noun*
1. Deep, thorough, or mature understanding : insight, profundity, sagaciousness, sagacity, sageness, sapience. *See* WISE. **2.** The ability to make sensible decisions : common sense, judgment, sense. *Informal:* gumption, horse sense. *See* ABILITY. **3.** That which is known; the sum of what has been perceived, discovered, or inferred : information, knowledge, lore. *See* KNOWLEDGE.

wise¹ *adjective*
1. Possessing or showing sound judgment and keen perception : knowing, sagacious, sage, sapient. *See* WISE. **2.** Possessing, proceeding from, or exhibiting good judgment and prudence : balanced, commonsensible, commonsensical, judicious, levelheaded, prudent, rational, reasonable, sagacious, sage, sane, sapient, sensible, sound[2], well-founded, well-grounded. *See* REASON, SANE. **3.** Having or showing a clever awareness and resourcefulness in practical matters : astute, cagey, canny, knowing, perspicacious, shrewd, slick, smart. *Informal:* savvy. *See* ABILITY, CAREFUL. **4.** Having or showing profound knowledge and scholarship : erudite, learned, lettered, scholarly. *See* KNOWLEDGE. **5.** Marked by comprehension, cognizance, and perception : alive, awake, aware, cognizant, sensible, sentient. *Slang:* hip. *Idiom:* on to. *See* KNOWLEDGE. **6.** *Slang.* Rude and disrespectful : assuming, assumptive, audacious, bold, boldfaced, brash, brazen, cheeky, contumelious, familiar, forward, impertinent, impudent, insolent, malapert, nervy, overconfident, pert, presuming, presumptuous, pushy, sassy, saucy, smart.

Informal: brassy, flip, fresh, smart-alecky, snippety, snippy, uppish, uppity. *See* ATTITUDE, COURTESY.

wise² *noun*
The approach used to do something : fashion, manner, method, mode, modus operandi, style, system, way. *See* MEANS.

wiseacre *noun*
Slang. One who is obnoxiously self-assertive and arrogant : malapert, witling. *Informal:* know-it-all, saucebox, smart aleck, smarty, smarty-pants, wisenheimer. *Slang:* wisecracker, wise guy. *See* GOOD.

wisecrack *noun*
Slang. A flippant or sarcastic remark : crack, dig, quip. *See* RESPECT, WORDS.

wisecracker *noun*
Slang. One who is obnoxiously self-assertive and arrogant : malapert, witling. *Informal:* know-it-all, saucebox, smart aleck, smarty, smarty-pants, wisenheimer. *Slang:* wiseacre, wise guy. *See* GOOD.

wise guy *noun*
Slang. One who is obnoxiously self-assertive and arrogant : malapert, witling. *Informal:* know-it-all, saucebox, smart aleck, smarty, smarty-pants, wisenheimer. *Slang:* wiseacre, wisecracker. *See* GOOD.

wisenheimer also **weisenheimer** *noun*
Informal. One who is obnoxiously self-assertive and arrogant : malapert, witling. *Informal:* know-it-all, saucebox, smart aleck, smarty, smarty-pants. *Slang:* wiseacre, wisecracker, wise guy. *See* GOOD.

wish *noun*
A strong wanting of what promises enjoyment or pleasure : appetence, appetency, appetite, craving, desire, hunger, itch, longing, lust, thirst, yearning, yen. *See* DESIRE.

wish *verb* **1.** To have the desire or inclination to : choose, desire, like[1], please, want, will. ***Idioms:*** have a mind, see fit. *See* DESIRE. **2.** To have a strong longing for : ache, covet, desire, hanker, long[2], pant, pine, want, yearn. *Informal:* hone[2]. *See* DESIRE.

wishy-washiness *noun*
Informal. The state or quality of being insipid : blandness, innocuousness, insipidity, insipidness, jejuneness, vapidity, vapidness, washiness, wateriness. *See* EXCITE, TASTE.

wishy-washy *adjective*
Informal. Lacking the qualities requisite for spiritedness and originality : bland, innocuous, insipid, jejune, namby-pamby, vapid, washy, waterish, watery. *See* EXCITE, GOOD.

wistful *adjective*
In low spirits : blue, dejected, depressed, desolate, dispirited, down, downcast, downhearted, dull, dysphoric, gloomy, heavy-hearted, low, melancholic, melancholy, sad, spiritless, tristful, unhappy. ***Idiom:*** down at (*or* in) the mouth. *See* HAPPY.

wit *noun*
1. The faculty of thinking, reasoning, and acquiring and applying knowledge : brain (often used in plural), brainpower, intellect, intelligence, mentality, mind, sense, understanding. *Slang:* smart (used in plural). *See* ABILITY, THOUGHTS. **2.** Skill in perceiving, discriminating, or judging : acumen, astuteness, clear-sightedness, discernment, discrimination, eye, keenness, nose, penetration, perceptiveness, percipience, percipiency, perspicacity, sagacity, sageness, shrewdness. *See* ABILITY, CAREFUL. **3.** A healthy mental state. Used in plural : lucidity, lucidness, mind, reason, saneness, sanity, sense (often used in plural), soundness. *Slang:* marble (used in plural). *See* SANE. **4.** The quality of being laughable or comical : comedy, comicality, comicalness, drollery, drollness, farcicality, funniness, humor, humorousness, jocoseness, jocosity, jocularity, ludicrousness, ridiculousness, wittiness, zaniness. *See* LAUGHTER. **5.** A person whose words or actions provoke or are intended to provoke amusement or laughter : clown, comedian, comic, farceur, funnyman, humorist, jester, joker, jokester, quipster, wag[2], zany. *Informal:* card. *See* LAUGHTER.

witch *noun*
1. A woman who practices magic : enchantress, hag, lamia, sorceress. *See* SUPERNATURAL. **2.** An ugly, frightening old woman : beldam, crone, hag. *Slang:* biddy. *Archaic:* trot. *See* BEAUTIFUL. **3.** *Informal.* A usually unscrupulous woman who seduces or exploits men : enchantress, femme fatale, seductress, siren, temptress. *Informal:* vamp. *See* SEX.

witch *verb* To act upon with or as if with magic : bewitch, charm, enchant, enthrall, entrance[2], spell[2], spellbind, voodoo. *See* PERSUASION.

witchcraft *noun*
The use of supernatural powers to influence or predict events : conjuration, magic, sorcery, sortilege, thaumaturgy, theurgy, witchery, witching, wizardry. *See* SUPERNATURAL.

witchery *noun*
1. The use of supernatural powers to influence or predict events : conjuration, magic, sorcery,

sortilege, thaumaturgy, theurgy, witchcraft, witching, wizardry. *See* SUPERNATURAL. **2.** The power or quality of attracting : allure, allurement, appeal, attraction, attractiveness, call, charisma, charm, draw, enchantment, enticement, fascination, glamour, lure, magnetism. *Informal:* pull. *See* LIKE.

witching *adjective*
1. Having, brought about by, or relating to supernatural powers or magic : fey, magic, magical, talismanic, thaumaturgic, thaumaturgical, theurgic, theurgical, wizardly. *See* SUPERNATURAL. **2.** Tending to seduce : alluring, bewitching, come-hither, enticing, inveigling, inviting, luring, seductive, siren, tempting. *See* LIKE, PERSUASION, SEX.
witching *noun* The use of supernatural powers to influence or predict events : conjuration, magic, sorcery, sortilege, thaumaturgy, theurgy, witchcraft, witchery, wizardry. *See* SUPERNATURAL.

withdraw *verb*
1. To move (something) from a position occupied : remove, take, take away, take off, take out. *See* MOVE. **2.** To pull back in : draw in, retract. *See* SHOW. **3.** To move or proceed away from a place : depart, exit, get away, get off, go, go away, leave[1], pull out, quit, retire, run (along). *Informal:* cut out, push off, shove off. *Slang:* blow[1], split, take off. ***Idioms:*** hit the road, take leave. *See* APPROACH. **4.** To move back in the face of enemy attack or after a defeat : draw back, fall back, pull back, pull out, retire, retreat. ***Idioms:*** beat a retreat, give ground (*or* way). *See* FORWARD. **5.** To remove from association with : abstract, detach, disassociate, disengage, dissociate. *See* ASSEMBLE. **6.** To disavow (something previously written or said) irrevocably and usually formally : abjure, recall, recant, retract, take back. *See* ACCEPT.

withdrawal *noun*
1. The act of leaving : departure, egress, exit, exodus, going. *See* APPROACH. **2.** The moving back of a military force in the face of enemy attack or after a defeat : fallback, pullback, pullout, retirement, retreat. *See* FORWARD. **3.** A formal statement of disavowal : abjuration, palinode, recantation, retractation, retraction. *See* ACCEPT.

withdrawn *adjective*
Not friendly, sociable, or warm in manner : aloof, chill, chilly, cool, distant, offish, remote, reserved, reticent, solitary, standoffish, unapproachable, uncommunicative, undemonstrative. *See* ATTITUDE, HOT.

wither *verb*
1. To make or become no longer fresh or shapely because of loss of moisture : dry up, mummify, sear, shrivel, wizen. *See* DRY. **2.** To waste away from longing or grief : languish, pine (away). *See* HEALTH. **3.** To render helpless, as by emotion : benumb, numb, paralyze, petrify, stun, stupefy. *See* AFFECT.

withhold *verb*
1. To hold oneself back : abstain, forbear, hold off, keep, refrain. *See* RESTRAINT. **2.** To have and maintain in one's possession : hold, hold back, keep, keep back, reserve, retain. *See* KEEP. **3.** To be unwilling to grant : deny, disallow, refuse, turn down. *See* ACCEPT.

with-it *adjective*
Slang. Being or in accordance with the current fashion : à la mode, chic, dashing, fashionable, mod, modish, posh, smart, stylish, swank, swanky, trig. *Informal:* classy, in, sharp, snappy, swish, tony, trendy. ***Idioms:*** all the rage, up to the minute. *See* STYLE, USUAL.

withstand *verb*
1. To oppose actively and with force : resist. ***Idioms:*** mount (*or* offer) resistance, put up a fight, stand up to (*or* against). *See* RESIST. **2.** To put up with : abide, accept, bear, brook[2], endure, go, stand (for), stomach, suffer, support, sustain, swallow, take, tolerate. *Informal:* lump[2]. ***Idioms:*** take it, take it lying down. *See* ACCEPT.

witless *adjective*
Displaying a complete lack of forethought and good sense : brainless, fatuous, foolish, insensate, mindless, senseless, silly, unintelligent, weak-minded. *See* ABILITY, PLANNED.

witling *noun*
One who is obnoxiously self-assertive and arrogant : malapert. *Informal:* know-it-all, saucebox, smart aleck, smarty, smarty-pants, wisenheimer. *Slang:* wiseacre, wisecracker, wise guy. *See* GOOD.

witness *noun*
1. Someone who sees something occur : eyewitness, seer, viewer. *See* SEE. **2.** Something visible or evident that gives grounds for believing in the existence or presence of something else : badge, evidence, index, indication, indicator, manifestation, mark, note, sign, signification, stamp, symptom, token. *See* SHOW. **3.** One who testifies, especially in court : attestant, attester, testifier. *Law:* deponent. *See* LAW. **4.** A formal declaration of truth or fact given under oath : testimony. *Law:* deposition. *See* LAW.

witness *verb* **1.** To give grounds for believing in the existence or presence of : argue, attest, bespeak, betoken, indicate, mark, point to, testify. *See* SHOW. **2.** To confirm formally as true, accurate, or genuine : attest, certify, testify, vouch (for). ***Idiom:*** bear witness to. *See* AFFIRM. **3.** To give evidence or testimony under oath : attest, swear, testify. *Law:* depone, depose. ***Idioms:*** bear witness, take the stand. *See* LAW.

witticism *noun*
Words or actions intended to excite laughter or amusement : gag, jape, jest, joke, quip. *Informal:* funny, gag. *Slang:* ha-ha. *See* LAUGHTER.

wittiness *noun*
The quality of being laughable or comical : comedy, comicality, comicalness, drollery, drollness, farcicality, funniness, humor, humorousness, jocoseness, jocosity, jocularity, ludicrousness, ridiculousness, wit, zaniness. *See* LAUGHTER.

witting *adjective*
Done or said on purpose : deliberate, intended, intentional, purposeful, voluntary, willful. *See* PURPOSE.

witty *adjective*
1. Intended to excite laughter or amusement : comedic, facetious, funny, humorous, jocose, jocular. *See* LAUGHTER. **2.** Amusing or pleasing because of wit or originality : clever, scintillating, smart, sparkling. *See* LAUGHTER.

wizard *noun*
A person with a high degree of knowledge or skill in a particular field : ace, adept, authority, dab hand, expert, master, past master, professional, proficient. *Informal:* whiz. *Slang:* crackerjack. *Chiefly British:* dab[2]. *See* ABILITY.

wizardly *adjective*
Having, brought about by, or relating to supernatural powers or magic : fey, magic, magical, talismanic, thaumaturgic, thaumaturgical, theurgic, theurgical, witching. *See* SUPERNATURAL.

wizardry *noun*
The use of supernatural powers to influence or predict events : conjuration, magic, sorcery, sortilege, thaumaturgy, theurgy, witchcraft, witchery, witching. *See* SUPERNATURAL.

wizen *verb*
To make or become no longer fresh or shapely because of loss of moisture : dry up, mummify, sear, shrivel, wither. *See* DRY.

wobble *verb*
1. To move back and forth or from side to side, as if about to fall : sway, teeter, totter, vacillate, waver, weave. *See* REPETITION. **2.** To walk unsteadily : falter, lurch, reel, stagger, stumble, teeter, totter, weave. *See* MOVE. **3.** To be irresolute in acting or doing : dither, falter, halt[2], hesitate, pause, shilly-shally, stagger, vacillate, waver. *See* DECIDE.

wobbliness *noun*
The quality or condition of being physically unsteady : instability, precariousness, ricketiness, shakiness, unstableness, unsteadiness. *See* FLEXIBLE.

wobbly *adjective*
1. Not physically steady or firm : precarious, rickety, shaky, tottering, tottery, unstable, unsteady. *See* FLEXIBLE. **2.** Lacking stability : infirm, insecure, precarious, shaky, tottering, tottery, unstable, unsteady, unsure, weak. *See* CHANGE, STRONG.

woe *noun*
1. A state of physical or mental suffering : affliction, agony, anguish, distress, hurt, misery, pain, torment, torture, wound, wretchedness. *See* HAPPY. **2.** A state of prolonged anguish and privation : misery, suffering, wretchedness. *See* HAPPY. **3.** A cause of suffering or harm : affliction, bane, curse, evil, ill, plague, scourge. *See* HELP.

woebegone *adjective*
1. Suffering from usually prolonged anguish : miserable, woeful, wretched. *See* HAPPY.
2. Full of or expressive of sorrow : doleful, dolorous, lugubrious, mournful, plaintive, rueful, sad, sorrowful, woeful. *See* HAPPY.

woeful also **woful** *adjective*
1. Suffering from usually prolonged anguish : miserable, woebegone, wretched. *See* HAPPY.
2. Full of or expressive of sorrow : doleful, dolorous, lugubrious, mournful, plaintive, rueful, sad, sorrowful, woebegone. *See* HAPPY.
3. Causing sorrow or regret : deplorable, doleful, dolorous, grievous, lamentable, mournful, regrettable, rueful, sad, sorrowful. *See* HAPPY.

woful *adjective* See **woeful.**

wolf *noun*
Slang. A man who philanders : Casanova, Don Juan, lady's man, philanderer, womanizer. *Slang:* lady-killer. ***Idioms:*** man on the make, skirt chaser. *See* SEX.

wolf *verb* To swallow (food or drink) greedily or rapidly in large amounts : bolt, down, englut, engorge, gobble, gulp, guzzle, ingurgitate, swill. *See* INGESTION.

wolfish *adjective*
Showing or suggesting a disposition to be

violently destructive without scruple or restraint : barbarous, bestial, cruel, fell[2], feral, ferocious, fierce, inhuman, savage, truculent, vicious. *See* KIND.

womanhood *noun*
Women in general : distaff, femininity, muliebrity, womankind, womenfolk. *See* GENDER.

womanish *adjective*
1. Of, relating to, or characteristic of women : distaff, female, feminine, womanly. *See* GENDER. **2.** Having qualities more appropriate to women than to men : effeminate, epicene, feminine, sissified, sissyish, unmanly. *See* GENDER.

womanishness *noun*
The quality of being effeminate : effeminacy, effeminateness, femininity, sissiness, unmanliness. *See* GENDER.

womanize *verb*
To be sexually unfaithful to another : philander. *Informal:* cheat, fool around, mess around, play around. *See* SEX.

womanizer *noun*
A man who philanders : Casanova, Don Juan, lady's man, philanderer. *Slang:* lady-killer, wolf. ***Idioms:*** man on the make, skirt chaser. *See* SEX.

womankind *noun*
Women in general : distaff, femininity, muliebrity, womanhood, womenfolk. *See* GENDER.

womanliness *noun*
The quality or condition of being feminine : femaleness, feminineness, femininity. *See* GENDER.

womanly *adjective*
Of, relating to, or characteristic of women : distaff, female, feminine, womanish. *See* GENDER.

womenfolk also **womenfolks** *noun*
Women in general : distaff, femininity, muliebrity, womanhood, womankind. *See* GENDER.

wonder *noun*
1. One that evokes great surprise and admiration : astonishment, marvel, miracle, phenomenon, prodigy, sensation, stunner, wonderment. ***Idioms:*** one for the books, the eighth wonder of the world. *See* GOOD. **2.** The emotion aroused by something awe-inspiring or astounding : amaze, amazement, astonishment, awe, marvel, wonderment. *Archaic:* admiration, dread. *See* EXCITE, FEELINGS. **3.** An event inexplicable by the laws of nature : miracle. *See* SUPERNATURAL. **4.** A lack of conviction or certainty : doubt, doubtfulness, dubiety, dubiousness, incertitude, mistrust, question, skepticism, suspicion, uncertainty. *See* CERTAIN.

wonder *verb* **1.** To have a feeling of great awe and rapt admiration : marvel. *See* EXCITE, FEELINGS. **2.** To be uncertain, disbelieving, or skeptical about : distrust, doubt, misdoubt, mistrust, question. ***Idiom:*** have one's doubts. *See* CERTAIN.

wonderful *adjective*
1. So remarkable as to elicit disbelief : amazing, astonishing, astounding, fabulous, fantastic, fantastical, incredible, marvelous, miraculous, phenomenal, prodigious, stupendous, unbelievable, wondrous. *See* GOOD. **2.** Particularly excellent : divine, fabulous, fantastic, fantastical, glorious, marvelous, sensational, splendid, superb, terrific. *Informal:* dandy, dreamy, great, ripping, super, swell, tremendous. *Slang:* cool, groovy, hot, keen[1], neat, nifty. ***Idiom:*** out of this world. *See* GOOD.

wonderment *noun*
1. The emotion aroused by something awe-inspiring or astounding : amaze, amazement, astonishment, awe, marvel, wonder. *Archaic:* admiration, dread. *See* EXCITE, FEELINGS. **2.** One that evokes great surprise and admiration : astonishment, marvel, miracle, phenomenon, prodigy, sensation, stunner, wonder. ***Idioms:*** one for the books, the eighth wonder of the world. *See* GOOD.

wondrous *adjective*
So remarkable as to elicit disbelief : amazing, astonishing, astounding, fabulous, fantastic, fantastical, incredible, marvelous, miraculous, phenomenal, prodigious, stupendous, unbelievable, wonderful. *See* GOOD.

wont *adjective*
In the habit : accustomed, habituated, used. *See* USUAL.
wont *noun* A habitual way of behaving : consuetude, custom, habit, habitude, manner, practice, praxis, usage, usance, use, way. *See* USUAL.
wont *verb* To make familiar through constant practice or use : accustom, condition, habituate, inure. *See* USUAL.

wonted *adjective*
Commonly practiced or used : accustomed, customary, habitual, regular, usual. *See* USUAL.

woo *verb*
To attempt to gain the affection of : court, pursue, spark[2]. *Informal:* romance. *See* SEEK, SEX.

wooden *adjective*
1. So rigidly constrained, formal, or awkward as to lack all grace and spontaneity : buckram, starchy, stiff, stilted. *See* FLEXIBLE. **2.** Lacking

responsiveness or alertness : benumbed, dull, insensible, insensitive, numb, stuporous, torpid, unresponsive. *See* AWARENESS.

wooer *noun*
A man who courts a woman : admirer, beau, courter, suitor, swain. *See* SEX.

woolgather *verb*
To experience dreams or daydreams : daydream, dream, fantasize, muse[1]. *See* REAL.

woolgathering *adjective*
Given to daydreams or reverie : dreamy, moony, visionary. *See* REAL.

woolly *adjective*
Covered with hair : fleecy, furry, fuzzy, hairy, hirsute, pilose. *See* SMOOTH.

wooziness *noun*
A sensation of whirling or falling : dizziness, giddiness, lightheadedness, vertiginousness, vertigo. *See* AWARENESS.

woozy *adjective*
Having a sensation of whirling or falling : dizzy, giddy, lightheaded, reeling, vertiginous. *See* AWARENESS.

word *noun*
1. A sound or combination of sounds that symbolizes and communicates a meaning : expression, locution, term. *See* WORDS. **2.** Something said : saying, statement, utterance. *See* WORDS. **3.** Something communicated, as information : communication, message. *See* WORDS. **4.** A declaration that one will or will not do a certain thing : assurance, covenant, engagement, guarantee, guaranty, pledge, plight[2], promise, solemn word, vow, warrant, word of honor. *See* OBLIGATION. **5.** An authoritative indication to be obeyed : behest, bidding, charge, command, commandment, dictate, direction, directive, injunction, instruction (often used in plural), mandate, order. *See* OVER, WORDS. **6.** New information, especially about recent events and happenings : advice (often used in plural), intelligence, news, tiding (often used in plural). *Informal:* scoop. *See* KNOWLEDGE, WORDS. **7.** Idle, often sensational and groundless talk about others : gossip, gossipry, hearsay, report, rumor, talebearing, tattle, tittle-tattle. *Slang:* scuttlebutt. *See* WORDS. **8.** A discussion, often heated, in which a difference of opinion is expressed. Used in plural : altercation, argument, bicker, clash, contention, controversy, debate, difficulty, disagreement, dispute, fight, polemic, quarrel, run-in, spat, squabble, tiff, wrangle. *Informal:* hassle, rhubarb, tangle. *See* CONFLICT.

word *verb* To convey in language or words of a particular form : couch, express, formulate, phrase, put. *See* WORDS.

wordage *noun*
1. Words or the use of words in excess of those needed for clarity or precision : diffuseness, diffusion, long-windedness, pleonasm, prolixity, redundancy, verbiage, verboseness, verbosity, windiness, wordiness. *See* EXCESS, STYLE, WORDS. **2.** Choice of words and the way in which they are used : diction, parlance, phrase, phraseology, phrasing, verbalism, wording. *See* WORDS.

wordbook *noun*
An alphabetical list of words often defined or translated : dictionary, glossary, lexicon, vocabulary. *See* WORDS.

word-for-word *adjective*
Employing the very same words as another : literal, verbal, verbatim. *See* SAME.

word-hoard *noun*
All the words of a language : lexicon, vocabulary. *See* WORDS.

wordiness *noun*
Words or the use of words in excess of those needed for clarity or precision : diffuseness, diffusion, long-windedness, pleonasm, prolixity, redundancy, verbiage, verboseness, verbosity, windiness, wordage. *See* EXCESS, STYLE, WORDS.

wording *noun*
Choice of words and the way in which they are used : diction, parlance, phrase, phraseology, phrasing, verbalism, wordage. *See* WORDS.

wordless *adjective*
1. Not voiced or expressed : silent, tacit, undeclared, unexpressed, unsaid, unspoken, unuttered, unvoiced. *See* WORDS. **2.** Conveyed indirectly without words or speech : implicit, implied, inferred, tacit, understood, unsaid, unspoken, unuttered. ***Idiom:*** taken for granted. *See* SHOW. **3.** Temporarily unable or unwilling to speak, as from shock or fear : dumb, inarticulate, mum, mute, silent, speechless, voiceless. *See* WORDS.

wordlessness *noun*
The avoidance of speech : dumbness, muteness, silence, speechlessness. *See* WORDS.

word of honor *noun*
A declaration that one will or will not do a certain thing : assurance, covenant, engagement, guarantee, guaranty, pledge, plight[2], promise, solemn word, vow, warrant, word. *See* OBLIGATION.

word-of-mouth *adjective*
Expressed or transmitted in speech : oral, spoken, unwritten, verbal. *See* WORDS.

wordy *adjective*
1. Relating to, consisting of, or having the nature of words : verbal. *See* WORDS. **2.** Using or containing an excessive number of words : diffuse, long-winded, periphrastic, pleonastic, prolix, redundant, verbose. *See* EXCESS, STYLE, WORDS.

work *noun*
1. Physical exertion that is usually difficult and exhausting : drudgery, labor, moil, toil, travail. *Informal:* sweat. *Chiefly British:* fag. ***Idiom:*** sweat of one's brow. *See* WORK.
2. Activity pursued as a livelihood : art, business, calling, career, craft, employment, job, line, métier, occupation, profession, pursuit, trade, vocation. *Slang:* racket. *Archaic:* employ. *See* ACTION. **3.** Something done : act, action, deed, doing, thing. *See* DO. **4.** Something that is the result of creative effort : composition, opus, piece, production. *See* MAKE. **5.** An issue of printed material offered for sale or distribution : opus, publication, title, volume. *See* WORDS. **6.** A building or complex in which an industry is located. Used in plural : factory, mill, plant. *See* MAKE, PLACE. **7.** The technique, style, and quality of working : craftsmanship, workmanship. *See* WORK.
8. *Informal.* An amount or quantity from which nothing is left out or held back. Used in plural : aggregate, all, entirety, everything, gross, sum, total, totality, whole. ***Idioms:*** everything but (*or* except) the kitchen sink; lock, stock, and barrel; the whole ball of wax (*or* kit and caboodle *or* megillah *or* nine yards *or* shebang). *See* PART.

work *verb* **1.** To exert one's mental or physical powers, usually under difficulty and to the point of exhaustion : drive, fag, labor, moil, strain[1], strive, sweat, toil, travail, tug. ***Idiom:*** break one's back (*or* neck). *See* WORK. **2.** To perform a function effectively : function, go, operate, run, take. *See* THRIVE. **3.** To react in a specified way : act, behave, function, operate, perform. *See* ACTION. **4.** To turn out well : come off, go, go over, pan out, succeed, work out. *Slang:* click. *See* THRIVE. **5.** To control or direct the functioning of : manage, operate, run, use. *See* CONTROL. **6.** To arrive at an answer to (a mathematical problem) : solve, work out. *Informal:* figure out. *See* REASON. **7.** To handle in a way so as to mix, form, and shape : knead, manipulate. *See* TOUCH. **8.** To introduce gradually and slyly : edge, foist, infiltrate, insinuate, wind[2], worm. *See* ENTER. **9.** To prepare (soil) for the planting and raising of crops : cultivate, culture, dress, tend[2], till. *See* PREPARED, TOUCH. **10.** To force to work : drive, task, tax. ***Idiom:*** crack the whip. *See* WORK.

work out *verb* **1.** To arrive at an answer to (a mathematical problem) : solve, work. *Informal:* figure out. *See* REASON. **2.** To plan the details or arrangements of : arrange, lay out, prepare, schedule. *See* PLANNED. **3.** To form a strategy for : blueprint, cast, chart, conceive, contrive, design, devise, formulate, frame, lay[1], plan, project, scheme, strategize. *Informal:* dope out. ***Idiom:*** lay plans. *See* PLANNED. **4.** To turn out well : come off, go, go over, pan out, succeed, work. *Slang:* click. *See* THRIVE. **5.** To subject to or engage in forms of exertion in order to train, strengthen, or condition : drill, exercise, practice, train. *See* WORK.

work up *verb* To stir to action or feeling : egg on, excite, foment, galvanize, goad, impel, incite, inflame, inspire, instigate, motivate, move, pique, prick, prod, prompt, propel, provoke, set off, spur, stimulate, touch off, trigger. *See* CAUSE, EXCITE.

workable *adjective*
1. Capable of being shaped, bent, or drawn out, as by hammering or pressure : ductile, flexible, flexile, flexuous, malleable, moldable, plastic, pliable, pliant, supple. *See* FLEXIBLE. **2.** Capable of occurring or being done : feasible, possible, practicable, viable. ***Idiom:*** within reach. *See* POSSIBLE.

workaday *adjective*
Of or suitable for ordinary days or routine occasions : everyday, quotidian, workday. *See* GOOD, USUAL.

workday *adjective*
Of or suitable for ordinary days or routine occasions : everyday, quotidian, workaday. *See* GOOD, USUAL.

worked up *adjective*
Feeling a very strong emotion : atingle, excited, fired up, thrilled. *Informal:* psyched. *Slang:* stoked, turned-on. *See* EXCITE.

worker *noun*
1. One who is employed by another : employee, hireling, jobholder. *Informal:* hire, hired hand. *See* OVER, WORK. **2.** One who labors : hand, laborer, operative, roustabout, working girl, workingman, workingwoman, workman, workwoman. *See* WORK.

workhorse *noun*
Informal. One who works or toils tirelessly : drudge, fag, grub, plodder, slave. *Informal:* grind. *See* WORK.

working *adjective*
1. In action or full operation : active, alive, functioning, going, operating, operative, running. *See* ACTION, AWARENESS. **2.** Having a job : employed, hired, jobholding, retained. *See* WORK.
working *noun* The way in which something functions. Often used in plural : behavior, functioning, operation, performance, reaction. *See* ACTION, MACHINE.

working girl *noun*
One who labors : hand, laborer, operative, roustabout, worker, workingman, workingwoman, workman, workwoman. *See* WORK.

workingman *noun*
One who labors : hand, laborer, operative, roustabout, worker, working girl, workingwoman, workman, workwoman. *See* WORK.

workingwoman *noun*
One who labors : hand, laborer, operative, roustabout, worker, working girl, workingman, workman, workwoman. *See* WORK.

workless *adjective*
Out of work : jobless, unemployed. *See* WORK.

workman *noun*
One who labors : hand, laborer, operative, roustabout, worker, working girl, workingman, workingwoman, workwoman. *See* WORK.

workmanship *noun*
The technique, style, and quality of working : craftsmanship, work. *See* WORK.

work out *verb* See **work.**

work up *verb* See **work.**

workwoman *noun*
One who labors : hand, laborer, operative, roustabout, worker, working girl, workingman, workingwoman, workman. *See* WORK.

world *noun*
1. The celestial body where humans live : earth (often uppercase). *See* PLACE. **2.** The totality of all existing things : cosmos, creation, macrocosm, nature, universe. *See* MATTER, PART. **3.** The human race : earth, flesh, Homo sapiens, humanity, humankind, man, mankind, universe. *See* CULTURE. **4.** A sphere of activity, experience, study, or interest : area, arena, bailiwick, circle, department, domain, field, orbit, province, realm, scene, subject, terrain, territory. *Slang:* bag. *See* TERRITORY. **5.** The totality of surrounding conditions and circumstances affecting growth or development : ambiance, atmosphere, climate, environment, medium, milieu, mise en scène, surroundings. *See* BE, LIMITED, PLACE. **6.** A great deal : abundance, mass, mountain, much, plenty, profusion, wealth. *Informal:* barrel, heap, lot, pack, peck[2], pile. *Regional:* power, sight. *See* BIG.

worldly *adjective*
1. Relating to or characteristic of the earth or of human life on earth : earthbound, earthen, earthly, earthy, mundane, secular, tellurian, telluric, temporal, terrene, terrestrial. *See* BODY, CULTURE, PLACE. **2.** Not religious in subject matter, form, or use : lay[2], profane, secular, temporal. *See* SACRED. **3.** Experienced in the ways of the world; lacking natural simplicity : cosmopolitan, sophisticated, worldly-wise. *See* KNOWLEDGE.

worldly-wise *adjective*
Experienced in the ways of the world; lacking natural simplicity : cosmopolitan, sophisticated, worldly. *See* KNOWLEDGE.

worldwide *adjective*
So pervasive and all-inclusive as to exist in or affect the whole world : catholic, cosmic, cosmopolitan, ecumenical, global, pandemic, planetary, universal. *See* LIMITED, SPECIFIC.

world without end *adjective*
Enduring for all time : amaranthine, ceaseless, endless, eternal, everlasting, immortal, neverending, perpetual, unending. *Archaic:* eterne. *See* CONTINUE.
world without end *noun* The quality or state of having no end : ceaselessness, endlessness, eternality, eternalness, eternity, everlastingness, perpetuity. *See* CONTINUE.

worm *verb*
1. To move or proceed with short irregular motions up and down or from side to side : squiggle, squirm, waggle, wiggle, wriggle, writhe. *See* MOVE, REPETITION. **2.** To move along in a crouching or prone position : crawl, creep, slide, snake. *See* MOVE. **3.** To introduce gradually and slyly : edge, foist, infiltrate, insinuate, wind[2], work. *See* ENTER. **4.** To make, achieve, or get through contrivance or guile : engineer, finesse. *Informal:* finagle, wangle. *See* GET, MAKE.

worn *adjective*
Pale and exhausted, as because of worry or sleeplessness : careworn, drawn, gaunt, haggard, hollow-eyed, wan. *See* TIRED.

worn-down *adjective*
Extremely tired : bleary, dead, drained,

exhausted, fatigued, rundown, spent, tired out, wearied, weariful, weary, worn-out. *Informal:* beat, bushed, tuckered (out). *Slang:* done in, fagged (out), pooped (out). ***Idioms:*** all in, ready to drop. *See* HEALTH, TIRED.

worn-out *adjective*

1. Without freshness or appeal because of overuse : banal, bromidic, clichéd, commonplace, corny, hackneyed, musty, overused, overworked, platitudinal, platitudinous, shopworn, stale, stereotyped, stereotypic, stereotypical, threadbare, timeworn, tired, trite, warmed-over, well-worn. *See* EXCITE, USUAL.
2. Extremely tired : bleary, dead, drained, exhausted, fatigued, rundown, spent, tired out, wearied, weariful, weary, worn-down. *Informal:* beat, bushed, tuckered (out). *Slang:* done in, fagged (out), pooped (out). ***Idioms:*** all in, ready to drop. *See* HEALTH, TIRED.

worrisome *adjective*

Troubling to the mind or emotions : disquieting, disruptive, distressful, distressing, disturbing, intrusive, perturbing, troublesome, troublous, unsettling, upsetting. *See* HAPPY, PAIN.

worry *verb*

1. To cause anxious uneasiness in : ail, cark, concern, distress, trouble. *See* CONCERN. **2.** To disturb by repeated attacks : annoy, bait, bedevil, beleaguer, beset, harass, harry, pester, plague, tease, torment. *See* FEELINGS, PAIN.
3. To focus the attention on something moodily and at length : brood, cark, dwell, fret, mope. *Informal:* stew. *See* CONCERN, THOUGHTS.

worry *noun* **1.** A troubled or anxious state of mind : angst, anxiety, anxiousness, care, concern, disquiet, disquietude, distress, nervousness, solicitude, unease, uneasiness. *See* FEELINGS. **2.** A cause of distress or anxiety : care, concern, trouble. *See* CONCERN.

worrywart *noun*

A prophet of misfortune or disaster : Cassandra, doomsayer, pessimist. *See* HOPE.

worsen *verb*

To become lower in quality, character, or condition : atrophy, decline, degenerate, descend, deteriorate, retrograde, sink. ***Idioms:*** go bad, go to pot, go to seed, go to the dogs. *See* BETTER.

worship *noun*

1. The act of adoring, especially reverently : adoration, idolization, reverence, veneration. *See* LIKE, LOVE, SACRED. **2.** Deep and ardent affection : adoration, devotion, love. *See* LIKE, LOVE.

worship *verb* **1.** To regard with great awe and devotion : adore, idolize, revere, reverence, venerate. *See* SACRED. **2.** To feel deep devoted love for : adore, love. *See* LOVE.

worshipful *adjective*

Feeling or showing reverence : reverent, reverential, venerational. *See* RESPECT.

worst *verb*

To win a victory over, as in battle or a competition : beat, best, conquer, defeat, master, overcome, prevail against (*or* over), rout, subdue, subjugate, surmount, triumph over, vanquish. *Informal:* trim, whip. *Slang:* ace, lick. ***Idioms:*** carry (*or* win) the day, get (*or* have) the best of, get (*or* have) the better of, go someone one better. *See* WIN.

worth *noun*

1. A measure of those qualities that determine merit, desirability, usefulness, or importance : account, valuation, value. *See* VALUE. **2.** A level of superiority that is usually high : caliber, merit, quality, stature, value, virtue. *See* GOOD, VALUE.

worthiness *noun*

The quality or state of being eligible : eligibility, fitness, qualification, suitability, suitableness. *See* ABILITY.

worthless *adjective*

1. Lacking all worth and value : drossy, good-for-nothing, inutile, no-good, nothing, valueless. *Informal:* no-account. *See* VALUE. **2.** Having no useful purpose : ineffectual, inutile, unusable, useless. *See* USED.

worthy *adjective*

1. Of great value : costly, inestimable, invaluable, precious, priceless, valuable. ***Idioms:*** beyond price, of great price. *See* VALUE.
2. Deserving honor, respect, or admiration : admirable, commendable, creditable, deserving, estimable, exemplary, honorable, laudable, meritorious, praiseworthy, reputable, respectable. *See* GOOD, PRAISE, RESPECT, VALUE.
3. Satisfying certain requirements, as for selection : eligible, fit[1], fitted, qualified, suitable. *See* ABILITY.

wound *noun*

1. Marked tissue damage, especially when produced by physical injury : trauma, traumatism. *See* HELP. **2.** A state of physical or mental suffering : affliction, agony, anguish, distress, hurt, misery, pain, torment, torture, woe, wretchedness. *See* HAPPY.

wound *verb* **1.** To cause physical damage to : hurt, injure. *See* HELP. **2.** To inflict physical or mental injury or distress on : shock[1], traumatize. *See* HELP. **3.** To cause suffering or painful sorrow to : aggrieve, distress, grieve, hurt, injure, pain. *See* HAPPY.

wow *noun*
Informal. A dazzling, often sudden instance of success : hit, sleeper. *Informal:* smash, smash hit, ten-strike. *Slang:* boff, boffo, boffola. *See* THRIVE.

wrack[1] *noun*
The act of destroying or state of being destroyed : bane, destruction, devastation, havoc, ruin, ruination, undoing, wreck, wreckage. *See* HELP, LEFTOVER.

wrack[2] *noun*
The remains of something destroyed, disintegrated, or decayed : debris, rubble, ruin, wreck, wreckage. *See* LEFTOVER.
wrack *verb* To cause the complete ruin or wreckage of : bankrupt, break down, cross up, demolish, destroy, finish, ruin, shatter, sink, smash, spoil, torpedo, undo, wash up, wreck. *Slang:* total. ***Idiom:*** put the kibosh on. *See* HELP.

wraith *noun*
A supernatural being, such as a ghost : apparition, bogey, bogeyman, bogle, eidolon, ghost, phantasm, phantasma, phantom, revenant, shade, shadow, specter, spirit, visitant. *Informal:* spook. *Regional:* haunt. *See* BEINGS, SUPERNATURAL.

wrangle *verb*
1. To quarrel noisily : brawl, broil[2], caterwaul, row[2]. *See* ATTACK. **2.** To engage in a quarrel : argue, bicker, contend, dispute, fight, quarrel, quibble, spat, squabble, tiff. *Informal:* hassle, tangle. ***Idioms:*** cross swords, have it out, have words, lock horns. *See* CONFLICT.
wrangle *noun* A discussion, often heated, in which a difference of opinion is expressed : altercation, argument, bicker, clash, contention, controversy, debate, difficulty, disagreement, dispute, fight, polemic, quarrel, run-in, spat, squabble, tiff, word (used in plural). *Informal:* hassle, rhubarb, tangle. *See* CONFLICT.

wrap *verb*
1. To cover completely and closely, as with clothing or bandages : enfold, envelop, enwrap, infold, invest, roll, swaddle, swathe, wrap up. *See* PUT ON. **2.** To put on warm clothes : bundle up, wrap up. *See* PUT ON. **3.** To cover and tie (something), as with paper and string : do up, package. *See* PUT ON. **4.** To surround and cover completely so as to obscure : cloak, clothe, enfold, enshroud, envelop, enwrap, infold, invest, shroud, veil. *See* SHOW.
wrap up *verb* **1.** To cover completely and closely, as with clothing or bandages : enfold, envelop, enwrap, infold, invest, roll, swaddle, swathe, wrap. *See* PUT ON. **2.** To put on warm clothes : bundle up, wrap. *See* PUT ON. **3.** To bring or come to a natural or proper end : close, complete, conclude, consummate, end, finish, terminate, wind up. *See* START.
wrap *noun* **1.** A garment wrapped about a person : cloak, shawl, stole. *See* PUT ON. **2.** The material in which something is wrapped : wrapper, wrapping (also used in plural). *See* PUT ON.

wrapper *noun*
The material in which something is wrapped : wrap, wrapping (also used in plural). *See* PUT ON.

wrapping *noun*
The material in which something is wrapped. Also used in plural : wrap, wrapper. *See* PUT ON.

wrap-up *noun*
1. A condensation of the essential or main points of something : recapitulation, rundown, run-through, sum, summary, summation, summing-up. *Informal:* recap. *See* WORDS. **2.** A concluding or terminating : cease, cessation, close, closing, closure, completion, conclusion, consummation, end, ending, end of the line, finish, period, stop, stopping point, termination, terminus, wind-up. *See* CONTINUE. **3.** The last part : close, conclusion, end, ending, finale, finish, last[1], termination, wind-up. *See* START.

wrap up *verb* See **wrap.**

wrath *noun*
Violent or unrestrained anger : furor, fury, irateness, ire, rage, wrathfulness. *See* FEELINGS.

wrathful *adjective*
Full of or marked by extreme anger : furious, irate, ireful, rabid. ***Idioms:*** fit to be tied, foaming at the mouth, in a rage (*or* temper), in a towering rage. *See* FEELINGS.

wrathfulness *noun*
Violent or unrestrained anger : furor, fury, irateness, ire, rage, wrath. *See* FEELINGS.

wreak *verb*
1. To cause to undergo or bear (something unwelcome or damaging, for example) : impose, inflict, play, visit. *See* GIVE, OVER, WILLING. **2.** *Archaic.* To exact revenge for or from : avenge, pay back, pay off, redress, repay, requite, vindicate. *Informal:* fix. ***Idioms:*** even the score, get back at, get even with, pay

back in kind (*or* in one's own coin), settle (*or* square) accounts, take an eye for an eye. *See* FORGIVENESS.

wreathe *verb*
To move or proceed on a repeatedly curving course : coil, corkscrew, curl, entwine, meander, snake, spiral, twine, twist, weave, wind[2]. *See* REPETITION, STRAIGHT.

wreck *noun*
1. The act of destroying or state of being destroyed : bane, destruction, devastation, havoc, ruin, ruination, undoing, wrack[1], wreckage. *See* HELP, LEFTOVER. **2.** A wrecking of a vehicle : crash, smash, smashup. *Informal:* crackup, pileup. *See* HELP. **3.** An abrupt disastrous failure : breakdown, collapse, crash, debacle, smash, smashup. *See* MONEY. **4.** The remains of something destroyed, disintegrated, or decayed : debris, rubble, ruin, wrack[2], wreckage. *See* LEFTOVER.

wreck *verb* **1.** To damage, disable, or destroy (a seacraft) : shipwreck. *See* HELP. **2.** To cause the complete ruin or wreckage of : bankrupt, break down, cross up, demolish, destroy, finish, ruin, shatter, sink, smash, spoil, torpedo, undo, wash up, wrack[2]. *Slang:* total. ***Idiom:*** put the kibosh on. *See* HELP. **3.** To pull down or break up so that reconstruction is impossible : demolish, destroy, dismantle, dynamite, knock down, level, pull down, pulverize, raze, tear down. *Aerospace:* destruct. *See* HELP.

wreckage *noun*
1. An act, instance, or consequence of breaking : breakage, damage, destruction, impairment. *See* HELP. **2.** The act of destroying or state of being destroyed : bane, destruction, devastation, havoc, ruin, ruination, undoing, wrack[1], wreck. *See* HELP, LEFTOVER. **3.** The remains of something destroyed, disintegrated, or decayed : debris, rubble, ruin, wrack[2], wreck. *See* LEFTOVER.

wrecker *noun*
Something that causes total loss or severe impairment, as of one's health, fortune, honor, or hopes : bane, destroyer, destruction, downfall, ruin, ruination, undoing. *See* HELP.

wrench *noun*
1. A sudden motion, such as a pull : jerk, lurch, snap, tug, twitch, yank. *See* MOVE, PUSH. **2.** A tool with jaws for gripping and twisting : *Chiefly British:* spanner. *See* MACHINE.

wrench *verb* **1.** To injure a (bodily part) by twisting : sprain, turn. *See* HEALTH. **2.** To move or cause to move with a sudden abrupt motion : jerk, lurch, snap, twitch, yank. *See* MOVE, PUSH. **3.** To alter the position of by a sharp, forcible twisting or turning movement : wrest, wring. *See* MOVE. **4.** To obtain by coercion or intimidation : exact, extort, squeeze, wrest, wring. *Slang:* shake down. *See* GET. **5.** To give an inaccurate view of by representing falsely or misleadingly : belie, color, distort, falsify, load, misrepresent, misstate, pervert, twist, warp, wrest. ***Idiom:*** give a false coloring to. *See* TRUE.

wrest *verb*
1. To alter the position of by a sharp, forcible twisting or turning movement : wrench, wring. *See* MOVE. **2.** To obtain by coercion or intimidation : exact, extort, squeeze, wrench, wring. *Slang:* shake down. *See* GET. **3.** To give an inaccurate view of by representing falsely or misleadingly : belie, color, distort, falsify, load, misrepresent, misstate, pervert, twist, warp, wrench. ***Idiom:*** give a false coloring to. *See* TRUE.

wrestle *verb*
1. To contend with an opponent at close quarters, as by attempting to throw him or her : grapple, scuffle, tussle. ***Idiom:*** go to the mat with. *See* CONFLICT, TOUCH. **2.** To strive in opposition : battle, combat, contend, duel, fight, struggle, tilt, war. *See* CONFLICT.

wretch *noun*
A person living under very unhappy circumstances : loser, miserable, underdog, underprivileged, unfortunate. *See* RICH.

wretched *adjective*
1. So objectionable as to elicit despisal or deserve condemnation : abhorrent, abominable, antipathetic, contemptible, despicable, despisable, detestable, disgusting, filthy, foul, infamous, loathsome, lousy, low, mean[2], nasty, nefarious, obnoxious, odious, repugnant, rotten, shabby, vile. *See* GOOD. **2.** Suffering from usually prolonged anguish : miserable, woebegone, woeful. *See* HAPPY. **3.** Having a painful ailment : afflicted, miserable, suffering. *See* HAPPY.

wretchedness *noun*
1. A state of physical or mental suffering : affliction, agony, anguish, distress, hurt, misery, pain, torment, torture, woe, wound. *See* HAPPY. **2.** A state of prolonged anguish and privation : misery, suffering, woe. *See* HAPPY.

wriggle *verb*
To move or proceed with short irregular

motions up and down or from side to side : squiggle, squirm, waggle, wiggle, worm, writhe. *See* MOVE, REPETITION.

wring *verb*
1. To alter the position of by a sharp, forcible twisting or turning movement : wrench, wrest. *See* MOVE. **2.** To obtain by coercion or intimidation : exact, extort, squeeze, wrench, wrest. *Slang:* shake down. *See* GET.

wrinkle *noun*
1. A line or an arrangement made by the doubling of one part over another : crease, crimp, crinkle, crumple, fold, pleat, plica, plication, pucker, rimple, ruck[2], rumple. *See* SMOOTH. **2.** An indentation or seam on the skin, especially on the face : crease, crinkle, furrow, line. *See* SMOOTH. **3.** *Informal.* A clever, unexpected new trick or method : gimmick, twist. *Informal:* kicker. *Slang:* angle[2], kick. *See* ABILITY, EXCITE, GOOD.

wrinkle *verb* To make irregular folds in, especially by pressing or twisting : crease, crimp, crinkle, crumple, rimple, rumple. *See* SMOOTH.

write *verb*
1. To form letters, characters, or words on a surface with an instrument : engross, indite, inscribe, scribe. *See* REMEMBER. **2.** To form by artistic effort : compose, create, indite, produce. *See* MAKE. **3.** To be the author of (a published work or works) : pen[1], publish. *See* WORDS.

write down *verb* **1.** To register in or as if in a book : book, catalog, enroll, inscribe, list[1], set down. *See* REMEMBER. **2.** To become or make less in price or value : cheapen, depreciate, depress, devaluate, devalue, downgrade, lower[2], mark down, reduce. *See* INCREASE, MONEY.

write-down *noun*
A lowering in price or value : depreciation, devaluation, markdown, reduction. *See* INCREASE, MONEY.

write down *verb* See **write.**

writhe *verb*
1. To twist and turn, as in pain, struggle, or embarrassment : agonize, squirm, toss, turn. *See* REPETITION. **2.** To move or proceed with short irregular motions up and down or from side to side : squiggle, squirm, waggle, wiggle, worm, wriggle. *See* MOVE, REPETITION.

written *adjective*
Of or relating to representation by means of writing : calligraphic, graphic, scriptural. *See* WORDS.

wrong *adjective*
1. Containing an error or errors : erroneous, fallacious, false, inaccurate, incorrect, mistaken, off, unsound, untrue. ***Idioms:*** all wet, in error, off base, off (*or* wide of) the mark. *See* CORRECT. **2.** Devoid of truth : counterfactual, false, specious, spurious, truthless, untrue, untruthful. *See* TRUE. **3.** Morally objectionable : bad, black, evil, immoral, iniquitous, peccant, reprobate, sinful, vicious, wicked. *See* RIGHT. **4.** Not in accordance with what is usual or expected : amiss, astray, awry, sour. *See* SURPRISE, THRIVE. **5.** Afflicted with or exhibiting irrationality and mental unsoundness : brainsick, crazy, daft, demented, disordered, distraught, dotty, insane, lunatic, mad, maniac, maniacal, mentally ill, moonstruck, off, touched, unbalanced, unsound. *Informal:* bonkers, cracked, daffy, gaga, loony. *Slang:* bananas, batty, buggy, cuckoo, fruity, loco, nuts, nutty, screwy, wacky. *Chiefly British:* crackers. *Law:* non compos mentis. ***Idioms:*** around the bend, crazy as a loon, mad as a hatter, not all there, nutty as a fruitcake, off (*or* out of) one's head, off one's rocker, of unsound mind, out of one's mind, sick in the head, stark raving mad. *See* SANE.

wrong *adverb* Not in the right way or on the proper course : afield, amiss, astray, awry. *See* THRIVE.

wrong *noun* **1.** A wicked act or wicked behavior : crime, deviltry, diablerie, evil, evildoing, immorality, iniquity, misdeed, offense, peccancy, sin, wickedness, wrongdoing. *See* RIGHT. **2.** That which is morally bad or objectionable : evil, iniquity, peccancy, sin, wickedness. *See* RIGHT. **3.** Lack of justice : inequity, iniquity, injustice, unfairness, unjustness. *See* LAW, RIGHT. **4.** An act that is not just : disservice, inequity, injustice, raw deal. *Law:* injury. *See* LAW, RIGHT.

wrong *verb* To do a wrong to; treat unjustly : aggrieve, oppress, outrage, persecute. *See* RIGHT.

wrongdoing *noun*
1. A wicked act or wicked behavior : crime, deviltry, diablerie, evil, evildoing, immorality, iniquity, misdeed, offense, peccancy, sin, wickedness, wrong. *See* RIGHT. **2.** Improper, often rude behavior : horseplay, misbehavior, misconduct, misdoing, naughtiness. *See* GOOD.

wrongful *adjective*
1. Prohibited by law : illegal, illegitimate,

illicit, lawless, outlawed, unlawful. *See* CRIMES, LAW. **2.** Of, involving, or being a crime : criminal, illegal, illegitimate, illicit, lawless, unlawful. *See* CRIMES.

wry *adjective*
Marked by or displaying contemptuous mockery of the motives or virtues of others : cynic, cynical, ironic, ironical, sardonic. *See* ATTITUDE, RESPECT.

·XYZ·

x *verb*
To remove or invalidate by or as if by running a line through or wiping clean. Also used with *out* : annul, blot (out), cancel, cross (off *or* out), delete, efface, erase, expunge, obliterate, rub (out), scratch (out), strike (out), undo, wipe (out). *Law:* vacate. *See* CONTINUE.

yahoo *noun*
An unrefined, rude person : barbarian, boor, chuff, churl, Philistine, vulgarian. *See* GOOD.

yak *verb*
Slang. To talk volubly, persistently, and usually inconsequentially : babble, blabber, chatter, chitchat, clack, jabber, palaver, prate, prattle, rattle (on), run on. *Informal:* go on, spiel. *Slang:* gab, gas, jaw. ***Idioms:*** run off at the mouth, shoot the breeze (*or* bull). *See* WORDS.
yak *noun Slang.* Incessant and usually inconsequential talk : babble, blab, blabber, chat, chatter, chitchat, jabber, palaver, prate, prattle, small talk. *Slang:* gab, gas. *See* WORDS.

yank *verb*
To move or cause to move with a sudden abrupt motion : jerk, lurch, snap, twitch, wrench. *See* MOVE, PUSH.
yank *noun* A sudden motion, such as a pull : jerk, lurch, snap, tug, twitch, wrench. *See* MOVE, PUSH.

yap *verb*
To utter a shrill, short cry : squeal, yawp, yelp, yip. *See* SOUNDS.
yap *noun* A shrill, short cry : squeal, yawp, yelp, yip. *See* SOUNDS.

yard *noun*
An area partially or entirely enclosed by walls or buildings : atrium, close, court, courtyard, enclosure, quad, quadrangle. *See* PLACE.

yardstick *noun*
A means by which individuals are compared and judged : benchmark, criterion, gauge, mark, measure, standard, test, touchstone. *See* USUAL.

yarn *noun*
Informal. An entertaining and often oral account of a real or fictitious occurrence : anecdote, fable, story, tale. *Informal:* tall tale. *See* WORDS.

yaup *verb & noun* See **yawp.**

yaw *verb*
1. *Nautical.* To turn aside sharply from a straight course : chop[2], cut, sheer[1], skew, slue[1], swerve, veer. *See* CHANGE. **2.** To lean suddenly, unsteadily, and erratically from the vertical axis : lurch, pitch, roll, seesaw. *See* MOVE, STRAIGHT.

yawn *verb*
1. To open the mouth wide with a deep inward breath, as when tired or bored : gape. *See* MOUTH. **2.** To open wide : gap, gape. *See* WIDE.

yawning *adjective*
Open wide : abysmal, abyssal, cavernous, gaping. *See* WIDE.

yawp also **yaup** *verb*
1. To utter a shrill, short cry : squeal, yap, yelp, yip. *See* SOUNDS. **2.** To speak or say very loudly or with a shout : bawl, bellow, bluster, call, clamor, cry, halloo, holler, roar, shout, vociferate, whoop, yell. *See* SOUNDS.
yawp also **yaup** *noun* A shrill, short cry : squeal, yap, yelp, yip. *See* SOUNDS.

yea *adverb*
It is so; as you say or ask : absolutely, agreed, all right, assuredly, aye, gladly, indubitably, roger, undoubtedly, unquestionably, willingly, yes. *Informal:* OK, uh-huh, yeah, yep. *Slang:* right on. *See* AFFIRM.
yea *noun* An affirmative vote or voter : aye, yes. *See* AFFIRM.

yeah *adverb*
Informal. It is so; as you say or ask : abso-

lutely, agreed, all right, assuredly, aye, gladly, indubitably, roger, undoubtedly, unquestionably, willingly, yea, yes. *Informal:* OK, uh-huh, yep. *Slang:* right on. *See* AFFIRM.

year *noun*
1. A period of time of approximately 12 months, especially that period during which the earth completes a single revolution around the sun : twelvemonth. *See* TIME. **2.** A period of origin : *Informal:* vintage. *See* TIME. **3.** Old age. Used in plural : age, agedness, elderliness, senectitude, senescence. *See* YOUTH. **4.** A long time. Used in plural : eon, eternity, long[1]. *Informal:* age (used in plural), blue moon. ***Idioms:*** forever and a day, forever and ever, month of Sundays. *See* TIME.

yearn *verb*
1. To have a strong longing for : ache, covet, desire, hanker, long[2], pant, pine, want, wish. *Informal:* hone[2]. *See* DESIRE. **2.** To experience or express compassion : ache, commiserate, compassionate, feel, pity, sympathize. ***Idioms:*** be sorry, have (*or* take) pity. *See* PITY.

yearning *noun*
A strong wanting of what promises enjoyment or pleasure : appetence, appetency, appetite, craving, desire, hunger, itch, longing, lust, thirst, wish, yen. *See* DESIRE.

yeast *noun*
1. A mass of bubbles in or on the surface of a liquid : foam, froth, head, lather, spume, suds. *See* SOLID. **2.** An agent that stimulates or precipitates a reaction, development, or change : catalyst, ferment, leaven, leavening. *See* CHANGE.
yeast *verb* To form or cause to form foam : bubble, cream, effervesce, fizz, foam, froth, lather, spume, suds. *See* SOLID.

yeasty *adjective*
Consisting of or resembling foam : foamy, frothy, lathery, spumous, spumy, sudsy. *See* SOLID.

yell *verb*
To speak or say very loudly or with a shout : bawl, bellow, bluster, call, clamor, cry, halloo, holler, roar, shout, vociferate, whoop, yawp. *See* SOUNDS.
yell *noun* A loud cry : call, halloo, holler, shout. *See* SOUNDS.

yellow *adjective*
Slang. Ignobly lacking in courage : chicken-hearted, cowardly, craven, dastardly, faint-hearted, lily-livered, pusillanimous, unmanly. *Slang:* chicken, gutless, yellow-bellied. *See* FEAR.

yellow-bellied *adjective*
Slang. Ignobly lacking in courage : chicken-hearted, cowardly, craven, dastardly, faint-hearted, lily-livered, pusillanimous, unmanly. *Slang:* chicken, gutless, yellow. *See* FEAR.

yellow-belly *noun*
Slang. An ignoble, uncourageous person : coward, craven, dastard, funk, poltroon. *Slang:* chicken. *See* FEAR.

yellowness *noun*
Slang. Ignoble lack of courage : chickenheartedness, cowardice, cowardliness, cravenness, dastardliness, faint-heartedness, funk, pusillanimity, unmanliness. *Slang:* gutlessness, yellow streak. *See* FEAR.

yellow streak *noun*
Slang. Ignoble lack of courage : chickenheartedness, cowardice, cowardliness, cravenness, dastardliness, faint-heartedness, funk, pusillanimity, unmanliness. *Slang:* gutlessness, yellowness. *See* FEAR.

yelp *verb*
To utter a shrill, short cry : squeal, yap, yawp, yip. *See* SOUNDS.
yelp *noun* A shrill, short cry : squeal, yap, yawp, yip. *See* SOUNDS.

yen *noun*
A strong wanting of what promises enjoyment or pleasure : appetence, appetency, appetite, craving, desire, hunger, itch, longing, lust, thirst, wish, yearning. *See* DESIRE.

yenta *noun*
Slang. A person habitually engaged in idle talk about others : blab, gossip, gossiper, gossipmonger, newsmonger, rumormonger, scandalmonger, tabby, talebearer, taleteller, tattle, tattler, tattletale, telltale, whisperer. *See* WORDS.

yep *adverb*
Informal. It is so; as you say or ask : absolutely, agreed, all right, assuredly, aye, gladly, indubitably, roger, undoubtedly, unquestionably, willingly, yea, yes. *Informal:* OK, uh-huh, yeah. *Slang:* right on. *See* AFFIRM.

yes *adverb*
It is so; as you say or ask : absolutely, agreed, all right, assuredly, aye, gladly, indubitably, roger, undoubtedly, unquestionably, willingly, yea. *Informal:* OK, uh-huh, yeah, yep. *Slang:* right on. *See* AFFIRM.
yes *noun* **1.** The act or process of accepting : acceptance, acquiescence, agreement, assent, consent, nod. *Informal:* OK. *See* ACCEPT. **2.** An affirmative vote or voter : aye, yea. *See* AFFIRM.

yes *verb* To respond affirmatively; receive with agreement or compliance : accede, accept, acquiesce, agree, assent, consent, nod, subscribe. *See* AGREE.

yesterday *noun*
A former period of time or of one's life : past, yesteryear, yore. ***Idioms:*** bygone days, days gone by, the good old days, the old days. *See* TIME.

yesteryear *noun*
A former period of time or of one's life : past, yesterday, yore. ***Idioms:*** bygone days, days gone by, the good old days, the old days. *See* TIME.

yet *adverb*
1. Up to this time : before, earlier, heretofore, previously. *See* PRECEDE. **2.** In addition : additionally, also, besides, further, furthermore, item, likewise, more, moreover, still, too. ***Idioms:*** as well, to boot. *See* INCREASE. **3.** To a more extreme degree : even[1], still. *See* BIG. **4.** In spite of a preceding event or consideration : all the same, however, nevertheless, nonetheless, still. *Informal:* still and all. ***Idiom:*** be that as it may. *See* AFFIRM.

yield *verb*
1. To bring forth (a product) : bear, give, produce. *See* RICH. **2.** To make as income or profit : bring in, clear, draw, earn, gain, gross, net[2], pay, produce, realize, repay, return. *See* MONEY. **3.** To let (something) go : abandon, cede, forgo, lay down, relinquish, surrender. *See* KEEP. **4.** To give up a possession, claim, or right : abandon, abdicate, cede, demit, forswear, hand over, quitclaim, relinquish, render, renounce, resign, surrender, waive. *See* KEEP. **5.** To cease opposition : concede, give in. *See* WIN. **6.** To give in from or as if from a gradual loss of strength : bow[1], buckle, capitulate, submit, succumb, surrender. *Informal:* fold. *See* RESIST. **7.** To conform to the will or judgment of another, especially out of respect or courtesy : bow[1], defer[2], submit. ***Idioms:*** give ground, give way. *See* PRECEDE, RESIST. **8.** To moderate or change a position or course of action as a result of pressure : ease off, relent, slacken, soften, weaken. ***Idiom:*** give way (*or* ground). *See* STRONG.

yield *noun* **1.** The amount or quantity produced : output, production. *See* BIG. **2.** The produce harvested from the land : crop, fruit, fruitage, harvest. *See* INGESTION.

yielding *adjective*
Yielding easily to pressure or weight; not firm : mushy, pappy[1], pulpous, pulpy, quaggy, soft, spongy, squashy, squishy. *See* RESIST.

yip *noun*
A shrill, short cry : squeal, yap, yawp, yelp. *See* SOUNDS.

yip *verb* To utter a shrill, short cry : squeal, yap, yawp, yelp. *See* SOUNDS.

yoke *noun*
1. Two items of the same kind together : brace, couple, couplet, doublet, duet, duo, match, pair, two, twosome. *See* GROUP, SAME. **2.** That which unites or binds : bond, knot, ligament, ligature, link, nexus, tie, vinculum. *See* CONNECT. **3.** A state of subjugation to an owner or master : bondage, enslavement, helotry, serfdom, servileness, servility, servitude, slavery, thrall, thralldom, villeinage. *See* OVER.

yoke *verb* To bring or come together into a united whole : coalesce, combine, compound, concrete, conjoin, conjugate, connect, consolidate, couple, join, link, marry, meld, unify, unite, wed. *See* ASSEMBLE.

yokel *noun*
A clumsy, unsophisticated person : bumpkin, clodhopper, rustic. *See* ABILITY.

yore *noun*
A former period of time or of one's life : past, yesterday, yesteryear. ***Idioms:*** bygone days, days gone by, the good old days, the old days. *See* TIME.

young *adjective*
Being in an early period of growth or development : green, immature, infant, juvenile, youthful. *See* YOUTH.

young *noun* **1.** Young people collectively : youth. *See* YOUTH. **2.** The offspring, as of an animal or a bird, for example, that are the result of one breeding season : brood, litter. *See* KIN.

youngster *noun*
A young person between birth and puberty : bud[1], child, innocent, juvenile, moppet, tot[1]. *Informal:* kid. *Scots:* bairn. *See* KIN, YOUTH.

youth *noun*
1. The time of life between childhood and maturity : adolescence, greenness, juvenescence, juvenility, puberty, salad days, spring, youthfulness. *See* YOUTH. **2.** A young person, usually between the ages of 13 and 19 : adolescent, teen, teenager. *Informal:* teener. *See* YOUTH. **3.** Young people collectively : young. *See* YOUTH.

youthful *adjective*
Being in an early period of growth or development : green, immature, infant, juvenile, young. *See* YOUTH.

youthfulness *noun*
The time of life between childhood and maturity : adolescence, greenness, juvenescence, juvenility, puberty, salad days, spring, youth. *See* YOUTH.

yowl *verb*
1. To utter or emit a long, mournful, plaintive sound : bay[2], howl, moan, ululate, wail. *See* SOUNDS. **2.** To make inarticulate sounds of grief or pain, usually accompanied by tears : bawl, blubber, cry, howl, keen[2], sob, wail, weep. *See* HAPPY, SOUNDS. **3.** To cry loudly, as a healthy child does from pain or distress : bawl, howl, wail. *See* SOUNDS.
yowl *noun* A long, mournful cry : bay[2], howl, moan, ululation, wail. *See* SOUNDS.

yucky *adjective*
Slang. Not pleasant or agreeable : bad, disagreeable, displeasing, offensive, uncongenial, unpleasant, unsympathetic. *Informal:* icky. *See* GOOD, PAIN.

yummy *adjective*
Slang. Highly pleasing, especially to the sense of taste : ambrosial, appetizing, delectable, delicious, heavenly, luscious, savory, scrumptious, tasteful, tasty, toothsome. *See* GOOD, INGESTION.

zaftig or **zoftig** *adjective*
Well-rounded and full in form : chubby, plump[1], plumpish, pudgy, roly-poly, rotund, round, tubby. *See* FAT.

zaniness *noun*
1. The quality of being laughable or comical : comedy, comicality, comicalness, drollery, drollness, farcicality, funniness, humor, humorousness, jocoseness, jocosity, jocularity, ludicrousness, ridiculousness, wit, wittiness. *See* LAUGHTER. **2.** Foolish behavior : absurdity, folly, foolery, foolishness, idiocy, imbecility, insanity, lunacy, madness, nonsense, preposterousness, senselessness, silliness, tomfoolery. *Informal:* craziness. *See* ABILITY.

zany *noun*
A person whose words or actions provoke or are intended to provoke amusement or laughter : clown, comedian, comic, farceur, funnyman, humorist, jester, joker, jokester, quipster, wag[2], wit. *Informal:* card. *See* LAUGHTER.
zany *adjective* **1.** Arousing laughter : amusing, comic, comical, droll, funny, humorous, laughable, risible. *See* LAUGHTER. **2.** So senseless as to be laughable : absurd, foolish, harebrained, idiotic, imbecilic, insane, lunatic, mad, moronic, nonsensical, preposterous, silly, softheaded, tomfool, unearthly. *Informal:* cockeyed, crazy, loony, loopy. *Slang:* balmy[2], dippy, dopey, jerky, sappy, wacky. *See* ABILITY, KNOWLEDGE.

zap *verb*
1. *Slang.* To cause the death of : carry off, cut down, cut off, destroy, dispatch, finish (off), kill[1], slay. *Slang:* waste. ***Idioms:*** put an end to, put to sleep. *See* HELP. **2.** *Slang.* To take the life of (a person or persons) unlawfully : destroy, finish (off), kill[1], liquidate, murder, slay. *Informal:* put away. *Slang:* bump off, do in, knock off, off, rub out, waste, wipe out. *See* HELP.

zeal *noun*
Passionate devotion to or interest in a cause or subject, for example : ardor, enthusiasm, fervor, fire, passion, zealousness. *See* CONCERN, FEELINGS.

zealot *noun*
1. One zealously devoted to a religion : devotee, enthusiast, fanatic, sectary, votary. *See* BELIEF, LOVE, RELIGION. **2.** A person who is ardently devoted to a particular subject or activity : bug, devotee, enthusiast, fanatic, maniac. *Informal:* buff[2], fan[2], fiend. *Slang:* freak, nut. *See* CONCERN. **3.** One who holds extreme views or advocates extreme measures : extremist, fanatic, radical, revolutionary, revolutionist, ultra. *See* EDGE, CONCERN, POLITICS.

zealous *adjective*
Showing or having enthusiasm : ardent, enthusiastic, fervent, keen[1], mad, rabid, warm. *Informal:* crazy. *Slang:* gung ho, nuts. *See* CONCERN.

zealousness *noun*
Passionate devotion to or interest in a cause or subject, for example : ardor, enthusiasm, fervor, fire, passion, zeal. *See* CONCERN, FEELINGS.

zenith *noun*
The highest point or state : acme, apex, apogee, climax, crest, crown, culmination, height, meridian, peak, pinnacle, summit, top. *Informal:* payoff. *Medicine:* fastigium. *See* HIGH.

zephyr *noun*
1. A gentle wind : breeze. *See* BREATH. **2.** A natural movement or current of air : air, blast, blow[1], breeze, gust, wind[1]. *Archaic:* gale. *See* BREATH.

zero *noun*
1. *Informal.* A totally insignificant person :

cipher, nebbish, nobody, nonentity, nothing. *Informal:* pip-squeak. *Slang:* shrimp, zilch. *See* IMPORTANT. **2.** *Informal.* No thing; not anything : nil, nothing, null. *Slang:* nix, zilch. *Archaic:* aught. *See* ABSENCE.

zero in *verb* To move (a weapon or blow, for example) in the direction of someone or something : aim, cast, direct, head, level, point, set¹, train, turn. *Military:* lay¹. *See* SEEK.

zero hour *noun*
A decisive point : climacteric, crisis, crossroad (used in plural), exigence, exigency, head, juncture, pass, turning point. *See* DECIDE.

zero in *verb* See **zero.**

zest *noun*
1. A distinctive property of a substance affecting the gustatory sense : flavor, relish, sapor, savor, smack², tang, taste. *See* TASTE. **2.** Spirited enjoyment : gusto, relish. *See* PAIN.

zesty *adjective*
Affecting the organs of taste or smell with a strong and often harsh sensation : piquant, pungent, sharp, spicy. *Archaic:* poignant. *See* SMELLS, TASTE.

zigzag *verb*
To move in a zigzag manner, as on a ski slope : traverse. *See* MOVE, RISE.

zilch *noun*
1. *Slang.* No thing; not anything : nil, nothing, null. *Informal:* zero. *Slang:* nix. *Archaic:* aught. *See* ABSENCE. **2.** *Slang.* A totally insignificant person : cipher, nebbish, nobody, nonentity, nothing. *Informal:* pip-squeak, zero. *Slang:* shrimp. *See* IMPORTANT.

zillion *noun*
Informal. An indeterminately great amount or number : jillion, million (often used in plural), multiplicity, ream, trillion. *Informal:* bushel, gob¹ (often used in plural), heap (often used in plural), load (often used in plural), lot, oodles, passel, peck², scad (often used in plural), slew, wad. *See* BIG.

zip *noun*
1. *Informal.* Capacity or power for work or vigorous activity : animation, energy, force, might, potency, power, puissance, sprightliness, steam, strength. *Informal:* get-up-and-go, go, pep, peppiness. *See* ACTION. **2.** A lively, emphatic, eager quality or manner : animation, bounce, brio, dash, élan, esprit, life, liveliness, pertness, sparkle, spirit, verve, vigor, vim, vivaciousness, vivacity. *Informal:* ginger, pep, peppiness. *Slang:* oomph. *See* ACTION.

zip *verb* **1.** To move swiftly and effortlessly : *Informal:* breeze. *Slang:* waltz. *See* EASY. **2.** To move swiftly : bolt, bucket, bustle, dart, dash, festinate, flash, fleet, flit, fly, haste, hasten, hurry, hustle, pelt², race, rocket, run, rush, sail, scoot, scour², shoot, speed, sprint, tear¹, trot, whirl, whisk, whiz, wing, zoom. *Informal:* hotfoot, rip. *Slang:* barrel, highball. *Chiefly British:* nip¹. ***Idioms:*** get a move on, get cracking, go like lightning, go like the wind, hotfoot it, make haste, make time, make tracks, run like the wind, shake a leg, step (*or* jump) on it. *See* MOVE.

zippy *adjective*
Disposed to action : active, brisk, driving, dynamic, dynamical, energetic, enterprising, lively, sprightly, spry, vigorous. *Informal:* peppy, snappy. *See* ACTION.

zoftig *adjective* See **zaftig.**

zone *noun*
A part of the earth's surface : area, belt, district, locality, neighborhood, quarter, region, tract. *Informal:* neck of the woods. *See* TERRITORY.

zonked *adjective*
1. *Slang.* Stupefied, intoxicated, or otherwise influenced by the taking of drugs : drugged. *Informal:* doped. *Slang:* high, hopped-up, lit (up), potted, spaced-out, stoned, turned-on, wiped-out. *See* DRUGS. **2.** *Slang.* Stupefied, excited, or muddled with alcoholic liquor : besotted, crapulent, crapulous, drunk, drunken, inebriate, inebriated, intoxicated, sodden, tipsy. *Informal:* cock-eyed, stewed. *Slang:* blind, bombed, boozed, boozy, crocked, high, lit (up), loaded, looped, pickled, pixilated, plastered, potted, sloshed, smashed, soused, stinking, stinko, stoned, tight. ***Idioms:*** drunk as a skunk, half-seas over, high as a kite, in one's cups, three sheets in (*or* to) the wind. *See* DRUGS.

zoom *verb*
To move swiftly : bolt, bucket, bustle, dart, dash, festinate, flash, fleet, flit, fly, haste, hasten, hurry, hustle, pelt², race, rocket, run, rush, sail, scoot, scour², shoot, speed, sprint, tear¹, trot, whirl, whisk, whiz, wing, zip. *Informal:* hotfoot, rip. *Slang:* barrel, highball. *Chiefly British:* nip¹. ***Idioms:*** get a move on, get cracking, go like lightning, go like the wind, hotfoot it, make haste, make time, make tracks, run like the wind, shake a leg, step (*or* jump) on it. *See* MOVE.

INTRODUCTION TO THE CATEGORY INDEX

The Category Index is designed to take the user from a synonym paragraph in the main body of the thesaurus to related words and words of opposite meaning elsewhere in the thesaurus. A category reference, which appears at the end of every synonym paragraph, leads from the main text to the Category Index.

> **favorite** *adjective*
> **1.** Being a favorite : favored, popular, preferred, well-liked. *See* LIKE. **2.** Given special, usually doting treatment : darling, fair-haired, favored, pet[1]. *See* TREAT WELL.

The category reference LIKE is a direction to turn to the entry **like** in the Category Index.

LIKE
dislike

like	**dislike**
noun	*noun*
admirer	disapproval
attraction	disgust
bent	dislike
bias	drip
delight	imposition
favorite	offense
liking	prejudice
lure	
public	*See also*
taste	desire
adjective	excite
agreeable	happy
attractive	likely
biased	love
delightful	praise

The lists of entries in the Category Index, such as the one at **like**, contain words related to the word looked up, in this case *favorite.* These related words are divided into groups by part of speech. In this list are found such words as the nouns *admirer, attraction,* and *bias* and the adjectives *agreeable, attractive,* and *biased.* These words are cross-references directing the reader back to entries in the thesaurus. At the entry for the adjective *agreeable,* for example, the user finds the group of synonyms for *agreeable* that ends with the category reference LIKE and searches through such synonyms as *congenial* and *good* to see if that list contains the desired word.

Most category references list two words as headwords, the second being opposite or contrastive in meaning to the first word, as with **like, dislike.** Under **dislike** appear words of opposite meaning grouped by part of speech. Looking up the entry for the noun *dislike* in the thesaurus the user finds the synonyms *disinclination, disrelish, distaste,* and *mislike.*

One or more additional headwords sometimes appear. For example in some cases there are three groups of words, the third group consisting of words that are neutral in meaning. At *excess* for example we find the headwords

EXCESS
insufficiency
enough

The group of words under **enough** are neutral in meaning.

Another type of headword group appears at **smells,** where the headword **smells** is followed by **good smells, bad smells** and **smell.**

Finally, many lists occur with only one headword, such as occurs at the headword **words.** Only a single undifferentiated list of words appears at such an entry.

In some cases more than one meaning of a thesaurus entry appears at the same entry and part of speech in the Category Index. This is indicated by a number enclosed in parentheses. For example at **sounds** *noun* is found

hearing (3)

This means that the entry for the noun *hearing* in the thesaurus contains three meanings with three different synonym lists that fit in the category **sounds.**

To offer the user even more choices most entries in the Category Index close with one or more cross-references to entries in the Category Index where more related words will be found. For example **like** as shown above offers the cross-references **desire, excite, happy, love,** and **praise.**

The Category Index opens up the thesaurus, offering many more choices than does the traditional alphabetical thesaurus.

ABILITY
inability

ability
noun
ability (2)
agility
comer
common sense
dexterity
discernment
expert
faculty
fluency
forte
grasp
hang
intelligence
invention
ken
mind
qualification
resilience
resource
tact
talent
trick
veteran
wrinkle

adjective
able
accomplished
artful
clever
delicate
dexterous
eligible
equal
experienced
expert
gifted
good
intelligent
inventive
methodical
neat
nimble
resourceful
shrewd
versatile

inability
noun
amateur
blunderer
clodhopper
dreamer
dullard
fool
foolishness
inability
inexperience
lump[1]

adjective
absent-minded
amateurish
artful
awkward
backward
doctrinaire
foolish
giddy
helpless
inadequate
incompetent
ineffectual
inefficient
inexperienced
mindless
stupid
tactless
through
unfit
unfortunate
unskillful
untried

verb
blunder
unfit

See also
awareness
industrious
means
wise

ABSENCE

noun
absence
nothing
nothingness

adjective
absent

pronoun
nobody

See also
accompanied
full

ACCEPT
reject

accept
noun
absorption
acceptance (2)
admission
adoption
initiation
openness
patience
tolerance

adjective
acceptable
accepted
patient
receptive
tolerant

verb
absorb
accept (2)
adopt
assume
confirm
endure
follow
initiate
pass
receive
reconcile

reject
noun
exile
refusal
retraction
snub

adjective
impatient
intolerant
nice

verb
banish
blackball
decline
refuse
repudiate
retract
snub
veto

See also
affirm
agree
forgiveness
give
keep
offer
request
resist

ACCOMPANIED

noun
accompaniment (2)
company

adjective
accompanying

verb
accompany
bring

adverb
together (2)

See also
absence
assemble

ACTION
inaction

action
noun
act
acting
activity
actor
behavior
bit[1]
business (2)
drive (2)
energy
feat
fuss
move
response
spirit
vigor

adjective
active
busy
energetic
lively
rough
spirited

(cont.)

ACTION *(cont.)*

action
vigorous

verb
act
activate
busy
establish
function
fuss
respond
shoot
tie up

inaction
noun
abeyance
inaction
lethargy

adjective
inactive
languid
latent
lazy
lethargic

verb
cancel

See also
attitude
awareness
continue
do
feelings
move
repetition
start
strong
thrive
time
tired
work

AFFECT
ineffectiveness

affect
noun
bias
effect
guidance
heritage
hold
impact
influence
wallop

adjective
influential
insensitive

verb
bias
dispose
nonplus
overwhelm
paralyze

ineffectiveness
noun
ineffectuality

adjective
ineffectual

See also
attitude
awareness
excite
feelings
move
persuasion
surprise
used

AFFIRM
deny
argue

affirm
noun
acknowledgment
argumentation
assertion
yes

adjective
favorable

verb
acknowledge (2)
assert
certify

adverb
still
yes

deny
noun
denial
no (2)

verb
deny
refute

adverb
no

argue
verb
argue

See also
accept
agree
certain
conflict

AGREE
disagree

agree
noun
agreement (4)
bargain
complement
compromise
concession
consistency
engagement
treaty
unanimity
unity

adjective
accepted
agreeable
complementary
convenient
custom
unanimous

verb
agree (2)
arrange
assent
complement
compromise
contract
fit[1] (2)
flatter
get along
harmonize
pledge (2)
settle
suit

disagree
noun
gap
impropriety

adjective
discrepant
improper
incongruous
inharmonious (2)

verb
conflict
differ
haggle

See also
accept
affirm
attack
conflict
right
same
support

ALLOW
prevent

allow
noun
license
permission

adjective
permissible

verb
authorize
conduct
enable
permit (3)

prevent
noun
forbiddance
prevention

adjective
forbidden
preventive (2)

verb
forbid
frustrate
head off
parry
prevent

See also
crimes
law

APPROACH
retreat

approach
noun
advance
approach
bent
charge
comeback
heading
talent

adjective
approachable

verb
accost
approach
bear
come
go
return

adverb
back

retreat
noun
bounce
defection
defector
departure
deviation
digression
emigrant
emigration
émigré
parting
recoil

adjective
digressive
parting

verb
bounce
defect
deviate
digress
double
eject
emigrate
flinch
go
pass
recede
run

See also
near
reach
touch

ASK
answer

ask
noun
appeal (2)
appealer
inquirer
inquiry
inquisitor

verb
appeal
ask (2)
hint

answer
noun
answer (2)
retort

verb
answer
resolve

See also
explain
investigate
request

ASSEMBLE
disassemble

assemble
noun
combination
convention
mixture

adjective
combinational

verb
attach
beat
combine
mix

disassemble
noun
analysis
breach
detachment
division (2)

verb
analyze
cut
detach (2)
divide (2)
separate
take down
tear[1]

See also
accompanied
connect
free
group
increase
near
part
put on

ATTACK
defend

attack
noun
accusation
accuser
aggression
aggressor
ambush
attack
barrage
beat
beating
belittlement
belligerence
blow[2]
brawl
defiance
force
indignity
invasion
libel
retaliation
sabotage
siege
slap
thug
tough

adjective
abusive
accusatorial
aggressive
belligerent (2)
biting
forcible
libelous
repressive

verb
accuse
afflict
ambush
attack
barrage
batter
bawl out
beat (2)
belittle
besiege (2)
bite (2)
blacken
brawl
call down
force
hit
implicate
insult
invade
lay for
libel
occupy
raid
retaliate
sabotage
seize
slap
slap around
thrash (2)

defend
noun
apology
cover
defense

adjective
tenable

verb
assert
defend

See also
agree
conflict
crimes
help
pain

(cont.)

ATTACK *(cont.)*

See also
strike
willing

ATTITUDE
good attitude
bad attitude
neutral attitude

good attitude
noun
amiability
benevolence
confidence
consideration
gallantry
gravity
modesty
posture
sentiment
temper

adjective
affectionate
aggressive
airy
amiable
approachable
benevolent
broad
companionable
confident
confidential
friendly
gallant
gracious
grave[2]
humanitarian
humble
outgoing
social

bad attitude
noun
arrogance
condescension
cruelty
cynic
detachment
impudence
malevolence
snob

adjective
abrupt
abusive
accusatorial
aggressive
arrogant
bleak
boastful
calculating
cold (2)
cold-blooded
contrary
cool
cynical
detached
dry
ill-tempered
impatient
impudent
insensitive
malevolent
pedantic
resentful
snobbish
tepid
unctuous

verb
condescend

neutral attitude
noun
posture
sentiment
temper

See also
action
affect
concern
feelings
happy
help
hot
kind
like
love
pity
tighten
treat well

AWARENESS
unawareness

awareness
noun
alertness
guard
lookout (2)
revival
sensation
sensitiveness
watch
watcher

adjective
active
alert
mindful
sensational
sensitive
wakeful (2)

verb
look out
revive
wake[1]
watch

unawareness
noun
blackout
daze
dizziness
nap
sleep
soporific
trance

adjective
absent-minded
absorbed
dead
dizzy
dull
giddy
sleeping
sleepy (2)
unconscious

verb
absorb
black out
daze
deaden
dull
inebriate
nap
retire
sleep
sleep in

See also
ability
action
affect
careful
drugs
feelings
knowledge
remember
see
strong
tired

BE

noun
air
bearing
behavior
character
condition (2)
disposition
effect
environment
existence
heart
identity
presence
quality (2)
self
soul
streak
texture
thing
timber

adjective
actual
constitutional
effective
essential
implicit
innate

verb
act
amount
be
constitute
exist
lead
run

See also
feelings
live
real
surface

BEAUTIFUL
ugly

beautiful
noun
adornment
beauty
elegance
glitter (3)
harmony
proportion

adjective
beautiful
becoming
clean
clear
elegant
fresh
glorious
harmonious
shapely
sleek
symmetrical

verb
adorn
flatter
grace (2)
harmonize

ugly
noun
defect
deformity
mess
ugliness
witch

adjective
ghastly
plain
ugly

verb
deform

See also
better
good
plain
rich

BEINGS
noun
boy
germ
ghost
giant
human being

adjective
human

BELIEF
unbelief

belief
noun
confidence (2)
devotee
doctrine
myth (2)
theory (2)

adjective
confident
presumptive
reputed
supposed

verb
repute
speculate
suppose

unbelief
noun
disbelief
skeptic

adjective
incredible
incredulous

verb
disbelieve

adverb
skeptically

See also
likely
opinion
thoughts

BETTER
worse

better
noun
advance
best
bloom[1] (3)
improvement
progress
remedy
soundness
stability
trim
welfare

adjective
best (2)
better[1]
choice
rare
ultimate

verb
bloom[1]
fix up
perfect
touch up

worse
noun
decay
defect
deterioration
lapse
reverse
tatter
tatterdemalion
weakness

adjective
bad
defective
deficient
inferior
ruinous
shabby
tattered
wasted

verb
debase
decay
deteriorate
injure
relapse
wilt

See also
beautiful
change
good
health
help
important
increase

BIG
small
amount

big
noun
body
bulk
crowd (2)
deal
enormousness
flood
giant
heap (2)
intensity
size (2)
weight

adjective
alive
best
big (2)
bulky (2)
burning
double
extreme
generous
giant
grand
implicit
incalculable
intense
many
profuse
proportional
roomy
several
severe
sharp
sizable
staggering
steep[1]
thick
thorough
towering
ultimate
utter[2]

verb
double
pour
shower
surpass
teem

adverb
better[1]

(cont.)

BIG *(cont.)*

big
completely
considerably
even[1]
fairly
usually
very

small
noun
bit[1] (2)
damn
drop
flash
modesty
peanut
shade (2)
adjective
brief (2)
delicate
fine[1]
humble
imperceptible
insufficient
little (2)
meager
minimal
moderate
qualified
remote
tiny

amount
noun
degree (2)
distance (2)
extent
measurement
quantity
yield
verb
measure

See also
fat
get
important
increase
limited
long
near
part

BLOOD
noun
blood
adjective
bloody (2)
verb
bloody

See also
body

BODY
spirit

body
noun
body
brawn
constitution
head
heart
matter
nose
physicality
adjective
bodily
earthly
materialistic
physical (2)
sensational
sensory

spirit
noun
spirit
adjective
immaterial
inner
spiritual

See also
blood
breath
matter

BREATH
breathlessness

breath
noun
breath (2)
breeze
inspiration
pull
wind[1]
adjective
airy (2)
verb
air
blow[1]
breathe (3)
gasp
pant

breathlessness
adjective
airless (2)
verb
choke (2)

See also
body

CALM
agitation

calm
noun
balance
calm
stillness
adjective
calm
cool
gentle
pastoral
still
verb
calm
pacify

agitation
noun
agitation (2)
agitator
disturbance
fuss
jitter
restlessness
state
stir[1]
throe
unrest
adjective
frantic
impatient
restless
rough
turbulent
verb
agitate (2)
boil
fuss (2)

See also
concern
easy
excite
feelings
happy
order
pain
peace
repetition
restraint
tighten

CARE FOR
neglect

care for
noun
care
food
verb
bring up
dress
grow
nurse
serve
support
tend[2]

neglect
noun
neglect
verb
neglect

See also
careful
help

CAREFUL
careless

careful
noun
care
discernment

prudence
thoroughness

adjective
acute
attentive
careful (2)
close
critical
economical
shrewd
thorough
wary

verb
ease
edge
look out

careless
noun
abandon
extravagance
haste
negligence
temerity

adjective
airy
careless (2)
extravagant
improvident
light[2]
mindless
negligent
rash[1]
thoughtless

See also
awareness
care for
knowledge
precise
thoughts
wise

CAUSE
effect

cause
noun
stimulus (2)

verb
exercise
get
provoke
urge

effect
noun
effect

verb
follow

See also
excite
help
kin
make
start

CERTAIN
uncertain

certain
noun
certainty
decision
fate (2)
sureness

adjective
certain (2)
decided
definite
fated
sure (2)

verb
fate (2)
guarantee

adverb
absolutely

uncertain
noun
chance (2)
doubt
qualm

adjective
ambiguous (2)
debatable
doubtful
indefinite

verb
doubt

adverb
maybe

See also
affirm
change
clear
continue
flexible
foresight
luck
move
same
surprise

CHANGE
persist

change
noun
adaptation (2)
agitator
catalyst
change (3)
conversion
development
instability
reversal
revision
revolution
rotation
shakeup
transition
turn
variation

adjective
adaptable
capricious
changeable
insecure
mobile

verb
adapt
adjust
become
change (3)
convert
go
overturn
reverse
revise
revolutionize
rotate
shuffle
swerve
swing
turn

persist
noun
monotony
stability

adjective
ageless
consistent
firm[1]
irrevocable

verb
keep
stabilize

See also
better
certain
continue
flexible
move
put in
same

CHOICE
noun
appointee
appointment
choice (2)
elect
elector

adjective
optional
select

verb
appoint
choose
elect

See also
free
necessary
willing

CLEAN
dirty

clean
noun
innocent
purification (2)
purifier
purity
sterility

(cont.)

CLEAN *(cont.)*

clean
adjective
clean
innocent
neat
pure
purgative
sterile
straight
thoroughbred

verb
purify
refine
scrub
sterilize

dirty
noun
contaminant
contamination
corruption
dirtiness
filth
impurity
pit[1]
slime

adjective
corrupt
crude
dirty
filthy
impure (2)
muddy
slimy
sticky

verb
adulterate
blacken
corrupt
dirty
muddy
pollute
stain
taint
violate

See also
crimes
marks

CLEAR
unclear

clear
noun
clarity

adjective
clear (2)
definite
frank
immediate
sharp
transparent
unsubtle

verb
clarify
clear

adverb
immediately

unclear
noun
ambiguity
equivocation
gibberish (2)
haze
vagueness

adjective
ambiguous (2)
confused
evasive
filmy
turbid (2)
unclear

verb
confuse
equivocate
obscure

See also
certain
light
open
put on
show

COLLECT
distribute

collect
noun
accumulation
assembly
assortment
hoard

adjective
concentrated

verb
accumulate
apply
assemble (2)
band[2]
confer
crowd
gather
glean
hoard

distribute
noun
allotment
distribution (2)

verb
allot
appropriate
assort
distribute (2)
lift
scatter

See also
edge
get
group
order

COLORS
colorless

colors
noun
color (2)
complexion
shade
tint

adjective
black
blackish
colorful
dark
fair (2)
multicolor
ruddy

verb
color
dip

colorless
adjective
dull
pale

verb
pale

COMFORT
discomfort

comfort
noun
amenity

adjective
livable

discomfort
noun
inconvenience (2)

adjective
bitter
inconvenient
uncomfortable

verb
inconvenience

See also
help

CONCERN
unconcern

concern
noun
care
concern
consideration
eager beaver
enthusiasm (2)
enthusiast
extremist
morale
thing

adjective
concerned
eager
enthusiastic
extreme

verb
brood
care
eat up
worry

unconcern
noun
detachment
indifference
neglect

adjective
detached
perfunctory

verb
ignore
neglect

See also
attitude
calm
feelings
happy
important
kind
love
treat well

CONFLICT
cooperation

conflict
noun
argument
argumentativeness
collision
combat
competition (2)
competitor
conflict (2)
fight (2)
fighter
tilt

adjective
argumentative
competitive

verb
argue
collide
compete
contend
engage
wrestle

cooperation
noun
cooperation

adjective
cooperative

verb
cooperate

See also
affirm
agree
attack
help
resist

CONNECT

noun
alliance
ally
associate
attachment
basis
bond (2)
boy
boyfriend
company
contact
joint
junction
relation
sympathy
touch

adjective
allied
mutual
social

verb
ally
associate
bond
engage
reciprocate
relate
see

See also
assemble
dependence
group
increase
love
near
put on
relevant

CONTINUE
stop
pause

continue
noun
continuation
endlessness
endurance
fidelity
immortality
insistence (2)
renewal
stability
thread
wait

adjective
bearable
chronic (2)
confirmed
continual
continuing
direct
endless
faithful
fast
hard
immortal
insistent
sound²
steady
stubborn
sure
tireless

verb
bear up
carry on
continue
endure (2)
follow up
harden
immortalize
insist (2)
keep
outlast
remain
renew

stop
noun
abolition
break
end
faithlessness
gap
grace
reversal
stop (2)
suppression
tie-up

adjective
capricious
faithless
uneven

verb
abandon
abolish
break
break up
cancel (2)
dry up
extinguish
lapse
lift
pause
quit
retire
separate
stop (2)
strike
suppress
suspend
tie up

pause
noun
break
rest¹
truce

adjective
intermittent
temporary (2)
transitory

verb
blink
break
interrupt
rest¹ (2)

adverb
intermittently

See also
action
certain
change
flexible
include
keep
move
same
start
strong
time
usual

CONTROL
uncontrol

control
noun
government
grip
monopoly

adjective
governable

verb
govern
handle
have
maneuver (2)
manipulate
operate
possess

uncontrol
noun
unruliness

adjective
naughty
runaway
unruly

See also
dependence
over
politics

CONVEX
concave

convex
noun
bill[2]
bulge
bump (2)
nose

verb
bulge
poke

concave
noun
cave
depression
hole

adjective
hollow

See also
geometry

CORRECT
incorrect

correct
noun
accuracy

adjective
accurate (2)
corrective

verb
correct

incorrect
noun
blunder
botch
deviation
error
fallacy (2)
lapse
miscalculation

adjective
errant
erroneous
fallacious

verb
botch
confuse
deviate
err
miscalculate
misjudge

See also
honest
real
right
true
usual

COUNT

noun
count
figure
score
total

verb
count
enumerate

See also
reason

COURTESY
discourtesy

courtesy
noun
amenity
bow[1]
ceremony
courtesy
gallantry
tact

adjective
ceremonious
correct
courteous
gallant
gracious

discourtesy
noun
impudence
thoughtlessness

adjective
coarse
impudent
rude
shameless
tactless
thoughtless

See also
grateful
include
respect
treat well

CRIMES
noun
accessory
annihilation
bribe
crime
criminal
illegality
larcenist
larceny
libel
plot
plunder
robbery
smuggler
thug
tough
trespass

adjective
corruptible
criminal
illegal
larcenous
libelous

verb
annihilate
break in
bribe
fix
implicate
kidnap
libel
plot
rob
sack[2]
smuggle
steal

See also
allow
attack
clean
help
law
right
treat well

CULTURE
nature

culture
noun
culture (2)
mankind

adjective
artificial
cultural
cultured
earthly
manlike

nature
adjective
natural
uncivilized

See also
wild

DECENT
indecent

decent
adjective
clean

indecent
noun
obscenity (2)
swearword

adjective
obscene
racy
unspeakable

verb
swear

See also
words

DECIDE
hesitate

decide
noun
crisis
decision
judge (2)

adjective
decisive (2)
definitive
fateful
set[1]

verb
decide
judge

hesitate
noun
hesitation

adjective
hesitant

verb
hesitate
swing

See also
important

DEPENDENCE
independence

dependence
noun
parasite

adjective
parasitic

verb
freeload

independence
noun
freedom
independence

adjective
free
independent (2)

See also
connect
control

DESIRE

noun
ambition
appetite
catch
desire (2)
envy
greed
sell
toast
vocation
voracity

adjective
ambitious
desirable
envious
greedy (2)
voracious

verb
choose
desire
drink
envy
lust

See also
like
sex

DO
not do

do
noun
accomplishment
act
fulfillment
function
part
performance
practice

verb
accomplish
act
commit
effect
fulfill
perform
practice
realize
satisfy
score
settle
wage

not do
noun
failure

adjective
insuperable
invincible

verb
defer[1]
fail
neglect
violate

See also
action
participate
work

DRUGS
temperance

drugs
noun
bender
drug (2)
drunkard
drunkenness
kick

adjective
drugged
drunk

verb
befuddle
drink
drug

temperance
noun
temperance

See also
awareness
transactions

DRY
wet

dry
adjective
absorbent
dry (2)
thirsty

verb
dry
dry up

wet
noun
branch
drink
drool
drop
swamp
sweat
tear[2]

adjective
damp
sticky
sweaty
wet

verb
drool
pour
steep[2]
sweat
tear[2]
wash (2)
wet

See also
solid

EASY
hard

easy
noun
breeze
ease

(cont.)

EASY *(cont.)*

easy
runaway

adjective
easy
light[2]

verb
breeze
ease (2)

hard
noun
bother
difficulty
predicament
problem
severity
trial

adjective
awkward
deep
delicate
difficult
heavy
severe
thorny
tight
troublesome

adverb
hard

See also
calm
heavy
pain
plain
simple

EDGE
center

edge
noun
border (2)
circumference
end
extreme
extremist
outline
skirt
verge

adjective
extreme (2)

verb
band[1]
border

center
noun
center (2)
concentration
moderation
thick

adjective
central
concentrated
inner (2)
middle
mild
moderate

verb
concentrate

See also
collect

ENTER
exit

enter
noun
admission
arrival
cut
entrance[1]
invasion
pass
plunge
trespass

verb
admit
break in
cut
dig
dip (2)
enter
insinuate
intrude
invade
muscle
penetrate
plunge

exit
verb
discharge

See also
move
open
participate
start
work

EXCESS
insufficiency
enough

excess
noun
excess (2)
surplus
wordiness

adjective
excessive
extravagant
heavy
profuse
superfluous
wordy

verb
exceed

adverb
unduly

insufficency
noun
absence
shortage

adjective
absent
deficient
inadequate
insufficient
meager
undermanned

verb
fail

enough
noun
enough
satiation

adjective
bare
sufficient

verb
satiate
serve

See also
full

EXCITE
bore
interest

excite
noun
absorption
attention
heat
infatuation
kick
sensation
thrill
trick
wonder
wrinkle

adjective
absorbed
attentive
dramatic
fervid
hot
infatuated
staggering
stimulating
thrilled

verb
absorb
arouse
carry away
climax
engage
fire
grip
interest
provoke
stagger
startle
tantalize
wonder

bore
noun
boredom
dullness
insipidity
monotony

adjective
boring
dry
dull
insipid

long[1]
realistic
trite

verb
bore

interest
noun
amusement (2)

adjective
amusing

verb
amuse

See also
affect
calm
cause
fear
feelings
help
like
surprise

EXPLAIN
baffle

explain
noun
account
excuse
explanation

adjective
explainable
explanatory

verb
account for
elaborate
explain

baffle
adjective
inexplicable
mysterious

See also
ask
knowledge
regret

EXPLOSION
collapse

explosion
noun
blast
eruption
load
outburst

verb
break
break out
burst
erupt
explode
fly

collapse
noun
breakdown

verb
cave in

See also
help

EXPRESS

noun
expression
face
frown
gesture
glare
smile
smirk
sneer

adjective
expressive

verb
blush
flourish
frown
gesture
glare
grimace
signal
smile
smirk
sneer

See also
show

FAIR
unfair

fair
noun
fairness

adjective
even[1]
fair
neutral
sportsmanlike

adverb
fair

unfair
noun
favor

adjective
favorable
unfair

verb
favor

See also
right

FAST
slow
velocity

fast
noun
haste

adjective
abrupt
brief
crash
fast
quick

adverb
fast
short

slow
noun
crawl
laggard

adjective
deliberate
gradual
slow

verb
crawl
delay

velocity
noun
speed

verb
speed

See also
time

FAT
thin

fat
noun
fat

adjective
fat
fatty
plump[1]
stocky

thin
adjective
gangling
thin

verb
reduce
thin

See also
big
thick

FEAR
courage

fear
noun
caution
complex
coward
cowardice
dismay
fear
jitter

adjective
afraid
cowardly
crawly
fearful
horrible
weird

verb
crawl
dismay

(cont.)

FEAR *(cont.)*

fear
fear
frighten

courage
noun
courage
hero
heroism

adjective
brave

See also
excite
feelings
surprise

FEELINGS

noun
anger
annoyance (3)
anxiety
apathy
balance
emotion
enthusiasm
fury
gloom
glow
heart
heat
mood
morale
passion
resentment
sentimentality
temper (2)
theatrics
wonder

adjective
angry
anxious
apathetic
awkward
emotional (2)
fervid
furious
insensitive
moody
neutral
passionate
pitying
sentimental
spirited
testy
unsympathetic

verb
anger (2)
annoy (2)
complain
confuse
emotionalize
feel
greet
rave
sentimentalize
wonder

See also
action
affect
attitude
awareness
be
calm
concern
excite
happy
hope
kind
pain
pity
religion
strong
surprise
tighten
tired

FLEXIBLE
rigid

flexible
noun
flexibility
unstableness

adjective
flexible (2)
limp
malleable
unstable

rigid
adjective
inflexible
pedantic
rigid
stiff

verb
stiffen

See also
certain
change
continue
move
resist
same
willing

FORESIGHT

noun
omen
precursor
prediction
prophecy
prophet
taste
threat
vision

adjective
predictive
prophetic
threatening
visionary

verb
adumbrate
foresee
predict
prophesy
threaten

See also
certain
precede
warn

FORGIVENESS
vindictiveness

forgiveness
noun
forgiveness
grace

adjective
justifiable
pardonable

verb
forgive

vindictiveness
noun
retaliation
vindictiveness

adjective
inexcusable
vindictive

verb
avenge
retaliate

See also
accept
kind
pity

FORWARD
backward

forward
noun
advance

verb
advance

backward
noun
retreat
reversion

verb
back
recoil
retreat

See also
precede

FREE
unfree

free
noun
escape
freedom
liberty
will

adjective
clear
free
loose

verb
clear
discharge
emit
escape
excuse
free

unfree

noun
bond
detention
entanglement
jail
jailer

adjective
tight

verb
bar
catch
commit
constrain
enclose
enslave
hamper
hold
imprison
involve
jail
kidnap

See also
assemble
choice
open
participate
restraint
tighten

FULL
empty
capacity

full

noun
plug
satiation

adjective
full
heavy

verb
charge
crowd
fill (2)
flood (2)
heap
satiate

empty

noun
emptiness (3)
nothingness

adjective
empty (3)
lonely
vacant

verb
empty

capacity

verb
accommodate

See also
absence
excess

GAMBLING

noun
bet
bettor
gamble
speculator

verb
bet
gamble (2)

See also
luck
transactions

GENDER

noun
effeminacy
femininity (2)

adjective
effeminate
feminine
manly

See also
sex

GEOMETRY

noun
circle
revolution

adjective
oval
parallel
round
square

See also
convex
horizontal
sharp
smooth
straight

GET
lose

get

noun
buy
catch
employment
gain
mercenary
recovery

adjective
available
profitable

verb
book
bring
buy
capture
catch
contract
develop
earn
employ
extort
find
get
hire
inherit
recover
run down
take
wangle

lose

noun
loss

adjective
lost

verb
drop
lose

See also
big
collect
money
pay

GIVE
take
reciprocity

give

noun
administration
attribution
benevolence
conferment
courtesy
delivery
donation
donor
generosity
gift
grant
gratuity

adjective
benevolent
generous (3)
gifted
sacred

verb
administer
attribute
confer
contribute
devote
donate
entrust
fix
furnish
gift
give (3)
grant
hand down
impose
inflict
leave[1]
lend
pass
play out
sacrifice
satisfy
shower
submit
transfer

(cont.)

GIVE *(cont.)*

take

noun
adoption
consumer
consumption
dependent
deprivation
draft
greed
miser
pirate
plunder
robbery
seizure
usurpation

adjective
greedy
stingy

verb
adopt
assume
claim
deplete
deprive
dip
draft
drink
earn
hoard
pirate
resume
rob
sack[2]
seize
steal

reciprocity

verb
exchange

See also
accept
keep

GOOD
bad

good

noun
amiability
chastity
delicacy
excellence
fire
marvel
masterpiece
merit
model
nonpareil
trick
virtue
wrinkle

adjective
acceptable
admirable
adorable
amiable
chaste
comfortable
convenient
decent
delicate
delicious
delightful
everyday
excellent
fabulous
good (2)
grand
ideal
marvelous
neat
ordinary
perfect
sound[2]
vintage

bad

noun
abnormality
boor
enormity
flagrancy
hole
infamy
joint
misbehavior
mischief (2)
prank[1]
shame
smart aleck

adjective
abnormal
affected
airy
bad
corrupt
deplorable
filthy
flagrant
impure
insipid
morbid
naughty
ponderous
rude
shoddy
terrible
unfortunate
unpleasant
unspeakable

verb
misbehave

See also
beautiful
better
important
right
thrive

GRATEFUL
ungrateful

grateful

noun
appreciation
grace

adjective
grateful

ungrateful

adjective
thankless (2)

See also
courtesy

GREETING

noun
greeting
regard

verb
accost
greet (2)

See also
meet

GROUP

noun
alliance
blast
circle
citizen
class (2)
combine (2)
common
company (2)
conference
countryman
couple
crowd (3)
detachment
detail
family
force
gang
group
kind[2]
line
pair
party
trio
union
web

adjective
common
domestic
social
societal

verb
class
socialize

See also
assemble
collect
connect
near
order

HANG

adjective
hanging

verb
hang (2)
slouch
trail

See also
posture

HAPPEN

noun
circumstance

event
history (2)
plot

verb
chance
come (3)
occur

See also
surprise

HAPPY
unhappy

happy
noun
delight
elation
exultation
fulfillment
happiness
heaven

adjective
cheerful
delightful
elated
exuberant
exultant
fulfilled
gay
glad (2)
light²
merry

verb
delight
elate
exult
light¹
rejoice

unhappy
noun
complaint
disappointment
distress
gloom
grief
grouch
misery
mutter

adjective
depressed
disappointing
disturbing
gloomy (2)
glum
lonely
miserable (2)
sad
sorrowful (2)
tearful

verb
complain
cry
depress
disappoint
distress
embitter
grieve
mutter
sulk

See also
attitude
calm
concern
feelings
hope
laughter
like
pain

HEALTH
sickness

health
noun
cure
health
recovery
treatment

adjective
curative
healthful
healthy

verb
cure
recover
treat

sickness
noun
black eye
disease
indisposition
seizure
sickness
tuberculosis

adjective
exhausted
sick
sickly (2)
tubercular
unwholesome

verb
collapse
languish
turn
upset

See also
better
help
strong

HEAVY
light

heavy
noun
burden¹ (2)
gravity
heaviness
seriousness
task

adjective
burdensome
grave²
heavy (2)
serious

light
adjective
light²

See also
easy
thick
tired

HELP
harm
harmless

help
noun
accessory
advantage (2)
assistant
capital
comfort
encouragement
favor
help
helper
interest
makeshift
panacea
patron
patronage
relief
renewal
rescue
resort
tonic
treatment
trump

adjective
auxiliary
beneficial
encouraging
obliging
positive
preservative
tonic

verb
adjust
advance
benefit
comfort
encourage (2)
energize
finance
fix
help
improve
oblige
patronize
profit
promote
refresh
renew
rescue (2)
restore
serve
sustain
treat

harm
noun
abuse
accident
annihilation
bar

(cont.)

HELP *(cont.)*

harm
black eye
breach
breakage
crash
curse
cut
defect
delay
destruction
disadvantage
disaster
distress
evil
harm
irritation
massacre
murder
murderer
poison
ruin
tear[1]
trauma
victim
weakness

adjective
cruel
destructive
fatal
grievous
harmful
helpless
murderous
poisonous
unfavorable
virulent

verb
abuse
afflict
annihilate (2)
batter
bend
blast
botch
break (3)
break up
bruise
chafe
consume
corrupt
crack
crash
cripple
crush (2)
cut
delay
destroy (2)
devastate
disable
discourage
eliminate
hamper
hang
hinder
hurt
injure
irritate
kill[1]
murder
overthrow
poison
shoot
slip
tamper
tear[1]
trample
trash
traumatize
wreck

harmless
adjective
harmless

See also
attack
attitude
better
care for
cause
comfort
conflict
crimes
excite
explosion
health
hope
kind
like
love
luck
make
support
treat well
used
value

HIGH
low

high
noun
air (2)
climax
elevation
height
hill
maximum

adjective
airy
climactic
elevated (2)
high (2)
higher
lofty
maximum
tall
top

low
noun
deep
low

adjective
low

verb
crouch

See also
over

HONEST
dishonest

honest
noun
honesty

adjective
accurate
artless
honest

dishonest
noun
act
affectation
art
cheat (2)
corruption
deceit
dishonesty
hypocrisy
hypocrite
indirection
insincerity
pretense (2)
trick

adjective
affected
artful
corrupt
dishonest
double
fallacious
hypocritical
insincere
plastic
shady
sly
unctuous
underhand
unscrupulous

verb
act
cheat
deceive
foist
pose
skin

See also
correct
performing arts
plain
respect
right
true

HOPE
despair

hope
noun
dream
dreamer
future
optimism
optimist

adjective
idealistic (2)
optimistic

despair
noun
despair
pessimist

adjective
despondent
gloomy
hopeless

verb
despair

See also
feelings
happy
help
surprise

HORIZONTAL
vertical
change of position

horizontal
adjective
flat
transverse

verb
lie[1]

vertical
adjective
erect
steep[1]
vertical

verb
erect

change of position
adjective
upside-down

verb
overturn
right

See also
geometry

HOT
cold
lukewarm

hot
noun
burn
fire
heat (2)

adjective
burning
fervid
hot (2)
sticky
tropical

verb
burn (3)
light[1]

cold
noun
cold
frigidness

adjective
bleak
cold (3)
cool
frigid

lukewarm
adjective
tepid

See also
attitude
kind

IMPORTANT
unimportant

important
noun
dignitary
eminence
emphasis
gravity
importance

adjective
big-league
decisive
essential
grave[2]
important
influential
pivotal
primary
ruling

verb
count
emphasize

unimportant
noun
nonentity
pettiness
trivia

adjective
petty

See also
beautiful
better
big
concern
decide
good
knowledge
over
strong

INCLUDE
exclude

include
noun
integration

adjective
built-in

verb
build in
contain (2)
embody
integrate (2)

exclude
noun
aloneness
detachment
erasure
individuality
isolation
seclusion
segregation
wall

adjective
alone
exclusive
individual
lone
mere
restricted
sacred
secluded
select
solitary

verb
censor
drop
exclude
isolate
seclude
sort
wall

adverb
alone
merely
separately
solely

See also
continue
courtesy
keep
limited
near
treat well

INCREASE
decrease

increase
noun
addition (2)
attachment
buildup
exaggeration
expansion
increase (2)
outbreak

adjective
accumulative
additional
auxiliary
coming
elevated
extensible
inflated

verb
add
amount
attach
deposit
double
elevate
exaggerate
explode
extend
gain
increase
intensify

(cont.)

INCREASE *(cont.)*

increase
lengthen
raise
restore (2)
return
rise
soar

adverb
additionally

decrease
noun
decrease
deduction
depreciation
fade-out
failure
fall
relief
wane

adjective
slow

verb
boil down
contract
cut back
decrease
deduct
deplete
depreciate
drain
exhaust
fade (3)
fade out
fall
go (2)
moderate
muffle
reduce
relieve
shade
shorten
slip
subside
thin

See also
assemble
better
big
connect
long
put on

INDUSTRIOUS
lazy

industrious
noun
diligence
efficiency

adjective
diligent
efficient

lazy
noun
laziness
wastrel

adjective
lazy

verb
idle (2)

See also
ability
thrive

INGESTION

noun
bite
cook
delicacy
drop
feast
food (2)
harvest
serving

adjective
delicate
delicious
edible
greedy
hard
heavy
nutritious
nutritive
ravenous
raw

verb
bite
boil
consume
cook
eat
gulp
live[1]
nourish
serve

See also
mouth
taste

INVESTIGATE

noun
analysis (2)
curiosity (2)
detective
examination (2)
exploration
feeler
inquirer
inquiry (2)
inquisitor
review
shakedown
snoop
spy
tail
test (3)

adjective
curious (2)

verb
analyze (2)
browse
examine
explore
feel out
interrogate
scour[1]
search
snoop
spy
tap[2]
test (3)

See also
ask
knowledge

KEEP
release

keep
noun
conservation
conservative
depository
grave[1]
hold
treasury

adjective
conservative
sticky

verb
bank[2]
carry
conserve (2)
grasp
have
hold
maintain
restore (2)
return
save
stockpile
tie

release
noun
abandonment
abdication
dismissal
disposal
ejection
elimination (2)

adjective
abandoned
eliminative

verb
abandon
abdicate
discard
discharge
dismiss (3)
drop
eject
eliminate (2)
relinquish
retire
rid

See also
accept
continue
give
include
usual

KIN

noun
ancestor

ancestry
baby
child
derivative
descendant
family
father
genealogy
illegitimacy
kin
nobility
progeny
relative
shoot
young

adjective
ancestral
derivative
domestic
fatherly
illegitimate
related

verb
derive
descend
develop
father

See also
cause
precede
start

KIND
cruel

kind
noun
benevolence (2)
consideration

adjective
benevolent (2)
gentle
gracious
humanitarian

cruel
noun
cruelty
fiend

adjective
cruel
fiendish
fierce
merciless

See also
attitude
concern
feelings
forgiveness
help
hot
like
love
pity
treat well

KNOWLEDGE
ignorance

knowledge
noun
ability
acknowledgment
acquaintance (2)
advertising
announcement (2)
awareness
celebrity
communication
education
eminence
fame
grasp
hint
information
informer
ken
knowledge
lore
news
notice
notoriety
presentation
promotion
recognition
table
tip3
veteran

adjective
artful
aware
contemporary
educated
eminent
familiar
famous
informed
learned
notorious
perceptible
practical
sophisticated
understandable

verb
acknowledge (2)
acquaint
advertise (2)
announce
break
come out (2)
communicate
feel
get around
inform (2)
know
notice
perceive
place
promote
recognize
register
usher in

ignorance
noun
ignorance (2)
innocent
nonsense
obscurity

adjective
anonymous
foolish
ignorant (3)
imperceptible
incomprehensible
mysterious
obscure
unfound
unscholarly
untried

verb
nonplus

See also
awareness
careful
explain
important
investigate
see
show
teach
thoughts
understand
wise
words

LAUGHTER

noun
celebration
gaiety (2)
giggle
humor
joke
joker
laugh
ribbing
ridicule
sarcasm
satire
scream
sneer
takeoff
taunt

adjective
amusing
clever
humorous
laughable
laughing
priceless
sarcastic

verb
break up
celebrate
chuckle
giggle
joke (2)
laugh
ridicule
sneer

See also
happy
work

LAW

noun
accusation
accused

(cont.)

LAW *(cont.)*

accuser
appeal
appealer
arrest
bond
bondsman
complainant
confirmation
court
exculpation
grant
guardian
holding
illegality
illegitimacy
informer
injustice (2)
judge
law (2)
lawsuit
lawyer
legality
libel
license
minor
minority
policeman
reversal
reward
ruling
sentence
sponsor
testimony
trial
witness

adjective
condemned
illegal
illegitimate
lawful
liable
libelous
litigable
minor

verb
accuse
arrest
clear
commit
condemn
confirm
hold
inform
inherit
judge
lapse
leave[1]
legalize
libel
lift
petition
police
present[2]
return
sign
sue
testify
transfer

See also
allow
crimes
order
politics

LEFTOVER

noun
balance
deposit
destruction
end
ruin
trace

adjective
remaining

LIGHT
darkness

light
noun
beam
blink
fire
glare
glitter
gloss
illumination
light[1]

adjective
bright
brilliant
glossy

verb
beam
blink
flash
glare
gloss
glow
illuminate

darkness
noun
dark
night
shade

adjective
black
dark
dull
gloomy
nightly
shady (2)

verb
shade

See also
clear
see

LIKE
dislike

like
noun
admirer
adoration (2)
attraction
bent
bias
delight
favorite
liking
lure (2)
public
taste

adjective
adorable
agreeable
attractive
biased
delightful
favorite
seductive

verb
admire
adore
attract
charm
delight
dispose
enjoy
like[1]
luxuriate
sweeten

dislike
noun
disapproval
disgust
dislike
drip
imposition
offense
prejudice
unwelcome
vociferation

adjective
bitter
crawly
damned
objectionable
offensive
unwelcome

verb
crawl
disapprove
disgust
dislike
offend

See also
attitude
desire
excite
happy
help
kind
likely
love
pain
praise
value

LIKELY
unlikely

likely
noun
chance
verisimilitude

adjective
inclined
liable
presumptive
probable

verb
tend[1]

unlikely
adjective
doubtful
implausible

See also
belief
like
opinion
possible
thoughts
true

LIMITED
unlimited

limited
noun
catch
environment
length
limit (2)
maximum
provision
restriction (2)

adjective
conditional
definite
local (2)
maximum
narrow
qualified
restricted (2)

verb
determine
limit

unlimited
noun
eternity
infinity

adjective
endless
eternal
implicit
indefinite
unconditional
universal (2)
utter[2]

adverb
absolutely
completely (2)

See also
big
include
necessary
relevant
specific

LIVE
die

live
noun
immortality
life

adjective
alive (2)
immortal

verb
quicken
revive
survive

die
noun
death
fatality (2)
fate

adjective
dead
deadly
ghastly
inanimate
vanished

verb
die
disappear
fate

See also
be

LONG
short

long
noun
extension

adjective
long[1] (3)

verb
lengthen

short
verb
shorten

See also
big
increase

LOVE
hatred

love
noun
admirer
adoration (2)
darling
devotee
friend
friendship
love (3)
reconciliation
sympathy

adjective
adorable
affectionate
darling
familiar
friendly

verb
adore (2)
reconcile

hatred
noun
enemy
enmity
estrangement
hate (2)

adjective
hateful
hostile
resentful

verb
estrange
hate

See also
attitude
concern
connect
help
kind
like
near
sex
support
value

LUCK
misfortune
chance

luck
noun
luck
opportunity

adjective
favorable
happy
opportune

misfortune
noun
fate
jinx
misfortune

adjective
bad
fateful
unfortunate

verb
fate
jinx

chance
verb
toss

See also
certain
gambling
help
supernatural
surprise
warn

MACHINE

noun
behavior
device
furnishing

(cont.)

MACHINE *(cont.)*

gadget
invention
stage
stick
tool
wrench

verb
govern

See also
means

MAKE
unmake

make
noun
builder (2)
building
composition
invention (2)
product
work

verb
build
compose
dig
establish
form
invent
make
produce
wangle

unmake
noun
annihilation

verb
annihilate (2)
lift

See also
cause
help

MARKS

noun
character
impression
mark
point
prick
score
smear
stain
stigma
ticket
trace
track
trail
welt

verb
engrave (2)
mark
point
speckle
spot
stain
stigmatize
streak
ticket
track

See also
clean
strike

MARRIAGE
unmarried

marriage
noun
engagement
intended
marriage
spouse
wedding

adjective
eligible
engaged
marital

verb
marry

unmarried
adjective
single

See also
sex

MATTER

noun
band[1]
beam
body
good
material
universe

adjective
earthy
physical

See also
body
solid
thing

MEANING

noun
idea
import
meaning
moral
subject
thrust

adjective
pithy
pregnant
thematic

verb
imply
mean[1]

See also
words

MEANS

noun
approach
art
go-between
mean[3]
outfit
tactic
ticket
tool
trick
way

adjective
artful

verb
maneuver

See also
ability
machine

MEET

noun
conferee
conference
confrontation

verb
come across
confer
confront
cross
encounter
engage
meet[1]

See also
greeting

MONEY

noun
bargain
bribe
buy
capital
collapse
combine
deposit
depreciation
failure
financier
fund
gain
living
money
peanut
speculator
take
tax
toll[1]

adjective
cheap
financial
free
independent
popular

verb
appropriate
bank[2]

bill[1]
bribe
buy
clean up
collapse
depreciate
earn
finance
return
ruin
secure

See also
get
owned
pay
rich
save
transactions
work

MOUTH

noun
bill[2]
drink
drool
mouth
swallow

verb
chew
drink
drool
swallow
vomit
yawn

See also
ingestion

MOVE
halt

move
noun
bounce (2)
constitutional
displacement
drive
driver
expedition
flow
jerk
jump (2)
motion
movement
removal
skip
smuggler
sneak
spate
spurt
stealth
throw
tourist
transportation
tread
tremor
trip
trot
walk
way

adjective
communicable
errant
migrant
migratory
mobile
nomadic
stealthy

verb
blunder
bounce (2)
communicate
cover
crawl
cross
disturb
drive (4)
edge
emit
flow (3)
fly (2)
glide
go
hike
jerk
journey
jump (2)
limp
lump[1]
lurch (2)
maneuver
migrate
mobilize
move (2)
ooze
overturn
plod
plunge
pour (2)
refer
remove
rove
run
rush
scramble
send
shed
shoot
shuffle
skip
slide (3)
slip
slither
slouch
smuggle (2)
sneak
spread (2)
spurt
stir[1] (2)
stride
stroll
strut
stumble
swing (2)
swirl
thrash
throw
toss
tramp
traverse (2)
trip
trot
turn (2)
walk
wallow
wash (2)
wiggle
wrench

halt
noun
catch

adjective
fixed
motionless

verb
catch
fasten
fix
land (2)

See also
action
affect
certain
change
continue
enter
flexible
push
put in
repetition
same
work

NATIVE
foreign

native
adjective
constitutional
domestic
indigenous
innate

foreign
noun
foreigner

adjective
foreign (2)

See also
near

NEAR
far
distance

near
noun
associate
association
environment
locality
neighborhood

adjective
adjoining
close (2)
coming
confidential
convenient
immediate
intimate[1]
last[1]
momentary

(cont.)

NEAR *(cont.)*

near

adjective
tactical
threatening

verb
adjoin
associate
coincide
snuggle
threaten

adverb
approximately
close
immediately
late

far

noun
detachment
distance

adjective
distant
remote

adverb
barely

distance

noun
remove

See also
approach
assemble
big
connect
group
include
love
native
touch

NECESSARY
unnecessary

necessary

noun
condition
demand
need

adjective
essential

verb
demand
must

unnecessary

adjective
unnecessary
wanton

See also
choice
limited
obligation

NEW
old

new

noun
contemporary
novelty (2)
renewal

adjective
contemporary
fresh
modern
new

verb
modernize
renew

old

noun
obsoleteness
obsoletism
square

adjective
high
obsolete
old (2)
old-fashioned
tacky[2]
vanished

verb
obsolesce

See also
time

OBLIGATION

noun
debt
duty
fidelity
guarantee
promise

adjective
obliged
required

verb
commit
enforce
guarantee
impose
pledge (2)
require
secure

See also
necessary
resist

OFFER

noun
offer
offering
proposal

verb
go
offer (2)
propose

See also
accept

OPEN
close

open

noun
breach
crack
gap
hole
prick
way

adjective
clear
open
passable

verb
air
breach
clear
open

close

noun
bar
blind alley

adjective
airless

verb
close (2)
close in
hinder
obstruct
surround

See also
clear
enter
free
put on
show

OPINION

noun
advice
adviser
belief (2)
guess
review
thesis

adjective
advisory
arbitrary

verb
advise
believe (3)
feel
guess
review

See also
belief
likely
perspective
reason
thoughts

ORDER
disorder

order

noun
arrangement
balance
law
method
order

rule
series

adjective
methodical
neat

verb
arrange
balance (2)
belong
dress up
fold
line
methodize
set[1]
shuffle
thread
tidy (2)

disorder
noun
botch
disorder (2)
disorderliness
disturbance
heap
unruliness
upset

adjective
confused
disorderly
messy
shapeless
unruly

verb
confuse
disorder
disrupt
entangle
heap
sprawl
tousle

See also
calm
collect
group
law
peace
planned
same
surface

OVER
under

over
noun
absolutism (2)
administration
advantage
authoritarian
authority (2)
boss (2)
bully
chief
command
demand
dictator
dominance
domination
employer
executive
muscle
nobility
society
superior
tyranny

adjective
absolute
administrative
authoritarian
authoritative
climactic
dictatorial
dominant
dominating
higher
highest
noble
principal

verb
administer (2)
bear
boss
command
conduct
control
demand
dictate
dominate (2)
enforce
govern
impose (2)
inflict
intimidate
seize
supervise
top
tyrannize

under
noun
base[1]
basis (2)
bearer
bottom (2)
burden[1] (3)
commonalty
employee
follower
pawn[2]
retinue
slavery
subordinate
sycophant
trash

adjective
bottom
lowly
minor
servile
subordinate

verb
base[1]
bear
carry
charge
condescend (2)
fawn

See also
control
high
important
politics
precede

OWNED
unowned

owned
noun
birthright (2)
claim
claimant
effect
holding
land
monopoly
owner
ownership
resource
riches

adjective
jealous

verb
carry
claim
command
enjoy

unowned
adjective
unreserved

verb
escape
lack

See also
pay
transactions

PAIN
pleasure

pain
noun
annoyance (3)
embarrassment
offense
pain
thorn
throe

adjective
disturbing
offensive
painful
thorny
tormenting
unbearable
unpleasant
vexatious

verb
annoy (2)
embarrass
hurt
insult
offend
sting
torture

pleasure
noun
enjoyment

(cont.)

PAIN *(cont.)*

pleasure
sensuousness
sybarite
zest

adjective
enjoyable
insinuating
sensuous
sybaritic

verb
please

See also
attack
calm
easy
feelings
happy
like

PART
whole

part
noun
branch (4)
complement
cut
division (2)
element (3)
extension
figure
interest
lump[1]
quarter
section (2)
subsidiary

adjective
complementary
concentrated
double
partial
subordinate

verb
branch
complement
divide

whole
noun
completeness
complex
system
unification
unity
universe
whole

adjective
complete (3)
round
whole

verb
integrate

adverb
completely
through

See also
assemble
big
start

PARTICIPATE
abstain

participate
noun
entanglement
meddler
meddling
part
participant
participation
snoop
voice

adjective
contributive
meddling
social

verb
contribute
engage
experience
involve
join
meddle
participate
play along
snoop

abstain
verb
secede

See also
do
enter
free

PAY
owe

pay
noun
deposit
payment
wage

adjective
even[1]

verb
compensate
pay
refund
reward
settle
treat

owe
noun
account
debt (2)
tax
toll[1]

adjective
due
unpaid

See also
get
money
owned
save
transactions
work

PEACE
conflict

peace
adjective
peaceable

conflict
noun
disorder
unrest
unruliness

adjective
disorderly
military (2)
unruly

verb
militarize

See also
calm
order

PERFORMING ARTS
noun
acting
actor
band[2]
booking
interpretation
lead
magic
mimic
player
scene
sketch
stage
vocalist

adjective
dramatic

verb
act
interpret
play (2)
stage

See also
honest
real

PERSPECTIVE
noun
phase
point of view
side

verb
regard

See also
opinion

PERSUASION
dissuasion

persuasion
noun
bribe
seducer

adjective
convincing
corruptible
seductive

verb
bribe
charm
coax
coerce
convince
persuade
seduce

dissuasion
verb
dissuade

See also
affect
suggest

PITY

noun
pity

adjective
pitiful
pitying

verb
feel

See also
attitude
feelings
forgiveness
kind

PLACE

noun
air
base[1]
bearing
court
earth
environment (2)
expanse
grave[1]
haunt
hide-out
locality (2)
place (3)
point
position (2)
room
scene
side
station
stay[1]
tenure
work

adjective
earthly
heavenly

verb
frequent
inhabit
keep
lay[1]
live[1]
position
set[1]
station
stay[1]

See also
put in
territory

PLAIN
fancy

plain
noun
modesty

adjective
bare
conservative
easygoing
humble
modest
quiet
rustic

fancy
noun
bombast
pretentiousness
theatricalism

adjective
affected
arty
elaborate
exclusive
fanciful
formal
genteel
inflated
ornate
pompous
showy
sonorous

verb
dress up

See also
beautiful
honest
put on
self-love
simple

PLANNED
unplanned

planned
noun
arrangement
design
draft
intention
line
plot
program (2)

verb
arrange
design (2)
draft
have
intend
plot
premeditate

unplanned
noun
improvisation

adjective
mindless
random
spontaneous
unintentional

verb
improvise

See also
order
prepared
purpose
surprise

POLITICS

noun
absolutism (2)
agitator
alarmist
alliance
ally
citizen
crisis
elector
extremist
government (2)
liberal
mission
patronage
possession
reactionary
state
tax
ticket
treaty
tyranny

adjective
absolute
allied
extreme
governmental
inner
liberal
popular
reactionary
unprogressive

verb
ally
elect
establish
secede
socialize

See also
control
law
over

POSSIBLE
impossible

possible
noun
possibility
potential

adjective
earthly

(cont.)

POSSIBLE *(cont.)*

possible
open
possible (2)
potential

impossible
adjective
impossible

See also
likely

POSTURE

noun
position
posture

verb
balance
pose
posture
slouch
sprawl
squat
stoop
stride

See also
hang

PRAISE
blame

praise
noun
acceptance
admirer
applause
boast
braggart
compliment
flattery
glory
praise
sycophant
testimonial

adjective
admirable
boastful
complimentary

verb
admire (2)
applaud
appreciate
approve
boast
compliment
flatter
honor
praise

blame
noun
accusation
accuser
blame
critic
rebuke
reflection
scapegoat
scold
smear
tirade
vituperation

adjective
accusatorial
blameworthy
critical
disparaging

verb
accuse
blame
call down
correct
deplore
nag
revile
slam

See also
like
religion
respect
reward
support
value

PRECEDE
follow

precede
noun
ancestor (2)
ancestry
façade
face (2)
front
future
lead
leader
precedence

adjective
advance
advanced
ancestral
future

verb
face
lead
precede

adverb
earlier (3)

follow
noun
back
follower
order
tail
train

adjective
back
backward (2)
consecutive
following
last[1]
late
later

verb
defer[2]
dog
follow (3)

adverb
backward
late
later

See also
foresight
forward
kin
over
seek

PRECISE
imprecise

precise
noun
discrimination

adjective
discriminating
even[1]
fine[1]
precise
round

adverb
directly
even[1]

imprecise
noun
estimate

adjective
loose

verb
estimate

See also
careful
wise

PREPARED
unprepared

prepared
noun
preparation

adjective
ready

verb
gird
prepare
till

unprepared
noun
improvisation

adjective
extemporaneous

verb
improvise

adverb
unawares

See also
planned

PROTECTION
exposure

protection
noun
bill[2]

hole
home (2)
shelter

verb
harbor (2)
shade

exposure
noun
exposure

adjective
open

verb
expose

See also
safety

PURPOSE
purposelessness

purpose
noun
intention

adjective
calculated
deliberate
firm[1]

verb
intend

purposelessness
adjective
aimless
erratic
mindless

See also
planned
reason
start
surprise

PUSH
pull

push
noun
pressure
push

verb
crowd
muscle
pressurize
push
urge

pull
noun
jerk
pull

verb
jerk
pull

See also
move
put in

PUT IN
take out

put in
verb
establish
introduce
load
ram

take out
verb
pull
unload

See also
change
move
place
push

PUT ON
take off

put on
noun
attire
dress (3)
habit
wrap
wrapper

verb
clothe
cover
don
dress
dress up
smear
top
wrap (3)

take off
noun
nudity
tatter

adjective
bare
nude

verb
bare
remove
scrape
scrub
shed
skin
strip[1]

See also
assemble
clear
connect
increase
open
plain
show

REACH
unreachable

reach
verb
extend
fall
reach (2)
snap

unreachable
adjective
inaccessible
inconvenient

See also
approach

REAL
imaginary

real
noun
actuality
circumstance
existence
fact

adjective
accurate
actual (2)
factual
real
realistic (2)

adverb
actually
really

imaginary
noun
character
dream
fiction
hallucination
illusion (2)
imagination
myth (2)

adjective
artificial
dreamy
fallacious
fictitious
idealistic (2)
illusive
illusory
imaginary
mythical
theoretical

verb
dream
sentimentalize

See also
be
correct
performing arts
true

REASON
unreason

reason
noun
argument
assumption
calculation
deduction
logic
reason *(cont.)*

REASON *(cont.)*

reason
sense
adjective
logical (2)
sane
sound[2]
verb
calculate
derive
infer
resolve
work

unreason
noun
unreason
adjective
unreasonable
adverb
unfoundedly

See also
count
opinion
purpose
sane
start
thoughts

REGRET
impenitence

regret
noun
apology
penitence
adjective
apologetic
remorseful
verb
regret

impenitence
adjective
remorseless

See also
explain

RELEVANT
irrelevant

relevant
noun
business
relevance
adjective
relevant
verb
apply
deal with

irrelevant
adjective
irrelevant

See also
connect
limited
specific

RELIGION
noun
devotee
devotion
faith
grace
holiness
inspiration
missionary
myth
novice
offering
praise
prayer[1] (2)
preacher
purification
religion
sacrifice
separatist
adjective
condemned
divine[1] (2)
heavenly
holy (2)
impure
missionary
purgative
spiritual
verb
praise
pray
preach
purify
sacrifice
sanctify
violate

See also
feelings
praise
respect
ritual
sacred
supernatural

REMEMBER
forget

remember
noun
celebration
list[1]
memorial
memory (2)
remembrance
toast
adjective
memorial
verb
celebrate
drink
immortalize
list[1]
memorialize
memorize
post[3]
recognize
remember (2)
schedule
time
write

forget
adjective
forgetful
verb
forget

See also
awareness

REPETITION
noun
beat
circle
dancer
haunt
lapse
recurrence
repetition
reversion
revolution
rhythm
tremor (2)
adjective
recurrent
repetitive
rhythmical
tautological
tremulous
winding
verb
agitate
beat (4)
blink
bump
dance
flap (2)
flutter
haunt
recur
relapse
repeat (2)
return
shake (3)
spin (2)
sway
swing
swirl
toss
turn
wag[1]
wiggle
wind[2]
writhe
adverb
anew

See also
action
calm
move

REPRODUCTION
barrenness

reproduction
noun
pregnancy
reproduction
adjective
pregnant
reproductive (2)

verb
grow
reproduce

barrenness
noun
sterility
sterilization

verb
miscarry
sterilize

See also
rich
sex

REQUEST

noun
beggar
claim
dare
demand
supplicant

verb
address
beg
bill[1]
call
claim
dare
demand
request

See also
accept
ask

RESIST
yield

resist
noun
defiance
disobedience
obstinacy
opponent
rebel
rebellion
resistance (3)
stubbornness
unruliness

adjective
defiant
disobedient
firm[1]
obstinate
rebellious
resistant (2)
stubborn
unruly

verb
defy
disobey
harden
rebel
resist
talk back

yield
noun
obedience (2)
surrender

adjective
deferential
obedient
passive
soft

verb
back down
defer[2]
give over
humor
succumb
surrender

See also
accept
conflict
flexible
obligation
respect
willing

RESPECT
contempt
standing

respect
noun
distinction
eminence
esteem
face
honor (2)
pride
trophy

adjective
admirable
eminent
holy
proud
reverent

verb
distinguish
pride

contempt
noun
condescension
crack
degradation
despisal
disgrace
disrespect
infamy
joke
mockery
ridicule
sarcasm
satire
sneer
stain
takeoff
taunt

adjective
biting
cynical
disdainful
disgraceful
disrespectful
sarcastic
shameless

verb
condescend
despise
disgrace
humble
ridicule
shame
sneer
stigmatize

standing
noun
reputation

See also
courtesy
honest
praise
religion
resist
reward
right
rise
sacred
value

RESTRAINT
unrestraint

restraint
noun
bit[2]
chastity
modesty
reserve
shyness
temperance

adjective
chaste
conservative
modest
repressive
reserved
taciturn
temperate

verb
compose
refrain
repress
restrain

unrestraint
noun
abandon
bender
binge
blast
ease
liberty
license
room

adjective
abandoned
impure
outspoken

verb
revel

See also
calm

(cont.)

RESTRAINT *(cont.)*

See also
free
tighten

REWARD
punish
deserve

reward
noun
decoration
reward (2)

verb
reward

punish
noun
beating
exile
fine[2]
hell
punishment
sanction

adjective
damned
punishing

verb
beat
fine[2]
punish
torture

deserve
noun
due

See also
praise
respect

RICH
poor

rich
noun
fertility
fortune
plenty
prosperity
riches

adjective
alive
big
fertile (2)
generous
luxurious
prosperous
rich

verb
bear (2)
bloom[1]
fertilize
teem

poor
noun
barren
beggary
depression
deprivation
hole
pauper
poverty
sterility
sterilization
tatterdemalion
trash
unfortunate

adjective
barren (2)
depressed
poor
sterile

verb
deplete
sterilize

See also
beautiful
money
reproduction

RIGHT
wrong

right
noun
decency
ethic (2)
good
innocent
justice

adjective
appropriate
ethical
exemplary
innocent (2)
just
justifiable

verb
call for
justify

wrong
noun
breach
crime (2)
evil
heavy
infamy
injustice (2)
outrage
pit[1]

adjective
evil
outrageous
shameless
sordid
unlawful
unwholesome

verb
fall
offend
shock[1]
wrong

See also
agree
correct
crimes
fair
good
honest
respect
usual

RISE
fall

rise
noun
advancement
ascent (2)
exaltation
inclination
jump
lift
rise
takeoff

adjective
elevated
exalted
gradual

verb
ascend
elevate
erect
exalt
get up (2)
jump
lift
promote
rise (2)
take off

fall
noun
condescension
demotion
descent
drip
drop
fall (2)

adjective
descending

verb
condescend (2)
cut
demote
descend
drip
drop (3)
fall (2)
flop
lower[2]
seat
set[1]
settle
sink
traverse

See also
respect

RITUAL

noun
ceremony
ritual
wake[1]

adjective
ritual

See also
religion

SACRED
profane

sacred
noun
adoration
sanctuary

adjective
sacred

verb
adore

profane
noun
sacrilege
swearword

adjective
impure
profane
sacrilegious

verb
swear
violate

See also
religion
respect

SAFETY
danger

safety
noun
cover
guard
refuge
safety
sanctity

adjective
safe (2)

danger
noun
adventure
adventurer
crisis
danger
daring
lure
pitfall
risk
threat

adjective
adventurous
critical
dangerous
helpless
insecure

verb
endanger
hazard
risk

See also
protection

SAME
different
compare

same
noun
copy
counterpart
couple
double
echo (2)
echoism
equivalence
integration
likeness
mate
mimic
mimicry
mockery
model
parallel
peer[2]
precedent
sameness
takeoff
tie

adjective
echoic
equal (2)
even[1] (2)
imitative
like[2]
literal
same
symmetrical
twin

verb
copy
echo
equal
equalize
favor
follow (2)
identify
imitate
integrate
liken
rival

adverb
even[1]

different
noun
contrast
difference
distinction
inequality
uniqueness
variation (2)
variety

adjective
different
distinct
distinctive
uneven
unique
various
versatile

verb
differ
distinguish (2)

compare
adjective
comparative
typical

verb
associate
compare (2)

See also
agree
certain
change
continue
flexible
move
order
substitute
support
true

SANE
insane

sane
noun
sanity

adjective
sane (2)

insane
noun
insanity

adjective
insane

verb
derange

See also
reason
usual
wise

SAVE
waste

save
noun
economy

adjective
economical

verb
economize
save
scrimp

waste
noun
extravagance
luxury
wastrel

adjective
extravagant

verb
spend
waste (2)

See also
money

(cont.)

SAVE *(cont.)*

See also
pay
transactions

SEA

noun
sailor

adjective
marine
nautical

SEE
not see

see
noun
appearance
eye
gaze
glance
glare
ken
look
notice
squint
view
visibility
vision
watch
watcher
witness

adjective
apparent
graphic
noticeable
squinty
unsubtle
visible
visual

verb
appear
catch
discern
foresee
gaze
glare (2)
glimpse
look
notice
see
squint
survey
watch

not see
noun
blindness
blink
fade-out

adjective
blind (2)
inconspicuous

verb
blink (2)
daze
fade
fade out

See also
awareness
knowledge
light

SEEK
avoid

seek
noun
applicant
application
aspirant
courtship
drive
insistence
pursuit (2)
target
visit

verb
accost
aim (2)
apply
aspire
catch up
court (2)
grope
hunt
insist
pursue
seek
target
track
visit

avoid
noun
cut
escape (2)
fugitive
recoil

adjective
evasive
fugitive
stray

verb
avoid
cut
evade
flinch
lose
skirt

See also
precede
try

SELF
other

self
noun
egoism
egotist
self

adjective
corrupt
egocentric
egotistic

other
adjective
selfless

See also
self-love

SELF-LOVE
modesty

self-love
noun
egotism (2)
egotist
snob

adjective
egotistic
snobbish
vain

verb
strut

modesty
noun
modesty

adjective
humble

See also
plain
self

SEX
asexual
sexual

asexual
noun
chastity
prude

adjective
chaste
frigid
innocent

sexual
noun
beau
boyfriend
courtship
desire
deviant
flirt
flirtation (2)
gallant
heat
infatuation
lecher
love (2)
lover
philanderer
prostitute
seducer
seductress
sensuality
slut
wanton

adjective
desirable
erotic (2)
flirtatious
gay
impure
infatuated

seductive
sensual
wanton

verb
court
flirt
neck
philander
rape
seduce
take
violate

See also
desire
gender
love
marriage
reproduction

SHARP
dull

sharp
noun
edge (2)
point
prick

adjective
acute
pointed
sharp
thorny

verb
sharpen

dull
adjective
dull

verb
dull

See also
geometry

SHOW
hide

show
noun
acknowledgment
display (2)
exhibition
expression
guide
hint
lead
nudity
precursor
reflection
representation
revelation
shade
sign (2)

adjective
designative
expressive
frank
nude

verb
adumbrate
air
bear
betray
come out
designate
develop
display
elaborate
evoke
express
guide
hint
indicate
instance
plot
prove
reflect
represent
reveal
scream
show (2)
strip[1]
uncover

hide
noun
belittlement
burial
confidant
disappearance
disguise
façade
hide-out
mystery
secrecy

adjective
blind
confidential (2)
expressionless
implicit (2)
latent
secluded
secret
ulterior

verb
belittle
block
bury
censor (2)
confide
cover
disappear
disguise
extenuate
hide[1]
hole up
lay for
obscure
soft-pedal
withdraw
wrap

adverb
secretly

See also
clear
express
knowledge
open
put on
surface
words

SIMPLE
complex

simple
adjective
elementary
pastoral

verb
boil down

complex
noun
complexity
tangle

adjective
busy
complex (2)

verb
complicate

See also
easy
plain

SMELLS
good smells
bad smells
smell

good smells
noun
fragrance

adjective
fragrant
pungent

verb
scent

bad smells
adjective
moldy
smelly

verb
smell

smell
noun
smell (2)
trail

verb
smell

SMOOTH
rough

smooth
adjective
even[1]
sleek
slick

verb
even[1]
press

rough
noun
fold
irregularity
line

(cont.)

SMOOTH *(cont.)*

rough
adjective
coarse (2)
hairy
irregular
rough
verb
fold
wrinkle

See also
geometry

SOLID
liquid
consistency

solid
verb
coagulate
harden

liquid
noun
foam
adjective
foamy
verb
evaporate
foam
melt
ooze

consistency
noun
viscosity
adjective
flat
thick
viscous
verb
thicken

See also
dry
matter

SOUNDS
pleasant sounds
unpleasant sounds
neutral sounds or silence

pleasant sounds
noun
laugh
melody
adjective
harmonious
laughing
melodious (2)
resonant
soft
verb
chuckle
laugh
listen
ring[2]
sing

unpleasant sounds
noun
beat
blast
clash
cry
hiss
howl
hum
mutter
noise
report
roar
scream
shout
snap
tread
vociferation
yelp
adjective
harsh
hoarse
inharmonious
loud
vociferous
verb
bang
bawl
blast
clash
crack
crackle
cry
grind
hiss
howl
hum
mutter (2)
rattle
roar
rumble
scrape
scream
snap
tramp
whine
yelp

neutral sounds or silence
noun
beat
drip
echo
echoism
hearing (3)
murmur
silence
sound[1]
tap[1]
tone (2)
voicing
adjective
echoic
high
low
silent
taciturn
vocal (2)
verb
beat
echo
hear
muffle
murmur
silence
tap[1]
thud
wash

See also
words

SPECIFIC
general

specific
noun
name
adjective
detailed
graphic
mere
personal
private
special
specific
verb
call
enumerate
name (2)
stipulate
adverb
merely
namely

general
noun
public
adjective
general (3)
popular
prevailing
public
universal (2)
verb
socialize
universalize

See also
limited
relevant

START
end

start
noun
beginner
beginning
birth (2)
blame
cause (3)
center
dawn
foundation
germ
introduction
origin
original
originator
seed (3)
adjective
beginning
constitutional
dependent
early (2)

elementary
first
introductory
original
pilot
preliminary
primitive
rough

verb
begin
break out
broach
cause
come
consist
contribute
dawn
depend on
found
introduce (2)
light[1]
seed
start
stem
usher in

end
noun
arrival
cause
end
evening
fate

adjective
last[1] (3)
through (2)

verb
address
aim
arrive
arrive at
carry
close
fate

adverb
last[1]
through
ultimately

See also
action
attack
cause
continue
enter
kin
part
purpose
reason
surface
time
work

STRAIGHT
bent

straight
adjective
accepted
direct

adverb
directly

bent
noun
bend
bias
inclination
irregularity
loop

adjective
bent
bias
biased
crooked
indirect
irregular
winding

verb
bend (2)
bias (2)
incline
lurch
manipulate
wave
wind[2]

See also
geometry

STRIKE
miss

strike
noun
beat
blow[2]
shock[1]
slam
slap

verb
batter
beat (2)
glance
hit
parry
slap
slap around
splash
sprinkle
thrash (2)

miss
adjective
clear

See also
attack
marks

STRONG
weak

strong
noun
character
decision
force
intensity
muscle
strength

adjective
authoritative
colorful
deep
emphatic (2)
firm[1]
forceful
hard
heavy
high
influential
intense
lusty
muscular
powerful
sound[2]
straight
strong (3)

verb
confirm
refresh
toughen

adverb
flatly
hard (2)

weak
noun
debilitation
ineffectuality
infirmity
instability

adjective
dilute
faint
fragile
gentle
ineffectual
infirm
insecure
light[2]
neutral
pale
tenuous
trick
vulnerable

verb
dilute
enervate
fade
weaken

See also
action
awareness
continue
feelings
health
important
tired

STYLE
good style
bad style
style

good style
noun
bearing
class
elegance
fashion
gravity
poetry

(cont.)

STYLE *(cont.)*

good style
taste

adjective
brief
elegant
elevated
fashionable
pithy
smooth
suave
tasteful
tight

bad style
noun
bombast
corruption
theatricalism
theatrics
wordiness

adjective
dramatic
gaudy
tacky[2]
wordy

style
noun
style

adjective
sonorous

See also
words

SUBSTITUTE

noun
acting
actor
change
compensation
copy
embodiment
example
flag[1]
makeshift
place
relief
representative
speaker
substitute
symbol

adjective
compensatory
symbolic
temporary

verb
act (2)
change (2)
compensate
embody
relieve
replace
represent (2)
substitute
supplant

See also
same

SUGGEST

noun
hint (2)
insinuation
suggestion

adjective
insinuating
suggestive

verb
hint
smack[2]

See also
persuasion

SUPERNATURAL

noun
charm
ghost
gibberish
magic
miracle
spell[2]
witch

adjective
magic
supernatural

See also
luck
religion
warn

SUPPORT
oppose

support
noun
endorsement
reference
sponsor
support

verb
back
confirm
defend
encourage
prove
support (2)

oppose
noun
objection
opponent
opposite
opposition

adjective
contrary
opposing
opposite

verb
contest
object
oppose
quibble

See also
agree
help
love
praise
same
treat well

SURFACE
depth

surface
noun
appearance
face (2)
form (2)
hide[2]
image
outline
shoal
skin (3)
terrain
trivia

adjective
apparent
frothy
glib
incidental
shallow
superficial

verb
appear
face
form

adverb
apparently

depth
noun
depth
essence

adjective
deep (3)
elemental
essential
radical
underground

adverb
essentially

See also
be
order
show
start

SURPRISE
expect

surprise
noun
accident
chance

adjective
abrupt
accidental
amiss
arbitrary (2)
dramatic
staggering

verb
backfire
stagger

startle
surprise
take

expect
noun
anticipation
cliché
expectation

adjective
common
due
expectant

verb
expect

See also
affect
certain
excite
fear
feelings
happen
hope
luck
planned
purpose
usual

TASTE
bad taste

taste
noun
flavor (2)
flavoring

adjective
pungent
sour
sweet

verb
flavor

bad taste
noun
insipidity

adjective
bad
bitter
flat (2)
unpalatable

See also
ingestion

TEACH
learn

teach
noun
education
educator
illumination

adjective
didactic
educable
educational
moral
pedantic

verb
educate
illuminate
impress
indoctrinate (2)
inform
moralize
socialize

learn
noun
discovery
student

adjective
studious

verb
discover
learn
study

See also
knowledge
understand

TERRITORY
noun
area (2)
basin
bay[1]
beat
border
home
lot
neighborhood
range
reservation
state
territory

adjective
territorial

See also
place

THICK
thin

thick
noun
thickness

adjective
thick

thin
adjective
filmy

See also
fat
heavy
wide

THING
noun
bouquet
matter
novelty
object
odds and ends
stick
thing
thread
wall
web

See also
matter

THOUGHTS
noun
advisement
depth
fancy
feeling
head
idea
imagination
inspiration
instinct
intelligence
psychology
survey
theory (2)
thinker
thought

adjective
instinctive
intellectual
mental
theoretical
thoughtful

verb
bear
brood
hear of
ignore
imagine
ponder
reconsider
review
speculate
think

See also
belief
careful
knowledge
likely
opinion
reason
wise

THRIVE
fail
exist

thrive
noun
efficiency
hit
prosperity
success

adjective
effective
efficient
flourishing
foolproof
good
prosperous

verb
clear
flourish (2)
prosper
succeed (2)

(cont.)

THRIVE *(cont.)*

fail

noun
decay
failure (3)
fall
futility

adjective
amiss
bad
futile
impractical

verb
decay
fail (3)
malfunction
miscarry

adverb
wrong

exist

verb
manage
mess around
muddle
work

See also
action
good
industrious
win

TIGHTEN

loosen

tighten

noun
constriction

adjective
edgy
taut
thick
tight (2)

verb
constrain
constrict
crowd (2)
squeeze (2)
tense
tie
tighten

loosen

noun
ease
freedom

adjective
easygoing
full
loose
thin

verb
ease
thin
undo

See also
attitude
calm
feelings
free
restraint

TIME

noun
age (2)
contemporary (2)
delay (2)
flash
future
instant
lateness
life
morning
now
occasion
past
period (2)
siege
spring
summer
term
time (2)
turn
vintage
year

adjective
consecutive
contemporary
distant
early
following
future
inconvenient
instant
late
modern
past
posthumous
present[1]
punctual
simultaneous
spring
transitory

verb
delay
follow
go (2)
serve
spend
time (2)

adverb
directly
early
just
late (2)
now (3)
slow
together
ultimately

See also
action
continue
fast
new
start
youth

TIRED

fresh

tired

noun
exhaustion

adjective
exhausted
haggard
languid
restless
sick
tiring
wasted

verb
exhaust
fatigue
run down

fresh

noun
drive
vigor

adjective
tireless

See also
action
awareness
feelings
heavy
strong

TOUCH

not touch

touch

noun
brush[1]
brush[2]
contact
dig
embrace
kiss
tangibility
touch (4)

adjective
affecting
tactile
tangible

verb
affect[1]
brush[1]
caress
contact
dig
embrace
fiddle
grope
kiss
tamper
till
touch
work
wrestle

not touch

adjective
clear

See also
approach
near

TRANSACTIONS

noun
bargain
cost (3)
dealer
good
gratuity
pass
patron
patronage (2)
pawn[1]
pusher
seller
store
toll[1]

adjective
costly

verb
cost
hire
lease
pawn[1]
peddle
push
sell
sell off

See also
gambling
money
owned
pay
save
work

TREAT WELL
treat badly
treat

treat well
noun
consideration

adjective
attentive
favorite

verb
baby
favor

treat badly
noun
abuse

verb
abuse (2)
bait

treat
verb
deal with

See also
attitude
concern
courtesy
crimes
help
include
kind
support

TRUE
false

true
noun
authenticity
certainty
confirmation
truth
veracity

adjective
accurate (2)
authentic
authoritative
believable
certain
genuine
true
truthful

verb
confirm
wash

adverb
actually
even[1]
really

false
noun
act
affectation
basis
counterfeit
fake
fallacy (2)
forger
liar
lie[2]
mendacity
pretense

adjective
affected
artificial
assumed
baseless
counterfeit
fallacious
false
fantastic
forced
perjurious

verb
act
assume
color
counterfeit
distort
equivocate
fake (2)
lie[2]
pretend

See also
correct
honest
likely
real
same
trust

TRUST
distrust

trust
adjective
dependable
faithful

verb
depend on
entrust

distrust
noun
betrayal
betrayer
defection
distrust
faithlessness
treachery
treason

adjective
distrustful
faithless
treasonous
undependable

verb
betray
defect
distrust

See also
true

TRY

noun
attempt
drive
try

adjective
aggressive

verb
attempt
presume

See also
seek

UNDERSTAND
misunderstand

understand
noun
sympathy

adjective
understanding

verb
interpret
sympathize
understand

misunderstand
noun
misunderstanding

verb
misunderstand

See also
knowledge
teach

URBAN
rural

urban
noun
city

adjective
city

verb
citify

rural
noun
country

adjective
country

USED
unused

used
noun
consumer
consumption
duty
exercise
use

adjective
practical
usable

verb
handle
resort
take
tie up
use

unused
noun
futility
obsoleteness
obsoletism
temperance

adjective
futile
idle
impracticable
obsolete
useless

verb
lose
obsolesce

See also
affect
help

USUAL
unusual

usual
noun
average
convention
custom
decency
fashion
grind
manner
ritual
routine
standard
usual
usualness

adjective
accepted
accustomed (2)
common
conventional
customary
decent
everyday
fashionable
ordinary
orthodox
strict
trite
typical

verb
accustom
conventionalize

adverb
usually

unusual
noun
abnormality
character
deviant
eccentricity
freak
impropriety (2)

adjective
abnormal
eccentric
fantastic
freakish
funny
improper (2)
infrequent
outrageous
preternatural
quaint
rare
steep[1]
unseasonable
unusual
weird

adverb
infrequently
unusually

See also
continue
correct
keep
right
sane
surprise

VALUE
worthlessness
evaluation

value
noun
treasure
worth

adjective
admirable
costly
valuable

verb
cherish

worthlessness
adjective
cheap
worthless

verb
discredit

evaluation
noun
class
critic
estimate
merit
quality

adjective
critical

verb
class
estimate
score

See also
help
like
love
praise
respect

WARN
invite

warn
noun
alarm
alarmist
example
omen
threat
warning

adjective
cautionary
dark
fateful
forbidding
malign

verb
warn

invite
noun
invitation

verb
invite

See also
foresight
luck
supernatural

WIDE
narrow

wide
noun
width

adjective
broad (3)

widespread
yawning

verb
broaden
spread
yawn

narrow
noun
constriction

adjective
narrow

verb
constrict

See also
thick

WILD
tame

wild
noun
wild

adjective
savage
uncivilized
wild

tame
adjective
domestic
gentle

verb
domesticate
gentle

See also
culture

WILLING
unwilling

willing
noun
volunteer
will

adjective
obliging
voluntary (2)
willing

adverb
voluntarily

unwilling
noun
imposition
indisposition

adjective
forced
indisposed

verb
impose (2)
inflict

adverb
helplessly

See also
attack
choice
flexible
resist

WIN
lose
recovery

win
noun
conqueror
conquest
defeat
favorite
runaway
suppression
trump
winner

adjective
invincible
victorious

verb
defeat
outwit
overwhelm
suppress
trump

lose
noun
degradation
surrender

verb
give in
humble
surrender

recovery
noun
comeback

verb
catch up

See also
thrive

WISE
foolish

wise
noun
sage[1]
wisdom

adjective
advisable
advised
wise[1]

foolish
noun
crackpot
dupe

adjective
easy
unwise

See also
ability
careful
knowledge
precise
sane
thoughts

WORDS

noun
application
argumentation
babble
bombast
book
call
chatter
command
comment
commentary (2)
communication
composition
conferee
conference (2)
confidant
conversation
conversationalist
coverage
crack
cry
curse
deliberation
dialect
discourse
draft
eloquence
entry
exclamation
expression (2)
feature
gibberish (2)
gossip (2)
head
history
impression
introduction
item
language (2)
letter
name
news
note
orator
oratory
paraphrase
pirate
plot
poem
poet
poetry
press
program
proverb
publication (2)
review
silence
speaker
speech (2)
stammer
story
summary
swearword
synopsis
talk
term

(cont.)

WORDS *(cont.)*

theme
thesis
vocabulary (2)
voicing
word
wordiness
wording
yarn

adjective
brief
conversational
descriptive
dumb
eloquent
glib
gossipy
graphic (2)
introductory
oral
oratorical
poetic
silent
sonorous
speechless
talkative
tautological
unspeakable (2)
verbal
wordy

verb
address (2)
air
announce
argue
babble
browse
call
chatter
command
comment
confer
confide
converse[1]
cover
curse
describe
discuss
draft
exclaim
gasp
ghost
gossip
introduce
name
paraphrase
phrase
pirate
present[2]
pronounce
publish (2)
rant
refer
review
say
signal
snap
speak
stammer
state
swear
talk back
telephone
translate

See also
decent
knowledge
meaning
show
sounds
style

WORK
play

work
noun
drudge
effort
employee
employer
employment (2)
labor
laborer
mission
practice (2)
project
seriousness
task (2)
volunteer
work

adjective
employed
serious
unpaid
workless

verb
apply
attack
bone
employ
exercise
grind
labor
practice (2)
work

play
noun
blast
dance
party
play (2)
playfulness
plunge
prank[1]
toy
vacation

adjective
playful

verb
dance
flirt
gambol
play

See also
action
do
enter
laughter
money
move
pay
transactions

YOUTH
age
maturity

youth
noun
baby (2)
child
minor
minority
squirt
teenager
young
youth

adjective
babyish
childish
minor
small
young

age
noun
age
senility
senior

adjective
senile

verb
age

maturity
noun
senior

adjective
aged
mature
senior

verb
mature

See also
time

CDEFGHIJK-RMV-99876